YOUR BIRTHDAY SIGN
THROUGH TIME
A Chronicle of the Forces that Shape Your Destiny

Skye Alexander, Frank Andrews, Rochelle Gordon,
Ronnie Grishman, Wendy C. Hawks, Jean Mars, Sophia Mason

✵

Editor-in-Chief – Rochelle Gordon
General Editor – Nadia Stieglitz

ATRIA BOOKS
New York London Toronto Sydney Singapore

ATRIA BOOKS

1230 Avenue of the Americas
New York, NY 10020

ISBN 0-7434-6261-0

Library of Congress Control Number: 2002110810

First Atria Books hardcover printing October 2002

10 9 8 7 6 5 4 3 2 1

ATRIA BOOKS is a trademark of Simon & Schuster, Inc.

For further information regarding special discounts for bulk purchases,
please contact Simon & Schuster Special Sales at 1-800-456-6798 or business@simonandschuster.com

Printed in the U.S.A.

This book was created and produced for Atria Books by
Pasteur Publishing Group, PO Box 3227, East Hampton, NY 11937

© 2002 Pasteur Publishing Group, Inc.

The authors wish to acknowledge the dedicated hard work of the following people,
without whom this book could never have come into being:

Contributors
Laura Boomer, Karen Christino, Stephanie L. Dempsey, Ronnie Gale Dreyer, Kim Farnell,
Nancy Frederick Sussan, Molly Hall, Madalyn Hillis-Dineen, Brenda Lewis, Kenneth Irving,
Bethea Jenner, Teresa H. Lamb, Michael O'Reilly, Marjorie Partch, Andrea Ploscowe, Christine Rakela,
Kim Rogers-Gallagher, Stefanie Iris Weiss

Assistant Editors
David Biello, Gigi Branch-Shaw, Dru-Ann Chuchran, Kathleen Crepeau, Susan Forney,
Paula Rollet de Fougerolles, Roya Ireland, Sonya Newland, Andrea Ploscowe

Publishing Consultancy, Layout and Production
The Foundry Creative Media Company,
Crabtree Hall, Crabtree Lane, Fulham, London, SW6 6TY

Development
Martin Branch Shaw, John Dunne, Rochelle Gordon, Greg Hill, Nadia Stieglitz

Special thanks to:
Ray Barnett, Anthony Cohen, David Crane, Mark Mobsby, Graham Stride, Nick Wells

Photography Credits
All pictures supplied courtesy of Topham Picturepoint
except page 185 (courtesy of Carnegie Hall Society)
and pages 585, 593, 601 (courtesy of the Findhorn Garden).

Contents

Introduction

"AS ABOVE, SO BELOW"

Astrologers have long debated the comparative influence of fate versus free will and heredity versus environment. The very nature of astrology as an esoteric science brings such issues to the forefront of the astrologer's work. Certainly, with the discoveries of modern medicine and psychology, no one can deny the influence of genetic makeup and environment upon human personality and experience. With these thoughts in mind, we thought it would be enlightening and entertaining to explore the interplay between history and astrology. This book is the result of our studies. Using both astrological and historical information from the twentieth century, we have done "readings" that combine these two significant factors. Now, for the first time, you can discover how your stars and your time and place in history come together in *Your Birthday Sign Through Time.*

Modern Astrology

Let us consider how astrology's focus comes into play. The premise of modern astrology is that the Universe makes a certain "imprint" on an individual, based on one's time and place of birth. Reflecting this imprint, the astrological natal chart (also known as one's personal horoscope) provides a sort of snapshot of the locations of the planets and their interrelationships at the moment of birth. Astrologers read this "map of the heavens" by interpreting the symbolism of the eight planets along with the Sun and the Moon. When accurately interpreted, this map can reveal the inherent character traits and potential experiences of an individual.

So, if you have been wondering whether you can learn anything new and valuable from your personal horoscope—information about yourself, the circumstances of your life, or the patterns at work in your "fate"—the answer is yes. Such information would be far more inclusive than an ordinary Sun-sign reading, which pertains only to one's sense of identity. A natal-chart interpretation by a qualified astrologer can indicate when you are likely to change jobs, find new love, relocate, or publish your new novel. Although we weren't able to be predictive when writing for you here, we have shown that the reading for a given Sun sign during your birth year (found by turning to the pages for your year of birth) differs from the same sign in other years. But you will discover more than your birth year's Sun sign. Because we want you to enjoy a broader range of astrological resources, we also provide information that allows you to locate the sign placements of the planets Venus, Mars, and Jupiter in your chart.

In the language of astrology, the planets, the Sun, and the Moon represent symbolic energies or forces. These planetary forces signify universal principles, which the Ancients summed up and personified as "gods." For example, Mars, the fiery "Red Planet," representing action, anger, aggression, drive, willpower, sex, and war, is named for the Roman god of war. If the planets are energies, then the signs of the zodiac can be thought of as coloring the expression of these energies. So, when Mars—signifying action—is located in its own fiery Sign of Aries in a birth chart, an individual will be quicker to act than he or she would be if Mars were in the gentler, patient sign of Taurus. This book provides you with the means to find out not only what sign your Venus, Mars, and Jupiter are located in, but also how this affects you.

The planet Venus indicates your love potential. It reveals much about your personal love nature, how you give and receive love, whom and what you love, and what you value in relationships. It also shows the kinds of people you are attracted to and with whom you are likely to be most compatible.

Mars tells a great deal about your drives, ambitions, and how you tend to assert yourself in the world. This dynamic, energetic planet reveals what gets you going and keeps you going until you reach a sought-after goal. Because Mars represents pure energy and desire, it also shows how you express your desires, particularly those of a sexual nature. Mars also suggests what excites you in a partner and how you are likely to pursue the object of your desires.

Life presents each of us with many opportunities to advance materially, mentally, emotionally, and spiritually. Your attitude and approach to life have a significant impact on how you will

4

take advantage of any luck that crosses your path. The planet Jupiter indicates what areas are likely to provide lucky opportunities for you, where you possess a sense of optimism and self-confidence, and how you can make your own luck.

The influence of the signs and planets obviously brings up the question of astrology's "predetermined" role in our lives versus free will. Modern astrologers prefer the concept of "meaningful coincidence" between the celestial events (the changing positions of the planets) and individual destinies, rather than the idea that the planets themselves "cause" events on earth. Astronomical research has verified that alterations in the magnetic fields of the planets, resulting from changes in their relative positions to one another, can directly influence solar-flare activity. Such changes (or "events") seem to coincide with variances in weather patterns, radio waves, and even human behavior on earth. But for most astrologers, the fact that changing planetary configurations are simply occurring "in sync" with events on earth is enough to provide them with useful information. The astrologer's job is to perceive and interpret the parallels between planetary and earthly events. Like gears working within gears, the various levels are all moving together at the same time.

Each astrologer brings his or her own individual perspective to the interpretation of these parallels—in effect, viewing the planets through the lens of his or her own personal horoscope—and so readings will be colored accordingly. The book you have in your hands was written by seven astrologers, each with his or her own expertise and personal style. Therefore, you may notice a different approach towards the readings throughout the book. These readings take into consideration all the planets except Mercury and the Moon. These two bodies move too quickly through the zodiac to pinpoint in this work.

Astrology and History

Now let us see how history fits into this picture. When we began this project, we wanted to know if we could intertwine history with astrology as a means of understanding the historical contexts into which people are born—as individuals, as generations, and as nations. While we do believe in free will and agree with Aristotle that "character is destiny," we also believe that all these levels of reality are layered on top of one another, a little bit like an onion. You can read more about this fascinating concept on the first page of each year's section, where we view history from an astrological perspective.

As an example of this idea, we can consider this question: was it "just a coincidence" that the planet Pluto was discovered in 1930, as the Nazi Party was coming into power in Germany? While some would say that it could have been a coincidence, astrologers would consider it a *meaningful* coincidence, because Pluto represents, first and foremost, power. The world had never before seen the likes of a Hitler, let alone a Stalin and a Mussolini. Nor had the world ever faced the possibility of atomic power and total annihilation. Pluto is also said to represent violent eruptions and destruction, as well as death and transformation. Thus it comes as no surprise that the development of the atom bomb was underway by 1939, within a decade of Pluto's discovery.

In undertaking this vast project, we wanted to provide our readers with an accurate and precise account of history. Thus we sought out reliable historical sources for our research, and we then fact-checked our findings to the best of our ability. Nevertheless, there were times when we found discrepancies in our reference material and even conflicting data with respect to certain historical events and birth dates of famous individuals. In these cases, we were forced to choose one historical source over another. We hope you will keep this in mind in the event that your own knowledge conflicts with a specific detail you may read.

We invite you to explore the wonders of the esoteric world here, along with our historical survey of the past century. We have given you a sampling of celestial influences in order to enrich your understanding of astrology, as well as the role it plays in your own life and the lives of those around you. Our work as professional astrologers has given us a window to monitor the many levels of our world—whether it be our global arena, or in the individual patterns of our own lives—and it confirms that we live in a complex but ultimately unified and meaningful Universe. We hope that we have successfully conveyed and shared this sense of unity—and meaning—with you.

SKYE ALEXANDER, FRANK ANDREWS, ROCHELLE GORDON, RONNIE GRISHMAN,
WENDY C. HAWKS, JEAN MARS, SOPHIA MASON

About the Authors

Rochelle Gordon

Rochelle has been a leading expert in astrology, tarot, acrophonology (alphabet/zodiac correspondences) and clairvoyance for over thirty years. Author of several books, including *Body Talk* and *Personal Power Is In Your Name*, and a former editor of *Body Mind Spirit* magazine, she is an influential voice both in popular astrology and the study of the mind/body connection. She was also editor of *Astro Signs Digest*, *Horoscope Guide* and *Astro Signs* magazines, and has contributed articles to *Cosmopolitan*, *Dell Horoscope*, *National Astrology*, and *American Astrology*. Rochelle is a member of the American Federation of Astrologers and past President of the Astra Guild for Education.

Skye Alexander

A highly respected astrologer, author, and advisor for over twenty years, Skye has published several books, including the classic *Planets In Signs* and the award-winning astrological mystery *Hidden Agenda*. She is a frequent contributor to the Llewellyn annual *Sun Signs* and *Moon Signs* books, and has written articles for *Better Homes and Gardens*, *Dell Horoscope* and *Magical Blend* magazines. Skye is also a well-known authority on Wicca and frequently speaks on magick and witchcraft at New Age conferences, workshops, and events. She recently appeared in a television program on magick for the Discovery Channel, filmed at Stonehenge.

Frank Andrews

World-renowned astrologer, tarot expert, lecturer, consultant, and columnist, Frank Andrews has advised so many famous people for so long that he is a celebrity in his own right. He has appeared on national TV shows including *Good Morning America*, *The Phil Donahue Show*, and *Fox News*, and has been featured on PBS. He writes the Sunday "Tarot To Go" column for *The New York Post* and writes a column for *Elegant Bride* magazine. He has been profiled by dozens of magazines including *Marie Claire*, *Cosmopolitan*, *Redbook*, and *Harper's Bazaar*, and *New York* magazine named him "Best Psychic in New York." Although he refrains from discussing current clients, Frank has been the advisor to a number of wealthy and famous people, including John Lennon, Princess Grace of Monaco, Perry Ellis, and Princess Aga Khan.

Wendy C. Hawks

Wendy has been a nationally published astrologer and consultant for over twenty-two years. She is the author of numerous popular horoscope booklets and three Mini-Mags, two including *An Astro Guide to Healing Herbs and Get Rich for the New Millennium*. Her book, *The Nuts and Bolts of Running an Astrology Practice*, is one of the American Federation of Astrologers' most in-demand titles. Wendy is perhaps best known for correctly predicting O. J. Simpson's acquittal in her *National Examiner* column in 1994, nearly a year before the trial ended. She also correctly predicted the outcome of the contested 2000 American presidential election several months before the controversy was settled.

Ronnie Grishman

Ronnie is the Editor-in-Chief of *Dell Horoscope* magazine and has over thirty years of experience in astrology and a broad range of metaphysical subjects, specializing in the I Ching. She studied comparative religion at Hunter College and esoteric philosophy at the School of Practical Philosophy, both in New York City. In her twenty-three years with Dell, Ronnie has also produced the popular *Annual Forecast Astrology* purse books, *Love Signs* purse books and, most recently, *Understanding Astrology*, a complete teaching guide for the beginner. She has written for *Cosmopolitan* magazine, *The Joy Of Outlet Shopping*, and the Internet Shopping Network's firstjewelry.com, and currently writes the monthly "Self-Guidance Chart," an aspect-by-aspect advice column for *Horoscope* magazine.

Jean Mars

A lifelong student of the prophecies of Nostradamus, Swiss astrologer and numerologist Jean Mars was for many years the resident astrologer for the French magazine *Ici Paris* and for Europe's Radio Monte Carlo. He has been a member of the American Mentalists Association for forty-five years and the American Federation of Astrologers for over twenty-five years. Jean is also a well-known figure on the international conference circuit, where he has given readings and telepathy demonstrations for many years. His *One Man Mental Show* is especially renowned as a "must-see" event!

Sophia Mason

A Master Astrologer, Sophia's passion for astrology spans over thirty years. She is a two-time winner of the American Federation of Astrologers' Best Astrologer, Lecturer, and Teacher award and specializes in "astrological detective" work and card divination. She lectures at astrology conferences throughout the U.S. and is the author of several books, including *Playing Your Cards Right: Finding Your Destiny in Playing Cards,* and *Sexuality*, an in-depth astrological study of sexual compatibility.

How to Use This Book

Your Birthday Sign Through Time gives combined historical and astrological readings for every sign, in every year from 1900 to 2001. The first page serves as an introduction to the main historical events and astrological occurrences within that year. It includes an astrological view of history, a general historical overview of the major events, and a feature on unusual incidents. This is intended to help you identify with the way historical and astrological forces,

in play at the time of your birth, may have struck an ongoing theme for you throughout your life. There are thirteen birthday-sign entries for each year, from January Capricorn to December Capricorn, analyzing your personal birth chart. At the end of each year, a Special Feature or a Star Profile allows you to read more about the key figures and events of the era. The elements contained within each year are outlined in more detail below.

A. Astrological View of History
The first page of every year includes a feature describing how the planets' energies corresponded with historical events during that year.

B. History
An overview of world history for each year is also outlined on the first page of each year section. All together, more than 3,000 important historical events of the last hundred years are noted in this book.

C. Unusual Incidents
The first page of some years contains a feature on an unusual or mysterious event that occurred in this year, including sightings of UFOs and other strange phenomena.

D. Birthday–Sign Readings
Following the first page for each year is an entry for each sign of the zodiac throughout the year. This gives an astrologer's analysis of how you would be affected by and react to the world events that occurred around the time of your birth, and the astrological factors in play at the time.

E. Your Personal Planets
You will find the sign positions of the personal planets listed in the side panel next to each Sun sign reading. This gives you the sign placement of Venus, Mars, and Jupiter, which will reveal your potential for love, drive and ambition, as well as luck magnetism. You can turn to page 826 for the astrologers' readings about these matters. If you were born when one of these planets was changing signs, please refer to *If You Were Born on the Cusp.*

F. World Events
By the side of each birthday-sign entry are listings of two of the main events that occurred in the world during the time of your birth, placing your birth in a global historical context.

G. Special Features

Located at the end of each year's section, these reports cover events that made a mark on history, bringing more detail to the historical overview.

H. Star Profiles

These Profiles are of people who made a mark on history. They bring more detail to the historical overview presented and discuss how astrological forces shaped such influential people as Sigmund Freud, Richard Nixon, Marilyn Monroe, and Princess Diana.

Finding Your Birthday-Sign Reading

Different astrology books can list varying dates for each Sun sign and may often give erroneous sign listings. This is because the Sun often moves from one sign to the next on different days from year to year (+/– one to two days).

To locate your personal reading, turn to the pages for your birth year. Exact dates and times for each sign are noted above each reading, so that you can determine your Sun-sign accurately.

If You Were Born on the Cusp

In case you were born on the "cusp" of two signs, that is, on the day the Sun moved into or out of a particular sign, you can determine your accurate Sun sign based on your time and place of birth in this book from our information.

For example, the date and time range for Aquarius of 1947 is January 20, 21:32 through February 19, 11:51. 21:32 and 11:51 are the times when the Sun moved from one sign to the next. So, say you were born in Miami, Florida, on February 19, 1947, at 7:15 a.m. To find out whether you are an Aquarius or a Pisces, you would first need to convert your birth time to Greenwich Mean Time. You can do this by consulting the Time Zone Map below. The Time Zone Map shows that Miami is in the Eastern Standard Time (EST) zone, and that the EST zone is five hours behind Greenwich Mean Time. Accordingly, to convert your birth time from EST to GMT, you would add five hours to your birth time. Here, that would be 7:15 + five hours = 12:15 GMT. Because your birth time is 12:15 GMT, it falls within the date and time range for Pisces of 1947. You are a Pisces!

Imagine now that you were born in Rome, Italy, on June 21, 1970 at 20:05 p.m. To find out whether you are a Cancer or a Gemini, you would need to convert your birth time to GMT. If you look at the Time Zone Map, you will see that Rome is in Central Europe Time (CET) and that the CET zone is one hour ahead of GMT; to find your birth time, therefore, you need to subtract one hour. So, 20:05 – one hour = 19:05 GMT, which falls in Gemini.

Your Personal Planets and What They Mean

In addition to individualized birthday-sign readings for 101 years, readers can determine the signs of certain personal planets, Venus, Mars, and Jupiter, in their charts, which affect their love life, their drive and ambition, and their luck potential.

You will find the sign positions of the personal planets listed in the side panel next to each Sun-sign reading. The information includes each planet's sign and the time it entered and left that sign. Again, just as you could determine your Sun sign with accuracy, you can also determine the exact sign placement of your personal planets based on the date, time, and place of your birth. Simply look to see whether your birth date falls within the date range for a given sign placement for a particular planet.

If you happen to have been born on a day Venus, Mars, or Jupiter was changing signs, please refer to the Time Zone Map below to determine your birth time zone, and make the appropriate

time adjustment from your local birth time to GMT. Once you have made the time-zone adjustments, you will be able to determine the positions of your personal planets.

Your Chinese Astrology Sign

Chinese Astrology can add much understanding about an individual's personality. This section gives details about your animal sign, as well as your Chinese "element," which lends a more individualized perspective to your Chinese animal sign. These signs and elements change at the Chinese New Year, which occurs at the New Moon in Aquarius each year. This event can fall on any day during either January or February. You can determine your true Chinese zodiac sign from the exact date and time listing of the sign/element changes from 1900 to 2001 on the Chinese Astrology Dates Chart on page 838. If you happened to be born on the day when the Chinese animal sign changed, you can refer to the Time Zone Map below to determine your birth time zone, and make the appropriate time adjustment from your local birth time to GMT time.

The Power of Your Mystical Cards

Astrology interacts with other seemingly unconnected areas of life. Most people don't know that there is a correspondence between an ordinary deck of playing cards and birth dates. It is also a little-known fact that these cards have mystical significance, much like the Tarot deck. Each card can be related to a birth date. The mystical meaning for each card is derived from an ancient esoteric system that combines the knowledge of astrology and numerology.

On page 858 of this volume, we present the meanings of the cards as they correspond to birth dates. Simply follow the chart on page 857 that lists birth dates until you find yours, and you can find the card that corresponds to your birth date. Once you find your card, you can look up its meaning.

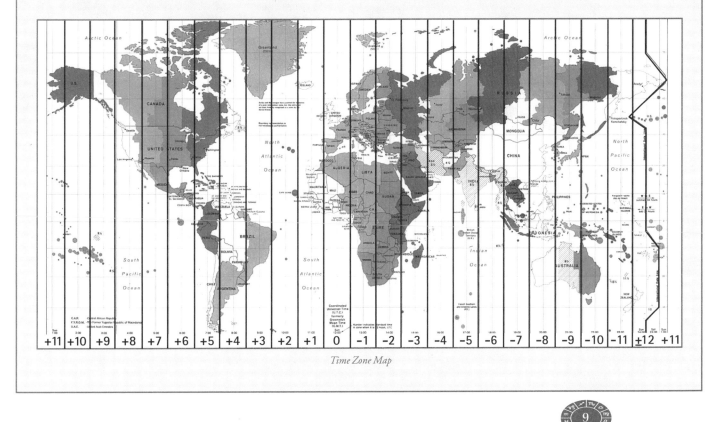

Time Zone Map

1900

Inventing the World Anew: Pluto in Gemini

As the century opened, stark changes swept through every area of life. The technology of the day exploded in ways that people had never imagined before. With Pluto, planet of transformation, in the sign of Gemini, ruler of the intellect, it's no wonder that inventors the world over were brimming with powerful new ideas that would alter our entire way of life. Henry Ford unveiled the first Detroit-made automobile in February of this year. The Paris Exhibition of 1900 opened on April 14. It covered 547 acres, and was larger than any previous European world fair. Among the many noteworthy attractions were the magnificent effects produced by electricity in the Château d'Eau and Hall of Illusions.

Also in 1900, there was much political activity, which is reflected by the placement of the planet Jupiter in the sign of Sagittarius. Jupiter is the planet of expansion, joy, and wisdom. When it slides into its natural sign, Sagittarius, it causes a stir. Sagittarius is the sign of liberty and freedom. With this position of Jupiter, dynamic tension was added to Pluto's need for revolution. Revolutionary Uranus was also in Sagittarius and "opposed" Pluto throughout the year. The dance that these two planets were performing could depict the contrast between traditional nineteenth century values of master and servant and the hope that a more egalitarian society was going to emerge. In January, labor revolts swept across Europe—steelworkers in Vienna, glass workers in Brussels—and there was a wave of strikes in coal basins. Although not the result of an organized movement, laborers made similar demands: an eight-hour day, pay increases, and better working conditions. While, on the other side of the Atlantic, in January, disturbed by U.S. military involvement in the Philippines, Andrew Carnegie and William Jennings Bryan emerged as vocal opponents of what they saw as U.S. imperialism.

In March of 1900, Pluto and Jupiter met up in the sky to make an angle that signaled spiritual regeneration through philosophy—the bettering of the human condition through constructive efforts. All over the world, people rallied optimistically to change the life of the common man.

The French Metropolitan Railway opens in Paris

Devastation left after the Boxer Rebellion

President McKinley wins a second term in office

BRIGHT HOPE FOR A NEW CENTURY

As 1900 dawned, there was widespread optimism that nothing was beyond the scope of rapidly advancing science and technology. War continued in South Africa between the British and Dutch Boers. Hopes of instant wealth brought thousands to the Canadian Klondike gold rush. In India, millions died from starvation, inducing the creation of the international food relief movement. British trade unions formed the Labour Representation Committee, later called the Labour Party. The Boxer Rebellion sprang from anti-foreign sentiment in China. The World Expo opened in Paris, featuring the latest developments in art, science, and technology. Australian colonies formed the Commonwealth of Australia. In the U.S., New York Mayor Van Wyck broke ground for the New York subway. Hawaii became a territory of the U.S. and President McKinley won a second term, with Theodore Roosevelt at his side. Moving pictures received a boost in popularity when the first viewing rooms opened. Two great minds were lost when Friedrich Nietzsche and Oscar Wilde died. British archaeologist Sir Arthur Evans began excavating the magnificent palace at Knossos, Crete.

➤ Read Sigmund Freud's Star Profile on page 17.

CAPRICORN

From January 01, 0:00 through January 20, 11:32

The Practical Adventurer

Your strong work ethic and sense of morality may have colored everything you have done throughout your life, January Capricorn of 1900. Even as a child, it is likely that you were diligent and studious, and only played with the other children after you had finished your homework and done your household chores. Around the time you were born, thousands in India were suffering due to widespread famine. Stories of such tragedies may have made you acutely aware of other, less-fortunate souls in the world. As a result, you probably never took things for granted, and always remained thankful for all that you had.

You understood early on that setting your goals and working hard were the best ways to earn security and prosperity. With your lively curiosity and ambitious streak, you may have chosen work that introduced you to distant cultures in some way. Even if you've never visited a foreign land, you've surely availed yourself of every opportunity to meet people from different backgrounds, or to read adventure books and travel guides.

Single-minded, focused, and determined, it's likely that you've always had relentless physical energy that enabled you to work hard—although the resulting long hours may have left you little time for fun. When you did take time off work, you were probably attracted to physical activities like running, walking, or climbing, rather than to mental pursuits.

Your ideal partner was someone who you could depend on through thick and thin and who would think the world of you regardless of your shortcomings. Fair-minded and loving, you'd have given the same unconditional love in return. Those with whom you share hard-working values are Pisceans, Taureans, Virgos, and Scorpios.

Your greatest challenge is putting your love of adventure to good use in practical activities. Your secret desire to conquer the world (or at least a small part of it) has always been the motivating force in your life, and your greatest strength has been the ability to pass that desire on to future generations, who would follow your example and carve out their own lasting niche.

AQUARIUS

From January 20, 11:33 through February 19, 2:00

The Determined Crusader

As a 1900 Aquarius, you were born just as the discontented Chinese sparked the Boxer Rebellion in China. The assertive spirit and belief in equal treatment seen in that event echoes your innate character, and hearing stories about it when you were young may have helped to solidify that part of your spirit early in your life.

Progressive, idealistic, and opinionated, you were raised during a time noted for political unrest and social reform in a variety of ways. This may have had a profound effect on your own convictions about human rights and decency, and your parents may have encouraged you to voice such concerns. In fact, you may have spent the greater part of your life trying to right the wrongs of others, even if only in a small and private way. At times, you can have almost a missionary zeal about instilling those beliefs in others, and the idea that everyone should respect human values probably made a great difference to your choice of work and friends.

Although you may have strong opinions about many issues, you have not just been all talk. You've probably always worked hard for a cause when the opportunity arose, and this could have led to an occupation that involved teaching, organizational or legal work, or involvement with journalism or the media. Even if "saving the world" was just an avocation for you, you were probably no stranger to political rallies, and your signature may have been at the top of more than a few petitions.

Your ideal mate is someone who shares your views, or at least respects your right to voice them. You can be very romantic and loving, but your mind needs to be involved in any relationship, along with your heart. You may naturally gravitate to Ariens, Geminis, Librans, and Sagittarians.

You have the faith of your convictions and a strong determination to leave a mark on this world. Your greatest challenge is to give the other person a chance to say what is on his or her mind. You're a crusader, and whether you've changed the world in large ways or small, you've certainly made a difference, and that is your true strength.

➤ Read about your Chinese Astrological sign on page 838. ➤ Read about your Personal Planets on page 826. ➤ Read about your personal Mystical Card on page 856.

CAPRICORN
Your Personal Planets

YOUR LOVE POTENTIAL
Venus in Aquarius, Jan. 01, 0:00 - Jan. 20, 1:38
Venus in Pisces, Jan. 20, 1:39 - Jan. 20, 11:32

YOUR DRIVE AND AMBITION
Mars in Capricorn, Jan. 01, 0:00 - Jan. 20, 11:32

YOUR LUCK MAGNETISM
Jupiter in Sagittarius, Jan. 01, 0:00 - Jan. 20, 11:32

World Events

Jan. 5 – Irish nationalist leader John Edward Redmond calls for a revolt against British rule.
Jan. 14 – Puccini's opera *Tosca* opens in Rome.

The international arbitration court at The Hague

AQUARIUS
Your Personal Planets

YOUR LOVE POTENTIAL
Venus in Pisces, Jan. 20, 11:33 - Feb. 13, 14:07
Venus in Aries, Feb. 13, 14:08 - Feb. 19, 2:00

YOUR DRIVE AND AMBITION
Mars in Capricorn, Jan. 20, 11:33 - Jan. 21, 18:50
Mars in Aquarius, Jan. 21, 18:51 - Feb. 19, 2:00

YOUR LUCK MAGNETISM
Jupiter in Sagittarius, Jan. 20, 11:33 - Feb. 19, 2:00

World Events

Feb. 6 – In Holland, the international arbitration court is created at The Hague.
Feb. 15 – The British threaten to use African natives in the Boer War.

1900

PISCES
Your Personal Planets

YOUR LOVE POTENTIAL

Venus in Aries, Feb. 19, 2:01 - Mar. 10, 18:07
Venus in Taurus, Mar. 10, 18:08 - Mar. 21, 1:38

YOUR DRIVE AND AMBITION

Mars in Aquarius, Feb. 19, 2:01 - Feb. 28, 22:14
Mars in Pisces, Feb. 28, 22:15 - Mar. 21, 1:38

YOUR LUCK MAGNETISM

Jupiter in Sagittarius, Feb. 19, 2:01 - Mar. 21, 1:38

World Events

Feb. 22 – Spanish film director and Surrealist Luis Buñuel is born.

Mar. 9 – In Germany, women petition the Reichstag for the right to take university entrance exams.

A ticket to the Paris Universal Exposition

ARIES
Your Personal Planets

YOUR LOVE POTENTIAL

Venus in Taurus, Mar. 21, 1:39 - Apr. 06, 4:14
Venus in Gemini, Apr. 06, 4:15 - Apr. 20, 13:26

YOUR DRIVE AND AMBITION

Mars in Pisces, Mar. 21, 1:39 - Apr. 08, 3:57
Mars in Aries, Apr. 08, 3:58 - Apr. 20, 13:26

YOUR LUCK MAGNETISM

Jupiter in Sagittarius, Mar. 21, 1:39 - Apr. 20, 13:26

World Events

Apr. 2 – In New York, the Automobile Club announces plans for a transcontinental roadway.

Apr. 14 – The Paris Universal Exposition, representing over forty countries, opens its gates to the public.

12

PISCES
From February 19, 2:01 through March 21, 1:38

The Good-Natured Dreamer

You may have been born with a deep compassion for the plight of others, Pisces of 1900. Around the time you arrived, workers in Great Britain united to form the Labour Party, giving them a voice in government for the first time. This signaled a trend that continued as you grew up, which might have deepened your empathy for those who were struggling against the status quo.

With your idealistic soul, you may have had the greatest admiration for those who pulled themselves up by their bootstraps. The novels of Charles Dickens could have been staples of your childhood and his own life the model of the kind of life you admired most. Your generous nature may have caused you to share what you had with everyone around you. As a result, you were probably ready with a helping hand whenever your advice was sought. As you matured, you may have used your keen intuition to spot those who really needed your help, but no matter whom you met, you'd always have retained your innate optimism.

You probably felt most at home devouring literature, listening to music, and admiring works of art, adding to an atmosphere that you found inspiring and uplifting. Even when wars and difficult economic times interrupted everyday life, reminding you that life isn't always fair or pleasant, you probably made it through the rough times because of your faith in humanity. You may have passed that message on to your colleagues, friends, and family, and it would have set you apart from others more cynical than yourself.

In relationships you sought someone who could be both romantic and spontaneous, yet who could bring you down to earth when you needed to attend to the practical matters of life. Those who are most likely to share your outlook are Taureans, Cancerians, Scorpios, and Capricorns.

Distinguishing between pipe dreams and what you can really achieve in life is your greatest challenge. Your strength is your unending belief that the goodness in people will always shine through. With that sense of faith and hope leading your way in life, you'd have made a lasting impression on everyone you met.

ARIES
From March 21, 1:39 through April 20, 13:26

The Enthusiastic Achiever

A confident self-starter with an entrepreneurial spirit, you might have grown up feeling that you could achieve just about anything you wanted, Aries of 1900. Your role models may have been the individuals who were at the helm of the huge corporations that were becoming enormously successful and profitable in your youth, and you may have hoped that you too could achieve the dream of financial success through persistence, hard work, and taking risks.

Around the time you were born, the World's Fair opened in Paris, France, ushering in the new century with spectacular displays of modern technology. Hearing about such marvels when you were a child may have made you dream of exploring the world and meeting exotic people. Since long-distance travel was difficult for most people in the early part of the twentieth century, these dreams could have guided you instead toward a profession where traveling plays a pivotal role.

Naturally enthusiastic, assertive, and driven, you may have dedicated your life to getting ahead, and you rarely looked back. You're more likely than most to have owned your own business. You may have found yourself a difficult person to work for, however, as a certain amount of impatience goes with your drive. It's likely that living through the Great Depression of the 1930s reinforced your perseverance even when your plans were frustrated.

In relationships you may have been bored easily, so your partner needed to share your love of travel, adventure, and variety. You may have a tough veneer, but underneath it you like having someone with whom you can share your life. Your ideal match is with Geminis, Leos, Sagittarians, or Aquarians.

Although you love starting new projects, you may not always be good at seeing them through. Your greatest challenge is to finish what you start, especially when the reality proves to be more ordinary than the dream. Your strength lies in tapping your great store of enthusiasm to renew your purpose. When you draw on that positive energy, even the simplest tasks have the mark of your pioneering individuality clearly stamped on them.

➤ Read about your Chinese Astrological sign on page 838. ➤ Read about your Personal Planets on page 826. ➤ Read about your personal Mystical Card on page 856.

TAURUS

From April 20, 13:27 through May 21, 13:16

The Affectionate Provider

As a Taurus of 1900, you entered the world at a turning point in history—the Austrian Emperor Franz Joseph I reasserted his alliance with German Kaiser Wilhelm II at around this time. The effects of this pact, which ultimately led to the divisions of world power, may have caused you to grow up feeling that danger was always on the horizon. As a result, feeling safe and secure may have been a high priority for you, and taking charge of your life the motivating force in most of your major decisions.

Gentle, steady, and determined, it's likely that you focused on finding someone with whom to share your life who could work hard, earn well, and enjoy raising a family. You may not have thought twice about leaving the place you called home in order to be with this person—especially if it also brought the promise of security and affluence. It's likely that you lived in several places throughout your adult life, following positions that netted your household the highest returns.

While you may have seemed set in your ways to those who knew you casually, in actuality you probably never hesitated to rearrange things to accommodate those who meant the most to you. If you had to provide for your family, you never even minded uninteresting jobs. As long as you were doing something that involved other people, you were never bored. In the end, taking care of those around you always came first, and the times you spent with your family were the ones you savored the most.

In love relationships, you can be warm and affectionate and, above all, provide a loving and secure environment. You may look for someone who tells you how important you are, as you can sometimes grow insecure if you do not hear the words often enough. You're usually most compatible with Cancerians, Virgos, Capricorns, and Pisceans.

Your challenge is to trust in the future, as otherwise your obsession with material security might overtake your life. Since you never know what life has in store, your strength is your ability to give and receive love, which has probably helped you through the darkest moments.

GEMINI

From May 21, 13:17 through June 21, 21:39

The Balanced Communicator

A defining moment in history occurred near the date of your birth, Gemini of 1900, with the founding of the International Ladies' Garment Workers' Union on New York's Lower East Side. Representing 2,300 workers in New York, Newark, Philadelphia, and Baltimore, the ILGWU paved the way for women to speak out loud and clear, making for a social climate that may have enhanced your innate belief that everyone's voice needs to be heard.

Restless, high-strung, and certainly talkative, you probably sought out friendships with people who were different from yourself, something that gave you a good education and an objective and fair perspective on the world. In turn, you probably had an opinion on everything and loved nothing more than a good debate with friends, family, and colleagues. You may have put your curious nature to work through a career in writing, teaching, or any job that encouraged research and communication.

Keeping abreast of current events may have been important to you, and going to the movies probably became a passion. From the newsreels that accompanied every feature to dramatizations of historical events and your favorite novels, you may have loved them all. Like many others born at the beginning of the new century, you might have had dreams about running away, changing your name, and becoming a star of the "silver screen."

In love relationships you could be most satisfied with a companion who provides the right blend of patience (listening intently to your every word) and stimulating repartee. While you love romance, having a true friendship with your partner, one that allows the two of you to agree as well as disagree, makes your relationships work best. The most ideal partnerships you can have will be with Leos, Librans, Aquarians, and Ariens.

Since you developed strong opinions, your greatest challenge is to remember to listen to others, and even to admit that you might be mistaken from time to time. Your strength comes from the fact that you are a truly fair-minded person. When you make a commitment, you're an extraordinarily loyal person as well.

➤ Read about your Chinese Astrological sign on page 838. ➤ Read about your Personal Planets on page 826. ➤ Read about your personal Mystical Card on page 856.

TAURUS
Your Personal Planets

YOUR LOVE POTENTIAL
Venus in Gemini, Apr. 20, 13:27 - May 05, 15:45
Venus in Cancer, May 05, 15:46 - May 21, 13:16

YOUR DRIVE AND AMBITION
Mars in Aries, Apr. 20, 13:27 - May 17, 9:04
Mars in Taurus, May 17, 9:05 - May 21, 13:16

YOUR LUCK MAGNETISM
Jupiter in Sagittarius, Apr. 20, 13:27 - May 21, 13:16

World Events

May 11 – After twenty-three rounds, James Jeffries knocks out James J. Corbett to retain the world heavyweight championship.

May 17 – In South Africa, British troops relieve Maj. Gen. Robert Baden-Powell at Mafeking, under siege since October 13, 1899.

The siege of Mafeking, South Africa

GEMINI
Your Personal Planets

YOUR LOVE POTENTIAL
Venus in Cancer, May 21, 13:17 - June 21, 21:39

YOUR DRIVE AND AMBITION
Mars in Taurus, May 21, 13:17 - June 21, 21:39

YOUR LUCK MAGNETISM
Jupiter in Sagittarius, May 21, 13:17 - June 21, 21:39

World Events

May 24 – Britain annexes the South African Orange Free State.

June 1 – In China, Boxer rebels conquer the key city of Tientsin.

CANCER

Your Personal Planets

YOUR LOVE POTENTIAL

Venus in Cancer, June 21, 21:40 - July 23, 8:35

YOUR DRIVE AND AMBITION

Mars in Taurus, June 21, 21:40 - June 27, 9:20
Mars in Gemini, June 27, 9:21 - July 23, 8:35

YOUR LUCK MAGNETISM

Jupiter in Sagittarius, June 21, 21:40 - July 23, 8:35

World Events

June 21 – General MacArthur offers amnesty to the Filipino rebels after their uprising.

July 9 – The British Parliament accepts the Commonwealth of Australia Act, uniting the Australian colonies under a federal government.

Peking ruins after Boxer Rebellion

LEO

Your Personal Planets

YOUR LOVE POTENTIAL

Venus in Cancer, July 23, 8:36 - Aug. 23, 15:19

YOUR DRIVE AND AMBITION

Mars in Gemini, July 23, 8:36 - Aug. 10, 1:14
Mars in Cancer, Aug. 10, 1:15 - Aug. 23, 15:19

YOUR LUCK MAGNETISM

Jupiter in Sagittarius, July 23, 8:36 - Aug. 23, 15:19

World Events

Aug. 5 – Anti-Jewish riots break out in Odessa, Russia.

Aug. 14 – International forces enter Peking, raising the fifty-six day siege of the Boxer rebels.

CANCER

From June 21, 21:40 through July 23, 8:35

The Creative Homebody

You were born at a time when the miracles of mass transit and around-the-world travel were fast becoming a reality, Cancer of 1900. Around the time you arrived, the first airship, built by the German Count Ferdinand von Zeppelin, made its maiden voyage (at a blazing fourteen miles an hour)—just one day after the grand opening of the Paris Subway. Events of this type made life exciting when you were growing up, and, like many children of your day, you may have dreamed of traveling the world and perhaps even living in far-away places.

Sentimental, kind, and often insecure, you may have shied away from anything competitive so that you could do things at your own pace. You may even have yearned for someone to take care of you so that you could indulge small passions such as creating gourmet meals or reading the futuristic novels of Jules Verne or H. G. Wells. Although you probably craved a secure lifestyle, you may have wanted a private escape-hatch where life was less ordinary and a bit more dramatic.

Your creative flair would have served you well if you followed the path of an artist or designer, or even if you just made crafts or clothes for yourself or your family. You've always known how to dress to get just the right effect, and may have favored a somewhat "daring" look that promoted your individuality on the outside and hid your shyness underneath.

In love, your ideal mate was probably someone who, like you, cherished romantic evenings filled with candlelit dinners, dim lights, and soft mood music. You loved taking care of those closest to you, and even when you had to be away from them, you always let them know that they were your first priority. The best relationships you can have are with Virgos, Scorpios, Pisceans, and Taureans.

You are a homebody at heart, and your greatest challenge is to maintain an independent streak while having a family you can call your own. Your warmth, caring, and capacity for love are your ultimate strengths, and it is through that commitment that you have always been able to move mountains, even if you did stay close to home.

LEO

From July 23, 8:36 through August 23, 15:19

The Dramatic Perfectionist

The British Parliament passed important legislation around the time you were born, Leo of 1900, that aimed to modernize the work environment by outlawing child labor, enhancing railway safety, and enacting workmen's compensation to protect workers who suffered injuries on the job. Hearing about such reforms when you were a child may have enhanced your natural inclination to favor the underdog. Although you may seem stubborn by some people's standards, whenever you applied your unyielding ways to a favorite cause, it's likely that everyone knew the job would get done in record time, and that those working for you would always know who was in charge.

You are probably known for your efficiency and detailed approach to life. You may have strived for perfection both professionally and personally, and even if you happened to find yourself between paying jobs, you'd always find something interesting and creative to do with your time.

As a Leo, you may have been most passionate about your love of the dramatic arts, and it's likely that you enjoyed spending your free time listening to music from classical to contemporary, going to the theater, or attending the ballet. Even in the 1930s, when money may have been tight, you probably satisfied your love of drama by going to the movies whenever you could, and getting lost in the romance of the silver screen.

Passionate, caring, and independent, you may have tried to juggle career, home and family at a time when few people would dream of such a thing. What is most important to you in a relationship is that your partner respects you for who you are and for the work that you do. In general, you'd be most compatible with Librans, Sagittarians, Ariens, and Geminis.

Deeply committed to family and friends, your greatest strength is finding the time for those who mean the most to you, while never letting down those who rely on you to champion their cause. Because you would never attempt anything unless you could do it perfectly, your greatest challenge is to find a way to be someone to everyone and have a little left over just for yourself.

➤ Read about your Chinese Astrological sign on page 838. ➤ Read about your Personal Planets on page 826. ➤ Read about your personal Mystical Card on page 856.

VIRGO
From August 23, 15:20 through September 23, 12:19

The Modest Educator

You may have found it difficult to comprehend the inhumanity and unkindness that you've seen in the world throughout the course of your life, Virgo of 1900. Yet, as critical as you can be about the way some people act, you probably still managed to be hopeful and optimistic about their ability to change. This may have led you to dedicate a good part of your time, and possibly your life, to education, healing, or the clergy—areas where you could make a difference and help things change for the better.

This optimism and deep compassion may have had its roots in a major event that occupied everyone's attention around the time you were born—the acquittal of Captain Alfred Dreyfus, whose "crimes" had been fabricated by anti-Semites in the French army. Although hearing stories about the case may have angered you when you were a child, it also could have reinforced your faith that people would always be called to account for their wrongdoings.

Sharp-minded and detail-oriented, you may have chosen to use your writing and teaching skills to help you spread the word about the values to which you aspire. Over your lifetime, it's likely that the slow but steady movement toward human rights and equality of opportunity gave you reason for hope, and you probably contributed your talents to aid such changes. No doubt you also encouraged those close to you to be model citizens and to treat people fairly.

Devoted yet practical, you probably formed lasting relationships with those who shared your values. You may have wanted someone in your life who was loving and attentive but who also extended tolerance and compassion to the world at large. You may be most compatible with Scorpios, Capricorns, and Taureans—however, home-loving Cancerians could be those whose values mesh with yours the best.

Your greatest challenge is to inspire people to develop the best within them. Despite your modesty, you are always at your best when utilizing your unique mentoring skills and sharing your life experiences with others. All whose lives you've touched will surely find them better for the experience.

LIBRA
From September 23, 12:20 through October 23, 20:54

The Engaging Persuader

Libra of 1900, around the time you were born, an alliance was formed between Germany and Great Britain to keep Chinese ports open for world trade. Later, you may have seen this as an appalling example of colonialism or an inspired attempt at peacemaking—or perhaps you had a hard time making up your mind which way you saw it. Librans tend to see both sides of an issue, which could be why even unsuccessful attempts at peacemaking, like the League of Nations after World War I, may have reaffirmed your belief that diplomacy and patience can bring people together.

You may be objective and fair-minded, with an innate talent for helping people work out their problems simply by listening and paying attention to them. You might have used your gift for words and your engaging manner in a career as a negotiator, or you may have worked on a personal level by helping people learn how to negotiate with and talk to each other.

Your charming manner and ability to make people listen could also have served you well as a professional sales person, especially in any industry that specializes in aesthetics and design. As fashion trends changed rapidly from the indulgent 1920s to the conservative thirties and forties, no doubt you were ahead of the curve and always looking good. You probably never minded putting in extra hours if you enjoyed the work, and never minded keeping things beautiful and harmonious on the home front either.

In relationships, you may always have wanted to fall in love and live happily ever after, and at times you may set aside your own desires to let your partner lead the way. The art of compromise comes easily to you, especially when it means preserving your relationship. You can be most comfortable with Sagittarians, Aquarians, Geminis, and Leos.

Your greatest challenge is to extend yourself beyond what is easy, to work just a little harder, and to communicate a little better. Your greatest strength is your love of helping people solve their problems. By helping people understand each other, you might not have changed the world, but you'd certainly have made a difference.

➤ Read about your Chinese Astrological sign on page 838. ➤ Read about your Personal Planets on page 826. ➤ Read about your personal Mystical Card on page 856.

VIRGO
Your Personal Planets

YOUR LOVE POTENTIAL
Venus in Cancer, Aug. 23, 15:20 - Sept. 08, 20:54
Venus in Leo, Sept. 08, 20:55 - Sept. 23, 12:19
YOUR DRIVE AND AMBITION
Mars in Cancer, Aug. 23, 15:20 - Sept. 23, 12:19
YOUR LUCK MAGNETISM
Jupiter in Sagittarius, Aug. 23, 15:20 - Sept. 23, 12:19

World Events

Aug. 25 - German philosopher Friedrich Nietzsche, author of *The Birth of Tragedy*, dies.
Sept. 8 - A hurricane sweeps through Galveston, Texas, claiming an estimated 8,000 lives.

Death of German philosopher Friedrich Nietzsche

LIBRA
Your Personal Planets

YOUR LOVE POTENTIAL
Venus in Leo, Sept. 23, 12:20 - Oct. 08, 13:35
Venus in Virgo, Oct. 08, 13:36 - Oct. 23, 20:54
YOUR DRIVE AND AMBITION
Mars in Cancer, Sept. 23, 12:20 - Sept. 26, 18:07
Mars in Leo, Sept. 26, 18:08 - Oct. 23, 20:54
YOUR LUCK MAGNETISM
Jupiter in Sagittarius, Sept. 23, 12:20 - Oct. 23, 20:54

World Events

Sept. 27 - In Paris, the International Socialist Congress ends.
Oct. 1 - The German Reichstag passes a Compensation Act which protects workers in case of accident or illness.

1900

SCORPIO
Your Personal Planets

YOUR LOVE POTENTIAL
Venus in Virgo, Oct. 23, 20:55 - Nov. 03, 21:32
Venus in Libra, Nov. 03, 21:33 - Nov. 22, 17:47

YOUR DRIVE AND AMBITION
Mars in Leo, Oct. 23, 20:55 - Nov. 22, 17:47

YOUR LUCK MAGNETISM
Jupiter in Sagittarius, Oct. 23, 20:55 - Nov. 22, 17:47

World Events

Nov. 5 - The Cuban constitutional convention opens in Havana.

Nov. 14 - American composer Aaron Copland is born.

Death of Oscar Wilde, British author of gothic novel, "The Picture of Dorian Grey"

SAGITTARIUS
Your Personal Planets

YOUR LOVE POTENTIAL
Venus in Libra, Nov. 22, 17:48 - Nov. 28, 21:54
Venus in Scorpio, Nov. 28, 21:55 - Dec. 22, 6:41

YOUR DRIVE AND AMBITION
Mars in Leo, Nov. 22, 17:48 - Nov. 23, 8:40
Mars in Virgo, Nov. 23, 8:41 - Dec. 22, 6:41

YOUR LUCK MAGNETISM
Jupiter in Sagittarius, Nov. 22, 17:48 - Dec. 22, 6:41

World Events

Nov. 30 - British author and playwright Oscar Wilde dies in exile in Paris.

Dec. 14 - Physicist Max Planck presents his quantum theory to the German Society of Physics in Berlin.

16

SCORPIO
From October 23, 20:55 through November 22, 17:47

The Determined Detective

As a Scorpio of 1900, you can be determined, passionate, and single-minded—qualities you may have shared with the team of William McKinley and Theodore Roosevelt, who won the U.S. presidential election around the time you were born. No matter where you grew up, stories of the heroic Teddy Roosevelt, famous for leading the Rough Riders in the Spanish-American War, may have inspired you, enhancing your own adventurous spirit and validating your desire to win at whatever you tried.

Your love of learning about everyone and everything around you probably extends to delving into the workings of the human mind, and you may have been fascinated by the intriguing psychological theories that became part of popular culture as you grew up. Your ability to assess other people's personalities may also have been an asset in the business world. Finance, banking, and other high-stakes endeavors could have been a welcome challenge that also brought financial rewards. Whatever work you chose, it's likely that its most important requirement was providing challenge and competition—both of which you may thrive on.

Your hobbies may have included reading detective stories or solving crossword puzzles. You might even have played detective yourself, always figuring out what those close to you were conjuring up. But you'd probably let them surprise you anyway so you wouldn't spoil their fun. You always demanded quality from your family and friends, and you provided them with great adventures in return.

With an intense love of life, you can be deeply passionate and do not like being idle. You may want a mate who is calm and serene and yet still loves adventurous, physical activities that you could do together. Your most harmonious relationships are with Capricorns, Pisceans, Cancerians, and Virgos.

With so much energy to burn, your life challenge centered on keeping yourself physically and mentally active without overdoing things. By utilizing your fierce determination to succeed at whatever you did, it's likely that you were always a powerful and influential force for good in people's lives.

SAGITTARIUS
From November 22, 17:48 through December 22, 6:41

The Daring Humorist

As a Sagittarius born in 1900, you can be a great competitor, and you may tend to "shoot for the Moon" in everything you do. You're probably passionate about learning, and have a great admiration for those who have made great scientific breakthroughs and discoveries, such as Max Planck, who presented his quantum theory to the Physics Society in Berlin around the time you were born.

While your brilliant mind at times wields a sharp tongue, it's likely that for the most part you are charming, witty, and engaging. A consummate performer, you probably love going to parties and you may be a great storyteller. And if you run out of stories, you just might spin a few tall tales out of your vivid imagination. The American humorist Mark Twain, who died in 1910, could easily have been a hero of yours. Like Twain, you'd have had the ability to command an audience, and your ease and rapport could have made you a wonderful teacher, performer, or writer.

With your strong sense of fairness, it's likely that you were a profound influence on others, especially children. You may not have traveled the world, but you instilled in those around you a passion for learning, and a zest for life. A loyal friend, you'd always have been someone who was fun to be around and a great companion for movies and sporting events.

In love relationships, you are an attentive partner who enjoys traveling, bicycling, or taking long walks with the one you love. You may have chosen someone who could make you laugh as well as give equal time to long-term planning and financial responsibilities. You are probably most at home with Aquarians, Ariens, Leos, and Librans.

You are athletic and daring, but you may find it impossible to "lose gracefully" at any game or competitive sport you engage in. Your greatest challenge is learning humility and accepting that while you don't always win, you emerge victorious just by trying. Your strength lies in bringing happiness to people who love being in your company. You may have been a great competitor but, in the end, you get a gold star for simply doing your best.

➤ Read about your Chinese Astrological sign on page 838. ➤ Read about your Personal Planets on page 826. ➤ Read about your personal Mystical Card on page 856.

CAPRICORN
From December 22, 6:42 through December 31, 23:59

The Silent Realist

As a December Capricorn of 1900, you may have taken on adult responsibilities at an early age. Perhaps you had to earn extra money by helping neighbors or doing errands for local merchants. It's likely that you learned to be pragmatic and realistic and felt that there were always people in the world worse off than you were.

Your awareness of life outside your childhood home could have stemmed from dinner-table discussions of political strife in places like South Africa, where during the very month you were born, British troops fought key battles with the Boers. As you matured, you may have added empathy to your list of commendable qualities as you heard bleak tales of peasants being mistreated in Russia.

Responsible and dedicated—yet intensely private—you may be known to others as the strong, silent type. You probably always had a select group of friends who often came to you for your good counsel and advice. If you parlayed that talent into work in fields like real estate, finance, insurance, or even the law, you could have had more clients than you could handle. Although you may not have been gregarious, or an aggressive go-getter, you were tenacious. You may prefer the tried and the true, the steady and the dependable, and probably stayed with any job you held over the course of many years.

Although you may seem reserved at first glance, you can really be quite affectionate and engaging, albeit more interested in being a friend and companion than anything else. Even so, once you fall in love your romantic nature and warmth come shining through. In general, those who make the most patient and understanding partners for you are Pisceans, Taureans, Virgos, and Scorpios.

You've probably had many occasions to be thankful that you could draw on your strength as a practical realist, making it possible for you to provide for your family even through tough economic times. Your greatest challenge is to firmly believe that you have made the right choices and, in moments of doubt, to be able to look over your life and be completely satisfied with all its accomplishments.

1900

CAPRICORN
Your Personal Planets

YOUR LOVE POTENTIAL
Venus in Scorpio, Dec. 22, 6:42 - Dec. 23, 7:47
Venus in Sagittarius, Dec. 23, 7:48 - Dec. 31, 23:59

YOUR DRIVE AND AMBITION
Mars in Virgo, Dec. 22, 6:42 - Dec. 31, 23:59

YOUR LUCK MAGNETISM
Jupiter in Sagittarius, Dec. 22, 6:42 - Dec. 31, 23:59

World Events

Dec. 23 – The Federal Party is formed in the Philippines, recognizing American sovereignty.

Dec. 26 – Race riots break out in Florida after a confrontation between a group of white women and a black woman.

Sigmund Freud
May 6, 1856 - September 23, 1939

SIGMUND FREUD
Taurus

Sigmund Freud, physician and neurologist, was the founder of psychoanalysis. He produced over twenty volumes of theory and clinical studies in which he originated concepts and terms, such as "libido," "subconscious," "inferiority complex," and many others that are now part of our culture.

With his Sun in determined and practical Taurus, Freud dedicated himself to developing his psychoanalytical techniques and to training his devotees in his methods. Uranus, the planet of radical ideas and brilliance, was also in Taurus and in close contact with Freud's Sun. He met with great antagonism to his theories and, later on, dissension among his own original circle. This is indicated by a stressful contact between his Jupiter (growth, expansion, learning) and his Mars (action/reaction). His Taurean stubbornness made him content to continue working alone in what he termed "splendid isolation."

With the investigative and profound sign of Scorpio rising in his chart, it is no surprise that Freud would be interested in unraveling the workings of the mind. It is interesting to note that both his Moon (emotions, the mother) and Saturn (discipline, the father) were in the eighth house. This is the natural home for Scorpio, and for issues of deep instinct, sex, death and, indeed, psychology. And it could hint at the basis of his Oedipal theory, which suggests that a child perceives the same sex parent to be his rival for the other parent's affection. Today, the "Oedipal complex" is regarded as more of an aberration than the norm. Perhaps it was really more of a personal issue.

With his Moon, the planet of emotion, in communicative Gemini, Freud recognized that everything people said, thought or dreamed had meaning, conscious or otherwise. Neptune, the planet of dreams and the subconscious, was placed in his fourth house of personal foundations. In what is probably his greatest work, *The Interpretation of Dreams*, he analyzed many of his own dreams recorded during a three-year period of self-analysis.

Neptune in its negative aspects can also indicate the irrational or hidden enemies. When he was three years old, his family was forced to leave their home in Freiberg, Moravia because of anti-Semitic riots. They eventually settled in Vienna. In 1938, the Germans occupied Austria, and Freud and his family fled to London, where he died in September of 1939.

➤ Read more about Freud in "Dreaming Through the Twentieth Century" on page 545.

1901

Consciousness Expanding: Neptune in Cancer

Creative and imaginative Neptune entered Cancer, sign of emotions and instinct, in July, and focus shifted toward fulfillment of ideals and mind expansion. Freud's *The Psychopathology of Everyday Life* was published, putting the idea of the Freudian "slip" into the collective consciousness. The study of psychology entered the public domain. The first purely abstract artist, Russian Wassily Kandinsky, showed his beautiful, moody paintings in Munich. Also in 1901, Constantin Stanislavsky, founder of the Moscow Art Theatre, formulated his revolutionary "Method" of acting, which requires actors to see and hear on stage as they do in real life. Stanislavsky stressed the importance of the actor's inner identification with the character and natural use of body and voice. With the dreamy planet Neptune shifting from intellectual Gemini into emotional Cancer, it was the perfect moment for art to turn inward.

There were several significant births this year. Clark Gable, the dashing star of Gone with the Wind, was born, as was Albert Giacometti, the Swiss-French painter and sculptor. On December 10, the first Nobel Peace Prize was jointly awarded to Jean Henri Dunant, the Swiss founder of the International Red Cross, and Frédéric Passy, the French founder of the International League of Peace. Andrew Carnegie announced that he would retire from business and spend the rest of his days giving away his fortune of more than $300 million. The influence of peace-loving Neptune's entry into sensitive Cancer affected both the worlds of art and commerce in powerful ways.

"La Danse Au Moulin Rouge" being painted by Toulouse-Lautrec

U.S. President McKinley was assassinated

Andrew Carnegie retires

WE ARE NOT ALONE

A young man in England made the first recorded contact with aliens in this year. In Bournbrook, a town in the West Midlands region of England, the young man encountered an object in a garden that resembled a "hut." He reported that it contained two small men, less than four feet tall, wearing khaki suits and helmets. He said that one of them walked toward him before turning around and returning inside. An electrical glow surrounded the object at its base and it whooshed as it launched suddenly into the sky.

THE VICTORIAN ERA ENDS

The death of Queen Victoria ended an era that had seen Britain rise to the pinnacle of world power. Filipinos rose against the U.S. annexation of their island nation, and the Boxer Rebellion in China was quelled by better-armed foreign forces. In Canada, Montreal was razed by a great fire. The U.S. stock market crashed, causing panic and a scurry to prevent total economic collapse. President McKinley was assassinated, and Theodore Roosevelt was sworn in as the new U.S. leader. J. P. Morgan formed the U.S. Steel Corporation, and Andrew Carnegie retired, to spend the rest of his life giving his fortune to charitable causes. An oil gusher in Texas promised a record output, exceeding America's need, and Oldsmobiles delivered the U.S. mail. In science, the source of radioactivity was discovered by Frenchman Henri Becquerel as atoms from the element uranium. Sweden awarded the first Nobel Prizes, to Wilhelm Roentgen, among others, for the discovery of X-rays. Marconi sent a telegraphic message across the Atlantic for the first time. The arts lost two brilliant geniuses in France's Henri Toulouse-Lautrec and Italy's Giuseppe Verdi.

18

➤ Read "Astrology Reigns Through the Ages: Powerful People Consulting the Stars" by Ronnie Grishman on page 25.

CAPRICORN

From January 01, 0:00 through January 20, 17:16

The Vulnerable Rock

Your reserved manner may often have fooled people into thinking you were aloof and uncaring, January Capricorn of 1901—something that could not be farther from the truth! Serious and persevering, it's likely that you're everyone's rock in times of need, yet still somewhat vulnerable. People may not know this as you probably rarely let anyone know when you are exhausted or your spirits are down.

During your birth month the New York Stock Exchange traded over two million shares for the first time, and oil fields discovered in Spindletop, Texas, established that state as the largest oil-producing region of the United States. These events changed the course of American business, adding another note to the message of progress and prosperity you would have heard when growing up in the century's first decade, no matter where you lived. Like all Capricorns, you may secretly have believed that if you spent your life putting in long, hard days, you'd find the pot of gold at the end of the rainbow!

It's likely that kindness and compassion always accompanied your reliability, and you may have worried when you were young that others couldn't get along without your help. Later in life, however, you may have been proud that you instilled independence into those close to you. Your professional choices more than likely targeted the world of finance and business, but you may also have flirted with the health and medical field since you care so deeply about others.

You may appear to be reticent, but behind closed doors you can be a most loving and ardent partner. You'd want someone who did not need constant attention, or endless reassurance of your love. Your best bet for an ideal partnership is with Pisces, Taurus, Virgo, or Scorpio.

With all you've done for others, your challenge has always been to make time for yourself and allow yourself to relax. Since you firmly believe that hard work will earn its just rewards, you should have had no problem allowing yourself to have fun as you matured. Seeing you having fun might actually be the greatest gift you can give to those you love.

AQUARIUS

From January 20, 17:17 through February 19, 7:44

The Inventive Rebel

As an Aquarius born in 1901, you came into the world at a time when Britons were mourning the loss of their beloved Queen Victoria, whose death (ending a sixty-year reign) marked the beginning of the end of the British Empire. Your life, too, may have been marked by its own transitions, with changes of jobs, location, or partners. Unlike those who are sentimental and long for the past, however, every time you faced change you forged ahead happily with no looking back.

Eccentric, inventive, and somewhat unpredictable, you can be wildly optimistic one day, and full of doubt the next. But you have never been dull, by any stretch of the imagination, and it's likely that you have been totally inspirational to those who needed a push in the right direction. In both your personal and professional life, you may always have been the one people looked up to and modeled themselves on.

You may have been a bit unconventional for the times in which you grew up. Due to a rebellious spirit, you might even have been labeled headstrong and excitable at school. Rather than be unhappy with that label, you may have used it to inspire and encourage others who were different or refused to accept things without questioning them. Not that you'd ever have thought that rules were made to be broken—you just may have believed it was appropriate to question the things that you found problematic.

In love, you probably want your partner to be your helpmate and friend, but in order for that to occur you would have to sit still long enough for the two of you to enjoy some quiet moments together! Of all the zodiacal signs, it's likely that you get along best with active Ariens, Geminis, Librans, and Sagittarians.

Perhaps your greatest challenge has been to harness the energy that has made you unable to stand in one place for very long. With eternal optimism and an eye toward the future, you probably reached a defining moment when you no longer needed to disrupt the status quo merely for the sake of trying something new. Once you did, you were more at peace, and could encourage others to be the same.

➤ Read about your Chinese Astrological sign on page 838. ➤ Read about your Personal Planets on page 826. ➤ Read about your personal Mystical Card on page 856.

1901

CAPRICORN
Your Personal Planets

YOUR LOVE POTENTIAL
Venus in Sagittarius, Jan. 01, 0:00 - Jan. 16, 11:28
Venus in Capricorn, Jan. 16, 11:29 - Jan. 20, 17:16

YOUR DRIVE AND AMBITION
Mars in Virgo, Jan. 01, 0:00 - Jan. 20, 17:16

YOUR LUCK MAGNETISM
Jupiter in Sagittarius, Jan. 01, 0:00 - Jan. 19, 8:32
Jupiter in Capricorn, Jan. 19, 8:33 - Jan. 20, 17:16

World Events

Jan. 1 – The Commonwealth of Australia is created.

Jan. 7 – In New York, trading on the Stock Exchange exceeds two million shares for the first time.

A scene from Chekhov's "Three Sisters"

AQUARIUS
Your Personal Planets

YOUR LOVE POTENTIAL
Venus in Capricorn, Jan. 20, 17:17 - Feb. 09, 13:06
Venus in Aquarius, Feb. 09, 13:07 - Feb. 19, 7:44

YOUR DRIVE AND AMBITION
Mars in Virgo, Jan. 20, 17:17 - Feb. 19, 7:44

YOUR LUCK MAGNETISM
Jupiter in Capricorn, Jan. 20, 17:17 - Feb. 19, 7:44

World Events

Jan. 23 – The first female intern is accepted in a Paris hospital.

Jan. 31 – Anton Chekhov's *Three Sisters* premières at the Moscow Art Theatre in Russia.

1901

PISCES
Your Personal Planets

YOUR LOVE POTENTIAL
Venus in Aquarius, Feb. 19, 7:45 - Mar. 05, 14:50
Venus in Pisces, Mar. 05, 14:51 - Mar. 21, 7:23

YOUR DRIVE AND AMBITION
Mars in Virgo, Feb. 19, 7:45 - Mar. 01, 19:27
Mars in Leo, Mar. 01, 19:28 - Mar. 21, 7:23

YOUR LUCK MAGNETISM
Jupiter in Capricorn, Feb. 19, 7:45 - Mar. 21, 7:23

World Events

Feb. 26 - Leaders of the Boxer Rebellion, Chi-Hsin and Hsu-Cheng-Yu, are executed in Peking.

Mar. 6 - In Bremen, Germany, an anarchist attempts to kill Kaiser Wilhelm II.

A graphic illustration of the time, depicting Boers starving in British concentration camps in South Africa

ARIES
Your Personal Planets

YOUR LOVE POTENTIAL
Venus in Pisces, Mar. 21, 7:24 - Mar. 29, 18:02
Venus in Aries, Mar. 29, 18:03 - Apr. 20, 19:13

YOUR DRIVE AND AMBITION
Mars in Leo, Mar. 21, 7:24 - Apr. 20, 19:13

YOUR LUCK MAGNETISM
Jupiter in Capricorn, Mar. 21, 7:24 - Apr. 20, 19:13

World Events

Mar. 23 - News reaches the rest of the world that Boers are starving in British concentration camps in South Africa.

Apr. 8 - In Belgium, the Congress of Social Democrats insists on the enforcement of universal suffrage.

PISCES
From February 19, 7:45 through March 21, 7:23

The Selfless Visionary

Caring, idealistic, and selfless almost to a fault, you may always have felt that your calling in life was to offer help whenever you sensed that it was needed, Pisces of 1901. And because it can mean a lot to you when somebody smiles and offers thanks for all that you've done for them, you probably also know another important secret—that helping others is truly the best way of helping yourself.

Perhaps it's no coincidence that American multi-millionaire Andrew Carnegie announced that he was retiring from business around the time you were born. Carnegie declared that he was becoming a philanthropist to give his fortune away. Although you may never have had Carnegie's vast wealth to work with, you probably shared his desire to provide for those less fortunate than yourself.

Even though you've dedicated a great deal of time to being an angel of mercy, you're probably still a dreamer at heart, and in your spare time you may have dreamed about taking a cruise ship to Europe, dining with royalty, or seeing an art exhibit in Paris. Those dreams may or may not have come true, but it's likely that you never stopped exercising your imagination, knowing that most of life's enjoyment comes from dreaming about the wonders you have yet to see. More than most Pisceans, you might have put this theory to the test by putting your energies into achieving at least some of your dreams.

You've probably always believed in love at first sight and, once you find someone who makes your heart skip a beat, chances are you'll be hooked for life. While you may hope that your romantic whimsy will be returned in kind, it's likely that your main concern is that the person of your dreams will be there to lean on in times of need. You might find something in every sign that is appealing, but those who may fit like a glove are Taurus, Cancer, Scorpio, and Capricorn.

Your challenge is to ask for help when you need it, so that you can continue serving others without draining your energies. Whether you are bringing a stray cat in from the rain or taking care of your family, your strength is your kind heart.

ARIES
From March 21, 7:24 through April 20, 19:13

The Venturesome Helper

Assertive and adventurous, you're probably ready to try anything once, Aries of 1901—daring yourself to go where others would not. A reflection of that attitude is found in a "shocking" event that happened around the time you were born: actors at the New York Music Academy were arrested for wearing costumes on Sunday! As a child, you probably played games in which you became the brave leader or dashing hero, rescuing those in distress.

While you can be competitive, you're also kind. You want to be respected for your integrity as well as your valor, and you'd never challenge someone you felt was not your equal or better. Seeing the world at war during much of your life may have reinforced your desire to do something both exceptional and humane. You may have dedicated your life to medicine, education, or politics, where you could leave your mark on the community in which you live. Whatever your profession, you'd have wanted to be recognized for doing something exemplary that no one before had ever attempted.

Although some may believe that you're oblivious to what other people think, you might actually need a great deal of approval, even admiration, especially from those you respect most. In fact, nothing can drain your boundless energy faster than a disapproving look from someone you admire. However, this trait may only have made you more sensitive to the feelings of others and helped you to be tactful and more respectful.

You may love the attention an intimate relationship brings, yet will also dote upon your partner in return. To make your relationships succeed, you may have worked hard to perfect the art of compromise, having learned the joys of giving and taking. Those who share your zest for life are Geminis, Leos, Sagittarians, and Aquarians.

You may seem to be full of fire and confidence when you charge into a room, but somewhere underneath it all you might still be a child waiting for approval. Your challenge is to learn humility and let someone else be first every once in a while. For you, the road to greatness lies in guiding others down that very same path.

► Read about your Chinese Astrological sign on page 838. ► Read about your Personal Planets on page 826. ► Read about your personal Mystical Card on page 856.

TAURUS

From April 20, 19:14 through May 21, 19:04

The Frugal Giver

Taurus of 1901, you might have been born believing that if you worked hard and kept a tight rein on the purse strings, you'd reap the rewards of financial prosperity and a secure life. The famine in India that claimed millions of lives around the time you were born could have impressed you very deeply when you heard about it as a child. It reflected an atmosphere that made you intent on finding security in your own life. Having developed an acute awareness of fiscal responsibility, you decided early in life that you would rather save prudently than spend foolishly.

Once you began to realize that the world could change at a moment's notice, you probably responded by looking for ways to control your own destiny. This led you to perfect the skills that helped you to be self-sufficient all your life and save what you earned.

The care you take with those close to you may always have guided your decisions and made you the best person to be around in tight situations. Although some may see your frugality as a lack of charity, this is far from true. Rather than give someone a fish, as the saying goes, you would rather teach them to fish so they can make do for themselves. You worked hard for what you earned, and while this may have made you a hard taskmaster, you also commanded the respect of your colleagues and the admiration of your family. Whether you're in charge or just part of the team, it's likely that you gave it everything you had and always turned in a job well done.

In love, you may show your emotions best with actions rather than words. Your favorite activity might be sharing a candlelit dinner for two and a movie, especially a romantic tearjerker where you can let your feelings show. Those with whom you can share your most intimate moments are Cancerians, Virgos, Capricorns, and Pisceans.

Probably your greatest challenge was learning to be more flexible, but once you had a chance to break free from habitual ruts, it's likely that you realized how great the rewards of change could actually be. Your desire to give your family a secure life is your greatest strength.

GEMINI

From May 21, 19:05 through June 22, 3:27

The Playful Companion

It's likely that your personality combines just the right blend of realistic outlook and vivid imagination to make your life both interesting and productive, Gemini of 1901. You might have loved having a steady job and a regular routine, but your eager curiosity may have led you to devour every mystery novel you could get your hands on. You could have felt a kinship with another 1901 Gemini—Anastasia, the daughter of Russian Tsar and Tsaritsa Nicholas and Alexandra. Later on, the mystery of whether Anastasia survived the 1917 Russian Revolution may have also been the type of romantic story that intrigued you.

You probably found a way to inject playfulness into everything you did, and you may never take life too seriously. What may have set you apart from your contemporaries was your ability to take ordinary circumstances and turn them into special events. You love being with children, and may have been a teacher or even the leader of a scout troop. You have a keen imagination and a wonderful way with words, and at some point you may even have flirted with creative writing.

Your home life had to have been a sparkling mixture of intellectual repartee and imaginative game playing. What you were most realistic about was being ready to offer your services to those in your community should the need ever arise.

In relationships, you love being in the company of someone with whom you can converse for hours, about any subject from politics to the latest movies. It's likely that your lifelong companion has been someone who has been able to support you when times became tough, and make you laugh in both good times and bad. You could be most compatible with Leos, Librans, and Ariens.

You probably like flitting from one activity to the next, something that may have prevented you from getting the best from your creative talents. Your challenge is to learn how to keep your versatility and curiosity from leading you into time-wasting distractions. Your strength is that, as talkative as you can be, you are also the most sympathetic listener and friend that anyone could ever have.

➤ Read about your Chinese Astrological sign on page 838. ➤ Read about your Personal Planets on page 826. ➤ Read about your personal Mystical Card on page 856.

1901

TAURUS
Your Personal Planets

YOUR LOVE POTENTIAL
Venus in Aries, Apr. 20, 19:14 - Apr. 22, 23:33
Venus in Taurus, Apr. 22, 23:34 - May 17, 7:33
Venus in Gemini, May 17, 7:34 - May 21, 19:04

YOUR DRIVE AND AMBITION
Mars in Leo, Apr. 20, 19:14 - May 11, 6:04
Mars in Virgo, May 11, 6:05 - May 21, 19:04

YOUR LUCK MAGNETISM
Jupiter in Capricorn, Apr. 20, 19:14 - May 21, 19:04

World Events

Apr. 29 – Jewish students clash with anti-Semites at the National University in Budapest.

Apr. 30 – In Manila, rebel leader Gen. Manuel Tinio surrenders to the U.S. army.

Queen Victoria's birthday, May 24, becomes a national holiday after her death

GEMINI
Your Personal Planets

YOUR LOVE POTENTIAL
Venus in Gemini, May 21, 19:05 - June 10, 17:36
Venus in Cancer, June 10, 17:37 - June 22, 3:27

YOUR DRIVE AND AMBITION
Mars in Virgo, May 21, 19:05 - June 22, 3:27

YOUR LUCK MAGNETISM
Jupiter in Capricorn, May 21, 19:05 - June 22, 3:27

World Events

June 12 – The Cuban Constitutional Convention votes sixteen to eleven to become a U.S. protectorate.

June 16 – Macedonian demonstrators in Sofia demand independence from Turkey.

1901

CANCER
Your Personal Planets

YOUR LOVE POTENTIAL
Venus in Cancer, June 22, 3:28 - July 05, 5:21
Venus in Leo, July 05, 5:22 - July 23, 14:23

YOUR DRIVE AND AMBITION
Mars in Virgo, June 22, 3:28 - July 13, 19:58
Mars in Libra, July 13, 19:59 - July 23, 14:23

YOUR LUCK MAGNETISM
Jupiter in Capricorn, June 22, 3:28 - July 23, 14:23

World Events

June 28 - The province of Manchuria rises in rebellion against Russian occupation.

July 12 - Members of the German Reichstag fail to force through a bill to outlaw dueling.

The Russian painter, Wassily Kandinsky

LEO
Your Personal Planets

YOUR LOVE POTENTIAL
Venus in Leo, July 23, 14:24 - July 29, 19:12
Venus in Virgo, July 29, 19:13 - Aug. 23, 12:32
Venus in Libra, Aug. 23, 12:33 - Aug. 23, 21:07

YOUR DRIVE AND AMBITION
Mars in Libra, July 23, 14:24 - Aug. 23, 21:07

YOUR LUCK MAGNETISM
Jupiter in Capricorn, July 23, 14:24 - Aug. 23, 21:07

World Events

July 31 - An uprising against President Castro in Venezuela gains 5,000 followers.

Aug. 15 - The paintings of Wassily Kandinsky go on display in Munich.

CANCER
From June 22, 3:28 through July 23, 14:23

The Emotional Ascetic

Nothing is more important to your sign than home and family, but you, Cancer of 1901, would probably be completely lost without the support of those you love. Emotional, moody, and shy, you may always have yearned for a simple life that included spending time with family or getting away quietly on your own. Near the time you were born, the liner *Deutschland* crossed the Atlantic in a record-breaking five-and-a-half days—an apt metaphor for someone like yourself, who has been known to move with record-breaking speed to a favorite retreat.

Music probably played an important part in your life, and your home may have been filled with rhythms as diverse as Scott Joplin's ragtime and Czech composer Antonin Dvoràk's opera *Rusalka*—both written in the year you were born. Dvoràk's piece, based on Hans Christian Andersen's *The Little Mermaid*, about a sea maiden who falls in love with a real man, might almost echo your own struggle of wanting to live in the world and, at the same time, escape from it.

The simple things in life probably appeal to you most, and situations in which you help or serve others have always been your forte. You'd have been just as comfortable in the role of caregiver as you would in the role of a cook who prepares lavish meals. In fact, inviting guests over for a home-cooked meal and pleasant conversation could be a favorite pastime.

Loyal, attentive, and affectionate, you may have perfected the art of nurturing those you love. In return, you'd want a partner who was as trustworthy, responsible, and sensitive to your emotional needs as you were to theirs. Your best chance for a perfect partnership probably lies with Virgos, Scorpios, Pisceans, and Taureans.

While you may be emotional and introverted, these have actually been your best and strongest qualities, the ones that kept you on track and on course. What you found most challenging is learning to feel as comfortable in social situations with new friends as you did with old ones. But finding the happy medium between your strengths and your challenges has always brought you the greatest rewards.

LEO
From July 23, 14:24 through August 23, 21:07

The Flamboyant Friend

You can be forceful and confident, Leo of 1901, and you've probably always been sure of yourself and your accomplishments. Extroverted, and with tastes that some might consider flamboyant, you may have had people wondering if there's a touch of royalty in your blood. You certainly made that kind of impression wherever you went.

Throughout your life, it's likely that you have been fascinated by those with glamorous, wealthy lifestyles. As a child, you were probably captivated by stories of both real and mythical kings and queens, including British King Edward VII, whose title was changed to make him ruler "of the British dominions beyond the Seas" around the time you were born. Your hope that you too might one day obtain wealth and power may have made you an optimist, even while you were growing up on the brink of World War I.

It's likely that you're a natural live wire, and there was probably no stopping you whenever you had an attentive audience. You may have acted professionally, but even if you just "performed" around the house, you would always have loved getting attention, especially if you could make people laugh at the same time. You probably never missed a chance to go to the theater, and it's a sure bet that you were always at the head of the line whenever a new movie opened.

When you fell in love, you probably did it with the same intensity as you approached everything else in life. You had to be in a relationship with someone who was as passionate and romantic as you are and who shared the same dream of an active and creative life. Those with whom you can share tender moments can include Librans, Sagittarians, Ariens, and Geminis.

You may have been overly dramatic at times, but most who know you admire your exuberant nature, and know you to be a magnanimous and loyal friend. Your strongest point is that you find a bit of greatness in everyone you meet and in everything you do. Your challenge is to make whatever you do in life interesting and exciting without letting your love of high drama distract you from the practicalities of what needs to be done.

➤ Read about your Chinese Astrological sign on page 838. ➤ Read about your Personal Planets on page 826. ➤ Read about your personal Mystical Card on page 856.

VIRGO

From August 23, 21:08 through September 23, 18:08

The Committed Worker

You may see yourself as upstanding, honest, and hardworking, Virgo of 1901—and it's likely that's the way others see you too. You've probably never been comfortable with competition, as you'd be more interested in doing a job and doing it right than in winning or losing. A good home and people to love are the best rewards for your labors. Some may think you a bit dull, but they're not the people who know you well! Anyway, it's likely that you never wanted to be a leader or an innovator. To be an upstanding citizen and a role model for family and friends is enough for you.

It would have been difficult to escape the fact that you were born at a momentous time in history, when one American President, William McKinley, was assassinated, and his successor, Theodore Roosevelt, rose to greatness. The tenor of the times might have made your parents think that you were born for greatness. At some level you may have felt they were right, but you would also have understood that where greatness is concerned, wishing doesn't make it so, work does.

By believing in yourself and developing skills that could be put to good use, you probably worked hard to follow the path to success. It's likely that your superb abilities to organize and communicate helped you work yourself to the top in any situation. Because of this, you may have fulfilled that dream of greatness—at least in your own eyes.

In love, it's likely that you are fully involved and enthusiastic about helping your partner to become all they can be. You may be self-conscious and reserved in the outside world, but behind closed doors you can be affectionate and loving. In long-term relationships, you're probably most at ease with Scorpios, Capricorns, Taureans, and Cancerians.

Your greatest challenge is to be willing to explore new ways of thinking and doing things. Although falling back on what is safe and secure may work sometimes, times and people change. You are well rounded and accomplished, but your strongest trait is that once you commit yourself to anything you can be counted on to see it through to the end.

LIBRA

From September 23, 18:09 through October 24, 2:45

The Confident Compromiser

Walk into a room, Libra of 1901, and heads turn. Just say a word or two, and smile, and you have people eating from your hand. You were probably born knowing that you're charming and attractive, and it's no accident that you take great pride in the way you look, as you can be thoroughly convinced that a winning image is the key to success. Your ability to be persuasive would have made work in fields like sales, public relations, or insurance natural for you.

Fair-minded and objective, it's likely that you've never made decisions or taken actions that make distinctions of class, religion, or race. Around the time you were born, U.S. President Theodore Roosevelt raised eyebrows by inviting Booker T. Washington—whose book *Up From Slavery* was published that very same year—to the White House. No matter where you lived, growing up in an era firmly stamped with Teddy Roosevelt's character probably helped to reinforce your belief in racial equality.

As confident an image as you project, you can still be put off balance sometimes, especially if you have to make a decision that might make someone angry with you. More than anything, you need to be loved and admired, so when someone disagrees with you, it could send you into a tailspin. You'd probably rather take the time to ask everyone what they think, than risk being on the losing end of a decision.

In love relationships, you know exactly how to make someone feel special—as if he or she were the only one in the room. You love the feeling of being in love, and more than anything, you want a partner who, like yourself, is a romantic at heart. Those with whom you could have a special union include Sagittarians, Aquarians, Geminis, and Leos.

No matter how far you've come in life, your constant challenge has been to realize that you cannot please everyone, no matter how much you try. If someone disagrees with you, you should not take it personally, nor does it mean you are not loved and respected. Your gift is your faithful heart and honorable instincts, and, by following them, you'll almost always make the right choices.

➤ Read about your Chinese Astrological sign on page 838. ➤ Read about your Personal Planets on page 826. ➤ Read about your personal Mystical Card on page 856.

VIRGO
Your Personal Planets

YOUR LOVE POTENTIAL
Venus in Libra, Aug. 23, 21:08 - Sept. 17, 11:28
Venus in Scorpio, Sept. 17, 11:29 - Sept. 23, 18:08

YOUR DRIVE AND AMBITION
Mars in Libra, Aug. 23, 21:08 - Aug. 31, 18:12
Mars in Scorpio, Aug. 31, 18:13 - Sept. 23, 18:08

YOUR LUCK MAGNETISM
Jupiter in Capricorn, Aug. 23, 21:08 - Sept. 23, 18:08

World Events

Sept. 7 – The Boxer uprising is officially ended in China by a treaty signed with a dozen foreign powers.

Sept. 9 – The French artist Henri de Toulouse-Lautrec dies.

"La Danse Au Moulin Rouge" by Toulouse Lautrec

LIBRA
Your Personal Planets

YOUR LOVE POTENTIAL
Venus in Scorpio, Sept. 23, 18:09 - Oct. 12, 19:14
Venus in Sagittarius, Oct. 12, 19:15 - Oct. 24, 2:45

YOUR DRIVE AND AMBITION
Mars in Scorpio, Sept. 23, 18:09 - Oct. 14, 12:47
Mars in Sagittarius, Oct. 14, 12:48 - Oct. 24, 2:45

YOUR LUCK MAGNETISM
Jupiter in Capricorn, Sept. 23, 18:09 - Oct. 24, 2:45

World Events

Oct. 16 – U.S. President Theodore Roosevelt arouses controversy by inviting African American leader Booker T. Washington to the White House.

Oct. 20 – The Belgian Parliament establishes a fund to assist the unemployed.

1901

SCORPIO
Your Personal Planets

YOUR LOVE POTENTIAL
Venus in Sagittarius, Oct. 24, 2:46 - Nov. 07, 19:24
Venus in Capricorn, Nov. 07, 19:25 - Nov. 22, 23:40

YOUR DRIVE AND AMBITION
Mars in Sagittarius, Oct. 24, 2:46 - Nov. 22, 23:40

YOUR LUCK MAGNETISM
Jupiter in Capricorn, Oct. 24, 2:46 - Nov. 22, 23:40

World Events

Oct. 25 - After a public outcry, Colonial Sec. Joseph Chamberlain defends the British treatment of Boers in South African concentration camps.

Oct. 28 - In New Orleans thirty-four people are killed during race riots sparked by African American leader Booker T. Washington's visit to the White House.

Cartoon of Joseph Chamberlain, accused of cruel treatment of Boers

SAGITTARIUS
Your Personal Planets

YOUR LOVE POTENTIAL
Venus in Capricorn, Nov. 22, 23:41 - Dec. 05, 13:31
Venus in Aquarius, Dec. 05, 13:32 - Dec. 22, 12:36

YOUR DRIVE AND AMBITION
Mars in Sagittarius, Nov. 22, 23:41 - Nov. 24, 4:43
Mars in Capricorn, Nov. 24, 4:44 - Dec. 22, 12:36

YOUR LUCK MAGNETISM
Jupiter in Capricorn, Nov. 22, 23:41 - Dec. 22, 12:36

World Events

Dec. 10 - Nobel Prizes are awarded for the first time in physics, chemistry, medicine, literature and peace.

Dec. 21 - In Norway, women are allowed to vote in communal elections for the first time.

24

SCORPIO
From October 24, 2:46 through November 22, 23:40

The Competitive Explorer

Serious and persistent, you may have spent hours tucked away in libraries when you were growing up, reading books about explorers, inventors, scientists, or anyone who had the courage to make a contribution to society against all odds. You may even have dreamed about being one of these glorious heroes or heroines yourself, Scorpio of 1901, and may have planned your life around that goal.

Medical and scientific breakthroughs could hold a particular fascination for you, and you may have worked in or been associated with one of these fields. You have considerable financial skills, and may have helped raise money to fund your own research, or the research of others. It's not surprising to learn that, around the time you were born, Dr. J. E. Gillman, of Chicago, Illinois, unveiled the first X-ray treatment for breast cancer—one of the earliest attempts to treat the disease in this way.

Your competitive spirit and enthusiasm for breaking down barriers may have extended to the realm of spectator sports. Going to a tennis match, baseball game, or other athletic event where you could let your hair down, has probably been a favorite pastime. It's likely that you admire those who play professionally, and may follow their careers closely, even though you may have been less inclined to play those sports yourself.

Intense and passionate, you have a warm and caring heart and can easily express your love for someone directly, clearly, and with few words. You may value your personal relationships, but you must take care to work as hard at them as you do at everything else in your life. When it comes to sharing your most intimate moments, you are probably most comfortable with Capricorns, Pisceans, Cancerians, and Virgos.

Given the level of intensity with which you live your life, it's no wonder that you can find it difficult to relax sometimes. Thus, your main challenge is not to get caught up in thinking that you're playing for high stakes each and every time you commit yourself to something. Your ability to commit yourself wholeheartedly and to persevere is your finest quality.

SAGITTARIUS
From November 22, 23:41 through December 22, 12:36

The Principled Giver

You were born at an exciting moment in history, Sagittarius of 1901. Italian physicist Guglielmo Marconi had just sent wireless telegraphic messages to Newfoundland, laying the foundations for the invention of radio and effectively making the world smaller. This kind of "instant" long-distance communication, pioneered in the year you were born, is a natural fit to your wide-ranging interests.

Principled and ethical, you've probably always focused on staying informed about world events. Because of the vast store of knowledge you've acquired, it's likely that you're rarely at a loss for words. You may have developed strong opinions about almost anything from a new law just passed in your city to the present state of the environment. You've always been willing to champion a worthy cause and to work long hours to help it along. All of these qualities would have worked beautifully when you became active in community affairs.

It's likely that this inspired attitude carried over into your personal relationships and that your friends and family knew they could count on you, even at a moment's notice. Still, you were always one to enjoy laughing with those close to you, and whenever there was a social occasion you were often the first to arrive and the last to leave. This may have led to a little too much eating and drinking, so weight watching may have been something you became accustomed to early on.

A loving and generous partner, you're never boring, and are likely to spend more than you can afford on lavish presents for your loved ones. You may have looked for someone who could be your anchor—perhaps someone who'd show you how to enjoy life on a smaller budget. Those who best complement your adventurous personality are Aquarians, Ariens, Leos, and Librans.

Your greatest challenge is to enjoy spending quiet times with your loved ones, without feeling that you need to conjure up elaborate and costly recreational activities. Giving of yourself to those closest to you has always been the greatest gift you can offer. Giving is, after all, your greatest and best strength.

➤ Read about your Chinese Astrological sign on page 838. ➤ Read about your Personal Planets on page 826. ➤ Read about your personal Mystical Card on page 856.

CAPRICORN

From December 22, 12:37 through December 31, 23:59

The Diligent Mountain-Climber

Around the time you were born, December Capricorn of 1901, Norwegian women were celebrating the fact that on December 21, they voted for the first time in communal elections. Hearing about women tenaciously and diligently fighting for their rights around the world may have struck a chord with you as you reached adulthood. After all, few are as persevering and diligent as you can be.

Cautious, determined, and methodical, you have probably always been patient in reaching the goals you set for yourself. Before you took on a job, large or small, it was most important that you learned everything you could about it. While others may get lost in side trips on their way to the top, it's likely that you set your sights higher than the average person could reach and climbed straight up the ladder from day one. Some are happy with a small piece of the pie, but you never settled for anything less than the top of the mountain.

Steady and security-minded, you probably weren't comfortable taking the type of financial risks that bring windfalls to some—and bankruptcy to others. Because of that, you'd nearly always come out ahead, even if it meant watching your money mature in a safe but low interest bank account. You may even be one of those people who literally have money tucked under your mattress for a rainy day. As long as you're in charge of the checkbook and bank account, your household finances are in safe hands.

In love relationships you can be loyal and faithful, and you may accept nothing less in return. While you could believe in falling madly in love, it's likely that you'd want your partner to share the values, spending habits, and work ethic you have. Those best suited to share your life are Pisceans, Taureans, and Virgos.

Controlling every step of your life is a wonderful thought, but life often gets in the way of even the best laid plans. Your great challenge is to have an alternate plan to follow whenever you meet with a tough obstacle. Your strength is understanding that, as important as your goals may be, what you learn by pursuing them is what matters most.

1901

CAPRICORN
Your Personal Planets

YOUR LOVE POTENTIAL
Venus in Aquarius, Dec. 22, 12:37 - Dec. 31, 23:59

YOUR DRIVE AND AMBITION
Mars in Capricorn, Dec. 22, 12:37 - Dec. 31, 23:59

YOUR LUCK MAGNETISM
Jupiter in Capricorn, Dec. 22, 12:37 - Dec. 31, 23:59

World Events

Dec. 25 – In the battle at Tweefontein in South Africa, the Boers launch a surprise attack on the British.

Dec. 27 – German film star and screen legend Marlene Dietrich is born.

Woodrow Wilson and his bride, Edith in the Presidential election campaign of 1916

Special Feature
Astrology Reigns Through the Ages: Powerful People Consulting the Stars

by Ronnie Grishman

More than a century before President and Mrs. Reagan were faithfully consulting with their astrologer, earlier occupants of the White House were doing likewise. President Lincoln's wife, Mary Todd Lincoln, sought out the advice of astrologers to advance her husband's progress into the White House. Once Lincoln had indeed become President, Todd began attending seances, in addition to visiting astrologers. It's even said that she had been advised that the charts of certain cabinet members, particularly Secretary of the Treasury Salmon Chase and Secretary of State William Seward, looked "injurious" to her husband. Astrologer Cranston Laurie reported strange premonitions in the hours just before Lincoln was assassinated—premonitions that sadly turned out to be right on target.

Mrs. Woodrow Wilson was also guided by the stars. Madame Marcia Champney, Washington, D.C.'s foremost astrologer at the time, was Mrs.

Wilson's private advisor. It is said that not only Mrs. Wilson, but many of Capitol Hill's élite, visited Champney at her residence on R Street in Washington. Edith Galt, the future Mrs. Woodrow Wilson, was told by Champney: "I can assure you that you will wield power in the White House."

Theodore Roosevelt was also known to have had a very strong interest in astrology. Roosevelt's father had consulted an astrologer to "see the tides of fortune" the universe would present to his son, the future President. According to an article by Jane C. Hunter entitled "Roosevelt and Astro-Science", the President was familiar with his natal chart and the aspects within it. Hunter goes on to say that Roosevelt had even drawn up his own horoscope and "had it mounted on a chessboard on a table in his room."

We know that at least two of the Founding Fathers of the United States, Thomas Jefferson

and Benjamin Franklin, were knowledgeable in astrology. Thomas Jefferson's own ephemeris (table of planetary positions) is housed in the Library of Congress. Franklin, a famous scientist, diplomat, and Freemason, also published *Poor Richard's Almanac*, which boasted an introduction by William Lilly, one of the most celebrated of English astrologers at the time. In his first Almanac, Franklin even accurately predicted the death of a friend, with the exact time and planetary aspects at the moment of death!

(Continued on page 33)

► Read "Astrology in the White House: The Reagans" on page 705. ► Read "Nostradamus: A Prophet Across Time" on page 785. ► Read "Money, Astrology, and the Crash of '29" on page 225.

1902

Triumph of the Will: Saturn in Capricorn

In the year 1902 Saturn took up residence in the sign of Capricorn, ruler of law and order, discipline, accomplishment, and worldliness. Capricorn is symbolized by the mountain goat, an animal fierce in its determination to get to the top, no matter how long it takes. The powerful energy of this sign is intensified when Saturn, Capricorn's ruling planet, comes to visit. Both Saturn and Capricorn insist on things that last. Nothing flimsy is born under this configuration. On August 22, German film director Leni Riefenstahl, director of the Nazi propaganda film *Triumph of the Will*, was born. The title of this film almost sounds like it could be a Saturn in Capricorn call to arms. A motto for Capricorn often quoted is, "I use." Because Jupiter, the most beneficent of the planets, was also in Capricorn for part of this year, most of the events that took place were useful and constructive.

This year in the U.S., the Bureau of the Census was established. It later became part of the Department of Commerce. Saturn likes to know exactly how many fish are in its bowl. Also this year, the Aswan Dam was completed in central Egypt, becoming the chief means of storing irrigation water for the Nile valley. On February 19, the smallpox vaccination became obligatory in France.

The fossilized remains of a Tyrannosaurus Rex were discovered by Barnum Brown in Hell Creek, Montana. Capricorn is the ruler of structures, including the skeleton and the skin. With its placement in its home sign of Capricorn, ruler of the bones of the body, Saturn could make way for a profound discovery that would come to change the way we understand history and evolution.

Mount Pelée on Martinique erupts repeatedly

The Boer War ends in South Africa with a British victory

The mile-long Aswan Dam is opened after nearly four years of construction

SPIRITUALISTS UNITE!

Mediumship is an ancient and universal practice used to prophesy, heal, and communicate with the divine or the spirits of the dead. Mediums have been known by a number of names, including oracle, channel, fortune-teller, and shaman, amongst others. Mediumship finally gained legal representation when the Spiritualists' National Union was created this year. Based in Manchester, England, the Spiritualists' National Union hoped to unite all Spiritualist churches and encourage research into mediumship and healing.

RAGTIME AND RUNAWAY PROFITS

The second Anglo-Boer war in South Africa ended with a hard-won British victory. Britain annexed the two Boer republics—the Orange Free State and Transvaal—as Crown Colonies. With this, the British gained rights to the South African gold mines. Mt. Pelée on Martinique erupted repeatedly. In the destroyed town of St. Pierre 40,000 died. The U.S. paid $40 million to develop the Panama Canal. In Egypt, the completion of the Aswan Dam created a two hundred mile long artificial lake on the River Nile, submerging some ancient sites. In the U.S., an Alaskan oil gusher created new excitement over this vast territory's riches. Morgan's U.S. Steel made record profits, and Oliver Wendell Holmes was appointed to the Supreme Court. Thomas Edison invented the battery, and it was found that yellow fever, the scourge of the tropics, is transmitted by mosquitoes. The curvilinear form of Art Nouveau was all the rage in Paris. Arthur Conan Doyle's *Hound of the Baskervilles* was published, while the song *In the Good Old Summertime* sold one million copies. Ragtime, spearheaded by black U.S. composer Scott Joplin, appealed to audiences of all races.

➤ Read "Astrology Reigns Through the Ages: Powerful People Consulting the Stars" by Ronnie Grishman on page 25.

CAPRICORN

From January 01, 0:00 through January 20, 23:11

The Dedicated Moralist

As a Capricorn born in January of 1902, you can be a dedicated worker, perfectionist, and, at times, overachiever. You can be your own worst critic, and may measure your life's accomplishments by the number of hours you put in. Around the time you were born, Frank Norris's novel *The Octopus* was enjoying widespread acclaim after its publication the previous year. It called attention to the greed of the railroad industry and carried the message that unrestrained power can at times go too far. You may have absorbed the spirit of this book, since you've never been ruthless and the goals you set for yourself were always challenging.

Although you can work exceptionally hard, your family and friends are likely to have been your top priority. Loyal and generous to a fault, you may have a very high sense of values, a system by which you weigh and measure everything and everyone. Those who did not measure up may never have seen the real you—to their great loss.

When you were young, you probably wanted not only to be the best but also to have the best. As you matured, however, you may have learned that getting where you wanted to go required time, commitment, and patience. While you might not have amassed as much wealth as others, you may have been happier knowing that you never compromised your values in order to do so.

In relationships, you can be romantic and charming, yet you may have found it difficult not to focus on mundane tasks like paying bills or mowing the lawn—sometimes to the detriment of having fun. But you probably looked for someone with a sense of humor who could remind you to enjoy life and share it with those you love. Good love matches for you are likely to be found among Pisceans, Taureans, and Scorpios.

Your challenge is discerning when to bring your high moral code to bear on a situation and when to leave it to others to figure out for themselves. But that dilemma is also your greatest strength and, in the end, your ethical sense and moral conscience is what makes people admire you most, even setting the standards by which they live their lives.

AQUARIUS

From January 20, 23:12 through February 19, 13:39

The Shining Example

You were born at a time when it seemed that medical breakthroughs were in the air. Around the time you were born, officials in France made the smallpox vaccination mandatory, while in the U.S. Major Walter Reed and Dr. James Carroll determined (and later published their findings) that the mosquito carried yellow fever, a dreaded tropical disease. The way that one discovery can help many people overcome great obstacles may have shaped your own way of thinking, Aquarius of 1902. You may have spent your life looking for mountains to move, but you still sought out the facts before pursuing the vision.

Those who know you may have been awed by your ability to see around corners and into the future. Although your well-honed intuition may not have been prophetic, it may have set you apart, and would have played a pivotal role in your ability to set idealistic and practical goals. In the prime of your life, you may have used your uncanny ability to project, plan, and organize in order to run a business, invest in the stock market, or manage an office for someone else.

Even when you weren't standing at the head of the pack calling the shots, you were probably the charismatic trendsetter. Without even trying, you set the example that others followed. When others saw you getting good results, they naturally tried to imitate your style. In rare cases where your way of doing things did not work as well as someone else's, you would have been the first to make adjustments by combining the best of both methods.

In relationships, you may be attracted to someone who shares your hopes and dreams. You could enjoy a Gemini's quick wit or a Libra's lightheartedness, but an adventurous Sagittarian might win your heart. Engaging and personable, you probably don't like being alone, and would want an extended family of friends to make your life complete.

Your strength lies in forever looking forward, envisioning a future that others do not see, and then making that future a reality. Your challenge is to place your personal relationships first, even while working toward those visionary goals.

➤ Read about your Chinese Astrological sign on page 838. ➤ Read about your Personal Planets on page 826. ➤ Read about your personal Mystical Card on page 856.

CAPRICORN
Your Personal Planets

YOUR LOVE POTENTIAL
Venus in Aquarius, Jan. 01, 0:00 - Jan. 11, 17:46
Venus in Pisces, Jan. 11, 17:47 - Jan. 20, 23:11

YOUR DRIVE AND AMBITION
Mars in Capricorn, Jan. 01, 0:00 - Jan. 01, 23:53
Mars in Aquarius, Jan. 01, 23:54 - Jan. 20, 23:11

YOUR LUCK MAGNETISM
Jupiter in Capricorn, Jan. 01, 0:00 - Jan. 20, 23:11

World Events

Jan. 7 – The Dowager Empress of China resumes power as the imperial court is re-established in the city of Peking.

Jan. 10 – The German Chancellor von Bulow leads an attack on British conduct in South Africa.

American aviator Charles Lindbergh is born under the sign of Aquarius

AQUARIUS
Your Personal Planets

YOUR LOVE POTENTIAL
Venus in Pisces, Jan. 20, 23:12 - Feb. 06, 22:54
Venus in Aquarius, Feb. 06, 22:55 - Feb. 19, 13:39

YOUR DRIVE AND AMBITION
Mars in Aquarius, Jan. 20, 23:12 - Feb. 08, 23:53
Mars in Pisces, Feb. 08, 23:54 - Feb. 19, 13:39

YOUR LUCK MAGNETISM
Jupiter in Capricorn, Jan. 20, 23:12 - Feb. 06, 19:30
Jupiter in Aquarius, Feb. 06, 19:31 - Feb. 19, 13:39

World Events

Feb. 4 – Pioneer American pilot Charles Lindbergh is born in Detroit, Michigan.

Feb. 15 – The Berlin subway is inaugurated.

1902

PISCES
Your Personal Planets

YOUR LOVE POTENTIAL
Venus in Aquarius, Feb. 19, 13:40 - Mar. 21, 13:16

YOUR DRIVE AND AMBITION
Mars in Pisces, Feb. 19, 13:40 - Mar. 19, 4:30
Mars in Aries, Mar. 19, 4:31 - Mar. 21, 13:16

YOUR LUCK MAGNETISM
Jupiter in Aquarius, Feb. 19, 13:40 - Mar. 21, 13:16

World Events

Feb. 22 – Maj. Walter Reed and Dr. James Carroll publish a report proving that yellow fever is transmitted by a species of mosquito.

Mar. 10 – In South Africa, the Boers score their last victory against the British, capturing General Methuen and 200 men.

Russian peasants eating in a communal dining room

ARIES
Your Personal Planets

YOUR LOVE POTENTIAL
Venus in Aquarius, Mar. 21, 13:17 - Apr. 04, 19:30
Venus in Pisces, Apr. 04, 19:31 - Apr. 21, 1:03

YOUR DRIVE AND AMBITION
Mars in Aries, Mar. 21, 13:17 - Apr. 21, 1:03

YOUR LUCK MAGNETISM
Jupiter in Aquarius, Mar. 21, 13:17 - Apr. 21, 1:03

World Events

Mar. 22 – Great Britain and Persia agree to link Europe and India by telegraph.

Apr. 1 – Russian peasants begin to loot landowners' barns, as famine persists in the countryside.

PISCES
From February 19, 13:40 through March 21, 13:16

The Quiet Rebel

As a 1902 Pisces, you were born into a world that was becoming ever more connected, as shown by the founding of the American Automobile Club in Chicago, with a mandate to lobby for good roads and uniform traffic laws across the United States. Authorities in Great Britain and Persia were also discussing the possibility of a telegraph system to link parts of the Middle East with Europe.

Although you may love the idea of being brought closer together, you were probably always the modest type and, even as a child, did not particularly like standing out in a crowd. Outwardly quiet and unassuming, it's likely that you didn't change much over the years, and frequently went your own way without much fanfare, secretly hoping others wouldn't notice you. That hardly meant that you were a shrinking violet, since nothing could be farther from the truth! You merely marched to the beat of a different drummer, followed your individual path, and listened to your own intuition.

If you worked for someone else, you probably did best with tasks on your own, especially if they involved a good deal of physical activity. Your quirky habits would have suited working from home, or being an independent writer or artist, as long as there was a right-hand person taking care of the nagging little details. Although you may have devoted a lot of time to your work, you would have managed to leave enough time to spare for volunteer work, or even mentoring others.

In relationships you can be sentimental, but you are forthright and passionate at the same time. When you love someone, your feelings rise quickly to the surface, and in a room full of people, it's likely that everyone knows exactly how you feel. You'd probably get along best with those that can match your ardor—Taureans, Cancerians, Scorpios, or Capricorns.

Your greatest challenge is to balance your personal and professional life. Your strength is your ability to see both sides of an issue and find a way for people with differing aims and interests to compromise. This is a quality that makes you the best friend that anyone could have.

ARIES
From March 21, 13:17 through April 21, 1:03

The Fiery Messenger

Around the time you were born, Aries of 1902, widespread famine in Russia caused peasants to take the desperate measure of looting landowners' estates. Events such as this, which shaped the years preceding the Russian Revolution of 1917, could describe your own passionate refusal to accept the status quo, especially if it involves class inequality or enforced silence. Throughout your life, it's likely that you not only refused to go along with such things, but let everyone know why it was that you wouldn't.

Because of your need to take the soapbox in one form or another, you could have been a good social activist, lecturer, or minister. You can be an exciting speaker, and your charisma may have inspired others to do more than they thought they could. As a follower, you'd have been the one who spoke up when things were heading in the wrong direction. As a leader, it's likely that you moved others through gentle persuasion.

You may have admired writers whose work furthered a cause or made an important social statement. As you grew older works such as Upton Sinclair's infamous novel *The Jungle*, which exposed the meatpacking industry and was published four years after your birth, may have appealed to you. You, too, probably liked influencing others, even if quietly within your community. You may have been naturally competitive, yet you would have felt strongly that everyone should start out on an equal footing, and have the opportunity to do so.

In love, there's probably nothing subtle about you. You may even tell your friends how you feel before you reveal it to the one you care for. You may have looked for someone who found your wild ways endearing, and who supported both you and your ideals. Those you connect with on a deep level are likely to be Geminis, Leos, Sagittarians, and Aquarians.

If there's one challenge you've faced more than another, it is keeping in mind that other people have opinions too, and that you may not have all the answers. Your capacity to do what needs to be done and stay the course is your greatest strength and what people admire most about you.

➤ Read about your Chinese Astrological sign on page 838. ➤ Read about your Personal Planets on page 826. ➤ Read about your personal Mystical Card on page 856.

TAURUS

From April 21, 1:04 through May 22, 0:53

The Spiritual Materialist

Around the time you were born, the volcanic eruption of Mt. Pelée destroyed St. Pierre, the bustling capital of Martinique, killing thousands, while in France, composer Claude Debussy celebrated the Paris opening of his opera *Pelléas and Mélisande*. You might remember your parents telling you of these tragedies and triumphs that surrounded your birth date, Taurus of 1902.

Practical and materialistic, yet charitable and generous, when you were a youngster you may have dreamed of the time when you would be financially well-off enough to donate time and money to worthy causes. As you matured, you may even have demonstrated your belief that tending to practical business matters could be a spiritual enterprise through the way you treated colleagues and employees. Your kindness could be legendary, and it's likely that no one who asked you for advice or help went away empty-handed.

You probably love anything that has a rich background and a story to tell, and you may have always admired antiques, from jewelry and clothing to furniture. Your own taste in fashion may have been rather conservative, and you probably stuck to dark colors, basic cotton, and simple tweed. You would treasure anything handed down to you from past generations, and you could take great pleasure in thinking about endowing these same heirlooms, along with your own valued possessions, to family members and beloved friends.

In love relationships, you may want a mate who shares the value you place on earning and saving money. Your partner must be someone who can be relied upon to reassure you in times of need and cheer you on when things go well. In general, you can be most compatible with Cancerians, Virgos, and Capricorns, but a mysterious Piscean could also fascinate you.

Your challenge is to balance the material and spiritual interests in your life, so that even while you're preoccupied with earning a living, you can make time for your family and take advantage of life's simple pleasures. Your gift is your ability to see the value of balancing your priorities, and to pass that lesson on to all who listen.

GEMINI

From May 22, 0:54 through June 22, 9:14

The Creative Conversationalist

You can be enthusiastic, energetic, and communicative, Gemini of 1902, and you probably leave a lasting impression on anyone you meet. It's interesting that around the time you were born, the "Reclamation Act" establishing the United States National Park System was passed. No matter where you lived, preserving expanses of natural wonder would fit well with your love of nature.

You may be a born educator, and even if you didn't take up teaching as a profession, your best moments in life probably occurred when presenting new information and simplifying complex ideas for a group of people. You may have incorporated these skills into print journalism or even radio, which was just catching fire as you entered adulthood in the late twenties. You may have also traveled for business or pleasure, and enjoyed meeting people from different cultures and backgrounds.

You could also have taken an interest in communication of a different kind, such as creative writing or performing comedy routines. Even if your goal wasn't to be a great novelist or short story writer, expressing yourself in this way has probably always been a pleasure for you. Few can match your ability to say things in just the way they need to be said, and as a letter writer it's likely that you had no equal.

When you are with someone you love, you can be not only a great companion but also a generous one. You have probably always adored giving little gifts that show in a real and concrete way how you feel about those you care most deeply about. You may be most at home with someone you can talk to easily, and you may have looked for a Leo, Libra, Aquarius, or Aries to share your life's conversation with.

Your challenge is to accept that some people may not want to listen to your words of wisdom or laugh at your jokes. Still, as the years passed and you mellowed, you would have learned to appreciate all types of people, and even agree that it takes all kinds to make a world. Your strength is the way you penetrate to the heart of any matter, and when the going gets rough, you always know exactly the right thing to do.

➤ Read about your Chinese Astrological sign on page 838. ➤ Read about your Personal Planets on page 826. ➤ Read about your personal Mystical Card on page 856.

1902

TAURUS
Your Personal Planets

YOUR LOVE POTENTIAL
Venus in Pisces, Apr. 21, 1:04 - May 07, 7:04
Venus in Aries, May 07, 7:05 - May 22, 0:53

YOUR DRIVE AND AMBITION
Mars in Aries, Apr. 21, 1:04 - Apr. 27, 10:48
Mars in Taurus, Apr. 27, 10:49 - May 22, 0:53

YOUR LUCK MAGNETISM
Jupiter in Aquarius, Apr. 21, 1:04 - May 22, 0:53

World Events

Apr. 30 – Claude Debussy's opera *Pélleas And Mélisande* premières in Paris.

May 5 – Women are denied the right to political association by the government in Prussia.

French opera composer, Claude Debussy

GEMINI
Your Personal Planets

YOUR LOVE POTENTIAL
Venus in Aries, May 22, 0:54 - June 03, 23:58
Venus in Taurus, June 03, 23:59 - June 22, 9:14

YOUR DRIVE AND AMBITION
Mars in Taurus, May 22, 0:54 - June 07, 11:19
Mars in Gemini, June 07, 11:20 - June 22, 9:14

YOUR LUCK MAGNETISM
Jupiter in Aquarius, May 22, 0:54 - June 22, 9:14

World Events

May 22 – The International Miners' Congress demands the nationalization of mines, but vetoes strikes in France and Belgium.

May 31 – The Boer War ends with the Treaty of Vereeniging; the Boers lose their sovereignty and British Rule in South Africa is established.

1902

CANCER
Your Personal Planets

YOUR LOVE POTENTIAL
Venus in Taurus, June 22, 9:15 - June 30, 6:27
Venus in Gemini, June 30, 6:28 - July 23, 20:09

YOUR DRIVE AND AMBITION
Mars in Gemini, June 22, 9:15 - July 20, 17:43
Mars in Cancer, July 20, 17:44 - July 23, 20:09

YOUR LUCK MAGNETISM
Jupiter in Aquarius, June 22, 9:15 - July 23, 20:09

World Events

June 28 – Germany, Austria-Hungary, and Italy renew the Triple Alliance for an agreed period of twelve years.

July 1 – Film director William Wyler is born.

Coronation of King Edward VII of Great Britain

LEO
Your Personal Planets

YOUR LOVE POTENTIAL
Venus in Gemini, July 23, 20:10 - July 25, 18:58
Venus in Cancer, July 25, 18:59 - Aug. 19, 18:27
Venus in Leo, Aug. 19, 18:28 - Aug. 24, 2:52

YOUR DRIVE AND AMBITION
Mars in Cancer, July 23, 20:10 - Aug. 24, 2:52

YOUR LUCK MAGNETISM
Jupiter in Aquarius, July 23, 20:10 - Aug. 24, 2:52

World Events

Aug. 9 – King Edward VII is crowned at Westminster Abbey in London.

Aug. 22 – German film director Leni Riefenstahl is born.

CANCER
From June 22, 9:15 through July 23, 20:09

The Indispensable Counselor

Around the time you were born, Cancer of 1902, French auto maker Marcel Renault beat the speed of his country's fastest train, the *Arlberg Express*, with his new lightning-quick racecar, which won the first Paris to Vienna motor race. Over your lifetime, the world has taken on even more speed than that, but you have probably taken the increase in speed all in your stride. That's because you may always have moved at your own pace and done things in your own time—the tortoise not the hare.

Although people might perceive you as one who went along with the crowd, you really maintained your independence in your own quiet way. You could enjoy being part of a group, as long as you calmly injected your own brand of individuality. More often than not, you probably left the leadership positions to other people, knowing intuitively that you were best suited to serve as an advisor or support to the person who held the spotlight. Although you may never have received the glory, or even the credit much of the time, you would have been content knowing that you had been an indispensable player.

Given these qualities, you might have gravitated toward working with people, perhaps in sales, hospitality, or in some capacity where service and communication were key components of the job. You could also have excelled at interviewing people or helping them work out their differences together. With your strong intuition leading the way, you probably always managed to sense someone else's feelings and respond to that person in just the right way.

In love relationships, you may have looked for someone who could draw out your innermost feelings and help you to express them in a positive way. You've always had an abundance of love to give and a lot of deep emotions to show to just the right person, so when you found that person you probably never looked back. Your best match can be made with Virgos, Scorpios, or Taureans.

Your challenge is to let people learn things for themselves—at least some of the time. Your gift is to do what you believe is right, never being swayed by what others think.

LEO
From July 23, 20:10 through August 24, 2:52

The Regal Transformer

Around the time you were born, Leo of 1902, British King Edward VII was crowned in Westminster Abbey in London, a fitting parallel to the birth of a regal Leo like yourself. And, like royalty, you may always have been benevolent, proud, and commanding. From the time you were very young, heads may have turned when you walked into a room. People may see an air of confidence and commanding presence about you that inevitably draws them to you. That dashing spirit has probably helped you work through the problem areas of life, taking the easy roads with gusto and meeting each obstacle as nothing less than an exhilarating challenge.

You were probably an outgoing child, and matured into a vibrant personality whose creative spirit would be evident to anyone who heard you speak, lecture, or perform before an audience. You were probably at your best in situations where you inspired others with your own life, or informed them by drawing on the well of special knowledge you had gained in one field or another. If something you did or said made the world a better place for others then that's all to the good.

You may have excelled at transforming ordinary things and situations into extraordinary ones, whether it was accessorizing a plain outfit, planning a surprise birthday party, or supervising a gala event. If you worked in the business world, you may have specialized in creating new, innovative companies by merging two longstanding but outdated ones.

In relationships, you'd be anything but boring, and you might initiate spontaneous outings, interesting dinners, and other surprises. You probably have a wonderful way of making those close to you feel special and, most importantly, loved. You fit like a glove with Librans, Sagittarians, Ariens, and Geminis.

Your greatest strength is your ability to find the creative best in any situation. While others may be content following old patterns or doing things in a safe way, your approach is always fresh, new, and sometimes downright amazing! Your greatest challenge is finding ways to innovate that are both interesting and practical.

➤ Read about your Chinese Astrological sign on page 838. ➤ Read about your Personal Planets on page 826. ➤ Read about your personal Mystical Card on page 856.

VIRGO

From August 24, 2:53 through September 23, 23:54

The Solid Healer

No matter where you were born, the major finds of gold and oil in Alaska, along with the biggest merger of railroad lines in United States history, would have served as a fascinating backdrop to your birth, Virgo of 1902. Your own reach in the world might have been a little more modest than panning for gold or wildcatting for oil, but in your own way you have probably been an explorer and a risk-taker all your life. Rather than scout the wilderness, however, your concern was probably the territory between family and the outside world.

Although your childhood years might have been idyllic, as you began to take on adult responsibilities there may have been pressures that pitted your interest in raising a family against those of having a career. Constructive and always busy, you probably managed to somehow do both, even if you had to take in work from the outside and do it from home. Your income might have been modest, but being home in time for family dinners was probably more important to you than building an empire.

That balanced approach is reflected in your other life activities, which is why you may have found yourself sought after to work in key positions in volunteer, charitable, and professional organizations. Especially where friends and colleagues were concerned, you considered all points of view, and tried to reconcile them whenever you could.

In love, it's likely that you focused on home and family. Although you may have admired dashing, romantic, or glamorous types from afar, you probably settled down with someone who could be a loyal, steadfast companion and who was mainly interested in building your life together. Signs that match up well with yours include Scorpio, Capricorn, Taurus, and Cancer.

Your challenge is to see the big picture, rather than getting lost in details that may only bog you down. Your strength is your ability to look at both sides of an issue, especially those that involve conflict within your family. In many ways, you have been a healer, and those who you've helped with your smiling face and compassionate nature may be more than grateful.

LIBRA

From September 23, 23:55 through October 24, 8:35

The Charming Harmonizer

Around the time you were born, the first Cadillac rolled off a Detroit assembly line, it was announced that Windsor Castle would be opened to the public, and the Crown Prince of Siam made a grand entry into New York. Snapshots of all these "elegant" events would have revealed a very lovely picture—and they made a most fitting backdrop for you, Libra of 1902, with your eye for beauty and desire to make sure it's included in your life.

It's likely that you've always appreciated quality and that, whatever your income level, you managed to create a harmonious home that is aesthetically pleasing. While you probably wouldn't insist that people had to be beautiful or perfect in a physical sense to be your friends, on the inside, where it counts most, you would have wanted your friends to have an element of nobility. Once you sensed the presence of that element, you would have treated that person in ways that made them feel beautiful.

You may have been drawn to pastimes and occupations that included artistic pursuits, and you probably loved spending hours in museums, galleries, theaters, and, of course, movie houses. But you probably also had an innate talent for dealing with people, making you a natural as a receptionist, tour guide, or working in publicity. You can charm anyone, largely because your interest in them is sincere and honest, never superficial. It's likely that everyone you've spent even a little time with remembers meeting you, often for the rest of their life.

When you were younger, you may have wanted a partner who would look good beside you, and who made you look good in turn. As you matured, however, you may have learned that looks fade, and what really matters is a true heart. You are a committed partner and a loyal family person, and could be most compatible with Aquarians, Geminis, and Leos. Your challenge is to remember that beauty is only skin deep, for that is something you can teach others only by example. Your strength is being able to see the good in anything, and it's something that has made you a poet at heart and a wonderful friend all your life.

➤ Read about your Chinese Astrological sign on page 838. ➤ Read about your Personal Planets on page 826. ➤ Read about your personal Mystical Card on page 856.

1902

VIRGO
Your Personal Planets

YOUR LOVE POTENTIAL
Venus in Leo, Aug. 24, 2:53 - Sept. 13, 7:17
Venus in Virgo, Sept. 13, 7:18 - Sept. 23, 23:54

YOUR DRIVE AND AMBITION
Mars in Cancer, Aug. 24, 2:53 - Sept. 04, 14:47
Mars in Leo, Sept. 04, 14:48 - Sept. 23, 23:54

YOUR LUCK MAGNETISM
Jupiter in Aquarius, Aug. 24, 2:53 - Sept. 23, 23:54

World Events

Sept. 9 – Miners discover gold in Alaska.

Sept. 22 – Tsar Nicholas II issues a decree abolishing autonomy in Finland.

Tsar Nicholas II

LIBRA
Your Personal Planets

YOUR LOVE POTENTIAL
Venus in Virgo, Sept. 23, 23:55 - Oct. 07, 12:05
Venus in Libra, Oct. 07, 12:06 - Oct. 24, 8:35

YOUR DRIVE AND AMBITION
Mars in Leo, Sept. 23, 23:55 - Oct. 23, 22:54
Mars in Virgo, Oct. 23, 22:55 - Oct. 24, 8:35

YOUR LUCK MAGNETISM
Jupiter in Aquarius, Sept. 23, 23:55 - Oct. 24, 8:35

World Events

Sept. 29 – French novelist Emile Zola dies.

Oct. 9 – Two-thirds of all mine workers go out on strike in France.

1902

SCORPIO
Your Personal Planets

YOUR LOVE POTENTIAL
Venus in Libra, Oct. 24, 8:36 - Oct. 31, 11:50
Venus in Scorpio, Oct. 31, 11:51 - Nov. 23, 5:35

YOUR DRIVE AND AMBITION
Mars in Virgo, Oct. 24, 8:36 - Nov. 23, 5:35

YOUR LUCK MAGNETISM
Jupiter in Aquarius, Oct. 24, 8:36 - Nov. 23, 5:35

World Events

Oct. 26 – American women's suffrage pioneer Elizabeth Cady Stanton dies.

Nov. 8 – In an attempt to improve relations between Britain and Germany, Kaiser Wilhelm II arrives in England for a twelve-day visit.

G. Marconi with an early wireless apparatus

SAGITTARIUS
Your Personal Planets

YOUR LOVE POTENTIAL
Venus in Scorpio, Nov. 23, 5:36 - Nov. 24, 9:05
Venus in Sagittarius, Nov. 24, 9:06 - Dec. 18, 5:31
Venus in Capricorn, Dec. 18, 5:32 - Dec. 22, 18:35

YOUR DRIVE AND AMBITION
Mars in Virgo, Nov. 23, 5:36 - Dec. 20, 3:32
Mars in Libra, Dec. 20, 3:33 - Dec. 22, 18:35

YOUR LUCK MAGNETISM
Jupiter in Aquarius, Nov. 23, 5:36 - Dec. 22, 18:35

World Events

Dec. 10 – The mile-long Aswan Dam is opened after nearly four years of construction by around 11,000 workers.

Dec. 21 – Guglielmo Marconi sends the first messages across the Atlantic by wireless.

32

SCORPIO
From October 24, 8:36 through November 23, 5:35

The Intense Planner

As a 1902 Scorpio, you were born in a time of transition signaled by the passing of Germany's wealthiest man, Friedrich Krupp, and America's most passionate crusader for women's rights, Elizabeth Cady Stanton. The empire that Krupp built continued after him, and Stanton's legacy became enshrined in law both in her own country and abroad. Although your life, your needs, and your interests may have been quite different from theirs, you have always been a builder in your own right, never letting up until you made your presence felt.

It's likely that your capacity for setting a goal and sticking to it until you achieved every aim you set for yourself is unmatched, and may have made you the one who set the standard for others. Whether you used that talent to build a small family, a big business, or something in between, it's likely that those who know you best see you as someone who is able to succeed where others have failed. You probably enjoyed building these successes on your own terms, and you may have stayed an entrepreneur as much as you could. If you worked for others, it was probably your independent mind that they valued.

You may not be what people think of as an intellectual, but it's likely that your engaging and probing mind is one of your most outstanding features. There's almost no detail that goes unnoticed, which is why you rarely have the wool pulled over your eyes. You don't take anything for granted, and thus check everything twice—then twice again.

In love, your relationships are probably somewhat intense, but it's likely that love never obscured the realities of surviving in a changing world. Your mate may have had to be someone who could carry their own weight in providing for the family living. Your ideal partners may be Capricorns, Pisceans, Cancerians, and Virgos.

Your greatest challenge is to view situations with your heart as well as your head. There's no doubting the importance of taking care of business, but love and friendship are important, too. Your greatest strength is your perseverance, and it's probably what people admire most about you.

SAGITTARIUS
From November 23, 5:36 through December 22, 18:35

The Boundless Seeker

Your birth coincided with the momentous event of the waters of Egypt's Nile River being tamed, as the Aswan Dam was officially declared complete. The idea of bringing an ancient river to heel perfectly reflects the optimistic and enterprising spirit that may have guided much of your life, Sagittarius of 1902. It's likely that no project was ever too big for you, and you probably tackled everything from getting good grades at school to getting ready for retirement with tremendous zeal.

Your direction in life may have been more varied than most, since seeing new places can be a lifelong passion for Sagittarians—whether it means taking long train rides or just going shopping in the next town. Teaching might have been your chosen occupation since you'd probably have loved the idea of molding young minds. Children under your tutelage would have learned to think and explore new ideas, and you may have encouraged these qualities in your family and friends as well.

If you tried your hand at business, it's likely that the details were left to others, and the big picture was reserved for you. You might have been most successful with a partner who could fill in the gaps left by your impatience with routine. You are a visionary and a planner, and you would always do best if you worked with someone who could follow through on the less exciting tasks.

Even in personal relationships, you would rather lead than follow, yet for you the real key to a successful relationship was to be with someone who shared your love of travel—and didn't mind listening to a good lesson or two along the way! You might find a happy love match with a Libran, but you could just as easily lose your heart to an Aquarian, Arien, or Leo.

Your strength is your seemingly limitless capacity for hard work when the chips are down, spurred by your boundless enthusiasm. Your greatest challenge is to realize that when other people cannot match your own energy, it's not due to lack of interest. Once you accept that everyone has their own uniqueness, you become the best teacher, friend, and partner anyone could have.

➤ Read about your Chinese Astrological sign on page 838. ➤ Read about your Personal Planets on page 826. ➤ Read about your personal Mystical Card on page 856.

CAPRICORN

From December 22, 18:36 through December 31, 23:59

The Bridge Builder

In the month you were born, December Capricorn of 1902, inventor Guglielmo Marconi was bringing his "wireless telegraphy" closer to practicality with another experiment in Newfoundland. What better event to herald the birth of someone like you, whose best talent may be building bridges between people and between institutions?

Your ability to find common purpose among groups of people in situations where others may only see chaos has probably stood you in good stead all your life. It's the kind of gift that would make you a great diplomat, no matter what field you went into. However, it also works well in daily life, helping you to heal the wounds caused by other people's disagreements, and your friends and family may rely on your clear vision almost without knowing that they're doing it.

Single-minded, ambitious, and idealistic, you may always have put your own individualistic stamp on anything you do. You've probably been known to transform assignments that involved a great deal of filing, accounting, or record keeping into creative positions that made you appear indispensable to the company or institution for which you worked. And when you've had to leave a job, or make a transition in your life situation, you probably left everything so well organized that anyone could take over and fill your shoes.

In love, it was probably important to you that your partner be on an equal footing with you both intellectually and emotionally, so you could share things and support one another through thick and thin. Your most harmonious partnerships can be with Pisceans, Taureans, and Virgos, but you could also find an intense, passionate Scorpio intriguing.

Your challenge is asking others for advice and even assistance. It's a good thing to be independent and do things in the way you know is best, but sometimes a second opinion adds objectivity. Your strength is your ability to see the true situation when others around you may be too caught up in the emotion of the moment to see things clearly. It is that level-headed objectivity that has won you admirers and made you a leader.

1902

CAPRICORN
Your Personal Planets

YOUR LOVE POTENTIAL
Venus in Capricorn, Dec. 22, 18:36 - Dec. 31, 23:59

YOUR DRIVE AND AMBITION
Mars in Libra, Dec. 22, 18:36 - Dec. 31, 23:59

YOUR LUCK MAGNETISM
Jupiter in Aquarius, Dec. 22, 18:36 - Dec. 31, 23:59

World Events

Dec. 22 – German psychiatrist Richard Freiherr von Krafft-Ebing dies.

Dec. 25 – Pope Leo XIII announces his endorsement of the European Christian Democratic movement as an alternative to Socialism.

Napoleon Bonaparte

Special Feature
Astrology Reigns Through the Ages: Powerful People Consulting the Stars

(Continued from page 25)

Adolf Hitler's use of astrology has also long been chronicled. Hitler's astrological advisor, Karl Ernst Krafft, was a fervent admirer of the *Führer*. Helping to cross Hitler's stars, Winston Churchill was himself seeing an astrologer, Louis de Wohl, to help him second-guess the strategies of the German dictator. On November 2, 1939, Krafft wrote to Hitler's infamous associate, Himmler, warning that between the 7th and the 10th of November, Hitler's life would be in danger because of "the possibility of an attempt at assassination—by what Krafft said would be "the use of an explosive material." The warning proved to have been right-on.

Hitler had been preceded by a number of other stargazing tyrants. The Mongol conqueror Genghis Khan was also known to have appointed astrologers to positions of prominence, including a Chinese forecaster named Ye Liu Chutsai—who, it's said, regularly advised Khan as he made his way triumphantly across Europe

and Asia. Other ancient astrologers of note included Julius Caesar's trusted astrologer, Spurina. Caesar turned to Spurina for counsel on matters of war—advice that apparently was quite good. Unfortunately, Caesar should have paid equal heed to Spurina's more personal predictions—for instance, that the planet Mars foretold violence toward him on the infamous Ides of March.

> Many of the Founding Fathers of the United States, including Thomas Jefferson and Benjamin Franklin, were astrologers.

Another dictator who became interested in astrology—or the "testimony of the planets," as he called it—was Napoleon Bonaparte. Regularly seeking out the predictions of the famous French seeress Mlle. Lenormand, Napoleon was repeatedly warned not to advance against the Russians—advice that, like Caesar before him,

the emperor should have taken. Italy's Catherine de Medici consulted Nostradamus, indisputably the most famous seer-astrologer of them all—who prophesied—among other things, the Great Fire of London in 1666, the French Revolution, and the rise of Napoleon.

Italy also had its astrologers—in particular, the famous Guido Bonatus, who was renowned for his uncannily accurate predictions. Bonatus was consultant to the Earl of Monserrat, for whom he chose auspicious battle times. Bonatus also once predicted that the Earl would receive "a slight wound to the knee." So sure was he of the accuracy of his forecast that he actually carried the necessary bandages to dress the wound—fortunately for the Earl, who did indeed receive a wound in just that spot.

(Continued on page 41)

➤ Read "Astrology in the White House: The Reagans" on page 705. ➤ Read "Nostradamus: A Prophet Across Time" on page 785. ➤ Read "Money, Astrology, and the Crash of '29" on page 225.

1903

Flying High: Mars and Uranus

In the year 1903, groundbreaking scientific discoveries came to light, and technological innovations astounded the masses. This was due, in part, to the celestial influences on the Earth. Mars, the planet of action, force and pure strength, was in the sign of Sagittarius this year. The centaur, half horse, half man, which symbolizes Sagittarius, is all power, endlessly shooting arrows into the future. When Mars is in Sagittarius, idealism and adventure are in the air. This year, Uranus, the planet of surprises, was also spending its time in fiery Sagittarius. When Uranus comes to visit the centaur, we can expect pyrotechnics and new concepts to emerge. When Mars met up with Uranus in the fall of 1903, everyone anticipated full speed ahead.

The first transcontinental trip by automobile took place this year from San Francisco to New York; 3,000 miles were covered in fifty-two days. On December 10, Pierre and Marie Curie shared the Nobel Prize in physics with Henri Becquerel, honoring for their work with radioactivity. Probably the most dazzling event of the year took place on December 17. On this day the Wright brothers achieved the first successful powered flight at Kitty Hawk, North Carolina. Aviation is favored when Mars meets Uranus in the sky, and nothing is more symbolic of Sagittarius than gazing from Earth to the star-filled heavens and wanting to be there! Sagittarius is the sign of expansion, both of the individual mind and the collective unconscious. With planets of such sheer force in this sign, it's no wonder that we took to the skies in 1903.

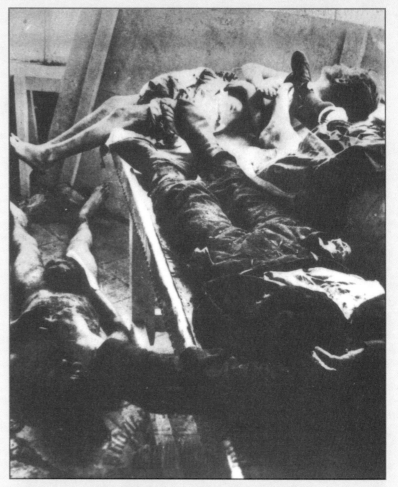

A wave of anti-semitic atrocities sweeps across Russia

Henry Ford begins the Ford Motor Company

The Wright brothers' first powered flight

BIGFOOT AND THE PRESIDENT

For years, Native Americans throughout North America had reported sightings of a man-like beast with a broad chest and shoulders as well as no neck. An explorer had discovered fourteen-inch long footprints believed to belong to this "Sasquatch" or "Bigfoot", as the creature became known, near Jasper, Alberta. Bigfoot's existence gained even more credibility this year when U.S. President Theodore Roosevelt recounted the story of two trappers in Idaho who survived an attack by this mysterious and giant creature.

TRANSITIONS AND FLYING MACHINES

Pope Leo XIII died after twenty-five years guiding the Catholic Church, while British King Edward VII was declared Emperor of India. Zionists pushed for a Jewish homeland in Palestine, preferring it to the site offered by Britain in Uganda. Meanwhile, dozens of Russian Jews were killed in a ferocious pogrom in Kishinev. Panama declared its independence from Colombia and was quickly recognized by the U.S. in its eagerness to build the Panama Canal. The Serbian king and queen were assassinated by the country's army, ending rule by the Obrenovich dynasty. American fortunes continued to grow, as Henry Ford began the Ford Motor Company. The new and lavish location of the New York Stock Exchange opened its doors, while Congress attempted to curtail immigration by imposing a $2 head tax on new immigrants. The Wright Brothers flew their aircraft *Flyer I* at Kitty Hawk, North Carolina, while French physicists Pierre and Marie Curie won the Nobel Prize for their research in radioactivity. Dutch researcher Einthoven unveiled his invention to monitor the heart, the electrocardiograph. The first World Series of baseball was played in Boston.

➤ Read "Astrology Reigns Through the Ages: Powerful People Consulting the Stars" by Ronnie Grishman on page 25.

CAPRICORN

From January 01, 0:00 through January 21, 5:13

The Unchanging Changer

As a Capricorn born in January of 1903, you arrived when the twentieth century was still new and just getting off to its start. Around the time you were born, the Bulgarian government renounced a commerce treaty with Austria-Hungary, causing some of the conflicts that eventually led to World War I. Possibly, growing up in an era filled with seriousness, even doom and gloom, made you even more sober-minded than your natural Capricorn earnestness would have. Also, providing a safe haven for you could have seemed important to your parents, and some of this concern may have rubbed off on you as well.

As a result, you can seem sturdy, stable, and reliable—perhaps excessively so by some people's standards. Because you may tend to be there whenever you're needed, people may have thought your routine was so predictable that they could say in advance what you would eat for dinner or what you would wear to work! You probably surprised them more often than not, but they may never have stopped believing that they knew what you would do next.

At home as well as at work, you were probably the organizer. You would have been the one who made the bank deposits and set up the budgets. Even though you would have kept your friends and co-workers focused on the practical side of life, they were probably appreciative of the lessons they learned. And they knew that whenever you praised them for a job well done, you did it with love and pride.

In love relationships, you may have looked for someone to provide emotional security above all. And when you were sure that you could trust your partner, you probably enjoyed revealing the real you—the fears and insecurities, as well as the steadiness and sensuality. You may be most comfortable relating to Pisceans, Taureans, and Virgos, but an intense Scorpio may fascinate you too.

Your challenge is to move past some of the routines that have made you feel safe but may have prevented you from just being a little bit silly every now and again. Your strength is your ability to explain the practical side of life to others in a way that they can understand.

AQUARIUS

From January 21, 5:14 through February 19, 19:40

The Truthful Transmitter

New and exciting information was in the air around the time you were born, Aquarius of 1903. Susan B. Anthony, nearing the end of a lifetime of championing women's rights, donated her collection of books on the subject to the U.S. Library of Congress in Washington, D.C. It probably comes as no surprise, then, that your own focus of interest over a lifetime may have been not only information-oriented, but also geared toward human-rights issues.

It's likely that people see you as honest, stubborn, and an original thinker. Even as a child, you may have been interested in how ideas are conveyed to others, and as you grew older you were probably eager to learn about each new medium of communication as it came along. You may have been the first in your town to experiment with radio and, later on, the first in your crowd to have a television set.

You may always have been a stickler for transmitting the truth, and you probably place a great deal of value on honesty. As an Aquarius, you might have a natural talent for writing, which may have suited you to work as an editor, proofreader, or teacher. Politics and the law may fascinate you, and you could even admire those who practice them, but you probably preferred to better the world by joining watchdog groups that monitored what the politicians and attorneys were doing. Small talk and idle chitchat are unlikely to amuse you for long, and you probably met your closest friends through your leisure-time activities, as you tend to be drawn to people whose interests are the same as yours.

Even in romance, you may value truth above all. You might have looked for someone who, like yourself, would be straightforward when things were not going well and complimentary when life was grand. Gemini and Libra are good love signs for you, but an adventurous Sagittarian might have been the one you settled down with.

Your challenge is to learn to listen with your heart, and appreciate that subtle shadings of truth and meaning do not always indicate bad intent. Your greatest strength is your ability to say what you mean and mean what you say.

➤ Read about your Chinese Astrological sign on page 838. ➤ Read about your Personal Planets on page 826. ➤ Read about your personal Mystical Card on page 856.

CAPRICORN
Your Personal Planets

YOUR LOVE POTENTIAL
Venus in Capricorn, Jan. 01, 0:00 - Jan. 11, 2:17
Venus in Aquarius, Jan. 11, 2:18 - Jan. 21, 5:13

YOUR DRIVE AND AMBITION
Mars in Libra, Jan. 01, 0:00 - Jan. 21, 5:13

YOUR LUCK MAGNETISM
Jupiter in Aquarius, Jan. 01, 0:00 - Jan. 21, 5:13

World Events

Jan. 3 - Revolutionaries in Venezuela are successfully crushed by government troops.

Jan. 19 - The imperial government in China announces that it will be unable to fulfill the reparation agreement for the Boxer uprising.

A map illustrating the dispute over the Alaskan border

AQUARIUS
Your Personal Planets

YOUR LOVE POTENTIAL
Venus in Aquarius, Jan. 21, 5:14 - Feb. 04, 0:46
Venus in Pisces, Feb. 04, 0:47 - Feb. 19, 19:40

YOUR DRIVE AND AMBITION
Mars in Libra, Jan. 21, 5:14 - Feb. 19, 19:40

YOUR LUCK MAGNETISM
Jupiter in Aquarius, Jan. 21, 5:14 - Feb. 19, 19:40

World Events

Jan. 24 - U.S. Secretary of State John Hay and British Ambassador Herbert create a joint commission to establish the Alaskan border.

Feb. 15 - The first teddy bear, named after President Theodore Roosevelt and created by Morris and Rose Michten, is introduced to America.

1903

PISCES
Your Personal Planets

YOUR LOVE POTENTIAL
Venus in Pisces, Feb. 19, 19:41 - Feb. 28, 3:02
Venus in Aries, Feb. 28, 3:03 - Mar. 21, 19:14

YOUR DRIVE AND AMBITION
Mars in Libra, Feb. 19, 19:41 - Mar. 21, 19:14

YOUR LUCK MAGNETISM
Jupiter in Aquarius, Feb. 19, 19:41 - Feb. 20, 8:34
Jupiter in Pisces, Feb. 20, 8:35 - Mar. 21, 19:14

World Events

Mar. 3 – The U.S. Congress passes a bill placing a $2 "head tax" on all incoming aliens and barring groups of people deemed to be "undesirables."

Mar. 18 – All Catholic religious orders in France are dissolved.

The mass murder of Jews in Russia

ARIES
Your Personal Planets

YOUR LOVE POTENTIAL
Venus in Aries, Mar. 21, 19:15 - Mar. 24, 11:52
Venus in Taurus, Mar. 24, 11:53 - Apr. 18, 6:40
Venus in Gemini, Apr. 18, 6:41 - Apr. 21, 6:58

YOUR DRIVE AND AMBITION
Mars in Libra, Mar. 21, 19:15 - Apr. 19, 20:45
Mars in Virgo, Apr. 19, 20:46 - Apr. 21, 6:58

YOUR LUCK MAGNETISM
Jupiter in Pisces, Mar. 21, 19:15 - Apr. 21, 6:58

World Events

Mar. 29 – A regular news service begins between New York and London through the wireless invented by Guglielmo Marconi.

Apr. 16 – A pogrom breaks out on Easter morning in Kishinev, Russia, after a Christian girl is killed; scores of Jews are murdered.

PISCES
From February 19, 19:41 through March 21, 19:14

The Intuitive Independent

Pisces of 1903, perhaps your life can be summed up as moving away from the insecurities of childhood and youth and journeying towards creative growth and belief in yourself—the kind that comes only with age and confidence. An example of this occurred around the time you were born, when painter Henri Matisse marked his debut, at the age of thirty-four, at the Salon des Indépendants in Paris.

You were probably working from a very early age to develop the sense of well-being and deep trust in the universe that may have been the hallmark of your later years. You have a tendency to be soft-spoken and gentle, and as a child it's possible that you were overly concerned about what others thought of you. As you grew older, however, you would have begun to realize that you were capable of making your own decisions. When you reached maturity, it's likely that your deeply intuitive nature allowed you to make the right moves at just the right time. And once you began paying attention to that kind of inner vision, you avoided jumping into situations that might have brought more problems than you could handle.

It's likely that you were more interested in being responsible for your own destiny than in controlling the fortunes of others. Although you were capable of accumulating wealth, it was probably more important to you to spend hours exploring your creative talents. You may have earned your living in the arts in some way, possibly working in a gallery, museum, or bookstore. You may have traveled widely, too—if only in your imagination.

In love relationships, you may have been willing to relinquish the control you guarded so carefully in other areas of your life. It may have taken a while, but once you knew you could trust someone, you would have had total faith in your partner to make decisions that were right for both of you. Your most compatible love signs can be Taurus, Cancer, Scorpio, and Capricorn.

Your challenge is to trust your intuition in situations when you need to rely on others. Your strongest asset is your ability to share your good fortune with those that you love.

ARIES
From March 21, 19:15 through April 21, 6:58

The Arts Patron

You were born at a time of great unrest, Aries of 1903. Students were rioting in several Spanish cities, and thousands of Jews were murdered during pogroms in Russia. Events like these dotted the era in which you grew up, and they may have inspired you to have sympathy for the underdog and become a supporter of creative freedom.

Passionate, vibrant, yet nonetheless structured, you may often have preferred to be on the side of the artist, perhaps even using the medium of music, painting, or literature to express your point of view. You may be unlike Ariens born in other years in that competition is probably not in your vocabulary. Instead of trying to outdo anyone, you might have been a patron of the arts and even of individual artists. At the very least, you would have collected small art objects, especially if they seemed inspired and whimsical. Whatever your income level, your love of all types of artistic expression was probably a constant throughout your life.

It's likely that you were responsible, pragmatic, and good at earning or managing money. You may have used those skills to become a professional bookkeeper, accountant, or auditor, and your talents in this area would have been obvious to anyone who knew you. Your well-organized mind would find a place for everything and insist that everything be returned to its place when you had finished using it, and this would have made for a very neat workspace or playroom.

Where close relationships are concerned, you can be committed, direct, and forthright. When looking for a mate, you may have wanted someone you could count on for a lifetime commitment from the start. You also realize that love requires space and room to grow, and needs to be kept fresh and surprising. Those who most share this perspective and with whom you may get along best are Geminis, Leos, and Aquarians.

Your challenge is to maintain the structure in your life while immersing yourself in the creative process. Your gift is that, by striking a balance between artistic endeavors and daily living, you have been an inspiration to all who know you.

► Read about your Chinese Astrological sign on page 838. ► Read about your Personal Planets on page 826. ► Read about your personal Mystical Card on page 856.

TAURUS

From April 21, 6:59 through May 22, 6:44

The Moral Compass

Around the time you were born, a new multi-million-dollar building opened to house the New York Stock Exchange. At the same time, a surging socialist movement took to the streets around the world. This fierce tug of war between capital and labor was to be a hallmark of the twentieth century, and it may have influenced you deeply, Taurus of 1903. It could even have been reflected later in your own struggle to acquire and manage money without becoming too materialistic and greedy in the process.

As a young person, you might have had lofty visions of imitating Andrew Carnegie. Determined, focused, and practical, you may have initially worked for a large corporation, perhaps finding a place in one of the behemoths run by the steel, oil, or railroad barons who had come to prominence just before the turn of the century. Whatever your field of endeavor, it's likely that you learned an invaluable lesson from it—money isn't everything.

Being a crusader is probably not your style, and you may have chosen to express your core values by going in the opposite direction to the urban migration. While others were moving to the cities, you may have decided to go back to the land—at least for a while. It's possible that you ran your own store, or with your brilliant business sense, you may have transformed a hobby into a profitable enterprise. You might have been tempted to succumb to pure materialism from time to time, but the value of work, to you, could always have been its spiritual aspect. It's likely that your hard-won ability to integrate the material and spiritual sides of life triumphed in the end.

Although you may have had no trouble attracting worthy admirers, it might have taken you a while to find the right one. Once you found someone who could meet your standards of kindness and compassion, making a lifelong commitment would have been easy for you. Your most compatible love signs may be Cancer, Virgo, Capricorn, and Pisces.

Your challenge is maintaining financial security without becoming obsessed with it. Your gift is your determination to make the world a better place.

GEMINI

From May 22, 6:45 through June 22, 15:04

The Inquisitive Motivator

Around the time you were born, Gemini of 1903, Paris and Rome were linked by telephone for the first time, and physicist Pierre Curie announced the discovery of a new radioactive element, Polonium (which he named after Poland to honor his wife, who was born there). These events gave an exciting edge to a still-new century, and it's likely that you felt that exhilaration when you were a child, and ran with it. Unlike many of your contemporaries, who were primarily concerned with day-to-day existence, you may always have been on the lookout for anything new and different to stimulate your quicksilver mind.

Restless, versatile, and upbeat, you probably craved excitement and variety when you were young, often looking like you would burst at the seams if you had to sit still. As you matured, your spirited personality may have quieted down a bit, but you thirsted for fresh ideas to satisfy your eager imagination. In adulthood, you could have grown into a serious, practical-minded person who was keenly aware that future possibilities could only materialize with accompanying hard work.

You may have excelled at conveying a sense of adventure to others, and motivating friends, family members, and people in your community to realize their dreams. In your job, you may have been equally encouraging to those who worked with you, or for you, allowing them to find their own particular niche, or discover a talent they did not know they had.

In love, you may have looked for a mate whose interests were as wide and varied as your own. And even though your individual interests may have differed, as long as you shared the same dreams of a lifetime surrounded by family and friends, your partnership could have succeeded where others failed. The most fulfilling love signs for you may be Leo, Libra, and Aquarius, but in the end fiery Aries may have won your mercurial heart.

Your challenge is to make the most of your time, accepting that you cannot pursue all your hobbies and passions. Your strength lies in helping people to discover the best in themselves, and use that best to improve their own lives.

➤ Read about your Chinese Astrological sign on page 838. ➤ Read about your Personal Planets on page 826. ➤ Read about your personal Mystical Card on page 856.

1903

TAURUS
Your Personal Planets

YOUR LOVE POTENTIAL
Venus in Gemini, Apr. 21, 6:59 - May 13, 16:22
Venus in Cancer, May 13, 16:23 - May 22, 6:44

YOUR DRIVE AND AMBITION
Mars in Virgo, Apr. 21, 6:59 - May 22, 6:44

YOUR LUCK MAGNETISM
Jupiter in Pisces, Apr. 21, 6:59 - May 22, 6:44

World Events

May 6 – Italy sends warships to Salonika to help the Turkish Sultan suppress the Macedonian rebellion.

May 8 – French artist Paul Gauguin dies.

French artist Paul Gauguin's "Te Raau Rahi"

GEMINI
Your Personal Planets

YOUR LOVE POTENTIAL
Venus in Cancer, May 22, 6:45 - June 09, 3:06
Venus in Leo, June 09, 3:07 - June 22, 15:04

YOUR DRIVE AND AMBITION
Mars in Virgo, May 22, 6:45 - May 30, 17:20
Mars in Libra, May 30, 17:21 - June 22, 15:04

YOUR LUCK MAGNETISM
Jupiter in Pisces, May 22, 6:45 - June 22, 15:04

World Events

June 8 – Nineteen people are killed as the Mississippi River floods in Missouri.

June 16 – Henry Ford sets up his automobile company in Detroit, Michigan.

1903

CANCER
Your Personal Planets

YOUR LOVE POTENTIAL

Venus in Leo, June 22, 15:05 - July 07, 20:35
Venus in Virgo, July 07, 20:36 - July 24, 1:58

YOUR DRIVE AND AMBITION

Mars in Libra, June 22, 15:05 - July 24, 1:58

YOUR LUCK MAGNETISM

Jupiter in Pisces, June 22, 15:05 - July 24, 1:58

World Events

June 25 - British author George Orwell is born.

June 26 - President Roosevelt's petition protesting Russian treatment of Jews is rejected by Czar Nicholas II.

"1984" author George Orwell is born under the sign of Cancer

LEO
Your Personal Planets

YOUR LOVE POTENTIAL

Venus in Virgo, July 24, 1:59 - Aug. 17, 21:50
Venus in Libra, Aug. 17, 21:51 - Aug. 24, 8:41

YOUR DRIVE AND AMBITION

Mars in Libra, July 24, 1:59 - Aug. 06, 16:26
Mars in Scorpio, Aug. 06, 16:27 - Aug. 24, 8:41

YOUR LUCK MAGNETISM

Jupiter in Pisces, July 24, 1:59 - Aug. 24, 8:41

World Events

Aug. 4 - Giuseppe Sarto is elected Pope Pius X.

Aug. 19 - The British government makes a formal protest against Belgian treatment of natives in the Congo.

CANCER
From June 22, 15:05 through July 24, 1:58

The Loving Relative

You may have been even more treasured than other newborns, Cancer of 1903. Around the time you were born, the birth rate was declining in England and elsewhere, causing alarm in some circles at the possible long-term consequences of descending population growth. As a result, you have probably been showered with affection—pampered and coddled in the bosom of your loving family.

In turn, you may have devoted much of your life to caring for your own family, which may have encompassed your extended family of friends and neighbors. Sending flowers, thoughtful notes, or simply saying "thank you" might have been your trademark, and would have endeared you to all. It's possible that your professional choices were made with your home and family in mind, and you may never have taken a job where you had to travel too far from home if you could help it. Although this may have seemed dull to some, you probably found it fulfilling in ways your more adventurous friends may never have known.

Caring and loving, you could have found great happiness in gardening, caring for animals, and other home-centered activities. When you did manage to take a break from your busy family life, you may have been involved in things like school organizing or community causes. It's likely that you were the one who held the group together, sorting out people's differences and finding ways for everyone to work together as one big family. You might be surprised to know how many of your colleagues are secretly grateful to you for pointing them in a new direction.

In relationships, you may always have been a person of few words, letting your meaningful gestures, hugs, and smiles say it all. You can be comfortable with someone else who does the talking, however, since you listen intently, and make others feel as if they have important things to say. You may have looked for and found your love match among the Virgos, Scorpios, or Pisceans of your acquaintance.

Your challenge is to keep your daily routine fresh and lively. Your strength lies in the way you let others know that you are thinking of them.

LEO
From July 24, 1:59 through August 24, 8:41

The Triumphant Visionary

As a Leo of 1903, you were probably born while the first United States transcontinental auto race from San Francisco to New York City was under way. Not until August 21, after two months and one day, did the winning car—a Model F Packard—finally cross the finish line. As you grew up you witnessed, and were probably transfixed by, communication and transportation breakthroughs of breathtaking proportions. As a Leo, you would have wanted to stand out from the crowd in any case, but hearing stories about the heroic drivers, pilots, and yachtsmen who broke record after record in your childhood could have prompted you to excel.

Exuding confidence and self-reliance, you've probably always impressed people with your certainty and ability to size up any situation. When you were a child, this may have translated into spending many hours alone so that you could develop your ideas unimpeded. As you matured, it's likely that you developed just the right touch to get people and their ideas moving when they ground to a halt. Contrary to what others may think, you've probably never been an initiator, or even a finisher, but rather a superb troubleshooter whose expertise can untangle any knots that develop in the middle of a project.

Although you may love being the center of attention, telling people what to do was probably never your style. Instead, you may have been more comfortable in a position where you could be inventive and original, but in your own time, and you probably chose to use your skills to handle your own day-to-day problems.

In love, you've always wanted a degree of privacy, yet you may be most fulfilled when you are needed. You can be a true helpmate, sharing in all the long-term plans and important decision-making of a committed relationship, and you may find your mate among the Sagittarians, Ariens, or Geminis that you know.

Your challenge is to let down your guard and ask others to be there for you when you need them. Your gifts are your enthusiasm and spirit, which can inspire everyone who knows you to bigger and better things.

➤ Read about your Chinese Astrological sign on page 838. ➤ Read about your Personal Planets on page 826. ➤ Read about your personal Mystical Card on page 856.

VIRGO

From August 24, 8:42 through September 24, 5:43

The Helpful Organizer

Turkish troops were exterminating thousands of Bulgarian citizens around the time you were born, and you may have heard stories about this massacre when you were a child. You may have been shy and sensitive, and these stories of brutality and inhumanity could have filled you not only with revulsion, but also with great sadness and empathy. You may have had to develop a thick skin early in life, Virgo of 1903, but you could have decided secretly that, even if the world were a cold, cruel place, you would do something to make a difference.

As you matured, you probably dealt with life's currents and crosscurrents in a way that seemed easy and graceful to those around you. Inside, you knew the hard work it took to get there, and it's likely that you always set yourself a high goal and then methodically worked to reach it. You probably never wasted time thinking about the in-between steps or worrying about whether they demanded more than you could muster. Because you probably don't like doing things over, it would be important that whatever you tackled be done right the first time.

You would have been a natural for a managerial position of some sort. When the going got rough or a crossroads was reached, you'd have been good at pointing out what the options were, and also the best way to exercise those options. It's likely that, wherever you were, everyone pitched in and helped everyone else, and you were the organizer. In your spare time, you might have started a collection of some kind—perhaps antique furniture or silver to add beauty to your home.

In your intimate relationships, you might have looked for someone who could be a real partner to you. You can be most compatible with Scorpios, Capricorns, and Taureans, who are likely to be people you could talk things out with, and who like hard work as much as you do.

With your infinite attention to detail, your challenge is to abandon at least some of the details so that you can complete the work in a reasonable amount of time. Your gift is your ability to attract a team of willing helpers who just want to be around you.

LIBRA

From September 24, 5:44 through October 24, 14:22

The Positive Promoter

Family outings, sporting events, and group activities may have filled your childhood, Libra of 1903. Around the time you were born, the first baseball World Series was played in Boston, Massachusetts. (The home team won in an upset.) Of course, only American teams played for the title of "world champion". Still, your parents might have used the example of baseball to instill good sportsmanship and teach you that winning isn't everything. They probably encouraged you to have fun while giving everything your best shot, and that could be why you learned early on not to take life too seriously.

A natural balance of charm and willingness to explore new ideas could have made you an asset to any creative team, and you might have used your talents in a profession such as advertising, sales, or public relations. But it's likely that you've never been ambitious, and work probably hasn't taken first place in your life. Even though you may have had the same personal and professional struggles as anyone else, you always had a smile on your face and some people may have thought that you didn't have a care in the world. Your co-workers might have loved helping you out now and then, but you probably shied away from sharing your feelings or asking for help.

You probably loved spending time talking and laughing with your friends, and plenty of invitations to parties, excursions, and sporting events could have come your way. You may have chosen hobbies that would keep you active, and you could have been a star player on any team you joined.

In love, you may have looked for someone who could enjoy lighthearted fun, and, while your only criterion wouldn't have been good looks, you may have loved the fact that people's heads turned when you walked down the street together. For this reason, you may have gravitated toward Sagittarians and Leos, who also love being in the spotlight.

Your challenge is to let down your guard and ask others to be there for you when you need them. Your gifts are your enthusiasm and spirit, which can inspire everyone who knows you to bigger and better things.

➤ Read about your Chinese Astrological sign on page 838. ➤ Read about your Personal Planets on page 826. ➤ Read about your personal Mystical Card on page 856.

VIRGO
Your Personal Planets

YOUR LOVE POTENTIAL
Venus in Libra, Aug. 24, 8:42 - Sept. 06, 2:27
Venus in Virgo, Sept. 06, 2:28 - Sept. 24, 5:43

YOUR DRIVE AND AMBITION
Mars in Scorpio, Aug. 24, 8:42 - Sept. 22, 13:51
Mars in Sagittarius, Sept. 22, 13:52 - Sept. 24, 5:43

YOUR LUCK MAGNETISM
Jupiter in Pisces, Aug. 24, 8:42 - Sept. 24, 5:43

World Events

Sept. 7 – U.S. troops are sent to Beirut to protect the Consulate from a threatened Muslim uprising.

Sept. 19 – King Leopold of Belgium denies foreign charges of cruelty in the Congo.

King Leopold of Belgium

LIBRA
Your Personal Planets

YOUR LOVE POTENTIAL
Venus in Virgo, Sept. 24, 5:44 - Oct. 24, 14:22

YOUR DRIVE AND AMBITION
Mars in Sagittarius, Sept. 24, 5:44 - Oct. 24, 14:22

YOUR LUCK MAGNETISM
Jupiter in Pisces, Sept. 24, 5:44 - Oct. 24, 14:22

World Events

Oct. 8 – Japan sends troops to Manchuria to force the Russian evacuation.

Oct. 13 – In northern France, 40,000 workers in the textile industry go on strike for shorter hours and wage hikes.

1903

SCORPIO
Your Personal Planets

YOUR LOVE POTENTIAL
Venus in Virgo, Oct. 24, 14:23 - Nov. 08, 14:43
Venus in Libra, Nov. 08, 14:44 - Nov. 23, 11:21

YOUR DRIVE AND AMBITION
Mars in Sagittarius, Oct. 24, 14:23 - Nov. 03, 5:30
Mars in Capricorn, Nov. 03, 5:31 - Nov. 23, 11:21

YOUR LUCK MAGNETISM
Jupiter in Pisces, Oct. 24, 14:23 - Nov. 23, 11:21

World Events

Oct. 28 – English novelist Evelyn Waugh is born.

Nov. 17 – In London, Lenin's radical views split the Russian Social Democratic Labor Party into two factions: Bolsheviks and Mensheviks.

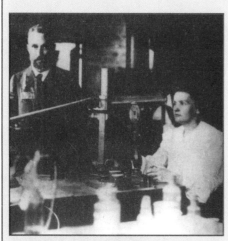

Pierre and Marie Curie, Nobel Prize winners for physics

SAGITTARIUS
Your Personal Planets

YOUR LOVE POTENTIAL
Venus in Libra, Nov. 23, 11:22 - Dec. 09, 14:41
Venus in Scorpio, Dec. 09, 14:42 - Dec. 23, 0:20

YOUR DRIVE AND AMBITION
Mars in Capricorn, Nov. 23, 11:22 - Dec. 12, 9:55
Mars in Aquarius, Dec. 12, 9:56 - Dec. 23, 0:20

YOUR LUCK MAGNETISM
Jupiter in Pisces, Nov. 23, 11:22 - Dec. 23, 0:20

World Events

Dec. 10 – Pierre and Marie Curie share the Nobel Prize for physics with Henri Becquerel for their experiments with radioactivity.

Dec. 17 – Orville and Wilbur Wright make four flights in a heavier-than-air plane at Kitty Hawk, North Carolina.

SCORPIO
From October 24, 14:23 through November 23, 11:21

The Objective Administrator

Around the time you were born, Scorpio of 1903, the United States signed the treaty that opened the way for building the Panama Canal. This remarkable engineering feat connecting the Atlantic and Pacific Oceans was completed in 1914, transforming the world economy by allowing goods to flow more easily from Europe and the Americas to the Far East. Building the canal was a monumental enterprise, and the scope and depth of this venture might illustrate the way you've always approached life. You were probably never afraid to dig deep and work long hours to get where you wanted to go, and once you set a goal for yourself there would have been little that could sway you from your path.

It's likely that things that others might have considered insurmountable obstacles did not easily daunt you. Although you too might want life to run in safe and familiar channels, you were rarely bothered when challenging situations arose, and simply worked through them until everything once again ran smoothly. For that reason, people could have wanted you to be on their team, and you would have made a valuable contribution no matter what your role, whether you were captain, partner, or supporting player.

In friendships, you were probably the one people came to for advice on everything from home improvement to handling heartache. Even though you may have been deeply concerned about and involved with those close to you, you could still look at their personal problems in an objective and unemotional way, and your advice was often the best.

In love, you may have displayed the same patience and ability to solve problems that you demonstrated in other areas of your life. You could have waited to make a commitment until you found a true soul mate who would understand you in a way that no one else did. You might find your mate among the Capricorns, Pisceans, or Cancerians in your life, but an organized Virgo could be a match for you too.

Your challenge is to let yourself be spontaneous more often. Your gift is the way you can break down even the most complicated task to a size you can handle with ease.

SAGITTARIUS
From November 23, 11:22 through December 23, 0:20

The Flying Ace

A truly monumental event occurred around the time you were born, 1903 Sagittarius. On December 17, the Wright brothers soared above the sands of Kitty Hawk in the first human-controlled powered flight ever made and, in an instant, changed the course of history. The power of invention illustrated by this historic incident may fit perfectly with your own optimism and exemplify the faith you've had in man's ability to change the world for the better.

This could be why you were always on the lookout for the unique and the interesting in everything. As a child, one of your favorite books might have been Mark Twain's *Life On The Mississippi*, and it may have inspired you to look for ways to put a fascinating spin on whatever you did.

You may have a knack for seeing through the masks people wear in public, and you may have used this ability to discover the unique skills and individuality that lies beneath. This talent may have made you invaluable in almost any line of work, from teaching to counseling to running a business. If you did go into business, it's likely that it had something to do with travel because you love adventure. And your team, or your employees, were probably the best that could be found. That's because you can find the "one thing" about anyone that sets them apart from the crowd and you have always been good at encouraging others to develop skills and interests that they otherwise might not. Your magnetic personality just seems to draw people to you, so maintaining close friendships that last many years may be the easiest part of life for you.

In relationships, you may have looked for a partner who was dynamic and who perhaps could confront you and challenge you at some level. The more interesting and unique a person is, the better for you. Good love signs for you may include Aquarius, Aries, and Leo, but you might lose your heart to a charming Libra.

Your challenge is to find a way to keep life exciting while at the same time maintaining some stability and security. Your gift is the ability to inspire others, as well as yourself, to get the most out of life.

➤ Read about your Chinese Astrological sign on page 838. ➤ Read about your Personal Planets on page 826. ➤ Read about your personal Mystical Card on page 856.

CAPRICORN

From December 23, 0:21 through December 31, 23:59

The Good-Natured Mediator

A tragic fire in the Iroquois Theater in Chicago, Illinois, marked the time you were born. No matter where you grew up, hearing about the fire as a child may have affected you deeply, especially if you learned that part of the reason nearly six hundred people had perished was the "every man for himself" stampede that took place when the fire was discovered. That's why, as a Capricorn born in December of 1903, you may have devoted much of your life to getting people to work together.

Your belief that there's always a way for people to get along is something you may have lived every day. Even if you never sought out situations to mediate, it's likely that they found you. It's possible that you used your skills later in life as a labor negotiator, lawyer, or investment banker, and you were probably the first person your friends turned to when an objective third party was needed to settle an argument. You'd always go a step beyond ruling on who was right and who was wrong and try to get the disputants to consider whether there was another viewpoint entirely, another way that could benefit both of them at the same time.

In your leisure time, you may enjoy outdoor activities, and it's likely that you can be found in the garden all summer long. Growing flowers can be fun for you, but your pragmatic side would also plant corn and beans—the kinds of vegetables that you could can or freeze to enjoy during the winter.

In love, you may feel that sharing the day-to-day responsibilities as well as the deep commitment of a loving partnership is the ideal recipe for a lasting relationship. You may look for a partner who would enjoy having family discussions and considering everybody's viewpoint on family decisions. In general, your best love signs are Pisces, Taurus, Virgo, and Scorpio.

Your challenge is trying to reason with people who think they are right and everyone else is wrong, no matter what the issue. Your greatest strength, and what people love you for, is the way you've learned to bring two people, two groups, or two opposing ideas together in a way that makes everyone a winner!

CAPRICORN
Your Personal Planets

YOUR LOVE POTENTIAL
Venus in Scorpio, Dec. 23, 0:21 - Dec. 31, 23:59

YOUR DRIVE AND AMBITION
Mars in Aquarius, Dec. 23, 0:21 - Dec. 31, 23:59

YOUR LUCK MAGNETISM
Jupiter in Pisces, Dec. 23, 0:21 - Dec. 31, 23:59

World Events

Dec. 28 – The French divide their part of the Congo into Ubangi-Shari, Chad, Gabon, and Middle Congo.

Dec. 31 – The Japanese Parliament is dissolved after publicly demanding that the country break diplomatic ties with Russia.

Jeanne Dixon

Special Feature
Astrology Reigns Through the Ages: Powerful People Consulting the Stars

(Continued from page 33)

Tycho Brahe, a colorful sixteenth-century Swede, was a royal astrologer in the Courts of Denmark and Germany. Brahe, who majored in stellar science, was often heard saying that, "The stars rule the lot of man." One of the most celebrated prophecies made by Brahe was based on his observations of a comet. Brahe predicted that "in the north of Finland, there will be born a prince who should lay waste to Germany and vanish in 1632." As history shows, Prince Gustavus Adolphus, a Finlander, did vanquish Germany during the Thirty Years' War. The *Encyclopedia Britannica* states that the "fulfillment of this prophecy suggests that Tycho Brahe had some basis of reason for his prediction"—but the Encyclopedia fails to credit astrology as that "reasonable" foundation.

Another famous sixteenth-century scientist, Johannes Kepler, taught astrology and the casting of horoscopes. From the planetary-motion tables he created, astrologers were able to easily calculate the positions of the planets at any point in time. Kepler's famous statement to theologians, physicians, and philosophers regarding astrology is still quoted: "While it is reasonable to reject star-gazing superstitions, the kernel should not be "thrown away with the shell," meaning that his esteemed colleagues should keep the parts of astrology that worked. Perhaps his most famous client was General Wallenstein. Kepler's original manuscript on this astrological prognostication is still preserved in the University of St. Petersburg, along with his predictions for the life and death of this general—all of which were accurately fulfilled.

Much more recently, American astrologer Jeanne Dixon (1918-1997) captivated astrology buffs the world over with both stunningly accurate—and inaccurate—prophecies. Her books, tabloid prognostications, and personal appearances made hers a household name. Decades earlier, another celebrity astrologer, Evangeline Adams, had taken New York's rich and famous by storm. In the early 1900s, Adams advised J. P. Morgan, Charlie Chaplin, and even world-famous tenor Enrico Caruso—who absolutely refused to cross the Atlantic without Adams's okay!

Clearly, it's easy to see that astrology has played a much larger role in the lives of the rich and powerful, famous and infamous—and ,therefore, in history itself—than we are ever likely to know. Unless, of course, we ask the astrologers... ☼

➤ Read "Astrology in the White House: The Reagans" on page 705. ➤ Read "Nostradamus: A Prophet Across Time" on page 785. ➤ Read "Money, Astrology, and the Crash of '29" on page 225.

41

1904

The Fires of Initiation: Aries and Leo

In the year 1904, the planets were involved in a fiery dance of forceful initiation and gusto. This was a year of new beginnings, due to the dynamic power of Jupiter in Aries. Jupiter in Aries provides the faith that man has the ability to overcome anything and everything. In March of this year, the planet Jupiter moved to a new sign—from emotional Pisces to sizzling Aries. Jupiter is the planet connected to philosophy and ideas. Aries is the sign of birth and leadership, and is ruled by Mars, the God of War. With Jupiter placed here in 1904, it is no wonder that the drumbeat toward confrontation sounded throughout the world. This was the year that the Russo-Japanese war began. During this conflict Russia and Japan fought over Manchuria and Korea. In July of this year, British warships were dispatched to protect merchant marine ships from harassment by the Russian navy. General strikes continued around the world as the aggressive planet Mars shifted into the royal sign of Leo. Leo is the sign of majesty, power and dignity. It is symbolized by the lion, king of the jungle. When Mars enters Leo, willpower skyrockets.

In August of 1904, these two strong planets made contact with each other across the sky, causing important projects to take off below. Initiation is the key when Mars and Jupiter prod each other on. This year, the New York City subway opened for business, and work on the Panama Canal finally began. These were just a few of the ventures that took off in this spectacular year. The live wire of the new was lit and making a grand conflagration.

A Russian poster of the Russo-Japanese War

Ivan Pavlov wins the Nobel Prize in physiology for his stimulus studies with dogs

Helen Keller, blind and deaf since infancy, is awarded a Bachelor's degree from Radcliffe College

THE KING OF HANDCUFFS

Master magician Harry Houdini had been a sensation in English vaudeville for many years, but in 1904 his European tour culminated in his most famous public escape yet. The British newspaper *The London Mirror* challenged the extraordinary magician to free himself from a specially designed pair of handcuffs complete with six sets of locks—dubbed "supercuffs." Houdini escaped in a little more than an hour, astonishing the huge crowd of four thousand spectators and earning himself the title of "King of Handcuffs."

GLOBALIZATION GROWS

The Russians and Japanese began fighting over Korea and Manchuria, with the Japanese winning decisive early battles, as other nations declared their neutrality. Fighting continued between the Dutch and Chinese in Sumatra, and the Germans and Herero tribes in southwest Africa. France severed ties with the Vatican in its continuing anti-clerical movement. King Leopold II of Belgium created an international commission in response to accusations of atrocities in the Congo. The incumbent US President, Theodore 'Teddy' Roosevelt, won another term in office. The New York subway officially opened and was immediately used by thousands. Helen Keller, blind and deaf since infancy, was awarded a Bachelor's degree from Radcliffe College. J.M. Barrie's *Peter Pan* was first published, while Puccini's *Madame Butterfly* and Ravel's *Scheherazade* premièred in Europe. The third modern Olympics were held in St. Louis, Missouri, with the U.S. winning most events. Bartholdi, sculptor of the Statue of Liberty, died, as did Sir Henry Stanley, the British explorer of Africa. Ivan Pavlov won the Nobel Prize for his studies of conditioned responses in dogs.

➤ Read J. P. Morgan's Star Profile on page 49.

CAPRICORN

From January 01, 0:00 through January 21, 10:57

The Conservative Reformer

As a Capricorn born in January of 1904, you came into a world that was starting to change very fast. Around the time you were born, Moscow saw the première of Anton Chekhov's play *The Cherry Orchard*, which centered on how landowners who knew nothing about business could lose their estates to the new, savvy working class. But old systems of class and wealth were being challenged everywhere, and ideas about equality of opportunity were in the air.

Throughout your life, these ideals may have been the bedrock of your thinking. No matter what your line of work was, it's likely that the main thing you required before becoming involved was a clear idea of what you would be paid. You're no stranger to volunteer work and charity, but you probably feel that those should come after you've done a good day's work for a good day's pay. Once you committed yourself to a project, however, you were probably a powerhouse who could handle projects big and small, finishing them on time and under budget.

You may enjoy being in the company of like-minded people, although you would reserve your greatest respect for those who shared your work ethic. You may have involved yourself with causes committed to reform of one kind or another. Because you can be dedicated to aiming forever higher, it's likely that you would work to change rules and institutions that you thought were unfair. However, you probably stayed with a reform movement only as long as it served a purpose. Your goal would have been to fix a problem, not to build an empire.

In love, you may have been drawn to someone who shared your traditional values and progressive ideals, yet who could follow a budget. A mystical Pisces may be able to calm you down when you get overexcited about some injustice you have seen. Other signs who share your values and with whom you could make a good match are Taurus, Virgo, and Scorpio.

Your challenge is to have patience with the people who don't catch on as quickly as you do, or work with the same type of exactitude. Your gift is your commitment to finding solutions that are fair to everyone.

AQUARIUS

From January 21, 10:58 through February 20, 1:24

The Patient Humanitarian

You were born around the time Japan and Russia declared war on each other, Aquarius of 1904—one of the many wars that would ravage the world during the twentieth century. As a child, hearing about man's inhumanity to man could have hurt you deeply, for you can have humanitarian instincts and a nurturing soul. Perhaps in an attempt to mitigate such human tragedies you might have devoted a good portion of your life to the care of others. If a friend or a neighbor was ill, or a family member needed help, you were probably the first person they called—and the first who pitched in.

When you were younger, you may have thought you were going to change the world, or even save it, and you might have dreamed of winning a Nobel Peace Prize or some other honor. As you matured, however, your dreams may have manifested closer to home, and you might have tried to help those in your own community who were in need. You may have found a way to do this professionally as a legal advocate or social worker, while working as a hospital volunteer may have been an activity you pursued in your leisure time.

You could tend to be basically happy, with an even disposition, although as a teenager you probably had quite a temper—one that was likely to flare up when someone disagreed with your point of view. You probably became more tolerant as an adult, gaining the facility to persuade others to your way of thinking and even to make them advocates of your point of view, and this ability to provide guidance may have become your hallmark.

In love, you may like being in a relationship in which you are needed, where your partner not only asks your advice but also respects your point of view. Talking about current events together, and sharing your dreams of how you can change the world, could have forged a strong bond between you and a Sagittarian, but you could also find a compatible love match with Ariens, Geminis, or Librans.

Your challenge is to balance your desire to save the world against your responsibilities to home and family. Your gift is your actions that have always spoken louder than words.

➤ Read about your Chinese Astrological sign on page 838. ➤ Read about your Personal Planets on page 826. ➤ Read about your personal Mystical Card on page 856.

1904

CAPRICORN
Your Personal Planets

YOUR LOVE POTENTIAL
Venus in Scorpio, Jan. 01, 0:00 - Jan. 05, 3:42
Venus in Sagittarius, Jan. 05, 3:43 - Jan. 21, 10:57

YOUR DRIVE AND AMBITION
Mars in Aquarius, Jan. 01, 0:00 - Jan. 19, 15:49
Mars in Pisces, Jan. 19, 15:50 - Jan. 21, 10:57

YOUR LUCK MAGNETISM
Jupiter in Pisces, Jan. 01, 0:00 - Jan. 21, 10:57

World Events

Jan. 13 - The Russian Foreign Minister denies Japanese interest in Manchurian affairs, stating that they concern only Russia and China.

Jan. 18 - American film star Cary Grant is born.

Battleships in the Suez Canal

AQUARIUS
Your Personal Planets

YOUR LOVE POTENTIAL
Venus in Sagittarius, Jan. 21, 10:58 - Jan. 30, 9:27
Venus in Capricorn, Jan. 30, 9:28 - Feb. 20, 1:24

YOUR DRIVE AND AMBITION
Mars in Pisces, Jan. 21, 10:58 - Feb. 20, 1:24

YOUR LUCK MAGNETISM
Jupiter in Pisces, Jan. 21, 10:58 - Feb. 20, 1:24

World Events

Feb. 3 - Colombian troops clash with U.S. Marines in Panama.

Feb. 10 - Russia and Japan declare war after a Japanese attack on Russian warships at Port Arthur two days previously.

1904

PISCES
Your Personal Planets

YOUR LOVE POTENTIAL
Venus in Capricorn, Feb. 20, 1:25 - Feb. 24, 3:07
Venus in Aquarius, Feb. 24, 3:08 - Mar. 19, 16:00
Venus in Pisces, Mar. 19, 16:01 - Mar. 21, 0:58

YOUR DRIVE AND AMBITION
Mars in Pisces, Feb. 20, 1:25 - Feb. 27, 3:11
Mars in Aries, Feb. 27, 3:12 - Mar. 21, 0:58

YOUR LUCK MAGNETISM
Jupiter in Pisces, Feb. 20, 1:25 - Mar. 01, 2:59
Jupiter in Aries, Mar. 01, 3:00 - Mar. 21, 0:58

World Events

Mar. 1 – American Big Band leader Glenn Miller is born in Clarinda, Iowa.

Mar. 3 – The first recording of a political document is made by Kaiser Wilhelm II on the Edison cylinder.

Wreckage of a Russian Battleship in Port Arthur Harbor

ARIES
Your Personal Planets

YOUR LOVE POTENTIAL
Venus in Pisces, Mar. 21, 0:59 - Apr. 13, 3:26
Venus in Aries, Apr. 13, 3:27 - Apr. 20, 12:41

YOUR DRIVE AND AMBITION
Mars in Aries, Mar. 21, 0:59 - Apr. 06, 18:05
Mars in Taurus, Apr. 06, 18:06 - Apr. 20, 12:41

YOUR LUCK MAGNETISM
Jupiter in Aries, Mar. 21, 0:59 - Apr. 20, 12:41

World Events

Mar. 24 – Japanese Vice Admiral Togo sinks seven Russian ships and strengthens the blockade of Port Arthur.

Apr. 2 – The rebelling Herero tribes are defeated by the German Major von Glasenapp near Okaharui in South-West Africa.

PISCES

From February 20, 1:25 through March 21, 0:58

The Whimsical Teacher

Around the time you were born a festival was held in London celebrating the work of the composer Edward Elgar, bringing his musical genius to a wide audience. Such events would have appealed to your creative side, Pisces of 1904. Unassuming, and at times timid, you might have wished for a simple life, one where you could exercise your imagination while occupying yourself with the everyday responsibilities of home and family. It's likely that these small dreams remained constant all your life, but that your life affected more people than you ever knew.

Your sweetness and your spontaneity might make you feel most comfortable when you're around children, so teaching or counseling children would have been a natural occupation for you. While a desire for security may have colored many of your decisions when you were younger, as you matured you might have become more involved in community life. You were probably more comfortable in small circles than in large groups, and you probably loved being left to yourself for hours to write, design clothing, or read.

Your ability to discover other people's hidden talents might have seemed uncanny, but it was just a result of your caring and loving heart, and you probably used your gifts to encourage others to do their very best. You could be a good coach and a supportive friend, as you bring out the best in people by guiding, never instructing. Interestingly, you may not be as good at seeing your own best talents, but will listen and learn from anyone who points them out to you.

In relationships, you probably strive to be supportive and help your partner feel that they are capable of doing anything at all. You may also want your mate to reassure you that the decisions you make are the right ones, both for yourself and your loved ones. You may be most compatible with Taureans, Cancerians, Scorpios, and Capricorns.

Your challenge is to believe that your whimsical imagination can be put to good use in the outside world and not just close to home. Your gift is the ability to make a real difference to everyone whose life you touch.

ARIES

From March 21, 0:59 through April 20, 12:41

The Bold Enthusiast

In the United States, Colorado authorities banished labor leader "Mother Jones" from their state around the time you were born. Her crime: stirring up striking coal miners. When you were growing up, hearing stories of the way she roused people to stand up for themselves may have inspired you, Aries of 1904, resonating with your natural independence. You may have loved to be first at anything. You probably excelled in your studies, and may have even won honors and gained recognition. You are an independent-minded person, but one who always works well with others. Later in your life, you may have dreamed about achieving something great and daring with a team, like climbing Mount Everest or swimming the English Channel.

Bold, fervent, and always ready to stand your ground, you may have been quite a handful as a youngster. With your infinite curiosity, you may have questioned much that your parents and teachers told you. As you matured, that rebelliousness may have been transformed into boundless enthusiasm, and your friends and family probably had trouble keeping up with your pace. Vacations were not likely to have been quiet times at the beach: long hikes and outdoor camping expeditions were probably more your style.

It's likely that there was always something just ahead that you set your sights on, even if you did not actually pursue each and every vision in a single-minded way. Eternally hopeful, you may have inspired others to follow their dreams, even the seemingly impossible ones.

In love, you may have looked for a partner who is as optimistic as you, someone who always looked on the bright side of life even in the most difficult times. Resolving problems quickly and then moving on to the next challenge is your style and you probably wanted your partner to feel the same. Those who share these sentiments and fit best with you are Geminis, Leos, Sagittarians, and Aquarians.

Your challenge is developing compassion for those who could not match your pace. Your strength is putting people at ease, especially in situations where you may have had a natural advantage.

➤ Read about your Chinese Astrological sign on page 838. ➤ Read about your Personal Planets on page 826. ➤ Read about your personal Mystical Card on page 856.

TAURUS

From April 20, 12:42 through May 21, 12:28

The Guiding Light

Around the time you were born, Czech composer Antonín Dvořák died. At the same time, two men who were destined to change history were born—physicist Robert Oppenheimer, the father of the atomic bomb, and Willem de Kooning, one of America's greatest painters—perhaps signaling that you too were born for greatness, Taurus of 1904. You probably never settled for anything less, and you may always have felt that if people tried just a little bit harder they would find success.

Determined, down to earth, and highly intuitive, you may have based your core values on an inner judgment of right and wrong. You've probably held firmly to your beliefs throughout your life, and while you have been known to change your mind, it's likely that you'll do so only in the face of solid evidence. It may have been difficult to persuade you to look at another point of view when you were younger, but as you matured you may have begun to understand how much you had learned from other people.

You may have been interested not only in ideas, but also in the best way to express them. Your own desire to be praised for your ideas and opinions may have challenged you to develop tactful ways to help people without criticizing them. This skill could have made you an exceptional manager, since the people who worked for you would feel that you appreciated their contributions. It's likely that you looked for clear-cut and straightforward ways of doing everything, and that friends and co-workers were comfortable with you because they knew where they stood.

In romance, you may have looked for someone who'd never settle for doing less than their best. You might enjoy a relationship that's based on repartee, perhaps preferring to argue about the small things as long as you agree about the things that matter. In general, you can get along famously with Cancerians, Virgos, and Capricorns, but don't rule out a mysterious Piscean.

Your challenge is to bend, not break, when the winds of change are strong. Your strength is your steady ideals, which are a beacon of hope and a guiding light for all who know you.

GEMINI

From May 21, 12:29 through June 21, 20:50

The Eternal Youth

You arrived at a hopeful moment in history, 1904 Gemini. China signed the Geneva Convention around the time you were born, and people could hope that peace would prevail. Charming, flighty, and eternally youthful, when you were growing up you probably viewed life with the type of innocence usually reserved for children. Friends may have teased that you had something in common with the title character of Sir James Barrie's play about a boy who refused to grow up, and it's probably no surprise to learn that *Peter Pan* premiered in the year you were born.

You may have needed very little sleep when you were young, and later on the song *I Could Have Danced All Night* might have reminded you of the days when you did just that. But getting old—and feeling old—was never in your game plan, and your feisty reluctance to defer to what others might deem inevitable would have drawn admirers all your life. With your drive to stay in top mental and physical shape, you probably worked hard to maintain your strength and stamina. What might have kept you going is your insistence that as long as you feel young, the numbers attached to your age make little difference.

Communication in all its forms could have been a lifelong passion, and you may have contributed to a community newspaper or possibly tried your hand at writing fiction at some time. Journalism could have suited you and would have held your interest over the long haul. You probably loved going to movies too, and you may have been more delighted than most when television arrived.

In love, you may have looked for someone who could keep up with your quicksilver mind and incredible pace. You'd probably also have wanted your mate to have a range of interests as wide as your own. If they could engage in conversations about anything and everything, so much the better! The best love signs for you can be Leo, Libra, Aquarius, and Aries.

Your challenge is to stay active so that your body keeps up with your mind. Your gift is your sense of eternal optimism that tells you there is no such thing as being "too old" for anything.

➤ Read about your Chinese Astrological sign on page 838. ➤ Read about your Personal Planets on page 826. ➤ Read about your personal Mystical Card on page 856.

1904

TAURUS
Your Personal Planets

YOUR LOVE POTENTIAL
Venus in Aries, Apr. 20, 12:42 - May 07, 14:51
Venus in Taurus, May 07, 14:52 - May 21, 12:28

YOUR DRIVE AND AMBITION
Mars in Taurus, Apr. 20, 12:42 - May 18, 3:34
Mars in Gemini, May 18, 3:35 - May 21, 12:28

YOUR LUCK MAGNETISM
Jupiter in Aries, Apr. 20, 12:42 - May 21, 12:28

World Events

May 4 - Work begins on the Panama Canal.
May 5 - Britain declares war on Tibet in an effort to end the country's isolation.

Work underway on the Panama Canal

GEMINI
Your Personal Planets

YOUR LOVE POTENTIAL
Venus in Taurus, May 21, 12:29 - June 01, 2:27
Venus in Gemini, June 01, 2:28 - June 21, 20:50

YOUR DRIVE AND AMBITION
Mars in Gemini, May 21, 12:29 - June 21, 20:50

YOUR LUCK MAGNETISM
Jupiter in Aries, May 21, 12:29 - June 21, 20:50

World Events

May 25 – The Russo-Japanese War sees 4,500 Japanese and 3,000 Russians killed at Nanshan in Korea; the Japanese seal off Port Arthur by land and sea.
June 2 – China signs the Geneva Convention.

1904

CANCER
Your Personal Planets

YOUR LOVE POTENTIAL

Venus in Gemini, June 21, 20:51 - June 25, 13:28
Venus in Cancer, June 25, 13:29 - July 19, 23:00
Venus in Leo, July 19, 23:01 - July 23, 7:49

YOUR DRIVE AND AMBITION

Mars in Gemini, June 21, 20:51 - June 30, 14:55
Mars in Cancer, June 30, 14:56 - July 23, 7:49

YOUR LUCK MAGNETISM

Jupiter in Aries, June 21, 20:51 - July 23, 7:49

World Events

June 24 – The Japanese sink a Russian battleship at Port Arthur.

July 14 – Russian author and playwright Anton Chekhov dies.

Anton Chekov

LEO
Your Personal Planets

YOUR LOVE POTENTIAL

Venus in Leo, July 23, 7:50 - Aug. 13, 6:52
Venus in Virgo, Aug. 13, 6:53 - Aug. 23, 14:35

YOUR DRIVE AND AMBITION

Mars in Cancer, July 23, 7:50 - Aug. 15, 3:21
Mars in Leo, Aug. 15, 3:22 - Aug. 23, 14:35

YOUR LUCK MAGNETISM

Jupiter in Aries, July 23, 7:50 - Aug. 08, 20:10
Jupiter in Taurus, Aug. 08, 20:11 - Aug. 23, 14:35

World Events

July 31 – The Trans-Siberian Railroad is completed after thirteen years; it stretches for over 4,500 miles, linking the Urals to the Pacific coast.

Aug. 3 – A British expedition reaches Tibet, causing the Dalai Lama to flee.

CANCER
From June 21, 20:51 through July 23, 7:49

The Sensitive Sustainer

Around the time you were born, Theodore Roosevelt was nominated unanimously by the Republican Party to run for a second term as President of the United States. Known for his fairness to all people, "Teddy" set a fine example to those who, like yourself, grew up in the twentieth century's first decade. Your own concern for others and identification with the underdog perhaps mirrors the best of the times in which you were raised, Cancer of 1904.

You can be tenacious, loyal, and vulnerable—a combination that could have made your life difficult at times. You might know intuitively what people are thinking, and while this could make the people whose minds you're reading feel special, it could also make you vulnerable to people's unspoken criticisms. When you were younger, this may have made you appear emotional and overly sensitive. However, as you matured, you probably stopped paying so much attention to what others thought of you.

As a child, you may have been more reclusive than your parents would have liked. You were probably overjoyed on rainy days when you could stay indoors and read, and you might have dreamed of becoming like the characters you met in fiction. It's possible that you were highly gifted in music, art, dance, or another creative medium, but you probably would have preferred pursuing them on your own to making a career of them. You may have become a librarian or a teacher, or you could have furthered the cause of literacy by teaching people to read. If music or art was your specialty, you might have taught that to others.

In love, you would probably want above all to be a true helpmate, sharing the joys and sorrows of life with your partner. As a Cancer, you can be the best nurturer in the zodiac, and it's likely that you'd be happiest in the role of caregiver and cheerleader. Your best partnerships may be with the austere Virgos, Scorpios, or Pisceans, but a luxury-loving Taurus just might win your heart.

Your challenge is to get past your insecurities and reach out to others. Your gift is your ability to make people feel at ease when they are with you.

LEO
From July 23, 7:50 through August 23, 14:35

The Indomitable Winner

Extroverted and magnanimous, you may be noted for the standards you set for yourself and for your ability to live up to them. Perhaps it's appropriate that Russia's Trans-Siberian Railroad was completed around the time you were born. Spanning almost an entire continent, this remarkable line linked the Ural Mountains in the west to Russia's Pacific seaports more than 4,500 miles to the east. Hearing about such majestic achievements at an impressionable age may have enhanced your indomitable will and your desire to succeed, Leo of 1904.

Being in the spotlight may come naturally to you, and this trait could have led you to the world of competitive sports, the performing arts, or even broadcasting, where radio would just have been coming into its own when you were pursuing job options. You were probably happy to learn something new if it meant broadening your horizons or expanding your talents, and later on, when television came along, you may have been among the first to see the potential of the fascinating new medium.

With your innate sense of style, you may also have turned to architecture, interior decorating, or clothing design. Even if you didn't pursue these talents in the professional arena, it's likely that your magnificently decorated home was the envy of all your friends. But your warm hospitality would have vanquished any feelings of jealousy they may have harbored and your friends and family may have gathered at your home more than any other. After all, that was where they would always have felt like royalty.

In romance, you may have wanted to feel special and needed, and anyone who couldn't put you in that position probably didn't get your attention. Generous in love, you always lifted the other person up rather than bringing him or her down. You can probably weave your magic spell most easily with Librans, Sagittarians, Ariens, and Geminis.

Your challenge is not to let the role of leader go to your head, and to continue to take pride in hard work and achieving great things. Your strength is your ability to create an enchanted atmosphere wherever you are.

➤ Read about your Chinese Astrological sign on page 838. ➤ Read about your Personal Planets on page 826. ➤ Read about your personal Mystical Card on page 856.

VIRGO

From August 23, 14:36 through September 23, 11:39

The Efficiency Expert

Around the time you were born, Helen Keller, who had been deaf and blind since the age of two, graduated with honors from Radcliffe College in Boston—a remarkable achievement both for Keller and for her teacher, Anne Sullivan. With Keller as a widely known role model during the era in which you were growing up, it's probably no surprise that you aspired to be as good as you could be at anything you took on, Virgo of 1904. You learned early in life that the secret to success is to do the job right, no matter how difficult it may seem.

Health-conscious, meticulous, and perhaps unfairly known as a perfectionist, you're probably used to working independently, and you can usually do a thorough job at breakneck speed. Despite your obvious ability, you may rarely have sought the responsibility of leadership, perhaps preferring the role of key team member—the boss's "right-hand" assistant who kept everything running smoothly. Bookkeeping, secretarial work, inventory maintenance, or any other detailed work was probably right up your alley, as was managing a shop, running a doctor's office, or being involved as a health-care practitioner yourself.

Staying physically active and keeping your body strong and flexible could have been priorities for you. When you were younger, you may have enjoyed sports like track and field, and as you matured, your physical regimen might have changed to include more activities like swimming and long walks. Keeping fit allowed you to continue working at a steady pace even as you got older.

In love, you may have sought total honesty and complete openness with the same fervor with which you pursued everything else in your life. Although you and a Scorpio might have taken the same enjoyment in running an efficient household, you could also find a compatible mate among the Capricorns and Taureans you know.

Your challenge is to remember to stop and smell the roses—things don't get done any faster just because you're always worrying about them. Your strength is your remarkable efficiency. Once you get rolling, no one is more effective than you are.

LIBRA

From September 23, 11:40 through October 23, 20:18

The Ideal Partner

Around the time of your birth, French sculptor Frédéric-August Bartholdi passed away. Presiding grandly over New York's harbor, his magnificent Statue of Liberty, France's gift to the United States, welcomed travelers from all over the globe. For your generation, and all that followed, this statue became a symbol of freedom. For you in particular, Libra of 1904, Lady Liberty may have reflected your lifelong respect for and fascination with art, as well as your ideals about how the world could be a better place.

Charming, loving, and always anxious to please, you've probably always done your best to ensure that everyone around you is happy and thriving. And you may have traded in your own secret yearnings in order to devote yourself to others. However, later in life, you may finally have had the freedom, and perhaps the opportunities, to do something that you might not have dared do earlier, namely, working in an art gallery, taking music lessons, or learning photography.

It's likely that you enjoy communicating with people, and exchanging ideas about almost anything under the Sun. You've probably never had any trouble making friends, and never had to worry about being alone. You would have been the person who others came to when they needed a sounding board or an objective viewpoint. In fact, you probably had to learn how to say "no" sometimes, as the most difficult thing for you would have been to shut others out.

Relationships are where you shine, and where you may always have been the ideal partner—one who listens yet does not judge. You may have looked for a partner who could encourage you to take the role of disciplinarian once in a while, and to make unpopular decisions when they were warranted. You may feel most at home with Sagittarians, Aquarians, and Geminis, but a dynamic Leo might be the sparkler that wins your heart!

Your challenge is to avoid superficiality, a natural result of courting the company of so many different types of people. Your gift is your ability to listen to the problems of others and teach them problem-solving skills of their own.

► Read about your Chinese Astrological sign on page 838. ► Read about your Personal Planets on page 826. ► Read about your personal Mystical Card on page 856.

1904

VIRGO
Your Personal Planets

YOUR LOVE POTENTIAL
Venus in Virgo, Aug. 23, 14:36 - Sept. 06, 13:49
Venus in Libra, Sept. 06, 13:50 - Sept. 23, 11:39

YOUR DRIVE AND AMBITION
Mars in Leo, Aug. 23, 14:36 - Sept. 23, 11:39

YOUR LUCK MAGNETISM
Jupiter in Taurus, Aug. 23, 14:36 - Aug. 31, 13:53
Jupiter in Aries, Aug. 31, 13:54 - Sept. 23, 11:39

World Events

Aug. 26 – The Japanese forces battle against the Russians, advancing on their line in Liao-Yang, Manchuria.

Sept. 21 – The Italian Socialist Party's nationwide general strike ends after weeks of violence.

The Russian cavalry marching to Manchuria

LIBRA
Your Personal Planets

YOUR LOVE POTENTIAL
Venus in Libra, Sept. 23, 11:40 - Sept. 30, 21:03
Venus in Scorpio, Sept. 30, 21:04 - Oct. 23, 20:18

YOUR DRIVE AND AMBITION
Mars in Leo, Sept. 23, 11:40 - Oct. 01, 13:51
Mars in Virgo, Oct. 01, 13:52 - Oct. 23, 20:18

YOUR LUCK MAGNETISM
Jupiter in Aries, Sept. 23, 11:40 - Oct. 23, 20:18

World Events

Oct. 3 – France and Spain sign a treaty agreeing spheres of influence in Morocco.

Oct. 20 – Bolivia and China sign a treaty ending the War of the Pacific.

1904

SCORPIO
Your Personal Planets

YOUR LOVE POTENTIAL
Venus in Scorpio, Oct. 23, 20:19 - Oct. 25, 5:36
Venus in Sagittarius, Oct. 25, 5:37 - Nov. 18, 16:39
Venus in Capricorn, Nov. 18, 16:40 - Nov. 22, 17:15

YOUR DRIVE AND AMBITION
Mars in Virgo, Oct. 23, 20:19 - Nov. 20, 6:23
Mars in Libra, Nov. 20, 6:24 - Nov. 22, 17:15

YOUR LUCK MAGNETISM
Jupiter in Aries, Oct. 23, 20:19 - Nov. 22, 17:15

World Events

Oct. 30 – The Japanese attempt another assault on Port Arthur, suffering heavy casualties under Russian machine-gun fire.

Nov. 21 – Motorized omnibuses are seen for the first time on the streets of Paris, replacing horse-drawn carriages.

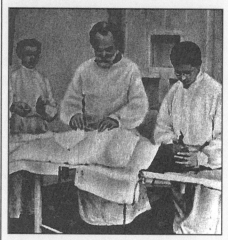

Ivan Pavlov, Nobel Prize winner

SAGITTARIUS
Your Personal Planets

YOUR LOVE POTENTIAL
Venus in Capricorn, Nov. 22, 17:16 - Dec. 13, 9:07
Venus in Aquarius, Dec. 13, 9:08 - Dec. 22, 6:13

YOUR DRIVE AND AMBITION
Mars in Libra, Nov. 22, 17:16 - Dec. 22, 6:13

YOUR LUCK MAGNETISM
Jupiter in Aries, Nov. 22, 17:16 - Dec. 22, 6:13

World Events

Dec. 5 – The Japanese destroy the Russian fleet at Port Arthur.

Dec. 10 – Ivan Pavlov wins the Nobel Prize for his stimulus studies with dogs.

SCORPIO
From October 23, 20:19 through November 22, 17:15

The Insightful Humanist

Around the time you were born, the New York City subway system went into operation. The underground home of this new form of mass transit could have mirrored your own way of delving beneath the surface and trying to make sense of things. In fact, as a Scorpio born in 1904, it's likely that people are astonished at your amazing insights into their actions. But then, you may have spent much of your life standing apart from the crowd, observing people and pondering why they think and behave as they do.

Introspective, intelligent, and unstoppable once you have a theory you want to prove, you were probably fascinated by the study of psychology, which was in its infancy when you were a child. Although job opportunities in this fascinating new field might have been few at the time you completed your education, the subject probably attracted your lifelong interest and you may have spent many hours poring over books and articles on the topic. Only the warmth of your heart matches the depth of your insights into people, so you probably had a chance to use your knowledge to help others on many occasions.

It's likely that working in an employment agency, as a guidance counselor, or as the key person in a company's personnel department would have been just right for you. Your ability to understand what others are thinking and feeling would have made you a loving and understanding disciplinarian, which is something that may have come in handy in your friendships too. Nobody succeeded in pulling the wool over your eyes!

As a person of few words, you may take great care in saying what you mean and expect nothing less from those with whom you share your life. In romance, you can be passionate and affectionate, and you put great value on loyalty and trust. This could make you most compatible with Capricorns, Cancerians, and Virgos.

Your challenge is to understand that introspection is not everyone's cup of tea, and accept people for who they are. Your strength is your understanding of human nature that has allowed you to be a compassionate friend to all who are lucky enough to know you.

SAGITTARIUS
From November 22, 17:16 through December 22, 6:13

The Peaceful Demonstrator

As a Sagittarius born in 1904, you may have grown up wanting to break with tradition and look to the future, and you probably didn't hesitate to alert people to what was going on in the world. It may be no surprise, therefore, to see that Russian students and workers who took to the streets in massive demonstrations against the Russo-Japanese War, and Ivan Pavlov's Nobel Prize for his stimulus studies with dogs topped the headlines around the time you were born. In its own way, each of these events conveyed dissatisfaction with the status quo. You too may have placed great emphasis on free speech and speaking one's mind, and you might have impressed those values on your friends and family as well.

As a child, you may have been just a bit more mature and worldly than most of your friends. Your brain may have raced like lightning, but you could concentrate it on the one issue that most concerned you. As an adult, you may have been a teacher or a school administrator. But even as a lay person, it's likely that you fought for better schools and always spoke up when you saw children being deprived of a good education.

Generous, idealistic, and social-minded, you probably found that keeping track of finances was never easy. You may have had to balance what you wanted to contribute to charities and causes against what you needed to keep for your home and family. On the occasions when you couldn't contribute as much as you would have liked, you may have offered your time and effort instead, and encouraged friends and family to volunteer along with you.

In love, you probably looked for someone who could help you control the purse strings. It would be fine if they viewed life a bit less colorfully than you do, as long as they had at least a little sense of adventure. You may be most comfortable with Aquarians, Leos, and Librans, who'd also find you charming.

Your challenge is to listen sincerely to what others have to say, even if it appears diametrically opposed to your own point of view. Your strength is that you are able to find some common ground with almost everyone you meet.

➤ Read about your Chinese Astrological sign on page 838. ➤ Read about your Personal Planets on page 826. ➤ Read about your personal Mystical Card on page 856.

CAPRICORN

From December 22, 6:14 'through December 31, 23:59

The Quirky Inventor

As a Capricorn born in December of 1904, you arrived at a time when the rights of the common man were beginning to be recognized. Around the time you were born, Tsar Nicholas II of Russia gave in to the growing unrest in his country, proposing a series of reforms that included more religious freedom and greater rights of the press. This did not stave off the eventual revolution, but the theme it struck of the rights of the working class reverberated for many years, and may have struck a chord that stayed with you your entire life.

Deliberate, determined, and unwilling to accept defeat, you may appear to the outside world as a strong, silent, and even pragmatic type. Yet underneath that cool exterior can be a mind that is unbelievably inventive, and often goes where others fear to tread. For example, it's likely that you were among the first to immerse yourself in the twentieth century technology and telecommunications revolution.

With a mind that can be both unique and practical, you probably had a very conservative profession that would allow you to pursue some remarkable hobbies in your leisure time. You could have excelled at learning languages, at doing impersonations, or at inventing secret ways of communicating. (These might even have included creating and deciphering codes, whether for fun or for more serious business.) You may also have enjoyed making up puzzles and brainteasers to amuse your friends and family.

You probably approached your relationships as you did everything else—conservatively, but with an unpredictable edge that made things interesting and exciting. You may have looked for a mate with an independent nature, whose patience and forbearance would give you the opportunity to retreat to your study from time to time. You probably feel most at ease with Pisceans, Virgos, and Scorpios, although you might also make a good match with a Taurus.

Your challenge is to find the balance between doing what is expected of you and doing the quirky things you love most. Your gift is your ability to encourage others to use their originality in any way they can.

1904

CAPRICORN
Your Personal Planets

YOUR LOVE POTENTIAL
Venus in Aquarius, Dec. 22, 6:14 - Dec. 31, 23:59

YOUR DRIVE AND AMBITION
Mars in Libra, Dec. 22, 6:14 - Dec. 31, 23:59

YOUR LUCK MAGNETISM
Jupiter in Aries, Dec. 22, 6:14 - Dec. 31, 23:59

World Events

Dec. 26 – Tsar Nicholas II proposes a series of reforms to offset growing unrest, although he does not acquiesce to a constitutional assembly.

Dec. 27 – W.B. Yeats' and Lady Gregory's play *On Baile's Strand* premieres in Dublin.

J. Pierpont Morgan
April 17, 1837 - March 31, 1913

J.P. MORGAN
Aries

J. Pierpont Morgan, the financier of America's Industrial Revolution, was born into wealth. But over the course of his life, the self-assured, daring, and willful Aries would amass an even greater fortune. With independent and unconventional Aquarius rising, he was a controversial figure who, depending on one's perspective, was either hailed as a financial genius or condemned as a robber baron.

Morgan's Aries Sun falls in the house of wealth. And joining in this crucial money area are Mercury, the planet of mental prowess, Venus, the planet of money and values, and Pluto, the planet of vast power. Morgan initiated a number of noteworthy mergers, including General Electric and International Harvester Corp. In 1901, he created U.S. Steel, the first billion-dollar company in the U.S.

Morgan wielded considerable power and could often be ruthless, as shown by his Mars, planet of action and aggression, in direct contact with Jupiter, the planet of expansion. While Morgan personally twice saved the United States from bankruptcy and acted as the unofficial "central banker" of the country, in his attempts to stabilize the economy he urged businesses to cut jobs and lower wages. But, a man of his word, he was trusted and revered in the rarefied world of wealth and privilege in which he lived.

In his personal life, with Uranus, the planet of the unexpected and unusual, prominently placed and at odds with his Moon (his emotional life), in the house of relationships, Morgan suffered tragedy and estrangement in his marital life. His first wife died of tuberculosis only a few months after their wedding, his second wife developed compulsions akin to agoraphobia, isolating herself from Morgan and society. Morgan himself battled with depression all of his life, but threw himself into work, travel, and collecting art to counteract it.

Morgan had first started to collect art at the age of fifteen. With Neptune, the planet of the arts and service, contacting his Mars (action) and Jupiter (generosity), he carried his enthusiasm into great acts of philanthropy. He was a founder of the American Museum of Natural History, the New York Botanical Garden, and the Metropolitan Museum. His personal collection of rare art, books, manuscripts and personal papers make up his legacy to his country, the Morgan Library.

▶ Read about J. P. Morgan in "Astrology Goes on Trial" on page 185. ▶ Read about J. P. Morgan and "Money, Astrology, and the Crash of '29" on page 225.

1905

Art and Science Overturned: Uranus in Capricorn

The year 1905 started with an important and auspicious planetary aspect. Uranus, the ruler of all things new and different, had just entered the stable and worldly sign of Capricorn. When Venus, the planet of love and art, entered the feisty sign of Aries in February, it formed a square with Uranus, causing radical ideas in art and science to be born. Squares are usually more difficult aspects, but not in this particular case. This year, the first ever movie theater opened in Pittsburgh, Pennsylvania. Isadora Duncan had established the first school of modern dance just the year before, radically altering dance as an art form forever more. Duncan's first visit to Russia came in 1905. She brought the dance to the attention of the art critic Sergey Diaghilev, who was soon to lead a resurgence of ballet throughout Western Europe Duncan is considered the mother of modern dance, dance to free the soul.

This year is regarded as Piscean Albert Einstein's "Miracle Year." Amongst other incredible achievements, the modest genius proposed his Special Theory of Relativity, changing our understanding of the physical universe forever. Soon after, his application of the theory to mass and enegy produced the now famous equation $e = mc^2$.

The Russian Revolution of 1905 also began under this influence, on "Bloody Sunday" on January 22. Revolution falls under the charge of Uranus and when Uranus is in Capricorn, people tend to fight to the death to put new ideas into action, particularly when these new ideas relate to our social values and the way we live. This was a year when the status quo was to change forever.

After "Bloody Sunday", Tsar Nicholas II establishes the legislative Duma

The Trans-Siberian Railway is inaugurated

President Roosevelt appoints several African Americans to high government positions

GHOST SHIP PROWLS THE SEAS

The legend of the *Flying Dutchman* began in the seventeenth century when a Dutch ship rounding the Cape of Good Hope experienced bad weather. The captain of the doomed vessel pressed on, declaring he would round the "damned" cape if it took until Doomsday. His ship sank. Official records in the British Admiralty preserve many sightings of the phantom vessel in the twentieth century. King George and his brother, as well as Hitler's commander in chief of U-boats and his crew, were among those terrified to behold the spectral ship.

RUSSIAN WOES AND TRANSPORTATION TRIUMPHS

The Russian-Japanese War ended with a treaty giving control of Korea and two Manchurian ports to Japan. Meanwhile, internal unrest continued to shake Russia, despite new civil liberties and the establishment of the legislative Duma. Jews, however, were subjected to increasing persecution, culminating in a massacre in Odessa. The Trans-Siberian Railway was inaugurated, allowing travel between Paris and Vladivostok. Europe grew uneasy as German Kaiser Wilhelm built naval forces and postured in Morocco. The French agreed to the separation of church and state, and the Belgians won a six-day working week. Sinn Fein, the Irish nationalist group, declared itself a political party. In the U.S., President Roosevelt gave a high customs position to an African-American, one of several to be appointed to government positions. A New York auto show displayed over one hundred current-model cars, with such innovations as lamps, speedometers, and tires. Professor James Breasted recorded ancient Nubian inscriptions. In Europe, Paris and Berlin were linked by telephone. Jules Verne, the science fiction author, died, as did the actor Maurice Barrymore.

➤ Read Pablo Picasso's Star Profile on page 57.

CAPRICORN

From January 01, 0:00 through January 20, 16:51

The Aspiring Accountant

As your birth year began, January Capricorn of 1905, the Tsar of Russia was massing troops to quell riots and rebellion, while at the same time the Trans-Siberian Railway went into service. This mingling of progress and dissatisfaction could have showed up in your feelings as an adult, for your aspirations always had you looking a little bit beyond today, down the road to tomorrow.

You are very much of a practical mind, and you've probably used this to good advantage over the years. When others were paying attention to details, you looked at the big picture; and when others were looking at nonessentials, you were examining the bottom line. For that reason, you would have been a great asset in business, but if you stayed at home and raised a family, that view and the skills that went with it would have served you and yours well.

Despite your practicality, you have also had an inner vision for much of your life. You understand that life has its creative as well as its practical side, and if you did not have the actual talent and vision, you probably sought the company of those who did. As much as possible, you made yourself a patron of the arts, whether that meant funding cultural events or simply buying a season ticket to the local opera or community theater.

In your romantic life, you probably sought partners who were good providers or those who could at least handle money well. Additionally, your ideal was someone who had some imagination and some culture, and thus could get you away from the humdrum of your daily existence, at least once in a while. Your best partner signs are Pisceans, Taureans, Virgoans, and Scorpios.

Your greatest challenge is to live up to your own expectations of yourself and what life is all about. It may have taken some time, but at some point in your life you probably came to realize that the things you have achieved are good in and of themselves, and that the reality is much better than the dream. Your greatest strength comes from the practical way with which you view life and your ability to communicate that to others at crucial times.

AQUARIUS

From January 20, 16:52 through February 19, 7:20

The Solid Citizen

Around the time you were born, Aquarius of 1905, the Russians struggled against the Japanese in Manchuria. These and other battles fought in foreign lands were also foreign to your nature, and growing up at a time when revolution and war seemed to loom over daily life might have influenced you to dedicate yourself to more peaceful pursuits. You can be quite a placid individual, in fact—not only because you can't stand the thought of people hurting each other, but also because you feel that war obstructs human progress.

You see yourself as a moral person, someone with a desire—even a mission—to let others know the right path to move along. This could have involved you with the ministry or even missionary work at some time, but even if you stayed at home and raised a family, you did your best to ensure that your children knew right from wrong, and behaved accordingly. You probably never scolded, but led others by the example you set.

Although you enjoy relaxation as much as the next person, your artistic tastes cannot shake your serious leanings. You may consider theater, film, and television relevant only if they have a serious message to convey. Your musical tastes lean more to the classical, and an ideal afternoon might be listening to chamber music, or going to a lecture at an art museum.

In matters of love, you tend to seek out a partner who is as serious and as dedicated as you are. Although your ideal match might be someone you could work together with on various humanitarian projects, you could be perfectly happy with someone who is just a good, solid citizen. Your best signs are Ariens, Geminis, Librans, and Sagittarians.

Your greatest challenge has always been to let yourself be lighthearted once in a while. Every now and again, it helps to laugh at life—and even at yourself—before you get on with more serious matters. Your greatest strength is that you are able to see clearly the consequences tomorrow of things done today, and because of that you have found that people always seek your advice and, moreover, listen closely to what you have to say.

➤ Read about your Chinese Astrological sign on page 838. ➤ Read about your Personal Planets on page 826. ➤ Read about your personal Mystical Card on page 856.

1905

CAPRICORN
Your Personal Planets

YOUR LOVE POTENTIAL
Venus in Aquarius, Jan. 01, 0:00 - Jan. 07, 14:37
Venus in Pisces, Jan. 07, 14:38 - Jan. 20, 16:51

YOUR DRIVE AND AMBITION
Mars in Libra, Jan. 01, 0:00 - Jan. 13, 19:25
Mars in Scorpio, Jan. 13, 19:26 - Jan. 20, 16:51

YOUR LUCK MAGNETISM
Jupiter in Aries, Jan. 01, 0:00 - Jan. 20, 16:51

World Events

Jan. 2 – The Russians surrender Port Arthur to the Japanese, after a six-month siege.

Jan. 11 – Belgian colonists in the Congo are slain in a native uprising.

In St. Petersburg, Tsarist troops fire on workers in a protest march

AQUARIUS
Your Personal Planets

YOUR LOVE POTENTIAL
Venus in Pisces, Jan. 20, 16:52 - Feb. 03, 4:48
Venus in Aries, Feb. 03, 4:49 - Feb. 19, 7:20

YOUR DRIVE AND AMBITION
Mars in Scorpio, Jan. 20, 16:52 - Feb. 19, 7:20

YOUR LUCK MAGNETISM
Jupiter in Aries, Jan. 20, 16:52 - Feb. 19, 7:20

World Events

Jan. 22 – In St. Petersburg, Tsarist troops fire on 100,000 workers during a peaceful protest march; 500 are killed, earning this event the name of "Bloody Sunday."

Feb. 8 – Colombia appeals to the U.S. to let Panama vote on independence.

1905

PISCES
Your Personal Planets

YOUR LOVE POTENTIAL
Venus in Aries, Feb. 19, 7:21 - Mar. 06, 5:25
Venus in Taurus, Mar. 06, 5:26 - Mar. 21, 6:57

YOUR DRIVE AND AMBITION
Mars in Scorpio, Feb. 19, 7:21 - Mar. 21, 6:57

YOUR LUCK MAGNETISM
Jupiter in Aries, Feb. 19, 7:21 - Mar. 07, 18:27
Jupiter in Taurus, Mar. 07, 18:28 - Mar. 21, 6:57

World Events

Mar. 3 – Tsar Nicholas II agrees to create an elected assembly and to undertake a series of religious and political reforms.

Mar. 14 – The British House of Commons urges the need to compete with Germany in naval strength.

U.S. President Roosevelt helps to bring peace to Russia and Japan

ARIES
Your Personal Planets

YOUR LOVE POTENTIAL
Venus in Taurus, Mar. 21, 6:58 - Apr. 20, 18:43

YOUR DRIVE AND AMBITION
Mars in Scorpio, Mar. 21, 6:58 - Apr. 20, 18:43

YOUR LUCK MAGNETISM
Jupiter in Taurus, Mar. 21, 6:58 - Apr. 20, 18:43

World Events

Mar. 30 – U.S. President Theodore Roosevelt is chosen to mediate in the Russo–Japanese peace talks.

Apr. 4 – The Kangra earthquake in India kills an estimated 19,000 people.

PISCES
From February 19, 7:21 through March 21, 6:57

The Hopeful Caregiver

Around the time you were born, Pisces of 1905, the British House of Commons announced that it had no choice but to compete with German naval strength. Events like this filled the news while you were growing up, and made a huge impact on the world in which you came of age. Still, in your own world, that impact might have seemed small and distant, if only because you're the kind of person who focuses on the here and now and on events closer to home, where you could make a difference.

Compassionate, sympathetic, and generous, you've always felt that everyone can influence the community they live in, but in choosing to get involved, you sometimes sacrificed your own interests to help others. Although you can be charitable and empathetic, you're concerned with helping others help themselves and grow impatient if someone takes advantage of your good nature just to get a free ride. When you feel your help is needed though, you go all out to do what you can.

If you were part of the working world, it's likely you worked for someone else rather than in your own business. You preferred leaving the office behind at the end of the day to spend valuable time at home with your loved ones. If you stayed home to raise a family, no one would have been a more attentive parent than you, as the same care you apply to helping others would have gone into helping your children and your spouse.

In relationships, you'd get along best with someone who needed your help and wanted your good counsel. More than anything, you and your partner would care deeply about each other and share intimate thoughts and feelings as true equals. In general, you can be most compatible with Taureans, Cancerians, Scorpios, and Capricorns.

Your greatest challenge has always been to learn to see each person clearly, to be there when needed, and to stand back when you are not. Your greatest strength has always been your caring nature, and in providing others with the tools they need to help themselves. It's likely that those whom you have coached to be the best people they can be will remember your influence always.

ARIES
From March 21, 6:58 through April 20, 18:43

The Enterprising One

Around the time you were born, Aries of 1905, Paris and Berlin were linked by telephone for the first time, while in England the past popularity of Sherlock Holmes brought about his revival from the dead. While the world remained basically the same in many respects, in some ways it moved forward quickly—a fact you were constantly reminded of while growing up in a new century.

Enterprising, assertive, and business-minded, you also favor moving forward quickly. Even though you're very much the go-getter, you had a unique way of combining making a living with raising a family. You may have worked in a family business of some sort, one where everyone could pitch in and help. Even if you didn't work outside the home, you likely had a business on the side, perhaps as a tailor or a decorator, and you probably made sure that the whole family participated in some way, even if it meant doing household chores while you were hard at work.

By the time you were in your mid-thirties, you had lived through the most prosperous decade, followed by the most depressed one. These economic life lessons only propelled your enterprising nature, and unlike other people who wallowed in self-pity, you pulled yourself and your family up by the bootstraps, and never looked back. This ability to move forward has gotten you through the hard times, and separated you from those who depended on others.

Your attitude towards relationships incorporated the good old-fashioned attributes of romance and partnership. In addition to sharing family life, you sought a partner who was on the same wavelength where money and how to make it are concerned. Your most compatible signs are Geminis, Sagittarians, and Aquarians.

Your greatest challenge in life has been to prevent economic and other mundane matters from monopolizing your time, and to remind yourself that a smile and a hug can go a lot farther than a lecture on how to earn a living. Your greatest strength is the way you have always been able to impart to others that life is a balance between practicality and the emotional bonds that tie us all together.

➤ Read about your Chinese Astrological sign on page 838. ➤ Read about your Personal Planets on page 826. ➤ Read about your personal Mystical Card on page 856.

TAURUS

From April 20, 18:44 through May 21, 18:30

The Cheerful Competitor

As a Taurus of 1905, you've probably tucked your competitive edge neatly under your practical, cautious, and kind demeanor. You may have even chuckled when you learned that Mata Hari, the dancer who later became an infamous spy, debuted in Paris to much acclaim around the time you were born. She too proved that looks could be deceiving! It's likely that those who know you can see that you've never been a pushover, and that you stick to your guns until you have either succeeded or admitted defeat.

Although you were certainly competitive, you were hardly cut-throat, and you probably challenged yourself at a mental level rather than a physical one. When you were younger you may have been involved in sports, but as you grew up, going one-on-one against someone else in a business situation or even in social life energized you. Running for president of a local club, for instance, was enough to focus your attention and get your blood racing.

Competing with you does not, however, mean winning at any cost, as it is more the love of the game than the result that you're interested in. You are a gracious loser as long as your opponent played fairly; you had a good time, and shook hands at the end. In raising your family, you made sure to impart to your children the importance of testing themselves in various ways, as well as the importance of knowing when the game was over.

In relationships, you sought a partner to challenge you and keep you on your toes, but one who could be sensitive and was unafraid to express true feelings. It does not hurt to be with someone who is good with money, since having enough to spare allows you to feel at ease. You are probably most comfortable with Cancerians, Virgos, Capricorns, and Pisceans.

Your greatest challenge has been to convince others that being on the losing end is not the worst thing that can happen, and can even teach you valuable lessons. Your greatest strength has been the helpful way in which you have provided support and encouragement to those who do not like playing "the game." Anyone who has you as a friend has been truly fortunate.

GEMINI

From May 21, 18:31 through June 22, 2:50

The Bold Evaluator

Around the time you were born, Gemini of 1905, land at the corner of Broadway and Wall Street in New York City was selling for as much as $2.75 a square inch! You yourself have always been fascinated by the idea of buying and selling, and may have spent a good part of your life in the world of sales, business, or even real estate. If you weren't able to buy and sell property on your own, you could have been a real estate agent, or perhaps you just put energy into decorating your own home. It wouldn't have mattered if you were on a shoestring budget—your tastes are simple, striking, and, above all, defined by quality.

Talkative, clever, and never shy, it's likely that you were always looking one step ahead and had your eye out for that job promotion or job change that would bring in just a bit more cash. You weren't shy about bringing up the subject of a raise to the boss, or about making a suggestion to your spouse about where the grass might be greener.

At home, you were probably the one who knew the value of money, and you made sure that your family understood this as well. Despite all of the above, you've never been obsessed with keeping up with the Joneses, and won't sacrifice everything to make a few dollars more. In fact, you may have an innate understanding that the best way to find a happy and productive balance in life is to make enough to save some, and to spend it on occasional frills.

In love relationships, you sought a partner who above all else would talk to you about plans and dreams for the future. You needed to be with someone who knew the value of feeling secure both materially and emotionally. Your most compatible signs are Leos, Librans, and Aquarians.

Your greatest challenge in life has been to keep from evaluating everything in terms of how much it costs. You have always been very much aware that money is not everything, but in the grind of everyday existence you may have had to struggle to keep that in mind at times. Your greatest strength is your understanding of real, true human values, and the way you have made that the central fact of your life.

TAURUS
Your Personal Planets

YOUR LOVE POTENTIAL
Venus in Taurus, Apr. 20, 18:44 - May 09, 10:36
Venus in Aries, May 09, 10:37 - May 21, 18:30

YOUR DRIVE AND AMBITION
Mars in Scorpio, Apr. 20, 18:44 - May 21, 18:30

YOUR LUCK MAGNETISM
Jupiter in Taurus, Apr. 20, 18:44 - May 21, 18:30

World Events

Apr. 25 – The Boers under Louis Botha condemn the new constitution offered by the British.

May 16 – American film star Henry Fonda is born.

American film star Henry Fonda is born under the sign of Taurus

GEMINI
Your Personal Planets

YOUR LOVE POTENTIAL
Venus in Aries, May 21, 18:31 - May 28, 11:17
Venus in Taurus, May 28, 11:18 - June 22, 2:50

YOUR DRIVE AND AMBITION
Mars in Scorpio, May 21, 18:31 - June 22, 2:50

YOUR LUCK MAGNETISM
Jupiter in Taurus, May 21, 18:31 - June 22, 2:50

World Events

May 31 – Anarchists in Paris attempt to assassinate President Loubet and the visiting Spanish King Alfonso.

June 10 – Santo Domingo rejects U.S. control over their economic affairs.

▶ Read about your Chinese Astrological sign on page 838. ▶ Read about your Personal Planets on page 826. ▶ Read about your personal Mystical Card on page 856.

53

1905

CANCER
Your Personal Planets

YOUR LOVE POTENTIAL
Venus in Taurus, June 22, 2:51 - July 08, 11:59
Venus in Gemini, July 08, 12:00 - July 23, 13:45

YOUR DRIVE AND AMBITION
Mars in Scorpio, June 22, 2:51 - July 23, 13:45

YOUR LUCK MAGNETISM
Jupiter in Taurus, June 22, 2:51 - July 21, 0:22
Jupiter in Gemini, July 21, 0:23 - July 23, 13:45

World Events

June 24 – A revolt in Lodz against the Russian occupation of Poland leaves 2,000 dead or wounded.

June 27 – In Chicago, the Industrial Workers of the World is formed by "Big Bill" Haywood with the motto "One big union for all."

Sun Yat-Sen, leader of the T'ung Meng Hui secret society

LEO
Your Personal Planets

YOUR LOVE POTENTIAL
Venus in Gemini, July 23, 13:46 - Aug. 06, 8:16
Venus in Cancer, Aug. 06, 8:17 - Aug. 23, 20:28

YOUR DRIVE AND AMBITION
Mars in Scorpio, July 23, 13:46 - Aug. 21, 19:32
Mars in Sagittarius, Aug. 21, 19:33 - Aug. 23, 20:28

YOUR LUCK MAGNETISM
Jupiter in Gemini, July 23, 13:46 - Aug. 23, 20:28

World Events

Aug. 12 - Japan and Britain draw up an agreement on spheres of influence in the Far East.

Aug. 20 - The Chinese doctor and revolutionary Sun Yat-Sen forms the T'ung Meng Hui secret society to fight the Manchu dynasty.

CANCER
From June 22, 2:51 through July 23, 13:45

The Responsible Server

Around the time you were born, Cancer of 1905, Commander Robert Peary set sail for the North Pole, and while this expedition was unsuccessful, he did eventually become the first man to reach that lonely spot on the Earth. While you may never have wanted to do anything that physically challenging or adventurous, you'd certainly have related to Peary's perseverance, and hearing about his journeys when you were a child may have inspired you and set a tone for your life.

You probably had an intuitive grasp of any hardships your parents may have encountered raising you, and your siblings may have thought of you as a goody two-shoes. Determined, intuitive, and ready to take on challenges, you were always a family person first, and a professional person second. If you had a job, it was purely to earn a living, never to inflate your sense of status or importance. It's likely that your duties to your family were always your true calling.

You're good at providing hospitality, so interacting with people and making them feel at home was right up your alley. If you did find your way into the professional arena, you were probably attracted to positions where you could interact with small groups of people, such as working in a department store, restaurant, or hotel. It's not likely you aspired to be in the front office of a big business, nor in a position of power. Your talent was always in caring for people, rather than directing them.

In love relationships, you looked for someone honest and warm, with whom you could cuddle after a long, hard day, and who'd be unafraid to share their thoughts and feelings with you. You wouldn't really care much about your partner's looks or finances, but want someone who was a nice person above all else. You are probably most comfortable with Virgos, Scorpios, Pisceans, and Taureans.

Your greatest challenge has been to accept others whose values may not have been as hardworking as your own. Your gift is your caring nature, which let you empathize with the problems they faced. You stuck by and helped them weather the bad times—and the good.

LEO
From July 23, 13:46 through August 23, 20:28

The Passionate Fund-Raiser

Leo of 1905, you may always have felt that the world was your oyster. You were the fearless leader, never afraid of anything, always heading up outdoor adventures or acting as President of an after-school club. Growing into a self-confident adult with a take-charge personality, you probably extended those qualities to management or finance positions, taking control of the purse strings either at the office or at home.

Charitable, proud, and magnanimous, giving makes you feel happy, so you've probably always been a great fund-raiser. (It might even have made you feel a little honored to learn that philanthropist John D. Rockefeller established a $10 million fund for higher education around the time you were born.) When you canvassed the neighborhood, knocking on doors, you'd never take no for an answer and the person who gave to your cause always felt good about it.

You probably love the performing arts and are especially attracted to great drama, opera, or anything that expresses passion intensely. If you are not in the arts yourself, you've probably kept journals during spare moments, in between commitments to family and community, and you may even have written some poetry or done some drawings. Although these artistic hobbies were hard to work into your busy schedule, you made the time, as they were always a welcome part of your day.

In relationships, you'd want someone to provide unconditional love and support after a whirlwind, hectic day. Underneath the brave exterior, you are deeply sensitive, and you want to know that you can let go of your public image and express your fears, anxieties, and doubts to someone who knows you inside and out. In general, you can be most at ease with Librans, Sagittarians, and Ariens.

It's likely that your most notable challenge came from thinking that your image as an infallible leader would be compromised if you did not appear in control at all times. Once you realized that your ability to lead was enhanced by your humanness, that "weakness" became your greatest strength, and those who mattered most would have respected you even more.

➤ Read about your Chinese Astrological sign on page 838. ➤ Read about your Personal Planets on page 826. ➤ Read about your personal Mystical Card on page 856.

VIRGO

From August 23, 20:29 through September 23, 17:29

The Yearning Pragmatist

As a Virgo born in 1905, you may always have felt as if you were following a destiny of your own, reaching for a star that others might not even be able to see. This was especially true when you were younger, and the feeling may have been heightened when you heard about a solar eclipse seen across the world around the time you were born. As you grew older and the practicalities of life became paramount, you may have put your dreams on hold, but still thought about them when you were alone.

Hard working, sensitive, and detailed, you may actually have invented the phrase "having it all," since you tried to combine professional and home life long before it became everyone's dream. If anyone could even come close to achieving that, it would be you, since you were never averse to working out of your home, if you had to. Bookkeeping or secretarial skills made it easy to find jobs you could do at home or at the office, and you were always one of those people who could turn drudgery into an enjoyable routine.

Due to your own inner vision, you may have devoted time to creative pursuits, especially those that involved writing. One way to be close to a dream is to write it down, or act it out, and you may have done both in one way or another. You may have done private journal writing, but it's also likely that your friends know you as someone who is eloquent and deeply expressive.

In love, you sought a partner who considered that the best decisions were those two of you made together. You would not want someone who wanted to be "the boss," although you can be willing to let your partner hold sway in areas where he or she does best. You share the same outlook on life with Scorpios, Capricorns, Taureans, and Cancerians.

Your challenge is to distinguish clearly between what is ideal and what is practical. Since you are somewhat driven by a secret longing, there may have been times, especially when you were younger, when you followed that to the detriment of everyday concerns. Your strength is the way in which you have learned to work with your dreams by turning them into reality.

LIBRA

From September 23, 17:30 through October 24, 2:07

The Music Maker

Around the time you were born, Sir Henry Irving, the first actor knighted by the King of England, and manager of the Lyceum Theatre, died. While this might not be a memorable event for some, you, Libra of 1905, would probably find it quite interesting—given your own propensity for and interest in the performing arts. Anything that is glamorous, dramatic, and creative would fit into the imaginative longings that are your constant companions.

Artistic, aesthetic, and harmonious, you probably learned to sing and dance before you could speak. If you did not grow up in an affluent family where you could have had formal music training, you probably wrote your own songs and stories, and put on shows for the entire neighborhood.

It's likely that singing in choirs and choral groups would have been a favorite activity for you as an adult. If you could not find a way to take up music as a profession, you probably filled your home with music. You might have also been a teacher, either in school or out of your home. Of course, you have many other talents, the best of which is your ability to listen to people and counsel them. Your objectivity and even-tempered disposition make you the perfect person to point out the source of problems and suggest workable solutions.

In love, your best partner would be someone with a creative sensibility who, like you, wants a home filled with beautiful paintings, music, and the sound of laughter. More than that, you value a love of family life, and the belief that together you can face anything. Your most harmonious relationships may be formed with Sagittarians, Aquarians, and Leos.

While you love any activity where you can be intuitive and sensual rather than analytical, you care most about people being happy, and, for you, creativity and the arts are the perfect means to help people forget their problems. Your greatest challenge has been to be able to balance the pragmatic side of your life with the creative side and its possibilities. When that balance is achieved, your true gifts and great strength as a loving, caring person shine through.

➤ Read about your Chinese Astrological sign on page 838. ➤ Read about your Personal Planets on page 826. ➤ Read about your personal Mystical Card on page 856.

VIRGO
Your Personal Planets

YOUR LOVE POTENTIAL
Venus in Cancer, Aug. 23, 20:29 - Sept. 01, 20:15
Venus in Leo, Sept. 01, 20:16 - Sept. 23, 17:29

YOUR DRIVE AND AMBITION
Mars in Sagittarius, Aug. 23, 20:29 - Sept. 23, 17:29

YOUR LUCK MAGNETISM
Jupiter in Gemini, Aug. 23, 20:29 - Sept. 23, 17:29

World Events

Sept. 5 - Japan and Russia sign the Treaty of Portsmouth, ending the war in Korea and Manchuria.

Sept. 18 - Film star Greta Garbo is born.

Film star Greta Garbo is born under the sign of Virgo

LIBRA
Your Personal Planets

YOUR LOVE POTENTIAL
Venus in Leo, Sept. 23, 17:30 - Sept. 27, 4:01
Venus in Virgo, Sept. 27, 4:02 - Oct. 21, 18:31
Venus in Libra, Oct. 21, 18:32 - Oct. 24, 2:07

YOUR DRIVE AND AMBITION
Mars in Sagittarius, Sept. 23, 17:30 - Oct. 08, 0:05
Mars in Capricorn, Oct. 08, 0:06 - Oct. 24, 2:07

YOUR LUCK MAGNETISM
Jupiter in Gemini, Sept. 23, 17:30 - Oct. 24, 2:07

World Events

Sept. 28 - A conference succeeds in reaching a Franco-German accord over Morocco.

Oct. 13 - The first English actor to be knighted, Henry Irving, dies.

1905

SCORPIO
Your Personal Planets

YOUR LOVE POTENTIAL
Venus in Libra, Oct. 24, 2:08 - Nov. 14, 22:39
Venus in Scorpio, Nov. 14, 22:40 - Nov. 22, 23:04

YOUR DRIVE AND AMBITION
Mars in Capricorn, Oct. 24, 2:08 - Nov. 18, 4:14
Mars in Aquarius, Nov. 18, 4:15 - Nov. 22, 23:04

YOUR LUCK MAGNETISM
Jupiter in Gemini, Oct. 24, 2:08 - Nov. 22, 23:04

World Events

Oct. 30 – Tsar Nicholas II issues the October Manifesto, granting a constitution and legislative power to the Duma and ending the general strike.

Nov. 5 – A Belgian commission established to investigate government of the Congo admits to misadministration in the colony.

Dr. Robert Koch wins the Nobel Prize for medicine

SAGITTARIUS
Your Personal Planets

YOUR LOVE POTENTIAL
Venus in Scorpio, Nov. 22, 23:05 - Dec. 08, 21:30
Venus in Sagittarius, Dec. 08, 21:31 - Dec. 22, 12:03

YOUR DRIVE AND AMBITION
Mars in Aquarius, Nov. 22, 23:05 - Dec. 22, 12:03

YOUR LUCK MAGNETISM
Jupiter in Gemini, Nov. 22, 23:05 - Dec. 04, 22:30
Jupiter in Taurus, Dec. 04, 22:31 - Dec. 22, 12:03

World Events

Nov. 28 – The Irish nationalist group Sinn Fein declares itself a political party.

Dec. 10 – Dr. Robert Koch is awarded the Nobel Prize for medicine for his discovery of the bacillus that causes tuberculosis.

SCORPIO
From October 24, 2:08 through November 22, 23:04

The Relentless Challenger

Around the time you were born, George Bernard Shaw's play *Mrs. Warren's Profession*, a satire on prostitution and incest, opened in New York City to harsh reviews and charges of indecency. Shaw's delight in shock and controversy rings a bell with you, Scorpio of 1905, since you too can thrive on getting a reaction—whatever it takes.

As a child, you were probably relentless at irritating people and getting under their skin. As you matured, however, you may have become less interested in shock value than in pushing people one step further, forcing them to use their minds, not their habits. That attitude led you to strive for bigger and better things, and you may have gone to work for a large company, or even a department store, where you saw a clear path to success. You easily could have been a lawyer whose every case was a challenge, or a researcher whose goal was to find the cure for some dreaded disease.

Whether you achieved greatness, or lived an ordinary life taking care of a family, it's likely that you always wanted to make your mark, and to be just a little different than the rest of the crowd. The emerging motion picture industry would have attracted you as you were growing up, and you may have pursued something connected with that field. You don't give up easily, so if you couldn't be in front of the cameras, it's likely that you created a world of glamour and inventiveness for yourself somewhere else.

In love relationships, you probably prefer someone very self-assured and confident, someone who loves mental and physical challenges. You want a person in your life who is not going to be shocked by anything you say or do, and who can perhaps dare you the way you do others. Those in whom you may have met your match are Capricorns, Pisceans, Cancerians, and Virgos.

Over the course of your life, your greatest challenge has come from your own need to urge yourself to greater heights, and to make yourself adapt to changing times. Your greatest gift has always been your passion for new ideas, and the even greater passion you would have for imparting them to others.

SAGITTARIUS
From November 22, 23:05 through December 22, 12:03

The Outspoken Storyteller

As a Sagittarius of 1905, you may believe deeply in camaraderie and the strength that emerges when you are part of a group. You know that it is not enough to have firm beliefs unless you can convince others to back you up. Being tactful and considerate of others' viewpoints while promoting your own ideas is what has enabled you to be influential.

Around the time you were born, the U.S. launched a campaign to help the Jews escape persecution in Russia. The appeals and marches on this issue reflect your own identity as a proponent of freedom of ideas, and one who has taught that ideal to others. You love a good philosophical or political debate, and although you can be quite fervent about your beliefs, you also encourage people to express their own. Anyone who discusses a hot issue with you knows that while you'll argue hard for your viewpoint, you can change your mind when you think it warranted.

You are a cultural enthusiast, and as a teacher, librarian, or parent, have probably been an inspiration to others. Whether you read from a book or related your own experiences about the "good old days," you always remained a wonderful storyteller and personality. As you matured, you may have read to other audiences—perhaps reading to someone who was visually impaired or recording books on tape for distribution to those with visual disabilities.

If your partner did not initially share your passion for artistic, musical, and literary achievements, it's likely that he or she eventually came around, if only because of your openness and your love. Sharing interests and giving support to one another are the two things you need most in a partner. You are probably most comfortable with Aquarians, Ariens, Leos, and Librans.

Your greatest asset has been your ability to provide inspiration to others by communicating, listening, and conveying your own personal tastes and life experiences. Your challenge has always been to learn to stand back from people who are set in their beliefs. In the end, even if others differ in their perspective, most will appreciate and remember your words.

➤ Read about your Chinese Astrological sign on page 838. ➤ Read about your Personal Planets on page 826. ➤ Read about your personal Mystical Card on page 856.

CAPRICORN

From December 22, 12:04 through December 31, 23:59

The Fun-loving Adventurer

As a 1905 December Capricorn, you were born in the same month as Howard Hughes, known more for his eccentric, reclusive lifestyle at the end of his life than for his career as an industrialist, film producer, and record-setting aviator when he was younger. Ambitious, conservative, and materialistic, you too may have tried to combine a yen for physical activity with a drive for material success.

Rather than taking undue physical or financial risks, you may have found your niche by managing other people's finances, owning a business, or finding work where you could make exciting deals for others. On the weekends, you may have let your hair down by competing in swim or track meets, sports car races, or anything that might bring speed and excitement into your life. If you could not actually participate yourself, it's likely that you either read stories about sports heroes or became an avid spectator.

In contrast to your adventurous spirit, you've probably felt uncertain when trying to express your feelings. You've never been much of a conversationalist, but instead communicated through shared experiences with friends, especially adventures in which you could be physically active together. Because of your fun-loving nature and passion for the outdoors, you were always ready to try new sports or new equipment the minute it was introduced.

In love relationships, you'd want someone who could share the great outdoors, whether through canoeing, swimming, or taking long camping trips. Alongside the fun and exploration, your ideal partner would also have to share the responsibilities of raising a family, perhaps even regarding that as an adventure in itself. Those who share your values and with whom you can be most suited are Pisceans, Taureans, Virgos, and Scorpios.

Your greatest challenge is accepting the natural change of pace that comes with age, and trading in physical for mental activities. However, those around you know that your greatest strength is reflected in the expression, "you're as young as you feel." Not only do you feel young, but you make others feel that way too.

1905

CAPRICORN
Your Personal Planets

YOUR LOVE POTENTIAL
Venus in Sagittarius, Dec. 22, 12:04 - Dec. 31, 23:59

YOUR DRIVE AND AMBITION
Mars in Aquarius, Dec. 22, 12:04 - Dec. 27, 13:49
Mars in Pisces, Dec. 27, 13:50 - Dec. 31, 23:59

YOUR LUCK MAGNETISM
Jupiter in Taurus, Dec. 22, 12:04 - Dec. 31, 23:59

World Events

Dec. 22 - One hundred twenty-five thousand strike in St. Petersburg as the Tsar revokes his promise of universal suffrage.

Dec. 24 - American industrialist Howard Hughes is born in Houston, Texas.

Pablo Picasso
October 25, 1881 - April 8, 1973

PABLO PICASSO
Scorpio

Pablo Picasso was probably the most influential artist of the twentieth century, achieving incredible fame and fortune in his lifetime. In an artistic career that spanned seventy-five years, he created thousands of works—paintings, sculptures, prints, theatrical sets and costumes, lithographs, collages, and ceramics. He pioneered the Cubist style and one of his most well-known paintings—*Guernica*—stands as a continuing indictment of war. He continued to develop his art in pace with the rapid technological and cultural changes of the twentieth century.

Personally, he was a difficult, moody, sarcastic man who could also suddenly dazzle with the force of his charm. With proud Leo rising, he was dramatic by nature. And with the Moon, planet of emotions, in fickle Sagittarius in the house of creativity and love affairs, he went through a succession of wives, mistresses, and children. A charming Venus, the planet of affection, in Libra gave him charisma from its contact with Pluto, the planet of mass appeal. But Venus also clashed with Mars, planet of sexual drive, in Cancer, which gave him an enormous power of will. And while his fiery Leo rising flowed well with his equally fiery Moon in Sagittarius, it was at odds with his basic personality of intense Scorpio, a water sign. Hence the kind of "love-hate" relationships he appeared to have with individual women or the idea of women as a whole.

Picasso's chart shows a remarkable cluster of planets, all in artistic Taurus, in his house of career. They are Saturn (discipline, achievement), Neptune (creativity), Jupiter (growth, good fortune), and Pluto (power, mass appeal). His Sun in Scorpio, providing him with a strong personality, made a dynamic contact to Saturn, representing the father. Picasso's father, an art teacher, recognized his son's genius at an early age and supported him. With Mercury expressing itself in Scorpio and sparking off Jupiter's expansion and Pluto's power, Picasso was able to be both prolific and profound in his creations.

Another key to his genius may be indicated by the planet Uranus, which represents the unusual, breaking new ground, technology, and the unexpected. Uranus supplied an easy flow to Jupiter, planet of success, and to Neptune, planet of inspiration. With action-oriented Mars energizing Uranus, Neptune, and achieving Saturn, his artistic drive was intense and lasted up to the end of his long life.

▶ Read Andy Warhol's Star Profile on page 665.

1906

Getting Lost in Art: Saturn in Pisces

In 1906, the planet Saturn, the most maligned of the celestial bodies, entered Pisces, sign of dreams, the unconscious, and karma. Because Saturn is also connected to karma, when these two forces meet, life unfolds exactly as it should. In this year, many beings came into the world that would come to deeply influence art, culture, and life itself. Neptune, the planet of mystical, spiritual and artistic experience, rules emotional and creative Pisces. Saturn brings those things that exist only in the imagination into being by giving them structure. This year, the first patent for talking film was issued to Eugène Lauste. All the visual arts, but especially film and photography, are connected to Neptune. When we get lost in the movies, we are having what astrologers call a "Neptunian experience."

This was a pivotal year for the film industry with the births of two important film directors who would have a profound influence on the movies. On August 5, screenwriter, actor and director John Huston was born. Part of a Hollywood dynasty, he directed his father Walter in *The Maltese Falcon* and *The Treasure of the Sierra Madre*, for which they both won Academy Awards. He was also nominated in 1985 for *Prizzi's Honor*, starring his daughter Angelica. June 22 was the birthday of Billy Wilder, Austro-Hungarian-born director of such quintessential American classics as *Double Indemnity*, *Sunset Boulevard*, and *Some Like It Hot*. In addition, several renowned writers were born in 1905. Clifford Odets, playwright and writer of *Golden Boy*, was born on July 18. Samuel Beckett, author of unorthodox plays such as *Waiting for Godot* and *Krapp's Last Tape* was born on April 13. Avant-garde composer Dmitri Shostakovitch was born on September 25. Brilliant and world-renowned painters Picasso, Matisse, and Roualt showcased their work this year. It seems that radical Uranus in tradition-loving Capricorn was beginning to make itself felt.

With Saturn in Pisces, all forms of art flourished and the world took notice. People sought to be transformed by visual images and the art world began to have an influence on popular culture that it never had before.

The battle for women's suffrage intensifies

Up to 1,000 die in an earthquake in San Francisco

French Impressionist painter Paul Cézanne dies

A STRUGGLE FOR NEW FREEDOMS

As the global naval arms race heated up, Britain launched the world's largest battleship, the *Dreadnought*. A survey of the British Empire found that Britain ruled one-fifth of the globe. The German government announced that the Kiel Canal would be widened to allow the passage of larger battleships. In South Africa, 1,047 rebels surrendered to the British. Finland became the first European country to give women the right to vote. In the U.S., the battle for women's suffrage became more violent. In Italy, Vesuvius erupted, killing hundreds and destroying the town of Ottaiano. The day after a cataclysmic quake, San Francisco was devastated by unstoppable flames, while another violent quake destroyed Valparaiso in Chile.In the U.S., Standard Oil was accused of creating a monopoly through corrupt business practices. The Pure Food and Drug Act was signed into law, protecting the American public from contaminants. The French Impressionist painter Paul Cézanne died, while Upton Sinclair published *The Jungle* and O. Henry penned *The Four Million*. The American stage was lit up by *Hedda Gabler*, written by Henrik Ibsen, who died this year.

➤ Read "East Meets Twentieth-Century West" by Ronnie Grishman on page 65.

CAPRICORN

From January 01, 0:00 through January 20, 22:42

The Gentle Touch

As a January Capricorn of 1906, you are single-minded and ready to face the rigors of life. Those who work with you may regard you as a hard task-master, though one with a kind-hearted, generous nature. Yet underneath that businesslike attitude, you are probably a pussycat, and a sucker for sentiment. Most likely known for your empathetic nature, you may wear your heart of gold on your sleeve, where others may often cry on it. Around the time you were born, the police in Berlin forbade Isadora Duncan—the free-spirited dancer who also wore her emotions on her sleeve—to dance in public. Though you may not be as uninhibited as she was, your emotions may rule many aspects of your life.

You may have limited advice to dinner parties, school functions, and friends and family, parlaying such advice into a career in social work or counseling. You may be tempted to believe that people can pick themselves up by their bootstraps, but you may also offer strength and support to other's efforts. Your children probably benefited from such lessons, bringing you great pleasure as they incorporated your wisdom into their lives.

When you were younger, you probably found it difficult to reconcile the different parts of your personality. You may have reserved your toughness for the business world and your sweetness for your family and friends. As you matured, you realized that people need a little of both and that you could be both compassionate and forgiving while maintaining high standards.

In relationships, you may have been somewhat reserved, needing someone more gregarious to make up for where you leave off. On the other hand, you also need someone who can put their foot down and teach you the meaning of the word no. In general, you share the same values with Pisceans, Taureans, Virgos, and Scorpios.

Your greatest challenge is allowing your humanity to shine through without thinking that it detracts from your effectiveness as a role model and leader. Sweetness can be your strength, a fact that enabled you to be more effective as a parent, partner, friend, and community leader.

AQUARIUS

From January 20, 22:43 through February 19, 13:14

The Committed Observer

Around the time you were born, suffragettes in Europe were risking prison sentences to fight for the right to vote, while their American counterparts presented demands for electoral reform to the authorities in Washington, D.C. Although this issue had been resolved by the time you, Aquarius of 1906, became a young adult, any activities that involve social reform and progressive ideals are probably right up your alley. You may have watched movements like these from the sidelines, or you could have actively supported at least one. Even if you were just an interested observer, what would have distinguished you was your passion.

Loyal and committed, you value honesty. Tact may not be your strong suit, but passion is—even if it sometimes takes you over the edge. You are most likely to have shown a dedicated commitment to reform, but that reform could be of the entire justice system or just improving the neighborhood or your house. You probably imparted the value of concern and commitment to your children, and by doing so you made your job as a parent that much more rewarding.

Although some might think you a pessimist, you are actually a realist who simply calls things as you see them. Even though you may be totally honest, you never judge people and have always tried to accept diversity in others. This makes you a good friend. Once someone has gained your trust, you are probably friends for life, and you will always be there for that friend, even when others are not.

In relationships, you have always sought out those who could provide a good friendship, as well as someone who could be a committed partner with whom you could share experiences. For you, honest communication may be just as important as affection. Those who share your values tend to be Ariens, Geminis, Librans, and Sagittarians.

One difficulty you may have struggled to accept throughout your life is that some people do not want the truth at all costs, especially when their truth is different from your truth. Your beliefs are your strength and, by following them, you may have left your mark on the world.

➤ Read about your Chinese Astrological sign on page 838. ➤ Read about your Personal Planets on page 826. ➤ Read about your personal Mystical Card on page 856.

1906

CAPRICORN
Your Personal Planets

YOUR LOVE POTENTIAL
Venus in Sagittarius, Jan. 01, 0:00 - Jan. 01, 18:22
Venus in Capricorn, Jan. 01, 18:23 - Jan. 20, 22:42

YOUR DRIVE AND AMBITION
Mars in Pisces, Jan. 01, 0:00 - Jan. 20, 22:42

YOUR LUCK MAGNETISM
Jupiter in Taurus, Jan. 01, 0:00 - Jan. 20, 22:42

World Events

Jan. 4 – Police in Berlin forbid dancer Isadora Duncan to perform in public.

Jan. 7 – Harry Houdini breaks out of a cell in Washington, DC, confirming his reputation as a great escapologist.

Britain launches the Dreadnought

AQUARIUS
Your Personal Planets

YOUR LOVE POTENTIAL
Venus in Capricorn, Jan. 20, 22:43 - Jan. 25, 15:11
Venus in Aquarius, Jan. 25, 15:12 - Feb. 18, 13:12
Venus in Pisces, Feb. 18, 13:13 - Feb. 19, 13:14

YOUR DRIVE AND AMBITION
Mars in Pisces, Jan. 20, 22:43 - Feb. 04, 23:44
Mars in Aries, Feb. 04, 23:45 - Feb. 19, 13:14

YOUR LUCK MAGNETISM
Jupiter in Taurus, Jan. 20, 22:43 - Feb. 19, 13:14

World Events

Feb. 10 – Britain launches the World's largest battleship, the *Dreadnought*, in Portsmouth, ushering in a new era of naval warfare.

Feb. 15 – Three hundred suffragettes present demands for electoral reform to legislators in Washington, DC.

1906

PISCES
Your Personal Planets

YOUR LOVE POTENTIAL
Venus in Pisces, Feb. 19, 13:15 - Mar. 14, 13:41
Venus in Aries, Mar. 14, 13:42 - Mar. 21, 12:52

YOUR DRIVE AND AMBITION
Mars in Aries, Feb. 19, 13:15 - Mar. 17, 11:53
Mars in Taurus, Mar. 17, 11:54 - Mar. 21, 12:52

YOUR LUCK MAGNETISM
Jupiter in Taurus, Feb. 19, 13:15 - Mar. 09, 21:47
Jupiter in Gemini, Mar. 09, 21:48 - Mar. 21, 12:52

World Events

Mar. 7 – Finland becomes the first European country to give women the vote, decreeing universal suffrage for all citizens over the age of twenty-four.

Mar. 13 – American women's suffrage pioneer Susan B. Anthony dies.

San Francisco is struck by a severe earthquake

ARIES
Your Personal Planets

YOUR LOVE POTENTIAL
Venus in Aries, Mar. 21, 12:53 - Apr. 07, 17:58
Venus in Taurus, Apr. 07, 17:59 - Apr. 21, 0:38

YOUR DRIVE AND AMBITION
Mars in Taurus, Mar. 21, 12:53 - Apr. 21, 0:38

YOUR LUCK MAGNETISM
Jupiter in Gemini, Mar. 21, 12:53 - Apr. 21, 0:38

World Events

Apr. 13 – Franco-Irish author Samuel Beckett is born near Dublin.

Apr. 18 – San Francisco is struck by a severe earthquake followed by a series of fires; up to 1,000 die, with damage estimates up to $200 million.

PISCES
From February 19, 13:15 through March 21, 12:52

The Compassionate Actor

Caring, compassionate, and sympathetic, as a Pisces of 1906, you may have taken on the caretaker role at quite a young age; this may have been with your siblings, or perhaps with other children in your neighborhood. Offering kind words of support, you probably had no idea that these traits, which you displayed so naturally in your childhood, would work to your advantage later in life, especially during difficult economic times.

You were born at a "catastrophic" time—more than 1,000 people were killed in a mining explosion in France, and a volcano erupted in Sicily, destroying the island of Ustica and taking many lives. In times of crisis in your own life, you will do just about anything, playing many different roles, each suited to the situation at hand. Though you had your own dreams, some may have been set aside so you could help others achieve their goals. You probably knew the right things to say to encourage others to make their secret longings real.

Words may not have come easily, but it probably hasn't been difficult for you to reach for a laugh, a smile, or a tear at a moment's notice. With your sensitivity to the inner needs and motivations of others, acting would have come naturally to you. You could have been involved in the theater, dance, or film as a professional or an amateur behind the scenes.

You may have been most at ease in relationships with those that understand your sensitivities and think before speaking. Most importantly, you want to be appreciated for the kind and caring person you are. You will always reciprocate since you are sensitive to other's needs. You are most compatible with Taureans, Cancerians, Scorpios, and Capricorns.

During your lifetime, you may have found it a challenge to keep your feelings in check and to take things less personally. If you are corrected or criticized, even in a tactful way, some may overreact. You probably find it difficult to see things from another's perspective. Your greatest strength lies in your sensitivity, compassion, and tolerance as each helps you to rise above pettiness and aim toward greatness.

ARIES
From March 21, 12:53 through April 21, 0:38

The Articulate Speaker

As a 1906 Aries, you have probably been independent, assertive, and articulate your whole life. People who've known you for a long time may be amazed at your continual and unwavering pace, and may have trouble keeping up with you. Because of your talent for going one step beyond what anyone else would even attempt, you may have been way ahead of the pack in whatever you did. This made you self-reliant, but also may have made it difficult for you to compromise with others.

You probably enjoy challenges, especially if you can work on them on your own terms and in your own time. Around the time you were born, an epic earthquake rocked San Francisco, devastating the entire Bay area. Stories of that event may have reverberated within you, reinforcing your desire to rely on your own talents and abilities. It also may have encouraged you to pack as much into one day as you possibly can, since you never know what life has in store.

Competitive, yet fair-minded, you also may have a talking streak that puts others to shame. You probably talk better than you listen, so your friends tend to be those who listen better than they talk. When you have an audience, you may like to weave magical tales conjured from your active imagination. Your ability to dramatize a story probably fascinated your children, making you the favored parent to read to them at bedtime.

In relationships, you have always sought an equal partner, rather than a competitor. Independence and respect come first and foremost with you, though you may have to remind yourself to reserve time for your partner to do the things you both enjoy. Those with whom you are likely most at ease are Geminis, Leos, Sagittarians, and Aquarians.

Since you are always three steps ahead of everyone else, your greatest challenge may have been to learn to slow down long enough to hear what others have to say. Going through life at breakneck speed can, after all, have its drawbacks at times. On the other hand, your uncompromising energy is your greatest strength, and it has probably made you an inspiration and an example to others.

► Read about your Chinese Astrological sign on page 838. ► Read about your Personal Planets on page 826. ► Read about your personal Mystical Card on page 856.

TAURUS

From April 21, 0:39 through May 22, 0:24

The Methodical Overseer

As a Taurus of 1906, you have probably always been an interesting blend of practicality and idealism, from the time you were a child with "impossible" dreams to your journey through adulthood with more realistic ones. Around the date you were born, the Simplon—the longest tunnel in the world—was completed, running through the Alps and connecting Switzerland and Italy by train. This project, started by Napoleon a century previously, reflects your own patience and perseverance, sticking with things that others give up on.

Stable and efficient, you may test the patience of others with your methodical way of working. Others may also find you controlling, but you are probably just someone who likes knowing every aspect of the job at hand. Whether as an employer or an employee, you probably made it your business to know everything about a job, from the minor details to the big picture.

Your thorough way of working also means that few people ever got anything past you. As a parent, you were certainly a match for your children, who may have thought at times that you had an extra pair of eyes and ears. These qualities have earned you the respect of your peers, friends, and family.

You need someone in your life that you can trust implicitly and who is as responsible as you are. In private life, when you are able to let your hair down just a little, you probably want to know that the person sharing your life can be loving, warm, and demonstrative with their affections. You may feel most comfortable with Cancerians, Virgos, Capricorns, and Pisceans.

Throughout your life, you have probably been the pillar of strength and the one who everyone knew would be there to pick up the pieces. Your challenge has been to hand over that responsibility and allow things to be just a little bit less than perfect. Your greatest strength is probably your even-handed view of life and the way in which you find every job useful, whether it is at the "bottom" of the ladder or at the top. It is this approach to life that has probably made you exemplary to all those that crossed your path.

GEMINI

From May 22, 0:25 through June 22, 8:41

The Avid Wordsmith

Extroverted, talkative, and truly interested in what others have to say, as a Gemini of 1906, you may have been easily distracted, with many interests. That is why you may have liked working in groups, since others may have helped to keep you focused. If you had a tangible goal in sight, you probably kept your eyes on the prize, with the encouragement of others.

Your love of words may have made you an avid reader as a child and a theater, film, and literature enthusiast as you matured. You may have tried writing yourself, maybe even as a journalist so that you could research, interview, and investigate. When you were born, Congress was finalizing the Pure Food and Drug Act, signed into law by President Theodore Roosevelt on June 30. This law was the result of Roosevelt reading Upton Sinclair's classic novel *The Jungle*, an exposé of the meatpacking industry published earlier that year. That is the kind of impact you probably sought with your own words, whether spoken or written.

As a young adult, you probably needed mental activities to fill your waking hours. If you became a stay-at-home parent, you probably devised creative ways to keep your children occupied. You probably benefited from the fact that there was no television when they were young, instilling them with your own love of words and reading, perhaps by acting out stories. This also allowed you to be an active parent, without ever being bored.

In relationships, you need someone calm, steady, and practical, who could balance your need for mental stimulation. You appreciate those who love learning but can also teach you how to enjoy moments of silence together. You may be most comfortable with Leos, Librans, Aquarians, and Ariens.

Your greatest challenge has probably been to learn how to stick with a project from beginning to end, even if it became boring at points. You may have had the gift of the gab and your greatest strength is probably your ability to convey wonderful thoughts and feelings to others through the use of words. This is the legacy you leave to your family, to your friends, and to the world.

TAURUS
Your Personal Planets

YOUR LOVE POTENTIAL
Venus in Taurus, Apr. 21, 0:39 - May 02, 3:12
Venus in Gemini, May 02, 3:13 - May 22, 0:24

YOUR DRIVE AND AMBITION
Mars in Taurus, Apr. 21, 0:39 - Apr. 28, 16:59
Mars in Gemini, Apr. 28, 17:00 - May 22, 0:24

YOUR LUCK MAGNETISM
Jupiter in Gemini, Apr. 21, 0:39 - May 22, 0:24

World Events

May 1 – Six thousand workers in Germany are fired after a May Day strike.

May 10 – Russia's first democratic Parliament, the Duma, is inaugurated by Tsar Nicholas II.

The Duma is inaugurated by Tsar Nicholas II

GEMINI
Your Personal Planets

YOUR LOVE POTENTIAL
Venus in Gemini, May 22, 0:25 - May 26, 18:16
Venus in Cancer, May 26, 18:17 - June 20, 16:35
Venus in Leo, June 20, 16:36 - June 22, 8:41

YOUR DRIVE AND AMBITION
Mars in Gemini, May 22, 0:25 - June 11, 19:38
Mars in Cancer, June 11, 19:39 - June 22, 8:41

YOUR LUCK MAGNETISM
Jupiter in Gemini, May 22, 0:25 - June 22, 8:41

World Events

May 23 – Norwegian poet and playwright Henrik Ibsen dies.

June 17 – Russian officials confess that an anti-Semitic pogrom at Bialystok had been sanctioned by the government.

➤ Read about your Chinese Astrological sign on page 838. ➤ Read about your Personal Planets on page 826. ➤ Read about your personal Mystical Card on page 856.

61

1906

CANCER
Your Personal Planets

YOUR LOVE POTENTIAL
Venus in Leo, June 22, 8:42 - July 16, 1:17
Venus in Virgo, July 16, 1:18 - July 23, 19:32

YOUR DRIVE AND AMBITION
Mars in Cancer, June 22, 8:42 - July 23, 19:32

YOUR LUCK MAGNETISM
Jupiter in Gemini, June 22, 8:42 - July 23, 19:32

World Events

June 22 – American film director Billy Wilder is born near Vienna, Austria.

July 21 – Alfred Dreyfus receives the Legion of Honor at the École Militaire, twelve years after being wrongly convicted for spying.

Alfred Dreyfus receives the Legion of Honor

LEO
Your Personal Planets

YOUR LOVE POTENTIAL
Venus in Virgo, July 23, 19:33 - Aug. 11, 3:20
Venus in Libra, Aug. 11, 3:21 - Aug. 24, 2:13

YOUR DRIVE AND AMBITION
Mars in Cancer, July 23, 19:33 - July 27, 14:12
Mars in Leo, July 27, 14:13 - Aug. 24, 2:13

YOUR LUCK MAGNETISM
Jupiter in Gemini, July 23, 19:33 - July 30, 23:11
Jupiter in Cancer, July 30, 23:12 - Aug. 24, 2:13

World Events

July 29 – Expelled members of the Duma incite rebellion amongst the Russian people.

Aug. 11 – The first patent for a talking film is issued to Eugène Lauste in France.

CANCER
From June 22, 8:42 through July 23, 19:32

The Team Player

Sensitive and emotional yet methodical and tenacious, as a Cancer of 1906, you are probably a complex blend of stay-at-home family person and take-charge manager. You may not be comfortable taking a back seat to others, yet you probably like the feeling of being part of a team. As a child and adolescent, you may have enjoyed competing in team sports of one kind or another, but, whether you played sports or not, group effort probably became more important to you.

As you matured, you probably grew to love making others feel welcome in your home, entertaining friends and family. If you worked in business, you may have been a manager or another position where you took charge and helped to build the team—you probably cherished your co-workers as if they were family. You are also probably sentimental and dislike change.

Around the time you were born, Captain Alfred Dreyfus—wrongly convicted in France of spying for Germany—received the French Legion of Honor, twelve years after being court-martialed and six years after being pardoned. Since Dreyfus was Jewish, this case helped bring to light the anti-Semitism in France. Hearing of this historic event in your youth may have confirmed your feeling that all kinds of people can live together peaceably. Perhaps considered idealistic at times, it is likely that you also tried to impart this idealism to your children.

Your perfect life partner may have been someone who could be sentimental and family-minded, yet strong and decisive. You probably enjoy taking the lead on important decisions, such as those affecting children and finances, so your partner has to be willing to let you be in charge—at least some of the time. You may be most comfortable with Virgos, Scorpios, Pisceans and Taureans.

Since you probably like being in control, your greatest challenge has been to learn flexibility—little in life happens exactly according to plan. Your strength is the way that you make other people feel that they are a part of your team. You may like to lead, but you know that the best effort requires many hands, hearts, and minds.

LEO
From July 23, 19:33 through August 24, 2:13

The Heroic Talent

As a Leo of 1906, you probably dreamed of scenarios in which your deeds could save the world. Though you are idealistic and humane, you also probably enjoy being the center of attention, and may have felt that no deed that you did should go unnoticed. This probably lay at the heart of a lifelong dilemma—there were times that you selflessly performed a good deed without thought of reward and other times when your willingness to help required recognition.

You may have had a wonderful flair for the dramatic, a talent that would have helped you as a performer, or even as a director. The great American film director John Huston was born around the same time that you were, and his great adventure masterpieces, *The African Queen* and *Moby Dick*, are just the kind of movies that might have been your personal favorites. But your dramatic urges may just as effectively have played out in a little theater group, teaching children how to express themselves creatively, or just around the home.

Your combination of dramatic flair and true selflessness may at times have left you in a tug of war with yourself, but you probably have tried to reserve time for others less fortunate than yourself. Such acts of kindness come straight from your heart, and you may have hoped your children would be inspired to follow the path you showed them.

In relationships, you probably need someone who could let you know from time to time how much you were respected, loved, and appreciated. In return, you probably work hard to provide that same warmth and an atmosphere of support in which you could both mature together. Those with whom you don't mind sharing the spotlight are Librans, Sagittarians, Ariens, and Geminis.

One of the challenges you face is to accept that while your name may not be in lights, true greatness often lies in the small and selfless deeds that are done for the sake of others. Though you may have secretly known this, you may not have accepted it until later in life. Your greatest gift and your strength is probably your ability to put aside your ego and just let your own humanity shine.

► Read about your Chinese Astrological sign on page 838. ► Read about your Personal Planets on page 826. ► Read about your personal Mystical Card on page 856.

VIRGO

From August 24, 2:14 through September 23, 23:14

The Problem Solver

There was probably nothing you loved more than tackling a tough problem and solving it, as long as the work on that problem could be your own. As a Virgo of 1906, you may have even felt a secret thrill when you proved another's theory wrong. It is interesting that rebellious activity was going on in Russia and Cuba at the time of your birth. Hearing of such things when you were young may have made you feel a twinge of sympathy for freedom fighters, especially if it seemed to you that they just wanted some control over their lives.

Also around this time explorer Roald Amundsen finally completed his journey around the North-West Passage of Canada—going the distance, no matter how long it takes, is something you understand. Once you accepted a challenge, you likely saw it through to the very end, sticking with it when others gave up. You may have enjoyed dares as such problems gave you a chance to devise new ways of solving them.

If you worked for a paycheck, you would have been good as a fact-checker, proofreader, or even auditor, especially if you investigated other people's "creative" bookkeeping. If you stayed home to raise a family, you probably had the whole place organized from top to bottom and applied your "investigative" skills to child-rearing problem solving. In your spare time, you might have been a crossword puzzle expert or a lover of murder mystery novels.

You probably looked for a partner who could challenge you to think and grow at all levels. When it came to running the household, however, you probably reserved control over that arena. You are most compatible with Scorpios, Capricorns, Taureans, and Cancerians.

Over your lifetime, you may have found that your greatest challenge was to know when to keep on with a task and when to set it aside. Even though your normal perseverance is a wonderful trait, it can sometimes get you in trouble by clouding your judgment. Your greatest strength has probably been your ability to find a new way to approach a problem. This has made you a valuable asset and ally to those you worked with and those you loved.

LIBRA

From September 23, 23:15 through October 24, 7:54

The Unifying Force

As a Libra of 1906, you may have always seen yourself as a peacemaker who could be a unifying and harmonizing force in the world, and you may have dreamt of having a wide-reaching effect in this way. You may have been good at getting others to think beyond their own interests and work together for a common purpose. Around the time you were born, the world was in turmoil, with German troops crushing an uprising in south-west Africa. Hearing of things like this may have made you sad and even more determined to bring people together.

If you were blessed with artistic or musical gifts, you may have tried to bring others together for a cooperative, creative effort. If your talents were not along those lines, you may have gravitated toward an occupation that allowed you to find creative ways to balance people's contending interests. You may have been a counselor, for example, or a mediator, or even a judge.

Perhaps you stayed home and raised a family, in which case you would have been very good at quieting the little squabbles between siblings. In fact, it's likely that more than one friend or acquaintance has remarked at the cooperative spirit evident in your children. Not only did you try to instill that spirit in them, but you were also very likely a calming force in your neighborhood or your social group, acting as mediator and peacekeeper.

No one can match you in love, as your life partner probably was showered with gifts or pleasantries each and every day. At some level, you need a partner who would do the same for you, but you probably are content if he or she just expressed gratitude and appreciation. You have always been in sync with Sagittarians, Aquarians, Geminis, and Leos.

Your biggest challenge in life has come whenever you met people who had negative attitudes toward life and acted accordingly. You could usually manage to win them over, at least to some degree, to your more positive viewpoint but it may not have been easy. Your greatest strength flows from that—your ability to find the best in everyone you meet and the best in every situation you face.

➤ Read about your Chinese Astrological sign on page 838. ➤ Read about your Personal Planets on page 826. ➤ Read about your personal Mystical Card on page 856.

1906

VIRGO
Your Personal Planets

YOUR LOVE POTENTIAL
Venus in Libra, Aug. 24, 2:14 - Sept. 07, 15:31
Venus in Scorpio, Sept. 07, 15:32 - Sept. 23, 23:14

YOUR DRIVE AND AMBITION
Mars in Leo, Aug. 24, 2:14 - Sept. 12, 12:52
Mars in Virgo, Sept. 12, 12:53 - Sept. 23, 23:14

YOUR LUCK MAGNETISM
Jupiter in Cancer, Aug. 24, 2:14 - Sept. 23, 23:14

World Events

Aug. 25 – In St. Petersburg, an assassin's bomb injures Premier Stolypin and thirty-three others, and kills twenty-eight, including Stolypin's daughter.

Sept. 7 – Rebel tribes attack Tangier during the revolution in Morocco.

Russian composer Dmitri Shostakovitch is born under the sign of Libra

LIBRA
Your Personal Planets

YOUR LOVE POTENTIAL
Venus in Scorpio, Sept. 23, 23:15 - Oct. 09, 10:30
Venus in Sagittarius, Oct. 09, 10:31 - Oct. 24, 7:54

YOUR DRIVE AND AMBITION
Mars in Virgo, Sept. 23, 23:15 - Oct. 24, 7:54

YOUR LUCK MAGNETISM
Jupiter in Cancer, Sept. 23, 23:15 - Oct. 24, 7:54

World Events

Sept. 25 – Russian composer Dmitri Shostakovitch is born.

Oct. 3 – In Berlin, the first conference on wireless telegraphy adopts SOS as a warning signal.

1906

SCORPIO
Your Personal Planets

YOUR LOVE POTENTIAL
Venus in Sagittarius, Oct. 24, 7:55 - Nov. 23, 4:53

YOUR DRIVE AND AMBITION
Mars in Virgo, Oct. 24, 7:55 - Oct. 30, 4:25
Mars in Libra, Oct. 30, 4:26 - Nov. 23, 4:53

YOUR LUCK MAGNETISM
Jupiter in Cancer, Oct. 24, 7:55 - Nov. 23, 4:53

World Events

Nov. 18 - Anarchists bomb St. Peter's Cathedral in Rome.

Nov. 22 - In Peking, the imperial government increases its efforts to solve the problem of opium abuse in China.

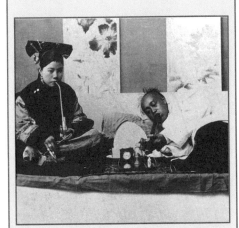

Opium abuse in China

SAGITTARIUS
Your Personal Planets

YOUR LOVE POTENTIAL
Venus in Sagittarius, Nov. 23, 4:54 - Dec. 15, 11:41
Venus in Scorpio, Dec. 15, 11:42 - Dec. 22, 17:52

YOUR DRIVE AND AMBITION
Mars in Libra, Nov. 23, 4:54 - Dec. 17, 12:06
Mars in Scorpio, Dec. 17, 12:07 - Dec. 22, 17:52

YOUR LUCK MAGNETISM
Jupiter in Cancer, Nov. 23, 4:54 - Dec. 22, 17:52

World Events

Dec. 10 - The Nobel Peace Prize is awarded to U.S. President Theodore Roosevelt for his work in bringing about the end of the Russo-Japanese War.

Dec. 12 - In Paris, the Pope's envoy is sent away from France and the state halts funding for churches.

SCORPIO
From October 24, 7:55 through November 23, 4:53

The Upbeat Futurist

A positive and upbeat atmosphere seemed to herald your birth, Scorpio of 1906, as President Theodore Roosevelt was "trust-busting" to preserve democracy and inventor Lee de Forest patented a key invention in the advancement of broadcasting technology. That kind of invention and progress echoes traits of your own you probably hold dear. You've always had your eye on the future and you may feel that the solution to the world's toughest problems lies around the corner.

Your forward-looking temperament may be matched by your feeling that there are also new worlds to be explored in the here and now. When you were younger, the idea of traveling to exotic countries and locations probably intrigued you. If you didn't get to go to all of the places you wanted to go, chances are you did as much traveling as you could in your adult years. Even if time and funds limited you, it's likely that you always found a way to get up and go someplace new every chance you got.

Your almost visionary perception of every situation you face would have helped you in any job that required you to define problems and inspire people to solve them. You would have done well in positions that required a positive attitude like sales, marketing, or even as a receptionist. If you stayed home and raised a family, your children probably had broader horizons and a longer-term view than their friends, as you always encouraged them to look outward and upward.

In love, you may have been attracted to those who were a bit different in one way or another. Someone from a foreign country, or someone skilled at telling stories would have been perfect for you, but they had to be willing to settle down when necessary. Your most compatible signs are Capricorns, Pisceans, Cancerians, and Virgos.

Your greatest challenge has been to accept the limitations of time—not going everywhere you wanted to go or learning all you wanted to learn. Your greatest strength is probably your ability to uplift others, encouraging them, making them dream and helping them to make some of those dreams come true.

SAGITTARIUS
From November 23, 4:54 through December 22, 17:52

The Merry Charger

If there's anything people know and remember you for, Sagittarius of 1906, it is most likely to be your dynamic drive and your ability to get where you want to go by your own efforts. A visit by President Theodore Roosevelt to the Panama Canal around the time you were born emphasized the kind of hard work and dedication to a goal that you probably admire. The opening of the canal during your youth may have inspired you to expand that ideal as you grew older.

You may have been motivated in equal parts by your love of doing something new and your need to be recognized for your achievements. Even though you enjoy the problems and challenges of working on something you find interesting, you also understand that the good feeling of a job well done fades over time, while recognition and your reputation have more staying power. You probably never want the limelight for yourself, however, and may be willing to share it with partners and co-workers who equally deserve it.

You would have done very well in professional fields like finance or even architecture, as you have both the talent and discipline to handle jobs of that nature. If you raised a family instead, you probably worked very hard to make sure your children understood responsibility and were willing to accept it. In your household, it's likely that everyone had a job assignment and was expected to get it done well and on time. You also probably made sure that work and play went hand in hand.

In your emotional life you want someone who understands hard work and responsibility, yet also knows how to have a good time. If you were the one who stayed home, you would have expected your mate to make a real and lasting mark in the outside world. You form meaningful relationships with Aquarians, Ariens, Leos, and Librans.

Your greatest challenge has been to find some balance between work and play. Although you're good at both, you occasionally need to be reminded to relax. Your greatest strength has been your ability to stretch your talents as far as they will go and, once you succeed, encouraging others to do the same.

➤ Read about your Chinese Astrological sign on page 838. ➤ Read about your Personal Planets on page 826. ➤ Read about your personal Mystical Card on page 856.

CAPRICORN

From December 22, 17:53 through December 31, 23:59

The Gracious Loner

You may have been something of a loner, December Capricorn of 1906, ready to do your own thing in your own time and in your own way. This is not to say that you don't like people or that you can't work with them if necessary, but you may have felt that you had a clear idea of what you wanted to do in life and that others could distract you from the path you had set for yourself.

Around the time you were born, the United States and Mexico signed a treaty providing for equitable distribution of the waters of the Rio Grande. This event may have mirrored your feeling that cooperation can involve sharing resources while working independently. Given your desire to be on your own as much as possible, you would have been most suited to a small business that you could run on your own. In your opinion, a small job well done is better than a grandiose project that is poorly executed.

If you worked at home and raised a family, your children probably marveled at your patience and dedication, especially when they were at their rowdiest, although they might not have appreciated this talent at the time. At the same time, they understood that there were times when you needed to be off somewhere by yourself, if only for an hour or so. You tried to teach your family the values of self-reliance and dependability; doubtless you were a good teacher on both scores.

Despite your need for privacy, you probably want to share, to cooperate, and to face life with a compatible partner. At the same time, you value a partner who intuitively knows when to hang around and when to give you a little breathing room. You share the same vision of life with Pisceans, Taureans, Virgos, and Scorpios.

Your biggest challenge has been to combine your efforts with others when necessary. Especially when younger, you may have balked at becoming involved in group activities. As time went on, however, you probably learned when it was best to be on your own, and when not. Your greatest strength is your sense of dedication and your ability to instill that in everyone who has been lucky enough to cross your path.

1906

CAPRICORN
Your Personal Planets

YOUR LOVE POTENTIAL
Venus in Scorpio, Dec. 22, 17:53 - Dec. 25, 23:48
Venus in Sagittarius, Dec. 25, 23:49 - Dec. 31, 23:59
YOUR DRIVE AND AMBITION
Mars in Scorpio, Dec. 22, 17:53 - Dec. 31, 23:59
YOUR LUCK MAGNETISM
Jupiter in Cancer, Dec. 22, 17:53 - Dec. 31, 23:59

World Events

Dec. 28 – Ecuador adopts its constitution.
Dec. 30 – British film director Carol Reed is born.

Traditional artwork of Indian gods

Special Feature
East Meets Twentieth-Century West
by Ronnie Grishman

Modern Western civilization can certainly be credited with advances unprecedented in human history, from democratic societies based upon the "inalienable rights of the individual," to mind-boggling quantum leaps in technology. The West's individualism has also produced great artists like Mozart, Shakespeare, and Picasso. Throughout history, however, the East has held a certain fascination for the Western mind, and many of us look to the East for spiritual replenishment. In this feature, we will concentrate on that influence in modern times.

In the mid-nineteenth century, a group of American philosophers and writers rejected the rigid Christian morality and dry scientific attitudes of their time. These early free-thinkers, a group that included Ralph Waldo Emerson and Henry David Thoreau, advocated human rights and a return to simple living, away from the newly emerging materialism and industrialism. Finding validation for their practical and poetic observations in newly available translations of

Hindu and Buddhist scriptures, they called themselves "American Transcendentalists." One hundred years later, their ideas are perhaps more relevant than ever; today's environmental movement is indebted to Thoreau's writings, which were influenced by Hindu teachings on ecology. Living for two years in rugged solitude in the woods of Massachusetts, Thoreau studied nature, meditated, read, and wrote.

At this time, in both Europe and the U.S., the pendulum was swinging away from the prevailing scientific reductionism. In seances held in the drawing rooms and salons of the bourgeoisie and nobility alike, spiritualists and mediums were probing "behind the veil," claiming to be not only contacting the dead but, much like psychics at the turn of this century, to be "channeling" spiritual guidance from higher beings.

In 1875, at the height of the Spiritualist Movement in England and the U.S., the Theosophical Society was established. The aim

of this international society, founded by Madame Helena Blavatsky and Colonel Henry S. Olcott was to introduce a universal brotherhood that would include, but not be limited to, elements of Western occultism, Hinduism, Buddhism, Sufism, Islam, and Christianity.

The Theosophical Movement had a seminal influence on Western culture of the twentieth century. The Irish poet W.B. Yeats was a member. The beloved 1939 American movie classic *The Wizard of Oz* was actually written by L. Frank Baum as a theosophical allegory in 1900.

(Continued on page 73)

➤ Read more about Jung in "Dreaming Through the Twentieth Century" on page 545. ➤ Read the Beatles' Star Profile on page 529. ➤ Read Einstein's Star Profile on page 169. ➤ Read the Dalai Lama's Star Profile on page 809.

1907

The Spirit of Protest: Uranus Opposes Neptune

In the year 1907, two of the most potent planets of the solar system formed an angle in the sky that influenced life on earth in numerous momentous ways. Uranus, the planet of rebellion and the unexpected, opposed Neptune, the planet of creativity and intuition. Because these are considered "outer" planets, they take a long time to traverse the zodiac, and have a generational affect. In 1907, they formed an exact opposition, an aspect that indicates some tension. With Cancer, the sign of home, hearth and family, and Capricorn, the sign of the world at large, involved in this configuration, events occurred that were both personal and political at once. Uranus opposite Neptune indicates a period of upheaval and general social unrest. People were out in force fighting for their rights in 1907. Women's suffrage was the *cause célèbre* for millions of women worldwide.

On February 13, in London, a crowd of suffragettes made several attempts to storm Parliament but were beaten back by police. On March 15, in Finland, women won their first seats in the Finnish Parliament. On December 31, American suffragettes opened their campaign for the vote with a rally in downtown New York City. Early feminist Susan B. Anthony had died the year before and women worked in her name to procure the rights they knew they deserved. Also this year and in the spirit of protest, the Irish group Sinn Fein proposed a boycott of British goods and businesses. Human rights are sacred and in 1907, people sought to protect and uphold humanity's highest aspirations.

Immigrants from Europe flood Ellis Island

The Lumière brothers discover a way to create color photographs

"The Girls of Avignon" by Pablo Picasso

THE PHANTOM IN THE THEATER

From Elizabethan times when Shakespeare penned his ethereal masterpiece, *Hamlet*, ghosts and other supernatural phenomena have been a popular subject for the stage. In 1907, *The Ghost Sonata*, which came complete with a ghost supper scene, opened in Stockholm, Sweden. It was the third of four chamber works that the playwright August Strindberg wrote for his Intimate Theater. The various unnatural characters in the play included a ghost, a mummy, a vampire, a dead body, and a child with supernatural powers.

HUMANITY ON THE MOVE

Following the treaty negotiated in 1905, the Russians and Japanese left Manchuria, but Japanese control of Korea became a bitter pill for Koreans to swallow, spawning incessant riots. In Norway, women were given the vote, while in Finland they won seats in Parliament. In South Africa, attorney Mahatma Gandhi led workers in peaceful protests against unfair labor laws. Riots in Vancouver, Canada, in response to the government's encouragement of Asian immigration, drove 2,000 Chinese from their homes. In the U.S., the stock market crashed even more deeply than in the Panic of 1901. Immigrants kept flooding Ellis Island from all over Europe, as they fled harsh economic or political conditions. In France, the Voisin brothers inaugurated the world's first ever aircraft manufacturing company. The Lumière brothers discovered a three-color process, a practical way to create color photographs. Thomas' *Sex and Society* advocated ending female subjection while the Ziegfeld Follies debuted in New York. In Britain, Sir Robert Baden-Powell started the Boy Scouts. Cubist art was introduced through the paintings of Picasso, Gris, and Braque.

▶ Read "East Meets Twentieth-Century West" by Ronnie Grishman on page 65.

CAPRICORN

From January 01, 0:00 through January 21, 4:30

The Self-Assured Doer

As a January Capricorn of 1907, you have always been very confident and firm in your own views and abilities. You may have never particularly sought or needed assurance or support—most of the time. Perhaps that is why people who do need encouragement and validation tend to gravitate to you, so that they can view first-hand how to be self-assured and take charge of their lives.

Being born and spending your early years in a time when women in many countries were stepping up their campaign for the right to vote would have struck a chord with you. You may not always have agreed with their sometimes extreme methods, but your judgment of human nature rests firmly on productivity rather than race or sex. You probably walked a straight line and from an early age tried to carve out a niche you could call your own. You were the type who could have created a business from scratch and, if you did, it was probably a success. Mathematical and organizational skills also may have made you a good manager, bookkeeper, or accountant.

It is unlikely that you have ever really worried about what other people thought of you or your methods. Whatever job you held should have been one that allowed you to think for yourself and work on your own. You raised your children according to your own dictates as well, and probably tried to teach them not to worry about what the neighbors said or what the other kids thought. Two characteristics you probably instilled in your children were independence and self-confidence.

Your romantic life was an area in which you sought someone to support you, at least on an emotional level. You may appear dry and intellectual but in fact you have quite a sensitive nature underneath your controlled exterior. You are most compatible with Pisceans, Taureans, Virgos, and Scorpios.

Your greatest challenge may have been to be able to accept and learn from well-meant criticism. In the end, your great strength is not so much your personal confidence, but the generous way in which you use it to strengthen the resolve and attitude of those who are not quite as sure as you.

AQUARIUS

From January 21, 4:31 through February 19, 18:57

The Counseling Risk-Taker

Even though you probably didn't climb Mount Everest or set new speed records in cars or planes, in your own way you liked trying new things and may have taken a few risks here and there, as an Aquarius of 1907. Some of this quiet innovation and muted need for adventure comes from a need for variety, but some of it comes from a need to keep your mind sharp by testing yourself when and where you can. Those who know you understand that if they want to be around you, they have to be ready to move at your pace and in your direction much of the time.

When you were born, suffragettes in London were coming head to head with the police as they tried to storm Parliament. In your own life, you were probably less interested in affecting others than proving to yourself that you could go beyond the limits others may have imposed. You could have entered a variety of occupations and done them well, but you needed them to involve an element of innovation that allowed you to do old things in new ways.

If you stayed home to raise a family, you probably channeled your creative needs into your children, instilling in them a desire not to follow the path of least resistance. You were probably the parent they always came to for advice and the one they looked to for support when they wanted to take on a task they hadn't tried before. You are also likely to have been the first to get the family out of the house to go to new places and see new things.

You would have sought out a partner who could love and support you, but challenge you at the same time. If you found someone who felt that life was an adventure but provided a safe cushion, then this would have been the person for you. You have always been most comfortable with Ariens, Geminis, Librans, and Sagittarians.

As a young adult, your greatest challenge was probably accepting that you might not have been destined to imitate those heroes you saw in newsreels or heard about on the radio. Your greatest contribution was probably closer to home, making everyday tasks exciting and guiding others into new ways to make their lives worthwhile.

➤ Read about your Chinese Astrological sign on page 838. ➤ Read about your Personal Planets on page 826. ➤ Read about your personal Mystical Card on page 856.

CAPRICORN
Your Personal Planets

YOUR LOVE POTENTIAL
Venus in Sagittarius, Jan. 01, 0:00 - Jan. 21, 4:30

YOUR DRIVE AND AMBITION
Mars in Scorpio, Jan. 01, 0:00 - Jan. 21, 4:30

YOUR LUCK MAGNETISM
Jupiter in Cancer, Jan. 01, 0:00 - Jan. 21, 4:30

World Events

Jan. 8 – A German committee on colonial policy demands more territorial acquisitions.

Jan. 14 – A huge earthquake in the West Indies causes widespread damage across Jamaica.

A crowd of suffragettes attempts to storm Parliament in London

AQUARIUS
Your Personal Planets

YOUR LOVE POTENTIAL
Venus in Sagittarius, Jan. 21, 4:31 - Feb. 06, 16:27
Venus in Capricorn, Feb. 06, 16:28 - Feb. 19, 18:57

YOUR DRIVE AND AMBITION
Mars in Scorpio, Jan. 21, 4:31 - Feb. 05, 9:28
Mars in Sagittarius, Feb. 05, 9:29 - Feb. 19, 18:57

YOUR LUCK MAGNETISM
Jupiter in Cancer, Jan. 21, 4:31 - Feb. 19, 18:57

World Events

Jan. 28 – Tsar Nicholas II informs the Chinese Emperor that Russian troops will evacuate Manchuria by March 22.

Feb. 13 – In London, a crowd of suffragettes makes several attempts to storm Parliament, but is beaten back by police.

1907

PISCES
Your Personal Planets

YOUR LOVE POTENTIAL
Venus in Capricorn, Feb. 19, 18:58 - Mar. 06, 20:43
Venus in Aquarius, Mar. 06, 20:44 - Mar. 21, 18:32

YOUR DRIVE AND AMBITION
Mars in Sagittarius, Feb. 19, 18:58 - Mar. 21, 18:32

YOUR LUCK MAGNETISM
Jupiter in Cancer, Feb. 19, 18:58 - Mar. 21, 18:32

World Events

Mar. 1 – The Salvation Army opens an anti-suicide bureau in New York.

Mar. 15 – In Finland, women are elected to Parliament for the first time.

The first anti-suicide bureau is created in New York

ARIES
Your Personal Planets

YOUR LOVE POTENTIAL
Venus in Aquarius, Mar. 21, 18:33 - Apr. 02, 1:27
Venus in Pisces, Apr. 02, 1:28 - Apr. 21, 6:16

YOUR DRIVE AND AMBITION
Mars in Sagittarius, Mar. 21, 18:33 - Apr. 01, 18:32
Mars in Capricorn, Apr. 01, 18:33 - Apr. 21, 6:16

YOUR LUCK MAGNETISM
Jupiter in Cancer, Mar. 21, 18:33 - Apr. 21, 6:16

World Events

Mar. 22 – Mahatma Gandhi organizes a campaign of civil disobedience in anger at the Asiatic Registration Act introduced in South Africa.

Apr. 15 – Japanese troops complete their evacuation of Manchuria.

PISCES
From February 19, 18:58 through March 21, 18:32

The Inspired Optimist

As a Pisces of 1907, you may be a dreamer, but you are one who understands that you have to apply yourself if you want to achieve any of those visions. Generally you are likely to be an optimist—someone rarely discouraged when life seems to place an obstacle in your path. When an obstacle does arise, you don't wonder if you can get past it but instead how you can move it out of the way. Most of the time, you defeat these obstacles best when you can work with someone you trust, someone who can give you the extra push you may need.

Around the time you were born, women in Finland won seats in Parliament for the first time—an event that underscores your feeling that with time and perseverance, a goal can always be reached, no matter how impossible it may appear at first. This attitude would have stood you in good stead if you worked in the world of business or retail, making you an asset to any company that employed you. Even in a subordinate position, you probably contributed that extra measure of intuitiveness and optimism that let others know they could solve whatever problem confronted them.

If your job was raising a family, your children would have found inspiration from your example. You most likely always encouraged your brood to follow both their hearts and their minds while setting lofty goals. When they were young, you may have read them heroic epics in addition to the regular fairy tales.

In love, you strive for the best and prefer a partner who is a cut above average, someone brimming with a good deal of self-confidence. Mutual support for each other's hopes, wishes, and dreams may have made every day of your time together as exciting as when you first met. You are most at ease with Taureans, Cancerians, Scorpios, and Capricorns.

The greatest challenge you have faced has been learning that some aspirations in life have to be set aside, or at least balanced against the hopes and dreams of other people. With the help of others, your ability to inspire proved your greatest strength, giving you a special place in the hearts and minds of those you love.

ARIES
From March 21, 18:33 through April 21, 6:16

The Road Guide

As an Aries of 1907, you are enterprising, active, and take the initiative long before others have even finalized their plan of action. A doer from start to finish, you have used these admirable traits in the service of other people—especially those you loved—for as long as you can remember. Around the time you were born, a young lawyer from India named Mohandas Gandhi followed a higher calling and launched a civil disobedience campaign in South Africa. This event may reflect your own desire to lead and Gandhi may have been an influence, representing the ideals to which you aspire.

While others lived according to their own grand visions, situations in which you helped others achieve drew you most strongly. Sometimes you may have done this by pointing out the right path, or you may have actually taken people under your wing. Teaching, social work, or counseling may have been the kind of careers that attracted you.

You have never been lazy and the more that you could sink your teeth into the better. You were probably one of the first to succeed at "having it all," long before the phrase became popular. As a parent, you helped your kids keep themselves on track as you worked subtly in the background to help them along.

You probably sought a life partner whom you could help in this way as well, keeping him or her on course with your advice, encouragement, and love. All you ask in return is to be treated with love and respect, and you have probably always been able to make important life decisions together. You are most compatible with Geminis, Leos, Sagittarians, and Aquarians.

Your greatest challenge has been to keep from losing yourself while helping others. Your personal dreams had merit and, though they may have been modest, you probably had to remind yourself to give them a chance. Your greatest strength has been your ability to serve in a subtle way that brings out the best in those around you. Some of those you helped over the years may not have been aware of the role you played, but the gratitude of those who did has been more than enough reward for you.

➤ Read about your Chinese Astrological sign on page 838. ➤ Read about your Personal Planets on page 826. ➤ Read about your personal Mystical Card on page 856.

TAURUS

From April 21, 6:17 through May 22, 6:02

The Touching Peacemaker

Some people are interested in big ideas, promoted loudly. You, Taurus of 1907, are more interested in small ideas, spoken well. You tend to think of anyone, rich or poor, as a human being, finding the common humanity that binds us together while ignoring the trappings that make us seem different. There may be nothing philosophical or political about this, it simply may be your natural way of looking at things.

Around the time you were born, government officials in Russia banned a revolutionary pamphlet written by author and pacifist Leo Tolstoy about the struggles between the haves and have-nots. Whether you read the pamphlet or not, you probably agree that at heart we are all the same and should all get along. This may have made you a natural mediator between friends and colleagues who couldn't see eye to eye. You may have followed a career in diplomacy, law, or some other field in which you were a go-between.

At home, you were probably the consoler and peacemaker. If your children argued over who would play with a favorite toy, your favored tactic may have been to distract and quiet them with a story, or some milk and cookies. When their minds returned to the original problem, the conflict had eased, and they would go quietly about their business. It may have taken them years to catch on!

You have been drawn emotionally to those who shared your feelings about harmony and humanity but could be firm and fill in the gaps left by your peaceable attitude. You also probably appreciated someone who could naturally sense when you needed quiet support. You feel most at ease with Cancerians, Virgos, Capricorns, and Pisceans.

Your greatest challenges have emerged when you had to maintain objectivity while helping others reach an accord. This may have been much more difficult as a young adult than when you matured and patience finally became a virtue. Your greatest strength has come from your ability to speak directly to someone's interests and concerns. Because you look right through the masks people wear, you can see their hearts and touch them in a way they will never forget.

GEMINI

From May 22, 6:03 through June 22, 14:22

The Charitable Companion

Friendly, open-minded, and charitable, you, Gemini of 1907, spent so much time trying to figure out how other people's minds' work that you may have sidestepped your own direction in life. Understanding that life is for living and that giving is an essential part of life, you tend to be generous—sometimes to a fault. While some appreciated your open heart and willingness to lend a hand, others may have taken advantage of your good nature.

Around the time you were born, the Lumière brothers in France had just invented a method for printing color pictures in magazines and newspapers, a sign that the world you grew up in had great depth and contrast. You were probably aware of those contrasts, especially wars and revolutions fought by people competing over limited resources. Your response to similar situations may have been to give your time, your money, or even yourself. This may have made work for a charitable organization natural for you. It was not important what job you had as long as you could integrate your personal desires with your professional life.

In raising a family, you were probably good at getting your children to share and care—you set a good example for them. Even if you had a problem child who never seemed to fit, eventually he or she would have been won over by your giving ways. You also probably emphasized ways to build family togetherness through group activities such as putting on plays for the neighborhood.

For a life partner you would have wanted someone who could balance your generous nature with an ability to keep an eye on the family balance sheet. This doesn't mean you sought someone cold and calculating, but rather someone who could gently remind you when your generosity exceeded your bank account. Your most compatible signs are Leos, Librans, Aquarians, and Ariens.

Your greatest challenge has been to distinguish between those who are true friends and those who take advantage of your good nature. Your greatest strength has been your openness and altruism and it is the thing that many who have encountered you will mention and remember always.

➤ Read about your Chinese Astrological sign on page 838. ➤ Read about your Personal Planets on page 826. ➤ Read about your personal Mystical Card on page 856.

TAURUS
Your Personal Planets

YOUR LOVE POTENTIAL

Venus in Pisces, Apr. 21, 6:17 - Apr. 27, 12:28
Venus in Aries, Apr. 27, 12:29 - May 22, 6:02

YOUR DRIVE AND AMBITION

Mars in Capricorn, Apr. 21, 6:17 - May 22, 6:02

YOUR LUCK MAGNETISM

Jupiter in Cancer, Apr. 21, 6:17 - May 22, 6:02

World Events

Apr. 27 – Threats of an uprising in the Punjab cause the British to arm volunteers.

May 14 – In Russia, twenty-eight people are arrested under suspicion of conspiring to kill the Tsar.

British actor Sir Laurence Olivier is born under the sign of Gemini

GEMINI
Your Personal Planets

YOUR LOVE POTENTIAL

Venus in Aries, May 22, 6:03 - May 22, 15:17
Venus in Taurus, May 22, 15:18 - June 16, 13:13
Venus in Gemini, June 16, 13:14 - June 22, 14:22

YOUR DRIVE AND AMBITION

Mars in Capricorn, May 22, 6:03 - June 22, 14:22

YOUR LUCK MAGNETISM

Jupiter in Cancer, May 22, 6:03 - June 22, 14:22

World Events

May 22 – British actor Sir Laurence Olivier is born in Dorking, Surrey.

June 14 – Legislation is passed in Norway granting women the vote.

CANCER
Your Personal Planets

YOUR LOVE POTENTIAL
Venus in Gemini, June 22, 14:23 - July 11, 6:41
Venus in Cancer, July 11, 6:42 - July 24, 1:17

YOUR DRIVE AND AMBITION
Mars in Capricorn, June 22, 14:23 - July 24, 1:17

YOUR LUCK MAGNETISM
Jupiter in Cancer, June 22, 14:23 - July 24, 1:17

World Events

July 1 – Britain grants self-government to the South African Orange Free State.

July 16 – American film star Barbara Stanwyck is born in Brooklyn, New York.

American film star Barbara Stanwyck is born under the sign of Cancer

LEO
Your Personal Planets

YOUR LOVE POTENTIAL
Venus in Cancer, July 24, 1:18 - Aug. 04, 19:07
Venus in Leo, Aug. 04, 19:08 - Aug. 24, 8:02

YOUR DRIVE AND AMBITION
Mars in Capricorn, July 24, 1:18 - Aug. 24, 8:02

YOUR LUCK MAGNETISM
Jupiter in Cancer, July 24, 1:18 - Aug. 18, 23:14
Jupiter in Leo, Aug. 18, 23:15 - Aug. 24, 8:02

World Events

Aug. 3 – Kaiser Wilhelm and Tsar Nicholas meet to discuss relations between their two countries.

Aug. 18 – The Women's International Socialist Congress in Stuttgart denounces German militarism and colonial policy.

CANCER
From June 22, 14:23 through July 24, 1:17

The Healing Aide

Ever the healer, as a Cancer of 1907, you have probably looked for ways to help others and gently remind them of their worth. Though you never thrust yourself and your good intentions on them, you let them know in a subtle way that you were available and ready to help out. The world you were born into may have seemed too centered on power for your taste, as illustrated by John D. Rockefeller testifying at the Standard Oil trial, which stretched over the month in which you were born.

The most effective way for you to help others has been simply by being there as a helpful companion. You probably were not someone who sought the limelight or the top spot, although you could have handled them if necessary. You may have tended to want and need less—you could be content helping, rather than trying to grab a brass ring for yourself.

You may have gravitated to a medical career as a doctor, nurse, or hospital volunteer. If you worked in a business setting, you probably assisted and supported the boss or partnered with someone who could take the lead. At home, you may have enjoyed preparing great meals and liked having the type of home where your children could bring their friends. Your most important accomplishment may have been instilling values of charity and friendliness in your children, then seeing them pass those values on to your grandchildren.

In relationships, you sought someone who could care for you, at least once in a while, since you usually took the lead in caring for others. You may even have attracted people who were moody, only because you understood the need to be alone and reflect. Those with whom you are most comfortable are Virgos, Scorpios, Pisceans, and Taureans.

Your greatest challenge has been to take care of yourself and stay healthy, something you do so naturally for others. When you have been able to balance your needs against those close to you, you were most satisfied with your life choices. Your greatest strength—your ability to soothe other people's anxieties and frustrations—has earned you the eternal gratitude of everyone who knows you.

LEO
From July 24, 1:18 through August 24, 8:02

The Deep Charmer

People often felt as if they knew all about you on first meeting, Leo of 1907, but the truth is that few probably managed to catch the depth of your mind or your feelings until they took the time to do so. This is not because you try to hide anything, but rather because of your engaging personality. Your pleasant charm has on more than one occasion led people to think you are a happy-go-lucky and optimistic person—which you are—but they neglected to see the deeper side of you.

Perhaps you're a little like the Peking to Paris auto race won by Prince Borghese that made splashy headlines around the time you were born. Behind the glamour of the race and its rich entrants was eight thousand miles and sixty-two days of hard work and intense driving. Underlying your sunny surface may be someone who knows that while we should meet life with a smile, nothing comes easy, so we have to be willing to put in extra hours when necessary.

You certainly worked hard, which is why anyone who employed you would have been more than grateful, especially if you worked in fields that required you to meet the public and keep them happy. On the other hand, if your full-time work was raising a family, you would have given your all for your kids. At the same time, you would have taught them to balance work and play, and look brightly toward the future, as you yourself probably did.

In love, you naturally gravitated toward a partner who knew how to take life seriously but also knew when to relax and savor each moment. You may have raised a family in difficult economic times and the perfect person would have been able to make you laugh in the more somber moments. Those who share your outlook on life and with whom you are most compatible are Librans, Sagittarians, Ariens, and Geminis.

Your greatest challenge has been to avoid the easy road of superficiality that you could go down when you wanted to avoid meeting life's difficulties head-on. Your greatest strength has probably been your good heart and your fundamentally cheery personality. Put simply, at your best, you make those around you feel happy.

➤ Read about your Chinese Astrological sign on page 838. ➤ Read about your Personal Planets on page 826. ➤ Read about your personal Mystical Card on page 856.

VIRGO

From August 24, 8:03 through September 24, 5:08

The Cooperative Critic

Grandness and glitz surrounded your birth, Virgo of 1907, as the luxury ocean liner *Lusitania*—later to be destroyed by a German warship—left London on its maiden voyage. Such events may seem rather remote, not just in time, but also in relation to who you are. You've probably seen life as a combination of happiness and hard work. The superficial show central to other people's lives has rarely distracted you.

You were probably at your best when you were cooperating with others on a serious project. Looking back, you realize that this was never an easy task. Good-natured though you may be, you can also be detailed, finicky, and perhaps critical of the way others do things, even when you do not mean to be. Yet your life featured many partnerships, some business and some social. You may have found that, although you were working overtime to balance the load and the politics of personalities, the rewards were well worth the effort.

You would have been very good as a partner in a law office or a similar professional situation where you could combine discipline and "people skills." Your approach to raising children may have been to make sure that they understood responsibility and, though you could understand if a child neglected his or her chores, you'd still make them do them even if the work had piled up. You also taught your children the importance of getting along with others.

In relationships, you probably favored someone who was well organized and could work with you to fit all the bits and pieces of life together. Deep down, however, you really are quite romantic and want the same in a spouse. You are likely to be most comfortable with Scorpios, Capricorns, Taureans, and Cancerians.

Your greatest challenge has been the tendency to favor your serious over your lighter side. You know how to laugh and let go, but it may be difficult for you to do so when you are concentrating on the task at hand. Your best talent and greatest strength has been to do for others what you sometimes forgot to do for yourself—show them the lighter side of life and help them to laugh.

LIBRA

From September 24, 5:09 through October 24, 13:51

The Idealistic Peace-lover

Around the time you were born, Libra of 1907, world powers were holding a major peace conference in The Hague. This did not end with the armaments agreement that they had originally gathered together to formalize, but instead laid out additional rules of war. Since your main concern in life may have been to maintain peace, the idea of having "rules of war" has probably seemed strange and you may have wondered, "Why not rules for peace instead?"

Idealistic and peace loving, you may have opted for a career as a missionary, teacher, or an administrator in a group promoting goodwill and understanding. Even if you did not seek a full-time career and stayed home to raise a family, you probably found the time to take on volunteer work so that your strong sense of purpose could find an outlet. As soon as your children were grown, you were probably the first to get involved with community service.

Fundamentally harmonious, you have probably always been skilled in getting people to squabble less and enjoy each other more. You probably promoted this in your own home, town, and neighborhood, and have been something of a peacemaker, at least in a small way. Whatever you could do to get people together, laughing and talking, you would do. You were not, however, just a social butterfly; you see human contact as essential to human existence. You communicated with your children instead of talking at them, and you encouraged them to talk to each other.

In love and marriage, you preferred a partner who was above all else open and honest and someone who was a good listener as well as a good talker. You probably didn't care about the size of someone's bank balance or family ties as long you could see into that person's heart. You are most comfortable with Sagittarians, Aquarians, Geminis, and Leos.

Your greatest challenge has been to accept that no matter how hard you try, there will always be those who settle disputes through fighting. Your great strength has been the way you tie and bind the people around you with your heart strings and, most significantly, your own "rules of peace."

➤ Read about your Chinese Astrological sign on page 838. ➤ Read about your Personal Planets on page 826. ➤ Read about your personal Mystical Card on page 856.

1907

VIRGO
Your Personal Planets

YOUR LOVE POTENTIAL
Venus in Leo, Aug. 24, 8:03 - Aug. 29, 2:29
Venus in Virgo, Aug. 29, 2:30 - Sept. 22, 5:51
Venus in Libra, Sept. 22, 5:52 - Sept. 24, 5:08

YOUR DRIVE AND AMBITION
Mars in Capricorn, Aug. 24, 8:03 - Sept. 24, 5:08

YOUR LUCK MAGNETISM
Jupiter in Leo, Aug. 24, 8:03 - Sept. 24, 5:08

World Events

Sept. 7 – Reports of the number of cholera cases in Russia raise fears of an epidemic.

Aug. 31 – Britain, Russia, and France sign the Triple Entente.

Count Zeppelin's dirigible

LIBRA
Your Personal Planets

YOUR LOVE POTENTIAL
Venus in Libra, Sept. 24, 5:09 - Oct. 16, 6:54
Venus in Scorpio, Oct. 16, 6:55 - Oct. 24, 13:51

YOUR DRIVE AND AMBITION
Mars in Capricorn, Sept. 24, 5:09 - Oct. 13, 14:28
Mars in Aquarius, Oct. 13, 14:29 - Oct. 24, 13:51

YOUR LUCK MAGNETISM
Jupiter in Leo, Sept. 24, 5:09 - Oct. 24, 13:51

World Events

Oct. 1 – The German army buys Count Zeppelin's dirigible.

Oct. 4 – U.S. President Theodore Roosevelt appeals to the public to increase the size of the U.S. navy.

1907

SCORPIO
Your Personal Planets

YOUR LOVE POTENTIAL
Venus in Scorpio, Oct. 24, 13:52 - Nov. 09, 7:07
Venus in Sagittarius, Nov. 09, 7:08 - Nov. 23, 10:51

YOUR DRIVE AND AMBITION
Mars in Aquarius, Oct. 24, 13:52 - Nov. 23, 10:51

YOUR LUCK MAGNETISM
Jupiter in Leo, Oct. 24, 13:52 - Nov. 23, 10:51

World Events

Oct. 29 – The Ottoman Sultan draws the attention of the Western powers to the agitation between the Bulgarians and Greeks in Macedonia.

Nov. 8 – A new discovery makes possible the reproduction of photographs by cable.

English Nobel Prize writer, Rudyard Kipling

SAGITTARIUS
Your Personal Planets

YOUR LOVE POTENTIAL
Venus in Sagittarius, Nov. 23, 10:52 - Dec. 03, 7:25
Venus in Capricorn, Dec. 03, 7:26 - Dec. 22, 23:51

YOUR DRIVE AND AMBITION
Mars in Aquarius, Nov. 23, 10:52 - Nov. 29, 4:29
Mars in Pisces, Nov. 29, 4:30 - Dec. 22, 23:51

YOUR LUCK MAGNETISM
Jupiter in Leo, Nov. 23, 10:52 - Dec. 22, 23:51

World Events

Nov. 26 – The Russian Tsar gains the support of the Duma after renouncing autocracy.

Dec. 10 – The Nobel Prize for literature is awarded to Rudyard Kipling.

SCORPIO

From October 24, 13:52 through November 23, 10:51

The Decisive Earner

One thing you have always understood, Scorpio of 1907, is the need to take decisive action when the time and place calls for it. This attitude is reflected in an event that began around your birth. As financial panic gripped the New York, markets financier J. P. Morgan was planning a solution; he later forced some of the richest men in America to donate $25 million to bring the country out of the disaster. Even though the world of the New York banker may have been far from your own, you probably admired Morgan's take-charge attitude.

Your own priorities centered more on earning enough to support your family without becoming caught up in the world of money or finance. Within that sphere, however, you were always ready to take action during tough times if you thought you were in danger of losing things that you cherished.

If you worked for a paycheck, doubtless you're the one who signed it for a business, possibly family-run, that you were in charge of yourself. If you were a stay-at-home parent, you may still have been in charge of the bookkeeping and, at the very least, were always aware of everything that came and went. You were probably a strict disciplinarian, teaching your children right from wrong and how to become responsible adults.

In relationships, you have probably freely and willingly given your time and your heart to your partner, asking for the same kind of strong commitment in return. Though you certainly can be romantic, it is high passion and not false sentimentalism that you show to the one you love. Those who share your values and with whom you are most compatible are Capricorns, Pisceans, Cancerians, and Virgos.

Your greatest challenge has been to find a way to deal with those around you who may have minimized your dedication. In particular, you may have had trouble understanding artistic types in your family and may have had to work doubly hard at reconciling your interests and theirs. Your greatest strength has been your commitment to anything you pursue. You never give up if the prize is worth it and others appreciate you for that most of all.

SAGITTARIUS

From November 23, 10:52 through December 22, 23:51

The Unrestricted Reacher

You may have felt that your reach should exceed your grasp, Sagittarius of 1907, and perhaps you were inspired by the fact that Rudyard Kipling, a man without formal education, won the Nobel Prize for literature around the time you were born. You were probably taken with stories about those who achieved a great deal in life without the perks and possibilities many take for granted. Whatever your start in life may have been, you never took it for granted.

Despite your serious and goal-oriented side, you have probably always approached life with a real zest and joy, meeting the challenges as they came and looking forward to the next one. Though you may not like competing against others in individual contests of will, you have, in fact, always competed against your last performance and set higher standards for yourself.

If you worked outside the home, you would have done well in occupations that involved travel and you may have even resided abroad for a time. If not, you probably traveled as much as you could, even if this was just on a local level. You may have occupied yourself with reading and watching films that took place in, or were about foreign lands—if you could not live out your dreams of seeing the world, you enjoyed pondering them nonetheless. You probably instilled that same sense of adventure and challenge in your children and encouraged them to pursue anything they wanted.

In love, you have sought someone who could allow you the freedom to move about and explore your environment. Even if that environment was fairly modest and close to home, you still wanted to be able to move on your own from time to time and looked for a partner without jealousy or the need to be attended by you. Your most compatible signs are Aquarians, Ariens, Leos, and Librans.

Your greatest challenge has come during those times when your freedom of movement was frustrated and restricted. Your great strength has been your ability, even in those physically limiting moments, to open up the world for yourself, your friends, and your family—even if only through your rich imagination.

► Read about your Chinese Astrological sign on page 838. ► Read about your Personal Planets on page 826. ► Read about your personal Mystical Card on page 856.

CAPRICORN

From December 22, 23:52 through December 31, 23:59

The Honest Leader

As a December Capricorn of 1907, you may have been one to go it alone, even during those times when you had no choice but to work with others. Like the suffragettes who took to the streets in the United States to campaign for voting rights around the time you were born, you've never minded taking on a big job when necessary. If you couldn't go it alone, you at least wanted to take the lead because you were more able to commit to the long term than others may have been—and certainly more able to stay focused on what needed to be done.

You may have been the one to stand up and point out what others were thinking to themselves, but never dared to say aloud. Tact may never have been your strong suit, but your ability to get right to the heart of the matter made you very good in an executive position, especially since you are likely to have been adept at handling money.

As a parent, you were much the same and your children may have thought you had eyes in the back of your head, as you always knew when they were trying to cut corners or get something past you one way or the other. Your no-nonsense approach was probably overstated in their eyes, as you made sure to balance their frivolous activities with the number of chores they had to accomplish.

In relationships, you looked for someone with as clear an eye as you, who could agree with you on how to teach your children the meaning of responsibility. You and your partner were probably both ambitious at the office but also affectionate and caring once the bedroom door was closed. You would have felt most at ease with Pisceans, Taureans, Cancerians, and Virgos.

Your greatest challenge has been to learn when to be serious and when to laugh as if you did not have a care in the world. You can be a bit too somber, but by mid-life, you may have realized that this attitude could actually dull your mental edge rather than sharpening it. Your greatest strength has been your ability to dedicate your efforts to one person or one project once you have put your mind to it. When someone needed commitment, they probably called on you first.

CAPRICORN
Your Personal Planets

YOUR LOVE POTENTIAL
Venus in Capricorn, Dec. 22, 23:52 - Dec. 27, 8:52
Venus in Aquarius, Dec. 27, 8:53 - Dec. 31, 23:59

YOUR DRIVE AND AMBITION
Mars in Pisces, Dec. 22, 23:52 - Dec. 31, 23:59

YOUR LUCK MAGNETISM
Jupiter in Leo, Dec. 22, 23:52 - Dec. 31, 23:59

World Events

Dec. 25 – American bandleader Cab Calloway is born.

Dec. 31 – For the first time a ball is dropped in New York's Times Square to signal the start of the new year.

Carl Jung

Special Feature
East Meets Twentieth-Century West
by Ronnie Grishman

(Continued from page 65)

The stream of teachings from East to West intensified when the Theosophical Society's headquarters were moved to India in 1882. The Society introduced a young Hindu but Western-educated teacher to the West in the 1920s. While not a yogi per se, Jiddu Krishnamurti, one of the first to "bridge" East and West, became one of last century's most influential spiritual teachers. Eventually leaving theosophy, Hinduism, and all "isms" behind, he taught that "Truth is a pathless land, and you cannot approach it by any path whatsoever, by any religion, by any sect." After his death in 1986, a library was established in his home in Ojai, California, where his talks, dialogues, journals, and letters have been preserved.

Paramahansa Yogananda, probably the first "guru to the West," was instructed by his own guru to come to the U.S. in 1922. Largely responsible for introducing yoga in the U.S., Yogananda settled in California, and in 1925 established the Self-Realization Fellowship in

Los Angeles to help spread the yoga teachings. His book *Autobiography of a Yogi* is considered a classic of spiritual literature.

> Eastern mystics have always said that "reality" is a concept, a dream, a shadow of the real; not the ultimate Reality.

C.G. Jung, the well-known Swiss psychologist, was also very drawn to Eastern thinking. Second to his theory of the "collective unconscious," in which he pointed out the similarities behind all the religions and mythologies of the world, and the linkage of all the *minds* of the world, Jung is known for his work on synchronicity, or "meaningful coincidence." To the Eastern mind, divine significance is found in all events, while for many Westerners, things just randomly happen, and even the most intriguingly meaningful "co-inciding" may be dismissed as coincidence. Jung's focus on the phenomenon of synchronicity helped awaken his fellow

Westerners to the grand, divine scheme of things. In 1949 Jung also brought new light to the mystery of all divinational methods when he wrote the foreword to a new translation of the ancient Chinese *I-Ching*. The *I-Ching*—or *Book of Changes*, in addition to being a divinational device, is seen as a repository of ancient Confucian and Taoist wisdom.

Jung's work on synchronicity, said to have been influenced by Albert Einstein's work on time and space, foreshadowed physicist Fritjof Capra's 1975 effort at East-West synthesis, *The Tao of Physics*. According to Capra, modern physicists confirm what Eastern mystics have always said about "reality"—that it's a concept, a dream, a shadow of the real; not the ultimate Reality.

(Continued on page 81)

➤ Read more about Jung in "Dreaming Through the Twentieth Century" on page 545. ➤ Read the Beatles' Star Profile on page 529. ➤ Read Einstein's Star Profile on page 169. ➤ Read the Dalai Lama's Star Profile on page 809.

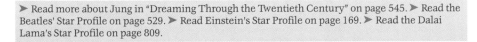

1908

Wreaking Havoc: Eclipse Events

A year of great cataclysm, due in part to the series of solar and lunar eclipses throughout the year. There were *seven* eclipses this year. Eclipses are thought to portend disaster and they are especially associated with earthquakes. The effects of an eclipse can be felt days, weeks or even months after they occur. In a solar eclipse the Moon blocks the Sun's light. During a lunar eclipse the shadow of the Earth passes over the moon. Eclipses happen when a New or Full Moon falls within about thirteen degrees of the Moon's Nodes. The last eclipse of the year occurred on December 23, and it was followed by a devastating earthquake. It fell on both sides of the Straits of Messina, killing some two hundred thousand souls. Earthquake aftershocks and resulting tsunamis killed seventy thousand to one hundred thousand in southern Italy and Sicily. This event still goes down as one of the most destructive earthquakes in history.

Natural disasters weren't the only thing to worry over in 1908. Also this year, on February 1, the King and the Crown Prince of Portugal were killed in Lisbon by an assassin as they were riding in a carriage. On March 3, in Washington, the government declared open war on U.S. anarchists. On June 4, in Paris, a military journalist shot and wounded Alfred Dreyfus at Émile Zola's bier. And on December 21 in German Samoa, natives threatened a revolt to gain their independence. Eclipses can wreak havoc on humanity, but they also bring necessary change. There's no reason to fear them.

The Young Turk movement frees Bulgaria from the Ottoman Empire

In the U.S., the state of Georgia bans the use of alcohol

Isadora Duncan's avant-garde dancing

SIBERIAN FIREBALL

On the morning of June 30, 1908, a fireball exploded in the air above the windswept tundra near the Tunguska River in Russia. The mysterious blast had the impact of a nuclear bomb, uprooting trees and destroying livestock and homes as far as 45 miles away. Survivors described a pillar of fire that resembled a mushroom cloud. Scientists have offered various theories—a meteorite, a comet, or a nuclear-powered spacecraft bursting in the atmosphere—but no provable explanation for the disaster has ever been found.

THE FALL OF EMPIRES

The Young Turk movement freed Bulgaria from the Ottoman Empire and forced Sultan Hamid II to grant basic constitutional freedoms elsewhere, while an assassin took the lives of Portugal's king and heir apparent. China's dowager empress and nephew emperor died suddenly and mysteriously, putting the two year-old puppet emperor Pu Yi on the throne. In Russia, Jewish peasants continued to be wiped out in pogroms. More than 200,000 died in southern Italy following its violent quake late in 1908. The U.S. state of Georgia passed a bill prohibiting the use of alcohol, as the Prohibition movement gathered steam. William Taft was elected president, and William Durant started a new mega-corporation in General Motors by combining Buick and Oldsmobile. Moving pictures were a $40 million industry, as fifty percent of Americans attended a film weekly, and French aviator Louis Blériot flew 30 feet in a monoplane. The London Olympics became a political hotbed, but the winners came from more diverse international locations. The American Isadora Duncan thrilled her audiences with her exotic classical dancing while Russian composer Rimsky-Korsakov died.

➤ Read "East Meets Twentieth-Century West" by Ronnie Grishman on page 65.

CAPRICORN

From January 01, 0:00 through January 21, 10:27

The Realistic Visionary

On the very first day of the year, January Capricorn of 1908, the head of the Rockefeller Institute for Medical Research stated that the day when disease could be healed by transplanting organs was not far off. Of course, it took much longer than anyone might have expected, but as you grew up, you probably responded to the hope that a newer and better world was near at hand and even imagined doing things when you grew up that would help humanity in one way or another.

You would probably be the first to admit that your hopes have often exceeded your ability to make them a reality. Even if your life was a relatively quiet and normal one, you likely admired those who dreamed great dreams and managed to work to attain them. You may have been active in a medical profession yourself and, if you did not become a doctor, nurse, or other medical practitioner, you may have worked as a hospital administrator or managing a doctor's office.

Dreamer though you may always have been, you excelled in getting down to brass tacks when you had a job to tackle; this characteristic made you a valuable asset to any organization you might have worked for throughout your life. Doing jobs around the office or managing others and training them are the tasks that you have always done best. You were probably also good at getting your children to concentrate on practical matters and learn skills and trades that would always put them in demand.

In relationships, you may have been most drawn to those who not only were visionary but also worked very hard to make whatever visions they had into realities. You would have been happy to make some sacrifices in order to help in this process, as long as your partner lived up to your own emotional and romantic ideals. You are most compatible with Pisceans, Taureans, Virgos, and Scorpios.

Your greatest challenge in life has been to find a way to achieve a measure of happiness even while taking into account other people's priorities. Your greatest strength has been your capacity to help others to sort out what is substantial, real, and useful in their own lives.

AQUARIUS

From January 21, 10:28 through February 20, 0:53

The Scientific Ethicist

Around the time you were born, Aquarius of 1908, a young lady named Katie Mulcahey was arrested and jailed in New York for violating a law that made it illegal for women to smoke. You too have probably been the quintessential rebel. When you were young, you may not have taken anything at face value and looked for ways to break down barriers. As you matured, you may have been inspired by the ever-changing world of communication and travel and learned as much as you could about the new technologies that made it all possible.

You may have sought work in the new field of radio and, later on, in the pioneering world of television. With your scientific gifts and skill as a teacher, your favorite place may have been a university or factory where you could master and use the many electronic marvels of that day. If nothing else, you liked to be on the inside of new and exciting developments and breakthroughs.

As a parent, your first priority was probably to instill your children with a lust for knowledge and the need to question everything that did not make sense. Though providing answers may have been tiring, your patience made you an excellent teacher, whether as a job or at home with your family. You may have even encouraged your children and students to read biographies of great men and women, to illustrate how anything is possible.

In relationships, you sought someone who shared your passion for new discoveries and, like you, was unafraid to forge ahead and leave the past behind. Since balancing the checkbook is not your favorite pastime, your partner probably had to budget the household income. You share the same values with Ariens, Geminis, Librans, and Sagittarians.

Your greatest challenge has been to balance the advances in technology with your strong value system. Though you tried your best, even in difficult economic times, to avoid jobs that didn't measure up in an ethical way, this was never easy to do. Your greatest strength has been not only that sense of ethics, but also how you demonstrated it in your own life, teaching others to live richer and fuller lives.

CAPRICORN
Your Personal Planets

YOUR LOVE POTENTIAL
Venus in Aquarius, Jan. 01, 0:00 - Jan. 20, 13:49
Venus in Pisces, Jan. 20, 13:50 - Jan. 21, 10:27

YOUR DRIVE AND AMBITION
Mars in Pisces, Jan. 01, 0:00 - Jan. 11, 4:38
Mars in Aries, Jan. 11, 4:39 - Jan. 21, 10:27

YOUR LUCK MAGNETISM
Jupiter in Leo, Jan. 01, 0:00 - Jan. 21, 10:27

World Events

Jan. 9 - Count Zeppelin announces his plans to build an airship that can carry one hundred passengers.

Jan. 12 - The first long-distance wireless message is sent from the Eiffel Tower in France.

King Carlos I and his son are assassinated

AQUARIUS
Your Personal Planets

YOUR LOVE POTENTIAL
Venus in Pisces, Jan. 21, 10:28 - Feb. 14, 2:54
Venus in Aries, Feb. 14, 2:55 - Feb. 20, 0:53

YOUR DRIVE AND AMBITION
Mars in Aries, Jan. 21, 10:28 - Feb. 20, 0:53

YOUR LUCK MAGNETISM
Jupiter in Leo, Jan. 21, 10:28 - Feb. 20, 0:53

World Events

Jan. 21 - In New York, the Sullivan Ordinance bars women from smoking in public facilities.

Feb. 1 - King Carlos I and the Crown Prince of Portugal are killed by assassins as they are riding in a carriage near the Home Office in Lisbon.

➤ Read about your Chinese Astrological sign on page 838. ➤ Read about your Personal Planets on page 826. ➤ Read about your personal Mystical Card on page 856.

1908

PISCES
Your Personal Planets

YOUR LOVE POTENTIAL
Venus in Aries, Feb. 20, 0:54 - Mar. 10, 8:05
Venus in Taurus, Mar. 10, 8:06 - Mar. 21, 0:26

YOUR DRIVE AND AMBITION
Mars in Aries, Feb. 20, 0:54 - Feb. 23, 3:24
Mars in Taurus, Feb. 23, 3:25 - Mar. 21, 0:26

YOUR LUCK MAGNETISM
Jupiter in Leo, Feb. 20, 0:54 - Mar. 21, 0:26

World Events

Mar. 2 – An international conference on arms reduction opens in London.

Mar. 2 – At the Academy of Sciences in Paris, Gabriel Lippman introduces three-dimensional color photography.

American film star Bette Davis is born under the sign of Aries

ARIES
Your Personal Planets

YOUR LOVE POTENTIAL
Venus in Taurus, Mar. 21, 0:27 - Apr. 05, 20:56
Venus in Gemini, Apr. 05, 20:57 - Apr. 20, 12:10

YOUR DRIVE AND AMBITION
Mars in Taurus, Mar. 21, 0:27 - Apr. 07, 4:05
Mars in Gemini, Apr. 07, 4:06 - Apr. 20, 12:10

YOUR LUCK MAGNETISM
Jupiter in Leo, Mar. 21, 0:27 - Apr. 20, 12:10

World Events

Apr. 5 – American film star Bette Davis is born.

Apr. 14 – In Denmark, Parliament grants the vote to men and women over twenty-five, except those supported by the state.

PISCES
From February 20, 0:54 through March 21, 0:26

The Soft Disciplinarian

Empathetic and emotional yet disciplined and serious, you, Pisces of 1908, were born around the time the United States government declared open war on American anarchists. In response to hearing about the detrimental effects of anarchy and the potential ensuing chaos, you probably developed the ability to complete each task carefully before turning your attention to anything else. When you were younger, this organization and attention to detail may have even been a source of amusement to adults as it made you seem older than your years.

As you grew up, you probably retained this ability, and those who knew you only casually might have thought you were a no-nonsense, unemotional character. Those close to you, however, always recognized your deep sensitivity and the difficulty you faced throughout your life in focusing your attention and keeping on track. This was especially true when you were around people who were upset or unhappy, as your natural empathy means that you often become sad as well, distracting you from anything else that demanded your attention.

Your compassion combined with your organizational skills would have made an excellent physician, nurse, or healthcare worker of one kind or another. If you stayed at home to raise a family, you probably used those very skills to fix wounds for the entire neighborhood as well as your own brood. Stern and sympathetic, you had the right combination to be a good disciplinarian yet a true confidant to friends and family.

Your ideal mate is someone who can be a good listener when you need to express your doubts, fears, and worries. On the other hand, your partner needs to be as passionate about life as you are and able to enjoy family outings and togetherness. You are most comfortable with Taureans, Cancerians, Scorpios, and Capricorns.

Your greatest challenge has been to keep your emotional nature in check, while still keeping it intact. Your greatest strength—your combination of sensitivity and discipline—has made you a good ally in a variety of situations and it's something those who know you depend on and love.

ARIES
From March 21, 0:27 through April 20, 12:10

The Perceptive Innovator

Around the time you were born, the first aircraft carrying a passenger took to the skies over Paris. The world you came of age in, Aries of 1908, was changing rapidly but you were never one to be afraid of moving ahead at a faster pace. In fact, among your family and friends, you were probably known as a champion of anything new and different. You may well have been aware of the latest technological innovations and had your finger on the pulse of news events that heralded change throughout the world.

Innovative and entrepreneurial, but also kind-hearted and generous, you have not embraced change simply for the sake of alleviating boredom, but have generally done so for the benefits promised by that change. You may be someone who has always had a great deal of business acumen and you would probably have done well owning your own company. As a result of your abilities, however, you may have taken financial risks that have not always been as successful as you envisioned. Still, you have a remarkable resiliency that others envy.

As a parent, you would have done everything you could to encourage independence in your children and provide them with the confidence to keep going after experiencing rejection or loss. With an eye toward the future, you wanted to be certain that they aimed for success and that their efforts would be even more successful than your own, benefiting from your experience and learning from your mistakes.

While you are attracted to friends who are bold and challenging, your recipe for a perfect partner includes someone with a sensitive touch. More than anything else, you need someone who can soften your hard edges and complement your more active personality. You are most comfortable with Geminis, Leos, Sagittarians, and Aquarians.

Your greatest challenge throughout your life has been savoring the private moments you enjoyed with friends and family rather than looking beyond your backyard for exciting adventures. Your great strength has been your ability to understand the unique talents of those around you and make the best use of them in any given situation.

➤ Read about your Chinese Astrological sign on page 838. ➤ Read about your Personal Planets on page 826. ➤ Read about your personal Mystical Card on page 856.

TAURUS

From April 20, 12:11 through May 21, 11:57

The Family Historian

A few days before you were born, Taurus of 1908, Winston Churchill was elected to the British House of Commons. While nobody could possibly imagine how much he would come to influence the course of history in years to come, you may have been intrigued by his career, even at its early stages. There is a definite parallel between his approach to life and your own—both of you looked the world straight in the eye but with a twist of humor. You feel that there is nothing so enjoyable as facing a new day, even when the road you may travel looks a bit rough.

What always gave you zest and confidence was your roots in your family and its traditions. As you grew up, you were probably the one who listened most intently when the "old folks" told tales of their youth, and you were the one to ask the most questions. You may have even approached your family history in an organized and almost scientific way—your passions may include history, architecture, and even genealogy. This interest in tradition and getting to the heart of the matter would have made you a good teacher, historian, lawyer, or police detective.

When raising your children, you probably managed to impart a sense of family history to them. You may have a natural way of telling a story, and may revel in passing on stories that you heard from various relatives in a way that both intrigues and enlightens those lucky enough to hear them. In a more literal sense, you made sure that your family ties were tight and strong.

Your emotional and romantic life required a strong partner who could be sensitive and supporting. At the same time, however, you may have wanted someone with just a bit of dash and adventure who could liven things up around the house from time to time. You share the same goals and values as Cancerians, Virgos, Capricorns, and Pisceans.

Your greatest challenge in life has been to accept everything your family has to offer, especially members whose values are different from your own. Your strong suit has been your ability to bind people together by helping them to transcend their differences.

GEMINI

From May 21, 11:58 through June 21, 20:18

The Communicative Arbitrator

Around the time you were born, the King of England, Edward VII, was paying a historic visit to Nicholas II, Tsar of Russia. The fact that two very important people were meeting and communicating for the very first time reflects your own interest in bringing people together to match their common interests and conquer their seemingly insurmountable differences.

People-oriented, objective, and communicative, your special gift has probably always been your ability to connect with people of diverse backgrounds—you are always able to find something, however small, that you have in common. This quality made you a wonderful event planner, either on a professional level or simply at home preparing fabulous parties and dinners for your friends and family. With your excellent leadership abilities, you also found it easy to mediate between differing viewpoints and solve problems between people.

As a parent, you probably attempted to nip sibling rivalries in the bud by teaching your children how to compromise; you also imparted to them your own skills at problem-solving and peacemaking, which stood them in good stead. You were proud to succeed on more than one occasion and it would have meant a lot to you that, as adults, your children still maintained close ties with each other

In relationships, you most want someone who could be a true partner, working things out with you on life's journey. Even though you may at times have been attracted to stronger, take-charge types, in the end you probably made the more satisfying choice of someone interested in being an equal rather than being the boss. Those with whom you are most compatible are Leos, Librans, Aquarians, and Ariens.

While you've earned the reputation of being able to get along with just about anybody, you still may find it challenging to connect with people unwilling to compromise, as this is a concept foreign to your nature. Your greatest strength has been the way in which you manage to calm troubled waters just by your presence. If there are problems to be solved or minds to be changed, everyone asks for you to be there.

▶ Read about your Chinese Astrological sign on page 838. ▶ Read about your Personal Planets on page 826. ▶ Read about your personal Mystical Card on page 856.

1908

TAURUS
Your Personal Planets

YOUR LOVE POTENTIAL
Venus in Gemini, Apr. 20, 12:11 - May 05, 17:43
Venus in Cancer, May 05, 17:44 - May 21, 11:57

YOUR DRIVE AND AMBITION
Mars in Gemini, Apr. 20, 12:11 - May 21, 11:57

YOUR LUCK MAGNETISM
Jupiter in Leo, Apr. 20, 12:11 - May 21, 11:57

World Events

Apr. 27 – The First International Congress of Psychoanalysis opens in Austria.

May 5 – Moving pictures become subject to copyright laws; royalties are to be paid.

Wright brothers, inventors of the first working airplane

GEMINI
Your Personal Planets

YOUR LOVE POTENTIAL
Venus in Cancer, May 21, 11:58 - June 21, 20:18

YOUR DRIVE AND AMBITION
Mars in Gemini, May 21, 11:58 - May 22, 14:13
Mars in Cancer, May 22, 14:14 - June 21, 20:18

YOUR LUCK MAGNETISM
Jupiter in Leo, May 21, 11:58 - June 21, 20:18

World Events

May 22 – The Wright brothers register their flying machine at the U.S. Patent Office.

June 4 – Alfred Dreyfus is shot and wounded by a military journalist at Émile Zola's bier in Paris.

1908

CANCER
Your Personal Planets

YOUR LOVE POTENTIAL
Venus in Cancer, June 21, 20:19 - July 23, 7:13

YOUR DRIVE AND AMBITION
Mars in Cancer, June 21, 20:19 - July 08, 3:53
Mars in Leo, July 08, 3:54 - July 23, 7:13

YOUR LUCK MAGNETISM
Jupiter in Leo, June 21, 20:19 - July 23, 7:13

World Events

June 26 – The Persian Shah orders an attack on the Parliament building, forcing deputies not killed to flee.

July 8 – Explorer Robert Peary departs for his Arctic voyage on the *Roosevelt*.

Explorer Robert Peary completes his Arctic voyage

LEO
Your Personal Planets

YOUR LOVE POTENTIAL
Venus in Cancer, July 23, 7:14 - Aug. 23, 13:56

YOUR DRIVE AND AMBITION
Mars in Leo, July 23, 7:14 - Aug. 23, 13:56

YOUR LUCK MAGNETISM
Jupiter in Leo, July 23, 7:14 - Aug. 23, 13:56

World Events

July 24 – Panic created by the Young Turk Movement forces Sultan Abdul-Hamid II to restore constitutional rule to the Turkish Empire.

Aug. 1 – Under American supervision, Cuba holds its first election.

CANCER
From June 21, 20:19 through July 23, 7:13

The Introspective Domesticate

As a Cancer of 1908, you grew up with a strong sense of "family values," long before the phrase became part of everyone's vocabulary. Domestic, loyal, and responsible, you were taught that despite professional aspirations, family came first. It was this axiom that is likely to have guided many of your choices in life. Once you matured and even had a family of your own, you made sure that both you and your spouse had jobs consisting of regular hours and infrequent travel. You probably looked forward to evening meals when you could gather as a family and discuss the day's events.

Around the time you were born, the Democratic Party nominated Williams Jennings Bryan to run against William Howard Taft in the United States presidential election. Your own interest in politics may have been limited to choosing the candidate whose economic policies would allow you to live comfortably and be paid well enough for whatever work you chose.

Your concern with supporting your family may have meant that the job you chose did not necessarily get your creative juices flowing, nor allow you to exercise original ideas. Instead, you probably worked for a large company that could ensure a steady job, health benefits, and a good retirement plan. If you stayed at home, you may have kept busy with bookkeeping, filing, or other detailed work for an outside business or company.

In relationships, you looked for someone who shared the same allegiance to home and hearth and who was willing to work hard to attain those goals, just as you were. The thing you most needed from a spouse, however, was loyalty, as a high priority for you has been to receive the same loyalty and devotion that you are willing to give to others. Those who share your values are Virgos, Scorpios, Pisceans, and Taureans.

Your greatest challenge in life has been learning to handle both family responsibilities and the financial demands that require you to earn a decent wage. Your greatest strength has been your ability to set a goal and then work firmly to achieve it. Other people have always relied on you because they know they can.

LEO
From July 23, 7:14 through August 23, 13:56

The Take-Charge Dynamo

The first Model T rolled off the assembly line at the Ford Motor Company in Detroit, Michigan, around the time you were born, Leo of 1908. Just as the world at that time was "ready to roll," so were you. Few people could match your dynamic, charging style. Even when you were young, you may have had a sense of mission and purpose that was matched only by your ability to take charge and set the agenda in any group.

Though you may have been a take-charge type, you were far from being bossy or dictatorial. Instead, your leadership skills were based on inspiration, partly by example, and partly by telling others what to do—if that happened to be absolutely necessary. You would have done very well as the owner of your own business or in a managerial position in the company of your choosing. A military career would also have suited you well.

As a parent, you probably saw yourself as the head of the family "troops," and may have assigned jobs to everyone to impart a sense of sharing and responsibility. Although you may not have been quite as efficient, your method of raising children could have been close to that of the father in the book *Cheaper By The Dozen*, which you probably loved reading and recommended to your children as a guide to managing their own lives.

In relationships, you sought someone to share the responsibility of raising a family as well as maintain lots of energy and a keen sense of purpose. More than anything you probably felt that life was an adventure and you needed someone who felt the same and was ready to share. Those with whom you share a vision are Librans, Sagittarians, Ariens, and Geminis.

Your greatest challenge in life has been to learn how to deal with those unwilling to handle their share of the load. Early on, such people may have been able to take advantage of you by appealing to your good heart but, as you matured, you finally learned to avoid them while maintaining your compassion. Your greatest strengths have been your enthusiasm and your drive. Both of these qualities are infectious, making other people feel good when they're around you.

► Read about your Chinese Astrological sign on page 838. ► Read about your Personal Planets on page 826. ► Read about your personal Mystical Card on page 856.

VIRGO

From August 23, 13:57 through September 23, 10:57

The Natural Talent

Around the time you were born, Virgo of 1908, Russian newspapers were praising eighty-year-old Count Leo Tolstoy as "the Shakespeare of the nineteenth century." This piece of trivia may have delighted you since you probably admire anyone who used creative talent to deliver an important message. As a young student, you may have fantasized about writing a great novel, short story, or even screenplay.

Practical, meticulous, and detailed, you probably have a remarkable ability to quickly switch gears and could have forged a career as a producer or even an accountant for a film company or other creative entity. You may have felt excitement at being involved, even from the business end, in a creative venture that the public would pay to enjoy. Whether or not you actually took up work in creative fields, you would have been a valuable asset to any company you joined forces with, as you came to the job each day ready to give your all.

Your children also benefited from your wonderful blend of creativity and practicality. You may have earned extra for your household by using your own natural creative talents on projects from painting to restoring furniture. You probably had the touch that could turn even a simple recipe or dress pattern into something quite unique and, when you needed more money, you may have called upon these natural talents to help you get it.

Quite apart from your practical bent, you may have been attracted to partners who were artistic or poetic. While you admired those who achieved great things, you also admired those who could express great things on a more emotional level. You are most comfortable with Librans, Sagittarians, Ariens, and Geminis.

The greatest challenge in your life has been to reconcile your great business sense with your creative drive. You may have discovered that you could do so by doing practical work for the performing arts or indulging a creative hobby. Whichever way you turned, your greatest strength has been your flexibility and keeping one foot in the world of the imagination and the other one firmly rooted in practical day-to-day living.

LIBRA

From September 23, 10:58 through October 23, 19:36

The Accommodating Cooperator

Around the time you were born, Libra of 1908, Bulgaria's Prince Ferdinand declared his country's independence from the Ottoman Empire. The sights and sounds of change, growth, and independence in the air both then and as you were growing up fit right in with your own natural inclinations to work cooperatively with others, yet maintain your own voice.

Your independent streak may have caused problems when you came up against hard-headed employers who liked to bark orders just to hear the sound of their own voice. For the most part though, you have found a way to get along with people through the art of compromise. This talent for working with others made you a good advocate and negotiator. It would have stood you in good stead in the legal profession, as a school counselor, or working for a charitable organization.

As a parent, you probably did everything you could to encourage a spirit of individuality among your children while also teaching them by example the value of communicating and cooperating. You were probably the type of parent who used reason and logic rather than "the rod" so popular in the early years of the century. Your main goal was to get your children to learn by experience—even by making mistakes—to learn things for themselves and to ask questions when unsure of themselves.

Since you find it difficult making decisions without asking others for advice, you are best suited to a life partner who is rational, logical, and capable of a quick decision. Inside, you are quite sensitive and your emotional currents run deep, so it is important that your partner is someone who can respond to you when you need to release fears and anxieties. You are most compatible with Sagittarians, Aquarians, Geminis, and Leos.

Due to your willingness to bend over backwards to accommodate others, your greatest challenge has been to deal with those situations in which you had to take firm control of someone else—no ifs, ands, or buts. The greatest strength you demonstrate has been drawing out the best in people, simply by encouraging them to stay just the way they are.

➤ Read about your Chinese Astrological sign on page 838. ➤ Read about your Personal Planets on page 826. ➤ Read about your personal Mystical Card on page 856.

VIRGO
Your Personal Planets

YOUR LOVE POTENTIAL
Venus in Cancer, Aug. 23, 13:57 - Sept. 08, 22:31
Venus in Leo, Sept. 08, 22:32 - Sept. 23, 10:57

YOUR DRIVE AND AMBITION
Mars in Leo, Aug. 23, 13:57 - Aug. 24, 6:43
Mars in Virgo, Aug. 24, 6:44 - Sept. 23, 10:57

YOUR LUCK MAGNETISM
Jupiter in Leo, Aug. 23, 13:57 - Sept. 12, 10:01
Jupiter in Virgo, Sept. 12, 10:02 - Sept. 23, 10:57

World Events

Sept. 19 - Doctors in Berlin announce the introduction of an electric knife for use in surgery.

Sept. 21 - In France, mathematician Herman Minkowski introduces the idea of time as a fourth dimension in his address "Time and Space."

Austrian soldiers in Herzegovina

LIBRA
Your Personal Planets

YOUR LOVE POTENTIAL
Venus in Leo, Sept. 23, 10:58 - Oct. 08, 6:12
Venus in Virgo, Oct. 08, 6:13 - Oct. 23, 19:36

YOUR DRIVE AND AMBITION
Mars in Virgo, Sept. 23, 10:58 - Oct. 10, 6:04
Mars in Libra, Oct. 10, 6:05 - Oct. 23, 19:36

YOUR LUCK MAGNETISM
Jupiter in Virgo, Sept. 23, 10:58 - Oct. 23, 19:36

World Events

Oct. 1 - Seven European nations compete in the first official international soccer tournament.

Oct. 6 - Austria-Hungary annexes Bosnia and Herzegovina, causing outrage in Turkey and Serbia.

79

1908

SCORPIO
Your Personal Planets

YOUR LOVE POTENTIAL
Venus in Virgo, Oct. 23, 19:37 - Nov. 03, 11:28
Venus in Libra, Nov. 03, 11:29 - Nov. 22, 16:34

YOUR DRIVE AND AMBITION
Mars in Libra, Oct. 23, 19:37 - Nov. 22, 16:34

YOUR LUCK MAGNETISM
Jupiter in Virgo, Oct. 23, 19:37 - Nov. 22, 16:34

World Events

Oct. 28 - Kaiser Wilhelm II cites German hostility to Britain in an interview with the *Daily Telegraph* in London.

Nov. 14 - Albert Einstein presents the quantum theory of light.

Scientist Albert Einstein

SAGITTARIUS
Your Personal Planets

YOUR LOVE POTENTIAL
Venus in Libra, Nov. 22, 16:35 - Nov. 28, 10:42
Venus in Scorpio, Nov. 28, 10:43 - Dec. 22, 5:33

YOUR DRIVE AND AMBITION
Mars in Libra, Nov. 22, 16:35 - Nov. 25, 14:17
Mars in Scorpio, Nov. 25, 14:18 - Dec. 22, 5:33

YOUR LUCK MAGNETISM
Jupiter in Virgo, Nov. 22, 16:35 - Dec. 22, 5:33

World Events

Nov. 26 - The Census Bureau reports that the divorce rate in the U.S. is higher than any other country.

Dec. 9 - A child labor bill is passed in the German Reichstag, prohibiting work for children under the age of thirteen.

SCORPIO
From October 23, 19:37 through November 22, 16:34

The Mystery Unraveler

As a Scorpio of 1908, you were born around the time that the scientist Professor Ernest Rutherford announced in London that he had isolated a single atom of matter, one of the most significant scientific advances of the era. Like Rutherford, who won the 1908 Nobel Prize in chemistry for his work on radioactivity, you probably had an intense need to get to the heart of the matter and to follow every last clue wherever it took you.

As a stickler for honesty and directness, you may have had an intuitive "nose" for little things that don't quite add up. Though you usually did not confront people when you caught them shading the truth, you probably didn't associate with them for too long either. Your ability to see through things and to piece odd facts together would have made you a perfect prosecutor or detective. Even if you opted for another career, you would have brought those unique skills to bear in any situation you encountered.

You probably had an amazing passion for solving mysteries and may have devoured novels, frequented films, and watched television shows with a "whodunit" plot, perhaps even guessing who committed the crime long before it was revealed. Your children learned at an early age that it was impossible to slip anything past you and, more importantly, the value of being open, honest, and above board. This wasn't anything you had to explain to them in so many words, since you taught them by your own example of being direct.

In relationships, you sought someone who could commit to you as deeply and sincerely as you did to them. Not one to do anything half way, you wouldn't accept anything less than a deep, honest, and caring relationship with someone who can carry his or her own weight at home and in the world. You are most compatible with Capricorns, Pisceans, Cancerians, and Virgos.

Your greatest challenge in life has been to learn when to hold other people to your high standards and when to be more tolerant. The greatest strength you possess has been your perception and vision, especially when you applied these to things beyond the realm of every-day life.

SAGITTARIUS
From November 22, 16:35 through December 22, 5:33

The Undaunted Searcher

Around the time you were born, Sagittarius of 1908, a full-scale excavation was underway at Chapelle-aux-Saints in France, where in August priests had discovered the earliest human remains. With a likely passion for history, anthropology, and the origins of religion, this discovery and others like it probably fascinated you. In a world that seemed to be hurrying ever onward toward an uncertain future, you may have lived your entire life fearing what would be left behind. For that reason, you may have decided early on not to have any regrets and to live each day as if it were your last.

You are likely to have been fascinated with history of all kinds, as well as other studies that delve into the past in one way or another. When you were young, your family may have felt you were overly serious, as you may have spent your free time reading books on "heavy" subjects such as philosophy and theology while others your age played outside or read simple fiction. This tendency may have led you into a college education at a time when few went that route and perhaps even to an academic career or a teaching position.

As a parent, you probably taught your children the alphabet, numbers, and colors well before they first set foot in a formal school. Even though all your children may not have had the same talent for learning that you did, you still made sure that they learned their school lessons well and did the best they could.

Your ideal life partner was one you considered a soul mate, who could communicate with you on an emotional, intellectual, and spiritual level. It didn't matter what your partner did but how they used his or her mind made all the difference in the world. You share the same values with Aquarians, Ariens, Leos, and Librans.

When you were young, you may have been unable to distinguish between which pipe dreams should be pursued and which ones were better left to the imagination. Your lifelong challenge has been to separate dreams from reality and your greatest strength has been your ability to eventually do so, and in so doing, make your greatest dreams come true.

➤ Read about your Chinese Astrological sign on page 838. ➤ Read about your Personal Planets on page 826. ➤ Read about your personal Mystical Card on page 856.

CAPRICORN

From December 22, 5:34 through December 31, 23:59

The Unstoppable Fighter

Within days of your birth, December Capricorn of 1908, Jack Johnson defeated Tommy Burns in Sydney, Australia, making him the first black man to win the world heavyweight boxing title. Officials actually had to call the bout short as Johnson outmatched his opponent in strength, ferocity, and endurance—a fact that reflects your own approach to life and most of the problems it set before you. You worked hard at everything you did and you never stopped until the job was done, showing unusual grit and determination.

The combination of drive, perseverance, and a talent for negotiating made you a natural in the field of business or the law. Few people have ever gotten the best of you in a bargain, whether it involved something as simple as haggling over the price of a used car or something as important as negotiating for months over a union contract. You worked all the angles and pulled the strings to get what you wanted and to go where you wanted.

Even raising a family gave you plenty of chances to use your talents in dealing with local shop owners and even your children. Not only could you probably stretch a household dollar further than anyone might imagine, but you could also outpace your children if they ever tried to pull the wool over your eyes. You were probably dedicated to shaping them up and making sure they were ready for life when it came time to go out on their own.

In love, you have been attracted to partners who are at least as strong as you are, if not stronger. At the same time, you want someone who can open you up emotionally and give you the opportunity to bring out feelings that you have to keep bottled up in other situations. Your most compatible partners are Pisceans, Taureans, Virgos, and Scorpios.

Your greatest challenge in life has been to know how and when to use your tenacity as not every situation you face calls for the full-on approach. Those times when subtlety was called for probably made you work the hardest. Your great strength has been not just your endurance, but also your sensitivity and grace. You try hard to win, but not at any cost.

1908

CAPRICORN
Your Personal Planets

YOUR LOVE POTENTIAL
Venus in Scorpio, Dec. 22, 5:34 - Dec. 22, 20:00
Venus in Sagittarius, Dec. 22, 20:01 - Dec. 31, 23:59

YOUR DRIVE AND AMBITION
Mars in Scorpio, Dec. 22, 5:34 - Dec. 31, 23:59

YOUR LUCK MAGNETISM
Jupiter in Virgo, Dec. 22, 5:34 - Dec. 31, 23:59

World Events

Dec. 26 – Texan Jack Johnson defeats Tommy Burns to become the first African American World heavyweight boxing champion.

Dec. 28 – The most devastating earthquake to hit Europe strikes on both sides of the Straits of Messina, killing nearly 300,000 people.

Ravi Shankar

Special Feature
East Meets Twentieth-Century West
by Ronnie Grishman

(Continued from page 73)

While the introduction and integration of esoteric and exoteric concepts from East and West were initially limited to a select audience of intellectuals, in the final four decades of the last century these ideas reached the general public. Perhaps it was the abrupt tearing open of inner vistas by the sixties drug culture that finally challenged the centuries-held rationalism of the West. Once again, the wisdom of the East was sought for understanding and balance.

Early pioneers of LSD, "consciousness explorers" like Ivy League professors Aldous Huxley (*Brave New World*, 1932; *The Doors of Perception*, 1954) and Dr. Timothy Leary, found parallels in Buddhism and Hinduism to the altered states they were experiencing. Their Harvard colleague, Professor Richard Alpert, (who changed his name to Ram Dass), did much to popularize Buddhism in his 1971 "hippie classic," *Be Here Now*." Jim Morrison named his popular band *The Doors*, after Huxley's title,

which the writer had himself taken from the eighteenth-century English mystical poet William Blake.

Beatle George Harrison had long been attracted to the Indian sitar music he first heard in England, and in 1967 it was the *Beatles* who brought sitarist Ravi Shankar and Transcendental Meditation™ founder Maharishi Mahesh Yogi to the West. Popular music culture thus became a powerful disseminator of ideas that had been rather obscure up until that point. If there was a defining moment, it was then that the Age of Aquarius was truly ignited.

In recent years the Western scientific community has recognized the benefits of yoga, meditation, martial arts, Indian ayurvedic medicine and nutrition, Chinese herbal medicine and acupuncture—the last, thanks to the ruptured appendix of a U.S. journalist traveling to China in 1971 with Henry Kissinger. After his operation with no anesthesia but acupuncture, he gave it a lot of favorable press.

The Dalai Lama's exile has brought, along with his cause to liberate Tibet, Buddhist teachings of compassion, peace, and understanding to a receptive Western audience. "Self-help guru" Deepak Chopra, M.D., a best-selling author and cultural icon now living in California, has become a household name. Chopra is very active in spreading the benefits of ayurvedic health practices and Hindu spiritual principles.

Understanding now flows easily between the mutually attractive poles of East and West. Like yin and yang, we are indeed complementary halves of one whole. And as we learn from one another, "global consciousness" evolves apace. The West has even been inspired to revive some of its own mystical practices, from Gregorian chant to Hebrew Kabbalah, and to explore the teachings of many indigenous cultures. This coming together of all spiritual paths is what the New Age is all about—and, as we can see, its roots lie in ages-old perennial wisdom. ☺

➤ Read more about Jung in "Dreaming Through the Twentieth Century" on page 545. ➤ Read the Beatles' Star Profile on page 529. ➤ Read Einstein's Star Profile on page 169. ➤ Read the Dalai Lama's Star Profile on page 809.

1909

Open Revolt Versus. Cautioned Resistance: Saturn Squares Uranus

At the start of the year of 1909, the planet Saturn, great teacher of discipline and restriction, had just entered the sign of Aries, arbiter of all things forceful and first. When Saturn takes up residence in Aries, people are compelled to learn the power of initiative, patience, and self-reliance. This astrological placement is connected to will and strength of character. This year, those who wanted to plunge ahead into uncharted territory had to take slower steps. On September 18, two suffragettes were sent to jail for throwing stones at British Prime Minister Asquith. On October 19th, Emmeline Pankhurst, a leading British suffragette, arrived in New York City to speak at a Carnegie Hall convention of suffragettes. On November 28, the French National Assembly offered working women eight weeks' vacation after childbirth. After many years of hard work, women were changing their circumstances by changing the world around them.

This year there was another very important celestial configuration related to the planet Saturn. Saturn in Aries squared Uranus in Capricorn. A square is often a difficult aspect to deal with. This was a blueprint for the opposition between conservative and radical forces across the globe. As many groups fought for their human rights and learned how to wage defiant yet practical protest, the powers at large tried to clamp down. On January 9 Colombia recognized Panama's autonomy. On May 8, France warned the U.S. that increased duties on luxuries would bring on a trade war.

The arms race accelerates as Germany's navy increases rapidly

Louis Blériot, the first man to fly across the English Channel

Sigmund Freud (front left) with disciples

WITHOUT A TRACE

Even in a scientific age, some incidents defy rational explanation. In the summer of 1909, the British ocean liner *Waratah* disappeared off the coast of South Africa. No wreckage or flotsam was found. All passengers and hands shared the boat's destiny, never to be seen again. The fate of the *Waratah* remains unknown, though oceanographers have cited "freak waves"—tall waves that form when storm waves collide with powerful currents and can reach heights of 100 feet—as one likely agent of the *Waratah*'s doom.

THE DRIVE FOR INDEPENDENCE CONTINUES

After Bulgaria's bid for freedom, Serbia declared itself independent of Ottoman rule and demanded rights to neighboring Bosnia and Herzegovina, once part of its domain. Ottoman ruler Hamid II was deposed in favor of his more compassionate brother, Mehmed V, but not before hiding $10 million offshore. Britain was shocked at the rapid build-up of Germany's navy under Kaiser Wilhelm II and vowed to build up its own. Japan's Prince Ito was assassinated by a Korean dissident in retaliation for his harsh rule of the annexed Korean peninsula. The U.S. Prohibition movement continued to spread, with many states banning alcohol, while W. E. B. Dubois spearheaded the effort to gain Negro suffrage. American farmers brought in bumper crops of corn, cotton, and wheat, and the Wright Brothers developed a commercial enterprise in airplane manufacture. Frederick Cook and Robert Peary disputed who made it to the North Pole first, but Cook's claim was rejected by experts. Sigmund Freud expounded his psychological theories in America, and the first movie-house newsreels fed world events to audiences. Apache leader Geronimo died peacefully at age eighty.

➤ Read Henry Ford's Star Profile on page 89.

CAPRICORN

From January 01, 0:00 through January 20, 16:10

The Structured Reformer

As a January Capricorn of 1909, you have always had progressive views about issues ranging from freedom of speech to racial equality. Despite your somewhat original ideas, however, you may have been most comfortable with a structured, some might even say conservative lifestyle. This probably never presented a conflict for you, since you put your personal stamp on everything you touched and, in your own way, asserted your individuality.

You probably had political interests and definite ideas about how you would reform the status quo if you were elected to office. You may have worked in government, maybe as an elected representative or as a civil servant, but you also might have simply held office in a professional club or organization. Whatever position you held, the chance to be around the excitement of political change gave you a great feeling. American senator and presidential candidate Barry Goldwater was born on the first day of the year. His brand of politics—combining conservative and libertarian values—may have echoed your own view of life.

If you did not work full-time then you may have taken up volunteer work for your favorite political party or become involved in parent-teacher associations. You enjoyed having a hand in making the future, although you stood against any tearing down of existing structures. Instead, you tried to introduce change slowly and steadily.

Your ideal partner would have been a blend of conservatism and idealism, combining a devotion to routine with a passion for discussing the issues of the day. Underneath the political affinities, however, you want someone kind and considerate, and most important, someone who is deeply fair-minded. You are most compatible with Pisceans, Taureans, Virgos, and Scorpios.

Despite your seeming ability to integrate two contradictory aspects of yourself into a strong core, it has not been easy for you, and it's a challenge you faced almost every day. Your greatest strength has been your ability to avoid being stereotyped by others, as you combine compassion and strong principles in your own unique way.

AQUARIUS

From January 20, 16:11 through February 19, 6:37

The Questioning Extrovert

As an Aquarius of 1909, you are probably extroverted and full of life, with an intense interest in the issues of the day. Around the time you were born, the fifty-story Metropolitan Life Insurance Company building was completed—the largest office building in New York at the time. The building also was notable because its owner funded its construction by offering life-insurance policies to the working class. This reflects your belief that creative thinking can make anything possible in an ever-changing world.

As a youngster, you may have had questions about everything. This is a trait that might have worn your parents' patience a bit thin. Once you got to secondary school and college (if you were fortunate enough to attend), you probably could not be kept away from debating teams, school newspapers, or any other forum where you were given the opportunity to speak your mind.

Although you may be stubborn and can be quite opinionated, you are also unpredictable. Nobody can ever really know for sure what side of the fence you will land on or what stand you might take on an issue. Your objectivity and your ability to consider each situation on its own terms make you a great researcher, editor, or writer. You would have been equally comfortable in the business world as a spokesperson or salesperson for anything from insurance to savings bonds.

In close relationships, you are drawn to someone who respects your individuality but who also is attentive to your emotional needs. You value your leisure time and, while it would be nice if your spouse also enjoyed socializing with diverse groups of people, it is only necessary that your partner not feel abandoned if you take center stage. Those with whom you are most comfortable are Ariens, Geminis, Librans, and Sagittarians.

With your penchant for speaking your mind, your most challenging moments have been those when you have expressed one too many opinions in mixed company. Your greatest strength has been your passion for your convictions, as you set an example for others who may be afraid to stand firm on their own beliefs.

➤ Read about your Chinese Astrological sign on page 838. ➤ Read about your Personal Planets on page 826. ➤ Read about your personal Mystical Card on page 856.

CAPRICORN
Your Personal Planets

YOUR LOVE POTENTIAL
Venus in Sagittarius, Jan. 01, 0:00 - Jan. 15, 23:19
Venus in Capricorn, Jan. 15, 23:20 - Jan. 20, 16:10

YOUR DRIVE AND AMBITION
Mars in Scorpio, Jan. 01, 0:00 - Jan. 10, 3:54
Mars in Sagittarius, Jan. 10, 3:55 - Jan. 20, 16:10

YOUR LUCK MAGNETISM
Jupiter in Virgo, Jan. 01, 0:00 - Jan. 20, 16:10

World Events

Jan. 1 - London astronomers hint at sightings of a planet beyond Neptune.

Jan. 3 - Statistics are released which reveal that moving pictures are a $40 million a year industry in the U.S.

Statistics reveal the spectacular growth of the U.S. movie industry

AQUARIUS
Your Personal Planets

YOUR LOVE POTENTIAL
Venus in Capricorn, Jan. 20, 16:11 - Feb. 09, 0:40
Venus in Aquarius, Feb. 09, 0:41 - Feb. 19, 6:37

YOUR DRIVE AND AMBITION
Mars in Sagittarius, Jan. 20, 16:11 - Feb. 19, 6:37

YOUR LUCK MAGNETISM
Jupiter in Virgo, Jan. 20, 16:11 - Feb. 19, 6:37

World Events

Feb. 8 - The British government announces its intention to construct six more Dreadnoughts.

Feb. 19 - U.S. President Theodore Roosevelt announces plans for a 1910 World conference on conservation at The Hague.

1909

PISCES
Your Personal Planets

YOUR LOVE POTENTIAL
Venus in Aquarius, Feb. 19, 6:38 - Mar. 05, 2:10
Venus in Pisces, Mar. 05, 2:11 - Mar. 21, 6:12

YOUR DRIVE AND AMBITION
Mars in Sagittarius, Feb. 19, 6:38 - Feb. 24, 2:12
Mars in Capricorn, Feb. 24, 2:13 - Mar. 21, 6:12

YOUR LUCK MAGNETISM
Jupiter in Virgo, Feb. 19, 6:38 - Mar. 21, 6:12

World Events

Feb. 24 – Austria considers declaring war on Serbia.

Mar. 15 – Italy proposes a European conference on the Balkans.

The "dreadnought" of Germany's aerial navy in flight

ARIES
Your Personal Planets

YOUR LOVE POTENTIAL
Venus in Pisces, Mar. 21, 6:13 - Mar. 29, 5:11
Venus in Aries, Mar. 29, 5:12 - Apr. 20, 17:57

YOUR DRIVE AND AMBITION
Mars in Capricorn, Mar. 21, 6:13 - Apr. 09, 20:33
Mars in Aquarius, Apr. 09, 20:34 - Apr. 20, 17:57

YOUR LUCK MAGNETISM
Jupiter in Virgo, Mar. 21, 6:13 - Apr. 20, 17:57

World Events

Mar. 31 – Serbia accepts Austrian control over Bosnia-Herzegovina.

Apr. 9 – Enrico Caruso makes a landmark broadcast from the Metropolitan Opera to the house of Lee de Forest, inventor of the three-element tube that made radio possible.

PISCES
From February 19, 6:38 through March 21, 6:12

The Free Spirit

Creative, free-spirited, and unflinchingly optimistic, you, Pisces of 1909, were born at a time when world events seemed anything but hopeful. For the first time in modern history, Britain's previously unprecedented naval power was matched by the build-up of Germany's fleet, creating a potentially dangerous situation in Europe. Yet despite the fact that the world of your early years was either preparing for war or at war, you probably retained a childlike faith in the good in people—and this faith is likely to have followed you throughout your life.

You have probably been good at giving people pep talks and renewing their commitment at critical times. Some may accuse you of being a Pollyanna who never sees the bad in people or situations, but you would counter by saying the bad in the world can be overcome by emphasizing the good. Your positive spirit would have made you a good public-relations specialist, press person, or salesperson.

Your need to express your imagination in a fresh and original way probably kept you busy. Whether you spent your spare moments painting, designing clothing, or writing poetry, you have left room in your life for creative activities. You also encouraged your children and your grandchildren to be spontaneous in their thinking, as well as their expression. You looked forward to your time with them as you appreciated the fresh way in which their young minds viewed the world.

In relationships, you need someone who has a handle on the practical side of life and thus can handle those necessities that you find tedious. While your spouse needs to balance the checkbook, he or she also needs to be spontaneous enough to have fun on the spur of the moment. You are most comfortable with Taureans, Cancerians, Scorpios, and Capricorns.

Your greatest challenge has always been to find the time for those precious private moments when you can indulge your imagination and test your creative depth. The ability to find something new and wondrous in the world around you has kept you young, and it is your strength that others admire in you, and to which they aspire.

ARIES
From March 21, 6:13 through April 20, 17:57

The Sure-footed Traveler

As an Aries of 1909, you probably felt as if you had your foot in the door of a new adventure, but caution and a sense of responsibility may have prevented you from going as far and fast as you would have liked. That is really not a bad thing since, rather than burning out at an early age, you have spread your achievements over a lifetime. Whereas some people have highs and lows, you moved steadily along, gaining speed with each advancing year.

Around the time you were born, United States Naval Commander Robert E. Peary landed at the North Pole, finally achieving a dream he had been pursuing for many years, after several unsuccessful expeditions. His courage, persistence, and adventurousness may have appealed to your own longing to be part of the action. Yet you are probably not someone to live with regret and, in the end, are happy with the choices you made to make time for the lesser adventures in your own life—your home, raising a family, and earning a steady income.

You might have earned that income from professions that required travel or contact with distant parts of the world. You are a good communicator and working for a company that imported and exported exotic products would have interested you. On the other hand, you would also have liked work in the trade and tourism industry, doing anything from working at a hotel to owning your own bed and breakfast. Whatever you chose, you managed to find something to do that offered opportunities to meet people and go places.

Your life partner is someone who can compete with your restless urges and can accompany you on spontaneous day trips or extended journeys. You like to be with someone who not only shares your interests, but also is warm, generous, and sensitive. You are most at ease with Geminis, Leos, Sagittarians, and Aquarians.

Your most challenging times have occurred when you have had to give up on a dream that you knew was unrealistic in the first place. The ability to recover quickly from disappointment and regroup has always been your greatest gift, and one that you have passed on successfully to others.

➤ Read about your Chinese Astrological sign on page 838. ➤ Read about your Personal Planets on page 826. ➤ Read about your personal Mystical Card on page 856.

TAURUS

From April 20, 17:58 through May 21, 17:44

The Grounded Idealist

Around the time that you were born, Taurus of 1909, ex-President Theodore Roosevelt was on safari in Africa, a trip sponsored by the Smithsonian Institute and the book publisher Scribner's, in exchange for stories of his adventures. You might have heard your parents talk about this event, and perhaps read the resulting publications, and the excitement it aroused may have stayed with you for a long time to come.

Stable, rooted, and predictable, perhaps too much so by some people's standards, you know deep inside that living by the rules can provide a solid foundation from which to do something wild and exciting—such as a trip around the world or a long sea cruise. Although the chance for travel may have been limited before you were an adult, you always saw distant places and the future as within your grasp. Unlike others who abandoned their early dreams, you knew how to plan for the time when you could make yours a reality.

Even if you were unable to visit the exotic places you saw in films or photographs, you may have learned to cook international cuisine or taken frequent trips to museums and art galleries. Your children and grandchildren probably inspired you to keep your dreams alive by asking you to tell them stories of the things you had accomplished and the things you still hoped to do.

In relationships, you need someone who, like yourself, is a realist but who also shares the idea that planning ahead is the best way to make time for your dreams. Over the years, you and your spouse would have worked together to balance a practical lifestyle with time off to enjoy cultural events like movies, theater, and concerts. Those who most share your values are Cancerians, Virgos, Capricorns, and Pisceans.

Your greatest challenge has been to keep your dreams alive throughout a lifetime of hard work, raising a family, and dealing with bad times and good. Your greatest gift has been your enduring patience and the belief that if you want something badly enough, you will eventually obtain it. This is the living example that you have always set for those who are close to you.

GEMINI

From May 21, 17:45 through June 22, 2:05

The Influential Speaker

You, Gemini of 1909, have believed in the power of words and that a meaningful message could have a profound effect on someone's life or even on a generation. Around the time you were born, the African-American educator W. E. B. Dubois convened the first meeting of the National Association for the Advancement of Colored People (NAACP), which fights racial prejudice to the present day. Hearing about this and similar organizations that started up during your formative years may have made you aware of your own ability to change things when you put your mind to it.

Conversational, witty, yet persistent and intense, you have a knack for getting to the heart of any matter, solving it, and moving on before most others have had time to think. Your mind works quickly and you are hungry to tackle any issues. You may not have been a shrinking violet, and as a child you were probably the one in your class who always had your hand raised or spoke out of turn when you knew you had the answer.

Whether you worked full time or stayed at home, there was probably always some new thing that you wanted to learn. In your professional career, you assuredly used your writing skills or speechmaking talents at some point. As a parent, you probably couldn't wait until your children came home from school so that you could help them with their homework and learn what they were learning.

In relationships, your ideal partner is a good listener and someone who always took you seriously whether or not the two of you agreed on the issues. The two of you had to be, however, of one mind when it came to raising your children and teaching them right from wrong. You are most compatible with Leos, Librans, Aquarians, and Ariens.

Your greatest challenge has been to focus your interests on one project or one cause when the situation really seemed to call for it so as not to diffuse your talents. In the end, your ability to get to the heart of the matter and use your power with words in order to persuade others to consider, if not adopt, your point of view, will be remembered by all those who have known you.

▶ Read about your Chinese Astrological sign on page 838. ▶ Read about your Personal Planets on page 826. ▶ Read about your personal Mystical Card on page 856.

TAURUS
Your Personal Planets

YOUR LOVE POTENTIAL
Venus in Aries, Apr. 20, 17:58 - Apr. 22, 10:34
Venus in Taurus, Apr. 22, 10:35 - May 16, 18:30
Venus in Gemini, May 16, 18:31 - May 21, 17:44

YOUR DRIVE AND AMBITION
Mars in Aquarius, Apr. 20, 17:58 - May 21, 17:44

YOUR LUCK MAGNETISM
Jupiter in Virgo, Apr. 20, 17:58 - May 21, 17:44

World Events

May 3 – The first wireless press message is sent from New York to Chicago.

May 15 – British film star James Mason is born.

American Big Band leader Benny Goodman is born under the sign of Gemini

GEMINI
Your Personal Planets

YOUR LOVE POTENTIAL
Venus in Gemini, May 21, 17:45 - June 10, 4:36
Venus in Cancer, June 10, 4:37 - June 22, 2:05

YOUR DRIVE AND AMBITION
Mars in Aquarius, May 21, 17:45 - May 25, 22:53
Mars in Pisces, May 25, 22:54 - June 22, 2:05

YOUR LUCK MAGNETISM
Jupiter in Virgo, May 21, 17:45 - June 22, 2:05

World Events

May 30 – American Big Band leader Benny Goodman is born.

June 12 – The British arms race with Germany gathers pace as 144 warships display British naval power.

1909

CANCER
Your Personal Planets

YOUR LOVE POTENTIAL
Venus in Cancer, June 22, 2:06 - July 04, 16:31
Venus in Leo, July 04, 16:32 - July 23, 13:00

YOUR DRIVE AND AMBITION
Mars in Pisces, June 22, 2:06 - July 21, 8:35
Mars in Aries, July 21, 8:36 - July 23, 13:00

YOUR LUCK MAGNETISM
Jupiter in Virgo, June 22, 2:06 - July 23, 13:00

World Events

July 13 - The great powers announce a plan to withdraw troops from Crete, but warn the Ottoman Empire they will protect their interests.

July 16 - The Persian Shah is deposed by nationalists; his twelve-year-old son Azad Mulk succeeds.

French Aviator Louis Blériot

LEO
Your Personal Planets

YOUR LOVE POTENTIAL
Venus in Leo, July 23, 13:01 - July 29, 6:41
Venus in Virgo, July 29, 6:42 - Aug. 23, 0:33
Venus in Libra, Aug. 23, 0:34 - Aug. 23, 19:43

YOUR DRIVE AND AMBITION
Mars in Aries, July 23, 13:01 - Aug. 23, 19:43

YOUR LUCK MAGNETISM
Jupiter in Virgo, July 23, 13:01 - Aug. 23, 19:43

World Events

July 25 - Frenchman Louis Blériot becomes the first person to fly across the English Channel.

Aug. 2 - British workers demonstrate at the start of Tsar Nicholas II's visit.

CANCER
From June 22, 2:06 through July 23, 13:00

The Enthusiastic Performer

Around the time you were born, impresario Sergei Diaghilev's acclaimed dance troupe *Ballet Russe* was enjoying one of its most successful seasons in Paris. Someone as romantic and imaginative as you, Cancer of 1909, probably responded to such creative milestones throughout your life. The more you heard about them as you were growing up, the more they may have invigorated your desire to immerse yourself in the world of the creative arts as much as your talents would allow.

Enthusiastic and passionate about music, dance, drama, and any other performing art that caught your fancy, you may have indulged that passion to excess—whether in your own practice sessions or seeing film after film after film. Once you become passionate about anything, there is no stopping you, and few people can keep up with your pace. You may have tried for a career in the performing arts, but even if you did not succeed you probably continued to enjoy playing the part of a serious amateur all your life. You may have become a teacher in a branch of the arts at some point in your life, since you wanted to encourage others to be as passionate as you were.

In your family life, you tried hard to make life around the house fun-filled and instilled in your children the need to combine academic excellence with creative imagination. Your own creative touches could probably be seen in any home you lived in, from the artwork on the walls and inventive meals to comfortable furnishings.

To provide the perfect balance, your ideal mate provided the foundation that enabled you to indulge your interests. He or she also has a love of the arts, since sharing what you love most with whom you love most is very important for you. Those who share your outlook in life are Virgos, Scorpios, Pisceans, and Taureans.

Your greatest challenge has been to accept the difference between life and art and to learn that art can often be less exciting than the inspiration underlying it. On the other hand, your gift—the unique thing that makes you so inspiring to be around—is your ability to find the magnificent in the mundane.

LEO
From July 23, 13:01 through August 23, 19:43

The Poised Champion

Direct, assertive, and poised, you, Leo of 1909, make a lasting impression on everyone you meet. Even as a child, something about your self-assured demeanor and air of experience probably made you seem older than your years. You may have learned at an early age that you could have a commanding presence and that you could convince people of just about anything. This not only gave you a competitive edge in life, but also made you someone who others would entrust to take charge and to get the job done.

Along with this leadership and executive power, you also have a strong moral conscience. You could easily have represented others as a union leader, city councilor, or community organizer. In any position, the most important quality you brought to the job was loyalty to those who trusted you.

Around the time you were born, Louis Blériot, a daring French aviator, became the first person to fly an airplane across the English Channel. In accomplishing this feat, he also won a cash prize offered by the London *Daily Mail*. While you were probably not a thrill-seeker and may have never tempted fate in a physical sense, you admire those who can do so. As a parent, you worked hard to teach your children that a confident attitude with some carefully crafted skill behind it can allow a person to accomplish anything.

In relationships, you want someone who can face life head on and who can share life's important responsibilities from earning a living to running a household and raising the children. High on your list of priorities is sharing those intimate moments with a significant other who feels things as deeply and who loves life as intensely as you do. You are most compatible with Librans, Sagittarians, Ariens, and Geminis.

Throughout life, your greatest challenge has been to hold back when the situation called for it and not simply to try your hand at everything just to prove that you could succeed. When carrying out an important task for other people, fighting others' battles as well as your own, you truly are at your best and the causes you undertake can have no greater champion.

➤ Read about your Chinese Astrological sign on page 838. ➤ Read about your Personal Planets on page 826. ➤ Read about your personal Mystical Card on page 856.

VIRGO

From August 23, 19:44 through September 23, 16:44

The Altruistic Interpreter

As a Virgo of 1909, you were born at a time when the British Parliament approved the South African constitution, establishing both English and Dutch as the official languages. This newsworthy item might have been interesting for you to learn about, since international relations and learning languages are both likely to have been interests of yours throughout your life.

Communicative, meticulous, and gregarious, you probably have a gift for interpreting and explaining things to others. This would have made you a great tutor, an understanding teacher, or simply an outstanding administrator for an organization that reaches out to people from different countries. You might even have been attracted to a service profession where you worked for a hotel or restaurant, allowing you to come into contact with people from different backgrounds.

Your most endearing characteristic may be your altruism, and the highlights of your life have probably involved using your skills to help and give to others. Working for a charitable organization would have been a wonderful way for you to make a living. If you could not find a job that paid enough to fulfill your financial needs, you probably volunteered in your spare time. You taught your children that charity always begins at home, and may have even done your service work at home where your kids could observe you in action.

In relationships, you probably looked for someone who is loyal, generous, and down-to-earth. You do not like pretension and as long as you know the person you share your life with sincerely believes in friendships and helping others, your own commitment is firm. Those who share your values are Scorpios, Capricorns, Taureans, and Cancerians.

You probably have been able to stick with an idea or project long after others have become bored and frustrated. While this is the greatest gift that you offer to others, it also has been your greatest challenge since it can separate you from others. Ultimately, your generous nature and your tireless efforts are the things that those who know you will admire and emulate for years to come.

LIBRA

From September 23, 16:45 through October 24, 1:22

The Loving Heart

Gentle, even-handed, and quite compromising, you, Libra of 1909, have taken the road of least resistance since you find confrontation a waste of time. Around the time you were born the High Court in Britain ordered an investigation into the force-feeding of suffragettes in prison. This event would have been of interest to you, because, despite your unwillingness to become involved in conflict, you are probably the first to take a firm stand when you see someone being treated unfairly or discriminated against for no reason. You cannot sit back and watch.

You may view conflict from a detached standpoint, allowing you to zero in on problems and pinpoint the best solutions. Your ability as a fabulous problem-solver is matched by your ability to get people to talk to one another. There may have been many times in your life when friends or colleagues have called on you to bring disparate parties together.

Loyal and non-judgmental, you likely have a wide circle of friends, mostly because you can tap into something to relate to in each person. You are one of those rare people who can see underneath anyone's persona, so you have never been fooled by those who are slick and charming, nor put off by those who are gruff and boisterous. As a parent, you taught your children how to speak to others from the heart. Your greatest pleasure in life has been witnessing your children and grandchildren blossom into compassionate people—the most important lesson you tried to teach them.

In relationships, you want someone who is charming on the outside and genuine on the inside. You admire honesty, loyalty, and fair-mindedness in others so the person you wish to share your life with needs to have these qualities in abundance. You are most comfortable with Sagittarians, Aquarians, Geminis, and Leos.

Your greatest challenge in life has been to learn to stand up and fight for what you want, even if it means that someone else might come in second place. Since you place so much emphasis on compassion and helping others, your greatest gift is teaching others those very same attitudes and ideals.

➤ Read about your Chinese Astrological sign on page 838. ➤ Read about your Personal Planets on page 826. ➤ Read about your personal Mystical Card on page 856.

VIRGO
Your Personal Planets

YOUR LOVE POTENTIAL
Venus in Libra, Aug. 23, 19:44 - Sept. 17, 0:20
Venus in Scorpio, Sept. 17, 0:21 - Sept. 23, 16:44

YOUR DRIVE AND AMBITION
Mars in Aries, Aug. 23, 19:44 - Sept. 23, 16:44

YOUR LUCK MAGNETISM
Jupiter in Virgo, Aug. 23, 19:44 - Sept. 23, 16:44

World Events

Sept. 7 – Lord Northcliffe, owner of the London *Times*, asserts that Kaiser Wilhelm is rushing preparations for war with Britain.

Sept. 13 – The Congress of Egyptian Youth demands the British evacuation of Egypt.

A new record for Orville Wright

LIBRA
Your Personal Planets

YOUR LOVE POTENTIAL
Venus in Scorpio, Sept. 23, 16:45 - Oct. 12, 9:27
Venus in Sagittarius, Oct. 12, 9:28 - Oct. 24, 1:22

YOUR DRIVE AND AMBITION
Mars in Aries, Sept. 23, 16:45 - Sept. 26, 21:18
Mars in Pisces, Sept. 26, 21:19 - Oct. 24, 1:22

YOUR LUCK MAGNETISM
Jupiter in Virgo, Sept. 23, 16:45 - Oct. 11, 23:32
Jupiter in Libra, Oct. 11, 23:33 - Oct. 24, 1:22

World Events

Sept. 25 – The First National Aeronautic Show opens at Madison Square Garden in New York.

Oct. 2 – Orville Wright sets a new record, flying at an altitude of 1,600 ft.

1909

SCORPIO
Your Personal Planets

YOUR LOVE POTENTIAL
Venus in Sagittarius, Oct. 24, 1:23 - Nov. 07, 12:10
Venus in Capricorn, Nov. 07, 12:11 - Nov. 22, 22:19

YOUR DRIVE AND AMBITION
Mars in Pisces, Oct. 24, 1:23 - Nov. 20, 20:47
Mars in Aries, Nov. 20, 20:48 - Nov. 22, 22:19

YOUR LUCK MAGNETISM
Jupiter in Libra, Oct. 24, 1:23 - Nov. 22, 22:19

World Events

Nov. 1 – Threat of a European conflict causes French deputies to seek the creation of a native colonial army.

Nov. 11 – Work begins on the new principal naval base at Pearl Harbor on Hawaii.

The Wright brothers establish a million-dollar corporation for the manufacture of planes

SAGITTARIUS
Your Personal Planets

YOUR LOVE POTENTIAL
Venus in Capricorn, Nov. 22, 22:20 - Dec. 05, 13:00
Venus in Aquarius, Dec. 05, 13:01 - Dec. 22, 11:19

YOUR DRIVE AND AMBITION
Mars in Aries, Nov. 22, 22:20 - Dec. 22, 11:19

YOUR LUCK MAGNETISM
Jupiter in Libra, Nov. 22, 22:20 - Dec. 22, 11:19

World Events

Nov. 23 – The Wright brothers establish a million-dollar corporation for the commercial manufacture of airplanes.

Dec. 17 – Germany criticizes the U.S., accusing the country of inciting rebellion in Nicaragua.

SCORPIO
From October 24, 1:23 through November 22, 22:19

The Savvy Reader

As a Scorpio of 1909, you are ardent and uncompromising yet sensitive and caring. Even as a young child you probably finished your assignments before the other children, which left you the time to explore beyond what was required of you. Reading may have become an intense passion and you may consider books to be your friends, as well as a means of escape from the world around you.

Around the time you were born, a report revealed that more than two million Americans owned corporate stock. This fact may reflect your own fascination with both the worlds of business and finance. Growing up in business-friendly times might have made you very business savvy and very aware of the value in being part of a growing economy. At some point in your life, you may have started your own business, even if it began as a sideline selling things from your home. On the other hand, you just as easily could have been a teacher or even a librarian due to your love of reading and of books.

As a parent, you tried to instill the value of money into your children and certainly had a hand in handling the family finances. There were always chores to be done around the house and chances are good that your kids took part in these tasks on a daily basis. At night, there was probably a bedtime story, as this gave you an opportunity to pass on your love of reading to your children and, later, to your grandchildren as well.

Your ideal spouse needed to be just the right blend of sensitivity and practicality. When you found yourself working overtime, planning for the future, he or she should have been able to get you into a different mood and to help you learn to relax. You are most compatible with Capricorns, Pisceans, Cancerians, and Virgos.

Your greatest challenge in life has been to learn to laugh a little more than you might be prone to do and not to take life so seriously all the time. You always had a knack for getting tough when the situation called for it and finding a niche in an uncertain world while still seeming hopeful and optimistic. More than anything, this is what those closest to you admire.

SAGITTARIUS
From November 22, 22:20 through December 22, 11:19

The Eloquent Spokesperson

As a Sagittarius of 1909, you have probably been adventurous and friendly, but you are also the person who will say things that others would like to say but do not dare. Your blunt honesty may have shocked those who did not know you at times, but once they saw how open your heart was they knew that everything you did and said was out of genuine concern and compassion. If anyone could present a controversial viewpoint or head a complaints committee effectively, you were definitely that person.

Around the time you were born, a labor conference in Pittsburgh ended with attendees and union leaders demanding an investigation of U.S. Steel's trade practices. Such public investigations during your youth may have convinced you that being articulate and speaking out for the truth was the right thing to do. In line with your social sense, you took life seriously and once you accepted a task you saw it through to a meaningful conclusion.

If you did not work full time while raising your children, you probably chose to work at home, utilizing your writing, editing, or even secretarial skills to supplement the household income. People around you learned quickly about your passion for getting involved in causes and your ability to speak eloquently for your beliefs, and encouraged your involvement. When your children were grown, you may have returned to the workplace where you could feel as if you were in the thick of things.

In relationships, you need someone who encourages you to speak your mind even if your viewpoint is totally different. Your partner is probably someone who is also sure of his or her beliefs and even looked forward to heated discussions—as long as they ended with the two of you kissing and making up. You have been most compatible with Aquarians, Ariens, Leos, and Librans.

Your greatest challenge has been to find value in quiet moments, when there was no struggle for justice nor cause to represent. At those times, you learned that even influencing one single person was just as valuable as influencing hundreds. Your ability to do that is your greatest strength.

➤ Read about your Chinese Astrological sign on page 838. ➤ Read about your Personal Planets on page 826. ➤ Read about your personal Mystical Card on page 856.

CAPRICORN

From December 22, 11:20 through December 31, 23:59

The Quiet Conscience

There are very few who are as dogged, persevering, and industrious as you, December Capricorn of 1909, and even fewer who can be so strong and supportive to those in need. Though you may not seem to have much to say a great deal of the time, you watch everything around you intently and feel everything deeply. Given your likely penchant for observing from the sidelines rather than jumping in at the deep end, most people who know you have learned that when you do have something to say it is truly worth listening to.

Around the time you were born, Frédéric Remington, painter and sculptor of scenes from the American West, passed away. As a lover of tradition, you probably admire the quiet hero or heroine who makes a country or a community great. You might even have seen yourself in that role—an ordinary person who can do great things and influence others by observing, being objective, and speaking your mind in a direct, effective manner.

Your sense of responsibility and your good head for business probably led you to the world of management or finance in terms of your career. You have an eye for the inspirational, so it would have made your life more interesting if the job you held was colorful and interesting. Most important, however, was that you could create a sense of financial security that let your children know that home was a safe haven.

Your ideal partner must be more than just a loving helpmate and family provider, but also a friend and confidante with whom you can share simple walks and quiet dinners. He or she must be compassionate, loving, and yet able to be a stern disciplinarian where the children are concerned. In general, you fit best with Pisceans, Taureans, Virgos, and Scorpios.

Since throughout your life you have been known as the serious person with a moral stance, you probably identify with that role. Your greatest challenge has been to let others also have their say where matters of conscience are concerned. You have taught many around you how to speak out about right and wrong and this is both your greatest strength and your lasting legacy.

1909

CAPRICORN
Your Personal Planets

YOUR LOVE POTENTIAL
Venus in Aquarius, Dec. 22, 11:20 - Dec. 31, 23:59

YOUR DRIVE AND AMBITION
Mars in Aries, Dec. 22, 11:20 - Dec. 31, 23:59

YOUR LUCK MAGNETISM
Jupiter in Libra, Dec. 22, 11:20 - Dec. 31, 23:59

World Events

Dec. 26 – The Ninth Zionist Congress opens in Hamburg.

Dec. 26 – American Western sculptor and painter Frédéric Remington dies.

HENRY FORD
Leo

Before Henry Ford, most Americans ventured no farther than twenty miles from home. With his development of the automobile, Ford got America out on the road and forever changed the dynamics of the U.S. An inventor and innovator, Ford was able to build a machine for the common man, due to the assembly-line method of auto fabrication, which he devised.

Mars, the planet of action—and automobiles—is prominently placed in Ford's horoscope, making him a dynamo and a leader. With Virgo rising, Ford was practical and orderly, and those two elements combined to create a man who wanted to automate factory production. In addition, Uranus, the planet of technology, appeared in Ford's house of career, so becoming an automotive engineer was quite a natural choice for this man. These planetary pictures also describe a man who was independent, self-motivated, and much happier working for himself than for anyone else.

His Moon, planet of emotions, was in Aquarius, and anyone with this planetary position wants to make the world a better place. Ford was an active philanthropist all his life. Contacts from Saturn, the planet of obligations, and idealistic Neptune further extended his desire to work hard to create his visions. We can also say that these planetary contacts contributed to the idea that, in ompartmentalizing the assembly tasks in his factory, more could be produced from less. In addition, a contact from domineering Pluto made Ford bossy. He got involved in every aspect of the lives of his workers, demanding they learn English, become citizens, and even began timing their movements to the minute on the assembly line.

Like all brilliant autocrats, Ford had a vision he wanted to create and he expected everyone in his world to play their assigned role on the stage he'd created. Leo is, after all, the sign of the showman, and Ford was confident in his ideas, his creativity, and his plan for a brave new world.

Henry Ford
July 30, 1863 - April 7, 1947

➤ Read J. P. Morgan's Star Profile on page 49. ➤ Read Bill Gates' Star Profile on page 737.

1910

Jumping Into Action: Mars in Aries

At the start of 1910, Mars, planet of fire and force, was in its very favorite place, the powerful arms of Aries. It set the tone for the whole year. When Mars goes into Aries, there is a stirring of the blood and everyone feels ready to jump into action. The Mexican revolution began this year, when Francisco Madero published his manifesto *La sucesión presidencial en 1910.* Japan formally annexed Korea this year as well. On October 4, in Lisbon, revolutionary troops crushed loyalist forces and King Manuel II fled to Gibraltar. On October 15 the French government arrested several editors of leftist and union newspapers, accusing them of fomenting national unrest. With feisty Mars conjunct with solid, strong Saturn, at year's start the Boy Scouts of America was incorporated. Mars is the initiator and Saturn is the teacher. Young men would learn the way of the warrior during their time in the Boy Scouts. Saturn makes things last a good, long time and the Boy Scout movement continues to flourish.

Mars was also opposite Jupiter in Libra at the beginning of this year. This aspect can sometimes lead to various holy crusades of self-aggrandizement, even by nations themselves. Many countries shored up their borders and refused to part with their colonies this year. On February 7, Belgium, Germany, and Britain fixed the borders in the Congo, Uganda, and German East Africa. On January 15, France reorganized its colonial territories into French Equatorial Africa. On August 4, in Spain, the insurrectionary movement spread to four provinces.

The Dalai Lama flees to India

Nursing pioneer Florence Nightingale with soldiers

Suffragettes continue the struggle for the right to vote

FRANKENSTEIN'S FILM DEBUT

In 1910, Thomas Alva Edison's film company in Orange, New Jersey produced the very first film version of Mary Shelley's 1818 novel *Frankenstein*. It was not, however, destined to be the definitive, or the last, version. Edison's *Frankenstein* is considered to be the forefather of thousands of subsequent horror and monster films. With a running time of just sixteen minutes, violence and mysticism fill this film deep—believed to be one of the oldest movies still in existence at the end of the twentieth century.

REVOLUTIONARY REFORMS

King Manuel II of Portugal was ousted by rebellious troops—subsequently Portugal became a constitutional republic. Supporters of Madero, a reformer who wanted to improve conditions in Mexico, overthrew Mexican President Diaz. South Africa became a British Empire Dominion with its own parliamentary government. Britain's King Edward VII died, to be replaced by his son King George V in a grand coronation. The Seine River reached record flood levels in Paris, endangering the Louvre's priceless art and causing death and hardship among residents. Boy Scouting was imported to the U.S., and suffragists doggedly pursued women's right to vote. After an effort of two years, Edison unveiled a new invention, the talking movie, promising color in a few years. Spurred by last year's earthquake, southern Italians led in the number of immigrants flooding the U.S. The year 1910 saw the deaths of the writers Leo Tolstoy, Mark Twain, and O. Henry, painters Henri Rousseau and Winslow Homer, and of Florence Nightingale, the founder of nursing. The tango was imported from Buenos Aires, and Stravinsky's *Firebird* was acclaimed in its Paris opening.

➤ Read Enrico Caruso's Star Profile on page 97.

CAPRICORN

From January 01, 0:00 through January 20, 21:58

The Time Sweeper

As a January Capricorn of 1910, you have seen the pace of daily life accelerate more rapidly than ever before in human history. Your Sun sign rules time, and Capricorn's long-term staying power is legendary. Members of your sign tend to be comfortable with stability and constancy in life and in world events. Possessed of qualities that enable you to confront and drive change, however, you are by no means typical.

In the year you were born, messages and travel occurred mostly via foot traffic, horseback, trains, or ships. Even sending or receiving telegraph messages required a trip to town. Mass production of automobiles was three years away; airplanes were barely challenging the speed of trains; telephones enjoyed only sporadic distribution. A phone call from London to Boston would have seemed like witchcraft to members of your parents' generation. Yet, like Albert Einstein—then a few years away from his theory of relativity, a breakthrough that would transform humanity's understanding of time—you are able to envisage and deploy new ideas, structures, and institutions to contain and channel the energy of humanity's ever-accelerating transactions.

Your lifetime included the development of global telephone service, domestic radio, television, car culture, facsimiles, jet planes, the Concorde, space rockets, and even email and the World Wide Web. A leader in a new era of human experience, you may have seen such innovations as tools for improving efficiency and productivity.

In relationships, partners who can share your vision provide an anchor in a sea of change. You honor the intrinsic value of commitment—your best partner evolves and grows with you. You may feel most comfortable with Virgos and Cancerians, but Ariens, Sagittarians, Geminis, and Librans may also give you a thrill.

Your challenge has been to accept and adapt to a rapidly changing world. As temporal boundaries dissolved around you, the hazards of rigidity may have come to you the hard way. Your talent for envisaging ways to manage innovation enabled you to take the bull of progress by the horns.

AQUARIUS

From January 20, 21:59 through February 19, 12:27

Real World Humanitarian

Aquarius of 1910 entered a world brewing with the potential for revolution over inequalities in the conditions of people's lives. In general, Aquarians have an acute sensitivity to matters of fairness and social justice. For those born in 1910, this sensitivity would literally materialize. That is, you would not have had the luxury of losing yourself in lofty ideals that defy real-life application. Rather, you may have found it impossible to ignore the suffering of those who lack the concrete basics of human subsistence.

Spending your tender years during the heyday of international socialism, you may have absorbed parental conversations expressing concern about the power of certain nations to dominate and take the natural resources of weaker, less developed countries. You may have heard similar concerns about worldwide inequities between the wealthy and the poor.

You may have directly experienced the homelessness, hunger, and scarcity prevailing during World War I, the worldwide depression of the 1930s, or the hardships of World War II. Having lived in an era of privation, the idea of wasteful excess might offend you to the marrow. Even in good times, to throw away food when others are starving constitutes the height of immorality. Aquarians of 1910 are most likely to have looked to governmental reform—from the New Deal to the outright overthrow of remaining monarchies—to provide system-wide solutions to globally endemic problems.

In relationships, your sense of security depends on having a sensible partner, someone not given to frivolity. On the other hand, a partner's sense of humor, creativity, and resourcefulness can bring out your capacity for joy in the midst of adversity. You may feel an easy compatibility with Leos and Librans, but Cancerians and Taureans also share important values with you.

Overemphasis on injustices can hamper your emotional and spiritual well being. Your Aquarian idealism and activism have enabled you to change things for the better. To avoid disillusionment, you owe it to yourself to exult in the abundance you have helped to create.

CAPRICORN
Your Personal Planets

YOUR LOVE POTENTIAL
Venus in Aquarius, Jan. 01, 0:00 - Jan. 15, 20:55
Venus in Pisces, Jan. 15, 20:56 - Jan. 20, 21:58

YOUR DRIVE AND AMBITION
Mars in Aries, Jan. 01, 0:00 - Jan. 20, 21:58

YOUR LUCK MAGNETISM
Jupiter in Libra, Jan. 01, 0:00 - Jan. 20, 21:58

World Events

Jan. 8 - The threat of the German military is raised in the British House of Commons.

Jan. 15 - France reorganizes its colonial territories into French Equatorial Africa.

The threat of German militarism

AQUARIUS
Your Personal Planets

YOUR LOVE POTENTIAL
Venus in Pisces, Jan. 20, 21:59 - Jan. 29, 9:11
Venus in Aquarius, Jan. 29, 9:12 - Feb. 19, 12:27

YOUR DRIVE AND AMBITION
Mars in Aries, Jan. 20, 21:59 - Jan. 23, 1:53
Mars in Taurus, Jan. 23, 1:54 - Feb. 19, 12:27

YOUR LUCK MAGNETISM
Jupiter in Libra, Jan. 20, 21:59 - Feb. 19, 12:27

World Events

Feb. 7 - Belgium, Germany, and Britain agree proprietorial borders in the Congo, Uganda, and German East Africa.

Feb. 19 - Jules Massenet's opera *Don Quixote* opens in Monte Carlo.

► Read about your Chinese Astrological sign on page 838. ► Read about your Personal Planets on page 826. ► Read about your personal Mystical Card on page 856.

1910

PISCES
Your Personal Planets

YOUR LOVE POTENTIAL
Venus in Aquarius, Feb. 19, 12:28 - Mar. 21, 12:02

YOUR DRIVE AND AMBITION
Mars in Taurus, Feb. 19, 12:28 - Mar. 14, 7:16
Mars in Gemini, Mar. 14, 7:17 - Mar. 21, 12:02

YOUR LUCK MAGNETISM
Jupiter in Libra, Feb. 19, 12:28 - Mar. 21, 12:02

World Events

Feb. 25 – The Dalai Lama flees to India to seek refuge from the Chinese in Tibet.

Mar. 8 – In France, Baroness Raymonde de la Roche becomes the first woman to be granted a pilot's license.

The Dalai Lama seeks refuge in India

ARIES
Your Personal Planets

YOUR LOVE POTENTIAL
Venus in Aquarius, Mar. 21, 12:03 - Apr. 05, 9:52
Venus in Pisces, Apr. 05, 9:53 - Apr. 20, 23:45

YOUR DRIVE AND AMBITION
Mars in Gemini, Mar. 21, 12:03 - Apr. 20, 23:45

YOUR LUCK MAGNETISM
Jupiter in Libra, Mar. 21, 12:03 - Apr. 20, 23:45

World Events

Apr. 2 – German Prof. Karl Harries perfects the process for the artificial synthesis of rubber.

Apr. 18 – A 500,000-signature petition is presented to the U.S. Congress by suffragists.

PISCES
From February 19, 12:28 through March 21, 12:02

Guardian of Delicacy

In 1910, the international art scene saw developments so dramatic, original, and enduring as to provide you with a lifetime supply of joy. You are built for total immersion in the delights of the arts. Interestingly, in January 1910, some of the greatest artwork in the world faced the danger of real immersion, when floodwaters in Paris threatened the Louvre museum. Causing hundreds of millions of dollars in damage, this disaster may have moved adults in your life to teach you to appreciate the fragility and irreplaceable nature of art.

The artwork of 1910 fed your appetite for beauty well into adulthood. Movements in Fauvism and Expressionism provided fanciful scenes, in colors pure, vivid, and bold. In 1910, Marc Chagall painted *The Wedding* in luscious shades of gold, green, and pale blue. In viewing this masterpiece in later years, you might have imagined yourself as the fairy alighting on the bride's shoulder.

Thomas Edison invented talking film in 1910, an innovation that would gain distribution in 1927—just in time for you to go out with friends to see *The Jazz Singer*. Russian influences in fashion may have inspired you to express the more eccentric sides of your personality. A career in the arts would have enabled you to initiate others into the wonders of modern creativity. You may have been an artist, poet, musician, or actor.

You simply must have a friend or lover to share the ecstasy you derive from fine arts, music, and just plain beauty. Your capacity for intense appreciation can reach spiritual dimensions, and it's a sin to worship alone. Cancerians, Taureans, Scorpios, and Librans are happy to join your aesthetic escapes.

A 1910 Pisces could have been among the team of art historians who lovingly dismantled and re-assembled the stained glass windows of the York Minster during and after World War II. In a cruel world rife with war and destruction, your challenge has been to preserve islands of delicacy and refinement for future generations. A Piscean ability to rescue and safeguard treasures may have enabled you to save a precious legacy for humankind.

ARIES
From March 21, 12:03 through April 20, 23:45

The Patient Warrior

Within days of your birth, Aries of 1910, mountaineers reached 12,000 feet on Mount McKinley. Perhaps this feat inspired your parents to have especially high hopes for your future. A flash of will in the cradle, an iron grip on your rattle, a precocious knack for walking and talking—these may have been the earliest clues that you, too, would have the strength, determination, and wit to scale great heights in life.

In 1910, all the elements were in place for the creation of a new world order. As the U.S. emerged as a world industrial power, suffragettes there and in Europe crusaded for political rights for women. King Albert opened the World Exhibition in Brussels, wishing to throw a spotlight on Belgium's international industrial prestige and ambitions. Worldwide attention was already fixed, however, on the personal and political intemperance of his predecessor, King Leopold, for his imperialist exploitation of the Congo. Other western colonial powers, such as England, France, and Italy, were also vulnerable to opposition by socialists and the international labor movement.

Once you seized upon the cause that mattered most to you, you pursued it with power, focus, ironclad determination, and unbreakable perseverance. Such qualities would prove essential to overcoming obstacles in long-running struggles that often faced violent resistance. Born under the sign of the warrior, Aries, you know that with change and growth, pain may be unavoidable. An Aries of 1910 would have been ideally suited to implement the Marshall Plan.

You have a natural talent for making empowering alliances. Your ability to link up with great partners might feel like good luck, but it's actually central to your personality. Because Librans, Geminis, and Capricorns know they can rely on you, they are happy to show their love by supporting you.

Your challenge has been to learn the power of patience. With maturity, you've come to understand that the ability to outlast your opponents is one of the most potent weapons in your Aries arsenal. The truth has been your strongest and most reliable partner.

➤ Read about your Chinese Astrological sign on page 838. ➤ Read about your Personal Planets on page 826. ➤ Read about your personal Mystical Card on page 856.

TAURUS

From April 20, 23:46 through May 21, 23:29

The Moral Banker

The bright red cape of economic inequality waved the bulls of 1910 into a head-on collision with some nasty bears. A signature event, occurring within days of your birth, foreshadowed the economic fate of the world—and you with it, Taurus. On May 6, 1910, King Edward VII of England died. A parade of royalty attended his funeral, including kings of Norway, Bulgaria, Portugal, Sweden, Spain, and Denmark. By 1950, all of these wealthy monarchies would be reduced to figurehead status or deposed outright. Today, the English monarchy draws an allowance, at the pleasure of the British taxpayer.

Your sign rules money and wealth, and economic issues would be prominent in your lifetime, on both personal and political levels. Although Taureans are usually slow to anger, the economic conditions of your first thirty-five years bore an impact too direct to ignore. From 1910 through the 1930s, the enormous discrepancy between the "haves" and the "have-nots" would play out in violent political and labor confrontations on a worldwide stage.

Perhaps you were a manual laborer seeking to unionize, a sweatshop worker needing safe conditions, a farmer fighting to save your family's livelihood, a budding professional wanting only the chance to advance. Even if your family owned a ten-ton mountain of gold, you might have been the one who empathized with the suffering of the poor and disempowered, packed into tenements, barely surviving the wages of hunger and disease. You may not believe in hand-outs, but you may have a burning conviction that everyone deserves a fair chance to succeed.

In relationships, values are much more important to you than material goods. You need a partner who is thrifty with finances and generous in love. Virgos, Scorpios, and Pisceans have an instinct for what truly matters to you.

Your challenge has been to get that charging bull under control. Early in the twentieth century, raw fury sometimes had its place in the struggle for democracy and economic equality. With maturity, your energy mellowed into the equally effective virtues of diplomacy and perseverance.

GEMINI

From May 21, 23:30 through June 22, 7:48

The Global Villager

What could be a better welcome into the world for Gemini than the race, on May 29, 1910, between a train and an airplane? The plane beat the train on the route from Albany to New York City, and neither the world nor you would ever be the same.

The air sign, Gemini, rules transportation, communication, and speed, and you have witnessed a dizzying revolution in these aspects of life. In ordinary interpretations, the sign Gemini rules only short distances. During the extraordinary span of your lifetime, however, dramatic developments in communications and transportation technologies turned long distances into short distances. Your parents waited months for answers to letters sent to Europe. In contrast, with today's telephone and Internet messaging, you can have instantaneous conversations with friends in Naples or Budapest. Your sign also rules neighborhoods. How appropriate, then, for you to have witnessed the evolution of the global village!

New feats of prowess on the ground or in the air carried the potential for danger and fear. At various intervals in every year, speedy Gemini needs to slow down and refuel. At these times, activities ruled by Gemini often experience interference and malfunctions. Robert Falcon Scott's ill-fated trek to the South Pole departed during one such unfavorable interval in 1910. Progress in travel technology may have intrigued you, but you may have felt nostalgic for the days when a slower pace allowed for leisurely walks and casual conversation over the back fence.

In relationships, you need an equal—someone who can listen while your internal twins dialogue their way to emotional clarity. An empathetic partner can help you negotiate the route between your head and your heart. Cancerians, Leos, Librans, and Pisceans can be very supportive, and they get a big kick out of the intricate meanderings of your exceptional mind.

Your challenge has been to help people—including yourself—to find their place in the march of progress. Your adaptable mind enables you to see that the global village is nothing more than a small world after all.

➤ Read about your Chinese Astrological sign on page 838. ➤ Read about your Personal Planets on page 826. ➤ Read about your personal Mystical Card on page 856.

1910

TAURUS
Your Personal Planets

YOUR LOVE POTENTIAL
Venus in Pisces, Apr. 20, 23:46 - May 07, 2:26
Venus in Aries, May 07, 2:27 - May 21, 23:29

YOUR DRIVE AND AMBITION
Mars in Gemini, Apr. 20, 23:46 - May 01, 20:48
Mars in Cancer, May 01, 20:49 - May 21, 23:29

YOUR LUCK MAGNETISM
Jupiter in Libra, Apr. 20, 23:46 - May 21, 23:29

World Events

Apr. 21 – American author Mark Twain dies.
Apr. 27 – Louis Botha and James Hertzog found the nationalist South African Party, calling for independence and equality for the Boers.

Death of American author Mark Twain

GEMINI
Your Personal Planets

YOUR LOVE POTENTIAL
Venus in Aries, May 21, 23:30 - June 03, 14:57
Venus in Taurus, June 03, 14:58 - June 22, 7:48

YOUR DRIVE AND AMBITION
Mars in Cancer, May 21, 23:30 - June 19, 3:29
Mars in Leo, June 19, 3:30 - June 22, 7:48

YOUR LUCK MAGNETISM
Jupiter in Libra, May 21, 23:30 - June 22, 7:48

World Events

May 31 – The Union of South Africa is established, although it remains part of the British Empire.
June 11 – French oceanographer Jacques Cousteau is born.

1910

CANCER
Your Personal Planets

YOUR LOVE POTENTIAL
Venus in Taurus, June 22, 7:49 - June 29, 19:31
Venus in Gemini, June 29, 19:32 - July 23, 18:42

YOUR DRIVE AND AMBITION
Mars in Leo, June 22, 7:49 - July 23, 18:42

YOUR LUCK MAGNETISM
Jupiter in Libra, June 22, 7:49 - July 23, 18:42

World Events

July 4 – Race riots break out throughout the U.S. after African American Jack Johnson successfully defends his World heavyweight title against Jim Jeffries.

July 16 – Riots break out in Spain during a miners' strike.

Death of nursing pioneer Florence Nightingale

LEO
Your Personal Planets

YOUR LOVE POTENTIAL
Venus in Gemini, July 23, 18:43 - July 25, 7:00
Venus in Cancer, July 25, 7:01 - Aug. 19, 5:55
Venus in Leo, Aug. 19, 5:56 - Aug. 24, 1:26

YOUR DRIVE AND AMBITION
Mars in Leo, July 23, 18:43 - Aug. 06, 0:57
Mars in Virgo, Aug. 06, 0:58 - Aug. 24, 1:26

YOUR LUCK MAGNETISM
Jupiter in Libra, July 23, 18:43 - Aug. 24, 1:26

World Events

Aug. 13 – Nursing pioneer Florence Nightingale dies.

Aug. 14 – A five-mile stretch of the Panama Canal is opened, giving access to the Atlantic Ocean.

CANCER
From June 22, 7:49 through July 23, 18:42

The Nostalgic Historian

In 1910, international events gave people good reason to pine for the safety and security of home. In that sense, all the world was a Cancer, the sign ruling nostalgia and patriotism. As the great industrialized countries jockeyed for position relative to their resource-rich colonial territories, refugees streamed out of their home borders and into countries like Israel, the United States, and Brazil, in pursuit of a better life. With unrest in countries such as Russia, China, and Portugal, people didn't even have to leave their homelands to yearn for a better place or better times.

1910 brought wonderful comfort for European expatriates in the Broadway debut of comedienne Fanny Brice, performing the songs of Irving Berlin (then just twenty-two), at the Ziegfeld Follies just weeks before your birth. Singing *Goodbye Becky Cohen* in a Yiddish accent, Brice connected with Jewish immigrants, but also with anyone who had left his or her homeland and loved ones behind.

Even if emigration was not part of your personal experience, the cataclysmic changes in the world during your lifetime may have made you nostalgic for slower and simpler times. And just as Fanny Brice enabled homesick immigrants to laugh at their plight, so too can you derive comfort from theater, entertainment, levity, singing—and children. Whether yours or simply future generations, children hold for you the promise of creating a world of peace, justice, and security for all.

In relationships, home and family mean everything to you, and you have Cancer's talent for creating a home wherever you go. You will protect your den and especially any children in your care with the fierceness of a lioness. Capricorns offer you stability, security, and a delightfully dry sense of humor. Pisceans, Leos, and Taureans can also be a comfort and a joy.

Safety and security have been in short supply throughout your life. Your challenge has been to adapt to a new world while it continually reinvented itself. Your Cancerian ability to adapt to the cycles of life has prepared you to evolve with the progress around you.

LEO
From July 23, 18:43 through August 24, 1:26

The Rebel Child

In 1910, the rebellious child provided the perfect symbol of the new world order, still in its infancy. Your sign, Leo, rules children and childhood rebellion. Prior to World War I, rebellious "children" were everywhere in evidence, embracing causes that would, in your lifetime, overturn the balance of powers in suffrage, labor, international relations, and governments.

One rallying cry of the child rebel born in 1910 might have been: "The king is dead! Long live democracy!" Campaigns for social justice were prevalent around the time of your birth, Leo of 1910: laborers were fighting for economic justice; 10,000 dockworkers were striking in Hamburg; and an unemployed civil servant attempted to assassinate the mayor of Hoboken, New Jersey. At that time, the enormous discrepancy between the wealthy and the poor mobilized masses of people to improve the desperate conditions in which they subsisted.

Your parents might have participated in anti-royalist or labor uprisings, but your generation would carry the torch forward, as a new middle class fought to establish itself and its place in the burgeoning industrializing world. If you were born between July 23 and August 6, a fiery and single-minded drive would make you a natural leader, with juggernaut-like momentum. 1910 Leos born after August 6 would have a natural empathy for "the working man" and deep resentment of any force withholding fair rewards for a job well done.

A 1910 Leo might have invented the phrase, "A man's home is his castle." If we forgive the saying's obliviousness to femininity, the democratic implication is forceful: every man or woman can be a sovereign. Virgos, Librans, and Geminis can see the king or queen in you and lavish you with proper adoration in your own private realm.

Your challenge has been to gain recognition based on your intrinsic value as a human being, as opposed to any advantage you may or may not have inherited or owned by virtue of your birth. The test of time has crowned you with hard-earned laurels of victory, reflecting Leo's courageous belief in the power of the individual.

► Read about your Chinese Astrological sign on page 838. ► Read about your Personal Planets on page 826. ► Read about your personal Mystical Card on page 856.

VIRGO

From August 24, 1:27 through September 23, 22:30

The Healing Mentor

Two great healers passed from this world just as you were arriving, Virgo of 1910. Your sign rules health and physical fitness, and the work of these seminal pioneers plays a role in promoting the wellness of billions of people today. Just before your time, on August 13, Florence Nightingale died; her role as a wartime nurse embodied Virgo's veneration of service and healing. William James, author of *Varieties Of Religious Experience*, passed away on August 26, 1910. James's theory on the healing power of spiritual surrender furnished the foundational principles for Alcoholics Anonymous, an organization founded by Bill Wilson in the early 1930s.

The work of James and Nightingale also shared the Virgoan virtue of pragmatism. Nightingale was a crusader for sanitary conditions, the most powerful, far-reaching, revolutionary, and yet humble development in the war on disease. Similarly, James's work led to a worldwide movement that brings hope and recovery to anyone whose life has been affected by alcoholism or addiction.

Helping others may give you a deep sense of satisfaction. You may have been a good mentor to others younger and less experienced than you. Likely to be thrifty but generous, you may be the kind of person friends and children call for pointers on simplifying and organizing their daily lives. You have a knack for picking out the key details that enable you to solve seemingly big problems.

Because Virgos like to feel needed, partners who need rescuing may have held a strong attraction for you—especially when you were young. Pisceans exude an irresistible vulnerability. With time and maturity, however, you may have come to prefer partners with discipline and stability, such as Taureans and Capricorns.Conditions in your lifetime have frequently challenged you to make do with less. Until mid-century, you could not afford to ignore the potential for famine, shortages, and epidemics. Your Virgoan gifts have enabled you to seize on the tiniest resources and turn them into something abundant, powerful, and beneficial for you, your family, and future generations.

LIBRA

From September 23, 22:31 through October 24, 7:10

The Open Opponent

Events of 1910 illustrate an infrequently noted, but valid, interpretation of certain matters ruled by your sign, Libra. While Libra rules partnership, marriage, and love, it also stands for open opponents—such as the revolutionary troops who ousted King Manuel of Portugal, in merely a few hours in the month of your birth. Libra rules diplomacy, and such matters were already reaching a heated pitch by the time of your birth. In the build-up to World War I, existing institutional authorities, such as monarchies, were dissolving under the pressure of internal insurgency and competing incursions by other nations.

Feverish diplomacy and open warfare among opponents would provide the backdrop to your life, right up until you reached thirty-five years of age. As boundaries between nations changed and rulers lost their grip on power, a whole new industry arose in diplomatic relations, based on the need to redefine international boundaries and systems of government. In times like these, you may have found it impossible to avoid having strong convictions or taking action to advance your beliefs and support others' rights. Careers in government, diplomacy, and law would have been ideal for you.

In general, Libra abhors war and conflict. You may be more than willing to fight, however, when fairness and justice are at stake. As a mature adult, you may have striven mightily to support the resolution of world conflicts through civil, diplomatic efforts. A 1910 Libran would have been ideally suited to draft constitutions for the new democracies blossoming mid-century.

Personal conflict can be painful for Libra, and you may tend to allow your partner to make all the decisions. Aries's clear point of view makes things easy, but Gemini, Sagittarius, and Cancer offer you the safety to open up about your true feelings and opinions.

Politics and world events loomed so large in your early life, you may have found it difficult to focus on personal relationships. Your challenge has been to define your own intimate territory, where you could express the very best parts of Libra's loving nature.

VIRGO
Your Personal Planets

YOUR LOVE POTENTIAL
Venus in Leo, Aug. 24, 1:27 - Sept. 12, 18:28
Venus in Virgo, Sept. 12, 18:29 - Sept. 23, 22:30

YOUR DRIVE AND AMBITION
Mars in Virgo, Aug. 24, 1:27 - Sept. 22, 0:14
Mars in Libra, Sept. 22, 0:15 - Sept. 23, 22:30

YOUR LUCK MAGNETISM
Jupiter in Libra, Aug. 24, 1:27 - Sept. 23, 22:30

World Events

Aug. 27 – Mother Theresa of Calcutta is born.

Aug. 27 – Thomas Edison demonstrates his latest invention to the press — the "kinetophone," a talking picture machine, part phonograph, part camera.

Thomas Edison's latest invention is a talking picture machine

LIBRA
Your Personal Planets

YOUR LOVE POTENTIAL
Venus in Virgo, Sept. 23, 22:31 - Oct. 06, 23:10
Venus in Libra, Oct. 06, 23:11 - Oct. 24, 7:10

YOUR DRIVE AND AMBITION
Mars in Libra, Sept. 23, 22:31 - Oct. 24, 7:10

YOUR LUCK MAGNETISM
Jupiter in Libra, Sept. 23, 22:31 - Oct. 24, 7:10

World Events

Oct. 4 – In Lisbon, revolutionary troops crush royalist forces and King Manuel II flees to Gibraltar.

Oct. 13 – American jazz pianist Art Tatum is born.

➤ Read about your Chinese Astrological sign on page 838. ➤ Read about your Personal Planets on page 826. ➤ Read about your personal Mystical Card on page 856.

1910

SCORPIO
Your Personal Planets

YOUR LOVE POTENTIAL
Venus in Libra, Oct. 24, 7:11 - Oct. 30, 22:52
Venus in Scorpio, Oct. 30, 22:53 - Nov. 23, 4:10

YOUR DRIVE AND AMBITION
Mars in Libra, Oct. 24, 7:11 - Nov. 06, 13:38
Mars in Scorpio, Nov. 06, 13:39 - Nov. 23, 4:10

YOUR LUCK MAGNETISM
Jupiter in Libra, Oct. 24, 7:11 - Nov. 11, 17:03
Jupiter in Scorpio, Nov. 11, 17:04 - Nov. 23, 4:10

World Events

Nov. 20 – Civil war breaks out in Mexico as dictator Porfirio Diaz runs for President.

Nov. 20 – Russian *War and Peace* novelist Leo Tolstoy dies.

Death of Russian novelist Leo Tolstoy

SAGITTARIUS
Your Personal Planets

YOUR LOVE POTENTIAL
Venus in Scorpio, Nov. 23, 4:11 - Nov. 23, 20:08
Venus in Sagittarius, Nov. 23, 20:09 - Dec. 17, 16:37
Venus in Capricorn, Dec. 17, 16:38 - Dec. 22, 17:11

YOUR DRIVE AND AMBITION
Mars in Scorpio, Nov. 23, 4:11 - Dec. 20, 12:15
Mars in Sagittarius, Dec. 20, 12:16 - Dec. 22, 17:11

YOUR LUCK MAGNETISM
Jupiter in Scorpio, Nov. 23, 4:11 - Dec. 22, 17:11

World Events

Dec. 3 – Mary Baker Eddy, founder of the Christian Science Church, dies.

Dec. 10 – In New York, Arturo Toscanini conducts Enrico Caruso in the World premiere of Puccini's *Girl Of The Golden West*.

SCORPIO
From October 24, 7:11 through November 23, 4:10

The Dare-Devil

It's a mystery, Scorpio, why so many people in 1910 seemed to have forgotten to have a healthy fear of death. Perhaps it was something in the stars—like the need to reach for them in one's own flying machine. Your parents might have spoken of the thrills and chills they experienced as the "Flying Ace Race" proceeded in the years around your birth. For you, however, the wonders of flying were tainted by the wartime use of airplanes as machines of death.

On November 17, 1910, aviator Ralph Johnstone, the world-record holder for altitude, died in a plane crash. He was not the only victim of what seemed to be a pathological competition for avian bragging rights during the year of your birth. In July 1910, Charles Stewart Rolls, the first pilot to make a round trip over the English Channel, perished in an eighty-foot fall during an in-flight competition, and disasters in the air dogged other flight pioneers around this time. Such ultimately tragic feats of daring capped a twenty-five year period in which rapid advances in transportation technologies brought on a catastrophic transformation of the world.

Because your sign rules transformation and death, you are intuitively aware of the potentially fatal hazards inherent when change comes on too rapidly. At the same time, you may share a hunger, similar to that of the flying daredevils of 1910, to make dramatic breakthroughs in occupations that stimulate your passions—no matter what the cost. The only thing more outrageous than your dreams is your burning desire to make them come true.

You would flourish with a partner who doesn't ruffle easily over the various matters commanding your absorption. Someone who calms your fears can win your heartfelt gratitude. Taurus provides Scorpio's traditional boulder of unshakeability, but Capricorn and Sagittarius can relate to and support any grand ambitions that you may have.

Your challenge has been to keep fighting when fear threatened to immobilize you. Your ideals may pressure you to make a difference. You know better than anyone that you cannot have courage unless you are afraid.

SAGITTARIUS
From November 23, 4:11 through December 22, 17:11

The Artistic Philosopher

At the start of the third millennium A.D., Sagittarius, you might be thrilled to see a brilliantly colored Kandinsky art poster hanging on the wall of your great grandchild's college dormitory room. In December 1910, Kandinsky released a treatise, *Concerning The Spiritual In Art*, which outlined Abstract theory—a rejection of the idea that artists had to paint recognizable real life objects. Abstract painting transformed the canvas from a "window" to a pure surface and the artist from a "mere copyist" to a pure creator. According to Kandinsky, the total freedom to combine color and form opened a path to the deeper realities of the artist's psyche and soul.

Because the sign of Sagittarius rules politics, fine arts, and the higher mind, you may be uniquely qualified to appreciate the significance of Kandinsky's theory. The freedom of the artist reflects the political rise of the individual, the same democratic revolution from which you were likely to benefit in the course of your own life, as monarchs fell from power, voting rights expanded and economic conditions improved. Under such circumstances, you were likely to feel free to take yourself more seriously.

You may have expressed your own sense of personal power by turning your attention inward, especially later in life, with the rise of popular psychology. Members of your sign tend to love exploration, and the realm of psyche and soul provided you with new opportunities for self-discovery, learning, and personal growth.

Sagittarians tend to seek partners who can share the pleasures of intellectual exploration. More inward-looking than the average Archer, you may have a hearty appetite for the proverbial "religious experience." Scorpio will indulge your desire to go into things deeply. Gemini, Leo, and Libra also love art and learning and will be happy to share intellectual pursuits.

You may have had to work to find others who could relate to your sophisticated and often complex point of view. Some might have dismissed you as too blunt or opinionated. Your strong teaching skills can raise others to your level.

➤ Read about your Chinese Astrological sign on page 838. ➤ Read about your Personal Planets on page 826. ➤ Read about your personal Mystical Card on page 856.

CAPRICORN

From December 22, 17:12 through December 31, 23:59

The Boundary Keeper

At the time of your birth in 1910, Capricorn, the boundaries between countries were dissolving all over the world. This trend would continue well into the present day. In December 1910, the Union of South Africa—having obtained dominion status following Britain's victory in the Boer War and precedents set by Canada and Australia—held its first session of Parliament. News accounts noted that while members of the indigenous black population were in the majority, they had no voice in government. By the late twentieth century, however, the last vestige of South African colonialism expired with the end of South African apartheid and the ascension of Nelson Mandela.

The sign Capricorn rules boundaries, borders, and limitations. Your motto might be, "Good fences make good neighbors." Having spent your childhood during World War I and much of your adulthood during World War II, you have seen how the fluidity of international borders could lead to insecurity and violent confrontation. Personal boundaries are important too, although that notion didn't come into vogue until the 1980s. Still, you have an instinctive regard for your own integrity as a person.

As the world constantly changed around you, life forced you to explore all the possibilities within yourself. You've had to become firm in your own principles, like something of a country unto yourself. You may or may not be a believer, but deep feelings about religion inform your sense of morality. As progress has marched on, your strong values have enabled you to lay a solid foundation for yourself, your family, and even your country.

Relationships can provide the spiritual grounding you need in unpredictable times. You may enjoy the safety of traditional family life. Cancerians, Scorpios, and Taureans can provide the private nurture that allows you to flourish in the public realm.

You can appreciate the virtues of progress. The broad changes you've lived through, however, may have caused you extreme anxiety at times. With maturity, you've learned to avoid rigidity, when flexibility could make for a softer ride.

1910

CAPRICORN
Your Personal Planets

YOUR LOVE POTENTIAL
Venus in Capricorn, Dec. 22, 17:12 - Dec. 31, 23:59

YOUR DRIVE AND AMBITION
Mars in Sagittarius, Dec. 22, 17:12 - Dec. 31, 23:59

YOUR LUCK MAGNETISM
Jupiter in Scorpio, Dec. 22, 17:12 - Dec. 31, 23:59

World Events

Dec. 30 – American author and composer Paul Bowles is born.

Dec. 31 – John Moisant and Archie Hoxsey, two of America's foremost aviators, die in separate airplane crashes.

ENRICO CARUSO
Pisces

Enrico Caruso was perhaps the greatest tenor of all time. With his Sun in dreamy and beguiling Pisces, Enrico mesmerized his audiences with both his magnificent voice and his charismatic personality. Mercury, the planet of communication, and the receptive Moon, which symbolizes the public, are in close contact in Pisces as well. Caruso was known for the rapport he had with his audiences. When there is a strong Piscean influence, boundaries seem to melt away. He had the ability to lift his audience to ecstatic heights. Even the great composer Giacomo Puccini was not immune to Caruso's magic. After hearing Caruso sing for the first time he said, "Who sent you to me? God?"

Jupiter, the planet of fame and fortune, makes a favorable contact with Caruso's Venus and Neptune in Aries, the sign of fiery passion. This combination gave Caruso his enormous talent and creativity and insured that he would be duly appreciated for his efforts. At the Metropolitan Opera House in New York alone, he performed in thirty-seven operas in eighteen years.

With ambitious Capricorn rising at the time of his birth, Caruso was as savvy in business as he was a natural performer. In fact, he was one of the highest paid performers of his time, making more than a million dollars in his lifetime from his record sales alone. His estate earned nearly twice that after his death. Not only was Caruso comfortable with his operatic career, but he also starred in two silent films. How ironic that his great voice could not be heard, but big names sold movie tickets and, even in those early years of film, profit was the bottom line. Caruso even has his own star on Hollywood's Walk of Fame.

Caruso consulted with Evangeline Adams, the famous astrologer, before making ocean crossings during World War I and she claims to have predicted his death from pleurisy two weeks before it occurred. With a young wife and new baby to live for, Caruso's premature death was both a personal tragedy and a great loss for music lovers throughout the world.

Enrico Caruso
February 27, 1873 - August 2, 1921

➤ Read more about Caruso in "Astrology Goes on Trial" on page 185. ➤ Read Isadora Duncan's Star Profile on page 129.

1911

Sleuths in Pursuit of Truth: Jupiter in Scorpio

When the jolly giant Jupiter rolls into the dark, secretive sign of Scorpio, as it did at the beginning of the year in 1911, deep investigation is at the center of everything. The truth is Jupiter's ultimate goal and the ultimate sleuths are apt to come out of the woodwork. People are willing to go to great lengths to find the answers that they seek. Unsavory behavior is possible under this astrological influence as well. In 1911, the Mona Lisa was suddenly stolen from the famous Louvre museum in Paris. Her smile, mysterious and sensual, has Scorpio written all over it. On August 3, in the first military use of aviation, Italian Commander Piazza flew reconnaissance missions over Tripoli. Obtaining secret information is the forte of Jupiter in Scorpio. Jupiter wants to know the whole story and Scorpio will dig deep into the dirt to root out the very essence of anything that has been buried, no matter how deep.

Also this year, U.S. explorer Hiram Bingham discovered the Incan city of Machu Picchu. A magical and previously hidden world was unearthed under the influence of Jupiter in Scorpio. Jupiter also rules travel and foreign cultures, so archaeology and exploration fall under its bright and ebullient umbrella. This aspect is also connected to large-scale involvement in financial prospects and legacies. It's no wonder that on May 1 of this year, J. P. Morgan paid $42,800 for the only perfect copy of *Le Morte d'Arthur*, printed by Caxton in 1485. Death and finances are two of Jupiter in Scorpio's favorite subjects.

George V, the new King of England

Italian ships vie for control of Tripoli

Growing unrest leads to revolution in China, led by Sun Yat-Sen

HOPE DIAMOND OFFERS DESPAIR

Originally embedded in a religious idol in seventeenth century Mandalay, this deep blue stone carried the Hindu goddess Sita's hex after it was stolen. The gem traveled from France to Russia and back, before passing to the Hope family in England, leaving tragedy, death, and misfortune in its wake. American Evalyn McLean was the last owner. She purchased the stone from Pierre Cartier in 1911 and lost both her children and husband in subsequent years. Ultimately, the jinxed jewel was donated to the Smithsonian.

EUROPE IS POISED FOR WAR

The edgy European powers began to assert rights in North African ports and coastal regions, as the naval arms build-up continued. Unrest in Morocco gave the French an excuse to intervene, spurring the Germans to counter by staking a claim in the southern part of the country. The Italians pushed the Turks out of Tripoli, and President Diaz gave up against rebel forces in Mexico. In China, child-emperor Pu Yi was powerless to prevent rebellion, and a republic was established under Sun Yat-Sen and his Kuomintang government. In the U.S., a fire in New York City's Triangle factory prompted indictments against the owners who had locked girls in workrooms, causing their deaths. Senators voted to make themselves directly accountable to the people, choosing to be directly elected rather than appointed. In a triumph of right over might, Standard Oil was found guilty of anti-trust violations. The Norwegian explorer Roald Amundsen reached the South Pole, beating his British rival Robert Falcon Scott. The Austrian composer Gustav Mahler died, while Russian Vaslav Nijinsky danced into the hearts of Parisian audiences in *The Spectre of the Rose*.

➤ Read "The Titanic: Prophecies, Legends, and Destiny" by Wendy C. Hawks on page 105.

CAPRICORN

From January 01, 0:00 through January 21, 3:50

The Progressive Industrialist

Capricorns born in January 1911 can state from experience that sixties radicals were hardly the first generation to defy "The Establishment." You were born near the beginning of a decade when labor revolts all over the world threatened to destroy capitalist businesses and the systems of government that supported them. Because members of your sign tend to be skilled in leading teams of people in productive enterprises, Capricorn is known as the "chief executive" of the zodiac. The events of 1911 set century-long trends in the relationship between governments, captains of industry, and the working people.

On January 14, 1911, the National Republican Club advocated uniform federal regulation of American business. The stated purpose for such laws was not, as one might expect, to limit unethical practices against workers or consumers, but rather to prevent "state socialism." The strategic idea behind this position revealed Capricorn-like shrewdness. By acting to regulate industry, the U.S. government could insulate itself from radical criticism and attack. Developments in Russia later in the century would tend to affirm such pre-emptive economic policy.

Your instinct for strategy, planning, and discipline enables you to start projects that can evolve into successful institutions. Whether from the labor or management side, the people of your generation made important contributions to the evolution of commerce and industry. Because you are good at reading the handwriting on the wall, you are able to innovate when times demand change. You work well in groups and can lead a diverse team to define and meet goals.

Capricorn needs partners who can push him or her to scale the greatest heights. Ariens have a talent for pioneering, but their egos may compete with yours. Taurus can point the way to rich resources, and Sagittarius can show you the big picture.

Your challenge has been to find a way to work with others without compromising your own best standards. For Capricorn, "Done is good!" Your clear vision and talent for leading by example can inspire others to get on your bandwagon.

AQUARIUS

From January 21, 3:51 through February 19, 18:19

The Outrageous Innovator

As any good Aquarius knows, if you aspire to be an innovator, you have to live with the risk that others just won't understand you. After all, your sign rules sudden technological breakthroughs. The scientific innovators of 1911 surely expected to be called eccentric and outrageous, but some of their claims were certainly kooky! Around the time you were born, doctors in Minnesota claimed that spinal injections of Epsom salts could cure tetanus; Professor Gabriel Petit of France reported that radium injections could rejuvenate horses; and Dr. Francis Rous of New York's Rockefeller Institute reported that a virus caused cancerous tumors.

Only Dr. Rous would gain professional vindication. Several tumors were eventually named for him, and his work would ultimately help clinicians to treat people suffering from AIDS-related cancers. Researchers owe a debt of gratitude to Dr. Rous for laying the foundation for the now uncontroversial theory that viruses play a role in the development of certain cancerous growths. You may well identify with poor Dr. Rous, who no doubt took a professional beating for his willingness to stake his reputation on what must have seemed an outrageous notion at the time.

You are willing to go out on a limb if it means helping people. You may even dream of saving the world, and no doubt the world has needed a lot of saving during your lifetime—especially in your first thirty-five years. When Martin Luther King, Jr. declared, "I have a dream," you may have heaved an enormous sigh of relief—at last, someone who gets it!

Friendships with like-minded souls are the best kind of relationships for Aquarius. Love and matrimony requires a spouse who is first and foremost a friend. Empathetic Pisceans can embrace your visions, and Cancerians can share your dreams. And Geminis will adore everything about you that is different.

Your challenge has been to find your niche, a place where you don't feel like an ugly duckling. But once you found your flock, you could feel admired and encouraged for your marvelous instincts for "thinking outside the box."

▶ Read about your Chinese Astrological sign on page 838. ▶ Read about your Personal Planets on page 826. ▶ Read about your personal Mystical Card on page 856.

CAPRICORN
Your Personal Planets

YOUR LOVE POTENTIAL
Venus in Capricorn, Jan. 01, 0:00 - Jan. 10, 13:27
Venus in Aquarius, Jan. 10, 13:28 - Jan. 21, 3:50

YOUR DRIVE AND AMBITION
Mars in Sagittarius, Jan. 01, 0:00 - Jan. 21, 3:50

YOUR LUCK MAGNETISM
Jupiter in Scorpio, Jan. 01, 0:00 - Jan. 21, 3:50

World Events

Jan. 3 – The Sydney Street home of anarchists in London burns down; Home Secretary Winston Churchill is at the scene.

Jan. 3 – American film director John Sturgee is born.

Winston Churchill at Sydney Street

AQUARIUS
Your Personal Planets

YOUR LOVE POTENTIAL
Venus in Aquarius, Jan. 21, 3:51 - Feb. 03, 12:02
Venus in Pisces, Feb. 03, 12:03 - Feb. 19, 18:19

YOUR DRIVE AND AMBITION
Mars in Sagittarius, Jan. 21, 3:51 - Jan. 31, 21:29
Mars in Capricorn, Jan. 31, 21:30 - Feb. 19, 18:19

YOUR LUCK MAGNETISM
Jupiter in Scorpio, Jan. 21, 3:51 - Feb. 19, 18:19

World Events

Jan. 23 – The French Academy of Sciences refuses to break the barrier of sex, electing Henri Becquerel rather than Marie Curie.

Jan. 26 – Richard Strauss's opera *Der Rosenkavalier* opens in Dresden.

1911

PISCES
Your Personal Planets

YOUR LOVE POTENTIAL
Venus in Pisces, Feb. 19, 18:20 - Feb. 27, 14:28
Venus in Aries, Feb. 27, 14:29 - Mar. 21, 17:53

YOUR DRIVE AND AMBITION
Mars in Capricorn, Feb. 19, 18:20 - Mar. 14, 0:06
Mars in Aquarius, Mar. 14, 0:07 - Mar. 21, 17:53

YOUR LUCK MAGNETISM
Jupiter in Scorpio, Feb. 19, 18:20 - Mar. 21, 17:53

World Events

Feb. 22 – The Canadian Parliament votes to remain part of the British Empire.

Mar. 12 – Dr. Fletcher of the Rockefeller Institute discovers the cause of infantile paralysis.

American playwright Tennessee Williams is born under the sign of Aries

ARIES
Your Personal Planets

YOUR LOVE POTENTIAL
Venus in Aries, Mar. 21, 17:54 - Mar. 23, 23:34
Venus in Taurus, Mar. 23, 23:35 - Apr. 17, 18:55
Venus in Gemini, Apr. 17, 18:56 - Apr. 21, 5:35

YOUR DRIVE AND AMBITION
Mars in Aquarius, Mar. 21, 17:54 - Apr. 21, 5:35
Jupiter in Scorpio, Mar. 21, 17:54 - Apr. 21, 5:35

World Events

Mar. 26 – American playwright Tennessee Williams is born.

Apr. 12 – The first non-stop London-to-Paris flight is completed by Frenchman Pierre Prier.

PISCES
From February 19, 18:20 through March 21, 17:53

The Compassionate Publicist

A Pisces of 1911 would not be known for his or her talent for public relations. Rather, most people might speak of your enormous energy for charitable pursuits. Still, you share all these qualities—charity, enormous energy, and a shrewd instinct for public relations—with Jane Addams, the celebrated founder of Hull House. In March 1911, Ms. Addams published a book describing the heartbreaks and breakthroughs she experienced in running the settlement home she founded for impoverished children in Chicago.

If you didn't hear about Ms. Addams from your parents, you may have read about her in the newspaper or perhaps in your school textbooks. By the 1970s, Ms. Addams was hailed as an American hero, and her tireless efforts on behalf of the poor and helpless may have served to inspire you in your own projects. In general, Pisceans have a soft spot for the wounded birds of this world. You would have to labor mightily to disown such an impulse.

Unlike most Pisceans, however, those of you born in 1911 are likely to have a stubborn drive to make a concrete difference and the ability to do so on an ambitious scale. Talents as a builder of institutions may have driven you to found a hospital, clinic, or other vehicle of public service. Dogged perseverance and resourcefulness with public relations have enabled you to rally masses of people to worthy enterprises.

In personal relationships, Pisces is usually the compassionate friend, who comes through in the clutch. Because commitment is important to you, you may be the kind of person who always stays in touch, via cards, telephone calls, and gentle unexpected gestures. Capricorns will admire, honor, and reciprocate your loyalty. Taureans can provide you with serene sanctuary. Scorpios can calmly absorb your most poignant horror stories, and Virgos will gladly support your compassionate missions.

Your challenge has been to avoid burnout. If you are giving selflessly of yourself at all times, eventually your Piscean well of tenderness will run dry. Take time to renew yourself, and remember, loved ones may be happy to provide assistance.

ARIES
From March 21, 17:54 through April 21, 5:35

The Humanitarian Activist

At the time of your birth, Aries, violent labor revolts throughout the world attracted tens of thousands of workers, each of whom accepted the potential for death or injury at the hands of management-paid thugs. One particular act of violence against workers permanently changed the course of labor history, although no protest provoked it and no manager ordered it.

On March 25, 1911, fire swept through the Triangle Shirtwaist Factory in New York City and caused the death of one hundred and forty-six workers, mostly young women. While managers on the tenth floor escaped to the roof, all exits from the ninth floor down were locked, except for one fire escape. When that collapsed, desperate workers, many with their dresses in flames, jumped to their deaths on the pavement below. To this day, reforms in occupational safety and fair labor practices owe their impetus to that fire. These include the certification of the International Ladies' Garment Workers' Union, the establishment of the federal Occupational Safety Hazard Administration, and today's ongoing battle against illegal sweatshops.

Like babies born the year President Kennedy was shot, you may have been continuously schooled in the lessons of the Triangle fire. Its story may have stoked the fires of humanitarian activism in you. Perhaps you have promoted unionization or supported other legal reforms to curb abusive corporate practices. Where you see pain or injustice, you are likely to jump in and seek to change the whole system.

In relationships, you may be a joiner and an organizer. You may assume the role of pulling together group field trips to rallies, art shows, or Bahamian cruises. Personable, gregarious signs such as Gemini, Aquarius, Sagittarius, and Libra are all good matches for you.

You were probably raised to have a healthy distrust of certain people's motives. In your lifetime, you have seen the very worst of what human beings can do to one another. Your challenge is to keep this from hardening your own heart and cutting you off from those who love and need you. Your strength is your profound love of your fellow beings.

➤ Read about your Chinese Astrological sign on page 838. ➤ Read about your Personal Planets on page 826. ➤ Read about your personal Mystical Card on page 856.

TAURUS

From April 21, 5:36 through May 22, 5:18

The Pleasure Collector

In the days surrounding your birth, several subjects near and dear to the pleasure-loving Taurean heart made news. The good news was announced that famed operatic tenor Enrico Caruso would fully recover from a malady affecting his vocal chords. Your sign rules the throat and singing, and many a home-alone Taurean has been spied warbling along with his or her favorite opera recordings. On May 18 the sad news was announced of the death, at age fifty, of Gustav Mahler, conductor of the New York Philharmonic and the Metropolitan Opera. Lauded as "one of the [world's] towering musical figures," Mahler's *Songs Of A Wayfarer* and *Songs Of The Earth* may have furnished an exquisitely lyrical and romantic backdrop to your childhood. His symphonies may be your sentimental favorites for their inclusion of song.

Because your sign also rules money, value, and possessions, you are likely to have a taste for collectibles. Around this time, American financier J. P. Morgan paid $42,800 for the only perfect copy of Sir Thomas Malory's *Le Morte d'Arthur*, printed by Caxton in 1485. Later in your life, you may have admired this and other priceless books, collected and displayed at the Morgan Library in New York City.

Like Morgan, you may gain a sense of security by maintaining your own collection of valuable objects. At some point in your life, you may have had to part with some of those treasured possessions. While such an experience may have been painful, it is likely to have strengthened your non-materialistic values.

Taureans tend to hold tightly to their loved ones. Partners who take commitment seriously can provide you with the comfort you need to feel safe and ease your grip. Committed Capricorn is in for the long haul. Cancer and Leo treasure the security of family and home life.

A hard pruning in winter allows the rosebush to flourish in spring. Your life may have followed this pattern. Loss in life may have made simple pleasures all the more precious to you. The comforts of home, music, and intimate family gatherings allow you to share the joys of what truly matters in life.

GEMINI

From May 22, 5:19 through June 22, 13:35

The High-Speed Racer

In general, Gemini has a need for speed, and 1911 brought the initiation of an event that reflected the accelerating pace of daily life, around the globe and throughout your lifetime. May 30, 1911, marked the first running of the Indianapolis 500, an automobile race that continues today. The winner of the race, Ray Harroun, could attribute his victory to several Gemini-like elements in his strategy. Because his was the only car that did not carry a mechanic as a passenger, Harroun had invented and employed a rearview mirror.

Like Harroun and Geminis in general, you may prefer to travel light. The lighter your load, the quicker you can go! Also, as a Gemini, you are likely to enjoy an inventiveness that enables you to devise clever solutions to problems. Because your thinking alternates between intuitive and practical modes, you are less likely than most Geminis to walk around with your cranium in the clouds.

Your vivid imagination and ability to visualize in sensuous ways makes for strong writing talents. Your Gemini versatility allows you to apply these gifts to either fiction or non-fiction, or to skip between different media as they evolve. If you started out in print journalism, you may have moved on to write novels or produce and broadcast stories for radio and television.

You may have required the freedom to roam before you became willing to settle down with one partner. The thrill of playing the field has less to do with your restlessness than with your highly sensitive nature. The gentle empathy of a Pisces, a Cancerian's tender nurture, or a Leo's sunny protectiveness can make you feel safe enough to expose your vulnerabilities.

Speeding through life may have enabled you to provide some protection for your sensitive side. Allowing charm and intellectual interests to carry you through your youth, you may have tended to skim across painful issues or the seemingly confining demands of others. Maturity may have brought the realization that you wanted to slow down, smell the roses, and enjoy the abundant rewards of emotional intimacy and family togetherness.

➤ Read about your Chinese Astrological sign on page 838. ➤ Read about your Personal Planets on page 826. ➤ Read about your personal Mystical Card on page 856.

1911

TAURUS
Your Personal Planets

YOUR LOVE POTENTIAL
Venus in Gemini, Apr. 21, 5:36 - May 13, 5:41
Venus in Cancer, May 13, 5:42 - May 22, 5:18

YOUR DRIVE AND AMBITION
Mars in Aquarius, Apr. 21, 5:36 - Apr. 23, 8:27
Mars in Pisces, Apr. 23, 8:28 - May 22, 5:18

YOUR LUCK MAGNETISM
Jupiter in Scorpio, Apr. 21, 5:36 - May 22, 5:18

World Events

Apr. 30 – Women are granted the right to vote by the Portuguese constitutional court.

May 1 – J.P. Morgan pays $42,800 for the only perfect first edition of *Le Morte d'Arthur*, printed by William Caxton in 1485.

J.P. Morgan, the multi-millionaire art collector

GEMINI
Your Personal Planets

YOUR LOVE POTENTIAL
Venus in Cancer, May 22, 5:19 - June 08, 18:47
Venus in Leo, June 08, 18:48 - June 22, 13:35

YOUR DRIVE AND AMBITION
Mars in Pisces, May 22, 5:19 - June 02, 21:47
Mars in Aries, June 02, 21:48 - June 22, 13:35

YOUR LUCK MAGNETISM
Jupiter in Scorpio, May 22, 5:19 - June 22, 13:35

World Events

May 22 – French Minister of War Berteaux is killed by a crashing airplane at the start of the Paris–Madrid aviation race.

May 30 – Ray Harroun wins the first Indianapolis 500.

1911

CANCER
Your Personal Planets

YOUR LOVE POTENTIAL
Venus in Leo, June 22, 13:36 - July 07, 19:03
Venus in Virgo, July 07, 19:04 - July 24, 0:28

YOUR DRIVE AND AMBITION
Mars in Aries, June 22, 13:36 - July 15, 16:00
Mars in Taurus, July 15, 16:01 - July 24, 0:28

YOUR LUCK MAGNETISM
Jupiter in Scorpio, June 22, 13:36 - July 24, 0:28

World Events

June 22 – King George V is crowned at Westminster Abbey in London.

June 28 – Samuel J. Battle becomes the first African American policeman in the U.S.

The coronation of George V in Westminster Abbey

LEO
Your Personal Planets

YOUR LOVE POTENTIAL
Venus in Virgo, July 24, 0:29 - Aug. 24, 7:12

YOUR DRIVE AND AMBITION
Mars in Taurus, July 24, 0:29 - Aug. 24, 7:12

YOUR LUCK MAGNETISM
Jupiter in Scorpio, July 24, 0:29 - Aug. 24, 7:12

World Events

Aug. 6 – American comedienne Lucille Ball is born.

Aug. 22 – Leonardo da Vinci's Mona Lisa is stolen from the Louvre in Paris.

CANCER
From June 22, 13:36 through July 24, 0:28

The Mobile Homemaker

A modest innovation, introduced within days of your birth, 1911 Cancer, would have a truly revolutionary effect. On July 1, 1911, Charles F. Kettering announced his invention of the electric starter for automobiles. Until that time, physical cranking had been the only way to start a car engine. By eliminating the necessity for brute force, Kettering's invention enabled women and the elderly to start cars.

Kettering's accomplishment exemplified Cancer's brand of leadership—one you're likely to possess—to introduce humble, unassuming measures that can revolutionize the world. Once anyone could drive, the automobile craze took off. Today, the automobile and "car culture" are ubiquitous. Your sign also rules the family, and the car is one form of transportation built to convey people one family at a time. Although often pegged as a homebody, Cancer can also be an avid traveler. Remember, the Crab carries its home on its back. As long as you can carry the comforts of home with you, you're free to go anywhere! Think of how perfectly the car does this. Your children may have fond memories of family road trips with you.

Your sign also rules women. That automatic starter may have done more for women than thousands of suffrage marches. The ability to drive without assistance made it possible for women to escape confinement at home. Cars enabled women to get out in the world to work and socialize, and even to leave unsatisfactory situations. From this perspective, the revolutionary impact of Cancer's brand of leadership is unmistakable.

You are likely to enjoy getting out and about. The journey of life is more fun with good companionship. Sagittarius generously replenishes your travel pack. Take walks in the forest with Taurus. Enjoy romance by the sea with Pisces.

In your lifetime, impersonal changes in technology have brought enormous changes in people's personal lives. Adapting to the changes, especially as they affected women's traditional roles, may have been your biggest challenge. But your greatest strength is your ability to grow with the times and flourish.

LEO
From July 24, 0:29 through August 24, 7:12

The Undiscovered Star

In the world of 1911, international events left little room for the usual amusements associated with your sign, Leo. World War I threatened to break out three years too early, with military confrontations between Italy and Turkey over Libya, and between France and Germany over Morocco. In this anxious atmosphere, the news pertaining to entertainment, a subject ruled by your sign, took on a desperate tenor. On August 22, the most famous painting in the world, the Mona Lisa, was stolen from the Louvre Museum. The crime triggered an instant sensation over the mystery of the pilfered Da Vinci masterpiece.

This event may have anticipated the exceptional circumstances you likely encountered as a youngster, growing up in the midst of global war. Leo rules childhood, a period normally filled with parental attention, playfulness, and the thrill of discovery. Many children of your generation were deprived of a normal childhood, however, having instead to evacuate their homes in fear for their safety. Even if you faced no direct exposure to danger, your parents most likely sensitized you to the plight of the thousands of other children who did.

You may have grown up feeling that, like the Mona Lisa, you had been spirited away from your rightful place in the spotlight. In adulthood, you may have compensated for this deprivation by relying on your career for recognition, respect, and rewards. You have a powerful drive to distinguish yourself and build a glorious reputation.

You thrive with partners who recognize the shining superstar within you. Aquarians and Geminis can draw you into social gatherings, where you can be the singular sensation. Because they are so truthful, Sagittarians' flattery gets them everywhere.

Your challenge has been to recover a sense of security in your own home. You may be one of those people who is always out—working, socializing, entertaining clients—anything to avoid being cooped up inside. As an older adult, in safer times, you may have summoned the courage to reclaim the sanctity of your own private enclave. After all, what is a lion without a den?

➤ Read about your Chinese Astrological sign on page 838. ➤ Read about your Personal Planets on page 826. ➤ Read about your personal Mystical Card on page 856.

VIRGO

From August 24, 7:13 through September 24, 4:17

The Benevolent Survivor

Many children grew up hearing their mothers recite some variation on the following: "You better eat everything on your plate. Children are starving in China!" In early September 1911, children really were starving in China, following devastating floods that caused crop failures, famine, and outbreaks of disease. The death toll from the pneumonic plague alone reached 30,000, and with the Yangtze River swelling to forty-five miles in width, death from starvation threatened the lives of millions.

Sadly, such circumstances were not unusual during your childhood or adulthood. The human toll of the two World Wars may have triggered and amplified your natural Virgoan desire to relieve the suffering of others. You may feel others' distress as if it were your own. If you personally survived disastrous conditions in your life, you were likely to have emerged with stronger survival skills and the desire to share them for the benefit of others: helping others is personally empowering for Virgo. You might have traveled great distances to aid the needy or focused on publicizing their plight to attract funds and support.

You have tremendous ingenuity and drive, and you may not be shy about shaking up the system if it means you can be more successful. Your sign rules agriculture, health, and cleanliness—skills you may have put to work as a nurse or medic in wartime, or in rebuilding farming and industry after 1945.

You may find yourself attracted to partners who can be practical, thrifty, and sensible. Such a match ensures that you will have emotional and material support for your chosen missions in life. Earthy Taurus and Leo offer reliability. Pisces vulnerability may prove irresistible.

Because Virgo needs to feel needed, you can be susceptible to overwork, burnout, or relationships with self-destructive people. Tending to lose yourself in worthy projects, you may have learned the hard way to direct a fair share of giving to yourself. You can't keep laying golden eggs for others if you've cooked your own golden goose! Self-care is as important as the care you give others.

LIBRA

From September 24, 4:18 through October 24, 12:57

The Conservative Suffragist

When you were born, Libra, enlistment of women in the military may have seemed like an impossible dream, but on October 7, 1911, London suffragette Ida Peploe announced plans to form an army consisting of Englishwomen.
Your sign rules relations between men and women, and as you were growing up, the battle of the sexes proceeded at a feverish pitch. Justice and equality are core Libran values. Whether you are male or female, you would have had a hard time finding valid reasons for denying women the vote. Your sentiments on other issues relating to equality may, however, be more complicated.

Romantic impulses may make you revere traditionally feminine virtues such as the ability to nurture others, to behave selflessly, and to create life. Your intellectual side may lead you to concede that those qualities may have more to do with gender socialization than genetic inevitability. Still, you would hate to see such good qualities fade from humanity, merely because they have been labeled "female." You might point out how wonderful it would be if men could play a greater role in nurturing others, without being labeled "weak."

Nevertheless, you might find it difficult to condone the formation of a women's army, not necessarily because of the gender factor, but because women historically have been advocates of peace. As a Libran, you recoil from ugly confrontations, violence, and war. You may have based your career on the pursuit and promotion of peace and cooperation among people and nations. You would be a good mediator, negotiator, lawmaker, or teacher.

You attach great value to partners who can provide you with a serene, harmonious atmosphere. This preference applies to your home, workplace, and even friends' homes. Gemini and Pisces share your need for a tranquil retreat while Cancer and Taurus specialize in creature comforts.

Your belief in justice and equality may compete with a somewhat conservative preference for the comfort of the status quo. Your strong Libran talent for synthesizing opposing positions enables you to find inner harmony through original thinking.

► Read about your Chinese Astrological sign on page 838. ► Read about your Personal Planets on page 826. ► Read about your personal Mystical Card on page 856.

VIRGO
Your Personal Planets

YOUR LOVE POTENTIAL
Venus in Virgo, Aug. 24, 7:13 - Sept. 24, 4:17

YOUR DRIVE AND AMBITION
Mars in Taurus, Aug. 24, 7:13 - Sept. 05, 15:20
Mars in Gemini, Sept. 05, 15:21 - Sept. 24, 4:17

YOUR LUCK MAGNETISM
Jupiter in Scorpio, Aug. 24, 7:13 - Sept. 24, 4:17

World Events

Sept. 18 – Russian premier Piotr Stolypin dies from an assassin's bullets four days after being shot at the Kiev Opera House.

Sept. 19 – Novelist William Golding is born.

Italian ships striving for control of Tripoli

LIBRA
Your Personal Planets

YOUR LOVE POTENTIAL
Venus in Virgo, Sept. 24, 4:18 - Oct. 24, 12:57

YOUR DRIVE AND AMBITION
Mars in Gemini, Sept. 24, 4:18 - Oct. 24, 12:57

YOUR LUCK MAGNETISM
Jupiter in Scorpio, Sept. 24, 4:18 - Oct. 24, 12:57

World Events

Sept. 29 – Italy declares war on Turkey, vying for the control of Tripoli.

Oct. 10 – Sun Yat-Sen leads the revolution in China.

1911

SCORPIO
Your Personal Planets

YOUR LOVE POTENTIAL
Venus in Virgo, Oct. 24, 12:58 - Nov. 09, 0:54
Venus in Libra, Nov. 09, 0:55 - Nov. 23, 9:55

YOUR DRIVE AND AMBITION
Mars in Gemini, Oct. 24, 12:58 - Nov. 23, 9:55

YOUR LUCK MAGNETISM
Jupiter in Scorpio, Oct. 24, 12:58 - Nov. 23, 9:55

World Events

Nov. 1 – Italy performs the first aerial bombing, on the Tanguira oasis in Libya.

Nov. 4 – A Franco-German treaty gives France their protectorate in Morocco while Germany gains territory in the French Congo.

Norwegian explorer Roald Amundsen reaches the South Pole

SAGITTARIUS
Your Personal Planets

YOUR LOVE POTENTIAL
Venus in Libra, Nov. 23, 9:56 - Dec. 09, 9:22
Venus in Scorpio, Dec. 09, 9:23 - Dec. 22, 22:52

YOUR DRIVE AND AMBITION
Mars in Gemini, Nov. 23, 9:56 - Nov. 30, 4:06
Mars in Taurus, Nov. 30, 4:07 - Dec. 22, 22:52

YOUR LUCK MAGNETISM
Jupiter in Scorpio, Nov. 23, 9:56 - Dec. 10, 11:34
Jupiter in Sagittarius, Dec. 10, 11:35 - Dec. 22, 22:52

World Events

Dec. 10 – Marie Curie is awarded the Nobel Prize in chemistry for her discovery of radium.

Dec. 14 – Norwegian explorer Roald Amundsen and four companions reach the South Pole, winning the race against Robert F. Scott's expedition.

SCORPIO
From October 24, 12:58 through November 23, 9:55

The Nuclear Tulip

You might be surprised to learn that the same sign that rules catastrophic, transformative power—Scorpio—also rules something as delicate and rarefied as tulips. Think of the power of a tulip sprout to push apart pavement bricks, and you have a vivid illustration of the kind of energy you possess within yourself. In 1911, a similar thrust of Scorpio's force enabled the common people of China to unseat the Manchu dynasty.

Emperor Pu Yi of China was the "Lord of Ten Thousand Years," but within days of your birth, the Manchu dynasty came to an end, with Pu Yi's granting of a constitution, a decisive rebel victory over the main Chinese army, and Sun Yat-Sen's proclamation of a republic. Your sign rules massive shifts in the balance of world power, often by violent means. Ultimately affecting billions of people in China, not to mention Japan, Korea, Vietnam, Cambodia, Russia, and the United States, the Chinese overthrow of the monarchy certainly qualifies as such a massive shift.

You may seem quiet and extremely private to others, but under the right conditions you can come forward with explosive power: from David Banner to the Incredible Hulk in under five seconds. You may identify strongly with people who are powerless to protect themselves against individuals or institutions with an unfair advantage. The one thing Scorpio of 1911 cannot abide is a bully. In those circumstances, the tender Scorpio tulip can shoot through bricks (and throw a few bricks, proverbial or otherwise). The courage of your convictions moves you to fight when necessary.

Dominating partners are most likely an excitement you dispensed with in your youth. You need someone trustworthy as an understanding ally. Pisces sympathizes with your deepest secrets; gentle Taurus will seal those secrets in a vault. Capricorn and you constitute the ultimate power couple.

You may have something of a temper. Perhaps you learned the hard way that being right doesn't always justify how you express your outrage. Instinctively, you know things work in cycles that eventually turn in your favor. Timing is everything.

SAGITTARIUS
From November 23, 9:56 through December 22, 22:52

The Colorful Conceptualist

Sagittarius rules the higher mind, fine arts, and cultural exchange. In 1911, a group of artists—Wassily Kandinsky of Russia, and Franz Marc and August Macke of Germany—founded the Expressionist movement *Der Blaue Reiter* ("The Blue Rider.") As allies, the three men sought to incorporate higher principles of spirituality and musicality into the fine art of painting, through the harmonization of color and light. Both Marc and Macke perished in World War I, but their paintings are exhibited and celebrated along with Kandinsky's throughout the world today.

As a Sagittarius, you may share many of the values and aspirations of the *Blaue Reiter* artists. The three traveled widely through Europe and North Africa, soaking in the influences of diverse cultures. Born under the sign ruling distant travel, you are likely to journey to exotic locales, in search of inspiration and self-expansion. You may also share the artists' belief in the creativity and innovation that comes from international cultural collaboration.

The idea of a correlation between color and music reflects the sophisticated thinking that Sagittarius adores. You may be fascinated by the intellectual exercise of comparing seemingly diverse phenomena. With the possibility of war staring these potential soldiers in the face, the relationship between the *Blaue Reiter* artists took on a passionate urgency. If you've ever bonded with a foreigner at home or abroad, you may have felt a similar romantic intensity.

The built-in problem of maintaining long-term relationships with foreigners may appeal to the happy wanderer in Sagittarius. You may feel safe to express strong feelings because the end is but a jet plane away. Busy with their own preoccupations, Pisceans, Geminis, and Virgos can hold on loosely enough to make you miss them when you're away.

You may have a strong hunger for risk and intensity. Eagerness to discover the next great thing can entice you to gamble with your safety. Your challenge has been to find a way to channel that energy without pushing yourself or your loved ones past the breaking point.

► Read about your Chinese Astrological sign on page 838. ► Read about your Personal Planets on page 826. ► Read about your personal Mystical Card on page 856.

CAPRICORN

From December 22, 22:53 through December 31, 23:59

The Self-Made Leader

The sign of Capricorn governs authority and its structure, and you grew up in a period when the very nature of governmental authority was redefined and transformed. On December 29, 1911, Sun Yat-Sen was announced as President of the provisional government of the nascent Republic of China and began to negotiate terms for the Manchu dynasty's abdication of power. Capricorn tends to revere tradition, but your childhood experiences exposed you to the dangers of excessive imperial power—be it China, England, or another world power. No parent could have completely shielded you from the anxieties of the international scene.

Some Capricorns of December 1911 might have responded to world events with nostalgia for the security of the old monarchies and imperial regimes. Having spent your tender years during World War I, however, and having seen in adulthood that the Communist alternative to the Manchu dynasty was neither benevolent nor just, you are most likely to believe that there is no more deadly assumption than that one has the divine right to lord over others—as emperor, party official, or otherwise.

While you may see some value in hierarchy as a necessary element of productivity, you may be an unconventional leader. In general, Capricorn likes to get the job done. You are unlikely, however, to demand respect for authority for authority's sake. Rather, you may believe that respect must be earned and that leadership is a matter of service to those being led. You may regard the so-called "trappings of authority" as excess baggage that merely detracts from the bottom line.

You are likely to maintain strong boundaries between your public and private life. To your intimates, the solemn leader becomes the romantic softy. Dreamy Pisceans, nurturing Cancerians, and sensual Taureans will gladly indulge your private fancies.

You may have found it difficult to find role models worth emulating—especially when the ruling authorities of your youth were being overthrown all the time! Capable of inventing new models, however, you have the freedom to become a truly self-made individual.

1911

CAPRICORN
Your Personal Planets

YOUR LOVE POTENTIAL
Venus in Scorpio, Dec. 22, 22:53 - Dec. 31, 23:59

YOUR DRIVE AND AMBITION
Mars in Taurus, Dec. 22, 22:53 - Dec. 31, 23:59

YOUR LUCK MAGNETISM
Jupiter in Sagittarius, Dec. 22, 22:53 - Dec. 31, 23:59

World Events

Dec. 29 – Sun Yat-Sen, leader of the rebellion against the Manchu dynasty, is elected President of the provisional government in China.

Dec. 31 – Hélène Dutrieu, known as the "Girl Hawk," wins the Femina aviation cup in Étampes, setting a distance record for women at 158 miles.

The Titanic sinks, killing 1,513 people

Special Feature
The Titanic: Prophecies, Legends and Destiny
by Wendy C. Hawks

Precisely at noon on April 10, 1912, the magnificent luxury liner *Titanic* set out on its maiden voyage across the Atlantic, with passengers and crew blissfully unaware that their fateful journey would end in a tragedy that would capture the imagination of generations to come. The *Titanic*, touted as the largest ship afloat, was believed by many to be unsinkable. But only four days later, *Titanic* would, nevertheless sink after colliding with an iceberg in the chilly North Atlantic. Instead of completing the first of many trips ferrying passengers across the sea, the *Titanic* came to rest 12,600 feet beneath the sea in the small hours of April 15, 1912. That same ocean would provide a watery grave for the more than 1,500 souls who perished along with the ship.

Titanic's passenger list included some of the most prominent members of society, as well as representatives of the White Star Line, owners of the *Titanic*. After all, there was considerable status attached to traveling on the lavish new ship, which was much more like a hotel than a sailing vessel. While there were only enough lifeboats for about half of the passengers, even fewer people used them. Such was the belief in the safety of the *Titanic*! It was only when it became apparent that the ship was definitely going down that many of the passengers realized that they were, indeed, in mortal peril. Fame and fortune offered no guarantee that your life would be spared: Among those who died were John Jacob Astor, builder of New York's famed Waldorf Astoria Hotel and Washington Augustus Roebling, named for his famous uncle who built the Brooklyn Bridge.

The story of the *Titanic* inspired a number of books and movies, including the 1958 film *A Night to Remember* with its unforgettable scene of the ship's band playing dutifully on as they and their unsinkable ship slipped beneath the icy waters of the Atlantic. And, nearly forty years later, James Cameron's *Titanic* won a staggering eleven Oscars, including Best Picture of 1997 (tying *Ben Hur* for the record), and dazzled millions of moviegoers with its compelling love story, haunting music, and special effects. Another film (and Broadway musical), *The Unsinkable Molly Brown*, is loosely based on the life of *Titanic* survivor Margaret Tobin Brown.

(Continued on page 113)

➤ Read about missing ships at sea in "The Mysterious Bermuda Triangle" on page 385.

1912

Fog of Deception: Mercury and Neptune

On April 15, the "unsinkable" Titanic sank with thousands of passengers on its maiden voyage. It was a tragedy of unimaginable proportions that could have been prevented if warning signs were heeded. The ship's engineers and captain ignored many signals that the Titanic was in deep trouble and not as seaworthy as it had been touted to be. There were several important aspects at work on that tragic day. First of all, the Sun in Aries, suggesting initiative without boundaries, was making a hard angle, a "square," to the planet Neptune. Neptune is the planet of deception and confusion and also ice and fog. It was placed in the sign of Cancer when the ship went down, suggesting that lies could lead to a watery grave. When the Titanic hit the iceberg that would cause its demise, Neptune obscured the truth. It would shock the world when it did eventually come out that the ship was traveling too fast and that its steel girders were not strong enough to protect it from splitting in two.

There were other planetary influences at work that day as well. Mercury is the planet of travel, communication, directions, crossroads, and messages. Mercury was the Roman messenger god who wore a winged hat and shoes. When Mercury is in retrograde motion (from earth, it appears to move backwards in the sky) everything that it rules goes awry. There are travel delays and often accidents. This event happens approximately three times each year, but when the Titanic went down, its effects were multiplied significantly by the other aspects of that day.

The Titanic sinks, killing 1,513 people

Serbian troops entering the fortress of Uskub

Woodrow Wilson wins the American election

PROPHECY OF DOOM

Before the sinking of the *Titanic*, a psychic warned William Stead, a famous newspaperman, that he would face grave danger if he were to travel, especially by water, during April 1912. He ignored the psychic's written warning and boarded the ill-fated, "unsinkable" *Titanic*, along with the other 2,227 passengers, most of whom were also destined to drown at sea. He perished in the ensuing tragedy. In his own bid at prognostication, Stead had written an article, months before, warning that such a disaster was possible.

TITANIC DISASTERS

While Turkey and Italy settled their conflict, the Balkan region exploded into war: allies Serbia, Greece, Montenegro, and Bulgaria sought to expel the weakened Ottoman Turks from their territories. The supposedly unsinkable liner *Titanic* hit an iceberg and went down in the north Atlantic: 1,513 people died. German Kaiser Wilhelm II boosted his nation's naval might by launching the world's largest ship, a luxury liner with safety features. Further weakness in the Russian monarchy was revealed when Tsar Nicholas' heir was found to suffer from the incurable hemophilia. In the presidential election, Theodore Roosevelt's Progressive (Bull Moose) Party and incumbent Taft split the Republican vote: Democrat Woodrow Wilson won. Arizona became a state and granted women the vote, in common with Oregon and Kansas. The bust of Nefertiti was discovered in Egypt's El-Amarna. French stage star Sarah Bernhardt acted in the films *Queen Elizabeth* and *La Dame aux Camélias*. Inspired by Baden-Powell's Boy Scouts, the American Girl Guides were founded by Juliette Gordon Low. The word vitamin was coined to identify the body-building chemicals.

➤ Read "The Titanic: Prophecies, Legends and Destiny" by Wendy C. Hawks on page 105.

CAPRICORN

From January 01, 0:00 through January 21, 9:28

The Civilized Laborer

Business and industry are matters falling firmly within Capricorn's jurisdiction, and, in 1912, both entities were undergoing radical challenges that would continue for decades. On January 12, 1912, thousands of workers, demanding pay increases and double-pay for overtime, commenced a violent strike at the textile mills of Lawrence, Massachusetts. The workers had been receiving an average of sixteen cents an hour for a fifty-six-hour working week. The Massachusetts militia attempted to restrain the striking workers, most of whom were women and children.

Only the exceptional January Capricorn of 1912 would have failed to hear a parent cry out against such harsh conditions. Indeed, in the decades that followed the Lawrence strike, you are likely to have been among the public servants, union leaders, and industrialists who worked to abolish child labor and to institute fair labor standards. The working world may owe you a debt of gratitude for such civilized innovations as the forty-hour week, the minimum wage, and mandatory overtime.

You may find it astonishing today to see how people, especially the young, take basic rights for granted. For your generation, the events in the news directly affected the welfare of ordinary people. It was impossible to avoid taking a strong position and doing something about it. You are likely to be a builder and a doer. Apathy was never an option for you. When problems arise, you fix them!

Lazy people probably drive you crazy. Even if you were to have a stay-at-home spouse, you would most likely expect them to tend the public good through charity fundraising or voluntary work. Hardworking Virgo is most likely to be your best match. The humanitarian and good-government projects of Aquarius and Sagittarius would also appeal to you.

Likely to proclaim, "If I don't do it, it won't get done," you may tend to overextend yourself. "Workaholism" is a challenge that a desperate spouse or family member may have brought to your attention. Sometimes the January Capricorn needs reminding that delegation is one of the great talents at their disposal.

AQUARIUS

From January 21, 9:29 through February 19, 23:55

The Fearless Engineer

With the "Flying Ace Race" speeding ahead at full throttle in 1912, the parachute could not have been far behind. During your youth, 1912 Aquarius, you may have frequently given loved ones reason to recall the famous last words of amateur parachute inventor, Franz Reichalt before he plummeted to his death from the heights of the Eiffel Tower around the time of your birth: "I am confident of success."

Gifted with exceptional inventiveness and intelligence, Aquarius of 1912 would quite correctly regard Reichalt's ill-fated plunge as merely an experiment gone wrong, not the indictment of an essentially good idea. On February 28, however, Albert Berry made the first successful in-flight parachute jump from an airplane. Like Reichalt and Berry, you are likely to have quite the daredevil in you and a propensity for addiction to your own adrenaline.

Family members might have often caught you jumping off the barn roof, into a soft mound of hay. In later years they might have beamed with pride as you competed for your country in Olympic Alpine Skiing or parachuted from a warplane on D-Day. A scientific sensibility enables you to reduce exposure to danger by engineering innovative solutions to any foreseeable problems. You also have the unique ability to relegate concrete objections and fears to the rear compartment of your cranium. Your motto is: "I know what I'm doing."

You are likely to hit the eject button on any partner who turns out to be a queasy worrywart. Your personals advertisement might say, "Iron stomach a plus." Stable, encouraging Leo will find your pursuits extremely entertaining. Gemini has the smarts to cheerfully assist with your inventions and to conceal any worries. Risk-loving Sagittarius sees your big picture and shares your aspirations of success.

Fearlessness and the drive for extreme physical challenge can add up to recklessness. A few broken bones may have been the price you've paid for any youthful impulsiveness. With the discipline and wisdom of maturity, however, you most likely learned to employ your ingenious mind as a truly effective parachute.

▶ Read about your Chinese Astrological sign on page 838. ▶ Read about your Personal Planets on page 826. ▶ Read about your personal Mystical Card on page 856.

CAPRICORN
Your Personal Planets

YOUR LOVE POTENTIAL
Venus in Scorpio, Jan. 01, 0:00 - Jan. 04, 18:37
Venus in Sagittarius, Jan. 04, 18:38 - Jan. 21, 9:28

YOUR DRIVE AND AMBITION
Mars in Taurus, Jan. 01, 0:00 - Jan. 21, 9:28

YOUR LUCK MAGNETISM
Jupiter in Sagittarius, Jan. 01, 0:00 - Jan. 21, 9:28

World Events

Jan. 6 – New Mexico becomes the 47th U.S. state.

Jan. 10 – Glenn Curtiss's flying-boat airplane — the first of its kind — makes its maiden flight at Hammondsport, New York.

Glenn Curtiss' flying-boat plane makes its maiden flight at Hammondsport, New York

AQUARIUS
Your Personal Planets

YOUR LOVE POTENTIAL
Venus in Sagittarius, Jan. 21, 9:29 - Jan. 29, 22:44
Venus in Capricorn, Jan. 29, 22:45 - Feb. 19, 23:55

YOUR DRIVE AND AMBITION
Mars in Taurus, Jan. 21, 9:29 - Jan. 30, 21:01
Mars in Gemini, Jan. 30, 21:02 - Feb. 19, 23:55

YOUR LUCK MAGNETISM
Jupiter in Sagittarius, Jan. 21, 9:29 - Feb. 19, 23:55

World Events

Jan. 29 – French suffragist Marguerite Durand leads a delegation to demand a place for women in the country's plans for electoral reform.

Feb. 5 – The British Arbitration League issues an appeal against air warfare; many famous figures back the petition.

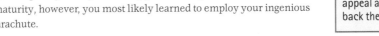

1912

PISCES
Your Personal Planets

YOUR LOVE POTENTIAL
Venus in Capricorn, Feb. 19, 23:56 - Feb. 23, 15:28
Venus in Aquarius, Feb. 23, 15:29 - Mar. 19, 3:48
Venus in Pisces, Mar. 19, 3:49 - Mar. 20, 23:28

YOUR DRIVE AND AMBITION
Mars in Gemini, Feb. 19, 23:56 - Mar. 20, 23:28

YOUR LUCK MAGNETISM
Jupiter in Sagittarius, Feb. 19, 23:56 - Mar. 20, 23:28

World Events

Mar. 15 - Italian King Victor Emmanuel III narrowly escapes an assassination attempt.

Mar. 15 - Yuan Shih-Kai succeeds Sun Yat-Sen as President of the Chinese Republic.

Crowds stand outside the White Star Line office in Leadenhall Street, waiting for news of the "Titanic"

ARIES
Your Personal Planets

YOUR LOVE POTENTIAL
Venus in Pisces, Mar. 20, 23:29 - Apr. 12, 14:49
Venus in Aries, Apr. 12, 14:50 - Apr. 20, 11:11

YOUR DRIVE AND AMBITION
Mars in Gemini, Mar. 20, 23:29 - Apr. 05, 11:30
Mars in Cancer, Apr. 05, 11:31 - Apr. 20, 11:11

YOUR LUCK MAGNETISM
Jupiter in Sagittarius, Mar. 20, 23:29 - Apr. 20, 11:11

World Events

Apr. 15 - In the early hours of the morning the liner *Titanic* sinks; more than 1,500 drown.

Apr. 16 - American aviator Harriet Quimby becomes the first woman to fly a plane across the English Channel.

PISCES
From February 19, 23:56 through March 20, 23:28

The Invisible Opponent

The ultimate consequences of events occurring at the time of your birth, Pisces of 1912, may have left you with an impression of the very subtle but penetrating power you possess. On February 27, 1912, Lord Kitchener celebrated the opening of a British rail line through the Sudan, a colonial territory over which he had previously served as Governor-General. Lionized for his military leadership in South Africa, India, and Egypt, Kitchener exemplified Great Britain's sense of manifest colonial imperative to rule over widespread dominions. Just four years later, Kitchener would be lost with the *HMS Hampshire*, in an underwater mine explosion off the Orkney Islands. By the end of the twentieth century, the British Empire too would fade, like Camelot, into the mists.

Your sign rules mists and fog, things that keep people from seeing clearly. In 1912, all the forces were in place for the ultimate demise of the British Empire, but—like Kitchener's ship, which sailed into a submerged minefield—its leaders failed to clearly see the opposition lurking in colonial territories.

Pisces born in 1912 also rule hidden enemies and self-undoing. In general, Pisceans are gentle, peace-loving folk, never ones for direct or violent confrontation. But should you have any opponents who are blinded by their own arrogance, you'll gladly stand aside and let their great expectations blow up in their faces. In other words, like Gandhi, you possess the power of passive resistance and the ability to read the invisible handwriting on the wall.

Relationships provide a sacred sanctuary for you. A peaceful home life is essential. Cancer offers security and easy compatibility. Virgo promises soft voices and relief from chaos. Libra will seduce you with harmonious atmosphere.

Passive resistance may wipe out empires or humiliate obnoxious co-workers, but loved ones might characterize Pisces' secret weapon as "passive aggression." Over time, Pisces of 1912, you may have learned to be more direct about your needs and desires. Your gentle way of asking virtually assures you a positive response.

ARIES
From March 20, 23:29 through April 20, 11:11

The Passionate Pioneer

You must have been mesmerized by stories about the pioneers of aviation, 1912 Aries, in the years before you were born. April 1912 brought two more stories about pilots who were pioneers in more ways than one. On April 2, Trehawke Davis became the first woman to co-pilot a dirigible across the English Channel. Fourteen days later, Harriet Quimby became the first woman to fly an airplane across the same stretch of water.

Aries is the ultimate pioneer of the zodiac. In general, members of your sign have a burning need to be first in pushing the limits of human possibilities. Like the early twentieth century aviators, you may feel compelled to blaze new trails through fields that arouse your passions, regardless of any dangers. The element of danger may make certain challenges all the more compelling. Power and speed are traditional objects of Arien affection. Born just as aviation emerged as the fastest form of transportation on Earth, Aries of 1912 are among the fastest of the speeding Rams. When pursuing a goal, you want to get where you're going! Heaven help any obstacle that gets in your way.

Conditions prevailing at the time of your birth virtually guaranteed that you would have extremely strong passions—like those that motivated activists for women's rights during your childhood. The female fliers' accomplishments may have inspired you to believe that anything was possible. Universal women's suffrage was one achievement that materialized before you reached adulthood.

If a relationship is not exciting, you may lose interest. You thrive with partners who can match your pace and push you to your next level of achievement. Jovial, competitive Sagittarius may be your dream come true. Gemini could outrace you, but would save victory for you and the story for your grandchildren.

In your youth, you might have had a tiny little problem with winning graciously. Patience might have been an issue too, but what else can you expect when absolutely everybody insists on getting in your way? Maturity brings out your gift for magnanimity and the ability to enjoy the ride.

➤ Read about your Chinese Astrological sign on page 838. ➤ Read about your Personal Planets on page 826. ➤ Read about your personal Mystical Card on page 856.

TAURUS

From April 20, 11:12 through May 21, 10:56

The Wise Financier

Apparently, Taurus of 1912, the issue of campaign finance reform is as perennial as springtime. The United States legislative and executive branches were arguing about this within days of your birth. Ninety years later, they were having the same argument. On April 20, 1912, the House of Representatives ordered public disclosure of campaign expenses for the President and Vice President. Your sign rules finance and springtime, and just about any Taurus will agree; there are few subjects easier to argue about than money.

Because most Taureans don't like to argue, and because a comfortable living is another important goal, you may have worked long and hard to accumulate enough resources to ensure your security. Early in life, you may have learned some hard financial lessons due to youthful impulsiveness, unforeseen risk, or trusting someone who turned out to be deceitful. Once burned, you may have become quite shy about parting with hard-earned cash. You may have adopted the Shakespearean wisdom to "neither a borrower nor a lender be," especially where family is involved.

You may prefer simple pleasures. In general, Taureans can be rather sedentary, but you are more likely than most to ascribe a high value to health and exercise. Fresh air and soft, damp soil can rejuvenate you. A brisk stroll through the neighborhood in springtime enables you to walk off anxieties, enjoy the wonders of nature, and stay in touch with nearby friends. If gardening is a favorite activity, you might even grow your own food.

You may be more sensitive and demonstrative than most Taureans. Partners who are stingy with criticism and generous with hugs will keep you smiling. Cancer always has an extra "Ah baby" on hand. Pisces feels like a gentle rain on freshly-planted soil. Scorpio's embrace can hold you until rapture.

Because you tend to trust what works, your comfort zone could get a little too comfortable. You may need to make sure your world doesn't get too small. Your talent for sharing the pleasures of this earth can aid in the acquisition of new and rewarding personal relationships.

GEMINI

From May 21, 10:57 through June 21, 19:16

The Cautious Navigator

You were born just as the world reached the end of the "Age of Gemini," a twenty-five-year period of frenzied progress in new transportation technologies. As the new developments dissolved spatial boundaries between countries, humanity faced the violent consequences of sudden insecurity. On May 28, 1912, the United States Senate ruled that negligent operation of the *Titanic* caused the luxury liner to sink. In fact, the *Titanic* disaster on April 15, 1912, epitomized the worldwide trend leading up to it and foreshadowed the next trend to come.

Prior to the *Titanic* disaster, transportation pioneers were making death-defying attempts to fly higher, faster, and longer, to build bigger ships, and to perform more impressive stunts. Your sign, Gemini, exemplifies that speedy progress, and aspects in your chart suggest a foreboding of future danger. By pushing the *Titanic* to its limits, the crew turned a maiden voyage into a test flight and passengers into pilots, speeding to their deaths. You might recast the frenzied pre-World War I negotiations among the great powers as merely "rearranging the seats on the *Titanic*."

Elders would have made sure to acquaint you with the myth of Icarus—the boy who stole his father's wings and flew fatally close to the Sun. The trauma framing your tender years, including the possible absence of your father, would have made you a more conservative Gemini than most. Too much movement and commotion can fray your sensitive nerves. Strong intuition may urge you to proceed with care and forethought.

Relationships, especially marriage and family, can provide a zone of stability and happiness for you. You may fiercely protect family ties, Gemini of 1912. Leo's den offers protection and joy. Sagittarius provides a positive outlook, and Cancer can make a cozy home anywhere.

The world you entered may have seemed dangerous and out of control. An overly cautious approach to life, however, can be suffocating to Gemini, a sign that needs plenty of air. Outgoing loved ones can inspire you to spread your wings and experience Gemini's joy of flying free.

➤ Read about your Chinese Astrological sign on page 838. ➤ Read about your Personal Planets on page 826. ➤ Read about your personal Mystical Card on page 856.

TAURUS
Your Personal Planets

YOUR LOVE POTENTIAL
Venus in Aries, Apr. 20, 11:12 - May 07, 1:56
Venus in Taurus, May 07, 1:57 - May 21, 10:56

YOUR DRIVE AND AMBITION
Mars in Cancer, Apr. 20, 11:12 - May 21, 10:56

YOUR LUCK MAGNETISM
Jupiter in Sagittarius, Apr. 20, 11:12 - May 21, 10:56

World Events

May 5 – The man later known as Joseph Stalin publishes the first issue of the Bolshevik political paper *Pravda*.

May 18 – The depths of the crater of Mt. Vesuvius are photographed for the first time by Professor Mallada of London's Royal Observatory.

Lenin reading an issue of the Bolshevik paper Pravda

GEMINI
Your Personal Planets

YOUR LOVE POTENTIAL
Venus in Taurus, May 21, 10:57 - May 31, 13:18
Venus in Gemini, May 31, 13:19 - June 21, 19:16

YOUR DRIVE AND AMBITION
Mars in Cancer, May 21, 10:57 - May 28, 8:15
Mars in Leo, May 28, 8:16 - June 21, 19:16

YOUR LUCK MAGNETISM
Jupiter in Sagittarius, May 21, 10:57 - June 21, 19:16

World Events

May 30 – American aviation pioneer Wilbur Wright dies.

June 8 – Carl Laemmele founds Universal Studios in Los Angeles.

1912

CANCER
Your Personal Planets

YOUR LOVE POTENTIAL
Venus in Gemini, June 21, 19:17 - June 25, 0:11
Venus in Cancer, June 25, 0:12 - July 19, 9:43
Venus in Leo, July 19, 9:44 - July 23, 6:13

YOUR DRIVE AND AMBITION
Mars in Leo, June 21, 19:17 - July 17, 2:42
Mars in Virgo, July 17, 2:43 - July 23, 6:13

YOUR LUCK MAGNETISM
Jupiter in Sagittarius, June 21, 19:17 - July 23, 6:13

World Events

July 1 – Female aviator Harriet Quimby dies in an airplane crash.

July 4 – Kaiser Wilhelm II and Tsar Nicholas II meet to reaffirm ties of loyalty between their two countries.

German cartoon of Kaiser Wilhelm's arrogant intervention in Morocco

LEO
Your Personal Planets

YOUR LOVE POTENTIAL
Venus in Leo, July 23, 6:14 - Aug. 12, 17:42
Venus in Virgo, Aug. 12, 17:43 - Aug. 23, 13:00

YOUR DRIVE AND AMBITION
Mars in Virgo, July 23, 6:14 - Aug. 23, 13:00

YOUR LUCK MAGNETISM
Jupiter in Sagittarius, July 23, 6:14 - Aug. 23, 13:00

World Events

Aug. 1 – An airmail service is inaugurated between Paris and London.

Aug. 11 – Morocco becomes a French protectorate after the Sultan abdicates.

CANCER
From June 21, 19:17 through July 23, 6:13

The Security Seeker

The subject of naval history may capture your interest, Cancer of 1912. Your sign rules history and the sea. In 1912, the British Admiralty redeployed its ships from the Mediterranean to the North Sea. This strategic move followed the failure of the Haldane Mission, negotiations in which Britain sought to limit rapid German militarization, and Germany sought to obtain mutual neutrality should either country go to war, both in vain. The outcome led to a further reshuffling of the international alliances that would ultimately plunge the world into war.

Your sign also rules family, and you might characterize this point in history as the world's entry into a protracted and ultimately violent family crisis. One of the root problems was paternalism, as the great powers negotiated for control over other countries, while leaving subject nations out of the discussion altogether. Having lived through this disastrous discord, you might agree that the world was in need of some serious family therapy!

In all seriousness, the onset of war may have ultimately realigned the dynamics in your own family life, especially as fathers were called away to military service. Mothers became the new heads of the household. Your sign also represents women, mothers, and their power. As European and American women gained the right to vote shortly after World War I, you may have wondered why they hadn't had it all along.

Romance and intimacy can take the edge off a tense day. You enjoy relationships with people who can whisk you away from it all. You can unwind when reliable Capricorn is at the wheel. Poetic Pisces fills your home with beautiful music. Sagittarius takes you on feel-good getaways.

Unlike the key players of 1912, you don't really want to control the world, but you may seek personal security by trying to anticipate everything that could possibly go wrong. Because Cancer is the most adaptable sign of the zodiac, you can flow with shifting situations. With maturity, you can enjoy the security of having a "Plan B" and still reap the benefits of a flexible approach to life.

LEO
From July 23, 6:14 through August 23, 13:00

The Exuberant Monarch

Just as you were arriving into a world poised on the brink of war, Leo of 1912, current events (including your birth) gave people reason for hope. On July 29, 1912, Danish Captain Enjar Mikkelson, believed to have perished in the Arctic, returned home to Copenhagen after spending three years stranded in Greenland. Your sign, Leo, rules resurrection in both the literal and the metaphorical sense. You instinctively know how to keep hope alive, even on your darkest days.

You are, of course, Leo the Lion, and the lion is the king of the beasts. For Leos of 1912, it can be very good to be king—or queen. Your temperament is likely to be sunny, genial, and contagious, regardless of external circumstances. Others may wonder about you sometimes. They just don't understand that you have your own way of directing and maintaining your formidable focus, so as not to dwell on matters that are upsetting or beyond your power to change.

As an adult, you may have enjoyed the work of your 1912 contemporary, entertainer Gene Kelly, born on the cusp of Leo and Virgo. Kelly's exuberance, flair, and cheerful aura may closely match yours. The thrilling physicality of his dance style may parallel your own enjoyment of dancing and physical exercise and all its forms. Although Kelly made his routines look easy, he worked hard to achieve perfection. For you, the secret of achieving perfection is to thoroughly enjoy what you do!

Your partnership theme song is "Love, love, hooray for love …!" For dramatic, romantic Leo, relationships are for sharing the joy. Hot dates with Sagittarius may break the bank, but the laughs alone are worth it! Gemini's charming flattery will have you floating home. Aquarius's social connections get you through every velvet rope.

You grew up in times so exceptionally trying that you may have had trouble being your sunny Leo self. If so, your challenge has been to exercise your ability to focus on the positive. Just like Gene Kelly's dancing, developing this mental discipline may take hard work, but the results will have you enjoying whatever it is you do!

➤ Read about your Chinese Astrological sign on page 838. ➤ Read about your Personal Planets on page 826. ➤ Read about your personal Mystical Card on page 856.

VIRGO

From August 23, 13:01 through September 23, 10:07

The Ready Preventer

Because your sign rules health, Virgo, a medical breakthrough serves as the perfect gift upon the occasion of your birth. That is exactly what you and the world got. On August 13, 1912, Dr. Gaston Odin of Paris announced his success in identifying, isolating, and reproducing cancer microbes. The discovery was hailed for creating the possibility of a cancer vaccine. At the time, of course, no one could have anticipated that a true vaccine for cancer would elude scientists well into the next millennium. Nevertheless, this discovery was essential in facilitating the development of increasingly effective treatments for the disease.

As far as you are concerned, Virgo of 1912, the best vaccine for cancer is prevention through healthy living. Now, not all Virgos succeed in living perfectly healthy lives. (In fact, it is rumored that three Virgos in Camden, New Jersey actually smoke.) But if you should succumb to the temptation of an unhealthy indulgence, you may feel very, very guilty.

At this point in your life you may be sick and tired of hearing that for your sign, "cleanliness is next to godliness," especially if you are one of those Virgos who lets it all hang out (and feels very, very guilty about it). Virgos tend to treat tidiness as an all-or-nothing proposition. Your sign also rules work, and you may be too busy to be a neatnik. If this is you, then tidiness may be the rule for you at work, melding together two of your greatest strengths—order and service.

You may prefer the traditional in relationships. Clearly defined roles afford you the comfort of knowing what to do and when to do it. Cancer and Taurus bring you all the comforts of home. To settle down with someone who is good for you, pick dutiful Capricorn or amenable Pisces.

Over-concern about other people's opinions can distract you. Your challenge is to do exactly what you want to do without feeling guilty. Appropriateness is high on Virgo's list of values. Once you realize how expert you are in doing the right thing, you'll see that you have plenty of room to compensate a little and have some fun!

LIBRA

From September 23, 10:08 through October 23, 18:49

The Natural Diplomat

It's a shame you didn't emerge into this world as a full-grown adult, Libra, because your diplomatic skills were desperately needed. October 1912 saw the beginning of an eight-month preview of World War I, as the Balkan allies—Greece, Montenegro, Serbia, and Bulgaria—declared war against the Ottoman Empire in Turkey. Once you were old enough to read, you may have eagerly studied the interactions that allowed an entire region to collapse into war. Perhaps you scoured your mind for alternative scenarios that might have averted not only the Balkan war of 1912, but World War I itself.

Discord among individuals or nations may be profoundly distressing for you. Restoration of harmonious relations is a high Libran priority. Likely to be a natural mediator, you may believe deeply in your ability to get opposing parties to understand and accept reasonable options. Hiding iron fists in velvet gloves, Libra is a natural leader. Members of this sign employ facts, persuasion, and positive incentives to build consensus.

Librans born September 23 to 28, 1912, are likely to have a gift for analytical thinking and an encyclopedic command of facts. Librans with birthdays after September 28 are likely to be highly skilled in synthesizing seemingly opposite views and coming up with compromises acceptable to all. Many Librans pursue careers in lawmaking, diplomacy, and mediation. Others may sow harmony through creative or artistic careers.

The quality of relationships can be a matter of pride for Libra. Long-term partners need to be willing to work through any issues that arise. Gemini is willing to talk through any concerns. Loyal Leo cheerfully takes ups and downs in stride. The optimism of Sagittarius assures you that everything will turn out well.

Because what you do can make such an important difference for other people, you may sacrifice your own needs. Sometimes, your own well-being requires devoting some time and effort to your relationship with yourself. Libra of 1912 knows better than anyone that caring for oneself enables that person to be a positive force for others.

➤ Read about your Chinese Astrological sign on page 838. ➤ Read about your Personal Planets on page 826. ➤ Read about your personal Mystical Card on page 856.

1912

VIRGO
Your Personal Planets

YOUR LOVE POTENTIAL
Venus in Virgo, Aug. 23, 13:01 - Sept. 06, 0:52
Venus in Libra, Sept. 06, 0:53 - Sept. 23, 10:07

YOUR DRIVE AND AMBITION
Mars in Virgo, Aug. 23, 13:01 - Sept. 02, 17:03
Mars in Libra, Sept. 02, 17:04 - Sept. 23, 10:07

YOUR LUCK MAGNETISM
Jupiter in Sagittarius, Aug. 23, 13:01 - Sept. 23, 10:07

World Events

Aug. 23 – American entertainer Gene Kelly is born.

Sept. 13 – Following an ancient custom, Gen. Nogi Maresuke and his wife commit suicide as a last tribute to the departed emperor of Japan.

Serbian troops entering the fortress of Uskub

LIBRA
Your Personal Planets

YOUR LOVE POTENTIAL
Venus in Libra, Sept. 23, 10:08 - Sept. 30, 8:25
Venus in Scorpio, Sept. 30, 8:26 - Oct. 23, 18:49

YOUR DRIVE AND AMBITION
Mars in Libra, Sept. 23, 10:08 - Oct. 18, 2:38
Mars in Scorpio, Oct. 18, 2:39 - Oct. 23, 18:49

YOUR LUCK MAGNETISM
Jupiter in Sagittarius, Sept. 23, 10:08 - Oct. 23, 18:49

World Events

Oct. 14 – Presidential candidate Theodore Roosevelt continues to give a speech in Milwaukee despite having been shot in the chest.

Oct. 17 – Bulgaria and Serbia declare war on the Ottoman Empire.

1912

SCORPIO
Your Personal Planets

YOUR LOVE POTENTIAL
Venus in Scorpio, Oct. 23, 18:50 - Oct. 24, 17:24
Venus in Sagittarius, Oct. 24, 17:25 - Nov. 18, 5:02
Venus in Capricorn, Nov. 18, 5:03 - Nov. 22, 15:47

YOUR DRIVE AND AMBITION
Mars in Scorpio, Oct. 23, 18:50 - Nov. 22, 15:47

YOUR LUCK MAGNETISM
Jupiter in Sagittarius, Oct. 23, 18:50 - Nov. 22, 15:47

World Events

Nov. 3 – The first all-metal plane takes to the skies over France.

Nov. 5 – Arizona, Wisconsin, and Kansas grant the vote to women.

The Balkans peace negotiations

SAGITTARIUS
Your Personal Planets

YOUR LOVE POTENTIAL
Venus in Capricorn, Nov. 22, 15:48 - Dec. 12, 22:22
Venus in Aquarius, Dec. 12, 22:23 - Dec. 22, 4:44

YOUR DRIVE AND AMBITION
Mars in Scorpio, Nov. 22, 15:48 - Nov. 30, 7:40
Mars in Sagittarius, Nov. 30, 7:41 - Dec. 22, 4:44

YOUR LUCK MAGNETISM
Jupiter in Sagittarius, Nov. 22, 15:48 - Dec. 22, 4:44

World Events

Dec. 6 – German archaeologist Ludwig Borchardt discovers the bust of Queen Nefertiti while excavating the ancient Egyptian city of El-Amarna.

Dec. 17 – Negotiations begin in London to achieve peace in the Balkans.

SCORPIO
From October 23, 18:50 through November 22, 15:47

The Instinctive Survivor

Born in late October and November of 1912, as war raged in the Balkans, Scorpio babies were likely to absorb the anxiety felt by adults around them. Such tensions may have been less severe in the United States, but American babies—especially Scorpios—would still have been sensitized to caregivers' fears about loved ones in Europe and the possibility of intervention. The immediate conflict would end in May 1913, but hostilities would brew into 1914, with the outbreak of World War I.

Scorpio rules psychology and the unconscious, and events occurring before you developed an active memory were therefore likely to affect you on the level of instinct and intuition. Today's psychologists refer to this kind of awareness as the "pre-conscious." The responses of your caregivers in your first year of life, Scorpio of 1912, may have caused you to become finely attuned to your surroundings and suspicious or wary of others.

Such a reaction, or "hyper-vigilance," would not be unhealthy if you grew up in the midst of war. In fact, having your survival instincts tuned to a high pitch may have given you a distinct advantage in coping with the extreme conditions of World War II. Later in life, your ability to "feel your way through the dark" would also have proven advantageous, especially if you were one of the millions who had to start life over again, either at home or in a new country. In work and your career, you don't let opportunities slip away.

You do best with nonjudgmental partners who can soothe your heightened sensitivities. Someone with a gentle spirituality can renew your soul. Serene Taurus is a rock of security and resourcefulness. Compassionate Pisces offers tender sanctuary. Nurturing Cancer will carry your dreams in a safe and loving place.

Even in times of peace and security, you may still worry that you have left an oven on somewhere. Constant anxiety like that can be debilitating and draining. Scorpio's connection to the deeper mysteries of life and death can lead you to a spiritual source of healing, redemption, and trust in the forces of life and goodness.

SAGITTARIUS
From November 22, 15:48 through December 22, 4:44

The Exotic Archaeologist

In 1922, when you were ten years old, the discovery of the tomb of Tutenkhamun captured the imagination of millions of Americans and Europeans and triggered a craze in "Egyptiana." In your likely eagerness to learn more about this fascinating subject, you might have stumbled across the story of another breakthrough discovery, occurring within days of your birth and providing the perfect birthday present for a Sagittarius. On December 6, 1912, archeologists at El-Amarna, Egypt, discovered the bust of Queen Nefertiti, the wife of King Akhenaton, who lived in the fourteenth century B.C.

Because your sign rules exploration in foreign countries, Sagittarians of 1912 would be particularly thrilled about the Egyptian excavations. You are likely to have a taste for the exotic, and it certainly doesn't hurt that Nefertiti's bust proved her to be exceedingly beautiful—so beautiful, in fact, that she set a standard of beauty that endures in the West, to this day. The incorporation of foreign influences into one's native culture is a process you're likely to find delightful, energizing, and fun.

Nefertiti's husband, Akhenaton, was regarded as a heretic for having founded and imposed a new, Sun-worshiping religion over Egypt. Your sign rules religion, and aspects of your chart suggest that you may get an intellectual kick out of unorthodox religious positions—the more outrageous, the better. You might even have a few of your own.

In relationships you may prefer a partner who can hold down the fort, while you are off exploring the planet. You may need someone who is willing to compromise on the amount of time you spend at home. Scorpio and Leo are generally happy to keep your home fires burning. Non-possessive Libra is certainly the master of compromise.

In your youth, authority figures may have interfered with your ability to get out and see the world. A talent for study and intellectual pursuits may have freed you to travel as far and as wide as your expansive mind could take you. With maturity, you could take the responsibility to account for and preempt any limiting reservations.

► Read about your Chinese Astrological sign on page 838. ► Read about your Personal Planets on page 826. ► Read about your personal Mystical Card on page 856.

CAPRICORN

The World Wonder

You might find it intriguing to ponder what it must have been like to build one of the wonders of the world. Of course, a Capricorn would imagine playing the role of chief executive for such an undertaking. Mapping out the execution of such a grand and complex project is the kind of challenge in which members of your sign excel. Just such a project made news on December 23, 1912, with the opening of the Aswan Dam canal in Egypt. Originally built in 1902, the Aswan Dam sought to meet Egypt's advancing industrial and agricultural needs. The opening of the canal in 1912 capped off a second round of building and progress.

You may have followed the news about later rounds of construction on the Aswan Dam, through 1956. December Capricorns of 1912 are likely to have a special interest in affairs concerning foreign countries. The building of infrastructure is also a matter ruled by your sign. When the two subjects come together in infrastructure projects affecting international commerce and the balance of power among nations, you are likely to find yourself riveted. To work on such a project might be a dream come true.

You are likely to have traveled to distant countries, and you may speak several foreign languages. Natural leadership skills may flow from your ability to spark others' enthusiasm (not to mention your own). Extremely persuasive, you may be entirely capable of getting people to move mountains and create new wonders.

You may have met close partners while you were traveling. Friendliness and an open-minded, can-do spirit appeal to you. Sagittarian optimism encourages you. Aquarians can help you expand your social network. Cancer can be delightfully resourceful on the road.

One hazard of pursuing grand schemes is that you are likely to encounter opposition from nay-sayers. In the course of your career, you may have had a few colossal clashes of will. Capricorn of 1912 has a wonderful ability to see the big picture. By sharing your broad visions, you can show others where and how they fit in. With this new perspective, you can win new converts to your cause.

1912
CAPRICORN
Your Personal Planets

YOUR LOVE POTENTIAL
Venus in Aquarius, Dec. 22, 4:45 - Dec. 31, 23:59

YOUR DRIVE AND AMBITION
Mars in Sagittarius, Dec. 22, 4:45 - Dec. 31, 23:59

YOUR LUCK MAGNETISM
Jupiter in Sagittarius, Dec. 22, 4:45 - Dec. 31, 23:59

World Events

Dec. 23 – The Aswan Dam canal is opened in Egypt.

Dec. 25 – Italy lands troops in Albania to protect its interests during the revolt that has broken out there.

Artist's impression of the sinking "Titanic"

Special Feature

The Titanic: Prophecies, Legends, and Destiny

(Continued from page 105)

Besides the myriad books and films inspired by the *Titanic's* ill-fated voyage, there is also a book that eerily foreshadowed what would occur in April 1912. In 1898, fourteen years before the demise of the *Titanic*, Morgan Robertson authored a novel titled *Futility*, about a seemingly unsinkable ship called the *Titan*. In this book, the unsinkable *Titan* does indeed sink, just like the real-life *Titanic*. Amazingly, the fictional *Titan* sinks on its April maiden voyage when it collides with an iceberg in the Atlantic. Again, just like *Titanic*! Not only were the circumstances similar, but the details of each of the ship's specifications were astonishingly alike. Both the fictional *Titan* and the real *Titanic* could hold a maximum of 3000 passengers; both had two masts and three propellers. While the *Titan* was 800 feet long and the *Titanic* was 882.5 feet long, both nevertheless moved at very high speeds; *Titan* at 25 knots and *Titanic* at 23 knots. And that's not all. In *Futility*,

Robertson's passenger list included the rich and famous, just like *Titanic's*. And, like *Titanic*, the *Titan* also lacked sufficient lifeboats, and a great number of people went down with the ship.

Despite the fact that on April 14 a total of six warnings about ice directly in its path were relayed to the *Titanic* from other ships, the crew never adjusted the ship's charted course. There is considerable doubt about whether this information was ever given to the bridge or plotted on the navigational maps because, if it had been, it would have been apparent that the *Titanic* had already entered the danger zone. Some speculate, however, that it was sheer arrogance, or the desire to break the speed record for crossing the Atlantic, that kept *Titanic* from changing her course. But these were not the only warnings that were received about impending disaster. There were also a number of psychic forewarnings that, if heeded, might have spared many lives.

Take, for instance, the case of William T. Stead and his protégé, Shaw Desmond. Stead, a British journalist and pacifist, was invited by President Taft to attend an international conference.

(Continued on page 121)

➤ Read about missing ships at sea in "The Mysterious Bermuda Triangle" on page 385.

1913

Innovation and Inauguration: Uranus in Aquarius

U ranus rules genius, science and the unexpected. In 1913, this planet had just moved into its home sign, Aquarius. When planets take up residence in their own constellation, they relax and get more comfortable and their influence is intensified. On December 15, the first telephone line was inaugurated between Berlin and New York. Also this year, Henry Ford developed the first moving assembly line, an innovation that would change the world of industrial production forever. Charles Richet of France won the Nobel Prize for medicine this year, for his work on anaphylaxy. On August 2, an international conference on cancer research opened in Brussels. Ernest Rutherford and Niels Bohr described atomic structure, leading to scientific revolutions that would ultimately come to alter society in far-reaching ways.

In February of 1913, Mars approached Uranus and locked arms in an aspect called a "conjunction". On January 31 in Turkey, the "Young Turks" and the military staged a coup d'état, removing the moribund Ottoman government and tossing peace negotiations into havoc. This aspect causes impulsiveness and rebellion against constraint. Revolution and sudden social change are in the air when Mars meets Uranus, particularly under the influence of Aquarius. Later in the year, in Ireland, 150,000 Ulstermen prepared for armed resistance to home rule proposed by British Liberals. Also, owing to the influence of this aspect on aviation, on October 9, French aviator Adolphe Pégoud became the first pilot to "loop the loop."

Greek wounded leave the front while their comrades rout the Bulgarians

Henry Ford production line

The "Mona Lisa" is recovered

REVOLUTION AND MURDER

Turkey's Ottoman regime fell to the radical Young Turks in a coup d'état backed by the military during peace negotiations over the Balkan confrontation: the peace was, however, signed all the same. Mexican revolutionary President Francisco Madero and his vice-president were murdered by forces loyal to previous President Porfirio Diaz: General Huerta succeeded as President. Britain, the United States, Germany, France, Japan, Russia, Italy, and Austria-Hungary continued their build-up of battleships and submarines in preparation for armed conflict. Suffragists upstaged President Wilson's inauguration with a protest march the day before. Ford opened the first moving assembly line for car manufacture. The 93-year old black freedom fighter, Harriet Tubman, died at her New York home. Financier John Pierpont Morgan, founder of the Metropolitan Museum of Art, also died. Isadora Duncan's two children drowned in the River Seine in Paris. The French aviator Roland Garros made the first flight across the Mediterranean. Stravinsky's 'scandalous' *The Rite of Spring* opened in Paris, and the *Mona Lisa*, stolen in 1911, was recovered undamaged.

➤ Read "The Titanic: Prophecies, Legends and Destiny" by Wendy C. Hawks on page 105.

CAPRICORN

From January 01, 0:00 through January 20, 15:18

The Ironic Humorist

A 1913 January Capricorn would be uniquely equipped to appreciate the irony of the inauguration of a telephone line between Berlin and New York on January 15, 1913. Over the next few years, transmissions over the wire might have made President-elect Woodrow Wilson wish he had had an economy-size pair of scissors. As rapid German militarization threatened to draw the European powers into war, Wilson could only wonder when that dreaded midnight call to battle would wake the United States from its dreams of neutrality.

Capricorn rules the building of infrastructure, like the international telecommunications network begun in the early 1910s, and members of your sign also tend to have a dark, dry, ironic sense of humor. Accordingly, as an adult looking back on this time, you were likely to see how bizarre it was to set up a connection between two countries that would soon want to annihilate each other. Of course, the situation was more complicated than that, but the Capricorn point of view rarely fails to flush out the twisted side of any story.

Such a perspective contributes to a strength you are likely to possess—the ability to see the humor in any situation, no matter how horrible it may be. This ability to laugh, if only to yourself, would enable you to maintain a sense of control in the most challenging of circumstances. Humor empowers you to hold to a difficult course over the long run because it allows you to see the light at the end of the rough stretch—even when that light is an oncoming train.

Quixotic and even flaky partners may have held an odd attraction for you. Perhaps they offer some (comic) relief from Capricorn's steady, serious tendencies. Light, mischievous Gemini has an irresistible charm. Sagittarius gets all your jokes. Virgo can even succeed at out-punning you!

In your youth, your strong point of view may have prompted others to respond with disapproval or intimidation. In general, 1913 January Capricorn has a solid sense of discretion. With experience, you were likely to perfect your feel for the right time and place for self-assertion.

AQUARIUS

From January 20, 15:19 through February 19, 5:43

The Extreme Humanitarian

You were born at a time, Aquarius, when it was not unusual for ordinary people to take extreme actions in pursuit of their goals. On February 8, 1913, British suffragettes destroyed a telephone line between London and Glasgow. This action was one among many attempts by the militant women's rights activists to attack and destroy symbols of governmental authority and industrial power.

Once you were old enough to look back on those times, you may have regarded the suffragettes' actions with sympathy and even nostalgia: "Those were the days when the revolutionary movements were serious!" Ruling rebellion, electricity, and sudden violent jolts, the sign of Aquarius puts the "volt" in revolting. You're unlikely to shy away from a vigorous protest when the cause is right. Worthy causes in your life may have included labor unionization, women's suffrage, pacifism, or anti-McCarthyism.

Strong humanitarian values, intellectual complexity, and forward thinking are characteristics most Aquarians share. Even as you reflect on the protests of the early twentieth century, your brilliant Aquarian mind might be thinking sideways and forward to a global perspective that envisions strategies for promoting fairness and equal rights for all people. As an elder, you may have encouraged younger activists to go all out in supporting humanitarian causes.

Having lived through the Depression and two global wars, you were unlikely to expect or accept a relationship in which either partner plays a gender-specific role. You may have chosen a partner who sought to bring out your individuality. Open-minded Geminis can be the ultimate progressives. Libra is willing to negotiate alternative arrangements. You might like the challenge of enticing Leo into a relationship that upholds the unique talents of each partner.

An Aquarian talent for advanced thinking can sometimes leave you feeling lonely and misunderstood. When you're ahead of your time, others may need a chance to catch up. Age and experience brings acceptance of this difference and the wisdom to find others who enjoy keeping up with you.

➤ Read about your Chinese Astrological sign on page 838. ➤ Read about your Personal Planets on page 826. ➤ Read about your personal Mystical Card on page 856.

CAPRICORN
Your Personal Planets

YOUR LOVE POTENTIAL
Venus in Aquarius, Jan. 01, 0:00 - Jan. 07, 5:26
Venus in Pisces, Jan. 07, 5:27 - Jan. 20, 15:18

YOUR DRIVE AND AMBITION
Mars in Sagittarius, Jan. 01, 0:00 - Jan. 10, 13:42
Mars in Capricorn, Jan. 10, 13:43 - Jan. 20, 15:18

YOUR LUCK MAGNETISM
Jupiter in Sagittarius, Jan. 01, 0:00 - Jan. 02, 19:45
Jupiter in Capricorn, Jan. 02, 19:46 - Jan. 20, 15:18

World Events

Jan. 15 – The first telephone line opens between Berlin and New York.

Jan. 18 – American comedian Danny Kaye is born.

Captain Scott is found dead in his tent in the Antarctic on February 10

AQUARIUS
Your Personal Planets

YOUR LOVE POTENTIAL
Venus in Pisces, Jan. 20, 15:19 - Feb. 02, 23:21
Venus in Aries, Feb. 02, 23:22 - Feb. 19, 5:43

YOUR DRIVE AND AMBITION
Mars in Capricorn, Jan. 20, 15:19 - Feb. 19, 5:43

YOUR LUCK MAGNETISM
Jupiter in Capricorn, Jan. 20, 15:19 - Feb. 19, 5:43

World Events

Jan. 22 – Turkey agrees to peace terms in the Balkans.

Jan. 27 – Jim Thorpe is stripped of his Olympic medals after confessing he had been a professional baseball player; the Olympics demand amateur status.

PISCES
Your Personal Planets

YOUR LOVE POTENTIAL
Venus in Aries, Feb. 19, 5:44 - Mar. 06, 17:08
Venus in Taurus, Mar. 06, 17:09 - Mar. 21, 5:17

YOUR DRIVE AND AMBITION
Mars in Capricorn, Feb. 19, 5:44 - Feb. 19, 7:59
Mars in Aquarius, Feb. 19, 8:00 - Mar. 21, 5:17

YOUR LUCK MAGNETISM
Jupiter in Capricorn, Feb. 19, 5:44 - Mar. 21, 5:17

World Events

Feb. 28 – American film director Vincente Minnelli is born.

Mar. 6 – The centenary of the Romanov Dynasty is celebrated throughout the Russian Empire.

American film director Vincente Minnelli is born under the sign of Pisces

ARIES
Your Personal Planets

YOUR LOVE POTENTIAL
Venus in Taurus, Mar. 21, 5:18 - Apr. 20, 17:02

YOUR DRIVE AND AMBITION
Mars in Aquarius, Mar. 21, 5:18 - Mar. 30, 5:52
Mars in Pisces, Mar. 30, 5:53 - Apr. 20, 17:02

YOUR LUCK MAGNETISM
Jupiter in Capricorn, Mar. 21, 5:18 - Apr. 20, 17:02

World Events

Mar. 29 – The German Reichstag raises taxes in order to fund its increased military.

Apr. 18 – Prof. Emil von Behring announces the discovery of a new diphtheria antitoxin.

PISCES
From February 19, 5:44 through March 21, 5:17

The Hidden Hero

You entered the world, Pisces of 1913, just as a hero of the anti-slavery movement was passing from it. In March 1913, Harriet Tubman died at the age of ninety-two. Having escaped slavery in 1849, Ms. Tubman returned to lead more than 300 black slaves to freedom through the Underground Railroad. A veteran of the Civil War, she served with the Union army as a cook, nurse, scout, and spy. If you learned of Ms. Tubman in your youth, you were blessed with a marvelous role model.

Harriet Tubman exemplified many of the best qualities associated with your sign. She risked life and limb to give compassionate service to others, an experience likely to be familiar to you. You may also share the "Piscean" nature of Ms. Tubman's strength. She worked quietly, invisibly, and relentlessly. Your personal style, too, may have been understated and covert but as effective as a trickling stream carving canyons through the mountains.

Pisces rules dark, hidden places, where efforts behind-the-scenes can yield buried treasure—such as personal freedom. The Underground Railroad was not a subterranean tunnel, but a series of safe-houses owned by compassionate people and linked together by Tubman's path of courage. You may have walked such a path in your own life. Many Pisceans of 1913 were no doubt among the unsung heroes of World War II who provided secret housing, false documentation, or that one fortuitous, lifesaving gesture to Jews fleeing Nazi persecution in Europe.

Serving others is likely to be a high priority for you. Because the identity of such "others" may extend beyond your immediate family, you need partners who can understand and share your values. Humanitarian Aquarius admires your commitment. Virgo feels needed when working beside you. Cancer can give you a spiritual refueling.

You may have felt that others have underestimated or even looked down on you. You have the Piscean power, however, to take personal pain or oppression and turn it into a drive to help others in similar straits. As you've lifted the downtrodden, you may have realized that you were lifting yourself.

ARIES
From March 21, 5:18 through April 20, 17:02

The Worthy Warrior

Aries rules battle and warfare and when you were born a new kind of warrior was in the news. On April 3, 1913, British suffragette Emmeline Pankhurst was sentenced to three years in prison for bombing the home of David Lloyd George, the Chancellor of the Exchequer. Intending to launch a hunger strike in prison, Ms. Pankhurst uttered the words of a true soldier, "I am probably going to my death."

You may by no means support terrorism, 1913 Aries, but the militancy of Ms. Pankhurst—a once respectable Victorian gentlewoman—speaks of the extremism of the times. And as you saw for yourself, the worldwide violence in the decades following would make the actions of the British suffragettes look like a tea party. Faced with unimaginable evil, members of your generation would ultimately have no choice but to fight—to the death, if necessary. Patterns in your chart suggest that not only would you be willing to fight the good war, but you also would be very good at doing so.

You are likely to have a bottomless well of fighting spirit, for actual battle, or for any challenge in life. If you served in the military, you may have truly believed you were saving the world. Ariens born on or before March 30 may have an ingenious mind for maneuvers and logistics. Ariens born on or after March 30 may have a seemingly mystical intuition for tactics; following your gut instincts to "go this way, not that" can lead to astonishing results. Such qualities may have aided you in achieving any objective.

You may have held family and home life to a romantic ideal. When you return from the cruel, hard world, all the comforts of home should be waiting. Taurus can lavish you with sweetness. Libra brings the blessings of peace and harmony. Leo is your ultimate resource for rest and relaxation.

Any warrior may have difficulty adjusting to peacetime, and you may have found it hard to "power down" after realizing important goals. Evidence of success in re-channeling your tremendous Arien energy is everywhere: in the post-war Baby Boom, in thriving economies, and in completely rebuilt countries.

➤ Read about your Chinese Astrological sign on page 838. ➤ Read about your Personal Planets on page 826. ➤ Read about your personal Mystical Card on page 856.

TAURUS

From April 20, 17:03 through May 21, 16:49

The Frugal Gourmand

The sign of Taurus rules income and finances, and Taureans tend to have a talent for providing financial advice and investment management services. On May 8, the United States House of Representatives passed a bill to impose the first graduated personal income tax following the ratification of the 16th Amendment to the Constitution on February 25, 1913. On May 2, five hundred letters between Robert Browning and Elizabeth Barrett Browning fetched $32,750 at an auction in London.

You may personally bristle at having to send any portion of your hard-earned cash to the government. In general, Taurus does not like to part with his or her money, at least not when the recipient is an impersonal institution. This antipathy may have moved you to become highly adept at figuring out, within the lines of the law, how to pay as little as possible in either taxes or ordinary expenses. Such skills would have made you extremely valuable to the buyer of the Browning letters or to wealthy industrialists like Henry Fricke. Having purchased Holbein's portrait of Oliver Cromwell for $235,000 around the time of your birth, Fricke would have needed to offset taxes owed on the appreciation in value of his investment.

Taureans can, on the other hand, be extremely generous with their funds and resources when it comes to lavishing loved ones with sumptuous gifts and treats. The joy of sharing the pleasures of the good earth outweighs the virtue of frugality where Taurus is concerned. You may also offer generous support to charities.

You may have felt tension between your traditional Taurean need for steady partnerships and a competing urge to be available for outside commitments. Absence makes Scorpio's heart grow fonder. Capricorn happily turns outside projects into a family business. Pisces is content to go with your flow.

You have lived through times when people often had to endure shattering losses of wealth. Because a gift for creating abundance is at the heart of your very being, you've had the ability to survive and rebuild with only the shirt on your back and the skills of your body and mind.

GEMINI

From May 21, 16:50 through June 22, 1:09

The Determined Aspirant

In general, Gemini is not known for undertaking projects involving long distances or extended periods of time but, Gemini of 1913, you may be an exception to this rule. Indicators in your chart show an ability to effect change in a steady, orderly way. Events at the time of your birth exemplify this character trait. On May 22, E.G. Baker set a new long-distance speed record by flying from the West Coast to New York in eleven days, seven hours, and fifteen minutes. And in Alaska on June 7, Hudson Stuck became the first to successfully scale the summit of Mount McKinley.

Once you set your mind to a task, you are likely to work with passion and determination until you get it done. Ordinarily, Gemini gets bored with long-term projects—unless they are interesting and challenging. Baker's cross-country plane trip and Stuck's conquest of the highest peak in North America easily satisfy the "must be interesting" requirement. Similarly, a worthy goal in and of itself may not be enough to engage you. The process of achieving it must arouse your passions and allow you to have some fun.

If you were born on or before May 28, you are likely to conceive new projects in your dreams and bring them to concrete completion in the real world. If you were born after May 28, you may enjoy exceptional capacities for original and disciplined thinking. Your methodical sensibility can hone your intellect to a laser-sharp focus. You have got what it takes to be an outstanding entrepreneur.

Gemini's double-sidedness allows you to be all over the place and firmly rooted, wherever you are. The stability of your relationships depends on your ability to allow them to grow and change steadily over time. Life with dramatic, entertaining Leo is never boring. Aquarius keeps you intellectually engaged. Capricorn challenges you to keep growing.

If you've ever fallen too much in love with an idea, you may have stuck with it, long after its viability proved hopeless; after that though, your adaptability may have helped you to snap out of such a rut and to move on to new and more promising ventures.

1913

TAURUS
Your Personal Planets

YOUR LOVE POTENTIAL
Venus in Taurus, Apr. 20, 17:03 - May 02, 5:11
Venus in Aries, May 02, 5:12 - May 21, 16:49

YOUR DRIVE AND AMBITION
Mars in Pisces, Apr. 20, 17:03 - May 08, 2:59
Mars in Aries, May 08, 3:00 - May 21, 16:49

YOUR LUCK MAGNETISM
Jupiter in Capricorn, Apr. 20, 17:03 - May 21, 16:49

World Events

Apr. 26 – The International Women's Peace Conference opens at The Hague.

May 13 – Russian engineer Igor Sikorsky completes and flies the first four-engine aircraft.

Composer Igor Stravinsky

GEMINI
Your Personal Planets

YOUR LOVE POTENTIAL
Venus in Aries, May 21, 16:50 - May 31, 9:44
Venus in Taurus, May 31, 9:45 - June 22, 1:09

YOUR DRIVE AND AMBITION
Mars in Aries, May 21, 16:50 - June 17, 0:37
Mars in Taurus, June 17, 0:38 - June 22, 1:09

YOUR LUCK MAGNETISM
Jupiter in Capricorn, May 21, 16:50 - June 22, 1:09

World Events

May 29 – Igor Stravinsky's *The Rite Of Spring* premières in Paris.

May 30 – The Treaty of London ends the first Balkan War; the second begins almost immediately.

➤ Read about your Chinese Astrological sign on page 838. ➤ Read about your Personal Planets on page 826. ➤ Read about your personal Mystical Card on page 856.

1913

CANCER
Your Personal Planets

YOUR LOVE POTENTIAL
Venus in Taurus, June 22, 1:10 - July 08, 9:15
Venus in Gemini, July 08, 9:16 - July 23, 12:03

YOUR DRIVE AND AMBITION
Mars in Taurus, June 22, 1:10 - July 23, 12:03

YOUR LUCK MAGNETISM
Jupiter in Capricorn, June 22, 1:10 - July 23, 12:03

World Events

July 4 – Rumania prepares to send troops to join the Greeks and Serbs in the Balkan war, after reports of Bulgarian atrocities.

July 23 – The "Second Revolution" breaks out in southern China.

The production line, invented by Henry Ford

LEO
Your Personal Planets

YOUR LOVE POTENTIAL
Venus in Gemini, July 23, 12:04 - Aug. 05, 23:32
Venus in Cancer, Aug. 05, 23:33 - Aug. 23, 18:47

YOUR DRIVE AND AMBITION
Mars in Taurus, July 23, 12:04 - July 29, 10:30
Mars in Gemini, July 29, 10:31 - Aug. 23, 18:47

YOUR LUCK MAGNETISM
Jupiter in Capricorn, July 23, 12:04 - Aug. 23, 18:47

World Events

Aug. 10 – The Treaty of Bucharest officially ends the second Balkan War.

Aug. 16 – Henry Ford announces that the forthcoming assembly line will quadruple automobile production.

CANCER

From June 22, 1:10 through July 23, 12:03

The Sensitive Patriot

Your sign rules patriotism and the sea and, at the time you were born, 1913 Cancer, these two subjects combined in ways that would ultimately plunge the world into the most deadly era in human history. The naval forces of the European powers and the United States were rapidly increasing, posing a severe threat to the Germans. War in the Balkans raged on between the former allies in the war against Turkey. Finally, the ugliest side of patriotism reared its head, as Bulgaria slaughtered thousands of Serbian and Greek civilians—and as reports of a "grave racial problem" in the U.S. characterized the foreign-born sector of its population (14.7 percent) as a "menace to our civilization."

To see world events cast in terms of the darker potentials of Cancerian qualities may be painful for you. You must hate for a value as dear as love for your country to be perverted and degraded by irrational hatred. Patterns in your own chart indicate a generous affection for foreign people, cultures, and languages. Well into adulthood, you were likely to find it upsetting to confront bigotry or national chauvinism among your neighbors and peers.

Even if you don't sympathize with such attitudes, you may understand how such hostilities could arise. As fast planes and telephone lines made national borders vulnerable, the potential for insecurity soared. Homeland security is a high Cancerian value, one you may have fought honorably to defend. Hatred and abuse, however, are deeply upsetting to emotional 1913 Cancer.

Your best partners have encouraged you to learn and grow. A marriage might have involved a foreigner or relocation to a different country. Taurus may have provided security, but the Bull's stubborn streak may have caused tension. Capricorn has the strength to start over. With Sagittarius, your relationship is a moveable feast.

Having lived through two world wars, you were likely to have felt extreme tension as the best of your values were distorted into something you could hardly recognize. Withdrawing into your Cancerian shell enabled you to protect your true feelings.

LEO

From July 23, 12:04 through August 23, 18:47

The Wonderful Dreamer

Your sign represents the irrepressible human urge to dream of newer, greater things and within days of your birth, 1913 Leo, several news items demonstrated that this spirit was still going strong. On July 28, 1913, Germany announced plans to build a railway linking Baghdad and Constantinople. On August 6, the British Parliament announced that it was considering building a tunnel under the English Channel. Leo rules the child in all who experience wonder and awe at projects as ambitious as a train through the desert or a tunnel under the sea.

You may fondly remember your first ride on a train. As you sped along, a parent might have told you about the new train through the desert. Decades later, the actual building and completion of the England-to-France "Chunnel" may have reawakened the child in you. Such a response may reach redemptive levels for you, given your firsthand experience in witnessing the blessings and curses that technology can bring.

In your tender years, you may have gained a painful acquaintance with the deadly capacities of airplanes, ships, and submarines. Even that perennial childhood fascination, trains, suffered an atrocious corruption under the Nazis. That poignant example captures the innocence robbed from children and adults in the World Wars, and you may have felt this loss acutely. Still, you and your children may have run outside to watch the planes flying during the Battle of Britain.

You may have had a taste for the unconventional in relationships. A series of close friendships may have preceded your readiness to settle down. Aquarius ensures you'll have an active social life. Butterfly-like Gemini might have captured you with charm. Romantic Pisces fills your den with passion.

The conditions you grew up in may have made it hard to preserve the part of you that is sunny and optimistic. Perhaps that is why 1913 Leo has the heart of a lion—to protect that hopeful, innocent, childlike spirit. When peacetime ushered in the opportunity to rebuild, you probably leapt at the chance to create something new, spectacular, and life affirming.

118

➤ Read about your Chinese Astrological sign on page 838. ➤ Read about your Personal Planets on page 826. ➤ Read about your personal Mystical Card on page 856.

VIRGO

From August 23, 18:48 through September 23, 15:52

The Principled Warrior

Born on September 12, 1913, Jesse Owens exemplified the very best characteristics of the sign he had in common with you, Virgo of 1913. The events of his life poignantly illustrate some of the most powerful aspects of your chart. Your sign rules athleticism, and Owens was perhaps the greatest athlete that ever lived. His four gold medals at the 1936 Olympics in Berlin were not merely a feat of physical wonder, they were a triumph over Adolf Hitler's terrible views on racial superiority. By publicly demonstrating that a person of African descent could outperform the best white athletes in the world, Owens forced the German *Fuhrer* from his own stadium in exasperated humiliation. The impact of that stunning moral victory endures today.

The chart for Virgo of 1913 reveals the unmistakable signature of a mighty warrior. You may, indeed, have grown up to serve as a brave soldier in World War II. And like Jesse Owens, you may have been a warrior for humanity. With great courage and conviction, you may have fought to defend a position that was not popular at the time. You may have stood up for others who could not stand up for themselves.

You are likely to have an incredible toughness and the ability to fight to the death, if necessary, to defend the defenceless. A heartfelt tenderness, idealism, and compassion for others—especially for those unfairly deprived of power—may have moved you to acts of heroism. If you were among those who suffered deprivation or injustice, your determination may have been even stronger.

Virgo needs to feel needed, and you are probably no exception. For 1913 Virgo, giving can be as good as getting. Pisces' tenderness allows you to express your own. Cancer appreciates your thoughtful gestures. Never one to forget acts of generosity, Scorpio will reward you in kind.

You may have had to work hard to resolve the seeming contradiction in your character between vulnerability and toughness. Your strong Virgo commitment to service—military, humanitarian, or both—may have provided the means for expressing both aspects of your personality.

LIBRA

From September 23, 15:53 through October 24, 0:34

The Empowered Partner

In this day and age, no one would argue that the right to vote jeopardizes the virtues of motherhood. But in the month of your birth, Libra of 1913, suffragettes in New York contended with just such a problem. On October 15, 1913, these crusaders for political equality held public baby shows to prove that they were good mothers. Their sense of the times was probably correct. Within a few days of the baby shows, British suffragette Emmeline Pankhurst had been deported on the grounds of moral turpitude.

As a Libran, you are likely to have an acute appreciation for the kind of double standard applied to the suffragettes, simply because they were women. "If one could besmirch the morals of a man who demanded fair representation," you might argue, "we'd have to deport the Founding Fathers of the United States!" One of Libra's most potent symbols is the blindfolded goddess, holding the scales of justice. The blindfold stands for the essential Libran principle that justice must be dispensed equally, without regard for color, gender, or other personal traits.

In your lifetime, you have witnessed astonishing changes in the rights and roles of women. By the time you reached the age of majority, women in most western countries gained the vote. If you are a man, your own nurturing tendencies may have gained more opportunities for expression, especially as women in the workforce needed help with child rearing.

Power dynamics in your relationships were likely to shift as women gained new status and men adjusted accordingly. Because women were no longer limited to a dependent role, your marriage may have become a truer partnership. Gemini cheerfully adapts to change. Progressive Aquarius enjoys the freedom from traditional roles. Sagittarius enjoys everything that two incomes can buy!

Your challenge has been to adapt to changing relationships as gender roles changed. As divorce rates soared in later generations, your Libran ability to understand all sides of any issue may have eased any panic. You may feel that individual happiness is more important than outmoded customs.

➤ Read about your Chinese Astrological sign on page 838. ➤ Read about your Personal Planets on page 826. ➤ Read about your personal Mystical Card on page 856.

1913

VIRGO
Your Personal Planets

YOUR LOVE POTENTIAL
Venus in Cancer, Aug. 23, 18:48 - Sept. 01, 9:18
Venus in Leo, Sept. 01, 9:19 - Sept. 23, 15:52

YOUR DRIVE AND AMBITION
Mars in Gemini, Aug. 23, 18:48 - Sept. 15, 17:17
Mars in Cancer, Sept. 15, 17:18 - Sept. 23, 15:52

YOUR LUCK MAGNETISM
Jupiter in Capricorn, Aug. 23, 18:48 - Sept. 23, 15:52

World Events

Sept. 1 - A streetcar strike riot breaks out in Dublin; 500 are injured.

Sept. 6 - Dr. Hideyo Noguchi isolates the rabies germ.

The Gambia Dike is blown up, allowing the waters of the Atlantic and Pacific to join

LIBRA
Your Personal Planets

YOUR LOVE POTENTIAL
Venus in Leo, Sept. 23, 15:53 - Sept. 26, 16:03
Venus in Virgo, Sept. 26, 16:04 - Oct. 21, 6:01
Venus in Libra, Oct. 21, 6:02 - Oct. 24, 0:34

YOUR DRIVE AND AMBITION
Mars in Cancer, Sept. 23, 15:53 - Oct. 24, 0:34

YOUR LUCK MAGNETISM
Jupiter in Capricorn, Sept. 23, 15:53 - Oct. 24, 0:34

World Events

Oct. 6 - Yuan Shih-Kai is re-elected President of the Chinese Republic.

Oct. 17 - An airship explodes over London, killing twenty-eight people.

1913

SCORPIO
Your Personal Planets

YOUR LOVE POTENTIAL
Venus in Libra, Oct. 24, 0:35 - Nov. 14, 9:54
Venus in Scorpio, Nov. 14, 9:55 - Nov. 22, 21:34

YOUR DRIVE AND AMBITION
Mars in Cancer, Oct. 24, 0:35 - Nov. 22, 21:34

YOUR LUCK MAGNETISM
Jupiter in Capricorn, Oct. 24, 0:35 - Nov. 22, 21:34

World Events

Nov. 2 – American film star Burt Lancaster is born.

Nov. 6 – Mahatma Gandhi, leader of the Indian Passive Resistance Movement, is arrested by British troops.

Indian Ranbindranath Tagore, Nobel Prize winner

SAGITTARIUS
Your Personal Planets

YOUR LOVE POTENTIAL
Venus in Scorpio, Nov. 22, 21:35 - Dec. 08, 8:37
Venus in Sagittarius, Dec. 08, 8:38 - Dec. 22, 10:34

YOUR DRIVE AND AMBITION
Mars in Cancer, Nov. 22, 21:35 - Dec. 22, 10:34

YOUR LUCK MAGNETISM
Jupiter in Capricorn, Nov. 22, 21:35 - Dec. 22, 10:34

World Events

Dec. 10 – Indian Ranbindranath Tagore wins the Nobel Prize for literature.

Dec. 13 – The Mona Lisa is found undamaged in Florence, after its theft from the Louvre two years previously.

SCORPIO
From October 24, 0:35 through November 22, 21:34

The Deserving Taxpayer

The sign of Scorpio rules death, taxes, and mysticism. With seemingly mystical exactitude, the first income tax law in the United States went into effect on November 30, 1913, within days of your birth. You don't need an ironic Capricorn to point out the humor that the first American income tax law should happen to become effective during Scorpio's birthday month. On a more ominous note, unemployment in Germany left 443,000 jobless, a situation that heightened volatility within the general populace and played a role in propelling that country towards war.

The sign of Scorpio rules debt and psychology as well. Because you came of age during the Great Depression, you are likely to have a special sensitivity to such matters. When you were a teenager, the crash of the stock market may have felt like a betrayal by those in power. Such an early loss of innocence and faith in powerful institutions may have left you wary of big business and reluctant to take on loans or any kind of financial exposure later in life.

Having survived World War I and worldwide depression, and having been a member of the generation that fought in World War II, you may feel strongly about your right to benefit from programs that rebuilt countries and economies in the post-war era. You may have supported or benefited from the GI Bill, New Deal, the Marshall Plan, or similar programs in other countries.

Family relationships are likely to be crucial to your sense of security. The importance of being able to trust your associates may have moved you to rule out anyone but close relations as partners in business. Taurus maintains a tight grip on the plus side of the family balance sheet. Keeping promises is a high priority for practical Capricorn. Family loyalty means everything to Cancer and Leo.

If you live your life assuming that resources will always be scarce, you may actually make such conditions more likely to materialize. Strong gut instincts enable Scorpio to know a sound investment from a get rich quick scam. By trusting yourself, you can afford to ease up on the tendency toward caution.

SAGITTARIUS
From November 22, 21:35 through December 22, 10:34

The Scrappy Competitor

When you were born, 1913 Sagittarius, the world gained two early holiday presents: one, of course, was you; the other was the recovery of the Mona Lisa. The celebrated painting had been stolen from the Louvre in August of 1911. The thief, Luigi Perugia, was caught when he tried to sell the painting to an antique dealer in Florence, Italy. Your parents might have laughed at Perugia's foolishness in thinking that he would be able to sell a painting as famous as Da Vinci's masterpiece.

The mystery of the missing Mona Lisa and its happy resolution provided a much-needed diversion in the months leading up to World War I. Although you would have been too young to remember most of those war years, you may have sensed the tension among adults around you. Likely to be an unusually perceptive child, you may have responded by telling stories or trying to amuse the grown-ups around you.

Having known only wartime in the earliest years of your life, you may not have realized that such events were terribly out of the ordinary. Such preparation may have equipped you to take adversity in stride in adulthood. Indeed, anger is likely to be emotionally energizing for you. Naturally competitive, you may have been one of the kids who liked to play rough. When it came to teasing, you probably could take as much as you could dish out. In adulthood, you might have acquired a taste for a good intellectual scrap.

You are likely to need hearty partners who can keep up with you. The ability to fight in a healthy way may be necessary to keep things interesting. Willing to go head-to-head, Aries appreciates the chance to let off steam. Mischievous Gemini enjoys a mental challenge. Aquarius welcomes your candor as well as the opportunity to shock you now and then.

In your youth, you may not have realized the force of your own personality. Others may have taken offense at times, when you thought you were only joking. Your dearest friends are likely to adore you for your candor and directness. With maturity, you may have learned how to adapt your tone to the sensitivities of your audience.

➤ Read about your Chinese Astrological sign on page 838. ➤ Read about your Personal Planets on page 826. ➤ Read about your personal Mystical Card on page 856.

CAPRICORN

From December 22, 10:35 through December 31, 23:59

The Resilient Manager

Within days of your birth, Capricorn, the President of the United States founded an institution that would play an integral role in the functioning of the world economy. On December 23, 1913, President Wilson founded the Federal Reserve System for banking. For years to come, the Federal Reserve would regulate the U.S. economy by raising or lowering interest rates as necessary to stimulate growth or slow down inflation. Financial markets in other countries would monitor the Federal Reserve for worldwide implications of the fluctuations in its policy.

The sign of Capricorn rules public institutions that provide for the orderly flow of commerce. For you, however, the most important developments would come in the 1930s and 1940s as governments passed legislation to regulate and rebuild corporate infrastructure. Having lived through the massive foreclosures and loss of savings in the Great Depression, you may have taken a keen personal interest in the development of regulatory schemes designed to protect middle class families and individual investors.

You are likely to be a talented businessperson with a gift for engaging in profitable negotiations. You may have taken some hard knocks in the course of your career, but your chart indicates an unusual resilience and resistance to intimidation. You may have also enjoyed a lot of luck in your business partnerships.

You've had to maintain your family and intimate relationships under the extreme conditions of war and economic depression. Staying together through the tough times is a high priority for Capricorn. Cancer's respect for traditional values enhances your sense of security. Taurus provides a firm foundation for family. Virgo affirms your sense of duty.

Early in adulthood, you may have suffered a sudden loss of assets due to unforeseen developments or the actions of an unscrupulous person. Such experiences may have made you wish you had listened to your instincts or taken control of things, yourself. Having learned your lesson, you were likely to rely on the strong management skills for which Capricorn is famous.

1913

CAPRICORN
Your Personal Planets

YOUR LOVE POTENTIAL
Venus in Sagittarius, Dec. 22, 10:35 - Dec. 31, 23:59

YOUR DRIVE AND AMBITION
Mars in Cancer, Dec. 22, 10:35 - Dec. 31, 23:59

YOUR LUCK MAGNETISM
Jupiter in Capricorn, Dec. 22, 10:35 - Dec. 31, 23:59

World Events

Dec. 23 – U.S. President Wilson creates the Federal Reserve System, a government-controlled banking system.

Dec. 30 – Britain and Germany agree to divide Portugal's African possessions.

"Titanic" survivors in a lifeboat

Special Feature
The Titanic: Prophecies, Legends, and Destiny

(Continued from page 113)

Even more exciting for Stead was the fact that he would sail to the U.S. on the *Titanic*! Days before, Shaw Desmond had the premonition that Stead would die in the very near future. Though the feeling was overwhelming, Desmond did not share his feelings with his mentor. He did, however, write down his premonition. Stead was, indeed, one of *Titanic's* casualties. Major Archibald Butt, a military aide to President Taft, was returning from his European vacation aboard the *Titanic*. Before leaving for Europe, Butt had an unshakable sense of approaching calamity and told several people about his trepidation. In fact, he even wanted to cancel his trip. But Taft was so convinced that Butt needed a rest that he insisted that his aide stick to his plans. Butt, too, perished on the *Titanic*.

Just as they do for people, astrologers cast horoscopes for events too. The astrological chart for the maiden voyage of the *Titanic* has its Sun in fiery, headstrong, and often reckless Aries.

With this Sun-sign placement, it's no wonder that the *Titanic* thrust full-throttle ahead to collide with its destiny. The Sun, which represents the ship and its voyage, is making a challenging and destructive contact with Neptune, symbol of the sea. Neptune is also associated with illusion, deception, psychic phenomena, and drowning, all of which are associated with *Titanic*. Certainly, the White Star Line fostered the illusion that the *Titanic* was "unsinkable" and, as a result, its passengers had a false sense of safety. Neptune is also making a challenging contact with the Nodes of the Moon, the points in a chart that have to do with group destiny, forever linking these 2,227 people through their shared experience at sea, whether they survived or perished. However the most chilling point is that Venus, the planet that in this chart governs the "end of the matter," is together with Scheat, a fixed star that the ancient Greeks associated with shipwreck.

Nearly one hundred years later, the story of the *Titanic* still fascinates many. Perhaps, its allure is that so much remains unexplained about the voyage. Or maybe we are collectively bound to this event through psychic forces that we have yet to understand. ✪

➤ Read about missing ships at sea in "The Mysterious Bermuda Triangle" on page 385.

1914

The Pain of War: Saturn and Pluto

On June 28, a nineteen-year-old Bosnian student, Gavrilo Princip, assassinated Archduke Franz Ferdinand and his wife in Sarajevo, lighting the spark that began the horrors of World War I. The significant astrological indicator was Saturn, planet of structure, moving towards Pluto, planet of deep and penetrating transformation. By August, both planets were in internal, moody Cancer, signifying change at the root of consciousness. Family and the home are also implicated in this aspect. During World War I, families were torn apart as young boys from all over the world died in battle. Millions died and the landscape of Belgium and northern France was devastated. It was the first time that global warfare touched everyone's life at the core. War was no longer understood as something that happened in other places to other people. Civilians far away from the frontline in England experienced aerial bombardment for the first time in history. Truly, this was a modern war and the previous rules of engagement had been thrown away.

Saturn and Pluto are often involved in the charts of wars. These planets seem to eviscerate life itself so that new ways of understanding can be born. During the first two world wars, at many points in the Israeli-Palestinian conflict, in Vietnam, and finally, on the fateful day of September 11, 2001, challenging aspects between these planets played a significant role. Saturn represents the status quo, structure and stability and when it contacts earth-shaking Pluto, the inevitable changes of life must be faced and accepted. During a period of darkness such as World War I, changes in the global scene were reflected by changes in the conscious minds of individuals. The pain felt at the loss of so much life touched every soul.

Saturn-Pluto contacts bring this depth to bear on a global scale so that people are forced to face their darkest demons. With so much loss of life, it is impossible not to confront one's own mortality. Under the complex and painful influence of Saturn and Pluto energies, people face their dark night of the soul, but they usually emerge on the other side transformed. There is indeed light at the end of this astrological tunnel.

Archduke Franz Ferdinand and his wife were assassinated

Germany invades Belgium

Zeppelins bomb London

ASSASSINATION TRIGGERS EUROPEAN WAR

Teetering on the edge of conflict, a series of alliances drove European nations closer to confrontation when a nineteen-year-old Serb student assassinated the Archduke Ferdinand, heir to the Austrian throne, and his wife, at Sarajevo. Already distrustful of each other, Austria and Russia staked rival claims in the Balkans, while Germany, France, and Britain engaged in an arms build-up. As Russia battled Germany and Austria on Germany's eastern boundary, Germany appeared unstoppable, assaulting Belgium, France, and Luxembourg in the west. Aerial combat introduced a new and deadly form of warfare. In the first three weeks of the war, 500,000 men on each side had been killed, wounded or captured. The Mexican Revolution wore on, and the U.S. intervened with a blockade aimed at preventing German armaments reaching Mexico. The U.S. remained neutral in the European war and the economy boomed. The Panama Canal opened for traffic. Ford assembly-line workers earned $5 per day plus profit share. Paramount Pictures, founded by Cecil B. De Mille and Sam Goldwyn, released its first movies. Charlie Chaplin made his first film, *Making a Living*.

▶ Read Isadora Duncan's Star Profile on page 129.

CAPRICORN

From January 01, 0:00 through January 20, 21:11

The Protective Innovator

As a Capricorn born in January of 1914, you might have invented the phrase "win-win proposition." Born after the development of key improvements in technology, your outlook may be quite different from your parents'. In 1913, industrialist Henry Ford had introduced the assembly line, an innovation that enabled him to multiply output and profits. Some might ask, "If it was his idea, why should he have to share the benefits?" But you'd have preferred measures that promote fairness, recognizing that even the most sophisticated production line couldn't run without workers.

In fact, any true blue Capricorn would probably appreciate the shrewd idea of preempting labor unrest by giving workers a fair wage and an interest in the future of their company. And that is exactly what Ford did within days of your birth, announcing on February 5, 1914, that he would pay his workers a minimum wage of $5 a day and a share in company profits. Looking back on this news, you might have wondered why it astounded the business world, given that violent labor riots involving thousands of workers were raging worldwide at the time.

In your career and your personal life, you're likely to feel that conflict is wasteful. You may have had occasion to persuade the old guard to adopt new ways, but you're likely to treat friends and colleagues as family and you probably enjoy taking care of people who depend on you. You may show your affection for others by doing business with them and finding jobs for their loved ones.

In love, it's likely that you'll be most compatible with Cancerians, who also view the world as one big family, or Taureans who also love to share the wealth. With you, Virgos would feel needed and appreciated. Needless to say, any of them could have felt fortunate if they had a chance to share their life with you.

Your challenge is to be sensitive to people's concerns about change, and to show them that the progress you seek would not come at anyone's expense. One of your greatest gifts is that you have often been able to defuse conflict and restore stability, even in the midst of change.

AQUARIUS

From January 20, 21:12 through February 19, 11:37

The Freedom Seeker

The art of movies may be a matter for Pisces, but the science of filmmaking is all Aquarius. Any Aquarian would be excited by the concept of an industry built upon ideas, energy charges, and modern technology, so it's probably no surprise to learn that the cornerstone of just such an industry was being laid as you were entering the world, Aquarius of 1914.

At this time, Cecil B. De Mille was taking the first steps in establishing Hollywood as the entertainment capital of the world. Perhaps few people would think of the tyranny of patent law as an instigating factor in the rise of Hollywood but, in fact, one of the reasons behind the emergence of the film industry in Hollywood was the desire of artists and producers to escape the monopoly control held by a certain innovator in motion picture technology in New Jersey—Thomas Edison.

Freedom of any kind can be a core value of your sign, and to you, it would probably make perfect sense to go west in search of creative freedom. Because you're likely to bridle against any kind of constraint on your creative or social freedom, you too may have been someone who would drop everything and head for new shores. You may have tried a number of different careers, and the idea of saving for the future probably didn't occur to you until relatively late in life. When it did, though, you may have saved enough in just a few years to take care of your old age.

In love, you may have been among the first to question traditional roles in relationships. You might have looked for a partner who is as original, forward thinking, and open minded as you are. It's likely you could find them among the Geminis of your acquaintance, who love to experiment with new ways of thinking, but a Leo also can elevate individualism to a high art, and an idealistic Pisces would never be an oppressive partner for you.

Your challenge is always to break away from the confines of tradition, and you may never feel comfortable among conservatives. Your gift is the ability to make new friends, which enables you to find a place among like-minded trendsetters wherever you are.

1914

CAPRICORN
Your Personal Planets

YOUR LOVE POTENTIAL
Venus in Sagittarius, Jan. 01, 0:00 - Jan. 01, 5:24
Venus in Capricorn, Jan. 01, 5:25 - Jan. 20, 21:11

YOUR DRIVE AND AMBITION
Mars in Cancer, Jan. 01, 0:00 - Jan. 20, 21:11

YOUR LUCK MAGNETISM
Jupiter in Capricorn, Jan. 01, 0:00 - Jan. 20, 21:11

World Events

Jan. 5 – Henry Ford astounds the business World by announcing a minimum wage of $5 a day.

Jan. 16 – Maxim Gorky is authorized to return to Russia after an eight-year exile for political dissidence.

Russian dissident, Maxim Gorky

AQUARIUS
Your Personal Planets

YOUR LOVE POTENTIAL
Venus in Capricorn, Jan. 20, 21:12 - Jan. 25, 2:08
Venus in Aquarius, Jan. 25, 2:09 - Feb. 18, 0:04
Venus in Pisces, Feb. 18, 0:05 - Feb. 19, 11:37

YOUR DRIVE AND AMBITION
Mars in Cancer, Jan. 20, 21:12 - Feb. 19, 11:37

YOUR LUCK MAGNETISM
Jupiter in Capricorn, Jan. 20, 21:12 - Jan. 21, 15:12
Jupiter in Aquarius, Jan. 21, 15:13 - Feb. 19, 11:37

World Events

Feb. 2 – In Mexico, Pancho Villa shoots Francisco Guzman, a messenger for President Diaz.

Feb. 3 – In Britain, suffragettes attempt to register to vote.

➤ Read about your Chinese Astrological sign on page 838. ➤ Read about your Personal Planets on page 826. ➤ Read about your personal Mystical Card on page 856.

123

1914

PISCES
Your Personal Planets

YOUR LOVE POTENTIAL
Venus in Pisces, Feb. 19, 11:38 - Mar. 14, 0:29
Venus in Aries, Mar. 14, 0:30 - Mar. 21, 11:10
YOUR DRIVE AND AMBITION
Mars in Cancer, Feb. 19, 11:38 - Mar. 21, 11:10
YOUR LUCK MAGNETISM
Jupiter in Aquarius, Feb. 19, 11:38 - Mar. 21, 11:10

World Events

Mar. 1 – American author Ralph Ellison is born.

Mar. 4 – Dr. Fillatre performs the first successful operation to separate Siamese twins in Paris.

British actor Alec Guinness is born under the sign of Aries

ARIES
Your Personal Planets

YOUR LOVE POTENTIAL
Venus in Aries, Mar. 21, 11:11 - Apr. 07, 4:47
Venus in Taurus, Apr. 07, 4:48 - Apr. 20, 22:52
YOUR DRIVE AND AMBITION
Mars in Cancer, Mar. 21, 11:11 - Apr. 20, 22:52
YOUR LUCK MAGNETISM
Jupiter in Aquarius, Mar. 21, 11:11 - Apr. 20, 22:52

World Events

Apr. 1 – Guglielmo Marconi conducts the first wireless tests from a train.

Apr. 2 – British actor Alec Guinness is born.

PISCES
From February 19, 11:38 through March 21, 11:10

The Sensitive Intuitive

An important contemporary of yours faced challenges that exemplify certain qualities and experiences you may have shared as a Pisces. Author Ralph Ellison was born on March 1, 1914, in Oklahoma City, Oklahoma. In 1952, he published *The Invisible Man*, a novel that set off a controversy over its depiction of events in the life of an African American man. Having grown up in radically changing times, you may identify with Ellison's depiction of the struggle to find one's own identity, Pisces of 1914.

Because your sign rules the realm of invisibility, the very title of Ellison's book evokes a quintessential Piscean theme. Just as Ellison's main character spoke about feeling invisible as a black man living in a white culture, Pisceans in the company of strongly assertive people may often feel that they're being treated as if they're not there. Because of this, you may have tended to emphasize others' needs and priorities to the detriment of your own.

With your sensitivity and keen intuition, it may have been difficult for you to feel at ease in the world of commerce. Your people skills may have led you to a career in teaching or counseling, where you would probably have been happy to let others take the credit if it would keep the spotlight away from you. Even your friends, who would have known how talented you are, might have given up trying to push you on stage when they saw how uncomfortable it made you.

When it comes to romance, joining up with a nurturing Cancer could have offered emotional validation. Or you may have gravitated toward partners with strong personalities, which you might have found among the fire signs of Aries, Leo, and Sagittarius. Capricorn is the best teacher of personal boundaries and integrity, and could well have offered you the support you need. But Aquarius respects your individuality, and may have been the one who won your heart.

Your challenge is to gain a solid self-image and find the courage to stand in your own truth. Your gift is your uncanny ability to see into people's minds and hearts, and your compassion for what you find there.

ARIES
From March 21, 11:11 through April 20, 22:52

The Patriotic Warrior

Your sign rules war, warriors, and military power, so it's probably no surprise that the beginning of World War I was the most significant event of your birth year, Aries of 1914. While war had not yet broken out, a sense of its inevitability was everywhere in the weeks leading up to your birth. All the great powers were arming themselves. Winston Churchill, then Britain's First Lord of the Admiralty, led a drive to build eight British squadrons for every five built by the Germans. Military expenditures consumed the majority of Austria-Hungary's budget. Russia planned a fourfold increase of its army. The U.S. had arranged for the prompt mobilization of 500,000 troops some months previously.

Indeed, it's likely that your earliest memories were formed amidst a world at war. As an Aries, you have the power to identify your objectives and work relentlessly until you reach them. But as an Aries of 1914, your key qualities may be your passionate convictions and willingness to put your life on the line. Many 1914 Ariens probably went on to careers in the military, and while some may have been fighting to promote their country's power-seeking ambitions, you might have been a warrior against nationalism, war, and man's inhumanity to man.

You're probably not known for your patience. However, in an effort to learn how to wait (only when you absolutely had to), you might have taken up a hobby that required it. You may have been a Sunday painter or an amateur horticulturist, and learned from nature how to let things develop at their own pace.

In love, you may have wanted a partner who was resilient enough to relocate and rebuild if necessary. You might be most compatible with a Sagittarius, who can maintain excellent morale while on the move, or a Leo, who is fiercely protective of home and family. But you'd also probably appreciate a Gemini's ability to learn new things quickly and lightning-fast repartee.

Your challenge is to make a secure place in the world. Your gift is that, having learned the lessons of history, you've gained the wisdom to avoid repeating its mistakes.

► Read about your Chinese Astrological sign on page 838. ► Read about your Personal Planets on page 826. ► Read about your personal Mystical Card on page 856.

TAURUS

The Unpretentious Noble

Taurus rules sumptuous displays and the breathless fascination people have with fabulous wealth. On April 21, 1914—in the midst of an international arms race, violent labor unrest, and militant suffrage agitation—hundreds of thousands of Parisians came out to catch a glimpse of King George and Queen Mary of Great Britain, making a public appearance in Paris as guests of the French government. Celebrating the friendship between the two nations, British and French flags decorated all the major streets. French citizens must have delighted in imagining themselves at the banquets that were held for the royal couple.

Perhaps, later on, when you learned in school about this royal visit, you might have found it amusing that the same country that once executed its own king and queen could so easily reveal its enchantment with pageantry and nobility. As a Taurus, however, you may understand the appeal of such events. The royal appearance provided a welcome diversion from otherwise unpleasant events in the news, and you too may rely on earthly pleasures for relief from life's challenges.

Your Taurean motto might be, "Every man a king, and every woman a queen." With the rise of the middle class in your lifetime, you could enjoy privileges that were once exclusive to the princely class, such as owning your own home. Having good manners afforded you the refinement of noble courtesy. Even in progressive times, such values may satisfy Taurus' conservative leanings.

You may have sought partners who could enjoy sharing the good life, and extravagance wouldn't be as important to you as an ability to stop and smell the roses. Like you, Scorpio takes pleasure in the good things in life, but a Leo, who brings a royal procession through your living room every night, may have won your heart.

You may have had to live through times of extreme scarcity in your life. Even through worldwide depression and war, you would always have had your Taurean ability to savor any good thing, no matter how modest. You can feed your soul by focusing on the pleasures of a sunset, a butterfly, a soft rain.

GEMINI

Publicist for Reform

Gemini favors free expression and the open flow of ideas, but remains neutral about the substance of messages. The life of Jacob Riis—who died on May 26, 1914—illustrates how open communication naturally promotes democratic and humanitarian aims. Having emigrated to New York City from Denmark, Riis went on to publish the books, *How The Other Half Lives* and *The Battle With The Slum*, each a moving indictment of urban poverty and economic inequality. Through vivid photography and textual observations, Riis allowed his subject matter to tell its own story. His work earned him the friendship of Teddy Roosevelt and laid the foundation for housing codes, urban renewal, and public housing.

You have been a witness to history, Gemini of 1914, having lived through the most extraordinary changes in the lifetime of humanity and their catastrophic consequences— inhumane labor conditions, women's political disenfranchisement, worldwide economic depression, two genocidal world wars. By giving voice to such matters, you could allow the truth of their horror to make the case for change.

In your lifetime, you have been able to select from an array of new technologies to spread awareness of these issues. You may have written books, articles, or letters. You may have spoken publicly in strikes or demonstrations, or taken your cause to the radio or television airwaves. In providing such publicity, Gemini abides by the credo: "The truth will out."

It's likely that your home resounded with spirited conversation and active intellectual exchanges, and you might have looked for a partner who shares your love of learning and knowledge. Compatible love signs for you can be Sagittarius, who values higher education, exploration, and truth, or Virgo who brings an encyclopedic knowledge base and a knack for research.

Later generations may have nagged you to stop taking world events so personally. They may not understand the personal impact such matters had in your day. Still, you have a vast and untapped capacity for emotional intimacy. Enjoying the love of family is a privilege you've earned.

➤ Read about your Chinese Astrological sign on page 838. ➤ Read about your Personal Planets on page 826. ➤ Read about your personal Mystical Card on page 856.

1914

TAURUS
Your Personal Planets

YOUR LOVE POTENTIAL
Venus in Taurus, Apr. 20, 22:53 - May 01, 14:10
Venus in Gemini, May 01, 14:11 - May 21, 22:37

YOUR DRIVE AND AMBITION
Mars in Cancer, Apr. 20, 22:53 - May 01, 20:30
Mars in Leo, May 01, 20:31 - May 21, 22:37

YOUR LUCK MAGNETISM
Jupiter in Aquarius, Apr. 20, 22:53 - May 21, 22:37

World Events

May 3 – Fights in the Russian Duma lead to the expulsion of Social Democratic members.

May 6 – The British House of Lords rejects the women's suffrage bill.

Jean Sibelius, Finnish composer, is awarded an honorary degree from Yale

GEMINI
Your Personal Planets

YOUR LOVE POTENTIAL
Venus in Gemini, May 21, 22:38 - May 26, 5:33
Venus in Cancer, May 26, 5:34 - June 20, 4:25
Venus in Leo, June 20, 4:26 - June 22, 6:54

YOUR DRIVE AND MAGNETISM
Mars in Leo, May 21, 22:38 - June 22, 6:54

YOUR LUCK MAGNETISM
Jupiter in Aquarius, May 21, 22:38 - June 22, 6:54

World Events

June 7 – The first boat passes through the Panama Canal.

June 20 – Germany launches the *Bismarck*, the largest liner yet built.

1914

CANCER
Your Personal Planets

YOUR LOVE POTENTIAL

Venus in Leo, June 22, 6:55 - July 15, 14:09
Venus in Virgo, July 15, 14:10 - July 23, 17:46

YOUR DRIVE AND AMBITION

Mars in Leo, June 22, 6:55 - June 26, 4:47
Mars in Virgo, June 26, 4:48 - July 23, 17:46

YOUR LUCK MAGNETISM

Jupiter in Aquarius, June 22, 6:55 - July 23, 17:46

World Events

June 27 – African American boxer Jack Johnson retains the heavyweight title, defeating Frank Moran in twenty rounds in Paris.

June 28 – A nineteen-year-old Bosnian student, Gavrilo Princip, assassinates Austrian Archduke Franz Ferdinand and his wife in Sarajevo.

Archduke Franz Ferdinand and his wife on the day they were assassinated

LEO
Your Personal Planets

YOUR LOVE POTENTIAL

Venus in Virgo, July 23, 17:47 - Aug. 10, 18:10
Venus in Libra, Aug. 10, 18:11 - Aug. 24, 0:29

YOUR DRIVE AND AMBITION

Mars in Virgo, July 23, 17:47 - Aug. 14, 14:09
Mars in Libra, Aug. 14, 14:10 - Aug. 24, 0:29

YOUR LUCK MAGNETISM

Jupiter in Aquarius, July 23, 17:47 - Aug. 24, 0:29

World Events

July 28 – Austria-Hungary declares war on Serbia, initiating World War I.

Aug. 4 – Germany invades neutral Belgium, causing Britain to enter the war.

CANCER
From June 22, 6:55 through July 23, 17:46

Survivor of the Flood

You may be far too modest to call yourself the mother or father of humanity, Cancer of 1914, but in a way you, like "Nuhu," are the first in a new generation. Nuhu is the hero of a pre-biblical account of the Great Flood that was inscribed on Babylonian tablets and deciphered by an Oxford University professor on June 14, 1914. In the ancient Babylonian version of the Noah story, Nuhu, a gardener, saved the world from disaster during the Flood and became the father of humankind. Similarly, your generation may have saved humanity—first in the Great Depression and then again in World War II.

Like Nuhu, you may have had to gather up your valuables and set out—literally or metaphorically—into the unknown. Cancer rules the home, family, and parenthood, and you would intuitively safeguard and preserve the precious values and customs of the past for the benefit of future generations. At the end of these crises, you may have had to build a new life, a new family, or a new home.

You may operate from instinct and you can have a knack of knowing how to make people feel at home when they're with you. This could have drawn people to you in droves, and finding time to do the things that you enjoyed may have been a challenge. Your "hobbies" may have been doing the things that were needed to take care of your home and the people who tended to fill it at all hours of the day and night. For this reason, you may have become a gourmet cook or a talented tailor in your "spare time."

Cancer of 1914 would need a partner who could be a rock of stability in difficult times. You may have looked to resourceful Capricorn, who keeps the faith over the long term, to Taurus, who would help you hold the family together and rebuild, or to Scorpio, who holds the power of life and regeneration.

After 1945, you may have had difficulty readjusting your assumptions about the world and continued habits founded on scarcity and imminent danger. Yet Cancer's role as guardian of tradition produces a miraculous reward—you can pass the torch to the next generation and perhaps bring security to the world.

LEO
From July 23, 17:47 through August 24, 0:29

Baptized by Fire

Around the time you were born, Leo of 1914, the world was having its baptism by fire. Following the assassination of Archduke Franz Ferdinand of Austria in June, declarations of war resounded all over the world. First Austria's against Serbia, on July 28, and then on through August, as one after the other of the great European powers, the Ottoman Empire, and even Japan plunged into the conflagration. With the introduction of mechanized warfare, World War I would prove to be the deadliest conflict yet known to humanity.

In the years ahead the world would suffer a tragic loss of innocence. In one day of warfare, thousands of bright-eyed boys might eagerly take their field positions—trenches fashioned after nineteenth-century conventions—only to see their ranks decimated under the murderous fire of machine guns, tanks, and warplanes. Occurring during your formative years, this rude shock to humanity's system could not but have affected your perception of the world and your sense of safety.

Even so, your love of the spotlight may have put you at the center of things as an adult, no matter what occupation you chose. You probably loved making an entrance, and would have dazzled any audience you found. Your friends may have been your biggest fans, and many would have followed you anywhere. You may have enjoyed giving little gifts to show people how much you appreciated them, and it's likely that those gifts were treasured keepsakes for years.

In love, you were likely to join up with a resourceful partner, preferably one who was wise enough to let you rule the roost (or at least think you did). You could probably make a good match with one of the Virgos, Cancerians, or Sagittarians of your acquaintance.

Since Leo rules children and the archetype of the child, it was your challenge to cope with the loss of innocence that marred the world into which you were born. In the course of your life, you may have had to find new causes or new countries that merited your loyalty. But Leos are known for loyalty, and finding them may have been your opportunity to recreate your innocence.

► Read about your Chinese Astrological sign on page 838. ► Read about your Personal Planets on page 826. ► Read about your personal Mystical Card on page 856.

VIRGO

From August 24, 0:30 through September 23, 21:33

The Fruitful Laborer

Within days of your birth, Virgo of 1914, the first crucial battles of World War I were fought at Mons and the Marne. The fighting culminated in victory by French and British troops over German forces in the Battle of the Marne. However, it would be a Pyrrhic victory. Just the first three weeks of World War I claimed the lives of more than 500,000 soldiers—250,000 allied soldiers and more than 250,000 on the German side.

The turning point of the battle came at Fère Champenoise, when a ragtag army of Moroccans, Senegalese, young boys, and old men held off the Second Army of German General Karl von Bulow. The clash poised the imperial aspirations of the German state against a group of soldiers whose motivations in defending France would become clearer in the light of history. As colonial subjects, the Moroccans and Senegalese had nothing to gain by fighting for France—except perhaps their liberty—and their gallantry in battle would in fact make the case for their liberation years later.

Similarly, as a Virgo, you may regard your own good works as the means of earning just rewards in life. Just as the colonial French subjects proved their loyalty to their "father country," you too may place a high premium on loyalty to those who have taken you into their care and may be extremely protective toward those who depend on you. As you find yourself among different groups of people, you may recreate family-like bonds and encourage emotional attachments to shared goals and achievements.

In relationships, you will probably work tirelessly to ensure the best for your loved ones. Compatible love signs for you include Cancer, who shows you that caring is a two-way street, Pisces, whose vulnerability can make you feel needed, and Capricorn, who admires your work ethic and honors your loyalty.

A tendency to see the world and relationships through family-oriented eyes may lead you to expect perfection for and from loved ones. Virgo is a fruitful, nurturing sign, though, and your loved ones may have taught you that your hugs have been as rich as the good living you have provided.

LIBRA

From September 23, 21:34 through October 24, 6:16

The Peaceful Negotiator

Librans often provide an island of sanity in the midst of chaos, and such a situation prevailed within days of your birth, 1914 Libra. On October 15, the U.S. Congress voted the Clayton Act into law. Hailed as "the Magna Carta for the Working Man," the Clayton Act exempted labor unions from prosecution under antitrust law and legitimized the union movement in the United States. Elsewhere in the world, massive labor revolts had ground to a sudden halt due to the overwhelming demands of World War I. But as the Russian Revolution would prove only three years later, even world war could not indefinitely quell laborers' demands for justice, equality, and a fair day's pay.

Libra rules contracts and negotiation, and the Clayton Act imposed a fundamental change in industrial labor relations. By legalizing the practice of collective bargaining, the Clayton Act made it possible for workers to gain bargaining power against management. You may have been among those who enjoyed the fair wage and hour standards and improved working conditions that collective bargaining won for workers and their families.

In general, Librans are gifted negotiators, and in your career you may have served as a union delegate or management negotiator. No one is more sociable or easier to get along with than you are, and it's likely that you would have worked to establish a legitimate and peaceful means for resolving conflicts between labor and management.

In love, you may have enjoyed greater equality in your relationships than others of your generation. You may have stunned your family by cohabiting with or divorcing a partner. Signs that fit well with you are rebellious Aquarius, who supports unconventional lifestyles, fiery Aries, often the first to set new relationship trends, or mercurial Gemini, who enjoys the freedom to nurture their partner's individuality.

Your challenge has been to devise new ways for relationships to function—whether in the workplace, between people, or between governments. Your gift is your ability to reconcile people's competing needs in ways that can work for everybody.

➤ Read about your Chinese Astrological sign on page 838. ➤ Read about your Personal Planets on page 826. ➤ Read about your personal Mystical Card on page 856.

1914

VIRGO
Your Personal Planets

YOUR LOVE POTENTIAL
Venus in Libra, Aug. 24, 0:30 - Sept. 07, 10:57
Venus in Scorpio, Sept. 07, 10:58 - Sept. 23, 21:33

YOUR DRIVE AND AMBITION
Mars in Libra, Aug. 24, 0:30 - Sept. 23, 21:33

YOUR LUCK MAGNETISM
Jupiter in Aquarius, Aug. 24, 0:30 - Sept. 23, 21:33

World Events

Sept. 5 – The first Battle of the Marne begins on the western front.

Sept. 7 – Scientist James Van Allen is born.

The destruction caused by the first Zeppelin raids on London

LIBRA
Your Personal Planets

YOUR LOVE POTENTIAL
Venus in Scorpio, Sept. 23, 21:34 - Oct. 10, 1:48
Venus in Sagittarius, Oct. 10, 1:49 - Oct. 24, 6:16

YOUR DRIVE AND AMBITION
Mars in Libra, Sept. 23, 21:34 - Sept. 29, 10:37
Mars in Scorpio, Sept. 29, 10:38 - Oct. 24, 6:16

YOUR LUCK MAGNETISM
Jupiter in Aquarius, Sept. 23, 21:34 - Oct. 24, 6:16

World Events

Oct. 4 – The first German zeppelin raids are made on London.

Oct. 9 – The Germans capture Antwerp after nearly two weeks of siege.

1914

SCORPIO
Your Personal Planets

YOUR LOVE POTENTIAL
Venus in Sagittarius, Oct. 24, 6:17 - Nov. 23, 3:19

YOUR DRIVE AND AMBITION
Mars in Scorpio, Oct. 24, 6:17 - Nov. 11, 10:46
Mars in Sagittarius, Nov. 11, 10:47 - Nov. 23, 3:19

YOUR LUCK MAGNETISM
Jupiter in Aquarius, Oct. 24, 6:17 - Nov. 23, 3:19

World Events

Oct. 27 – British poet Dylan Thomas is born.

Oct. 29 – The Turkish government declares war on the Allies by bombarding Odessa, Sevastopol and Theodosia.

Admiral Von Spee's ships at the Falkland Islands

SAGITTARIUS
Your Personal Planets

YOUR LOVE POTENTIAL
Venus in Sagittarius, Nov. 23, 3:20 - Dec. 05, 23:19
Venus in Scorpio, Dec. 05, 23:20 - Dec. 22, 16:21

YOUR DRIVE AND AMBITION
Mars in Sagittarius, Nov. 23, 3:20 - Dec. 22, 3:48
Mars in Capricorn, Dec. 22, 3:49 - Dec. 22, 16:21

YOUR LUCK MAGNETISM
Jupiter in Aquarius, Nov. 23, 3:20 - Dec. 22, 16:21

World Events

Dec. 8 – Admiral Von Spee's fleet is destroyed by British Admiral Sturdee at the Falkland Islands, emphasizing British naval supremacy.

Dec. 9 – The Turks halt the British offensive in Mesopotamia and occupy Akaba.

SCORPIO
From October 24, 6:17 through November 23, 3:19

The World Transformer

Scorpio rules war and world trends. Combine these, and you have the most prominent historical event occurring at the time of your birth, Scorpio of 1914—World War I. Over your lifetime, however, you may have been concerned with events occurring on a deeper level. The 1914 chart for Scorpio shows something more at stake than the competing claims to supremacy among the Great Powers. In fact, World War I marked the beginning of a massive transformation in the structure and dynamics of world power, a process that would continue into the twenty-first century.

You belong to a generation that spearheaded the most dramatic period of change in human history. As you saw for yourself, even the winning side of the "war to end all wars" would lose to larger forces that ultimately brought an end to imperialist forms of government. At the close of the twentieth century, the great powers, stripped of their colonial subjects, had become just plain democratic countries, whose governments derived their legitimacy from the people.

As a Scorpio, you may have had an intuitive understanding of the way progress was affecting everything. You would have seen that gaining political rights ultimately would saddle you with the power and responsibility to decide what to do with yourself and your life. On the other hand, the sense that anything was possible may have made you feel a part of humanity's evolution.

As the world changed, relationships changed with it. Your best partners would be able to grow and evolve with you. Bold, pioneering Aries may have dazzled you with a passion for new possibilities. Leo's courage may have emboldened you to take on new challenges. Cancer's ability to move with new cycles of growth can inspire you.

Members of your sign may tend to expect progress to go hand in hand with fear. In fact, a Scorpio might have inspired U.S. President Franklin D. Roosevelt's famous declaration, "The only thing we have to fear is fear itself." By tapping into your deepest wells of strength, though, you have been uniquely qualified to conquer any challenge that has confronted you.

SAGITTARIUS
From November 23, 3:20 through December 22, 16:21

The Wise Diplomat

By the time of your birth, Sagittarius of 1914, long-simmering tensions among countries had boiled over into the raging conflagration of World War I. Much of the conflict involved competing claims by the major European powers for dominion over other countries. For example, on December 16, in a move to protect its interests in the Suez Canal, Britain declared Egypt a protectorate—an action that would incite the hostilities of the Ottoman Empire.

Because your sign rules matters of government and foreign countries, Sagittarius might be called the "Secretary of State" of the zodiac. When you were old enough to study the Great War, you were likely to be fascinated by the interaction among countries and how the war itself set in motion certain long-term trends, in which the "vassal countries," such as Egypt, India, and Morocco, secured their independence later in the century.

Other indicators in your chart suggest that you may have talents usually described as Libran. You may be a talented negotiator, able to appreciate both sides of a conflict and devise winning compromises. Although you may be competitive, you are likely to be a gracious winner. Sagittarius generally has a knack for legal thinking. You might have had a career as a transactional attorney, contract mediator, or foreign relations expert.

Intellectually sophisticated partners are likely to have appealed to you. Your home is likely to be lined with books and resound with stimulating conversation. Libra's ability to think on your wavelength can win your romantic interest. You may graciously attribute some of your best ideas to an ingenious, idealistic Aquarian partner. Gemini and you may share a mutual admiration for each other's exceptional minds.

As much as world events may have fascinated you, they may also have affected you personally. Providing security for your family in a changing world may have been the greatest challenge of your life. By drawing upon your Sagittarian wisdom and Libra-like sense of fairness, you could harmonize private needs with those of your community and the public at large.

➤ Read about your Chinese Astrological sign on page 838. ➤ Read about your Personal Planets on page 826. ➤ Read about your personal Mystical Card on page 856.

CAPRICORN

From December 22, 16:22 through December 31, 23:59

The Responsible Leader

As a Capricorn born in December of 1914, you entered the world at a time when the human race was learning an extremely painful lesson. Christmas in 1914 could not have held much cheer. The news reported enormous casualty counts—exceeding two million in the first few months of World War I. Combatant countries had introduced mechanized offensive weapons while deploying ground troops in outdated and utterly indefensible field positions. It's likely, though, that these lessons wouldn't sink in fully until your generation had made its own terrible sacrifices for humanity in World War II.

Your sign rules sacrifice and decisions made in the light of maturity. In many respects, you and members of your generation bore the burden of helping the world to recover from the horrible shocks to humanity in the World Wars. Your sign rules strategy, planning, boundaries, and standards. Accordingly, you may have endorsed and promoted efforts in the decades ahead to improve defensive measures for soldiers, to set humanitarian standards for warfare, and to outlaw certain kinds of weapons.

Capricorns tend to be highly disciplined leaders and workers. If you served in World War II or any subsequent war, you may have been a brilliant military tactician or a brave and efficient leader of nurses or defense plant workers. It's likely that your ability to learn from experience and think ahead enables you to accomplish your goals with focus and efficiency.

You are likely to be willing to make great sacrifices for the welfare of your family and country. Partners who value commitment and traditional values enhance your sense of security. Patriotic Cancer's love of home wins your respect, as does Virgo's sense of duty. Pisces provides precious moments of private tenderness.

Having lived through two World Wars and the Great Depression, you may have wished you could simply slow down the world and go back to a simpler, safer place and time. In general, Capricorn enjoys a strong ability to set limits and create stable foundations. By drawing on such resources, you could restore a sense of control.

CAPRICORN
Your Personal Planets

YOUR LOVE POTENTIAL
Venus in Scorpio, Dec. 22, 16:22 - Dec. 30, 23:14
Venus in Sagittarius, Dec. 30, 23:15 - Dec. 31, 23:59

YOUR DRIVE AND AMBITION
Mars in Capricorn, Dec. 22, 16:22 - Dec. 31, 23:59

YOUR LUCK MAGNETISM
Jupiter in Aquarius, Dec. 22, 16:22 - Dec. 31, 23:59

World Events

Dec. 25 – An unofficial truce is called by soldiers of both sides on the western front, as Christmas is celebrated in the trenches.

Dec. 25 – World War I takes to the skies as two German airplanes are engaged by the British over London.

ISADORA DUNCAN
Gemini

Free-spirited and rebellious, Isadora Duncan was born in San Francisco, California. With her Sun in versatile and lively Gemini, she is credited with reshaping the art of dance in the twentieth century. Unlike classical ballet, which relied on strict positions and stiff postures, Isadora's idea of the dance freed the body from imposed constraints and stressed "natural" movement. She took her inspiration from ideas of ancient Greece and the rhythms she observed in nature.

Known for her free-flowing and sometimes revealing costumes, Isadora also had Mercury, the planet of movement, and Venus, the planet of artistic expression, in unconventional and ethereal Gemini. Gemini often blesses one with a gift for teaching and Isadora opened a number of dance schools throughout Europe and Russia based on her unorthodox ideas of movement. She believed that awakening her students to their spirit was the first step in teaching them to dance.

With the headstrong sign of Aries rising, Mars,

the planet of action and courage, ruled Isadora's chart. She dared to challenge convention both with her radical approach to her art and in her personal life, taking many lovers and choosing not to marry the fathers of her two children. Four planets are involved in a network of dynamic contact with each other: Mars, the Moon, which rules the nurturing, feminine principle, Uranus, the planet of revolutionary ideas, and Pluto, the planet of deep transformation. These forces gave Isadora her defiant attitudes towards the traditions of society, the power to innovate a new form of dance, and a sense of fateful tragedy.

For the circumstances of Isadora's life were as tragic as they were exciting. Uranus, the planet of accidents, fell in the part of her chart that governs children. In 1913, both of her children along with their governess were drowned when their driverless car rolled into the Seine River. And, ironically, her own death came in 1927 when her long shawl became caught in the wheel of a car and instantly snapped her neck. Just before she got into the car, she

Isadora Duncan,
May 26, 1877—September 14, 1927

had waved to her friends and said lightheartedly, "Good-bye, my friends. I am off to glory!"

► Read Martha Graham's Star Profile on page 297. ► Read Josephine Baker's Star Profile on page 217.

1915

Art and Soul Unbound: Jupiter in Pisces

Despite the roar of war whirring all around, in the year 1915 many souls were brought into the world that would bring great joy to all of us. Under the influence of the planet Jupiter, in the artistic and creative sign of Pisces, many significant artists from all genres were born. Jupiter represents the urge for personal growth and self-expression. Pisces is the sign that represents the urge to transcend the mundane and reach the incredible. On April 7, heartbreaking and poignant Blues singer Billie Holiday, famous for the tragic and beautiful song *Strange Fruit*, was born. On May 6, brilliant film director and actor Orson Welles was born. On August 29, film actress Ingrid Bergman, star of *Casablanca*, *For Whom the Bell Tolls*, and *Spellbound*, was born. On October 17, playwright Arthur Miller, creator of *The Crucible* and *Death of a Salesman*, was born. And on December 19, French singer Edith Piaf, singer of *La Vie en Rose* and known as "The Little Sparrow" was born. In terms of artistic and musical creativity 1915 was an extremely rich year indeed.

Jupiter in Pisces delivered to the world the souls of artists whose work would come to enrich and transform our lives on so many different levels. Performance of all sorts is powered by the sign of Leo, and with Neptune stationed in this sign as well, it's no wonder that the actors, singers, and writers born this year would affect our culture so profoundly. No one knew it in 1915, but forces were at work that would elicit tremendous joy and passion for all those that would come to experience the art of those born that year.

The Lusitania, a British civilian ship, sinks

Einstein announces his relativity theory

British and Australian troops assault Gallipoli in Turkey

RAISING CONSCIOUSNESS

Russian philosopher P.D. Ouspensky began teaching the "Gurjieffian system" in St. Petersburg this year. Mystic G. I. Gurjieff had devised his own occult teaching based on the belief that most humans were "asleep." His system focused on self-realization through self-observation, hypnotism, and efforts to penetrate the self's normal state of consciousness to reach true consciousness. "True spiritual growth cannot begin unless each individual becomes aware that each moment could be his last," Gurjieff commented.

A WORLD GONE MAD

Zeppelin airships bombed British cities. Germany ordered total submarine warfare, sinking the British civilian ship *Lusitania*, which had 128 Americans on board. British and Australian troops assaulted Gallipoli in Turkey, but retreated, with horrific losses, before ferocious Turkish counter-attacks. Germany was condemned for using poison gas in France and Russia. Bulgaria declared war on Serbia and backed Germany and Austria. The fighting spread to Africa, where colonies of the European nations became involved in the war. Mexico continued to be wracked by revolution. Haiti also exploded into violence, prompting the U.S. to take control. The European war ignited nationalistic passions in Bohemia and Moravia (Czech Republic/Slovakia), Poland. Italy was wracked by earthquake and conflict with Austria. In Britain, anti-German fever led to violence in the streets. In Germany, Albert Einstein announced his general theory of relativity. Somerset Maugham's *Of Human Bondage* was published, as was Franz Kafka's *The Metamorphosis*. D.W. Griffiths' opulent film *Birth of a Nation* was marred by blatant racism and faced a ban in the U.S.

➤ Read Tsar Nicholas II's Star Profile on page 137.

CAPRICORN

From January 01, 0:00 through January 21, 2:59

The Decent Bulwark

It is an unwritten law of warfare to treat houses of worship as neutral sanctuaries, off-limits from attack—a tradition honored more often in the breach, as demonstrated within days of your birth, Capricorn. On January 4, 1915, German soldiers detained Belgian Cardinal Mercier upon publication of his pastoral letter, "Patriotism And Endurance," a condemnation of World War I and Germany's violation of Belgium's neutrality. Having destroyed 15,000 copies of the letter, interrogated the Cardinal, and demanded a retraction, the Germans provoked the outrage of the Pope and the entire Catholic world.

The brazenness of the attack on Cardinal Mercier and its occurrence near the time of your birth increased the probability that you would eventually learn about it from your parents. A strong regard for tradition and respect for authority are quintessential Capricorn qualities that your parents have likely reinforced in you. Because members of your sign feel strongly about appropriate boundaries, any military incursion into places of worship is likely to offend your sense of decency.

Unfortunately, you would see all too many violations of decency in your life, the worst during World War II. Indicators in your chart suggest that such matters can trigger your anger and resistance. You may have been a partisan or soldier against Nazism or the worst abuses of Communism. You may have felt sorrow over the deterioration of family values later in your life.

You may regard a traditional family as the last bulwark against a world gone insane. Loyal partners who respect commitment and sacrifice would be your best match. Cancerians share your feelings about the sanctity of the home. Taurus's sturdy conservatism makes you feel safe. Libra's regard for decorum wins your admiration.

You have an acute intellectual ability to identify customs and traditions that may have exhausted their usefulness. Still, you have also seen and paid the price for overly rapid progress in your lifetime. With maturity, you were likely to learn how to pick your battles and know when certain changes made sense.

AQUARIUS

From January 21, 3:00 through February 19, 17:22

The Conscientious Innovator

The sign of Aquarius favors innovation and technological progress in the service of humanitarian goals. Within days of your birth, Aquarius, two technological milestones would make headlines—one of which you would approve and one that would deeply offend your Aquarian values. In New York City, on January 25, 1915, Alexander Graham Bell would succeed in placing a phone call to his esteemed partner, Thomas Watson, in San Francisco, setting a telephonic long-distance record. In horrific contrast, on January 31, at Bolimov, on the eastern front of World War I, the German Ninth Army used poison gas against Russian troops.

Later in life, you would certainly have gladly embraced long-distance telephony as a way to stay in touch from afar with family members and loved ones. But you were just as likely, as a conscientious Aquarian, to lead protests against chemical and biological warfare and to advocate for treaties banning forms of weaponry so hideous and cruel.

Growing up in wartime may have forced you to forfeit the pleasures of childhood and grow up too quickly. As an adult, you may have advocated against war altogether. Patterns in your chart indicate sympathy with Libran sentiments against violent confrontation. You may have been a conscientious objector and a peacemaker. Nostalgic feelings for family might have won your approval of the Vietnam-era saying, "War is not healthy for children and other living things."

In general, Aquarius is not afraid to swim against the current of popular opinion. Your life partner may have been a non-conformist, whom you met at a meeting for a cause you shared. Libra's commitment to justice and fairness would earn your respect. Sagittarius's mind for politics would excite your interest. Pisces' compassion for the disempowered would soften your heart.

Although you have a strong ability to make friends, you may have felt lonely or misunderstood in your youth. Your views may have triggered angry reactions from peers or authority figures. Once you were older, you could enjoy the freedom to head out into the world to find your niche.

➤ Read about your Chinese Astrological sign on page 838. ➤ Read about your Personal Planets on page 826. ➤ Read about your personal Mystical Card on page 856.

1915

CAPRICORN
Your Personal Planets

YOUR LOVE POTENTIAL
Venus in Sagittarius, Jan. 01, 0:00 - Jan. 21, 2:59

YOUR DRIVE AND AMBITION
Mars in Capricorn, Jan. 01, 0:00 - Jan. 21, 2:59

YOUR LUCK MAGNETISM
Jupiter in Aquarius, Jan. 01, 0:00 - Jan. 21, 2:59

World Events

Jan. 1 - A German U-24 submarine sinks the British battleship *Formidable* in the English Channel.

Jan. 3 - In the Caucasus, the Turkish army is decimated by Russian troops at the Battle of Sarikamis.

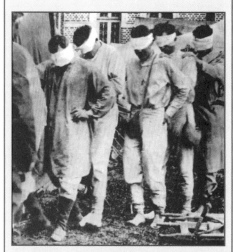

First World War gas victims

AQUARIUS
Your Personal Planets

YOUR LOVE POTENTIAL
Venus in Sagittarius, Jan. 21, 3:00 - Feb. 06, 15:56
Venus in Capricorn, Feb. 06, 15:57 - Feb. 19, 17:22

YOUR DRIVE AND AMBITION
Mars in Capricorn, Jan. 21, 3:00 - Jan. 30, 6:11
Mars in Aquarius, Jan. 30, 6:12 - Feb. 19, 17:22

YOUR LUCK MAGNETISM
Jupiter in Aquarius, Jan. 21, 3:00 - Feb. 04, 0:43
Jupiter in Pisces, Feb. 04, 0:44 - Feb. 19, 17:22

World Events

Jan. 31 - The German Ninth Army deploys poison gas against the Russians at Bolimov.

Feb. 8 - DW Griffith's silent movie *Birth Of A Nation* opens in Los Angeles.

PISCES
Your Personal Planets

YOUR LOVE POTENTIAL
Venus in Capricorn, Feb. 19, 17:23 - Mar. 06, 13:14
Venus in Aquarius, Mar. 06, 13:15 - Mar. 21, 16:50

YOUR DRIVE AND AMBITION
Mars in Aquarius, Feb. 19, 17:23 - Mar. 09, 12:55
Mars in Pisces, Mar. 09, 12:56 - Mar. 21, 16:50

YOUR LUCK MAGNETISM
Jupiter in Pisces, Feb. 19, 17:23 - Mar. 21, 16:50

World Events

Mar. 13 – The Germans defeat the British at the Battle of Neuve Chapelle.

Mar. 14 – The German warship *Dresden* is sunk by the British navy off the coast of Chile.

International Women's Peace Conference

ARIES
Your Personal Planets

YOUR LOVE POTENTIAL
Venus in Aquarius, Mar. 21, 16:51 - Apr. 01, 15:18
Venus in Pisces, Apr. 01, 15:19 - Apr. 21, 4:28

YOUR DRIVE AND AMBITION
Mars in Pisces, Mar. 21, 16:51 - Apr. 16, 20:41
Mars in Aries, Apr. 16, 20:42 - Apr. 21, 4:28

YOUR LUCK MAGNETISM
Jupiter in Pisces, Mar. 21, 16:51 - Apr. 21, 4:28

World Events

Mar. 28 – The International Socialist Women's Conference in Bern issues a peace proposal.

Apr. 5 – Jack Johnson, the first African American heavyweight champion, loses his title to Jess Willard in Havana.

PISCES
From February 19, 17:23 through March 21, 16:50

The Instinctive Empathizer

The sign of Pisces rules the cinema and hidden enemies, two subjects that seem not so odd in light of news events around the time of your birth. March 3, 1915 marked the first New York showing of D. W. Griffith's groundbreaking film, *Birth of a Nation*. Meanwhile, thousands of miles away, off the coast of Britain, German submarines lurked in the Atlantic, following Berlin's February announcement of total submarine warfare. With astonishing technical sophistication that would revolutionize filmmaking for decades to come, *Birth of a Nation* would have been a movie-loving Piscean's dream-come-true; except for the fact that the film featured certain hidden enemies as dangerous and insidious as the Germans lurking in their submarines.

Griffith's film cast the hooded members of the Ku Klux Klan as unmistakable heroes, forever tarnishing this breakthrough cinematic achievement with the obscenity of racism. Indeed, once you were old enough to go to the movies, your folks may have forbade you from seeing *Birth of a Nation*. Pisces can be impressionable. Your knowledge about certain subjects may have come from films.

Having lived through two world wars, exposure to propaganda films may have left you vulnerable to guilt and remorse later on, in the light of time and better information. The compassion for which Pisces is famous would make you likely to empathize deeply with others, even those you had been led to believe were your enemies.

Early on, you may have preferred decisive partners who had strong points of view. With maturity, however, you may have turned to partners who would trust you to know your own mind. Taureans and Scorpios could give you the security of a sure thing—even if it was the wrong thing. Virgos, Sagittarians, and Librans could gently guide you to find your own truth.

Your ability to escape into the world of imagination may have helped you to survive the atrocities of worldwide war and depression. Your challenge has been to find secure grounding once the worst of the danger has passed. With maturity, you have learned to trust and affirm your own best instincts.

ARIES
From March 21, 16:51 through April 21, 4:28

The Underdogs' Champions

Within days of your birth, Aries, the news was punctuated with a lot of hot air. On March 22, 1915, a German zeppelin made a night raid on Paris railway stations. On April 20, President Woodrow Wilson urged strict neutrality for the United States in a speech at New York's Waldorf Astoria hotel. By late 1916, the zeppelins would prove cumbersome, mostly ineffective, and vulnerable to the bullets of the British. Of course, American neutrality was also cumbersome, mostly ineffective, and vulnerable to German aggression, as the sinking of the *Lusitania* would demonstrate in May.

The sign of Aries rules force and aggression, but your chart indicates some kind of inhibition, preventing the full expression of your energy and power. Extreme frustration was likely to have made you rebel against any such limitations. Later in life, you may have found a better way to cope with such feelings. Championing the underdog in various causes may have helped you to relieve your own sense of powerlessness.

You may have suffered serious losses in your life—financial or familial—due to either war or the Great Depression. Putting the pieces of your life back together again may have consumed much of your attention and effort. You were likely to work hard to regain independence and to safeguard your loved ones from danger. Again, working for your community may have empowered you to give to yourself by giving to others.

An active social life would have provided you with the stimulation you needed to blow off steam. Community service was a likely setting for finding a life partner. Aquarians enjoy serving humanity in a group setting. Generous Pisces inspires your best instincts. Virgo's commitment to service ensures a steady stream of activities that make you feel good about yourself.

You have a virtually bottomless well of energy, but at times you may have struggled to find positive ways to express yourself. The circumstances of your early life may have challenged you just to survive. In your thirties, however, you could exercise your outstanding talent for making glorious new beginnings.

➤ Read about your Chinese Astrological sign on page 838. ➤ Read about your Personal Planets on page 826. ➤ Read about your personal Mystical Card on page 856.

TAURUS

From April 21, 4:29 through May 22, 4:09

The Deliberate Pacifist

In the early years of World War I, the United States shared a lot of characteristics with the sign of Taurus. Steadfast in its neutrality, the country was like a large bull, grazing contentedly in its pasture, unmoved by battles raging on distant horizons. Not even the sinking of the *Lusitania* by a German submarine on May 7, 1915 could rouse the U.S. from its peaceful repast—despite the loss of 128 American lives. President Wilson protested the attack to the German government, but a statement he made in April controlled the U.S. reaction: "There is such a thing as a man being too proud to fight; there is such a thing as a nation being so right that it does not need to convince others by force that it is right."

Without a doubt, Wilson's position was inspired by the most honorable intentions. The U.S. was just coming into its own as an industrial power, and the war was already proving to be an unprecedented bloodbath. Similarly, Taureans tend to move very slowly before making any changes in their lives. When a change requires you to depart from a position of comfort, your deliberation process may be even more steady, methodical, and time-consuming.

Your home is your castle, a welcome retreat where you can recharge your energy and enjoy some creature comforts. In the safety of privacy, you may show a more playful, fun-loving side of your personality. You may enjoy entertaining at home on happy occasions, including your extended family and their children.

You may have a subtle and extremely seductive appeal to others. A glimpse of the true force of your personality may intrigue potential partners. Your quiet strength can be enchanting to Pisces. Your peaceful, stable disposition makes Cancer feel secure. The challenge of catching you can move Aries to chase you down.

Your preference for steady, considered judgment may have protected you from making foolish decisions on impulse. At the same time, loved ones may have accused you of being stubborn from time to time. With maturity, you may have discovered the benefits of giving new opportunities a fair chance.

GEMINI

From May 22, 4:10 through June 22, 12:28

Seeker of Truth

At the time of your birth, Gemini, events in the news would provoke furious and enduring debate. On June 17, 1915, German sources reported mass slaughter of Turkey's minority Armenian population by the Ottoman government. On June 21 in the United States, the governor of Georgia commuted the death sentence of Leo Frank. Convicted of the murder of Mary Phagan, Frank's trial spurred nationwide protest claiming that the proceedings were motivated by anti-Semitism. Frank would be lynched by a mob in Atlanta in August, but the identity of his attackers would not emerge until the end of the twentieth century. Similarly, although the Armenian population of Turkey (estimated at 1.5 million) was virtually wiped out by 1916, defenders of Turkey fiercely deny charges of genocide to this day.

The sign of Gemini rules reporting and storytelling. Members of your sign tend to feel strongly that all sides of a story deserve a fair hearing. At the same time, you may believe that, although there may be many stories, there can only be one truth. You may nevertheless regard free, unfettered expression as the most reliable route to discovering that one truth.

Your sign rules the rational mind and the ability to think logically. Over time, as you pondered stories of Leo Frank or the Armenian slaughter, you may have concluded "you cannot reason someone out of something they were not reasoned into." You may be sensitive to emotional motives in people's stories.

You value learnedness in your partners. You may equate someone's trustworthiness with their ability to embrace the truth—warts and all. Sagittarius and Aries may be blunt and abrasive, but you may find their candor truly comforting. Taurean deliberateness and Virgo's fealty to the facts let you know where you stand.

Your appreciation for different points of view enhances your intellectual integrity, but you may have had to make a decision when respecting all opinions was too much of a good thing. Having lived through the most disturbing stories in human history, you may have learned a painful lesson about the dangers of moral relativism.

➤ Read about your Chinese Astrological sign on page 838. ➤ Read about your Personal Planets on page 826. ➤ Read about your personal Mystical Card on page 856.

1915

TAURUS
Your Personal Planets

YOUR LOVE POTENTIAL
Venus in Pisces, Apr. 21, 4:29 - Apr. 27, 0:55
Venus in Aries, Apr. 27, 0:56 - May 22, 2:55
Venus in Taurus, May 22, 2:56 - May 22, 4:09

YOUR DRIVE AND AMBITION
Mars in Aries, Apr. 21, 4:29 - May 22, 4:09

YOUR LUCK MAGNETISM
Jupiter in Pisces, Apr. 21, 4:29 - May 22, 4:09

World Events

May 6 – American film director and actor Orson Welles is born.

May 7 – A German U-20 submarine torpedoes the liner *Lusitania* ten miles off the Irish coast; over 1,000 souls drown.

The Lusitania, a British civilian ship, sinks

GEMINI
Your Personal Planets

YOUR LOVE POTENTIAL
Venus in Taurus, May 22, 4:10 - June 16, 0:20
Venus in Gemini, June 16, 0:21 - June 22, 12:28

YOUR DRIVE AND AMBITION
Mars in Aries, May 22, 4:10 - May 26, 3:07
Mars in Taurus, May 26, 3:08 - June 22, 12:28

YOUR LUCK MAGNETISM
Jupiter in Pisces, May 22, 4:10 - June 22, 12:28

World Events

May 23 – Italy declares war on Austria-Hungary and enters the European conflict.

May 28 – In Berlin, women demonstrate for peace.

1915

CANCER
Your Personal Planets

YOUR LOVE POTENTIAL
Venus in Gemini, June 22, 12:29 - July 10, 17:30
Venus in Cancer, July 10, 17:31 - July 23, 23:25

YOUR DRIVE AND AMBITION
Mars in Taurus, June 22, 12:29 - July 06, 6:22
Mars in Gemini, July 06, 6:23 - July 23, 23:25

YOUR LUCK MAGNETISM
Jupiter in Pisces, June 22, 12:29 - July 23, 23:25

World Events

June 30 – French troops fail in their objective of capturing the Vimy Ridge.

July 17 – Thirty thousand British women organize a march to demand they be allowed to assist in the war effort by taking on male jobs.

Failure of the second Gallipoli landing

LEO
Your Personal Planets

YOUR LOVE POTENTIAL
Venus in Cancer, July 23, 23:26 - Aug. 04, 5:46
Venus in Leo, Aug. 04, 5:47 - Aug. 24, 6:14

YOUR DRIVE AND AMBITION
Mars in Gemini, July 23, 23:26 - Aug. 19, 9:09
Mars in Cancer, Aug. 19, 9:10 - Aug. 24, 6:14

YOUR LUCK MAGNETISM
Jupiter in Pisces, July 23, 23:26 - Aug. 24, 6:14

World Events

Aug. 5 – German troops smash through Russian defensive lines and take Warsaw.

Aug. 8 – The second Allied landing at Gallipoli fails after three days due to lack of naval support.

CANCER
From June 22, 12:29 through July 23, 23:25

The Responsible Patriot

The sign of Cancer rules parenthood, patriotism, and love for one's homeland. Within days of your birth, such values had an ominous presence in the news. On June 23, 1915, German industrialists and the Kaiser issued a joint declaration of Germany's aims in World War I: the annexation of Poland, the Baltic region, and the Ukraine. Shortly thereafter, 1,347 German intellectuals issued a manifesto in support of the annexation policy. Apparently, the Kaiser, the industrialists, and the intellectuals had a passion for the Fatherland so strong that they wanted to pull as much of the world as possible into Germany. Socialist Democrats in Germany strenuously condemned this policy, but their will would not prevail.

Taken to their ultimate extreme, the qualities of any sign can manifest in abusive ways. Astrological patterns leading into the Great War indicated massive worldwide insecurity that raised nationalism to pathological levels in certain quarters. But just as mere citizenship did not destine all Germans to embrace notions of supremacy, neither does your identity as a Cancer destine you to act on the negative potentials of your sign in your own life.

Because the sign of Cancer rules parenting, you are likely to embrace the principle of personal responsibility, holding individuals accountable for their choices and actions, regardless of the circumstances of their birth. Your sign also rules childbearing and care-taking—qualities likely to move you to celebrate, preserve, and nurture all life on Earth.

Family loyalty may be extremely important to you. You may seek partners who will be your ally in creating an island of security in the midst of a dangerous world. Capricorn and Scorpio can assure you that everything is under control. Taurus can be an excellent provider.

Your self-discipline has enabled you to protect yourself and your family in chaotic times. Loved ones may have bridled under the yoke of excessive control. Having learned that fearful assumptions about life can turn into self-fulfilling prophecies, you may hold on more loosely to the ones you love most.

LEO
From July 23, 23:26 through August 24, 6:14

The Undercover Dramatist

Your sign is associated with the Sun, Leo, and within days of your birth, certain information—once secret—saw the light of day. On August 16, 1915, President Wilson was informed of German espionage plans. One month earlier, in New York, U.S. agents discovered a briefcase belonging to a German propaganda minister. Undertaking an inquiry, the Americans began arresting German spies later in August.

Suspicion of hidden enemies may be a strong element of your personality, but you may enjoy the thrill of cloak-and-dagger pursuits. Leos tend to have an affinity for drama and theatre, and indicators in your chart suggest that you would be especially skilled as an actor or in role-playing. Likely to have a talent for adapting yourself to meet others' needs and expectations, you might have made an excellent spy, undercover detective, or investigative reporter. Your intuition about others' motives can be acutely sensitive, and you may have worked hard in your life to sharpen your powers of perception.

You may have highly persuasive writing skills or a flair for public speaking. Perhaps you applied these skills in advocating for causes important to you. You may have written exposés on governmental or business abuses. Your chart suggests that you have the ability to flush out major scandals. Or you may simply get a kick out of reading gossip columns.

You're likely to team up with partners who are happy to let you shine. Mates who take family life seriously are okay, so long as they don't frown on levity or playfulness within the four walls of home. Mercurial Gemini can keep up with your changes and may have written some of your best lines. Pisces and Libra share Leo's affection for good theatre, and they'll support you generously behind the scenes.

You can spot dishonesty or a con game from a mile away, but this skill may have come at a price. Early in life, you may have been deceived or betrayed; having learned your lesson, you were less likely to be taken in and more likely to turn the experience to your own advantage. You may be very careful about whom you trust.

► Read about your Chinese Astrological sign on page 838. ► Read about your Personal Planets on page 826. ► Read about your personal Mystical Card on page 856.

VIRGO

From August 24, 6:15 through September 24, 3:23

Cultivator of Life

At a meeting held on September 5, 1915, European Socialists gathered at Zimmerwald, Switzerland, to articulate their opposition to World War I. The Socialists regarded competition by the European powers over lesser countries and their resources as directly at odds with laborers' interests in the means of production and the ability to earn a decent living. Such matters fall within the realm of Virgoan concern. Not all Virgos are necessarily Socialists. One might also view American resistance to entering the war through a "Virgoan" lens. As the war began, the United States was enjoying increasing productivity and prosperity. Legalization of unions, a minimum wage and profit-sharing at Ford plants, and other trends proved that benefits for workers could benefit capitalists.

The sheer destructiveness of war is at odds with the Virgoan need to cultivate life. You may have witnessed such devastation during either World War. To see once-fertile fields blasted to dust and poisoned with lead would weigh especially heavily on your Virgoan heart. You may have eagerly joined efforts to rejuvenate the postwar landscape. Hoping to leave a better world for your children, you may have supported environmental causes later in life.

Your motto might be "live and let live." Attempts to force one way of life on others may strike you as arrogant and spiritually offensive. Ironically, you may be willing to fight to defend against those who elevate their own cause, values, or country *"über alles."*

You may feel that all things are better when they're shared. Gratitude for health and the wealth of the good earth may be the central values of your household. Taurus lives to share the simple, sensual pleasures of nature. Cancer will gladly cook up your garden goodies. Pisces' appreciation multiplies your horn of plenty.

Nobody works with more dedication than Virgo. Too much focus on the details of productivity and organization can blind you to larger issues that may affect you. Hard shocks in your life may have taught you the pointlessness of watering one tree when the whole forest is on fire.

LIBRA

From September 24, 3:24 through October 24, 12:09

The Secure Lover

You entered a world engulfed in war, Libra. Within days of your birth, the Central Powers decimated Serbia; French and British were called to invade Greece; and with Russian troops in desperate straits, Tsar Nicholas II took command of the eastern front. Although Germany had promised to cease submarine attacks on American vessels, German-sponsored sabotage still aimed to undermine American industry. In the midst of all the chaos, destruction, and danger, there was still time for love. On October 6, 1915, U.S. President Wilson, widowed in 1914, announced his engagement to Edith Bolling Galt.

Libra rules love, marriage, and partnership. As a Libra and member of the generation that fought World War II, you may have an acute awareness of the strange way in which war and the nearness of death can increase one's desire to marry and start a family. Because your sign also rules contracts, you can see the pragmatic benefits of formalizing romantic relationships. In times of war, marriage ensures certain rights and benefits in the event of the death or disability of either partner.

Europe saw the catastrophic loss of a generation of men in the Great War. The loss of your father, uncles, or even older brothers, may have left the women of your family struggling just to hold the family together. As an adult, you may have married and pursued a standard of living that would ensure security for your family, no matter what happened.

If one of your own parents passed before his or her time, you may regard marriage as a sacred reaffirmation of life. Protecting your family by properly providing for them may be paramount. Taurus maintains extra reserves in the event of emergency. Cancer shares your devotion to family bonds. Leo fiercely defends your children and homestead.

Because Libra is expert in relationship care, you may have had strong support in hard times. The urgency of wartime, however, may have made you enter relationships out of pragmatic concerns. With maturity, you may have devoted more energy to the love and emotion in your relationships—or sought new ones altogether.

➤ Read about your Chinese Astrological sign on page 838. ➤ Read about your Personal Planets on page 826. ➤ Read about your personal Mystical Card on page 856.

VIRGO
Your Personal Planets

YOUR LOVE POTENTIAL
Venus in Leo, Aug. 24, 6:15 - Aug. 28, 13:05
Venus in Virgo, Aug. 28, 13:06 - Sept. 21, 16:30
Venus in Libra, Sept. 21, 16:31 - Sept. 24, 3:23

YOUR DRIVE AND AMBITION
Mars in Cancer, Aug. 24, 6:15 - Sept. 24, 3:23

YOUR LUCK MAGNETISM
Jupiter in Pisces, Aug. 24, 6:15 - Sept. 24, 3:23

World Events

Aug. 29 – Swedish film star Ingrid Bergman is born.

Sept. 8 – Tsar Nicholas II takes over the leadership of the Russian army.

Tsar Nicholas inspects the Russian army

LIBRA
Your Personal Planets

YOUR LOVE POTENTIAL
Venus in Libra, Sept. 24, 3:24 - Oct. 15, 17:41
Venus in Scorpio, Oct. 15, 17:42 - Oct. 24, 12:09

YOUR DRIVE AND AMBITION
Mars in Cancer, Sept. 24, 3:24 - Oct. 07, 20:47
Mars in Leo, Oct. 07, 20:48 - Oct. 24, 12:09

YOUR LUCK MAGNETISM
Jupiter in Pisces, Sept. 24, 3:24 - Oct. 24, 12:09

World Events

Oct. 12 – British nurse Edith Cavell, accused of harboring Belgians of military age and aiding Allied soldiers' escape, is shot by the Germans.

Oct. 17 – American playwright Arthur Miller is born.

1915

SCORPIO
Your Personal Planets

YOUR LOVE POTENTIAL
Venus in Scorpio, Oct. 24, 12:10 - Nov. 08, 18:06
Venus in Sagittarius, Nov. 08, 18:07 - Nov. 23, 9:13

YOUR DRIVE AND AMBITION
Mars in Leo, Oct. 24, 12:10 - Nov. 23, 9:13

YOUR LUCK MAGNETISM
Jupiter in Pisces, Oct. 24, 12:10 - Nov. 23, 9:13

World Events

Nov. 19 – The Allies seek China's support in the war.

Nov. 21 – The HMS *Endurance* sinks in the Antarctic; expedition leader Ernest Shackleton and his crew escape.

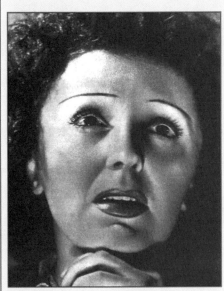

French singer Edith Piaf is born under the sign of Sagittarius

SAGITTARIUS
Your Personal Planets

YOUR LOVE POTENTIAL
Venus in Sagittarius, Nov. 23, 9:14 - Dec. 02, 18:37
Venus in Capricorn, Dec. 02, 18:38 - Dec. 22, 22:15

YOUR DRIVE AND AMBITION
Mars in Leo, Nov. 23, 9:14 - Dec. 22, 22:15

YOUR LUCK MAGNETISM
Jupiter in Pisces, Nov. 23, 9:14 - Dec. 22, 22:15

World Events

Nov. 25 – Col. William J. Simmons revives the Ku Klux Klan in Atlanta.

Dec. 19 – French singer Edith Piaf is born.

SCORPIO
From October 24, 12:10 through November 23, 9:13

The Conscientious Objector

Your sign rules the human will, Scorpio, and you were born at a time when conflicts of wills resulted in the most devastating bloodshed yet known to humankind. The news within days of your birth focused on two individuals whose fortitude and perseverance may have inspired you to follow their example. November 14, 1915 marked the passing of Booker T. Washington, the former slave who went on to found the Tuskegee Institute in Alabama. Washington stood for the principle that the best route to liberation for African Americans was through education, occupational training, and self-improvement. On November 22, Mohandas Gandhi returned to India, where he began his campaign for Indian independence from British rule.

Your sign rules legacies. Whereas the Great War left your generation a legacy of further violence in World War II, Gandhi and Washington left an uplifting legacy of human liberation. As a Scorpio, you may have marveled at Gandhi's power to do what the Germans could not—defeat the British Empire. You may personally believe in the power that comes from humility, non-violent resistance, and trust in the truth.

The sign of Scorpio stands not only for war but also for the power of deeper truth. Having survived two wars, you may have been eager to heal the ignorance and spiritual deficits that could lead to violence. Seeking to promote understanding, you may have worked for a religious establishment or in a university setting.

You may find blustery, domineering partners repellent. Strength so secure it needs no proving is the kind of quality you were likely to seek in a life partner. Cancerians and Librans are both natural leaders, who abhor the idea of staring down or humiliating others. Taurus may be your favorite strong, silent type.

You have an abiding, ironclad ability to see and stand up for deeper principles and higher truths. Such beliefs may have set you apart from others in your family or even your own country. With the potential to be the ultimate conscientious objector, you may have been willing to wait as long as it took for history to prove you right.

SAGITTARIUS
From November 23, 9:14 through December 22, 22:15

The Tolerant Humanist

The sign of Sagittarius rules those from countries abroad, religion, art criticism, and popular culture. Within days of your birth, news from Atlanta, Georgia reported a bizarre and tragic convergence of these subjects. On November 25, 1915, William J. Simmons, a Methodist minister, held a Thanksgiving Day revival of the Ku Klux Klan, a group first founded after the American Civil War by ex-soldiers of the Confederacy. Inspired by the depiction of Klansmen in the film *Birth of a Nation*, released earlier in the year, Simmons advertised his meeting in a local newspaper, alongside advertisements for the film. Like its predecessor, the new Klan reviled African Americans, but its hostility also extended to Jews, Communists, labor unionists, and immigrants to the U.S.—many of them Catholic.

Sagittarius is wise, tolerant, and celebrates the diverse beauty of all cultures. You may find the Klan's timing of its meeting appallingly ironic, given that Thanksgiving marks the arrival of a population of immigrants to American shores! Simmons' introduction of the flaming cross, as a religious symbol for the Klan's mission, may strike you as an abomination.

As a Sagittarian, you are likely to be fascinated and repulsed by the ability of popular culture—such as a film about the Klan—to influence real world developments. Later in life, you may have focused your critical abilities on similar influences in new media, such as sex and violence in art and on television.

Compassionate, open-minded partners are likely to appeal to you. The spirit of generosity may grace your home, and you may enjoy frequent house guests. Pisces' giving, tender soul inspires your love. Leo captivates you with romance. Gemini shares your passion for diversity.

Sagittarius stands for the belief that everyone benefits when all are allowed to contribute to the best of their abilities. Dealing with intolerance—by the Klan, Nazism, or your peers—may have been the most painful challenge of your life. Your own shining example of tolerance may have proven to be your most potent weapon against hatred and bigotry.

➤ Read about your Chinese Astrological sign on page 838. ➤ Read about your Personal Planets on page 826. ➤ Read about your personal Mystical Card on page 856.

CAPRICORN
From December 22, 22:16 through December 31, 23:59

The New Physicist

Because your sign rules the structure of things, Capricorn, you could not have received a more perfect birthday present than a new theory on the composition of the Universe. In December 1915, Albert Einstein announced his development of the General Theory of Relativity. This new explanation of the force of gravity would ultimately overthrow Newtonian theory, the system by which physicists had understood the natural world since the seventeenth century. Einstein would have to wait until after the conclusion of World War I to complete the research necessary to test relativity against Newtonian theory. As you would see in your studies later in life, relativity would indeed prevail and utterly transform the science of physics.

Indicators in your chart suggest that you would also have a fine mind for higher education and, indeed, the ability to make your own breakthroughs and discoveries. Doing research may energize you, and you may get a thrill as you discover new facts to add to your collection. You also have the ability to stick with a problem until you resolve it to your satisfaction.

Impulsive action and wasted energy in your youth may have provided some tough but valuable learning experiences. A mentor may have helped you to develop discipline and efficiency. Likely to be methodical in approach, you tend to think through challenges and plan a course of action.

Important relationships may have changed drastically in your lifetime, or a partner may have been instrumental in compelling you to make changes in yourself. Cancer can commit for the long term, while growing and evolving with all the seasons of your life. Relations with Leo or Pisces may bring on a transformation in how you see yourself, opening you to new possibilities.

You entered a world in desperate need of problem-solvers and, as a Capricorn, you are likely to have the skills to answer this need. Having lived through global wars, depression, and massive technological progress, you were uniquely equipped to restore comfort and predictability by adapting old structures to handle new and unprecedented circumstances.

CAPRICORN
Your Personal Planets

YOUR LOVE POTENTIAL
Venus in Capricorn, Dec. 22, 22:16 - Dec. 26, 20:20
Venus in Aquarius, Dec. 26, 20:21 - Dec. 31, 23:59

YOUR DRIVE AND AMBITION
Mars in Leo, Dec. 22, 22:16 - Dec. 31, 23:59

YOUR LUCK MAGNETISM
Jupiter in Pisces, Dec. 22, 22:16 - Dec. 31, 23:59

World Events

Dec. 29 – Peter I and the Serbian army seek refuge on the island of Corfu.

Dec. 31 – Germans torpedo the British liner *Persia* without warning; 335 are drowned.

TSAR NICHOLAS II
Taurus

Tsar Nicholas II was the last ruler of the Romanov dynasty. With his Sun in tradition-oriented Taurus, Nicholas fully intended to carry on the autocratic government established by his ancestors in 1613. But rather than continuing the reign of the Romanovs, the royal line would end with the brutal execution of Nicholas and his entire family.

Neptune, the planet of illusion, made challenging contacts to Venus (self-expression) and Uranus (the unexpected, change). This shows how—though he was quite charming—Nicholas eventually gained the reputation of being two-faced or deceitful. It was more a matter of not wanting to offend someone by disagreeing, as well as a personal dislike of argument. So he would give the impression that he was in accord, which his subsequent actions would contradict. And, with Mercury (the planet of ideas), in a difficult aspect with Saturn (the planet of restriction) Nicholas could, on the one hand, doubt his own convictions and listen to poor advice, or on the other hand, stick stubbornly to his convictions, despite good advice or proof to the contrary. Further, with his Moon in the sometimes self-absorbed sign Aries, Nicholas was unable to identify with his subjects except in the most autocratic manner.

Mars, the planet of action, was also in impulsive Aries, giving Nicholas a quick temper and a tendency to act precipitously. With his Mars making a contact with his Neptune, the planet of deceit and confusion, his ill-considered actions adversely impacted on his own fortunes as well as those of his family and his nation.

Nicholas' impressionability and lack of political judgment were disastrous in the rapidly changing times. During World War I, Nicholas joined his troops in battle, leaving his wife, Alexandra, and her much-hated advisor Rasputin in charge. Meanwhile the internal unrest in Russia worsened, and in 1917 Nicholas was forced to abdicate and his entire family was placed under arrest. They were executed in July 1918.

Tsar Nicholas II
May 18, 1868—July 17, 1918

➤ Read more about Nicholas II in "The Birth and Rebirth of a Nation" on page 145.

1916

Women Take Control: Saturn in Cancer

Margaret Sanger, a true Virgo, dedicated her life to the service of humanity. (Virgo is the sign of the handmaiden, the helper, and the one who works tirelessly for whatever worthy cause arises.) Sanger's work as a visiting nurse focused her interest in sex education and women's health. In 1912 she began writing a column on sex education for the *New York Call* entitled "What Every Girl Should Know." She was censored for her ideas and her column on venereal disease was deemed obscene and suppressed. Her ideas, at that time, were just too radical for the mainstream. Sanger worked in New York's Lower East Side with poor women suffering the pain of frequent childbirth, miscarriage, and abortion. She was quite influenced by the beliefs of anarchist and advocate of "free love" Emma Goldman. Sanger began to vociferously argue for the need for family limitation as a tool by which working-class women would liberate themselves from the economic burden of unwanted pregnancy.

She opened the first birth control clinic in New York in October of 1916. This marked an extraordinary moment in our collective history, as women were finally able to take control of their reproductive destiny. The astrological indicators at this time signaled a profound change in women's ideas about home and childrearing. At this time, the serious and steadfast planet Saturn was in the emotional sign of Cancer, constellation of motherhood in all its manifestations. Pluto was also in Cancer, indicating a revolution in family life. Cancer is indeed the sign of the home, the mother and early childhood. Mars was in intense Scorpio this month making a gentle angle to Saturn. This helped create the boundless energy that allowed Sanger's radical act to manifest.

All of these astrological aspects boded well for the inauguration of a clinic dedicated to freeing women from the limitations of traditional marriage and enforced pregnancy. It was a time for women to begin to reclaim their power, and the stars offered just the right kind of assistance in 1916.

President Wilson favors women's suffrage

The Battle of Verdun begins under a German offensive

Emperor Franz Joseph of Austria dies

EUROPE FIGHTS AND AMERICA HOPES

The war was centered around the French fortress of Verdun, where some 700,000 casualties were suffered by both sides in a 10-month struggle. In the battle of the Somme, the British suffered 60,000 casualties on the first day. German zeppelins dropped more bombs on England. The British introduced the first tanks into warfare in an attempt to break the gridlock of trench fighting. The Austrian Emperor Franz Joseph, whose reign was marked by his struggles to unite the 17 nationalities in his empire, died after 68 years of rule. Russia's politics changed when assassination broke the stranglehold that Grigori Rasputin had exerted over the Tsar's family. The campaign slogan "He kept us out of war" helped U.S. President Woodrow Wilson to be re-elected. Meanwhile, the U.S. economy boomed. The senate passed a bill introducing an 8-hour working day. Rockefeller, founder of Standard Oil, was worth $1 billion as share prices exploded. Wilson favored women's suffrage, and although women did not have the vote in many states, Jeannette Rankin was elected to represent Montana in Congress. U.S. writers Henry James and Jack London died.

➤ Read "The Birth and Rebirth of a Nation: Russia" by Frank Andrews on page 145.

CAPRICORN

From January 01, 0:00 through January 21, 8:53

The Wry Strategist

One of the most infamous fiascoes of World War I concluded within days of your birth, January Capricorn. Given Capricorn's taste for wry humor, you might appreciate the irony that the one strategic masterpiece of the Allies' campaign in the Dardenelles was their retreat from Gallipoli on January 8, 1916. Removing troops over a period of weeks, while fooling the Turks into believing that Allied lines were still secure, the Allies were able to complete their withdrawal with only one casualty. The rest of the campaign, begun in February 1915, had been an utter disaster for both sides, with the total number of losses exceeding half a million, with as many deaths from dysentery as from fighting.

Once you were old enough to study this campaign, you may have found it irresistible to play armchair General. Your chart shows a capacity for strategic thinking far superior to that of the Allied generals at Gallipoli—like the genius who ordered 600 Australian Light Horsemen out to attack the Turks at the Nek, without protective shelling or infantry cover. In contrast, if you fought in World War II, you were likely to have been an outstanding field officer.

On the field of battle, at work, or in community projects, you are likely to have a talent for leading teams with discipline and focus. You may also have a wonderful ability to get people to sacrifice self-interest, in favor of the group's greater goals. You, of course, can set your own inspiring example of self-sacrifice for the sake of a cause.

With appropriate boundaries, a Capricorn can be quite the saucy spouse. Privacy is important to you, but behind closed doors you can be a most affectionate companion. Taurus brings an unlimited hug supply. Your playful affection is Cancer's favorite emotion. Virgo shares your respect for privacy and your ideas of what to do with it.

You are likely to have won great admiration for your ability to bear awesome responsibilities, but all work and no play may have left some feeling dour and humorless. With time, you could relax and enjoy the eccentric, creative side of your personality.

AQUARIUS

From January 21, 8:54 through February 19, 23:17

The Wise Nonconformist

If you have grandchildren, Aquarius, you may have watched with amusement as they traded prized goodies with each other and sealed the exchange by crying out, "No backsies!" Not long after, you may have had to settle things when one child sought to undo the deal. In the days surrounding your birth, no one was amused when Germany revealed the petulance of a five-year-old in its dealings with the United States. On February 6, 1915, Germany admitted its full liability for reparations to the U.S., for the loss of American life in the sinking of the *Lusitania*. A mere ten days later, Germany ordered the sinking of armed neutral ships.

The potential for similar disillusionment appears in your chart. Early in life, you may have encountered someone who promised one thing but did something else. For example, many people in your generation—wanting only good things, such as fair pay and decent conditions for workers—affiliated themselves with Socialist or Communist causes, only to suffer bitter disappointment later on, in the era of Stalin.

Individualism and non-conformism are classic Aquarian traits, and you are likely to exude such qualities with greater intensity than the average member of your sign. Guided by a passionate idealism, you may have sought to peel away outmoded traditions and value systems, or you may have held on to the security of the old ways with even greater vigor.

Likely to model your relationships in line with your own ideals, you may have been attracted to partners who shared your values about what marriage and family should be in a changing world. Leo may have brought you a soaring sense of romantic elevation. Pisces or Cancer would bring an enduring intensity of passion. In later years, you may have been drawn to the conscious devotion and friendship of Sagittarius.

Strong Aquarian principles may have been your most reliable compass through life, but dealing with real, fallible people may have been another story. Later in life, your spirituality may have enabled you to become more accepting of others and, therefore, less vulnerable to disappointment.

► Read about your Chinese Astrological sign on page 838. ► Read about your Personal Planets on page 826. ► Read about your personal Mystical Card on page 856.

CAPRICORN
Your Personal Planets

YOUR LOVE POTENTIAL
Venus in Aquarius, Jan. 01, 0:00 - Jan. 20, 1:40
Venus in Pisces, Jan. 20, 1:41 - Jan. 21, 8:53

YOUR DRIVE AND AMBITION
Mars in Leo, Jan. 01, 0:00 - Jan. 21, 8:53

YOUR LUCK MAGNETISM
Jupiter in Pisces, Jan. 01, 0:00 - Jan. 21, 8:53

World Events

Jan. 8 – The allied forces of Great Britain and France evacuate the Gallipoli Peninsula in the Dardanelles.

Jan. 14 – British authorities seize German attaché Franz von Papen's financial records, confirming espionage activities in the U.S.

Britain and France evacuate Gallipoli

AQUARIUS
Your Personal Planets

YOUR LOVE POTENTIAL
Venus in Pisces, Jan. 21, 8:54 - Feb. 13, 15:23
Venus in Aries, Feb. 13, 15:24 - Feb. 19, 23:17

YOUR DRIVE AND AMBITION
Mars in Leo, Jan. 21, 8:54 - Feb. 19, 23:17

YOUR LUCK MAGNETISM
Jupiter in Pisces, Jan. 21, 8:54 - Feb. 12, 7:10
Jupiter in Aries, Feb. 12, 7:11 - Feb. 19, 23:17

World Events

Feb. 6 – Germany takes full responsibility for the sinking of the *Lusitania*.

Feb. 9 – The Military Service Acts are enforced in Britain, introducing conscription.

1916

PISCES

Your Personal Planets

YOUR LOVE POTENTIAL

Venus in Aries, Feb. 19, 23:18 - Mar. 09, 21:48
Venus in Taurus, Mar. 09, 21:49 - Mar. 20, 22:46

YOUR DRIVE AND AMBITION

Mars in Leo, Feb. 19, 23:18 - Mar. 20, 22:46

YOUR LUCK MAGNETISM

Jupiter in Aries, Feb. 19, 23:18 - Mar. 20, 22:46

World Events

Feb. 21 – The Battle of Verdun begins under a German offensive.

Feb. 28 – American–British novelist Henry James dies.

The Battle of Verdun

ARIES

Your Personal Planets

YOUR LOVE POTENTIAL

Venus in Taurus, Mar. 20, 22:47 - Apr. 05, 13:30
Venus in Gemini, Apr. 05, 13:31 - Apr. 20, 10:24

YOUR DRIVE AND AMBITION

Mars in Leo, Mar. 20, 22:47 - Apr. 20, 10:24

YOUR LUCK MAGNETISM

Jupiter in Aries, Mar. 20, 22:47 - Apr. 20, 10:24

World Events

Mar. 31 – Gen. John J. Pershing leads an army into Mexico to capture Pancho Villa.

Apr. 4 – Pope Benedict XV meets with British Prime Minister Herbert Henry Asquith at the Vatican.

PISCES

From February 19, 23:18 through March 20, 22:46

The Spiritual Deflector

The sign of Pisces rules spirituality and universal truths. At the time of your birth, Pisces, the news of World War I would tragically bear out a certain variation on the Golden Rule. On February 21, Germany attacked Verdun, France. The commander of the German army, General Falkenhayn, intended to pursue a strategy *Weissbluten* ("white blood"), so taxing as to literally bleed the French dry. By the conclusion of the Battle of Verdun, however, the Germans ended up doing to themselves what they had intended to do to the French. Having driven so forcefully into French territory, they were unable to re-supply themselves from the rear, and the French drove the Germans back to their original position. After ten months of fighting and the loss of 700,000 men, neither side gained any ground.

Every other year, a certain planetary pattern brings extreme disfavor on the initiation of combat. The Battle of Verdun was a textbook illustration of the power of this cosmic phenomenon. As a child, you were likely to hear many retellings of this story. Because the "Verdun pattern" is in your chart, you were uniquely prone to internalize the lesson of the futility of war.

Tending to avoid overt confrontation, Pisceans have the spiritual power to deflect hostile energy and let antagonists hoist themselves with their own petards. This gift may have made you an effective warrior in World War II or an advocate for peace and humanitarian aid. An ability to see through others' illusions may also give you an advantage.

Wartime conditions may have increased the intensity of your relationships. Passionate, expressive partners were likely to attract you. Cancer creates a safe place for your feelings. Dramatic Leo can raise your emotional temperature. Scorpio's depth and power recharges your energy.

Your Gandhi-like gift for passive resistance can vanquish empires, but such martial artistry may be counterproductive in a family environment. With maturity, you were likely to realize that loved ones treasured your happiness. If directly told what you wanted, they would gladly give it to you.

ARIES

From March 20, 22:47 through April 20, 10:24

The Sporting Warrior

Events within days of your birth, Aries, underscored the hopelessness of a world engulfed in violence. In Paris, on April 10, 1916, the President of the Interim Olympic Committee canceled the 1916 Olympic Games. The situation involved an unfortunate reversal of a sacred Olympic tradition. Instead of a worldwide cease-fire for the duration of the Games, the Games themselves ceased for the duration of the war. When you grew old enough to understand, the adults in your life may have told you about this tragic cancellation, coming as it did in the midst of the legendary Battle of Verdun.

The sign of Aries rules power, competition, and athleticism, and you were likely to be an able athlete. Because your sign also rules war and combat, you may have been just as able a warrior. Life likely furnished you the opportunity to be both: to play hard from the twenties to the thirties, and to fight hard from the thirties into the forties.

You may have been fiery and impulsive in your youth, but hard experiences may have forced you to temper your reactions with discipline and forethought. The loss of someone in your family or your wartime "band of brothers and sisters" may have brought about a dramatic change in your perspective. Time and experience likely taught you to be a strong and respected leader on the battlefield, in your career, or in your community.

You may go for the kind of partner who can enjoy playful sparring. A lively back-and-forth keeps things interesting and serves as a healthy pressure release. Sagittarius is competitive, enjoys sports, and knows when to let you win. Playful Leo's strong will can give you a thrilling challenge, so long as you both agree on the ground rules. Cancer's game of hard-to-get never fails to arouse your hunter spirit.

Your energy and vigor has been indispensable in protecting your family and country, but the requirements of your life probably changed as you went from wartime to peacetime. With maturity, you learned to direct your power toward creation and rebuilding. You may have come to feel tremendous gratitude for having survived such hard times.

► Read about your Chinese Astrological sign on page 838. ► Read about your Personal Planets on page 826. ► Read about your personal Mystical Card on page 856.

TAURUS

From April 20, 10:25 through May 21, 10:05

The Resourceful Procurer

The sign of Taurus rules resources and supplies, and news within days of your birth demonstrated the influence of provisions in World War I. One of the most deadly forces in that war was not a weapon, but the lack of adequate food, drinking water, and other vital supplies. On April 29, 1916, British troops in Mesopotamia (now Iraq) surrendered *en masse* to the Turks at Kut-el-Amara. Starvation and the failure of re-supply efforts were the critical factors in the surrender. Similarly, on May 4, Germany agreed to limit its submarine warfare if the United States would oppose an Allied blockade. Preventing foodstuffs from reaching the German homeland, the blockade contributed to shortages, hunger, and protests in Berlin. Hunger and thirst would also be a decisive factor in Germany's eventual defeat at Verdun.

Hunger and starvation may have affected you personally during World War I, the Great Depression, or World War II. To deal with such a crisis, you may have devoted tremendous energy to locating, storing, and hiding supplies. Loved ones may admiringly attest to the marvels of your secret stockpiles. In your military unit or hometown, you may have been the go-to person for procuring precious items.

Your chart indicates an unusual ability to improvise solutions with whatever materials might be on hand. A flair for mechanical creativity may have inspired you to rig up Rube Goldberg-like contraptions. Your resourcefulness is one of your greatest assets.

Tenacious with relationships, you may be the kind of person who stays in touch with every person who was ever dear to you. You may have married a childhood sweetheart. Leo shares your heartfelt loyalty. Drinking from Scorpio's deep waters infuses you with life-giving force. Cancer's tender loving care is your ultimate comfort food.

Your survival skills probably saved your family in times of crisis, but scrimping and saving can be inappropriate under normal conditions. Grandchildren may have winced to see you stashing away a potato after a restaurant meal. With time, you could learn to trust the abundance in your life.

GEMINI

From May 21, 10:06 through June 21, 18:23

The Verbal Acrobat

Gemini rules the making of agreements, a sensitive issue for aspiring pan-Arab nationals in World War I. On June 5, 1916, Hussein, Grand Sherif of Mecca, led Arabs in a revolt against the Turks in the Hejaz. To induce the Arabs to join the war against the Turks, Britain and France had promised Arab control over certain regions of the Middle East upon defeat of the Turks. From a purely astrological perspective, Hussein's revolt consummated this agreement during the worst time for making a clear and enforceable contract. Later in the war, Arab leaders would charge the British with duplicity, especially with respect to Britain's support of Zionism in Palestine. Clearly, the British were willing to play to both sides of the age-old conflict between the Arabs and the Zionists, as Britain's own interests dictated.

While planetary conditions at the time of your birth compromised Britain's promises to Hussein, they play a different role in your personal chart. You may enjoy an offbeat, unusual, and creative way of thinking and perceiving the world. In today's vernacular, you are the kind of person who can "think outside the box."

In evaluating a problem, the last thing you want to hear from others is, "But we've always done it this way!" You have the ability to see all sides of any issue. A command of details affords you the capacity for excellence in studies, career, and challenges requiring brain power.

You're likely to be close to people from a variety of backgrounds. Friendships were likely to lead to your most valuable relationships in life, including your life partner. Sagittarius shares your taste for a wide range of people and cultures. Aries can be an energizing friend or mate. Aquarius brings you the thrill of exotic and unusual experiences.

As a Gemini, you're likely to have a flair for words and language. While you may enjoy wordplay, others may not be able to keep up with your mental speed and verbal acrobatics. With maturity, you've learned to tailor your words and presentation to be more straightforward, especially when ambiguity might cause insecurity.

► Read about your Chinese Astrological sign on page 838. ► Read about your Personal Planets on page 826. ► Read about your personal Mystical Card on page 856.

TAURUS
Your Personal Planets

YOUR LOVE POTENTIAL
Venus in Gemini, Apr. 20, 10:25 - May 05, 20:36
Venus in Cancer, May 05, 20:37 - May 21, 10:05

YOUR DRIVE AND AMBITION
Mars in Leo, Apr. 20, 10:25 - May 21, 10:05

YOUR LUCK MAGNETISM
Jupiter in Aries, Apr. 20, 10:25 - May 21, 10:05

World Events

Apr. 22 - American violin virtuoso Yehudi Menuhin is born.

Apr. 24 – Irish nationalists stage the Easter Rising in Dublin, capturing the General Post Office, St. Stephen's Green, and adjacent houses.

American violin virtuoso Yehudi Menuhin is born under the sign of Taurus

GEMINI
Your Personal Planets

YOUR LOVE POTENTIAL
Venus in Cancer, May 21, 10:06 - June 21, 18:23

YOUR DRIVE AND AMBITION
Mars in Leo, May 21, 10:06 - May 28, 18:41
Mars in Virgo, May 28, 18:42 - June 21, 18:23

YOUR LUCK MAGNETISM
Jupiter in Aries, May 21, 10:06 - June 21, 18:23

World Events

May 25 - David Lloyd George is sent on a peace-seeking mission to Ireland.

June 10 - Turkish-controlled Mecca falls into Arab hands during the Arab Revolt.

1916

CANCER
Your Personal Planets

YOUR LOVE POTENTIAL
Venus in Cancer, June 21, 18:24 - July 23, 5:20

YOUR DRIVE AND AMBITION
Mars in Virgo, June 21, 18:24 - July 23, 5:20

YOUR LUCK MAGNETISM
Jupiter in Aries, June 21, 18:24 - June 26, 1:31
Jupiter in Taurus, June 26, 1:32 - July 23, 5:20

World Events

July 1 – The first day of the Battle of the Somme on the western front sees unprecedented casualties.

July 7 – David Lloyd George replaces Lord Kitchener as British Minister of Defense.

Death of Sir Roger Casement, an Irish nationalist and rebel

LEO
Your Personal Planets

YOUR LOVE POTENTIAL
Venus in Cancer, July 23, 5:21 - Aug. 23, 12:08

YOUR DRIVE AND AMBITION
Mars in Virgo, July 23, 5:21 - July 23, 5:22
Mars in Libra, July 23, 5:23 - Aug. 23, 12:08

YOUR LUCK MAGNETISM
Jupiter in Taurus, July 23, 5:21 - Aug. 23, 12:08

World Events

Aug. 3 – Sir Roger Casement, one of the leaders of the Irish Easter Rising, is hanged in London.

Aug. 5 – American chewing gum is introduced in France.

CANCER
From June 21, 18:24 through July 23, 5:20

The Human Tank

The symbol for the sign of Cancer is the Crab, a creature that carries its own fortress on its back. In June 1916, the British announced the development of the tank, a technology mirroring your symbol. In the wake of battlefield bloodbaths, in which troops charged from trenches into hailstorms of bullets, the machine-gun-proof tank was desperately needed by rank-and-file soldiers. Without the protection of tanks, field movement was measured in feet and inches, and one battle could claim hundreds of thousands of lives. Tragically, the tank was not put into use in time to prevent the greatest casualties—60,000 on July 1 alone—in the Battle of the Somme.

Your sign rules protection and security, benefits conferred by the tank's defensive capabilities. In a way, every Cancer has his or her own "tank." Of course, barring other influences in your chart, your personal tank does not come equipped with a small cannon on the top. Rather, when confronted with stressful circumstances or an emotional attack, you tend to withdraw. You may physically take yourself to a safe place, preferably home, or you may shut down, pulling your emotions deep within yourself.

Indicators in your chart suggest that you may be more emotionally vulnerable than other Cancerians, especially those born in peacetime. Because you may have been sensitized to the wartime anxiety of your caretakers, your feelings and intuition are likely to be more intense.

A secure family life may be your highest priority. You are likely to seek partners who honor commitment for better, for worse, for richer, for poorer, no matter what. Capricorn respects tradition and is "in it for the long haul." Taurus provides sturdy shoulders to lean on and strong arms to hold you close. Nothing can penetrate the safety of Leo's royal den.

Your capacity for self-protection has enabled you to survive the harrowing circumstances of two World Wars and the Great Depression. Problems can arise, however, if withdrawal lasts too long. With time, you may have learned to rely on loved ones to help you give your feelings a healthy airing.

LEO
From July 23, 5:21 through August 23, 12:08

The Marketing King

The sign of Leo represents children and the prerogative to lord over others. The news within days of your birth touched on both subjects. On August 5, 1916, American chewing gum was introduced to French markets. This new product might have lent some comfort to the boys on the warfront. Adding chewing gum to the list of military provisions, however, was not going to earn the United States respect in the arena of World War I. Europe was losing patience with the United States' determined neutral stance and staying out of the conflict was becoming an impossibility. Eight months later, the U.S. would join the war effort on the side of the Allies.

The Americans had other tricks up their sleeves, and the child in you certainly admires tricks. In the decades ahead, other products would join chewing gum in the pantheon of U.S. exports, and the French would be among the first to decry American cultural imperialism. Using the power of marketing is certainly one way to become king in a democratic country.

Indicators in your chart reveal a combination of ingenuity and razzle-dazzle. Members of your sign tend to be sunny, charismatic, and inventive. You may have made an outstanding salesperson: you could make a mint selling snowshoes in the Sahara desert. The force of your personality may be so great, people just feel special around you. You may have been a politician or celebrity.

You're likely to be fiercely protective of your family and their privacy. You may have sought strong partners who respect the sanctity of the royal Leo den. Cancer lavishes you with comfort and emotional security. Libra is happy to watch out for you behind the scenes. Pisces soaks in the glory of your grandeur, while Aquarius keeps your head from swelling to unhealthy proportions.

You may have charmed your way out of many a tough spot, but even appealing Leo cannot live on glamour alone. Jarring wake-up calls in life may have left you longing for something deeper, substantial, and meaningful. With maturity, you may have found glory in a child's graduation from college or a grandchild's first steps.

➤ Read about your Chinese Astrological sign on page 838. ➤ Read about your Personal Planets on page 826. ➤ Read about your personal Mystical Card on page 856.

VIRGO

From August 23, 12:09 through September 23, 9:14

The Devoted Friend

Virgo rules workers, and within days of your birth, the news reported several developments that benefited laborers in the United States. On September 1, 1916, the U.S. Congress enacted the Keating-Owens Act, which barred goods made by children from interstate trade. On September 3, President Wilson signed a bill mandating an eight-hour day for railroad workers. And on September 7, the U.S. Congress enacted the Worker's Compensation Act, providing work-related injury coverage for 500,000 federal employees. Such measures contrasted with the often violent conflicts over workers' rights in Europe, where countries' involvement in World War I may have triggered radicalization on the labor side and greater outrage on the government side. The contrast was starker still when one considers that the Russian Revolution was but six months away.

The U.S. had good astrological timing, as planetary patterns prior to September 8 favored peaceful resolution of potential conflicts. Similarly, if you are a Virgo born on or before September 8, you may prefer negotiation and political lobbying to overt conflict. If you were born after September 8, you may be willing to stand up and fight for your beliefs and demands.

No matter when you were born, group affiliations are likely to be very important to you. You may have been a devoted union member or a brave soldier on the battlefield. Your highest priorities may be to provide a safe home for your family and to put food on the table. Working hard is a part of you.

You are likely to be a devoted friend who remembers birthdays and sends cards. You may have settled down with a trusted companion who makes you feel safe. Cancer shares your family values. Steady, peaceful Taurus loves to share the fruits of your labors. Reliable Capricorn values your work ethic.

Having worked long and hard to provide for your loved ones, you deserve every benefit you've earned. Sometimes, though, your sense of self-worth may depend more on what you do than on who you are. With maturity, you can learn to trust in the unconditional love of those dear to you.

LIBRA

From September 23, 9:15 through October 23, 17:56

Liberator of Love

Your sign rules love and relationships, Libra, and the news within days of your birth included an item that promised to revolutionize relations between men and women in the decades to come. On October 16, 1916, Margaret Sanger, a public health nurse, argued that family planning was a necessary component of fighting poverty and promoting social progress. Having studied with Havelock Ellis in London, Sanger returned to Brooklyn, New York, where she opened the first birth-control clinic outside of Holland. Jailed for opening the clinic and indicted for distributing birth-control literature, Sanger focused her educational efforts on new immigrants to the United States.

Represented by the symbol of the Scales, Librans are likely to favor equality among all people. Because women gained the vote and greater reproductive rights during your lifetime, the personal was truly political for you. Having seen marked changes in your own family life, you might reason that birth control did more for gender equality than the vote.

The ultimate success of Sanger's crusade may have made a dramatic difference between your parents' family and your own. Likely to have had far fewer children than your parents, you may have enjoyed more disposable income. As freedom from serial pregnancy enabled women to pursue education and work, men and women in your family may have taken on new roles. Yours may have been one of the first two-income families.

Sanger's work may have freed you to enjoy greater intimacy in your marriage. The quality of relationships is very important to Libra, and you may not be happy unless you feel truly in love with your partner. Scorpio satisfies your need for closeness and passion. Leo lavishes you with romantic attention. Sagittarius makes every vacation a honeymoon.

The ability to work out compromises is a classic Libran talent. The late twentieth century brought such dramatic changes to relationships, even you may have had a hard time adjusting. Divorce among your children may have caused you sorrow. In time, you may have learned to withhold judgment and provide support.

➤ Read about your Chinese Astrological sign on page 838. ➤ Read about your Personal Planets on page 826. ➤ Read about your personal Mystical Card on page 856.

VIRGO
Your Personal Planets

YOUR LOVE POTENTIAL
Venus in Cancer, Aug. 23, 12:09 - Sept. 08, 22:25
Venus in Leo, Sept. 08, 22:26 - Sept. 23, 9:14

YOUR DRIVE AND AMBITION
Mars in Libra, Aug. 23, 12:09 - Sept. 08, 17:43
Mars in Scorpio, Sept. 08, 17:44 - Sept. 23, 9:14

YOUR LUCK MAGNETISM
Jupiter in Taurus, Aug. 23, 12:09 - Sept. 23, 9:14

World Events

Aug. 29 – Field Marshal von Hindenburg is appointed Chief of the German General Staff.

Sept. 20 – The German Spartacus League publishes the first edition of the underground newspaper *Die International.*

Sergei Diaghilev (right) in St. Mark's Square

LIBRA
Your Personal Planets

YOUR LOVE POTENTIAL
Venus in Leo, Sept. 23, 9:15 - Oct. 07, 22:10
Venus in Virgo, Oct. 07, 22:11 - Oct. 23, 17:56

YOUR DRIVE AND AMBITION
Mars in Scorpio, Sept. 23, 9:15 - Oct. 22, 2:57
Mars in Sagittarius, Oct. 22, 2:58 - Oct. 23, 17:56

YOUR LUCK MAGNETISM
Jupiter in Taurus, Sept. 23, 9:15 - Oct. 23, 17:56

World Events

Sept. 27 – Greece declares war on Bulgaria.

Oct. 16 – Sergei Diaghilev's Ballets Russes opens at the Manhattan Opera House in New York.

143

1916

SCORPIO
Your Personal Planets

YOUR LOVE POTENTIAL
Venus in Virgo, Oct. 23, 17:57 - Nov. 03, 0:58
Venus in Libra, Nov. 03, 0:59 - Nov. 22, 14:57

YOUR DRIVE AND AMBITION
Mars in Sagittarius, Oct. 23, 17:57 - Nov. 22, 14:57

YOUR LUCK MAGNETISM
Jupiter in Taurus, Oct. 23, 17:57 - Oct. 26, 14:52
Jupiter in Aries, Oct. 26, 14:53 - Nov. 22, 14:57

World Events

Oct. 24 – Henry Ford awards equal pay to women – $5 per day.

Nov. 7 – Jeanette Rankin becomes the first woman to be elected to the U.S. Congress.

David Lloyd George, Prime Minister of Great Britain

SAGITTARIUS
Your Personal Planets

YOUR LOVE POTENTIAL
Venus in Libra, Nov. 22, 14:58 - Nov. 27, 23:06
Venus in Scorpio, Nov. 27, 23:07 - Dec. 22, 3:58

YOUR DRIVE AND AMBITION
Mars in Sagittarius, Nov. 22, 14:58 - Dec. 01, 17:09
Mars in Capricorn, Dec. 01, 17:10 - Dec. 22, 3:58

YOUR LUCK MAGNETISM
Jupiter in Aries, Nov. 22, 14:58 - Dec. 22, 3:58

World Events

Dec. 5 – David Lloyd George becomes Britain's new Prime Minister.

Dec. 18 – U.S. President Wilson asks for the peace terms of the European powers.

SCORPIO
From October 23, 17:57 through November 22, 14:57

The Intense Energizer

Your sign rules sex and power, Scorpio, and at the time of your birth, breakthroughs involving both subjects were in the news. Margaret Sanger's crusade to bring birth control to women was well under way. On October 24, 1916, the Ford Motor Company awarded equal pay to its women workers. On November 7, Jeannette Rankin became the first woman elected to the U.S. House of Representatives. And in Europe, women were manufacturing munitions, driving trams, and working on the railroad. These surges in progress coincided with long-term planetary patterns that favored the worldwide empowerment of women, especially after men's power shifted from the homeland to the warfront.

The sign of Scorpio rules radical power politics. Women's gains in reproductive freedom and public stature affected everything from the economic and political interests of countries to the private welfare of families. A sweetly perfumed version of radical revolution was in the air. Throughout your life, women joined the workforce in ever-increasing numbers.

Because birth control removed the risk of pregnancy from private marital pleasure, its availability had a direct impact upon Scorpionic concerns. As an adult, you could enjoy worry-free intimacy with your mate, but you may have been concerned about threats to the integrity of your family. As sexuality seeped into popular culture, later in your life you may have wished you could stuff that genie back into a private bottle.

Sharing the blessings of prosperity may be your ultimate aim in relationships. Hard working partners were necessary to reach your goal. Taurean resourcefulness brings comfort. Cancer cares deeply about providing for family needs. Sagittarius shoots for lofty goals with perfect aim.

In times of radical change, Scorpio tends to thrive on the intensity of the shifting dynamics. And while you may have felt energized by the new possibilities of modernity, developments later in your life may have shocked even you. With maturity, you may have come to trust that the pendulum of progress would ultimately swing back toward greater discretion.

SAGITTARIUS
From November 22, 14:58 through December 22, 3:58

The Philosophical Optimist

The sign of Sagittarius rules international affairs and state governance. You were born at a time of turning points in such matters. After the death of Emperor Franz Josef, Austria was confronting the truth of its declining hold over the seventeen nationalities it once ruled. December 15, 1916, marked France's victory in the Battle of Verdun, with losses of 700,000 German and French men. Germany's costly and failed attempt to drive through Verdun undermined its absolute confidence on the western front. On the eastern front, Russia was reaching a different kind of turning point. Egregiously undersupplied both at home and on the warfront, the minds of the Russian people were turning from the overthrow of Germany to the overthrow of their own government.

When you were old enough to study World War I and its effects, you may have had a tragic appreciation for all its unforeseen consequences, such as the ultimate dissolution of its imperial participants. Because Sagittarius is the sign of the higher mind, you are likely to have a more sophisticated understanding of most things going on in the world.

The obsolescence of the nineteenth century empires may have brought drastic changes to your prospects in life. You may have faced new challenges—surviving the Great Depression and fighting World War II—that may have severely tested your religious views. You may have adopted a more agnostic, philosophical perspective.

Realistic, intelligent partners are likely to appeal to you. Yours is probably a home where world affairs dominate dinner-table discussion. Aries shares your eagerness to get to the point of a matter. Pisces offers spirituality you can accept. Gemini shares your regard for knowledge.

The Sagittarian ability to see the big picture allows you to remain optimistic under stress—a gift severely tested in your lifetime. Your generation produced the French Existentialists who declared, "God is dead," in the midst of World War II. Still, just as the imperative to defy evil enabled these same people to find the will to go on, so too were you inspired to say "yes" to life.

► Read about your Chinese Astrological sign on page 838. ► Read about your Personal Planets on page 826. ► Read about your personal Mystical Card on page 856.

CAPRICORN

From December 22, 3:59 through December 31, 23:59

The Pragmatic Realist

The sign of Capricorn rules confrontations with hard cold reality, two instances of which made news within days of your birth. On December 23, United States Secretary of State Robert Lansing suggested that the U.S. might have to discard its policy of avoiding "entangling foreign alliances." With American ships "entangling" themselves on German torpedoes in the Atlantic, the days of ignoring such provocations would soon end. A more harrowing reality confronted Tsar Nicholas II on December 30, with the assassination of the infamous royal family advisor, Grigori Rasputin. An astonishing expression of contempt for the Tsar, the murder of Rasputin opened the floodgates to the Russian Revolution.

When you were old enough to study these events, you may have wondered how the U.S. and Nicholas could have been so out of touch. For Capricorn, the safest way to live and survive is to maintain an unvarnished view of reality, warts and all. Preferring to know where any threat may be lurking, you may feel incapable of ignoring an enemy.

For one who had to live through the most murderous fifty years in human history, such a survival strategy was sensible and healthy. Indeed, the ability to read the handwriting on the wall may have given you an advantage in fleeing or coping with potentially deadly situations. Likely to be practical and unsentimental, you may respect similar qualities in others.

Solid relationships may have been a matter of life and death for you. You were likely to trust only the most honest, reliable partners. Both Cancer and Virgo would share your need for ultimate security and discretion. Scorpio and Taurus would safeguard your secrets and lock down all resources.

As a member of the generation that fought in and survived two world wars, the Great Depression, and the Holocaust, your pragmatism may have saved your life and that of your family. In peacetime, recognizing the absence of danger may have been one of the most difficult challenges of your life. With time to heal and restore your faith, you could regain a sense of trust and enjoy the fruits of your labors.

1916
CAPRICORN
Your Personal Planets

YOUR LOVE POTENTIAL
Venus in Scorpio, Dec. 22, 3:59 - Dec. 22, 7:49
Venus in Sagittarius, Dec. 22, 7:50 - Dec. 31, 23:59

YOUR DRIVE AND AMBITION
Mars in Capricorn, Dec. 22, 3:59 - Dec. 31, 23:59

YOUR LUCK MAGNETISM
Jupiter in Aries, Dec. 22, 3:59 - Dec. 31, 23:59

World Events

Dec. 22 – British forces occupy Sinai.

Dec. 30 – Grigori Rasputin, the Siberian monk who was reputed to have the Russian royal family in his power, is assassinated.

The storming of the Winter Palace in St. Petersburg

Special Feature
The Birth and Rebirth of a Nation: Russia
by Frank Andrews

Conditions in Russia in 1917 were ripe for revolution. Tsar Nicholas II had abdicated in February. A provisional government was in place, but its solid middle-class base was at odds with the growing number of workers' groups, set up as "soviets," and demanding food and the end of the slaughter of Russian troops in World War I. Bolshevist leaders hurried back home to Russia from their exile abroad, deeming their time had come, and set the wheels in motion.

The turning point was the capture of the former Tsar's Winter Palace in St. Petersburg, where the provisional government had made its headquarters. In the early morning hours of November 8, 1917, ministers were hiding in an upstairs room, still issuing orders by telegraph. The revolutionaries had overrun the streets and were storming the palace.

After a brief struggle, the ministers surrendered. A stray bullet hit a royal clock, stopping it at 2:12 a.m., freezing this moment in time. This same stopped clock remains a favorite tourist attraction at St. Petersburg's Hermitage Museum, where it forever points to the moment the new Russian state was born. Astrologers need a date, time, and place to draw up a horoscope, so the "birth data" for what was to become the Soviet Union became November 8, 1917, 2:12 a.m., St. Petersburg.

This new nation was a Scorpio—keenly interested in power, and what can be done when power is harnessed. Scorpio energy has the capacity to go to extremes in attempting to control its environment. A nation with its Sun in Scorpio is capable of swift and deep transformations, because Scorpio is ruled by Pluto, the planet of regeneration. The influence of Pluto steps in when deep changes are called for. A destruction of the old must occur to make way for the birth of the new. Plutonian energies are changes on a grand scale, affecting masses of people.

In the horoscope of the Soviet Union, Pluto is in the tenth house, representing in a nation's chart the chief executive or ruler. Directly opposite Pluto is Venus in the fourth house, which represents the interests of the people, as distinguished from the interests of the government, and representing democratic as opposed to autocratic tendencies. These are in direct opposition to each other.

(Continued on page 153)

➤ Read the Tsar Nicholas II's Star Profile on page 137.

1917

The Lion's Roar Enters Karma's Door: Saturn in Leo

During the volatile year of 1917 the world was still at war; as the King of Karma the planet Saturn made his way from the emotional sign of Cancer into the constellation of the mighty lion, Leo. Saturn in Leo gives rise to the need for self-importance and can bring to the masses a compulsive need for control of the environment. Dictatorial and dogmatic attitudes tend to flourish under the influence of Saturn in Leo. World leaders made defiant displays of this kind of behavior in the year of 1917. In the United Kingdom, on June 19, 1917, anti-German feeling led the government to advise the British royal family to change its German name to the House of Windsor. On November 7, 1917, the Bolsheviks seized power in Russia. On December 24, 1917, the Kaiser warned Russia that he would use an "iron fist" and "shining sword" if peace was spurned. Big egos abounded this year and most people in charge had no compunction about expressing them. The world was at war, and aggressive leaders gave new meaning to the word "bold". Under the intense energy of Saturn in Leo, many were enervated, and some in rather unpleasant ways. (This was also the time before the rise to power of Adolf Hitler, when he was beginning to foment his ideas.)

There are other ways to understand the influence of Saturn placed in the sign of Leo. Probably the most telling event of all during this unstable period was the birth of ultra-charismatic future President John F. Kennedy, the absolute worldliest Gemini born in the twentieth century. He represents the ultimate Saturn in Leo persona and, certainly, the less destructive manifestation of the energy. People born with Saturn in Leo tend to seek positions of power and leadership, and Kennedy exemplified this. The laws of principle and justice are high when Saturn is in Leo, and Kennedy's life attests to this function of the aspect. A great deal of attention is sought by those born with Saturn in Leo, and history confirms that there is a deep need for respect by those living under the influence of the aspect. In 1917, when world leaders didn't get exactly what they wanted, they lashed out.

Alexander Kerensky becomes premier in Russia

Mata Hari is executed for espionage

America enters the war

CLIMAX AND REVOLUTION

Germany proclaimed unrestricted submarine warfare and its U-boats sank dozens of Allied ships in the waters around Britain. President Wilson asserted that "The world must be made safe for democracy" and declared war on Germany. The U.S. mobilized swiftly, leading to hopes of a quick end to the war, but the year closed with no peace yet in sight. Revolution in Russia forced Tsar Nicholas II to abdicate. A moderate Menshevik government was established, but was soon overthrown by communist Bolsheviks, led by Lenin. British Foreign Secretary Arthur Balfour declared his support for a Jewish homeland in Palestine. To deploy American troops, the Selective Draft Act was passed, requiring men between twenty-one and thirty (later eighteen to forty-five) to register for military service. Food, fuel, and war supplies came under government control, halting nearly all exports. In the U. S., the first of the New Orleans Dixieland jazz recordings created a sensation across the country. Buffalo Bill (William F. Cody) and sculptor Auguste Rodin passed on, while the Dutch dancer Mata Hari (Marghereta Zelle) was executed for espionage.

➤ Read "The Birth and Rebirth of a Nation: Russia" by Frank Andrews on page 145.

CAPRICORN

From January 01, 0:00 through January 20, 14:36

The Honorable Team Player

The sign of Capricorn rules industrial productivity. At the time of your birth, the news told a tale of two countries. As of January 1, 1917, the U.S. celebrated the conclusion of the most prosperous year in its history. While World War I raged across the Atlantic, the U.S. enjoyed a record year in domestic trade, foreign trade, and output of steel and iron. In tragic contrast, Russia faced starvation, strikes in munitions factories, and the loss of millions of its men in the war. Within the year, Russia would be out of the war, and the U.S. would be in it.

You had just reached adulthood when war again broke out in Europe and began to spread across the world. Once again, the U.S. lagged behind other world powers in getting involved. Your position on entry into World War II—on an individual or national level—was a matter of responsibility and honor. You may have enlisted in the military, signed up to work at the defense plant, or joined up with a pacifist or other political organization. Likely to be courageous but not impulsive, you may judge yourself and others by the willingness to serve a cause greater than oneself.

Personal sacrifice and teamwork are likely to be among your highest values. Members of your sign tend to be natural leaders with a respect for organization and a chain of command. The higher the stakes—in military campaigns, emergency triage, or quarterly production goals—the better you tend to perform.

Your respect for commitment extends to relationships. Drawn to stable, reliable companions, you likely enjoy an affectionate family life within the comfort of privacy. Aquarius shares your regard for principle. Not easily ruffled, Taurus provides a secure foundation for marriage and raising children. Leo's spirituality can bring out the best in you.

Friends and loved ones may have come to rely on your dependability and devotion. At some point in your life, however, you may have reached the point of exhaustion. With maturity, you may have realized that the better you care for yourself, the better prepared you will be to care for others.

AQUARIUS

From January 20, 14:37 through February 19, 5:04

The Electrifying Champion

The sign of Aquarius rules the spark that lights a conflagration, and within days of your birth, sparks were flying between Germany and the United States. With its overtures of peace rejected by the U.S. and the Entente, Germany once again launched unrestrained submarine warfare on neutral ships. On February 3, Germany sank the U.S.S. *Housatonic* off the coast of Sicily. On that same day, the U.S. broke off diplomatic relations with Germany. On February 7, Germany announced that it was holding all American citizens within its borders hostage. In the face of such blatant provocation, U.S. entry to the war became imminent.

Your personality may reflect the volatile times in which you were born. Even as a baby, you may have absorbed the anger and stress of the adults who cared for you. You may have had an explosive temper, especially in your youth. Such a characteristic may have been an asset if you were among the members of your generation who fought in World War II. Heaven help the enemy who crossed you or any authority figure who tried to unjustly squelch you.

Your chart reveals the potential for electrifying genius, with your peak performance under pressure. Still, you may also feel a basic, intuitive allegiance to certain traditional standards of patriotism and decency. Your sense of spirituality may bring out a selfless, humanitarian impulse in you. You may have championed causes to help the displaced, homeless, and disadvantaged.

You may have teamed up with partners who were attracted to your energy. Any long-term relationship would require an active pace and constant growth. Hardworking Virgo values service and provides plenty of projects to keep you busy. With Leo, you can make romantic fireworks. Aries' speedy, competitive pace can keep you happily on the move.

The strong Aquarian influences in your chart gave you the kind of personal power that could fuel revolutions. If you operated at peak capacity for too long, however, you may have blown a few gaskets. With maturity, you may have learned to avoid burnout by making time to recharge your batteries.

➤ Read about your Chinese Astrological sign on page 838. ➤ Read about your Personal Planets on page 826. ➤ Read about your personal Mystical Card on page 856.

CAPRICORN
Your Personal Planets

YOUR LOVE POTENTIAL
Venus in Sagittarius, Jan. 01, 0:00 - Jan. 15, 10:45
Venus in Capricorn, Jan. 15, 10:46 - Jan. 20, 14:36

YOUR DRIVE AND AMBITION
Mars in Capricorn, Jan. 01, 0:00 - Jan. 09, 12:54
Mars in Aquarius, Jan. 09, 12:55 - Jan. 20, 14:36

YOUR LUCK MAGNETISM
Jupiter in Aries, Jan. 01, 0:00 - Jan. 20, 14:36

World Events

Jan. 9 – Russian Premier Trepov resigns; Prince Golitzin succeeds.

Jan. 10 – Wild West showman "Buffalo Bill" Cody dies.

The British Labour Delegation among Russian soldiers

AQUARIUS
Your Personal Planets

YOUR LOVE POTENTIAL
Venus in Capricorn, Jan. 20, 14:37 - Feb. 08, 11:50
Venus in Aquarius, Feb. 08, 11:51 - Feb. 19, 5:04

YOUR DRIVE AND AMBITION
Mars in Aquarius, Jan. 20, 14:37 - Feb. 16, 13:32
Mars in Pisces, Feb. 16, 13:33 - Feb. 19, 5:04

YOUR LUCK MAGNETISM
Jupiter in Aries, Jan. 20, 14:37 - Feb. 12, 15:57
Jupiter in Taurus, Feb. 12, 15:58 - Feb. 19, 5:04

World Events

Feb. 3 – Germany declares total submarine warfare, causing the U.S. to break diplomatic relations.

Feb. 10 – International Zionist leaders meet with the British government in London to discuss the Jewish settlement in Palestine.

1917

PISCES
Your Personal Planets

YOUR LOVE POTENTIAL
Venus in Aquarius, Feb. 19, 5:05 - Mar. 04, 13:08
Venus in Pisces, Mar. 04, 13:09 - Mar. 21, 4:36

YOUR DRIVE AND AMBITION
Mars in Pisces, Feb. 19, 5:05 - Mar. 21, 4:36

YOUR LUCK MAGNETISM
Jupiter in Taurus, Mar. 19, 5:05 - Mar. 21, 4:36

World Events

Feb. 25 – British author Anthony Burgess is born.

Mar. 16 – Tsar Nicholas II is forced to abdicate due to high war losses and widespread political unrest.

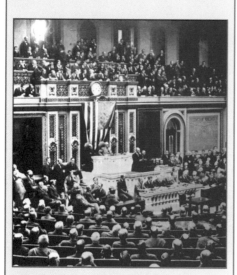

President Wilson reads the declaration of war against Germany to Congress

ARIES
Your Personal Planets

YOUR LOVE POTENTIAL
Venus in Pisces, Mar. 21, 4:37 - Mar. 28, 16:00
Venus in Aries, Mar. 28, 16:01 - Apr. 20, 16:16

YOUR DRIVE AND AMBITION
Mars in Pisces, Mar. 21, 4:37 - Mar. 26, 17:39
Mars in Aries, Mar. 26, 17:40 - Apr. 20, 16:16

YOUR LUCK MAGNETISM
Jupiter in Taurus, Mar. 21, 4:37 - Apr. 20, 16:16

World Events

Apr. 6 – U.S. President Wilson signs a declaration of war against Germany.

Apr. 7 – President Valdez of Panama promises to aid the U.S. in defending the Panama Canal.

PISCES
From February 19, 5:05 through March 21, 4:36

The Seafaring Hero

As a Piscean, you have a natural affinity for water, but when you were born, the sea was a deadly destination. In the three weeks ending February 26, 1917, German submarines had sunk 134 non-belligerent Allied ships in the Atlantic, the English Channel, and the North Sea. This was the salvo that would finally propel the United States to enter World War I on the side of the Allies. Because members of your sign tend to love anything to do with ships, adults in your life would have made sure to tell you about the submarine warfare at the time of your birth.

Likely to have studied naval history in your youth, you may have joined the navy or the marines in World War II. While you are likely to have the Piscean trait of compassion, your chart also reveals a fierce, courageous energy. Without a doubt, more than a few Pisceans of 1917 landed on Omaha Beach. If you are female, you may have joined the military to serve on a hospital ship or in other support capacities.

You were likely to pursue a career that involved saving others from peril. You may have been a wartime hero for your bravery in saving the lives of civilians or fellow soldiers. A rebellious streak in your chart suggests a personality type like those who defied Hitler by hiding Jews and helping them to escape to safety. In peacetime, you may have been a firefighter, a social worker, or even an animal rescue worker.

Your relationships may be filled with emotional intensity. Affectionate, demonstrative partners are most likely to attract you. Moved by your tenderness, Cancer honors your feelings. Taurus offers you peaceful refuge and indulgently dotes on you. Leo fires up your romantic side. Aquarius shares your devotion to others.

You may have repeatedly proved your ability to rise to any occasion, no matter how perilous. With your tender Piscean soul, however, it may have been difficult for you to shield your feelings from the impact of violence, warfare, and human suffering. With time and experience, you may have developed healthy emotional filters to protect yourself from overexposure to painful situations.

ARIES
From March 21, 4:37 through April 20, 16:16

The Personal Powerhouse

As you've no doubt been repeatedly advised, Aries, when you were born, all hell broke loose. The Russian Revolution was underway. On April 16, 1917, Vladimir Ilyich Lenin, Marxist leader of the Bolsheviks, arrived in Russia, following the abdication of Tsar Nicholas II on March 16. On April 6, the United States declared war on Germany. Upon joining the Allies in World War I, President Wilson exclaimed, "The world must be made safe for democracy."

The Russian Revolution and America's entry into the war were long in coming. The chart for Ariens born in 1917 reflects a similar dynamic, in which simmering energies shift into open expression. If you were born before March 26, you may express anger or willfulness in a restrained, indirect way. Although you are calm and peaceful on the outside, others may find you intimidating. In dealing with conflict, secret negotiations may be more in line with your style. You would have made an outstanding intelligence officer in World War II.

If you were born on or after March 26, you are more likely to be openly forceful, willing to stare down an opponent, and charge ahead if necessary. When diplomats had given up on a recalcitrant opponent, they might have called you into play. By way of introduction, you might have announced, "Hello. I'm your worst nightmare." All Ariens of 1917 are likely to enjoy the benefit of fearlessness, tempered and focused by discipline.

On the home front, you may have sought a partner who was strong enough to keep you in line. A well-ordered family life made it easier to deal with the upheaval of worldwide wars and economic depression. Cancer gives you the security of tradition. Capricorn provides excellent survival planning. Loyal Leo protects the family lair.

You spent the first twenty-eight years of your life during the most violent and deadly period in human history. To redirect your remarkable power in a post-1945 world, you had to remake yourself. With all the rebuilding needed in peacetime, you may have become a human Marshall Plan, forging a new infrastructure for progress and prosperity.

➤ Read about your Chinese Astrological sign on page 838. ➤ Read about your Personal Planets on page 826. ➤ Read about your personal Mystical Card on page 856.

TAURUS

From April 20, 16:17 through May 21, 15:58

The Creative Financier

The sign of Taurus rules critical resources. At the time of your birth, the Allies were preparing to tap into a newly available cache of supplies, desperately needed in the fight against Germany in World War I—Yankees. On May 18, 1917, American troops received their orders to ship out to France. The failed Nivelle Offensive had ended April 20, with French casualties totaling 120,000. With native manpower badly depleted, France had turned to its colonies for recruits. That, combined with the imminent arrival of thousands of brand-spanking-new "doughboys" from the States—not to mention $200 million in U.S. war loans—would markedly change the character of the war: from a contest for dominance among imperial powers, to a campaign for worldwide democratization.

In general, the Taurean personality is placid, peace-loving, and happy—so long as conditions of abundance prevail. You are likely to associate adequate income with security. At some point in your life, you may have lost money to an outright swindler or someone who could not deliver on promises. Any wrongful incursion on your finances is a red flag, inciting you to charge full-force.

You are likely to think in concrete, vivid ways. In business, you may have a flair for "creative financing." Concepts may come to you in visual patterns. In brainstorming sessions, you may jump up and sketch diagrams on the drawing board. When someone has a new idea, you may ask what it looks like.

Security is as important in your relationships as it is in your bankbook. You are likely to seek out partners who can grow with you over time. Thoughtful Virgo realizes the value of small, loving gestures. Capricorn is willing to invest in long-term happiness. Everything you give to Cancer comes back to you in sweet new forms.

You may have learned that if something sounds too good to be true, it probably is. Hesitation in trusting others may have protected you and your family from potentially disastrous losses. With the return of prosperity, you could afford to be more generous in sharing the finer things in life with your loved ones.

GEMINI

From May 21, 15:59 through June 22, 0:13

The Historical Orator

The sign of Gemini rules dialogue and oratory, and within days of your birth a debate of historic proportions was taking place in Petrograd. On June 16, 1917, the Pan-Russian Congress of Workman's and Soldiers' Delegates voted to reject Austria's proposal for a separate peace in World War I. This resolution followed the position, advocated by Minister of War Alexander Kerensky, that to agree to peace would be "fraternizing with the enemy." Challenging Kerensky was none other than Vladimir Ilyich Lenin, leader of the Bolsheviks, who contended that involvement in the war was "treason to the interests of international Socialism."

If you studied these events in school, you may have wished you could have been a fly on the wall for that showdown! The competition of ideas can be extremely energizing for Gemini, especially when the stakes are high. In the confrontation between Kerensky and Lenin, two ideologies—liberal democracy and radical socialism—competed for control over Mother Russia.

Members of your sign tend to be excellent writers and speakers. The chart for Gemini of 1917 indicates exceptional creativity along with a passion for history. You might have been inspired to write and perform plays, songs, or epic poems that recreated dramatic episodes of the past. Likely to prefer works of fiction to non-fiction, you may have crafted artistic compositions in any number of media.

You may have met your mate at a poetry reading, an art gallery, or even a cafe frequented by intellectuals. You may seek relationships that can broaden your horizons. Sagittarians share your passion for ideas. Creative Librans relate to your intelligence. Leos' flair for romance and drama can bring out the best in you.

Your talents for expression and artistry may have provided a healthy outlet for coping with the challenges of living through the Great Depression and World War II. Sometimes, however, the stress of real life may have overwhelmed your delicate Gemini nerves. With time, you may have gotten in the habit of retiring to a safe retreat, where you could relax and rejuvenate yourself.

➤ Read about your Chinese Astrological sign on page 838. ➤ Read about your Personal Planets on page 826. ➤ Read about your personal Mystical Card on page 856.

1917

TAURUS
Your Personal Planets

YOUR LOVE POTENTIAL
Venus in Aries, Apr. 20, 16:17 - Apr. 21, 21:16
Venus in Taurus, Apr. 21, 21:17 - May 16, 5:07
Venus in Gemini, May 16, 5:08 - May 21, 15:58

YOUR DRIVE AND AMBITION
Mars in Aries, Apr. 20, 16:17 - May 04, 22:13
Mars in Taurus, May 04, 22:14 - May 21, 15:58

YOUR LUCK MAGNETISM
Jupiter in Taurus, Apr. 20, 16:17 - May 21, 15:58

World Events

May 12 – Béla Bartok's ballet *The Wooden Prince* opens in Budapest.

May 18 – President Wilson signs the Selective Service Act, requiring all men between the age of twenty-one and thirty to register for possible military service.

John F. Kennedy, thirty-fifth U.S. President, is born under the sign of Gemini

GEMINI
Your Personal Planets

YOUR LOVE POTENTIAL
Venus in Gemini, May 21, 15:59 - June 09, 15:14
Venus in Cancer, June 09, 15:15 - June 22, 0:13

YOUR DRIVE AND AMBITION
Mars in Taurus, May 21, 15:59 - June 14, 20:57
Mars in Gemini, June 14, 20:58 - June 22, 0:13

YOUR LUCK MAGNETISM
Jupiter in Taurus, May 21, 15:59 - June 22, 0:13

World Events

May 29 – John F. Kennedy, 35th U.S. President, is born.

June 19 – King George V adopts the new name of Windsor for the British royal family.

149

1917

CANCER
Your Personal Planets

YOUR LOVE POTENTIAL
Venus in Cancer, June 22, 0:14 - July 04, 3:19
Venus in Leo, July 04, 3:20 - July 23, 11:07

YOUR DRIVE AND AMBITION
Mars in Gemini, June 22, 0:14 - July 23, 11:07

YOUR LUCK MAGNETISM
Jupiter in Taurus, June 22, 0:14 - June 29, 23:50
Jupiter in Gemini, June 29, 23:51 - July 23, 11:07

World Events

June 26 – Maj. Gen. John J. Pershing and his troops arrive in France.

July 20 – Alexander Kerensky becomes premier of Russia.

Mata Hari is executed for espionage

LEO
Your Personal Planets

YOUR LOVE POTENTIAL
Venus in Leo, July 23, 11:08 - July 28, 17:51
Venus in Virgo, July 28, 17:52 - Aug. 22, 12:18
Venus in Libra, Aug. 22, 12:19 - Aug. 23, 17:53

YOUR DRIVE AND AMBITION
Mars in Gemini, July 23, 11:08 - July 28, 3:59
Mars in Cancer, July 28, 4:00 - Aug. 23, 17:53

YOUR LUCK MAGNETISM
Jupiter in Gemini, July 23, 11:08 - Aug. 23, 17:53

World Events

July 25 – A court-martial in France sentences Dutch dancer MataHari to death for espionage.

Aug. 14 – China declares war on Germany and Austria.

CANCER
From June 22, 0:14 through July 23, 11:07

The Parental Nurturer

The sign of Cancer rules parents, feeding, and security—all themes in the news within days of your birth. On June 29, 1917, the Ukraine, known as the breadbasket of Mother Russia, declared its independence. Riots sparked by widespread starvation had already led to the Tsar's abdication. Succeeding to the position of Prime Minister of the provisional government in July, Alexander Kerensky could afford neither to lose the Ukraine, nor to allow unrest there to inspire defiance in other ethnic regions. In the United States, President Wilson nationalized exports of food, fuel, and war supplies. To ensure that no such necessities would reach the enemies of the U.S., special licenses were required to ship such provisions out of the country.

Both Wilson and Kerensky acted as parents over their countries. Like Kerensky in Russia, the viability of your own family might have depended on the struggle to find adequate food in the world wars. Wilson's role was like the parent who declares the neighborhood bully unwelcome at the family dinner table. For you too, sharing meals may be a way to define relationships and express affection.

You are likely to be handy, the great fixer around the house. Home renovations may provide an outlet for your restlessness. You are also likely to be the kind of Cancerian who enjoys travel. Taking great care to outfit your means of transportation with the most luxurious accommodations, you may carry a smaller version of home with you.

Nothing is liable to be as dear to you as family. You may seek a partner who shares your insistence on perfect attendance at the supper table. Capricorn shares your regard for traditional ties of togetherness. Taurus shares your dreams of abundance. Pisces never fails to compliment your cooking.

Your parental instincts were likely to be the factor that ensured the survival of your loved ones in challenging times. Sometimes, however, Cancerians tend to equate acceptance of what they give with whether they are truly loved. With maturity, you may have come to trust in the unconditional love of those dearest to you.

LEO
From July 23, 11:08 through August 23, 17:53

The Rebellious Royal

Your sign puts the "child" in childhood rebellion, Leo, and the news within days of your birth reflected this theme. On August 15, 1917, the removal from St. Petersburg of Tsar Nicholas II—once revered as the "Little Father" of the Russian people—was the starkest example. As the prospects for victory in World War I grew dim, men of the German naval fleet mutinied *en masse* at Wilhelmshaven in early August 1917. President Wilson held a tighter reign in the United States, declaring that draft resisters could be executed. Because the U.S. could afford to outfit its soldiers like little kings—each with 168 articles of arms, clothing, and eating utensils—discipline was easier to maintain.

Leo is the sign of the King, but the nature of official royalty went into radical dissolution during your lifetime. The chart for Leo of 1917 shows that, like the common people at the time of your birth, you too were likely to gain personal power by rebelling against or overthrowing authority figures. You may pride yourself on your rugged individualism.

In every aspect of your life, you were likely to team up with others in order to realize your goals. You may have been a union organizer or started a business with a trusted partner. Maintaining balance and fairness in such relationships may have been one of your highest priorities. You have a special genius for taking challenging situations and turning them to your benefit.

You may have met your life partner through social circles or by working together on a shared cause. You may refer to him or her as "my best friend." Aquarians share your love for exciting activities and people. Libra's artistic touch ensures your home will be fit for a king. Gemini may be the only sign that can sweet talk you into happy submission.

Leo's confidence and charisma can capture others' attention, but you may have sometimes doubted your ability to deliver on your promises. Your challenge in life has been to learn to truly believe in yourself. With maturity, you came to depend less on how others responded to you and more on the power of your own convictions.

► Read about your Chinese Astrological sign on page 838. ► Read about your Personal Planets on page 826. ► Read about your personal Mystical Card on page 856.

VIRGO

From August 23, 17:54 through September 23, 14:59

The Dedicated Egalitarian

A basic Virgoan rule holds that a job well done deserves to be rewarded. A tragic violation of this principle occurred within days of your birth, Virgo. The news on August 24, 1917, told of a race riot involving African American soldiers quartered in Houston. Having objected when a white police officer slapped a black woman on the street, one of the black soldiers was beaten, along with a fellow soldier who tried to help him. The riot erupted from there. Similar scenes occurred in other southern cities in the United States, despite the fact that 2,291,000 African Americans had volunteered to fight for the U.S. in World War I—200,000 of those with the French army. The 369th Regiment, the "Hell Fighters," was the first Allied regiment to break through German lines to the Rhine. To America's shame, ten black soldiers, several still in uniform, were lynched in the year after the war ended.

The sign of Virgo rules people in service. Members of your sign tend to judge others by the quality of their work—not by color, family of birth, or social standing. You are likely to believe that everyone deserves a fair chance to work for fair compensation. You may feel shame when others receive unjust treatment.

Virgos are often meticulous in their habits, but if you were born during the period from August 27 to September 15, you may care more about maintaining balance and flexibility in your life. You may be more willing than most Virgos to break personal routines, especially if friends or partners need help.

You are likely to be attracted to people who need you. Vulnerable partners can give you the security of feeling indispensable. Pisces knows how to show gratitude for all your support. Reclusive Aquarius relies on you to manage routine business. Scorpio treasures your discretion with secrets.

Your faith in common decency may have shamed others into doing the right thing, but you may have gotten yourself in trouble by too often taking on responsibility for others' sins. With maturity, you may have learned to simply be your own best example of the high ideals you embrace.

LIBRA

From September 23, 15:00 through October 23, 23:43

The Charismatic Leader

A Libran might have coined the phrase, "all's fair in love and war." Such a philosophy summed up the tragic career of Mata Hari, executed as a spy on October 15, 1917. Born Margaretha Zelle in 1876 in Holland, Mata Hari became a celebrated exotic dancer and courtesan in Paris. Recruited as a spy for the French in World War I, Mata Hari pursued romantic adventures with high-ranking German officials. Such dangerous liaisons may have backfired. Historians today contend that suspicious German officials purposely incriminated Mata Hari as a German spy, by sending messages in a code they knew had been broken by the Allies. Arrested by the French in February 1917, she was found guilty by a military tribunal.

Represented by the symbol of the Scales, Libra is a double-sided sign. Tending to be equivocal, Librans can easily relate to opposing parties in a dispute. You may be able to sympathize with people who hold mutually hostile positions. The story of Mata Hari, however, illustrates the old proverb that the middle of the road can be the most dangerous place to be.

You may be idealistic and extremely charismatic. Even in the toughest circumstances, you may strongly believe in your ability to inspire others to rise above themselves. Your chart shows an ability to put concrete results behind your beliefs, and a record of good results may have been your saving grace. Others may find you to be a gracious and compelling leader.

You are not likely to be willing to compromise on the necessity for romance in love and marriage. You may have chosen a partner who took your breath away from across the room. Leo dazzles you with hearts and flowers. Cancer fills your nights with passion. Music-loving Pisces may have you dancing in the kitchen.

Having sympathy with others has always enabled you to play the peacemaker. Sometimes, however, the failure to take a strong position can get you into trouble. People may distrust you if they don't know where you stand. With maturity, you may have realized that you could stand firm in your own truth while respecting others' right to disagree.

➤ Read about your Chinese Astrological sign on page 838. ➤ Read about your Personal Planets on page 826. ➤ Read about your personal Mystical Card on page 856.

1917

VIRGO
Your Personal Planets

YOUR LOVE POTENTIAL
Venus in Libra, Aug. 23, 17:54 - Sept. 16, 12:59
Venus in Scorpio, Sept. 16, 13:00 - Sept. 23, 14:49

YOUR DRIVE AND AMBITION
Mars in Cancer, Aug. 23, 17:54 - Sept. 12, 10:51
Mars in Leo, Sept. 12, 10:52 - Sept. 23, 14:49

YOUR LUCK MAGNETISM
Jupiter in Gemini, Aug. 23, 17:54 - Sept. 23, 14:49

World Events

Sept. 15 - Alexander Kerensky declares Russia a republic.

Sept. 18 - The San Francisco shipping industry is threatened as 3,500 go on strike.

Death of French painter Edgar Degas

LIBRA
Your Personal Planets

YOUR LOVE POTENTIAL
Venus in Scorpio, Sept. 23, 15:00 - Oct. 11, 23:32
Venus in Sagittarius, Oct. 11, 23:33 - Oct. 23, 23:43

YOUR DRIVE AND AMBITION
Mars in Leo, Sept. 23, 15:00 - Oct. 23, 23:43

YOUR LUCK MAGNETISM
Jupiter in Gemini, Sept. 23, 15:00 - Oct. 23, 23:43

World Events

Sept. 27 - French painter Edgar Degas dies.

Oct. 21 - Jazz trumpeter Dizzy Gillespie is born.

1917

SCORPIO
Your Personal Planets

YOUR LOVE POTENTIAL
Venus in Sagittarius, Oct. 23, 23:44 - Nov. 07, 5:00
Venus in Capricorn, Nov. 07, 5:01 - Nov. 22, 20:44

YOUR DRIVE AND AMBITION
Mars in Leo, Oct. 23, 23:44 - Nov. 02, 10:59
Mars in Virgo, Nov. 02, 11:00 - Nov. 22, 20:44

YOUR LUCK MAGNETISM
Jupiter in Gemini, Oct. 23, 23:44 - Nov. 22, 20:44

World Events

Nov. 7 – The Bolsheviks, led by Vladimir Ilyich Lenin, seize power in Russia.

Nov. 10 – Forty-one U.S. suffragettes are arrested during a demonstration outside the White House.

Lawrence of Arabia, the "uncrowned king"

SAGITTARIUS
Your Personal Planets

YOUR LOVE POTENTIAL
Venus in Capricorn, Nov. 22, 20:45 - Dec. 05, 13:13
Venus in Aquarius, Dec. 05, 13:14 - Dec. 22, 9:45

YOUR DRIVE AND AMBITION
Mars in Virgo, Nov. 22, 20:45 - Dec. 22, 9:45

YOUR LUCK MAGNETISM
Jupiter in Gemini, Nov. 22, 20:45 - Dec. 22, 9:45

World Events

Dec. 9 – British General Allenby enters Jerusalem with seven infantry and three cavalry divisions.

Dec. 10 – The Nobel Peace Prize is awarded to the International Red Cross.

SCORPIO
From October 23, 23:44 through November 22, 20:44

The Radical Missionary

Your sign rules radical shifts in world power, Scorpio. You were born within days of two events that would influence world history into the next millennium. On November 2, 1917, the British government issued the Balfour Declaration, supporting the establishment of a Jewish homeland in Palestine. Although the ambiguous wording of the statement has fueled argument to this day, the Balfour Declaration laid the foundation for the State of Israel. As if the future of the Holy Land was not enough, on November 7, the Bolshevik Party overthrew the Provisional Government of Russia in a bloodless revolution. Leon Trotsky was appointed head of the new revolutionary government, but Vladimir Ilyich Lenin exercised true control.

You may have felt energized to learn of the developments that coincided with your birth. Scorpios tend to be quiet but intense people with steely focus. The "October Revolution" succeeded without a fight because the Bolsheviks simply harnessed the power of government troops already on the verge of mutiny. You may be similarly astute, able to sense the undercurrent of any situation and turn it to your advantage.

You lived through the most murderous period in human history, but your chart shows a deep capacity for rekindling life. Your sign rules birth and death, and you may see the two as i nextricably intertwined. Reverence for life may be your foremost religious value, one for which you may have risked your own life.

Unlikely to intellectualize the reasons for your relationships, you may have chosen a life partner because ... well, just because. Cancer can fulfill your needs, based on intuition alone. You and Pisces can finish each other's sentences. Virgo understands your need for discretion.

Scorpio's cool instinct for power dynamics can bring life to influential new movements. The mission can become hopelessly corrupted, however, if leaders allow honorable ends to justify illegitimate means. If you ever found yourself in such a situation, you may have become disillusioned. With experience, you may have resolved never to compromise certain values.

SAGITTARIUS
From November 22, 20:45 through December 22, 9:45

The Passionate Professor

The sign of Sagittarius rules foreign adventure. About a month before your birth, a certain foreign adventurer played a crucial role in General Edmund Allenby's World War I victory in Palestine. He was not T. E. Lawrence, but Richard Meinertzhagen. Planning thrusts at Gaza and Beersheba, Allenby ordered Meinertzhagen, a Zionist Christian, to fool the Turks into expecting the main blow at Gaza. Riding out on horseback, Meinertzhagen lured the Turks to give chase. As he fled, he dropped a sack containing false plans. Falling for the ruse, the Turks left Beersheba lightly guarded. On October 31, Allenby took Beersheba before the Turks could destroy its wells, thus affording British troops a chance at refreshment before proceeding north. On December 9, 1917, Allenby took Jerusalem, as a Christmas present for British Prime Minister Lloyd George.

Sagittarius rules the discipline of learning. Once a subject captures your interest, you are likely to research it to the fullest extent. If an interest in foreign adventure moved you to study Lawrence of Arabia, you may have gone on to learn about the equally fascinating Meinertzhagen and how he softened the remaining Turkish forces at Beersheba by arranging an airdrop of opium-laced cigarettes.

Likely to have a strong capacity for discipline and imagination, you would make a great teacher, diplomat, or politician. A flair for vivid description of subjects that ordinarily seem dry and inaccessible may enable you to convey knowledge and opinions with compelling charisma.

You may seek relationships that expand your horizons. Your life partner may have found you traveling in a foreign country. With Gemini you can feast on food for thought. Libra has as much elegance as intelligence. Leo inspires you to reach your greatest potential.

Intellectual Sagittarius can grasp subtle but important details about the world and its processes. Your enthusiasm for such pursuits can be contagious, but loved ones may wish to connect on a more personal level. With maturity, you may have come to give your heart with as much emphasis as your mind.

► Read about your Chinese Astrological sign on page 838. ► Read about your Personal Planets on page 826. ► Read about your personal Mystical Card on page 856.

CAPRICORN

From December 22, 9:46 through December 31, 23:59

The Patient Founder

Within days of your birth, Capricorn, the news reported the death of a woman who exemplified many of the best characteristics of your sign. December 22, 1917, marks the passing of Frances Xavier Cabrini, the first American citizen to be canonized as a saint (in 1946). Born in 1850, Mother Cabrini was a native of Santangelo, Italy. Pope Leo directed her to found a mission to help Italian immigrants in the United States. When she arrived, the archbishop of New York, citing a breakdown in plans, told her to go back to Italy. Ignoring the archbishop, Mother Cabrini went on to found sixty-seven institutions, including schools, hospitals, and orphanages, in the U.S., Europe, and South America.

Whatever your religious background, you may find Mother Cabrini's achievements inspiring. Capricorn rules the creation of new institutions, and you may share the patience, resourcefulness, and stubborn resolve of this ordinary peasant woman from Italy. Mother Cabrini's success is a story of upward mobility based on hard work—a Capricorn dream come true.

At key junctures in her life, Mother Cabrini humbly surrendered herself to her mission, worked hard, and trusted that what she needed would turn up. In other words, she was the perfect embodiment of the evolved Capricorn. You are likely to enjoy similar qualities. The chart for Capricorn of 1917 reveals a beautiful combination of creativity, duty, and discipline.

Your life partner may have been the answer to your prayers. You were likely to seek a helpmate to share the burdens and rewards of life. Cancer brings an iron will to make your dreams come true. Leo brings a joyous, can-do attitude. Taurus makes sure the bottom line always supports your plans.

Your greatest challenge has been to maintain a positive outlook, even as you survived two World Wars, the Great Depression, and the Holocaust. If you lost the belief in your own ability to rebuild and rekindle life, your gifts as a visionary and creator would have been wasted. In peacetime, you could revive your talents by using them, working hard, and trusting that help would come.

CAPRICORN
Your Personal Planets

YOUR LOVE POTENTIAL
Venus in Aquarius, Dec. 22, 9:46 - Dec. 31, 23:59

YOUR DRIVE AND AMBITION
Mars in Virgo, Dec. 22, 9:46 - Dec. 31, 23:59

YOUR LUCK MAGNETISM
Jupiter in Gemini, Dec. 22, 9:46 - Dec. 31, 23:59

World Events

Dec. 22 – Frances X. Cabrini dies; she is later canonized as the first American saint.

Dec. 24 – Kaiser Wilhelm II warns Russia that he will use an "iron fist" and "shining sword" if attempts at peace are spurned.

The storming of the Winter Palace in Petrograd

Special Feature
The Birth and Rebirth of a Nation: Russia

(Continued from page 145)

The Soviet chart indicates that, although the autocratic rule of the tzars was over, in fact a strong minority would be ruling the country and would seek to rule through imposing conformity and control over the masses. So, although the ideal was a communist, or workers' communal, state, what occurred was that power again was wielded by a few over the many. Two tyrannical men were to play pivotal roles in the development of the country—Lenin and Stalin.

One of the ways power was wielded was through the control of all forms of communication. In the chart of the Soviet Union, the Scorpio Sun is joined by Mercury (the planet of communication), which is also in Scorpio, and both are in the third house of communication. The art of propaganda reached its zenith in the Soviet Union.

In the birth chart we also find that the Scorpio Sun and Mercury are at odds with Uranus, planet of the unexpected, sudden upheavals,

technology, and humanitarian ideals, indicating the ideological power plays carried out by both Lenin and Stalin. Uranus also forms a difficult contact with Saturn, the planet of discipline, restriction, structure, and achievement. There was rapid development of technology and industrialization to make the new nation on a par with the rest of the world. Under Lenin, Scorpio Russia began a dramatic conversion to a new socialist order. Lenin moved the capital to Moscow, abolished private property, and suppressed the Church's power. The Bolshevist forces executed Tsar Nicholas II and his family and by 1920, after three more years of civil war, established a monopoly on power. Later, Stalin was ruthless in "purging" the country of those who disagreed, or had different ideas about how the State should operate.

The Moon in a national horoscope represents the common people and their psychological and material needs. The Soviet Moon is in proud and regal Leo, and it makes a close contact to the

planet Mars in Virgo. Weaponry, violence, and aggression are some of the keywords associated with Mars, the war planet. Mars is located in the service-oriented sign of Virgo, and represents the workers who played such an integral part in the Revolution. This is emphasized even more with Virgo rising at the time of the birth of the Soviet Union. Mars in Virgo also symbolizes soldiers and the military. So, the pride of the Russian people, formerly symbolized by the double-headed eagle, now lay in their communal efforts, military forces, and weapons technology, symbolized by the hammer and sickle on their new flag.

(Continued on page 161)

➤ Read the Tsar Nicholas II's Star Profile on page 137.

1918

Calming the Waters of War: Mars in Capricorn

On November 11, 1918, the war was officially over, as the Armistice was signed by the Germans. The position of Mars in the zodiac can indicate how the collective feels about war, hostility, and the use of force in general. Aggressive behavior is usually heightened when Mars is in fire signs. When Mars moves into earthy Capricorn—the sign of rational thought and careful planning—this feisty planet is reigned in, and logic can take over. When Mars moved into solid and structure-oriented Capricorn on November 12, 1918, it made a hard angle to Pluto, the planet of transformation. When Mars opposes Pluto in the sky, it opens the door to evolutionary forces, and there is a choice, either the path of good or evil can be chosen. On November 23, the U.S. War Department reported that 50,585 Americans had died in the ravages of World War I. World leaders chose peace in this case, possibly due to Pluto's position in Cancer at this time. Cancer is the most nurturing and emotional sign, and explosive Pluto may have understood, finally, that enough was most definitely enough. Sometimes hard astrological angles can have very positive outcomes.

Mars is exalted in Capricorn. This means that Capricorn is Mars' favorite place to spend his time. When Mars is in Capricorn, it makes the most efficient use of its unbounded, forceful energy. Mars can do just about anything it wants to do, but there is rarely ever any sort of method to his madness. In Capricorn, Mars's energy can truly be used for the best, as we see demonstrated with the end of World War I in November of 1918.

The Armistice is signed

British and Arab forces push the Turks out of Palestine

Max Planck wins the Nobel Prize for physics

CONTACTING THE DEAD

The Ouija board had been used for centuries to divine the future, gain spiritual insight, and communicate with the spirits of the dead. Its name derived from the French and German words for yes, *oui* and *ja* consecutively. During and after World War I, the Ouija board experienced an enormous surge in popularity, coinciding with the revival of Spiritualism. This renewed interest could be attributed to those who were desperate to talk with loved members of family or friends who had tragically been killed in the war.

WAR AND PEACE

The new Russian communist government made a separate peace with Germany. Tsar Nicholas II and his family were massacred and civil war broke out between the communists (Reds) and the Tzarist supporters (Whites). The German Kaiser initiated a fierce offensive in Western Europe. In the air war, the much-feared "Red" Baron von Richthofen was shot down and killed. Exhausted Germans were pushed back by American and French troops. British and Arab forces pushed the Turks out of Palestine. Ottoman Turkey, Austria, and Germany crumpled. The Armistice was signed, and the war ended. The German Kaiser abdicated. The Hapsburg empire of Austria-Hungary broke up as Austrians and Hungarians declared separate republics. By the war's end, the U.S. had sent 4 million troops to the front. A lethal influenza epidemic killed 21 million people worldwide. In the U.S. alone, 80,000 died, including many soldiers who contracted the disease before leaving for Europe. German physicist Max Planck won the Nobel Prize for physics for his work on energy. Chaplin's feature film *A Dog's Life* was released, while Spengler's *Decline of the West* disturbed readers.

➤ Read "The Birth and Rebirth of a Nation: Russia" by Frank Andrews on page 145.

CAPRICORN

From January 01, 0:00 through January 20, 20:24

The Institution Builder

Within days of your birth, Capricorn, United States President Woodrow Wilson issued a Fourteen Point proposal for ending World War I. The terms of the statement included: "[i]mpartial adjustment of all colonial claims, giving equal weight to the interests of colonial peoples," and the formation of a league of nations "to guarantee independence and territorial integrity to all." British Prime Minister Lloyd George's statement of January 5 anticipated Wilson's, but also called for "adoption of a really democratic constitution by Germany." A war that had begun as a competition for dominance among colonial powers seemed poised to end in a movement for international democracy and independence. But the Great War had spawned a violent offspring: socialist revolution, which was rising like a Frankenstein monster in the East.

The sign of Capricorn rules reform and institution building. Wilson's statement laid the foundation for the League of Nations and, ultimately, for the United Nations. Your sign rules things that endure, and you have the power to take the energy of destruction and turn it toward the creation of institutions, industry, and, indeed, nations.

Tending to think in concrete, pragmatic terms, you are likely to have a respect for the past and realistic expectations for the new. Idealism may compel you to build upon the new possibilities you envisage. You were unlikely to expect your life to be like that of your parents and grandparents.

You probably sought a life partner to forge a new life by your side. Together you would endure the worst and go on to create the best. Virgo works tirelessly to cultivate life. Libra brings harmony to home life. With Cancer, you reap the best of every season.

Able to bring structure from ruins, you helped to rebuild civilization from the ashes of the Great Depression and World War II. But later developments—rising divorce rates, rampant sexuality, drug culture—may have seemed like a new Frankenstein monster in your eyes. Having lived through the worst, you would have to trust the cycles of life to work out such excesses.

AQUARIUS

From January 20, 20:25 through February 19, 10:52

The Scrupulous Rebel

The sign of Aquarius rules rebellion and revolution, and when you were born, 1918 Aquarius, Bolshevism was tightening its stranglehold over Russia. Elsewhere in Europe, as World War I ground to a finish, democratic reform of former imperial powers had seemed the natural next step in any peace settlement. Overthrow of the Tsar had seemed a means to greater democracy, but within a year Russia had vaulted from the autocracy of the Tsar to the dictatorship of the proletariat. On January 28, 1918, Lenin ordered his newly formed Red Guard to forcibly dissolve the assembly, after it rejected his motion to form *soviets* or workers' councils.

The Soviet Union was your contemporary, and as soon as you were old enough, you may have felt personally invested in its progress. Many idealistic people supported socialist organizations, and you may have been one of them. Aquarians tend to favor protest and activism. In the wake of Stalin's purges and the Nazi-Soviet Non-Aggression Pact of 1939, however, you may have become disillusioned and questioned how the cause could become so egregiously divorced from its founding principles.

You are likely to be sociable, persuasive, and open to new ideas. You may have an interest in justice and the law. Your chart shows the potential to be critical of individualism or to embrace a spirituality that seeks to dissolve ego concerns. Whatever form your personal beliefs take, you may have a severe allergy to selfishness.

You may forge partnerships as a way to give and receive support, in a material, spiritual, and ideological sense. You might have rejected prospective mates who had overly restrictive expectations of relationships. Gemini's open-mindedness can be refreshing. Equality-loving Libra gives you room to breathe. Pisces' selflessness can inspire you.

The Aquarian tendency to care about others has been the driving force behind important humanitarian reforms. Your desire to help and support others, however, may have caused you to betray your own sense of what was right. With experience, you may have resolved to stand firmly in your own truth.

➤ Read about your Chinese Astrological sign on page 838. ➤ Read about your Personal Planets on page 826. ➤ Read about your personal Mystical Card on page 856.

CAPRICORN
Your Personal Planets

YOUR LOVE POTENTIAL
Venus in Aquarius, Jan. 01, 0:00 - Jan. 20, 20:24

YOUR DRIVE AND AMBITION
Mars in Virgo, Jan. 01, 0:00 - Jan. 11, 8:54
Mars in Libra, Jan. 11, 8:55 - Jan. 20, 20:24

YOUR LUCK MAGNETISM
Jupiter in Gemini, Jan. 01, 0:00 - Jan. 20, 20:24

World Events

Jan. 7 – The Germans move 75,000 troops from the eastern front to the western front.

Jan. 19 – Bolshevik deputies under Lenin order the constituent assembly to be dissolved after it rejects the motion to form soviets (workmen's councils).

The mobilization of German troops

AQUARIUS
Your Personal Planets

YOUR LOVE POTENTIAL
Venus in Aquarius, Jan. 20, 20:25 - Feb. 19, 10:52

YOUR DRIVE AND AMBITION
Mars in Libra, Jan. 20, 20:25 - Feb. 19, 10:52

YOUR LUCK MAGNETISM
Jupiter in Gemini, Jan. 20, 20:25 - Feb. 19, 10:52

World Events

Feb. 6 – Austrian artist Gustav Klimt dies.

Feb. 14 – Leon Forrest Douglass demonstrates a method for producing motion pictures in color.

1918

PISCES
Your Personal Planets

YOUR LOVE POTENTIAL
Venus in Aquarius, Feb. 19, 10:53 - Mar. 21, 10:25

YOUR DRIVE AND AMBITION
Mars in Libra, Feb. 19, 10:53 - Feb. 25, 18:59
Mars in Virgo, Feb. 25, 19:00 - Mar. 21, 10:25

YOUR LUCK MAGNETISM
Jupiter in Gemini, Feb. 19, 10:53 - Mar. 21, 10:25

World Events

Mar. 5 – The Russians move their capital from St. Petersburg to Moscow.

Mar. 13 – Women are to march in the St. Patrick's Day Parade in New York due to a shortage of men.

Recruitment poster for World War I

ARIES
Your Personal Planets

YOUR LOVE POTENTIAL
Venus in Aquarius, Mar. 21, 10:26 - Apr. 05, 20:10
Venus in Pisces, Apr. 05, 20:11 - Apr. 20, 22:04

YOUR DRIVE AND AMBITION
Mars in Virgo, Mar. 21, 10:26 - Apr. 20, 22:04

YOUR LUCK MAGNETISM
Jupiter in Gemini, Mar. 21, 10:26 - Apr. 20, 22:04

World Events

Apr. 1 – The first day of daylight saving is reported as a big success for fuel conservation in the U.S.

Apr. 9 – British Prime Minister Lloyd George orders conscription for Ireland, sparking angry protest.

PISCES
From February 19, 10:53 through March 21, 10:25

The Wary Survivor

Pisceans tend to be peace-loving people, but there was not much to love about the peace treaty ending the World War I enmity between Russia and the Central Powers. On March 14, 1918, the All-Russian Congress of Soviets ratified the Treaty of Brest-Litovsk. Lithuania, Poland, and the Ukraine were the price the Soviets paid for peace—a bargain that amounted to a betrayal for the Ukraine. Wanting independence from any colonial occupation, Ukrainian resentment of this deal would drain German troops from offensives on the western front, planned for the spring.

The sign of Pisces rules hidden dangers. At the time you were born, every new development in World War I seemed to trigger a chain reaction of unforeseen consequences. You may look to learning and education as a way of gaining emotional comfort. As an adult, you may have looked to the lessons of the Great War in order to understand the oncoming dangers of World War II. If you were left with a feeling of foreboding and helplessness, you were certainly not alone.

Likely to believe that violence leads to violence, you may be uncomfortable with open hostility and confrontation. During World War II, you may have worked for peace or did your best to save people from peril. You may be emotionally intense—a trait that can magnify small pleasures in good times. Performing routine chores can be soothing for you.

If you lost a parent in the Great War, you may have felt that having a family was a way to reaffirm life. You may have sought a partner committed to giving your children a better life. Cancer's faith in the cycles of life can reassure you. Dutiful Virgo makes you feel safe. Leo's optimism strengthens your hope.

You may have wondered how you could possibly survive the hellish challenges of your young adulthood. You may have wished you could hide somewhere and come out once World War II had ended. But you have an astounding supply of inner power. In maturity, you may have realized that you never knew how strong you were until you were tested. The pain you suffered made you more able to help and comfort others.

ARIES
From March 21, 10:26 through April 20, 22:04

The Uncommon Warrior

Aries is the sign of the warrior, and you were born during the final pivotal battle of World War I. In March 1917, Germany mounted a massive offensive, bombing Paris and attacking British lines at Feiurbaix-Armentières. Throwing 3,000,000 German troops onto the western front at once, the Kaiser called this "the most decisive moment of the war," and it was just that. While Germany gained some ground, it failed to meet its objectives, and eventually ran short on men, armaments, and power. If the Germans weren't having flashbacks to Verdun, they should have, because the offensive of spring 1918 was begun under the same planetary pattern that brings extreme disfavor on the initiation of combat. Ultimately, the Allies rallied and forced the Germans into an armistice by November.

You have this same planetary pattern in your chart, but its influence in a personal chart differs from its effects on transitory world events. You may express your "fighting spirit" in unconventional and creative ways. The "anti-instigation" pattern occurs every other year. At those times you may feel strangely energized, while other Ariens wander around feeling like Superman on Kryptonite.

You are likely to be athletic and health-conscious, but you may prefer contests of strength, endurance, or grace—distance events, dog sledding, figure skating—to contact sports. You may enjoy moments in the spotlight, but a need for regular hard work is more likely to drive you. You may feel out of sorts when you break your routine.

Relationships may have taught you a good lesson about give-and-take. The structure of commitment may paradoxically open you to greater romanticism in private. Loyal sunny Leo can be an inspirational mate. Virgo is giving and supports healthy habits. Sagittarius helps you realize your greatest potentials.

Your creative energies enabled you to set an example for new ways of living, a talent badly needed in a world changing more rapidly, year by year. With time and experience, you may have eagerly worked to serve humankind, by building on the ashes of the old and obsolete ways.

➤ Read about your Chinese Astrological sign on page 838. ➤ Read about your Personal Planets on page 826. ➤ Read about your personal Mystical Card on page 856.

TAURUS

From April 20, 22:05 through May 21, 21:45

The Adoring Songsmith

Within days of your birth, Taurus, the world marked the death of an infamous hero and the birth of another kind of hero who became beloved throughout the world. On April 22, Germany's greatest flying ace, Manfred von Richthofen, was shot down and killed in the Battle of the Somme. Known as the "Red Baron" for the color of his Fokker triplane, von Richthofen had the highest aerial kill rate of any pilot on either side of World War I. While your parents might have celebrated the death of the Red Baron, you would be more likely in later years to have celebrated the birth of Ella Fitzgerald. Like the Red Baron, Ella Fitzgerald had a way of sending people to heaven, but she sent them there on the wings of song.

The Red Baron owed his effectiveness to patience in waiting for the enemy to advance before firing. "Let the customer come into the store," he would say. You, too, are likely to be content to let excitement go to the trouble of finding you—especially if it involves any unpleasantness. You may consider yourself a lover, not a warrior—but if certain lines are crossed, you will charge.

The sign of Taurus rules the throat, vocal chords, and song, and you may have been a great admirer of Ella Fitzgerald's glorious voice. You may have a lovely singing voice yourself. Music calms the savage Bull, and you are likely to rely on music and various songs to set your emotional tone or to work out feelings.

In relationships, you are likely to be dutiful but romantic, reliable but original. You enjoy partners who can improvise creative variations in your domestic routine. Virgo welcomes warm, furry pets, and grows luscious plants and vegetables in the garden. Pisces makes for a melodious marriage. Capricorn brings you the finest furnishings.

The Taurean adoration for the simple things in life may have brought you contentment, even in times of scarcity. The World Wars and the Great Depression may have forced you to contend with violence and evil beyond your wildest imaginings. Restoring order, peace, and abundance may have given you a sense of mission and satisfaction.

GEMINI

From May 21, 21:46 through June 22, 5:59

The Rejuvenating Hero

The sign of Gemini rules youthfulness, speed, and aviation. When you were born, American troops were rejuvenating Allied forces in World War I. On May 25, 1918, the first American-built warplanes took off into French skies to do battle with Germany. The top flying ace for the American Army Air Service was former racecar driver Eddie Rickenbacker. A captain in the 94th Aero Pursuit Squadron, Rickenbacker shot down twenty-six enemy aircraft and was awarded the French Croix de Guerre and the Congressional Medal of Honor. After the war, he went on to own Indianapolis Speedway and ran Eastern Air Lines from 1938 to 1959.

Captain Rickenbacker may have been one of your childhood heroes. Like him, you too may have had a fascination for technology and speed. Members of your sign tend to eagerly gather up knowledge on subjects of interest. Stories of Rickenbacker's exploits may have inspired you to learn about the contests for speed, altitude, and distance among the pioneers of aviation in the decades prior to your birth.

Likely to be mechanically inclined, you may have a gift for fine-tuning a machine for optimum performance. You may love to go as fast as possible. You might have been a fighter pilot or worked among the thousands of women who manufactured American warplanes in World War II. The grandchildren of a Gemini of 1918 were likely to enjoy weekend spins in Granny's or Grandpa's muscle car.

You may have sought a partner to share the joys of getting out in the world and learning new things. When children joined the picture, you were likely to make regular field trips into family affairs. Sagittarius shares your love of exploration. Aries shares your need for speed. Aquarius is happy to help out in your workshop.

Your sharp mind and can-do spirit boost the morale of all who share the privilege of working with you. Your challenge has been to make it through the difficult circumstances of worldwide war and depression and to come out with your optimism intact. In tough times, you may have discovered that you had untapped capacities for pragmatism and resourcefulness.

➤ Read about your Chinese Astrological sign on page 838. ➤ Read about your Personal Planets on page 826. ➤ Read about your personal Mystical Card on page 856.

TAURUS
Your Personal Planets

YOUR LOVE POTENTIAL
Venus in Pisces, Apr. 20, 22:05 - May 06, 20:57
Venus in Aries, May 06, 20:58 - May 21, 21:45

YOUR DRIVE AND AMBITION
Mars in Virgo, Apr. 20, 22:05 - May 21, 21:45

YOUR LUCK MAGNETISM
Jupiter in Gemini, Apr. 20, 22:05 - May 21, 21:45

World Events

Apr. 25 – American Jazz singer Ella Fitzgerald is born.

Apr. 28 – Gavrilo Princip, Archduke Franz Ferdinand's assassin, dies of tuberculosis in a prison hospital.

American singer Ella Fitzgerald is born under the sign of Taurus

GEMINI
Your Personal Planets

YOUR LOVE POTENTIAL
Venus in Aries, May 21, 21:46 - June 03, 5:26
Venus in Taurus, June 03, 5:27 - June 22, 5:59

YOUR DRIVE AND AMBITION
Mars in Virgo, May 21, 21:46 - June 22, 5:59

YOUR LUCK MAGNETISM
Jupiter in Gemini, May 21, 21:46 - June 22, 5:59

World Events

June 2 – The destroyer *Ward* is launched just seventeen days after construction on it begins, setting a new record.

June 11 – The Soviets create a peasants' committee to oversee the distribution of land.

CANCER
Your Personal Planets

YOUR LOVE POTENTIAL
Venus in Taurus, June 22, 6:00 - June 29, 8:11
Venus in Gemini, June 29, 8:12 - July 23, 16:50

YOUR DRIVE AND AMBITION
Mars in Virgo, June 22, 6:00 - June 23, 19:18
Mars in Libra, June 23, 19:19 - July 23, 16:50

YOUR LUCK MAGNETISM
Jupiter in Gemini, June 22, 6:00 - July 13, 5:53
Jupiter in Cancer, July 13, 5:54 - July 23, 16:50

World Events

July 14 - Swedish film director Ingmar Bergman is born.
July 16 - The Bolsheviks execute Tsar Nicholas II, his family, and servants.

Leon Trotsky addresses the Red Army from a tank

LEO
Your Personal Planets

YOUR LOVE POTENTIAL
Venus in Gemini, July 23, 16:51 - July 24, 18:43
Venus in Cancer, July 24, 18:44 - Aug. 18, 17:05
Venus in Leo, Aug. 18, 17:06 - Aug. 23, 23:36

YOUR DRIVE AND AMBITION
Mars in Libra, July 23, 16:51 - Aug. 17, 4:15
Mars in Scorpio, Aug. 17, 4:16 - Aug. 23, 23:36

YOUR LUCK MAGNETISM
Jupiter in Cancer, July 23, 16:51 - Aug. 23, 23:36

World Events

July 26 - President Wilson demands an end to lynchings in the U.S. in the midst of race riots in Pennsylvania.
Aug. 8 - Leon Trotsky's Red Army takes Kazan from the White Russians.

CANCER
From June 22, 6:00 through July 23, 16:50

The Sensitive Patriot

The sign of Cancer rules parents and family. Within days of your birth, one of the most famous families in history met with tragedy. On July 16, 1918, the Bolsheviks brought the Romanov dynasty to an end with the murder of Tsar Nicholas II, Tzarina Alexandra, and their five children, including the heir to the Russian throne, Alexis. Exiled to Siberia following Nicholas' abdication in March 1917, the entire family was shot to death. Rumors of the survival of certain family members—such as the youngest daughter, Anastasia—persisted until 1995, when DNA testing confirmed that bodies found in Ekaterinburg included all the members of Nicholas' family.

Cancerians tend to be emotional people, who have a high regard for history and patriotism. Involving all these elements, the murder of the Romanovs may have been the most haunting subject in all of your history studies. The Tsar was not only a father to his children; the Russian populace endearingly called him "Little Father." To love the Tsar was to love Russia itself. You may have regarded his murder as the ultimate act of patricide by hateful, treasonous children.

You may have an emotional intensity about the people and things that matter most to you. When anything poses a threat to your children or your country, you may devote all your power to restoring safety and security. If the situation requires fighting, your chart reveals a capacity for shutting down all softer instincts and unleashing a shocking current of energy.

Your ideal relationship requires spiritual devotion and loyalty. You are likely to seek a partner who respects your sensitivity and enjoys your passion. Libra provides a harmonious environment for family life. Capricorn provides you with a secure commitment. Scorpio offers you a bottomless well of strength.

Deep Cancerian sensitivities can enable you to scale the heights of joy in life. Having lived through historically traumatic times, you may have emerged with emotional scars. As you reopened yourself to the joys of peacetime, the depth of earlier pain may have increased your capacity for joy.

LEO
From July 23, 16:51 through August 23, 23:36

The Children's Benefactor

The sign of Leo rules children, and news items within days of your birth reflected this theme. In August 1918, the United States Department of Education reported that states had begun establishing kindergartens for pre-school age children. The distinction between the welfare of children in America and Russia could not have been starker. While American parents sought to give their children a head start in learning, making friends, and civil participation, Russian parents were desperate to adequately feed, clothe, and house their little ones. The Bolshevik regime, still in its infancy itself, was engaged in civil war with opposing forces known as the "White Army." On August 15, 1918, the United States joined France, Great Britain, and Japan in sending troops to support the White forces.

Good parenting may have been a crucial value to you. After all, your generation had to raise its children under the challenging circumstances of World War II. If you lived with the constant possibility of sudden disruption, you may have had to be a strict disciplinarian. You may have made the supreme sacrifice of removing your children from danger by sending them far away from battle zones.

You are likely to have a pragmatic perspective on daily life. A keen eye for detail may make you capable of producing outstanding work. You may be inventive and good at problem-solving. Likely to work well on team efforts, you may set an inspirational example for colleagues.

A good relationship can energize and empower you. You may seek partners you can trust with your deepest emotions. Cancer can help you work through strong feelings. Pisces helps you find spiritual strength. Scorpio brings out the treasures buried deep within your soul.

In your early adulthood, your survival may have depended on your ability to take everything very seriously. With the arrival of peacetime, you may have felt as if a part of you was missing. Indeed, it is natural for Leo to be childlike and fun-loving. Spending time around children may have made it easier for you to get back to your playful, joyous self.

➤ Read about your Chinese Astrological sign on page 838. ➤ Read about your Personal Planets on page 826. ➤ Read about your personal Mystical Card on page 856.

VIRGO

From August 23, 23:37 through September 23, 20:45

The Vital Warrior

The sign of Virgo rules health and nutrition, and you were born at a time when these factors had begun to play a pivotal role in the outcome of World War I. By September 12, 1918, American and British victories in France had left German lines in a state of total collapse. But the Allies had assistance from certain microscopic forces. A virulent influenza epidemic was raging among the German troops and would soon spread to Allied troops and civilians as well. On the nutrition front, a ten-day drive to recruit women for farm labor began in New York. The harvest was in, and with millions of men serving in Europe, extra hands were needed to bring in wheat, corn, and other produce essential to American nourishment and trade.

Like any good Virgo, you are likely to feel especially energized at harvest time. Your sign rules the harvest, and every year you may look forward to biting into a crisp apple, fresh off the tree. Likely to be instinctively in tune with the seasons, you may be a gardening aficionado. Planting and tilling can be a wonderful way for you to work off steam and feel in touch with the forces of nature.

Virgos often embrace public service, and you may be a diligent member of a charity. Indicators in your chart suggest that you may be a talented fundraiser. You may also be dedicated to providing relief funds to immigrants from your homeland; if you emigrated yourself, you may have sent funds to those you left behind. You may have funded a new hospital or even an entire country.

Virgos value an active, healthy family life. Your life partner was likely someone with an appealing vitality. Passionate Scorpio attracts you like a magnet. Cancer can be a generous, nurturing mate. Leo enchants you with a romantic playfulness.

An iron will and dedication to helping others may have made you a hero in the eyes of the many whose lives you touched. You may have risen to the occasion during World War II. After the war, wide open swaths of unstructured time may have been profoundly uncomfortable for you. With practice, you could enjoy simple pleasures with loved ones.

LIBRA

From September 23, 20:46 through October 24, 5:32

The Balancing Diplomat

The sign of Libra rules diplomacy, and the days surrounding your birth were literally buzzing with urgent *communiqués* and machinations. In late September and early October of 1918, leaders of the Axis nations were dropping like dominoes, as the inevitability of defeat in the Great War became more and more apparent. When you were old enough to study this period, you may have been quite amused by the action taken by Brazil on September 25—declaring war on Austria eleven days after Austria-Hungary had petitioned to the Allies for peace.

All Librans are likely to take an interest in the interactions leading to the end of World War I, but if you were born on or after October 1, 1918, you may have an especially brilliant flair for international affairs. Because your sign rules equality and justice, you are likely to have a keen awareness of the American influence over the war aims of the Allies. Indeed, in the settlement of the war, your own country may have gained its independence, yielded control over colonial territories, or become more democratized.

Striving for balance tends to be a central element of the Libran mission in life. You may have gone through periods in which you needed to balance a need for structure, security, and predictability against an equally strong need for creativity, originality, and the excitement of the new. You may be constitutionally incapable of holding a job that holds no promise of advancement or new challenges.

You were likely to require your relationship to be built like a palazzo with airy porticos. You may have chosen a solid partner who could give you plenty of breathing room. Loyal Leo can bring you constant rejuvenation. Aquarius offers solid friendship and respect for your individuality. Aries enjoys the thrill of constant growth.

You have the ability to grow and reform yourself as you evolve through new seasons of life. Gaining a sense of your own rhythms may have been one of your greatest challenges, especially as you dealt with disruptive world events. Experience likely strengthened your instinct for the right time to make changes.

➤ Read about your Chinese Astrological sign on page 838. ➤ Read about your Personal Planets on page 826. ➤ Read about your personal Mystical Card on page 856.

VIRGO
Your Personal Planets

YOUR LOVE POTENTIAL
Venus in Leo, Aug. 23, 23:37 - Sept. 12, 5:22
Venus in Virgo, Sept. 12, 5:23 - Sept. 23, 20:45

YOUR DRIVE AND AMBITION
Mars in Scorpio, Aug. 23, 23:37 - Sept. 23, 20:45

YOUR LUCK MAGNETISM
Jupiter in Cancer, Aug. 23, 23:37 - Sept. 23, 20:45

World Events

Aug. 25 - American composer Leonard Bernstein is born.

Sept. 12 - German lines are in total collapse on the western front as the British recapture Havrincourt, Moeuvres, and Trescault.

American composer Leonard Bernstein is born under the sign of Virgo

LIBRA
Your Personal Planets

YOUR LOVE POTENTIAL
Venus in Virgo, Sept. 23, 20:46 - Oct. 06, 9:59
Venus in Libra, Oct. 06, 10:00 - Oct. 24, 5:32

YOUR DRIVE AND AMBITION
Mars in Scorpio, Sept. 23, 20:46 - Oct. 01, 7:41
Mars in Sagittarius, Oct. 01, 7:42 - Oct. 24, 5:32

YOUR LUCK MAGNETISM
Jupiter in Cancer, Sept. 23, 20:46 - Oct. 24, 5:32

World Events

Oct. 1 - British and Arab troops take Damascus along with 7,000 Turkish prisoners.

Oct. 17 - American actress Rita Hayworth is born.

1918

SCORPIO
Your Personal Planets

YOUR LOVE POTENTIAL
Venus in Libra, Oct. 24, 5:33 - Oct. 30, 9:42
Venus in Scorpio, Oct. 30, 9:43 - Nov. 23, 2:37

YOUR DRIVE AND AMBITION
Mars in Sagittarius, Oct. 24, 5:33 - Nov. 11, 10:12
Mars in Capricorn, Nov. 11, 10:13 - Nov. 23, 2:37

YOUR LUCK MAGNETISM
Jupiter in Cancer, Oct. 24, 5:33 - Nov. 23, 2:37

World Events

Nov. 4 – British poet Wilfred Owen dies in battle.

Nov. 11 – An armistice is signed by the Germans acknowledging the Allied victory; World War I is officially over.

World War I is officially over

SAGITTARIUS
Your Personal Planets

YOUR LOVE POTENTIAL
Venus in Scorpio, Nov. 23, 2:38 - Nov. 23, 7:01
Venus in Sagittarius, Nov. 23, 7:02 - Dec. 17, 3:33
Venus in Capricorn, Dec. 17, 3:34 - Dec. 22, 15:41

YOUR DRIVE AND AMBITION
Mars in Capricorn, Nov. 23, 2:38 - Dec. 20, 9:04
Mars in Aquarius, Dec. 20, 9:05 - Dec. 22, 15:41

YOUR LUCK MAGNETISM
Jupiter in Cancer, Nov. 23, 2:38 - Dec. 22, 15:41

World Events

Dec. 1 – U.S. troops occupy Germany.

Dec. 10 – Max Planck, the celebrated German physicist, is awarded the Nobel Prize in physics for his quantum theory about the nature of energy.

SCORPIO
From October 24, 5:33 through November 23, 2:37

The Postwar Psychologist

The world was heaving and shifting as you entered this world, Scorpio. On November 11, 1918, Germany signed an armistice, ending World War I in favor of the Allies. Austria signed its armistice on November 3, and in the midst of widespread insurrection, the Habsburg Empire came to an end. The client nations constituting Austria-Hungary scrambled to form new governments. Turkey surrendered on October 31. Kaiser Wilhelm abdicated the German throne on November 9. The specter of Bolshevik revolution hovered over the new German republic. But nature made a fool of everyone: although the war had claimed 10 million lives, it was only half of the death toll the Spanish Influenza epidemic of 1918 had claimed worldwide.

The sign of Scorpio rules massive trends that change the world. When you were old enough to study history, you may have urgently reviewed the events following the end of the Great War. Members of your sign are often given to mysticism, and you may have found it irresistible to ponder whether a higher intelligence had been the animating force behind the devastating efficiency of the influenza epidemic—perhaps divine punishment for human arrogance in making war?

As you would see, two decades were all that was required for the lessons of World War I to fade. Scorpio rules psychology, and you are likely to know the phenomenon of denial when you see it. You might have contended that a deep insanity, more deadly than the Spanish Influenza, afflicted humanity in World War II.

For you, marriage and family provided a way to affirm the value of life. Urgent circumstances may have contributed to your choice in partners. Taurus and Scorpio make for a passionate match. Pisces shares your intensity. Cancer grows with the cycles of life.

Intuitive Scorpionic insight may have helped you to deal with hard questions about human nature. The insanity of World War II may have left you feeling as if the weight of the world was on your shoulders. With time and experience, your deep connection to the mysteries of life and death may have regenerated your faith in humankind.

SAGITTARIUS
From November 23, 2:38 through December 22, 15:41

The Ideological Cartographer

The sign of Sagittarius rules foreign countries and matters of state, and when you were born, such matters were of critical importance. By the end of November 1918, each of the Axis powers had signed an armistice, conceding defeat in World War I, and in the months ahead, the map of the world would be entirely redrawn. The Ottoman, German, and Habsburg Empires were now in dissolution. Client nations of the colonial empires were in the process of redefining themselves as independent republics. The very nature of international relations was transforming before the eyes of the world. The contest for hegemony among imperialist powers—the force behind the onset of the war—now bowed to a new, budding contest between free market democracy and socialism.

International relations and statecraft are Sagittarian concerns. When you were old enough to study history, you were likely to be utterly fascinated by the aftermath of the Great War. A diplomacy-minded Libran friend might have been your best study buddy. Members of your sign tend to find maps utterly absorbing, and you might have poured over maps reflecting the shifting geography of the Great War period.

As far as you are concerned, what people believe is just as important as what they do. You may firmly believe that idealism and ideology go hand-in-hand with concrete consequences. After all, you grew up in a time when the world was divided up and governments could rise and fall, based on the prevailing ideology.

Intellectual compatibility may be an important element in your relationships. You may choose a life partner who shares a fascination with world politics and foreign cultures. Gemini and Virgo share your love of variety and knowledge. Leo's sunny faith in renewal stokes your optimism.

Sagittarians tend to be very talented teachers, but when the world plunged into World War II, you may have felt helpless and unheard. Later in your life, the optimism of your sign may have allowed your hope to spring anew. You may have worked tirelessly to teach the lessons of peace, if only because it was the right thing to do.

➤ Read about your Chinese Astrological sign on page 838. ➤ Read about your Personal Planets on page 826. ➤ Read about your personal Mystical Card on page 856.

CAPRICORN

From December 22, 15:42 through December 31, 23:59

The Responsible Citizen

The sign of Capricorn rules new foundations and infrastructure, and when you were born, the largest reconstruction project yet known to humanity stood before the world, as the Great War came to a conclusion. As of late December 1918, the Allies had won the war. The great colonial powers that started the war, including the victors, were about to undergo the radical redrawing of their boundaries. New countries were coming into existence. The terrible devastation of the war—the deracination of landscape and farmland, the destruction of transportation and communications networks, the economies in collapse—everything had to be rebuilt.

Your sign rules boundaries and borders. When you were old enough to study the Great War and its aftermath, you may have taken a keen interest in the reconstruction of institutions and the impact on the well being of the people affected—virtually all of humanity. The lessons of World War I may have informed your perceptions and responses when your generation inherited the task of rebuilding after World War II.

The world would transform itself repeatedly throughout your lifetime. Indicators in your chart show that you had the power and vision to steer such changes in a positive direction. Likely to be idealistic and driven to apply your ideals to constructive projects, you lived through times when world events had a direct impact on your personal life. For you, it was impossible not to take a position on the world's direction.

Pragmatic factors may have influenced the quality of your relationships. You may choose a life partner who would make sacrifices for the benefit of your family and others. Aquarius and Virgo work tirelessly to serve others. Cancer's parental instincts make you feel safe. Taurus makes sure that essential family needs are met.

As a Capricorn of 1918, you were likely to exemplify responsible citizenship in the world. After 1945, you may have found it difficult to settle into the comforts of private life. In time, you may have realized that enjoying the fruits of your labor was very much a healthy way to show gratitude.

CAPRICORN
Your Personal Planets

YOUR LOVE POTENTIAL
Venus in Capricorn, Dec. 22, 15:42 - Dec. 31, 23:59

YOUR DRIVE AND AMBITION
Mars in Aquarius, Dec. 22, 15:42 - Dec. 31, 23:59

YOUR LUCK MAGNETISM
Jupiter in Cancer, Dec. 22, 15:42 - Dec. 31, 23:59

World Events

Dec. 25 – Revolt erupts in Berlin.
Dec. 25 – Egyptian statesman Anwar al-Sadat is born.

Lenin arrives in Moscow

Special Feature
The Birth and Rebirth of a Nation: Russia

(Continued from page 153)

When a horoscope for a nation has been drawn up, it can be used to monitor and even predict important events by tracking the current movement of the planets and the angles they make to the original position of the planets in the birth chart. The most important planetary movement began when Pluto started to contact the Soviet Union's Scorpio Sun, beginning in December 1988. Pluto, the planet symbolizing destruction and transformation, shook the foundations laid by the Bolshevik Revolution. Communism could no longer compete with Western affluence and influence. The charismatic leader Mikhail Gorbachev introduced the controversial policy of *perestroika*—a restructuring—in an attempt to save the Soviet Union; but this failed. Pluto demands a complete breaking down and building anew. Gorbachev was the last Soviet leader. Pluto went on to contact the Soviet Scorpio Mercury, and by September 5, 1991, started to

move past the point of contact, to finish the transforming process. On December 8, 1991, President Boris Yeltsin announced the signing of the Minsk Declaration, proclaiming the new Russian Federation at 7:45 p.m. Moscow time. A horoscope drawn up using this date, time, and place shows a radically different Russia. Now, instead of the powerful and driven Sun in Scorpio, the Russian Federation Sun is a searching, idealistic Sagittarius, concerned with the establishment of law.

The influence of Pluto steps in when deep changes are called for. A destruction of the old must occur in order to allow the birth of the new

It's especially interesting that there is no longer an opposition between the will of the rulers and the will of the people. Both Venus and Pluto are in the same house and in the

same sign of Scorpio, indicating a united drive to establish the country's foundation. Jupiter, in a prominent position in the second house of wealth, appears to be the challenge facing the new nation. With contacts from six other planets, it emphasizes the need to establish a strong economy—a capitalistic one—and a complete turnaround from its revolutionary origins. So we find that the massive changes that occurred in Russia in the twentieth century are a perfect example of the transforming power of Pluto. ☉

➤ Read Tsar Nicholas II's Star Profile on page 137.

1919

Core Transformation: Pluto In Cancer

In January, 1919, the powerful and explosive planet Pluto was transiting the nurturing, emotional sign of Cancer. (It first knocked on this constellation's door in 1914, at the very beginning of World War I.) The energy of Pluto completely breaks down everything that it touches, so that a "rebirth" of a new form can take place. It disintegrates things that are no longer of use so that new, more evolved forms can take their place. When Pluto visits the sensitive, fertile, hearth-loving and life-giving sign of Cancer, it can be a volatile combination. Pluto also rules obsession, and during the years when Pluto was in Cancer and war ravaged Europe, people were consumed with protecting their homes and homelands.

Although the war ended officially the year before, nationalism remained rampant during the post-war years. The rising tensions of this kind, of overblown ethnic pride, in part set up the conditions that eventually led to World War II some twenty years later. The world was not yet ready to learn its bloody lesson. The Treaty of Versailles enforced serious, humiliating restrictions on Germany after the war. This included payment of reparations, loss of territory, and the trial of its leaders as war criminals. Resentments and regrets started to build at this very early stage and the relentless pressure and humiliation meted out to Germany was another factor that made conditions ripe for the emergence of Adolf Hitler and his extreme ideas.

The Treaty also established the League of Nations in a futile effort to create lasting peace. It was unfortunately only an idealistic pipe dream at that time. The ethnocentric values imposed by the placement of Pluto in Cancer lasted many years, from war to war. Similarly harsh terms were applied to Turkey and these laws provoked resistance by nationalist forces. Russia exploded in still greater chaos. The spark of fascism was lit when Mussolini began an aggressive, destructive, nationalistic political movement in economically depressed post-war Italy. This was just a small taste of the destruction to come in the future, unbound by Pluto's long stay in Cancer. The cycles of history unfolded in a manner that could have served as a warning, if only the powers that be had looked up at the stars for answers.

Clemenceau, Lloyd George and Wilson after signing the Treaty of Versailles

Lady Astor after her election

Charlie Chaplin, Mary Pickford, Douglas Fairbanks and D. W. Griffith

PEACE CREATES A NEW MAP

The so-called "war to end all wars" was over but retribution followed. The Treaty of Versailles imposed humiliating restrictions on Germany, including guilt for causing the war, payment of reparations, loss of territory, and war crime trials for its leaders. President Wilson's brainchild League of Nations was established, though without the U.S., to work for lasting peace. Similar treaties applied to Turkey but provoked resistance from nationalist forces. The spark of fascism was lit as Mussolini started an aggressive, nationalist, political movement in Italy's post-war economic vacuum. In Britain, American-born Nancy Astor became the first woman to be elected to Parliament. In the U.S., screen stars Charlie Chaplin, Mary Pickford, and Douglas Fairbanks Snr. joined with director D.W. Griffiths to form the United Artists film company. Roads were seen as the pathway to economic growth, and rags-to-riches millionaire Andrew Carnegie died, leaving many monuments to his generosity. The first Paris-to-London commercial flight was inaugurated, and Impressionist painter Renoir died. Shorter styles for women became fashionable.

➤ Read Albert Einstein's Star Profile on page 169.

CAPRICORN

From January 01, 0:00 through January 21, 2:20

The Ethical Reformer

Your sign rules conservatism, Capricorn, and within days of your birth, events revealed how extreme insecurity can corrupt and turn conservative tendencies into reactionary brutality. On January 15, 1919, Karl Liebknecht and Rosa Luxemburg, founders of the German Communist Party, were murdered by government officers. In the wake of Germany's World War I surrender, Kaiser Wilhelm had abdicated, and liberal Social Democrats took over the government. More radical socialists, such as Luxemburg and Liebknecht, agitated for position and attempted to incite mutiny, or "socialist revolution," in the military. Panic over the prospect of Bolshevik revolution was a likely motive for the double murder.

Capricorn represents conservatism in its classic sense: the regard for long-standing values and organizational structures. Capricorn does not oppose change, but rather supports and triggers reform when necessary for healthy growth. A good metaphor for Capricornian reform is the pruning of the rosebush to promote more prolific flowering in a later season. In contrast, a radical orientation rips out the bush altogether because a few shoots have gotten out of control.

You have the ability to "revolutionize" a company, industry, or profession, but if you've done so, you were likely to take models that worked in the past and adapt them to meet current needs. Such a strategy enables you to win the support of people who might be affected because you can preserve the comfort of the familiar for them.

You are likely to see your relationship as a joint venture for pursuing family goals. You would need a mate who provides you with essential resources and behind-the-scenes support. Cancer provides nurture and private sanctuary. Taurus provides the means to meet your objectives. Virgo keeps track of the details essential to a healthy family life.

Capricornian conservatism preserves order in times of chaos, but if you allow fear or terror to distort your perception, you may lash out in reactionary and counterproductive ways. True security requires refusal to compromise on core ethical values.

AQUARIUS

From January 21, 2:21 through February 19, 16:47

The Adaptable Pragmatist

The sign of Aquarius rules rapid change, and when you were born, history was moving faster than greased lightning. The Prohibition amendment to the U.S. Constitution, banning alcohol, was ratified just days before your birth-month began. January 18 marked the opening of the peace conference at Versailles. On January 21, twenty-five Sinn Fein members were elected to the British House of Commons, refused to take their seats, formed their own parliament in Dublin, and pronounced an Irish Republic. One week later, 200,000 went on strike in England and Ireland. February 9 marked the first commercial round-trip flight between London and Paris. The International Women's Suffrage Conference opened in Paris on February 12.

Because your sign rules science and electricity, orthodox Aquarians are likely to cite the February 8 announcement of the first electrocardiogram as their favorite news item of this period. You may regard technology as a more effective way to revolutionize the world. Had you been an adult in 1919, you might have been just as satisfied to retire to the relative quiet of your basement laboratory.

Your personality reflects the tension of conflicting traits. You are likely to be a visionary, eager to solve problems. But you also have a practical, conservative streak. You may be a walking dialectic, synthesizing opposing positions into something new and different. Change alone may not be good enough for you—unless it leads to tangible benefits.

You may have had unconventional relationships that were shocking to some. Perhaps you dispensed with conventional roles in a marriage or dispensed with marriage altogether and maintained convention in other senses. Leo can provide excitement and loyalty. Cancer combines tradition and changeability. Pisces moves with your pace and tone.

Ingenious Water-Bearers, Aquarians tend to be way ahead of their times. Able to see the flaws in the positions of your own revolutionary contemporaries, you may have had to wait for history to prove them wrong. The price paid in human lives would have reinforced your stance even more.

► Read about your Chinese Astrological sign on page 838. ► Read about your Personal Planets on page 826. ► Read about your personal Mystical Card on page 856.

CAPRICORN
Your Personal Planets

YOUR LOVE POTENTIAL
Venus in Capricorn, Jan. 01, 0:00 - Jan. 10, 0:27
Venus in Aquarius, Jan. 10, 0:28 - Jan. 21, 2:20

YOUR DRIVE AND AMBITION
Mars in Aquarius, Jan. 01, 0:00 - Jan. 21, 2:20

YOUR LUCK MAGNETISM
Jupiter in Cancer, Jan. 01, 0:00 - Jan. 21, 2:20

World Events

Jan. 1 – American author J.D. Salinger is born.
Jan. 15 – Karl Liebknecht and Rosa Luxemburg, leaders of the German Communist Party, are killed while in government custody.

Punch cartoon illustrates the widespread lack of confidence in the League of Nations

AQUARIUS
Your Personal Planets

YOUR LOVE POTENTIAL
Venus in Aquarius, Jan. 21, 2:21 - Feb. 02, 23:07
Venus in Pisces, Feb. 02, 23:08 - Feb. 19, 16:47

YOUR DRIVE AND AMBITION
Mars in Aquarius, Jan. 21, 2:21 - Jan. 27, 11:19
Mars in Pisces, Jan. 27, 11:20 - Feb. 19, 16:47

YOUR LUCK MAGNETISM
Jupiter in Cancer, Jan. 21, 2:21 - Feb. 19, 16:47

World Events

Jan. 25 – The Paris Peace Conference discusses the possibility of forming a league of nations.
Feb. 17 – Germany signs an agreement ceding much of its Polish territory.

1919

PISCES
Your Personal Planets

YOUR LOVE POTENTIAL
Venus in Pisces, Feb. 19, 16:48 - Feb. 27, 1:42
Venus in Aries, Feb. 27, 1:43 - Mar. 21, 16:18

YOUR DRIVE AND AMBITION
Mars in Pisces, Feb. 19, 16:48 - Mar. 06, 18:47
Mars in Aries, Mar. 06, 18:48 - Mar. 21, 16:18

YOUR LUCK MAGNETISM
Jupiter in Cancer, Feb. 19, 16:48 - Mar. 21, 16:18

World Events

Mar. 3 – The World's war bill is estimated at nearly $200 billion.

Mar. 17 – American jazz singer Nat "King" Cole is born.

Charlie Chaplin, Mary Pickford, Douglas Fairbanks and D. W. Griffith sign to form United Artists

ARIES
Your Personal Planets

YOUR LOVE POTENTIAL
Venus in Aries, Mar. 21, 16:19 - Mar. 23, 11:07
Venus in Taurus, Mar. 23, 11:08 - Apr. 17, 7:02
Venus in Gemini, Apr. 17, 7:03 - Apr. 21, 3:58

YOUR DRIVE AND AMBITION
Mars in Aries, Mar. 21, 16:19 - Apr. 15, 4:59
Mars in Taurus, Apr. 15, 5:00 - Apr. 21, 3:58

YOUR LUCK MAGNETISM
Jupiter in Cancer, Mar. 21, 16:19 - Apr. 21, 3:58

World Events

Mar. 23 – Benito Mussolini organizes a new movement in Italy to fight liberal and Communist influences; it becomes known as fascism.

Apr. 5 – Eamon de Valera becomes President of Ireland.

PISCES
From February 19, 16:48 through March 21, 16:18

The Hopeful Romantic

The sign of Pisces rules romance. When you were born, hopeful news was issued from the most romantic city in the world. On March 8, 1919, sources in Paris reported that 6,000 Americans had married French women since 1918.

Flight and getaways also fall within Piscean purview. For young people living with the constant trauma of death and destruction, a few hours in another's arms must have seemed an exquisite escape. When every embrace could be the last, the emotional intensity of a relationship soars.

As a Piscean, you are likely to enjoy being in love and all the intoxicating trappings of romance—music, poetry, sweet perfume, dreamy thinking. Your sign also rules alcohol and intoxicating substances. If you grew up in the United States, Prohibition came in 1919, and went, before you reached drinking age. As an adult, you may have indulged in the occasional drink, to smooth over jagged edges and soothe raw emotions, but you may have had to be careful. Pisceans can be vulnerable to alcoholism and addiction.

You may enjoy love stories in films and novels; tear-jerkers can bring you emotional catharsis. To fully express your feelings, you may listen to sentimental songs or read or write poetry. The theatre may also be a passion for you, as a spectator or an actor. Many Pisceans can be excellent actors because role-playing involves escaping into other characters.

Like lovers in war, you may have regarded your relationships as a welcome escape from the hardships of everyday life. Partners who provide comfort and sanctuary are likely to appeal to you. Leo loves to keep you entertained. Your every wish is Virgo's command. You may discover a garden of wonder hidden within Cancer's walls.

You may know the secret of how to escape without actually running away, 1919 Pisces, and this talent may have enabled you to survive the trauma, ugliness, and insanity of World War II. In peacetime, however, you may have found it difficult to regain your focus and concentration. Establishing a normal routine and pursuing activities you adore were likely to revive your sense of joy in life.

ARIES
From March 21, 16:19 through April 21, 3:58

The Ambitious Dreamer

Aries is the first sign of the zodiac, and Ariens are all about getting new things started. March 23, 1919, marked a new and historically significant development in Italy—the formation of the Italian Fascist Party by Benito Mussolini. Pride and militarism are traits associated with Aries. As fears of Bolshevism spread throughout postwar Europe, Italians eagerly embraced the nationalistic pride and military discipline of the fascist movement.

Ariens are known for being pioneers of new frontiers. Also in March, physicist Robert A. Goddard published an article claiming that his experiments with rocket technology would one day enable a man to fly to the Moon. His peers responded with ridicule. Like Goddard, you may dare to dream ambitious dreams and to believe that your dreams can come true. You most likely lived to have the last laugh on Goddard's behalf—in 1969, when Neil Armstrong took that first "giant leap for mankind" on the Moon.

You may have participated in a mass trend of the twentieth century, in which many people rejected traditional religion and placed their faith in scientific knowledge. You may be agnostic or atheistic—or at least willing to break bread with people who do not believe in an almighty spiritual being. An ethical outlook or personal moral compass may be more important to you than membership in any particular faith.

In relationships, you were probably determined to live the good life. You were likely to be upwardly mobile and to seek partners who would join you in the active pursuit of career goals and family recreation. Proud Leo glories in your every achievement. Cancer happily holds down the fort while you're out conquering the world. Sagittarius shares and supports your greatest ambitions for yourself and your family.

You probably had no idea just how much the world would need your ability to think big and to go on believing, in spite of everything. To rebuild the world after the devastation of the Great Depression and World War II was likely the greatest challenge anyone has ever faced. You were well equipped to rise to that occasion.

➤ Read about your Chinese Astrological sign on page 838. ➤ Read about your Personal Planets on page 826. ➤ Read about your personal Mystical Card on page 856.

TAURUS

From April 21, 3:59 through May 22, 3:38

The Resilient Investor

The sign of Taurus rules financial power and, when you were born, the United States seemed to enjoy a rapidly rising "currency" in the world. The Allies had welcomed President Wilson as a peace negotiator at Versailles. On May 6, 1919, Belgium requested a $500 million loan from the U.S. Wilson enjoyed lavish ceremonies in France, but in reality, Lloyd George and Clemenceau shared a thinly-veiled contempt, rejecting most of Wilson's proposed terms and exacting harsh vengeance on Germany. Their position was understandable, relative to their losses. For every man lost to the U.S., Britain had lost nine, and France thirteen. Ultimately, the U.S. Congress refused to ratify the Treaty of Versailles and America receded back into isolationism.

In your life, you may have invested a lot of time and resources toward making the "Big Score," and you may have seen some attractive returns. You may have learned some hard lessons, however, about the long-term costs of short-term gains. You may have also suffered setbacks when something that was too-good-to-be-true turned out to be exactly that. Fortunately, your chart shows a surplus of energy to regenerate losses.

You may have been an entrepreneur, and good friends may have partnered up with you in launching new ideas. Two wars ensured a high demand for the creation of infrastructure, and you may have made a career in industries involving communications, transportation, and domestic or international trade.

In relationships, you are likely to be indulgent toward partners and children. You may be generous with gifts and sometimes a bit possessive. Cancer will stick with you through lean seasons. Capricorn serves as a pragmatic sounding board. Virgo appreciates the thought behind the loving gestures you make.

Your irrepressible faith allows you to take occasional setbacks in stride, but sometimes you may stick with a decision, no matter how vigorously a loved one may object. With maturity, you may have learned the importance of listening. Others may support you with greater enthusiasm when they feel they've been given a fair hearing.

GEMINI

From May 22, 3:39 through June 22, 11:53

The Technological Tourist

What could be a more perfect birthday present for the first Gemini babies born after World War I, than the resumption of the pre-war trend in competitive aviation? On May 27, 1919, Lt. Com. A. C. Read completed the first transatlantic air flight in a U.S. Navy seaplane NC-4. Taking off from Rockaway, New York, Read stopped over in Massachusetts, Nova Scotia, and Newfoundland, before final takeoff for Lisbon. On June 15, a two-man team from Britain and the U.S. made the first non-stop transatlantic flight in a Vickers-Vimy biplane. Less than a month later, a British dirigible would make the first round-trip flight across the Atlantic. Not until you reached eighteen would Charles Lindbergh fly solo across the Atlantic for you.

The sign of Gemini rules transportation and aviation. When you were old enough to study aviation history, the pre-and-post-war pioneers of the skies may have fascinated you. By 1919, the emphasis was on long distances, not usually a matter within Gemini's purview. Your sign rules speed, and the new developments—including commercial flights—would speed the pace of ordinary people's lives by allowing for distant travel in manageable stretches of time.

Technological advances in your lifetime would likely inspire you to dream. Friends may have encouraged you to believe that anything is possible. You may have written or enjoyed reading science fiction novels. You are likely to have pursued a career in communications, radio, or television.

Collecting many friends and experiences before you finally settled down, you may have had an active and enjoyable single life. You were likely to seek a partner who likes to be on the move. Like you, Sagittarius seeks a knowledgeable travel buddy. Leo takes you on romantic getaways. The bottomless capacity of Cancer's knapsack never fails to astound you.

A finely-tuned Gemini mind can elevate your perception and intelligence. You probably know why ignorance is bliss—because dull people don't have to worry about nervous sensitivity! With time, you've learned to take time out to recharge and smooth out your raw edges.

➤ Read about your Chinese Astrological sign on page 838. ➤ Read about your Personal Planets on page 826. ➤ Read about your personal Mystical Card on page 856.

TAURUS
Your Personal Planets

YOUR LOVE POTENTIAL
Venus in Gemini, Apr. 21, 3:59 - May 12, 18:58
Venus in Cancer, May 12, 18:59 - May 22, 3:38

YOUR DRIVE AND AMBITION
Mars in Taurus, Apr. 21, 3:59 - May 22, 3:38

YOUR LUCK MAGNETISM
Jupiter in Cancer, Apr. 21, 3:59 - May 22, 3:38

World Events

Apr. 25 – Walter Gropius founds the Bauhaus school in Weimar, Germany.

May 7 – Argentinian first lady Eva Perón is born.

Eva Perón is born under the sign of Taurus

GEMINI
Your Personal Planets

YOUR LOVE POTENTIAL
Venus in Cancer, May 22, 3:39 - June 08, 10:34
Venus in Leo, June 08, 10:35 - June 22, 11:53

YOUR DRIVE AND AMBITION
Mars in Taurus, May 22, 3:39 - May 26, 9:37
Mars in Gemini, May 26, 9:38 - June 22, 11:53

YOUR LUCK MAGNETISM
Jupiter in Cancer, May 22, 3:39 - June 22, 11:53

World Events

June 7 – New York inaugurates a written test for driver's license applicants.

June 8 – Britain finishes work on the largest airplane in history: the triplane carries fifty people and four tons of explosives.

1919

CANCER
Your Personal Planets

YOUR LOVE POTENTIAL
Venus in Leo, June 22, 11:54 - July 07, 18:16
Venus in Virgo, July 07, 18:17 - July 23, 22:44

YOUR DRIVE AND AMBITION
Mars in Gemini, June 22, 11:54 - July 08, 17:13
Mars in Cancer, July 08, 17:14 - July 23, 22:44

YOUR LUCK MAGNETISM
Jupiter in Cancer, June 22, 11:54 - July 23, 22:44

World Events

June 28 – Five years to the day that gunshots in Sarajevo sparked the beginning of World War I, a peace treaty is signed in Versailles.

July 15 – Irish novelist Iris Murdoch is born.

Iris Murdoch is born under the sign of Cancer

LEO
Your Personal Planets

YOUR LOVE POTENTIAL
Venus in Virgo, July 23, 22:45 - Aug. 24, 5:27

YOUR DRIVE AND AMBITION
Mars in Cancer, July 23, 22:45 - Aug. 23, 6:16
Mars in Leo, Aug. 23, 6:17 - Aug. 24, 5:27

YOUR LUCK MAGNETISM
Jupiter in Cancer, July 23, 22:45 - Aug. 02, 8:38
Jupiter in Leo, Aug. 02, 8:39 - Aug. 24, 5:27

World Events

July 30 – The military is called in to help deal with race riots in Chicago.

July 31 – Germany adopts its first constitution.

CANCER
From June 22, 11:54 through July 23, 22:44

The Reflective Powerhouse

The sign of Cancer rules parents and country, subjects that figured strongly in the post-World War I disposition of Germany. On June 28, 1919, Germany signed the Treaty of Versailles—in a room known, interestingly, as the Hall of Mirrors. In future decades, people would look into the Treaty of Versailles for a reflection of the root causes of Nazism and World War II. The treaty itself required total demilitarization, billions of dollars in reparations, and massive loss of territory. The father-figure of Germany, Kaiser Wilhelm, faced possible prosecution as a war criminal. Clearly the intent of the treaty—which ultimately proved unenforceable—was to wreak vengeance on Germany's security, economic viability, and its father figure.

Whether or not Germany deserved all this, you may see the danger of allowing a resisted opponent to set the tone for one's own choices and actions. The Hall of Mirrors is a telling metaphor vis-à-vis Cancer, a sign also known as the Moonchild. Deriving its light from the Sun, the Moon is a heavenly mirror. Similarly, Cancerians can be human mirrors of others' actions, expressions, and moods.

Your feelings can be a powerful compass for you in the midst of challenging situations. You are likely to have a sixth sense for the deeper implications of events and a nose for danger or deception. Able to maneuver in accordance with your intuition, you may have had a career as an investigator, a detective, a spy, or a mystery writer.

You are likely to take the lead in your family or relationship, but your influence is subtle, never overt. You and your partner are likely to enjoy a deep, heartfelt understanding. Loyal Leo protects you and your family with ferocity. You and Scorpio can finish each other's sentences. Pisces brings you a tender spiritual bond.

Cancerian sensibilities may allow you to navigate through life with precision, but your ability to pick up on other people's energies can throw you off course. With experience, you may have learned to filter out external influences, tune in to your best instincts, and follow your own lodestar.

LEO
From July 23, 22:45 through August 24, 5:27

The Big-Hearted Benefactor

Leos are known for their strength, generosity, and confidence. You were born within days of the passing of a man who exemplified these qualities. On August 11, 1919, steel magnate Andrew Carnegie died at his home in Lenox, Massachusetts. Born in Dunfermline, Scotland, Carnegie immigrated to America at age thirteen. Starting as a telegrapher at the Pennsylvania Railroad, Carnegie parlayed his savings into stocks and investments, and ultimately founded the Carnegie Steel Corporation, a company that would bring the United States to preeminence in the steel industry. In 1901, Carnegie sold his company to the U.S. Steel Corporation for $400 million, and commenced a new career in philanthropy, giving away $350 million before he died.

The sign of Leo rules the heart, and you may understand completely when, in speaking on the true meaning of wealth, Carnegie said, "My heart is in the work." Monetary wealth is unlikely to be your greatest ambition. Rather, you are happiest when immersed in work you love. Ideally, Leo can make a living in his or her favorite hobby or cause.

You are likely to agree heartily with Carnegie's dictum, "The man who dies thus rich, dies disgraced." Members of your family are likely to be the well-indulged beneficiaries of your generosity. And you are likely to have an extremely expansive definition of your extended family. Likely to remember the smallest gesture, the extra effort, you may reply to others' loyalty with a handsome reward.

In the privacy of your relationships, you are likely to express your emotions through grand gestures. You may be drawn to partners who can be gracious hosts to friends and family. Sagittarius brings happy laughter to your home. Cancer can be as giving as you are. Libra keeps a harmonious home.

You may have started out in life with limited resources but, like Andrew Carnegie, you were likely to have confidence in your abilities and the willingness to work hard for your dreams. Success alone is empty if you don't love what you do. In maturity, you were likely to please yourself by pursuing work that was its own reward.

► Read about your Chinese Astrological sign on page 838. ► Read about your Personal Planets on page 826. ► Read about your personal Mystical Card on page 856.

VIRGO

From August 24, 5:28 through September 24, 2:34

The Dedicated Worker

The sign of Virgo rules workers, and within days of your birth, conflicts involving workers made news in the United States. During World War I, labor leaders had desisted from protests, in deference to the need for unity in wartime. In the postwar period, however, labor activism emerged from dormancy. Throughout August 1919, railway workers had been striking for higher wages, profit sharing, and government ownership. On September 9, police officers went on strike in Boston, leaving the streets to riots, looters, and chaos. To restore order Governor Calvin Coolidge called in the state militia. The police officers were protesting poor pay, inadequate working conditions, and the suspension of nineteen patrolmen for engaging in union activities.

The union movement came into its own during your adulthood, particularly after World War II. In 1919 union organizing was far from mainstream acceptance, especially in light of widespread fear of communist and anarchist terror. You are likely to be sympathetic with laborers' demands, provided you are satisfied that they are working hard and do their jobs well.

You may place high priority on the quality of your own work. A command of detail can make you capable of excellence. You may also have an appreciation for the finer points of others' work. Nothing is likely to give you greater pleasure than a virtuoso performance in music, dance, or theatre. Possessed of great discipline, you would make an outstanding director, manager, or coach.

You are likely to devote a lot of effort to your relationship, and you may expect the same from your partner. Your mate may have lavished you with attention. Pisces senses your needs and gladly fulfills them. Cancer knows what you like and how you like it. Aquarius works hard to fulfill shared goals.

Perfectionism can make you capable of mastery, but overemphasis can lead you to be overcritical of others and to beat up on yourself. You may need to ease up and be human. With maturity, you've learned to be glad when you know you've done your best, as opposed to the best imaginably possible.

LIBRA

From September 24, 2:35 through October 24, 11:20

The Harmonious Promoter

The sign of Libra rules brotherly love, something that seemed in short supply at the time of your birth. Civil war between Bolshevik and Cossack forces was tearing Russia apart. In America, 1919 was named the "Red Summer" for a different reason. Between May and September 1919, race riots were rife all over the United States. On September 28, a mob in Nebraska, claiming that African Americans were attacking white women, lynched Willie Brown, a black man, and burned the Omaha courthouse. At the time, any show of friendliness between black men and white women could trigger a lynching. Exaggerated fears of rape or attacks on "our women" is the quintessential rationalization for racist vigilante violence.

As a Libran, you are likely to be sensitive to the interplay of the issues of romantic love and racism. When you were old enough to learn about lynching in America, you may have been mortified. Hateful discrimination violates every value Libra stands for. True to your sign, you are likely to promote harmonious relationships among human beings. You may have been heartened in 1958, when the U.S. Supreme Court overthrew laws banning interracial marriage.

Your own experience may have predisposed you to be respectful of people's need to feel okay about themselves, even when their behavior needs improvement. You would probably never dream of criticizing someone in front of others. Your attunement to saving face and avoiding ego clashes may have made you an excellent team player or manager.

You may be drawn to attractive, charismatic partners—someone who looks good with you. You may enjoy going out together to glamorous or entertaining events. Leo and you can be a striking power couple. Jovial Sagittarius fills your home with laughter and enlightenment. Open-minded Gemini charms you with witty repartee.

The Libran desire to make sure everyone is happy may have made you popular with friends and colleagues, but you may have cheated yourself out of getting your own needs met. With maturity, you may have learned to be more direct by asking nicely to get what you wanted.

➤ Read about your Chinese Astrological sign on page 838. ➤ Read about your Personal Planets on page 826. ➤ Read about your personal Mystical Card on page 856.

VIRGO
Your Personal Planets

YOUR LOVE POTENTIAL
Venus in Virgo, Aug. 24, 5:28 - Sept. 24, 2:34
YOUR DRIVE AND AMBITION
Mars in Leo, Aug. 24, 5:28 - Sept. 24, 2:34
YOUR LUCK MAGNETISM
Jupiter in Leo, Aug. 24, 5:28 - Sept. 24, 2:34

World Events

Sept. 2 – U.S. Congress passes a bill banning railroad strikes.
Sept. 21 – The *Orient Express* resumes its service from Constantinople to Paris.

The Orient Express

LIBRA
Your Personal Planets

YOUR LOVE POTENTIAL
Venus in Virgo, Sept. 24, 2:35 - Oct. 24, 11:20
YOUR DRIVE AND AMBITION
Mars in Leo, Sept. 24, 2:35 - Oct. 10, 3:52
Mars in Virgo, Oct. 10, 3:53 - Oct. 24, 11:20
YOUR LUCK MAGNETISM
Jupiter in Leo, Sept. 24, 2:35 - Oct. 24, 11:20

World Events

Oct. 8 – The first German enters the U.S. since it came into the war in April 1917.
Oct. 15 – The Soviets ban the practice of giving Christian names to children.

SCORPIO
Your Personal Planets

YOUR LOVE POTENTIAL
Venus in Virgo, Oct. 24, 11:21 - Nov. 09, 8:04
Venus in Libra, Nov. 09, 8:05 - Nov. 23, 8:24

YOUR DRIVE AND AMBITION
Mars in Virgo, Oct. 24, 11:21 - Nov. 23, 8:24

YOUR LUCK MAGNETISM
Jupiter in Leo, Oct. 24, 11:21 - Nov. 23, 8:24

World Events

Oct. 28 - U.S. Congress passes the Volstead Act.

Nov. 1 - The U.S. opens Indian reservations in Arizona to prospectors.

Lady Astor, first woman in the British Parliament

SAGITTARIUS
Your Personal Planets

YOUR LIVE POTENTIAL
Venus in Libra, Nov. 23, 8:25 - Dec. 09, 3:28
Venus in Scorpio, Dec. 09, 3:29 - Dec. 22, 21:26

YOUR DRIVE AND AMBITION
Mars in Virgo, Nov. 23, 8:25 - Nov. 30, 12:09
Mars in Libra, Nov. 30, 12:10 - Dec. 22, 21:26

YOUR LUCK MAGNETISM
Jupiter in Leo, Nov. 23, 8:25 - Dec. 22, 21:26

World Events

Nov. 28 - Lady Astor becomes the first woman in the British Parliament.

Dec. 10 - Captain Ross Smith is the first person to fly half way round the World, from England to Australia.

SCORPIO
From October 24, 11:21 through November 23, 8:24

The Strategic Operator

The sign of Scorpio rules shifts in power so necessary and inevitable that to hold them back can result in violence. At the time of your birth, laborers' need for fair wages, decent work conditions, and organized representation had become so urgent, and indeed inevitable, that labor riots had broken out in Germany, the United States, and elsewhere. In October of 1919, federal troops were sent to quell rioting by thousands of steelworkers in Gary, Indiana. The strike began after company management refused to negotiate with union leaders. Rioting broke out when the strikers, led by World War I veterans in uniform, came upon scabs hired by the U.S. Steel Company. In the U.S. Congress, charges flew that the workers were in league with Bolshevik forces aiming to overthrow the government. Given that communists had taken over governments in Europe, the Congressional fears were not so outrageous.

The mere idea of soldiers taking up the banner of the proletariat was likely to strike terror across America and Europe. Your parents were likely to speak vividly of these times, and you were likely to find their stories riveting. Scorpios tend to be fascinated by worldwide shifts in power. As an adult, you may have risen high in the ranks of laborers, during unionism's heyday, after World War II.

You are likely to be someone who works hard and with a great deal of discipline. Methodical and analytical, you may have an excellent mind for strategy. You would have made an excellent field officer in war, or a highly productive supervisor or manager in a factory.

You may be willing to give everything for your spouse and children and to fiercely guard your family's privacy. Virgo works hard by your side. Capricorn shares your willingness to make sacrifices for a better future. Taurus ensures you material means of independence.

You may have been a shrewd and successful operator early in life, but even if you enjoyed admiration, you may also have become isolated. It's lonely at the top. With experience and maturity, you may have decided that it was far better to be loved than to be feared.

SAGITTARIUS
From November 23, 8:25 through December 22, 21:26

The Principled Optimist

The sign of Sagittarius rules higher education, foreign travel, and academic cooperation. Within days of your birth, these subjects combined to produce a scientific breakthrough of momentous import. In December 1919, verification of Albert Einstein's General Theory of Relativity is issued from London. To test Einstein's theory, teams of British astronomers made expeditions to Brazil and West Africa to observe a solar eclipse and measure the angle of the path of light. The British scientists confirmed results predicted by Einstein, a German, and announced that his work was "perhaps the greatest ... in the history of human thought." This affirmation was significant due to the lingering enmity between Britain and Germany in the wake of the Great War.

When you were old enough to learn of this development, you might have seen the breakthrough in humanitarian terms. The British astronomers cared not that Einstein was a German. His greatness as a scientist was all that mattered. Sagittarians tend to regard race, nationality, or ethnicity as irrelevant. You are likely to abide by higher principles that enable people to rise above their petty fixations.

Having lived through the Holocaust, you know that Adolph Hitler might just as well have sent Einstein, who was Jewish, to perish in a concentration camp. Any kind of bigotry is antithetical to Sagittarian values, and you may have dedicated your life to promoting tolerance. You may have been a lawyer, politician, or educator.

You may look to relationships for sympathetic support. Your mate was likely to be open minded and eager to share the joys of cultural and educational pursuits. Gemini brings you a world of knowledge. Libra brings a passion for harmony and beauty. Leo sees the highest potential in all people.

Your Sagittarian optimism enables you to see the best in others, but in your lifetime, you witnessed the most unimaginable atrocities. You may have had to struggle just to survive. Working to ensure that such evil would never recur may have enabled you to meet inspiring people who could revive your faith in humanity.

➤ Read about your Chinese Astrological sign on page 838. ➤ Read about your Personal Planets on page 826. ➤ Read about your personal Mystical Card on page 856.

CAPRICORN

From December 22, 21:27 through December 31, 23:59

The Constructive Visionary

The sign of Capricorn rules the application of economic theory to the business of running industry and countries. In December 1919, John Maynard Keynes published *The Economic Consequences Of The Peace*, which he wrote after resigning in frustration from his role as representative to the British Treasury at Versailles. Maintaining that Germany would be unable to pay even a fraction of the economic reparations required in the Treaty of Versailles, Keynes predicted that the treaty would lead to worldwide economic disaster. He also criticized the vengeful intentions of Lloyd George and Clemenceau—and Wilson's capitulation to them.

You, of course, grew up to witness and suffer the fulfillment of Keynes' predictions in the Great Depression of the 1930s. Keynes would continue to play a role in your life, due to his influence in the creation of the New Deal, the International Monetary Fund, and the thirty-year economic boom in Western industrial countries following the end of World War II. You may have played a role "on the ground" in helping to lead postwar rebuilding efforts.

You are likely to have a mind for complex ideas and an ability to apply conceptual schemes in the real world. Indicators in your chart suggest a talent for leading cooperative efforts to meet ambitious goals and objectives. As an inventor, entrepreneur, or manager, you may have encouraged others to come up with revolutionary ideas for every day usage. The word, "constructive" is likely to be your mantra.

Relationships may have been a matter of solemn but joyful duty. You may have chosen a partner who saw family and children as an affirmation of life and belief in the future. Cancerians grow with you through the cycles of life. Leo supports the ideals and best potentials of family members. Scorpio brings a deep and empowering faith.

Diligent and reliable, Capricorns tend to believe that good work is its own reward. So much needed to be done during your lifetime that you may have felt uncomfortable in quieter times. Even if you retired, you were likely to stay young by staying active in worthy causes.

1919

CAPRICORN
Your Personal Planets

YOUR LOVE POTENTIAL
Venus in Scorpio, Dec. 22, 21:27 - Dec. 31, 23:59

YOUR DRIVE AND AMBITION
Mars in Libra, Dec. 22, 21:27 - Dec. 31, 23:59

YOUR LUCK MAGNETISM
Jupiter in Leo, Dec. 22, 21:27 - Dec. 31, 23:59

World Events

Dec. 23 – Britain publishes a new constitution for India.

Dec. 30 – Reports in France indicate that births have doubled since the start of the year.

Albert Einstein
March 14, 1879 - April 18, 1955

ALBERT EINSTEIN
Pisces

Albert Einstein, the greatest scientist of the twentieth century, changed our understanding of the universe. With his Sun in mystical and intuitive Pisces, Einstein believed that scientific theory and religious beliefs could co-exist. In 1941, at a symposium on "Science, Philosophy, and Religion" he said, "Science without religion is lame; religion without science is blind." And with the Moon, ruler of his chart, in philosophical and probing Sagittarius, Einstein would spend a lifetime seeking to unravel the mysteries of the cosmos.

Einstein's Mercury, the planet of ideas and thinking, is in fiery and inspired Aries and made a contact with Saturn, the planet of discipline and order. Einstein believed in the intrinsic order of the universe, eschewing the theory of chaos, which became popular in his later years. "I cannot believe that God would choose to play dice with the universe," said Einstein, who spent the last twenty-five years of his life in a futile search for a unified field theory.

But Saturn is also the planet of delay and limits. Ironically, the man whose name has become synonymous with genius actually had a hard time finding a job. It was while working at the patent office in 1905 that he wrote three landmark papers on theoretical physics, including one that led to his famous "Theory of Relativity." His scientific writings are indicated by his Jupiter in its natural placement in the house of higher learning in the scientific sign of Aquarius. And Jupiter contacts Uranus, the planet ruling science, in the third house of communication. In 1921, Einstein was awarded the Nobel Prize for physics. The young man who hadn't been able to get a university professorship became a sought-after lecturer, at the world's most prestigious universities, finally settling at the Institute for Advanced Study in Princeton, New Jersey.

With sensitive Cancer rising along with his empathetic Pisces Sun, Einstein lived a quiet life. He was fond of the classical music and played the violin. And while he devoted much of his energy to supporting pacifism and Zionism, for him, science always came first. He felt that only the discovery of the nature of the universe would have lasting meaning.

➤ Read about Einstein in "Dreaming Through the Twentieth Century" on page 545. ➤ Read about Einstein and Jung in "East Meets Twentieth-Century West" on page 65.

1920

Impractical Idealism, Inspired Intuition: Uranus in Pisces

U ranus is the planet of shock and surprise. It makes its appearance suddenly, and then slips away again to invent something new. Pisces is the sign of intuition, dreams, compassion, and the pink fog that can sometimes cloud our logic. In January of 1920, Prohibition took effect in the United States. Wine and liquor were banned by the 18th Amendment. This sent American culture into an endless spiral of post-war decadence that became the wild and crazy flapper era. Uranus also rules rebellion, and while it was tuned into the vibrations of artistic Pisces at the start of the twenties, people found ways to radicalize art and culture in a new and exciting manner.

In true Uranian fashion, skirts got shorter, and women's hair was shorn to then shockingly boyish lengths. People danced and drank with abandon, and even though these activities were looked upon with shame by authorities, Dionysus himself would have looked on with pride. Several souls with new and radical ideas were born this year as well. On January 20, brilliant avant-garde Italian filmmaker Frederico Fellini, creator of *Juliet of the Spirits* and *8½*, was born. On July 24, American lawyer, radical feminist, and Congresswoman Bella Abzug, was born. She was known for her eccentric hats, which were a vivid expression of her arty Uranus in Pisces placement.

On August 26, the 19th Amendment was finally ratified, giving women the right to vote. This was the first of many revolutionary triumphs for women in the years to come, inspired by the shift of quirky Uranus into compassionate Pisces. Popular culture reflected the drive toward rebellion inspired by this inspirational transit. The energy was felt in everyone's lives, as people recovered from the war and regained the comfort that they had lost as a result of living under the gun. Now they could relax, kick back, and learn to finally enjoy life once again. Although there was still much to do to repair broken lives, many felt that it was time for some rollicking fun. Drinking and dancing were the key tension-releasing activities for the generation that came of age in the twenties.

The League of Nations headquarters in Geneva

Executed White Army soldiers   *Illegal barrels of beer confiscated during Prohibition*

NEW POLITICAL REALITIES EMERGE

The League of Nations met for the first time in Paris. The German population, dissatisfied by last year's peace settlement, was fertile ground for political chaos. An anti-Semitic, anti-government political movement headed by Adolf Hitler found support among war veterans, and uprisings occurred in Berlin, Munich, and the Ruhr. Mexican revolutionary Pancho Villa surrendered to President Huerta, vowing to become a quiet rancher. Russia experienced more chaos as the Red Army, created by Trotsky, overpowered the White pro-Tzarist forces. Lenin's efforts to subsume Poland in the Communist empire were curtailed when the Red Army was stopped short of Warsaw. In the U.S., after the 18th Amendment was approved by three-quarters of the states in 1919, prohibition of alcohol possession and consumption went into effect. In Congress, the majority of Democrats failed to ratify the Treaty of Versailles. American women finally won the right to vote when the 19th Amendment was ratified. As clothing prices soared, so did hemlines, and the 'flapper' dress was the height of fashion. Joan of Arc was canonized by the Roman Catholic Church.

➤ Read Coco Chanel's Star Profile on page 177.

CAPRICORN

From January 01, 0:00 through January 21, 8:03

The Stoic Pragmatist

People born under the sign of Capricorn are often described as serious, stoic, strict, and—apropos of the news within days of your birth—sober. On January 16, 1920, the 18th Amendment to the Constitution, mandating Prohibition of beer, wine, and liquor, went into effect in the U.S. Fortunately, New Yorkers were able to toast the Yankee's acquisition of Babe Ruth eleven days before Prohibition became law. Elsewhere in the world, the Treaty of Versailles went into effect, and the League of Nations held its first meeting in Paris. Because Congress had failed to ratify the treaty, America remained technically at war with Germany.

History would prove Prohibition's inability to guarantee the sobriety of anybody, even serious, stoic, and strict Capricorns. Certain values associated with your sign—such as surrender to a higher power, discipline, responsibility, and rigorous honesty—do, however, constitute the foundational values of most twelve-step sobriety programs. Whether you are a teetotaler or not, you may embrace such values as a pathway to a healthy life.

You may have a pragmatic respect for tradition, authority, and chains of command, but your support may rapidly expire if leaders fail to devote as much effort as they expect from others. In group projects, you may feel that everyone should have a fair chance to do their best. When you're in charge, you're likely to run a well-disciplined operation and allow everyone to share equally in both the credit and rewards.

In relationships, you are likely to seek a peaceful retreat from the world. You may have chosen a life partner who was honest, good-humored, and agreeable. Shunning acrimony, Libra creates a harmonious household. Pisces turns your home into a soothing, peaceful sanctuary. Taurus makes sure you have the finest creature comforts.

You are likely to have an excellent work ethic, but at times you may have taken responsibility for certain things beyond your control. With maturity, you were able to trust that others could handle things just as well, even if they did not do things the way you would have.

AQUARIUS

From January 21, 8:04 through February 19, 22:28

The Universal Individualist

Your sign stands for universal human rights, Aquarius, and on February 3, 1920, the Allies demanded that 890 German military leaders stand trial for commission of war crimes during World War I. Shortly afterwards the Allies accepted a German offer to conduct the trials in Leipzig. Historians criticize the Leipzig trials for being politicized. Indeed, the Allies abandoned the hearings before their completion. Leipzig did, however, set a precedent for the much-respected Nuremberg trials after World War II. The prosecution of war criminals laid a foundation for the concept of crimes against humanity and a new jurisprudence of international human rights.

Individualism is a basic Aquarian value, and you are likely to have an instinctive sympathy for universal notions of right and wrong. An interest in law, politics, or diplomacy may have led you to join with the pioneers of international human rights law, or you may have donated funds or personal time to humanitarian campaigns.

Having witnessed the atrocities of World War II, you may have sought to understand how people could find it acceptable to condone or perpetuate such cruelty against other human beings. You may have pursued studies or a career in psychology. Private moments may have found you engaging in deep soul-searching. Struggling to find a source of goodness in a world seemingly abandoned by God, you may have been among the members of your generation who wrote groundbreaking works on theology and spirituality.

Traditional relationships may have seemed antiquated to you. You were likely to choose a partner who could bring an original approach to intimacy and family life. Leo shares your commitment to being true to yourself. Pisces respects your freedom of conscience. Scorpio can be a sympathetic companion on spiritual journeys.

Aquarians have an uncanny way of seeing through the flawed belief systems of their societies. The label of "heretic" or "blasphemer" may not be unfamiliar to you. With maturity, you may have learned to recast your message so as to make it accessible to those who most needed to hear it.

► Read about your Chinese Astrological sign on page 838. ► Read about your Personal Planets on page 826. ► Read about your personal Mystical Card on page 856.

CAPRICORN
Your Personal Planets

YOUR LOVE POTENTIAL
Venus in Scorpio, Jan. 01, 0:00 - Jan. 04, 9:19
Venus in Sagittarius, Jan. 04, 9:20 - Jan. 21, 8:03

YOUR DRIVE AND AMBITION
Mars in Libra, Jan. 01, 0:00 - Jan. 21, 8:03

YOUR LUCK MAGNETISM
Jupiter in Leo, Jan. 01, 0:00 - Jan. 21, 8:03

World Events

Jan. 14 – More than one hundred people are killed or injured as 40,000 radicals attack the Reichstag in Berlin; the city is placed under marshal law.

Jan. 16 – Prohibition begins in the U.S. as the 18th Amendment bans the sale of beer, wine, and liquor.

A demonstration in Berlin is dispersed by machine gun fire

AQUARIUS
Your Personal Planets

YOUR LOVE POTENTIAL
Venus in Sagittarius, Jan. 21, 8:04 - Jan. 29, 11:54
Venus in Capricorn, Jan. 29, 11:55 - Feb. 19, 22:28

YOUR DRIVE AND AMBITION
Mars in Libra, Jan. 21, 8:04 - Jan. 31, 23:17
Mars in Scorpio, Jan. 31, 23:18 - Feb. 19, 22:28

YOUR LUCK MAGNETISM
Jupiter in Leo, Jan. 21, 8:04 - Feb. 19, 22:28

World Events

Feb. 1 – The Royal Mounted Police are established in Canada.

Feb. 3 – Allied representatives demand that nearly 900 German military leaders are tried for war crimes.

1920

PISCES
Your Personal Planets

YOUR LOVE POTENTIAL
Venus in Capricorn, Feb. 19, 22:29 - Feb. 23, 3:46
Venus in Aquarius, Feb. 23, 3:47 - Mar. 18, 15:30
Venus in Pisces, Mar. 18, 15:31 - Mar. 20, 21:58

YOUR DRIVE AND AMBITION
Mars in Scorpio, Feb. 19, 22:29 - Mar. 20, 21:58

YOUR LUCK MAGNETISM
Jupiter in Leo, Feb. 19, 22:29 - Mar. 20, 21:58

World Events

Mar. 8 – Syrian independence is proclaimed.

Mar. 19 – The U.S. Senate rejects the terms of the Treaty of Versailles for the second time.

A meeting of a new political group, the Nazis

ARIES
Your Personal Planets

YOUR LOVE POTENTIAL
Venus in Pisces, Mar. 20, 21:59 - Apr. 12, 2:06
Venus in Aries, Apr. 12, 2:07 - Apr. 20, 9:38

YOUR DRIVE AND AMBITION
Mars in Scorpio, Mar. 20, 21:59 - Apr. 20, 9:38

YOUR LUCK MAGNETISM
Jupiter in Leo, Mar. 20, 21:59 - Apr. 20, 9:38

World Events

Mar. 23 – Britain criticizes the U.S. for its hesitation in joining the League of Nations.

Apr. 1 – The German Workers' Party becomes the Nationalist Socialist German Workers' (Nazi) Party.

PISCES
From February 19, 22:29 through March 20, 21:58

The Conscientious Rebel

Although the course of history can reflect the dark side of a sign, it does not necessarily mean that all members of that sign will exhibit the same qualities. The sign of Pisces rules intoxication, obliviousness, and hidden enemies, and these three factors played a role in the rise of the man who began his career as propaganda chief of the German Workers' Party—Adolf Hitler. On February 24, 1920, Hitler announced the anti-Semitic platform of that party. In America, New Jersey legalized 3.5-proof beer on March 2, and a federal agent killed the first violator of the Prohibition laws that month. History would attest to Hitler's intoxicating effect over his followers, and one might argue that a kind of obliviousness allowed good people to ignore nagging apprehensions about Hitler as he continued to rise on the German political scene.

Pisceans tend to enjoy feelings of intensity, and your sign rules things that are spellbinding. Just because Pisceans can be easily influenced does not necessarily mean that Pisceans were convinced by the hypnotic character of Hitler. Indeed, indicators in your chart show the potential for fierce compassion and rebellion, in accordance with the dictates of your conscience. You may have been among those who risked grave consequences in order to save innocents from the evil schemes of Hitler in World War II and the Holocaust.

You may have extremely high ideals and may be self-abnegating. With a spirituality that is likely to reflect your individuality, you may be driven to give yourself in service to others. You may have been a nurse, a social worker, or some other helping professional.

Mutual aid is likely to be your main purpose in relationships. You may seek partners who need you and provide support in return. Virgo shares your commitment to service. You may follow Leo's rising star. Cancer appreciates your emotional validation.

A tendency for self-sacrifice can be invaluable to a worthy cause, but over-emphasis of this virtue can turn it into the vice of vanity. With maturity, you may have learned that giving is its own reward.

ARIES
From March 20, 21:59 through April 20, 9:38

The Loyal Opposition

The sign of Aries rules competition for power, and you were born as new conflicts emerged in the aftermath of World War I. On March 28, 1920, Admiral Nicholas Horthy de Nagybanya seized leadership of Hungary in an anti-revolutionary coup against the communist regime of Béla Kun. Across the Atlantic, the United States was in the throes of the Red Scare. On April 1, the New York State Assembly expelled five socialist members. Later that month, with 50,000 railway workers out on strike, U.S. Attorney General Palmer charged that the Industrial Workers of the World (a labor union) had instigated the strike as part of an international communist conspiracy.

What you learned of the Red Scare in childhood likely colored your opinions about it and the Cold War in your adulthood. Certainly, in both instances, Communists were out to seize as much control as possible over unstable nations. You may have questioned, however, the actual risk to the United States and whether breaches of civil rights were justifiable. You may have believed that overreaction by the U.S. government was as dangerous to democracy as any communist conspiracy.

Indicators in your chart suggest a capacity for loyal dissent. As a member of the generation that supported and fought in World War II, you may have felt that the state of the world had immediate and personal consequences. Even as you defended your country with your life, your personal conscience was just as compelling.

In relationships there may be certain people with whom you simply cannot break bread. You were likely to choose a mate who shared your convictions and instilled them in your children. Taurus runs a home that is rich in values. Leo shares your high ideals and ambitions. Pisces respects your capacity for independent thought.

"All talk and no action" is rarely a criticism that can be applied to Aries. You may feel that you cannot help but stand strongly for your beliefs. Heated arguments with your children, however, may have moved you to soften your stances. With maturity, you could afford to be more receptive to other points of view.

➤ Read about your Chinese Astrological sign on page 838. ➤ Read about your Personal Planets on page 826. ➤ Read about your personal Mystical Card on page 856.

TAURUS

From April 20, 9:39 through May 21, 9:21

Embracer of Values

The sign of Taurus rules values, and within days of your birth, a controversy arose that would provoke debate over the core values espoused by the United States. May 5, 1920, marked the arrest in Massachusetts of Niccolò Sacco and Bartolomeo Vanzetti—both poor Italian immigrants and radical anarchists— for payroll robbery and murder. Pointing to Red Scare hysteria, defenders of Sacco and Vanzetti claimed that the prosecution of the case was irredeemably biased and that the men had been framed. Worldwide belief in their innocence included voices as distinguished as future U.S. Supreme Court Justice Felix Frankfurter. Still, the men were executed on August 23, 1927.

You may have felt disillusioned when you learned about the Sacco and Vanzetti case. You or members of your family may have been among the immigrants to America, who prized freedom of speech and assembly as highly as the opportunity for financial stability. Perhaps you lived in a country that looked to the democratic example of the U.S. Nothing could compromise the value of American freedom more than the execution of two men, based on their beliefs and the group with whom they associated.

You may be introspective and hesitant to take a strong position at the first hint of strong disagreement. Indeed, you may avoid open conflict. Fairness may be an important value for you. You may not believe that everybody has a right to equal wealth, but you would likely fight hard to defend the right to equal opportunity to earn one's fair share.

In relationships, you are likely to be a passionate partner. You may have chosen a mate who was affectionate and generous with hugs. Scorpio indulges your sensuous nature. Libra tends diligently to the health of your relationship. Leo enriches your home life with romance.

Abundance tends to come naturally to Taurus. Early in your life, you may have worked hard to accumulate material wealth, but losses in hard times may have forced you to re-evaluate those things most precious to you. With maturity, you may have put greater store in family health, personal principles, and love.

GEMINI

From May 21, 9:22 through June 21, 17:39

Master of Wordplay

You entered this world, Gemini, as a new art movement emerged on the world stage. June 1, 1920, marked the opening in Berlin of the first international exposition of artworks representing Dadaism, an art movement that opposed movements and declared that art was dead. This self-contradictory description may delight you; Geminis tend to appreciate anything that engages their mind on a conceptual level, even when the concept is the rejection of concepts. Dadaism was about the denial and destruction of meaning. But the very act of denying and destroying meaning actually created new meaning. Cerebral processes that twist meaning into a tasty pretzel may send you into paroxysms of delirium. After all, Gemini is the master of trickery, wordplay, and mind games.

Perhaps you discovered Dadaism on a childhood fieldtrip to a local art gallery. If so, you probably related to it more easily than adults did. When you saw the Mona Lisa with a moustache, you may have laughed. As an adult, you were likely to retain this fresh, ingenuous perspective. Geminis tend to be youthful, open-minded, and energized by originality and irreverence. You may have an unorthodox sense of beauty.

Likely to be imaginative and wildly creative, you may be a gifted artist or writer yourself. An unusual ability to put intuitive or sensory signals into words may have led to a career in cultural or artistic criticism. Because you have the discipline to do complex research, you may have worked in academia.

You may have found romance in a community rich in intellectual activity. Your mate was likely to be someone who could stimulate your mind and inspire your best ideas. You may have admired Libra's flair for art and beauty. Sagittarius turns you on to a world of culture. Leo brings you to glamorous salons and creative circles.

The agile Gemini mind is matchless, but your blessing can be a curse when others fail to keep up with you or to get your jokes. To stay out of trouble, you have probably learned to gear your words to your audience and to fashion your language to be accessible but never condescending.

➤ Read about your Chinese Astrological sign on page 838. ➤ Read about your Personal Planets on page 826. ➤ Read about your personal Mystical Card on page 856.

1920

TAURUS
Your Personal Planets

YOUR LOVE POTENTIAL
Venus in Aries, Apr. 20, 9:39 - May 06, 12:54
Venus in Taurus, May 06, 12:55 - May 21, 9:21

YOUR DRIVE AND AMBITION
Mars in Scorpio, Apr. 20, 9:39 - Apr. 23, 20:28
Mars in Libra, Apr. 23, 20:29 - May 21, 9:21

YOUR LUCK MAGNETISM
Jupiter in Leo, Apr. 20, 9:39 - May 21, 9:21

World Events

May 16 - Switzerland is accepted into the League of Nations.

May 16 - Joan of Arc, originally burned at the stake for heresy in 1431, is canonized.

Joan of Arc

GEMINI
Your Personal Planets

YOUR LOVE POTENTIAL
Venus in Taurus, May 21, 9:22 - May 31, 0:04
Venus in Gemini, May 31, 0:05 - June 21, 17:39

YOUR DRIVE AND AMBITION
Mars in Libra, May 21, 9:22 - June 21, 17:39

YOUR LUCK MAGNETISM
Jupiter in Leo, May 21, 9:22 - June 21, 17:39

World Events

June 1 - The Communist Party is established in Spain.

June 20 - Race riots cause havoc in Chicago.

1920

CANCER
Your Personal Planets

YOUR LOVE POTENTIAL

Venus in Gemini, June 21, 17:40 - June 24, 10:52
Venus in Cancer, June 24, 10:53 - July 18, 20:25
Venus in Leo, July 18, 20:26 - July 23, 4:34

YOUR DRIVE AND AMBITION

Mars in Libra, June 21, 17:40 - July 10, 18:13
Mars in Scorpio, July 10, 18:14 - July 23, 4:34

YOUR LUCK MAGNETISM

Jupiter in Leo, June 21, 17:40 - July 23, 4:34

World Events

July 11 – Actor Yul Brynner is born.

July 12 – Soviet Russia approves Lithuania's independent status.

Mexican rebel leader Pancho Villa

LEO
Your Personal Planets

YOUR LOVE POTENTIAL

Venus in Leo, July 23, 4:35 - Aug. 12, 4:30
Venus in Virgo, Aug. 12, 4:31 - Aug. 23, 11:20

YOUR DRIVE AND AMBITION

Mars in Scorpio, July 23, 4:35 - Aug. 23, 11:20

YOUR LUCK MAGNETISM

Jupiter in Leo, July 23, 4:35 - Aug. 23, 11:20

World Events

July 28 – Pancho Villa surrenders to the Mexican government on the condition his life is spared.

Aug. 1 – The Communist Party is founded in Great Britain.

CANCER
From June 21, 17:40 through July 23, 4:34

The Underdogs' Sympathizer

The sign of Cancer rules the care and feeding of dependents. When you were born, the reign of Pancho Villa, the Mexican revolutionary and legendary Robin Hood figure to his people, was waning. July 28, 1920, marked Villa's retirement, with a general's pension awarded by the Mexican government. Having begun his career as a laborer-turned-bank-robber and cattle rustler, Villa went on to recruit thousands of men—including noteworthy Americans such as John Reed—to fight in the revolutionary forces of Francisco I. Madero in 1910. After Madero's assassination, Villa remained in Chihuahua and became a warlord over northern Mexico. He gained his reputation as a Robin Hood by breaking up the plantations of wealthy local landowners and giving out parcels of land to the widows and children of his fallen soldiers.

The exploits of Pancho Villa, published worldwide, may have captured your imagination in your childhood. Indicators in your chart suggest a streak of rebelliousness in your personality, and as an adult, you may have enjoyed other romantic adventure stories. Likely to sympathize with the underdog, you may find it hard to get incensed when the wealthy and powerful lose out to the disadvantaged.

You may have had to fight or go to extreme lengths to protect or provide for your own family. In challenging times, you were likely to do what was practical and made sense in tough situations. You may often play the role of the team member who comes through in the clutch.

The vitality of your relationship may involve the feeling that it's you and your partner against the world. You may have fallen in love with a romantic person who defies convention. Pisces shares your dream of "making it work against all odds." Scorpio's iron will may thrill you. Leo plays the part of your shining hero or heroine.

The ability to live out your dreams may have kept you energized at times when reality was altogether unpleasant. Your greatest challenge may have been to avoid boredom when circumstances returned to normalcy. In maturity, creative pastimes may have fed your hunger for love and romance.

LEO
From July 23, 4:35 through August 23, 11:20

Champion of Children

The sign of Leo rules children, and within days of your birth, news items focused on an activist who championed children. On August 2, 1920, J. William Lloyd was found guilty in Chicago of conspiracy to overthrow the government. In the late nineteenth century, Lloyd had been an anarchist, but he quit that movement in reaction to the position of some of its leaders that children were property. A millionaire and a gentleman scholar, Lloyd wrote an article, "The Anarchist Child," in which he ardently expressed his belief in the integrity, freedom, and individuality of children, despite their dependent status. In the dramatic conclusion of another article on the subject, Lloyd declared: "Henceforth I am no Anarchist, but a Free Socialist!" No doubt, Lloyd's pursuits as a Socialist made him vulnerable to persecution in the midst of the Red Scare.

Lloyd faded into obscurity, but you may instinctively share his view on the status of children. As a Leo, you may have always felt unique and somehow special. Charismatic and enthusiastic, you are likely to reject any movement that requires effacement of one's individuality. "To thine own self be true" may be your motto.

You may also share Lloyd's affection and respect for children. As a Leo, you are likely to be playful and ever youthful. Time spent with children may keep you feeling refreshed and energized. Your own children may inspire your best ideas. You may have been an outstanding teacher, parent, or coach.

Challenges in your early life may have forced you to create your own model of marriage and family. You may have chosen a partner who shared your ideals on family life. Agreeable Libra makes compromise feel painless. Pisces finds your charisma enchanting. Aquarius likes to play relationships by ear.

The supreme self-confidence of Leo may have enabled you to become a self-made person, and you have every reason to be proud. To get along with others, however, you may have had to develop some self-awareness about the impact of your strong personality. With maturity, you may have made sure to share the spotlight with others.

➤ Read about your Chinese Astrological sign on page 838. ➤ Read about your Personal Planets on page 826. ➤ Read about your personal Mystical Card on page 856.

VIRGO

From August 23, 11:21 through September 23, 8:27

The Respected Breadwinner

A Virgo might have thought up the saying, "A woman's work is never done." Within days of your birth, women in America were able to vote for elected officials. It was a "burden" that women would bear with joy. On August 26, 1920, Secretary of State Bainbridge Colby signed the certification to ratify the 19th Amendment to the United States Constitution, granting the right to vote to women. In Britain, only women over thirty had the right to vote; the age dropped to twenty-one in 1928. France and Belgium had granted women the vote in 1919.

Thanks to the efforts of suffragists in the generations before you, the women of your generation would be spared the indignity of having to fight for the simple right to vote. Born under the sign that rules laborers, Virgos tend to believe that hard work makes one worthy of respect and rewards. Indeed, during the Great War, women had entered the workforce in great numbers, to build armaments and support their countries on the home front. Gaining the vote was a virtually inevitable consequence of such instrumental service.

You are likely to be a diligent worker, and the quality of your service may have helped you to get ahead. You may feel at your best when you are at your busiest. Indeed, your motto may be, "If you want to get anything done, give it to a busy person." If you were born in August, others' praise may be your chief motivation. If you were born in September, your work may be its own reward.

Your relationship may provide a nice change from the workaday world. Your partner was likely to interest you in cultural or humanitarian activities. Compassionate Pisces brings the spiritual gifts of giving. Sagittarius opens your mind to culture and the arts. Aquarius enlists you in making the world a better place.

Virgoan respect for rules and order can bring manageability to chaotic situations, but if your expectations are rigid, you can be vulnerable to disappointment. Greater flexibility in maturity allowed you to go with the flow.

LIBRA

From September 23, 8:28 through October 23, 17:12

Advocate of Fairness

The sign of Libra rules the scales of justice. September 28, 1920, marked the indictment of eight men from the Chicago White Sox in one of the greatest sports scandals ever. Accused of conspiring with gamblers to fix the 1919 Baseball World Series, the eight men became known as the Black Sox, despite being acquitted in criminal court. The new Commissioner of Baseball, Judge Kenesaw Mountain Landis banned the players from professional baseball for life.

When you were old enough to learn of the Black Sox story, you may have felt offended by the unsportsmanlike behavior of the players, had they indeed been guilty of play-fixing. The scandal left a permanent stain on the national sport that symbolized American wholesomeness; it was the subject of discussion and derision for many years to come. Members of your sign tend to have a virtually religious faith in fair play. If you are a baseball fan, you may have regarded the conduct of the Black Sox as a personal betrayal—even decades after the act.

Even if you could not forgive the Black Sox for throwing the games, you still may have some sympathy for the fact that the ball players had been horribly exploited and underpaid as laborers. Librans tend to sympathize with both sides of a conflict and can see when and how both sides can be wrong. You might have had a career in law, as an attorney, mediator, or judge, or you may have worked as a labor negotiator for unions or management.

For Librans, the good things in life are so much sweeter when they can be shared and to this end you may have chosen a partner whose interests and pursuits complemented your own. Sagittarius indulges your taste for the arts and exotic creativity. With children, Leo ensures fun and learning for the whole family. Scorpio encourages you to cultivate your passions.

The Libran ability to understand both sides of any issue may have endowed you with a truly judicious temperament. Sometimes Librans can insist on being equivocal when a friend just needs you to be on their side. With maturity, you may have learned that not everything needs to be weighed.

► Read about your Chinese Astrological sign on page 838. ► Read about your Personal Planets on page 826. ► Read about your personal Mystical Card on page 856.

VIRGO
Your Personal Planets

YOUR LOVE POTENTIAL
Venus in Virgo, Aug. 23, 11:21 - Sept. 05, 11:52
Venus in Libra, Sept. 05, 11:53 - Sept. 23, 8:27

YOUR DRIVE AND AMBITION
Mars in Scorpio, Aug. 23, 11:21 - Sept. 04, 20:26
Mars in Sagittarius, Sept. 04, 20:27 - Sept. 23, 8:27

YOUR LUCK MAGNETISM
Jupiter in Leo, Aug. 23, 11:21 - Aug. 27, 5:28
Jupiter in Virgo, Aug. 27, 5:29 - Sept. 23, 8:27

World Events

Aug. 10 – Turkey and the Allied powers sign the Treaty of Sèvres, by which Turkey loses the majority of its territory.

Aug. 26 – The 19th Amendment is ratified, granting American women the right to vote.

American women are granted the right to vote

LIBRA
Your Personal Planets

YOUR LOVE POTENTIAL
Venus in Libra, Sept. 23, 8:28 - Sept. 29, 19:44
Venus in Scorpio, Sept. 29, 19:45 - Oct. 23, 17:12

YOUR DRIVE AND AMBITION
Mars in Sagittarius, Sept. 23, 8:28 - Oct. 18, 13:21
Mars in Capricorn, Oct. 18, 13:22 - Oct. 23, 17:12

YOUR LUCK MAGNETISM
Jupiter in Virgo, Sept. 23, 8:28 - Oct. 23, 17:12

World Events

Sept. 28 – Eight Chicago White Sox baseball players are charged with fixing the 1919 World Series.

Oct. 14 – Finland and the USSR agree Finland's independence.

1920

SCORPIO
Your Personal Planets

YOUR LOVE POTENTIAL

Venus in Scorpio, Oct. 23, 17:13 - Oct. 24, 5:10
Venus in Sagittarius, Oct. 24, 5:11 - Nov. 17, 17:27
Venus in Capricorn, Nov. 17, 17:28 - Nov. 22, 14:14

YOUR DRIVE AND AMBITION

Mars in Capricorn, Oct. 23, 17:13 - Nov. 22, 14:14

YOUR LUCK MAGNETISM

Jupiter in Virgo, Oct. 23, 17:13 - Nov. 22, 14:14

World Events

Oct. 25 – The Greek King Alexander I dies after being bitten by his pet monkey.

Nov. 21 – Bloody Sunday in Ireland as the police open fire at Croke Park stadium in Dublin.

Nobel Peace Prize winner, Woodrow Wilson

SAGITTARIUS
Your Personal Planets

YOUR LOVE POTENTIAL

Venus in Capricorn, Nov. 22, 14:15 - Dec. 12, 11:45
Venus in Aquarius, Dec. 12, 11:46 - Dec. 22, 3:16

YOUR DRIVE AND AMBITION

Mars in Capricorn, Nov. 22, 14:15 - Nov. 27, 13:37
Mars in Aquarius, Nov. 27, 13:38 - Dec. 22, 3:16

YOUR LUCK MAGNETISM

Jupiter in Virgo, Nov. 22, 14:15 - Dec. 22, 3:16

World Events

Dec. 6 – Finland's independent status is ratified in the Dorpart Treaty.

Dec. 10 – Woodrow Wilson is awarded the Nobel Peace Prize for his work in restoring war-torn Europe.

SCORPIO

From October 23, 17:13 through November 22, 14:14

The Fearless Idealist

The sign of Scorpio rules willfulness and matters of life and death. On October 25, 1920, the mayor of Cork, Ireland, Terence MacSwiney, died in Brixton Prison after a seventy-four-day hunger strike. A leader in Sinn Fein and the Irish Republican Army, MacSwiney had been charged with seditious speech and possession of police code and a resolution recognizing Irish independence. He was convicted by court martial and sentenced to two years in jail. His hunger strike inspired protest worldwide: from longshoremen in Brooklyn, New York, to Irish soldiers serving in India, to South American Catholics, who appealed to the Pope for intervention. Responding to possible release by the British government, MacSwiney declared, "I am confident that my death will do more to smash the British Empire than my release."

When you were old enough to learn about the fighters for Irish independence, you may have recognized their unshakable commitment to their cause. Regardless of how you feel about the IRA, the steely will expressed in MacSwiney's statement has much in common with the Scorpionic temperament, known for its fearlessness and shrewd political instinct. When you believe in the absolute righteousness of a cause or position, your fear of death may also evaporate.

Likely to pursue a career that allowed you to promote your highest ideals, you may have found it impossible to work for an employer who required moral compromises. You may work well with groups and may have served in a leadership role in humanitarian causes.

You may regard relationships as a safe haven in a dangerous world. Trustworthiness may be an essential trait in any partner. Reliable and discreet, Capricorn encloses your family within firm boundaries. Taurus assures you the comfort of material independence. Cancer shares your vigilance about security.

A strong Scorpionic will may have enabled you to survive the most murderous period in human history. Powering down in peacetime may have been surprisingly stressful for you and your family. With time and healing, you could regenerate your faith in the goodness of life.

SAGITTARIUS

From November 22, 14:15 through December 22, 3:16

The World's Surveyor

The sign of Sagittarius rules the international arena and institutions of state. On December 10, Woodrow Wilson won the Nobel Peace Prize for his work in bringing peace to Europe and in founding the League of Nations in the wake of the Great War. The United States' rejection of participation in the League of Nations was heartbreaking for Wilson. Still, his impassioned advocacy of democracy and self-rule for former colonial territories had helped new nations to emerge after the war. Late December brought further evidence of the dissolution of even those great powers that had won the war. On December 23, the Government of Ireland Act was passed—a much-disputed but important step toward the establishment of an Irish Republic.

When you were born, the established world order was in flux. When you reached adulthood, you or members of your family would have to fight to restore order to the world. Throughout your youth, you witnessed the breakdown and transformation of traditional institutions. You might not have realized the severity of the situation until things truly fell apart in the Great Depression and World War II.

Sagittarians have a talent for taking a survey of the world around them and seeing the big picture. Yours was the generation that literally saved and rebuilt the world. In your career, you may have taken on the laying of new foundations, the framing of new laws for new countries, and the rebuilding of industries and national infrastructure.

You may look to relationships for new beginnings. Your mate was likely to be youthful, energetic, and able to share your visions of a better world. Aquarius helps you frame an optimistic vision for the future. Gemini can help you think through the details of your schemes. Capricorn supports you in realizing your goals.

Your ability to understand world events in personal terms enabled you to make a difference when it really mattered. The rebellions of your own children may have made you fear for the future. In time, you could come to see that they, too, were driven by conscience and an awareness of their world.

► Read about your Chinese Astrological sign on page 838. ► Read about your Personal Planets on page 826. ► Read about your personal Mystical Card on page 856.

CAPRICORN

From December 22, 3:17 through December 31, 23:59

The Enlightened Factualist

The sign of Capricorn rules the call of reality, and within days of your birth, the winds finally left the sails of one very dogged, quixotic romantic. On December 31, 1920, the poet, warrior, proto-fascist, and loose cannon Gabriele D'Annunzio finally gave up on his fifteen-month occupation of the Adriatic coastal city of Fiume. Infuriated with Italy's loss of Fiume in the aftermath of World War I, D'Annunzio led a regiment of black-shirted legionnaires in taking over the city, declaring its independence, and insisting on occupying Fiume until formal annexation by Italy. D'Annunzio declared himself the de facto "Commandante" of Fiume. He surrendered when 20,000 Italian and Allied forces marched on Fiume and took it back, pursuant to the Treaty of Rapallo.

In years to come, Mussolini would assimilate many of D'Annunzio's romantic, nationalist ideas and themes in building the Fascist movement. One of the lessons of your lifetime has been recognition of the ways in which murderous movements dressed themselves in the glamour of patriotic nostalgia. An appreciation for "just the facts" may have rendered you less susceptible to mob mentality.

Capricorns tend to be practical, pragmatic people. Indicators in your chart show the power of enlightenment, a strong ability to read the handwriting on the wall, and to take appropriate action. You are likely to know how to get others to snap out of whatever delusions they may be harboring. If necessary, you may also be able to disappear into thin air, for safety's sake.

Wartime may have made your relationships unusually intense and passionate. You were likely to choose a mate as practical and plain-dealing as you are. Cancer gives you shelter and security. Aquarius can always provide a clarity check. Virgo keeps track of important little details you might miss.

Capricorn's ability to grasp plain facts may have enabled you to maintain your focus in chaotic times. The safety of taking things at face value may have forced you to sacrifice your sense of humor. With maturity, you may have learned to ease up and laugh at crazy things.

CAPRICORN
Your Personal Planets

YOUR LOVE POTENTIAL
Venus in Aquarius, Dec. 22, 3:17 - Dec. 31, 23:59

YOUR DRIVE AND AMBITION
Mars in Aquarius, Dec. 22, 3:17 - Dec. 31, 23:59

YOUR LUCK MAGNETISM
Jupiter in Virgo, Dec. 22, 3:17 - Dec. 31, 23:59

World Events

Dec. 24 – Enrico Caruso gives his last public performance, at the Metropolitan Opera House in New York.

Dec. 30 – The Communist Party is established in France.

Coco Chanel,
August 19, 1883 - January 10, 1971

COCO CHANEL
Leo

When we think of the essence of the French woman, we envision someone with style and flair, a personal elegance, and an ability to carry flawlessly whatever vision is hers alone. Many women fill some of these criteria, but Coco Chanel remains the quintessence of that expectation. Determinedly individualistic, uniquely stylish, her innovative visions defined fashion across the world for years during her lifetime, and she remains an important presence decades after her death in 1971.

Chanel single-handedly changed the face of fashion in her own times and she confidently adhered to her own vision of what is beautiful. In a period of fashion excess, Chanel created the boyish look of the flapper, put women in trousers, and developed signature scents that are still prized. She broke new ground and shocked a few people along the way, but she stuck to her beliefs. As a Leo, Chanel had a natural interest in fashion, enhanced by a contact from Venus, planet of beauty. A difficult contact from Neptune often creates identity and security

problems or a drinking problem, but Chanel used that energy to refine her senses, to intuit what would be the next fashion craze, and to create perfumes that would be adored around the world. Neptune is one of the most creative of planetary energies, and its influence in her chart helped Coco to be the true artist and visionary she was.

In a time of frilly excess, Chanel created fashion in which less was more and that bespoke a sense of elegant austerity. With the Moon, planet of feelings, in sensitive Pisces, Coco was quite emotional, but a contact from responsible Saturn inclined her to be practical, to channel her creativity into saleable products. This is also an indication of hard work, and Chanel worked virtually all her life.

Her attitude was always to design for herself and to allow other people to accept her vision or not, as they chose. This degree of confidence and independence is both admirable and indeed quite rare, and is described by a prominently placed Mars, the planet of action. She was assertive,

even on those days when she felt a pang of insecurity. In addition, a contact from Uranus (planet of independence) to Mars increased her willingness to swim against the current and to find her own sense of expression and to make it work for her. Like all great artists, Chanel found her own vision and shared it with the world.

➤ Read Jacqueline Kennedy Onassis' Star Profile on page 649.

Jupiter and Saturn in Virgo: Service and Sacrifice

Virgo is the sign of work, detail, health, and spiritual service. It is ruled by the planet Mercury, whose domain is thought and the intellectual sphere. When planets spend time in this sign, their efficiency is increased tremendously. Saturn was in Virgo in 1921, and accuracy and precision became benchmarks of collective cultural progress. Saturn represents structure and mastery, and when it meets up with Virgo, painstaking attention must be paid to each and every detail. On July 30, 1921, Canadian scientists discovered insulin, one of the most important breakthroughs in the field of medicine of the century. Also this year, Vitamin D was discovered and it was shown to prevent rickets. Frederick Soddy of the United Kingdom was awarded the Nobel Prize in chemistry, for investigations into origin and nature of isotopes. And Albert Einstein of Germany was awarded the Nobel Prize in physics for his discovery of the law of photoelectric effect.

The planet Jupiter also spent time in the sign of Virgo in 1921, expanding our ideas about work and service. Eight million American women were counted among the employed this year, and they worked mainly as teachers and secretaries. But still, they were paid much less than men in the same positions. The meeting of Jupiter and Saturn can cause a serious outlook on life to emerge, and discipline can become a central focus. Against the backdrop of the roaring twenties, many people around the world had to work harder than they ever had done before in the postwar era. Unfortunately, not everyone was busy doing the Charleston.

Demonstration of the unemployed in London

Members of the Sinn Fein Parliament

Insulin is isolated by Frederick Grant Banting

THE GREAT WAR CASTS A SHADOW

A Europe deeply scarred by the war continued to suffer due to hunger and unemployment, but a prosperous America rushed to their aid under the helmsmanship of Herbert Hoover. The dire straits of its peasants brought Russia's premier Lenin to limit socialization in favor of limited free enterprise. From all over Europe, refugees attempted to enter the U.S., prompting restrictions on immigration. In response to Irish demands, Britain created the Irish Free State in southern Ireland, self-governing but loyal to the British crown. New, daring styles of dress and dance were popular in the U.S., raising fears of a deep moral crisis. A vicious race riot broke out in Tulsa, Oklahoma, after the arrest of an African American accused of attacking a white woman. Eight million American women were counted among the employed, finding their vocation as teachers and secretaries, but still being paid less than men in the same positions. Douglas Fairbanks Snr. broke cinema records in *The Mark of Zorro*, while the golden throat of tenor Enrico Caruso was permanently silenced. In medicine, diabetics gained a new lease on life when insulin was isolated.

➤ Read "Astrology Goes on Trial: Evangeline Adams" by Rochelle Gordon on page 185.

CAPRICORN

From January 01, 0:00 through January 20, 13:54

The Able Achiever

The sign of Capricorn rules the foundation of any investment in the future, and within days of your birth, such matters were clearly on the mind of Joseph H. Defrees, President of the Chamber of Commerce of the United States. The Great War was over; the American economy was struggling due to costs of the war, but Mr. Defrees was focusing on America's future—its children. On January 16, 1921, Defrees called attention to America's deficit in skilled teachers. Poor training and low pay had caused teaching standards to fall below every other civilized country in the world, leaving the U.S. vulnerable to long-term competitive disadvantage. Defrees envisaged that education would provide the firm foundation upon which the U.S. could develop into an international force to be reckoned with.

Like Defrees, you have the ability to articulate a vision, to map out a long-term strategy for development, and to work hard to make it happen. Indicators in your chart suggest that you have a spirit for dreaming, a heart for commitment, a head for planning, and hands for building. You may be the kind of person who simply must work, who will push a broom just to get one foot in the door and the other foot on the ladder to the top.

Colleagues and subordinates may find you an accessible, inspiring leader, someone who is never too proud to roll up your sleeves and take on any job, however humble. You have the ability to rally a team by making everyone feel proud to have one small part in the creation of something greater than themselves.

You and your mate were liable to be a power couple, deeply involved in each other's passions and projects. Together you may enjoy showing a public face of devotion and support. Cancer satisfies your private needs. Pisces inspires and cultivates your dreams. Virgo works tirelessly to fulfill your highest aspirations.

Your commitment to projects enables you to make dreams come true, but you can be susceptible to overworking yourself. With maturity, you may have learned to tune in to early warning symptoms of work addiction and to set a healthy, livable pace.

AQUARIUS

From January 20, 13:55 through February 19, 4:19

The Idealistic Dreamer

The sign of Aquarius rules revolution, and when you were born, one great revolutionary was arriving in this world as another one was leaving it. February 4, 1921, marked the birth of Betty Friedan, whose book, *The Feminine Mystique*, set off the Second Wave of feminism in the United States and elsewhere in the world. A founder of the National Organization for Women, Friedan played an instrumental role in the legalization of abortion rights and the campaign for equal pay for equal work. February 8 marked the passing of Russian revolutionary and anarchist theorist Prince Peter Kropotkin, whose writings articulated the anarchist's dream—a classless society, in which material resources belonged to everyone. From exile in Western Europe, Kropotkin returned to Russia in 1917. Disillusioned by the totalitarianism of the Bolsheviks, he withdrew from public life.

Like Friedan and Kropotkin, you may think in new and unconventional ways, and you are likely to be among the most idealistic of revolutionaries. Indicators in your chart suggest that you are compassionate, humane, and quite the dreamer. For you, selfless service to others can reach spiritual dimensions. Your acts of devotion may truly be acts of devotion.

Vivid imagery may fill your mind, and you may be a talented poet or storyteller. You may also have an interest in psychology. The works of Carl Jung—rich in evocative archetypes and mythology—may have special appeal for you. You may have profound insight into the collective unconscious of humanity.

Your life may revolve around relationships and an active social life. Your life partner was probably a good friend, who graduated to best friend and mate for life. Leo inspires you and keeps you smiling. Pisces shares your devotion to others. Virgo supports the purity of your ideals.

The best of Aquarian intentions can lead to marvelous improvements for humanity, but like Kropotkin, you may have run into conflict over the execution of your ideals. When the means threaten to corrupt your ends, you may withdraw your support and retire to the safety of private life.

➤ Read about your Chinese Astrological sign on page 838. ➤ Read about your Personal Planets on page 826. ➤ Read about your personal Mystical Card on page 856.

1921

CAPRICORN
Your Personal Planets

YOUR LOVE POTENTIAL
Venus in Aquarius, Jan. 01, 0:00 - Jan. 06, 20:32
Venus in Pisces, Jan. 06, 20:33 - Jan. 20, 13:54

YOUR DRIVE AND AMBITION
Mars in Aquarius, Jan. 01, 0:00 - Jan. 05, 7:38
Mars in Pisces, Jan. 05, 7:39 - Jan. 20, 13:54

YOUR LUCK MAGNETISM
Jupiter in Virgo, Jan. 01, 0:00 - Jan. 20, 13:54

World Events

Jan. 3 – India convenes its first Parliament.

Jan. 6 – In an attempt to encourage commercial flight, the U.S. navy orders the sale of 125 flying boats.

Philanthropist John D. Rockefeller grants $1 million to aid Europe's destitute

AQUARIUS
Your Personal Planets

YOUR LOVE POTENTIAL
Venus in Pisces, Jan. 20, 13:55 - Feb. 02, 18:34
Venus in Aries, Feb. 02, 18:35 - Feb. 19, 4:19

YOUR DRIVE AND AMBITION
Mars in Pisces, Jan. 20, 13:55 - Feb. 13, 5:20
Mars in Aries, Feb. 13, 5:21 - Feb. 19, 4:19

YOUR LUCK MAGNETISM
Jupiter in Virgo, Jan. 20, 13:55 - Feb. 19, 4:19

World Events

Jan. 21 – John D. Rockefeller grants $1 million to aid Europe's destitute.

Jan. 28 – Albert Einstein suggests it might be possible to measure the Universe.

1921

PISCES
Your Personal Planets

YOUR LOVE POTENTIAL
Venus in Aries, Feb. 19, 4:20 - Mar. 07, 9:17
Venus in Taurus, Mar. 07, 9:18 - Mar. 21, 3:50

YOUR DRIVE AND AMBITION
Mars in Aries, Feb. 19, 4:20 - Mar. 21, 3:50

YOUR LUCK MAGNETISM
Jupiter in Virgo, Feb. 19, 4:20 - Mar. 21, 3:50

World Events

Mar. 8 – Spanish Premier Eduardo Dato is assassinated.

Mar. 12 – Edith Cowan becomes the first woman to be elected to the Western Australian Parliament.

British actor Peter Ustinov is born under the sign of Aries

ARIES
Your Personal Planets

YOUR LOVE POTENTIAL
Venus in Taurus, Mar. 21, 3:51 - Apr. 20, 15:31

YOUR DRIVE AND AMBITION
Mars in Aries, Mar. 21, 3:51 - Mar. 25, 6:25
Mars in Taurus, Mar. 25, 6:26 - Apr. 20, 15:31

YOUR LUCK MAGNETISM
Jupiter in Virgo, Mar. 21, 3:51 - Apr. 20, 15:31

World Events

Mar. 23 – A new parachuting record is set by Arthur G. Hamilton — 24,400 ft.

Apr. 16 – British actor Peter Ustinov is born.

PISCES
From February 19, 4:20 through March 21, 3:50

The Fantastic Voyager

The sign of Pisces rules fashion and motion pictures, and within days of your birth, both subjects were in the news. On March 6, 1921, the new fashion of shorter skirts was causing public alarm in Sunbury, Pennsylvania. In response to complaints from a dozen residents, the chief of police issued an edict requiring women to wear skirts at least four inches below the knee. Elsewhere in the U.S., the National Association of Moving Picture Industry announced a plan to introduce censorship to movies. Europeans must have laughed at the puritanical impulses of the Americans. Shorter skirts were the latest in couture to issue from Paris, and as much as genteel American burghers howled, the craze for shorter skirts and sleeves would prevail throughout the twenties, in the U.S. and throughout the world.

Fashion and movies share at least one very important quality with the sign of Pisces—the power of seduction. You may enjoy the movies for their ability to captivate and transport you into another reality. You are likely to enjoy the feeling of being absorbed in fantasy—a state that can leave you vulnerable to the power of suggestion.

Fashion offers you another means of fantasy and escape. Pisceans enjoy a gift for disguise, and you may dress yourself to make a specific impression on others. Likely to have a seductive, compelling personality, you might have charmed the spots off quite a few leopards in your day. Creative and original, you may have pursued a career in the arts, design, or entertainment.

For you, sharing everything in life tends to magnify your pleasure. You were likely to choose a partner willing to live out your dreams. Virgo is devoted to helping you realize your greatest potential. Aries brings energizing initiative. Cancer indulges your hunger for emotional intensity.

The Piscean penchant for dreams and fantasy can produce inspiring creativity, but if your feet are not planted firmly on the ground, some may become spaced out and unreliable. With maturity, you may have developed a discipline for keeping promises and backing up ideas with results.

ARIES
From March 21, 3:51 through April 20, 15:31

The Foremost Competitor

The sign of Aries rules competition for sports titles and bragging rights, and both subjects were in the news within days of your birth. On April 10, 1921, the United States Reclamation Service announced a plan to build the world's highest dam in Boulder Canyon. Construction on the project, the Hoover Dam, began in 1931 and was completed in four years. It was the largest government contract of its time. April 11 marked the first radio broadcast of a sports event, a boxing match. Again, the U.S. could claim bragging rights for the milestone. Elsewhere in the world, Europe was enduring severe postwar aftershocks. England was paralyzed, with one million miners on strike and another million railway and transport workers threatening a walkout.

You may not personally enjoy boxing, but it is the quintessential sport for the sign of Aries, ruler of pugilistic confrontations. In general, Ariens aspire to be the biggest, the strongest, the fastest, and the first! You may have admired the ambitious architecture projects in your lifetime—from the Empire State Building, to the reconstruction of post-World War II Europe, to the Petronas Towers in Malaysia.

If you were born on or before March 25, 1921, you are more likely to be a classic Arien—powerful, competitive, confrontational, direct, athletic, fiercely competitive. If you were born after March 25, you are more likely to be aggressive about investing, accumulating wealth, and defending your values.

Relationships allow you to express your passion and energy. You may choose a partner who can be as energetic as you or who can provide a comfy retreat for powering down. Sensuous Taurus channels your energy in an affectionate direction. Gemini shares your need for speed. Virgo keeps you busy on rewarding projects.

Ariens can be brave and fearless, but if you have ever found yourself playing chicken with an opponent, you may have landed in a lose-lose situation. With maturity, you were likely to mellow and become less impulsive. Once you learned to pick your battles wisely, you could avoid having to waste any of your energy.

► Read about your Chinese Astrological sign on page 838. ► Read about your Personal Planets on page 826. ► Read about your personal Mystical Card on page 856.

TAURUS

From April 20, 15:32 through May 21, 15:16

Maximizer of Life

The sign of Taurus rules value and beauty, and art exhibits occurring within days of your birth demonstrated the varying esteem that the viewing public accorded certain kinds of art over time. On May 2, 1921, New York's Metropolitan Museum of Art held a grand opening for an exhibition of Impressionist artworks. The reverent approval voiced by attendees contrasted markedly with the outrage and disapproval expressed toward the Impressionist artists in the nineteenth century. Still, the viewing public was not quite ready for the Cubist works of Pablo Picasso, included in the Metropolitan show. And the Dadaist compositions of Max Ernst aroused protest and controversy when he opened his first exhibit on May 2, 1921, in Paris.

Like the art show audiences of the late nineteenth and early twentieth centuries, you too may take time to warm up to new styles, trends, and influences. In general, Taureans are a conservative breed who tend to reject change as an initial matter, but you may have more exotic tastes than most members of your sign. Things that appeal to your senses—lovely colors, velvety textures, sweet scents, robust flavors—can win you over.

You may have a lot of energy and drive, but a built-in brake on impulsiveness enables you to take on challenges with discipline and focus. Projects requiring methodical diligence may be comforting. For relaxation, you may enjoy sewing, knitting, gardening, or woodworking. Singing, writing, or music may provide you with an outlet for spiritual expression.

You may feel that relationships are for sharing the abundance of the good earth. You may have chosen a mate who has a taste for the finer things in life. Pisces woos you with poetry, music, and fine wine. Virgo cultivates a fertile garden. Cancer babies you with all your favorite things.

Indicators in your chart suggest that you were made to go for the maximum joy in life. The conditions your generation faced likely forced you to endure horrific challenges before enjoyment was even an option. Your Taurean determination likely empowered you to build heaven on Earth from the ashes of war.

GEMINI

From May 21, 15:17 through June 21, 23:35

The Mischievous Intellectual

The sign of Gemini rules matters that have two sides. Within days of your birth, this principle appeared to affect issues concerning women. On June 5, 1921, famed American stunt pilot Laura Bromwell died as she had lived—in the air—after losing control of her airplane while performing a loop. In May 1921, she had broken women's records for air speed (135 mph) and consecutive loops (199). On June 11, Penn State graduated its first female engineer. On June 20, Congresswoman Alice Robinson proved her competence as a public servant by becoming the first woman to preside over the United States House of Representatives—albeit for only thirty minutes. This was certainly a month when women were hitting the headlines.

You may have a healthy sense of humor about all the crazy contradictions life can throw in your path. Members of your sign tend to have a sophisticated intellect, and you are likely to have a refined sensibility for paradox and irony. Unlike people who see the world in literal, black-and-white terms, you may feel that a little inconsistency adds spice to life.

You are likely to rebel against any routine that gets too regular or any job that gets too repetitive. Rigid or overly meticulous people may catch a glimpse of your mischievous side. A playful imagination may make you a bit of a practical joker, an irrepressible punster, or a talented member of literary circles. You are nothing if not complex.

Before settling down, Gemini tends to take plenty of time to sample a variety of friends and experiences. The perfect partner may have appeared in a magic moment, when you recognized your soul mate. Sagittarius elevates your sense of endless possibilities. Capricorn's ironic point of view may tickle your funny bone. Leo knows just how to capture your heart.

The Gemini personality can overflow with sparkle and charm. In certain circumstances, this can lighten up a sagging spirit, but at other times a joke may go over like a lead balloon. With maturity, you may have gained a stronger sensitivity to the gravity of a situation and how to respond appropriately.

➤ Read about your Chinese Astrological sign on page 838. ➤ Read about your Personal Planets on page 826. ➤ Read about your personal Mystical Card on page 856.

TAURUS
Your Personal Planets

YOUR LOVE POTENTIAL
Venus in Taurus, Apr. 20, 15:32 - Apr. 25, 23:45
Venus in Aries, Apr. 25, 23:46 - May 21, 15:16

YOUR DRIVE AND AMBITION
Mars in Taurus, Apr. 20, 15:32 - May 06, 1:44
Mars in Gemini, May 06, 1:45 - May 21, 15:16

YOUR LUCK MAGNETISM
Jupiter in Virgo, Apr. 20, 15:32 - May 21, 15:16

World Events

May 2 – The first Dadaist exhibition opens in Paris.

May 14 – Fascists win thirty-five seats in the Italian Parliament.

Fascists' influence grows in Italy

GEMINI
Your Personal Planets

YOUR LOVE POTENTIAL
Venus in Aries, May 21, 15:17 - June 02, 4:20
Venus in Taurus, June 02, 4:21 - June 21, 23:35

YOUR DRIVE AND AMBITION
Mars in Gemini, May 21, 15:17 - June 18, 20:33
Mars in Cancer, June 18, 20:34 - June 21, 23:35

YOUR LUCK MAGNETISM
Jupiter in Virgo, May 21, 15:17 - June 21, 23:35

World Events

May 25 – In Dublin, the Customs House is burned to the ground by Sinn Fein rebels.

June 16 – Sun Yat-Sen approaches the U.S. for official recognition of the South China Republic.

1921

CANCER
Your Personal Planets

YOUR LOVE POTENTIAL
Venus in Taurus, June 21, 23:36 - July 08, 5:56
Venus in Gemini, July 08, 5:57 - July 23, 10:29

YOUR DRIVE AND AMBITION
Mars in Cancer, June 21, 23:36 - July 23, 10:29

YOUR LUCK MAGNETISM
Jupiter in Virgo, June 21, 23:36 - July 23, 10:29

World Events

June 25 – In Germany, coal is successfully liquefied into oil by scientist Friedrich Bergius.

July 18 – Astronaut John Glenn is born.

Adolf Hitler, leader of the Nazi Party

LEO
Your Personal Planets

YOUR LOVE POTENTIAL
Venus in Gemini, July 23, 10:30 - Aug. 05, 14:41
Venus in Cancer, Aug. 05, 14:42 - Aug. 23, 17:14

YOUR DRIVE AND AMBITION
Mars in Cancer, July 23, 10:30 - Aug. 03, 11:00
Mars in Leo, Aug. 03, 11:01 - Aug. 23, 17:14

YOUR LUCK MAGNETISM
Jupiter in Virgo, July 23, 10:30 - Aug. 23, 17:14

World Events

July 29 – Adolf Hitler takes over as President of the Nationalist Socialist German Workers' (Nazi) Party.

Aug. 11 – American author Alex Haley is born.

CANCER
From June 21, 23:36 through July 23, 10:29

The Parental Provider

The sign of Cancer rules women, providers, and parents. When you were born, news items focused on women's status as wage earners in the United States. On July 19, 1921, Mills College President Dr. Amelia Reinhardt reported that 8 million women were employed in the American workforce. Of these, fifty percent were teachers; thirty-seven percent were secretaries. Dr. Reinhardt emphasized the inroads that still needed to be made in traditionally male professions, especially in medicine and law. In other news, parents everywhere could look forward to the benefits of a new medical breakthrough in France. On July 18, 1921, Albert Calmette and Camille Guérin vaccinated a baby for tuberculosis.

Women's participation in the workforce had increased dramatically by the time you reached adulthood, especially during World War II. Women in your family may have worked outside the home, especially if they were unmarried. In maturity, you probably supported your daughters or nieces in pursuing educational and career equality.

You are likely to have a non-traditional outlook. Your grandchildren might often marvel at how young at heart you are. Cancerians are not often thought of as leaders, but you may have set a new standard for leadership. You may be nurturing and fiercely protective toward people who depend on you. At home or in the workplace, people with no biological relationship to you whatsoever may regard you as a parental figure or treasured mentor.

You are likely to be deeply loyal and willing to work hard on the quality of your relationships. You may have chosen a partner who was slightly eccentric but endearing—someone you might call "a real character." Pisces delights you with dreamy originality. Gemini exudes a youthful charm. Sunny Leo brings playful fun to family life.

Cancerians can be compelling, deeply emotional people, and your feelings may flow through you with great intensity. Occasional moodiness may have caused those dearest to you to walk on eggshells. In maturity, you may have helped your loved ones cope with the natural ebb and flow of your moods.

LEO
From July 23, 10:30 through August 23, 17:14

The Compelling Charmer

Within days of your birth, Leo, women in Connecticut might have wished they could wash the government right out of their hair. On August 22, 1921, the State Barber's Commission ruled that women couldn't bob their own hair without a state barber's license. The bob had recently come into fashion and was especially convenient for women working in industry, where long hair could be a nuisance and a hazard. Many people saw the ruling as a reaction against women's greater freedom in the political realm and the workplace. The bob was treated as a symbol of rebellion that was associated with public smoking, private drinking, scanty clothing, and too much makeup.

By the time you reached adulthood in the forties, the reaction to the bob might have seemed antiquated and silly. Whether you are male or female, any interference in the care and grooming of your royal mane, Leo, is likely to make you roar with rage. In general, Leos like to cut a striking image in public, and you are unlikely to take kindly to anybody trying to dictate how you should look or who should cut your hair.

You are likely to be glamorous and to have an enchanting, even seductive, personality. Leos born before August 4 may be sensitive to what other people think about them, but if you were born on or after August 4, you may be especially rebellious and willful. Your independence may have become especially fierce once you became able to support yourself financially. Pride may fuel your determination to get by on your own.

For Leo the Lion, relationships are truly a matter of the heart. You may have chosen a partner for reasons you can hardly explain: a magical attraction, a romantic coincidence. When you shine, Cancer glows with pride. Gemini charms you with sweet talk. Lovely Libra soothes the savage lion.

Your sunny personality and winning ways can be so compelling, you may have gotten away with mischief on numerous occasions. You can get into trouble, however, with people who are less susceptible to your natural charm. With maturity, you may have become more humble and less likely to push your luck.

➤ Read about your Chinese Astrological sign on page 838. ➤ Read about your Personal Planets on page 826. ➤ Read about your personal Mystical Card on page 856.

VIRGO

From August 23, 17:15 through September 23, 14:19

The Charitable Organizer

The sign of Virgo rules health and nutrition. You were born at a time when conditions were extremely bad in Russia. Starvation was threatening 18 million people, and cholera had afflicted 50,000. On August 27, 1921, news stories reported that Russian peasants were eating soup made from grass. The U.S. managed to feed 20,000 children in St. Petersburg by September 21, but nothing short of an overnight bumper crop could have saved millions of Russian people from starvation, malnutrition, and disease.

If you were born in post-war Europe, your family may have struggled with homelessness, scarcity of staples, hunger, or disease. The tragedies that you may have learned about or experienced as a child repeated themselves again in the horror of World War II. Even if you were born to abundance, the idea of others lacking sustenance may be deeply distressing to you. As an adult, you may have resolved to devote all your might to ensuring a decent living for yourself and your family and to helping as many people as humanly possible. You may also have a soft spot for animals in distress.

Indicators in your chart suggest that charitable impulses are a driving force in your life, ones that may operate on a subconscious level. You also have what it takes to give generously of yourself and to organize effective campaigns in the service of humanity. Your personal philosophy likely moves you to give a needy person a fishing pole, not just a fish.

You may define relationships expansively; if someone is dear to you, he or she may be as good as family. You are likely to have chosen a partner who would welcome all the lost souls you were likely to bring home. Pisces' compassion is your perfect complement. Aquarius shares your concerns about the world. Sagittarian generosity and good humor keeps you going.

People are often astounded by the Virgoan capacity for service to others. While helping others may be energizing, even you can reach the point of exhaustion. With maturity, you may have learned to recognize the warning signals of burnout and to take the time necessary to revive yourself.

LIBRA

From September 23, 14:20 through October 23, 23:01

Reconciler of Equality

The sign of Libra rules marriage and the politics of relationships. When you were born, evidence was mounting that progress in women's equality was affecting the stability of marriages. On October 16, 1921, the St. Louis Court of Domestic Relations reported that the number of divorces in the state of Missouri—700 in a recent term—had increased by one hundred percent since 1896. The court attributed the rise in the divorce rate to lower birth rates and increases in women's earning power. Still, women were earning half of what men were earning for equivalent work.

Fifty years later, divorce rates would make those of 1921 look statistically insignificant. Such changes might have inspired some people to claim that the St. Louis court was prophetic in blaming women's independence, but you were unlikely to share that viewpoint. In general, Librans stand for equality in matters concerning relations between the sexes. And, by the 1970s, the entire discourse on women's rights would undergo such a fundamental shift, there was no going back.

Like all good Librans, you may believe deeply in fairness, and you may regard change as, if not a good thing, then an inevitable thing. You may welcome any opportunity that allows men and women to fully realize their potential as individuals. Likely to sow harmony and beauty in the world, you may have supported human rights and free artistic expression. You may have pursued a career in law, mediation, or the arts.

Although you may not judge others who seek a divorce, you are likely to have a stable and long marriage. You were likely to choose a partner with whom you could live in peace and friendship. Virgo tends to the little things that keep a relationship going. Aries keeps you moving forward as a couple. Leo illuminates your bond with sunshine and romance.

Although Librans respect fairness and equality, the application of such principles to new populations can create unanticipated upheaval. You may find the process of change to be disconcerting. In maturity, you may have come to accept that a little tumult goes with the territory.

➤ Read about your Chinese Astrological sign on page 838. ➤ Read about your Personal Planets on page 826. ➤ Read about your personal Mystical Card on page 856.

VIRGO
Your Personal Planets

YOUR LOVE POTENTIAL
Venus in Cancer, Aug. 23, 17:15 - Aug. 31, 22:23
Venus in Leo, Aug. 31, 22:24 - Sept. 23, 14:19

YOUR DRIVE AND AMBITION
Mars in Leo, Aug. 23, 17:15 - Sept. 19, 11:39
Mars in Virgo, Sept. 19, 11:40 - Sept. 23, 14:19

YOUR LUCK MAGNETISM
Jupiter in Virgo, Aug. 23, 17:15 - Sept. 23, 14:19

World Events

Aug. 25 – After months of deliberation, the U.S. finally agrees peace terms with Germany.

Sept. 7 – *Tarzan Of The Apes* opens on Broadway, with a performance that uses live jungle animals.

Tarzan of the Apes opens on Broadway with live jungle animals

LIBRA
Your Personal Planets

YOUR LOVE POTENTIAL
Venus in Leo, Sept. 23, 14:20 - Sept. 26, 4:07
Venus in Virgo, Sept. 26, 4:08 - Oct. 20, 17:34
Venus in Libra, Oct. 20, 17:35 - Oct. 23, 23:01

YOUR DRIVE AND AMBITION
Mars in Virgo, Sept. 23, 14:20 - Oct. 23, 23:01

YOUR LUCK MAGNETISM
Jupiter in Virgo, Sept. 23, 14:20 - Sept. 25, 23:09
Jupiter in Libra, Sept. 25, 23:10 - Oct. 23, 23:01

World Events

Oct. 4 – The League of Nations refuses to send relief to the Russian famine.

Oct. 8 – Indian nationalists go on strike as the Prince of Wales arrives in Bombay.

1921

SCORPIO
Your Personal Planets

YOUR LOVE POTENTIAL
Venus in Libra, Oct. 23, 23:02 - Nov. 13, 21:10
Venus in Scorpio, Nov. 13, 21:11 - Nov. 22, 20:04

YOUR DRIVE AND AMBITION
Mars in Virgo, Oct. 23, 23:02 - Nov. 06, 16:12
Mars in Libra, Nov. 06, 16:13 - Nov. 22, 20:04

YOUR LUCK MAGNETISM
Jupiter in Libra, Oct. 23, 23:02 - Nov. 22, 20:04

World Events

Nov. 2 – The American Birth Control League is formed by Margaret Sanger and Mary Ware Dennett.

Nov. 7 – Benito Mussolini becomes leader of the National Fascist Party in Italy.

Benito Mussolini becomes leader of the National Fascist Party in Italy

SAGITTARIUS
Your Personal Planets

YOUR LOVE POTENTIAL
Venus in Scorpio, Nov. 22, 20:05 - Dec. 07, 19:46
Venus in Sagittarius, Dec. 07, 19:47 - Dec. 22, 9:06

YOUR DRIVE AND AMBITION
Mars in Libra, Nov. 22, 20:05 - Dec. 22, 9:06

YOUR LUCK MAGNETISM
Jupiter in Libra, Nov. 22, 20:05 - Dec. 22, 9:06

World Events

Nov. 25 – Hirohito becomes ruler of Japan.

Dec. 6 – British and Irish representatives sign a treaty creating the Irish Free State as a dominion of the British Empire.

SCORPIO
From October 23, 23:02 through November 22, 20:04

The Magnetic Delver

The sign of Scorpio rules animal magnetism, insanity, and the macabre, and when you were born, a worldwide "made-for-Scorpio" film festival seemed to be in progress. October 31, 1921, marked the New York premier of *The Sheik*, starring Rudolph Valentino, an actor with the power to make women swoon. Focusing on Valentino's lithe body and androgynous aura, men were dumbounded by the star's appeal. November 14 marked the Paris premiere of *The Cabinet of Dr. Caligari*, the landmark expressionist film by German director Robert Wiene. *Caligari* told the story of a serial killer psychiatrist who uses hypnotism in murdering his victims.

Every sign has a dark side, and Scorpio has the darkest of all. This does not mean, however, that you were destined to take after the dark side of your sign. When you were old enough to be allowed to see movies with adult appeal, like *The Sheik* or *Caligari*, talking movies had left silent films in the dust. You are likely, however, to exude your own animal magnetism, to have a compelling personality, and to be fascinated by mental pathology, criminology, and mysteries. The passion of the Expressionist movement in art may also hold great appeal for you. Scorpios tend to have a taste for intensity.

You may have pursued a career in psychology, criminology, forensics, or detective work. You may be compelled to study the underbelly of human nature—an interest that others may find puzzling. But Scorpios happen to be puzzling, inscrutable, mysterious, compelling people.

In relationships, you may draw a bright line between mere friends and a love interest. Your partner is likely to be the one person whom you trust with your deepest, darkest secrets. Non-judgmental Pisces shares your eccentric interests. Capricorn is discreet, with a bawdy side that comes out in private. Taurus protects your secrets and indulges your sensual side.

Your ability to plumb the depths of human nature can help prevent future tragedies. To preserve your sanity, hope, and faith, you may have learned to balance your exposure to the dark side with healthy spiritual pursuits.

SAGITTARIUS
From November 22, 20:05 through December 22, 9:06

The Generous Ambassador

The sign of Sagittarius rules politics and generosity, a virtue the President of the U.S. appeared to lack late in 1921. On November 22, President Warren Harding gave a speech in Des Moines, Iowa, where he warned of danger to the nation if women voters were to unite as a class. The alleged danger was promptly demonstrated on November 24, as the first American women arrived in Moscow to aid victims of the Russian famine.

When you were old enough to learn of Harding's warning, you might have laughed out loud. No good Sagittarian could miss the humor in Harding's fear of a future political force that might run around inspiring people to have compassion and—heaven forbid—to help feed and care for millions of poor, starving people. Like the feminine ambassadors of goodwill, you may believe that the more one shares, the more there is to go around. At some point in your life, you may have traveled to foreign locales to aid people in need.

You are likely to demand fairness and justice, and believe in the universal humanity of all people. Likely to be skilled in negotiation and arbitration, you may have a gift for resolving differences. You may have been a judge, statesperson, or champion for human rights. A deep sense of compassion may augment your political instincts. A creative approach to intractable problems can enable you to bring long-opposed adversaries together. You may have chosen to enlighten others through writing or artistic endeavors.

Your relationship may serve as the focal point for both public and private pursuits. You were likely to choose a mate who would be a true partner and ally in realizing your goals. Libra shares your desire for harmonious relationships. Aquarius shares your sense of a larger mission in the world. Pisces shares your compassion for others.

Sagittarians tend to have a strong drive to elevate the best potentials of humankind. Your lifetime brought quite the opposite reality in World War II. To avoid depression and disillusionment, you may have found strength by helping people who had been wounded, rejected, and forgotten.

► Read about your Chinese Astrological sign on page 838. ► Read about your Personal Planets on page 826. ► Read about your personal Mystical Card on page 856.

CAPRICORN

From December 22, 9:07 through December 31, 23:59

The Practical Reformer

The sign of Capricorn rules hard work, sacrifice, and diligent campaigns that bear fruit over time. On December 23, 1921, the President of the United States granted clemency to Eugene Debs, champion of working men and women around the world and founder of the first industrial union in the United States, the American Railway Union. Debs, who began his career as a railroad fireman, spent his life fighting for the conditions and rights that ordinary people take for granted today. In late December of 1921, Debs was serving a ten-year sentence in federal prison. He had been convicted of espionage in 1918, for making a speech against the Great War. For exercising his freedom of speech, Debs was stripped of his citizenship and his right to vote.

A certain element of your sign is all about truth and inevitability—the simple reality that some people don't want to acknowledge but just plain *is*. Capricorn is often regarded as a conservative sign, but you may support reform in certain situations when promoting change is just the right thing to do. You are doubtlessly smart enough to see when resistance will only breed further tension, conflict, and pain.

If you run a business, you may provide generous benefits to employees because their happiness and loyalty brings greater productivity. You are likely to see no sense in lose-lose propositions. Nor would you demand submission purely for the sake of proving your own authority. You may be dedicated to the belief that compassion, fairness, and practicality can coexist in harmony.

You are likely to regard your relationship as your rock and salvation. You may have chosen a mate who was loyal and even-tempered. Libra creates a peaceful home life. Pisces gives you tender affection. Taurus provides material security and a solid shoulder to lean on.

As a Capricorn, you have the ability to persevere when things get difficult. Another strand in your personality needs everything to be peaceful and beautiful. Having lived through the devastation and ugliness of World War II, your faith and staying power enabled you to survive and rebuild.

CAPRICORN
Your Personal Planets

YOUR LOVE POTENTIAL
Venus in Capricorn, Dec. 22, 16:31 - Dec. 31, 23:59

YOUR DRIVE AND AMBITION
Mars in Libra, Dec. 22, 9:07 - Dec. 26, 11:47
Mars in Scorpio, Dec. 26, 11:48 - Dec. 31, 23:59

YOUR LUCK MAGNETISM
Jupiter in Libra, Dec. 22, 9:07 - Dec. 31, 23:59

World Events

Dec. 23 – U.S. President Harding frees Eugene Debs and twenty-three other political prisoners.
Dec. 26 – British troops enter Cairo to suppress the riots.

Astrologer Evangeline Adams
January 31, 1899 - November 10, 1932

Special Feature
Astrology Goes on Trial: Evangeline Adams

by Rochelle Gordon

Aquarius is famous for being radical, rebellious, and totally unconventional. It's also the sign that's said to rule astrology. It's no surprise, then, that Evangeline Adams, thought of by many as the "mother of astrology," made her planetary debut under that Sun sign on February 8, 1868, in Jersey City, New Jersey. Adams chose her unusual career at a time when it was thought of as even odder—during the early 1900s. Appropriately enough, in true Aquarian style, she also found herself in court—not once, but twice—quite literally "fighting City Hall" for the right to pursue her profession.

Adams was arrested in 1914—but it's a good bet that those who had charged her with "fortune-telling" had absolutely no idea what they were in for. She began her defense by establishing astrology's validity through a full rundown of its long and rich history. She then testified that she did not "predict actual outcomes" for her clients, but rather that she

simply "interpreted astrological symbolism." The judge who officiated was sufficiently impressed to acquit her of all charges. In fact, among the comments he made were these: "The defendant raises astrology to the dignity of an exact science. She uses the relative position of the planets at the time of birth, basing the horoscope on the well-known and fixed science of astronomy. As such, she has violated no law." Further, he went on to say that although "Every fortune-teller is a violator of the law, every astrologer is not a fortune-teller." The verdict set a precedent for how this "fortune-telling" law would be interpreted in New York City in the future—and didn't hurt Adams's reputation one bit. As if she hadn't already proved her point well enough, she was arrested yet again—in 1923—and, once again, the charges were dismissed.

Adams began her astrology practice in earnest after relocating to New York in 1905. She had

quite an impressive client list, which, over the course of her life, would come to include financiers Charles Schwab and J. P. Morgan, along with a host of celebrities from all walks of life. Eugene O'Neill, Enrico Caruso, Joseph Campbell, Charlie Chaplin, and Gloria Vanderbilt were also said to have consulted with her.

Over the course of a career that would span nearly four decades, Adams showed her talent for astrology in many ways. She wrote four astrology texts, all of which are on astrologers' bookshelves to this day. She hosted a nationally syndicated radio show that was among the most popular of its time. In fact, "Radio Round-Ups of 1932" noted that her program, "Your Stars," had "taken the country by storm," receiving more fan mail than any other in 1931.

(Continued on page 193)

➤ Read about the 1929 Crash in "Money, Astrology, and the Crash of '29" on page 225. ➤ Read more about Adams in "Astrology Reigns Through the Ages" on page 25. ➤ Read Caruso's Star Profile on page 97.

Jupiter in Libra: Genuine Justice

One of the world's most famous Piscean politicians was born on March 1, 1922. Yitzhak Rabin, Israeli general, statesman and Prime Minister—until he was killed in 1995—was born under the influence of Jupiter in Libra. When Jupiter settles in Libra, justice is the key phrase. People born with this aspect are generally popular and magnanimous. There is an inherent nobility to this placement. Jupiter is the planet of big ideas and expansion. Everything that comes under the spell of Jupiter grows and grows. So when this planet moves into the intellectual and refined sign of Libra, we feel like grappling with life's bigger questions. In 1922, artists Joan Miró and Marc Chagall were very popular, as was Hermann Hesse's *Siddhartha*. Also this year, Sinclair Lewis's *Babbit* and James Joyce's *Ulysses* intrigued readers. People were interested in mind expansion, in the arts, politics, and the sciences.

Reader's Digest published its first edition of a pocket-sized magazine this year. This gave the lay public the ability to learn more about current events and literature, quests of interest under the influence of Jupiter in Libra.

On February 7, Marie Curie was elected to the French Academy of Sciences. On February 27, the U.S. Supreme Court unanimously upheld the Women's Suffrage Amendment, in the ultimate expression of Libran justice. President Harding dedicated the Lincoln Memorial on May 30 of this year, under the influence of Jupiter in Libra. Lincoln, although he was an Aquarius, expressed the energy of the scales of justice through his actions again and again.

Fascists in Italy take over the government in a bloodless revolution

Mahatma Gandhi's trial at Gujarat

The death mask of Tutankhamen

THE CURSE OF THE MUMMY

In 1922, archeologists Lord Carnarvon and Howard Carter discovered Egyptian Pharaoh Tutankhamen's tomb, filled with priceless treasures. The entrance to the tomb bore a warning: "Death will come on swift wings to he who violates the tomb of the Pharaoh." Mysterious deaths in the archeological team soon led some to suspect that Tut's spirit sought his revenge. Within a year, thirteen members of the expedition, including Carnarvon himself, had died; by the end of the decade, sixteen others also had perished.

A DELICATE BALANCE OF POWER

The Ottoman Empire came to an end as its Sultan was forced to abdicate by the Turkish Grand National Assembly. Mussolini's fascist forces took over Italy's government in a bloodless revolution facilitated by fears of a communist take-over. The Irish Free State suffered two setbacks when its leaders were felled, one by a heart attack, the other by an assassin. Following the 1920 San Remo agreement, Britain assumed its mandate to rule Palestine, angering Arabs with its favor toward the Jewish state. Mahatma Gandhi, who headed peaceful opposition to British rule in India, was sentenced to six years in prison, increasing the popularity of his cause. The U.S. extended its ban on alcohol to ships in port, causing some traffic to divert to Canada, while officials find prohibition hard to enforce. *The Readers Digest*, offering condensed magazine articles, began publication. The untouched 3,259-year-old tomb of Pharaoh Tutankhamen was found in the Valley of the Kings near Luxor, Egypt, full of splendiferous riches. Artists Miró and Chagall were popular, while Hesse's *Siddhartha*, Lewis's *Babbit*, and Joyce's *Ulysses* intrigued readers.

➤ Read "Astrology Goes on Trial: Evangeline Adams" by Rochelle Gordon on page 185.

CAPRICORN

From January 01, 0:00 through January 20, 19:47

The Crisis Manager

January 5, 1922 marked the passing of Sir Ernest Shackleton, the British polar explorer, who died of a heart attack on his final expedition, another voyage to Antarctica. He had failed to reach Antarctica in 1914 when his ship—prophetically named the *Endurance*—became trapped in ice and sank after 281 days. Shackleton's goal then became getting his crew to civilization. With supplies dwindling, he and his men crossed perilous miles of ice hauling three lifeboats salvaged from the ship. Reaching open water, they made first for a tiny, uninhabited island. Leaving most of the men there, on Elephant Island, Shackleton and five men crossed 800 miles of the stormiest waters in the world, bound for the whaling station at South Georgia Island from which the *Endurance* had departed three years earlier. Arriving on the wrong side of the mountainous island, Shackleton crossed it on foot. At the whaling station, a ship was quickly outfitted and Shackleton retrieved his crew from Elephant Island. Every man survived.

Capricorn rules character-building crises, and Shackleton's perseverance in the face of adversity exemplifies the best traits of your sign, January Capricorn of 1922—the ability to solve problems without wasting time or energy on recriminations.

When facing a challenge, you're likely to be a take-charge kind of person who can inspire absolute confidence. You're probably able to reckon with reality, innovate on the spot, and work with steadfast determination and endurance toward meeting any objective.

In your most meaningful relationships, you may trust your partner with your life, and you're likely to write off anyone who shows the slightest sign of unreliability. Scorpio's depth and strength wins your confidence. Taurus brings stability and resourcefulness. Leo shows you loyalty and courage.

The ability to make and act upon concrete decisions endows you with excellent crisis management skills. Under normal conditions, however, your steadfastness can turn into rigidity. Your greatest challenge is to be more flexible in your evaluation of people and circumstances.

AQUARIUS

From January 20, 19:48 through February 19, 10:15

The Civilizing Force

The civilizing trends of the latter twentieth century are indebted to the ideals associated with your sign, Aquarius of 1922. Aquarius rules rebellion and innovation, and you were born during the career of one of the most innovative rebels in human history. In early February, Mahatma K. Gandhi was leading the people of India in a campaign of civil disobedience against British colonial rule. A firm believer in *ahimsa*, or non-violence, Gandhi proved true to his principles following the February 5 incident at Chauri Chaura, where villagers attacked a police station and killed the constables. Horrified, Gandhi unilaterally called off the civil disobedience campaign. Still, the British arrested him in March for sedition—an interesting charge in light of Gandhi's rejection of British jurisdiction over India.

By the time you reached adulthood, Gandhi had succeeded in bringing the mighty British Empire to its knees, and he did it by scrupulously peaceful means. Likely to have been inspired by his example, you may have engaged in non-violent resistance in support of a cause dear to you.

Aquarians are literally revolted by oppression and injustice. In America, Aquarians born in 1922 may well have marched for civil rights alongside Martin Luther King, Jr., another great disciple of Gandhi's ideals. You also may share a certain political astuteness often attributed to Gandhi—reckoning that when hundreds of millions are on your side, overt violence is not necessary. Your intelligence, shrewd instincts, and sense of fairness may have made you an effective negotiator, diplomat, politician, or activist.

Relationships may bring you inspiration and the reason to carry on in life. You might look for a life partner who supports you in realizing your highest ideals. Pisces wields the power of compassion. Virgo works hard to help the needy. Libra cultivates a harmonious home and a serene, peaceful world.

Your challenge is to control the inner demons that threaten to betray the very values you embrace. Your strength is the discipline and patience to find a peaceful way through any situation.

➤ Read about your Chinese Astrological sign on page 838. ➤ Read about your Personal Planets on page 826. ➤ Read about your personal Mystical Card on page 856.

CAPRICORN
Your Personal Planets

YOUR LOVE POTENTIAL
Venus in Capricorn, Jan. 01, 0:00 - Jan. 20, 19:47

YOUR DRIVE AND AMBITION
Mars in Scorpio, Jan. 01, 0:00 - Jan. 20, 19:47

YOUR LUCK MAGNETISM
Jupiter in Libra, Jan. 01, 0:00 - Jan. 20, 19:47

World Events

Jan. 5 – British Antarctic explorer Sir Ernest Shackleton dies.

Jan. 6 – The Allies agree to a deferment of the reparation payments to be made by Germany.

German bank notes are worth less than wallpaper

AQUARIUS
Your Personal Planets

YOUR LOVE POTENTIAL
Venus in Capricorn, Jan. 20, 19:48 - Jan. 24, 13:12
Venus in Aquarius, Jan. 24, 13:13 - Feb. 17, 11:05
Venus in Pisces, Feb. 17, 11:06 - Feb. 19, 10:15

YOUR DRIVE AND AMBITION
Mars in Scorpio, Jan. 20, 19:48 - Feb. 18, 16:14
Mars in Sagittarius, Feb. 18, 16:15 - Feb. 19, 10:15

YOUR LUCK MAGNETISM
Jupiter in Libra, Jan. 20, 19:48 - Feb. 19, 10:15

World Events

Feb. 5 – The first volume of the pocket-sized magazine *Reader's Digest* is published.

Feb. 7 – Marie Curie is elected to the Academy of Sciences.

1922

PISCES
Your Personal Planets

YOUR LOVE POTENTIAL
Venus in Pisces, Feb. 19, 10:16 - Mar. 13, 11:29
Venus in Aries, Mar. 13, 11:30 - Mar. 21, 9:48

YOUR DRIVE AND AMBITION
Mars in Sagittarius, Feb. 19, 10:16 - Mar. 21, 9:48

YOUR LUCK MAGNETISM
Jupiter in Libra, Feb. 19, 10:16 - Mar. 21, 9:48

World Events

Feb. 27 – In the U.S., the women's suffrage amendment is unanimously upheld by the Supreme Court.

Mar. 18 – Mahatma Gandhi is sentenced by the British government to six year's imprisonment for sedition.

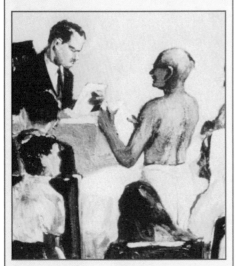

A painting of Mahatma Gandhi's trial at Gujarat

ARIES
Your Personal Planets

YOUR LOVE POTENTIAL
Venus in Aries, Mar. 21, 9:49 - Apr. 06, 15:49
Venus in Taurus, Apr. 06, 15:50 - Apr. 20, 21:28

YOUR DRIVE AND AMBITION
Mars in Sagittarius, Mar. 21, 9:49 - Apr. 20, 21:28

YOUR LUCK MAGNETISM
Jupiter in Libra, Mar. 21, 9:49 - Apr. 20, 21:28

World Events

Apr. 12 – The Russian Council of Commissars restores its citizens' right to own motor vehicles.

Apr. 16 – Annie Oakley sets a new women's shooting record — one hundred targets in a row.

PISCES
From February 19, 10:16 through March 21, 9:48

The Working Vacationer

Pisces rules dancing, music, and intoxication, and within days of your birth, news items reported that such matters were causing international anxiety. On February 26, 1922, the periodical *La Revue Mondiale* warned that a dance craze was interfering with the postwar reconstruction of France and threatening American willingness to provide aid. At the time, jazz music and the tango had become wildly popular, and French club-goers were also consuming drugs imported from Germany. Synthetic cocaine and heroin from Germany were also flooding into America.

Your sign's association with escapist activities and substances doesn't mean that you're a dance fiend or a drug user, 1922 Pisces. In fact, when you reached adulthood, you may have been quite aware of the need to exercise moderation in such matters. As a member of the generation that fought World War II, however, you may have turned to music or dancing as a way to relax and relieve stress. A passion for theater, poetry, and other arts may have inspired your career choices, perhaps leading to a career in writing or teaching.

If anything, you may need to watch out for the potential to overwork yourself. Indicators in your chart suggest that you have the capacity to become completely absorbed in your work. When you are pursuing a calling or a relationship, you may give it all your undivided attention and effort. In projects requiring teamwork, you can be selfless and sacrificing. You may even identify with the people or causes that matter most to you.

Your level of devotion in relationships can be very high, and you can tend to merge emotionally with your partner. You're likely to choose a mate who needed you or was willing to take the lead. Sagittarius can lead you to exciting new places. Libra takes charge in a gentle way. Leo's charisma may be irresistible.

Selfless devotion can make you an asset to any project or relationship. Constant self-sacrifice, however, can be too much of a good thing. Over-extending yourself may have forced you to forswear martyrdom, and ultimately you may have perfected the art of saying, "No."

ARIES
From March 21, 9:49 through April 20, 21:28

First and Best

The sign Aries is often associated with warfare and martial themes, but in 1922, as the world returned to peacetime amusements, there emerged a certain warrior bearing a bow and cello. Celebrated as "the best that draws a bow," Spanish musician Pablo Casals appeared at Carnegie Hall on April 7, 1922. To the delight of the crowd in attendance, Casals revealed yet another weapon in his arsenal, a conductor's baton, with which he demonstrated his virtuosity as a then-emerging orchestral conductor. Leading performances of pieces by Beethoven, Brahms, and Wagner, Casals won repeated ovations from the audience.

Casals' performance exemplifies certain virtues of your sign, Aries, that you are likely to share. Just as Casals topped his field as a solo musician, Aries is driven to be the best in his or her chosen field. And just as Casals succeeded in leading an entire orchestra, Aries has an exceptional gift for taking diverse contributions from a group of individuals and orchestrating them into one harmonious and spectacular enterprise.

Likely to have a taste for music, poetry, and other arts, you may even perform or compose yourself. Foreign and avant-garde influences may be especially energizing and inspiring for you. As Aries tends to be first in all things, you may have been the first to learn the newest dance, to wear the latest fashions, or to start the most modern trend.

The ability to let off steam may be exactly what lends stability to your relationships. Ariens born in 1922 thrive with partners who can maintain an active pace and a sense of humor. Playtime with Leo provides healthy exercise for Aries. Sagittarius offers the joys of travel and laughter. Libra balances excitement with rest time.

Early in life, a certain willfulness may have caused you to "butt heads" with parents or other adults in positions of authority. As you got older, you may have come to understand the method to their madness. With maturity, a greater capacity for discipline would have enabled you to focus that Aries energy, increase your effectiveness, and reap the rewards of mastery.

► Read about your Chinese Astrological sign on page 838. ► Read about your Personal Planets on page 826. ► Read about your personal Mystical Card on page 856.

TAURUS

From April 20, 21:29 through May 21, 21:09

The Lucrative Collaborator

During the twentieth century, innovations in motion pictures paved the way for a new and highly lucrative industry. On April 21, 1922, Lee De Forest demonstrated a new technology, Phonofilm, that recorded sound directly on to film. A different technology, the Vitaphone system, was used in the first talkies, however. Vitaphone sought to synchronize a vinyl record player with a film projector. The awkwardness of Vitaphone led the descendants of the Phonofilm technique to prevail in the industry. De Forest's invention had been the wave of the future—just a bit further into the future than expected—and in 1959 he was awarded an honorary Oscar for his contribution to the science of motion pictures.

By the forties when you came of age, the motion picture industry was in a golden age itself, and its glamour and opportunity may have attracted you. If the artist's life seemed too insecure, you may have pursued a career as a film accountant, a producer, or an intellectual property lawyer. You may have a talent for presiding over complex collaborative projects—and your sign does rule profitable artistic enterprises, after all.

Copyright and trademark licensing is a perfect vocation for Taurus because it allows you to harvest revenue from artistic works. You may enjoy foreign travel and exotic cultures. Later in life, you might have wandered the galleries of the world in search of promising investments.

You may express your most romantic ideals in your relationships. It's likely that your life partner leads you on pleasant getaways from the drudgery of daily life. Sunny Leo brings you rest and recreation. You can escape with Pisces into the magic of the silver screen. Libra's refined tastes provide a valuable artistic perspective.

Taureans can tend to have an excellent instinct for the next great breakthrough, and you may have jumped at the chance to get in on a few potential "gold mines" in your day. Although rose-colored glasses may have led to some disappointments, it is most likely that experience quickly taught you how to tell the difference between a rising star and a dud.

GEMINI

From May 21, 21:10 through June 22, 5:26

The Multifaceted Talent

Gemini of 1922, you were born within days of another celebrated member of your sign. June 10 marked the birth of Judy Garland, the legendary actress and singer. Best known as Dorothy in MGM's *The Wizard Of Oz*, Garland gained worldwide renown for her work in film. In general, Geminis have multifaceted personalities and lives. Garland was one of the greatest all-around entertainers in history—an actress, singer, dancer, and cabaret persona. She is also well known for the two sides of her life. Her career was wildly successful, but her personal life was often sad. She received several Oscar nominations, and won numerous Grammy and Emmy awards, but she also had five marriages, struggled with drug abuse, and died at the age of forty-seven. In death, as in life, her fans adored her, and thousands gathered outside the funeral home in New York City to pay their respects.

You are also likely to enjoy unusual creativity, which you may express through a variety of outlets. You may have achieved celebrity in your field as a performing artist or professional expert. Indicators in your chart suggest that you could parlay your talents into handsome financial rewards and public prominence.

You may be happiest when you can make a living doing something that you would otherwise do just for fun. In general, financial rewards alone are rarely enough to motivate a Gemini. You may have a vivid imagination and an ability to express feelings and ideas that others find uplifting.

You may seek relationships that allow you the freedom to seek new challenges and exciting experiences. Sagittarius brings the allure of an experienced world traveler. Charismatic Leo promises fun and glamour. Libra brings a more subtle, sophisticated appeal that may offer greater staying power.

Your charm and ability to articulate moving sentiments may have won you many admirers. Like Judy Garland, however, you may have experienced an imbalance between the glamour of your public persona and the quality of your private life. With maturity, you may have turned your back on rewards that turned out to be fleeting.

➤ Read about your Chinese Astrological sign on page 838. ➤ Read about your Personal Planets on page 826. ➤ Read about your personal Mystical Card on page 856.

TAURUS
Your Personal Planets

YOUR LOVE POTENTIAL
Venus in Taurus, Apr. 20, 21:29 - May 01, 1:21
Venus in Gemini, May 01, 1:22 - May 21, 21:09

YOUR DRIVE AND AMBITION
Mars in Sagittarius, Apr. 20, 21:29 - May 21, 21:09

YOUR LUCK MAGNETISM
Jupiter in Libra, Apr. 20, 21:29 - May 21, 21:09

World Events

Apr. 21 - Lee De Forest demonstrates the first instrument on which image and voice appear on the same film.

Apr. 23 - Ireland goes on strike to protest the presence of the military.

American actress and singer Judy Garland is born under the sign of Gemini

GEMINI
Your Personal Planets

YOUR LOVE POTENTIAL
Venus in Gemini, May 21, 21:10 - May 25, 17:03
Venus in Cancer, May 25, 17:04 - June 19, 16:31
Venus in Leo, June 19, 16:32 - June 22, 5:26

YOUR DRIVE AND AMBITION
Mars in Sagittarius, May 21, 21:10 - June 22, 5:26

YOUR LUCK MAGNETISM
Jupiter in Libra, May 21, 21:10 - June 22, 5:26

World Events

May 30 - Ecuador is granted independence.

June 10 - American actress and singer Judy Garland is born.

1922

CANCER
Your Personal Planets

YOUR LOVE POTENTIAL
Venus in Leo, June 22, 5:27 - July 15, 3:21
Venus in Virgo, July 15, 3:22 - July 23, 16:19

YOUR DRIVE AND AMBITION
Mars in Sagittarius, June 22, 5:27 - July 23, 16:19

YOUR LUCK MAGNETISM
Jupiter in Libra, June 22, 5:27 - July 23, 16:19

World Events

June 28 – Troops of the Irish Free State come into conflict with the Irish Republican Army in Dublin.

July 18 – Joseph O'Sullivan and Reginald Duncan receive the death penalty for the murder of Northern Ireland deputy Henry Wilson.

Troops of the Irish Free State

LEO
Your Personal Planets

YOUR LOVE POTENTIAL
Venus in Virgo, July 23, 16:20 - Aug. 10, 9:29
Venus in Libra, Aug. 10, 9:30 - Aug. 23, 23:03

YOUR DRIVE AND AMBITION
Mars in Sagittarius, July 23, 16:20 - Aug. 23, 23:03

YOUR LUCK MAGNETISM
Jupiter in Libra, July 23, 16:20 - Aug. 23, 23:03

World Events

Aug. 2 – Scottish inventor Alexander Graham Bell dies.

Aug. 22 – Michael Collins, chief of the provisional government of the Irish Free State and commander of the Irish National Army, is killed in an ambush.

CANCER
From June 22, 5:27 through July 23, 16:19

The Caring Communicator

Cancer rules patriotism, nationalism, and xenophobia. Within days of your birth, news items illustrated the deadly consequences such impulses can breed. On June 22, 1922, in London, two members of the Irish Republican Army shot and killed Field Marshall Sir Henry Wilson, a member of Britain's Parliament from Ulster. It was the first time that the conflict over Ireland had exported violence to the British homeland. On June 24, in Berlin, nationalist forces assassinated German Foreign Minister Walter Rathenau. Rathenau, who was Jewish, had been the subject of anti-Semitic attacks by German reactionaries. The attack on Rathenau was a ripple that anticipated the tidal wave of genocide to come.

Every sign has its own dark side, but other conditions determine whether a mere potential will manifest in extreme behavior. Free will is foremost among those other conditions. As a Cancer of 1922, you are likely to respect all people as equals and to have a strong revulsion to conflict. You may have been absolutely traumatized and heartbroken about the violence of your early adulthood.

Indicators in your chart suggest that you are a hard worker, and that you may have had a career that involved communications. You may write wonderful letters, and you were likely attracted to the writings of the dissident writers of your times. You may also have strong charitable impulses that you back up with concrete action to help others.

Maintaining a harmonious home life may have been a high priority for you in relationships. You may have looked for a partner who is enlightened and caring. Leo enjoys entertaining in a welcoming family lair. Sagittarius can be a good-humored trooper. Pisces reaches out for you with tenderness.

The caring nature of Cancer may have compelled you to defend people in need during the most violent period in human history. Your sensitivity may have forced you to shut down emotionally, just to cope with the devastation around you. However, in maturity, you may have learned to lower your defenses when your intuition assured you that all threats of danger had passed.

LEO
From July 23, 16:20 through August 23, 23:03

The Playful Performer

In general, Leos are creative people who enjoy entertainment and love being in the spotlight. In 1922, radio was on its way to becoming a staple of family entertainment, one that would occupy center stage at home until the advent of television in the fifties. Leo rules playfulness, and within days of your birth, a radio station in Schenectady, New York broadcast the first sound effect—somebody smacked two blocks of wood together to create the sound of a slamming door. From there, many more innovations in radio would evolve as the result of people experimenting with sounds and having fun.

By the time you reached adulthood, radio programs were being performed before live audiences. As you listened, you might have imagined yourself on the stage, soaking up the glamour and excitement. With a healthy curiosity for travel and foreign cultures, you may have relied on radio to keep apprised of world events and to help you undertake distant journeys and adventures in your mind. Later in life, it's likely that you enjoyed travel and exploration in the real world.

Indicators in your chart suggest that you can have a vivid imagination and enjoy heartwarming stories, tales of romance, and tearjerker movies. You may also be artistically talented. Many Leos become actors and entertainers, and you may have a flair for performing on the stage. Perhaps you were one of the pioneers of the emerging television industry.

In relationships, you're likely to be both romantic and a loyal, lifelong friend. Your partner may regard you as a dear old softy. Pisces finds you endlessly entertaining. Sagittarius would gladly accompany you to the ends of the Earth. Libra adores your artistic temperament.

Your charismatic appeal and shining personality may have won you many admirers, 1922 Leo, but your propensity for drama can sometimes get you into trouble. When you get bored, you may become argumentative, if only to provide your active mind with a diversion. With maturity, it's likely that you realized that you needed no additional agitation—life would provide more than enough excitement!

➤ Read about your Chinese Astrological sign on page 838. ➤ Read about your Personal Planets on page 826. ➤ Read about your personal Mystical Card on page 856.

VIRGO

From August 23, 23:04 through September 23, 20:09

The Prudent Nature-Spirit

Your sign rules plants and their properties, and within days of your birth, Virgo of 1922, news items reflected apprehension about the dangers of certain forms of vegetation. In America, fears were expressed about the potential for certain plants to compromise the virtue of young ladies. August 28 brought the announcement that fragrant flowers and perfume would be banned from the Miss America pageant in Atlantic City. Officials worried that sweet perfumes might seduce the public or judges in the competition. Meanwhile, in France, a news item on August 29 reported an infestation of mushrooms, which threatened to engulf the Palace of Versailles.

In general, prudishness is a quality associated with Virgos. While your attitude may not be so extreme as to bring on flower-phobia, you're likely to be prudent and discreet, especially with respect to your private affairs. You're probably soft-spoken and avoid being seen by others as loud, obnoxious, or confrontational. In the sixties and seventies, you may have found the overt sexuality in behavior and popular culture to be distasteful.

Your sign also has an ancient association with the medicinal properties of certain forms of vegetation. You may be a gardening buff, someone who knows which mushrooms are safe to eat. You may have extensive knowledge of helpful hints for home and health, and members of your family may have come to you for folk remedies for headaches, stress, and colds.

Your relationships may let you take certain liberties that you might not allow yourself when left to your own devices. Extroverted partners may have attracted you. You can rely on Sagittarius to say what you're thinking but are too nice to say. Aquarius encourages you to take a public stand on your private beliefs. Cancer supports you in pursuing your passions.

Because Virgo tends to be discreet and understated, people are likely to find you agreeable, cooperative, and pleasant. Sometimes, however, you may feel like others are ignoring you. But by learning to speak up for yourself, in maturity you were less likely to let others take you for granted.

LIBRA

From September 23, 20:10 through October 24, 4:52

The High Flier

Libra is associated with equality and the element of air. On October 8, 1922, Lilian Gatlin became the first woman to cross the American continent by airplane. Flying from San Francisco to Long Island in twenty-seven hours and eleven minutes, she performed the stunt to urge governmental commemoration of the aviators who lost their lives "on the altar of patriotism and progress in pursuit of an ideal." In Europe, Germany was struggling with more earthbound concerns as high food prices and the collapse of the mark brought the country to the brink of bankruptcy. "Bread first, then reparations," the German Chancellor had earlier pleaded, as compliance with the Treaty of Versailles looked ever-more remote.

Librans can tend to be sympathetic to others, even those who might bear the responsibility for their own plight. When you were old enough to learn about the conditions that prevailed after World War I, you may have felt for the German people. The humanitarian in you can appreciate the difficulty of fulfilling international obligations on an empty stomach.

During your lifetime, you witnessed the march of women's equality. In America, "suffragettes" fought to obtain the vote for women during the year you were born. Later on you may have supported such reforms for the sake of future generations, and you may have been a proud onlooker at graduations for the lady doctors and lawyers in your family.

Your relationships could have gone through their own evolution, reflecting the shifts and advances in roles between men and women, and you're likely to appreciate the greater freedom that equality brings to both partners. Sagittarius likes a forward-moving relationship. Capricorn appreciates growth within understood boundaries. Scorpio exults in the realization of human potential.

Your respect for equality can create healthy conditions for human well-being. The realities of World War II may have forced you to realize that equality without justice was an empty proposition. With maturity, you may have found a way to be fair, without reflexively splitting everything down the middle.

➤ Read about your Chinese Astrological sign on page 838. ➤ Read about your Personal Planets on page 826. ➤ Read about your personal Mystical Card on page 856.

VIRGO
Your Personal Planets

YOUR LOVE POTENTIAL
Venus in Libra, Aug. 23, 23:04 - Sept. 07, 7:14
Venus in Scorpio, Sept. 07, 7:15 - Sept. 23, 20:09

YOUR DRIVE AND AMBITION
Mars in Sagittarius, Aug. 23, 23:04 - Sept. 13, 13:01
Mars in Capricorn, Sept. 13, 13:02 - Sept. 23, 20:09

YOUR LUCK MAGNETISM
Jupiter in Libra, Aug. 23, 23:04 - Sept. 23, 20:09

World Events

Aug. 30 – Southern Russia revolts against the spread of Bolshevism.

Sept. 11 – The Arabs declare a national day of mourning as the British mandate begins in Palestine.

Bolsheviks make themselves comfortable in the house of a bourgeois

LIBRA
Your Personal Planets

YOUR LOVE POTENTIAL
Venus in Scorpio, Sept. 23, 20:10 - Oct. 10, 22:32
Venus in Sagittarius, Oct. 10, 22:33 - Oct. 24, 4:52

YOUR DRIVE AND AMBITION
Mars in Capricorn, Sept. 23, 20:10 - Oct. 24, 4:52

YOUR LUCK MAGNETISM
Jupiter in Libra, Sept. 23, 20:10 - Oct. 24, 4:52

World Events

Oct. 8 – Lilian Gatlin becomes the first woman to cross the continental U.S. by airplane, flying from San Francisco to Long Island in twenty-seven hours and eleven minutes.

Oct. 9 – In Britain, Members of Parliament call for the resignation of Prime Minister David Lloyd George.

1922

SCORPIO
Your Personal Planets

YOUR LOVE POTENTIAL
Venus in Sagittarius, Oct. 24, 4:53 - Nov. 23, 1:54

YOUR DRIVE AND AMBITION
Mars in Capricorn, Oct. 24, 4:53 - Oct. 30, 18:54
Mars in Aquarius, Oct. 30, 18:55 - Nov. 23, 1:54

YOUR LUCK MAGNETISM
Jupiter in Libra, Oct. 24, 4:53 - Oct. 26, 19:15
Jupiter in Scorpio, Oct. 26, 19:16 - Nov. 23, 1:54

World Events

Oct. 31 – Benito Mussolini seizes power in Italy.
Nov. 18 – French novelist Marcel Proust dies.

Benito Mussolini

SAGITTARIUS
Your Personal Planets

YOUR LOVE POTENTIAL
Venus in Sagittarius, Nov. 23, 1:55 - Nov. 28, 21:46
Venus in Scorpio, Nov. 28, 21:47 - Dec. 22, 14:56

YOUR DRIVE AND AMBITION
Mars in Aquarius, Nov. 23, 1:55 - Dec. 11, 13:09
Mars in Pisces, Dec. 11, 13:10 - Dec. 22, 14:56

YOUR LUCK MAGNETISM
Jupiter in Scorpio, Nov. 23, 1:55 - Dec. 22, 14:56

World Events

Nov. 26 – Archaeologists Lord Carnarvon and Howard Carter open the door to the Pharaoh Tutankhamen's tomb.

Dec. 10 – Niels Bohr of Denmark receives the Nobel Prize in physics for using the quantum theory to explain the internal structure of the atom.

SCORPIO
From October 24, 4:53 through November 23, 1:54

The Introspective Dreamer

Within days of your birth, 1922 Scorpio, the world bade farewell to a French writer who found the inspiration for his books by mining the depths of his psyche. November 18 marked the death of Marcel Proust, the reclusive and somewhat obsessive author of *Remembrance Of Things Past*, a 3,000-page novel in seven volumes. Proust propounded the stream-of-consciousness style of writing, a technique that triggers intuitive thought processes and reads like a waking dream. *Remembrance* is probably best known for the madeleine cake that triggered the voluminous flood of memories.

Scorpios can be intensely introverted, inward-looking people, and the dense, internalized content of Proust's books may be an apt example of your own mental state. Overexposure to stimulation from the unconscious mind could be difficult for you to cope with, however, and you may have protected yourself from it by acting outgoing and extroverted. Even your close friends may be surprised to learn the depth of your insights, when you choose to share them.

Your dream life may be vivid and filled with evocative images. Like Proust, you may believe that life itself is the dream, and you may draw only the filmiest of borders between the two. You may have been an exquisite poet, musician, filmmaker, or photographer. A career in the field of psychiatry, social work, or psychology could also have been open to you.

You may look to your personal relationships to balance out your internal orientation. You were likely to choose a more extroverted partner, who assured you good grounding and a rational point of view. Taurus keeps you safely anchored on the earthly plane. Capricorn gives you a reality check. Aquarius offers crystal clarity and a friendly wake-up call.

Your sign rules psychology and the unconscious. The sumptuous furnishings of the Scorpionic imagination may have inspired astonishing creations, but your deepest fear might have been that you would end up secluded in a sound-proofed flat, like Proust. With maturity, it's likely that you learned to balance your inner world with an equally vibrant outer life.

SAGITTARIUS
From November 23, 1:55 through December 22, 14:56

The Thrill Seeker

Your sign rules exploration and exotic places, and you were born within days of the greatest archeological find of the twentieth century. On November 26, 1922, Lord Carnarvon and Howard Carter opened the tomb of King Tutankhamen in Egypt's Valley of the Kings. In two rooms, next to the crypt of Ramses VI, Carnarvon, and Carter discovered an astonishing collection of priceless antiquities dating back to 1337 bc. Objects included gold figurines, chariots, and furniture—all magnificently carved and inlaid with semi-precious stones. News of this discovery created an international sensation in Egyptian fashion and design, and later in the century, the collection would travel the world.

When you reached school age, the discovery of King Tutankhamen's tomb may have fascinated you. Sagittarians tend to enjoy studying, especially when it allows you to learn about foreign lands and exotic cultures. You are also likely to enjoy a good mystery, and the "King Tut" story was loaded with controversy, from the "Secret of the Mummy's Curse" to the debate among scholars over whether Tutankhamen had been murdered.

You are likely to be a thrill-seeker, and you may enjoy high-stakes gambling with money or opportunities. An indicator in your chart (one you share with Chuck Yeager) suggests that you have the constitution of a flying ace or test pilot. You may even have an addiction to your own adrenaline, a trait that would have served you well if you had to take on sensitive missions in World War II.

You may prefer relationships that provide plenty of breathing space and elbowroom, and you might have chosen a mate who wouldn't cramp your adventurous style. Freedom-respecting Gemini can be a breezy companion. Taurus stoically holds down the fort without complaint. Even-tempered Libra adores the bounty of your travels.

More than a few Sagittarians of 1922 may have assumed leadership roles on D-Day in 1944. A taste for danger and flying by the seat of your pants can be a dazzling response in dangerous times, but with maturity, you were likely to be more respectful of loved ones' blood pressure.

► Read about your Chinese Astrological sign on page 838. ► Read about your Personal Planets on page 826. ► Read about your personal Mystical Card on page 856.

CAPRICORN

From December 22, 14:57 through December 31, 23:59

The Jazzy Mogul

Capricorn rules foundations that evolve into new institutions, and when you arrived, the foundation was being laid for a new form of music that would trigger a worldwide craze. Around the time you were born, December Capricorn of 1922, a young trumpet player was making his debut with King Oliver and his seven-piece band in Chicago, Illinois. That trumpet player was the now-legendary Louis "Satchmo" Armstrong, and jazz was the music he played. Reflecting the improvised blending of a variety of instruments, rhythms, and melodies, no other musical form represented the American character or generated worldwide appeal better than jazz.

If you didn't love jazz as a kid, you may have enjoyed its offspring: rhythm and blues, soul, country music, rock 'n roll. You grew up alongside the technologies that parlayed and conveyed music: record labels, radio stations, vinyl disks, reel-to-reel tape players, high-fidelity stereo. Throughout your life, popular entertainment offered new opportunities, and as a good Capricorn, it's likely that you got in on the ground floor. You may have become an industry mogul, a promoter, talent scout or manager, or even a performer.

Indicators in your chart suggest that you have a good mind for mechanics, electronics, and logistics. You may have an instinct for the "wave of the future," the drive to make it happen, and the smarts to capitalize on it. A strong sense for trends and what people want may have inspired you to employ the new media in innovative marketing campaigns.

You probably regard your personal relationships as a private source of emotional nurture and support, and you're likely to choose a mate who is absolutely trustworthy. Scorpio may be the power behind your throne. Virgo works hard by your side. Taurus locks joint resources in a vault.

You may tend to have the instinctive ability to weave dreams into profitable ventures. Early in life you may have discovered the hazards of falling too much in love with any one dream. With maturity, you may have learned to set minimum standards for projects worthy of your time, money, or effort.

1922

CAPRICORN
Your Personal Planets

YOUR LOVE POTENTIAL
Venus in Scorpio, Dec. 22, 14:57 - Dec. 31, 23:59

YOUR DRIVE AND AMBITION
Mars in Pisces, Dec. 22, 14:57 - Dec. 31, 23:59

YOUR LUCK MAGNETISM
Jupiter in Scorpio, Dec. 22, 14:57 - Dec. 31, 23:59

World Events

Dec. 24 – Pope Pius XI issues his first encyclical, in which he urges World peace.

Dec. 30 – Lenin renames Soviet Russia the Union of Soviet Socialist Republics (USSR).

Special Feature
Astrology Goes On Trial: Evangeline Adams

(Continued from page 185)

And although Adams adamantly defended herself against being labeled a "fortune-teller," she also predicted a series of events that made her quite famous, the first concerning the then-worst disaster in New York City history—the Windsor Hotel fire. The story begins in Boston, in 1899, when Adams left via train for the long journey to New York. When she arrived, the proprietor of the hotel she had initially registered with would not allow her to practice astrology under his roof. Adams, of course, never easily dissuaded from doing what she believed in, moved on—to the upscale Windsor, where Andrew Carnegie, General Ulysses S. Grant and President McKinley had all stayed. This time, the owner, Warren Leland, had no problem with Adams as a guest. In fact, since he played the stock market, he asked for an astrology reading immediately. Evangeline was quoted as saying that she saw disaster in Leland's horoscope—which, unfortunately, he didn't take very seriously.

> *Every fortune-teller is a violator of the law; every astrologer is not a fortune-teller.*

The next day, St. Patrick's Day, saw many hotel guests gathered by the windows to watch the annual parade. Suddenly, a guest's cigar ignited a curtain; the hotel quickly burned to the ground. More than sixty people died in this terrible disaster, including Leland's wife and daughter. Adams was quoted in the *New York World* a few days later, and wrote a feature for the *New York Journal* shortly thereafter, being sure to mention her forecast each time.

In a 1927 lecture, she made yet another uncanny prediction that would soon become famous. While discussing the cycles of Uranus,

Enrico Caruso, who consulted Evangeline Adams

she warned her audience to "be extremely cautious in investment and money matters," especially from 1927 to 1929.

(Continued on page 201)

➤ Read about the 1929 Crash in "Money, Astrology, and the Crash of '29" on page 225. ➤ Read more about Adams in "Astrology Reigns Through the Ages" on page 25. ➤ Read Caruso's Star Profile on page 97.

1923

Jupiter Conjunct Saturn: Tecumseh's Curse

Inflation in Germany; the 1 billion mark note is worth only $5

While he was sitting for a portrait, it is said that Tecumseh, a Native American prophet, predicted the death of each sitting American President that was to be elected every twenty years. Tecumseh predicted President Harrison's death, and said "And after him, every Great Chief chosen every 20 years thereafter will die." There is indeed an astrological connection to this strange and eerie phenomenon, which has frighteningly proved itself authentic over the years. Since President Harrison's death in 1841, each President inaugurated every twenty years, except for Ronald Reagan, has died in office either by assassination or from natural causes—there was a serious assassination attempt against Reagan, which was unsuccessful. Jupiter and Saturn have been in conjunction with one another in relation to either the election of each of these Presidents, or during their term.

In 1923, Warren Harding came down with intestinal cramps and then pneumonia, after visiting Alaska—he was the first president to visit this state. While convalescing in San Francisco, California, he suffered an apparent stroke and died on August 2, 1923. While he was preparing to run for President in March of 1919, there was a Jupiter/Saturn conjunction in Cancer. The conjunction of these two planets infers a kind of destiny. There is an inescapable karma linked to this aspect. President George Bush Jr. lives under the threat of this very curse. Only time will tell its true wisdom. Some astrologers predict that there will be at least one attempt on George Bush Jr.'s life during his term as President.

An earthquake in Japan kills 300,000   *Ku Klux Klan members in Oklahoma*

ANTHROPOSOPHY

Rudolph Steiner established the General Anthroposophical Society in 1923 as an international organization for esoteric research. Originally based in Basel, Switzerland, it now has branches all over the world. Steiner described anthroposophy as a path for personal spiritual development on four levels: the senses, imagination, inspiration, and intuition. Education was integral to Steiner's philosophy. His greatest legacy is the Waldorf School movement, the largest non-sectarian system of education in the world.

STRUGGLES IN GERMANY

Tensions in Europe heightened as Germany became increasingly restive under post-war constraints and the low value of its currency. The feeling of rebellion in Germany was crystallized by the rise of Hitler's Nazi Party, which attempted an unsuccessful coup. Soviet leader Lenin suffered a massive stroke and relinquished control to Stalin, Zinoviev, and Kamenev. Mexican Pancho Villa was gunned down in revenge for killings perpetrated during the Revolution. The Turkish-Greek War was ended by treaty, displacing Armenians, who had to seek refuge elsewhere. Tokyo was decimated by a quake which killed 300,000 and left 2.5 million homeless. Without warning, U.S. President Harding died of a stroke, and Coolidge became head of state. Oklahoma Governor Walton was impeached for declaring martial law in efforts to rid the state of the Ku Klux Klan. Dance marathons were popular, and the first nonstop cross-continental flight was achieved. More exquisite treasures were found in Tutankhamen's tomb, although the sponsor of the archeological dig, Lord Carnarvon, died amidst rumors of a pharaoh's curse. Blues singer Bessie Smith made records.

➤ Read "Astrology goes on Trial: Evangeline Adams" by Rochelle Gordon on page 185.

CAPRICORN

From January 01, 0:00 through January 21, 1:34

The Ethical Tactician

The sign of Capricorn rules consequences. Certain "what if" celestial scenarios, occurring within days of your birth, defy one to imagine whether worldwide tragedy might have been avoided, had events turned out differently. On January 4, 1923, Vladimir Lenin sought to dismiss Joseph Stalin from the Soviet government, for his repressive treatment of comrades. One can only wonder how many lives might have been spared Stalin's purges had Lenin been more cold-blooded in disposing of him. On January 11, the French army entered the Ruhr Valley and commenced an occupation that would provoke violent nationalist backlash in Germany, including the January 13 march of 5,000 storm troopers led by Adolf Hitler.

You belong to the generation that inherited the consequences of events set in motion in the years surrounding your birth. Indicators in your chart suggest that you had the decisiveness and resolve to do what was necessary to save the world and to learn the lessons essential to preventing a recurrence of murderous insanity. You are likely to have a strong ethical backbone and the determination to follow through on your beliefs.

You may have powers of anticipation that enable you to evaluate a situation and see where it could lead. Although you might characterize yourself as "a lover, not a fighter," you are unlikely to stand by in the face of injustice or oppression. Passive resistance or clandestine tactics may be your preferred weapon. Compassionate motives may drive you to take risks for the sake of righteousness.

Wartime may have stoked the passion of your first relationships. Indeed, your generation created the boom in postwar babies. Scorpio regenerates your faith in the power of life. Pisces and Leo offer romantic escape. Libra offers the beginning of a beautiful relationship.

As a Capricorn, you may have the endurance and strength to promote the betterment of the world. Your challenge was the unimaginable degree to which the world required your services. In maturity, you could take pride in the enormous scope of your accomplishments and enjoy the blessings of peace.

AQUARIUS

From January 21, 1:35 through February 19, 15:59

The Responsible Individual

The sign of Aquarius rules scientific discovery and innovation. February 10, 1923, marked the passing of William Conrad Roentgen, known for his 1895 discovery of X rays. X-ray technology revolutionized the practice of medicine, by allowing for non-invasive internal examination of the body. For his breakthrough, Roentgen was awarded the first Nobel Prize in physics. Just as Roentgen's life ended in Munich, the same city served as the setting for the birth of the Nazi Party. On January 27, 1923, Adolf Hitler presided over the first public congress of the National Socialist Party, where he called for immediate repeal of the Treaty of Versailles.

This strange coincidence of noteworthy events in Munich illustrates the potential for members of every sign to use their inborn talents for good or for evil. Roentgen used his powers of discovery and innovation to create a technology that spared millions death and suffering. Hitler invoked the same powers to engineer the Final Solution. As an Aquarian, you are likely to place great emphasis upon the individual's responsibility to resist evil and promote humanitarian goals.

You are likely to think in unusually creative and inventive ways. Aquarians tend to be rebellious and resist unfairness and oppression. Indicators in your chart suggest that you have a powerful store of fighting spirit. You may have been a brilliant warrior in World War II or served the forces of resistance. A tendency toward introversion may have drawn you to a career in psychology or mysticism.

You may rely on your relationship for a feeling of spiritual connectedness. Mutual devotion with your partner may have provided an escape from the harsh realities of the world. Pisces' love offers you sanctuary. Leo offers romantic inspiration. Scorpio offers divine ecstatic union.

Aquarian resistance to the status quo can provide a powerful check on abuses by those in authority. The classic Aquarian challenge has been to maintain compassion after you've prevailed. By staying true to your best principles you were able to prevent tragic repetitions of history.

CAPRICORN
Your Personal Planets

YOUR LOVE POTENTIAL
Venus in Scorpio, Jan. 01, 0:00 - Jan. 02, 7:26
Venus in Sagittarius, Jan. 02, 7:27 - Jan. 21, 1:34

YOUR DRIVE AND AMBITION
Mars in Pisces, Jan. 01, 0:00 - Jan. 21, 1:34

YOUR LUCK MAGNETISM
Jupiter in Scorpio, Jan. 01, 0:00 - Jan. 21, 1:34

World Events

Jan. 9 – Novelist Katherine Mansfield dies.

Jan. 10 – The last of the U.S. forces are withdrawn from Germany.

Death of novelist Katherine Mansfield

AQUARIUS
Your Personal Planets

YOUR LOVE POTENTIAL
Venus in Sagittarius, Jan. 21, 1:35 - Feb. 06, 14:33
Venus in Capricorn, Feb. 06, 14:34 - Feb. 19, 15:59

YOUR DRIVE AND AMBITION
Mars in Pisces, Jan. 21, 1:35 - Jan. 21, 10:06
Mars in Aries, Jan. 21, 10:07 - Feb. 19, 15:59

YOUR LUCK MAGNETISM
Jupiter in Scorpio, Jan. 21, 1:35 - Feb. 19, 15:59

World Events

Feb. 12 – Italian film director Franco Zefirelli is born.

Feb. 13 – The first man to break the sound barrier, Charles "Chuck" Yeager, is born.

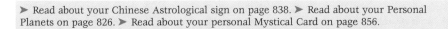➤ Read about your Chinese Astrological sign on page 838. ➤ Read about your Personal Planets on page 826. ➤ Read about your personal Mystical Card on page 856.

1923

PISCES
Your Personal Planets

YOUR LOVE POTENTIAL

Venus in Capricorn, Feb. 19, 16:00 - Mar. 06, 5:37
Venus in Aquarius, Mar. 06, 5:38 - Mar. 21, 15:28

YOUR DRIVE AND AMBITION

Mars in Aries, Feb. 19, 16:00 - Mar. 04, 0:41
Mars in Taurus, Mar. 04, 0:42 - Mar. 21, 15:28

YOUR LUCK MAGNETISM

Jupiter in Scorpio, Feb. 19, 16:00 - Mar. 21, 15:28

World Events

Mar. 2 – Mussolini makes a statement acknowledging the right of women to the vote, although he makes no move to introduce such legislation.

Mar. 5 – The first old-age pensions are introduced in the U.S. – a sum of $25 per month.

The women's section of the Balilla march into Rome to pay homage to Mussolini

ARIES
Your Personal Planets

YOUR LOVE POTENTIAL

Venus in Aquarius, Mar. 21, 15:29 - Apr. 01, 5:15
Venus in Pisces, Apr. 01, 5:16 - Apr. 21, 3:05

YOUR DRIVE AND AMBITION

Mars in Taurus, Mar. 21, 15:29 - Apr. 16, 2:53
Mars in Gemini, Apr. 16, 2:54 - Apr. 21, 3:05

YOUR LUCK MAGNETISM

Jupiter in Scorpio, Mar. 21, 15:29 - Apr. 21, 3:05

World Events

Mar. 26 – Actress Sarah Bernhardt dies.

Apr. 19 – In Egypt, King Fuad I promulgates a new constitution.

196

PISCES
From February 19, 16:00 through March 21, 15:28

The Gentle Champion

The sign of Pisces rules hidden enemies. When you were born, open enemies abounded all over the world. The Turks hated the Greeks. The French hated the Germans. Fascists hated liberal democrats. And everybody hated the Communists. With so much in the world to hate, America neglected to hate one very important thing—the corruption stewing under President Harding's nose. March 2, 1923, marked the beginning of a Congressional inquiry into corruption in the Veterans Bureau under Charles R. Forbes. The investigation uncovered bribery, contract kickbacks, embezzlement, and even bootlegging of federally held liquor stocks. On March 15, Forbes's General Counsel Charles F. Cramer committed suicide. Speculators linked the scandal to President Harding's untimely death in August 1923.

While your sign rules the dangers of unacknowledged enemies, it also represents the power and healing that comes from facing the things you'd least like to confront. At key points in your life, you may have been the force behind the exposure of corrosive secrets and scandals.

Indicators in your chart suggest an ability to inspire upsets of dominating powers—from sports teams to governments. You may see yourself as a champion of the underdog. Repelled by acts of humiliation, you may work hard to impose your power as painlessly as possible. Although you are likely to be diplomatic and soft-spoken, you may carry a big stick. You could have pursued a career in diplomacy, education, or the arts.

You may look to your relationship as a source of inspiration and renewal. A healthy, uncluttered home can help you soothe tattered nerves at the end of the day. Virgo watches out for your fitness and maintains an immaculate living space. Leo rejuvenates you with playful exercise. Cancer loves to baby you.

Peaceful Pisceans tend to shun aggressive or domineering behavior, but your generation learned the most painful lesson imaginable about the potentially deadly consequences of denial. After World War II, you may have resolved never to remain politely silent in the face of certain red flags of trouble.

ARIES
From March 21, 15:29 through April 21, 3:05

The Enduring Competitor

The sign of Aries rules the start of new trends and athletic challenges. You were born within days of the beginning of a new fad that pushed participants to the limits of their endurance. This year marked the beginning of a new craze, imported to the U.S. from Europe—the dance marathon. On March 31, New York City hosted the first dance marathon in America; Alma Cummings set a world record of twenty-seven hours of uninterrupted dancing. Before the end of April, marathons were held in Houston, Baltimore, and Cleveland. The rich purse for winners motivated the young participants to push themselves beyond exhaustion. Recalling medieval legends in which towns had lost entire populations of children to dancing fevers, the marathon fad provoked anxiety among elders in the U.S.

You were a bit young to participate in the dance marathons of the twenties or the Depression era, but you might have a talent for long-distance sports. As an Aries, you may have endurance, a bit of stubbornness, and a taste for a challenge. Regular exercise can provide you with a healthy outlet for channeling excess energy.

Indicators in your chart suggest that you may have more than a bit of the Midas touch. You may have lost everything during the Depression, World War II, or after taking big risks that promised big payoffs. Even with such setbacks, you are likely to be extremely resilient and able to more than offset your losses. A willingness to work as long and as hard as necessary may be your secret.

Over time, you may have become a steady, reliable partner in relationships. Finding the right person may have made the difference for you. Libra is lovely and gives you plenty of breathing space. Leo lavishes you with romance and playful fun. Gemini can satisfy your varying needs for speed and rest time.

Ariens are natural leaders, with spirited powers of motivation. Early in life, impulsive tendencies may have brought you nose-to-nose with disapproving authority figures. With maturity, you may have tempered your drive with discipline, thoughtful planning, and diplomacy.

➤ Read about your Chinese Astrological sign on page 838. ➤ Read about your Personal Planets on page 826. ➤ Read about your personal Mystical Card on page 856.

TAURUS

From April 21, 3:06 through May 22, 2:44

The Thrifty Thinker

The sign of Taurus rules the value of money and, at the time of your birth, runaway inflation was devaluing currency in the U.S. and Europe. On May 2, 1923, British housewives initiated a boycott to protest the high cost of sugar and tea. On May 15, Paris reported the highest bread prices since 1870. In Germany, the mark was plummeting out of control. By late June, it would take 136,000 marks to buy an American dollar. Coal miners in Germany had cut production to protest the French and Belgian occupation of the Ruhr. As a result, Germany lost any income it might have made on coal exports and was unable to meet even domestic needs.

By the time you were old enough to study the history behind these developments, your family would have been struggling to survive the Great Depression. You are a member of the generation that learned to conserve and reuse everything. The idea of wasting resources or throwing away food may strike you as a mortal sin. The experience of loss and poverty may have had an impact on you emotionally.

You were likely to become an avid pursuer of food for thought. Intellectual challenges may have diverted and energized you, and you may have become an excellent thinker, writer, or speaker. You may have a message and a mission to make it known. Popularizing ideas may be a passion for you. If you were born on or after May 8, 1923, you may think in unorthodox patterns or have a talent for criticism and analysis.

Your chart suggests that you have wonderful relationship skills. You may be "the marrying type" and enjoy the benefits of partnership. If you ever suffered a loss, you were likely to start over again. Cancer appreciates your resourcefulness. Gemini shares your love of knowledge. Even when you're broke, Scorpio enriches you with passion.

Taureans have an extraordinary ability to make do with what they have, and to make what they have stretch beyond all expectation. The experience of scarcity in your early adulthood may have left a lasting imprint. In maturity, you could enjoy resilience in productivity and resist any need for hoarding.

GEMINI

From May 22, 2:45 through June 22, 11:02

The Decisive Debater

The sign of Gemini rules debate and the quest for knowledge. One of the great debates of the early twentieth century reached a minor crescendo within days of your birth. On May 22, 1923, the Presbyterian General Assembly in Indianapolis defeated a motion by William Jennings Bryan to prohibit the teaching of evolution in church schools. Bryan contended that the theory of biological evolution undermined biblical authority for Christian doctrine and threatened to fray the moral fiber of American culture. Bryan was on a collision course with destiny, in the form of Clarence Darrow, at the Scopes Monkey Trial in 1925. Darrow's cross-examination must have been withering, as Bryan died shortly after the conclusion of the trial.

As a Gemini you are probably clever enough to argue either side of a debate, but—unlike your Libran friends—you are not as prone to remain impartial. Members of your sign tend to have a strong bias for values such as academic freedom, intellectual integrity, and scientific objectivity. While you certainly respect people's right to their religious beliefs, you may feel that faith and dogma are incompatible with the pursuit of secular knowledge.

Colleagues may consider you one of the most original and ingenious thinkers they know. An unorthodox point of view may inspire you to marvelous feats of creativity. You are likely to have the intellectual mega-wattage to spark new trends in popular consciousness. A strong sense of family loyalty may move you to defend your loved ones and country with your life.

Geminis tend to enjoy a variety of relationships before settling down. Your mate's allure may have hit you on an indescribable emotional level. Sagittarius provides you with an intellectual challenge. Cancer captures your imagination. Leo simply melts your heart.

You are likely to be just plain smart—so smart, in fact, you may even intimidate others. As you get older, however, you may discover that the quest for happiness may launch you on a mission to live life from the neck-down. That is, your greatest satisfaction may come from connections of the heart.

➤ Read about your Chinese Astrological sign on page 838. ➤ Read about your Personal Planets on page 826. ➤ Read about your personal Mystical Card on page 856.

1923

TAURUS
Your Personal Planets

YOUR LOVE POTENTIAL
Venus in Pisces, Apr. 21, 3:06 - Apr. 26, 13:35
Venus in Aries, Apr. 26, 13:36 - May 21, 14:49
Venus in Taurus, May 21, 14:50 - May 22, 2:44

YOUR DRIVE AND AMBITION
Mars in Gemini, Apr. 21, 3:06 - May 22, 2:44

YOUR LUCK MAGNETISM
Jupiter in Scorpio, Apr. 21, 3:06 - May 22, 2:44

World Events

Apr. 28 – The first non-stop flight is made across the U.S., from New York to San Diego.

May 1 – American author Joseph Heller is born.

American statesman Henry Kissinger is born under the sign of Gemini

GEMINI
Your Personal Planets

YOUR LOVE POTENTIAL
Venus in Taurus, May 22, 2:45 - June 15, 11:45
Venus in Gemini, June 15, 11:46 - June 22, 11:02

YOUR DRIVE AND AMBITION
Mars in Gemini, May 22, 2:45 - May 30, 21:18
Mars in Cancer, May 30, 21:19 - June 22, 11:02

YOUR LUCK MAGNETISM
Jupiter in Scorpio, May 22, 2:45 - June 22, 11:02

World Events

May 27 – American statesman Henry Kissinger is born.

June 8 – The British House of Commons passes a bill equalizing the terms of divorce for men and women.

1923

CANCER
Your Personal Planets

YOUR LOVE POTENTIAL
Venus in Gemini, June 22, 11:03 - July 10, 4:35
Venus in Cancer, July 10, 4:36 - July 23, 22:00

YOUR DRIVE AND AMBITION
Mars in Cancer, June 22, 11:03 - July 16, 1:25
Mars in Leo, July 16, 1:26 - July 23, 22:00

YOUR LUCK MAGNETISM
Jupiter in Scorpio, June 22, 11:03 - July 23, 22:00

World Events

July 20 - Mexican bandit Pancho Villa is killed.

July 21 - An equal rights amendment is drafted at a meeting of the National Women's Party in Seneca Falls, U.S.

New U.S. President, Calvin Coolidge

LEO
Your Personal Planets

YOUR LOVE POTENTIAL
Venus in Cancer, July 23, 22:01 - Aug. 03, 16:41
Venus in Leo, Aug. 03, 16:42 - Aug. 24, 4:51

YOUR DRIVE AND AMBITION
Mars in Leo, July 23, 22:01 - Aug. 24, 4:51

YOUR LUCK MAGNETISM
Jupiter in Scorpio, July 23, 22:01 - Aug. 24, 4:51

World Events

July 29 - Albert Einstein marches in a pacifist demonstration in Berlin.

Aug. 2 - U.S. President Warren G. Harding dies suddenly in San Francisco.

CANCER
From June 22, 11:03 through July 23, 22:00

The Family Guardian

The sign of Cancer rules motherhood, women, and love of country. Within days of your birth, the latter value was being pushed to hateful extremes as fascism took root in Italy, Germany, and even in America. On June 30, 1923, Ku Klux Klan Imperial Wizard H. W. Evans announced that the Klan—a secret society violently opposed to minorities, immigrants, and foreign alliances—had more followers in the northern United States than in the South. On July 10, Mussolini dissolved all non-fascist parties in Italy. Another news item illustrated the highest potentials of your sign. On July 21, the National Women's Party held a convention at Seneca Falls, New York, where participants drafted an Equal Rights Amendment to the U.S. Constitution.

Because your sign rules security and providing for others, you are likely to see how feelings of insecurity and deprivation can make people susceptible to xenophobia and bigotry. While you may combat such ills once they arise, you are also uniquely equipped to anticipate and prevent them. After all, your generation not only fought World War II; it also implemented the Marshall Plan.

While the sign of Cancer traditionally rules mothers and women, the women's movement freed all Cancerians to be themselves. Likely to have strong emotions and parental instincts, Cancerian men are often seen as being in touch with their "feminine side," but you may believe that care-giving and compassion are just plain human.

Family life and child rearing are likely to be important priorities in your relationship. You may have chosen a partner who shared your devotion to a safe and secure home life. Libra respects the contributions of both parents. Capricorn honors long-term commitments. Children are precious to Leo.

Cancerians gain strength by nurturing and caring for others, especially children, but you reached adulthood in times and conditions that were extremely hostile to such virtues. Bringing an end to hatred, violence, and scarcity may have been a driving force in your life. Your efforts may have been instrumental in making the world safe for families.

LEO
From July 23, 22:01 through August 24, 4:51

The Wise Seer

Strange events occurred within days of your birth, Leo. On July 23, 1923, President Warren Harding was stricken with ptomaine poisoning and pneumonia while touring the U.S. Pacific Coast. On 2 August, Harding died of an apoplectic fit. No autopsy was ever performed and conspiracy theorists still speculate as to what really killed him. Evidence of scandals abounded after Harding's death. Senate investigations of Harding's administration uncovered extensive graft and corruption. Harding had appointed his cigar-smoking, bootleg-whiskey-drinking poker buddies to high offices in his administration. But on his final tour, he repeatedly asked trusted advisors and reporters what a President should do when his friends have betrayed him.

During his final tour, Harding cut a tragically childlike figure in his helpless, hypothetical questioning of what to do when friends turn out to be big jerks. The sign of Leo rules children and childlike qualities in adults. Unlike Harding, however, you are likely to roar with rage at disloyal friends who even think of making you look bad.

You may have phenomenal intuition. Like an eagle searching for prey, you may survey a broad situation, get your bearings, and then zero in on your target. You are likely to have excellent "people sense"—just a nose for knowing who can be trusted and who "smells bad." The people in your inner circle probably feel like family to you.

A relationship enables you to fully enjoy your capacity for fun, entertainment, and companionship. You may have been attracted to a playful, nurturing partner. Sagittarius's generosity and good humor keep your spirits high. Protective Cancer makes you feel safe. Serious and responsible in public, Capricorn loosens up in private.

Likely able to back up expectations of loyalty with a good sense of people's character, you may have gone through some rough patches while learning how to hear and understand your own intuition. While you may have suffered some let downs early in life, over time you could sharpen your ability to decode the signals of your inner instincts and wisdom.

➤ Read about your Chinese Astrological sign on page 838. ➤ Read about your Personal Planets on page 826. ➤ Read about your personal Mystical Card on page 856.

VIRGO

From August 24, 4:52 through September 24, 2:03

The Diligent Organizer

The sign of Virgo rules human interaction with and vulnerability to the natural world. Within days of your birth, a wave of natural disasters occurred all over the world. On September 1, 1923, the greatest earthquake in Japanese history leveled Tokyo and Yokohama. On September 12, a tidal wave wiped out the town of San José de Cabo on the southern California coast. On September 18, earthquakes shook Sicily and Malta. The Japan quake, measuring 8.3 on the Richter scale, left 300,000 dead, 500,000 injured, and 2.5 million homeless. Thirst, starvation, and a cholera epidemic threatened those who had managed to survive.

In the wake of natural disasters, people often reconsider the management of their local habitat. Because the sign of Virgo has an ancient mythological connection to natural cycles, Virgos tend to have a special sense of respect and awe for the environment. As a Virgo, you are more likely to be attuned to natural factors in deciding how you will live your life. While others may infrequently wash their hands or build their homes on a flood plain, the dangers of such practices are unlikely to seem quite so remote to you.

Likely to be among the more forward-thinking members of your sign, you may have supported the early pioneers of the environmental movement. Deeply passionate and willing to work hard, you may have been an activist, educator, or local organizer. You may make it your business to monitor developments in your community and to take action that can benefit all.

Involvement in meaningful activities may have provided the setting for your closest relationships. You were likely to choose a partner who shared your passions and convictions. Aquarius shares a humanitarian devotion. Pisces inspires you with vision and compassion. Scorpio renews your awe at creation.

Virgoan diligence makes you likely to keep track of important details that other people tend to let slide. At times you may have gotten tired of always working for everybody else. With maturity, you may have decided that you were content to maintain healthy habits for your own good reasons.

LIBRA

From September 24, 2:04 through October 24, 10:50

The Creative Peacemaker

The sign of Libra rules open enemies and justice. Within days of your birth, Germany was splintering in an explosion of regional violence among Communists, Socialists, National Socialists (Nazis), and supporters of the Social Democratic government. By the time you were born Chancellor Gustav Stresemann had been given dictatorial powers over Germany and sought to rein in separatist movements in Saxony and Bavaria. By November 8, the unrest peaked in Adolf Hitler's Beer Hall putsch, an unsuccessful attempt to take over the German government, for which Hitler was arrested. By November 23, Stresemann and his cabinet were ousted in a no-confidence vote in the Reichstag.

When you studied these developments in school, their relevance was still immediate, as Hitler's rise continued throughout your childhood. World War II began as you were reaching adulthood; you or your friends may have joined the war effort. In general, fighting is not the Libran way, but the conditions of your young adulthood forced you to reckon with the justice of self-defense against aggression.

You may be an unusually creative thinker, unlikely to allow common assumptions to limit your perspective. You may express your idealism through political activism, teaching, or artistic pursuits. Willing to risk criticism, your work may have challenged others to see things in a new and original way. You may be eager to elevate others' consciousness beyond their prejudices to new possibilities.

Your closest relationship might have started as a friendship that suddenly turned romantic. Companionship and mutual support were likely to form the foundation of your bond. Pisces inspires your creativity. Leo woos in an irresistibly playful way. Aries offers energizing passion.

You may have felt like an inside-out Libran in your early adulthood. Only after World War II ended could you shift your focus to the peacemaking and reconciliation favored by members of your sign. To its credit, your generation showed true Libra-like enlightenment by rejecting the vengeful model of the Treaty of Versailles in postwar resolutions.

➤ Read about your Chinese Astrological sign on page 838. ➤ Read about your Personal Planets on page 826. ➤ Read about your personal Mystical Card on page 856.

1923

VIRGO
Your Personal Planets

YOUR LOVE POTENTIAL
Venus in Leo, Aug. 24, 4:52 - Aug. 27, 23:58
Venus in Virgo, Aug. 27, 23:59 - Sept. 21, 3:28
Venus in Libra, Sept. 21, 3:29 - Sept. 24, 2:03

YOUR DRIVE AND AMBITION
Mars in Leo, Aug. 24, 4:52 - Sept. 01, 0:56
Mars in Virgo, Sept. 01, 0:57 - Sept. 24, 2:03

YOUR LUCK MAGNETISM
Jupiter in Scorpio, Aug. 24, 4:52 - Sept. 24, 2:03

World Events

Aug. 27 – Mexico is formally recognized by the U.S.

Sept. 1 – An earthquake in Japan destroys Tokyo, Yokohama, and towns for hundreds of miles around.

Tokyo is destroyed by an earthquake

LIBRA
Your Personal Planets

YOUR LOVE POTENTIAL
Venus in Libra, Sept. 24, 2:04 - Oct. 15, 4:48
Venus in Scorpio, Oct. 15, 4:49 - Oct. 24, 10:50

YOUR DRIVE AND AMBITION
Mars in Virgo, Sept. 24, 2:04 - Oct. 18, 4:17
Mars in Libra, Oct. 18, 4:18 - Oct. 24, 10:50

YOUR LUCK MAGNETISM
Jupiter in Scorpio, Sept. 24, 2:04 - Oct. 24, 10:50

World Events

Oct. 4 – American actor Charlton Heston is born.

Oct. 9 – The World Disarmament Conference opens in Geneva.

1923

SCORPIO
Your Personal Planets

YOUR LOVE POTENTIAL
Venus in Scorpio, Oct. 24, 10:51 - Nov. 08, 5:22
Venus in Sagittarius, Nov. 08, 5:23 - Nov. 23, 7:53

YOUR DRIVE AND AMBITION
Mars in Libra, Oct. 24, 10:51 - Nov. 23, 7:53

YOUR LUCK MAGNETISM
Jupiter in Scorpio, Oct. 24, 10:51 - Nov. 23, 7:53

World Events

Nov. 8 – The British Empire Conference rules that dominions have the right to decide their own foreign policies.

Nov. 12 – Adolf Hitler is arrested after an attempted coup against the German national government, in what comes to be known as the "Beer-Hall Putsch."

W. B. Yeats wins the Nobel Prize for literature

SAGITTARIUS
Your Personal Planets

YOUR LOVE POTENTIAL
Venus in Sagittarius, Nov. 23, 7:54 - Dec. 02, 6:05
Venus in Capricorn, Dec. 02, 6:06 - Dec. 22, 20:52

YOUR DRIVE AND AMBITION
Mars in Libra, Nov. 23, 7:54 - Dec. 04, 2:10
Mars in Scorpio, Dec. 04, 2:11 - Dec. 22, 20:52

YOUR LUCK MAGNETISM
Jupiter in Scorpio, Nov. 23, 7:54 - Nov. 24, 17:30
Jupiter in Sagittarius, Nov. 24, 17:31 - Dec. 22, 20:52

World Events

Nov. 25 – The first regular broadcast between Britain and the U.S. comes into effect.

Dec. 10 – The Nobel Prize for literature is awarded to Irish poet W.B. Yeats.

SCORPIO
From October 24, 10:51 through November 23, 7:53

The Mystery Maven

The sign of Scorpio rules mysteries, curses, and the dead. In late 1922, archeologist Howard Carter had discovered the tomb of King Tutankhamᵒn near Luxor, Egypt. On November 23, 1923, Carter uncovered an inner shrine, containing additional riches. Meanwhile, stories of "The Mummy's Curse" were fueling a press sensation. Lord Carnarvon, sponsor of the expedition, had been taken ill and died suddenly in Cairo in April. According to legend, at the moment Carnarvon died, a power outage triggered a blackout in Cairo, and his favorite dog yowled and dropped dead back in England. The story of the curse was further elaborated over the years, with accounts of premature death among members of Carter's team. Examination of Tutankhamen's body in the late twentieth century inspired another mystery, as Egyptologists uncovered evidence that he had been murdered.

You may have been riveted as the mystery of "The Mummy's Curse" evolved during your childhood. Scorpios tend to enjoy mysteries, and you are likely to have a special fascination for the ancient past. Indeed, you might have pursued your own favorite mysteries in foreign travel or academic research.

Your interests might have jumped from crypts to cryptology. Scorpios tend to love puzzles and have a gift for deciphering encoded messages. Subliminal influences, mind control, and propaganda may also have been favorite subjects of study or practice. You might have been a great spy or counter-intelligence officer.

Your romantic relationships may have begun with love at first sight that deepened over time. You may have been attracted to eccentric or exotic partners but settled down with someone more conservative. Pisces has seductive allure. Aquarius exudes a challenging defiance. Cancer may intrigue you, but is a safe choice for the long term.

Scorpios have a talent for unearthing secrets and unraveling mysteries, but over-immersion in cloak-and-dagger affairs can distort your perspective and make you needlessly distrustful of people. In maturity, you may have relaxed your guard and allowed others to prove their reliability.

SAGITTARIUS
From November 23, 7:54 through December 22, 20:52

The Philosopher Poet

The sign of Sagittarius rules the high arts, religion, and politics. On December 10, 1923, the poet and playwright William Butler Yeats received the Nobel Prize for literature. A native of Dublin, Ireland, Yeats's pride in his country was a driving force in his works. At the turn of the century, Yeats drew on the inspiration of Irish mythology and folklore, and he had an abiding interest in mysticism and the occult. Indeed, he urged the same kind of polite respect for mysticism that atheists might accord the church. During the Great War, his works became more overtly political, and he served as a senator of the Irish Free Republic in 1922. The awarding of the Nobel Prize to Yeats may have been a nod to the cause of Irish independence.

You may have studied Yeats's poems and plays in school. Sagittarians tend to enjoy the high arts of poetry and theatre. When religion or politics furnish the themes for such works, you are liable to be even more interested. Your own views on religion and politics may differ from those of your parents. In fact, you may have made a point of rebelling against their views.

You may have idealized the philosopher poets, such as Yeats, and sought to follow in their footsteps. Your quest in life may be to explore the brilliant mosaic of human experience. You may feel compelled to travel the world to discover the customs, rituals, and ways of diverse cultures. You may be a marvelous teacher, mentor, politician, or diplomat.

The joy of exploration, discovery, and learning is twice as good when you can share it. You may have chosen an open-minded partner with common interests. Gemini provides intelligent, fun-loving companionship. Aquarius dazzles you with ingenious insights. Aries challenges you with fast-paced passion.

Sagittarians are the gifted seekers of truth. Focusing only on profound resources, however, can make you miss the glimmers of insight in your own backyard. In maturity, you may have renewed your sense of wonder and awe by adopting the practice of always looking at the most humble elements of daily life, as if for the first time.

➤ Read about your Chinese Astrological sign on page 838. ➤ Read about your Personal Planets on page 826. ➤ Read about your personal Mystical Card on page 856.

CAPRICORN

From December 22, 20:53 through December 31, 23:59

Twentieth-Century Industrialist

The sign of Capricorn rules the ineluctable march of progress. Two powerful symbols of this process were in the news within days of your birth. December 28, 1923, marked the death of Gustav Eiffel, engineer and builder of the famous Parisian landmark bearing his name. Although the Eiffel Tower, built for the Paris Exposition of 1889, was supposed to be a purely temporary structure, it became a permanent symbol of France. The tower reflected and celebrated industrial progress in the nineteenth century—a time of mechanics, steel, engines, and rails. In contrast, a new and different kind of industry was growing in the twentieth century—one made of celluloid, glamour, imagination, and dreams. On December 31, the U.S. film industry reported a new milestone in investment; producers raised $750 million in 1923.

In childhood, you may have enjoyed making occasional escapes to the silver screen. As an adult, you were equipped to think of innovative ways to exploit the potential of the rapidly expanding entertainment and communications industry. Indicators in your chart show the potential makings of a mogul.

First, however, you would have to survive World War II, an experience that may have been deeply wounding for you. Losses of home, possessions, family, or friends may have completely rearranged your priorities in life. You may have emerged determined to erect a wall of protection around your loved ones.

In relationships, you may seek to balance commitment with passion and drive. You may have chosen a partner who also had a certain determination to maximize family power and influence. Taurus ensures ample financial and material resources. Safety and security are Cancer's primary goals. Scorpio has an iron will to recoup all losses and exceed all expectations.

Capricorns tend to set firm boundaries for self protection, but the trauma of World War II may have caused you to throw up walls. Blocking out pain also blocks out the capacity to feel joy, passion, and pleasure. By facing your pain in maturity, you could transform it into a bottomless well of empathy and strength.

1923

CAPRICORN
Your Personal Planets

YOUR LOVE POTENTIAL
Venus in Capricorn, Dec. 22, 20:53 - Dec. 26, 8:02
Venus in Aquarius, Dec. 26, 8:03 - Dec. 31, 23:59

YOUR DRIVE AND AMBITION
Mars in Scorpio, Dec. 22, 20:53 - Dec. 31, 23:59

YOUR LUCK MAGNETISM
Jupiter in Sagittarius, Dec. 22, 20:53 - Dec. 31, 23:59

World Events

Dec. 27 – In Japan, Hirohito escapes an assassination attempt.

Dec. 31 – A car crosses the Sahara Desert for the first time.

J. P. Morgan, who consulted Evangeline Adams

Special Feature
Astrology Goes on Trial: Evangeline Adams

(Continued from page 193)

Needless to say, when the stock market crashed in 1929, Evangeline Adams was inundated with even more clients. She repeatedly forecast a period of war for the U.S. from 1942 to 1944, also based on Uranus, but died before she could see it come to pass.

As her Sun sign also suggests, Adams's personal life was every bit as amazing as her professional life. She was also quite unpredictable in relationships, born with that strong, independent streak of Aquarian energy. She broke off an engagement with an older, quite well-to-do gentleman while still quite young. Then, a few years later, Franklin Simmons, a famous sculptor who was thirty years her senior, also proposed. His intention was to marry her and take her away to a life of leisure in his lushly furnished palazzo in Rome. Evangeline needed her work, however, and eventually turned him down. She remained single, independent, and self-supporting at a time when

most women's fondest dreams consisted of marriage and family. She eventually did marry, however, at the age of fifty-five, choosing George E. Jordan Jr., who, in Aquarian tradition, was "different"—he was much younger than she.

In addition to being a Sun-sign Aquarius, Adams was born with several planets in the compassionate sign of Pisces, showing gentleness, impressionability, and strong intuition—as well as an untiring urge to help others. She had originally found astrology during a long period of illness, while still in her teens. Her doctor, amused by her rather unconventional ideas, introduced her to Dr. J. Hebert Smith, a homeopathic physician who taught Adams the astrology she would come to know and love. She also studied with Dr. George S. Adams, another Aquarian, who used astrology to help his patients at the Westborough Insane Asylum. The time she

spent studying the charts of these patients made her an important pioneer in the field of astro-psychology.

By the end of her career, she had actually become wealthy by the standards of those days, charging $50 per half-hour for personal consultations—which, in 1930, was the price of a three-piece bedroom set. Her estate was valued at about $60,000 in 1932—equivalent to nearly two million dollars today. She died on November 10, 1932 from a cerebral hemorrhage—and it's said that she'd actually predicted her own death. ✪

➤Read about the 1929 Crash in "Money, Astrology, and the Crash of '29" on page 225. ➤ Read more about Adams in "Astrology Reigns Through the Ages" on page 25. ➤ Read Caruso's Star Profile on page 97.

1924

Pluto Trine Uranus: Changes Big and Small

In 1924, Pluto was still in Cancer, and Uranus continued its stay in Pisces. Both of these are water signs, linked to intuition, emotion, the arts, and the instincts. Pluto represents the deepest changes we experience, those that occur over time and completely restructure us. Uranus represents sudden change, the things that shock us out of complacency. When these two powerful outer planets tickle one another in the harmonious aspect called a trine, we can expect cultural evolution and dynamic progress to take place. In 1924, Wall Street had its biggest boom ever. No one could foresee the plunge that would take place five years into the future, and speculators were riding high. The revolt against prohibition was in full swing, and speakeasies abounded. Flappers danced and people had fun. A postwar cultural sea change was in full force.

This year also saw the birth of the actor Marlon Brando on April 3. His intense performances are Plutonian to the core. The writer James Baldwin was born on August 2 of 1924. His books would transform our understanding of race and class, and had a deep impact on the way Americans viewed themselves and the society that they lived in. Jimmy Carter, the thirty-ninth American President, was born on October 1. His work on the Camp David accords in the late seventies helped to create a bit of peace in the Middle East. The world lost two important authors this year as well: Franz Kafka and Joseph Conrad both died in 1924. Also this year, radio waves were used to broadcast communication for the first time, sending a signal 7,000 miles.

Bolshevik leader Vladimir Lenin dies

George Gershwin performs his "Rhapsody in Blue"

The first ever radio broadcast is made

THE BERMUDA TRIANGLE

There have been more than thirty vessels reported lost in the Bermuda Triangle. In 1924, a Japanese freighter called the *Raifuku Maru* joined that list. Unlike some of the other vessels, the *Raifuku Maru* did manage a last radio message before it disappeared between the Bahamas and Cuba. The bizarre message left by the terrified pilot was: "Danger like dagger. Come quick!" No explanation has ever been found for what kind of object or incident could have had the distinctive shape or character of a dagger.

WORLD POWERS RE-STABILIZE WHILE GERMANY STRUGGLES

The Russian communist leader Lenin died, leaving Stalin and Trotsky vying for power; Stalin prevailed. In Britain, the Labour Party gained control of the government for the first time, showing the power of workers recently given the vote. New Turkish leader Kemal (Ataturk) introduced innovations, banning hereditary leadership, polygamy, and traditional clothing. In Greece, King George II was deposed in favor of a republic. Germany, in dire economic straits, reformed its currency, formerly exchanged at four trillion to the dollar. Although imprisoned for high treason, Hitler was treated royally and released after eight months. Hollywood saw the birth of Metro Goldwyn Mayer film studios. U.S. President Coolidge was elected to his first full term, and Wall Street enjoyed its biggest boom. Radio waves were used to make the first ever broadcast, sending a signal 7,000 miles. The first Winter Olympics were launched in Chamonix, France, where Scandinavian participants were prominent. Italian Puccini, composer of *La Bohème* and *Tosca*, died, as did authors Joseph Conrad and Franz Kafka. George Gershwin performed his *Rhapsody in Blue*.

➤ Read F. Scott Fitzgerald's Star Profile on page 209.

CAPRICORN

From January 01, 0:00 through January 21, 7:27

The Conservative Liberator

The sign of Capricorn rules limits and restrictions. On January 18, 1924, the New York State Motion Picture Censorship Board accused Hollywood of glorifying vice. The statement echoed worries voiced worldwide about dancing, fashion, and the increasing liberties enjoyed by women. Across the U. S., Hollywood projected an image of the most frightening force since the Red Army—the flapper. Sporting bobbed hair, makeup, and short skirts while smoking, dancing, and staying out late, the flapper threatened to fulfill the prophecy of the late President Harding—women voters united as a class. There was indeed something delectably dangerous about the flapper.

In general, members of your sign tend to be conservative, comforted by rules and regulations. Known in legal parlance as "prior restraint," censorship might seem a force favored by Capricorns. On the contrary, many Capricorns, including you, are likely to have even greater respect for constitutional restraints on governmental interference with free speech and other liberties.

Likely to be open-minded—while ever the pragmatic, business-oriented Capricorn—you may entrust the competition between good and bad speech to the marketplace of ideas. Capricorns may be conservative, but prudish you are not. You are likely to have a raucous, bawdy side. The key distinction is that it emerges only when the time and place are right.

Relationships provide the privacy that allows your inner wild man or flapper to emerge. You may have chosen a partner who could be discreet and proper in public but very affectionate behind closed doors. Cancerians can be old-fashioned but very loving. Scorpios know how to keep passionate secrets. Taureans are solid, discreet, and very sensuous.

You may be fairly liberal, as far as Capricorns go, but your greatest strength may be a sense of propriety and a capacity for self-regulation that others just don't possess. Striking a healthy balance between personal and external restraints may have been your greatest challenge. When chaos threatens to break out, you may favor greater regulation.

AQUARIUS

From January 21, 7:28 through February 19, 21:50

The True Idealist

The sign of Aquarius rules revolution and the vanquishing of tyrannical regimes. January 21, 1924 marked the death of Vladimir Lenin, the father of the Russian Revolution. In letters publicized at a party congress in May 1924, Lenin asserted his wish to remove Joseph Stalin as General Secretary of the Communist Party and to promote Leon Trotsky as his successor. Stalin allied with Grigori Zinoviev and Lev Kamenev to engineer the ouster and subsequent murder of Trotsky. In time, Stalin would demonize Zinoviev and Kamenev as Jews and purge them from the party. Ultimately, Stalin's reign would become a bloodbath as purges, forced starvation, and the gulag claimed millions of lives throughout the Soviet empire.

In studying the progression of the Russian Revolution, you may have sympathized with its initial aims. Most Aquarians would favor nice ideas such as eliminating tyranny, ending selfishness, sharing everything, and fairness to workers. But the lessons of Stalinism may have made you suspicious of wolves in activist clothing.

In your own lifetime, you may have suffered heartbreaking disillusionment at the hands of opportunists who used needy people as pawns in their own power trip. Indicators in your chart show a potential for nuclear-strength rage. You may have directed this power against the Nazis in World War II or in other campaigns against oppression and injustice.

Romance and idealism may fuel your relationships. Seductive, charismatic partners may have attracted you in your youth, but maturity may have brought a preference for truthfulness and candor. Leo's exciting personality can dazzle you. Scorpios exude a hypnotic magnetism. Capricorns' integrity and Sagittarians' bluntness provide more reliable alternatives.

Your greatest strength may be your tendency to combat oppression from any source, but your drive to make a difference can cause some to inadvertently hurt the ones you want to help. With maturity, you may have become more conscious of the need to check your motives, making sure you're serving a worthy cause and not a need for self-aggrandizement.

CAPRICORN
Your Personal Planets

YOUR LOVE POTENTIAL
Venus in Aquarius, Jan. 01, 0:00 - Jan. 19, 13:44
Venus in Pisces, Jan. 19, 13:45 - Jan. 21, 7:27

YOUR DRIVE AND AMBITION
Mars in Scorpio, Jan. 01, 0:00 - Jan. 19, 19:05
Mars in Sagittarius, Jan. 19, 19:06 - Jan. 21, 7:27

YOUR LUCK MAGNETISM
Jupiter in Sagittarius, Jan. 01, 0:00 - Jan. 21, 7:27

World Events

Jan. 3 – The sarcophagus of the Pharaoh Tutankhamen is discovered in the fifth shrine of his tomb.

Jan. 9 – Sun Yat-Sen appeals for international pressure to effect peace in China.

The sarcophagus of Tutankhamen

AQUARIUS
Your Personal Planets

YOUR LOVE POTENTIAL
Venus in Pisces, Jan. 21, 7:28 - Feb. 13, 4:09
Venus in Aries, Feb. 13, 4:10 - Feb. 19, 21:50

YOUR DRIVE AND AMBITION
Mars in Sagittarius, Jan. 21, 7:28 - Feb. 19, 21:50

YOUR LUCK MAGNETISM
Jupiter in Sagittarius, Jan. 21, 7:28 - Feb. 19, 21:50

World Events

Jan. 21 – Bolshevik leader Vladimir Ilyich Lenin dies.

Feb. 8 – The gas chamber is used as a method of execution for the first time in the U.S.

➤ Read about your Chinese Astrological sign on page 838. ➤ Read about your Personal Planets on page 826. ➤ Read about your personal Mystical Card on page 856.

1924

PISCES
Your Personal Planets

YOUR LOVE POTENTIAL

Venus in Aries, Feb. 19, 21:51 - Mar. 09, 11:54
Venus in Taurus, Mar. 09, 11:55 - Mar. 20, 21:19

YOUR DRIVE AND AMBITION

Mars in Sagittarius, Feb. 19, 21:51 - Mar. 06, 19:01
Mars in Capricorn, Mar. 06, 19:02 - Mar. 20, 21:19

YOUR LUCK MAGNETISM

Jupiter in Sagittarius, Feb. 19, 21:51 - Mar. 20, 21:19

World Events

Mar. 7 – In a landmark broadcast, signals from station WJZ in New York are relayed across the country to San Francisco, and then to a station in Manchester, England.

Mar. 13 – The German Reichstag is dissolved.

American actor Marlon Brando is born under the sign of Aries

ARIES
Your Personal Planets

YOUR LOVE POTENTIAL

Venus in Taurus, Mar. 20, 21:20 - Apr. 05, 6:45
Venus in Gemini, Apr. 05, 6:46 - Apr. 20, 8:58

YOUR DRIVE AND AMBITION

Mars in Capricorn, Mar. 20, 21:20 - Apr. 20, 8:58

YOUR LUCK MAGNETISM

Jupiter in Sagittarius, Mar. 20, 21:20 - Apr. 20, 8:58

World Events

Mar. 25 – The Greek King George II is deposed and the country is declared a republic.

Apr. 16 – Film company Metro-Goldwyn-Mayer is formed from the merger of Metro Pictures, Goldwyn Pictures, and the Louis B. Mayer Company.

PISCES
From February 19, 21:51 through March 20, 21:19

The Pedestal Repudiator

The sign of Pisces rules disguises and unseen dangers. On March 10, 1924, the United States Supreme Court upheld a New York state law that forbade women from working late-night shifts. The measure purported to protect women but its actual effect was to limit their earning power, interfere with their freedom of movement, and reduce them to children in need of protection. Members of the women's movement argued that to idealize women on a pedestal was as oppressive as an open display of hostility. Indeed, if legitimate work did not exist as a reason for women to be out and about, those who dared to venture outside in off-hours would be vulnerable to accusations of prostitution.

Aid, support, or an advantage you once enjoyed may have turned out to be oppression in disguise. Many supporters of the Communist Party, seeking relief from tyrannical governments and exploitative industrialists, ended up horrified by the tyranny of purported liberators. Perhaps a spouse supported you and treated you like gold. A sudden loss, possibly in war, may have forced you to face your own inability to fend for yourself.

Such a painful lesson may have been the first step in taking control over your own life. Indicators in your chart show the potential for a phenomenally successful career. Higher education or travel may have allowed you to develop precious skills. You may have worked as an academic or in politics, or you may have started your own business.

Relationships may have given you the impetus to reach your full potential as a human being. Early partners may have been doting caretakers, likely to become or be replaced by reliable companions. A Cancerian can be a generous provider. Virgos thrive on mutual service. Capricorns respect your personal integrity.

You have the potential to wield tremendous personal power, but the challenge for you may be to dispense with false illusions. But the shattering of tenaciously held rationalizations may have been your moment of greatest strength and the signature moment in your personal evolution. In maturity, the truth truly set you free.

ARIES
From March 20, 21:20 through April 20, 8:58

The Bully Fighter

The sign of Aries rules naked aggression, intimidation, and leadership by bullies. On April 1, 1924, Adolf Hitler was sentenced to five years imprisonment for his attempted takeover of the German government. Hitler turned the sentencing hearing into a propaganda opportunity for the Nazi Party. He interrupted the proceedings at will, invoking Wagner and nationalist mythology to undermine the legitimacy of the court. The punishment was a slap on the wrist, as Hitler would be eligible for parole in six months. On April 17, Benito Mussolini won control of the Italian Parliament with the support of the popular vote, despite the campaign being clouded by suspicions of fraud.

Every sign has a dark side. Just because you are an Aries, you are not destined to become a Fascist, a bully, or an aggressor. (In fact, Hitler was born under the peace-loving sign of Taurus.) Your natural access to the martial energies of your sign may invest you with a sense of mission to promote awareness of the potential for violence in all human beings.

You are unlikely to share the fear that made people vulnerable to the appeal of fascism. Your chart shows an ability to respond with courage and fighting spirit. Yours may exemplify your generation's destiny—displayed during the Great Depression and World War II—as the preservers and parents of the future. Possessed of great powers of vision and initiative, you could have founded new industries or even new nations.

Relationships provided a structure in which you could give and receive love and nurture. Your partner may have been gentle but firm. Librans softly tell you what you need to hear—even if it's not what you want to hear. Aquarians' social instincts keep you from feeling lonely. Capricorns and Virgos can finish what you begin.

You may have seen fear as the breeding ground for bigotry, abuses of power, and corruption. After all, bullies are opportunistic cowards. To stand against such diseases of the human soul may have been the signature challenge of your life. Your greatest strength is the ability to rise to the occasion.

➤ Read about your Chinese Astrological sign on page 838. ➤ Read about your Personal Planets on page 826. ➤ Read about your personal Mystical Card on page 856.

TAURUS

From April 20, 8:59 through May 21, 8:39

The Creative Mediators

The sign of Taurus rules financial resources and income. In April of 1924, the German government indicated its support for a proposal to settle the issue of World War I reparations. Charles Dawes headed a committee of the Reparations Commission of the Allied nations that came up with a plan to enable Germany to meaningfully comply with the reparations demanded under the Treaty of Versailles. Through his proposal, which provided a $200 million foreign loan to Germany, Dawes sought to restore the reign of common sense and blunt Fascists' opportunistic attempts to exploit the issue of reparations.

Like Dawes, you are likely to be generous and willing to strike compromises between people who are too invested in their positions to be objective. This ability may enable you to undo damage by stripping away obstacles to reason and peace. You may often feel like a parent resolving a fight among children. The Marshall Plan was exactly the kind of program you would have been likely to endorse.

You may feel that your personality has much in common with your Gemini friends. You are likely to be insightful, intelligent, and sensitive to the impact of ideology in human affairs. Able to account for disparate factors, you may be able to improvise creative solutions to stubborn problems. Likely to be innovative, individualistic, and highly disciplined, you may have been a diplomat, a deal-maker, or an entrepreneur.

Relationships may have been a motivating force in your life. You may have chosen a partner who was loyal but gave you room to breathe. Librans would satisfy your need for a beautiful and harmonious home. Capricorns could provide long-term stability and healthy boundaries. Pisceans cling loosely and make you eager for moments of private tenderness.

Your patience and creativity are a wonderfully productive combination, one that may have come over the years. Early impulsiveness might have been a challenge, landing a few disapproving feet on your bright-eyed bushy tail. With maturity, you may have polished up your great strengths: presentation, discipline, and compromise.

GEMINI

From May 21, 8:40 through June 21, 16:58

The Soulful Intellectual

Gemini rules intellectualism and duos. May 21, 1924 marked the kidnapping and murder of thirteen-year-old Bobby Franks by the infamous duo, Nathan Leopold and Richard Loeb. The nineteen-year-old suspects were geniuses, college graduates, and children of millionaires. Apparently, the two had read too much Friedrich Nietzsche and not enough of his contemporary, Fyodor Dostoyevsky. Invoking Nietzsche's nihilistic philosophy, the duo saw themselves as intellectual supermen above morality. Like Raskolnikov, Dostoyevsky's anti-hero in *Crime and Punishment*, Leopold and Loeb committed murder based on a purely rational calculus. But Raskolnikov was redeemed through his acceptance of punishment and soulful suffering; these two failed to express remorse. Loeb was murdered in prison in 1936; historians are divided over whether Leopold's thirty-three years in jail softened his soul.

Every sign has a dark side. Mere identity as a Gemini does not doom you to become a psychopath. Geminis are readers, and you may regard *Crime and Punishment* as a great novel. Its message underscores the emptiness of intellect without soul. While you may be utterly brilliant, the circumstances of your life were likely to emphasize matters of the heart and spirit.

Likely to be an outstanding student, you may speak many languages. A generous mentor may have made a difference in your life. You may have enjoyed the challenge of foreign travel and acquired a love of exotic cultures. You may be a teacher, writer, and a humanitarian.

Relationships may have allowed you to become a well-rounded person. Your partner was likely to love you for who you were as a person. Sagittarians nurture your highest potential. Virgos frank feedback keeps you down to Earth. Pisceans offer you a soulful inspiration.

A Gemini's typical superior intellect could be your greatest strength, bringing success, but one cannot live on brains alone. To avoid alienation and loneliness, your challenge may have been to reach out to others. In maturity, you may have resolved that most knowledge was worthless if it did not help others.

➤ Read about your Chinese Astrological sign on page 838. ➤ Read about your Personal Planets on page 826. ➤ Read about your personal Mystical Card on page 856.

TAURUS
Your Personal Planets

YOUR LOVE POTENTIAL
Venus in Gemini, Apr. 20, 8:59 - May 06, 1:48
Venus in Cancer, May 06, 1:49 - May 21, 8:39

YOUR DRIVE AND AMBITION
Mars in Capricorn, Apr. 20, 8:59 - Apr. 24, 15:57
Mars in Aquarius, Apr. 24, 15:58 - May 21, 8:39

YOUR LUCK MAGNETISM
Jupiter in Sagittarius, Apr. 20, 8:59 - May 21, 8:39

World Events

Apr. 21 – Italian actress Eleonora Duse dies.

May 10 – J. Edgar Hoover becomes head of the FBI at the age of only twenty-nine.

American Indians are given full U.S. citizenship

GEMINI
Your Personal Planets

YOUR LOVE POTENTIAL
Venus in Cancer, May 21, 8:40 - June 21, 16:58

YOUR DRIVE AND AMBITION
Mars in Aquarius, May 21, 8:40 - June 21, 16:58

YOUR LUCK MAGNETISM
Jupiter in Sagittarius, May 21, 8:40 - June 21, 16:58

World Events

June 2 – American Indians are finally granted full citizenship of the U.S.

June 8 – George Leigh Mallory and Andrew Irvine are last seen alive as they set off on the last stage of their expedition to conquer Mt. Everest.

1924

CANCER
Your Personal Planets

YOUR LOVE POTENTIAL
Venus in Cancer, June 21, 16:59 - July 23, 3:57

YOUR DRIVE AND AMBITION
Mars in Aquarius, June 21, 16:59 - June 24, 16:26
Mars in Pisces, June 24, 16:27 - July 23, 3:57

YOUR LUCK MAGNETISM
Jupiter in Sagittarius, June 21, 16:59 - July 23, 3:57

World Events

July 7 - U.S. President Calvin Coolidge's sixteen-year-old son Calvin Jr. dies of septicemia.

July 14 - Three thousand people are killed in a clash between the military and rebels in São Paulo.

American author James Baldwin is born under the sign of Leo

LEO
Your Personal Planets

YOUR LOVE POTENTIAL
Venus in Cancer, July 23, 3:58 - Aug. 23, 10:47

YOUR DRIVE AND AMBITION
Mars in Pisces, July 23, 3:58 - Aug. 23, 10:47

YOUR LUCK MAGNETISM
Jupiter in Sagittarius, July 23, 3:58 - Aug. 23, 10:47

World Events

Aug. 2 - American author James Baldwin is born.

Aug. 7 - Japan and Russia resume negotiations to improve relations between the countries.

CANCER
From June 21, 16:59 through July 23, 3:57

The Traveling Homebody

The sign of Cancer rules homecomings. At the time of your birth, speculation swirled around a mystery involving the most hazardous homecoming known to humanity. News items from late June reported the disappearance of Andrew Irvine and George Mallory, last seen on June 8, as they launched an attempt to be the first to reach the summit of Mount Everest. The question of whether Mallory and Irvine died while ascending or descending has fueled controversy to this day. Members of a 1999 expedition discovered Mallory's body and certain items that supported the theory of a fatal fall after reaching the summit. Decisive evidence remains elusive. In subsequent assaults on Everest, three-quarters of all deaths occurred on the descent when the eagerness to make the summit consumed precious time for the return to a home base.

Although Cancerians are often regarded as homebodies, your sign is also linked to travel. Like the crab—and the 1924 mountaineers—you may take fantastic journeys with essential provisions affixed to your back. A desire to bring back souvenirs for loved ones may ensure that your load will be heavier upon your return.

You may be a relationship-mender, the person people look to as the mediator of family feuds. A compelling personality may enable you to persuade others to surrender their own selfish interests. You may have had a career as a divorce or labor mediator, a family counselor, a psychologist, or a diplomat.

You may be passionate and tenacious in relationships and likely to choose a partner who could give you an ironclad commitment. Capricorns could stick with you for the long term. Scorpios afford you a bottomless well of love. Taureans can indulge your need for reassurance.

Your strength may have been your generosity with signs of affection but your giving may have come with strings attached. When someone did not respond as expected, your challenge could have been to prevent disappointment from spiraling into feelings of abandonment. With maturity, you may have gradually learned to cling more loosely and enjoy the gift of giving for its own sake.

LEO
From July 23, 3:58 through August 23, 10:47

The Playful Dreamer

The sign of Leo rules games, diversions, and drama. When you were born the 1924 Olympics in Paris provided all of these things. Paavo Nurmi of Finland turned in the greatest individual performance with five gold medals in track and field. You may have paid your own visit to the 1924 Olympics through the magic of the silver screen. The 1981 Oscar-winning film *Chariots of Fire* told the story of the winning British track team. The story illustrated the struggles of Harold Abrahams who braved anti-Semitism on his way to winning a gold medal in the 100-meter race in world-record time. Also featured was Eric Liddel, the Scottish missionary and 400-meter gold medalist who, in maintaining his religious duty to honor the Sabbath, surrendered his chance to run as the favorite in the 200-meter.

You are likely to be playful and animated. Because your dreams may be vivid and elaborate, children may get a charge out of you. You may be able to shift into "child mind," a state of psychological innocence and receptivity that can inspire marvelous creative works. You may be a compelling storyteller, actor, photographer, or teacher.

You may enjoy competitive athletics, but having fun would be your first priority. Good sportsmanship may be important to you. At some point in your life, feelings of compassion for another's circumstances may have moved you to allow an opponent to win.

Your relationship may have filled your need for a loyal companion. You may have chosen an adoring partner, willing to give you plenty of attention. Sagittarians offer a generous supply of fun, admiration, and good humor. Pisceans share a taste for romance and drama. Librans are likely to have a strong need to meet your needs.

Boyish or girlish charm may have made you irresistibly endearing but life may have jarred you into adulthood. You grew up during the Great Depression and came of age as World War II raged around you. The need to safeguard your own children was the factor most likely to bring out the strength of the fiercely protective lion in you. Your challenge may have been to tame your ferocity.

➤ Read about your Chinese Astrological sign on page 838. ➤ Read about your Personal Planets on page 826. ➤ Read about your personal Mystical Card on page 856.

VIRGO

From August 23, 10:48 through September 23, 7:57

The Identity Keeper

Ancient mythology links the sign of Virgo with matrilineal identity. The Roman story of Ceres, goddess of the harvest, and her daughter Persephone explained the origin of the seasons. When Pluto, god of the underworld, seized Persephone from her mother, Ceres' grief cloaked the world in wintry cold. On September 15, 1924, in Washington, D.C., the National Women's Party protested a ruling requiring female federal employees to go by their husbands' surnames for payroll purposes. The protesters argued that the loss of women's maiden names amounted to the stripping away of their identity, integrity, and validity as self-determining political beings.

Virgos tend to have strong opinions about "what's in a name." After all, the sign of Virgo is associated with words and their practical impact in the world. You are likely to believe that one's identity is inextricably intertwined with one's name. Indeed, "your good name" may be your dearest asset. Virgos tend to care deeply about reputation and what others think of them. For you, words and thoughts may be as real as the things they represent.

The symbol for Virgo, the Virgin, represents more than mere physical chastity. In ancient times a virgin was one who had never been *possessed* by another. Whether you are male or female, your personal sanctity, inner solitude, and freedom—that part of you that no one can reach, change, or control—may be central to your sense of self and well being.

Your relationship may have transformed as rapidly as the times in which you lived. You and your partner were likely to nurture and respect each other's individuality. Aquarians worship all that is unique about you. Pisceans understand the need for "alone time." Cancerians care for you through life's passages.

Virgos tend to be competent and self-reliant—these are your greatest strengths. You may be perfectly happy when left to your own devices. Too much solitude can become isolation, however, and your challenge may have been to recognize this. With maturity, you may have become more of a social being, enjoying the blessings of cooperation.

LIBRA

From September 23, 7:58 through October 23, 16:43

The Goodwill Ambassador

The sign of Libra rules goodwill missions and the promotion of peaceful relationships. September 28, 1924 marked the successful conclusion of the first round-the-world journey by air. Landing outside Seattle, Washington, a team of aviators from the United States army had flown three planes through twenty-one foreign countries and twenty-five states. The mission began on April 6, 1924, and proceeded in fifty-seven increments; crowds came out to cheer the fliers at every stop. Earlier in the century, advances in aviation technology had rendered national borders porous, provoking the insecurity that played no small role in triggering World War I. But for five months in 1924, people the world over turned out to celebrate the wonders of new technology and human aspiration.

Librans tend to have an instinctive sense for the values and experiences that can unify people in common wonderment and respect. You may have a special talent in helping people to rise above themselves or commit to a larger goal. Indicators in your chart suggest that you would not shy away from ambitious projects.

Like the great explorers and innovators of the early twentieth century, you may feel a tension to take on unusual and unprecedented challenges. Going through ordinary channels and climbing the ladder may not be for you. You are likely to need to start at the top. You may have been an entrepreneur, a clergy member, a statesperson, or an adventurer.

Relationships may provide you with a sense of strength and validation. You were likely to choose a partner who would accompany and inspire you in the world as well as at home. Sagittarians share affection for big ambitions. Aquarians share your aspirations to find a better world. Leos offer you encouragement.

Librans tend to have an easy and natural appeal to others, and your strength may be an infectious enthusiasm. A desire to aim high and start big may have challenged you, leaving your feet on a few of the wrong toes. With maturity, you may have polished your diplomatic pitch and charmed more than a few resisters into seeing things your way.

➤ Read about your Chinese Astrological sign on page 838. ➤ Read about your Personal Planets on page 826. ➤ Read about your personal Mystical Card on page 856.

1924

VIRGO
Your Personal Planets

YOUR LOVE POTENTIAL
Venus in Cancer, Aug. 23, 10:48 - Sept. 08, 21:42
Venus in Leo, Sept. 08, 21:43 - Sept. 23, 7:57

YOUR DRIVE AND AMBITION
Mars in Pisces, Aug. 23, 10:48 - Aug. 24, 15:37
Mars in Aquarius, Aug. 24, 15:38 - Sept. 23, 7:57

YOUR LUCK MAGNETISM
Jupiter in Sagittarius, Aug. 23, 10:48 - Sept. 23, 7:57

World Events

Sept. 4 – American Indians vote in a U.S. election for the first time.

Sept. 23 – Germany asks to become a member of the League of Nations.

Two U.S. Army planes are visited by admiring crowds a day before takeoff

LIBRA
Your Personal Planets

YOUR LOVE POTENTIAL
Venus in Leo, Sept. 23, 7:58 - Oct. 07, 14:15
Venus in Virgo, Oct. 07, 14:16 - Oct. 23, 16:43

YOUR DRIVE AND AMBITION
Mars in Aquarius, Sept. 23, 7:58 - Oct. 19, 18:41
Mars in Pisces, Oct. 19, 18:42 - Oct. 23, 16:43

YOUR LUCK MAGNETISM
Jupiter in Sagittarius, Sept. 23, 7:58 - Oct. 23, 16:43

World Events

Sept. 28 – The first round-the-world flight is completed by six American pilots in three U.S. army planes; the trip took twenty-two days.

Oct. 16 – In Canton, China, workers stage an uprising against Sun Yat-Sen's rule.

1924

SCORPIO
Your Personal Planets

YOUR LOVE POTENTIAL
Venus in Virgo, Oct. 23, 16:44 - Nov. 02, 14:43
Venus in Libra, Nov. 02, 14:44 - Nov. 22, 13:45

YOUR DRIVE AND AMBITION
Mars in Pisces, Oct. 23, 16:44 - Nov. 22, 13:45

YOUR LUCK MAGNETISM
Jupiter in Sagittarius, Oct. 23, 16:44 - Nov. 22, 13:45

World Events

Nov. 6 – *Boris Godunov* opens to acclaim at the Metropolitan Opera in New York.

Nov. 22 – Actress Geraldine Page is born.

Gershwin's "Lady Be Good" makes its debut in New York

SAGITTARIUS
Your Personal Planets

YOUR LOVE POTENTIAL
Venus in Libra, Nov. 22, 13:46 - Nov. 27, 11:47
Venus in Scorpio, Nov. 27, 11:48 - Dec. 21, 19:55
Venus in Sagittarius, Dec. 21, 19:56 - Dec. 22, 2:44

YOUR DRIVE AND AMBITION
Mars in Pisces, Nov. 22, 13:46 - Dec. 19, 11:08
Mars in Aries, Dec. 19, 11:09 - Dec. 22, 2:44

YOUR LUCK MAGNETISM
Jupiter in Sagittarius, Nov. 22, 13:46 - Dec. 18, 6:24
Jupiter in Capricorn, Dec. 18, 6:25 - Dec. 22, 2:44

World Events

Nov. 25 – Charlie Chaplin weds sixteen-year-old Lita Grey in Mexico City.

Dec. 20 – Adolf Hitler is released from prison, after serving only eight months of a five-year sentence for treason.

SCORPIO
From October 23, 16:44 through November 22, 13:45

The Willful Survivor

The sign of Scorpio rules the underworld and the dark side of human nature. November 10, 1924, marked the death of underworld boss Dion O'Banion, Chicago florist, bootlegger, gang leader, and murderous psychopath. In a way, O'Banion and other mob leaders represented the dark side of the American character. The Volstead Act, outlawing alcoholic beverages, was the product of the puritan streak running through American culture. Instead of creating universal sobriety, Prohibition facilitated the development of criminal syndicates across the country. The lucrative potential of bootlegging attracted European immigrants who faced discrimination in legitimate businesses. As each gang competed for dominance over the illegal alcohol trade, the body count multiplied. Indeed, O'Banion's death triggered a war.

Scorpio is not the only sign that has a dark side and your birth under it by no means destines you for an underworld existence. You are likely, however, to have an instinctive appreciation of the havoc that can break out when healthy impulses are repressed. Unlike O'Banion, however, you may channel impulses with focus and discipline.

Indicators in your chart suggest that you have a powerful will and harbor intense feelings about the things you create, particularly children. You are liable to defend your family with your life. Likely to be deeply insightful, compassionate, and intuitive, you may have been a psychologist, detective, or theologian.

Once you commit to a relationship, you are likely to hold on with everything you've got. You may have been drawn to a partner who was adventurous and challengingly defiant. Taureans' stubbornness can be madly exciting. Pisceans' disappearing act can be romantically intriguing. Capricorns offer surprising passion behind closed doors.

The iron will and magnetic personality of Scorpio may have been your strength, enabling you to survive challenging circumstances and stare down opponents. Coming out with all guns blasting, however, could prove counterproductive. With maturity you may have learned when to use a more subtle approach.

SAGITTARIUS
From November 22, 13:46 through December 22, 2:44

The Wise Strategist

The sign of Sagittarius rules international relations and statecraft. The year of 1924 brought momentous changes in the Arab world as the British Empire withdrew from the area and competition between local dynasties produced enduring results. On December 5, 1924, Ibn-Saud occupied Medina and led the Ikhwan, a Muslim military brotherhood, in deposing King Hussein. Hussein was the father of Faisal, then King of Iraq and better known to today's westerners as the wise Arabian king played by Alec Guiness in *Lawrence of Arabia*. Ibn-Saud's occupation of Medina was a crucial victory in a campaign that led to the unification of the Arabian Peninsula under the Saud clan—the country we know today as Saudi Arabia.

Ibn-Saud was both a brilliant military strategist and politician, having had the wisdom to win over the support of religious leaders. The sign of Sagittarius rules religion, politics, and wisdom, and your chart shows the potential for wielding the potent combination of wisdom, inspirational zeal, and revolutionary force. You may have expressed this kind of power in warfare, in pursuing a career, or in tackling any challenge.

Your emotional energy may be explosive at times, especially if you do not find healthy and vigorous ways of expressing it. If you hold in your feelings, they are likely to emerge like a lightning strike. Possibly accident prone early in life, you would need a career that allows passionate self-expression and physical labor. You may have pursued dance, music, or foreign exploration.

Your relationships may have been passionate and occasionally tempestuous. You would need a hardy partner who would find you energizing. Leos may succeed at taming you. Pisceans and Scorpios tend to enjoy the energy of a high-intensity partner.

Geminis know what a fire can do; Sagittarians remember the burn. You may have suffered several burns on your journey, challenging you to overcome any fear. Lucky for you, your greatest strength may be a bottomless sense of optimism and possibility. With maturity, you could enjoy the benefits of your wide-ranging experiences.

► Read about your Chinese Astrological sign on page 838. ► Read about your Personal Planets on page 826. ► Read about your personal Mystical Card on page 856.

CAPRICORN

From December 22, 2:45 through December 31, 23:59

The Artful Innovator

The sign of Capricorn rules industry, productivity, and functionality. December 26, 1924, was a sad day for the art world. Taken over by right-wing elements, the government of Thuringia, Germany, dealt a death blow to the Bauhaus art movement by withdrawing financing for the Weimar-based school of architecture and design founded by Walter Gropius. Reflecting ideals of the German left, Bauhaus promoted productive workshops and functional design in architecture, pottery, painting, weaving, metal and wood working, and more. With eminent artists such as Paul Klee, Lyonel Feininger, and Wassily Kandinsky teaching at the Bauhaus school, the movement combined brilliant aesthetic values with practical, accessible applications.

Bauhaus absolutely reflects the aesthetics and ideals of the sign of Capricorn. Members of your sign embrace practicality, usability, and accessibility. Designer labels are meaningless without first-rate craftsmanship. You might like the Bauhaus branded line of ready-to-wear products, however, because it was geared for mass use and industrial scale production. Indeed, the Bauhaus movement gave birth to the field of industrial design.

Indicators in your chart show the capacity to lead new movements and innovate as necessary. Adversity may energize you. A deliciously wicked sense of humor can empower you to surmount challenges. You may have climbed the ladder in industry, statecraft, or construction and development.

Relationships may give you a comfort zone, where you can let down your guard and relax. Your partner may have been someone who could be trusted to see the wilder side of your personality. Taureans are faithful, solid, and indulgent. Scorpios love to share naughty secrets. Cancerians provide safe refuge at home.

As someone likely to thrive in challenging circumstances, your greatest test may have been to get others to surrender their objections and fall in line with you. You needed to find a way to win support without beating people over the head. In maturity, a successful track record may have been your most valuable asset and strength.

1924

CAPRICORN
Your Personal Planets

YOUR LOVE POTENTIAL
Venus in Sagittarius, Dec. 22, 2:45 - Dec. 31, 23:59

YOUR DRIVE AND AMBITION
Mars in Aries, Dec. 22, 2:45 - Dec. 31, 23:59

YOUR LUCK MAGNETISM
Jupiter in Capricorn, Dec. 22, 2:45 - Dec. 31, 23:59

World Events

Dec. 26 – The Weimar Bauhaus in Germany closes down.

Dec. 29 – John D. Rockefeller makes a million-dollar donation to the Metropolitan Museum of Art.

F. Scott Fitzgerald,
September 24, 1896 - December 21, 1940

F. SCOTT FITZGERALD
Libra

Flappers, the "Lost Generation," the Jazz Age—all were chronicled by F. Scott Fitzgerald. His writings mirrored the times in lyrical prose, wit, and keen social observation. At 23, he won "overnight" success with his first novel. He and his wife, Zelda, became media darlings of the day. Stories of their escapades, and later drunken fights and self-destruction, became widespread until, like the stock market crash of 1929, their lives suffered a "crack-up." By the time he died at the young age of 44, Fitzgerald considered himself a has-been and public opinion seemed to agree.

With six of his planets in air signs (communication) and his Libra Sun and Taurus Moon, both ruled by artistic Venus, Fitzgerald was born to be a writer. The Taurean Moon in the house of communication indicated his realistic style as well as his fascination with wealth and the popularity of his short stories. Energetic Mars and inspired Neptune were joined in quick-witted Gemini in his house of creativity, giving him great ambition to write and a vivid imagination. Negatively, contacts with Mars and Neptune may often indicate seeking escape in drugs—in his case, alcohol.

But with taskmaster Saturn in close contact with erratic Uranus, no matter how extreme his behavior became, he applied discipline and fine craftsmanship in his writing. These same planets in his house of travel indicated the kind of gypsy life he and his family led. He revised his masterwork *The Great Gatsby* in Rome and it was published while they were en route to Paris.

Fitzgerald's writing life was closely tied to his personal life. His Sun (personality), Mercury (thought) and Venus (affection) were all in gracious, loving Libra, but placed in the eighth house, ruled by Scorpio, were deepened and made more passionate. His Libran need for a partner was emphasized by Jupiter, the planet of expansion, in his house of relationships. And Jupiter's ruler Pluto, the planet of transformation, in the house of personal foundations indicated the power struggles with his wife, Zelda, who was a source of material for

him as well as a creative rival with artistic ambitions of her own. With her mental breakdown and his increased drinking, their lives fell apart.

When his unfinished novel *The Last Tycoon* was published after his death, however, his reputation rose and he took his place among the great American authors of the twentieth century.

➤ Read Salman Rushdie's Star Profile on page 697.

1925

Saturn in Scorpio: *Mein Kampf* is Published

On July 18, 1925, Adolph Hitler's anti-Semitic treatise, *Mein Kampf* was published. The planet Saturn was in Scorpio at this time. Scorpio is ruled by both Pluto and Mars and is considered by many to be the most powerful sign of the zodiac. It is connected to intense emotion, desire, and true transformation. Possessiveness, jealousy, and violence are within the domain of Scorpio. Under the influence of Saturn in Scorpio there can be a tendency to scheme and plot. This placement can cause deep resentment and fanaticism. Hitler outlined his plans for the decimation of the Jews of Germany in his evil tract. In it, he said, "And so I believe today that my conduct is in accordance with the will of the Almighty Creator. In standing guard against the Jew I am defending the handiwork of the Lord." Saturn's residence in Scorpio encouraged the public to be open to such ugliness and rage in the name of German nationalism.

Hitler's book was written while he was in prison, where he formulated his plans for world-domination. When Saturn enters Scorpio, there is a serious emotional sensitivity that can have a heavy, burdensome quality to it. When people are affected by this placement they desire authority and will go to any lengths to attain their desires and ambitions. There is a desire for revenge when Saturn meets Scorpio. There is also a relentless drive toward perfectionism, evidenced by Hitler's ghastly ideas of the Aryan race. The publishing of *Mein Kampf* was the first step in Hitler's rise to power; what would follow would change the world forever.

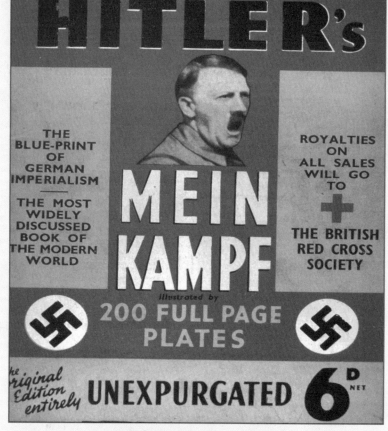

Hitler's "Mein Kampf" is published

Josephine Baker becomes the toast of Paris

Forty-thousand Ku Klux Klansmen march on Washington

LEY LINES

In 1925, Alfred Watkins published *The Old Straight Track* in which he established his theory of "leys." He described leys as the alignments and patterns of powerful, invisible earth-energy, designed by ancient peoples to connect various sacred sites, such as churches, temples, stone circles, megaliths, holy wells, burial sites, and other locations of spiritual or magical importance. Although controversial, adherents to this theory believe that ley lines mark the path of an energy that can be detected by dowsing.

JAZZ AND *MEIN KAMPF*

Adolf Hitler revived his banned Nazi party and revealed his anti-Semitic, anti-Communist policies in the newly published *Mein Kampf*, which roused nationalist fervor among Germans. In Soviet Russia, a determined Stalin ousted Trotsky. A demilitarized zone was set up along the Rhine by the Locarno Agreement, in which six nations, including Germany, pledged to uphold peace. Germany was later admitted to membership of the League of Nations. Tennessee banned the teaching of evolution in public schools, because it contradicted the Bible creation story. In the largest open display ever, 40,000 white-robed Ku Klux Klansmen marched on Washington, but the event was washed out by heavy rain. The smallpox vaccine spread confidence in the battle against disease. Slighted in the U.S. because of her race, dancer and singer Josephine Baker became the toast of Paris in *The Negro Review*. The Charleston, a dance named for its town of origin, was the craze of all age groups. Charlie Chaplin's *The Gold Rush* amused movie audiences, while Lon Chaney Snr. frightened them in *The Phantom of the Opera*. F. Scott Fitzgerald published *The Great Gatsby*.

➤ Read Josephine Baker's Star Profile on page 217.

CAPRICORN

From January 01, 0:00 through January 20, 13:19

The Principled Leader

The sign of Capricorn rules the consolidation of power. Within days of your birth, Benito Mussolini was tightening his grip over Italy and Joseph Stalin was taking control of the Soviet Union. On January 5, 1925, Mussolini bullied two Liberal ministers into leaving his cabinet. In a campaign to remove all opposition from his government, Mussolini dispatched police to search the homes of dissident ministers, seize documents, and forcibly disband political and press organizations that presented any challenge to Fascism. On January 16, Leon Trotsky was ousted from the Soviet War Council, a development that increased the influence of Stalin, Grigori Zinoviev, and Lev Kamenev in the Communist party.

You are likely to be an ambitious and an effective leader but the ruthless tactics of Stalin or Mussolini would have horrified you. Still in power by the time you reached adulthood, the two dictators may have served as your model of how not to behave. The suffering and destruction caused by the Fascists or Soviets may have moved you to fight such regimes and the values they represent.

Indicators in your chart suggest that brutality and intimidation would be repellant to you. Likely to be compassionate, inspiring, and principled, you can wield the power of positive motivation. Practical problem-solving skills may have brought you success in organizing and running businesses in your community.

Relationships may bring out your tenderness, a feeling that may trigger a fiercely protective instinct. You were likely to choose a partner who was sympathetic and reliable. Scorpios help you turn pain into power. Cancerians calm your fears and provide a safe space for your feelings. Sagittarians recharge your sense of optimism and good humor.

You may have an extraordinary ability to rebuild from the ashes of hard experience. As a member of the generation that survived the Depression and World War II, the early years of your life may have been quite painful. Your challenge may have been to regenerate your capacity for a joyful family life with time and the opportunity to create better conditions.

AQUARIUS

From January 20, 13:20 through February 19, 3:42

The Original Thinker

The sign of Aquarius rules scientific breakthroughs with revolutionary implications. On February 3, in South Africa, Australian anthropologist Raymond Dart announced the discovery of a fossilized skull that represented the earliest human being. Dating the fossil to two to three million years in the past, Dart claimed that this human ancestor, "Australopithecus," was the "missing link" between humans and the apes. The theory of a relationship between humans and apes would trigger one of the greatest debates between science and religion, a controversy that would culminate in the Scopes Monkey Trial in May of 1925.

The conflict between evolution theory and creationism may have been among your most interesting subjects of study in school. Aquarians tend to credit the validity of scientific inquiry. This does not mean that you lack spirituality, but you may draw a bright line between earthly reality and matters of faith. Likely to think in practical, concrete terms, you may strenuously resist any religion-related attempts to limit your freedom.

Some of your best ideas may have come to you in your sleep. If you found yourself unable to let go of a confounding problem, your dreams may have furnished the solution by morning. Solving puzzles and unraveling mysteries may thrill you. You may have had a career in applied science, research, or any field involving the pursuit of original ideas.

Relationships may have provided a safe place for expressing your spiritual and romantic side. You were likely to choose a partner who shared your unique sense of idealism. Leos encourage you to pursue your aspirations. Ariens offer the excitement of trying new things. Pisceans watch out for the spiritual side of your humanitarian values.

You may have gone through your own trials in overturning entrenched systems and obsolete values that, from your perspective, had outlived their purpose. "But that's the way we've always done it," is the statement most likely to enrage you. Your challenge may be to let go of the frustrating obstacles along the way and take pride in your accomplishments.

▶ Read about your Chinese Astrological sign on page 838. ▶ Read about your Personal Planets on page 826. ▶ Read about your personal Mystical Card on page 856.

1925

CAPRICORN
Your Personal Planets

YOUR LOVE POTENTIAL
Venus in Sagittarius, Jan. 01, 0:00 - Jan. 14, 22:27
Venus in Capricorn, Jan. 14, 22:28 - Jan. 20, 13:19

YOUR DRIVE AND AMBITION
Mars in Aries, Jan. 01, 0:00 - Jan. 20, 13:19

YOUR LUCK MAGNETISM
Jupiter in Capricorn, Jan. 01, 0:00 - Jan. 20, 13:19

World Events

Jan. 5 – Nellie Taylor Ross becomes the first woman governor in the U.S., in Wyoming.
Jan. 14 – Japanese author Yukio Mishima is born.

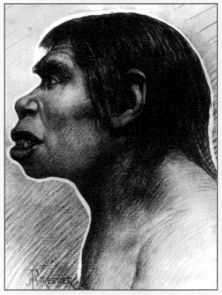

A sketch of an early man who could be the "missing link"

AQUARIUS
Your Personal Planets

YOUR LOVE POTENTIAL
Venus in Capricorn, Jan. 20, 13:20 - Feb. 07, 23:15
Venus in Aquarius, Feb. 07, 23:16 - Feb. 19, 3:42

YOUR DRIVE AND AMBITION
Mars in Aries, Jan. 20, 13:20 - Feb. 05, 10:16
Mars in Taurus, Feb. 05, 10:17 - Feb. 19, 3:42

YOUR LUCK MAGNETISM
Jupiter in Capricorn, Jan. 20, 13:20 - Feb. 19, 3:42

World Events

Jan. 21 – British comedian Benny Hill is born.
Feb. 3 – A fossilized skull of early man, believed to be the "missing link," is found in South Africa.

1925

PISCES
Your Personal Planets

YOUR LOVE POTENTIAL
Venus in Aquarius, Feb. 19, 3:43 - Mar. 04, 0:20
Venus in Pisces, Mar. 04, 0:21 - Mar. 21, 3:11

YOUR DRIVE AND AMBITION
Mars in Taurus, Feb. 19, 3:43 - Mar. 21, 3:11

YOUR LUCK MAGNETISM
Jupiter in Capricorn, Feb. 19, 3:43 - Mar. 21, 3:11

World Events

Feb. 20 – American film director Robert Altman is born.

Mar. 12 – Chinese rebel leader Sun Yat-Sen dies.

F. Scott Fitzgerald with his wife Zelda and their daughter

ARIES
Your Personal Planets

YOUR LOVE POTENTIAL
Venus in Pisces, Mar. 21, 3:12 - Mar. 28, 3:03
Venus in Aries, Mar. 28, 3:04 - Apr. 20, 14:50

YOUR DRIVE AND AMBITION
Mars in Taurus, Mar. 21, 3:12 - Mar. 24, 0:41
Mars in Gemini, Mar. 24, 0:42 - Apr. 20, 14:50

YOUR LUCK MAGNETISM
Jupiter in Capricorn, Mar. 21, 3:12 - Apr. 20, 14:50

World Events

Apr. 1 – The Hebrew University of Jerusalem opens in the face of Arab protest demonstrations.

Apr. 10 – F. Scott Fitzgerald's *The Great Gatsby* is published in New York.

212

PISCES

From February 19, 3:43 through March 21, 3:11

The Compassionate Rebel

The sign of Pisces rules illusions and deception. On February 27, 1925, Adolf Hitler, out of jail for two months, organized an assembly in Munich's Hofbrau Haus, where he announced "a new beginning" for the German National Socialist Workers' Party. The year of your birth was truly springtime for Hitler. This time he promised to renounce the use of force and to rebuild his movement through purely legal aims. He lied.

Every sign has its dark side and your identity as a Pisces does not destine you to become a liar. The greatest risk for Pisceans, who can be impressionable, is to be taken in by others or to harbor illusions themselves. Indeed, many good people of all signs allowed themselves to harbor illusions about Hitler because the alternative was too horrible—more violence in a world that had been thoroughly devastated and exhausted by World War I and its turbulent aftermath.

Likely to be romantic and idealistic, you may tend to believe the best about people. If you ever made the mistake of assuming that all people were as kind and decent as you are, the discovery of those who were not may have moved you to take dramatic action. You may have been a resistance fighter, a relief worker, a medic, or someone who preserved delicacy through music or poetry.

Relationships may have provided you with spiritual solace and encouragement. You were likely to choose a partner who protected all that was tender and refined about you. A safe haven awaits you in Cancerians' arms. Leos can keep you smiling on your darkest days. Virgos keep you busy with productive activities.

Your chart shows the potential for a challenge similar to that of people who felt uneasy about Hitler but failed to take decisive action against him early on. You may have sometimes felt strong urges to take harsh action or to show initiative, but self doubt and reservations may have held you back. Later in life, you may have struck a compromise between these two forces. By proceeding thoughtfully and with a well-organized strategy, you could channel anger and energy into a highly focused laser beam of power.

ARIES

From March 21, 3:12 through April 20, 14:50

The Intellectual Warrior

The sign of Aries rules epic battles and March 23, 1925, marked the first step in what would become one of the epic intellectual battles of the twentieth century. On that day, the governor of Tennessee signed a law banning the teaching of evolutionary theory in state-supported schools. On May 25, 1925, the indictment of John T. Scopes, a Tennessee high-school teacher, for teaching Darwinian theory would lead to the Scopes Monkey Trial. Arrayed against Scopes and evolution were prosecutor William Jennings Bryan and the Creationist movement. On Scopes' side were the international scientific community, the doctrine of separation of Church and State, the ghost of Charles Darwin, and Clarence Darrow. Scopes would lose the battle, but the war would go to evolution, science, and the United States Constitution.

You may get a charge out of a good intellectual battle. The contest between evolution and creationism unfolded throughout your life and may have affected your own schooling. The U.S. Supreme Court did not throw out laws against evolution theory until 1968.

Likely to be a crusader for academic freedom, you may pursue information with a passion. Knowledge is power, and you may resist attempts to limit your free access as fiercely as you would resist attempts to dominate or control you. A talent for networking may have enabled you to promote profitable social, educational, and industry connections. You may have worked in business, academia, or communications.

Relationships may provide you with a private source of empowerment and advancement. You were likely to choose a partner who would encourage your ambitions. Scorpios channel inner power into your outer drive. Geminis encourage your quest for knowledge. Sagittarians push you to realize your greatest aspirations.

Your drive to learn may have empowered you to become an expert in many fields. While a good intellectual scrap may have been energizing for you, your "desk-side manner" may have been intimidating to people with thinner skins. Your greatest challenge may have been to learn to state your case with greater diplomacy.

➤ Read about your Chinese Astrological sign on page 838. ➤ Read about your Personal Planets on page 826. ➤ Read about your personal Mystical Card on page 856.

TAURUS

From April 20, 14:51 through May 21, 14:32

The Healthy Skeptic

The sign of Taurus rules creature comforts and conservative leanings. When you were born, news items suggested a conflict between these two values. In May of 1925, doctors in Britain were preparing to publish an article on the hazards silk stockings posed to women. An article in the *British Medical Journal* warned that wearing silk stockings in cold weather resulted in chafing and puffiness of the skin. Doctors attributed this condition to the scanty covering of the exposed portion of the leg between the tops of ladies' shoes and the bottom of their skirts.

Given the frequency with which doctors of this era diagnosed hysteria in women, the neurotic fixation on women's clothing and hairstyles was not remarkable. When you reached adulthood, you may have appreciated the seeming coincidence between women's political freedom and the increasing attention that doctors and politicians paid to women's fashion and habits. You may have a keen understanding of psychology and a natural suspicion of ulterior motives.

Taureans tend to enjoy clothing and furnishings that are sumptuous, lovely, and pleasant to the touch. You may feel that fashion is not as important as comfort and ease of movement. Once you find clothing or furnishings that work for you, new trends are unlikely to change your preferences or habits. You may be highly creative, sensuous, and indulgent. You may have worked as a designer, artist, or therapist.

Your closest relationship may have been an emotional world unto itself, filled with privately expressed passion. You were likely to choose a partner who shared your intensity of commitment. The comfort of a long-term bond allows Capricorns to become more vulnerable. Scorpios may feel like your long lost soul mate. Cancerians offer deep devotion to family.

You have a healthy streak of skepticism that may have protected you and your resources. Sensible distrust may have saved you from being hoodwinked, but it also might have prevented you from enjoying profitable opportunities. With maturity, you may have become better attuned to the subtleties of your instincts.

GEMINI

From May 21, 14:33 through June 21, 22:49

The Passionate Student

Gemini rules transportation and aviation. May 21, 1925, saw the departure of Roald Amundsen, famed polar explorer, to reach the North Pole by plane. Amundsen's six-member team took off in two Dornier Wal flying boats from Kings Bay on the island of Spitzbergen. On June 18, Amundsen returned to Spitzbergen after a four-week ordeal that began with an emergency landing 250 kilometers short of his goal. One of the planes was badly damaged by the landing and could not be repaired. Fierce weather further interfered with the building of a runway on the polar ice. Toward the end of June, all six members of the expedition packed themselves into the remaining plane and made it back to Spitzbergen.

When you were old enough to learn about Amundsen's attempt to fly to the North Pole, you may have become fascinated by the amazing stories of polar exploration in the decades prior to your birth. While you may have a fascination with death-defying stunts, you are more likely to pursue them in the pages of history than real life. Some people may find history boring but your powers of imagination may enable you to feel what conditions and events were really like for the people who experienced them.

You may have a willful and dynamic personality. Geminis can have sensitive nerves, and you may have adopted an athletic discipline to channel excess energy and maintain good health. Likely to be a team player and a devoted co-worker, you may have pursued a career involving research, detective work, or psychological analysis.

Relationships offer you the chance to collaborate in public and at home. You were likely to choose a partner eager to offer another point of view. Scorpios offer a deep, emotional perspective. Sagittarians help you see the big picture. You may enjoy Capricorn's sense of humor.

Your passion for your favorite subjects or activities may have brought you a large measure of success. Your challenge may have been not to feel misunderstood if others failed to share your enthusiasm. Gravitating to people equally as intense as you may have helped you avoid isolation and loneliness.

➤ Read about your Chinese Astrological sign on page 838. ➤ Read about your Personal Planets on page 826. ➤ Read about your personal Mystical Card on page 856.

TAURUS
Your Personal Planets

YOUR LOVE POTENTIAL
Venus in Aries, Apr. 20, 14:51 - Apr. 21, 8:13
Venus in Taurus, Apr. 21, 8:14 - May 15, 16:03
Venus in Gemini, May 15, 16:04 - May 21, 14:32

YOUR DRIVE AND AMBITION
Mars in Gemini, Mar. 20, 14:51 - May 09, 22:43
Mars in Cancer, May 09, 22:44 - May 21, 14:32

YOUR LUCK MAGNETISM
Jupiter in Capricorn, Apr. 20, 14:51 - May 21, 14:32

World Events

May 1 – The island of Cyprus becomes a British colony.

May 19 – Civil rights activist Malcolm X (Malcolm Little) is born.

An anti-evolution Fundamentalist bookshop in Tennessee

GEMINI
Your Personal Planets

YOUR LOVE POTENTIAL
Venus in Gemini, May 21, 14:33 - June 09, 2:13
Venus in Cancer, June 09, 2:14 - June 21, 22:49

YOUR DRIVE AND AMBITION
Mars in Cancer, May 21, 14:33 - June 21, 22:49

YOUR LUCK MAGNETISM
Jupiter in Capricorn, May 21, 14:33 - June 21, 22:49

World Events

May 25 – Tennessee schoolteacher John Scopes is indicted under an anti-evolution law on a charge of teaching Darwin's theories.

June 11 – The first murder in the skies takes place when a London gem dealer is thrown from an airplane.

1925

CANCER
Your Personal Planets

YOUR LOVE POTENTIAL
Venus in Cancer, June 21, 22:50 - July 03, 14:30
Venus in Leo, July 03, 14:31 - July 23, 9:44

YOUR DRIVE AND AMBITION
Mars in Cancer, June 21, 22:50 - June 26, 9:07
Mars in Leo, June 26, 9:08 - July 23, 9:44

YOUR LUCK MAGNETISM
Jupiter in Capricorn, June 21, 22:50 - July 23, 9:44

World Events

July 18 - Adolf Hitler's book *Mein Kampf* is published.

July 21 - John Scopes is found guilty of teaching Darwin's theories of evolution; he is fined $100.

Charlie Chaplin in "The Gold Rush"

LEO
Your Personal Planets

YOUR LOVE POTENTIAL
Venus in Leo, July 23, 9:45 - July 28, 5:24
Venus in Virgo, July 28, 5:25 - Aug. 22, 0:27
Venus in Libra, Aug. 22, 0:28 - Aug. 23, 16:32

YOUR DRIVE AND AMBITION
Mars in Leo, July 23, 9:45 - Aug. 12, 21:11
Mars in Virgo, Aug. 12, 21:12 - Aug. 23, 16:32

YOUR LUCK MAGNETISM
Jupiter in Capricorn, July 23, 9:45 - Aug. 23, 16:32

World Events

Aug. 16 - Charlie Chaplin's film *The Gold Rush* opens in the U.S.

Aug. 20 - Leon Trotsky takes over as leader of the Soviet Economic Council.

CANCER
From June 21, 22:50 through July 23, 9:44

The Precocious Caretaker

The sign of Cancer has an association with women and travel. In 1925, the Automobile Association of America announced that women were as competent behind the wheel as men. Both women and Cancerians have often been stereotyped as homebodies. In 1925, women were expanding their roles and identities beyond the home. Similarly, while the sign of Cancer rules the home, members of this sign tend to enjoy travel so long as they can bring along a smaller, moveable version of their living quarters. Designed to convey a family unit with plenty of room for provisions, the car is the perfect Cancerian mode of transportation. Membership in automobile associations responds to Cancerian concerns by providing protection, direction, and rescue in case of emergency.

Likely to be highly parental in disposition, you may be a firm disciplinarian and stern taskmaster. Challenging circumstances early in your life may have forced you to take on a serious, stoic approach to life. Growing up through the Great Depression may have required you to stretch limited resources. Then, the threat of starvation and death multiplied to unimaginable proportions during World War II.

You may have played the role of "little adult" in your family. If your parents were coping with their own anxieties, you may have worked hard to bring comfort and encouragement to them and your siblings. Your caretaker skills may have made you a talented social worker, doctor, nurse, or clergy member.

Relationships can give you an opportunity to regain your childhood. You may have chosen a partner who needed you, but the tables may have turned later in your lives. Capricorn's fun-loving side may surprise you. Scorpios can help you transcend the pain of the past. Leos can rejuvenate your sense of wonder and your ability to be playful.

Your strong discipline and ability to act responsibly may have enabled you to survive adversity. But all work and no play make a Cancerian an unhappy creature. Over time, you were likely to find that the challenges you endured could also increase your appreciation for the good things in life.

LEO
From July 23, 9:45 through August 23, 16:32

The Spotlight Seeker

The sign of Leo rules entertainment and childlike characters and, within days of your birth, a certain little tramp was charming film audiences around the world. *The Gold Rush* was released on August 16, 1925, starring British native and Hollywood legend Charlie Chaplin. The film—regarded as Chaplin's best and his personal favorite—included classic scenes often honored through mimicry in films by later artists. Set in the Klondike of Alaska during the Gold Rush, the film featured scenes such as Chaplin's dancing dinner rolls, two starving prospectors eating a shoe for Thanksgiving, a cabin teetering on the edge of a cliff, and Chaplin running into the wind and getting nowhere.

By the time you were old enough to go to the movies, the "talkies" were threatening to blow silent films into oblivion. Still, Chaplin was likely to be among the favorite of children everywhere for his mastery of pantomime, his ingenious sight gags, and the emotional appeal of his films. The movies offered a pleasant escape during the Great Depression. After you grew up, movies provided a getaway from the stresses of your workday.

Perhaps you dreamed of seeing your name in lights. Leos tend to enjoy being in the spotlight where they can be noticed and applauded. You were likely to work long and hard to make your dream come true. You may have participated in amateur theater productions, pursued a career in acting, or sought recognition as an expert in your profession.

In relationships, you are likely to be dramatic and romantic. You may have been attracted to a partner who provided enough tension to keep passions running high. Scorpios can provide a willful tug-of-war. The roving routines of Geminis and Sagittarians render reunions all the more romantic.

Once you set your heart on a certain course of action, your determination can be unbeatable. Your ambitions may have invited the disapproval of your parents or guardians, challenging your choices. Others' support and encouragement matters to you. With maturity, however, you were likely to demand respect for your need to be true to yourself.

► Read about your Chinese Astrological sign on page 838. ► Read about your Personal Planets on page 826. ► Read about your personal Mystical Card on page 856.

VIRGO

From August 23, 16:33 through September 23, 13:42

The Dancing Organizer

The sign of Virgo rules health, nutrition, and physical exercise. Food shortages had plagued Europe in the wake of World War I but in the late summer of 1925, a drought threatened to create crop failures in the United States. The news on September 5, 1925, reported that water was being sold by the gallon to farmers. On the lighter side, with the Jazz Age in full swing, a new dance craze was sweeping the country. The signature dance of the Roaring twenties, the Charleston, had people of all ages raising their hands in a hallelujah sparkle and swinging their legs from front to back. By autumn, the Charleston would create a sensation, first in Paris, then all over Europe.

The art of dance is a Piscean matter, but its physicality and health benefits are all yours, Virgo. The Charleston owed its popularity to its simplicity. The dance became an American classic, enjoying a longevity that extended well into the future. At family celebrations, you may have danced the Charleston with your grandchildren and they may have marveled at your vigor. Likely to have had an abundance of vitality, you may have channeled excess energy through dance, exercise routines, or hard work.

Paying attention to details may come to you effortlessly, and you may have excellent organizational skills. Approximately every three months, you may feel that your mental sharpness has left you. Treat this as a signal of your need for some rest and relaxation. Virgos of 1925 born before September 5 may actually feel better and more highly attuned at this time.

Good communication may be the secret to the longevity of your relationship. You may be happiest with a partner who expresses love through thoughtful gestures and words. Taureans lavish you with gifts. Pisceans know just what you need and when. Librans know the right thing to say.

Attention to detail invests you with a capacity for excellence, but overemphasis on perfectionism can alienate loved ones and leave you vulnerable to chronic disappointment. Maturity may have graced you with a greater appreciation for progress and a sincere show of effort.

LIBRA

From September 23, 13:43 through October 23, 22:30

The Creative Iconoclast

Ancient mythology links the sign of Libra with Venus, the goddess of love, beauty, and the arts. In October 1925, a beautiful black Venus descended upon the Paris Theatre des Champs-Elysees. Casting an enchanting spell with the Jazz Age rhythms of Harlem, New York, the goddess appeared in the form of legendary singer and dancer Josephine Baker, starring in *La Revue Nègre*. Making a stunning entrance clothed only in a pink flamingo feather, Ms. Baker introduced the audience to the latest dance rage in the U.S., the Charleston. New Yorker correspondent Janet Flanner described Ms. Baker as "an unforgettable female ebony statue" who aroused a "scream of salutation" from the audience. Ms. Baker's appearance triggered a craze in Paris for African-American culture and launched her on a career that lasted into her late sixties.

Many people were offended by the flamboyance of Ms. Baker's act, but the longevity of her celebrated career easily eclipsed the objections of her detractors. You are likely to have a passion for cutting edge art that defies convention and arouses controversy.

In fact, you may be somewhat rebellious and iconoclastic in every area of your life. As a diplomatic Libran, you also have the ability to ease people's fears about shocking trends in art or politics. Drawn to careers that allowed you to pioneer, promote, and popularize new and innovative movements, you may have worked as an artist, critic, educator, or gallery curator.

Relationships provide you with an opportunity to collaborate in romantic and other aspects of life. You were likely to choose a partner who would provide a competing but respectful point of view. Aquarians offer defiantly eccentric tastes. Sagittarians have an open mind. Ariens invented the avant-garde.

Your hunger for artistic inspiration can cause you to gravitate to the fringes of society, a fertile ground for breakthroughs and important innovations. Your enlightened point of view can help to focus attention on neglected contributors to culture. With maturity you may have learned to deftly counter censorious objections.

► Read about your Chinese Astrological sign on page 838. ► Read about your Personal Planets on page 826. ► Read about your personal Mystical Card on page 856.

VIRGO
Your Personal Planets

YOUR LOVE POTENTIAL
Venus in Libra, Aug. 23, 16:33 - Sept. 16, 2:04
Venus in Scorpio, Sept. 16, 2:05 - Sept. 23, 13:42

YOUR DRIVE AND AMBITION
Mars in Virgo, Aug. 23, 16:33 - Sept. 23, 13:42

YOUR LUCK MAGNETISM
Jupiter in Capricorn, Aug. 23, 16:33 - Sept. 23, 13:42

World Events

Sept. 8 – Germany is accepted into the League of Nations.

Sept. 16 – American blues singer B. B. King is born.

British politician Margaret Thatcher is born under the sign of Libra

LIBRA
Your Personal Planets

YOUR LOVE POTENTIAL
Venus in Scorpio, Sept. 23, 13:43 - Oct. 11, 14:09
Venus in Sagittarius, Oct. 11, 14:10 - Oct. 23, 22:30

YOUR DRIVE AND AMBITION
Mars in Virgo, Sept. 23, 13:43 - Sept. 28, 19:00
Mars in Libra, Sept. 28, 19:01 - Oct. 23, 22:30

YOUR LUCK MAGNETISM
Jupiter in Capricorn, Sept. 23, 13:43 - Oct. 23, 22:30

World Events

Oct. 12 – Germany and the USSR sign a treaty of commerce.

Oct. 13 – British politician Margaret Thatcher is born.

1925

SCORPIO
Your Personal Planets

YOUR LOVE POTENTIAL
Venus in Sagittarius, Oct. 23, 22:31 - Nov. 06, 22:33
Venus in Capricorn, Nov. 06, 22:34 - Nov. 22, 19:34

YOUR DRIVE AND AMBITION
Mars in Libra, Oct. 23, 22:31 - Nov. 13, 14:01
Mars in Scorpio, Nov. 13, 14:02 - Nov. 22, 19:34

YOUR LUCK MAGNETISM
Jupiter in Capricorn, Oct. 23, 22:31 - Nov. 22, 19:34

World Events

Oct. 30 - Scottish inventor John Logie Baird makes the first television broadcast.

Nov. 14 - The first collective exposition of the Surrealists opens in Paris, featuring works by Max Ernst, Man Ray, Joan Miro, and Pablo Picasso.

Nobel Prize winner George Bernard Shaw

SAGITTARIUS
Your Personal Planets

YOUR LOVE POTENTIAL
Venus in Capricorn, Nov. 22, 19:35 - Dec. 05, 15:08
Venus in Aquarius, Dec. 05, 15:09 - Dec. 22, 8:36

YOUR DRIVE AND AMBITION
Mars in Scorpio, Nov. 22, 19:35 - Dec. 22, 8:36

YOUR LUCK MAGNETISM
Jupiter in Capricorn, Nov. 22, 19:35 - Dec. 22, 8:36

World Events

Dec. 1 - British troops begin to move out of the Cologne region of Germany; they have been a presence there since the last year of World War I.

Dec. 10 - George Bernard Shaw is awarded the Nobel Prize for literature.

SCORPIO
From October 23, 22:31 through November 22, 19:34

The Dreamy Dynamo

The sign of Scorpio rules psychology and psychoanalysis. When you were born, a new artistic movement was drawing its inspiration from the subconscious minds of its creators. November 14, 1925, marked the first collective exhibition of the Surrealists at the Pierre Loeb Gallery in Paris. The canvases of surrealist painters such as Man Ray, Giorgio De Chirico, and Joan Miro opened a window into a world of dreams, fantasy, nightmares, and inner demons. The poet, Andre Breton, presented works created through "automatic writing," a technique in which the writer attempted to work himself or herself into a trance state that allowed words to flow by free association, without forethought or rational argument.

When you were old enough to discover the Surrealists, their works and philosophies may have struck you as a revelation. Surrealist paintings and writings reflect Scorpio-like concerns, which are likely to figure large in your life: involuntary urges, deep feelings, metaphysical perception, and subconscious imagery. You may have struggled to get such input under control.

You may have a compelling, magnetic personality that some may find hypnotic. Indicators in your chart show powerful unconscious stimuli that can create tremendous tension if you do not channel them in healthy ways. Writing, art, or psychotherapy can help you transform this tension into a geyser of creative inspiration. You may have pursued a career as an artist, writer, therapist, or theologian.

Your relationships are likely to be passionate and exciting. You may have chosen a partner who could handle you without turning every tiny issue into a full-blown power struggle. Intuitive Cancerians and compassionate Pisceans easily navigate through your world of dreams. Taureans keeps you from venturing too far from the material world.

You may be a dynamo of subconscious inspiration and motivation. Your greatest challenge may have been to assert some control over all that fire in your belly. Maturity was likely to bring you the insight and discipline necessary to channel your energy into a beneficial force.

SAGITTARIUS
From November 22, 19:35 through December 22, 8:36

The Master Strategist

The sign of Sagittarius rules politics, ideology, and propaganda. You were born at a time of tremendous worldwide political instability. In the wake of World War I, borders and governments remained fluid in Europe, North Africa, and the Middle East. New political groups vied for power and position. Tending to draw fine ideological distinctions, the groups often splintered into factions and sub-factions. It was common for average people to have strong and very specific opinions. Leaflets and position papers flew like confetti. In December of 1925, Representative Hamilton Fish introduced a bill in Congress warning Italy against distributing fascist propaganda in the United States.

You came of age at a time when all these forces boiled over into the conflagration of World War II. You, your friends, and loved ones may have fought against Mussolini and Hitler and witnessed the devastation and atrocities their ideologies wrought. As a Sagittarian, you already have an instinctive appreciation for the political impact of words and arguments. Your lived experience, however, may have reinforced your instinct with concrete evidence and personal pain.

Your chart shows all the elements of a master strategist. Just as Mozart walked around with complete symphonies in his head, you may walk around with professional treatises in yours. You are likely to have an intuitive understanding of power dynamics in the world, in the workplace, or in the family. You may have had a career in politics, academia, industry, or the military.

Early relationships may have been intense and volatile. You would have succeeded best with a partner who could help you work through emotional challenges. Geminis are willing to listen. Pisceans bring spiritual insight. Librans can mediate and defuse strong feelings.

You may have the power, drive, and discipline to lead armies and found new nations. The exceptional influences in your chart may have proven a blessing or a daunting burden. With maturity, you may have learned to moderate the amount of responsibility you were willing or prepared to handle.

► Read about your Chinese Astrological sign on page 838. ► Read about your Personal Planets on page 826. ► Read about your personal Mystical Card on page 856.

CAPRICORN

From December 22, 8:37 through December 31, 23:59

The Enterprising Innovator

The sign of Capricorn rules sobriety, realistic thinking, and the principle of supply and demand. At the end of December, the Mexican government outlawed the cultivation of marijuana and sent health department inspectors on a mission across the republic to destroy all crops and arrest persistent growers. The received wisdom at the time maintained that smoking marijuana cigarettes produced a murderous delirium and reduced its addicts to insanity. If America's experience with alcohol prohibition offered any indication about Mexico's prospects, the new law was likely to create a bonanza in market share for illicit Mexican growers. The drug wars would continue in America and Mexico up to the present day.

Prohibition would be repealed by the time you reached drinking age, and your children and grandchildren may have experimented with marijuana. In general, Capricorns have a pragmatic outlook and an appreciation for the laws of the marketplace. You are likely to personally believe in moderation in all things, including moderation.

In addressing complex challenges, you are likely to be the kind of person who can "think outside the box." Entrepreneurial ventures may have suited you best, as they would have allowed you to exercise your own initiative while building productive enterprises. Your discipline is strong, and you may have a good instinct for picking out powerful business allies. You may have been a pioneer in technology, research and development, or engineering.

In relationships, a deep, enduring friendship may have blossomed into a romance. You were likely to choose an optimistic partner who had a good sense of humor. Sagittarians take ups and downs in stride. Aquarians value your individuality. Scorpios offers you empowering insights to help you realize your ambitions.

You can commit strongly to projects in your long-term interest and yet, if developments warrant, you may change direction on a dime. People with a stake in your projects may react negatively to sudden reversals. Your challenge may have been to learn to prepare others for evolving circumstances.

1925

CAPRICORN
Your Personal Planets

YOUR LOVE POTENTIAL
Venus in Aquarius, Dec. 22, 8:37 - Dec. 31, 23:59

YOUR DRIVE AND AMBITION
Mars in Scorpio, Dec. 22, 8:37 - Dec. 28, 0:35
Mars in Sagittarius, Dec. 28, 0:36 - Dec. 31, 23:59

YOUR LUCK MAGNETISM
Jupiter in Capricorn, Dec. 22, 8:37 - Dec. 31, 23:59

World Events

Dec. 24 – Mussolini announces that he is second only to the King in Italy.

Dec. 26 – Six U.S. warships are sent to China in an effort to protect American interests in the civil war raging there.

JOSEPHINE BAKER
Gemini

Josephine Baker was the African-American performer who achieved far greater success and recognition in Europe than she ever could have in America. Limber, lanky, and a gyrating marvel on the stage, her African-inspired dances, in which she often wore nothing more than a skirt made of bananas, made her the toast of Paris and an icon of liberality and free-wheeling sensationalism.

Baker began performing in her teens and was singlemindedly devoted to building a career as an entertainer. Her Sun, planet of identity, was in Gemini, a sign noted for its speed, intelligence, and agility. Connections from both Mercury, planet of movement, and expansive Jupiter further increased her physical agility and gave her the unselfconscious, outgoing nature that allowed her to dance nude with *joie de vivre*. In addition, Baker's horoscope shows two other planets in Gemini, and this stellium, or cluster of energy, made her a true Gemini. Mars, the planet of action, is there, activated by

intense, sexy Pluto, and that is another reason for her unselfconscious nudity as well as her well-documented sex appeal.

With all this intense energy, there was much more to Baker than a sensational dancer. She was a determined and optimistic person, someone who felt she could be a force for change in the world, and she participated in the famous march on Washington at which Martin Luther King gave his celebrated "I have a dream" speech. Her vision of the world was so positive that she couldn't imagine failure. Even when her financial situation became troubled, she maintained her course of action.

With Venus, planet of love, in the tender, emotional sign of Cancer, Baker was a nurturing person. A contact from idealistic Neptune made her a bit of a dreamer where love is concerned, and she had quite a few failed marriages and relationships. Her real love was children, and she put her financial security on the line to adopt twelve children of mixed ethnicity, whom she

Josephine Baker
June 3, 1906 - April 12, 1975

dubbed her "Rainbow Tribe." With true grace and generosity, she opened her heart toward humanity in the hope of making the world a more hospitable place.

➤ Read Isadora Duncan's Star Profile on page 129. ➤ Read Martha Graham's Star Profile on page 297.

1926

Naïve Choices, Monetary Mayhem: Jupiter and Uranus

In 1926, the planet Jupiter, ruler of limitless expansion and joy, was in the inventive sign of Aquarius, ruler of independence, humanitarianism and brotherhood. As Jupiter floated through this intelligent air sign, it made an "opposition" in the sky to the planet Uranus, ruler of brand new ideas and the home sign for Aquarius. This occurred as Uranus was taking a long vacation in the fiery sign of Leo. When Jupiter opposes Uranus, we can expect restlessness and unwise decisions in the financial realm. As France struggled with its post-war problems, the value of the franc suffered a drastic fall and Raymond Poincaré formed a new coalition government. This aspect can cause an overabundance of optimism that can sometimes lead to naïve speculation with money. This risky energy was in full effect in 1926, an important year in the lead up to the market crash of 1929 that preceded the Great Depression. Overconfidence and idealism on Wall Street stoked the fires of public consumption and the scene was set for a downfall, the likes of which had never been experienced before in the United States.

Economic highs such as the ones experienced during the mid-twenties are almost always followed by lows that are equally intense. Sailing into the lofty air on the wings of Jupiter in Aquarius, the public had no idea of the global economic crisis that was to come.

The position of Jupiter in Uranus had some less damaging effects as well. In fact, wherever Jupiter is concerned, there is almost always a jolly buoyancy, against all odds. On January 1, New York and London celebrated the New Year together over the radio. Uranus unfurls new ideas in science and technology, and Jupiter expands everything it comes into contact with. It's no wonder that under the influence of Jupiter in Uranus, a ground-breaking technological event like this would take place. Also this year, on April 1, a check from London crossed the ocean by radio to be cashed in New York. This was the first time in history something like this had occurred. Aquarius represents brotherhood and this sharing of the bounty between nations is indicative of the influence of this astrological placement.

Prohibition is finally repealed in Canada

Agatha Christie goes missing　　　　*Film star Rudolph Valentino dies*

A TIME OF DEATH AND NEAR–DEATH

As France struggled with post-war problems, the value of the franc suffered a drastic fall and Raymond Poincaré formed a new coalition government. Britain granted new freedoms to its Empire dominions, including Ireland, Australia, and Canada. An attempt on the life of the Italian dictator Mussolini was unsuccessful. Instead of reducing problems, the prohibition of alcohol use in the U.S. increased them, with a 1000 percent rise in alcoholism as well as a higher level of crime. Prohibition ended in Canada after the 'wets' won their ten-year struggle to re-legalize alcohol. A hurricane destroyed Miami, Florida, with 130 mph winds. New Yorker Gertrude Ederle became the first woman to swim the English Channel. A long-lost Mayan city was found in the jungles of Mexico's Yucatan Peninsula. Audiences swooned at the Swedish actress Greta Garbo but mourned the loss of Rudolph Valentino and Harry Houdini; both died as a result of ruptured appendixes. Two impressionist painters, the French Claude Monet and the American Mary Cassatt, died, while British crime writer Agatha Christie disappeared but was later found suffering from amnesia.

➤ Read "Money, Astrology, and the Crash of '29" by Sophia Mason on page 225.

CAPRICORN

From January 01, 0:00 through January 20, 19:11

The Dynamic Builder

The 1926 world you emerged into could have used more Capricorn qualities, such as common sense and structure. Many countries were still reeling from the devastating impact of World War I and some, including France, were on the verge of declaring bankruptcy. This was a time of planning and laying new foundations, both of which are specialties of the astute Capricorn. It was also a vulnerable year for unstable countries where dictators, such as Greek Premier Pangalos, could come to power. In the January 1926 Capricorn, the natural drive for authority is complemented by a compassionate, yet detached warmth toward all kinds of people.

Your horoscope holds outgoing Sagittarian influences that can drive you into surprisingly bold actions. In 1926, New York and London celebrated New Year's Eve together over the radio. This technological triumph was a celebration of the Sagittarian desires to communicate with and "travel" to other lands. With intelligent Aquarian astrological elements as well as these Sagittarian influences, you probably have an innovative mind that is open to the new and unusual. Emerging from this year, you may have enjoyed both the mundane and otherworldly technological advances of the time. You may well have been inspired by the futuristic vision of Fritz Lang's *Metropolis*, which opened in Berlin in this month.

With your ability to create form out of chaos, others could look to you for guidance in times of change. You have the qualities of leadership that would fare well in the financial world. You could thrive in environments where many people of all types pass through your door. When you set goals that inspire you to do your best, you are unstoppable.

Though others might find you reserved at first, you are quite open to the full spectrum of humanity. Your companions could be other open-minded and eclectic types such as Aquarians, Sagittarians, or Geminis.

Your gift has been your open-mindedness toward others and your ability to bring focus and structure to any pursuit. Your challenge has been to delve below the surface of life to discover deeper truths.

AQUARIUS

From January 20, 19:12 through February 19, 9:34

The Opinionated Friend

The 1926 Aquarian might appreciate the desire for independence that led to Great Britain granting new freedom to its dominions of Ireland, Australia, and Canada. Like these modern-day countries, yours is a sign destined to forge its own path in life. And with many planets in your birth sign, you came into this world fully empowered to seek your own personal truth. Also in this month, the Mexican government took possession of all Church property. Whatever your opinion on political matters, people can surely count on you to have a strong one. However, the 1926 Aquarian is just as likely to take the opposing view at a later time. Those around you have to learn to expect the unexpected and to avoid making demands on your time. They may not always understand you, but they will grow to appreciate your unique way of navigating through life.

With the planet of good-luck, Jupiter, in your birth sign, it could be said that your were born under a "lucky star." It may seem that the right doors open for you throughout your life. Of course, it's always up to you to make the most of these cosmic gifts. And to add yet more Aquarian energy to the mix, Venus, the planet of relationships, in your birth sign brings an easy, yet detached social persona and a desire to meet new and interesting people. Though you treasure your Aquarian independence, such factors indicate a steady flow of comrades flowing through your life.

You emerged with a mind tuned like a radio transmitter to everything around you. It would surely suit you to be in public life or other arenas where diverse people gather. Your Aquarian mind seeks sparks from others through the sharing of ideas and observations.

As a 1926 Aquarian, you could favor social groups rather than one-on-one connections. In relationships, you could shine with the vibrant minds of those with signs in Aquarius, Gemini, or Sagittarius.

Your gift has been your quirky sense of humor and objective acceptance of others. Your challenge has been to find a balance between spending time in the social sphere and retreating into your treasured solitude.

CAPRICORN
Your Personal Planets

YOUR LOVE POTENTIAL
Venus in Aquarius, Jan. 01, 0:00 - Jan. 20, 19:11

YOUR DRIVE AND AMBITION
Mars in Sagittarius, Jan. 01, 0:00 - Jan. 20, 19:11

YOUR LUCK MAGNETISM
Jupiter in Capricorn, Jan. 01, 0:00 - Jan. 06, 1:00
Jupiter in Aquarius, Jan. 06, 1:01 - Jan. 20, 19:11

World Events

Jan. 1 – New York and London are united by radio for the New Year celebrations.

Jan. 10 – Fritz Lang's film *Metropolis* premières in Berlin.

Fritz Lang directs "Metropolis"

AQUARIUS
Your Personal Planets

YOUR LOVE POTENTIAL
Venus in Aquarius, Jan. 20, 19:12 - Feb. 19, 9:34

YOUR DRIVE AND AMBITION
Mars in Sagittarius, Jan. 20, 19:12 - Feb. 09, 3:34
Mars in Capricorn, Feb. 09, 3:35 - Feb. 19, 9:34

YOUR LUCK MAGNETISM
Jupiter in Aquarius, Jan. 20, 19:12 - Feb. 19, 9:34

World Events

Feb. 6 – Germany is threatened by Italian dictator Mussolini over unrest in the Tyrol region.

Feb. 18 – Five ancient Mayan cities are discovered by archeologists in Mexico.

► Read about your Chinese Astrological sign on page 838. ► Read about your Personal Planets on page 826. ► Read about your personal Mystical Card on page 856.

1926

PISCES
Your Personal Planets

YOUR LOVE POTENTIAL
Venus in Aquarius, Feb. 19, 9:35 - Mar. 21, 9:00

YOUR DRIVE AND AMBITION
Mars in Capricorn, Feb. 19, 9:35 - Mar. 21, 9:00

YOUR LUCK MAGNETISM
Jupiter in Aquarius, Feb. 19, 9:35 - Mar. 21, 9:00

World Events

Mar. 10 – Brazil vetoes Germany's application to join the League of Nations.

Mar. 16 – Physicist Robert H. Goddard launches the first liquid-fueled rocket.

Robert H. Goddard with his first liquid-fueled rocket

ARIES
Your Personal Planets

YOUR LOVE POTENTIAL
Venus in Aquarius, Mar. 21, 9:01 - Apr. 06, 3:58
Venus in Pisces, Apr. 06, 3:59 - Apr. 20, 20:35

YOUR DRIVE AND AMBITION
Mars in Capricorn, Mar. 21, 9:01 - Mar. 23, 4:38
Mars in Aquarius, Mar. 23, 4:39 - Apr. 20, 20:35

YOUR LUCK MAGNETISM
Jupiter in Aquarius, Mar. 21, 9:01 - Apr. 20, 20:35

World Events

Apr. 3 – Twelve people are killed in a fracas between Muslims and Hindus in Calcutta.

Apr. 20 – The first check to be transmitted by radio travels from London to New York, where it is cashed.

PISCES

From February 19, 9:35 through March 21, 9:00

The Subtle Rationalist

In the year you entered the world, the impressionist artists Claude Monet and Mary Cassatt were leaving it. Both died in 1926, leaving behind enduring art that gave the world a timeless "impression" of their time. As a Pisces of 1926, you hold the sensitivity to fully embrace the essence and magic of art, music, and literature. You are tuned in to the subtler moments that others often miss and you are uniquely able to spark a sense of wonder. Whether it is a walk in the park or time spent with a child, you have the ability to savor each and every nuance of a moment like an artist. With the rise of cinema, perhaps you engaged your imagination in a captivating movie house as you came of age. In your birth year, Greta Garbo was the star of the day. She was among the only stars to make the transition from silent pictures to "talkies," revealing to the world her husky, resonant voice. As a 1926 Pisces, you have a creative mind that borders on the mystical with the ability to "give voice" to your own observations of life.

You were graced with the planet of action, Mars, passing through the practical sign Capricorn in your birth chart. This bestowed upon you both discipline and fortitude, which brings the balance of logic to your "head in the clouds," Piscean nature. With Aquarius, sign of friendship, transiting Venus, the planet of love and beauty, in your horoscope, you are likely blessed with many social contacts. You can share your nonjudgmental and compassionate nature with a diverse and eclectic circle of friends.

You could shine in artistic fields, where your intuitive impressions would be your greatest asset. If you surround yourself with sensitive people who respect your gentle nature, you can't lose.

Though you are likely to find the good in every person you meet, you could find special harmony with Pisceans, Scorpios, and Aquarians.

Your gift has been the quality of presence you bring to each moment, as well as your artistic, intuitive gifts. Your challenge has been to trust your impressions and to cultivate a sense of an "internal compass" to guide your life.

ARIES

From March 21, 9:01 through April 20, 20:35

The Bold Instigator

In 1926, the Prohibition movement in North America backfired; alcoholism rose to a staggering 1,000 percent and crime became rampant in the major cities. In Canada, Prohibition ended after the "wets" won their ten-year struggle to make alcohol legal again. Goodness knows, many Aries love both a good fight and a good time. The 1926 Aries also entered the world when landmark events bridged the continental gap. A check from London crossed the ocean by radio and was cashed in New York. The 1926 Aries would see many such "firsts,", continuing today with the World Wide Web. With a drive toward the new and novel, the 1926 Aries came into an exciting era when pioneering advances in communication were just beginning.

With Mercury, the planet of communication, also in honest Aries, your wit is likely to be sharp and your tongue even sharper. You are likely to enjoy good-natured arguments and competitions among friends, which sometimes lead to voices raised. Perhaps you have had to do your fair share of apologizing for hurtful words. You shine with those who can spar with you without taking it to heart. Key planets in socially aware Aquarius, including Mars, the planet of action, can temper that primal Arien fire with respect for others. However, you will find it wise to cultivate harmonious working relationships as your best achievements could come in group situations, where a lively exchange of ideas can lead to innovative collaborations.

You could be drawn to occupations that allow you to be the pioneer communicator. With the right motivation, you can inspire others with your dynamic presence. Be wary of situations that seem to reign in your vibrant personality.

Your blazing spirit requires the company of people who can entertain your bright mind with endless conversation. Your bold approach will find friends among Sagittarians, Aquarians, and of course, other Ariens.

Your gift has been the inspiration you bring to others through your enthusiasm and willingness to try new things. Your challenge has been to cultivate patience and compassion for the sensitivities of others.

➤ Read about your Chinese Astrological sign on page 838. ➤ Read about your Personal Planets on page 826. ➤ Read about your personal Mystical Card on page 856.

TAURUS

From April 20, 20:36 through May 21, 20:14

The Loyal Stabilizer

You, 1926 Taurus, were born in the same sign as the future Queen of England, Elizabeth II. And while you might not necessarily be a royal-watcher, the sense of continuity provided throughout history as represented by the British monarchy could appeal to your Taurean love of tradition. Growing up with Elizabeth II, you saw the tumult of war and social unrest herald enormous change, just as she did. In the year of Elizabeth's birth, trade unions had begun a general strike in Britain, which laid-off four million workers and threatened to provoke a civil war. Across the world, in India, Hindu women finally won the right to seek elected office under the British Raj. The Taurus of 1926 has likely sought to carve out a sense of stability amid these and other turbulent changes. You have likely employed the patient, careful planning of a structured life to create a life of meaning and substance.

With Saturn, the planet of limitations, in turbulent Scorpio, the 1926 Taurus may find particular challenges in the area of control. Scorpio's intensity can be restricted under Saturn, causing a feeling of repression. The Taurean tendency of holding on to possessions and structures long after they serve their purpose could also unwittingly enhance this feeling of repression. And yet, your love of the sensual pleasures of life can be employed to overcome any rigidity in your life. "Eat, drink, and be merry," could be your mantra.

At work, you have probably been the reliable and consistent one, always willing to work hard if the rewards are there. Others likely respect your dedication and commitment to the tasks at hand. You could thrive in occupations where there is a respect for tradition, such as in a university or medicine.

In relationships, you are likely to seek loyal, steadfast partners who are as reliable as you are. Good matches for your temperament are Pisceans, Taureans, and Capricorns.

Your gift has been your patient, consistent determination to build a life that has meaning. Your challenge has been allowing yourself to enjoy the abundance that you have brought to your life.

GEMINI

From May 21, 20:15 through June 22, 4:29

The Mercurial Explorer

You, 1926 Gemini, can claim film legend Marilyn Monroe among those who share the traits of your particular birth year and sign. It has been suggested that a self-destructive shadow dwelt within Monroe, which led to her early death of a drug overdose. The 1926 Gemini is also no stranger to the mercurial nature of the sign, and you can likely claim multiple selves on any given day. While it can be confusing to those who know you, it probably has been even more confusing to you, the 1926 Gemini. Your social side requires ample stimulation, while your more retiring, inward "twin" requires restful solitude. Finding the balance in the inherent dual nature of this sign is the key to harnessing your often frenetic Gemini energy.

In December 1926, the writer Agatha Christie disappeared, only to be found later under the spell of amnesia from an automobile accident. You are probably a lover of the written and spoken word and, perhaps, of mysteries. With Saturn, the planet of karma, placed in probing Scorpio, the Gemini of 1926 has likely been challenged to explore the hidden and mysterious in a disciplined way. With Jupiter, the planet of expansion, in rebellious Aquarius, some of your best opportunities could involve bringing needed changes in established areas. You also have the detachment and cool head to be a diplomat in times of change.

Some fields of interest could include writing, which would give the brilliant 1926 Gemini mind ample room to roam and grow. You may be an engaging storyteller and you may discover enraptured audiences for your tales. With your desire for continual education, you might enjoy teaching as a profession or as a volunteer.

You are a social creature by nature, and you are likely to enjoy witty banter and joyful gatherings. Among your most compatible cohorts are Ariens, Aquarians, and other Geminis.

Your gift has been your unique way with words, which can be a catalyst to help others put their thoughts into form. Your challenge has been to avoid simply being busy and find ways to settle into a state of restful activity that has a deeper purpose.

➤ Read about your Chinese Astrological sign on page 838. ➤ Read about your Personal Planets on page 826. ➤ Read about your personal Mystical Card on page 856.

TAURUS
Your Personal Planets

YOUR LOVE POTENTIAL
Venus in Pisces, Apr. 20, 20:36 - May 06, 15:12
Venus in Aries, May 06, 15:13 - May 21, 20:14

YOUR DRIVE AND AMBITION
Mars in Aquarius, Apr. 20, 20:36 - May 03, 17:02
Mars in Pisces, May 03, 17:03 - May 21, 20:14

YOUR LUCK MAGNETISM
Jupiter in Aquarius, Apr. 20, 20:36 - May 21, 20:14

World Events

May 3 – Trade unions begin a general strike in Britain, with four million workers off the job, paralyzing the country.

May 9 – Richard Byrd and Floyd Bennett become the first people to fly over the North Pole.

American film star Marilyn Monroe is born under the sign of Gemini

GEMINI
Your Personal Planets

YOUR LOVE POTENTIAL
Venus in Aries, May 21, 20:15 - June 02, 19:58
Venus in Taurus, June 02, 19:59 - June 22, 4:29

YOUR DRIVE AND AMBITION
Mars in Pisces, May 21, 20:15 - June 15, 0:49
Mars in Aries, June 15, 0:50 - June 22, 4:29

YOUR LUCK MAGNETISM
Jupiter in Aquarius, May 21, 20:15 - June 22, 4:29

World Events

June 1 – American film star Marilyn Monroe is born.

June 12 – Brazil withdraws from the League of Nations over Germany's admission to the organization.

1926

CANCER
Your Personal Planets

YOUR LOVE POTENTIAL
Venus in Taurus, June 22, 4:30 - June 28, 21:04
Venus in Gemini, June 28, 21:05 - July 23, 15:24

YOUR DRIVE AND AMBITION
Mars in Aries, June 22, 4:30 - July 23, 15:24

YOUR LUCK MAGNETISM
Jupiter in Aquarius, June 22, 4:30 - July 23, 15:24

World Events

July 2 – The U.S. Army Air Corps is established.
July 4 – In Germany, the Nazi Party convenes its first congress since its reorganization.

Swimmer Gertrude Ederle

LEO
Your Personal Planets

YOUR LOVE POTENTIAL
Venus in Gemini, July 23, 15:25 - July 24, 6:41
Venus in Cancer, July 24, 6:42 - Aug. 18, 4:34
Venus in Leo, Aug. 18, 4:35 - Aug. 23, 22:13

YOUR DRIVE AND AMBITION
Mars in Aries, July 23, 15:25 - Aug. 01, 9:13
Mars in Taurus, Aug. 01, 9:14 - Aug. 23, 22:13

YOUR LUCK MAGNETISM
Jupiter in Aquarius, July 23, 15:25 - Aug. 23, 22:13

World Events

Aug. 6 – Gertrude Ederle becomes the first woman to swim the English Channel.
Aug. 13 – Cuban revolutionary leader Fidel Castro is born.

CANCER
From June 22, 4:30 through July 23, 15:24

The Fiery Protector

At the time of your birth, Adolf Hitler's Nazi Party held its first congress since its February 1925 reorganization in Weimar, Germany. It was also the time when Mussolini was hinting that Italy sought to expand its territorial boundaries. The 1926 Cancer emerged into a world when anxieties caused some leaders to aggressively protect their homelands. As history later recorded, they felt their best defense was a good offense.

The 1926 Cancerian entered the world with ample will and ambition to create the kind of home they wanted. A sheltering home environment is essential to protect the emotional sensitivity of the 1926 Cancer. With Mars, the planet of action and its ruling planet, in bold Aries, the 1926 Cancer has more than enough tenacity to pursue his or her interests. With all that fiery protectiveness, you might find it wise to avoid confrontations or situations that make you defensive. It is likely that the 1926 Cancer has unusual energy stores, ready for the right moment. With careful planning, there is nothing out of reach. Your wisdom comes in balancing your personal interests, with those of the wider community. Peace-loving Aquarius' influence on Jupiter, the planet of expansion, could open doors for the 1926 Cancer to show compassion to a wider and wider spectrum of humanity.

When you are at ease, you can be unusually productive. This could mean that your most inspiring environment is right at home. Bringing others into your home could be the key to enlarging your life. You might find it rewarding to work in some capacity at home with another person or two. Working to better the lives of others could give your generous heart an outlet and lighten the spirits of others.

You can be patiently cautious in your goal of creating a loyal circle of trustworthy people in your life. Good matches for your sensitive, yet strong sensibility, are Taureans, Pisceans, and Scorpios.

Your gift has been a compassionate heart to those in your intimate sphere and even beyond it. Your challenge has been to continue to open your heart and life to new people and situations.

LEO
From July 23, 15:25 through August 23, 22:13

The Enthusiastic Inspirer

In the year of your birth, Leo of 1926, an American company named Vitaphone premiered a motion picture with sound—a "talkie"—featuring music by Henry Hadley, head of the New York Philharmonic Orchestra. It is an appropriate setting for you to emerge, since you arrived to be both seen and heard. The 1926 Leo has the flair and finesse to star in any movie or simply in his or her own life. Another event at the time of your birth was the discovery of the largest diamond mines ever near Johannesburg, South Africa. The 1926 Leo doesn't necessarily need precious jewels to shine, but you would perhaps appreciate a little glamour from time to time. You have likely always known how best to attract attention, with or without the glitter of gold. The key is knowing how and when to take center stage to achieve your goals.

The 1926 Leo gets a double dose of leonine pride and power with Mercury, the planet of communication, also in your own birth sign. Your way of expressing yourself may be noticeably theatrical and engaging. Your star quality may draw others to you, which is only a bad thing if you can't say no to their requests. If you are accused of trying to steal the show, you can surely blame it on the planets. You can also seek ways to search out the spotlight through productive, growth-inducing activities.

Your talent for showmanship could emerge in any number of fields, from teaching to a life in theater or the movies. By linking your enthusiasm to your compassion for others, you can be a great motivator for people of all ages. If you give yourself free reign, you can be a delight to those in your circle of friends and family.

Though you give a bold and outgoing presentation, you are likely to seek the company of gentle, reliable souls. You are likely anchored by those who operate more from the head than from the heart. You could find compatibility with Cancerians, Pisceans, and other Leos.

Your gift has been your enthusiastic *joie de vivre*, which infuses excitement into everything you do. Your challenge has been to cultivate the humility to see your own faults.

➤ Read about your Chinese Astrological sign on page 838. ➤ Read about your Personal Planets on page 826. ➤ Read about your personal Mystical Card on page 856.

VIRGO

From August 23, 22:14 through September 23, 19:26

The Steady Achiever

The 1926 Virgo was born in the same time that film idol Rudolph Valentino died of a ruptured appendix at the age of thirty-one. As a silent film star, his smoldering presence had enchanted millions. Though not oblivious to the world stage, the 1926 Virgo was more likely to grow into a nature that was more absorbed in the daily routine of his or her life. You can be counted on to keep life in order, even in times of great flux and change. You are probably a steady sort, who is also prone to sudden, inexplicable bursts of enthusiasm. To those who prove themselves worthy, the 1926 Virgo is a loyal friend and trusted advisor on matters big and small.

The planet of action, Mars, was in steady, consistent Taurus, enhancing your already present love of stability and order. You are likely drawn to activities that you are confident will bring tangible rewards. You might have a harder time making sense of the ineffable or intangible aspects of life. Still, with Saturn, the planet of limitations, in Scorpio, a sign known for explorations of all that is unknown and hidden, you could be drawn toward activities that encourage expressing the deeper mysteries of life.

You might enjoy activities where your attention to detail is rewarded and of benefit to others. The goals that you set for yourself are usually achieved, since you know few equals in determination and persistence. You could enjoy physical activities that are also creative, such as sculpting or gardening. You are also someone who likely desires cleanliness in appearance and home environment. This gives you the polished air of someone in control of your life.

You are discerning in your choice of company and you are attracted to those who appreciate your fastidious nature. Yet you also may enjoy exuberant companions who bring out your fiery side. Some good matches for your prudent personality are other Virgos, Taureans, and sometimes Leos.

Your gift has been the practical and sound advice you give as a trusted friend. Your challenge has been avoiding the trap of perfectionism and embracing a lighter, carefree lifestyle.

LIBRA

From September 23, 19:27 through October 24, 4:17

The Trusted Leader

You were born at a time when fascist dictators were tightening their grip on power in many parts of the world. In Poland, Marshal Pidulski set himself up as head of the new Polish cabinet following a military coup. Mussolini abolished all political opposition in Italy at this time, making the Fascist Party into the state Party. For you, 1926 Libra, this type of grasping imposition would surely have rankled your innate sense of what is just and balanced. Whatever your political views, as a Libra, you have the ability to see both sides of an issue and often offer objective ways to compromise.

With the active planet Mars in steady Taurus, you're likely to be both a dreamer and a doer. The 1926 Libra seeks ways to bring tangible progress to any given pursuit. Your realistic Taurean influence gives the balance of determination to your grand ideas of bettering the world. This likely gave credibility and weight to any plans you put forward over the years. You have had the goals along with the realistic path to achieving them. This makes you, 1926 Libra, an ideal choice to lead people, groups, or companies.

Any organization or group could benefit from the 1926 Libra's leadership skills. Lucky circumstances in your work life could come about through laboring to help others. Coming of age at the height of World War II, you might have been inspired to enlist your services for a cause. A natural diplomat, you could find that your mediation skills go far in professions such as counseling or teaching. You could also do well as an attorney. In fact, you may have found that your air of judicious leadership thrust you into the public eye on more than one occasion.

You bring harmony and trust to many of your relationships, as long as you feel respected and loved. You could find happy connections with those with planets in Taurus, Virgo or Libra.

Your gift has been your generosity in trying to find the balance in unsettling situations, as well as your natural sense of beauty and grace. Your challenge has been finding ways to spread your wealth around, rather than in one partnership.

➤ Read about your Chinese Astrological sign on page 838. ➤ Read about your Personal Planets on page 826. ➤ Read about your personal Mystical Card on page 856.

VIRGO
Your Personal Planets

YOUR LOVE POTENTIAL
Venus in Leo, Aug. 23, 22:14 - Sept. 11, 16:36
Venus in Virgo, Sept. 11, 16:37 - Sept. 23, 19:26

YOUR DRIVE AND AMBITION
Mars in Taurus, Aug. 23, 22:14 - Sept. 23, 19:26

YOUR LUCK MAGNETISM
Jupiter in Aquarius, Aug. 23, 22:14 - Sept. 23, 19:26

World Events

Aug. 23 – Film idol Rudolph Valentino dies at the age of thirty-one.

Sept. 6 – Forces under Chiang Kai-Shek reach the key city of Hankow as the civil war continues in China.

Chiang Kai-shek leads the civil war in China

LIBRA
Your Personal Planets

YOUR LOVE POTENTIAL
Venus in Virgo, Sept. 23, 19:27 - Oct. 05, 21:06
Venus in Libra, Oct. 05, 21:07 - Oct. 24, 4:17

YOUR DRIVE AND AMBITION
Mars in Taurus, Sept. 23, 19:27 - Oct. 24, 4:17

YOUR LUCK MAGNETISM
Jupiter in Aquarius, Sept. 23, 19:27 - Oct. 24, 4:17

World Events

Oct. 17 – In the USSR, Leon Trotsky concedes Stalin's leadership.

Oct. 18 – American musician Chuck Berry is born.

1926

SCORPIO
Your Personal Planets

YOUR LOVE POTENTIAL
Venus in Libra, Oct. 24, 4:18 - Oct. 29, 20:49
Venus in Scorpio, Oct. 29, 20:50 - Nov. 22, 18:11
Venus in Sagittarius, Nov. 22, 18:12 - Nov. 23, 1:27

YOUR DRIVE AND AMBITION
Mars in Taurus, Oct. 24, 4:18 - Nov. 23, 1:27

YOUR LUCK MAGNETISM
Jupiter in Aquarius, Oct. 24, 4:18 - Nov. 23, 1:27

World Events

Oct. 31 – Master of magic and escape artist Harry Houdini dies.

Nov. 19 – Leon Trotsky and Grigori Zinoviev are thrown out of the Soviet Politburo by Joseph Stalin.

Death of escape artist Harry Houdini

SAGITTARIUS
Your Personal Planets

YOUR LOVE POTENTIAL
Venus in Sagittarius, Nov. 23, 1:28 - Dec. 16, 14:47
Venus in Capricorn, Dec. 16, 14:48 - Dec. 22, 14:32

YOUR DRIVE AND AMBITION
Mars in Taurus, Nov. 23, 1:28 - Dec. 22, 14:32

YOUR LUCK MAGNETISM
Jupiter in Aquarius, Nov. 23, 1:28 - Dec. 22, 14:32

World Events

Dec. 1 – Prohibition is finally repealed in Canada.

Dec. 14 – Mystery writer Agatha Christie is found alive but suffering from amnesia after being missing for nine days.

SCORPIO
From October 24, 4:18 through November 23, 1:27

The Intuitive Explorer

Around the time of your birth, a massive hurricane with 130 mph winds moved through Miami, destroying most of that city along the United States Eastern Seaboard. You emerged, 1926 Scorpio, with all the intensity of a hurricane and with a nature that promotes both creation and destruction as part of the requirements for your growth. In your lifetime, you have seen your share of dead wood falling away so that new life may emerge. The 1926 Scorpio is uniquely attuned to the natural rhythm of life, and you are able to "die" to the past only to be reborn in new and improved forms.

With Mars, the planet of action, in careful Taurus, you have an anchor to steady the turbulence of your Scorpio nature. With Saturn, the planet of limitations, in your own sign, your quest for selfhood likely has been a struggle to harness your intensity to structured pursuits. Nevertheless, the 1926 Scorpio is well equipped to go deep within and emerge with something to share with the world. In fact, such a cycle of death and rebirth is a key for the continued progress of the 1926 Scorpio. As you go inward and seek new answers, you let go of the things you no longer need.

With the ability to spend time alone being diligently productive, you are likely to succeed at any task you can claim as a priority. And for the 1926 Scorpio, it must be your decision to proceed, as you are likely to be uninspired to follow others. You can bring your talent for "soul mining" to bear in many fields. Your insights into human nature could lead you into psychology or other helping professions. Other possible pursuits lie in the artistic fields, including painting or drama.

You bring passionate intensity to your connections with others and take an interest in getting to know people very intimately. Those with signs in Cancer, Scorpio, or Libra could be harmonious.

Your gift has been your ability to dive into whatever you are doing and emerge with new stories to tell those around you. Your challenge has been not allowing yourself to get derailed by intrigues and entanglements that don't serve your best interests.

SAGITTARIUS
From November 23, 1:28 through December 22, 14:32

The Restless Adventurer

In the year you were born, 1926 Sagittarius, the ruins of a Mayan city were found in the jungles of Mexico's Yucatán Peninsula. The rumors of the existence of this ancient city were finally proven to be true. The artifacts shed light on the fascinating Mayan civilization, which lived in harmony with nature and, some scholars would say, the planets. Your adventurous Sagittarian spirit would likely revel in such a fantastic voyage or quest to re-discover lost worlds.

You may be full of wanderlust and the desire to explore the planet. Traveling to new countries could be one of your favorite things to do. Your keen interest in learning about other cultures could lead you to learn a language or two. Many other planets in Sagittarius give the 1926 Sagittarius an amplification of the traits of the sign. You can be vital, fiery, active, and always on the move. It may seem that you always have five kettles on the stove, constantly brewing new ideas and activities. Luckily for you, this is given balance by Mars, the planet often responsible for setting events in motions, in cautious Taurus. This gives the 1926 Sagittarius the ability to know how best to direct that restless energy.

You can be easily motivated if something piques your curiosity. You enjoy experiencing things firsthand, rather than reading about it in a book. This should keep you always moving since there is so much you have yet to discover. It is wise to stay active with work that stimulates your mind and, perhaps, your body. With a vital constitution, you could be drawn toward vigorous physical pursuits. Your high-energy can be inspiring to others, especially as you got older and wiser.

Often called "the friend of the zodiac," your Sagittarian openness attracts an eclectic circle of interesting mates. In particular, you could find common ground with other Sagittarians as well as Capricorns and Aquarians.

Your gift has been your wide-eyed search for further knowledge and experience, which is inspiring to behold. Your challenge has been settling into one pursuit so that you can gain proficiency in one area.

► Read about your Chinese Astrological sign on page 838. ► Read about your Personal Planets on page 826. ► Read about your personal Mystical Card on page 856.

CAPRICORN

From December 22, 14:33 through December 31, 23:59

The Curious Innovator

When you came into being, 1926 December Capricorn, the year was coming to a close. The beloved German poet and mystic Rainer Maria Rilke died around the time you were born, as did the Japanese Emperor Yoshihito. The world was between wars, enjoying a time of fragile peace and uncertainty. It was on the brink of some major changes. Germany and Italy signed an arbitration treaty at the time of your birth, a foreshadowing perhaps of the later alliance of the two countries. You emerged into this world of 1926 with plenty of the fortitude that Capricorns are famous for, along with a delightfully curious and inquisitive mind.

The influence of Mercury, the planet of communication, in dynamic Sagittarius gives the 1926 Capricorn the ability to engage anyone around them in stimulating conversation. The cherished goal of respect and authority is likely reached by winning admirers, those who recognize the brilliance of mind that the 1926 Capricorn possesses. This prominent Sagittarian influence also brings humor and optimism to temper your tendency toward melancholy. You are likely happy, as long as you are satisfying your curiosity and moving toward reaching your goals.

The 1926 Capricorn has the drive and ambition to have made a mark on the world. You could have found enjoyment through a stable work life that offers ample room to evolve and grow. A desire for status and recognition could have led you into careers working with the public, such as a doctor or politician. Your talent for communication would be well served in situations where you meet many different types of people. You can absorb information from almost everyone you meet.

You are likely very discriminating in your choice of close companions and possibly easily bored by many of the people you meet. You could delight in the company of other Capricorns, Sagittarians, and Aquarians.

Your gift has been your innovative approach to building things in your life, whether it is a career or a relationship. Your challenge has been to avoid alienating those around you by acting defensively or in a stubborn manner.

CAPRICORN
Your Personal Planets

YOUR LOVE POTENTIAL
Venus in Capricorn, Dec. 22, 14:33 - Dec. 31, 23:59

YOUR DRIVE AND AMBITION
Mars in Taurus, Dec. 22, 14:33 - Dec. 31, 23:59

YOUR LUCK MAGNETISM
Jupiter in Aquarius, Dec. 22, 14:33 - Dec. 31, 23:59

World Events

Dec. 29 – Germany and Italy sign an arbitration treaty.

Dec. 29 – German poet Rainer Maria Rilke dies.

Panic in Wall Street

Special Feature
Money, Astrology, and the Crash of '29
by Sophia Mason

Mostly everyone involved in the speculative boom of the late twenties knew that eventually the stocks would drop. In the heat of the moment, though, few could foresee when the bubble would burst. Investing in the stock market had become almost a craze. "Everybody's doing it," as the song went. You could get "tips" on the stock market from your barber or the bellboy at a hotel. And, just as you could buy new electronic appliances and furniture "on credit," you could also go to a broker and purchase stock "on margin." This meant that, instead of paying for the stocks outright, you could purchase them with cash down and the rest on credit. Then you could sell off shares at a profit before paying what you owed.

Not that there weren't warnings beforehand. The legendary financial analyst W. D. Gann, using mathematical principles and astrology, warned his clients in November 1928 that a collapse was imminent.

Investors who cared to listen also heard the dire prediction from eminent British banker Paul Warburg. In March 1929, he predicted that unless the colossal volume of loans and "the orgy of unrestrained speculation" were checked, stocks would eventually crash, leading to "a general depression involving the entire country." The Stock Exchange actually peaked on September 3, and began drifting downward over the next two months.

The first wave of panic hit on October 23, and hit hard. The market was lackluster for most of the day until the blue-chip radio and automotive stocks began to plummet in mid-afternoon, with the rest of the stocks following them downward. About $3,000,000,000 in paper values was lost in just an hour—an average of about $50,000,000 a minute.

The next day, October 24, 1929, now known as Black Thursday, was the most frantic day of stock trading in history. The hurricane of liquidation so overwhelmed the Edison ticker tape that the last quotation couldn't be read until four hours after the market had closed. A record 12,894,650 shares traded, with hundreds of stocks selling at or near low levels for the year. Rumors fueled the fire. One report said at least eleven speculators had committed suicide. Panic spread to other exchanges and markets, including the Chicago Commodities Exchange.

(Continued on page 233)

➤ Read Morgan's Star Profile on page 49. ➤ Read Cayce's crash prediction in "The First New Age Psychic" on page 265. ➤ Read Evangeline Adam's crash prediction in "Astrology goes on Trial" on page 185.

225

1927

Behind the Scenes: Saturn meets Neptune

The placement of Saturn in Sagittarius can encourage serious pursuit of philosophy, truth, and justice. This is because Saturn is the planet that gets down to business and Sagittarius is the sign of expansion of the mind. Because boisterous Sagittarius is an energetic fire sign, when planets make contact with it, there can sometimes be momentous results. Correspondingly, when Saturn sends a beam of energy to dreamy planet Neptune, there can be interesting results. In 1927, Saturn in Sagittarius made a "trine", usually a rather light and pleasant astrological aspect, to Neptune in Leo, also a bright and feisty fire sign. In this case, the stars seemed to work in a curious way.

This placement of the planets is all about the hidden forces in the universe. Secret government projects fall under the domain of Saturn making a trine to Neptune. Adolf Hitler's first Nazi Party meeting in Berlin took place on May 1. Trotsky was expelled from the Communist Party this year. Portugal quelled a revolution months after Carmona had established his military dictatorship. There was clandestine activity everywhere. Months and years later the results of these secret activities would come out, but in the mean time, under the influence of hard-working Saturn and mystical Neptune, they remained behind the scenes.

Neptune is the ruler of the image-making capacity of the mind. It is connected to art and imagination, and movies come under the ethereal Neptunian sphere of influence. With Saturn blowing kisses to Neptune in the sky, this dreamy sensibility is given some serious structure. Saturn provides the form and it helps the meeker, more sensitive planets do their work. Leo is the sign most connected to drama, so it's not surprising that innovations linked to film photography and drama occurred while Leo was highlighted. On January 5, Fox Studios first exhibited *Movietone*, a new invention that synchronized sound and motion pictures. On September 8, television inventor John Logie Baird sent his own image from Leeds to London. On October 6, Al Jolson opened in his first talking film, *The Jazz Singer*. Also this year, *National Geographic* published its first beautiful underwater color photographs.

Soviet leader Stalin expels Trotsky and Zinoviev

Charles Lindbergh flies non-stop from New York to Paris

Violinist Yehudi Menuhin performs at ten years old

THE DAWN OF THE AUTOMOBILE AGE

Twelve thousand British soldiers moved into China after xenophobic riots in Shanghai endangered British residents. Austria was convulsed by a revolt incited by communists. Stalin claimed greater control of the Soviet Union by expelling Trotsky and Zinoviev, both of whom were critical of his policies. Portugal quelled a revolution months after Carmona had established his military dictatorship. Hitler continued to gain power, as Germany removed the ban on his public speeches. A survey found that 39 percent of the world's cars were owned by Americans and the Mississippi River flooded thirty million acres along its mid-western route, making 200,000 homeless. Ten-year-old Russian violin virtuoso Yehudi Menuhin created a sensation in Paris with his performance of Lalo's *Symphonie Espagnole*. Telephone service smoothed business between San Francisco and London. Charles Lindbergh gained worldwide fame when he flew alone from New York to Paris, while the U.S. Army pilots Maitland and Hagenberger made the pioneering ocean flight from California to Hawaii. New Paris fashions gave women more freedom of movement, and Clara Bow was the 'It' girl.

➤ Read "Money, Astrology, and the Crash of '29" by Sophia Mason on page 225.

CAPRICORN

From January 01, 0:00 through January 21, 1:11

The Achiever

Stability and security are probably strong motivating factors for you, January Capricorn of 1927. Born between world wars, you were probably influenced by those who wanted to put strife behind them and get on with the business of living. As a result, your efforts may be largely devoted to producing material goods and providing financial security for you and your loved ones—and you have likely been very successful.

You probably see wealth and material accomplishments as marks of your value and have worked hard to acquire possessions, status, and stability. Through determination, you overcame obstacles. Whether you followed in the footsteps of your forebears in a family business or made your money in the World Stock Market, established the year you were born, your decisions were based on a special combination of pragmatism and hopeful speculation.

Despite your inclination to proceed with caution and use accepted methods, you may have sought to expand your reach beyond the limits set by tradition. You keep your feet planted firmly on the ground, yet your sights are set on the distant horizon. You instinctively know which modern advances are likely to have a measurable impact on society, like the release of the first sound news film and the connection of telephone service between London and San Francisco in the year of your birth.

In your relationships—personal as well as professional—you probably need to establish a clearly defined system where everyone knows and accepts his or her place. You value traditional attitudes and can be rather formal. You may sometimes see relationships as contracts and establish partnerships for practical reasons rather than romantic ones. Once you make a commitment, you uphold it and the people close to you know that they can rely on you. You are usually most compatible with Taureans, Virgos, and other Capricorns who value tradition as much as you do.

Your greatest strengths have been your determination and practicality. Your challenge is to remain open to new approaches and ideas that could not only benefit you but advance society as well.

AQUARIUS

From January 21, 1:12 through February 19, 15:33

Champion of Equality

Like most Aquarians, you have always strived to create a balance between the haves and the have-nots. You know that unless there is economic parity, there cannot be fairness in other areas. Aquarius of 1927, you might have been influenced by the awareness of women's and workers' rights that was growing when you were born. You probably believe people should have a say in matters that concern them, as well as a right to be heard.

Idealistic and independent, you may have rebelled against the restrictions of a materialistic society. At the same time, however, you might have enjoyed the "good life" and the pleasures that money could buy. Born during a period of relative peace between two World Wars, you may understand society's emphasis on personal comfort, stability, and happiness. However, your own dreams likely extend beyond your own well-being. Your humanitarianism could have been well used in fields such as social services.

Though you may value peace and cooperation, your outspoken, unconventional nature can stir up tension between you and others, particularly authority figures. You probably have a temper and don't mind a good argument—in fact, you find it stimulating. Freedom of speech is likely important to you and you want to express your views candidly.

Born during the Jazz Age, you may have an affinity for artists, intellectuals, and the politically progressive who, like you, tend to be unconventional in their lifestyles and want to make the world a better place. Perhaps you were part of the Beat Generation in your youth. Your friends and associates may be from all walks of life—you choose your acquaintances for their inner beauty rather than their wealth or social standing. For the most part, you get along best with intelligent, friendly types such as Geminis, Librans, and Sagittarians; imaginative Pisceans might also interest you.

Your greatest strength has been your ability to transcend the limited scope of your society and to form your own values independent of others. Your challenge is to reach a happy medium between idealism and practicality.

► Read about your Chinese Astrological sign on page 838. ► Read about your Personal Planets on page 826. ► Read about your personal Mystical Card on page 856.

CAPRICORN
Your Personal Planets

YOUR LOVE POTENTIAL
Venus in Capricorn, Jan. 01, 0:00 - Jan. 09, 11:47
Venus in Aquarius, Jan. 09, 11:48 - Jan. 21, 1:11

YOUR DRIVE AND AMBITION
Mars in Taurus, Jan. 01, 0:00 - Jan. 21, 1:11

YOUR LUCK MAGNETISM
Jupiter in Aquarius, Jan. 01, 0:00 - Jan. 18, 11:43
Jupiter in Pisces, Jan. 18, 11:44 - Jan. 21, 1:11

World Events

Jan. 5 - Fox Studios in New York exhibits Movietone, a new invention which synchronizes sound and motion pictures.

Jan. 7 - The first commercial telephone line opens between New York and London.

British troops march through Shanghai

AQUARIUS
Your Personal Planets

YOUR LOVE POTENTIAL
Venus in Aquarius, Jan. 21, 1:12 - Feb. 02, 10:32
Venus in Pisces, Feb. 02, 10:33 - Feb. 19, 15:33

YOUR DRIVE AND AMBITION
Mars in Taurus, Jan. 21, 1:12 - Feb. 19, 15:33

YOUR LUCK MAGNETISM
Jupiter in Pisces, Jan. 21, 1:12 - Feb. 19, 15:33

World Events

Jan. 24 - British troops embark for China to protect the British concession at Shanghai.

Feb. 13 - The U.S. deploys warships to China.

1927

PISCES
Your Personal Planets

YOUR LOVE POTENTIAL
Venus in Pisces, Feb. 19, 15:34 - Feb. 26, 13:15
Venus in Aries, Feb. 26, 13:16 - Mar. 21, 14:58

YOUR DRIVE AND AMBITION
Mars in Taurus, Feb. 19, 15:34 - Feb. 22, 0:42
Mars in Gemini, Feb. 22, 0:43 - Mar. 21, 14:58

YOUR LUCK MAGNETISM
Jupiter in Pisces, Feb. 19, 15:34 - Mar. 21, 14:58

World Events

Feb. 20 - American actor Sidney Poitier is born.

Mar. 12 - Eleven-year-old violinist Yehudi Menuhin debuts at Carnegie Hall in New York.

Mae West is found guilty of indecency

ARIES
Your Personal Planets

YOUR LOVE POTENTIAL
Venus in Aries, Mar. 21, 14:59 - Mar. 22, 22:55
Venus in Taurus, Mar. 22, 22:56 - Apr. 16, 19:24
Venus in Gemini, Apr. 16, 19:25 - Apr. 21, 2:31

YOUR DRIVE AND AMBITION
Mars in Gemini, Mar. 21, 14:59 - Apr. 17, 1:28
Mars in Cancer, Apr. 17, 1:29 - Apr. 21, 2:31

YOUR LUCK MAGNETISM
Jupiter in Pisces, Mar. 21, 14:59 - Apr. 21, 2:31

World Events

Apr. 19 - Communists in China declare war on Chaing Kai-Shek.

Apr. 19 - Leading Broadway actress Mae West is found guilty of indecency, given a ten-day sentence, and fined $500.

PISCES

From February 19, 15:34 through March 21, 14:58

The Artful Communicator

Expressing yourself in an imaginative way is important for you, Pisces of 1927. Born when the movie industry began making talking films and the Jazz Age was in full swing, you were influenced by the creative culture that surrounded you. All artistic media may appeal to you and you probably possess your share of natural talent. Whether or not you mastered an instrument, you probably enjoy listening to the great composers and performers, such as Igor Stravinsky, whose *Oedipus Rex* debuted the year of your birth.

Painting, photography, fashion design, and movies could be favorite pastimes. You might even have chosen to pursue a career in fine or commercial arts, where your special combination of sensitivity and daring, set you apart from the pack. You probably favor bold, colorful, inventive approaches to self-expression and have less appreciation for staid, traditional styles.

A natural teacher, you have a knack for conveying information, probably because you may find learning so exciting yourself. Your curious mind and expansive nature could lead you to travel in search of knowledge and experience. Born in a year that saw the auto industry make travel easier and Charles Lindbergh complete the first solo, non-stop flight from New York to Paris, you probably want to see the world.

You might also be an inspired writer, investing your compositions with flair and feeling. At the least, you enjoy sharing your ideas with all who will listen—you might be an avid letter writer or popular public speaker. Most likely, your companions are original individuals with whom you can discourse on art, music, and literature. In all your relationships, you value independence and intelligence and don't want to waste time with unadventurous people. Ariens, Geminis, Scorpios, Taureans, and other Pisceans could be interesting companions for you.

Your greatest strength has been your passionate creativity, which expresses itself in such an exciting way. Your challenge is to overcome a tendency to be impatient so you can develop your self-expressive abilities fully and use them productively.

ARIES

From March 21, 14:59 through April 21, 2:31

The Outspoken Individual

When it comes to giving an opinion, Aries of 1927, you rarely hold your tongue. Even if your ideas are a bit provocative, you probably express them openly and enthusiastically. You were born at a time when strong political ideologies were rocking nations: Germany witnessed clashes between Socialists and Communists; China was engulfed in civil war; and the Russian regime was teetering on dissolution. Your psyche was likely impressed with the spirit of controversy.

But your special form of daring intellect is needed to bring new ideas to the fore. Independent and original in your approach to problem solving, you rarely shy away from a dilemma. You quickly assess the problem, then take decisive action. Your inventiveness might have been an asset in fields such as electronics, aviation, engineering, advertising, or telecommunication.

You need outlets for your abundant energy, and you may pursue a number of activities that allow you to assert yourself physically and mentally. Sports are probably one of your interests and you might possess more than your share of athletic ability. You enjoy a good contest that challenges your strength, speed, agility, and wits. The martial arts might also interest you; they pit you against an obvious adversary and keep your adrenaline flowing.

Your associates on the playing field or in the boardroom probably admire your special combination of aggression and determination. However, you can be a bit abrasive at times, for you don't always think before you speak and might offend others without realizing it. For the most part, you enjoy the company of active, uninhibited people who can keep up with you mentally and physically. Geminis, Aquarians, Sagittarians, and Leos, who are as independent and outgoing as you, are usually your best matches. In romantic relationships, though, you might benefit from the stabilizing influence of a Taurean partner.

Your greatest strength has been your ability to make things happen. Your challenge is to accept the input and ideas of others sometimes, rather than insisting on always having your own way.

➤ Read about your Chinese Astrological sign on page 838. ➤ Read about your Personal Planets on page 826. ➤ Read about your personal Mystical Card on page 856.

TAURUS

From April 21, 2:32 through May 22, 2:07

The Secure Loyalist

At the time you were born, unrest circled the globe as revolt or pending conflict upset nations such as China, Germany, and Austria. As a result, you may have a strong desire for security and stability, Taurus of 1927. You probably try to establish a safe environment for yourself and your loved ones, and you will fiercely defend what you value. However, your conservative nature might cause you to see different lifestyles as threats.

You love nice things and probably are quite proud of your possessions. You might even see your worldly goods as measures of your success and, to some extent, judge people by their ability to provide. Having grown up when economic hardship plagued many parts of the world, you understand the value of money and are willing to do whatever is necessary to ensure that you have enough of it. A job with a large, well-established firm where you felt like family probably suited you best—you might have stayed at the same company your entire career.

Your home and family are likely to be the center of your universe, and your home might be something of a show place. Interior decorating could be an interest of yours because you have a natural sense of color, texture, and form. At the very least, your living environment is comfortable and inviting—friends and family tend to gather at your home for holidays and get-togethers. With your green thumb, you might grow your own vegetables and herbs. Your culinary skills could have led you to choose a career in the restaurant, grocery, or food industry.

To those you love, you are generous, caring, and devoted, but also perhaps possessive. You are always there to help out. For the most part, you prefer to surround yourself with people who are similar to you in heritage, culture, ideology, and economic standing. Loyalty in all your relationships is essential. You are generally most compatible with Cancerians, Virgos, and Pisceans who are gentle and compassionate like yourself.

Your greatest strengths have been your unfaltering loyalty and steadfastness. Your challenge is to become more open-minded and less stubborn.

GEMINI

From May 22, 2:08 through June 22, 10:21

The Creative Thinker

You think therefore you are, Gemini of 1927. In fact, your ideas may define you, rather than your job, heritage, or social standing. Your restless mind is always busy and your thoughts may be quite inspired. Quite likely, you are rather attached to your ideas and want to express them, perhaps creatively. You possess a good imagination and might excel as a story or script-writer. Born as the first "talkies" were being produced, you might have been influenced by this medium—and by the advent of television during your youth.

You probably place a high value on knowledge and intelligence. If your educational opportunities weren't the best, you probably taught yourself and sought to learn everything you could. Most likely, you are an avid reader and collect information through all forms of communication. You might even have chosen a career in one of the communication fields, such as journalism, computers, advertising, or publishing. Teaching could also be a good avenue for you; you love sharing ideas and can inspire young minds.

Growing up during the dawn of the automobile age may have encouraged your restless nature; you tend to be on the go much of the time. Whether or not you reach distant lands, you are probably an "armchair traveler." *National Geographic*, which published the first color underwater pictures the year of your birth, might be one of your favorite magazines. You might even combine work and travel.

For the most part, you are friendly and good-natured, attracting many companions. Your social calendar is usually full for you have so many interests and activities that you can barely fit them all in. In relationships, you prefer people who are easy to talk to and have a creative way of looking at the world, such as artists and writers who can inspire your own imagination. In love and in work, you want the people close to you to be friends too. Leos, Aquarians, and Librans are usually among your best matches.

Your greatest strength is your rich and colorful way of expressing yourself. Your challenge is to distinguish between useful and superfluous information.

➤ Read about your Chinese Astrological sign on page 838. ➤ Read about your Personal Planets on page 826. ➤ Read about your personal Mystical Card on page 856.

1927

TAURUS
Your Personal Planets

YOUR LOVE POTENTIAL
Venus in Gemini, Apr. 21, 2:32 - May 12, 8:32
Venus in Cancer, May 12, 8:33 - May 22, 2:07

YOUR DRIVE AND AMBITION
Mars in Cancer, Apr. 21, 2:32 - May 22, 2:07

YOUR LUCK MAGNETISM
Jupiter in Pisces, Apr. 21, 2:32 - May 22, 2:07

World Events

May 9 – Canberra is made the new capital of Australia.

May 21 – Charles Lindbergh completes the first solo non-stop flight from New York to Paris.

The Duke and Duchess of York at the opening of the new parliament house in Canberra, Australia

GEMINI
Your Personal Planets

YOUR LOVE POTENTIAL
Venus in Cancer, May 22, 2:08 - June 08, 2:50
Venus in Leo, June 08, 2:51 - June 22, 10:21

YOUR DRIVE AND AMBITION
Mars in Cancer, May 22, 2:08 - June 06, 11:35
Mars in Leo, June 06, 11:36 - June 22, 10:21

YOUR LUCK MAGNETISM
Jupiter in Pisces, May 22, 2:08 - June 06, 10:13
Jupiter in Aries, June 06, 10:14 - June 22, 10:21

World Events

May 31 – The last Model T Ford comes off the production line.

June 4 – The Indonesian Nationalist Party is founded.

1927

YOUR LOVE POTENTIAL

Venus in Leo, June 22, 10:22 - July 07, 18:54
Venus in Virgo, July 07, 18:55 - July 23, 21:16

YOUR DRIVE AND AMBITION

Mars in Leo, June 22, 10:22 - July 23, 21:16

YOUR LUCK MAGNETISM

Jupiter in Aries, June 22, 10:22 - July 23, 21:16

World Events

June 29 – A total eclipse of the Sun is witnessed from the north of England.

July 4 – American playwright Neil Simon is born.

Thomas Edison celebrates the fiftieth anniversary of his invention, the phonograph

LEO
Your Personal Planets

YOUR LOVE POTENTIAL

Venus in Virgo, July 23, 21:17 - Aug. 24, 4:04

YOUR DRIVE AND AMBITION

Mars in Leo, July 23, 21:17 - Aug. 25, 7:46
Mars in Virgo, Aug. 25, 7:47 - Aug. 24, 4:04

YOUR LUCK MAGNETISM

Jupiter in Aries, July 23, 21:17 - Aug. 24, 4:04

World Events

Aug. 6 – American pop artist Andy Warhol is born.

Aug. 11 – Eamon de Valera and forty-four other Irish deputies swear allegiance to the British Crown and take their seats in the Irish Parliament.

CANCER

From June 22, 10:22 through July 23, 21:16

The Benevolent Leader

Your sense of identity is linked with your heritage, Cancer of 1927. Where you came from and the legacy you leave are matters of great importance to you. You see yourself as a strong link in a long chain, carrying the traditions, responsibilities, and hopes of the past on to future generations. You were born at a time when the structures, established orders, and traditions of many nations were being called into question, which may have given you a desire for continuity and connection.

In one sense, you may believe that might makes right. However, you also understand that those in power have an obligation to protect those who are entrusted to their care. You are particularly concerned with caring for the young, realizing that they are the future. In your own circle, you may be the one people turn to for advice, direction, or encouragement—family members and friends know they can rely on you.

Although you may accept the status quo, you may also find it necessary to adapt to a changing world occasionally. You might benefit from taking some risks that require you to reach beyond your comfort level. A born leader, you can inspire others to follow your direction for you engender trust. Instinctively, you probably know what others want and need. You also possess natural creative ability that enables you to breathe new life into old structures and practices. These talents could have served you well in a career in politics, entertainment, advertising, or architecture.

You are loyal and devoted to your loved ones. Generous, warm, and supportive of the people you care about, you may be the matriarch or patriarch of your clan. Your home is your castle, and most likely everyone tends to gather there. People who share your creative interests are often your favorite companions. You usually get along well with Pisceans, Leos, and Taureans, who share your love of beauty and desire for close personal ties.

Your greatest strength is your loyalty to the people and land that you love. Your challenge is to broaden your horizons and take chances in areas beyond your own territory.

LEO

From July 23, 21:17 through August 24, 4:04

The Meticulous Artist

Like violinist Yehudi Menuhin, whose flawless performance as a child virtuoso created a sensation in New York and elsewhere in the world the year you were born, you seek perfection in your art, whatever it may be. And your best is quite remarkable, Leo of 1927. With your rare combination of imagination, drive, and discipline, you excel at even the most daunting tasks. Whether your path takes you into the world of art, business, or politics, you set the standard to which others aspire.

One of the secrets to your success is your belief in yourself. You take risks because you are confident that you can handle whatever situation might arise. You take the road less traveled when you think it will lead you to your goal faster. Your occasionally unconventional ideas distinguish you in the crowd. Perhaps you broke new ground in theater, music, graphic design, or fashion. Born as films with sound wowed the world, you might have made your own contributions to the movies.

Not only do you have great ideas, you are practical and persistent enough to get your creations into the real world. You want people to benefit from your efforts and use what you devise. Therefore, you might turn your talents toward creating practical products that are beautiful as well. Nevertheless, regardless of how good your work is, you are constantly refining and improving it.

Not only do you expect a great deal of yourself, you have high standards for other people and you choose your associates carefully. At times, however, the people close to you may feel you are too critical of them. Quite likely, your friends and loved ones might share an interest in your work, and a partner could be a valuable asset in advancing your career. Ariens and Sagittarians are often your best matches, for they are energetic and self-confident like you. However, you might benefit from allying yourself with Virgos in close personal relationships.

Your greatest strength is your ability to produce creative work of a very high caliber. Your challenge is to not look down on other people who can't perform at your level.

➤ Read about your Chinese Astrological sign on page 838. ➤ Read about your Personal Planets on page 826. ➤ Read about your personal Mystical Card on page 856.

VIRGO

From August 24, 4:05 through September 24, 1:16

The Perfection Seeker

No one could ever fault you for not doing your best, Virgo of 1927. Conscientious and hard working, you strive for perfection—in your work and at home—making sure you don't overlook any details. Never one to shirk your duty, you sometimes take on more than your share and may push yourself too hard. Because you want to feel needed, you sometimes allow others to take advantage of you.

Practical matters probably interest you more than philosophical ones—what good is a nice idea unless someone else can use it? You have a knack for making the best of whatever materials you have at hand, whether you are fixing a meal or a carburetor. You make up for what you may lack in creativity with effort, diligently honing your skills to a degree that few can match. You could have been successful at accounting, engineering, editing, or any other job that requires meticulous attention to detail. However, it's important for you to set priorities. Otherwise, your perfectionism can cause you to rework the same issue over and over instead of moving ahead.

Born at a time when malaria, tuberculosis, and trachoma ravaged areas of the USSR and infectious diseases threatened the health of all people, you may have a fear of contagion. Your concern for your own health and others' might have led you to work in the field of medicine, nutrition, biology, or sanitation. Social services, too, may have interested you, for you want to help make the world a better place for all.

Your critical nature probably shows itself in relationships, too, for you are quite discriminating and particular about the people you let into your life. However, you are usually devoted to your loved ones and put a great deal of selfless effort into caring for them. Most compatible with people who, like yourself, are hard-working, meticulous, and restrained, you generally get along well with Capricorns, Cancerians, Scorpios, and other Virgos.

Your greatest strength is your dedication to improving everything you touch. Your challenge is to appreciate when something is good enough so you don't grind the diamond into dust.

LIBRA

From September 24, 1:17 through October 24, 10:06

Injustice Fighter

Justice and fairness are important to you, Libra of 1927, and you are willing to fight to make sure people are treated decently. Born when cruel dictators and military regimes were seizing power in Europe and other parts of the world, you may have a strong dislike of tyranny. Like most Librans, you attempt to establish harmony in all areas of your life, but unlike other Librans, you can be quite forceful at times: you might not initiate a fight, but you won't run away from one either.

Your keen sense of right and wrong could lead you to champion a wide range of causes in business or social affairs. At the time you were born fear of unconventional views ran high in many countries—demonstrated by the controversial execution of anarchists Sacco and Vanzetti in the U.S.—and this xenophobia might have influenced you deeply. You may not always agree with other people's ideas, but you support their right to express them.

You usually attempt to see both sides of any issue and often can help opposing factions reach a compromise. You might also be called upon to settle disputes between friends, family members, or co-workers. You know how to make a good argument and can be a persuasive orator. This special talent could be an asset in professions such as law or politics.

Although you rarely act without considering how your behavior will affect others, you ultimately rely on your own judgment. Relationships of all kinds are important to you, and you understand the value of sharing both work and pleasure with others. You are likely to maintain a large network of friends and associates, who enjoy your outgoing charm and respect your leadership qualities. Although you can get along with almost anyone, you are usually most compatible with Aquarians, Geminis, Sagittarians, and other Librans. You might also find Virgos to be good partners in business and love; they are as orderly and hard working as you are.

Your greatest strengths are your willingness to fight the good fight and your knack for motivating people. Your challenge is to know when to fight and when to make peace.

➤ Read about your Chinese Astrological sign on page 838. ➤ Read about your Personal Planets on page 826. ➤ Read about your personal Mystical Card on page 856.

1927

VIRGO
Your Personal Planets

YOUR LOVE POTENTIAL
Venus in Virgo, Aug. 24, 4:05 - Sept. 24, 1:16

YOUR DRIVE AND AMBITION
Mars in Virgo, Aug. 24, 4:05 - Sept. 10, 14:18
Mars in Libra, Sept. 10, 14:19 - Sept. 24, 1:16

YOUR LUCK MAGNETISM
Jupiter in Aries, Aug. 24, 4:05 - Sept. 11, 3:42
Jupiter in Pisces, Sept. 11, 3:43 - Sept. 24, 1:16

World Events

Aug. 27 – Riots break out in Paris over the executions of Italian anarchists Nicola Sacco and Bartolomeo Vanzetti.

Sept. 14 – Dance pioneer Isadora Duncan dies when her scarf becomes caught in the wheel of a car.

The first talking picture, "The Jazz Singer"

LIBRA
Your Personal Planets

YOUR LOVE POTENTIAL
Venus in Virgo, Sept. 24, 1:17 - Oct. 24, 10:06

YOUR DRIVE AND AMBITION
Mars in Libra, Sept. 24, 1:17 - Oct. 24, 10:06

YOUR LUCK MAGNETISM
Jupiter in Pisces, Sept. 24, 1:17 - Oct. 24, 10:06

World Events

Sept. 30 – Babe Ruth, holder of the World Series record for consecutive scoreless innings pitched, adds to his legend by scoring his sixtieth home run of the season.

Oct. 6 – *The Jazz Singer*, starring Al Jolson, ushers in the era of the talking picture show.

1927

SCORPIO
Your Personal Planets

YOUR LOVE POTENTIAL
Venus in Virgo, Oct. 24, 10:07 - Nov. 09, 13:25
Venus in Libra, Nov. 09, 13:26 - Nov. 23, 7:13

YOUR DRIVE AND AMBITION
Mars in Libra, Oct. 24, 10:07 - Oct. 26, 0:19
Mars in Scorpio, Oct. 26, 0:20 - Nov. 23, 7:13

YOUR LUCK MAGNETISM
Jupiter in Pisces, Oct. 24, 10:07 - Nov. 23, 7:13

World Events

Oct. 27 - The world's first sound news film, Fox Movietone News, is shown in New York.

Oct. 29 - Russian archeologist Peter Kozloff uncovers the tomb of Genghis Khan in the Gobi Desert.

Chiang Kai-Shek marries Meling Soong

SAGITTARIUS
Your Personal Planets

YOUR LOVE POTENTIAL
Venus in Libra, Nov. 23, 7:14 - Dec. 08, 21:25
Venus in Scorpio, Dec. 08, 21:26 - Dec. 22, 20:18

YOUR DRIVE AND AMBITION
Mars in Scorpio, Nov. 23, 7:14 - Dec. 08, 11:00
Mars in Sagittarius, Dec. 08, 11:01 - Dec. 22, 20:18

YOUR LUCK MAGNETISM
Jupiter in Pisces, Nov. 23, 7:14 - Dec. 22, 20:18

World Events

Dec. 1 - Chinese General Chiang Kai-Shek marries Meling Soong, sister-in-law to former President of the republic Sun Yat-Sen.

Dec. 12 - Communist forces seize Canton in China.

SCORPIO
From October 24, 10:07 through November 23, 7:13

Conqueror of Obstacles

No matter how great the obstacle, you can usually find a way to overcome it, Scorpio of 1927. During your youth, you witnessed the ultimate power struggle as war gripped the planet. As a result, you believe that you must use your own power if you are going to succeed—and use it you do. You possess an amazing ability to marshal your formidable forces and no one had better get in your way.

Behind your controlled exterior beats a passionate heart. This combination may manifest as ruthlessness when necessary. In business, you could be a dynamic leader, an agent of transformation, or both. The year you were born events—such as television inventor John Baird's transmission of his own image from Leeds to London—changed our view of the world forever and could have caused you to see life as constantly changing. Although you may try to control things, you've probably undergone many shifts during your life. The insights you've gained enable you to transform the lives of others.

You may have an almost uncanny intuition. Therefore, you could be a master at psychiatry, detective work, or espionage. Your desire to plumb the depths might also have sparked an interest in mining, surgery, oceanography, or archeology—much like Russian Peter Kozloff, who uncovered the tomb of Genghis Khan around the time of your birth. When it comes to handling financial and human resources, you possess remarkable instincts that could make money.

While many people probably respect you, you may not always be the easiest person to like. You tend to be serious and skeptical. In relationships, you don't allow many people into your inner circle. Learning to trust and open up to those you love can be difficult for you. However, once you do let someone get close, you are a devoted and loyal companion. Intensely emotional, you are usually most comfortable with other sensitive, private types, such as Cancerians, Virgos, and Pisceans.

Your greatest strength is your ability to focus all your energy, commitment, and passion on any objective. Your challenge is to learn to be more trusting and objective.

SAGITTARIUS
From November 23, 7:14 through December 22, 20:18

The Hard Working Dreamer

Like all Sagittarians, you are a dreamer, Sagittarius of 1927, but you also have what it takes to make your dreams come true. You understand the necessity of hard work and realize that success, as Albert Einstein said, is ten percent inspiration and ninety percent perspiration.

Your inventive and forward-thinking mind is never at a loss for clever ideas. You want to learn and experience everything you possibly can. Even if you didn't have a chance to attend a first-rate college you have probably educated yourself and consider learning a lifelong pursuit. Much of your knowledge may have come through personal experience, not through books. With your knowledge and wit, you can be a fascinating conversationalist and even could have been an inspired teacher.

You probably enjoy traveling and may have had an opportunity to visit many places. Quite likely, some of your excursions were taken for work or were connected with some type of duty, such as military service. Like Charles Lindbergh, who completed the first solo non-stop flight from New York to Paris in the year of your birth, you might be willing to endure some hardships in order to expand your horizons. You might have chosen a career that involved traveling, such as pilot, journalist, truck driver, or sales representative. When you're not actually on the move, you may enjoy watching travel shows on television or reading about distant lands.

Although you do have a somewhat shy and serious side, you are generally an outgoing and cheerful individual who enjoys the company of friends and family. People find your pleasant personality and sense of humor attractive, and your circle of acquaintances might include people from various cultures, ideologies, and walks of life. For the most part, you get along well with outgoing types, such as Ariens, Leos, Librans, and Aquarians, though imaginative Pisceans might also be drawn to you.

Your greatest strength is your ability to combine imagination with pragmatism. Your challenge is to overcome the obstacles and limitations that life presents to you, so that your dreams bear fruit.

► Read about your Chinese Astrological sign on page 838. ► Read about your Personal Planets on page 826. ► Read about your personal Mystical Card on page 856.

CAPRICORN

From December 22, 20:19 through December 31, 23:59

The Idealistic Realist

You possess a special blend of realism and idealism that has probably allowed you to accomplish a great deal, Capricorn of 1927. Like other Capricorns, you take a practical and orderly approach to life. Once you know where you're going, you can move at a fairly rapid pace but you aren't rigid or narrow about following the course you've set.

Although you tend to be rather conservative, on occasion you are willing to take a risk—albeit a calculated one. You know a good thing when you see it and can usually capitalize on it, as Fox studio did when it released the first dialogue film the year of your birth. You know how to fit the pieces of the big picture together so the end result matches your vision. These valuable qualities could have enabled you to be quite successful at whatever you undertook—especially when your persistence and common sense are factored into the equation.

Money is important to you and you might have worked hard to acquire as much as possible. While you have dreams, you can put your idealism aside for the greater economic good, like Mexico did when it opened land to foreign investment the year of your birth. Business is your ideal arena where you could have profited from your practicality and foresight. With your natural managerial skills, you know how to make the best use of time, money, people, and other resources. You might also have earned money for other people who recognized your talents and invested in you. A career in banking, insurance, investments, international trade, or manufacturing could have suited you well.

In relationships, you tend to be serious and a bit cautious. You don't let many people get close, but once you do let them in you are a loyal and devoted companion. Business relationships can be easier for you in some ways—you might even meet many of your friends through your work. Usually you are most compatible with Scorpios, Virgos, Taureans, and Pisceans.

Your greatest strength is your ability to bring your dreams down to earth and apply them in practical ways. Your challenge is to be more trusting of other people.

CAPRICORN
Your Personal Planets

YOUR LOVE POTENTIAL
Venus in Scorpio, Dec. 22, 20:19 - Dec. 31, 23:59

YOUR DRIVE AND AMBITION
Mars in Sagittarius, Dec. 22, 20:19 - Dec. 31, 23:59

YOUR LUCK MAGNETISM
Jupiter in Pisces, Dec. 22, 20:19 - Dec. 31, 23:59

World Events

Dec. 27 – The musical *Show Boat*, with music by Jerome Kern, premieres on Broadway.

Dec. 28 – Charles Lindbergh lands in Mexico City, having broken another aviation record.

Wall Street stock exchange during the panic of the stock market crash

Special Feature
Money, Astrology, and the Crash of '29

(Continued from page 225)

That afternoon on Black Thursday, a hurried meeting of top Wall Street bankers was convened at J. P. Morgan & Co., and a reassuring statement issued by one of the Morgan partners temporarily halted the plunging prices. Still, the report that was carried across the U.S. and around the globe described the dramatic climax to this era of avid speculation as "the most terrifying stampede of selling ever experienced." Over the next few days, the feeling of panic subsided as investors were lulled into a sense of security by small rallies.

Then, on Black Tuesday, October 29, 1929, the Crash began in earnest. Within the first few hours of trading, prices fell enough to wipe out all the gains made in the previous year. Blocks of stock were dumped at any price they could fetch. There was a general loss of confidence in the market and not one person or group of individuals could stem the torrent of selling. It was reported that hotel clerks were asking customers if they wanted a room "for sleeping or jumping." On October 30, *Variety* ran its now-famous headline: "Wall St. Lays an Egg."

The selling continued through November 13 when stocks hit bottom and over $30 billion disappeared from the American economy. Most stocks wouldn't recover their 1929 highs for another twenty-five years. But the 1929 Crash, as it turned out, was only the beginning. The market wouldn't hit absolute bottom until March 1933, by which time stocks had lost eighty percent of their value. The fall in share prices meant that entrepreneurs couldn't raise the money to run their companies, and soon 100,000 American companies were forced to close. A worldwide depression set in, with global manufacturing down by forty percent, and 33 million persons out of work.

The worst crash since 1929 occurred in October 1987 when once again Saturn was in Sagittarius. Saturn's next sojourn will be in 2015.

In the aftermath of the Crash and the Great Depression that followed, economists tried to understand what had happened, and how to prevent it from happening again. One of the most popular theories on the subject came from John Kenneth Galbraith's best-selling book *The Great Crash of 1929*. He theorized that the Crash was caused by the speculative mania and misguided policies. The hard times that followed brought the inevitable consequences of giddy excess.

(Continued on page 241)

➤ Read Cayce's crash prediction in "The First New Age Psychic" on page 265.
➤ Read Evangeline Adam's crash prediction in "Astrology goes on Trial" on page 185.

233

1928

Blazing New Trails: Uranus in Aries

Aries is the first sign of the zodiac. It is initiative incarnate, the beginning of all things, the arbiter of self-expression, assertion, and aggression. Imagine the baby's very first cry. That is the very essence of the astrological sign of Aries. The key phrase associated with Aries is "I AM". When mighty, electrified Uranus meets Mars, the God of War and also the ruler of Aries, we can expect a pretty dynamic firework display. It is an explosive combination of intense energies, sure to brand changes into the hearts of many. Social reform is usually a key factor when Uranus goes into Aries. On May 7, the age for women voters in Britain was finally reduced from thirty to twenty-one. This was a gigantic leap forward in democratic progress for the women of Great Britain, and by extension, women around the world. Their victory would obviously have implications for other women hungry to make political and social leaps forward in their own countries.

Feisty Leo Amelia Earhart became the first woman passenger to fly over the Atlantic on June 18. On November 20, Mrs. Glen Hyde became the first woman to dare Grand Canyon rapids in a scow, which is a large flat-bottomed boat with broad, square ends. It was a daring mode of transportation, to be sure. Richard E. Byrd, American aviator and polar explorer, started an expedition to the Antarctic this year. He was not to return until 1930. Adventure was in the air all over the world when Uranus entered Aries in 1928.

Sagittarian anthropologist and strong proponent of women's rights Margaret Mead published her ground-breaking work *Coming of Age in Samoa* in 1928. It was a psychological study of youth and is still recognized as a scientific classic. The New York Stock Exchange went wild with trading volume so high—6.6 million—that it had to be closed to record transactions initiated by enthusiastic traders. And Japanese Emperor Hirohito was crowned in Kyoto, "by divine decree." All in all, the astrological influence of Uranus in Aries signified a wildly energized march toward the new and unexplored in life.

Alexander Fleming discovers penicillin

Anastasia, daughter of the last tsar of Russia

Emperor Hirohito is crowned in Japan

NEW KINGS AND RULERS

China was united under the Nationalist flag of Chiang Kai-Shek, who became president, while Hirohito ascended the Japanese throne as emperor. Stalin introduced his first five-year plan to establish communist principles for the gradual takeover of industry and agriculture. Kemal Ataturk introduced more reforms in Turkey, adopting the Roman alphabet and separating the state from the faith of Islam. Republican Herbert Hoover was elected U.S. President. As Prohibition continued, deaths rose due to poisoning from unregulated liquor and enforcement was increased. The New York Stock Exchange went wild with trading volume so high that it had to be closed to give time for recording transactions initiated by enthusiastic traders. A young woman arrived in New York claiming to be Anastasia, the Tsar's youngest daughter who had "survived" the family massacre of 1918. In Britain, penicillin was accidentally discovered by Alexander Fleming, and the anthropologist Margaret Mead wrote on the culture of Samoa. Gershwin performed his *An American in Paris* to a sell-out New York crowd, while Ravel's *Bolero* was given its very first performance.

234

➤ Read "Money, Astrology, and the Crash of '29" by Sophia Mason on page 225.

CAPRICORN

From January 01, 0:00 through January 21, 6:56

The Playful Worker

Like most Capricorns, once you undertake a task you see it through. But just because you take your work and other responsibilities seriously doesn't mean you can't have fun too. You are a firm believer in the saying "all work and no play makes you dull," and you wouldn't let that happen.

You were born when the New York Stock Exchange was enjoying a period of record gains. The optimism that existed the year of your birth may have given you an innate confidence in your ability to earn money. As a result, you might be willing to take a few risks in financial areas. Of course, those risks are calculated ones, you study the odds and make your decisions based on a combination of facts and instincts. Money is important to you, after all.

Your management and finance skills could have served you well in banking, investments, real estate, manufacturing, or economics. However, your special blend of pragmatism and vision could be valuable in virtually any field of business. One of your talents is being able to take a small operation or project and build it into something outstanding. Like Bell Laboratories,·hard at work developing revolutionary new television technology, released the year after you were born, you have a knack for spotting a promising idea and turning it into a real winner.

Once you've taken care of business, you usually do something that affords you pleasure, such as attending an athletic event or going dancing. Listening to or playing music could be a favorite pastime, for you were born during the exciting Jazz Age. You probably play as hard as you work. Your usually outgoing and pleasant personality is likely to attract many companions. Taureans and Pisceans are often your best choices as friends and partners; however, you could also have fun with lively Sagittarians.

Your greatest strength is your ability to combine vision with practicality, in order to make dreams realities. Your challenge is to communicate your plans, desires, and ideas clearly and openly with other people. That way, they can participate in working and playing with you.

AQUARIUS

From January 21, 6:57 through February 19, 21:18

The Intellectual Pioneer

Never one to follow convention, you rush ahead where few people dare to go, at least mentally. Your explorations into uncharted territory are likely to turn up some unique and intriguing new ideas. You need to find answers to life's perplexing questions through independent study and personal experience rather than taking someone else's word for it. Some of your own discoveries have probably been boons to humankind much like penicillin, which was discovered this year.

Some of your intellectual adventures may take you into the realm of science and technology. Your inventiveness and ability to "think outside the box" can be real assets here. Perhaps you even pursued a career in a technological or scientific field; it's likely that you have a real aptitude in these areas. Aviation might also have been of interest and you may have admired pioneers in the field such as Amelia Earhart. She became the first woman passenger to fly over the Atlantic in 1928.

One of your special qualities is your ability to take a novel idea and find useful applications for it. You might even have turned some of your brainstorms into cash. When it comes to making money, you tend to be practical and persistent, and, when a concept captures your imagination, you are willing to put in the necessary effort to bring it to fruition.

Although you enjoy going your own way, you tend to be outgoing and sociable as well. Consequently, you probably have some very good friends who share your interests. You might also be involved with one or more organizations or groups, for you enjoy the stimulation of intellectual give and take. Friendship is important to you, and the people you care about know they can rely on you. You choose your companions carefully, so your relationships are likely to endure for many years. Usually you get along best with Ariens, Geminis, Librans, and Sagittarians, but you might also appreciate a Capricorn's loyalty and common sense.

Your greatest strength is your unique combination of ingenuity and determination. Your challenge is to learn from others' experiences as well as your own.

1928

CAPRICORN
Your Personal Planets

YOUR LOVE POTENTIAL
Venus in Scorpio, Jan. 01, 0:00 - Jan. 04, 0:05
Venus in Sagittarius, Jan. 04, 0:06 - Jan. 21, 6:56

YOUR DRIVE AND AMBITION
Mars in Sagittarius, Jan. 01, 0:00 - Jan. 19, 2:01
Mars in Capricorn, Jan. 19, 2:02 - Jan. 21, 6:56

YOUR LUCK MAGNETISM
Jupiter in Pisces, Jan. 01, 0:00 - Jan. 21, 6:56

World Events

Jan. 3 – The U.S. sends 1,000 additional Marines to Nicaragua to fight the guerilla leader General Sandino.

Jan. 11 – English poet and novelist Thomas Hardy dies.

Nicaraguan leader General Sandino

AQUARIUS
Your Personal Planets

YOUR LOVE POTENTIAL
Venus in Sagittarius, Jan. 21, 6:57 - Jan. 29, 1:12
Venus in Capricorn, Jan. 29, 1:13 - Feb. 19, 21:18

YOUR DRIVE AND AMBITION
Mars in Capricorn, Jan. 21, 6:57 - Feb. 19, 21:18

YOUR LUCK MAGNETISM
Jupiter in Pisces, Jan. 21, 6:57 - Jan. 23, 2:53
Jupiter in Aries, Jan. 23, 2:54 - Feb. 19, 21:18

World Events

Feb. 7 – The U.S. and France sign an arbitration treaty.

Feb. 15 – After seventy years of work, the new *Oxford English Dictionary* is finally completed.

➤ Read about your Chinese Astrological sign on page 838. ➤ Read about your Personal Planets on page 826. ➤ Read about your personal Mystical Card on page 856.

YOUR LOVE POTENTIAL

Venus in Capricorn, Feb. 19, 21:19 - Feb. 22, 16:14
Venus in Aquarius, Feb. 22, 16:15 - Mar. 18, 3:24
Venus in Pisces, Mar. 18, 3:25 - Mar. 20, 20:43

YOUR DRIVE AND AMBITION

Mars in Capricorn, Feb. 19, 21:19 - Feb. 28, 6:29
Mars in Aquarius, Feb. 28, 6:30 - Mar. 20, 20:43

YOUR LUCK MAGNETISM

Jupiter in Aries, Feb. 19, 21:19 - Mar. 20, 20:43

World Events

Feb. 20 – Japan's first universal suffrage elections take place in Tokyo.

Feb. 28 – Communist forces attack Peking.

A Medal of Honor for Charles Lindbergh

ARIES
Your Personal Planets

YOUR LOVE POTENTIAL

Venus in Pisces, Mar. 20, 20:44 - Apr. 11, 13:34
Venus in Aries, Apr. 11, 13:35 - Apr. 20, 8:16

YOUR DRIVE AND AMBITION

Mars in Aquarius, Mar. 20, 20:44 - Apr. 07, 14:26
Mars in Pisces, Apr. 07, 14:27 - Apr. 20, 8:16

YOUR LUCK MAGNETISM

Jupiter in Aries, Mar. 20, 20:44 - Apr. 20, 8:16

World Events

Mar. 21 – Charles Lindbergh is awarded the Congressional Medal of Honor.

Apr. 4 – American poet and novelist Maya Angelou is born.

PISCES
From February 19, 21:19 through March 20, 20:43

The Humanitarian Advocate

A true humanitarian, your kindness and compassion know no bounds. You are not only concerned about the well being of your loved ones, you want everyone in the world to have a better life and you are willing to do your part to improve the lot of those less fortunate than yourself. You believe everyone deserves a fair chance; you might champion the cause of animals as well.

Despite your gentle outward demeanor, you can be a staunch advocate for change. You don't mind bucking the system and usually take the side of the underdog. Your causes tend to be progressive—issues such as peace, ecology, equality, and feeding the hungry might be important to you. Born the year Mexico abolished summary executions and England lowered the voting age for women from thirty to twenty-one, you may have been influenced psychologically by the tenor of the times. Occasionally, though, you may be more idealistic than realistic. You might also hold so strongly to your beliefs that at times you have trouble compromising.

Perhaps you chose to express your humanitarian nature by working for charity, social services, government, or as a teacher. A job in health care or with a spiritual organization, ministering to the needs of those who sought your assistance, might also have appealed to you. Being of service is more important to you than earning a lot of money. Later in life, you may volunteer your time to a worthy cause. You want to feel that your efforts have had a beneficial effect on others.

With loved ones, you are loyal, compassionate, and selfless. Your kind and friendly personality attracts many people, especially those who have a humanitarian bent. Your circle of associates is likely to include unconventional types, activists, idea people, and perhaps some artists or musicians. Usually, you get along well with Cancerians, Taureans, and other sensitive, caring sorts, but you might find idealistic and individualistic Aquarians and Ariens to be stimulating companions.

Your greatest strength is your whole-hearted concern for one and all. Your challenge is to choose your battles wisely.

ARIES
From March 20, 20:44 through April 20, 8:16

The Fearless Adventurer

You need to be free to experience everything the world has to offer. Perhaps you were influenced by the expansive energy of the year you were born in which the first commercial aircraft, the *Graf Zeppelin* dirigible, crossed the Atlantic. With your restless and inquisitive nature, you tend to rush forward into uncharted territory. Even though you occasionally go way out on a limb, things seem to work out for you, perhaps because you believe they will.

However, you'd be wise to use care rather than rushing headlong into risky situations. You possess a strong sense of your own abilities. You enjoy challenges that force you to stretch until you reach a new personal best. With your tremendous energy and enthusiasm, you can usually accomplish more than three people—if you don't lose interest before you finish. Restless and impatient, you may tend to be more concerned with the next activity than the one you're involved in right now.

Good luck seems to come to you, although it's true that you also make your own luck. Your entrepreneurial spirit may have served you well in a job in sales, exploration, journalism, or inventing. You might also have started one or more small businesses. Sports probably interest you for you like a clearly defined opponent and challenge. With your natural athletic ability, you could even have made a career of sports. The military, police work, or fire fighting might also have been good choices for you, allowing you to express your combativeness and desire for excitement constructively.

You may not spend much time with loved ones due to your individualistic nature and your strong need for freedom. However, you probably have buddies with whom you do things, such as fishing, camping, playing golf, or watching sporting events. Generally you get along with other outspoken, active, independent people including Aquarians, Leos, Geminis, and Sagittarians. But in one-to-one relationships, you might benefit from the quiet, calming influence of a Piscean.

Your greatest strengths are your energy and courage. Your challenge is to learn to finish what you start.

➤ Read about your Chinese Astrological sign on page 838. ➤ Read about your Personal Planets on page 826. ➤ Read about your personal Mystical Card on page 856.

TAURUS

From April 20, 8:17 through May 21, 7:51

The Persistent Partner

Your success is due, in large part, to your persistence and patience. More like the tortoise than the hare, you proceed in a slow, steady manner until you reach your goal. Your special combination of strength and focus keeps you from giving up when the going gets tough. You may not capture as much attention as the flashier types, but your accomplishments have a better chance of enduring.

In fact, many of your projects may have been undertaken with permanence in mind. The ultimate realist, you place a high value on things you can touch, measure, and use. Money and the material goods it can buy are important to you and with your drive and talent you might have managed to acquire your share. You also have a fondness for things that appeal to the senses: good food, creature comforts, art, and music. Born during the Jazz Age, you might enjoy performers such as Louis Armstrong, popular the year you were born. Perhaps you have musical talent yourself.

You might be better at implementing other people's brainstorms than coming up with your own. With your appreciation for beauty, you give whatever you produce a touch of artistry. Your skills and creativity could have been well used in a career in interior decorating, architecture, fashion, carpentry, landscaping, or theater. Your interest in food might have led you to work as a cook, restaurateur, farmer, or grocer.

Over the years you have probably benefited from partnerships and cooperative ventures such as the merger between Chrysler and Dodge that made automotive history this year. Although you can be stubborn at times, you are usually willing to compromise to keep the peace. You are likely to be drawn to creative types, especially Pisceans, and those whose loyalty and reliability make you feel secure, including Cancerians and Capricorns. Generous toward your loved ones, you enjoy the companionship of others and your easygoing nature attracts many. When friends and family gather at your home, you always make them feel welcome.

Your greatest strength is your tenacity. Your challenge is to be flexible when necessary.

GEMINI

From May 21, 7:52 through June 21, 16:05

The Earnest Thinker

Your mind is always busy, examining, contemplating, and inventing. When you aren't deep in thought, you are probably gleaning information from others. Just about any subject interests you and you can discourse on a wide variety of topics. You see learning as an adventure and pursue it with great enthusiasm, as did prizefighter Gene Tunney who quit the ring this year to study philosophy at the Sorbonne in Paris.

A diligent student, you might be self-taught in many areas and have continued educating yourself throughout your life by reading, attending lectures, and watching educational television. At times you may have experienced obstacles or delays that interfered with your learning, at least temporarily.

Some of your ideas are probably a bit unconventional. You may not even understand where some of your brainstorms come from—they just pop into your head, seemingly out of nowhere. You possess a special blend of originality and pragmatism that allows you to find solutions to problems that stump other people. Your inventiveness and imagination could have been valuable assets in a career in advertising, technology, the media, sales, or communication. With your lively oratory style and wealth of knowledge, you might also have been an inspired teacher. Writing, too, is likely to be a favorite pastime of yours, whether you simply record your experiences in a journal or compose a novel.

Although you highly prize ideas, you know these treasures are not to be locked away in a vault. They are meant to be shared and share them you do. One of your favorite activities is probably chatting with friends and loved ones, perhaps over a game of cards. A natural teacher, you enjoy inspiring others to think about things in new ways. You have an outgoing personality that attracts many companions who can teach you a thing or two, as well. Usually you enjoy the lively banter of Aquarians, Ariens, and other Geminis, though you might also be compatible with Librans.

Your greatest strength is your fertile and perceptive mind. Your challenge is to use your mental ability for the good of all.

➤ Read about your Chinese Astrological sign on page 838. ➤ Read about your Personal Planets on page 826. ➤ Read about your personal Mystical Card on page 856.

1928

TAURUS
Your Personal Planets

YOUR LOVE POTENTIAL
Venus in Aries, Apr. 20, 8:17 - May 06, 0:02
Venus in Taurus, May 06, 0:03 - May 21, 7:51

YOUR DRIVE AND AMBITION
Mars in Pisces, Apr. 20, 8:17 - May 16, 21:34
Mars in Aries, May 16, 21:35 - May 21, 7:51

YOUR LUCK MAGNETISM
Jupiter in Aries, Apr. 20, 8:17 - May 21, 7:51

World Events

Apr. 23 – American child actress and future diplomat Shirley Temple is born.

May 14 – Revolutionary Che Guevara is born.

Shirley Temple is born under the sign of Taurus

GEMINI
Your Personal Planets

YOUR LOVE POTENTIAL
Venus in Taurus, May 21, 7:52 - May 30, 10:59
Venus in Gemini, May 30, 11:00 - June 21, 16:05

YOUR DRIVE AND AMBITION
Mars in Aries, May 21, 7:52 - June 21, 16:05

YOUR LUCK MAGNETISM
Jupiter in Aries, May 21, 7:52 - June 04, 4:50
Jupiter in Taurus, June 04, 4:51 - June 21, 16:05

World Events

June 14 – Leading British suffragette Emmeline Pankhurst dies.

June 18 – Norwegian polar explorer Roald Amundsen is killed when his seaplane crashes near Spitzbergen during an attempt to rescue the crew of a downed Italian dirigible.

1928

CANCER
Your Personal Planets

YOUR LOVE POTENTIAL
Venus in Gemini, June 21, 16:06 - June 23, 21:41
Venus in Cancer, June 23, 21:42 - July 18, 7:15
Venus in Leo, July 18, 7:16 - July 23, 3:01

YOUR DRIVE AND AMBITION
Mars in Aries, June 21, 16:06 - June 26, 9:03
Mars in Taurus, June 26, 9:04 - July 23, 3:01

YOUR LUCK MAGNETISM
Jupiter in Taurus, June 21, 16:06 - July 23, 3:01

World Events

July 6 – The first all-talking movie, *The Lights Of New York*, premières in the city of its title.

July 21 – Queen of the London stage Dame Ellen Terry dies; her last request is for "no funeral gloom," but smiles and joyful music.

Gene Tunney's last fight

LEO
Your Personal Planets

YOUR LOVE POTENTIAL
Venus in Leo, July 23, 3:02 - Aug. 11, 15:28
Venus in Virgo, Aug. 11, 15:29 - Aug. 23, 9:52

YOUR DRIVE AND AMBITION
Mars in Taurus, July 23, 3:02 - Aug. 09, 4:09
Mars in Gemini, Aug. 09, 4:10 - Aug. 23, 9:52

YOUR LUCK MAGNETISM
Jupiter in Taurus, July 23, 3:02 - Aug. 23, 9:52

World Events

July 29 – Prizefighter Gene Tunney gives his last fight before quitting to study philosophy at the Sorbonne in Paris.

Aug. 9 – A stash of diamonds is retrieved from the wreck of the Belgian steamship *Elizabethville*, sunk during the war.

CANCER

From June 21, 16:06 through July 23, 3:01

The True Homebody

Cancers are known for being domestic, but you are probably the quint-essential homebody. You are so comfortable in your nest that you prefer to have other people to come to you. Your home may be the center of your universe. Once you put down roots, you aren't likely to pull them up again. If you can live near your family or your place of birth, all the better.

When it comes to making your home beautiful, you spare no effort or expense. You probably possess natural decorating talent and could even have used it professionally as an interior designer, architect, or carpenter. A job in real estate also might have appealed to you. Even if your home isn't grand or expensive, you have a knack for making it comfortable and welcoming. Your love of good food and your talents in the kitchen might have landed you a job in a restaurant or bakery. Perhaps you even grow your own food, for it's likely that you have a green thumb.

Financial security is very important to you too. Born during a year of wildly expansive trading on Wall Street that preceded the crash and Great Depression, you may have been convinced at an early age to hold on to your money. As a result, you may have squirreled away cash or made some careful investments that have provided you with a nest egg. Your desire to take care of your loved ones and to own nice things might have led you to work for a large, well-established firm where you could rely on a steady income.

Like the many nations who signed the Kellogg-Briand Treaty to outlaw war this year, you strive to create harmony and unity. You tend to surround yourself with other peace-loving individuals and often get along well with Pisceans, Taureans, and Virgos. Many of your companions are likely to come from backgrounds that are similar to yours, for you tend to feel uncertain around people who are very different.

Cautious and conservative, you are a good example of an upstanding citizen. Your greatest strength is your unwavering loyalty to your loved ones. Your challenge is to expand your horizons and your understanding of the world beyond your own doorstep.

LEO

From July 23, 3:02 through August 23, 9:52

The Creative Leader

Leo is the sign of royalty and you probably have a touch of the king or queen in you. Like the Japanese Emperor Hirohito who ascended to the throne this year, you may feel that you were born to rule. It's likely that you possess a sense of style that sets you apart from the masses. You certainly appreciate beautiful and luxurious things. Your home is your castle and you do your best to make it a place that is truly fit for royalty. With your good taste and creativity, you can turn even a modest dwelling into a showplace.

You might express your artistry in other ways too. Quite likely, you possess an abundance of creativity and might have chosen to pursue a career in commercial or fine art. Perhaps you have musical talent as well. The theater could have been ideal for you, allowing you to shine in the spotlight. Even if you didn't use your artistic ability professionally, you probably dabble in one or more creative areas, such as painting, photography, writing poetry, singing, or designing and making your own clothes.

Other people tend to see you as a leader, for you project confidence and strength. Your vitality and personal magnetism also may have helped you to create a good impression. You may have found it relatively easy to rise to the top. Because you believe you can succeed at whatever you undertake, you often do. However, you don't expect something for nothing. Perhaps you have the Midas touch, which would be very useful to someone with your tastes.

With those you care about, you are inclined to be generous with your time and money and you may shower the people you love with gifts. Like the lion, which is your zodiac animal, you are loyal and fiercely protective of your friends and family. In return, you expect their devotion and respect. You tend to enjoy the company of other creative people who can inspire you and often get along well with Ariens, Geminis, and Sagittarians.

Your greatest strengths are your artistic ability and your powerful will, which enables you to accomplish a great deal. Your challenge is to learn to rule with fairness and integrity.

➤ Read about your Chinese Astrological sign on page 838. ➤ Read about your Personal Planets on page 826. ➤ Read about your personal Mystical Card on page 856.

VIRGO

From August 23, 9:53 through September 23, 7:05

The Diligent Problem-Solver

You possess the skills and determination to accomplish a great deal. You are so diligent that you are busy most of the time. Once you set out to do something, you invest plenty of time and energy in it and, as a result, you usually succeed. Conscientious and hard-working, you strive for perfection and have high expectations of others as well. Like Hilda Sharp, who swam the English Channel this year, you know the value of discipline and persistence. However, you can sometimes suffer from stress because you try to do too much.

A real do-it-yourself-er, you pride yourself on handling challenges. With your keen analytic ability, you can generally figure out a way to fix just about any problem. Most likely, you've had to face some obstacles or limitations in your lifetime and you've succeeded by overcoming them one step at a time.

Your undertakings are likely to be of a practical nature, though your interests might also include some broad-reaching matters. What's most important to you is that your efforts serve a worthy cause. A career in social services or health care could have been a good choice for you. Born just as Alexander Fleming discovered penicillin, your psyche may have been influenced by the importance of fighting germs. Consequently, you are probably careful about cleanliness, your diet, and your environment. This fastidiousness can be helpful, especially if you experience problems with your digestion or other stress-related conditions.

Your many interests and activities are likely to bring you into contact with lots of people, but you are quite particular about those you consider friends. To your loved ones, you are caring and kind. Though at times you might seem a bit too critical or over-protective, your heart is always in the right place. You are usually best matched with other intelligent, practical, unassuming individuals and tend to get along with Taureans, Capricorns, Cancers, and Librans.

Your greatest strength is your willingness to be of help to others. Your challenge is to give yourself a break now and again to take time to smell the flowers.

LIBRA

From September 23, 7:06 through October 23, 15:54

The Smooth Operator

Librans are known for their charm and congeniality and you certainly project these qualities. But you aren't as gentle as you might seem at first glance. Underneath your pleasant and refined exterior, you are quite determined. You know what you want and can use your wonderful people skills to accomplish your aims. But because you always consider others' needs as well as your own, you aren't likely to use force or underhanded tactics.

A natural diplomat, you can be a skillful negotiator who settles disputes and works out compromises. You might even have used these special talents professionally as a lawyer, mediator, agent, or counselor. At times, however, you may surprise other people with a show of temper or unexpected assertiveness. You will fight back if pushed too far or if you feel aggression is necessary, but usually you try to avoid conflict, seeking peaceful ways to resolve difficulties. Like prizefighter Gene Tunney, who put down his gloves the year you were born, you prefer to use your brain rather than your brawn to overcome your adversaries.

You possess a unique combination of intellect and insight that can be advantageous to you in both personal and professional areas. Outwardly, you appear calm and detached. However, you are quite intuitive. You also have a special knack for understanding what's going on beneath the surface. As a result, not much gets by you. Perhaps you could have been a very effective detective, psychiatrist, financial analyst, politician, or surgeon.

Although you are usually even-tempered, you have a deeply emotional side that shows itself in your relationships. Relationships are very important to you and once you commit, you take the commitment seriously. You may even be rather possessive of your loved ones. Though you might enjoy an intellectual rapport with Geminis, Sagittarians, and Aquarians, you may prefer more sensitive, feeling types, such as Scorpios or Pisceans.

Your greatest strength is your ability to assert yourself without creating animosity. Your challenge is to achieve a balance between your head and your heart.

➤ Read about your Chinese Astrological sign on page 838. ➤ Read about your Personal Planets on page 826. ➤ Read about your personal Mystical Card on page 856.

VIRGO
Your Personal Planets

YOUR LOVE POTENTIAL
Venus in Virgo, Aug. 23, 9:53 - Sept. 04, 23:04
Venus in Libra, Sept. 04, 23:05 - Sept. 23, 7:05

YOUR DRIVE AND AMBITION
Mars in Gemini, Aug. 23, 9:53 - Sept. 23, 7:05

YOUR LUCK MAGNETISM
Jupiter in Taurus, Aug. 23, 9:53 - Sept. 23, 7:05

World Events

Aug. 27 – The U.S., France, Great Britain, Germany, and eleven other nations sign the Kellogg-Briand Treaty in Paris.

Sept. 15 – Bacteriologist Alexander Fleming discovers a bacteria-killing compound, penicillin.

Soviet leader Stalin

LIBRA
Your Personal Planets

YOUR LOVE POTENTIAL
Venus in Libra, Sept. 23, 7:06 - Sept. 29, 7:17
Venus in Scorpio, Sept. 29, 7:18 - Oct. 23, 15:54

YOUR DRIVE AND AMBITION
Mars in Gemini, Sept. 23, 7:06 - Oct. 03, 3:45
Mars in Cancer, Oct. 03, 3:46 - Oct. 23, 15:54

YOUR LUCK MAGNETISM
Jupiter in Taurus, Sept. 23, 7:06 - Oct. 23, 15:54

World Events

Oct. 1 – Joseph Stalin's first five-year plan goes into effect in the Soviet Union; its aim is to expand industrial production, take farms out of private hands, and create schools.

Oct. 12 – The first iron lung is used on a girl with infantile paralysis at Children's Hospital in Boston.

1928

SCORPIO
Your Personal Planets

YOUR LOVE POTENTIAL
Venus in Scorpio, Oct. 23, 15:55 - Oct. 23, 17:11
Venus in Sagittarius, Oct. 23, 17:12 - Nov. 17, 6:08
Venus in Capricorn, Nov. 17, 6:09 - Nov. 22, 12:59

YOUR DRIVE AND AMBITION
Mars in Cancer, Oct. 23, 15:55 - Nov. 22, 12:59

YOUR LUCK MAGNETISM
Jupiter in Taurus, Oct. 23, 15:55 - Nov. 22, 12:59

World Events

Nov. 10 – Japanese Emperor Hirohito is crowned in Kyoto, vowing to work for world peace.

Nov. 18 – *Steamboat Willie*, the first animation featuring Mickey Mouse, premieres in New York.

The first Mickey Mouse animation

SAGITTARIUS
Your Personal Planets

YOUR LOVE POTENTIAL
Venus in Capricorn, Nov. 22, 13:00 - Dec. 12, 1:24
Venus in Aquarius, Dec. 12, 1:25 - Dec. 22, 2:03

YOUR DRIVE AND AMBITION
Mars in Cancer, Nov. 22, 13:00 - Dec. 20, 5:22
Mars in Gemini, Dec. 20, 5:23 - Dec. 22, 2:03

YOUR LUCK MAGNETISM
Jupiter in Taurus, Nov. 22, 13:00 - Dec. 22, 2:03

World Events

Dec. 11 – Presidential candidate Herbert Hoover escapes an assassination attempt while visiting Buenos Aires.

Dec. 13 – Gershwin's musical *An American In Paris* opens at Carnegie Hall in New York.

240

SCORPIO

From October 23, 15:55 through November 22, 12:59

The Powerful Detective

You possess great power to achieve just about anything. Not only are you blessed with natural strength and fortitude, you may have a unique ability to focus all your energy and attention on a goal. Consequently, you have probably managed to accomplish things that would have stymied other people. You don't back down from challenges, though you sometimes approach them via a circuitous route, and it's a rare individual who gets the better of you.

Most likely, you have experienced many transformations during your lifetime, some of them quite dramatic. Born when some nations were unifying and others were splitting apart, your psyche may have been imprinted with a sense that nothing lasts forever. Each shift you've undergone has led to personal growth and, like a snake shedding its old skin, you have probably had to strip away old parts of yourself periodically in order to move ahead.

You have remarkable powers of observation and are quite intuitive; you can practically read other people's minds. Your keen insights help you understand the inner machinations of the social, political, or business world. Like the Italian diver who recovered a fortune in diamonds from the wreck of a Belgian steamship this year, you often delve deep beneath the surface to get at the hidden treasure. You might have been successful as a police officer, detective, spy, miner, or psychiatrist. With your perception and shrewdness, you might have been able to earn a good deal of money in financial fields too.

Scorpios are known for being possessive of the people they care about and you are certainly not frivolous with your affection. However, you might tend to be a bit more outgoing and flexible in this area than other Scorpios. You do have a sensitive and private side to your personality, but you also enjoy socializing with friends. Though you usually tend to get along with Pisceans, Cancers, Virgos, and Capricorns, you might also have fun with optimistic Sagittarians.

Your greatest strength is your indomitable willpower and sense of purpose. Your challenge is to keep from overpowering other people.

SAGITTARIUS

From November 22, 13:00 through December 22, 2:03

The Serious Seeker

You pursue knowledge in an earnest, orderly manner. Regardless of your age, you want to learn as much as you can, perhaps continuing your education throughout your life. If you weren't able to get as much formal schooling as you wanted, you might have undertaken a self-education program. While you value knowledge for its own sake, you want to be able to apply what you know in practical ways. Therefore, you might choose to study subjects that will advance you financially or are useful in your daily life.

Your quest may take you far away from your home. Most likely, you are interested in other countries and cultures. You might have been inspired by the writings of anthropologist Margaret Mead, whose work on the Samoans was published this year. A job as a foreign correspondent, traveling salesperson, truck driver, or aviator could have been interesting to you. If you can't travel as much as you'd like, you may expand your horizons by reading about distant lands or watching television travel shows.

Your special blend of optimism and pragmatism could have served you well in many areas of life. Born when the New York Stock Exchange was racking up record sales only to crash, your psyche may have been imprinted with a sense of caution that keeps you from being overly idealistic. You are willing to take some chances, but you aren't foolhardy.

You possess a good imagination and might be a wonderful storyteller. Although you enjoy socializing and probably have many friends, you can be rather shy or reserved at times. You take relationships seriously and your loved ones know that they can depend on you. In fact, you may have known many of your companions for a very long time. Partnerships could be advantageous to you, financially or socially. Usually you get along well with Leos, Ariens, and Aquarians, but in close relationships you might appreciate a Capricorn's steadfastness.

You are able to dream while still keeping your feet on the ground and this is your greatest strength. Your challenge is to share your knowledge with others so that you help them to advance as well.

➤ Read about your Chinese Astrological sign on page 838. ➤ Read about your Personal Planets on page 826. ➤ Read about your personal Mystical Card on page 856.

CAPRICORN

From December 22, 2:04 through December 31, 23:59

The Steady Achiever

You move forward at a sure and steady pace, like a mountain goat carefully scaling a rocky cliff. Your measured motion usually gets you where you want to go while keeping you from suffering too many pitfalls. Security is certainly important to you and you do your best to get ahead and stay there. Because you aren't inclined to take unnecessary risks, you generally hold on to your gains and probably established a secure position.

Even if you don't have a Midas touch, you might have been financially successful. Your grew up when the U.S. was in the midst of the Great Depression and many countries were experiencing economic hardship. Quite likely, this climate encouraged you to acquire as much money as possible. With your head for business and your strong work ethic, you certainly have what it takes to succeed. You might also have enjoyed a little luck.

Other people are likely to see you as a strong and capable leader, or at least a responsible manager. You know the value of setting goals and working in an orderly manner to accomplish them, like fellow Capricorn Joseph Stalin, who introduced a five-year plan for industrializing Russia this year. Through your special combination of vision and determination, you have probably risen to a position of respect. Fields such as engineering, banking, law, or science might have appealed to you, but any business could have profited from your common sense and organizational skills.

Despite your rather serious and reserved personality, you enjoy getting together with friends and can be quite a lively companion. The older you get, the more easygoing you become. Your circle of acquaintances might include some unconventional types: people who can teach you something of value intrigue you. Generally, you get along well with Taureans and Virgos but you might also be drawn to the outgoing and adventurous spirit of Aquarians.

Your greatest strength is your ability to determine what's really important. Your challenge is to take a broader view of life, perhaps becoming more philosophical, instead of focusing too much on material things.

1928

CAPRICORN
Your Personal Planets

YOUR LOVE POTENTIAL
Venus in Aquarius, Dec. 22, 2:04 - Dec. 31, 23:59

YOUR DRIVE AND AMBITION
Mars in Gemini, Dec. 22, 2:04 - Dec. 31, 23:59

YOUR LUCK MAGNETISM
Jupiter in Taurus, Dec. 22, 2:04 - Dec. 31, 23:59

World Events

Dec. 23 – The RAF begins an evacuation program of citizens caught in the attack on Kabul in Afghanistan.

Dec. 25 – Summary executions are abolished in Mexico.

Depositors besiege a merchant bank following the Wall Street crash

Special Feature
Money, Astrology, and the Crash of '29

(Continued from page 233)

Financial astrologers have some good insights into the Crash and the Great Depression. The key planet in these events is Saturn, sometimes known as the "Grim Reaper," but more constructively as the "Teacher" or "Taskmaster." Saturn's influence is restrictive and consolidating. When Saturn is prominent in the horoscope for an event, the tendency is to tighten up and to take responsibility for actions.

Saturn can be particularly difficult when going through the zodiac in Sagittarius, a sign that is naturally exuberant and fiery. When other planets go through Sagittarius, they are filled with enthusiasm and excitement. When heavy Saturn goes through Sagittarius, the feeling can also be enthusiastic, but with an underlying fear that the reasons for the excitement are false or overly optimistic. This was exactly the atmosphere in 1929, when Saturn was in Sagittarius.

Astrologers believe that whenever Saturn goes through Sagittarius, it can have a heavy influence over a nation's wealth—a kind of "reality check." Saturn takes about 29 years to make one orbit around the Sun, and every 29 years Saturn returns to Sagittarius. American financial astrologers have recognized that this Saturn cycle closely corresponds to a regular, predictable economic cycle. After the Crash of '29, the next time Saturn was in Sagittarius was in 1958, when the United States experienced a recession and an unusually high unemployment rate. The worst crash since 1929 occurred in October 1987, when once again Saturn was in Sagittarius. Saturn's next sojourn there will be in 2015.

The global Great Depression that followed was indicated by what are termed the "outer planets"—Saturn and the planets farthest away from the Sun. These planets take a relatively long time to orbit, and periodically they form stressful angular relationships to each other. Whenever this happens, major wide-ranging social, political, and economic changes can occur.

In the early 1930s Saturn, Uranus, and Pluto were all involved in a tight formation, with each one stressfully related to the other. This three-planet configuration is relatively rare, and it is suggested that it led to the inevitable downward financial spiral, reaching its climax around the time the market hit absolute bottom in 1933.

The most severe link-up was Saturn and Pluto exactly opposite each other as seen from the Earth. Financial astrologers see this event as triggering another major economic cycle. Every 35 years Saturn and Pluto oppose each other, and every 35 years some global economic situation threatens to become as traumatic as the Great Depression. The most recent occurred from 2001 through 2002. ✪

Black Thursday: the Moon Meets Pluto

The Great Depression truly began on October 24, 1929, on what came to be known as Black Thursday, when stock values in the United States dropped rapidly. Thousands of stockholders lost large sums of money in an instant. The bloated markets of the twenties were eviscerated. Many stockholders were wiped out completely. Banks, factories, and stores closed and left millions of Americans jobless and penniless. Many people had to depend on the government or charity to provide them with food. Rising stock values had encouraged many people to speculate during the second half of the twenties, and this led to the disaster of Black Thursday. Because the market was already out of control, an aspect that might be ordinary on any other day, it became the breaking point for the moment of the crash. The implications of longer-term aspects in the years before the crash created the conditions that made the Depression possible. Jupiter opposed Uranus in 1926, and Pluto had been deeply ensconced in Cancer since 1914. When the emotional, unstable moon entered its own sign, Cancer, on October 24, 1929, it hit Pluto directly. This minor aspect was the straw that broke the weary camel's back.

Thousands upon thousands of people lost huge sums of money as stock values fell far below the prices paid for the stock. Banks and businesses had also bought stock, and many lost so much that they had to close. Stock values fell almost steadily for the next three years. Because there was already such a stark disparity between rich and poor, recovery from this economic crisis was slow and painful.

Arabs in Palestine rise up against Jewish access to Jerusalem's Wailing Wall

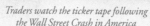

Traders watch the ticker tape following the Wall Street Crash in America

The "Graf Zeppelin" begins a round-the-world flight

THE GLASTONBURY ZODIAC

In 1929, sculptor Katherine Maltwood discovered that natural land formations at Glastonbury—one of the oldest sacred sites in England—formed the twelve signs of the zodiac spread out over a ten-mile area, creating a giant terrestrial zodiac. Similar zodiacs have been found in England and France since then, and they seem to be very precisely placed—the result of careful surveying. Some experts believe that such surveying was a pagan way of dividing the country into areas similar to dioceses in the Christian era.

CHAOS AND COLLAPSE

In Yugoslavia, ethnic enmities obliged King Alexander to stave off chaos by dissolving Parliament and assuming dictatorial control. Italy signed the Lateran Agreement with the Vatican, granting sovereignty to the Pope. President Obregon of Mexico was assassinated. In France, Premier Poincaré resigned and was succeeded by Briand. Arabs in Palestine rose up against Jewish access to Jerusalem's Western (Wailing) Wall, and were quelled by British troops. The first Academy Awards were held in Hollywood, California; Janet Gaynor won as Best Actress. *Wings* was named Best Picture. The U.S. stock market crashed on Black Thursday October 24, as investors panicked and sold, deciding to be safe rather than sorry. Seven Chicago gangsters were gunned down in the Valentine's Day massacre, ordered by Al Capone, who was jailed in June for carrying a gun. The airship *Graf Zeppelin* flew round the world in twenty-one days. Actress and one-time mistress of King Edward VII, Lillie Langtry, died. Lawman Wyatt Earp, a participant in the famous gunfight at the OK Corral in 1881, died peacefully at age eighty. The first full-color TV image was shown in New York.

➤ Read Amelia Earhart's Star Profile on page 249.

CAPRICORN

From January 01, 0:00 through January 20, 12:41

The Powerful Authority

Never one to stand by and let others call the shots, you usually like to be in charge, January Capricorn. With your careful, orderly manner and common sense, you are well-qualified to be the boss. You earn your reputation through your own efforts, so other people have learned to trust your judgment in most things. Like King Alexander, who took control in Yugoslavia and staved off chaos between the Serbs and the Croats around the time of your birth, you strive to establish order and stability through perseverance and hard work.

Although you are usually conservative and cautious, you are still willing to entertain a range of possibilities and don't always rely on tried and true methods. In short, if an idea is logical, you'll consider it and probably be just as enthused with someone else's brainstorms as with your own.

Because you are quite down-to-earth in most respects, you like to see the results of your efforts manifest tangibly. You are often the one who gives form to other people's ideas, and you are undoubtedly quite successful at this. Your special brand of talents could have come in handy in a career as an engineer, architect, builder, manufacturer, or banker. Money is one important measure of your success, and you might have devoted much effort to earning a good living. Having grown up during a period when many countries were experiencing economic hardship, you were likely influenced by the insecurity of the times and will seek to create stability for yourself and your loved ones.

You tend to be quite protective of the people you care about, but at times, you may seem to be a bit too controlling or domineering. Try to allow others to stand on their own two feet. Even though you are practical and quite reserved at times, you might enjoy the company of more creative types who help to open you up to new ways of thinking. Pisceans and Taureans are often your favorite companions, though you may be intrigued by unconventional Aquarians.

Your strength is your ability to size up a situation and make the best of it. Your challenge is to learn when to delegate authority.

AQUARIUS

From January 20, 12:42 through February 19, 3:06

The Free Thinker

You really believe in "doing your own thing," Aquarius of 1929. Even though your views aren't in keeping with the mainstream, you want to have room to express them openly and can't bear to have anyone place limits on you. You often "push the envelope," and you are probably curious about all sorts of unusual subjects, such as alternative medicine or astrology. You tend to have an opinion on everything, from politics to religion—and that opinion is rarely the same as that of the majority. You also enjoy a lively debate now and again.

Born the same year as civil rights leader Martin Luther King Jr., you believe in equality for all and may be quite a champion of the underdog. Just as you rebel against people or institutions that restrict your independence, you uphold others' rights to live free of social or political controls. While your idealism is well-intended, some may have trouble seeing other viewpoints and perhaps need to learn to compromise. Your frank and feisty manner can also ruffle feathers at times.

Your free thinking and unconventional approach to life often leads you to unique discoveries, and you may find solutions to problems that more conservative types miss. With your inventive and original mind, you may be successful at engineering, electronics, computers, aviation, or science. Perhaps you were inspired by the ideas of Albert Einstein, who introduced his theory that united gravity and electromagnetism the year you were born.

Born at a time when sexual censorship was on the rise and performers like dancer Josephine Baker were being banned from the stage for indecency, when it comes to relationships, your ideas are equally avant-garde. You absolutely demand freedom and equality in your relationships, and won't put up with people who try to fence you in. For this reason, you usually get along best with other independent types, such as Geminis, Ariens, and Sagittarians.

Your strength is your willingness to break rules that need to be broken. Your challenge is to find ways to win over your adversaries and change their attitudes rather than alienating them.

➤ Read about your Chinese Astrological sign on page 838. ➤ Read about your Personal Planets on page 826. ➤ Read about your personal Mystical Card on page 856.

1929

CAPRICORN
Your Personal Planets

YOUR LOVE POTENTIAL
Venus in Aquarius, Jan. 01, 0:00 - Jan. 06, 12:00
Venus in Pisces, Jan. 06, 12:01 - Jan. 20, 12:41

YOUR DRIVE AND AMBITION
Mars in Gemini, Jan. 01, 0:00 - Jan. 20, 12:41

YOUR LUCK MAGNETISM
Jupiter in Taurus, Jan. 01, 0:00 - Jan. 20, 12:41

World Events

Jan. 10 – The cartoon character Tintin first appears in the Belgian paper *The 20th Century*.

Jan. 15 – U.S. civil rights leader Martin Luther King Jr. is born.

Martin Luther King Jr. is born under the sign of Capricorn

AQUARIUS
Your Personal Planets

YOUR LOVE POTENTIAL
Venus in Pisces, Jan. 20, 12:42 - Feb. 02, 14:33
Venus in Aries, Feb. 02, 14:34 - Feb. 19, 3:06

YOUR DRIVE AND AMBITION
Mars in Gemini, Jan. 20, 12:42 - Feb. 19, 3:06

YOUR LUCK MAGNETISM
Jupiter in Taurus, Jan. 20, 12:42 - Feb. 19, 3:06

World Events

Feb. 11 – The Lateran Treaty is signed, in which Italy acknowledges the sovereign status of Vatican City.

Feb. 14 – The St Valentine's Day Massacre takes place between the warring gangs of Al Capone and Bugs Moran.

1929

PISCES
Your Personal Planets

YOUR LOVE POTENTIAL
Venus in Aries, Feb. 19, 3:07 - Mar. 08, 7:28
Venus in Taurus, Mar. 08, 7:29 - Mar. 21, 2:34

YOUR DRIVE AND AMBITION
Mars in Gemini, Feb. 19, 3:07 - Mar. 10, 23:17
Mars in Cancer, Mar. 10, 23:18 - Mar. 21, 2:34

YOUR LUCK MAGNETISM
Jupiter in Taurus, Feb. 19, 3:07 - Mar. 21, 2:34

World Events

Feb 23 – The Chinese capture the city of Hunan.

Mar. 11 – Maj. Henry Seagrave breaks the land speed record at Daytona Beach, reaching an average of 223.2 mph.

The first musical comedy movie, "Broadway Melody," is released in the U.S.

ARIES
Your Personal Planets

YOUR LOVE POTENTIAL
Venus in Taurus, Mar. 21, 2:35 - Apr. 20, 2:04
Venus in Aries, Apr. 20, 2:05 - Apr. 20, 14:09

YOUR DRIVE AND AMBITION
Mars in Cancer, Mar. 21, 2:35 - Apr. 20, 14:09

YOUR LUCK MAGNETISM
Jupiter in Taurus, Mar. 21, 2:35 - Apr. 20, 14:09

World Events

Apr. 7 – The U.S. postal service intercepts a package containing a bomb, addressed to President Roosevelt.

Apr. 8 – Belgian singer and composer Jacques Brel is born.

244

PISCES
From February 19, 3:07 through March 21, 2:34

The Boundless Idealist

No matter what disappointments or hardships life has presented you with, Pisces of 1929, you continue to believe that good will conquer evil and that the power of love can overcome the love of power. This positive attitude often gets you through rough times and enables you to rebound from setbacks. Although you were born at a time when many nations were experiencing economic difficulties, and witnessed a world war during your youth, you saw those crises give way to peace and prosperity later on. Some might call you a "Pollyanna," but your optimism will attract good fortune.

Born the year Roman Catholicism became Italy's official religion and Mexico modified its anti-religious laws, you might have been influenced by strong spiritual views from an early age. Whether or not you are traditionally religious, you likely have a strong faith in a higher power. This faith may inspire you to care for others—in fact, your compassion may lead you to social work, health care, psychology, or the ministry.

An imaginative person, you have a rich inner life and may express your visions through some creative outlet. Perhaps you possess talent at painting, poetry, photography, fashion design, or music. You might even choose to follow a career in one of the commercial or fine arts. Film-making would also be an ideal profession for you, allowing you to use your substantial imagination to create "a world of your own." Born during the year the first Academy Award ceremonies were held in Hollywood, you might be quite the movie buff and likely enjoy escaping into the world of glamor and fantasy whenever possible.

Your optimism and compassion will attract a varied array of admirers to you. You have a unique ability to see the good in others and to bring out their best. Others may take advantage of your kindness, but you would rather give too much than not enough. You tend to get along with Cancerians, Taureans, and Scorpios, equally sensitive souls.

Your ability to see the silver lining in every cloud is your strength. Your challenge is to be realistic without sacrificing your high ideals.

ARIES
From March 21, 2:35 through April 20, 14:09

The Unpredictable Innovator

Unpredictable is a good word to describe you, Aries of 1929. In fact, as Picasso once said, "If you know exactly what you're going to do, what's the good of doing it?" You may start out in one direction, then suddenly go off in an entirely new direction. While your spontaneity can be unsettling to more orderly types, things are never dull when you're around.

This ability to live in the moment enables you to stay open to new ideas and experiences and to keep a fresh outlook on life. You also might be very inventive, coming up with original and unique ways of solving problems or building a better mousetrap. Born the year the first color television was released, you might have a fascination with technology and gadgets. With your adventurous spirit, you are always ready to take a chance and frequently, your wild schemes pay off.

Daring and assertive, you go after what you want and don't worry much about the risks or consequences. You love a good challenge, most especially the sense of adventure that comes from taking on a formidable adversary or daunting project. Full speed ahead is the only speed you know. Once your interest is piqued, your energy and enthusiasm are boundless. Babe Ruth, who hit his 500th major league home run the year you were born, may have been one of your idols. Usually, you are more successful if you can finish something quickly for your attention span is rather short.

Despite your strong independent streak, you probably have a lively and varied array of friends. Your socializing generally revolves around a particular activity; you aren't much interested in just chatting. Family is important to you and you are probably good with children. You may have a bit of a temper, but your anger usually subsides as quickly as it comes on. You'll likely get along well with other outgoing individuals, such as Aquarians or Sagittarians, but you would also benefit from the stabilizing influence of Taureans.

Your strength is a zest for life. Your challenges are to learn to look before you leap and to consider the needs and feelings of others before you act.

➤ Read about your Chinese Astrological sign on page 838. ➤ Read about your Personal Planets on page 826. ➤ Read about your personal Mystical Card on page 856.

TAURUS

From April 20, 14:10 through May 21, 13:47

The Domestic Sensualist

You're a lover, not a fighter, Taurus of 1929. In fact, it likely takes quite a lot to upset you. You don't see the sense in getting upset about petty things, especially when there is so much in life to enjoy—and enjoy it you will! You know how to live well and appreciate all the good things money can buy. You may have been influenced by being raised during the time of the Great Depression in the U.S., so in your later years, you want to get the most out of life.

Your love of luxury may inspire you to stretch your budget every now and then to have what you want. Earning money has probably been important to you and your choice of a job might have hinged largely on how much it paid. Most likely, you have a knack for making money, too, and could be successful in banking, real estate, or manufacturing. Because you take it slow and steady, you may not achieve success overnight, but your perseverance and fortitude, coupled with an innate sense of where to invest your resources, will enable you to hold onto your goals.

Quite likely, you have an artist's eye and might possess talent in one or more creative areas. You may express yourself through sculpture, interior decorating, landscaping, fashion design, or a career in the arts. Music and/or the theater might be also be among your passions. The first Academy Awards were held on May 15, 1929, and this may have influenced a fondness for the movies at a young age.

You take particular pride in your home and family; you are highly protective and devoted. You likely enjoy gathering at your home with friends and relatives and dazzling them with your culinary skills. In fact, you may even be a professional chef. You are affectionate and generous toward the people you care for, who'll never have cause to doubt your love. You are likely most compatible with Pisceans, Cancerians, and other Taureans. In friendships, seek out the fire of Ariens or Sagittarians.

Your strength is your easygoing disposition, which will bring you the unending devotion of your loved ones. Your challenge is to never connect self-worth with material worth.

GEMINI

From May 21, 13:48 through June 21, 22:00

The Enthusiastic Teacher

You have a great deal to offer the world in terms of ideas, Gemini of 1929. In fact, your mind is so full of interesting information that you probably aren't able to keep your thoughts to yourself—and please don't! Nothing pleases you more than sharing your thoughts and engaging in lively discourses with interesting, unusual friends, but they enjoy you just as much as you enjoy them. Whether or not you actually choose teaching as a profession, you will be a natural teacher, with an intellectual passion capable of inspiring anyone and everyone.

You are inventive and original. In fact, you may also find that ideas pop into your head out of the blue. You'll often see things in new ways, putting a unique spin on accepted concepts. Albert Einstein, who introduced the theory that united gravity and electromagnetism during the year you were born, perhaps inspired you. In that case, you may have chosen to pursue a profession in science or technology.

You possess a good imagination, and you would excel in any area that allows you to express your creativity. Because you love language and have a way with words, you may be drawn to writing as a career or a hobby. Quite likely, you've always dreamed of writing an important novel. Writing for television may also appeal to you, since you grew up during the time when the first color TV was unveiled. Your clever wit would also make you a natural in the fields of advertising or marketing, though journalism would be a fine choice as well. You could also put your innate teaching skills to work for you by successfully authoring textbooks or pursuing technical writing.

Sociable and good-natured, you really shine when you are in the company of other intellectually oriented folks who enjoy listening to your bold, clever ideas. An enthusiastic conversationalist, you are never at a loss for words—in fact, you likely have a famous "gift of the gab." You'll probably get along best with the air signs: Aquarians, Librans, and other Geminis.

Your strength is your rich, fertile imagination. Your challenge is to focus on one project at a time.

➤ Read about your Chinese Astrological sign on page 838. ➤ Read about your Personal Planets on page 826. ➤ Read about your personal Mystical Card on page 856.

1929

TAURUS
Your Personal Planets

YOUR LOVE POTENTIAL
Venus in Aries, Apr. 20, 14:10 - May 21, 13:47

YOUR DRIVE AND AMBITION
Mars in Cancer, Apr. 20, 14:10 - May 13, 2:32
Mars in Leo, May 13, 2:33 - May 21, 13:47

YOUR LUCK MAGNETISM
Jupiter in Taurus, Apr. 20, 14:10 - May 21, 13:47

World Events

May 4 – Actress Audrey Hepburn is born.
May 16 – The first Academy Awards are held at the Roosevelt Hotel in Hollywood.

Actress Audrey Hepburn is born under the sign of Taurus

GEMINI
Your Personal Planets

YOUR LOVE POTENTIAL
Venus in Aries, May 21, 13:48 - June 03, 9:47
Venus in Taurus, June 03, 9:48 - June 21, 22:00

YOUR DRIVE AND AMBITION
Mars in Leo, May 21, 13:48 - June 21, 22:00

YOUR LUCK MAGNETISM
Jupiter in Taurus, May 21, 13:48 - June 12, 12:19
Jupiter in Gemini, June 12, 12:20 - June 21, 22:00

World Events

June 7 – The sovereign state of Vatican City comes into effect.
June 12 – Dutch Jewish refugee Anne Frank is born.

CANCER
Your Personal Planets

YOUR LOVE POTENTIAL
Venus in Taurus, June 21, 22:01 - July 08, 1:59
Venus in Gemini, July 08, 2:00 - July 23, 8:52

YOUR DRIVE AND AMBITION
Mars in Leo, June 21, 22:01 - July 04, 10:02
Mars in Virgo, July 04, 10:03 - July 23, 8:52

YOUR LUCK MAGNETISM
Jupiter in Gemini, June 21, 22:01 - July 23, 8:52

World Events

June 27 – Bell Laboratories gives a demonstration of full-color television transmission.

July 1 – The British sign a treaty agreeing to support Chinese naval development.

The "Graf Zeppelin" aims to set a new record for a round-the-world flight

LEO
Your Personal Planets

YOUR LOVE POTENTIAL
Venus in Gemini, July 23, 8:53 - Aug. 05, 5:38
Venus in Cancer, Aug. 05, 5:39 - Aug. 23, 15:40

YOUR DRIVE AND AMBITION
Mars in Virgo, July 23, 8:53 - Aug. 21, 21:51
Mars in Libra, Aug. 21, 21:52 - Aug. 23, 15:40

YOUR LUCK MAGNETISM
Jupiter in Gemini, July 23, 8:53 - Aug. 23, 15:40

World Events

Aug. 11 – The Jewish Agency for Palestine is founded in Zurich under the leadership of Chaim Weizmann.

Aug. 18 – The best-selling World War I novel *All Quiet On The Western Front* is banned from army libraries in Austria.

CANCER
From June 21, 22:01 through July 23, 8:52

The Inventive Homebody

Born at a time of both union and conflict, Cancer of 1929, you witnessed in your youth a world war that caused many to leave their homelands. You may even have been one of them. As a result, you likely put a high value on stability and security. Even if you live far from your place of birth, you'll still hold your heritage quite dear to your heart.

Because your home is so important to you, you'll want your domestic life to be as comfortable and pleasant as possible. With your natural talent for decorating, you can create an attractive and comfortable living environment—in short, a cozy nest. A "do-it-your-self-er," you might be handy at fixing things, making you a skilled architect, carpenter, interior designer, or antique dealer.

Your desire for security may be rooted in your earliest moments, since you were born the year the New York Stock Exchange crashed and the Great Depression began. In fact, you may attempt to ensure your security by earning and saving as much money as possible. Occasional upsets or unexpected situations may cause financial ups and downs, but your instincts will enable you to turn these seeming setbacks into opportunities. Your keen intuition may also serve you well in advertising, investments, or real-estate development.

You likely love nothing more than gathering your clan around you, especially during holidays. If family members live far away, you'll undoubtedly stay in touch, remain close in heart, and travel regularly to visit them. Friends and neighbors, as well as blood relatives, will all be included in your circle of extended family, but your ties to your community will likely also be quite strong, involving you in a variety of local or neighborhood projects. Your friends will probably include creative and intelligent types, particularly Taureans, Virgos, and Pisceans with whom you are usually compatible.

Your greatest strength is your sense of community, which you express as love of home, family, and country. Your challenge is to be tolerant and open-minded toward those whose backgrounds or beliefs are different from your own.

LEO
From July 23, 8:53 through August 23, 15:40

The Careful Creator

Leo is the sign best known for creativity, and you, Leo of 1929, certainly possess your share. Unlike most creative souls, however, you were given the qualities of self-discipline and persistence. You take your work seriously and strive to do your best, always improving on previous efforts. You'll likely also devote considerable time and energy to detail, constantly refining your techniques and turning out high caliber products that endure.

One of your special talents is your ingenuity, allowing you to inspire others, who'll see you as their mentor, guru, or patron. Perhaps you were a pioneer in the television industry, since you grew up as this new creative medium was just beginning to take off— the first color TV was introduced the year you were born. The movies, too, may have captured your imagination; in fact, you may remember being inspired in your youth by the early days of talking films. Careers in these fields, or in other areas that combine creativity and technology such as computer graphics or advertising, could be good choices for you.

Communication is another of your specialties, so you have probably tried your hand at creative or technical writing, or chosen to communicate through music, singing, composing, or playing an instrument. Colorful musical productions, such as *Babes In Toyland* or Gershwin's *Strike Up The Band*, both of which opened in New York the year of your birth, might have struck your fancy. In fact, you may have been drawn to sound engineering.

Many of your friends are probably artistic or literary types, and you enjoy collaborating with them even if it's only on an informal, fun basis. Geminis, Sagittarians, and Ariens are usually your favorite companions, but you'd also appreciate the devotion of a Cancerian partner. Although you may seem to be a bit critical of the ideas of others at times, your suggestions can help them improve. The same is true with family members toward whom you will likely be quite encouraging and supportive.

Your strength is the care you invest in your work. Your challenge is to guard against being overly critical.

► Read about your Chinese Astrological sign on page 838. ► Read about your Personal Planets on page 826. ► Read about your personal Mystical Card on page 856.

VIRGO

From August 23, 15:41 through September 23, 12:51

The Meticulous Peacemaker

Whether you are ironing a shirt or painting a masterpiece, Virgo of 1929, you'll undoubtedly do it with the highest level of care. There are no rough edges on your creations—in fact, you'll be sure to polish them until they sparkle.

Even if you don't think of yourself as an artist, your creativity is likely quite substantial, allowing you to excel in any craft from carpentry to fashion design. You give even the most basic tasks that special dash of elegance that elevates them from ordinary to unique. Meticulous and exacting, both personally and professionally, you firmly believe that anything worth doing is worth doing right—the first time. This trait would make you a good editor, architect, software designer, or draftsperson. The care with which you handle responsibility sets you apart from others, enabling you to reach a high level of expertise and success in any field. Like professional golfer Arnold Palmer, who shares your birth sign and year, you exhibit precision and cool control, even under stress.

You dislike upsets or arguments, and you will go to great lengths to keep the peace. Perhaps your psyche was influenced by the turmoil of the world war that you witnessed in your youth. A deft communicator, you have a knack for smoothing out disagreements between other people and may be called upon to mediate disputes now and again. You attempt to be fair to all concerned and can usually arrive at a workable, practical solution. This skill may serve you well in a career as a lawyer, agent, or counselor.

In social situations, you are the perfect host, equally skilled in decorating, food preparation, and keeping a conversation flowing smoothly. Your companions are likely to be creative, intelligent people who share your appreciation for the finer things in life. Usually you get along best with Taureans, Cancers, and Capricorns, but friendly Librans, Leos, and Geminis would make good companions as well.

Your strength is your artfulness, infusing all your creations with aesthetic beauty and balance. Your challenge is to allow yourself to take credit for your achievements.

LIBRA

From September 23, 12:52 through October 23, 21:40

The Skillful Navigator

You have a special knack for handling tough times, Libra of 1929, and you'll likely be called on often throughout life to use it. You were born during a period when many nations were experiencing economic distress and the U.S. was reeling from a crash on Wall Street. During your youth, you also witnessed World War II. These early challenges, however, have fostered the skills you needed to establish balance in your personal and professional life.

You rarely let your emotional feelings influence your decisions or impel you into action, choosing instead to weigh matters carefully before you set a course. At times, you can also be surprisingly forceful, taking charge in a way that may seem harsh to those who are accustomed to only seeing your more gentle, tactful side.

You probably possess a keen intellect and a respect for knowledge. Learning any subject will come easily to you—in fact, you have probably managed to become both objective and analytical in your thinking. You have the capacity to see what's important and what isn't, allowing you to focus your energy only on achieving your goals. This valuable quality would make you a fine lawyer, doctor, teacher, accountant, or manager—but you also have the eye of an artist. This special blend of creativity and meticulousness could bring you success as an architect, engineer, literary agent, editor, conductor, or graphic artist.

You are ordinarily quite outgoing and even-tempered and at your best in social situations. You like people and enjoy surrounding yourself with intelligent, talented, sophisticated companions. Relationships are quite important to you, in fact, so you are likely not often found without a companion. Speaking of companions, when it's time to choose one for life, you may often find you're in the company of Geminis, Sagittarians, Leos, and Aquarians—but Virgos who'll share your penchant for analytical thinking and order would also make fine choices.

Your strength is your diplomacy, allowing you to step in and soothe even the most troubled waters. Your challenge is to be both realistic and compassionate.

➤ Read about your Chinese Astrological sign on page 838. ➤ Read about your Personal Planets on page 826. ➤ Read about your personal Mystical Card on page 856.

VIRGO
Your Personal Planets

YOUR LOVE POTENTIAL
Venus in Cancer, Aug. 23, 15:41 - Aug. 31, 11:23
Venus in Leo, Aug. 31, 11:24 - Sept. 23, 12:51

YOUR DRIVE AND AMBITION
Mars in Libra, Aug. 23, 15:41 - Sept. 23, 12:51

YOUR LUCK MAGNETISM
Jupiter in Gemini, Aug. 23, 15:41 - Sept. 23, 12:51

World Events

Aug. 23 – Anne Morrow Lindbergh makes her first solo flight, in Hicksville, Long Island.

Aug. 23 – The Hebron Massacre begins between Jews and Arabs in Jerusalem.

Fritz Von Opel strapped into his rocket-propelled plane

LIBRA
Your Personal Planets

YOUR LOVE POTENTIAL
Venus in Leo, Sept. 23, 12:52 - Sept. 25, 16:12
Venus in Virgo, Sept. 25, 16:13 - Oct. 20, 5:11
Venus in Libra, Oct. 20, 5:12 - Oct. 23, 21:40

YOUR DRIVE AND AMBITION
Mars in Libra, Sept. 23, 12:52 - Oct. 06, 12:26
Mars in Scorpio, Oct. 06, 12:27 - Oct. 23, 21:40

YOUR LUCK MAGNETISM
Jupiter in Gemini, Sept. 23, 12:52 - Oct. 23, 21:40

World Events

Sept. 30 – Fritz von Opel's rocket plane—the first of its kind—is successfully tested.

Oct. 3 – The Kingdom of Serbs, Croats, and Slovenes becomes Yugoslavia.

1929

SCORPIO
Your Personal Planets

YOUR LOVE POTENTIAL
Venus in Libra, Oct. 23, 21:41 - Nov. 13, 8:34
Venus in Scorpio, Nov. 13, 8:35 - Nov. 22, 18:47

YOUR DRIVE AND AMBITION
Mars in Scorpio, Oct. 23, 21:41 - Nov. 18, 13:28
Mars in Sagittarius, Nov. 18, 13:29 - Nov. 22, 18:47

YOUR LUCK MAGNETISM
Jupiter in Gemini, Oct. 23, 21:41 - Nov. 22, 18:47

World Events

Oct. 24 - "Black Thursday"—Wall Street plunges into financial crisis as the stock market crashes.

Nov. 12 - Actress and later Princess of Monaco Grace Kelly is born.

Frenzy in Wall Street

SAGITTARIUS
Your Personal Planets

YOUR LOVE POTENTIAL
Venus in Scorpio, Nov. 22, 18:48 - Dec. 07, 7:02
Venus in Sagittarius, Dec. 07, 7:03 - Dec. 22, 7:52

YOUR DRIVE AND AMBITION
Mars in Sagittarius, Nov. 22, 18:48 - Dec. 22, 7:52

YOUR LUCK MAGNETISM
Jupiter in Gemini, Nov. 22, 18:48 - Dec. 22, 7:52

World Events

Nov. 28 - Adm. Richard Byrd becomes the first person to fly over the South Pole.

Dec. 10 - Thomas Mann is awarded the Nobel Prize for literature.

SCORPIO
From October 23, 21:41 through November 22, 18:47

The Determined Force

Once you set a goal for yourself, Scorpio of 1929, you don't let anything stand in your way. You have tremendous strength and willpower, allowing you to be quite an assertive person when you need to be. In fact, other people may often see you as a force to be reckoned with.

Your commanding presence may enable you to succeed in quite challenging fields such as professional sports, politics, or international trade, but you'd also do well as a police officer, crisis intervention counselor, soldier, or detective. You're never afraid to take risks and don't shy away when the going gets rough, which makes you a natural leader though you may prefer to wield your power from behind the scenes. The New York stock market crash during the year of your birth, the onset of the Great Depression, and living your early years through World War II would all contribute to your incredible inner strength.

Most likely, your life has undergone several quite dramatic changes, but you've undoubtedly learned how to rise above difficulties. You know that when one door closes, another opens. In addition to transforming yourself, however, you have likely also had a deep effect on others, perhaps through psychiatry or surgery. You may also have the urge to transform your physical environment, perhaps through working as a renovator, miner, demolition expert, or construction worker. One of your special talents is your ability to recycle old things into new, useful ones.

You are likely quite a private person—in fact, you can be a bit of a loner at times. This doesn't mean, however, that relationships don't matter to you—once you do form an emotional bond, you'll give it your all. Though you have strong feelings, you may not allow "just anyone" to see your more sensitive side. You'll likely be most comfortable with emotional, intuitive people such as your water-sign cousins, Pisceans and Cancerians, but you could also benefit from the emotional balance and objectivity of a Libran partner.

Your strength is your powerful determination. Your challenge is to know when to bend—so you won't break yourself.

SAGITTARIUS
From November 22, 18:48 through December 22, 7:52

The World Explorer

Your unbridled curiosity and sense of adventure, Sagittarius of 1929, will likely lead you to explore many places. A rolling stone at heart, you might have been influenced by travel and exploration developments during your formative years that enhanced future travel possibilities. Admiral Richard Byrd, for example, became the first person to fly over the South Pole, around the time of your birth. You may even have chosen to make a career out of traveling, choosing work as an aviator, truck driver, foreign correspondent, or travel agent. Even when you aren't happily globetrotting, however, your restless nature will keep you on the go through short trips to visit your many friends or just hitting the hot spots around your hometown.

You need to be free to stretch your imagination as well as your legs. In fact, you likely see learning as a lifelong adventure and your education has probably taken a few unconventional turns. You have a strong independent streak and prefer to learn from experience. As such, life itself was probably your principal teacher. With your wealth of knowledge and experience, you would be an inspired teacher, since you have a knack for making learning exciting.

With your abundant energy and quick reflexes, you might have been an outstanding athlete, like Babe Ruth, who hit his 500th major league home run in 1929. Fast-paced games and those that utilize the legs may be your favorites. You enjoy competition and physical activity, but unless you manage to discipline your restless spirit, you may find it difficult to fulfill your potential.

It's likely that you have many friends and acquaintances, since your outgoing personality and lively sense of humor are appealing to people of all ages, from all over the world. In relationships, as with all else, you'll need your freedom, and won't allow anyone to "fence you in." Aquarians, Ariens, and other Sagittarians will share those sentiments, as will intellectually oriented Geminis.

Your strength is your unstoppable quest for truth. Your challenge is to stay on track, taking life one goal at a time.

➤ Read about your Chinese Astrological sign on page 838. ➤ Read about your Personal Planets on page 826. ➤ Read about your personal Mystical Card on page 856.

CAPRICORN

From December 22, 7:53 through December 31, 23:59

The Practical Visionary

With your special blend of vision and practicality, December Capricorn of 1929, you have a gift for spotting good things and making the most of them. Like Bell Laboratories, which demonstrated the first full-color television during the year of your birth, your foresight, combined with common sense and hard work, has probably paid off quite well for you.

In financial areas, your natural understanding of the material world could bring you a great degree of success. Born during the onset of the Great Depression, you may have been influenced by your parents' struggles to seek financial security above all else. As a result, you'll likely choose to work in a field that will allow you to earn a steady, reliable income. Banking, real estate, manufacturing, construction, or law might be good areas for you to pursue, but your managerial skills and organizational ability would be well appreciated in any field.

Although you tend to be quite conservative and cautious in most areas, you possess an inventive streak that often inspires you to take a risk. You also have a flexibility that many born under your sign do not have. This unique quality will allow you to take a novel approach to problem solving when the usual methods fail and to take advantage of unexpected twists of fate rather than being upset by them. You may also be a skilled engineer, scientist, or technologist.

When in the company of friends and loved ones, your jovial side will emerge. In fact, among your inner circle, you are probably known to be humorous, sociable, and popular. That circle of companions is probably quite diverse—in fact, you'll enjoy a wide range of friends from a variety of backgrounds and ideologies. A firm believer that everyone you meet will teach you something, you're only too happy to reciprocate. You may get along best with practical Taureans and Virgos, but you can also have fun with lively Sagittarians and Geminis.

Your strength is the ability to give form to ideas in order to create something useful and enduring. Your challenge is to make the best of changes rather than resisting them.

1929

CAPRICORN
Your Personal Planets

YOUR LOVE POTENTIAL

Venus in Sagittarius, Dec. 22, 7:53 - Dec. 31, 3:43
Venus in Capricorn, Dec. 31, 3:44 - Dec. 31, 23:59

YOUR DRIVE AND AMBITION

Mars in Sagittarius, Dec. 22, 7:53 - Dec. 29, 10:44
Mars in Capricorn, Dec. 29, 10:45 - Dec. 31, 23:59

YOUR LUCK MAGNETISM

Jupiter in Gemini, Dec. 22, 7:53 - Dec. 31, 23:59

World Events

Dec. 22 – Soviet troops leave Manchuria after a truce is agreed between the two countries.

Dec. 23 – The operetta *Babes In Toyland* opens in New York.

Amelia Earhart
July 24, 1897 - July 2, 1937

AMELIA EARHART
Leo

Born in Atchison, Kansas, Amelia Earhart was the first woman ever awarded the Distinguished Flying Cross by the United States Congress. With her Sun in regal and courageous Leo, Amelia was comfortable both in the spotlight and the cockpit. But it is the mystery surrounding her disappearance in the Pacific that makes Amelia Earhart one of the twentieth century's most unforgettable figures.

With her Mars, the planet of daring, and Jupiter, the planet of confidence, in the part of her chart that tells about risk, Amelia knew she wanted to fly after her first $1 ride in an airplane at a flying show. She broke the women's flight altitude record, but celebrity came when she became the first woman to cross the Atlantic, albeit as a passenger. Embarrassed by the prominence afforded her for what she considered to be a nonachievement, she realized her ambition to fly solo across the Atlantic a few years later.

It was her husband, the famous New York publisher George Putnam, who selected her to be a passenger on that first transatlantic flight. Friendship and love developed between them, even though George was a married man. A lineup of planets, including the Moon, symbolic of our feeling nature, and Venus, the planet of love, in unconventional Gemini gave Amelia her less than traditional attitudes toward relationship. Reluctant to ever marry at all, Amelia agreed to marry George with the stipulation that he would let her leave in a year if they were unhappy.

Besides the feminine Moon and Venus in Gemini, Neptune, the planet that is often beyond our understanding, and Pluto, the planet that is often beyond our control, are symmetrically aligned in that air sign as well. And, on the day of her disappearance, now-you-see-it, now-you-don't Neptune was making a challenging contact to that crucial array of planetary energies. We may never know what happened to Amelia Earhart and her airplane on that mysterious, fateful day in 1937. But we do know that the importance of her legacy is the courageous example she set for women to dare to reach the impossible.

► Read about Coco Chanel, another exceptional woman of her time, on page 177.

1930

Opening Freedom's Doors: Saturn and Uranus

With Pluto, often called the transformer, in globally energizing Cancer, a New World economy was being born, but the rules of engagement had not yet been invented to manage it. Although nations still acted autonomously, government and people were becoming aware of how their actions and experiences affected each other. Jupiter, the planet of economic expansion, was in the jumpy sign of Gemini for half the year. The world's separate economies echoed last year's crash like so many dominoes, continuing to create financial difficulty for millions. However, Gemini's gift for travel and connections brought advances in transportation and communication. Traffic lights made life safer for New York pedestrians and Dumont's television broadcasting from New York brought visual images to many homes for the first time. Movies could talk and delighted audiences were impressed that Greta Garbo sounded as sultry as she looked.

A drive for freedom was being born, when Saturn, the planet of status-quo structure, was challenged by Uranus, the reformer. As old structures crumbled around the world, people saw their opportunity to free themselves from ancient oppressions. They seeded rebellions in Germany, China, and Russia; Gandhi led the Salt March to protest British rule, leading the British government to consider giving India more independence as a federation. Saturn in its guise as scientist resonated with creative Neptune throughout the year, highlighting new technologies into practical use: synthetic rubber was commercialized, and Birdseye flash-froze foods to keep them fresh.

Marlene Dietrich in "The Blue Angel"

The U.S. suffers huge unemployment

Riots across Spain erupt in revolution

E.S.P. PROVED

Joseph Banks Rhine, sometimes called the father of modern parapsychology, used a special deck of cards—called Zener cards—to test psychic abilities. Each card displayed one of five symbols: a plus sign, a circle, a star, a square, and wavy lines. During the test, the cards were placed face down in front of a subject who guessed the hidden symbol. Subjects scored better than would be expected by the mathematical law of averages—proving to Rhine that something else (extra sensory perception or E.S.P.) was at work.

NEW WORRIES, NEW FRONTIERS

After last year's market crash, the world teetered on the brink of economic disaster. Those in the U.S. suffered acutely, with 4.8 million people unemployed; Europe's workers were also made idle at the highest rate ever. In Russia, Stalin ordered the collectivization of farms. World powers put brakes on their naval rivalry, and signed the London Naval Treaty. In elections, Germany, still furious at their post-World War I reparations, voted the Nazi Party the second largest in the new Reichstag. Baseball fans cheered Babe Ruth to national hero status as he hit home run after home run. The film *The Blue Angel* scandalized audiences but made Marlene Dietrich a star. In her first talkie, *Anna Christie*, Greta Garbo sounded as sultry and sexy as she looked. Famed U.S. labor leader Mother Jones (Mary Harris Jones) and Arthur Conan Doyle, creator of Sherlock Holmes, died. The discovery of the planet Pluto confirmed the source of Neptune's orbital irregularities. Freud's *Civilization and its Discontents*, and Dasheill Hammett's *The Maltese Falcon* were published, as the blues favorite *Georgia On My Mind* wooed some away from their worries.

➤ Read Franklin Delano Roosevelt's Star Profile on page 257.

CAPRICORN

From January 01, 0:00 through January 20, 18:32

The Efficient Achiever

As a Capricorn, you were born under one of the most ambitious signs of the zodiac. And, just like the goat that symbolizes your sign, there is no mountain too high for you to climb! You thrive on new challenges, January Capricorn of 1930, and have the patience and willpower to fulfill your personal vision quest. Whether it's your family, your work, or a hobby, you approach every task with focus, attention to detail, and a determination to reach your goal. You have an inventive mind and, born near the time of the first diesel engine automobile trip, you came of age during a time of rapid technological advance.

Although you were probably a bit rebellious as a youth, you eventually found the way to reconcile your desire for freedom with your strong sense of duty. While there may have been times you dreamed of escaping to a tropical isle, with your steadfastness and need to achieve you are not likely to have veered off course for long. Growing up in the 1930s taught you the value of hard work and restraint. Your life has embodied these principles, much like Grant Wood's *American Gothic*, which was exhibited in the year of your birth.

Born with extraordinarily good taste, you have a deep appreciation for the best that life has to offer. Never flamboyant or garish, you have lots of charisma. You may be rather conservative in your likes and dislikes and prefer a classic, elegant style. And, once you set your mind on what you want, whether it's the right car, home, spouse, or job, you are unlikely to let anything stand in your way.

You have excruciatingly high standards for yourself and for others. In relationships, you are probably reserved in public yet quite passionate behind closed doors. Once you have decided on a mate, your ardor is unmatched by anyone. Look to Taurus, Virgo, Scorpio, or Pisces to find a kindred spirit.

Your life challenge is to use your formidable personal power in a positive manner. Others may experience your decisiveness as a need to control the people and situations around you. Your greatest strength lies in your enormous capacity for self-discipline.

AQUARIUS

From January 20, 18:33 through February 19, 8:59

A True Visionary

Resourceful, inventive, and creative are just a few of the words that describe you, 1930 Aquarius. You enjoy marching to a different drummer and have always been just a bit ahead of your time. Just like Vannevar Bush's "differential analyzer," a prototype of the first analog computer that was built in the year of your birth, you pride yourself on your ability to find the solution to any dilemma with your logical and practical mind.

In your youth, you may have relished defying authority. And, you probably enjoyed being thought of as an outrageous non-conformist. Yet, with age, you learned to respect the rules of society. You are likely to have found that having structure and being responsible did not hem you in. Rather, these qualities gave you the foundation you needed to be truly innovative and to fulfill your personal potential.

While your family was busy welcoming you into their world, the rest of the planet was celebrating Clyde Tombaugh's discovery of Pluto. The discovery of a new, though tiny member of the Solar System was just another reminder that the Universe is far vaster than the human mind can grasp. You have a deep appreciation for the wonders of the Universe and you like using your intellect to stretch beyond your limits.

There is no zodiacal sign more freedom-loving than yours, and you need to be able to pull your own strings, no matter the cost. Above all, you need space in a relationship. Once you have found a partner who can give you the room to be yourself and to pursue your own interests, you can be as faithful and devoted as anyone. Ultimately, building an intimate and enduring relationship is likely to be one of the high points of your life. You can find contentment and happiness with those born during the time of Gemini, Libra, and Sagittarius.

Throughout your life, your biggest challenge has been to be flexible. Your tendency to see only your own point of view may be a cause of distress for your friends and loved ones. Rely on your greatest strength, your visionary ideas, to help you to accept change and to embrace the future with open arms.

➤ Read about your Chinese Astrological sign on page 838. ➤ Read about your Personal Planets on page 826. ➤ Read about your personal Mystical Card on page 856.

CAPRICORN
Your Personal Planets

YOUR LOVE POTENTIAL
Venus in Capricorn, Jan. 01, 0:00 - Jan. 20, 18:32

YOUR DRIVE AND AMBITION
Mars in Capricorn, Jan. 01, 0:00 - Jan. 20, 18:32

YOUR LUCK MAGNETISM
Jupiter in Gemini, Jan. 01, 0:00 - Jan. 20, 18:32

World Events

Jan. 3 - A second conference at The Hague convenes to discuss war reparations.

Jan. 15 - Amelia Earhart sets a world aviation record for women, flying at 171 mph in her Lockheed Vega.

American Admiral Richard Byrd

AQUARIUS
Your Personal Planets

YOUR LOVE POTENTIAL
Venus in Capricorn, Jan. 20, 18:33 - Jan. 24, 0:21
Venus in Aquarius, Jan. 24, 0:22 - Feb. 16, 22:10
Venus in Pisces, Feb. 16, 22:11 - Feb. 19, 8:59

YOUR DRIVE AND AMBITION
Mars in Capricorn, Jan. 20, 18:33 - Feb. 06, 18:20
Mars in Aquarius, Feb. 06, 18:21 - Feb. 19, 8:59

YOUR LUCK MAGNETISM
Jupiter in Gemini, Jan. 20, 18:33 - Feb. 19, 8:59

World Events

Jan. 22 - Adm. Richard Byrd becomes the first person to map a large section of the Antarctic.

Feb. 18 - American astronomer Clyde Tombaugh discovers Pluto, the ninth planet in the Solar System.

1930

PISCES
Your Personal Planets

YOUR LOVE POTENTIAL
Venus in Pisces, Feb. 19, 9:00 - Mar. 12, 22:33
Venus in Aries, Mar. 12, 22:34 - Mar. 21, 8:29

YOUR DRIVE AND AMBITION
Mars in Aquarius, Feb. 19, 9:00 - Mar. 17, 5:54
Mars in Pisces, Mar. 17, 5:55 - Mar. 21, 8:29

YOUR LUCK MAGNETISM
Jupiter in Gemini, Feb. 19, 9:00 - Mar. 21, 8:29

World Events

Mar. 2 – British author D.H. Lawrence dies.

Mar. 12 – Mahatma Gandhi begins his 200-mile "march to the sea" in defiance of the British tax on salt.

Mahatma Gandhi breaking the salt law in India

ARIES
Your Personal Planets

YOUR LOVE POTENTIAL
Venus in Aries, Mar. 21, 8:30 - Apr. 06, 2:56
Venus in Taurus, Apr. 06, 2:57 - Apr. 20, 20:05

YOUR DRIVE AND AMBITION
Mars in Pisces, Mar. 21, 8:30 - Apr. 20, 20:05

YOUR LUCK MAGNETISM
Jupiter in Gemini, Mar. 21, 8:30 - Apr. 20, 20:05

World Events

Mar. 22 – American composer Stephen Sondheim is born.

Apr. 1 – Josef von Sternberg's film *The Blue Angel*, starring Marlene Dietrich and Emil Jannings, premières in Germany.

PISCES
From February 19, 9:00 through March 21, 8:29

The Beautiful Dreamer

For you, 1930 Pisces, the world is your own magical kingdom, not unlike a Disney theme park. Interestingly enough, Mickey Mouse first appeared in a cartoon strip in the year of your birth. Imaginative, sensitive, and eternally hopeful, you believe that fairy tales come true. As far as you are concerned, anything is possible—world peace, an end to poverty, or even winning the lottery!

Of course, you also have had your share of disappointments and dark moments. You are blessed with the capacity to feel deeply, whether it is agony or ecstasy. Life has been like a roller-coaster ride with dizzying heights and plummeting depths. But, seeing the world as a cold, dark, and cruel place for any prolonged length of time is simply contrary to your essential nature.

Growing up as you did during the Great Depression, you have a great sense of compassion for those in need. Mahatma Gandhi began his famous "march to the sea" for Indian independence just as you were entering the world. These influences had a profound and remarkable effect on your life. You see yourself as a champion of the underdog, a savior and a superhero, born to right the wrongs of an unjust society. You are someone who believes that one person can make a difference and you try to live your life that way.

When it comes to those close to you, you find it hard to set limits or boundaries. If you love someone, you give them all your faith, trust, and support. Your greatest desire is to merge with another. Relationships have a mystical and spiritual quality, and you believe that love can conquer all. But, losing yourself in the process is a real danger, as is attempting to save another, or trying to make their life better. Relationships work best between equal partners and you may find that Taureans, Capricorns, and Virgos give you the stability that you need.

Your biggest challenge in life is to keep the faith during difficult times. You may have a tendency to despair when the harsh realities of life have to be faced. Use your great capacity for love and understanding to forgive and to move ahead with hope.

ARIES
From March 21, 8:30 through April 20, 20:05

The Fiery Innovator

You were born to lead, 1930 Aries. You are a trailblazer and a pioneer, daring to break new ground without reservation. Around the time of your birth, some rather significant technological advances changed the way we live: Clarence Birdseye developed a method for quick-freezing food and synthetic rubber was first produced. These forces are reflected in your own personality—you, too, have a bit of the revolutionary in your soul and it is unlikely that you were ever comfortable with the status quo.

You are always ready for action and enjoy new challenges. If you fail, you don't lick your wounds for long. As an innovator, it is in your nature to pick yourself up, dust yourself off, and move on. If truth be told, beginning anew is more your style than seeing things through to the end. It's not that you don't intend to finish what you begin, but something usually comes along to divert your attention midstream. After all, there are so many places to go, people to see, and adventures to be experienced.

Impulsive and unpredictable, you are full of surprises and are exciting to be around. However, you may be erratic and unreliable on occasion. Nor are you a stranger to adversity. Like other children of the Depression era who experienced the gloominess of hard times, you need financial security. But, you are not interested in money for its own sake, but for the freedom that it can buy. Your worst moments occur when you fear that you may lose your autonomy.

You need a partner who enjoys excitement as much as you do and who is ready to do things at the spur of the moment. You may find that Geminis and Sagittarians provide you with the stimulus that you need to keep a relationship fresh and exciting. Leos and Aquarians may also keep your interest, and they can help to keep you on track, too.

Your principal life challenge is to learn to enjoy the moment, without looking forward to the next pursuit. Try to find as much joy in the old and familiar as you do in the fresh and new. Use your greatest strength, your genius for seeing the possibilities, to keep the wonder alive.

➤ Read about your Chinese Astrological sign on page 838. ➤ Read about your Personal Planets on page 826. ➤ Read about your personal Mystical Card on page 856.

TAURUS

From April 20, 20:06 through May 21, 19:41

The Dependable Provider

You are as solid and dependable as Earth itself, 1930 Taurus. Your life has been filled with responsibility, which you have embraced wholeheartedly. Capable of establishing and following a routine, you derive a great deal of comfort from the predictable and don't appreciate the surprise roadblocks that sometimes arise in the flow of everyday life. Just like Babe Ruth, who hit three consecutive homers in one game during the 1930 baseball season, you are consistent and can be counted on to do your best under every circumstance.

Practical and resourceful, you have an uncanny ability to make the best of any situation. You may also be quite lucky in financial matters. When you were growing up in the thirties and forties, resources were scarce, and it is likely that these early experiences cultivated your natural ability to make the most of what you have. You truly understand what it means to work for what you have achieved. And you can rest easy knowing that you have done your best.

Like most Taureans, you are a sensual being who derives a great deal of pleasure from the creature comforts of life. But, you also crave mental stimulation. With your quick mind and dogged determination, you are a master at working through the most difficult puzzles. And, when you need to make a decision, you carefully mull through all the possibilities. Once you decide upon a course of action, you are likely to move forward with surety and confidence.

Home and family are of paramount importance to you. They provide the impetus for all that you do and for all you have built. You are devoted to those you care for and can be counted on to live up to your word. Once you find a mate, you willingly share your love as well as your talents and resources. Those born under the signs of Cancer, Virgo, Capricorn, and Pisces are able to return your love and loyalty.

Your greatest challenge is to feel safe and secure in your material abundance. You need to develop trust that your needs will always be met. When you become doubtful, rely on your ability to persevere to reassure yourself that all will be well.

GEMINI

From May 21, 19:42 through June 22, 3:52

The Thoughtful Communicator

Known for your quick wit and your charming demeanor, 1930 Gemini, you are the messenger of the zodiac. A talented wordsmith, you were born to communicate. However, you may not be as glib as most Geminis, since you are careful about what you say, and how and when you say it. Taking time to think before you speak makes you an excellent communicator, and others typically find your conversations stimulating, informative, and enjoyable.

You have a youthful attitude and you delight in a variety of interests. Whether it is politics or pop culture, you usually know what is happening in the world. Never one to eschew controversy, you may find that your opinions are a bit avant-garde. In bold moves for 1930, the *New York Times* agreed to capitalize the "n" in the word Negro, and nudist colonies opened in the U.S. and UK. Such daring events, occurring in the year of your birth, are markedly symbolic of your own broad-mindedness.

Like the twins that represent your Gemini Sun sign, you may have two distinct personalities: one that is highly social, and one that enjoys solitude or the company of a close few. Although it may seem paradoxical, you need to experience both ends of the spectrum in order to be at your best. For, while you may have a myriad of activities to keep you busy, you have a strong need for affection and camaraderie. And, it is from your relationships with family and friends that you find a real sense of satisfaction as well as the security that you need.

In intimate relationships, you are a charming and fun-loving companion. Even when you are fully committed to one partner, you are still flirtatious at heart. You need to find a partner who is secure in his or her own right and who can allow you the space that you need to be yourself. Fellow Geminis, Ariens, Leos, and Librans can provide both the mental stimulation and the physical attraction to keep you interested for a good, long while.

Your primary challenge in life is to be able to reconcile the seemingly contradictory aspects of your persona. Trust in your greatest strength, your superlative mental abilities.

➤ Read about your Chinese Astrological sign on page 838. ➤ Read about your Personal Planets on page 826. ➤ Read about your personal Mystical Card on page 856.

TAURUS
Your Personal Planets

YOUR LOVE POTENTIAL
Venus in Taurus, Apr. 20, 20:06 - Apr. 30, 12:36
Venus in Gemini, Apr. 30, 12:37 - May 21, 19:41

YOUR DRIVE AND AMBITION
Mars in Pisces, Apr. 20, 20:06 - Apr. 24, 17:26
Mars in Aries, Apr. 24, 17:27 - May 21, 19:41

YOUR LUCK MAGNETISM
Jupiter in Gemini, Apr. 20, 20:06 - May 21, 19:41

World Events

Apr. 30 – The Soviet Union suggests a military alliance with Britain and France.

May 15 – American artist Jasper Johns is born.

Pilot Amy Johnson

GEMINI
Your Personal Planets

YOUR LOVE POTENTIAL
Venus in Gemini, May 21, 19:42 - May 25, 4:35
Venus in Cancer, May 25, 4:36 - June 19, 4:38
Venus in Leo, June 19, 4:39 - June 22, 3:52

YOUR DRIVE AND AMBITION
Mars in Aries, May 21, 19:42 - June 03, 3:14
Mars in Taurus, June 03, 3:15 - June 22, 3:52

YOUR LUCK MAGNETISM
Jupiter in Gemini, May 21, 19:42 - June 22, 3:52

World Events

May 24 – Amy Johnson completes a solo flight from London to Australia in nineteen-and-a-half days.

June 11 – A new diving record is set by New Yorker William Beebe—1,426 ft.

1930

CANCER
Your Personal Planets

YOUR LOVE POTENTIAL
Venus in Leo, June 22, 3:53 - July 14, 16:33
Venus in Virgo, July 14, 16:34 - July 23, 14:41

YOUR DRIVE AND AMBITION
Mars in Taurus, June 22, 3:53 - July 14, 12:53
Mars in Gemini, July 14, 12:54 - July 23, 14:41

YOUR LUCK MAGNETISM
Jupiter in Gemini, June 22, 3:53 - June 26, 22:41
Jupiter in Cancer, June 26, 22:42 - July 23, 14:41

World Events

June 30 – France withdraws its troops from the German Rhineland.

July 7 – British author of the "Sherlock Holmes" stories Sir Arthur Conan Doyle dies.

American astronaut Neil Armstrong is born under the sign of Leo

LEO
Your Personal Planets

YOUR LOVE POTENTIAL
Venus in Virgo, July 23, 14:42 - Aug. 10, 0:53
Venus in Libra, Aug. 10, 0:54 - Aug. 23, 21:25

YOUR DRIVE AND AMBITION
Mars in Gemini, July 23, 14:42 - Aug. 23, 21:25

YOUR LUCK MAGNETISM
Jupiter in Cancer, July 23, 14:42 - Aug. 23, 21:25

World Events

July 30 – The National Union Party is formed by fascists in Portugal.

Aug. 5 – The first man to walk on the Moon, astronaut Neil Armstrong, is born.

CANCER
From June 22, 3:53 through July 23, 14:41

The Sentimental Protector

You are a born nurturer and protector, 1930 Cancer. You have an intense need to create a family and you will sacrifice to make sure that your loved ones have all that they desire. You do best when you feel that you belong and are needed, especially in the workplace. A true patriot, you love your homeland and treasure your roots.

Sentimental and often moody, you recognize just how powerful your emotions are. However, you came of age during a time when children were not encouraged to express how they felt. Therefore, becoming comfortable with your feelings may have taken a good deal of work. Early in life, you may have feared that once you open the floodgate to your emotions, you will drown in them. Much like the Hoover Dam, which was begun when you were taking your first breaths, you eventually learned that you were a storehouse of powerful emotional energy that could feed all those around you.

There may have been times in your life when you felt that you have had the rug pulled out from under you and were left alone to face a crisis. Just when you needed them most, the people you always believed would be there turned up "missing in action." Fortunately, you have a good deal of resiliency, enabling you to survive the harshest circumstances. Perhaps growing up during the Great Depression steeled you for the twists and turns of your tumultuous life.

You can be dramatic at times, especially when it comes to your love relationships. You are very demonstrative and you expect your adoration to be returned by your partner. Just be careful not to overwhelm your mate with your devotion. You can find an ardent partner in those born during the time of Taurus, Virgo, Scorpio, and Capricorn. You can mutually explore the world of feelings with Pisces.

Your greatest challenge is to avoid becoming resentful at life's disappointments. It's likely that some of these events have indelibly scarred you, and your memory is flawless, making it difficult to forget. However, use your great gift of empathy to help you to see the other side and to release your anger.

LEO
From July 23, 14:42 through August 23, 21:25

The Levelheaded Entertainer

Like the lion that symbolizes your sign, 1930 Leo, you rule over your own personal kingdom with pride and with fearlessness. You radiate warmth and, for that reason, people naturally gravitate toward you. For the most part, you enjoy the attention and have a flair for entertaining. The welcome mat is always out at your door and you naturally make everyone feel special and comfortable.

You can really relate to the phrase "all the world's a stage." Like the Dumont Co., which aired its first TV broadcast for home reception around the time of your birth, you don't mind sharing your thoughts with others. While you may not have a talent for acting, you are most assuredly an engaging conversationalist. You are not only a great talker, but also an excellent listener. For this reason, it is likely that you are a much sought-after confidante.

Your approach to life is quite sensible. Perhaps, you learned your practicality during your early childhood in the Depression years. While you are very generous at heart, you may be quite thrifty. You also dislike waste and these frugal ways probably have their origin in your formative years, as well. However financially secure you may be now, you may still practice those early lessons, though the need to do so is long past.

You are a perfectionist and you may worry about making mistakes. Your pride may keep you from trying new things. You have a great deal of faith in human nature. Setting incredibly high standards for yourself and for others, your greatest disappointments in life have been when people failed to live up to your ideals. In relationships you are loyal and loving. You may need to learn the art of compromise, however. Lasting partnerships can be made with Ariens, Geminis, Librans, and Sagittarians.

Your greatest challenge in life is to avoid being overly self-critical. There is nothing more difficult for a Leo to deal with than low self-esteem. When you are not feeling good about yourself, you may tend to become tyrannical. Your greatest strength is your warm and generous spirit. Use that gift to be kind to yourself.

► Read about your Chinese Astrological sign on page 838. ► Read about your Personal Planets on page 826. ► Read about your personal Mystical Card on page 856.

VIRGO

From August 23, 21:26 through September 23, 18:35

The Detailed Planner

Blessed with a sharp mind and a practical nature, 1930 Virgo, you are a master of details. You can take a myriad of facts and integrate them into a unified hypothesis. Moreover, you can make your ideas readily understandable to others. With your uncanny ability to assess another's position, you are much like a master chess player, constantly strategizing and synthesizing. Your thinking processes are thorough and you will not express an opinion unless you are quite certain that you are correct. Rarely do you make a mistake but, if you do, you are not likely to make it a second time.

You have witnessed significant technological advances over the course of your life. In fact, the first non-stop airplane flight from Europe to the U.S. occurred around the time of your birth. Your parents were quite likely to be inspired by this accomplishment and may have encouraged your knack for spotting future trends. It is likely that you are very interested in scientific and medical topics, as well.

Besides witnessing the changes in the world around you, you may have also experienced significant personal transformations of one kind or another. Perhaps, you had to let go of your high standards and learn to be less precise and exacting. Or, you may have had to discover how to be less critical and more understanding of your own shortcomings and the limitations of others, too. In the end, these changes are likely to have accentuated your talents even more.

Although you have strong opinions, you are not likely to force your point of view on to another. With your firm feelings about the attributes you want in another person, it may take some time to find a partner. But, once you have found your mate, you are likely to be quite loyal and even possessive. You may find the qualities you are looking for in a Taurus, Cancer, Scorpio, or Capricorn.

Feeling loved and accepted may be your life's greatest challenge. You may fear that others are as disapproving of you as you are of yourself. Use your great analytical abilities to recognize that your strengths definitely outweigh your weaknesses.

LIBRA

From September 23, 18:36 through October 24, 3:25

The Great Peacemaker

Beauty and harmony are essential for you to be happy in your environment, 1930 Libra. Appearances are very important to you and you place great value in how things look. This is not to say that you are superficial; you simply believe that the outer world mirrors the inner. You may feel quite unsettled when faced with disorder. Restoring harmony in your environment gives you the tranquility you need to function at your highest level.

You were born in the same year that the Nazi party gained a foothold in the German Parliament, Japan invaded Manchuria, and Chinese Nationalists attempt to rid themselves of Mao and his Red Army. The effect of growing up during wartime is sure to have made your instinctual desire for peace even stronger. You not only require an inner serenity, but you also often assume the role of mediator when faced with disagreements. Because you have an ability to see both sides of a question, you may find that others often seek out your wisdom and that you can hit upon a fair and simple solution.

Like many Librans, you may have learned about balance and harmony by vacillating between two extremes. Perhaps you fluctuated between asserting yourself strongly and not asserting yourself at all. Or, you may shift between being overly generous and solicitous and not being able to give at all. Through trial and error, you learned how to find that happy balance between all and nothing.

You love to be in love and finding the right partner is paramount in your life. You exude charm and grace and it is essential to you that your partner does as well. You know how to set the stage for romance, creating just the right atmosphere for intimacy. A suitable match may be found with Geminis, Leos, Sagittarians, or Aquarians.

Your greatest challenge may be to learn how to be decisive. It pains you to know that once you have made a choice, you may be closing the door on other options. Although not choosing at all leaves all your options open, you may never move forward. Use your gift for rational and sound judgment, your greatest asset, to assess the best course to follow.

➤ Read about your Chinese Astrological sign on page 838. ➤ Read about your Personal Planets on page 826. ➤ Read about your personal Mystical Card on page 856.

1930

VIRGO
Your Personal Planets

YOUR LOVE POTENTIAL
Venus in Libra, Aug. 23, 21:26 - Sept. 07, 4:04
Venus in Scorpio, Sept. 07, 4:05 - Sept. 23, 18:35

YOUR DRIVE AND AMBITION
Mars in Gemini, Aug. 23, 21:26 - Aug. 28, 11:26
Mars in Cancer, Aug. 28, 11:27 - Sept. 23, 18:35

YOUR LUCK MAGNETISM
Jupiter in Cancer, Aug. 23, 21:26 - Sept. 23, 18:35

World Events

Aug. 25 – Scottish actor Sean Connery is born.

Sept. 21 – Archeologists working on a site in Ecuador uncover a horde of Incan treasure worth $15 million.

Scottish actor Sean Connery is born under the sign of Virgo

LIBRA
Your Personal Planets

YOUR LOVE POTENTIAL
Venus in Scorpio, Sept. 23, 18:36 - Oct. 12, 2:44
Venus in Sagittarius, Oct. 12, 2:45 - Oct. 24, 3:25

YOUR DRIVE AND AMBITION
Mars in Cancer, Sept. 23, 18:36 - Oct. 20, 14:42
Mars in Leo, Oct. 20, 14:43 - Oct. 24, 3:25

YOUR LUCK MAGNETISM
Jupiter in Cancer, Sept. 23, 18:36 - Oct. 24, 3:25

World Events

Oct. 1– Irish delegates demand freedom from British rule at a meeting in London.

Oct. 10 – British playwright Harold Pinter is born.

SCORPIO
Your Personal Planets

YOUR LOVE POTENTIAL
Venus in Sagittarius, Oct. 24, 3:26 - Nov. 22, 7:43
Venus in Scorpio, Nov. 22, 7:44 - Nov. 23, 0:33

YOUR DRIVE AND AMBITION
Mars in Leo, Oct. 24, 3:26 - Nov. 23, 0:33

YOUR LUCK MAGNETISM
Jupiter in Cancer, Oct. 24, 3:26 - Nov. 23, 0:33

World Events

Nov. 2 – Haile Selassie is crowned Emperor of Ethiopia.

Nov. 15 – Riots break out in Madrid in Spain.

Troops leave Seville to combat military revolution in Spain

SAGITTARIUS
Your Personal Planets

YOUR LOVE POTENTIAL
Venus in Scorpio, Nov. 23, 0:34 - Dec. 22, 13:39

YOUR DRIVE AND AMBITION
Mars in Leo, Nov. 23, 0:34 - Dec. 22, 13:39

YOUR LUCK MAGNETISM
Jupiter in Cancer, Nov. 23, 0:34 - Dec. 22, 13:39

World Events

Dec. 3 – French film director Jean-Luc Godard is born.

Dec. 12 – A month of strikes and riots across Spain erupts into revolution.

SCORPIO
From October 24, 3:26 through November 23, 0:33

The Charismatic Survivor

Intense and inquisitive, you are the detective of the zodiac. With a natural flair for digging beneath the surface, 1930 Scorpio, you love to peel through the layers of a person or a situation until you reach the core. You take nothing at face value, recognizing that things are seldom as they appear. Appropriately, just as you were making your entrance on the planet, the first tunnel between two countries, the U.S. and Canada, opened for vehicular traffic.

Others may sense that you are profound and deep. Perhaps it is because you carry all of your past experiences, good and bad, with you. As a child of the Great Depression, you may have internalized the grief and misery around you. These early imprints remained with you throughout your life, giving you an enormous capacity for compassion. You take great pride in your ability to surmount any difficulty and have a ready reservoir of inner strength at your disposal.

Persuasive and dynamic, you have a great deal of personal charisma. You often get what you want, mostly because you don't give up very easily. You assume responsibility well and make the most of every opportunity to advance, be it in the workplace or in the social sphere. You understand the importance of power and how to use it. Dependable and trustworthy, you always fulfill what you promise to do.

You enjoy living on the edge and conquering new horizons. Never content with the mundane or ordinary, you seek out the exotic and unusual. Others are inexplicably drawn to your compelling and mysterious demeanor. Be careful not to smother those you love with your passion and devotion. In relationships, you need a partner who is honest and faithful, as well as stimulating and different. You can find a satisfying and meaningful union with Cancer, Capricorn, and Pisces.

Learning to trust may be the biggest challenge of your life. Once betrayed, you find it hard to allow yourself to be vulnerable again. But, self-protection is a lonely road. Draw on your greatest strength, your capacity to overcome any obstacle, to find the courage to have faith in others again.

SAGITTARIUS
From November 23, 0:34 through December 22, 13:39

The Lifelong Traveler

You are the explorer of the zodiac, 1930 Sagittarius, always looking forward to life's next journey. You were born in a year when great aviators sought to conquer the sky, such as Laura Ingalls, the first woman to complete a transcontinental flight. Architects like William Van Allen who designed the Chrysler Building in New York City looked skyward, too.

While you are fond of travel and would like to traverse the far corners of the globe, your personal search has little to do with excitement or adventure. You are, first and foremost, a seeker of the real meaning of life. In the final analysis, you probably found that the answer lies deep within rather than in the stratosphere. Once you made this realization, you probably found contentment in staying close to home.

Learning is a lifelong pursuit and your thinking is both revolutionary and visionary. You are focused on the big picture, sometimes missing the finer details. Not content with accepting the conventional wisdom, you often question why things are the way they are. During your childhood years, dictators such as Hitler and Mussolini counted on people to follow them blindly. Perhaps this initial exposure to life reinforced your innate tendency to try to comprehend the reasons behind acting in a particular way. While this may have been disconcerting at times for your parents, they were also likely to have a deep respect for your quest for understanding.

Much of your life was probably spent in search of a deep and abiding love. Though you may show the world a carefree attitude, you have a real need for affection. Here, again, looking inward and learning to love yourself is the first, necessary step in finding a fellow voyager for the journey of life. You need someone who can keep you interested and make the ordinary moments of day-to-day life remarkable. You may find Ariens, Leos, Librans, and Aquarians to be fascinating and interesting partners.

Your greatest challenge is to find happiness and contentment in your own backyard. Rely on your greatest strength, your love of knowledge, to stay interested in life.

➤ Read about your Chinese Astrological sign on page 838. ➤ Read about your Personal Planets on page 826. ➤ Read about your personal Mystical Card on page 856.

CAPRICORN

From December 22, 13:40 through December 31, 23:59

The Confident Decision-Maker

With your strong opinions and a mind like a steel-trap, you are a formidable adversary to anyone who would dare to challenge your will, December Capricorn of 1930. You are quite confident in your decision-making prowess and are not reticent about making your thoughts known. In the year of your birth, William Hays, head of the Motion Picture Producers and Distributors of America, established a code of decency that outlines what is acceptable in films. You, too, have a strong sense of propriety and have determined for yourself what is acceptable in your life.

Your powerful convictions are matched by your very perceptive intellect. You don't take much at face value, and you have a thorough and deep understanding of any topic you choose to explore. Sly and secretive, you are a master at allowing people to know only as much as you want to reveal. Like Arthur Conan Doyle, creator of Sherlock Holmes, who passed away in the year you were born, you enjoy getting to the bottom of any complex and mystifying situation.

Though you are usually quite predictable, every so often you may break out of your typical routine. You can have flashes of inspiration or you may just enjoy shaking things up. However, if you become too complacent, you may find that circumstances conspire to force change upon you. Your presence is larger than life and you have a tendency to think big. While you are capable of accomplishing a great deal, you also need to stay realistic and not bite off more than you can chew.

In relationships, you can be quite passionate, protective and, at times, possessive. You would go to the ends of the Earth to please a loved one. But, you demand absolute loyalty in return. Taureans, Cancers, Scorpios, and Pisces possess the high degree of intensity and sensuality that you require in a mate.

Your greatest challenge in life is to learn how to express your anger constructively. The danger is that you may either misdirect your rage or turn it inward. Instead, use your greatest strength, which is your laser-like capacity to focus your attention, to go to the heart of the matter.

1930

CAPRICORN
Your Personal Planets

YOUR LOVE POTENTIAL
Venus in Scorpio, Dec. 22, 13:40 - Dec. 31, 23:59

YOUR DRIVE AND AMBITION
Mars in Leo, Dec. 22, 13:40 - Dec. 31, 23:59

YOUR LUCK MAGNETISM
Jupiter in Cancer, Dec. 22, 13:40 - Dec. 31, 23:59

World Events

Dec. 23 – In the Punjab, the British governor is injured in an assassination attempt.

Dec. 31 – Brewery heir Adolphus Busch is kidnapped.

Franklin Delano Roosevelt
January 30, 1882 - April 12, 1945

FRANKLIN D. ROOSEVELT
Aquarius

Franklin Delano Roosevelt, a son of high society who was a victim of polio at the age of thirty-nine, was elected to the presidency when the country was in deep economic crisis. The Great Depression was raging and Roosevelt had to reopen the banks, help the farmers, and get the country back to work. His New Deal brought him a landslide reelection and eventually an unprecedented third term as president, where he worked to lead the Allies to victory in World War II.

Roosevelt was an Aquarius, a sign noted for its innovation and sense of brotherhood. With his Sun, the planet of identity, in the house of pleasure and creativity, Roosevelt connected well with many different kinds of people, a trait that was emphasized by a contact from Venus, planet of affection. Uranus, the ruler of Aquarius and the planet of eccentricity, was prominently placed in his horoscope, further encouraging a nature that was creative and innovative. Roosevelt developed social security and many other social reforms. His intentions to go into politics were strong, and right from the beginning of his career he informed people of his desire to be president.

His Sun received a contact from responsible Saturn, the planet of hard work, as well as from Jupiter, planet of expansion. A contact from Neptune gave him the idealism and great vision that allowed him to lead the U.S. through the Great Depression and World War II.

In his house of career, Roosevelt had Mars, the planet of action and war. From the start of his education, he had wanted to attend Annapolis, but family demands required that he go to Harvard instead. He was an ardent military strategist, which helped him steer the U.S. through war. Also in his house of career is the Moon, planet of emotions, located in the sensitive sign of Cancer. He had a strong connection with the people of his nation and was reelected because of an ability to tap into the public needs and desires for security. With the Moon here, it was quite natural for him to marry a wife who could be a true partner in his work, his cousin Eleanor.

➤ Read "The Presidential Death Cycle" on page 657. ➤ Read Churchill's Star Profile on page 337. ➤ Read "Astro Twins: Hitler and Chaplin" on page 345.

257

Experimentation and Innovation: Saturn Opposes Pluto

A s Saturn, symbolizing rules and structures, faced off with Pluto, the planet of deep change, the world began to respond to the cataclysmic economic events of the past two years. Whenever these two planets connect, big changes are afoot, but it is not always evident immediately because it is happening at a deeper level. These transformations often take place on the highest level of human functioning such as government, institutions, and civilization. In 1931, people were becoming aware of themselves as members of a global community and governments were following suit. Spain rejected its long-standing monarchy, opting for a system of constitutional republicanism. Pluto, in the nurturing sign of Cancer, saw upheaval in the way people and governments took care of themselves and each other and the means they devised to survive. Accordingly, the citizenry of many countries, desperate for something new to provide opportunity embraced communism or fascism because they offered hope. Communism promised that workers would gain control of the state through revolution, symbolized by Pluto, while fascism reassured those already in control that chaos among the working people would be contained through patriarchal authoritarianism, reflecting Saturn's energies.

Cancer is also associated with women and food, both a part of nurturing. Pluto's position in Cancer heralded changes in the role of women, as they frequently found themselves more employable than their husbands. Food became a central focus when workers could not buy what they needed. Hunger marchers demonstrated in the U.S., and frustrated laborers rioted in London. The positive side of Pluto's influence was highlighted by advances in healing and home conveniences. Penicillin saw its first clinical use, giving hope to those with tuberculosis, while Frigidaire™ made refrigerators safe for domestic use.

Fun-loving Jupiter also moved through Cancer in 1931, correlating with light-hearted distractions like the motion picture *Platinum Blonde*. However, as it moved close to Pluto, mythological Lord of the Underworld, a darker side was revealed through now-classic versions of *Frankenstein* and *Dracula*, and the German murder mystery *M*.

Gandhi on the occasion of meeting King George V in London

Spain's first president, Niceto Alacara Zamora

Al Capone

DESPAIR GIVES WAY TO HOPE AND INNOVATION

The Great Depression deepened as bank closures caused unemployment across the world. Germany and Britain were in crisis, as civil unrest and economic failure prompted stringent austerity measures. Individual rights were affirmed and peace was in the air when republican Spanish voters forced King Alfonso XIII to abdicate and elected Zamora to lead their new republic. While Gandhi was in London for a conference on Indian self-government, Britain's King George V met the Mahatma, who was clad in his trademark loincloth, shawl, and sandals. The sad saga of the Scottsboro boys, young black men accused of rape, showed how little had been done to advance racial justice in the U.S. The motion picture double feature provided refuge from economic hardship, while the first TV broadcasts were relayed from Canada. Technological innovations accelerated the modernization of society, as the first refrigerators came into use. The public was impressed by the opening of the Empire State Building, the world's tallest building. Justice was served when Al Capone, the liquor baron, was convicted for tax evasion in this eleventh year of Prohibition.

➤ Read "The First New Age Psychic: Edgar Cayce" by Wendy C. Hawks on page 265.

CAPRICORN

From January 01, 0:00 through January 21, 0:17

The Resilient Go-Getter

You are a heroic and grand figure to your family and friends, Capricorn of January 1931, and love to do things in a big way. You are not content with half-measures, and can usually be counted on to run the gauntlet of life with pride and courage. Decisive and forthright, you can be trusted to tell it like it is. And, like the Goat you are, once you have stated your position, you are not likely to back off.

In spite of your enormous drive and talents, there may have been times when you doubted your vision or lacked the self-confidence to see plans through. Perhaps others told you that you were too grandiose or unrealistic. And, at times, the skeptics may have been right. But, when it was crucial, your resolve and purposefulness helped you to overcome your uncertainty. Like Lucille Thomas who, around the time of your birth, became the first woman ever to purchase a baseball team, you are unafraid to chart a new course.

Growing up in the thirties and forties, you had the chance to develop your considerable inner strength and character. The old adage "when the going gets tough, the tough get going" may have been written with you in mind. Thanks to your remarkable resiliency, nothing gets you down for long. As you overcame each obstacle in life, your ability to handle crisis grew as well. Your sturdiness is an asset that you can rely on, and one that others will come to admire and have confidence in as well.

In relationships, you can be a fortress of strength for your partner. But, you also need someone who will embark on the adventures of life as persistently and spiritedly as you do. Your ideal mate will face life's challenges unafraid, and you will derive a great deal of power from each other. For a kindred spirit, look to those born under the signs of Taurus, Virgo, Scorpio, and Pisces.

One of your life's greatest challenges has been to overcome disappointment in yourself, or others. You may expect a little too much from life and set too-high standards that may never be met. Use your remarkable ability to rebound to give you the fortitude to accept all shortcomings.

AQUARIUS

From January 21, 0:18 through February 19, 14:39

The Tenacious Idealist

Far-reaching ideas and a love of humanity have been the hallmark of your life, 1931 Aquarius. You pride yourself on your personal integrity and noble principles. Faced with many obstacles over the course of your life, you have had to make considerable adjustments in order to survive. At times, it may have been a struggle to hold on to your dreams and ideals. However, born around the time of the release of the first *Dracula* movie, you tend to approach life in a stranglehold fashion, never letting go.

In your birth year, there were worldwide bank failures, and money and resources were as scarce as at any time in history. These tumultuous times taught you how to get beyond any impasse either by going around it, climbing over it, digging under it, or simply plowing right through it. Still, there may have been times when you experienced considerable frustration, feeling as if you were taking two steps backwards for every step forward. As you matured, however, you may have learned to appreciate the art of taking things slowly and methodically in order to reach your goals.

The early days of your life saw Germany seek withdrawal from the League of Nations, in a move that sowed the seeds of disquiet for the rest of the decade. Growing up as you did with a world at war, you would find that your search for serenity took many turns. You are not always able to express your anger constructively and may have turned your dissatisfaction inward.

Your approach to relationships is unafraid and tenacious. You seek a partner who can share your high ideals and single-mindedness. Even though you highly value personal freedom and individuality, you also desire the companionship of a true friend and partner to share life's journey. Ariens, Geminis, Librans, and Sagittarians may offer you the right mix of togetherness and independence.

Life has presented you with many challenges, but perhaps the most significant has been to learn how to gracefully accept life's inevitable changes. You can depend upon your great ability to face life realistically to help you adapt to any new circumstances.

➤ Read about your Chinese Astrological sign on page 838. ➤ Read about your Personal Planets on page 826. ➤ Read about your personal Mystical Card on page 856.

1931

CAPRICORN
Your Personal Planets

YOUR LOVE POTENTIAL
Venus in Scorpio, Jan. 01, 0:00 - Jan. 03, 20:02
Venus in Sagittarius, Jan. 03, 20:03 - Jan. 21, 0:17

YOUR DRIVE AND AMBITION
Mars in Leo, Jan. 01, 0:00 - Jan. 21, 0:17

YOUR LUCK MAGNETISM
Jupiter in Cancer, Jan. 01, 0:00 - Jan. 21, 0:17

World Events

Jan. 2 – The Panama government is overthrown.
Jan. 5 – American choreographer Alvin Ailey is born.

American movie star James Dean is born under the sign of Aquarius

AQUARIUS
Your Personal Planets

YOUR LOVE POTENTIAL
Venus in Sagittarius, Jan. 21, 0:18 - Feb. 06, 12:24
Venus in Capricorn, Feb. 06, 12:25 - Feb. 19, 14:39

YOUR DRIVE AND AMBITION
Mars in Leo, Jan. 21, 0:18 - Feb. 16, 14:26
Mars in Cancer, Feb. 16, 14:27 - Feb. 19, 14:39

YOUR LUCK MAGNETISM
Jupiter in Cancer, Jan. 21, 0:18 - Feb. 19, 14:39

World Events

Jan. 26 – Mahatma Gandhi is released from jail after eight months of imprisonment for civil disobedience.
Feb. 8 – American movie icon James Dean is born.

1931

PISCES
Your Personal Planets

YOUR LOVE POTENTIAL
Venus in Capricorn, Feb. 19, 14:40 - Mar. 05, 21:45
Venus in Aquarius, Mar. 05, 21:46 - Mar. 21, 14:05

YOUR DRIVE AND AMBITION
Mars in Cancer, Feb. 19, 14:40 - Mar. 21, 14:05

YOUR LUCK MAGNETISM
Jupiter in Cancer, Feb. 19, 14:40 - Mar. 21, 14:05

World Events

Mar. 11 – The USSR bans the import or sale of the Holy Bible.

Mar. 11 – Australian media magnate Rupert Murdoch is born.

King Alfonso of Spain before his exile

ARIES
Your Personal Planets

YOUR LOVE POTENTIAL
Venus in Aquarius, Mar. 21, 14:06 - Mar. 31, 19:03
Venus in Pisces, Mar. 31, 19:04 - Apr. 21, 1:39

YOUR DRIVE AND AMBITION
Mars in Cancer, Mar. 21, 14:06 - Mar. 30, 3:47
Mars in Leo, Mar. 30, 3:48 - Apr. 21, 1:39

YOUR LUCK MAGNETISM
Jupiter in Cancer, Mar. 21, 14:06 - Apr. 21, 1:39

World Events

Apr. 1 – An earthquake in Managua, Nicaragua claims an estimated 2,000 lives.

Apr. 14 – Spain becomes a republic with the overthrow and exile of King Alfonso XIII.

PISCES
From February 19, 14:40 through March 21, 14:05

The Practical Visionary

You are a marvelous blend of sensitivity and practicality, Pisces of 1931, making you a much sought after advisor and confidante. Blessed with the ability to recognize the needs of others, you are also able to offer some very real solutions. You have a personal vision of how things should be, and you strive to turn that dream into a reality. To that end, you can put your powerful imagination and creativity to use for the betterment of yourself, your loved ones, and the world as a whole.

Just like the sentiments expressed in the "Star-Spangled Banner," which was declared the national anthem of the U.S. around the time of your birth, you are a true believer. Growing up as you did during the Depression and World War II, you have faith in the notion that with an indomitable spirit and personal sacrifice, good can triumph over any evil. And, over the course of your life, you have been quite capable of the sacrifice and moral fiber needed to live your life on your own terms.

Ever waiting for your "ship to come in," you are blessed with unbridled optimism and an ability to view any situation positively. Perhaps it is no coincidence, then, that gambling was legalized in Nevada around the time of your birth. In the casino of life, you believe that at any moment you can hit the jackpot. You are not afraid to take a risk in the hope that the rewards will be great.

People are naturally drawn to your common sense and kind demeanor. Thanks to your visionary beliefs and sensible nature, you have great leadership qualities. Charismatic and romantic, relationships are easy for you. You are both passionate and affectionate, and you enjoy all the sensual pleasures life has to offer. Taureans, Cancerians, Scorpios, and Capricorns make ideal partners that can enchant and delight you for a lifetime.

Your greatest challenge in life is to learn how to use your considerable personal magnetism for the greatest good. You could easily lead others astray, or fall prey to fly-by-night, get-rich-quick schemes. Use your strong sense of right and wrong to keep you on the straight and narrow.

ARIES
From March 21, 14:06 through April 21, 1:39

The Enthusiastic Fighter

Strong-willed and feisty, Aries of 1931, you are the warrior of the zodiac, ever willing to fight for your beliefs. Much like Little Orphan Annie, who made her radio debut around the time you were born, you insistently pursue what you want. You can be counted on to rally the troops, beginning a momentum that leads inevitably to triumph. Spontaneous, creative, and often dramatic, you provide the spark and excitement in any situation.

A born innovator, you have a fondness for anything new or unusual. Living life on the cutting edge, you are quite enthusiastic, especially at the beginning of new ventures. At times, you can be unconventional and even revolutionary. Freedom and independence are important to you, just as they were to those Spaniards who voted to overthrow their monarchy as you were entering the world. You will fight for your right to make your own choices and determine your own fate.

You have a quick mind and rarely hold back from speaking your thoughts. It's not in your nature to soft-pedal an issue, and the more you try to do so, the more likely you will erupt and blow things out of proportion. Worse yet, you may simply bolt and run, never to return. When you were young and impetuous, you may have been more apt to lose your temper. With wisdom and maturity, you probably learned how to be both direct and tactful, and to say what you mean at the appropriate time.

Fun-loving and exciting, being around you is rarely boring. Others are naturally attracted to your effervescent personality. But, you also have a dreamy and romantic side, and are quite capable of turning on the charm when an opportunity presents itself. To keep your interest, your partner needs to be spontaneous and have a sense of adventure. Geminis, Leos, Librans, and Sagittarians may possess the qualities you need to stay happily engrossed over the long haul.

Your greatest challenge is to keep going, even when your plans are interrupted by unexpected and unwelcome obstacles. Remember, you cannot control every situation. Rely on your enthusiasm to keep you working toward your desired goal.

➤ Read about your Chinese Astrological sign on page 838. ➤ Read about your Personal Planets on page 826. ➤ Read about your personal Mystical Card on page 856.

TAURUS

From April 21, 1:40 through May 22, 1:14

The Cautious Achiever

You have a realistic perspective and a cautious nature, Taurus of 1931. While you may be slow to make a decision, once made, you stick to your chosen course. You don't care how long a project takes, as long as you make continual progress. From your point of view, slow and steady definitely wins the race. You made your entrance into the world just as the Empire State Building opened its doors. Just like that building—which symbolizes one of the greatest architectural accomplishments of modern man—achievement is important to you and you strive to be the best in all your endeavors.

You tend to be introspective and may have trouble expressing your feelings. Consequently, people may find you reticent or uncommunicative. You also need more time to absorb what is being said. The more you are hurried, the more likely you are to stubbornly resist being rushed. You dislike change and need sufficient time and consideration to embrace the new. When you were younger, you may have had to be dragged, kicking and screaming, into new situations. But, as you've grown older, you surely learned that change is inevitable.

As a child of the Depression era, you understand the importance of financial security. During the course of your life, financial ups and downs are likely to have had a great impact on you, making it difficult for you to place your trust in anyone else's hands. Though you are proud of making it on your own and are quite self-reliant, you may still have lingering fears about your financial condition.

Relationships can provide you with a great sense of security and help to heal your childhood fears. You need a mate who not only is sensitive to your deep needs and able to restore your trust in the world, but is also passionate and loyal. Cancerians, Virgos, Capricorns, and Pisceans may offer you the love you so strongly desire.

Your greatest challenge is to learn how to overcome your stubbornness. Obstinately holding on to ideas or situations that have outlived their usefulness is counterproductive. Use your great gift of common sense to help you know when to let go.

GEMINI

From May 22, 1:15 through June 22, 9:27

The Gifted Raconteur

Versatile and youthful, Gemini of 1931, you have a real gift for communication and a wonderful sense of humor. Your way with words makes even the most mundane incident compelling. While at times you may exaggerate, it is only to make your point more forcefully. Your intention is not to mislead or bamboozle, but rather to delight your audience with your story-telling ability.

Perhaps it was growing up in the difficult years of the thirties and forties that taught you to live in the moment, rather than the future or the past. In your youth, you may have been a bit reckless, never thinking of the future. Like Al Capone, who was finally indicted for his criminal activities around the time of your birth, you too, finally took responsibility for your actions. Once you accepted life's inevitable restrictions, it's likely that you used your natural light-heartedness to live each day to its fullest.

You are generous and giving, almost to a fault, and may find that your financial situation fluctuates as a result. But, whether up or down, you have the capacity to accept life on life's terms. There is a serious, down-to-earth side to your personality, and you can adapt to any situation. While you take pleasure in the simple things of life, like good conversation, a home-cooked meal, and the company of family and friends, you can be equally comfortable with a glamorous night out on the town.

Flirtatious and witty, you have probably enjoyed a number of romantic associations over the course of your life. While you may have been a bit fickle in your youth, you ultimately desired a close relationship with one person. However, to keep your interest, your partner needs to be as multi-faceted and as easygoing as you are. Look for a kindred spirit among Ariens, Leos, Librans, and Aquarians.

Your greatest challenge over the years has been to stay positive amidst all your frustrations and changes in fortune. You're on top of the world one day; the next, you're downtrodden. Use your incredible talent to see the absurdity of the moment—it will help you to laugh at yourself and get back on an even keel.

➤ Read about your Chinese Astrological sign on page 838. ➤ Read about your Personal Planets on page 826. ➤ Read about your personal Mystical Card on page 856.

TAURUS
Your Personal Planets

YOUR LOVE POTENTIAL
Venus in Pisces, Apr. 21, 1:40 - Apr. 26, 2:09
Venus in Aries, Apr. 26, 2:10 - May 21, 2:37
Venus in Taurus, May 21, 2:38 - May 22, 1:14

YOUR DRIVE AND AMBITION
Mars in Leo, Apr. 21, 1:40 - May 22, 1:14

YOUR LUCK MAGNETISM
Jupiter in Cancer, Apr. 21, 1:40 - May 22, 1:14

World Events

Apr. 22 – Egypt signs a treaty of friendship with Iraq, the first of its kind to be drawn up between Egypt and an Arab state.

May 1 – The Empire State Building, the world's tallest structure to date, is formally opened in New York City.

The Empire State Building in New York City

GEMINI
Your Personal Planets

YOUR LOVE POTENTIAL
Venus in Taurus, May 22, 1:15 - June 14, 23:03
Venus in Gemini, June 14, 23:04 - June 22, 9:27

YOUR DRIVE AND AMBITION
Mars in Leo, May 22, 1:15 - June 10, 14:57
Mars in Virgo, June 10, 14:58 - June 22, 9:27

YOUR LUCK MAGNETISM
Jupiter in Cancer, May 22, 1:15 - June 22, 9:27

World Events

June 10 - Maestro Arturo Toscanini is granted permission to leave Italy after nearly a month of house arrest for his refusal to play the fascist anthem "Giovinezza."

June 12 - Gangster Al Capone and sixty-eight henchmen are charged with violating Prohibition laws in the U.S.

1931

CANCER
Your Personal Planets

YOUR LOVE POTENTIAL

Venus in Gemini, June 22, 9:28 - July 09, 15:34
Venus in Cancer, July 09, 15:35 - July 23, 20:20

YOUR DRIVE AND AMBITION

Mars in Virgo, June 22, 9:28 - July 23, 20:20

YOUR LUCK MAGNETISM

Jupiter in Cancer, June 22, 9:28 - July 17, 7:51
Jupiter in Leo, July 17, 7:52 - July 23, 20:20

World Events

July 1 – French actress and dancer Leslie Caron is born.

July 1 – Wiley Post and Harold Gatty complete a round-the-world flight in a record eight days, fifteen hours and fifty-one minutes.

French actress and dancer Leslie Caron is born under the sign of Cancer

LEO
Your Personal Planets

YOUR LOVE POTENTIAL

Venus in Cancer, July 23, 20:21 - Aug. 03, 3:28
Venus in Leo, Aug. 03, 3:29 - Aug. 24, 3:09

YOUR DRIVE AND AMBITION

Mars in Virgo, July 23, 20:21 - Aug. 01, 16:37
Mars in Libra, Aug. 01, 16:38 - Aug. 24, 3:09

YOUR LUCK MAGNETISM

Jupiter in Leo, July 23, 20:21 - Aug. 24, 3:09

World Events

Aug. 3 – The Yangtze River in China floods, killing nearly 200,000 people.

Aug. 14 – Lithuanian dictator Woldemaras appears before a military tribunal on charges of treason.

CANCER
From June 22, 9:28 through July 23, 20:20

The Loving Guardian

You are guided by your emotions, Cancer of 1931, and have a strong attachment to family and home. Affectionate and sympathetic, your greatest pleasure is to be surrounded by those you love. When faced with a problem or a decision, you respond with your feelings, rather than your logical mind. You have great instincts about people and can learn how to use your intuitive powers to your advantage.

Growing up during the Depression and World War II took its toll on your psyche. Fiercely protective, you may sometimes believe that your entire life has been spent safeguarding what you have. For a watery and sensitive soul, there is little choice but to become firmer and stronger. And so, just like ice, which was first sold through vending machines at the time of your birth, you hardened over time. But, given the right circumstances, you can also melt and soften, opening your heart again when only your special care will suffice.

Your achievements have not come without difficulty; even when you thought you were on solid ground, the foundation would unexpectedly crumble beneath your feet. You may feel that your life has been spent pushing an enormous boulder uphill, without assistance of any kind. But, in the process you have learned about your own inner strength, and probably recognize that the hard knocks of life taught you how to be of real service to others.

When it comes to love and romance, you are prepared to give yourself totally to another. But, you must first feel totally safe and secure in the knowledge that your loved one returns your affections. In your younger days, you may have been a bit manipulative or secretive about what you wanted but, as you matured, you learned how to be more direct about your desires. Look to Taureans, Virgos, Scorpios, Capricorns, and Pisceans to find a lifelong partner.

Life has handed you many challenges, but perhaps the greatest has been to learn how to overcome your fear of loss. Your greatest strength is your ability to nurture others. When you are anxious or worried, use this gift to look after yourself, and allay your fears.

LEO
From July 23, 20:21 through August 24, 3:09

The Spirited Leader

Self-assured and courageous, 1931 Leo, you are capable of shining as bright as the Sun itself. The warmth that you generate can light up a city, and those around you cannot help but want to bask in your dazzling glow. Just as the Sun is the center of our Solar System, you are the focus of any group, and are likely to have a legion of admiring followers wherever you go. Over the course of your life, your boundless energy and radiant spirit is likely to have been a source of inspiration for your loved ones.

However, just as too much Sun can scorch and burn, others may resent your impressive demeanor and mistake it for arrogance or self-importance. In your youth, you may have been a bit self-absorbed, vying for attention and always needing to be on center stage. But, with maturity, you are likely to have learned that your true greatness lies in connecting with your powerful inner core—your heart. You also understand that real self-esteem comes from being true to yourself.

You exude confidence and have a way of helping others feel more capable in your presence. Perhaps surviving the Great Depression helped you to believe in yourself and your ability to prevail. Along with being quite competent, you are blessed with endurance and determination. Around the time you were born, Ernest Lassy completed a 6,102-mile canoe journey without stopping at any port. Like Lassy, your resolve and fortitude make it possible for you to achieve just about any goal you set for yourself.

Popular and affable, you have had many friends and admirers throughout your life. But, when it comes to an intimate relationship, you want the love and attention of just one special person. You are loyal and generous, and you need a partner who can return your considerable passion. Ariens, Geminis, Librans, and Sagittarians are likely to delight you and keep your fiery warmth ablaze.

In life, your greatest challenge has been to learn to relax and take life one day at a time. You may even have been a bit of a workaholic. Your greatest strength lies in your ability to bring out the best in other people.

➤ Read about your Chinese Astrological sign on page 838. ➤ Read about your Personal Planets on page 826. ➤ Read about your personal Mystical Card on page 856.

VIRGO

From August 24, 3:10 through September 24, 0:22

The Fastidious Organizer

You are resourceful, independent, and self-reliant, 1931 Virgo. Meticulous in both your appearance and your approach to work, your careful manner makes you suited for tasks where accuracy and precision count. You are also quite well disciplined and organized, and find it easy to stick to a routine. Analytical and detailed, you enjoy gathering facts and figures and rely on reason, rather than emotion, when making decisions. You have strong opinions about how things should be done, though you may be somewhat reticent about expressing them.

You may also be a bit of perfectionist, holding yourself to very exacting standards. Even in early childhood, you always strived to do everything well. But no one, not even yourself, can ever meet your high expectations. This reality may have led you to be quite self-critical and to doubt your capabilities. Hopefully, you eventually learned to be more forgiving of your own shortcomings as well as those of others.

When it comes to taking action, you can go to extremes. At times, you may be overly cautious and fail to act, even though you should. There may also be occasions when you act impetuously and regret your behavior afterwards. However, it's likely that in due course you've learned how to balance these contradictory impulses and to achieve your objectives. Your ability to take risks and your precise nature are much like the qualities that airplane daredevil Jimmy Doolittle needed in his record-breaking flight across America around the time you were born.

While you are quite self-contained and competent, you still have the desire for an intimate relationship. However, it's hard for you to allow yourself to need or trust anyone else. Once you get over this fear of dependence on another, you can obtain sweet satisfaction in love. You may find a loyal and devoted partner among Taureans, Cancerians, Scorpios, and Capricorns.

Learning how to let go of control is one of your great challenges. When you attempt to manipulate a situation, you often find yourself considerably frustrated. Rely on curiosity to help you go with the flow.

LIBRA

From September 24, 0:23 through October 24, 9:15

The Serenity Seeker

Cooperation and diplomacy come naturally to you, 1931 Libra, and your life has been spent trying to create a pleasant environment for yourself and your loved ones. Artistic and creative, your tastes are eclectic. You are just as comfortable with modern furnishings and works of art as you are with the more traditional. Chester Gould's groundbreaking *Dick Tracy* comic strip made its debut right around the time you were making your entrance into the world. Just like you, it is highly stylized and striking in its appearance.

Born during a time when the world was in financial crisis, it's likely that you have quite a few insecurities about money. Growing up during the Depression, you understood scarcity and lack all too well. Consequently, you may feel that you don't deserve wealth, or may feel guilty about having too much. As you matured, you probably realized that if you have money, it does not diminish that possibility for others. At times, you may also have worried about not having enough. Finding the right balance in your attitude toward money may be a lifelong task.

When you were young, you may have relied on the exterior trappings of life to make you happy. As a result, contentment may have been elusive. Once your happiness ceased to depend on things outside yourself, and you recognized that true value is found within one's own soul, you finally gained the inner peace that Librans so desperately need.

Relationships are all important to you, and you need the company of others more than any other sign. You are very sociable and blessed with many friends. But, you may have had a more difficult time in your romantic life because you may not have always believed that you are worthy of love and affection. You could find the love you need with someone born under the sign of Gemini, Leo, Sagittarius, or Aquarius.

Your biggest challenge is to be true to yourself and your values. Because you fear confrontation, you may accede to others in order to keep the peace. Rely on your sense of fairness, your greatest strength, to help you balance your needs with those of others.

VIRGO
Your Personal Planets

YOUR LOVE POTENTIAL
Venus in Leo, Aug. 24, 3:10 - Aug. 27, 10:41
Venus in Virgo, Aug. 27, 10:42 - Sept. 20, 14:14
Venus in Libra, Sept. 20, 14:15 - Sept. 24, 0:22

YOUR DRIVE AND AMBITION
Mars in Libra, Aug. 24, 3:10 - Sept. 17, 8:42
Mars in Scorpio, Sept. 17, 8:43 - Sept. 24, 0:22

YOUR LUCK MAGNETISM
Jupiter in Leo, Aug. 24, 3:10 - Sept. 24, 0:22

World Events

Sept. 18 – Japan invades Manchuria, a direct breach of treaty terms.
Sept. 21 – Britain goes off the Gold Standard.

Mahatma Gandhi with Charlie Chaplin in London

LIBRA
Your Personal Planets

YOUR LOVE POTENTIAL
Venus in Libra, Sept. 24, 0:23 - Oct. 14, 15:44
Venus in Scorpio, Oct. 14, 15:45 - Oct. 24, 9:15

YOUR DRIVE AND AMBITION
Mars in Scorpio, Sept. 24, 0:23 - Oct. 24, 9:15

YOUR LUCK MAGNETISM
Jupiter in Leo, Sept. 24, 0:23 - Oct. 24, 9:15

World Events

Oct. 7 – South African archbishop Desmond Tutu is born.
Oct. 18 – American scientist and inventor Thomas Alva Edison dies.

➤ Read about your Chinese Astrological sign on page 838. ➤ Read about your Personal Planets on page 826. ➤ Read about your personal Mystical Card on page 856.

263

1931

SCORPIO
Your Personal Planets

YOUR LOVE POTENTIAL
Venus in Scorpio, Oct. 24, 9:16 - Nov. 07, 16:31
Venus in Sagittarius, Nov. 07, 16:32 - Nov. 23, 6:24

YOUR DRIVE AND AMBITION
Mars in Scorpio, Oct. 24, 9:16 - Oct. 30, 12:45
Mars in Sagittarius, Oct. 30, 12:46 - Nov. 23, 6:24

YOUR LUCK MAGNETISM
Jupiter in Leo, Oct. 24, 9:16 - Nov. 23, 6:24

World Events

Nov. 12 – Mahatma Gandhi attends the second Round Table Conference at the Ritz Hotel in London.

Nov. 8 – American chemist Frederick Allison discovers the element halogen.

Chinese leader Chiang Kai-Shek

SAGITTARIUS
Your Personal Planets

YOUR LOVE POTENTIAL
Venus in Sagittarius, Nov. 23, 6:25 - Dec. 01, 17:28
Venus in Capricorn, Dec. 01, 17:29 - Dec. 22, 19:29

YOUR DRIVE AND AMBITION
Mars in Sagittarius, Nov. 23, 6:25 - Dec. 10, 3:10
Mars in Capricorn, Dec. 10, 3:11 - Dec. 22, 19:29

YOUR LUCK MAGNETISM
Jupiter in Leo, Nov. 23, 6:25 - Dec. 22, 19:29

World Events

Dec. 7 – A report is released stating that the Nazis will ensure "Nordic dominance" through the sterilization of certain races.

Dec. 12 – Chiang Kai-Shek resigns as President of the Nanking government.

SCORPIO
From October 24, 9:16 through November 23, 6:24

The Powerful Enigma

Mysterious and complex, you are not an easy person to get to know, Scorpio of 1931. You seem to enjoy keeping others guessing about what you'll do or say next. Although you project a serene and strong exterior, you may be hiding a whole host of insecurities. However, when you start to overcome your fears, you can finally get in touch with the magnitude of your own personal power. Once you've learned how to use that power to serve others rather than to get what you want, you are truly a force to be reckoned with.

Your far-reaching ideas and your thirst for knowledge make you an inspiration to those around you. You have a commanding presence and others are attracted to your intellect and ability to quietly lead the way. Just like Gandhi, who visited Buckingham Palace during a trip to England to discuss his campaign of peaceful protest around the time of your birth, you are not content with surface solutions. Rather, you seek to find the root of a problem.

For you, life is an exploration, of both yourself and the outer world. You seek to discover the secrets of your psychological makeup, to know exactly what makes you tick. Restless and intense, you also yearn to discover all there is to know about other people, places, and things. As you grew, you developed internal radar that gives you the ability to quickly assess the true motivations of those around you and enables you to act accordingly. You have a way of honing in on the hot spots or triggers in any person or situation.

Being so familiar with the darker aspects of the personality, you may be distrustful of others. As a result, you may find it difficult to reveal yourself to another person, making true intimacy very hard to achieve. You need to find a partner who can help restore your faith in the nobler aspects of human nature. Look to Cancerians, Virgos, Capricorns, and Pisces to find a partner with whom you can share every aspect of your being.

Your greatest challenge is to learn openness. Develop your greatest strength, your ability to understand others, to overcome your fear of illuminating your true nature.

SAGITTARIUS
From November 23, 6:25 through December 22, 19:29

The Optimistic Teacher

Playful and spontaneous, Sagittarius of 1931, you love adventure and freedom. You have a natural enthusiasm for life and all it has to offer. Friendly and out-going, your effervescent personality bubbles like a child's when you're interested in something new. Interestingly, you were born right around the time that Alka-Seltzer, the fizzy cold remedy, was introduced.

An excellent communicator, you are a born teacher and can clearly express your thoughts. In fact, in your youth, you may have been too direct, blurting out exactly what you were thinking without regard for the impact your words might have. As you matured, you probably developed your diplomatic skills. For the most part, you are respected for your ability to see the truth and "tell it like it is."

It is important for you to maintain your faith and optimism. This may not always have been easy, especially growing up during the turbulent years of the thirties and forties. But, perhaps you learned that while you may not always have material possessions, no one could take your spirituality from you. Your strong beliefs give you the power to transform any adversity into opportunity. The lessons of your early years may also have helped you to develop more of a social conscience than you might have had ordinarily. Perhaps people like Jane Addams, the activist who, around the time of your birth, became the first U.S. woman ever awarded a Nobel Peace Prize, also influenced your humanitarian leanings.

Your integrity is one of your most endearing qualities, and it is essential that in a relationship your partner also shares your code of ethics. You also need someone who can revel in the simple things of life, those wonderful moments that only nature can give us: a beautiful sunrise, or the shimmering reflection of the moon's glow on a mountain lake. You can find a kindred spirit among Ariens, Geminis, Leos, Librans, or Aquarians.

Putting yourself in another's shoes may be one of the greatest challenges of your life. You can transform the way you think by using your love of the truth to help you to see another point of view.

► Read about your Chinese Astrological sign on page 838. ► Read about your Personal Planets on page 826. ► Read about your personal Mystical Card on page 856.

CAPRICORN

From December 22, 19:30 through December 31, 23:59

The Grateful Rebel

You are a lover of tradition and history, and want to know all you can about the past, Capricorn of December 1931. Patriotic and courageous, you have a deep respect for the sacrifices of our forebears. In fact, the Pulitzer Prize-winning play *Of Thee I Sing* opened on Broadway, just as you were making your debut in the world. Seeking to make your own mark in history, you have a lot of ambition both for yourself and your loved ones.

As a youth, you may have been a bit rebellious. It's not that you wanted to flaunt authority. In fact, you place a high value on obedience and the rule of law. Rather, you may have had a tendency to act upon your impulses without thinking through the consequences. As you matured, however, you probably learned how to use your incredible energy to make positive and innovative changes. Expressing your anger constructively may also be a problem for you. You may tend to fly off the handle at very small things, or allow big problems to fester inside of you until you erupt like a volcano.

Because material security is very important for Capricorns, it was quite difficult for you to grow up during the Depression years. As a result, you have a good deal of gratitude for all that you have accomplished in your life. Because you experienced events like the collapse of the worldwide banking system, you simply recognize that work and opportunity is not always available. Thus, when given the chance to make your own way in life, you made the most of it. In fact, you may even be a bit of a workaholic.

You have a tendency to want to control every situation. This may be fine when you are in the workplace or managing a household but, in close relationships, you need to learn flexibility. Truth and honesty is also very important to you, and you will simply walk away if you are betrayed. You may find that Taureans, Virgos, Scorpios, and Pisceans can make suitable life partners.

Overcoming selfishness and arrogance may be one of your life's greatest challenges. Let your enormous capacity to love help you to be more giving and sensitive to the needs of others.

1931

CAPRICORN

Your Personal Planets

YOUR LOVE POTENTIAL

Venus in Capricorn, Dec. 22, 19:30 - Dec. 25, 19:43

Venus in Aquarius, Dec. 25, 19:44 - Dec. 31, 23:59

YOUR DRIVE AND AMBITION

Mars in Capricorn, Dec. 22, 19:30 - Dec. 31, 23:59

YOUR LUCK MAGNETISM

Jupiter in Leo, Dec. 22, 19:30 - Dec. 31, 23:59

World Events

Dec. 22 – The foreign debt moratorium is ratified by the U.S. Senate.

Dec. 26 – The second Round Table Conference about Indian independence in London collapses as a stalemate is reached.

Special Feature

The First New Age Psychic: Edgar Cayce

by Wendy C. Hawks

He could speak in two dozen foreign languages, was known worldwide for his uncanny accuracy at psychically diagnosing illnesses, and provided believers with fascinating stories about the ancient kingdoms of Atlantis and Lemuria—all while in a trance. Born on March 18, 1877, in Hopkinsville, Kentucky, this very religious and humble man became a legend in his own time—and, to many people, he still is one.

At first glance, it would seem that Cayce's intellect was remarkable, especially since his formal education didn't go beyond grammar school. However, what he had could not be learned in school. Cayce considered it a gift from God. In the course of his lifetime, he gave almost 15,000 readings—sessions in which he "dictated" information about an individual—half of which were health-related, and based on specific medical conditions. His readings also included both spiritual and psychological advice, as well as information about past lives and dream interpretation. However, his "dictations"—often of a predictive nature—were not restricted to the lives of individuals. Six months before the Crash of 1929, he warned investors to sell everything they held. He predicted the beginning and end of both World Wars, and in 1935, he predicted the Holocaust.

Like many psychics, Cayce was born with his gift. At thirteen, while reading, he heard a humming sound. He looked up and saw a woman in white with wings on her back. She said to Cayce, "Your prayers have been answered, little boy. Tell me what it is you want most of all, so that I may give it to you." Though frightened, he told her, "Most of all I would like to be helpful to other people, especially children." Upon that, the vision vanished. Shortly after, young Cayce found a new way to study. He slept on his schoolbooks, waking up with a crystal-clear, photographic memory of their entire contents. Cayce discovered he could use self-hypnosis to travel to other dimensions, and while there, obtain psychic information on anything. He also claimed that anyone with the proper training and attunement could do what he did.

For forty-three years Cayce lay on a couch each day with his head to the south, responding to questions.

(Continued on page 273)

Edgar Cayce
March 18, 1877 - January 3, 1943

➤ Read more about Cayce in "Ancient Secrets of the Great Pyramid" on page 305. ➤ Read about the 1929 Crash in "Money, Astrology, and the Crash of '29" on page 225.

1932

Inventiveness Relieves Chaos: Jupiter, Uranus, and Pluto Interact

Coinciding with a crescendo of cultural change, revolutionary Uranus made a challenging contact with transformative Pluto all year. This was seen in the aggressive approaches, both positive and negative, that leaders took to current issues. Ethiopian Emperor Haile Selassie ended slavery, while El Salvador's army initiated a bloodbath among protesting farmers. Pressure was relieved through inventive approaches, as Jupiter, the planet of exploration, contacted Uranus harmoniously. This combination came in the fiery signs of Aries and Leo, emphasizing the use of new ideas and approaches. In the U.S., the promise of a New Deal to end the Depression dazzled the public and swept Franklin D. Roosevelt into the Presidency. In Germany, Adolf Hitler's popularity continued to rise as he offered hope to humiliated war veterans and the unemployed.

New uses of technology were in the offing, as telecommunications and the use of electricity, also in Uranus's domain, expanded, lighting a fire in the economy of the industrialized world that was to come—automation. The airwaves bristled as several European broadcasting services offered overseas radio, and London's Piccadilly Circus was electrically illuminated, giving a new glow to its allure. Despite the Depression, the Los Angeles Olympic Games set records for attendance and athletic prowess, suggested by the symbolism of Jupiter's position in Leo of "more, bigger, and better," no matter what! The Shakespeare Memorial Theatre opened in Stratford-on-Avon, England, a clear expression of Jupiter in creative Leo.

Franklin D. Roosevelt wins a landslide victory in his run for U.S. President

Hitler fails to take over as Chancellor

Charles Lindbergh's son is kidnapped

BRAVE NEW WORLD

Aldous Huxley's *Brave New World*, published in 1932, portrayed a dystopian world in approximately the twenty-seventh century. It rapidly became one of the most famous science fiction novels to date. The tribulations faced by Huxley's hero in the sterile world of the future offered the author's sharp indictment of the faults of the twentieth century and his grim predictions of where such mistakes would lead humanity. His "feelies" anticipated virtual reality and the treatment of "soma" in the novel showed how drugs could be used to control behavior and society.

LIGHT DAWNS IN A DARK AGE

Roosevelt's promise of a New Deal produced a landslide win in his first run for U.S. President. The League of Nations suspended German reparations due to the parlous state of the German economy. In Germany, Chancellor von Papen blocked Hitler's attempts to take over his post. The Olympic Games held in Los Angeles captured the hearts and minds of audiences around the world, a tribute to human excellence. In Los Angeles, Gandhi went on hunger strike in protest at the lack of representation for the Untouchables. The world was shocked when aviator Lindbergh's son was kidnapped and murdered: the killer, Bruno Hauptmann, was not arrested until 1934. In Britain, unemployment was blamed for a 1100 percent crime rise. Gangster Al Capone was depicted in the cinema with *Scarface*; other hits included *Tarzan*, *Dr. Jekyll and Mr. Hyde*, and *A Farewell to Arms*. Huxley's *Brave New World* showed the dangers of taking science too far. Erskine Caldwell's *Tobacco Road* and William Faulkner's *Light in August* were published. Shakespeare's birthday, 23 April, was marked by the opening of a new Shakespeare Memorial Theatre in Stratford-on-Avon.

➤ Read "The First New Age Psychic: Edgar Cayce" by Wendy C. Hawks on page 265.

CAPRICORN

From January 01, 0:00 through January 21, 6:06

The Uncompromising Reformer

Like most people born under your sign, 1932 Capricorn, you are skillful and steady, able to persevere through the most arduous situations. But, you also have a flair for the dramatic and can be uncharacteristically spontaneous at times. Your personal freedom is of paramount importance to you and, while you are devoted to your family and friends, you still need to be able to chart your own destiny. Much like Hattie T. Caraway who, around the time of your birth was sworn in as the first woman ever elected to the U.S. Senate, you are a trailblazer.

Blessed with profound insight, you quite possibly have a strong interest in politics, law, philosophy or religion. A bit of a social reformer, you are adept at identifying the need for change and using your great inventiveness to make your vision a reality. Growing up as you did during World War II, you appreciate courage and bravery and believe in fighting for a just cause. This is not to say that you will go to your death defending an abstract idea or principle. Rather, you are much more likely to do battle when you perceive that the security of your home, family, or country is threatened.

A direct and forceful communicator, you are not particularly tolerant of those who disagree with you. Because of your strong opinions and your outspokenness, others may be intimidated by your blunt and no-nonsense manner. In your younger years, you most likely were quite overbearing and uncompromising, even with those close to you. But, as you matured, you undoubtedly learned that you could gain the cooperation of others by becoming more willing to see another point of view.

When it comes to romance, you enjoy a mate who is bright, ingenious and shares your strong ideas about life. Most of all, you need someone who can be a loyal and trusted friend as well as a passionate partner. Taureans, Virgos, Scorpios, and Pisceans may offer you an enduring relationship.

Swallowing your enormous pride and listening to the advice of others may be one of your greatest challenges in life. Your greatest strength may very well be your unrelenting and determined spirit.

AQUARIUS

From January 21, 6:07 through February 19, 20:27

The Freedom Fighter

A true original, 1932 Aquarius, you are inventive, determined, and sometimes quite stubborn. Never satisfied with the ordinary, you can be rather eccentric and enjoy being thought of as different or unusual. Because you thrive on mental stimulation, you are at your best in the company of others. And, with your strong humanitarian instincts, you will generally favor the underdog in any situation. You abhor hypocrisy and elitism of any kind and you have your own personal moral code by which you live your life.

You are a person of action and you need to do things in your own inimitable way. Gifted with both intelligence and good organizational skills, you take work very seriously and tend toward perfectionism. As a result of your diligence, you may be a bit nervous or apprehensive, even though you show a calm exterior to the world. In your youth, you probably believed that you were better off working alone, rather than compromising your ideas of how things should be done. But, with maturity, it is likely that you learned the value of teamwork and group cooperation.

Blessed with compassion and sensitivity, you are in touch with the pain and suffering of humanity. Around the time of your birth, the El Salvadoran army killed 4,000 protesting farmers. It is events such as these that have colored your life, making you conscious of social injustice and willing to speak against it. Due to your strong spirituality, you are able to tap into universal ideals for inspiration and creativity. You have an enormous appreciation for art, music, and other artistic endeavors and may even be a gifted artist in your own right.

When it comes to relationships, you need a loving, close partnership with one person as well as maintaining friendships with others. You have a strong romantic streak and really believe in the power of love. Geminis, Leos, Librans, and Sagittarians all may provide the right blend of intimacy and freedom.

Your greatest challenge is to deal with responsibility, restrictions, and the rules of society. When you feel hemmed in, you use your great imagination to set you free.

▶ Read about your Chinese Astrological sign on page 838. ▶ Read about your Personal Planets on page 826. ▶ Read about your personal Mystical Card on page 856.

CAPRICORN
Your Personal Planets

YOUR LOVE POTENTIAL
Venus in Aquarius, Jan. 01, 0:00 - Jan. 19, 1:51
Venus in Pisces, Jan. 19, 1:52 - Jan. 21, 6:06

YOUR DRIVE AND AMBITION
Mars in Capricorn, Jan. 01, 0:00 - Jan. 18, 0:34
Mars in Aquarius, Jan. 18, 0:35 - Jan. 21, 6:06

YOUR LUCK MAGNETISM
Jupiter in Leo, Jan. 01, 0:00 - Jan. 21, 6:06

World Events

Jan. 4 – The British authorities have Mahatma Gandhi arrested and imprisoned in Bombay.

Jan. 5 – Italian novelist Umberto Eco is born.

General Myeda is among those injured by the Japanese attack on Shanghai

AQUARIUS
Your Personal Planets

YOUR LOVE POTENTIAL
Venus in Pisces, Jan. 21, 6:07 - Feb. 12, 16:57
Venus in Aries, Feb. 12, 16:58 - Feb. 19, 20:27

YOUR DRIVE AND AMBITION
Mars in Aquarius, Jan. 21, 6:07 - Feb. 19, 20:27

YOUR LUCK MAGNETISM
Jupiter in Leo, Jan. 21, 6:07 - Feb. 19, 20:27

World Events

Jan. 28 – The Japanese launch an attack on Shanghai in China, placing the city under marshal law.

Feb. 6 – French film director François Truffaut is born.

1932

PISCES
Your Personal Planets

YOUR LOVE POTENTIAL
Venus in Aries, Feb. 19, 20:28 - Mar. 09, 2:06
Venus in Taurus, Mar. 09, 2:07 - Mar. 20, 19:53

YOUR DRIVE AND AMBITION
Mars in Aquarius, Feb. 19, 20:28 - Feb. 25, 2:35
Mars in Pisces, Feb. 25, 2:36 - Mar. 20, 19:53

YOUR LUCK MAGNETISM
Jupiter in Leo, Feb. 19, 20:28 - Mar. 20, 19:53

World Events

Feb. 22 – Adolf Hitler stands for presidential elections on behalf of the Nazi Party in Germany.

Mar. 1 – Charles Lindbergh's twenty-month-old son, Charles Jr., is kidnapped from his home in New Jersey.

Charles Lindbergh, Jr. is kidnapped from his home in New Jersey

ARIES
Your Personal Planets

YOUR LOVE POTENTIAL
Venus in Taurus, Mar. 20, 19:54 - Apr. 05, 0:18
Venus in Gemini, Apr. 05, 0:19 - Apr. 20, 7:27

YOUR DRIVE AND AMBITION
Mars in Pisces, Mar. 20, 19:54 - Apr. 03, 7:01
Mars in Aries, Apr. 03, 7:02 - Apr. 20, 7:27

YOUR LUCK MAGNETISM
Jupiter in Leo, Mar. 20, 19:54 - Apr. 20, 7:27

World Events

Apr. 4 – Vitamin C is first isolated by chemists C. C. King and W. A. Waugh in Pittsburgh.

Apr. 10 – Field Marshal Paul von Hindenburg is elected as the first German President.

PISCES
From February 19, 20:28 through March 20, 19:53

The Sensitive Worrier

Like a sponge on the depths of the ocean floor, 1932 Pisces, you absorb the feelings and emotions of those around you. More often than not, this occurs without your even being aware of it. Your mood can shift like the tide as you encounter another person or place. Just as water takes the shape of its container, you are able to adapt to your surroundings. Sometimes you are hard to pin down and, at other times, you can be very precise and exacting.

You may have a hard time separating fantasy from reality and your dreamy and trusting quality leaves you vulnerable to those who might seek to take advantage of you. At times, you may find yourself confused about what course to take and you find it hard to make a decision. Likewise, there are times when you confuse others because you may give off mixed signals about your intentions.

The kidnapping of the Lindbergh baby, perhaps the most notorious crime of the twentieth century, occurred right around the time of your birth. The abduction of the child of such a famous and heroic figure created dread in the hearts of parents all over the world, and your heart was probably no exception. It is likely that their fears were unconsciously transmitted to you and you may find that you have gone through life with a nebulous apprehension about what may happen next. Your tendency to worry could impact your health and you need to learn to be a bit more lighthearted.

You have an empathetic nature and may find that others will mistake your compassion for weakness. In relationships, you can be rather headstrong and you may jump into a liaison with carefree abandon. Sensitive and sensual, you enjoy both the spiritual and physical aspects of intimacy. You can find a suitable partner among Taureans, Cancerians, Scorpios, and Capricorns.

Your greatest challenge in life is to discover how to get what you want in a forthright way. Because of the manner in which you approach things, others may be suspicious of you, even when you have the best of intentions. Rely on your greatest strength, your remarkable gift of intuition, to help illuminate your path.

ARIES
From March 20, 19:54 through April 20, 7:27

The Tempestuous Adventurer

Confident, assertive, and enthusiastic, Aries of 1932, you are capable of accomplishing whatever you set out to do once you master the art of self-discipline. In your younger years, you may have found that you did not have the resolve to see a project through to the finish. However, as you matured, you developed the strength of will needed to complete what you start.

Quick-witted and fast-moving, your family and friends probably have a hard time keeping up with your frenetic pace. Impatient and energetic, once you've made up your mind that you want something, others are best advised to stay out of your way. You can be like a tornado, moving fiercely through your surroundings, wreaking havoc in your wake. Perhaps, as a result of your growing up during the uncertain and troubled years of the thirties and forties, this same mayhem exists inside you. The psychological impact of a world in financial collapse and then at war makes it hard for you to ever feel calm and secure.

You thrive on competition and like nothing better than to be the first on your block to try something new. Throwing caution to the wind, you often act impulsively and recklessly. A lover of adventure, you are always attempting to conquer new horizons. Just like Amelia Earhart who became the first woman to fly solo across the Atlantic in the month after you were born, you are daring, courageous, and you seek to be the best at whatever you do.

While you are likely to have many acquaintances, you may find that you are close to only a few people. You love to act on the spur of the moment and may find most people too staid and serious. Romantically, you require a partner who enjoys your madcap approach to life but who also can bring you back to Earth when necessary. You also need someone who can remain undaunted by your insistent manner. Find a soul mate under the signs of Gemini, Leo, Sagittarius, and Aquarius.

Your biggest challenge in life is to avoid trying to make others over to your liking. Rely on your greatest strength, your ability to be yourself, to help you to respect the right of others to do the same.

➤ Read about your Chinese Astrological sign on page 838. ➤ Read about your Personal Planets on page 826. ➤ Read about your personal Mystical Card on page 856.

TAURUS

From April 20, 7:28 through May 21, 7:06

The Original Achiever

A lover of beauty, 1932 Taurus, appearances and physical form are very important to you. It is not only essential that things look good, but also smell, taste, feel, and sound good too. You take great pleasure in exercising all your senses but you especially enjoy the soft and silky textures found in the finest of clothing and furnishings. In your judgment, success in life is measured through the material possessions that one acquires and you are quite satisfied with all that you have obtained. Born in a year when unemployment in the U.S. reached a staggering level of 13,000,000 people, you are especially sensitive about your position in life.

Though you are generally cautious, at times, you can be rather impetuous and headstrong. You communicate in a compelling manner and may be fond of dramatization. It is no coincidence then that the Shakespeare Memorial Theatre opened at Stratford-on Avon around the time that you were born. Quick and original in your thinking, you have many splendid ideas as well as the resolve to carry them through. Easily frustrated with delays and obstacles, you are prone to making hasty decisions.

You are a person of action and will typically stop at nothing to attain your ends. When you want something, diplomacy and careful planning take a back seat to the sheer force of your resolute, unwavering manner. In your youth, you probably were prone to tactless remarks and may have felt intellectually superior to others, but, with age, you hopefully found out how to transform your bull-headed obstinacy into genuine wisdom and profound insight.

Naturally curious about people and their motivations, you have a varied group of friends and associates. When it comes to romance, your partner needs to have a sharp intellect as well as a penchant for sensual pleasure. Look to Cancerians, Virgos, Capricorns, and Pisces to find a mate who can satisfy all your needs.

One of your life's greatest challenges is to learn to avoid alienating others with your egotistical behavior. Instead, use your greatest strength, your sharp, creative mind to inspire others.

GEMINI

From May 21, 7:07 through June 21, 15:22

The Intellectual Homebody

Versatile, talented, and intelligent, 1932 Gemini, you are also a bit of a non-conformist. You are quite proud of your individuality and, in fact, you rarely go along with convention, unless you really want to do so. Because of your ability to shift gears at a moment's notice, you are quite good in an emergency. Perpetually on the go, you tend to spend a lot of time in your car or walking around your neighborhood. With automobiles having become fairly commonplace in the U.S., the first federal gasoline tax was enacted around the time of your birth.

Affectionate and sensitive, your home and family life is more important to you than it is to most Geminis. Easily hurt, you tend to hide your vulnerable side beneath a mask of charm and affability. It is likely that your household is a warm and comfortable place for folks to congregate, making it the focus of the neighborhood social activities. You are happiest when your home is filled with people enjoying sumptuous food and sparkling conversations.

Though you may be a quick thinker, you are a bit slower to act. Once you do start on a project, however, you have the determination to see it through. You are excellent at anything that requires you to use both your careful attention to detail and your natural dexterity. Both practical and clever, you are a resourceful and inventive individual who can find a solution to most any problem. And, you have used your talents to earn money, not for its own sake, but for the financial security that it provides for you and your family.

Never at a loss for companionship, others appreciate your sense of humor, your all-around intelligence as well as your kind and gentle side. Devoted to your relationship, you cherish your partner fully and may even be a bit possessive. Look for a kindred spirit among Ariens, Leos, Librans, and Aquarians.

Your biggest life's challenge is to feel comfortable with your deepest emotions. You are much more at ease with facts and figures than with feelings. Try using your greatest strength, your ability to conceptualize, to help you to understand yourself.

➤ Read about your Chinese Astrological sign on page 838. ➤ Read about your Personal Planets on page 826. ➤ Read about your personal Mystical Card on page 856.

TAURUS
Your Personal Planets

YOUR LOVE POTENTIAL
Venus in Gemini, Apr. 20, 7:28 - May 06, 9:03
Venus in Cancer, May 06, 9:04 - May 21, 7:06

YOUR DRIVE AND AMBITION
Mars in Aries, Apr. 20, 7:28 - May 12, 10:52
Mars in Taurus, May 12, 10:53 - May 21, 7:06

YOUR LUCK MAGNETISM
Jupiter in Leo, Apr. 20, 7:28 - May 21, 7:06

World Events

Apr. 28 – Wilbur Sawyer, Wray Lloyd, and Stuart Kitchen develop the first yellow fever vaccine for humans.

May 12 – The dead body of the Lindbergh baby is discovered in a wooded area less than five miles from the family's home.

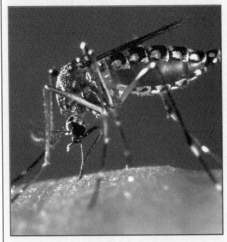

A yellow fever mosquito feeding on a human host

GEMINI
Your Personal Planets

YOUR LOVE POTENTIAL
Venus in Cancer, May 21, 7:07 - June 21, 15:22

YOUR DRIVE AND AMBITION
Mars in Taurus, May 21, 7:07 - June 21, 15:22

YOUR LUCK MAGNETISM
Jupiter in Leo, May 21, 7:07 - June 21, 15:22

World Events

June 14 – Representative in favor of the U.S. bonus bill for veterans, Edward Eslick, dies on the floor of the House while pleading for the bill's passage.

June 16 – Franz von Papen lifts the ban on Nazi storm troopers.

1932

CANCER
Your Personal Planets

YOUR LOVE POTENTIAL
Venus in Cancer, June 21, 15:23 - July 13, 10:32
Venus in Gemini, July 13, 10:33 - July 23, 2:17

YOUR DRIVE AND AMBITION
Mars in Taurus, June 21, 15:23 - June 22, 9:18
Mars in Gemini, June 22, 9:19 - July 23, 2:17

YOUR LUCK MAGNETISM
Jupiter in Leo, June 21, 15:23 - July 23, 2:17

World Events

June 24 – A coup brings to an end the absolute monarchy in Siam.

July 18 – The U.S. and Canada sign an agreement for the development of the St. Lawrence Seaway.

Indian writer V. S. Naipaul is born under the sign of Leo

LEO
Your Personal Planets

YOUR LOVE POTENTIAL
Venus in Gemini, July 23, 2:18 - July 28, 12:35
Venus in Cancer, July 28, 12:36 - Aug. 23, 9:05

YOUR DRIVE AND AMBITION
Mars in Gemini, July 23, 2:18 - Aug. 04, 19:51
Mars in Cancer, Aug. 04, 19:52 - Aug. 23, 9:05

YOUR LUCK MAGNETISM
Jupiter in Leo, July 23, 2:18 - Aug. 11, 7:15
Jupiter in Virgo, Aug. 11, 7:16 - Aug. 23, 9:05

World Events

Aug. 14 – Canine actor Rin Tin Tin dies.

Aug. 17 – Indian writer V. S. Naipaul is born.

CANCER
From June 21, 15:23 through July 23, 2:17

The Unconditional Lover

You know what it means to love unconditionally, 1932 Cancer, and you have probably spent most of your life taking care of others. Even as a child growing up during the difficult years of the Depression and World War II, you may have been a source of consolation to those around you. At times, especially during a crisis, it seems as if you possess the strength of Hercules. But, there are other moments when you are just as helpless as an infant. You may feel especially powerless when you recognize that you cannot protect those you love from the perils of life.

A wellspring of emotional potency, you may unconsciously affect the moods of those around you by your frame of mind. If you are feeling good, then those around you will too. But, when you are depressed, it becomes difficult for anyone else to feel joyful or happy. And, your emotional lows can be as severe as the lows of the stock market, which hit its Depression bottom around the time of your birth. You also need to realize that your powerful feelings and negative thoughts may impact your health adversely. Therefore, both for your own sake as well as for those around you, you should try to be positive and upbeat.

Even though you may sometimes lack the motivation, activity and exercise are very important for your well-being. Quite capable of doing two or more things at once, it is likely that you have had a variety of jobs or interests throughout your lifetime. However, because of your restless nature, you may find it hard to see your tasks through to completion.

Shy and somewhat reserved, you can be rather reticent. But, once you feel comfortable and safe, you are a lively participant in any group, large or small. In relationships, you must be absolutely certain that you are loved before you can give yourself entirely to another. Taureans, Virgos, Scorpios, and Pisceans can provide you with the security you so desperately need.

Your major challenge is to avoid smothering those you love with your powerful feelings. Rely on your greatest gift, your storehouse of inner strength, to give you the ability to let go.

LEO
From July 23, 2:18 through August 23, 9:05

The Magnificent Protector

When you enter a room, 1932 Leo, you illuminate it with your splendor, just as the Sun eradicates darkness with its light. Majestic and noble, you preside over your own private domain with affection and authority.

Attracting attention wherever you go, you are a charismatic figure, who can give selflessly of your time, talents, and, most importantly, love. You are utterly devoted to those close to you and you give of yourself without reservation. Heaven help anyone who would dare to hurt someone that you care about, for you would stop at nothing to safeguard your loved ones.

Blessed with a high degree of integrity, you are also ready and able to stand up for your principles. Your personal dignity is quite important to you and you fear making a fool of yourself. Therefore, you are very careful about what you say and how you say it. In a group or work situation, you must have all the facts before you will offer an opinion. But, when it comes to discussions of a more emotional nature, you are passionate and effusive about your feelings.

Determined to succeed, you are a brave and spirited competitor. And, like the Olympic athletes who gathered in Los Angeles around the time of your birth, you consistently make every effort to do your personal best. In triumph, you are a magnanimous winner. And, though you rarely lose anything you really want, in the face of defeat, you respond with grace, courage, and strength.

Because of your protective and nurturing demeanor, other people feel safe and secure in your presence. In most situations, you have a tendency to dominate and you need to let others take the spotlight at times. Also, you are so willing to help that you may not let your loved ones take care of themselves, even when they can. In relationships, you need a partner who can return your adoration. Look to Geminis, Cancerians, Librans, and Sagittarians for a lifelong partner.

Using your personal magnetism for the greatest good is one of your life's great challenges. You can rely on your greatest strength, your sense of fairness and integrity to keep your intent pure.

➤ Read about your Chinese Astrological sign on page 838. ➤ Read about your Personal Planets on page 826. ➤ Read about your personal Mystical Card on page 856.

VIRGO

From August 23, 9:06 through September 23, 6:15

The Dedicated Helper

You are passionate about many things, 1932 Virgo, but most of all about work. You are detailed, organized, and enjoy creating order out of chaos. A firm believer in the work ethic, you abhor laziness and have little respect for anyone who isn't gainfully employed. Whether you are in a helping profession or not, you are still committed to selfless service to others. You are the one that everyone in your circle counts on to help whenever there is a need. You are much like Gandhi who, around the time you were born, began yet another hunger strike against the inhumane treatment of the so-called Untouchables.

Even though you have worked hard throughout your life, you probably haven't amassed a great deal of money. Though you are fairly self-disciplined in most respects, when it comes to your finances you tend to go to extremes of thriftiness and spending freely. A discerning and discriminating critic, you have a definite appreciation for the best that life has to offer—good food, cozy furnishings, and fine clothing.

Growing up during the turbulent depression and war years, your perception is that life is, at best, uncertain. Just when you thought that you had all you ever hoped for, unexpected events may have rocked your world. Likewise, though you are an excellent strategist, you would either fail to anticipate what could go wrong or an unexpected calamity would upset your careful planning. Though generally even-tempered, you can occasionally explode, shocking others with your pent up feelings.

You have a strong desire for an intimate relationship. But, your tendency to seek perfection in others, coupled with your inescapable attraction to people who are unattainable may make it difficult for you to find a truly satisfying partnership. As you mature, you are more likely to understand that perfection is but an illusion. Your soul mate may be found among Taureans, Cancerians, Scorpios, and Pisceans.

Ever concerned about losing what you have, your greatest challenge is to enjoy happiness when it occurs. Take solace in your great strength, your commitment to helping others.

LIBRA

From September 23, 6:16 through October 23, 15:03

The Reluctant Compromiser

Justice and fairness are of paramount importance to you, 1932 Libra, and you consider it your role in life to balance both sides of an issue. You are an excellent communicator and know how to foster cooperation with others. Because you are interested in bringing people together, you try to understand their psychological motivations. As a result, you make an excellent therapist, either professionally or just for those lucky few who know you.

You are a student of the art of compromise and recognize that you can get what you want by finding a middle ground. But, making concessions for the sake of agreement also necessitates that you give up some of what you want. However, this puts you in danger of losing yourself as well as becoming resentful in the process. There are times when it is utterly crucial for you to stand firm and hold your ground. Peace, at any price, rarely endures in the long run. It is interesting that around the time of your birth, Iraq finally gained its independence from Great Britain and joined the League of Nations.

At times, you can be rather headstrong, acting without regard to the consequences. When you were young, it may have been especially difficult to reconcile your need to exert your self-will with your desire for cooperation. However, this struggle was probably short-lived because your need for approval is so strong. You may have also believed that you could influence others to change but, eventually, you would realize that the only person you can change is yourself.

Artistic and creative, your tastes may range from conventional to avant-garde. But, what is most important to you is quality, and you are proud of the fact that you can spot excellence. Your friends are sure to be varied and interesting as well as accomplished. In romance, you need a partner who meets your high standards. Look to Geminis, Leos, Sagittarians, and Aquarians to decorate your life with their love.

Your greatest challenge in life is to express your anger constructively. Deal with your resentment by using your greatest strength, your desire to understand human nature.

➤ Read about your Chinese Astrological sign on page 838. ➤ Read about your Personal Planets on page 826. ➤ Read about your personal Mystical Card on page 856.

VIRGO
Your Personal Planets

YOUR LOVE POTENTIAL
Venus in Cancer, Aug. 23, 9:06 - Sept. 08, 19:44
Venus in Leo, Sept. 08, 19:45 - Sept. 23, 6:15

YOUR DRIVE AND AMBITION
Mars in Cancer, Aug. 23, 9:06 - Sept. 20, 19:42
Mars in Leo, Sept. 20, 19:43 - Sept. 23, 6:15

YOUR LUCK MAGNETISM
Jupiter in Virgo, Aug. 23, 9:06 - Sept. 23, 6:15

World Events

Aug. 30 – Hermann Goering becomes President of the German Reichstag.

Sept. 1 – Jimmy Walker resigns—the first New York City Mayor to leave office under fire; he was charged with corruption during his first and second terms in office.

German physicist Albert Einstein

LIBRA
Your Personal Planets

YOUR LOVE POTENTIAL
Venus in Leo, Sept. 23, 6:16 - Oct. 07, 5:45
Venus in Virgo, Oct. 07, 5:46 - Oct. 23, 15:03

YOUR DRIVE AND AMBITION
Mars in Leo, Sept. 23, 6:16 - Oct. 23, 15:03

YOUR LUCK MAGNETISM
Jupiter in Virgo, Sept. 23, 6:16 - Oct. 23, 15:03

World Events

Oct. 9 – The Soviets open the world's largest hydroelectric plant on the Dnieper River.

Oct. 16 – Albert Einstein estimates the age of the Earth to be ten billion years.

1932

SCORPIO
Your Personal Planets

YOUR LOVE POTENTIAL
Venus in Virgo, Oct. 23, 15:04 - Nov. 02, 4:00
Venus in Libra, Nov. 02, 4:01 - Nov. 22, 12:09

YOUR DRIVE AND AMBITION
Mars in Leo, Oct. 23, 15:04 - Nov. 13, 21:24
Mars in Virgo, Nov. 13, 21:25 - Nov. 22, 12:09

YOUR LUCK MAGNETISM
Jupiter in Virgo, Oct. 23, 15:04 - Nov. 22, 12:09

World Events

Nov. 8 – Franklin D. Roosevelt beats Herbert Hoover to the U.S. presidency.

Nov. 21 – President von Hindenburg offers Hitler a limited chancellorship, but Hitler refuses.

New U.S. President Franklin D. Roosevelt

SAGITTARIUS
Your Personal Planets

YOUR LOVE POTENTIAL
Venus in Libra, Nov. 22, 12:10 - Nov. 27, 0:05
Venus in Scorpio, Nov. 27, 0:06 - Dec. 21, 7:42
Venus in Sagittarius, Dec. 21, 7:43 - Dec. 22, 1:13

YOUR DRIVE AND AMBITION
Mars in Virgo, Nov. 22, 12:10 - Dec. 22, 1:13

YOUR LUCK MAGNETISM
Jupiter in Virgo, Nov. 22, 12:10 - Dec. 22, 1:13

World Events

Dec. 5 – German physicist Albert Einstein is granted a U.S. visa.

Dec. 19 – The BBC launches its Empire Service, its first overseas transmission and the forerunner of the World Service.

272

SCORPIO
From October 23, 15:04 through November 22, 12:09

The Compassionate Transformer

Intuitive and magnetic, 1932 Scorpio, you are a fascinating and complex creature. You have piercing eyes that yearn to see to the core of any situation. And, you have an unsurpassed understanding of both good and evil, of the light and dark sides of existence. You have a strong will and immense personal power. Though you seek to understand the inner workings of others, others may find you hard to comprehend. Prone to secrecy, you only reveal exactly what you want others to know about you.

Because of your ability to feel intensely, you have probably experienced extremes of both great joy and profound sorrow. As a result, you are genuinely compassionate, especially when it comes to those whom you perceive to be in real need. However, you won't tolerate weakness in yourself or in others. Like Franklin D. Roosevelt, who was elected to his first term as President around the time you were born, you truly believe that we have "nothing to fear but fear itself." Conquering your inner demons may be a lifelong struggle, especially when life seems particularly unjust.

Your manner of communication is frank and powerful. You have a high regard for the truth and though you may not consciously hurt anyone, you may still, nonetheless, offend others with your candor when articulating your incisive thoughts. Over time, you may have learned to keep silent when your ideas will fall on deaf ears. But, if you believe that there is any possibility to effect a change in someone else, you will not hesitate to share your beliefs.

Because of your considerable mystique, others are magically drawn to you. Like a moth to a flame, you attract those who are daring enough to want to explore and experience all the facets of life with a seasoned and practiced tour guide. Your ideal partner is someone who can match your strength and you may find that quality in Cancerians, Virgos, Capricorns, and Pisces.

Overcoming your tendency to seek vengeance when you or anyone you love is wounded is one of life's greatest challenges. The power to transform a problem into a possibility is your greatest strength.

SAGITTARIUS
From November 22, 12:10 through December 22, 1:13

The Lifelong Philosopher

Philosophical and reflective, 1932 Sagittarius, you often find yourself lost in thought. Your thirst for knowledge is difficult to quench. You always want to know more about a subject, until you have completely mastered the topic. Then, you are free to move on to the next fascination. You dream of faraway places and long to know about the customs of other cultures. Interestingly, the British Broadcasting Company began transmitting overseas around the time of your birth, taking a key step in making the world a smaller place and fostering understanding among its people.

There are two rather distinct sides to your personality. One is the introspective thinker, full of aspiration to higher ideals and concerned with your fellow man. Your other side is carefree, impulsive, and indifferent to what others may think. Throughout your life, you have had to reconcile these two opposing aspects to your nature. You are also in danger of becoming fanatical about your beliefs and you are not likely to shy away from trying to impose your values on others. Needless to say, this can cause resentment for both you and those you are trying to convert.

Managing your time in an efficient way may also be a problem for you. You tend to dissipate your energy by either taking on too much or getting involved in trivial and unimportant details. Frustration is inevitable once you realize that you are not making as much headway as you might like. Try delegating responsibilities to others or scale down the scope of your undertakings.

In relationships, you have a highly attuned sensitivity to the needs and feelings of your partner. You take your commitments very seriously and so you may play the field before settling on a mate. Once you do take a partner, you are loyal and trustworthy and may even be a bit possessive. Ariens, Leos, Librans, and Aquarians may spark your interest and hold your attention for a lifetime.

Your greatest challenge in life has been to find the discipline to plan ahead for the future, rather than living entirely in the moment. Your greatest strength is your integrity.

➤ Read about your Chinese Astrological sign on page 838. ➤ Read about your Personal Planets on page 826. ➤ Read about your personal Mystical Card on page 856.

CAPRICORN

From December 22, 1:14 through December 31, 23:59

The Spiritual Achiever

As you grow older, you seem to get younger, 1932 December Capricorn. It's as if each of your accomplishments takes a weight off of your shoulders, as you grow more confident with each achievement. And, achieve you must. Your quest for success, however, has more to do with the need to develop something that will endure rather than with fame or fortune. Around the time you were born, Radio City Music Hall opened its doors for the first time; through the years that theater has endured as a showcase for the Art Deco style of architecture that was so popular in the thirties.

Hard-working and ambitious, you are quite shrewd when it comes to financial affairs. Money represents both status and security to you. This financial safety net is quite important for your state of mind. You truly believe that it is vital to save for a rainy day and you may even have a reputation for your thriftiness. Certainly, the struggle of coming of age during the Depression taught you many valuable lessons about making the most of what you have.

Spiritual and philosophical, you are a person of honor, possessing high ethical standards. Others may find your abstract ideas difficult to understand or fail to grasp your vision of the future. You may also be a bit forgetful, especially when it comes to small details. Because you have a highly developed imagination, you may also fall prey to get-rich-quick schemes or be taken advantage of by someone with a sympathetic hard-luck story.

Dreamy and sensitive, you may have had some disappointments when it comes to love. In your youth, you may have idealized your partners, seeing them through proverbial "rose-colored" glasses. But, as you matured, you probably came to understand the importance of honesty from both sides in a relationship. Taureans, Cancerians, Virgos, and Pisceans can provide the tenderness you need for an enduring relationship.

Your greatest challenge in life is to learn to be less irritable and frustrated when people fail to understand you. Rely on your greatest strength, your patience, to help you to communicate your thoughts more clearly.

1932

CAPRICORN
Your Personal Planets

YOUR LOVE POTENTIAL
Venus in Sagittarius, Dec. 22, 1:14 - Dec. 31, 23:59

YOUR DRIVE AND AMBITION
Mars in Virgo, Dec. 22, 1:14 - Dec. 31, 23:59

YOUR LUCK MAGNETISM
Jupiter in Virgo, Dec. 22, 1:14 - Dec. 31, 23:59

World Events

Dec. 27 – Radio City Music Hall, the largest of its kind with 6,000 seats, opens in New York City.

Dec. 29 – The USSR prohibits food aid for housewives under the age of thirty-six, declaring they must work for their living.

Gloria Swanson, who consulted Edgar Cayce

Special Feature
The First New Age Psychic: Edgar Cayce

(Continued from page 265)

Hands over stomach, tie and shoelaces loosened, he waited to receive the "go" signal from the universe—a flash of brilliant white light. Once seen, Cayce would fall into a trance and answer any question posed. His responses contained insights so valuable that thousands of individuals found practical help for everything they needed—from maintaining a balanced diet, to overcoming life-threatening illness, to making peace with their enemies.

Cayce's health-related "readings" were often dismissed by the medical community of his day. Nevertheless, physicians were amazed at his ability to correctly diagnose and offer accurate treatment to those with chronic illnesses, especially considering the fact that he had no formal medical training. One of the earliest readings Cayce did was for Aime Dietrich, who had been ill for three years. At age two, after an attack of flu, her mind stopped developing. Dietrich was racked with constant convulsions, her mind nearly a blank. Cayce read for her, and

announced that her problem had actually begun a few days before catching the flu—she had injured her spine in a fall and germs had settled there. Dietrich's doctor did follow Cayce's suggestions for a cure and within three months, she was healed.

His responses contained insights so valuable that thousands of individuals found practical help for everything they needed—from maintaining a balanced diet to overcoming life-threatening illness.

People from all walks of life came to him for help and counseling. Among his clients, in fact, were Nelson Rockefeller, Woodrow Wilson, Thomas Edison, Irving Berlin, George Gershwin, and Gloria Swanson. The majority who sought Cayce's advice didn't have the opportunity to meet with him. Most of his patients, some of them from other countries, made their requests through the mail. All Cayce needed to give a

reading was the client's name, address, and where he or she would be at the time of the reading. When entering his trance, Cayce would often mumble, as though searching for something. Soon after, he would clear his throat—and begin an amazingly accurate half-hour discussion of the individual's physical and/or mental condition.

One of the biggest obstacles with Cayce's readings was finding doctors to carry out the recommended treatments. Eventually, he did find support from many health practitioners. Cayce dreamed of having a hospital and staff to help implement his work. He began looking for financial backing, and finally started accepting donations for his readings—previously, he'd given them for free.

(Continued on page 281)

► Read more about Cayce in "Ancient Secrets of the Great Pyramid" on page 305. ► Read about the 1929 Crash in "Money, Astrology, and the Crash of '29" on page 225.

1933

Dreams Shaken by Reality: Mars in Virgo

The heavens were alight as optimistic Jupiter joined idealistic Neptune in Virgo, the sign of the common people. Around the world many approached 1933 with bright hope. New U.S. President Roosevelt promised an end to economic suffering and Germans pinned their hopes on the rising politico, Adolf Hitler. However, as Mars, symbolizing action and aggression, began a six-month sojourn in Virgo at the beginning of the year, these hopes were tempered by reality. Mars in Virgo interacted with Jupiter and Neptune, highlighting the gaps between what was wished for, a Jupiter-Neptune association, and what was possible, signified by Mars. As this planetary pattern unfolded, the mutation of the dream into reality did not always meet the citizenry's expectations. The newly empowered Nazi regime expressed its ideals by consolidating authoritarian control over Germany, banning books and imposing martial law, to the chagrin of peaceful nations.

However, this Mars-Jupiter-Neptune contact also symbolized the increased drive to escape the realities of modern life. Movies promoted romantic idealism through films such as *Little Women*, *King Kong*, and the perfect symbol of Neptune's illusions, *The Invisible Man*, and audiences eagerly bathed in cinematically induced dreams—pure escapism. These sources of pleasure were supplemented as Americans' right to drink alcohol was restored with the repeal of Prohibition. Neptune's contact with supportive Jupiter through most of 1933 heralded the opening of soup kitchens and government aid to feed and clothe America's needy.

Dancer Fred Astaire becomes a Hollywood star

People celebrate the new appointment of Hitler as the Chancellor of Germany

The ancient Persian city of Persepolis is excavated

NESSIE CAUGHT ON FILM

The first two photographs of the Loch Ness monster aroused international attention and offered credibility to believers in a creature in the Scottish lake. In November 1933, Hugh Gray took the first photograph of "Nessie." It showed a blurred, sinewy, snake-like shape swimming through the lake's water. The following April, Robert Wilson, a gynecologist, snapped a picture showing a long neck—reminiscent of an aquatic dinosaur—gliding through the lake. The latter photo has become famous as the "surgeon's picture."

DARK CLOUDS AND BRIGHT PROSPECTS

In Germany, Hitler finally succeeded in being named Chancellor, and active persecution of liberals and Jews began. The Dust Bowl hit the Great Plains of the U.S., heralded by drought and the Great Black Blizzard. In Japan, the Sanriku earthquake and tsunami killed 3,064 people. Two British biplanes made the first flight over Mt. Everest. Mass catering came to Britain with the opening of the first Lyon's Corner House. Despite Nazism in Germany, 1933 was a year of outstanding progress. After his inauguration, Franklin D. Roosevelt and Congress speedily adopted plans to put America back to work; with the National Industrial Recovery Act, they funded farm relief and public works projects. Banks were closed temporarily while new regulations were drafted to ensure their stability. Prohibition of alcohol was repealed. It was a splendid year for entertainment, with the showing of memorable films, *The Private Life of Henry VIII*, *King Kong*, and *Little Women*, starring Katharine Hepburn. Irving Berlin produced his joyous *Easter Parade*. Dancer Fred Astaire emerged as a new Hollywood star. The ancient Persian city of Persepolis was excavated.

➤ Read "The First New Age Psychic: Edgar Cayce" by Wendy C. Hawks on page 265.

CAPRICORN

From January 01, 0:00 through January 20, 11:52

The Intrepid Traveler

The 1933 January Capricorn usually has their luggage packed and ready, eager to explore foreign lands at the drop of a hat. You came into this world intent on learning as much about it as possible. As you grew older, television offered tantalizing glimpses of different countries, although, knowing you, you probably also started reading about other lands at an early age. The first issue of *Newsweek* was published in your birth year, and in all probability you grew up thumbing through such periodicals as a means of armchair travel.

You're intensely interested in learning how other people think. Although you have a strong personal philosophy, you enjoy hearing about other people's religious, cultural, and political views. The older you get, the more you realize that people are essentially the same all over the world. This must be tremendously comforting to a person who was born between two World Wars.

It's very important for you to be of service to others and you derive great satisfaction from helping people in need. Your missionary zeal is profound and impressive. Even if you aren't able to travel, you have a tremendous intellectual capacity. You may have used it to learn foreign languages and customs, so that you can enlighten others who may be reluctant to look beyond their own personal experience. Your open-minded attitude has probably made you an excellent spiritual advisor, teacher, or mentor.

For you, relationships are what make life worth living. You're best suited to a person who shares your love of learning. Geminis, Sagittarians, Aquarians, and Pisceans can prove loving companions. In marriage, try not to let things get too cerebral. There's a lot to be said for following your heart, especially where your beloved is concerned.

Goats born in January 1933 are challenged to put their knowledge to good use. Studying and reading are exemplary pursuits; so is applying what you've learned. Take every opportunity to travel around—experience is the best teacher. Your greatest strength is your love of humanity; use it to shine light into shadowy corners of society.

AQUARIUS

From January 20, 11:53 through February 19, 2:15

The Diehard Detective

As a 1933 Aquarius, you're determined to get to the bottom of things. Secrets of any kind make you uneasy; the year you were born, Germany's Nazi Party won a majority in Parliament. Their underhanded dealings set a horrifying example for the world, and no doubt you took the lessons of the Holocaust to heart. You're intent on learning as much as you can about people and institutions so that you can make informed decisions about them; consequently, intimacy may be a problem for you.

Some people may accuse you of having a dark outlook, but exploring the seamy side of life gives you great pleasure and you may be a mystery buff. Water-bearers of 1933 know how sweet life can be because they're able to face its horrors, too. Nobody will ever accuse you of being naïve. Your serious approach to life is immediately apparent to everyone you meet; consequently, you can pose an intimidating picture to more light-hearted folks.

Few people realize that you have an intense need to love and be loved. You have a romantic streak a mile wide. Gothic novels and soap operas may give you a thrill, as they reflect your own view of relationships. You want to experience the height of ecstasy and depths of despair with your partner. For you, a passionate relationship provides a welcome respite from the drudgery of day-to-day life.

You're drawn to people who share your love of drama. Cancerians, Leos, Virgos, and Pisceans hold a special appeal. Although you yearn for an intense relationship, take care that things don't get too dramatic with your partner, or you could do irreparable damage to your bond. Contrary to what the movies suggest, the healthiest unions always feature stretches of calm.

Your greatest challenge as a 1933 Aquarius is to lighten up a bit. Try not to think the worst of people. When brooding gets the best of you, rent a screwball comedy. Blessed with tremendous sensitivity, you need to give yourself a break from time to time, or you could fall victim to depression. Use your intuition to form loving relationships that will sustain and uplift you in both good times and bad.

➤ Read about your Chinese Astrological sign on page 838. ➤ Read about your Personal Planets on page 826. ➤ Read about your personal Mystical Card on page 856.

1933

CAPRICORN
Your Personal Planets

YOUR LOVE POTENTIAL
Venus in Sagittarius, Jan. 01, 0:00 - Jan. 14, 9:55
Venus in Capricorn, Jan. 14, 9:56 - Jan. 20, 11:52

YOUR DRIVE AND AMBITION
Mars in Virgo, Jan. 01, 0:00 - Jan. 20, 11:52

YOUR LUCK MAGNETISM
Jupiter in Virgo, Jan. 01, 0:00 - Jan. 20, 11:52

World Events

Jan. 3 – Japanese forces capture Shuagyashan in China.

Jan. 8 – Physicist Dr. Irving Langmuir successfully measures the force of a single atom.

The new cabinet after Hitler is elected Chancellor of Germany

AQUARIUS
Your Personal Planets

YOUR LOVE POTENTIAL
Venus in Capricorn, Jan. 20, 11:53 - Feb. 07, 10:29
Venus in Aquarius, Feb. 07, 10:30 - Feb. 19, 2:15

YOUR DRIVE AND AMBITION
Mars in Virgo, Jan. 20, 11:53 - Feb. 19, 2:15

YOUR LUCK MAGNETISM
Jupiter in Virgo, Jan. 20, 11:53 - Feb. 19, 2:15

World Events

Jan. 21 – The League of Nations rejects the settlement plans proposed by Japan to achieve peace in China.

Jan. 30 – After a month of secret negotiations, Adolf Hitler becomes Chancellor of Germany.

1933

PISCES
Your Personal Planets

YOUR LOVE POTENTIAL
Venus in Aquarius, Feb. 19, 2:16 - Mar. 03, 11:23
Venus in Pisces, Mar. 03, 11:24 - Mar. 21, 1:42

YOUR DRIVE AND AMBITION
Mars in Virgo, Feb. 19, 2:16 - Mar. 21, 1:42

YOUR LUCK MAGNETISM
Jupiter in Virgo, Feb. 19, 2:16 - Mar. 21, 1:42

World Events

Mar. 4 – Franklin D. Roosevelt is inaugurated as U.S. President.

Mar. 12 – German President von Hindenburg orders that the empire flag and the swastika should be flown side by side.

The filming of Fritz Lang's movie "Metropolis"

ARIES
Your Personal Planets

YOUR LOVE POTENTIAL
Venus in Pisces, Mar. 21, 1:43 - Mar. 27, 13:57
Venus in Aries, Mar. 27, 13:58 - Apr. 20, 13:17

YOUR DRIVE AND AMBITION
Mars in Virgo, Mar. 21, 1:43 - Apr. 20, 13:17

YOUR LUCK MAGNETISM
Jupiter in Virgo, Mar. 21, 1:43 - Apr. 20, 13:17

World Events

Mar. 29 – Film director Fritz Lang leaves Germany in disapproval at the Nazi regime.

Apr. 3 – The British Marquis of Clydesdale and RAF Lieutenant David MacIntyre perform the first flight over Mt. Everest.

PISCES
From February 19, 2:16 through March 21, 1:42

The Hopeless Romantic

If there's anybody who believes in the concept of soul mates, it's a 1933 Pisces. You may always be on the lookout for the perfect mate. It's easy for you to fall head-over-heels in love, but harder to sustain your ardor; that's because you have very high standards. You may expect your beloved to scale the highest mountain and swim the deepest river—after all, you'd do the same for them! Consequently, you may either have a lot of partners, or an extremely patient one!

Despite your desire for a mate, you still enjoy spending long periods of time on your own. Solitary pursuits give you an opportunity to recharge your batteries. You expend an awful lot of energy on others, so it's only natural that you may burn out quickly. Working on creative projects helps you to regain a sense of self, as does praying and meditating. You're quite a spiritual person, but may prefer to keep your beliefs private.

An "easy come, easy go" attitude toward money may get you into financial difficulties from time to time. Growing up during the Depression may have made you wary of investments, thereby limiting your earning power. In all likelihood, you've become more responsible about money as you've grown older. Still, you've never been excited about acquiring wealth. To your credit, you've always cared more about people than possessions.

As a 1933 Pisces, you need friends who are eager to please. You'd be wise to surround yourself with Cancerians, Virgos, Librans, and fellow Pisceans. In relationships, you're very loving as a general rule. Bear in mind that praise will help your partner live up to your expectations far better than criticism.

Your greatest challenge, 1933 Pisces, is to develop a strong sense of self apart from your mate. While love is the ultimate experience, it doesn't always have to be experienced with another person. Loving yourself is a good place to start. This will create a solid foundation for a warm, fruitful relationship that can last a lifetime. Your biggest strength is your profound spirituality; take every opportunity to develop, nurture, and enjoy it.

ARIES
From March 21, 1:43 through April 20, 13:17

The Ardent Humanitarian

Born during a time of worldwide financial hardship, 1933 Aries, you understand that there is strength in numbers. While most Rams are die-hard individualists, you're an exception to this rule. True, you value your independence, but you also understand that having strong ties to your family and community can help you withstand any deprivation.

The year you were born, U.S. President Franklin Roosevelt intoned, "We have nothing to fear but fear itself." This could well be your motto—anything is possible, provided you stick with kith and kin. Whenever you achieve success in life, you long to share it with those less fortunate than you. It's a kind of insurance policy against personal deprivation. You're firmly convinced that if you share your wealth with others, you will never be completely destitute. For the most part, this philosophy has worked remarkably well for you.

A favorite form of escape for you may be fashion. No matter how much or how little money you have, you always try to look fabulous. Your biggest fashion influences probably come from the movies. Dapper movie stars like Clark Gable and Fred Astaire hold special appeal for male Rams, while glamour queens like Ava Gardner and Joan Crawford inspire female Aries.

In relationships, you need someone who will stick with you through good times and bad. Fair-weather friendships are an anathema to you. Consequently, you prefer the company of loyal Virgos, Leos, and Sagittarians. Fellow Aries also appeal to your love of bravery. All this emphasis on courage can drive a wedge between you and your loved ones if you're not careful, though. Don't be afraid to comfort a partner or pal if they express fear or anxiety. Being tender is no crime!

As a 1933 Aries, your challenge is to be less wary about the future. Your nostalgia can prevent you from enjoying the benefits of modern society. Don't discount a new gadget or service just because you did without it as a youth. Your greatest strength is undeniably your humanitarian spirit. So long as you continue to obey your generous instincts, you'll never lack for love.

➤ Read about your Chinese Astrological sign on page 838. ➤ Read about your Personal Planets on page 826. ➤ Read about your personal Mystical Card on page 856.

TAURUS

From April 20, 13:18 through May 21, 12:56

The Secret Sensualist

A 1933 Taurus is one playful Bull. Unfortunately, the circumstances surrounding your birth didn't encourage levity. The Great Depression and Adolf Hitler's rise to power cast a long shadow on your generation. Still, being the Bull that you are, you probably managed to have a bit of fun whatever the circumstances surrounding your youth.

Even though it may seem like a burden at times, your natural capacity for joy is a true gift. Some folks simply can't understand how you can manage to smile through adversity. Don't bother making excuses for yourself. The truth is that you understand that life itself is the ultimate experience, and you're not going to waste a single moment of it brooding over silly concerns. It's no mistake that some of the greatest screwball comedies of all time were made during your formative years. *Duck Soup*, *It Happened One Night*, and *Bringing Up Baby* brought the world much needed laughter just when darkness threatened to shroud it in misery.

Reputation means everything to you. That's probably why you fight so hard to suppress giggles during serious public events. If you'd let your humor come to the surface more often, though, you'd surprise and delight onlookers. You've got a knack for coming up with brilliant, witty remarks just when things start to get too serious. When you let this talent shine through, your popularity soars.

Your love of fun draws you to people who can appreciate a good joke. Cancerians, Leos, Sagittarians, and Capricorns have special appeal for you. Resist the urge to team up with folks simply because they might advance your personal and professional prospects—you're better off mixing with people who know how to have a good time.

The greatest challenge for 1933 Bulls is to let go of the need to be respected and admired for superficial reasons. Instead of wasting time on acquiring status symbols, focus on expressing your creativity. Your greatest strength is your humor. By integrating it into artistic endeavors, you'll achieve tremendous happiness. For a joyous soul like you, there can be no better achievement.

GEMINI

From May 21, 12:57 through June 21, 21:11

The Unabashed Homebody

Nobody loves the comforts of home more than the 1933 Gemini. Generally, your sign is associated with intellectual curiosity and adventure. Although that's still true of you, you'd rather do your explorations from the comforts of home. When you were born, the world was an unpredictable, scary place. Chances are, you grew to yearn for a home where everything was safe, secure, and predictable.

It's no accident that The Century of Progress World's Fair opened the month you were born. Most of its exhibitions featured gadgets for making the home a virtual utopia—what a comforting prospect for somebody born between two World Wars! You're probably eager to try the latest time-saving devices and welcomed the many technological advances that so characterized the twentieth century.

For a Gemini, you may be hesitant about discussing controversial topics in public. The rise of fascism taught you all too well the dangers of dogma, whether religious or political. You're extra scrupulous about respecting other people's beliefs, to the point that you'd rather remain silent than openly disagree. However, you do have a strong moral code that immediately becomes apparent when you're confronted with injustice. Your considerable verbal abilities are best applied when championing the underdog. You have the makings of a great lawyer.

You thrive best in relationships that value personal integrity above all else. Cancerians, Librans, Aquarians, and Pisceans probably dominate your social circle. You and your friends may run the risk of being too accommodating of each other, though. Don't be afraid to push your agenda when it's really important, or it will be impossible to move forward.

As a 1933 Gemini, your greatest challenge is to assert your will. Don't be afraid of stepping on people's rights; a conscientious person like you rarely makes such transgressions. Your biggest strength is your love of home—use it to create a harmonious domestic life. Coming home to a peaceful household puts all the world's problems in perspective. If there's anybody who can make their own bliss, it's you.

➤ Read about your Chinese Astrological sign on page 838. ➤ Read about your Personal Planets on page 826. ➤ Read about your personal Mystical Card on page 856.

1933

TAURUS
Your Personal Planets

YOUR LOVE POTENTIAL
Venus in Aries, Apr. 20, 13:18 - Apr. 20, 18:59
Venus in Taurus, Apr. 20, 19:00 - May 15, 2:46
Venus in Gemini, May 15, 2:47 - May 21, 12:56

YOUR DRIVE AND AMBITION
Mars in Virgo, Apr. 20, 13:18 - May 21, 12:56

YOUR LUCK MAGNETISM
Jupiter in Virgo, Apr. 20, 13:18 - May 21, 12:56

World Events

May 10 – Books labeled "un-German" are burned in front of Berlin University.

May 16 – The ban on jazz music is lifted in Moscow.

British jazz ensemble in Pushkin Square after the ban on jazz is lifted in Moscow

GEMINI
Your Personal Planets

YOUR LOVE POTENTIAL
Venus in Gemini, May 21, 12:57 - June 08, 13:00
Venus in Cancer, June 08, 13:01 - June 21, 21:11

YOUR DRIVE AND AMBITION
Mars in Virgo, May 21, 12:57 - June 21, 21:11

YOUR LUCK MAGNETISM
Jupiter in Virgo, May 21, 12:57 - June 21, 21:11

World Events

June 16 – The National Industrial Recovery Act (NRA) is signed into law, giving the U.S. government control over industry in an effort to curb the economic depression.

June 19 – Soviet political exile Leon Trotsky is granted asylum in France.

1933

CANCER
Your Personal Planets

YOUR LOVE POTENTIAL
Venus in Cancer, June 21, 21:12 - July 03, 1:28
Venus in Leo, July 03, 1:29 - July 23, 8:04

YOUR DRIVE AND AMBITION
Mars in Virgo, June 21, 21:12 - July 06, 22:02
Mars in Libra, July 06, 22:03 - July 23, 8:04

YOUR LUCK MAGNETISM
Jupiter in Virgo, June 21, 21:12 - July 23, 8:04

World Events

July 12 - The U.S. Congress passes the first minimum-wage law.

July 14 - All political parties in Germany are outlawed—except the Nazi Party.

Polish film director Roman Polanski is born under the sign of Leo

LEO
Your Personal Planets

YOUR LOVE POTENTIAL
Venus in Leo, July 23, 8:05 - July 27, 16:44
Venus in Virgo, July 27, 16:45 - Aug. 21, 12:22
Venus in Libra, Aug. 21, 12:23 - Aug. 23, 14:51

YOUR DRIVE AND AMBITION
Mars in Libra, July 23, 8:05 - Aug. 23, 14:51

YOUR LUCK MAGNETISM
Jupiter in Virgo, July 23, 8:05 - Aug. 23, 14:51

World Events

Aug 18 - Polish film director Roman Polanski is born.

Aug 21 - British opera singer Janet Baker is born

CANCER
From June 21, 21:12 through July 23, 8:04

The Passionate Patriot

As a 1933 Cancer, you are intensely loyal to origins. You're willing to fight and, if necessary, to die for your country. Chances are, you've got your nation's flag displayed prominently in your home. Woe be unto anyone who dares criticize the land of your birth—you never shy away from a political debate. In fact, you'd rather hash things out publicly than keep your feelings a secret. This is a strange attribute for a Cancer, but life experience has shown you that intrigues can be dangerous. After all, 1933 was the year that the German Secret Police (the Gestapo) was created.

You're probably used to being called an atypical Cancer. That's because, unlike other members of your sign, you enjoy calling attention to yourself. As far as you're concerned, there's nothing worse than being boring. You want to communicate your ideas in an unusual, compelling way. It's no surprise, then, that the first singing telegram was sent during your birth year! Those who rely on you, like employees and children, may on occasion be embarrassed by your behavior, but who cares? At least your individuality sets you apart from the crowd.

If there's anything you can't stand, it's being dependent on someone or something. Unfortunately, this fear can undermine your relationships. While it's admirable that you want to pull yourself up by your own bootstraps, it's important to ask for help when you need it. Practice communicating your needs to others. If voicing your needs aloud is too difficult, you can always put them down in a note. Nobody writes a better love letter than you!

In relationships, you need to surround yourself with people who are followers, not leaders, lest ego-clashes result. Chances are, you have a great many Geminis, Virgos, Librans, and Pisceans for friends. When you let those who love and support you shine, everyone benefits.

Your challenge is to become more open-minded to different ideas. Make time to listen to proposals that reflect principles other than you own. Your greatest strength is your individuality. Learn to appreciate and celebrate it in others.

LEO
From July 23, 8:05 through August 23, 14:51

The Enterprising Idealist

As a 1933 Leo, you're always looking for a new way to make money. It's not that you're greedy; it's just that you like the luxury that wealth can bring. Having a good source of income is very important to you, probably because you saw the effects of the Great Depression. It's no coincidence that the game Monopoly was invented in the year of your birth. Every 1933 Leo has the makings of a tycoon, and you are no different—whether you realize it or not.

Your love of financial security may make you wary about the marriage institution. As a Leo, you're probably in love with the idea of love. Unfortunately, putting this ideal into practice may be a different story. It's possible that the responsibility of supporting another person scares you. Perhaps you're afraid of being a drain on your partner's income. Whatever your fears, it's important to remember that abundance comes in many different forms. The emotional support you can get and give is more precious than gold.

When a relationship gets too intense, you're liable to take off for parts unknown. Travel affords you the sense of freedom you crave. Even if you haven't taken many trips in your lifetime, there's a good chance that you've read many books about foreign cultures and faraway places. In fact, you could have considerable success in the import-export business, as you've got a good eye for what the public lacks and craves.

As far as relationships go, you need to be involved with people who will constantly reassure you of their love and loyalty. Steadfast friends and lovers include Taureans, Cancerians, and Capricorns. You also do well with fellow Lions, although occasional power struggles are bound to ensue. If you're willing to be a little more giving of your time and affection, you'll find the love you deserve and desire.

The greatest challenge you face is to learn to trust more. Under the facade of that adversary you see may lurk the heart of a friend. Opening your heart may lead to untold rewards. You've been blessed with an adventurous spirit. Use it to reach out to people who can enrich your life.

► Read about your Chinese Astrological sign on page 838. ► Read about your Personal Planets on page 826. ► Read about your personal Mystical Card on page 856.

VIRGO

From August 23, 14:52 through September 23, 12:00

The Adaptable Achiever

All Virgos are born with the need to serve in some way. Virgos born in 1933, however, may experience this desire as a curse. Too often, you may feel loaded down with drudge work and boring tasks. At times your work-load may even have threatened your health. Your problem may be that your vocabulary lacks one small but important word: "no."

Before taking on another thankless job, remember that the minimum wage law was passed this year in the U.S. That means getting an honest day's wage for an honest day's work. You don't have to be a martyr in order to win acceptance; in fact, the opposite is true. The sooner you set firm boundaries, the faster you'll earn respect. Everybody deserves some time to kick back, relax, and have fun. As a child growing up during the Depression, this may have been a difficult lesson for you to learn.

Sudden changes have had a way of transforming your life. Great highs have probably followed tremendous lows, and vice versa. Instead of dreading this roller-coaster ride, learn to love it. Virgos have a tendency to get bogged down in routine. Being forced to deal with radical changes has made you a much more interesting, adaptable person. In addition, you have an air of mystique that is most captivating—use it to get others to do your bidding, it may be a refreshing change for you!

As far as relationships go, you need friends and lovers who will bolster your confidence. Effusive Geminis, Leos, Sagittarians, and Pisceans will appreciate your considerable talents, especially when your self-esteem needs a lift. Resist the urge to criticize their shortcomings, however. Your words may be more cutting than you realize. Remember, you catch more flies with honey than you do with vinegar.

1933 Virgos are challenged to set firm personal boundaries, both at work and at home. Fortunately, you have been blessed with loads of charisma, talent, and an amazing adaptability. By using them to your best advantage, you'll feel more in control. You have much more power over your Destiny than you realize. Make it your mission to forge your own path in life.

LIBRA

From September 23, 12:01 through October 23, 20:47

The Dynamic Charmer

As a 1933 Libra, you're even more charming than most folks born under your sign, and that's saying a lot! You have an expansive, jolly personality that draws admirers like bees to a flower. Somehow you manage to be fun-loving without losing your dignity. Your popularity never fails to bring people together. Is it any wonder that work began on the Golden Gate Bridge the year you were born? It's a virtual symbol of your diplomatic talents.

Strangely, although you have many admirers, you may be secretly worried that you're not really worthy of their love. Things seem to come more easily to you than to other people. Don't feel guilty about your good fortune. Instead, use it to shine light in the world. Fellow Libran Eleanor Roosevelt became First Lady in 1933. She used her wealth and privilege to benefit others. There's no reason you can't do the same with your natural born talents. Performing volunteer work can boost your self-esteem enormously.

You may have a reputation for being a "love 'em and leave 'em" kind of person. It's not that you don't want a long-lasting relationship; it's just that you have so many chances for love! Settling down should have been easier for you later in life. You'll have done best with a partner who is spontaneous. You need someone with whom you'll never be bored.

As far as friends and lovers go, you're best suited to the adventurous and free-spirited. You're probably most comfortable with Ariens, Geminis, Sagittarians, and Aquarians. Make sure you have at least some different interests, though—you need to retain your own identity in any relationship. Taking separate vacations can actually strengthen your bond to loved ones.

The greatest challenge for you as a 1933 Libra is to settle down. While it's admirable that you want to lead an interesting life, every relationship needs an element of stability to survive. Your strength is that you can charm anybody who crosses your path. Use it to woo your partner from time to time, just to keep the magic alive. Even the oldest relationships can be romantic—it's all a matter of willpower!

➤ Read about your Chinese Astrological sign on page 838. ➤ Read about your Personal Planets on page 826. ➤ Read about your personal Mystical Card on page 856.

1933

VIRGO
Your Personal Planets

YOUR LOVE POTENTIAL
Venus in Libra, Aug. 23, 14:52 - Sept. 15, 14:53
Venus in Scorpio, Sept. 15, 14:54 - Sept. 23, 12:00

YOUR DRIVE AND AMBITION
Mars in Libra, Aug. 23, 14:52 - Aug. 26, 6:33
Mars in Scorpio, Aug. 26, 6:34 - Sept. 23, 12:00

YOUR LUCK MAGNETISM
Jupiter in Virgo, Aug. 23, 14:52 - Sept. 10, 5:09
Jupiter in Libra, Sept. 10, 5:10 - Sept. 23, 12:00

World Events

Aug. 25 – Italy and the USSR agree terms for a treaty of non-aggression.

Sept. 21 – President Roosevelt signs an authorization for the distribution of $75 million of surplus food and clothing to those considered to be the most in need.

Albert Einstein is exiled from Germany

LIBRA
Your Personal Planets

YOUR LOVE POTENTIAL
Venus in Scorpio, Sept. 23, 12:01 - Oct. 11, 4:31
Venus in Sagittarius, Oct. 11, 4:32 - Oct. 23, 20:47

YOUR DRIVE AND AMBITION
Mars in Scorpio, Sept. 23, 12:01 - Oct. 09, 11:34
Mars in Sagittarius, Oct. 09, 11:35 - Oct. 23, 20:47

YOUR LUCK MAGNETISM
Jupiter in Libra, Sept. 23, 12:01 - Oct. 23, 20:47

World Events

Oct. 14 – Germany leaves the League of Nations.

Oct. 17 – Albert Einstein lands in the U.S. in exile from Germany.

SCORPIO
Your Personal Planets

YOUR LOVE POTENTIAL
Venus in Sagittarius, Oct. 23, 20:48 - Nov. 06, 16:01
Venus in Capricorn, Nov. 06, 16:02 - Nov. 22, 17:52

YOUR DRIVE AND AMBITION
Mars in Sagittarius, Oct. 23, 20:48 - Nov. 19, 7:17
Mars in Capricorn, Nov. 19, 7:18 - Nov. 22, 17:52

YOUR LUCK MAGNETISM
Jupiter in Libra, Oct. 23, 20:48 - Nov. 22, 17:52

World Events

Nov. 14 – The Nobel committee in Stockholm decides not to award the Peace Prize for 1933.

Nov. 16 – The U.S. officially recognizes the Communist government of the Soviet Union.

James Joyce, author of "Ulysses"

SAGITTARIUS
Your Personal Planets

YOUR LOVE POTENTIAL
Venus in Capricorn, Nov. 22, 17:53 - Dec. 05, 17:59
Venus in Aquarius, Dec. 05, 18:00 - Dec. 22, 6:57

YOUR DRIVE AND AMBITION
Mars in Capricorn, Nov. 22, 17:53 - Dec. 22, 6:57

YOUR LUCK MAGNETISM
Jupiter in Libra, Nov. 22, 17:53 - Dec. 22, 6:57

World Events

Dec. 5 – The 21st Amendment repealing Prohibition becomes effective; Utah is the last of thirty-six states to ratify it.

Dec. 6 – In the U.S., the ban on James Joyce's *Ulysses* is lifted.

SCORPIO
From October 23, 20:48 through November 22, 17:52

The Restless Wanderer

Any Scorpio born during 1933 has a bad case of wanderlust. Growing up during World War II didn't make you fear foreign lands; rather, it whetted your appetite to visit them. It's no surprise, really—your sign is famous for its insatiable curiosity. Often, the only way for you to satisfy this craving is to do a little detective work. If that means traveling to parts unknown, so be it. As far as you're concerned, there's no better way to learn about a culture than to experience it firsthand.

If you haven't been able to travel, it's probably because domestic responsibilities have prevented you from doing so. You feel a tremendous obligation toward your family. Your deepest wish may be to break free of these ties, though you'd never admit it to others. Maybe that's why folks suspect you of harboring a deep, dark secret. When personal responsibilities get to be too much, you often head for the movies as a means of escape—luckily for you, the first drive-in theater opened in 1933.

Your restless spirit draws you to work that can be performed independently. If there's anything you can't stand, it's a micromanager breathing down your neck. There's a good chance that you've either held a variety of jobs throughout your lifetime, or picked one that afforded plenty of personal freedom. Functioning under pressure holds a special appeal for you; a 1933 Scorpio is well-suited for working in an emergency room.

In relationships, you do best with people who provide a stabilizing influence. In general, this means that Taureans, Cancerians, Virgos, and Capricorns suit you well. Don't let jealousy get in the way of your partner's personal development, though. Trust is the cornerstone of any fruitful relationship. For your own peace of mind, learn to let go of your fears of betrayal.

Creating a solid, fulfilling foundation may be your greatest challenge. Life can't always be an adventure, no matter how much you wish it. You've been blessed with a curious mind. Use it to learn as much as you can about the subjects that interest you. Let expanding your mind be a lifelong pursuit.

SAGITTARIUS
From November 22, 17:53 through December 22, 6:57

The Colorful Butterfly

There's an old proverb that says, "Nothing is constant but change," and this saying applies beautifully to the 1933 Sagittarius. Born with powerful psychic ability, you can sense momentous changes before they actually happen, and are able to adapt accordingly. This gift came in especially handy during your formative years, when the entire map of the world was rewritten to reflect the radical political changes of the time. Social changes inevitably followed political shifts—Prohibition was repealed in the year of your birth. While most people were thrown off balance by these upheavals, you thrived on them.

When the going gets rough, your vivid imagination comes to the rescue. During World War II, you probably had lots of heroic fantasies about beating the bad guys. Adults probably shook their heads and called you a wild-eyed dreamer, but there's a good chance that your creative spirit served you well in your work. You probably have a reputation for being wonderfully imaginative.

Your creative drive comes in spurts and should never be forced. The more freedom you allow your imagination, the more fruitfully it will serve you. You're probably prone to change your look every few months or so. You absolutely hate to look dated, and go in for the latest fads; nobody could ever accuse you of being stuffy or predictable.

With regard to relationships, you need a partner who is willing to move with the times. You're most compatible with Ariens, Geminis, and Aquarians, though pairing up with another Sagittarius would be fun, too. It's easy for you to fall in and out of love quickly, so you'd be wise to pick a partner who is able to hold your attention.

The greatest challenge for a 1933 Sagittarius is to not be intimidated by well-educated people. This can be a problem even for Archers with advanced degrees. For some reason, you're convinced that everybody else is smarter than you. Not so! You've got an excellent mind; in fact, it's perhaps your biggest strength. Finding a practical application for your intellectual power will give you a terrific sense of accomplishment.

➤ Read about your Chinese Astrological sign on page 838. ➤ Read about your Personal Planets on page 826. ➤ Read about your personal Mystical Card on page 856.

CAPRICORN

From December 22, 6:58 through December 31, 23:59

The High Roller

Life is rarely boring for the 1933 December Capricorn. You're the type who thrives on giddy highs and subterranean lows. Actually, it's hard for you to relax when things are on an even keel. That's because you're a gambler at heart. Most folks are probably surprised to learn that you are a Capricorn, as Goats are famous for their steadfast reliability. The only thing reliable about you may be your risky behavior!

The year you were born, an earthquake, the most powerful in centuries, hit Japan. That's the kind of upheaval your loved ones may have experienced as a result of your many escapades. Fortunately, you were blessed with considerable charm, and are usually able to talk your way out of any situation. You may get a thrill out of seeing how much you can get away with, and enjoy baiting authority figures. You absolutely glow when you manage to beat the system.

When things go wrong, 1933 Capricorn, you may try to sweep your actions under the rug. This can cause serious rifts in your relationships if you're not careful. You've got a hidden source of energy that helps you overcome obstacles despite incredible odds. Somehow, you manage to elude trouble—but it often involves a lot of work.

Because of your wild heart, you need to surround yourself with people who are capable of unconditional love. Taureans, Cancerians, Leos, and Pisceans are good prospects for you, both as friends and partners. In marriage, it would be wise to keep your bank accounts separate, if only to give your partner a needed sense of security. It would also be wise to do things your spouse enjoys, even if their favorite activities seem boring to you.

As a 1933 December Capricorn, your greatest challenge is to understand the consequences of your actions. Although you thrive on taking big risks, your behavior can actually age your loved ones. Try not to involve friends and family in your intrigues. Your greatest strength is your zest for life—use it to inspire folks who deprive themselves of pleasure. Life is the ultimate adventure, and you can teach others to enjoy it to the fullest.

1933

CAPRICORN
Your Personal Planets

YOUR LOVE POTENTIAL
Venus in Aquarius, Dec. 22, 6:58 - Dec. 31, 23:59

YOUR DRIVE AND AMBITION
Mars in Capricorn, Dec. 22, 6:58 - Dec. 28, 3:42
Mars in Aquarius, Dec. 28, 3:43 - Dec. 31, 23:59

YOUR LUCK MAGNETISM
Jupiter in Libra, Dec. 22, 6:58 - Dec. 31, 23:59

World Events

Dec. 23 – The Pope condemns the Nazi sterilization program on women deemed to be unfit to have children.

Dec. 27 – Stalin refers to Japan as "a grave danger."

(Continued from page 273)

Special Feature
The First New Age Psychic: Edgar Cayce

In 1928, the Edgar Cayce Hospital opened its doors in Virginia Beach to patients from all over the world. Then in 1930, Atlantic University was started so that others could study his teachings. Unfortunately, the Depression took a toll on both the hospital and university, and they were forced to close for lack of funds.

During World War II, sacks of letters and requests for readings continued to arrive at an ever-growing rate. In an effort to keep up with the increasing demand, Cayce began giving as many as eight readings a day, despite the warnings he'd received in readings for himself not to do more than two a day. During this period, Cayce was booked for two years in advance. But by 1944, he was a year behind, suffering from overexertion and edema of the lungs. Shortly afterwards, Cayce had a stroke, was partially paralyzed, and died.

Astrologically speaking, virtually everything in Cayce's horoscope points to visionary experiences as well as the ability to make practical, realistic use of these gifts. He has important points stressing spiritual and psychic abilities, including the Sun in Pisces in the eighth house of the occult and the esoteric. In addition, Pisces' ruling planet, ultra-sensitive Neptune, is tightly aligned with Cayce's Moon in Taurus in the ninth house of dreams and visions. It's easy to see how Edgar Cayce became the world's most celebrated psychic of his time.

Cayce once confided to a friend—after having used his powers successfully for 33 years—that he couldn't explain how he did what he did! It is believed that Cayce obtained his information by tapping into the subconscious mind of the person asking for information, as well as tapping into what are called "the Akashic Records"—complete spiritual records of every person's soul-history, written in space and time. Drawing from these sources, Cayce could speak on literally any subject. Fortunately, people continue to benefit from his psychic legacy through the many books that have been written

Nelson Rockefeller, who consulted Edgar Cayce

about him, as well as the vast body of his readings, now housed at the ARE—Association for Research and Enlightenment, a Virginia Beach, Virginia-based organization founded by Cayce in 1931. ✺

➤ Read more about Cayce in "Ancient Secrets of the Great Pyramid" on page 305. ➤ Read about Atlantis in "The Mysterious Bermuda Triangle" on page 385.

1934

Freedom and Disruption: Jupiter Opposes Uranus

Throughout most of the year, Jupiter, the planet of expansion and enterprise, opposed Uranus, the planet of rebellion and innovation, signaling an escalation of political and social tensions. Although they reached their maximum contacts in February and October, they were interconnected until November, and several tense political situations came to a head over the intervening months. In January, Paris saw fighting between communists and their right-wing opponents. In November, Germany, headed by Fuhrer Hitler, shocked the international community when it admitted to secretly violating the Treaty of Versailles by aggressively rebuilding its army, navy, and air forces. Instability was also experienced in other European nations as a reaction to the Nazi movement, while Nicaragua, Bolivia, and Paraguay had internal conflicts of their own.

With Jupiter in conciliatory Libra, this contact also saw the birth of new freedoms, as some nations expressed the combination's lighter side. Protesting Filipinos were promised the independence of their island nation from the U.S. and Tunisia began its own drive for independence. Saturn, symbolizing solid structure, in the socially progressive sign of Aquarius, resonated happily with Jupiter and Uranus, suggesting that reforms initiated at this time would be robust and produce stable governments from this moment's inspiration. The sciences, also Saturn's domain, were highlighted and this triumvirate of planetary harmony supported technological advances and their practical application for the benefit of society. The first streamlined steam locomotive was christened in New York, while Edwin Hubble photographed a galaxy-filled universe.

Although Uranus was in Aries for most of the year, in June it briefly entered Taurus for the first time in 165 years, starting a seven-year period of focus on wealth and beauty, as well as a tendency to resist change which would truly begin in 1935. This placement correlated with a greater level of stubborn resistance, and many political factions now hardened their positions, taking dramatic measures to bring about change. Mao Tse-Tung's Chinese communists began the Long March, while Nazi insurgents killed Austrian Chancellor Dollfuss.

Hitler makes himself President on the death of Hindenburg

Mao Tse-Tung begins his long march to escape Chiang Kai-Shek's Nationalists

Salvador Dali becomes known for his stark, neurotic surrealism

DICTATORS, GANGSTERS, AND PATRIOTISM

International attitudes hardened as, in the midst of economic crisis, Hitler gained uncontested control of Germany, making himself President on the death of the aged incumbent, Hindenberg. A socialist uprising in neighboring Austria was brutally crushed and Nazis assassinated the Chancellor, Dollfuss. In China, Communist Mao Tse-Tung began his Long March to elude the reach of Chiang Kai-Shek's Nationalists. Stalin's purges continued in the USSR, as he rid himself of those whose power he feared. In Spain, Catalan separatists made a bid for independence, but the revolt was brutally put down and martial law was declared. King Alexander of Yugoslavia was assassinated in Marseilles, France. Amidst these tempestuous events, a war against organized crime triumphed in the U.S.: John Dillinger, Baby Face Nelson, Bonnie and Clyde, and Pretty Boy Floyd were wiped out by the forces of justice. The U.S. relinquished its right to intervene in Cuba's internal affairs. In the arts, Georgia O'Keeffe's soft sensual style contrasted with Salvador Dali's stark neurotic surrealism. A dimpled Shirley Temple rose to fame in *Little Miss Marker*.

➤ Read Clark Gable's Star Profile on page 289.

CAPRICORN

From January 01, 0:00 through January 20, 17:36

The Enterprising Sage

Any 1934 Capricorn born in the month of January is determined to make his or her own way in life. Even if you were born into a well-off family, you probably wanted to be a success on your own terms. The year that you were born, the U.S. ended its occupation of Haiti after nearly twenty years. You were similarly determined to assert your independence, even if it meant breaking away from a strong power base. Although they may not understand it at times, people do admire you for your self-sufficiency.

Always thinking about the future, you are more of a saver than a spender. Chances are you had a well-filled piggy bank as a child. It's easy for you to put off fleeting pleasures in favor of long-term security. At times, folks may have accused you of being overly cautious about money, but growing up during the Depression has taught you some valuable lessons. At times, your financial prudence may have seemed more like a burden than a blessing. You may have had to grant loans to friends and relatives throughout your life.

Blessed with good instincts about the future, you were probably quick to learn about computers, the Internet, and other emerging technologies long before they became commonly used. You've always been perfectly willing to pack up and move to places that might be more financially promising. This may have caused friction with family members who wanted to lead a more settled life. Power struggles with your loved ones may not have been uncommon.

You're best suited to adaptable people who are willing to take risks in order to achieve greater goals. Ariens, Geminis, Leos, and Aquarians are very compatible with you. You still may have to check your impulses from time to time, if only to appease your loved ones. It's important to remember that relationships are all about give and take.

The greatest challenge you face is your eagerness for results. This can cause you to rush ahead, without considering how people who depend on you may be affected by your behavior. Your biggest strength is your foresight, which gives you a decided advantage over more conventional types.

AQUARIUS

From January 20, 17:37 through February 19, 8:01

The Resourceful Adventurer

As a 1934 Aquarius, you've never let money stand in the way of your dreams. You learned how to make your resources stretch during the Depression. These pragmatic habits have enabled you to enjoy exotic adventures that have shaped your personality. Your childhood heroes were probably the vagabonds who rode boxcars during the Depression. The year you were born, Clark Gable and Claudette Colbert won Oscars for their roles in the comedy *It Happened One Night*. Their cross-country hitchhiking jaunt is probably your idea of a fantastic trip. Is it any wonder your friends think you're a little eccentric?

Part of the reason you're so willing to see far-off places is to learn how other people live. You may have witnessed some sobering scenes during the course of your life, which gives you an air of seriousness. It may be difficult for you to enjoy the simpler pleasures of life, knowing how others are suffering throughout the world. While it's wonderful that you are so conscientious, you must not deprive yourself of amusement. Forgoing fun won't solve the social problems that weigh on your heart.

You're capable of hard work, and never shy away from difficult jobs. In 1934, the National Labor Relations Board was created in the U.S. to regulate collective bargaining between workers and employers. There's a good chance that you've spent a great deal of your life negotiating better working conditions for you and your colleagues. At the very least, you demand appreciation for the duties you perform, whether domestic or professional.

As a 1934 Water-bearer, you get along best with people who share your vagabond ways. Chances are you know many Geminis, Sagittarians, and Pisceans, as well as fellow Aquarians. These folks understand your restless heart, although they may not be willing to "rough it" to the extent that you are!

Your greatest challenge is a tendency to be too serious. Try not to put the weight of the world on your shoulders. Life is too short for that. Your biggest strength is your willingness to try anything once. Don't let age dampen your adventurous spirit.

➤ Read about your Chinese Astrological sign on page 838. ➤ Read about your Personal Planets on page 826. ➤ Read about your personal Mystical Card on page 856.

CAPRICORN
Your Personal Planets

YOUR LOVE POTENTIAL
Venus in Aquarius, Jan. 01, 0:00 - Jan. 20, 17:36

YOUR DRIVE AND AMBITION
Mars in Aquarius, Jan. 01, 0:00 - Jan. 20, 17:36

YOUR LUCK MAGNETISM
Jupiter in Libra, Jan. 01, 0:00 - Jan. 20, 17:36

World Events

Jan. 1 – The former U.S. army fort at Alcatraz officially becomes a federal prison.

Jan. 16 – American opera singer Marilyn Horne is born.

U.S. Federal prison Alcatraz

AQUARIUS
Your Personal Planets

YOUR LOVE POTENTIAL
Venus in Aquarius, Jan. 20, 17:37 - Feb. 19, 8:01

YOUR DRIVE AND AMBITION
Mars in Aquarius, Jan. 20, 17:37 - Feb. 04, 4:12
Mars in Pisces, Feb. 04, 4:13 - Feb. 19, 8:01

YOUR LUCK MAGNETISM
Jupiter in Libra, Jan. 20, 17:37 - Feb. 19, 8:01

World Events

Feb. 6 – Angry anti-republican and fascist mobs fight with police throughout Paris, tearing up sidewalks and setting buses on fire.

Feb. 11 – Pianist Vladimir Horowitz makes his first appearance in New York with the Philharmonic Orchestra.

1934

PISCES
Your Personal Planets

YOUR LOVE POTENTIAL
Venus in Aquarius, Feb. 19, 8:02 - Mar. 21, 7:27

YOUR DRIVE AND AMBITION
Mars in Pisces, Feb. 19, 8:02 - Mar. 14, 9:08
Mars in Aries, Mar. 14, 9:09 - Mar. 21, 7:27

YOUR LUCK MAGNETISM
Jupiter in Libra, Feb. 19, 8:02 - Mar. 21, 7:27

World Events

Feb. 23 – British composer Sir Edward Elgar dies.

Mar. 8 – An Edwin Hubble photograph opens up the mysteries of space by showing thousands of galaxies.

Shirley Temple appears in her first movie

ARIES
Your Personal Planets

YOUR LOVE POTENTIAL
Venus in Aquarius, Mar. 21, 7:28 - Apr. 06, 9:22
Venus in Pisces, Apr. 06, 9:23 - Apr. 20, 18:59

YOUR DRIVE AND AMBITION
Mars in Aries, Mar. 21, 7:28 - Apr. 20, 18:59

YOUR LUCK MAGNETISM
Jupiter in Libra, Mar. 21, 7:28 - Apr. 20, 18:59

World Events

Apr. 12 – F. Scott Fitzgerald's *Tender Is The Night* is first published in New York.

Apr. 19 – Shirley Temple appears in her first movie, *Stand Up And Cheer.*

PISCES

From February 19, 8:02 through March 21, 7:27

The Eternal Romantic

Look up the word "romantic" in the dictionary and you may well find beside it a picture of the 1934 Pisces. You've been blessed with boundless enthusiasm, which never fails to attract admirers. If truth be told, you enjoy falling in love. As you've grown older, you've probably become more scrupulous about whom you flirt with, but that hasn't quenched your desire to romance everybody in your path. Growing up, you may have idealized fellow Piscean Elizabeth Taylor, not only for her acting ability, but also for her romantic exploits and charm.

Blessed with tremendous creativity, you're not above reinventing yourself year after year. Quite often, you change artistic media, experiencing various degrees of success with each. As with most Pisces, you're particularly gifted at dance, photography, and poetry. However, you probably possess talent in the fields of acting, singing, and painting as well.

While you can seem happy-go-lucky on the surface, there is a more somber dimension to your personality. It's possible that very few people know about this side of you, because you're uncomfortable putting it on display. Perhaps you're uncomfortable with these pessimistic thoughts, or are reluctant to burden your friends with them. Hopefully, assuming a perpetually sunny image has become less important to you as you've gotten older. A sensitive person like you needs to be true to their feelings.

As a 1934 Pisces, you need friends who accept you unconditionally. You probably find great kinship with Taureans, Cancerians, Leos, and Sagittarians. Don't be afraid to discuss serious subjects with your pals, as they can help ease you through difficult periods of your life. Contrary to what you may think, they love you for who you are, not how you act.

The greatest challenge you face is to fuse the light part of your personality with its darker component. Once you succeed in doing this, the admiration you seek will be your own. Your biggest strength is your artistic ability. Never stop exploring your different interests. They will never fail to take you down fascinating paths in life.

ARIES

From March 21, 7:28 through April 20, 18:59

The Generous Extremist

"Neither a lender nor a borrower be" is a piece of advice that every 1934 Aries should remember. Extravagant to a fault, you may not be above borrowing funds from friends when your own resources are running low. That said, your motives are entirely innocent. You're interested in having a good time at all costs, even if it means taking out a few loans. You're no hypocrite, however. When you've got money, you share it generously with anyone and everyone.

Growing up during the Great Depression, you understand just how fleeting fortune can be. Therefore, you're determined to milk every last drop from life that you can. Some folks may call your behavior extreme, but you'd rather cause a stir than remain a nonentity. Your wild behavior can cause trouble at home, however. When that happens, you're quick to make up for any transgressions with handsome gifts and effusive apologies. It's hard to stay mad at you for long; you're just so darned likable!

Breaking away from your family may have been a big issue for you. Although you greatly cherish intimate relationships, your need for independence is too strong to ignore. The year that you were born, the U.S. declared that the Philippines were to become independent in 1945. This gradual move toward self-determination may mirror your own experience with your relatives or guardians.

In general, personal relationships have brought you great fortune. You need somebody calm, cool, and collected to balance out your exuberance. Pairing up with charming, tactful people has always brought you luck. Geminis, Cancerians, Librans, and Pisceans have probably played favorable roles in your life. You must admit, it's nice to have somebody to rein you in from time to time!

As a 1934 Aries, your greatest challenge is to temper your will with prudence. Having fun is important, but not at the risk of your future security. Fortunately, you're a generous person who thinks nothing of helping people in need. This trait has helped you get through hard times, and is sure to serve you for years to come. When in doubt, it's better to be charitable.

➤ Read about your Chinese Astrological sign on page 838. ➤ Read about your Personal Planets on page 826. ➤ Read about your personal Mystical Card on page 856.

TAURUS

From April 20, 19:00 through May 21, 18:34

The Intuitive Helper

There's no better friend than the 1934 Taurus. That's because you have a knack for knowing just what people need, and when they need it. You're always providing kind services without being asked, and people love you for it. Folks who don't know you very well may be surprised by how down-to-earth you really are, as you may have a reputation for being a saint. However, once they're admitted into your social circle, they soon appreciate your wicked sense of humor.

For all your friends, there are times when you really want to be alone. Going off on lone nature walks or solo vacations helps to recharge your batteries. Even a service-oriented person like you needs private time. You may especially enjoy visiting exotic places to give you added perspective on your own life. The year that you were born, Franklin D. Roosevelt made a tour around Columbia. He was the first sitting U.S. President to visit South America and his pioneering spirit may be reflected in your occasional jaunts to parts unknown.

You have a vivid imagination that demands expression. Teaching art to children may give you lots of pleasure, as could holding quilting bees, pottery parties, or writing workshops. When you're not working on a craft project of some sort, you feel restless and anxious. Do your best to spend at least a half an hour each day on some creative pursuit. This will give you more energy to help the many folks who rely on you.

Throughout your life, you have probably attracted many admirers. You prefer people like yourself—serious and thoughtful at first glance, with a biting wit lurking just beneath the surface. Over the years, you've probably amassed a great many friends who are Cancerians, Scorpios, and Capricorns. Fellow Taureans are also congenial company for you.

Blessed with many gifts, the greatest challenge to the 1934 Taurus is an eagerness to serve. As you've gotten older, you've learned how to pick and choose your causes with more discretion. Your strongest gift is your imagination. Use it as a means to escape the mundane daily realities that sometimes weigh on your heart.

GEMINI

From May 21, 18:35 through June 22, 2:47

The Fair-Minded Judge

Every Gemini is born with admirable intellectual ability, but the 1934 Twins are doubly blessed. Not only are you smart, you're insightful—you're able to apply your knowledge in practical ways. Figuring out solutions to complex problems is something of a hobby for you. You especially enjoy working out larger social dilemmas. As far as you're concerned, people were put on this planet to benefit one another. When folks are able to overcome their differences, miracles can happen; you've seen it time and time again.

You're capable of organizing and executing huge projects, bringing together friends, family and neighbors to get the job done. People are eager to pitch in, as you manage to make any group endeavor fun and fulfilling. Your talent for bringing out the best in others makes you a very popular figure. People admire your drive, and would be a little afraid of it if you weren't so friendly. Your determination does come in handy when dealing with strangers. It's hard to say "no" to somebody as willful as you.

Sometimes your loyalty to friends and family can get in the way of what you really want to do. The year that you were born, Mahatma Gandhi suspended his campaign of civil disobedience in India for the greater good of his country. You've used similar strategies throughout your life, with varying degrees of success. It wouldn't hurt for you to be more selfish, especially when it comes to expanding your horizons.

Over the years, you've come to realize that you're most compatible with people who share your love of justice. Librans, Sagittarians, and Pisceans probably make up a good part of your social circle, as do fellow Geminis. Resist the urge to put your loved ones on pedestals: it can be very difficult for them to live up to such exalted expectations.

Your greatest challenge, 1934 Gemini, is to reconcile your ideals with reality. Although your desire for justice is admirable, human beings are flawed creatures and are prone to disappointing behavior. Your greatest strength is your resourcefulness. Use it to make others feel productive, happy, and healthy.

► Read about your Chinese Astrological sign on page 838. ► Read about your Personal Planets on page 826. ► Read about your personal Mystical Card on page 856.

TAURUS
Your Personal Planets

YOUR LOVE POTENTIAL
Venus in Pisces, Apr. 20, 19:00 - May 06, 8:53
Venus in Aries, May 06, 8:54 - May 21, 18:34

YOUR DRIVE AND AMBITION
Mars in Aries, Apr. 20, 19:00 - Apr. 22, 15:39
Mars in Taurus, Apr. 22, 15:40 - May 21, 18:34

YOUR LUCK MAGNETISM
Jupiter in Libra, Apr. 20, 19:00 - May 21, 18:34

World Events

Apr. 23 – British fascist leader Oswald Mosley meets with Italian leader Benito Mussolini in Rome.

May 3 – Yemen is invaded by Arabian forces under the orders of King Ibn Saud.

Bank robbers Bonnie Parker and Clyde Barrow

GEMINI
Your Personal Planets

YOUR LOVE POTENTIAL
Venus in Aries, May 21, 18:35 - June 02, 10:10
Venus in Taurus, June 02, 10:11 - June 22, 2:47

YOUR DRIVE AND AMBITION
Mars in Taurus, May 21, 18:35 - June 02, 16:20
Mars in Gemini, June 02, 16:21 - June 22, 2:47

YOUR LUCK MAGNETISM
Jupiter in Libra, May 21, 18:35 - June 22, 2:47

World Events

May 23 – Bank robbers Bonnie Parker and Clyde Barrow are killed in a police ambush.

June 8 – Oswald Mosley is heckled and fighting breaks out at a fascist demonstration in the Olympia Auditorium in London.

1934

CANCER
Your Personal Planets

YOUR LOVE POTENTIAL

Venus in Taurus, June 22, 2:48 - June 28, 9:37
Venus in Gemini, June 28, 9:38 - July 23, 13:41

YOUR DRIVE AND AMBITION

Mars in Gemini, June 22, 2:48 - July 15, 21:32
Mars in Cancer, July 15, 21:33 - July 23, 13:41

YOUR LUCK MAGNETISM

Jupiter in Libra, June 22, 2:48 - July 23, 13:41

World Events

June 30 – In the "Night of the Long Knives," Hitler orders the execution of several officials and storm-trooper leaders he believes to be planning a revolt.

July 4 – Physicist and Nobel Prize winner Marie Curie dies.

General Von Schleicher and his wife are shot by the Gestapo

LEO
Your Personal Planets

YOUR LOVE POTENTIAL

Venus in Gemini, July 23, 13:42 - July 23, 18:21
Venus in Cancer, July 23, 18:22 - Aug. 17, 15:44
Venus in Leo, Aug. 17, 15:45 - Aug. 23, 20:31

YOUR DRIVE AND AMBITION

Mars in Cancer, July 23, 13:42 - Aug. 23, 20:31

YOUR LUCK MAGNETISM

Jupiter in Libra, July 23, 13:42 - Aug. 23, 20:31

World Events

Aug. 2 – Adolf Hitler becomes President as well as Chancellor of Germany, on the death of Paul von Hindenburg.

Aug. 10 – Baseball great Babe Ruth announces his final season as a full-time player.

CANCER
From June 22, 2:48 through July 23, 13:41

The Determined Reformer

The 1934 Cancer was born with a mission in life. Growing up during World War II, you witnessed the worst of humanity—you are determined to do your part to reverse that trend. The year you were born, Arthur Henderson won the Nobel Peace Prize for arranging the International Disarmament Conference. Always looking for opportunities to make the world a better place, you share this reformatory zeal.

An intense spiritual life gives you a hidden core of energy that kicks in at the most valuable times. Just when it looks like you're down and out, you're able to overcome seemingly insurmountable obstacles. Even people who have known you for years are astonished by your ability to overcome adversity. You probably feel as though you're being watched by a divine presence. This makes it easy for you to deal with problems that would overwhelm folks who don't share your faith in a beneficent universe.

You have a forceful personality that seems emotionally intense to others. Sometimes you can't figure out why it takes so long for people to warm up to you. Frankly, they're scared! As you've grown older, you've learned to lighten up. You've got terrific sex appeal, which accounts for your many admirers. However, you've never been interested in making a lot of conquests. Monogamy is very important to you, and if you can't settle down with a single partner, you'd rather be alone.

As a 1934 Cancer, you're not interested in talking about the weather. You'd rather converse about important topics like politics, religion, and culture. You get along very well with Leos, Scorpios, Sagittarians, and Aquarians. These signs share your desire for making the world a better place, and will probably be eager to join any of your reform efforts.

Your greatest challenge is to avoid snap judgments. It can be disillusioning when others don't seem to be living up to their end of the bargain, but not everybody has your boundless energy and courage. Your biggest strength is your ability to enforce positive changes in the world. By refusing to back down from challenges, you can accomplish great things.

LEO
From July 23, 13:42 through August 23, 20:31

The Irrepressible Rebel

Nobody could ever accuse the 1934 Leo of being boring. Just when somebody thinks they've got you figured out, you do something utterly shocking. At first glance, nobody would peg you for a rebel. That's because you enjoy putting on an air of respectability, just so you call lull folks into a false sense of security. Then, when they least expect it, you do something startling enough to make everybody run for cover.

The reason you like controversy so much is that you prize individuality above all else. If there's anything you've learned over the years, it's that people are utterly unpredictable. You want a life filled with thrills, chills, and surprises, even if it means getting an unpleasant shock every now and then. The year you were born, Edwin Hubble took a photograph which showed that there are as many galaxies as the Milky Way has stars. That's the way you see human beings—each one is utterly unique, and can never be replicated.

Because you like doing things your own way, it may have been difficult for you to make a serious commitment. The prospect of a permanent relationship can seem stifling to a 1934 Leo. If you do decide to settle down, it's for better or for worse. You can't stand it when couples split up just because circumstances are bad. If you've had an unsuccessful marriage, it probably hit you very hard. You strongly believe in the concept of "soul mates."

As a general rule, you enjoy making friends with people who are respected and experienced in some way. It's quite possible you've married someone older than you. At the very least, your social circle is comprised of some pretty impressive people. You get along best with ambitious types like Ariens, Taureans, Leos, and Capricorns.

One of the biggest challenges for the 1934 Leo is your ego. You may at times be so focused that you forget the feelings of others. As you've grown older, you've learned when to speak your mind and when to remain silent. Your greatest strength is your boundless enthusiasm. No matter where you go or what you do, you'll never cease to be thoroughly engaged in life.

➤ Read about your Chinese Astrological sign on page 838. ➤ Read about your Personal Planets on page 826. ➤ Read about your personal Mystical Card on page 856.

VIRGO

From August 23, 20:32 through September 23, 17:44

The Ever-Shifting Mystic

Talking about the 1934 Virgo is like trying to describe an impressionist watercolor. It's impossible to completely discern all its forms and colors, because they blend so closely together. Virgos born in this year have moods and attitudes that are ever-shifting—and that includes you! One minute you're happy; the next, you're blue. Sometimes you're conservative, other times liberal. It all depends on what is happening around you. You soak up your environment like a sponge!

People often describe you as being psychic. You have a knack for knowing how situations are going to play out, and have learned to follow your hunches over the years. Your sensitivity may be something of a sore spot. You tend to see it as a liability, when really it's a strength. When life gets too intense, you usually head for the movies. The year you were born, Shirley Temple starred in the film *Stand Up and Cheer*. Wholesome entertainment like this made it possible for you to enjoy cinema from a very early age.

You prefer living in an idealized world of pink smoke and gossamer clouds—facing reality may not be your strong suit. Still, you don't shy away from hard work. You've probably been involved with various volunteer projects throughout your life. On some deep level, you understand that the secret to receiving grace is to give it to others on a regular basis.

Although you're more practical than you appear, it's still a good idea to team up with down-to-earth people. Earthy types like Taureans and Capricorns can help you deal with day-to-day chores, although you secretly prefer the company of fanciful Librans and Pisceans, because they invite you to build castles in the air. Remember to praise your loved ones; everyone needs to be adored!

As a 1934 Virgo, you need to have more confidence in your abilities. Your greatest challenge is a tendency to underplay your talents. Hopefully, you've come to appreciate your sensitivity over time. Your biggest strength is that you understand how folks feel without their saying a word. No wonder so many people seek you out when they are in trouble.

LIBRA

From September 23, 17:45 through October 24, 2:35

The Restless Romantic

The charms of the 1934 Libra are legendary. Although you're quick to fall in love, you've got a restless heart, even by Libran standards. There are simply too many romantic opportunities for you to stay focused on one person for too long. As you've gotten older, your wild heart may have been tamed, but there will always be a corner of it that yearns for greener pastures. Although some of your disappointed admirers may accuse you of being fickle, the truth is that you're really searching for a romantic ideal.

There is one topic you take very seriously: creativity. "Go forth and prosper" may be your motto. The year that you were born, the famous Dionne quintuplets were born in Canada. Whether your particular form of creativity is having lots of children or making works of art is immaterial. So long as you have something tangible to show for your efforts, you're satisfied. Sometimes your devotion to your creative pursuits can take time away from your friendships, which can cause resentment.

You have a profound love of the arts, and may have many friends who share this passion. Probably one of your favorite pastimes is debating your favorite artists, musicians, and writers. There's nothing you love more than a stimulating argument over your greatest love—creative expression.

As a general rule, you like to keep your relationships light. Intimacy may be difficult for you. Therefore, you gravitate toward people who take an intellectual, rather than emotional, approach to life. Geminis, Virgos, and Aquarians respect your rational handling of sticky situations, as do fellow Librans. It wouldn't hurt, though, to occasionally open up to the ones you love.

As a 1934 Libra, your greatest obstacle is your disinclination to settle down. As you've grown older, this has become less of an issue, although your eye may still wander from time to time. Still, this is part of your charm: your insatiable curiosity to find out what's new, different, and interesting. If you apply this open-minded approach to creative pursuits, you just might realize the happiness you've always sought.

➤ Read about your Chinese Astrological sign on page 838. ➤ Read about your Personal Planets on page 826. ➤ Read about your personal Mystical Card on page 856.

VIRGO
Your Personal Planets

YOUR LOVE POTENTIAL
Venus in Leo, Aug. 23, 20:32 - Sept. 11, 3:31
Venus in Virgo, Sept. 11, 3:32 - Sept. 23, 17:44

YOUR DRIVE AND AMBITION
Mars in Cancer, Aug. 23, 20:32 - Aug. 30, 13:42
Mars in Leo, Aug. 30, 13:43 - Sept. 23, 17:44

YOUR LUCK MAGNETISM
Jupiter in Libra, Aug. 23, 20:32 - Sept. 23, 17:44

World Events

Sept. 18 – The USSR is admitted to the League of Nations.

Sept. 20 – Italian actress Sophia Loren is born.

Italian actress Sophia Loren is born under the sign of Virgo

LIBRA
Your Personal Planets

YOUR LOVE POTENTIAL
Venus in Virgo, Sept. 23, 17:45 - Oct. 05, 7:55
Venus in Libra, Oct. 05, 7:56 - Oct. 24, 2:35

YOUR DRIVE AND AMBITION
Mars in Leo, Sept. 23, 17:45 - Oct. 18, 4:58
Mars in Virgo, Oct. 18, 4:59 - Oct. 24, 2:35

YOUR LUCK MAGNETISM
Jupiter in Libra, Sept. 23, 17:45 - Oct. 11, 4:54
Jupiter in Scorpio, Oct. 11, 4:55 - Oct. 24, 2:35

World Events

Oct. 4 - Enrico Fermi measures the speed of the neutron.

Oct. 9 - King Alexander of Yugoslavia is assassinated during a state visit to France.

1934

SCORPIO
Your Personal Planets

YOUR LOVE POTENTIAL
Venus in Libra, Oct. 24, 2:36 - Oct. 29, 7:36
Venus in Scorpio, Oct. 29, 7:37 - Nov. 22, 4:58
Venus in Sagittarius, Nov. 22, 4:59 - Nov. 22, 23:43

YOUR DRIVE AND AMBITION
Mars in Virgo, Oct. 24, 2:36 - Nov. 22, 23:43

YOUR LUCK MAGNETISM
Jupiter in Scorpio, Oct. 24, 2:36 - Nov. 22, 23:43

World Events

Oct. 24 – Mahatma Gandhi quits the Indian National Congress after disagreements over methods of practice.

Nov. 9 – American astronomer Carl Sagan is born.

American scientist and author Carl Sagan is born under the sign of Scorpio

SAGITTARIUS
Your Personal Planets

YOUR LOVE POTENTIAL
Venus in Sagittarius, Nov. 22, 23:44 - Dec. 16, 1:38
Venus in Capricorn, Dec. 16, 1:39 - Dec. 22, 12:48

YOUR DRIVE AND AMBITION
Mars in Virgo, Nov. 22, 23:44 - Dec. 11, 9:31
Mars in Libra, Dec. 11, 9:32 - Dec. 22, 12:48

YOUR LUCK MAGNETISM
Jupiter in Scorpio, Nov. 22, 23:44 - Dec. 22, 12:48

World Events

Nov. 28 – Bolivian President Daniel Salamanaca is ousted.

Dec. 10 – Italian existentialist playwright Luigi Pirandello wins the Nobel Prize for literature.

SCORPIO
From October 24, 2:36 through November 22, 23:43

The Spiritual Artist

No matter what obstacles you face in life, Scorpio of 1934, you will always manage to express yourself creatively, in one form or another. Whether it's doodling on a scratch pad at the office or painting into the wee hours of the morning, you're determined to channel your imagination in a positive direction. Art is a religion to you. Without it, life would have very little meaning. Growing up during the Great Depression, you felt an intense need for beauty in an otherwise bleak landscape. Art provided you with that beauty at a very early age.

As a 1934 Scorpio, you're somewhat of an escapist. You hate constraints of any kind, whether physical, emotional, or cultural. The year that you were born, bank robbers Clyde Barrow and Bonnie Parker were shot to death by lawmen in Louisiana. Gangster John Dillinger was killed by the FBI outside a Chicago movie theater. Not only that, Alcatraz prison opened its doors in San Francisco. These events may have planted a seed in your subconscious, one that flowered into a healthy fear of confinement in your later years. The minute you begin to feel constrained, out comes the paintbrush and canvas.

You have an intense, magnetic nature that draws people to you in droves. Once you make a friend, it's for life. Since you were young, pals probably confided their deepest secrets and fears; that's because very little shocks you. Coming of age during World War II, you learned very quickly that human beings are capable of some shocking behavior. No matter what transgressions your friends make, you're able to see their good qualities, too.

With regard to relationships, you've always had a great need for light-hearted friends. You may have a tendency to brood that isn't always healthy. Consequently, you've probably been drawn to a great many Geminis, Leos, Librans, and Sagittarians. These folks can lift you out of even the darkest moods.

Your greatest obstacle in life is pessimism. It may be difficult, but try to give people the benefit of the doubt. You've been blessed with a great love of art, which can easily hold depression at bay.

SAGITTARIUS
From November 22, 23:44 through December 22, 12:48

The Magnetic Go-Getter

By hook or by crook, the 1934 Sagittarius is determined to win. Ever since you were little, you probably imagined accepting a big award, appearing in spotlight before the public, or seeing your name in newspaper headlines. Leading a "normal" life holds very little appeal for you. You have big dreams, and will pursue them relentlessly, regardless of the obstacles before you. The year that you were born, baseball's African-American National League pitcher Satchel Paige broke Dizzy Dean's thirty-game winning streak. It is this kind of drive and determination that characterizes many of your exploits.

The secret to your success is your self-sufficiency. Whenever life becomes too hectic, you go off on your own. You probably gain a great deal of solace and energy through prayer, meditation, and other solitary pursuits. After you've recharged your batteries, you're raring to go again. Many people have probably commented that you have enough energy for an entire army, and that's true to a great extent.

When you're in competitive mode, you take on a do-or-die attitude that is very effective. Still, over the years, you've learned to accept the fact that you can't win every time. This lesson has not come easy to you, but it has made your victories much sweeter. The best contests focus not on annihilating your rivals but on testing your own limits. Remember that being a graceful loser is even more important than being a regular champion.

As far as relationships go, 1934 Sagittarians need friends who enjoy a bit of rivalry. Ariens, Geminis, and Leos probably dominate your social circle. You may have several Sagittarian pals, too, though these friendships may be plagued by the "anything you can do, I can do better" syndrome.

Your challenge is to overcome your need to be the best in everything. While it's true you have the heart of a champion, it's impossible to win every single contest. When the chips are down, engage in a hobby that serves no other purpose than to bring you pleasure. Your biggest strength is your appreciation for all life's delights, whether great or small.

➤ Read about your Chinese Astrological sign on page 838. ➤ Read about your Personal Planets on page 826. ➤ Read about your personal Mystical Card on page 856.

CAPRICORN

From December 22, 12:49 through December 31, 23:59

The Demanding Executive

As a 1934 December Capricorn, you don't want to be bothered with the little details. You'd rather be calling the shots, while others take care of the grunt work. From a very early age, you knew you were meant for greatness. This attitude may have caused some run-ins with authority figures, as you hate taking orders. Chances are you spent a great deal of time being disciplined by your elders because you failed to respect their age. You judge folks not by their rank, but by their ability.

Growing up during World War II, you were probably inspired by great leaders like Franklin D. Roosevelt, Winston Churchill, Charles de Gaulle, and Harry Truman. You've always been fascinated by larger-than-life figures. The year that you were born, Babe Ruth played his final game as a Yankee. To this day, Ruth is still considered one of the greatest baseball players of all time. It's this level of success that you've always yearned for, even at the expense of your relationships.

In your youth, you were probably quite bossy, although this tendency has mellowed over time. Deep down, you're convinced that you can do a better job than anybody else, and you're probably right. As you've grown older, though, you've learned to give both loved ones and colleagues a bit of breathing room. This has improved your relationships enormously, although you still wish you had an extra pair of hands so you could do all the work yourself.

Surrounding yourself with agreeable people is important to you. You particularly enjoy the company of Geminis, Virgos, Librans, and Pisceans. Don't forget to praise your loved ones for their talents, especially when they perform services for you. Taking such acts for granted can hurt even the healthiest relationships.

Your greatest challenge is your love of fame. While it's nice to be recognized for your accomplishments, it's also important to appreciate life's simpler pleasures. Slow down and smell the flowers, even if you have to force yourself to do so. Your biggest strength is your formidable power. There's nothing you can't do, so long as you set your mind to it.

CAPRICORN
Your Personal Planets

YOUR LOVE POTENTIAL
Venus in Capricorn, Dec. 22, 12:49 - Dec. 31, 23:59

YOUR DRIVE AND AMBITION
Mars in Libra, Dec. 22, 12:49 - Dec. 31, 23:59

YOUR LUCK MAGNETISM
Jupiter in Scorpio, Dec. 22, 12:49 - Dec. 31, 23:59

World Events

Dec. 26 – The Yomiuri Giants, Japan's first professional baseball team, is formed.

Dec. 28 – British actress Maggie Smith is born.

Clark Gable
February 1, 1901 - November 16, 1960

CLARK GABLE
Aquarius

In an era when actors were refined and almost dandified, Clark Gable toiled along unappreciated, in search of his niche and his success. It took time and the efforts of female mentors who became his wives, but ultimately Gable's confident, roguish masculine presence catapulted him to the top of the Hollywood hierarchy, earning him the nickname, "the King." To this day he remains an American icon of strength, substance and masculinity.

Gable was an Aquarius, a sign noted for its intelligence, innovation, and eccentricity. Aquarian men are among the most masculine, and because electric Uranus, ruler of Aquarius, contacted his Sun, planet of identity, it expanded further those Aquarian energies. Another contact from magnetic, sexy Pluto increased Gable's sex appeal, power and intensity. The ascendant is the point at which the rest of the world feels our energy; and as both of these intense planets contacted Gable's ascendant, he could walk into a room and immediately

project that quality of the sexy rogue, the thing that made him so appealing as Rhett Butler.

Mars is the planet of action, and it's also what defines a man's masculinity. Gable's Mars was in practical, earthy Virgo, making him reliable and capable. Because Mars was contacted by six of the remaining nine planets, his energy was quite electric, giving him many different variations on his masculinity—he was charged with energy and pizzazz!

Despite his winsome masculine presence, Gable's emotional life wasn't always happy. His Moon, the planet of emotions, was in Cancer, a sign noted for sensitivity and tenderness. A contact from chaotic Uranus made it difficult to create a stable emotional life, and Gable was quite devastated when he lost Carole Lombard, the love of his life, in a tragic plane crash. Venus, the planet of love, was in earthy Capricorn, and that could indicate an attraction to older, more experienced women. This tendency is further magnified by a contact from responsible Saturn,

and because both Saturn and Venus contact the sensitive Moon, we can see how those several early liaisons with older women provided the vehicle for Gable's career advancement.

➤ Read Marilyn Monroe's Star Profile on page 489.

1935

Bold New Perspectives: Saturn and Uranus

When 1935 began, two important planets were about to change signs, signaling a new cycle and the beginning of a new way of perceiving the world and responding to its challenges. Saturn, the planet of responsibility and the lessons of life, was moving from Aquarius, the sign of the social reformer to humanitarian-oriented Pisces. Saturn's final weeks in Aquarius were ultimately signified in maverick Louisiana Senator Huey Long's dictatorial control over his state, as well as his "Every Man is a King" social reform program. In mid-February when Saturn entered Pisces, the sign of selfless surrender, the focus of humanity's lessons shifted to managing the outcasts, victims, and underdogs of society. Neptune, ruler of Pisces, in the opposite sign of Virgo, reinforced the quality of this Saturn position.

This placement was admirably exemplified in the U.S. with the ratification of the Social Security Act, by which the weak and elderly would be cared for. This spot for Saturn is also connected with a fear of being victimized, or the desire to victimize others. In March, this dilemma was apparent on both sides of the fray as Western European allies fumbled for a response to long-feared German aggression.

Uranus, planet of disruption and sudden change, also changed locations in 1935, from assertive Aries to materialistic Taurus. In Aries since April 1927, Uranus's sojourn there coincided with the rise of fascism, an egotistical political movement reflecting Aries' potential for self-absorption. Until Uranus entered Taurus in March, fascist leaders were content to exert their influence on home soil. Once in Taurus, their attention turned to exerting power for material and territorial gains. German and Italian desire for land and wealth began to move in a much more worrying direction. Hitler made a grab for French territory in March, while in October, Italy's Mussolini invaded Abyssinia, or Ethiopia as it is now known.

A poster for the Gershwin musical "Porgy and Bess"

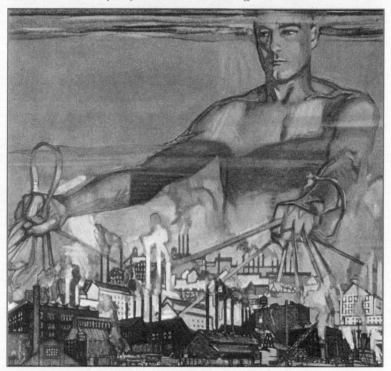

Roosevelt's New Deal policy

PROGRESS AGAINST DEMONS OLD AND NEW

Still battling depression, the global economy was in the throes of re-invention. The opening of the Iraq-Mediterranean oil pipeline and the introduction of driving tests in Britain signaled the growing incidence of car ownership. In the U.S., there was a welcome boom in the auto industry. The New Deal continued to revive the economy, putting citizens to work building roads and bridges. In Nazi Germany, the citizenship of Jews was revoked and the Luftwaffe was officially inaugurated. The three-year Chaco War between Bolivia and Paraguay over rights in the border region came to an end. The U.S. granted the Philippines self-government as a precursor to full independence within ten years. In France, the socialist Popular Front vowed to oppose fascism. There were anti-fascist demonstrations in Britain and Spain. Mussolini, the Italian fascist dictator, invaded Abyssinia (Ethiopia). Women's rights were recognized at an Istanbul world congress. The first practical radar system was produced by the British physicist Sir Robert Watson-Watt. In the arts, *Porgy and Bess* made its stage debut. Baseball icon Babe Ruth retired at age forty.

➤ Read Martha Graham's Star Profile on page 297.

CAPRICORN

From January 01, 0:00 through January 20, 23:27

The Resolute Realist

When you were born January Capricorn of 1935 there were faint signs of the light at the end of the Great Depression. Still, you probably learned to rely on your own initiative—you've never been handed anything. Your family may have taught you that while religious convictions are important, they don't necessarily put food on the table. Faith in religious or political dogma can often let you down—far better to rely on your own resourcefulness. In other words, you may hope for the best but prepare for the worst.

The urge to control your own fate led you to develop many practical skills. Driven by ambition, you no sooner reached one objective than you headed for the next. Mindful of a time when resources were precious you may have always held something back. Your skeptical outlook made you unlikely prey for get-rich-quick schemes and you are probably wary of the easy credit on offer today. The crooked path does not tempt you either; you know it rarely pays, as evidenced by Bruno Hauptman's trial for the murder of the Lindbergh baby during the month of your birth.

The automobile and oil industries were expanding when you were young. The oil pipeline from Iraq to the Mediterranean opened in your birth month, symbolizing your belief that the Earth's bounty is for our benefit. You may have worked in industry but your affinity for the land could also have led you to farming or real estate. Whatever the sphere, your urge to succeed was balanced by your concern for fair play. You may be combative but never underhand.

You may be more at home with what you can see and touch, but you also probably realized that suppressing emotions affects your level of performance. Stable relationships helped you to honor the importance of these emotions. Scorpios, Taureans, Virgos, and Cancerians may all have contributed to your emotional growth.

You may have learned through your life that the intangible can have a bearing on the physical and your challenge may have been to accept this. Your strength is your conviction that you alone are responsible for your failures and your successes.

AQUARIUS

From January 20, 23:28 through February 19, 13:51

The Intellectual Explorer

First impressions can be deceptive, Aquarius of 1935. You may come across as less unconventional than the typical Aquarian, but in your quiet way you may still have been ahead of your time. Modern life probably holds few fears for you as you have always ensured your control of your immediate environment. You are likely more able than many of your peers to accept the changes in attitude and behavior that have occurred during your lifetime. You may not often let your emotions cloud your judgment, therefore you might have understood the rationale behind Iceland's decision to legalize abortion this month—still a contentious issue. Your original thinking could help you see both sides of many difficult questions.

Your leadership qualities have been obvious from early on and you may have preferred to work on your own initiative. Intellectual inspiration probably motivated you at work and your ability to incorporate new methods could have put you at the cutting edge of your chosen field. The spectacular new techniques that have revolutionized existing industries—such as the innovative *March of Time* newsreel that presented an alternative to newspapers in the month of your birth—may have enthralled you.

While you may have relied on your flashes of insight for problem solving, you'd rather have the chance to study your interests in depth. You may find that you now have the time to investigate more esoteric and unusual disciplines that intrigue you.

You have always been happy mixing with a wide variety of people, their background of much less importance than their ideas. You have a talent for drawing people out of their shells and may still enjoy the company of younger people as well as your contemporaries. While you may be more comfortable with matters of the mind than those of the heart, you are a loyal and devoted partner. Generally you click with Librans, Geminis, Sagittarians, and Ariens.

Your refusal to be dominated is a great strength, but sometimes your adherence to your own path could have intimidated potential allies and may have been your greatest challenge to overcome.

➤ Read about your Chinese Astrological sign on page 838. ➤ Read about your Personal Planets on page 826. ➤ Read about your personal Mystical Card on page 856.

CAPRICORN
Your Personal Planets

YOUR LOVE POTENTIAL
Venus in Capricorn, Jan. 01, 0:00 - Jan. 08, 22:43
Venus in Aquarius, Jan. 08, 22:44 - Jan. 20, 23:27

YOUR DRIVE AND AMBITION
Mars in Libra, Jan. 01, 0:00 - Jan. 20, 23:27

YOUR LUCK MAGNETISM
Jupiter in Scorpio, Jan. 01, 0:00 - Jan. 20, 23:27

World Events

Jan. 8 – American rock-and-roll pioneer Elvis Presley is born.

Jan. 17 – The League of Nations votes to award Germany the area of the Saar Basin.

Bruno Hauptmann is sentenced to death for the murder of the Lindbergh baby

AQUARIUS
Your Personal Planets

YOUR LOVE POTENTIAL
Venus in Aquarius, Jan. 20, 23:28 - Feb. 01, 21:35
Venus in Pisces, Feb. 01, 21:36 - Feb. 19, 13:51

YOUR DRIVE AND AMBITION
Mars in Libra, Jan. 20, 23:28 - Feb. 19, 13:51

YOUR LUCK MAGNETISM
Jupiter in Scorpio, Jan. 20, 23:28 - Feb. 19, 13:51

World Events

Jan. 28 – Iceland becomes the first country to legalize abortion.

Feb. 13 – Bruno Hauptmann is found guilty of the kidnap and murder of the Lindbergh baby.

1935

PISCES
Your Personal Planets

YOUR LOVE POTENTIAL

Venus in Pisces, Feb. 19, 13:52 - Feb. 26, 0:29
Venus in Aries, Feb. 26, 0:30 - Mar. 21, 13:17

YOUR DRIVE AND AMBITION

Mars in Libra, Feb. 19, 13:52 - Mar. 21, 13:17

YOUR LUCK MAGNETISM

Jupiter in Scorpio, Feb. 19, 13:52 - Mar. 21, 13:17

World Events

Mar. 16 – Hitler rejects those parts of Versailles Peace Treaty which limit German arms.

Mar. 19 – In India, British troops are ordered to fire on a crowd of protesting Muslims; twenty-three are killed.

Dust storms in the U.S. cause severe destruction

ARIES
Your Personal Planets

YOUR LOVE POTENTIAL

Venus in Aries, Mar. 21, 13:18 - Mar. 22, 10:28
Venus in Taurus, Mar. 22, 10:29 - Apr. 16, 7:36
Venus in Gemini, Apr. 16, 7:37 - Apr. 21, 0:49

YOUR DRIVE AND AMBITION

Mars in Libra, Mar. 21, 13:18 - Apr. 21, 0:49

YOUR LUCK MAGNETISM

Jupiter in Scorpio, Mar. 21, 13:18 - Apr. 21, 0:49

World Events

Mar. 30 – Britain and Russia agree on measures to halt the threat of the German Reich.

Apr. 11 – Severe dust storms over much of the U.S. decimate wheat crops, force people to flee from their farm homes, and destroy livestock.

PISCES
From February 19, 13:52 through March 21, 13:17

The Devoted Dreamer

As a Pisces of 1935, your sympathetic outlook allows you to feel others' pain as though it were your own; sometimes you let your needs take second or even third place if necessary. Significantly, Robert Watson-Watt first demonstrated the usefulness of RADAR around the time of your birth. With your radar-like sensitivity you feel rather than think your way forward in life. As a result, you may have worked hard to expand your practical skills as a counterbalance to your vivid imagination. Routine doesn't come naturally to you and your own set of personal guidelines and criterion may be crucial—not unlike the driving tests introduced by the British government at this time.

You probably attempt to derive meaning from difficult circumstances but the miserable conflicts that have marred the twentieth century may have tested even your faith in human goodness. The current emphasis on materialism and individuality may be something you still find difficult to understand. In your personal relationships, however, you are always prepared to give others the benefit of the doubt. Working in the caring professions may have provided an outlet for your empathy while allowing you to maintain a sense of personal responsibility and balance.

Paradoxically, while you are generous toward the shortcomings of others you can be much harder on yourself. It may only be when family and work commitments are not so pressing that you are able to allow yourself the freedom to explore your own creative and imaginative impulses.

Devotion to family and friends may be central to your happiness and you have never shirked responsibility for their well being. Romantic and impulsive, you may have sometimes found that love's reality didn't always match your expectations. Scorpios, Cancerians, and Taureans may have provided the emotional security you craved, but other Pisceans may have been in tune with your more private world.

Sometimes prey to negative thinking your challenge has been to keep a balanced perspective. Your strength is your ability to retain your faith in life even when others disappoint you.

ARIES
From March 21, 13:18 through April 21, 0:49

The Inspired Original

The dramatic changes you have witnessed during your lifetime have dramatically colored your outlook, Aries of 1935. You weren't content to accept the value systems you inherited from your family and tradition; instead you continually sought to create your own. You may have suffered many setbacks and reversals, both personal and financial, and during the early seventies and nineties you may have had to dig deep into your reserves of energy. Like the ancient kingdom of Persia, which renamed itself Iran in the month of your birth, you may have expertly reinvented yourself when necessary.

Subtler than many Ariens, your fighting spirit may have benefited others more than yourself. You would have been a supportive and energizing colleague, able to transmit your enthusiasm and ideas. With your commitment to justice you would probably have approved of President Roosevelt's prospective New Deal and the approval by Congress of the Works Progress Administration. You could have found your professional niche as a spokesperson for those lacking a voice. In your private life you may still be ready to speak up on behalf of others.

Your initiative and motivation may have led you to go it alone professionally, but you may have preferred to join with others to maximize the potential for change. You may have used your financial skills to create and distribute funds for charity or the public services instead of fulfilling any greed on your part.

Dynamic and forthright in relationships you are happiest with people that respond to your warmth and spontaneity. You may find that you have less of a connection with more timid or introverted souls. Leos, Sagittarians, Geminis, and Aquarians likely have the energy and confidence to match yours.

In your haste to reach your objectives you may have concentrated on the forest while overlooking the individual trees. Your challenge Aries has been to remember that "the devil is in the detail." Your main strength has been your ability to draw on your deep reserves of energy. You may have come to realize that you function best when your back is to the wall.

► Read about your Chinese Astrological sign on page 838. ► Read about your Personal Planets on page 826. ► Read about your personal Mystical Card on page 856.

TAURUS

From April 21, 0:50 through May 22, 0:24

The Charming Dissenter

As a Taurus born in 1935, determination and dependability coexist with your desire to stand out. This may manifest simply in the way that you dress or act, but it is also clear that you are an original thinker and far from the usual traditional, conservative Taurean. You may have stubbornly pursued your own independent path, probably only conforming when it suited you. After all, independence and reform were in the air when you were born. The World Congress for Women's Rights concluded in Istanbul this month and an independence agreement was ratified by plebiscite in the Philippines.

Loathing hypocrisy you may have worked tirelessly to expose it. You understand the power of words and can be a thorn in the side of those that seek to conceal the truth. You could have been a formidable writer or broadcaster and once you state your position you are still as immovable as the Boulder Dam, completed this month. Even if you found yourself in a nine to five job you still maintained your high standards of honesty. The movement for social change of the sixties and seventies could have inspired you to take to the streets. However, your charm may have been a better instrument than any bomb to undermine institutions of which you disapproved.

You are responsive to beauty and art but creative self-expression may have had to take second place to professional, political, or family commitments. You may find that now that you are older there is more time to explore the artist within you.

You love to widen your knowledge of different cultures and you may continue to seek groups and organizations that can expand your horizons. In your personal relationships you can be very romantic—forever in love with love. While you crave intimacy and closeness, you also need some space to pursue your own interests. Partners that understand these twin needs can be found among Virgos, Pisceans, Cancerians, and Capricorns.

You usually prefer to take the lead and your challenge may have been to value the contribution of those that follow. Your strength is your stubborn refusal to take no for an answer.

GEMINI

From May 22, 0:25 through June 22, 8:37

The Agile Playmate

As a Gemini born in 1935 you may be proud of your social standing as well as your professional achievements. While you always may have had clear-cut goals, your progress was probably hampered by many setbacks along the way. Known as the communicator of the zodiac, Gemini, you may be amused to know that this month, Senator Huey Long of Louisiana delivered the U.S. Senate's longest speech on record, comprised of 150,000 words and lasting for fifteen hours. Your ideal career may have involved promotion and publicity for companies, organizations, or even individuals.

You may have been motivated by the prospect of a healthy bank balance and enhanced status when you were younger, but in later years you realized that you really felt most satisfied and comfortable when working in the service of others. You could have become a proficient teacher and, as you will always remain young in your outlook, you may still enjoy the company of different generations.

You may have taken on so much that setting aside time for yourself was a huge project in itself. Relaxation was not something that came easily but competitive sport would have provided an ideal outlet for your excess energy. Much-loved baseball player Babe Ruth announced his retirement when you were born.

A consummate flirt, you probably have attracted many admirers with your sparkling conversation. You may have played the game of love with verve but underneath the flippant façade you have been looking for a soul mate. You value constancy but you also hate to be confined and you may have felt most comfortable with Sagittarians, Aquarians, Leos, and Ariens.

You have spent much of your life carving out your identity through your work and, while ambition may have had its charms, you don't need to prove anything now. You may be exploring more spiritual and esoteric subjects. You are a chameleon and you have already played many roles. Your challenge may have been to see projects through all the way to the end. However, your strength may be that with your child-like enthusiasm you are able to turn the dreariest of chores into fun.

➤ Read about your Chinese Astrological sign on page 838. ➤ Read about your Personal Planets on page 826. ➤ Read about your personal Mystical Card on page 856.

TAURUS
Your Personal Planets

YOUR LOVE POTENTIAL
Venus in Gemini, Apr. 21, 0:50 - May 11, 22:00
Venus in Cancer, May 11, 22:01 - May 22, 0:24

YOUR DRIVE AND AMBITION
Mars in Libra, Apr. 21, 0:50 - May 22, 0:24

YOUR LUCK MAGNETISM
Jupiter in Scorpio, Apr. 21, 0:50 - May 22, 0:24

World Events

May 6 – The Works Progress Administration (WPA) is created by the executive order of President Roosevelt, to provide jobs for workers of all kinds.

May 19 – Col. T. E. Lawrence, known as "Lawrence of Arabia," dies from injuries received in a motorcycle accident near his home in Dorset, England.

Death of "Lawrence of Arabia"

GEMINI
Your Personal Planets

YOUR LOVE POTENTIAL
Venus in Cancer, May 22, 0:25 - June 07, 19:10
Venus in Leo, June 07, 19:11 - June 22, 8:37

YOUR DRIVE AND AMBITION
Mars in Libra, May 22, 0:25 - June 22, 8:37

YOUR LUCK MAGNETISM
Jupiter in Scorpio, May 22, 0:25 - June 22, 8:37

World Events

May 29 – The French liner *Normandie* sets out on her maiden voyage.

June 10 – Alcoholics Anonymous is founded in New York City.

293

1935

Death of American comedian Will Rogers

CANCER
From June 22, 8:38 through July 23, 19:32

The Wise Confidante

As a Cancer of 1935 it may have been hard for you to learn to look forward positively in life. As you have grown older, however, you have managed to adapt your traditional values to fit modern life. Your attachment to the good in the past does not prevent you from making sweeping personal changes if and when necessary, much like city elders in Amsterdam, who approved plans for that city's growth until the year 2000. You would have approved as the future is far less alarming if you feel you can maintain a degree of control.

You like to put your natural common sense and rich imagination to practical use. Others often turn to you for advice as your store of wisdom and ability to conceal disapproval make you an ideal sounding board, especially with finances. When it comes to spending you probably go for quality over quantity, preferring to save rather than squander. Symbolically, President Roosevelt ordered the building of a new federal gold vault this month and its name, Fort Knox, has become a byword for security.

You may have preferred to work for a large organization rather than go it alone as this could supply the job security with which you felt most comfortable. You probably don't envy today's work force as they grapple with professional insecurity. But work may have been mainly a means to an end as your home was where the real action really took place. Family life may have suited you and provided the base from which to launch your professional aspirations.

Along with your family you enjoy wide and diverse friendships. You may have found that you still love entertaining, your home often filled with guests. While unconventional types may intrigue you, you probably preferred a partner who reflected your need for commitment and a conservative attitude to family life. Taureans, Scorpios, Virgos, and Capricorns may all have contained qualities you appreciate.

Learning to adapt to the rapid changes during your lifetime may have been your challenge, Cancer of 1935. Your strength is your ability to draw on your deep reserves of wisdom and to pass this on to others.

LEO
From July 23, 19:33 through August 24, 2:23

The Steadfast Protector

As a Leo of 1935 you may have always felt that you had to be in control of your own destiny. Your ambition and will to succeed is equaled only by your stubborn refusal to fall into line and your career may have stalled when you clashed with those in authority. You have always been aware that agreeing with everybody else is sometimes the wrong thing to do. The noose was tightening in Germany when you were born. The Nazis staged a demonstration against German Jews, the swastika became the German national flag, and the government took control of the media.

While you may be an individualist, you need others to bounce your ideas off of as well as for the support and encouragement that they can offer. Personally creative, and with a feeling for public tastes, you could have excelled in the media. With a thoroughly modern outlook you would have been excited at the opportunities that the first Penguin paperback offered when it was published this month—more people now had a chance to enjoy both the classics and new works as the reduction in price meant the wider availability of books.

A stable home life has always helped you to pursue your dreams. Your awareness of life's dangers made you very protective of those you love. When you were starting out in the 1950s, the Cold War may have made you even more determined to keep your loved ones as safe as possible. Now that you are older, however, you may have come to realize that the best protection is to live every day as if it were your last and give your all.

You are a generous friend and partner, although your need for self-protection may mean that you require others to demonstrate their loyalty before you allow them a peek at the real you. You may demand devotion from your partner but you are more than willing to repay that devotion a thousandfold. You may find that you are most comfortable with Ariens, Sagittarians, Librans, and, unusually, Scorpios.

Your challenge in life may have been to accept that change is inevitable sometimes and not always bad. Your greatest strength is still your steadfast loyalty to those you love.

➤ Read about your Chinese Astrological sign on page 838. ➤ Read about your Personal Planets on page 826. ➤ Read about your personal Mystical Card on page 856.

VIRGO

From August 24, 2:24 through September 23, 23:37

The Conscientious Objector

As a Virgo born in 1935, your modesty and tendency to stay in the background has never prevented you from speaking out against injustice. The 1960s may have been an exhilarating time when you felt that the people had the power to make positive changes. When you were born, the Nuremberg Laws deprived German Jews of their citizenship—a horrifying example of the authoritarian attitude you detest.

You are convinced that ignorance, far from being bliss, is a real handicap. In addition to your own insatiable desire to know and understand, you are passionate about passing information to others. You may have been drawn to teaching or journalism where your ability to communicate in a fresh and engaging manner would have been a huge asset. You also may have found that you have a healing effect on others, perhaps leading you to great satisfaction in helping them to explore their own creative potential. The growing interest in complementary medicine and personal growth could have attracted your attention in later life.

But it was never all books and learning for you. Travelling may be one of your passions and the increased availability of car ownership when you reached your teenage years would have put more of the world within your reach. Speed probably thrills you and you may like to know that the millionaire Howard Hughes designed his own plane and flew it at an astonishing 352.46 mph this month.

Reaching the top may never have been as important for you, Virgo of 1935, as your relationships with others. You may have sacrificed your ambitions, choosing instead to encourage your friends and family. Your dedicated support makes you a caring and dependable partner. You may have found that you are most compatible with Taureans, Scorpios, Cancerians, and Pisceans who all appreciate and respond to you.

With a unique approach to practical matters, your strength may be your adaptability and willingness to guide others through their difficulties. Having the confidence to express your own creativity may have been your greatest challenge—you surely are your own biggest critic.

LIBRA

From September 23, 23:38 through October 24, 8:28

The Forthright Diplomat

You, Libra of 1935, like others of your sign, appreciate beauty and you may be interested to know that the Hayden Planetarium opened in New York this month, giving thousands the chance to examine the stars. This is a lovely symbol of your desire to transcend the limits of this world. Fairness and justice have been high on your list of priorities and your professional objectives have been guided by a strong sense of morality. Practicality may not be your strong point and you were most suited to a job where your ingenuity and inventiveness were an advantage. You may have come up with the ideas and allowed someone else to turn them into reality.

Libran concern with balance is well known; a sad, strange, and sinister example of this balance occurred when you were born. In New York, George Gershwin's musical *Porgy and Bess* premiered. With its poignant tale of the lives of African Americans in the South it may have helped open American eyes to the injustice within their own society. As an unpleasant counter balance, Nazi Germany banned jazz from its airwaves this year. You may have expressed your hatred of this kind of bigotry with uncharacteristic directness during your life.

Money may have never been an end in itself for you, Libra of 1935, and you may have seen cash as purely a means to acquire beautiful objects to enhance your environment. You can also be unexpectedly and spontaneously generous—your sense of fairness makes you ready to share your good fortune with others.

Relationships are likely still the prime source of interest for you. You are fascinated by people and constantly seek to learn all you can from your interactions with those from every walk of life. You have gained insight and a sense of completion from your most important connections. Often most comfortable with Aquarians and Geminis, you also love the warmth of fiery Leos and Sagittarians.

In aiming for perfection you may have overlooked your own special qualities Libra of 1935. Balancing this weakness is your flair for looking beyond the limits of the daily grind and continuing to reach for the stars.

➤ Read about your Chinese Astrological sign on page 838. ➤ Read about your Personal Planets on page 826. ➤ Read about your personal Mystical Card on page 856.

VIRGO
Your Personal Planets

YOUR LOVE POTENTIAL
Venus in Virgo, Aug. 24, 2:24 - Sept. 23, 23:37

YOUR DRIVE AND AMBITION
Mars in Scorpio, Aug. 24, 2:24 - Sept. 16, 12:58
Mars in Sagittarius, Sept. 16, 12:59 - Sept. 23, 23:37

YOUR LUCK MAGNETISM
Jupiter in Scorpio, Aug. 24, 2:24 - Sept. 23, 23:37

World Events

Sept. 13 - Millionaire Howard Hughes flies a plane designed by himself at 352.46 mph.

Sept. 15 - The Nuremberg Laws deprive German Jews of citizenship and make the swastika the official symbol of Nazi Germany.

Howard Hughes at the controls in the cockpit of "The Spruce Goose"

LIBRA
Your Personal Planets

YOUR LOVE POTENTIAL
Venus in Virgo, Sept. 23, 23:38 - Oct. 24, 8:28

YOUR DRIVE AND AMBITION
Mars in Sagittarius, Sept. 23, 23:38 - Oct. 24, 8:28

YOUR LUCK MAGNETISM
Jupiter in Scorpio, Sept. 23, 23:38 - Oct. 24, .8:28

World Events

Oct. 2 - Mussolini's forces invade Ethiopia.

Oct. 10 - *Porgy And Bess*, by George Gershwin, opens at the Alvin Theater in New York.

1935

SCORPIO
Your Personal Planets

YOUR LOVE POTENTIAL
Venus in Virgo, Oct. 24, 8:29 - Nov. 09, 16:33
Venus in Libra, Nov. 09, 16:34 - Nov. 23, 5:34

YOUR DRIVE AND AMBITION
Mars in Sagittarius, Oct. 24, 8:29 - Oct. 28, 18:21
Mars in Capricorn, Oct. 28, 18:22 - Nov. 23, 5:34

YOUR LUCK MAGNETISM
Jupiter in Scorpio, Oct. 24, 8:29 - Nov. 09, 2:55
Jupiter in Sagittarius, Nov. 09, 2:56 - Nov. 23, 5:34

World Events

Nov. 13 – Anti-British riots break out in Egypt.
Nov. 15 – The Commonwealth of the Philippines is inaugurated as Manuel Luis Quezon is sworn in as its first President.

Chiang Kai-Shek, President of China

SAGITTARIUS
Your Personal Planets

YOUR LOVE POTENTIAL
Venus in Libra, Nov. 23, 5:35 - Dec. 08, 14:35
Venus in Scorpio, Dec. 08, 14:36 - Dec. 22, 18:36

YOUR DRIVE AND AMBITION
Mars in Capricorn, Nov. 23, 5:35 - Dec. 07, 4:33
Mars in Aquarius, Dec. 07, 4:34 - Dec. 22, 18:36

YOUR LUCK MAGNETISM
Jupiter in Sagittarius, Nov. 23, 5:35 - Dec. 22, 18:36

World Events

Dec. 1 – Chiang Kai-Shek becomes President of China.
Dec. 1 – American comedian and film director Woody Allen is born.

SCORPIO
From October 24, 8:29 through November 23, 5:34

The Purposeful Visionary

 As a Scorpio born in 1935 you are a master of strategy, knowing that the best way to avoid the disorder you hate is to ensure that you have covered every angle. While this may mean that you aim for self-control, it doesn't mean that you have a narrow outlook. Far from it—you have striven all your life to expand your horizons through any means at your disposal. Travel may have been a real eye-opener and the opportunities we now enjoy for visiting distant lands are a great contrast to those when you were young.

You like to study subjects in great depth, always trying to get beneath the surface rather than skimming superficially. You would have soon seen that although the Nazis promised to remove anti-Jewish signs during the forthcoming Olympic Games in Berlin, it was only a cosmetic change and had no bearing on their real intentions.

Your ability to get right to the heart of the matter may have had a bearing on your choice of career. Medicine and research are both traditionally associated with Scorpio and both fields offer the chance to transform chaos into order by finding its root cause. Regardless of your career choice, it has been important for you to have professional control as well as personal. While you accept that people have a right to protest you may have been uneasy at the violent social upheavals of the late 1960s. You prefer change to be orderly, like the inauguration of the Philippines as an independent commonwealth at the time of your birth.

Paradoxically, while security is crucial in your closest relationships, you may have often been attracted to unconventional types. They may have broadened your perspective and helped you to relax and enjoy the moment. Generally though you have felt most at home with Capricorns, Pisceans, Virgos, and Taureans.

While life may not always have matched your high expectations you have probably remained optimistic. Your challenge may be to recognize that the things that really matter are just as often up close as they are far away. Your strength has been your desire to know the truth even if it wasn't what you'd hoped.

SAGITTARIUS
From November 23, 5:35 through December 22, 18:36

The Versatile Extremist

 As a Sagittarius of 1935 you share the philosophical outlook traditionally associated with your sign. You may have explored many avenues in your search for a religious or political framework that you could believe and follow. Always yearning to know more, your search is far from over. You may have veered from left to right or right to left over the years—at the time of your birth the question, "which side are you on," was being whispered all over the world. In China, the dedicated anti-Communist Chiang Kai-shek was named President and anti-Communism reared its head in many western countries, including the U.S.

You may have found it difficult to diligently follow one vocation. Your versatility and hatred of routine could have led you to try your hand at many different occupations. Always enthusiastic at first, you could find that your interest sometimes waned just as suddenly as it emerged. You probably hate to go without the material pleasures of life, however, and you would have always ensured that you weren't lacking an income for too long.

Your humor is one of your most obvious assets and even when things weren't looking too bright you could probably still summon up a smile. You may have found that during the 1970s, the decade dedicated to navel gazing, even you were tempted to look inward for the answers. Filmmaker Woody Allen, almost as famous for his fascination with analysis as his brilliant humor, was born this month with you.

Impulsive and ardent in relationships you may have found it hard to settle down. Even now you may have a twinkle in your eye and the ability to charm the birds from the trees. Anyone that took you on could have been in for an emotional roller coaster. You may have found that Ariens, Leos, Aquarians, and Geminis could hold your interest the longest.

Your expansive personality may have meant that you sometimes undertook way too much. Your challenge may have been to deliver exactly what you promised. However, your buoyancy and unfailing good cheer may be your strength and it may have metaphorically allowed you to "get away with murder."

➤ Read about your Chinese Astrological sign on page 838. ➤ Read about your Personal Planets on page 826. ➤ Read about your personal Mystical Card on page 856.

CAPRICORN

From December 22, 18:37 through December 31, 23:59

The Prudent Gambler

As a December Capricorn of 1935 your cautious and disciplined outlook is balanced and expanded by a willingness to take a few gambles. It's to be expected from your sign that your approach to money matters would be rational and clear-headed but you understand more than many fellow Capricorns that the occasional calculated risk can pay off. While you probably take the view that our fate is in our own hands, you may also accept that luck can play a part in our success.

You may be conservative where your finances are concerned but you are also a believer in progress. In December the National Council of Negro Women was formed in the U.S.—an example of how people with very little influence were beginning to realize that joining with others enabled them to initiate positive change. You probably wanted all the good things that a secure career offered but not if it meant trampling over someone else.

The new technology that has revolutionized the banking and business worlds would have delighted you. You have the mental agility to grasp new ideas and the practical skills to put them to use. You may never have thought of yourself as creative but you are—just not in the traditional sense. You would never stick with tradition for its own sake and you may have been the first one to try a new approach.

While you may have chosen a partner who shared your ambitions for a comfortable home and bank balance, mixing with people with very different lifestyles may have always had a stimulating effect. You probably love gourmet food and may be a fantastic cook. You may enjoy a good glass of wine as well but you are moderate in most of your appetites. You might be amused to know that when you were born, Russia announced that vodka consumption had plummeted by fifty percent since 1913. You probably are most compatible with Taureans, Virgos, Cancerians, and Scorpios.

You can sometimes be contrary, December Capricorn 1935, and your challenge may have been to learn how to co-operate with others less forward-looking. Your main asset is your faith that you've always got an ace in the hole.

1935

CAPRICORN
Your Personal Planets

YOUR LOVE POTENTIAL
Venus in Scorpio, Dec. 22, 18:37 - Dec. 31, 23:59

YOUR DRIVE AND AMBITION
Mars in Aquarius, Dec. 22, 18:37 - Dec. 31, 23:59

YOUR LUCK MAGNETISM
Jupiter in Sagittarius, Dec. 22, 18:37 - Dec. 31, 23:59

World Events

Dec. 23 – Charles Lindbergh and his family leave the U.S. for England.

Dec. 25 – Austrian composer Alban Berg dies.

Martha Graham
May 11, 1894 - April 1, 1991

MARTHA GRAHAM
Taurus

Martha Graham was the world's leading exponent of modern dance. A dancer and choreographer, she wanted to reach deep into the psyche and explore all of its complex and discordant themes, and then to embody them through movement that challenged the typical dance notions of fluidity and beauty. Graham liked to see motion that was angular, chaotic, filled with the intensity of emotion that inspired it. She understood the turmoil in the human soul and expressed it through dance. The works she created and the schools she founded were instrumental in making modern dance what it is today.

Graham was a Taurus, a sign noted for its earthiness. Her Sun, the planet of identity, was contacted by Uranus, planet of eccentricity, and that inspired her to reach beyond the ordinary in her mode of self-expression.

Mars, the planet of action, lay in her house of career, which makes a lot of sense in a career devoted to movement. In addition, other planetary contacts emphasized her career and

provided a sense of rhapsodic, dynamic energy whose promise was fulfilled in the intensity and lifelong devotion to dance and her lifelong devotion to the art form that defined her life.

With three planets contacting each other in Gemini in her first house, Martha was indeed a powerhouse and pioneer. Expansive Jupiter provided that larger-than-life, confident quality to her work. Intense Pluto provided a sexual undercurrent and raw force. And Neptune, planet of music and illusion, offered grace and the chameleon ability to translate an emotional impulse into movement.

Graham's personal life was far less important to her than her career, and although her Moon, planet of emotions, was located at the lower part of her chart where emotions thrive, a contact from eccentric Uranus inclined her to maintain independence and keep people at arm's length. Planets close to the cusp of the fourth house, the point of mother and the foundation of life, are quite intense and

significant. With her lunar energy at this point, it formed the wellspring of feelings that provided Graham with her inspiration for dance.

➤ Read Isadora Duncan's Star Profile on page 129. ➤ Read Josephine Baker's Star Profile on page 217.

1936

Communism and Fascism: Saturn-Neptune Connect

Throughout 1936, Saturn and Neptune opposed each other, reflecting a standoff between the competing political ideologies of communism and fascism. Saturn, associated with authoritarianism and control in political systems, was in a tension-inducing relationship with Neptune, champion of the underdog. Here Neptune symbolized communism, a political system that favors the worker. Nations took action to support or forestall these factions. Fascist Germany, Italy, and Japan consolidated their efforts and objectives by forming the Axis military alliance against the threat of communism. Austria's leader combined power under one political party and Spain was torn by a civil war between fascist nationalists and the ruling republican socialists.

With these planets in the balancing signs of healthy Virgo and idealistic Pisces, the challenge was on to find a way to avoid another World War and its atrocities. The Olympics seemed to present that opportunity: a peaceful gathering of athletes from around the world ideally devoid of politics. Held in Hitler's Berlin, the games were politicized, but this did not prevent spirits from soaring in response to other acts of international kindness and co-operation. Out of the darkest times, opportunity flies on gossamer wings. With Neptune in Virgo, the sign of employees and work, laborers in economically depressed nations received financial relief when they were mobilized to build war machines and armaments, an element of Saturn's tie with large equipment. As Saturn was in watery Pisces, the emphasis was on building naval strength.

King Edward VIII making his abdication speech

A poster for the Berlin Olympic Games depicting the Aryan Hero

Margaret Mitchell, author of "Gone With The Wind"

PRIZE-WINNING DREAMS

In 1936, physiologist Otto Loewi won the Nobel Prize for his discovery of the chemical transmission of nerve impulses. Loewi reported that his discovery occurred to him in two dreams. Awaking from the second dream, Loewi went directly to his laboratory to perform the experiments suggested to him. Scientists agree Loewi's story proves that ideas—including ideas for important scientific research—can indeed arrive during sleep. Imagination appears to be most active in the dream-state.

LOVE AND TRUTH BRIGHTEN A DARKENING WORLD

On the death of the English King George V, his son Edward VIII succeeded, but after eleven months, he abdicated for the sake of American divorcée Wallis Simpson. Meanwhile, Mussolini's invasion of Abyssinia resulted in victory over weak opposition. Germany, Italy, and Japan formed the Axis, raising fears of worldwide military action. The Nazis flaunted their disregard for the Versailles Treaty by invading the demilitarized Rhineland. The Spanish Civil War began between Nationalists and the incumbent republicans. In Paraguay, a totalitarian government took power. Hitler's hopes to prove Aryan superiority at Berlin's Olympic Games were marred when black U.S. athlete Jesse Owens won four gold medals, but even so German medal-winners figured prominently. Proving the success of his New Deal, Roosevelt was re-elected U.S. President by a landslide. The swing gave an exhilarating outlet for young people, while Margaret Mitchell's *Gone With the Wind* was published and Prokofiev's *Peter and the Wolf* received its premiere. Crystal Palace in London was destroyed by fire, while Frank Lloyd Wright's novel architectural style was all the rage.

➤ Read "Ancient Secrets of the Great Pyramid" by Jean Mars on page 305.

CAPRICORN

From January 01, 0:00 through January 21, 5:11

The Successful Independent

When you were born, January Capricorn of 1936, economic hardship was still prevalent but there were signs of improvement. As a result, you may have always believed that faith in the future combined with no-nonsense hard work is the best recipe for success.

A media first was announced right at the very start of the year in which you were born. This month, *Billboard* magazine published the first "Hit Parade", listing the sales performance of current albums. Little did they know how enduring a tradition the Billboard chart would become and—more importantly in your eyes Capricorn—what an enormous global money-spinner the music industry would become. Meanwhile, your sound business sense and ability to make decisions quickly would have made you a brilliant salesperson. Your ability to spot a window of opportunity and then go straight through it also may have meant you preferred to be in at the start of a new company rather than join a more established one.

Whatever projects you have undertaken it may have been important for you that success or failure was in your hands. Nothing would have irritated you more than being held back by the inefficiency or recalcitrance of others. You have always had the courage to stick by your decisions and take the consequences.

You may have been just as single-minded in your attitude to relationships. When you liked the look of someone you probably homed in on your target regardless of your chances of success. You may be more of a realist than a romantic but you have probably experienced sudden, inexplicable passion that seemed to appear out of nowhere. You may have been attracted to those that could offer emotional security but also honored your independent spirit. Generally, you may have had your most satisfying relationships with Taureans, Scorpios, Virgos, and Pisceans.

You hate to be misunderstood and you are generally plain speaking, but occasionally you may have confronted situations head-on when a more subtle approach would have worked better. Your enduring strength is that you continue to welcome new concepts and ideas.

AQUARIUS

From January 21, 5:12 through February 19, 19:32

The Detached Idealist

As an Aquarius born in 1936, it has probably been crucial for your self-esteem that any success you have achieved was entirely a result of your own hard work. You may have striven extra hard to develop your natural skills and to learn new ones. Concentration may have sometimes been difficult, as there are just so many fascinating subjects to explore.

Aquarius is often linked to science and you may be interested to know that radium E, the first radioactive substance to be produced synthetically, made its debut this month. However, your inventiveness may have been best used in the creative world, perhaps in film, photography, or animation. Felix the Cat, a new member of the popular cast of cartoon characters amusing the public, was introduced this year, too.

Staying too close to your roots may have felt wrong and carrying forward the same values as your parents may not have appealed to you. An example of this is the British monarchy— King George V died in 1936 and was succeeded immediately by his eldest son. Perhaps your unconventional outlook sometimes made you feel like a fish out of water while growing up. The 1960s counterculture that explored new ways of living together may have initially seemed baffling but then probably began to make perfect sense. Now that you are older you may still feel slightly out of step with your peers.

Love may have been difficult to sustain when you were younger—there seemed to be so many enticing prospects available. You may have felt that you needed a best friend rather than a partner, as friendship is very high on your list of priorities. You are capable of great loyalty but, loathing petty jealousy, you needed a partner who was as independent as yourself. You may have always found that Sagittarians, Geminis, Ariens, and possibly Virgos understood you best.

You may have wandered far and wide in your search for understanding, only to find the answer was right under your nose. Accepting this may have been your challenge. Always contributing to the greater good rather than just lining your own pockets may be your greatest strength.

▶ Read about your Chinese Astrological sign on page 838. ▶ Read about your Personal Planets on page 826. ▶ Read about your personal Mystical Card on page 856.

1936

CAPRICORN
Your Personal Planets

YOUR LOVE POTENTIAL
Venus in Scorpio, Jan. 01, 0:00 - Jan. 03, 14:15
Venus in Sagittarius, Jan. 03, 14:16 - Jan. 21, 5:11

YOUR DRIVE AND AMBITION
Mars in Aquarius, Jan. 01, 0:00 - Jan. 14, 13:58
Mars in Pisces, Jan. 14, 13:59 - Jan. 21, 5:11

YOUR LUCK MAGNETISM
Jupiter in Sagittarius, Jan. 01, 0:00 - Jan. 21, 5:11

World Events

Jan. 18 – British author and Nobel Prize winner Rudyard Kipling dies.

Jan. 20 – King George V dies; he is succeeded by Edward VIII.

Death of British author Rudyard Kipling

AQUARIUS
Your Personal Planets

YOUR LOVE POTENTIAL
Venus in Sagittarius, Jan. 21, 5:12 - Jan. 28, 13:59
Venus in Capricorn, Jan. 28, 14:00 - Feb. 19, 19:32

YOUR DRIVE AND AMBITION
Mars in Pisces, Jan. 21, 5:12 - Feb. 19, 19:32

YOUR LUCK MAGNETISM
Jupiter in Sagittarius, Jan. 21, 5:12 - Feb. 19, 19:32

World Events

Feb. 8 – Jawaharlal Nehru is elected President of the Indian National Congress.

Feb. 11 – Charlie Chaplin's *Modern Times* opens in London.

1936

PISCES
Your Personal Planets

YOUR LOVE POTENTIAL
Venus in Capricorn, Feb. 19, 19:33 - Feb. 22, 4:13
Venus in Aquarius, Feb. 22, 4:14 - Mar. 17, 14:52
Venus in Pisces, Mar. 17, 14:53 - Mar. 20, 18:57

YOUR DRIVE AND AMBITION
Mars in Pisces, Feb. 19, 19:33 - Feb. 22, 4:08
Mars in Aries, Feb. 22, 4:09 - Mar. 20, 18:57

YOUR LUCK MAGNETISM
Jupiter in Sagittarius, Feb. 19, 19:33 - Mar. 20, 18:57

World Events

Feb. 26 - Ferdinand Porsche's Volkswagen (the "people's car") is introduced.

Mar. 7 - Hitler violates the treaties of Versailles and Lorcano by invading the Rhineland.

Hitler sends troops into the Rhineland

ARIES
Your Personal Planets

YOUR LOVE POTENTIAL
Venus in Pisces, Mar. 20, 18:58 - Apr. 11, 0:40
Venus in Aries, Apr. 11, 0:41 - Apr. 20, 6:30

YOUR DRIVE AND AMBITION
Mars in Aries, Mar. 20, 18:58 - Apr. 01, 21:29
Mars in Taurus, Apr. 01, 21:30 - Apr. 20, 6:30

YOUR LUCK MAGNETISM
Jupiter in Sagittarius, Mar. 20, 18:58 - Apr. 20, 6:30

World Events

Mar. 25 - Britain, France, and the U.S. sign a naval agreement.

Apr. 18 - The Pan-Am Clipper begins regular passenger flights from San Francisco to Honolulu.

PISCES
From February 19, 19:33 through March 20, 18:57

The Dramatic Visionary

You may have been more capable of focusing on your goals and objectives than more traditional Pisceans, Pisces of 1936. Conventional education may not have suited you; your way of looking at life may be slightly off center. You probably preferred to go along with the creative flow rather than trying to force it in your direction. Nevertheless, you have an uncanny knack for homing in on vital information without always having to go the long way.

Your experience with education may have led you to explore the ways in which it can be improved and mentor those who don't fit into the standard model. You may know intuitively that there is no right or wrong way of learning and everyone has his or her own individual way of absorbing and understanding information. Your ability to tap into the collective mood could also have made advertising or public service a good career choice.

It may be irrelevant what field you chose, so long as you could act independently but also be of benefit to the wider society. You may have always loved to travel, your imagination stimulated by exploring different cultures. It's become a great deal easier since your youth and it may amuse you that the much-loved Volkswagen was introduced this month—perhaps the one good thing to come out of Nazi Germany. Sadly, the ill-fated *Hindenberg* airship also took its maiden flight this month.

It may have been in relationships that the more sensitive and dreamy side of you emerged. Your compassion is easily aroused especially if those you care about are unhappy in some way. You may still let your needs lag far behind those of your family and friends. You may have found mutual support with Taureans, Virgos, Capricorns, and Scorpios.

Your challenge may have been to overcome any disappointment at not achieving everything you hoped for in life. The 1980s may have been the decade when you reached your peak professionally but then you possibly changed direction to explore the diverse interests you never had time for before. Your strength is still the dramatic flair you bring to the mundane tasks of everyday life.

ARIES
From March 20, 18:58 through April 20, 6:30

The Bold Adventurer

As an Aries born in 1936 you have always relied on your own initiative, vitality, and sense of adventure to get you out of many a tight spot. You may firmly believe that you make your own luck and have often taken risks knowing that they may not always pay off. However, you probably did not take the kind of risks that appealed to racketeer Lucky Luciano whose crimes finally caught up with him this month.

You could have been a pioneer in any chosen field and may have operated best when allowed to do things your way. Having someone breathing down your neck was always guaranteed to get you hot under the collar. Routine work may have held little attraction for you—you liked to provide the impetus and then let someone else deal with the details. Sometimes though you may have found that you had to put some kind of structure in place before you lost track of the main objective. Working to a self-imposed routine or perhaps learning to delegate may have been the answer.

Being a big fish in a small pond would never have been enough for your ambitious aspirations. The big wide world probably always held more of an attraction than your local neighborhood for you. Symbolically, Pan-Am Airline began operating regular passenger flights from San Francisco to Honolulu in Hawaii this month. Probably convincing your family that all the time you spent away from home to further your career would ultimately benefit them could have been a career in itself.

You were most likely an enthusiastic player in the game of love. You may have loved the warmth and security that a family provided but you needed a lot of space in which to operate. You may find that you enjoy your family even more now, especially when your children or grandchildren tell you of their hopes and dreams. You may have felt most at home with Leos, Sagittarians, Aquarians, and other Ariens.

You may sometimes have alienated potential allies by your impatient attitude; learning to employ tact and patience may have been your greatest challenge. Your strengths have always been your resourcefulness and belief in mind over matter.

➤ Read about your Chinese Astrological sign on page 838. ➤ Read about your Personal Planets on page 826. ➤ Read about your personal Mystical Card on page 856.

TAURUS

From April 20, 6:31 through May 21, 6:06

The Patient Creative

You may have found that everyday life left you little time to explore the wider world, Taurus of 1936. In any case, you probably found quite enough to fascinate you in your immediate location and using your imagination inside your own head. You may have earned your living in a variety of different ways, using your talent for communicating or your brilliant financial skills. While Taureans generally prefer to make their way slowly and steadily, you may have found that self-improvement came most readily when you pounced on unexpected opportunities.

Your tendency to be preoccupied with your own thoughts might have found an outlet in creative writing. Many novelists and poets produce their best work by writing directly from their own experience. A. E. Housman, the poet who wrote so beautifully about the English landscape, died this month. Your roots could be very strong and you may feel that you function best from home territory. You would have sympathized with Emperor Haile Selassie who was forced by Mussolini's invasion of Abyssinia, now named Ethiopia, to flee his own country.

The need to provide for your family may have meant that your creativity was put on hold and only emerged later in life. Even at an older age you may have faced the common artistic dilemma—keeping your creations to yourself or allowing the wider world to peek. Creativity comes in many forms; with your affinity for nature you may find that the simple pleasure of creating a garden is fulfillment enough.

You are probably the kind of person who prefers a few reliable and trusted friends that you have known for a long time to a whirl of brief acquaintances. It may have been important that you felt valued in your closest relationships and an ideal partner would have been as tolerant of your quirks as you are of theirs. You may have felt comfortable with Virgos, Capricorns, Pisceans, and Cancerians.

Normally placid, you can sometimes fly off the handle and your challenge may have been learning self-control during these moments of fury. Your strength is your willingness to take care of business before you indulge in your own pleasure.

GEMINI

From May 21, 6:07 through June 21, 14:21

The Eloquent Communicator

As a Gemini of 1936 you have a fantastic ability to take in information, quickly assimilate it, and then pass it on to others. Teaching, writing, and the media in general were all fields that may have attracted you. Television's easy availability from the 1950s onward would have delighted you and you must be in seventh heaven now that satellites beam hundreds of programs into our living rooms.

Your timing may be your greatest asset. Your ability to be in the right place at the right time may have been responsible for much of your professional success. Those people that had tickets for the world heavyweight championship fight between U.S. favorite Joe Louis and German Max Schmeling would not have known that they were going to witness a piece of sporting history this month—unexpectedly Louis was knocked out.

You've probably still got tons of energy and hate to be restricted. Driving is often a Gemini pleasure and today's endless road restrictions may infuriate you. You may be amused that the prototype for parking meters was invented now. Gemini Paul McCartney even wrote a song about them. But while you have never lost any of your interest in the world and its ways you may find that a whole new source of fascination has opened up recently. You could now be applying your versatile mind to figuring out the meaning of life rather than the mastering of it.

Ever optimistic in your relationships with others you are a quick-witted and playful companion. When it came to settling down with just one partner the number of available candidates was probably the only problem. You may still be delighted at the prospect of new playmates and all you can learn from them. You may have found commitment without shackles with Aquarians, Sagittarians, Ariens, or other Geminis.

With so many interests your challenge may have been to take the time to learn more than just the superficial facts about each subject. However, your greatest strength has to be your continuing desire to know about as many things as possible. That may be a contradiction but that is the essence of you Gemini of 1936.

➤ Read about your Chinese Astrological sign on page 838. ➤ Read about your Personal Planets on page 826. ➤ Read about your personal Mystical Card on page 856.

1936

TAURUS
Your Personal Planets

YOUR LOVE POTENTIAL
Venus in Aries, Apr. 20, 6:31 - May 05, 10:52
Venus in Taurus, May 05, 10:53 - May 21, 6:06

YOUR DRIVE AND AMBITION
Mars in Taurus, Apr. 20, 6:31 - May 13, 9:16
Mars in Gemini, May 13, 9:17 - May 21, 6:06

YOUR LUCK MAGNETISM
Jupiter in Sagittarius, Apr. 20, 6:31 - May 21, 6:06

World Events

Apr. 30 – British poet A. E. Housman dies.
May 9 – Mussolini annexes Ethiopia and proclaims himself Emperor.

Death of Soviet author Maxim Gorky

GEMINI
Your Personal Planets

YOUR LOVE POTENTIAL
Venus in Taurus, May 21, 6:07 - May 29, 21:38
Venus in Gemini, May 29, 21:39 - June 21, 14:21

YOUR DRIVE AND AMBITION
Mars in Gemini, May 21, 6:07 - June 21, 14:21

YOUR LUCK MAGNETISM
Jupiter in Sagittarius, May 21, 6:07 - June 21, 14:21

World Events

June 8 – Parking meters are invented.
June 14 – Soviet author and revolutionary Maxim Gorky dies.

YOUR LOVE POTENTIAL

Venus in Gemini, June 21, 14:22 - June 23, 8:15
Venus in Cancer, June 23, 8:16 - July 17, 17:50
Venus in Leo, July 17, 17:51 - July 23, 1:17

YOUR DRIVE AND AMBITION

Mars in Gemini, June 21, 14:22 - June 25, 21:52
Mars in Cancer, June 25, 21:53 - July 23, 1:17

YOUR LUCK MAGNETISM

Jupiter in Sagittarius, June 21, 14:22 - July 23, 1:17

World Events

July 14 - Britain begins the mass production of gas masks—one for each citizen—in anticipation of World War II.

July 18 - Gen. Francisco Franco lands in Cadiz with foreign legion troops from Morocco, signaling the start of the Spanish Civil War.

Jesse Owens breaks the record for the 200-meter race at the Olympics in Berlin

LEO
Your Personal Planets

YOUR LOVE POTENTIAL

Venus in Leo, July 23, 1:18 - Aug. 11, 2:10
Venus in Virgo, Aug. 11, 2:11 - Aug. 23, 8:10

YOUR DRIVE AND AMBITION

Mars in Cancer, July 23, 1:18 - Aug. 10, 9:42
Mars in Leo, Aug. 10, 9:43 - Aug. 23, 8:10

YOUR LUCK MAGNETISM

Jupiter in Sagittarius, July 23, 1:18 - Aug. 23, 8:10

World Events

Aug. 1 - Adolph Hitler opens the 11th Olympic Games in Berlin.

Aug. 25 - Sixteen of Stalin's political opponents, all said to be Trotskyites, are executed.

CANCER

From June 21, 14:22 through July 23, 1:17

The Shrewd Conservative

As a Cancer born in 1936 your driving ambition may have been to put down solid roots. Often you may have experienced the disruption of moving homes during your childhood, but it may also just be that you are at your best knowing that you have a stable home and family behind you. While you may prefer life to be comfortable rather than dramatically eventful, you adjust rather more easily than many fellow Cancerians do. You have probably coped rather well with the changes during your lifetime, even if you'd rather that they hadn't always happened quite so quickly. You use both your intuition and your shrewd common sense to help you with tricky decisions. A bit like Rhett Butler and Scarlett O'Hara in *Gone with the Wind*, published this month, you hang on to what you can, but let go of what you can't.

You have probably been very hard working, sometimes to the point of overload. You may not know but it was only in 1936 that the U.S. federal law stipulating a forty-hour working week was approved. You may have considered working for yourself but your need to feel secure may have meant you chose not to attempt it. With your creative but disciplined mind you may have worked in advertising or even publishing—possibly cookbooks as Cancer and cooking often go together.

Traditionally Cancer is linked to mothering and whatever vocation you chose you would have nurtured and protected it like a mother hen. Your caring nature could have led you toward a profession where you took care of others. You are undoubtedly sympathetic but you may be a believer in tough love rather than endless handouts.

Generally sociable, you may enjoy mixing with creative people who lead a very different lifestyle. Family comes first, however, and you may get the most pleasure from catching up with your children and grandchildren. You may have found Virgos, Pisceans, Taureans, and Scorpios like you—both conventional and broad minded.

Occasionally you may have tended toward pessimism and overcoming it may have been a challenge. Your strength could be an uncanny sixth sense that is increasing with age.

LEO

From July 23, 1:18 through August 23, 8:10

The Confident Strategist

As a Leo of 1936 you really come into your own when all eyes are focused on you. You may always have been the first to try something new, but this did not mean that you didn't love to share your discoveries with your friends.

Both sport and entertainment appealed to your colorful sense of drama. The eleventh Olympic Games opened in Berlin this month. Hitler hoped the Games would be a glorious demonstration of Aryan achievement. No one told Jessie Owens, however, the brilliant African-American athlete who stole the show, much to Hitler's annoyance.

While you have never liked blending into the background, you may have been an expert at concealing your motivations and the real effort involved in producing results. You wanted praise for your accomplishments, not for the methods used in achieving them. You have probably made things look far too easy, although your casual appearance conceals a tenacious will.

You could have succeeded in many careers but you probably always enjoyed an element of risk. You may have been a player in the financial markets as your love of strategy and your ability to conceal your hand would have been a great asset. However, accumulating money could have been a sideline compared to the thrill you got simply from the process of speculation.

In your relationships with others you also prosper. Your stylish manner and your warmth may have brought you endless admirers. You are comfortable expressing your emotions and sometimes have found that they have more importance than material things. While you may sometimes have been happy to live on a diet of kisses and starlight, your partner may have demanded a much more practical approach. You have probably found that you have been most compatible with Ariens, Sagittarians, Librans, and Pisceans.

Sometimes you may have been carried away by your fantasies, and keeping your feet on the ground while continuing to gaze up at the heavens may have been a challenge. Your strength may be that while you love to be adored you are never afraid to reciprocate—those you love are never left in the slightest doubt.

➤ Read about your Chinese Astrological sign on page 838. ➤ Read about your Personal Planets on page 826. ➤ Read about your personal Mystical Card on page 856.

VIRGO

From August 23, 8:11 through September 23, 5:25

The Quiet Crusader

Your practical skills ands your diplomatic approach have probably made you the most efficient of organizers, Virgo of 1936. Whatever vocation you followed, those skills have been instrumental in your success. Your modesty means that you could sometimes find praise a bit hard to handle and you may have occasionally allowed others to take the credit for your efforts. Your satisfaction came from a job well done rather than a pat on the back or a golden handshake. You could have been particularly suited to working in the public services, where you could feel that your contribution was vital.

While not overly materialistic, you may have found it difficult to relax if your home was threatened or insecure. It was important for you to set down your own roots as soon as you could. You could still feel intense sympathy for anyone that lost his or her home. In Berlin by this year, twenty-five percent of Jewish properties had been seized by the state—boding ill for the future. While you may appear quite docile and even dreamy, you would be prepared to fight for your family's security.

You are inspired by the diversity in the world and like nothing more than to immerse yourself in foreign culture. You emerge refreshed and renewed, ready to appreciate the wealth of interest in your everyday life, such as the fact that English aviatrix, Beryl Markham, became the first woman to fly solo east-west across the Atlantic this month.

You may appear self-contained but you are probably not a loner. What's more, you can take the responsibility that comes with relationships very seriously. Your quiet charm may have meant you were more attractive to others than you realized. A stable family life may have been crucial to your peace of mind and you may have felt most comfortable with Cancerians, Scorpios, Capricorns, and Taureans.

Letting your actions speak for themselves may have been your general attitude and your challenge may have been to accept your full measure of credit. You are generous to a fault and your main strength is that you are willing to share your good fortune with others.

LIBRA

From September 23, 5:26 through October 23, 14:17

The Agreeable Debater

As a Libra of 1936 you share the traditional Libran qualities of cooperation, fair-mindedness, and impartiality. However, you are also quite outspoken and sometimes impulsive. You probably love a debate and, knowing that you can't make an omelet without breaking eggs, you sometimes like to stir up a little controversy. Radio was first used during a presidential campaign this year and may have led to many of the kinds of discussions you love as more and more people were able to hear the politicians speak in their own homes.

You have great organizing ability. Your willingness to start at the bottom and work your way steadily up in your chosen career would have impressed your superiors. Your good taste would have made you an asset to the art world and you may have had an eye for the next big thing before it happened. In your own home you may enjoy being surrounded by beautiful things and prefer them to be unique one-offs.

Your local neighborhood probably holds almost as much interest for you as the wider world and you may have been involved in local politics or interest groups from time to time. This year also President Roosevelt gave the FBI the authority to pursue Fascists and Communists as well as common criminals. Growing up in the 1940s you may have been intrigued and a little alarmed at the idea of "Reds under the Bed."

Socially you may prefer small groups of friends or cozy one-to-ones rather than large noisy parties. You may feel a little nervous or overwhelmed if there is too much noise and too many people. In close relationships you loved the mystery of romance and probably still do. However, good conversation is something you really crave and you and your partner may still find plenty to talk about. You may generally feel most comfortable with Sagittarians, Geminis, Aquarians, and Leos.

Maintaining a balance between your work and your home life may sometimes have been a bit tricky. Your challenge may have been to create realistic routines and stick to them. Your knack of drawing people out and making them feel comfortable is one of your greatest strengths.

➤ Read about your Chinese Astrological sign on page 838. ➤ Read about your Personal Planets on page 826. ➤ Read about your personal Mystical Card on page 856.

VIRGO
Your Personal Planets

YOUR LOVE POTENTIAL
Venus in Virgo, Aug. 23, 8:11 - Sept. 04, 10:01
Venus in Libra, Sept. 04, 10:02 - Sept. 23, 5:25

YOUR DRIVE AND AMBITION
Mars in Leo, Aug. 23, 8:11 - Sept. 23, 5:25

YOUR LUCK MAGNETISM
Jupiter in Sagittarius, Aug. 23, 8:11 - Sept. 23, 5:25

World Events

Sept. 7 – American rock legend Buddy Holly is born.

Sept. 21 – The German army begins a series of maneuvers.

American rock legend Buddy Holly is born under the sign of Virgo

LIBRA
Your Personal Planets

YOUR LOVE POTENTIAL
Venus in Libra, Sept. 23, 5:26 - Sept. 28, 18:35
Venus in Scorpio, Sept. 28, 18:36 - Oct. 23, 4:59
Venus in Sagittarius, Oct. 23, 5:00 - Oct. 23, 14:17

YOUR DRIVE AND AMBITION
Mars in Leo, Sept. 23, 5:26 - Sept. 26, 14:50
Mars in Virgo, Sept. 26, 14:51 - Oct. 23, 14:17

YOUR LUCK MAGNETISM
Jupiter in Sagittarius, Sept. 23, 5:26 - Oct. 23, 14:17

World Events

Sept. 24 – Creator of the Muppets Jim Henson is born.

Sept. 26 – Spanish rebels take Toledo.

1936

SCORPIO
Your Personal Planets

YOUR LOVE POTENTIAL
Venus in Sagittarius, Oct. 23, 14:18 - Nov. 16, 18:35
Venus in Capricorn, Nov. 16, 18:36 - Nov. 22, 11:24

YOUR DRIVE AND AMBITION
Mars in Virgo, Oct. 23, 14:18 - Nov. 14, 14:51
Mars in Libra, Nov. 14, 14:52 - Nov. 22, 11:24

YOUR LUCK MAGNETISM
Jupiter in Sagittarius, Oct. 23, 14:18 - Nov. 22, 11:24

World Events

Nov. 1 – Mussolini describes the alliance between Italy and Germany as an "axis" running between Rome and Berlin.

Nov. 2 – The BBC's television service is inaugurated—the world's first regular high-definition service.

The BBC's television service officially opens

SAGITTARIUS
Your Personal Planets

YOUR LOVE POTENTIAL
Venus in Capricorn, Nov. 22, 11:25 - Dec. 11, 14:50
Venus in Aquarius, Dec. 11, 14:51 - Dec. 22, 0:26

YOUR DRIVE AND AMBITION
Mars in Libra, Nov. 22, 11:25 - Dec. 22, 0:26

YOUR LUCK MAGNETISM
Jupiter in Sagittarius, Nov. 22, 11:25 - Dec. 02, 8:38
Jupiter in Capricorn, Dec. 02, 8:39 - Dec. 22, 0:26

World Events

Nov. 25 – Germany signs a pledge with Japan, agreeing support against the Soviet Union.

Dec. 10 – Edward VIII abdicates the British throne over his affair with twice-divorced American Wallis Simpson.

304

SCORPIO
From October 23, 14:18 through November 22, 11:24

The Passionate Enigma

As a Scorpio of 1936 you've always been aware of the need to make life as secure as possible for those you love. You probably cannot be shocked and you have an awareness that not everyone is always on the level. You have probably been pretty good at concealing your motivations until the time was right to reveal your master plan. When you were born Mussolini, in a bid to put himself center stage, announced that the alliance between Italy and Germany was now an axis.

You may have found yourself working in typical Scorpio occupations like research, the military, or even as an undercover agent. However, your contrary streak may have meant that you hated any kind of external authority. You could be hard enough on yourself as it was. It has always been crucial for your self-esteem that you could control your career path and you may have felt it was better for you to be your own boss. It may have meant hard work—but that has never proved to be a problem.

You could lighten up sometimes, however, and take a break from building your empire. You love to be entertained, especially if there is a deeper message underneath the main story line. While film and television may have their faults, you may love the way that you can just get lost and let your imagination have free reign. The BBC made the very first high definition television broadcast this month, paving the way for the fantastic pictures we are now able to see.

Before you let others in to your world you have to trust them; nothing hurts you more than betrayal. You need to feel secure and you may find that your closest relationship has become even more passionate and intense as the years have gone by. Nonetheless, a partner with an independent streak may have been the one to finally claim you. Virgos, Pisceans, Capricorns, and Cancerians are often the people with whom you have the most in common.

Your ability to direct your formidable energy to where it can be of the most use is probably one of your most enduring strengths. Your challenge may have been to distinguish between being independent and just plain obstinate.

SAGITTARIUS
From November 22, 11:25 through December 22, 0:26

The Mental Traveler

As a Sagittarius born in 1936 you are broad-minded and forward-looking. You love to socialize and your big-hearted enthusiasm is only enhanced by your surprising courtesy. You may occasionally be a bit tactless but at least you are aware of it—for the most part.

Curious about what is happening around you, you always have been so busy with what is up close that the wider world remains a tantalizing mystery. You could be the classic armchair traveler, and to help you in this quest, *Life* magazine published its first issue in 1936 and brought the outside world a lot closer to people that never had the opportunity—or wanted—to travel further than the next town.

You may have spent your working life in a variety of different jobs but you were probably happiest when you were doing something you cared about deeply. You give the impression of being laid back but you have strong opinions and principles, which you have stuck by all your life. Edward VIII, the new King of England who had not even been crowned, was forced to make a momentous choice between love and duty. Very few people have to decide between their partner and their job but you probably would have gone for the partner like Edward, as people may be more important than status to you. Regardless, your optimism and ingenuity would probably be working overtime trying to figure out how you could have both.

Friendship comes in many guises and you are always intrigued by other people's stories. You've always known that you can learn something from everyone and that humanity has rarely let you down. You may have sometimes liked to rail against the restrictions of family life but you probably wouldn't want to face life alone and you are probably quite comfortable letting your partner know how much you value them. Aquarians, Leos, Ariens, and Geminis would all have known how to handle your wandering ways.

You have a relaxed attitude to life and your challenge may have been in taking the opportunity to stretch yourself mentally. Your undoubted strength is your optimism and ability to bounce back from your setbacks.

➤ Read about your Chinese Astrological sign on page 838. ➤ Read about your Personal Planets on page 826. ➤ Read about your personal Mystical Card on page 856.

CAPRICORN

From December 22, 0:27 through December 31, 23:59

The Careful Speculator

Not all Capricorns are happy to be a small cog in the great wheel and you, Capricorn of 1936, have aimed to stand out from the crowd. You may have those qualities of self-discipline and determination that usually aid success, but you've also always looked at life from a very wide perspective. You may be pretty passionate about making money but you are also passionate about fairness. When you were born, workers staging sit-down strikes shut down seven of General Motors' automobile plants. You may have soon learned that an unhappy workforce has the potential to bring disaster to even the most thriving business. If you have found yourself in a position of power during your life you probably used it wisely.

Whether you were your own boss or worked for large companies you have always been capable of making snap decisions. In general, however, you preferred to go over every question with a fine-toothed comb before you reached your conclusions. Attention to detail and a good deal of foresight may have characterized every enterprise you undertook.

It's never been all work and no play for you, and you may have enjoyed unusual and even risky leisure pursuits. You may have an interest in science and technology even if you work in a completely different field. The first time radioactive isotopic medicine was administered was in Berkley, California this month. You may have often wanted to get away from the rat race and, while long holidays may have appealed, a few hours of uninterrupted contemplation may have been all you needed.

Although you are a generous friend and partner you can sometimes be shy when expressing your feelings. With your courtesy and good manners you are the consummate gentleman or real lady and may feel that the best way to express your love is through actions rather than words. Generally, you are most compatible with Cancerians, Scorpios, Virgos, and Taureans.

Your challenge, December Capricorn, may be to sometimes let others know when you are anxious—they may be able to help. Your strength is your ability to respond cheerfully to those that seek your help.

1936

CAPRICORN
Your Personal Planets

YOUR LOVE POTENTIAL
Venus in Aquarius, Dec. 22, 0:27 - Dec. 31, 23:59

YOUR DRIVE AND AMBITION
Mars in Libra, Dec. 22, 0:27 - Dec. 31, 23:59

YOUR LUCK MAGNETISM
Jupiter in Capricorn, Dec. 22, 0:27 - Dec. 31, 23:59

World Events

Dec. 24 – The first radioactive isotope medicine is administered in Berkeley, California.

Dec. 30 – Seven General Motors plants are closed by sit-down strikes in a dispute over collective bargaining.

The Pyramids of Giza, Egypt

Special Feature
Ancient Secrets of the Great Pyramid
by Jean Mars

The Great Pyramid of Giza, one of the Seven Wonders of the World, continues to baffle experts as to its origins and the manner in which it was constructed. In the course of the last century, the ancient monument has inspired many new scientific, religious, and mystical beliefs about its architectural achievement, the ancient Egyptians, and by extension, the origins of the human race. A wide variety of experts and mystics developed intriguing and often contradictory explanations about the Great Pyramid, and none of them could be proven right or wrong.

The big question remains: how could the ancient Egyptians have possessed such sophisticated astronomy, geography, mathematics, and engineering skills in their construction and design of this pyramid? This mystery is even more puzzling given the fact that traditional science recognizes only primitive hunters and gatherers as the cultures predating the ancient Egyptians and their Sumerian neighbors.

Let's consider some of the amazing details surrounding this architectural marvel. Even though it is the oldest and largest single structure on Earth, the Great Pyramid is also the most accurately oriented, with its four huge facets laid out almost exactly due north, south, east, and west. In addition, the physical location of the Great Pyramid is extraordinary since it is found at the exact geometric center of the world's land mass. Its latitude (east-west line) is right on the longest land parallel, extending through Africa, Asia, and America. Its longitude is on the longest land meridian, going through Asia, Africa, Europe, and Antarctica. There is only one building site and one structure on Earth that offers this unique placement.

The Great Pyramid also reveals the advanced mathematical knowledge applied in its design. The base perimeter measures 36,524 inches and the height of the structure is 5,813 inches. What is so interesting about these two numbers is that they are proportionally the same as the radius of a circle to its circumference, and

define the ratio pi as 3.14159. Plus, by moving the perimeter's decimal over two places, one gets the number of days in a year (365.24), which is as exact as modern science can figure it.

Uncanny precision of design and coordinates makes the Great Pyramid the world's best example of sacred architecture, which means that it acts as a bridge between heaven and Earth. For in addition to its unique geographical location, the Great Pyramid also embodies a symbolic relationship to the larger cosmos, notably in the alignment of its airshafts with the star Sirius, which is part of the Orion constellation.

(Continued on page 313)

➤ Read about UFOs in "The Extraterrestrial Highway" on page 465. ➤ Read "Gaia's Mystical Power Places" on page 745. ➤ Read "The First New Age Psychic: Edgar Cayce" on page 265.

1937

Unfriendly Relations: Venus, Mercury, and Mars in Discord

U.S. workers on strike

Even though the tense relationships found between the slow-moving planets—Saturn, Uranus, Neptune, and Pluto—of the past few years were fading, the other planets were now spotlighted, correlating with dramatic actions in the human sphere. Venus, the planet of love and relationships; Mercury, the planet of communication; and Mars, the planet of action and war, did just that in 1937 when each made its closest orbital swing by the earth in March through June. This coincided with a time when opposing factions had the opportunity to clear up differences but often found it difficult to come to agreements. This tendency was highlighted by Venus's contact with rebellious Uranus in potentially stubborn Taurus, while Mercury and Mars faced off with each other across the heavens, increasing the likelihood of alienation. In the U.S., workers shut down automobile plants across the Midwest, but striking auto workers and Chrysler officials came to an agreement that ended a massive sit-down strike as Venus's conciliatory energies received emphasis. Violence, the most extreme expression of alienation, was expressed in the destruction of Guernica by German bombing during the Spanish Civil War, as Venus slipped back into angry Aries—her least favorite place.

During the same period, Saturn, the planet of rules and responsibilities, ended its journey through compassionate Pisces, signaling a shift from when the focus was on victims and victimization. This energy was exemplified in the selfless generosity of Andrew Mellon, who founded the National Art Gallery with $40 million in art and funds for all to enjoy. In April Saturn entered self-oriented Aries, suggesting a change toward more selfish, but also more blatant, actions. Nazi forces in Germany took increasingly brutal action and in Soviet Russia, Stalin continued his purges, killing real and imagined rivals, however unlikely they were to challenge his power.

The Spanish Civil War became the dress rehearsal for the impending World War, as Saturn made a supportive connection with potentially subversive Pluto. The revolutionary forces, symbolized by Pluto, were being covertly aided by Germany and Italy, the dictatorial governments of which can be linked to the disciplinary side of Saturn.

The Spanish Civil War

The Hobbit by J.R.R. Tolkien is published

GLOBAL CONFLICT LOOMS OMINOUSLY

The world braced itself for global conflict, as war raged in China and Spain. Spain's Civil War became a symbol of fascist aggression and a proxy for the struggle between free and authoritarian governments. The German Luftwaffe was accused of, but denied, bombing the historic Basque town of Guernica. Stalin's second round of purge trials resulted in high-level executions. The necessities of war created strange bedfellows, as Nationalist and Communist forces united in China to stop Japan's advance on Chinese soil. King George VI was crowned in London, with daughter Elizabeth as his heir. U.S. workers flexed their muscles, striking successfully in the automotive, steel, and entertainment industries, the three new powerhouses driving the economy. A near-complete braincase of Java Man was discovered. Joe DiMaggio became the people's hero with his first grand slammer. *Of Mice and Men* and *The Hobbit* were published, animation took off in Hollywood, and the Marx Brothers spent *A Day at the Races*. With little vegetation to hold waters after the Dust Bowl drought, the U.S. Great Plains flooded, destroying the homes of nearly one million.

➤ Read "Ancient Secrets of the Great Pyramid" by Jean Mars on page 305.

CAPRICORN

From January 01, 0:00 through January 20, 11:00

The Genial Philosopher

You were born, January Capricorn of 1937, with high expectations and strong motivations. Confident and combative in your dealings with others, your parents may have striven to set standards of decency and excellence. They also may have noted your obstinate will. American citizens who served in the Spanish Civil War despite a government ban symbolized a similar determination around the time of your birth. While Capricorns can be conservative, you are not afraid to tread your own path.

Your natural self-control helps you maintain a cheerful exterior during times of disappointment. Your desire to explore life's mystery could lead you to travel the Earth in your quest for personal growth. You need to make up your own mind about the big questions and this could lead to a lifelong interest in politics and religion.

Political and religious beliefs can be dangerous, however. Leon Trotsky, one of the architects of the Russian Revolution, fled to Mexico this month to plead for an impartial trial of his alleged crimes against Joseph Stalin after falling out of favor. While you may not have had to face that kind of challenge you are likely to continue to stand up for your beliefs no matter what the circumstances. You may no longer be in full time work but your agile mind shows that you won't be content with a lazy retirement. You may still be involved in business, convinced of your unique contribution.

You may have delighted in somewhat unusual people who had their own slant on life. You may not be one of life's true eccentrics but you aren't a typically staid Capricorn either. You meet each new acquaintance with friendly curiosity. Your intimate relationships, while passionate, could tend toward possessiveness. You may find most compatibility with Virgos, Taureans, Pisceans, and Scorpios.

Your challenge, January Capricorn of 1937, could be to learn how to really listen without prejudice, as you are sometimes so convinced of your own viewpoint that you could miss vital information. Your strength is your ability to brush off disappointments and face each new challenge with joy.

AQUARIUS

From January 20, 11:01 through February 19, 1:20

The Orderly Eccentric

You were born, Aquarius of 1937, with your sign's typical curiosity and interest in all things modern—this month DuPont patented nylon, an exciting and versatile new material. Your early home life may have been slightly unorthodox and your family may have stressed the importance of individual freedom of expression. They may have been comforted by Hitler's recent pledge to honor the neutrality of Holland and Belgium.

While you may march to the beat of a different drum, you are careful and cautious when expressing your views. While you are unafraid to defend your ideas, you may not wish to court controversy. Nevertheless, you have a lot to say to those that care to listen and you can set out your arguments with order and precision. You may have a deep-rooted conviction that personal freedom is of overwhelming importance and you are willing to support those who fight against oppression.

Your career may have been marked by single-minded determination to succeed. Although you are able to harness and concentrate your energy you may not always have gained the financial rewards you deserved. You may sometimes have hesitated when contemplating a professional risk. Luckily, you have an innate spiritual awareness and faith that everything will turn out right in the end. You probably learned early on to value happiness over material success.

You may have had to work hard at combining your love of freedom with your need for intimacy. The seeming shackles of commitment will be easier to bear if your partner shares your outlook. An open mind and a willingness to continually refresh your relationship could be two vital requirements in relationships for you. More practical than many Aquarians, you could be willing to stick with it during the bad times. You may have found love with someone born under Gemini, Libra, Aries, or Sagittarius.

One challenge you may continue to face is maintaining confidence in your ability to communicate, Aquarius of 1937. You are perceptive and opinionated and it's a pity to conceal it. Your strength is your faith in the humanity's underlying goodness.

➤ Read about your Chinese Astrological sign on page 838. ➤ Read about your Personal Planets on page 826. ➤ Read about your personal Mystical Card on page 856.

1937

CAPRICORN
Your Personal Planets

YOUR LOVE POTENTIAL
Venus in Aquarius, Jan. 01, 0:00 - Jan. 06, 3:17
Venus in Pisces, Jan. 06, 3:18 - Jan. 20, 11:00

YOUR DRIVE AND AMBITION
Mars in Libra, Jan. 01, 0:00 - Jan. 05, 20:38
Mars in Scorpio, Jan. 05, 20:39 - Jan. 20, 11:00

YOUR LUCK MAGNETISM
Jupiter in Capricorn, Jan. 01, 0:00 - Jan. 20, 11:00

World Events

Jan. 9 – Trotsky and his wife arrive in Mexico, seeking an impartial retrial for alleged crimes against Stalin.

Jan. 13 – The U.S. forbids Americans from serving in the Spanish Civil War.

Capture of Bilbao by Franco's forces

AQUARIUS
Your Personal Planets

YOUR LOVE POTENTIAL
Venus in Pisces, Jan. 20, 11:01 - Feb. 02, 10:38
Venus in Aries, Feb. 02, 10:39 - Feb. 19, 1:20

YOUR DRIVE AND AMBITION
Mars in Scorpio, Jan. 20, 11:01 - Feb. 19, 1:20

YOUR LUCK MAGNETISM
Jupiter in Capricorn, Jan. 20, 11:01 - Feb. 19, 1:20

World Events

Jan. 30 – Hitler gives an address guaranteeing the neutrality of Belgium and Holland.

Feb. 16 – Du Pont obtains a patent on a versatile new plastic called nylon.

1937

PISCES
Your Personal Planets

YOUR LOVE POTENTIAL
Venus in Aries, Feb. 19, 1:21 - Mar. 09, 13:18
Venus in Taurus, Mar. 09, 13:19 - Mar. 21, 0:44

YOUR DRIVE AND AMBITION
Mars in Scorpio, Feb. 19, 1:21 - Mar. 13, 3:15
Mars in Sagittarius, Mar. 13, 3:16 - Mar. 21, 0:44

YOUR LUCK MAGNETISM
Jupiter in Capricorn, Feb. 19, 1:21 - Mar. 21, 0:44

World Events

Mar. 15 – The first blood bank is opened at the Cook County Hospital in Chicago.

Mar. 16 – Communist and fascist riots break out throughout Paris.

Trotsky calls for a new revolution to overthrow Stalin

ARIES
Your Personal Planets

YOUR LOVE POTENTIAL
Venus in Taurus, Mar. 21, 0:45 - Apr. 14, 4:18
Venus in Aries, Apr. 14, 4:19 - Apr. 20, 12:18

YOUR DRIVE AND AMBITION
Mars in Sagittarius, Mar. 21, 0:45 - Apr. 20, 12:18

YOUR LUCK MAGNETISM
Jupiter in Capricorn, Mar. 21, 0:45 - Apr. 20, 12:18

World Events

Apr. 14 – The musical *Babes In Arms* opens in New York, launching songs such as "The Lady Is A Tramp."

Apr. 18 – The exiled Trotsky declares that a new revolution is necessary to overthrow Joseph Stalin and his Soviet bureaucracy.

PISCES
From February 19, 1:21 through March 21, 0:44 ▶

The Idealistic Reformer

As a Pisces of 1937 you have had to face dramatic changes in your lifetime with fortitude. Your sympathetic nature has withstood a severe battering as the brutality of war during your childhood gave way to the rise of materialism in your adult life. Although you may sometimes be disillusioned, you try to retain your basic faith in human nature.

While you probably possess artistic and creative talent, you may have turned to science as a career. Medicine would have offered the opportunity to combine your need to serve with your visionary outlook. Blood banks became such an integral component of hospital resources that it's hard to comprehend that the first one was opened in Chicago during your birth month. Pisceans rarely have been described as radical but you have a knack for asking awkward questions and pinpointing hypocrisy wherever you find it. You can be a thorn in the side of those that seek to hide the truth.

You may have felt that your ultimate contribution to society was pursuing quiet enlightenment in your chosen field. You may feel uneasy with violent upheaval, preferring to improve the establishment from within, but you are unafraid to fight for your beliefs. While possibly in sympathy with 1960s protesters you were more likely to be waving a first-aid kit than a banner. When you were born, rioting in Paris between Communists and Fascists led to many deaths and injuries.

Your relationships may be characterized by a tendency to place friends and partners on a pedestal. You are a romantic and may sometimes be saddened when reality falls short of your ideal. Having had your fingers burnt once or twice you quickly learned to distinguish between fantasy and the real deal. You may have found that Cancerians, Scorpios, Virgos, and Taureans all met your requirements.

You may sometimes fear that life is moving too quickly. Trying to maintain your integrity in our superficial age could be an ongoing struggle and your challenge is to look optimistically to the future. You may find that your power to see the positive qualities in humanity is your main strength.

ARIES
From March 21, 0:45 through April 20, 12:18

The Brave Struggler

While many of your generation, Aries of 1937, may be apprehensive of the speed of progress, you are ever-ready to embrace change. Never one to avoid a challenge you continue to stride forth, certain that you are invincible. You have cheerfully overcome the obstacles that have littered your path. Your impetuosity may have contributed to some of your setbacks, but you'd rather pick yourself up and start again than waste time mired in regret. You much prefer to live in the present—the past is a country you'd rather not revisit.

Your natural courage could have been put to good use in the fire or ambulance services or you may have been drawn to the military. There has been enough conflict during your lifetime to satisfy even the most aggressive Arien. You may have struggled with the discipline required by many such institutions, however, as you are always happier giving rather than taking the orders.

Financial and professional reversals may have dogged your life, but they have enabled you to empathize with those in difficulties. When you were born, economic depression was a fact of life. Movies and music allowed people to forget their troubles but only for a short time. Those enduring cartoon characters Daffy Duck and Elmer J. Fudd made their first appearances in 1937 and the Rodgers and Hart musical *Babes in Arms* contained the classics "My Funny Valentine" and "The Lady Is A Tramp."

Emotionally vibrant, Aries of 1937, the thrill of the chase will always intrigue you. You may be devoted to your partner but you can still enjoy a little harmless flirting. You could be happiest when surrounded by people that match your childlike enthusiasm. Leos, Sagittarians, Geminis, and Aquarians are all capable of singing from the same song sheet.

Your impetuosity is an asset but sometimes you can be a little domineering. Your need to win can sometimes backfire. By incorporating the needs of others into your plans you may find that the journey is more fun than the destination. Your greatest strength could be your willingness to understand changing circumstances and adjust accordingly.

▶ Read about your Chinese Astrological sign on page 838. ▶ Read about your Personal Planets on page 826. ▶ Read about your personal Mystical Card on page 856.

TAURUS

From April 20, 12:19 through May 21, 11:56

The Flexible Controller

Adjusting to the dramatic changes of your lifetime may not have been easy for you, Taurus of 1937, but your success is a tribute to your realism and your strength of character. You may prefer to control your immediate environment and you have come to understand that burying your head in the sand usually works against you. You may have learned to face life's dilemmas head on. German warplanes bombed the Basque town of Guernica this month, demonstrating to western governments that Fascism was not going to disappear because they were ignoring it. Earlier refusals to assist the beleaguered Spanish government signaled an unwillingness to counter the military threat posed by Germany, effectively giving them a green light.

While you may have preferred the peaceful life you often have had to take a more assertive stance. The best form of defense is offense and you have been unafraid to raise your voice in anger if your family or your principles were threatened.

Travel may excite you but you are equally enthralled by mental exploration. Zealously continuing to pursue knowledge, you are unwilling to give up on a subject until you have exhausted every angle. Your ability to create order out of chaos made you an asset in any form of administration. Your foresight and ability to detect public enthusiasms could have led you toward publishing. Margaret Mitchell's epic *Gone with the Wind* won the Pulitzer Prize this month. Its theme of stoic adjustment to dramatically altered circumstances could be the story of your life.

While you may claim friends from all walks of life your closest relationships probably are based on shared values of loyalty and a love for the good life. Personal betrayal is one crime you can never forgive. Capricorns, Virgos, Cancerians, and Scorpios could have met your desire for a comfortable home and loving family.

Your ability to spot the glint of gold at the bottom of the pan is one of your greatest strengths. One challenge that may have followed you in life is a tendency to sometimes browbeat others rather than convince them with measured argument.

GEMINI

From May 21, 11:57 through June 21, 20:11

The Joyful Seeker

As a Gemini born in 1937 the polarized thinking of your formative years would surely have gone against the grain. Film star Jean Harlow, who provided a tragic example of someone who tried to challenge the hypocritical morality of the film industry, died this month. Tired of struggling to suppress your unconventional way of seeing the world you probably breathed a huge sigh of relief as the 1960s unfolded. You may have gleefully embraced the breaking down of ideological and artistic boundaries as you and your peers explored new ways of relating to one another and the wider world. You may continue to maintain your youthfully inquisitive outlook into maturity.

Your fascination with what motivates others could have led you to explore diverse forms of therapy, either as a career or for your own personal growth. The startling rise to prominence of the new technology must have thrilled you and you may still be following developments with interest. You may be one of the original silver surfers on the Internet.

You may have a spiritual awareness not typical of your sign; part of your quest is to figure out your place in the grand plan. You may have explored many belief systems. Your need to challenge orthodoxy for its own sake may keep you outside the religious mainstream, however, even if you are convinced that we are far more than the sum of our parts.

That you can harbor deep and passionate feelings may not always be apparent from your light-hearted persona. You could be capable of giving up a great deal in the pursuit of love. Like King Edward VIII, who sacrificed his kingdom to be with his chosen partner the previous year, your security could be found in your partner rather than bricks and mortar. Librans, Aquarians, Leos, and Sagittarians could all share your mental agility and love of novelty.

Your refusal to compromise can sometimes result in some lonely periods. Being a pioneer often means a solitary path and your challenge may have been to search long and hard for your ideal home. Your determination to stubbornly maintain your self-reliance has been your main strength.

➤ Read about your Chinese Astrological sign on page 838. ➤ Read about your Personal Planets on page 826. ➤ Read about your personal Mystical Card on page 856.

1937

TAURUS
Your Personal Planets

YOUR LOVE POTENTIAL
Venus in Aries, Apr. 20, 12:19 - May 21, 11:56

YOUR DRIVE AND AMBITION
Mars in Sagittarius, Apr. 20, 12:19 - May 14, 22:51
Mars in Scorpio, May 14, 22:52 - May 21, 11:56

YOUR LUCK MAGNETISM
Jupiter in Capricorn, Apr. 20, 12:19 - May 21, 11:56

World Events

Apr. 27 – German warplanes attack the town of Guernica in Spain; the fascists deny responsibility.

May 6 – The German dirigible *Hindenburg* bursts into flames over New Jersey, killing thirty-six of the people on board.

The German dirigible "Hindenburg" ablaze

GEMINI
Your Personal Planets

YOUR LOVE POTENTIAL
Venus in Aries, May 21, 11:57 - June 04, 6:40
Venus in Taurus, June 04, 6:41 - June 21, 20:11

YOUR DRIVE AND AMBITION
Mars in Scorpio, May 21, 11:57 - June 21, 20:11

YOUR LUCK MAGNETISM
Jupiter in Capricorn, May 21, 11:57 - June 21, 20:11

World Events

June 3 – In France, the Duke of Windsor marries Wallis Simpson.

June 7 – The "Platinum Blonde" Jean Harlow dies at the age of twenty-six.

1937

CANCER
Your Personal Planets

YOUR LOVE POTENTIAL

Venus in Taurus, June 21, 20:12 - July 07, 21:12
Venus in Gemini, July 07, 21:13 - July 23, 7:06

YOUR DRIVE AND AMBITION

Mars in Scorpio, June 21, 20:12 - July 23, 7:06

YOUR LUCK MAGNETISM

Jupiter in Capricorn, June 21, 20:12 - July 23, 7:06

World Events

July 2 - Female aviator Amelia Earhart disappears during a flight over the Pacific.

July 11 - American musical composer George Gershwin dies.

Amelia Earhart's Lockheed plane is lost at sea

LEO
Your Personal Planets

YOUR LOVE POTENTIAL

Venus in Gemini, July 23, 7:07 - Aug. 04, 20:13
Venus in Cancer, Aug. 04, 20:14 - Aug. 23, 13:57

YOUR DRIVE AND AMBITION

Mars in Scorpio, July 23, 7:07 - Aug. 08, 22:13
Mars in Sagittarius, Aug. 08, 22:14 - Aug. 23, 13:57

YOUR LUCK MAGNETISM

Jupiter in Capricorn, July 23, 7:07 - Aug. 23, 13:57

World Events

Aug. 8 - Japanese occupy the key Chinese city of Peking.

Aug. 8 - American actor Dustin Hoffman is born.

CANCER
From June 21, 20:12 through July 23, 7:06

The Devoted Protector

You possess an indomitable will but also the conviction that life is fragile and precious. Composer George Gershwin died prematurely and aviatrix Amelia Earhart disappeared in the skies. Seemingly unassuming, you can summon up enormous reserves of energy when your security is threatened. Family life is traditionally a Cancerian concern and current levels of divorce may be difficult for you to accept. Nevertheless, you probably have come to realize through your faith in human nature that, while the family unit may be reinvented, qualities of loyalty and integrity remain intact.

Because of your conciliatory approach and your respect for others' feelings you may avoid most confrontation. You probably don't enjoy debate for its own sake and argue from an emotional rather than an intellectual base. You are not afraid, however, to fly in the face of popular fashion if your principles are at stake. Your stubborn independence must sometimes have left you feeling like an alien within your own culture.

Born at a time of economic uncertainty you never forget the true value of money and may have had more than one financial iron in the fire. Your ability to nurture may have led you to any profession that involves taking care of people's needs. An affinity with the public would have made you an enterprising shopkeeper. Whatever professional path you have followed you know that success is usually ten percent inspiration and ninety percent perspiration.

Relationships are where you truly flourish. It may take a little while for you to open up and you probably favor a few trusted friends over an army of acquaintances. Your commitment to mutual support is without question and makes you a rock in troubled times. Scorpios, Pisceans, Taureans, and Capricorns may share your faith in the importance of family.

You have lived through a time of changing attitudes and shifting morals. Your challenge may be to retain your respect for traditional values while recognizing that not all new ideas are wrong or dangerous. Your greatest strength could be your empathy with those less fortunate.

LEO
From July 23, 7:07 through August 23, 13:57

The Loyal Maverick

You were born, Leo of 1937, with all the dynamic qualities associated with your sign—and then some. Your lust for life and determination to have as much fun as possible will have seen you through the good years and the bad. Your stubborn refusal to fade into the background is probably just as evident now as it was during your teens. It's no surprise that many entertainers are Leos, including Dustin Hoffman, born this year.

You may have hated the drab post-war austerity but as you reached your young adulthood the explosion of avant-garde art and design as well as the emerging counter-culture must have seemed like gifts from heaven. This would have been far more exciting for you than the consumer boom that was gathering pace at the same time. Money may not be your main motivation even now—you value the freedom to express yourself physically, intellectually, and spiritually. You know that when freedom of expression is suppressed it has a nasty habit of turning on itself and creating havoc. In your birth month King George VI narrowly escaped injury from a bomb in Belfast—part of a conflict that remains unresolved.

You may not have had to worry too much about job security and rather than buckle into a humdrum nine-to-five job you may have tried to earn your living from your own creativity— even on the fringes of the art or entertainment world. No matter if the work seemed insignificant you probably tried to instill it with some kind of magic. Your main concern may have been a congenial atmosphere and a cause you believed in.

You adore company and prefer to be the central point of the group rather than an outsider. Passion and an unwavering loyalty may have marked your intimate relationships and you would always be drawn to creative and unpredictable partners. You may have found love with Ariens, Sagittarians, Aquarians, and even Pisceans.

Your desire to follow your own star regardless of the practical is admirable but may have meant you were challenged by some lean times over the years. That you never give less than your best to any undertaking is your greatest strength.

➤ Read about your Chinese Astrological sign on page 838. ➤ Read about your Personal Planets on page 826. ➤ Read about your personal Mystical Card on page 856.

VIRGO

From August 23, 13:58 through September 23, 11:12

The Responsible Radical

As a Virgo born in 1937 you might be expected to fit the dutiful and responsible Virgo mold. This may even have been how you spent your early years but, as you matured, a small but significant streak of rebellion probably began to emerge. You never rebel out of contrariness—it's just that you are so receptive to new ideas that each one merits investigation. You love to create order from chaos—a process that still needs help. In the month of your birth Arabs and Jews in Palestine began the complicated process of partition.

You are naturally intuitive but your need to gather detailed information may have led you to doubt your own gift. Perhaps you have realized that your first impressions and gut reactions are more important than endless reams of data. Your need to maintain boundaries between yourself and the world may be of less importance now as well.

When not pondering the big political and religious questions you may enjoy a host of creative hobbies; you hate to be idle. You may prefer to make practical use of your creative flair—art for art's sake may not appeal. Your vivid imagination is easily stimulated and you could still be enthralled by fantasy worlds like that created in J. R. R. Tolkien's *The Hobbit*, published this month. Your ability to absorb and reflect images and ideas could have found an ideal outlet in television, increasingly dominating our lives in the 1950s. You would have felt very comfortable in the media so long as you were behind the scenes; you probably preferred not to be the focus of attention.

Your need to rebel may have been reflected in your choice of partners. You may have been attracted by the fascinating and unconventional. You are capable of great devotion and you may sometimes have sacrificed your needs for those of your partner. Capricorns, Taureans, Cancerians, and Pisceans may all have had a profound effect on your life.

Eternally youthful, your strength may be your willingness to shed outmoded or rigid ideas as you gain more insight. Your challenge may have been to develop the confidence to express your views in public.

LIBRA

From September 23, 11:13 through October 23, 20:06

The Hidden Powerhouse

Libra of 1937, your entire life may have been a process of integrating and reconciling those aspects of your personality that just don't seem to fit. On the one hand you place great emphasis on rational and balanced thought. On the other, you just can't help sometimes being overwhelmed by visionary but contradictory ideas and concepts. At least you come equipped to constantly shed any out-of-date thought patterns and your interest in new ventures won't have diminished with age. You could be the epitome of the skateboarding old-timer.

You may have been saddened that the world does not live up to your high ideals or your concern for fairness. This month, the magnificent blues singer, Bessie Smith, died needlessly in Mississippi because her color tragically barred her from receiving emergency treatment at the nearest hospital after a car crash. Sometimes the only way conflicting ideologies—like those you carry—can be united is to fight a common foe. Rival Chinese leaders Mao Tse-Tung and Chiang Kai-Shek set aside their differences and united in an attempt to force the Japanese from China.

You hate to be limited by others and your career may have been characterized by driving ambition and an ability to take difficult decisions that others may shy away from. Your need to be fully engaged with your work may have led you into science or medicine but in any career the Twin's need to be in total control and produce excellence shone through.

Your need for partnerships that are stable and secure may sometimes have been at odds with your need for freedom. It may not have been until the 1960s—when the whole sphere of love and relationship was undergoing a radical rethink—that you finally found a way of reconciling your contrasting needs. Ariens, Leos, Sagittarians, and Capricorns may all have helped you honor your feelings.

Your challenge may have been to acknowledge, accept, and then redirect any angry feelings you experience. No one can be nice all the time. Your strength may be your ability to renew and refresh yourself by focusing on the beauty of our world during times of difficulty.

➤ Read about your Chinese Astrological sign on page 838. ➤ Read about your Personal Planets on page 826. ➤ Read about your personal Mystical Card on page 856.

VIRGO
Your Personal Planets

YOUR LOVE POTENTIAL
Venus in Cancer, Aug. 23, 13:58 - Aug. 31, 0:07
Venus in Leo, Aug. 31, 0:08 - Sept. 23, 11:12

YOUR DRIVE AND AMBITION
Mars in Sagittarius, Aug. 23, 13:58 - Sept. 23, 11:12

YOUR LUCK MAGNETISM
Jupiter in Capricorn, Aug. 23, 13:58 - Sept. 23, 11:12

World Events

Aug. 23 - Jews request powers of direct negotiation with the Arabs before the partition of Palestine.

Sept. 21 - J.R.R. Tolkien's *The Hobbit* is published.

Works and letters by J. R. R. Tolkien

LIBRA
Your Personal Planets

YOUR LOVE POTENTIAL
Venus in Leo, Sept. 23, 11:13 - Sept. 25, 4:02
Venus in Virgo, Sept. 25, 4:03 - Oct. 19, 16:32
Venus in Libra, Oct. 19, 16:33 - Oct. 23, 20:06

YOUR DRIVE AND AMBITION
Mars in Sagittarius, Sept. 23, 11:13 - Sept. 30, 9:07
Mars in Capricorn, Sept. 30, 9:08 - Oct. 23, 20:06

YOUR LUCK MAGNETISM
Jupiter in Capricorn, Sept. 23, 11:13 - Oct. 23, 20:06

World Events

Sept. 26 - Blues singer Bessie Smith dies of injuries sustained in a car crash; she had been refused treatment at hospital because she was African American.

Oct. 6 - The U.S. states that it supports China in its fight against the Japanese.

1937

SCORPIO
Your Personal planets

YOUR LOVE POTENTIAL
Venus in Libra, Oct. 23, 20:07 - Nov. 12, 19:42
Venus in Scorpio, Nov. 12, 19:43 - Nov. 22, 17:16

YOUR DRIVE AND AMBITION
Mars in Capricorn, Oct. 23, 20:07 - Nov. 11, 18:30
Mars in Aquarius, Nov. 11, 18:31 - Nov. 22, 17:16

YOUR LUCK MAGNETISM
Jupiter in Capricorn, Oct. 23, 20:07 - Nov. 22, 17:16

World Events

Nov. 7 – In Moscow, a parade is held to mark the twentieth anniversary of the Bolshevik revolution.

Nov. 17 – Britain's Lord Halifax makes a peacekeeping visit to Nazi Germany.

The Lindberghs return to the U.S.

SAGITTARIUS
Your Personal Planets

YOUR LOVE POTENTIAL
Venus in Scorpio, Nov. 22, 17:17 - Dec. 06, 18:05
Venus in Sagittarius, Dec. 06, 18:06 - Dec. 22, 6:21

YOUR DRIVE AND AMBITION
Mars in Aquarius, Nov. 22, 17:17 - Dec. 21, 17:45
Mars in Pisces, Dec. 21, 17:46 - Dec. 22, 6:21

YOUR LUCK MAGNETISM
Jupiter in Capricorn, Nov. 22, 17:17 - Dec. 20, 4:04
Jupiter in Aquarius, Dec. 20, 4:05 - Dec. 22, 6:21

World Events

Dec. 5 – The Lindberghs return to the U.S. after a two-year voluntary exile in England.

Dec. 11 – Italy withdraws from the League of Nations.

SCORPIO
From October 23, 20:07 through November 22, 17:16

The Steely Utopian

You have got a lot to say Scorpio of 1937. You can be quick-thinking and opinionated; your habit of forthright self-expression may sometimes have placed you up to your neck in hot water. You could have made an excellent teacher or broadcaster as you grab any opportunity to broaden your own and others' perspectives. Never content to rest on your laurels, you may continue to pursue your quest for knowledge and understanding into old age.

You have always been convinced that you can make a vital difference, possibly by joining with others who shared your political, educational, or humanitarian ideals. You were one of the first of a new generation dedicated to empowering the self and, while past the first flush of youth, you may have approved of the growing tide of political and social activism in the sixties and seventies.

Your enthusiasm for utopian ideals of brotherhood and understanding has never prevented you from sticking to your guns when necessary. When you were born Hitler revealed his expansionist military intentions. Despite this, the British government continued to tread the path of appeasement, sending Lord Halifax to Germany on yet another futile diplomatic mission. You probably know instinctively when to take a stand and when to compromise. When you do dig in your heels nothing short of an earthquake will knock your off your feet.

Scorpios are often described as possessive and while you may sometimes have been prey to jealous feelings, you also could have learned early on that the harder you try to hold on to someone the more they want to escape. Recognition of your own need for personal freedom may have allowed you to be less insecure with others. You probably found that not only are you compatible with Pisceans, Capricorns, and Cancerians but possibly Aquarians as well.

Independent through and through, your challenge may still be to accept help from others with grace. Ironically, this independence may also be your greatest strength, as you refuse to take no for an answer; you insist on continually confronting prejudice and sloppy thinking wherever you encounter it.

SAGITTARIUS
From November 22, 17:17 through December 22, 6:21

The Unpretentious Mystic

As a Sagittarius born in 1937 you must have worked hard to maintain your famous good cheer when young. The gathering storm of war edged a little closer as Japan officially recognized Franco's fascist government in Spain and Italy withdrew from the League of Nations—alliances were being made crystal clear. You may have learned to rely on yourself at an early age as those around you may have been unable or unwilling to devote themselves to your endless curiosity. The most fascinating route on life's journey for you could be through the far reaches of your own imagination as you seek meaning to our existence.

Loathing routine, it may have been difficult to settle on a career. You may not have been interested in making huge amounts of money, having faith that it always appears when you need it. It was always far more important that your work was absorbing and even better if you felt you were serving others in at least some small a way. While education could have tempted you, so could some form of healing. You could have changed direction frequently, as your restless and spontaneous nature would never allow you to continue with something that had lost its meaning. You may not have found your true purpose until you were older.

In some ways you were born too early. If the explosion of interest in alternative therapies and oriental philosophies that happened when you were older had occurred earlier, you might have felt less like a square peg in a round hole. But then you still may be ahead of your time.

Your approach to others is friendly and uncomplicated. You may sometimes seem a little detached, living as you do in the mind rather than the feelings. Occasionally you need to be brought back down to Earth. But when your closest partner can attract your attention you can be a lively, entertaining, and above all honest companion. You may have had your happiest relationships with Leos, Ariens, Geminis, and Pisceans.

Your childlike curiosity may still be your strongest asset but your greatest challenge may have been to acknowledge that sometimes you just can't avoid reality.

► Read about your Chinese Astrological sign on page 838. ► Read about your Personal Planets on page 826. ► Read about your personal Mystical Card on page 856.

CAPRICORN

From December 22, 6:22 through December 31, 23:59

The Respectable Nonconformist

It's possible, December Capricorn of 1937, that anyone meeting you now would see a well-heeled and successful individual. They probably would have no idea that beneath the impeccable face you show the world is concealed a far more complicated personality. Not only do you have an unorthodox streak but you may also still get a kick out of shocking people. While you appreciate the material benefits that came with playing the corporate game you also value freedom of expression. You may have toned this down as you got older but your tolerant outlook endured. You would have approved of Mae West who made it her life's work to push the limits of decency to the point of collapse. She was banned from NBC radio this month after performing a racy "Adam and Eve" sketch.

You may have spent your youth exploring all the possibilities available to you, not really connecting with your powerful ambition until you reached maturity. By then you may have been able to reconcile your security needs and your unconventional mindset. Once decided on a course of action, your practical skills and determination would have allowed you to shape your life almost exactly the way you wanted.

You may have found your niche working in the industries that developed in the wake of the new technologies just emerging, satisfying both your fascination with novelty and your creative side. Alternately, anyone who initially resisted your sales pitch would have soon surrendered.

In relationship you are deeply sensual and appreciate mental stimulation and spontaneity. Maurice Ravel, who died at this time, was a master of romantic piano music, but is remembered most for his stirring *Bolero*. You may not be traditionally romantic but your unique gestures would have touched your partner deeply. You may have been most comfortable with Taureans, Virgos, Pisceans, and Scorpios.

Boredom may have been your greatest enemy and you may have often had to use all your powers of concentration to focus on your immediate priorities. Your strength is your continuing tolerance for others right to the freedom of self-expression.

1937

CAPRICORN
Your Personal Planets

YOUR LOVE POTENTIAL
Venus in Sagittarius, Dec. 22, 6:22 - Dec. 30, 14:41
Venus in Capricorn, Dec. 30, 14:42 - Dec. 31, 23:59

YOUR DRIVE AND AMBITION
Mars in Pisces, Dec. 22, 6:22 - Dec. 31, 23:59

YOUR LUCK MAGNETISM
Jupiter in Aquarius, Dec. 22, 6:22 - Dec. 31, 23:59

World Events

Dec. 27 – Mae West performs the "Adam and Eve" skit that gets her banned from NBC radio.

Dec. 28 – French composer Maurice Ravel dies.

The view from atop the Great Pyramid, Egypt

Special Feature
Ancient Secrets of the Great Pyramid

(Continued from page 305)

How can we account for such advanced mathematical expertise and geographic sophistication? The explanations are many. Edgar Cayce, the man known as the Sleeping Prophet, offered one popular theory. He claimed that the Great Pyramid was built 12,000 years ago by priest-magicians from the lost continent of Atlantis. Between 1920 and 1944, Cayce gave many readings about the ancient civilization of Atlantis, including details about the Great Pyramid. When asked how the Great Pyramid was built, he said, "By the use of those forces in nature as make for iron to swim. Stone floats in the air in the same manner."

In addition to its unique geographical location, the Great Pyramid also embodies a symbolic relationship to the larger cosmos.

Some twentieth-century Christians maintained that the Great Pyramid was built with supernatural assistance. In the 1920s a few complex theories began to appear that related specific measurements in the pyramid's grand gallery passageway to actual historical events. Using the supposed construction date of 2623 B.C. and equating one year to one inch, the Grand Gallery represented a chronological mapping of God's plan for humanity. The greatest events were shown by geometric relationships of the queen's chamber floor, the ascending passageway, and other intersecting lines and angles. This group believed biblical prophecies were encoded in these measurements, including the End Times as the entrance doorway to the antechamber.

A more radical theory arose in the 1960s, claiming that the Great Pyramid was built by beings from other planets. Erich von Daniken kicked off the ancient-astronauts theory with his book *Chariots of the Gods*. He scoffed at the widely accepted mainstream theories that some 2,300,000 stone blocks, weighing up to nine tons each, were moved up steep inclines using wooden rollers. "Could it be true that extraterrestrial space travelers helped with their highly developed technology?"

One of the most popular advocates of the extraterrestrial theory is Zecharia Sitchin, who asserts that the Great Pyramid was built by the Anunnaki, people who live on a twelfth planet he proposed for our solar system. Using his command of ancient languages and other archeological oddities, Sitchin proposed that the Anunnaki manufactured humans through genetic manipulation. What's more, this alien intelligence created the Great Pyramid as a landing beacon for incoming spacecraft.

(Continued on page 321)

► Read more about Cayce in "The First New Age Psychic" on page 265. ► Read about UFOs in "The Extraterrestrial Highway" on page 465. ► Read "Gaia's Mystical Power Places" on page 745.

1938

Global Holding Pattern: Pluto Enters Leo

The planets lost their closer connections with each other in 1938 and the world held its breath. The subtly aggressive actions played out on the international stage prompted no decisive reactions. Saturn, the planet of discipline and control, winged its way through wayward but pioneering Aries, but only connected awkwardly with Neptune, the planet of imagination and deception. As Germany allied with Italy and annexed neighboring areas, its potential opponents were telling themselves that it was probably best not to interfere. Opportunistic and entrepreneurial Jupiter traveled rapidly this year, sweeping quickly through Aquarius, the sign of social reform, by mid-May. When Jupiter squared off with Uranus, symbolizing anarchistic tendencies, in January and February, Hitler again gave himself a boost of power by seizing command of the German army. The real story, however, was played out as Jupiter touched off transformative Pluto in April, May, and early January 1939. Together, these planets symbolize the potential for megalomania and, more positively, constructive social growth. Hitler exhibited such grandiose behavior when he declared dominion over Austria and part of Czechoslovakia, solidifying his power base while free nations looked on in stunned silence.

Pluto, the planet of hidden factors, made astrological news by entering creative and expressive Leo, signaling a shift in the global perspective away from mere survival and toward excellence of experience. This occurred as film, radio, and the newly marketed television began to dramatically change lives.

120,000 stormtroopers are reviewed by Hitler at Nuremberg

Neville Chamberlain, Edward Daladier, Adolf Hitler, and Benito Mussolini at the Munich Conference

Hitler Youth burn books at Salzburg

HITLER'S ASTROLOGERS

After the outbreak of World War II, the British left no stone unturned trying to uncover Hitler's plans. Knowing him to be an avid occultist who employed astrologers, the British Secret Service hired their own astrologers. These astrologers tried to determine what the German astrologers were telling their boss. Unfortunately for their British counterparts, the German astrologers could not just follow the stars—if they failed to keep their client Hitler happy, or made an incorrect prediction, they risked losing their lives.

TERRIBLE FEARS AND ROMANTIC FANTASIES

As the threat of fascist power increased, each nation reacted in its own way. King Carol II of Romania declared a personal dictatorship. Mexico seized all foreign-owned oil holdings. Sudetenland Germans in Czechoslovakia greeted the Nazi invasion, while Austria united with Germany in the *Anschluss*. British Prime Minister Neville Chamberlain made what he declared to be a peace agreement with Germany and Italy. Nazi Germany continued to prepare for war and occupied the Sudetenland of Czechoslovakia. On *Kristallnacht* (Crystal Night), 9 November, Nazis burned synagogues, looted Jewish shops, and killed hundreds of Jews throughout Germany. The isolationist U.S. wanted to avoid conflict and refrained from European alliances. In the U.S., eight million remained jobless despite government projects. An escapist social movement attempted to dream away the world's woes: Humphrey Bogart, Spencer Tracy, Jimmy Cagney, and Bette Davis all scored hits on the silver screen, but Errol Flynn stole most hearts in *The Adventures of Robin Hood*. Nylon was produced by Du Pont in the U.S. and nylon-based toothbrushes were marketed to consumers.

➤ Read "Ancient Secrets of the Great Pyramid" by Jean Mars on page 305.

CAPRICORN

From January 01, 0:00 through January 20, 16:58

The Dignified Toiler

As a January Capricorn born in 1938 you can pride yourself on your original mind. Tradition has its place, but you know that the good old days were often only good in retrospect. While you share the typical Capricorn urge for material security, you would have been unlikely to compromise your principles for the sake of a quick buck. It's possible that you opted for a career that combined a comfortable income while contributing some significant benefit to society. The medical profession is one obvious choice. You might be horrified to know that in Germany, Jewish doctors lost their license to practice this month, depriving them of their income and their patients of medical care.

Your disciplined and dependable approach inspired confidence in others, whatever your profession. You have always been able to convince people that you know what you are talking about on your given subject. With your commitment to excellence you may have worked long and hard to deliver the goods.

Taking care of business probably took precedence over allowing yourself some time to unwind in daily life. You may have realized, however, that it was crucial to put aside at least some time each day for a little recreation. Music could be one of your passions and you may have been overjoyed at the invention of the personal stereo—it allowed you to cut off from everyday pressures wherever and whenever you chose. A prominent jazz musician was in the news this month. Benny Goodman refused to play Carnegie Hall when the African-American members of his band were barred from performing—an example of how bad the good old days could be.

With friends and family you can be a sucker for a sob story, offering practical advice as well as a sympathetic ear. It almost goes without saying that security has always been crucial and a happy family life is your bedrock. You may have felt most comfortable with Virgos, Taureans, Scorpios, and Cancerians.

You may have had numerous goals. Learning to accept that you may not achieve every one could have been a challenge. Your enduring strength is your open and inquiring mind.

AQUARIUS

From January 20, 16:59 through February 19, 7:19

The Objective Liberal

As an Aquarian born in 1938 your independent attitude is underlined by an obstinate refusal to go along with the majority if you disagree with them. Indeed, you may love to play the devil's advocate just to stir up some excitement. Your favorite phrase may have been "Why don't we do it this way?" Your ingenuity has probably meant that your way was often the best in any case. Your only motive was probably to get the job done in the most efficient and beneficial way. Your friendly and impartial approach made even the most reluctant of colleagues eager to help out.

You have always worked best when unfettered by petty restrictions and you are pretty good at holding both the big picture and the minor details in your mind's eye. Your leadership qualities have always been underpinned by your humane ideals. You may have found that you grew as a person when your work involved giving something back to the wider society. You have never been afraid of speaking your mind and accepting any responsibility that goes along with it.

An example of a person taking responsibility and having the courage to speak out occurred this month. In Britain, Foreign Secretary and future Prime Minister Anthony Eden resigned in disgust at the policy of appeasement that Chamberlain's government followed. In the long run his came to be the majority view—a sequence of events with which you might be familiar. This month also, Hitler named himself supreme military commander and assumed control of foreign policy.

Settling down may have been the last thing on your mind and you can be somewhat insecure even now at expressing your feelings. However, when stirred into action your emotions may sometimes have completely overwhelmed you. Sagittarians, Leos, Ariens, and Librans may all have let you feel comfortable enough to express your deeper feelings.

When you make up your mind, it often stays made up. Your challenge Aquarius of 1938 may have been to know when to gracefully back down. Your extraordinary powers of concentration, enabling you to solve the most complex problems, may be your greatest strength.

1938

CAPRICORN
Your Personal Planets

YOUR LOVE POTENTIAL
Venus in Capricorn, Jan. 01, 0:00 - Jan. 20, 16:58

YOUR DRIVE AND AMBITION
Mars in Pisces, Jan. 01, 0:00 - Jan. 20, 16:58

YOUR LUCK MAGNETISM
Jupiter in Aquarius, Jan. 01, 0:00 - Jan. 20, 16:58

World Events

Jan. 1 – Jewish doctors in Germany lose their insurance under the Nazi Nuremburg Laws.

Jan. 16 – Benny Goodman performs his legendary concert at Carnegie Hall in New York.

Neville Chamberlain's foreign policy causes Anthony Eden to resign

AQUARIUS
Your Personal Planets

YOUR LOVE POTENTIAL
Venus in Capricorn, Jan. 20, 16:59 - Jan. 23, 11:15
Venus in Aquarius, Jan. 23, 11:16 - Feb. 16, 8:59
Venus in Pisces, Feb. 16, 9:00 - Feb. 19, 7:19

YOUR DRIVE AND AMBITION
Mars in Pisces, Jan. 20, 16:59 - Jan. 30, 12:43
Mars in Aries, Jan. 30, 12:44 - Feb. 19, 7:19

YOUR LUCK MAGNETISM
Jupiter in Aquarius, Jan. 20, 16:59 - Feb. 19, 7:19

World Events

Feb. 4 – Hitler names himself Supreme Commander of the German army and seizes direct control of foreign policy.

Feb. 20 – British Foreign Secretary Anthony Eden resigns in disapproval of Prime Minister Neville Chamberlain's policy of appeasement towards Italy and Germany.

► Read about your Chinese Astrological sign on page 838. ► Read about your Personal Planets on page 826. ► Read about your personal Mystical Card on page 856.

1938

PISCES
Your Personal Planets

YOUR LOVE POTENTIAL
Venus in Pisces, Feb. 19, 7:20 - Mar. 12, 9:19
Venus in Aries, Mar. 12, 9:20 - Mar. 21, 6:42

YOUR DRIVE AND AMBITION
Mars in Aries, Feb. 19, 7:20 - Mar. 12, 7:47
Mars in Taurus, Mar. 12, 7:48 - Mar. 21, 6:42

YOUR LUCK MAGNETISM
Jupiter in Aquarius, Feb. 19, 7:20 - Mar. 21, 6:42

World Events

Mar. 12 – German troops invade Austria and Hitler enters Vienna, proclaiming the *Anschluss* (union) of the two countries.

Mar. 17 – Russian choreographer and ballet dancer Rudolf Nureyev is born.

Russian ballet dancer Rudolf Nureyev is born under the sign of Pisces

ARIES
Your Personal Planets

YOUR LOVE POTENTIAL
Venus in Aries, Mar. 21, 6:43 - Apr. 05, 13:45
Venus in Taurus, Apr. 05, 13:46 - Apr. 20, 18:14

YOUR DRIVE AND AMBITION
Mars in Taurus, Mar. 21, 6:43 - Apr. 20, 18:14

YOUR LUCK MAGNETISM
Jupiter in Aquarius, Mar. 21, 6:43 - Apr. 20, 18:14

World Events

Apr. 4 – Franco's assault on Tortosa is reported to have devastated the U.S. volunteer regiment Lincoln-Washington.

Apr. 12 – Russian basso Feodor Chaliapin dies.

316

PISCES
From February 19, 7:20 through March 21, 6:42

The Compassionate Seeker

As a Pisces of 1938 you may have the dreamy quality associated with your sign, but you also possess a powerful and energetic will. You have the kind of quick-fire intelligence that cuts through confusion and homes in on the point.

You may have been drawn to work in the healing professions or within institutions that try to benefit humanity. Your creativity could have been used effectively in the field of art therapy that began to be explored from the 1970s onwards.

To follow your dreams you may have had to break with your past. You may have felt that the expectations of your family and the society you grew up in restricted you and to really explore your potential you had to distance yourself. Rudolf Nuryev, the brilliant ballet dancer who famously defected from the Soviet Union in the 1960s, was born this month. Like him, you may have been subject to the "divine discontent" that insists that the perfect place for you might be just over the horizon or around the next bend.

You may have moved around a lot during your life, but it was usually out of choice. You sympathize greatly with those people that are unable to control their own destiny. The German army invaded Austria this month and Hitler announced *Anschluss* or "union" between the two countries. Many Austrians were happy with this, but any that felt uneasy had to prepare to either leave the country or make rapid changes to their lifestyle.

Personal relationships are where your clear thinking may have been clouded by your emotions. Your sympathetic nature may have meant that you were often a soft touch for some unscrupulous types. You may have often been carried away by romance but Taureans, Virgos, Scorpios, and Cancerians may have valued your kindness and given you a sense of security.

Sometimes you may find yourself overtaken by nostalgia or lost in your vision of the future. Your challenge, Pisces of 1938, may have been to live fully in the present. Some of the decisions you have made during your life may not have turned out as you hoped and your strength is that you have never put the blame elsewhere.

ARIES
From March 21, 6:43 through April 20, 18:14

The Bold Adventurer

Your courage and sense of adventure, Aries of 1938, may have made you far more of a leader than a follower. You may have always been impulsive and idealistic. While organization may never have been your strong point, you've always been fantastic at rallying the troops.

Your outlook may have been radical, progressive, and almost always on the side of the underdog. Preferring direct action to gradual change you may have been at the forefront of demonstrations in the sixties and seventies. Whatever your pet causes, you wanted them to be noticed by the silent majority. The continuing horror of the war in Spain was being noticed that way when you were born. The American Lincoln-Washington battalion, one of the brave and idealistic International Brigades that volunteered to fight with the legitimate Spanish government, was all but destroyed in fierce fighting at Tortosa with Franco's troops.

You may be less active nowadays, but you probably still maintain your individualistic opinions and you are more than happy to share them with anyone that cares to listen. Whatever you have done in life, second place was never good enough—you have always wanted to give your best. While singing may not be your passion or even your interest, Feodor Chaliapin, operatic bass who was considered by many to be the world's greatest singer of all time, died this month.

Just as impulsive in relationships, you may have jumped straight in and worried about the consequences later. You may have loved the idea of being swept off your feet by passion and once you found your ideal partner you probably worked hard to maintain the original spark. Leos, Sagittarians, Aquarians, and Geminis have all responded to your dynamic and straightforward need to give and receive love.

You may have often jumped so far and so fast, Aries of 1938, that you sometimes landed in hot water. Your challenge may have been to appreciate the value of stopping and thinking before you acted. The sense of enterprise, imagination, and above all fun that you have brought to all you have undertaken, has always been your greatest strength.

➤ Read about your Chinese Astrological sign on page 838. ➤ Read about your Personal Planets on page 826. ➤ Read about your personal Mystical Card on page 856.

1938

TAURUS

From April 20, 18:15 through May 21, 17:49

The Earthy Opportunist

As a Taurus of 1938 you may hate sudden changes—unless of course you have decided to make them yourself. You may have had to work hard to develop a relaxed attitude to the changing ways of life around you. After all, you were born at a time when many people were adjusting to rapid changes to their way of life, over which few of them had any control. Fearing for national security, Czechoslovakia placed 400,000 troops on its border with Germany this month. This brave but ultimately futile gesture showed how desperately that country feared for its safety. You may have always felt that maintaining control over your immediate environment was of the utmost importance. The rapid acceleration of change in the late twentieth century probably made you uneasy.

The need to have some say in what goes on around you in your locale may have meant that you were a dynamic force in your own neighborhood. You may have been an active member of your local council or organizations dedicated to improving and promoting your hometown. Your love of music and the arts could have meant that your contribution was most appreciated in these areas—Thornton Wilder's classic play, *Our Town*, opened in New York this year.

Paradoxically, you may have always been an expert at making the little adjustments necessary to succeed at your chosen career. While you are capable of the steady, patient plodding that Taureans are famous for, you may also have demonstrated an admirable eye for the main chance. You are an articulate and efficient communicator and may have talked your way into plum positions on occasion.

In relationships you are tolerant and trustworthy and may often surprise your partner with loving and romantic gestures. Scorpios, Virgos, Pisceans, and Capricorns may all have combined the sensuality and the mental spark to which you respond.

You can occasionally manufacture Mount Everest from a tiny molehill, Taurus of 1938, and gaining a clearer sense of perspective may have been your main challenge. Your strength is your skill at spotting a window of opportunity and then diving through, head first.

GEMINI

From May 21, 17:50 through June 22, 2:03

The Eloquent Thinker

As a Gemini born in 1938 your curiosity about the world around you remains undiminished. You may be as inquisitive now as when you were a child, and each new subject to which you are introduced enhances your sense of accomplishment. Your sense of security may have been linked to what you knew and understood rather than status or a large bank balance.

Your verbal dexterity and fascination with words and language could have led you toward a career in teaching, journalism, or broadcasting. You may have loved the introduction of the remote control for television, allowing you to flip backwards and forwards between channels and not missing out on anything. Game shows have enduring popularity and the BBC broadcast the very first television game show, *Spelling Bee*, this month. This is a great symbol that combines both your joy in language and your love of risk taking.

You can be dogged when searching for the truth and have always been aware that sometimes what you are being told may not be the whole story. Highlighting this, the U.S. House of Representatives formed a committee to purge activities deemed to be "un-American." When you were growing up in the 1950s many people were punished for their suspected words or deeds and some bitter divisions remain to this day.

You may have many casual acquaintances thanks to your interest in people and your ability to communicate but you probably allowed only a small band of trusted friends in your inner circle. Your chosen partner would have had to be as intrigued by the world as you were. You would have wanted to share your life with someone that contributed a unique viewpoint to the relationship and was continually able to surprise you. You may generally have felt most compatible with Aquarians, Librans, Ariens, and Sagittarians.

"How much can I take in and understand?" This may have been your constant question through life. Your challenge may have been to realize that the quality of information was more useful than the quantity. Your strength is that your curiosity and openness to new experience keeps your outlook young.

TAURUS
Your Personal Planets

YOUR LOVE POTENTIAL
Venus in Taurus, Apr. 20, 18:15 - Apr. 29, 23:34
Venus in Gemini, Apr. 29, 23:35 - May 21, 17:49

YOUR DRIVE AND AMBITION
Mars in Taurus, Apr. 20, 18:15 - Apr. 23, 18:38
Mars in Gemini, Apr. 23, 18:39 - May 21, 17:49

YOUR LUCK MAGNETISM
Jupiter in Aquarius, Apr. 20, 18:15 - May 14, 7:45
Jupiter in Pisces, May 14, 7:46 - May 21, 17:49

World Events

May 2 – In London, the House of Commons ratifies the Anglo-Italian Pact.
May 21 – The Czechs mobilize and place troops on the German border.

The BBC broadcasts "Spelling Bee," made possible by John Logie Baird, inventor of the television

GEMINI
Your Personal Planets

YOUR LOVE POTENTIAL
Venus in Gemini, May 21, 17:50 - May 24, 15:55
Venus in Cancer, May 24, 15:56 - June 18, 16:36
Venus in Leo, June 18, 16:37 - June 22, 2:03

YOUR DRIVE AND AMBITION
Mars in Gemini, May 21, 17:50 - June 07, 1:27
Mars in Cancer, June 07, 1:28 - June 22, 2:03

YOUR LUCK MAGNETISM
Jupiter in Pisces, May 21, 17:50 - June 22, 2:03

World Events

May 26 – The Committee of House Un-American Activities is formed in Washington.
May 31 – The BBC broadcasts *Spelling Bee*, the first game show on television.

➤ Read about your Chinese Astrological sign on page 838. ➤ Read about your Personal Planets on page 826. ➤ Read about your personal Mystical Card on page 856.

317

1938

CANCER
Your Personal Planets

YOUR LOVE POTENTIAL
Venus in Leo, June 22, 2:04 - July 14, 5:43
Venus in Virgo, July 14, 5:44 - July 23, 12:56

YOUR DRIVE AND AMBITION
Mars in Cancer, June 22, 2:04 - July 22, 22:25
Mars in Leo, July 22, 22:26 - July 23, 12:56

YOUR LUCK MAGNETISM
Jupiter in Pisces, June 22, 2:04 - July 23, 12:56

World Events

June 25 – Douglas Hyde becomes the first Irish President under the revised constitution.

July 14 – Millionaire aviator Howard Hughes sets a new record for round-the-world flight: three days, nineteen hours, seventeen minutes.

Howard Hughes sets a new record for flying around the world

LEO
Your Personal Planets

YOUR LOVE POTENTIAL
Venus in Virgo, July 23, 12:57 - Aug. 09, 16:25
Venus in Libra, Aug. 09, 16:26 - Aug. 23, 19:45

YOUR DRIVE AND AMBITION
Mars in Leo, July 23, 12:57 - Aug. 23, 19:45

YOUR LUCK MAGNETISM
Jupiter in Pisces, July 23, 12:57 - July 30, 3:01
Jupiter in Aquarius, July 30, 3:02 - Aug. 23, 19:45

World Events

July 29 – Denmark's Jenny Kammersgaad becomes the first woman to swim the Baltic Sea.

Aug. 7 – Constantin Stanislavsky, founder of the Moscow Art Theatre and initiator of the famous "Stanislavsky method" of acting, dies.

CANCER
From June 22, 2:04 through July 23, 12:56

The Kind Conservative

As a Cancer of 1938 you sincerely believe that life's bounty is there for the taking. While you have never been greedy, you know that emotional security can be damaged by material deprivation. You may have used your ambition to succeed primarily to provide stability for those you love most. You may have had to work hard to maintain your routines as your receptivity to external influences sometimes means that you undertake too much at once. You've always worked best in an orderly environment—Ireland finally gained one this month with a new constitution and President, Douglas Hyde, after years of chaos and civil war.

You spend so much of your energy nurturing your family and friends that sometimes you may have to remind them that you need affection too. Sometimes you need time away from them, however, if only to do your own thing. While you may enjoy typical Cancerian hobbies like gourmet cooking, you may also have enjoyed traveling. Millionaire Howard Hughes arrived in New York this month after setting a new round the world flight record of three days, nineteen hours, and seventeen minutes. You would have loved to be in the crowd that welcomed him home.

You have always had a style of your own and you appreciate a glamorous touch. Immaculately turned out and possessing a beautiful home, you may not have felt comfortable with the denim-and-cheesecloth look of the sixties and seventies—the return to dressing up in the eighties would have been much more appealing to you.

The home and family have always been the most important aspect of your life. Without those you love close at hand you may feel that there is something missing. You have never been afraid to express your emotions openly and encourage others to reciprocate. You may have had the closest rapport with Taureans, Scorpios, Pisceans, and Virgos.

Sometimes your immediate environment may become a little chaotic. Your challenge may have been to turn a blind eye and go with the flow a bit more. Your strength, which may be increasing with age, is using your intuition and imagination to guide you toward your decisions.

LEO
From July 23, 12:57 through August 23, 19:45

The Magnetic Enigma

As a Leo of 1938 your bubbling enthusiasm and your desire for new and fascinating experiences may have meant that your life often veered far from your intended course. That just means you have ended up in much more interesting circumstances than you originally planned—unlike the German army, on war maneuvers this month, which usually had a pretty good idea of its direction.

Despite your enigmatic charm and your glamorous appearance you could sometimes fall prey to self-doubt. Your analytical mind sometimes bogged you down in interminable detail, so much so that you lost sight of your main objectives. However, your Leo determination usually won out in the end and you were always capable of getting yourself back on the right track. As you have grown older these lapses in self-confidence may have become fewer and fewer. No one would have noticed when you were nervous anyway as you put on such a good show.

Your work needed to be stimulating, engaging, and, above all, not dull. You probably preferred a job where your own personality was your prime asset. You could have been a fabulous salesperson and you may have been in at the start of the explosion in public relations and promotions in the late 1970s and early 1980s. If the company you worked for had a high public profile, so much the better. Everything you do is tinged with a theatrical flourish. You probably wouldn't have felt at home with the downbeat dramatic method of Stanislavsky, who died this month.

In relationships you are powerfully passionate. The magic has to be present or you lose interest very quickly. You are capable of great loyalty and generosity to your family and your many friends. You needed a partner that continually surprised you and never forgot just how special you are. You may have found the love you wanted with Ariens, Sagittarians, Librans, or Pisceans.

Sometimes you may have been carried away by your own fantasies and your challenge may have been to remain grounded while not losing sight of your dreams. Your enduring strength is your child-like joy when you realize how much you are loved.

► Read about your Chinese Astrological sign on page 838. ► Read about your Personal Planets on page 826. ► Read about your personal Mystical Card on page 856.

VIRGO

From August 23, 19:46 through September 23, 16:59

The Hardworking Philosopher

As a Virgo of 1938 you are an eternal seeker after knowledge. Your approach to the mysterious business of life is typical of your sign: you like to analyze and categorize each new piece of information. Your world may resemble a giant jigsaw puzzle where each piece that fits into place enhances your sense of spiritual and emotional security. You may have developed an interest in natural or unorthodox forms of healing and you may even have made it your career. The growing interest in alternative subjects during your lifetime means that you may still be spreading the alternative message in some capacity, possibly in the role of a teacher.

You may, however, have worked in a less esoteric environment, possibly in administration where your organizational skills would have made you indispensable. Nevertheless, you still might feel that retirement equals death and you are not ready for that yet. You know that the only way to remain youthful is to keep on striving.

Your open outlook and your firm belief that we should all work to live as harmoniously as possible stand in great contrast to the world into which you were born. The fascist Italian government was busy expelling Jews that had settled there since 1919. On the other side of the world, Japan announced that it would back Germany and Italy with arms if the need arose. Gentle Virgo of 1938 you were born into a dangerous world.

Typically, Virgos are known for their independence, sometimes shunning marriage as too much of a compromise. You however may have felt incomplete without a partner and beneath your cool and calm exterior runs a stream of fiery passion. What excites you most, though, is a meeting of minds and you still delight when you come into contact with new people that can teach you something you didn't know. You may have found compatibility with Pisceans, Scorpios, Taureans, and Capricorns.

You have sometimes bitten off more than you could chew and your challenge may have been to stop and smell the roses more often. Your strength is that you remain as cheerfully willing to be useful to your fellow men as ever.

LIBRA

From September 23, 17:00 through October 24, 1:53

The Diplomatic Provocateur

As a Libra of 1938 you may appear to be the epitome of agreeable diplomacy. Behind the easygoing exterior, however, you conceal a core of assertive energy. You may have always related to Theodore Roosevelt's motto "Speak softly and carry a big stick." You probably believe passionately that everyone has a right to the freedom of self-expression and you may have been active in the movement for political and social equality that was the keynote of the sixties and seventies.

Despite your preference for peace and harmony as well as your conciliatory approach, you can pack a heavyweight punch if necessary. You would never have approved of Neville Chamberlain's appeasement of Hitler in Munich over the issue of Czechoslovakia. You probably thought that giving in to bullies only sows the seeds of more trouble. While Charles Lindbergh was undoubtedly an American hero you may have felt that by accepting the Service Cross from Hitler this month, he did himself a great disservice.

When you weren't busy changing the world you probably found time to carve out a successful career, hopefully in work that had a purpose other than simply making money. You needed to have some degree of authority and a good deal of space in which to operate to feel comfortable. You love good quality and may always have had slightly offbeat tastes. You may still dress beautifully in your own unique style.

While you may enjoy a wide circle of friends who share your humanitarian ideals, you may have been more discriminating in your choice of partner. You may have approached long-term relationships with caution, needing to be absolutely certain that it would last before you made any commitments. You may generally have been most compatible with Aquarians, Geminis, Sagittarians, and Ariens.

You have sometimes been guilty of putting two and two together and coming up with five. Your challenge in life may have been to check your facts before you came to your conclusions. Your greatest strength has always been your breadth of vision—you know that positive change can always be achieved if enough minds focus on it.

➤ Read about your Chinese Astrological sign on page 838. ➤ Read about your Personal Planets on page 826. ➤ Read about your personal Mystical Card on page 856.

1938

VIRGO
Your Personal Planets

YOUR LOVE POTENTIAL
Venus in Libra, Aug. 23, 19:46 - Sept. 07, 1:35
Venus in Scorpio, Sept. 07, 1:36 - Sept. 23, 16:59

YOUR DRIVE AND AMBITION
Mars in Leo, Aug. 23, 19:46 - Sept. 07, 20:21
Mars in Virgo, Sept. 07, 20:22 - Sept. 23, 16:59

YOUR LUCK MAGNETISM
Jupiter in Aquarius, Aug. 23, 19:46 - Sept. 23, 16:59

World Events

Sept. 15 – Adolf Hitler and British Prime Minister Neville Chamberlain meet to discuss methods of avoiding war.

Sept. 21 – A hurricane sweeps through New York and New England, killing more than 600 people.

Neville Chamberlain on his return from Germany with Hitler's "piece of paper"

LIBRA
Your Personal Planets

YOUR LOVE POTENTIAL
Venus in Scorpio, Sept. 23, 17:00 - Oct. 13, 18:48
Venus in Sagittarius, Oct. 13, 18:49 - Oct. 24, 1:53

YOUR DRIVE AND AMBITION
Mars in Virgo, Sept. 23, 17:00 - Oct. 24, 1:53

YOUR LUCK MAGNETISM
Jupiter in Aquarius, Sept. 23, 17:00 - Oct. 24, 1:53

World Events

Oct. 3 - German troops occupy the Czech Sudetenland.

Oct. 19 - Hitler decorates the aviator Charles Lindbergh with the Service Cross.

1938

SCORPIO
Your Personal Planets

YOUR LOVE POTENTIAL
Venus in Sagittarius, Oct. 24, 1:54 - Nov. 15, 16:06
Venus in Scorpio, Nov. 15, 16:07 - Nov. 22, 23:05

YOUR DRIVE AND AMBITION
Mars in Virgo, Oct. 24, 1:54 - Oct. 25, 6:19
Mars in Libra, Oct. 25, 6:20 - Nov. 22, 23:05

YOUR LUCK MAGNETISM
Jupiter in Aquarius, Oct. 24, 1:54 - Nov. 22, 23:05

World Events

Oct. 30 – Orson Welles panics America with a broadcast of his book *The War Of The Worlds*.

Nov. 9 – In what becomes known as "Kristallnacht," Nazis go on the rampage, killing Jews and destroying their property.

Pearl Buck, Nobel Prize winner for literature

SAGITTARIUS
Your Personal Planets

YOUR LOVE POTENTIAL
Venus in Scorpio, Nov. 22, 23:06 - Dec. 22, 12:12

YOUR DRIVE AND AMBITION
Mars in Libra, Nov. 22, 23:06 - Dec. 11, 23:24
Mars in Scorpio, Dec. 11, 23:25 - Dec. 22, 12:12

YOUR LUCK MAGNETISM
Jupiter in Aquarius, Nov. 22, 23:06 - Dec. 22, 12:12

World Events

Nov. 26 – Poland renews its pact on non-aggression with the USSR.

Dec. 10 – Pearl Buck is awarded the Nobel Prize for literature.

SCORPIO
From October 24, 1:54 through November 22, 23:05

The Purposeful Independent

As a Scorpio of 1938 you have endless self-control and the gleam in your eye of someone that has always known where they were going. You have let very little stand in your way, especially when ensuring you or your family's security. You could be a shrewd financial operator, knowing that a solid foundation allowed you the freedom to decide how you wanted to live. Whatever your vocation, you probably coped well with positions of authority. You may even have enjoyed devising strategies to ensure you won the boardroom battles or the shop-floor power struggles. You would have been fascinated by Orson Welles' famous radio broadcast of *The War of the Worlds* this month. The panic he induced in the American public may have outraged some, but you probably would have been amused.

Your intuition has allowed you to see the writing on the wall, often before the ink was dry. You always have been adept at making speedy decisions or abrupt changes of direction if it was necessary to protect your interests. Those German Jews who had failed to foresee the coming horror and were unwilling or, more likely, unable to leave Germany could cling to no further illusions after the month you were born. Nazis set about killing them and destroying their homes, businesses, and synagogues on what infamously became known as *Kristallnacht*.

Home and family have always supplied you with your sense of security. You may also be a staunch believer in the merit of regular routines. Your family may have teased you, setting their watches by your habits, but you have never been afraid to cut things out of your life that no longer served any useful purpose.

You have always brought passion and intensity to relationships. While you did not give your trust easily, once you did you were always a generous and steadfast friend or partner. You may feel most comfortable with Taureans, Capricorns, Virgos, and Cancerians.

You may be a pretty serious type, Scorpio of 1938, and your challenge may have been to let a little frivolity into your life. Never flinching from your commitments remains your most enduring strength.

SAGITTARIUS
From November 22, 23:06 through December 22, 12:12

The Jovial Prophet

You may have always preferred to face the future rather than dwell on the past, Sagittarius of 1938. For you the journey was always so much more exciting than the final destination. You may have tried a multitude of different careers, often leaving them with no idea what you would do next. Like Charles Dickens' Mr. Micawber, you were always confident that something would turn up. You would have made a fantastic traveling salesperson with your love of movement; also, you had enough charm to sell ice to the Eskimos.

The main reason for any wandering may have been that you have always had to find a meaning in what you did. This search for the meaning of our existence underpins your entire approach to life. You may have been able to stomach routine if you understood and agreed with its purpose. In Britain this month, as war loomed, officials planned a national register so that every citizen would know what part they had to play when hostilities finally broke out.

Comradeship and the joining of groups to exchange ideas and promote your schemes may have formed a big part of your life. You could be a powerful communicator but it is also possible that it wasn't until your fifties that you had the confidence to try your hand at writing. It may only have been at that age that you felt that you had enough experience to pass on to others. Like Pearl Buck, this year's winner of the Nobel Prize for literature, what you want to communicate may be inextricably bound up with your own personal philosophy.

You may have enjoyed playing the romantic field and your engaging charm meant that you had plenty of opportunity. Your chosen partner needed to understand that while you were a fabulous companion you also needed your own interior space. Aquarians, Ariens, Geminis, and Librans may all have provided the right combination of closeness and space.

You get so enthusiastic that you can sometimes overdo it. Your challenge may have been to learn that sometimes less is more. Ever the optimist, your strength is that you are always able to see something positive even in the most disastrous events.

➤ Read about your Chinese Astrological sign on page 838. ➤ Read about your Personal Planets on page 826. ➤ Read about your personal Mystical Card on page 856.

CAPRICORN

From December 22, 12:13 through December 31, 23:59

The Serious Humorist

As a December Capricorn born in 1938 you may have realized early that you always gained the most satisfaction from seeing your efforts benefit others. Working purely to line your own pockets may never have held much appeal for you. You may have believed that it's every generation's duty to make improvements to the world that they inherited. You probably wanted to leave something valuable for your grandchildren and great-grandchildren. You may not be an inventor but you are comfortable with new technology and you may be amused to know that the prototype breath test, quaintly named the Drunkometer, was introduced this month in Indiana.

You've always understood that the material world needs to be balanced with spiritual understanding. You may not adhere to a specific religious doctrine and you accept all forms of worship. You are broad-minded and respectful of others' beliefs. If this sounds dull, you also number a playful sense of humor and an expertise at practical jokes among your attributes.

You also have a contrary streak that can sometimes put you at odds with others. Every Hollywood actress wanted to play the part of Scarlett O'Hara in *Gone with the Wind* but George Cukor gave it to Vivien Leigh, primarily a star of theater from England. Well suited to the part, Scarlett's wayward and willful character exactly mirrored Leigh's own—you would have approved.

You really enjoyed the dance of love and may still possess a magnetic attraction for others. Far more obviously passionate than typical Capricorns you may have fallen in love very deeply. Your commitment was unshakeable once you found the partner you wanted. You may have felt that Scorpios, Taureans, Pisceans, and Cancerians were the most likely to light your fire.

You may sometimes have felt that you didn't always measure up to your own exacting standards, December Capricorn of 1938. Your challenge may have been to strive not only for self-improvement but also to give yourself enough pats on the back. Your strength has always been your ability to see the funny side during even the most difficult setbacks.

1938

CAPRICORN
Your Personal Planets

YOUR LOVE POTENTIAL
Venus in Scorpio, Dec. 22, 12:13 - Dec. 31, 23:59

YOUR DRIVE AND AMBITION
Mars in Scorpio, Dec. 22, 12:13 - Dec. 31, 23:59

YOUR LUCK MAGNETISM
Jupiter in Aquarius, Dec. 22, 12:13 - Dec. 29, 18:33
Jupiter in Pisces, Dec. 29, 18:34 - Dec. 31, 23:59

World Events

Dec. 29 – American actor Jon Voigt is born.

Dec. 31 – Dr. R.N. Harger's "drunkometer," the first breath tester, is introduced in Indiana.

The Pyramids of Giza, Egypt

Special Feature
Ancient Secrets of the Great Pyramid

(Continued from page 313)

In the 1970s the next phase in pyramidology arrived, once again turning upside down twentieth-century concepts about the Great Pyramid's function and significance. According to this view, the Great Pyramid is the source of mysterious energy that has magical healing and regenerative properties. An explorer in the Pyramid's inner chambers noticed that stray cats, that must have wandered inside, were perfectly mummified. Further experiments suggested that the shape of the pyramid seemed to be focusing and accumulating electromagnetic energy, or some other unknown energy, that influenced the biological and chemical processes taking place inside the pyramid.

Karel Drbal obtained the first patent issued for a device based on this pyramid-power for the Cheop's Pyramid Razor Blade Sharpener. Using a six-inch pyramid oriented due north, he could get 200 shaves from one Gillette Blue Blade™. The pyramid shape was soon found to keep food fresher longer, reduce headache pain, and increase sexual potency. All kinds of pyramid products began showing up, including pyramid tents, energy generators, and pyramids to expand consciousness and cure illness. The 1973 book *Pyramid Power, The Millennium Science* became a bestseller by explaining how the pyramid's shape produces biocosmic energy.

One of the difficulties in solving the pyramid mystery is the disagreement over its construction date. Cayce, Sitchin, and others favor a construction date of 12,000 years ago. However, in the late 1990s, archaeologists discovered the tombs of the workers who supposedly built the pyramids. They also discovered the bakery, rock quarry, and other evidence that points to a completion date around 2566 B.C. In 1994, Robert Bauval's *The Orion Mystery* described how the Great Pyramid and its two companion pyramids are exact reflections of the stars in the belt of the Orion constellation, and depicts the Nile River as an analogue to the Milky Way. In his view, now shared by many followers and related theorists, the Pyramid is not merely a tomb but a metaphysical device to assist the Pharaoh's soul in its journey to distant stars. This interpretation would explain why the Pyramid's airshafts were constructed to align with different stars. In 10,500 B.C., these airshafts would have been perfectly lined up with the stars in Orion's Belt.

Is the Great Pyramid 4,500 years old or 12,000 years old? Was it created by aliens, Atlanteans, God, or ordinary Egyptians? Like a dream, the Great Pyramid is open to numerous interpretations, but in the final analysis, your thoughts on it depend on what you believe about the nature of reality and the origins of humanity. ✪

➤ Read more about Cayce in "The First New Age Psychic" on page 265. ➤ Read about UFOs in "The Extraterrestrial Highway" on page 465. ➤ Read "Gaia's Mystical Power Places" on page 745.

Talk Becomes Action: Uranus and Pluto Are Eclipsed

Eclipses, which amplify the symbolic expressions of planets and signs, in late 1938 connected with Uranus, the planet of chaos and upheaval, in stalwart Taurus. The stage was set for spontaneous and ruthless behavior. War, although undeclared, seemed inevitable as Germany claimed Czechoslovakia in March. The solar eclipse in April highlighted Pluto, planetary symbol of power spotlighting the compulsion to seize absolute control. War fears escalated when Hitler conscripted boys over age 9 in April and signed a war pact with Italy in May. Some leaders scrambled to ally themselves with whomever they thought was stronger. Stalin signed a treaty with Germany but Britain had vowed to defend Poland against invasion. As Mars began its biennial swing closest to earth in June, action stalled and taut emotions relaxed. However, when it was spotlighted by the Sun at the end of July, Hitler again threatened to invade Poland. When he made his move on September 1, allies Britain and France had no option but to declare war.

The times were not without their grace and beauty in 1939, however. Uranus, also associated with innovation, moved into a harmonious tie with Neptune, linked to the loftiest ideals and flights of fancy. The New York World's Fair proclaimed the stability and prosperity of a world emerging from the Great Depression and celebrated the wealth of global diversity. *The Wizard of Oz* dazzled cinema audiences with the fairy-tale beauty of the brilliant Emerald City, as well as the deeper moral lessons of living with ethics and heart demonstrated in the film.

Germany invades Poland, September 30, 1939

Britain and France declare war on Germany

Psychologist Sigmund Freud dies

IS THAT YOUR AURA, KIRLIAN?

Russian inventor-electrician Semyon Kirlian began his experiments in bio-electrophotography in 1939. Kirlian shot high voltage electricity through a metal plate upon which rested animate objects to produce photographic images instead of using a camera. Some researchers claim that the resulting pictures reveal auras and prove the physical existence of psychic energy. Kirlian photographs are also said to reveal health and emotion by changes in color. This type of photography has been used for diagnostic work.

WAR BEGINS IN EUROPE

Franco's Nationalist forces triumphed in the Spanish Civil War, while the rest of Czechoslovakia was overrun by Nazi Germany. Hitler and Mussolini signed the Pact of Steel, committing Germany and Italy to mutual support in war. Germany signed a Non-aggression pact with Russia. The Nazis invaded Poland with a decisive *blitzkrieg* (lighting war) campaign. In response, Britain and France declared war on Germany and made a mutual assistance pact with Turkey. Latvia signed a mutual aid pact with Russia. The U.S. maintained neutrality, and even though its population remained focused internally, President Roosevelt escalated efforts to create better wartime preparedness, approving a record military budget. Standard Oil agreed with Saudi Arabia to drill its oil, based on King Ibn Saud's faith in the U.S. Hollywood produced *The Wizard of Oz* with Judy Garland and released *Gone with the Wind*, which won eight Oscars including Best Picture and Best Actress (Vivien Leigh). Joyce's *Finnegan's Wake* and Steinbeck's *The Grapes of Wrath* were published. Psychologist Sigmund Freud died, leaving the world wiser for his insights into the human psyche.

➤ Read The Duke of Windsor's (Edward VIII) Star Profile on page 329.

CAPRICORN

From January 01, 0:00 through January 20, 22:50

Resolute Realist

Capricorns are noted for their determination and slow, steady progress, but you, January Capricorn of 1939, are even more persistent than most. Once you set a goal for yourself, you don't quit until you've achieved it. You have an ability to determine what's important, then you focus all your energy on it. Other people may have trouble separating the wheat from the chaff—but not you.

You don't let obstacles stand in your way; you, 1939 Capricorn, find ways to overcome them. At times, you might appear a bit ruthless, but you always get the job done. Especially in the business world, you can excel due to a combination of common sense and hard work. You may expect a lot from other people, but even more of yourself. You have what it takes to rise to the top and to earn a good living, perhaps by working for a large, established company. Law or science also might appeal to you.

Because you were born on the brink of war, the harsh reality of death might have influenced you. You take personal and professional matters very seriously. You don't waste time on things that are inconsequential. While you are mainly devoted to matters close to home—earning a living, family, and community—you are also interested in issues of a broader scope. Despite your down-to-earth approach, you also look beneath the surface for answers.

Reserved and shy in most areas of life, you still let down your guard at times and enjoy good times with loved ones. You will probably be happiest if you surround yourself with good-natured Taureans or Sagittarians, who have a way of bringing out your lighter side. Going to movies with friends might be one of your favorite forms of entertainment—especially films that allow you to escape from reality, such as *The Wizard of Oz* or *Gone with The Wind*, which were produced the year you were born.

Your rather severe exterior can sometimes be intimidating to those who don't know you well. Your challenge is to lighten up and look on the positive side. Your strength is your determined, persevering nature that keep you going when other, weaker sorts fail to keep going.

AQUARIUS

From January 20, 22:51 through February 19, 13:08

The Independent Thinker

You have a strong sense of right and wrong, Aquarius of 1939, perhaps because the twin forces of Hitler and Mussolini oppressed Europe when you were born. You are quick to spot injustices and don't hesitate to speak out against them. Even if your views are ahead of the times or unpopular with others—and they often are—you champion them with passion and determination. Most likely, you've ruffled a few people's feathers in your time.

Because you think for yourself rather than simply accepting what you are told, you can make some original discoveries. Science was changing the world at the time you were born—the first uranium atom was split in the month you were born after years of experimentation—and you may have developed an interest in science or technology as a result. Quite likely, you have an inventive mind and are always in the vanguard.

In both professional and personal areas, you are likely to exhibit your humanitarianism. You want to see people everywhere treated fairly and might become involved in movements for social change, labor reform, or human rights. John Steinbeck's novel, *The Grapes of Wrath*, published the year of your birth, might be one of your favorite books.

Although you are sure to upset conventional types, others admire you for your refreshing uniqueness. You probably have a large circle of friends and might be a member of one or more organizations of like-minded individuals. Drawn to people from all walks of life, your companions are likely to be lively, intelligent, and uninhibited people. You usually get along well with Ariens, Geminis, and Sagittarians.

A career in electronics, medicine, or engineering could have appealed to you and you might have had a hand in bringing about some important technological advances. You need change, stimulation, and an opportunity to make your own decisions in order to do your best. Your challenge is to temper your independent spirit with pragmatism, so you can usher in constructive changes without alienating other people. Your strengths are your ingenuity and your original method for solving problems.

► Read about your Chinese Astrological sign on page 838. ► Read about your Personal Planets on page 826. ► Read about your personal Mystical Card on page 856.

CAPRICORN
Your Personal Planets

YOUR LOVE POTENTIAL
Venus in Scorpio, Jan. 01, 0:00 - Jan. 04, 21:47
Venus in Sagittarius, Jan. 04, 21:48 - Jan. 20, 22:50

YOUR DRIVE AND AMBITION
Mars in Scorpio, Jan. 01, 0:00 - Jan. 20, 22:50

YOUR LUCK MAGNETISM
Jupiter in Pisces, Jan. 01, 0:00 - Jan. 20, 22:50

World Events

Jan. 1 – The Hewlett-Packard Company is established.
Jan. 4 – The fascist Baron Hiranuma becomes ruler of Japan.

Baron Hiranuma, ruler of Japan

AQUARIUS
Your Personal Planets

YOUR LOVE POTENTIAL
Venus in Sagittarius, Jan. 20, 22:51 - Feb. 06, 9:19
Venus in Capricorn, Feb. 06, 9:20 - Feb. 19, 13:08

YOUR DRIVE AND AMBITION
Mars in Scorpio, Jan. 20, 22:51 - Jan. 29, 9:48
Mars in Sagittarius, Jan. 29, 9:49 - Feb. 19, 13:08

YOUR LUCK MAGNETISM
Jupiter in Pisces, Jan. 20, 22:51 - Feb. 19, 13:08

World Events

Jan. 26 – Cheering crowds welcome Gen. Francisco Franco's troops into Barcelona.
Jan. 28 – Irish poet W. B. Yeats dies.

1939

PISCES
Your Personal Planets

YOUR LOVE POTENTIAL

Venus in Capricorn, Feb. 19, 13:09 - Mar. 05, 13:28
Venus in Aquarius, Mar. 05, 13:29 - Mar. 21, 12:27

YOUR DRIVE AND AMBITION

Mars in Sagittarius, Feb. 19, 13:09 - Mar. 21, 7:24
Mars in Capricorn, Mar. 21, 7:25 - Mar. 21, 12:27

YOUR LUCK MAGNETISM

Jupiter in Pisces, Feb. 19, 13:09 - Mar. 21, 12:27

World Events

Mar. 12 – Eugenio Pacelli is crowned Pope Pius XII.

Mar. 15 – On Hitler's orders, the German army invades Czechoslovakia and enters Prague.

Cardinal Pacelli becomes Pope Pius XII

ARIES
Your Personal Planets

YOUR LOVE POTENTIAL

Venus in Aquarius, Mar. 21, 12:28 - Mar. 31, 8:33
Venus in Pisces, Mar. 31, 8:34 - Apr. 20, 23:54

YOUR DRIVE AND AMBITION

Mars in Capricorn, Mar. 21, 12:28 - Apr. 20, 23:54

YOUR LUCK MAGNETISM

Jupiter in Pisces, Mar. 21, 12:28 - Apr. 20, 23:54

World Events

Mar. 28 – Franco captures Madrid, effectively concluding the Spanish Civil War.

Apr. 7 – Italy invades Albania.

PISCES
From February 19, 13:09 through March 21, 12:27

The Beautiful Dreamer

The real world doesn't hold much appeal for you, Pisces of 1939. Instead, you dream of exciting adventures and magical places that let you get away from your everyday existence. Born when war raged in Europe, you might have desired to escape into the realm of fantasy where the good guys always win—as in the Superman comic strip, which debuted the year of your birth.

Your creativity might have led you to choose a career in commercial or fine arts. Music, theater, or poetry might also interest you. Even if you don't earn a living at these pursuits, you probably enjoy dabbling in artistic activities in your spare time. Your keen sense of color and harmony can enable you to transform your living environment into a place of beauty or turn the plainest outfit into something glamorous.

Your idealism can make you restless, and you don't have much tolerance for routine. Distant horizons call to you—you want to see and experience as much of the world as possible. If you do travel, a peaceful ocean voyage may soothe your soul. Spiritual journeys could also be beneficial to you. Most likely, you have a mystical side, and whether or not you are conventionally religious, you probably have faith in something beyond the physical world.

Extremely sensitive, your emotions are easily engaged. Less sensitive people may bruise your tender feelings without realizing it. Therefore, you might be wise to surround yourself with others who, like yourself, are gentle and considerate, such as Cancerians or Taureans—even though you may admire more outspoken and independent sorts such as Aquarians and Sagittarians.

Your sensitivity gives you a keen intuition, too; you seem to be able to sense what other people are thinking and feeling. Consequently, you could be a natural at psychology or the healing arts. Social services might be a good field for you—with your compassionate nature, you want to help those in need. Your strength is your kindheartedness and desire to make the world a better place. Your challenge is to bring your dreams down to Earth where they can benefit you and others.

ARIES
From March 21, 12:28 through April 20, 23:54

The Fearless Defender

One of the things people admire about you, Aries of 1939, is your willingness to stand up for what you believe. Born during a period when the Nazis were committing atrocities in Europe, you want to combat evil in the world. You have strong opinions and you act on them. With zeal and forthrightness, you confront bogus authority and attempt to bring about changes in systems that you feel are outdated or oppressive.

Your fighting spirit is likely to show from the playing field to the workplace. This spirit might have led you to become an outstanding athlete, like boxer Joe Louis who won the heavyweight title the year of your birth. You go head-to-head with adversaries and often win through a unique combination of assertiveness and determination. With your quick temper, you might have made your share of enemies but you also have what it takes to accomplish a great deal for yourself and others. As a result, you've undoubtedly attracted many friends and supporters.

You tend to jump in before you know exactly what you're getting into. It seems that you are always ready to take a risk and might pursue things that other, more cautious individuals avoid. However, you can rein in your restless nature when necessary to achieve your goals. Perhaps you excelled as an entrepreneur, stockbroker, salesperson, or in some other field that allowed you to operate independently. Jobs that require lots of action and even danger, such as police work, the military, or fire fighting, might also appeal to you.

Many of your battles may be waged in the name of a good cause; you have quite a compassionate side. Loved ones know they can depend on you to defend and protect them. In relationships, you are quite idealistic and tend to get along best with Aquarians or Sagittarians who share your optimism and high ideals.

As you matured, any hot-headedness mellowed and you might actually accomplish more than you did in your youth, without wasting so much energy. Your courage and enthusiasm are your strengths. Your challenge is to find constructive ways to work within the system to implement change.

➤ Read about your Chinese Astrological sign on page 838. ➤ Read about your Personal Planets on page 826. ➤ Read about your personal Mystical Card on page 856.

TAURUS

From April 20, 23:55 through May 21, 23:26

The Energetic Builder

You have a strong appreciation for the material world and, like most Taureans, you use your energy in ways that will produce tangible, lasting results. But, unlike your fellow Bulls, Taurus of 1939, you aren't a plodder. Instead, you might even behave in a spontaneous or unpredictable manner at times. While you value structure, order, and stability, you also understand the need for change.

You particularly favor updates that improve quality of life, like the air conditioning in cars that was introduced the year of your birth. Your home probably showcases the latest and finest gadgetry—as soon as a newer, better model comes out, you want it and don't mind paying for quality. You may also be a dedicated follower of fashion.

Fortunately, you possess the instincts to attract money and sometimes know which investments will pay off before the experts do. You may have experienced some financial ups and downs, for you are willing to take a risk now and again. With your determination, abundant energy, and strong work ethic, however, you usually find yourself secure.

You may appear quiet and even a bit lethargic at first glance, but it doesn't take long before you reveal your uninhibited side. You have to be pushed before you show your temper and these occasional bursts dissipate quickly. There is nothing devious or manipulative about you. You build relationships with enthusiasm and expect them to last a lifetime. Capricorns and Pisceans, whose company wears well, are probably the people with whom you are most compatible.

With your creative ability, you might have been successful as an architect or engineer. Or you might have chosen to express yourself tangibly as an interior decorator, fashion designer, carpenter, landscaper, or beautician. Cooking is likely to be a favorite pastime of yours, and whether or not you do it professionally, you possess skills in this area that your loved ones enjoy. Your strength is your ability to give an original twist to whatever you do. Your challenge is not to try to do everything yourself—let other people shoulder some of the load.

GEMINI

From May 21, 23:27 through June 22, 7:38

The Forward Thinker

You were born during a period of rapid technological growth that influenced you and the people around you at a profound level. As a result, Gemini of 1939, you are an inventive and forward-thinking individual. Always in the vanguard, your original ideas may break new ground or change the way people perceive things forever. You energetically seek new approaches to old problems and your quick mind can usually come up with a clever solution.

You pursue learning with gusto and are rarely without a book, magazine, or newspaper. John Steinbeck, whose influential novel *The Grapes of Wrath* was published the year of your birth, might be one of your favorite authors. Your range of interests is vast and diverse, and you probably know a little bit about everything.

Consequently, you can converse on nearly any subject. You like nothing better than a lively discourse with other original thinkers. Of course, few people are as mentally deft as you, but you are eager to bring them up to speed. You could have been an inspired teacher or thought-provoking writer. Computers, too, might have offered you a challenging career.

You are the quintessential networker and may have a web of contacts with which you stay in touch via phone, email, and letters. With your outgoing, upbeat personality, you tend to attract many friends who enjoy sharing ideas and good times with you. You are loyal and devoted to those you love and always have time for them. Sociable and talkative Aquarians, Librans, and Sagittarians are often your favorite companions.

Restless and changeable, you are always on the go and grow bored quickly with anything routine. You have so many interests, activities, and hobbies that you need several calendars to keep track of all your engagements. Although you want to try everything and hate thinking that you might miss out on something, you can run the risk of spreading yourself too thin or starting more projects than you can finish. Your challenge is to set priorities and stay focused on them. Your strengths are your flexibility and ability to adapt to changing circumstances.

➤ Read about your Chinese Astrological sign on page 838. ➤ Read about your Personal Planets on page 826. ➤ Read about your personal Mystical Card on page 856.

1939

TAURUS
Your Personal Planets

YOUR LOVE POTENTIAL
Venus in Pisces, Apr. 20, 23:55 - Apr. 25, 14:27
Venus in Aries, Apr. 25, 14:28 - May 20, 14:12
Venus in Taurus, May 20, 14:13 - May 21, 23:26

YOUR DRIVE AND AMBITION
Mars in Capricorn, Apr. 20, 23:55 - May 21, 23:26

YOUR LUCK MAGNETISM
Jupiter in Pisces, Apr. 20, 23:55 - May 11, 14:07
Jupiter in Aries, May 11, 14:08 - May 21, 23:26

World Events

Apr. 30 – "The World of Tomorrow" – the New York World's Fair – is opened by President Roosevelt.

May 19 – Britain signs an anti-Nazi agreement with the USSR.

Hitler and Mussolini agree to the "Pact of Steel"

GEMINI
Your Personal Planets

YOUR LOVE POTENTIAL
Venus in Taurus, May 21, 23:27 - June 14, 10:10
Venus in Gemini, June 14, 10:11 - June 22, 7:38

YOUR DRIVE AND AMBITION
Mars in Capricorn, May 21, 23:27 - May 25, 0:18
Mars in Aquarius, May 25, 0:19 - June 22, 7:38

YOUR LUCK MAGNETISM
Jupiter in Aries, May 21, 23:27 - June 22, 7:38

World Events

May 22 – Hitler and Mussolini sign what becomes known as the "Pact of Steel," agreeing a military alliance.

May 23 – The British Parliament approves a plan for Palestinian independence in ten years, with power divided between Arabs and Jews.

1939

CANCER
Your Personal Planets

YOUR LOVE POTENTIAL
Venus in Gemini, June 22, 7:39 - July 09, 2:24
Venus in Cancer, July 09, 2:25 - July 23, 18:36

YOUR DRIVE AND AMBITION
Mars in Aquarius, June 22, 7:39 - July 21, 19:30
Mars in Capricorn, July 21, 19:31 - July 23, 18:36

YOUR LUCK MAGNETISM
Jupiter in Aries, June 22, 7:39 - July 23, 18:36

World Events

June 24 - Three thousand German Jewish refugees find asylum in Brazil.

July 10 - The first passenger flight over the Atlantic is completed by the *Yankee Clipper*.

Judy Garland as Dorothy in "The Wizard of Oz"

LEO
Your Personal Planets

YOUR LOVE POTENTIAL
Venus in Cancer, July 23, 18:37 - Aug. 02, 14:10
Venus in Leo, Aug. 02, 14:11 - Aug. 24, 1:30

YOUR DRIVE AND AMBITION
Mars in Capricorn, July 23, 18:37 - Aug. 24, 1:30

YOUR LUCK MAGNETISM
Jupiter in Aries, July 23, 18:37 - Aug. 24, 1:30

World Events

Aug. 2 - Albert Einstein writes to President Roosevelt explaining that the creation of an atomic bomb is possible.

Aug. 15 - The *Wizard Of Oz* premieres in New York.

CANCER
From June 22, 7:39 through July 23, 18:36

The Outspoken Patriot

The nations of the world into which you were born, Cancer of 1939, were forming alliances as World War II raged in Europe. The intense political fervor of the times—and the patriotism that the situation engendered—no doubt imprinted itself upon you. As a result, you have a strong sense of patriotism and support your country. You also pledge your allegiance to your community and family.

You hold strong, emotionally-fueled beliefs and speak out in support of them. While you value the traditions in which you were raised, you also understand the need to embrace new developments in technology, science, and social systems. You believe people can rise above their backgrounds through education, becoming valuable contributors to their society.

You will go to great lengths to establish a secure environment for yourself and those you love. Although you have a tendency to be outspoken and idealistic, your views often parallel those of the establishment. Periodically, however, your independent nature and your desire for security may clash.

Despite your rather conservative nature, you take risks in business and economic areas. Your intuition allows you to sense and tap the zeitgeist to your advantage. A career in advertising, fashion, entertainment, or politics might have been ideal for you. You also possess a unique ability to gauge what the future holds, trusting your instincts is likely to pay off for you.

Family oriented, you usually prefer to spend time at home with a few close loved ones rather than going out on the town. However, you probably have a diverse assortment of contacts and associates whom you consider to be an extended family. While you may be drawn to independent types such as Aquarians, Geminis, and Ariens, these people might be too abrasive for you to be totally comfortable. Pisceans, Taureans, and other Cancerians are more likely to offer you the understanding and comfort you desire. Your challenge is to unite your head and heart, so they work together in harmony. Your greatest strength is your ability to ascertain what others need and provide it for them.

LEO
From July 23, 18:37 through August 24, 1:30

The Enduring Star

Your unique vision, Leo of 1939, has such depth and richness that it transcends its own time. As a result, your creations are likely to appeal to future generations as much as they do your own. Like *The Wizard of Oz* and *Gone With The Wind*, which were produced the year you were born, the products of your fertile imagination touch something fundamental in all of us.

Regardless of whether you consider yourself to be an artist, you infuse everything you do with grandeur and drama. You may have excelled in a career in one of the commercial, fine, or performing arts, where you had an opportunity to shine and express your special talents. But any position that allows you to be a star, such as politics, sports, or the entertainment industry, would also suit you well. When the spotlight is on you, you rise to the occasion.

You claim authority as if you were born to it. Other people admire your charisma and style, and are willing to let you take charge. With your unique combination of courage, determination, and responsibility, you could succeed as the head of a corporation or nation. Although some tend to be a bit self-centered and have a strong individualistic streak, Leos don't shirk their duty.

A romantic at heart, you bring drama and excitement to all your relationships. One might say you are in love with love. You enjoy the attention of other people and like showing generosity to your loved ones. To your faithful followers, you bestow largesse and undying loyalty. You are usually most compatible with other energetic, colorful people such as Ariens and Sagittarians, but could also get along with Geminis and Librans.

Unlike many creative people, you don't just dream beautiful dreams, you make your visions realities. Along the way, you might inspire others and you are willing to help them fulfill their potential. You know that behind every overnight success lies years of dedicated effort. Your challenge is to find practical applications for your talents and creativity. Your greatest strength is your ability to create artistic works that can stand the test of time.

► Read about your Chinese Astrological sign on page 838. ► Read about your Personal Planets on page 826. ► Read about your personal Mystical Card on page 856.

VIRGO

From August 24, 1:31 through September 23, 22:48

The Efficiency Expert

No one has a better sense of order than you, Virgo of 1939. You understand the meaning of the saying "a place for everything and everything in its place." You aren't just being fussy, you know that good organization saves time and money. You always manage to make things function efficiently, perfecting the tools and systems around you. When a problem arises, you are usually the one who is called in to fix it.

Hard-working and conscientious, you do your best at every task you undertake. Some might call you a perfectionist, for you set high standards for yourself and others. Jobs that require precision, such as accounting, editing, computer programming, or engineering, could be good choices for you. Process-oriented, you may be less interested in the result than you are in the steps necessary to get there.

You have a compassionate, humanitarian side too, and want to do what you can to alleviate suffering in the world. You were born the year the Social Security Administration approved unemployment compensation and food stamps were issued for the first time in the U.S. Being of service is important to you, and you may choose to work in the field of health care or social services to help those in need.

Despite your obvious skills, you tend to be rather modest, preferring to work behind the scenes in a support position. Your shyness and reserve are apparent in personal relationships as well. Usually, you wait for the other person to make the first move. You tend to judge yourself too harshly and probably think others are more critical of you than they really are. In fact, many people are drawn to your kindness and your quiet, unassuming nature. Capricorns, Taureans, Cancers, and other Virgos usually make the best companions for you.

Although you are able to resolve many problems with your practicality and efficiency, you have a tendency to rely on tried and true methods and may avoid anything you don't understand. Your challenge is to try to be more daring, trusting that you will succeed. Your greatest strength is your careful and meticulous way of approaching life.

LIBRA

From September 23, 22:49 through October 24, 7:45

The Inspired Coordinator

You are an expert at coordinating people and organizing group endeavors because you understand all sides of any issue or problem, Libra of 1939. You can usually assuage people's egos and design solutions that keep everyone happy. You have a special talent for finding the right person for the right job.

You also possess a knack for inspiring others. Your sense of fairness and your willingness to give everyone a chance encourages them to get behind your plans. People know they can come to you if they have a problem, and you can usually offer good advice. You also realize that the carrot works better than the stick in most situations, and you use positive incentives to bring out the best in others.

The tension and chaos that surrounded your formative years may have caused you to place a high value on peace. You abhor discord and often go to great lengths to bring about harmony. A skillful negotiator, you are frequently called in to solve disputes and might have been successful as a lawyer, counselor, mediator, personnel manager, or diplomat.

You want everything to be peaceful in your personal life as well. At times, your desire for harmony may cause you to compromise too readily. You rarely offend or alienate anyone, partly because you want to be liked. A real people person, you hate being alone and probably have a large circle of friends and associates. Relationships of all kinds are important to you and you might identify yourself by the company you keep. You may even stay in a partnership that is less than satisfactory rather than risk being lonely. Sociable, intellectually oriented people such as Geminis, Aquarians, Leos, and Sagittarians are usually your favorite companions.

You appreciate beauty and nice things. You might possess creative talent but, whether you have pursued a career in the arts or not, you probably surround yourself with art and your home is a place of grace and refinement. Your greatest strength is your ability to find beauty in everything and everyone. Your challenge is to know your own mind and not allow yourself to be swayed by others.

➤ Read about your Chinese Astrological sign on page 838. ➤ Read about your Personal Planets on page 826. ➤ Read about your personal Mystical Card on page 856.

VIRGO
Your Personal Planets

YOUR LOVE POTENTIAL
Venus in Leo, Aug. 24, 1:31 - Aug. 26, 21:23
Venus in Virgo, Aug. 26, 21:24 - Sept. 20, 1:01
Venus in Libra, Sept. 20, 1:02 - Sept. 23, 22:48

YOUR DRIVE AND AMBITION
Mars in Capricorn, Aug. 24, 1:31 - Sept. 23, 22:48

YOUR LUCK MAGNETISM
Jupiter in Aries, Aug. 24, 1:31 - Sept. 23, 22:48

World Events

Sept. 1 - German forces march into Poland, instigating World War II.

Sept. 3 - Britain and France declare war on Germany.

Britain and France declare war on Germany

LIBRA
Your Personal Planets

YOUR LOVE POTENTIAL
Venus in Libra, Sept. 23, 22:49 - Oct. 14, 2:40
Venus in Scorpio, Oct. 14, 2:41 - Oct. 24, 7:45

YOUR DRIVE AND AMBITION
Mars in Capricorn, Sept. 23, 22:49 - Sept. 24, 1:12
Mars in Aquarius, Sept. 24, 1:13 - Oct. 24, 7:45

YOUR LUCK MAGNETISM
Jupiter in Aries, Sept. 23, 22:49 - Oct. 24, 7:45

World Events

Sept. 23 - German pioneering psychoanalyst Sigmund Freud dies.

Oct. 6 - In an address to the Reichstag, Hitler states he had no intention of waging war with Britain and France.

1939

SCORPIO
Your Personal Planets

YOUR LOVE POTENTIAL
Venus in Scorpio, Oct. 24, 7:46 - Nov. 07, 3:40
Venus in Sagittarius, Nov. 07, 3:41 - Nov. 23, 4:58

YOUR DRIVE AND AMBITION
Mars in Aquarius, Oct. 24, 7:46 - Nov. 19, 15:55
Mars in Pisces, Nov. 19, 15:56 - Nov. 23, 4:58

YOUR LUCK MAGNETISM
Jupiter in Aries, Oct. 24, 7:46 - Oct. 30, 0:44
Jupiter in Pisces, Oct. 30, 0:45 - Nov. 23, 4:58

World Events

Oct. 24 – Nylon stockings go on sale in the U.S.

Nov. 18 – The IRA detonates three bombs in London's Piccadilly Circus.

"Gone With The Wind" premieres in Atlanta, Georgia

SAGITTARIUS
Your Personal Planets

YOUR LOVE POTENTIAL
Venus in Sagittarius, Nov. 23, 4:59 - Dec. 01, 4:51
Venus in Capricorn, Dec. 01, 4:52 - Dec. 22, 18:05

YOUR DRIVE AND AMBITION
Mars in Pisces, Nov. 23, 4:59 - Dec. 22, 18:05

YOUR LUCK MAGNETISM
Jupiter in Pisces, Nov. 23, 4:59 - Dec. 20, 17:02
Jupiter in Aries, Dec. 20, 17:03 - Dec. 22, 18:05

World Events

Nov. 24 – In Czechoslovakia, the Gestapo executes 120 students accused of anti-Nazi plotting.

Dec. 15 – *Gone With The Wind* premières in Atlanta, Georgia.

SCORPIO
From October 24, 7:46 through November 23, 4:58

The Intuitive Powerbroker

Powerful forces were at work at the time of your birth and during your formative years, Scorpio of 1939. Hitler and Mussolini were trying to take over Europe and the world was poised for a power struggle of monumental proportion. As a result, you have a strong need to control your environment, perhaps because you fear that things will degenerate into chaos if you don't keep your hand on the wheel.

Although you have strong emotions, you generally keep them under control. To the outside world, you present an image of a powerful, capable leader. Indeed, you are better than most people at remaining cool under pressure. However, you do have a fiery temper and when you let it out, other people would be wise to stay out of your way. You can be a fierce foe or a powerful ally.

No doubt, your life has been a series of changes and challenges. Perhaps you have experienced many ups and downs in your career or your economic position. You manage to handle these upsets and tensions better than most people could, and you muster your tremendous resources to overcome obstacles. You have a unique ability to turn setbacks into advantages. With your special talent for transforming old practices, systems, ideas, and structures into new, improved ones, you could have excelled in a career as a demolitions expert, building renovator, psychiatrist, political reformer, or plastic surgeon.

Most likely you insist on having power and control in your relationships as well. Your keen intuition and observation enable you to understand what makes people tick, and you can use this knowledge to your advantage. Some individuals may be intimidated by your commanding personality, but those who know you appreciate your loyalty, passion, and protectiveness. You may not have many friends, but the ones you do have are dear to you. Usually you get along best with Cancers and Pisceans, who are intuitive and emotional like you.

Your strength lies in your ability to transform the world around you and to bring about radical changes. Your challenge is to do this in a constructive, rather than a destructive way.

SAGITTARIUS
From November 23, 4:59 through December 22, 18:05

The Restless Seeker

Your restless nature might lead you to travel in search of happiness, wisdom, and freedom, Sagittarius of 1939. With your boundless curiosity, you probably rush from place to place, activity to activity, and person to person in pursuit of adventure. Like New York's La Guardia Airport, which began operations at the same time you were born, you attract people of all kinds from faraway lands. You might even make a career of traveling as a pilot, tour guide, truck driver, or foreign correspondent.

Like fellow Sagittarian, Walt Disney, you possess a wonderful imagination and sense of humor. One of your special talents may be storytelling. You may use your inventiveness to weave fascinating tales of a futuristic or magical nature, like the *Superman* stories that first appeared in 1939. You may also have a knack for knowing what the public will want in the near future. This quality could prove a valuable asset in the fields of fashion design, entertainment, publishing, or investments.

Hungry for knowledge, you are probably a lifelong student. Religion or philosophy might be special interests of yours. You could also be intrigued by the mysteries of the human psyche, inspired by psychology pioneer Sigmund Freud who died the year you were born. Your education, however, may often come through experience rather than books. You enjoy sharing what you know with other people and could be an enthusiastic teacher.

Friendly, buoyant, and versatile, you collect people the way you collect adventures. However, your restlessness and idealism may make it difficult for you to commit to a life partner—someone better suited might come along. Lively and adventurous Ariens, Leos, and Aquarians usually make the best companions for you; however, a Capricorn partner could help you keep reality in sight.

While you may roam the globe in your quest for experience and knowledge, the real quest lies within you. Only there will you find the meaning of life that you seek. Your expansiveness and vision are your greatest strengths. Your challenge is to remain focused on a goal long enough to reach it.

➤ Read about your Chinese Astrological sign on page 838. ➤ Read about your Personal Planets on page 826. ➤ Read about your personal Mystical Card on page 856.

CAPRICORN

The Inspired Manager

Like most Capricorns, you possess the gifts of common sense and determination that can help you succeed in virtually any undertaking. You know instinctively how to manage people, resources, and time so that you can accomplish your goals. You can be depended on to get the job done and set a good example for your associates. Your special skills can serve you particularly well in the business world, although law, banking, medicine, venture capitalism, or real estate might also appeal.

Unlike some Capricorns, you also exhibit insight and ingenuity, December Capricorn of 1939. You respect the past and draw on traditional methods, but you also look for new, inspired ways to accomplish tasks. Your willingness to think beyond safe tradition often puts you ahead of your competition. Like the makers of the Packard automobile who installed air conditioning in their cars for the first time in 1939, you know a good thing when you see it. Your ability to "think outside the box" has probably helped you profit in many ways.

Born as Europe was in the midst of a war that would ultimately change the order of the continent, you were probably imprinted with a sense that change is both inevitable and, at times, desirable. Thus you developed a willingness to change with changing times, though you prefer to make adjustments at a slow, steady, comfortable pace.

Although you are ambitious, you are practical enough to know you can't do everything yourself. You surround yourself with capable people and delegate authority to them. Thus, you garner respect from those who know you in business and personally. You are loyal, understanding, and supportive to friends, loved ones, and colleagues alike. Although you have a serious side, you can also enjoy meeting new people from all walks of life. You usually get along well with Taureans and Pisceans, though you might be inspired by the lively minds of Aquarians and Sagittarians.

Your greatest strength is your ability to blend new ideas and procedures into traditional practices. Your challenge is to achieve a comfortable balance between work and home life.

1939

CAPRICORN
Your Personal Planets

YOUR LOVE POTENTIAL
Venus in Capricorn, Dec. 22, 18:06 - Dec. 25, 7:24
Venus in Aquarius, Dec. 25, 7:25 - Dec. 31, 23:59

YOUR DRIVE AND AMBITION
Mars in Pisces, Dec. 22, 18:06 - Dec. 31, 23:59

YOUR LUCK MAGNETISM
Jupiter in Aries, Dec. 22, 18:06 - Dec. 31, 23:59

World Events

Dec. 22 – "Mother of the Blues" singer and composer Ma Rainey dies.
Dec. 27 – Earthquakes across Turkey claim 11,000 lives.

Duke of Windsor
June 23, 1894 - May 28, 1972

DUKE OF WINDSOR
(Edward VIII)
Cancer

One of the most dramatic love stories of the twentieth century was the King of England abdicating his throne "for the woman he loved." However, when we look at the horoscope of the former King Edward VIII, who became the Duke of Windsor, we see a more complicated person than first impressions may suggest.

Much has been written about the fact that "David," as he was intimately known, was a strong-willed Cancer, and with Moon, planet of emotions, in Pisces, the ultimate sign of feeling, he was the tender, emotional sort of person not well suited for the public life of a royal. But there was more to David than his emotional side. A connection from Uranus, planet of boldness, freedom and eccentricity, to both Sun (his ego) and Moon (his heart), gave him an individualistic and independent nature along with the determination to express himself as he chose without royal restrictions. His need for

self-determination is further emphasized by Mars, the planet of assertiveness, in impetuous Aries, strengthening his reticent, gentle Cancer Sun. The man may well have been sensitive and playful, but those who felt he was merely weak or puppet-like were completely wrong.

With the Sun in his horoscope's fifth house of pleasure, David loved to socialize and enjoy life, but the key to this royal's choice of love over the throne lies in his fourth house of personal emotional foundation. Both illusory Neptune and dominating Pluto are placed there, making it hard for him to find happiness living the life for which he was bred. He felt stifled and needed freedom to do as he pleased. Interestingly, Wallis shared these traits with her true love, creating an emotional resonance between them.

In choosing his dazzling divorcee over duty, David opted to be where he was most comfortable—with someone who understood

him at the core and with whom he could create a life for which he was truly suited. This pairing allowed David to preside more adroitly over sparkling international social circles than he ever would have done in his limited capacity on the throne of England.

➤ Read about Queen Elizabeth II in "An Astrology Family Tree: The British Royal Family" on page 425. ➤ Read Princess Diana's Star Profile on page 689. ➤ Read Queen Elizabeth's Star Profile on page 449.

1940

Holy Crusades: Planets in Fire Signs

At the start of the year in 1940, three important planets were holding court in the first sign of the zodiac, the feisty and unstoppable Aries. Mars, Jupiter, and Saturn were warmly ensconced in the fiery belly of the sign of the Ram as the year opened. Because Mars is right at home in Aries and Jupiter is ruled by another fire sign, the philosophical Sagittarius, the events of this year tended to be conflagrations, not just tiny brush fires. Saturn in Aries gives substance to the initiative that Aries inspires. With all this Aries energy in the air, events happened in blazing ways.

World War II was exploding all over Western Europe and North East Africa. Later in the year, in May, Winston Churchill, 65, a trailblazing Sagittarian with a vision, became British Prime Minister. It was just in time, too, because his wise leadership was needed to fight the war. Churchill's chart was all lit up in 1940. With his Sun in Sagittarius and his Moon in Leo, he was a true firebrand. Mars, planet of action and force; Jupiter, planet of truth-seeking adventure; and Saturn, planet of reason and karma, were all activating his major planets. This is because Sagittarius and Leo, just like Aries, are fire signs. Churchill's natal Venus was also in Sagittarius and when these three planets contacted his Venus, it made Churchill not only look like the man of the hour but enabled him to actually become it. Venus is the planet that rules attractiveness. In 1940 Churchill certainly looked the attractive leader to his embattled nation as it struggled to resist German aggression.

Winston Churchill succeeds Neville Chamberlain as Prime Minister of Britain

The RAF fight the Battle of Britain against the German Luftwaffe

Prehistoric cave paintings are discovered at Lascaux

DOUBLE LIFE

Biological factors explain physical similarities between twins but sometimes the similarities in the details of their lives are extraordinary even if they do not grow up together. Two separate sets of parents each adopted one twin boy shortly after their birth in 1940. Forty years later the twins reunited and discovered they both had been christened James, married a woman named Linda, and had one son named James Alan. Each had subsequently divorced and remarried a woman named Betty; and both had a dog named Toy.

THWARTING THE ENEMY

In April and May, the forces of Nazi Germany invaded and overran Belgium, the Netherlands, Luxembourg, and France. Despite isolationist anti-war sentiment, American President Roosevelt ordered the training of 50,000 war pilots and supplied arms and munitions to the Allies. Occupied France was divided between a German-ruled north and the collaborationist Vichy regime in the south. Italy entered the war on the German side. Winston Churchill succeeded Chamberlain as British Prime Minister. The Royal Air Force, helped by RADAR, ferociously fought the German Luftwaffe in the Battle of Britain. German bombers raided British towns, but the RAF, helped by RADAR, ultimately prevailed. Hitler postponed his planned invasion of Britain "indefinitely". In Tibet, the new five-year-old Dalai Lama was enthroned. The 9,000-year-old mummified body of a "white" human was discovered at Spirit Cave in Nevada and a cave containing significant prehistoric art was found at Lascaux in France. Leo Trotsky was murdered in Mexico by Stalin's assassins, while a more natural death claimed Swiss artist Paul Klee and U.S. novelist F. Scott Fitzgerald.

➤ Read Sir Winston Churchill's Star Profile on page 337.

CAPRICORN

From January 01, 0:00 through January 21, 4:43

The Devoted Worker

As a Capricorn born in January of 1940, you arrived in a world filled with uncertainty for many people. Europe was once again embroiled in war and it wouldn't be long before other nations were also drawn into the conflict. Around the time you were born, Britain began wartime rationing of bacon, butter, and sugar. This parallels the essence of Capricorn, which is the efficient and resourceful use of your property, your time, and your talents. There were also many uplifting influences in effect for January 1940 Capricorns. One that was particularly exciting occurred on January 5, when the U.S. FCC heard the first transmission of radio with a clear, static-free signal—the event that marked the beginning of FM radio.

As a Capricorn, you may exemplify the character traits of strength of will and dogged determination, and it's likely that your best rewards come through discipline and hard work. Yet, as a 1940 Capricorn, you may also carry with you a quality of excitement and of ways to be pioneering and bold. Growing up, you probably showed many assertive tendencies, as well as a focus on how to interact with others in ways that represent compromise and service when faced with anxiety over an uncertain world. When your energy feels too low to take the initiative yourself, you can let others carry the ball. You could succeed in almost any occupation that calls for you to manage people.

Your uncertainties might color your friendships, and sometimes the sacrifices you make in order to serve others may prompt you to let go rather than persevere.

In love, you might seek a partner who would make home and family high priorities. You may believe that there are no guarantees in life, and you would want your partner to be mature enough to respect your need for structure and order, to keep the ever-present threat of chaos at bay. A Virgo, Taurus, or another Capricorn may be the most likely to fulfill these requirements.

Your challenge is to dedicate your efforts to a cause that benefits others as well as yourself. Your strengths are your determination, dedication, and compassion.

AQUARIUS

From January 21, 4:44 through February 19, 19:03

The True Individualist

As an Aquarius born in 1940, your cosmic indicators include an abundance of planets in the action-oriented fire signs, as well as your Sun in airy, intellectual Aquarius. This combination can give you a powerful drive for freedom and independence, both of thought and of movement. It's likely that you march to the rhythm of your own drummer, Aquarius of 1940, and you always will!

On February 8, 1940, a Nazi decree ordered the establishment of a Jewish ghetto in Lodz, Poland—the first of many to spring up over the next few years—casting a huge shadow on the world and especially upon those who became victims of this rigid, authoritarian rule. This might explain why you can strive hard for tolerance in your speech and for humanitarian ideals to counteract any leanings toward authoritarianism you encounter. Aquarius is the eccentric and individualistic rebel—with or without a cause—and you might have had a few outstanding examples of this as your role models when you were growing up. Frank Sinatra made his singing debut with the Tommy Dorsey Orchestra while the Sun was in Aquarius in 1940. Aquarius is also the sign of intellectual freedom and unconventional thinking, so you may have sought out a work environment that encouraged imagination and innovation, where your sense of whimsy and make-believe could have put you at the top.

In relationships, enjoying true friendship can be as important to you as emotional intimacy—if not more so—and your friends are likely to be your admiring fans much if not all of the time. Where you lead, a Virgo or a Taurus could follow, whereas a fellow Aquarian would probably rather meet you there.

Your ideal mate may be equal parts romantic lover and action hero, ready to take a stand for a noble cause, and it's likely that your best matches can be found among the Geminis, Sagittarians, and Leos of your acquaintance.

Your challenge is to employ mediation and intervention as tools to resolve conflicts, instead of issuing a "cease and desist" order. Your gift is your capacity to overcome whatever obstacles life may put in your way.

➤ Read about your Chinese Astrological sign on page 838. ➤ Read about your Personal Planets on page 826. ➤ Read about your personal Mystical Card on page 856.

1940

CAPRICORN
Your Personal Planets

YOUR LOVE POTENTIAL
Venus in Aquarius, Jan. 01, 0:00 - Jan. 18, 13:59
Venus in Pisces, Jan. 18, 14:00 - Jan. 21, 4:43

YOUR DRIVE AND AMBITION
Mars in Pisces, Jan. 01, 0:00 - Jan. 04, 0:04
Mars in Aries, Jan. 04, 0:05 - Jan. 21, 4:43

YOUR LUCK MAGNETISM
Jupiter in Aries, Jan. 01, 0:00 - Jan. 21, 4:43

World Events

Jan. 8 – Britain orders that meat, sugar, and butter should be rationed.

Jan. 11 – Sergei Prokofiev's ballet *Romeo And Juliet* premières in Leningrad.

Coupons are required to buy food in Britain

AQUARIUS
Your Personal Planets

YOUR LOVE POTENTIAL
Venus in Pisces, Jan. 21, 4:44 - Feb. 12, 5:50
Venus in Aries, Feb. 12, 5:51 - Feb. 19, 19:03

YOUR DRIVE AND AMBITION
Mars in Aries, Jan. 21, 4:44 - Feb. 17, 1:53
Mars in Taurus, Feb. 17, 1:54 - Feb. 19, 19:03

YOUR LUCK MAGNETISM
Jupiter in Aries, Jan. 21, 4:44 - Feb. 19, 19:03

World Events

Feb. 5 – Glenn Miller and his orchestra record "Tuxedo Junction."

Feb. 7 – Britain nationalizes its railroads.

1940

PISCES
Your Personal Planets

YOUR LOVE POTENTIAL
Venus in Aries, Feb. 19, 19:04 - Mar. 08, 16:24
Venus in Taurus, Mar. 08, 16:25 - Mar. 20, 18:23

YOUR DRIVE AND AMBITION
Mars in Taurus, Feb. 19, 19:04 - Mar. 20, 18:23

YOUR LUCK MAGNETISM
Jupiter in Aries, Feb. 19, 19:04 - Mar. 20, 18:23

World Events

Feb. 21 – The Germans begin constructing the concentration camp at Auschwitz.

Feb. 22 – The five-year-old Dalai Lama is enthroned in Tibet.

Booker T. Washington

ARIES
Your Personal Planets

YOUR LOVE POTENTIAL
Venus in Taurus, Mar. 20, 18:24 - Apr. 04, 18:09
Venus in Gemini, Apr. 04, 18:10 - Apr. 20, 5:50

YOUR DRIVE AND AMBITION
Mars in Taurus, Mar. 20, 18:24 - Apr. 01, 18:40
Mars in Gemini, Apr. 01, 18:41 - Apr. 20, 5:50

YOUR LUCK MAGNETISM
Jupiter in Aries, Mar. 20, 18:24 - Apr. 20, 5:50

World Events

Apr. 7 – Booker T. Washington becomes the first African American to appear on a U.S. postage stamp.

Apr. 20 – The Radio Corporation of America demonstrates its new electron microscope to the public.

PISCES
From February 19, 19:04 through March 20, 18:23

The Passionate Dreamer

In addition to your compassionate nature, you may possess a strong strain of common sense that stems from the earthy influences in effect for Pisces in 1940. In this year, Richard Wright's groundbreaking book *Native Son* was published. Focusing on themes of racial frustration, hopelessness, and lack of opportunity for blacks in a white-dominated world, this book raised awareness of racial inequality throughout the world and helped to plant the seeds of rebellion against oppression. Growing up under the influence of voices such as Wright's could be one reason why you, who might tend to be a dreamer under ordinary circumstances, have also been known to take action to create an enduring legacy of freedom.

As a Pisces, you could be tuned into unseen realms with your exceptional psychic sensitivity. You may even have dedicated your life to spiritual forces rather than worldly ones, and it's possible that you used your abilities to help others as a counselor or spiritual director. Being a 1940 Pisces, you may also have a highly developed sense of fair play that could have been expressed in the fields of human rights advocacy or civil rights law.

You may head to the water for relaxation and might especially enjoy sailing. You can have a zest for living that draws friends to you by the dozen, so socializing in large groups could be best for you, as finding time to visit with everyone individually could be difficult over the long haul. Your closest friends are likely to be very spiritual Virgos, Librans, or Aquarians, and they could be some of the same people you were in school with when you were a child.

In relationships, you will probably seek out a mate who shares your concern for doing what is right, and you would probably want to be with someone who accepts your occasional need to withdraw from social activity. A Virgo, Cancer, or Capricorn could make an excellent match for you.

Your challenges include being open to compromise and keeping your sense of humor in the midst of adversity. Your strengths are your sensitivity to others' sufferings and your determination to make dreams come true.

ARIES
From March 20, 18:24 through April 20, 5:50

The Iron-Willed Optimist

As an Aries, you're not likely to back down when it comes to what you believe is right, and you can be the first to question the status quo in favor of change. However, as an Aries born in 1940, your strong-willed independence could be tempered by a focus on practical necessity, material security, and property rights. Historic developments around the time you were born were worthy of admiration and of shame. On the dark side, Himmler ordered the building of the concentration camp at Auschwitz in spring this year. The evil intent and outcome of this order expressed the worst of human nature, under the guise of seeking the best, at the expense of all humanity. Ariens born in 1940 carry within them the dynamic tensions associated with the need to work tirelessly to overcome evil with goodness.

On the bright side, on April 7 the United States issued a postage stamp bearing the likeness of Booker T. Washington—the first African American ever to receive that honor. Born on April 5, 1856, Washington was the son of a slave. His remarkable achievements advanced the cause of blacks in America, both socially and economically. Like him, you may wish to inspire others by your example. Teaching, writing, performing, or any endeavor that puts you in the public eye could be good career choices for you. Whatever your profession, it's likely that your desire for personal advancement would be subordinated to your desire to create a better world.

When it comes to your leisure time, you may believe that conversation is a contact sport, so you might not be surprised to find that there's an abundance of the voluble fire signs of Leo, Sagittarius, and Aries among your closest friends.

In romance, you don't want to be fenced in so you're likely to need a lot of space. You'd also want a partner who would cheer you on enthusiastically. Favorable love signs for you can be Aquarius, Pisces, Gemini, and Libra.

Your challenge is to overcome the temptations of your lower nature in favor of more noble pursuits. Your greatest strengths are your courage, your devotion to duty, and your resourcefulness.

➤ Read about your Chinese Astrological sign on page 838. ➤ Read about your Personal Planets on page 826. ➤ Read about your personal Mystical Card on page 856.

TAURUS

From April 20, 5:51 through May 21, 5:22

The Determined Builder

You were born during a time that brought a few causes to celebrate, even amidst a world of uncertainty and confusion. On May 11, the New York World's Fair reopened. Its theme of "Building the World of Tomorrow" expressed the essence of Taurus the builder, and as a 1940 Taurus you may have a passion to turn visions into reality. A fabulous manifestation of Taurus sensuality came on May 15, when nylon stockings went on sale for the first time in the U.S. While this event might be minor in the context of human fate, it certainly typified Taurean voluptuousness.

On the world stage, Europe's political drama turned an important new page. Neville Chamberlain, Britain's Prime Minister, resigned, and on May 10 Winston Churchill became Britain's new Prime Minister at Buckingham Palace. Taurus being a sign of will and power—worldly power—it was fitting that Churchill rose to power at this time.

Your childhood may have been shaped by the shortages of World War II, but you were probably among the first to enjoy the relative affluence of life in the sixties and seventies. Taurus is the sign of material wealth, consumption, sensual delights, and practical common sense—all qualities you may have employed in choosing a career. You would appreciate how technology and science can foster greater prosperity and personal freedom through convenience, and the emerging computer field might have been your chosen path. You could also enjoy exploring technology in your leisure time, and you can probably rely on your Virgo, Scorpio, and Capricorn friends to go along if you want company in your excursions into the limitless possibilities of technology.

In romance, you would be likely to find the greatest happiness with a partner who is as passionate as you are. An intuitive Pisces or an insightful Cancer could provide a window to the inner life that you may want but not take time to seek out for yourself.

Your challenge is to balance your dogged stubbornness with tolerance for those whose convictions are not as strong as yours. Your gift is your steadfast devotion to the values that matter most to you.

GEMINI

From May 21, 5:23 through June 21, 13:35

The Winged Messenger

History was at a turning point around the time you were born, 1940 Gemini. German forces had entered Paris on June 14. Churchill responded with his stirring "We shall fight on the beaches..." speech, broadcast that night on BBC radio. As the world held its breath, tiny Britain girded itself for the onslaught of a seemingly unstoppable Nazi war machine. The burden of history may have seemed too heavy for your quicksilver sign to bear. Yet, in the end, it may only have made your complex personality even more intriguing.

Gemini is an air sign, highly "mental" in character. You may feel that it's your obligation to gather and spread news, and it's probably no coincidence that radio was so important in the forties when you were a child. Growing up with instant access to news and entertainment via the airwaves may have inspired you to make a career in the field of communications when you got older, and doubtless encouraged the early development of your natural brilliance with words.

You could be known for your wit, curiosity, and vast network of friends and acquaintances. Some people might take you for a lightweight, at first, but they probably wouldn't make that mistake twice. Your mind can be as quick as a whip, and nobody can learn their way around a new place or a new idea faster than you can. Unlike some of your stodgier friends, you love variety, novelty, and new experiences. It might be hard to sustain long-term friendships with Taureans and Scorpios because they may never understand why you change your mind so much. But you'd probably get along fine with Virgos and Sagittarians, and Aquarians could fascinate you.

In romance, you could want a mate with a passion for information. However, you might also seek someone who is as serious as you are lighthearted—opposites attract, after all. Favorable love signs for you can be Libra, Aquarius, and Leo.

Your challenge is to leave a record of your life so that others can learn from the history you can teach. Your gift is your keen awareness of your connection with others and your desire to preserve the best in human nature.

➤ Read about your Chinese Astrological sign on page 838. ➤ Read about your Personal Planets on page 826. ➤ Read about your personal Mystical Card on page 856.

TAURUS
Your Personal Planets

YOUR LOVE POTENTIAL
Venus in Gemini, Apr. 20, 5:51 - May 06, 18:46
Venus in Cancer, May 06, 18:47 - May 21, 5:22

YOUR DRIVE AND AMBITION
Mars in Gemini, Apr. 20, 5:51 - May 17, 14:44
Mars in Cancer, May 17, 14:45 - May 21, 5:22

YOUR LUCK MAGNETISM
Jupiter in Aries, Apr. 20, 5:51 - May 16, 7:53
Jupiter in Taurus, May 16, 7:54 - May 21, 5:22

World Events

Apr. 25 – American actor Al Pacino is born.
May 10 – Winston Churchill becomes Prime Minister of Britain.

Al Pacino is born under the sign of Taurus

GEMINI
Your Personal Planets

YOUR LOVE POTENTIAL
Venus in Cancer, May 21, 5:23 - June 21, 13:35

YOUR DRIVE AND AMBITION
Mars in Cancer, May 21, 5:23 - June 21, 13:35

YOUR LUCK MAGNETISM
Jupiter in Taurus, May 21, 5:23 - June 21, 13:35

World Events

May 28 – Belgium surrenders to the Nazis, two weeks after the Netherlands succumbs to the relentless barrage of Germany's Blitzkrieg.
June 5 – The synthetic rubber tire is unveiled.

1940

CANCER
Your Personal Planets

YOUR LOVE POTENTIAL
Venus in Cancer, June 21, 13:36 - July 05, 16:16
Venus in Gemini, July 05, 16:17 - July 23, 0:33

YOUR DRIVE AND AMBITION
Mars in Cancer, June 21, 13:36 - July 03, 10:31
Mars in Leo, July 03, 10:32 - July 23, 0:33

YOUR LUCK MAGNETISM
Jupiter in Taurus, June 21, 13:36 - July 23, 0:33

World Events

June 29 – Swiss-born artist Paul Klee dies.

July 7 – Beatles drummer Ringo Starr is born Richard Starkey.

Beatle Ringo Starr (Richard Starkey) is born under the sign of Cancer

LEO
Your Personal Planets

YOUR LOVE POTENTIAL
Venus in Gemini, July 23, 0:34 - Aug. 01, 2:19
Venus in Cancer, Aug. 01, 2:20 - Aug. 23, 7:28

YOUR DRIVE AND AMBITION
Mars in Leo, July 23, 0:34 - Aug. 19, 15:57
Mars in Virgo, Aug. 19, 15:58 - Aug. 23, 7:28

YOUR LUCK MAGNETISM
Jupiter in Taurus, July 23, 0:34 - Aug. 23, 7:28

World Events

Aug. 6 – The British retreat from China, leaving Shanghai under the control of the Japanese.

Aug. 21 – Russian revolutionary Leon Trotsky is assassinated in Mexico City.

CANCER
From June 21, 13:36 through July 23, 0:33

The Devoted Protector

The season of your birth was filled with crucial developments for the world, Cancer of 1940. On June 22, France fell to Nazi Germany. With General Charles DeGaulle and the "Free French" in exile in England, the collaborationist government at Vichy signed an armistice agreement subjugating France to occupation and domination by German and Italian forces. Meanwhile, Hitler at last ordered the invasion of England. On July 10, as Nazi forces attacked by air, the Battle of Britain began.

It was beginning to seem that no place would be safe from war for very long, and even in the "neutral" countries people may have begun to wonder what would happen if their country were drawn into it. Because your sign rules the home and emotions, the mere threat of having your homeland invaded when you were a child could have had a lasting influence on you. As a result, home and family can mean even more to you than they do to Cancers who were born in other years.

You may feel life's ups and downs more keenly than most people do, and your impulse to nurture others can be highly developed. You may be exceptionally sensitive to what people are feeling and would instinctively respond with caring and concern. You can be good at keeping secrets—your own and others'—and people may have opened their hearts to you almost before they know it. Counseling, teaching, and writing are fields you may have succeeded in. In your leisure time, you probably enjoy projects that make your home more comfortable.

In relationships, you can be vulnerable and easily hurt, and you may look to your mate for the same emotional security that you provide. You take great care to protect the ones you love—in fact, you probably express your feelings for people by taking care of them and tending to their needs. Virgo or Scorpio could be a good love match for you, but a Capricorn in particular would appreciate your sense of stability, propriety, and tradition.

Your challenge is to make peace with the past. Your strength is your devotion to those you love, and your willingness to act unselfishly to protect them.

LEO
From July 23, 0:34 through August 23, 7:28

The Proud Warrior

An event that took place around the time you were born may have changed the course of history. On August 21, 1940, while attending an international workers' conference in Mexico, socialist revolutionary Leon Trotsky was attacked by an ice pick-wielding assassin, probably on Stalin's orders. He was mourned by millions, for he was a friend of the oppressed and the voice of the common man. With the death of the last leader of the revolution, no one in the USSR was powerful enough to challenge the ascendancy of Josef Stalin, whose brutal abuses of power only later would become known to the world.

On August 8, the RAF shot down thirty-one German aircraft in a fierce battle in the skies over England, showing that the Nazi war machine could be defeated. On August 20, British Prime Minister Winston Churchill uttered his famous words in praise of the RAF: "Never in the field of human conflict was so much owed by so many to so few."

These men may have been your role models as you were growing up, Leo of 1940. Like them, you can be moved to answer the callings of your heart to act with courage—their heroics could have fueled your innate sense of pride and determination. You might have enjoyed any work that called for you to be at the center of things. You may have chosen a career that allowed you to act on your convictions, but it's likely that you would have collected adoring fans no matter what you did. You could have many outlets for expressing yourself creatively in your leisure time, but performing on stage in amateur theatricals is something you probably wouldn't do without.

It's likely that you admire your friends as much as they admire you, and you may tend to choose friends whose interests complement your own. In romance, you might have high standards when it comes to choosing a mate. Again, the qualities you look for could be those that balance your own. Libra and Sagittarius can be good love signs for you, along with impulsive Aries or quicksilver Gemini.

Your challenge is to be gracious in accepting help when it is offered. Your gift is your clear sense of self.

➤ Read about your Chinese Astrological sign on page 838. ➤ Read about your Personal Planets on page 826. ➤ Read about your personal Mystical Card on page 856.

VIRGO

From August 23, 7:29 through September 23, 4:45

The Adaptable Critic

An amazing event that occurred around the time you were born may have convinced many people that, truly, nothing was impossible. On September 12, 1940, four teenagers followed their dog into a hole in the ground near Lascaux, France, and were surprised to find themselves inside a cave that had lain unknown and untouched for 17,000 years. Even more astonishing, its walls were covered with beautiful and lifelike drawings of huge bison, deer, and other animals. Speculation about this remarkable archeological find, known as the Lascaux Cave Paintings, would have filled the news during your childhood years, and would ultimately change how anthropologists think about our ancestors.

In other respects, the world may have seemed to be coming apart at the seams. War developments continued unabated, as thousands of retaliatory bombings of Britain and Germany wreaked havoc on both peoples. On September 10, a German bomb hit Buckingham Palace. No matter where you grew up, you would have seen the shocking images of war, either in newsreels or on the front pages of the newspaper.

The worries that pervaded that time may have influenced you profoundly, Virgo of 1940, and could explain why you would seek to repair what has been damaged whenever possible. In you, the perfectionism that your sign is famous for can be softened by a quality of caring that attracts people to you. Your sign rules the parts that make up the whole, so you can have an uncanny ability to focus on the small details. Your precision and technical skill, combined with your concern for health, could have drawn you to the helping professions, and you may have made a career in medicine or the ministry.

In relationships, you may find that happiness in love comes from sharing a spiritual quest with your mate to put compassion and service into effect. Good partners for you may include Pisces, Taurus, Capricorn, and Scorpio.

Your challenge is to recognize that everyone makes mistakes, and to forgive them in yourself as well as others. Your strength is your ability to analyze any situation and pinpoint the problem.

LIBRA

From September 23, 4:46 through October 23, 13:38

The Trusted Partner

Although it is not widely known, Libra is the sign that rules the military. Certainly, the events that unfolded while the Sun was in Libra in 1940 had a militaristic bent. On September 27, Germany, Italy, and Japan signed a formal ten-year axis alliance, making them full partners in war. On October 4, Hitler and Mussolini met in person at the Brenner Pass in the Alps. Several other history-making events occurred in October: the world witnessed a lunar eclipse on October 16; although not yet involved in the fighting, the U.S. army held its first lottery for World War II draftees; and the Warsaw Ghetto was formed.

As a Libra born in 1940, your sense of fair play could be even stronger than that of Librans born in other years. As a child, you might have been a student of history, and history may have shown that creating alliances with those whose interests and talents complement your own can magnify your power. You probably wouldn't have been interested in the kind of shifting alliances based on self-interest that political coalition-building usually spawns, and that's why finding people you can rely on could have been a priority for you.

You might have chosen a career in the helping professions so that you would be sure these services were available to people whose needs might have been overlooked otherwise. In your spare time, you may enjoy working with children, perhaps in a kindergarten or coaching a team sport. Aquarians could be your best bet when choosing close friends, as you like to have a clear sense of definition within your friendships, with each person's role and responsibilities spelled out.

In romance, you have much to offer, and you may find settling on a partner difficult. Your most compatible signs include Leo, Aquarius, and Sagittarius. But yours is the sign of love, beauty, and appreciation, so you'd probably find something to admire about any sign in the zodiac!

Your challenge is to see that only you can define your life purpose, regardless of your desire to please others. Your strength is understanding that, with others, you can accomplish great things.

► Read about your Chinese Astrological sign on page 838. ► Read about your Personal Planets on page 826. ► Read about your personal Mystical Card on page 856.

VIRGO
Your Personal Planets

YOUR LOVE POTENTIAL
Venus in Cancer, Aug. 23, 7:29 - Sept. 08, 16:58
Venus in Leo, Sept. 08, 16:59 - Sept. 23, 4:45

YOUR DRIVE AND AMBITION
Mars in Virgo, Aug. 23, 7:29 - Sept. 23, 4:45

YOUR LUCK MAGNETISM
Jupiter in Taurus, Aug. 23, 7:29 - Sept. 23, 4:45

World Events

Sept. 4 – Hitler steps up the aerial bombardment of Britain after RAF bombing in Germany.

Sept. 12 – Switzerland reasserts its neutrality in the midst of European conflict.

The RAF fight against the German Luftwaffe in the Battle of Britain

LIBRA
Your Personal Planets

YOUR LOVE POTENTIAL
Venus in Leo, Sept. 23, 4:46 - Oct. 06, 21:09
Venus in Virgo, Oct. 06, 21:10 - Oct. 23, 13:38

YOUR DRIVE AND AMBITION
Mars in Virgo, Sept. 23, 4:46 - Oct. 05, 14:20
Mars in Libra, Oct. 05, 14:21 - Oct. 23, 13:38

YOUR LUCK MAGNETISM
Jupiter in Taurus, Sept. 23, 4:46 - Oct. 23, 13:38

World Events

Oct. 16 – A peacetime draft is held in the U.S. for the first time.

Oct. 23 – Brazilian soccer star Pélé is born Edson Arantes do Nascimento.

1940

SCORPIO
Your Personal Planets

YOUR LOVE POTENTIAL
Venus in Virgo, Oct. 23, 13:39 - Nov. 01, 17:23
Venus in Libra, Nov. 01, 17:24 - Nov. 22, 10:48

YOUR DRIVE AND AMBITION
Mars in Libra, Oct. 23, 13:39 - Nov. 20, 17:15
Mars in Scorpio, Nov. 20, 17:16 - Nov. 22, 10:48

YOUR LUCK MAGNETISM
Jupiter in Taurus, Oct. 23, 13:39 - Nov. 22, 10:48

World Events

Nov. 5 - Franklin D. Roosevelt is elected for a third term.

Nov. 9 - Former British Prime Minister Neville Chamberlain dies.

Walt Disney's movie "Fantasia" is released

SAGITTARIUS
Your Personal Planets

YOUR LOVE POTENTIAL
Venus in Libra, Nov. 22, 10:49 - Nov. 26, 12:31
Venus in Scorpio, Nov. 26, 12:32 - Dec. 20, 19:35
Venus in Sagittarius, Dec. 20, 19:36 - Dec. 21, 23:54

YOUR DRIVE AND AMBITION
Mars in Scorpio, Nov. 22, 10:49 - Dec. 21, 23:54

YOUR LUCK MAGNETISM
Jupiter in Taurus, Nov. 22, 10:49 - Dec. 21, 23:54

World Events

Dec. 16 - Joe Louis KOs Al McCoy in the sixth round to win the heavyweight boxing title in Chicago.

Dec. 21 - Jazz-age novelist F. Scott Fitzgerald dies.

SCORPIO
From October 23, 13:39 through November 22, 10:48

The Equitable Extremist

On October 24, 1940, the forty-hour work week mandated by the Fair Labor Standards went into effect in the United States, ensuring more rights and freedoms to U.S. workers. A different but perhaps equally significant event also occurred while the Sun was in Scorpio that year. On November 13, Walt Disney studios released *Fantasia*, the first feature-length animated film ever made. It captures extremes of imagination and remains a classic to this day. The fact that these events illustrated opposite ends of the spectrum from work to play may come as no surprise to you, Scorpio of 1940—in fact, you'd probably expect nothing less!

Intensity is the hallmark of your sign, and the liberation of imagination represented by these events may explain why you could be even more intense than other Scorpios. You would go to extremes, rather than take the middle of the road, and you can be relentless in whatever you do, whether your focus is work or leisure time activities. You may have a knack for seeing what lies under the surface, and you can sense what's going on and send out subtle signals to shape things to your way of thinking. Friends may have a hard time keeping up with you, and co-workers may wonder how you can get so much done in a day.

You may tend to feel things deeply, and your ardent nature would lead you to live your life to the fullest. However, you may balance your passionate adherence to a cause or goal with a great love of beauty. It's likely that you play a musical instrument, which you probably enjoy because it gives you a way to express your feelings.

In love, you would probably seek a partner who appreciates your sense of passion and your ability to embrace change. Because you may tend to go to extremes, you might do best with a mate who is steady and reliable, with a more moderate temperament than your own. Good love signs for you include Taurus, Virgo, and Capricorn, although nurturing Cancer and mystical Pisces could also intrigue you.

Your challenge is to appreciate the lighter side of life. Your strength is the depth of your insight into human nature.

SAGITTARIUS
From November 22, 10:49 through December 21, 23:54

The Rarest Adventurer

Sagittarius is known for its warm, expansive, sometimes jolly personality. It is a sign of vision, higher education, travel, and hope. Some of the events that took place during the Sun's passage through Sagittarius in 1940 were good expressions of those qualities.

On November 30, the unlikely couple of comedienne Lucille Ball and Cuban crooner Desi Arnaz were married. This wedding certainly highlighted cross-cultural connections and, interestingly enough, Sagittarius rules foreign relations. In Pasadena, California, the first McDonald's hamburger stand opened, beginning what ultimately became a fast food trend that, like Sagittarius, fosters an interest in enjoying travel conveniences. On December 6, the Gestapo arrested German resistance fighter and poster artist Helen Ernst, whose work was an uncompromising testimony to the truth of what she observed, very Sagittarian-like. Honesty is also the highest value for you, as you prize your insights and judgment above nearly all else.

Some of the features prevalent during this period included a focus on the ways in which power could be used or abused, and how to educate oneself and others to achieve the broadest possible perspective. One of your key words is "perception" and it comes naturally to you to set your sights on the future and to expand your understanding of yourself and others.

Your happiness probably involves going beyond the routine of tradition. When it comes to love, you may want a partner with whom you can enjoy exploring life together, venturing into as yet uncharted territories. Being a sign that loves sports, romance for you may represent a chance for a chase from time to time. Once caught, however, the object of your affection may be less appealing to you. Suitable mates may include Aries, Gemini, and Leo, but harmonious Libra and visionary Aquarius could also win your heart.

Your challenge is to stay with the present even when the future, or "greener pastures," may look more promising. Your strength is your sense of optimism in the face of hardship and your faith in the basic goodness of others.

➤ Read about your Chinese Astrological sign on page 838. ➤ Read about your Personal Planets on page 826. ➤ Read about your personal Mystical Card on page 856.

CAPRICORN

From December 21, 23:55 through December 31, 23:59

The Industrious Worker

Like most Capricorns, your strength is your great sense of pride and self-reliance. However, as a Capricorn born in December of 1940, you came into a world that was on the brink of a global conflagration. In the United Kingdom, people were already growing war weary, and many may have been looking ahead, wondering what it would take to rebuild when the destruction of war was finally over. Then, on December 27, Germany began dropping incendiary bombs on London. The devastation caused by this event was considered to be the second Great Fire of London.

In the United States, an ocean away from the war, songbird Judy Garland graced the covers of many popular magazines in December of 1940. Like many MGM stars of the forties, she would later lend her captivating voice to the war effort in films and radio shows—but, for the moment, her girl-next-door appeal probably reassured people that things were going to be all right, at least in the U.S.

You grew up during the war years, and striving to make the best use of your resources may have been a big part of your childhood. As a result, you may have an extraordinary appreciation for the rewards that come from hard work. Capricorn being a sign of industriousness and productivity, you can probably take pride in your well-earned achievements. No matter what field you entered, you would have headed straight for the top. That's in your nature. And you might excel at team sports, where your leadership abilities would ensure that you'd be at the center of things.

In romance, you may look for a mate who respects the traditions that are important to you. And if your mate is someone who is mindful of their station in life, so much the better. Good love signs for you include Virgo, Taurus, and Cancer, but Pisces and Scorpio could be just different enough from what you'd expect to fascinate you.

Your challenge is to be patient with those who don't have your self-assurance and to be compassionate with those who need help. Your strength is your persistence—you're not afraid to make a commitment to what you believe is worth doing.

1940

CAPRICORN
Your Personal Planets

YOUR LOVE POTENTIAL
Venus in Sagittarius, Dec. 21, 23:55 - Dec. 31, 23:59

YOUR DRIVE AND AMBITION
Mars in Scorpio, Dec. 21, 23:55 - Dec. 31, 23:59

YOUR LUCK MAGNETISM
Jupiter in Taurus, Dec. 21, 23:55 - Dec. 31, 23:59

World Events

Dec. 26 - *The Philadelphia Story*, starring Katharine Hepburn, opens in New York.

Dec. 27 - More than one hundred German bombers launch a night attack on London.

Winston Churchill
November 30, 1874 - January 24, 1965

SIR WINSTON CHURCHILL
Sagittarius

Winston Churchill was the stalwart leader of Great Britain during World War II. As you would expect from his philosophical and truth-seeking Sagittarius Sun, Churchill stood fearlessly against fascism and demonstrated that the inherent virtues of democratic principles can ultimately defeat the destructive forces of tyranny.

Due to Saturn, the planet of status and achievement, making a challenging contact with Uranus, the planet of sudden change, Churchill experienced considerable ups and downs in his political career. And with Saturn, the planet that relates to fathers, under stress, it is not surprising that Churchill had a difficult relationship with his father, who was a political failure. Though his father died in 1895, Churchill spent his life trying to succeed where his father had failed. With his Moon, representing emotions and the public, in dramatic Leo, he used that sign's leadership qualities and personal bravery in his own "finest hour," leading Britain through World War II as Prime Minister.

Erratic Uranus made challenging contacts with Mercury, the planet of the mind, and Pluto, the planet of profound intensity, in his chart. From this we can see how Churchill was subject to severe bouts of depression throughout his life, which he called the "black dog."

However, Uranus in its aspect of originality also made fortunate contacts with his Sun (personality) and Venus (the arts), both in the sign of witty and scholarly Sagittarius, in his house of communication. The eloquent, forthright power of his speeches during wartime will not be forgotten. Churchill also was a writer, producing several volumes of biography, memoirs, and history. In 1953, he was awarded the Nobel Prize for literature (history), "for his mastery of historical and biographical description, as well as for brilliant oratory in defending exalted human values.

With critical and tense Virgo rising, Churchill fought illness throughout his life. But Churchill lived to age 90. With aggressive Mars placed prominently in the part of his chart symbolizing the self, Churchill fought to live just as fiercely as he fought to keep his political life alive and as surely as he struggled to keep Great Britain free during the war.

➤ Read more about Churchill in "Astrology Reigns through the Ages" on page 25. ➤ Read F. D. Roosevelt's Star Profile on page 257. ➤ Read "Astro Twins: Hitler and Chaplin" on page 345.

1941

Surprise Attack: Saturn Conjunct Uranus

On December 7, 1941, at 7:55 a.m. local time, Japan launched a surprise attack on Pearl Harbor, leading the United States into World War II once and for all. At this time, the planet Uranus was in Taurus, making an astrological angle called a "conjunction" to the planet Saturn, also in Taurus. Saturn in Taurus indicates holding on to things past their due and the United States indeed held out as long as it could before it joined the war. The attack on Pearl Harbor was the straw that broke the camel's back so to speak. When Uranus meets Saturn in the sky, surprise attacks are indicated. There are accidents and mishaps. There are sudden intrusions and threats to security. Under this kind of influence, everyone should be alert, but sadly, at Pearl Harbor, the U.S. Navy was not.

In the chart of the United States, Scorpio is considered by many astrologers to be the rising sign, or ascendant. With this chart, we can see how easily the Japanese were able to launch their sneak attack. Scorpio is opposite Taurus in the sky, so both Uranus and Saturn were opposing the first house of the U.S. chart. When any planet opposes the ascendant of the chart of a person, it can mean that their self-image is negatively affected. Uranus is the planet of surprises and Saturn is the planet of careful planning. The Japanese made careful preparations for their attack, which was meant to neutralize the U.S. Navy at Pearl Harbor. The attack shook the very soul of America, and awoke the United States from the cushy *laissez-faire* snooze it had been taking up until that fateful day.

Japanese raid on Pearl Harbour, December 7, 1941

German forces invade Russia

Irish author James Joyce

THE SOUL OF THINGS

Psychometry is the ability to detect an object's history and the emotions of those who handled it by psychic means. In 1941, a London psychometrist was given a sealed package and asked to describe its contents. He saw two Chinese bowls and envisioned the modern kerosene lamps of the workshop where they were made. This was apparently impossible as the Chinese bowls in the package were reputed to be 300-year-old antiques. Years later, experts determined that they were forgeries—the psychometrist was proved correct.

ATTACK, SIEGE, AND SURVIVAL

In preparation for his invasion of Russia, Hitler made treaties with Hungary, Romania, and Bulgaria, but invaded and occupied Yugoslavia which refused to cooperate. German forces rescued the failing Italian campaign in Greece and overran the country. Japan attacked the U.S. Pacific fleet at Pearl Harbor and the U.S. declared war. Japan invaded French Indochina and attacked Singapore and Hong Kong. The British Army retrieved Abyssinia, throwing out the Italians and restoring Emperor Haile Selassie to his throne. The Germans invaded Russia on June 22 and rapidly advanced toward Moscow, ferociously resisted by the Russians. The prestigious German battleship *Bismarck* was sunk by the Royal Navy. General MacArthur was appointed Commanding General of U.S. Army forces in the Far East. Two literary greats, James Joyce and Virginia Woolf, died, while Orson Welles' masterwork, *Citizen Kane*, premièred. The USO began operations to entertain armed forces, and the first successful clinical trial in penicillin initiated a new era in medicine. U.S. President Roosevelt signed Executive Order 8802 prohibiting racial discrimination in employment.

338

➤ Read "Astro Twins: Hitler and Chaplin" by Jean Mars on page 345.

CAPRICORN

From January 01, 0:00 through January 20, 10:33

The Benevolent Dictator

You were born during a time when "rationing" was about to become an accepted way of life, 1941 January Capricorn. World War II would require everyone to cut back at least a little, so you're probably quite familiar with the concept of frugality. Still, your generous heart—and your optimistic spirit—probably would not allow you to deny a request, no matter how difficult it might be for you to fulfill. As a result, it's likely that you're known for your ability to forget your own needs in favor of the greater good. However, the admiration of those around you—as well as their willingness to return a favor as soon as they could—may have kept you afloat even during the most difficult of times.

Your tolerance and objectivity may have put you in the spotlight throughout your life, but your innate modesty would never be overcome by pride. In short, you have a rare talent for quiet accomplishment, and despite your efforts to remain behind the scenes, you could become quite well known in your circles because of it.

You're probably skilled in the ways of management, which means that being at the head of any group, whether it has gathered for recreational or business purposes, would suit you just fine—and could bring kudos from your contemporaries. You may have chosen a career that allowed you to make a contribution to the world, and when it comes to your leisure time, you may also turn to avocations that benefit the world in some way. Your love of nature would draw you to long walks in the countryside, and collecting rare plants that could have medicinal value is something that might intrigue you.

In friendships, it's likely that you would be drawn to other Capricorns, whose grounded, stable nature can make you feel secure. But, in love, you would probably seek out a Taurus, Cancer, or Virgo, who could provide you the emotional and spiritual confidence you need to attain your goals.

Your challenge is to keep your eye on your goal, never allowing yourself to be distracted by temporary rewards. Your gift is the ability to inspire loyalty and love, even as you command respect.

AQUARIUS

From January 20, 10:34 through February 19, 0:55

The Uneasy Humanitarian

As an Aquarius, your mission is to keep an open mind and accept everyone equally, but the troubled times into which you were born could have provided many challenges to doing that, Aquarius of 1941. You arrived on the planet during a most contentious time—one that seemed to foster dissension rather than cooperation. Around the time you were born, the Nazis had begun a campaign to close Jewish businesses in Amsterdam, aiming to follow Holland with the rest of the world, and the stress of war was felt everywhere. Although this didn't necessarily mean that life was hard for you as a child, it's likely that growing up against the backdrop of World War II had a defining effect on you.

On the negative side, the uncertainty of the times may have taught you to protect yourself from those who might take advantage of you. On the positive side, it may have pushed you to hone your intuition and develop the ability to understand others' motives, no matter how thickly veiled they might be. In any case, these are the *leitmotifs* that may have reappeared most consistently throughout your life.

Your Aquarian love of technology could have drawn you to a career in the emerging information industry, either in computers or in one of the applied sciences. However, you would have kept your intuitive skills sharp by choosing an avocation that called for them—possibly as an amateur actor or playwright. You might have been fascinated by stage magic as a child, and you may still enjoy amazing friends or co-workers with your feats of prestidigitation.

In relationships, this uncertainty may have made bonding quite difficult for you, at least initially. As you grew older, however, you've probably learned that your "antennae" will never fail you—and that ignoring them is where you may get into trouble. You may find that Sagittarians and Taureans provide you with the greatest sense of trust and security, since they're famous for their honesty—but a Capricorn lover may also show you the path to success.

Your challenge is to learn unconditional acceptance. Your gift is your amazingly accurate insight.

➤ Read about your Chinese Astrological sign on page 838. ➤ Read about your Personal Planets on page 826. ➤ Read about your personal Mystical Card on page 856.

1941

CAPRICORN
Your Personal Planets

YOUR LOVE POTENTIAL
Venus in Sagittarius, Jan. 01, 0:00 - Jan. 13, 21:28
Venus in Capricorn, Jan. 13, 21:29 - Jan. 20, 10:33

YOUR DRIVE AND AMBITION
Mars in Scorpio, Jan. 01, 0:00 - Jan. 04, 19:41
Mars in Sagittarius, Jan. 04, 19:42 - Jan. 20, 10:33

YOUR LUCK MAGNETISM
Jupiter in Taurus, Jan. 01, 0:00 - Jan. 20, 10:33

World Events

Jan. 6 – U.S. President Franklin D. Roosevelt delivers his "Four Freedoms" address: freedom of speech and worship; freedom from want and fear.

Jan. 9 – American folk singer Joan Baez is born.

American folk singer Joan Baez is born under the sign of Capricorn

AQUARIUS
Your Personal Planets

YOUR LOVE POTENTIAL
Venus in Capricorn, Jan. 20, 10:34 - Feb. 06, 21:48
Venus in Aquarius, Feb. 06, 21:49 - Feb. 19, 0:55

YOUR DRIVE AND AMBITION
Mars in Sagittarius, Jan. 20, 10:34 - Feb. 17, 23:31
Mars in Capricorn, Feb. 17, 23:32 - Feb. 19, 0:55

YOUR LUCK MAGNETISM
Jupiter in Taurus, Jan. 20, 10:34 - Feb. 19, 0:55

World Events

Feb. 12 – The USSR signs a treaty with Germany by which it agrees to assist against the British blockade.

Feb. 19 – American singer/songwriter Smokey Robinson is born.

1941

PISCES
Your Personal Planets

YOUR LOVE POTENTIAL
Venus in Aquarius, Feb. 19, 0:56 - Mar. 02, 22:32
Venus in Pisces, Mar. 02, 22:33 - Mar. 21, 0:19

YOUR DRIVE AND AMBITION
Mars in Capricorn, Feb. 19, 0:56 - Mar. 21, 0:19

YOUR LUCK MAGNETISM
Jupiter in Taurus, Feb. 19, 0:56 - Mar. 21, 0:19

World Events

Mar. 11 - President Roosevelt authorizes the sending of war supplies to the Allies through the Lend-Lease Bill.

Mar. 13 - Hitler issues an edict calling for the invasion of the USSR.

Death of British author Virginia Woolf

ARIES
Your Personal Planets

YOUR LOVE POTENTIAL
Venus in Pisces, Mar. 21, 0:20 - Mar. 27, 0:57
Venus in Aries, Mar. 27, 0:58 - Apr. 20, 5:52
Venus in Taurus, Apr. 20, 5:53 - Apr. 20, 11:49

YOUR DRIVE AND AMBITION
Mars in Capricorn, Mar. 21, 0:20 - Apr. 02, 11:45
Mars in Aquarius, Apr. 02, 11:46 - Apr. 20, 11:49

YOUR LUCK MAGNETISM
Jupiter in Taurus, Mar. 21, 0:20 - Apr. 20, 11:49

World Events

Mar. 28 - British feminist writer Virginia Woolf commits suicide.

Apr. 13 - The Germans capture Belgrade.

PISCES
From February 19, 0:56 through March 21, 0:19

The Sensitive Student

During the spring of 1941, Germany was planning its attack on England. This would be a major step in the expansion of World War II, and it was also an episode that's likely to have shaped your family's attitude toward safety and security. As a result, you may have felt a certain sense of insecurity when you were a child, not necessarily from your family, but from the general tenor of the world. The positive side of these childhood experiences is that they may have helped to educate you in the ways of the world—a lesson that could come in handy for a sign as potentially vulnerable and eternally sensitive as yours is known to be. While your birth year gave you the gift of discretion—and a sense of caution that can be invaluable—as you grew older, you probably learned to see the best in others, a trait your sign can also be famous for.

In fact, as a Pisces born in 1941, you might have become an expert at "reading" people, making you invaluable in any line of work that requires solid people-skills. You may also have grown up with a very strong work ethic, and you could have made a big splash in sales, advertising, or public relations. Whether you're formally educated or not, life experiences alone may have left you with the spiritual belief that all things are possible—regardless of how uncertain the final outcome seems.

You could have an amazingly open heart. You may feel pulled toward helping those who are less fortunate, either professionally or by donating your time, goods, or a bit of extra cash to the needy. If you're an animal-lover, several strays may have already found their way into your home.

Look to Cancerians, Sagittarians, and other Pisceans for your most intimate partnerships—and keep in mind that, while challenging, relationships with Aquarians could bring you the objectivity you need to guard your tender heart.

Your quest is to learn everything there is to learn about life and people—and to remember that your best-learned lessons are often the hardest ones. Your gift is your ability to spot a pure heart and an honest soul—no matter what shape it takes.

ARIES
From March 21, 0:20 through April 20, 11:49

The Reluctant Believer

Aries of 1941, it would appear that your feisty spirit was presented with a series of challenges right off the bat to help you hone your boldness. At the time you were born, the famous Nazi "Blitz" of England was well underway, spotlighting the two major powers whose bitter conflict would soon involve many of the world's nations. As a result, your early years might have been fraught with worry, and your family may have been quite doubtful about the prospect of peace. The good news is that your fiery disposition and innate optimism were undimmed, and you may have learned a lot about the power of faith from the world's struggle.

That faith in tomorrow, regardless of how cloudy the horizon seems, could be what keeps your red-hot engine running on high. And when presented with an appropriate battle—especially on behalf of an underdog—you'd be even more passionate. Channel this potent energy into worthy causes and your life can be as rewarding as it is exciting.

You may have found the secret of combining work and play by insisting on doing only what you love. Staying physically active can be important—otherwise, your need for action could turn to stress—and you may have chosen work that keeps you outdoors. You might be better at starting projects than at finishing them, so Virgos or Taureans, who enjoy untangling knots and pinning down details, could be compatible partners or co-workers for you. They'll have to learn to keep up with you, though, for you may have only one speed—go!

In love, you may be attracted to Librans, whose knowledge, skill at socializing, and knack for restoring balance can help to bring you peace of mind. But you'll probably always be drawn to Leos and Sagittarians, the other fire signs. These impulsive, passionate folks will prove worthy allies, and one of them could steal your heart.

Your challenge is to defend your ideals and retain your individuality, even in the face of seemingly no-win situations. Your gifts are your courage, your love of taking action swiftly, and your absolute belief that things will always work out just as they should.

➤ Read about your Chinese Astrological sign on page 838. ➤ Read about your Personal Planets on page 826. ➤ Read about your personal Mystical Card on page 856.

TAURUS

From April 20, 11:50 through May 21, 11:22

The Deliberate Laborer

By the late spring of 1941, World War II had spread even further across Europe. The Nazi occupation of France continued; thousands of Parisian Jews had already been arrested. It's likely that being born into this difficult moment in history gave you a strong backbone, Taurus of 1941, and an even stronger dislike of those who prey upon the weak. But the heavens were also fairly bursting with your particular brand of fixed, focused energy at the time of your birth—and it is this determination and persistence that is your heritage.

In fact, your patience can be legendary, along with your reputation for stubbornness. These traits may have drawn you into situations that require hard work and long hours, possibly in the service of an ideal that's dear to your heart. You may also have a gift for making money easily—especially when your heart is involved in what you're doing. Working on behalf of the poor or downtrodden could give you a sense of satisfaction, and you may have chosen a career as a social worker, legal advocate, or financial counselor. Your love of fine food could have made gourmet cooking one of your favorite leisure-time activities.

There may be a few Pisceans among your co-workers, but your relationship is likely to be all business. Your friends will probably be few, chosen carefully over time. You may particularly enjoy spending time with your closest friends, whose guidance and loyalty keep you grounded. Anyone who can count you as more than an acquaintance is quite fortunate—your devotion to your dear ones never wavers.

In romance, you might look for someone who's willing to commit for the long haul. As a result, you could be best suited to other earth signs—practical Virgo and permanence-loving Capricorn—but home-loving Cancer could also be a good match. Above all, you would want a mate who appreciates life's finer things as much as you do.

Your challenge is to take time to enjoy life, no matter how stressed or overwhelmed you may feel. Your gift is your ability to keep at a task until it's done—no matter how many roadblocks are tossed in your way.

GEMINI

From May 21, 11:23 through June 21, 19:32

The Adaptable Changeling

A major shift occurred in the heavens around the time you were born, Gemini of 1941, reflected by an equally major shift here on Earth. Nazi Germany banned all Catholic publications, exhibiting to the rest of the world just how easily a basic right could be taken away by brute force.

Regardless of where you were raised, this issue may have caused quite a bit of subconscious stress to your family—especially if they had formerly taken a strong religious, political, or societal stance. They may suddenly have become fearful of being persecuted, judged, or simply ostracized by others because of the opinions they held. As a result, you probably learned the virtue of tact—and the ability to keep your opinions to yourself. In short, you're well equipped to deal with contention, emergencies, and even life-threatening circumstances. You can also think fast enough—and confidently enough—to make decisions that will affect lives, and possibly save them.

Used in your professional dealings with others, this trait would no doubt gain you admiration for your objectivity and authoritative detachment, 1941 Gemini, when urgent situations present themselves. Your great courage and knack for shape shifting would allow you to infiltrate the ranks of any group you choose, easily mingling with anyone. It could also give you the opportunity to plead your cause without seeming to be emotionally attached to it—and this type of stark logic could prove to be invaluable throughout your life.

When it comes to companions, you'll probably be most comfortable with Aquarians, Sagittarians, and other Geminis—but anyone who can keep up with your versatile mind and adaptable personality is likely to become a friend. Look to a responsible Capricorn for financial guidance and sound advice on business matters.

Your challenges, Gemini of 1941, are to show the world an impartial face, even as you keep a firm hold on your ideals, and to never confuse diplomacy with weakness or lack of conviction. Your special gifts are your knack for sizing up a situation quickly—and the ability to fit into any circle almost immediately.

➤ Read about your Chinese Astrological sign on page 838. ➤ Read about your Personal Planets on page 826. ➤ Read about your personal Mystical Card on page 856.

TAURUS
Your Personal Planets

YOUR LOVE POTENTIAL
Venus in Taurus, Apr. 20, 11:50 - May 14, 13:35
Venus in Gemini, May 14, 13:36 - May 21, 11:22

YOUR DRIVE AND AMBITION
Mars in Aquarius, Apr. 20, 11:50 - May 16, 5:04
Mars in Pisces, May 16, 5:05 - May 21, 11:22

YOUR LUCK MAGNETISM
Jupiter in Taurus, Apr. 20, 11:50 - May 21, 11:22

World Events

May 1 - Orson Welles' masterwork film *Citizen Kane* premières in New York.

May 10 - In Britain, Prime Minister Neville Chamberlain resigns and is succeeded by Winston Churchill as head of a coalition government.

Orson Welles and Dorothy Comingore in "Citizen Kane"

GEMINI
Your Personal Planets

YOUR LOVE POTENTIAL
Venus in Gemini, May 21, 11:23 - June 07, 23:52
Venus in Cancer, June 07, 23:53 - June 21, 19:32

YOUR DRIVE AND AMBITION
Mars in Pisces, May 21, 11:23 - June 21, 19:32

YOUR LUCK MAGNETISM
Jupiter in Taurus, May 21, 11:23 - May 26, 12:47
Jupiter in Gemini, May 26, 12:48 - June 21, 19:32

World Events

May 26 - The German battleship *Bismarck* is sunk by the British navy.

June 13 - Allied troops surround the city of Damascus.

1941

CANCER

Your Personal planets

YOUR LOVE POTENTIAL

Venus in Cancer, June 21, 19:33 - July 02, 12:32
Venus in Leo, July 02, 12:33 - July 23, 6:25

YOUR DRIVE AND AMBITION

Mars in Pisces, June 21, 19:33 - July 02, 5:16
Mars in Aries, July 02, 5:17 - July 23, 6:25

YOUR LUCK MAGNETISM

Jupiter in Gemini, June 21, 19:33 - July 23, 6:25

World Events

July 2 - Noël Coward's play *Blithe Spirit* premières at the Piccadilly Theatre in London.

July 10 - Pianist and composer Jelly Roll Morton dies.

Roosevelt and Churchill meet in Newfoundland

LEO

Your Personal Planets

YOUR LOVE POTENTIAL

Venus in Leo, July 23, 6:26 - July 27, 4:11
Venus in Virgo, July 27, 4:12 - Aug. 21, 0:28
Venus in Libra, Aug. 21, 0:29 - Aug. 23, 13:16

YOUR DRIVE AND AMBITION

Mars in Aries, July 23, 6:26 - Aug. 23, 13:16

YOUR LUCK MAGNETISM

Jupiter in Gemini, July 23, 6:26 - Aug. 23, 13:16

World Events

Aug. 9 - Roosevelt and Churchill meet in Newfoundland to produce the Atlantic Charter, declaring hopes for a better future.

Aug. 20 - Hitler authorizes the development of a new missile, the V-2.

CANCER

From June 21, 19:33 through July 23, 6:25

The Nest Builder

Ordinarily, your sign isn't happy when it's not sleeping in its own bed, Cancer, but being born in 1941 probably gave you the ability to be a bit more adaptable. Basically, you can create a comfortable nest wherever your travels take you—and you may do quite a bit of traveling throughout life, both for business and recreation.

You arrived at a time when Nazi Germany seemed to be unbeatable, and thousands of Jews in the Baltic States made a difficult choice: to leave their homes, or face wearing the infamous "gold star," the sacred Star of David, a beloved symbol which would now put them in great peril. Forced to pack up only what was most dear to them, they fled, hoping to find the most precious thing of all: safety. As a result, you probably grew up in an atmosphere that reinforced the importance of family, and the security of home-base—no matter where that happened to be.

Since your sign's symbol is the crab, who carries its home on its back wherever it goes, you have an innate understanding of the importance of safety and security—and of the necessity of finding it. As a result, one of your top priorities is probably your own home—and your skill at making your loved ones feel at ease there is most likely famous. Even while traveling, you may have a way of making everywhere feel like home—even the starkest hotel room. You're probably also quite protective about your family, putting their well being first and taking their side in any battle—regardless of your own feelings about the issue.

Your best friends will probably arrive early in your life, and stay there—your sign has never been known to forget a kindness or desert a loved one in need. In love, your home-loving nature and knack for creature comforts could attract the admiring attention of Taureans over the years, but Virgos and Scorpios would also find you appealing—and the feeling is likely to be mutual.

Your challenge, Cancer of 1941, is to trust that the Universe will provide. Your strength is your flexibility and adaptability to sudden change—and your contagious appreciation for the little things in life.

LEO

From July 23, 6:26 through August 23, 13:16

The Team Player

A mighty alliance was formed around the time you were born, Leo of 1941—one that would ultimately lead to the end of Nazi rule. British Prime Minister Winston Churchill and U.S. President Franklin D. Roosevelt met in secret in Newfoundland and together drew up the Atlantic Charter, which clarified the goals of the two governments with regard to World War II. This powerful coalition, forged while the Sun was in Leo in 1941, led eventually to an era of peace.

As a result, you may carry within you the seeds of peace and compromise. In family situations, you're probably often called on to settle differences, offer advice on matters of fairness, and help put an end to ancient disputes—and you're well equipped to handle it all. It's likely you've been given an eye for detail, a fiery spirit, and a relentless drive toward equality. Put them to good use and you gain the lasting admiration of your dear ones, who no doubt will be more than happy to return your kindness when the need arises—just don't forget to ask for their help when you need it.

You also understand the meaning of teamwork. As such, you can be a welcome addition to any workplace and you're often quite popular with co-workers, who'll admire your determination to keep at a task until it's done. This same quality will be appealing to friends and lovers alike. In friendships, Sagittarius and Aries may always be your best bets. They're happy to provide you with the inspiration to forget your duties and be playful sometimes—something your fun-loving sign really needs. In love, Taurus, Scorpio, and Capricorn, all famous for their determination and long-term focus, could be the most appealing to you.

You may be challenged throughout life to face the fact that you can't be responsible for everything, and to delegate to others. Although this may be difficult for you, 1941 Leo, keep in mind that the power of many is far greater than the power of one—in short, there's strength in numbers. Your gift is to speak your truth, uncensored, unabridged, and completely—the only real way to form a legitimate, long-lasting peace.

► Read about your Chinese Astrological sign on page 838. ► Read about your Personal Planets on page 826. ► Read about your personal Mystical Card on page 856.

VIRGO

From August 23, 13:17 through September 23, 10:32

The Intellectual Rebel

Born during a time when most citizens of the world were forced to think hard about the rights they'd formerly taken for granted—and how to defend those rights—you're probably known for your verbal skills, Virgo of 1941. And those who are willing to take you on in this department may be brave, indeed. You can have a quicksilver mind and the ability to wield words like weapons, making you quite formidable when you're angry—and deliciously witty when you're in the company of friends.

You were born at a time of ceaseless communication. As World War II continued to sweep across Europe, citizens all over the globe listened anxiously for news, and meetings were held on both sides of the Atlantic in the hope of ending the carnage. Unfortunately, peace was not to come just yet, and your family was probably trying to accept the fact that force would necessarily have to continue until that peace was achieved. This may have meant that your parents ruled your home with an iron hand, and during your early years you may have felt that you were held back by the authorities around you. Later on, that perceived repression may have led to rebellion.

As freethinking as you can be, you may also have been in disputes involving your personal independence. These conflicts probably led you to form a strong and well-grounded sense of self, and this could have served you well in your work, for you would be the bastion of strength in any organization.

In friendships, aim for the other earth signs—Taurus and Capricorn. In love relationships, you may prefer Aquarians or Sagittarians, who'll happily allow you to lead your own life, follow your own rules, and express your ideals as passionately as you feel them. If you're up for a bit of drama, however, a Leo or Scorpio might also make a good mate—and you certainly wouldn't be bored!

Your challenge, Virgo of 1941, is to be sure there's a legitimate reason to say "no" before you say it. It may be all too easy for you to be a rebel without a cause. Your gift is the ease with which you state your case—no matter how seemingly radical the subject is.

LIBRA

From September 23, 10:33 through October 23, 19:26

The Balance Seeker

As a Libra born in 1941, you arrived around the time Nazi Germany stepped up its assault on the Soviet Union. Even as these two massive powers clashed in battle, Japan was planning a surprise attack on the U.S. naval base at Pearl Harbor, Hawaii. All over the world, people may have wondered when their lives might come under threat, and, for many, such fears would turn out to be justified. At a moment in history as uncertain as this one, tending to the small rituals of daily life may have been a great source of comfort to your parents. This could be why tending to the familiar details of your own life can often be what puts your mind at ease.

Yet, even as your parents tried to maintain a semblance of normalcy, the possibility that they would need to have an escape route handy undoubtedly put them under stress. They may have sent out mixed messages with regard to the future—and you may have picked up on the tension, even as an infant. As a result, you may have felt a vague sense of unease about the future as you were growing up—without quite being able to put your finger on the reason. You may also sometimes feel that nothing is ever really set in stone, or that promises made to you would be broken.

The positive outcome of this could be that the juggling you may have had to do to restore your emotional balance honed your Libran skills. You might have become an expert at finding an outcome to every situation that's fair, equitable, and acceptable to all parties concerned—and you may have applied this skill by choosing a career as a politician, labor negotiator, or office manager.

In romance, it's likely that you value security and above all look for someone you can trust, no matter what life tosses your way. A Taurus, Virgo, or Capricorn could provide you with that secure feeling—and the deep connection you would need to stay committed.

Your challenge, 1941 Libra, is to learn that it is possible to trust—and to develop a keen eye for choosing those who are worthy of your devotion. Your gift is the ability to see exactly what compromises are needed to bring about a happy ending.

VIRGO
Your Personal Planets

YOUR LOVE POTENTIAL
Venus in Libra, Aug. 23, 13:17 - Sept. 15, 4:00
Venus in Scorpio, Sept. 15, 4:01 - Sept. 23, 10:32

YOUR DRIVE AND AMBITION
Mars in Aries, Aug. 23, 13:17 - Sept. 23, 10:32

YOUR LUCK MAGNETISM
Jupiter in Gemini, Aug. 23, 13:17 - Sept. 23, 10:32

World Events

Sept. 2 – The Motion Picture Academy of Arts and Sciences copyrights the Oscar statuette.

Sept. 6 – The German secret police states that Jews are forbidden to appear in public without wearing the Jewish star.

American civil rights leader Jesse Jackson is born under the sign of Libra.

LIBRA
Your Personal Planets

YOUR LOVE POTENTIAL
Venus in Scorpio, Sept. 23, 10:33 - Oct. 10, 19:20
Venus in Sagittarius, Oct. 10, 19:21 - Oct. 23, 19:26

YOUR DRIVE AND AMBITION
Mars in Aries, Sept. 23, 10:33 - Oct. 23, 19:26

YOUR LUCK MAGNETISM
Jupiter in Gemini, Sept. 23, 10:33 - Oct. 23, 19:26

World Events

Oct. 3 – Film classic *The Maltese Falcon*, starring Humphrey Bogart, opens.

Oct. 8 – American politician and civil rights leader Jesse Jackson is born.

➤ Read about your Chinese Astrological sign on page 838. ➤ Read about your Personal Planets on page 826. ➤ Read about your personal Mystical Card on page 856.

343

1941

SCORPIO
Your Personal Planets

YOUR LOVE POTENTIAL
Venus in Sagittarius, Oct. 23, 19:27 - Nov. 06, 10:16
Venus in Capricorn, Nov. 06, 10:17 - Nov. 22, 16:37

YOUR DRIVE AND AMBITION
Mars in Aries, Oct. 23, 19:27 - Nov. 22, 16:37

YOUR LUCK MAGNETISM
Jupiter in Gemini, Oct. 23, 19:27 - Nov. 22, 16:37

World Events

Oct. 31 – The monument at Mount Rushmore, depicting U.S. Presidents Washington, Jefferson, Lincoln, and Theodore Roosevelt, is completed.

Nov. 16 – Half a million Polish Jews are sealed inside the Warsaw Ghetto.

The monument at Mount Rushmore

SAGITTARIUS
Your Personal Planets

YOUR LOVE POTENTIAL
Venus in Capricorn, Nov. 22, 16:38 - Dec. 05, 23:03
Venus in Aquarius, Dec. 05, 23:04 - Dec. 22, 5:43

YOUR DRIVE AND AMBITION
Mars in Aries, Nov. 22, 16:38 - Dec. 22, 5:43

YOUR LUCK MAGNETISM
Jupiter in Gemini, Nov. 22, 16:38 - Dec. 22, 5:43

World Events

Dec. 7 – The Japanese launch an attack on the naval base at Pearl Harbor, drawing the U.S. into World War II.

Dec. 9 – China declares war on Japan, Germany, and Italy.

SCORPIO
From October 23, 19:27 through November 22, 16:37

The Determined Defender

The season of your birth was marked by powerful fixed astrological energies—energies that may have been reflected in the world's equally fixed determination to bring about justice for those being persecuted. Around the time you were born, 1941 Scorpio, the United States was finalizing arrangements to lend $1 million to the Soviet Union to aid them in driving the Nazis from their homeland, and this alliance between onetime enemies may have left a profound imprint on your nature.

This could explain why you're often the person your loved ones turn to in an emergency, confident that you'll be willing to help—anytime, anywhere. In fact, regardless of your age, sex, or actual position in the family, you could be perceived as the head of your family since you take on the role of "protective parent" so easily and you're never afraid to risk your own safety for those you love.

Your willingness to put yourself in the line of fire for those you love is an outer symbol of the bravery that lies at your core, and it wouldn't be surprising if you also gravitated to a career where you would have had a lot of responsibility. You might have chosen to serve the public as a police officer or firefighter. In your time off, you may tend to seek out your quieter friends to unwind with. Pisces, Cancer, or Virgo could provide the steady shoulder even you might need to lean on, every now and again. It's likely that your friends will share at least some of your enthusiasms, but you could also seek out those whose interests diverge from your own so that you would be able to learn from them.

In love, you may want a partner who's equally skilled at sheltering and safeguarding the life you've built. Look to Taureans, Leos, and Capricorns to fulfill those substantial requirements—and give you the unconditional loyalty and faithfulness you need.

You can be a true friend or an implacable foe, Scorpio of 1941. Your challenge is to learn to use only the force you need to ensure the preservation of what you hold dear. Your gifts are your unwavering determination and your fearlessness in the face of adversity.

SAGITTARIUS
From November 22, 16:38 through December 22, 5:43

The Great Uniter

Sagittarius of 1941, you were born during a time that was marked by a hostility unfamiliar to your benevolent sign. The bombing of Pearl Harbor on December 7 was an event that plunged the United States into World War II and greatly escalated the existing conflict. No matter where you were born, this incident probably colored your childhood, but perhaps not in a negative way. Surprisingly, it's likely that your famously sunny outlook on life remained intact—and your raffish sense of humor as well.

During your childhood, patriotism and nationalism ran high in countries all over the world. Pulling together to get through difficult times would have required people to put aside petty differences, and you may have learned early on to cooperate, compromise, and let minor issues slide—especially when it came to immediate family and long-term friends. This capacity for finding common ground in virtually any gathering would make you a welcome addition to any group, and it's likely that you always had more invitations than you could handle.

Your knack for communicating with people from any social background may also make you the perfect negotiator, mediator, and peacemaker—a trait that might bring you a motley crew of friends, to say the least! At work, you may take the lead without seeming to. You've probably mastered the art of delegating, so people could naturally turn to you for direction. In your time off, you can make sure to get the physical exercise you need to stay happy.

Your ability to entertain and amuse with your wit could be one of the reasons your dear ones adore you. In love, you may be drawn to Librans, the sign that's famous for its ability to bring balance to any situation, but Aquarians and Leos could appeal to your fiery, independent temperament, too. It's likely that your personal freedom is important to you, so regardless of what sign you choose for a mate, make sure they understand that you're going to need plenty of space.

Your challenge is to stand up for yourself no matter what. Your strength is your ability to see both the forest and the trees.

➤ Read about your Chinese Astrological sign on page 838. ➤ Read about your Personal Planets on page 826. ➤ Read about your personal Mystical Card on page 856.

CAPRICORN

From December 22, 5:44 through December 31, 23:59

The Cautious Optimist

You may have grown up in an environment of extreme caution, December Capricorn of 1941. Germany and Italy had declared war on the U.S. and her allies earlier in the month, and your family would undoubtedly have felt the strains most families did. Gasoline and many foodstuffs were in short supply, and in some cases would be strictly rationed for the duration of the war. But any hardships you experienced during your youth probably brought you even closer to your dear ones, enabling you to see things objectively yet look to the future with a positive attitude. This inner confidence, despite adversity or stress, might be your strongest character trait and may have brought you admiration and respect throughout life.

It's likely that you displayed leadership qualities early on, and they, in combination with your stable attitude, won you the approval of authority figures. In fact, you may automatically be put behind the steering wheel, regardless of where you are or what kind of group you're part of. Your talents can be as varied and unpredictable as your sense of humor, and you probably surprise others on a continuous basis, both with your dry wit and your skill at so very many things. Above all else, however, you can be an organizational genius. You may be capable of directing and coordinating even the most diverse group of individuals, bringing them together to achieve a collective goal.

Friendship can be a lifelong affair for you. You may admire the effortless daring of your Aries friends, but another Capricorn could be your best pal over the long haul.

In romance, you may find yourself most often in the company of Taurus, Virgo, or Sagittarius lovers. These signs are famous for their earthiness and honesty—traits your reputable sign values highly. But don't ignore an Aquarius with a radical new idea who happens to cross your path. He may have much to teach you about breaking those rules you've mastered.

Your challenge is to put aside your discriminating eye when you feel yourself obsessing over minor details. Your gift is your innate understanding of how things work.

1941

CAPRICORN
Your Personal Planets

YOUR LOVE POTENTIAL
Venus in Aquarius, Dec. 22, 5:44 - Dec. 31, 23:59

YOUR LOVE POTENTIAL
Mars in Aries, Dec. 22, 5:44 - Dec. 31, 23:59

YOUR LUCK MAGNETISM
Jupiter in Gemini, Dec. 22, 5:44 - Dec. 31, 23:59

World Events

Dec. 26 – In an address to a joint meeting of Congress, Winston Churchill warns that "the Axis powers will stop at nothing."

Dec. 29 – President Roosevelt claims that the U.S. is the "arsenal of democracy."

Charlie Chaplin in "The Great Dictator"

Special Feature

Astro Twins: Hitler and Chaplin
by Jean Mars

Charlie Chaplin's 1940s film *The Great Dictator* is a prophetic satire of Hitler and his Third Reich. While Chaplin's ability to foresee the political future is certainly commendable, an astrologer might not find it so out of the ordinary. Some might even consider the two men to have been "astro twins!" This term generally refers to people born on the same day, or very close to the same day as these two were. When you have very close horoscopes, you are bound to have very similar life circumstances—and these two are no exception. As you will see, their family backgrounds and early years closely mirror one another.

Both Chaplin and Hitler had questionable Jewish ties in their family backgrounds and both had difficulties with that aspect of their lives. Initially, Chaplin admitted to his Jewish heritage, later denying it. Hitler's family name is an adopted name, and his real father was said to have been the illegitimate son of a Jewish man. Hitler was born into an ordinary middle-class family, while Chaplin's parents were music hall

entertainers. Their families enjoyed relatively comfortable positions, and both men would exchange that comfort—due to circumstances beyond their control—for tragedy early on. Hitler's father, a difficult and domineering man, died in 1903, and his mother died in 1907. Hitler seems to have spent his adolescent years as a vagabond, wandering aimlessly, trying to make ends meet and dreaming of becoming a great painter. Chaplin's parents divorced when he was an infant. After that, he had little contact with his father, who died when Chaplin was five. Around this same time he lost his mother to a nervous breakdown, and he and his half-brother became street urchins, going in and out of charity homes.

Interestingly enough each of these men, in his own way, would pull himself out of a difficult and desperate situation. Both had a powerful drive to succeed and needed to prove themselves to the world. As a young man, Hitler's artistic talents proved to be mediocre, and he found himself drawn to an unstable political

world. It was also at this time that he came in contact with certain thinkers and philosophers of the era who believed firmly in the superiority of a "pure" Aryan race. While he was certainly influenced—even manipulated—by their dogmatic concepts, Hitler managed to reformulate these racist ideas to his own preconceptions and to manipulate others to join his campaign. It was at this time that he discovered his true talent: a charisma and magnetism that enabled him to inspire and influence others.

(Continued on page 353)

➤ Read more about Hitler in "Astrology Reigns through the Ages" on page 25. ➤ Read about an astrologer Chaplin consulted on page 185.

1942

Danger and Destruction: Pluto Meets Mars

Devastation touched every corner of the earth in 1942. The Allies fought the Axis powers on three continents. Hitler rattled his saber ever more wildly. In summer of that year, Mars, the planet of war and ambition, linked arms with Pluto, the planet of destruction and degeneration. This is a volatile combination with far-reaching consequences for all. In 1942, Nazi leaders attended the Wanssee Conference to coordinate the "Final Solution"—the ghastly blueprint for the utter decimation of the Jews of Europe. Because Pluto was in Leo at this time, it was making an aspect called a "sextile" to Hitler's Libra ascendant. Oftentimes male volent Saturn and warmongering Mars were hitting his Sun and angry Mars in Taurus during the first month of the year and the same month as the fateful Wanssee Conference.

On June 9, 1942, the Nazis liquidated the village of Lidice in Czechoslovakia to avenge the assassination of Reinhard Heydrich, protector of Bohemia and Moravia. Throughout the month, mass deportations of Jews took place in Europe. All Jewish schools in Germany were closed at the end of the month. Power-hungry Pluto and fear-producing Mars were brothers in arms during this period, helping to inspire a deepening lust for power of the Nazis, and pumping up their greed and egotism. Leo is the sign of self-aggrandizement, and with two power planets perched in the constellation of the lion, obsessive, deluded movements can gain ground. Adolf Hitler, as a stubborn Taurus, would do whatever it took to transform the world into his own warped and nightmarish vision.

British troops surrender to the Japanese in Singapore

The Allies gain ground with a victory at El Alamein in Egypt

Enrico Fermi making progress in the project to build an atomic bomb

BELIEVE THIS

Mediums claim that the presence of skeptics at séances tended to inhibit their powers. gertrude Schmeidler of New York City University was the first researcher to investigate the relationship between ESP and the effects of belief and disbelief. Her findings proved to be a landmark in parapsychology. Using test-groups made up from her students, Schmeidler's research showed a definite correlation between ESP and an individual psychology. Belief was clearly indicated to be conducive to psychic ability.

THE TIDE OF WAR TURNS

In southeast Asia, the Japanese captured Singapore, the Netherlands East Indies (Indonesia), and the Philippines. The crack German Afrika Korps led by "Desert Fox" General Rommel arrived in North Africa. The U.S. imposed rationing to preserve resources. Japanese Americans were interned. At the Wansee (Berlin) conference, the Nazis planned the Final Solution to the Jewish Question, or the extermination of the Jews. However, the Allies began to gain ground with the British victory over the Afrika Korps at El Alamein in Egypt, a severe blow from which the Germans never recovered. The Americans scored a decisive triumph over the Japanese at the Battle of Midway. In Russia, the Germans occupied Stalingrad but became trapped there. Eisenhower was appointed Allied commander of the European Theatre of Operations. U.S. forces landed in North Africa. Enrico Fermi led fellow physicists to the first controlled nuclear chain reaction, a vital step in the secret Manhattan Project to build an atomic bomb. Franz Boas, father of American anthropology, died at eighty-four, while film actress Carole Lombard and her mother were killed in a plane crash.

➤ Read "Astro Twins: Hitler and Chaplin" by Jean Mars on page 345.

CAPRICORN

From January 01, 0:00 through January 20, 16:23

The Great Uniter

Born during January of 1942, Capricorn, your arrival was marked by two major alliances, both of which most likely shaped your personality in powerful ways. First, the twenty-six nations who had bonded together to wage war against "the Axis" (Nazi Germany and its supporters) pledged that there would be no peace until it was shared by the entire world. Also during your birth month, however, the Nazis and their allies held a conference, the beginning of the infamous "Final Solution"—basically, a plan for the systematic extermination of every European Jew.

Although the motivation behind each of these events was starkly contrasted, the intention was the same: to unite to achieve a common end. As a result, it's likely that you were influenced at a very young age to value the power of partnership.

This innate understanding of the strength of fellowship has probably grown stronger over the years, turning you into an expert at the art of delegation. It may also have given you the capacity to see where an individual's talents may be used toward a collective purpose. Along with your sign's famous ability to lead, this may mean you're continuously put in charge of just about every group you become involved with—including both personal and business relationships.

In love, your propensity to accept a position of authority may require that you find a mate who's equally responsible and hard-working. As a result, the other earth signs—Virgos and Taureans—will probably always find their way into your life. Librans could also teach you to fine-tune your ability to negotiate peace. The curiosity your birth year endowed you with probably also means you'll enjoy the company of cerebral Aquarians and Geminis.

Your challenge, January Capricorn, is to learn that you can't "fix" every unhappy situation—especially those involving individuals or entities that refuse to compromise and pool their efforts. Your greatest gifts are your knack for finding a fair compromise in any situation and your ability to find the right person for the right position—and you'll undoubtedly be well respected for it.

AQUARIUS

From January 20, 16:24 through February 19, 6:46

The Freedom Fighter

You, as a 1942 Aquarius, were born at a time when thousands of Japanese were detained and interned in the U.S., following the bombing of Pearl Harbor. Although this may not have affected you directly in the country of your birth, the news of this event was broadcast all over, raising concerns about freedom in every corner of the globe.

As a result, you may have been raised in an early environment that bolstered a trait your sign is famous for: the determination to have complete independence and autonomy over your life. This innate thirst for self-expression and the pursuit of your own particular moral standards may have heightened the rebellious streak your sign is also known to possess, especially during your adolescent and teenage years. But even as you mature, your defense of your right to live every moment exactly as you believe you should will only grow stronger. In fact, the one thing that you probably cannot tolerate, above all else, is the repression of your personal uniqueness. Over time, you may even become a champion for those whose rights have been squelched in some way, whether through their personal relationships or their philosophical beliefs.

As such, being subjected to confinement or restrictions of any kind, as well as being forced to make choices that aren't based solely on your own morals, are situations you'll rebel against with a vengeance—as your co-workers, family, and dear ones have probably already learned.

This innate, unwavering insistence on personal freedom will probably lead you to keep company with Sagittarians, both for love and friendship. Geminis and Librans will also make good partners, however, both romantically and platonically, since these Sun signs share your love of chatting, mingling, and socializing with kindred spirits.

Your challenges are to learn cooperation, and to understand that agreeing to compromise isn't a threat to your independence. Your gift is your ability to allow others to love you and to have a strong place in your heart, even as you encourage them to live their own lives in an equally free fashion.

► Read about your Chinese Astrological sign on page 838. ► Read about your Personal Planets on page 826. ► Read about your personal Mystical Card on page 856.

CAPRICORN
Your Personal Planets

YOUR LOVE POTENTIAL
Venus in Aquarius, Jan. 01, 0:00 - Jan. 20, 16:23

YOUR DRIVE AND AMBITION
Mars in Aries, Jan. 01, 0:00 - Jan. 11, 22:20
Mars in Taurus, Jan. 11, 22:21 - Jan. 20, 16:23

YOUR LUCK MAGNETISM
Jupiter in Gemini, Jan. 01, 0:00 - Jan. 20, 16:23

World Events

Jan. 11 – Japan declares war in the Netherlands and invades the Dutch East Indies.

Jan. 17 – American boxer Muhammad Ali is born Cassius Clay.

American boxer Muhammad Ali is born under the sign of Capricorn

AQUARIUS
Your Personal Planets

YOUR LOVE POTENTIAL
Venus in Aquarius, Jan. 20, 16:24 - Feb. 19, 6:46

YOUR DRIVE AND AMBITION
Mars in Taurus, Jan. 20, 16:24 - Feb. 19, 6:46

YOUR LUCK MAGNETISM
Jupiter in Gemini, Jan. 20, 16:24 - Feb. 19, 6:46

World Events

Feb. 1 – Planes of the U.S. Pacific fleet attack the Japanese bases on the Marshall and Gilbert Islands.

Feb. 15 – British forces under Lt. Gen. Arthur Percival surrender to Gen. Tomoyuki Yamashita in Singapore.

1942

PISCES
Your Personal Planets

YOUR LOVE POTENTIAL
Venus in Aquarius, Feb. 19, 6:47 - Mar. 21, 6:10

YOUR DRIVE AND AMBITION
Mars in Taurus, Feb. 19, 6:47 - Mar. 07, 8:03
Mars in Gemini, Mar. 07, 8:04 - Mar. 21, 6:10

YOUR LUCK MAGNETISM
Jupiter in Gemini, Feb. 19, 6:47 - Mar. 21, 6:10

World Events

Mar. 2 – American novelist John Irving is born.

Mar. 17 – Gen. Douglas MacArthur lands in Australia to take over as Supreme Commander of the Allied forces in the south-west Pacific.

American soul singer Aretha Franklin is born under the sign of Aries

ARIES
Your Personal Planets

YOUR LOVE POTENTIAL
Venus in Aquarius, Mar. 21, 6:11 - Apr. 06, 13:13
Venus in Pisces, Apr. 06, 13:14 - Apr. 20, 17:38

YOUR DRIVE AND AMBITION
Mars in Gemini, Mar. 21, 6:11 - Apr. 20, 17:38

YOUR LUCK MAGNETISM
Jupiter in Gemini, Mar. 21, 6:11 - Apr. 20, 17:38

World Events

Mar. 25 – American soul singer Aretha Franklin is born.

Apr. 15 – The citizens of Malta are awarded the George Cross by King George VI.

PISCES
From February 19, 6:47 through March 21, 6:10

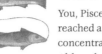

The Devout Defender

You, Pisces of 1942, were born during a time when the horrors of World War II reached a horrifying peak. Thousands of Jews arrived at the Auschwitz concentration camp, forced from their homes in France by the Nazis. Although most had no idea of what awaited them, their piteous situation undoubtedly touched your family members in a deeply emotional way.

As such, your early years were probably influenced by this collective compassion. And since compassion is a trait your Sun sign is already famous for, your innate sensitivity to the plight of the helpless was tremendously heightened. You may also have picked up on the anger, outrage, and fear your family felt. Fortunately, your softness was astrologically tempered during the time of your birth by several planets in air signs, giving you the ability to mentally detach—an armor of sorts for your tender heart. In fact, you'll always find the strength to carry on in the interest of keeping those dear to you safe—even as you and your peers may have thought constantly about what you might do to help.

The influence of this time has probably turned you into an extremely committed defender of the unfortunate—and an even more resolute champion of your dear ones in times of danger. You've been given the simultaneous ability to offer sympathy, understanding, and a soothing touch—even as you ardently pursue retribution on behalf of who and what you love. As such, you've probably become involved with causes and organizations that do battle for the rights of those powerless to fight in their own defense.

In love, your sensitive, wistful personality means you'll probably feel most comfortable with the other water signs—Scorpios and Cancerians. If you're intent on building a solid home base, you might also consider the attentions of a Taurean or Libran. When you're after justice, seek out the advice and support of Aquarian friends, the zodiac's experts at initiating huge societal changes.

Your gift, Pisces of 1942, is your ability to feel what others feel. Your challenge is to detach from those feelings when life requires you to be strong.

ARIES
From March 21, 6:11 through April 20, 17:38

The Blunt Communicator

You, 1942 Aries, were born into a world that was searching for truth, a trait you inherited from the astrological influences of your Sun sign as well as the world events that reflected them. Around the time you were born, the "Office of War Information" was in the final planning stages. An agency initiated by U.S. President Roosevelt and formed on June 13, its goal was to make the facts of war available—and its influence probably shows in your blunt, forceful style of communication.

Your sign has never been famous for beating around the bush or sugarcoating the truth—but you, as an Aries born in 1942, may be especially adept at this brutal honesty. As a result, your skill at leadership and management is probably unparalleled, making you a natural candidate for tough jobs—especially when it comes to replacing someone who may have been too nonchalant with co-workers or employees in the past. When you arrive, it's likely that you'll put your foot down immediately, and whether you're popular or not with those around you probably won't matter to you. What is important in your determined mind is that all parties concerned are honest, reputable, and forthcoming in their dealings with one another—and with the people who depend on them.

In friendships, you may be attracted to Sagittarians, who will always keep your intellectual fire burning brightly. The Archers will also allow you to experience depth and independence in relationships—something that will help you hone your talent for directing others.

In romance, your search for someone whose mind and mouth move as quickly as yours—and whose spirit is equally bold—will probably lead you to Geminis, Leos, and Aquarians. A Gemini's quicksilver mind and incisive wit could intrigue you, but it could be a Leo's commanding temperament and regal bearing that draws your lasting attention.

Your challenge, Aries of 1942, is to wield your verbal skills carefully and not to bully or belittle those who aren't as fast thinking as you are. Your gift is your intuitive understanding of which individual is suited to which particular task.

➤ Read about your Chinese Astrological sign on page 838. ➤ Read about your Personal Planets on page 826. ➤ Read about your personal Mystical Card on page 856.

TAURUS

From April 20, 17:39 through May 21, 17:08

The Provident Investor

Born in 1942, Taurus, you arrived during a time that became famous for rationing. As a result of World War II, the U.S. and its allies began to dole out gasoline, electricity, and even food—and these cutbacks were mandatory. As such, in your early years, your parents probably taught you to get by on very little—and to enjoy what you did have. Although this may have been difficult at the time, the experience later instilled in you the ability to appreciate your possessions and to work diligently to make life easier for yourself and your dear ones.

As a result, you've probably learned over the years to invest both your time and your resources wisely. You won't waste either on personal or financial situations that aren't solid, grounded, and reliable—and your keen sense of timing will never let you down. In fact, you're probably well known for your instinct with regard to both business and personal ventures, and well trusted as an advisor.

When you decide to take a chance, it's undoubtedly because you've taken the time to figure the odds—and through meticulous calculation, found them to be in your favor. Whenever you opt not to take up an opportunity that's offered, there's a good reason. As such, you'd make a wonderful counselor and negotiator, regardless of the situation. Your skills at budgeting, saving toward a long-term goal, and meting out your assets in times of scarcity can always help you achieve the end you seek.

When it comes to relationships, Taurus of 1942, you're probably in search of a mate who'll fulfill all your fantasies—mainly by keeping you fascinated. It's likely that you'll find Pisceans, Scorpios, and Geminis particularly interesting. But if you're after a long-term, stable partnership, look to the other earth signs—Virgo and Capricorn—whose goals will most likely mirror your own.

Your gift lies, 1942 Taurus, in your ability to make do with exactly what you have—no matter how much or how little that happens to be. Your challenge is to continue believing that you'll always have what you need—in short, to trust that the Universe will always provide.

GEMINI

From May 21, 17:09 through June 22, 1:15

The Trusted Trouble-Shooter

You, 1942 Gemini, were born during a most monumental and inspirational time. As World War II continued to storm through Europe, thousands of Jews were being forced to either hide or submit to the atrocities that awaited them in concentration camps. The distribution of real, factual information about what was actually occurring was continually sabotaged by the Nazis—but one little girl was given a blank book that was destined to change all that. Anne Frank received a diary as a birthday gift, a journal now known as the most detailed and accurate personal account of the Holocaust ever written.

Your sign's innate skill at communication is already famous, Gemini—but the particular timing of your birth may have added substantially to that trait. You may possess the ability to notice the little things most of us miss—and to put those details to use, no matter what project you're working on. Through this knack for spotting even the tiniest flaws in any situation, you've probably also developed a talent for trouble-shooting. As a result, you may be drawn to work that allows your keen intellect and shrewd eye to stop those tiny potential problems from becoming major roadblocks.

In friendships and business partnerships, 1942 Gemini, you'd do well to connect with the earth signs—Taurus, Virgo, and Capricorn—whose ability to understand the importance of every tidbit of information rivals even your own.

In love, your search for a partner will probably lead you straight into the arms of Ariens, Sagittarians, or Aquarians, whose trustworthy natures and devotion to honesty could touch your heart. These signs also perfectly provide you with the freedom and spontaneity you need to keep your lighthearted spirit amused.

Your challenge, Gemini of 1942, is to overcome pettiness in relationships—to see your dear ones' intentions, rather than becoming sidetracked by any annoying idiosyncrasies. You have two substantial gifts: the ability to intuitively pick up on both the silent strengths and the Achilles heels of others in any circumstance—and the wisdom to know when those little things matter.

➤ Read about your Chinese Astrological sign on page 838. ➤ Read about your Personal Planets on page 826. ➤ Read about your personal Mystical Card on page 856.

TAURUS
Your Personal Planets

YOUR LOVE POTENTIAL

Venus in Pisces, Apr. 20, 17:39 - May 06, 2:25
Venus in Aries, May 06, 2:26 - May 21, 17:08

YOUR DRIVE AND AMBITION

Mars in Gemini, Apr. 20, 17:39 - Apr. 26, 6:17
Mars in Cancer, Apr. 26, 6:18 - May 21, 17:08

YOUR LUCK MAGNETISM

Jupiter in Gemini, Apr. 20, 17:39 - May 21, 17:08

World Events

Apr. 24 – American singer and actress Barbra Streisand is born.

Apr. 28 – A nightly "dim-out" begins along the East Coast of America.

The RAF launches bombing raids on German cities

GEMINI
Your Personal Planets

YOUR LOVE POTENTIAL

Venus in Aries, May 21, 17:09 - June 02, 0:25
Venus in Taurus, June 02, 0:26 - June 22, 1:15

YOUR DRIVE AND AMBITION

Mars in Cancer, May 21, 17:09 - June 14, 3:55
Mars in Leo, June 14, 3:56 - June 22, 1:15

YOUR LUCK MAGNETISM

Jupiter in Gemini, May 21, 17:09 - June 10, 10:35
Jupiter in Cancer, June 10, 10:36 - June 22, 1:15

World Events

May 30 – The RAF launches a 1,000-plane raid of major German cities.

June 4 – The aerial Battle of Midway begins over the Pacific.

1942

CANCER
Your Personal Planets

YOUR LOVE POTENTIAL

Venus in Taurus, June 22, 1:16 - June 27, 22:17
Venus in Gemini, June 27, 22:18 - July 23, 6:09
Venus in Cancer, July 23, 6:10 - July 23, 12:06

YOUR DRIVE AND AMBITION

Mars in Leo, June 22, 1:16 - July 23, 12:06

YOUR LUCK MAGNETISM

Jupiter in Cancer, June 22, 1:16 - July 23, 12:06

World Events

July 9 – Thirteen-year-old Jewish girl Anne Frank goes into hiding in Amsterdam with her family.

July 18 – The first jet-propelled combat aircraft, the German Me-262, makes its inaugural flight.

Anne Frank's diaries

LEO
Your Personal Planets

YOUR LOVE POTENTIAL

Venus in Cancer, July 23, 12:07 - Aug. 17, 3:03
Venus in Leo, Aug. 17, 3:04 - Aug. 23, 18:57

YOUR DRIVE AND AMBITION

Mars in Leo, July 23, 12:07 - Aug. 01, 8:26
Mars in Virgo, Aug. 01, 8:27 - Aug. 23, 18:57

YOUR LUCK MAGNETISM

Jupiter in Cancer, July 23, 12:07 - Aug. 23, 18:57

World Events

July 24 - Italian troops attack the rebels in Yugoslavia.

Aug. 9 - Mahatma Gandhi and other All-Indian Congress leaders are arrested in Bombay during their continuing campaign to end British rule.

CANCER
From June 22, 1:16 through July 23, 12:06

The Discriminating Care-Giver

As a 1942 Cancer, you arrived into a world still plagued by a wave of racial hatred. Around the time you were born, 300,000 Jews from Warsaw were sent to Treblinka, an "extermination camp"—a chilling example of the Nazis' lack of compassion for those weaker than themselves. Growing up in the shadow of these horrible events may have refined your already sympathetic nature, influencing you later in life to become a champion of the weak and underprivileged.

You may have developed a knack for spotting individuals who really want and need help, and are willing to work hard to make something of themselves—as opposed to those who attempt to take advantage of the generosity of others.

This doesn't mean that you've ever been jaded or unappreciative of the plight of those less fortunate than yourself—only that you've most likely become an expert at spotting a con-artist from someone who's legitimately in need of assistance. In fact, you may find yourself drawn to organizations or causes that defend the abandoned, whether they're people or animals. Your generous, unselfish nature probably also means you've been moved, at one time or another, to donate your time and resources to helping others to get back on their feet. That goes double for the empathy you show toward family and friends who've hit a rough spot in the road.

It's likely that you were raised in a family structure that placed compassion, understanding, and maintaining a safe home base at the top of their priorities. That could be why, in romance, your home-loving sign will probably look for happiness and security with Taureans, other Cancerians, and Virgos. These three signs are stable and permanence-oriented—all of them willing to work hard to keep a long-term relationship intact. In platonic partnerships, look to Pisceans and Capricorns to inspire you to express your emotions and rely on your instinct.

Your challenge, Cancer of 1942, is to never allow your tender heart to be taken advantage of by those who'd seek to use you. Your greatest gift lies in your ability to separate the frauds from those legitimately in need.

LEO
From July 23, 12:07 through August 23, 18:57

The Fiery Freedom-Fighter

The time of your birth, 1942 Leo, was marked by the arrests of Mahatma Gandhi and fifty kindred sprits in Bombay, an event that occurred after the "quit India" campaign to overturn British rule was upheld by the All-India Congress. This stunning example of the determination of humanity to escape from the shackles of oppression probably inspired in you a deep-seated need for personal freedom—also at any cost.

In later life, you may have fought off attempts by peers to force you to bow to their rules, especially if you viewed these rules as oppressive or illogical. The senselessness of certain customs may have caused you to become known as a rebel. In fact, you may feel as if you've been put here on Earth to break traditions—most especially those that were handed down to you without any logical reason for your adherence.

Your willingness to change the world around you, even if that only pertains to your family's ways, has probably put you in battle with even blood relatives at times—and with "City Hall" quite often. Never let this independent streak go ignored. You were blessed with a way of "just knowing" when others are trying to keep you under their thumbs—no matter how persuasive their arguments. You're probably quite skilled at countering those arguments, regardless of the cost to your relationships. Your unyielding spirit may put you in difficult emotional situations at times, but if you pursue your beliefs as adamantly as your conscience advises, you'll be true to yourself—the most important thing any of us can do. And after all, self-respect is far more important than the applause of the crowd.

In love, your fondness for entertainment might draw you to Sagittarians, Librans, and Geminis, but an Aquarius friend may have a thing or two to teach you about remaining true to yourself even while committed.

Your challenge, Leo of 1942, is to keep on doing battle against oppression, regardless of whether it's on behalf of yourself or others. Your gift is your stubborn rebelliousness that will never allow you to submit to a dogma or belief system you're ardently opposed to.

➤ Read about your Chinese Astrological sign on page 838. ➤ Read about your Personal Planets on page 826. ➤ Read about your personal Mystical Card on page 856.

VIRGO

From August 23, 18:58 through September 23, 16:15

The Cautious Confidante

As a 1942 Virgo, you arrived at a moment when the world around you probably left your parents quite reluctant to invest their complete confidence in anyone or anything. After Japan suddenly bombed Pearl Harbor in December 1941, citizens the world over were forced to consider just how risky it was to trust another country—even a formerly friendly one. Conversely, alliances sprung up between the most unlikely of entities—such as the U.S. and the USSR.

You probably sensed the uncertainty your elders felt during your early years, and you may have learned to hold back your own trust until you were absolutely sure it was deserved. In fact, this doubtfulness may have made its way into even your closest relationships—especially your earliest ones. As time went by, however, you may have realized that what you were given was the virtue of discrimination, and the ability to protect yourself from false friends. This gift will make it less likely for you to be taken advantage of—and your notoriously tenderhearted sign often needs that sense of caution. Difficult or not, then, those subtle messages you received during childhood have probably done you a great service.

In addition, the loyalty and need for closeness that you innately possess as an earth sign, 1942 Virgo, would inevitably need to surface—as would your search for your soul-mate. And once someone does manage to earn your confidence—no easy task, but a truly worthwhile one—they will never lose it. You are the truest of friends, and the most devoted of mates.

Still, you probably prefer spending time alone to socializing with "just anyone." You may become involved with those who are equally particular about the company they keep—other Virgos, Capricorns, and Taureans. A Piscean whose gift for creating magic in everyday life may attract your attention, too, and your long-term affection, as well.

Your gift, Virgo of 1942, is your discretion—the ability to spot a true friend immediately. Your challenge is to let go of doubt and skepticism that may keep you from enjoying the best that intimate friendships have to offer.

LIBRA

From September 23, 16:16 through October 24, 1:14

The Elegant Connoisseur

You arrived as the heavens were fairly bursting with the energy of your sign, Libra of 1942. Despite the fact that World War II was spreading, even to the shores of northern Africa, a quality your sign is famous for managed to take center stage: the appreciation of beauty—in all its forms. Theaters, art galleries, and concert halls the world over were sold out, providing a welcome respite from war and the horrors of the Holocaust, and tickets for all the aesthetic arts were at a premium.

As a result, you were probably raised in an early environment that placed great value on enjoying the finer things in life—and that love of creature comforts may have stayed with you all your life. You may be known for your elegance, and a unique sense of style that no one could ever quite succeed in copying.

Your taste for good music, fine art, and quality entertainment has probably developed throughout your life, giving you an added boost to develop the respect for and love of beauty your sign virtually owns. In fact, you may be known among your friends as the best person to talk to about the weekend's plans, whether it's where to dine, which movie to see, or which gallery shows to peruse. You're undoubtedly very popular, then, and you'll do well to always surround yourself with companions who are equally pleasing to the senses: charming, witty, well-dressed, and cultured.

Taking all this into account makes it easy to see that your best bet for romance and long-term relationships, 1942 Libra, absolutely must be the signs who share your appreciation for the best—and who, like you, will settle for nothing less. In that respect, look to Leos, Sagittarians, and Capricorns, all of whom will always make any evening out an experience to remember.

Your gifts, Libra of 1942, are your innate sense of artistic balance, your well-tuned ear, and your discriminating palate—all of which will help you to enjoy each and every moment you spend on this wonderful playground we call the Earth. Your challenge is to keep a tight rein on your desires, never letting any physical pleasure take control of you.

➤ Read about your Chinese Astrological sign on page 838. ➤ Read about your Personal Planets on page 826. ➤ Read about your personal Mystical Card on page 856.

VIRGO
Your Personal Planets

YOUR LOVE POTENTIAL
Venus in Leo, Aug. 23, 18:58 - Sept. 10, 14:37
Venus in Virgo, Sept. 10, 14:38 - Sept. 23, 16:15

YOUR DRIVE AND AMBITION
Mars in Virgo, Aug. 23, 18:58 - Sept. 17, 10:10
Mars in Libra, Sept. 17, 10:11 - Sept. 23, 16:15

YOUR LUCK MAGNETISM
Jupiter in Cancer, Aug. 23, 18:58 - Sept. 23, 16:15

World Events

Aug. 23 - The Battle of Stalingrad begins between German and Russian troops.

Sept. 15 - In the Pacific, U.S. troops repel the Japanese at Guadalcanal.

The Battle of Stalingrad begins

LIBRA
Your Personal Planets

YOUR LOVE POTENTIAL
Venus in Virgo, Sept. 23, 16:16 - Oct. 04, 18:57
Venus in Libra, Oct. 04, 18:58 - Oct. 24, 1:14

YOUR DRIVE AND AMBITION
Mars in Libra, Sept. 23, 16:16 - Oct. 24, 1:14

YOUR LUCK MAGNETISM
Jupiter in Cancer, Sept. 23, 16:16 - Oct. 24, 1:14

World Events

Oct. 16 - A cyclone sweeps through the Bay of Bengal in India, claiming an estimated 40,000 lives.

Oct. 16 - Aaron Copland's ballet *Rodeo* premières in New York City.

351

1942

SCORPIO
Your Personal Planets

YOUR LOVE POTENTIAL
Venus in Libra, Oct. 24, 1:15 - Oct. 28, 18:39
Venus in Scorpio, Oct. 28, 18:40 - Nov. 21, 16:06
Venus in Sagittarius, Nov. 21, 16:07 - Nov. 22, 22:29

YOUR DRIVE AND AMBITION
Mars in Libra, Oct. 24, 1:15 - Nov. 01, 22:35
Mars in Scorpio, Nov. 01, 22:36 - Nov. 22, 22:29

YOUR LUCK MAGNETISM
Jupiter in Scorpio, Oct. 24, 1:15 - Nov. 22, 22:29

World Events

Nov. 8 - The Allied forces under the command of Dwight D. Eisenhower seize control of French North Africa.

Nov. 13 - The minimum draft age in the U.S. is lowered from twenty-one to eighteen.

American rock guitarist Jimi Hendrix is born under the sign of Sagittarius

SAGITTARIUS
Your Personal Planets

YOUR LOVE POTENTIAL
Venus in Sagittarius, Nov. 22, 22:30 - Dec. 15, 12:52
Venus in Capricorn, Dec. 15, 12:53 - Dec. 22, 11:39

YOUR DRIVE AND AMBITION
Mars in Scorpio, Nov. 22, 22:30 - Dec. 15, 16:50
Mars in Sagittarius, Dec. 15, 16:51 - Dec. 22, 11:39

YOUR LUCK MAGNETISM
Jupiter in Cancer, Nov. 22, 22:30 - Dec. 22, 11:39

World Events

Nov. 27 - American rock guitarist Jimi Hendrix is born.

Dec. 2 - The first controlled nuclear chain reaction is demonstrated at the University of Chicago, leading to the development of the atomic bomb.

SCORPIO
From October 24, 1:15 through November 22, 22:29

The Hopeful Thinker

You arrived at a moment in history that perfectly reflects the intensity of your sign, 1942 Scorpio—and the innate optimism. The Soviet retaliation at the city of Stalingrad began around the time you were born. Although World War II was destined to continue for almost three more years, this historic siege was a surprising testimony to enduring perseverance in the face of impossible odds.

As a result, although your family members were probably still reeling from the reports they heard on a daily basis concerning the atrocities and horrors of the war, a ray of light may have been instilled in your young soul, infusing you with an equally optimistic bent on life. In times of emotional, political, or social turbulence, that trait has most likely carried you through it all. In addition, your faith in the future has probably inspired many of your dear ones to keep going, strengthened by your powerful example.

It's likely that you face each and every hurdle and roadblock life presents to you with inner peace and an understanding of the inevitability of change. You're perceptive enough to realize that although we may not be able to change the circumstances that the Universe tosses our way, we can make the best of any situation—even the unpleasant ones—by changing our attitude.

As passionate, intense, and intuitive as you are, you're probably looking for a mate who'll be able to return the depth you need. If you choose Pisceans, Librans, or other Scorpios, you'll no doubt find these qualities you find so important in a mate. Look to Sagittarian friends to provide you with philosophical inspiration, challenging conversation, and the chance to let your cares slide in favor of just having some fun.

Your greatest gift is your unfailing certainty that everything that has ever happened has put you right where you are at this moment—and that if you're happy with who you are, you've got to give thanks for it all, regardless of whether it seemed "bad" or "good" at the time. Your challenge, Scorpio of 1942, is to allow others to make their own mistakes—and never say "I told you so."

SAGITTARIUS
From November 22, 22:30 through December 22, 11:39

The Eternal Optimist

As a 1942 Sagittarius, you arrived in a world that was sorely in need of your humor, understanding, and ability to see the bright side of any situation. The world was dealing with the grim reality of World War II—a conflict that may have seemed endless, especially to the countries that were directly involved in the fighting. The war was particularly stressful and taxing around the time you were born, as the Allied forces launched the largest daylight raid from the sky the war had so far seen.

It's likely that your family considered you a blessing, as you probably displayed the positive attitude your sign is famous for at a very young age. This trait may have grown more powerful over time, and those who are lucky enough to have you near them on a daily basis can be touched by your sunny disposition as well as your generous soul. It's possible, however, that you may have had to learn at some point that you couldn't save everyone, and that, often, the best lessons are the ones that force people to confront their weaknesses.

This understanding could have led you to a career in teaching or counseling, where your innate compassion would give you the ability to provide good advice, and to be totally honest when you were asked for it. Later in life, someone you had helped may even have let you know that not allowing them to shirk their responsibilities gave them the opportunity they needed to grow and change.

In romance, your need for freedom means that your most compatible signs are probably other Sagittarians, Aquarians, and Geminis. These three signs are cerebral equals who'll be able keep up with your keen sense of humor—and they'll also provide you with the intellectual challenge you love. But a fiery Leo could match your love of adventure, and that could win your heart.

Your challenge is to reel in any tendency toward continually bailing your loved ones out of tough situations—especially if they've brought these problems on themselves. Your gift is your ability to raise the spirits of those around you with your philosophical, optimistic, and keenly witty personality.

► Read about your Chinese Astrological sign on page 838. ► Read about your Personal Planets on page 826. ► Read about your personal Mystical Card on page 856.

CAPRICORN

From December 22, 11:40 through December 31, 23:59

The Noble Egalitarian

Born during late December of 1942, Capricorn, you arrived in a world that was divided by conflict. But as a result, the need to work together was probably quite strongly reinforced by those around you during your early years. This time period marked the beginning of an enormous social change that came about as a result of the ongoing conflict of World War II. While young men the world over commonly expected to be sent off to fight for their country, now, for the first time, women became involved in the war effort. In fact, many women found themselves in positions that were formerly "male only"—both through their employment in war industries and sometimes through actual military support.

As a result, you were probably raised in an environment that unknowingly fostered sexual equality. This subtle message you received regarding the value of every individual's efforts—regardless of gender—was a powerful one. In fact, you may have gone on to become a strong advocate of that cause, and of racial and religious equality as well. You may also often feel it necessary for you to personally convince others to put aside prejudice and bias, and work toward attaining a joint purpose.

This powerful capacity to remain neutral and impartial, along with the innate candor the Universe gave you, probably made you a force to be reckoned with when discrimination you view as unfair and ungrounded occurred around you, and it could have made you a lot of friends in the process.

Your fair mind and egalitarian soul will lead you to search for a lover who shares your beliefs—which may lead to a long-term relationship with a Libran, the sign whose impartiality is famous. Scorpios, Virgos, or Cancerians, however, will share your fondness for home—and your intense, lifelong dedication to family.

Your greatest challenge may be to learn that separation and disconnection are often necessary—especially with regard to intimate relationships. Your gift is your ability to bring about cooperation between individuals and entities who hold deeply ingrained but illogical biases.

CAPRICORN
Your Personal Planets

YOUR LOVE POTENTIAL
Venus in Capricorn, Dec. 22, 11:40 - Dec. 31, 23:59

YOUR DRIVE AND AMBITION
Mars in Sagittarius, Dec. 22, 11:40 - Dec. 31, 23:59

YOUR LUCK MAGNETISM
Jupiter in Cancer, Dec. 22, 11:40 - Dec. 31, 23:59

World Events

Dec. 25 – Allied troops capture Rathedaung in Burma.

Dec. 29 – The Russians retake the key area of Kotelnikovo near the besieged city of Stalingrad.

Adolf Hitler

Special Feature
Astro Twins: Hitler and Chaplin

(Continued from page 345)

Chaplin and Hitler were born four days apart. All of their planets are in the same signs except for the luminaries—the Sun and Moon. Hitler's Sun is Taurus and his Moon Capricorn; Chaplin's is an Aries Sun sign with a Scorpio Moon. Still this difference is not so different. Both Taurus and Scorpio are "fixed" astrological signs energized by great wealth and power, with enough staying power to accomplish great feats. Aries and Capricorn are "cardinal" signs that have the wherewithal to generate activity to achieve success. Cardinal signs are the movers and the shakers of the zodiac.

Each of these men, in his own way, was able to pull himself out of a difficult and desperate situation.

Both men were very popular with their "fans," and outspoken in expressing their views, as can be seen by the strength of their respective moons. Hitler's serious Capricorn Moon is aligned with philosophical and expansive Jupiter, thus enabling him to spread his propaganda to the masses. Chaplin shared the same Capricorn Jupiter in his natal horoscope. His Moon was also nicely aligned with this planet that deals in beliefs. While living in Hollywood, Chaplin was very expressive of his strongly liberal political and social views, which during the reign of Senator McCarthy resulted in Chaplin's leaving America to reside in Switzerland. This magnetic Scorpio Moon is located in his chart's first house of personality, reflecting his immense popularity.

Both had Mercury, the planet of the mind, in the bright, quick and clever sign of Aries. Mercury placed in Aries is considered a very fortunate position for this mental planet. The intellectuals who surrounded Hitler were amazed by his sponge-like ability to absorb their demagogic ideas. Only too late would they discover to what degree he had made these ideas his own. Meanwhile, Chaplin was considered a creative genius. Actor, director, screenwriter, composer, and producer, he was truly one of Hollywood's most innovative pioneers.

Oddly enough, Chaplin had the more somber personality. Chaplin's intense Scorpio Moon, the planet of the emotions, in his house of personality might incline him toward a definite dark side, stimulated by a dominating temperament and a complex emotional life. He obviously possessed strong creative energies, but dealings with him were most likely strained. He didn't like to be contradicted and kept a strong, governing hand over his professional and familial dealings.

(Continued on page 361)

➤ Read more about Hitler in "Astrology Reigns through the Ages" on page 25. ➤ Read about an astrologer Chaplin consulted on page 185.

1943

Chaos Building: Neptune in Libra

At the beginning of 1943, the nebulous planet Neptune had just floated into the diplomatic sign of Libra. Neptune, planet concerned with visions, dreams, art, and the unfathomable realms of life, also rules chaos and confusion. Libra is the sign of fairness, diplomacy, and relationships. When the planet of the imagination enters the sign of social relations, new paradigms are struck. The babies born under the influence of Neptune in Libra became the colorful hippies of the late sixties—the flower children that defied everything that was socially conventional. One of the striking events of 1943 took place when British Prime Minister, Winston Churchill, and American President, Franklin D. Roosevelt, held the Casablanca Conference in Morocco. (Libra rules treaties and peace-building.) Because of the influence of Neptune, the conference did not yield the results that were hoped for. The rival French generals Giraud and de Gaulle were also at the Casablanca conference but each refused to accept subordination to the other.

At the beginning of the year, the war planet, Mars, was in feisty, philosophical Sagittarius, giving it an extra edge, just the motivation that the freedom fighters of the Warsaw ghetto needed to plan their revolution. Uranus, planet of surprise, pulled into the intellectual sign of Gemini, was making an aspect called an "opposition" to Mars. This created the necessary tension to invoke the ghetto-dwellers to rise up in rage against their Nazi oppressors. Although it was suppressed, the Warsaw Ghetto Uprising was a valiant protest against oppression.

Soviet troops complete the rout of the Germans from Stalingrad

Atrocities continue in concentration camps

The Allied leaders meet at the Tehran Conference

ALLIED POWER ON THE RISE

Having seized the initiative, Allied superiority in the war became manifest. After the surrender of the German Sixth Army at Stalingrad, the Russian Army began to push the Germans gradually eastward. In North Africa, German and Italian forces surrendered. The Germans surrendered at Stalingrad. MacArthur's "island hopping" campaign continued to push them back across the Pacific toward their home islands. Atrocities continued with the wanton slaughter of European Jews, gypsies, and others in concentration camps. In the air war, British and German bombing campaigns continued. The Allies invaded Sicily and moved on to Italy, which surrendered almost at once. Mussolini was ousted. The Allied leaders, Roosevelt, Churchill, and Stalin met at Teheran (Iran) and planned the postwar world. However, the wartime demand for raw materials made rationing an increasing necessity, addressing shortages of such commodities as sugar, coffee, canned foods, and shoes. African-American scientist George Washington Carver died, as did Russian composer Sergei Rachmaninov; British actor Leslie Howard was killed while flying from Portugal to Britain.

➤ Read "Astro Twins: Hitler and Chaplin" by Jean Mars on page 345.

CAPRICORN

From January 01, 0:00 through January 20, 22:18

The Influential Traveler

As a Capricorn born in January of 1943, you would have been blessed with the ability to communicate with a wide variety of individuals—and to have a strong influence over them all. The heavens were hosting a pack of air energies at the time you entered the world, and they are quite an intellectually formidable crew.

The event that exemplifies the substantial strength your birth time gave you occurred on January 14, when U.S. President Franklin D. Roosevelt joined the Prime Minister Churchill in Casablanca, Morocco. The journey was the first ever made by a U.S. President to foreign shores during wartime; its urgent purpose was a meeting of the Allied nations, all of whom were aiming at ending the Nazis' rule of terror. The countries who participated were there to plan their joint strategies—but in the process, they also agreed to ask for nothing less than unconditional surrender from the Axis nations.

When you arrived, then, the heavens were primed to show you the necessity of reaching successful consensus, regardless of language or cultural barriers. The skill you inherited from your birth time's influence has probably shown itself through your expertise at strategy. In fact, you may often find yourself mediating potent disputes—and it's likely that you won't leave the bargaining table until the end you're after is accomplished. One problem you may encounter due to this quality, however, could be the inability to either extend or accept apologies—especially in times of stress. But if you resolve to listen before you speak to your adversary, you may learn that they're not nearly as rigidly fixed in their ways as you'd first thought.

When it comes to partners, none but the strongest and most secure individuals will do—and that's not an easy shoe to fill. The depth, intensity, and focus of Scorpios may attract you, however, and Cancerians and Taureans, both famous for their solid emotional natures, will also appeal.

Your gift is your surety and confidence, even in the most doubtful and perilous situations. Your challenge, Capricorn of 1943, is to learn the art of bargaining.

AQUARIUS

From January 20, 22:19 through February 19, 12:39

The Efficient Administrator

Aquarians born in 1943 arrived with a unique assemblage of intellectual tools. And at the same time, several equally cerebral forces were assembled to combat the Axis powers in the course of World War II. U.S. General Dwight D. Eisenhower was selected by the Allied nations to head the march against Hitler's Germany, and in the United States, President Franklin D. Roosevelt ordered a mandatory minimum work week of forty-eight hours for those employed in the war industries.

The steely determination and shrewd planning demonstrated by these major authority figures is mirrored in you, 1943 Aquarius, through your innate talent for organization, delegation, and direction. In fact, you may find that life has often presented you with the opportunity to take charge of situations that had been previously botched or left undone by others.

As a result, it's likely that you're equal parts administrator and worker, as willing to lead as you are to work alongside those you manage. And speaking of management, your people skills are probably second to none. Your way of letting each and every person understand the important part they play in the whole—no matter how menial their job—will no doubt gain you their admiration, respect, and loyalty. In more personal relationships, you'll also find it easy to win the hearts of those you admire—and even easier to extract true and faithful commitments, perhaps even lifelong bonds.

When choosing a life partner, it's likely that you'll look for someone whose self-respect and integrity is as intact as your own. You'll find just those qualities in Capricorns, Taureans, and Sagittarians, all of whom place honesty at the top of their priority lists. In platonic partnerships, these signs will also prove trustworthy, as will Librans and other Aquarians.

Your challenge is to give praise only where and when it's merited—and to give constructive criticism when necessary, no matter how difficult you find that task. Your greatest gifts are your managerial astuteness and your knack for inspiring the respect and fidelity you need to get the job done.

➤ Read about your Chinese Astrological sign on page 838. ➤ Read about your Personal Planets on page 826. ➤ Read about your personal Mystical Card on page 856.

1943

CAPRICORN
Your Personal Planets

YOUR LOVE POTENTIAL
Venus in Capricorn, Jan. 01, 0:00 - Jan. 08, 10:02
Venus in Aquarius, Jan. 08, 10:03 - Jan. 20, 22:18

YOUR DRIVE AND AMBITION
Mars in Sagittarius, Jan. 01, 0:00 - Jan. 20, 22:18

YOUR LUCK MAGNETISM
Jupiter in Cancer, Jan. 01, 0:00 - Jan. 20, 22:18

World Events

Jan. 5 – American chemist and botanist George Washington Carver dies.

Jan. 9 – Soviets drop leaflets into the besieged city of Stalingrad, demanding the Germans' surrender.

The Battle of the River Don

AQUARIUS
Your Personal Planets

YOUR LOVE POTENTIAL
Venus in Aquarius, Jan. 20, 22:19 - Feb. 01, 9:01
Venus in Pisces, Feb. 01, 9:02 - Feb. 19, 12:39

YOUR DRIVE AND AMBITION
Mars in Sagittarius, Jan. 20, 22:19 - Jan. 26, 19:09
Mars in Capricorn, Jan. 26, 19:10 - Feb. 19, 12:39

YOUR LUCK MAGNETISM
Jupiter in Cancer, Jan. 20, 22:19 - Feb. 19, 12:39

World Events

Feb. 10 – In India, Gandhi begins a hunger strike to protest his imprisonment.

Feb. 13 – The U.S. Women's Marine Corps is created.

1943

PISCES
Your Personal Planets

YOUR LOVE POTENTIAL
Venus in Pisces, Feb. 19, 12:40 - Feb. 25, 12:03
Venus in Aries, Feb. 25, 12:04 - Mar. 21, 12:02

YOUR DRIVE AND AMBITION
Mars in Capricorn, Feb. 19, 12:40 - Mar. 08, 12:41
Mars in Aquarius, Mar. 08, 12:42 - Mar. 21, 12:02

YOUR LUCK MAGNETISM
Jupiter in Cancer, Feb. 19, 12:40 - Mar. 21, 12:02

World Events

Mar. 9 – American chess champion Bobby Fischer is born.

Mar. 10 – German Field Marshall Rommel, the Desert Fox, leaves Africa, defeated, ill, and exhausted.

American chess champion Bobby Fischer is born under the sign of Pisces

ARIES
Your Personal Planets

YOUR LOVE POTENTIAL
Venus in Aries, Mar. 21, 12:03 - Mar. 21, 22:23
Venus in Taurus, Mar. 21, 22:24 - Apr. 15, 20:11
Venus in Gemini, Apr. 15, 20:12 - Apr. 20, 23:31

YOUR DRIVE AND AMBITION
Mars in Aquarius, Mar. 21, 12:03 - Apr. 17, 10:24
Mars in Pisces, Apr. 17, 10:25 - Apr. 20, 23:31

YOUR LUCK MAGNETISM
Jupiter in Cancer, Mar. 21, 12:03 - Apr. 20, 23:31

World Events

Mar. 28 – Russian composer Sergei Rachmaninov dies.

Apr. 19 – Jews in the Warsaw Ghetto stage an uprising that lasts almost a month.

PISCES
From February 19, 12:40 through March 21, 12:02

The Spiritual Gladiator

You arrived just as it appeared that the tide of World War II was beginning to turn, Pisces of 1943. The Allies had won the Battle of the Bismarck Sea, the first of many losses the Nazis would endure over the course of this year. For the first time, it seemed that the end of World War II might be in sight—and regardless of the expected length and hardships of this road toward peace, the world breathed a tiny sigh of relief.

As a result, you may have been raised in an atmosphere that was newly hopeful and increasingly optimistic, giving you a sense that all things were possible. The hopeful enthusiasm you experienced as a child may have given you the energy necessary to attain your goal—no matter how difficult or far-off the end seemed—even as you would give thanks for each minor accomplishment along the path. You probably don't hesitate to celebrate your small personal victories. You will do what it takes to keep your inner fire burning bright—and that includes giving yourself time off to enjoy what you've achieved.

You are capable of blessing others by showing them how simple faith and perseverance can conquer situations that might initially seem to be hopeless. This could make you an excellent health care practitioner, social worker, physical therapist, or spiritual counselor. In your leisure hours, you may offer your time to organizations that work to help others, both in your community and around the world. It's also likely that you traveled to see the places where your organization's efforts might have made a difference.

In relationships, you'll probably find a happy match in the company of most Scorpios, Cancerians, and Taureans—three kindred spirits whose loyalty and loving applause for each of your victories will fuel your passion and determination. In friendships, Sagittarians' innate optimism and *joie de vivre* will keep your mood upbeat and your heart full.

Your challenge, 1943 Pisces, is to remain positive, even when life seems to be targeting you with obstacles to success. Your greatest gift is your conviction that right will always prove the victor over might.

ARIES
From March 21, 12:03 through April 20, 23:31

The Thoughtful Rebel

You, 1943 Aries, were born during a period that was infused with planets in fire and air signs—the heavens' own recipe for genius. These energies played a strong part in the events of your birth time, influencing you to develop your own particular brand of genius—no matter how radical or rebellious your chosen path seems. During April of 1943, Great Britain and the United States, leading the other Allied nations, came together in Africa to wrest control from the Nazis. The far-sighted strategies they employed would be successful in early May, in another victory against Hitler's oppressive regime, and yet another sign that the end of World War II seemed to be in sight.

The astrological influences of this time were primed for this type of detailed, meticulous planning, and you inherited them all. As a result, you've probably gained a well-deserved reputation for carefully assessing risks before you attack in any situation—something that Ariens born in other years aren't famous for! Far from proving a hindrance, however, your ability to think before you storm off into battle will always be a great strength.

Once your plan is in place, however, you won't hesitate to initiate the steps necessary to accomplish your aims. You probably also aren't afraid to take a distinctly different path from those who went before you, regardless of the lessons of those experiences. In short, you learned how important it was to learn the rules before you broke them—but break them you will. In fact, you are probably the kind of person who inspired the phrase "question authority"—a trait which ironically often places you in just that position.

In romance, you'll probably do best with those whose fiery independence and willingness to break tradition match your own—Aquarians and Sagittarians. But the keen insights of Scorpio and the quicksilver mind of Gemini will provide you with valuable feedback and wise advice.

Your gifts, 1943 Aries, are your fast-moving mind and your respect for tried-and-true techniques. Your challenge is to curb your natural love of immediate action in any battle you face.

➤ Read about your Chinese Astrological sign on page 838. ➤ Read about your Personal Planets on page 826. ➤ Read about your personal Mystical Card on page 856.

TAURUS

From April 20, 23:32 through May 21, 23:02

The Diligent Bridge-Builder

The period of your birth saw several further major victories for the Allied nations, 1943 Taurus. The Axis forces, under the direction of the Nazis, were driven from North Africa's Cape Bon peninsula, surrendering to the Allied forces on May 12, when General Jurgen von Arnim, the German commander who took Rommel's place, was captured—along with several other high-ranking Axis officers.

This monumental victory helped citizens of the world to keep their faith in peace intact—even though the persecution of the Jews was continuing in the concentration camps in Germany and Poland. The ability to enjoy the taste of success while simultaneously remaining steadfastly committed to a long-term goal is a quality your fixed, earthy sign has always enjoyed—but your birth year's planetary influences gave you a double-dose of it. In fact, this combination of determination, vision, and the understanding of how important it is to give praise when it's due means you're a natural candidate for a position of authority—and that's most likely just where you want to be in life.

You're probably well known among those close to you for being the "strong, silent type" who works quietly and persistently until a project is finished—no matter how long it takes. Still, however, your sign is also famous for its love of creature comforts, and for its innate belief in the reward system—which means you've probably never been frugal when it comes to spoiling yourself or your dear ones on special occasions, either.

In love relationships, Taurus of 1942, you may look for those who share your drive and dedication. Other Taureans, as well as Capricorns, Scorpios, and Virgos, will share your stubborn persistence and refusal to abort any mission—regardless of how tough the last few steps may be.

Be careful, however, of a tendency to set goals for yourself that are unreasonably difficult to attain. Your greatest challenge, 1942 Taurus, is to treat yourself with the same respect and understanding you offer to others. Your greatest gift is your quiet diligence—and your total disregard for the applause of the crowd.

GEMINI

From May 21, 23:03 through June 22, 7:11

The Thoughtful Hero

The Allied forces continued to gain ground against Nazi Germany, taking the Italian island of Lampedusa in one of many similar victories in the Mediterranean. Battles like this would have made news around the time you were born, 1943 Gemini. In addition, the astrological influences in effect at your birth time would have provided you with a substantial mix of cerebral and physical energy, both of which can be virtually bottomless reservoirs of strength for you.

Basically, 1943 Gemini, you possess the stuff that's necessary to fulfill long-term, heroic goals—and life has probably presented you with several opportunities to show those talents off. When it comes to taking the side of your dear ones, you can be even more steadfast—and you might be unwilling to give in even if you secretly believe that they are in the wrong.

In battle, then, you're a worthy adversary—to say the very least—whether you're wielding words or influence. But you're also quite the peacemaker, instinctively gifted with the capacity to listen well and assimilate the wisdom of others into your own vast storehouse of knowledge. As a result, you're probably unbeatable at word games, riddles, and puzzles—and that goes double for arguments. One thing you would never do is "pull rank" on your dear ones, or use your intimidating verbal skills on anyone who's not quite up for the challenge. You know that being fair is the only way to truly win a battle, and that "winning" over opponents you know you can easily outdo isn't really winning at all.

In relationships, you'll probably do best to stay by the side of Librans, Aquarians, and Taureans—especially those who prove their loyalty to you through never asking you to take on their defense when they don't deserve it. Your best friendships will probably come through affiliations with other Geminis and with Sagittarians, whose wide-angle view of the world will help you to learn objectivity.

Your challenge, Gemini of 1943, is to learn when it's appropriate to attack—and when it's not. Your gifts are your ability to learn and absorb quickly, and your endless curiosity.

▶ Read about your Chinese Astrological sign on page 838. ▶ Read about your Personal Planets on page 826. ▶ Read about your personal Mystical Card on page 856.

TAURUS
Your Personal Planets

YOUR LOVE POTENTIAL
Venus in Gemini, Apr. 20, 23:32 - May 11, 11:55
Venus in Cancer, May 11, 11:56 - May 21, 23:02

YOUR DRIVE AND AMBITION
Mars in Pisces, Apr. 20, 23:32 - May 21, 23:02

YOUR LUCK MAGNETISM
Jupiter in Cancer, Apr. 20, 23:32 - May 21, 23:02

World Events

Apr. 30 – Noël Coward's *This Happy Breed* premières in London.

May 12 – German troops surrender to Allied forces in North Africa.

The Dambusters raid on the Eder and Moehne Dams

GEMINI
Your Personal Planets

YOUR LOVE POTENTIAL
Venus in Cancer, May 21, 23:03 - June 07, 12:08
Venus in Leo, June 07, 12:09 - June 22, 7:11

YOUR DRIVE AND AMBITION
Mars in Pisces, May 21, 23:03 - May 27, 9:24
Mars in Aries, May 27, 9:25 - June 22, 7:11

YOUR LUCK MAGNETISM
Jupiter in Cancer, May 21, 23:03 - June 22, 7:11

World Events

June 1 – British Actor Leslie Howard is killed when his plane is shot down by German raiders.

June 11 – U.S. President Roosevelt appeals to the Italian people to overthrow Mussolini.

1943

CANCER
Your Personal Planets

YOUR LOVE POTENTIAL
Venus in Leo, June 22, 7:12 - July 07, 23:55
Venus in Virgo, July 07, 23:56 - July 23, 18:04

YOUR DRIVE AND AMBITION
Mars in Aries, June 22, 7:12 - July 07, 23:04
Mars in Taurus, July 07, 23:05 - July 23, 18:04

YOUR LUCK MAGNETISM
Jupiter in Cancer, June 22, 7:12 - June 30, 21:44
Jupiter in Leo, June 30, 21:45 - July 23, 18:04

World Events

June 22 – W. E. B. DuBois becomes the first African American member of the National Institute of Letters.

July 10 – Allied forces launch a new offensive on the coast of Sicily.

American actor Robert De Niro is born under the sign of Leo

LEO
Your Personal Planets

YOUR LOVE POTENTIAL
Venus in Virgo, July 23, 18:05 - Aug. 24, 0:54

YOUR DRIVE AND AMBITION
Mars in Taurus, July 23, 18:05 - Aug. 23, 23:57
Mars in Gemini, Aug. 23, 23:58 - Aug. 24, 0:54

YOUR LUCK MAGNETISM
Jupiter in Leo, July 23, 18:05 - Aug. 24, 0:54

World Events

July 25 – Mussolini resigns as Italian premier.
Aug. 17 – American actor Robert De Niro is born.

CANCER
From June 22, 7:12 through July 23, 18:04

The Mother Lion

Cancer of 1943, you arrived during a time that would later become famous for the Allies' invasion of Italy, a move that would ultimately push the Nazis further back toward Germany. In the process, the beautiful island of Sicily and even Rome, "The Holy City" herself, became battlegrounds. The astrological influences you inherited are shown through the perseverance of those who were fighting to bring World War II and Nazism to a halt—and these energies are potent, long lasting, and volatile.

As such, although your sign's reputation for sensitivity and sympathy remains intact in you, you were given the added gift of fire—the astrological formula for immediate action. You probably seem quite fiery to those who love you, and like your fire-sign cousins, your devotion to your dear ones might know no boundaries. In times of need, you'll pull out all the stops to see that your loved ones have everything they need—including a sound and reliable defender—and you'll probably stop at nothing to keep them happy. You may seem much like a defensive mother lioness, who'll sacrifice herself willingly to save the lives of her young—and battle fiercely to ensure their safety.

Your family members and friends alike will appreciate your devotion, however, and return it to you tenfold. Co-workers may rely on you to be the spokesperson in any situation where leadership is called for, and unlike Cancers born in other years, you might relish such opportunities to be in the spotlight.

Your search for the ultimate soul mate might lead you into the arms of a fire sign like Leo, Sagittarius, or Aries, equally ardent kindred spirits who'll share your unconditional devotion to family and long-term friends. When all is said and done, it's likely that you'll have a strong circle of supportive people around you, all eager to gain your approval.

Your greatest challenges, Cancer of 1943, are to keep your calm in all situations—even in the most urgent of times—and never to forget to fulfill your own needs: they are just as important as the needs of others. Your gift is your surefire willingness to do whatever it takes to protect and provide shelter to those you love.

LEO
From July 23, 18:05 through August 24, 0:54

The Dedicated Protector

You arrived just as the first steps to Italy's fall were taken with the resignation of Benito Mussolini as the premier of Italy. In addition, an inmate uprising at the Bialystok concentration camp completely destroyed the crematorium, showing that the Nazis may have severely underestimated the courage of their supposedly well-intimidated detainees. One lesson the world learned from these events was that nothing—including the fear of physical harm or even death—can overcome humanity's innate love of life.

It's likely that being raised in these powerful times gave you an equally powerful spirit, Leo of 1943—and you probably show that spirit most especially when times of emergency arise. During these moments, your bravery and ability to take action swiftly can be unparalleled, as is your determination to win. Along the way, you may have learned to live each moment as if it were your last, loving every breath you take, learning from every person you cross paths with, and gaining wisdom from every event that life tosses your way.

You've probably never backed down from a challenge to your quest for experience, either—no matter how intimidating your adversaries were. In life, you may have truly exemplified the unswerving bravery of the lion—given the title of "King of the Jungle" because of its noble devotion to the care of the pride. Your family, then, is probably the most important thing in your life—and it's likely that providing for those connected to you by blood will always be your top priority.

In love relationships, your fervent devotion to those close to you will be matched well by the intensity and passion of Scorpios, the bravery of Ariens, or the constant fire of Sagittarians. As for friendships and business associates, you'll probably do best to keep a Capricorn or Virgo by your side. Those sturdy, reliable earth signs will probably never do you wrong or let you down.

Your challenge, Leo of 1943, lies in determining whether passivity or aggression is called for to protect your interests. Your gift is your unwavering devotion to the defense of those in your care.

► Read about your Chinese Astrological sign on page 838. ► Read about your Personal Planets on page 826. ► Read about your personal Mystical Card on page 856.

VIRGO

From August 24, 0:55 through September 23, 22:11

The Great Illuminator

Virgo of 1943, you came along just as Italy surrendered to the Allied nations—the start of the defeat of Nazism in Europe. This victory wasn't just a military one, however. Rather than resting in sullen defeat, the Italians subsequently switched sides, joining the Allies in the battle against the Axis forces. This showed how important the revelation of truth really is—under all circumstances—and your early upbringing probably reinforced this trait. It's likely that your parents placed a high premium on honesty, 1943 Virgo, and whatever minor transgressions you made during your younger years were probably met with understanding and compassion—but also strict punishment.

As a result, you probably learned at an early age to speak the truth—and that the consequences of your actions would always be lessened if you remained honest. Your strict adherence to the virtue of integrity has probably been tested—but it's likely that you've always been able to rise to the occasion. The good news is that life situations will always show that your best path is the straightforward one.

When it comes to your encounters with others, this quality will prove to be invaluable—both professionally and personally. Those around you will learn that you say only what you mean and that they can always expect a truthful answer to an earnest question. It's likely that the long-term trust and confidence this behavior inspires in others will come back to you many times over. In short, you always let your personal integrity be your guide—even if it's not the easiest path to follow.

In love, you'll probably be drawn to others who share your desire to be honest and aboveboard in all your words and deeds. As a result, Sagittarians and Aquarians will attract your respect—and your affections, as well. In friendships, join up with Capricorns and Taureans, your solid earth-sign cousins whose love of respectability rivals your own.

Your challenge, Virgo of 1943, is not to allow yourself to be drawn into less than reputable relationships or situations. Your gift is your commitment to complete and total candor.

LIBRA

From September 23, 22:12 through October 24, 7:07

The Versatile Defender

An important shift occurred around the time you were born, Libra of 1943. After surrendering to the Allied nations, Italy joined hands with its former adversaries and declared war on Germany, its former Axis partner, because of the treatment it received at the hands of the Germans. This change brought thousands more troops onto the side of the Allies in World War II, greatly increasing the Allies' strength.

This could explain why being flexible, versatile, and adaptable was important to you, even in your early years. Far from being a weakness, this ability to shift gears when you discover a problem with your current position is a tremendous strength—one that may have proved invaluable over the years. It's possible that, in the course of life, glaring flaws in your belief systems cropped up when you least expected them—but that didn't mean that you would ignore them due to pride, timidity, or the need to coddle those close to you. If you believed you were wrong about something, you would always be brave enough to admit it and move on, without allowing others to intimidate you into backtracking.

In addition, your sign's innate capacity for understanding the motives of all parties concerned—and seeing both sides of any issue—may have helped to hone your skills at mediation, negotiation, and peacemaking. You may also turn into quite the determined advocate—regardless of which side of the fence you find yourself on—and these traits may have drawn you into the field of politics, teaching, or the law.

In love relationships, your partner-loving sign is naturally drawn close to others who share your desire for a long-term commitment. It's likely that dutiful Capricorns, steady, solid Taureans, and emotionally intense Scorpios will always be your best bets. In friendships, however, look to Geminis and Sagittarians to provide you with another side to every coin.

Your challenge, Libra of 1943, is to learn when it's time to leave a lost cause behind. Your gift is your instinctive ability to know when to maintain your courage and follow your path—no matter where it may lead you.

► Read about your Chinese Astrological sign on page 838. ► Read about your Personal Planets on page 826. ► Read about your personal Mystical Card on page 856.

VIRGO
Your Personal Planets

YOUR LOVE POTENTIAL
Venus in Virgo, Aug. 24, 0:55 - Sept. 23, 22:11

YOUR DRIVE AND AMBITION
Mars in Gemini, Aug. 24, 0:55 - Sept. 23, 22:11

YOUR LUCK MAGNETISM
Jupiter in Leo, Aug. 24, 0:55 - Sept. 23, 22:11

World Events

Aug. 24 – French philosopher Simone Weil dies.

Sept. 8 – It is announced that Italy has surrendered to the Allies.

Italy surrenders to the Allies

LIBRA
Your Personal Planets

YOUR LOVE POTENTIAL
Venus in Virgo, Sept. 23, 22:12 - Oct. 24, 7:07

YOUR DRIVE AND AMBITION
Mars in Gemini, Sept. 23, 22:12 - Oct. 24, 7:07

YOUR LUCK MAGNETISM
Jupiter in Leo, Sept. 23, 22:12 - Oct. 24, 7:07

World Events

Sept. 29 – Polish Solidarity leader Lech Walesa is born.

Oct. 12 – The U.S. air fleet launches a surprise attack on Rabaul in the South Pacific.

1943

SCORPIO
Your Personal Planets

YOUR LOVE POTENTIAL
Venus in Virgo, Oct. 24, 7:08 - Nov. 09, 18:24
Venus in Libra, Nov. 09, 18:25 - Nov. 23, 4:21

YOUR DRIVE AND AMBITION
Mars in Gemini, Oct. 24, 7:08 - Nov. 23, 4:21

YOUR LUCK MAGNETISM
Jupiter in Leo, Oct. 24, 7:08 - Nov. 23, 4:21

World Events

Nov. 7 – Canadian singer/songwriter Joni Mitchell is born.

Nov. 9 – American artist Jackson Pollock's work goes on display at the Guggenheim Gallery in New York.

The Allied leaders at the Tehran Conference

SAGITTARIUS
Your Personal Planets

YOUR LOVE POTENTIAL
Venus in Libra, Nov. 23, 4:22 - Dec. 08, 7:44
Venus in Scorpio, Dec. 08, 7:45 - Dec. 22, 17:28

YOUR DRIVE AND AMBITION
Mars in Gemini, Nov. 23, 4:22 - Dec. 22, 17:28

YOUR LUCK MAGNETISM
Jupiter in Leo, Nov. 23, 4:22 - Dec. 22, 17:28

World Events

Dec. 1 – Roosevelt, Churchill, and Stalin agree to Operation Overlord (D-Day).

Dec. 15 – American jazz pianist Thomas W. "Fats" Waller dies.

SCORPIO
From October 24, 7:08 through November 23, 4:21

The Holy Warrior

Scorpio of 1943, your arrival coincided with an event that would change the free world's mood from fearful to furious—the bombing of the Vatican. Regardless of your family's religious beliefs, this attack on a place as holy, sacred, and peaceful as the seat of Catholicism outraged citizens of all faiths the world over. It's likely that it also increased their determination to end World War II—and to stop the wave of religious hatred the Nazis seemed intent on perpetuating.

The astrological energies that assembled during that time were equally resolute—and just as startling. A host of planets in fast-moving fire and air signs turned up the thermostat on the world's collective urge to act swiftly—and since you own this pack of energies, you've probably continued to exhibit these traits throughout life. As time goes on, in fact, you may even exhibit the qualities of a crusader, regardless of whether religion, philosophy, or romantic love is the reason for your battle.

You may have a strong religious belief, or you may simply consider yourself a "spiritual" person—either way, it's likely that you'll never back down from defending what you believe in. You may have chosen a career that gives you the chance to fight for something you believe in, perhaps by writing about or photographing the lives of the oppressed or the underprivileged. You may also have been active in some of the anti-establishment movements of the sixties and seventies, marching for civil liberties and against war.

When it comes to finding a committed relationship, you might be looking for someone as deeply spiritual as yourself. In this regard, it's likely that mysterious Pisces and nurturing Cancer will be your best bet. When it comes to friendships, look to Virgos, Capricorns, and other Scorpios to provide you with the camaraderie and reassurance you can only get from a platonic kindred spirit.

Your greatest challenge, 1943 Scorpio, is to hold back your intense passion and your strong opinions when necessary to keep the peace. Your greatest gift is your ability to stand up on behalf of a cause you believe to be just.

SAGITTARIUS
From November 23, 4:22 through December 22, 17:28

The International Networker

Born during 1943, Sagittarius, you arrived at a time when the exchange of information was becoming more and more important to the cause of the Allied nations and the free world itself—that cause being to put an end to World War II and Hitler's reign of terror. Around the time you were born, in fact, three major leaders met to swap strategies: U.S. President Franklin D. Roosevelt, British Prime Minister Winston Churchill, and Soviet Premier Joseph Stalin.

This important meeting focused on the defeat of the Nazis, and was destined to have powerful consequences. This was portrayed beautifully by the arrangement of energies in the heavens at the time, which you inherited. Virtually every planet held court in fire and air signs, the elements that inspire action, communication, and assertiveness—and it's likely that you've learned to use those energies in the manner in which they were intended. In fact, your already feisty nature has undoubtedly been heightened, inspiring you to become an expert at long-distance communication—as well as a skilled and confident traveler, no matter where your wanderlust may lead you.

Your sign is already famous for its love of boldly going where you've never gone before—in fact, you may live for the thrill of a completely new horizon and the challenges of making your way through entirely new surroundings. But your particular breed of Sagittarian was also endowed with a special blessing. You are likely to have the capacity for making your point, regardless of language or cultural differences—and the ability to understand the viewpoints of others as well.

In love, you may seek out a partner who's as adventurous as you are—and just as willing to wake up in another state, on another coast, or in another country. As a result, you'll probably be drawn to Leo and Aries, the other fire signs, whose spirit and passion will fan your own flames—and who'll always make brave and eager playmates.

Your challenge, Sagittarius of 1943, is to dole out facts with an eye toward helping—not manipulating. Your gift is your ability to recognize the difference.

► Read about your Chinese Astrological sign on page 838. ► Read about your Personal Planets on page 826. ► Read about your personal Mystical Card on page 856.

CAPRICORN

The Respected Commander

Born during December of 1943, Capricorn, you arrived as the Allied nations' ultimate victory over Nazism was edging closer—although it would not be close enough for the thousands of Jews, Gypsies, Slavs, and others who remained in German concentration camps. Around the time you were born, U.S. General Dwight D. Eisenhower, after his successes in Europe, was given supreme command over the entire army of Allied forces, including the U.S., Great Britain, Holland, France, and Poland.

Being raised in this monumental era probably gave you a tremendous respect for the authority and experience necessary to battle tyranny—whether an individual or an organization is the source of it. In addition, your sign's already hard-working disposition received the benefits of a mixed bundle of astrological energies, endowing you with versatility, adaptability, and mental agility. But your capacity to break the rules that Capricorns born in other years might follow unquestioningly probably arises from the fact that you carry within you the seeds of an era that displayed just how necessary rebellion can be.

It's likely that the times you were born into helped to sharpen the skills of leadership within yourself. Your Capricorn desire to climb to the top of any mountain could also put you at the top of an organization, and if you were part of the anti-establishment in the sixties, you were probably in charge of something. Along the way, you'd learn to choose your battles, and determine for yourself when to follow the established order and when to take steps to defeat it.

In love, it's likely that you're well-suited to partner up with fixed yet rebellious Aquarians, philosophical Sagittarians, or determined Taureans—but the passion and unwavering focus of intense Scorpios could appeal to you most. Look to Virgos and other Capricorns for friendship and business alliances—their advice will usually prove to be sound.

Your challenge, 1943 Capricorn, lies in developing an impeccable sense of timing. Your gift is your innate knack for taking charge of huge projects, and bringing them to successful conclusions.

CAPRICORN
Your Personal Planets

YOUR LOVE POTENTIAL
Venus in Scorpio, Dec. 22, 17:29 - Dec. 31, 23:59

YOUR DRIVE AND AMBITION
Mars in Gemini, Dec. 22, 17:29 - Dec. 31, 23:59

YOUR LUCK MAGNETISM
Jupiter in Leo, Dec. 22, 17:29 - Dec. 31, 23:59

World Events

Dec. 22 - Beatrix Potter, author of the "Peter Rabbit" books, dies.

Dec. 30 - The Russians seize the city of Kazatin, south-west of Kiev.

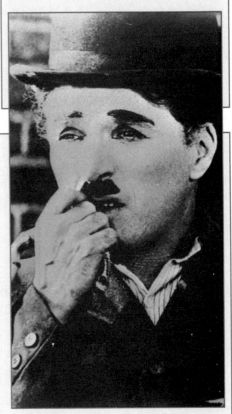

Charlie Chaplin

Special Feature
Astro Twins: Hitler and Chaplin

(Continued from page 353)

Chaplin's chart reveals a propensity for intolerance, and he obviously had a tyrannical side. Fortunately for him, he was able to filter his intense emotions as well as his ability to intuit emotions of those around him through his work. Like many artists, Chaplin used the materials of his own life to produce a body of art that illuminated the human condition.

On a more intimate level, both Hitler and Chaplin experienced turbulence in their emotional lives. To an astrologer, this fact comes as no surprise as both of their charts reveal a tough astrological relationship in that area: Mars, the planet of sex, is tightly aligned with Venus, the planet of love. This alliance is in a difficult configuration with the oftentimes depressive and restrictive planet Saturn, which can bring about strange difficulties in matters of love and sex. It seems to have affected them differently. With Hitler, it came through as sexual dysfunction which included impotence and sexual perversion.

Chaplin's emotional life was by far the more "normal" of the two men. However, he was known in Hollywood for his penchant for younger women. In the course of his life, he married four times (all teen brides), was the father of 10 children from two wives, and is rumored to have had other children out-of-wedlock.

With astro twins, along with similar life paths, similar life circumstances occur around the same time. In 1914, after being refused entrance into the Austrian military, Hitler crossed the border into Germany and volunteered for their army. In that same year, Chaplin signed with the American film producer Mack Sennet and began his illustrious career. From soldier to dictator and from actor to studio producer, this would be their point of departure toward the apex of their careers.

Fate, it would seem, is unknowable, yet astrology tries to explain or understand it—sometimes using hindsight, sometimes using predictive techniques. It is said that Hitler had a vulgar sense of humor. It makes one wonder if, had circumstances been slightly different, Hitler

might have found his place in a cabaret in Berlin! And Chaplin, with his strong political leanings, might just as easily have gone into politics. We will never know. Two men, whose destinies on the outside look so different, were actually, in many ways, similar. Yet, there is a fine—but definite—line drawn between these two geniuses: one on the side of good, and the other on the side of evil. ✪

➤ Read more about Hitler in "Astrology Reigns through the Ages" on page 25. ➤ Read about an astrologer Chaplin consulted on page 185.

1944

Winning the War with Words: Uranus in Gemini

On June 6, 1944, the invasion of Europe began at 6.30 in the morning, when the first Allied troops landed in different parts of Normandy, on the northern coast of France. Planning for this invasion, which came to be known as "D-Day," had started as far back as September 1941. Despite terrible initial losses on the beaches, the campaign, known as Operation Overlord, pressed on until August of 1944 and was ultimately successful. At this time, the planet Uranus was in the same degree of Gemini as when the Declaration of Independence was written and signed, when Lincoln was elected and the Civil War began. In fact, General Eisenhower's Libran sun was receiving a positive beam of energy from Uranus at this very time. This aspect is called a "trine" and it can bode well for action. World War II was nearing its end, though there was a great deal of hard fighting still yet to come.

When Uranus enters Gemini, intuitive, intelligent decision-making is possible. Uranus rules Aquarius, which is the most forward-thinking sign of the zodiac. Gemini is the sign of the mind, of communications, and information. Both are air signs, related to the generation of ideas. These zodiac signs are cerebral rather than emotional. In World War II, the Allies scored major breakthroughs with their ability to intercept German and Japanese intelligence messages. Elaborate code-breaking systems were used to find out what the enemy was planning. Navaho "code talkers" kept Japanese and German code-breakers from learning Allied battle plans. These tools lie within the domain of Uranus in Gemini.

American planes bomb Monte Cassino Abbey

D-Day landings in Normandy, France

Paris is liberated by the Allied forces

CODE NAME: PUZZLED

As the Allies prepared to invade Europe, military planners used code words in communications. The invasion was named "Overlord" and "Mulberry" was the code word for the harbor used. The naval attack was "Neptune;" "Utah" and "Omaha" were the Normandy beaches. Four days before the assault was set to begin, all the code words appeared as answers in *The Daily Telegraph* crossword puzzle. When military intelligence raided the paper's offices, they expected to find German spies, but instead found a mystified schoolteacher.

BRUTALITY AND SUCCOR

World War II burned across Europe and in the Pacific, where U.S. forces began staging B-29 raids on Japan. The Russians recaptured German-occupied areas of their country and advanced into Poland. Warsaw, the Polish capital, was destroyed by the Germans. The Axis powers were on the run everywhere. On D-Day, June 6, Allied forces landed on the beaches of Normandy in northern France and began to move towards Germany, freeing France, Belgium, the Netherlands, and Luxembourg. Paris was triumphantly liberated by French forces. MacArthur kept his promise to return to the Philippines, coming ashore in October. The Germans launched their "Vengeance weapons"—the V-1 flying bomb and V-2 rocket—against England and targets in France and Belgium. An attempt was made to assassinate Hitler, but failed to kill him. The building of the first atomic bomb proceeded in the U.S. In London, the Allies made arrangements for the division of Germany after the end of the war. Quinine, the malaria preventive, was synthesized. French pilot Antoine de St. Exupéry went missing on a flight, but not before he wrote a masterpiece, *The Little Prince*.

➤ Read Eva Péron's Star Profile on page 369.

CAPRICORN

From January 01, 0:00 through January 21, 4:06

The Cautious Adventurer

As a Capricorn born in 1944, you arrived just before Allied troops landed at Anzio in Italy on January 22. This was a move designed to bring a substantially greater army to the door of a major German defensive point—the "Gustav Line," which extended through central Italy and served as the railway passage over which thousands of Jews would travel toward the concentration camps in Germany and Poland. Possibly, the Allies had realized that the way to stop the transportation of more innocent souls was to place roadblocks in the path the Germans had chosen to bring them there. And now, although the Allied Nations were not able to advance just yet, and the Nazis retained control of the area, the assault had finally begun.

This means that your birth month was a time of simultaneous risk and caution—and this is a trait you may have displayed throughout your life. You probably developed a keen sense of timing early on—a quality that could prove invaluable to you in both personal and professional situations. This knack for knowing when to act and when to wait can make you a valuable addition to any team, and you may have been put in positions of authority by those above you who sensed your uncanny skill at gauging the temperature of your surroundings.

Your special connection with nature may have led you to a career that put you out of doors. However, if your work didn't keep you in touch with the earth, you might have chosen activities such as hiking, rock climbing, and cross country skiing to get out as often as possible. Friends may rely on your sense of knowing when to act, and would almost always follow your lead in any situation.

In love, your search for a partner with equally sharp instincts could lead you into the arms of Sagittarians, other Capricorns, or Taureans, who would also give you the blessings of their candor, humor, and ability to translate life experiences into wisdom.

Your gift is your capacity to blend action with patience, knowing when each is appropriate. Your challenge is to learn the virtue of letting go—and letting the Universe lead you where it will.

AQUARIUS

From January 21, 4:07 through February 19, 18:26

The Stalwart Inventor

You arrived just as the Allies recorded a major victory in the Pacific, Aquarius of 1944. Around the time you were born, Roi Island, one of the Marshall Islands, was taken by the U.S. Fourth Marine Division, which secured positions on Namur and Kwajalein. This was the first time Allied troops had triumphed on territory previously held by the Japanese, and the news could have given people hope that World War II might actually be coming to an end. There was no way they could have known how bloody these "victories" were, or how casualties would mount into the thousands as Allied troops clawed their way from one tiny island to the next across the trackless ocean.

Your early years may have been infused with a charge of optimism and energy that would later be tempered by an understanding of the costs of victory. The astrological influences you inherited were primed to foster the virtues of hope, bravery, and bold initiative. Life itself could have taught you the merits of hard work and determination. You may have lived the maxim, "Success is ten percent inspiration and ninety percent perspiration," and you may value yourself and your achievements even more as a result.

Your innate ability to sense where and when a new idea will be most welcome makes you an inventive, resourceful, and creative worker, a welcome addition to any staff. Your knack for finding a brand new solution to a nagging problem could keep your relationships with dear ones stable, no matter what turbulent conditions you're forced to endure together. Those you call friends may have been in your life for as long as you remember. They're probably Geminis and Librans, whose airy dispositions keep your mind moving.

In love, you may be after a partner who's as clever and imaginative as you are—which means you might look to the fire and vitality of Leo, Sagittarius, and Aries, the three fire signs. But it may be a Cancer whose warmth and caring wins your heart.

Your challenge is to use your creative talents to further the good of the whole. Your gift is your ability to sense the best time to reveal an original idea.

➤ Read about your Chinese Astrological sign on page 838. ➤ Read about your Personal Planets on page 826. ➤ Read about your personal Mystical Card on page 856.

1944

CAPRICORN
Your Personal Planets

YOUR LOVE POTENTIAL
Venus in Scorpio, Jan. 01, 0:00 - Jan. 03, 4:42
Venus in Sagittarius, Jan. 03, 4:43 - Jan. 21, 4:06

YOUR DRIVE AND AMBITION
Mars in Gemini, Jan. 01, 0:00 - Jan. 21, 4:06

YOUR LUCK MAGNETISM
Jupiter in Leo, Jan. 01, 0:00 - Jan. 21, 4:06

World Events

Jan. 4 – Ralph Bunche becomes the first African American in the U.S. State Department.

Jan. 16 – Dwight D. Eisenhower becomes Supreme Commander of the Allied Expeditionary Forces in Europe.

The U.S. forces going ashore at Anzio, Italy

AQUARIUS
Your Personal Planets

YOUR LOVE POTENTIAL
Venus in Sagittarius, Jan. 21, 4:07 - Jan. 28, 3:10
Venus in Capricorn, Jan. 28, 3:11 - Feb. 19, 18:26

YOUR DRIVE AND AMBITION
Mars in Gemini, Jan. 21, 4:07 - Feb. 19, 18:26

YOUR LUCK MAGNETISM
Jupiter in Leo, Jan. 21, 4:07 - Feb. 19, 18:26

World Events

Jan. 23 – Norwegian artist Edvard Munch dies.

Jan. 29 – The largest warship ever built, the *Missouri*, is launched in New York.

1944

PISCES
Your Personal Planets

YOUR LOVE POTENTIAL
Venus in Capricorn, Feb. 19, 18:27 - Feb. 21, 16:39
Venus in Aquarius, Feb. 21, 16:40 - Mar. 17, 2:45
Venus in Pisces, Mar. 17, 2:46 - Mar. 20, 17:48

YOUR DRIVE AND AMBITION
Mars in Gemini, Feb. 19, 18:27 - Mar. 20, 17:48

YOUR LUCK MAGNETISM
Jupiter in Leo, Feb. 19, 18:27 - Mar. 20, 17:48

World Events

Feb. 29 – U.S. forces begin their drive through the Pacific Islands under the command of Gen. Douglas MacArthur.

Mar. 3 – French singer Yves Montand makes his debut in Paris.

French singer and actor Yves Montand

ARIES
Your Personal Planets

YOUR LOVE POTENTIAL
Venus in Pisces, Mar. 20, 17:49 - Apr. 10, 12:08
Venus in Aries, Apr. 10, 12:09 - Apr. 20, 5:17

YOUR DRIVE AND AMBITION
Mars in Gemini, Mar. 20, 17:49 - Mar. 28, 9:53
Mars in Cancer, Mar. 28, 9:54 - Apr. 20, 5:17

YOUR LUCK MAGNETISM
Jupiter in Leo, Mar. 20, 17:49 - Apr. 20, 5:17

World Events

Apr. 3 – Blacks are permitted to vote in all elections in the U.S.

Apr. 10 – In the U.S., Robert B. Woodward and William Doering synthesize quinine, the drug used to prevent malaria.

364

PISCES
From February 19, 18:27 through March 20, 17:48

The Righteous Warrior

The war in Europe reached an important turning point around the time you were born, Pisces of 1944. On March 6, for the first time, the Allied forces carried their campaign to end Nazi rule to the very seat of Hitler's power—Berlin. More than 2,000 tons of bombs were dropped over the German capital, and as a result, the Nazis' belief that their campaign would reach its inevitable triumph—unchallenged—was shaken to its very roots.

The tenacity of the Allies probably meant that your early upbringing was infused with a strong respect for doing battle with a clear conscience when you believe your cause is just. At the same time, your sign's intrinsic need to find a spiritual purpose to life was given an encouraging boost by the heavens. Pisces is one of the three water signs, the element that's famous for bestowing compassion on those born under its influence. But Pisceans who were born in 1944 were also given a potent dose of intellectual resolve, and the ability to put that resolve to use to make major changes in the world around you. This can make you a firm and righteous fighter for the causes you believe in. You may also have been given the ability to keep a steady hand on the wheel, even when conditions might seem to make it impossible to go on.

It's likely that your courage has won you a host of admirers throughout your life, and that friends and co-workers would have looked to you for leadership in challenging times. However, spending time alone can also be important to you, and you probably enjoy the hours which you spend thinking about your experiences and exploring their deeper meaning.

In love relationships, you'll probably search out those whose emotions are tempered by a strong mind and a determined heart. It's likely that Scorpios, Sagittarians, and Taureans will prove worthy allies, while a home-loving Cancer would encourage you to let your feelings show.

Your challenge, 1944 Pisces, is to put your tenderness and empathy aside in urgent times, allowing your keen mind to find practical solutions. Your gift is your ability to mix compassion with objectivity.

ARIES
From March 20, 17:49 through April 20, 5:17

The Unbeatable Debater

Your year's events show the seeds of your bravery and intellectual acuity, Aries of 1944. Russian forces made spectacular gains against Hitler and his Nazi army—although those gains cost thousands of Russian lives. Shortly afterwards, U.S. forces set out on the major invasion of Dutch New Guinea, landing on April 24, in another military assault that brought home a strong message to Germany—its reign of terror would not continue unchallenged.

You made your entrance at a moment in history when the heavens were ready, willing, and able to pass on the ability to take action—quickly, forcefully, and firmly—and since your sign is here to learn just those qualities, you're probably quite a true example of your Sun sign. In addition, a host of mighty planets in your own element, fire, helped you develop another of your sign's most famous traits: courage under fire. You were also given the ability to voice that courage, and you may often choose your words as carefully as you'd choose a weapon to take into battle.

You probably possess all the traits your Sun sign suggests—several times over. That list includes assertiveness, bravery, eagerness, and rapid-fire decision-making—but possibly aggressiveness and impatience, too. In fact, throughout life, you've probably had to learn how o wait—something your sign has never been fond of. But your innate impetuosity makes you decisive when others might waver, and you're probably no stranger to being first. As a result, it's likely that friends and family members instinctively turn to you when they need guidance, and willingly follow your lead.

Your love of debate—and your year's particular skill with words and concepts—probably means you're looking for a partner who won't back down from a challenge either. In that case, you're best-suited to Leos and Sagittarians, the other fire signs, whose equally feisty natures should give you all the support you need.

Your gifts are many—but they can be summed up in two words: courage and swiftness. Your challenge, Aries of 1944, is to keep your temper at bay, even in situations that merit it.

➤ Read about your Chinese Astrological sign on page 838. ➤ Read about your Personal Planets on page 826. ➤ Read about your personal Mystical Card on page 856.

TAURUS

From April 20, 5:18 through May 21, 4:50

The Stalwart Combatant

Your arrival was marked by a tremendous victory for the Allied forces in World War II, Taurus of 1944. They launched a new attack on Monte Cassino, the key point of Germany's "Gustav line" in Italy, eventually breaking the German army's hold there on May 25. Since the Gustav line had been the route along which thousands of Jewish "detainees" were coldly and callously shuttled off to concentration camps in Germany, this battle further showed the world's unswerving determination to stop the Nazis' destructive campaign against Jews and other minority groups.

At the same time, the heavens were full of your own sign's stubborn, resolute energies, making you a perfect example of the qualities your Sun sign is noted for. You can be steadfast, persistent, and focused, able to mete out your substantial energy in carefully-measured doses. You're probably a whiz at finances and career objectives, able to make both your resources and your interest last until the end of any project. This endurance may have won you the approval of higher-ups time and time again—and your ability to finish what you've started would make you a welcome member of any team.

Throughout life, you'll probably find this stick-to-it-iveness an invaluable asset. You may also find that—in both spiritual and practical matters—you help others to keep their faith by the strength of your example. In fact, it's likely that your refusal to stop working until your duties are complete will inspire those around you to keep their own determination just as strong—and their energies well-focused on the end result.

In love relationships, intense Scorpios might engage your passionate side, but you'll probably find that steady Virgos and earthy Capricorns, the other earth signs, will give you the stability and quiet commitment you need to feel secure.

Your greatest challenges, 1944 Taurus, are to avoid becoming obsessed with a project that may need to be aborted and to avoid a tendency toward being over-possessive with your dear ones. Your greatest gifts are your integrity and solid perseverance to finish what others may abandon.

GEMINI

From May 21, 4:51 through June 21, 13:01

The Avid Learner

Despite the war news that continued to shock and sadden the world you arrived into, Gemini of 1944, you somehow managed to develop your sign's most famous traits: the need to gather information, and the ability to share what you know. In fact, information became vastly more affordable and accessible around the time you were born, when publishers began to print and market soft-cover books for mass consumption.

Your early years were probably colored by this new flood of information, which may only have whetted your appetite for education. In addition, with Mercury speeding through your chart at the same time, the heavens would have been pouring curiosity down upon you. Your parents may have noticed your early attraction to books and encouraged you to keep reading and absorbing—and possibly to write, as well. One way or the other, your sign's innate knack for communication was given a mighty boost—and your thirst for knowledge about a huge variety of subjects was stirred.

Far from being intellectually wounded by the times you were born into, your eager mind was probably bolstered by it, and it's likely that your skills as a word-wizard have made you an expert at communicating in many ways. You may have been one of the first to own a personal computer, and your personal library may be huge and varied. Regardless of where you currently get your information, you probably enjoy a good conversation more than anything—and a healthy debate, as well. And speaking of debate, your skills in that department are probably quite substantial!

In love relationships, you may be drawn to others who share your never-ending inquisitiveness, such as Aquarians, Sagittarians, and other Geminis. In platonic situations, you'll probably seek out the company of those who will challenge, educate, and inform you—which could also bring you into contact with other Geminis, as well as plenty of Sagittarians.

Your challenge is to keep at a subject until you know absolutely everything there is to know about it. Your gifts are your love of knowledge and ability to use it to communicate in many different ways.

➤ Read about your Chinese Astrological sign on page 838. ➤ Read about your Personal Planets on page 826. ➤ Read about your personal Mystical Card on page 856.

TAURUS
Your Personal Planets

YOUR LOVE POTENTIAL
Venus in Aries, Apr. 20, 5:18 - May 04, 22:03
Venus in Taurus, May 04, 22:04 - May 21, 4:50

YOUR DRIVE AND AMBITION
Mars in Cancer, Apr. 20, 5:18 - May 21, 4:50

YOUR LUCK MAGNETISM
Jupiter in Leo, Apr. 20, 5:18 - May 21, 4:50

World Events

May 6 – Soviet troops capture the key city of Sevastopol.

May 13 – Hitler orders a full German withdrawal from the USSR.

D-Day in Normandy

GEMINI
Your Personal Planets

YOUR LOVE POTENTIAL
Venus in Taurus, May 21, 4:51 - May 29, 8:38
Venus in Gemini, May 29, 8:39 - June 21, 13:01

YOUR DRIVE AND AMBITION
Mars in Cancer, May 21, 4:51 - May 22, 14:15
Mars in Leo, May 22, 14:16 - June 21, 13:01

YOUR LUCK MAGNETISM
Jupiter in Leo, May 21, 4:51 - June 21, 13:01

World Events

June 6 – D-Day — Allied forces invade the coast of Normandy in France.

June 17 – Iceland proclaims itself to be an independent republic.

1944

CANCER
Your Personal Planets

YOUR LOVE POTENTIAL

Venus in Gemini, June 21, 13:02 - June 22, 19:11
Venus in Cancer, June 22, 19:12 - July 17, 4:46
Venus in Leo, July 17, 4:47 - July 22, 23:55

YOUR DRIVE AND AMBITION

Mars in Leo, June 21, 13:02 - July 12, 2:53
Mars in Virgo, July 12, 2:54 - July 22, 23:55

YOUR LUCK MAGNETISM

Jupiter in Leo, June 21, 13:02 - July 22, 23:55

World Events

July 1 – Representatives from forty-four nations attend the Bretton Woods Conference in New Hampshire.

July 20 – A group of Nazi officers fail in their plan to assassinate Hitler.

French author and pilot Antoine de Saint-Exupéry

LEO
Your Personal Planets

YOUR LOVE POTENTIAL

Venus in Leo, July 22, 23:56 - Aug. 10, 13:12
Venus in Virgo, Aug. 10, 13:13 - Aug. 23, 6:45

YOUR DRIVE AND AMBITION

Mars in Virgo, July 22, 23:56 - Aug. 23, 6:45

YOUR LUCK MAGNETISM

Jupiter in Leo, July 22, 23:56 - July 26, 1:03
Jupiter in Virgo, July 26, 1:04 - Aug. 23, 6:45

World Events

July 21 – Guam is completely recaptured as Japanese troops surrender in the Pacific.

July 31 – French author of *The Little Prince* and pilot Antoine de Saint-Exupéry is reported missing, presumed dead.

CANCER
From June 21, 13:02 through July 22, 23:55

The Proud Defender

As a Cancer born in 1944, it's likely that your caring nature was heightened through the influence of your family. When you were born, the world was listening for news of the success of the Allied forces in Normandy—and hoping, for the sake of the millions of innocent lives at stake, that success would come quickly. The Nazis' efforts toward the infamous "Final Solution" had shocked and horrified the world, but these terrible events may have drawn your family closer together. In the long run, this might have made your entire circle of relatives a tightly-knit clan—and anyone who dared to take issue with one of you probably found himself dealing with all of you.

Being raised during the postwar years may only have reinforced something your sign is already famous for—the urge to protect and nurture those you love. In addition, the astrological influences of your birth time gave you a powerful sense of pride in the accomplishments of those you love. As a result, your concern for and categorical guardianship of your dear ones' safety and happiness probably outranks your concern for your own needs.

You may have chosen a career that would give you power behind the scenes, letting others stand in the glare of the spotlight. In your leisure time, too, you may enjoy quiet activities that you can do on your own. Your home is probably brimming with snapshots of friends and family—however, given your desire to stay out of the spotlight (and behind the camera), you may have taken most of the pictures, leading more than one acquaintance to scrutinize the photographs intently before asking, "Where are you?"

Your search for a mate might bring you to Scorpios and Pisceans, whose sensitive natures can make you feel comfortable enough to express even your deepest feelings. However, your strongest allies in the fight to keep your dear ones safe will probably be practical, objective Capricorns, meticulous Virgos, and determined Taureans.

Your gift is your special knack for tender loving care. Your challenge, 1944 Cancer, is to guard your tender heart against those who would abuse your kindness.

LEO
From July 22, 23:56 through August 23, 6:45

The Dedicated Mastermind

Born during the summer of 1944, you arrived just as Saint Lo, a major link in the German railroad line, was brought to its knees by the American First Army. This event was especially significant because this railroad connection was part of the route along which thousands of European Jews were transported to their ultimate death in Germany's concentration camps. It's likely that the news of this collapse, at a point of such major importance to the Nazis' campaign of terror, gave your family—as so many others—yet more hope that the tide of World War II was beginning to turn.

The astrological significators of your birth time also have a tale to tell about your personality, Leo of 1944. They included a sky full of planets in solid, meticulous, and eminently practical Virgo—which can make you a force to be reckoned with in the department of planning.

As such, you may have developed expertise in planning and executing large-scale events, both personal and business in nature, and you're probably the one who puts together the family reunions or plans the company's annual sales meeting. Or you may have been drawn into a career that allows you to use your substantial skills in these areas, such as work that involves the shaping of political, non-profit, or civic-minded organizational affairs, where your knack for delegation should come in handy.

In love relationships, it's likely that you're looking for a very particular type of partner—and no one else will do. Your search might lead you to Capricorns, Geminis, or Taureans, all of whom will share your careful regard for details. However, you'll probably find the passion and fire you're longing for in the company of Ariens or Sagittarians—both of whom will prove worthy companions and equally worthy colleagues.

Your strengths are your ability to dissect a project and see exactly what needs to happen to make it all come together, and your knack for delegating the right duties to the right talent. Your challenge, Leo of 1944, is your desire to be perfect—despite the fact that imperfections are what make a masterpiece noteworthy.

► Read about your Chinese Astrological sign on page 838. ► Read about your Personal Planets on page 826. ► Read about your personal Mystical Card on page 856.

VIRGO

From August 23, 6:46 through September 23, 4:01

The Humble Helper

You arrived at a monumental time in modern history, Virgo of 1944. After more than four years of occupation by the German army, Paris was at last liberated from Nazi control. The courage of the Allies, as well as their willingness to do unrelenting battle on behalf of those who were unable to defend themselves, probably colored your early upbringing with a strong sense of justice—and the ability to spot an unfair situation as soon as it occurred.

The astrological indicators of your birth time were equally keen: of the ten heavenly bodies astrologers take into consideration, five were in your own help-oriented sign. And since yours is the Sun sign that's famous for its humility, it's possible that many of the heroes who performed so bravely during your early years would have shrugged off the applause of the crowd, seeking only to achieve a greater good. As such, you may have inherited an innate distaste for the spotlight. Efficient and methodical, it may be out of character for you to step onstage and take a bow—even when you richly deserve it!

While you're probably not the picky perfectionist your sign is famous for being, you can be extremely critical of your own efforts. You see how you could have done things better, and that may be why you shy away from allowing others to give you the recognition and rewards you've earned. Although you might enjoy acting because it would allow you to bury yourself in a role and "become someone else," you might have a hard time accepting an Oscar without saying, "I could have done it better."

In love, you're probably looking for a partner who is as capable of long-term devotion and unconditional love as you are. In that case, Librans and Sagittarians will probably be good choices, since their devotion can rival even your own. In friendships, look to the other earth signs—Capricorns and Taureans—for the solid support and steady encouragement you need.

Your challenge is to learn to be less critical of yourself. Your gift is your unending energy in service to others—regardless of whether or not public recognition awaits you.

LIBRA

From September 23, 4:02 through October 23, 12:55

The Decisive Diplomat

Yet another Allied victory of World War II occurred around the time you entered the world, Libra of 1944. In the Battle of Leyte Gulf, the Japanese forces, unable to halt the United States' invasion of the Philippines, suffered an extremely heavy military defeat. This was the most substantial naval battle of World War II, and brought home the Allies' firm determination to win the war in the Pacific.

At the same time, the heavens boasted a large dose of your sign's peace-loving energies. This is ironic, considering that the war was going on at a fast and furious pace. Still, the resoluteness of Britain, the U.S., and their allies would ultimately prove successful. And although your sign is known for its ability to restore balance, it's likely that you were born with the knowledge that balance can sometimes only be achieved by tipping the scales—especially in times of tyranny.

As a result, you could be an unparalleled advocate for the underprivileged, the handicapped, or the poor. Over the course of your life, this devotion to the plight of the underdog may have drawn you to working on behalf of under represented groups all over the world. You may have learned early on to keep a happy balance between work and your personal life, however, so you'd probably be the last person to get over-stressed or burned out, no matter how taxing your work might be. You may also enjoy team sports, rather than individual sports like skiing or tennis, because relying on your teammates can actually be relaxing for you.

In love relationships, your sense of justice and your never-ending search for fairness will probably lead you into the arms of other Librans—but generous, benevolent Sagittarians can also be good choices. With regard to friendships, you may be drawn to Virgos, Taureans, and Capricorns, all of whom will provide you with the sound advice and objective opinions you seek.

Your greatest challenge is to forgive yourself when your efforts are to no avail. Your gift, 1944 Libra, is your ability to make a decision and stick to it, regardless of the effort it may take to attain your goals.

VIRGO
Your Personal Planets

YOUR LOVE POTENTIAL
Venus in Virgo, Aug. 23, 6:46 - Sept. 03, 21:15
Venus in Libra, Sept. 03, 21:16 - Sept. 23, 4:01

YOUR DRIVE AND AMBITION
Mars in Virgo, Aug. 23, 6:46 - Aug. 29, 0:22
Mars in Libra, Aug. 29, 0:23 - Sept. 23, 4:01

YOUR LUCK MAGNETISM
Jupiter in Virgo, Aug. 23, 6:46 - Sept. 23, 4:01

World Events

Aug. 25 – Paris is liberated from Nazi occupation by the Allies.

Aug. 31 – The French provisional government returns to Paris after its liberation.

The Allied forces liberate Paris

LIBRA
Your Personal Planets

YOUR LOVE POTENTIAL
Venus in Libra, Sept. 23, 4:02 - Sept. 28, 6:11
Venus in Scorpio, Sept. 28, 6:12 - Oct. 22, 17:06
Venus in Sagittarius, Oct. 22, 17:07 - Oct. 23, 12:55

YOUR DRIVE AND AMBITION
Mars in Libra, Sept. 23, 4:02 - Oct. 13, 12:09
Mars in Scorpio, Oct. 13, 12:10 - Oct. 23, 12:55

YOUR LUCK MAGNETISM
Jupiter in Virgo, Sept. 23, 4:02 - Oct. 23, 12:55

World Events

Sept. 27 – The Battle of Arnhem commences, part of Operation Market Garden.

Oct. 8 – Samuel Barber's *Capricorn Concerto* premières.

➤ Read about your Chinese Astrological sign on page 838. ➤ Read about your Personal Planets on page 826. ➤ Read about your personal Mystical Card on page 856.

367

1944

SCORPIO
Your Personal Planets

YOUR LOVE POTENTIAL
Venus in Sagittarius, Oct. 23, 12:56 - Nov. 16, 7:25
Venus in Capricorn, Nov. 16, 7:26 - Nov. 22, 10:07

YOUR DRIVE AND AMBITION
Mars in Scorpio, Oct. 23, 12:56 - Nov. 22, 10:07

YOUR LUCK MAGNETISM
Jupiter in Virgo, Oct. 23, 12:56 - Nov. 22, 10:07

World Events

Nov. 1 - Mary Coyle Chase's play *Harvey* premières in New York.

Nov. 9 - The Red Cross is awarded the Nobel Peace Prize.

Winston Churchill with Charles de Gaulle in Paris

SAGITTARIUS
Your Personal Planets

YOUR LOVE POTENTIAL
Venus in Capricorn, Nov. 22, 10:08 - Dec. 11, 4:46
Venus in Aquarius, Dec. 11, 4:47 - Dec. 21, 23:14

YOUR DRIVE AND AMBITION
Mars in Scorpio, Nov. 22, 10:08 - Nov. 25, 16:10
Mars in Sagittarius, Nov. 25, 16:11 - Dec. 21, 23:14

YOUR LUCK MAGNETISM
Jupiter in Virgo, Nov. 22, 10:08 - Dec. 21, 23:14

World Events

Nov. 29 - The first open-heart surgery is performed at the John Hopkins hospital.

Dec. 16 - An airplane carrying Big Band leader Glenn Miller and two companions disappears en route from England to France.

SCORPIO
From October 23, 12:56 through November 22, 10:07

The Passionate Savior

Scorpio of 1944, you were born at a time that foreshadowed the final victory of the Allied forces over Nazi Germany. Planning for the Battle of the Bulge, which would prove to be the last major German offensive of the war, was already underway—in just six months, the Nazis' reign of terror would be forced to a halt. Your family may have begun to sense that they were nearing the end of the long, dark tunnel that became known as World War II, and their fervent capacity to keep hope alive is a flame that has probably burned brightly within you all your life.

The astrological influences of your birth time were equally ardent, as the heavens played host to several planets in your passionate sign, famous for its all-or-nothing attitude. This "do or die" quality probably shows up in everything you do, regardless of how seemingly minor or menial the event. In fact, there's no situation or circumstance in which you're likely to settle for anything less than exactly what you want—and you'll show your determination gladly. This may win you a few adversaries as you go through life, but you'll thrive on such challenges for, rather than setting out to destroy an enemy, it's likely that you'll try to make him your friend instead.

Your attention to detail may be second to none—as is your acute investigative reasoning ability. You're probably a natural-born detective and an expert at the tactics and strategies necessary to win any game. It's likely that you possess the capacity to right a wrong when you find one, no matter how deep the cut goes. You'd be a wise judge, but you could also be a passionate and persuasive advocate.

When it comes to love relationships, you'd do well in the company of Leos and Sagittarians, whose fire and passion will keep yours alive. In friendships, turn to Taureans, Capricorns, and Aquarians, who can be valuable sounding boards for your ideas.

Your challenge is to follow your heart regardless of what others may do to dissuade you. Your gift is your ability to sense weakness or treachery around you—and deal with it before it damages your aims.

SAGITTARIUS
From November 22, 10:08 through December 21, 23:14

The Ardent Gladiator

In typical Sagittarian style, you made your entrance at a time that would become famous for the enormity of the event it hosted, 1944 Sagittarius. On December 16, Allied and German forces clashed in the cold, bloody battle that became known as the Battle of the Bulge. The bitter fighting continued for days, and when at last the battle was decisively won by the Allies, it signaled to the world that Nazi Germany was far from invincible.

As people around the world learned that the wave of terror that had held Europe hostage since the late 1930s was beginning to ebb, a new sense of hope was born as well. News of the Allies' stunning success probably brought your family both optimism and a renewed sense of security, perhaps infusing your first days and weeks with a joyfulness your parents may not have felt in years—a joyfulness you might have exhibited throughout your life.

As a result, you may be known for your ability to keep your chin up, Sagittarius. However, since your nature can be basically fiery, you would also show a willingness to do battle for justice when necessary. It's likely that you joined one or more of the anti-establishment movements in your early adulthood, and you may have maintained a lifelong commitment to the causes you embraced in the sixties. Your passionate pursuit of fairness may have made you "famous" in one way or another as a leader in the fight for equality. Your friends and co-workers might count on you to speak up against prejudice and injustice, or you might have chosen a career where your love of justice would frequently put you in the public eye.

In relationships, you may want a partner who shares your lack of prejudice—and Aquarians and Geminis will probably always answer your call. Your best friends may also be people who were born under these signs, as well as fair-minded Librans and, of course, other Sagittarians.

Your challenge is to stay on course, despite any societal or emotional roadblocks that threaten to deter you. Your gift is your passion, an inner fire that's absolutely unbeatable when your sense of fairness is aroused.

➤ Read about your Chinese Astrological sign on page 838. ➤ Read about your Personal Planets on page 826. ➤ Read about your personal Mystical Card on page 856.

CAPRICORN

From December 21, 23:15 through December 31, 23:59

The Covenant Builder

As you made your planetary debut, and even as World War II was drawing to its protracted, bitter, and bloody conclusion, the seeds of hope were beginning to sprout, December Capricorn of 1944. Peace may have been only a dream when you were born, but the governments of the world were laying their plans to achieve that dream. Already, a forum for the world's nations to meet to work out their differences was being created—it was to be called the United Nations.

The heavens were primed to inspire what the world had fervently desired for so long—the opportunity to end segregation, repression, and persecution, especially when they were based on religious or racial intolerance. As such, your birth time's astrological influences included patience, discipline, and the ability to follow a plan to fruition. Fortunately, you were born at a time that would also allow you to hone all those skills—and more.

You may have learned early on the importance of pledging your loyalty—and you would have the innate capacity to hold true to what you promise, even under changing circumstances or unstable outside influences. You can be a true ally, an even truer friend, and a formidable enemy when your dear ones' interests are challenged. Those close to you are quite fortunate, then, to call you their own, and it's likely that their constant support throughout your life will make all things possible for you—even the things that you may initially feel are all but impossible to achieve.

In love relationships, you'd probably do well to seek out the company of other Capricorns, Virgos, and solid, stable Taureans, whose desire for commitment will match your own. These same signs, along with family-oriented Cancerians and adventure-loving Sagittarians, will also provide the kind of long-term friendships you enjoy most.

Your challenge, 1944 Capricorn, is to stay positive even when you feel somewhat melancholy—especially if those feelings are caused by outside circumstances. Your gift is your ability to combine your innate ambition with the calmness, frugality, and objectivity necessary to achieve your goals.

1944

CAPRICORN
Your Personal Planets

YOUR LOVE POTENTIAL
Venus in Aquarius, Dec. 21, 23:15 - Dec. 31, 23:59

YOUR DRIVE AND AMBITION
Mars in Sagittarius, Dec. 21, 23:15 - Dec. 31, 23:59

YOUR LUCK MAGNETISM
Jupiter in Virgo, Dec. 21, 23:15 - Dec. 31, 23:59

World Events

Dec. 22 – The Vietnamese People's Army is founded in Indochina.

Dec. 31 – General Eisenhower orders General Montgomery's troops to launch an attack on the German lines at Ardennes.

EVA PERÓN
Taurus

Eva Perón was the working-class, much younger wife and political partner of Argentine president, Juan Perón. Popular and influential with the people of her nation, she was politically active and responsible for women's suffrage in 1947. She was a tireless supporter of workers' rights, gave audiences to the poor, and worked to help the ill receive better care. As loved as she was by the Argentine poor and downtrodden, she was reviled by the ruling classes, and they ultimately were successful in putting her husband out of power. She tragically died of cancer at the young age of thirty-two.

Eva was a Taurus, a sign known for practical resourcefulness, financial acumen, and stability. Her Sun, planet of identity, was prominently placed in her horoscope, making people notice her from the moment she walked into the room. A contact from Mars, planet of action and sex appeal, made her seem dynamic and exciting.

The Moon, planet of emotions, was in luxury-loving Leo, which could account for her glamour and charisma. The location of the Moon, in addition to a difficult contact from Saturn, planet of limits, describes the poverty and difficulty of her childhood. Her chart indicates a sense of emotional limitation and the desire to rise up from her humble beginnings and to make more of herself than her family might ever have imagined. In addition, there is a feeling of loneliness and the desire to be loved and protected. The placement of Neptune, planet of insecurity, also indicates a woman who feels that she hasn't as much as she needs and that she must try harder.

With Venus, the planet of pleasure, in her house of money, it was understandable for her to like nice things, but it was also a sign of generosity. She enjoyed the luxuries of her own life but never lost sight of the needs of other people. Her insecurities and humble background were an emotional stumbling block, but from

Eva Perón
May 7, 1919 - July 26, 1952

them she found the strength to help those even more in need than herself, and in so doing she created an improved sense of identity as well as a personal power base.

1945

Darkness Unbound: Pluto in Leo

The war in Europe ended on May 7, 1945, when the German forces surrendered. Europe was in ruins and the full horror and atrocities of the concentration camps began to emerge. Three months later, the world's future was irrevocably altered when an atomic bomb was dropped on the Japanese industrial city of Hiroshima. At 2:45 a.m. on August 6, the B-29 "Enola Gay," with a specially modified bomb bay, took off from Tinian Island, carrying a 9,000 pound bomb called "Little Boy." The bomb, dropped at 8.25 a.m., detonated 1,980 feet above Hiroshima and leveled the city. Three days later, a second atomic bomb "Fat Man" was dropped on Nagasaki. Faced with the prospect of complete and utter destruction, Japan surrendered on August 14.

The planet Pluto rules atomic energy. When it first moved into the sign of Leo, a few years earlier, Robert Oppenheimer and the other engineers of the Manhattan Project were hard at work creating the technology necessary to build an atomic bomb. Pluto is sometimes described as an astrological representation of the Hindu God Shiva—he is the master of destruction but he is also the lord of rebirth. For the first time in history, the world at large was faced with the concept of total annihilation of civilization. Leo is a fire sign and also one of the most intense and expressive signs of the zodiac. During the era of Pluto in Leo, awesome forces in the universe were faced by all in the course of World War II. Human beings were made aware of their ability for destruction and evilness and were also forced to confront their own fragile mortality.

The concentration camp at Auschwitz is liberated

Smoke from the atomic bomb above Hiroshima

Prime Minister Winston Churchill greets a crowd of 50,000 on VE day

TRIANGLE SWALLOWS FLIGHT 19

In December, five Avenger torpedo bombers left the U.S. Navy base in Fort Lauderdale, Fla., on a routine target practice run and headed toward the Bahamas. Suddenly, Lt. Charles Taylor radioed base; "We seem to be lost... Everything is wrong, strange... We can't be sure of any direction... Even the ocean doesn't look as it should." Despite a thorough search with hundreds of planes and ships, no trace of the planes or their pilots was found. The notorious Bermuda Triangle had notched another mysterious disappearance.

THE WAR IS OVER!

As the Russians liberated Auschwitz in January, the horror of the concentration camps began to be revealed. Allied planes wrought destruction on the beautiful city of Dresden. Mussolini was executed, and Hitler committed suicide. U.S. President Roosevelt died, though he knew an Allied victory was imminent. Nazi Germany surrendered in May. Japan continued its resistance, and new President Truman sanctioned the dropping of atomic bombs on Hiroshima and Nagasaki, finally bringing its surrender. The "living hell" of Japanese prisoner of war camps was revealed. After the war, Britain, the U.S., Soviet Russia and France divided Germany into occupation zones. The U.S. introduced the Marshall Plan to rehabilitate devastated Europe, but also to keep countries from Soviet communist influence. The Nuremberg Trials began to assess the crimes of twenty-two Nazi leaders. In response to wartime pan-Arabism and the inter-community problems in Palestine, the Arab League was formed. The United Nations took over from the League of Nations. The International Monetary Fund and the World Bank were established to promote healthy world trade.

➤ Read Mahatma Gandhi's Star Profile on page 377.

CAPRICORN

From January 01, 0:00 through January 20, 9:53

The Practical Engineer

You were born at the beginning of a year of triumph and tragedy, January Capricorn of 1945. Your birth year would mark the end of World War II, but the fighting had not yet abated when you arrived. In Europe, Hitler's troops were waging fierce rear-guard actions as Allied forces began to push eastward toward Germany. Meanwhile, the Soviet army was preparing to race across Poland, crushing the Nazis in an ever-tightening pincer grip. With its main forces heavily engaged on two fronts, the defense of the German homeland was left to the very young and the very old. Before summer came, thousands of German boys and old men would shoulder shotguns and hunting rifles and die in defense of the Fatherland.

Even more than Capricorns born in other years, you may realize how fragile life is. However, as a new, more cosmopolitan world emerged from the ashes of war, you would also have seen the potential for rebirth that exists even in the worst of times. As you grew up, it's likely that you were impressed by the speed of technological development. It must have seemed that there was something new to learn every day, and the uneasy ambiance of the Cold War may have made you even more determined to master all that you could.

Like most other sturdy mountain goats, you're an independent thinker by nature. While you can be a reliable business partner, it is easier for you to work alone at times. You'd probably make an excellent engineer, designer, or investment banker. Jobs in the fields of international law, finance, and accounting could also be good choices for you.

In love, you may want to know that there's someone looking out for your comfort and creating a peaceful sanctuary for you while you build the world from the ground up. You might look to a sensitive Piscean to provide the kind of warmth you need to give you a supportive home life. Romantic sparks can also come from Aquarians and Sagittarians, while Librans make great friends.

Your challenge is to work alone without allowing yourself to become isolated. Being able to place your work in a global context is your greatest gift.

AQUARIUS

From January 20, 9:54 through February 19, 0:14

The Optimistic Futurist

Your birth was probably the most precious of the things your parents celebrated during the year you were born, 1945 Aquarius, because you represented the hope of the future after the darkness of World War II. This spirit of celebration and optimism fueled the internationalism that flourished with the founding of the United Nations that same year. Along with the hope of a world without war came a new sense of unity among the world's nations.

The products of the postwar boom in industry and technology may have fascinated you as a child—movies, television, transistor radios, the first manmade satellite to orbit the Earth! It might have seemed that anything was possible, and that science was the way to get there. In school, you may have sought out the subjects that would allow you to engage in innovative and original thinking. Always marching to a different drummer, you may have been the first in your crowd to hear about Elvis, not to mention The Beatles and the Rolling Stones. From the jitterbug to the twist, you probably danced your way into adulthood, never happy unless "doing your own thing" meant that you thought of it yourself.

The freeform structure of the New Age that dawned while you were in your twenties seemed customized to fit your futuristic vision of the world. While the radicalism of the 1960s may not have been for you, becoming an adult smack dab in the middle of the Age that is named for your sign could have been right up your alley. You may have felt that you had many of the answers, and your determined mind rarely allowed the thought that anyone else's opinion could be more enlightened than your own. In the 1980s you may have helped lead your generation into the information age.

There's little doubt that your loved ones think of you as a true original. Leo's daring and showmanship can attract you into permanent relationships. You enjoy intellectual Gemini and fun-loving Sagittarius, who both can be good for you.

Your challenge is to accept positive feedback for your new ideas. Your gift is the ability to keep faith in the possibilities of the future.

➤ Read about your Chinese Astrological sign on page 838. ➤ Read about your Personal Planets on page 826. ➤ Read about your personal Mystical Card on page 856.

1945

CAPRICORN
Your Personal Planets

YOUR LOVE POTENTIAL
Venus in Aquarius, Jan. 01, 0:00 - Jan. 05, 19:17
Venus in Pisces, Jan. 05, 19:18 - Jan. 20, 9:53

YOUR DRIVE AND AMBITION
Mars in Sagittarius, Jan. 01, 0:00 - Jan. 05, 19:30
Mars in Capricorn, Jan. 05, 19:31 - Jan. 20, 9:53

YOUR LUCK MAGNETISM
Jupiter in Virgo, Jan. 01, 0:00 - Jan. 20, 9:53

World Events

Jan. 7 – Boris Karloff signs with RKO Radio in Hollywood to star in three horror shows.
Jan. 9 – U.S. troops under General MacArthur land on the island of Luzon in the Pacific.

Dresden in ruins after Allied air raids

AQUARIUS
Your Personal Planets

YOUR LOVE POTENTIAL
Venus in Pisces, Jan. 20, 9:54 - Feb. 02, 8:06
Venus in Aries, Feb. 02, 8:07 - Feb. 19, 0:14

YOUR DRIVE AND AMBITION
Mars in Capricorn, Jan. 20, 9:54 - Feb. 14, 9:57
Mars in Aquarius, Feb. 14, 9:58 - Feb. 19, 0:14

YOUR LUCK MAGNETISM
Jupiter in Virgo, Jan. 20, 9:54 - Feb. 19, 0:14

World Events

Feb. 3 – The Battle of Manila begins.
Feb. 4 – Churchill, Roosevelt, and Stalin meet at the Yalta Conference to discuss war aims.

1945

PISCES
Your Personal Planets

YOUR LOVE POTENTIAL
Venus in Aries, Feb. 19, 0:15 - Mar. 11, 11:16
Venus in Taurus, Mar. 11, 11:17 - Mar. 20, 23:36

YOUR DRIVE AND AMBITION
Mars in Aquarius, Feb. 19, 0:15 - Mar. 20, 23:36

YOUR LUCK MAGNETISM
Jupiter in Virgo, Feb. 19, 0:15 - Mar. 20, 23:36

World Events

Feb. 23 – Turkey declares war on Germany and Japan.

Mar. 6 – Federico Garcia Lorca's *La Casa de Bernardo Alba* premières in Buenos Aires.

Spanish writer Federico Garcia Lorca

ARIES
Your Personal Planets

YOUR LOVE POTENTIAL
Venus in Taurus, Mar. 20, 23:37 - Apr. 07, 19:14
Venus in Aries, Apr. 07, 19:15 - Apr. 20, 11:06

YOUR DRIVE AND AMBITION
Mars in Aquarius, Mar. 20, 23:37 - Mar. 25, 3:42
Mars in Pisces, Mar. 25, 3:43 - Apr. 20, 11:06

YOUR LUCK MAGNETISM
Jupiter in Virgo, Mar. 20, 23:37 - Apr. 20, 11:06

World Events

Apr. 11 – The concentration camp Buchenwald is liberated and the extent of the Holocaust atrocities is revealed.

Apr. 12 – Franklin D. Roosevelt dies on the eve of Allied victory.

PISCES
From February 19, 0:15 through March 20, 23:36

The Compassionate Dreamer

The social upheavals that occurred during your lifetime illustrate how much the world needed the compassion you brought with you, 1945 Pisces. Certainly, it's no surprise to learn that racial injustice began to be healed during your birth year. In America, the first decrees (by New York State) prohibiting discrimination in employment came into being at the same time you did, and you've probably been helping along such equality ever since. No matter what language you spoke, you'd have understood U.S. Senator Robert F. Kennedy when he said in 1968 (quoting Buckminster Fuller), "Others see what is, and ask 'why?' I see what can be, and ask 'why not?'"

It's likely that these words perfectly captured your idealistic perspective. However, by the time you heard them, the world had already seen a dozen of its finest leaders assassinated, including Mahatma Gandhi, Patrice Lumumba, and John F. Kennedy. The death of U.S. civil rights leader Dr. Martin Luther King, Jr. in April of 1968, followed shortly by the murder of RFK himself, may have hit you very hard. As you entered the decade of the seventies, you probably felt that the world was a sadder, poorer place.

As a result, you may have chosen work that would allow you to spread your love and care to the greatest number of people. With your global outlook, you could have been an effective administrator in international relief efforts, anti-poverty programs, or world health organizations. Or you may have worked as a doctor or nurse, where you could become more directly involved in the acts of compassion you identified with. If you stuck close to home, you'd almost certainly have joined some of the anti-establishment protests of the time, perhaps marching for civil rights, women's rights, or against war.

In love, a Virgo mate would help you keep your feet on the ground, while Cancerians and Scorpios would share your sensitivity. It is also easy for you to admire the courage of your Aries friends.

While it might be a challenge for you to know that others are suffering, you may also have the greatest gift of all—being able to heal them.

ARIES
From March 20, 23:37 through April 20, 11:06

The Unabashed Pioneer

Although you can be impatient and strong-willed, you can also embody a fresh view on the world, coupled with unparalleled enthusiasm, 1945 Aries. Nothing can stop you from moving forward, and this could be because the world you were born into may have seemed to offer limitless possibilities. Having made your entrance as the long, dark night of World War II was finally drawing to a close, it's likely that you enjoyed quite a few of life's luxuries when you were growing up, especially when compared to the wartime privations your parents probably had experienced.

Movies may have been among the favorite entertainments for you and your family. In Europe, the postwar film industry would gear up to produce a spate of film-noir classics in the fifties, but in Hollywood, film production had hardly slowed during the war years. In fact, one of the films that premiered the year you were born would become an instant classic—*Mildred Pierce*, starring Joan Crawford, a fellow Arien.

As you grew older, your pioneering spirit could have made you the first in your group to explore Existentialism, perhaps studying the works of Camus, Sartre, and de Beauvoir. American "Beat generation" writers like Kerouac and Corso could also have intrigued you, and you might have wanted to follow their example when you came of age in the sixties. You may have put off choosing a career while you saw some of the world, but when you did decide, being the first to do just about anything probably would have suited you fine. Although money might not have been your only concern, you may have fared well in the fast-paced eighties, when you probably reached your pinnacle of financial success.

In relationships, your fun-loving personality can mingle well with Leo and Sagittarius, and you can also be fast friends with Scorpio. Cancer and Capricorn are practical self-starters who appreciate your ability to take the initiative, and they could make worthy life-mates for you.

Waiting for the right time to make your move is your biggest challenge. Your gift is your ability to get up and go wherever your ambition takes you.

➤ Read about your Chinese Astrological sign on page 838. ➤ Read about your Personal Planets on page 826. ➤ Read about your personal Mystical Card on page 856.

TAURUS

From April 20, 11:07 through May 21, 10:39

The Persistent Pragmatist

The war in Europe ended around the time you were born, and the return to peace probably helped to form your stable and secure personality, Taurus of 1945. The part of you that seeks pleasure would have been relieved that the end of World War II eventually meant an end to rationing. Although you may remember a few of the wartime privations, you probably delighted in the many material goods your family could provide as you were growing up. As a child in the 1950s, even if your family wasn't rich, you still enjoyed more affluence than any generation before you. It is this domestic prosperity that may have made you so dependable as an adult.

You probably equate excellence with hard work, yet you may also like to make things look easy and effortless—as fellow Taurean Bing Crosby illustrated when he won the Academy award during the year you were born. When it comes to other people, it isn't likely that you take much on faith—you want people to show you what they've got before you believe that it exists.

Your passion might turn you toward the arts, 1945 Taurus, especially sculpture. But when it comes to making a living, sales or communications could have an important role in your life. You may not have been the first one to change your style in the turbulent sixties, but you probably owned a few pairs of bell bottoms —the revolution in thinking exemplified by The Beatles' *Sgt. Pepper* album was pretty strong! In the eighties, you might have been among the first to see the bull market coming, and you may have done well financially as a result.

In love relationships, you value stability, which means that once you're settled you'd tend to stay put. Scorpios, for example, are very attracted to this trait in you, since you satisfy their need for security. You can be feistier in romance than Taureans born during other years, but your soft heart can tend to balance out any impetuous tendencies. Librans make good friends for you.

Your challenge is to speak from your heart without abandoning your inner direction. Your gift is an ability to make money under the strangest of circumstances.

GEMINI

From May 21, 10:40 through June 21, 18:51

The Inquisitive Inventor

As a Gemini born in 1945, you may be endowed with a unique way of looking at the world. Certainly things had changed a lot by the time you were born, especially the face of world politics. Four-term U.S. President Franklin D. Roosevelt died suddenly in April and Winston Churchill resigned as British Prime Minister just as you were entering the world. These transitions may have shaken your parents, who might have felt that the free world was entering the difficult postwar years without a proven leader.

As you got older, you may have sensed some good in the changes going on around you. Industry was finding peacetime uses for technology developed during the war, and because you'd love the idea of being in touch with the world at all times, you may have been among the first of your friends to have a transistor radio. Later on, you would have marveled at other new inventions, like the microwave oven, which was patented during your birth year.

All the excitement over technology probably gave you extra confidence to go out and do new and unusual work, as well. You think more quickly than Bugs Bunny, and this could have led you to a career in science, mathematics or computers, or in the entertainment world. Writing and speaking are two of the things that you do very well, so you may have acted more than once as spokesperson for a group that wanted to institute change, especially during the turbulent sixties.

In relationships, you need someone who will stimulate you and give you enough freedom to pursue life on the wild side—at least mentally. Spirited Sagittarius is a good bet for a mate, but you'll probably flirt seriously with Aries or Taurus before you settle down. Stick with Virgo friends when you want someone around who will fully support your latest escapades.

You need to believe that anything is possible, Gemini of 1945, and you won't give up on a project until you've tried your hand at it—at least once. Your challenge is to stay in one place long enough to make meaningful connections, and your gift is to be able to do this while still managing to think "outside the box."

➤ Read about your Chinese Astrological sign on page 838. ➤ Read about your Personal Planets on page 826. ➤ Read about your personal Mystical Card on page 856.

TAURUS
Your Personal Planets

YOUR LOVE POTENTIAL
Venus in Aries, Apr. 20, 11:07 - May 21, 10:39

YOUR DRIVE AND AMBITION
Mars in Pisces, Apr. 20, 11:07 - May 02, 20:28
Mars in Aries, May 02, 20:29 - May 21, 10:39

YOUR LUCK MAGNETISM
Jupiter in Virgo, Apr. 20, 11:07 - May 21, 10:39

World Events

Apr. 30 – Adolf Hitler and his wife Eva Braun commit suicide in Berlin.

May. 21 – American actors Lauren Bacall and Humphrey Bogart wed.

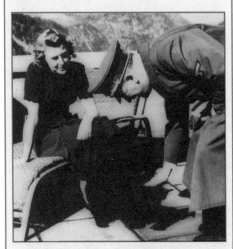

Adolf Hitler and Eva Braun at their retreat in Berchtesgaden

GEMINI
Your Personal Planets

YOUR LOVE POTENTIAL
Venus in Aries, May 21, 10:40 - June 04, 22:57
Venus in Taurus, June 04, 22:58 - June 21, 18:51

YOUR DRIVE AND AMBITION
Mars in Aries, May 21, 10:40 - June 11, 11:51
Mars in Taurus, June 11, 11:52 - June 21, 18:51

YOUR LUCK MAGNETISM
Jupiter in Virgo, May 21, 10:40 - June 21, 18:51

World Events

June 7 – Benjamin Britten's opera *Peter Grimes* premieres in London.

June 21 – Pan Am announces an around-the-world flight in eighty-eight hours and at a cost of $700.

1945

CANCER
Your Personal Planets

YOUR LOVE POTENTIAL
Venus in Taurus, June 21, 18:52 - July 07, 16:19
Venus in Gemini, July 07, 16:20 - July 23, 5:44

YOUR DRIVE AND AMBITION
Mars in Taurus, June 21, 18:52 - July 23, 5:44

YOUR LUCK MAGNETISM
Jupiter in Virgo, June 21, 18:52 - July 23, 5:44

World Events

July 11 – Napalm is first used as a weapon of war by the U.S. forces against the Japanese.

July 16 – The first atomic bomb is tested in the Los Alamos desert in New Mexico.

Japan surrenders to the Allies

LEO
Your Personal Planets

YOUR LOVE POTENTIAL
Venus in Gemini, July 23, 5:45 - Aug. 04, 10:58
Venus in Cancer, Aug. 04, 10:59 - Aug. 23, 12:34

YOUR DRIVE AND AMBITION
Mars in Taurus, July 23, 5:45 - July 23, 8:58
Mars in Gemini, July 23, 8:59 - Aug. 23, 12:34

YOUR LUCK MAGNETISM
Jupiter in Virgo, July 23, 5:45 - Aug. 23, 12:34

World Events

Aug. 9 – The U.S. drops the atomic bomb on the Japanese city of Nagasaki; around 75,000 people are killed.

Aug. 15 – Japan surrenders to the Allies; World War II is over.

CANCER
From June 21, 18:52 through July 23, 5:44

The Responsible Protector

Much of the world was divided into winners and losers at the time you arrived, Cancer of 1945, and this may have had a lifelong effect on you. In Germany, the vaunted thousand-year Reich had been defeated, and many of its leaders were dead or in captivity. Some escaped to lives of hiding in countries that would accept them, while others —particularly scientists—were quickly and secretly being recruited by British, Russian, and American agents to work in the military, industrial, and scientific establishments of their own countries. While war still raged in the Pacific, in Europe "peace" was already beginning to turn into the Cold War.

Raised in the edgy, uneven 1950s, it's likely that you're always ready for an emergency, and you do what it takes to make yourself and your loved ones feel safe and secure. This early training, combined with your innate qualities as a nurturer, may have suited you later in life to a career in office management, real estate, or public relations, where your natural instincts as a "firefighter" would prepare you to put out a blaze no matter where it pops up.

To distract yourself from some of your worries, you may have listened to music like the soundtrack from *Kiss Me Kate*, and Ella Fitzgerald's unique song stylings, both of which made their debut the year you were born. Surely, having such strong and vibrant tunes resonating through the world you grew up in would have reassured you, allowing you to feel better about reaching out to people.

The traditional idea of "opposites attract" never applied more than it does to you, 1945 Cancer. It's very important that you have at least one solid Capricorn in your life to make you feel protected. Librans make diverting friends, because you both tend to like variety in the activities you share. Pisces and Taurus understand and appreciate your sensitivity, which make it likely that they'll listen when you talk.

Your challenge is to prevent your responsibilities from holding you back as you pursue your goals. Your gift is your ability to contribute your skills and caring to the community around you.

LEO
From July 23, 5:45 through August 23, 12:34

The Reluctant Leader

The world learned about the destructive power of the atom when U.S. President Harry S. Truman authorized the bombing of Hiroshima on August 6, 1945. This was an event of enormous seriousness. Now it appeared that man might have the power to destroy the whole world. It is said that when J. Robert Oppenheimer, one of the fathers of the atom bomb, saw the first nuclear detonation in the U.S. desert, just weeks before the bomb was dropped, he was overwhelmed with sadness. He quoted Hindu scripture: "I am Shiva, destroyer of worlds."

You were born at a time when everyone was asked to sacrifice, and as a child you may have accepted this with more humility than your sign's stereotype would suggest. But it's likely that your flamboyant side emerged as you grew up and witnessed the possibilities that prosperity can bring. You may also have an enterprising side, Leo of 1945, and when you hit mid-life during the 1980s, you were probably very much in tune with the materialistic mood of the times.

You think big, but you may stop short of taking foolish risks, remembering the privations your parents had lived through. Nevertheless, the pride that influences your thinking demands that you own your sense of power and use it without reservation. This attribute can make you a natural leader, so a career as a business executive, a politician, a teacher, or a performer could suit you well. You enjoy bringing out the best in people, and the power of your attention could turn even the lowliest lump of coal into a brilliant diamond.

In love relationships, you relish a person who appreciates your strength. Aquarius is self-sufficient enough to stand up to you, so long as you don't mistake your mate's independent behavior for abandonment. Fast-thinking Geminis appeal to your intellect, while Virgos share your desire to be practical. Although a Scorpio probably won't defer to your authority, there's a good chance that one could fascinate you just the same.

Your challenge is to believe that you are as powerful as you pretend to be. Your desire to bring out the best in others is your greatest gift.

➤ Read about your Chinese Astrological sign on page 838. ➤ Read about your Personal Planets on page 826. ➤ Read about your personal Mystical Card on page 856.

VIRGO

From August 23, 12:35 through September 23, 9:49

The Effective Innovator

Just before you were born, Emperor Hirohito of Japan surrendered in a solemn ceremony aboard a U.S. naval vessel. The last combatants of World War II had laid down their arms. For you, it's likely that the end of war meant you were destined to live a life of opportunity. Perhaps that's why you really know how to roll up your sleeves and get the job done, Virgo of 1945. Where others may see insurmountable obstacles, you might see openings for financial reward and personal gratification, and you probably make the most of every chance you get to shine.

You are always thinking about ways to make things more efficient and practical, and because you are a 1945 Virgo, you can even be optimistic about changing other people's bad habits. During the year you were born, Grand Rapids, Michigan became the first community to add fluoride to its water, and Raymond Libby developed an oral form of penicillin. These revolutionary developments worked to ensure that the postwar generation you grew up in would be the healthiest ever.

You were probably eager to rise to the challenge of the stringent standards that were imposed on you in school. You are the kind of person who finds ways to use technology and other innovations to improve communication and performance in your work place, as well as to help collect all the detailed information and data that you love to work with. You might be attracted to a career in the sciences or even broadcasting, and you'll probably be known for your ability to adapt easily to many different circumstances. This may have been very useful to you in the nineties, when the world changed faster than anyone ever imagined.

In love, you need someone who can roll with the punches as easily as you do, so Pisces, Sagittarius, and Gemini make your best life-mates. Libra makes you laugh, and Taurus makes a solid, like-minded business partner for you.

Your challenge is to accept that things will never be as perfect as you want them to be. Your gift is your ability to believe that no matter how good things already are, if people try harder, they can be even better.

LIBRA

From September 23, 9:50 through October 23, 18:43

The Hopeful Romantic

As a 1945 Libra, you were born when the world seemed to have shifted in a way that assured your freedom and safety. As a child, you may have admired the men and women whose victories in World War II permitted you to grow up in a time of peace and prosperity. This could be why the exotic world of international trade has been a subject of intrigue for you. To you, the ideas that come from other cultures can be beams of light that help us see ourselves in new and creative ways.

Once you master the art of judging people for what they are rather than what you wish them to be, you can enjoy a career in the arts, writing, or the law. When the technology revolution of the seventies hit full stride, you might have integrated a scientific element into your work, or perhaps experimented with an electronic database of the information you had gathered to make it easier for you to keep track of and use.

All Librans are natural artists, but as a 1945 Libra you could have a particular gift for channeling the muse of creativity. You can also be extremely optimistic, and you may tend to see the best features of people's personalities, rather than their flaws. This makes you a very pleasant person to be around, and you probably have a legion of friends and fans who adore you. Other Librans can make good friends for you, as can Taureans, with their earthy, pragmatic view of the world.

In love, it may seem vital to you to find your soul mate—the person with whom you can share your innermost thoughts and dreams. This is because, in love as in all things, you seek the perfect balance—the right combination of assertion and compassion that results in a thing of beauty. You might seek someone who would counterbalance your even-tempered ways. Brilliant, elusive Gemini could hold enough fascination for a lifetime, while a fiery Aries could be the epitome of honesty, which you would probably appreciate for the treasure that it is.

Your life challenge is to see things as they truly are. Your greatest gift is the ability to take ordinary life experiences and purify them until they become works of art.

► Read about your Chinese Astrological sign on page 838. ► Read about your Personal Planets on page 826. ► Read about your personal Mystical Card on page 856.

1945

VIRGO
Your Personal Planets

YOUR LOVE POTENTIAL
Venus in Cancer, Aug. 23, 12:35 - Aug. 30, 13:04
Venus in Leo, Aug. 30, 13:05 - Sept. 23, 9:49

YOUR DRIVE AND AMBITION
Mars in Gemini, Aug. 23, 12:35 - Sept. 07, 20:55
Mars in Cancer, Sept. 07, 20:56 - Sept. 23, 9:49

YOUR LUCK MAGNETISM
Jupiter in Virgo, Aug. 23, 12:35 - Aug. 25, 6:04
Jupiter in Libra, Aug. 25, 6:05 - Sept. 23, 9:49

World Events

Aug. 31 – Israeli Violinist Itzhak Perlman is born.
Sept. 18 – One thousand whites walk out of schools in Indiana to protest against integration.

Argentine leader Juan Perón

LIBRA
Your Personal Planets

YOUR LOVE POTENTIAL
Venus in Leo, Sept. 23, 9:50 - Sept. 24, 16:05
Venus in Virgo, Sept. 24, 16:06 - Oct. 19, 4:08
Venus in Libra, Oct. 19, 4:09 - Oct. 23, 18:43

YOUR DRIVE AND AMBITION
Mars in Cancer, Sept. 23, 9:50 - Oct. 23, 18:43

YOUR LUCK MAGNETISM
Jupiter in Libra, Sept. 23, 9:50 - Oct. 23, 18:43

World Events

Sept. 24 – At a meeting in London, British and U.S. representatives agree an oil treaty.
Oct. 17 – Juan Perón stages a coup to become dictator of Argentina.

1945

SCORPIO
Your Personal Planets

YOUR LOVE POTENTIAL
Venus in Libra, Oct. 23, 18:44 - Nov. 12, 7:04
Venus in Scorpio, Nov. 12, 7:05 - Nov. 22, 15:54

YOUR DRIVE AND AMBITION
Mars in Cancer, Oct. 23, 18:44 - Nov. 11, 21:04
Mars in Leo, Nov. 11, 21:05 - Nov. 22, 15:54

YOUR LUCK MAGNETISM
Jupiter in Libra, Oct. 23, 18:44 - Nov. 22, 15:54

World Events

Nov. 13 – The French elect Charles de Gaulle as their new President.

Nov. 20 – Nazi war criminals go on trial at Nuremberg in Germany.

The microwave oven is patented

SAGITTARIUS
Your Personal Planets

YOUR LOVE POTENTIAL
Venus in Scorpio, Nov. 22, 15:55 - Dec. 06, 5:21
Venus in Sagittarius, Dec. 06, 5:22 - Dec. 22, 5:03

YOUR DRIVE AND AMBITION
Mars in Leo, Nov. 22, 15:55 - Dec. 22, 5:03

YOUR LUCK MAGNETISM
Jupiter in Libra, Nov. 22, 15:55 - Dec. 22, 5:03

World Events

Dec. 6 – The microwave oven is patented.

Dec. 15 – Baritone Robert Merrill makes his debut at the Metropolitan Opera House in New York.

SCORPIO
From October 23, 18:44 through November 22, 15:54

The Entranced Reformer

A fellow Scorpio, Swedish beauty Ingrid Bergman, ran away with the Oscar for Best Actress the year you were born, and the world was listening to another Scorpio's paean to American idealism—Aaron Copland's *Appalachian Spring*. The pride and patriotism that swept the world just after your birth may have made you highly idealistic, 1945 Scorpio, and willing to believe that people were essentially good—until and unless they proved otherwise.

Although you arrived in a world where the wounds of war were still tender, it's likely that the times you were born into protected your high-minded perspective. As a result, you might be more intuitive and less calculating than is usual for your sign. You probably view the world in a highly spiritual way, and as a child you may have had little trouble accessing your unconscious mind whenever you needed answers to pressing questions.

It's possible that this ability to tune in to the unseen did not disappear at childhood's end. You may have been drawn to the "occult" studies that emerged in the sixties, such as astrology, Tarot, and ESP. Since you can also have an impulse to "fix" the hurts that you see in your fellow human beings, you may have used your own powers of perception to create a career for yourself as a psychologist, social worker, or physician. In later years, if you revealed your interest in psychic studies to your peers, you might have been surprised by how many of them shared your perspective!

In love relationships, you might enjoy flirting with Librans and Cancerians, but when it comes to true love, a Leo or a Taurus could be the one that proves they are with you for the long haul. Your Gemini and Libra friends could be the ones who are most interested in working with the mysterious unseen forces you can have access to.

Your challenge is to believe that the spiritual work you do has concrete and beneficial effects in the material world, and that it is all right to receive monetary rewards for it if you want them. Your gift is the ability to see beyond the scope of your own lifetime and hold out hope for a brighter future.

SAGITTARIUS
From November 22, 15:55 through December 22, 5:03

The Team Player

Enjoying life might come easily to you, 1945 Sagittarius, and you've probably never had a problem connecting to groups of people who bolster your good mood. As you grew up, you probably enjoyed balancing your outdoor activities and sports with intensive studies of foreign countries. And with your sense of global community, you may seem to embody the spirit of the United Nations, which was founded during the year that you were born.

You probably tend to think broadly and deeply, and it's likely that your sense of optimism is focused on the success of groups and the world at large. To you, the things that you do for a living are meaningless unless they make some sort of impact on the collective. This would invite you to use your interest in the law, higher learning, religion, philosophy, or politics to make a living. It's likely that your sense of fair play was shocked many times, however, as it might have seemed that social justice took one step forward and two steps back during your lifetime.

As an adventure-loving Sagittarius, travel can be the most rewarding leisure-time activity for you. Maps and atlases might be your favorite decorations, and if you haven't seen the whole world, chances are you've covered at least one continent rather thoroughly. Swimming, dancing, and active forms of exercise help you stay fit and happy. Enjoying dinner and a movie (preferably a travelogue) with friends can be a favorite weekend ritual.

In love relationships, you'd probably do best with someone who loves to travel and see the world as much as you do. The Geminis you would normally pair up with might come across to you as being unreliable, so perhaps you would prefer a more stable Capricorn or a sensuous Cancer. In friendship, Libra shares your desire to perform deeds of kindness, while visionary Aquarius inspires you to dream even bigger dreams.

Your challenge is to balance your need to assert yourself against the sensibilities of the people who are closest to you. Your gift is your ability to sacrifice your own gratification for the sake of the greater good of the community.

376

➤ Read about your Chinese Astrological sign on page 838. ➤ Read about your Personal Planets on page 826. ➤ Read about your personal Mystical Card on page 856.

CAPRICORN
From December 22, 5:04 through December 31, 23:59

The Bashful Planner

Going out on a limb probably isn't for you, December Capricorn of 1945. You were born when the world was just beginning to understand the enormity of the destruction wrought by World War II. Berlin, Dresden, Hiroshima, and Nagasaki were in ruins. London was badly damaged by years of German air raids and long-range bombing. Much of Russia had been laid to waste, first by the German invaders and again as Soviet troops drove westward toward Berlin. Millions had lost their land, their homes—sometimes even their families—in one of the biggest population dislocations humanity had ever experienced.

The world you entered was radically different from the one your parents had inherited, and they may never have adjusted completely to the changing rules. As a result, you may have learned early on to play your cards close to your vest—and you might have done so most of your life. You tend to think in practical terms, and although you were born during a festive time of year, you probably appreciate the more solemn moments that come with the onset of winter. Although you may not appear to be as confident as Capricorns born in other years, when you do act you have faith that what you're doing is the right thing.

It's likely that authority figures have been good to you during your life. As a teenager, you probably rebelled less than most of your classmates. You may have waited until the late eighties before you allowed yourself to dabble in matters that bordered on the less-than-concrete. By then, you had the wisdom to discern whether the inspiration you received was genuine or just a flash in the pan.

In love relationships, you may have a tendency to attract people who are overly emotional and hypersensitive. Although Cancer is usually a good match for you, you could also be drawn to saucy Leos and good-looking Librans. Taurus is your most reliable friend, and you may love to flirt with Scorpios and Sagittarians.

Your challenge is to stand up to the people you work with in one-to-one relationships. Being able to see the big picture without losing the details is your greatest gift.

CAPRICORN
Your Personal Planets

YOUR LOVE POTENTIAL
Venus in Sagittarius, Dec. 22, 5:04 - Dec. 30, 1:55
Venus in Capricorn, Dec. 30, 1:56 - Dec. 31, 23:59

YOUR DRIVE AND AMBITION
Mars in Leo, Dec. 22, 5:04 - Dec. 26, 15:03
Mars in Cancer, Dec. 26, 15:04 - Dec. 31, 23:59

YOUR LUCK MAGNETISM
Jupiter in Libra, Dec. 22, 5:04 - Dec. 31, 23:59

World Events

Dec. 27 – The International Monetary Fund and World Bank are established by the Bretton Woods Conference.

Dec. 31 – The Germans begin their retreat from Czechoslovakia.

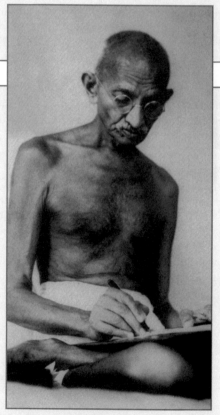

Mahatma Gandhi
October 2, 1869 - January 30, 1948

MAHATMA GANDHI
Libra

Mahatma Gandhi was a lawyer who never felt comfortable in that role until he began to embrace a more spiritual form of living. Rather than sacrificing his life to material gain, Gandhi's goal was to serve others and to share his religious beliefs, which encouraged love and a non-violent form of civil disobedience. He was determined to remove the British from his native India and spent decades inspiring his countrymen to protest with him. He held fast to his beliefs in love and forgiveness and inspired others to abandon the caste system and embrace all as God's children. He is considered a role model for others desiring political change without bloodshed. Although he lived by love, he died by an assassin's bullet.

Gandhi was a Libra, a sign noted for its people skills and charm. His Sun, the planet of identity, was not in a prominent place in his horoscope, accounting for his early shy and awkward personality.

Gandhi's Moon, the planet of emotions and women, was in warmhearted Leo. The Moon received a number of contacts from other planets, heightening Gandhi's emotional inclinations. Contacts from both Venus and Mars, the planets of affection and action respectively, made him intense and passionate. A contact from expansive Jupiter provided a sense of personal, emotional security, making it easy for him to devalue the importance of money. Another contact from domineering Pluto indicated personal power struggles. Gandhi said many times that, in the early days of his marriage, he was autocratic, controlling, and considered himself superior to his wife. As time passed and he saw that, despite his bad behavior, her love remained steady, he realized that she was his teacher, not his subordinate.

A final contact to his Moon from Neptune, planet of idealism, bestowed a psychic and spiritual ability. He came to be revered as a

"Mahatma," someone with a great soul and wisdom, a master. Gandhi's philosophy no doubt grew out of his ability to meditate and to connect with the forces of the universe, the greater good, and the universal powers of love.

➤ Read Martin Luther King's Star Profile on page 537. ➤ Read "East Meets Twentieth-Century West" on page 65.

1946

Justice for All: Jupiter and Neptune in Libra

In the year of 1946, the eyes of the world were trained on the aftermath of World War II. The suffering of the war years seemed incomprehensible. The governments of the nations involved in the war and the people that dwelled within those nations were focused on healing and repair. A fundamental part of this process was charging those responsible for the Holocaust for their crimes against humanity. Jupiter and Neptune were both placed in Libra in 1946, giving seekers of justice just the push they needed to move beyond blind rage. When two planets occupy a particular sign, the energy of that sign is greatly intensified. Jupiter is the planet of hope and promise and it helps to move things into action. Jupiter signifies the future, learning, culture and "Big Ideas." When Libra became Jupiter's resting-place in 1945, people began once again to invest their hopes in the idea of a just world. The astrological symbol for Libra is the scales of justice. It is the sign of peace, consensus, and balance. Neptune represents the dream world and in 1946, everyone seemed to share one big dream—that of a world without evil.

The first meeting of the United Nations General Assembly opened in London on January 10, 1946. Twelve Nazi leaders (including one tried *in absentia*) were sentenced to death, seven were imprisoned, and three were acquitted in the Nuremberg trials that began on October 1 the same year. The Sun had also moved into Libra by this time of the year, influencing the drive toward international diplomacy with even greater gusto. Resolution seemed to be at hand.

War criminals are sentenced at the Nuremberg Trials

A UNICEF car on a field inspection

An underwater atom bomb test is held at Bikini Atoll

MYSTERY ROCKETS

Strange objects streaking across the sky terrorized Northern Europe in 1946. Witnesses described one as a sparkling pinwheel that spat orange and green flames, made eerie whistling sounds, then crashed into a lake. Although the war had ended, some speculated that the Nazis were still experimenting with new weapons. Others thought that the Soviets were behind the "ghost rockets" or suspected extraterrestrials. Although the Swedish government investigated, the shower of fast-moving lights remains unexplained.

THE SHAPE OF THINGS TO COME

Political events of this year revealed the shape of the future. The United Nations held its first optimistic session, but the U.S. and Russia were already at odds, presaging the Cold War. At the Nuremberg trials, twelve Nazi leaders were sentenced to death, seven were imprisoned, and three acquitted. There was civil war between Mao Tse-Tung's Communists and Chiang Kai-shek's Nationalists in China. A provisional Indian government was established, by Muslim leader Jinnah, which held out for a separate Muslim state. Violent Hindu-Muslim riots broke out. The King of Italy was dethroned and a republic established. De Gaulle was installed as France's first postwar Prime Minister. Greece voted for the return of its King, George II—not an entirely popular move. Peron was overwhelmingly elected President of Argentina. France held its first Cannes Film Festival, Ethel Merman hit it big in *Annie Get Your Gun. Road To Utopia*, the fourth 'road' film, was released. U.S. industry suffered strikes for better conditions and pay. Smoking and cancer were linked for the first time. TV pioneer John Logie Baird and U.S. author Damon Runyon died.

➤ Read "The Mysterious Bermuda Triangle" by Sophia Mason on page 385.

CAPRICORN

From January 01, 0:00 through January 20, 15:44

The Grand Planner

You arrived just as a major force for peace was also making its debut, January Capricorn of 1946. Around the time you were born, the United Nations General Assembly met for the first time in London (it wasn't decided until the end of the year that the UN would be headquartered in New York). This significant assembly of nations aimed to safeguard the world against another global conflagration such as the one that was just concluding. With the news of the founding of such a world body, your family, like many others, may have felt a profound sense of relief, and this may have colored your early years with optimism, faith, and hope—things the world had not allowed itself to expect for a very long time.

The astrological factors influencing your birth time were equally strong. The heavens were full of planets in both your own dutiful, conscientious sign and its opposite—home- and family-loving Cancer. This combination of energies is the basis for creating sound foundations, both personally and professionally. As such, you'd have inherited both the urge to build a strong home base and the solid work ethic for which your sign is famous.

You may have followed a rather conservative life-path, then, especially when compared to others of your generation. You might have a lifelong commitment to family and community, and you could tend to travel as much for the pleasure of coming home as for the journey itself. Your responsible attitude has probably put you at the head of many groups over your lifetime, both family-oriented and social. In fact, your skills at leadership, organization, and careful preparation may be quite substantial.

In love relationships, you'll probably seek out someone who shares your need to create an unshakeable foundation. The other earth signs, Virgos and Taureans, as well as other Capricorns, are logical choices—but protective, tenacious Cancerians will also appeal to you.

Your challenge is never to become so wrapped up in your plans for the future that you forget to enjoy the present. Your gift is your innate ability to build a firm and unswerving foundation.

AQUARIUS

From January 20, 15:45 through February 19, 6:08

The Unconditional Altruist

Your arrival coincided with a time of great humanitarianism, 1946 Aquarius—a much-needed blessing after the display of inhumanity the world had witnessed during recent years. Around the time you were born, people were beginning to comprehend the financial and emotional toll World War II had taken on the citizens of Europe. Residents of New York City reached out to help thousands they had never met—and probably would never meet—by donating millions of pounds of clothing to those who had been stricken by poverty and food shortages as a result of the Nazis' campaign of terror. And that was just the start of a worldwide wave of generosity that eventually reached historic proportions.

This outpouring of kindness infused the time of your birth with qualities your sign is already famous for: unselfishness, friendly concern, and the strong desire to shelter and protect the underdog. The heavens certainly reflected both the spirit of the times and your own philanthropic tendencies. A host of planets in your own sign intermingled with two more in peace-loving Libra, the sign best known for its fairness and sense of justice.

As a result, you probably grew up in an early environment infused with strong liberal views. Even if you considered yourself to be quite conservative later in life, it's likely that the virtues of altruism, kindness, and compassion you learned in childhood continued to motivate your actions. As such, you can be a mighty ally and an even better friend. You may also be an outspoken advocate for the rights of others—regardless of race, sex, or religious preference, all of which you no doubt find completely unimportant when choosing your friends.

In love relationships, it's likely that you'll want someone by your side who is as impartial and fair-minded as you are, and you may be drawn to generous Sagittarians, justice-loving Librans, and compassionate Pisceans.

Your challenge is to separate your own interests from those of others—and to take care of yourself as well as you take care of your dear ones. Your gift is your unconditional acceptance—a rare quality indeed.

▶ Read about your Chinese Astrological sign on page 838. ▶ Read about your Personal Planets on page 826. ▶ Read about your personal Mystical Card on page 856.

1946

CAPRICORN
Your Personal Planets

YOUR LOVE POTENTIAL
Venus in Capricorn, Jan. 01, 0:00 - Jan. 20, 15:44

YOUR DRIVE AND AMBITION
Mars in Cancer, Jan. 01, 0:00 - Jan. 20, 15:44

YOUR LUCK MAGNETISM
Jupiter in Libra, Jan. 01, 0:00 - Jan. 20, 15:44

World Events

Jan. 6 – Ho Chi Minh is elected President of North Vietnam.

Jan. 10 – The first General Assembly of the United Nations is convened in London.

Ho Chi Minh, new President of North Vietnam

AQUARIUS
Your Personal Planets

YOUR LOVE POTENTIAL
Venus in Capricorn, Jan. 20, 15:45 - Jan. 22, 22:27
Venus in Aquarius, Jan. 22, 22:28 - Feb. 15, 20:10
Venus in Pisces, Feb. 15, 20:11 - Feb. 19, 6:08

YOUR DRIVE AND AMBITION
Mars in Cancer, Jan. 20, 15:45 - Feb. 19, 6:08

YOUR LUCK MAGNETISM
Jupiter in Libra, Jan. 20, 15:45 - Feb. 19, 6:08

World Events

Feb. 1 – Yugoslavia and Hungary declare themselves to be republics.

Feb. 14 – IBM introduces the first electronic calculator.

1946

PISCES
Your Personal Planets

YOUR LOVE POTENTIAL
Venus in Pisces, Feb. 19, 6:09 - Mar. 11, 20:31
Venus in Aries, Mar. 11, 20:32 - Mar. 21, 5:32

YOUR DRIVE AND AMBITION
Mars in Cancer, Feb. 19, 6:09 - Mar. 21, 5:32

YOUR LUCK MAGNETISM
Jupiter in Libra, Feb. 19, 6:09 - Mar. 21, 5:32

World Events

Mar. 5 – Winston Churchill delivers his famous "Iron Curtain" speech.

Mar. 12 – American singer and actress Liza Minnelli is born.

American singer and actress Liza Minnelli is born under the sign of Pisces

ARIES
Your Personal Planets

YOUR LOVE POTENTIAL
Venus in Aries, Mar. 21, 5:33 - Apr. 05, 1:00
Venus in Taurus, Apr. 05, 1:01 - Apr. 20, 17:01

YOUR DRIVE AND AMBITION
Mars in Cancer, Mar. 21, 5:33 - Apr. 20, 17:01

YOUR LUCK MAGNETISM
Jupiter in Libra, Mar. 21, 5:33 - Apr. 20, 17:01

World Events

Mar. 28 – Juan Perón is elected President of Argentina.

Apr. 18 – The League of Nations is dissolved.

PISCES

From February 19, 6:09 through March 21, 5:32

The Empathetic Idealist

The world really seemed to be getting smaller when you arrived, 1946 Pisces. You were born into a time that was marked by an unprecedented need for union, the consolidation of interests, and the end of political isolation. In Europe, millions had been left homeless and poverty-stricken as a result of World War II. Fortunately, people all over the globe heard their call for help—and answered with shipments of food, clothing, and other basic necessities the war had taken away.

Even as people reached out to help their European brothers and sisters, they faced major problems of their own. In postwar America, thousands faced the specters of spiraling inflation, a dangerous shortage of suitable housing, and labor disputes that would threaten not just the American economy, but the world's economy as well. In a move to prevent a global financial collapse, Great Britain took over the Bank of England just before you were born.

The astrological influences of your birth time may also have served to hone your innate unselfishness and your belief in the virtue of sharing with others. In addition to a pack of energies in your own sign, the heavens played host to planets in equally compassionate, empathetic areas of the zodiac: fair-minded Libra, nurturing Cancer, and ardent, generous Leo. As a result, your inherently gentle, mystical nature could have been infused with idealism, integrity, and honesty. This combination may have made you a powerful force in your adult years. You may have been among those who worked to change society in the sixties, and you could have chosen a career that would let you continue to help people.

Your search for a mate may lead you into the arms of benevolent, generous Sagittarians, sympathetic, caring Cancerians, or emotionally determined Scorpios. In friendships, you'll probably seek out the companionship of altruistic Aquarians and justice-loving Librans, who'll be more than happy to help you spread your charitable beliefs to the world.

Your challenge is to give only as much as you can afford—not all you have. Your gift is your incredible unselfishness.

ARIES

From March 21, 5:33 through April 20, 17:01

The Assertive Reformer

You were born during a time of significant change in the way people saw the world, 1946 Aries. The major powers, now beginning to be known as "Superpowers," realized that isolationism was a luxury they could no longer afford. The recent ending of World War II, and the subsequent assimilation of the consequences of that conflict, had demonstrated to these world leaders how important it was to dominate in their sphere of influence. Meanwhile, the existence of the atom bomb was forcing ordinary people to contemplate the presence of a weapon that was capable of destroying huge numbers of lives—and perhaps of endangering the future of the planet itself.

Your ruling planet, Mars, is the ancient god of war, but growing up at a time when the two nations that could do so—the U.S. and the USSR—were building nuclear arsenals as fast as possible, probably instilled in you the knowledge that war was folly. As a result, your aggressive, warrior-like qualities would have been tempered by an understanding of how important peace really is. In addition, you were gifted with the astrological components necessary for change, decisive action, and courage. For you, the lesson to be learned from the Cold War was the one your sign is here to achieve: assertion without destruction.

You may have chosen a career in teaching, writing, or broadcasting, but any work that allowed you to influence people would probably suit you. The heavens showed your mighty determination—as well as your ardent spirit—and it's likely that you would have succeeded no matter what you turned your energies to.

In love, you'll probably seek out kindred spirits who share your fire, passion, and wide-angle vision. As such, optimistic, open-minded Sagittarians, ingenious Aquarians, and self-reliant Leos may answer your call. In friendships, look to other Ariens, lighthearted Geminis, and subtly powerful Librans.

Your challenge is to realize that you can only make changes one step at a time, and to remain patient in the process. Your gifts are your amazing courage and your unwillingness to give up on what's important to you.

➤ Read about your Chinese Astrological sign on page 838. ➤ Read about your Personal Planets on page 826. ➤ Read about your personal Mystical Card on page 856.

TAURUS

From April 20, 17:02 through May 21, 16:33

The Frugal Builder

You were born into a world that was reeling from the emotional and financial shocks of World War II. Shortages of housing were prompting builders to experiment with new types of homes, aimed at making ownership more affordable and more available to a larger number of families. The "ranch-style" home—a sprawling one-story house—gained popularity in America, while slender two- and three-story domiciles were thrown up in Great Britain and Europe, where land was at a premium.

The astrological indicators of your birth time also pointed to frugality, 1946 Taurus—but to the need for solid foundations, as well. A host of planets were on hand in your own grounded sign, as well as in home-oriented Cancer. These energies are the astrological recipe for establishing deep emotional roots—regardless of how difficult the groundbreaking might be. You probably wouldn't forget the value of your immediate family—and you'd never let pride interfere with accepting or extending an apology when one is warranted.

As a result of these influences, you were probably raised in an environment that reinforced the values of budgeting, saving for the future, and meting out resources carefully—all of which your practical sign is innately skilled in. However, your love of comfort would allow you to turn the humblest dwelling into a cozy nest, and you'd probably find a way to put something aside for the little luxuries you love.

In love, you'll look for someone as practical and solid as you are, which is no easy task. Cautious Capricorns and stable Virgos, both earth signs like yourself, are famous for their skill as meticulous planners. Balance-oriented Librans and home-loving Cancerians could also fit the bill. In friendships, upbeat, cheerful Sagittarians will always help to keep your spirits high and your attitude positive.

Your challenges are to build steadily throughout life, to constantly add on to what you've already got, and to release the fear that what you value will be taken from you. Your gift is your ability to make the best of what you have—no matter how much or how little it may seem to be.

GEMINI

From May 21, 16:34 through June 22, 0:43

The Benevolent Uniter

You arrived at a moment in history that was remarkable for the unity of purpose it exhibited, Gemini of 1946. In the United States, the Supreme Court had just ruled that racial segregation on buses was unconstitutional, a move aimed at uniting citizens who had been at odds over the race issue since the Civil War. At the same time, in Europe, the Jews who had escaped Hitler's murderous reach were working hard to restore some semblance of normalcy to their lives and to reintegrate themselves into postwar society—despite the indignities and horrors they had suffered.

Meanwhile, the skies above you were full of planets in fire and air signs, classically known for their dislike of grudges, animosity, and resentment. These influences probably inspired you to become the type of person who finds it easy to let go of the past, preferring instead to focus your energy on what lies ahead.

You probably grew up in an early environment marked by solid, family-oriented values—including, most especially, the great virtue of forgiveness. Your family may have taught you to respect everyone you crossed paths with, regardless of what had recently been seen as "differences." As a result, your tendency to let go of anger was probably reinforced by these early days, as were your innate flexibility, adaptability, and acceptance. Your natural curiosity may have been encouraged, too, as your parents might have tried to explain what the world had recently been through in terms your young mind could understand.

In love relationships, your quest for a mate may have instinctively led you to be attracted to peace-loving Librans, benevolent Sagittarians, and perhaps other Geminis, whose equally clever minds and thirst for answers are likely to hold your interest over the long term. In friendships, you may find yourself attracted to the company of open-minded Aquarians and Cancerians, whose belief in the power of forgiveness will allow the softer side of your cerebral personality to emerge.

Your challenge is to inspire others to be as open-minded and forgiving as you are. Your gift is your ability to make everyone feel comfortable in your presence.

► Read about your Chinese Astrological sign on page 838. ► Read about your Personal Planets on page 826. ► Read about your personal Mystical Card on page 856.

1946

TAURUS
Your Personal Planets

YOUR LOVE POTENTIAL
Venus in Taurus, Apr. 20, 17:02 - Apr. 29, 10:58
Venus in Gemini, Apr. 29, 10:59 - May 21, 16:33

YOUR DRIVE AND AMBITION
Mars in Cancer, Apr. 20, 17:02 - Apr. 22, 19:30
Mars in Leo, Apr. 22, 19:31 - May 21, 16:33

YOUR LUCK MAGNETISM
Jupiter in Libra, Apr. 20, 17:02 - May 21, 16:33

World Events

May 11 - The first Cooperation for American Remittances to Europe (CARE) packages reach Le Havre in France.

May 18 - U.S. baseball star Reggie Jackson is born.

Singer Barry Manilow is born under the sign of Gemini

GEMINI
Your Personal Planets

YOUR LOVE POTENTIAL
Venus in Gemini, May 21, 16:34 - May 24, 3:38
Venus in Cancer, May 24, 3:39 - June 18, 4:59
Venus in Leo, June 18, 5:00 - June 22, 0:43

YOUR DRIVE AND AMBITION
Mars in Leo, May 21, 16:34 - June 20, 8:30
Mars in Virgo, June 20, 8:31 - June 22, 0:43

YOUR LUCK MAGNETISM
Jupiter in Libra, May 21, 16:34 - June 22, 0:43

World Events

June 10 - Italy overthrows its monarchy and established itself as a republic.

June 17 - American singer and pianist Barry Manilow is born.

CANCER
Your Personal Planets

YOUR LOVE POTENTIAL
Venus in Leo, June 22, 0:44 - July 13, 19:21
Venus in Virgo, July 13, 19:22 - July 23, 11:36

YOUR DRIVE AND AMBITION
Mars in Virgo, June 22, 0:44 - July 23, 11:36

YOUR LUCK MAGNETISM
Jupiter in Libra, June 22, 0:44 - July 23, 11:36

World Events

July 1 – The U.S. detonates an atomic bomb near the Bikini atoll in the Marshall Islands.

July 13 – American photographer Alfred Stieglitz dies.

The U.S. detonates an atomic bomb near Bikini Atoll

LEO
Your Personal Planets

YOUR LOVE POTENTIAL
Venus in Virgo, July 23, 11:37 - Aug. 09, 8:33
Venus in Libra, Aug. 09, 8:34 - Aug. 23, 18:25

YOUR DRIVE AND AMBITION
Mars in Virgo, July 23, 11:37 - Aug. 09, 13:16
Mars in Libra, Aug. 09, 13:17 - Aug. 23, 18:25

YOUR LUCK MAGNETISM
Jupiter in Libra, July 23, 11:37 - Aug. 23, 18:25

World Events

Aug. 1 – The Atomic Energy Commission is established.

Aug. 19 – William (Bill) Jefferson Clinton is born.

CANCER
From June 22, 0:44 through July 23, 11:36

The Detached Caregiver

Cancer of 1946, you were born during a time made famous for retribution—characteristics that your ordinarily compassionate sign is never fond of. Throughout July, the U.S. presided over the trial of SS officers for war crimes in Nuremberg. For many of these Nazi prisoners, the punishment for the atrocities they had ordered and committed would be a heavy one: death. The heavens perfectly reflected this difficult period in time, as well as the emotionally wrenching events that occurred. Your own sign was strongly represented—but so were fiery Leo and fairness-seeking Libra. Although every sign is quite capable of compassion and understanding, these two are firm believers in justice—especially on behalf of helpless victims.

Being raised during this time of retribution may have had a lifelong influence on you, in that you may have learned to pull back your tender heart in order to keep your objectivity intact. As a result, those closest to you know that they can trust you to be fair, neutral-minded, and impartial in all situations—no matter what your personal feelings and opinions might be.

Your innate capacity to love, sympathize, and unconditionally accept things, combined with the ability to keep your wits about you, may have led you to work in the helping professions, where you might be put in charge of emergency care. All those in your charge would know that your decisions are based on the facts as you see them, never on favoritism. In your leisure time, you could put your talents to work as a scoutmaster or coach of children's sports.

In love, it's likely that you'll seek out the stability and comfort of your fellow water signs—focused Scorpio and romantic, sensitive Pisces. But the practical-minded earth signs—Taurus, Virgo, and Capricorn—could also prove worthy of your tender heart and long-lasting affection. In friendships, look to Geminis, Leos, and Librans, who'll entertain and amuse you, and keep your mood upbeat.

Your challenge is to remain emotionally detached when situations call for it. Your gift is your unswerving devotion to those you love and trust.

LEO
From July 23, 11:37 through August 23, 18:25

The Cautious Protector

Around the time you were born, 1946 Leo, the U.S. Atomic Energy Commission was created—a monumental organization that would end up affecting not only the United States, but also its allies. This mighty step toward regulating and controlling the development of nuclear power may have restored your parents' hope that, somehow, the world would be a safe place to raise you after all. Therefore, your early years may have been infused with a sense of security, despite the fact that the atomic bomb had been perfected, and was in fact ready to be used.

The astrological energies above you were equally potent—and equally full of caution. Several planets in determined earth and sensitive water signs would have provided you with an innate understanding of how important it is to keep safety and security in mind at all times—especially with regard to your loved ones.

As such, you may be quite concerned with planning for the future, and installing "safety-nets" in your life—emotionally, financially, and professionally. You'd probably never leave a job until you have a new one to go to, and you'd always encourage those closest to you to have a plan in mind before they make changes. This conservative side of your personality stands in drastic contrast to your sign's famous love of taking action quickly, but throughout life you may have found that it's wise to listen to your inner voice of caution. As a result, you'll probably never find yourself without options—and your dear ones will learn the value of planning for the future.

In love relationships, you'll be on the lookout for those who share your caution and discretion, so earthy Virgos, Capricorns, and Taureans will probably appeal to you. In friendships, the fire and passion of Ariens and Sagittarians—the other fire-signs—will inspire you to let the more impulsive side of you emerge and help you find a happy medium between vigilance and spontaneity.

Your challenge is to find that happy medium—to know when to wait, and when to take action immediately. Your gift is the ability to inspire others to protect themselves and their dear ones.

➤ Read about your Chinese Astrological sign on page 838. ➤ Read about your Personal Planets on page 826. ➤ Read about your personal Mystical Card on page 856.

VIRGO

From August 23, 18:26 through September 23, 15:40

The Methodical Peacemaker

Born in 1946, Virgo, you arrived into a world that was fervently trying to restore peace, order, and camaraderie. In fact, around the time you were born, the British Prime Minister called for a "United States of Europe." Although that vision wasn't to be realized immediately, the citizens of the free world did become more focused on unity—regardless of racial, philosophic, or religious differences. As a result, your parents may have placed great importance on the virtues of peace and reconciliation, and they are likely to have taught you to use your intellect to bring about these ends.

The astrological energies in effect at the time you were born were equally dedicated to peace. A host of planets in peace-loving Libra added a knack for restoring balance to your already helpful nature, making you an expert negotiator, moderator, and judge. You may find yourself drawn to professions that require you to use these qualities—as a labor negotiator or a children's advocate, for example—where you may become known as the person to talk to when an honest and unbiased viewpoint is needed.

It's likely that you'll always enjoy the blessings of self-confidence, self-respect, and the strength of character that holding tight to your convictions bestows. Your hobbies, too, may be activities that you share with others, where your ability to foster harmony and agreement could be useful, rather than solitary pursuits—conducting a community orchestra rather than birdwatching.

In love relationships, you may seek someone who's as honest as you are. As such, Aquarians, Librans, and Sagittarians will probably appeal to you, since these three signs have always been famous for their open-mindedness, fairness, and gift for cooperation. In friendships and business situations, you'll probably find that earthy Capricorns, Taureans, and other Virgos will provide you with the stability you need, even as they help you to further your personal goals.

Your challenge is to accept others, no matter how "imperfect" or self-involved they seem to be. Your gift is the ability to bring out the best in everyone.

LIBRA

From September 23, 15:41 through October 24, 0:34

The Even-Handed Judge

Although Libra is known for its mercy and tolerance, your natural inclination toward bringing about balance and fairness may have been reinforced by the cosmic influences in effect when you were born, 1946 Libra. In addition to three planets in your own principled sign, the skies hosted several in intense Scorpio—famous for its belief in retribution and in enforcing a punishment suitable to the crime. It may not be surprising to learn that, around the time you were born, ten Nazi leaders were hanged as war criminals in Nuremberg as a result of the part they played in the murder of thousands of innocent Jews in World War II.

When you were growing up, it's likely that your parents impressed upon you the necessity of accepting the consequences of one's actions. Your ordinarily peaceful nature was probably tempered by an even stronger need for justice—especially when an innocent, helpless, or underprivileged individual has been harmed.

You may choose to work with people or animals that have been preyed upon or unfairly treated by others in some way, and be a dedicated guardian of their rights. Whether you pursue this as a career or simply find yourself drawn to these types of circumstances on a personal basis, you'd be a persuasive ally, ready to spring to the defense of anyone or anything who's being unfairly handled. You may have joined groups that speak for preserving endangered species or against polluting the air or water.

In love relationships, this probably created a need for you to be involved with those who'll give you the respect and candor you value. As such, Sagittarians, famously honest and as fair-minded as your own sign, will probably appeal to you, as will other Librans, stolid Capricorns, and perhaps thoughtful Virgos. In friendships and business relationships, look to Geminis and Aquarians. They'll encourage you to stay true to yourself and find a partner who's perfect for you.

Your challenge is to put your feelings aside and dispense appropriate justice in all situations, no matter how difficult you find it. Your gift is your ability to forgive and forget.

► Read about your Chinese Astrological sign on page 838. ► Read about your Personal Planets on page 826. ► Read about your personal Mystical Card on page 856.

VIRGO
Your Personal Planets

YOUR LOVE POTENTIAL
Venus in Libra, Aug. 23, 18:26 - Sept. 07, 0:15
Venus in Scorpio, Sept. 07, 0:16 - Sept. 23, 15:40

YOUR DRIVE AND AMBITION
Mars in Libra, Aug. 23, 18:26 - Sept. 23, 15:40

YOUR LUCK MAGNETISM
Jupiter in Libra, Aug. 23, 18:26 - Sept. 23, 15:40

World Events

Aug. 29 – Afghanistan, Iceland, and Sweden become members of the United Nations.

Sept. 13 – The promise of wage increases brings the strike in Italy to an end.

George Orwell's "Animal Farm" is published

LIBRA
Your Personal Planets

YOUR LOVE POTENTIAL
Venus in Scorpio, Sept. 23, 15:41 - Oct. 16, 10:44
Venus in Sagittarius, Oct. 16, 10:45 - Oct. 24, 0:34

YOUR DRIVE AND AMBITION
Mars in Libra, Sept. 23, 15:41 - Sept. 24, 16:34
Mars in Scorpio, Sept. 24, 16:35 - Oct. 24, 0:34

YOUR LUCK MAGNETISM
Jupiter in Libra, Sept. 23, 15:41 - Sept. 25, 10:18
Jupiter in Scorpio, Sept. 25, 10:19 - Oct. 24, 0:34

World Events

Oct. 9 – The first electric blanket is manufactured; it sells for $39.50.

Oct. 9 – Eugene O'Neill's *The Iceman Cometh* premières at the Martin Beck Theater in New York.

1946

SCORPIO
Your Personal Planets

YOUR LOVE POTENTIAL
Venus in Sagittarius, Oct. 24, 0:35 - Nov. 08, 8:55
Venus in Scorpio, Nov. 08, 8:56 - Nov. 22, 21:45

YOUR DRIVE AND AMBITION
Mars in Scorpio, Oct. 24, 0:35 - Nov. 06, 18:21
Mars in Sagittarius, Nov. 06, 18:22 - Nov. 22, 21:45

YOUR LUCK MAGNETISM
Jupiter in Scorpio, Oct. 24, 0:35 - Nov. 22, 21:45

World Events

Nov. 5 – John F. Kennedy is elected to the House of Representatives.

Nov. 13 – The first artificial snow is produced from a natural cloud at Mt. Greylock in Massachusetts.

A UNICEF car on a field inspection

SAGITTARIUS
Your Personal Planets

YOUR LOVE POTENTIAL
Venus in Scorpio, Nov. 22, 21:46 - Dec. 22, 10:52

YOUR DRIVE AND AMBITION
Mars in Sagittarius, Nov. 22, 21:46 - Dec. 17, 10:55
Mars in Capricorn, Dec. 17, 10:56 - Dec. 22, 10:52

YOUR LUCK MAGNETISM
Jupiter in Scorpio, Nov. 22, 21:46 - Dec. 22, 10:52

World Events

Dec. 11 – The United Nations International Children's Emergency Fund (UNICEF) is established.

Dec. 21 – Frank Capra's *It's A Wonderful Life* premières.

SCORPIO
From October 24, 0:35 through November 22, 21:45

The Protective Administrator

Born in 1946, Scorpio, you arrived at a moment that found the world's Superpowers in the midst of pursuing what may have looked like contradictory goals: restoring peace, yet endeavoring to perfect weapons of mass destruction. The month after you were born, the Nobel Peace Prize was awarded to Americans John Raleigh Mott and Emily Greene Balch—two leaders who had worked tirelessly with a score of international churches to bring relief and restore basic human rights to those who had been unfairly imprisoned during World War II.

At the same time, German rocket engineers began work in the USSR, aiding that nation in its goal of arming and defending itself against future military attacks. Again, although these events may seem contradictory, they had a common denominator: to make sure that those who needed protection received it.

Meanwhile, in the heavens, several planets in your own intense, committed sign may have provided you with the ability to sense when danger is near and take steps to safeguard yourself and those you love against it. A host of planets were also on duty in Sagittarius, the sign that's famous for its open-mindedness and ability to see "the big picture." As a result, your sign's tendency to focus its considerable energies on only one project at a time was probably broadened, allowing you to develop both insight and perspective—and making you an expert administrator and organizer.

In love, it's likely that you won't settle for anyone who isn't as precise, methodical, and broad-minded as you are—quite an assembly of virtues for one personality to possess. If you direct your attention toward those born under Sagittarius, Aquarius, and Scorpio, however, you may find what you're after. In friendships and business relationships, you could find the business acuity of Taureans and the precision of Virgos most helpful and supportive.

Your challenge is to learn to balance your gift for details with your ability to see the greater whole—basically, to see both the forest and the trees. Your gift is the capacity for bringing order and structure to every situation.

SAGITTARIUS
From November 22, 21:46 through December 22, 10:52

The Focused Achiever

Born during 1946, you, Sagittarius, may have been given a special talent: to combine your sign's famous broad-mindedness with the ability to set boundaries. The events of the day perfectly mirrored this gift. In mid-December, the UN General Assembly voted to locate its permanent headquarters in New York City, a place that's world famous for its diverse ethnic and social population.

The astrological energies in effect at this time included several planets in your own sign, long known for its ability to embrace a variety of cultures, philosophies, and concepts. But an equal number of planets in shrewd, perceptive Scorpio also added depth, a talent for analysis, and unwavering concentration to the mix. As a result, your sign's tendency to occasionally scatter its energies may have been tempered by an intense desire to scrutinize, consider details, probe into the real meaning of things—a welcome addition, especially in situations where you may be emotionally involved in the outcome.

Your symbol, the Archer, shows your need to aim your energies toward a goal, but your innate curiosity and restlessness often means you become distracted along the way. Adding this substantial heap of Scorpio to your birth time's astrological influences, however, means you'll be able to focus, work hard, and complete everything you start.

In love relationships, you'll probably find yourself in the company of other Sagittarians, but Scorpios and Leos will also fascinate you—and fulfill your innate need for a partner who's involved in every corner of your life, even as they encourage you to maintain your independence. Your friends will most likely be Aquarians, Geminis, and Ariens, whose spontaneity and cheerfulness will provide a welcome distraction from the complete and total focus you'll exhibit on every project you pursue.

Your challenge is to take a break from work when you need it. This allows you to keep your mind active and your curiosity whetted. Your gift is a knack for surrounding yourself with interesting, intelligent acquaintances who'll continually educate, amuse, and inspire you.

➤ Read about your Chinese Astrological sign on page 838. ➤ Read about your Personal Planets on page 826. ➤ Read about your personal Mystical Card on page 856.

CAPRICORN

From December 22, 10:53 through December 31, 23:59

The Confirmed Believer

As a Capricorn born during December of 1946, you arrived as the world was still in recovery from World War II, both financially and emotionally, but the prospects for success in both categories were high. The optimism and release from fear that citizens of every country would have felt around the time of your birth probably influenced your early environment, causing your parents to be optimistic—and to pass that optimism on to you. As a result, you no doubt developed the ability to recover quickly from negative or unpleasant events.

In the heavens, as on Earth, faith and hope were also prevalent when you made your entrance, Capricorn. Several planets in optimistic Sagittarius and fiery Leo brought a sense of expectation to your personality, perfectly balancing your sign's usual caution with a sense of adventure—all based on an unshakeable faith in the future.

Your ability to find the silver lining behind every storm-cloud, even as you maintain your sign's famous realism and practicality, could make you a gifted advisor, and it's likely that others will recognize this talent, thinking of you first when they need advice, counsel, or an objective opinion. You're probably not known for sugarcoating your ideas, either, so your dear ones know that they will always get an honest answer when they turn to you. You may be drawn to careers that allow you to use your knack for straightforward communicating. It's possible that inspirational speaking, professional consulting, and business management could all appeal to you.

In love relationships, you'll probably seek out others who have a similar knack for combining faith with discretion, such as Pisceans, Aquarians, and Librans. In friendships, you may find that other Capricorns, Virgos, and Taureans will be your unswerving allies.

Your greatest challenge is to learn when to be silent and allow others to learn certain lessons for themselves, without continuously feeling the need to manage the outcome for them. Your greatest gift is the capacity to combine sound advice with positive encouragement and solid emotional support.

1946
CAPRICORN
Your Personal Planets

YOUR LOVE POTENTIAL
Venus in Scorpio, Dec. 22, 10:53 - Dec. 31, 23:59

YOUR DRIVE AND AMBITION
Mars in Capricorn, Dec. 22, 10:53 - Dec. 31, 23:59

YOUR LUCK MAGNETISM
Jupiter in Scorpio, Dec. 22, 10:53 - Dec. 31, 23:59

World Events

Dec. 25 – American comedian W. C. Fields dies.

Dec. 31 – U.S. President Harry S. Truman formally ends World War II.

Special Feature
The Mysterious Bermuda Triangle
by Sophia Mason

The five U.S. *Avenger* torpedo bombers of Flight 19, with twenty-seven crew members on board, took off from Fort Lauderdale, Florida, at 14:10 hours on December 5, 1945. This was a training flight, with a route that took the aircraft on a triangular course over the Atlantic Ocean before returning to base. However, Flight 19 turned out to be something quite extraordinary and very sinister.

At around 15:00 hours on that winter afternoon, the flight commander, Lieutenant Charles Taylor, reported that his compass wasn't working properly. Before long, all contact with Taylor had been was lost. It grew dark. The *Avengers* were running low on fuel. The weather was getting rough. Communications between Flight 19 and Fort Lauderdale grew weaker and weaker and after 19:04 hours, they ceased. Three aircraft were sent out to find the *Avengers*, but despite a diligent search, there was no sign of them—neither then nor since. Flight 19 had vanished and its crew along with it.

This tragedy occurred in an area of the Atlantic Ocean known today as the Bermuda Triangle. Its other, more graphic, names are the Triangle of Death and the Hoodoo Sea. Covering roughly 500,000 square miles, it extends over a triangular expanse of water between Bermuda, Florida, and Puerto Rico. It has a long history of strange happenings, inexplicable sights, and unaccountable disappearances.

The toll of casualties has been considerable. Between 1947 and 1972 alone, thirteen aircraft have disappeared, along with four freighters, one of them a vessel of 20,000 tons: all vanished without trace. An area similar to the Triangle exists off the east coast of Japan—the Devil's Sea, where fishermen have reported disappearances of the same type.

The concept of the Bermuda Triangle is fairly recent. It received its name in 1964 from Vincent Gaddis in his article in "Argosy: A Magazine of Masterpiece Fiction." Ten years later, the story was popularized by Charles Berlitz in his book *The Bermuda Triangle*. These publications,

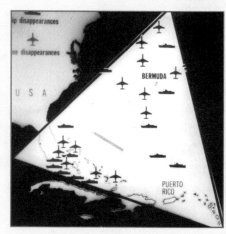

The Bermuda Triangle

together with a mass of books, dozens of articles, and a number of television programs and Internet websites, have spawned scores of theories, some of which are considered distinctly far-fetched. One theory of this kind blames the disappearances on giant sea creatures, such as a mammoth octopus. Another explanation has been abduction by aliens, and a similar one has it that the ships and aircraft somehow got caught up in vortices that warped them to other places and times.

(Continued on page 393)

➤ Read more about aliens in "The Extraterrestrial Highway" on page 465.

1947

Saturn and Pluto in Leo

The planet Saturn, ruler of responsibility and order, has a very special relationship with the planet Pluto, ruler of the Underworld. Whenever these two cross each other's paths in the sky and form the angles known in astrology as "aspects," there are deep implications for life on Earth. Astrologers often use the expression "as above, so below". This is a simple way of saying that when the planets dance together, people experience events in their personal and collective lives that carry great weight. Of particular importance is the relationship between Saturn and Pluto. In the twentieth century, almost every time there has been an aspect between these two large and looming outer planets, there has been a heavy-duty consequence, usually related to war. The reason for this is that Saturn contracts and Pluto explodes. Saturn prepares maps and goals with exacting accuracy and Pluto bulldozes over them and rips the heart from any matter at hand.

In 1947, Saturn met Pluto directly, as they both occupied the self-aggrandizing sign of Leo, giving extra power to the mighty strength of these two planets. Leo can be self-defensive and egoistic; loss of face is sometimes its biggest fear. In 1947 the Cold War was just beginning. Winston Churchill had given his "Iron Curtain" speech just the year before and the arms race was taking off with all due speed. The Truman Doctrine proposed containment of the communist threat. The Soviet Union rejected a U.S. plan for United Nations atomic-energy control. The race of the Superpowers was on and all dukes were at the ready.

British troops screening residents of Jerusalem in preparation for "Operation Eviction"

Hindu-Muslim violence before India and Pakistan are granted independence

The Duke of Edinburgh and Princess Elizabeth leave Westminster Abbey after their wedding

THE BODY OF CHRIST

After a vision, Italian monk Padre Pio began bleeding from his hands, feet, and side, replicating the wounds of Christ. In agony for years, he believed his stigmata strengthened him to "fend off the devil." Many doubted his sincerity and he was banned from saying Mass. But in 1947, the Pope visited Pio and accepted him back into the Church with the name "The Venerable." When a hospitalized woman recovered after praying for Padre Pio's help, the Vatican saw it as extraordinary evidence of his authenticity.

RED THREAT RISING

Treaties took territory from Germany's wartime allies. The U.S. and Russia were divided over terms for Germany. In Palestine, the British experienced difficulties due to growing strife between Jews and Arabs. These difficulties were typified by the British refusal to allow 4,500 Jewish refugees aboard the *Exodus* from Europe to enter Palestine. Britain finally handed back its mandate in Palestine to the United Nations, which voted for a Jewish state (Israel) and an Arab state. The independence of India and Pakistan in August was marked by horrific Hindu-Muslim violence. In the U.S., the GI Bill sent more than one million war veterans to college. The House Committee on Un-American Activities scrutinized Hollywood artists as fears of Communism rose: seventy-nine were declared subversive and ten who refused to testify were blacklisted. In London, the future Queen Elizabeth married Philip Mountbatten. Carbon-14, effective in dating archaeological remains, was discovered. In Paris, Christian Dior's New Look took the fashion world by storm. Jackie Robinson became the first African American to play in U.S. major-league baseball.

➤ Read "The Mysterious Bermuda Triangle" by Sophia Mason on page 385.

CAPRICORN

From January 01, 0:00 through January 20, 21:31

The Strong-Willed Commander

Your high energy level must have confused your parents, who, if they were expecting a typical Capricorn, were probably better prepared for an even-tempered child with a penchant for order and serenity. What they didn't realize was that, as a Capricorn born in January of 1947, you would have an almost Arien iron will and an unusual drive to excel. The world you arrived in seemed to be hanging in the balance between peace and all-out destruction, with Mahatma Gandhi starting a non-violent march in East Bengali and the Soviets implying that the USSR had developed its own version of the atom bomb.

In much the same way, you may struggle to maintain peace in your own life by balancing your intense energy with even-tempered common sense. Although you can be kind and patient with those who are doing their best, you can become testy when you detect mediocrity. Your standards may be exceptionally high, and it would be surprising to find that you have not achieved much in your life.

Your forceful personality probably makes you an excellent executive. You are fair, but it's likely that you would insist that your charges forfeit their own selfish interests for the good of the organization. Even if you never become a CEO, you may need to run something, so joining a club and volunteering to serve on its board of directors could be a good thing for you to do in your spare time. Your "big-picture" outlook would steer any organization to a secure and productive future.

Your friends must also meet your standards of excellence, and you probably like to play active sports with at least some of them. Ariens and Sagittarians make good team-mates, and it's likely that you keep an Aquarian or two around to share your thoughts with. In romance, you may be attracted to intense Scorpios and, of course, other Capricorns. However, you and a Cancer— astrological opposites—could combine to create a cozy home together.

Your challenge is to accept that not everyone has the same priorities that you do. Your gift is your global view and your love for humankind. With this, you bring out the best in people.

AQUARIUS

From January 20, 21:32 through February 19, 11:51

The Determined Idealist

Once you get an idea, Aquarius of 1947, you stick to it, which is probably why you remain faithful to your youthful ideals. You may follow a doctrine of right and wrong that is exceptionally idealistic, as the events of your birth year reflect. In 1947 people of color were making the news by taking jobs from which they had previously been barred. In the U.S., the first black reporter entered the Congressional press gallery within a few weeks of your birth. Also this year, Arabs and Jews continued the debate over whether—and how—to split Palestine.

From a young age, you seemed determined to carry out this same desire for fairness. Once you make a decision that something is the right thing to do, you embark upon a campaign to ensure that it gets done, and it's likely that you have met with much success over the years as a result of sheer determination.

You may have a strong affinity for working in committees and groups, and you can be an enthusiastic team player. You could work on a design team, in a personnel office, or even perform as part of an orchestra. The way you see it, we are all the same, and everyone deserves a chance to do his or her best work—as long as it contributes to the benefit of the group.

Your huge heart and wide-open mind easily earn you an abundance of friends, and you enjoy the time you spend with them. You might like to sit and talk with a Gemini, or you may get into intellectual sparring matches with a Sagittarius. Your considerable physical energy indicates an interest in team sports, and you probably love to compete with Leos and Scorpios. If you don't play sports, you might cheer from the sidelines—for the underdog, of course! In love, it's likely that you're attracted to Scorpios' supportive presence and the pioneering spirit of Ariens. Although you admire them, you might find that Leos are too demanding over the long haul.

Your challenge is to be patient with the fact that change comes slowly over time. Your gift is your ability to embrace everyone you meet and identify the talents they have—probably even before they notice they have them.

► Read about your Chinese Astrological sign on page 838. ► Read about your Personal Planets on page 826. ► Read about your personal Mystical Card on page 856.

CAPRICORN
Your Personal Planets

YOUR LOVE POTENTIAL
Venus in Scorpio, Jan. 01, 0:00 - Jan. 05, 16:44
Venus in Sagittarius, Jan. 05, 16:45 - Jan. 20, 21:31

YOUR DRIVE AND AMBITION
Mars in Capricorn, Jan. 01, 0:00 - Jan. 20, 21:31

YOUR LUCK MAGNETISM
Jupiter in Scorpio, Jan. 01, 0:00 - Jan. 20, 21:31

World Events

Jan. 2 - Mahatma Gandhi begins a march for peace in East Bengali.

Jan. 5 - Coal mines are the latest industry to undergo nationalization in Britain.

Mahatma Gandhi

AQUARIUS
Your Personal Planets

YOUR LOVE POTENTIAL
Venus in Sagittarius, Jan. 20, 21:32 - Feb. 06, 5:40
Venus in Capricorn, Feb. 06, 5:41 - Feb. 19, 11:51

YOUR DRIVE AND AMBITION
Mars in Capricorn, Jan. 20, 21:32 - Jan. 25, 11:43
Mars in Aquarius, Jan. 25, 11:44 - Feb. 19, 11:51

YOUR LUCK MAGNETISM
Jupiter in Scorpio, Jan. 20, 21:32 - Feb. 19, 11:51

World Events

Jan. 29 - Arthur Miller's *All My Sons* premieres in New York.

Jan. 25 - American gangster Al Capone dies.

1947

PISCES
Your Personal Planets

YOUR LOVE POTENTIAL
Venus in Capricorn, Feb. 19, 11:52 - Mar. 05, 5:08
Venus in Aquarius, Mar. 05, 5:09 - Mar. 21, 11:12

YOUR DRIVE AND AMBITION
Mars in Aquarius, Feb. 19, 11:52 - Mar. 04, 16:45
Mars in Pisces, Mar. 04, 16:46 - Mar. 21, 11:12

YOUR LUCK MAGNETISM
Jupiter in Scorpio, Feb. 19, 11:52 - Mar. 21, 11:12

World Events

Feb. 21 – The first instant camera is demonstrated by E. H. Land in New York City.

Mar. 13 – At the nineteenth Academy Awards *The Best Years Of Our Lives*, Olivia de Havilland, and Frederic March win Oscars.

Olivia de Havilland, Oscar winner

ARIES
Your Personal Planets

YOUR LOVE POTENTIAL
Venus in Aquarius, Mar. 21, 11:13 - Mar. 30, 22:13
Venus in Pisces, Mar. 30, 22:14 - Apr. 20, 22:38

YOUR DRIVE AND AMBITION
Mars in Pisces, Mar. 21, 11:13 - Apr. 11, 23:02
Mars in Aries, Apr. 11, 23:03 - Apr. 20, 22:38

YOUR LUCK MAGNETISM
Jupiter in Scorpio, Mar. 21, 11:13 - Apr. 20, 22:38

World Events

Apr. 7 - American automobile pioneer Henry Ford dies.

Apr. 10 - Selected for the Dodgers, Jackie Robinson becomes the first African American in major-league baseball.

PISCES
From February 19, 11:52 through March 21, 11:12

The Master Craftsman

The world remembers your birth year as an exciting one, 1947 Pisces, because so many new things came along at almost exactly the same time as you did. In this one month, the Truman Doctrine was put into action, launching America's fight against Communism, and E. H. Land fascinated the world with his first demonstration of the instant-developing camera—which would become famous as the "Polaroid."

Like Land, you might be focused on the things you can invent or make that will be of use to the world. An exceptional talent for making things with your hands might accompany this power of invention you have. If you don't feel that you're gifted this way, then maybe you collect things that others have made by hand. To you, the unique human touch that identifies items that are not mass-produced is worth the premium in price.

With talents like these, there are many things that you could do for a living. You might be part of a research and development team, or you could be involved in producing images through movies, photography, or the graphic arts. You have a very strong sense of duty, and since you want the things that you create to be useful, you spend a lot of time trying to find practical applications for your ideas. You can become obsessive about work, so you may want to set a timer when you go into the office or the studio, just in case you get lost in your work and forget to come out before bedtime!

Relaxing with friends is the best way for you to recharge your batteries. You like to socialize with Cancerians and Capricorns, maybe because they share your love of life's basics. You might take a cooking class together, or enjoy sumptuous meals in restaurants where you can all talk. In love, you may feel passionate about Scorpios, as they lift your spirits and stimulate your curiosity. Gemini is an interesting match too, but only if you don't mind spending some time alone.

Your challenge is to maintain your personal ties no matter how wrapped up in your work you get. Your gift is the ability to appreciate fine craftsmanship, and see it as an expression of human ingenuity.

ARIES
From March 21, 11:13 through April 20, 22:38

The Gentle Powerhouse

As an Aries born in 1947, it's likely that your rush toward progress is slowed somewhat by the deep compassion you feel toward your fellow human beings. The events that took place during the year of your birth—such as John D. Rockefeller's donation of land in New York City to house the United Nations organization—exemplified the idea of sharing. With such magnanimous gestures providing the background for your arrival, it's probably no surprise that you find it nearly impossible to step on anyone's toes, no matter how much such delicacy of feeling might deter you from keeping to your schedule.

Your ideas may come to you in flashes of inspiration, and at times it could be hard for even you to understand where they come from. You could also have dreams that help you work out problems, or that give you insight into how you can improve your relationships. Since you're so full of ideas, you might find a gratifying career in advertising, PR, or magazine production. You would make a good leader, and your desire to help people could be good for a job in a non-profit organization or in the helping institutions like hospitals. It's likely that you'll want your co-workers to be the ones who are meticulous and highly organized—freeing you up to initiate new projects.

You take your leisure time very seriously, and it's possible that you spend a lot of time with children, even if they are not your own. You also like parties, and your Leo friends may invite you to plenty of them. They know they can always count on you to liven things up and share some entertaining stories drawn from your own experiences. You may like Geminis, too, and you'll also have a lot in common with Pisceans.

In romance, you may be most comfortable with Pisces and Libra—but you could also find yourself falling for an intense, compelling Scorpio, who can be sensitive, passionate, and irresistibly attractive to you.

Your challenge is to slow down your pace so that you can accomplish one thing before you start something new. Your gift is the ability to generate excitement over big projects that help people in need.

➤ Read about your Chinese Astrological sign on page 838. ➤ Read about your Personal Planets on page 826. ➤ Read about your personal Mystical Card on page 856.

TAURUS

From April 20, 22:39 through May 21, 22:08

The Practical Pioneer

As a Taurus, you are likely to be a person of action, and being born in 1947 only added to your innate desire to get results. Several practical inventions were introduced during the year you were born, and the technical innovations of that time—things like the transistor and the use of radar for aircraft—created a host of new possibilities that you still benefit from. While you were growing up, it may have seemed that the world provided a growing selection of opportunities for an ambitious, action-oriented person like yourself.

Although you never waver from the pragmatic doctrine you subscribe to, you probably think in a much more aggressive manner than the stereotype of your sign suggests. You can usually carry a large workload, perhaps toiling behind the scenes to realize your ideas and put them to work for the good of all. If you do step on stage, prosecuting the bad guys or defending the innocent as an attorney might be the way you put your ideas to work. You have that uncanny ability to think "outside the box," finding new uses for things that have been around for centuries. You can also be forward thinking, and may always be on the lookout for the next profitable trend. These talents could make you an excellent scientist, information technology specialist, or industrial designer.

Even when it's time to relax, you probably look for action. It's likely that you need to work off your energy physically, and you may enjoy walking through the scenic countryside, or even on a treadmill—provided you're supplied with a good book.

In friendships, it's likely that you'll enjoy a few hours of intellectual sparring with an Aries friend every now and then. Sagittarians may also be interesting to you, as you'd like trying to keep up with their mental as well as their international travels. In romance, you may be attracted to Ariens and Scorpios, but you could also enjoy a stable life with another Taurus, a Cancer, or a Pisces.

Your challenge is to put your rapid-fire mental processes to good use. Your gift is your ability to be of service to a cause that's larger than you are.

GEMINI

From May 21, 22:09 through June 22, 6:18

The Global Utopian

You were born into a world that was focused on maintaining peace, Gemini of 1947. The environment in which you grew up was one that encouraged awareness of the different countries and cultures of the world, so it should be no surprise that your mind darts in many different directions. In school, there would have been many new political realities for you to learn about. During the month you were born, the Marshall Plan was drafted, and the monumental task of rebuilding war-scarred Europe began. In many countries, wartime rationing ended around the time you were born, so your arrival may have seemed especially sweet to your family.

Indeed, your disposition can be sensual and earthy, which is remarkable in a sign that is known for its mental detachment. You also have an aura that draws people to you. While you enjoy collecting information, you probably hope that what you learn can be used to help the cause of bringing the world together.

You may feel that you already have the right balance of imagination and practicality, and you would feel constricted by authority. This may mean that you would do best in a situation that allows you the freedom to act on your own ideas—perhaps working on your own as a writer, artist, or craftsperson. Given the opportunity to lead, you could become a politician, or you might want to run an organization that helps the underprivileged in some way. It is very important to you that you teach others that they need not be constrained by limitations—their own or those that others might try to impose on them.

Your lightning-quick mind and independent streak can make you fast friends with Sagittarians and Aquarians. You might like to talk about taking trips together, or you could create a partnership that provides a framework for your idealistic dreams. In love, Taurus could make a surprisingly good match for you, although Libra holds an attraction that you may find hard to resist.

Your challenge is to keep yourself centered so that you can accomplish one thing at a time. Your gift is your ability to visualize a world that celebrates human diversity.

➤ Read about your Chinese Astrological sign on page 838. ➤ Read about your Personal Planets on page 826. ➤ Read about your personal Mystical Card on page 856.

TAURUS
Your Personal Planets

YOUR LOVE POTENTIAL

Venus in Pisces, Apr. 20, 22:39 - Apr. 25, 3:02
Venus in Aries, Apr. 25, 3:03 - May 20, 2:05
Venus in Taurus, May 20, 2:06 - May 21, 22:08

YOUR DRIVE AND AMBITION

Mars in Aries, Apr. 20, 22:39 - May 21, 3:39
Mars in Taurus, May 21, 3:40 - May 21, 22:08

YOUR LUCK MAGNETISM

Jupiter in Scorpio, Apr. 20, 22:39 - May 21, 22:08

World Events

Apr. 28 – Norwegian Thor Heyerdahl leads the *Kon Tiki* expedition.

May 8 – The House Un-American Activities Committee is convened to track down Communists in Hollywood.

Salman Rushdie is born under the sign of Gemini

GEMINI
Your Personal Planets

YOUR LOVE POTENTIAL

Venus in Taurus, May 21, 22:09 - June 13, 21:34
Venus in Gemini, June 13, 21:35 - June 22, 6:18

YOUR DRIVE AND AMBITION

Mars in Taurus, May 21, 22:09 - June 22, 6:18

YOUR LUCK MAGNETISM

Jupiter in Scorpio, May 21, 22:09 - June 22, 6:18

World Events

June 11 – The All-Indian Congress accepts the British plans for the partition of India.

June 19 – Salmān Rushdie is born.

1947

CANCER
Your Personal Planets

YOUR LOVE POTENTIAL
Venus in Gemini, June 22, 6:19 - July 08, 13:29
Venus in Cancer, July 08, 13:30 - July 23, 17:13

YOUR DRIVE AND AMBITION
Mars in Taurus, June 22, 6:19 - July 01, 3:33
Mars in Gemini, July 01, 3:34 - July 23, 17:13

YOUR LUCK MAGNETISM
Jupiter in Scorpio, June 22, 6:19 - July 23, 17:13

World Events

July 2 – An object crashes near Roswell in New Mexico, giving rise to speculation about alien spacecraft.

July 9 – The engagement of Britain's Princess Elizabeth to Lt. Philip Mountbatten is announced.

Celebrations for India's independence

LEO
Your Personal Planets

YOUR LOVE POTENTIAL
Venus in Cancer, July 23, 17:14 - Aug. 02, 1:05
Venus in Leo, Aug. 02, 1:06 - Aug. 24, 0:08

YOUR DRIVE AND AMBITION
Mars in Gemini, July 23, 17:14 - Aug. 13, 21:25
Mars in Cancer, Aug. 13, 21:26 - Aug. 24, 0:08

YOUR LUCK MAGNETISM
Jupiter in Scorpio, July 23, 17:14 - Aug. 24, 0:08

World Events

Aug. 15 – India is granted its independence after more than 200 years of British rule.

Aug. 24 – The first Edinburgh Festival opens.

CANCER
From June 22, 6:19 through July 23, 17:13

The Resolute Teacher

As a Cancer born in 1947, you probably came into the world knowing that taking care of others is the way to make yourself feel secure. It might seem shocking, then, that a brutal event like the British seizure of a ship carrying Jewish émigrés to Palestine occurred around the time you were born. Surely if you had had a say in the outcome of that incident, you'd have struggled to help those people to the place they wanted to call home.

Because of your strong desire to defend the weak and protect the young, you'd probably have been an excellent teacher. Believing that the love a child receives from adults at an early age is the key to unlocking its individual potential, you may have been drawn to working with young children. Whatever the age of the children in your care, you would have been able to talk about history and tell stories in a way that made them seem personal. In fact, your subjective spin on current events may have inspired a lifelong thirst for knowledge in even the most lackadaisical students.

You may have become politically active in children's causes in your later years. With your intuitive grasp of the meaning behind any situation, you'd make an equally excellent editorial writer or political advocate. You might have been tempted, at one time or another, to put your beliefs aside in favor of personal gain. However, it probably took only one quick dip into that world to cure you of the desire to work for anything other than the people and causes you believe in.

You can have as much fun as a kid when you allow yourself to. You may like games and structured activities, and you might enjoy going on vacations to places where you can play cards, bingo, or other games of chance. Scorpio can be a great friend to you. Your most interesting love matches may be Taurus and Gemini, because they make you feel needed and appreciated, but a Libra is also capable of capturing your heart.

Your challenge is to remember that you cannot take care of other people the whole time. Your gift is your ability to make loving sacrifices as a promise to the future of humankind.

LEO
From July 23, 17:14 through August 24, 0:08

The Quiet Dynamo

As a Leo born in 1947 you could face many constrictions, but you can also be very powerful. It might not be surprising to learn that the U.S. Department of Defense shares your Sun sign. Created by the postwar consolidation of the American War Department with the air force and the navy, the Department of Defense constituted a core of power that was awesome to ponder. Then, on August 15, India gained her independence after 150 years of British rule. These two events aptly illuminate the tug-of-war between accumulation of power and resistance to oppression that you seem to embody.

Perhaps because you think in broad terms, it may not be as easy for you to actualize your ideas as it is for Leos born in other years. You might feel like you have a powerful rocket strapped to your back but you're stuck in a very small room. However, as you've no doubt learned from experience, the trick is understanding that you need to work within the structural framework that you keep banging your head against, rather than gnashing your teeth and wishing it wasn't there.

As a younger person, you may have shied away from accepting positions where your work was closely monitored or your creativity restricted. It's likely that your ability to see the big picture and attention to detail makes you a good manager, and you may excel at bringing out people's hidden talents. It can be very important to you that people respect you for your hard work. As a result, you could also succeed in publishing or retail sales, or perhaps become a successful entrepreneur.

In friendships, it's possible that Ariens make ideal friends for you. You'd also enjoy Geminis because they have an ability to live in freedom regardless of the restrictions people try to put on them. In love, an intuitive Pisces or a nurturing Cancer could be the kind of mate who knows when you need to be alone and when you need someone to listen to you.

Your challenge is to remember that you are not alone in your struggle. Your gift is your ability to pick yourself up and get back to work, even when it seems like you're running against the wind.

➤ Read about your Chinese Astrological sign on page 838. ➤ Read about your Personal Planets on page 826. ➤ Read about your personal Mystical Card on page 856.

VIRGO

From August 24, 0:09 through September 23, 21:28

The Compassionate Observer

Virgo of 1947, you arrived at a time when nations strove to maintain the fragile peace that had come from the end of World War II—and it was not always easy. India had only just thrown off the yoke of colonial rule, and now two factions were battling for control of the new nation. Around the time you were born, thousands of people died in fierce fighting between Muslims and Hindus around the Indian state of Punjab. In its weariness following the long years of war, the rest of the world turned a blind eye to the slaughter, hoping that the two sides would be able to work it out on their own.

This low moment in the history of humanity was the tragic backdrop to your birth. As a result, you may have made it your mission in life to come to others' aid whenever you can, vowing never to turn away from anyone who needs your help. As a teenager, you may have joined some of the protest movements of the sixties, perhaps working for human rights, women's rights, or against war. With your organizing skills, it's likely that you'd get any group running smoothly, no matter how chaotic things may have looked when you arrived.

You detect flaws that no one else can find by analyzing complex operations and breaking them down into small components. It's a good thing that you are so capable, because you may tend to work for people who are not organized at all. You could be a good accountant, designer, financial analyst, or electronics technician. Recognizing that co-workers resent it if you point out their mistakes, you would avoid their wrath by finding the pleasantest way to tell people how you think their work can be improved, and by being more tolerant of their flaws, especially when they're not crucial ones.

Your friends have to be as serious as you are about life, so Capricorn and Taurus are probably the most compatible choices for you. Another Virgo would be an excellent romantic choice for you, as you both keep a tidy house and would be devoted to each other.

Your challenge is to speak your truth without coming across as critical. Your gift is your ability to create order out of chaos.

LIBRA

From September 23, 21:29 through October 24, 6:25

The Charming Achiever

As a Libra born in 1947, you can have a great deal of confidence in your ideas, as well as the tenacity to see things through. You were born in the year the first helicopter airmail and express service went into business, and you may have been rocked to sleep while your parents watched the first live television programs ever broadcast. In fact, the events that took place while the Sun passed through your sign were success stories that foreshadowed the technological explosion that would take place in your lifetime.

You may have a great deal of ambition and a drive for professional success, and it's likely that you've rarely, if ever, had a problem finding a suitable job. You may also possess great financial insight, which enhances your ability to perceive hidden opportunities to generate income. You can be extremely generous with your money, and you probably believe in donating to charities that allow disadvantaged people to experience something beautiful, like fine music or art.

You may be happy working as an administrator or fund-raiser for a philanthropic organization. Your personal charm and your ability to tune in to what appeals to other people will also take you far if you choose to become a counselor or teacher. Sales is another natural profession for you to pursue, since you probably love meeting new people and finding out what makes them tick.

You share this love of networking with Geminis, and you might befriend many of them as a result of some of their own connection-making expeditions. You might enjoy long drives in the country with Sagittarian friends, and since you're likely to be a person that people who have money and power gravitate to, you might also count an abundance of Capricorns among your acquaintances. But when you fall in love, it could be the raw energy of Aries or the loving devotion of Cancer that wins your heart.

You face the challenge of balancing your desire to donate your services with your need to retain some of your resources for yourself. Your gift is your ability to treasure your friends as though they were the finest jewels on Earth.

➤ Read about your Chinese Astrological sign on page 838. ➤ Read about your Personal Planets on page 826. ➤ Read about your personal Mystical Card on page 856.

1947

VIRGO
Your Personal Planets

YOUR LOVE POTENTIAL

Venus in Leo, Aug. 24, 0:09 - Aug. 26, 8:16
Venus in Virgo, Aug. 26, 8:17 - Sept. 19, 12:00
Venus in Libra, Sept. 19, 12:01 - Sept. 23, 21:28

YOUR DRIVE AND AMBITION

Mars in Cancer, Aug. 24, 0:09 - Sept. 23, 21:28

YOUR LUCK MAGNETISM

Jupiter in Scorpio, Aug. 24, 0:09 - Sept. 23, 21:28

World Events

Sept. 9 – Argentina grants the vote to women.
Sept. 22 – The first automatic-pilot flight over the Atlantic is made by a Douglas C-54 Skymaster.

Charles "Chuck" Yeager breaks the sound barrier

LIBRA
Your Personal Planets

YOUR LOVE POTENTIAL

Venus in Libra, Sept. 23, 21:29 - Oct. 13, 13:48
Venus in Scorpio, Oct. 13, 13:49 - Oct. 24, 6:25

YOUR DRIVE AND AMBITION

Mars in Cancer, Sept. 23, 21:29 - Oct. 01, 2:30
Mars in Leo, Oct. 01, 2:31 - Oct. 24, 6:25

YOUR LUCK MAGNETISM

Jupiter in Scorpio, Sept. 23, 21:29 - Oct. 24, 2:59
Jupiter in Sagittarius, Oct. 24, 3:00 - Oct. 24, 6:25

World Events

Oct. 7 – French troops in Indochina launch Operation Lea against the Viet Minh.

Oct. 14 – Charles "Chuck" Yeager breaks the sound barrier in his Bell XS-1 aircraft.

1947

SCORPIO
Your Personal Planets

YOUR LOVE POTENTIAL
Venus in Scorpio, Oct. 24, 6:26 - Nov. 06, 14:58
Venus in Sagittarius, Nov. 06, 14:59 - Nov. 23, 3:37

YOUR DRIVE AND AMBITION
Mars in Leo, Oct. 24, 6:26 - Nov. 23, 3:37

YOUR LUCK MAGNETISM
Jupiter in Sagittarius, Oct. 24, 6:26 - Nov. 23, 3:37

World Events

Nov. 4 – Indian troops invade Pakistan.
Nov. 20 – Princess Elizabeth weds Lt. Philip Mountbatten in a ceremony in Westminster Abbey, London.

Film director Steven Spielberg is born under the sign of Sagittarius

SAGITTARIUS
Your Personal Planets

YOUR LOVE POTENTIAL
Venus in Sagittarius, Nov. 23, 3:38 - Nov. 30, 16:22
Venus in Capricorn, Nov. 30, 16:23 - Dec. 22, 16:42

YOUR DRIVE AND AMBITION
Mars in Leo, Nov. 23, 3:38 - Dec. 01, 11:43
Mars in Virgo, Dec. 01, 11:44 - Dec. 22, 16:42

YOUR LUCK MAGNETISM
Jupiter in Sagittarius, Nov. 23, 3:38 - Dec. 22, 16:42

World Events

Dec. 3 – Tennessee Williams' *A Streetcar Named Desire* premières in New York.
Dec. 18 – Film director Steven Spielberg is born.

SCORPIO
From October 24, 6:26 through November 23, 3:37

The Ambitious Detective

As a Scorpio born in 1947, you probably caught the curious postwar wave of mass consciousness that probed deeply into the mind—for memory of trivia as well as essential knowledge. The world began to make a game out of guessing during the year you were born—especially the United States, with radio shows like *You Bet Your Life* permitting the masses to try their hand at answering tricky questions from acerbic host Groucho Marx. You might also possess an amazing amount of intuition, and when you were growing up "quiz" shows like these would have demonstrated that you could have a lot to gain by using this talent.

During your youth, as the tools of spies and counterspies became more popular and accessible to the public, you may have taken up a hobby like ham radio, which allowed you to eavesdrop on conversations taking place thousands of miles away. You are likely to be proficient at mathematics and the sciences, and you may have developed a knack for breaking codes as a result of taking on work that requires the careful examination and analysis of subtle clues.

At work, you may exhibit a core of energy that helps you adapt to changing situations. It's likely that you're more aggressive and ambitious than Scorpios born in other years, and while your motives are pure, you probably don't like to share information with your competitors. This could make you a valued employee of a research center, or perhaps a talented psychiatrist, a police detective, or even an international spy.

Your personal involvements can also be quite intense, due to the fact that you want to know others who are as successful as you. You'll probably enjoy other Scorpios—as long as you're not in competition with them. Cancer and Libra might also make good friends for you. Your traditional love match is Taurus, but Leo could also score well with you—this is the one sign in your year that can be as single-minded as you are!

Your challenge is to allow yourself enough time away from work to refresh yourself. Your gift is the ability to know what you want, and to cross barriers that are outmoded and arbitrary.

SAGITTARIUS
From November 23, 3:38 through December 22, 16:42

The Dedicated Partner

Tennessee Williams' sizzling drama *A Streetcar Named Desire* premiered in America just as you were born, Sagittarius of 1947, and it was this revolutionary play that set the stage for the kind of psychological drama you may have seen in movies and on television when you were growing up. Like Blanche DuBois, one of Williams' most memorable characters, you may have "relied on the kindness of strangers" quite frequently in your life—and you would rarely assume that people had ulterior motives or would be out to deliberately hurt you.

You may have a natural inclination toward partnership, both wanting and needing the support of a partner whose strengths complement your own. This could make you a successful entrepreneur, but if you chose to work for a company—rather than start your own—you may have thrived in an area such as sales, where your unparalleled dedication to your clients' success would ensure your own. Like all Sagittarians, your thirst for knowledge might seem insatiable, but unlike Sagittarians born in other years, you may find that you can learn something new every day simply by getting to know people.

You may have many friends who share your desire to enjoy life to its fullest, and the Leos among them might have this endeavor perfected. You'd enjoy a Scorpio's sense of humor, and you might find Pisces to be even more blissfully innocent than you are.

Your innocent's perspective on life may have stood you in good stead not only in choosing your business partnerships and client relationships but in romance as well. If you found the perfect relationship without even looking for it, it's probably because the astrological influences in effect at your birth blessed you with an abundance of love. While fiery Leo could intrigue you, it's likely that Scorpio or Capricorn are the signs whose burning intensity would win your heart.

Your challenge is to focus your curious mind long enough to learn all you can about one thing before moving on to another. Your gift is your knowledge that every episode in life is a learning experience that, eventually, you're going to cherish.

➤ Read about your Chinese Astrological sign on page 838. ➤ Read about your Personal Planets on page 826. ➤ Read about your personal Mystical Card on page 856.

CAPRICORN

From December 22, 16:43 through December 31, 23:59

The Master Strategist

As a Capricorn born in December of 1947, you arrived at a time when tensions were building between the nations that split the spoils of World War II. The struggle between the communist bloc and the western world—known as the Cold War—shifted into high gear when American Congressional committees began scrutinizing U.S. citizens suspected of having Soviet sympathies.

Because you were born near the beginning of this period of global political mistrust and suspicion, you may tend to ponder your position in life even more deeply than other Capricorns. You probably managed to maintain your belief that ultimately the people who were on the side of right would prevail. Still, you'd want to get to the bottom of events and people rather than simply accept them at face value.

People can be hard to predict, but you may enjoy trying to find patterns in their seemingly erratic behavior. At work, you probably enjoy studying your co-workers to see if you can anticipate their next moves. Corporate law might interest you, as you could enjoy dissecting the character of an organization almost as much as you enjoy analyzing individuals. It goes without saying that you'd make a good therapist or spiritual counselor. You could also excel at anything that requires precision, like playing an instrument or painting in a realistic style.

It's likely that your disciplined mind attracts Scorpios and Leos. You might have plenty of Scorpio friends, but you could have more trouble relating to Leos, as they'll head straight for the spotlight and want to drag you along with them. Romantically speaking, you could easily become enmeshed with another Capricorn, although it would probably be one born in another year. You find Geminis exciting, but their hard-to-pin-down personalities can make it difficult for you to become passionate about them. However, your interest in an elusive Aquarius could last a lifetime.

Your gift is knowing what people really mean when they talk, giving you antennae that some may call a nonsense detector. Your challenge is not to allow your sensitivity to weaken your resolve.

CAPRICORN
Your Personal Planets

YOUR LOVE POTENTIAL
Venus in Capricorn, Dec. 22, 16:43 - Dec. 24, 19:12
Venus in Aquarius, Dec. 24, 19:13 - Dec. 31, 23:59

YOUR DRIVE AND AMBITION
Mars in Virgo, Dec. 22, 16:43 - Dec. 31, 23:59

YOUR LUCK MAGNETISM
Jupiter in Sagittarius, Dec. 22, 16:43 - Dec. 31, 23:59

World Events

Dec. 24 – Gen. Markas Vafthiades announces the Free Greek Government in northern Greece.

Dec. 30 – King Michael of Romania is forced into exile when Communists take over control of the country.

Christopher Columbus

Special Feature
The Mysterious Bermuda Triangle

(Continued from page 385)

A romantic theory links disappearances in the Bermuda Triangle area to the legendary city of Atlantis, which supposedly sank beneath the waters of the Triangle, bequeathing its name to the ocean where the disaster occurred. There are divers who claim to have seen debris lying on the seabed, which they believe to be the sunken buildings of Atlantis. Some theorize that the Triangle effect is caused by the fire-crystals that provided Atlantis with its heat, lighting, and other energy: the crystals—so the theory goes—are still emitting energy beams powerful enough to crash a low-flying plane or suck down an entire ship.

Sailors have known for centuries that the area covered by the Bermuda Triangle is both dangerous and mysterious.

However, on the wider canvas of man's ages-old encounter with the sea, stories of the Bermuda Triangle and its Japanese equivalent have given a new face to a very ancient story. Sailors

have known for centuries that the area covered by the Bermuda Triangle is both dangerous and mysterious. During his first voyage to America in 1492, Christopher Columbus reported seeing strange lights in the sky that suddenly and mysteriously disappeared. Columbus also noted that he was having compass trouble; since his time, many others have found that in the Bermuda Triangle readings can be undependable.

Normally, compass readings point to magnetic north, but the Triangle is one of only two areas on Earth—the other is the Devil's Sea— where magnetic north aligns with true north. This causes variations that can place a craft up to one hundred miles off course: considerable distance must be compensated for if a route is to be accurately reckoned. Unfortunately, airplane pilots and ships' captains have not always been aware that their compass may be "lying" to them. Combined with the swift and turbulent Gulf Stream, which can itself drive a craft off course, it is possible that "victims" of

the Bermuda Triangle actually met their fate well away from the area. No wonder, then, that they have never been found.

(Continued on page 401)

➤ Read more about aliens in "The Extraterrestrial Highway" on page 465.

1948

The Birth of Israel: Scorched by Fire Signs

On May 14th, 1948, the state of Israel was officially created by a mandate of the British government. On this historic day, four major planets were lined up in fire signs. Fire signs are spontaneous, enthusiastic, and sometimes dangerous. They are the most dynamic signs of the Zodiac. When planets enter any of the fire signs, Aries, Leo, or Sagittarius, their power principle is ignited and conflagrations are possible. When the ardent "God of War", Mars, enters any of the fire signs, one can expect major fireworks with lasting effects. Mars was placed in Leo at this time in history. Mars represents the aggressive urge, the animal nature, and sheer force. When it enters fire-sign Leo, sign of the roaring lion, everyone tends to feel their power, no matter how deeply buried it is.

Also at this time in history, lofty Jupiter was placed in idealistic Sagittarius, its natural sign, and a feisty fire-sign at that. When Jupiter enters Sagittarius, hope for the future is paramount. People feel bigger than their britches, and after the ravages of World War II, the creation of Israel seemed to be the perfect solution to the unimaginable horrors that were foisted on the Jews of Europe. Israel was intended to be a home for refugees, a place where those whose lives had been ripped apart could begin the process of healing. This idealistic and somewhat naïve attitude is indicative of Jupiter in Sagittarius. When the legions of European Jews were brought to the promised land without regard for the Palestinian Arabs who already lived there, Jupiter in Sagittarius had clearly put a blind spot in the lens of the political leaders of the day.

Saturn was also in Leo at that time, making a soft aspect called a trine to Jupiter, and a strong contact to both planets Pluto and Mars. When Saturn makes a hard connection to Pluto, history has shown us that everything explodes. Throughout the 20th century, many of the major events that have taken place in the Middle East have been linked to connections made by the planets Saturn and Pluto. 1948 was no exception. Because these two heavy hitting planets were placed in a fierce fire sign, the embers of history were stoked and burst into a lasting blaze.

Crowds on the streets of Tel Aviv after the Jewish State of Israel is proclaimed

Children watch a U.S. Airforce plane bringing supplies to Berlin

Farewell gathering for the retiring Governor General of India, Lord Mountbatten

ISRAEL IS BORN

Mahatma Gandhi was assassinated by a Hindu extremist, who believed he had made too many concessions to the Muslims. As Jewish immigration to Palestine increased, so did Arab resistance. The State of Israel was proclaimed, but countries of the Arab League responded by attacking the Jewish state. As the rift between the communist 'East' and the democratic 'West' built up, the Soviets blockaded its sector of Berlin, preventing goods and services from reaching the city. In response, Berlin was supplied by an Anglo-American airlift. Yugoslavia's new communist leader Marshal Tito angered Russia by forging his own brand of Communism. The push to automate the home was on, as U.S. women were encouraged to use electrical appliances to make life easier. President Truman called for an end to racial inequality and followed this up by ordering the integration of the U.S. armed forces. The search for communist spies pressed on, demoralizing federal employees and the public alike. The first operation inside the heart was performed. Michener's first novel, *Tales Of The South Pacific* won the Pulitzer Prize. The pioneer of flight, Wilbur Wright died.

► Read "The Mysterious Bermuda Triangle" by Sophia Mason on page 385.

CAPRICORN

From January 01, 0:00 through January 21, 3:17

The Tireless Pioneer

As a Capricorn born in January of 1948, you arrived just as a year full of "firsts" was starting. The consolidation of government services and conveniences hit the UK during your birth month, when Britain nationalized the railway system and opened its first self-service supermarket. At the same time, athletes in the U.S. were preparing for their first Winter Olympics—they'd soon be home with several medals.

The energy and focus it took to make these things happen may be a natural part of your personality as well, along with the Olympian urge to bring the world together. You probably have an avid interest in higher learning, international travel, or languages. Even if you never leave home, you'll find ways to bring the outside world to you—probably through long-distance acquaintances. Over the years, it's likely that your practical mind and skill at making money will never fail you. Even when you don't succeed at something, you probably land on your feet in the midst of an even better project. It's called luck, Capricorn—and whether you have a charm in your pocket or just a hunch, rest assured that when you need it most, magic will happen.

Because you are so blessed, you probably find many ways to share your good fortune, possibly through the work that you do. You may be a financial advisor or credit counselor, or a wise investor who helps others realize their dreams. Your organizational skills and your empathy have probably led you at least once down the path of leadership in your community.

You often make friends through your business and professional affiliations, and may count many Sagittarians among your close friends. After all, their concern for humanity is well-known. You might also enjoy the travel companionship of Virgos, who share your uncanny knack for being in the right place at the right time. In love, you could gravitate toward other Capricorns, who will always understand you.

Your challenge is to reserve some of your energy for your personal life, and to take care of your own needs as well as you take care of others. Your gift is your amazing endurance.

AQUARIUS

From January 21, 3:18 through February 19, 17:36

The Sentimental Lover

Born in 1948, Aquarius, you could possess qualities that take you beyond the world of hard, cold facts—even though typically Aquarian events, like the development of the tape recorder and the first flight by a radio-controlled airplane, occurred around the time you were born. By the time you grew up, you probably took these new inventions for granted, saw them as less than impressive, and made no connection between you and them—but your family did. It's likely that they saw you as a wonderfully unique "human innovation" who arrived especially for them to love—and they were absolutely right.

You are truly an original. You possess a brilliant mind and a unique view of the future, while somehow also managing to be sentimental and close to others in a deep, spiritual way. You have an unusually "soft" way of expressing yourself, and may be interested in distinctly non-scientific subjects, such as music, ESP, and dream analysis. You may also have a strong urge to form alliances, and a gift for drawing powerful people to you.

This appreciation for both logic and intuition means that work in the field of psychoanalysis could be ideal for you, allowing you to use your insight to unlock the secrets of the unconscious. You may also be interested in pursuing a career in communications, where your knack for blending emotion and logic would come in handy.

As if to dispel the myth that all Aquarians are cold and heartless, your co-workers will probably find you amusing, unique, and endearing. You may attract friends easily, and it's likely that you'll enjoy Pisceans and Scorpios, who'll be more than willing to listen to your futuristic dreams and give you useful feedback. In love, you might try to tame a Leo, but the relationship may run hot and cold—until you make it clear that you need attention, too. Spontaneous, variety-loving Gemini is another good match—sure to keep you on your toes.

Your challenge is to accept the sensitive part of yourself without abandoning your ideals. Your gift is the ability to understand people on a deep level after only a few brief words are exchanged.

CAPRICORN
Your Personal Planets

YOUR LOVE POTENTIAL
Venus in Aquarius, Jan. 01, 0:00 - Jan. 18, 2:13
Venus in Pisces, Jan. 18, 2:14 - Jan. 21, 3:17

YOUR DRIVE AND AMBITION
Mars in Virgo, Jan. 01, 0:00 - Jan. 21, 3:17

YOUR LUCK MAGNETISM
Jupiter in Sagittarius, Jan. 01, 0:00 - Jan. 21, 3:17

World Events

Jan. 4 – Britain grants Burma independence.
Jan. 5 – The first color newsreel is filmed in Pasadena, California.

Death of Mahatma Gandhi

AQUARIUS
Your Personal Planets

YOUR LOVE POTENTIAL
Venus in Pisces, Jan. 21, 3:18 - Feb. 11, 18:50
Venus in Aries, Feb. 11, 18:51 - Feb. 19, 17:36

YOUR DRIVE AND AMBITION
Mars in Virgo, Jan. 21, 3:18 - Feb. 12, 10:27
Mars in Leo, Feb. 12, 10:28 - Feb. 19, 17:36

YOUR LUCK MAGNETISM
Jupiter in Sagittarius, Jan. 21, 3:18 - Feb. 19, 17:36

World Events

Jan. 27 – The first tape recorder is sold.
Jan. 30 – Mahatma Gandhi is assassinated.

► Read about your Chinese Astrological sign on page 838. ► Read about your Personal Planets on page 826. ► Read about your personal Mystical Card on page 856.

395

1948

PISCES
Your Personal Planets

YOUR LOVE POTENTIAL
Venus in Aries, Feb. 19, 17:37 - Mar. 08, 6:58
Venus in Taurus, Mar. 08, 6:59 - Mar. 20, 16:56

YOUR DRIVE AND AMBITION
Mars in Leo, Feb. 19, 17:37 - Mar. 20, 16:56

YOUR LUCK MAGNETISM
Jupiter in Sagittarius, Feb. 19, 17:37 - Mar. 20, 16:56

World Events

Feb. 25 – The Communists seize power in Czechoslovakia.

Mar. 4 – French actor and playwright Antonin Artaud dies.

An Anglo-American airlift brings supplies to Berlin

ARIES
Your Personal Planets

YOUR LOVE POTENTIAL
Venus in Taurus, Mar. 20, 16:57 - Apr. 04, 12:39
Venus in Gemini, Apr. 04, 12:40 - Apr. 20, 4:24

YOUR DRIVE AND AMBITION
Mars in Leo, Mar. 20, 16:57 - Apr. 20, 4:24

YOUR LUCK MAGNETISM
Jupiter in Sagittarius, Mar. 20, 16:57 - Apr. 20, 4:24

World Events

Apr. 1 – The Berlin Airlift begins.

Apr. 7 – World Health Organization is founded.

PISCES
From February 19, 17:37 through March 20, 16:56

The Adaptable Innovator

As a 1948 Pisces, you were born into a moment that would help you hone the skill of adaptability. Social and political conflicts on a grand scale probably caused your parents to realize that peace was a precarious—and precious—condition. Arab attacks on Jerusalem and the seizure of Czechoslovakia by communist forces spread concern about maintaining order throughout the world. In the U.S., secularity returned, through the Supreme Court's ban on religious instruction in public schools. This legal separation of Church and State may reflect your ability to honor both science and spirituality, even more than Pisceans born in other years.

As a result, you somehow manage to be simultaneously emotional and logical, with a gift for translating the mystical into the comprehensible. Appropriately enough, two great communicators were applauded during your birth year. James Michener and Tennessee Williams were both awarded the Pulitzer Prize. Whether or not you achieve a similar fame to these men, you probably have the ability to communicate powerfully through your chosen work. It's possible that you'll be drawn to work with science. In particular, chemistry, veterinary medicine, or mathematics are likely to capture your interest.

You probably like to share your happiness, and welcoming people into your home can be as natural as breathing for you. It's likely that you're famous in your circle of friends for being the perfect host or hostess.

In committed relationships, you're probably looking for someone who'll be equal parts friend and lover. Precision-oriented Virgo may be the right sign for you to spend your life with, since they will undoubtedly appreciate your unique blend of talents. Aquarius is another good match, since you see "the big picture" in such similar ways. When it comes to friendship, you probably have a collection of Scorpios, whose ability to perceive the motivations of others will amaze and delight you.

Your challenge is to take hold of your abilities and use them for the greater good. Your gift is an appreciation of both logic and mystery—and the ability to communicate either with ease.

ARIES
From March 20, 16:57 through April 20, 4:24

The Cerebral Dynamo

You're an energetic person born at an exciting time, 1948 Aries—and the news of the day shows that you arrived along with a few other symbols of brilliance. Scientists observed a flash of light emanating from the lunar crater Plato around the time you were born, while here on the ground, the United Nations formed the World Health Organization. Like the individuals behind these events, you are probably inspired by the search for truth and compassion, and you'll follow your curious mind's lead to places no one else has dared to explore before.

Your mind can be extremely active, allowing you to relate to anyone—and, more importantly, to understand them. You are probably far more intellectual than Ariens born in other years, and you may be able to use your highly charged creative energies to produce remarkable results under pressure. Deadlines might be your specialty—especially if they've been pushed back a few times. You can be a great moneymaker, too—as long as you enjoy what you're doing. You are likely to have a knack for instantly knowing what to do with a new device that befuddles your friends.

When you're not off trying to find new ways to dazzle the world, you probably engage in a very active social life. At some point, you may have been involved in contact sports like football or field hockey—but in calmer moments acting and dancing might interest you, fulfilling your need to perform. The friends you choose are likely to be rough-and-tumble types. Leo and Sagittarius are your likely companions, as their fiery temperaments keep you stimulated.

When it comes to romance, it's likely that you won't want to settle for less than the person of your dreams. Pisceans and Taureans will probably attract you with their enticing inner beauty and passion, as well as their well-groomed beauty, but an intense Scorpio could win your heart.

Your challenge is to allow yourself to slow down and enjoy the best life has to offer—even if it sometimes means you're not first in line at the theater when it opens. Your gift is your stamina, which is at least equal to your mental brilliance.

➤ Read about your Chinese Astrological sign on page 838. ➤ Read about your Personal Planets on page 826. ➤ Read about your personal Mystical Card on page 856.

TAURUS

From April 20, 4:25 through May 21, 3:57

The Diligent Justice-Seeker

As a 1948 Taurus, it's likely that justice is very important to you—just as it was to the victims of the Holocaust who, around the time you were born, were avenged when Hans Rauter of the Nazi secret service was called to task for his horrendous acts. As a result of growing up when the wrongs of World War II were being redressed, it's possible that a concern with fairness and equality may have stayed with you all your life.

A sign as security-conscious as yours will do whatever needs to be done to attain this, and you're probably a force to be reckoned with when you're protecting your turf, your family, or your prized possessions. With such tremendous struggles taking place in the world around you, you probably also had to be quite self-sufficient as a child—and that, too, may have carried over into your adult life. This would have made you an excellent worker—perhaps the one on whom the concept of a "self-starter" might have been based.

At the same time, however, you can have a way of encouraging people to cooperate, and the ability to instill a high moral standard in your fellow workers. Even if you aren't initially in charge at your job, your "team-player" attitude would undoubtedly get you noticed by the higher-ups sooner or later—and financial rewards may soon follow. You might be drawn to fields such as beauty, cosmetics, or the arts—all of which would be perfectly suited to your ability to scrutinize, analyze, and perfect.

Your friends are probably like family, and extremely devoted to you. You may automatically trust fellow Taureans and admire Librans' ability to be pleasant even under stress. In love relationships, it's likely that you would want passion as well as companionship, and you'd probably gravitate toward fiery, lavish Leo, intense, charming Scorpio, or fun-loving Sagittarius. Then again, it's possible that one of the visionary air signs—Aquarius, in particular—might dazzle you with their unpredictable ways!

Your challenge is to realize that you simply can't control everything. Your gifts are your way with people and your reputation as a hard worker.

GEMINI

From May 21, 3:58 through June 21, 12:10

The Compassionate Intellectual

Your parents might have been concerned about the world they were bringing you into, Gemini of 1948. Even as the UN issued its Declaration of Human Rights, a policy of racial separation known as "apartheid" was defined by the new government in South Africa. In Europe, the Iron Curtain began to materialize when the USSR blocked the road to West Berlin, effectively isolating the city from its allies in the West. Although your parents' safety may not have been directly threatened, the entire world was affected by these events. As a result, your family probably put a strong emphasis on the value of human rights, shaping your future outlook by sensitizing you to what could happen when political power was abused.

Your personal priority can be to nurture and protect those who are dear to you. It's likely that you have a passionate way of expressing yourself—a quality that can make you an excellent public speaker and may also mean that you're involved in an occupation such as teaching, writing, or politics, that allows you to speak to an audience. In one way or another, your work will probably require you to write or speak on behalf of an organization. It's not likely that you would settle for just any job, however. You can feel quite strongly about doing only what you believe in, and you probably wouldn't work for any group whose policies don't reflect your strong sense of morality.

Your knack for cooperation shows in your affiliation with a variety of individuals. You probably adore Librans, since that sign is famous for the ability to state its case delicately yet firmly.

Your ideal partner is someone who can be both friend and lover, so you may also find many Sagittarians in your life. Since it's so important for you to be on the same intellectual wavelength as your mate, Aquarius and Capricorn, both known for their objectivity, are also good choices.

Your challenge is to accept that the line between right and wrong is not always as clear to others as it is to you. Your strength is your ability to stand up for your beliefs, and communicate them with energy and confidence.

➤ Read about your Chinese Astrological sign on page 838. ➤ Read about your Personal Planets on page 826. ➤ Read about your personal Mystical Card on page 856.

TAURUS
Your Personal Planets

YOUR LOVE POTENTIAL
Venus in Gemini, Apr. 20, 4:25 - May 07, 8:26
Venus in Cancer, May 07, 8:27 - May 21, 3:57

YOUR DRIVE AND AMBITION
Mars in Leo, Apr. 20, 4:25 - May 18, 20:53
Mars in Virgo, May 18, 20:54 - May 21, 3:57

YOUR LUCK MAGNETISM
Jupiter in Sagittarius, Apr. 20, 4:25 - May 21, 3:57

World Events

May 1 – The People's Democratic Republic of Korea is declared in the north of the country.

May 14 – Israel declares its independence from British administration and David Ben-Gurion is proclaimed Prime Minister of the new state.

The Jewish State of Israel is proclaimed

GEMINI
Your Personal Planets

YOUR LOVE POTENTIAL
Venus in Cancer, May 21, 3:58 - June 21, 12:10

YOUR DRIVE AND AMBITION
Mars in Virgo, May 21, 3:58 - June 21, 12:10

YOUR LUCK MAGNETISM
Jupiter in Sagittarius, May 21, 3:58 - June 21, 12:10

World Events

June 6 – French photography pioneer Louis Lumière dies.

June 14 – New York publisher Lee Wagner launches his *TeleVision Guide*.

1948

CANCER
Your Personal Planets

YOUR LOVE POTENTIAL
Venus in Cancer, June 21, 12:11 - June 29, 7:57
Venus in Gemini, June 29, 7:58 - July 22, 23:07

YOUR DRIVE AND AMBITION
Mars in Virgo, June 21, 12:11 - July 17, 5:24
Mars in Libra, July 17, 5:25 - July 22, 23:07

YOUR LUCK MAGNETISM
Jupiter in Sagittarius, June 21, 12:11 - July 22, 23:07

World Events

July 5 – The National Health Service goes into effect in Britain.

July 12 – Delegates from sixteen nations attend the Marshall Plan Conference in Paris.

Albert Camus, French author of "The Plague"

LEO
Your Personal Planets

YOUR LOVE POTENTIAL
Venus in Gemini, July 22, 23:08 - Aug. 03, 2:14
Venus in Cancer, Aug. 03, 2:15 - Aug. 23, 6:02

YOUR DRIVE AND AMBITION
Mars in Libra, July 22, 23:08 - Aug. 23, 6:02

YOUR LUCK MAGNETISM
Jupiter in Sagittarius, July 22, 23:08 - Aug. 23, 6:02

World Events

July 29 – The Olympic Games are opened in London by King George VI.

Aug. 1 – Albert Camus' *The Plague* is published in the U.S.

CANCER
From June 21, 12:11 through July 22, 23:07

The Financial Crusader

As a 1948 Cancer, you may have been aware of the value of money from a very early age. The world you were born into was not at its most stable, and it's likely that your parents taught you to gather enough resources to tide you over should that mythical "rainy day" suddenly arrive. Israel and Egypt were at military odds around the time you were born, illustrating that there would always be conflict in the world. But at about the same moment, some people, such as those who founded Alcoholics Anonymous in Britain at the time you were born, took control over their lives in a way that brought hope to others who may have believed that their own lives were hopeless.

Through your acquisition of wealth, both materially and spiritually, you probably seek to share with others a deeply held concept—that there is always hope. You may tend to work very well on your own, which can mean that fields like independent stock speculation or freelance writing could be ideal career paths for you. You may also use your wealth to help someone who has not been treated fairly, or to help others get ahead by lending them a hand, an ear, or even the cash they need to get them through a rough spot.

You probably have an easy time making friends, since you have a way of letting people know immediately that you are willing to take care of them. Pisceans, Sagittarians, and Virgos are likely to reciprocate your kindness, and unlikely to abuse it.

In love relationships, you'll probably want someone who will be able to pool resources with you, so look to signs who have sound material credentials—like the earth signs, Capricorn, Taurus, and Virgo. It's likely that you'll date a lot of Scorpios, too, and one of those intense individuals could be the lucky person with whom you'll forge a partnership that will bring both of you stability and lifelong happiness.

Your challenge is to accept the fact that you will often be fairer to others than you are to yourself—and to learn to think of yourself first sometimes. The love and appreciation you're given in return for your efforts toward fairness is your greatest gift.

LEO
From July 22, 23:08 through August 23, 6:02

The Cautious Caretaker

Leos of 1948 possess a mixed bag of emotions that perfectly reflect events happening around the world at this particular time. Just as you arrived, the Summer Olympics opened in London—a celebration of global unity, teamwork, and friendly competition that continues to this very day. Conversely, on the other side of the globe, Communists formed the North China People's Republic, ushering in an era of centralized government control in China—which still exists today. This contradictory mix of segregation and incorporation probably shows in your ability to erect or let down your own personal boundaries as you intuitively feel it's appropriate.

You're likely to show your care and concern for people who don't have your self-confidence, making them comfortable enough to open up to you and ask your advice. Your magnanimous personality creates a comfort zone that draws others to you—and to your warm heart. This personal magnetism gives you the ability to be an outstanding supervisor, counselor, or teacher.

You can be quite diplomatic and charming, too, so it's also possible that you may work as a protocol expert or social organizer. With your regal presence, you doubtless have no trouble feeling like "one of the gang" among society's elite, but despite the ability to rub elbows with important folks, you have friends from all walks of life. You've probably enjoyed the friendship of Geminis, Librans, and Scorpios throughout your life, as well as one special Aquarian who'll be in your heart forever.

In love, you may be looking for someone who's as outgoing and sociable as you are. You need look no further than Gemini, Sagittarius, or Aquarius, who will understand your need to share your ideas with others, and welcome the personal freedom a relationship with you allows. It's also possible that a Libra friendship could become a lifelong partnership.

Your challenge is to soften any tendency toward pessimism and choose, instead, to keep your chin up as you follow a cautious, patient, and hard-working path. Your gift is the ability to make people feel truly special and appreciated.

➤ Read about your Chinese Astrological sign on page 838. ➤ Read about your Personal Planets on page 826. ➤ Read about your personal Mystical Card on page 856.

VIRGO

From August 23, 6:03 through September 23, 3:21

The Social Activist

You 1948 Virgos can possess a political astuteness that sets you apart from Virgos born in other years. You were born during a time when the news was filled with revolutionary "firsts." For example, in 1948 a woman from the U.S. House of Representatives was elected to the Senate—the first female ever to have held a seat in both houses of Congress. The ceremony to inaugurate construction at the United Nations world headquarters in New York City broke new ground, too—both literally and figuratively. The world you were born into was growing in global consciousness, 1948 Virgo, and as you matured it's likely that you also became involved in the world community in some way.

You may tend to have an orderly mind and a soft heart—in fact, you're probably known for all but adopting your co-workers in an effort to organize them. At times, you may feel that you're carrying more than your share of the workload, but you also realize that you are far more capable of doing it than others might be. You might find a career as a customer service specialist, in quality control, or as a consultant. It's also possible that your love of the Earth could draw you to a job in the environmental sciences.

Your friends will probably always be a motley crew, each one entirely different from any other—and you'll love the varied opinions and new ideas every one of them will bring to the table. Cancer and Libra are comfortable companions, very committed to their word, and eager to keep their promises.

When it comes to romance, you'll probably always have plenty of admirers to choose from. It's likely that you'll find Pisces and Scorpio to be attractive companions, with the capacity to make you feel like family—and treat you every bit as well. But another Virgo or a Capricorn can probably give you the kind of stability you're after in a long-term relationship.

Your challenge is to avoid taking on responsibilities that aren't yours, keeping in mind that doing other people's work for them is really interfering in their growth process. Your gifts are your faith in the power of community and your diligence.

LIBRA

From September 23, 3:22 through October 23, 12:17

The Caring Environmentalist

Libra of 1948, you arrived just as uranium was found in the Belgian Congo, a discovery that led to fears that more countries would be able to construct the atom bomb. The subject of just who had "The Bomb" was probably a conversation you heard over and again while you were growing up, inspiring your Libran tendency to resolve conflict. And as you grew older, you probably thought often that it must be possible to handle disputes through technology rather than warfare. As a result, you may be drawn to groups and organizations that work to make life safer, and taking care of the environment can be very important to you.

You may have very deep powers of perception and the urge to break new ground in your career—which may focus on Earth sciences. Teachers may have seen scientific talent in you—in fact, your parents probably gave you a chemistry set or a microscope at an early age. Later on, you may have been drawn to the field of computers, following your interest in finding ways to make life easier through technology. You could also make a successful career at writing or research. Making money probably won't be your main goal, which paradoxically could make having all you need seem easy for you.

In friendships, you may feel as if you're always put in a position of leadership—in which case, you'll be eager to share the load with a partner. As a result, you'll probably gravitate naturally toward Leos, who'll guide you in a new and bold direction and be willing to help hold the pack together. But keep a Capricorn close by—after all, who's better to advise you about finding a comfortable way to take charge?

In love, you want someone who's bold and fiery yet deeply perceptive, someone who'll notice your mind as much as your physical beauty. Leo might be able to provide a good balance of strength and consideration, but don't overlook another Libran if you're after understanding and long-term commitment.

Your challenge is to handle the authority life hands you. Your gifts are your scientific and creative inspiration, and your ability to find useful applications for your ideas.

> ➤ Read about your Chinese Astrological sign on page 838. ➤ Read about your Personal Planets on page 826. ➤ Read about your personal Mystical Card on page 856.

VIRGO
Your Personal Planets

YOUR LOVE POTENTIAL
Venus in Cancer, Aug. 23, 6:03 - Sept. 08, 13:39
Venus in Leo, Sept. 08, 13:40 - Sept. 23, 3:21

YOUR DRIVE AND AMBITION
Mars in Libra, Aug. 23, 6:03 - Sept. 03, 13:57
Mars in Scorpio, Sept. 03, 13:58 - Sept. 23, 3:21

YOUR LUCK MAGNETISM
Jupiter in Sagittarius, Aug. 23, 6:03 - Sept. 23, 3:21

World Events

Sept. 9 - The People's Democratic Republic of Korea is proclaimed.

Sept. 13 - Republican Margaret Chase Smith is elected Senator — the first woman to serve in both houses of Congress.

Nazi propagandist Mildred Gillars, known as "Axis Sally"

LIBRA
Your Personal Planets

YOUR LOVE POTENTIAL
Venus in Leo, Sept. 23, 3:22 - Oct. 06, 12:24
Venus in Virgo, Oct. 06, 12:25 - Oct. 23, 12:17

YOUR DRIVE AND AMBITION
Mars in Scorpio, Sept. 23, 3:22 - Oct. 17, 5:42
Mars in Sagittarius, Oct. 17, 5:43 - Oct. 23, 12:17

YOUR LUCK MAGNETISM
Jupiter in Sagittarius, Sept. 23, 3:22 - Oct. 23, 12:17

World Events

Sept. 24 - Mildred Gillars pleads innocent of charges of being "Axis Sally," the Nazi propagandist.

Sept. 26 - Singer Olivia Newton-John is born.

399

1948

SCORPIO
Your Personal Planets

YOUR LOVE POTENTIAL
Venus in Virgo, Oct. 23, 12:18 - Nov. 01, 6:41
Venus in Libra, Nov. 01, 6:42 - Nov. 22, 9:28

YOUR DRIVE AND AMBITION
Mars in Sagittarius, Oct. 23, 12:18 - Nov. 22, 9:28

YOUR LUCK MAGNETISM
Jupiter in Sagittarius, Oct. 23, 12:18 - Nov. 15, 10:37
Jupiter in Capricorn, Nov. 15, 10:38 - Nov. 22, 9:28

World Events

Nov. 4 – T. S. Eliot wins the Nobel Prize for literature.

Nov. 16 – Operation Magic Carpet sees the first airplane carrying Jews from Yemen to Israel.

Literature Nobel Prize winner, T. S. Eliot

SAGITTARIUS
Your Personal Planets

YOUR LOVE POTENTIAL
Venus in Libra, Nov. 22, 9:29 - Nov. 26, 0:54
Venus in Scorpio, Nov. 26, 0:55 - Dec. 20, 7:27
Venus in Sagittarius, Dec. 20, 7:28 - Dec. 21, 22:32

YOUR DRIVE AND AMBITION
Mars in Sagittarius, Nov. 22, 9:29 - Nov. 26, 21:58
Mars in Capricorn, Nov. 26, 21:59 - Dec. 21, 22:32

YOUR LUCK MAGNETISM
Jupiter in Capricorn, Nov. 22, 9:29 - Dec. 21, 22:32

World Events

Nov. 29 – The first opera to be televised, *Otello*, is broadcast from the Metropolitan Opera House in New York.

Dec. 12 – Reports state that Communist forces are only fifty miles from Nanking.

SCORPIO

From October 23, 12:18 through November 22, 9:28

The Inconspicuous Executive

As a 1948 Scorpio, you arrived along with some shocking developments in the world, and this could be shown in the way you keep your friends and loved ones guessing—in much the way the news did back then. Around the time you were born, U.S. President Harry S. Truman was locked in a battle for re-election. He faced strong opposition from Republican Thomas E. Dewey, and the election was a race to the wire. Many citizens went to bed believing that Dewey had won, only to wake up to the news that Truman had triumphed in a photo finish—literally. In a photograph that became famous around the world, a smiling Truman held aloft a newspaper that had got it wrong. "Dewey Wins!" read the banner headline.

Like these amazing events, you can be a constant source of surprise to others, working quietly in the shadows only to emerge with a solution in sight—and the knowledge that you're in charge of it all. You are probably more objective than Scorpios born in other years, but you still retain the eerie perceptive qualities your sign is famous for. You probably like direct action, and have a way of disarming one and all with your wit and shrewdness. Needless to say, you'd make an excellent attorney or public advocate, but if you prefer to work behind the scenes, you could end up as a strategist for a company or as a political advisor. You like to play games that involve intricate rules and strategy—or anything that challenges you and really raises your heartbeat.

In friendships, you probably enjoy Virgo and Gemini most. Capricorns and Aquarians will be fun for you too, however, since they share your global view—and your wit.

You may be drawn to Librans when it comes to romance, the perfect sign for permanence. Regardless of which sign you choose for life, you'll want a partner who appreciates your keen powers of analysis and shares your ability to sweeten every moment with a laugh—and a warm embrace.

Your challenge is to channel your intensity and passion, and to keep your curious mind occupied with mysteries. Your gifts are your detective-like abilities and your keen observations.

SAGITTARIUS

From November 22, 9:29 through December 21, 22:32

The Smiling Worker

You've probably had plenty of chances to exercise your belief in truth and justice, Sagittarius of 1948. The battle has gone on for most of your life, inspired by the indictment of Algier Hiss around the time you were born. A former U.S. State Department official, Hiss was indicted by a federal grand jury on two counts of perjury. Your arrival, coinciding with a time when truth was quite literally on trial, reveals a lot about your character—and your love of honesty.

The fact that you can be a mighty adversary when it comes to what you believe in hasn't stopped you, however, from developing the warm heart and exuberant desire to have fun that makes your sign the most boisterous, adventurous, and fun-loving of them all. But there's a more serious side to you. You'll probably never back down from a challenge—and the harder the job is, the more determined you'll be to complete it.

You distinguish yourself from Archers born in other years by being a single-minded and disciplined worker. Once you get your mind on a task, not even a free trip to the Canary Islands can distract you—at least not until you get that work done.... The fact that you can concentrate during distracting times—along with your legendary sense of humor—makes you a valuable employee, especially well-suited to the restaurant business. In fact, you may love having an extra-large share of work to do so you won't be bored. In your spare time, too, staying busy is important to you, and if you don't work out at the gym you probably work at a hobby of some kind.

You may want your friends to be exciting, so you probably count plenty of Ariens, Geminis, and Leos among them. As for love, Virgo makes you feel protected but drives you crazy with details and what you think of as petty concerns. You may find Scorpio and Taurus sexy but equally hard to deal with in the long-term. Aries and Libra may be your best matches.

Your challenge is to know the difference between fighting for a cause and being a rebel without one. Your ability to enjoy physical pleasures and laugh at your troubles are your greatest gifts.

➤ Read about your Chinese Astrological sign on page 838. ➤ Read about your Personal Planets on page 826. ➤ Read about your personal Mystical Card on page 856.

CAPRICORN

From December 21, 22:33 through December 31, 23:59

The Ingenious Teacher

As a 1948 December Capricorn, you're probably a firm believer in the old adage that we reap what we sow in life. Still, you may have a happy-go-lucky attitude that doesn't seem to fit the stereotype of a Capricorn—which will probably please and delight you. Born during a time when scientific discoveries helped revolutionize basic fields of endeavor, you can be full of surprises—and probably quite the revolutionary genius yourself. Consider the fact that the "key starter" was introduced on cars this year, and the first Land Rover was produced. Over the years, you've probably retained the fiery, electric initiative your birth month provided, and maintained a fast-paced lifestyle to keep you from becoming bored.

You can have a keen curiosity that urges you to leave no stone unturned, and the personal confidence to find ways around any obstacles that block your path to success. In short, you're an expert at boldly going where you've never gone before—and at immediately being completely comfortable there. An adventurous spirit may have given you a taste for aeronautics, long-distance travel, or daredevil leisure-time activities—but you may also have a spiritual mission. You may long to visit a sacred site, or help lost souls find their way back to love and community. A natural teacher and businessperson, you may enjoy work that allows you to make presentations and speeches, such as public relations or corporate training.

Your best students, however, will always be your friends—and it's likely that Sagittarians will be right at the top of that list. Just don't forget that they may be able to teach you a thing or two. It's likely that your fellow Capricorns and sturdy Taurus playmates will be the ones you call on when you're in need of guidance.

In love, Leos will probably appeal to you most, but they'll also present you with challenges. Regardless of whom you choose for a mate, however, there's no limit to the things you'll want to see and experience together.

Your challenge is to focus on one dream at a time. Your gifts are your wit, humor, and splendid sense of adventure.

1948

CAPRICORN
Your Personal Planets

YOUR LOVE POTENTIAL
Venus in Sagittarius, Dec. 21, 22:33 - Dec. 31, 23:59

YOUR DRIVE AND AMBITION
Mars in Capricorn, Dec. 21, 22:33 - Dec. 31, 23:59

YOUR LUCK MAGNETISM
Jupiter in Capricorn, Dec. 21, 22:33 - Dec. 31, 23:59

World Events

Dec. 23 – Japanese Prime Minister Hideki Tojo and six others are executed in Tokyo.

Dec. 30 – Cole Porter's musical *Kiss Me Kate* opens on Broadway.

U.S. Navy Ship 'Cyclops', disappeared en route to the West Indies, 1918

Special Feature
The Mysterious Bermuda Triangle

(Continued from page 393)

Another explanation for the Bermuda Triangle has been giant methane bubbles rising up from the ocean bed and pulling craft down to their doom. Recent underwater surveys have proved that this phenomenon, known as "ocean flatulence," can put oil rigs, ships, and low-flying aircraft at risk. Pockets of the gas, derived from organic matter on the seabed, build up beneath the surface, and when the pressure becomes too great, the methane rises and produces a "blowout effect." This lowers the buoyancy of the water and any ship within reach will sink in a matter of minutes. Once on the surface, the gas continues to rise and can rob aircraft engines of oxygen or produce explosions from the highly flammable mixture of methane and air. Either way, the aircraft will crash and sink.

Nevertheless, the possibility can never be discounted that tales of strange disappearances in the Bermuda Triangle have been tailored in the telling. A case in point is DC-3 aircraft NC-16002, with thirty-two passengers and crew

aboard, which disappeared on December 27, 1948, while on a commercial flight from San Juan, Puerto Rico, to Miami, Florida. In the lore of the Bermuda Triangle, the story went like this: The plane was fifty miles from Miami and in visual contact with the control tower when the pilot, Captain Robert Lindquist, radioed for landing instructions. Miami sent the instructions, but there was no acknowledgment from Lindquist. Flight NC-16002 was never seen or heard from again.

However, subsequent investigation turned up circumstances not included in the story. Lindquist was evidently having compass trouble, because the position he radioed to the Miami tower was only an approximation of where he thought he was: his true and his imagined positions could have been at least fifty miles apart. The Miami tower transcripts made no mention of Lindquist sighting Miami. Lindquist radioed that he was flying due south, but his proper position, had he been on course, was east-south-east of Miami. In addition, a

change in wind direction had occurred, another factor that could make the DC-3 drift off course. All this suggests that Flight NC-16002 was nowhere near the Bermuda Triangle when it disappeared: it's much more likely that it crashed far away to the west, in the Gulf of Mexico.

There have been at least as many skeptics who try to defuse tales of the Triangle in scientific terms as there are those who adhere to paranormal explanations. This means that there can be no universally acceptable truth on the subject and only one certainty—the ages-old fact that strange things happen at sea.

➤ Read more about aliens in "The Extraterrestrial Highway" on page 465.

1949

Birth of Free Will: Uranus in Cancer

In 1949, Uranus, the planet of freedom, excitement, and ruler of all that is new, moved into the sign of Cancer, linked to motherhood, home, hearth, and the emotions. In this year, those with radical ideas about the home environment began to incarnate. Uranus remains in each sign for approximately seven years. The generation that came to be born in the year before the relatively bland era of the 1950s started would begin to shake things up a few years later when they reached maturity. Those born under the influence of Uranus in Cancer were those who became the flower children of the late 1960s. Their ideas about marriage, home, and family were sometimes even truly remarkable—and they caused a major paradigm shift when they began to take root.

And take root they did, because Cancer rules one's roots, the foundation, even birth itself. When Uranus comes to visit this sometimes rather traditional sign, things may go awry. The element of surprise is the key, but because Cancer can sometimes prefer the status quo, this isn't always the best combination. There can be conflict, as was seen in the late 1960s when the flower-power generation opposed their parents. Many of them left home early, and struck out on their own in true Uranian fashion. This generation also came to be known for its quirky taste in home décor; this is because Cancer is connected to interior decoration—the way people's homes reflect their characters and spirits. Black light posters, futuristic furniture, and beaded doorways were *de rigueur* for children born under the influence of Uranus in Cancer.

Mao Tse-Tung proclaims the People's Republic of China

Russians lift the blockade on Berlin

Katharine Hepburn and Spencer Tracy in "Woman Of The Year"

EXORCISMS

Douglas Deen, a fourteen-year-old boy from suburban Washington, DC endured all the drama of *The Exorcist* in 1949. The boy began hearing increasingly weird noises and experiencing strange disturbances in his room. When his family could find no other solution, they summoned a Catholic priest to exorcise the supposed demons from their home. During the exorcism ceremony, the boy screamed and shook violently. The ritual had to be performed thirty times over two months before the young boy's life returned to normal.

THE COLD WAR ESCALATES

East and West Berliners were more and more rigidly separated from each other by the Soviet blockade, until a compromise was negotiated by the United Nations. Germany divided into two states—communist East Germany and the Federal Republic of Germany. Tensions mounted when the Soviets revealed that they had the atomic bomb, increasing Cold War tensions. In China, Mao Tse-Tung's communist forces finally defeated the Nationalists, who withdrew to the offshore island of Formosa (Taiwan). The veteran anti-Nazi Konrad Adenauer was elected Chancellor in Germany. Wartime clothes rationing ended in Britain. In the U.S., Truman tried to calm fears about communist infiltration. The construction of United Nations headquarters on New York's East River commenced. Columbia's 33 rpm 'long playing' record was rivaled by RCA's 45 rpm record. George Orwell painted a bleak picture of a totalitarian future in *1984*. Katharine Hepburn and Spencer Tracy once more thrilled audiences, appearing in *Adam's Rib*, while Miller's play *Death Of A Salesman* received its first performance. De Beauvoir's thought-provoking book, *The Second Sex*, was published.

➤ Read Walt Disney's Star Profile on page 409.

CAPRICORN

From January 01, 0:00 through January 20, 9:08

The Practical Inventor

As a Capricorn born in January of 1949, you arrived as the world received news of a breakthrough in the music history—RCA introduced the first 45 rpm record this month. Lighter and smaller than the hefty vinyl discs that had been in use, this new format allowed records to be distributed quickly and easily to radio stations and jukeboxes around the world. This was the first of many breakthroughs this year, including the discovery of cortisone, which was developed to bring relief to sufferers of rheumatoid arthritis. The first non-stop around-the-world flight, requiring four in-flight refuelings, would also be completed in 1949. This focus on experimentation in all fields showed that the horrors of World War II were now—finally—being consigned to history.

You may have been born with a mixture of practicality and inventiveness by virtue of the fact that your conservative, traditional sign was equally represented in the heavens by visionary, futuristic Aquarius. It's likely that this blend of opposite forces gave you a respect for the mastery that comes from learning the rules, and the simultaneous urge to push past them in the pursuit of genius.

As such, you may be very learned, whether you come by that expertise through education or life experience. In any case, it's likely that you devoted your life to achieving proficiency in one particular field, and your greatest success may come from employing your unique mixture of traits equally. You can also be a good teacher, a wise mentor, and a worthy advisor, never offering advice if you're not completely convinced of its validity.

In romance, you'd do well to seek out the company of the other earth signs. Virgos and Taureans could provide you with a solid home base to return to after you're finished with your studies. In friendships, you might look to the cerebral air signs—Gemini, Libra, and Aquarius—for intellectual support and innovative ideas.

Your challenge is to maintain a balance between your quest to make new discoveries and your need for emotional stability. Your gift is your ability to stay focused on your goals.

AQUARIUS

From January 20, 9:09 through February 18, 23:26

The Calm Problem-Solver

You, 1949 Aquarius, were born during a time that would demonstrate the need for calmness and emotional detachment—two distinctly Aquarian traits. When *The War Of The Worlds* was rebroadcast in Quito, Ecuador, thousands of listeners panicked. The plot, a Martian invasion, provoked the same reaction from Ecuadorians as it had from Americans in 1938—for similar reasons. In both cases, due to widespread violence and rebellion, the real future may have seemed uncertain, and ordinarily sensible people were likely to believe anything. The lesson taught to the people of both times and places was the same, as well: that rational thought and objectivity were absolutely necessary in times of turmoil. Fortunately, you probably were born with both those attributes in abundance—and you do, indeed, demonstrate them most especially when crises arise.

The astrological influences in the heavens during your birth time also describe your capacity for sound reasoning and logical reaction. There were several planets in both your sign and in Capricorn, known for being sensible, reasonable, and deliberate. As such, you're not easily shaken—and that solid attitude has probably helped both you and those you love to weather life's stormier times.

It's likely that your unshakeable ability to cope with anything that comes your way has earned you the respect and confidence of those around you, from family members and friends to co-workers and employers. Whether the crisis is business or personal, you'll be able to provide comfort, candor, and practical solutions. In fact, you may be drawn to work that allows you to use these qualities, either by trouble-shooting, handling emergencies, or problem-solving—and you'll be good at all of it.

In love, you may look for a partner who's equally steadfast, solid, and practical—which describes the traits of Taureans, Capricorns, and Scorpios. You may also enjoy Geminis and Librans, the other air signs, whose cerebral, intellectual natures are bound to appeal to you.

Your challenge is to combine kindness with practicality. Your gift is your unshakeable courage.

➤ Read about your Chinese Astrological sign on page 838. ➤ Read about your Personal Planets on page 826. ➤ Read about your personal Mystical Card on page 856.

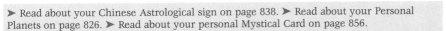

1949

CAPRICORN
Your Personal Planets

YOUR LOVE POTENTIAL
Venus in Sagittarius, Jan. 01, 0:00 - Jan. 13, 9:00
Venus in Capricorn, Jan. 13, 9:01 - Jan. 20, 9:08

YOUR DRIVE AND AMBITION
Mars in Capricorn, Jan. 01, 0:00 - Jan. 04, 17:49
Mars in Aquarius, Jan. 04, 17:50 - Jan. 20, 9:08

YOUR LUCK MAGNETISM
Jupiter in Capricorn, Jan. 01, 0:00 - Jan. 20, 9:08

World Events

Jan. 7 – The first photograph of genes is taken at the University of Southern California.

Jan. 15 – Chinese Communists seize Tientsin after a day-long battle with nationalist troops.

American actor Lee J. Cobb plays the part of Willy Loman in "Death of a Salesman"

AQUARIUS
Your Personal Planets

YOUR LOVE POTENTIAL
Venus in Capricorn, Jan. 20, 9:09 - Feb. 06, 9:04
Venus in Aquarius, Feb. 06, 9:05 - Feb. 18, 23:26

YOUR DRIVE AND AMBITION
Mars in Aquarius, Jan. 20, 9:09 - Feb. 11, 18:04
Mars in Pisces, Feb. 11, 18:05 - Feb. 18, 23:26

YOUR LUCK MAGNETISM
Jupiter in Capricorn, Jan. 20, 9:09 - Feb. 18, 23:26

World Events

Feb. 1 – Hungary proclaims the People's Republic.

Feb. 10 – Arthur Miller's *Death Of A Salesman* opens at the Morosco Theater on Broadway.

1949

PISCES
Your Personal Planets

YOUR LOVE POTENTIAL
Venus in Aquarius, Feb. 18, 23:27 - Mar. 02, 9:37
Venus in Pisces, Mar. 02, 9:38 - Mar. 20, 22:47

YOUR DRIVE AND AMBITION
Mars in Pisces, Feb. 18, 23:27 - Mar. 20, 22:47

YOUR LUCK MAGNETISM
Jupiter in Capricorn, Feb. 18, 23:27 - Mar. 20, 22:47

World Events

Mar. 4 – Israel is voted into the United Nations by the Security Council.

Mar. 15 – Clothes rationing is finally brought to an end in Britain.

The formal inauguration of Eire takes place in Dublin

ARIES
Your Personal Planets

YOUR LOVE POTENTIAL
Venus in Pisces, Mar. 20, 22:48 - Mar. 26, 11:53
Venus in Aries, Mar. 26, 11:54 - Apr. 19, 16:43
Venus in Taurus, Apr. 19, 16:44 - Apr. 20, 10:16

YOUR DRIVE AND AMBITION
Mars in Pisces, Mar. 20, 22:48 - Mar. 21, 22:01
Mars in Aries, Mar. 21, 22:02 - Apr. 20, 10:16

YOUR LUCK MAGNETISM
Jupiter in Capricorn, Mar. 20, 22:48 - Apr. 12, 19:17
Jupiter in Aquarius, Apr. 12, 19:18 - Apr. 20, 10:16

World Events

Apr. 4 – The North Atlantic Treaty Organization (NATO) treaty is signed by twelve nations.

Apr. 13 – Eire becomes the Republic of Ireland.

PISCES
From February 18, 23:27 through March 20, 22:47

The Treaty-Maker

Pisces of 1949, you were born into a time that was marked by the agreement of a major peace-seeking organization, when a group of nations came together, aiming to unite their efforts to promote world peace through both negotiation and military assistance. Among the nations of this coalition—which was known as the North Atlantic Treaty Organization (NATO), and which had been planned over many years—were the U.S., Great Britain, France, and Canada. The organization officially came into being on April 4. Arriving at this time in history may have instilled in you a lifelong love of peace and a keen understanding of the steps required to achieve it.

The astrological factors influencing your birth time were planets in your own idealistic sign and in humanitarian Aquarius. This powerful meeting of compassion and vision may show most especially in your ability to keep the peace within your own family and work relationships. As such, you're probably the person everyone turns to when there's a difficult situation to be ironed out.

Although this is a demanding and exhausting mission, your determination to keep volatile circumstances from spiraling out of control has probably kept more than one unpleasant incident from escalating. You also have an innate knack for helping opposing parties to understand how strongly the other side feels about their stance—which is the first step toward compromise. You may have begun using your talents at a young age, especially if your keen intuition told you there were serious problems brewing among family members. While you may always have a tendency to help in any unbalanced situation, it's also likely that you'll need to remember to keep your own needs in mind, as well as those of others.

In love, you'll probably be drawn to Scorpios and Cancerians, the other water signs, whose capacity for sympathy and understanding rivals your own. However, Taureans, Capricorns, and Virgos—the steady earth signs—could also win your affections.

Your challenge is to be as patient and understanding of yourself as you are of others. Your gift is your intuitive vision.

ARIES
From March 20, 22:48 through April 20, 10:16

The Uncompromising Judge

You were born into a world that was in the process of finishing up the last of World War II's business, Aries of 1949—exacting punishment on the Nazi war criminals who had not yet been called to account for the atrocities they had perpetrated. In 1949, the final judgments of the International Military Tribunal at Nuremberg were passed, sentencing Nazi leaders to death as retribution for the horrors they had helped to exact on the innocent. As such, your being may be infused with the strong seeds of justice—and your natural fire may have been fueled by the urge to achieve fairness for all. Although you may or may not have supported the death penalty in your later years, it's likely that you'll always have an innate urge to protect the interests of the weak—and you may become a powerful defender on their behalf.

The astrological factors that fueled your already substantial fire and passion for justice included several planets in your own sign, all of which are under the rulership of Mars, the ancient god of war. This stern, uncompromising warrior is an apt "patron planet" for you, since when your passion is aroused, there's absolutely no one who's potentially more volatile. But you were also given the powerful gift of Jupiter's presence in Capricorn, the inspiration behind the phrase "benevolent dictator." As such, while you're a formidable enemy and a determined defender, you also possess a sense of fairness that you extend to all.

You can have a strong personal power, and the ability to wield that strength impartially. You may be drawn to occupations that involve work with law enforcement, politics, or civil defense. Regardless of the field you choose, you'll be a capable and resolute defender when you feel the weak have been victimized—and you'll have no sympathy for those who use their power and strength for selfish or cruel purposes.

In romance, fair-minded Librans may appeal to you, as could objective Aquarians and justice-seeking Sagittarians.

Your gift is your ability to champion a cause with never-ending passion. Your challenge is to never stifle your emotions.

➤ Read about your Chinese Astrological sign on page 838. ➤ Read about your Personal Planets on page 826. ➤ Read about your personal Mystical Card on page 856.

TAURUS

From April 20, 10:17 through May 21, 9:50

The Educated Entrepreneur

Optimism and hope probably dominated your early upbringing, Taurus of 1949. You were born into a time marked by increasing prosperity for many people, as the world began to show signs of financial recovery from the poverty and deprivation caused by World War II. The increasing popularity of books on religion, world affairs, and philosophy, as well as the revival of the motion picture industry, showed that entertainment was no longer a luxury confined to the privileged classes. In fact, for the first time in years, it's likely that your parents had most of what they needed, and you may have been raised in a family that placed high regard on education and entrepreneurial goals, and that encouraged you to strike out on your own and go after your dreams.

The astrological influences of your birth time included several planets in your own sign, famous for its love of creature comforts, physical pleasures, and social amenities. But you also inherited an appreciation for the more cerebral side of life, such as works like Arthur Miller's *Death Of A Salesman*, which was awarded the Pulitzer Prize around the time you were born.

Your equal fondness for work and play has probably brought you the best in life, both materialistically and emotionally. Although you may not shy away from working hard to have what you want, you're also not afraid to enjoy the fruits of your labors. It's probably your home that your family and friends frequent most on holidays and special occasions—the place where many of your dear ones' warmest and happiest memories have been created. You may have a substantial collection of art and literature, but since your aim is not only to feed the mind but also to amuse the body and spirit, you probably have an equal number of games.

In love, it's likely that home-loving Cancerians, emotionally strong Scorpios, meticulous Virgos, or steady Capricorns can be good matches for you.

Your challenge is to enjoy the lifestyle you create with as much energy as you put into earning it. Your gift is your knack for balancing the needs of your spirit and emotions, mind and body.

GEMINI

From May 21, 9:51 through June 21, 18:02

The Inventive Story-Teller

The ingenuity and mental acumen that combined at the time of your birth are exemplified by the unveiling of the gas turbine electric locomotive in the United States, as well as the publication of two works of fiction destined to become classics—*The Greatest Story Ever Told* and *A Rage To Live*, both published in 1949. This combination of inventiveness and intellectual prowess might also describe you, for it's likely that you received a generous helping of your sign's cerebral aptitude.

This blend of scientific ability and imagination also showed in the astrological factors that were prevalent at your birth time. Several planets in your own sign worked together with other planets in the mental air signs to give you the potential not just for intelligence, but for genius. In fact, you're probably well known in your circles for being the "idea person," the one who comes up with the most entertaining, resourceful, and clever theories. As a result, it's likely that your company is sought out by many, either because of your wit or your technical expertise, and you may have a diverse group of friends.

This ease in socializing, added to your fast mind and faster wit, means you may be drawn to employment in fields that allow you to work one-on-one with others, or to lead groups. You'll still manage to find time to mingle with co-workers, though. You may also be an expert with computers or other electronics. One way or the other, it's likely that you'll be known as a "people person," preferring to strike up a conversation with a stranger rather than sit silently in a public place or on public transportation.

Your choice of partner, then, should necessarily lead you to the side of signs that are also well known for sociability. As a result, Librans, Pisceans, and other Geminis will likely be your first choices for romance. In friendships, look to Sagittarians and inventive Aquarians for companions who can keep up with your fast-moving mind.

Your challenge is to learn to enjoy your own company as much as you enjoy others'. Your gift is your ability to make friends with everyone you meet.

➤ Read about your Chinese Astrological sign on page 838. ➤ Read about your Personal Planets on page 826. ➤ Read about your personal Mystical Card on page 856.

TAURUS
Your Personal Planets

YOUR LOVE POTENTIAL
Venus in Taurus, Apr. 20, 10:17 - May 14, 0:24
Venus in Gemini, May 14, 0:25 - May 21, 9:50

YOUR DRIVE AND AMBITION
Mars in Aries, Apr. 20, 10:17 - Apr. 30, 2:32
Mars in Taurus, Apr. 30, 2:33 - May 21, 9:50

YOUR LUCK MAGNETISM
Jupiter in Aquarius, Apr. 20, 10:17 - May 21, 9:50

World Events

May 11 - The first Polaroid camera is sold for $89.95.

May 17 - The British government recognizes the Republic of Ireland.

Movie star Rita Hayworth becomes Princess Aly Khan

GEMINI
Your Personal Planets

YOUR LOVE POTENTIAL
Venus in Gemini, May 21, 9:51 - June 07, 10:46
Venus in Cancer, June 07, 10:47 - June 21, 18:02

YOUR DRIVE AND AMBITION
Mars in Taurus, May 21, 9:51 - June 10, 0:56
Mars in Gemini, June 10, 0:57 - June 21, 18:02

YOUR LUCK MAGNETISM
Jupiter in Aquarius, May 21, 9:51 - June 21, 18:02

World Events

May 23 - The Federal Republic of Germany (West Germany) officially comes into existence.

June 14 - The State of Vietnam is established with Bao Dai as its Emperor.

1949

CANCER
Your Personal Planets

YOUR LOVE POTENTIAL
Venus in Cancer, June 21, 18:03 - July 01, 23:39
Venus in Leo, July 01, 23:40 - July 23, 4:56

YOUR DRIVE AND AMBITION
Mars in Gemini, June 21, 18:03 - July 23, 4:56

YOUR LUCK MAGNETISM
Jupiter in Aquarius, June 21, 18:03 - June 27, 18:29
Jupiter in Capricorn, June 27, 18:30 - July 23, 4:56

World Events

June 22 - American actress Meryl Streep is born.
June 28 - The last U.S. troops leave Korea.

American actress Meryl Streep is born under the sign of Cancer

LEO
Your Personal Planets

YOUR LOVE POTENTIAL
Venus in Leo, July 23, 4:57 - July 26, 15:42
Venus in Virgo, July 26, 15:43 - Aug. 20, 12:38
Venus in Libra, Aug. 20, 12:39 - Aug. 23, 11:47

YOUR DRIVE AND AMBITION
Mars in Gemini, July 23, 4:57 - July 23, 5:53
Mars in Cancer, July 23, 5:54 - Aug. 23, 11:47

YOUR LUCK MAGNETISM
Jupiter in Capricorn, July 23, 4:57 - Aug. 23, 11:47

World Events

Aug. 3 - The National Basketball Association (NBA) is formed.
Aug. 14 - The last of the Nuremberg war-crime trials are concluded.

406

CANCER
From June 21, 18:03 through July 23, 4:56

The Liberal Practitioner

You arrived at a momentous time for the women of the world, Cancer of 1949. On June 23, the first twelve women were graduated with degrees from Harvard Medical School. This event gave a sense of authority back to women caregivers—some who may even have remembered that midwives were the primary physicians in days of old. Eliminating gender prejudice from the modern medical profession was an important step toward creating equal opportunities for everyone in every field. You too can be a gifted and instinctive nurturer who knows exactly what to do and say to offer comfort to those in need, and it's likely that you were born with respect for skill, professionalism, and ability—regardless of the sex, race, or religion of those who possessed them.

The astrological factors involved in your birth time were also well balanced and nurturing. While several planets wore your own sign, an equal number of earth, air, fire, and water planets presided, giving you a fair and even-keeled disposition. Your commitment to home and family, as well as career, may keep you busy, but you'll somehow manage to tend to both the personal and professional sides of your life with equal care.

You can be impartial in all matters, preferring to see the good in everyone—and, in fact, this faith will often bring out the best in others. As a result, if you're put in a position of authority, it's likely that your co-workers will strive to do their very best for you. You may choose to work from your home, turning a well-loved hobby into a profession. But no matter what you decide to do with your life, you'll always find time to be a devoted caretaker to your friends and family members.

When it comes to committing your heart, you'll probably be on the lookout for someone who's as stable, well-adjusted, and responsible as you are, and that means you may find yourself in the company of Capricorns, Librans, and Taureans.

Your challenge is to guard against being deceived by anyone who sees your capacity for fairness and unconditional acceptance as a weakness. Your gifts are your magnanimity and kindness.

LEO
From July 23, 4:57 through August 23, 11:47

The Proficient Performer

Leo of 1949, you were born at a time when theater, motion pictures, and music were booming. Since your sign has such strong connections to entertainment, you probably spent much of your early years at the movies—which means you may have developed an interest in performing yourself. It's probably no surprise to learn that a number of famous actors and actresses were born under the same sign as you—Robert DeNiro, Dustin Hoffman, Robert Redford, Madonna, and Melanie Griffith, to name but a few.

The heavens at the time of your birth show a versatile array of talents, as well as the diligence with which you'll pursue your chosen path. But it's likely that a rather "theatrical" quality will be present, even in your daily life. You may also have a knack for impersonation or mimicry. At any rate, you'll probably be the star of the show in just about any situation—and the person your family, friends, and co-workers will turn to for a smile after a tough day. This doesn't mean you can't also be very somber when the occasion calls for it—and extremely caring as well. In fact, it's likely that you'll take the matter of defending your loved ones very seriously. In times of trouble, they will undoubtedly come to you for support, advice, and solid answers—and you'll never let them down.

Your attention to detail means you may often turn a discriminating eye on yourself, however, never giving yourself credit for what you've accomplished unless someone else mentions it first—and even then, you may tend to be quite self-deprecating. Still, you'll never do anything half way or put less than your whole self into any project—so you need to learn to be as gentle and accepting of yourself as you are of others.

When it comes time to choose a partner, it's likely that you'll opt for an Aries or Sagittarius, one of the other fire signs. But no matter who you choose, you'll have what it takes to be a devoted spouse and a loving parent.

Your challenge is to never take yourself too seriously. Your gifts are your wisdom, humor, and laughter, which will deservedly earn you the admiration of others.

► Read about your Chinese Astrological sign on page 838. ► Read about your Personal Planets on page 826. ► Read about your personal Mystical Card on page 856.

VIRGO

From August 23, 11:48 through September 23, 9:05

The Diligent Worker

Born during 1949, Virgo, you arrived in an election season that showed the politicians' renewed interest in labor. In fact, in virtually every democratic country, candidates were taking great care to draw up platforms that would attract the votes of working-class men and women. This resurgence of interest in the opinions of the working class showed the power that its members held. And since your sign rules the issue of work, your pride in your chosen profession, as well as your need to stand up and be counted, was doubtless heightened by the energy of your birth time. In short, you're not afraid to work for what you want—but you may also crave recognition for your efforts.

You made your debut to a sky that held planets in a "cross" formation. Astrologically, this can indicate friction, high energy, and determination to accomplish—characteristics for which your hard-working sign is already well known. Still, these astrological factors reinforced your innate diligence and attention to detail, qualities which may mean you'll often take on jobs that others have left undone, or tasks others refuse to tackle. Regardless of what you're given to do, you won't stop until it's finished—a trait that means you're likely to climb rapidly in any field.

This responsible, practical side of you means you make a welcome addition to any gathering, whether for business or social purposes. You make as good a friend as you do an employee—and the trust you'll earn in both departments is unparalleled.

Your choice in a life-partner should definitely be someone whose work ethic and perseverance rivals your own. As such, Taureans and Capricorns, the other earth signs, could prove good choices for you. In business and friendships, look to the fixed signs—Taurus, Leo, Scorpio, and Aquarius—who always enter into a commitment with an eye toward keeping it.

Your challenge is to work with only those who appreciate your industriousness—otherwise, you may rapidly lose interest in your project. Your gift is the ability to take on jobs others might try to avoid, and to not stop until they're accomplished.

LIBRA

From September 23, 9:06 through October 23, 18:02

The Committed Judge

You, 1949 Libra, arrived at a moment that would demonstrate the need for two of your sign's most respected traits: grace under fire and a commitment to justice. In the United States, the fight to expose and punish those who had been indicted and found guilty of conspiring to overthrow the government had reached a peak. Despite the cost to his reputation, presiding federal judge Harold Medina oversaw the sentencing of twelve accused leaders of the Communist Party. Appropriately, Libra is represented by the scales of justice, making this event a perfect symbol of your sign's high regard for that quality. Regardless of whether he was right or wrong in his determination, Medina's commitment to justice, in the midst of personal attacks, became legendary.

The unwavering belief in justice for all also shows up in the astrological factors that presided over the Sun's thirty-day passage through your sign. Several planets were in your own high-minded, equality-seeking sign. And these energies combined with those of Jupiter—the mythical King of the gods and the ultimate impartial judge—in no-nonsense, dispassionate Capricorn, a sign also long associated with integrity and honor. In all, you were given a firmness of purpose, regardless of the cost to your personal popularity. It's likely that you're known for your principles and ideals, and you can be the person others seek out for suggestions on how to solve difficult moral and ethical questions.

All this may mean that you are involved in work with the legal system, but no matter what vocation you choose, your adherence to the rules and standards of that profession will undoubtedly put you in the well-deserved position of leadership.

In relationships, you may look for a partner whose scruples and exemplary character matches your own. As such, you may choose Sagittarians, Capricorns, Virgos, or other Librans, those that you feel you will always be able to stand by.

Your challenge is to ignore personal criticism and continue to pursue the truths you hold dear. Your gift is your complete impartiality in controversial issues.

➤ Read about your Chinese Astrological sign on page 838. ➤ Read about your Personal Planets on page 826. ➤ Read about your personal Mystical Card on page 856.

1949

VIRGO
Your Personal Planets

YOUR LOVE POTENTIAL
Venus in Libra, Aug. 23, 11:48 - Sept. 14, 17:11
Venus in Scorpio, Sept. 14, 17:12 - Sept. 23, 9:05

YOUR DRIVE AND AMBITION
Mars in Cancer, Aug. 23, 11:48 - Sept. 07, 4:50
Mars in Leo, Sept. 07, 4:51 - Sept. 23, 9:05

YOUR LUCK MAGNETISM
Jupiter in Capricorn, Aug. 23, 11:48 - Sept. 23, 9:05

World Events

Aug. 24 – The U.S. joins NATO.

Sept. 22 – The USSR detonates its first atomic bomb.

Mao Tse-Tung proclaims the People's Republic of China

LIBRA
Your Personal Planets

YOUR LOVE POTENTIAL
Venus in Scorpio, Sept. 23, 9:06 - Oct. 10, 10:17
Venus in Sagittarius, Oct. 10, 10:18 - Oct. 23, 18:02

YOUR DRIVE AND AMBITION
Mars in Leo, Sept. 23, 9:06 - Oct. 23, 18:02

YOUR LUCK MAGNETISM
Jupiter in Capricorn, Sept. 23, 9:06 - Oct. 23, 18:02

World Events

Oct. 1 – The People's Republic of China is proclaimed by Mao Tse-Tung.

Oct. 16 – The civil war in Greece ends with the defeat of the rebels.

1949

SCORPIO
Your Personal Planets

YOUR LOVE POTENTIAL
Venus in Sagittarius, Oct. 23, 18:03 - Nov. 06, 4:52
Venus in Capricorn, Nov. 06, 4:53 - Nov. 22, 15:15

YOUR DRIVE AND AMBITION
Mars in Leo, Oct. 23, 18:03 - Oct. 27, 0:57
Mars in Virgo, Oct. 27, 0:58 - Nov. 22, 15:15

YOUR LUCK MAGNETISM
Jupiter in Capricorn, Oct. 23, 18:03 - Nov. 22, 15:15

World Events

Nov. 7 - Konstantin Rokossovsky is appointed Minister of Defense in Poland.

Nov. 19 - Prince Rainier III is crowned King of Monaco.

Prince Rainier III, King of Monaco

SAGITTARIUS
Your Personal Planets

YOUR LOVE POTENTIAL
Venus in Capricorn, Nov. 22, 15:16 - Dec. 06, 6:05
Venus in Aquarius, Dec. 06, 6:06 - Dec. 22, 4:22

YOUR DRIVE AND AMBITION
Mars in Virgo, Nov. 22, 15:16 - Dec. 22, 4:22

YOUR LUCK MAGNETISM
Jupiter in Capricorn, Nov. 22, 15:16 - Nov. 30, 20:07
Jupiter in Aquarius, Nov. 30, 20:08 - Dec. 22, 4:22

World Events

Nov. 25 - Popular Tap dancer Bill "Bojangles" Robinson dies.

Dec. 8 - *Gentlemen Prefer Blondes* opens at the Ziegfeld Theater in New York.

SCORPIO
From October 23, 18:03 through November 22, 15:15

The Truthful Spokesperson

You were born during a time that would attest to your sign's propensity for expressing opinions in blunt, frank, and candid fashion, 1949 Scorpio. Although you may be criticized at times for this somewhat intimidating quality, your need to be honest makes you a noble and high-minded individual—someone who can always be trusted to speak the truth without sugar-coating it. During the thirty-day passage of the Sun through your sign, the second trial of Algier Hiss opened in New York City, and the issue of perjury—lying under oath—was broached to the entire world.

In addition to the strength of your Sun sign's conviction, several other astrological factors that influence your personality were equally bent on inspiring bluntness and candor in you. Mercury, the ancient messenger of the gods and the ruler of communication, was posited in direct, straightforward Sagittarius, and Jupiter, the ultimate mythical judge, held court in prudent, conscientious Capricorn. Like your 1949 Libran neighbors, you may actually be drawn to an occupation that allows you to profess your truth and serve as judge or legal enforcer. No matter what your vocation, however, it's likely that your commitment to the truth, and nothing but the truth, will gain you the admiration, respect, and support of your contemporaries.

It is probably this powerful trait that inevitably wins you friendships with others whose strong backbones make them worthy of your companionship. Although your strong personality is definitely not for the faint of heart, those who stick by you and remain loyal will earn your lifelong devotion—and your unwavering willingness to brave any storm for them.

In relationships, you probably wouldn't be able to settle down with anyone who shirks their responsibility for telling the truth. As such, honest Sagittarians, high-principled Capricorns, and objective Aquarians will be most likely to appeal to you.

Your challenge is to express exactly what's on your mind, regardless of public opinion, and never back down from the truth. Your gift is your ability to cut to the chase in all matters.

SAGITTARIUS
From November 22, 15:16 through December 22, 4:22

The Lifelong Student

Sagittarius of 1949, you arrived during a time that provided a perfect example of your sign's determination to teach, travel, and acquire experiences that broaden your intellectual horizons. Mao Tse-tung, premier of the newly formed People's Republic of China, was received at the Kremlin (a visit that displayed the bravery and adventurousness your sign is also known for), where he delivered a strong message about the importance of seeking out and expressing one's personal truths.

Astrologically speaking, your Sun-sign's period in 1949 provided you with a strong curiosity, but unlike those born under your sign in other years, you may also have a knack for assimilating details with precision and meticulousness. Energetic Mars, the most action-oriented planet in the heavens, was posited in Virgo, known for its connection to accuracy and exactitude. This can give you the ability to understand equally the importance of the details and the big picture. Combined with your love of distant places, this means you may end up traveling in order to study, teach, or learn the customs of a foreign place—and it's likely that you'll absorb every experience and new piece of knowledge with equal enthusiasm. Your love of wisdom may make you a lifelong student, and whether or not you pursue a degree or certification, you'll probably often be found in classes.

Your communication gifts can be substantial and quite exact. Rather than exaggerating for effect, you strive to relate what you know with care and discretion—which can make you a powerful speaker, a wonderful teacher, and a wise mentor. You may possess a gift for mingling with anyone, from any background and any walk of life, and your natural versatility and adaptability means that you're usually welcome in any social circle.

In romance, it's likely that you'll be after someone who shares your love of travel, new experiences, and educational adventures. This could mean other Sagittarians, or possibly cerebral Geminis and Aquarians.

Your gift is your endless thirst for knowledge. Your challenge is to keep from scattering your energy.

➤ Read about your Chinese Astrological sign on page 838. ➤ Read about your Personal Planets on page 826. ➤ Read about your personal Mystical Card on page 856.

CAPRICORN

From December 22, 4:23 through December 31, 23:59

The Impartial Juror

As a Capricorn born in December of 1949, you arrived during a period when the world's attention was focused on a trial that was being held for the second time that year—that of Algier Hiss, whose first perjury trial had ended in a deadlock in July. Charged with two counts of perjury relating to his testimony to a U.S. federal grand jury on alleged espionage activities, Hiss would eventually be found guilty. During the process of this second round of testimony, however, the job of the jurors—no easy task—was to impartially separate themselves from the frenzied media reports in the hope of arriving at a fair and impartial verdict. That quest for fairness and impartiality may be reflected in your own need to pursue your truth, and never to allow your ambition to get in the way of your conscience.

In addition to the influence of this event, however, the astrological factors of your birth time were also quite symbolic of your urge to get to the bottom of every moral and ethical question that troubles you. Your Capricorn intelligence and aptitude ensures that you'll make a name for yourself through reputable and righteous accomplishments, while keeping your self-respect and personal integrity.

In fact, you may find that you have an avid interest in legal matters, perhaps even to the extent that you pursue work within the legal or judicial system. And if called to serve on a jury yourself, it's likely that you'll listen carefully, follow the rules of determination, and make what you believe is a fair and honest judgment—regardless of your personal feelings.

In both personal and business situations, you may find that this same integrity and strength of character will draw you to the companionship of Virgos and Taureans, the other earth signs. But it's just as likely that Libra, the sign that's affiliated with the scales of justice, will appeal to you.

Your challenge is to live every moment of your life by the high scruples and ethics you own, never "selling out" for fame or professional success. Your gift is your keen and unbiased mind, which should make that job an easy one.

1949

CAPRICORN
Your Personal Planets

YOUR LOVE POTENTIAL
Venus in Aquarius, Dec. 22, 4:23 - Dec. 31, 23:59

YOUR DRIVE AND AMBITION
Mars in Virgo, Dec. 22, 4:23 - Dec. 26, 5:22
Mars in Libra, Dec. 26, 5:23 - Dec. 31, 23:59

YOUR LUCK MAGNETISM
Jupiter in Aquarius, Dec. 22, 4:23 - Dec. 31, 23:59

World Events

Dec. 28 – Hungary announces the nationalization of all its key industries.

Dec. 30 – India recognizes the People's Republic of China.

Walt Disney
December 5, 1901 - December 15, 1966

WALT DISNEY
Sagittarius

Walt Disney, the ruler of his own magic kingdom, was the winner of thirty-two Academy Awards and the creator of Mickey, the world's most famous Mouse. With his Sun in Sagittarius, the sign of exploration, Disney took his audiences along on his personal journey of creativity and imagination. His Sun closely contacted Uranus, the planet of technology, and it was the use of new technologies that fascinated him. The attractions in Disneyland and later Disney World were built with what he termed "imagineering," the combination of imagination and engineering. He was the first to add a music and effects track to a cartoon, and he risked everything on his first feature *Snow White And The Seven Dwarfs*.

With Neptune, the planet of imagination and film, placed in the career sector of his chart, Disney stands as a creative genius. His Moon in the first house in creative Libra also indicated his ability to please the public with his creations. With Jupiter, the planet that magnifies

everything that it touches, contacting Saturn, the planet of achievement, as well as energetic Mars, all in solid and business-like Capricorn, Disney built an empire that combined animation, movies, television, theme parks, and merchandizing.

The happy image he projected on TV was not all that it seemed, though. With the latter three important planets in the fourth house of foundations, Disney had had an emotionally and materially deprived childhood, further indicated by the difficult aspect these planets make to his Moon (the emotions, nurturing). In animation he found a perfect little world that he could control and shape in the way he liked. He could celebrate the uncomplicated sweetness of an ideal small-town life that he longed for.

Virgo, the sign of precision, is rising in his chart, making him a stickler for meticulous detail and a perfectionist. When asked late in life what he was proudest of, he said: "The whole thing.

The fact that I was able to build an organization and hold it." But Walt Disney is more than the sum of his achievements; he is a piece of Americana itself and his creations have endured as a symbol of American culture.

Mars and Jupiter Spotlight Uranus

In 1950, Uranus, planet of disruption and shocking surprises, had recently entered Cancer, the sign of home, hearth, and family. With this position, people felt more protective, even fearful of alien threat, and they wanted to build a dream world for their children—one that, with the Depression and two world wars behind them, they had not experienced themselves. With the assertive and aggressive planet Mars in a challenging contact to Uranus in January-February and June, paranoid protectiveness peaked as Senator Joseph McCarthy began his crusade to remove the communist "Red Threat" from American soil. This connection culminated in the ominous invasion of South Korea by communist North Korea in the month of June.

Saturn, the planet of responsible action and fierce drive, was highlighted in September by a challenging connection with Mercury, the planet of communication and foreign travel. This was felt when, after long debate, the United Nations decided to come to the aid of South Korea and invaded the country in September. In November, the Chinese communist army joined in the war on North Korea's side, as combative Mars also squared off with Saturn, then lent its volatility to Uranus once more later in the month. When war-mongering Mars raises his fist to taskmaster Saturn, you can be sure that the sparks that fly will catch fire and start a long, painful blaze. Usually a great lesson comes from the conflagration, though.

But all was not lost to darkness, as jolly Jupiter in idealistic and loving Pisces made a harmonious and creative "trine" with Uranus. A trine is one of the loveliest astrological aspects, bringing with it the best of both planets involved in the cosmic connection. This angle highlights the majesty of human ingenuity, courtesy of Uranus, from artistic to technological expressions, to the heights of humor, courtesy of Jupiter. As this link came into focus in April, RCA unveiled a new technology for color television, and Bob Hope made his first TV appearance. With both planets also symbolic of open-mindedness, racial barriers dissolved in several sports.

A soldier carries a small girl to safety in South Korea

Thor Heyerdahl's Kon-Tiki expedition leaves Peru

Atom spy Klaus Fuchs is released from jail

COMMUNISM SPREADS

Halfway through the century, the people of the world had two horrific wars behind them and the means to destroy the planet, but there was also a strong drive for peace. Despite this, war broke out in Korea between the communist North and the democratic South, and the Viet Minh fought the French in Vietnam. The U.S. headed a United Nations force supporting the South Korean government and sent troops and supplies to the war. China joined in on the North Korean side. The United Nations was used by Russia to promote East-West rivalries. Atom spy Klaus Fuchs was sentenced to fourteen years' imprisonment in Britain for supplying atom-bomb secrets to Russia. Pakistan and India came to an accord regarding the treatment of minorities, while communist China and the Soviet Russia signed a secret pact. A majority of U.S. schoolchildren were found to watch twenty-seven hours of television per week. RCA produced an experimental color TV, and the freedom of drive-in theaters attracted moviegoers in droves. Bradbury's *Martian Chronicles* was published. Norwegian anthropologist Thor Heyerdahl crossed the Pacific on the balsa-wood raft *Kon Tiki*.

➤ Read Mao Tse-Tung's Star Profile on page 417.

CAPRICORN

From January 01, 0:00 through January 20, 14:59

The Financial Warrior

As a 1950 January Capricorn, you were born at a time when battle lines were being drawn in many new kinds of struggle. Even as your parents welcomed in the New Year, they may have felt uneasy about the news from around the world. Alger Hiss, a former top State Department official, was sentenced to five years imprisonment for perjury for denying that he had passed top government secrets to Whittaker Chambers, a former agent for the Communists. The Red Scare in the United States was just one of many fronts in the newly emerging Cold War.

This could explain why you take on the task of amassing your fortune as if it were a battle, and why you see being the boss as winning the war. It goes without saying that you would make a good executive. And if you start out a little bit smaller—as an executive's assistant or a supervisor—you could still work your way into a position where you are the one in charge, even if you have only one employee. You probably have an easy time staying focused, and your interests naturally drift toward the things that allow you to make money. You may also tend to manage people and mentor others, encouraging them to be the same kind of achiever you are.

Personal relationships may not always be easy for you, Capricorn of 1950. Trust can be difficult if you have to ask yourself whether people want you as a friend or for the things you can do for them, and you may need to use the diplomatic skills you learned from your work to sort out the honest ones from those who may take advantage. Sagittarians, Taureans, and Virgos can be good choices as friends to have fun with.

In romance, you're likely to seek someone who's unique or unusual, and you most certainly need someone who can put up with your work schedule. An Aquarian could suit you as a partner, as you can share the world of ideas. Also, the two of you can be so efficient together, you could build a house in half the time it would take any other couple!

Your challenge is to allow yourself to relax. Your gift is the ability to get past your fears and feel certain that if you try, you will win.

AQUARIUS

From January 20, 15:00 through February 19, 5:17

The Circumspect Teacher

The year that you were born marked a halfway point for the century, and this could be why you may be concerned about the way the rest of it would turn out. You were born at a time when Senator Joe McCarthy was starting to identify "Communists" in the U.S. government; at the same time, Albert Einstein warned the world against the dangers of developing the hydrogen bomb. As you began your school years, the possibility that chaos would prevail was becoming frighteningly real. In the turbulent sixties and seventies, many Aquarians would wind up leading the anti-establishment rallies, but your unique perspective as an Aquarius of 1950 may have taken you on a different route.

You like to think of yourself as a person who learns from the past, and it wouldn't be surprising to find that you love to study history, anthropology, or archaeology. You can feel connected to the yearnings of your ancestors, and you may want to ensure that they are not forgotten. You want to build on what was left to you and create a legacy that can be passed on to a new and more enlightened generation. Teaching would certainly suit you as a profession, as would investigating the past through science. You might also enjoy writing, drawing, or music, since your ability to appreciate the arts is rooted in your sense of balance and precision.

A Virgo could make an excellent friend for you, especially at times when you need someone who will be stable, like the "rock" we all need in our lives from time to time. You enjoy fellow Aquarians too, and you might encounter them in a group that meets to play games as diverse as softball and chess.

In romance, Librans may attract you with their zesty attitude and enjoyment of life's finer points. For a long-term partner, though, look to Capricorn to calm your mind and help you to realize that all the world's problems do not rest on your shoulders—they probably think they rest on theirs.

Your challenge is to light a spark of awareness in the people you can influence. Your gift is the ability to assure everyone that the world will go on—as long as we make the right choices.

▶ Read about your Chinese Astrological sign on page 838. ▶ Read about your Personal Planets on page 826. ▶ Read about your personal Mystical Card on page 856.

1950

CAPRICORN
Your Personal Planets

YOUR LOVE POTENTIAL
Venus in Aquarius, Jan. 01, 0:00 - Jan. 20, 14:59

YOUR DRIVE AND AMBITION
Mars in Libra, Jan. 01, 0:00 - Jan. 20, 14:59

YOUR LUCK MAGNETISM
Jupiter in Aquarius, Jan. 01, 0:00 - Jan. 20, 14:59

World Events

Jan. 6 – The British government announces its official recognition of the Communist government of China.

Jan. 15 – Four thousand people attend the National Emergency Civil Rights Conference in Washington, DC.

U.S. Senator Joseph McCarthy

AQUARIUS
Your Personal Planets

YOUR LOVE POTENTIAL
Venus in Aquarius, Jan. 20, 15:00 - Feb. 19, 5:17

YOUR DRIVE AND AMBITION
Mars in Libra, Jan. 20, 15:00 - Feb. 19, 5:17

YOUR LUCK MAGNETISM
Jupiter in Aquarius, Jan. 20, 15:00 - Feb. 19, 5:17

World Events

Jan. 26 – India proclaims itself a republic and appoints Rajendra Prasad as its leader.

Feb. 9 – Senator Joseph McCarthy asserts that more than 200 Communists are working in the U.S. State Department.

PISCES
Your Personal Planets

YOUR LOVE POTENTIAL
Venus in Aquarius, Feb. 19, 5:18 - Mar. 21, 4:34

YOUR DRIVE AND AMBITION
Mars in Libra, Feb. 19, 5:18 - Mar. 21, 4:34

YOUR LUCK MAGNETISM
Jupiter in Aquarius, Feb. 19, 5:18 - Mar. 21, 4:34

World Events

Mar. 14 - The FBI's "Ten Most Wanted Fugitives" program begins.

Mar. 18 - Nationalist forces land on the Chinese mainland and seize the Communist stronghold of Sungmen.

Death of Russian ballet dancer Vaslav Nijinski

ARIES
Your Personal Planets

YOUR LOVE POTENTIAL
Venus in Aquarius, Mar. 21, 4:35 - Apr. 06, 15:12
Venus in Pisces, Apr. 06, 15:13 - Apr. 20, 15:58

YOUR DRIVE AND AMBITION
Mars in Libra, Mar. 21, 4:35 - Mar. 28, 11:04
Mars in Virgo, Mar. 28, 11:05 - Apr. 20, 15:58

YOUR LUCK MAGNETISM
Jupiter in Aquarius, Mar. 21, 4:35 - Apr. 15, 8:57
Jupiter in Pisces, Apr. 15, 8:58 - Apr. 20, 15:58

World Events

Apr. 8 - Celebrated Russian ballet dancer Vaslav Nijinsky dies.

Apr. 12 - American singer and actor David Cassidy is born.

PISCES
From February 19, 5:18 through March 21, 4:34

The Gentle Worrywart

As a 1950 Pisces, you were born into a world that talked openly of spies and counterspies and criminals who sought to evade the law. In an effort to show that society was at least trying to gain control over its renegades, the FBI had conveyed its determination that justice would prevail by instituting its list of "Ten Most Wanted Fugitives." In the rest of the world, such shows of Establishment power seemed to demand that citizens choose between right and wrong.

Later in life, you may have come to see such either/or choices as overly simple. But wondering what might happen next may in fact be one of your favorite pastimes, and it's possible that as a child you developed nail-biting to a state of high art. On the other hand, you are probably not the kind of Piscean who wants to save the whole world. Being born at the beginning of the first decade since the end of World War II gave you a unique perspective, perhaps, and you could be happy just making your corner of the world a little more peaceful. You might do this by taking on jobs that require someone to tend to everything down to the last detail. Catering, interior design, and editing a magazine are three good examples of careers that need the kind of dedication that you instinctively give.

You may have sought out friends who build your confidence—Aquarians to boost your ego and Librans to inspire you to find beauty in all things. You and a Taurus may well enjoy finding the best restaurants in town and sampling all that they have to offer. In love, the best partner for you is someone who is interested in the details of your life. But they should understand that you almost need a tiny bit of crisis to keep you going and that that isn't always a bad thing. Even if it might seem like a great relief at first, the last thing you want is a partner who solves all your problems for you!

Your challenge is to feel secure in your own little corner of the world and trust that the rest will ultimately take care of itself. Your gift is the ability to care about those little things that often matter more than we might realize.

ARIES
From March 21, 4:35 through April 20, 15:58

The Team Leader

You were born at a time when the world was getting smaller, Aries of 1950. Avro, the first turbojet transport plane, flew from Toronto to New York in one hour. Travel and commerce grew more convenient, especially for people in the western world, while in Korea war broke out between the communist North and the non-communist South. For you, growing up during the Cold War may only have underlined the necessity that people must learn to live together in a new way—as citizens of one planet. This could explain why you tend to shun status and power. You may be concerned with the collective, and how you might change things to gather resources together for peaceful purposes. You may be much more interested in progress than you are in politics, and you're more likely than not to have gotten in on the ground floor when it comes to science and technology. Your home may be filled with electronic gadgets, which you love to experiment with, hoping to make your own life more convenient and civilized.

If you were swept up in the electronic revolution of the 1970s and eighties, it's likely you were a manager who worked on ways to use technology to improve the well-being of the people who worked for you. Or you may have an interest in labor negotiations or in the field of ergonomics. You might feel most comfortable in groups, and you want to make your teammates comfortable and keep them safe.

Your friends admire your ability to get the whole gang together for fun, and the parties and networking events you put together can attract people from a variety of fields. Aquarians can appeal to you because they share your sense of being part of a larger tribe than simply one family circle. A Libran or Arien friend could also be a suitable business partner—you'll inspire each other to keep working when the rest of the world is taking a holiday!

In love, you tend to seek out people whose comparatively relaxed and soothing attitude helps to keep you calm.

Your challenge is to form even closer bonds with the ones you love. Your gift is the ability to make almost any location into a comfortable home.

➤ Read about your Chinese Astrological sign on page 838. ➤ Read about your Personal Planets on page 826. ➤ Read about your personal Mystical Card on page 856.

TAURUS

From April 20, 15:59 through May 21, 15:26

The Stubborn Romantic

As a Taurus of 1950, you were born during a time of sweeping social change and a simultaneous movement toward more traditional family values. The Baby Boom was just getting started, and the collective gaze was turned homeward—domestic life was at the center of everything. As the world watched, the People's Republic of China banned traditional religious observances, attempting to govern its citizens' behavior in the realm of religion. Also this year, a new Marriage Law in China abolished forced and arranged marriages, and made divorce easier.

All of the focus on family values at the time you were born might explain why you embody the ideas of tradition in relationship, Taurus of 1950. But it's hardly likely that you need an authority to force you to comply with ideals like love and loyalty! You have an idealistic view of love that transcends the physical plane. You may feel that you were destined to find your soul mate, and you probably began looking for that perfect partner very early in life.

You may even have been able to make your living by matching people up, Taurus of 1950. With your keen intuition and eye for talent, you could do well as a personnel recruiter, an agent for entertainers or models, or running a dating service. It's likely that you enjoy mixing business with pleasure: you like to work with friends, and you almost never leave a party without having made at least one new acquaintance.

You probably believe in love at first sight, but your steady nature may have kept you from acting impulsively during the many times you've fallen "in love." You may like to flirt with Cancerians and Geminis, but when you settle down it's likely to be with a fellow Taurus. You like the feeling of being with someone who makes you feel as though you have known each other forever. And, with your desire to never let go of a lover even after the passion fizzles, you just might!

Your challenge is to realize that sometimes it's best to leave people to their own devices rather than push them together. Your gift is your ability to see how everyone has at least a little good within.

GEMINI

From May 21, 15:27 through June 21, 23:35

The Social Equalizer

Gemini of 1950, you were born at a time when archaic social traditions were beginning to crumble. In the United States, the Supreme Court barred segregation in two colleges, marking important victories in the fledgling civil rights movement of the 1950s and sixties. In large ways and small, people were just beginning to rise up against oppression. This could be why the idea of bringing in new ideas and dissolving the forces that promote unfair practices can be so important to you. You may work very hard to ensure that no one gets less than a fair share, and if you perceive that people need help accessing the resources they need to thrive, you may offer to help by showing them how to do it.

Such characteristics mean that you may not be especially interested in personal financial gain—you could be an excellent social worker or government policymaker, such as the head of a human rights agency. You might also work in a school as a counselor or on the medical staff, where you could ensure that the advantages are being meted out to the people in your charge in fair and equal portions.

People earn your friendship by showing you that they too are filled with compassion. Librans can be your closest match, because they have an inherent sense of equality that transcends human law. Pisces is your next closest match, because this sign, too, has a way of seeing the world that puts everyone on equal footing. Because you like to be around people who care about social issues as much as you do, you might also find that you work with quite a few Pisceans and even some visionary Aquarians.

In love, a steadfast Virgo would work hard to make sure that you have a peaceful and attractive home life. Since Virgo's life mission is about being of service, it's also likely that you and your mate would share the same ideology. Even if your home may be humble in material terms, it can be full of the kind of love that can't be bought at any price.

Your challenge is to give yourself permission to have the things you need. Your gift is your ability to get along with just enough to make you comfortable.

➤ Read about your Chinese Astrological sign on page 838. ➤ Read about your Personal Planets on page 826. ➤ Read about your personal Mystical Card on page 856.

TAURUS
Your Personal Planets

YOUR LOVE POTENTIAL
Venus in Pisces, Apr. 20, 15:59 - May 05, 19:18
Venus in Aries, May 05, 19:19 - May 21, 15:26

YOUR DRIVE AND AMBITION
Mars in Virgo, Apr. 20, 15:59 - May 21, 15:26

YOUR LUCK MAGNETISM
Jupiter in Pisces, Apr. 20, 15:59 - May 21, 15:26

World Events

Apr. 23 – The nationalist invasion in China fails and Chiang Kai-Shek orders a withdrawal.

May 1 – Gwendolyn Brooks becomes the first black woman to receive the Pulitzer Prize, for her book of poetry *Annie Allen*.

French climbers Maurice Herzog and Francis De Noyelle

GEMINI
Your Personal Planets

YOUR LOVE POTENTIAL
Venus in Aries, May 21, 15:27 - June 01, 14:18
Venus in Taurus, June 01, 14:19 - June 21, 23:35

YOUR DRIVE AND AMBITION
Mars in Virgo, May 21, 15:27 - June 11, 20:26
Mars in Libra, June 11, 20:27 - June 21, 23:35

YOUR LUCK MAGNETISM
Jupiter in Pisces, May 21, 15:27 - June 21, 23:35

World Events

June 3 – A French expedition reaches the top of the Himalayan peak of Annapurna in Nepal.

June 10 – Soviet proposals for German re-unification are rejected by the West.

1950

CANCER
Your Personal Planets

YOUR LOVE POTENTIAL

Venus in Taurus, June 21, 23:36 - June 27, 10:44
Venus in Gemini, June 27, 10:45 - July 22, 17:49
Venus in Cancer, July 22, 17:50 - July 23, 10:29

YOUR DRIVE AND AMBITION

Mars in Libra, June 21, 23:36 - July 23, 10:29

YOUR LUCK MAGNETISM

Jupiter in Pisces, June 21, 23:36 - July 23, 10:29

World Events

June 25 – Communist North Korea invades the South, instigating three years of war.

July 22 – King Leopold returns to Belgium after six years in exile.

King Leopold of Belgium

LEO
Your Personal Planets

YOUR LOVE POTENTIAL

Venus in Cancer, July 23, 10:30 - Aug. 16, 14:17
Venus in Leo, Aug. 16, 14:18 - Aug. 23, 17:22

YOUR DRIVE AND AMBITION

Mars in Libra, July 23, 10:30 - Aug. 10, 16:47
Mars in Scorpio, Aug. 10, 16:48 - Aug. 23, 17:22

YOUR LUCK MAGNETISM

Jupiter in Pisces, July 23, 10:30 - Aug. 23, 17:22

World Events

Aug. 3 – The United Nations Security Council vetoes Communist China's entry to the union.

Aug. 5 – Florence Chadwick breaks the record for swimming the English Channel in thirteen hours and twenty-two minutes.

CANCER
From June 21, 23:36 through July 23, 10:29

Everybody's Loving Sibling

The summer of 1950 was a time when the sanctity of the homeland was being acknowledged by governments around the world. In the U.S., President Truman signed a law allowing citizens of Puerto Rico to write their own constitution, while in Israel, the Law of Return was passed, guaranteeing all Jews the right to live in the Jewish state. Even if you see the world as one large community, Cancer of 1950, all the "nesting" that was going on when you were born could explain why you can also relate to the concept that people everywhere want a section of it to call home.

You may have a highly developed political consciousness, and much of this might rest with the idea of allowing people to keep their traditions. You can probably be found haunting ethnic restaurants, asking the proprietor about the food. You may also want to know more about the culture and learn which holidays call for the various dishes to be served. You might even have become one, as you grew older, to actively resist the forces of homogenization that caused some of the peoples of the world to melt into one bland mass.

Your desire to embrace people for their unique qualities can draw you to Aquarians, Pisceans, and Scorpios. You may like to make a family out of your friends, especially if some aspects of your own home life were not particularly pleasant. You might have had to move a lot when you were young, or there could have been some disputes that disturbed your sense of comfort at home. Due to such disruptions, you may have taken to carrying your home with you wherever you go, and you can probably feel at home in a variety of traditions.

In love, you seek out steadiness and security, and this may well draw you to a Taurean. Taurus doesn't take commitment lightly, so make sure you're ready for a long relationship if you're involved with someone of this sign—they're no more likely than you to put up with disloyalty or intolerance.

Your challenge is to understand that you need to look out for yourself as much as you protect others. Your gift is your ability to relate to people from all walks of life and almost every culture.

LEO
From July 23, 10:30 through August 23, 17:22

The Soft-Pedaled Transformer

You may not be as outspoken as all the astrology books say you're supposed to be, Leo of 1950. In fact, you might prefer working on one person at a time to trying to change the world all at once—and this is a wise choice for you, no matter how unlike a typical Leo it might be. Like the earthquake in India that burst from the bowels of the Earth at the time you were born, you may feel that your energy can sometimes overwhelm the people in your midst. If you were to let out the true force of your power, it could be difficult for you to put a stop to it. This is why you can have a way of quietly working behind the scenes to effect the change that you are after.

You may think a lot about how you can protect yourself from the world's harsh realities, and at the same time you can also strive to bring out the best in others. It's likely that you prefer fighting with words than weapons, and you may well be a capable debater. You would be a good prosecutor or law-enforcement officer, and you could also do well in sales. Most of all, however, you are gifted with the ability to see behind the façade that people put forth, and you can get to the core of their being, well before they are willing to reveal it to you. This could make you a talented psychotherapist or perhaps a counselor.

When it comes to your leisure time, you're likely to prefer going out on the town to a quiet evening at home. A Sagittarian can be a great friend or date, while Cancerians may interest you—but can also make you nervous. You may have much in common with Scorpios, who can compare notes with you on the finer points of people's psychic lives. The two of you could make jokes about the subliminal messages in people's conversations for an entire evening.

When it comes to finding a life partner, you can be extremely attracted to Pisces and Gemini. Both of these signs have an adaptable nature that you may appreciate, and they give you a feeling of hope as well as inner beauty.

Your challenge is to find good ways to release tension. Your gift is the ability to see beyond the evidence and discover the truth.

➤ Read about your Chinese Astrological sign on page 838. ➤ Read about your Personal Planets on page 826. ➤ Read about your personal Mystical Card on page 856.

VIRGO

From August 23, 17:23 through September 23, 14:43

The Poetic Communicator

It's possible that the background music for the time of your birth (songs like "Mona Lisa" and "Sentimental Me") inspired a desire to communicate what is in your heart, Virgo of 1950. This might also explain why you can be more emotionally aware than other Virgos. In fact, it's likely that you are able to soften the criticism for which your sign is known with the diplomacy that helps people take it much more easily.

You may think on the detail level and yet be very diplomatic with others. In addition, you can have considerable writing talent and the ability to make even the most mundane idea sound like poetry. This can make you a good speechwriter or screenwriter, as well as a person who works behind the scenes in television broadcasting or motion pictures. You may not have a great deal of ambition when it comes to earning money, and you also want the luxury of indulging yourself in projects that don't necessarily earn you a lot of money. It's likely that you have a strong work ethic, so you might work a day job and do something artistic during your off-hours.

Your friends are not very numerous, but that's not because you are not well liked. You may prefer to keep to a small circle of people, and because you are so busy, you don't have a lot of time to keep up superficial relationships. You may treasure your deep and heady conversations with Librans and your fellow Virgos. Like you, they're not likely to miss a detail and yet they can be very accepting of others.

You play for keeps in love, and it's possible that you could do very well through your partner's ability to take care of you. The only difficulty you might have here is that you may feel you do not contribute enough. Look to a Pisces to help you find a way of accepting this kind of relationship—surely you will be appreciated for your ability to keep your Piscean grounded in reality and feeling safe.

Your challenge is to learn to measure your contribution in ways other than wealth. Your gift is the ability to see beauty in the simplest of things, and love shining in the eyes of everyone you encounter.

LIBRA

From September 23, 14:44 through October 23, 23:44

The Clever Idealist

The world you were born into needed some healing, 1950 Libra. Surprise attacks filled the news. While the U.S.-led UN forces were pushing the North Koreans all the way to the Chinese border, Chinese forces invaded Tibet. These disconcerting shocks of war troubled a world in which so many people longed for peace.

Such uncertainties occurring around the time you were born could be why you might have even more trouble than other Librans in decision-making. As far as you're concerned, you may never have all the information, so you could be constantly putting your finger to the wind to see which way it's blowing. You may be an excellent political advisor or "spin doctor," as you probably have no trouble finding a multitude of different ways to express the same idea. At the same time, the idealism you were born with could make you want to work for peace. You may have felt that working for a newspaper or television news station would ensure that the messages that express ways of spreading peace throughout the world are sent out in every direction. You could also work with organizations that support political causes, or you might be a company designate for lobbying and canvassing politicians in power.

Since you can be a natural politico yourself, you tend to keep a lot of people around you, and you do like them all. But the ones you wouldn't want to do without would be the Leos, because their high self-esteem helps you to feel even more empowered about the things you do every day. You may also gravitate toward your fellow Librans. Like you, they may believe that there are better ways than killing to settle disputes over land. When you're with them, you can express your global insights and display your intuitive understanding of politics.

In love, you like the passion of Sagittarius, but you could also be gratifyingly joined with a Cancer or Aries. It would be good if at least one of you in the household were able to make quick decisions!

Your challenge is to see the truth before you get lost in someone else's cause. Your gift is the ability to find peaceful solutions.

➤ Read about your Chinese Astrological sign on page 838. ➤ Read about your Personal Planets on page 826. ➤ Read about your personal Mystical Card on page 856.

VIRGO
Your Personal Planets

YOUR LOVE POTENTIAL
Venus in Leo, Aug. 23, 17:23 - Sept. 10, 1:36
Venus in Virgo, Sept. 10, 1:37 - Sept. 23, 14:43

YOUR DRIVE AND AMBITION
Mars in Scorpio, Aug. 23, 17:23 - Sept. 23, 14:43

YOUR LUCK MAGNETISM
Jupiter in Pisces, Aug. 23, 17:23 - Sept. 15, 2:22
Jupiter in Aquarius, Sept. 15, 2:23 - Sept. 23, 14:43

World Events

Aug. 29 – The first British troops land in Korea as part of the United Nations effort to assist South Korea.

Sept. 15 – United Nations forces arrive at Inchon and begin to march on Seoul.

Soldiers in South Korea had many peace-keeping duties

LIBRA
Your Personal Planets

YOUR LOVE POTENTIAL
Venus in Virgo, Sept. 23, 14:44 - Oct. 04, 5:50
Venus in Libra, Oct. 04, 5:51 - Oct. 23, 23:44

YOUR DRIVE AND AMBITION
Mars in Scorpio, Sept. 23, 14:44 - Sept. 25, 19:47
Mars in Sagittarius, Sept. 25, 19:48 - Oct. 23, 23:44

YOUR LUCK MAGNETISM
Jupiter in Aquarius, Sept. 23, 14:44 - Oct. 23, 23:44

World Events

Oct. 14 – The Rev. Sun Young Moon is liberated from Hung Nam prison.

Oct. 19 – United Nations forces enter Pyongyang, the North Korean capital.

1950

SCORPIO
Your Personal Planets

YOUR LOVE POTENTIAL

Venus in Libra, Oct. 23, 23:45 - Oct. 28, 5:32
Venus in Scorpio, Oct. 28, 5:33 - Nov. 21, 3:02
Venus in Sagittarius, Nov. 21, 3:03 - Nov. 22, 21:02

YOUR DRIVE AND AMBITION

Mars in Sagittarius, Oct. 23, 23:45 - Nov. 06, 6:39
Mars in Capricorn, Nov. 06, 6:40 - Nov. 22, 21:02

YOUR LUCK MAGNETISM

Jupiter in Aquarius, Oct. 23, 23:45 - Nov. 22, 21:02

World Events

Oct. 26 - Mother Theresa founds the Mission of Charity in Calcutta, India.

Nov. 10 - The Nobel Prize for literature is awarded to William Faulkner.

Mother Theresa in Calcutta

SAGITTARIUS
Your Personal Planets

YOUR LOVE POTENTIAL

Venus in Sagittarius, Nov. 22, 21:03 - Dec. 14, 23:53
Venus in Capricorn, Dec. 14, 23:54 - Dec. 22, 10:12

YOUR DRIVE AND AMBITION

Mars in Capricorn, Nov. 22, 21:03 - Dec. 15, 8:58
Mars in Aquarius, Dec. 15, 8:59 - Dec. 22, 10:12

YOUR LUCK MAGNETISM

Jupiter in Aquarius, Nov. 22, 21:03 - Dec. 01, 19:56
Jupiter in Pisces, Dec. 01, 19:57 - Dec. 22, 10:12

World Events

Dec. 5 - The North Koreans drive the UN forces out of their capital Pyongyang.

Dec. 16 - U.S. President Truman proclaims a state of emergency against "Communist imperialism."

SCORPIO

From October 23, 23:45 through November 22, 21:02

The Decisive Winner

The technology explosion was in full swing when you were born, Scorpio of 1950, and this could explain why you're usually the first to try anything new. Life in the fast lane may appeal to you, so it's fitting that around the time you were born, jet planes were bringing new speed and power to the business of war in Korea. Growing up in the 1950s and sixties, you probably loved the new aerodynamic styling of the cars, too!

It's likely that you were impressed by humanity's material progress as you grew up, and you may even have gone into in overdrive when it came to making your fortune. You may be extremely aggressive about earning money, and you might have succeeded beyond your ambitious expectations. You could be an excellent investor for your own portfolio, or you might be the one who is in charge of investing money for a company that deals with machines or energy. You would be very good at working with contracts or as an arbiter, as well, since you're able to see both sides of an issue and resolve disputes easily. You can be charming, so it's also likely that you'd do well in a field like client development or sales. Seeing the world could appeal to you, and you probably can be ready to leave the country at a moment's notice, either for business or for the sole purpose of unwinding.

Your friends admire your versatility, and they are attracted to your inner radiance and your intensity. You like to play with Librans and Cancerians, especially if they enjoy traveling with you. You can be intent on ensuring that your status in the community is never questioned, so keeping a powerful Leo around is always a good idea.

You would be likely to choose a mate based on his or her ability to be flexible and willing to help you enjoy the fruits of your labor. An Aquarian could be a friend and a lover to you, as well as a person you can count on to share your fervor for excitement. The home you might make together would be sure to be beautiful.

Your challenge is to slow down every so often so that you can incubate fresh ideas. Your gifts are your incisive mind and winning personality.

SAGITTARIUS

From November 22, 21:03 through December 22, 10:12

The Patriotic Speculator

When the Sun was in Sagittarius in the year you were born, as the war in Korea wore on, U.S. President Harry S. Truman declared a state of emergency against "Communist Imperialism." His Economic Stabilization Agency imposed new wage and price controls in response to the shocking setbacks in Korea. Such events may have inspired you later in life, Sagittarius of 1950, to amass the resources that could protect you and the people you love in the event of an emergency.

You can be extremely ambitious, with a drive to succeed that's likely to have made you stand out at an early age. You may be a natural athlete, but when you were a child you probably also loved to play Monopoly or other board games because you could pretend to make deals and count money. It's not that you're cold and calculating, it's just that the principles you grew up with may have taught you that it was important to acquire the resources you need to survive when you live in an uncertain world. As a result, you may feel that it is your responsibility to be prosperous. You could be a speculator, dealing in commodities, or in the energy business exploring the Earth for new resources. If you like to keep things on a smaller scale, you might work with gardening supplies or help to facilitate the sale of municipal bonds and other securities.

Your friends are likely to be as ambitious as you are, and you probably have plenty of Ariens and Leos among them. Capricorns and Taureans may also appeal to you, as they appreciate the things that money can buy and enthusiastically join you in enjoying them.

You might need another Sagittarian as a lover just so that you can be assured of having enough passion to keep you satisfied. You can have a great love of being alone, though, so you may also require a partner who will understand when you retire to the TV room for a weekend afternoon of old movies. A Cancer might even make you some popcorn!

Your challenge is to remember to share the things that you have with others who need them. Your gift is the ability to polish a diamond in the rough and make it your fortune.

➤ Read about your Chinese Astrological sign on page 838. ➤ Read about your Personal Planets on page 826. ➤ Read about your personal Mystical Card on page 856.

CAPRIC●●N

From December 2● ●through December 31, 23:59

The ●●pable Engineer

In th● ●●days of 1950, when U.S. and South Korean troops withdrew in th● ●●a Chinese offensive in Korea, it might have seemed that the ●●●democracy would be unable to withstand the advance of Co●●●●. Events like this would have been in the news when you were born, December Cap●●●●1950, and could explain why you may have grown up wanting to escape from a wo●●●as growing increasingly threatening. As a youth, you may have wondered if life rea●●d on other worlds, and perhaps you lost yourself in magazines like *Galaxy*, one of ●●●science-fiction publications. You may still enjoy thinking and reading about the ●●●●

Your capacity f●●●ng your interests in your work can be phenomenal. You could be something of a ti●●●●o wound up becoming an inventor or software designer. Or you could be involve●●●●tics or bioengineering. If you chose a less heady career, it's likely that you used e●●●●that didn't even exist at the time that you were born, and that you adopt new tech●●●●as soon as you see how they can contribute to your financial well-being. At work ●●●●robably the one who takes the lead, often offering your help to employees or co-workers who want to learn how to use technology to their greater benefit.

You might enjoy explaining your work to your friends, especially if they're not the most technologically advanced people in the world. But your Taurus pals are good at helping you make money from your ideas, so you're usually anxious to see what they have to say. If you want to forget about work, you might call one of your Pisces friends, who can tell you stories that allow you to see the world in a new and creative way.

In love, you can be attracted to deeply passionate people. A Sagittarian could make a good confidante for you. You need someone to provide for, and this sign at least lets you think that they could not get along without your help!

Your challenge is to develop your capacity to have fun. Your gift is your ability to make progress when others would stay stuck behind obstacles.

1950

CAPRICORN
Your Personal Planets

YOUR LOVE POTENTIAL
Venus in Capricorn, Dec. 22, 10:13 - Dec. 31, 23:59

YOUR DRIVE AND AMBITION
Mars in Aquarius, Dec. 22, 10:13 - Dec. 31, 23:59

YOUR LUCK MAGNETISM
Jupiter in Pisces, Dec. 22, 10:13 - Dec. 31, 23:59

World Events

Dec. 25 – The Coronation Stone, taken from Scone in Scotland by English King Edward I in 1296, is stolen from Westminster Abbey and smuggled back to Scotland.

Dec. 27 – Spain and the U.S. resume diplomatic relations after a hiatus.

Mao Tse-Tung
December 26, 1893 - September 9, 1976

MAO TSE-TUNG
Capricorn

Mao, a key figure in China in the twentieth century, desired equality for all in his country. During the turbulent years after World War I, he searched for an ideology that would match his vision for a reformed China. As the teachings of Marx and Lenin came out of Russia, Mao felt that they might be the answer to the imperialist, warlord mentality in his nation. Considered undereducated by China's rulers and their Russian allies, Mao turned to the peasant population and organized a revolt that ultimately led to his election to power and the spread of his personal ideology.

Mao was a Capricorn—a sign noted for its practical, hardworking nature. Saturn, the ruler of Capricorn and the planet of hard work, achievement, and life lessons, was prominently placed in his horoscope, indicating a long but steady battle toward success. Mao's rise to power wasn't swift and for most of life he fought those who

attempted to unseat him. Uranus, the planet of upheavals, was in his house of career and perhaps this further explains his many drives for power and the equal number of setbacks he suffered.

Mao's chart features a precise geometrical configuration highlighting Mercury, the planet of thought and communication. This might explain why, although he was a relatively uneducated man, he sought deep ideas and worked tirelessly to share them with the people of his nation. With Mercury in egalitarian Sagittarius, it's no wonder that Mao's philosophies were built on a desire to strip China of its rigid, tradition-bound power structure and introduce a new regime.

Mercury received many contacts in Mao's chart. It was aspected by the Moon, planet of emotions, giving him the ability to communicate from the heart. A contact from controlling Pluto bestowed deep thought as well as a verbally domineering style and the

willingness to argue for his beliefs. A contact from Neptune, planet of idealism, helped him beyond the reality that surrounded him in order to seek something he considered better. Without doubt, he remains an influential figure in China as well as one of the most important reformers worldwide.

➤ Read Richard Nixon's Star Profile on page 577.

417

1951

Limiting Power: Jupiter Opposes Saturn

Jupiter, the planet of expansion, contrasted with Saturn, the planet of contraction, coinciding with the establishment of new, often beneficial, limits on business and government. Together, these planets demarcate the balance of power, especially when they are linked from opposite positions in the heavens, where they were twice in 1951 and once in 1952. As they came into contact in April, the U.S. presidency was term-limited to reduce the control of the administrative branch and increase the powers of the legislative and judicial branches of government. Iran curbed British control of its oil, a constriction of its business presence, which the Iranian government felt was too intrusive. The excesses of racism were also curtailed in the U.S., as both New York and Washington prohibited discrimination. The planets' second contact, in October, was in the opposing signs of Aries and Libra. Aries, in its fiery forwardness, must be balanced with Libra's urge for peace and harmony. This link coincided with intensified peace talks between North Korean Communists and United Nations representatives of South Korea to end the Korean conflict. These efforts were successful in realizing a truce, but the war continued.

Progressive Jupiter also contacted ground-breaker Uranus in May, coinciding with a march for peace and freedom among 600,000 Germans. But Jupiter's placement in headstrong Aries clashed with Uranus's in protective Cancer, suggesting difficulty in seeing others' points of view: The war in Korea escalated temporarily as this occurred, while China finally asserted overt control over Tibet after years of soft-pedaling.

Despite conflicts both open and covert among world powers, Saturn's movement into the peace-loving sign of Libra this year signaled a new international concern for peace in the wake of atomic power. The power of the United Nations was being proven as a global consensus was slowly forming on the proper conduct of international affairs. In particular, it was increasingly less acceptable for one nation to gratuitously invade or control another. While not all nations were willing participants in the emerging limitations, they all felt constrained by them.

Charles de Gaulle wins the French parliamentary election

Tickertape showers on General MacArthur during a parade in his honor in New York

Winston Churchill is re-elected as Britain's Prime Minister

THE COMMUNIST SCARE CONTINUES

UN forces halted the North Koreans in their drive south in January, but ceasefire talks took place in May. President Truman fired U.S. General MacArthur, UN forces commander in Korea. The Chinese occupied the Tibetan capital of Lhasa, but sanctioned religious freedom in the country. Israel and the state of Jordan, independent since 1946, remained at the center of the Arab-Israeli dispute, while a repentant West German Parliament voted reparations to the Jewish state of Israel. Japan became a sovereign nation again after the end of the American occupation, signing a treaty with forty-eight nations, and becoming demilitarized. The 22nd Amendment to the U.S. Constitution prevented a single individual from serving more than two terms as President. The U.S. tested an atomic bomb in Nevada and the first hydrogen bomb at Eniwitok Atoll in the Pacific. Ethel and Julius Rosenberg were sentenced to death for divulging nuclear secrets to the Russians. Jet aircraft were tested by the U.S. military and achieved height and speed records. *The King and I* drew appreciative audiences in New York. The lavish Festival of Britain was staged in London.

➤ Read "An Astrological Family Tree: The British Royal Family" by Wendy C. Hawks on page 425.

CAPRICORN

The Connected Communicator

As a 1951 January Capricorn, you were born at the same time that the world's largest natural-gas pipeline was opened, connecting Brownsville, Texas, to New York City. At the time, the pipeline was considered an engineering marvel. This might explain why "making connections" can give you so much joy!

You may have grown up in a neighborhood where it was possible to walk into almost any house and be welcomed like extended family, and your energy can be pure and simple, reflecting the family values that were in vogue then. As you got older, you may have developed the ability to fine-tune your thoughts so that they can be universally understood. Combined with a charming and clever style, this could make you an excellent writer, either in the entertainment business or in a more traditional corporate setting. You can be a poised and self-possessed spokesperson, too, making you the likely candidate for putting the public face on private enterprises. Or you might have used this skill to teach children their ABCs. To you, there is nothing too fundamental, so long as what you are teaching helps people clarify their thoughts. This could also make you a good technical trainer or driving instructor.

You probably like to get down to the basics with friends too, and that's why you may favor straightforward people like Ariens and Sagittarians when you're out to have fun. As an earth sign, you may enjoy running through the countryside or digging in the garden when you're looking for some solitary diversions. You might like trying to figure out what makes people tick, so you may spend some time alone in public places, guessing at a person's "story" or speculating about what they might do for a living.

In romance, you may feel that you lack the ability to break the ice, so "think warm" when it comes to looking for a partner. You and a Leo could have a lot of fun together. Being traditional won't stop you from being a little rowdy when you're with the most flamboyant sign in the zodiac!

Your challenge is to be able to accept change. Your gift is the ability to remember the good things about the past.

AQUARIUS

The Explosive Pacifist

Born at the time that the United States was expanding its experiments with nuclear tests at a site in Nevada, you may have found yourself dropped into a rather inconsistent environment, 1951 Aquarius. As you grew older, your enthusiasm for technology may have stopped short at condoning futuristic and frightening weapons of war. In fact, you would probably have preferred that atomic energy be restricted to generating electricity—if it had to be a force in your life at all.

It's likely that you think not only about what is good for you, but what would benefit the rest of the world as well. At one time you may even have believed that you had the answers that could save the world! This could have gone against the grain of your teachers, who might have preferred that you keep your far-out ideas in the science lab. As an adult, you might have shunned the professions that dealt with technology, since you can have a healthy respect for the harm many man-made devices can do. Working for a company or group that is connected to the arts could have been right up your alley. Later in life, it may have been hard for you to keep your ideas about the importance of peace to yourself, and you could have gravitated toward working for a philanthropic or political organization.

Your friendships can be based upon how well you feel you can trust the other person. Your biggest fear may be that people will try to change your mind when it comes to the way that you think about world politics. If you do have someone you especially enjoy talking with, it's likely to be an open-minded Gemini. For fun, you may enjoy places with high noise levels, like nightclubs and sporting events.

In romance, you may tend to be set in your ways, so flexibility can be a big attraction for you. Cancer or Sagittarius probably fit the bill here. You may also relate well to the softness of Pisces, and you can relax in the presence of their calm and peaceful energy.

Your challenge is to accept that the world will have problems that peace cannot resolve. Your gift is your faith that one day there will be no more war.

► Read about your Chinese Astrological sign on page 838. ► Read about your Personal Planets on page 826. ► Read about your personal Mystical Card on page 856.

1951

CAPRICORN
Your Personal Planets

YOUR LOVE POTENTIAL
Venus in Capricorn, Jan. 01, 0:00 - Jan. 07, 21:09
Venus in Aquarius, Jan. 07, 21:10 - Jan. 20, 20:51

YOUR DRIVE AND AMBITION
Mars in Aquarius, Jan. 01, 0:00 - Jan. 20, 20:51

YOUR LUCK MAGNETISM
Jupiter in Pisces, Jan. 01, 0:00 - Jan. 20, 20:51

World Events

Jan. 4 - Communist forces attack and capture the city of Seoul.

Jan. 11 - In Vietnam the Viet Minh launch an attack on the French in Tonkin.

Boxer "Sugar" Ray Robinson wins in a fight against Jake La Motta in Chicago

AQUARIUS
Your Personal Planets

YOUR LOVE POTENTIAL
Venus in Aquarius, Jan. 20, 20:52 - Jan. 31, 20:13
Venus in Pisces, Jan. 31, 20:14 - Feb. 19, 11:09

YOUR DRIVE AND AMBITION
Mars in Aquarius, Jan. 20, 20:52 - Jan. 22, 13:04
Mars in Pisces, Jan. 22, 13:05 - Feb. 19, 11:09

YOUR LUCK MAGNETISM
Jupiter in Pisces, Jan. 20, 20:52 - Feb. 19, 11:09

World Events

Feb. 3 - Tennessee Williams' *Rose Tattoo* premières in New York.

Feb. 11 - UN forces in Korea push beyond the 38th Parallel once again.

1951

PISCES
Your Personal Planets

YOUR LOVE POTENTIAL
Venus in Pisces, Feb. 19, 11:10 - Feb. 24, 23:25
Venus in Aries, Feb. 24, 23:26 - Mar. 21, 10:04
Venus in Taurus, Mar. 21, 10:05 - Mar. 21, 10:25

YOUR DRIVE AND AMBITION
Mars in Pisces, Feb. 19, 11:10 - Mar. 01, 22:02
Mars in Aries, Mar. 01, 22:03 - Mar. 21, 10:25

YOUR LUCK MAGNETISM
Jupiter in Pisces, Feb. 19, 11:10 - Mar. 21, 10:25

World Events

Feb. 26 – The 22nd Amendment is ratified in the U.S., limiting the presidential office to two terms.

Mar. 13 – Israel demands 6.2 billion German marks ($1.2 billion) as compensation from Germany for helping war refugees.

Americans Julius and Ethel Rosenberg wait for judgement to be passed on them for espionage

ARIES
Your Personal Planets

YOUR LOVE POTENTIAL
Venus in Taurus, Mar. 21, 10:26 - Apr. 15, 8:32
Venus in Gemini, Apr. 15, 8:33 - Apr. 20, 21:47

YOUR DRIVE AND AMBITION
Mars in Aries, Mar. 21, 10:26 - Apr. 10, 9:36
Mars in Taurus, Apr. 10, 9:37 - Apr. 20, 21:47

YOUR LUCK MAGNETISM
Jupiter in Pisces, Mar. 21, 10:26 - Apr. 20, 21:47

World Events

Apr. 5 – U.S. spies Ethel and Julius Rosenberg are given the death penalty.

Apr. 11 – Gen. Douglas MacArthur is relieved of his command in Korea by President Truman.

PISCES
From February 19, 11:10 through March 21, 10:25

The Fervent Believer

You may have a lot of faith in humanity, and at the time of your birth it probably appeared to some people that the world was moving toward an uneasy balance. In the U.S., "atomic spies" Julius and Ethel Rosenberg were convicted and condemned to death after a sensational trial. In Korea, the U.S.-led United Nations forces recaptured Seoul. Such was the tenor of the world you grew up in, 1951 Pisces.

As a child, your quiet demeanor may have belied a strong desire to take action in order to effect change. You can be the kind of person who goes along with the rules, or at least appears to do so from the outside. On the inside, though, you may be seething at all the restrictions. In fact, intellectual and artistic freedom are probably as necessary for you as air. You might have been the class poet—but with an edge that would set you apart from the gentle and passive stereotype of your sign. You may have been a good dancer, cheerleader, or team booster in high school, and these would have been excellent ways for you to work off your excess energy. Finding fun ways to let your energy out can be essential to you—otherwise you could become highly nervous and unhappy—and you could have done well in any job that requires you to use your body, such as a dance teacher or gym instructor. You might like sports you can enjoy in the water, such as water skiing, yachting, or fishing.

One way to decompress is through your friendships. Your Cancerian friends may not be the usual common-or-garden variety: they can be scientific, or perhaps they have eclectic tastes. In any case, they'll be engaged in things you love learning about from them. You also enjoy doing active things with Ariens, so look out for them on any team you might play on or in a local softball or bowling league.

In love, you can require plenty of attention. You might create a lifetime full of adventure with a Sagittarian or another Pisces, who would share your enthusiasms.

Your challenge is to maintain your belief even when your arguments are being challenged. Your gift is the ability to create your own reality.

ARIES
From March 21, 10:26 through April 20, 21:47

The Crisis Manager

Events in the news at the time you were born reflect a no-nonsense attitude and a decisive sense of knowing what to do. While the Sun was in Aries in the year 1951, President Truman fired General Douglas MacArthur, commander of the UN forces in Korea and on April 12, the Israeli Knesset designated an official Holocaust Day. The dramatic events that occurred around the time of your birth could explain why you tend to get past problems quickly and take decisive action.

You may have an unconscious faith that you will prevail when the pressure is on, and you could even seek out high-pressure occupations. You might work as an air-traffic controller or a computer operations executive. You can be aggressive about obtaining work that pays well, and you earn your pay by commanding authority in times of crisis. In fact, you might love to be sitting at the desk where the buck stops because you love to save the day. Home can be the one place where you don't handle chaos well, but letting your home life be somewhat unpredictable is usually okay with you. You might even use it as a training ground for the next predicament you encounter on the job!

When you're not working, you can be zealous about having fun. You're probably a sports fan, and you may have played a sport into your adult years. Martial arts can interest you, and you could get a lot of benefit from releasing energy in a Tai Chi class. Your friends are likely to be active too, and there are probably a few other Ariens among them. The Leos you know might extend invitations to the kind of parties and events that you may not otherwise be able to attend.

In romance you might have to look hard for someone who can keep up with you, but Leo and Scorpio would have a pretty good chance at it. Your physical desires are not the only things that need to be satisfied. You demand from your partner enough stamina to keep up with the hectic schedule you like to keep, even on vacations.

Your challenge is to learn patience so you can stop creating crisis situations. Your gift is your ability to let off steam and get past your anger.

➤ Read about your Chinese Astrological sign on page 838. ➤ Read about your Personal Planets on page 826. ➤ Read about your personal Mystical Card on page 856.

TAURUS

From April 20, 21:48 through May 21, 21:14

The Thoughtful Speechmaker

You could have the gift of gab, Taurus of 1951, and using it to gather people together for a good cause probably pleases you greatly. Certainly, things of this nature were a big part of the news at the time you were born. In Germany, 600,000 people gathered to march for peace. They had a reason to worry about keeping the peace, too, having just heard about the first H-bomb tests being conducted by the U.S. at Los Alamos. As a lover of peace also, you believe in the power of the pen and the spoken word and you have a talent for persuading others to do things your way.

In addition, using words to expose people to new ideas could have been a major preoccupation in your life. You may have striven to bring light to the world, helping people to see that there can be a way to enjoy material prosperity and maintain global peace at the same time. There could have been times in your life when even you didn't believe this was possible, but your perseverance would have allowed you to keep working for the forces that you felt were on the side of right. This may have led to a fairly high-profile career. You would be good at any kind of debate, including courtroom litigation. You could also be a politician, although probably not the flamboyant kind.

While the people you work with might be preoccupied with utopian models that are unlikely to ever become reality, you are the kind of leader who can roll up your sleeves and get on with the work necessary. Although your friends admire this quality in you, they're probably especially thankful when you choose to take some time off to spend with them. In friendships, your favorite people are probably Geminis and Cancerians, because they are most likely to be able to help you get out of your rut.

In love, it's important to find a mate who shares your love of comfort, and another Taurus could suit you best. No one else would really appreciate the things you love so much!

Your challenge is to not allow frightening circumstances to cause you to waver from your goals. Your gift is the ability to translate the most sublime ideas into plain English.

GEMINI

From May 21, 21:15 through June 22, 5:24

The Intrigued Spectator

You might like to hear at least two sides of every conversation, Gemini of 1951, so perhaps it's no surprise to find that a famous case involving three nations was decided around the time you were born. The Haya de la Torre Case, which involved a refugee from Colombia being protected in Peru by a treaty signed in Cuba, had the kind of many-sided intrigue that you'd enjoy. Sometimes you can be the embodiment of the trickster, who, wishing to avoid being caught, hides behind the scenes, causing just enough mischief to create an interesting show!

You may have an incredibly bright mind and a showy way about you that could lead you to a career in the entertainment business. You may be capable of doing more than one job at a time, so it's possible that you would also pursue the arts while using your substantial verbal talents in a field like journalistic writing or broadcasting. No matter what your job is, you're probably the one who keeps everyone up on the news in your office or family. You may particularly enjoy getting groups of people together, and you could be the one who organizes the office picnics and family reunions.

You never forget a friend, and you probably maintain connections that go back to childhood. Your favorite friends are likely to be Cancers, Leos, and Pisceans, who also honor old bonds and enjoy meeting new people to add to their families. Your own family life might have been made difficult by a stern relative who ruled the roost with an iron hand. If this was the case, you were probably likely to rebel all the more, because you value your freedom so much.

This could also be the case in love, and it's possible that you waited to settle down until you finished sampling the population of potential partners. Cancerians around your age are just independent enough to sustain a busy schedule that doesn't always require your presence, yet their attentiveness can be something you treasure.

Your challenge is to be sensitive to the needs of the people who look to you for reassurance. Your gift is the ability to juggle many things, yet keep your eye on all of them.

► Read about your Chinese Astrological sign on page 838. ► Read about your Personal Planets on page 826. ► Read about your personal Mystical Card on page 856.

1951

TAURUS
Your Personal Planets

YOUR LOVE POTENTIAL
Venus in Gemini, Apr. 20, 21:48 - May 11, 1:40
Venus in Cancer, May 11, 1:41 - May 21, 21:14

YOUR DRIVE AND AMBITION
Mars in Taurus, Apr. 20, 21:48 - May 21, 15:31
Mars in Gemini, May 21, 15:32 - May 21, 21:14

YOUR LUCK MAGNETISM
Jupiter in Pisces, Apr. 20, 21:48 - Apr. 21, 14:56
Jupiter in Aries, Apr. 21, 14:57 - May 21, 21:14

World Events

May 1 - The U.S.'s Radio Free Europe is transmitted behind the Iron Curtain into the Eastern Bloc.

May 4 - The long-awaited Festival of Britain opens in London.

The Festival of Britain

GEMINI
Your Personal Planets

YOUR LOVE POTENTIAL
Venus in Cancer, May 21, 21:15 - June 07, 5:09
Venus in Leo, June 07, 5:10 - June 22, 5:24

YOUR DRIVE AND AMBITION
Mars in Gemini, May 21, 21:15 - June 22, 5:24

YOUR LUCK MAGNETISM
Jupiter in Aries, May 21, 21:15 - June 22, 5:24

World Events

June 13 - Swedish movie actor Stellan Skarsgard is born.

June 18 - Charles De Gaulle wins the French parliamentary election.

1951

CANCER
Your Personal Planets

YOUR LOVE POTENTIAL
Venus in Leo, June 22, 5:25 - July 08, 4:53
Venus in Virgo, July 08, 4:54 - July 23, 16:20

YOUR DRIVE AND AMBITION
Mars in Gemini, June 22, 5:25 - July 03, 23:41
Mars in Cancer, July 03, 23:42 - July 23, 16:20

YOUR LUCK MAGNESTISM
Jupiter in Aries, June 22, 5:25 - July 23, 16:20

World Events

June 25 – The first color TV broadcast is made; CBS's Arthur Godfrey is beamed from New York to four other cities.

July 16 – J. D. Salinger's novel *The Catcher In The Rye* is published.

Walt Disney and Kathryn Beaumont at the world première of "Alice in Wonderland"

LEO
Your Personal Planets

YOUR LOVE POTENTIAL
Venus in Virgo, July 23, 16:21 - Aug. 23, 23:15

YOUR DRIVE AND AMBITION
Mars in Cancer, July 23, 16:21 - Aug. 18, 10:54
Mars in Leo, Aug. 18, 10:55 - Aug. 23, 23:15

YOUR LUCK MAGNESTISM
Jupiter in Aries, July 23, 16:21 - Aug. 23, 23:15

World Events

July 28 – Walt Disney's animated film *Alice In Wonderland* is released.

Aug. 5 – Reports of Communist soldiers in neutral areas of Korea bring peace negotiations to a standstill.

CANCER
From June 22, 5:25 through July 23, 16:20

The Family Peacemaker

Color was in the news in the summer of 1951 when you were born. In the U.S., the *Arthur Godfrey Show* was making history with the first color TV broadcasts from the CBS New York studios to four other cities. But in Cicero, Illinois, a white mob tried to prevent a black family from moving into their new home. The fact that the family had been able to buy the property at all was unusual. Because of practices like "redlining," banks had been able to quietly refuse loans to blacks who wanted to buy in white neighborhoods. Even though no one seemed to have a problem accepting color TV, in its own way it showed that the world was shrinking. With less room between them, people would need to find ways to live together in peace.

You probably liked this idea when you were growing up, Cancer of 1951, since it would be hard for you to comprehend how anyone could see another human being as anything but a part of one big family—and you may have been extremely vocal about your desire to bring people together. You might also like taking the lead in a family environment, so you would make an excellent entrepreneur. Or you might work in a business that serves families, like food production or education.

You could have many friends, but you might need to be careful about meddling too much in their lives. You probably don't like to be intruded upon either, so you understand perfectly when your Leo and Virgo friends tell you that they can do without your advice!

You can be extremely sexy, and it's possible that you would continue to attract admirers even after you settle down. But straying from your relationship wouldn't have much appeal for you, and you'd probably be content just to flirt a little every now and again. Joining up with a Gemini or a Sagittarius could pay big dividends, since they're likely to understand that, although you like to be admired by other people, your loyalty will win out over your roving eye every time.

Your challenge is to accept people's need for privacy. Your gift is the ability to understand prejudice, in the hope of transforming it into universal harmony.

LEO
From July 23, 16:21 through August 23, 23:15

The Sympathetic Organizer

Your roar can be a lot worse than your bite, Leo of 1951, so you may find that you are more weepy and emotional than the astrology books would lead you to believe. Floods killed almost 5,000 people in China and ruined 850,000 acres of farmland in the United States at the time of your birth. It's possible that being born with all that destructive weather around gave you extra empathy for others, as well as a strong sense of duty and service. At any rate, your sense of pride probably comes more from what you do than from how many people know about it.

You can have an extremely orderly mind and may handle detailed work very well. It may please you to make contributions in little ways, and you could enjoy a hobby painting miniatures or a job in the silicon-processor industry. You may like to be very active physically, and your ideas could come to you in flashes of inspiration, so you might be in a field that has you working in spurts, such as management consulting or grant writing. You can have a commanding presence that puts you in high demand, and you probably don't need to worry about your income if you work on an as-needed basis. You can be great at managing money, so the budgets you make are likely to be airtight and you'd rarely have to worry about covering your expenses.

It's likely that you conserve your friendships, and some of them may have had their beginnings in your grade-school years. It can please you to know that people who have known you that long still admire and respect you. You probably have many birthdays to remember—especially the birthdays of your Virgo friends—and you may also have some active Cancerians around to play sports with.

In love, someone who appreciates your special qualities and who can keep you calm may be the best choice for you. A Virgo, who also wants to help and pays attention to detail, would never go over the budget and could shower you with devotion!

Your challenge is to let yourself accept compliments gracefully. Your gift is the ability to feel for people, and then take action to help them find a way out of their dilemmas.

➤ Read about your Chinese Astrological sign on page 838. ➤ Read about your Personal Planets on page 826. ➤ Read about your personal Mystical Card on page 856.

VIRGO

From August 23, 23:16 through September 23, 20:36

The Quiet Crusader

Around the time you were born, U.S. President Harry S. Truman made the first live transcontinental TV broadcast, reaching thousands of homes. Similarly, you can usually get your message out to a lot of people when you need to, 1951 Virgo. And while you probably prefer working behind the scenes, once you get your thoughts together you can have a commanding way of getting your point across. This combination of unassuming hard work and powerful presentation can make you a valuable asset to your superiors.

You may have an extra dose of intellectual artisanship, even more than a typical Virgo, and you might like to incorporate ideas from the past into your present-day studies. This can make you a good historian or archeologist, or you might be an anthropologist who turns scientific discoveries into tantalizing documentaries. You may also be a fine therapist, taking patient encounters and incorporating them into a self-help book that can school a whole generation in a better way of life. If you have chosen a less public career path, you may be the person in your company or group who is in charge of packaging annual earnings and activity reports. It would be very difficult for you to avoid being a writer of some kind, even if you only occasionally write music, film, or art reviews.

Friends may come to you to have things explained to them, and many of them might even use you as a consultant. People can be kind to you in general, but it may take you a little bit longer than most to let your friends get close to you. Other Virgos would understand this, as would the many Scorpios who would be enticed by your formidable skills as a communicator.

In love, you may seek the refuge of a gentle soul who understands your need to be alone from time to time. Both Pisceans and Scorpios would be able to comfort you, but a Scorpio could be stronger and less likely to complain when you were not there to cuddle with.

Your challenge is to get past shyness and feel free to invite people into your world. Your gift is the ability to clear out all the contradictions and come to your own conclusions.

LIBRA

From September 23, 20:37 through October 24, 5:35

The Courageous Protector

You may be shy and reluctant to stick up for yourself, 1951 Libra, but you'll come to the aid of another like a warrior going into battle. Like the U.S. troops in Korea who retook "Heartbreak Ridge" around the time you were born, you may have a fearless quality that enables you to charge forth heedlessly—as long as you're fighting for someone else. There's much to be said for this, as it can come from a solid sense of justice, and you may have a natural reserve that can keep you from being seen as pompous or egotistical. One well-known Libran attribute you may share, though, is a dislike of arguments, especially if it is your idea or opinion that is being disputed.

You may spend a lot of time thinking about what you can do for others, and this desire to help can permeate not only your mental activity but also your professional calling. No one would make a better lawyer or public advocate than you. You have an ability to deal with detail to create airtight cases on your client's behalf, and you would be a champion of justice. You might lean more toward being a public defender than a prosecutor or commercial attorney. You could take pride in your ability to earn money, but it isn't the most important thing to you. You might have a partner, however, who is more outgoing than you are, and able to pull in lucrative accounts and lure high-profile people into your practice. If you are not in the legal profession, it's likely that you work in a capacity that allows you to assist others in some way, perhaps as a customer-service representative.

You may have many friends as a result of your compassion, and most of them admire you as much as they seek solace in your protective aura. Pisceans may be the most likely to understand where you're coming from when it comes to doing for others.

In love, you may need someone you can lean on, at least some of the time. Seek out an Aries—no one could bring you more enthusiasm or luck!

Your challenge is to do something nice for yourself every once in a while. Your gift is the ability to see the value in protecting the weak from the greedy.

▶ Read about your Chinese Astrological sign on page 838. ▶ Read about your Personal Planets on page 826. ▶ Read about your personal Mystical Card on page 856.

1951

VIRGO
Your Personal Planets

YOUR LOVE POTENTIAL
Venus in Virgo, Aug. 23, 23:16 - Sept. 23, 20:36

YOUR DRIVE AND AMBITION
Mars in Leo, Aug. 23, 23:16 - Sept. 23, 20:36

YOUR LUCK MAGNETISM
Jupiter in Aries, Aug. 23, 23:16 - Sept. 23, 20:36

World Events

Sept. 9 – Chinese soldiers occupy the Tibetan town of Lhasa.

Sept 11 – Igor Stravinsky's opera *The Rake's Progress* premières in Venice.

British troops search natives for arms during the Suez crisis

LIBRA
Your Personal Planets

YOUR LOVE POTENTIAL
Venus in Virgo, Sept. 23, 20:37 - Oct. 24, 5:35

YOUR DRIVE AND AMBITION
Mars in Leo, Sept. 23, 20:37 - Oct. 05, 0:19
Mars in Virgo, Oct. 05, 0:20 - Oct. 24, 5:35

YOUR LUCK MAGNETISM
Jupiter in Aries, Sept. 23, 20:37 - Oct. 24, 5:35

World Events

Oct. 15 – American comedy show *I Love Lucy* debuts on CBS TV.

Oct. 15 – The Egyptian Parliament denounces the Suez Canal Treaty.

1951

SCORPIO
Your Personal Planets

YOUR LOVE POTENTIAL
Venus in Virgo, Oct. 24, 5:36 - Nov. 09, 18:47
Venus in Libra, Nov. 09, 18:48 - Nov. 23, 2:50

YOUR DRIVE AND AMBITION
Mars in Virgo, Oct. 24, 5:36 - Nov. 23, 2:50

YOUR LUCK MAGNETISM
Jupiter in Aries, Oct. 24, 5:36 - Nov. 23, 2:50

World Events

Oct. 26 – Winston Churchill is re-elected as Britain's Prime Minister.

Nov. 10 – The first long-distance telephone call without operator assistance is made from New Jersey to California.

Winston Churchill makes the sign of victory

SAGITTARIUS
Your Personal Planets

YOUR LOVE POTENTIAL
Venus in Libra, Nov. 23, 2:51 - Dec. 08, 0:18
Venus in Scorpio, Dec. 08, 0:19 - Dec. 22, 15:59

YOUR DRIVE AND AMBITION
Mars in Virgo, Nov. 23, 2:51 - Nov. 24, 6:10
Mars in Libra, Nov. 24, 6:11 - Dec. 22, 15:59

YOUR LUCK MAGNETISM
Jupiter in Aries, Nov. 23, 2:51 - Dec. 22, 15:59

World Events

Dec. 11 – Baseball great Joe DiMaggio announces his retirement from the game.

Dec. 13 – Future British Prime Minister Margaret Roberts marries Denis Thatcher.

SCORPIO
From October 24, 5:36 through November 23, 2:50

The Community Leader

While the Sun was in Scorpio in 1951, the first long-distance telephone call was made without operator assistance. The fact that many telephone users became more independent around the time you were born might explain why you can be so independent, Scorpio of 1951. You may enjoy working with groups, and your independent nature might be what enables you to lead the people who need your decisive direction. In fact, in leading you may even teach people to rely on themselves—not on you—and in this way get your deeply perceptive and hard-working attitude to spread amongst your peers.

You probably have very high standards and don't skimp when it comes to providing resources, whether they are material, mental, or emotional. You may be able to find the best people to work with in any field you enter, but your desire to get to the truth and your knack for detail suggests that you would enter the medical field or the area of detective work. The people who work for you can be extremely helpful. They'll respond to your capable leadership with a "can-do" attitude and higher-than-average output. If you don't have anyone working under your supervision, you might notice that your co-workers could be more cheerful and cooperative than the ones your friends may complain about.

The people you like to be around are full of optimism and very focused on their work. Aries and Virgo might be your best bets for supportive and interesting friendships, and both would make good work partners. They could support you should you decide to pursue community work or volunteer for social committees and they would probably be willing to help you develop your ideas.

Love can be very important to you, and you may require a great deal of support from your partner. Aries and Sagittarius both make interesting matches for you. They can stop you from becoming too serious, yet they are able to provide the sounding board you need if you are to avoid becoming moody and withdrawn.

Your challenge is to learn that it's all right to rely on your partners. Your gift is your ability to keep a slow and steady pace.

SAGITTARIUS
From November 23, 2:51 through December 22, 15:59

The Lonely Traveler

You were born at a time when the Golden Gate Bridge had to be closed due to high winds, and hearing stories about this event when you were older might have made you notice how many similar situations had occurred in your life. You can tend to be a courageous traveler, Sagittarius of 1951, and might enjoy adventures that most people don't even have the nerve to think about. But this may not be the only reason that you travel alone. You may be the original dancer to the different drummer, and it might seem that the things you want to do—even something as mundane as crossing a bridge—somehow just come out sounding dangerous!

You may think about how much you can be learning from the world at all times, and you've probably found a way to incorporate travel and learning into your life. You might have traveled abroad, even when you were in high school, or chosen to take a year off to discover a different country or continent before you decided what to do with the rest of your life. To you, learning about the world and your place in it can be the only thing that really matters, and it may have been difficult to find others who felt as strongly about this as you do. You may have found them by choosing a daring line of work, for they are likely to be a very elite group. You could do well as a flight attendant, a pilot, or an international businessperson who spends a lot of time on airplanes.

If you do not work in one of those fields, then you probably try to save your money so that you can visit the four corners of the world on fabulous vacations. You can make friends easily, and many of them may be from distant lands. Aries and Leo, who have some semblance of a sense of adventure, could be your happiest companions.

In love, you may need to have someone who understands the concept of being loved from afar. Capricorn or Aquarius could do this for you, since they wouldn't need to have a lover around every minute of the day.

Your challenge is to learn how to find at least one place that you can call home. Your gift is the ability to find something you love about everyone you meet.

➤ Read about your Chinese Astrological sign on page 838. ➤ Read about your Personal Planets on page 826. ➤ Read about your personal Mystical Card on page 856.

CAPRICORN

From December 22, 16:00 through December 31, 23:59

The Efficient Problem-Solver

It's likely that you are an intense soul, December Capricorn of 1951. You have the kind of motivation that generates positive change in the people you interact with. On December 31, 1951, these same Capricorn qualities manifested in the scientific world: it was announced that a battery had been able to convert radioactive energy into electrical energy. When challenged, however, you've been known to smolder. Since you're known to be as persistent as the goat of your zodiac glyph, it's no coincidence that one of the top records on the Hit Parade the year you were born was, "On Top Of Old Smokey."

You may tend to go over what has happened in the recent past when searching for a solution to a problem. This ability to track the path of the past would make you an excellent operations manager or a technician who could troubleshoot computers and other equipment. Or you might be an essayist whose commentary on politics and current events incorporates past as well as present quagmires. You could have considerable skill at writing and a love of working on committees. You can enjoy assembling other great minds to help unravel the puzzles you are presented with, and it's likely that your cohorts rely on your intuition.

You may choose your friends from among the soft, intuitive types like Pisces and Cancer, who would nurture your ability to "read" situations and support your efforts to succeed. For fun, you probably like to get out into the world of nature. As a youth you may have enjoyed rock climbing, but as you got older you may have adjusted your leisure activities to something a little easier on your muscles, like hiking in the mountains or walking through the hills.

In love you can be deeply emotional, and you may need to have a person in your life who is dependable. Cancerians of your era might not fit this criterion, so you might look to Librans and Pisceans to give you a soft place to land after a hard day's work.

Your challenge is to think of ways to reduce the stress that you put on yourself. Your gift is the ability to empower others to use their own problem-solving skills.

1951

CAPRICORN
Your Personal Planets

YOUR LOVE POTENTIAL
Venus in Scorpio, Dec. 22, 16:00 - Dec. 31, 23:59

YOUR DRIVE AND AMBITION
Mars in Libra, Dec. 22, 16:00 - Dec. 31, 23:59

YOUR LUCK MAGNETISM
Jupiter in Aries, Dec. 22, 16:00 - Dec. 31, 23:59

World Events

Dec. 24 – The UN grants the United Kingdom of Libya independence from Italy.

Dec. 31 – The first battery to convert radioactive energy to electrical energy is demonstrated.

The Royal Family

Special Feature

An Astrological Family Tree: The British Royal Family

by Wendy C. Hawks

While we are all individuals, you may find that you share many characteristics with other members of your family. Is it nature or nurture that leads members of a family to look at life from similar perspectives and share similar traits? Astrological counselors note, when looking at the birth charts of different members of a single family, that patterns are often repeated in each person's chart. A birth or "natal" chart is a map of the planetary positions in the sky at the exact moment of birth. These repeated patterns can be as simple as the predominance, down through the generations, of one sign. For example, perhaps one or more of the personal planets—Mercury, Venus, and Mars, as well as the Sun or Moon—of each member of the family are in the same sign.

In a natal chart, the personal planets represent our individual characteristics. Planets can be described as energies or

activators. The signs they fall into at the moment of birth describe the manner or style in which each planet asserts its energy. It is not only signs that may be repeated in family member charts, but also links, referred to as aspects, between planets. For example Mars, the planet representing assertion and aggression, would behave very differently if linked to kind-hearted Venus or the gentle Moon than if it was connected to stern Saturn or power-hungry Pluto.

If your most obvious family traits are generosity and a laid-back attitude to life, you may find that each member has one of the personal planets in Sagittarius, the sign exemplifying these traits, or that personal planets are in aspect to Jupiter, the planet promoting these traits. If your family tends to worry a lot or has a need to be in control, you may find that the oftentimes somber, responsibility oriented sign of Capricorn or the

serious planet Saturn is strongly represented in your family's birth charts.

The "houses" the planets occupy in the natal chart further modify the planets' energy. The "houses" (numbered one to twelve) are astrological symbols for different areas of our lives, such as home, career, and so on. Sometimes there may be an emphasis on specific houses in the family members' charts. The first house starts with the sign that was rising on the horizon at the time and place of birth. It, along with the rest of the houses, can only be determined by an accurate time of birth.

(Continued on page 433)

➤ Read about your Chinese Astrological sign on page 838. ➤ Read about your Personal Planets on page 826. ➤ Read about your personal Mystical Card on page 856.

425

1952

Structures Change: Saturn, Uranus, and Neptune

The interplay of Saturn, Uranus, and Neptune correlated with a dramatic unfolding of events in 1952. Uranus, associated with both innovation and upheaval, was beginning its "square" to imaginative but often deceptive Neptune. While not in full focus until 1953, or completed until 1957, Saturn's contact brought the processes that these planets symbolize into the forefront. This combination is often seen symbolically in unusual events and advances, from inventive ways of solving long-standing problems, to surges in technology, to sudden catastrophic events. With Uranus in nurturing Cancer and Neptune in diplomatic Libra, barriers to social harmony were challenged. Progress was made in U.S. racial equality, and television raised the awareness of everyman, spawning a new accountability in government. In South Africa, a new segregation law spawned political conflict and was quashed by their Supreme Court.

Saturn, the planet of manifest lessons, connected with both Uranus and Neptune from its position in Libra. Thus the darker side of human affairs could be exposed, allowing an eventual shift in consciousness. However, in 1952, that shift was yet to come. The growing pains of a world under threat of nuclear war continued as the Soviets and Britain revealed that they had the bomb, and the Korean War ground on. With changes of leaders in key nations like Britain with a new monarch, and the U.S. with a new President, the future seemed uncertain, the uneasy postwar peace imperiled. Still, the great promise of this planetary combination was exhibited through the ultimately peaceful transitions of power in all these countries.

Although it added to the planetary tension through April, Jupiter, the planet of enterprise, was in stabilizing Taurus by May. It made a harmonizing link with Uranus in Cancer, signifying an increase in the human desire for comfort and security. This shows that, while some nations continued to engage in contentious actions, others were less willing to react. Despite troubles in hot spots like French Indochina and Egypt, people were eager to focus on the pleasures of watching the Helsinki Olympics or the suspense and social conflict of Ivanhoe played out on the silver screen.

The veiled Queen Elizabeth II mourns the death of her father King George VI

General Batista seizes control of the Cuban government

Maria Montessori dies at 81

LONG LIVE THE QUEEN!

In Britain, George VI died, and his daughter succeeded him as Elizabeth II. Following a truce, fighting resumed in Korea. Hussein succeeded his unstable father as King of Jordan; after a military coup ousting Egypt's King Farouk II, General Naguib seized control. Argentine Evita Péron, despot and workers' champion, died of ovarian cancer at thirty-three. Cuba's instability resurfaced as Batista regained control in a lightning coup, suspending freedoms and canceling elections. Tornadoes in six U.S. states left more than 200 dead and many towns devastated; steel workers went on strike for higher wages. The enormously popular war hero Dwight Eisenhower won the election by a landslide to become President, with Nixon as his Vice-President. Soviet Russia returned to the Olympics at Helsinki after forty years' absence, but the U.S. still dominated events. George Jorgensen became Christine after a sex-change operation. In the U.S., an artificial heart was used for the first time. Italian Maria Montessori, champion of developmentally appropriate education, died at eighty-one in the Netherlands. Anne Frank's diary was published.

➤ Read "An Astrological Family Tree: The British Royal Family" by Wendy C. Hawks on page 425

CAPRICORN

From January 01, 0:00 through January 21, 2:37

The Responsible Reformer

January-born 1952 Capricorns tend to be a bit wilder and crazier than their astrological brethren of other years. A far cry from the usual Capricorn, who is 100 percent cautious, conservative, and traditional, you come across more like an Aquarius in many ways. You have an unusual share of that sign's qualities of freedom-loving nonconformity and spontaneity. In all likelihood, you exhibit traits of both, and struggle to find a happy medium between these opposite ends of the spectrum.

In your younger years, you may have felt especially torn between contradictory post-war values. On the one hand, you felt attached to your conventional roots in what are popularly called the Eisenhower years, as Ike announced his intention to run on the Republican ticket in January 1952. And then, at the other end of the spectrum, nonconformist Mad Magazine made its loony debut in the year of your birth. Unable to ignore either influence, you have embodied both a serious sense of decency and duty (your usual mode), and rebellious zaniness. This is not a bad thing at all, by the way—far from it.

As you've matured, you've learned how to preserve what ought to be preserved, while also recognizing when rebellion or a call for change can bring in a new vision for the future, and expansive progress. Your gift for establishing order and structure has been enhanced by your appreciation for individuality and inventiveness. These elements combine well to create an entrepreneurial spirit which utilizes your independence as well as your natural organizational abilities and business sense.

When seeking a mate, you may feel particularly drawn to Cancerians, whose warm, nurturing emotionality complements your practicality. Cancers born between 1949 and 1955 combine your sense of vision for a better future with your traditional family values. Also compatible are Aquarians, Taureans, Virgos, Scorpios, and Pisceans.

Your greatest strength is your ability to balance judiciously the status quo with inevitable progress. Your greatest challenge is to find the fine line between social responsibility and individual autonomy.

AQUARIUS

From January 21, 2:38 through February 19, 16:56

The Ambitious Visionary

As a 1952 Aquarian, you are less laid back than your Sun-sign alone would suggest. You are unusually driven to succeed and to make your mark through some public endeavor. You bring your humanitarian concerns to your career, which you then pursue just as passionately as any more personally motivated sign. The difference is that you truly seek to benefit humanity and you have the personal power to succeed on both fronts, personal and collective. You may be perceived as a formidable warrior, fighting the good fight. It's a matter of perspective: to those on your side, you will be a welcome ally; but your enemies may regret crossing your path.

Jackie Robinson, groundbreaking African-American baseball player, signed a contract with WNBC and WNBT to serve as Director of Community Activities in February of 1952, in a fine example of personal ambition serving a larger vision. This is the kind of achievement and statement of which you are capable.

In addition to media and communications, politics would be a natural career choice. Any of these, or any combination of them, would bring together your love of group activities and your ambition to make a powerful impact. Your egalitarian vision for a better world assures that you seek innovative, win-win solutions to age-old social problems. You know that knowledge is power, and were among the first to anticipate the far-reaching social implications of the Information Age. You mature alongside technology, which you understand as a means of personal and political liberation.

Scorpios on the same mission will prove to be either excellent comrades, or (should they have a different agenda) worthy opponents. Freedom-loving Sagittarius is a companionable choice for a close friend or mate, while fiery Leo's passion intrigues you. Gemini shares your gift of the gab and cool detachment, and Libra's diplomatic charm helps your cause.

Your greatest asset, 1952 Aquarius, is your incredible passion to succeed, not only for yourself, but also for the greater good. Your greatest challenge is to maintain a vigilant watch over your true motives, making sure always to check in with others and their goals.

➤ Read about your Chinese Astrological sign on page 838. ➤ Read about your Personal Planets on page 862. ➤ Read about your personal Mystical Card on page 856.

CAPRICORN
Your Personal planets

YOUR LOVE POTENTIAL
Venus in Scorpio, Jan. 01, 0:00 - Jan. 02, 18:43
Venus in Sagittarius, Jan. 02, 18:44 - Jan. 21, 2:37

YOUR DRIVE AND AMBITION
Mars in Libra, Jan. 01, 0:00 - Jan. 20, 1:32
Mars in Scorpio, Jan. 20, 1:33 - Jan. 21, 2:37

YOUR LUCK MAGNETISM
Jupiter in Aries, Jan. 01, 0:00 - Jan. 21, 2:37

World Events

Jan. 7 – Dwight D. Eisenhower, Supreme Allied Commander in Europe, announces that he will run for the U.S. presidency.

Jan. 20 – British troops invade Ismalia in Egypt.

Princess Elizabeth becomes Queen of England

AQUARIUS
Your Personal Planets

YOUR LOVE POTENTIAL
Venus in Sagittarius, Jan. 21, 2:38 - Jan. 27, 15:57
Venus in Capricorn, Jan. 27, 15:58 - Feb. 19, 16:56

YOUR DRIVE AND AMBITION
Mars in Scorpio, Jan. 21, 2:38 - Feb. 19, 16:56

YOUR LUCK MAGNETISM
Jupiter in Aries, Jan. 21, 2:38 - Feb. 19, 16:56

World Events

Feb. 6 – King George VI dies; his daughter becomes Queen Elizabeth II.

Feb. 16 – The FBI captures ten members of the Ku Klux Klan in North Carolina.

1952

PISCES
Your Personal Planets

YOUR LOVE POTENTIAL
Venus in Capricorn, Feb. 19, 16:57 - Feb. 21, 4:41
Venus in Aquarius, Feb. 21, 4:42 - Mar. 16, 14:17
Venus in Pisces, Mar. 16, 14:18 - Mar. 20, 16:13

YOUR DRIVE AND AMBITION
Mars in Scorpio, Feb. 19, 16:57 - Mar. 20, 16:13

YOUR LUCK MAGNETISM
Jupiter in Aries, Feb. 19, 16:57 - Mar. 20, 16:13

World Events

Mar. 7 – A military aid agreement is signed by the U.S. and Cuba.

Mar. 20 – At the 24th Academy Awards *An American In Paris*, wins an Oscar.

Gene Kelly and Leslie Caron in "An American in Paris"

ARIES
Your Personal Planets

YOUR LOVE POTENTIAL
Venus in Pisces, Mar. 20, 16:14 - Apr. 09, 23:16
Venus in Aries, Apr. 09, 23:17 - Apr. 20, 3:36

YOUR DRIVE AND AMBITION
Mars in Scorpio, Mar. 20, 16:14 - Apr. 20, 3:36

YOUR LUCK MAGNETISM
Jupiter in Aries, Mar. 20, 16:14 - Apr. 20, 3:36

World Events

Apr. 1 – The "Big Bang" theory of the universe is proposed by Alpher, Bethe, and Gamow in the Physical Review.

Apr. 15 – The first B-52 prototype test flight takes place.

PISCES
From February 19, 16:57 through March 20, 16:13

The Financial Wizard

As a Pisces born in 1952, you have a special gift for acquiring wealth and resources. While most Pisceans aren't particularly materialistic, you possess a magic wand for molding your wildest financial imaginings into physical form. You probably do not amass great sums of money simply for its own sake, but rather to fuel your typical Piscean creative, spiritual and philanthropic dreams. You prove to be surprisingly practical in bringing your visions down to Earth, even if they seem far-fetched and too romantic to less idealistic souls.

When it comes to generating your own income, you are not only a magnet for lucky opportunities, you seem also to magically materialize resources from other quarters, be they loans, grants, prize winnings, inheritances, or insurance settlements. You have an uncanny ability to turn apparent disappointments and losses into gains, mystifying those around you. The more altruistic your pursuits, the more this seems to be the case. However, you are not required to live a life of sacrifice in order to contribute to the greater good. You are simply a magnificent conduit for distributing wealth, in ways that benefit both yourself and others.

You excel in any field that calls these attributes into play: fundraising for an art therapy program in a children's hospital would be ideal. Or, you could help sponsor a movie or a theater, endow a museum, or initiate yoga classes or day-care services. The bigger you can imagine, the bigger you can create. It's no coincidence that the first plastic lens for cataract patients was fitted in Philadelphia in your birth month. Like those physicians, the sky's the limit!

Capricorn and Aries make good partners in business, romance, or both. Capricorn supports you to take practical steps to organize your vision, and Aries inspires faith and confidence. Also compatible are nurturing Cancer and passionate Scorpio, whose sexy personal power and drive stimulate your imagination.

Your greatest asset is your ability to bring your visions down to Earth, and your greatest challenge is to think big—really big.

ARIES
From March 20, 16:14 through April 20, 3:36

The Independent Partner

All Aries value their self-reliance, and Ariens born in 1952 are exceptionally self-confident. Born as the Big Bang theory was first proposed, you, too, are a human dynamo. However, you are also learning the profound lessons of partnership, and are continually pulled to stretch beyond the safety of your self-contained equilibrium. At first, the drills in cooperation and give-and-take may have felt like extra weight, throwing you off-balance. But, as you've matured, you've found that the stretching has made you not only more flexible, but also, ironically, even more self-sufficient. The exact opposite of a vicious circle, this is called a positive-feedback loop.

All your close one-to-one relationships—be they romantic, business partnerships, or clients—pull you, like taffy, out of your self-referential, singular universe. Then, bang: by rising to a series of challenges, you are sent back home as a fuller and more expanded version of yourself. As you have learned to meet yourself and your partner with greater responsibility, compassion, and more realistic expectations, you've grown even stronger. This, in turn, has served you well in your next encounter. Over time, you've learned that this is your greatest source of growth, and that you are gaining far more than you ever thought you were giving up.

You love a good debate, and law would be a good arena for your ever-expanding ability to see two sides to every question. You know the importance of collaboration, even with your clients. You've had to learn to make limitations work for you, and you realize that external requirements actually provide a helpful outline.

You may find an ideal partner in Libra, whose gentleness and empathy disarm your best defenses. Compassionate Pisces can also melt your heart. Leo and Sagittarius share your fiery enthusiasm, and Aquarius lends an interested ear to your loftiest ideas.

Your greatest strength is your robust self-confidence. Your greatest challenge is to learn to trust that a partner can help you accomplish even more and, in a paradoxical way, also enhance your independence.

► Read about your Chinese Astrological sign on page 838. ► Read about your Personal Planets on page 826. ► Read about your personal Mystical Card on page 856.

TAURUS

From April 20, 3:37 through May 21, 3:03

The Practical Mystic

Taureans are known for their pragmatic, methodical approach to life, and as a Taurus born in 1952, you are no less down-to-Earth. However, your area of concern is a bit unusual: what you are bringing down to Earth are spiritual structures. Taurus is the master builder of the zodiac: the mason, the carpenter, the architect, and pyramid designer. With your particular gifts, 1952 Taurus, you would make a great builder of temples and cathedrals. If all this sounds too grand for your tastes, know that you are, at the very least, a great builder of dreams, able to give form to your highest ideals.

Taureans tend also to be fond of money and material possessions. In your case, they may tend to slip through your fingers if you are amassing them only for your own ends, or you lose sight of your higher aspirations. However, when you are gathering resources to finance a spiritual goal or a philanthropic service, then you seem to have the golden touch. This distinction between owning and using resources may challenge your natural possessiveness. But because so much of your creative energy is directed toward service, you are usually able to let go and be a powerful channel for the spirit.

As you develop inner security, you blossom, revealing your hidden talent for words. In your birth month, the Pulitzer Prize was awarded to Herman Wouk for his novel *The Caine Mutiny*. Like Wouk, your confidence expands as you find your proper niche, and allow yourself to be guided by your mystical muse. Once you align yourself with your true avocation, your imagination seems to grow right along with your discipline, and you are richly rewarded for your efforts.

Aries inspires you to reach for the stars and Pisces whispers gentle encouragement in your ear. If they are directing their intensity toward similar goals, Scorpios make passionate allies (on many levels), while Virgos and Capricorns support you in grounding your dreams.

Your greatest strength, 1952 Taurus, is your ability to turn your highest visions into concrete reality. Your greatest challenge is to surrender control to a higher power.

GEMINI

From May 21, 3:04 through June 21, 11:12

The Secret Lover

As a 1952 Gemini, you have an unusual need for security. Luckily, you are also exceptionally intuitive, and your hunches give you uncanny practical advice when it comes to material resources. The only caveat is that if you try to cash in on these Tips from Beyond for your own gratification, they tend to backfire. When you serve some purpose higher than yourself, they grow and expand. Try as you may to outwit this catch to the Aladdin's Lamp you possess, you'll find that you're bound to its law. You're left with no choice but to figure out how to match your own needs with those of a larger cause.

Your cleverness pays handsome dividends for all concerned, yourself included. Where many Geminis prefer to be free agents, you may be happiest serving some large organization whose purpose is aligned with your own values. This will satisfy your need for security, and give you a stable outer structure within which to work.

All Geminis love to talk and flirt; you, however, also harbor an unusual desire for physical intimacy and affection. Under that playful persona, you are surprisingly warm. Your hidden sensuality is a delightful secret waiting to be discovered by those who make it past your detached intellectual front. And it's not only cuddling we're talking about—although there's plenty of that. It's passion and excitement, too. You don't wear your heart on your sleeve. Rather, you put your phenomenal memory and gift for the gab up front and center, reserving your inner riches for the select few able to penetrate your veil of cleverness. When it comes to love, you're not only less cool, calm, and collected than you seem, you're also a lot more possessive.

Taurus can key right into your secret emotions and sensuality, while Aquarius stimulates your main erogenous zone—your mind. Libra balances your verbal gymnastics with grace. Leo is a classic match, as with Jackie O and Gemini Jack Kennedy, who became a senator in 1952.

Your greatest strength is your intuitive knowledge of what's beneath the comfortable surface of life. Your greatest challenge is to trust what you know.

➤ Read about your Chinese Astrological sign on page 838. ➤ Read about your Personal Planets on page 826. ➤ Read about your personal Mystical Card on page 856.

1952

TAURUS
Your Personal Planets

YOUR LOVE POTENTIAL
Venus in Aries, Apr. 20, 3:37 - May 04, 8:54
Venus in Taurus, May 04, 8:55 - May 21, 3:03

YOUR DRIVE AND AMBITION
Mars in Scorpio, Apr. 20, 3:37 - May 21, 3:03

YOUR LUCK MAGNETISM
Jupiter in Aries, Apr. 20, 3:37 - Apr. 28, 20:49
Jupiter in Taurus, Apr. 28, 20:50 - May 21, 3:03

World Events

Apr. 25 – Juan Perón is re-elected as President of Argentina.

May 5 – The Pulitzer Prize is awarded to Herman Wouk for his novel *The Caine Mutiny*.

Eva Perón with President Perón on the balcony at the Plaza de Mayo

GEMINI
Your Personal Planets

YOUR LOVE POTENTIAL
Venus in Taurus, May 21, 3:04 - May 28, 19:18
Venus in Gemini, May 28, 19:19 - June 21, 11:12

YOUR DRIVE AND MAGNETISM
Mars in Scorpio, May 21, 3:04 - June 21, 11:12

YOUR LUCK MAGNETISM
Jupiter in Taurus, May 21, 3:04 - June 21, 11:12

World Events

May 26 – Eight countries, including the U.S., Britain, and West Germany, form the European Defense Community.

June 18 – Isabella Rossellini, Italian actress and daughter of Ingrid Bergman, is born.

1952

CANCER
Your Personal Planets

YOUR LOVE POTENTIAL
Venus in Gemini, June 21, 11:13 - June 22, 5:45
Venus in Cancer, June 22, 5:46 - July 16, 15:22
Venus in Leo, July 16, 15:23 - July 22, 22:06

YOUR DRIVE AND AMBITION
Mars in Scorpio, June 21, 11:13 - July 22, 22:06

YOUR LUCK MAGNETISM
Jupiter in Taurus, June 21, 11:13 - July 22, 22:06

World Events

June 26 - Nelson Mandela and fifty-one others infringe a curfew in South Africa in protest against apartheid laws.

July 21 - American actor Robin Williams is born.

ANC leader Nelson Mandela protests against apartheid

LEO
Your Personal Planets

YOUR LOVE POTENTIAL
Venus in Leo, July 22, 22:07 - Aug. 09, 23:57
Venus in Virgo, Aug. 09, 23:58 - Aug. 23, 5:02

YOUR DRIVE AND AMBITION
Mars in Scorpio, July 22, 22:07 - Aug. 23, 5:02

YOUR LUCK MAGNETISM
Jupiter in Taurus, July 22, 22:07 - Aug. 23, 5:02

World Events

July 25 - The first U.S. commonwealth is created in Puerto Rico.

July 26 - Argentina's first lady, Evita Perón, dies of cancer.

430

CANCER
From June 21, 11:13 through July 22, 22:06

The Family Clanner

All Cancerians love family, but a Cancer born in 1952 just can't get enough of it. If you don't come from a large family, you have probably created one, either literally or in your community. Think of Nelson Mandela: in your birth month, he and fifty-one other activists disobeyed South Africa's curfew, for the greater good of the nation. Regardless of your gender, you are probably one of life's nurturers. If you don't greet your guests with overflowing pots of spaghetti, you feed them emotionally. People come to you with their problems, and you are only too happy to help.

House calls present no problems for you, of course, but your doors are also always open, even to passing acquaintances. However, you will usually find that most new acquaintances don't pass by; they stick around and become friends for life.

You also possess great originality and imagination, along with a strong independent streak. You have the creative vision to be in business for yourself. Something in the food-service industry would suit you well, like a family owned restaurant or supermarket. If you do not work with your family, you would most definitely make efforts to turn your business into an extended family. Even your clients are welcomed into the fold and consider your office a second home. You also have the gift of seeing the big picture, so you would make an excellent consultant to the distribution industry or similar. When you've got bad news to deliver, your loony sense of humor helps the medicine go down and softens your criticism and advice.

At some point in your life, you may decide that you want to get as far away as possible from all this emotion. You may choose to come up for air with a detached Aquarius for a mate, or a freedom-loving Sagittarius. These signs can take you on wild adventures away from the clan. You may find that fellow water signs Pisces and Scorpio may drown you out with their intensity and sensitivity.

Your greatest challenge, Cancer, is to find yourself as an individual, and your greatest strength is your ability to build community and family wherever you go.

LEO
From July 22, 22:07 through August 23, 5:02

The We Generation

Leos born in 1952 love the limelight even more than most, so if your mother wanted you to go into movies, it wasn't simply parental pride. Your mother has probably been an especially powerful force in your life, and harbored a lot of ambition for you from the day you were born. And, Momma was right. You are a natural star, whether on stage or screen, or just strolling about the neighborhood. You need an outlet for your larger-than-life emotions, and professional drama can temper personal dramas, allowing your strong personality to be a positive role model for shyer types.

Fortunately, your fiery nature is stabilized by your serious commitment to fairness and justice. As we all know, life isn't fair, and your sense of honor compels you to try to do something about the inequities. In this way, you would make an excellent litigator—what could be more dramatic than life-or-death courtroom battles?

You could do quite well for yourself financially if you apply your leadership abilities to serve a larger group. Besides, what greater service to a group is there than leadership? The leader is the vision-holder, the light-bearer who embodies the group's purpose. You have the kind of charisma that can allow you to carry this load without becoming burdened. The group could be fellow cast members, or your clients; anyone, in fact, with any common goal at all. You further everyone's best interests by taking the lead. However, while it is important to take others into account, you do nobody any good by hiding your light under a bushel. You can be a team player, but don't be afraid to show your personal best.

An Aquarian mate helps balance your healthy sense of self with a larger vision, supporting your karmic growth. As comrades-in-arms, Geminis make helpful suggestions, while Librans diplomacy smoothes over any ruffled feathers. Aries and Sagittarius relate to your passionate nature.

Your greatest challenge, Leo of 1952, is to look to the larger purpose of a group endeavor, and your most admirable strengths are the courage, confidence, and generosity you contribute to the cause.

➤ Read about your Chinese Astrological sign on page 838. ➤ Read about your Personal Planets on page 826. ➤ Read about your personal Mystical Card on page 856.

VIRGO

From August 23, 5:03 through September 23, 2:23

The Student-Teacher

Virgos live to serve, and 1952 Virgos are more torn than most between serving family or career. Your ideal would be to find a way to combine both, allowing you to have your cake and eat it, too. Working at home might be one configuration; home-schooling your children might be another. You also have quite a hankering to travel, mentally as well as physically. Different periods of your life may reflect different aspects of these contradictions.

Education is very important to you, whether it is the pursuit of your own intellectual interests, or teaching others. There is a saying that we teach what we need to learn, and teachers are blessed in that their learning is continual. You love the world of words and ideas, and in fact Hemingway's *Old Man And The Sea* was published as you came into the world. You may share not only his gift for language, but also his taste for refined simplicity and cut-to-the-chase style. Your own intellectual prowess is considerable, giving you x-ray vision into much that is hidden from others. Your penetrating insights, born of your well-known aptitude for research and getting to the bottom of things, may surprise even you, at times.

Even if you aren't a professional teacher, you are probably a natural teacher to those around you. Your nurturing style is steady, consistent, and empathetic. You have the patience to polish your diamonds in the rough into shape, gently pointing out the details they are likely to overlook. You would also make an excellent healer or psychologist. This would mix your astute perceptiveness with your call to service and gentle compassion. Good therapy involves teaching, and good teaching often involves healing.

Taurus makes a simpatico mate, sharing your pragmatic priorities, and inspiring you as a possible mentor figure. Aquarius makes for a stimulating combination, matching your analytical abilities and leading you toward a more liberated approach to your duties.

Your greatest challenge is to learn to season your perfectionism with praise, and your greatest gift is your ability to encourage hidden potential.

LIBRA

From September 23, 2:24 through October 23, 11:21

The Dutiful Dreamer

Libra of 1952 combines high ideals and imaginative vision with the commitment necessary to make such dreams come true. While other people may think your crazy ideas impossible, by combining responsibility with idealism and method with madness, you are well equipped to succeed where others can only fantasize. All dreams are fantasies before they come true; they only become illusions if we do not take the practical steps to make them happen. You are gifted with this ability.

While all Libras will do anything to keep the peace, you tend to be especially self-sacrificing in your approach to friendship, love, and life itself. Your diplomatic skills demonstrate that healthy confrontation clears the air, and as you've matured you've learned to trust that conflict can be just as creative as harmony. In this way, life's inevitable tests and disappointments have guided your growth and helped you develop your conviction and willpower. You may have learned the most from your early mistakes and disappointments, paving the way for your eventual successes.

Right before you were born, a supersonic fighter plane exploded during a London air show, killing the pilot and twenty-five spectators. But in October, on the heels of this aviation tragedy, New York began its helicopter mail and parcel postal service. These are the kinds of setbacks, sacrifices, and breakthroughs that accompany great dreams like the Wright brothers' flight of 1903. In barely fifty years, supersonic jets had become a reality.

Your perseverance and idealism pay off in matters of the heart as well as your creative aspirations, bringing you a lasting bond perhaps later in life, but deeper than many. If you don't give in to their stronger egos, Aries and Leo offer fiery examples of healthy self-interest. Capricorn shares your sense of duty and purpose, while Pisces understands your compassionate love nature.

Your greatest challenge is to remember to fill your own well before everyone else's. This gives you the strength you need to support others. Your greatest asset is your ability to see two sides to every question.

➤ Read about your Chinese Astrological sign on page 838. ➤ Read about your Personal Planets on page 826. ➤ Read about your personal Mystical Card on page 856.

VIRGO
Your Personal Planets

YOUR LOVE POTENTIAL
Venus in Virgo, Aug. 23, 5:03 - Sept. 03, 8:16
Venus in Libra, Sept. 03, 8:17 - Sept. 23, 2:23

YOUR DRIVE AND AMBITION
Mars in Scorpio, Aug. 23, 5:03 - Aug. 27, 18:52
Mars in Sagittarius, Aug. 27, 18:53 - Sept. 23, 2:23

YOUR LUCK MAGNETISM
Jupiter in Taurus, Aug. 23, 5:03 - Sept. 23, 2:23

World Events

Aug. 28 – Germany and Israel reach an accord about reparation payments.

Sept. 8 – Ernest Hemingway's *The Old Man And The Sea* is published.

American novelist Ernest Hemingway in Venice

LIBRA
Your Personal Planets

YOUR LOVE POTENTIAL
Venus in Libra, Sept. 23, 2:24 - Sept. 27, 17:35
Venus in Scorpio, Sept. 27, 17:36 - Oct. 22, 5:01
Venus in Sagittarius, Oct. 22, 5:02 - Oct. 23, 11:21

YOUR DRIVE AND AMBITION
Mars in Sagittarius, Sept. 23, 2:24 - Oct. 12, 4:44
Mars in Capricorn, Oct. 12, 4:45 - Oct. 23, 11:21

YOUR LUCK MAGNETISM
Jupiter in Taurus, Sept. 23, 2:24 - Oct. 23, 11:21

World Events

Oct. 1 – In Kenya, emergency measures are introduced to eliminate the secret Mau Mau society.

Oct. 22 – Iran officially breaks off relations with Britain during the oil dispute.

1952

SCORPIO
Your Personal Planets

YOUR LOVE POTENTIAL
Venus in Sagittarius, Oct. 23, 11:22 - Nov. 15, 20:02
Venus in Capricorn, Nov. 15, 20:03 - Nov. 22, 8:35

YOUR DRIVE AND AMBITION
Mars in Capricorn, Oct. 23, 11:22 - Nov. 21, 19:38
Mars in Aquarius, Nov. 21, 19:39 - Nov. 22, 8:35

YOUR LUCK MAGNETISM
Jupiter in Taurus, Oct. 23, 11:22 - Nov. 22, 8:35

World Events

Nov. 1 – The first test of the hydrogen bomb is carried out at Enewetak Atoll.

Nov. 4 – Dwight D. Eisenhower is elected 34th President of the U.S.

Dwight D. Eisenhower celebrates his election victory

SAGITTARIUS
Your Personal Planets

YOUR LOVE POTENTIAL
Venus in Capricorn, Nov. 22, 8:36 - Dec. 10, 18:29
Venus in Aquarius, Dec. 10, 18:30 - Dec. 21, 21:42

YOUR DRIVE AND AMBITION
Mars in Aquarius, Nov. 22, 8:36 - Dec. 21, 21:42

YOUR LUCK MAGNETISM
Jupiter in Taurus, Nov. 22, 8:36 - Dec. 21, 21:42

World Events

Dec. 1 – Adolfo Ruiz Cordines becomes President of Mexico.

Dec. 17 – Yugoslavia breaks off relations with The Vatican.

SCORPIO
From October 23, 11:22 through November 22, 8:35

The Ambitious Strategist

Combining a chess master's careful planning with concentration and intensity, 1952 Scorpios are especially equipped to mastermind their own success. Not only do you know how to think and plan big, you attract the right partners to bring financial resources to the table. You know people in high places, and it would be surprising if you were not a mover and shaker in your own right. Politics would be a natural choice for your powerful ambition, and your ambition to power.

The man who was to Israel what Washington was the U.S. died in November 1952. Fondly remembered as a great humanitarian, President Chaim Weizmann was also a world-class chemist. Your own prodigious intellect serves your determined ambition well. However, it is entirely open to question what purpose your ambition will serve. In itself, power is neither good nor evil; it is merely an instrument to be used toward a given end. You see that, contrary to the old adage that the ends justify the means, the means can also justify the ends.

You were born at the historical moment when Dwight Eisenhower, Allied Supreme Commander in Europe in World War II, was elected U.S. President, heralding a decade or so of relative peace and prosperity. Your parents no doubt welcomed this respite from the Depression and the war, and America, at least, seemed to embrace the wholesome materialism that Ike represented. Provided your parents were not extremely unconventional or Communists, the climate of self-assured affluence was conducive to your success. No matter where you grew up, you exhibited unusual ambition and success, ferreting out opportunities hidden amongst life's challenges. And you do love a challenge, particularly a mental challenge. "Strength in adversity" could be your motto.

Capricorn spurs you on as a mate—a running mate, perhaps? Taurus fills the coffers, gives supportive backrubs, and is an enthusiastic cheerleader for your aspirations. Friendly Sagittarius helps you lighten up a bit.

Your greatest challenge is to decide what you want to do with all the power you are capable of acquiring. Your greatest gift is your ability to acquire it.

SAGITTARIUS
From November 22, 8:36 through December 21, 21:42

The Intrepid Explorer

Sagittarius is the sign of the teacher, and a love of both learning and teaching is especially strong in those of this sign born in 1952. Travel, both long-distance and short, is probably a must in your life, as you thrive on expanding both your mental and literal horizons. Driven to learn and to share what you learn with others, you not only love a good adventure, party, book, and cause as all Archers do, but you will also go to any lengths to combine them all into one satisfying whole. If you do not spend at least part of your life teaching English in China or running New-Age cruises around the world, you will no doubt join the local PTA and sponsor class trips to mind-expanding museums for youngsters, exposing them to cultures different from their own.

Anthropology would be a good career or hobby for you, as you have an objective eye for your own culture and its power structures. You tend to question the powers that be, and have been known to challenge academic and religious assumptions and taboos. While you understand the power of these cultural institutions to shape public opinion and government policy, the value of tradition may elude you for quite some time.

If you had been born a generation earlier, you might have voted for Adlai Stevenson, the liberal intellectual who was defeated by Dwight D. Eisenhower in November 1952. It was such a landslide victory for Eisenhower that Stevenson has been virtually eclipsed from history. Stevenson was known for his sharp and rebellious wit. You too are gifted with a quick mind and a sharp tongue.

Aquarius adds fuel, perhaps dangerously, to the fire of your free-thinking imagination, while Capricorn's seriousness and loyalty move and ground you. You find Gemini amusing, but it might be hard for you two wanderers to settle into a routine together.

Your greatest challenge throughout your life is to focus your energies and find balance. Your greatest gift is your free-spirited curiosity. You are a perennial student of life.

➤ Read about your Chinese Astrological sign on page 838. ➤ Read about your Personal Planets on page 826. ➤ Read about your personal Mystical Card on page 856.

CAPRICORN

From December 21, 21:43 through December 31, 23:59

The Freelance Artist

As a December-born 1952 Capricorn, you can fit the conservative tenor of your times—but only sometimes. You are able to generate your own income in highly unorthodox and creative ways and you may be an independent consultant or freelancer rather than an employee—and it is highly probable that you are paid quite well for your efforts.

You easily attract grants, loans, investors, sponsors, and patrons for your work, which is likely to be very individualistic and artistic. You are also able to sell your creations and ideas outright, which are appreciated for their originality and novelty. You have the mark of a skilled craftsperson—your work reflects patience, discipline, and attention to detail. You probably like to master traditional techniques before you develop more innovative approaches.

Although you were born during the conservative Eisenhower years, your tastes run to the orthodox, and you favor avant-garde ideas, like some of the great artists of the time. You are able to bridge the best of both worlds, linking the originality of a Jackson Pollock or a Samuel Beckett with your sensible outlook. In 1952, Pollock gave his first show in Paris and Beckett published *Waiting For Godot*. Challenged by these contradictory traits of tradition and novelty, your true values may battle your sense of who you are supposed to be. Your contradictions may also disconcert others: rebels hold your success suspect, while conventional types suspect your originality and freedom. Ultimately, you are able to fit in anywhere—the more you follow your own drummer, the more you earn respect from both camps.

An Aquarius would make an excellent client and muse for your work, as well as excite your passion, but you may be too possessive for such a free spirit. You balance your need for freedom and commitment better with a Libra. Taurus makes an excellent benefactor, and, as a fellow earth sign, appreciates your practicality and decency.

Your greatest asset is your ability to blend innovation in your work with technique and tradition. Your greatest challenge is to integrate them within your identity.

CAPRICORN
Your Personal Planets

YOUR LOVE POTENTIAL
Venus in Aquarius, Dec. 21, 21:43 - Dec. 31, 23:59

YOUR DRIVE AND AMBITION
Mars in Aquarius, Dec. 21, 21:43 - Dec. 30, 21:34
Mars in Pisces, Dec. 30, 21:35 - Dec. 31, 23:59

YOUR LUCK MAGNETISM
Jupiter in Taurus, Dec. 21, 21:43 - Dec. 31, 23:59

World Events

Dec. 22 – Oscar Wilde's *The Importance of Being Ernest* premières in New York.

Dec. 31 – The Argentine government signs a trade agreement with Britain.

Special Feature
An Astrological Family Tree: The British Royal Family

(Continued from page 425)
(Continued from page 425)

To demonstrate how astrological signs and houses can be highlighted in families, we will examine the natal charts of the British royal family, whose dates, times, and places of birth are all well documented. Let's begin with the royal sign of Leo. The late Queen Mother's Sun and Mercury are in Leo, as are the Moons of her daughter Queen Elizabeth II and Elizabeth's husband, Prince Phillip. The rising sign of two of their sons—Prince Charles and Prince Andrew—are also in Leo. Their late aunt, Princess Margaret, and sister Anne both are Leo Sun Signs. Leaving the immediate family and going back further, relatives George V and George VI have Mars in Leo and Jupiter in Leo respectively.

Taurus and its opposite sign Scorpio—signs of wealth and power—are represented in the chart of every monarch from Queen Victoria to Prince William, now second in line to the British throne. Queen Victoria had Mercury in Taurus, her grandson George V, Mercury and Venus in Taurus, great-grandson George VI, Moon and Venus in Scorpio, and Prince William has Venus in Taurus and Jupiter in Scorpio. Queen Elizabeth II was born under Taurus and both her great-grandfather Edward VII and her son Prince Charles were born under Scorpio. Zodiacal signs are measured in degrees, thirty to each sign. To add even more to the mix, Queen Elizabeth's Taurus Sun is at zero degrees of the sign, as is Prince Charles's Moon. (Some astrologers consider zero degrees to be a "critical" or powerful degree.) In-laws Prince Phillip and Princess Diana also have Venus in Taurus. Venus is the planet that "rules" Taurus and symbolizes both love and money in a horoscope.

Taurus and Scorpio all figure in the charts of Queen Elizabeth's other children. Prince Edward has Venus in Taurus, while Prince Andrew's Moon and Princess Anne's Mars are

Princess Elizabeth and Prince Phillip on their wedding day

in Scorpio. Even the next generation follows suit, with Prince William's Venus and his younger brother Prince Harry's Moon in Taurus. Can all this be coincidence?

Jupiter is the planet that signifies royalty. It is associated with Sagittarius as well as the ninth house. If we look at Queen Victoria, the three kings, one queen and two kings-in-waiting that have followed her, we can see that Jupiter is prominent in every chart, either because of its house position or because it is in Sagittarius. In the charts of Queen Victoria and great-grandson George VI, Jupiter sits in the tenth house of career and status.

(Continued on page 441)

▶ Read Princess Diana's Star Profile on page 689. ▶ Read Queen Elizabeth's Star Profile on page 449.
▶ Read the Duke of Windsor's Star Profile on page 329.

433

1953

Truths are Revealed: Saturn and Neptune

Saturn, the planet of status quo and institutions, conjoined Neptune, planet of the underprivileged, in Libra, sign of balance and harmony, from late 1952 through September 1953. Whenever these planets connected, Communism—which, in its ideal and purest form is intended to uplift the underdog working masses—became stronger and received more global attention. Communist regimes ruled the great powers of China and the Soviet Union and threatened to spread their dominion in nations around the world. Southeast Asian governments, weakened by decades of instability, were under assault and European powers were uneasy with the Eastern European governments still under Soviet post-war control. Through Neptune's association with deception, secret activities were highlighted. Spies and espionage both frightened and intrigued, as the Rosenbergs were executed for betraying atomic secrets to Russia and readers were titillated by Ian Fleming's debut James Bond novel, *Casino Royale*.

Saturn and Neptune were also associated with social issues affecting the ideals of the masses (Neptune) and the freedoms of the oppressed (Saturn). The legality of women's contraception was debated, while the exodus of families to the suburbs allowed them to fulfill the dream of owning a home with a patch of lawn. As Jupiter, planet of entertainment, made a harmonious contact with Saturn and Neptune from communicative Gemini, the arts portrayed serious social issues through masterpieces like Miller's *The Crucible*, but people also found fertile ground for laughter in the top-rated TV show *I Love Lucy*.

A Soviet tank disperses demonstrators during riots in East Berlin

Sherpa Tensing and Edmund Hillary on their return from climbing Mount Everest

Soviet leader Joseph Stalin dies

ENGRAM ANYONE?

L. Ron Hubbard founded the Church of Scientology, expanding his teaching of dianetics, a new approach to mental health. Scientology techniques purport to enable people to overcome negative aspects of prior experience and rid the world of drugs, war, pollution, and other ills. The religion acknowledged both reincarnation and extraterrestrial life. Although Scientology has caused controversy and experienced problems with governments worldwide, its initial aim was to raise humankind to a higher level of consciousness.

A BRIGHT NEW WORLD OF FREEDOM AND PEACE

Soviet leader Joseph Stalin died of a brain hemorrhage, ending a ruthless and paranoid regime. The Korean conflict came to an end, but left North and South still divided along a demilitarized 38th Parallel. After last year's coup in Egypt, Naguib abolished the monarchy and named himself President and Premier of a new republic. Cambodia's King Sihanouk negotiated independence from France. A popular uprising in East Berlin protested increased production quotas, but Russian tanks put an end to the unrest, leaving hundreds killed and injured. Jacqueline Bouvier married Senator John F. Kennedy, the future President. *Ozzie And Harriet*, which idealized traditional family values, was America's favorite TV show. Britain's east coast was devastated by floods. U.S. scientist Watson and British biologist Crick discovered the structure of DNA, the building block of life. The world of art was diminished by the deaths of Sergei Prokofiev, Russian composer of *Peter And The Wolf*, and French master of color, Raoul Dufy. British Sir Edmund Hillary and Sherpa Tensing became the first to reach the summit of Mount Everest, the world's highest mountain.

➤ Read "An Astrological Family Tree: The British Royal Family" by Wendy C. Hawks on page 425.

CAPRICORN

From January 01, 0:00 through January 20, 8:20

The Dichotomy Buster

While most Capricorns tend to put business before pleasure, those of you born in January 1953 are romantic at heart. Free-spirited partners liberate you from formality and cautious practicality. Born as the alienated Irishman Samuel Beckett's play *Waiting For Godot* premièred at the Left Bank Theater of Babylon in Paris, you are drawn to eccentric nonconformists and creative types. You may never burn all your suits and ties, but you share a playful sense of the absurd with your bohemian pals and sweethearts.

On one hand you (perhaps unconsciously) need a lot of freedom and may tend to pick partners who seem reluctant to commit. On the other hand, you are quite old-fashioned, and long for serious love. If this is an inner conflict, you may chase after unavailable lovers and wait and wait and wait. Once you've sown your own wild oats and come to understand your own duality, you may forge a bond with someone of similar complexity. Deep passion is not necessarily mutually exclusive of space. One or both of you could travel in connection with work or other duties, which are never far away for Capricorn.

You are also extremely creative, and hopefully you realize in time that you don't have to work nine-to-five to make a living. In your case, pursuing your artistic dreams could prove to be quite practical and lucrative. This becomes another opportunity to synthesize a dichotomy: creativity and poverty do not necessarily go together, and success does not have to preclude pleasure. This is a huge lesson for Capricorn, who tends to finish every last soggy vegetable on life's plate before moving on to dessert. Life is sweet indeed when you pay your rent (more likely a mortgage in your case) by pursuing your heart's desire.

Once you work out the pesky freedom/commitment problem, you may mate for life. Romantic Libra supports your creative endeavors and values loyalty as much as you do. Cancer also needs room to move, and a nest to come home to.

Your greatest challenge is to create mutuality rather than exclusivity, and your greatest gift is your ability to combine oil and water.

AQUARIUS

From January 20, 8:21 through February 18, 22:40

The Miracle Worker

As a 1953 Aquarius, you are surprisingly sentimental and mushy. You may feel torn between your need for cool detachment and independence, and your out-of-character urge to merge. You enjoy candlelit dinners and flowers more than you may care to admit, even to yourself. This may be embarrassing to other Aquarians, who prefer a stimulating intellectual discussion to mistily gazing into someone else's eyes. But you can't resist—yours is the stuff of soul-mate reunions and dreamy knights and maidens.

You were born just as Walt Disney's *Peter Pan* premièred, and this reflects the aura of fantasy with which your love nature is imprinted. But as much as nay-sayers may tease, the message of that story is true: miracles can happen, when we believe (and when we take the practical steps to make our dreams come true). You instinctively know that if we don't dream, we don't strive; and if we don't strive, we don't succeed. The only real danger is pretending that a wish has come true before it really has: that's an illusion. Your natural ability to step back and look at the big picture keeps you honest and on track.

You may have real healing abilities, because your compassion and empathy are as boundless as your idealism and belief in people's potential. It has been said that there is nothing more important for our development than someone believing in us. You are that kind of believer, which is a tremendous gift. In your life, money moves in mysterious ways. It seems to come out of nowhere quite miraculously and to vanish just as mysteriously. The more you can trust this as a flow rather than a controlled substance, the more reliable it will be. Again, you tend to prove the realists wrong, always having exactly what you need when you need it.

Romantically, you couldn't find a better match than a Pisces, provided you both look outside the relationship for much-needed reality checks. A wealthy Taurus helps you keep both feet on the ground.

Your greatest challenge is to distinguish potential from reality. Your greatest gift is your ability to see the best, and thereby bring it out.

➤ Read about your Chinese Astrological sign on page 838. ➤ Read about your Personal Planets on page 826. ➤ Read about your personal Mystical Card on page 856.

CAPRICORN
Your Personal Planets

YOUR LOVE POTENTIAL
Venus in Aquarius, Jan. 01, 0:00 - Jan. 05, 11:09
Venus in Pisces, Jan. 05, 11:10 - Jan. 20, 8:20

YOUR DRIVE AND AMBITION
Mars in Pisces, Jan. 01, 0:00 - Jan. 20, 8:20

YOUR LUCK MAGNETISM
Jupiter in Taurus, Jan. 01, 0:00 - Jan. 20, 8:20

World Events

Jan. 5 – Samuel Beckett's *En Attendant Godot* (*Waiting For Godot*) premières in Paris.

Jan. 12 – Nine Jewish "physicians" are arrested on charges of terrorist activities in Moscow

American playwright Arthur Miller

AQUARIUS
Your Personal Planets

YOUR LOVE POTENTIAL
Venus in Pisces, Jan. 20, 8:21 - Feb. 02, 5:53
Venus in Aries, Feb. 02, 5:54 - Feb. 18, 22:40

YOUR DRIVE AND AMBITION
Mars in Pisces, Jan. 20, 8:21 - Feb. 08, 1:06
Mars in Aries, Feb. 08, 1:07 - Feb. 18, 22:40

YOUR LUCK MAGNETISM
Jupiter in Taurus, Jan. 20, 8:21 - Feb. 18, 22:40

World Events

Jan. 22 – Arthur Miller's *The Crucible* premières on Broadway.

Feb. 9 – The French attack six Viet Minh war factories hidden in the Vietnamese jungle.

1953

PISCES
Your Personal Planets

YOUR LOVE POTENTIAL
Venus in Aries, Feb. 18, 22:41 - Mar. 14, 18:57
Venus in Taurus, Mar. 14, 18:58 - Mar. 20, 22:00

YOUR DRIVE AND AMBITION
Mars in Aries, Feb. 18, 22:41 - Mar. 20, 6:53
Mars in Taurus, Mar. 20, 6:54 - Mar. 20, 22:00

YOUR LUCK MAGNETISM
Jupiter in Taurus, Feb. 18, 22:41 - Mar. 20, 22:00

World Events

Mar. 5 - Soviet leader Joseph Stalin dies.

Mar. 20 - Nikita Khrushchev is appointed Secretary of the Soviet Communist Party.

Death of Soviet leader Joseph Stalin

ARIES
Your Personal Planets

YOUR LOVE POTENTIAL
Venus in Taurus, Mar. 20, 22:01 - Mar. 31, 5:16
Venus in Aries, Mar. 31, 5:17 - Apr. 20, 9:24

YOUR DRIVE AND AMBITION
Mars in Taurus, Mar. 20, 22:01 - Apr. 20, 9:24

YOUR LUCK MAGNETISM
Jupiter in Taurus, Mar. 20, 22:01 - Apr. 20, 9:24

World Events

Mar. 26 - Dr. Jonas Salk announces the discovery of a vaccine to prevent polio.

Apr. 10 - The first three-dimensional movie, *House of Wax*, is shown in New York.

PISCES
From February 18, 22:41 through March 20, 22:00

The Self-Made Capitalist

Pisces of 1953 is driven to succeed as independently and as rapidly as possible. Unusually oriented toward making a fast buck, you probably did chores or ran errands for sick neighbors, or had a thriving baby-sitting business by the age of ten. Your birth coincided with Joseph Stalin's death, marking the end of his tyrannical reign. While your altruistic side sympathizes with the ideal of sharing equally and sacrificing for a larger purpose, there's something too competitive and driven about you to completely surrender your individualistic flair for generating capital.

You are not especially motivated to trample anyone else in your pursuit of money, nor are you seeking to exploit others. However, neither are you one to entirely eschew personal wealth, as many Pisceans seem to do. More an athlete of affluence than a greedy imperialist, you are probably extremely generous. You would also never try to impose your values on others, let alone brutally enforce them. You simply want to be free to achieve your personal best, and to be handsomely rewarded for it.

If you are a parent, your children are a source of inspiration and delight. You learn as much from them as you teach, and the appreciation is mutual. Even if they introduce a little chaos into your routine, they stimulate your thinking with fresh ideas.

You are not at all shy or passive when it comes to romance. Regardless of your gender, you tend to charge your prey at full tilt. Your idealism really shows when it comes to love, and you are attracted to ladies and gentlemen in distress. And they may rescue you as much as you rescue them. Aries turns you on, and spurs you on to succeed. Taurus understands your appreciation for money, but doesn't get why the making of it is more fun for you than the having or the spending of it.

Your greatest challenge is to integrate your sensitivity with your ambition, and your greatest strength is your inventive approach to the game. Your creative thinking leads you to take risks others would pale before, but your gambles tend to pay off. When you leap, a net gain usually appears.

ARIES
From March 20, 22:01 through April 20, 9:24

The Persistent Pioneer

Aries of 1953's fiery enthusiasm is grounded in more perseverance than the typical Ram shows. Always great at initiating new endeavors, you possess the determination to finish what you begin. Not content to rest on the laurels of your great ideas, you are a slow and steady builder who works methodically to achieve your ends. You still love an unconquered horizon, and the call of uncharted territory will always beckon, but your endurance matches your pioneering spirit.

Dr. Jonas Salk reported in March 1953 that his experimental vaccine against polio had been successfully tested in ninety individuals. In addition to conceiving the notion of a vaccine, Salk labored methodically to develop the concept, patiently testing it for many years. Rather than seeking instant success and gratification, you learn to adjust your expectations to a realistic level and find, simultaneously and paradoxically, that you tend to come closer to your ideal. Early disappointments may have taught you the importance of persistence, and this helps you rise to the occasion every time. This becomes an uncanny ability to turn challenges into opportunities.

You are also unusually diplomatic for an Aries, and able to take deft and bold action to ease tensions between sparring partners. In a surprising move that broke the deadlock between the Soviet Union and the U.S., the UN elected Swedish Minister of State Dag Hammarskjold as Secretary-General around this time. You are similarly gifted at imaginative compromises.

It might just motivate you further to earn all the more, but a Libran partner may well spend your money as fast as you can make it. You tend to put your mate on a pedestal, which brings out the best in them—and perhaps in you as well. As a lover you are not only ardent, but also sensuous and earthy. You can share with a Taurus, who is also likely to help you hold on to your winnings and invest them wisely. A powerful Leo can meet you toe-to-toe.

Your greatest challenge is to balance your taste for quick action with your perseverance. Your greatest strength is your persistent action.

➤ Read about your Chinese Astrological sign on page 838. ➤ Read about your Personal Planets on page 826. ➤ Read about your personal Mystical Card on page 856.

TAURUS

From April 20, 9:25 through May 21, 8:52

The Selfless Aristocrat

1953 Taurus is a Taurus Taurus, a mega-Taurus, embodying your signs traits in every way possible. When you're not gardening or amassing huge fortunes, you're throwing pots or building great pyramids. On your breaks from your comfortable routines, you are surrounded by lush velvets and brocades, purring with satisfaction in your cozy nest.

You have enviable timing and reliable hunches that may lead you to consistently fortunate opportunities. You are blessed with a golden touch, and generally land on your feet where others stumble and fall. The only thing that may tend to mar your charmed existence is what looks like a karmic call to service. But these stints of duty need not be all drudgery and sacrifice. You are still allowed your indulgences. You are just required to contribute in one area of your life with no direct visible return. Keep in mind what they say: the highest form of charity is anonymous. In all other areas of your life, you are richly rewarded for your efforts.

Romance may be what requires some degree of altruism on your part. Positively, this spiritualizes your love nature. You may have to care for a partner with a serious health problem, for example. But this does not have to be a burden, because you have the potential to develop a more rarefied, selfless kind of love that brings you to a greater understanding of the divine. You are ideally qualified to receive the gift of the higher love that fate may have in store for you.

Speaking of destiny, DNA was finally unravelled in your birth month—finally understood to be a double rather than a single helix. The two bands dance around each other, linked by gossamer strands of hydrogen, in an intricate design based on the incredibly simple principle of duality. You may replicate a similar dance with a delicate Libra or a dreamy Pisces. Don't even try to decipher the mystery.

Your greatest challenge is to realize that sacrifice is not necessarily self-denial. The former leads to a greater gain, while the latter may not serve any true purpose. Your greatest gift is your ability to generate resources to share with others.

GEMINI

From May 21, 8:53 through June 21, 16:59

The Mercenary of Words

You enjoy beating the odds and achieving great firsts. All Geminis tend to be somewhat eager gallants, but 1953 Geminis take this to new lengths. You were born as Edmund Hillary and Sherpa Tensing scaled Mount Everest. Announcement of this feat was delayed until June 2, Queen Elizabeth II's coronation day. You, too, aspire to lofty heights, albeit intellectually more than literally. If you find the right patron, client, or cause to which to dedicate your mighty pen as your sword, you could make a gifted attorney, an arguer-for-hire, or a warrior of words.

With your love of adventure and your talent for words, you could bring sword and pen together as Ernest Hemingway did. Known as a great outdoorsman and fearless soldier who wrote about his own exploits, Hemingway was gaining recognition as a fearless writer as you came into the world. In May, he won a Pulitzer Prize for his tall tale of a great fishing feat, *The Old Man And The Sea*, continuing his themes of Man Against Man, Man Against Nature, and Man Against All Odds. You may be drawn to similar adversarial themes in your life.

Public speaking or writing is even better choices for you than for most Geminis. Beyond simply being charming and clever, you communicate forcefully, seeing the big picture and gauging the impact of your words. This translates into excellent timing, meaning you know when to speak to get what you want. The old caveat applies, though: be careful what you ask for, you just might get it.

After a possible period of learning love's lessons the hard way, you developed compassion. But you are a quick student, whatever the subject. You soon figure out that the more you give, the more you get. Commitment liberates you. Look for love in a creative group situation. An Aries attracts you and inspires you, but pushes your freedom/commitment buttons. You might reach a happier synthesis with a Cancer, or avoid the dilemma with fellow free spirit Aquarius.

Your greatest challenge is to choose your battles with your heart rather than your head. Your greatest gift—or weapon—is what's inside your head.

➤ Read about your Chinese Astrological sign on page 838. ➤ Read about your Personal Planets on page 826. ➤ Read about your personal Mystical Card on page 856.

TAURUS
Your Personal Planets

YOUR LOVE POTENTIAL
Venus in Aries, Apr. 20, 9:25 - May 21, 8:52

YOUR DRIVE AND AMBITION
Mars in Taurus, Apr. 20, 9:25 - May 01, 6:07
Mars in Gemini, May 01, 6:08 - May 21, 8:52

YOUR LUCK MAGNETISM
Jupiter in Taurus, Apr. 20, 9:25 - May 09, 15:32
Jupiter in Gemini, May 09, 15:33 - May 21, 8:52

World Events

Apr. 24 - Winston Churchill is knighted by Queen Elizabeth II.
Apr. 25 - James Watson and Francis Crick define the structure of DNA.

Queen Elizabeth II's coronation

GEMINI
Your Personal Planets

YOUR LOVE POTENTIAL
Venus in Aries, May 21, 8:53 - June 05, 10:33
Venus in Taurus, June 05, 10:34 - June 21, 16:59

YOUR DRIVE AND AMBITION
Mars in Gemini, May 21, 8:53 - June 14, 3:48
Mars in Cancer, June 14, 3:49 - June 21, 16:59

YOUR LUCK MAGNETISM
Jupiter in Gemini, May 21, 8:53 - June 21, 16:59

World Events

May 29 - Edmund Hillary and Sherpa Tensing become the first people to conquer Mt. Everest.
June 2 - Queen Elizabeth II is crowned in Westminster Abbey, London.

1953

CANCER
Your Personal Planets

YOUR LOVE POTENTIAL
Venus in Taurus, June 21, 17:00 - July 07, 10:29
Venus in Gemini, July 07, 10:30 - July 23, 3:51

YOUR DRIVE AND AMBITION
Mars in Cancer, June 21, 17:00 - July 23, 3:51

YOUR LUCK MAGNETISM
Jupiter in Gemini, June 21, 17:00 - July 23, 3:51

World Events

June 22 - The trial of John Christie, charged with the Rillington Place murders, begins in England.

July 4 - Imre Nagy becomes leader of Hungary.

Cuban rebel Fidel Castro

LEO
Your Personal Planets

YOUR LOVE POTENTIAL
Venus in Gemini, July 23, 3:52 - Aug. 04, 1:07
Venus in Cancer, Aug. 04, 1:08 - Aug. 23, 10:44

YOUR DRIVE AND AMBITION
Mars in Cancer, July 23, 3:52 - July 29, 19:24
Mars in Leo, July 29, 19:25 - Aug. 23, 10:44

YOUR LUCK MAGNETISM
Jupiter in Gemini, July 23, 3:52 - Aug. 23, 10:44

World Events

July 26 - Fidel Castro begins a rebellion against Fulgencio Batista's regime in Cuba.

July 27 - The Korean War is officially concluded after three years of conflict.

CANCER
From June 21, 17:00 through July 23, 3:51

The Reluctant Leader

Cancer of 1953 is more forceful than most. Almost an honorary Aries, you are bold, ambitious, and competitive. Not one to back down from a challenge or a confrontation, you can even be aggressive when your rights are at stake. Your lightning-quick temper surprises people who think they can take advantage of your patience and willingness to share. But that "almost" is very important: you remain at heart a gentle soul looking to nurture and care for your friends and family—even the world at large.

As you were born, both these traits were seen surrounding a sudden workers' strike-turned-riot in East Berlin. The protest began over the government increase in production quotas, and an angry crowd of 100,000 workers gathered. Soviet troops and tanks were called in to quell the violence. The strike, which the government blamed on western provocateurs, continued to expand among disgruntled workers throughout the country. In response, the U.S., Britain, and France quickly condemned the Soviet military. The U.S., playing the Cancerian role of paternalistic breadbasket nation, sought to assert influence by sending 5.5 million food parcels to East Berlin. The Soviets later demanded that the U.S. halt its attempt to intervene.

Anarchy may taste like freedom when you're young, but as you've matured, you've learned that chaos holds you back. You've realized that constantly reconfiguring your life can be a distraction, delaying your growth. Leadership is another strong quality for you. Perhaps a bit reluctantly, you will probably lead something, somewhere, sometime. You do so because you are best suited to support the groups endeavor—and you will probably be of enormous benefit to your family or community, which is what you really care about.

Libra helps you reinvent yourself without destroying everything you've built. Aries matches your drive and high energy level, but you have the deepest connection with passionate Scorpio.

Your greatest challenge is to balance your forcefulness with your gentleness, and your greatest gift is your willingness to step up to bat for those you love.

LEO
From July 23, 3:52 through August 23, 10:44

Your Own Write

It's show time, and 1953 Leo is ready. Never a shy one, you are especially happy to model healthy self-confidence for the more timid types. Your charm and charisma bring you many friends and admirers, and you gain on all levels from group affiliations. Your goodwill and generosity go far to promote your efforts, and you are a networking king or queen. Your personal courage encourages others to shed their fears and join you in the spotlight.

You probably have extraordinary creative writing ability, combining imagination and discipline with sheer talent. Your love of life and generosity of spirit come across vividly in your words, which you virtually sculpt into form. You would also make an inspired teacher, bringing out the latent talent in your students. You'd excel at designing and leading creative workshops—inspired creations in their own right. Theater would be a natural forum for your love of language and gift of drama. You can write the plays and star in them, or use your coaching ability to direct. You would also make a gifted event planner.

You can be surprisingly tough and quick to anger. Like a cat's retractable claws, your temper flares when you are crossed. You were born during one of the largest strikes in history. It was staged, so to speak, in France in response to the government's attempt to sneak through austerity measures during the country's vacation month. It was the government that was surprised, though, when four million workers marched off the job in anger, demanding raises. That is precisely how you defend your human rights: quickly, hotly, and effectively.

A sunny Sagittarius could light up your life, sharing your confidence and enthusiasm, while a chatty Gemini brings you delightful conversation and companionship. In a classic combo, Gemini American Senator J. F. Kennedy married lovely Leo Jackie in 1953. An Aquarius brings you out of yourself and expands your circle even further.

Your greatest challenge is to learn to balance your devotion with your own creativity and that of others, and your greatest strength is your powerful personality.

➤ Read about your Chinese Astrological sign on page 838. ➤ Read about your Personal Planets on page 826. ➤ Read about your personal Mystical Card on page 856.

VIRGO

From August 23, 10:45 through September 23, 8:05

Fire Under Water

There is much hidden power behind the 1953 Virgo's clever disguise as a mild-mannered perfectionist. Your scientific mind is quick, sharp, and penetrating, and like a shark, it needs to keep moving. Your attention to detail and legendary memory help you compile and sort through vast catalogs of raw data. You can argue your theories cogently, and your sharp tongue intimidates your opponents—but your refinement won't allow you to become ruthless. With your insight and determination to get to the bottom of things, you would make an excellent journalist, or criminal investigator. Probing psychological depths would be another strong possibility. They say every good detective is part psychologist, and every psychologist is part detective.

You are like Jacques Cousteau meets C. G. Jung. A natural-born explorer of the workings of the unconscious, you came into the world the same year that the inventor of the aqualung published his remarkable account of his deep-sea dives throughout the world. It was like discovering another planet right here on Earth. While the 1950s were dominated by Freudian thinking, Jung's ideas were also beginning to emerge. Jung stressed the importance of a strong ego when exploring archetypal realms, using the image of a glass-bottomed boat. Your strong powers of discrimination and earthy common sense serve you well in your own investigations of inner space.

You are a human dynamo, with ninety percent of your power submerged below the horizon of your personality. But rather than ice, you are hiding fire under your mysterious waters. You are able to call on vast reserves of strength when crisis strikes. You have both a tendency to experience crises and the ability to turn them into opportunities.

Perceptive Scorpio relates to your depths and intensity, while a Leo may come too close to your own secrets for comfort. You may want to run away from homey Cancer's nest into Aquarius's more open arms.

Your greatest challenge is to bring your hidden power to light for productive purposes, and your greatest asset is that rumbling underground volcano of yours.

LIBRA

From September 23, 8:06 through October 23, 17:05

The Great Equalizer

Libra's usual diplomacy and peacekeeping efforts were heightened in 1953, reflecting the world's growing weariness with the Cold War. At the same time, people all over the world were growing wary of programmed thinking. Whether this suppression took the blatant form of fascist pogroms, communist propaganda, or the anti-communist propaganda of the American McCarthy era witch hunt, the world was clearing its throat to utter your favorite line: "On the other hand... ."

You have a great ability to see two sides to every question, and you understand the need for freedom of thought and expression. Within your astrological month alone, 1953 Libra, a British TV movie of George Orwell's *1984* was released and Ray Bradbury's novel *Fahrenheit 451* was published. The sheer lack of demand in the marketplace would probably have blocked their arrival any earlier.

Both works ironically express a growing concern about our tendency to regiment society, and the accompanying thought control and "us vs. them" thinking. Arriving in this climate of more open questioning and debate, your own thirst for knowledge and understanding may have made you an excellent teacher. Far more than a mere disseminator of rhetoric, you would challenge your students to think for themselves. You may also feel called to the law—as one of the potentially highest expressions of civilization. Your inherent sense of fairness compels you to action and, whether in the public arena or your personal life, you find it hard to accept arbitrary authority. But neither are you an arbitrary rebel. You seek to balance autonomy and responsibility, working as a conscious individual in partnership and community with others.

An idealistic Gemini supports your vision of a fair system, and an Aries with a fighting spirit might help you to be a little more straightforward. You find a powerfully connected political ally in Virgo, and a surprising passion behind their analytical front.

Your greatest challenge is to remember to love yourself as well as your neighbor. Your greatest strengths are your open-mindedness and sense of perspective.

➤ Read about your Chinese Astrological sign on page 838. ➤ Read about your Personal Planets on page 826. ➤ Read about your personal Mystical Card on page 856.

VIRGO
Your Personal Planets

YOUR LOVE POTENTIAL
Venus in Cancer, Aug. 23, 10:45 - Aug. 30, 1:34
Venus in Leo, Aug. 30, 1:35 - Sept. 23, 8:05

YOUR DRIVE AND AMBITION
Mars in Leo, Aug. 23, 10:45 - Sept. 14, 17:58
Mars in Virgo, Sept. 14, 17:59 - Sept. 23, 8:05

YOUR LUCK MAGNETISM
Jupiter in Gemini, Aug. 23, 10:45 - Sept. 23, 8:05

World Events

Sept. 12 - Senator John F. Kennedy marries Jacqueline Bouvier.

Sept. 13 - Nikita Khrushchev is appointed Secretary-General of the USSR.

John F. Kennedy and his wife Jacqueline cut the cake after their marriage

LIBRA
Your Personal Planets

Your Love Potential
Venus in Leo, Sept. 23, 8:06 - Sept. 24, 3:47
Venus in Virgo, Sept. 24, 3:48 - Oct. 18, 15:26
Venus in Libra, Oct. 18, 15:27 - Oct. 23, 17:05

YOUR DRIVE AND AMBITION
Mars in Virgo, Sept. 23, 8:06 - Oct. 23, 17:05

YOUR LUCK MAGNETISM
Jupiter in Gemini, Sept. 23, 8:06 - Oct. 23, 17:05

World Events

Sept. 30 - A new diving record is set at 10,330 ft by Swissman August Piccard.

Oct. 16 - Fidel Castro is sentenced to fifteen years imprisonment for his involvement in the Cuban rebellion; he claims "History will defend me."

1953

SCORPIO
Your Personal Planets

YOUR LOVE POTENTIAL
Venus in Libra, Oct. 23, 17:06 - Nov. 11, 18:11
Venus in Scorpio, Nov. 11, 18:12 - Nov. 22, 14:21

YOUR DRIVE AND AMBITION
Mars in Virgo, Oct. 23, 17:06 - Nov. 01, 14:18
Mars in Libra, Nov. 01, 14:19 - Nov. 22, 14:21

YOUR LUCK MAGNETISM
Jupiter in Gemini, Oct. 23, 17:06 - Nov. 22, 14:21

World Events

Nov. 5 – The Nobel Prize for physics is awarded to Frederik Zernicke.

Nov. 9 – British poet and novelist Dylan Thomas dies.

Death of author Dylan Thomas

SAGITTARIUS
Your Personal Planets

YOUR LOVE POTENTIAL
Venus in Scorpio, Nov. 22, 14:22 - Dec. 05, 16:23
Venus in Sagittarius, Dec. 05, 16:24 - Dec. 22, 3:30

YOUR DRIVE AND AMBITION
Mars in Libra, Nov. 22, 14:22 - Dec. 20, 11:21
Mars in Scorpio, Dec. 20, 11:22 - Dec. 22, 3:30

YOUR LUCK MAGNETISM
Jupiter in Gemini, Nov. 22, 14:22 - Dec. 22, 3:30

World Events

Dec. 9 – In the U.S., General Electric announces that all Communist employees will be dismissed.

Dec. 17 – Chinese premier Nguyen Van Tam resigns after disagreements with Bao Dai.

SCORPIO
From October 23, 17:06 through November 22, 14:21

The Lamaze Methodist

Never a particularly frivolous type, 1953 Scorpio brings new meaning to the word intense. You have the focus and precision of a laser, and the potency, too. Your intuition matches your penetrating intellect, giving you extraordinary insight into the workings of the human mind as well as its deepest heart. November 1953 was marked by the deaths of two incredibly intense writers, both well acquainted with the lizard on the windowpane—American playwright Eugene O'Neill and Welsh poet Dylan Thomas. You too are able to render your deepest emotions in words, but need not succumb to the raging alcoholism that escorted them both into that good night. In fact, by the time you were coming of age, the psychological understanding of addiction created another possible niche for you. You could put your prolific verbal talents to great use helping others with similar wounds to heal.

Transformation is one of your keywords, and you are especially likely to experience many identities within one lifetime. You are also likely to facilitate a healing process of rebirth for others. Able to articulate what some can only vaguely sense and might prefer to avoid, your integrity inspires others to work hard to improve their lives. Your supportive presence brings steadiness and compassion to your insights.

It is specifically through your words that you are able to help others restructure their realities into new forms which enhance their spirits, rather than trying to force square pegs into round holes. Your words give power and form to what would otherwise remain idle imaginings and inarticulate longings.

Taurus helps you ground your thinking in emotional truth. Capricorn holds down the fort while Cancer points out interesting forays into uncharted territory. Virgo introduces you to kindred spirits. Group activities bring you healing support, and activate your leadership abilities.

Your greatest challenge, 1953 Scorpio, is to be true to your deepest truth and dive to your truest depths. Your greatest asset is your ability to put your experience into words that everyone can relate to.

SAGITTARIUS
From November 22, 14:22 through December 22, 3:30

The Lucid Dreamer

Sagittarius rules the rainbow, and on December 18, 1953, the FCC ruled in favor of transmitting color-TV signals over the airwaves. In the years to come, images of the world on television would transform from drab black-and-white into vivid Technicolor®, much like Dorothy's shift from Kansas to Munchkinland in *The Wonderful Land Of Oz*, a program you may have enjoyed upon its American première in 1969. Never one to miss a call to adventure, 1953 Sagittarius is raring to go. You can also be private and glad to return to Home Sweet Home. Inner spiritual journeys continually renew your familiar outer surroundings.

Behind your happy-go-lucky exterior, you are also a philosophical soul, often given to profoundly secret midnight ruminations and insights. Your poetic way with words has a mystical tint. You may keep your more serious musings under wraps well into maturity, not wanting to blow your cool daytime image. But behind the façade of easy bonhomie and carefree fun and adventure, a quiet creature lurks, given to not only thoughtful introspection but also hidden passion.

As you mature, there is less of a split between your insightful depths and your good-natured enthusiasm. You are a fine example of how to decline co-membership in the Mental Depression club, which is automatically extended to anyone who can See Beneath the Surface. You simply refuse to be miserable, preferring to be amused by the absurdities of life.

You achieve your greatest growth and learning through partnerships of all kinds—creative, business, and romantic. Partners expand your horizons and your wealth, helping you to articulate and objectify the inner workings of your imagination, giving form to your visions. A Scorpio readily discovers your buried treasure and an adventurous, playful Gemini helps you explore inner and outer territory. Kindred fire sign Leo helps you plumb your greatest depths and scale your greatest heights, adding the flesh of experience to your theories.

Your greatest challenge is to integrate your entire spectrum of possibilities, and your greatest strength is your eternal optimism.

➤ Read about your Chinese Astrological sign on page 838. ➤ Read about your Personal Planets on page 826. ➤ Read about your personal Mystical Card on page 856.

CAPRICORN

From December 22, 3:31 through December 31, 23:59

The Silly Goat

Like Groucho Marx in a tuxedo, straight-faced 1953 December Capricorn's twinkling eyes belie a clown behind a formal front. Your humorous wit and sly way with words add a good-natured dimension to your solemn persona, rounding out your traditional seriousness. It may take people a while to see beyond your poker face, but you are winking behind the deadpan mask. You are especially inclined to liven up a humdrum work routine with humor. You may initially come off as a bit of a curmudgeon, but you are secretly warm-hearted underneath.

Skilled at choreographing group dynamics, you are gifted in presiding over meetings. Competing agendas can elevate ego energies, but your easygoing humor helps diffuse struggles for power or control. In December 1953, leaders of the U.S., France, and Britain attended the "Big Three Conference" in Bermuda. You may have a gut sense for how the location of a meeting sets the tone among participants. In stressful gatherings, your flair for impromptu repartee can ease tensions. You also quickly learn that simply letting go of your own end of the rope promptly ends any tug of war. Sensitive antennae usually help you to tune into and short-circuit rising tempers before they explode. Because you tend to control your own emotions, others look to you for leadership and guidance.

In work and love, you seem to attract restless and rebellious partners until you recognize this as a part of yourself. Once you can accept your own inner rebel, you are able to balance your own need for freedom with your more conscious need for commitment. You eventually see that the simple trust of giving others room to move is the greatest gift you can give, which keeps them coming back.

A zany Cancer helps you stretch in ways that liberate you emotionally, while a determined Scorpio helps you focus your intentions. Playful Sagittarius sees right through your serious facade and tickles your funny bone while eliciting your best bons mots.

Your greatest challenge is to lighten up—let the chips fall where they may. Your greatest strength is your delightful sense of humor.

1953
CAPRICORN
Your Personal Planets

YOUR LOVE POTENTIAL

Venus in Sagittarius, Dec. 22, 3:31 - Dec. 29, 12:52
Venus in Capricorn, Dec. 29, 12:53 - Dec. 31, 23:59

YOUR DRIVE AND AMBITION

Mars in Scorpio, Dec. 22, 3:31 - Dec. 31, 23:59

YOUR LUCK MAGNETISM

Jupiter in Gemini, Dec. 22, 3:31 - Dec. 31, 23:59

World Events

Dec. 28 – Joseph Beck is appointed premier of Luxembourg.

Dec. 29 – Viet Minh forces arrive at the Mekong River on the Thai–Laos border.

Special Feature

An Astrological Family Tree: The British Royal Family

(Continued from page 425)

Queen Elizabeth II and her great-grandfather Edward VII have Jupiter in the first house of self-expression, and George V, Elizabeth's grandfather, and her son Prince Charles have Jupiter in Sagittarius. Prince William's Jupiter may not be in Sagittarius, but it is in Scorpio, positioned in a "power zone" of a horoscope. In this case, at the time of the Prince's birth, his Jupiter was only two degrees from the highest point it could reach in the heavens and is thus in a power zone. Add to this the fact that his Jupiter is at zero degrees of Scorpio—exactly opposite his grand-mother's Taurus Sun and his father's Taurus Moon—and we can see an astrological family patterntaking shape through three generations.

What makes this Jupiter astrological trait in the family so very interesting is neither Victoria nor George VI were, strictly speaking, "heirs to the throne." Victoria was crowned because there was no direct heir when her uncle William IV died, and George VI became king upon the abdication of his brother King Edward VIII in 1936. As such neither had been groomed as a future monarch. At the time of the abdication, Jupiter was in the sign of Sagittarius and unpredictable Uranus, the planet that often brings about abrupt reversals in our lives, was in Taurus. Both George VI, and therefore his little daughter Elizabeth, had their lives changed forever by this fact.

> Taurus and its opposite sign Scorpio—signs of wealth and power—are represented in the charts of every monarch from Queen Victoria to Prince William, now second in line to the British throne.

As we've noted, Jupiter is the planet of royalty; and as Prince Charles's Jupiter is in

Members of the Royal Family

Sagittarius, this is a good sign that he will one day take the throne. Yet his Jupiter is also in opposition aspect to his natal Uranus, making one wonder how long he might reign. Does unpredictable Uranus portend another unexpected event in the lives of the royal family? Only time will tell! ✪

► Read Princess Diana's Star Profile on page 689. ► Read Queen Elizabeth's Star Profile on page 449. ► Read the Duke of Windsor's Star Profile on page 329.

1954

Dreams Actualized: Jupiter Contacts Uranus and Neptune

Jupiter, the planet linked to education, expansion, and enterprise, moved quickly through both Gemini and Cancer during 1954. It completed its transit of sprightly Gemini by the end of May, but not before it harmonized poetically with imaginative Neptune in artistic Libra. From *The Caine Mutiny* and *The Lord Of The Rings* to Elvis Presley or the ground-breaking "Disneyland," the arts were expressed in their finest efflorescence. While expressive Jupiter remained in loquacious Gemini, Senator Joseph McCarthy was given full rein to destroy the lives of blacklisted Americans. On its last gasp in the sign, its loftiest symbolism was manifested in the U.S. Supreme Court decision to offer equal education to African Americans through school integration.

When Jupiter entered emotive Cancer, it began to build dynamic tension with Uranus, the planet of sudden change, also in Cancer. Rock 'n' roll gave voice to the exuberance of a generation. Bill Haley rocked around the clock, and the great Elvis thrilled audiences with *That's All Right*. Science provided the perfect metaphor for this combination, as astronomers first realized that the Universe may have been created in a Big Bang. Jupiter also swept by Neptune—still in Libra—giving flight to a whole range of new heroic fancies and fantasies. Finally, the voices of moderation prevailed in the Joseph McCarthy investigation, and he was censured by year's end. Air Force One made its first presidential take-off, while the small screen saw the première of *The Tonight Show* and the pageantry of the Miss America beauty contest.

IT'S RAINING FROGS AGAIN, DEAR

Hundreds of frogs fell from the sky, landing on people's umbrellas during a shower in the Sutton Park neighborhood of Birmingham, England. Frogs falling out of the sky during rainstorms has occurred throughout history in Europe and North America. One of the more bizarre explanations offered for this phenomenon is that solar evaporation could carry frogspawn from the water of the marshes and into the atmosphere. The spawn might survive in the vapor of the clouds and mature into frogs and toads that would then fall to the Earth like rain.

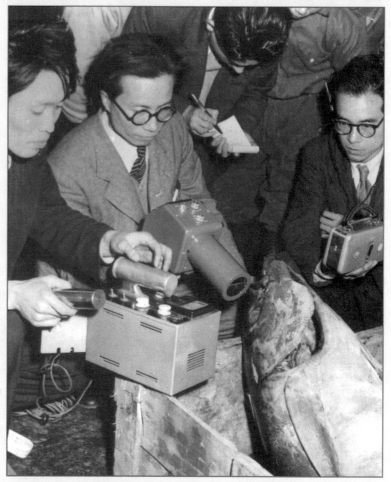

Japanese fishing boat affected by H Bomb test

Joseph McCarthy during a recess of his sub-committee's hearing at Albany

The French suffer a disastrous defeat at Dien Bien Phu

COMMUNIST VICTORY

Fighting in Indochina escalated between Ho Chi Minh's North Vietnamese Communists and the French, who suffered a disastrous defeat at Dien Bien Phu. A peace treaty was signed and Ho Chi Minh became Prime Minister and President of North Vietnam. A power struggle took place in Russia between Stalin's successor Malenkov and Nikita Khrushchev. Anti-French nationalist riots took place in Algeria. Communist witch-hunter Joseph McCarthy, exposed on TV as a bully, was indicted by Congress for conduct unbecoming a Senator. Although Indian Prime Minister Nehru proposed halting nuclear bomb tests, the U.S. tested a hydrogen bomb 600 times more powerful than the bomb dropped on Hiroshima, contaminating the crew of a Japanese fishing vessel. The Supreme Court ordered racial integration in schools. With developments in computers, a 'second Industrial Revolution' was proclaimed. Boeing's 707 'Jumbo' jet made its first flight. The Salk vaccine brought poliomyelitis under control. Marilyn Monroe married the baseball player Joe DiMaggio. Tolkien's trilogy *Lord Of The Rings* was published, as was Golding's morality tale *Lord Of The Flies*.

➤ Read Queen Elizabeth II's Star profile on page 449.

CAPRICORN

From January 01, 0:00 through January 20, 14:10

Back to the Future

You came into the world, 1954 January Capricorn, as your fellow Capricorn Elvis Presley celebrated his nineteenth birthday by making his very first recording. Far from being a late-bloomer, you are likely to show similar talent and moxie—and success—from quite an early age. Like Presley, while you are disciplined and ambitious, you are probably also somewhat rebellious against the traditional backdrop of both your times and your sign. You can be surprisingly individualistic and eccentric.

Black leather is not necessarily your style, however, and your originality may well take a more cerebral form. Like the English poet W. H. Auden, who won the Bollingen Prize in January 1954, you have a serious regard for the beauty of formal language. Not one to completely overthrow tradition, Auden was nevertheless said to be the first poet writing in English who felt at home in the twentieth century. Instead of nursing nostalgia for a lost golden era, Auden was passionately concerned with the present and the future. Whatever your medium, you are blessed with a similar gift to breathe new life into existing frameworks, expanding them to encompass change and growth. You are also likely to share Auden's concern about the larger social picture, and to use your well-honed voice to transform external structures.

You have the drive and discipline to achieve your ambitions, whatever they may be, and the right combination of technical skill and ingenuity to be truly creative. Whether you are designing a work of art or a business deal, you understand that the act of creation is an act of limitation, rather than a state of unbridled freedom. You know that in order to bring any possibility into actuality, you must let go of some potentialities. You are able to focus your activities based on this principle.

In love, an influential Scorpio brings you powerful connections and awakens your passion, while a Cancer can nurture your unconventional streak.

Your greatest challenge is to bridge the past and the future, and your greatest gift is your ability to transform not by destroying, but by rebuilding.

AQUARIUS

From January 20, 14:11 through February 19, 4:31

The Electrified Inventor

In January 1954, it was announced that the fifty millionth customer was added to America's power lines: all this from experiments by Thomas Edison no more than a generation earlier. As a 1954 Aquarius, you share this inventor's lightning-quick ingenuity and originality. You are hardwired to perceive the big picture, and have a special affinity for abstract systems, be they technological, mathematical, or physical. Even if you were not directly involved in the development of the Internet, by the time it evolved it made intuitive sense to you, and you are able to use it for yourself, and to communicate with others.

To mark the seventy-fifth anniversary of Edison's invention of the light bulb, a 75,000-watt bulb was lit in Rockefeller Center on February 11. Like Edison's, your greatest inspirations come out of left field like bolts of lightning. And like Edison and the classical Greek inventor Archimedes for whom they were named, you are able to ground these "eureka" moments in everyday life with practical, useful applications.

Networking maven that you are, you are expert at weaving webs of relationships, between people, ideas, or physical locations. Talented at languages and other symbolic systems, you are well suited to a career in hi-tech communications. Linguistics is another distinct possibility, as is the occult. You were born as the seminal recordings of African American blues folksinger Leadbelly were released on Folkway Records. Born in 1888, Leadbelly was said to be the grandfather of rock 'n' roll. You are similarly gifted to bring a timeless voice to traditional forms, and to the humanitarian cause of the liberation of the oppressed.

As you continue to evolve (well into your youthful old age, by the way), you will acknowledge hidden truths: steady Capricorns can actually help you ground your loftiest concepts, while ambitious, possessive Scorpios encourage you to succeed and make an impact.

Your greatest challenge is to maximize existing systems while giving free reign to your originality, and your greatest strength is your intuitive grasp of the big picture.

➤ Read about your Chinese Astrological sign on page 838. ➤ Read about your Personal Planets on page 826. ➤ Read about your personal Mystical Card on page 856.

1954

CAPRICORN
Your Personal Planets

YOUR LOVE POTENTIAL
Venus in Capricorn, Jan. 01, 0:00 - Jan. 20, 14:10

YOUR DRIVE AND AMBITION
Mars in Scorpio, Jan. 01, 0:00 - Jan. 20, 14:10

YOUR LUCK MAGNETISM
Jupiter in Gemini, Jan. 01, 0:00 - Jan. 20, 14:10

World Events

Jan. 4 - Elvis Presley records a ten-minute demo at a studio in Nashville, Tennessee.

Jan. 14 - Joe DiMaggio and Marilyn Monroe marry in San Francisco.

Joe DiMaggio marries Marilyn Monroe

AQUARIUS
Your Personal Planets

YOUR LOVE POTENTIAL
Venus in Capricorn, Jan. 20, 14:11 - Jan. 22, 9:19
Venus in Aquarius, Jan. 22, 9:20 - Feb. 15, 7:00
Venus in Pisces, Feb. 15, 7:01 - Feb. 19, 4:31

YOUR DRIVE AND AMBITION
Mars in Scorpio, Jan. 20, 14:11 - Feb. 09, 19:17
Mars in Sagittarius, Feb. 09, 19:18 - Feb. 19, 4:31

YOUR LUCK MAGNETISM
Jupiter in Gemini, Jan. 20, 14:11 - Feb. 19, 4:31

World Events

Jan. 26 - Preparation begins on the site that will become Disneyland.

Feb. 3 - Queen Elizabeth II arrives in Australia on her first royal visit there.

1954

PISCES
Your Personal Planets

YOUR LOVE POTENTIAL
Venus in Pisces, Feb. 19, 4:32 - Mar. 11, 7:21
Venus in Aries, Mar. 11, 7:22 - Mar. 21, 3:52

YOUR DRIVE AND AMBITION
Mars in Sagittarius, Feb. 19, 4:32 - Mar. 21, 3:52

YOUR LUCK MAGNETISM
Jupiter in Gemini, Feb. 19, 4:32 - Mar. 21, 3:52

World Events

Feb. 25 - Abdul Nasser is appointed President of Egypt.

Mar. 8 - Talks begin in Paris between the French and Vietnamese to establish the state of Indochina.

Gamal Abdel Nasser, President of Egypt

ARIES
Your Personal Planets

YOUR LOVE POTENTIAL
Venus in Aries, Mar. 21, 3:53 - Apr. 04, 11:54
Venus in Taurus, Apr. 04, 11:55 - Apr. 20, 15:19

YOUR DRIVE AND AMBITION
Mars in Sagittarius, Mar. 21, 3:53 - Apr. 12, 16:27
Mars in Capricorn, Apr. 12, 16:28 - Apr. 20, 15:19Your Luck Magnetism
Jupiter in Gemini, Mar. 21, 3:53 - Apr. 20, 15:19

World Events

Apr. 10 - French cinema pioneer Auguste Lumière dies.

Apr. 13 - Scientist Robert Oppenheimer is accused of being a Communist.

PISCES
From February 19, 4:32 through March 21, 3:52

The Relativity Prodigy

Creative 1954 Pisces, you are often gifted at abstractions like calculus but challenged by simplicities like making change at a cash register. You are thus frequently misunderstood, like Piscean Einstein, who was told he had a learning disability. What your less inspired teachers may not have realized is that you were actually a step ahead and—much to their chagrin—devising new approaches to old methods. You have been cursed with a learning super-ability, based in intuitive, non-linear thinking. Distinctly right-brained, you probably excel at spatial concepts and abstract relationships.

Einstein admitted that all his greatest ideas came to him through inspiration, which he later worked out laboriously through mathematics. Like him, you have a genius for overarching principle rather than the collection of detailed data. Leave that task to others. Like Einstein, who declined the post of Prime Minister of Israel shortly before you were born, you may be a reluctant leader. Groups and partnerships, however, tend to bring you the stability to achieve your goals. If you haven't already, it pays to establish these external structures.

Not unlike the political game of musical chairs in Egypt at the time of your birth, your baffling chameleon nature leaves onlookers wondering "who's in charge?" Things at last settled into place there as Lieutenant Colonel Gamal Abdel Nasser took the helm in February 1954. Once he did, he established stability and was to play a pre-eminent role in the country's, and region's, leadership until 1970. Likewise, once you finally make up your own changeable mind, you do settle down to the matters at hand, and energetically rise to the occasion—even leadership, sometimes.

You find ambitious, charismatic Sagittarius to be highly stimulating, but perhaps a steady Capricorn better invites you to share a vision for the future and ultimately to settle down.

Your greatest challenge is to decide who's in charge of your life (who else could it be?), and your greatest gift is your ability to embrace the relativity of reality. Reality? What a concept...

ARIES
From March 21, 3:53 through April 20, 15:19

The Opportunity Magnet

Rather than being action-based, 1954 Aries, you tend to be pleasure-oriented and hope to magnetize good fortune without a whole lot of effort. Travel and adventure issue a rousing call from time to time, but nothing too taxing. Your birth coincided with the first sale of frozen TV dinners by Swanson & Sons. This dovetailed perfectly with the release of color TV shortly before. So hey, by the time you were growing up, you could even travel from home. Why ever leave the couch? Well, until remotes came out, you did have to get up to change the channel, or delegate that task to someone else, so you did get some exercise!

The thing is, you do tend to attract opportunity, right from the comfort of your own home. And, being highly charismatic and attractive, you have tended to attract lots of romantic interest as well. It could even be said that you have been downright lucky in this life. You have the gift of excellent timing, helping you make the most of whatever comes your way. And you have the knack of intercepting any opportunities that might be passing by, before they pass you by. If anything holds your interest long enough, you are likely to be successful at it.

You are intensely creative and original, and have an appreciation for art, even if you haven't engaged in the making of it. That said, it's never too late—Grandma Moses was in her seventies when she started painting. You bring your creativity, and a deeply personal perspective, to whatever you do. Even your home decor is likely to be somewhat eccentric, reflecting your unique individuality.

In romance, accommodating Libra is a good match, but you two may tend to overdo it in the pleasure department, for better and for worse. Let's put it this way: a Libra would probably not make a good exercise or diet partner. A Sagittarius is most likely to get a rise out of you, and to get you moving. You may even be somewhat competitive, which may not be such a bad thing.

Your greatest challenge is to allow something to motivate you. Your greatest asset is your ability to attract opportunities, friends, and lovers.

➤ Read about your Chinese Astrological sign on page 838. ➤ Read about your Personal Planets on page 826. ➤ Read about your personal Mystical Card on page 856.

TAURUS

From April 20, 15:20 through May 21, 14:46

The Armchair Tourist

Never a sign to take life particularly lightly, the 1954 Taurus is even more serious than the usual Bull. You approach both your ideals and partnerships of all kinds with a high degree of commitment and integrity, 1954 Taurus. You were born as the U.S. Supreme Court outlawed racial segregation in the nation's public schools. Like the civil rights activists who fought long and hard for this victory, you are the kind of visionary who can launch a well-organized battle for your ideals, whatever they may be.

You are motivated to excel intellectually, and may feel drawn to the academic or publishing fields. Your mind has a restless quality, which makes for an interesting contrast with your otherwise steady, stable nature. In work, you are able to establish a cozy niche that also allows your intellect free reign, perhaps even involving travel to foreign cultures. You have a special gift for establishing structures that allow you the freedom to explore new vistas, mentally if not physically.

You are attracted to partners, in business and love, who share your seriousness and sense of responsibility. As a youngster, you may have tended to latch on to older friends, and as your life has unfolded, this trend has continued. If they are not chronologically older than you, your close friends and partners may be people you respect a lot, and perhaps even look up to. Your intense seriousness may translate into caution about love, and it may take you quite a while to commit. But when you do make up your mind, its 200 percent forever. Learning to trust others may be a lifelong lesson for you. The more you can trust your own strength and resilience, which you have in abundance, the less you need to worry about others.

Both a Capricorn and a Scorpio mate (especially those born between 1953 and 1955) would share your seriousness. Your solidness grounds Scorpios intensity, and their need for transformation can help unstick you from any Taurean ruts you may fall into.

Your greatest challenge is to learn to trust, yourself and others. Your greatest strength is your own loyalty and trustworthiness.

GEMINI

From May 21, 14:47 through June 21, 22:53

The Diversification Specialist

It may be hard for you, Gemini of 1954, to settle down into any kind of routine, unless you are lucky enough to discover a role in life that is constantly changing, ever-stimulating, and which feeds your insatiable appetite for knowledge. Even more of an information junkie than others of your sign, you read everything, from history books, to phone books, to cereal boxes. Your mind is a lot like IBM's first mass-produced computer, sold in May 1954. The vacuum-tube electronic brain boasted it could perform more than ten million operations an hour. Coming of age with computers, communications technology, and the resulting Information Age, you may have made an excellent programmer.

You are likely to be quick-moving, agile and athletic, both mentally and physically. In addition to being a highly skilled verbal gymnast, you might also enjoy running. As you were born, two men broke the record for running a mile in under four minutes: Englishman Roger Bannister in May, and Australian John Landy in June. You also have a highly developed competitive streak, and an iron will to go with it. As long as a particular endeavor holds your interest, your focused willpower and discipline are bound to bring you many victories.

Your natural curiosity and supernatural diversification may lead you to live many lifetimes within one lifetime. A Renaissance Man or Woman par excellence, you tend to explore many avenues of discovery and expression. You would do well in many different fields, at the same time or at different times: from sales, to writing, to business, to sports, to fine craftsmanship. You are a perennial student of life, and you will probably keep moving and learning long after your peers have grown sedentary.

A grounded Capricorn helps you organize priorities and set goals, perhaps leading to financial support such as grants, sponsorships, and loans. A philosophical Sagittarius stimulates your mind.

Your greatest challenge in life is to keep up with your own restlessly inquiring mind, following its lead in many changing directions. Your greatest gift is your genius—use it wisely.

➤ Read about your Chinese Astrological sign on page 838. ➤ Read about your Personal Planets on page 826. ➤ Read about your personal Mystical Card on page 856.

TAURUS
Your Personal Planets

YOUR LOVE POTENTIAL
Venus in Taurus, Apr. 20, 15:20 - Apr. 28, 22:02
Venus in Gemini, Apr. 28, 22:03 - May 21, 14:46
YOUR DRIVE AND AMBITION
Mars in Capricorn, Apr. 20, 15:20 - May 21, 14:46
YOUR LUCK MAGNETISM
Jupiter in Gemini, Apr. 20, 15:20 - May 21, 14:46

World Events

May 6 – In Britain, Roger Bannister breaks the four-minute mile.

May 18 – The European Convention on Human Rights goes into effect.

Runner Roger Bannister crosses the tape

GEMINI
Your Personal Planets

YOUR LOVE POTENTIAL
Venus in Gemini, May 21, 14:47 - May 23, 15:03
Venus in Cancer, May 23, 15:04 - June 17, 17:03
Venus in Leo, June 17, 17:04 - June 21, 22:53
YOUR DRIVE AND AMBITION
Mars in Capricorn, May 21, 14:47 - June 21, 22:53
YOUR LUCK MAGNETISM
Jupiter in Gemini, May 21, 14:47 - May 24, 4:42
Jupiter in Cancer, May 24, 4:43 - June 21, 22:53

World Events

May 26 – In Egypt, archaeologists discover the Ship of the Dead at the Great Pyramid of Cheops.

June 11 – Iris Murdoch's first novel *Under the Net* is published in London.

1954

CANCER
Your Personal Planets

YOUR LOVE POTENTIAL

Venus in Leo, June 21, 22:54 - July 13, 8:42
Venus in Virgo, July 13, 8:43 - July 23, 9:44

YOUR DRIVE AND AMBITION

Mars in Capricorn, June 21, 22:54 - July 03, 7:22
Mars in Sagittarius, July 03, 7:23 - July 23, 9:44

YOUR LUCK MAGNETISM

Jupiter in Cancer, June 21, 22:54 - July 23, 9:44

World Events

July 3 – Food rationing finally comes to an end in Britain.

July 5 – Elvis Presley records his first hit, *That's All Right.*

American singer and actor, Elvis Presley

LEO
Your Personal Planets

YOUR LOVE POTENTIAL

Venus in Virgo, July 23, 9:45 - Aug. 09, 0:33
Venus in Libra, Aug. 09, 0:34 - Aug. 23, 16:35

YOUR DRIVE AND AMBITION

Mars in Sagittarius, July 23, 9:45 - Aug. 23, 16:35

YOUR LUCK MAGNETISM

Jupiter in Cancer, July 23, 9:45 - Aug. 23, 16:35

World Events

Aug. 11 – Peace is formally established in Indochina after seven years of conflict between the French and Viet Minh.

Aug. 18 – Assistant Secretary of Labor James E. Wilkins becomes the first black man to attend a U.S. Cabinet meeting.

446

CANCER

From June 21, 22:54 through July 23, 9:44

The Fledgling Flyer

Like all Cancers, those born in 1954 have a deep attachment to home and family. Because of a special astrological emphasis, you may face a significant challenge at some point in your life—one which calls for you to re-evaluate your family values in order to commit more fully to your partner. This is not to say that your partner has to preclude your family, but you may need to decide which to make your priority. You realize that your greatest growth lies with your mate, and not with your family of origin and your roots. Once you've clarified your commitment to your partnership, however, the two can come together in a truly complementary way, each balancing and enhancing the other. Elvis Presley, who recorded his first hit in July, *That's All Right*, expressed that sentiment.

Your own children, if you have them, may also call for an unusually significant commitment. If not your own children, then children you work with or associate with will bring a test of some kind. And if you do not parent or midwife literal, human children, then you may do so with other creations: your brain children. This call to duty is likely to bring forth amazing support from both your family and your partner, and could even be a unifying force between them, as they put this common cause first.

As a great nurturer and lover of food, it is fitting that you were born as post-war food rationing ended in Britain. You are warm, nurturing, enthusiastic, and caring, so you are a people-magnet, drawing people of all kinds to you, including vulnerable souls who need a little extra care. Your original thinking keeps you open-minded, and you accept people of all stripes, including the rebels. You take all comers under your kind wing, and treat them all like family.

A highly motivated Capricorn pulls you forward, out of the path of least resistance—your family background. A Scorpio mate supports your creative endeavors with intense commitment.

Your greatest challenge is to leave the safe nest of your original family, and your greatest asset is your ability to forge partnerships that inspire you to fly.

LEO

From July 23, 9:45 through August 23, 16:35

The Great Defender

As a 1954 Leo, you exhibit many emotional traits—perhaps unconsciously. In addition to your sign's usual high-profile potential for leadership, you are likely to show a fond concern for your family's well-being. Your ancestral roots may fascinate you. There may be some question, challenge, or mystery surrounding this matter, which you undertake to uncover or defend. You identify strongly with your clan and probably seek a leadership role within that context, rather than breaking free of this influence entirely. You gladly accept the duties and responsibilities that go along with this call to service, and the role you play can become healing not only for yourself, but also for others.

On August 17, President Eisenhower committed the U.S. to stop China from invading Formosa (Taiwan) and possibly averted an all-out war between the Nationalists and the Communists in China. This turning point exemplifies the kind of achievement of which you are capable, springing from your loyalty to family, tradition, community, and nation, as embodied by the leadership of President Eisenhower. Like "Ike," you function best from a position of authority. Others naturally look to you for direction and you often rise to upper management level in the business world.

Politics and community service are excellent outlets for your leadership abilities and your profound commitment to family and community. Born as Assistant Secretary of Labor James Wilkins became the first African American to attend a U.S. Cabinet meeting, even if you are not actively engaged in combat or politics, you are likely to be engaged in a struggle of ideas and ideals at some point in your life. Your nurturing protectiveness, combined with your courage, honor, and willingness to sacrifice, make for a classic champion of the oppressed. You happily commit to the cause.

A Cancer reminds you of the importance of where you've come from, and a Capricorn urges you toward the future.

Your greatest challenge is to find your own purpose within your family's historical context, and your greatest asset is your natural leadership ability.

➤ Read about your Chinese Astrological sign on page 838. ➤ Read about your Personal Planets on page 826. ➤ Read about your personal Mystical Card on page 856.

VIRGO

From August 23, 16:36 through September 23, 13:54

The Discriminating Nurturer

As a Virgo born in 1954, you bring your analytical abilities to bear on group endeavors that affect your home soil, from your family to, by extension, your community at large or nation. At the time of your birth, President Eisenhower signed the Communist Control Act, outlawing the Communist Party in the U.S. He explained that the American people were determined to protect themselves from any organization that was actually a conspiracy dedicated to the violent overthrow of the entire form of government. You might grow up to ponder the constitutionality of such an edict, given that the Constitution specifically allows for a complete change in the form of government, if the people wish it.

Group activities of all kinds are hugely important to you, motivating you to expand beyond your limits at all stages of your life. Regardless of your gender, you tend to look after your colleagues and associates, clucking over their welfare like a mother hen. President Eisenhower signed a bill to extend Social Security to ten million more on September 1, 1954, so that America could care for its sick and elderly as an extended family. There were those who objected to this as a nearly communistic measure, but this kind of public policy is likely to suit your humanitarianism.

You bring attention to detail to whatever question you choose to subject to your investigative powers. You are an expert researcher, able to marshal vast warehouses of information. You seem to arrange your data in alphabetical order in your head, so highly organized is your thinking. You also have great manual dexterity and skill, which you bring to crafts and fine handiwork with a delicate aesthetic sensibility. You would also make an expert research technician.

A Cancer shares your fondness for extended families, be they political organizations or support groups, while a Sagittarius spurs you on, to explore old and new possibilities at home.

Your greatest challenge is to not lose the forest for the trees in your perfectionist attention to detail, and your greatest asset is your ability to transcend the particulars.

LIBRA

From September 23, 13:55 through October 23, 22:55

The Mountain-Mover

As a Libra born in 1954, you may have even more trouble than usual making up your mind. While all Librans are gifted to perceive two sides to every question, you are like an honorary Piscean, seeing an infinite number of possibilities. Its all relative, you may say—but to what? The very idea of standards may not seem to apply at all, or they may be completely unrealistic. As a youngster, you were much better at imagistic poetry than you were at clear-cut judgments and decisions.

You came into the world along with the epitome of the "aw-shucks" fantasy family TV show, *Father Knows Best*. This set-piece of Americana—a misty vision of the American Dream—was to become an unrealistic standard against which many families were to measure their normalcy for years to come. Needless to say, most real-life families failed miserably against the shows fantasy-level of old-fashioned homey simplicity, and folksy wholesomeness and functionality.

Along with your idealism, you have the potential to learn to ground yourself and, working with the limitations of reality, are well equipped to bring your visions down to Earth. And one of your ambitions is to build a secure home base and, if not a literal family, then a community that feels like family. You have what it takes to create much more than a fantasy family; you can build a community reality. As you were born, Mao Tse-Tung was re-elected as Chairman of the People's Republic of China. Whatever else may be said about some of his methods, this was a man who could move mountains to realize his vision for a better community.

You are surprisingly serious and passionate when it comes to love. This may cause you to delay commitment, but when you do, you mean it for life. This is true for friendships as well as romance. You may tend to have a few good friends; casual is not really for you. A Scorpio or Capricorn mate best understands the depth of your passion and commitment.

Your greatest challenge is to learn the difference between aspiration and fantasy. Your greatest strength is your practical ability to make your dreams come true.

➤ Read about your Chinese Astrological sign on page 838. ➤ Read about your Personal Planets on page 826. ➤ Read about your personal Mystical Card on page 856.

1954

VIRGO
Your Personal Planets

YOUR LOVE POTENTIAL
Venus in Libra, Aug. 23, 16:36 - Sept. 06, 23:28
Venus in Scorpio, Sept. 06, 23:29 - Sept. 23, 13:54

YOUR DRIVE AND AMBITION
Mars in Sagittarius, Aug. 23, 16:36 - Aug. 24, 13:21
Mars in Capricorn, Aug. 24, 13:22 - Sept. 23, 13:54

YOUR LUCK MAGNETISM
Jupiter in Cancer, Aug. 23, 16:36 - Sept. 23, 13:54

World Events

Aug. 24 – President Eisenhower signs the Communist Control Act, outlawing the Communist Party in the U.S.

Aug. 25 – American musician Elvis Costello is born Declan Patrick McManus.

U.S. President Eisenhower

LIBRA
Your Personal Planets

YOUR LOVE POTENTIAL
Venus in Scorpio, Sept. 23, 13:55 - Oct. 23, 22:06
Venus in Sagittarius, Oct. 23, 22:07 - Oct. 23, 22:55

YOUR DRIVE AND AMBITION
Mars in Capricorn, Sept. 23, 13:55 - Oct. 21, 12:02
Mars in Aquarius, Oct. 21, 12:03 - Oct. 23, 22:55

YOUR LUCK MAGNETISM
Jupiter in Cancer, Sept. 23, 13:55 - Oct. 23, 22:55

World Events

Sept. 30 – Germany is admitted to the North Atlantic Treaty Organization (NATO).

Oct. 19 – Britain cedes the Suez Canal to Egypt in the Suez Canal Treaty.

1954

SCORPIO
Your Personal Planets

YOUR LOVE POTENTIAL
Venus in Sagittarius, Oct. 23, 22:56 - Oct. 27, 10:41
Venus in Scorpio, Oct. 27, 10:42 - Nov. 22, 20:13

YOUR DRIVE AND AMBITION
Mars in Aquarius, Oct. 23, 22:56 - Nov. 22, 20:13

YOUR LUCK MAGNETISM
Jupiter in Cancer, Oct. 23, 22:56 - Nov. 22, 20:13

World Events

Nov. 3 - French artist Henri Matisse dies.

Nov. 12 - French troops are ordered to Algiers to deal with rising unrest in the region.

Death of Nobel Prize winner Enrico Fermi

SAGITTARIUS
Your Personal Planets

YOUR LOVE POTENTIAL
Venus in Scorpio, Nov. 22, 20:14 - Dec. 22, 9:23

YOUR DRIVE AND AMBITION
Mars in Aquarius, Nov. 22, 20:14 - Dec. 04, 7:40
Mars in Pisces, Dec. 04, 7:41 - Dec. 22, 9:23

YOUR LUCK MAGNETISM
Jupiter in Cancer, Nov. 22, 20:14 - Dec. 22, 9:23

World Events

Nov. 24 - Italian scientist Enrico Fermi dies.

Dec. 2 - Johannes Strydom is appointed premier of South Africa.

SCORPIO
From October 23, 22:56 through November 22, 20:13

The Artful Bomber

As a 1954 Scorpio, you have even more ability to focus your laser-like intensity than usual. Born as the U.S. Air Force authorized the B-58, you are not unlike this first supersonic bomber. Whatever you do, you bring colossally concentrated energy to the task, in a lightning flash. In your youth, you may have displayed a hair-trigger temper with shocking ground-zero explosions that frightened even the adults around you. But, as you developed self-control, you learned to harness and direct the energy, turning your explosive bombs into power tools for transformation.

Also born as the first atomic power plant was built, you do learn to come up with constructive civilian purposes for your pure force. Thankfully, you have great vision for a liberated community and society, which calls you to serve a cause greater than yourself. Because freedom and justice are more important to you than power and control, the latter serve the former.

On a very different note—creatively—your sense of liberation might be compared to Matisse's joyfully free sense of color and shape. He died on November 3, after a lifetime of exploration, discovery, and playful rebellion against the restrictive rules of formal art. But rather than confronting, disturbing, or destroying, his creative expression liberated other artists and even his viewers to experiment with new forms, new media, and new ideas. This kind of self-liberation opens up creative possibilities for the rest of us mortals. You are thus able to complete the cycle of transformation with positive examples of what to do in the void left by destroying outworn forms.

Romantically, a visionary Cancer may be best suited to share your dreams, nurturing them with open-minded enthusiasm. A Capricorn colleague can help you structure your thinking more clearly when discrimination is called for.

Your mission, after first learning how not to self-destruct, is to determine where to direct your potent energies. Whether you choose to use it for destruction or creation—or creative destruction—your greatest gift is the great power you have at your disposal.

SAGITTARIUS
From November 22, 20:14 through December 22, 9:23

The Passionate Explorer

Beneath the easy-going, good-natured front you present to the world, 1954 Sagittarius, your typical Sagittarian bonhomie belies an almost Scorpionic depth and intensity. You are intense and possessive, especially when it comes to love. This is not always comfortable for your Sagittarian nature, which usually prefers a casual friendliness in even your most intimate relationships.

As you came into the world, Simone de Beauvoir won the prestigious Prix Goncourt. Perhaps ironically better known as the paramour of the French Existentialist Jean Paul Sartre, De Beauvoir wrote the seminal feminist work *The Second Sex*. During their decades-long association, she and Sartre had separate but adjacent apartments and an open relationship, never codified by marriage. It is said that while she publicly accepted Sartre's other lovers, inwardly de Beauvoir suffered. This may be the case for you, 1954 Sagittarius—wanting to be a free spirit, but deep down, longing for the emotional depth for which you are secretly programmed. Hopefully, as your life has unfolded you have learned to be true to your inner self.

You were also born in the year that the erudite Princeton philosopher and author Aldous Huxley wrote *The Doors Of Perception*. With a title taken from the mystical poet William Blake (later adopted by Jim Morrison), Huxley made public an unprecedented exploration of consciousness of both literary and psychological merit. Using himself as subject, he shared his own experiments with hallucinogens, before they were popular enough to be illegal. You share this proclivity for the mystical and psychological depths of the psyche, and you seek to expand your mind and your consciousness. You also have the sense of focus to develop a disciplined meditation practice, bypassing the dangerous side-effects of artificial substances.

A passionate Scorpio helps you unlock your hidden depths and matches your intensity, while a Leo may encourage you to aspire to hidden heights.

Your greatest challenge is to be true to your innermost feelings and your greatest strength is the depth of your experience.

➤ Read about your Chinese Astrological sign on page 838. ➤ Read about your Personal Planets on page 826. ➤ Read about your personal Mystical Card on page 856.

CAPRICORN

From December 22, 9:24 through December 31, 23:59

The Strategic Ally

You can be quite the social butterfly, Capricorn born in December 1954. Far from the somewhat reclusive Mountain Goat, you forge fierce allegiances with both groups and partners. And your enmities can be just as fierce.

Actually, your group commitments may run deeper than your one-to-one associations, to your mate's dismay. You encompass a piquant blend of Scorpionic emotional intensity and Aquarian open-minded exploration. Depending on your associate's point of view, you may combine the best, or the worst, of both.

You were born as the hatchet between the Allied and Axis Forces was finally buried. On December 30, France, which had harbored deep fears about the Germans after they had been invaded three times in seventy years, approved West Germany's re-armament and recognized its membership of NATO, which had been approved two months earlier. While you, too, can hold a suspicious grudge, you are not above letting bygones be bygones and forming new strategic alliances, once they have been shown to be truly in your favor. You are an unusual Capricorn in that you are quite open to old forms morphing into new configurations.

Observations released on December 27, 1954, seemed to confirm the Big Bang theory that the Universe as we know it came out of a giant primeval explosion, from which the pieces are still flying. New evidence suggested that the Universe continues to expand at a rate of one-fifth the speed of light, indicating that everything is continually moving a little farther away from everything else. Your own growth seems to stem from cycles of contraction, which build concentration and intensity, until there is an explosion, followed by an expansion. You may need a similar cyclical rhythm of waxing and waning in your relationships, allowing your emotions to ebb and flow.

A free-spirited Cancer can crack your quirky combination of freedom and passion, while a possessive Scorpio may balk at your need to explore new horizons.

Your greatest challenge in life is to balance your need for intensity with your need for expansion. Your greatest strength is your wide-open mind.

1954
CAPRICORN
Your Personal Planets

YOUR LOVE POTENTIAL
Venus in Scorpio, Dec. 22, 9:24 - Dec. 31, 23:59
YOUR DRIVE AND AMBITION
Mars in Pisces, Dec. 22, 9:24 - Dec. 31, 23:59
YOUR LUCK MAGNETISM
Jupiter in Cancer, Dec. 22, 9:24 - Dec. 31, 23:59

World Events

Dec. 24 – The National Assembly in France approves proposals for Germany's re-armament.
Dec. 28 – African-American actor, Denzel Washington, is born.

*Queen Elizabeth II
Born April 21, 1926*

QUEEN ELIZABETH
Taurus

Queen Elizabeth II, monarch of Great Britain since 1952, shows no sign of easing up on her busy schedule or wanting to retire. Although the British monarchy no longer has the power to govern the nation as it did in former days, Elizabeth remains actively involved in the affairs of her country and her people, and she has kept herself informed of political matters virtually all her life. A mother of four and grandmother of six, the Queen travels extensively as the most beloved and respected representative of her nation.

Elizabeth is a Taurus, a sign noted for its stability, endurance, and practical approach to life. The Sun, the planet of identity, had barely entered Taurus at the moment of her birth, and had she been born less than an hour earlier, she would have been an impetuous Aries. Although the Sun is prominently placed in her horoscope, near the point of home and emotional foundations, it receives virtually no contact from the other planets in her chart. This creates an individual who can put her own needs aside in favor of the expectations of other people. That, combined with the steadiness of the Taurus sign, makes her ideal as a long-reigning monarch.

The Queen's Moon, the planet of emotions, resides in a house that deepens its sensitivity and is placed in the regal sign of Leo. Her emotions are not only deep and intense, but she realizes that she must preserve appearances, so she shows her true feelings only when appropriate. We might also say that with the Moon in the luxury-loving sign Leo, Elizabeth has an emotional attachment to all her jewels and finery—and who can blame her?

With Mars, the planet of action, in altruistic Aquarius, it feels quite comfortable to her to work on behalf of the welfare of her subjects. A contact from beneficent Jupiter gives her courage and a bit of spunk. Finally, with Saturn, the planet of obligation, in her house of career, it's no wonder that Elizabeth has worked so determinedly at her job as monarch. She is a woman for whom the royal way of life is not just a comfortable lifestyle but something that defines her very essence as a person.

➤ Read about Queen Elizabeth II in "An Astrology Family Tree: The British Royal Family" on page 425.
➤ Read Princess Diana's Star Profile on page 689. ➤ Read the Duke of Windsor's Star Profile on page 329.

449

1955

Creature Comforts: Jupiter-Uranus Trine Saturn

The best of modern technology reached the marketplace in 1955, as Jupiter, associated with pleasure and opportunity, joined Uranus, linked with innovation and invention. Both were positioned in Cancer, sign of home and family. The situation was supported and strengthened by Saturn, which made a harmonious "trine" from Scorpio to them. Saturn is tied to business, science and government—bringers of rules, laws, and structures into our lives. When it is in deep and mysterious Scorpio, the inner workings of the universe—expressed as scientific breakthroughs—are often revealed. In 1955, this planetary combination manifested in new scientific understandings, which led to technological innovations benefiting homemakers and their families. Magazine and television advertisements extolled the virtues of the latest conveniences for the household. "Dacron" clothing freed women from the tedium of ironing, while microwave ovens and convenience foods like instant oatmeal and potato patties made cooking a breeze.

The darker events of the year were related to a challenging Saturn-Pluto contact. When Pluto, sometimes called the reformer, contacted structural Saturn, power plays in government are often afoot. In 1955, Soviet leader Khrushchev confirmed Western fears as he revealed his plans to control Eastern bloc nations through the Warsaw Pact, a Soviet-commanded military alliance. This resulted in new perceptions of the USSR's intentions, influencing foreign and domestic policy decisions world wide for years to come.

Churchill retires from his second term as Prime Minister

American film star James Dean dies in a car accident

Einstein dies at the age of 76

CURSED CAR PARTS

After film star James Dean died in a car crash, his Porsche Spyder 550 was divided into pieces that were sold off one by one. Mysteriously, anyone who owned a part of the car suffered an accident or mishap. The doctor who bought the engine was killed in an auto race; another car incorporating Dean's drive shaft rolled over, injuring the driver. Tires exploded and brakes failed. Finally, as the body of the car was put on display as a highway safety warning, it broke an onlooker's hip and then disintegrated.

EAST-WEST TENSIONS MOUNT

Eastern-bloc nations signed the Warsaw Pact, an alliance to match NATO. Britain, France, the U.S. and the USSR held an inconclusive summit conference. Meanwhile, the Soviets exploded an h-bomb. Soviet Communist Party leader Khrushchev pushed out Premier Malenkov in favor of Bulganin. The USSR reconciled with maverick Communist leader Tito of Yugoslavia. The U.S. agreed with France and South Vietnam to send personnel to train the South Vietnamese army. Argentine President Péron was ousted and fled to Spain. West Germany gained full sovereignty and began building an army. In Morocco, the French declared martial law after mob violence in Casablanca. Israelis and Arabs battled in the Gaza Strip. In the U.S., Disneyland opened in California and the *Mickey Mouse Club* wooed kids with the singing and dancing Mouseketeers. President Eisenhower was hospitalized with a heart attack, but recovered. Teens mourned twenty-four-year-old film star James Dean who was killed in a car crash. In Britain, Churchill retired from his second term as Prime Minister, and Relativity genius Albert Einstein died in New Jersey at the age of seventy-six.

➤ Read Elvis Presley's Star Profile on page 457.

CAPRICORN

From January 01, 0:00 through January 20, 20:01

The Enterprising Professional

With deeply hidden resources to tap when the going gets tough, you could have the means to make it to the top in any area of life you choose, 1955 January Capricorn. All Capricorns like to be recognized for their achievements, but what makes you special is that you have an extraordinary insight into the hearts and minds of other people, without giving away your own plans. You are a master of strategy who's nearly impossible to beat in the "end game."

Although you can have the unique ability to change course suddenly, bound for broader horizons, you also have an understanding of human psychology, which can make you superb at business. You may also go further than most when working with others you implicitly trust, whether that person is a family member or just someone you believe in. As a result, you could enjoy the fabulous benefits that working closely with a partner can bring. A case in point is Elvis Presley—a fellow Capricorn who made his first TV appearance in the year you were born. When Elvis was drafted into the U.S. army, he left his career in the hands of his trusted advisor "Colonel" Tom Parker and returned to civilian life as big a star as he had been when he left.

Your family could be seen as unusual, particularly as you look back now. Perhaps this is due to growing up when the "nuclear family" became the norm, and the traditional support of the extended family, which you thrive under, slipped into social history. However, looking further afield for backing may have had its rewards, as it probably helped you explore your imagination and turned you into a visionary with far-reaching ideals.

In relationships, a Cancer could encourage the creative thinker within you to experiment more, while Virgo and Taurus could provide you the stability and security you enjoy.

Your greatest strength is that you can be outspoken on issues that offend your sense of justice, yet others could tell you their deepest secrets and they would be safe with you. Your challenge is to keep your goals in perspective, without distancing yourself from your support network or your family.

AQUARIUS

From January 20, 20:02 through February 19, 10:18

The Progressive Player

Nearly all Aquarians possess a brilliant mind that borders upon genius, and you are no exception, 1955 Aquarius. In fact, you may set the standard from which that generalization comes! With an unusual capacity to see the bigger picture and form abstract ideas, your brainpower could astound. You may even be among your generation's most advanced thinkers. This may come as a surprise to you, for you might see yourself as shy and introverted, someone who has to constantly revise and refine ideas to make them work. But that doesn't mean you don't have a feel for the future!

RCA demonstrated the first music synthesizer around the time you were born, and since then, techno tunes have become popular around the world, as computer technology makes massive headway year by year. You and your friends are probably all computer literate, and you know how important it is to stay ahead of the competition. You're also likely to be a spirited team player, one who understands that it is important to give your all in order to triumph, be that individually or with your team-mates.

Filled with intellectual ideals and brotherly love, you're the rebel with a cause—quite unlike movie icon James Dean, whose film *Rebel Without A Cause* was released in 1955. It portrayed youths who lived fast to die young, as he himself did, tragically killed in a road crash only months after finishing the film in which he was immortalized on the silver screen.

As an individualist, you appreciate being with others who have their own interests. If they have a wicked sense of adventure, so much the better! An independent Aries might make a perfect partner, if a little feisty. Fortunately, you may enjoy an occasional bout of intellectual sparring. A quick-witted Gemini may also stimulate your inquiring mind.

Because you are mentally gifted, it's easy for you to dominate without realizing it. Your challenge is to be considerate and respectful of authority, and allow others to air their ideas. Your strength is being able to visualize a better world, and make it a reality—a reality that can only benefit humanity.

► Read about your Chinese Astrological sign on page 838. ► Read about your Personal Planets on page 826. ► Read about your personal Mystical Card on page 856.

CAPRICORN
Your Personal Planets

YOUR LOVE POTENTIAL
Venus in Scorpio, Jan. 01, 0:00 - Jan. 06, 6:47
Venus in Sagittarius, Jan. 06, 6:48 - Jan. 20, 20:01

YOUR DRIVE AND AMBITION
Mars in Pisces, Jan. 01, 0:00 - Jan. 15, 4:32
Mars in Aries, Jan. 15, 4:33 - Jan. 20, 20:01

YOUR LUCK MAGNETISM
Jupiter in Cancer, Jan. 01, 0:00 - Jan. 20, 20:01

World Events

Jan. 15 - The USSR reaches an agreement with the Federal Republic of Germany, ending the state of war between the countries.

Jan. 19 - The board game Scrabble first appears on the market.

The Panama Canal Treaty is signed

AQUARIUS
Your Personal Planets

YOUR LOVE POTENTIAL
Venus in Sagittarius, Jan. 20, 20:02 - Feb. 06, 1:14
Venus in Capricorn, Feb. 06, 1:15 - Feb. 19, 10:18

YOUR DRIVE AND AMBITION
Mars in Aries, Jan. 20, 20:02 - Feb. 19, 10:18

YOUR LUCK MAGNETISM
Jupiter in Cancer, Jan. 20, 20:02 - Feb. 19, 10:18

World Events

Jan. 25 - The U.S. and Panama sign the Panama Canal Treaty, guaranteeing cooperation.

Feb. 9 - Communist China introduces compulsory military service.

1955

PISGES
Your Personal Planets

YOUR LOVE POTENTIAL
Venus in Capricorn, Feb. 19, 10:19 - Mar. 04, 20:21
Venus in Aquarius, Mar. 04, 20:22 - Mar. 21, 9:34

YOUR DRIVE AND AMBITION
Mars in Aries, Feb. 19, 10:19 - Apr. 26, 10:21
Mars in Taurus, Apr. 26, 10:22 - Mar. 21, 9:34

YOUR LUCK MAGNETISM
Jupiter in Cancer, Feb. 19, 10:19 - Mar. 21, 9:34

World Events

Feb. 28 – Israel launches a lightning attack on the Gaza Strip, held by the Egyptians.

Mar. 11 – British bacteriologist Alexander Fleming dies.

Death of Alexander Flemming

ARIES
Your Personal Planets

YOUR LOVE POTENTIAL
Venus in Aquarius, Mar. 21, 9:35 - Mar. 30, 11:29
Venus in Pisces, Mar. 30, 11:30 - Apr. 20, 20:57

YOUR DRIVE AND AMBITION
Mars in Taurus, Mar. 21, 9:35 - Apr. 10, 23:08
Mars in Gemini, Apr. 10, 23:09 - Apr. 20, 20:57

YOUR LUCK MAGNETISM
Jupiter in Cancer, Mar. 21, 9:35 - Apr. 20, 20:57

World Events

Mar. 24 – Tennessee Williams' *Cat On A Hot Tin Roof* premières on Broadway.

Apr. 5 – Winston Churchill resigns as British Prime Minister; he is succeeded by Anthony Eden.

PISCES
From February 19, 10:19 through March 21, 9:34

The Philanthropic Inventor

As a Pisces born in 1955, it's likely that you're in tune with your generation's passion for improvement. Feeling the plight of others can have a deep impact upon your psyche, so the greatest happiness for the greatest number is an ideal you have probably work tirelessly toward throughout your life so far—and will continue to do so.

Compassion is your keyword, dear Pisces. You have a deep capacity for understanding the wounds of others, and you are willing to go to any lengths to aid those in need. Any perceived inequality—be it racial, sexual, physical, or ageist—could move you to alert the relevant authorities to the unfairness. This altruistic streak runs through most things you do. You also can be extremely musical, and your faith in human nature is the instrument you play in order to win freedom and reduce conflict in your family, with your friends, in your society, and in your country. Indeed, you could feel proud to be born in the year when WINS radio announced it would not play "copycat" white cover versions from such artists as Pat Boone, playing the original Fats Domino recording of "Ain't That A Shame" instead.

Although you are deeply responsive, always encouraging others to fulfill their potential, you can be objective too. You're unlikely to fetter anyone with dogma, preferring the free flow of humanitarianism. Letting others have their say is no threat to your inventiveness, for you innately know how freedom, and therefore free enterprise, generates financial security.

In love relationships, you may enjoy building empires with a Capricorn, whose solid financial skills you probably admire. As you enjoy the good life, sharing life with a Taurus could provide economic stability. Cancer and Scorpio, however, will always relate to the philanthropist in you and empathize with any show of feeling.

As a 1955 Pisces, your greatest strength lies in being able to take care of others without getting overwhelmed by emotion, as others of your sign often do. Your challenge is to combine intuition and reason, and realize how powerful an image you create when you do.

ARIES
From March 21, 9:35 through April 20, 20:57

The Even Pacer

What makes the action-oriented 1955 Aries so special is a hidden sensitivity that underlies his or her personality. You're still highly competitive, as all Ariens are, but the difference is that while you go for gold (and often get it), you can still feel sympathetic to those who lose— a compassionate streak rarely found in the sign of the Ram. With you, all that potential "me-first" selfishness can be turned into charitable selflessness. Consider the valiant Johnny Podres, a man of humble origin and sportsman of the year in 1955. Practically single-handedly, he brought Brooklyn its first-ever baseball championship over the New York Yankees. In doing so, he gave something to the whole world, not just to Brooklyn.

While you get your kicks behaving like the daredevil who enjoys having rivals to pit your skills against, you can have a sensible streak that stops you from going too far, too fast. You're endowed with the smarts to put on the brakes and prevent disastrous events, such as the one that took place in the 1955 Le Mans motor race, when a Mercedes spun out of control, killing eighty spectators.

Being prudent could even stretch to the way you handle finances. Although most Aries have a propensity for impulse shopping, on the odd occasion you may hold yourself back to the point of being economical—unheard of by Arien standards! You may be in tune with a legacy of World War II, as rationing still existed in Europe when you were born.

In love, you could be surprisingly interested in your home. You might have a "do-it-yourself" approach to home improvement to create a style that could be ultra modern or cozily old-fashioned. Either way, Leo or Sagittarius appreciates your dreamy but wild initiative. Gemini, however, could keep you entertained, while Pisces brings out a tenderhearted spirituality.

Your challenge is to allow relationships to take you deeper into the mysterious world of emotions to discover a cosmic kind of love. Your strength is that rare mix of vigor and endurance—a quality you can use to pace yourself in all activities, including relationships.

➤ Read about your Chinese Astrological sign on page 838. ➤ Read about your Personal Planets on page 826. ➤ Read about your personal Mystical Card on page 856.

TAURUS

From April 20, 20:58 through May 21, 20:23

The Clever Strategist

More ambitious than most Taureans, the 1955 Taurus has grand designs, and the thrill of going after what you want can be just as satisfying as the end result. Consequently, you can be a force to be reckoned with—a no holds barred opponent. It's likely that you're extremely smart, too.

Always looking for the quickest way to achieve your goals, you might consider entering a quiz show, just to prove how clever you are. Also, it's a chance to get your hands on some ready money that Taureans simply cannot live without! It's probably no surprise to learn that a quiz show called *$64,000 Question* premièred on CBS-TV the year you were born. Of course, it had been called $64 Questions when it was a radio show, but with inflation being what it is, you'd probably see the sense in upping the stakes.

Such are the sights of the 1955 Taurus. In the end, though, you might be too shy, and rely on another of your other gifts—that of being a master strategist—to win your honors. You know how important it is to keep the lines of communication open, and ultimately, you strive for peace, not war. A significant event that parallels your need for constant contact, particularly with the powers that be, is that in the year of your birth the Warsaw Pact was signed by the Eastern Bloc nations and the USSR, to create a powerful equivalent of the West's NATO alliance. You are the kind of person that has simply an instinct for making the right alliances.

When it comes to love relationships, you're playful, talkative, and sometimes gullible. Your main topics of conversation may have familial or work concerns, as these can be the areas in your life that are subject to constant flux. A Cancer will help to crystallize your vision and clear confusion, while Virgo and Capricorn offer the stability you need.

Your challenge is to accept the power of your own authority, and not fear it. You're mentally and physically very strong and others have been known, on occasion, to mistake your assertiveness for aggression. It helps to use brains rather than brawn to win allies, and then you will realize your many objectives.

GEMINI

From May 21, 20:24 through June 22, 4:30

The Informed Sentinel

Famed for having a sharp mind and quick wit, Gemini is clever, bright, and cunning. Few are as on the ball as a 1955 Gemini, however. With an innate need to stay up to date, you probably love being seen as knowledgeable and your mind is always full of fascinating facts and figures. Did you know that in the year you were born, the very first edition of The Village Voice was published in New York City? It set the trend for hip young communities to keep in touch with a weekly newspaper and to know what was going on in their town.

Fleet-footed as you are, you may always be one step ahead of the game. You like to get around quickly, and although you were born at the time of the "American Dream," the "Italian Dream" could also appeal to you. As a teenager, a short shopping trip probably meant zipping around town on a sporty motor scooter the way Audrey Hepburn did in *Roman Holiday*. Interestingly, Britain put the pedal to the metal as it started work on new motorways in this period, too.

With a widespread network, you're probably a "people person" with a love of media. Part of you also maintains links with all that has gone before. By all celestial accounts you have a brilliant memory that files away endless information. You may enjoy keeping journals and old snapshots, never to throw them away.

With as many ideas as spin around in your gray matter, you may need someone special to help you sift through your thoughts. As a double-sided Gemini, with one eye on the future and another on the distant past, you might attract a cultured Libran to be your life partner. Aquarians also thrive on constant mental stimulation, so the Water Bearer might bring love into your life. You need to watch your finances, though, and a thrifty Taurus could help to maintain a fiscal balance.

Keeping your fantasies in perspective is your biggest challenge. Daydreams of an opulent, movie-star lifestyle are well and good, and all things are possible, but you'd do well to get yourself comfortable first. Prosperity lies with your greatest strength: to assimilate data and keep a waiting world informed.

➤ Read about your Chinese Astrological sign on page 838. ➤ Read about your Personal Planets on page 826. ➤ Read about your personal Mystical Card on page 856.

TAURUS
Your Personal Planets

YOUR LOVE POTENTIAL
Venus in Pisces, Apr. 20, 20:58 - Apr. 24, 15:12
Venus in Aries, Apr. 24, 15:13 - May 19, 13:34
Venus in Taurus, May 19, 13:35 - May 21, 20:23

YOUR DRIVE AND AMBITION
Mars in Gemini, Apr. 20, 20:58 - May 21, 20:23

YOUR LUCK MAGNETISM
Jupiter in Cancer, Apr. 20, 20:58 - May 21, 20:23

World Events

May 2 – Tennessee Williams is awarded the Pulitzer Prize for *Cat On A Hot Tin Roof*.

May 14 – The Soviet Union, Albania, Bulgaria, Czechoslovakia, East Germany, Hungary, Poland, and Romania sign the Warsaw Pact.

Tennessee Williams' "Cat on a Hot Tin Roof" premières on Broadway

GEMINI
Your Personal Planets

YOUR LOVE POTENTIAL
Venus in Taurus, May 21, 20:24 - June 13, 8:37
Venus in Gemini, June 13, 8:38 - June 22, 4:30

YOUR DRIVE AND AMBITION
Mars in Gemini, May 21, 20:24 - May 26, 0:49
Mars in Cancer, May 26, 0:50 - June 22, 4:30

YOUR LUCK MAGNETISM
Jupiter in Cancer, May 21, 20:24 - June 13, 0:05
Jupiter in Leo, June 13, 0:06 - June 22, 4:30

World Events

June 16 – Argentine President Juan Péron is excommunicated by Pope Pius XII.

May 31 – The U.S. Supreme Court orders school integration "with all deliberate speed."

1955

CANCER
Your Personal Planets

YOUR LOVE POTENTIAL
Venus in Gemini, June 22, 4:31 - July 08, 0:14
Venus in Cancer, July 08, 0:15 - July 23, 15:24

YOUR DRIVE AND AMBITION
Mars in Cancer, June 22, 4:31 - July 11, 9:21
Mars in Leo, July 11, 9:22 - July 23, 15:24

YOUR LUCK MAGNETISM
Jupiter in Leo, June 22, 4:31 - July 23, 15:24

World Events

June 29 - The USSR sends troops to Poland to help quell anti-Communist riots.

July 17 - Disneyland opens its doors in California.

American Donald Campbell sets a new world water speed record in Bluebird

LEO
Your Personal planets

YOUR LOVE POTENTIAL
Venus in Cancer, July 23, 15:25 - Aug. 01, 11:42
Venus in Leo, Aug. 01, 11:43 - Aug. 23, 22:18

YOUR DRIVE AND AMBITION
Mars in Leo, July 23, 15:25 - Aug. 23, 22:18

YOUR LUCK MAGNETISM
Jupiter in Leo, July 23, 15:25 - Aug. 23, 22:18

World Events

Aug. 12 - Thomas Mann, German author of *Death in Venice*, dies.

Aug. 20 - Riots against French control break out in Morocco and Algiers.

CANCER
From June 22, 4:31 through July 23, 15:24

The Visionary Guardian

Every once in a while, a true visionary comes into the world, who has the potential to make significant reforms where freedom is lacking. You are one of these visionaries, 1955 Cancer. Nurturing others comes naturally to those of your sign, but 1955 Cancer may see the whole world as his or her family, and has the added incentive of individual liberty to fight for.

Injustice of any sort riles you, and you often support the underdog, or those whose freedoms are oppressed in some way. You may wholeheartedly identify with an incident that took place in the year of your birth—one that had far-reaching effects for the civil rights movement. In 1955, in the heart of the U.S.'s segregated South, a black woman, Rosa Parks, refused to give up her seat on a bus to a white man. She was forced off the bus to walk home, but her brave act sparked a boycott that cost the bus company thousands of dollars and eventually brought an end to segregation in America. No matter where you lived, this milestone must have had a huge impact on your parents, and it's likely that you were brought up to believe all human beings are equal, regardless of their color.

You can be a home lover at heart and you adore taking care of your immediate family. Even so, a 1955 Cancer tends to travel more than other Cancerians. You may often experience sudden opportunities to take trips, which could not only broaden your horizons, but also give you the chance to live out some of your dreams.

Whatever you do is done with style. Going dramatically over the top, even in your relationships, can be a common occurence for you. A Taurean's steady personality could temper your wild side, while Scorpio or Pisces might encourage your outrageous imagination to outdo itself.

It's not always easy for society's conservatives to understand a person with your breadth of vision, for those in authority are often locked in tradition. Therein is your challenge. Your global perspective and spiritual understanding are strengths you can rely upon to rouse the humanitarian in everyone you meet, and make the world one big happy family.

LEO
From July 23, 15:25 through August 23, 22:18

The Dependable Sovereign

Leos tend to act royal, think big, and walk tall, and the 1955 Leo is probably one of the most majestic Lions ever to roam the Earth. Theatrics may come naturally to you—everything you do is bigger and better than most. If you've got anything, you've got flair and unsurpassed glamour.

Think drama. Think Elizabeth Taylor. Then recall her part in the movie version of a play that was first performed in 1955, *Cat On A Hot Tin Roof,* by Pulitzer Prize-winner Tennessee Williams. In the movie, Liz, as Maggie the Cat, fights to save her marriage to her husband Brick (played by Paul Newman). She's as caring, loving, and loyal as you are, and the character she played lived in opulence—just as you would like to do, if you don't already!

On the subject of Liz, think of a glittering ten-carat diamond! Leos love to sparkle. Even if you can't afford to splash out on the real thing, a 1955 Leo can still twinkle, as the first pilot plant to produce man-made diamonds was announced in the year you were born.

You must, however, choose partners, friends, and associates with care. This is because you come up against opposition, which is often undeserved, but can, nonetheless, slow down personal development. Surrounding yourself with optimistic people such as Sagittarians or Ariens could help you to reverse any negativity that might come from feeling you have to prove yourself all the time. When you combine your positive outlook with forethought and reason, and take your time over things, you achieve much more—more respect, more work, and more money! Ultimately, you go far when you listen to the still, small voice that whispers certain wisdom, urging you to expand or draw back at the right time. A Gemini or Libra could help you to hear that voice.

You have the potential to be extremely polished in all you do. Your challenge is to watch for inflated self-importance and avoid foolish risks, and at the same time, overcome limitations. Your nerve, confidence, and utter self-belief will give you the strength to help you to do just that, as well as to discover your truly magnificent majesty.

➤ Read about your Chinese Astrological sign on page 838. ➤ Read about your Personal Planets on page 826. ➤ Read about your personal Mystical Card on page 856.

VIRGO

From August 23, 22:19 through September 23, 19:40

The Respectful Healer

A Virgo's incisive mind is brought to the fore in your year. Although you might not agree, and you may think of others as intellectually superior, it's important not to underrate yourself, 1955 Virgo. It's likely that you have the makings of a brilliant mind—one that has the ability to cut right to the heart of any situation. Teaching may also come naturally to you, as you rarely embellish the truth. Unless a story is called for to illustrate a point, you can usually be counted upon to tell it like it is.

You could have a sharp tongue sometimes, and it's possible that others' shocked reaction to your insights may cause you to believe that your ideas are not worthwhile—but nothing could be further from the truth. You can be a gifted researcher in your own right, someone who leaves no stone unturned. In fact, it might hearten a health-oriented Virgo to know that in 1955 Dr. Jonas Salk successfully tested the polio vaccine, protecting millions of children from infantile paralysis.

You were also born in what could politely be referred to as "paranoid times." In the mid-1950s, the Cold War raged, albeit quietly. The threat of nuclear war had an impact upon those around you, and they could have been apprehensive of what the future might bring. It may be a coincidence, but you probably tend to worry a lot too. Thankfully, the only "nuclear weapons" employed were those that were used to fight cancer.

All your fretting, nonetheless, is probably only due to your wanting to perfect an imperfect world, and much of your time may be spent trying to improve situations— be it a physical healing that's needed, or a mental one. A Taurus or Virgo could provide the stability you need to progress, as well as give you the space you require to further your education. A Scorpio could appreciate your ability to tell fact from fantasy.

To be as forgiving with yourself as you are with others, and let compassion be your guide as you fulfill your daily duties, is your greatest challenge. With insight as your greatest strength, you may well enhance and heal the lives of everyone you meet.

LIBRA

From September 23, 19:41 through October 24, 4:42

The Artistic Advisor

Being in tune with your generation's ideals of personal transformation through meaningful relationships, you could be better equipped than most to actually achieve that makeover, 1955 Libra. All Librans live for love and function best when in partnership. As such, you may be a born diplomat—someone to be relied upon to mediate should the going get tough. Interestingly, fellow Libran President Dwight D. Eisenhower sent the first advisers to Vietnam in the year of your birth—the beginning of years of American involvement there.

Decision-making is always a Libran dilemma. A 1955 Libra could have a tougher time than most making up their mind, due to their intellectual ability to see all sides of any story. You're extremely clever, but brilliance has it drawbacks if you wake up with existential angst over the choices you have to make. This is why you need friends and loved ones to be honest with you, as your mind spins around the proverbial ball of confusion. Although relying upon loved ones is a way out of quandaries, ultimately it's your own intuition that should be adhered to.

Librans also have artistic sensibilities. You know how powerfully an image can affect people's lives, seeping deep into the psyche to shape later decisions. It's no surprise to learn that, in 1955, the Libran U.S. President was the very first to be televised in glorious living color. You may even work in TV, film, or the arts.

A relationship-oriented Libra could also appreciate a phenomenon in 1955 movie theaters—"couples seats," where the central armrest was removed. In Britain these were popularly called "love seats," as courting couples would often use the cinema for dates. Sounds like Libra heaven—with a good film to watch and a gorgeous someone, perhaps a Gemini or an Aquarian, at your side!

You also have a spiritual side which, in the end, is your greatest strength, as it not only feeds your soul but nourishes others' too. Your challenges are to say "no" to intoxicants that could affect your judgment and to avoid getting mystified by future plans, particularly your own.

► Read about your Chinese Astrological sign on page 838. ► Read about your Personal Planets on page 826. ► Read about your personal Mystical Card on page 856.

VIRGO
Your Personal Planets

YOUR LOVE POTENTIAL
Venus in Leo, Aug. 23, 22:19 - Aug. 25, 18:51
Venus in Virgo, Aug. 25, 18:52 - Sept. 18, 22:40
Venus in Libra, Sept. 18, 22:41 - Sept. 23, 19:40

YOUR DRIVE AND AMBITION
Mars in Leo, Aug. 23, 22:19 - Aug. 27, 10:12
Mars in Virgo, Aug. 27, 10:13 - Sept. 23, 19:40

YOUR LUCK MAGNETISM
Jupiter in Leo, Aug. 23, 22:19 - Sept. 23, 19:40

World Events

Aug. 27 - *The Guinness Book Of World Records* is first published.

Sept. 19 - President Perón is ousted by Argentina's armed forces.

Death of American film star James Dean

LIBRA
Your Personal Planets

YOUR LOVE POTENTIAL
Venus in Libra, Sept. 23, 19:41 - Oct. 13, 0:38
Venus in Scorpio, Oct. 13, 0:39 - Oct. 24, 4:42

YOUR DRIVE AND AMBITION
Mars in Virgo, Sept. 23, 19:41 - Oct. 13, 11:19
Mars in Libra, Oct. 13, 11:20 - Oct. 24, 4:42

YOUR LUCK MAGNETISM
Jupiter in Leo, Sept. 23, 19:41 - Oct. 24, 4:42

World Events

Sept. 26 - The New York Stock Exchange experiences the worst price decline since the Wall Street Crash of 1929.

Sept. 30 - American film icon, James Dean dies in a car accident.

1955

SCORPIO
Your Personal Planets

YOUR LOVE POTENTIAL
Venus in Scorpio, Oct. 24, 4:43 - Nov. 06, 2:01
Venus in Sagittarius, Nov. 06, 2:02 - Nov. 23, 2:00

YOUR DRIVE AND AMBITION
Mars in Libra, Oct. 24, 4:43 - Nov. 23, 2:00

YOUR LUCK MAGNETISM
Jupiter in Leo, Oct. 24, 4:43 - Nov. 17, 3:58
Jupiter in Virgo, Nov. 17, 3:59 - Nov. 23, 2:00

World Events

Oct. 28 – Microsoft billionaire William Henry (Bill) Gates is born.

Oct. 31 – After months of speculation, Princess Margaret announces she will not marry Captain Peter Townsend.

Rosa Parks with her attorney after her arrest

SAGITTARIUS
Your Personal Planets

YOUR LOVE POTENTIAL
Venus in Sagittarius, Nov. 23, 2:01 - Nov. 30, 3:41
Venus in Capricorn, Nov. 30, 3:42 - Dec. 22, 15:10

YOUR DRIVE AND AMBITION
Mars in Libra, Nov. 23, 2:01 - Nov. 29, 1:32
Mars in Scorpio, Nov. 29, 1:33 - Dec. 22, 15:10

YOUR LUCK MAGNETISM
Jupiter in Virgo, Nov. 23, 2:01 - Dec. 22, 15:10

World Events

Dec. 1 – African-American, Rosa Parks, is arrested in Alabama for refusing to move to the back of a bus.

Dec. 11 – Israel launches an attack on Syria at the Sea of Galilee.

SCORPIO
From October 24, 4:43 through November 23, 2:00

The Deep Psychologist

Insight is a Scorpio's gift, and one that a 1955 Scorpio could be especially well aware of. You can have an amazing ability to understand the deeper workings of an individual's mind, as well as to make sense of a world in psychological turmoil. With the ability to rise above situations, you may have an eagle-eye view, but you might not like everything you survey. Sometimes you see how the shadowy, more extreme side of human nature operates, in all its stark reality.

In the year you were born, for example, the USSR exploded a powerful megaton h-bomb, equal to one million tons of TNT. You recognize that it is deeply problematic to try and solve the moral dilemmas that can arise from a scientific discovery, and you might relate to an eyewitness physicist who said, "No one who saw the atom bomb could forget it, a foul and awesome display." You too can probably see how there could be a peculiar beauty in dangerous and difficult situations.

It has to be said though, that if anyone can make good from a complex state of affairs, it's you, 1955 Scorpio, for you have the uncanny ability to be like the beautiful phoenix that will always rise from the ashes, unscathed and stronger. This dynamic inner strength shines through in all you do.

You may also enjoy life's mysteries and might be interested to know that *Alfred Hitchcock Presents* premièred in 1955, bringing mystery and intrigue to television. You may have intense, all-or-nothing relationships. However, you also know that it's important not to get too involved with a relationship, and you may surround yourself with supportive friends. Cancer or Pisces can relate to the profound emotions you feel. But Taurus or Virgo could offer stability, especially when dealing with burdensome circumstances.

Your challenge is to use your ability to see the bigger picture for the realization of wisdom and not wield your power just for fame or fortune. You are a formidable character, but perhaps your most effective strength is that, when you embark upon self-improvement, you also improve the world around you—and that is a mighty talent to own.

SAGITTARIUS
From November 23, 2:01 through December 22, 15:10

The Generous Leader

Sagittarius of 1955 is ever the optimist, with a permanently sunny outlook even when facing problems. This may be because you recognize the need to control a potentially large ego, and you do so by being of service to others. This doesn't mean that you don't fulfill your own dreams or ambitions, simply that you choose to avoid potentially destructive power games, and go for the healing power of positive thinking instead. You can be magnanimous to the point of stepping away from power, if you feel the greater good demands it. Such traits are exemplified by fellow Sagittarian Winston Churchill, who resigned as British Prime Minister on the grounds of ill health in 1955. As wartime Prime Minister, he often displayed typical Sagittarian traits, such as impulsive strategy.

You too have the potential to make decisions that work out for the best—unlike contentious Argentine leader Juan Péron, who also had to resign as President in 1955. He was ousted in a revolt by the Argentine army and navy, and excommunicated from the Catholic Church. The people backed the Pope, and Péron was forced into exile. Luckily, you may be more like Churchill, a sound statesman with a knack for seeing the bigger picture.

You also have the gift, often found in politics, of being able to translate your big ideas into action. Amazingly, you have the ability to bring your ideas to fruition in almost exactly the way you imagine them in your mind. To round out your professionalism, it's likely that you're also more organized than most Sagittarians.

You could work well with Leo or Aries, who quickly recognize your (sometimes crazy) wisdom and spur you on to greater insights. On the whole, you're level-headed, though, and an Aquarian or Libra could help you to streamline your thoughts.

Ultimately, it's when helping others that you discover your power. As an aide-de-camp, you grow intellectually and spiritually. Your challenge is to keep working, steadily and deliberately, towards the highest possible standards. Also, keep an open mind—it's your upbeat outlook that is the strength that takes you to the top.

➤ Read about your Chinese Astrological sign on page 838. ➤ Read about your Personal Planets on page 826. ➤ Read about your personal Mystical Card on page 856.

CAPRICORN

From December 22, 15:11 through December 31, 23:59

The Cautious Administrator

A Capricorn needs a structure to life in order to achieve its aims, and it can be especially important to a 1955 December Capricorn to know there is a self-subscribed grand design to fall back on should the going get tough. Not that you are afraid of the hard work needed to succeed in today's society—it's the murky realm of feelings that could threaten to swamp or overwhelm you, particularly if you find it hard realizing your ambitions.

Consequently, you may need a protective veneer that shields you if and when you feel besieged by pressures (which may be self-imposed). On occasion, you might decide to be your own ruler and get rid of whoever and whatever you feel is blocking you. The Federal Republic of West Germany became a sovereign state in 1955 and East Germany joined the Warsaw Pact in that year as well; the Pact was a symbol of the hold the USSR retained—often by force—over all its satellites. You know how to lead, and you know also know when to break out and be independent. That's why people like to work with you. It's your nature to take responsibility seriously, so others may rely upon you, sometimes without considering your well-being.

To avoid becoming cynical or resentful, you may have developed a deep faith in your intuition, for deep in your heart you know that your better judgment never lets you down. The dollar being the emerging world currency, it's significant that in the year of your birth the U.S. Congress authorized the addition of the words "In God We Trust" to all currency!

You may do well, in either a business or love relationship, with a fellow Capricorn. Like you, a Taurus would know that money makes the world go round. Prudent Virgo could provide you with a dependable stability. Encouragement from an Aquarian might help you remain detached from mawkish sentiment.

Your challenge is to allow profound feelings to feed your soul and not destroy the spirit. Your strength lies in having an incisive mind. It will enable you to safeguard your interests, as well attain a lasting and beneficial transformation in both the material and emotional arenas.

CAPRICORN
Your Personal Planets

YOUR LOVE POTENTIAL
Venus in Capricorn, Dec. 22, 15:11 - Dec. 24, 6:51
Venus in Aquarius, Dec. 24, 6:52 - Dec. 31, 23:59

YOUR DRIVE AND AMBITION
Mars in Scorpio, Dec. 22, 15:11 - Dec. 31, 23:59

YOUR LUCK MAGNETISM
Jupiter in Virgo, Dec. 22, 15:11 - Dec. 31, 23:59

World Events

Dec. 22 - Syria demands that Israel is expelled from the UN.

Dec. 28 - Reports reveal that Britain is preparing to send arms to Egypt and Israel.

Elvis Presley
January 8, 1935 - August 16, 1977

ELVIS PRESLEY
Capricorn

Elvis Presley was the husky-voiced southerner whose rockabilly renditions of rhythm-and-blues favorites helped him give birth to a new kind of music that a generation of teens claimed as their own. Presley's magnetism and sex appeal, good ol' boy persona, and scandalous on-stage pelvic gyrations almost instantly turned him into the King of rock 'n' roll.

Presley was a Capricorn, a sign known for practical abilities and business acumen. With his Sun, the planet of identity, in his house of money, Presley was a natural to achieve success and he lived a luxurious—some may say decadent—lifestyle. With Venus, the planet of affection, also in his house of money, it's easy to comprehend Presley's legendary generosity. He gave Cadillacs away as gifts as though they were trinkets, and it made him happy to do so.

In addition, Venus was contacted by Uranus, the planet of eccentricity, located in Elvis's house of romance, so it's no wonder that his love life was a bit odd. Another contact from sexy and magnetic Pluto gave him The King appeal, but also made him a bit of a romantic despot. He spotted the young Priscilla, his future wife, when she was just a teenager, and he persuaded her family to allow him to take custody of her until she was old enough to marry him. Eventually they divorced after she became weary of his attempts to dominate every phase of her life.

Elvis's Moon, the planet of emotions, was in sensitive Pisces, a very nice placement that made him tender-hearted and loving. A contact from venerable Saturn gave him emotional maturity and created the much-publicized attachment to his mother.

Most important in Presley's chart is Neptune, the planet of music, movies, drugs and alcohol, very prominently placed. In

Elvis's case, as with many musicians, Neptune provided a sort of win-lose scenario. It gave him the wonderful singing and acting ability that made him an enduring star, but also produced the susceptibility to drugs and alcohol that ultimately ended his life at only forty-two.

➤ Read The Beatles' Star Profile on page 529. ➤ Read Janis Joplin's Star Profile on page 569.

1956

New Perspectives Emerge: Four Planets Change Signs

When one of the slow-moving planets—Saturn, Uranus, Neptune, and Pluto—changes signs, it signals a corresponding change in attitudes and perspectives. Fresh solutions to old problems arise and there is an overriding feeling of optimism. In 1956, all these planets moved and the shifts in consciousness were reflected in a series of dramatic events.

When Saturn, planet of responsibility, entered truth-seeking Sagittarius in January, people began to feel they could no longer compromise on truth, integrity, and justice. African American Rosa Parks illustrated this when she refused to sit in the back of the bus in Alabama, violating segregation laws but upholding her right to equality with all others.

Explosive and excitable Uranus entered Leo in June, bringing out the urge to act courageously. Two weeks after its ingress, Egyptian President Nasser boldly asserted control of the country's vital Suez Canal, ousting foreign interests for refusing to finance a proposed Nile River dam. Talk did not become action until Pluto, often tied to revolutionary change, entered business-oriented Virgo on October 21. On October 29, British, French, and Israeli troops invaded, leading to UN control of the canal.

Neptune's entry into Scorpio, like Neptune itself, was more subtle. Neptune is tied to shifts in cultural awareness, such as changes in musical taste or fashion trends. Scorpio is linked to deeply felt passionate emotions. When Neptune passed into Scorpio, rock 'n' roll music entered its heyday. Little Richard reached the top with *Tutti Frutti*, and Elvis was never more popular.

Egyptian President Abdel Gamal Nasser after nationalizing the Suez Canal

Tanks in Budapest during the Hungarian Insurrection   *"My Fair Lady" star Julie Andrews*

AMERICAN PSYCHIC

American psychic Jeanne Dixon had been making successful predictions of world events for years, but she won fame this year when she said that the 1960 election would be won by a Democrat who would die in office, "although not necessarily in his first term." Her precognition of JFK's death came to her in a vision, as did the deaths of his brother Robert, Martin Luther King, and Gandhi. She also foresaw the launching of Sputnik and Khrushchev's rise to power in Russia, as well as Nixon's destiny as U.S. President.

REBELLION AND RETRIBUTION

Khrushchev denounced Stalin and his "paranoid" politics before Communist Party officials, calling his decisions during World War II "military stupidity." As Khrushchev consolidated his power, he initiated a de-Stalinization program of liberal reforms in Russia. Polish workers went on strike for higher wages but lost out in the subsequent street fighting. The Hungarians rebelled against Russian control, but were crushed by Russian tanks; Russian troops shot hundreds of unarmed demonstrators. Egypt's Nasser nationalized the Suez Canal, provoking armed retaliation by Britain and France, in alliance with Israel. Segregation on buses in Alabama was declared illegal. The Baby Boom of the late 1940s was followed by a housing boom in newly built suburban paradises, while funds to construct the U.S. interstate highway system were approved. *My Fair Lady* premièred on Broadway to an enthusiastic reception. Elvis Presley appeared on Ed Sullivan's TV show, *Toast Of The Town*, before screaming fans. Grace Kelly married Monaco's Prince Rainier. Playwright Arthur Miller married film star Marilyn Monroe. Frozen-food pioneer Clarence Birdseye died.

➤ Read "The Extraterrestrial Highway: Exploring UFOs" by Jean Mars on page 465.

CAPRICORN

From January 01, 0:00 through January 21, 1:47

The Reserved Explorer

As a 1956 January Capricorn, you may have been born knowing that you need to combine talent, luck, and hard work to realize your ambitions. Perhaps you were inspired as a young child by U.S. President Dwight D. Eisenhower, who was elected to a second term in the late fall of your birth year. People felt safe with him, as they often do with you. This could be what gives you the ability to work effectively within an already established framework, and you could be the one to make major changes within your family, your friends, your work, and even society, and seem to do it with remarkable ease.

When you put your mind to it, you can also be a networker par excellence—it's only a matter of having the confidence to use your people skills. True, there may be times when you feel as though you're all alone, out on a limb. But when it's called for, you'll probably move smoothly with the times, all the while maintaining a conservative approach so you're never seen as rebellious or pushy. You're also philosophical, accepting that while fate and flair might account for five percent of the success equation, the other ninety-five percent is plain old hard work. But, for you, this could be where the greatest rewards lie.

That people turn to you for advice may constantly surprise you, but it's likely that your wisdom is well and truly valued. As the sign of the Mountain Goat with an extended twirly fish's tail, you would naturally gravitate to the top in your chosen profession and could excel in any leadership position. And, once set, very little could stop you from reaching your goal, even if it takes you a lifetime.

In love, a Taurus or Virgo could help you to appreciate your intelligence, and a Sagittarius or Pisces may take you to unexplored territory. However, you just might decide to settle down with another Capricorn and climb the heights together.

Having the staying power to remain on course is your great strength. Your challenge lies in knowing when to expand and when to rest. Timing is the key, and understanding your place in relation to others is the door of perception.

AQUARIUS

From January 21, 1:48 through February 19, 16:04

The Intellectual Philosopher

Because an Aquarian is usually a prolific thinker, it's likely that the inner workings of the mind fascinate you, 1956 Aquarius. With flashes of brilliance, you may be prone to deep realizations, such as how a dualistic nature invades the human mind with ease. Consequently, people get caught up in situations that are good or bad, negative or positive. But what's special about you is a non-judgmental prevailing optimism, keeping your thoughts helpful, your feelings buoyant, and your actions constructive.

You are also likely to have a great love of gadgets. Although it's a long way from an e-mail videophone, it may interest you to know of a computer breakthrough that took place in the year of your birth. Helping to retain information and, consequently, encourage a researcher—such as yourself—to look further afield, the first direct keyboard input into a computer was introduced in 1956.

Deep within your personality lies a hidden wealth—not only can you be a crazy rebel, but you're also prepared to prove it. Bear in mind how Elvis Presley appeared on the *Ed Sullivan Show* in this year. Because his dancing was thought too outrageous, he was only televised gyrating from the waist up, and even then there was public protest! You can sometimes be cut off in your prime too. Just when you think you're turning up trumps, you often need to reconsider your plan, going over the same idea until you get it right, which you nearly always do.

You have the potential to be a powerful and influential person. Few can touch the lives of others with as much impact as you do. As such, you need to be around those who can handle dynamism. Gemini, Libra, or Leo has a strong sense of self that could only add to your vitality, and encourage you to play a useful role in society, while you broaden your horizons at the same time.

Your challenge is to use your authority wisely, without manipulating others for personal gain, be that financial or psychological. Your strength lies in your brainpower, which could move mountains. For you, anything is possible, especially when you remain focused.

► Read about your Chinese Astrological sign on page 838. ► Read about your Personal Planets on page 826. ► Read about your personal Mystical Card on page 856.

CAPRICORN
Your Personal Planets

YOUR LOVE POTENTIAL
Venus in Aquarius, Jan. 01, 0:00 - Jan. 17, 14:21
Venus in Pisces, Jan. 17, 14:22 - Jan. 21, 1:47

YOUR DRIVE AND AMBITION
Mars in Scorpio, Jan. 01, 0:00 - Jan. 14, 2:27
Mars in Sagittarius, Jan. 14, 2:28 - Jan. 21, 1:47

YOUR LUCK MAGNETISM
Jupiter in Virgo, Jan. 01, 0:00 - Jan. 18, 2:03
Jupiter in Leo, Jan. 18, 2:04 - Jan. 21, 1:47

World Events

Jan. 8 – Elvis Presley's double A-side single "Don't Be Cruel/Hound Dog" reaches Number One in the Hit Parade and remains there for a record eleven weeks.

Jan. 16 – Islam is declared to be the state religion of Egypt.

Death of Alexander Korda

AQUARIUS
Your Personal Planets

YOUR LOVE POTENTIAL
Venus in Pisces, Jan. 21, 1:48 - Feb. 11, 7:45
Venus in Aries, Feb. 11, 7:46 - Feb. 19, 16:04

YOUR DRIVE AND AMBITION
Mars in Sagittarius, Jan. 21, 1:48 - Feb. 19, 16:04

YOUR LUCK MAGNETISM
Jupiter in Leo, Jan. 21, 1:48 - Feb. 19, 16:04

World Events

Jan. 23 – Hungarian-born film director Alexander Korda dies.

Feb. 16 – Britain abolishes the death penalty.

1956

PISCES
Your Personal Planets

YOUR LOVE POTENTIAL
Venus in Aries, Feb. 19, 16:05 - Mar. 07, 21:30
Venus in Taurus, Mar. 07, 21:31 - Mar. 20, 15:19

YOUR DRIVE AND AMBITION
Mars in Sagittarius, Feb. 19, 16:05 - Feb. 28, 20:04
Mars in Capricorn, Feb. 28, 20:05 - Mar. 20, 15:19

YOUR LUCK MAGNETISM
Jupiter in Leo, Feb. 19, 16:05 - Mar. 20, 15:19

World Events

Feb. 23 – West German authorities ban the goose-step in the army.

Mar. 2 – Morocco gains independence from French rule.

*The wedding of Grace Kelly and
Prince Rainier of Monaco*

ARIES
Your Personal Planets

YOUR LOVE POTENTIAL
Venus in Taurus, Mar. 20, 15:20 - Apr. 04, 7:22
Venus in Gemini, Apr. 04, 7:23 - Apr. 20, 2:42

YOUR DRIVE AND AMBITION
Mars in Capricorn, Mar. 20, 15:20 - Apr. 14, 23:39
Mars in Aquarius, Apr. 14, 23:40 - Apr. 20, 2:42

YOUR LUCK MAGNETISM
Jupiter in Leo, Mar. 20, 15:20 - Apr. 20, 2:42

World Events

Mar. 23 – Pakistan becomes the first wholly Islamic republic.

Apr. 19 – Actress Grace Kelly marries Prince Rainier of Monaco.

PISCES
From February 19, 16:05 through March 20, 15:19

The Sensitive Intellectual

As a 1956 Pisces, you could well be one of those lucky beings who blend logic and intuition with relative ease. You may come up against a brick wall when wanting to express yourself, however—particularly in professional situations or when you're dealing with authority, which can make you feel hemmed in and uncomfortable. Pisces is a water sign, and as such you need to be allowed to go with the flow. But a key event of your birth year—the 1956 war in Egypt over the newly nationalized Suez Canal, in which Britain had a large number of shares— brought this vital passage between the Mediterranean and the Persian Gulf to a standstill. This was a serious threat to the supply of oil to the West, which had previously been trafficked through the Canal.

Like the players in the Suez drama, you, too, may need to reassess your power base occasionally. But this can be a handy gift to have, not just when dealing with difficult or taciturn people, but also for messy situations. You may have the ability to pre-empt problems, and when life gets knotty, you could have an uncanny knack of knowing how to unravel each thread tenderly, with a care rarely seen in other signs.

Although you're cheerful in most actions, you're also very sensitive, some might even say spiritual. Even if you don't make a career in the arts, you may be musical or love to dance, or visit the theater. You're probably also very forgiving—finding life's harsh realities quite brutal, and at times wondering how people could be so apparently cruel. It may help to know that others also see how two wrongs don't make a right. No matter what, you are always kind.

In romance, it may be a Cancer or Scorpio whose unique perspective helps you to see the other options open to you, and it's also likely that you'll have mutual interests that require perception and understanding.

A highly tuned "sixth sense" is your great strength which, when adhered to, will help you to avoid troublesome obstacles. Your challenge is to maintain a deeply supportive faith and, in the face of adversity, use your delightful charm and powerful compassion.

ARIES
From March 20, 15:20 through April 20, 2:42

The Professional Dynamo

A multi-faceted 1956 Aries is a rare, many-sided gem, as there are many areas of life where you can shine. You're probably a great communicator and financially shrewd. You can be professional and humanitarian, self-confident and philosophical. In short, you've got a lot going for you! Since you know how to mix artistic sensibilities with animal passion, it's probably no surprise that the story of another wild creature, King Kong, was first televised in the year you were born.

John Osborne's first play *Look Back In Anger* premièred around this time, too. The play dealt with domestic quarrels in a realistic, hard-hitting manner that had never been attempted in theater before. Osborne is often seen as the spokesman of a generation of "Angry Young Men" and, like him, you may be first in many areas of life, and have consequent leadership qualities.

While most Ariens are born ahead of the game, wanting to rise to the top quickly in their field of interest, many can be clumsy or careless, which often prevents them from reaching their goal. You, on the other hand, are likely to be calculating and smart. With skills of strategy and war you're not the foot soldier, you're the Major General, who plans a campaign to be fought without bloodshed—quite unlike the Hungarian Freedom Fighters of 1956, who killed many Soviet secret police that were operating in Hungary, only to have Khrushchev, Russia's party leader, swiftly counter-revolutionize as he sent troops and tanks to quash the uprising.

Khrushchev was brave. At home in Russia, he dared to attack the memory of Stalin, who had maintained the tough party-line corruption of Communism. In love relationships you, too, are probably the fearless hero. As such, a Leo or Sagittarius, who will appreciate your pluck and valor, could adore you. A Gemini or an Aquarian could also make a good partner, for they can be excellent sounding boards.

Your greatest challenge is to keep a willful temper under wraps. Courageousness is your strength, and facing up to situations in a cool, calm, and collected manner will win your battles every time.

➤ Read about your Chinese Astrological sign on page 838. ➤ Read about your Personal Planets on page 826. ➤ Read about your personal Mystical Card on page 856.

TAURUS

From April 20, 2:43 through May 21, 2:12

The Sensational Campaigner

Born into a rock 'n' roll generation, you may prefer to rock the political boat rather than dance the night away, 1956 Taurus, using your natural exuberance to create waves of unrest until the authorities right basic wrongs. Significantly, in 1956 Nelson Mandela was arrested and charged with treason: after a six-year trial, he was acquitted, but he remained under suspicion for his anti-apartheid activities—a situation that may have inspired you to take action later on.

You were born in the early days of space discovery, and you may have a scientific bent that loves unusual artifacts or state-of-the-art technology. All kinds of electronic developments took place in 1956. Around the time you were born a laboratory in the U.S. detected high-temperature microwave radiation from Venus, which is actually the ruling planet of Taurus.

Taureans tend to attach great importance to material wealth. As a 1956 Taurus, you may also see the sense in looking after all you treasure. Because, if truth be told, no matter how good you think you are with money, you're likely to be a bit of a spendthrift, who needs to exercise tighter control on the purse strings! You may want to take a solid-gold leaf out of fellow Taurean Liberace's book. As fans across the world adored the piano-playing showman, Liberace would ask his audience if they liked his diamonds, proffering a hand dripping in twenty-four carat jewels. "You should," he'd boldly say. "You paid for them!" Not that you would be so cheeky, but the point is to maintain fiscal balance, and control your love of glitz and glamour.

When it comes to your love life, you may be attracted to a nurturing Cancer, who could galvanize you into romantic action. You may also be attracted to Virgo or Capricorn, both of whom could help your work find greater acceptance.

Separating fact from fiction is your greatest challenge. Your communication skills are the strength which keeps your feet on the ground, for when you talk things through with others you're less likely to get lost in romantic ideals that could otherwise have you chasing rainbows.

GEMINI

From May 21, 2:13 through June 21, 10:23

The Thoughtful Communicator

Born on the eve of the Space Race between the U.S. and the USSR, your brain probably assimilates information at the speed of light, 1956 Gemini. You may also be more of a family person than most Geminis—although letting loved ones know you care when you're light years apart wasn't as easy back in the 1950s as it is zipping along the information superhighway today. In the year of your birth, small steps to link continents, rather than planets, were being taken, as the very first transatlantic telephone cable opened, carrying telephone traffic between Britain and the U.S. and Canada.

With a talent for communication, you may also be a brilliant storyteller and writer. Relating every fact and figure to others may be a way for you to store information in your memory. Recording your life might be a project you've either toyed with or already done, and it may fascinate you to know that one of the most famous diaries of all time, the play based on *The Diary of Anne Frank* won the 1956 Pulitzer Prize. Anne was also a Gemini, hence her marvelous writing ability.

What was inspirational about the young diarist was her sensitive example of a teenager's aspirations. Unfortunately, as she died in a wartime concentration camp in 1945, Anne's hopes of a writing career were never fulfilled. For you, the fact that you were growing up in the fifties and sixties, after World War II was over, gave you the opportunity to fulfill your dreams—and you often do.

In relationships, you know how opposites attract. Take Marilyn Monroe and Arthur Miller, who married in 1956: she a Gemini movie star, and he a Sagittarian playwright. Both professions demand clear communication skills. Indeed, Miller even wrote Marilyn's last film, aptly titled *The Misfits*. Sagittarians will make you think, although Libran or Aquarian could make a more pertinent connection.

It's likely that you're on the ball, and run on rocket fuel. Your strength is your inquiring mind, to make light of the frivolous or probe the profound. Your challenge is to avoid superficiality and to seize the momentous opportunities that come your way.

➤ Read about your Chinese Astrological sign on page 838. ➤ Read about your Personal Planets on page 826. ➤ Read about your personal Mystical Card on page 856.

TAURUS
Your Personal Planets

YOUR LOVE POTENTIAL
Venus in Gemini, Apr. 20, 2:43 - May 08, 2:16
Venus in Cancer, May 08, 2:17 - May 21, 2:12

YOUR DRIVE AND AMBITION
Mars in Aquarius, Apr. 20, 2:43 - May 21, 2:12

YOUR LUCK MAGNETISM
Jupiter in Leo, Apr. 20, 2:43 - May 21, 2:12

World Events

May 9 - John Osborne's diatribe against the British establishment *Look Back in Anger* premières in London.

May 13 - Stirling Moss wins the Monaco Grand Prix.

Egyptian President Abdel Gamal Nasser nationalizes the Suez Canal

GEMINI
Your Personal Planets

YOUR LOVE POTENTIAL
Venus in Cancer, May 21, 2:13 - June 21, 10:23

YOUR DRIVE AND AMBITION
Mars in Aquarius, May 21, 2:13 - June 03, 7:50
Mars in Pisces, June 03, 7:51 - June 21, 10:23

YOUR LUCK MAGNETISM
Jupiter in Leo, May 21, 2:13 - June 21, 10:23

World Events

June 13 - Real Madrid wins the first European Cup, held in Paris.

June 13 - Britain hands over control of the Suez Canal to Egypt.

1956

CANCER
Your Personal Planets

YOUR LOVE POTENTIAL

Venus in Cancer, June 21, 10:24 - June 23, 12:09
Venus in Gemini, June 23, 12:10 - July 22, 21:19

YOUR DRIVE AND AMBITION

Mars in Pisces, June 21, 10:24 - July 22, 21:19

YOUR LUCK MAGNETISM

Jupiter in Leo, June 21, 10:24 - July 07, 19:00
Jupiter in Virgo, July 07, 19:01 - July 22, 21:19

World Events

June 28 – Israeli Prime Minister David Ben-Gurion states his intention to respond with force to Jordan's attacks.

July 9 – Academy Award-winning American actor Tom Hanks is born.

Marilyn Monroe marries Arthur Miller

LEO
Your Personal Planets

YOUR LOVE POTENTIAL

Venus in Gemini, July 22, 21:20 - Aug. 04, 9:48
Venus in Cancer, Aug. 04, 9:49 - Aug. 23, 4:14

YOUR DRIVE AND AMBITION

Mars in Pisces, July 22, 21:20 - Aug. 23, 4:14

YOUR LUCK MAGNETISM

Jupiter in Virgo, July 22, 21:20 - Aug. 23, 4:14

World Events

July 26 – Egyptian President Nasser nationalizes the Suez Canal.

Aug. 11 – American artist Jackson Pollock dies.

CANCER

From June 21, 10:24 through July 22, 21:19

The Imaginative Powerhouse

A telling characteristic of a 1956 Cancer is that they may often appear frivolous and fun while in their hearts they are really the opposite—deep and profound. With an undercurrent of hidden feelings that glide unnoticed, you may be a bit like the USS *Nautilus*, the first nuclear-powered submarine commissioned into the U.S. navy in the year you were born. The similarity is that you too can be powerful and often unfathomable. So subterranean are your feelings that even you might not be aware of them. All Cancers tend to be passionate, but your quiet exterior may mask the ticking of an awesome emotional bomb, Cancer of 1956.

Should you insist upon burying what is really a hidden treasure—i.e., your immense inner power—then you're not using your resources as best you can. It may be that you, or other people, find this intensity too much, or too threatening to handle, and you may prefer to keep it under wraps until you really need it. Interestingly, Britain also had to ration a form of power during the year you were born, when oil had to be transported the long way round via the Horn of Africa, because of the Suez Canal crisis.

Confidential information may have a habit of coming your way, and you might know all kinds of mysterious things about people, situations, and ideas. Perhaps it's because you come across as caring and loving that others respond accordingly and shower their secrets upon you. You are one of the few signs that can usually put your feelings into words. With communication skills that other people appreciate, you may write for a living or for pleasure.

You may also have artistic or musical gifts, like fellow Cancerian Louis Armstrong, who did blow his own trumpet—and how! A Scorpio or a Pisces will always empathize and jazz up how you feel, but it may be a conscientious Virgo who can pry you out of your shell.

With an exceptional imagination, your challenge is to make something real from the chimerical world of illusion. A quick and discerning intellect is the strength you can rely on to make your life a work of art and realize your enormous potential.

LEO

From July 22, 21:20 through August 23, 4:14

The Refined Stylist

To be born a Leo in 1956 is truly special, and not just because the mid-1950s offered many wondrous effects that could have influenced those around you to be extra playful, and really bring out a Leo's creativity. The year 1956 was a time when America seemed to have it all, and people everywhere wanted to be a part of the great American Dream.

"Lurex" had just celebrated a tenth anniversary, and life in America glittered with soda fountains and coffee bars where, with jukebox music to rock 'n' roll to, pony-tailed bobby-soxers jived with guys in drainpipe trousers. Surprisingly, you can be a touch nostalgic, and you may enjoy retro periods of fashion—particularly back in the seventies, when dressing up in vintage clothes would have been thoroughly in vogue.

A Leo always has style, wanting to travel first class all the way. Not that you're a snob, but you may be glad to hear how Britain abolished third-class rail carriages the year you were born! You also have a strong value system. Believing you should be remunerated handsomely for any effort you make, you would probably support the U.S. steel workers who went on strike in 1956.

While others may live to work, you live for love. A creative Leo, Ted Hughes (who later became the British Poet Laureate, the highest honor paid to a poet), met and married fellow wordsmith Sylvia Plath at Cambridge. With two young children, they appeared to be a happy family for a while, until sadly Ted fell in love with someone else. Tragically, Plath succumbed rather quickly to Scorpionic self-destruction. The moral of the story: steer clear of old scimitar-tail, Scorpio. Best stick to Aries or Sagittarius, who are loyal, loving, and a good laugh. Gemini might also keep you romantically entertained.

With a discerning mind as your great strength, you could find that riches come easily. Although money can't buy love, your challenge is to invest wisely. Ultimately, your life is a psychologically revealing, transformational journey of self-discovery. You have enormous reserves of energy at your disposal, and your mission is to use them wisely.

➤ Read about your Chinese Astrological sign on page 838. ➤ Read about your Personal Planets on page 826. ➤ Read about your personal Mystical Card on page 856.

VIRGO

From August 23, 4:15 through September 23, 1:34

The Energetic Healer

Virgo of 1956 was indeed born under a lucky star. You probably have a knack for being in the right place at the right time, talking to the right person. Somehow things just seem to fall into your lap, like gifts from the gods. It's likely that you're a wholesome nature lover who may have the gift of healing, and that the well-being of all God's creatures means a great deal to you. It may concern you that, around the time you were born, the necessity for testing medicines and scientific space gadgets on animals meant that concern for animal welfare wasn't as widespread as it is today.

With cheerful optimism and a broader vision that stops you from getting bogged down in petty detail (as so many other Virgos can), it's likely that you're always up for travel and adventure. In your exploits, you could take more risks than most. You may win with a once-in-a-while flier, but you're asking for trouble if you move to Las Vegas. Interestingly, in Britain, ERNIE, the Electronic Random Number Indicating Equipment, came into use in 1956, to pick prize-winners among the owners of Premium Bonds. Since you also like longevity and hate to waste, you may be pleased to know that ERNIE is still in use today! Couple your love of conserving ecological resources with your need to be understood, and you may also take pride in the fact that the first solar-powered radios came into existence in 1956.

There are astral indications of a deep spirituality that you might not feel comfortable about showing in public. Not that you would behave like the British, who, in order to control the island of Cyprus, deported Archbishop Makarios, the leader of the Greek-Cypriot community, to an island in the Indian Ocean in 1956.

In love, a Taurus or Capricorn would respect your privacy and rarely invade your inner sanctum. A Cancer, however, brings out your need to care for others.

Organizing yourself and others is your aid to deep spiritual development which, once realized, is your ultimate strength. Your challenge is to utilize your remedial skills for the benefit of humanity without getting drained in the process.

LIBRA

From September 23, 1:35 through October 23, 10:33

The Inspired Diplomat

As a lover of all things gorgeous, 1956 Libra, it may interest you to know that a Libran beauty began her international career the year you were born. Cast by her then-husband, French director Roger Vadim, in the film *And God Created Woman*, Brigitte Bardot brought French sensuality to the screen. Librans love to languish dreamily, pose with poise, and attract the attention of a partner. Like Bardot, you may work best in association with another. Another creative partnership also began in 1956, when a young John Lennon (also a Libra) met Paul McCartney for the first time. Impressed because Paul knew how to play chords on the guitar, John asked him to join his band, The Quarrymen, and a music phenomenon was born. The Quarrymen were soon joined by George Harrison and Ringo Starr and re-named The Beatles. When the band, and the Lennon-McCartney songwriting team split up, you were in your teens—it wasn't just the end of a collaboration, it was the end of an era.

Because you're naturally diplomatic and tactful, you may find arguments or quarrels upsetting. Keeping the peace is important, as you are at your most creative when calm abides. Unfortunately, fighting broke out in many places across the world in 1956. Tanks were deployed against racist demonstrators in Clinton, Tennessee; the IRA began a six-year campaign against the Northern Ireland border with the Irish Republic; and trouble continued in the Middle East as Israel invaded Egypt as far as the Suez. It was the latest in an ongoing series of confrontations. You probably find that long-standing conflicts such as these disturb your equilibrium.

You could make your mark through world affairs, but in your personal life it might be a Gemini or Aquarian that restores balance and harmony. Should you mix fate and fondness with a Leo, they could bring luck with love.

Relationships are both your challenge and your strength. Although it's sometimes tough to get others to listen to you, it's important that you do, because what you say counts, and your influence is inspirational, particularly to those in authority.

➤ Read about your Chinese Astrological sign on page 838. ➤ Read about your Personal Planets on page 826. ➤ Read about your personal Mystical Card on page 856.

VIRGO
Your Personal Planets

YOUR LOVE POTENTIAL
Venus in Cancer, Aug. 23, 4:15 - Sept. 08, 9:22
Venus in Leo, Sept. 08, 9:23 - Sept. 23, 1:34

YOUR DRIVE AND AMBITION
Mars in Pisces, Aug. 23, 4:15 - Sept. 23, 1:34

YOUR LUCK MAGNETISM
Jupiter in Virgo, Aug. 23, 4:15 - Sept. 23, 1:34

World Events

Sept. 8 – Harry Belafonte's album *Calypso* goes to Number One and remains there for thirty-one weeks.

Sept. 13 – Igor Stravinsky's *Canticum Sacrum* premières in Venice.

Tanks in Budapest during the Hungarian insurection

LIBRA
Your Personal Planets

YOUR LOVE POTENTIAL
Venus in Leo, Sept. 23, 1:35 - Oct. 06, 3:11
Venus in Virgo, Oct. 06, 3:12 - Oct. 23, 10:33

YOUR DRIVE AND AMBITION
Mars in Pisces, Sept. 23, 1:35 - Oct. 23, 10:33

YOUR LUCK MAGNETISM
Jupiter in Virgo, Sept. 23, 1:35 - Oct. 23, 10:33

World Events

Sept. 24 – The first transatlantic telephone cable goes into use between Newfoundland and Scotland.

Oct. 23 – Demonstrators in Hungary demand independence from Soviet control.

1956

SCORPIO
Your Personal Planets

YOUR LOVE POTENTIAL
Venus in Virgo, Oct. 23, 10:34 - Oct. 31, 19:39
Venus in Libra, Oct. 31, 19:40 - Nov. 22, 7:49

YOUR DRIVE AND AMBITION
Mars in Pisces, Oct. 23, 10:34 - Nov. 22, 7:49

YOUR LUCK MAGNETISM
Jupiter in Virgo, Oct. 23, 10:34 - Nov. 22, 7:49

World Events

Nov. 5 - French and British troops arrive in Egypt during the Suez Crisis.

Nov. 15 - Elvis Presley's first film, *Love Me Tender*, premières.

South African activist, Nelson Mandela, is arrested

SAGITTARIUS
Your Personal Planets

YOUR LOVE POTENTIAL
Venus in Libra, Nov. 22, 7:50 - Nov. 25, 13:00
Venus in Scorpio, Nov. 25, 13:01 - Dec. 19, 19:06
Venus in Sagittarius, Dec. 19, 19:07 - Dec. 21, 20:58

YOUR DRIVE AND AMBITION
Mars in Pisces, Nov. 22, 7:50 - Dec. 06, 11:23
Mars in Aries, Dec. 06, 11:24 - Dec. 21, 20:58

YOUR LUCK MAGNETISM
Jupiter in Virgo, Nov. 22, 7:50 - Dec. 13, 2:16
Jupiter in Libra, Dec. 13, 2:17 - Dec. 21, 20:58

World Events

Dec. 6 - Nelson Mandela and 156 others are arrested for political activities in South Africa.

Dec. 18 - Japan joins the League of Nations.

SCORPIO
From October 23, 10:34 through November 22, 7:49

The Productive Influence

Being born in 1956 could enhance even a Scorpio's ability to dream and fantasize, and it's likely that you have an uncanny ability to tap into the unspoken rhythm of life and make some sense of it all. In psychological terms, you may have a gift for tuning into the zeitgeist, able to feel the undercurrent of your generation's needs and wants. You can be deep and thoughtful, able to understand people's psyches, making you a good psychologist or researcher.

You were born at a time when science made extraordinary headway, not only in outer space, but also in studying the subatomic particles found in cosmic rays (radiation from outer space)—a field that may fascinate you more. In 1956, the neutrino, the subatomic particle, was first detected. Space was crowded with more artificial satellites that were revealed as you grew up. As a 1956 Scorpio, you too could have the mysterious x-factor, for it's likely that there is more to you than meets the eye, and this can literally mesmerize others.

Once under your spell, people may be captivated. Prince Rainier of Monaco is an example of one bewitched by a Scorpio; he married the enchanting Grace Kelly, princess of the silver screen, and made her a real-life princess in 1956. You are also drawn to glamour, and you could find the thought of fairy-tale romance rather seductive.

While the allure of lighthearted glitz appeals, you're also drawn to profound relationships where the mystery of love takes you on a heartfelt exploration of yourself. Scorpio understands that sensation and emotion are powerful forces which, when harnessed positively, can provide an unparalleled source of energy. A Cancer or Pisces could help you to achieve the power and self-knowledge you seek.

In due course, you discover your potency, if you haven't already. But it's what you do with all that power that is the 1956 Scorpio's lesson. Your challenge is to transform the world around you to be healthier, cleaner, and wiser—no easy task. Your strength is the way you combine sympathy with action, which brings about sensitive behavior that others truly respect.

SAGITTARIUS
From November 22, 7:50 through December 21, 20:58

The Diplomatic Explorer

Born with a love of travel, 1956 Sagittarius, you might get a kick out of knowing that the Best Film Oscar of your birth year was awarded to *Around The World In Eighty Days!* You too might want to explore the world, but it's likely that you'd travel light and not be weighed down by anything that could hinder your progress. You may seem ruthless sometimes in the way you offload things, ideas, or people that you might think aren't worth the risk. However, you discard such things only for practical reasons and are not intentionally cruel or thoughtless.

With an independent streak that runs through almost everything you do, you might also empathize with all the smaller countries that began, in the mid-1950s, to pull away from the empires of old-style imperialism. In 1956, for example, Egypt nationalized the Suez Canal, while Sudan, Tunisia, and Morocco finally achieved independence from colonial status. Also in Africa, Algerian freedom fighters began a six-year war of independence against the French. Because you were born in such a year, perhaps you innately know how much more can be achieved through discussion, rather than rushing into situations with all guns blazing.

You may also show the skills of diplomacy and tact—rare for a fiery Sagittarian, who is famed for gauche indiscretion. This insight is an excellent quality to use at work, at home, and in relationships, for it allows you to bring a balance into all your affairs. Working with diligence and patience, you have much to achieve in the way of change, be that a revolution within yourself, your family, or the world around you.

You could also appear quite suave and sophisticated to others. Consequently, an Aries or Leo might fall for you in a big way. However, it's likely to be a Libra who can really help you to grow and develop all your skills.

As you're more disciplined and organized than most other Sagittarians, this is one of your greatest strengths. To bring in the new, without threatening the old, is a masterful skill and a challenge you must live up to, without reneging on anyone's authority, including your own.

► Read about your Chinese Astrological sign on page 838. ► Read about your Personal Planets on page 826. ► Read about your personal Mystical Card on page 856.

CAPRICORN

From December 21, 20:59 through December 31, 23:59

The Adventurous Originator

Being born in December of 1956 makes you an unusual kind of Capricorn, as you're probably much more passionate and tempestuous than the usually reserved Mountain Goat. You have fire in your soul and, as such, you're likely to be an adventurous person who hears the call of the wild and loves to be free.

By all astral accounts, your interests are many and varied. In contrast to a typical Capricorn, who shares a fairly traditional mind-set, you can be curious and open-minded, willing to accept others as they are rather than passing judgment. Although you know there isn't much new under the Sun left to be discovered, you may still seek out new worlds and you might travel just to see how other people live. It's comparing the way that every culture has different ideologies, different recipes, and even different gods, that could fascinate you. Although Pakistan was already independent by the time of your birth, it declared the Islamic Republic in 1956, which may have interested you later in life.

With a firm belief that all people are created equal, you could be a strong believer in human rights. Any affront to personal freedom could rile you into action. The fact that Martin Luther King, Jr.'s home was bombed in 1956 is just the kind of fuel to make your blood boil. But as if to restore your faith in human nature, the U.S. Supreme Court ended segregation on buses in your birth year.

Confronting situations head on—sometimes with an awesome fearlessness—makes you a formidable opponent to deal with. You're not someone to shy away from anything or anyone, unless, of course, you get bored or restless, which is rare for a Capricorn. You may need to share life with others who are as dynamic as you are, such as a Sagittarius. On the other hand, you may do well with those who have a taming, earthy influence like a Taurus or Virgo.

The challenge you face is to stick to your game plan without thinking you know it all. Your strength lies in being a practical Capricorn, enabling you to broaden your horizons at the same time as you secure your status within a competitive society.

1956
CAPRICORN
Your Personal Planets

YOUR LOVE POTENTIAL
Venus in Sagittarius, Dec. 21, 20:59 - Dec. 31, 23:59

YOUR DRIVE AND AMBITION
Mars in Aries, Dec. 21, 20:59 - Dec. 31, 23:59

YOUR LUCK MAGNETISM
Jupiter in Libra, Dec. 21, 20:59 - Dec. 31, 23:59

World Events

Dec. 22 – The first gorilla born in captivity is announced at the Columbus Zoo in Ohio.

Dec. 26 – Japan and the USSR officially bring their state of war to an end.

A UFO picture taken by a US government worker in New Mexico

Special Feature
The Extraterrestrial Highway: Exploring UFOs

by Jean Mars

It all began on a clear, brilliant Pacific Northwest afternoon, June 24, 1947. Kenneth Arnold had just left Chehalis, Washington, en route to his home in Boise, Idaho, undoubtedly enjoying the picture-perfect flying weather from the cockpit of his small private plane. A little before 3:00 p.m., however, Arnold suddenly noticed that he was not alone. He'd been joined by a sky full of shining objects—nine in all—unlike anything he'd ever seen. The gleaming pack made its way south through the Cascade Mountains, easily weaving in and out among the craggy peaks. Hardly able to believe his eyes, when he stopped to refuel in Pendleton, Oregon, he related his story to a local editor. The objects he described were roughly circular, he said, somehow flying in an undulating pattern, "like a saucer would if you skipped it across the water."

That story was the first of many that would be told to the American media over the next few weeks, all describing flying objects of similar appearance and talents. When all was said and done, reports of the strange new phenomenon had come in from thirty-six states—and they kept on coming. In Portland, Oregon, dozens of ordinary citizens and even police officers swore they had seen a "formation of flying saucers." A United Airlines commercial pilot said his plane was "buzzed" by several of these "flying discs." Then, on July 5, 1947, the *Seattle Post-Intelligencer* made history when it published a UFO photograph taken by Yeoman Frank Ryman of the U.S. Coast Guard.

The wave of sightings peaked on July 8, 1947, when the U.S. Army reported that a crashed flying saucer had been found near Roswell, New Mexico. The incident made headlines around the world, but by the next day the army was issuing retractions. At a press conference in Fort Worth, army General Roger Ramey displayed debris from a wrecked weather balloon. He insisted that the balloon was what officials had really found, not a "flying saucer," as had been stated previously.

The occurrence literally put Roswell on the map as the starting point for modern "ufology," which is the study of "Unidentified Flying Objects" (UFOs). The incident also immediately sparked rumors of a government cover-up, especially since not just the Roswell event, but virtually every eyewitness account from all thirty-six states, were soon to be disputed by army officials. These government denials, along with increasingly skeptical news accounts, fueled what was soon termed "the UFO craze."

(Continued on page 473)

➤ Read "Ancient Secrets of the Egyptian Pyramids" by Jean Mars on page 305. ➤ Read "The Enigma of Crop Circles" by Frank Andrews on page 673.

1957

The Space Race: Uranus in Leo

Russian satellite "Sputnik I" is launched

After the Suez Canal crisis brought back fears of war, people were eager to find a more uplifting focus for their attention. This came in the form of the drive to conquer the frontiers of space. With Uranus, ancient god of the heavens, in Leo, known for its competitive winner-take-all spirit, the Space Race was its ultimate expression. The Soviet Union made news on October 4 by launching the *Sputnik* unmanned satellite. This coincided with a resonance-creating "trine" from Saturn, the planet which reveals our limitations. Uranus breaks up old patterns and leads us beyond previous limitations when it interacts with Saturn. With space exploration, humanity embarked on a new adventure that expressed this Saturn-Uranus blend precisely and with seeming ease.

Saturn also connotes business, and Uranus electronics and automation. Together they suggest technology, and this year was a boom time for new devices and developments. The first large-scale nuclear power plant went on-line in the U.S., while the "Tang" breakfast drink and frozen pizzas first hit store shelves this year.

By the end of 1957, the Uranus-Neptune contact of the past five years was dissipating, but the cultural upheaval that this represented lingered on. Neptune is the symbol of cultural compassion, consciousness, and ideals regarding what it means to be part of civilization. Uranus symbolizes experiences that awaken us; when it contacted Neptune in an abrasive "square" connection, people woke up to the ways in which their culture did not fulfill its ideals. They saw how racial and religious minorities, women, workers, and others were disenfranchised by their society. The highest form of this Uranus-Neptune contact was fulfilled when the first major civil-rights bill for nearly one hundred years was passed by the U.S. Congress this year—one more step on a long path.

The struggle to meet the needs of the powerless continued around the world. Progress accelerated once Jupiter, the great entrepreneur, entered Libra, the sign of justice and equality, in August. For example, Little Rock Central High School in Arkansas was forcibly integrated over the military-backed objections of the governor.

Bill Haley and the Comets

National guard protects an African American school girl

THE SPACE RACE BEGINS

Soviet leader Khrushchev snuffed out a Stalinist plot to remove him from power. The world was taken by surprise when the Russians made it into Space with the launch of *Sputnik I*. The European Economic Community was formed when six European nations signed the Common Market treaty. The Gold Coast, formerly a British colony in West Africa, became independent as the Republic of Ghana. Jordan's King Hussein severed relations with Egypt, after Egyptian calls for his death. In Haiti, "Papa Doc" Duvalier became President and in Cuba, Fidel Castro's guerrillas defied the government. Defying federal law, Arkansas Governor Faubus sent state militia troops to stop African American students from entering a white high school, prompting President Eisenhower to send in federal troops. Greece refused a NATO plan for peace in Cyprus. Jack Kerouac promoted the Beat Generation, and Theodor "Dr. Seuss" Geisel brought the kid out in everyone with *The Cat In The Hat*. The Everly Brothers topped the charts with *Bye Bye Love*, while Joanne Woodward brought *The Three Faces Of Eve* to the cinema. Rockers Bill Haley and the Comets wowed London audiences.

➤ Read "The Extraterrestrial Highway: Exploring UFOs" by Jean Mars on page 465.

CAPRICORN

From January 01, 0:00 through January 20, 7:38

The Courageous Traditionalist

Events around the time of your birth illustrated the potential benefits of Capricorn virtues, such as restraint and advance planning. In January 1957, U.S. President Eisenhower proposed a two-year ban on nuclear weapons testing. Such restraint gained general acceptance decades later. In the same month Sir Anthony Eden was forced to resign as Prime Minister of Britain over the Suez crisis, a botched incursion against Egypt over which Khrushchev threatened nuclear retaliation. Eisenhower complained that Britain and its allies had failed to inform the U.S. of the venture. To add insult to injury, the tankers built to deliver oil while the canal was closed turned out to be too big navigate the canal anyway. Capricorns tend to anticipate engineering and communications problems before they mushroom into career-ending disasters.

Few commodities are more valuable to you than time. Interestingly, the first electric watch was introduced in the U.S. in your birth month. Most Capricorns would agree that time really is money. For you, killing time is also a waste of valuable energy. It's just too easy to miss opportunities while sitting and twiddling your thumbs. With your get-up-and-go approach, you are likely to keep appointments and avoid boredom.

You tend to walk around with a lot on your mind. An impulsive streak may drive you to rush into situations with headstrong gusto, but snap decisions can get you into trouble. You can spare yourself a lot of aggravation by relying on your native Capricorn reserve and mulling things over before you jump into action.

You may seek a partner who shares your standards at home, supports your goals at work, and recognizes your talent for leadership and achievement. Often fearless and in command of your feelings, you may attract a Virgo or Taurus who enjoys your stable disposition. Aries may admire your drive, ambition, and taste for competition.

In relationships, work, and life in general, your challenge is to produce high-quality creations that can endure. The ability to work hard, with patience and precision, is your greatest strength

AQUARIUS

From January 20, 7:39 through February 18, 21:57

The People's Protector

Aquarius is a forward-thinking sign, so it's interesting how often a 1957 Aquarian will take time to revise ideas before moving on. What stops you from advancing quickly may be a lack of presumption on your part. To thoroughly discuss, research, or reassess certain deals or situations before giving anything the go-ahead is, in fact, wisely circumspect.

Being so circumspect, however, may make you seem pessimistic at times. Because you nearly always resolve your problems, you have the potential to be a policy maker par excellence. You can even make friends with old enemies, provided you believe the time is right. Indeed, in your birth month, Chou En-Lai announced that the friendship between the USSR and China was eternal and unbreakable.

Improving the world we live in is a main motivation for you. Because you tend to know what others need but may fail to follow your own advice, the common rejoinder, "do as I say and not as I do," may sometimes apply to you. In a similar vein, two authoritarian governments made headlines in your birth year. François "Papa Doc" Duvalier was elected President in Haiti and proclaimed himself President for life. His dictatorship began a fourteen-year reign of terror. Conversely, Honduras ratified a new constitution and elected its first liberal President in twenty-five years.

Because Aquarians tend to work tirelessly for democracy and equality, your most intimate relationships may evolve against a backdrop of activist causes. You are likely to gravitate to partners who share your convictions and humanitarian passions. A Libran can help you balance the extreme circumstances you sometimes face. A Gemini can provide intellectual clarity. A fiery Aries or an adventurous Sagittarius will help you to unblock your wilder energies

Stubbornness is your downfall, as it can create barriers. Your challenge is to deal with boundaries positively and effectively, and to shield yourself and others from disruptive situations. Wisdom, self-reliance, determination, and objectivity are your greatest strengths. Use them for your own self-protection.

➤ Read about your Chinese Astrological sign on page 838. ➤ Read about your Personal Planets on page 826. ➤ Read about your personal Mystical Card on page 856.

1957

CAPRICORN
Your Personal Planets

YOUR LOVE POTENTIAL
Venus in Sagittarius, Jan. 01, 0:00 - Jan. 12, 20:22
Venus in Capricorn, Jan. 12, 20:23 - Jan. 20, 7:38

YOUR DRIVE AND AMBITION
Mars in Aries, Jan. 01, 0:00 - Jan. 20, 7:38

YOUR LUCK MAGNETISM
Jupiter in Libra, Jan. 01, 0:00 - Jan. 20, 7:38

World Events

Jan. 1 - Benjamin Britten's ballet *The Prince And The Pauper* premieres in London.

Jan. 9 - British Prime Minister Anthony Eden resigns in the wake of the Suez disaster; he is replaced by Harold Macmillan.

Harold Macmillan and family in Downing Street

AQUARIUS
Your Personal Planets

YOUR LOVE POTENTIAL
Venus in Capricorn, Jan. 20, 7:39 - Feb. 05, 20:15
Venus in Aquarius, Feb. 05, 20:16 - Feb. 18, 21:57

YOUR DRIVE AND AMBITION
Mars in Aries, Jan. 20, 7:39 - Jan. 28, 14:18
Mars in Taurus, Jan. 28, 14:19 - Feb. 18, 21:57

YOUR LUCK MAGNETISM
Jupiter in Libra, Jan. 20, 7:39 - Feb. 18, 21:57

World Events

Jan. 22 - Israeli troops evacuate Egypt, maintaining a token presence only in the Gaza Strip.

Jan. 26 - India annexes Kashmir.

1957

PISCES
Personal Planets

YOUR LOVE POTENTIAL
Venus in Aquarius, Feb. 18, 21:58 - Mar. 01, 20:38
Venus in Pisces, Mar. 01, 20:39 - Mar. 20, 21:15

YOUR DRIVE AND AMBITION
Mars in Taurus, Feb. 18, 21:58 - Mar. 17, 21:33
Mars in Gemini, Mar. 17, 21:34 - Mar. 20, 21:15

YOUR LUCK MAGNETISM
Jupiter in Libra, Feb. 18, 21:58 - Feb. 19, 15:37
Jupiter in Virgo, Feb. 19, 15:38 - Mar. 20, 21:15

World Events

Feb. 25 - Buddy Holly and the Crickets record "That'll Be The Day."

Mar. 20 - African-American film director Spike Lee is born.

Buddy Holly and the Crickets

ARIES
Your Personal Planets

YOUR LOVE POTENTIAL
Venus in Pisces, Mar. 20, 21:16 - Mar. 25, 22:45
Venus in Aries, Mar. 25, 22:46 - Apr. 19, 3:27
Venus in Taurus, Apr. 19, 3:28 - Apr. 20, 8:40

YOUR DRIVE AND AMBITION
Mars in Gemini, Mar. 20, 21:16 - Apr. 20, 8:40

YOUR LUCK MAGNETISM
Jupiter in Virgo, Mar. 20, 21:16 - Apr. 20, 8:40

World Events

Mar. 25 - The Treaty of Rome is signed, establishing the European Economic Community.

Apr. 3 - Samuel Beckett's *Endgame* premieres in London.

PISCES
From February 18, 21:58 through March 20, 21:15

The Cosmic Connector

With compassion as your loadstar, Pisces, you can be wonderful with people. Like bees to the honey pot, others gravitate to you. As nice as you are, though, you're no pushover. Rather, you're a sturdy soul who can't help but be guided by loving kindness. Deep faith in the human spirit carries you through all your endeavors. You can be a guiding light in your community.

In 1957 Parisians had an opportunity to witness an example of spiritual courage in the letters of Jean Muller, quoted in an article published in the communist daily, *L'Humanité*. The letters gave an eyewitness account of torture performed by French officers and their subordinates against Algerian prisoners. French authorities responded by shutting down *L'Humanité*. Muller and L'Humanite took a moral stand at a time when French mainstream opinion was not yet ready for such an indictment. You too have the potential to stand strong in your convictions when others are being hurt.

For many Pisceans, music provides a connection with the sacred. You may have musical talent, as a performer or connoisseur. Born at the height of the rock 'n' roll years, you may have had parents who combined Peekaboo with Hand Jive. "That'll Be The Day" by Buddy Holly and The Crickets was climbing the charts in the month of your birth. In all probability, this tuneful exuberance rubbed off on you. Pisceans love to escape the humdrum of the everyday world. Seeing movies and going to the theatre may also be a favorite pastime. Director Spike Lee, who shares your birth month, likes the movies so much he makes them!

Cancer may enjoy accompanying you on frequent getaways—at home or elsewhere. Scorpio can help you realize your many dreams. Capricorn, on the other hand, offers practical insight and the opportunity for an excellent working partnership.

You have a gifted imagination, Pisces, and you need to express it wisely. Your challenge is to focus your creativity by channeling it through your sharp, incisive mind. Your strength lies in letting a cosmic kind of love flow through your heart, in the light of conscious choice.

ARIES
From March 20, 21:16 through April 20, 8:40

The Dynamic Communicator

All Ariens love to be first on the block; being ahead of the game satisfies their competitive leadership spirit. Ariens also tend to enjoy sports. Born at the beginning of the Space Race and when alien saucers flew through the movies, 1957 Aries could look forward to a childhood with flying disks hovering in their own backyards. In 1957, Californian inventor Walter F. Morrison dreamt up the Frisbee. Initially crafting their product in metal, manufacturers of the Frisbee would soon make the smart and successful shift to the wave of the future, plastics.

The Frisbee wasn't the only pioneering subject in 1957. A major political breakthrough also took place in your birth month. The Treaty of Rome, signed by France, West Germany, Italy, Belgium, Luxembourg, and the Netherlands, established the European Common Market. The EEC enhanced the economic power of Europe. The Euratom, the European Atomic Energy Authority, also came into being at this time. Why is all this pertinent to you? Having sufficient bargaining power may be an issue for you in managing your finances. Making smart alliances also provides you with the structure and support you need to channel your abundant supply of personal energy. Interaction with others helps you to vent feelings that might otherwise turn to anger.

While all Ariens are fiery at the best of times, you are positively turbo-charged, and burn brighter and faster than most. You may also spend a lot of time in your head, thinking. Physical exercise and workouts help you to avoid spiraling worries. Grab that Frisbee now! You will release pent-up energy and stay fit.

Outdoor types like Sagittarius or fun-loving Leo help you ease stress or pressure by balancing intellectual needs with physical activities. Libra or Aquarius appreciate your independent spirit and provide many opportunities for social interaction.

Your greatest challenge is to express your ideas without overwhelming others. Your quick mind and dynamic drive can make you a compelling and powerful leader. A dash of diplomacy readies others to welcome and promote your ideas.

➤ Read about your Chinese Astrological sign on page 838. ➤ Read about your Personal Planets on page 826. ➤ Read about your personal Mystical Card on page 856.

TAURUS

From April 20, 8:41 through May 21, 8:09

The Thoughtful Evaluator

Often depicted as leisurely and serene, Taureans tend to have an air of deliberation about them, and others may see you as considerate, thoughtful, and reflective. You may not show the slightest sign that a million light bulbs are flashing above your head. Slowing down the pace of your ideas affords you the comfort of scrutinizing each one. Finding the right information is important to you, for you know how easy it is to be misunderstood. Scanning a bus timetable may bring you as much contentment as reading the winner of the 1957 Pulitzer Prize, *Profiles In Courage* by John F. Kennedy.

Because down-to-earth is a favorite Taurean destination, you may enjoy hobbies like gardening, walking in the woods, or bird watching. Such pastimes allow you to center yourself. While you may stubbornly stick to your own tried-and-tested techniques, you may also appreciate that everyone tweaks geraniums in a different way.

Issuing a seeming invitation to free expression, China's Chairman Mao Tse-Tung declared, "Let a thousand flowers bloom," in 1957. But the Chinese cracked down soon thereafter when open debate produced protest, criticism, and open dissidence. The critics were labeled as reactionary, and totalitarian rule returned. Because you belong to a generation that seeks equality, you may vehemently object to repression and single-party rule.

In the interest of fairness, you prefer to study every angle, however long it takes, before joining any group. It may hearten you to know that women's rights took another step forward in 1957: Tunisia, Egypt, and Malaysia gave women the right to vote. In your own quest for freedom of choice, a Virgo or Capricorn may be your kindred spirit. Surprisingly, you can be impulsive in love. A Cancer can help you to harmonize your need for caution with passion.

Your challenge is to develop insight and new motivation, without turning it into self-defeating anxiety, particularly when dealing with finances. Your strength lies in helping yourself and others to realize that opportunities abound. You can trust that when one door closes, another one opens.

GEMINI

From May 21, 8:10 through June 21, 16:20

The Sparkling Wit

Facts, figures, and symbols (even funny, scientific-looking squiggles) tend to fascinate natives born under the sign of the Twins. Open and curious, Gemini of 1957 likes to know what others are doing. Born at the height of the Cold War, you spent your tender years at a time when intelligence played an urgent role in international security. The sign of Gemini also rules broadcasting, and in your birth month, Khrushchev became the first Soviet premier to appear on television in the United States. You may keep a television or radio on for background noise at home, and you're likely to maintain your own eclectic collection of books.

The Nobel Prize-winning physicist and principal developer of the Soviet hydrogen bomb Andre Sakharov was also a Gemini. Members of this sign tend to be talented with their hands. Uniquely ambidextrous, Sakharov could write a sentence with one hand while making a mirror image of the sentence with his other hand. In 1957, Sakharov first expressed his opinions, in what would be long career as a leader in the international nuclear disarmament movement and as a critic of Soviet tyranny.

The sign of Gemini rules the arms and hands. You may enjoy exceptional dexterity, as well as excellent hand-eye coordination. Perhaps you enjoy conducting or playing music, like the famous classical composer Igor Stravinsky, another Russian Gemini. In the mid-1950s, Stravinsky made a stylistic change, in which he adopted a more sympathetic view of Arnold Schoenberg's innovative twelve-tone musical system.

Intellectual stimulation can be the driving force in your relationships. An experimental Aquarian or a cultured Libran can keep your thinking moving forward and help you refine new ideas. Competitive Aries makes a good match for sports and love. Sagittarius helps you broaden your horizons and maintain a mischievous sense of humor.

Knowledge is not the same thing as wisdom. Your challenge is to apply what you know on a deeper level. Blessed with an incisive mind, extensive learning, and expressive gifts, you have the ability to sow understanding among people.

➤ Read about your Chinese Astrological sign on page 838. ➤ Read about your Personal Planets on page 826. ➤ Read about your personal Mystical Card on page 856.

TAURUS
Your Personal Planets

YOUR LOVE POTENTIAL
Venus in Taurus, Apr. 20, 8:41 - May 13, 11:07
Venus in Gemini, May 13, 11:08 - May 21, 8:09

YOUR DRIVE AND AMBITION
Mars in Gemini, Mar. 20, 8:41 - May 04, 15:21
Mars in Cancer, May 04, 15:22 - May 21, 8:09

YOUR LUCK MAGNETISM
Jupiter in Virgo, Apr. 20, 8:41 - May 21, 8:09

World Events

May 2 – U.S. Senator Joseph McCarthy dies.

May 6 – The Pulitzer Prize is awarded to John F. Kennedy for his *Profiles In Courage*.

John F. Kennedy wins the Pulitzer Prize

GEMINI
Your Personal Planets

YOUR LOVE POTENTIAL
Venus in Gemini, May 21, 8:10 - June 06, 21:34
Venus in Cancer, June 06, 21:35 - June 21, 16:20

YOUR DRIVE AND AMBITION
Mars in Cancer, May 21, 8:10 - June 21, 12:17
Mars in Leo, June 21, 12:18 - June 21, 16:20

YOUR LUCK MAGNETISM
Jupiter in Virgo, May 21, 8:10 - June 21, 16:20

World Events

June 1 – The USSR announces that its first space satellite is ready to be launched.

June 3 – The U.S. joins the Baghdad Pact on order to fight Communism.

1957

CANCER
Your Personal Planets

YOUR LOVE POTENTIAL
Venus in Cancer, June 21, 16:21 - July 01, 10:41
Venus in Leo, July 01, 10:42 - July 23, 3:14

YOUR DRIVE AND AMBITION
Mars in Leo, June 21, 16:21 - July 23, 3:14

YOUR LUCK MAGNETISM
Jupiter in Virgo, June 21, 16:21 - July 23, 3:14

World Events

June 27 – The Great Mecca Pilgrimage begins at the new Moon in the Middle East.

July 17 – African-American jazz star John Coltrane dies.

Althea Gibson is the first African-American woman to win Wimbledon

LEO
Your Personal Planets

YOUR LOVE POTENTIAL
Venus in Leo, July 23, 3:15 - July 26, 3:09
Venus in Virgo, July 26, 3:10 - Aug. 20, 0:43
Venus in Libra, Aug. 20, 0:44 - Aug. 23, 10:07

YOUR DRIVE AND AMBITION
Mars in Leo, July 23, 3:15 - Aug. 08, 5:26
Mars in Virgo, Aug. 08, 5:27 - Aug. 23, 10:07

YOUR LUCK MAGNETISM
Jupiter in Virgo, July 23, 3:15 - Aug. 07, 2:10
Jupiter in Libra, Aug. 07, 2:11 - Aug. 23, 10:07

World Events

July 29 – The International Atomic Energy Agency is established.

Aug. 17 – The first particle accelerator in Europe opens in Geneva.

CANCER
From June 21, 16:21 through July 23, 3:14

The Nourishing Dramatist

Most Cancerians need a handy shelter, particularly when the going gets tough. As a Cancer born in 1957, however, you're unusual in that you can stand your ground and put up a fierce front should anyone try to intimidate you. A home sweet home remains important to you. A cozy family life provides a setting where you can discover and fully express your true self.

You're not as shy as most other Cancerians. Indeed, a part of you may be dramatic, theatrical, and flamboyant. You may have a surprising bravado that cries out, "Look at me, everybody!" Of course, after spending some time in the spotlight, you may need to retreat into the familiar safety of your shell. Behind your tough exterior lies a soft and tender heart of gold. Take Patty Smyth, for instance, a New York City rocker who shares your birth month. Her defiant dignity can't camouflage her vulnerability.

Cancer of 1957 has an inspiringly vivid imagination. Your talents can lead you, quite unwittingly, down the path to fame. In 1957, the Chilean poet Pablo Neruda was arrested during a visit to Buenos Aires. He was given a poem by one of the policemen who also happened to be a fan. It read: "Poetry is a deep inner calling in man; from it came liturgy, the psalms, and also the content of religions."

In relationships, you may seek acceptance of all the facets of your personality. You may have chosen partners or friends who would be sensitive to your changing moods. Scorpios instinctively know how to delve into your deepest emotions. Pisceans have the ability to share profoundly spiritual experiences. Virgos can tune into subtle changes in your demeanor.

Water, the element associated with Cancer, reflects your deeply emotional nature. It's important for you to keep your emotions flowing and to avoid becoming mired in negativity. Powerful intuition is your strength. Armed with style, sensitivity, and magnanimity, your challenge is to distinguish self from ego and to develop relationships built of heartfelt connections. By looking beyond prestige, protection, or passion, you can create bonds that last a lifetime.

LEO
From July 23, 3:15 through August 23, 10:07

The Noble Mind

There's a childlike innocence to the 1957 Leo, no matter what your age. This is mainly due to your lighthearted cheerfulness. It should come as no surprise, then, that in your birth year no less than three timeless toys hit the market. Wham-O gave us the Frisbee and the Hula-Hoop. And the Pogo Stick enjoyed a popular revival, giving a certain bounce to mid-fifties life!

Leo rules youthful self-expression. In 1957, *American Bandstand*, the long-running popular dance and music show, emceed by the eternally youthful Dick Clarke, premiered on network TV. In the 1950s British youth enjoyed a craze in skiffle, a form of jazz or folk music played on jugs, washboards, banjos, and guitars. And rock 'n' roll was taking over the world. At the time, one's taste in music defined whether you were hip or a square. Growing up while those around you were rocking around the clock, you may enjoy openly celebrating your own favorite music.

You are vivacious and sensible. Your practicality often comes through for you in tricky situations. Intelligent and able to offer swift solutions in a crisis, you may enjoy problem-solving. You're at your best when you can offer ideas that are both innovative and useful. In 1957, Albuquerque, New Mexico gained the distinction of unveiling the first building to be heated by solar power. Because the life-giving Sun rules the sign of Leo, you may feel a special sense of pride in that particular milestone.

Members of your sign tend to be childlike, but for Leo of 1957, life is not just one big playground. You can be very responsible in both business and romantic relationships. You may be choosy about potential partners. Aries or Sagittarius can be great playmates. Libra is elegant and helps you strike the right balance between maturity and youthful indulgence.

With a powerful sense of reason at your command, a noble decorum is one of your greatest strengths. Your challenge is to promote creative change in the world, in a measured and controlled manner. A disciplined approach allows you to triumph peacefully over adversity, with style, panache, and finesse.

► Read about your Chinese Astrological sign on page 838. ► Read about your Personal Planets on page 826. ► Read about your personal Mystical Card on page 856.

VIRGO

From August 23, 10:08 through September 23, 7:25

The Judicious Intellect

Virgos tend to reflect before they take action—an approach often mistaken for worry. The 1957 Virgo may exhibit this characteristic more than other members of this sign. It's your nature to re-think, re-do, and re-organize. For you, an alteration here and there can make a world of difference—and not just to you, but to everyone else. Others might think you're fussy, but a command of detail is the secret to your success.

To your mind, few things are perfect on first presentation. If you had your way, half the products on the market would be safer. When you reached adulthood, you may have learned of the tragedy that began in late 1957, when the drug thalidomide was first marketed in Europe. Prescribed to counteract morning sickness in pregnant women, the drug was ultimately linked to horrific birth defects and removed from the world market in the 1960s. You may be very sensitive about your health, diet, and what you put in your body.

Eager to correct basic wrongs, you may have absorbed the influence of an incident that took place in your birth month. In September, 1957, the governor of Arkansas violated a federal court order for desegregation when he called in the state militia to bar nine African-American children from entering a high school in Little Rock. President Eisenhower sent in the National Guard to escort the children.

In relationships you need partners who understand your need to make things right. You are likely to be happiest when you connect with partners who are as diligent and reliable as you are. Taurus and Capricorn provide sturdy support. A Cancerian can sympathize with your occasional need to retreat into the safety of solitude.

One of your major strengths is a discerning mind that conveniently signals when ideas, things, or relationships need re-adjusting. Too much idealism, however, can cause you to set standards that are impossible to satisfy. You have both the mental discipline and the physical energy to take good care of yourself and your loved ones. You'll enjoy the greatest success when you aim for progress, as opposed to perfection.

LIBRA

From September 23, 7:26 through October 23, 16:23

The Expansive Teacher

When you look around and see the lives of others, 1957 Libra, you might realize how lucky you are. Not that everything goes your way, though—others' needs almost always figure into your decisions. This is especially true for 1957 Librans, who have the potential to be perfect arbitrators. The Broadway musical *West Side Story* premiered during your birth month. When you were old enough to see a revival of the play or the film version, you may have reacted strongly to the conflict between the Jets and the Sharks. You prefer one-on-one relationships and easily see both sides of every story.

The Space Race officially began in your zodiacal month, when the Russians launched the first satellite, *Sputnik I*. Distant horizons beckoned, and a contest to orbit Earth began. You, too, may have an instinctive need to travel and discover new worlds. Even if you stay home, you may want to expand your awareness of the world, at the very least. You may teach, and you may also be a perennial student. For you, there's always much more to learn in the world.

Informed, and with a highly charged energy, you may be interested to learn that Eveready batteries produced the AA size in your birth year, for use in the new personal transistor radios. Good health tends to follow you, as it does with people who are generally lively, happy, and optimistic. When old age inevitably catches up with you, you are likely to take it in your stride. Understanding the bigger picture, you find it easy to put life into perspective.

Love and relationships feed your soul, and friendships help you to envisage bigger and brighter possibilities in life. Although you may have the odd disagreement, you're philosophical about relationships. You may find that you have much in common with a truth-seeking Sagittarian. A knowledge-loving Aquarius or Gemini can send you to seventh heaven.

Your strength lies in your ability to see beauty in everything and everyone, but an overly rose-colored perspective can lead you to make reckless choices in relationships or financial matters. You can learn to balance sympathy with truth.

➤ Read about your Chinese Astrological sign on page 838. ➤ Read about your Personal Planets on page 826. ➤ Read about your personal Mystical Card on page 856.

1957

VIRGO
Your Personal Planets

YOUR LOVE POTENTIAL
Venus in Libra, Aug. 23, 10:08 - Sept. 14, 6:19
Venus in Scorpio, Sept. 14, 6:20 - Sept. 23, 7:25

YOUR DRIVE AND AMBITION
Mars in Virgo, Aug. 23, 10:08 - Sept. 23, 7:25

YOUR LUCK MAGNETISM
Jupiter in Libra, Aug. 23, 10:08 - Sept. 23, 7:25

World Events

Aug. 29 - The U.S. Congress passes the Civil Rights Act.
Aug. 30 - Malaysia becomes an independent state.

Leonard Bernstein's "West Side Story" premieres in New York

LIBRA
Your Personal Planets

YOUR LOVE POTENTIAL
Venus in Scorpio, Sept. 23, 7:26 - Oct. 10, 1:15
Venus in Sagittarius, Oct. 10, 1:16 - Oct. 23, 16:23

YOUR DRIVE AND AMBITION
Mars in Virgo, Sept. 23, 7:26 - Sept. 24, 4:30
Mars in Libra, Sept. 24, 4:31 - Oct. 23, 16:23

YOUR LUCK MAGNETISM
Jupiter in Libra, Sept. 23, 7:26 - Oct. 23, 16:23

World Events

Sept. 26 - Leonard Bernstein's musical *West Side Story* premieres in New York.
Oct. 4 - The USSR launches *Sputnik 1*, the first artificial Earth satellite.

1957

SCORPIO
Your Personal Planets

YOUR LOVE POTENTIAL
Venus in Sagittarius, Oct. 23, 16:24 - Nov. 05, 23:45
Venus in Capricorn, Nov. 05, 23:46 - Nov. 22, 13:38

YOUR DRIVE AND AMBITION
Mars in Libra, Oct. 23, 16:24 - Nov. 08, 21:03
Mars in Scorpio, Nov. 08, 21:04 - Nov. 22, 13:38

YOUR LUCK MAGNETISM
Jupiter in Libra, Oct. 23, 16:24 - Nov. 22, 13:38

World Events

Oct. 24 - French fashion designer Christian Dior dies.

Nov. 3 - The USSR launches *Sputnik II*, containing the dog Laika.

"Sputnik II" is launched carrying a dog called Laika

SAGITTARIUS
Your Personal Planets

YOUR LOVE POTENTIAL
Venus in Capricorn, Nov. 22, 13:39 - Dec. 06, 15:25
Venus in Aquarius, Dec. 06, 15:26 - Dec. 22, 2:48

YOUR DRIVE AND AMBITION
Mars in Scorpio, Nov. 22, 13:39 - Dec. 22, 2:48

YOUR LUCK MAGNETISM
Jupiter in Libra, Nov. 22, 13:39 - Dec. 22, 2:48

World Events

Nov. 25 - Mexican artist Diego Rivera dies.

Dec. 18 - *Bridge On The River Kwai* premières at the Palace Theater in New York.

SCORPIO
From October 23, 16:24 through November 22, 13:38

The Powerful Reactor

Scorpio is considered to be one of the mightiest signs of the zodiac. What's interesting about the 1957 Scorpio is the degree to which you may direct your intense energy in affecting the lives of others. You can have an impact that enhances or detracts. The kind of potency you possess can go either way—the choice is yours.

Your sign is often linked to nuclear power. During your birth year, the nuclear energy industry expanded at a frenzied pace. In 1957, the Windscale nuclear plant in Britain had to shut down after a serious fire occurred. In that same year, the first large-scale nuclear plant began operating in Shippingport, Pennsylvania; the first nuclear chain-reaction took place in Brazil; and Japan produced the first current from its nuclear reactor. Your caretakers knew that all this power could change the world, for better or worse. This insight may have rubbed off on you. Indicators in your chart suggest an acute awareness of your own ability to affect people and situations in powerful and decisive ways.

Whatever your public reputation may be, intimate friends know you as a darling. You are likely to express empathy with and tolerance of those who are down-on-their luck. Your personal acquaintance with the extreme highs and lows in life may have intensified your capacity for compassion. You may even feel for the dog, Laika, who shot into space in your birth month, on a one-way voyage in Russia's *Sputnik II*, never to return to Earth. The Space Race was underway.

In 1957 America's magazine for the modern home, *Better Homes & Gardens*, printed its first microwave recipe. Today, a Cancerian may be the hot dish in your kitchen. Sympathetic Pisces brings out the best of your benevolence. Taurus provides stable grounding for your energy.

With potent resources at your disposal, your challenge is to share your power in love or business relationships. Let everyone benefit from your wealth in worldly goods or deep, psychological treasures. Your strength lies in bravely making dynamic transformations that will not only benefit your life, but the lives of others, too.

SAGITTARIUS
From November 22, 13:39 through December 22, 2:48

The Progressive Benefactor

A trailblazing Sagittarian is usually a step ahead of the crowd. As a 1957 Sagittarian, your trend-setting may extend to the wardrobe as well as the mind. At the time of your birth, fashion was evolving in exciting, daring, and revolutionary ways. French couturier Christian Dior died in 1957, not long after he came out with a new version of the above-the-knee, A-line dress. In the same year, English designer Mary Quant, godmother of the mini-skirt, opened her first boutique, Bazaar. She would influence fashion through the 1970s.

Beat writer Jack Kerouac would kick off an important social movement at the time of your birth. His infamous book, *On The Road*, was first published in 1957. The Beat Generation lived to be hip. Poetry, drugs, music, overt sexual experimentation, and even Zen Buddhism took them to "Antsville" (1950s-speak for a place with lots of people). You, too, tend to get your kicks from being around the *beau monde*. In your quest for knowledge, you may often gravitate to places with diverse people. You may pursue experiences that can stimulate your enquiring mind.

Another innovation during your birth year offers a potent symbol for the expansive reach of your mind. The world's first giant radio telescope opened at Jodrell Bank in the north of England. The powerful 250-ft telescope allowed unprecedented observations to be made, initiating further advances in mankind's knowledge of the stars.

Born under the sign of the Centaur—half-man, half-horse—you might enjoy a certain movie genre, the Western. In the mid-1950s, cowboy shows were all the rage on television, and your birth year marked the United States premier of *Wagon Train*. You may be happiest traveling into new frontiers with a fiery Aries or Leo by your side.

The sign of Sagittarius rules bachelorhood, and you may enjoy the freedom to go about your happy wanderings, unencumbered by marriage or children. Your challenge is to make meaningful connections while remaining true to yourself. You can develop your greatest potential through the give-and-take of loving relationships.

➤ Read about your Chinese Astrological sign on page 838. ➤ Read about your Personal Planets on page 826. ➤ Read about your personal Mystical Card on page 856.

CAPRICORN

From December 22, 2:49 through December 31, 23:59

The Considerate Teacher

While most Capricorns are interested in claiming new territories, the 1957 December Capricorn was born as old European empires crumbled and former colonial territories declared independence. Ghana, Tunisia, and Malaya all gained sovereignty in your birth year. You may also enjoy self-regulation and personal liberty. Wary about getting involved with others, you may prefer to take your time in getting to know people, before you'll invite them to become fast friends.

Capricorns tend to frown upon frivolity and tackiness, but you have a healthy sense of humor. You may find it amusing that the ultimate icon of American tackiness—the plastic Pink Flamingo—first graced a Florida homestead in 1957. You are likely to have an internal optimism that keeps you buoyant and fuels your drive and ambition. You may have a lot in common with fellow Capricorn Humphrey Bogart, whose hangdog expression masked his sassy style. This beloved Hollywood star, who passed away in 1957, may have appeared to be a jaded cynic, but he was actually deeply insightful and sensitive, just like you.

You were born at the height of the Cold War, when the Iron Curtain was firmly drawn across Eastern Europe. In 1957, both the U.S. and the USSR launched ICBMs, Inter-Continental Ballistic Missiles. The tension between the two countries was a constant presence in the daily news. You may pursue an interest in international affairs through education, travel, or your career.

With a mind to match the skill of a brilliant chess player, you can plan ahead with foresight and care. In 1957, Bobby Fischer became U.S. Open Chess Champion at the age of fourteen. You may take relationships seriously, but you appreciate the importance of having fun. In the game of love, Scorpio and Taurus can serve as friendly opponents. If you're looking to learn some new moves, you can rely on Cancer or Virgo.

You have the grace, wisdom, and compassion to understand other people's foibles. Your challenge is to be more forgiving of your own idiosyncrasies. With maturity you can recast setbacks and shortcomings as learning experiences.

CAPRICORN
Your Personal Planets

YOUR LOVE POTENTIAL
Venus in Aquarius, Dec. 22, 2:49 - Dec. 31, 23:59

YOUR DRIVE AND AMBITION
Mars in Scorpio, Dec. 22, 2:49 - Dec. 23, 1:28
Mars in Sagittarius, Dec. 23, 1:29 - Dec. 31, 23:59

YOUR LUCK MAGNETISM
Jupiter in Libra, Dec. 22, 2:49 - Dec. 31, 23:59

World Events

Dec. 25 – The Queen makes her first televised Christmas speech.

Dec. 27 – In tennis, Australia beats the U.S. to keep hold of The Davis Cup.

UFO in Ohio, 1966

Special Feature
The Extraterrestrial Highway: Exploring UFOs

(Continued from page 465)

To satisfy the public, the U.S. Air Force kept track of all credible UFO sightings, giving them various code names. By 1952, reports were coming in at an average of 150 a year. In all, roughly 700 reports were logged. Suddenly, during April and May of 1952, a surge in UFO sightings occurred, heralding

> The most astounding stories of activity occurred over Washington, DC, on the nights of July 19, July 26, and August 2, 1952. UFOs were seen flying over the White House, the Capitol, and the Pentagon.

the second wave of intense UFO activity. Reports poured in throughout June and July, by telephone, teletype, mail, and messenger service. Over 400 sightings were reported during July alone, some even from jet interceptor pilots responding to radar or visual sightings from the ground.

The most astounding stories of activity that year, however, occurred on the nights of July 19, July 26, and August 2, over Washington, D.C. UFOs were seen flying over the White House, the Capitol, and the Pentagon. They were tracked on radar from the ground and from flight control towers. The Air Force sent two fighter jets to chase them down, but the UFOs slipped away, only to reappear after the jets had landed. Military pilots estimated the crafts flew at speeds of 100 mph, but, in an instant, could accelerate to an unbelievable 2,100 mph.

After intense criticism, the Air Force finally held a press conference on July 29, 1952. Probably the most-asked question was how these UFOs could possibly have flown over the nation's capital. Attendance at the press conference was the highest since the war

years. The presiding officer, Air Force Intelligence Chief Major General John Samford, insisted that this most recent rash of sightings was caused by "an unusual temperature inversion," which is the same phenomenon that causes mirages. The press left the conference confused, but ufologists became more certain than ever that the government did indeed have a plan to cover up and discredit all sightings.

(Continued on page 481)

➤ Read "Ancient Secrets of the Egyptian Pyramids" by Jean Mars on page 305. ➤ Read "The Enigma of Crop Circles" by Frank Andrews on page 673.

1958

Drama and Peace: Jupiter Contacts

Expansive Jupiter made contact with all four of the outermost planets—Saturn, Uranus, Neptune, and Pluto—in 1958, and these interactions were played out on Earth in powerful and action-packed events. Jupiter made harmonious connections to Saturn, linked to business and government, and to Pluto, harbinger of change. Together, they represent the opportunity for easy transition to new forms in business and government and no one took better advantage of this impetus than Nikita Khrushchev. A bombastic and influential Soviet party leader, he had insinuated himself into increasingly powerful positions over the previous few years. With the promise to "conquer Capitalism" he wooed his way to the top slot in the country.

Jupiter did not quite connect with Uranus and Neptune until late summer. Uranus, the planet of shocking events, and Neptune, linked to loss of boundaries, symbolized the ongoing colonial crisis in Africa. This was played out in French-ruled Algeria, where unrest reached explosive levels in May, prompting the panicked French government to recall the great Charles de Gaulle to solve the problem. However, as Jupiter contacted these planets, the prevailing beneficent energies of the year reached this situation. De Gaulle astonished everyone with a plan to let Algeria and all other French colonies determine their future. In the fall, Jupiter carried to Neptune the positive structural changes suggested by its Saturn-Pluto contacts, signifying a harmonious loss of governmentalcontrol. This was shown in the Algerian vote for autonomy and the peace that ensued.

ELECTRONIC YOGA

Biofeedback research began when Joe Kamiya announced his hypothesis that people might be able to regulate and alter the physiological responses—such as heart rate and temperature—brought on by emotional states, by controlling their thoughts. This discipline became a therapeutic tool used in the treatment of a wide variety of psychological problems and symptoms. Sometimes called "electronic yoga," biofeedback proved very successful in reducing stress and anxiety as well as alleviating psychosomatic symptoms.

General de Gaulle becomes President of France

John XXIII becomes the new Pope

Boris Pasternak is forced to refuse the Nobel Prize for literature

KHRUSHCHEV REIGNS SUPREME

Fiery leader Khrushchev eclipsed Bulganin and became sole leader in Russia. The Russians lent Egypt $100,000 for the construction of the Aswan Dam on the Nile. As Algerian nationalists fought to oust their French colonial rulers, General de Gaulle was called in to solve the problem: he became President of France. Following the coup in pro-western Iraq, the U.S. sent troops to Lebanon to protect it from the same fate, angering Moscow. Pope Pius XII died, to be succeeded by John XXIII. In Baghdad, King Faisal of Iraq was murdered in a coup by army officers. Elvis Presley joined the army. The splendid steel-blue Hope Diamond was safely installed at the Smithsonian Institute after a checkered career in private ownership. Michigan's five-mile Mackinac Bridge, joining its upper and lower peninsulas, was named the world's longest suspension bridge. Boris Pasternak, Russian author of *Dr. Zhivago*, was coerced into refusing the Nobel Prize for literature. Thalidomide, used to counteract morning sickness, was condemned for causing severe birth defects in babies. Two British-born film actors, Ronald Colman and Robert Donat, died.

➤ Read "The Extraterrestrial Highway: Exploring UFOs" by Jean Mars on page 465.

CAPRICORN

From January 01, 0:00 through January 20, 13:27

The Disciplined Sage

Bringing people together to work in a structured and logical manner is a gift that Capricorns born in 1958 may enjoy. Within days of your birth, a new organization emerged to perform a similar function. On January 1, 1958, the European Economic Community officially opened for business. Seeking to promote balanced economic development, elevated living standards, and closer relations between member states, the EEC institutionalized the benefits of cooperation.

You are sensible and have an altruistic heart. You may also have a fascination for technology, such as television and the Internet. In your birth month, the U.S. Congress banned subliminal advertising, images flashed on a TV screen for 1/20th of a second. Experts claimed that such techniques could be used to brainwash the masses for political purposes. Also in 1958, Pope Pius XII declared St. Clare of Assisi to be the patron saint of television.

In popular culture, the late 1950s gave birth to "kitsch," the aesthetic of tackiness or "sickly sentimentality." Capricorns tend to have a taste for only the finest art, jewelry, or furniture, but campy kitsch may appeal to your wickedly ironic sense of humor. You may enjoy the old sci-fi B movies, such as 1958's *IT, The Terror From Beyond Space*. And you're not one to argue with the value of kitsch in retro collectables.

For a sign that is traditionally conservative, a part of you, 1958 January Capricorn, is surprisingly unconventional. You may enjoy bizarre or fanciful diversions. In January 1958, e.e. cummings, famous in part for using small letters in his name and for his whimsical works, won the Bollingen Prize for poetry. A Sagittarian or Pisces can understand your sometimes eccentric point of view. A Taurus or Virgo, on the other hand, may relate to your old-fashioned side.

Your challenge is to take complex and sometimes conflicting ideas and influences and to recast them in productive applications. Perseverance, discipline, and wisdom are strengths that enable you to make positive progress that can affect not only your life, but also the lives of many others.

AQUARIUS

From January 20, 13:28 through February 19, 3:47

The Exciting Explorer

Aquarians tend to fall into two categories: one is traditional and sticks to the tried and tested; the other can be rebellious and innovative. Because you are likely to propose interesting new ideas that galvanize others into action, you may belong to the latter group.

With its modern outlook, Aquarius of 1958 has the ability to come up with exciting new propositions. When you mention your ideas, others may smack their heads and shout, "Why didn't I think of that!" Many of the events of your birth year may excite your expansive and enquiring imagination. 1958 saw the formation of the National Aeronautics and Space Administration, in direct competition with Russia. In your birth month, the United States won a lap in the Space Race, as NASA successfully launched *Explorer 1*. This satellite provided evidence that Earth was surrounded by the Van Allen radiation belts, named for the man who designed *Explorer's* instrumentation.

The best of your unique personality comes out in relationships. Being with loved ones brings out your talents and humanitarian nature. Fellow Aquarian Paul Newman had an especially good year in 1958. He won the Cannes Film Festival's Best Actor award for *The Long Hot Summer* and was nominated for an Oscar for *Cat On A Hot Tin Roof*. Newman also married Joanne Woodward in your birth month. Nominated for seven more Oscars during his long acting career, he went on to serve humanitarian causes. Newman donated the profits from his gourmet food business to worthy charities, such as African drought relief and treatment for alcoholism.

Aquarian Newman and Piscean Woodward celebrated their fortieth wedding anniversary in 1998. You, too, may find Pisces a loving partner. Adventurous Sagittarians, loving Librans, and intellectual Geminis like your wild ideas.

Your greatest challenge is to create change while keeping the potential for chaos to a minimum. Some old orders may need disrupting, but you may need to moderate any desire for instant results. You can inspire personal or public revolution when you communicate objectively. A clear and concise mind is your strength.

➤ Read about your Chinese Astrological sign on page 838. ➤ Read about your Personal Planets on page 826. ➤ Read about your personal Mystical Card on page 856.

CAPRICORN
Your Personal Planets

YOUR LOVE POTENTIAL
Venus in Aquarius, Jan. 01, 0:00 - Jan. 20, 13:27

YOUR DRIVE AND AMBITION
Mars in Sagittarius, Jan. 01, 0:00 - Jan. 20, 13:27

YOUR LUCK MAGNETISM
Jupiter in Libra, Jan. 01, 0:00 - Jan. 13, 12:51
Jupiter in Scorpio, Jan. 13, 12:52 - Jan. 20, 13:27

World Events

Jan. 3 - Britain establishes the West Indian federation.

Jan. 4 - *Sputnik I* burns up as it reenters Earth's atmosphere.

Dr. George Hass inspects the U.S.'s first satellite "Explorer I"

AQUARIUS
Your Personal Planets

YOUR LOVE POTENTIAL
Venus in Aquarius, Jan. 20, 13:28 - Feb. 19, 3:47

YOUR DRIVE AND AMBITION
Mars in Sagittarius, Jan. 20, 13:28 - Feb. 03, 18:56
Mars in Capricorn, Feb. 03, 18:57 - Feb. 19, 3:47

YOUR LUCK MAGNETISM
Jupiter in Scorpio, Jan. 20, 13:28 - Feb. 19, 3:47

World Events

Jan. 29 - Actors Paul Newman and Joanne Woodward wed.

Jan. 31 - The U.S. launches its first artificial satellite, *Explorer 1*.

1958

PISCES
Your Personal Planets

YOUR LOVE POTENTIAL
Venus in Aquarius, Feb. 19, 3:48 - Mar. 21, 3:05

YOUR DRIVE AND AMBITION
Mars in Capricorn, Feb. 19, 3:48 - Mar. 17, 7:10
Mars in Aquarius, Mar. 17, 7:11 - Mar. 21, 3:05

YOUR LUCK MAGNETISM
Jupiter in Scorpio, Feb. 19, 3:48 - Mar. 20, 19:13
Jupiter in Libra, Mar. 20, 19:14 - Mar. 21, 3:05

World Events

Feb. 23 - Five-times world driving champion Juan Fangio is kidnapped by Cuban rebels.

Mar. 19 - Nationalist China breaks off trade relations with Japan over its dealings with the Communists.

World champion racing driver Juan Manuel Fangio

ARIES
Your Personal Planets

YOUR LOVE POTENTIAL
Venus in Aquarius, Mar. 21, 3:06 - Apr. 06, 15:59
Venus in Pisces, Apr. 06, 16:00 - Apr. 20, 14:26

YOUR DRIVE AND AMBITION
Mars in Aquarius, Mar. 21, 3:06 - Apr. 20, 14:26

YOUR LUCK MAGNETISM
Jupiter in Libra, Mar. 21, 3:06 - Apr. 20, 14:26

World Events

Mar. 24 - Elvis Presley joins the army.

Apr. 14 - *Sputnik II*, with dog Laika on board, burns up in the atmosphere.

PISCES
From February 19, 3:48 through March 21, 3:05

The Perceptive Scientist

Pisceans tend to be aware of situations before they happen. While a 1958 Pisces may deny having psychic abilities, you are likely to have deep sensitivity that can evolve into a finely-tuned intuition or even extra-sensory perception. With practice, you can increase your conscious attunement with signals others tend to miss.

In 1958, the Nobel Prize for physics went to Soviet scientists for their contribution to the cosmic-ray counter, a technology ultimately used in satellites. The physicists clarified method for detecting particles zooming through a medium, faster than the speed of light. Picking up energy from outer space may be out of your league, but your ability to sit next to someone and sense the way they feel can be all too real.

A 1958 Pisces may often take a feeling, a dream, or a gut impulse and make it into something real. In your birth month, a group of British geologists crossed the surface of the Antarctic in ninety-nine days. The adventure produced not only discoveries but also the fulfillment of a dream. Another exploratory voyage took place in 1958, at the other pole, as the nuclear missile submarine, USS *Nautilus*, prowled under the Arctic icecap. You, too, can be a bit like that Arctic icecap, as you sometimes put up a cool front that covers deep undercurrents of unfathomable feelings.

The symbol for the sign of Pisces is the Fish. In 1958, the film, *South Pacific* triggered a fashion trend in Hawaiian shirts. In the U.S. tropical fish were voted the most popular house pet of the year. You could while away the hours watching the multi-colored flow of an exotic fish-tank, should you make a home with Cancer. Because Scorpio's still waters run deep, a relationship with the Scorpion can help you get in touch with your intuitive perception.

When intense, momentous feelings rise up deep within you, your challenge is to fearlessly delve into them. Doing so can empower you to transform your life, by developing greater self knowledge and inner strength. By taking command of your instinctive gifts, you can become capable of astonishing creativity.

ARIES
From March 21, 3:06 through April 20, 14:26

The Game-Playing Guide

If anyone is bold enough to hold their nose and jump into the unknown, Aries is. While you, 1958 Aries, are just as brave, you may be a little more circumspect. You may test situations and ask for relevant facts before you act. Born at the time of China's Great Leap Forward, you may have been taught the dangers of rushing into action without regard for the consequences. Mao Tse-Tung's policy of organizing millions of people into farming communes, combined with a drought, resulted in a terrible famine. By the early 1960s, twenty million Chinese faced starvation.

Like most Ariens, you can be impatient and impulsive, easily distracted by novelties and fads. You have plenty of energy to burn. Exercise can help you relieve excess tension and regain a clearer perspective on any business at hand. During your childhood, you may have taken advantage of an innovative toy that came on the market in 1958—the skateboard. At a time when surf music was also a new craze, the skateboard enabled California surfers to test their skills when they couldn't go into the water.

You may gravitate to social events, where you can enjoy an endless stream of new people to talk to and befriend. If you joined the military, you may have made some of your closest friends during your tours of service. During your birth month, Elvis, the king of rock 'n' roll, enlisted as a G.I.

Egalitarian values may govern the division of roles in your personal relationships. You may seek to connect with someone who will enjoy an action-packed lifestyle. Gemini offers fast-paced fun. Sagittarius enjoys a hearty competition. And loyal Leo just loves to play. You might make a good match with a Scorpio, like the great footballer Pelé, who won his first World Cup in 1958. The Scorpion could share strategic moves with you.

When unfinished thoughts whir through your mind, others may find it hard to keep up with you. Your challenge is to bring ideas and situations to a conclusion. You have wonderful people skills and the ability to communicate clearly. Take time to let these strengths emerge and you'll enjoy success.

➤ Read about your Chinese Astrological sign on page 838. ➤ Read about your Personal Planets on page 826. ➤ Read about your personal Mystical Card on page 856.

TAURUS

From April 20, 14:27 through May 21, 13:50

The Tender Pioneer

Taureans born in 1958 can be more sensitive to people's feelings than other Bulls. You have a mega-kind heart, and you may be a little impulsive at times and restlessness is one thing that can lead you astray.

You may need to learn to focus on your aspirations more intently. Mulling things over is a classic Taurean method for centering yourself and building concentration. Centering yourself over a good meal is another option for the pleasure-loving Bull. Frank and Dan Carney made food history in your birth year: borrowing $600 from their mother, they opened the first Pizza Hut in Kansas and triggered a teenage passion. The year marked the television debut of the Jolly Green Giant, complete with his famous tag, "Ho, ho, ho! Good things come from the garden!" Earthy Taureans often have green thumbs of their own. Your garden goodies may beat anything you could fetch from your grocer's freezer.

Many Taureans have a creative side. In 1958, Orson Welles made the *film noir* production *A Touch Of Evil*. Famed for its legendary opening sequence lasting over three minutes, Welles pioneered the use of a camera-crane tracking shot and panoramic vision. Critics marveled as the film followed the heroes, Charlton Heston and Janet Leigh, through a seedy Mexican border town. *Touch Of Evil* was also noted for its advocacy of civil rights. You may follow Welles' visionary example in creativity and social justice.

Keeping equality in mind, you may be in touch with your feminine side, even if you're a guy! You may be pleased to know that Spain finally recognized women's right to own their own property in your birth month. Although traditional, you're not that old-fashioned. Capricorn, Cancer, or Scorpio could share a happy homestead with you.

You tend to work hard, even doggedly, to reach a cherished goal. Your challenge is to be flexible with plans and people without losing sight of your target. Your strength lies in the fact that you come from the heart. Your devotion to your projects enables you to build firm foundations that can endure.

GEMINI

From May 21, 13:51 through June 21, 21:56

The Mercurial Pioneer

Born under the sign of the Twins, Gemini of 1958 has twice the wit, character, and charm of the rest of humanity. The first stereo recording was made in 1958, bringing twice the music to everyone's ears. The gramophone industry produced 45 rpm singles and 33 rpm long-playing record albums by artists such as Peggy Lee, Little Richard, Eddie Cochran, Sam Cooke, Miles Davis, and Smokey Robinson and The Miracles. By 1958 sales of 78m rpm albums had dropped precipitously. The 45 rpm single was the new popular hit.

Musical talent abounded in your birth year. In 1958 your caretakers may have rock 'n' rolled to Chuck Berry's "Sweet Little Sixteen." Berry's influence certainly rubbed off on another Gemini born in 1958—the artist now known as Prince was born on June 7, 1958. You may share Prince's love of music. In another musical sign of the times, the tools of the music trade struck another deep chord in 1958: the famous Les Paul model of Gibson guitars made its market debut, to the delight of strummers everywhere.

Your forward-thinking mind may have earned you a place in the vanguard of your generation. Although you tend to go with the thought-flow, you can change your plans in midstream. NASA's Project Mercury, initiated in 1958, was subject to some mercurial flux (Mercury is Gemini's ruling planet). The objective was to put a man in space, orbit the Earth, and safely delivered him back home, all within two years. It took twice as long, however, to reach that goal.

In your personal affairs, Librans or Aquarians are compatible free spirits, willing to join you in riding the wind, wherever it may blow. A Sagittarian could really take you places, however, as you share a love of travel and intellectual pursuits.

Born under the speediest sign of the zodiac, you may need to develop patience in your relationships and business affairs. When you present your ideas in a logical, patient manner, you stand a greater chance of gaining support. Boundless energy enhances your versatile mind. Adapting to accommodate the need of other enables you to gain trust, influence, and authority.

➤ Read about your Chinese Astrological sign on page 838. ➤ Read about your Personal Planets on page 826. ➤ Read about your personal Mystical Card on page 856.

1958

TAURUS
Your Personal Planets

YOUR LOVE POTENTIAL
Venus in Pisces, Apr. 20, 14:27 - May 05, 11:58
Venus in Aries, May 05, 11:59 - May 21, 13:50

YOUR DRIVE AND AMBITION
Mars in Aquarius, Apr. 20, 14:27 - Apr. 27, 2:30
Mars in Pisces, Apr. 27, 2:31 - May 21, 13:50

YOUR LUCK MAGNETISM
Jupiter in Libra, Apr. 20, 14:27 - May 21, 13:50

World Events

May 13 – French forces take control of Algiers.

May 20 – The Austin Healey Sprite is launched in Britain by the BMC.

French soldiers in Algiers

GEMINI
Your Personal Planets

YOUR LOVE POTENTIAL
Venus in Aries, May 21, 13:51 - June 01, 4:06
Venus in Taurus, June 01, 4:07 - June 21, 21:56

YOUR DRIVE AND AMBITION
Mars in Pisces, May 21, 13:51 - June 07, 6:20
Mars in Aries, June 07, 6:21 - June 21, 21:56

YOUR LUCK MAGNETISM
Jupiter in Libra, May 21, 13:51 - June 21, 21:56

World Events

June 1 – French premier Charles de Gaulle is called in to deal with the escalating problems in Algiers.

June 16 – Hungarian premier Imre Nagy dies.

1958

CANCER
Your Personal Planets

YOUR LOVE POTENTIAL
Venus in Taurus, June 21, 21:57 - June 26, 23:07
Venus in Gemini, June 26, 23:08 - July 22, 5:25
Venus in Cancer, July 22, 5:26 - July 23, 8:49

YOUR DRIVE AND AMBITION
Mars in Aries, June 21, 21:57 - July 21, 7:02
Mars in Taurus, July 21, 7:03 - July 23, 8:49

YOUR LUCK MAGNETISM
Jupiter in Libra, June 21, 21:57 - July 23, 8:49

World Events

June 28 - Pélé helps Brazil win the soccer World Cup in Sweden.

July 23 - The first women to be elected to the peerage are announced in Britain.

Pélé weeps as Brazil beats Sweden 5-2 in the World Cup final

LEO
Your Personal Planets

YOUR LOVE POTENTIAL
Venus in Cancer, July 23, 8:50 - Aug. 16, 1:27
Venus in Leo, Aug. 16, 1:28 - Aug. 23, 15:45

YOUR DRIVE AND AMBITION
Mars in Taurus, July 23, 8:50 - Aug. 23, 15:45

YOUR LUCK MAGNETISM
Jupiter in Libra, July 23, 8:50 - Aug. 23, 15:45

World Events

Aug. 16 - "Like A Virgin" pop singer Madonna is born.

Aug. 18 - Vladimir Nabokov's controversial novel *Lolita* is published in the U.S.

478

CANCER
From June 21, 21:57 through July 23, 8:49

The Lighthearted Authority

Most Cancerians are ambitious in their own unique way. Go-getting 1958 Cancer is special because you have goals and the turbo-charged drive to go the top, via the fastest, most direct route possible. Unless, that is, you get distracted. Sometimes Cancer can lose forward momentum and sidestep into trivial matters. In that case, your dreams may trail behind you when you could be blazing trails instead.

You may have oodles of style and an enchanting capacity for wit. If you also like to be enchanted, take note of Truman Capote's heroine in *Breakfast At Tiffany's*, published in your birth year. Flashy and flippant, Holly Golightly is always looking for the real thing—love. Casual relationships may hold a certain appeal, and you may enjoy water-cooler chatter. As Miss Golightly learned, an attractive face may be alluring, but beauty is only skin-deep. And it fades.

You are likely to be a romantic at heart. Endowed with generous helpings of charm and persuasiveness, you have the ability to get whatever you're after in life. You tend to hang on tenaciously until you reach your goals. Brave and fearless, you can hold your own in any battle. You're also a powerful ally. It may interest you to know that Eisenhower, at President Chamoun's request, sent the U.S. Marines into Lebanon in July 1958 to help re-establish the government after civil war had broken out.

Yet for all your verve and vitality, you can sometimes be a Cancerian chocoholic! Nearly all Cancerians have a sweet tooth. Thanks to the 1958 introduction of Sweet & Low, you can indulge your cravings, without paying an enormous price in excess calories. Taurus may share your love of all things naughty but nice. Pisces and Scorpio can understand the seemingly unfathomable emotions that can sometimes engulf you.

Your tough Cancerian shell is there to protect you, not to keep others from reaching the true you. Your challenge is to know the right time to wear or shed your armor. Maturity and experience can help you learn to listen to your gut reactions. Your own instincts will tell you who and what you can trust.

LEO
From July 23, 8:50 through August 23, 15:45

The Entertaining Investor

Hip-swinging, cool-talking, finger-snapping Leo! With style and panache, the 1958 Leo can have it all—a whole lot of soul, looks, brains, and the ability to make bundles of lovely loot!

One side of you can be playful, but another tends to be cautious—repeatedly reviewing plans and double-checking your progress. Too much worry can take the zing out of a naturally colorful lifestyle and may ultimately defeat your purposes. The characters of *77 Sunset Strip*, a television detective show that debuted in 1958, seemed to strike the right balance between fun and responsibility. The young private eyes rode around in brand-new sports cars and hung out in a rat-pack bar. For them, life was a caper, with cases that needed to be solved.

You may be drawn to the exotic or groovy, and perhaps you pay for your leonine escapades with plastic. In 1958 Visa and American Express launched their credit facilities, although you may prefer cold, hard cash. You're likely to have a gift for handling money. Not only can you make investments wisely, with an eye to future returns, but you're also likely to invest in items that you actually like. Another famous Leo of 1958, the singer Madonna, follows this asset-management pattern. Leos tend to appreciate art. Along with her traditional investments in real estate, Madonna collects modern paintings. Interestingly, one of Madonna's dance teachers, noted choreographer Alvin Ailey, started the American Dance Theatre in 1958.

Like Madonna, you like to be the undisputed boss. You thrive when working with others. Glamour comes naturally to you, and you may dream of walking down a runway to an awards ceremony, escorted of course by an equally glamorous partner. The very first Grammy was awarded in your birth year. You might belt out "Volare"—voted 1958's Best Single, with a loved one, preferably an Arien or Sagittarian.

Your challenge, 1958 Leo, is to have a deeply loving relationship in which both partners can nurture and express your unique identities. With your kind heart, smart mind, and plenty of talent, meeting this challenge will be fun!

► Read about your Chinese Astrological sign on page 838. ► Read about your Personal Planets on page 826. ► Read about your personal Mystical Card on page 856.

VIRGO

From August 23, 15:46 through September 23, 13:08

The Positive Perfectionist

With the ability to classify and analyze, a 1958 Virgo can be an asset to any company. You may be a bit of a worrier, but you're not too shy to ask for help when you need it. To deal with anxiety, you may be a list-maker par excellence. You know that order makes sense. On the whole, you're cheerful. Even when you're feeling apprehensive, you're likely to muster a smile. Because Virgos tend to be nature lovers, you may get a kick out of Chlorophyll Toothpaste, a green gel that became popular in the late fifties.

Rarely do you take things on face value. You're likely to believe that certain situations need constant appraisal to make sure they are still viable. Your penchant for criticism may kick in when people in authority, for whatever reason, get something wrong. In 1958, the Dean of UCLA declared that nuclear radiation had little chance of causing leukemia, cancer, or tumors. Health is an area of interest to most Virgos. A breakthrough in the field of medicine took place in 1958: a team of American scientists won the Nobel Prize for their discovery of the role of genes in the transmission of hereditary characteristics.

The threat of nuclear war loomed in 1958, and the Cold War may have had a profound effect upon your caretakers. It is likely that the era you were born in left an uneasy impression upon your psyche. People in western countries became very alarmed in 1958, not only because China mounted a heavy artillery bombardment against Taiwan, but also because China built its first heavy-water nuclear reactor.

When the balance of power shifts at work or at home, you may do your best to keep any crazed dramatics to a minimum. You tend to aim for perfect harmony, even when your chances for complete success are remote. You may appreciate art, nature, and beauty. A Taurean or Capricorn who shares these affinities can make a wonderful partner.

Your challenge is to take pride in all you do. Your active mind enables you to see a variety of alternatives. Your gifts of discernment empower you to reject negative self-deprecation and embrace endearing, positive modesty.

LIBRA

From September 23, 13:09 through October 23, 22:10

The Objective Mind

Most Librans enjoy a certain intellectual sophistication. As a 1958 Libra, you may be a culture vulture—as much at ease with street-savvy pop as you are with high art. As such, you're probably a mine of information; a walking encyclopedia, with an admiration for works of art that show a unique understanding of human relationships.

Author Boris Pasternak showed this sensitivity to the human condition. He won the Nobel Prize for literature in 1958 for the classic *Dr. Zhivago*. In this absorbing study of relationships during the Russian Revolution, Pasternak told the story of a man, his family, and his lover as they struggled through the chaos and violence surrounding them. As if to realize and compound the fictionalized suffering, the Soviet government forced Pasternak to refuse his prize.

Unfairness disturbs your higher sensibilities. Injustice can spur you into action. At some time in your life, you may be called upon to make judgments or to help build bridges between groups. The civil rights movement had begun its turbulent evolution. Martin Luther King, Jr. was stabbed at a book signing. In the UK, horrendous race riots took place in Notting Hill, London. Racial tension was deepening in South Africa. Your sympathy goes out to those who deal with discrimination, even today. The cause of gender equality took a turn for the better in 1958; for the first time, women were allowed to enter Britain's House of Lords.

Caring about others is a Libran gift, but overemphasis on your partner can strain intimate affairs. Your most successful relationships involve a fair balance that allows you to express and satisfy your own needs, too. Aquarius and Leo can be trustworthy friends as well as lovers. Exchanging ideas with Geminis can be stimulating as the Twins tend to bring out your competitive side.

You tend to exercise leadership authority in a way that wins the admiration and loyalty of those who follow you. Your greatest challenge is to wield power with impartiality, while developing your deeply spiritual nature. Your Libran sensibility helps you strike the right balance.

➤ Read about your Chinese Astrological sign on page 838. ➤ Read about your Personal Planets on page 826. ➤ Read about your personal Mystical Card on page 856.

1958

VIRGO
Your Personal Planets

YOUR LOVE POTENTIAL
Venus in Leo, Aug. 23, 15:46 - Sept. 09, 12:34
Venus in Virgo, Sept. 09, 12:35 - Sept. 23, 13:08

YOUR DRIVE AND AMBITION
Mars in Taurus, Aug. 23, 15:46 - Sept. 21, 5:25
Mars in Gemini, Sept. 21, 5:26 - Sept. 23, 13:08

YOUR LUCK MAGNETISM
Jupiter in Libra, Aug. 23, 15:46 - Sept. 07, 8:51
Jupiter in Scorpio, Sept. 07, 8:52 - Sept. 23, 13:08

World Events

Sept. 5 - Boris Pasternak's *Doctor Zhivago* is published in the U.S.

Sept. 12 - The U.S. Supreme Court orders integration at the high school at Little Rock, Arkansas.

Boris Pasternak, author of "Doctor Zhivago"

LIBRA
Your Personal Planets

YOUR LOVE POTENTIAL
Venus in Virgo, Sept. 23, 13:09 - Oct. 03, 16:43
Venus in Libra, Oct. 03, 16:44 - Oct. 23, 22:10

YOUR DRIVE AND AMBITION
Mars in Gemini, Sept. 23, 13:09 - Oct. 23, 22:10

YOUR LUCK MAGNETISM
Jupiter in Scorpio, Sept. 23, 13:09 - Oct. 23, 22:10

World Events

Oct. 1 - The U.S. National Aeronautical and Space Administration (NASA) is inaugurated.

Oct. 9 - Pope Pius XII dies after suffering a stroke.

1958

SCORPIO
Your Personal Planets

YOUR LOVE POTENTIAL
Venus in Libra, Oct. 23, 22:11 - Oct. 27, 16:25
Venus in Scorpio, Oct. 27, 16:26 - Nov. 20, 13:58
Venus in Sagittarius, Nov. 20, 13:59 - Nov. 22, 19:28

YOUR DRIVE AND AMBITION
Mars in Gemini, Oct. 23, 22:11 - Oct. 29, 0:00
Mars in Taurus, Oct. 29, 0:01 - Nov. 22, 19:28

YOUR LUCK MAGNETISM
Jupiter in Scorpio, Oct. 23, 22:11 - Nov. 22, 19:28

World Events

Oct. 28 – Angello Giuseppe Roncalli is elected Pope John XXIII.

Oct. 29 – Boris Pasternak refuses to accept the Nobel Prize for literature under pressure from Soviet authorities.

New Pope: John XXIII

SAGITTARIUS
Your Personal Planets

YOUR LOVE POTENTIAL
Venus in Sagittarius, Nov. 22, 19:29 - Dec. 14, 10:54
Venus in Capricorn, Dec. 14, 10:55 - Dec. 22, 8:39

YOUR DRIVE AND AMBITION
Mars in Taurus, Nov. 22, 19:29 - Dec. 22, 8:39

YOUR LUCK MAGNETISM
Jupiter in Scorpio, Nov. 22, 19:29 - Dec. 22, 8:39

World Events

Nov. 30 – Khrushchev attends the opening of the Hungarian Party Congress in Budapest.

Dec. 4 – The USSR and Japan sign a new trade agreement, promising a twenty-five per cent increase by the end of the decade.

480

SCORPIO
From October 23, 22:11 through November 22, 19:28

The Sparkling Gem

While Scorpios are generally recognized to be powerful and full of insight, a 1958 Scorpio positively takes command by firing on all cylinders. With dynamic high-octane energy, you rarely waste fuel upon meaningless activity. You've got places to go, people to see, and a waiting world to explore.

Whether for business or pleasure, you are likely to travel more than most Scorpios. Travel technology took a dramatic leap forward when you were an infant. In 1958 the first passenger jet, the Boeing 707, crossed the Atlantic from bustling New York to glamorous Paris. Also in 1958, the air force introduced the Phantom aircraft. Able to serve as both an interceptor and a ground support bomber, the Phabulous Phantom remained in use until 1996, after many successful missions.

You are likely to be optimistic, even lucky. In the course of your life, you may encounter sudden opportunities to broaden your horizons, through foreign travel or by studying and taking classes. You may see yourself as the perennial student, always exploring and investigating a variety of subjects. Scorpios tend to be talented researchers. You may be fearless about delving into the underworld and rummaging for buried treasures. Your sign is associated with minerals, rocks, and supernatural powers. In 1958 the notorious Hope Diamond was donated to the Smithsonian museum. Originating in seventeenth-century India, this 45-carat gem was reputed to bring tragedy to each of its owners.

You have the potential to make good money, and you may treat loved ones as precious possessions. You may sympathize with the heroine of the 1958 Oscar-winning film Gigi. Based on a novel by Colette, the film tells of a girl raised to be a courtesan but who chooses marriage. In making your choices in love, you can enjoy romance and companionship with a Cancer or a Pisces.

Freedom in relationships is important to you. Your challenge is to express your passions while avoiding intense drama. You have the strength and determination to create open, honest, and sincere partnerships that offer the depth, trust, and happiness you seek.

SAGITTARIUS
From November 22, 19:29 through December 22, 8:39

The Visionary Itinerant

With an enduring love of travel, either in the world or in the mind, most Sagittarians enjoy the free-flowing lessons that materialize when they're on the road. As a 1958 Sagittarian, you can take this desire for mind-expansion even further and become a truth-seeker.

With that aim in sight, timing is the key to your success. As your mind processes thoughts quickly, 1958 Sagittarius, you may need to slow down now and then. Because you may tend to move on too soon and too quickly, you may miss the benefits of the moment unfolding before you. Sometimes you need to pull over and park or stable the horses—to use 1950s parlance—and ponder the universal truths that fascinate you. By strange coincidence, parking meters were introduced in the UK in 1958 and in the same year, drive-in movies reached their all-time peak in popularity in the U.S. Wherever you may go, you may sometimes need to find a place where you can hide away and philosophize to your hearts content.

Members of your sign tend to take a broad perspective on international affairs. One Sagittarian saw the bigger picture from a political point of view. In 1958 the illustrious statesman Charles de Gaulle became President of France. During his term in office, de Gaulle addressed the Algerian question. After a series of diplomatic journeys, de Gaulle offered a "peace of the brave." He proposed independence for Algeria. Like de Gaulle, who was a soldier, writer, statesman, and architect of France's Fifth Republic, you are also capable of playing many different roles.

Because you enjoy travel and varied experiences, you rarely stay in one place for too long. You will do best by choosing partners who will not feel offended when you take off on journeys. A relationship with an Aries or Gemini accords you ample freedom of movement. Leo shares your joy of learning and discovery.

Ultimately, your challenge is to develop patience and discipline in all you do. While you have everyone's highest good in mind, by using the knowledge you spend your life seeking, you have the strength to make an effective mark upon society.

➤ Read about your Chinese Astrological sign on page 838. ➤ Read about your Personal Planets on page 826. ➤ Read about your personal Mystical Card on page 856.

CAPRICORN

From December 22, 8:40 through December 31, 23:59

The Practical Philosopher

People tend to put a great deal of responsibility upon Capricorns, and 1958 Capricorn is no exception. The difference is that while other Mountain Goats may feel burdened, you take it in your stride. While you may still feel the weight, it doesn't distract you from taking your duty seriously.

Indeed, you're deeply philosophical about most things in life. You were born in a year that, like most, had its highs and lows. It had been a difficult year in the U.S.: Nixon had a disastrous foreign tour, unemployment was up, and, along with the rest of the world, your caretakers looked on anxiously as Fidel Castro led a rebel movement in waging guerrilla warfare, including political kidnappings, in Cuba.

It was the middle of the Cold War. Countries with nuclear missiles had drafted an approved Test Ban Treaty, and the world heaved a sigh of relief, praying they would never again see an atomic bomb, let alone a nuclear one. Knowing all this could have led to a sensible upbringing, so the saner aspect of your personality had the opportunity to develop alongside your accepting nature. In 1958, good news came from space; America's Earth-orbiting satellite was successfully launched and new horizons beckoned. A Christmas message from President Eisenhower, the first voice in space, echoed over the globe. Your actions also have far-reaching effects. Like the space scientists, you see things through a telescopic lens. Understanding the paucity of life, you can put your troubles into perspective, particularly when you consider the greater scheme of things.

You tend to inspire, and be inspired by, fellow truth seekers, such as Sagittarius or Aquarius. Yet it is with more gentle folk, such as Cancer, Taurus, or Virgo, that you might find a furrowed brow soothed.

You're a pragmatist who asks big questions. The challenge is to find answers to uncertainties: Why are we here? Where did we come from? Where are we going? Life is no small task for you, then, but you have an ability to approach it in an organized manner and with a smile on your face. Ultimately, this is a mighty strength.

1958

CAPRICORN
Your Personal Planets

YOUR LOVE POTENTIAL
Venus in Capricorn, Dec. 22, 8:40 - Dec. 31, 23:59

YOUR DRIVE AND AMBITION
Mars in Taurus, Dec. 22, 8:40 - Dec. 31, 23:59

YOUR LUCK MAGNETISM
Jupiter in Scorpio, Dec. 22, 8:40 - Dec. 31, 23:59

World Events

Dec. 22 – The USSR agrees to send aid to the United Arab Republic.

Dec. 27 – Cuban rebel Che Guevara and his rebel forces attack Santa Clara.

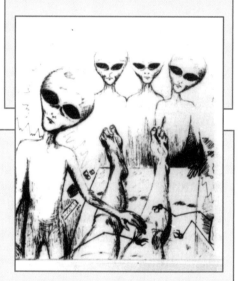

Illustration of aliens drawn by abducted people

Special Feature
The Extraterrestrial Highway: Exploring UFOs

(Continued from page 473)

More waves of sightings occurred, and continue to this day. However, the most startling story of all describes actual alien bodies found near the crash site at Roswell, which were said to have undergone autopsies at the hands of government agents. The creatures were amazingly similar to the "aliens" familiar to movie-watchers the world over, with large, gray heads, small bodies, and huge, dark eyes. In January 1953, according to actual documents released under the Freedom of Information Act, the CIA created a secret panel of five prominent scientists to discuss the UFO situation. Establishing the Robertson Panel, as it came to be called, was the first of many steps taken by the U.S. government to debunk the sightings, despite reputable witnesses and photographic evidence that continue to emerge.

Ufologists point out that both the Roswell incident and the Arnold sighting took place around facilities related to the army's top-secret "Manhattan Project." Roswell was home to an army air force facility, which at the time was the only military base on the planet with the capacity to actually detonate an atom bomb. Central Washington state, where Kenneth Arnold was when he flew over those nine shining discs, is the home of Hanford, where plutonium for "the bomb" was then being produced.

Area 51, located ninety-five miles north of Las Vegas, is a testing ground for top-secret military aircraft, but ufologists believe that to this day, the U.S. Air Force stores its downed UFOs there. In 1989, Bob Lazar came forward to tell the story of his part in helping to dismantle and reverse-engineer a UFO in a secret underground complex near Area 51. The U.S. government officially disavows any knowledge, but private individuals as well as media news teams continue to videotape

brightly-lit craft in the night sky that demonstrate fantastic maneuverability, far beyond even the most sophisticated of military aircraft. So many sightings were reported in this area that in 1996, Nevada's governor officially renamed the desolate stretch "The Extraterrestrial Highway."

In the more than fifty years since the Roswell Incident, this and other UFO sightings continue to mystify and amaze even the hardiest of skeptics. Still, UFO believers hold conferences worldwide, Internet sites attract tens of thousands every month, and membership in organizations such as MUFON (Mutual UFO Network, Inc.) is on the increase. Meanwhile, UFO sightings continue. ☉

➤ Read "Ancient Secrets of the Egyptian Pyramids" by Jean Mars on page 305. ➤ Read "The Enigma of Crop Circles" by Frank Andrews on page 673.

1959

Stability and Progress: Saturn in Capricorn

It was difficult to imagine life getting any better in western society in 1959. Although bad news could be found, it was hard to focus on it when there was so much to celebrate. French leader Charles de Gaulle reigned over a peaceful French community. The U.S. welcomed the hottest and coldest states into its union: Hawaii and Alaska. The Hula-Hoop had kids and adults doing cartwheels in Australia and America, and both the U.S. and Soviets pushed the envelope in space. These were all manifestations related to the placement of Saturn in Capricorn and its links to other planets. Saturn's expression is especially harmonious in Capricorn. Saturn is tied to structures both external and internal, from governments and institutions to manmade and scientific laws. Capricorn is expressed in the administration of laws and the establishment of structures to create stability, so Saturn in this sign can be expressed fully and easily.

What's more, Saturn made ease-inducing contacts with both Neptune and Pluto in 1959. Neptune, the ancient god of the seas, signifies the subtle influences around us. Pluto represents hidden, powerful forces of humanity and nature that periodically well up to the surface of our experiences to create great change. With Saturn making flowing contacts to each of these planets, people tended to feel a sense of general well-being, since both subtle and dramatic changes occurred without crisis.

Yet, this combination also permitted insidious difficulties to grow, as they slipped unnoticed by people eager for peace. Tibetans rose up against occupying Chinese forces but were brutally put down, culminating in the flight of the Dalai Lama to India. The growing strength of Communism was masked by a visit from Soviet Premier Khrushchev to the West.

Still, these events did not upset the global balance, reflecting the general planetary harmony. The uses of science also received a boost through Saturn's association with the laws of physics and their application in human affairs: the St. Lawrence Seaway was completed, linking the Great Lakes and the Atlantic Ocean; and the microchip was invented, spurring the development of multiple miniaturized products in the coming years.

The 14th Dalai Lama seeks asylum in India

Vice President Nixon with the Soviet premier Khrushchev

Soviet space probe "Luna I" is launched

FLYING HIGH

After years of struggle, Fidel Castro's revolutionary forces finally ousted President Batista in Cuba. The Soviets continued their space exploration successes, sending three Luna rockets to the Moon, while the U.S. launched the *Pioneer 4* space probe, which became the first Sun orbiter. After years of Chinese violence against peaceful Tibetans, the Dalai Lama sought asylum in India. U.S.-Soviet relations began to warm after Vice President Nixon visited Moscow, and Khrushchev reciprocated. Twelve nations agreed to make the Antarctic continent an international scientific preserve. Little Rock in Arkansas still seethed with anger and violence, as State Governor Faubus continued to refuse integration of public schools, despite orders from the U.S. Supreme Court. Alaska and Hawaii became the forty-ninth and fiftieth states to join the Union. Hula-Hoops, exported from Australia to the U.S., became a fad. *The Sound Of Music* was a big success on Broadway. The pop music world was saddened when three rock 'n' roll icons, Buddy Holly, Richie Valens, and the Big Bopper, J.P. Richardson, died in a plane crash. Crime novelist Raymond Chandler died.

➤ Read Marilyn Monroe's Star Profile on page 489.

CAPRICORN

From January 01, 0:00 through January 20, 19:18

The Playful Producer

January Capricorn of 1959 is smart, great at organizing, ambitious, and brilliant in exercising authority. In other words, you have the credentials to succeed. If you keep an open mind and avoid getting distracted by the allure of material wealth, you could discover spiritual happiness.

Not everyone feels good about how they earn their daily bread, but it's important to know that you are making a positive contribution to the world. Otherwise, your spirit could wilt. Capricorns need to avoid situations that render them jaded or cynical. Likely to have exceptional business acumen and accounting skills, you can also make people smile. In your birth month, businessman Larry Harmon franchised Bozo the Clown to various American networks. You might argue that Harmon wasn't the first businessman to make a living working with a bunch of clowns. Your fellow Capricorn Berry Gordy also enjoyed the privilege of making money by bringing joy to himself and millions of music-lovers worldwide. In 1959, he started Hitsville USA, later known as the legendary Motown record label.

Like Harmon, you have an eye for talent and the ability to attract influential people into your sphere. With the backing of important figures, you can be a force to reckon with. Indeed, building empires and creating coalitions are what Capricorn is all about. Another kind of coalition—the U.S.—expanded during your birth month, when Alaska became the forty-ninth state. Aiding Americans' ability to navigate the cold Alaskan environment, the first commercial snowmobile came on to the market the same year.

In personal relationships, you may vacillate between being cool and sweetly sentimental. A Taurean or Virgo can take these fluctuations in their stride. Cancer also has an intuitive understanding of the waxing and waning of emotional cycles.

While making your dreams concrete, your challenge is to not be too hard on anyone, including yourself. To embrace life with a compassionate heart is a mighty strength, one that enables you to include all beings into an ever-expanding circle of friends and loved ones.

AQUARIUS

From January 20, 19:19 through February 19, 9:37

The Global Conscience

Maintaining individuality in the midst of a social situation is important to any Aquarian, and the 1959 Aquarian tends to boldly assert his or her uniqueness with flair and ingenuity. Indeed, few have enough confidence in their talents to hold their own in the midst of the hustle and bustle of the writhing masses. Your awareness of your brilliance in no way detracts from your ability to use your gifts for the greater glory of the collective. Your self knowledge tends to inspire others' admiration.

Your vision is usually altruistic. You may be aware of how one can shape the future and how thought can influence action. You are likely to have a clear understanding of the interconnectedness of life, including the way human beings interact with machines. In your everyday world, you may have a love of technology and computers. In 1959, the computer engineers Jack St. Clair Kilby and Robert Noyce, represented by separate companies, filed for patents on their virtually simultaneous invention: the integrated circuit board.

You may feel it is important for people to work together in peace, and you like to make sure that the people close to you are happy. Your modus operandi is quite unlike that of Marxist revolutionary Fidel Castro who violently seized control over Cuba from Batista in your birth month. Castro had no compunction about swiftly nationalizing all American business in Cuba. In doing so, he exacerbated an already tense relationship with his next-door neighbor, the United States.

In your personal relationships, you may prefer to keep a Leo, like Castro, as a pal rather than a lover. With a Gemini or Libra, who encourage you to talk about everything under the Sun, you can formulate all the plans you have to make the world a better place.

You are aware, clever, and highly knowledgeable. What counts, however, is that you walk your talk and put your ideas into action. Your strength lies in being able to delve into the inner workings of the psyche and come out with a globally conscious manifesto. You have what it takes to be a founding parent of planetary citizenship.

➤ Read about your Chinese Astrological sign on page 838. ➤ Read about your Personal Planets on page 826. ➤ Read about your personal Mystical Card on page 856.

CAPRICORN
Your Personal Planets

YOUR LOVE POTENTIAL
Venus in Capricorn, Jan. 01, 0:00 - Jan. 07, 8:15
Venus in Aquarius, Jan. 07, 8:16 - Jan. 20, 19:18

YOUR DRIVE AND AMBITION
Mars in Taurus, Jan. 01, 0:00 - Jan. 20, 19:18

YOUR LUCK MAGNETISM
Jupiter in Scorpio, Jan. 01, 0:00 - Jan. 20, 19:18

World Events

Jan. 1 – The Cuban dictator Fulgencio Batista flees the country, leaving it in the hands of Che Guevara's rebels.

Jan. 3 – Alaska becomes the 49th U.S. state.

New Cuban president Manuel Urrutia and rebel leader Fidel Castro at the Presidential Palace

AQUARIUS
Your Personal Planets

YOUR LOVE POTENTIAL
Venus in Aquarius, Jan. 20, 19:19 - Jan. 31, 7:27
Venus in Pisces, Jan. 31, 7:28 - Feb. 19, 9:37

YOUR DRIVE AND AMBITION
Mars in Taurus, Jan. 20, 19:19 - Feb. 10, 13:56
Mars in Gemini, Feb. 10, 13:57 - Feb. 19, 9:37

YOUR LUCK MAGNETISM
Jupiter in Scorpio, Jan. 20, 19:19 - Feb. 10, 13:44
Jupiter in Sagittarius, Feb. 10, 13:45 - Feb. 19, 9:37

World Events

Feb. 3 – Buddy Holly, Ritchie Valens, and the Big Bopper are killed in a plane crash.

Feb. 19 – Cyprus gains its independence in a treaty signed by Britain, Turkey and Greece.

1959

PISCES
Your Personal Planets

YOUR LOVE POTENTIAL
Venus in Pisces, Feb. 19, 9:38 - Feb. 24, 10:52
Venus in Aries, Feb. 24, 10:53 - Mar. 20, 21:54
Venus in Taurus, Mar. 20, 21:55 - Mar. 21, 8:54

YOUR DRIVE AND AMBITION
Mars in Gemini, Feb. 19, 9:38 - Mar. 21, 8:54

YOUR LUCK MAGNETISM
Jupiter in Sagittarius, Feb. 19, 9:38 - Mar. 21, 8:54

World Events

Feb. 28 - Britain and the UAR finally agree settlement of claims from the Suez Crisis.

Mar. 9 - The first known radar contact is made with Venus.

Tony Curtis and Marilyn Monroe in "Some Like It Hot"

ARIES
Your Personal Planets

YOUR LOVE POTENTIAL
Venus in Taurus, Mar. 21, 8:55 - Apr. 14, 21:07
Venus in Gemini, Apr. 14, 21:08 - Apr. 20, 20:16

YOUR DRIVE AND AMBITION
Mars in Gemini, Mar. 21, 8:55 - Apr. 10, 9:45
Mars in Cancer, Apr. 10, 9:46 - Apr. 20, 20:16

YOUR LUCK MAGNETISM
Jupiter in Sagittarius, Apr. 21, 8:55 - Apr. 20, 20:16

World Events

Mar. 29 - The classic movie *Some Like It Hot*, starring Marilyn Monroe, Jack Lemmon, and Tony Curtis premieres.

Apr. 9 - American architect Frank Lloyd Wright dies in Arizona at the age of ninety-one.

PISCES
From February 19, 9:38 through March 21, 8:54

The Logical Dreamer

Having the time and space to daydream, as well as to tune into those mysterious messages of the night, is important to Pisceans, and none more so than the Pisces born in 1959. You may have a natural ability to channel fantasies into real-world creations. Your talent is to bring realism to whimsy and to harvest wealth from all your ideas.

While you appreciate the need to escape the everyday world, you may also see the commercial goldmine in that little doll, that mini-glamour queen with plastic proportions no more than eleven and a half inches tall, who ignited the imaginations of twenty million baby-boomers. That's right—your time-twin Barbie, the Mattel money-magnet, was born in 1959, in the same zodiacal sign as you. Call it coincidence, but Disney's *Sleeping Beauty* also kissed her prince in 1959.

Fantasy and fairy tales—anything that affords a dreamy escape from reality—tend to thrill Pisces. Music can also take you out of this world, and many Pisceans adore musical theater. In 1959, *The Sound Of Music* opened on Broadway, in New York City. You can also be deeply philosophical about life, the Universe, and spirituality. Although you were not yet born, you may feel sadness and loss when you think about "the day the music died." In early February of 1959, three of rock 'n' roll's young heroes—Buddy Holly, Richie Valens, and the Big Bopper, J. P. Richardson—died in a plane crash.

Relationships that take you into mysterious worlds of passion tend to excite you. So, cue the spooky music, and let a Cancer or Scorpio escort you into the *Twilight Zone*, a television series that happened to begin broadcasting in your birth year. When your head is floating in the clouds, a Capricorn can help you keep your feet firmly on the ground.

Your challenge is simply to let your love and light shine for the world to see. Although you may find it hard to realize this goal on a daily basis, you have the spiritual awareness to follow a regular outlook-brightening discipline. Yoga, meditation, art, music, and dance provide a variety of methods for achieving an ever-expanding consciousness.

ARIES
From March 21, 8:55 through April 20, 20:16

The Lively Mind

Ariens are born leaders and the astral indications unique to your chart show a special gift for courageous initiative. As you've risen to life's challenges, you may have felt like you've had your work cut out for you. Along the way, you might have developed an ironic appreciation for the Chinese curse, "may you live in interesting times."

When you were born, the Cold War was raging on between Russia and the West. Tibet had erupted in rebellion against China's brutal occupation. On March 20, 1959, the fourteenth Dalai Lama, forced to flee his beloved Tibetan homeland, escaped across the Himalayan mountains and sought sanctuary in India. You may relate to the bravery of His Holiness. The Dalai Lama's practice of compassion and non-violence may also be an inspiration for you to use brains, not brawn, to get what you want in life.

A man or woman of valor, you may have a powerful musculature. With maturity, however, you may have come to believe in negotiation rather than the use of force, in realizing your goals. Your sense of personal power may be so secure that you can afford to be magnanimous. Friends and family may regard you as a marvelously generous soul. As a leader, you have the ability to make team members feel lucky to be a part of something greater than themselves. From time to time, you may burst out in hearty laughter, a gift that others are likely to find positively infectious.

Your can be quite the charmer and a bit of a social butterfly, flitting from one fascinating subject or person to the next. You may work in the world of communication. Likely to have a high-powered intellect, you enjoy the original juxtapositions of ideas. Librans offer you creative inspiration. Aquarians offers thought-provoking conversation.

You can be as fast on your feet as you are with your mind. You are likely to be a high-energy person, with a fiery spirit. Your challenge is to seize every moment and live in the present. You excel in engaging your open mind in the exchange of ideas. Your active awareness empowers you to capture the best potential of every opportunity.

➤ Read about your Chinese Astrological sign on page 838. ➤ Read about your Personal Planets on page 826. ➤ Read about your personal Mystical Card on page 856.

TAURUS

From April 20, 20:17 through May 21, 19:41

The Enchanting Creator

Taureans work best when they have a goal they can pursue. Some seek to build a beautiful home, to grow a fruitful garden, or to establish a successful business. As a Taurus of 1959, you may pursue happiness and pleasure not only for yourself, but for others as well. You may be willing to devote all your energy towards the realization of this dream.

Near the time of your birth, the Campaign for Nuclear Disarmament (CND) came to life in Britain. Carrying placards with the now-famous peace sign, demonstrators marched from Aldermasterton to Trafalgar Square in London. The Cold War threat of nuclear war was looming over the world. Interestingly, the CND sign is actually a runic symbol connoting death. In 1959, Richard Nixon and Nikita Khrushchev met for the Kitchen Debate to discuss Capitalism and Communism. Such meetings may have helped to reduce the tension between the two countries and the danger to humanity. Because the sign of Taurus is associated with the Earth, you are likely to care deeply about the world's fate.

A desire to build a better world is likely to remain a powerful motivating force in your life. Bright and inspired, you may hearken back to nature for inspiration in your creations—even your own house. You are also likely to appreciate art and design. You may admire the organic architecture of the Guggenheim Museum in New York, which opened 1959. Its architect, Frank Lloyd Wright, passed away that same year.

You may also admire your fellow Taurean, singer Bobby Darin. Taurus rules the throat, and many singers share your sign. Darin's hit, "Mack The Knife" won a Grammy Award in 1959. A Capricorn or Virgo could provide you with an appreciative audience. Together, you could win a lifetime achievement award for romance!

As a realistic sensualist, Taurus of 1959, your challenge is to avoid seeking material gratification at your own or others' expense. You have a strong ability to nurture others and to give unconditional love. You reap unquantifiable benefits when you help others to be the best they can be. What you give truly inures to your honor.

GEMINI

From May 21, 19:42 through June 22, 3:49

The Dashing Caperer

Clever and resourceful, the 1959 Gemini has a bright mind. Most Geminis are smart, but you may have a memory that recalls it all. Your mind can work like the string used by the ancient Greek Theseus when he needed to retrace his path and make his way out of the Minotaur's labyrinth.

Finding it easy to figure your way through the maze of life, with all its twists and turns, you move smoothly from one place to the next, swapping ideas and information along the way. Not that you're fickle; indeed, you are fiercely loyal to your cause. You may appreciate the production of a certain automobile of the late 1950s, the British Mini, which made movement slick and easy. Like the Mini, you have the ability to maneuver through tight spots and enough power to match a Buick.

You may also find it interesting that the godfather of Beat, Allen Ginsberg, first took LSD during your birth month, an experiment that gave the Beat Poets a psychedelic perspective as they entered the early 1960s. Perhaps Ginsburg used the newly marketed Bic ballpoint pen in drafting his poetry. What matters is that, like Ginsberg, you share an understanding of the power of the word. Like him, you have no axiom to grind!

In relationships, you are likely to seek partners who can enjoy your wit and penchant for wild capers. In a fabulous 1959 film about bizarre relationships, two of the three leading actors shared your sign. *Some Like It Hot* featured Geminis Marilyn Monroe and Tony Curtis facing off in quite an entanglement. Curtis played a dual role that involved cross-dressing, along with Aquarian Jack Lemmon. You won't get the fuzzy end of the lollipop (Marilyn Monroe's words for bad luck) with Aquarians. You are more likely find that they—along with Librans—make great partners.

With an ability to view serious subjects with a light heart, you could also have a knack for enjoying the spiritual side of life without forgoing material wealth, and this is a great strength an inspiration for all those around you. Your challenge is to keep your sense of humor under all circumstances, without seeming frivolous.

➤ Read about your Chinese Astrological sign on page 838. ➤ Read about your Personal Planets on page 826. ➤ Read about your personal Mystical Card on page 856.

TAURUS
Your Personal Planets

YOUR LOVE POTENTIAL
Venus in Gemini, Apr. 20, 20:17 - May 10, 15:44
Venus in Cancer, May 10, 15:45 - May 21, 19:41

YOUR DRIVE AND AMBITION
Mars in Cancer, Apr. 20, 20:17 - May 21, 19:41

YOUR LUCK MAGNETISM
Jupiter in Sagittarius, Apr. 20, 20:17 - Apr. 24, 14:10
Jupiter in Scorpio, Apr. 24, 14:11 - May 21, 19:41

World Events

Apr. 22 – The Queen Mother and Princess Margaret visit the Pope at The Vatican.

May 11 – The "Big Four" meet in Geneva to discuss the reunification of Germany.

The Queen Mother and Princess Margaret at the Vatican

GEMINI
Your Personal Planets

YOUR LOVE POTENTIAL
Venus in Cancer, May 21, 19:42 - June 06, 22:41
Venus in Leo, June 06, 22:42 - June 22, 3:49

YOUR DRIVE AND AMBITION
Mars in Cancer, May 21, 19:42 - June 01, 2:25
Mars in Leo, June 01, 2:26 - June 22, 3:49

YOUR LUCK MAGNETISM
Jupiter in Scorpio, May 21, 19:42 - June 22, 3:49

World Events

June 3 – Singapore becomes an independent state within the British Commonwealth.

June 5 – The NATO nations convene in London to reaffirm their unity.

CANCER
Your Personal Planets

YOUR LOVE POTENTIAL
Venus in Leo, June 22, 3:50 - July 08, 12:07
Venus in Virgo, July 08, 12:08 - July 23, 14:44

YOUR DRIVE AND AMBITION
Mars in Leo, June 22, 3:50 - July 20, 11:02
Mars in Virgo, July 20, 11:03 - July 23, 14:44

YOUR LUCK MAGNETISM
Jupiter in Scorpio, June 22, 3:50 - July 23, 14:44

World Events

June 26 – The St. Lawrence Seaway is officially opened.

July 17 – Dr. Leakey discovers the oldest human skull; it is estimated to be 600,000 years old.

Archeologists Dr. Leakey and his wife

LEO
Your Personal Planets

YOUR LOVE POTENTIAL
Venus in Virgo, July 23, 14:45 - Aug. 23, 21:43

YOUR DRIVE AND AMBITION
Mars in Virgo, July 23, 14:45 - Aug. 23, 21:43

YOUR LUCK MAGNETISM
Jupiter in Scorpio, July 23, 14:45 - Aug. 23, 21:43

World Events

July 24 – The first elected Parliament opens in Nepal.

Aug. 21 – Hawaii becomes the 50th U.S. state.

CANCER
From June 22, 3:50 through July 23, 14:44

The Spectacular Preserver

As a 1959 Cancerian, you may strongly relate to tradition, customs, heritage, and genealogy. You may identify with the plight of the Tibetan leader and fellow Cancerian the Dalai Lama. Forced to escape from his homeland in 1959, he found refuge in India from the brutal occupation by the Chinese.

Kith and kin mean a great deal to you, too, and tracing your family history may be a hobby. You are likely to ascribe great importance to the preservation of your particular cultural heritage. You may regard certain rituals, objects, or practices as being to the birthright of your children or grandchildren. Interestingly, the United Nations issued its Declaration of the Rights of the Child in 1959. A part of you is also sweetly sentimental; you may mourn the passing of blues singer Billie Holiday, who died this year. Another side of you may adore her glamour and the way she pushed the boundaries of her time.

There is no greater frontier for humankind to conquer than space. As a Cancerian born in the midst of the Space Race, you may have a particular fascination with the Moon. The first unmanned rocket to reach the Moon, the Russian *Lunik II*, landed in 1959. Any space exploration involving the Moon may be all the more significant to you because la Luna rules the sign of Cancer. The Moon controls the tides. Because water is the most prominent element in the physical composition of human beings, many astrologers contend that the phases of the Moon can affect people's emotions. In 1959, scientists got their first look at the dark side of the Moon. Examination of the mysterious world of personal feelings is another story, though.

It's important for you to respect your own feelings. Doing so enables you to make valuable connections, both internal and external, that enhance your personal and professional relationships. As a mate, a Pisces or Scorpio can sympathize with your deep emotions.

Intuition is your greatest strength, and using it with timely wisdom is your challenge. A sixth sense is a priceless commodity; note how and when it speaks, and you will never go wrong.

LEO
From July 23, 14:45 through August 23, 21:43

The Refined Performer

Although occasionally accused of being showy and full of razzamatazz, a 1959 Leo is not as likely as most Leos to seek validation from admiring others. You may enjoy your place in the spotlight, but you tend to gauge people's responses with a certain reserve—as food for thought. You may not feel any particular need to prove yourself.

A part of you adores the allure of stage, screen, and podium. Dressing up as a character from a movie may even be fun for you. Although you might prefer a classic look, you may go glitzy now and then. A Lion of 1959, though, would draw the line at looking like the Hula Doll which graced the dashboard of many an American car in the fifties. Back then, all things tropical were fashionable. Hawaiian shirts became all the rage after Hawaii's admission as the fiftieth U.S. state.

You are a star in your own right, but you tend to be quietly confident. You like your personal productions to run smoothly. Like the actor who has to learn his or her lines, going over them time and time again, you, too, may need to revise what you are doing, so that you are never caught unprepared. By making lists and organizing life to the infinitesimal detail, you stand a greater chance of being able to take time out to play and enjoy those spontaneous forms of self-expression you hold so dear.

Ready to make your glamorous entrance and receive your public, it's "Lights! Camera! Action!" Your fellow Leo Cecil B. de Mille was the master of the film extravaganza. He left the world a film heritage including the spectacula, *The Greatest Show On Earth*, when he died in 1959. While de Mille was famed for being dictatorial, you might prefer relationships with a little more earthy realism and equality. Ariens or Sagittarians could provide excitement as well as make loving companions. You may also settle with a Gemini who can stimulate your mind.

You are among the bravest of beings, and your challenge is to honor your principles with dignity, charm, and love. Being able to communicate in a direct and thoughtful manner is a strength that enhances your wide-ranging talents.

➤ Read about your Chinese Astrological sign on page 838. ➤ Read about your Personal Planets on page 826. ➤ Read about your personal Mystical Card on page 856.

VIRGO

From August 23, 21:44 through September 23, 19:07

The Perfect Communicator

Enjoying a gift for conceptual organization, Virgos tend to store a vast quantity of data in their minds. The year of your birth marked the introduction of postal codes in Britain. Encoding locations in an elegant and logical pattern, the postal code scheme provides a metaphor for the way in which you grasp and process information. Fitting facts and figures together and imparting knowledge are your specialties.

Like all Virgos, you like forward planning. You may relate to *Mercury 7*, the NASA space mission that began in 1959. Paving the way for the later Apollo program, *Mercury 7* conveyed the United States along a celestial highway that would ultimately lead to Neil Armstrong's Moon walk in 1969. Although daring test pilots flew the *Mercury* spacecraft, it was the scientists who had the right stuff—Virgo-like know-how on the details of space travel.

Anything is possible under the auspices of *Mercury*, the planet that rules travel and, coincidentally, the sign of Virgo. The mythological god Mercury helped people to make transitions between different spheres, like Earth and the Moon. In this way, the name for the space mission, Mercury, resonates symbolically for you. You have a special ability that allows you to go anywhere, get information, and send the message where it needs to go. Consequently, you can connect the brain with the heart or the spiritual with reality.

Being able to converse, exchange, and express ideas is important. Those in relationships with you have to constantly sharpen their communication skills. It doesn't matter if someone is attractive, or from the same background. If you can't connect, you're unlikely to fall in love with that person. You may relate to Crown Prince Akihito of Japan, who married a commoner in 1959: her fine mind was what captivated him. A Capricorn or Taurean has the ability to enthrall you.

Your challenge, Virgo of 1959, is to balance the demands of the mundane world with your intellectual and spiritual needs. Practicality, prudence, and an endearing sense of humor are the strengths that can help you reach for the stars.

LIBRA

From September 23, 19:08 through October 24, 4:10

The Assertive Diplomat

Sitting on the fence is a Libran prerogative. From such a vantage point, you are able to see both sides, and it is here that we expect to find that marvelous moderator, the 1959 Libran. You're great to have around when arguments need resolving or laws need interpretation. With your high principals and sound morals, you are very well qualified to offer sound advice without imposing too harsh a penalty.

Librans prefer to resolve or avoid disputes. Born in the era of the Cold War and a growing anti-nuclear movement, you may sympathize with both sides: the cold combatants and the peace protesters. On an intellectual level, you can understand how opponents could arrive at their respective positions. You are most comfortable when people work together. In 1959, the Pan African Congress was formed; the U.S. signed cooperation agreements with Turkey, Iran, and Pakistan; a European Free Trade Association was formed to counteract the Common Market; and no less than twelve nations agreed to keep Antarctica a military-free zone.

You could make an excellent politician, able to diffuse conflict and sow consensus. While some 1959 Librans will be spokespeople for others, each and every one of you may live for one thing only: love.

Looking for a combination of looks and intellect, a 1959 Libran may seem fussy in his or her choice of partner. Why settle for less than the best? The 1959 Nobel Prize for medicine went to American scientists who discovered the vital role chromosomes play in heredity. Librans don't need advanced degrees to know that beautiful partners make beautiful babies. Glamour, glitz, and style can captivate you, but remember this: in 1959 *Cosmopolitan* editor Helen Gurley married a man with the plain name Mr. Brown. Once she had him, she had it all. A Gemini or Aquarian could be the one for you.

Purity, selflessness, and grace are strengths you bring to any relationship. You give of yourself wholeheartedly and expect others to reciprocate faithfully. Your challenge is to bring an inspired kind of love into the world, the power of which will always overcome difficulty.

► Read about your Chinese Astrological sign on page 838. ► Read about your Personal Planets on page 826. ► Read about your personal Mystical Card on page 856.

VIRGO
Your Personal Planets

YOUR LOVE POTENTIAL
Venus in Virgo, Aug. 23, 21:44 - Sept. 20, 3:00
Venus in Leo, Sept. 20, 3:01 - Sept. 23, 19:07

YOUR DRIVE AND AMBITION
Mars in Virgo, Aug. 23, 21:44 - Sept. 05, 22:45
Mars in Libra, Sept. 05, 22:46 - Sept. 23, 19:07

YOUR LUCK MAGNETISM
Jupiter in Scorpio, Aug. 23, 21:44 - Sept. 23, 19:07

World Events

Sept. 14 - The model X-15 rocket makes its first flight.

Sept. 17 - Soviet space probe *Luna 2* becomes the first man-made object to touch the surface of the Moon.

President Eisenhower (right) talks with Nikita Krushchev

LIBRA
Your Personal Planets

YOUR LOVE POTENTIAL
Venus in Leo, Sept. 23, 19:08 - Sept. 25, 8:13
Venus in Virgo, Sept. 25, 8:14 - Oct. 24, 4:10

YOUR DRIVE AND AMBITION
Mars in Libra, Sept. 23, 19:08 - Oct. 21, 9:39
Mars in Scorpio, Oct. 21, 9:40 - Oct. 24, 4:10

YOUR LUCK MAGNETISM
Jupiter in Scorpio, Sept. 23, 19:08 - Oct. 05, 14:38
Jupiter in Sagittarius, Oct. 05, 14:39 - Oct. 24, 4:10

World Events

Sept. 25 - Camp David talks begin between Eisenhower and Khrushchev.

Oct. 7 - The Soviet space probe *Luna 3* sends back images of the far side of the Moon—the first time it has been seen.

1959

SCORPIO

Your Personal Planets

YOUR LOVE POTENTIAL
Venus in Virgo, Oct. 24, 4:11 - Nov. 09, 18:10
Venus in Libra, Nov. 09, 18:11 - Nov.

YOUR DRIVE AND AMBITION
Mars in Scorpio, Oct. 24, 4:11 - Nov. 23, 1:26

YOUR LUCK MAGNETISM
Jupiter in Sagittarius, Oct. 24, 4:11 - Nov. 23, 1:26

World Events

Oct. 21 – The Guggenheim Museum, designed by Frank Lloyd Wright, opens in New York.

Nov. 18 – *Ben Hur* premieres in New York.

The Guggenheim Museum opens in New York

SAGITTARIUS

Your Personal Planets

YOUR LOVE POTENTIAL
Venus in Libra, Nov. 23, 1:27 - Dec. 07, 16:40
Venus in Scorpio, Dec. 07, 16:41 - Dec. 22, 14:33

YOUR DRIVE AND AMBITION
Mars in Scorpio, Nov. 23, 1:27 - Dec. 03, 18:08
Mars in Sagittarius, Dec. 03, 18:09 - Dec. 22, 14:33

YOUR LUCK MAGNETISM
Jupiter in Sagittarius, Nov. 23, 1:27 - Dec. 22, 14:33

World Events

Nov. 26 – Che Guevera is appointed President of the National Bank of Cuba.

Dec. 1 – Twelve nations sign an international agreement making the Antarctic a preserve for scientific research.

SCORPIO

From October 24, 4:11 through November 23, 1:26

The Shrewd Investigator

Because you have an uncanny knack for seeing beneath any veneer, absolutely nothing escapes a 1959 Scorpio. While most Scorpios can be great detectives, a 1959 Scorpio embodies stealth. Skillfully covering up any tracks, you're a master at concealment.

Hidden and forbidden subjects tend to fascinate you. These include sex, other people's finances, and the biggest taboo of all—death. You may also have an innate understanding of the never-ending cycle of life and rebirth. As one amazing detective left the planet in your birth year, another arrived. Writer Raymond Chandler passed on, leaving behind his private-eye creation Philip Marlow, who uttered the famous line, "Trouble is my business." This year marks the debut of the popular television series *The Untouchables*, based on the exploits of G-man Elliot Ness. Critics considered the show to be excessively violent. While you're unlikely to be overtly aggressive, you can sometimes appear fierce and others may find you intimidating.

Capable of brilliance in business, you could make it to the top of any profession. Likely to have a nose for hidden treasures, you may be have a great talent for handling money, especially when it belongs to someone else. When you apply your talents on a broader scale, you can help to create a stable economy. You may be intrigued by certain odd financial practices that came to light in the year of your birth. In 1959, forged £5 notes were retrieved from an Austrian lake, where the Nazis had dumped them years before. You may also be puzzled by Fidel Castro's 1959 decision to entrust the Bank of Cuba to a warrior like Che Guevara.

You might like to settle down with someone like Taurus, who can make a comfortable home. You can also have a loving bond with Cancer or Pisces, who will happily share their deepest secrets with you.

Trust may be an issue, Scorpio of 1959. Your challenge is to share your secrets and let others see your tenderness, without giving in to suspicion or fear. You possess a mighty powerful life force, an inner strength you can draw upon, as you walk along the path of renewal.

SAGITTARIUS

From November 23, 1:27 through December 22, 14:33

The Lucky Adventurer

Most Sagittarians are born winners, but the stars for 1959 Sagittarius truly blessed you with the potential for supreme good fortune. Indicators in your chart suggest an ability to seize any opportunity and make the most if it. As a result, you could take the kind of risks that others wouldn't dream of. A little gamble here and there usually pays off for you. And if you should suffer a setback, you'll probably smile, shrug it off with philosophical optimism, and move on without so much as a backward glance.

You are thoughtful and enjoy a quick mind. This combination allows you to understand the broadest of concepts and the wildest of ideas. You also enjoy the birthright of all Sagittarians—an appreciation of the big picture and the ability to envision wondrous possibilities. It's no coincidence that the first picture of planet Earth, taken from *Explorer 6*, a U.S. space satellite, came through in your birth year.

In the same year, scientists developed terrestrial radio telescopes powerful enough to detect radio signals from outer space. As the 1950s came to a close, the Space Race fueled a popular fascination with aliens in flying saucers. The search for extra-terrestrial beings flourishes to this day. Because members of your sign love adventure and exploration, a Sagittarian just might be the first human being to discover those little green men from Mars!

Having the means to get where you want to go is important to you. This was a landmark year for travel. A hovercraft made its maiden voyage across the English Channel, and a Soviet space probe landed on the Moon. An Aries or Leo could send you into orbit anytime! An Aquarian values the freedom you hold so dear.

Sagittarians tend to live life to the max. Your challenge is to keep your perspective and ambitions down to a manageable size, or you may scatter your energy. Your commitment to truth is your strength. You intuitively accept that many roads can lead to the same place and that many cultural beliefs can reach the same universal understanding. Your tolerance and gratitude can be a shining example for all.

➤ Read about your Chinese Astrological sign on page 838. ➤ Read about your Personal Planets on page 826. ➤ Read about your personal Mystical Card on page 856.

CAPRICORN

From December 22, 14:34 through December 31, 23:59

The Daring Mastermind

Capricorns tend to be cautious characters, planning ahead carefully to build a firm and solid future. But the 1959 December-born Capricorn has faith in life. Without forgoing material ambitions, you tend to be more adventurous and philosophical than most others who share your sign.

An ability to delegate is your special gift. Practical and efficient, you seek economical ways to get work done. The first commercial robot went into production in 1959. With the United States and the Soviet Union competing to send a man to the Moon, the Space Race of the 1950s inspired all kinds of new inventions. In that year the U.S. sent two monkeys, Able and Baker, into orbit. Although Able died shortly after her return from the trip, Baker went on to live until 1984.

You may be adventurous enough to try to reach the Moon. At the very least, you enjoy flirting with the stars. You like to know those with influence and may have a network of reliable friends. To keep trade and the exchange of ideas flowing smoothly, you may work hard to maintain open lines of communication. In 1959, Queen Elizabeth II and President Eisenhower made a joint appearance at a ribbon-cutting ceremony, to celebrate the opening of the St. Lawrence Seaway, which linked the Great Lakes to the Atlantic.

Growing up as a member of the Baby Boom generation, you were likely to enjoy unprecedented prosperity. While you may have had deep concern about civil rights and Cold War conflicts, members of your parents' generation may have resonated with Harold Macmillan's slogan, "You've never had it so good!" Elected as Prime Minister of the UK in 1959, Macmillan was known to the public as "Super Mac." You may also have a big, bright, and energetic presence—and no shortage of courageous plans. A Virgo would work well with you. An affectionate Taurean can help you stay financially fit.

Self-contained, disciplined, and confident, you may exude determination. Your challenge is to carry out your responsibilities while allowing others some leeway to make their own judgment calls. Effective delegation empowers you and others.

1959
CAPRICORN
Your Personal Planets

YOUR LOVE POTENTIAL
Venus in Scorpio, Dec. 22, 14:34 - Dec. 31, 23:59

YOUR DRIVE AND AMBITION
Mars in Sagittarius, Dec. 22, 14:34 - Dec. 31, 23:59

YOUR LUCK MAGNETISM
Jupiter in Sagittarius, Dec. 22, 14:34 - Dec. 31, 23:59

World Events

Dec. 25 – Khrushchev demands an East-West summit to be convened the following spring.

Dec. 29 – West Berlin mayor Willy Brandt announces he is able to hold off the Soviet blockade for another entire year before supplies begin to dwindle.

Marilyn Monroe
June 1, 1926 - August 5, 1962

MARILYN MONROE
Gemini

Marilyn Monroe was the "blonde bombshell"—the screen goddess who was both adored and ridiculed for her blatant and shimmering sexuality. When she was onscreen, it was almost impossible to watch anyone else; and although she has actually been dead longer than she lived, no other actress has come close to replacing her as the premier sexual icon in the whole history of the silver screen. Although Monroe owned her sexuality, she hated being regarded as a joke and desperately wanted to be taken seriously as an actress and a person—something that a woman with her appearance and personality found it difficult to achieve in the times in which she lived.

Monroe was a Gemini, a sign known for its intelligence and the ability to make clever and witty retorts. With her Sun, the planet of identity, in her house of career, she sought success and respect. With Neptune, the planet of illusion and film, prominently placed in her horoscope, she was a natural for the movies. Monroe's mother suffered from mental illness, and it's quite likely that Marilyn had some of the same problems as well, another possibility with such a strong Neptune influence. In addition, with Saturn, the planet of limitations, in her house of childhood foundations, it was easy to see how she was ill prepared to assume the status to which she rose. Tragically, she simply lacked the self-esteem to force people to accept her on her own terms.

The Moon, the planet of emotions, was placed in friendly Aquarius, in Monroe's house of marriage, and a contact from expansive Jupiter would normally have indicated a permanent and happy marriage to a supportive spouse. But with both Saturn and Neptune limiting that promise, it was very difficult for Marilyn to attract a mate liberated enough to offer her the sort of unequivocal support she needed. Her marriages were tumultuous and short-lived. In the days before women's liberation, it was normal to see her as a sex object without a soul. If she were alive today, she might still be playing a sexy goddess, but she'd also be producing the movie.

► Read Clark Gable's Star Profile on page 289.

1960

To Be of Use: Pluto in Virgo

The decade that would come to be known for hippies, flower power, the infamous Vietnam War, and social upheaval started quietly rather than with a huge bang. However, changes were afoot. John F. Kennedy narrowly defeated Richard Nixon in the thrilling race for the presidency in the United States. The civil rights movement continued to gain strength and put down roots. Nazi murderer Adolf Eichmann was captured in Argentina and later tried and executed in the state of Israel. Pluto, planet of the deepest kind of transformation, was placed in the serious sign of Virgo this year. Virgo stands for work, health, and analysis, and as Pluto had just moved into this earth sign a few years earlier, the powerful and sweeping changes it inspired were gradually becoming visible. Under the influence of Pluto in Virgo, the practical application of scientific theories can begin to take place and did so at this time.

In 1960, the first working laser was built by T. H. Maiman in the United States. *Echo 1*, the very first communications satellite, was launched. (Virgo is ruled by the planet Mercury, master of communication.) NASA, the American space program, launched *Tiros 1* this year, the first weather satellite, owing perhaps to Pluto in Virgo's push toward the practical. Also in 1960, Sir Macfarlane Burnet of Australia and Peter Brian Medawar of the United Kingdom won the Nobel Prize for medicine for their discovery of acquired immunological tolerance. Discoveries in science and medicine were far more than theory in 1960. They would all have important and positive implications in the years to come.

John F. Kennedy becomes the youngest elected U.S. President

Moslems demonstrate in Algiers during De Gaulle's Algerian tour　　*French writer Albert Camus*

FREEDOM AND EQUALITY FOR ALL

French settlers in Algeria revolted against de Gaulle's policy of self-determination for native Algerians. Ceylon (Sri Lanka) elected the world's first woman leader, Sirimavo Bandaranaike, as Prime Minister. In Cuba, Castro nationalized all privately owned businesses. U.S.-Soviet relations were once more strained with the downing of a U.S. U-2 spy plane by Soviets in their airspace, and Soviet premier Khrushchev disrupted UN proceedings, pounding the table with his shoe. Fifteen new African states achieved independence, redrawing the map of the continent. In Sharpeville, South Africa, fifty-six African demonstrators were killed by police. John F. Kennedy became the second youngest President, narrowly defeating Nixon and sweeping a new generation into leadership. Racial inequities continued to be attacked, as African Americans "invaded" a North Carolina lunch counter and a "whites only" beach in Mississippi. Deaths this year included actor Clark Gable, lyricist Oscar Hammerstein II, and French author Albert Camus, who was killed in a car crash. Ancient Biblical texts, 1,700 years old, were discovered in the Judean desert.

➤ Read The Kennedy Family's Star Profile on page 497.

FOLLOW THE ANIMALS

One of the worst earthquakes in history happened in Agadir, Morocco, killing 15,000 people in 1960. Before the earthquake hit, stray animals were seen streaming away from the village, displaying erratic behavior, and screaming. Similar stories from other disaster sites suggest that animals may have an internal mechanism for detecting natural disasters such as earthquakes that is more sensitive than scientific instruments. It has not been proven yet how they are receiving the signals of impending catastrophe.

CAPRICORN

From January 01, 0:00 through January 21, 1:09

The Thoughtful Optimist

Capricorns tend to take the world of big business very seriously. But as a 1960 January Capricorn, you may be attracted to a more flexible career track, a departure from the usual nine-to-five routine. Born at the dawning of the sixties, you spent your formative years seeing the dreams of children born decades before you actually come true in the Space Race. The possibilities realized before your eyes may have inspired a forward-looking perspective in you. An expanding universe is out there, waiting to be explored.

A conventional workaday job may not be ideal for someone like you. Likely to seek adventure and activity, you may make your way in the world by freelancing, self-employment, or entrepreneurial ventures. You may have a reputation as someone who is perceptive, visionary, and reliable. Your self-discipline and sense of direction enable you to put your freedom to profitable use.

Sincerity may be the bedrock of your personality. In business matters, you probably have a zero-tolerance policy toward breaches in the truth. You may be surprised to learn that disk jockey Alan Freed was a fellow Capricorn. Known for coining the phrase, "rock 'n' roll," Freed was accused in 1960 of taking bribes from record companies to play their artists' records. Some people may do anything for money, but you are unlikely to be one of them. You've got principles and people to protect.

With perseverance and patience, you can rise to a leadership position and attract the support of others with your open, approachable style. You may admire witty, personable Geminis, like John F. Kennedy, who announced his candidacy for the Democratic presidential nomination in January of 1960. In relationships, Gemini and Virgo offer flexibility and ingenuity. Taurus can provide material stability.

You have the potential to be a major player with big picture ambitions. Your challenge is to make the most of opportunities that open up along the way. Your sense of discretion protects you from offers that are too good to be true. Your work ethic ensures you'll be prepared when the real deal comes your way.

AQUARIUS

From January 21, 1:10 through February 19, 15:25

The Independent Spirit

An Aquarian could have conceived the French motto, "Liberty, Equality, Fraternity!" Aquarians of 1960 are likely to aspire to the creation of a society that promotes freedom, fairness, and respect for all members.

You might identify with fellow Aquarian, British Prime Minister Harold Macmillan, who gave his famous "Winds of Change" speech to the South African Parliament in 1960. Announcing Britain's support for black majority rule in the Union of South Africa, the speech reflected a change in British policy and the rejection of apartheid. White-dominated South Africa soon left the British Commonwealth and withdrew into progressive isolation. Elsewhere in Africa, a growing number of countries declared independence under black-majority ruled government. In 1960 fifteen African countries joined the United Nations.

The winds of change were blowing elsewhere in the world at the time. In the United States, four African-American students, having been refused service at a Woolworth's lunch counter in North Carolina, staged the first sit-in of the 1960s. Members of your sign tend to support humanitarian causes, and you may find it impossible to do nothing when injustice rears its ugly head. Idealistic, public-spirited, and willing to get involved, the Aquarian of 1960 is likely to take his or her politics very personally.

The Aquarian penchant for non-conformism necessarily narrows the pool of people who can understand you. You're happiest among supportive, like-minded souls who admire your willingness to go against the grain. Libra shares your commitment to justice and equality. Open-minded Gemini shares your enthusiasm for new ideas. Challenge-loving Sagittarius finds Aquarian rebelliousness exciting and loves a good political debate.

Ultimately, your challenge is to innovate and initiate change while remaining true to your ideals. You possess a brilliant mind packed with original ideas. Your sense of universal responsibility stands out as your greatest strength. Able to live in accordance with the ideals you embrace, you can bring enlightenment to all who encounter you.

➤ Read about your Chinese Astrological sign on page 838. ➤ Read about your Personal Planets on page 826. ➤ Read about your personal Mystical Card on page 856.

CAPRICORN
Your Personal Planets

YOUR LOVE POTENTIAL
Venus in Scorpio, Jan. 01, 0:00 - Jan. 02, 8:42
Venus in Sagittarius, Jan. 02, 8:43 - Jan. 21, 1:09

YOUR DRIVE AND AMBITION
Mars in Sagittarius, Jan. 01, 0:00 - Jan. 14, 4:58
Mars in Capricorn, Jan. 14, 4:59 - Jan. 21, 1:09

YOUR LUCK MAGNETISM
Jupiter in Sagittarius, Jan. 01, 0:00 - Jan. 21, 1:09

World Events

Jan. 2 – U.S. Senator John F. Kennedy announces his candidacy for President.

Jan. 4 – French writer of *The Plague* Albert Camus dies in a car crash.

A new record for deep-sea divers

AQUARIUS
Your Personal Planets

YOUR LOVE POTENTIAL
Venus in Sagittarius, Jan. 21, 1:10 - Jan. 27, 4:45
Venus in Capricorn, Jan. 27, 4:46 - Feb. 19, 15:25

YOUR DRIVE AND AMBITION
Mars in Capricorn, Jan. 21, 1:10 - Feb. 19, 15:25

YOUR LUCK MAGNETISM
Jupiter in Sagittarius, Jan. 21, 1:10 - Feb. 19, 15:25

World Events

Jan. 23 – Deep-sea divers Piccard and Walsh set a new record of 3,350 ft in the Pacific Ocean.

Jan. 28 – Burma signs a treaty of cooperation with China.

1960

PISCES
Your Personal Planets

YOUR LOVE POTENTIAL
Venus in Capricorn, Feb. 19, 15:26 - Feb. 20, 16:46
Venus in Aquarius, Feb. 20, 16:47 - Mar. 16, 1:52
Venus in Pisces, Mar. 16, 1:53 - Mar. 20, 14:42

YOUR DRIVE AND AMBITION
Mars in Capricorn, Feb. 19, 15:26 - Feb. 23, 4:10
Mars in Aquarius, Feb. 23, 4:11 - Mar. 20, 14:42

YOUR LUCK MAGNETISM
Jupiter in Sagittarius, Feb. 19, 15:26 - Mar. 01, 13:09
Jupiter in Capricorn, Mar. 01, 13:10 - Mar. 20, 14:42

World Events

Mar. 4 - American comedy actress Lucille Ball files for divorce from Desi Arnaz.

Mar. 6 - In Switzerland, women are granted the right to vote in municipal elections.

Lucille Ball and Desi Arnaz divorce

ARIES
Your Personal Planets

YOUR LOVE POTENTIAL
Venus in Pisces, Mar. 20, 14:43 - Apr. 09, 10:31
Venus in Aries, Apr. 09, 10:32 - Apr. 20, 2:05

YOUR DRIVE AND AMBITION
Mars in Aquarius, Mar. 20, 14:43 - Apr. 02, 6:23
Mars in Pisces, Apr. 02, 6:24 - Apr. 20, 2:05

YOUR LUCK MAGNETISM
Jupiter in Capricorn, Mar. 20, 14:43 - Apr. 20, 2:05

World Events

Mar. 21 - The Sharpeville Massacre in South Africa leaves sixty-nine protesters dead.

Apr. 10 - The U.S. Senate passes a landmark Civil Rights Bill.

PISCES
From February 19, 15:26 through March 20, 14:42

The Philanthropic Dreamer

Tending to have vivid imaginations, Pisceans can play movies in their minds in glorious Technicolor. A 1960 Pisces is likely to have wide-screen, panoramic vision. Your dreams may be inspired not only by your personal life, but by world events. You may strongly empathize with the suffering of others; their trials and tribulations may feel like your own. Impressionable Pisceans often have an acute sensitivity to the physical or emotional environment, in which they find themselves. In 1960 the first weather satellite, *Tiros I*, was launched into orbit.

Your deep empathy for humanity could inspire you to champion equal rights. This was an important year for human rights: the second wave of the women's liberation movement was beginning to gain momentum; the contraceptive pill came on the market; Switzerland finally gave women the vote; schools in the United States began to integrate; and Sirimavo Bandaranaike became the first woman Prime Minister of Ceylon. In 1972, she changed the country's name to Sri Lanka.

Learning to draw the line and say "enough is enough" is important for Pisces. Otherwise you can be overwhelmed by the enormity of what you see, hear, or feel. You might worry about alienating loved ones by drawing boundaries around yourself. Such an outcome is a virtual impossibility for Pisces. Your empathetic nature moves you to take account of others' needs without even thinking about it. Loved ones may need to get used to hearing the word "no" issue from your lips. Rest assured, they'll adjust.

In friendships or love, Scorpio and Cancer make sympathetic partners. Capricorn can help you to assert healthy boundaries, without worrying about excluding or hurting anyone.

Your challenge as a 1960 Pisces is to assess when, where, and how to be altruistic. Your particular kind of compassionate humanitarianism can sometimes border on martyrdom. Your strength comes from being a truly kind, loving spirit. When you enter into heart-to-heart relationships, your true light of understanding shines through. You illuminate not only yourself, but also the world around you.

ARIES
From March 20, 14:43 through April 20, 2:05

The Spiritual Warrior

While most Aries gladly become the traditional kind of soldier, willing to bear arms, a 1960 Aries would rather sit calmly and talk things over. It's no surprise that you were born as the sit-ins of 1960s were getting underway. The civil rights anthem "We Shall Overcome" may have been the background music to your tender years. The peaceful protests of your birth year were the first in a movement that would bring important progress in the decades to come.

You may resonate with the words of Martin Luther King, "I believe that unarmed truth and unconditional love will have the final word. We have flown the air like birds and swum the sea like fishes, but have yet to learn the simple act of walking the Earth as brothers." In 1960 King pledged to support SNCC, the Students Nonviolent Coordinating Committee. United States President Eisenhower signed the 1960 Civil Rights Act, which levied penalties for interference with anyone's attempt to register to vote or with the act of voting itself.

Your compassionate streak can come through relationships, ideas, and actions. Cool and rhythmic, you prefer the sound of music to the noise of guns blazing. In your birth year, police broke up a peaceful demonstration against ID cards for Africans in Sharpeville, South Africa. This outrage left fifty-six dead and 162 wounded. Not only are you peaceful, you're brave. Others are receptive to your approach. You could become the pioneering conscience for your generation. Others may call upon you to speak, act, and think for those who find it difficult to present themselves in a relaxed, serene manner, like you.

While your compassion for others is immeasurable, when it comes to work and personal projects you like to have boundaries. An Aquarian can help you set reasonable limits. A Sagittarian or Leo can make an excellent partner for laughter and love.

Your courage and confidence have a sense of genius and magic to them, 1960 Aries, and they are your strength. Your challenge is to use this power for the benefit of others as well as for yourself. Your dreams could show you the way to begin.

➤ Read about your Chinese Astrological sign on page 838. ➤ Read about your Personal Planets on page 826. ➤ Read about your personal Mystical Card on page 856.

TAURUS

From April 20, 2:06 through May 21, 1:33

The Romantic Hero

If truth be known, most Taureans are old-fashioned romantics, and none more so that the 1960 Taurus. Loving relationships mean everything to you, and you may become extremely upset if things fail to go well; you might even throw the odd petulant tantrum to get your way.

You are, however, extremely brave and may go where angels fear to tread. In your birth month, U-2 pilot Gary Francis Powers was shot down by the Soviets while flying over Russia. Bono, lead singer of the rock group U2, was born at the same time as this event! Powers admitted he was working for the CIA, and it led to a breakdown of the Paris Peace Talks, also taking place during in your birth month. The Cold War between the U.S. and USSR a turn for the worse.

You may vent excess energy in competitive sports or an exercise regime. With your stubborn Taurean persistence, you can keep fit well into your senior years. At the 1960 Rome Olympics, a young American reaped the rewards of her own stubborn persistence. Celebrated athlete Wilma Rudolph won three gold medals, despite having contracted polio as a child. After six years in a brace, she came back and excelled in basketball and track. You may not have that kind of difficulty to overcome, but you probably share Wilma's tenacity of spirit. Once you set your mind on a goal, you will not allow anything to get in your way.

Taureans sometimes have a soft spot for chivalry and royal romance. Your birth month marked the wedding of Britain's Princess Margaret to commoner Anthony Armstrong-Jones, a famous society photographer. In your own relationship, a Virgo or a Capricorn could be your beautiful queen or your knight in shining armor.

Courage combined with caution, is a strength that keeps you from going too far, too fast. Sometimes, however, your caution can tip the balance in favor of total inaction. If you find yourself wanting for motivation—not an uncommon issue for Taureans—you can break free by indulging your passions. Once engaged by something you love, you will have no shortage of projects that are worthy of your astounding power and fortitude.

GEMINI

From May 21, 1:34 through June 21, 9:41

The Bright Spark

Geminis often live by their wits, and as a 1960 Gemini, you may mix artful skill with intelligent action. The fastest learner under the Sun, you can pick up new ideas and carry them forward in your life, testing their various applications as you go. You're super-smart, with guile and cunning to match, and you gain enormous satisfaction from beating your rivals.

You may admire the intelligence of the Israeli secret service, the Mossad, which sent agents to Argentina in 1960 on a mission to find and capture Adolf Eichmann, Nazi war criminal and director of the "Final Solution," the systematic murder of the Jews of Europe during World War II. The agents smuggled Eichmann out of the country and took him to Israel, where he was put on trial. Found guilty in a unanimous verdict, Eichmann was later executed aboard a ship at sea.

While you have a strong sense of justice, you also like to learn all sides of an issue. Geminis tend to believe that communication is the key to understanding. The first communications satellite went into orbit in 1960. Called *Echo 1*, the satellite received and sent information back to Earth. You, too, are singularly gifted in getting your message across to anyone, anywhere. You might enjoy learning Lincos— the artificial language designed in 1960 to communicate with aliens—just for kicks! You were brought up in an era of space-age pop, where everyone would "twist again like we did last summer." Lovers of novelty, Geminis are often quite intellectual, but intellectual snobs they are not!

In personal relationships, you may seek a partner who is happy to let you be a motivating force. While you like convenience, you're really interested in people who have a lust for life. Often restless, you may find it hard to stay in one place for too long. Your feelings tend to display themselves on your face and in your bearing. A Libran, Arien, or Aquarian may appreciate your stimulating influence.

When you're in your element, you can laugh at yourself and find humor in every situation. Your challenge is to use your dynamic optimism to take mistakes in stride.

➤ Read about your Chinese Astrological sign on page 838. ➤ Read about your Personal Planets on page 826. ➤ Read about your personal Mystical Card on page 856.

TAURUS
Your Personal Planets

YOUR LOVE POTENTIAL
Venus in Aries, Apr. 20, 2:06 - May 03, 19:55
Venus in Taurus, May 03, 19:56 - May 21, 1:33

YOUR DRIVE AND AMBITION
Mars in Pisces, Apr. 20, 2:06 - May 11, 7:18
Mars in Aries, May 11, 7:19 - May 21, 1:33

YOUR LUCK MAGNETISM
Jupiter in Capricorn, Apr. 20, 2:06 - May 21, 1:33

World Events

May 6 - Princess Margaret marries Anthony Armstrong-Jones in a ceremony held at Westminster Abbey, London.

May 7 - Leonid Brezhnev is elected leader of the Soviet Union.

Princess Margaret marries Anthony Armstrong-Jones

GEMINI
Your Personal Planets

YOUR LOVE POTENTIAL
Venus in Taurus, May 21, 1:34 - May 28, 6:10
Venus in Gemini, May 28, 6:11 - June 21, 9:41

YOUR DRIVE AND AMBITION
Mars in Aries, May 21, 1:34 - June 20, 9:04
Mars in Taurus, June 20, 9:05 - June 21, 9:41

YOUR LUCK MAGNETISM
Jupiter in Capricorn, May 21, 1:34 - June 10, 1:52
Jupiter in Sagittarius, June 10, 1:53 - June 21, 9:41

World Events

May 27 - The democratic government of Turkey is overthrown in a military coup.

June 16 - Alfred Hitchcock's *Psycho* opens in New York.

1960

CANCER
Your Personal Planets

YOUR LOVE POTENTIAL
Venus in Gemini, June 21, 9:42 - June 21, 16:33
Venus in Cancer, June 21, 16:34 - July 16, 2:10
Venus in Leo, July 16, 2:11 - July 22, 20:36

YOUR DRIVE AND AMBITION
Mars in Taurus, June 21, 9:42 - July 22, 20:36

YOUR LUCK MAGNETISM
Jupiter in Sagittarius, June 21, 9:42 - July 22, 20:36

World Events

July 1 - Italian Somaliland gains independence and unites with the Somali Republic.

July 8 - In Nairobi, police capture more than one hundred people suspected of associations with the Mau Mau secret society.

Sirima Bandaranaike leader of the Sri Lanka Freedom Party

LEO
Your Personal Planets

YOUR LOVE POTENTIAL
Venus in Leo, July 22, 20:37 - Aug. 09, 10:53
Venus in Virgo, Aug. 09, 10:54 - Aug. 23, 3:33

YOUR DRIVE AND AMBITION
Mars in Taurus, July 22, 20:37 - Aug. 02, 4:31
Mars in Gemini, Aug. 02, 4:32 - Aug. 23, 3:33

YOUR LUCK MAGNETISM
Jupiter in Sagittarius, July 22, 20:37 - Aug. 23, 3:33

World Events

July 30 - Sixty thousand Buddhists in South Vietnam stage a protest against the Diem government.

Aug. 3 - In Britain, Sir Roger Casement is hanged for treason.

494

CANCER
From June 21, 9:42 through July 22, 20:36

The Imaginative Romantic

A 1960 Cancerian is among the most original, resourceful, and creative of all beings. Gifted with an emotionally enriched imagination, you may be a poet or artist-craftsman. Likely to appreciate the fictional and rhapsodic, the expression of love can be an inspiring force in your creative works.

Experimental art flourished in 1960. You were born during the heyday of the Pop Art movement. Andy Warhol and Roy Lichtenstein were creating works inspired by comic-book superheroes. Yves Klein created paintings by covering models in blue pigment and directing them to roll on his oversized canvases. Everybody could get in on the art action, thanks to the introduction of the Etch-A-Sketch, designed by Frenchman Arthur Granjean. The Japanese brought out the felt-tip pen.

Likely to pursue a career as an artist or professional designer, you may be a connoisseur of the good life. Frederico Fellini's masterpiece *La Dolce Vita* depicted the sweet life of 1960 Italy and won the 1960 Academy Award for best foreign film. Cancerian's claim to fame can often be found in the kitchen; you may be a superb, inventive cook, who happily feeds friends as if they were family.

Personal relationships can mean everything to you. Home is where the Cancerian heart is. Eager to help your loved ones, you may have excellent money-management skills and can be an economic whiz. Security is important to Cancerians. Likely to maintain savings for a rainy day, you may dip into your nest egg for an occasional round of shopping therapy. In partnerships, you might attract a Taurean who shares your passion for love and luxury. A Pisces or Scorpio can appreciate your artistic temperament and may escort you into a world of fantasy and dreams.

Your challenge, 1960 Cancer, is to give love for the purest of reasons, without expectations or strings. You have a deeply healing touch. Others entering your orbit cannot help but feel your emotional power, sensitivity, and sensuality. Your strength lies in your sense of simplicity, faithfulness, and harmony, all of which open you to a continuous flow of inspiration.

LEO
From July 22, 20:37 through August 23, 3:33

The Smart Sensationalist

Leos often gain renown for their special skill, and the Leo of 1960 has gifts reflecting its capacity for genius. A brilliant performer can attract the loyalty of repeat audiences—an achievement that suits Leo just fine! Members of your sign tend to have a flair for drama. You may have an intuitive sense of how to play to the back row. Indicators in your chart suggest a mega-buck talent.

Loving and loyal, you can come from the heart in all you do. Likely to be a unique character, with a marvelous gift of the gab, you know how to make a point. Your fellow Leo, Fidel Castro, holds the record for the longest speech ever given to the United Nations—more than four hours—in 1960! When you occupy the stage, your listeners are never bored; people rally round to hear a good story. With your penchant for a clever turn of phrase, even the mundane sounds interesting.

You may have unusual insight into the workings of people's minds. Music may provide an absorbing channel into spirituality. In 1960, the fiery queen of soul, Aretha Franklin, moved to New York City, where her gospel voice and Pentecostal beat began to attract national attention. This year also marked the protest march by 60,000 Buddhists against the Diem government of South Vietnam. At the same time, the National Liberation Front, alleged to be communist-controlled, was founded; its aim was to oust the Catholic Diem. Events in Vietnam formed the backdrop to your tender years, as the United States escalated its intervention in the former French colony into a full-blown war.

You may sympathize with people those who cannot share the freedoms you enjoy. For all your self-confidence, you can also be altruistic and a loyal friend to many. Your fierce sense of pride comes through in relationships. Your charisma and courage appeal to Ariens. Sagittarians adore your enthusiasm for learning and discovery.

Powerful, devoted and gentle, you can offer an example of inspired leadership through service to a higher cause. Your challenge is to prove that authority can be exercised with generosity, graciousness, and humanity.

► Read about your Chinese Astrological sign on page 838. ► Read about your Personal Planets on page 826. ► Read about your personal Mystical Card on page 856.

VIRGO

From August 23, 3:34 through September 23, 0:58

The Formidable Marvel

The chart for Virgo of 1960 shows an enquiring mind, a marvelous intellect, and the capacity to conceive ideas that can transform situations and relationships for the better. More intense than most Virgos, you have more influence than you may think. But then, people often don't see themselves as others do—not even discerning, insightful Virgo. With make-or-break abilities in business or love, you can be a powerhouse. Your life may be filled with extremes—all or nothing, good or bad. Half-measures are not a part of your behavioral repertoire. You were born at a time when the nuclear power industry was also in its infancy—you were two babies with awesome energy!

Because members of the sign of Virgo tend to be environmentally conscious, you are likely to devote your energy towards the control, if not the complete elimination of nuclear power. Plutonic power can be mightily threatening, and radioactive waste has a half-life of a quarter of a million years. Virgo is the ultimate waste-hater of the zodiac!

The United States, the first country to equip its submarines with nuclear weapons, successfully fired its first Polaris missile in 1960. The same year marked the launch of the *USS Enterprise*, the first aircraft carrier to run on nuclear power and, consequently, free of any need for portside refueling. Strong, powerful, and self-contained, you too have a deep reservoir of resources to call upon, should you so need.

In relationships, you need partners who can handle such commanding energy. Taurus or Capricorn may be attracted to your compelling and passionate personality. The depth of your character provides endless hours of fascination for Gemini, while Cancer can go with the flow of your emotions.

With an air of mystery and magnetic sexual allure, you can be an intuitive, curious soul. Because you can exhibit fearlessness in exploring uncharted frontiers, you have the potential to serve as a guide for others. Your challenge is to apply your brilliant communication skills in bringing facts, ideas, and unconscious desires into the light, where they can be understood.

LIBRA

From September 23, 0:59 through October 23, 10:01

The Image-Maker

Librans tend to accord great importance to making a good impression. As a Libran of 1960, you might also spend time carefully preparing yourself or your work for presentation. People may not judge a book by its cover, but as far as Libra is concerned, a nice cover couldn't hurt. Members of your sign tend to take pride in their appearance, and your sense of taste is likely to be exquisite: timeless, elegant, and classic.

The first televised debates for the United States presidential election took place during your zodiacal birth month, before an audience of ninety million viewers. Given the power of the medium, the first presidential debate constituted a landmark in television programming. The most memorable aspect of the four televised contests, held between John F. Kennedy and Richard Nixon, over the course of two months, was not the issues discussed but rather the impression each candidate made on the small screen. Many commentators attributed Nixon's loss of the election to the vividness of his five o'clock shadow in the debates.

A caring person, you may help others find positive opportunities. Librans tend to be peace-makers. Candidate Kennedy first proposed the Peace Corps in your birth month. Likely to be a good money manager, you may encourage people to cooperate to promote their economic interests. The fall of 1960 marked the formation of OPEC, the Organization of Petroleum Exporting Countries.

Financial security and a happy home life may be important goals for you. Your ability to bring harmony and balance to both material and emotional matters enables you to have it all. Geminis and Aquarians appreciate your style and make good companions. Cancerians admire your nerve, courage, and mental agility. You can make a striking impression when you appear arm-in-arm with spotlight-loving Leo.

You derive personal strength from seeing the wonder in everything. You can appreciate the inner beauty that shines within all people. Accepting yourself for who you are is your challenge. Nurturing the best of your own abilities empowers you to bring out the best in others.

➤ Read about your Chinese Astrological sign on page 838. ➤ Read about your Personal Planets on page 826. ➤ Read about your personal Mystical Card on page 856.

VIRGO
Your Personal Planets

YOUR LOVE POTENTIAL
Venus in Virgo, Aug. 23, 3:34 - Sept. 02, 19:28
Venus in Libra, Sept. 02, 19:29 - Sept. 23, 0:58

YOUR DRIVE AND AMBITION
Mars in Gemini, Aug. 23, 3:34 - Sept. 21, 4:05
Mars in Cancer, Sept. 21, 4:06 - Sept. 23, 0:58

YOUR LUCK MAGNETISM
Jupiter in Sagittarius, Aug. 23, 3:34 - Sept. 23, 0:58

World Events

Aug. 25 – The Olympics open in Rome.
Sept. 4 – Iraq, Iran, Kuwait, and Saudi Arabia form the Organization of Petroleum Exporting Countries (OPEC).

Boxer Cassius Clay, later Muhammad Ali, wins the Olympic Gold medal in Rome

LIBRA
Your Personal Planets

YOUR LOVE POTENTIAL
Venus in Libra, Sept. 23, 0:59 - Sept. 27, 5:12
Venus in Scorpio, Sept. 27, 5:13 - Oct. 21, 17:11
Venus in Sagittarius, Oct. 21, 17:12 - Oct. 23, 10:01

YOUR DRIVE AND AMBITION
Mars in Cancer, Sept. 23, 0:59 - Oct. 23, 10:01

YOUR LUCK MAGNETISM
Jupiter in Sagittarius, Sept. 23, 0:59 - Oct. 23, 10:01

World Events

Sept. 24 – The first nuclear-powered aircraft, the USS *Enterprise*, is launched in Virginia.
Oct. 1 – Nigeria gains its independence.

1960

SCORPIO
Your Personal Planets

YOUR LOVE POTENTIAL
Venus in Sagittarius, Oct. 23, 10:02 - Nov. 15, 8:56
Venus in Capricorn, Nov. 15, 8:57 - Nov. 22, 7:17

YOUR DRIVE AND AMBITION
Mars in Cancer, Oct. 23, 10:02 - Nov. 22, 7:17

YOUR LUCK MAGNETISM
Jupiter in Sagittarius, Oct. 23, 10:02 - Oct. 26, 3:00
Jupiter in Capricorn, Oct. 26, 3:01 - Nov. 22, 7:17

World Events

Nov. 2 - Penguin Books releases D. H. Lawrence's novel *Lady Chatterley's Lover*, after a thirty-year ban on its publication.

Nov. 8 - John F. Kennedy beats Richard Nixon to the presidency.

Senator Kennedy and Vice President Nixon during their television debate

SAGITTARIUS
Your Personal Planets

YOUR LOVE POTENTIAL
Venus in Capricorn, Nov. 22, 7:18 - Dec. 10, 8:33
Venus in Aquarius, Dec. 10, 8:34 - Dec. 21, 20:25

YOUR DRIVE AND AMBITION
Mars in Cancer, Nov. 22, 7:18 - Dec. 21, 20:25

YOUR LUCK MAGNETISM
Jupiter in Capricorn, Nov. 22, 7:18 - Dec. 21, 20:25

World Events

Dec. 18 - A general meeting of the United Nations condemns apartheid.

Dec. 20 - The National Liberation Front is formed by guerrillas in South Vietnam.

496

SCORPIO
From October 23, 10:02 through November 22, 7:17

The Mysterious Magnet

Glitz and glamor may captivate a 1960 Scorpio, but not for long. Your depth and vision enables you to see through the diaphanous veil of illusion that covers the celebrity circus. You are likely to have more meaningful ambitions. If fame catches up with you, so be it. You know that talent speaks for itself, and you have nothing to prove to anyone but yourself. You probably have a healthy perspective that holds spiritual well-being above the fleeting rewards of the material world.

You may express your spirituality through music, yoga, meditation, dance, or art. You may seek mystical experiences that take you out of yourself and allow you to transcend mundane preoccupations. Admirers of rock 'n' roll guitarist Eddie Cochran will attest that his music was out of this world. An icon of his generation, Cochran devoted all his attention and energy to making the music he loved. Credited for influencing the music of The Beatles, he died tragically in a car crash in 1960, at the age of twenty-one.

Compelled to explore the darker side of unconscious desire, you may be drawn to thrillers such as the film *Psycho*, made in your birth year by that master of suspense, Alfred Hitchcock. The movie focuses on the psychopathic killer Norman Bates, and his preoccupation with his mother. The famous shower scene—considered shocking in its day—still succeeds in thrilling and chilling movie audiences. Another shocker received vindication in 1960, the year the obscenity ban was lifted from *Lady Chatterley's Lover*, by D. H. Lawrence.

Scorpio's can be sexually magnetic, but love is likely to be more important to you. You may relate to the words of D. H. Lawrence: "Love is the flower of life, and blossoms unexpectedly and without law, and must be plucked where it is found, and enjoyed for the brief hour of its duration." A Cancer or Pisces may captivate you with poetically poignant romance.

Your challenge is to avoid power-struggles in personal relationships. The ability to see past superficiality is your strength. With wisdom as your guide, you can bravely walk the path of transformation.

SAGITTARIUS
From November 22, 7:18 through December 21, 20:25

The Nurturing Mentor

Teaching others is a Sagittarian gift. Imparting knowledge is second nature to Archers. Sometimes you may not even realize that you're educating others. A Sagittarian of 1960 is likely to care deeply about world events. You may feel drawn to an active role in creating a sound basis for the future. Attractive careers may involve reform of higher education, civil law, or religious values and institutions.

You may have an affinity for crazy eclectic objects, unusual cars, wild looking people, exotic religious artifacts. Comparative cultural studies could be a perfect choice for you in higher education. You may be compelled and inspired by the diversity and idiosyncrasies of humans all over the world. Members of your sign often have an interest in politics. You were born in the month John F. Kennedy was elected to the office of President of the United States. You would be a perfect candidate for President Kennedy's innovative program, the Peace Corps.

In 1960, the UN condemned apartheid and admitted fifteen newly independent African nations into its fold. Cyprus also gained independence from Britain. Civil war brought tragedy to the Congo; border disputes between China and the Soviet Union compounded an already tense relationship; the Laos government fled to Cambodia, as the capital raged with war. Vietnam was engulfed in combat.

The freedom to move around at will is important to Sagittarius. You are likely to support the building of new infrastructures that can afford maximum mobility for all. In 1960, a midair collision of two planes over Staten Island, New York provided the impetus for Project Beacon, the overhaul of U.S. air traffic control. As freewheeling as you may be, you may realize the necessity for reasonable regulation of local and international travel. A Leo can be an encouraging partner as you travel through life. Aries shares your taste for adventure.

You can serve as an excellent leader or mentor, for you interact easily and enjoy teamwork. Serving the good of society is a challenge that encourages you to share your invaluable wisdom and insight.

➤ Read about your Chinese Astrological sign on page 838. ➤ Read about your Personal Planets on page 826. ➤ Read about your personal Mystical Card on page 856.

CAPRICORN

From December 21, 20:26 through December 31, 23:59

The Humanitarian Traditionalist

The December-born Capricorn of 1960 has the talent to become a roaring success. Even with all the trials and tribulations in life, you have the ability to combine a keen mind with an enormous capacity for hard work. Clearly defined goals and careful planning provide a recipe for victory. These may be old-fashioned principles, but to your mind they are time-tested methods for success. You have the potential to be a cheerfully bright and optimistic character, with a hefty amount of realism thrown in for good measure!

As a family-oriented person with an interest in history, you might be amused to know that a very special pre-historic family hit the airwaves in your birth year. In 1960, Fred and Wilma Flintstone transported American children to Bedrock, a place with abundant dinosaurs, fossils, and "yabadabadoo" times. In a more serious development, by 1960, archaeologists had assembled a treasure trove of pre-Christian biblical artifacts, first discovered in caves on the shore of the Dead Sea in 1947. Consisting of fragments from a total of 800 scrolls, the Dead Sea Scrolls revolutionized biblical scholarship.

You work hard and give credit where credit is due. While you may honor conservative values, you are also a philanthropic champion of human rights. You may sympathize with fellow Capricorn, Mohammed Ali (or Cassius Clay, as he was known back in 1960). Clay won an Olympic gold medal for boxing earlier in the year, but when refused service at a restaurant, he threw his medal into the Ohio River. You, too, may sometimes act dramatically when you want to make a point.

Taureans can help to even out your tempo, and Virgoans are at your service. A Cancerian, on the other hand, can seduce you with good old apple pie and down-home nurturance.

In due course, your challenge is to balance the urge to expand with the desire to hold back and draw the line. Your sense of timing lets you know when it's right to expand or contract. Practical judgment, combined with an ability to see the bigger picture, is the strength that enables you to apply your talents to most profitable effect.

CAPRICORN
Your Personal Planets

YOUR LOVE POTENTIAL
Venus in Aquarius, Dec. 21, 20:26 - Dec. 31, 23:59

YOUR DRIVE AND AMBITION
Mars in Cancer, Dec. 21, 20:26 - Dec. 31, 23:59

YOUR LUCK MAGNETISM
Jupiter in Capricorn, Dec. 21, 20:26 - Dec. 31, 23:59

World Events

Dec. 27 – The French use the Sahara Desert as a testing ground for their third atomic bomb.

Dec. 29 – Laos appeals to the UN for assistance against invasions from North Vietnam.

THE KENNEDY FAMILY

Everything achieved by the Kennedy children can be seen as a tribute to their father, Joseph Kennedy, Sr., a son of Irish immigrants, and a brilliant financier who worked all his life to gain the acceptance of the upper-crust society of his day. He encouraged his children to climb to greater heights than he felt he would ever be able to, and was rewarded in this aim by seeing John elected President, Robert Attorney General, and Ted a senator. He also suffered the agony of seeing not one but two of his children assassinated, and Ted involved in a scandal that cut short any chances he might have had to become President. In addition, his eldest son, Joe, Jr., was killed in World War II and his daughter Kathleen perished in a plane crash. The larger-than-life existence of this powerful family, replete with huge success and terrible tragedy, has caused some people to wonder if perhaps there was a curse on the whole clan.

Joseph, considered by many to be a controversial figure, had Uranus, the planet of the unexpected, prominently placed in his horoscope. Generally speaking, this is not the best augur for someone in public office. As a Virgo, with neither the Sun, planet of identity, nor the Moon, planet of emotions, placed prominently in his chart, Joe Sr. was a much more effective person working behind the scenes on behalf of other people. With his Mars, planet of action, contacted by both expansive Jupiter and power-oriented Pluto, it was clear that this was a man who knew how to wield power.

By contrast, all three brothers have a prominently placed Saturn, the planet of obligation. It's clear that, from an early age, they understood what was expected of them and they were committed to fulfilling their duty. Neptune, the planet of idealism, is strongly placed in John's chart and provided him with the sense that what he was doing

Joseph P. Kennedy - Virgo
September 6, 1888 - November 19, 1969
John F. Kennedy - Gemini
May 29. 1917 - November 22, 1963
Robert F. Kennedy - Scorpio
November 20, 1925 - June 4, 1968
Edward Kennedy - Pisces
Born February 22, 1932

for the world was far more important than focusing on his needs as an individual. It is expressed in one of his most famous speeches, "Ask not what your country can do for you but what you can do for your country".

➤ Read about John F. Kennedy in "Cartography and the Planets" by Rochelle Gordon on page 505. ➤ Read "The Presidential Death Cycle" by Rochelle Gordon on page 657. ➤ Read Martin Luther King, Jr.'s Star Profile on page 537.

1961

Tug o' War: Saturn and Jupiter in Capricorn

The year 1961 marked the height of the Cold War. The United States broke off diplomatic relations with Cuba on January 3. One thousand two hundred United States-sponsored anti-Castro exiles invaded Cuba at the infamous Bay of Pigs operation on April 19. The attackers were all killed or captured by Cuban forces. East Germany erected the Berlin Wall dividing East and West the city into East and West on August 13 in an attempt to halt the flood of refugees escaping from the communist East to the capitalist West. The USSR detonated a fifty-eight megaton hydrogen bomb in the largest man-made explosion ever seen on October 30. During this year, the planet Saturn resided in its home sign of Capricorn. Because Saturn is connected to ambition, power, status, and authority, it's no wonder that nations would exhibit their most grandstanding behavior at this time. This is a very strong astrological placement: the struggle to attain security is very much heightened under this influence. When Saturn enters Capricorn the preservation instinct is activated.

During this year, Jupiter was also in the sign of Capricorn. Because Jupiter symbolizes expansion and Saturn represents contraction, there seemed to be a cosmic tug of war between these two forces. The struggle between Capitalism and Communism is akin to the struggle between Jupiter and Saturn. On one hand, The United States and Soviet Union sought to increase their influence by rivaling each other in the outside world. On the other hand, each nation carried out this work in the name of self-preservation.

Yuri Gagarin, the first man in space

East Berlin authorities build a wall dividing the city

Rudolf Nureyev speaking to journalists in Paris after asking for political asylum

CLOSE ENCOUNTERS

As Betty and Barney Hill drove home one night in 1961 they claimed to have seen a bright light following them. Mr Hill stopped the car and walked towards the light before discovering humanoid shapes staring at him. Panic-stricken, they fled back to the car and drove off. They further stated they were haunted by dreams and fears afterwards and sought help. Regression hypnosis determined that they believed they had been stopped by a flying saucer and taken aboard, where they were subjected to a medical examination by the alien creatures.

U.S.–SOVIET TENSIONS INCREASE

Exiled anti-Castro revolutionaries, backed by the U.S., unsuccessfully invaded the Bay of Pigs in Cuba. East Berlin authorities erected a wall dividing the city to prevent their citizens from escaping to West German zones. Russian Yuri Gagarin became the first man in space, followed by Gherman Titov. U.S. astronaut Alan Shepherd became the first American in space and Virgil Grissom piloted the *Liberty Bell 7* spacecraft. UN Secretary-General Dag Hammarskjold was killed in a suspicious plane crash while on a peace mission in Africa. John F. Kennedy inspired America at his inaugural address, declaring, "Ask not what your country can do for you; ask what you can do for your country." A fresh assault on segregation began as African American and white Freedom Riders violated bus segregation rules, sparking violence. At Olduvai Gorge, anthropologist Mary Leakey found remains of *Homo Habilis*, the first human tool-user, and geologists worked on verifying the theory of continental drift. While visiting Paris to perform, Russian ballet star Rudolf Nureyev defected to the West and Disney hit it big with his animated feature *101 Dalmatians*.

➤ Read "Cartography and the Planets" by Rochelle Gordon on page 505.

CAPRICORN

From January 01, 0:00 through January 20, 7:00

The Familial Patriot

Born in the month of the inauguration of United States President John F. Kennedy, the January-born Capricorn of 1961 is likely to grow up feeling an enormous sense of responsibility. Indicators in your chart show that you can be dependable, reliable, and trustworthy. You are likely to be a leader in your own right. Sensing your dutiful nature, bosses and colleagues may often refer projects to you. Chances are, you have an intimate acquaintance with the old saying: "If you want to get something done, give it to a busy person."

Having a sense of belonging may be essential to your sense of well-being. You may treat anyone with a regular presence in your life—colleagues, friends, subordinates—as a member of your family. You'll work hard to build a stable future, and you may look forward to a cozy retirement. On the home front, you can be traditional and sentimental. At work, however, you may be the very picture of professionalism. A conservative approach may serve you well in business. Bosses, colleagues, and clients may admire your practical, hands-on style.

Overwork can be an issue. A physical fitness routine eases stress, enhances your health and stamina, and boosts your energy. You may even have a memory like a steel trap. A wonderful example of someone with excellent recall is the poet Robert Frost, who was invited to recite at President Kennedy's inauguration. Asked to read one of his poems from a sheet of paper, Frost found the print was faded and two small. Instead, he quoted "The Gift" outright from memory.

Not one to waste time, you may feel that every moment in life is precious. Such an outlook can lead to great success and public recognition, but you're not one to believe your own press. Rather, you take pride in your work on its own merits. A Taurus or Virgo could help you climb to ambitious heights.

With awareness and understanding, your challenge is to empower others with the wisdom of your experience. Gentle caution and determination are strengths that enable you to lay the foundations for a fruitful career and for an equally satisfying home life.

AQUARIUS

From January 20, 7:01 through February 18, 21:15

The Cosmic Preserver

Renowned for their futuristic perspectives, Aquarians are usually well ahead of their time. And an Aquarian of 1961 is no exception, indeed they can project to the stratosphere and beyond! A dual-perspective distinguishes you from other Water Bearers. While you can offer a prophetic vision that looks to future progress, you are also able to appreciate the past and you may desperately strive to preserve the best of what has gone before.

Aquarius is the sign most directly associated with the future of humanity. In 1961, Britain and the United States saw mass demonstrations to protest the nuclear arms race. The eighty-nine-year-old mathematician, philosopher, and Nobel Prize-winner Lord Bertrand Russell was imprisoned for leading the demonstration in London. In that same year, U.S. President John F. Kennedy suggested the building of bomb shelters for the University of California at Berkeley. The protection of humanity from nuclear annihilation is the quintessential Aquarian cause. Because bomb shelters create the illusion of the survivability of nuclear war, your acute intellect is likely to recognize the futility of such a measure and to dismiss it as ridiculous.

High technology is a traditional area of Aquarian interest. You're likely to have a natural aptitude for any technology that imparts knowledge, such as television, the Internet, and satellite communications. The first U.S. presidential press conference was televised during your birth month. The Soviet Union produced its first live TV show in 1961, and at the end of the year, a satellite with the capacity for world link-up went into orbit. Such events mirror your special ability to employ the mass media in artistic or scientific projects. You may also have a flair for creating media events, publicizing humanitarian causes.

A Libra or Gemini could join you to make Aquarian heaven. With your bright intellect and determined ambition, you could also do well with an Aries or Pisces.

With your tendency to build castles in the air, your greatest challenge is to keep both feet firmly on the ground, which you must do if you want to make the most of your abilities and see your dreams of a better future become a reality.

▶ Read about your Chinese Astrological sign on page 838. ▶ Read about your Personal Planets on page 826. ▶ Read about your personal Mystical Card on page 856.

CAPRICORN
Your Personal Planets

YOUR LOVE POTENTIAL
Venus in Aquarius, Jan. 01, 0:00 - Jan. 05, 3:30
Venus in Pisces, Jan. 05, 3:31 - Jan. 20, 7:00

YOUR DRIVE AND AMBITION
Mars in Cancer, Jan. 01, 0:00 - Jan. 20, 7:00

YOUR LUCK MAGNETISM
Jupiter in Capricorn, Jan. 01, 0:00 - Jan. 20, 7:00

World Events

Jan. 3 - The U.S. severs diplomatic relations with Cuba.

Jan. 20 - John F. Kennedy becomes the youngest President in U.S. History.

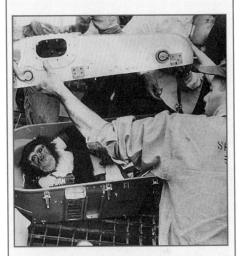

The space chimp "Ham" after his journey above earth

AQUARIUS
Your Personal Planets

YOUR LOVE POTENTIAL
Venus in Pisces, Jan. 20, 7:01 - Feb. 02, 4:45
Venus in Aries, Feb. 02, 4:46 - Feb. 18, 21:15

YOUR DRIVE AND AMBITION
Mars in Cancer, Jan. 20, 7:01 - Feb. 05, 0:21
Mars in Gemini, Feb. 05, 0:22 - Feb. 07, 5:24
Mars in Cancer, Feb. 07, 5:25 - Feb. 18, 21:15

YOUR LUCK MAGNETISM
Jupiter in Capricorn, Jan. 20, 7:01 - Feb. 18, 21:15

World Events

Jan. 31 - David Ben-Gurion resigns as Prime Minister of Israel.

Jan. 31 - "Ham," the first U.S. astrochimp, returns from space after an eighteen-minute flight, 420 miles through space.

PISCES
Your Personal Planets

YOUR LOVE POTENTIAL
Venus in Aries, Feb. 18, 21:16 - Mar. 20, 20:31

YOUR DRIVE AND AMBITION
Mars in Cancer, Feb. 18, 21:16 - Mar. 20, 20:31

YOUR LUCK MAGNETISM
Jupiter in Capricorn, Feb. 18, 21:16 - Mar. 15, 8:00
Jupiter in Aquarius, Mar. 15, 8:01 - Mar. 20, 20:31

World Events

Feb. 26 - King Hassan II succeeds to the throne of Morocco.

Mar. 15 - South Africa announces that it will withdraw from the British Commonwealth of Nations over its apartheid policy.

Yuri Gagarin makes the first-ever flight in space

ARIES
Your Personal Planets

YOUR LOVE POTENTIAL
Venus in Aries, Mar. 20, 20:32 - Apr. 20, 7:54

YOUR DRIVE AND AMBITION
Mars in Cancer, Mar. 20, 20:32 - Apr. 20, 7:54

YOUR LUCK MAGNETISM
Jupiter in Aquarius, Mar. 20, 20:32 - Apr. 20, 7:54

World Events

Apr. 12 - Soviet cosmonaut Yuri Gagarin becomes the first human in space.

Apr. 17 - Organized by the CIA, anti-Castro exiles invade the Bay of Pigs in Cuba, hoping to overthrow the Castro government.

PISCES
From February 18, 21:16 through March 20, 20:31

The Passionate Defender

Emotionally sensitive Pisceans have an instinctive empathy for others. While you may feel for humanity, 1961 Pisces, you may also need to follow up on feelings with concrete action. You're likely to be one brave, proactive, and motivated Piscean.

You may identify with a fellow Pisces who made tremendous sacrifices in order to pursue his artistic career. In 1961, dancer Rudolph Nureyev defected to the West while in Paris with the Bolshoi Ballet. Nureyev hungered for the creative freedom that simply could not be found in the Soviet Union—of course, the defection humiliated the USSR. Ballet is a distinctive Piscean art form; dance and movement may provide you with a liberating means for expressing your feelings, creativity, and spirituality.

Philanthropic urges may move you to help others. This year marked the inauguration of the Peace Corps, a program first proposed by U.S. President John F. Kennedy. Its first project involved the development of roads in Tanganyika, Africa. With the issue of highway safety gaining prominence in the U.S., seat belts were introduced in your zodiacal month. Indicators in your chart suggest a penchant for fast driving. Increased safety features in automobiles afford you the freedom to put your pedal to the metal.

In love, you can be a wild child. You could grow bored if your partner isn't adventurous. Variety may be the spice of your love life. A caring Cancerian may encourage you to mingle with a range of friends and associates. Aries shares your taste for adventure and speed. Scorpio adores the depth of your personality.

You're a complex character, with the ability to look past superficial preoccupations and to dive into a world of profound and crystal-clear emotion. Your challenge is to find ways to bring your empathy and spirituality into your daily life. A career that involves helping others, creative expression, or spreading inspiration may be perfect for you. You can be an outstanding social worker, health-care provider, artist, or clergy member. Intimate family life can also benefit from your emphasis on empathy and giving.

ARIES
From March 20, 20:32 through April 20, 7:54

The Space-Age Pioneer

Ariens of 1961 may feel proud to know that the very first human being launched into space in their zodiacal month. Ariens tend to love being first, as it reflects your natural leadership qualities. In April of 1961, the Soviet Major Yuri Gagarin shot into the stratosphere in the spaceship Vostok I and orbited for 108 minutes.

Gagarin was known as the "Columbus of the Cosmos." Such an adventurous act could serve as an inspiring ideal for you. You may indeed break into new and exciting frontiers, but you'll do it in accordance with your own brand of pioneering—one that involves originality and a bold imagination.

With a strange mixture of enthusiasm and unconventionality, you can inspire others to commit acts of outrageous creativity. Your birth year marked a number of firsts. The godfather of Beat, William S. Burroughs, initiated a wildly inventive writing style called "cut-ups," (later copied by David Bowie). Burroughs literally cut up words and rearranged them for his book, *The Soft Machine*. Diana Ross signed with Tamala Records for the first of her fifty-eight albums. And modern guru Ram Dass, or Professor Richard Alpert as he was known back then, got involved with the psychedelic hallucinogen experiments conducted by Timothy Leary at Harvard University. Because Aries of 1961 is likely to live every moment to the maximum degree, you may relate to Ram Dass's book, *Be Here Now*.

You can be self-sufficient and may have a healthy appreciation of your own company. Leo can show you the pleasure of spontaneity in your relationship and life in general. Sagittarius shares your adventurous flair for exploration and discovery.

You may lose interest if a job or relationship fails to incite your passion. Your challenge is to resist the urge to cut bait and run at the first sign of declining energies. You may later regret giving up on something that was once dear to you, especially if you didn't make a concerted effort to remedy your reasons for dissatisfaction. Experience and maturity can enhance your understanding of the natural cycles of intimate and business connections.

➤ Read about your Chinese Astrological sign on page 838. ➤ Read about your Personal Planets on page 826. ➤ Read about your personal Mystical Card on page 856.

TAURUS

From April 20, 7:55 through May 21, 7:21

The Ardent Lover

Taurus of 1961 can be hot, hot, hot! You have a powerful capacity for ardent passion, tingling excitement, and fervent love! Members of your sign tend to have a deeply sensual nature, but you could go one step further. Romance can infuse you with a permanent case of spring fever.

Moderating this tendency is a practical sensibility that can keep your feet on the ground when your head is floating in the clouds. The quintessential American movie hero Gary Cooper, who was also a Taurean, provided an example of cool comportment, even when temptation called. After thirty-five Hollywood years of besting bad guys and getting the girl, Cooper passed away in your birth month.

You can be a homebody, content to stay in and enjoy cozy creature comforts. During 1960s, timesaving innovations in appliances made the kitchen a more inviting place. You may also have a rebellious, libertarian side that seeks to promote fairness and equality in the public sphere. You could become actively involved in social and political issues—a bit of a departure from the traditional personality profile of the staid Taurus. Your birth month marked the embarkation of the famous Freedom Riders, multiracial activists who rode across America to protest against segregation on buses and in terminals. Although the Freedom Riders were attacked, beaten, burnt, arrested, and jailed, they carried on, against all odds, and succeeded in winning President Kennedy's support for legislation (eventually passed) outlawing segregation on interstate buses.

In your personal life, you may find an Aquarian can bring out the freedom fighter within you. A Virgo shares your devotion to service and enjoying abundance at home. Capricorn may be eager to cater to your desires and satiate your appetite for the good life.

Vigor, courage, and determination are strengths that enable you to develop a well-balanced approach to life. Your challenge is to resist going overboard, and that includes keeping an eye on relationships as well as spending. You may find that the place to live is with your loved one, and just within your income.

GEMINI

From May 21, 7:22 through June 21, 15:29

The Clear-Headed Champion

Communication is a Gemini skill. Words, ideas, and data flow easily both within you and from you. A Gemini of 1961 has the added talent of being able to speak and perform publicly, with confidence, flair, and wit. In short, you're a class act!

An ultimately legendary Gemini burst on to the scene in 1961. Bob Dylan, musician, wordsmith, and spokesperson for a generation, signed with Columbia Records in that year. Dylan revolutionized the field of folk music and youth culture, with poetic lyrics that packed a stunning wallop. No history of rock music can be complete without noting the moment, later in his career, when Dylan went electric. You, too, have the ability to describe life with drama, poetry, and impact.

Super-smart, you're quick on the uptake and impress others with your nimble mind and stylish appearance. John and Jackie Kennedy were a big hit in the European style magazines of 1961, with just the character combinations that you may share in common. Jack was a bright, talkative Gemini, and his Leonine First Lady brought beauty, elegance, and culture to the White House. Gemini is the sign of the Twins, so it's interesting that Kennedy worked closely with another Gemini, Henry Kissinger, whom he named as a consultant to the Department of State in 1961. You may also share Kennedy's ability to keep a firm grip on situations. In 1961, at the Vienna summit, Kennedy made progress over Laos, but the Berlin issue deepened. You may not be as moderate as Kennedy was.

Like the astronauts of your childhood, you may have "the right stuff," rocketing ambitions,boundless energy, and the urge to push the outer envelope of possibility. In intimate relationships, Aquarians can match your pace and brilliance. A Libran's sense of style makes for fabulous nights on the town.

You may love to soak in splendor and pleasure. Flattery and opulence can be seductive, but your challenge is to rise above such mundane temptations. With your enormous capacity for bighearted inspiration, you have the ability to empower others to believe in themselves and fulfill their highest ideals.

➤ Read about your Chinese Astrological sign on page 838. ➤ Read about your Personal Planets on page 826. ➤ Read about your personal Mystical Card on page 856.

1961

TAURUS
Your Personal Planets

YOUR LOVE POTENTIAL
Venus in Aries, Apr. 20, 7:55 - May 21, 7:21

YOUR DRIVE AND AMBITION
Mars in Cancer, Apr. 20, 7:55 - May 06, 1:12
Mars in Leo, May 06, 1:13 - May 21, 7:21

YOUR LUCK MAGNETISM
Jupiter in Aquarius, Apr. 20, 7:55 - May 21, 7:21

World Events

Apr. 21 - The French army revolts in Algiers.
May 5 - Navy Cmdr. Alan B. Shepard Jr. becomes the first U.S. astronaut, making a 302-mile trip into space.

Rudolf Nureyev, ballet dancer

GEMINI
Your Personal Planets

YOUR LOVE POTENTIAL
Venus in Aries, May 21, 7:22 - June 05, 19:24
Venus in Taurus, June 05, 19:25 - June 21, 15:29

YOUR DRIVE AND AMBITION
Mars in Leo, May 21, 7:22 - June 21, 15:29

YOUR LUCK MAGNETISM
Jupiter in Aquarius, May 21, 7:22 - June 21, 15:29

World Events

June 6 - Swiss psychiatrist Carl Jung dies at the age of eighty-five.
June 16 - Russian ballet dancer Rudolph Nureyev defects to the West.

1961

CANCER
Your Personal Planets

YOUR LOVE POTENTIAL
Venus in Taurus, June 21, 15:30 - July 07, 4:31
Venus in Gemini, July 07, 4:32 - July 23, 2:23

YOUR DRIVE AND AMBITION
Mars in Leo, June 21, 15:30 - June 28, 23:46
Mars in Virgo, June 28, 23:47 - July 23, 2:23

YOUR LUCK MAGNETISM
Jupiter in Aquarius, June 21, 15:30 - July 23, 2:23

World Events

July 1 – British troops arrive in Kuwait in preparation for an attack by Iraq.

July 2 – American Author Ernest Hemingway commits suicide.

East Berlin authorities build a wall dividing the city

LEO
Your Personal Planets

YOUR LOVE POTENTIAL
Venus in Gemini, July 23, 2:24 - Aug. 03, 15:27
Venus in Cancer, Aug. 03, 15:28 - Aug. 23, 9:18

YOUR DRIVE AND AMBITION
Mars in Virgo, July 23, 2:24 - Aug. 17, 0:40
Mars in Libra, Aug. 17, 0:41 - Aug. 23, 9:18

YOUR LUCK MAGNETISM
Jupiter in Aquarius, July 23, 2:24 - Aug. 12, 8:53
Jupiter in Capricorn, Aug. 12, 8:54 - Aug. 23, 9:18

World Events

Aug. 6 – Soviet cosmonaut Gherman Titov is launched on a mission that will see him orbit the Earth seventeen times.

Aug. 13 – East German authorities erect the Berlin Wall between the eastern and western zones of the city to halt the flood of refugees.

CANCER
From June 21, 15:30 through July 23, 2:23

The Impressive Protector

As a Cancer of 1961, you may put up a cool front, but you can be a sentimental softie at heart. In 1961, your cradle may have rocked to the rhythm of Henry Mancini's *Moon River*. Because the Moon has a special connection with your sign, Mancini's song may have a place in your heart. In your birth year, Mancini won two Academy Awards and four Grammies for his musical accomplishments. Diana, Princess of Wales, was also born in your zodiacal month. Known as "The People's Princess," Diana was a tenderhearted soul. Reflecting the best qualities of the sign of Cancer, she devoted her career to giving care and dignity to underprivileged, needy, and forgotten people.

Cancerians tend to revere the past, and you may be an avid collector of antiques or fossils. In 1961, Dr. Louis Leakey discovered hominid bones, believed to be over one million years old, in Tanganyika. You may exhibit Leakey-like zeal on your own expeditions through flea markets and second-hand stores.

You may be fiercely loyal and protective of your home, resources, and dependents. Britain ended its protectorate over Kuwait in your birth month. Iraq quickly claimed sovereignty and sent troops to Kuwait's boarder. With full Kuwaiti support, Britain retaliated and succeeded in gaining a complete Iraqi withdrawal. Most Cancerians deal with conflict by retreating to a safe place. When someone crosses your particular line in the sand, however, you may stand and fight with deadly determination.

While you may envision a world where everyone has adequate care, ample food, and shelter, you may also believe that charity begins at home. Nurturing family members may get first priority, but your circle of care tends to expand to include everyone you know. Scorpio and Pisces share and support your spirit of tender generosity.

Hard times in life can either harden your shell or deepen your sensitivity. Your challenge is to choose to pursue the latter course of action. Time and experience can show you the needlessness of taking misfortune personally. With maturity you can transform personal pain into wisdom and compassion.

LEO
From July 23, 2:24 through August 23, 9:18

The Light-Hearted Individual

Leos tend to have a live-and-let-live attitude. Freedom may be an especially important value for Leo of 1961. The idea of anyone cramping your style is anathema to you. August 1961 marked the beginning of construction of the Berlin Wall, a barrier designed to halt the flow of East Berliners to the West. With the erection of this concrete section of the metaphorical Iron Curtain, personal freedoms were further curtailed, causing relations between the U.S. and the Soviet Union to deteriorate even further.

Indicators in your chart show a brilliant capacity for thinking outside the box. A big-picture perspective and exceptional intelligence enables you to devise original and ingenious solutions to seemingly complex dilemmas. Your insights and suggestions may leave others slapping their heads and declaring "why didn't I think of that?"

The ability to interact freely with others is crucial to your intellectual and personal growth. Teamwork and partnerships will tend to magnify your effectiveness and potential for success. You are simply not the type to be secretive or possessive about your accomplishments and discoveries. Rather, you may believe that the more input and appraisal you can get, the merrior your endeavours and results will be. Other's perspectives nicely complement your talent for flushing out important details.

One of your greatest survival skills may derive from a talent for divining humor from even the most horrible of situations. You may seek partners who can appreciate your unorthodox point of view and challenge you to grow. Gemini can be your equal in intellect and humor. Able to respect your need for breathing room, Aries and Sagittarius can bring an exciting competitive edge to your partnership. An Aquarian's lively individuality and confidence can keep relationships interesting and exciting.

As a 1961 Leo, your challenge is to allow for flexibility and compromise from time to time, especially when your partner needs your support. Choosing to give generously of your heart can be liberating for you and reassuring for your significant other.

➤ Read about your Chinese Astrological sign on page 838. ➤ Read about your Personal Planets on page 826. ➤ Read about your personal Mystical Card on page 856.

VIRGO

From August 23, 9:19 through September 23, 6:41

The Smooth Operator

Your cool exterior may hide a fiery and hot-blooded heart. The Virgo of 1961 may be more passionate than others who share your sign. With a tranquil demeanor to camouflage your powerful core, you are loyal and loving. Your often-hidden inner strength can be an asset to any relationship.

Not everyone can maintain a poised self-assurance while going through the heartache and tragedies of life. Country-pop singer and fellow Virgo Patsy Cline is revered for having done just that. Miss Cline released her famous songs, "Crazy" and "I Fall To Pieces," in your birth year. She described herself as "trouble and honey."

Your air of composure may come from being highly organized and methodical. In contrast, the CIA made some disastrous miscalculations in your birth year, with respect to its involvement in Cuba. The CIA played a key role the U.S' attempt to overthrow Castro's communist-Marxist government by organizing anti-Castro exiles and landing them at the Bay of Pigs. The whole affair was a fiasco, prompting the U.S. to cut off diplomatic relations with Cuba, which deepened the rift between communist East and capitalist West. In the winter of 1961, the Cold War became very chilly indeed.

Possessed of analytical skills and keen perceptive abilities, you can understand the complexities of the human personality. Because you can be deeply insightful, the inner workings of the mind may fascinate you. You may have an interest in psychology, and relate to the work of Carl Gustav Jung, who died in 1961. Jung made tremendous contributions to his field, such as the four types of personality: thinking, feeling, intuiting, and sensing. Likely to be intuitive and sensual, you may fare well with partners who have a similar mix of characteristics, such as Taurus, Leo, or Libra.

By combining patience and stillness with a generous, warm nature, you create an atmosphere that encourages diplomacy and tact, and this is your major strength. Because you are intellectually competitive, your challenge is to choose your strategy carefully and ensure that you won't be caught unprepared.

LIBRA

From September 23, 6:42 through October 23, 15:46

The Perceptive Peacekeeper

In general, Librans take their time in making decisions. The possibility of making the wrong choice can feel potentially disastrous. Avoiding snap decisions can be a healthy strategy for you, especially when others' well-being depends on the outcome. Libra of 1961 strives for the careful assessment of any situation—and this takes time.

When you do finally render your decisions, others are likely to appreciate your perceptiveness and wisdom. You can come up with real buried treasure. Sometimes your tendency to hesitate can result in a lack of confidence in your own authority. With time, you can learn to become a better listener to your own instincts. And the more you listen to your instincts, the easier it becomes to trust them. Your record of good results proves the good quality and validity of your inner voice.

Like most Librans, you may be a peacekeeper, a diplomat who tirelessly helps others find harmony and agreement. Like Dag Hammarskjold, the Secretary-General for the United Nations in 1961, you can bring light and concord to demanding situations involving embattled parties. Unfortunately, while on his way to negotiate a peace treaty in the civil war in the Congo, Hammarskjold was killed in a plane crash in northern Rhodesia. He was posthumously awarded the Nobel Peace Prize in 1961.

In the end, though, a peaceful existence is nothing without love. Librans tend to live for relationships. In your birth year, the toy company Mattel introduced the pink plastic princess, Barbie, to a new companion—the handsome, chisel-cheeked Ken! While you might be swayed by dashing good looks, you want more than mere superficial infatuation. You may prefer a deep, meaningful, and magnetic romance. An Aquarian, Virgo, or Gemini may be the one for you.

You have a sharp and incisive mind. Your challenge is to combine the compelling forces of your intelligence and intuition. With such a power working on your side, you can see through any attempt to deceive you. Impervious to glamorous enticements, you can render judgments that are fair and beneficial both to you and to others.

➤ Read about your Chinese Astrological sign on page 838. ➤ Read about your Personal Planets on page 826. ➤ Read about your personal Mystical Card on page 856.

VIRGO
Your Personal Planets

YOUR LOVE POTENTIAL
Venus in Cancer, Aug. 23, 9:19 - Aug. 29, 14:17
Venus in Leo, Aug. 29, 14:18 - Sept. 23, 6:41

YOUR DRIVE AND AMBITION
Mars in Libra, Aug. 23, 9:19 - Sept. 23, 6:41

YOUR LUCK MAGNETISM
Jupiter in Capricorn, Aug. 23, 9:19 - Sept. 23, 6:41

World Events

Aug. 26 – Burma becomes the world's first Buddhist republic.

Sept. 18 – Secretary-General of the United Nations Dag Hammarskjold is killed in a plane crash.

Yves St. Laurent opens his own fashion firm

LIBRA
Your Personal Planets

YOUR LOVE POTENTIAL
Venus in Leo, Sept. 23, 6:42 - Sept. 23, 15:42
Venus in Virgo, Sept. 23, 15:43 - Oct. 18, 2:57
Venus in Libra, Oct. 18, 2:58 - Oct. 23, 15:46

YOUR DRIVE AND AMBITION
Mars in Libra, Sept. 23, 6:42 - Oct. 01, 20:01
Mars in Scorpio, Oct. 01, 20:02 - Oct. 23, 15:46

YOUR LUCK MAGNETISM
Jupiter in Capricorn, Sept. 23, 6:42 - Oct. 23, 15:46

World Events

Sept. 30 – Syria removes itself from the United Arab Republic in protest against Egypt's domination of the area.

Oct. 17 – Khrushchev banishes Albania from the Soviet bloc.

1961

SCORPIO
Your Personal Planets

YOUR LOVE POTENTIAL
Venus in Libra, Oct. 23, 15:47 - Nov. 11, 5:32
Venus in Scorpio, Nov. 11, 5:33 - Nov. 22, 13:07

YOUR DRIVE AND AMBITION
Mars in Scorpio, Oct. 23, 15:47 - Nov. 13, 21:49
Mars in Sagittarius, Nov. 13, 21:50 - Nov. 22, 13:07

YOUR LUCK MAGNETISM
Jupiter in Capricorn, Oct. 23, 15:47 - Nov. 04, 2:48
Jupiter in Aquarius, Nov. 04, 2:49 - Nov. 22, 13:07

World Events

Oct. 30 - The USSR detonates a fifty-megaton hydrogen bomb in the largest man-made explosion in history.

Nov. 3 - U Thant of Burma is elected interim Secretary-General of the United Nations.

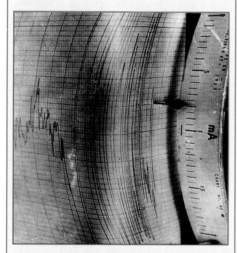

A seismograph chart measures the huge Soviet bomb blast

SAGITTARIUS
Your Personal Planets

YOUR LOVE POTENTIAL
Venus in Scorpio, Nov. 22, 13:08 - Dec. 05, 3:39
Venus in Sagittarius, Dec. 05, 3:40 - Dec. 22, 2:18

YOUR DRIVE AND AMBITION
Mars in Sagittarius, Nov. 22, 13:08 - Dec. 22, 2:18

YOUR LUCK MAGNETISM
Jupiter in Aquarius, Nov. 22, 13:08 - Dec. 22, 2:18

World Events

Nov. 30 - The USSR vetoes Kuwait's application for membership of the United Nations.

Dec. 21 - President Moishe Tshombe of Katanga agrees to the unification of the Congo.

504

SCORPIO
From October 23, 15:47 through November 22, 13:07

The Diplomatic Powerhouse

Able to carefully assess and unravel complicated situations, the 1961 Scorpio has the potential to reach a powerful position in life. You may have charm and wit, but most of all, you can be relentless in pursuing a goal that is crucial to you. You may find time-wasting intolerable. You are likely, however, to make time for lucrative pursuits and meaningful relationships.

You may also have a certain cultural refinement. Art and beauty may bring you deep pleasure. In your birth month the New York Metropolitan Museum paid a record price for Rembrandt's *Aristotle Contemplating The Bust Of Homer*. Such ambitious acquisitions may not be in your stars, but you may own works of art that are dear to you. Making wise investments comes naturally to Scorpio. Couple your business skills with an eye for the unusual, and you may find yourself relaxing in a stylish home.

Born during the Cold War era, you may have a formidable and sometimes intimidating presence. Like all Scorpios, you can be powerful and fierce. Within days of your birth, the Soviet Union detonated a fifty-eight megaton hydrogen bomb. The explosion broke a three-year moratorium on nuclear testing. You too may have a storehouse of immense personal power that has the potential to burst out of control. Fierce words can fly when you lose your temper—a situation which can cause as much harm to you as to others.

You are likely to have a sharp eye for promising opportunities and the courage to seize the moment. In your zodiacal month, Brian Epstein spotted The Beatles at the Cavern club in Liverpool, England. Epstein went on to make the mop-tops into world-famous mega-stars. You may enjoy your own wonderful prospects for wealth and romance with Cancer, Taurus, or Pisces.

Your challenge, Scorpio of 1961, is to transform any destructive elements that come to light, be they within or around you. Your ultimate strength is a perceptive mind that sees right to heart of any matter. When a certain relationship or behavior ceases to serve you, you can let it go—an act of courage that allows you to continuously evolve and prosper.

SAGITTARIUS
From November 22, 13:08 through December 22, 2:18

The Excitable Extrovert

As one of the fieriest signs of the zodiac, Sagittarians can burn with excitement. The chart for Sagittarius of 1961 shows an exceptional flow of personal energy. You have a luminous mind that needs constant stimulation and demands variety. You can take even the most predictable job and make it into something thrilling and wonderful. Likely to be attracted to a career involving information, technology, or communication, you may constantly seek opportunities to make new and exciting discoveries. Blessed with a learning curve that can spirals ever onwards and upwards, you may inspire awe in others with your achievements. You can exude a wild, almost crazy, enthusiasm for life.

As merry a soul as you may be, you are perfectly capable of carrying out your responsibilities and satisfying the demands of the most taciturn bosses or authority figures. Ideally, however, you are likely to pursue a career that allows you to be free and experimental. Your fellow Sagittarian, jazz legend and composer Dave Brubeck, released his classic *Take Five* in your birth year. You too may be capable of inspired improvisations, in music or other venues.

Sagittarians tend to adore travel. The allure of different peoples, places, and cultures may inform your choices in education, career, and home decor. Discrimination is the only idea likely to be truly foreign to you. Within days of your birth, the United States Supreme Court overturned the convictions of civil rights workers, who had been arrested for participating in sit-ins against segregation.

Your tendency to fly from one thing to the next may keep loved ones guessing about your next move. Itinerant intimacy can be tough to maintain. You may have friends from all walks of life. You may choose a partner like Scorpio, who's content to hold down the fort while you are away. Aries and Gemini tend to savor life on the move.

Truth is the banner you brandish, and your challenge is to make sense of life's big questions. You may wonder why we are here; your answers may be found in religion or philosophy, where your honesty is a significant strength.

➤ Read about your Chinese Astrological sign on page 838. ➤ Read about your Personal Planets on page 826. ➤ Read about your personal Mystical Card on page 856.

CAPRICORN

From December 22, 2:19 through December 31, 23:59

The Knowledgeable Expert

Members of the sign of Capricorn tend to be cautious, hardworking, and organized. While the December-born Capricorn of 1961 is likely to share these traits, you can also be liberally inventive. Interestingly, you may take a conservative approach in espousing wild or unorthodox ideas. You may insist on proper proof and testing in your pursuit of novel theories.

Although broadminded, you like to keep your feet on the ground. In 1961 the scientific community engaged in heated debate over the phenomenon of continental drift. American geologist Harry Hess proposed the theory of plate tectonics, attributing earthquakes, oceanic trenches, and other geological formations to the movement of large sections of the Earth's crust, upon which the continents rest. Following years of independent testing by Hess's peers in the field, his theory ultimately gained general acceptance. You may feel most comfortable in promoting change by working within the system and going through established channels.

You tend to respect authority, but you also regard leadership as a sacred trust. When you attain a position of power, you may see your role as the bearer of responsibility to those who depend on you. In this interesting and revolutionary perspective, the boss is also a servant. People probably feel incredibly lucky to work for you because everything you do together serves a higher principle, a shared goal, something larger than any one person or even the group itself.

You may be sporting and competitive. In 1961, New York Yankee Roger Maris exceeded the home-run record of his fellow Yankee Babe Ruth, by hitting his sixty-first home run in a single season. With the help of a loving partner who supports your goals and dreams, you could make your own mark in history. Taurus can provide the resources you need. Virgo will work hard by your side.

Determination, sound judgment, and earthiness are personal strengths, which can help you to realize your objectives. Your challenge is to strike the right balance between your traditional style of handling things and your often unconventional values.

1961

CAPRICORN
Your Personal Planets

YOUR LOVE POTENTIAL
Venus in Sagittarius, Dec. 22, 2:19 - Dec. 29, 0:06
Venus in Capricorn, Dec. 29, 0:07 - Dec. 31, 23:59

YOUR DRIVE AND AMBITION
Mars in Sagittarius, Dec. 22, 2:19 - Dec. 24, 17:49
Mars in Capricorn, Dec. 24, 17:50 - Dec. 31, 23:59

YOUR LUCK MAGNETISM
Jupiter in Aquarius, Dec. 22, 2:19 - Dec. 31, 23:59

World Events

Dec. 22 – James Davis becomes the first U.S. soldier to be slain in the Vietnam conflict.

Dec. 29 – In a speech given in Paris, Charles de Gaulle promises French troops will withdraw from Algeria in 1962.

Special Feature
Cartography and the Planets
by Rochelle Gordon

Locality astrology, or astro-mapping, an astrological technique that seeks to discover the connection between your geographical location(s)—where you live—and your planetary influences, is a uniquely twentieth-century phenomenon. After all, for ancient astrologers, the idea of moving more than several hundred miles from one's birthplace was as inconceivable as the automobile, the jet plane, or space travel.

When astro-maps first came into fashion, they were used for mundane astrology—the astrology of world events and the horoscopes of nations. It was the exceptionally gifted astrologer Jim Lewis who popularized the technique by applying it to the charts of individuals. Through his amazingly popular Astro*Carto*Graphy™ maps, Lewis introduced a sophisticated technique that anyone can use to find out what it would be like to visit, work, or live at any location on the globe. Even a fictional daytime soap-opera character once

went off to have her Astro*Carto*Graphy map read to see if there was somewhere on Earth where she could finally find true happiness. Though enduring contentment is unlikely to happen on a soap opera, many thousands of people consult locality astrologers each year to help them find a favorable place for romance, career, retirement, or any desired pursuit. This technique can also let you know where to stay away from, and when to do so!

While the actual idea of astro-maps is relatively new, the theory upon which the maps are based is really quite ancient. From time immemorial, astrologers have placed great significance on the rising and setting of the planets, believing that when planets are at these "angles, " their influence is most powerful. In addition to the angles of rising and setting, astrologers also look at planets that are at the highest point in the sky (culminating planets), as well as those at the

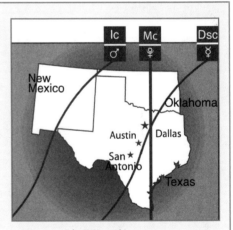

John F. Kennedy's astro-map

opposite point of—anti-culmination. The most easily understandable image is the movement of the Sun from sunrise (rising, or ascending) to high noon (culminating), to sunset (setting) and, finally, to midnight (anti-culminating). You can think of the angles of a horoscope wheel as the north, south, east, and west points on a compass.

(Continued on page 513)

➤ Read The Kennedy Family's Star Profile on page 497.

1962

Working for Change: Saturn in Aquarius

Saturn is the planet of structure and work. When it enters any sign of the zodiac, it focuses daily life on the energy of that sign. In 1962, Saturn was placed in Aquarius, sign of freedom, social relations, and all that is new and different. The revolutionary planet Uranus rules Aquarius. The civil rights movement broke through in powerful ways in 1962.

On October 1, 1962, James H. Meredith, an African-American civil rights leader, lodged a protest against segregation as he registered at the University of Mississippi. He did so despite the opposition of Governor Ross R. Barnett and the prevailing attitude in the southern United States. A mob gathered and attacked the contingent of several hundred federal marshals assigned to protect Meredith; two people were killed in the ensuing fracas. The next day federal troops occupied Oxford, Mississippi, and restored order. Meredith had earlier become the first African American to attend a Mississippi public school with white students in accordance with the groundbreaking 1954 court decision of Brown versus Board of Education. When Saturn is in Aquarius, institutions and progressive movements—as well as the concept of justice itself—come under the spotlight and radical shake-ups are inevitable. On the very day that Meredith registered at the University of Mississippi, Saturn in Aquarius was making a positive angle, called a "trine", to the Sun in Libra. Libra is the arbiter of all that is just and fair in the Universe. Under this influence, the civil rights movement took a giant step forward into new territory.

John F. Kennedy with his wife, Jackie

Nazi Adolf Eichmann is executed

Bombers aboard the Soviet ship, the Kasimov, at sea off Cuba

SPACE ODDITY

In the Mercury I mission spacecraft, the *Friendship 7*, astronaut John Glenn became the first American to orbit Earth successfully. He reported seeing the lights of Perth, Australia; residents there had turned on all their house lights when he passed overhead. Completing the first orbit, he noted thousands of luminous particles in the sunrise over the Pacific, clustered near the capsule. Glenn also brought back a photo of a "cigar-shaped object with a bright light next to it" that some say could have been a UFO.

NUCLEAR WAR IS AVERTED

The Cuban missile crisis strained U.S.-Russian relations and caused the world to collectively hold its breath as, under threat of nuclear war, Khrushchev and Kennedy faced off over the installation of Russian nuclear missiles in Cuba. After fourteen days, Khrushchev backed down. France granted Algeria its independence. Nazi Adolf Eichmann was executed by Israel for orchestrating the deaths of millions of Jews during World War II. John Glenn became the first American to orbit the Earth, and First Lady Jackie Kennedy became a celebrity, offering a televised tour of the White House. Rev. Martin Luther King, Jr. met President Kennedy to urge for American-African civil rights, but was jailed this same year for holding a prayer meeting. With the Education TV Facilities Act, the federal government funded public TV in the U.S. for the first time. The U.S. spacecraft Mariner 2 flew by and scanned the planet Venus. Telstar, the first active communications satellite, was launched and transmitted TV pictures from the U.S. to France. William Faulkner, chronicler of the American South, died, while Marilyn Monroe died of an overdose of barbituates.

➤ Read "Cartography and the Planets" by Rochelle Gordon on page 505.

CAPRICORN

From January 01, 0:00 through January 20, 12:57

The Experimental Tactician

Capricorns come in two varieties—both are ambitious, but there are subtle differences. One is traditionally conservative, rarely willing to change established rules. The other welcomes radical new systems, albeit in a tentative manner. January Capricorn of 1962 is likely to lean in the latter direction. Altruistic tendencies may inspire you to look to the future, with an aim to making it better for all.

Back in 1962, the Space Race was on, and new technologies opened a wide range of possibilities to humanity. You may have an avid interest in the world of high technology and mass communication. Machines that were unimaginable in the first half of the century now play an utterly unremarkable role in your everyday life.

In 1962, two American engineers, Charles E. Molnar and Wesley A. Clark, developed the first personal computer. Employing their machine in medical research, the advanced operating system was simple to use. You, too, may be able to devise new innovations to serve the needs of your chosen field. Liable to share character traits with your Aquarian friends, you are likely to be a unique character, endearingly eccentric. Actor Jim Carrey, an expert player of outrageous roles, shares your zodiacal birth month.

Equal opportunity just makes good sense to you. You were born the year Nelson Mandela was sentenced to five years imprisonment. Martin Luther King also did a stint in jail that year. After four tries to enroll in the University of Mississippi, an African-American student, James Meredith, succeeded in gaining admission—albeit accompanied by troops from the National Guard. You value fairness in personal relationships, too. You may prefer a partnership that has practical workability. The love of a Taurus or Virgo could offer you a solid foundation that can last.

Your challenge is to work with others to build a strong foundation for the future while maintaining your wonderful individuality. Forward-looking wisdom gives you the strength to achieve your hopes and wishes. You have the confidence to be independent and the compassion to reach out to others.

AQUARIUS

From January 20, 12:58 through February 19, 3:14

The World Citizen

The laser, invented in 1958, was used to bounce a beam off the Moon in 1962. Get ready, all you hipsters, to groove to the chorus: "This is the dawning of the Age of Aquarius, the Age of Aquarius, Aquarius!" You were born during the biggest astrological event of the century, which makes you among the world's most forward-thinking individuals.

Aquarians of 1962 tend to have distinctive qualities that can make you stand out in a crowd. Even if you have a regular job, you're likely to give it your unique stamp and make it more interesting. In your zodiacal month, the First Lady of the United States, Jacqueline Kennedy, took Americans on a nationally televised tour of the White House, in which she displayed her hand in renovating this historical landmark. Anything exhibiting state-of-the-art workmanship is likely to appeal to you.

Working with others, however, comes naturally. You've got team spirit. The ability to be yourself, to cooperate with others, and appreciate their uniqueness makes you a very special person. You may believe that independence is a human birthright. In 1962, after years of violence and strife, Algerian rebels agreed to de Gaulle's proposed truce with France. Algeria gained its independence that year, after 132 years of French rule. Burundi, Uganda, Kenya, Western Samoa, Trinidad and Tobago, and Jamaica also gained sovereignty in 1962, making it quite a year for nations to break free of colonialism.

Freedom is likely to be one of your most precious ideals. You need to ally yourself with intimate partners who will respect your need for autonomy. Hardly the needy or dependent type, Aries likes to pursue a variety of interests. Libra and Gemini have an intellectual sophistication that you may find endlessly stimulating.

Aquarians tend to be idealistic. Your challenge is to make your humanitarian dreams come true, without giving in to disillusionment along the way. Imperfect people need time to get used to perfect goals. With single-minded focus, you can maintain a clear vision of your ultimate goal. Patience and persistence will take you there.

➤ Read about your Chinese Astrological sign on page 838. ➤ Read about your Personal Planets on page 826. ➤ Read about your personal Mystical Card on page 856.

CAPRICORN
Your Personal Planets

YOUR LOVE POTENTIAL
Venus in Capricorn, Jan. 01, 0:00 - Jan. 20, 12:57

YOUR DRIVE AND AMBITION
Mars in Capricorn, Jan. 01, 0:00 - Jan. 20, 12:57

YOUR LUCK MAGNETISM
Jupiter in Aquarius, Jan. 01, 0:00 - Jan. 20, 12:57

World Events

Jan. 4 - The U.S. offers aid to Saigon as a commitment to its future.

Jan. 18 - The Dominican junta of Rafael Rodriguez Echavarria is ousted.

The north face of the Matterhorn is conquered

AQUARIUS
Your Personal Planets

YOUR LOVE POTENTIAL
Venus in Capricorn, Jan. 20, 12:58 - Jan. 21, 20:30
Venus in Aquarius, Jan. 21, 20:31 - Feb. 14, 18:08
Venus in Pisces, Feb. 14, 18:09 - Feb. 19, 3:14

YOUR DRIVE AND AMBITION
Mars in Capricorn, Jan. 20, 12:58 - Feb. 01, 23:05
Mars in Aquarius, Feb. 01, 23:06 - Feb. 19, 3:14

YOUR LUCK MAGNETISM
Jupiter in Aquarius, Jan. 20, 12:58 - Feb. 19, 3:14

World Events

Feb. 3 - U.S. President Kennedy announces a trade embargo with Cuba.

Feb. 4 - Hilti von Allmen and Walter Etter successfully scale the north face of the Matterhorn in winter.

1962

PISCES
Your Personal Planets

YOUR LOVE POTENTIAL
Venus in Pisces, Feb. 19, 3:15 - Mar. 10, 18:27
Venus in Aries, Mar. 10, 18:28 - Mar. 21, 2:29

YOUR DRIVE AND AMBITION
Mars in Aquarius, Feb. 19, 3:15 - Mar. 12, 7:57
Mars in Pisces, Mar. 12, 7:58 - Mar. 21, 2:29

YOUR LUCK MAGNETISM
Jupiter in Aquarius, Feb. 19, 3:15 - Mar. 21, 2:29

World Events

Feb. 20 - John Glenn becomes the first American to orbit the Earth.

Mar. 4 - The island of Malta gains full independence.

American astronaut John Glenn

ARIES
Your Personal Planets

YOUR LOVE POTENTIAL
Venus in Aries, Mar. 21, 2:30 - Apr. 03, 23:04
Venus in Taurus, Apr. 03, 23:05 - Apr. 20, 13:50

YOUR DRIVE AND AMBITION
Mars in Pisces, Mar. 21, 2:30 - Apr. 19, 16:57
Mars in Aries, Apr. 19, 16:58 - Apr. 20, 13:50

YOUR LUCK MAGNETISM
Jupiter in Aquarius, Mar. 21, 2:30 - Mar. 25, 22:06
Jupiter in Pisces, Mar. 25, 22:07 - Apr. 20, 13:50

World Events

Apr. 8 - The Bay of Pigs prisoners are convicted of treason and sentenced to thirty years imprisonment; they are later released on payment of $62 million.

Apr. 14 - Georges Pompidou becomes French Prime Minister.

508

PISCES
From February 19, 3:15 through March 21, 2:29

The Compassionate Visionary

The Space Race skyrocketed during your childhood, Pisces. In 1962 the very idea, that someone could blast beyond the atmosphere and look back to see a little blue ball called Earth, was breathtaking. Imaginative Pisceans have the kind of vision that can foresee travel in space and dimensions beyond. In order to focus more clearly upon the bigger picture, you may sometimes distance yourself from others.

Technology and the Internet may appeal to you. Working online allows you to share your particular brand of brilliance with a worldwide audience. You have a talent for working with group dynamics and may be a networker extraordinaire. Friends mean a lot to you. In your birth year, American astronaut John Glenn orbited the globe three times in his spaceship *Friendship 7*. He returned to a hero's welcome. In 1998 Glenn returned to space, via the space shuttle *Discovery*, when he was seventy-seven years old.

You can be a cool character. Pisceans tend to understand intuitively that all life is linked and interdependent. You may also appreciate the individuality of every person—and perhaps every animal, plant, and thing—each with its own unique talents. You have a talent for making others feel special. You may also have an interest in science. In 1962, the Nobel Prize for medicine went to the team that discovered DNA (deoxyribonucleic acid), the ladder-like framework of molecules that store genetic information and provide the unique blueprint for every living thing.

Spiritual and empathetic, Pisceans can soar to the heights of cosmic love. You need partners who will encourage you to maintain your own personal interests. Otherwise, you can lose yourself in another's needs. Aquarians share your ideals and respect your need for quiet alone-time. Cancerians and Scorpios can understand feelings you may find hard to articulate.

You tread upon a path of constant change. To help you process events and ideas, your challenge is to focus your energy where you can be most effective. Your emotional intelligence and great insight give you the strength to derive wisdom from tough experiences.

ARIES
From March 21, 2:30 through April 20, 13:50

The Benevolent Dreamer

Eager to be the first in all things, ardent Ariens often assert themselves with gusto and verve. As an Aries born in 1962, however, you may champion causes that underscore altruistic tendencies. You may be incredibly selfless, eager to help others more than you help yourself.

This admirable trait can sometimes lead others to take advantage. You may have to guard against such exploitation throughout your life. With the bravery of the firefighter, who runs in when everybody else is running out, you will remain wholeheartedly true to your mission. You may derive inspiration from your fellow Aries, Gregory Peck. He earned the 1962 Academy Award for Best Actor for his portrayal of the heroic defense lawyer Atticus Finch in the film version of *To Kill A Mockingbird*. In the movie, Peck's character defends an African-American man against an unjust rape charge. In real life Peck campaigns for cancer research and gun control.

Your sense of decency and morality may inspire you to make the world a better place. Although you may not be the orthodox churchgoer, you are likely to engage in activities that make your life meaningful. You may engage in prayer or meditation, but you are more likely to take action consistent with your sense of right and wrong. You may admire the courage of holy men like the Panchen Lama, a senior Tibetan Buddhist cleric, second only to the Dalai Lama. In 1962 he witnessed mass starvation, torture and other abuses inflicted on the Tibetans by the Chinese.

In personal confrontations, you may struggle between fight or flight. Aries can be a warrior. At heart, though, you're a peaceful soul. Your relationships may help you work out your options. Leo can nurture your courage. Sagittarius can lead you to a bottomless font of wisdom.

Your passion can sometimes rouse you to anger—an emotion that can sometimes hinder your positive personal development. Your challenge, Aries of 1962, is to give of yourself responsibly, with love in your heart. Your untold compassion and deep intuition are strengths that protect you from any impulsive tendencies.

➤ Read about your Chinese Astrological sign on page 838. ➤ Read about your Personal Planets on page 826. ➤ Read about your personal Mystical Card on page 856.

TAURUS

From April 20, 13:51 through May 21, 13:16

The Valuable Enthusiast

Considered to be the zodiac's bankers, Taureans tend to be good with money. Indicators in your chart suggest a flair for finance. You may help others make investments, too.

Taurus of 1962 tends to appreciate the value of things, events, and people. Blessed with an uncanny ability to assess talent and the bank-ability of an act, you may be shocked to learn that the record company Decca refused to sign the Beatles in 1962—not the kind of mistake you'd make! You may have an eye for art—as an appreciator, not a dilettante. You can recognize a priceless commodity when you see it. The early sixties saw a burgeoning of culture for lovers of the classics (which you may be) and the modern. In your birth year, the New York Philharmonic performed for the first time in its new home at Philharmonic Hall (later renamed Avery Fischer Hall), the first venue to open, in 1962, at the newly constructed Lincoln Center for the Performing Arts. In Britain, the Royal Shakespeare Company was formed in 1960.

With the ability to focus upon a goal, and to hold it in mind, you're determined and resolute. While most Bulls tend to take their time getting anywhere, you prefer the fast lane. Your unusual speed keeps you ahead of the game. A fellow Taurean, the singer, songwriter, and producer Stevie Wonder, illustrates Bullish creative genius and the will to succeed. Blinded in an accident at birth, he credits his disability for the development of his listening skills and his evolution into musical genius by 1962, at age twelve. Like Stevie Wonder, you could also be multi-talented. You may enjoy many means of expression and the ability to make extra cash in a variety of ways.

A Capricorn or Virgo can be a compatible partner at work and in love. Pisces or Cancer, however, can bring out your deeply sympathetic side and teach you how to dream.

You are a potentially powerful person. You may, however, tend to lose yourself in romantic fantasies. Your challenge is to transform love from the rush of infatuation to the commitment of a sacred union. Valuing yourself brings the strength and insight necessary to reach this goal.

GEMINI

From May 21, 13:17 through June 21, 21:23

The Glamorous Idealist

Among the world's fastest thinkers, Geminis assess situations at the speed of light. As a 1962 Gemini, you also have a quick mind, but you may see the sense in slowing down to carefully assess each stage of any process, just in case something might go wrong. For all your smarts, you see that speed isn't a virtue in and of itself. The more important the matter, the less likely you are to rush to judgment.

When you take your time, nothing can slip through your net. In your birth month, three men escaped from the prison at Alcatraz and disappeared forever in the San Francisco Bay. You may have seen the 1979 Clint Eastwood film based upon this event. Your restless imagination might be as capable of engineering such an impossible escape as preventing it. Able to play out the various outcomes of every situation in your mind, you can be a master strategist.

When you need to give your razor-sharp mind a rest, you may enjoy celebrity gossip and silly factoids. You may be amused to know that in your zodiacal month, one extremely glamorous Gemini expressed best wishes to another. Perhaps you have seen the footage of Marilyn Monroe, in that skintight beaded dress, breathlessly singing "Happy birthday Mr. President...." to John F. Kennedy.

Feelings of compassion and tragedy are likely to overshadow any sense of romantic enchantment you may have toward Marilyn Monroe. As a Gemini you may have made it your business to educate yourself about the true story behind the cliché of fallen beauty. Your common sense teaches you that passions pursued too hard, too fast, and too long, can be destructive. Should you overcompensate on the side of caution, Leo can encourage you let go, give your all, and win! Libra or Aquarius may be your inspirational muse.

A thirst for knowledge and careful planning are strengths that empower you to reach your goals. Your challenge is to avoid power games. It's one thing to conceive of effective strategies; it's quite another to test the patience of others who are willing to help you. Gemini can be mischievous, but maturity tends to blunt such tendencies.

➤ Read about your Chinese Astrological sign on page 838. ➤ Read about your Personal Planets on page 826. ➤ Read about your personal Mystical Card on page 856.

TAURUS
Your Personal Planets

YOUR LOVE POTENTIAL
Venus in Taurus, Apr. 20, 13:51 - Apr. 28, 9:22
Venus in Gemini, Apr. 28, 9:23 - May 21, 13:16

YOUR DRIVE AND AMBITION
Mars in Aries, Apr. 20, 13:51 - May 21, 13:16

YOUR LUCK MAGNETISM
Jupiter in Pisces, Apr. 20, 13:51 - May 21, 13:16

World Events

Apr. 23 - The U.S. launch the unmanned spacecraft *Ranger 4* to investigate the surface of the Moon.

Apr. 30 - Pablo Picasso shares the Lenin Peace Prize with the President of Ghana.

Lenin Peace-Prize winner Pablo Picasso

GEMINI
Your Personal Planets

YOUR LOVE POTENTIAL
Venus in Gemini, May 21, 13:17 - May 23, 2:45
Venus in Cancer, May 23, 2:46 - June 17, 5:30
Venus in Leo, June 17, 5:31 - June 21, 21:23

YOUR DRIVE AND AMBITION
Mars in Aries, May 21, 13:17 - May 28, 23:46
Mars in Taurus, May 28, 23:47 - June 21, 21:23

YOUR LUCK MAGNETISM
Jupiter in Pisces, May 21, 13:17 - June 21, 21:23

World Events

May 31 - Israel executes the infamous war criminal Adolf Eichmann.

June 17 - Brazil retains the soccer World Cup trophy.

1962

CANCER
Your Personal Planets

YOUR LOVE POTENTIAL
Venus in Leo, June 21, 21:24 - July 12, 22:31
Venus in Virgo, July 12, 22:32 - July 23, 8:17

YOUR DRIVE AND AMBITION
Mars in Taurus, June 21, 21:24 - July 09, 3:49
Mars in Gemini, July 09, 3:50 - July 23, 8:17

YOUR LUCK MAGNETISM
Jupiter in Pisces, June 21, 21:24 - July 23, 8:17

World Events

July 3 - France transfers sovereignty to the new republic of Algeria.
July 6 - American novelist William Faulkner dies.

Death of American icon Marilyn Monroe

LEO
Your Personal Planets

YOUR LOVE POTENTIAL
Venus in Virgo, July 23, 8:18 - Aug. 08, 17:12
Venus in Libra, Aug. 08, 17:13 - Aug. 23, 15:11

YOUR DRIVE AND AMBITION
Mars in Gemini, July 23, 8:18 - Aug. 22, 11:36
Mars in Cancer, Aug. 22, 11:37 - Aug. 23, 15:11

YOUR LUCK MAGNETISM
Jupiter in Pisces, July 23, 8:18 - Aug. 23, 15:11

World Events

Aug. 5 - American film star Marilyn Monroe dies of an overdose.
Aug. 12 - The USSR sets another space record by launching two manned spacecraft into orbit side by side.

CANCER
From June 21, 21:24 through July 23, 8:17

The Tasteful Tantalizer

With a love of home and family, Cancerians enjoy comfort. Graced with style and imagination, a 1962 Cancer can make others feel at ease. Catering and cooking may be a hobby. Fellow Cancerian and celebrated 1960s astronaut John Glenn performed the first eating experiments while in orbit. Glenn dined on sticky protein bars, but you probably prefer gourmet fare, an indulgence that became easier with the 1962 introduction of the non-stick pan. DuPont discovered that space-age polyamide withstood 750 degrees Fahrenheit! Post-feast cleanup need never again doom you to dishpan hands.

Members of your sign tend to entertain a high regard for history. Combine this trait with your gustatory refinement, and you may find yourself waxing nostalgic over a very good year for grapes. Your birth year marked the opening at France's Chateau Mouton Rothschild of a priceless collection of artwork, relating to wine and wine tasting. Likely to have expensive tastes, you may put them to good use in the pursuit of old-fashioned romance.

Although you might not admit to it, a flirtatious twinkle in your eye tells the world you're ready for love. Others may find you as appealing as your fellow 1962 Cancerian Tom Cruise. His Oscar-nominated portrayal of a motivational speaker in *Magnolia* illustrated another potential aspect of your personality—petulance. The same was true of Bette Davis' 1962 Oscar-nominated performance in *Whatever Happened To Baby Jane?*

In relationships, you may have a weakness for a handsome or pretty face. You may seek partners who are easy to talk to. Your need to reach out to another and feel understood is paramount. Don't forget, you were born at the time when the Telstar Satellite transmitted the first transatlantic television show—a development reflecting your need for long-distance connections. Scorpio or Pisces can help you expand your ability to express yourself and be heard.

You challenge is to guard all you have without being miserly. While territorial, you gain strength by welcoming others into your personal space, where they can enjoy your charm and wisdom.

LEO
From July 23, 8:18 through August 23, 15:11

The Brilliant Superstar

Fiery Leos burn brightly. And a Leo of 1962 lights up any room that he or she graces. You've got star quality, a versatile mind, eye-catching style, and high-octane energy. When you're at your best, you can shine like the Sun. True to your Leonine legacy, you are likely to enjoy being at the center of attention.

The sun is the celestial body associated with the sign of Leo. In 1962, the first radar signals were bounced off the surface of the Sun, allowing mathematicians to calculate the size of the Solar System. The Sun symbolizes your sense of self, vis à vis your circle of friends, colleagues, and loved ones.

Your fellow lionhearted Leo Peter O'Toole spent a lot of time under the Sun when he made Lawrence Of Arabia, winner of the Academy Award for Best Film of 1962. Drama, theatre, and the movies hold a strong attraction for Leos, and you may dream of pursuing a career in the entertainment industry. Your intelligence and strong sense of self can protect you from the hazards of stardom. Your birth month marked the tragic and controversial death of Marilyn Monroe. Likely to care about your health, you may maintain habits that enhance your physical and spiritual fitness. This year also saw the debut of fashionable holistic health centers. Esalen in Big Sur, California and Findhorn in Scotland offered programs to harmonize mind, body, and soul.

Group activity and socializing are important to you. You may rely on your friends to stimulate your mind and keep you in tune with the world around you. Your friends' support can ease demands on your romantic partner. Communication is your key to a successful relationship. A Libran can keep you happily chatting for hours. Passionate romance is likely to blossom between you and an Arien or Sagittarian.

Whether or not you have material wealth, you are definitely rich in spirit. Your challenge is to make positive, healthy decisions about how you will share your treasures. A bright mind, loyal heart, and generous spirit provide the key to good timing, wise choices in love and friendship, and positive ways to share your gifts.

➤ Read about your Chinese Astrological sign on page 838. ➤ Read about your Personal Planets on page 826. ➤ Read about your personal Mystical Card on page 856.

VIRGO

From August 23, 15:12 through September 23, 12:34

The Ecological Powerhouse

Health, happiness, and intelligence are Virgo's gifts. A Virgo of 1962 is likely to pursue a lifestyle that encourages wellness by working to make the world a better place. You are a member of a generation raised as the movement in planetary consciousness gained momentum. In the Virgoan perspective, the survival of humanity depends on the well-being of the Earth.

In 1962 Rachel Carson informed the world of the horrors of toxic chemical pesticides in her revolutionary book *Silent Spring*. Carson's work is famous for its gently devastating exposé of human responsibility for damage to wildlife ecosystems, notably to birds. For Virgo, environmental ills reflect moral failings.

The Virgoan call for a cleaner and healthier world applies down to the level of the individual body. Virgos tend to insist upon good hygiene and healthy habits. You are likely to practice moderation in all things, including moderation. You're not one to drive yourself crazy by scrubbing every miniscule bit of dirt. You may appreciate the body's miraculous capacity to build resistance to everyday bugs through its own natural defenses. In 1962, the Nobel Peace Prize was awarded to anti-war activist and chemist Linus Pauling, who later proposed Vitamin C as a valuable anti-cancer agent.

Another agent who smoothed his way on to the scene in your birth year was Bond, James Bond, Agent 007. Physical perfection personified, and unsurprisingly a fellow Virgo, Sean Connery captivated imaginations across the globe with his action-oriented hero, surrounded by beautiful girls. In *Dr No*, a Piscean Ursula Andress emerged rather fittingly from the sea, to play opposite the Virgo Bond. Pisces is also your opposite sign: you, too, may find that Pisces could be a perfect mate. A Taurus or Capricorn provides you with an earthier kind of love.

Your challenge is to network, helping others become aware how personal transformation is the beginning of making other, bigger changes that affect the world. Making conscious choices to actively shape the future is your strength, for you could be a true custodian of planet Earth.

LIBRA

From September 23, 12:35 through October 23, 21:39

The Friendly Confidant

With an ability to see another's point of view, a 1962 Libra has a balanced mind. You may have an instinctive grasp of how others think and process personal experiences. Psychology could be a field of interest. One way or another, Libra of 1962, you enjoy sharing, solving problems, and helping people. Likely to be stylish, but not one to put on airs, you have the grace to make others feel at ease. While you have a bright intellect, you're also incredibly sensitive. Others respond well to your comforting presence. You may find that total strangers open up and reveal all in your company.

During your birth year, religion was in the news. The Vatican called an ecumenical council to discuss how a reforming spirit might best serve the needs of a modern world. When you were old enough to learn about these developments, you may have appreciated the clergy's need to reorganize and emphasize counseling skills. You too often hear many people's intimate confessions. Likely to be a non-judgmental people-person, you may find yourself at the beck and call of friends and neighbors. They may appreciate your incisive mind, which always gets to the heart of any matter, no matter how long it may take you.

On a lighter note, The Beatles released their classic "Love Me Do" in your birth month. You too may hanker after love. At the time, The Beatles were thought of as radical. The song was nowhere near as groundbreaking as the Declaration of Human Rights, drafted by fellow Libran Eleanor Roosevelt, whose passing was mourned by the world in the autumn of 1962.

You could find a lifetime of personal pleasure and untold happiness with an Aquarian. Geminis and Scorpios may also be inspiring.

Your challenge, Libra of 1962, is to be philosophical about relationships. Partnership provides as a means for discovering the deeper aspects of sharing emotion by giving, not possessing. Strength comes when you release the past and see each day as a starting point for the future. Learning to be at peace is a statement to others. You can offer a shining example of how to achieve lasting happiness.

➤ Read about your Chinese Astrological sign on page 838. ➤ Read about your Personal Planets on page 826. ➤ Read about your personal Mystical Card on page 856.

VIRGO
Your Personal Planets

YOUR LOVE POTENTIAL
Venus in Libra, Aug. 23, 15:12 - Sept. 07, 0:10
Venus in Scorpio, Sept. 07, 0:11 - Sept. 23, 12:34

YOUR DRIVE AND AMBITION
Mars in Cancer, Aug. 23, 15:12 - Sept. 23, 12:34

YOUR LUCK MAGNETISM
Jupiter in Pisces, Aug. 23, 15:12 - Sept. 23, 12:34

World Events

Sept. 10 – Australian Rod Laver wins the tennis Grand Slam.

Sept. 16 – The Malaysian Federation comes into effect.

Tennis player Rod Laver

LIBRA
Your Personal Planets

YOUR LOVE POTENTIAL
Venus in Scorpio, Sept. 23, 12:35 - Oct. 23, 21:39

YOUR DRIVE AND AMBITION
Mars in Cancer, Sept. 23, 12:35 - Oct. 11, 23:53
Mars in Leo, Oct. 11, 23:54 - Oct. 23, 21:39

YOUR LUCK MAGNETISM
Jupiter in Pisces, Sept. 23, 12:35 - Oct. 23, 21:39

World Events

Oct. 8 – Algeria becomes part of the United Nations.

Oct. 11 – Pope John XXIII convenes the Second Vatican Council.

1962

SCORPIO
Your Personal Planets

YOUR LOVE POTENTIAL
Venus in Scorpio, Oct. 23, 21:40 - Nov. 22, 19:01

YOUR DRIVE AND AMBITION
Mars in Leo, Oct. 23, 21:40 - Nov. 22, 19:01

YOUR LUCK MAGNETISM
Jupiter in Pisces, Oct. 23, 21:40 - Nov. 22, 19:01

World Events

Oct. 28 – The Cuban Missile Crisis comes to an end.

Nov. 20 – The Soviet Union closes its missile bases in Cuba and President Kennedy lifts the blockade.

John Steinbeck after being awarded the Nobel Prize for literature

SAGITTARIUS
Your Personal Planets

YOUR LOVE POTENTIAL
Venus in Scorpio, Nov. 22, 19:02 - Dec. 22, 8:14

YOUR DRIVE AND AMBITION
Mars in Leo, Nov. 22, 19:02 - Dec. 22, 8:14

YOUR LUCK MAGNETISM
Jupiter in Pisces, Nov. 22, 19:02 - Dec. 22, 8:14

World Events

Nov. 27 – The Boeing 727 makes its first flight.

Dec. 14 – The *Mariner 2* spacecraft returns the first close-up photographs of Venus.

SCORPIO
From October 23, 21:40 through November 22, 19:01

The Dynamic Force

Always powerful, Scorpio is mysterious, with a depth of feeling often difficult to fathom. Scorpio of 1962 can be somewhat secretive and your requirements are manifold. Your needs can be complex, not easily defined, and therefore tough to satisfy. One of your greatest lessons is to see that you have the innate power to manifest whatever your heart desires, simply by adopting the right intention. You're best off seeking the right direction, as opposed to the right result.

Strategy is of the utmost importance in all your affairs. You were born at the time of the Cuban Missile Crisis, the incident marking the closest the world had come to nuclear war. In October of 1962, United States reconnaissance planes revealed that the Soviet Union, under Nikita Khrushchev, had installed nuclear missiles in Cuba, with the consent of Fidel Castro. President Kennedy imposed a naval blockade to quarantine Cuba while diplomats brokered a deal in which U.S. missiles would be removed from Turkey in exchange for the immediate removal of all Soviet offensive weapons from Cuba.

Luckily for the world, leaders in the United States and Soviet Union enjoyed a moment of clarity in which they could appreciate the meaning of "mutually-assured destruction." The incident offers some lessons for you. You may have tremendous, dynamic power that, if abused, can hurt others and you. Take care not to underestimate opponents, but don't be afraid to turn back if catastrophe threatens.

Your compassion helps you to accept humanity with all its flaws. In relationships, you can evolve personally by loving deeply, which is, after all, what you really want. As a partner, a Cancerian or Piscean can offer you nurturance, understanding, and a sense of belonging.

In all relationships, your challenge is to remember that retreat is not the same as defeat. A hard exterior can sometimes mask your sense of vulnerability, but too much pride can prevent loved ones from reaching you. Maturity brings the wisdom that tells you when it's safe to let down your guard and allow your big-hearted, generous spirit to shine through.

SAGITTARIUS
From November 22, 19:02 through December 22, 8:14

The Perceptive Traveler

Rarely still for a minute, energetic Sagittarians love to explore new horizons, in the world or in their minds. The Sagittarian of 1962 can be especially restless. Indicators in your chart suggest the potential for flamboyance and flair. You can be bold and beautiful.

While you are audacious and dynamic, love can make you feel shy and reticent—but not for long. Because your style can be strong and sassy, you can make a striking impression. In 1962 Yves Saint Laurent opened his first boutique in Paris. Your fashion sense may be chic and unique. Even if you have gotten your haute couture from a thrift shop, your individual taste may distinguish you as a trendsetter, rather than a follower of fashion.

In clothing and other more weighty matters, you may like to try things out several times, until you get it just right. This need for repeated practice and revisions may be a constant theme in your relationships. Interestingly, in 1962 a new Prime Minister, Georges Pompidou, began to work with French President de Gaulle. Because the French government resigned just months after Pompidou gained office, he was installed twice. He took his position for the second time during your zodiacal month.

In your birth month, the *Mariner 2* flew within 21,600 miles of Venus. Measurements of the planet's surface and atmosphere revealed that the planet of love was hot, hot, hot! You, too, can be warm-hearted and hot to handle. You can sizzle with Leo or be a firecracker with Aries. Another side of you likes relationships to be magical. Romantic Pisces can take you on endless, dreamy adventures.

Your challenge is to explore the depths of your soul and to realize the wisdom that comes from within. Enlightenment need not involve magical, metaphysical rituals. Rather, revelations may come to you through travel to distant lands or during the course of your everyday life. Mindfulness enables you to derive deep meaning from ordinary experiences. By combining insights with the higher perspective that comes naturally to Sagittarius, you can discover the spiritual source of your strength

➤ Read about your Chinese Astrological sign on page 838. ➤ Read about your Personal Planets on page 826. ➤ Read about your personal Mystical Card on page 856.

CAPRICORN

From December 22, 8:15 through December 31, 23:59

The Dignified Worker

The December-born Capricorn of 1962 can be serious, ambitious, and quite competitive. Members of this sign have a talent for precision planning. Careful calculations play an important role in your pursuits, but you may also have an enthusiastic, gung-ho spirit. Once you've fixed your mind on a project, you may throw yourself into it, heart and soul. Killer instincts and a magnetic personality can make you a powerhouse.

In 1962, Alexander Solzhenitsyn published *One Day In The Life of Ivan Denisovitch*, an account of life for political prisoners condemned to exile in the Soviet gulag, forced labor camps, in the 1950s. The American writer John Steinbeck won the Nobel Prize for literature in 1962. Both Solzhenitsyn and Steinbeck created sympathetic and heroic depictions of working men and women, who manage to survive under extreme duress while keeping their dignity intact.

Profound respect for anyone who works hard is a core Capricornian value. Like Solzhenitsyn, you are likely to believe that working is its own reward. You may feel at your best when busy with productive activities. You can also be vulnerable to "workaholism," as your loved ones might attest. Long stretches of idle, unstructured time can be intensely uncomfortable for you. The first few days of even the most well-earned vacation time may find you struggling with feelings of anxiety and guilt. Your unconscious, flustered to find itself in a state of un-busy-ness, may need some time to get used to the wonders of rest, relaxation, and intimacy.

Early in life, your relationships may exhibit a pattern of attraction and repulsion. A love-hate dynamic can emerge in highly passionate affairs. Steely Scorpio has the stamina and strength to reach the highest heights and weather the occasional depths. The gentle patience of Taurus or Virgo can provide a stable and enduring connection that can be quiet but just as precious.

Your greatest challenge is to temper your drive to achieve with discipline. Insight and love are the tools that help you to maintain self-esteem, and, at the same time, keep all expectations in check.

1962

CAPRICORN
Your Personal Planets

YOUR LOVE POTENTIAL
Venus in Scorpio, Dec. 22, 8:15 - Dec. 31, 23:59

YOUR DRIVE AND AMBITION
Mars in Leo, Dec. 22, 8:15 - Dec. 31, 23:59

YOUR LUCK MAGNETISM
Jupiter in Pisces, Dec. 22, 8:15 - Dec. 31, 23:59

World Events

Dec. 26 – Eight people escape from East Berlin by charging through the gates in an armor-plated bus.

Dec. 30 – President Tsombe flees Katanga after UN forces invade the region.

Special Feature
Cartography and the Planets

(Continued from page 505)

In creating an astro-map, lines are drawn on a map of the world showing exactly where, at a precise moment in time, the planets are located at their four angles. So, while the Sun may be rising in New York City, it is culminating in Baghdad, setting in Perth, and at its lowest point, or anti-culmination, in the Yukon Territory. For an individual, an astro-map is made by overlaying their birth planets on to a flattened image of the globe and locating them in geographical longitude and latitude.

> Though he was President for only 1,000 days, there are certain places in the world that are forever identified with Kennedy.

John F. Kennedy's astro-map is a fascinating example of the power of this astrological method. Let's look at one of the very first places in the world that brought Kennedy to fame—the location in the South

Pacific where the patrol torpedo boat he commanded, the PT-109, sank during World War II. A few of the crew members perished and Kennedy, who sustained a chronic back injury, managed to save the life of one of his crew, towing the man several miles to shore by holding the strap of the fellow's life jacket in his teeth.

The location of this event, quite close to Gizo, Solomon Islands, is under the influence of three of Kennedy's planetary lines: the Sun and Venus-rising lines, and the Moon at anti-culmination. The Sun represents the hero in us all, and places where sunrises afford us an opportunity to shine. Certainly, Kennedy acted bravely and the situation truly brought out the best in him. And, with benefic Venus rising nearby as well, the incident ultimately boosted Kennedy's popularity with the electorate that would soon send him to the House, Senate and the presidency. With the Moon, representing one's nurturing and

John F. Kennedy

traditions, at anti-culmination, it is likely that Kennedy's Catholic upbringing played a part in the extraordinary effort he made to save his shipmate. Kennedy went on to gain even more fame as a result of the incident. While recuperating from back surgery necessitated by his injuries, he penned the 1957 Pulitzer Prize-winning *Profiles In Courage*, a book about two senators who risked their careers to do what they believed to be right.

(Continued on page 521)

➤ Read The Kennedy Family's Star Profile on page 497.

1963

Presidential Death: Pluto and the Moon

On November 22, 1963, the world watched in horror as American President John F. Kennedy was assassinated while riding in a motorcade in Dallas, Texas. The Warren Commission, appointed by Kennedy's successor, Lyndon B. Johnson, to investigate his death, eventually announced that he had been killed by a single assassin named Lee Harvey Oswald. This was a cathartic event in American history. Americans mourned as if they had lost one of their own, and the promise of Camelot encapsulated in Kennedy, was destroyed.

On that day, the Sun was in Scorpio, making an "opposition" to Kennedy's bright and mercurial Gemini Sun. Kennedy was born on May 29, 1917, in Brookline, Massachusetts. When the Sun opposes the Sun of one's natal, or birth, chart, it can cause weakness and susceptibility to trauma. The heavy Sun in Scorpio often portends that darkness concealed beneath the surface is about to rise to the surface. Scorpio rules secrets, and the secrets that abounded after Kennedy's assassination continue to fascinate conspiracy theorists worldwide. The planet Pluto, ruler of Scorpio and King of the Underworld, was making an aspect known as a "conjunction" to Kennedy's natal Moon in Virgo. Pluto symbolizes destruction and rebirth and the Moon represents one's innermost emotional life, the raw territory of the psyche. Pluto transits, or planetary aspects, to the Moon often herald a transformation at the very root of one's being, a kind of psychological overhaul. For Kennedy, this transit meant total transformation—a trip from the Earth plane to whatever lies beyond it.

Martin Luther King Jr. waves to the crowd during a civil rights demonstration

President Kennedy on the day of his assassination

The Fermi Prize is awarded to atomic scientist Robert Oppenheimer

RADIO STARS

For many years astronomers had been baffled by point-like objects similar to stars that also emitted radio waves. In 1963, Maarten Schmidt of the Mount Palomar Observatory in California realized that these objects—which he dubbed "quasars"—were emitting very energetic hydrogen and hurtling away from Earth at a tremendous speed. He determined that these intense sources of radiation were extremely distant objects, on the edge of the cosmos, probably formed billions of years ago in the early days of the Universe.

CIVIL RIGHTS AND CAMELOT LOST

Although the USSR removed its nuclear missiles from Cuba as promised, its troops remained, causing further U.S.-Soviet tension. Russian Valentina Tereshkova became the first woman in space. Kennedy visited Berlin to pledge his commitment to the freedom of East Berliners. In Iran, Ayatollah Khomeini was arrested for fomenting revolution against the Shah and his pro-American, pro-Israel policies. President Kennedy was assassinated in Dallas. While under arrest, the alleged killer, Lee Harvey Oswald was himself killed by Jack Ruby while TV audiences watched. Four African-American girls were killed in an explosion in a Birmingham, Alabama church, prompting Martin Luther King Jr. to charge the pro-segregationist Governor Wallace with having "blood on his hands." The civil rights movement staged a peaceful demonstration in Washington, DC, where Rev. Martin Luther King Jr. proclaimed, "I have a dream"—a dream of equality. Britain was rocked by the Profumo scandal, which caused Prime Minister Macmillan to resign. British novelist Aldous Huxley died, as did U.S. blues singer Dinah Washington and German composer Paul Hindemith.

➤ Read "Cartography and the Planets" by Rochelle Gordon on page 505.

CAPRICORN

From January 01, 0:00 through January 20, 18:53

The Old-Fashioned Progressive

With good old-fashioned sensibilities, Capricorns tend to be traditionalists at heart. The same can be said about the 1963 January Capricorn—except that you can also be a radical revolutionary who sees that new ideas are usually worth a second look. Because of this forward-thinking trait, you may often appear to be ahead of the game.

You were born at a time when racial and gender equality was making headlines. The Ku Klux Klan terrorized the American south, and women across the world began crusading for equal pay. These issues may have exerted an important influence in your life, and you may strive for fairness in all situations and relationships.

Former colonies of the European great powers were reconstituting as nations in the 1960s. Independence may be an important personal value and goal for you. As African countries gained independence, thirty new nations came together in 1963 to form the Organization of African Unity (OAU), an institution dedicated to the eradication of colonialism and the promotion of mutual defense and economic and social welfare. Personal self-governance may also be important for you. At the same time you may make advantageous alliances with others who share your values and objectives.

In personal relationships, you may enjoy taking the lead. As your bond grows, you find a natural balance of power may evolve. Healthy give-and-take can increase the depth of feeling, breadth of vision, and height of passion for both partners. A little mystery could also intrigue you. The Mona Lisa, by Leonardo da Vinci, traveled to American and was unveiled by President Kennedy in your zodiacal month. With her enigmatic smile, this famous painting enthralled the U.S. You, too, can have a profound impact upon others, for you rarely give your feelings away.

Your challenge is to minimize the potential for power struggles. An open mind and clear, direct communication help to reduce the tension of unsatisfied needs. With rock-solid personal integrity that can inspire others, you have a talent for organizing large groups of people into effective, goal-oriented teams.

AQUARIUS

From January 20, 18:54 through February 19, 9:08

The Liberated Policy-Maker

While a professional career suits most Aquarians, a 1963 Aquarius may struggle with the degree to which career demands may force one to compromise on personal ideals or goals. You have the ability to be authoritative and could run a business extremely well—which may very well be your own— but you may sense that something bigger and truer is out there. Balancing two distinct needs, to succeed and have a meaningful life, can lead you to walk a fine line between making it big and doing something that really matters to you.

Aquarians tend to have an affinity for science. In entertainment and literature, you may appreciate science fiction and fantasy! This year marked the premier of two television series that focused on new technology and the mysteries of the Universe. In the United States, *The Outer Limits* combined the themes of space technology with social issues. Britain saw the debut of *Doctor Who*, involving a continuing storyline about a Time Lord, who solved problems as he moved in and out of time. Aquarians tend to have a futuristic perspective, and you may often imagine new and far-out possibilities.

Fairness and equality may be important values for you. In 1963 Betty Friedan, a forward-thinking Aquarian, kick-started the second wave of the women's liberation movement with her book *The Feminine Mystique*.

Your sign rules friendship. Mutual respect for boundaries can enhance the quality of your relationships. In 1963, France and Germany made a pact to be friends, after centuries of fighting. Likely to excel in group dynamics, you may work hard to help diverse groups get along with each other, even at a distance. For Aquarians, romance often blossoms from friendly beginnings. Both Gemini and Libra find it easy to like, understand, and love you.

Your challenge is organize your life to provide enough time to relax and enjoy yourself. Overwork can leave you vulnerable to depression. Even a mind as brilliant and alert as yours needs to recharge now and then. Striking a healthy balance can empower you to pursue your most important goals and realize your dearest dreams.

➤ Read about your Chinese Astrological sign on page 838. ➤ Read about your Personal Planets on page 826. ➤ Read about your personal Mystical Card on page 856.

1963

CAPRICORN
Your Personal Planets

YOUR LOVE POTENTIAL
Venus in Scorpio, Jan. 01, 0:00 - Jan. 06, 17:34
Venus in Sagittarius, Jan. 06, 17:35 - Jan. 20, 18:53

YOUR DRIVE AND AMBITION
Mars in Leo, Jan. 01, 0:00 - Jan. 20, 18:53

YOUR LUCK MAGNETISM
Jupiter in Pisces, Jan. 01, 0:00 - Jan. 20, 18:53

World Events

Jan. 15 - Katanga and the Congo are reunited after the UN forces President Tsombe to concede.

Jan. 17 - Nikita Khrushchev pays a visit to the Berlin Wall.

British Labour Party leader Harold Wilson

AQUARIUS
Your Personal Planets

YOUR LOVE POTENTIAL
Venus in Sagittarius, Jan. 20, 18:54 - Feb. 05, 20:35
Venus in Capricorn, Feb. 05, 20:36 - Feb. 19, 9:08

YOUR DRIVE AND AMBITION
Mars in Leo, Jan. 20, 18:54 - Feb. 19, 9:08

YOUR LUCK MAGNETISM
Jupiter in Pisces, Jan. 20, 18:54 - Feb. 19, 9:08

World Events

Jan. 29 - British poet and Pulitzer Prize-winner Robert Frost dies.

Feb. 14 - Harold Wilson is elected leader of the Labour Party in Britain.

PISCES
Your Personal Planets

YOUR LOVE POTENTIAL
Venus in Capricorn, Feb. 19, 9:09 - Mar. 04, 11:40
Venus in Aquarius, Mar. 04, 11:41 - Mar. 21, 8:19

YOUR DRIVE AND AMBITION
Mars in Leo, Feb. 19, 9:09 - Mar. 21, 8:19

YOUR LUCK MAGNETISM
Jupiter in Pisces, Feb. 19, 9:09 - Mar. 21, 8:19

World Events

Feb. 22 - A revolutionary metal tennis racket is patented by French tennis champion Rene Lacoste.

Mar. 13 - Mao Tse-Tung extends an invitation to Khrushchev to visit Peking.

Communist leader Mao Tse-Tung

ARIES
Your Personal Planets

YOUR LOVE POTENTIAL
Venus in Aquarius, Mar. 21, 8:20 - Mar. 30, 0:59
Venus in Pisces, Mar. 30, 1:00 - Apr. 20, 19:35

YOUR DRIVE AND AMBITION
Mars in Leo, Mar. 21, 8:20 - Apr. 20, 19:35

YOUR LUCK MAGNETISM
Jupiter in Pisces, Mar. 21, 8:20 - Apr. 04, 3:18
Jupiter in Aries, Apr. 04, 3:19 - Apr. 20, 19:35

World Events

Apr. 5 - The Fermi Prize is awarded to J. Robert Oppenheimer for his research in nuclear energy.

Apr. 12 - Martin Luther King Jr. is arrested in Alabama while leading a civil rights march.

PISCES
From February 19, 9:09 through March 21, 8:19

The Inspired Explorer

Interacting with others in a sensitive manner is a Piscean gift. A 1963 Pisces cares about people, and you also care about your environment. You may dream of being at one with your surroundings. Pisces' symbol is the Fish and its planetary ruler is Neptune, the planet named after the tempestuous Roman god of the sea. The deep holds a special allure for Pisceans, and you may feel compelled to plunge into emotional depths with others and on your own.

In 1963, the famed underwater explorer Jacques Cousteau speculated that human evolution would lead to *Homo Aquaticus*, a half-human, half-fish, who would live in the sea all the time! Attracted to the mysteries of the marine world, Cousteau began a series of experiments in the early 1960s to see if aquanauts could survive submersion over extended periods of time. (They did, but only for a month!) According to Cousteau, humanity needs only to sink beneath the surface to discover true freedom. In 1963, the USS *Thresher*, a nuclear submarine, sank, resulting in the total loss of its payload and crew. While you would feel deep sympathy for the sailors' families, you might also feel concern over the military hardware left to pollute the seabed.

Whatever you do, you do freely. Recognizing the truth of this dictum—even respecting choices you may regret—can be highly liberating for Pisceans. Your positive outlook and resilience enable you keep tragedy and hardship from defeating you.

Your abiding conscience and unshakeable faith in humanity may move you to pursue utopian ideals. In your birth year the United States Supreme Court ruled that all poor people facing criminal charges were entitled to a lawyer. You may believe that all people should be seen as children of the Universe—with a basic right to happiness. A Cancerian will be glad to accompany you in questing after bliss. A Scorpio can teach you effective ways to express your power.

Your challenge is to show compassion to others without sacrificing your basic well-being. Your empathy for all living beings can help you to fulfill your wish to bring joy to the world.

ARIES
From March 21, 8:20 through April 20, 19:35

The Turbo-Charged Pioneer

Often recognized by the wake of creative energy they leave behind, Ariens are quick off the mark and easily burn past the competition. A 1963 Aries also rides the fast track—in mind as well as body. You may assimilate information at the speed of light. The Porsche 911, capable of going over 100 mph, appeared on the market in your birth year!

Likely to be glamorous, you may be attracted to show-business hype and celebrity culture. You have what it takes to be a trendsetter. One of Hollywood's hottest young filmmakers, Quentin Tarantino, shares your zodiacal birth month. While Tarantino's works can be wry and witty, critics have objected to his slapstick depiction of violence. Ariens tend to have no fear of provoking controversy, especially when they want to make a point.

With Cuba, the Soviet Union, and the United States at loggerheads in 1963, you were born when nuclear war was a serious threat. You may have developed the ability to remain positive in the midst of potential madness. This sunny disposition in the face of adversity can afford you with an advantage in life. Easter of 1963 saw 70,000 demonstrate in Britain against nuclear weapons, and Algiers insisted that the French cease nuclear testing in the Sahara Desert. At the same time, American J. Robert Oppenheimer was given a Fermi Award for research into nuclear energy. Ironic developments such as Oppenheimer's award can bring a sardonic smile to your face.

You may live life on an express roller coaster, but you can also be a sweetheart with deep empathy for others' feelings. You may have an irrepressible habit of taking an instant liking to everyone you meet—at least as an initial matter. You could shower kisses upon a Leo, who adores the attention. You could make a truly loving connection with a Sagittarian, who can share the thrill of adventure.

Your finger is on the pulse of the times. Your challenge is to let your talents and abilities shine, while allowing helpful others to share in the glory. Deriving strength from the loving support of others, your gratitude makes you an even bigger person.

➤ Read about your Chinese Astrological sign on page 838. ➤ Read about your Personal Planets on page 826. ➤ Read about your personal Mystical Card on page 856.

TAURUS

From April 20, 19:36 through May 21, 18:57

The Artistic Protector

Almost preternaturally aware of the connection between humanity and the seasons, Taureans are often gifted at giving the loving care that, apart from light and water, helps to make things grow. As a 1963 Taurus, you may feel blessed to share the Earth with all beings, including plants and animals. Your planetary consciousness can make you a special kind of nurturer—a cultivator par excellence.

As a child, the Taurean of 1963 was likely to respond extremely well to caring cultivation and nurturance by caretakers. If you were properly cherished in your childhood, you were like to grow up to be a tender, generous, and loving soul. You may have rocked in your cradle to the sound of The Beatles and the newly formed Rolling Stones. If such lullabies provided the background music to your tender years, you may truly "rock 'til you drop."

Sharing the wealth of the good earth with friends and families is a classic Taurean virtue. You are likely to enjoy the strong devotion of loved ones. Indicators in your chart suggest marvelous creative and artistic abilities and a dramatic, imaginative streak. You may also appreciate the monetary value of art. The year 1963 marked the passing of Georges Braque and Jean Cocteau—two artists who enriched the world with their daring and brilliant innovations.

You may count fiery personalities among your friends. Adding sizzle and pop to life, such people reflect the passionate side of your personality. In your zodiacal month, Fidel Castro, a Leo, visited Nikita Khrushchev, an Aries, in the Soviet Union. Coming on the heels of the Cuban Missile Crisis, meeting turned up the heat a notch in the Cold War. Although you may have wonderful friendships with Leos, you might choose someone less fiery as a lifelong mate. Virgo and Capricorn adore your creativity, affectionate nature, and abundant generosity.

Especially if you faced a difficult childhood, your challenge is to bring out the confident, giving soul that lies within you. Graced with a kind and generous heart, you can develop the confidence to overcome any obstacle that may fall in your path.

GEMINI

From May 21, 18:58 through June 22, 3:03

The Disciplined Genius

Gemini of 1963 enjoys gifts generally common to the sign of The Twins, such as curiosity, a bright mind, and intellectual brilliance. While you also have the common Geminian capacity to be a jack of all trades, a certain tension may nag at you until you decide to become the master of one.

A lack of discipline can leave Gemini vulnerable to the dangers of gossip and scandal. You were born as the Profumo Affair rocked the British government. Minister for War John Profumo was accused of having an affair with Christine Keeler, a young model who had also been intimate with a Russian naval attaché. Denying the charges at first, Profumo confessed the truth to the British Parliament ten weeks later. When you devote yourself to weighty principles like truth, commitment, and propriety, you can enjoy freedom on a surprisingly rewarding scale. Paradoxes like this never fail to delight intellectual Gemini.

While other Geminis hop from one place to another, you can rocket through the stratosphere like Valentina Tereshkova, the Soviet cosmonaut who became the first woman in space. Your chart is configured to invest you with discipline, focus, and unbelievable power. Once you set your mind on one thing, you can make it happen.

In relationships, you may flit from one person to the next until that gas-pedal-brake-pedal tension forces you to make a choice. You may feel fearful at first, but the joys of an evolving partnership will surprise you. Aquarius can delight you with electrifying insights. A harmonious home life with Libra provides a welcome balm for frazzled Gemini nerves.

A pattern in the chart for Gemini of 1963 shows the potential for "driving through life with one foot on the gas and the other on the brakes." Early in life, you may have plunged into projects with great enthusiasm, only to run into obstacles or discouragement. By the time you reached your thirties, you were likely to find ways to turn this pattern to your advantage. By applying your brilliant mind to strategizing and advance planning, you can channel your energy with laser focus and astounding effectiveness.

➤ Read about your Chinese Astrological sign on page 838. ➤ Read about your Personal Planets on page 826. ➤ Read about your personal Mystical Card on page 856.

TAURUS
Your Personal Planets

YOUR LOVE POTENTIAL
Venus in Pisces, Apr. 20, 19:36 - Apr. 24, 3:38
Venus in Aries, Apr. 24, 3:39 - May 19, 1:20
Venus in Taurus, May 19, 1:21 - May 21, 18:57

YOUR DRIVE AND AMBITION
Mars in Leo, Apr. 20, 19:36 - May 21, 18:57

YOUR LUCK MAGNETISM
Jupiter in Aries, Apr. 20, 19:36 - May 21, 18:57

World Events

Apr. 27 - Fidel Castro arrives in the USSR to meet with Khrushchev.

May 16 - U.S. astronaut Maj. Gordon Cooper returns to Earth after twenty-two orbits of the Earth in the *Faith 7* capsule.

British Secretary of State John Profumo

GEMINI
Your Personal Planets

YOUR LOVE POTENTIAL
Venus in Taurus, May 21, 18:58 - June 12, 19:56
Venus in Gemini, June 12, 19:57 - June 22, 3:03

YOUR DRIVE AND AMBITION
Mars in Leo, May 21, 18:58 - June 03, 6:29
Mars in Virgo, June 03, 6:30 - June 22, 3:03

YOUR LUCK MAGNETISM
Jupiter in Aries, May 21, 18:58 - June 22, 3:03

World Events

June 5 - British Secretary of War David Profumo resigns his office over a scandal that involving twenty-one-year-old prostitute Christine Keeler.

June 16 - Soviet Lt. Valentina Tereshkova becomes the first woman in space.

1963

CANCER
Your Personal Planets

YOUR LOVE POTENTIAL
Venus in Gemini, June 22, 3:04 - July 07, 11:17
Venus in Cancer, July 07, 11:18 - July 23, 13:58

YOUR DRIVE AND AMBITION
Mars in Virgo, June 22, 3:04 - July 23, 13:58

YOUR LUCK MAGNETISM
Jupiter in Aries, June 22, 3:04 - July 23, 13:58

World Events

June 29 – Pope Paul VI is crowned in Rome.

July 1 – British newspaper correspondent Kim Philby is named as a Soviet spy.

Police investigate the Great Train Robbery in Britain

LEO
Your Personal Planets

YOUR LOVE POTENTIAL
Venus in Cancer, July 23, 13:59 - July 31, 22:37
Venus in Leo, July 31, 22:38 - Aug. 23, 20:57

YOUR DRIVE AND AMBITION
Mars in Virgo, July 23, 13:59 - July 27, 4:13
Mars in Libra, July 27, 4:14 - Aug. 23, 20:57

YOUR LUCK MAGNETISM
Jupiter in Aries, July 23, 13:59 - Aug. 23, 20:57

World Events

Aug. 8 – The world's greatest train robbery is carried out on a British train traveling from London to Glasgow; $5 million in cash and jewelry is stolen.

Aug. 13 – A seventeen-year-old Buddhist monk burns himself to death in Saigon as a protest against the Diem government.

CANCER
From June 22, 3:04 through July 23, 13:58

The Healing Homebody

The Crab is famed for having claws that can hold on for dear life. Cancer of 1963 may also posses a healing touch that can nurture a living being back to full strength. Born under the sign that rules parenting, you may admire Mother Teresa. A native of Yugoslavia, Mother Teresa went to India as a young nun and worked with the poor of Calcutta for most of her life. In 1963, the Padmashiri Award for Services to the People of India recognized Mother Teresa's efforts. Although this great woman exhibited the dedication of a saint, you too can be capable of great commitment. Mother Teresa's peaceful approach may have inspired you to help others.

In order to bring the greatest good to the greatest number, you may be willing to make profound sacrifices. Your fellow Cancerian Sir Alexander Douglas-Home took over as Britain's Prime Minister in 1963. To take this position, he renounced his title to an earldom. Because heritage and legacies mean a great deal to Cancerians, you may understand how difficult that choice must have been.

Members of your sign tend to have a sentimental attachment to history and family. Tracing your family roots may mean a great deal to you. The further back the connections goes, the greater your sense of identity and belonging. In your birth year, archeologists unearthed Viking remains in Canada, predating the arrival of Columbus by 500 years.

Your sign rules cooking. When you were born, the modern kitchen included all kinds of new time-saving gadgets. Nineteen sixty-three marked the introduction of the blender, a now indispensable addition to the culinary arts. Frozen fruit drinks, guacamole, gazpacho—you may have an endless list of gourmet delights you've whipped up on the blender. To capture the heart of a Taurus, Scorpio, or Pisces you may treat his or her stomach to one of your gastronomic specialties.

While your desire to help others is a precious gift, your challenge is to avoid rushing into potentially overwhelming situations, where you could wind up feeling helpless. With maturity, you can learn to pick your battles and manage your commitments.

LEO
From July 23, 13:59 through August 23, 20:57

The Inspired Stylist

Leos tend to have a dramatic flair, and the Leo of 1963 can positively glow with glossy, gorgeous glamour. You were born just as Pop Art and Op Art were beginning to dazzle people's retinas all over the world. Mods and Rockers embodied the early 1960s ideal of hip British youth in groovy gear. The playful and daring art movements of this era may have exerted an influence on you, one that freed you to define your own unique style. You are likely to be fashionable, but you're no slave to fashion.

For all your dash, you're also likely to be daring. You may be capable of masterminding high-risk plans. August 1963 witnessed the Great Train Robbery, the largest heist in the history of Britain. The robbers killed a guard and made off with over $5 million. Your own big ambitions do not extend to illegal activities. You have the talent to earn big money on the up-and-up. You have the advantage of a mind that swiftly drills down to the heart of any problem and solves the matter just as quickly.

You are likely to have a passionate belief in human rights. This year marked the beginning of a shocking and tragic form of protest, as Buddhist monks self-immolated in Saigon to protest the repressive policies of the Diem government in South Vietnam. Your birth year also marked the first surgical implantation of a permanent pacemaker for the heart. The sign of Leo rules the heart—symbol of power, courage, and leadership. You can let all these qualities shine from within you.

No one likes to turn away admirers, and you're likely to have many. In relationships, however, you can be a loyal and fiercely protective partner. Sagittarius tends to think highly of your creativity, courage, and intelligence. Ariens stand in awe of your courageous exploits and fiery inspiration. Your unique sense of style and maturity (a rarity among Leos) exerts a powerful allure for Libra.

Your ability to imagine infinite possibilities can be both a gift and a curse. You have the courage and strength to imagine the unimaginable and explore new realms. Your challenge is to choose wisely among your dreams.

➤ Read about your Chinese Astrological sign on page 838. ➤ Read about your Personal Planets on page 826. ➤ Read about your personal Mystical Card on page 856.

VIRGO

From August 23, 20:58 through September 23, 18:23

The Peaceful Communicator

To communicate clearly and concisely is Virgos talent, but being able to communicate in a manner that brings peace and harmony can be the unique gift of Virgo of 1963. Near the time of your birth, United States President John F. Kennedy unexpectedly announced a proposal for the U.S. and the Soviet Union to undertake a joint mission to the Moon. You, too, have a talent for promoting cooperation among once-hostile parties.

A hotline was set up between Russia and America. The "red phone" made famous in the movies of the sixties kept lines of communication open in case of military movement. The first analog cellular phones were also invented in 1963. The descendents of such a device may have proved invaluable to you later in life. Receiving and dispatching information can be vital for Virgo.

While you are likely to be well-spoken, you can also be a very good listener. On August 28, 1963, in Washington, DC, Martin Luther King Jr. stood on the steps of the Lincoln Memorial and uttered the immortal words "I have a dream." King had led 250,000 people in the March on Washington for Jobs and Freedom. While King was primarily concerned with the rights of African Americans, his words inspired people of all colors, across the world and throughout time. Another man gained prominence in the arena of human rights during this fateful year: Malcolm X, whose call for black self-dependence was never fairly appreciated in American mainstream culture until after his untimely death. Like Malcolm X, you may value order, discipline, and self-possession.

Your dedication to service can gain full expression in relationships. You can derive great fulfillment from taking care of a beloved partner. Still, you need to create a balance in your affairs. If you end up doing everything, you may feel resentful. Taurus or Capricorn can be true a helpmate for you.

Your strength lies in bringing harmony, laughter, and joy into relationships. Your challenge is to allow others to nurture you. Asserting your needs can feel awkward. Think of it this way: your loved ones deserve the joy of giving to you!

LIBRA

From September 23, 18:24 through October 24, 3:28

The Insightful Judge

As a Libra of 1963, you were born at time when novelty existed side-by-side with serious global turmoil. In the year you were born, a French nun hit the top of the music charts with her sprightly tune "Dominique"; the United States committed more military advisers to South Vietnam, and the superpowers signed a nuclear test ban treaty. Such diverse events are enough to make anyone stop in his or her tracks and think. But if anyone could make sense of them, a Libra of 1963 would.

Balancing is a Libran art, and you have a skill for taking diverse input and forming a sensible opinion. Your exceptional critical faculties enable you to bring order to chaotic situations. Indeed, you may review situations repeatedly before you become willing to render any judgments.

With astounding insight into others' thought processes and behavior, you can pave the way for peaceful solutions. The Nuclear Test Ban Treaty between the U.S. and the USSR, signed in your zodiacal month, reflects such a diplomatic sensibility.

Helping others to overcome problems may come naturally to you. People may rely on your ability to give excellent advice. In personal relationships, you may prefer the give-and-take of equal partnership. The Beatles sang "Please, Please Me" in 1963, but you know that being a pleaser can often lead to a one-sided affair! Fellow Libran John Lennon employed his whimsical sensibility and witty insights to promote a serious message against war and hatred. In classic Libran form, he sought whole-heartedly to help people to "come together." His famed remark, "Those in the front row can clap, while those at the back can rattle their jewelry!" showed his talent for diffusing tension with humor. You are likely to enjoy relationships with an ingeniously rebellious Aquarius or an intellectually playful Gemini.

The combination of caution and courage makes you a formidable character. You know that working together is paramount for harmony. Your challenge is use your keen sensibilities to champion peace and love through positive measures and share your perceptions when others need help.

➤ Read about your Chinese Astrological sign on page 838. ➤ Read about your Personal Planets on page 826. ➤ Read about your personal Mystical Card on page 856.

VIRGO
Your Personal Planets

YOUR LOVE POTENTIAL
Venus in Leo, Aug. 23, 20:58 - Aug. 25, 5:48
Venus in Virgo, Aug. 25, 5:49 - Sept. 18, 9:42
Venus in Libra, Sept. 18, 9:43 - Sept. 23, 18:23

YOUR DRIVE AND AMBITION
Mars in Libra, Aug. 23, 20:58 - Sept. 12, 9:10
Mars in Scorpio, Sept. 12, 9:11 - Sept. 23, 18:23

YOUR LUCK MAGNETISM
Jupiter in Aries, Aug. 23, 20:58 - Sept. 23, 18:23

World Events

Aug. 28 - Martin Luther King delivers his "I have a dream" speech in front of 250,000 people demonstrating for the passage of civil rights legislation.

Aug. 30 - The diplomatic "hot-line" goes into operation between the U.S. and Moscow to reduce the risk of accidental war.

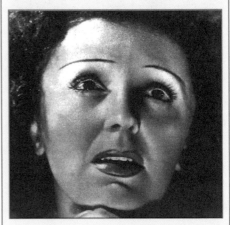

French singer Edith Piaf

LIBRA
Your Personal Planets

YOUR LOVE POTENTIAL
Venus in Libra, Sept. 23, 18:24 - Oct. 12, 11:49
Venus in Scorpio, Oct. 12, 11:50 - Oct. 24, 3:28

YOUR DRIVE AND AMBITION
Mars in Scorpio, Sept. 23, 18:24 - Oct. 24, 3:28

YOUR LUCK MAGNETISM
Jupiter in Aries, Sept. 23, 18:24 - Oct. 24, 3:28

World Events

Oct. 7 - President Kennedy signs the Atomic Test Ban Treaty.

Oct. 11 - Paris mourns the deaths of Edith Piaf and Jean Cocteau.

SCORPIO
Your Personal Planets

YOUR LOVE POTENTIAL
Venus in Scorpio, Oct. 24, 3:29 - Nov. 05, 13:24
Venus in Sagittarius, Nov. 05, 13:25 - Nov. 23, 0:48

YOUR DRIVE AND AMBITION
Mars in Scorpio, Oct. 24, 3:29 - Oct. 25, 17:30
Mars in Sagittarius, Oct. 25, 17:31 - Nov. 23, 0:48

YOUR LUCK MAGNETISM
Jupiter in Aries, Oct. 24, 3:29 - Nov. 23, 0:48

World Events

Nov. 2 – President Ngo Dinh Diem of South Vietnam is killed during an American-supported military coup.

Nov. 22 – President John F. Kennedy is assassinated while riding in an open-topped car in Dallas.

President John F. Kennedy before his assassination

SAGITTARIUS
Your Personal Planets

YOUR LOVE POTENTIAL
Venus in Sagittarius, Nov. 23, 0:49 - Nov. 29, 15:20
Venus in Capricorn, Nov. 29, 15:21 - Dec. 22, 14:01

YOUR DRIVE AND AMBITION
Mars in Sagittarius, Nov. 23, 0:49 - Dec. 05, 9:02
Mars in Capricorn, Dec. 05, 9:03 - Dec. 22, 14:01

YOUR LUCK MAGNETISM
Jupiter in Aries, Nov. 23, 0:49 - Dec. 22, 14:01

World Events

Nov. 24 – President John F. Kennedy's assassin, Lee Harvey Oswald, is shot and killed by Jack Ruby.

Dec. 12 – Kenya is granted independence.

SCORPIO
From October 24, 3:29 through November 23, 0:48

The Insightful Philosopher

Born when the world was gripped by the Cold War, a 1963 Scorpio may have the rare ability to ward off any threat, be it real or imagined. Whether you throw yourself into the material world or develop deep spiritual connections, your sense of optimism can help you cope with the fears to which Scorpios can be vulnerable.

Themes of suspicion and terror were all too present in your birth year: John le Carre published *The Spy Who Came In From The Cold*; a Mafia killer named the heads of organized crime; Kim Philby was identified as the third man in a British spy scandal, and *The Fugitive* began its long run on American television. The threats faced by members of your generation—nuclear annihilation, environmental degradation—were more remote than those that confronted your parents. While you were spared the horrors of World War II, the Depression, and McCarthyism, you may have had a perfectly valid sense of concern.

You may have philosophical attitude that can help to buoy others' spirits. Espousing a positive perspective, you can encourage others. Likely to be a natural psychologist, you could pursue a career in this field. In 1963, two Harvard professors were dismissed for their extremely unorthodox methods in examining the mind. Richard Alpert and Timothy Leary conducted experiments with the psychedelic drug LSD. Leary administered LSD to the dying Aldous Huxley in the winter of 1963.

The sign of Scorpio is associated with mystical experiences that can involve the ritualized use of intoxicants. The Native American vision quest involved the use of peyote. You may be critical of people who ape such rituals in order to justify recreational drug abuse. You may connect to the mystical through meditation, music, or relationships. A Cancer or Pisces can support your efforts to delve into the divine.

Able to fearlessly probe the depths, your strength lies in your willingness to seek the truth and live a meaningful life. You can be good with money too. Your challenge is to balance your need for material independence with your equally important need for spiritual fulfillment.

SAGITTARIUS
From November 23, 0:49 through December 22, 14:01

The Truthful Authority

Honest and forthright, a Sagittarian tells it straight. The Sagittarius of 1963 can sometimes be a bit blunt. While your dearest friends may rely on this quality, new acquaintances may shut down before they get a chance to know and love you. The value of tact and diplomacy may be a lesson you learned in your youth. People of good character admire someone with the nerve to stand firmly on moral principle.

You probably have leadership qualities that encourage others to believe they can make a difference in the world. One man who inspired optimism around the globe was the dashing young President of the United States, John F. Kennedy. On November 22, 1963, President Kennedy was assassinated as his motorcade moved through the streets of Dallas, Texas. In one day, a country lost its President and its innocence. Your caretakers surely told you stories of that shocking day, but you may remain committed to the social good, if only to prove that such faith is possible.

You may sometimes get caught up in situations unfolding so quickly, your need to act outweighs the nicety of sparing others' feelings. When challenges arise, you may resolve to do as much and as best you can under the circumstances. You may not be able to provide the ideal solution, but you can have the satisfaction of knowing you gave your all. Keeping expectations down to a manageable proportion may be the secret to your positive outlook.

For a freewheeling Sagittarian, you may exercise authority in new and innovative ways. In your career, you can be a popular boss by leading by example, insisting that everybody abide by the same set of fair rules, and by investing the members of your group with the belief that they are playing a part in something larger than themselves. In personal relationships, you can enjoy an enduring bond with Leo. Aries finds your ambition inspiring.

Dependability, responsibility, and unshakeable integrity make you a sober kind of Sagittarian. Your challenge is to live up to your principles in all your affairs. Your ethics and faith in yourself give you the strength to pursue your ambitions.

➤ Read about your Chinese Astrological sign on page 838. ➤ Read about your Personal Planets on page 826. ➤ Read about your personal Mystical Card on page 856.

CAPRICORN

From December 22, 14:02 through December 31, 23:59

The Diplomatic Organizer

Families and family feuds were making headlines worldwide around the time you were born. During Christmas of 1963—for the first time since the Berlin Wall went up in 1961—Germans were allowed to pass through its checkpoint to visit relatives and friends for the holidays. When you were old enough to learn of this story, it may have pulled at your heartstrings. In good times and bad and through the years, *family* means a great deal to Capricorn.

Capricorn can be super-organized, super-capable, and super-skilled. You are likely to have a mind built to solve big problems and to put together mega-deals. You may also have the potential to be a policy-maker *par excellence* and to tackle the trickiest business challenges. You may sometimes wonder whether people are paying attention to what you say. Not to worry—you speak with the authority of someone in command. People may often call upon you to bring order to disorganized situations. In your career, you could have a future as a corporate turnaround specialist.

Your leadership skills can have the effect of setting you apart from others. You can be calm and cool under pressure, and this trait can sometimes be misinterpreted as an impersonal style. Capricorns tend to be stoic, not easily given to showing their emotions. When conditions call for a break in the tension, you may occasionally show a softer or even a humorous side of your personality to colleagues and team members.

In intimate relationships, you are likely to have a more demonstrative side that only loved ones are allowed to see. Your secrets are safe with Scorpio. You may seek a long-term relationship with a Virgo or Taurus, who respect your discretion and admire your practical, no nonsense style.

Able to earn the admiration of others, you may excel in weaving a network of helpers, colleagues, and friends. Delegating your workload is your challenge. Capricorns tend to have high standards, and you may feel that if you don't do something, it won't be done right. With experience you learn to trust that others can be relied upon to take pride in their work.

CAPRICORN
Your Personal Planets

YOUR LOVE POTENTIAL

Venus in Capricorn, Dec. 22, 14:02 - Dec. 23, 18:52
Venus in Aquarius, Dec. 23, 18:53 - Dec. 31, 23:59

YOUR DRIVE AND AMBITION

Mars in Capricorn, Dec. 22, 14:02 - Dec. 31, 23:59

YOUR LUCK MAGNETISM

Jupiter in Aries, Dec. 22, 14:02 - Dec. 31, 23:59

World Events

Dec. 23 – More than 900 people are rescued from the Greek liner Lakonia after fire breaks out on board during a two-week holiday cruise.

Dec. 28 – German avant-garde composer Paul Hindemith dies.

Special Feature
Cartography and the Planets

(Continued from page 513)

John F. Kennedy in Berlin

Though he was President for only 1,000 days, there are certain places in the world that are forever identified with Kennedy. One is Berlin, where he showed solidarity with the citizens of that city who found themselves divided by the Berlin Wall, when he uttered the famous words, "Ich bin ein Berliner." And, while the Cold War sizzled, Kennedy's birth chart astro-map showed that his Venus setting line in Berlin ensured that he would be much loved by the people of West Berlin. Also, Mars, the planet of war, in Kennedy's astro-map is at its low point in Moscow, seat of Nikita Khrushchev's Russian government. With this placement, Kennedy saw Russia and communism as a threat to his heritage as an American. After all, Khrushchev did vow to "bury" democracy. But it was in Cuba where the battle between Kennedy and Khrushchev would be largely resolved during the Cuban Missile Crisis. Here we find the Moon's South Node, a point in a horoscope

that often indicates negative conditions, suggesting that Kennedy's presidency might be inextricably connected to this place. In addition, Saturn, the planet of leadership and discipline, is also culminating nearby, indicating that he could achieve greatness with this locale. Certainly, Kennedy's diplomatic and cool-headed handling of the crisis averted what could easily have become a third world war, while at the same time, safeguarding the western hemisphere from the constant threat of Soviet attack.

Kennedy's quest for the presidency began with his winning the Democratic nomination in Los Angeles, a location along his Sun culmination line. Here, the hero achieves his career aspirations and, in Kennedy's case, he also realizes the goals that his father, represented by the Sun, had set for him. But perhaps there is no place more associated with John Kennedy than Dallas, the city where he was assassinated. Found close to the line

where Pluto, the planet of power, transformation, and death, culminates, Kennedy's death not only ended his presidency but also began his legacy as the much-loved, martyred President.

For astrologers who study world events, astro-mapping gives important clues about where in the world significant events may take place. And, in our fast-paced, global society, astro-mapping gives people valuable and practical insights about where to live, vacation, do business, retire, or even find love. ✪

➤ Read The Kennedy Family's Star Profile on page 497.

1964

Freedom and Sacrifice: Saturn in Pisces

During the summer of 1964, known as "Freedom Summer" by civil rights workers, three young men, Michael Schwerner, Andrew Goodman, and James Cheney, prematurely met their deaths in Mississippi. They had gone down to the South to help fight for the rights of African Americans. In the same year, Lyndon B. Johnson signed the Civil Rights Act of 1964. This prohibited discrimination on the grounds of color, race, religion, or national origin in places of public accommodation covered by interstate commerce, such as restaurants, hotels, motels, and theaters. The Act also dealt with the desegregation of public schools.

In 1964, the planet Saturn had just moved into the sign of Pisces. Pisces is the sign of karma, transformation, dreams, and compassion. The whole of human suffering is situated within the realm of Pisces. Pisces is the most unselfish, tender, and loving sign of the zodiac. When the planet Saturn, connected to work, structure, and purpose, fell under the spell of Pisces in 1964, these three idealistic boys—Schwerner, Goodman, and Cheney—set out to change the world. Instead, they became sacrificial lambs for their cause. They were murdered simply because they believed that people of color should have the same rights and access to freedom as whites. The Age of Pisces is said to have started during the time of Christ, and his suffering is the ultimate symbol for Piscean compassion. In 1964, great changes were made, but not without great sacrifices. These three boys become modern symbols of Piscean valor and compassion, and martyrs for their cause.

Sidney Poitier wins an Oscar for his role in "Lilies of the Field"

The Beatles take America by storm

U.S. President Johnson with Martin Luther King after signing the Civil Rights Bill

THE SOUND OF THE BIG BANG

When Arno Penzias and Robert Wilson, scientists at Bell Laboratories, modified a radio antenna during ordinary studies on radio signals from outer space, they kept hearing strange noises. After removing all the terrestrial background radio signals, they found that they could not remove a residual radiation "noise." After much consideration and consultation, they realized that the noise had the energy equal to the radiation left over from the Big Bang. What they were listening to was the birth of the Universe!

GOOD–BYE KHRUSHCHEV, HELLO BEATLES

In the USSR, Khrushchev was discredited and deposed for "hare-brained scheming" and was replaced by Kosygin and Brezhnev. A heart attack killed India's first Prime Minister, Nehru, who was succeeded by Lal Bahadur Shastri. China became a nuclear power, exploding its first atom bomb in Sianking province. In Egypt, work began on moving the ancient temples of Abu Simnel which were threatened by the building of the Aswan Dam. U.S. President Johnson signed the Civil Rights Act, which outlawed racial discrimination. The North Vietnamese attacked U.S. ships in the Gulf of Tonkin, prompting greater U.S. involvement in Vietnam's civil war. The Beatles' harmonies in "I Wanna Hold Your Hand" took American teens by storm, and Detroit's Motown sound got a move on with the Supremes' "Where Did Our Love Go?" Scots actor Sean Connery played the lead in the second James Bond thriller *Goldfinger*, while Audrey Hepburn charmed in the film of *My Fair Lady*. Environmentalist Rachel Carson, author of *Silent Spring*, died. Sidney Poitier was the first African American to win a Best Actor Oscar. Martin Luther King Jr. won the Nobel Peace Prize.

➤ Read The Beatles' Star Profile on page 529.

CAPRICORN

From January 01, 0:00 through January 21, 0:40

The Responsible Campaigner

Enjoying a knack for organization, Capricorns tend to rise to positions of leadership. The chart for the January-born Capricorn of 1964 shows a capacity for leadership on a large scale. As your career progresses, you could find yourself leading a campaign to promote a cause of great importance to you and, possibly, of great benefit to society. In January, 1964, President Lyndon B. Johnson delivered his State of the Union address, in which he declared the beginning of the war on poverty in the United States.

Progressive innovations, like this social campaign, are likely to appeal to Capricorn of 1964. You are not one to adopt a cause on impulse or for purely sentimental reasons. Before you throw your support behind any new project you may take your time to give it due consideration. Your mind is built to ponder weighty, deep, and far-reaching matters. In 1964 scientists discovered cosmic radiation that lent credence to the Big Bang theory, an explanation of the origin of the Universe.

Capricorns tend to respond with great caution when confronted with revolutionary ideas. In your birth month, anti-American rioting broke out in Panama over the flying a U.S. flag over the Canal Zone. Years later the U.S. transferred control over the canal to Panama. While rioting may be one of your least favorite ways to get things done, you may also fiercely resent being subjected to the control of someone who has only the most remote connection with the incidents and conditions of your daily life.

Occasionally enjoying solitude, you may rely on your friends to pluck you out of isolation and to look out for your romantic interests by playing matchmaker. Your fellow Capricorn Carol Channing played a matchmaker in *Hello Dolly*, the musical that hit Broadway in January 1964. Aquarians bring out your individuality. Taurus or Virgo can be your true equal.

Information is power, and your challenge is trust your ability to enlighten and persuade others. You may not realize the authority of your words and ideas. Your credibility rests on the solid foundation of practical, time-tested experience.

AQUARIUS

From January 21, 0:41 through February 19, 14:56

The Unconventional Modernist

Aquarians tend to fall into two categories. One prefers to work within the confines of convention while the other likes to run wild and free. Indicators in the chart for Aquarius of 1964 suggest that you may have an unconventional, alternative, perhaps even eccentric personality.

In the early 1960s, the *Mersey Beat* newspaper took notice of those revolutionary trendsetters, the mop-topped Beatles. Your birth month marked the arrival of the Fab Four in the United States, where they were promptly mobbed by delirious girls. In culture and the arts, you may gravitate to little-known venues, where you can catch avant-garde creativity at its most "avant."

Unlikely to accept old-school beliefs at face value, you may do your utmost to advocate an alternative point of view. In politics, visionary and sometimes utopian views may land you on the side of the loyal opposition. In your birth month Yasser Arafat became head of the Palestine Liberation Organization (PLO). Your humanitarian convictions will never allow you to abandon the hope for a just and peaceful world.

While you may keep colleagues at a cordial distance, you can be passionate in personal relationships. Your feelings may run hot and cold, and you may be perfectly comfortable with that. Modern-day technology may play a role in your personal and professional interactions. Early 1964 marked the beginning of the second generation of IBM computers. Likely to feel at home in the hi-tech cyber world, you may have been the first in your extended family to stay in touch via e-mail. You could meet the Gemini or Libra of your dreams by surfing the World Wide Web!

The challenge for Aquarius of 1964 is to avoid worrying about your position within group situations. Because your ideas can be so far ahead of the times, Aquarians often feel misunderstood. Work steadily and don't let others divert your focus. Clarity and brilliance are your major strengths. Use them to help others open their minds to new possibilities. At times, your flashes of inspiration astound others, and the breakthrough you've awaited suddenly occurs.

➤ Read about your Chinese Astrological sign on page 838. ➤ Read about your Personal Planets on page 826. ➤ Read about your personal Mystical Card on page 856.

CAPRICORN
Your Personal Planets

YOUR LOVE POTENTIAL
Venus in Aquarius, Jan. 01, 0:00 - Jan. 17, 2:53
Venus in Pisces, Jan. 17, 2:54 - Jan. 21, 0:40

YOUR DRIVE AND AMBITION
Mars in Capricorn, Jan. 01, 0:00 - Jan. 13, 6:12
Mars in Aquarius, Jan. 13, 6:13 - Jan. 21, 0:40

YOUR LUCK MAGNETISM
Jupiter in Aries, Jan. 01, 0:00 - Jan. 21, 0:40

World Events

Jan. 9 - Anti-American rioting breaks out in the Panama Canal Zone.
Jan. 13 - Skirmishes break out between Muslims and Hindus in Calcutta.

Cuban Premier Fidel Castro and Soviet Premier Nikita Kruschev make the 'Suger Deal'

AQUARIUS
Your Personal Planets

YOUR LOVE POTENTIAL
Venus in Pisces, Jan. 21, 0:41 - Feb. 10, 21:08
Venus in Aries, Feb. 10, 21:09 - Feb. 19, 14:56

YOUR DRIVE AND AMBITION
Mars in Aquarius, Jan. 21, 0:41 - Feb. 19, 14:56

YOUR LUCK MAGNETISM
Jupiter in Aries, Jan. 21, 0:41 - Feb. 19, 14:56

World Events

Feb. 2 - The space probe *Ranger 6* crash lands on the Moon, but unfortunately it fails to transmit any information.
Feb. 7 - British pop band The Beatles arrive in America.

1964

PISCES
Your Personal Planets

Your Love Potential
Venus in Aries, Feb. 19, 14:57 - Mar. 07, 12:37
Venus in Taurus, Mar. 07, 12:38 - Mar. 20, 14:09

YOUR DRIVE AND AMBITION
Mars in Aquarius, Feb. 19, 14:57 - Feb. 20, 7:32
Mars in Pisces, Feb. 20, 7:33 - Mar. 20, 14:09

YOUR LUCK MAGNETISM
Jupiter in Aries, Feb. 19, 14:57 - Mar. 20, 14:09

World Events

Mar. 6 - King Constantine XII of Greece is crowned at the age of twenty-three.

Mar. 14 - Jack Ruby, Lee Harvey Oswald's killer, is sentenced to death.

Oscar winner Sidney Poitier

ARIES
Your Personal Planets

YOUR LOVE POTENTIAL
Venus in Taurus, Mar. 20, 14:10 - Apr. 04, 3:02
Venus in Gemini, Apr. 04, 3:03 - Apr. 20, 1:26

YOUR DRIVE AND AMBITION
Mars in Pisces, Mar. 20, 14:10 - Mar. 29, 11:23
Mars in Aries, Mar. 29, 11:24 - Apr. 20, 1:26

YOUR LUCK MAGNETISM
Jupiter in Aries, Mar. 20, 14:10 - Apr. 12, 6:51
Jupiter in Taurus, Apr. 12, 6:52 - Apr. 20, 1:26

World Events

Apr. 3 - The U.S. and Panama agree to resume diplomatic relations.

Apr. 13 - Sidney Poitier becomes the first African American to win an Oscar, for his role in *Lilies Of The Field*.

PISCES

From February 19, 14:57 through March 20, 14:09

The Deep Dreamer

Pisceans have a cosmic connection that can tune into the mysterious messages hovering in the night sky. Because your gift for visualizing is likely to be strong, the Pisces of 1964 may also be prone to daydreaming. In your mind's eye, you may see paradise, where everyone is treated equally, regardless of race, sex, or creed. In 1964 Sidney Poitier received the Academy Award for Best Actor for the movie *Lilies Of The Field*. He was the first African American to win the prestigious award—and the last until Denzel Washington won his Best Actor award in 2002 for *Training Day*.

Movies, art, photography, meditation, swimming—all these activities can enhance your vivid imagination. Extraordinary theme parks can captivate a child's fancy, as they could yours. Pisceans tend to love experiences that allow them to escape from this world and into fantasy. Because your symbol is the Fish, you might appreciate Sea World, which opened in 1964 in San Diego, California.

Others may see you as a magical being, a bit like Samantha from 1964's hit television show, *Bewitched*. Even if you're a guy, all you apparently have to do is twitch your nose and things happen! When you wish to change or influence your world, you may practice the spiritual discipline of defining an intention with a cosmic love in your heart and then focusing your attention with detachment. The best results follow when you refrain from imposing expectations on events, things, or people. When things do go your way, your sense of the miraculous enjoys a big boost.

You can be a cool character with cool ideals. Authority figures might find you a bit radical. You can be sensitive but very powerful. Your intelligence and compassion can renew the faith of even the worst cynic. Your personal relationships could be very rewarding. Love may blossom for you with Aries, Taurus, Cancer, or Scorpio.

Your challenge is to use your dynamism for the benefit of humanity. You are fluid yet focused, determined yet vital, alert, and prepared. Your spiritual strength empowers you to champion your own goals and those of others in need.

ARIES

From March 20, 14:10 through April 20, 1:26

The Loving Instigator

Aries loves to be present at the start of any event. And if it isn't happening already, an eager 1964 Aries makes things happen—and fast. Another speedy Aries, Donald Campbell, became the first and only person to break the land and water speed records in the same year in Australia this year. Despite careful planning, Campbell's ambitions ended in tragedy a few years later. While trying to surpass this record, he fatally crashed in the *Bluebird*, a jet-powered water craft in 1967. The Aries personality tends to include a stoic acceptance of risk and an enormous capacity for courage. Like Campbell, you are driven to plan for every contingency. No failure will result from a lack of effort on your part.

That said, you are a maverick. That Ford Motors brought out the Mustang in 1964 only reflects your ability to put your pedal to the metal and kick-start the action. Because you are energetic and love to burn up the racetrack, you might share a certain rallying cry, "Just Do It!" with the famous sporting goods company that began trading in 1964—Nike.

You may make the Earth move in your relationships. Aries passion can generate energy similar to the earthquake—the largest ever recorded in America, with an ensuing tsunami and fires—that rocked Alaska in your zodiacal month. Loved ones might attest to the power of your ardor. While you have a gift for leadership on the career front, you also have a fiery flair for romance.

You know what you like, and you don't mess around. Heaven help people who stand in your way. You're likely to give them the short shrift and put them in their place. A Taurean can stand his or her ground, and a fleet-footed Gemini can match your pace. With a Leo or Sagittarius, you can find that love runs true.

Maintaining influential friends can be a challenge for someone so self-sufficient. Instead of going it alone, you could become richer by working with others. Cooperation enables you to benefit from the contributions of friends, family, and society. Your astounding confidence, courage, and determination empower you to set and meet ambitious goals.

► Read about your Chinese Astrological sign on page 838. ► Read about your Personal Planets on page 826. ► Read about your personal Mystical Card on page 856.

TAURUS

From April 20, 1:27 through May 21, 0:49

The Philosophical Romantic

Taureans have an uncanny ability to maintain their cool under almost any circumstance. At some point, the accumulation of pent-up feelings, thoughts, and energy becomes too strong. To keep the Bull from charging would be impossible. Taurus of 1964 tends to keep his or her composure by adopting a philosophical attitude toward incidents and accidents. You usually have no problem putting things into the right perspective.

The repeated assaults made on *The Little Mermaid* statue, however, might merit a one-angry-Bull stampede. In April 1964 this statue—housed in and symbolizing Copenhagen, Denmark—suffered a decapitation. In fact, vandals have repeatedly attacked *The Little Mermaid* before and after the 1964 incident. In 1998, she was decapitated yet again. Such assaults on works of art are likely to offend your sense of decency and respect for creative works.

Sometimes Taureans can be stubborn. Born in the era of the 1960s sit-ins, you may refuse to budge when staunch convictions are at stake. In 1964 a group of Lakota (Sioux) Native Americans peacefully occupied the abandoned Alcatraz Island, claiming it belonged to them pursuant to nineteenth-century treatises. Earthy Taurus appreciates the value of land. You may also feel for the First Nation Americans, tribes in the U.S. and Canada who pleaded to recover territory in the early 1960s. Like you, they have a shamanic connection to nature. For Taureans the loss of land and possessions can feel like the loss of a part of yourself.

Practical and sympathetic, you tend to seek peaceful solutions to difficult predicaments. In relationships, your main focus is sweet love. An incurable romantic, you love to please those dear to you. Virgo and Capricorn respond well to your protective loyalty.

Making adjustments and compromises in partnerships can be challenging. With your charm, sensitivity, and thoughtfulness, you can summon the flexibility necessary to prove your love, not only to your intimate partner, but also to your family, colleagues, and the world. Your kindness ensures that you will be cherished in return.

GEMINI

From May 21, 0:50 through June 21, 8:56

The Thoughtful Enthusiast

Geminis are often too busy flitting about to concentrate upon family concerns. As a 1964 Gemini, however, you have strong family ties, making it unlikely that you will fly too far away. Keeping those at home happy while you merrily achieve your goals shows how you value yourself. By cherishing yourself, others will too.

Because learning to treasure personal talent boosts self-esteem, having the freedom to express your ideas is also important. On June 13, 1964, one hundred people turned out to protest the arrest of fast-talking comedian Lenny Bruce. In that same zodiacal month, Nelson Mandela, already in jail in South Africa for incitement to strike, was sentenced to life imprisonment. You may shake your head at the degree to which these men suffered for exercising rights we take for granted today. In light of their vindication in the eyes of history, you may admire both of these men as heroes.

You were born during the height of the global civil rights movement. The progress made at that time may support your natural tendency to question authority. Members of your sign tend to be too smart and perceptive to blindly accept propaganda. When others suffer an unfair disadvantage, you may struggle with an irresistible impulse to speak up and take action against the perpetrators.

Your personal relationships are enhanced when you can claim the support of those who encourage you to dream. You're thoughtful by nature and may share a love of the past with a Cancerian, who appreciates the way you care about others. In business, you may also do well with a Taurean, whose money sense matches your canny mind. When it comes to the real thing, however, you might settle with a Libran or Aquarian, who will always give you space to develop skills and process ideas.

Your challenge is to proceed along the path of transformation, while at the same time balancing your personal needs with those of others (without negating either party's gifts or opinions). Endowed with a vivid imagination and able to visualize each stage of growth, you can be like the caterpillar that emerges from the cocoon as a beautiful butterfly.

➤ Read about your Chinese Astrological sign on page 838. ➤ Read about your Personal Planets on page 826. ➤ Read about your personal Mystical Card on page 856.

TAURUS
Your Personal Planets

YOUR LOVE POTENTIAL
Venus in Gemini, Apr. 20, 1:27 - May 09, 3:15
Venus in Cancer, May 09, 3:16 - May 21, 0:49

YOUR DRIVE AND AMBITION
Mars in Aries, Apr. 20, 1:27 - May 07, 14:40
Mars in Taurus, May 07, 14:41 - May 21, 0:49

YOUR LUCK MAGNETISM
Jupiter in Taurus, Apr. 20, 1:27 - May 21, 0:49

World Events

May 4 – It is decided that the Pulitzer Prize will not be awarded this year.

May 19 – U.S. diplomats find more than forty hidden microphones in their Moscow embassy.

Indian leader Jawaharlal Nehru dies

GEMINI
Your Personal Planets

YOUR LOVE POTENTIAL
Venus in Cancer, May 21, 0:50 - June 17, 18:16
Venus in Gemini, June 17, 18:17 - June 21, 8:56

YOUR DRIVE AND AMBITION
Mars in Taurus, May 21, 0:50 - June 17, 11:42
Mars in Gemini, June 17, 11:43 - June 21, 8:56

YOUR LUCK MAGNETISM
Jupiter in Taurus, May 21, 0:50 - June 21, 8:56

World Events

May 27 – Indian leader Jawaharlal Nehru dies.

June 12 – Nelson Mandela is sentenced to life imprisonment in South Africa.

1964

CANCER
Your Personal Planets

YOUR LOVE POTENTIAL
Venus in Gemini, June 21, 8:57 - July 22, 19:52

YOUR DRIVE AND AMBITION
Mars in Gemini, June 21, 8:57 - July 22, 19:52

YOUR LUCK MAGNETISM
Jupiter in Taurus, June 21, 8:57 - July 22, 19:52

World Events

June 28 – Malcolm X founds the Organization for Afro-American Unity.

July 6 – The Beatles' first film, *A Hard Day's Night*, premieres.

Malcolm X, leader of the Black Muslims organization

LEO
Your Personal Planets

YOUR LOVE POTENTIAL
Venus in Gemini, July 22, 19:53 - Aug. 05, 8:52
Venus in Cancer, Aug. 05, 8:53 - Aug. 23, 2:50

YOUR DRIVE AND AMBITION
Mars in Gemini, July 22, 19:53 - July 30, 18:22
Mars in Cancer, July 30, 18:23 - Aug. 23, 2:50

YOUR LUCK MAGNETISM
Jupiter in Taurus, July 22, 19:53 - Aug. 23, 2:50

World Events

July 31 - *Ranger 7* relays the first close-up photographs of the Moon.

Aug. 2 - Communist PT boats attack a U.S. destroyer in the Gulf of Tonkin.

CANCER
From June 21, 8:57 through July 22, 19:52

The Bright Inspiration

Often depicted as homebodies who rarely leave their shell, Cancerians have rightly won a reputation as creators of domestic bliss. The 1964 Cancerian, however, can be a rambling Crab. While a happy home life remains important, you may also love to go out and socialize with others outside your family circle.

In 1964 the Summer Olympics were held in Japan, where the high-speed Shinkansen bullet train had just been introduced. A traveling Cancerian of 1964 can leave others in the dust, which is quite an accomplishment given that you are likely to be carrying a miniature version of your house on your back. You move fast, and a competitive streak may drive you to succeed in sports, especially ball games. You also have a strong belief in fair play. In 1964, South Africa was barred from entering the Olympics because of its apartheid policy.

You'll accord respect to authority where such respect is due. Freedom of thought and expression are also important priorities. You can be creative, inspired, and ingenious. Open-minded and imaginative, you may enjoy the works of avant-garde artists like Yoko Ono. In 1964, Ono presented the performance artwork, *Cut Piece in Japan*.

Female Cancerians can exude sexual magnetism. In 1964, British actress and fellow Cancerian Diana Rigg landed the plum role of Emma Peel in the British television series *The Avengers*. "M appeal" stood for "man appeal" way back then! You may appreciate the *double entendre*; wordplay can turn you on and make you laugh. Bright, witty conversation may be part of a fulfilling relationship for you. Gemini will love your mind and your imaginative, intuitive spirit. Pisces can weave your words into romantic poetry. Scorpio will be more than happy to give you a few pointers on body language.

Your challenge is to resist the allure of mental distractions in times of stress. Blessed with a nimble mind, you can recast any difficult situation as a learning experience. You can combine the advantages of a brilliant intellect with highly sensitive gut instincts. Guided by head, heart, and gut, you can improvise as you go.

LEO
From July 22, 19:53 through August 23, 2:50

The Sensitive Fun-Lover

You are one very considerate Lion, Leo of 1964. You may be modest and fairly shy—traits that are somewhat unusual in members of your sign. Even if you enjoy the occasional Leonine turn in the spotlight, you may look forward to returning to the safety and security of a private retreat. A compassionate person who loves deeply, you may gravitate to homemaking and intimate companionship.

Because you have the sensitivity of an artist, you may also thrive on visual entertainment. Abstract and Pop Art dominated culture in your birth year. Bacon, De Kooning, Lichtenstein, Rauchenberg, Hockney, Reilly, and Warhol all unveiled famous works in 1964. You may adore history and genealogy. Speaking of old roots—a pine tree in Nevada, chopped down in 1964, turned out to be no less than 4,900 years old! You may like to relax with lighthearted entertainment. *Top Of The Pops* premiered on British television in 1964, with songs like "I Get Around" by the newly-formed Beach Boys.

Another reason for the social and political upheaval of the late 1960s was taking root at the time of your birth. The Gulf of Tonkin Resolution prompted an escalation of America's involvement in the conflict in Vietnam. By the end of the year, Australia was also involved. The Cold War and its extension in Vietnam may have made a strong impression upon you during your tender years. By simply watching television and through exposure to the young adults around you, you may have tuned out from mainstream values and developed a fundamental distrust of government and authority.

Relationships enable you to fully experience and express your deepest, heartfelt emotions. Cancer can return your nurturing in kind. With Aries or Sagittarius, romance can become a spiritual adventure.

The challenge for Leo of 1964, is to integrate your emotional, intuitive side with your powerful creative drive. You have the talent to weave beauty through everything you do. Courage and faith in the power of love can ignite the fire in your soul. A compassionate soul, you can reach out and bring inspiration to others through good works.

➤ Read about your Chinese Astrological sign on page 838. ➤ Read about your Personal Planets on page 826. ➤ Read about your personal Mystical Card on page 856.

VIRGO

From August 23, 2:51 through September 23, 0:16

The Wholesome Organizer

The sign of Virgo rules health—physical, mental, spiritual, global. Virgo of 1964 is likely to take a wholesome approach to life. Your personal mission may be to carefully eliminate all negative or destructive influences. You may avoid negative thoughts, unhealthy food, or hurtful people. Purity may be an important ideal for you, and you care deeply about preventing any harm to others.

In 1964 the United States Surgeon General initiated an anti-smoking campaign, following distribution of the famous report linking cigarette smoking to cancer. But that didn't stop Bob Dylan from sharing a joint with a Beatle in a New York hotel room in that year!

Advising that "a spoonful of sugar helps the medicine go down," the title character of Oscar-winning *Mary Poppins*, which came out in 1964, could well be a Virgo! You might share Miss Poppins' ability to swiftly organize life, as if by magic, into neat little bundles, sorted by degree of importance and urgency. Sometimes prone to worry, you may constantly run through a mental list of things to do, or ideas to fulfill. Virgo doesn't like to come up short under any circumstances.

While you display the usual Virgoan traits of organization, order, and skill, you retain your own distinctive individuality. You may have an exceptionally open mind with respect to alternative points of view. Able to take a big-picture perspective, you may espouse a global consciousness, especially where ecology or world health is involved. Your personality can be magnetic and compelling. So, while you may take personal responsibility for creating a safer, pollution-free planet, you may also see the need to enlist support from conventional quarters. With a Cancerian's love to back you up, all things are possible. Taurus, Leo, or Virgo can help you to lead the way to the greater good.

Your challenge is to recognize that for all your problems, solutions always lie within your grasp. Taking the needs of others into account is your strength. Maturity and experience will teach you the value of pausing to think things through before you plunge into action.

LIBRA

From September 23, 0:17 through October 23, 9:20

The Stylish Peacemaker

Classic Libran goals include seeking balance in life, promoting equality and justice, and ensuring peace and harmony for all. Friendship and good will are also important to Libra of 1964. In your birth year, civil rights campaigner Martin Luther King Jr. was awarded the Nobel Peace Prize, making him the youngest person ever to receive it.

Librans tend to be competitive, but not confrontational. You're not one to lust after success. The desire to do the right thing is more likely to be a driving force for you. Members of your sign care deeply about being fair and reasonable. You may have strong opinions about the right way to do things, but you somehow manage to impose your judgment without seeming judgmental.

In 1964, the Soviets became the first to launch a three-man crew in a space rocket. Also, the Warren Commission officially announced that Lee Harvey Oswald had acted alone. You prefer your information to be like your food—easily digestible and pretty to look at, too. Unfortunately, 1964 had its horrors: China detonated a nuclear bomb—the fifth country to do so—and fighting in Vietnam escalated. None of this would be your ideal, for although you're loyal, you're also loving and romantic.

Librans tend to have a fabulous fashion sense. Your style may reflect the latest trends, but you may avoid flamboyant or exhibitionistic fashion statements. Three women were arrested in swinging London in 1964 for wearing topless dresses! Librans like a look that is elegant and tasteful, but you're not too modest to create a striking impression. You may enjoy turning heads with a limelight-loving Leo on your arm. A Gemini or Aquarian may admire your modern elegance and creative sensibility.

Life may not be perfect all the time, but that won't stop you from throwing out the ugly 1960s troll doll to improve and beautify your environment. In ideas, projects, and relationships, your contribution is usually the one element that can untangle knotty problems. You have a gift for enhancing your environment with sophisticated touches, harmonious creativity, and pleasant ambiance.

➤ Read about your Chinese Astrological sign on page 838. ➤ Read about your Personal Planets on page 826. ➤ Read about your personal Mystical Card on page 856.

VIRGO
Your Personal Planets

YOUR LOVE POTENTIAL
Venus in Cancer, Aug. 23, 2:51 - Sept. 08, 4:52
Venus in Leo, Sept. 08, 4:53 - Sept. 23, 0:16

YOUR DRIVE AND AMBITION
Mars in Cancer, Aug. 23, 2:51 - Sept. 15, 5:21
Mars in Leo, Sept. 15, 5:22 - Sept. 23, 0:16

YOUR LUCK MAGNETISM
Jupiter in Taurus, Aug. 23, 2:51 - Sept. 23, 0:16

World Events

Sept. 18 - Irish dramatist Sean O'Casey dies.

Sept. 23 - The Paris Opera unveils its new ceiling, painted by Marc Chagall.

Death of Irish dramatist Sean O'Casey

LIBRA
Your Personal Planets

YOUR LOVE POTENTIAL
Venus in Leo, Sept. 23, 0:17 - Oct. 05, 18:09
Venus in Virgo, Oct. 05, 18:10 - Oct. 23, 9:20

YOUR DRIVE AND AMBITION
Mars in Leo, Sept. 23, 0:17 - Oct. 23, 9:20

YOUR LUCK MAGNETISM
Jupiter in Taurus, Sept. 23, 0:17 - Oct. 23, 9:20

World Events

Oct. 16 - Communist China becomes the world's fifth nuclear power.

Oct. 22 - French existentialist writer Jean-Paul Sartre refuses the Nobel Prize for literature.

527

1964

SCORPIO
Your Personal Planets

YOUR LOVE POTENTIAL
Venus in Virgo, Oct. 23, 9:21 - Oct. 31, 8:53
Venus in Libra, Oct. 31, 8:54 - Nov. 22, 6:38

YOUR DRIVE AND AMBITION
Mars in Leo, Oct. 23, 9:21 - Nov. 06, 3:19
Mars in Virgo, Nov. 06, 3:20 - Nov. 22, 6:38

YOUR LUCK MAGNETISM
Jupiter in Taurus, Oct. 23, 9:21 - Nov. 22, 6:38

World Events

Nov. 2 - King Saud of Saudia Arabia is deposed and replaced by his brother.

Nov. 19 - South Vietnam launches its biggest attack of the war so far.

Martin Luther King Jr. wins the Nobel Peace Prize

SAGITTARIUS
Your Personal Planets

YOUR LOVE POTENTIAL
Venus in Libra, Nov. 22, 6:39 - Nov. 25, 1:24
Venus in Scorpio, Nov. 25, 1:25 - Dec. 19, 7:01
Venus in Sagittarius, Dec. 19, 7:02 - Dec. 21, 19:49

YOUR DRIVE AND AMBITION
Mars in Virgo, Nov. 22, 6:39 - Dec. 21, 19:49

YOUR LUCK MAGNETISM
Jupiter in Taurus, Nov. 22, 6:39 - Dec. 21, 19:49

World Events

Dec. 2 - Juan Péron attempts to return to Argentina, but he is captured and sent back to Spain.

Dec. 10 - Martin Luther King Jr. accepts the Nobel Peace Prize.

528

SCORPIO
From October 23, 9:21 through November 22, 6:38

The Perceptive Dreamer

The sign of Scorpio rules power and control, but the Scorpio of 1964 is highly likely to reject a notion of leadership that implies dominating others. Going with the flow suits your lifestyle far better. While you might enjoy directing situations and leading people in goal-oriented activities, you may tend to follow the promptings of your active imagination, vivid dreams, and deep intuition.

Scorpios can be very perceptive—usually there's little that escapes you. You'd be good at espionage. Robert Vaughn, a.k.a. Napoleon Solo in the *Man From U.N.C.L.E.*, is also a Scorpio. The popular television show premiered in the fall of 1964. On the subject of spies, forty hidden microphones were found bugging the American Embassy in Moscow in your birth year! Nothing, however, can be hidden from you for long.

While the western world sang along to "Leader Of The Pack," by the Shangri-Las, a pack of world leaders were shuffling positions during your birth month. Brezhnev ousted Khrushchev as First Secretary of the Soviet Union, and Aleksei Kosygin became Chairman of the Council of Ministers. Labour Leader Harold Wilson won the UK elections, ousting the Tory leader Sir Alec Douglas-Home. Lyndon B. Johnson was elected in his own right as President of the U.S.

The world of glamour can exert a powerfully seductive influence over you, even now. Film, music, theatre, and television provide a means for escaping the real world of politics and intrigue. As your loved ones might attest, Scorpionic tastes, thoughts, and sense of humor, can sometimes run on the dark side. *The Munsters* and *The Addams Family* had their television premieres in 1964. Cancerians and Pisceans appreciate your irony and your spooky sense of fun.

No matter how accomplished, educated, or worldly you may be, Scorpio of 1964, your ultimate challenge lies in relationships. The realm of intimacy provides a zone of safety that allows you to delve into the real depths of your soul. With insight and acute perception, you can summon the courage to express your mighty Scorpionic power, with all its psychic and sexy sensitivity.

SAGITTARIUS
From November 22, 6:39 through December 21, 19:49

The Mystical Adventurer

Without a backward glance, a Sagittarian happily takes off to explore new horizons. As a Sagittarian of 1964, you share the same drive. Because you are more likely to be a truth seeker, spiritual adventures may be most compelling for you. Archers tend to be intrigued by religion and philosophy, and you may pursue a career that involves sharing your learning on these subjects with others. You may dedicate your life to looking for the perfect belief system.

In 1964, space science began to explore the question of life on Mars. Back on Earth, Pope Paul VI, decreed it permissible to celebrate Catholic Mass in the English language. He also paid an eleven-hour visit to Israel—without, however, recognizing the country's statehood. Sagittarians have a reputation for tolerance of different peoples with different religions.

Mystery and intrigue may appeal to a certain side of you. In your birth month, celebrated crooner and fellow Sagittarian Frank Sinatra paid nearly a quarter of a million dollars as ransom for his kidnapped son. True crime stories may offer you fascinating insights into the human mind.

You are likely to exude a personal magnetism that others find hypnotic. Your depth may attract romantic interest. While most Sagittarians tend to be charismatic and gregarious, you may be serious, understated, and irresistibly mysterious. Likely to be more sensitive to intoxicants than others, you may need to moderate your intake. Sipping does for you what gulping does for others. Indicators in your chart suggest that you have a potent intellect. In love and romance, fiery Aries and Leo can be exciting partners. Taurus and Scorpio offer a bond that is enduring and deeply fulfilling.

Your challenge is to resist the temptation to idolize others. In your travels and studies, you may come to admire many gurus, guides, or teachers, and you may be tempted to invest all your dreams in them. By remembering that they are only human, you can spare yourself from disappointment. You can rely on your honesty, intellect, and insight to keep your expectations down to a realistic size.

➤ Read about your Chinese Astrological sign on page 838. ➤ Read about your Personal Planets on page 826. ➤ Read about your personal Mystical Card on page 856.

CAPRICORN

From December 21, 19:50 through December 31, 23:59

The Smart Philosopher

Capricorns are usually cool, calm, and collected. As a 1964 December-born Capricorn, you're a little bit wilder than most other members of your sign. Other Mountain Goats may seem like stuck-in-the-mud traditionalists in comparison with you.

Capricorns often exhibit a serious interest in politics and foreign affairs. The world of 1964 was full of upheaval. Kenya became a republic, and Tanganyika joined up with Zanzibar to become Tanzania. A British development may appeal to your lighthearted nature—1964 marked the premiere of the groundbreaking Beatles film, *A Hard Day's Night*.

Bringing an action-packed touch of James Bond class to your own earthly debut, the film *Goldfinger* also opened in December. Perhaps the most encouraging event of your birth month was Britain's abolition of the death penalty after years of debate. Tending to be philosophical, a Capricorn of 1964 is likely to appreciate the fact that important ideas take time to yield results. You may have an instinctive understanding of what it takes to bring about a shift in public opinion. Because you like your topics to be big and mind-boggling, you may appreciate the importance of the Cesium Beam Clock built in 1964, an advance on the atomic clock of sixteen years earlier.

In relationships, you might travel miles to be with loved ones. A fascination with exotic cultures may have inspired a romantic involvement with someone from a foreign country. Sagittarius shares a passion for all things international. Pisces brings spiritual balance. Taurus and Cancer, on the other hand, like to keep the home fires burning, especially when you're traveling on business.

The most important challenge for 1964 December-born Capricorn is to see that spiritual development is just as significant as material wealth. You may achieve this realization through relationships, or, more likely, through activity, such as music, dance, swimming, or sailing. Connecting to something as deep as the azure-blue sea might be scary, but it's a learning experience that can enrich your spirit and enhance your profound strength of character.

1964

CAPRICORN
Your Personal Planets

YOUR LOVE POTENTIAL
Venus in Sagittarius, Dec. 21, 19:50 - Dec. 31, 23:59

YOUR DRIVE AND AMBITION
Mars in Virgo, Dec. 21, 19:50 - Dec. 31, 23:59

YOUR LUCK MAGNETISM
Jupiter in Taurus, Dec. 21, 19:50 - Dec. 31, 23:59

World Events

Dec. 25 - A hurricane in the Indian Ocean claims 7,000 lives.

Dec. 30 - Five hundred alleged Chinese spies are apprehended in India.

George Harrison - Pisces
February 25, 1943 - November 29, 2001
John Lennon - Libra
October 9, 1940 - December 8, 1980
Paul McCartney - Gemini
Born June 18, 1942
Ringo Starr – Cancer
Born July 7, 1940

THE BEATLES:
John, Paul, George and Ringo

The Beatles burst on to the music scene after the relative complacency of the 1950s and their mop-top looks and exciting music created a revolution in rock 'n' roll that will probably never be equaled. Arguably the most successful band of all time, The Beatles dominated the music scene for an entire decade. As the sixties wound to a close, The Beatles began to experience some strife and disagreement within their group and, with the tragic death of manager Brian Epstein from an accidental overdose, they ultimately chose to go in separate directions. Each has had many measures of success as an independent and with other collaborators, but as individuals none of them caused a furor to match the phenomenon that was known as "Beatlemania."

One astrological element shared by all four Beatles is the planet Neptune, prominently placed in their individual horoscopes. Neptune is the planet of music, of idealism, of film, and of illusion, and the music of The Beatles features the best possible expression of this Neptunian energy. They wanted us to give peace a chance, sing silly love songs, and to learn to imagine.

Ringo Starr has an intense planetary configuration in his house of pleasure. With the sensitive Moon in close contact with assertive Mars as well as thundering Pluto, it is no wonder that he loves to play the drums!

John Lennon was killed outside his New York home by the bullet of an insane assassin. With Mars, planet of action, contacted by idealistic Neptune, and his Moon, planet of emotions, challenged by controlling Pluto, Lennon liked strong women and was devoted to peace and love as an ideal in life.

George Harrison died of cancer in 2001. His Venus, planet of creativity, was contacted by intense Pluto, helping him express the healing power of love in his many touching and memorable songs.

Paul McCartney remarried in 2002 after a long and celebrated marriage to Linda Eastman, who died of cancer. Paul's outgoing Moon in Leo is contacted by Venus, the planet of love, making him passionate and someone who appreciates the best qualities of the women in his life. It also brings a sense of *joie de vivre* to his daily life and the ability to sing those silly love songs we all adore.

➤ Read about The Beatles in "East Meets Twentieth-Century West" by Ronnie Grishman on page 81.
➤ Read Janis Joplin's Star Profile on page 569. ➤ Read Elvis Presley's Star Profile on page 457.

1965

Vietnam Exploding: Mars, Pluto, and Uranus Merge

U.S. planes began combat missions over South Vietnam in 1965. North Vietnam rejected the U.S. offer of economic aid in exchange for peace. Two weeks later, President Lyndon B. Johnson raised America's combat strength in Vietnam to more than 60,000 troops—thereby breaking the promise that he had made to the American people. Allied forces from Korea and Australia were also added as a sign of international support. In June, 23,000 Americans were committed to combat and by the end of the year over 184,000 U.S. troops had landed in the area.

In April of 1965, three major planets were residing in the sign of Virgo, making an aspect called a "conjunction" to one another. These three planets were locked in an embrace, infecting one another with their energy and pushing one another's boundaries. Virgo is the sign of selfless service, and at this point in the war the soldiers served their country proudly and without questioning why they were there. The anti-war movement had not yet revealed the moral complexities and savagery of the war. Mars is the warrior planet representing aggression and force. Pluto is the planet of transformational changes, forcing through the soul-shaking energies that linger beneath the surface. And Uranus, the planet of sudden reversals, shocks us with his unexpected turn of events. The war in Vietnam escalated in a surprising way in April of 1965. Despite the uncertainty inherent in the march toward war, President Johnson upped the ante and sent thousands of young American soldiers into the jungles of Vietnam to meet their fate—often death.

Two American rockets, "Gemini VI" and "Gemini VII", rendezvous in space

Winston Churchill's funeral procession

U.S. forces become more fully engaged in the Vietnam War

SPACE WALK

On March 18, 1965, astronaut Alexei Leonov, a member of the Russian *Voskhod 2* mission, became the first man to walk in space. He remained outside his spacecraft for ten minutes, during which time he managed a somersault. He described the experience: "What struck me most was the silence. It was a great silence, unlike any I have encountered on Earth, so vast and deep that I began to hear my own body. My heart beating, my blood vessels pulsing, even the rustle of my muscles moving over each other seemed audible."

VIETNAM PROTESTS AND PSYCHEDELIC SOUNDS

Sir Winston Churchill, the great British World War II leader, died. U.S. forces became fully engaged in the Vietnam War, with air strikes, ground troops, and the first use of napalm. When President Cabral of the Dominican Republic was deposed by communist rebels, U.S. marines were sent to protect American citizens. Russian cosmonaut Alexei Leonov became the first man to walk in Space, followed by the first American astronaut, Ed White. Meanwhile, two American spacecraft rendezvoused in orbit. Actions in support of civil rights intensified to fight segregation and voting rights violations in the American South. The Watts Riots in Los Angeles left thirty dead, hundreds injured and caused 1,000 fires: 300 of them major blazes. President Johnson christened the Great Society, emphasizing his war on poverty and racism. Protests began against U.S. involvement in Vietnam, as draft cards were burned. The Astrodome, the first indoor, air-conditioned football stadium, was opened in Houston, Texas. Britain's tallest building, the 620-ft. Post Office Tower, was opened in London. The Byrds scored a big hit with "Mr. Tambourine Man."

➤ Read Martin Luther King Jr.'s Star Profile on page 537.

CAPRICORN

From January 01, 0:00 through January 20, 6:28

The Favorite Teacher

Blessed with a quick wit and keen curiosity, the 1965 January Capricorn is a pleasure to know. You can amass huge amounts of information with relative ease, although you never lord this knowledge over others. People delight in talking with you, as they always come away learning something new. You're especially good at putting complicated concepts into simple language, making it easy for folks to join any conversation. You've never been the kind of student who locked yourself in a room piled with books. You want to air ideas through vigorous discussion.

Although you respect tradition, you are willing to challenge the status quo. In 1965, eighteen were arrested in Mississippi for the murder of the voting-rights workers James Cheney, Andrew Goodman, and Michael Schwerner. Like these martyrs for civil rights, you may feel that the integrity of any system of democracy depends on its inclusiveness. You've probably made quite a few accurate predictions about the future that seemed absurd at the time.

When you're not studying, you're indulging in sensual pleasures. You love a good meal, and may have a tendency to gain weight if you're not careful. Most Capricorns dislike physical displays of affection—but not you. You're probably famous for giving bear hugs, tousling hair, and pecking friends on the cheek. Beware of bad habits jeopardizing your health. As you get older, you will realize the need to treat your body like a temple, but this is one lesson that may not come easy to you.

You like well-balanced people who treat life as the ultimate adventure. Taureans share your love of luxury, while Geminis are always good for a chat. Leos are always ready for fun, while Pisceans appreciate your philosophical bent. Pessimists are the bane of your existence; you simply refuse to give in to negativity.

Your greatest challenge is perfectionism. Don't berate yourself if you turn in a sub-standard performance. Everybody has bad days, including you. Your biggest strength is your love of learning and it's one of the many reasons you're so popular with people from all walks of life.

AQUARIUS

From January 20, 6:29 through February 18, 20:47

The Sensual Artist

The creative intensity of the 1965 Aquarius is breathtaking to behold. You send shockwaves through every room you enter; it's utterly impossible to ignore your presence. The year you were born, forty-eight tornadoes struck the U.S. and three devastating cyclones hit eastern Pakistan. The force of your personality can be cyclonic. You have a knack for stirring up the atmosphere while maintaining a calm center. While people marvel at your serenity, they can sometimes find it a little unnerving.

You have the soul of an artist, and will never feel fulfilled unless you give yourself over to your creative impulses. Your work manages to be profound without being depressing. Although you enjoy exploring the big issues (life, death, and sex), you manage to do so with a sense of humor. Although you may not realize it, you've been blessed with writing talent, and would do equally well producing novels and non-fiction works. You're the farthest thing from a tortured artist there is. As far as you're concerned, there's no point to work unless its fun.

A healthy sexual appetite is one of the leading characteristics of the 1965 Aquarius. You'll probably never want for partners, although you want a relationship that is profoundly meaningful. Merging souls is just as important as merging bodies, and you probably derive lots of artistic inspiration from your romantic exploits. Money can be a problem for you, and it's a good idea to keep your bank account separate from your partner's.

In relationships, you gravitate toward people who are both imaginative and sensual. Taureans, Librans, Scorpios, and Pisceans are good company for you. For lovers, you'd do well with fellow artists, so long as their self-esteem is good. It may be hard for your partner when others compare his or her work to your ingenious creations.

Your biggest challenge is financial instability. While your imagination can fill a studio or laboratory, it can also fill your pocketbook, as distasteful as this may sound. Trust your artistic impulses, as they can take you to astounding personal and professional heights.

➤ Read about your Chinese Astrological sign on page 838. ➤ Read about your Personal Planets on page 826. ➤ Read about your personal Mystical Card on page 856.

CAPRICORN
Your Personal Planets

YOUR LOVE POTENTIAL
Venus in Sagittarius, Jan. 01, 0:00 - Jan. 12, 7:59
Venus in Capricorn, Jan. 12, 8:00 - Jan. 20, 6:28

YOUR DRIVE AND AMBITION
Mars in Virgo, Jan. 01, 0:00 - Jan. 20, 6:28

YOUR LUCK MAGNETISM
Jupiter in Taurus, Jan. 01, 0:00 - Jan. 20, 6:28

World Events

Jan. 7 – Gangster twins Ronnie and Reggie Kray are arrested in London.

Jan. 16 – Eighteen people are arrested in Mississippi on charges of murdering three civil rights workers.

Gangster twins Reggie and Ronnie Kray

AQUARIUS
Your Personal Planets

YOUR LOVE POTENTIAL
Venus in Capricorn, Jan. 20, 6:29 - Feb. 05, 7:40
Venus in Aquarius, Feb. 05, 7:41 - Feb. 18, 20:47

YOUR DRIVE AND AMBITION
Mars in Virgo, Jan. 20, 6:29 - Feb. 18, 20:47

YOUR LUCK MAGNETISM
Jupiter in Taurus, Jan. 20, 6:29 - Feb. 18, 20:47

World Events

Jan. 24 – Former British Prime Minister Winston Churchill dies.

Feb. 7 – The U.S. begins regular bombing and strafing of North Vietnam.

1965

PISCES
Your Personal Planets

YOUR LOVE POTENTIAL

Venus in Aquarius, Feb. 18, 20:48 - Mar. 01, 7:54
Venus in Pisces, Mar. 01, 7:55 - Mar. 20, 20:04

YOUR DRIVE AND AMBITION

Mars in Virgo, Feb. 18, 20:48 - Mar. 20, 20:04

YOUR LUCK MAGNETISM

Jupiter in Taurus, Feb. 18, 20:48 - Mar. 20, 20:04

World Events

Feb. 21 - Civil rights campaigner Malcolm X is shot and killed by African Americans.

Mar. 19 - Rembrandt's *Titus* sells for over $3 million.

Malcolm X is shot dead

ARIES
Your Personal Planets

YOUR LOVE POTENTIAL

Venus in Pisces, Mar. 20, 20:05 - Mar. 25, 9:53
Venus in Aries, Mar. 25, 9:54 - Apr. 18, 14:30
Venus in Taurus, Apr. 18, 14:31 - Apr. 20, 7:25

YOUR DRIVE AND AMBITION

Mars in Virgo, Mar. 20, 20:05 - Apr. 20, 7:25

YOUR LUCK MAGNETISM

Jupiter in Taurus, Mar. 20, 20:05 - Apr. 20, 7:25

World Events

Mar. 21 - Martin Luther King Jr. leads 3,200 people on a freedom march from Selma to Montgomery.

Apr. 9 - Border skirmishes break out between India and Pakistan.

532

PISCES
From February 18, 20:48 through March 20, 20:04

The Powerful Partner

The 1965 Pisces realizes their full potential through the help of a partner. Although you are blessed with considerable talent in your own right, it takes the influence of another to bring it to fruition. The year you were born, Bill Cosby launched the television series *I Spy*, which marked the first time an African American shared top billing with a white co-star. The pairing brought the talented comedian into the mainstream entertainment industry, where he has remained ever since. Partnerships are similarly lucky for you, particularly in the early stages of your work.

Although you like working with others, your unions can hardly be called conventional. You may be the type who has a business partner who seems more like a spouse, or a best friend who acts more like a parent. You put great energy into your relationships, and refuse to let public opinion hamper them in any way. Besides, it's not important what people think of your work methods, so long as they are effective in the long run.

You have an idealistic outlook that is not easily shattered. Traveling is a comfort to you, as it reminds you that, whatever our differences, human beings are essentially the same in wants and needs. You may enjoy studying world religions, which help define your own beliefs. It's very important for you to believe in something that is bigger than yourself, be it God, Nature, or Fate. Beware of shrugging off all responsibility for your behavior, though. No matter what your outlook, it should include an element of self-determination.

In relationships, you flourish with people who like working in pairs. Gemini's, Virgos, Librans, and fellow Pisceans bring out the best in you. Be careful not to give up too much of your power to friends and lovers, though. As you get older, it will be easier to assert yourself, but only after some hard lessons.

Your greatest challenge is modesty. Don't be afraid to speak up when you disagree with a plan, or have another that you feel is better. Your biggest strength is your adaptability. You can work under any condition, so long as you feel valued and appreciated.

ARIES
From March 20, 20:05 through April 20, 7:25

The Dutiful Soldier

As a 1965 Aries, you need to devote your life to a cause. Coming of age during the Vietnam War, political demonstrations may have made a big impression on you. It doesn't matter which side you sympathized with; you identified with the need to debate issues openly and honestly. You have more respect for the opposition than you do for apathetic folks who don't hold anything sacred.

The year you were born, India and Pakistan were engaged in a fight over Kashmir. While you're certainly no warmonger, you can understand the need to draw clear distinctions between people who have different beliefs. Chances are you belong to several clubs and organizations devoted to doing good works. This gives you a chance to be useful, as well as meet people who share your sense of duty—it gives you a sense of security to be with your own people.

You've been blessed with considerable business acumen, and may be the treasurer of one of your many clubs. People trust you with publicly held money. You're not the type to spend hard-earned resources on flashy status symbols; you'd rather invest for the future. If there's ever any drudge work to be done, there's a good chance it will be put into your capable hands. Sometimes these responsibilities drain you of energy. When you feel overwhelmed, you should take some time to be by yourself. Many Rams enjoy the public eye, but 1965 Aries are more private than the rest of the herd.

In relationships, you may feel a strong attraction to Scorpios, whose passionate beliefs resonate with your own do-or-die attitude. Such a pairing is bound to be volatile but stimulating. You also get along well with hard workers like Taureans, Virgos, and Capricorns, although earth signs don't satisfy your fiery penchant for political protests.

Your greatest challenge is to look for commonalities among people, instead of differences. Often, your beliefs prevent you from making friends with people who can give you a different perspective on the world. Your biggest strength is your admirable work ethic. You can accomplish more in a day than most folks can in a week!

➤ Read about your Chinese Astrological sign on page 838. ➤ Read about your Personal Planets on page 826. ➤ Read about your personal Mystical Card on page 856.

TAURUS

From April 20, 7:26 through May 21, 6:49

The Lucky Lover

Born with tremendous energy and courage, the 1965 Taurus is a good friend to have. That's because you have a knack for spinning straw into gold. No matter how bleak a situation appears, you manage to turn it to advantage. Far be it for you to feel discouraged by obstacles. When confronted by a closed door, the wheels in your mind start spinning, and pretty soon you've found a way to pick the lock.

You understand the power of positive thinking, and use it to advantage all the time. People have a very hard time saying no to you, and that includes romantic prospects. Over the course of your life, you've probably had quite a few relationships, but very few of them ended on bitter terms. Even when the spark has died out of a romance, partners want to stay friends with you. You definitely benefited from the sexual revolution; the year you were born, the U.S. Supreme Court overturned a ban on contraceptives. Consequently, you've been able to romance with a light-hearted attitude that was impossible for your predecessors.

While you like to have fun, you do value the people in your life. A tendency to idealize loved ones can lead to occasional disappointments, but for the most part, folks flourish under your adoring gaze. You're the type who believes in love at first sight, and it's probably happened to you several times. Both your business and romantic partnerships have a fated quality to them. Within the first few seconds of meeting someone, you know whether or not you were meant to be together.

As a 1965 Taurus, you do best with fellow romantics. You delight in the company of Leos, Librans, and Pisceans, and probably have many Bulls in your social circle, too. You need friends who encourage you to build castles in the air. If there's anything you hate, it's a cynic.

Your greatest challenge may be satisfying your legions of your friends. Your enthusiasm and creativity act like a magnet on people. It can be difficult to balance your own needs with theirs at times. Your biggest strength is your sunny outlook. Even the darkest days hold promise for an optimist like you.

GEMINI

From May 21, 6:50 through June 21, 14:55

The Ambitious Homebody

Torn between personal desires and professional ambitions, total contentment can be elusive for the 1965 Gemini. Nobody appreciates the comforts of home like you. Chances are you don't keep the back door locked, as people are always dropping by for a visit. If you don't have a huge biological family, you probably treat your huge circle of friends as kin. The year you were born, the film *The Sound Of Music* opened to rave reviews. If you had your way, you'd have a home life a lot like the von Trapps: filled with laughter, music, love, and lots of children!

Your love of home is rivaled by your desire for personal success. From childhood, you felt destined for greatness in some way. Holding a prominent position in society is very important to you, and this desire has probably taken you far from home at times. Often, you'd rather be home when you're out, and out when you're home. For a person with divided loyalties, striving for a happy medium is essential.

Perhaps you can start a home-based business, or earn money by helping out in other people's homes. You could do very well running a catering or cleaning business. With your innate sense of order, organizing other people's lives may come naturally to you, too. At the very least, your professional life should have a distinctly domestic feel to it, or you won't feel comfortable. Ideally, you should work with people who feel more like kin than colleagues.

In relationships, you work best with ambitious, family-oriented, people. Taureans, Cancerians, Leos, and Capricorns are all good bets, as either friends or romantic partners. Watch out for a tendency to treat friends like employees and vice-versa. It can cause problems in both realms of your life if you're not careful.

Your greatest challenge is balance. You're the type who needs a rewarding private and public life simultaneously. This requires making sacrifices in both spheres. Though your choices will be difficult at times, they will be necessary for leading a well-rounded life. Your biggest strength is your ability to build close friendships in every circumstance.

➤ Read about your Chinese Astrological sign on page 838. ➤ Read about your Personal Planets on page 826. ➤ Read about your personal Mystical Card on page 856.

TAURUS
Your Personal Planets

YOUR LOVE POTENTIAL
Venus in Taurus, Apr. 20, 7:26 - May 12, 22:07
Venus in Gemini, May 12, 22:08 - May 21, 6:49

YOUR DRIVE AND AMBITION
Mars in Virgo, Mar. 20, 7:26 - May 21, 6:49

YOUR LUCK MAGNETISM
Jupiter in Taurus, Apr. 20, 7:26 - Apr. 22, 14:31
Jupiter in Gemini, Apr. 22, 14:32 - May 21, 6:49

World Events

May 11 - Windstorms in Bangladesh kill thousands and render millions homeless.

May 12 - Israel and West Germany exchange letters indicating a resumption of diplomatic relations.

King Hassan II of Morocco

GEMINI
Your Personal Planets

YOUR LOVE POTENTIAL
Venus in Gemini, May 21, 6:50 - June 06, 8:38
Venus in Cancer, June 06, 8:39 - June 21, 14:55

YOUR DRIVE AND AMBITION
Mars in Virgo, May 21, 6:50 - June 21, 14:55

YOUR LUCK MAGNETISM
Jupiter in Gemini, May 21, 6:50 - June 21, 14:55

World Events

June 7 - Absolute monarchy is restored in Morocco under King Hassan II.

June 8 - U.S. troops are ordered to launch an offensive in Vietnam.

1965

CANCER
Your Personal Planets

YOUR LOVE POTENTIAL

Venus in Cancer, June 21, 14:56 - June 30, 21:58
Venus in Leo, June 30, 21:59 - July 23, 1:47

YOUR DRIVE AND AMBITION

Mars in Virgo, June 21, 14:56 - June 29, 1:11
Mars in Libra, June 29, 1:12 - July 23, 1:47

YOUR LUCK MAGNETISM

Jupiter in Gemini, June 21, 14:56 - July 23, 1:47

World Events

July 4 - At an assembly in Washington, Martin Luther King Jr. demands an end to the Vietnam War.

July 14 - The U.S. space probe *Mariner 4* flies past Mars and beams back twenty-two pictures of the planet.

U.S. forces in the Vietnam War

LEO
Your Personal Planets

YOUR LOVE POTENTIAL

Venus in Leo, July 23, 1:48 - July 25, 14:50
Venus in Virgo, July 25, 14:51 - Aug. 19, 13:05
Venus in Libra, Aug. 19, 13:06 - Aug. 23, 8:42

YOUR DRIVE AND AMBITION

Mars in Libra, July 23, 1:48 - Aug. 20, 12:15
Mars in Scorpio, Aug. 20, 12:16 - Aug. 23, 8:42

YOUR LUCK MAGNETISM

Jupiter in Gemini, July 23, 1:48 - Aug. 23, 8:42

World Events

Aug. 9 - Singapore proclaims its independence from the Malaysian Federation.

Aug. 19 - U.S. forces defeat the Viet Cong and capture the stronghold of Van Tuong in South Vietnam.

CANCER

From June 21, 14:56 through July 23, 1:47

The Star Pupil

The chief characteristic of a 1965 Cancer is a keen, probing mind. You rarely have to be shown how to do something twice; you have an almost photographic memory. You probably stood out in school, because teachers considered you either a fantastic or a terrible student: people with your intellectual abilities are often labeled geniuses or dullards at an early age. If you were lucky, your instructors recognized your gift and helped nurture it. If you were less fortunate, mediocre teachers sensed your superior intellect and resented you for it.

The year you were born, Peter Jennings became the anchor of ABC's nightly news at the young age of twenty-six. His ability to deliver news in an intelligent, compassionate way probably mirrors your own style. You have a knack for communicating complicated ideas in a way that puts people at ease. If you aren't a teacher, you could easily become one, thanks to your easy rapport with young people.

Philosophy, religion, and foreign cultures may have a special hold on your imagination. At some point in your life, you will probably visit Nepal, Jerusalem, Mecca, or some other place of spiritual significance. You've always had a sense that there is something beyond the physical plane, and may study metaphysical subjects later in life. Your interests may not sit well with friends and family who don't share your thirst for information. It's important for you to make friends with folks who share your interests.

Intellectual types suit your temperament best. A great number of your friends may be Geminis, Virgos, Librans, and Aquarians. Don't be afraid to touch on emotional subjects from time to time. Although your penchant for study is admirable, not everything you need to know can be found in books.

Your greatest challenge is to link head and heart. Water signs rule the emotions, and you're no exception. Until you learn to trust your heart, it may feel as though you're working at half your capacity. Your biggest strength is your quick mind. No matter what you do or where you go in life, you'll always be an eager and willing student.

LEO

From July 23, 1:48 through August 23, 8:42

The Cherished Friend

Some people worship power, others money; the 1965 Leo prizes friends above all else. Maybe that's why you have so many loved ones. People want to feel appreciated, and you do a marvelous job of it. You're firmly convinced that love can heal any wound, no matter how deep. The year you were born, Israel and West Germany began diplomatic relations. This impressive example of diplomacy reflects your own desire to build rather than to burn bridges.

Although some Leo's can have a rather aggressive way of expressing themselves, you still manage to be charming. Others are attracted by your feisty debating style; you'd make a terrific trial lawyer. You prefer keeping things on an intellectual level, though. You like to draw a distinct line between your personal and private lives, and admit very few people into your confidence. Leos of 1965 may have claustrophobic family relationships. It can take a while to break away from these constraints, but when you do, trust will be less of a problem.

You have a tendency to spend money as fast as you make it. As far as you're concerned, abundance should be enjoyed—you don't see much sense in tucking vast sums into a savings account. Fortunately, you have many friends who are looking out for you. You'll always have a roof over your head and plenty to eat, thanks to your extensive network of friends. Nobody could ever accuse you of being a leech. All the riches you enjoy are a reward for having an open, loving heart.

You get along with just about every sign. However, you have particular success with steadfast Taureans, nurturing Cancerians, loving Leos, and sensitive Pisceans. The only risk you run in relationships is coddling your loved ones. Sometimes you have to state painful truths in order to salvage a damaged union. Be honest about your feelings.

Your biggest challenge is to temper love with justice. Don't look the other way at people's bad behavior, especially if it's hurting you. Your biggest strength is your capacity to love. So long as there are 1965 Leos in the world, there will always be hope for harmony and bliss.

➤ Read about your Chinese Astrological sign on page 838. ➤ Read about your Personal Planets on page 826. ➤ Read about your personal Mystical Card on page 856.

VIRGO

From August 23, 8:43 through September 23, 6:05

The Respected Communicator

The 1965 Virgo makes a powerful impression on everyone they meet. You have a forceful, inventive personality that sets you apart from the crowd. When you talk, people listen. Even when folks disagree with you, they respect what you say. The year you were born, Britain held a state funeral for Winston Churchill. The esteem with which he was held is similar to the kind you enjoy. While you weigh your words carefully, you never censor your opinions. You're not one to sugar-coat unpleasant truths.

You are destined to hold a position of prominence, although it may take many years before you reach the pinnacle of your success. At some point, you could be put in charge of large groups of people. This could put strain on intimate relationships. It's hard to focus on a single person when you're responsible for so many others. There's a chance you will marry late in life. Alternately, you could pair up with someone who is mature enough to realize that you have serious priorities outside of your primary relationship.

Visualization is a valuable technique that every 1965 Virgo should learn. Images have a powerful effect on your subconscious. Whenever you want to achieve something, draw a picture of your goal and put it where you will see it on a regular basis, or play a movie of your achievement in your mind before you go to sleep. The older you get, the better this method will work for you.

In relationships, you get along best with people who are willing to work behind-the-scenes. You're too powerful a personality to share the spotlight with others. Quiet, unassuming friends like Taureans, Capricorns, and Pisceans are good matches for you. You also work very well with fellow Virgos, provided they weren't also born in 1965.

Your greatest challenge is your tendency to dominate weaker people. Resist the urge to steamroll folks who are timid about expressing their opinions. If you take the time to listen, you could learn something valuable. Your biggest strength is your leadership ability. Use it to enact great changes to the world. You have the power to move mountains!

LIBRA

From September 23, 6:06 through October 23, 15:09

The Intuitive Politician

Sweet and unassuming on the outside, the 1965 Libra appears as gentle as a lamb. However, anybody who takes the trouble to know you will realize that you're nobody's fool. Beneath your gentle surface lurks the heart of a warrior. One of your favorite pastimes is to lull folks into a sense of security, than shock them with a shrewd observation or show of courage.

You have the makings of a great politician. That's because you can play one side against the other, with remarkable results. The year you were born, President Lyndon Johnson asked the U.S. Congress to guarantee every citizen voting rights. Only a shrewd politician could have achieved this remarkable act of bravery. Sure enough, LBJ soon signed the Voting Rights Act, despite massive opposition in the South. You're able to pull off similar feats wherever you go, thanks to your uncanny instincts. And you're perfectly willing to hit a person's weak spot in order to get the job done.

A persuasive manner of speech makes it easy to convert others to your point of view. You've got a wicked sense of humor, and are probably an excellent mimic. If it's not mean-spirited, your mocking behavior comes as a delight to onlookers. Try not to offend more sensitive acquaintances, though, or you could get a reputation for being malicious. It's important for you to enjoy good relationships with colleagues, as your work environment has a strong effect on your health.

In relationships, you fare best with people who can shelter you from your busy public life. Taureans, Cancerians, and Pisceans can provide you with a safe haven. You can also form lasting relationships with fellow Librans, who share your love of beauty and refinement.

Your greatest challenge is a tendency toward cynicism. You've probably witnessed some pretty unsavory behavior—mostly because people think that they can misbehave in front of you without fear of reprisal. Do your best to surround yourself with people who have impeccable ethics. Your greatest strength is your iron will. If you try hard enough, you can overcome even the most pessimistic thoughts.

➤ Read about your Chinese Astrological sign on page 838. ➤ Read about your Personal Planets on page 826. ➤ Read about your personal Mystical Card on page 856.

VIRGO
Your Personal Planets

YOUR LOVE POTENTIAL
Venus in Libra, Aug. 23, 8:43 - Sept. 13, 19:49
Venus in Scorpio, Sept. 13, 19:50 - Sept. 23, 6:05

YOUR DRIVE AND AMBITION
Mars in Scorpio, Aug. 23, 8:43 - Sept. 23, 6:05

YOUR LUCK MAGNETISM
Jupiter in Gemini, Aug. 23, 8:43 - Sept. 21, 4:38
Jupiter in Cancer, Sept. 21, 4:39 - Sept. 23, 6:05

World Events

Aug. 27 – Swiss-born architect and designer Le Corbusier dies.

Sept. 9 – Tibet becomes an autonomous region of China.

Le Corbusier in his arbor

LIBRA
Your Personal Planets

YOUR LOVE POTENTIAL
Venus in Scorpio, Sept. 23, 6:06 - Oct. 09, 16:45
Venus in Sagittarius, Oct. 09, 16:46 - Oct. 23, 15:09

YOUR DRIVE AND AMBITION
Mars in Scorpio, Sept. 23, 6:06 - Oct. 04, 6:45
Mars in Sagittarius, Oct. 04, 6:46 - Oct. 23, 15:09

YOUR LUCK MAGNETISM
Jupiter in Cancer, Sept. 23, 6:06 - Oct. 23, 15:09

World Events

Sept. 26 – The Beatles receive the Order of the British Empire.

Oct. 4 – The USSR launches *Luna 7*, which eventually crash lands on the Moon.

1965

SCORPIO
Your Personal Planets

YOUR LOVE POTENTIAL
Venus in Sagittarius, Oct. 23, 15:10 - Nov. 05, 19:35
Venus in Capricorn, Nov. 05, 19:36 - Nov. 22, 12:28

YOUR DRIVE AND AMBITION
Mars in Sagittarius, Oct. 23, 15:10 - Nov. 14, 7:18
Mars in Capricorn, Nov. 14, 7:19 - Nov. 22, 12:28

YOUR LUCK MAGNETISM
Jupiter in Cancer, Oct. 23, 15:10 - Nov. 17, 3:07
Jupiter in Gemini, Nov. 17, 3:08 - Nov. 22, 12:28

World Events

Nov. 9 - The most extensive power failure in history occurs across New England in the U.S. and Ontario, Canada.

Nov. 11 - Prime Minister Ian Smith declares Southern Rhodesia independent of Britain.

Rhodesian Prime Minister Ian Smith

SAGITTARIUS
Your Personal Planets

YOUR LOVE POTENTIAL
Venus in Capricorn, Nov. 22, 12:29 - Dec. 07, 4:36
Venus in Aquarius, Dec. 07, 4:37 - Dec. 22, 1:39

YOUR DRIVE AND AMBITION
Mars in Capricorn, Nov. 22, 12:29 - Dec. 22, 1:39

YOUR LUCK MAGNETISM
Jupiter in Gemini, Nov. 22, 12:29 - Dec. 22, 1:39

World Events

Dec. 1 - An airlift of refugees from Cuba to the U.S. begins.

Dec. 16 - British novelist W. Somerset Maugham dies.

SCORPIO
From October 23, 15:10 through November 22, 12:28

The Open-minded Humanitarian

As 1965 Scorpio, you have a deep love of philosophy, religion, and higher education. These subjects have granted you insight into humanity. You're always looking for ways to connect with others, no matter how different their background. The disturbing images of the Vietnam War probably made a deep impression on you. You can't abide people being ugly or cruel, and may devote your life to promoting kindness and understanding. The year you were born, the United Nations Children's Fund (UNICEF) was awarded the Nobel Peace Prize. This organization's noble mission reflects your own desire to bring comfort to powerless, dispossessed people, regardless of politics.

You have an innate talent for making money during good times and bad. A natural-born fund-raiser, you could have a very successful career in the nonprofit industry. Very few people can say no to your passionate pleas for justice and mercy. Sometimes your social conscience can undermine your happiness. As you grow older, you will learn that it's not a sin to amuse yourself in a world filled with strife. You'll be able to perform acts of kindness more easily if you lead a joyous life.

When depression threatens to settle in, you can always call on your friends. Most Scorpios are a bit reclusive, but you're an exception to this rule. You probably have quite a few eccentrics among your acquaintance, as well as some powerful authority figures. Let them comfort and cheer you when the weight of the world threatens to press you down.

In relationships, you do best with people who are deeply committed to peace and understanding. Librans, Sagittarians, Aquarians, and Pisceans are among your favorite friends, although you manage to get along with just about anybody. You even have respect for belligerent Ariens; you can identify with their ardent passion and courage.

Your greatest challenge as a 1965 Scorpio is a tendency toward seriousness. As you get older, you'll have a greater appreciation of the absurd. Your biggest strength is your love of people. No matter where you go or what you do, you will never lack for friends.

SAGITTARIUS
From November 22, 12:29 through December 22, 1:39

The Courageous Leader

As a 1965 Sagittarius, you were born with a special mission: to strip the world of injustice. If this sounds like an awesome task, you're right. The year you were born, Dr. Martin Luther King Jr. began a drive to register African-American voters in the U.S. His revolutionary work may have left its mark on you. Injustice of any kind offends you deeply, and there's a good chance that you'll be involved with many moral crusades throughout the course of your life.

Often, you're willing to sacrifice your personal life for the sake of work. If you're not careful about balancing your public and private sides, your loved ones may feel that they are your second priority. The older you get, the more you'll realize just how important a happy home life is to an ardent crusader like yourself. Intimate partnerships can be problematic for you, as you tend to expect too much from the ones you love. If you remember that you get out of relationships what you put into them, you'll avoid the heartache you may have experienced in your young adulthood.

Although you usually like being in the spotlight, you do need to withdraw from public life at times. You're an extraordinarily sensitive person, and soak up the atmosphere like a sponge. When you're exposed to toxic environments, try to get off on your own for a few hours. Developing a solitary hobby like painting, woodwork, writing, or gardening can help cleanse you of noxious influences.

As far as relationships go, you get along best with people who are diligent but humble. Virgos, Aquarians, and Pisceans probably make up a large part of your social circle. So do fellow Sagittarians, although you may have some ego clashes with Archers who were also born in 1965. Your personalities are simply too strong to be compatible.

As a 1965 Sagittarius, your greatest challenge is to temper justice with mercy. You have a tendency to castigate people whose politics do not match your own—this will only escalate the intolerance you hate. Your biggest blessing is your ability to break down outmoded institutions to make way for ones that are more just.

➤ Read about your Chinese Astrological sign on page 838. ➤ Read about your Personal Planets on page 826. ➤ Read about your personal Mystical Card on page 856.

CAPRICORN

The Quiet Philosopher

Secret and solitary, the 1965 December Capricorn is a delicious mystery. Very few people know the real you, and that's just the way you like it. Tabloid journalism and reality television leave a bad taste in your mouth—speculating about the private lives of others feels like a waste of time. You'd rather discuss concepts, not people. Ideas can't disappoint you the way human beings can. The year you were born, black nationalist leader Malcolm X was shot and killed, silencing one of the most provocative political voices of his time. For you, the destruction of thought is just as tragic as the loss of human life.

Still, you do enjoy finding out what makes people tick, although you keep your views to yourself. Subjects like body language, handwriting analysis, and astrology can give you valuable insight into human behavior. Few people realize you're something of an amateur psychologist. You may feel compelled to write a book about your observations one day, although you'll probably want to publish it under a pseudonym. You hate giving yourself away, even through artistic media.

At some level, you may never feel satisfied with your education. There's so much to learn, and so little time to study. Ideally, you should devote a year or two solely to scholarship. If money is a problem, apply for a grant. Your diligence and common sense should be enough to impress anyone. You're a natural-born student, although people may have been slow to recognize this. Perhaps you had a learning disability that prevented teachers from recognizing your potential. As you get older, educational opportunities will become more readily available.

In relationships, you're most compatible with quiet, thoughtful people. You delight in the company of Taureans, Cancerians, Librans, and Pisceans, as their easy companionship suits your reserve.

Your greatest challenge is an intellectual inferiority complex. Don't be too intimidated by experts with lots of degrees; you're just as capable of profound thought. Your biggest strength is your calm nature, which helps you to weather considerable storms.

CAPRICORN
Your Personal Planets

YOUR LOVE POTENTIAL
Venus in Aquarius, Dec. 22, 1:40 - Dec. 31, 23:59

YOUR DRIVE AND AMBITION
Mars in Capricorn, Dec. 22, 1:40 - Dec. 23, 5:35
Mars in Aquarius, Dec. 23, 5:36 - Dec. 31, 23:59

YOUR LUCK MAGNETISM
Jupiter in Gemini, Dec. 22, 1:40 - Dec. 31, 23:59

World Events

Dec. 22 – Director David Lean's *Doctor Zhivago* premieres.

Dec. 30 – Ferdinand Marcos is inaugurated as President of the Philippines.

MARTIN LUTHER KING, Jr.
Capricorn

Martin Luther King, Jr. was a Baptist minister who devoted his life to Christian activism and improving society through non-violent means. Influenced in his studies by Mahatma Gandhi and Henry David Thoreau, King became a leader in the early civil rights movement, as well as in the anti-war protests during the U.S. involvement in Vietnam. He became the youngest recipient of the Nobel Peace Prize. While on his campaign against economic inequalities, he was assassinated by a white supremacist.

King was a Capricorn, a sign noted for its unwavering devotion to hard work and success. With his Sun, the planet of identity, near the cusp of the house of career, King projected a sense of authority and was a force to be reckoned with. A difficult contact from Pluto, planet of manipulation, explains the power struggles King faced and the difficulty he experienced within his own ranks as he preached non-violence to those who were longing to act out their anger and frustration.

Looking at his chart, it is no surprise that he devoted his life to others. Jupiter, the planet of opportunity, in the house of the underprivileged made positive contacts with both his Neptune, planet of ideals, in the house of creative energy, and Saturn, the planet of leadership, in the house of deep changes. His Moon (emotional life) was in compassionate Pisces in the house of others, with positive contact to his Pluto (transformation) in the house of communication, drawing him to speak out and work for social change. This placement of Pluto indicated King's gift of oratory. He was mesmerizing and his words inspired a nation to walk beside him in the march for freedom, equality and justice. His stirring and inspirational "I have a dream" speech still touches all who hear it and is as fresh as the day he delivered it.

Martin Luther King Jr.
January 15, 1929 - April 4, 1968

In addition, Neptune, the planet of idealism, provides yet another significant aspect, making King both photogenic and inspirational. With a contact from Saturn to Mars, planet of action, King was aware of his responsibilities and willing to perform whatever duty seemed meaningful and appropriate, to the point of risking his life.

➤ Read Mahatma Gandhi's Star Profile on page 377.

1966

The Fires of Idealism: Uranus meets Neptune

In late March 1966, 25,000 people demonstrated through the streets of New York City against America's involvement in the war in Vietnam. There were simultaneous marches in seven other American cities and seven foreign cities. Opposition to the war in Vietnam was going global as aggression increased under President Lyndon B. Johnson's leadership. The year before, Norman Morrison and Alice Herz had immolated themselves to protest the war, in the ultimate form of dissent. Anti-establishment fervor continued to grow.

At this time, the planet Uranus was making an aspect called a "sextile" to the planet Neptune in the heavens. A sextile is usually a positive aspect, indicating opportunities. Uranus is the planet of humanitarianism and rebellion. Neptune is the planet of illusion, delusion, and spirituality. When they met in the sky in 1966, the fires of idealism were lit. Neptune was in the sign of Scorpio at this time, symbolizing the unknown worlds and the unconscious mind. This is a very emotional placement and the personal really did become the political. Uranus was in Virgo at this time, sign of service and people were clearly prepared to take to the streets to express solidarity with their brothers and sisters who were dying thousands of miles away. Protest movements exploded in every area. This was the time of the Student Non-Violent Coordinating Committee and the Black Panthers. As Uranus blew soft kisses to Neptune, the youth of the world responded with the sound of footsteps pounding the pavement to make a powerful statement.

Thousands of anti-Vietnam War demonstrators in New York

The first B-52 bombing on North Vietnam

China's Chairman Mao proclaims the Cultural Revolution

CULTURAL REVOLUTION

Nehru's daughter, Indira Gandhi became Prime Minister of India. China's Chairman Mao proclaimed the Cultural Revolution and his drive to eradicate bourgeois thinking by purging the educated from society's upper echelons. In Africa, there were violent changes of leadership in Ghana and Uganda. British Bechuanaland became independent, as did Botswana. Heavy rains in Italy caused floods which destroyed many of Florence's priceless art treasures. Vigorous anti-Vietnam war protests continued in the U.S. and elsewhere, while sniper Charles Whitman killed thirteen and wounded thirty-one at Austin's University before being shot dead himself. Ralph Nader denounced the lack of safety in automobiles. Super-slim British model Twiggy became the symbol of a new youthful fashion movement. Women felt more liberated in the climate of freedom brought about by the civil rights movement and the birth control pill. John Fowles' *The Magus* struck the right chord with mystically oriented youth, while Jacqueline Susann's *Valley Of The Dolls* told it like it was in the desperate world of lonely women. U.S. Manhattan Project scientist J. Robert Oppenheimer died.

➤ Read "Dreaming Through the Twentieth Century" by Skye Alexander on page 545.

CAPRICORN

From January 01, 0:00 through January 20, 12:19

The Industrious Do-Gooder

The Capricorn born in January 1966 is always looking for ways to be of service. Whether its running small errands for friends or assisting over-burdened colleagues, you derive a divine feeling of purpose from being useful. Your industrious attitude has paid off over the years. You believe in an honest day's work for an honest day's pay, and wouldn't dream of overcharging for services.

Although you may not be the most learned person in your social circle, you're one of the most respected. This is because you have so much common sense. Folks often come to you for home-spun advice, and you're happy to dispense it. You'd never dream of sugar-coating the truth, or lying to spare someone's feelings. The year you were born, all U.S. cigarette packs were forced to carry warning labels cautioning consumers about the dangers of smoking. You're not above issuing similar warnings, and folks respect you for it.

You derive a great deal of strength from your many friends. There's a good chance you belong to several community organizations, and this makes you very well-connected. You're the type who can solve problems with a single phone call. It's not that you take advantage of your friends; it's just that you have many loved ones who are willing (and able) to help in a crisis. You may have been shy about asking for assistance in the past, but this has grown easier with time.

As a 1966 Capricorn, you get along best with folks who share your profound respect for work. Taureans, Virgos, Scorpios, and Capricorns are good matches for you, both as friends and lovers. Take care that your relationships don't solely revolve around work, though, or you could miss out on some precious moments. Take a break now and again!

Although you know what it takes to get the job done, you may lack a creative approach. Don't feel pressured to always do things by the book. Your greatest challenge is to let your imagination take over when the routine starts to pall. Your biggest strength is your willingness to speak the truth. Use it to build strong, trustworthy friendships that will last a lifetime.

AQUARIUS

From January 20, 12:20 through February 19, 2:37

The Pragmatic Rebel

At first glance, the 1966 Aquarius doesn't look like a rebel. You prefer not to draw attention to yourself and this helps you to size up your environment before taking action. Once you get a grasp of the surroundings, though, you become a force to be reckoned with. Aquarians are always anxious to improve their circumstances, and you're no exception. You take a more subtle approach to reform than most Water Bearers, though, and this gives you a decided advantage over the establishment.

The year you were born, Henry Ford accused Ralph Nader of being ignorant about car safety. Authority figures tend to underestimate your reform efforts too, only to be proven wrong in the end. This never fails to give you a thrill, although your primary goal is to make the world a better place. You have a healthy suspicion of corporations, as they tend to sacrifice human need for profit. Reforming the business world may be one of your favorite causes, although you are interested in many other humanitarian issues.

Your deceptively innocent appearance belies a sensual nature. Many people would be surprised to learn of your considerable sexual appetite. This side of you comes out quite unexpectedly. You're irresistibly drawn to mad geniuses, and become a shameless flirt in such company. Willing to try anything once, you often surprise lovers with your daring behavior. Prudes are quickly crossed out of your little black book.

Relationships are a bit difficult for you, as you're easily bored. You're best suited to people with strong intellects. Geminis, Virgos, Librans, and fellow Aquarians stimulate your imagi-nation. Beware of withholding your emotions from your romantic partner, though, or alienation could ensue.

Although you're quite brilliant, you're totally confounded when people act illogically. Your biggest challenge is to examine your own heart. Once you understand the effect of the heart on the brain, your relationships will become much more rewarding. Your greatest strength is your gift for strategy. You can get around anyone or anything when you put your mind to it.

➤ Read about your Chinese Astrological sign on page 838. ➤ Read about your Personal Planets on page 826. ➤ Read about your personal Mystical Card on page 856.

CAPRICORN
Your Personal Planets

YOUR LOVE POTENTIAL
Venus in Aquarius, Jan. 01, 0:00 - Jan. 20, 12:19

YOUR DRIVE AND AMBITION
Mars in Aquarius, Jan. 01, 0:00 - Jan. 20, 12:19

YOUR LUCK MAGNETISM
Jupiter in Gemini, Jan. 01, 0:00 - Jan. 20, 12:19

World Events

Jan. 2 – The first Jewish child is born in Spain since the expulsion of the Jews in 1492.
Jan. 19 – Indira Gandhi becomes Prime Minister of India.

Indira Gandhi becomes Prime Minister of India

AQUARIUS
Your Personal Planets

YOUR LOVE POTENTIAL
Venus in Aquarius, Jan. 20, 12:20 - Feb. 06, 12:45
Venus in Capricorn, Feb. 06, 12:46 - Feb. 19, 2:37

YOUR DRIVE AND AMBITION
Mars in Aquarius, Jan. 20, 12:20 - Jan. 30, 7:00
Mars in Pisces, Jan. 30, 7:01 - Feb. 19, 2:37

YOUR LUCK MAGNETISM
Jupiter in Gemini, Jan. 20, 12:20 - Feb. 19, 2:37

World Events

Feb. 11 – American Vice-President Hubert Humphrey embarks on a tour of Vietnam.
Feb. 16 – The World Council of Churches calls for peace in Vietnam.

1966

PISCES
Your Personal Planets

YOUR LOVE POTENTIAL
Venus in Capricorn, Feb. 19, 2:38 - Feb. 25, 10:54
Venus in Aquarius, Feb. 25, 10:55 - Mar. 21, 1:52

YOUR DRIVE AND AMBITION
Mars in Pisces, Feb. 19, 2:38 - Mar. 09, 12:54
Mars in Aries, Mar. 09, 12:55 - Mar. 21, 1:52

YOUR LUCK MAGNETISM
Jupiter in Gemini, Feb. 19, 2:38 - Mar. 21, 1:52

World Events

Feb. 24 – President Nkrumah of Ghana loses his job through a military coup while away in China on a Vietnam peace mission.

Mar. 18 – General Suharto forms a government in Indonesia.

Indonesian General Suharto

ARIES
Your Personal Planets

YOUR LOVE POTENTIAL
Venus in Aquarius, Mar. 21, 1:53 - Apr. 06, 15:52
Venus in Pisces, Apr. 06, 15:53 - Apr. 20, 13:11

YOUR DRIVE AND AMBITION
Mars in Aries, Mar. 21, 1:53 - Apr. 17, 20:34
Mars in Taurus, Apr. 17, 20:35 - Apr. 20, 13:11

YOUR LUCK MAGNETISM
Jupiter in Gemini, Mar. 21, 1:53 - Apr. 20, 13:11

World Events

Mar. 29 – Leonid Brezhnev becomes First Secretary of the Communist Party in the USSR.

Apr. 12 – The first B-52 bombing is launched on North Vietnam.

540

PISCES
From February 19, 2:38 through March 21, 1:52

The Wistful Homebody

The 1966 Pisces is no stranger to mood swings. One second you're on the top of the world; the next you're in the depths of despair. This is because you judge your progress by how other people react to you. As a child, you were probably always trying to please parents, teachers, and authority figures—with varying results. The urge to please others will diminish as you get older, but until you become more confident, you may frequently fall victim to a fickle public.

Ideally, you should spend lots of time at home, in the company of friends and family. However, you have a restless spirit and often dream of visiting distant lands. The year you were born, the television show Star Trek debuted, inviting viewers to go where no man has gone before. While travel can be broadening, its important not to use adventure as a substitute for contentment.

You may always be on the lookout for a strong partner who will shield you from life's harsh realities. Be careful not to relinquish too much power, though, or you could wind up feeling suffocated. People may be surprised to learn how independent you really are. In fact, you may love your freedom so much that you refuse to work in an office. You probably work better as a freelancer, anyway. Creative occupations like photography, fashion, and dance may appeal to you, although you'd do equally well in a job promoting health and well-being.

Sensitive and romantic, you enjoy people who share your idealistic view of the world. Taureans, Cancerians, Librans, and Pisceans will do this best. Joining forces with such friends can make it difficult to do business, though. Your social life may eclipse career concerns, getting you into trouble at work.

Pleasing yourself is your biggest challenge, 1966 Pisces. Don't worry about whether other people will approve of your decisions. Its impossible to satisfy everybody all the time, anyway. Your greatest strength is your ability to create a wonderful, nurturing home. Like Dorothy in *The Wizard Of Oz*, you can find happiness in your own back yard, if you'd only take the trouble to look for it.

ARIES
From March 21, 1:53 through April 20, 13:11

The Habitual Enthusiast

The 1966 Aries refuses to let any grass grow under their feet, and for good reason. You've always got a million projects going on at once. Idleness is an anathema to you. Very often, you stretch your schedule to the limit, so when one thing goes wrong, there's a dreadful domino effect. Your immediate impulse is to throw a temper tantrum at the first sign of disaster. The year you were born, the Fermi nuclear reactor melted down in Detroit, Michigan. You've probably experienced many emotional meltdowns throughout the course of your life. As you grow older, its vital that you develop coping strategies, or you could forever alienate the people on whom you rely.

You need a career with plenty of variety, perhaps one with an intellectual element to it. You have the makings of a wonderful journalist, paramedic, or sales analyst. In your later years, homeopathy could become a growing interest, and may get integrated into your career in some way. Strengthening the mind-body connection can help you stave off nervous exhaustion, which can be an issue for you.

You have a spiritual side of which you may be unaware. At some point in your life, you may be tempted to study religions, searching for one that feels right for you. As a 1966 Aries, you expend a great deal of physical and emotional energy. Having a rich spiritual life will guard against burn-out, although you could probably also stand to take more vacations.

Eager and enthusiastic, you need friends who want to live life to the fullest. Ariens, Geminis, Leos, and Sagittarians prove wonderful playmates for you. Take care not to lash out at your loved ones when things don't go according to plan. Learn to channel your anger in more positive directions, like aerobic exercise.

The greatest challenge you face is your formidable temper. The sooner you come to terms with disappointments, the easier life will be. Your biggest strength is your willingness to tackle tough jobs. If you play your cards right, you can accomplish a great deal at a very young age. You'll rarely be sad if you keep setting new challenges for yourself.

➤ Read about your Chinese Astrological sign on page 838. ➤ Read about your Personal Planets on page 826. ➤ Read about your personal Mystical Card on page 856.

TAURUS

From April 20, 13:12 through May 21, 12:31

The Tasteful Romantic

Possessing tremendous sensuality, the 1966 Taurus is a quite a dish. You love all the pleasures of the flesh, and can be quite dogged about pursuing them. When you're not indulging yourself with food, drink, or sex, you're probably busy acquiring beautiful objects. Your taste in clothes, furniture, and antiques is impeccable, and you would do very well as a designer or decorator of some sort. Herb Alpert's *What Now My Love?* won a Grammy award in 1966. That's what you're searching for at all times—a taste of honey to make life a little sweeter.

Although most Taureans are noted for their steadfast loyalty, you may be a bit flighty when it comes to romance. You have a healthy appreciation for other people's beauty, and are somewhat liable to leave one partner for a better-looking one at the drop of a hat. Some people accuse you of being heartless, but you're actually just eager to sample every offering from the buffet table of life.

Just when you think you'll be a permanent singleton, you are likely to fall for someone like a ton of brinks. Your serious partnerships seem fated. When you spot the person you're supposed to be with for the rest of your life, you'll feel it to the very core of your being.

Partnerships can drastically alter the course of your life, so be careful with whom you associate. Mature, refined people understand your need for beauty. Fellow Bulls, nurturing Cancerians, dignified Virgos, and sophisticated Libras are good candidates as lovers, business partners, or both. Try to develop interests together, as you need a lasting bond that will sustain you. When the fires burn low, taking trips out in nature can rekindle the spark between you. Any close relationship you enjoy will probably have a spiritual element to it.

Your impeccable taste may make you a bit of a snob—you may shy away from people on the basis of how they look or behave. The greatest challenge you face is overcoming such prejudices. In terms of strengths, your biggest is your *joie de vive.* Continue to treat yourself to the finer things in life; goodness knows you're worth it!

GEMINI

From May 21, 12:32 through June 21, 20:32

The Passionate Debater

The 1966 Gemini shows a passion for facts and figures from a very early age. You were probably the kind of kid who asked weary authority figures "why?" morning, noon, and night. In 1966, the U.S. Supreme Court ruled that suspects must be read their rights before being taken into custody. You put the same demands on anybody who wields power over you. You've never been the type to blindly follow orders, no matter what the pressure. At times, people accuse you of being deliberately difficult, but that's not true. You're simply watching after your own interests, which makes manipulators uneasy.

Extraordinarily sensitive, you are eager to work hard on another's behalf. Whether its bringing beauty into the world, healing physical or emotional wounds, or promoting a greater sense of spirituality, you need a job that allows you to connect with people profoundly. There's a very good chance that you'll gain recognition for your efforts, although it could take many years before you reach the pinnacle of your career.

Chances are your home life is pretty unusual. You're the type who refuses to accept that you can pick your friends, but you can't choose your family. If you don't get along with kin, you simply treat your pals like honorary relatives. Watch for a tendency to boss your loved ones. You may be smart as a whip, but you can't make decisions for others, no matter how sorely you're tempted. That being said, you are incredibly generous with your possessions, and would never let a loved one go without when you have adequate resources.

You get along best with rabble-rousers who have a healthy suspicion of authority. Ariens, Geminis, Sagittarians, and Aquarians may play a prominent role in your life. You may want to add a sensible member to your group, though, if only to talk you out of crazier schemes.

Impatient and restless, your greatest challenge is to slow down. Racing through life will deprive you of its most profound pleasures. Your biggest strength is your fine mind. If you use it to analyze, assess, and discern everything you do, you'll rarely make a bad decision.

➤ Read about your Chinese Astrological sign on page 838. ➤ Read about your Personal Planets on page 826. ➤ Read about your personal Mystical Card on page 856.

TAURUS
Your Personal Planets

YOUR LOVE POTENTIAL
Venus in Pisces, Apr. 20, 13:12 - May 05, 4:32
Venus in Aries, May 05, 4:33 - May 21, 12:31

YOUR DRIVE AND AMBITION
Mars in Taurus, Apr. 20, 13:12 - May 21, 12:31

YOUR LUCK MAGNETISM
Jupiter in Gemini, Apr. 20, 13:12 - May 05, 14:51
Jupiter in Cancer, May 05, 14:52 - May 21, 12:31

World Events

May 6 – Myra Hindley and Ian Brady are convicted of the "Moors Murders" in Britain.

May 21 – Muhammad Ali retains the heavyweight title, beating Henry Cooper in six rounds.

French artist and sculptor Jean Arp dies

GEMINI
Your Personal Planets

YOUR LOVE POTENTIAL
Venus in Aries, May 21, 12:32 - May 31, 17:59
Venus in Taurus, May 31, 18:00 - June 21, 20:32

YOUR DRIVE AND AMBITION
Mars in Taurus, May 21, 12:32 - May 28, 22:06
Mars in Gemini, May 28, 22:07 - June 21, 20:32

YOUR LUCK MAGNETISM
Jupiter in Cancer, May 21, 12:32 - June 21, 20:32

World Events

June 7 – French sculptor and artist Jean Arp dies.

June 14 – Sixty people are injured when the Dutch police attack and beat construction workers.

1966

CANCER
Your Personal Planets

YOUR LOVE POTENTIAL
Venus in Taurus, June 21, 20:33 - June 26, 11:39
Venus in Gemini, June 26, 11:40 - July 21, 17:10
Venus in Cancer, July 21, 17:11 - July 23, 7:22

YOUR DRIVE AND AMBITION
Mars in Gemini, June 21, 20:33 - July 11, 3:14
Mars in Cancer, July 11, 3:15 - July 23, 7:22

YOUR LUCK MAGNETISM
Jupiter in Cancer, June 21, 20:33 - July 23, 7:22

World Events

July 4 - The Beatles are attacked while on a visit to the Philippines after they insult Imelda Marcos.

July 17 - Ho Chi Minh orders a partial mobilization in North Vietnam as a reaction against U.S. air attacks.

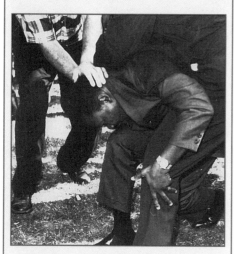

Martin Luther King, Jr. is struck by a rock

LEO
Your Personal Planets

YOUR LOVE POTENTIAL
Venus in Cancer, July 23, 7:23 - Aug. 15, 12:46
Venus in Leo, Aug. 15, 12:47 - Aug. 23, 14:17

YOUR DRIVE AND AMBITION
Mars in Cancer, July 23, 7:23 - Aug. 23, 14:17

YOUR LUCK MAGNETISM
Jupiter in Cancer, July 23, 7:23 - Aug. 23, 14:17

World Events

July 30 - England wins the soccer World Cup.
Aug. 5 - Martin Luther King Jr. is stoned during a rally in Chicago.

CANCER
From June 21, 20:33 through July 23, 7:22

The Cuddly Crab

Gentle, caring, and oh-so-cute, the 1966 Cancerian is indeed a popular figure. You've got a kind word for everyone, and can elicit a smile from the most die-hard depressive. However, you're no pushover. Anybody who tries to pull one over on you is in for a nasty surprise. You've got good instincts when it comes to people, and can spot an opportunist from a mile away.

The year you were born, Mrs. Indira Gandhi, who was Nehru's daughter, became Prime Minister of India. Backers believed their new leader would be a convenient puppet, then sat back helplessly as she became one of the most powerful figures in that country's history. You share this same quality: you look like a lamb but behave like a lion. To you, though, power is less important than people. Family is the cornerstone of your life. If you're forced to choose between a prestigious job and a happy home, you'll choose the latter every time.

You have a serious interest in spiritual matters, and may study religions throughout the course of your life. Although you're more emotional than philosophical, you do need plenty of intellectual stimulation. At some point, you may feel tempted to write a book, which could be an incredibly cathartic experience. Although you are unquestionably loyal to your loved ones, its important for you to examine your relationships, if only as a means to overcome stubborn problems. And, writing can help you forge a better relationship with yourself.

A strong desire for romance draws you to dreamy, artistic people with vivid imaginations. Many of your loved ones look like bedraggled waifs— they never fail to bring out your nurturing instincts. Your most rewarding relationships are with people who like plenty of physical affection. Taureans, Scorpios, Pisceans, and fellow Cancerians bask in the glow of your company.

A tendency to idealize your loved ones can lead to trouble in your personal life. Your greatest challenge is to accept your friends' flaws, as well as their charms. Your biggest strength is your lovable personality. Very few people can resist your charms, and you know it!

LEO
From July 23, 7:23 through August 23, 14:17

The Glamorous Recluse

Greta Garbo may be the patron saint of the 1966 Leo. Like the glamorous movie star, you want to be alone. This comes as an unpleasant shock to your admirers, who never tire of your company. The more you withdraw from public life, the greater peoples desire to pin you down. It feeds their frenzy.

In 1966, Simon and Garfunkel released the hit single "The Sound Of Silence." Silence may play an important role in your life. It invites you to find the truth within your heart. Working independently gives you a profound sense of satisfaction. You'd make a wonderful landscaper, researcher, or department store buyer. As there's a good chance you prefer the company of animals to people, being a veterinarian would also be a good career choice. Make no mistake— you would be miserable in the capacity of office drone. There has to be an element of glamour to your work, although you'd prefer to perform it behind closed doors.

Intimacy may scare the living daylights out of you. Your profound distrust of people makes it hard for you to trust even the most giving individuals. It's quite possible you got a lot of mixed messages from your family growing up, which made you wary about relationships. Unless you come to terms with this fear, it could dog you for many years. Unfortunately, you may lack the motivation to form close bonds, as you're quite solitary by nature. Still, the sight of happy couples can give you a strange sense of longing from time to time.

As a 1966 Leo, you need people who make you feel secure, but not suffocated. Select Virgos, Sagittarians, Aquarians, and Pisceans can fit the bill, but it takes a long time to get relationships off the ground with you. Anybody who wants to gain your confidence should have lots of patience. A good sense of humor wouldn't hurt, either.

Learning to trust people is your greatest challenge. Yes, you're wonderfully self-sufficient, but being alone becomes less and less satisfying with age. Your biggest strength is your rich imagination. Draw upon it to create beautiful works of art, even if they'll never be shown to the public.

➤ Read about your Chinese Astrological sign on page 838. ➤ Read about your Personal Planets on page 826. ➤ Read about your personal Mystical Card on page 856.

VIRGO

From August 23, 14:18 through September 23, 11:42

The Forceful Friend

Intensely self-aware, the 1966 Virgo has a will of iron. You may be so intent on getting your way that you can't bear to be tied down by anyone. That being said, you're not shy about ordering around your friends. You see it as your mission to straighten out other people's lives. Few are as organized and determined as you. Helping them out is the least you can do for humanity! The year you were born, Mao Tse-Tung began the Cultural Revolution in China as a means to purge the country of dead weight. Your reformatory zeal can be just as extreme at times and this might cause problems in your private and professional lives.

The sciences have a special appeal for you, as they have the power to transform lives for the better. You'd do well as a doctor, nurse, chemist, or biologist. If you don't have a medical degree, you probably possess a great deal of knowledge about illness and pharmaceuticals. The most prized volume on your bookshelf may be the *Merck Manual*. Whatever your job, it's bound to have an aspect of humanitarianism. Ridding the world of poverty and disease is a very serious goal for Virgos born in 1966.

You have a strong sense of responsibility towards others, and have many friends despite a sometimes overbearing manner. You're often in a position to assist pals, and think nothing of writing recommendations and handing out loans. If a rogue manages to take advantage of your giving nature, you could spend years plotting a masterful revenge.

In relationships, you like to surround yourself with people who need your help. Willing recipients may include accident-prone Ariens, scatterbrained Geminis, slapdash Sagittarians, and unfocused Pisceans. Don't patronize your loved ones, or a deep-seated resentment may eventually undermine even the strongest relationships.

A hopeless perfectionist, your greatest challenge is to live and let live. Some of your most attractive qualities are your flaws; don't despair when they surface from time to time. Your biggest strength is your natural philanthropy. The world is a far better place because of giving people like you.

LIBRA

From September 23, 11:43 through October 23, 20:50

The Sociable Psychic

The 1966 Libra has a big heart with an address book to match. You have profound insight into human foibles, and can see the promise in even the most flawed characters. On some deep level, you believe that everything in the Universe is somehow linked, and you seek to understand this connection. This enlightened attitude wins you lots of friends from various walks of life. You're not one to divide the world into saints and sinners; as far as you're concerned, everyone has value, and you treat people accordingly.

This was also the year that the U.S. Department of the Interior published its first rare and endangered species list, spurring a brand-new conservation movement. You have a strong investment in a complex, varied world, and seek to promote peoples individual talents whenever possible. You'd make a wonderful guidance or career counselor. A strong religious bent could draw you toward spiritual work. You're always willing to help in any capacity. Nobody could accuse you of being a prima donna.

You have a tendency to worry, which drains you of valuable energy. Part of the problem is that you're extraordinarily intuitive, and can sense danger before it occurs. Practice relaxation techniques like meditation and controlled breathing as a means to keep anxiety at bay. As you get older, your hunches will feel more like a blessing than a burden. It's all a matter of learning to go with the flow.

Kind and considerate, you need friends who are convivial and outgoing. Ariens, Geminis, Leos, and Sagittarians are enjoyable company. When it comes time to pick a romantic partner, though, make sure your beloved isn't afraid to show affection. Although you're quite reserved in public, behind closed doors you like lots of kissing and cuddling. Steer clear of cold fish.

Your greatest challenge is to live in the moment. Too often, you undermine your own happiness by worrying about the future. Your biggest strength is your sympathetic nature. Use it to connect with a wide variety of people. The more people you know, the more convinced you are that the world is a beautiful place.

➤ Read about your Chinese Astrological sign on page 838. ➤ Read about your Personal Planets on page 826. ➤ Read about your personal Mystical Card on page 856.

VIRGO
Your Personal Planets

YOUR LOVE POTENTIAL
Venus in Leo, Aug. 23, 14:18 - Sept. 08, 23:39
Venus in Virgo, Sept. 08, 23:40 - Sept. 23, 11:42

YOUR DRIVE AND AMBITION
Mars in Cancer, Aug. 23, 14:18 - Aug. 25, 15:51
Mars in Leo, Aug. 25, 15:52 - Sept. 23, 11:42

YOUR LUCK MAGNETISM
Jupiter in Cancer, Aug. 23, 14:18 - Sept. 23, 11:42

World Events

Sept. 6 – South African Prime Minister Hendrik Verwoerd is assassinated in Parliament.

Sept. 16 – The New Metropolitan Opera House opens at the Lincoln Center in New York.

Dr. Hendrik Verwoerd, the South African Premier

LIBRA
Your Personal Planets

YOUR LOVE POTENTIAL
Venus in Virgo, Sept. 23, 11:43 - Oct. 03, 3:43
Venus in Libra, Oct. 03, 3:44 - Oct. 23, 20:50

YOUR DRIVE AND AMBITION
Mars in Leo, Sept. 23, 11:43 - Oct. 12, 18:36
Mars in Virgo, Oct. 12, 18:37 - Oct. 23, 20:50

YOUR LUCK MAGNETISM
Jupiter in Cancer, Sept. 23, 11:43 - Sept. 27, 13:18
Jupiter in Leo, Sept. 27, 13:19 - Oct. 23, 20:50

World Events

Oct. 6 – Hanoi demands that U.S. air strikes should cease before peace talks can commence.

Oct. 21 – A landslide in Aberfan in Wales lands on a school, killing 116 children.

1966

SCORPIO
Your Personal Planets

YOUR LOVE POTENTIAL
Venus in Libra, Oct. 23, 20:51 - Oct. 27, 3:27
Venus in Scorpio, Oct. 27, 3:28 - Nov. 20, 1:05
Venus in Sagittarius, Nov. 20, 1:06 - Nov. 22, 18:13

YOUR DRIVE AND AMBITION
Mars in Virgo, Oct. 23, 20:51 - Nov. 22, 18:13

YOUR LUCK MAGNETISM
Jupiter in Leo, Oct. 23, 20:51 - Nov. 22, 18:13

World Events

Nov. 4 - The River Arno floods, causing havoc across Florence.

Nov. 8 - Movie actor Ronald Reagan is elected Governor of California.

Ronald Reagan, Governor of California

SAGITTARIUS
Your Personal Planets

YOUR LOVE POTENTIAL
Venus in Sagittarius, Nov. 22, 18:14 - Dec. 13, 22:08
Venus in Capricorn, Dec. 13, 22:09 - Dec. 22, 7:27

YOUR DRIVE AND AMBITION
Mars in Virgo, Nov. 22, 18:14 - Dec. 04, 0:54
Mars in Libra, Dec. 04, 0:55 - Dec. 22, 7:27

YOUR LUCK MAGNETISM
Jupiter in Leo, Nov. 22, 18:14 - Dec. 22, 7:27

World Events

Dec. 12 - Frances Chichester arrives in Sydney, Australia, after making the longest solo sea voyage in history.

Dec. 15 - American film producer and animation pioneer Walt Disney dies.

544

SCORPIO
From October 23, 20:51 through November 22, 18:13

The Magnetic Star

Dramatic and expressive, the 1966 Scorpio is always eager to perform for the public. This comes as a surprise to those who know your sign, as it is famous for secrecy. The 1966 Scorpio is the exception to this rule, however. Granted, there is an air of mystery about you, but you use it to draw attention to yourself. You probably have a signature article of clothing to distinguish yourself from the pack. Slouchy hats, filmy scarves, and dark sunglasses are probably standard elements of your ensemble.

The year you were born, John Lennon declared that The Beatles were more popular than Jesus. You desire a similar level of acclaim, and aren't shy about admitting it. Sometimes your ego can get in the way of relationships—pals can tire of feeding your ego twenty-four hours a day. If you want to sustain friendships, install a full-length mirror and pelt yourself with compliments. In the end, it will save everybody a lot of anguish!

Despite your demanding ways, people do like you. You're the unquestionable leader of a large pack of friends, and draw a great deal of sustenance from their company. Joining a theater troupe or artistic enclave can give you the support and inspiration you need. If you're not a professional artist, you'd be a great union leader. You have a knack for promoting a spirit of unity wherever you go. People trust that you will act in the best interests of the entire group, and often elect you as their spokesperson.

In relationships, you like people who are willing to play second fiddle to your lead. Geminis, Virgos, Librans, and Pisceans are content to stand in your shadow, but take care you don't neglect your loved ones. An expressive person like you should have no trouble lavishing friends and lovers with hugs, kisses, and cuddles.

Deep down inside, you may feel unworthy of public adulation, although you're perpetually in search of it. Your greatest challenge is to love yourself, regardless of what others think of you. You have an impressive ability to bring people together in a spirit of unity. This—not your popularity—is your biggest strength.

SAGITTARIUS
From November 22, 18:14 through December 22, 7:27

The Absent-Minded Professor

The 1966 Sagittarius manages to be objective and analytical without being cold or unfeeling. You like to examine people from every angle before passing judgment, and you always leave room for the possibility of change. The year you were born, movie actor Ronald Reagan was elected Governor of California. Transformations like these only serve to underscore your theory that the human race is the most unpredictable species on Earth.

Folks enjoy your open-minded attitude, and may seek your friendship in droves. And while your popularity is gratifying, you don't put too much stock in it. You're well aware of how fickle the public can be. The only thing that is within your control is your own behavior. Therefore, you take pains to develop a strong code of ethics, and follow it at all costs. People respect your impeccable standards, though are a little puzzled by them at times. Taking the moral high ground may seem out of date in the twenty-first century, but it will never be out of fashion for you.

You have a love of learning that will probably draw you to the educational field. Whatever your job, you are destined to achieve a strong level of success. Unfortunately, your duties may take you away from home a lot, which can create an unsettled domestic atmosphere. You may be forced to choose between your private and public lives throughout the course of your life. If you're smart, you'll err on the side of domestic bliss whenever possible. You can't afford to alienate your loved ones, no matter how tempting the professional opportunity.

Your favorite companions are folks with an intellectual bent. Geminis, Virgos, Librans, and Aquarians may be among your closest friends. Take care that your interactions don't become too cerebral, however. Even egg-heads need healthy doses of physical affection!

Although you try to see the good in everything and everyone, you have a decidedly maudlin streak. Your greatest challenge is to rise above black moods that threaten to spoil your enjoyment of life. Your biggest strength is your fine mind. Use it to enlighten your many admirers.

➤ Read about your Chinese Astrological sign on page 838. ➤ Read about your Personal Planets on page 826. ➤ Read about your personal Mystical Card on page 856.

CAPRICORN

From December 22, 7:28 through December 31, 23:59

The Beneficent Royal

The December-born 1966 Capricorn can be quite formidable without even trying. There's something about you that makes people stand at attention. It's not that you have a bad temper—far from it! It's just that folks want you to think well of them. Your opinion means more than virtually anybody else's, probably because you hold yourself with such regal dignity. The year you were born, author Paul Bowles published *Up Above The World*. That title well describes your position in society.

You have the makings of an excellent judge, diplomat, or ambassador. There's a very good chance you will be involved with human relations in some capacity. People trust you implicitly you're probably famous for keeping secrets. Making a name in your desired field is terribly important to you. Work gives you a sense of purpose and accomplishment. Beware of deferring important decisions to the last minute, though, or your authority could be undermined.

People would be astonished to learn of your prodigious sex drive. It's rather difficult to picture such a dignified person in the throes of passion! No matter—your partner is in for a delightful surprise when your relationship moves to the bedroom stage. Friends have a way of becoming lovers with you. It takes a long time for you to develop intimate feelings for another person, but when you do, there's no turning back.

You prefer the company of people who are quiet and dignified. Taureans, Virgos, Librans, and fellow Goats are all good companions for you. Beware of being too reserved with your mate, especially when you're angered. It isn't healthy to keep your emotions bottled up. You need to dispense with politeness for the sake of your health, at least occasionally.

Your greatest challenge as a 1966 Goat born in December may be finding friends. Too often, people are scared to approach you because you seem to be out of their league. Make a concerted effort to reach out to folks who tickle your fancy. Your elegance is your strongest point. Thanks to you, there will always be an element of grace around, even in the twenty-first century!

1966 CAPRICORN
Your Personal Planets

YOUR LOVE POTENTIAL
Venus in Capricorn, Dec. 22, 7:28 - Dec. 31, 23:59
YOUR DRIVE AND AMBITION
Mars in Libra, Dec. 22, 7:28 - Dec. 31, 23:59
YOUR LUCK MAGNETISM
Jupiter in Leo, Dec. 22, 7:28 - Dec. 31, 23:59

World Events

Dec. 24 – The Soviet research station arrives on the Moon.

Dec. 28 – Australia beats India to keep the Davis Cup for the third year in a row.

"The Dream" by painter Henri Rousseau

Special Feature

Dreaming Through the Twentieth Century
by Skye Alexander

Everyone dreams, but how many of us remember our dreams or are able to decipher their meaning? For some, dreams can be a mysterious source of creativity and problem-solving, or even precognition, while for the psychoanalyst, dreams provide a window to the subconscious and its repressed desires. For still others, dreams can be a pathway to spiritual growth, or a gateway into the parallel worlds of the shaman.

Dreams can also provide artistic inspiration and ideas for inventions and musical compositions. German composer Richard Wagner found his inspiration for the opera *Tristan und Isolde* in a dream. "For once you are going to hear a dream," he wrote to a friend. "I dreamed all this. Never could my poor head have invented such a thing purposely."

Or consider how the Theory of Relativity first came to the young Albert Einstein. Einstein dreamt it was nighttime and that he was with friends, sledding down a hill. On one trip down he noticed that he was going faster and faster until finally the sled was approaching the speed of light. He looked up and saw the twinkling stars of the night refracted into a brilliant spectrum of colors. Einstein awoke with a numinous sense of awe, and knew immediately that he had just witnessed an event containing his calling in life. "I knew I had to understand that dream," Einstein told an interviewer, "and you could say, and I would say, that my entire scientific career has been a meditation on that dream."

Over the course of the twentieth century, our understanding of dreams underwent a complex evolution. Sigmund Freud's *The Interpretation Of Dreams* proved to be a breakthrough. Published in 1900, this work became the cornerstone for psychoanalysis and a therapeutic tool for treating mental illness using the techniques of free association and hypnosis. Although Freudian psychotherapy is no longer seen as an effective way to heal a disturbed mind, it did open the door for dreams to become the subject of scientific research. One of Freud's most important discoveries remains a central psychological premise. Emotions buried in the unconscious surface in disguised forms in dreams, and working with the dream symbolism can help uncover the buried feelings.

(Continued on page 553)

➤ Read Sigmund Freud's Star Profile on page 17. ➤ Read Albert Einstein's Star Profile on page 169. ➤ Read more about Jung and Einstein in "East Meets Twentieth-Century West" by Ronnie Grishman on page 25.

1967

Altered Consciousness: Chiron Trine Neptune

Neptune rules glamour, dreams, illusion, spirituality, the sea, mystery, and escapism. This is why drugs, alcohol, and addiction fall under the rulership of the planet Neptune. Chiron is considered to be the "wounded healer" of the zodiac, bringing individuals into closer touch with that which makes them whole. In 1967, Neptune made an aspect called a "trine" to the planet Chiron in the sky. Under this influence, it seemed as if people didn't want to live in the real world. Experimentation with LSD and marijuana became *de rigueur* for everyone under thirty. Dr. Timothy Leary, dubbed the "Galileo of Consciousness," had made his call to the youth of the era to "tune in, turn on, drop out". And they followed him in droves.

The psychedelic experience became the tribal glue that brought the hippie movement together. When young people weren't taking to the streets to protest the war, they were dropping acid and exploring far-flung dimensions. Chiron was in the Neptune-ruled sign of Pisces at this time, and Neptune was in Scorpio, another water sign. Many sought the promise of psychological healing through the use of mind-altering drugs. The summer of 1967 became the "Summer of Love". With these two emotional planets spending time in transcendental water signs, the power of love was primary. It was easy to escape into the nebulous realm of music, drugs, and illusion. The youth of the world set out in search of the holy grail of sex, drugs, and rock 'n' roll. They descended on Haight-Ashbury in San Francisco, and New York City's Greenwich Village. Many of them left home unexpectedly. Young people lived collectively, often in communal societies, and felt that they were witnesses to the dawning of a new age and in many ways, it was. The Beatles turned the wider culture on to the ideas of the ancient yogis through their relationship with Maharisha Mahesh Yogi in India. Psychedelics became a tool for the explosion of a new cultural paradigm, a global culture that embraced history—ancient and new.

Israeli troops occupy Bethlehem

U.S. planes step up their bombing of targets in North Vietnam

British actress Vivien Leigh dies

WAR AND PEACE RALLIES

Israel blunted the power of Egypt, Syria, and Jordan in one fell swoop during the Six-Day War, taking the cities of Jerusalem, Gaza, Bethlehem, Hebron, and Sharm el Sheikh. A region of southern Nigeria declared independence as the Republic of Biafra, prompting conflict. Stalin's daughter, Svetlana Alliluyeva, defected from Soviet Russia. Montreal's Expo 67 extolled the marvels of the Space Age with sleek, spare architecture and displays reproducing the lunar surface. The war in Vietnam escalated as more U.S. troops, equipment, and armaments were sent in. Stokely Carmichael became leader of the Black Panther movement. Thurgood Marshall was the first African American to be named to the Supreme Court over the objections of southern Senators. U.S. astronauts Grissom, White, and Chaffee died in a launch-pad flash fire. Hippies gathered peacefully in New York's Central Park for a Be-In, while the Monterrey Pop Festival featured the acid and hard rock of artists Jimi Hendrix, Jefferson Airplane, Janis Joplin, and The Who. Former German Chancellor Konrad Adenauer, Belgian surrealist Magritte and British actress Vivien Leigh died.

➤ Read "Dreaming Through the Twentieth Century" by Skye Alexander on page 545.

CAPRICORN

From January 01, 0:00 through January 20, 18:07

The Irrepressible Flirt

Utterly irresistible and extremely ambitious, Capricorns who were born under the sign of the Goat in January 1967 know how to charm their way to the top. You know just what to say to win people over and use this talent to advance your own reputation. Men and women alike respond to your Capricorn magnetism. Although you have many admirers, it is possible that very few people feel close to you. You don't wear your heart on your sleeve.

You really do like people and want to make them feel comfortable and appreciated; it's just that you have a hard time integrating the serious and light sides of your personality. The year you were born, the famous film *The Graduate* had its première. The cynical view of suburban life illustrated in this movie is an accurate mirror of your personality. At first glance, you're prim, proper, and respectable, but a little probing reveals more complex facets—like your liberal views of love and marriage. As you grow older, you'll be less concerned with what other people think of you, and your unconventional side will surface more often.

You have a strong sensual side that comes across in your personal life. You're a master of public relations and would do well in advertising or sales. Blessed with impeccable taste, you'd also do well as an interior decorator, fashion designer, or florist. Ultimately, your work should involve putting people at their ease, whether it's selling them a product or idea, or creating a beautiful environment in which they can live.

Your ideal partner is someone steadfast, true, and non-judgmental. Taureans, Cancerians, Virgos, and fellow Capricorns will help you lay a solid foundation for a rich, happy life. However, you have got the right qualities to make friends with every sign in the zodiac, thanks to your ability to appreciate the good points of each individual.

Your greatest challenge as a January-born 1967 Capricorn is to overcome your fear of public opinion. Act to suit yourself. Your biggest strength is your ability to be gracious. Use it to make the world a more enjoyable place in which to live.

AQUARIUS

From January 20, 18:08 through February 19, 8:23

The Sympathetic Philosopher

The Aquarian born in 1967 has tremendous powers of concentration and is capable of profound thought. That's why topics like religion, philosophy, and spirituality may have special appeal for you. From a very early age, you may have been occupied with the idea of transcendence and the attractions of the non-physical Universe. Overcoming emotional and physical limitations will help you lead a life of utter contentment, but it won't be quick or easy—for you, the process will last a lifetime.

The year you were born, there were vigorous protests against the Vietnam War in the United States and Europe. You, too, are interested in making people aware of what's going on in the wider world and will probably hold a teaching job at some point in your life. You have an optimistic attitude that makes people responsive to your message. However, your optimism doesn't go too far and nobody could ever accuse you of being a "cock-eyed optimist." That's because your beliefs come from a secure, well-grounded source—your own spiritual core.

When you were younger, you may have divided the world rather too neatly into haves and have-nots. Your sympathy was clearly with the underprivileged. As you grow older, your worldview will become more complex. Money—or rather the love of it—isn't the root of all evil; rather, it's a form of energy that can be applied to good as well as bad purposes. You will come to respect wealthy philanthropists.

As a 1967 Aquarius, you get along best with people who share your idealism. Geminis, Aquarians, and Pisceans probably make up the greater part of your social circle. In love, you need a mate who is playful and physically affectionate. Hugs and kisses make you positively glow with pleasure; don't hesitate to ask for them when you feel the weight of the world on your shoulders.

Because you're prone to thinking in "black and white," your greatest challenge is to recognize the many shades of gray in between. Your biggest strength is your belief that anything is possible. Rely on this attitude to get you through the rough periods in your life.

► Read about your Chinese Astrological sign on page 838. ► Read about your Personal Planets on page 826. ► Read about your personal Mystical Card on page 856.

CAPRICORN
Your Personal Planets

YOUR LOVE POTENTIAL
Venus in Capricorn, Jan. 01, 0:00 - Jan. 06, 19:35
Venus in Aquarius, Jan. 06, 19:36 - Jan. 20, 18:07

YOUR DRIVE AND AMBITION
Mars in Libra, Jan. 01, 0:00 - Jan. 20, 18:07

YOUR LUCK MAGNETISM
Jupiter in Leo, Jan. 01, 0:00 - Jan. 16, 3:49
Jupiter in Cancer, Jan. 16, 3:50 - Jan. 20, 18:07

World Events

Jan. 3 - Jack Ruby, convicted of the murder of Lee Harvey Oswald, dies.

Jan. 11 - The Society for the Protection of Unborn Children is established in Britain.

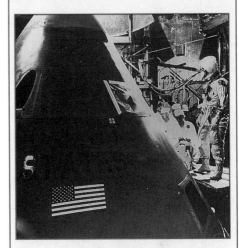

Apollo astronauts take altitude tests

AQUARIUS
Your Personal Planets

YOUR LOVE POTENTIAL
Venus in Aquarius, Jan. 20, 18:08 - Jan. 30, 18:52
Venus in Pisces, Jan. 30, 18:53 - Feb. 19, 8:23

YOUR DRIVE AND AMBITION
Mars in Libra, Jan. 20, 18:08 - Feb. 12, 12:19
Mars in Scorpio, Feb. 12, 12:20 - Feb. 19, 8:23

YOUR LUCK MAGNETISM
Jupiter in Cancer, Jan. 20, 18:08 - Feb. 19, 8:23

World Events

Jan. 27 - Fire breaks out in the capsule of *Apollo 1* during a routine test on the launch pad; the three astronauts on board are killed.

Feb. 5 - Anastasio Somoza becomes President of Nicaragua.

1967

PISCES
Your Personal Planets

YOUR LOVE POTENTIAL
Venus in Pisces, Feb. 19, 8:24 - Feb. 23, 22:29
Venus in Aries, Feb. 23, 22:30 - Mar. 20, 9:55
Venus in Taurus, Mar. 20, 9:56 - Mar. 21, 7:36

YOUR DRIVE AND AMBITION
Mars in Scorpio, Feb. 19, 8:24 - Mar. 21, 7:36

YOUR LUCK MAGNETISM
Jupiter in Cancer, Feb. 19, 8:24 - Mar. 21, 7:36

World Events

Feb. 20 - American rock star Kurt Cobain is born.

Mar. 12 - Indira Gandhi is reelected Prime Minister of India.

Playwright Tom Stoppard

ARIES
Your Personal Planets

YOUR LOVE POTENTIAL
Venus in Taurus, Mar. 21, 7:37 - Apr. 14, 9:53
Venus in Gemini, Apr. 14, 9:54 - Apr. 20, 18:54

YOUR DRIVE AND AMBITION
Mars in Scorpio, Mar. 21, 7:37 - Mar. 31, 6:09
Mars in Libra, Mar. 31, 6:10 - Apr. 20, 18:54

YOUR LUCK MAGNETISM
Jupiter in Cancer, Apr. 21, 7:37 - Apr. 20, 18:54

World Events

Mar. 29 - The first French nuclear submarine is launched.

Apr. 11 - Tom Stoppard's *Rosencrantz And Guildenstern Are Dead* premieres in London.

PISCES
From February 19, 8:24 through March 21, 7:36

The Creative Mystic

The 1967 Pisces is so shy and retiring that only a few people really know what they're about. Perhaps this is because you're not quite sure of yourself. To compensate, you may well have taken to expressing yourself through games of pretence.

Whether it was play-acting with toys or miming to your favorite records, you probably led a rich fantasy life of which no one else was aware. You were born with great artistic talent, so art was probably your favorite subject in school. You take a lot of pride in your creative work. The year you were born, The Rolling Stones appeared on *The Ed Sullivan Show*. However, their lyrics for "Let's Spend The Night Together" were considered too racy for television audiences and had to be altered. This wouldn't have suited you at all—you dislike having your own work tampered with or criticized. Even so, as the years go by, you'll worry less about the opinions of others and that will make it easier for you to show off the fruits of your labor.

Pisceans born in 1967 possess a profound sense of mysticism and that mysticism will probably influence the work you do. Being a holistic healer, astrologer, tarot card reader, or spiritual advisor may appeal to you. Chances are your job will involve constant research and study, which should suit you since you are destined to be a perpetual student. In particular, there's something about research that naturally appeals to your probing curiosity. You may hold several advanced university degrees; it's easy for you to succeed in institutions of higher learning.

Your greatest strength is your ability to see life in mystical terms. Throughout your own life, you'll be comforted by the knowledge that there is a grand order to things that unites the entire Universe.

Relationships can be a bit difficult for you as you may tend to put too much pressure on your loved ones. Whenever a friend or partner disappoints you, your first instinct is to get away from them. This is why, as a 1967 Pisces, you fare best with people who are patient and persevering, like Taureans, Cancerians, Virgos, and Capricorns.

ARIES
From March 21, 7:37 through April 20, 18:54

The Capable Peace-Maker

The 1967 Aries is so cool, calm, and collected that people often find them a bit of a mystery: few of them can guess your birth sign correctly because you don't offer many clues. As a 1967 Aries, you're far less aggressive than other Rams. If you get angry, you don't lash out. Perhaps you look back on the violent demonstrations of the 1960s with apprehension, preferring to resolve problems through compromise not rebellion. 1967 was indeed a tumultuous year. One hundred and thirty separate race riots took place in the U.S. in the summer of 1967. In addition, there was a brutal civil war in Nigeria and a military coup in Greece. Perhaps this is why you go to great lengths to suppress your anger.

All the same, as an Aries, you are quite ambitious. Work probably plays an important role in your life as it gives you a chance to relieve built-up pressure. Fortunately, you have remarkable powers of concentration, and that helps you to do well in stressful situations. You would also be a great police officer, judge, or customer service representative, as you're at your best when it comes to defusing tense situations.

In your personal relationships, you're passionate and need to feel profoundly connected to your partner. When you're at home with the one you love, you probably turn the telephone off so you won't be disturbed. When you aren't in a relationship, you may retreat to a romantic fantasy world. You're a sucker for a good love story and may read romance novels on a regular basis.

As a 1967 Aries, you get along best with people who are articulate and expressive. Ariens, Geminis, Virgos, and Leos are marvelous company for you. Romantically, you are best suited to a creative partner who has a gift for sweet talk.

Fear of anger is the greatest challenge for the 1967 Aries, but it doesn't do any good to suppress it. Find ways to express your pent-up energy, whether it's running marathons or doing scream therapy. Your biggest strength is remaining calm under pressure. If there's anybody who can withstand the stresses and strains of today's society, it's you.

➤ Read about your Chinese Astrological sign on page 838. ➤ Read about your Personal Planets on page 826. ➤ Read about your personal Mystical Card on page 856.

TAURUS

From April 20, 18:55 through May 21, 18:17

The Efficient Nurturer

The 1967 Taurus is brisk and efficient on the outside but soft and tender on the inside. You're a hard worker who knows how to be compassionate, and your services are much in demand. You have a knack for making people feel wonderful even when they're going through difficult times. The year you were born, the world's first heart transplant was performed in South Africa. Perhaps this medical breakthrough had a psychic impact on you, since you may frequently perform spiritual heart transplants on discouraged people.

It is likely you are attracted to the healing professions. You would certainly shine as a doctor, nurse, physical therapist, or psychologist. Your abilities go beyond the actual job, though; you have the knack of becoming an integral part of a team and the ability to take the sting out of personality clashes. Whatever job you perform, you are sure to be a valued member of the team.

Children occupy a special place in your heart. Spending time with young people helps to sustain your own enthusiasm. If you don't have kids of your own, you've probably got nieces and nephews who look up to you. A part of you wants to recapture your youth; some of your favorite places probably include the zoo, the park, and the circus. Secretly, you love to play at dressing up and enjoy clothes shopping for fancy occasions.

You tend to idealize your loved ones, but nobody's perfect, so this could lead to disappointment. As a 1967 Taurus, you want a storybook romance that will allow you to live happily ever after. This is probably why you're drawn to fellow romantics like Ariens, Taureans, Cancerians, and Pisceans. In love, you need a partner who is loyal and passionate. You are especially attracted to goal-oriented people.

You're so kind and considerate yourself that your biggest challenge is to separate worthy friends from scheming opportunists. You shouldn't waste valuable energy on people who don't have your best interests at heart. Your greatest strength is your healing power. Apply it to people who are worthy of your help, but don't forget to treat yourself, too.

GEMINI

From May 21, 18:18 through June 22, 2:22

The Ceaseless Wanderer

Because you're always in search of greener pastures, the 1967 Gemini is hard to pin down. Although you have a strong need for a secure home life, there's a part of you that always needs to be on the move, looking for a better situation. You're inspired by love and pleasure and if you find yourself in unfulfilling circumstances, your instinct is to pack up and move on.

The year you were born, *Cabaret* won a Tony award for being the best musical on Broadway and, in the subsequent film, Liza Minnelli won a Best Actress Oscar for her performance as the heroine, Sally Bowles. Possibly, this wasn't a coincidence because, for the 1967 Gemini, real life is very much a cabaret. You never tire of going to parties and would rather do without sleep than miss the fun. Thanks to your sizeable social circle, you've always got somewhere to go and something to do. Quite often, you have to choose between several different events and may offend some of your friends as a result. It can't be helped, though; you're just too popular for your own good!

Because you like to be constantly on the move, you need work that allows you lots of freedom. You'd make a great airline flight attendant, travel writer, or foreign correspondent. A job that moves you around the globe—for example as a travel company representative—would also suit you very well. The best way to further your career prospects and also gain the freedom you need is to learn foreign languages. Fortunately, this shouldn't be a problem for you: you've got a good ear and a talent for mimicry.

You like to surround yourself with zany, outgoing friends. Ariens, Geminis, Sagittarians, and Aquarians share your zest for life and make good pals for you. Romantically, you need a partner who is adventurous and flexible. You may be strongly attracted to exotic-looking foreigners.

Your greatest challenge is to find contentment when you can't be on the go. Take pleasure in day-to-day delights—like good food and loyal friends. A love of adventure is your greatest strength; you'll never pass up an opportunity to expand your horizons.

➤ Read about your Chinese Astrological sign on page 838. ➤ Read about your Personal Planets on page 826. ➤ Read about your personal Mystical Card on page 856.

TAURUS
Your Personal Planets

YOUR LOVE POTENTIAL
Venus in Gemini, Apr. 20, 18:55 - May 10, 6:04
Venus in Cancer, May 10, 6:05 - May 21, 18:17

YOUR DRIVE AND AMBITION
Mars in Libra, Apr. 20, 18:55 - May 21, 18:17

YOUR LUCK MAGNETISM
Jupiter in Cancer, Apr. 20, 18:55 - May 21, 18:17

World Events

Apr. 28 – Muhammad Ali refuses induction into the army and is stripped of his heavy-weight boxing title.

May 1 – The king of rock 'n' roll Elvis Presley marries Priscilla Beaulieu.

Elvis Presley with Priscilla

GEMINI
Your Personal Planets

YOUR LOVE POTENTIAL
Venus in Cancer, May 21, 18:18 - June 06, 16:47
Venus in Leo, June 06, 16:48 - June 22, 2:22

YOUR DRIVE AND AMBITION
Mars in Libra, May 21, 18:18 - June 22, 2:22

YOUR LUCK MAGNETISM
Jupiter in Cancer, May 21, 18:18 - May 23, 8:19
Jupiter in Leo, May 23, 8:20 - June 22, 2:22

World Events

June 5 – The Six-Day War erupts in the Middle East as Israel attacks Egyptian military targets.

June 16 – Fifty thousand people attend the Monterey International Pop Festival.

1967

CANCER
Your Personal Planets

YOUR LOVE POTENTIAL
Venus in Leo, June 22, 2:23 - July 08, 22:10
Venus in Virgo, July 08, 22:11 - July 23, 13:15

YOUR DRIVE AND AMBITION
Mars in Libra, June 22, 2:23 - July 19, 22:55
Mars in Scorpio, July 19, 22:56 - July 23, 13:15

YOUR LUCK MAGNETISM
Jupiter in Leo, June 22, 2:23 - July 23, 13:15

World Events

June 28 – Israel announces the reunification of Jerusalem.

July 8 – British actress and star of *Gone With The Wind* Vivien Leigh dies.

British actress Vivien Leigh

LEO
Your Personal Planets

YOUR LOVE POTENTIAL
Venus in Virgo, July 23, 13:16 - Aug. 23, 20:11

YOUR DRIVE AND AMBITION
Mars in Scorpio, July 23, 13:16 - Aug. 23, 20:11

YOUR LUCK MAGNETISM
Jupiter in Leo, July 23, 13:16 - Aug. 23, 20:11

World Events

July 24 – Race riots break out in Detroit in the U.S.

Aug. 15 – Belgian Surrealist artist Rene Magritte dies.

CANCER
From June 22, 2:23 through July 23, 13:15

The Busy Bee

As with most Crabs, home is where the heart is for the 1967 Cancer. If you had your way, you'd spend most of your days just lazing around the house. Unfortunately, this can clash with your considerable abilities as a leader. If, for example, professional responsibilities keep you away from home, you find it frustrating. One of the main struggles of your life is balancing your public and private lives. While it's gratifying to be in demand, you can't help wishing folks were less dependent on your talent.

Working hard does, of course, bring its rewards. You love the finer things in life so you need a job that earns plenty of money. You have the makings of a great manager, sports coach, or executive. The secret of your success lies in your ability to plan long-range strategies. Consequently, any ventures you undertake will succeed—whether it's boom time or slump. Ideally, you should start a business that can be run from home. It's much easier for you to flourish when you're in familiar surroundings.

Although you're remarkably practical in business, you're hopelessly romantic in love. Falling head over heels for somebody is a familiar experience for you. You have a particular weakness for artistic types. If someone mentions they're into painting, sculpture, or dance, this appeals to you straight away. Things don't always work out, though, and after a few disappointments, you'll learn to separate a person's work from their character.

Ideally, you need friends who are willing to keep the home fires burning for you while you're at the office. Taureans, Virgos, and Scorpios keep you on an even keel, although you get along best with fellow Cancerians. It's always comforting to be around someone who understands your every mood. In love, you are attracted to the strong, silent type.

As a 1967 Cancer, your greatest challenge is to find work that is meaningful to you. Otherwise, you'll be constantly distracted by thoughts of home. You're sensitive and intuitive and your greatest strength is your ability to create an environment that's peaceful for all who enter it.

LEO
From July 23, 13:16 through August 23, 20:11

The Generous Giant

Larger than life, the 1967 Leo does everything in a big way. You're too busy making a giant splash to worry about small details. Everything from your flashy dress to your booming voice commands attention. Fortunately, people find this attractive; they can't help it because they're responding to your animal magnetism. You probably identify with gorgeous creatures from the wild—like the noble tiger or the glamorous lion—and you may be especially proud of your mane. Is it any coincidence that the musical *Hair* had its premiere on Broadway in 1967?

Friendly and benevolent, you are extremely well-liked. People find that your company is like sitting in the Sun. You draw wealth like a magnet, and you like sharing your riches with others. Some people may think you're a little too generous with cash, but you never worry about going broke. The flow of money isn't always consistent. So there will be long stretches when you'll have to make sacrifices, but these will be followed by fun periods of extravagance. Even so, you always manage to have fun, regardless of your financial situation.

You're a born salesperson because of your ability to inspire confidence in others. You'd also do well as a real-estate agent, art dealer, or movie producer. Anything that involves an element of risk appeals to you. Working in a casino is also a possibility for you, as you enjoy the highly charged atmosphere of gambling houses. However, after a hard day's work, you want to come home to a quiet, sensuous retreat. Your domain is probably filled with lots of sensual fabrics.

When it comes to relationships, you like people who are utterly loyal. Taureans, Leos, Scorpios, and Aquarians make you feel adored, in both good times and bad. In love, you need a partner who is intelligent, original, and unconventional.

The greatest challenge for a 1967 Leo is to defer to others from time to time. Handing over the spotlight someone else, at least occasionally, will considerably improve your relationships. Your biggest strength is your generosity. You enjoy your possessions more when you share.

➤ Read about your Chinese Astrological sign on page 838. ➤ Read about your Personal Planets on page 826. ➤ Read about your personal Mystical Card on page 856.

VIRGO

From August 23, 20:12 through September 23, 17:37

The Star Debater

The 1967 Virgo is born with the gift of the gab. From a very early age, you probably talked the ear off anybody who would listen. As a child, teachers repeatedly asked you not to blurt out answers to questions in class. Their efforts were probably in vain because you couldn't contain your love of learning. Chances are you've become more disciplined with age, although you still tend to interrupt others out of sheer enthusiasm.

You have an incredibly retentive mind. It's even possible that you have a photographic memory. You'd make an excellent lawyer, reporter, or political analyst. You love arguing about controversial subjects like politics and religion, and usually win every debate. Putting your thoughts down on paper is therapeutic for you. If you don't have a satisfying job, you should keep a diary. You can later weave your observations into a novel if you're so inclined.

Because you concentrate so much on intellectual matters, you have a hard time with physical displays of affection. Sexually, you may have been a late developer. It's hard for you to make yourself vulnerable to others. Fortunately, as you grow older, you'll become more comfortable about all this and displays of affection will come more easily to you. You could even initiate lovemaking on a regular basis. The key is to find a partner who is kind, patient, and accepting. You are actually quite sensual.

You're most comfortable with outgoing, talkative people. Ariens, Geminis, Virgos, and Sagittarians are good company for you. When it comes to choosing a romantic partner, make sure you pick somebody who isn't intimidated by your argumentative nature. It's more stimulating to be at odds with someone than always be in perfect agreement. For you, a good debate is a form of foreplay.

As a 1967 Virgo, your greatest challenge is to listen as much as you speak. If you continue to dominate every conversation, you'll never learn anything new. Fortunately, your love of learning, which is your biggest strength can help you overcome this tendency and it shouldn't prove too much of an effort, either.

LIBRA

From September 23, 17:38 through October 24, 2:43

The Intelligence Gatherer

Considering it's such a social sign, the 1967 Libra spends a lot of time in the background. Many people would be surprised to know just how shy you really are. On the outside, you're all smiles and laughter, but your true personality is quite different. You'd rather curl up with a good book than attend a noisy, rollicking party. Usually, you end up going out to please your hordes of admirers.

When you do attend a social occasion, you like to stand in the corner and observe everybody else. This vantage point gives you a hidden sense of power. You've mastered the art of blending in with the woodwork while others babble away but, quite often, you hear and see things you shouldn't. This makes you a valuable, discreet friend or a fearful enemy, depending on your mood. If you're wise, you'll use this talent for intelligence gathering for a positive purpose. You'd make an excellent detective, job recruiter, or auditor.

Although you have many friends, you like to keep them at arm's length, which makes it very hard for them to know the real you. In 1967, Frank Sinatra's "Strangers In The Night" was the Record of the Year. That's the way some of your relationships appear to go—two strangers meet briefly for a romantic interlude, only to part forever afterwards. When you do decide to settle down, it will probably be with someone who is mature, rather than a young upstart.

Surprisingly enough, you're attracted to aggressive folks. It seems strange that a polite person like you should team up with such bombastic types, but there's method to your madness. Quite often, your gruff pals take up your causes and fight for them while you sit quietly in the background and let them get on with it. No wonder you have so many Ariens, Leos, Sagittarians, and Aquarians as friends! Romantically, you are best suited to a fiery, affectionate partner who is a bit of a challenge.

Your biggest challenge is to overcome your shyness for the purpose of making friends. This will become easier with practice. Your greatest strength is your love of the truth. Living in denial is not for you.

➤ Read about your Chinese Astrological sign on page 838. ➤ Read about your Personal Planets on page 826. ➤ Read about your personal Mystical Card on page 856.

VIRGO
Your Personal Planets

YOUR LOVE POTENTIAL
Venus in Virgo, Aug. 23, 20:12 - Sept. 09, 11:57
Venus in Leo, Sept. 09, 11:58 - Sept. 23, 17:37

YOUR DRIVE AND AMBITION
Mars in Scorpio, Aug. 23, 20:12 - Sept. 10, 1:43
Mars in Sagittarius, Sept. 10, 1:44 - Sept. 23, 17:37

YOUR LUCK MAGNETISM
Jupiter in Leo, Aug. 23, 20:12 - Sept. 23, 17:37

World Events

Aug. 29 – Shirley Temple announces that she will be running for Congress.

Sept. 1 – The oil embargo imposed during the Six-Day War is lifted.

Cuban rebel Che Guevara dies

LIBRA
Your Personal Planets

YOUR LOVE POTENTIAL
Venus in Leo, Sept. 23, 17:38 - Oct. 01, 18:06
Venus in Virgo, Oct. 01, 18:07 - Oct. 24, 2:43

YOUR DRIVE AND AMBITION
Mars in Sagittarius, Sept. 23, 17:38 - Oct. 23, 2:13
Mars in Capricorn, Oct. 23, 2:14 - Oct. 24, 2:43

YOUR LUCK MAGNETISM
Jupiter in Leo, Sept. 23, 17:38 - Oct. 19, 10:50
Jupiter in Virgo, Oct. 19, 10:51 - Oct. 24, 2:43

World Events

Oct. 2 – Thurgood Marshall is sworn in as the first black Supreme Court Justice in the U.S.

Oct. 9 – Cuban rebel Che Guevara is shot and killed in Bolivia.

1967

SCORPIO
Your Personal Planets

YOUR LOVE POTENTIAL
Venus in Virgo, Oct. 24, 2:44 - Nov. 09, 16:31
Venus in Libra, Nov. 09, 16:32 - Nov. 23, 0:03

YOUR DRIVE AND AMBITION
Mars in Capricorn, Oct. 24, 2:44 - Nov. 23, 0:03

YOUR LUCK MAGNETISM
Jupiter in Virgo, Oct. 24, 2:44 - Nov. 23, 0:03

World Events

Oct. 28 - *Pretty Woman* actress Julia Roberts is born.

Nov. 9 - The first successful *Saturn V* rocket is launched aboard *Apollo 4*.

American actress Julia Roberts is born under the sign of Scorpio

SAGITTARIUS
Your Personal Planets

YOUR LOVE POTENTIAL
Venus in Libra, Nov. 23, 0:04 - Dec. 07, 8:47
Venus in Scorpio, Dec. 07, 8:48 - Dec. 22, 13:15

YOUR DRIVE AND AMBITION
Mars in Capricorn, Nov. 23, 0:04 - Dec. 01, 20:11
Mars in Aquarius, Dec. 01, 20:12 - Dec. 22, 13:15

YOUR LUCK MAGNETISM
Jupiter in Virgo, Nov. 23, 0:04 - Dec. 22, 13:15

World Events

Dec. 3 - South African Dr. Christiaan Barnard performs the first human heart transplant.

Dec. 14 - DNA is created in a test tube.

SCORPIO
From October 24, 2:44 through November 23, 0:03

The Faithful Friend

Scorpios born in 1967 are usually surrounded by an extensive circle of friends. However, your crowd is far from normal and probably includes some pretty strange characters. But then you've always been attracted to offbeat types. Maybe it's because you were born just when the alternative culture really started to take off. After all, 1967 was the year "Flower Power" first appeared and with it the certainty that love could conquer all. Peace and love was the order of the day, even though it was sometimes synonymous with drugs. Also, in the year you were born, the first *Rolling Stone* magazine was published in San Francisco and that ushered in a whole new way of talking and thinking about popular music. This is the kind of thing that appeals to you. You like people with revolutionary spirit and probably shun conventional types like the plague.

Although you don't like toeing the company line, you're a hard worker. You flourish in difficult conditions and would make a splendid relief worker, emergency service technician, or soldier. Working in the great outdoors may also appeal to you, especially when you can operate as member of a large team. Consequently, construction work could be a viable option for you.

You tend to underplay your talents. Surrounding yourself with supportive people bolsters your confidence. It also helps to create an uplifting office environment. Fill your workspace with bright colors and inspirational pictures; these will fend off defeatist thoughts that could undermine your progress.

People with integrity have your undying admiration. You're smart enough to value character over looks and are rarely deceived by rogues, however charming they may be. Taureans, Cancerians, Virgos, and Capricorns make up a large part of your social circle. Romantically, you need a partner who is tasteful and artistic.

Your greatest challenge as a 1967 Scorpio is a tendency toward escapism. By surrounding yourself with practical people, you can keep your feet on the ground. Your biggest strength is your loyalty, which has helped to build lasting friendships.

SAGITTARIUS
From November 23, 0:04 through December 22, 13:15

The Captivating Leader

Whenever a 1967 Sagittarius enters the room, the whole place goes quiet. This is because you possess a remarkable, arresting presence that commands the attention of everyone within your orbit. Gregarious yet intimidating, you enjoy holding positions of power. Part of the secret to your success is your ability to keep people guessing. Nobody can ever predict what you're going to do next, but one thing is certain—whatever you do, it's bound to be captivating.

Your greatest chance for success is probably in the health and human services field. Medicine or nutrition may appeal to you, although heading a non-profit-making organization could be equally rewarding. The important thing is that you are providing a valuable service to people in need. You're perfectly willing to start at the bottom of the ladder and work your way to the top, provided the work you're doing is meaningful for you.

You sometimes find it hard to relax. You may feel guilty about having a good time when there's so much trouble in the world. However, you need to cultivate hobbies or you will quickly burn out. Cooking, playing music, and painting landscapes can help you unwind. The more varied your interests, the easier it will be for you to blow off steam. Aerobic sports like jogging, tennis, and soccer can also keep tension at bay.

Close relationships can be problematic for you. You usually attain such a high level of authority that it's hard for you to make friends at work. What you need to do is socialize outside the office. Philosophical types suit you best. You have lots in common with Geminis, Virgos, Librans, and Aquarians and may enjoy discussing current events with these opinionated signs. In love, you need a mate who is witty, smart, and a little irreverent.

The 1967 Sagittarius tends to be driven and determined, so your greatest challenge is to enjoy life's smaller pleasures. Pause to enjoy simple delights like a good meal, a sunny day, or a fragrant flower. Your biggest strength is your impulse to help others. Use it to form lasting bonds with family, friends, and neighbors.

➤ Read about your Chinese Astrological sign on page 838. ➤ Read about your Personal Planets on page 826. ➤ Read about your personal Mystical Card on page 856.

CAPRICORN

From December 22, 13:16 through December 31, 23:59

The Prolific Learner

Any 1967 Capricorn born in the month of December possesses a deep love of learning. There's a good chance you did very well in school and studied subjects outside the curriculum in your spare time. Teachers were probably your greatest heroes, and you may have looked forward to going to school every day. On the other hand, if you didn't enjoy school, it was likely that you weren't able to study the subjects you wanted. In that case, you should make every effort to get the kind of education you always desired now.

Born too late to take part in the "Swinging Sixties," you grew up in the aftermath in the 1970s—a more serious-minded decade because people had witnessed what too much freedom and too little discipline could do to a generation. In the 1970s, people began to pay the price of the 1960s—drug addiction spiraled out of control and many marriages broke up. Your youthful experience may have made you reluctant to venture too far and test your own boundaries. However, if you loosen up just a bit, you can have a good time and still promote a wholesome family life.

Smart and considerate, you would make an excellent educator. Whether you're a kindergarten teacher or college professor, you're sure to derive lots of pleasure from your students. Alternately, you could be a very successful writer, journalist, or editor thanks to your admirable writing ability. Whatever your job, it should have an intellectual flavor.

As a 1967 Capricorn, you're drawn to people who have a strong spiritual side. Scorpios, Sagittarians, Aquarians, and Pisceans probably dominate your social circle. In love, you need a mate who is ambitious and hard-working. There's a good chance you'll settle down with a self-made person.

Your deeply ingrained love of family means that your greatest challenge could be creating an identity that's separate from it. Your biggest strength is your love of learning. Channel this passion into gathering as much knowledge as you can about your favorite subjects. There's a good chance you can become a respected scholar in whatever field you happen to choose.

1967

CAPRICORN
Your Personal Planets

YOUR LOVE POTENTIAL
Venus in Scorpio, Dec. 22, 13:16 - Dec. 31, 23:59

YOUR DRIVE AND AMBITION
Mars in Aquarius, Dec. 22, 13:16 - Dec. 31, 23:59

YOUR LUCK MAGNETISM
Jupiter in Virgo, Dec. 22, 13:16 - Dec. 31, 23:59

World Events

Dec. 22 – The Pope exhorts peace in Vietnam.
Dec. 26 – The North Vietnamese launch an attack on Laos.

Carl Jung, Swiss psychiatrist

Special Feature
Dreaming Through the Twentieth Century

(Continued from page 545)

Psychiatrist Carl Jung was greatly intrigued by Freud's revolutionary theories. The two exchanged letters, and in 1906 they finally met, striking up an instant rapport by discussing the psychology of dreams for thirteen consecutive hours. Their closeness became evident in 1908 at the First International Congress of Psycho-Analysis, where Freud confided to Jung that he considered him as an eldest son, and chose him as his successor in the new movement.

However, Jung's fascination with parapsychology and precognition eventually precipitated an end to their professional and personal relationship. According to Freud, the unconscious is filled with repressed memories invariably linked to sexual themes. His theory of the Oedipus Complex fit his own Victorian psyche, and perhaps many of his contemporaries', but Jung could see from the beginning that this theory was too limiting for the

unbounded potential of the psyche. For Jung, Freud's Oedipal Complex was a myth for one culture in one moment in history.

Dreams provide a channel of communication for our psyche, helping us to understand our very being.

In Jung's view, dreams are natural reactions to current situations, and offer clues that may lead to insight and personal growth. They may be forward-looking as well as retrospective. Dreams may tap into a mysterious reservoir of mythological images, presenting symbols and archetypes that share a fundamental essence with those of all other cultures. Most importantly, dreams provide a channel of communication for our psyche, helping us to understand our very being. Jung developed an entirely new vocabulary to analyze dreams and the structure of the psyche.

With its broad and complex view of dreams, Jung's work inspired much further research. In 1953, scientists first attached electroencephalograms (EEGs) to the eyes of test subjects and discovered that everyone spends part of each night in a sleep state characterized by rapid eye movements (REM). They then discovered that most dreams occur during this REM phase, especially the longer, more vivid dreams. The phenomenon of dreams was moving beyond the psychoanalytical arena of phobias, neuroses, and schizophrenia. During the social upheavals of the 1960s, working with dreams became part of the New Age experience. At this time, people began talking about lucid dreaming, astral traveling, and out-of-body experiences (OBEs).

(Continued on page 561)

► Read Sigmund Freud's Star Profile on page 17. ► Read Albert Einstein's Star Profile on page 169. ► Read more about Jung and Einstein in "East Meets Twentieth-Century West" by Ronnie Grishman on page 25.

553

1968

Prague Spring: Jupiter and Uranus in Virgo

By 1968, Czechoslovakia had been under communist rule for twenty years, ever since the democratic President Edouard Benes had been overthrown. Alexander Dubcek had been a seemingly faithful follower of party politics until he experienced a total transformation in 1968. He became the hero of the freedom movement that came to be called the Prague Spring. The Czech people revolted against communist rule without a single instance of violence in the spring of 1968. Rampant democracy broke out everywhere. Press censorship was ended and criticism of the Soviet regime was enjoyed. This was only to last a few months, as the Soviets drove in with tanks to smash the revolution in August of the same year.

Revolution was in the air all around the world in 1968. At this time, the planet Uranus, ruler of resistance and freedom fighter of the zodiac, was in Virgo, sign of integrity and conscientiousness. In addition, the planet Jupiter, ruler of idealism, hope, and promise, was also in the sign of Virgo. Virgo holds sway over work and service. At the start of the Prague Spring, Dubcek was dedicated to working for his people, until his movement was crushed so brutally. The placement of these two forward-marching planets in the steady sign of Virgo signified a progressive and easy movement toward freedom. When aggressive Mars moved into fiery Leo in August and made a hard angle to the planet Neptune, the Soviets were able to mount their attack. The passive resistance of a people who wanted only the promise of democratic Socialism was met with determined and inflexible military occupation.

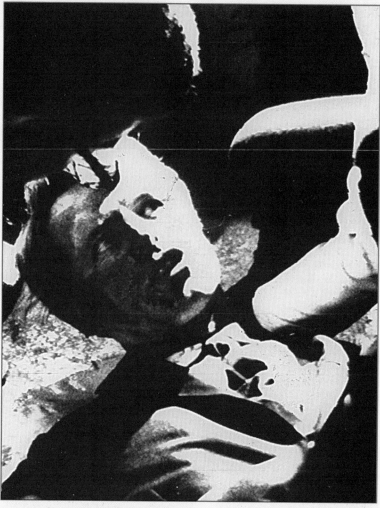
Senator Robert F. Kennedy moments after being shot

Martin Luther King Jr. is assassinated

Barbara Streisand in London to open her show "Funny Girl"

THE SURGEON WITH THE RUSTY KNIFE

Psychic surgery is the paranormal treatment of medical conditions. A psychic surgeon opens and closes the patient's body without the use of surgical instruments, instead using just bare hands or simple objects. One of the most famous such psychic surgeons, Ze Arigo of Brazil, used a rusty penknife for his surgical work. Arigo said the channeled spirit of a Dr. Fritz guided him. In 1968, American doctors investigated Arigo for fraud but admitted that he was really able to control an unknown form of life energy.

A WORLD GONE CRAZY

The American public learned the stark truth about the Vietnam War as the Viet Cong's ferocious Tet Offensive was shown on TV. Liberal reformer Alexander Dubcek became Czech President and launched a democratic experiment, leading to a Soviet crackdown. In the first jet hijacking, Palestinian extremists seized an Israeli El Al jet, diverting it to Rome. The Biafran people starved as Nigeria turned down aid for the secessionist region. A cavalcade of violence, as well as peaceful protests, was sparked when civil rights leader Martin Luther King Jr was fatally shot in Memphis in April. The world was further stunned when presidential candidate Robert Kennedy was assassinated in Los Angeles. Rioting students and strikers clashed with police in Paris. Pope Paul VI refused to sanction artificial birth control. Republican Nixon narrowly won the presidency, after incumbent Johnson refused to run. A U.S. B-52 bomber with four nuclear bombs on board crashed in Greenland. The astronauts of *Apollo 8* orbited the Moon. *The Lion In Winter* and *Funny Girl* were box office hits. The first man in space, Yuri Gagarin, was killed in a plane crash.

➤ Read "Dreaming Through the Twentieth Century" by Skye Alexander on page 545.

CAPRICORN

From January 01, 0:00 through January 20, 23:53

The Gentle Philosopher

High standards and a humble attitude characterize the January-born 1968 Capricorn. Work gives you a sense of purpose, and you never offer up anything less than a stellar performance. You especially enjoy repetitive tasks, as they allow your mind to wander. Your quiet introspection is intriguing, drawing admirers wherever you go. However, very few people can push past the dignified air that puts distance between you and the rest of the world.

Your zeal to help others could prompt you to undertake a great deal of volunteer work. You may not be above adopting a passive-aggressive attitude to get your goals met. People look into your helpless eyes and melt into submission. Actually, you're not helpless at all—you just like to appear that way, as it brings fabulous results. Aggressive, blustery types blush with pleasure when you give them a prim thank you for their assistance. Everybody wants to come to your rescue.

Many folks would be shocked to know that underneath your calm exterior beats the heart of a die-hard reformer. The year you were born, Dr. Benjamin Spock was indicted for conspiring to violate the draft law. You're willing to fight tooth and nail for what you believe, and your cause is usually peace-oriented. You could have a successful career in the nonprofit industry. Medicine and scientific research may also appeal to you. Whatever job you take, it should help others in some material way.

Your introspective attitude draws you to people who are similarly pensive. Taurus, Cancer, Virgo, and Pisces are content to sit in silence with you, speaking only when the mood strikes. You can't abide chatterboxes—they make you nervous and irritated. It wouldn't hurt to be more forthcoming with your partner, though. Some things do have to be verbalized, like "I love you."

Passive and shy, your greatest challenge is to defend yourself when others take advantage of you. Too often, you look the other way when people abuse your gentle nature. A fine eye for detail is your biggest strength. This makes you an especially good worker—certainly one who is always in demand.

AQUARIUS

From January 20, 23:54 through February 19, 14:08

The Sexy Spendthrift

According to the 1968 Aquarius, money is meant to be spent, not saved. You love the good things in life, like rich fabrics, fragrant flowers, and gourmet food. The concept of self-deprivation is alien to you; you intend to live each moment as if it were your last. This attitude makes your loved ones worry about your welfare, but you don't waste time on imagined fears. If you come up short at the end of the month, a friend is usually willing to help you out. Its hard to resist your charms. Besides, you're so generous with your time and attention, most friends treat loans to you as repayment for services rendered.

An uncanny intuition should play an important part in your career. Chances are you will have many different jobs throughout the course of your life. Ironically, you'll probably be a success at everything you try. Your problem is that you get bored easily. Unconventional jobs related to metaphysics might suit you best. You'd make a terrific ghost-buster, psychic detective, or astrologer.

You have a tremendous sex drive that makes the air positively crackle. The year you were born, the first international exhibition of erotic art toured Sweden and Denmark. Part of the reason you're so randy might be that you were raised in a prudish environment. Quite often, strong sexual beings are the product of a repressed upbringing. Have all the fun you want, provided you take the necessary health precautions. Ultimately, you're looking for a committed partner who is just as adventurous as you when it comes to pleasures of the flesh.

You need friends and lovers who seek to merge the body with the spirit. Scorpios, Sagittarians, Aquarians, and Pisceans will be eager to explore the deeper questions of life with you. Beware, however, of neglecting mundane responsibilities, like balancing your checkbook!

Always looking for a new experience, your greatest challenge is to be more selfless. Sometimes its more important to serve others than to indulge your own whims. Your biggest strength is your desire to live life to the fullest. Regret isn't part of your vocabulary.

➤ Read about your Chinese Astrological sign on page 838. ➤ Read about your Personal Planets on page 826. ➤ Read about your personal Mystical Card on page 856.

CAPRICORN
Your Personal Planets

YOUR LOVE POTENTIAL
Venus in Scorpio, Jan. 01, 0:00 - Jan. 01, 22:36
Venus in Sagittarius, Jan. 01, 22:37 - Jan. 20, 23:53

YOUR DRIVE AND AMBITION
Mars in Aquarius, Jan. 01, 0:00 - Jan. 09, 9:48
Mars in Pisces, Jan. 09, 9:49 - Jan. 20, 23:53

YOUR LUCK MAGNETISM
Jupiter in Virgo, Jan. 01, 0:00 - Jan. 20, 23:53

World Events

Jan. 1 - Cecil Day-Lewis is appointed as Britain's Poet Laureate.

Jan. 10 - John Gorton becomes Australia's Prime Minister.

Poet Laureate Cecil Day-Lewis

AQUARIUS
Your Personal Planets

YOUR LOVE POTENTIAL
Venus in Sagittarius, Jan. 20, 23:54 - Jan. 26, 17:34
Venus in Capricorn, Jan. 26, 17:35 - Feb. 19, 14:08

YOUR DRIVE AND AMBITION
Mars in Pisces, Jan. 20, 23:54 - Feb. 17, 3:17
Mars in Aries, Feb. 17, 3:18 - Feb. 19, 14:08

YOUR LUCK MAGNETISM
Jupiter in Virgo, Jan. 20, 23:54 - Feb. 19, 14:08

World Events

Jan. 31 - The infamous Tet Offensive is launched in Vietnam.

Feb. 6 - Charles de Gaulle opens the winter Olympics in Grenoble.

PISCES
Your Personal Planets

YOUR LOVE POTENTIAL
Venus in Capricorn, Feb. 19, 14:09 - Feb. 20, 4:54
Venus in Aquarius, Feb. 20, 4:55 - Mar. 15, 13:31
Venus in Pisces, Mar. 15, 13:32 - Mar. 20, 13:21

YOUR DRIVE AND AMBITION
Mars in Aries, Feb. 19, 14:09 - Mar. 20, 13:21

YOUR LUCK MAGNETISM
Jupiter in Virgo, Feb. 19, 14:09 - Feb. 27, 3:32
Jupiter in Leo, Feb. 27, 3:33 - Mar. 20, 13:21

World Events

Feb. 24 – Pulsars in space are discovered by astronomer Jocelyn Bell.

Mar. 16 – U.S. troops massacre a group of Vietnamese civilians in the village of My Lai, in one of the worst atrocities of the war.

Death of Martin Luther King, Jr.

ARIES
Your Personal Planets

YOUR LOVE POTENTIAL
Venus in Pisces, Mar. 20, 13:22 - Apr. 08, 21:47
Venus in Aries, Apr. 08, 21:48 - Apr. 20, 0:40

YOUR DRIVE AND AMBITION
Mars in Aries, Mar. 20, 13:22 - Mar. 27, 23:42
Mars in Taurus, Mar. 27, 23:43 - Apr. 20, 0:40

YOUR LUCK MAGNETISM
Jupiter in Leo, Mar. 20, 13:22 - Apr. 20, 0:40

World Events

Apr. 4 – Civil rights leader Martin Luther King Jr. is assassinated.

Apr. 11 – U.S. President Johnson signs the Civil Rights Act, just a week after Martin Luther King Jr's assassination.

PISCES

From February 19, 14:09 through March 20, 13:21

The Strident Saver

Financial security is the foremost concern of the 1968 Pisces. You're determined to have the finer things in life, even if it means working your fingers to the bone. As a child, you probably saved your allowance, rather than spent it on candy. If you didn't have an allowance, you probably had an after-school job that was more important than school. Sitting in a classroom felt like a waste of time—why learn your lessons when you could make cash?

You may find money in marriage. The year you were born, Jacqueline Kennedy married shipping magnate Aristotle Onassis. If you decide to go this route, be prepared to live with the consequences. Such a union would mean renouncing a great deal of your personal power. You may be better off accumulating your own wealth. Blessed with an eye for beauty, you'd make a fabulous fashion designer, set designer, or makeup artist. The key is to enter a field about which you feel passionate. Do what you love, and the money will follow, may be a good guiding principle for you.

As you get older, an interest in mysticism could play an increasing role in your life. Developing a meaningful moral code is important for you. This will help you balance your material and spiritual needs. The more wealth you accumulate, the less important it will seem to you. Believe it or not, there's a good chance you will give away a great part of your fortune in your later years. You have the makings of a respected philanthropist.

People who are powerful and unusual excite your imagination. Your social circle is probably comprised of extraordinary people. Cancerians, Scorpios, Aquarians, and Pisceans never fail to hold your interest. Don't let your friends accomplishments diminish your own ego, however. Be sure to choose a romantic partner who fully appreciates your talents, or you may suffer from an inferiority complex.

Hard-working and ambitious, your greatest challenge is to overcome your material desires. Making money shouldn't be your sole aim. Your biggest strength is your artistic flair. The more you develop it, the less important wealth will seem.

ARIES

From March 20, 13:22 through April 20, 0:40

The Dedicated Idealist

Above all else, the 1968 Aries needs to feel needed. You want to be of service to others, to improve their lives in some fundamental way. The year you were born, both Dr. Martin Luther King Jr. and Robert Kennedy were assassinated. You may be very conscious of the sacrifices such people made for future generations, and may want to make a similar contribution. You want to leave the world a better place than you came into it.

Although you have a serious side, you also have a great capacity for joy. Children hold a special place in your heart. You think nothing of getting down on the floor and making funny faces at a crawling baby. Young people sense your love for them, and seek out your company whenever possible. You would make a fabulous athletic coach, art teacher, or child psychologist. Working with children makes you feel less self-conscious, which comes as a welcome relief to a shy person like you.

Your self-effacing humor is a form of armor. You'd rather criticize yourself than have others point out your faults. This humble attitude makes you a popular figure, although you're the last one to realize it. If you surround yourself with kind, demonstrative people, you can overcome feelings of unworthiness. Steer clear of nitpickers and micromanagers, or you will fall prey to their abuse. You're all too aware of your own shortcomings—you don't need somebody else to point them out.

A sensitive person like you needs tactful and intuitive friends. Reach out to Taureans, Cancerians, Librans, and Pisceans. These folks sense when you need an ego boost, and dispense hugs and kisses on a regular basis. Your ideal romantic partner will share your love of service, and will probably want to work alongside you.

As a 1968 Aries, your greatest challenge is shyness. Force yourself to make overtures toward strangers. The more you practice being social, the easier it becomes. Your biggest strength is your concern for others. As long as you're helping humankind, you'll have a profound sense of contentment. Find a cause that's close to your heart, and devote yourself to it.

➤ Read about your Chinese Astrological sign on page 838. ➤ Read about your Personal Planets on page 826. ➤ Read about your personal Mystical Card on page 856.

TAURUS
From April 20, 0:41 through May 21, 0:05

The Joyful Giver

Resourceful and imaginative, the 1968 Taurus is always looking for ways to help others. You have a knack for putting others at ease, and are probably famous for throwing terrific parties. You're the first person to show up at a sick person's home with a pot of soup, and are happy to pet-sit when your pals go on vacation. Although this generous attitude makes you a lot of friends, that isn't your motive for being kind. You simply enjoy sharing what you have with others. The year you were born, The Poor People's March on Washington was launched, protesting the problem of hunger in the U.S. The thought of anybody going to bed hungry profoundly disturbs you, and you do your best to correct such inequities.

Folks love coming to your home, which is warm and inviting. In fact, you have a hard time getting rid of guests. You'd be wise to go into the hotel or restaurant business. Running a bed-and-breakfast might appeal to you, especially if you run your business from an old-fashioned house. You've got great instincts when it comes to interior decorating, and could have lots of fun restoring a crumbling mansion to its original glory.

You love totally and unselfishly, and have many rewarding relationships. Occasionally, a nasty opportunist will slip beneath your radar, but you don't let this poison your belief that human beings are basically good. You're a born romantic who loves to be wined, dined, and seduced. If a prospective partner forgets a birthday, anniversary, or Valentines Day, you'll probably send them packing.

Affectionate, optimistic people comprise the bigger part of your social circle. Cuddly Cancerians, loving Librans, and peaceful Pisceans are among your favorite signs. An ardent Scorpio would make a good romantic partner for you, though jealousy could be a problem. Don't apologize for your effusive nature.

A tendency to daydream is your greatest challenge as a 1968 Taurus. You have to accept that life isn't always a fairy tale. Your biggest strength is your selflessness. If you continue to honor this instinct, you'll lead a rich and satisfying life.

GEMINI
From May 21, 0:06 through June 21, 8:12

The Fact-Gatherer

Bursting with facts and figures, the 1968 Gemini always has some interesting piece of information to share. Your favorite volumes probably include *The Guinness Book Of World Records*, *The People's Almanac*, and *The Book Of Lists*. Few people can beat you at Trivial Pursuit, and you're a whiz at crossword puzzles and other types of quiz. Some folks collect antiques—you collect information. Chances are, you've got at least one filing cabinet bursting with news clippings. Your magazine collection isn't too shabby, either.

You love a good debate, and express your ideas quite forcefully. The year you were born, demonstrators clashed with police at the Democratic National Convention in Chicago. You're probably no stranger to political protests yourself. You give your opinion often and loudly, even to the point of shouting over others. While people admire the scope of Gemini's knowledge, they sometimes wish that they weren't quite such a showoff about it. Fortunately, most have been blessed with a great sense of humor, and often poke fun at themselves as a means of apologizing for boorish behavior.

As far as careers go, you'd make a terrific fact-checker, librarian, or museum archivist. Your restless mind makes it hard to concentrate on the job. Going into an office every day could bore you to tears. Being a traveling salesperson can hold your interest, as it allows you to meet different people on a regular basis. If you're not interested in doing work, you could always make a fortune on a quiz show!

Leading an active social life is important to you. You like well-established people who are experts in some way. Geminis, Virgos, Capricorns, and Aquarians are among your favorite folk. Make an effort to listen as much as you speak, especially in romantic relationships, otherwise, your loved ones may tire of your company.

Although you're undeniably bright, at times you may lord your knowledge over others. Your greatest challenge is to treat less educated people with respect; books aren't the only way to attain wisdom. Your biggest strength is your fine mind. Use it to form friendships, not rivalries.

➤ Read about your Chinese Astrological sign on page 838. ➤ Read about your Personal Planets on page 826. ➤ Read about your personal Mystical Card on page 856.

1968

TAURUS
Your Personal Planets

YOUR LOVE POTENTIAL
Venus in Aries, Apr. 20, 0:41 - May 03, 6:55
Venus in Taurus, May 03, 6:56 - May 21, 0:05

YOUR DRIVE AND AMBITION
Mars in Taurus, Apr. 20, 0:41 - May 08, 14:13
Mars in Gemini, May 08, 14:14 - May 21, 0:05

YOUR LUCK MAGNETISM
Jupiter in Leo, Apr. 20, 0:41 - May 21, 0:05

World Events

May 5 – Spain seals off its front with British-owned Gibraltar.

May 6 – Widespread student riots cause havoc in Paris.

Robert Kennedy moments before his assassination

GEMINI
Your Personal Planets

YOUR LOVE POTENTIAL
Venus in Taurus, May 21, 0:06 - May 27, 17:01
Venus in Gemini, May 27, 17:02 - June 21, 3:19
Venus in Cancer, June 21, 3:20 - June 21, 8:12

YOUR DRIVE AND AMBITION
Mars in Gemini, May 21, 0:06 - June 21, 5:02
Mars in Cancer, June 21, 5:03 - June 21, 8:12

YOUR LUCK MAGNETISM
Jupiter in Leo, May 21, 0:06 - June 15, 14:42
Jupiter in Virgo, June 15, 14:43 - June 21, 8:12

World Events

June 5 – Sen. Robert F. Kennedy dies after being shot in Los Angeles by Sirhan Bishara Sirhan.

June 17 – Britain endorses sanctions against Rhodesia.

1968

CANCER
Your Personal Planets

YOUR LOVE POTENTIAL
Venus in Cancer, June 21, 8:13 - July 15, 12:58
Venus in Leo, July 15, 12:59 - July 22, 19:06

YOUR DRIVE AND AMBITION
Mars in Cancer, June 21, 8:13 - July 22, 19:06

YOUR LUCK MAGNETISM
Jupiter in Virgo, June 21, 8:13 - July 22, 19:06

World Events

July 1 – Thirty-six nations, including the U.S. and the USSR, sign the Nuclear Non-Proliferation Treaty.

July 4 – The radio-astronomy satellite *Explorer 38* is launched.

Richard Nixon supporters at the party convention in August 1968

LEO
Your Personal Planets

YOUR LOVE POTENTIAL
Venus in Leo, July 22, 19:07 - Aug. 08, 21:48
Venus in Virgo, Aug. 08, 21:49 - Aug. 23, 2:02

YOUR DRIVE AND AMBITION
Mars in Cancer, July 22, 19:07 - Aug. 05, 17:06
Mars in Leo, Aug. 05, 17:07 - Aug. 23, 2:02

YOUR LUCK MAGNETISM
Jupiter in Virgo, July 22, 19:07 - Aug. 23, 2:02

World Events

July 26 – A guerilla group attack a U.S. airbase in Thailand.

Aug. 20 – Warsaw Pact nations begin invading Czechoslovakia as a reaction against the "Prague Spring."

CANCER
From June 21, 8:13 through July 22, 19:06

The Emotive Speaker

The 1968 Cancer is as emotive as an opera singer. You have intense, passionate feelings that cannot be contained. When you love somebody, it's all-consuming. Sometimes you confuse mothering with smothering. Try to give your friends and relatives more freedom. The year you were born, the Soviet Union invaded Czechoslovakia, fearful that the satellite nation was becoming too independent. Don't make the same mistake in your relationships, or resentment may ensue.

You are determined to be a success. Status means a lot to you. Chances are you'll work very hard to live in a nice neighborhood, drive a fancy car, and wear designer clothes. Blessed with excellent communication skills, you'd make a great best-selling novelist, motivational speaker, or advertising executive. Putting your ideas before the public gives you a great deal of satisfaction. You'd probably be a great talk-show host, too. Starting out at the bottom of a company doesn't bother you. You know that through sheer work and determination, you will rise to the top.

A born romantic, you delight in listening to love songs, watching old movies, and touring ancient cities. Although your career takes up a great deal of time, you still manage to indulge your creative impulses. Hobbies such as restoring antiques may be a welcome outlet for your imagination. Such pastimes soften the hard-edged executive in you, making you a well-rounded, interesting person.

You like people who allow you to fuss over them. Cancerians, Leos, Librans, and Pisceans satisfy your nurturing instincts. Don't forget to let your loved ones wait on you, though, otherwise your relationships will seem one-sided and unsatisfactory. Even a strong leader like you needs to be babied, at least once in a while.

Strong-willed and passionate, your greatest challenge is to accept the good with the bad. Try not to get carried away when things don't go your way. It's just part of life! Your biggest strength is your ability to connect with people on a grand scale. Use this gift to spread a message of love and compassion throughout the world. What a beautiful legacy!

LEO
From July 22, 19:07 through August 23, 2:02

The Zealous Organizer

"A place for everything, and everything in its place" is the motto of the 1968 Leo. You have an innate sense of order that governs everything you do. Perhaps it's because your upbringing was somewhat chaotic. Growing up during the free-wheeling seventies, you may have felt constantly uprooted. As a result, you became incredibly organized. You take very good care of your property, and invest in only quality items that will last a lifetime. If everyone were as resourceful as you, there would be very little waste in the world.

You've got a great head for business, and can make a fortune at almost anything you do. You could have especially strong luck in real estate, banking, or commodities. Its important to vary your investments, as you can build and lose wealth rather quickly. Spreading your money around can guard against massive loss. Be sure to have several tax shelters, too, or your obligation to the government could become prohibitive.

A rigid moral code may prevent you from making as many friends as you'd like. As you get older, you'll be less picky. Try to meet people from many different walks of life, as they can expand your understanding of the Universe. Too often, you may assume your way is the only way, which drives love from your door. Being miserly with your money or affection will ultimately backfire.

In relationships, you need people who will encourage you to loosen up a little. Geminis, Sagittarians, Aquarians, and Pisceans can teach you the value of having fun. Not everything you do has to be geared toward making money. As you get older, you will recognize that the most precious things in life are friends, not status symbols. You could use a romantic partner with a strong spiritual side. Such a centered person can show you that the road to contentment isn't paved with gold.

Enterprising and resourceful, your greatest challenge is to stop living solely on the physical plane. Your emotional and spiritual sides are equally important. Your biggest strength is your sense of organization. Making order out of chaos is your special talent—be proud of it!

➤ Read about your Chinese Astrological sign on page 838. ➤ Read about your Personal Planets on page 826. ➤ Read about your personal Mystical Card on page 856.

VIRGO

From August 23, 2:03 through September 22, 23:25

The Practical Powerhouse

The 1968 Virgo knows what needs to be done, and the fastest way to do it. Confident of your abilities, you don't waste time running plans past a committee. You formulate a strategy and move forward with it. The year you were born, the North Vietnamese launched a daring attack on South Vietnamese cities. The Tet Offensive marked an astonishing turning point in the Vietnam War, suggesting the little guys had bested a major military power. You're capable of staging similar upsets, thanks to your unshakeable confidence.

You have a deep concern for needy people that draws you toward the helping professions. Teaching in underprivileged communities, building houses for the poor, or providing health care for the indigent may appeal to you. Big bureaucracies don't daunt you. In fact, you've got a knack for cutting through even the stickiest red tape. The Miracle Worker is probably an apt nickname for you.

Sex may be a bit of a taboo subject for you. It may be difficult to abandon yourself to physical pleasure. Perhaps this is the result of being so preoccupied with other people's troubles. If it is, don't deprive yourself physical intimacy. Sex is a valuable means to connect with another human being. The older you get, the more you'll appreciate how good it feels to be stroked, hugged, and kissed. Depriving yourself of joy is no way to go through life.

Caring and kind, you like people who share your love of humanity. Virgos, Sagittarians, Aquarians, and Pisceans understand your need to serve. When it comes to romance, you'd be wise to pick a demonstrative partner. Being swept into a loving embrace puts you in touch with your physical needs, which are considerable. (Earth signs have the strongest sex drives!)

An addiction to work is your greatest challenge. You don't have to be saving the world all the time. Treat yourself to a movie marathon when your energy starts to wane. If there's anybody who deserves a break, its you! Your biggest blessing is your resourcefulness. If there's a way out of trouble, you will find it. No wonder everybody wants you on their team!

LIBRA

From September 22, 23:26 through October 23, 8:29

The Charming Lover

Tasteful and selective, it's hard to live up to a 1968 Libra's standards. You demand only the best, not only from products, but from people as well. When you do meet someone who meets your expectations, you're slavishly devoted. Until that happens, however, you're content to play the field. Your past is probably littered with heartbroken admirers. The year you were born The Beatles' *Sergeant Pepper's Lonely Hearts Club Band* was the album of the year. If your lovers formed a similar club, it might be sizable indeed.

You may be reluctant to form a lasting relationship for another reason: fear of commitment. Freedom is important to the 1968 Libra. You couldn't abide amending your behavior for the sake of somebody else. Many people accuse you of being flighty, and they're probably right. You're always looking for greener pastures, better lovers, and happier circumstances. If that means burning all the bridges behind you, so be it.

In work, you need a job that keeps you on the move. You'd make a great importer/exporter, photo-journalist, or translator. Working behind the scenes suits you best. You hate being scrutinized by anybody, much less a bossy authority figure. Colleagues can't figure out why a charmer like you would want to spend so much time alone. People enjoy speculating about your private life, and you do everything in your power to fuel their curiosity.

You prefer dealing with friends on an individual basis. Mixing with a big group makes you nervous. Older, mature people appeal to your sense of dignity—your contemporaries probably seem childishly naïve to you. Your best bet for a fruitful partnership is with a Taurean, Cancerian, Virgo, or Capricorn. Anybody who can keep you grounded is a good candidate for romance.

Fussiness is your greatest obstacle. You can't expect to have things perfect all the time. Learn to make allowances, especially when everybody else is forced to deal with substandard conditions. Your biggest strength is your impeccable taste. Apply it toward things that really matter: dinner parties, beautiful clothes, and enjoyable company.

VIRGO
Your Personal Planets

YOUR LOVE POTENTIAL
Venus in Virgo, Aug. 23, 2:03 - Sept. 02, 6:38
Venus in Libra, Sept. 02, 6:39 - Sept. 22, 23:25

YOUR DRIVE AND AMBITION
Mars in Leo, Aug. 23, 2:03 - Sept. 21, 18:38
Mars in Virgo, Sept. 21, 18:39 - Sept. 22, 23:25

YOUR LUCK MAGNETISM
Jupiter in Virgo, Aug. 23, 2:03 - Sept. 22, 23:25

World Events

Aug. 31 – Earthquakes in Iran are estimated to have killed 12,000 people.

Sept. 9 – Arthur Ashe defeats Tom Okker to win the U.S. Tennis Open.

Tennis player Arthur Ashe

LIBRA
Your Personal Planets

YOUR LOVE POTENTIAL
Venus in Libra, Sept. 22, 23:26 - Sept. 26, 16:44
Venus in Scorpio, Sept. 26, 16:45 - Oct. 21, 5:15
Venus in Sagittarius, Oct. 21, 5:16 - Oct. 23, 8:29

YOUR DRIVE AND AMBITION
Mars in Virgo, Sept. 22, 23:26 - Oct. 23, 8:29

YOUR LUCK MAGNETISM
Jupiter in Virgo, Sept. 22, 23:26 - Oct. 23, 8:29

World Events

Oct. 11 – The first manned Apollo mission—*Apollo 7*—is launched from Cape Canaveral.

Oct. 12 – The Olympics opens in Mexico City.

➤ Read about your Chinese Astrological sign on page 838. ➤ Read about your Personal Planets on page 826. ➤ Read about your personal Mystical Card on page 856.

1968

SCORPIO
Your Personal Planets

YOUR LOVE POTENTIAL
Venus in Sagittarius, Oct. 23, 8:30 - Nov. 14, 21:47
Venus in Capricorn, Nov. 14, 21:48 - Nov. 22, 5:48

YOUR DRIVE AND AMBITION
Mars in Virgo, Oct. 23, 8:30 - Nov. 09, 6:09
Mars in Libra, Nov. 09, 6:10 - Nov. 22, 5:48

YOUR LUCK MAGNETISM
Jupiter in Virgo, Oct. 23, 8:30 - Nov. 15, 22:43
Jupiter in Libra, Nov. 15, 22:44 - Nov. 22, 5:48

World Events

Oct. 27 - Londoners demonstrate in the capital against the Vietnam War.

Nov. 5 - Richard Nixon is elected thirty-seventh President of the U.S., defeating Hubert Humphrey in the election race.

Richard Nixon wins the Presidential election

SAGITTARIUS
Your Personal Planets

YOUR LOVE POTENTIAL
Venus in Capricorn, Nov. 22, 5:49 - Dec. 09, 22:39
Venus in Aquarius, Dec. 09, 22:40 - Dec. 21, 18:59

YOUR DRIVE AND AMBITION
Mars in Libra, Nov. 22, 5:49 - Dec. 21, 18:59

YOUR LUCK MAGNETISM
Jupiter in Libra, Nov. 22, 5:49 - Dec. 21, 18:59

World Events

Nov. 28 - British author Enid Blyton dies.

Dec. 20 - American novelist John Steinbeck, author of *The Grapes Of Wrath*, dies.

560

SCORPIO
From October 23, 8:30 through November 22, 5:48

The Gregarious Do-Gooder

Friendly and outgoing, the 1968 Scorpio never wants for friends. You're always happy to set extra places at the table for unexpected visitors. "The more the merrier" is your motto. The commune mentality of the sixties and seventies probably rubbed off on you as a child. For you, sharing food with friends is one of the supreme pleasures in life. You also like working in a collective, and may live on a kibbutz at some point in your life. You're not afraid of hard work, so long as its applied to the benefit of a group.

You have a gift for making people feel special and valued, regardless of their surroundings. Working in a prison, hospital, or reform school may appeal to you. It's your belief that every human being has potential. You feel it's your mission to bring out the best in everybody, and take a special interest in problem cases. The 1968 Scorpio is destined to perform difficult but vital jobs that require great moral fiber.

Your strength comes from a hidden source. Chances are you are a very spiritual person, but keep your beliefs secret. Religion is a private matter which you rarely discuss, even with close friends. Yoga, meditation, and other forms of mysticism probably play a role in your life, and give you great strength when worldly pressures weigh heavily on your shoulders. An intense, powerful imagination can also help you escape reality. Painting, writing, and sculpting can offer a strong measure of comfort.

Although you have friends from many walks of life, you prefer people who are capable of profound introspection. Cancerians, Scorpios, Aquarians, and Pisceans are sympathetic to your way of thinking. At times, it seems as though these loved ones can read your thoughts. Resist the urge to suppress anger toward your mate, or it could flare up in hurtful ways.

Your greatest challenge is a desire for sainthood. Above all things, you are human. As you get older, it will be easier identify and come to terms with your flaws. Your biggest strength is your ability to shine light on impossibly dark situations. The world is a better place because of people like you.

SAGITTARIUS
From November 22, 5:49 through December 21, 18:59

The Gracious Host

The guest room of a 1968 Sagittarius is rarely empty. You have an enormous number of friends, all of whom love to visit. Your parties are famous. The food is always good, the guests charming, and the music rollicking! The year you were born, dour Richard Nixon appeared on the comedy show *Laugh-In*, hoping to lighten his image. Even the Grim Reaper would seem downright friendly at one of your parties—the upbeat atmosphere is that infectious!

Of course, you'd be a great success as an event planner. Other jobs that might appeal to you are disc jockey, cruise director, or tour guide. Any career that involves showing folks a good time would suit you well. Working alongside congenial people is important to you. You can't abide gossipy back-stabbers. If you find yourself in such a situation, look for other opportunities. You have a knack for finding well-paying jobs, even in the worst economic times. Maybe it's because you've got so many friends who are willing to put in a good word for you.

Having children may be a scary prospect for you. It's not that you dislike young people—it's just that they involve so much responsibility. You're really a big kid at heart, and it may be difficult to assume serious burdens, even in late adulthood. If you're determined not to have children, make your intentions known before embarking on a serious romance. You wouldn't want to disillusion your partner; you're too truthful for that.

You get along best with folks who appreciate your independent spirit. Ariens, Geminis, Librans, and Sagittarians are eager to join you on madcap adventures. When it comes to romance, though, you may want to calm down a bit, if only for the sake of creating a stable home life. If you want excitement, you can always head for the bedroom!

Fun and free-wheeling, your greatest challenge is to accept responsibility. You can't always do as you like, although you manage to most of the time. Creating a joyous atmosphere is your biggest strength. When you enter it room, it feels like a burst of sunshine. Beam your warmth on lonely folks who could use a lift.

➤ Read about your Chinese Astrological sign on page 838. ➤ Read about your Personal Planets on page 826. ➤ Read about your personal Mystical Card on page 856.

CAPRICORN

From December 21, 19:00 through December 31, 23:59

The Respected Authority

Any 1968 Capricorn born in December commands a great deal of respect. You have a dignified air that makes people stand at attention. While others are frantically trying to wave down a waiter, you've got five at your elbow, all anxious to serve you. Fortunately, you're not likely to abuse your power. Instead, you use it to organize people into formidable workforces. You have big dreams, and need help to make them come true. Consequently, you only surround yourself with superior people who know what they're doing. Anybody in your employ should be proud of themselves—you're an expert at spotting talent.

Positions that involve a great deal of responsibility suit you best. You'd make a great military leader, politician, or company president. Ultimately, it doesn't matter if you're in charge of an army or a household, your leadership qualities are evident wherever you go. The year you were born, U.S. President Lyndon B. Johnson announced that he would not be standing for re-election. Established leaders feel insecure in your presence, and may step down voluntarily if they sense a challenge from you.

Domestic responsibilities may feel more like a burden than a blessing. Beware of neglecting your loved ones, as they can provide you with valuable emotional support. Being admired by your co-workers is pleasant, but it's more important to have the respect of your family. Force yourself to take an extended vacation every year—it won't kill you to relax! Don't be afraid to pass the reins of responsibility to your subordinates.

Let nurturing people make up the greater part of your social circle. You already know enough experts, authorities, and prodigies—what you really need are friends who know how to administer tender loving care. Taureans, Cancerians, Virgos, and Pisceans invite you to put your feet up and let your hair down. What better recipe for bliss?

Exacting and dedicated, your greatest challenge is to relax. Fun isn't a four-letter word, you know! Your biggest strength is your ability to spot talent and reward it. Working for you is sure to be a labor of love.

CAPRICORN
Your Personal Planets

YOUR LOVE POTENTIAL
Venus in Aquarius, Dec. 21, 19:00 - Dec. 31, 23:59

YOUR DRIVE AND AMBITION
Mars in Libra, Dec. 21, 19:00 - Dec. 29, 22:06
Mars in Scorpio, Dec. 29, 22:07 - Dec. 31, 23:59

YOUR LUCK MAGNETISM
Jupiter in Libra, Dec. 21, 19:00 - Dec. 31, 23:59

World Events

Dec. 27 – *Apollo 8* returns to Earth.

Dec. 29 – The launch of the luxury liner *QE2* is postponed as the ship is not completed.

Picasso's "The Dream"

Special Feature
Dreaming Through the Twentieth Century

(Continued from page 553)

In the early 1970s anthropologist Carlos Castaneda popularized another evolutionary step in the New Age movement—the path of the warrior. Through his published conversations with the mysterious sorcerer Don Juan, Castaneda described a magical world of alternate realities and taught the sorcerer's techniques to attaining magical powers. One of the methods outlined by Don Juan took advantage of a state known as lucid dreaming. In this type of dream, a person is aware he is dreaming, and is thus able to take control of what happens in the dream. This is believed to bring more control (or power) to the person's waking life.

Another New Age personality showed how to blend the best of Hindu mysticism with twentieth-century psychology. In his book *The Psychology Of The Esoteric*, Bhagwan Shree Rajneesh developed a logical framework for explaining the range of dreams, from the ordinary to the extraordinary. In Rajneesh's system, dreams occur at seven levels, with the first level being psychological. The second level is known as the etheric body, and in this state a person may experience spiritual visions. The third level is the astral level, in which the dreamer may experience past lives and the knowledge that was gained during the passage of these lives. At the fourth level, the dreamer is able to travel into both the past and future. The fifth, sixth, and seventh levels all connect the individual with the transpersonal, the place at which dreams and waking reality become the one and the same. An understanding of all seven levels, with their seven types of reality, is very rare. However, it is believed that experiencing at least the first four levels clarifies the meaning of most dreams.

Rajneesh's system of dreams lends an eastern perspective to our views on dreams.

Over the course of the last hundred years, our understanding of dreams had undergone a thorough transformation. Consequently, we can now appreciate the beauty of their rich symbolic language as well as their invaluable messages, which speak to us personally, culturally and spiritually. Perhaps in this century, we can work toward merging the Eastern esoteric knowledge with our Western scientific studies for the advancement of consciousness and our lives. ☉

➤ Read Sigmund Freud's Star Profile on page 17. ➤ Read Albert Einstein's Star Profile on page 169. ➤ Read more about Jung and Einstein in "East Meets Twentieth-Century West" by Ronnie Grishman on page 25.

1969

Neptune, Uranus and Jupiter in the Spotlight

I n 1969, the astrological stage was set for the ultimate hippy rock festival. The planet Neptune had been in the sign of Scorpio since the mid-1950s, bringing new ideas about sexual openness and spirituality into the consciousness. Neptune's placement in Scorpio signified the power and pleasure of rock 'n' roll. Neptune rules all forms of art, especially music and poetry, and Scorpio signifies sex. Groups like Led Zeppelin and the Doors, with their explicit lyrics and amorous and sexy front men, became icons of this unprecedented and decadent era. Uranus had just moved into Libra, indicating renewed beliefs about marriage, partnership, and social conduct. Libra is the sign of justice, fairness, and friendship. In addition, Jupiter, planet of hopes and the higher mind, had also moved into Libra in 1968. Idealism and abundant joy ran rampant despite the continued pain of the war in Vietnam. The culture of the hippies had become an antidote to the anguish of the war.

When Woodstock opened in August 1969, no one could have guessed at the historic milestone that it would become. Many of the bands that came to symbolize the era of Flower Power and hippydom appeared in front of many thousands of fans on Max Yasgur's muddy farm in Saugerties, New York, and somehow managed to change the world forever. It was the largest rock concert ever conceived. More than 450,000 people attended. It was a counter-cultural mini-nation, erected for three days and three nights. Neptune, Uranus, and Jupiter came together to attend the party and all had a wonderful time.

Crowd playing their own music at the Woodstock Festival

The first Moon landing

Women and children lie dead in the road after the Mylai Massacre, Vietnam

THE PRESIDENT AND THE UFO

In Leary, Georgia, in the U.S. on January 6, while waiting outside for the meeting of the local Lions Club to begin, future President Jimmy Carter and ten other club members were surprised by a sharply outlined light in the sky. According to Carter, it showed "bluish at first, then reddish, but not solid.... It appeared as bright as the Moon." All men believed that what they had seen was a UFO and Carter went so far as to boldly and publicly discuss the sighting when he became Governor later in his career.

A WALK ON THE MOON

The U.S. were first to land a craft on the Moon when crewmen from *Apollo 11* touched down, and civilian astronaut Neil Armstrong became first to walk on the lunar surface. Around the world, an audience of 600 million watched the epoch-making event on TV. Rising tensions in Northern Ireland finally flared to life, resulting in a three-day riot in Belfast. Libya's King Idris was ousted in a coup which placed an army subaltern, Muammar Khadaffi, in control. After last year's Paris riots, France's de Gaulle resigned as President, to be replaced by Pompidou. In Britain, anti-apartheid protesters disrupted the rugby tour by the South African Springboks. Sirhan Bishara Sirhan was convicted of killing Bobby Kennedy for pro-Israel policies. Charles Manson and his "family" massacred actress Sharon Tate and four others at her home in Beverly Hills. U.S. army Lt. William Calley was charged with the Mylai massacre in Vietnam. In New York, the Woodstock Music and Arts Festival drew a young audience, estimated at around half a million. China's Cultural Revolution came to an end. North Vietnam's Ho Chi Minh and U.S. author Jack Kerouac died.

➤ Read Janis Joplin's Star Profile on page 569.

CAPRICORN

From January 01, 0:00 through January 20, 5:37

The Born Organizer

Popular, friendly, and just a little bit sassy, the January-born 1969 Capricorn is destined to lead. You've got friends from all walks of life and move easily among several social circles. Although these groups are very different, they have one thing in common—you as their leader. Your strong, vivacious personality causes you to rise to the top of any organization. Your schedule is jam-packed. Often, you're busy putting together fund-raisers, committee meetings, and office parties, all at the same time. Still, you love being in demand and would feel restless if you didn't have something to manage.

The year you were born, the Woodstock Music and Art Fair opened in New York state. Thousands of people came from miles around to hear their favorite artists. You're similarly capable of bringing hordes of folks together in a spirit of harmony. Your upbeat attitude is utterly infectious. If you propose a gathering, folks will try their best to be there. You come alive in large groups and love entertaining crowds with funny stories. One thing is for sure: you're a fantastic host!

You need to work with people. Your tact and discretion may draw you to the service industry. You'd make a great hotel manager, health spa owner, or corporate event planner. Coming up with clever gimmicks and desirable services is easy for you. You like to give the public something that it didn't even know it wanted. Running an advertising agency is also a good possibility for you. Your job should have flair.

Partnerships are very important to you. Chances are, you have a best friend on whom you strongly rely. You want to be married but may hold out until the perfect partner comes along. You get along best with congenial types like Geminis, Leos, Librans, and Sagittarians. Anybody who can lure you away from work is a good companion for you.

Hard-working and determined, your greatest challenge is to develop a rewarding personal life that is separate from the office. Your biggest strength is your outgoing personality. Apply it toward making friends who have nothing to do with your job.

AQUARIUS

From January 20, 5:38 through February 18, 19:54

The Creative Genius

You can spot a 1969 Aquarius by their busy hands. You're always painting, writing, sculpting, or crafting. Normally, you have several projects going on at once. When you get bored of one, you pick up another. Being idle is beyond the scope of your prodigious imagination. There are simply too many intriguing ideas that need to be realized! Much of your inspiration comes from dreams. If you don't keep pencil and paper by your bed, you should start doing so. You've been blessed with a highly developed subconscious. Draw upon it whenever you feel stuck or confused.

Unconventional art forms may suit you best. The year you were born, The Who released their rock opera *Tommy*. Putting new twists on old media gives you a tremendous sense of pleasure. That's why you may never hold down a conventional job—you need work that allows you to flex your creative muscles. Filmmaking, performance art, or photography may prove fulfilling. You probably have strong musical talent, too.

A strong intellect draws you to clever, inventive people. One of your favorite pastimes may be sitting up all night discussing religion, philosophy, and ethics. You may pose moral dilemmas to yourself, wondering what you would do in difficult situations. Some folks find these mind games stressful, but they are your way of relaxing. Travel provides you with lots of food for thought. You love to see the way other people exist, comparing and contrasting their lives with your own.

Ariens, Geminis, Librans, and fellow Aquarians are among your companions. Rebellious types also find favor with you. You can't go along with folks who insist on doing things the proper way all the time. In love, you need a partner who is both noble and generous. It wouldn't hurt if your mate had a playful sense of humor, too. You love a good joke!

Your greatest challenge is boredom. You're always looking to conquer new lands and that's not always possible. Blessed with tremendous creativity, you like to show people new ways of looking at things. The world will always be an interesting place thanks to visionaries like you.

➤ Read about your Chinese Astrological sign on page 838. ➤ Read about your Personal Planets on page 826. ➤ Read about your personal Mystical Card on page 856.

CAPRICORN
Your Personal Planets

YOUR LOVE POTENTIAL
Venus in Aquarius, Jan. 01, 0:00 - Jan. 04, 20:06
Venus in Pisces, Jan. 04, 20:07 - Jan. 20, 5:37

YOUR DRIVE AND AMBITION
Mars in Scorpio, Jan. 01, 0:00 - Jan. 20, 5:37

YOUR LUCK MAGNETISM
Jupiter in Libra, Jan. 01, 0:00 - Jan. 20, 5:37

World Events

Jan. 9 - Neil Armstrong and Edwin "Buzz" Aldrin are selected as the men who will walk on the Moon.

Jan. 15 - The Soviets launch the *Soyuz 5* spacecraft, which later docks with *Soyuz 4* in an unprecedented maneuver.

Newly elected PLO leader Yasser Arafat with Gamul Abdel Nasser

AQUARIUS
Your Personal Planets

YOUR LOVE POTENTIAL
Venus in Pisces, Jan. 20, 5:38 - Feb. 02, 4:44
Venus in Aries, Feb. 02, 4:45 - Feb. 18, 19:54

YOUR DRIVE AND AMBITION
Mars in Scorpio, Jan. 20, 5:38 - Feb. 18, 19:54

YOUR LUCK MAGNETISM
Jupiter in Libra, Jan. 20, 5:38 - Feb. 18, 19:54

World Events

Feb. 4 - Yasser Arafat takes over as Chairman of the Palestinian Liberation Organization.

Feb. 9 - The first flight of a Boeing 747 airplane takes place.

1969

PISCES
Your Personal Planets

YOUR LOVE POTENTIAL
Venus in Aries, Feb. 18, 19:55 - Mar. 20, 19:07

YOUR DRIVE AND AMBITION
Mars in Scorpio, Feb. 18, 19:55 - Feb. 25, 6:20
Mars in Sagittarius, Feb. 25, 6:21 - Mar. 20, 19:07

YOUR LUCK MAGNETISM
Jupiter in Libra, Feb. 18, 19:55 - Mar. 20, 19:07

World Events

Mar. 10 - James Earl Ray pleads guilty to the murder of Martin Luther King Jr.

Mar. 12 - Beatle Paul McCartney marries Linda Louise Eastman in London.

Paul McCartney shields his bride Linda from the crowds outside Marylebone Registry Office

ARIES
Your Personal Planets

YOUR LOVE POTENTIAL
Venus in Aries, Mar. 20, 19:08 - Apr. 20, 6:26

YOUR DRIVE AND AMBITION
Mars in Sagittarius, Mar. 20, 19:08 - Apr. 20, 6:26

YOUR LUCK MAGNETISM
Jupiter in Libra, Mar. 20, 19:08 - Mar. 30, 21:36
Jupiter in Virgo, Mar. 30, 21:37 - Apr. 20, 6:26

World Events

Mar. 25 - John Lennon and his wife Yoko Ono begin a "bed-in" as a plea for peace in Vietnam.

Apr. 17 - Sirhan Bishara Sirhan is convicted of assassinating Sen. Robert F. Kennedy.

PISCES
From February 18, 19:55 through March 20, 19:07

The Good-natured Comedian

Always quick with a joke, the 1969 Pisces wants to make folks smile. You've got a delicious sense of humor that is never mean-spirited. People don't tense up when you enter the room; they're more likely to give a delighted cry. You love to hold court at large parties, doing uncanny imitations of all the guests. It's hard to keep up with you—you may bounce around the room with a boundless energy. Friends would be wise to put away their breakables before you come over, as you may tend to wave your hands around a lot.

In 1969, the Children's Television Workshop launched *Sesame Street*. You're probably a big fan of Ernie, that merry prankster who always manages to get the best of his good pal, Bert. Like Ernie, you've got a distinctive laugh that can be immediately identified. Your laugh is the sexiest thing about you. Legions of admirers have been attracted to your irrepressible giggle.

Caring and compassionate, you need a job that affords emotional fulfillment. You'd make an excellent social worker, spiritual advisor, or veterinarian. The chances are you have many pets, most of them strays. If you don't have any animals, it's probably because you travel too much to provide them with a stable home life. Working in foreign countries provides you with the stimulation you need to stay focused. It's not easy for you to stay in one place for long. Outdoor work is also a good possibility for you as it allows you to move about freely.

Relationships have the power to transform you. You're attracted to intellectual types because they provide a nice counterbalance to your dreamy, intuitive approach. Nevertheless, you get along best with brainy Geminis, Virgos, Librans, and Aquarians. In love, you need a partner who is attentive and kind.

Your greatest challenge is to take pride in your accomplishments. Try to surround yourself with people who appreciate your gifts. Your biggest strength is your humor. Wherever you go and whatever you do, you'll always find something amusing. Give the world the gift of laughter whenever possible. We could all stand to smile a little more!

ARIES
From March 20, 19:08 through April 20, 6:26

The Humble Helper

Most Rams are noted for being leaders, but not the 1969 Aries. You're more interested in getting the job done right than standing in the spotlight. Abundantly clever, you've got a knack for solving problems. You're always looking for ways to improve existing conditions, whether at work or at home. Chances are, you've come up with some cunning inventions that save time, money, and labor. Folks marvel at your inventiveness, though you tend to brush off the praise. Somehow, you don't see how valuable your contributions are. You need to learn to savor praise instead of dismissing it.

The year you were born, the electron microscope was invented. You have a similar gift for spotting tiny details that escape everybody else's notice. Under your meticulous care, mistakes are rarely—if ever—made. That's why you're often entrusted with pivotal jobs like proofreading, fact checking, and product testing. Given your talent, you would make an excellent editor, lab technician, or electrician. Working on a small scale pleases you as it demands tremendous concentration. If you're looking for a hobby, try making dollhouse furniture in your spare time. This could even become a lucrative business for you.

You have a serious side to your personality that comes out in public. It may be hard for people to warm up to you as you have such a dignified manner. Meeting you is a bit like encountering royalty. As you get older, you'll find it easier to loosen up. You may even start wearing jeans on casual Fridays! Stranger things have happened.

You like unconventional people who keep you guessing. Spontaneous Ariens, mercurial Geminis, impulsive Leos, and unpredictable Aquarians are among your favorite friends. When it comes to love, you need a partner who likes to be protected and cherished. Select a lovable mate who inspires you to kiss, cuddle, and hug.

Your greatest challenge is to be more outgoing. Make more of an effort to meet people, especially at social occasions. Your biggest blessing is your dedication to work. Whatever job you perform, be sure that it speaks to your soul.

➤ Read about your Chinese Astrological sign on page 838. ➤ Read about your Personal Planets on page 826. ➤ Read about your personal Mystical Card on page 856.

TAURUS

From April 20, 6:27 through May 21, 5:49

The Admirable Visionary

The 1969 Taurus never lacks for art supplies. That's because you integrate natural materials into all of your work. As far as you're concerned, Mother Nature is the most brilliant artist of all time. Drawing on her bounty provides you with endless inspiration. If you feel unhappy, do so some gardening; take up pottery; draw with charcoals. As a 1969 Bull, you have a profound connection to the earth, combined with a strong desire to create. If you disobey these instincts, emotional paralysis could be the consequence.

The first in vitro fertilization of a human egg was performed the year you were born. You're similarly interested in using unconventional methods to create something new. You'd make an excellent special education teacher as you're good at presenting information in compelling ways. You'd also be a terrific landscaper, inventing ways to integrate man-made structures with the environment. Making household products out of recycled materials is also a good option for you.

You have unique gifts that set you apart from the crowd. Sometimes you wish you could be more ordinary, if only to escape people's curiosity. Eventually, you'll have to accept the fact that your work will always attract attention. You could achieve great success in the entertainment industry. While other actors, singers, and dancers struggle to gain recognition, you'll have an easy time getting noticed. You would also make a great artist.

Unconventional types comprise the biggest part of your social circle. Energetic Ariens, quirky Geminis, offbeat Aquarians, and kooky Pisceans appreciate your unique way of doing things. When it comes to romance, though, you like to do things the old-fashioned way. Make sure your partner is an expert in the art of lovemaking as your physical needs are strong.

Your greatest challenge is an inordinate respect for the status quo. Try to appreciate your extraordinary gifts on their own terms—you're too special to compare yourself to others. A vivid imagination is your biggest strength. Let it carry you away on a cloud of pink smoke; reality is overrated!

GEMINI

From May 21, 5:50 through June 21, 13:54

The Contented Homebody

The 1969 Gemini is definitely a domestic creature. You'd rather curl up in bed with a good book than go on an exotic vacation. Chances are you had a pretty happy childhood. If you didn't, you're making up for it now. You treat your home like a big playpen and love it when friends come to join the fun. The year you were born, John Lennon and Yoko Ono staged a bed-in for peace. That's definitely an idea you can get behind. You think that if people had happier domestic lives, they'd be less prone to commit violence.

You dislike typical office environments, feeling they are sterile and impersonal. Consequently, it's a good idea for you to work in somebody else's home. Being a cook, nanny, gardener, or personal assistant might be enjoyable for you, provided your employer treats you like a member of the family. Better yet, you could open a home office of your own, doing business over the Internet while lounging around in your pajamas.

It's quite possible that your family is unusual in some way. You may have a combined household, featuring children from two separate marriages. Perhaps you live in a commune or artists' colony. You're not the type to put up with suffocating conditions for long. If a place doesn't suit you, you'll simply look for a better opportunity. Ideally, you should live in an area that has lots of grass and trees. Nature has a therapeutic effect on you. Take a walk through your favorite park on those rare days you get cabin fever.

Blessed with democratic instincts, you like people who prize equality. Librans, Sagittarians, and Aquarians are good company for you. As far as romance goes, you need a nurturing partner who excels at the domestic arts. You can actually be seduced by a person's cooking.

Steady and predictable, your greatest challenge is to take more risks. Make an effort to try something new, at least once in a while. Who wants to eat meatloaf five days a week, even if it is your favorite food? Your biggest strength is your hospitality. It's a good idea to always have a pot of soup on the stove. You never know who might come over!

➤ Read about your Chinese Astrological sign on page 838. ➤ Read about your Personal Planets on page 826. ➤ Read about your personal Mystical Card on page 856.

TAURUS
Your Personal Planets

YOUR LOVE POTENTIAL
Venus in Aries, Apr. 20, 6:27 - May 21, 5:49

YOUR DRIVE AND AMBITION
Mars in Sagittarius, Apr. 20, 6:27 - May 21, 5:49

YOUR LUCK MAGNETISM
Jupiter in Virgo, Apr. 20, 6:27 - May 21, 5:49

World Events

May 10 – The Battle of Hamburger Hill begins in Vietnam.

May 11 – The Monty Python comedy troupe is formed in Britain.

The Monty Python team

GEMINI
Your Personal Planets

YOUR LOVE POTENTIAL
Venus in Aries, May 21, 5:50 - June 06, 1:47
Venus in Taurus, June 06, 1:48 - June 21, 13:54

YOUR DRIVE AND AMBITION
Mars in Sagittarius, May 21, 5:50 - June 21, 13:54

YOUR LUCK MAGNETISM
Jupiter in Virgo, May 21, 5:50 - June 21, 13:54

World Events

May 25 – The government in Khartoum is overthrown by a military coup.

June 1 – Canada bans the advertisement of tobacco on television and radio.

CANCER
Your Personal Planets

YOUR LOVE POTENTIAL
Venus in Taurus, June 21, 13:55 - July 06, 22:03
Venus in Gemini, July 06, 22:04 - July 23, 0:47

YOUR DRIVE AND AMBITION
Mars in Sagittarius, June 21, 13:55 - July 23, 0:47

YOUR LUCK MAGNETISM
Jupiter in Virgo, June 21, 13:55 - July 15, 13:28
Jupiter in Libra, July 15, 13:29 - July 23, 0:47

World Events

June 22 – American actress Judy Garland dies.

July 21 – Neil Armstrong steps on to the surface of the Moon as millions watch on television around the world.

The first Moon landing

LEO
Your Personal Planets

YOUR LOVE POTENTIAL
Venus in Gemini, July 23, 0:48 - Aug. 03, 5:29
Venus in Cancer, Aug. 03, 5:30 - Aug. 23, 7:42

YOUR DRIVE AND AMBITION
Mars in Sagittarius, July 23, 0:48 - Aug. 23, 7:42

YOUR LUCK MAGNETISM
Jupiter in Libra, July 23, 0:48 - Aug. 23, 7:42

World Events

July 25 – Edward Kennedy pleads guilty to leaving the scene of an accident a week after the Chappaquiddick car accident that killed Mary Jo Kopechne.

Aug. 9 – Actress Sharon Tate and her friends are brutally murdered—an incident that shocks the Hollywood world.

CANCER
From June 21, 13:55 through July 23, 0:47

The Town Crier

More reliable than the town newspaper, the 1969 Cancer is a valuable source of information. You've got your finger on the pulse of the entire neighborhood. If a baby is born or a marriage splits up, you're usually the first to know. That's because you're friendly with everybody from the mail carrier to the mayor. You love to hear about other people's lives and have a knack for drawing secrets from even the most tight-lipped folks.

The year you were born, Ralph Nader set up a consumer organization designed to inform the public about faulty products. You're a regular fount of information, too. Blessed with a retentive memory, you never forget a face or story. Given your excellent recall, you'd make an effective historian, lawyer, or detective. Very few details escape your notice. At some point, you may decide to write a book about all you've observed. If you do, be sure to heavily disguise any characters that are based on real-life acquaintances.

Friends play an important part in your life. Honor them by refusing to betray their secrets, no matter how juicy. After all, you expect the same consideration. You are the type of person who has pals from every stage of your life and manages to integrate new ones into your old crowd. You're probably an expert matchmaker, too, and may have set up several couples.

You like people who are sensitive and intuitive. Librans, Scorpios, Pisceans, and fellow Crabs are pleasing company, although you've probably got friends from every sign of the zodiac. Your ideal romantic partner should be spiritual, sensitive, and creative. There is a very good chance that at least one of your children will be a talented artist.

Your greatest challenge is to become more organized. At times you can let mundane responsibilities pile up, causing you undue stress later on. Make a greater effort to take care of small jobs as they crop up; this will give you more time to engage in your favorite leisure time pursuits, like reading and writing. Your biggest strength is your powerful memory. Use it to provide future generations with a link to the past.

LEO
From July 23, 0:48 through August 23, 7:42

The Star Pupil

The 1969 Leo is a born scholar. You've got an incredibly quick mind and may be an authority on a variety of subjects. Getting good grades was probably no problem for you, unless teachers resented your irreverent approach to learning. You're fond of jokes and probably enjoyed making your classmates laugh. The year you were born, the satirical comedy show *Monty Python's Flying Circus* was first aired on British TV. Its silly brand of humor is very similar to yours.

You are very serious about one thing: your career. You want a job that provides plenty of financial security. Banking, real estate, and finance are fields you may explore. You've got good instincts about market trends and leadership positions suit you best. You're an expert at providing guidance without making folks feel bullied. Furthermore, people enjoy working for you because you are an appreciative employer. You always make it a point to praise a job well done.

In love, you are very determined. You like to pursue the object of your affection. This technique works remarkably well, with a few exceptions. If you find yourself chasing someone who is immune to your charms, back off. A strategic retreat can be just as effective as a frontal assault. It's very important for you to have romance in your life at all times. Just because you're in a committed partnership doesn't mean you can take your mate for granted! Whomever you pick for a permanent partner is very lucky indeed.

You like witty, smart people with a dash of flair. Geminis, Librans, Leos, and Sagittarians are your chief delight. When you decide to get married, it will be for keeps. All Lions are loyal, but the 1969 Leo is especially devoted. You'd be wise to stay away from flirtatious types—they'll only cause you heartache and worry. A quiet, adoring partner would suit you very well.

Dealing with authority figures is your greatest challenge. Giving your superiors respect is a smart strategy for your own long-term success. Your biggest strength is your fine mind. Use it to open doors for yourself, both personally and professionally.

➤ Read about your Chinese Astrological sign on page 838. ➤ Read about your Personal Planets on page 826. ➤ Read about your personal Mystical Card on page 856.

VIRGO

From August 23, 7:43 through September 23, 5:06

The Relentless Collector

The 1969 Virgo is destined to live the good life. You have a strong appreciation for beautiful clothes, objects, and furnishings. There's probably one special thing you collect: stamps, coins, shells ... it doesn't matter. Gathering objects in a series appeals to your acquisitive, orderly mind. You probably keep your collection in a special display case and have dreams of finding that one elusive object that would make your cache complete.

You may have expensive tastes, which may also extend to restaurants. The year you were born, *Oliver!* won an Oscar for best picture. You're likely to break into a chorus of "Food, Glorious Food" when you pull up to the table of a five-star restaurant. Succulent meals and luscious desserts make your eyes gleam with delight. Make sure you integrate a half-hour of exercise into your daily routine or you will come to curse your cravings. Outdoor sports like hiking, rock climbing, and biking may especially appeal to you.

Your love of possessions will probably draw you to sales. You'd make an excellent store buyer, antique-shop owner, or mystery shopper. Gracious and diplomatic, you'd also do well in customer service. You could also use your gift with words to write a restaurant column for your local newspaper. Getting paid to eat, what could be better? Whatever your job, it should involve your impeccable taste.

Relationships are easy for you so long as they are with people whose background is similar to yours. You may be shy with people from other cultures, although you will become more relaxed with such folks as you get older. People with traditional values put you at ease. Taureans, Leos, Virgos, and Capricorns make up the bigger part of your social circle. As far as love is concerned, you're most attracted to gentle, poetic types who bring out your protective instincts.

Your greatest challenge as a 1969 Virgo is to develop a spiritual practice. This can give you a more balanced appreciation for money. Your biggest blessing is your thorough enjoyment of physical pleasure. Life is the ultimate buffet—fill your plate and dig in!

LIBRA

From September 23, 5:07 through October 23, 14:10

The Tasteful Free-Spirit

Sociable and refined, the 1969 Libra seeks to spread beauty throughout the entire world. You have exquisite taste and are always trying to make your surroundings fresh and inviting. You also have a knack for making friends wherever you go. It's easy for you to blend your talents with other people's gifts. The year you were born, Simon and Garfunkel's "Mrs. Robinson" won Record of the Year. Deep down inside, you want to create beautiful harmonies with someone special, just like that famous singing duo.

Your home is your castle. Chances are, you spend a great deal of time shopping for it. People love to visit you, although they're reluctant to bring rambunctious kids lest they ruin the fragile knickknacks and elegant fabrics that grace your abode. If you have pets, they are definitely housebroken. Naturally, you'd make an excellent decorator, although any career that involves visual arts would suit you well. Ever the diplomat, you could also work as a receptionist, hotel manager, or customer service representative. Whatever your job, it should involve an element of grace.

You don't like being held down to routines and enjoy having lots of free, unstructured time. When you get into a good book, you don't want to put it down to fix dinner or go to sleep. You get similarly wrapped up when pursuing your favorite hobbies. Keeping a fluid schedule helps keep your spirits high; try not to make too many firm commitments, especially on the weekends. It's better to go with the flow.

In relationships, you work best with people who have strong egos. Ariens, Leos, Scorpios, and Sagittarians make your eyes sparkle with admiration. Deep down inside, you may wish you could be as forceful and aggressive as they are. Finding romance with one of these signs is also a good idea. You're especially attracted to people with athletic builds.

Your greatest challenge as a 1969 Libra is to become less self-conscious. Don't worry what people think if your hair isn't perfect or the house isn't spotless. Your biggest strength is your tact. Your kind words act as a balm for blistered egos.

➤ Read about your Chinese Astrological sign on page 838. ➤ Read about your Personal Planets on page 826. ➤ Read about your personal Mystical Card on page 856.

VIRGO
Your Personal Planets

YOUR LOVE POTENTIAL
Venus in Cancer, Aug. 23, 7:43 - Aug. 29, 2:47
Venus in Leo, Aug. 29, 2:48 - Sept. 23, 3:25
Venus in Virgo, Sept. 23, 3:26 - Sept. 23, 5:06

YOUR DRIVE AND AMBITION
Mars in Sagittarius, Aug. 23, 7:43 - Sept. 21, 6:34
Mars in Capricorn, Sept. 21, 6:35 - Sept. 23, 5:06

YOUR LUCK MAGNETISM
Jupiter in Libra, Aug. 23, 7:43 - Sept. 23, 5:06

World Events

Aug. 31 - Former heavyweight boxing champion Rocky Marciano dies in a plane crash.
Sept. 3 - President of North Vietnam Ho Chi Minh dies.

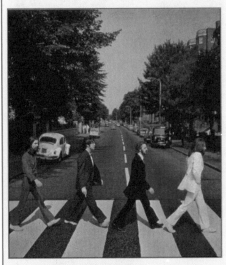

The cover for the Beatles' "Abbey Road" album

LIBRA
Your Personal Planets

YOUR LOVE POTENTIAL
Venus in Virgo, Sept. 23, 5:07 - Oct. 17, 14:16
Venus in Libra, Oct. 17, 14:17 - Oct. 23, 14:10

YOUR DRIVE AND AMBITION
Mars in Capricorn, Sept. 23, 5:07 - Oct. 23, 14:10

YOUR LUCK MAGNETISM
Jupiter in Libra, Sept. 23, 5:07 - Oct. 23, 14:10

World Events

Sept. 26 - The Beatles release their final album, *Abbey Road*.
Oct. 21 - The War of Attrition begins between Israel and Egypt.

567

1969

SCORPIO
Your Personal Planets

YOUR LOVE POTENTIAL
Venus in Libra, Oct. 23, 14:11 - Nov. 10, 16:39
Venus in Scorpio, Nov. 10, 16:40 - Nov. 22, 11:30

YOUR DRIVE AND AMBITION
Mars in Capricorn, Oct. 23, 14:11 - Nov. 04, 18:50
Mars in Aquarius, Nov. 04, 18:51 - Nov. 22, 11:30

YOUR LUCK MAGNETISM
Jupiter in Libra, Oct. 23, 14:11 - Nov. 22, 11:30

World Events

Nov. 10 – Children's TV show *Sesame Street* premieres on PBS television.

Nov. 19 – The second Moon landing is made by *Apollo 12*.

Beatle John Lennon and his wife Yoko after staying in bed for a week as a protest against world violence

SAGITTARIUS
Your Personal Planets

YOUR LOVE POTENTIAL
Venus in Scorpio, Nov. 22, 11:31 - Dec. 04, 14:40
Venus in Sagittarius, Dec. 04, 14:41 - Dec. 22, 0:43

YOUR DRIVE AND AMBITION
Mars in Aquarius, Nov. 22, 11:31 - Dec. 15, 14:21
Mars in Pisces, Dec. 15, 14:22 - Dec. 22, 0:43

YOUR LUCK MAGNETISM
Jupiter in Libra, Nov. 22, 11:31 - Dec. 16, 15:54
Jupiter in Scorpio, Dec. 16, 15:55 - Dec. 22, 0:43

World Events

Nov. 25 – John Lennon returns his OBE in protest against British support of the Vietnam War.

Dec. 18 – In Britain, the death penalty for murder is abolished.

SCORPIO
From October 23, 14:11 through November 22, 11:30

The Mysterious Rebel

The only party that a 1969 Scorpio may want to attend is a masquerade ball. Then, just before the stroke of midnight, when everybody is supposed to reveal his or her true identity, you slip out the back door. You love to have a good time; you just don't want to do it in public. You'd rather serenade yourself in the mirror than jump onstage at a karaoke bar. It's really a shame because you have a kind of movie-star mystique that is rare and compelling.

You have a daring sense of humor that either delights or shocks people. The year you were born, Philip Roth published *Portnoy's Complaint*. The book's relentless mocking of sexual taboos mirrors your own humor. You enjoy challenging social conventions and probably admire comedians like George Carlin and Lenny Bruce. Your "take-no-prisoners" style would make you an excellent film critic, political journalist, or cultural commentator. You're also good at spotting trends. You could have great success in the stock market, either as a trader or casual investor.

Solitary pursuits bring you joy. Meditation, prayer, and spiritual exploration make you feel centered and strong, though you must watch for extremes. Maintaining a close-knit circle of pals will only add to your physical, emotional, and spiritual well being. By balancing your private and social lives, you can get both the peace and support you need to be content.

Quiet, introspective people suit you best. Taureans, Cancerians, Virgos, and Scorpios probably make up a majority of your friends. Do your best to honor their presence in your life. When the chips are down, you will need a shoulder to cry on. Romantically, you are best suited to a partner who is affectionate but self-sufficient. You appreciate self-motivated people and respect their resourceful behavior.

Your greatest challenge as a 1969 Scorpio is to become more outgoing. Push yourself to go out with friends, even when your first instinct is to stay home with a good book. A love of truth is your greatest strength. Folks know they can trust your version of the facts because you rarely embellish stories.

SAGITTARIUS
From November 22, 11:31 through December 22, 0:43

The Popular Optimist

Eminently popular, the 1969 Sagittarius is a shoo-in for public office. Your phone is constantly ringing, and your welcome mat is worn thin. Every neighborhood committee wants you for a member, and you probably head at least one social club. The secret to your success is your vivacity. You infuse the air with energy; even die-hard couch potatoes are stirred to action in your presence. The year you were born, the first humans walked on the Moon. People feel a similar sense of "anything is possible" when working with you.

In terms of a career, you need a position that places you in the spotlight. You'd make an excellent politician, entertainer, or news anchor. People trust you and look to you for inspiration. Consequently, you might also want to look into work as a motivational speaker, spiritual leader, or civil rights lawyer. You could also be a popular exercise guru, as you have a serious interest in the mind-body connection. When stress starts to weigh down on you, head for the gym. Exercise is tremendously beneficial to you mentally, spiritually, and physically.

Blessed with tremendous faith, you know when to give way to your higher power. Many folks in the public spotlight think they can control their destinies but you may know better. The older you get, the easier it will be to open yourself to the fabulous surprises life has to offer. Instead of steering the speedboat, you're content to water ski behind it. Neurosis is not part of your vocabulary; you know that worry accomplishes nothing.

Although you get along with every sign in the zodiac, your favorite folks are friendly and outgoing. Ariens, Geminis, Leos, and Sagittarians help maintain your high spirits. Ideally, your romantic partner will share your love of adventure and enjoy traveling as much as you do.

Loving and giving, your greatest challenge as a 1969 Archer is to put limits on your accessibility. If this means cutting yourself off from the world at times, so be it. Your biggest strength is your vivacity. Keep it high by surrounding yourself with optimistic, can-do people like yourself.

➤ Read about your Chinese Astrological sign on page 838. ➤ Read about your Personal Planets on page 826. ➤ Read about your personal Mystical Card on page 856.

CAPRICORN
From December 22, 0:44 through December 31, 23:59

The Hopeful Humanitarian

Idealistic and determined, the December-born 1969 Capricorn is always looking to improve his or her surroundings. From a very early age, you were conscious of injustice and demanded to know the reasons behind inequities. Your fair-minded attitude makes you a popular figure, and you probably have friends from all walks of life. Traveling in large groups gives you comfort, and you may be a member of several social clubs.

You share many qualities with the characters in the television series, *Mission: Impossible*, that was enjoying so much popularity during the year you were born. Mundane tasks do not interest you so much as those that are truly challenging and you thrive in doing work that involves helping others. You'd be a great union organizer, health advocate, or scientist. Although your methods are unconventional, they are effective. At first, your colleagues may question your sanity, but after they've worked with you a while, they will understand that there is a method to your madness.

You have a persuasive way of talking that wins over even the grumpiest opponents. Sympathetic and understanding, you know how to structure an effective argument. The more resistant your opponent, the harder you try to change their mind. People admire your tenacity and will give you a chance even when the odds are against you. You're the type who makes luck rather than stumbles upon it.

Although you love all sorts of people, your favorites are honest and hard-working. Taureans, Cancerians, Virgos, and Capricorns make up most of your inner circle. Romantically, you need someone tender, compassionate, and nurturing. You delight in coming home to loving hugs, kisses, and caresses after a hard day's work.

As a December-born 1969 Capricorn, your greatest challenge lies in asking for the love you deserve. The only way to overcome this problem is through practice. Your greatest strength is your humanitarian spirit. So long as you keep working to make life better for others, you'll always be satisfied in yourself. Your services are desperately needed and appreciated; keep up the good work.

1969
CAPRICORN
Your Personal Planets

YOUR LOVE POTENTIAL
Venus in Sagittarius, Dec. 22, 0:44 - Dec. 28, 11:03
Venus in Capricorn, Dec. 28, 11:04 - Dec. 31, 23:59
YOUR DRIVE AND AMBITION
Mars in Pisces, Dec. 22, 0:44 - Dec. 31, 23:59
Your Luck Magnetism
Jupiter in Scorpio, Dec. 22, 0:44 - Dec. 31, 23:59

World Events

Dec. 22 - German film director Joseph von Sternberg dies.

Dec. 24 - Four people, including cult leader Charles Manson, are arrested and charged with the murder of Sharon Tate.

Janis Joplin
January 19, 1943 - October 4, 1970

JANIS JOPLIN
Aquarius

Janis *was* the blues. When she rose to take the stage, the power of her transcendent voice made hearts pound and souls rise. The planet Venus rules love, beauty, and art. Janis's Venus was placed in her twelfth house of secrets and the subconscious at the moment of her birth in Port Arthur, Texas, in 1943. This positioning emphasized her great sensitivity to the world around her. Janis's amazing talent is indicated all through her chart. Mercury was making a special angle to Venus when she was born, endowing her with astonishing singing skills. Her abilities were recognized by The Village Voice after her performance at the Monterey Pop Festival in 1967: "She sure projects.... She jumps and runs and pounces, vibrating the audience with solid sound. The range of her earthy dynamic voice seems almost without limits," the papers reported. It was just one of many rave reviews she would receive through her short life.

The world took notice of her after the Monterey Pop Festival. Her fiery performance on that day was helped by the placement of feisty Jupiter. Jupiter is the planet of luck and grace. On June 16, 17, and 18 of 1967, Jupiter was charged up in the sign of Leo, ruler of fame and performance. It was making a positive aspect by sign to Janis's Mars in Sagittarius. Mars is power and drive, and Sagittarius is the home sign of Jupiter. This was a very good forecast indeed for Janis Joplin's short but intense bout with fame and glory. She burned like a flame for a few great years but, sadly, her light was extinguished too soon.

Janis was known for her hard drinking and passionate romantic involvements. At her birth, her Moon, in the watery, emotional sign of Cancer, was in contact with Neptune, planet of fantasy, self-delusion, and dreams. Besides the artistic accomplishments this can

bring, it can also lead to addictions of all sorts. Janis died of a heroin overdose at age twenty-seven. The clash of these contradictory characteristics combined to bring this young woman, seething with great potential, to a tragically early demise.

➤ Read Elvis Presley's Star Profile on page 457   ➤ Read The Beatles' Star Profile on page 529

1970

Hopeful New Decade: Neptune in Sagittarius

In 1970, as spiritual Neptune began to move into high-minded Sagittarius, the world was filled with idealism. Society was dazzled by the building of the massive World Trade Center. Books and movies had happy endings and music spoke of love. There was hope that humanity would conquer its worst tendencies and join hands in universal brotherhood. Revolutionary Pluto in the last of hard-working Virgo continued to be felt. In the 1960s, this was seen in social and political catharsis. In 1970, it still carried the revolutionary ghosts that remained unappeased. The Vietnam War dragged on despite global protests. Crosby, Stills, Nash, and Young echoed the outcry against the invasion of Cambodia: "Four Dead In Ohio." Positively, the first Earth Day was celebrated. Entrepreneurial Jupiter, planet of leadership, "opposed" Saturn, planet of structure and limitation. Together, these planets symbolize changes in leadership, both popular and political. This was seen when pop culture was rocked by the Beatles' break-up, George Harrison reincarnating with "My Sweet Lord." In politics, French President de Gaulle's death marked an era's end, while Egyptian President Nasser fell to a heart attack, to be succeeded by moderate Sadat.

With disruptive Uranus in Libra, linked to equality and co-operation, being nice was replaced by being "real." Women were gaining more equal recognition and U.S. President Nixon reduced the voting age to eighteen. Uranus's irreverence was expressed as Robert Altman's *M*A*S*H* exposed the ugly underbelly of war, spawning the black-comedy movement.

American rock star Jimi Hendrix dies of an overdose

The Aswan Dam is completed

U.S. soldiers returning from the invasion of Cambodia

EVERY PLOT OF GROUND HAS A HISTORY

Paranormal activity occurs regularly at the Toys`R'Us store built over the old Murphy ranch in Sunnyvale, California. Mornings bring scattered books and toys; aisle 15C smells of fresh flowers; and water faucets turn themselves on and off. In May 1970, psychic Sylvia Brown discovered the ghost "Crazy Johnny"—a ranch hand who died in 1884—was responsible for the disturbances. Johnny had no intention of leaving as he was still waiting for his true love Beth, who had left the ranch to marry an East Coast lawyer.

CHANGING OF THE GUARD

Starved and exhausted after thirty months of fighting, Biafra was crushed and became part of Nigeria again. Skyjackings proliferated, as Palestinian extremists attempted to gain objectives through terror. In Egypt, the Aswan Dam was completed with Russian financial aid. In Jordan, Palestinian terrorists blew up three hijacked jets on the ground at Amman airport. During a protest against the sending of U.S. troops to Cambodia, the National Guard killed four people and injured another seven at Kent State in Ohio. The gay rights movement took a giant step forward as protesters marched in New York for liberalization of discriminating laws. Similar protests took place in Britain and Australia. The first Boeing 747 "Jumbo" jet in Britain landed at London's Heathrow airport. The fabulously popular Beatles disbanded and Paul McCartney struck out on his own, releasing the Omega album, *McCartney*. Drugs killed both Janis Joplin and Jimi Hendrix. British publisher Allen Lane, pioneer of the paperback, died. Several world leaders departed the scene with the deaths of Portugal's Salazar, Egypt's Nasser, and France's de Gaulle.

➤ Read Richard Nixon's Star Profile on page 577.

CAPRICORN

From January 01, 0:00 through January 20, 11:23

The Thoughtful Builder

As a Capricorn born in January 1970, you have more physical energy than most people—energy that fuels your natural drive to be the best and to get to the top. However, unlike the typical Capricorn, you may be torn by ethical or emotional dilemmas that reflect the social strife of your birth year. Periodic setbacks make your lifestyle a natural "two steps forward, one step back" advance.

When you came into this world, segregation issues and massive anti-war rallies like the 60,000 demonstrators who met in Washington, DC, were commonplace, pitting conservative and liberal factions of society vehemently against each other. These events form an integral part of your psyche so that questions of right and wrong constantly influenced your moral compass through your developmental years.

You are lucky to have an intense passion about something in life, and often this finds expression in your career. You have an unusual ability to penetrate to the truth of matters, and this makes you good at anything that requires research, deep thought, or persuasion. You have the ambition and drive to become very successful, as long as you aren't too troubled by any hypocrisy that may be lurking in your place of work.

In your personal relationships, you tend toward the more traditional side, and are likely to honor holiday seasons, birthdays, and family gatherings as best you can. Although you may have been a late-starter in romance, you are likely to be a highly sensual and loving person. You may have a subtle wild side which finds expression through your selection of friends, who may seem out of sync to your family. In general, your best partners are Taureans, Virgos, Scorpios, and Pisceans.

A challenge in your life may have been established by the intense moral confrontations that took place in 1970. You may speak out for your cause and sacrifice personal goals, or you may build a personal career but sacrifice your principles. Ultimately, neither will be satisfying. Your special gift is that when you find the balance, you are setting a standard that helps make the world a better place.

AQUARIUS

From January 20, 11:24 through February 19, 1:41

The Lively Visionary

Aquarius of 1970 has an unusually bold and confident personality that enjoys a good challenge, especially one that takes on authority figures or bucks tradition. You may be driven to maintain your personal independence in the face of overwhelming odds, and this increases your willingness to take risks and to find new friends.

Your personal convictions were formed in the crucible of tumultuous 1970 events—such as Arthur Ashe being denied a visa to play tennis in South Africa because of the apartheid laws that banned blacks. This feeling of injustice lives with you, so that you seek fair treatment within the system. Sometimes you may blurt out an uncomfortable truth, although you have likely adopted a cool or trendy style.

As a 1970 Aquarius you have a strong sense of aesthetics and fashion. This can be usefully translated into a career as an artist, graphic designer, or in advertising and marketing. You may enjoy the high-risk environment of creating new technologies, and may also be adept at networking. However, your innate sense of perfection may intrude on a steady working situation, so being a freelancer or having a skill that can provide you with work anywhere would be beneficial.

With friends and family you have a genuinely loving disposition, and as long as you aren't forced into family functions, you regard relatives as friends. However, if you are told what to do, your first reaction is to do the opposite. Making a commitment may be difficult for you since it interferes with your need to come and go as you please. If you have found a good partnership, it may be rocked by constant change. You tend to get along best with Ariens, Geminis, Librans, and Sagittarians.

Your challenge as a 1970 Aquarius is that you have an activist's desire for peace, both in your personal relationships and in the world around you. Yet when others don't live up to your hopes or expectations, it can drive you into loneliness or isolation. Your gift is that you have the vision to help usher in the New Age, plus a lively spirit to push beyond those traditions and people tied to the past.

➤ Read about your Chinese Astrological sign on page 838. ➤ Read about your Personal Planets on page 826. ➤ Read about your personal Mystical Card on page 856.

CAPRICORN
Your Personal Planets

YOUR LOVE POTENTIAL
Venus in Capricorn, Jan. 01, 0:00 - Jan. 20, 11:23
YOUR DRIVE AND AMBITION
Mars in Pisces, Jan. 01, 0:00 - Jan. 20, 11:23
YOUR LUCK MAGNETISM
Jupiter in Scorpio, Jan. 01, 0:00 - Jan. 20, 11:23

World Events

Jan. 1 – The age of majority is reduced from twenty-one to eighteen in the U.S.
Jan. 15 – Lt-General Philipp Efiong, commander of the Biafran forces surrenders.

End of the Nigerian Civil War

AQUARIUS
Your Personal Planets

YOUR LOVE POTENTIAL
Venus in Capricorn, Jan. 20, 11:24 - Jan. 21, 7:25
Venus in Aquarius, Jan. 21, 7:26 - Feb. 14, 5:03
Venus in Pisces, Feb. 14, 5:04 - Feb. 19, 1:41
YOUR DRIVE AND AMBITION
Mars in Pisces, Jan. 20, 11:24 - Jan. 24, 21:28
Mars in Aries, Jan. 24, 21:29 - Feb. 19, 1:41
YOUR LUCK MAGNETISM
Jupiter in Scorpio, Jan. 20, 11:24 - Feb. 19, 1:41

World Events

Jan. 28 – Arthur Ashe is denied a visa to play tennis in South Africa due to apartheid laws.
Feb. 2 – The first nerve transplant is performed in Munich.

1970

PISCES
Your Personal Planets

YOUR LOVE POTENTIAL
Venus in Pisces, Feb. 19, 1:42 - Mar. 10, 5:24
Venus in Aries, Mar. 10, 5:25 - Mar. 21, 0:55

YOUR DRIVE AND AMBITION
Mars in Aries, Feb. 19, 1:42 - Mar. 07, 1:27
Mars in Taurus, Mar. 07, 1:28 - Mar. 21, 0:55

YOUR LUCK MAGNETISM
Jupiter in Scorpio, Feb. 19, 1:42 - Mar. 21, 0:55

World Events

Mar. 5 - The Nuclear Non-Proliferation Treaty comes into effect between the U.S., the USSR, and forty-one other nations.

Mar. 18 - Postal workers go on strike for the first time in U.S. history.

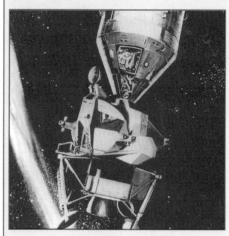

A serious electrical fault is discovered aboard "Apollo 13"

ARIES
Your Personal Planets

YOUR LOVE POTENTIAL
Venus in Aries, Mar. 21, 0:56 - Apr. 03, 10:04
Venus in Taurus, Apr. 03, 10:05 - Apr. 20, 12:14

YOUR DRIVE AND AMBITION
Mars in Taurus, Mar. 21, 0:56 - Apr. 18, 18:58
Mars in Gemini, Apr. 18, 18:59 - Apr. 20, 12:14

YOUR LUCK MAGNETISM
Jupiter in Scorpio, Mar. 21, 0:56 - Apr. 20, 12:14

World Events

Apr. 10 - British pop band The Beatles splits up.

Apr. 17 - The U.S. spacecraft *Apollo 13* successfully splashes down after its abortive mission to the Moon.

PISCES
From February 19, 1:42 through March 21, 0:55

The Universal Lover

As a 1970 Pisces, you carry with you the urge for transcendence that an entire counter-culture hoped to experience. You may feel the rhythms of life as a struggle between the harsh realities of daily living, and the enjoyable awareness of a more beautiful place or state of mind. You are likely to have a highly developed sense of compassion and caring for the well-being of others, and an instinctive understanding of Mother Nature.

On March 5, 1970, the Nuclear Non-Proliferation Treaty came into effect between the U.S., the USSR, and forty-one other nations. This event underscores your desire to overcome individual differences for the benefit of the larger group. The 1970 hits "Let It Be" by Paul McCartney and "Bridge Over Troubled Water" by Simon and Garfunkel were also instrumental vibes in shaping your developing personality.

You probably carry a deep desire to help the underprivileged, handicapped, or those who are otherwise at a disadvantage, and may have developed a career out of this natural instinct. Dealing with financial needs may be a struggle, as the obligation of making a living can distract you from your spiritual side. Your interest in the newest technologies may find a career outlet in biotechnology, the pharmaceutical industry, or in New Age professions.

Family means a lot to you—more than to most Pisceans. You may have become a parent at an early age, or perhaps your relationship with your parents is an ongoing, mutually rewarding connection. You learn about yourself through the mirror of relationship, and every confrontation or meaningful encounter helps shape your personality. In general, you get along best with Cancerians, Scorpios, Virgos, and Taureans.

You have a deep faith in the Universe, and a profound respect for the mystery of life. Yet this personal attunement to the invisible realms may challenge your ability or willingness to fulfill daily tasks. You may feel it's easier to escape into music or other self-indulgences. Your gift and strength is your ability to translate your spiritual perception into concrete form for others to recognize.

ARIES
From March 21, 0:56 through April 20, 12:14

The Steady Pioneer

As a 1970 Aries, you have a strong drive to make an impact on the world, and to assert your natural optimism while others get bogged down in hopelessness or entrenched patterns from the past. You are likely to have absorbed the moral and social dilemmas of 1970, and push to make progress with a better plan—one that hasn't been explored by others. You can be a trendsetter and pioneer.

On April 10, 1970, the British pop group The Beatles split up. This event reflects the cosmic energy prevalent during your birth month, and features the willingness and desire to go your own way when status-quo situations are too unhealthy or unsafe for the common good. As in the case of The Beatles, issues of moral right and wrong will probably pop up frequently in your life, giving you the opportunity to pioneer a new path.

In your professional life, you are likely to understand the value of consistent, steady work, for which you can be well paid. You have an indomitable stamina that can persevere with diligence long after others have quit. One area that might bring difficulty is in your relations with co-workers or bosses, since you strive to be as independent as possible. Owning a small business, or being a freelancer or consultant, might work best.

In your relationships, you may find that your allegiance to traditional modes of interaction competes with your urge to explore new friendships and possible romances. The sexual morality of 1970 was breaking new ground, and from time to time you, too, may find yourself in morally questionable situations. You get along best with Geminis, Leos, and Sagittarians, while Librans may give you pleasure or pain.

One of your greatest challenges is to build a safe bridge to the future without leaving the past embittered and out in the cold. Likely as not, you have a great desire to move forward, but can get caught up in personal battles that only make situations worse. Your strength is that when you help build a harmonious interface between the people who represent the past and future, you are heroically moving us all along the path of steady progress.

➤ Read about your Chinese Astrological sign on page 838. ➤ Read about your Personal Planets on page 826. ➤ Read about your personal Mystical Card on page 856.

TAURUS

From April 20, 12:15 through May 21, 11:36

The Reliable Trendsetter

Taureans from 1970 have a great interest in social interactions and are likely to have many friends from diverse backgrounds. From time to time, you may be uniquely placed to recognize some problem or difficulty that can only be resolved through major change, and you may feel a responsibility to enlist others to help make those changes. You can take care of others by showing them their independence.

Two historical events took place in your birth month that reflect your unique astrological strengths. The first Earth Day was held on April 22, 1970; and four students were shot dead in Kent State, Ohio, on May 4, while protesting the U.S. invasion of Cambodia. Earth Day and the student teach-ins that followed the Kent State incident both demonstrated the power of ideas to change a system heading in the wrong direction.

Your professional life may be strengthened both by your ability to take care of resources and by your interest in disseminating information and new ideas. You have an unusual amount of personal charisma, and can get along well with others—two personal assets that will take you far in your business or work environment. You are also capable of handling great responsibility, and this can lead you to top management positions.

In your personal relationships, communication can be very important to you. You enjoy sharing ideas and plans, and you may find traveling together a wonderful way to enjoy good times. While you were younger, you may have experimented with different kinds of relationships, but by thirty you probably felt ready to make a serious commitment. In general, you get along best with Geminis, Virgos, Librans, and Capricorns.

One significant challenge for you is that you frequently have to change your plans after arrangements have been finalized. You may be constantly under pressure to redefine your goals, your travel plans, and your finances, as new people or information arrives. Your strength is that you are unusually flexible for a Taurus, and can bend with the wind as the situation demands. You are capable of instituting fundamental changes.

GEMINI

From May 21, 11:37 through June 21, 19:42

The Twin Paths

As a 1970 Gemini, you have a naturally inventive mind that can lead you down paths that are different from your family heritage or social traditions. You're capable of seeing things from angles that others haven't considered, and this can give you a quick wit, a facility with words, and an ability to receive and transmit original ideas. You are likely to question everything, including authority and the way things have been done in the past.

On June 3, 1970, Lars Gorbind of the University of Wisconsin synthesized the first artificial gene. This scientific breakthrough is characteristic of the tenor of your birth month, in that an entirely new direction was established. In the same way, through your curiosity and steadfast purpose, you may open up new vistas for fruitful exploration. While your specialty may not be biotechnology, you have the same keen interest in finding new paths.

In your professional life, you are likely to enjoy diversity, and are able to move easily between one task or project and the next. You have a great restlessness, and unless you are busy making significant breakthroughs, or teaching and spreading new ideas, you may find it difficult to stay in one job for very long. At times you may find yourself with two jobs, one for personal interest and the other to pay the bills.

In your relationships you value stability. You also enjoy interacting with many different kinds of people—and herein lies a dilemma. Moving between commitment and personal freedom can be a tricky process for you, as can finding companions that both your family and your circle of friends can enjoy. In general, you get along best with Cancerians, Leos, Librans, and Sagittarians.

A major challenge for you may be settling on a life path that satisfies your desire to explore new frontiers and to enjoy financial security and stable relationships. If you can't find the balance point, you may find yourself either flitting about aimlessly or caught in a rut. Your gift is that once you have found it, you may become a source of inspiration to others and help to create positive change.

➤ Read about your Chinese Astrological sign on page 838. ➤ Read about your Personal Planets on page 826. ➤ Read about your personal Mystical Card on page 856.

TAURUS
Your Personal Planets

YOUR LOVE POTENTIAL
Venus in Taurus, Apr. 20, 12:15 - Apr. 27, 20:32
Venus in Gemini, Apr. 27, 20:33 - May 21, 11:36

YOUR DRIVE AND AMBITION
Mars in Taurus, Apr. 20, 12:15 - May 21, 11:36

YOUR LUCK MAGNETISM
Jupiter in Scorpio, Apr. 20, 12:15 - Apr. 30, 6:43
Jupiter in Libra, Apr. 30, 6:44 - May 21, 11:36

World Events

Apr. 22 – The first Earth Day, organized to draw attention to the dangers posed by pollution to the environment, is celebrated in the U.S.

May 15 – Elizabeth Hoisington and Anna May Hays become the first women to be nominated as U.S. Generals.

Death of British author E.M. Forster

GEMINI
Your Personal Planets

YOUR LOVE POTENTIAL
Venus in Gemini, May 21, 11:37 - May 22, 14:18
Venus in Cancer, May 22, 14:19 - June 16, 17:48
Venus in Leo, June 16, 17:49 - June 21, 19:42

YOUR DRIVE AND AMBITION
Mars in Gemini, May 21, 11:37 - June 02, 6:49
Mars in Cancer, June 02, 6:50 - June 21, 19:42

YOUR LUCK MAGNETISM
Jupiter in Libra, May 21, 11:37 - June 21, 19:42

World Events

June 4 – The islands of Tonga receive independence from Britain.

June 7 – British author E. M. Forster dies.

1970

CANCER
Your Personal Planets

YOUR LOVE POTENTIAL
Venus in Leo, June 21, 19:43 - July 12, 12:15
Venus in Virgo, July 12, 12:16 - July 23, 6:36

YOUR DRIVE AND AMBITION
Mars in Cancer, June 21, 19:43 - July 18, 6:42
Mars in Leo, July 18, 6:43 - July 23, 6:36

YOUR LUCK MAGNETISM
Jupiter in Libra, June 21, 19:43 - July 23, 6:36

World Events

June 22 - U.S. President Nixon reduces the voting age from twenty-one to eighteen.

July 21 - The Aswan Dam on the Nile River is completed.

The Aswan Dam is completed

LEO
Your Personal Planets

YOUR LOVE POTENTIAL
Venus in Virgo, July 23, 6:37 - Aug. 08, 9:58
Venus in Libra, Aug. 08, 9:59 - Aug. 23, 13:33

YOUR DRIVE AND AMBITION
Mars in Leo, July 23, 6:37 - Aug. 23, 13:33

YOUR LUCK MAGNETISM
Jupiter in Libra, July 23, 6:37 - Aug. 15, 17:56
Jupiter in Scorpio, Aug. 15, 17:57 - Aug. 23, 13:33

World Events

July 27 - Portuguese leader Antonio d'Oliviera Salazar dies.

Aug. 10 - For the first time in 116 years, New York bar McSorley's opens its doors to women, after the signing of a bill banning sexual discrimination in public places.

CANCER
From June 21, 19:43 through July 23, 6:36

The Natural Defender

As a 1970 Cancer, you have a strong instinct to protect your family and loved ones, and you are always willing to fight for those who come under your protection, if the situation calls for it. You may find that your family interests are much larger than the nuclear family, and include a favorite faction within the larger society. You are likely to be unusually sensitive and reactionary, and have a need to establish clear boundaries.

On June 22, 1970, President Nixon lowered the voting age from twenty-one to eighteen. Then, on July 21, the Aswan Dam on the Nile was completed. Both these events reflect an astrological theme of your birth month—and that is the proud awakening of a new era within the collective society. In the same way, you take great pride in defending your family or your people, whoever they might be.

Championing the underprivileged or disenfranchised may be a part of your professional career or vocation. You may get a head start through family connections, or enjoy working in a family-run business. If you work outside your inherited family, your co-workers may eventually become like family members to you. You have a strong aesthetic awareness, and may be gifted in the arts, music, or fashion worlds.

In your relationships, your shared living conditions are likely to be a top priority for you. You have a strong desire to take charge within the household, and your relationship status probably depends on how well others let you do this. You can be very moody at times, and if your partner can go with the flow, then you are lucky. You get along best with Virgos, Scorpios, and Pisceans. Librans can either drive you bananas or help keep you emotionally balanced.

A major life challenge for you might be knowing when to fight for your rights, and when to let things slide. Perhaps you get bogged down in trivial arguments by blowing up minor incidents into huge disputes. Or, you may get overly defensive when no insult was intended. Your strength is your willingness to fight for the underdog, and to bring justice to those harmed by cruelty, ignorance, or bigotry.

LEO
From July 23, 6:37 through August 23, 13:33

The Talented Hero

You take great pride in doing things in a big way and with a big heart, 1970 Leo. You are probably more self-confident and spirited than most Leos of the twentieth century, and are likely to have exquisite taste in your lifestyle choices. Fiery, dramatic, and occasionally presumptuous, you enjoy being the center of attention through your great acts of creativity or generosity.

Portuguese dictator Antonio Salazar died on July 27, 1970. His forty-two years in power represent a vibration prevalent during your birth month, and can be characterized by its enduring strength, but also by the notion of personal superiority. Another series of events which took place during the month you were born offers a more constructive image— the concerted effort by the U.S., the UN, and world leaders to find a lasting peace in the Middle East.

Your career is likely to carry with it these same traits of doing even small things in a big way, and being willing to tackle seemingly insurmountable financial obstacles or competition. You are a doer; you can see the big picture, and have grand ideas about how to proceed. You have a driving ambition to make a lot of money, so how well you meet others' objections or envy may determine your level of prosperity. You do best when you are your own boss.

In your personal life, you love to be in love. Fine dining and expensive entertainment is probably a favorite romantic evening. You are likely to place a high value on performance, and that can include your choices in sports, theater, or in bed. You need a partner that appreciates your most outstanding talents, and you are not shy about expressing them. You may get along best with Librans, Sagittarians, and Ariens.

A major challenge in your life is to get along with others while being the best, most creative, strongest person you can be. Your ability to rise above others can generate much hostility and jealousy. Your gift is that when you tone down your brilliance, you can be a magnificent example of independence and self-sufficiency, leading others to break away from the inconsequential and subservient.

➤ Read about your Chinese Astrological sign on page 838. ➤ Read about your Personal Planets on page 826. ➤ Read about your personal Mystical Card on page 856.

VIRGO

From August 23, 13:34 through September 23, 10:58

The Focused Technician

As a 1970 Virgo, your consistent attention to practical matters and ability to discriminate between what's useful and what's pointless has served you well following the social chaos of your birth era. While others have waffled over various moral issues, or flamed out by taking unhealthy risks, you have the work ethic and drive for stability that brings personal security and national pride.

You have a highly analytical, probing mind. This characteristic was part of the cosmic forces in play during the month of your birth and was reflected by the first computer chess tournament held in August 1970. The same integrated logic required to understand computer chess became part of your psyche—and a natural asset in helping develop your job skills.

You have tremendous capacity for hard work, and would enjoy a career where you feel you are being helpful or are serving others' needs. Any health profession, especially one that incorporates advanced technology, is particularly suitable. Your keen analytical skills would be adept at computer technology, biotechnology, or any profession where you could feel appreciated for your expertise and attention to details. You also have unusually good people skills and might prosper in sales.

The sexual revolution of your era may have tempted you to experiment with different partners as you were growing up, and you have strong powers of attraction and a romantic streak. But, as you matured, you probably realized your greatest need was for a committed relationship. Stable relationships with co-workers, family, and friends are also a high priority for you, for which you would sacrifice much. You get along best with Taureans, Cancerians, Scorpios, and Capricorns.

Your challenge is to use your intense mental power for constructive use, perhaps in research, communications, or in managing your work. The tendency might be to become too focused on a personal problem, or to obsess about a situation until you lose track of what's really important. Your gift is your inherent belief in infinite intelligence, which can always lead you out of the darkness.

LIBRA

From September 23, 10:59 through October 23, 20:03

The Faithful Lover

As a 1970 Libra, you have a keen interest in maintaining your personal freedom within relationships. Unlike most Librans, you are probably not very willing to sacrifice your own needs for the sake of a partner. If you do subjugate your own priorities to your mate's, you tend to become depressed or combative. You may be attracted to many different kinds of people, including the sexually ambivalent or those much older or younger than you.

Janis Joplin died of a drug overdose on October 4, 1970, a victim of her own depression and a failed affair. Of course your karma is not as hopeless as this rock star's, but this event reflects some of the celestial currents prevalent during your birth month. The willingness to explore sexual alternatives to mainstream morality is one theme, as is the need to control your own intense desires to maintain a feeling of balance.

You have unusually good people skills, which puts you at great advantage in the business world. You probably have a strong work ethic and would do well at any job that requires a methodical, careful, and detailed approach. With your efficient and pleasant manner at work, you would be an asset to any business or professional work environment. In a small-business situation, you would work well with an open-minded partner.

Naturally, relationships mean a lot to you, but for any long-term arrangement you need to be able to come and go as you please. You have a unique spiritual connection with the infinite (though probably not through the traditional religions), and your faith is critical to all your endeavors, especially finding a compatible significant other. In general, you get along best with Geminis, Virgos, Scorpios, and Aquarians.

A major challenge for you may be loss of faith. You have a powerful drive to discover spiritual truth, but may also be brought down by the greed, grimness, or selfishness found in everyday living. Your gift and special strength is that once you have established a solid channel with your deity, you are given an especially keen sense of justice and become a beacon for others to follow.

➤ Read about your Chinese Astrological sign on page 838. ➤ Read about your Personal Planets on page 826. ➤ Read about your personal Mystical Card on page 856.

1970

VIRGO
Your Personal Planets

YOUR LOVE POTENTIAL
Venus in Libra, Aug. 23, 13:34 - Sept. 07, 1:53
Venus in Scorpio, Sept. 07, 1:54 - Sept. 23, 10:58

YOUR DRIVE AND AMBITION
Mars in Leo, Aug. 23, 13:34 - Sept. 03, 4:56
Mars in Virgo, Sept. 03, 4:57 - Sept. 23, 10:58

YOUR LUCK MAGNETISM
Jupiter in Scorpio, Aug. 23, 13:34 - Sept. 23, 10:58

World Events

Sept. 13 – Margaret Court becomes the first woman since 1953 to win the tennis Grand Slam.

Sept. 18 – American rock star Jimi Hendrix dies from a drug overdose.

Death of American singer Janis Joplin

LIBRA
Your Personal Planets

YOUR LOVE POTENTIAL
Venus in Scorpio, Sept. 23, 10:59 - Oct. 23, 20:03

YOUR DRIVE AND AMBITION
Mars in Virgo, Sept. 23, 10:59 - Oct. 20, 10:56
Mars in Libra, Oct. 20, 10:57 - Oct. 23, 20:03

YOUR LUCK MAGNETISM
Jupiter in Scorpio, Sept. 23, 10:59 - Oct. 23, 20:03

World Events

Oct. 4 – American singer Janis Joplin dies from a drug overdose.

Oct. 5 – Anwar al-Sadat is elected to succeed Abdul Nasser as President of Egypt.

1970

SCORPIO
Your Personal Planets

YOUR LOVE POTENTIAL
Venus in Scorpio, Oct. 23, 20:04 - Nov. 22, 17:24

YOUR DRIVE AND AMBITION
Mars in Libra, Oct. 23, 20:04 - Nov. 22, 17:24

YOUR LUCK MAGNETISM
Jupiter in Scorpio, Oct. 23, 20:04 - Nov. 22, 17:24

World Events

Nov. 2 - Strategic Arms Limitation Talks (SALT) between the U.S. and USSR resume in Helsinki.

Nov. 9 - French President Charles de Gaulle dies.

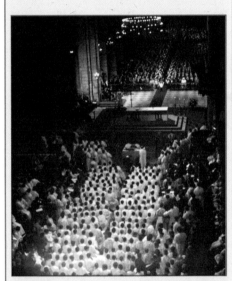

French President Charles de Gaulle's funeral

SAGITTARIUS
Your Personal Planets

YOUR LOVE POTENTIAL
Venus in Scorpio, Nov. 22, 17:25 - Dec. 22, 6:35

YOUR DRIVE AND AMBITION
Mars in Libra, Nov. 22, 17:25 - Dec. 06, 16:33
Mars in Scorpio, Dec. 06, 16:34 - Dec. 22, 6:35

YOUR LUCK MAGNETISM
Jupiter in Scorpio, Nov. 22, 17:25 - Dec. 22, 6:35

World Events

Dec. 2 - The Environmental Protection Agency (EPA) is established, with William Ruckelshaus as its head.

Dec. 4 - Mexican-American labor leader Cesar Chavez is jailed for failing to call off the "lettuce boycott."

SCORPIO
From October 23, 20:04 through November 22, 17:24

The Financial Wizard

As a 1970 Scorpio, you are likely to have great ambitions for your life, and a burning desire to change or reform the world in some manner. Unfortunately, you may also experience great opposition to your plans. While you may see this take a variety of forms in your life, it will usually relate to those who prefer the status quo and the tried-and-true ways of doing business.

On November 3, 1970, the newly elected President of Chile, Salvador Allende Gossens, took office despite the CIA's best efforts to stop him and his socialist reforms from challenging the economic plutocracy. The same desire to make broad, radical reforms is an astrological condition of your birth month, as is the desire to overcome all limitations, as when the Concorde SST exceeded twice the speed of sound for the first time on November 4, 1970.

In your professional life, you may have unusually keen insights into economic or financial affairs which would make you a successful financial planner, investment adviser, or manager of other people's money. You may find personal fulfillment as a reformer, lawyer, or advocate—careers in which you must deal with the entrenched interests of others. Your job may depend on making clients more prosperous or healthy, or in challenging some existing order.

You have a highly sexual temperament, but unlike most Scorpios, you may be willing to experiment with the status of your closest partnership. This might mean being friends rather than lovers, or being lovers rather than friends. Your love nature may find expression in your professional world, and you may enjoy having affairs with co-workers or clients. In general, you get along best with Cancerians, Scorpios, and Pisceans, and Capricorns.

A great challenge for you is to find the right battle and the just confrontation. You may think long and hard about good versus evil, and periodically feel hapless over how powerful the enemy is. You may fall victim to larger social or economic forces. Once you realize your true limitations and that you can't control everything, you are on the road to being the financial wizard.

SAGITTARIUS
From November 22, 17:25 through December 22, 6:35

The Grounded Wanderer

Sagittarius of 1970 tends to be more settled or stable than most Sagittarians of the twentieth century, though you still have a cosmopolitan view and a compelling urge to expand your horizons, both inner and outer. Forming enduring relationships keeps you anchored to some places, and you may have developed a fascination with resources and with finding the meaning of real security.

The Environmental Protection Agency was activated on December 2, 1970—an institutional breakthrough inspired by the first Earth Day earlier in the year. The underlying planetary forces allowing this event to unfold also influence your own life path, including the ecological vision of interconnectivity. In the social sense, you probably feel like a global citizen, and seek ways of managing our collective resources, both natural and economic.

You are likely to be one of the more practical Sagittarians, and this keeps you grounded in the business world. Occasionally, you may run into moral dilemmas because of your job, and this may force you to seek more fulfilling work. For example, you wouldn't have wanted a job at the tuna industry on December 15, 1970, when millions of cans of tuna were recalled because of mercury contamination.

Another area where you may find interesting ethical issues is in your personal relationships. Part of you wants a long-term, stable commitment, but another part is a romantic adventurer. Secret liaisons are possible, but can wreak havoc with your sense of stability. You may find that questions of loyalty, friendship, and non-attachment are frequently competing in your mind as to which has the highest value. In general, you get along best with Ariens, Leos, Librans, and Scorpios.

A major life challenge for you is coming to terms with commitment and personal freedom. In both your relationships and work environment you want to escape from boring routine, but being rootless is not satisfying either. Your gift is that once you understand the many paradoxes discovered along your path, you may find meaning in life's most mundane tasks, and feel comfortable in one place.

➤ Read about your Chinese Astrological sign on page 838. ➤ Read about your Personal Planets on page 826. ➤ Read about your personal Mystical Card on page 856.

CAPRICORN
From December 22, 6:36 through December 31, 23:59

The Strategic Builder

As a Capricorn born in December 1970, you probably live with a great ambition to overcome insurmountable obstacles. In all likelihood, you want to achieve something quite unusual or spectacular, which will demonstrate your strength and vitality. You are a natural builder and can make lasting achievements, if you start from a firm foundation. You may be irritated much of the time if you don't learn to deal creatively with resistance.

On December 23, 1970, the north tower of the World Trade Center was completed, making it the world's tallest building at the time. This monumental drive to be the best, the highest, and the most impressive is the dominant astrological theme during the last ten days of December 1970, when you were born. In the same way, you have this overwhelming urge to make something big happen in your life, and only sound planning and patience can achieve this goal.

In your professional life, you may be known for your aggressive strategies and willingness to take on powerful competition. You may take on too much financial risk to achieve your goals, or jump in too soon or too late when dealing with negotiations or clients. Getting a feel for the right time to act is your ticket to success, but it may mean holding back when you want to charge forward.

In your personal relationships, you may have a strong desire to be with the most beautiful, talented, and admired people. You have an incredibly strong sex drive, but if you feel that you don't match up to the ideal image, you may sabotage yourself through poor eating or health habits which will negatively affect your relationships. In general, you get along best with Taureans, Virgos, and Scorpios, and sometimes Ariens.

A big challenge in your life may be how to live up to your own expectations. Your intense drive to be the best will naturally run into major obstacles along the way, leading to much frustration and stress. You may press your luck and build a house of cards, but your strength is that if you learn patience and timing you may indeed become the best at something, especially if it benefits everyone.

1970
CAPRICORN
Your Personal Planets

YOUR LOVE POTENTIAL
Venus in Scorpio, Dec. 22, 6:36 - Dec. 31, 23:59

YOUR DRIVE AND AMBITION
Mars in Scorpio, Dec. 22, 6:36 - Dec. 31, 23:59

YOUR LUCK MAGNETISM
Jupiter in Scorpio, Dec. 22, 6:36 - Dec. 31, 23:59

World Events

Dec. 28 – The murderers of Canadian Prime Minister Pierre Laport are apprehended.

Dec. 31 – Paul McCartney initiates a suit against the other former Beatles to dissolve their company Beatles and Co.

Richard M. Nixon
January 9, 1913 - April 22, 1994

RICHARD M. NIXON
Capricorn

Richard Milhouse Nixon won his first political office as a staunch anti-communism crusader. During his candidacy for the vice-presidency alongside Eisenhower, he was accused of fiduciary misconduct. In a televised speech, he rebutted those charges and the American audience got a glimpse of the unattractive self-pity to which he was prone. Defeated by JFK in his initial run for the presidency, he and running-mate Spiro Agnew eventually gained the Oval Office in 1969. Once President, he was a controversial figure in the U.S., but was regarded as an excellent statesman abroad. He negotiated SALT I, the nuclear arms control agreement, and made his historic trip to China to establish relations in 1972. He also ended the Vietnam War. However, in 1973, Agnew was forced to resign on charges of federal income tax evasion and accepting kickbacks. In 1974, the ultimate scandal—Watergate—forced Nixon himself to resign to avoid impeachment.

Nixon was a Capricorn, a sign noted for its practicality and need for success and high achievement. In the early seventies, he worked to rebalance the American economy with price controls and the devaluation of the dollar. With his Sun, the planet of identity, receiving a contact from Saturn, the ruler of Capricorn, he was a hard worker and certainly believed in success. A difficult aspect from Neptune, planet of confusion, could account for Nixon's insecurity as well as the use of deception and undercover work behind the scenes.

Nixon's Mercury, the planet of communication, received a contact from expansive Jupiter, making him an outgoing and talkative person. Another contact from Mars, the planet of aggression, could explain his assertiveness and tendency to use "smear tactics" as part of his campaign strategy. These planets all together may perhaps explain his desire to record everything going on in the White House for posterity. Unfortunately, a difficult contact from Pluto, planet of manipulation and power struggles, in his house of career describes only too well the consequences that resulted from those infamous tapes.

➤ Read about John F. Kennedy in the Kennedy Family's Star Profile on page 497. ➤ Read Franklin D. Roosevelt's Star Profile on page 257. ➤ Read George W. Bush's Star Profile on page 817. ➤ Read Mao Tse-Tung's Star Profile on page 417.

1971

Freedom and Fantasy: Jupiter, Saturn, and Neptune

Jupiter, Saturn, and Neptune came together in 1971, correlating with dramatic events around the world. Jupiter, symbolizing growth and expansion, met with Neptune, representing unseen influences. At the same time, Saturn, the planet of structure and limitation, "opposed" them from across the heavens, inciting a dynamic interplay between constriction and expansion. With the addition of Neptune, people sensed an added element of fantasy or confusion, perhaps by choice. One manifestation of this was a noticeable upsurge in drug use. Drug searches were ordered for U.S. troops stationed in Vietnam and the Doors' Jim Morrison died of a drug overdose—the third rock legend to die this way in the space of a year. A study revealed that one-third of college students had tried marijuana. Epidemics, an expression of Neptune amplified by Jupiter's energy, were seen in the cholera and smallpox that hit refugees in the newly formed state of Bangladesh in the wake of civil war. Neptune also can be expressed positively as compassion to uplift the downtrodden. When rock star George Harrison responded by raising money to benefit the homeless Bengalis, he was spearheading its finest fulfillment.

The formation of Bangladesh was also signified in this planetary combination. Both Jupiter and Neptune are associated with religion. The polarity of Jupiter and Saturn can be seen to represent two factions in long-term disagreement or conflict. In this case, Saturn represented the old state of Pakistan. Jupiter and Neptune are shown in the religion-inspired founding of the new Bangladesh.

An "Apollo 15" astronaut saluting by the lunar module

Residents flee from a blazing street in Belfast

Russian composer Igor Stravinsky dies

CORRECTING THE BALANCE OF POWER

East Pakistan declared itself a separate nation as Bangladesh, but suffered brutal reprisals from west Pakistani armed forces. Famine and disease among Bangladeshis spurred rock stars George Harrison, Eric Clapton, and Bob Dylan to spearhead a gala benefit to aid victims. Communist China joined the United Nations and Britain joined the European Common Market. Violence and protest in Northern Ireland continued after the arrest of leaders of the Irish Republican Army. Fighting continued in Cambodia as communist forces occupied the ancient temple at Angkor Wat, which was damaged by artillery fire. *The Pentagon Papers*, a government study of the Vietnam War, was published. A bomb exploded in the Senate wing of the Capitol. U.S. astronauts Scott and Irwin went for a drive on the Moon. Three Russian cosmonauts were found dead in their Soyuz spacecraft after it returned to Earth. A quake measuring 6.6 on the Richter Scale hit San Fernando, California. Igor Stravinsky, Russian composer of *The Rite Of Spring*, died in New York. Sino-American relations warmed over the ping-pong table when a U.S. table-tennis team visited China.

➤ Read "Findhorn's Magical Garden" by Skye Alexander on page 585.

METEORIC LIFE

The analysis of an Australian meteorite found in 1971 indicated that the conditions for life to survive existed in space. Meteorites formed early in the history of the Solar System; some are believed to be fragments of minor planets. They may have been the originators of life on Earth. Researchers believe that many of the bodies in interplanetary space are rich in carbon-based organic chemicals which, when carried to the hot, wet conditions of early Earth, could have become the raw material for primitive life.

CAPRICORN

From January 01, 0:00 through January 20, 17:12

The Determined Hunter

As a 1971 January Capricorn, you have tremendous capacity to realize your goals and are fully able and willing to overcome any and all obstacles to get there. You can be very passionate about what you believe, and with a consistency and efficiency that leave others in your dust, you can zoom ahead with single-minded focus and determination.

The Vietnam War sharply divided people in your birth year, over the morality of the war, as well as lifestyle choices. On January 6, 1971, the commander of the U.S. forces in Vietnam ordered searches for marijuana users and growers. This event reflects in your own personality as an ability to find things that are hidden, and the need to demonstrate with determined action the rightness of your cause.

Born during an era of uncertainty, when much of the world was divided into opposing factions, you probably developed a strong desire to persuade others of the truth of your opinions and convictions. This mental edge can be used to great effect in your career choice. You may excel at research, and have a talent for finding important information, key people, and critical resources. The truth is that you can do anything you want to do in your professional life; you have the inner resources to reach for the stars.

Your personal relationships are extremely passionate, which makes life interesting but sometimes too intense. A tendency to spend too much time with mental preoccupations can challenge your commitments, diverting intimacy and love with communication "snafus." You need someone who understands your relentless approach to life. In general, you get along best with Taureans, Scorpios, Virgos, and Cancerians.

Your challenge is to find something worth fighting for, perhaps a cause or professional goal that makes good use of your personal power. You may get sidetracked by trivial but seemingly important problems that are not worth your time in the long run. Your strengths are many, and include a deep religious faith or spiritual awareness. If you have found the right path, you may achieve widespread recognition and great accomplishments.

AQUARIUS

From January 20, 17:13 through February 19, 7:26

The Restless Seeker

As an Aquarian born in 1971, you have an unusually powerful drive to find the truth and to convey your understanding in a unique or unusual manner. You were born at the beginning of the Age of Gurus, and carry a celestial mandate to seek out gifted teachers, and in your own way, to spread the news. You have an instinctive understanding that we are all essentially interconnected.

On February 11, 1971, a treaty banning nuclear weapons from the seabed beyond the standard twelve-mile coastal limit was signed by sixty-two nations. This event demonstrates a particular quality that is encoded in your sign, and that is the recognition of the big picture and how mutual accords can aid everyone. You are astrologically favored to see how the individual fits into the larger collective, and to take constructive action for everyone's mutual benefit.

Your career may have developed along lines that utilize your natural ability for abstract thinking. This may include technological development, social work, or any position where you can help move the world in a more progressive and innovative direction. You have a great restless spirit, and may change jobs regularly, always seeking better opportunities and new ways of expressing your knowledge.

Your personal relationships may revolve around your need to travel and to find the latest developments in your chosen field of work. Part of you enjoys a stable relationship, but you are always ready to expand your personal horizons. You may have developed a cosmopolitan philosophy through your studies and travels, and undoubtedly have met some great friends and lovers along the path. In general, you get along best with Geminis, Leos, Sagittarians, and Capricorns.

Your challenge is that you may drift too much in life, never finding a place to call home or a lifestyle that feels just right. Your special gift is that you have the potential to access cosmic truth, and can be a trendsetter in your special area of expertise. You have an inner mystic that can find the meaning of life, or more mundanely, the inventive solution to chronic social problems.

➤ Read about your Chinese Astrological sign on page 838. ➤ Read about your Personal Planets on page 826. ➤ Read about your personal Mystical Card on page 856.

CAPRICORN
Your Personal Planets

YOUR LOVE POTENTIAL
Venus in Scorpio, Jan. 01, 0:00 - Jan. 07, 0:59
Venus in Sagittarius, Jan. 07, 1:00 - Jan. 20, 17:12

YOUR DRIVE AND AMBITION
Mars in Scorpio, Jan. 01, 0:00 - Jan. 20, 17:12

YOUR LUCK MAGNETISM
Jupiter in Scorpio, Jan. 01, 0:00 - Jan. 14, 8:48
Jupiter in Sagittarius, Jan. 14, 8:49 - Jan. 20, 17:12

World Events

Jan. 15 – Presidents al-Sadat and Podgorny officially open the Aswan High Dam.
Jan. 10 – French fashion designer Coco Chanel dies.

Death of fashion designer Coco Chanel

AQUARIUS
Your Personal Planets

YOUR LOVE POTENTIAL
Venus in Sagittarius, Jan. 20, 17:13 - Feb. 05, 14:56
Venus in Capricorn, Feb. 05, 14:57 - Feb. 19, 7:26

YOUR DRIVE AND AMBITION
Mars in Scorpio, Jan. 20, 17:13 - Jan. 23, 1:33
Mars in Sagittarius, Jan. 23, 1:34 - Feb. 19, 7:26

YOUR LUCK MAGNETISM
Jupiter in Sagittarius, Jan. 20, 17:13 - Feb. 19, 7:26

World Events

Jan. 25 – Idi Amin seizes power in Uganda in the midst of a bloodbath.
Feb. 15 – Britain goes decimal; the pound changes from 240 pence to 100 pence.

1971

PISCES
Your Personal Planets

YOUR LOVE POTENTIAL
Venus in Capricorn, Feb. 19, 7:27 - Mar. 04, 2:23
Venus in Aquarius, Mar. 04, 2:24 - Mar. 21, 6:37

YOUR DRIVE AND AMBITION
Mars in Sagittarius, Feb. 19, 7:27 - Mar. 12, 10:10
Mars in Capricorn, Mar. 12, 10:11 - Mar. 21, 6:37

YOUR LUCK MAGNETISM
Jupiter in Sagittarius, Feb. 19, 7:27 - Mar. 21, 6:37

World Events

Feb. 28 – Women in Lichtenstein are refused the right to vote.

Mar. 20 – The Northern Ireland premier James Clark resigns under pressure from the Protestants.

Charles Manson, Susan Atkins, Patricia Krewnwinkel, and Leslie van Houten are sentenced to death

ARIES
Your Personal Planets

YOUR LOVE POTENTIAL
Venus in Aquarius, Mar. 21, 6:38 - Mar. 29, 14:01
Venus in Pisces, Mar. 29, 14:02 - Apr. 20, 17:53

YOUR DRIVE AND AMBITION
Mars in Capricorn, Mar. 21, 6:38 - Apr. 20, 17:53

YOUR LUCK MAGNETISM
Jupiter in Sagittarius, Mar. 21, 6:38 - Apr. 20, 17:53

World Events

Mar. 29 – Charles Manson, Leslie van Houten, Susan Atkins and Patricia Krewnwinkel are sentenced to death for the murder of Sharon Tate and four others.

Apr. 6 – Russian composer of "The Rite of Spring" Igor Stravinsky dies.

PISCES
From February 19, 7:27 through March 21, 6:37

The Conscientious Objector

The 1971 Pisces has an inside track on the value of passive resistance, knowing that direct confrontation often leads to more conflict. You have a highly developed sense of spiritual matters, and your faith in transcendent realities noticeably guides you in many of your earthly endeavors. Still, you are much more grounded than most Pisceans, although meeting the demands of the material world may be a steady challenge to your beliefs.

The entire world was focused on this Piscean dilemma when the U.S. Supreme Court ruled on March 8, 1971 that disagreement with a particular war—such as the Vietnam War—rather than war itself, was not sufficient grounds for conscientious objection. You are often caught between the dictates of your beliefs, and the pressure to get involved in controversial situations. Your conundrum is this: do you work for security and stability, or, if they conflict with these, for your higher values?

In your career, you have great earning capacity. You may have executive abilities as well, and there are significantly more Piscean CEOs than any other sign. You have the vision and empathy that allow you to rise quickly in your chosen profession. You tend to identify with something larger than yourself, and this could be a corporation, a sacred principle, or a cause.

You want to take care of others, financially as well as spiritually, by providing the values that you hold so dear. This can lead to confusing or chaotic relationships—you can't really make a commitment until you feel secure, but getting to that point may mean bruising your conscience. You get along best with Cancerians, Taureans, Scorpios, and Sagittarians.

Your greatest challenge is emotional duality because you are blessed with extraordinary insights into mystical realms, yet also have a driving ambition to achieve a very solid sense of place. You can get psychologically caught between these two, and waste much time and energy through unhealthy indulgences. Your gift is that when you can bridge your religious ideals with the existing system, you will lead us all into a more harmonious world.

ARIES
From March 21, 6:38 through April 20, 17:53

The Energetic Pioneer

As a 1971 Aries, you like to do things in a big way. You tend to see compromises, wishy-washiness, and ill-defined goals as signs of weakness, so you take great pride in your directness and forcefulness. More so than other Ariens, you have a robust manner and self-confidence that can be pioneering and competitive, as well as reliable, patient, and disciplined.

Like others born in 1971, you have a deep urge to improve the world. In March 1971, the U.S. Senate, bowing to environmental and international concerns, stopped funding the SST (supersonic transport), leaving France and Britain free to develop the Concorde without U.S. competition. This event reflects your own willingness and ability to take on very large forces for the sake of a principle—which is the only thing stronger than your intensely competitive spirit.

You have a keen interest in being the first in business or your chosen profession. This makes computer technology, medical research, and owning and running your own small business good outlets. You may also excel at sales, environmental work, and anything related to the health field, whether it's traditional medical or holistic health. Your greatest enemy is yourself: not waiting until the time is ripe is the only thing holding you back from immense success.

You probably enjoy interacting with many different kinds of people from diverse backgrounds and lifestyles, and these connections make for an interesting and diverting group of friends. You undoubtedly desire an intimate and long-term relationship, yet may have had painful experiences due to past betrayals or abandonment. Still, you can rise above the past to find a deep sense of caring companionship. You get along best with Geminis, Leos, Sagittarians, and Pisceans.

As a keen competitor, you have an indomitable drive to win and have likely attracted a number of rivals. Your greatest challenge is to find a personal path that uses your drive for a larger good rather than focusing solely on individual goals. Your gift is that you may lead the way out of entrenched interests that hold progress back.

➤ Read about your Chinese Astrological sign on page 838. ➤ Read about your Personal Planets on page 826. ➤ Read about your personal Mystical Card on page 856.

TAURUS

From April 20, 17:54 through May 21, 17:14

The Creative Connoisseur

As a Taurus born in 1971, you have an unusually colorful sense of place and an energetic drive for social reform. While you cherish traditional values, you may find in them the rationale and strength to overcome current trends that may be unhealthy or unwise. Born in an era of social unrest, you are likely to have a keen interest in building a stable culture that is rooted in lofty principles.

On May 3, 1971, U.S. Public Radio introduced *All Things Considered*, a quality news commentary that endures to this day. Your personality carries many of the astrological components of that historical debut, and these include creativity, originality, class, and staying power—you may also have a desire to pioneer something that is socially relevant and that will last a long time.

More so than other Bulls, 1971 Taureans have a powerful drive to attain financial security. Whatever your career path, it must provide you with a healthy income so you can enjoy the finest things in life, as well as support those who rely on you ... and there may be a few of those! You are endowed with a strong work ethic, and the physical energy and vision to accomplish your long-term goals. In your leisure time you may enjoy outdoor activities such as gardening or hiking.

Your family relationships are likely to be an important part of your life. You may have a good idea of where your roots lie, and how they have shaped who you are today. In personal relationships, you are not shy about telling your partner or a romantic interest what you want. You love flirting and the intrigue of new possibilities, but have probably learned to appreciate the value of commitment. In general, you get along best with Virgos, Cancerians, Capricorns, and other Taureans.

A major challenge in your life is that you can get on to a safe track that provides financial security, but not enough meaning or personal fulfillment. Born during an era of great social upheaval, at times you may resist settling for a traditional job or relationship. Your gift is that you have creative intelligence at your disposal in your most inspired moments.

GEMINI

From May 21, 17:15 through June 22, 1:19

The Talented Communicator

Gemini of 1971 has great interest in information and communications, and likes to share what they've learned through a variety of media. Your natural curiosity favors the unusual, eccentric, and socially relevant—especially if what you have to say or write about gets noticed and fosters change. You're likely to be adept at making connections that others miss and are capable of thinking in great abstractions.

On June 13, 1971, the first installment of the "Pentagon Papers" was printed in the *New York Times*: it was a turning point in the era of the Vietnam War, detailing how the government had consistently lied to the American people. This event arose from the same astrological factors that shape your life, and reveals your belief in the power of the press and freedom of speech.

Since you thrive anywhere that communications play a central role, your career may have developed along these lines. Perhaps you feel comfortable working in telecommunications, computer technology, writing and publishing, or teaching. You have the gift of gab, and may also excel at sales, marketing, or public speaking. Anything related to the transportation industry is also right up your alley, including a career as a travel agent. You are likely to be multi-talented but require freedom of movement and expression in your work.

In your relationships, you enjoy many different kinds of people—rich and poor, business-oriented and artistic, foreigners and locals. You enjoy sharing opinions and exchanging ideas, and when this rapport wears off, you're ready to move on. You are likely to have many friends, but may feel like a lone wolf at times without a committed relationship. You get along best with Leos, Libras, Sagittarians, and Aquarians.

A major challenge for you may be to find stability in your life. Your restless nature and revolutionary spirit keeps you detached and cool, so you may feel aloof about people and places. Your special gift is your ability to gather important information and to spread the word; you may be a talented writer or communicator who helps others grow by relaying the facts.

➤ Read about your Chinese Astrological sign on page 838. ➤ Read about your Personal Planets on page 826. ➤ Read about your personal Mystical Card on page 856.

TAURUS
Your Personal Planets

YOUR LOVE POTENTIAL
Venus in Pisces, Apr. 20, 17:54 - Apr. 23, 15:43
Venus in Aries, Apr. 23, 15:44 - May 18, 12:47
Venus in Taurus, May 18, 12:48 - May 21, 17:14

YOUR DRIVE AND AMBITION
Mars in Capricorn, Apr. 20, 17:54 - May 03, 20:56
Mars in Aquarius, May 03, 20:57 - May 21, 17:14

YOUR LUCK MAGNETISM
Jupiter in Sagittarius, Apr. 20, 17:54 - May 21, 17:14

World Events

Apr. 25 - Secessionists in Pakistan establish the new nation of Bangladesh.

May 3 - In Washington, DC 10,000 march in a protest against the Vietnam War.

Anti-war protesters are arrested in Washington

GEMINI
Your Personal Planets

YOUR LOVE POTENTIAL
Venus in Taurus, May 21, 17:15 - June 12, 6:57
Venus in Gemini, June 12, 6:58 - June 22, 1:19

YOUR DRIVE AND AMBITION
Mars in Aquarius, May 21, 17:15 - June 22, 1:19

YOUR LUCK MAGNETISM
Jupiter in Sagittarius, May 21, 15:15 - June 05, 2:11
Jupiter in Scorpio, June 05, 2:12 - June 22, 1:19

World Events

June 13 - Frank Sinatra gives his last concert before retiring.

June 13 - François Mitterand is elected leader of the new Socialist Party in France.

1971

CANCER
Your Personal Planets

YOUR LOVE POTENTIAL
Venus in Gemini, June 22, 1:20 - July 06, 22:01
Venus in Cancer, July 06, 22:02 - July 23, 12:14

YOUR DRIVE AND AMBITION
Mars in Aquarius, June 22, 1:20 - July 23, 12:14

YOUR LUCK MAGNETISM
Jupiter in Scorpio, June 22, 1:20 - July 23, 12:14

World Events

June 30 – The U.S. Supreme Court overrules the government attempt to prevent the Pentagon Papers being published by the New York Times and the Washington Post.

July 3 – American rock star Jim Morrison of The Doors dies.

Death of rock star Jim Morrison

LEO
Your Personal Planets

YOUR LOVE POTENTIAL
Venus in Cancer, July 23, 12:15 - July 31, 9:14
Venus in Leo, July 31, 9:15 - Aug. 23, 19:14

YOUR DRIVE AND AMBITION
Mars in Aquarius, July 23, 12:15 - Aug. 23, 19:14

YOUR LUCK MAGNETISM
Jupiter in Scorpio, July 23, 12:15 - Aug. 23, 19:14

World Events

July 25 – South African Dr. Christiaan Barnard performs the first heart and lung transplant.

July 31 – *Apollo 15* astronauts take mankind's first ride on the Moon in a four-wheel rover.

CANCER
From June 22, 1:20 through July 23, 12:14

The Sentimental Bridge-Builder

As a 1971 Cancer, you have an abiding interest in family, the home, and your national or ethnic roots. You enjoy protecting those close to you by providing emotional support and physical security, and this may include a circle of friends who you prefer to think of as family. During your life you may find that you wrestle with great moral or religious issues, especially when they divide those close to you.

Your domestic skills are well known. Even when far from your nest, you'll strive to create a homey atmosphere. On July 7, 1971, the Soviet spacecraft *Soyuz* made the first successful docking with the space station *Salyut*, launched early that spring. In addition to working space, *Salyut* contained areas for dining, recreation, food and water storage, and exercise. The *Soyuz* crew spent twenty-two days there, enjoying the Cancerian benefits of their home away from home.

Professionally, you have a caring, nurturing instinct that fits in well with health care, teaching children, real estate, or consulting. You may find that your family connections bring work opportunities, or that your co-workers become like brothers and sisters to you. You have strong people skills, and may be adept at sales or social work. A family owned small business would neatly combine many of your interests.

You are likely to have a highly romantic nature, and enjoy flirting and talking with new acquaintances. In your closest relationships, you may have boundary issues, such as who is a friend, and who is a potential love interest. If you find yourself emotionally involved with more than one person, it's probably because you aren't ready to make a commitment. In general, you get along best with Geminis, Scorpios, Capricorns, and Pisceans.

As a 1971 Cancer, a major challenge that you have is how to bring your romantic or creative imagination into concrete form. At times, you may have a tendency to get lost in your fantasies or feel deluged by inexplicable events. Your strengths are your abilities to encourage and inspire the less fortunate, and to bring people together over a common cause or goal.

LEO
From July 23, 12:15 through August 23, 19:14

The Creative Protagonist

As a 1971 Leo, you have a deep sense of compassion and a flair for the dramatic. Your natural showmanship is modified by a need to accomplish something worthwhile in your life, and this works best when you are a team player, even if you are the most valued or talented member in the group. You have an unusually serious attitude that reflects your determination to overcome great adversity.

Former Beatle George Harrison organized a spectacular benefit concert for Bangladeshis suffering from famine and disease on August 1, 1971—an event that suggests some of your own personality traits. During this gala affair, Harrison was the modest center of attention, ably supported throughout by many of his rock-star friends. Harrison's efforts were cause-oriented, fabulously extravagant, thought-provoking, trendy, and innovative—and all these characteristics might be applied to you.

In your professional life, you probably have a strong desire to create something worthwhile, something that makes people reflect or that has an enduring influence in the larger community or culture. You probably prefer to be your own boss, or have arranged a great deal of independence for yourself within the work environment. There may be times during your career when you bump into rivals or competitors with mediocre talents who don't understand your genius.

Your mental attitude plays a big part in how well you get along with others. At times you may be moody or thoughtful as you work on your various projects, and this can cause difficulties in your romantic life. You love to be in love, and if your present situation is less than ideal you may harbor fantasies about certain individuals. In general, you get along best with Librans, Sagittarians, and Ariens. You may find in Aquarians either partners or worthy opponents.

One of your greatest challenges is mental focus. Perhaps you slip into deep thoughts or feelings of confusion because conditions seem so difficult. The flip side of this coin is your special gift: when you see a tough situation, you have the talent, vision, and plan of action to achieve a meaningful solution.

➤ Read about your Chinese Astrological sign on page 838. ➤ Read about your Personal Planets on page 826. ➤ Read about your personal Mystical Card on page 856.

VIRGO

From August 23, 19:15 through September 23, 16:44

The Holistic Practitioner

As a 1971 Virgo, you have a keen ability to focus on details while keeping in mind how all the pieces fit into the larger whole. This magical awareness allows you to see how every part or every person is an integral component of the larger function or social group. You are likely to have a broad range of interests, but may also be a master of a particular art form or craft.

On September 8, 1971, the Kennedy Center for the Performing Arts opened for the first time, with Leonard Bernstein conducting his beautiful, intricate Mass. This event reflects many of the astrological qualities that were present in your birth month, including the professional musicians' heightened sense of craftsmanship, and the state of perfection that can exist when all the individual pieces are orchestrated into a harmonious pattern. The result is gorgeous, thanks to the attention you've paid to the constituent parts along the way.

Your quest for perfection, for creating the ideal product or service, is likely to be a major consideration for you in your career. You enjoy feeling useful, and like to know that the tasks and services you provide are helping to make the world a better place. You would do well in any health profession, especially one that uses alternative or holistic perspectives. You may also excel at accounting or other financial work.

The work environment is likely to provide you with a major source of companionship. Your co-workers may be your closest friends, or possibly you have found a love interest through your work. You prefer your most intimate companions to be healthy and clean, and you have a tendency to show your affection through practical gestures like cooking or massaging. In general, you get along best with Taureans, Cancerians, Capricorns, and Pisceans.

A big challenge for you may be to use your analytical mind for constructive advice rather than blunt criticism. You can get lost in the details and lose sight of the big picture. Your unique gift is your holistic awareness, and your ability to show others how everyone—no matter how seemingly insignificant—matters.

LIBRA

From September 23, 16:45 through October 24, 1:52

The Independent Partner

As a 1971 Libra, you have a love of beauty and an aesthetic awareness that graces almost everything you set your hand to, whether in work, in play, or in your many relationships. Lifestyle matters a lot to you, and your personal presentation is likely to be tailored to appeal to a very specific group of friends or social faction. You probably have a strong sense of who's in and who's out, as well as the harmony or turmoil that results.

On October 19, 1971, the final issue of *Look* magazine hit the newsstands after some thirty-eight years of publishing the best of American photography and art. This event in your birth month reflects on several levels what you are all about: you want to be seen, you want a good look around, and you have probably fine-tuned your own "look." You may also be an artist with a practical knowledge of some advanced or modern technique.

In the business world, you are likely to be a capable team player. Your people skills are your best asset, along with your appreciation for balance and harmony. Social work, office management, anything to do with the fashion or glamour industries, and any job where you can be around influential people are good career choices. If you are in a small business, you would do best with a trusted partner.

While you enjoy a variety of social interactions and appreciate having a partner around, you may not want to be dominated. Since you need a great deal of personal freedom, you will most likely run away from anyone who tries to control or smother you. Emotional scenes frighten or repulse you, and you tend to leave behind friendships that get bogged down in muddy feelings. In general, you get along best with Ariens, Geminis, Sagittarians, and Aquarians.

A challenge for you is the world of emotions and feelings, which you may find undefined and frightening. You prefer civil discussions to heated arguments, but this strategy may backfire if you walk away from overly emotional people before the air can be cleared. Your own emotions may confuse or disorient you. Your strength is your ability to be objective in all matters.

➤ Read about your Chinese Astrological sign on page 838. ➤ Read about your Personal Planets on page 826. ➤ Read about your personal Mystical Card on page 856.

VIRGO
Your Personal Planets

YOUR LOVE POTENTIAL
Venus in Leo, Aug. 23, 19:15 - Aug. 24, 16:24
Venus in Virgo, Aug. 24, 16:25 - Sept. 17, 20:24
Venus in Libra, Sept. 17, 20:25 - Sept. 23, 16:44

YOUR DRIVE AND AMBITION
Mars in Aquarius, Aug. 23, 19:15 - Sept. 23, 16:44

YOUR LUCK MAGNETISM
Jupiter in Scorpio, Aug. 23, 19:15 - Sept. 11, 15:32
Jupiter in Sagittarius, Sept. 11, 15:33 - Sept. 23, 16:44

World Events

Aug. 27 - American photographer Margaret Bourke-White dies.

Sept. 11 - Former Soviet leader Nikita Khrushchev dies.

Emperor Hirohito with his wife Empress Nagako and family

LIBRA
Your Personal Planets

YOUR LOVE POTENTIAL
Venus in Libra, Sept. 23, 16:45 - Oct. 11, 22:42
Venus in Scorpio, Oct. 11, 22:43 - Oct. 24, 1:52

YOUR DRIVE AND AMBITION
Mars in Aquarius, Sept. 23, 16:45 - Oct. 24, 1:52

YOUR LUCK MAGNETISM
Jupiter in Sagittarius, Sept. 23, 16:45 - Oct. 24, 1:52

World Events

Sept. 25 - A declaration asserting Yugoslav independence is signed by Marshal Tito and Leonid Brezhnev.

Oct. 9 - Emperor Hirohito of Japan makes a tour of Europe as a "trip of penance."

1971

SCORPIO
Your Personal Planets

YOUR LOVE POTENTIAL
Venus in Scorpio, Oct. 24, 1:53 - Nov. 05, 0:29
Venus in Sagittarius, Nov. 05, 0:30 - Nov. 22, 23:13

YOUR DRIVE AND AMBITION
Mars in Aquarius, Oct. 24, 1:53 - Nov. 06, 12:30
Mars in Pisces, Nov. 06, 12:31 - Nov. 22, 23:13

YOUR LUCK MAGNETISM
Jupiter in Sagittarius, Oct. 24, 1:53 - Nov. 22, 23:13

World Events

Oct. 28 – The British Parliament approves England's membership of the European Economic Community (EEC).

Nov. 15 – The People's Republic of China joins the United Nations.

British Prime Minister Edward Heath

SAGITTARIUS
Your Personal Planets

YOUR LOVE POTENTIAL
Venus in Sagittarius, Nov. 22, 23:14 - Nov. 29, 2:40
Venus in Capricorn, Nov. 29, 2:41 - Dec. 22, 12:23

YOUR DRIVE AND AMBITION
Mars in Pisces, Nov. 22, 23:14 - Dec. 22, 12:23

YOUR LUCK MAGNETISM
Jupiter in Sagittarius, Nov. 22, 23:14 - Dec. 22, 12:23

World Events

Nov. 26 – Corporal punishment in schools is outlawed in Britain.

Nov. 28 – The first two Anglican women priests are ordained.

SCORPIO
From October 24, 1:53 through November 22, 23:13

The Invincible Catalyst

As a 1971 Scorpio, you hold a unique position of influence in many of your affairs, both business and personal. You can use your talents, perspective, and insights into others' behavior to advance your own cause, or if it suits you, to get the better of your rivals. Since your influence is considerable and you can have a tendency to go overboard in your actions, your task is how to use your power in a responsible way.

On October 28, 1971, the British Parliament voted to join the European Economic Community. This pivotal event came about through very favorable celestial influences—the same ones under which you were born. With this vote, the historical split between the continental nations and the United Kingdom suddenly became a formidable union, and in the same way you have the survival instincts to stand alone or to create a powerful combined effort.

This process of strong individualism leading eventually to beneficial unions may be evident in your career. Developing your personal skills and your ability to be independent has likely been a high priority for you. However, you also have a strong urge to work within a group, as a team player. Your source of personal power is your ability to act as the situation demands, and developing this leverage is your ticket to success.

Close, intimate relationships mean a lot to you, and when you do get involved, it tends to be all or nothing. You may find that your sexual demands and your partner's are frequently out of sync, and this could create emotional distance. Tilting back and forth between intense partnerships and dealing with solitude might be a natural rhythm for you. In general, you get along best with Cancerians, Librans, Sagittarians, and Pisceans.

A great challenge for you is learning how to balance intellectual detachment with emotional intensity. You may swing from one to the other as a chaotic reaction to random events. Your gift is that once you can control both your objective analysis and your invincible willpower, you may become the small catalyst that transforms everything around you for the benefit of all.

SAGITTARIUS
From November 22, 23:14 through December 22, 12:23

The Spiritual Warrior

As a 1971 Sagittarius, you are likely to be a restless traveler and a seeker of truths. You may be compelled to understand ethical behavior and moral issues, and to do something about what you believe in your heart is right. Of all the Sagittarians of the twentieth century, you, more than most, are on a spiritual quest, but you face a world caught in regressive religious and legal traditions.

Two historical events stand out in your birth month, and both reflect your inherited cosmic itch. On November 26, 1971, London outlawed the caning of schoolchildren as punishment. However this ban was not placed for all British schools until 1998. Overcoming traditional barriers to outmoded or unjust practices is a tedious process, but your commitment to the noble struggle between right and wrong sustains you on your life path.

In the career department, you have probably run up against social expectations and standards that test your convictions. If you are to keep a steady job, you may have to make serious compromises with your personal beliefs. Any career that allows you to express your strong opinions or progressive principles will work for you. Telecommunications, mass media, publishing, the travel industry, transportation jobs, and teaching are also favored.

You probably have a great ability to adapt to circumstances wherever you are, and this is true also in your personal relationships. You can be a chameleon, responding effortlessly to your partner's every mood or astral message. You probably cherish good communication when partnered, but as you have such strong opinions, you may fall into discord over philosophical principles. In general, you get along best with Ariens, Leos, Librans, and sometimes Geminis.

As we live in an imperfect world, one of your greatest challenges is to accept people and society as they are. You tend to dream or fantasize a lot, but when you apply your idealized world to actual situations that need changing, you are fulfilling your mission in life. Your gift is your ability to do the right thing—when you do, the world becomes a better place.

➤ Read about your Chinese Astrological sign on page 838. ➤ Read about your Personal Planets on page 826. ➤ Read about your personal Mystical Card on page 856.

CAPRICORN

From December 22, 12:24 through December 31, 23:59

The Energized Professional

As a 1971 Capricorn born in December, you are likely to have a take-charge attitude, and a strong urge to help overcome the forces of chaos in our collective society. Your natural ability to take small steps toward achieving a worthwhile goal shows that you can achieve success in a timely manner. Not everyone has the staying power that you do, 1971 December Capricorn. And you get stronger as you get older, especially as you learn the value of patience and a cautious, but direct approach.

On December 24, 1971, President Nixon signed into law the National Cancer Act that authorized the then enormous amount of $1.5 billion per year to combat cancer. This landmark program came into being under the same celestial influences that guide your life. Even though the program yielded few results in its first decade, the hope and vision were there, and that's what you have as well, supported by a long-term plan of action.

Along your career path, you are likely to have an indomitable drive to get to the top of your chosen profession. If you work in the business world, you are lucky to have tremendous physical energy and stamina, allowing you to push through the competition and all obstacles in your way. You make friends easily, and have good people skills when you choose to use them.

You are likely to have great sex appeal, and romantic escapades help you escape the real world. Other escapes, perhaps in alcohol or drugs, may play a strong role in your personal relationships, but if you have this under control, you can find a faithful companion. Your partner probably comes with an odd assortment of friends, family, and acquaintances, and they help you to be more carefree. In general, you get along best with Taureans, Cancerians, Virgos, and Aquarians.

One of your greatest challenges is to climb the ladder of success doing something that you find meaningful or purposeful in a larger social sense. Without this sense of having a significant objective, you may flounder or even run into skilled enemies. Once you find a worthy goal, you may still attract enemies, but also powerful allies.

1971

CAPRICORN
Your Personal Planets

YOUR LOVE POTENTIAL
Venus in Capricorn, Dec. 22, 12:24 - Dec. 23, 6:31
Venus in Aquarius, Dec. 23, 6:32 - Dec. 31, 23:59

YOUR DRIVE AND AMBITION
Mars in Pisces, Dec. 22, 12:24 - Dec. 26, 18:03
Mars in Aries, Dec. 26, 18:04 - Dec. 31, 23:59

YOUR LUCK MAGNETISM
Jupiter in Sagittarius, Dec. 22, 12:24 - Dec. 31, 23:59

World Events

Dec. 26 – U.S. forces resume attacks on targets in North Vietnam.

Dec. 31 – Thousands of Iranians are expelled from Iraq.

The Findhorn Garden

Special Feature
Findhorn's Magical Garden

by Skye Alexander

Imagine a broccoli head so big it could feed a family of six for four months. Or a forty-pound head of cabbage growing in your back yard! Such garden marvels were common experiences in northern Scotland in the late 1960s and early 1970s, even though the soil was nothing more than sand and gravel, and the North Sea's bitter-cold climate created wretched growing conditions. The giant vegetables were cultivated at Findhorn, a community of like-minded people "communicating" and "cooperating" with nature spirits.

The Findhorn Community began quite by accident on November 17, 1962, when Peter and Eileen Caddy set up camp at Findhorn Bay Caravan Park. For the previous five years, Peter had been a successful manager of a prestigious hotel nearby. That job ended, and while he searched for new work, he and Eileen, their three sons, and their friend Dorothy MacLean lived in their mobile home (caravan) by the ocean. These founders all shared a strong sense of spiritual guidance, and messages Eileen received in her meditations revealed that they had all been led to this place for a reason. When the ground began to thaw in February and March 1963 Peter cleared an area to grow a garden. Although they had little gardening experience, through their metaphysical insights they lived "in the moment," and enjoyed beautifying their environment. Peter later recalled, "We were 'told' that Findhorn would be of importance to the world, that there was a plan behind it."

With spiritual guidance from what they felt was the angelic realm, Dorothy began receiving messages directly from the nature spirits, or devas. The first deva to talk to her was from the sweet pea, which was her favorite vegetable. This deva wished that human beings would use their abilities to work with nature. She learned that the sweet pea deva was the group angel for all the garden peas in the world, and it told her exactly what to do to maximize their growth. Peter's guide explained that devas are part of the angelic hierarchy that holds the pattern for each plant species and directs energy to bring the plant into physical form.

Soon Dorothy was getting messages from the landscape deva, which was a different consciousness than the sweet-pea deva. Then the Tibetan blue-poppy deva jumped in, followed by the rose deva, the rain deva, and many more. These devas all had great gardening advice, and after a while the garden became incredibly productive. The devas told them to make hotbeds, gather specific materials for compost, and when to sow, plant, thin, weed, and water.

(Continued on page 593)

➤ Read "Gaia's Mystical Power Places" by Wendy C. Hawks on page 745. ➤ Read "Gaia's Mystical Power Places" by Wendy C. Hawks on page 673.

1972

Explosive Changes Bring Benefits: Jupiter and Pluto

Jupiter and Pluto put their stamp on the events of 1972 from start to finish. Jupiter, the planet of expansion, magnifies the effect of every other planet. Pluto signifies powerful changes that stem from long-term transformative processes in human awareness. In 1972, these two planets formed a challenging "square" angle to each other, imparting dynamism to events that, with Pluto in the co-operative sign of Libra, brought much-needed changes in foreign relations. Chief among these was a thaw of the relationships between the U.S. and the nations of the communist world, China and the Soviet Union. This culminated by the end of the year in a series of agreements between the U.S. and USSR, including a pivotal arms agreement, as well as other accords to share technology and U.S. wheat. However, this combination often manifests in violence—a fact evidenced this year when the Munich Olympics were marred by a terrorist attack on Israelis in the Olympic Village.

This combination also fostered dreams of grandeur, with Jupiter enlarging upon the urge to gain power that Pluto often represents. Campaign organizers working for the re-election of U.S. President Richard Nixon responded to his desire to gain a resounding win by sabotaging his opponents with a series of "dirty tricks". The first to be detected was a break-in at the Watergate office complex, launching the investigation that ultimately prompted him to leave office prematurely. Still, altruism was also possible, as Marlon Brando sacrificed his Best Actor Oscar to protest government treatment of Native Americans..

American film star Liza Minelli in "Cabaret"

Richard Nixon visits China on a peace-building mission

Terrorists kill eleven Israeli athletes at the Munich Olympics

AIRLINE HAUNTINGS

An Eastern Airlines flight in an L-1011 plane crashed over the Florida Everglades, killing pilots Bob Loft and Don Repo in 1972. However, soon crew members were reporting apparitions of the pilots saying they would "never allow another L-1011 to crash." Later, an unidentified man warned a pilot about a fire risk. The pilot assumed the man was an airline engineer. The warning proved correct and disaster was averted, but when the pilot went to thank the engineer he had vanished. Descriptions confirmed it was Repo.

THE WATERGATE ERA BEGINS

President Nixon visited China, bringing an end to decades of icy Sino-U.S. relations. Northern Ireland was placed under direct rule from London to stop sectarian violence. The U.S. stepped up bombing of North Vietnam, but U.S. combat troops began to pull out four months later—in August. Egypt's leader Anwar Sadat ordered Soviet advisors and troops to leave. Terrorists killed eleven Israeli athletes at the Munich Olympic Games. In the U.S., five burglars with CIA ties were caught in the Watergate offices of the Democratic National Committee in Washington, leading to the indictment of former White House aides Hunt and Liddy. In the wake of airline hijackings, airlines decided to adopt more diligent inspection of luggage. After signing an arms agreement with Russia, Nixon was re-elected to the presidency by a landslide. An assassination attempt crippled Alabama governor George Wallace. Bob Fosse's picture of pre-World War II Germany *Cabaret* made Liza Minnelli a star. Bobby Fischer was the new world chess champion, defeating Russian Boris Spassky. The Duke of Windsor, who abdicated as King of England in 1936, died in Paris.

586

➤ Read "Findhorn's Magical Garden" by Skye Alexander on page 585.

CAPRICORN

From January 01, 0:00 through January 20, 22:58

The Patient Dynamo

You have an unusually strong capacity for creating constructive change, 1972 January Capricorn. Your natural disciplined attention to duty and a steady, patient approach to life is augmented by a boldness and spontaneity that can make you unbeatable. You are likely to have a dynamic lifestyle: you enjoy challenges, and feel comfortable initiating and taking charge of activities. When you combine your innate wisdom with your high energy, you can move mountains.

On January 5, 1972, President Nixon signed a bill authorizing a $5.5 billion six-year program to develop the Space Shuttle. The vision, patience, and adventurous spirit behind this landmark event reflect some of the best astrological qualities available to those born in your birth month. You, too, have this drive to overcome traditional limitations, and are fueled by a can-do attitude and the persistence to make it possible.

In your career, these personal assets will help in your ambition to be successful. You will likely become adept at managing your more impulsive side as you get older, but until then you may have some clashes with co-workers or bosses. In truth, you need strong competition or challenging goals to fire up your talents. You're at your best when allowed free rein and may prosper in a more independent business or professional role.

Your personal relationships are likely to be highly charged with energy, both emotional and physical. You need a great deal of personal freedom within any long-term relationship, as well as someone who appreciates your various heroic battles in the business world. Friendship is a high priority for you, and will enhance your most intimate encounters. In general, you get along best with Taureans, Virgos, Sagittarians, and Aquarians.

A major challenge for you is how to channel your high spirits and drive to be the best into a constructive position or project. You may bolt from well-established roles when you feel oppressed by others, but when you have found your unique lifestyle and professional mode, everything else—relationships, recognition, and achievements—will follow.

AQUARIUS

From January 20, 22:59 through February 19, 13:10

The Team Player

As a 1972 Aquarius, you have a keen interest in promoting the highest values of the Aquarian Age, generally regarded as freedom, equality, and brotherhood (or sisterhood). This celestial mandate inspires you to stick up for those who aren't treated equally, and to establish links between factions of society that are disconnected from each other. Through your lifestyle choices you show your allegiance to your favorite group or cause.

Several historical events during your birth month mirror the Aquarian desire to reconcile opposing sides. Following "Bloody Sunday" in Londonderry, the citizens of Northern Ireland marched in protest of internment laws. You, too, are willing to fight for what you feel is right. On February 12, 1972, Senator Edward Kennedy advocated amnesty for Vietnam draft dodgers in an attempt to gain respect for those youths condemned for their convictions.

You undoubtedly have strongly held convictions about the social order, 1972 Aquarius, and perhaps you have found work that helps you express your progressive views. You have great people skills, and could work well in an organization or corporation with others of like mind. You are also capable of pioneering a small business or profession that breaks into new social territory or perhaps relies on new technology.

Teamwork and partnerships give you inspiration. While you know that by yourself you can do nothing, you do have an independent nature that prefers being with equals or friends rather than being subordinate to someone else. You love to work with others toward a common goal, and from this your closest relationships develop. In general, you get along best with Ariens, Geminis, Librans, and Sagittarians.

A big challenge for you is how to deal with people whose actions are driven by their emotions rather than their rational side. Also, you respect everyone's unique talents and beauty, and this can get you into trouble with your romantic interests. Your gift is that you embody some of the ideals that are ushering in the New Age, and the people-problems that you help solve are moving us all forward.

➤ Read about your Chinese Astrological sign on page 838. ➤ Read about your Personal Planets on page 826. ➤ Read about your personal Mystical Card on page 856.

CAPRICORN
Your Personal Planets

YOUR LOVE POTENTIAL
Venus in Aquarius, Jan. 01, 0:00 - Jan. 16, 15:00
Venus in Pisces, Jan. 16, 15:01 - Jan. 20, 22:58

YOUR DRIVE AND AMBITION
Mars in Aries, Jan. 01, 0:00 - Jan. 20, 22:58

YOUR LUCK MAGNETISM
Jupiter in Sagittarius, Jan. 01, 0:00 - Jan. 20, 22:58

World Events

Jan. 1 - French actor Maurice Chevalier dies.
Jan. 9 - The miners' strike begins in Britain.

Death of French entertainer Maurice Chevalier

AQUARIUS
Your Personal Planets

YOUR LOVE POTENTIAL
Venus in Pisces, Jan. 20, 22:59 - Feb. 10, 10:07
Venus in Aries, Feb. 10, 10:08 - Feb. 19, 13:10

YOUR DRIVE AND AMBITION
Mars in Aries, Jan. 20, 22:59 - Feb. 10, 14:03
Mars in Taurus, Feb. 10, 14:04 - Feb. 19, 13:10

YOUR LUCK MAGNETISM
Jupiter in Sagittarius, Jan. 20, 22:59 - Feb. 06, 19:35
Jupiter in Capricorn, Feb. 06, 19:36 - Feb. 19, 13:10

World Events

Feb. 4 - Britain officially recognizes the independent state of Bangladesh.
Feb. 12 - Senator Edward Kennedy calls for amnesty for Vietnam draft dodgers.

1972

PISCES
Your Personal Planets

YOUR LOVE POTENTIAL
Venus in Aries, Feb. 19, 13:11 - Mar. 07, 3:24
Venus in Taurus, Mar. 07, 3:25 - Mar. 20, 12:20

YOUR DRIVE AND AMBITION
Mars in Taurus, Feb. 19, 13:11 - Mar. 20, 12:20

YOUR LUCK MAGNETISM
Jupiter in Capricorn, Feb. 19, 13:11 - Mar. 20, 12:20

World Events

Feb. 21 - Nixon arrives in China on an historic peace-building mission.

Feb. 29 - The new premier of Bangladesh, Sheik Mujibur Rahman, embarks on a tour of friendship to the USSR.

Richard Nixon makes an historic visit to China

ARIES
Your Personal Planets

YOUR LOVE POTENTIAL
Venus in Taurus, Mar. 20, 12:21 - Apr. 03, 22:47
Venus in Gemini, Apr. 03, 22:48 - Apr. 19, 23:36

YOUR DRIVE AND AMBITION
Mars in Taurus, Mar. 20, 12:21 - Mar. 27, 4:29
Mars in Gemini, Mar. 27, 4:30 - Apr. 19, 23:36

YOUR LUCK MAGNETISM
Jupiter in Capricorn, Mar. 20, 12:21 - Apr. 19, 23:36

World Events

Mar. 22 - The Equal Rights Amendment is passed by the U.S. Senate, prohibiting discrimination on the basis of sex.

Mar. 30 - The North Vietnamese invade South Vietnam, crossing the DMZ and launching the heaviest bomb attack in four years.

PISCES
From February 19, 13:11 through March 20, 12:20

The True Believer

As a 1972 Pisces, you have the warmth and practical know-how to create and maintain a stable lifestyle. Unlike many twentieth-century Pisceans, you are endowed with a keen business sense; you know the value of money and how to get it. And you know the value of forming enduring relationships to build a secure family life and community. You are likely to have a heightened sense of right and wrong.

A cultural breakthrough occurred during the week of February 21–28, 1972, when President Nixon made an historic visit to China. Nixon's America and Mao's China were religious, political, and cultural competitors, yet each saw an advantage to bridging the gap. In the same way, you were born with this ability to overcome religious and other cultural differences for the sake of business or other practical concerns.

These traits are great resources in your professional life. You have the vision to get past personal differences, and a steady reliability that makes you an asset to any business firm. You need work that can provide you with an opportunity to rise, both in terms of income and responsibility. You are likely to have an excellent financial touch, and can realize good earnings through shrewd investments.

In your personal relationships, you tend to warm up slowly to new encounters. Once you've established a rapport, however, your connections can last a long time. You may have friends you've known your whole life, and you prefer that your committed relationships last forever as well, but this will only work if your beliefs or religion are compatible. In general, you get along best with Taureans, Cancerians, Scorpios, and Capricorns.

A major life challenge for you concerns your belief system. Perhaps you were born into a particular religion, or you have intense feelings about certain ethical principles. You may be periodically faced with people or situations that challenge your faith. As you discover the difference between provincial doctrine and universal truth, your beliefs are also your strength. Then you can be unshakeable in your determination to make spiritual progress.

ARIES
From March 20, 12:21 through April 19, 23:36

The Restless Pioneer

You are likely to have a strong urge to travel, communicate, and keep abreast of the latest news and information, 1972 Aries. You may be skilled in several areas, and capable of disarming your rivals with a quick remark or a hail of words. However, you may be more cautious or thoughtful than the typical Aries of the twentieth century. You are likely to have many interests, and this includes your social interactions as well as your professional expertise.

On April 20, 1972, *Apollo 16* landed on the Moon's surface. The Apollo astronauts stayed for a record seventy-one hours and returned to earth with 217 lbs of lunar rocks. This groundbreaking event reflects an astrological condition of your birth month that is embodied in your own life. These conditions include the restless urge for adventure, especially in travel to distant lands, and the urge to gain knowledge.

These same qualities probably help shape your professional role, making you a fast learner at any new technique, and an eager participant in the Information Age. Any career dealing with writing, teaching, or expressing new ideas or technologies would be appropriate for you. You probably like work that allows you to come and go, or offers frequent travel. Having two jobs may also fit your lifestyle, giving you the diversity you enjoy.

You are likely to have a great deal of personal magnetism, and a fascination with beauty and romance. Staying in a traditional marriage or commitment may be difficult for you since you enjoy meeting new people and moving around a lot. When you find a worthy partner or romantic interest, the passion that keeps you going may need constant renewal and shared interests to endure. In general, you get along best with Geminis, Leos, Librans, and Sagittarians.

A significant challenge for you may be having too many interests, sticking to just one job, or having just one romantic partnership. To become a master, to be first or the best at something, you need to focus and narrow your interests. Your strength is your agility, speed, and grasp of new ideas that helps us all move forward.

➤ Read about your Chinese Astrological sign on page 838. ➤ Read about your Personal Planets on page 826. ➤ Read about your personal Mystical Card on page 856.

TAURUS

From April 19, 23:37 through May 20, 22:59

The Calm Center

As a 1972 Taurus, you have a constructive, practical approach to the fast-paced modern era which keeps you and those around you well grounded. Like many born during the turbulent year of 1972, you have a keen interest in new ideas and technologies, and in participating in the rapid changes they create. Unlike many of your peers, you are uniquely positioned to provide a useful and enduring form to the flood of innovations.

In April 1972, Japan opened a 103-mile railroad linking two metropolitan centers with commuter trains speeding along at 155 mph. This revolutionary engineering project characterizes the astrological tenor of your birth month, and is a vibration characteristic of your life. You have the same interest in new technologies, especially those that prove useful in travel and communications. You may find opportunities and prosperity in similar projects.

In your work environment, you have a charming ability to engage others, smoothing inter-office relations. You have a fortunate blend of curiosity for the new, and a practical approach that businesses rely on. While others venture out on a limb, you can see clearly what works and what doesn't. And while others may fall behind in outdated traditions or technologies, you are up on the latest and ready to advance.

In your personal relations, you are likely to have intense desires that lead to passionate and deeply sensual experiences. You may also have run into romantic triangles, been confused by jealousy, or otherwise encountered complex questions of loyalty and commitment. Once you are certain that you want one— and only one—person as your true partner, these issues clear up. You get along best with Geminis, Cancerians, Virgos, and Capricorns.

A big challenge for you is how to accept your early family life for what it was, and then move on to find your place in the world, a place that enlarges your sense of family to include a community or even a people. You have mystical tendencies, and this can be a gift once you have found inner silence. Then you radiate with a calmness that influences everyone around you.

GEMINI

From May 20, 23:00 through June 21, 7:05

The Bridge Builder

As a 1972 Gemini, you have an interest in communications, new ideas, and travel, and are naturally inclined to build metaphorical bridges between the old and the new. The socially chaotic era you were born in is often characterized as a generation gap, but you have the unique traits that link the traditional with the experimental. Family life may be tempestuous at times, but it is still very important to you.

On May 22, 1972, President Nixon made a first-time visit to the Soviet Union. This historic event reveals the celestial influences of your birth month, and shows how you are willing to take big steps to bridge differences. On June 17, 1972, five burglars were caught at the Watergate hotel, kicking off a huge political scandal. The USSR visit and the Watergate break-in were both high-risk ventures, the difference being the intention in each case—one conciliatory, the other criminal.

In your career, you can make great strides toward success when your motivations are for mutual progress. You may have a tendency to get sidetracked by suspicious actions from your co-workers or competitors, especially when money is involved. A natural defensiveness is best used to protect your professional interests and those who depend on you. Your love of risk can be a double-edged sword.

You have great passions in your love life, and tend to go to extremes when involved with an intimate partner. While this can be a good thing, allowing you to experience the most intense of bonding experiences, it can also lead to emotional entanglements that demand full-time attention. In general, you get along best with Cancerians, Librans, and Aquarians.

A great challenge for you is to develop a sense of non-attachment in your personal relationships. You have the potential to gain an objectivity that can take you far in your professional life, but it means getting a handle on your personal life. You may find yourself in difficult mood swings, but your gift is that once you recognize your higher purpose of bridging differences, you find the serenity and trust to create healthy relationships.

TAURUS
Your Personal Planets

YOUR LOVE POTENTIAL
Venus in Gemini, Apr. 19, 23:37 - May 10, 13:50
Venus in Cancer, May 10, 13:51 - May 20, 22:59

YOUR DRIVE AND AMBITION
Mars in Gemini, Apr. 19, 23:37 - May 12, 13:13
Mars in Cancer, May 12, 13:14 - May 20, 22:59

YOUR LUCK MAGNETISM
Jupiter in Capricorn, Apr. 19, 23:37 - May 20, 22:59

World Events

Apr. 22 – Britons John Fairfax and Sylvia Cook become the first people to row across the Pacific, landing on the Hayman Islands in Australia.

Apr. 28 – Five Oxford colleges decide to open their doors to women from 1974.

The scene of the Watergate break-in, which led to Richard Nixon's resignation

GEMINI
Your Personal Planets

YOUR LOVE POTENTIAL
Venus in Cancer, May 20, 23:00 - June 11, 20:07
Venus in Gemini, June 11, 20:08 - June 21, 7:05

YOUR DRIVE AND AMBITION
Mars in Cancer, May 20, 23:00 - June 21, 7:05

YOUR LUCK MAGNETISM
Jupiter in Capricorn, May 20, 23:00 - June 21, 7:05

World Events

May 22 – President Nixon visits the USSR to meet with Leonid Brezhnev, the first U.S. President in history to meet with any Soviet leader.

June 17 – Five burglars are caught in the Watergate offices of the Democratic National Committee.

➤ Read about your Chinese Astrological sign on page 838. ➤ Read about your Personal Planets on page 826. ➤ Read about your personal Mystical Card on page 856.

1972

CANCER
Your Personal Planets

YOUR LOVE POTENTIAL
Venus in Gemini, June 21, 7:06 - July 22, 18:02

YOUR DRIVE AND AMBITION
Mars in Cancer, June 21, 7:06 - June 28, 16:08
Mars in Leo, June 28, 16:09 - July 22, 18:02

YOUR LUCK MAGNETISM
Jupiter in Capricorn, June 21, 7:06 - July 22, 18:02

World Events

June 29 - The U.S. Supreme Court determines that capital punishment is unconstitutional.

July 9 - Stan Smith beats Ilie Nastase, and Billie Jean King beats Evonne Goolagong to take the Wimbledon titles.

Wimbledon winner Stan Smith

LEO
Your Personal Planets

YOUR LOVE POTENTIAL
Venus in Gemini, July 22, 18:03 - Aug. 06, 1:25
Venus in Cancer, Aug. 06, 1:26 - Aug. 23, 1:02

YOUR DRIVE AND AMBITION
Mars in Leo, July 22, 18:03 - Aug. 15, 0:58
Mars in Virgo, Aug. 15, 0:59 - Aug. 23, 1:02

YOUR LUCK MAGNETISM
Jupiter in Capricorn, July 22, 18:03 - July 24, 16:42
Jupiter in Aquarius, July 24, 16:43 - Aug. 23, 1:02

World Events

Aug. 4 - Archaeologists in China report that they have uncovered a tomb believed to date from the Han dynasty.

Aug. 11 - The last U.S. ground troops leave Vietnam, although B-52 bombers continue their raids.

CANCER

From June 21, 7:06 through July 22, 18:02

The Quick Wit

As a 1972 Cancer, you have unusually persuasive opinions that were shaped during an unusually vibrant era of social change. Unlike many twentieth-century Cancerians, you probably have a relatively even emotional life—one that relies on your intellectual side and ability to reason. You are likely to have a protective instinct that can reach far beyond your natural family, and take great pride in your abundant talents and abilities.

The first issue of *Ms.* magazine appeared in July 1972, an event that came about through the same astrological influences that shape your life. Just like the founders of *Ms.*, you have a strong independent streak, one that fearlessly takes on the status quo in order to present a new lifestyle. You may also share a well-protected emotional side that fares better in business than in intimate relationships.

In your professional life, you have tremendous talents and generosity of spirit that can facilitate a quick rise to the top. You probably have several creative abilities, artistic as well as in writing and communicating, and these can be developed into valuable career assets. On the cautionary side, you may need to develop a diplomatic touch. But you are no doubt good with money, and have the poise and self-confidence to succeed.

In the relationship department, you are likely to have great personal charisma, and favor honesty and good communications as top priorities. Your astrological predisposition is for making commitments, since you prefer someone around who you can count on. If this doesn't work, you like to spend time with friends or family, and for leisure activities probably enjoy lavish meals and entertainment. In general, you get along best with Leos, Scorpios, Pisceans, and Geminis.

A big challenge for you may be finding true love. You have an intensely romantic side, but can spend too much time in your work to allow intimate relationships to blossom. You may find that partnership comes easily, but that the empathy doesn't happen until you relax your mind. Your gift is that you have leadership qualities that can open up new horizons.

LEO

From July 22, 18:03 through August 23, 1:02

The Radiant Talent

As a 1972 Leo, you are likely to have a hero's courage and sense of purpose, driven on by strong convictions and the need to persuade others. Since you see the necessity for profound changes, you don't like to be bothered by trivial or meaningless events. You may have some unusual creative talents that help you along, and an ability to inspire others to action.

A good example of your innate sense of self-confidence and resolve arrived on August 1, 1972, when two *Washington Post* reporters, Bob Woodward and Carl Bernstein, began to crack the Watergate affair. In their investigation, they wrote about having discovered a link between the break-in and the GOP re-election committee. The same celestial influences shaped their heroic efforts and your birth personality. No one paid much attention to this first story, and you, too, may have to wait for the big break.

In your professional life, you may find success in many fields, but will feel most fulfilled when you are expressing your creative talent. You may have to sacrifice some financial considerations until you are recognized, but eventually influential people will favor your best efforts. You can excel when unsupervised and can follow your own intuition. Being your own boss works best, or having an open-ended job description.

In your love life, you are likely to be generous and full of optimism, unless you are criticized. You tend to melt under adverse comments, and puff up when flattered. A favorite activity with a friend or mate is to travel to exotic and expensive retreats where you can be treated like royal guests. In general, you get along best with Librans, Sagittarians, Ariens, and Geminis.

A worthy challenge for you is to learn patience. It may be some time before others recognize your talent and the truth that you are expressing. Your strongly held beliefs in yourself and your cause may give others the impression you are too full of yourself. Your gift is your natural radiance that brings cheer and warmth to otherwise dreary lives. Your lifestyle shows by example the power of autonomy and self-determination.

➤ Read about your Chinese Astrological sign on page 838. ➤ Read about your Personal Planets on page 826. ➤ Read about your personal Mystical Card on page 856.

VIRGO

From August 23, 1:03 through September 22, 22:32

The Discriminating Warrior

As a 1972 Virgo, you have a strong sense of power, as well as understanding who has it and who doesn't. In your natural urge to be of service to others, you would resent being under the control of someone who enforces arbitrary rules, but you are motivated by seemingly impossible challenges. You have a driving need to overcome resistance, and may often encounter people or situations that test your personal strength and will.

On September 4, 1972, American swimmer Mark Spitz won a record seven gold medals at the Olympics. The underlying astrological influences present during his record-setting success also shape your own life and personality. Physical strength may be a high priority for you, or the need to demonstrate your mastery over competitors. You also have great pride and seek to do your best in difficult circumstances.

In the work environment, your analytical or technical skills may be a terrific source of job security. Since you are willing to confront authority at any moment, you need a career or work environment where you trust and respect your supervisors and peers. You can prosper and find success when the challenges you seek are outside your work team, in the form of business rivals or difficult goals. Then you are unstoppable.

In your personal relationships, you need a partner who can test you and stand up to you. You wouldn't be satisfied with a mate who never disagreed with you. You need the struggle to stay excited and fuel the passions. Guarding against being too critical can help you ease the interactions—just remember that no one's perfect. In general, you get along best with Scorpios, Capricorns, Taureans, and Cancerians.

A major life challenge for you is in managing your frustration levels. You may repeatedly run into immoveable people or conditions, like a ram smacking into a brick wall. Your task is to know when you can get where you want to go, and when to try something else. Your strength is in your discrimination, especially in choosing your battles. Then your intelligence and analytical abilities can achieve seemingly impossible goals.

LIBRA

From September 22, 22:33 through October 23, 7:40

The Informed Mediator

As a 1972 Libra, you are more than willing to fight for peace. You have an inherent diplomatic side that seeks to make order of chaos and to disable hostility. On the other hand, you don't like it when people get too comfortable and polite, and are perfectly capable of starting a rousing debate to spark up a social gathering. You are especially active when people are expressing their religious or political ideology.

Your birth year was an exceptionally threatening time in the Cold War. However, on October 3, 1972, the USSR and U.S. entered into an agreement—the Strategic Arms Limitation Treaty— that sought to contain the nuclear arms race. In this event, favored by the astrological influences of your birth month, the most powerful forces were brought into an uneasy balance through negotiation. This mediating dynamic is also present in your life as a prominent motivation.

You have terrific people skills, and although this social awareness is not taught or tested in school, it's a big plus in the job market. You have the grace, confidence, and communication skills to take you far in any professional or business environment. You also have an instinct for smelling where the power is and where the big money comes from, which you can use to your own advantage.

You probably prefer a mate who can help you socialize in the most influential circles. You naturally gravitate toward the biggest game in town, and like discussing the most important issues. A partner who is well informed and not too emotional would suit you well—though since that's what you are, you may opt for the opposite. In general, you get along best with Sagittarians, Aquarians, Geminis, and Leos.

A big challenge for you may be to avoid sacrificing your own needs for the sake of your partnership. You have a tendency to be totally in sync with your significant other, but this can take you out of touch with what you want as an individual. Eventually, repressed personal needs will disrupt your harmony. Your gift is your keen interest in ideological differences, and your talent in moving toward mutual progress.

➤ Read about your Chinese Astrological sign on page 838. ➤ Read about your Personal Planets on page 826. ➤ Read about your personal Mystical Card on page 856.

VIRGO
Your Personal Planets

YOUR LOVE POTENTIAL
Venus in Cancer, Aug. 23, 1:03 - Sept. 07, 23:26
Venus in Leo, Sept. 07, 23:27 - Sept. 22, 22:32

YOUR DRIVE AND AMBITION
Mars in Virgo, Aug. 23, 1:03 - Sept. 22, 22:32

YOUR LUCK MAGNETISM
Jupiter in Aquarius, Aug. 23, 1:03 - Sept. 22, 22:32

World Events

Sept. 4 – American swimmer Mark Spitz wins a record seven gold medals at the Olympics.

Sept. 5 – Arabs terrorists massacre eleven Israeli Olympic athletes in Munich.

Helicopter wreckage after police intervention against terrorism at the Munich Olympic Games

LIBRA
Your Personal Planets

YOUR LOVE POTENTIAL
Venus in Leo, Sept. 22, 22:33 - Oct. 05, 8:32
Venus in Virgo, Oct. 05, 8:33 - Oct. 23, 7:40

YOUR DRIVE AND AMBITION
Mars in Virgo, Sept. 22, 22:33 - Sept. 30, 23:22
Mars in Libra, Sept. 30, 23:23 - Oct. 23, 7:40

YOUR LUCK MAGNETISM
Jupiter in Aquarius, Sept. 22, 22:33 - Sept. 25, 18:18
Jupiter in Capricorn, Sept. 25, 18:19 - Oct. 23, 7:40

World Events

Oct. 3 – An arms agreement is signed by the U.S. and the USSR—a significant achievement in restraining the arms race.

Oct. 15 – The U.S. beats Rumania to keep the Davis Cup for the fifth straight year.

1972

SCORPIO
Your Personal Planets

YOUR LOVE POTENTIAL
Venus in Virgo, Oct. 23, 7:41 - Oct. 30, 21:39
Venus in Libra, Oct. 30, 21:40 - Nov. 22, 5:02

YOUR DRIVE AND AMBITION
Mars in Libra, Oct. 23, 7:41 - Nov. 15, 22:16
Mars in Scorpio, Nov. 15, 22:17 - Nov. 22, 5:02

YOUR LUCK MAGNETISM
Jupiter in Capricorn, Oct. 23, 7:41 - Nov. 22, 5:02

World Events

Nov. 1 – American poet Ezra Pound dies.

Nov. 7 – U.S. President Nixon is reelected by the greatest Republican landslide in history.

Richard Nixon is re-elected President of the U.S.

SAGITTARIUS
Your Personal Planets

YOUR LOVE POTENTIAL
Venus in Libra, Nov. 22, 5:03 - Nov. 24, 13:22
Venus in Scorpio, Nov. 24, 13:23 - Dec. 18, 18:33
Venus in Sagittarius, Dec. 18, 18:34 - Dec. 21, 18:12

YOUR DRIVE AND AMBITION
Mars in Scorpio, Nov. 22, 5:03 - Dec. 21, 18:12

YOUR LUCK MAGNETISM
Jupiter in Capricorn, Nov. 22, 5:03 - Dec. 21, 18:12

World Events

Dec. 10 – The anti-militarist German writer Heinrich Böll wins the Nobel Prize for literature.

Dec. 19 – The final Apollo Moon mission comes to an end as *Apollo 17* returns to Earth.

592

SCORPIO
From October 23, 7:41 through November 22, 5:02

The Modern Shaman

As a 1972 Scorpio, you have an intense interest in the larger, perhaps hidden forces that shape society. Your own goals, in both your career and personal relationships, may be deeply altered from time to time by mysterious historical, economic, or cultural shifts. Understanding or mastering these forces means becoming a modern-day shaman, so that you have more control over your own destiny and can assist others in the same way.

The poet Ezra Pound died on November 1, 1972, and he was also born a Scorpio in 1885. His life and death exemplify the path of the modern shaman, and include controversial theories on Capitalism, a stint as a respected educator and founder of the Imagist movement, and a twelve-year stay in an insane asylum. In the same way, you are in tune with the most creative and destructive forces of the psyche.

In your professional life, you may have a keen grasp of financial markets or some other esoteric science. Like Pound, you have an aesthetic awareness that can also be translated into an art form. You may have a strong ideology that will shape your chosen profession according to the associates you work with or against. You also have excellent social skills, and can engage anyone in meaningful discussion.

In your personal relationships, you are likely to enjoy an active social life. The friends and acquaintances you choose to spend time with may live on the fringe or otherwise be considered out of the mainstream. This is your connection to the unknown, where you can find the offbeat psychic or ignored genius, and perhaps a love interest. In general, you get along best with Capricorns, Pisceans, Cancerians, and Librans.

A challenge for you is to put your mystical awareness to practical use in the civilized world. You may be a healer or a misfit, depending on how well you integrate the visible and invisible realms. Your gift is that once you have become the modern shaman, you can transform yourself into a success story, and then help others find the same inner resources. Your personal path may also help transform the larger community or social order.

SAGITTARIUS
From November 22, 5:03 through December 21, 18:12

The Strong Clairvoyant

As a 1972 Sagittarius, you have a great imagination and an ability to see meaning in the most obscure events. Unlike many Sagittarians, you also have an iron will and can be very determined to achieve your envisaged goals. Some of your greatest ideas are likely to face strong opposition from mediocre minds or those preoccupied by their own self-interests. Seeing the big picture is your gift, but implementing it means overcoming the momentum of tradition.

On December 18, 1972, President Nixon ordered a full-scale bombing attack against the North Vietnamese after peace talks in Paris had stalled. This event reflects the underlying power available to those born in your birth month, as well as the difficulties in getting others to see your point of view. While you don't have a fleet of B-52 bombers at your disposal, you may be very forceful at times when you feel you are right.

In your professional life, you are likely to have a great resourcefulness and consistency that mark you as an effective, can-do worker. If you have a job in which you can't invest your heart and soul, you may be prone to mental drifting. You probably have great ambitions, and don't want to waste time in trivial work. You may see opportunities that others miss, and can use this talent to advance your own career.

You are likely to have a strong sex drive and plenty of charisma. Intimate relationships are very important to you, but may also be a major source of personal growth since in them you tend to attract what you most need to learn about yourself. You may feel comfortable with someone significantly older or younger than yourself. In general, you get along best with Ariens, Leos, Librans, and Scorpios.

A big challenge for you is to avoid saying things or proposing ideas that you may later regret. While you have great vision, perhaps even psychic talent, what comes to you is filtered through your own desires and cultural mindset. When you know the difference between your own subconscious thoughts and what may be channeled from a higher source, then you have the precious gift of clairvoyance.

➤ Read about your Chinese Astrological sign on page 838. ➤ Read about your Personal Planets on page 826. ➤ Read about your personal Mystical Card on page 856.

CAPRICORN

From December 21, 18:13 through December 31, 23:59

The Protected Reformer

As a Capricorn born in December 1972, you have a strong sense of responsibility and duty, and a respect for law and order. Your may feel that you have a special calling in life, and that you are favored to bring improvements to unfortunate situations or people. You are a doer, and will undoubtedly face great personal struggles, but are favored to help make profound changes in the community around you.

The conservative astrological influences taking place during your birth month can be seen in the death of Harry Truman on December 26, 1972. Truman guided the United States and the world through difficult times by virtue of his steadfast determination to follow his moral compass. Then, on December 31, 1972, the EPA ordered a total ban on DDT, an event that further reflects your reliance on the laws to make radical, but necessary, changes.

In your career, you have a powerful drive to make constructive changes, perhaps as a reformer or health specialist. You will likely come across strong rivals or competitors from time to time who challenge your status and have a vested interest in undermining your mission. They won't succeed if you are on the right path, because you have a unique astrological marker that promises success when you do the right thing.

Casual relationships may provide you with an opportunity to travel and enjoy life more. You probably prefer a traditional partnership to short-term serial affairs, but keeping the romance going with a committed partner requires a lot of patience and honest communication. Your partner may be years older or younger than you, and may remind you of one of your parents. In general, you get along best with Taureans, Virgos, Scorpios, and Sagittarians.

A major challenge for you is to not get discouraged while you go about your daily tasks. The difficult situations that you inevitably find in life are testing your resolve and faith in your mission. When you accept these obstacles and turn them into stepping-stones, they will lead you to your gift in life, which is the realization and satisfaction that you are doing the Universe's work.

1972

CAPRICORN
Your Personal Planets

YOUR LOVE POTENTIAL
Venus in Sagittarius, Dec. 21, 18:13 - Dec. 31, 23:59

YOUR DRIVE AND AMBITION
Mars in Scorpio, Dec. 21, 18:13 - Dec. 30, 16:11
Mars in Sagittarius, Dec. 30, 16:12 - Dec. 31, 23:59

YOUR LUCK MAGNETISM
Jupiter in Capricorn, Dec. 21, 18:13 - Dec. 31, 23:59

World Events

Dec. 26 – Former U.S. President Harry S. Truman dies.

Dec. 29 – The last issue of weekly *Life* magazine is published.

Findhorn Harvest Festival

Special Feature
Findhorn's Magical Garden

(Continued from page 585)

In addition to practical advice, the gardeners also realized that their pinpoint concentration was needed to make the garden grow. Theyneeded heightened intuition to know where to place various plants. Eileen's spirit guide said, "The garden is rather like a crossword puzzle, and when you get the right plant in the right place, you will see where the next plant should go. Now, this may not be the usual way of gardening, but this is not the usual garden."

In 1964 Peter was strongly prompted to grow lettuce, and not just a patch of lettuce, but thousands of seedlings, far more than they could use. As it turned out, that summer there was shortage of lettuce in the area, and individuals and shop owners came from all over to buy their lush, organically grown lettuce. While they were there, visitors also bought spinach, parsley, and radishes, and word spread fast about the special taste and quality of the produce.

Many outsiders erroneously assumed that the fantastic vegetables and fruits had been grown using artificial fertilizers. In 1967 the group began planting flowers, and these too grew into spectacular specimens, radiant with light and uniformly far above standard heights. Experts were baffled, while visitors

> Findhorn is not just about raising fabulous vegetables and flowers; it is about providing the world a natural model of cooperation between the plant and human kingdoms.

were mesmerized. Foxgloves, which normally reach three to four feet, were growing to eight and nine feet. All these wonders are chronicled and photographed in several books, including The Findhorn Garden by the Findhorn Community.

Eileen then received the message that Findhorn was not just about raising fabulous vegetables and flowers; it was about providing

the world a natural model of cooperation between the plant and human kingdoms. As word spread about the miraculous garden, guests began arriving to learn about the principles behind it, and they were invited to share in the experience. By the end of the sixties, residents viewed themselves as the vanguard of a New Age, a new society based on cooperation between humans and the natural world. In 1970 a young David Spangler joined the Findhorn Community to help begin an educational process for this work that was called a "university of light." By this time, around 300 others were participating in the communal experience, and David became co-director during his stay through 1973. David brought his own ideas about the New Age, and they blended easily with what was happening at Findhorn.

(Continued on page 601)

➤ Read "Gaia's Mystical Power Places" by Wendy C. Hawks on page 745. ➤ Read "The Enigma of Crop Circles" by Frank Andrews on page 673.

1973

Tensions Increase: Mars and Saturn

Mars and Saturn were activating planets in 1973 and troubles erupted around the globe. In the early part of the year, a brief encounter between expansive Jupiter and disruptive Uranus set the stage for later, more profound challenges. The U.S. agreed to evacuate Vietnam, leaving local governments to their own devices. Quietly, one by one, Nixon's closest aides were being picked off in the Watergate investigation. In April, inflammatory Mars and Jupiter, both in justice-seeking Aquarius, contacted Pluto, opening the floodgates of information on Watergate and it became front-page news, a harbinger of coming events. In July, as Mars, linked to law enforcement, began its cyclic swing closest to Earth, it triggered Uranus, planet of rebellion and electronics: Nixon's Oval-Office tapes were subpoenaed, marking the beginning of the end. Nixon rebelled, refusing to turn them over despite repeated court orders. At the same time, an Arab-Israeli dispute flared over lands taken by Israelis in 1967's Six Day War. Arab forces, acting out Mars's aggressive nature, struck suddenly in October, an expression of Uranus.

However, as the year ended, restrictive Saturn came into play, contacting transformative Pluto. When these two planets interact, sieges between powerful nations can develop. This was the case in late 1973, when the Arab nations imposed an oil embargo on Israel's supporters. At the same time, the Watergate scandal reached the President and talk of impeachment began in Congress. As Saturn and Pluto continued to interact in 1974, these situations would be resolved.

A Peace Declaration is signed between North and South Korea

Chilean President Augusto Pinochet

The World Trade Center is completed

A NOVEL COINCIDENCE

Anthony Hopkins was cast in the movie *The Girl From Petrovka* based on the novel by George Feifer. Wanting to read the book, he searched but could not find a copy in any bookstore. Then, while waiting for a train, he found a book lying on the bench next to him—it was *The Girl From Petrovka*. When filming began, Hopkins met Feifer and told him the story. Feifer said he had lost his only copy with notes scribbled in it two years earlier. Amazingly, they discovered that it was the very same book Hopkins had found.

THE ARAB OIL EMBARGO STRIKES

Egyptian and Syrian forces staged a surprise attack on Israel on Yom Kippur, the Jewish Day of Atonement, but the Israelis defeated them. In retaliation, Arab states imposed an embargo on oil shipments to countries supporting Israel until lands seized in the 1967 war were returned. A possibly U.S.-backed coup headed by General Pinochet ousted Chilean president Allende. Eighteen years after being exiled, Juan Peron returned as President of Argentina, with wife Isabel as Vice-President. The world's oldest head of state, ninety-year old de Valera, resigned without accomplishing his goal of unifying Ireland. In the Vietnam War, the U.S. signed a truce in Paris and prisoners-of-war were exchanged. In the U.S., the drive for equality continued, as the Native American Movement seized the town of Wounded Knee and took ten hostages to protest their plight. Investigation of the Watergate break-in was pursued by The *Washington Post's* Bernstein and Woodward, implicating White House officials. The Arab oil embargo caused fuel prices to rise sharply, and the World Trade Center was completed, giving new majesty to the New York skyline.

➤ Read "Findhorn's Magical Garden" by Skye Alexander on page 593.

CAPRICORN

From January 01, 0:00 through January 20, 4:47

The Cosmopolitan Conservative

As a January Capricorn of 1973, you have exquisite taste, and a more cosmopolitan view than most. Unlike many Capricorns, you are a natural risk-taker; you may look and act fairly mainstream, but you have an underlying independent streak that compels you to be original, creative, and stylish. At times, your interest in freedom of expression can run into conflict with your more restrained cultural or religious background.

On January 7, 1973, Adolf Hitler's automobile was sold at auction for a record $153,000. This event took place under the same astrological influences that shape your life, and shows how pursuing elegance and freedom of expression can conflict with popular values, in this case anti-Nazi sentiment. On January 9, 1973, with the same general principle in effect, the military government of Brazil banned the sale of Picasso's erotic prints.

Your career will probably afford you many opportunities to pursue a more conservative lifestyle. Still, you may ignore these in favor of work in which you feel more liberated. You may falter if you are too free, not finding steady work. On the other hand, you are likely to rebel in any job in which you can't speak your mind. Once you've found a way to reconcile these two impulses, your march toward success is assured.

In relationships, your outgoing attitude probably attracts many friends and romantic interests. You may have an idealistic view of the perfect partner, and wonder if there is a soul mate for you. Naturally, long-term relationships with ordinary human beings need compromises to endure. In general, you get along best with Taureans, Virgos, Scorpios, and Sagittarians.

A significant challenge for you is expressing your strong opinions without alienating the people who mean the most to you. Your broad views on many subjects may indeed represent an excellent route toward progress, but debating these with your mate or boss may not be the best outlet. Your gift is that once you find an appropriate venue for your insights, perhaps a professional role, you may help humanity move toward a more enlightened worldview.

AQUARIUS

From January 20, 4:48 through February 18, 19:00

The Social Progressive

As a 1973 Aquarius, you are likely to have an unusually strong yearning to help create a more progressive, holistic, and egalitarian society. You can see the big picture, how the world is shaping up, and what needs to change. The era you were born in represents an historical transition from the old to the new, and likewise, you harbor this desire to see more humane conditions at work, in play, and in the community around you.

Your birth month is exceptional in an exceptional year. On January 21, 1973, the Supreme Court protected a woman's right to abortion with its decision in the case of Roe vs. Wade. Then, the Vietnam War officially ended with a truce signed on January 23. On January 30, two top Nixon aides were convicted of spying on the Democratic National Committee headquarters at the Watergate Building.

In the same way that these landmark events brought a sense of justice and liberation, you, too, seek to personify these qualities in your professional life. Perhaps you have found yourself in a well-heeled place of work, but have felt unsatisfied by its regressive mentality. Your unique astrological connection to some of the most powerful and influential people around helps you move things from the old to the new.

When in love, friendship is a high priority for you, perhaps even more than sexual compatibility. Your egalitarian attitude allows for more open relationships than society generally recognizes, but this, too, is a way to achieve change. Though you are generally tolerant of others, you're probably most attracted to those who share your worldview. You tend to get along best with Geminis, Librans, Sagittarians, and Capricorns.

A big challenge for you, Aquarius of 1973, is to find the professional role that allows you to help change the world. Since your birth month represents a pivotal point in history, you are psychologically encoded to help usher in the New Age. You won't be satisfied with ordinary work or social relationships. Once you have found your special task, your gift lies in being the committed individual who sets the example for us all.

➤ Read about your Chinese Astrological sign on page 838. ➤ Read about your Personal Planets on page 826. ➤ Read about your personal Mystical Card on page 856.

1973

CAPRICORN
Your Personal Planets

YOUR LOVE POTENTIAL
Venus in Sagittarius, Jan. 01, 0:00 - Jan. 11, 19:14
Venus in Capricorn, Jan. 11, 19:15 - Jan. 20, 4:47

YOUR DRIVE AND AMBITION
Mars in Sagittarius, Jan. 01, 0:00 - Jan. 20, 4:47

YOUR LUCK MAGNETISM
Jupiter in Capricorn, Jan. 01, 0:00 - Jan. 20, 4:47

World Events

Jan. 1 - Great Britain, Ireland, and Denmark join the European Economic Community.

Jan. 9 - The sale of Picasso's erotic prints is banned in Brazil.

British Prime Minister Edward Heath on deciding to join the EEC

AQUARIUS
Your Personal Planets

YOUR LOVE POTENTIAL
Venus in Capricorn, Jan. 20, 4:48 - Feb. 04, 18:42
Venus in Aquarius, Feb. 04, 18:43 - Feb. 18, 19:00

YOUR DRIVE AND AMBITION
Mars in Sagittarius, Jan. 20, 4:48 - Feb. 12, 5:50
Mars in Capricorn, Feb. 12, 5:51 - Feb. 18, 19:00

YOUR LUCK MAGNETISM
Jupiter in Capricorn, Jan. 20, 4:48 - Feb. 18, 19:00

World Events

Jan. 23 - A volcano erupts in Iceland, causing widespread panic and destruction.

Jan. 27 - A peace treaty is signed by North and South Korea.

1973

PISCES
Your Personal Planets

YOUR LOVE POTENTIAL
Venus in Aquarius, Feb. 18, 19:01 - Feb. 28, 18:44
Venus in Pisces, Feb. 28, 18:45 - Mar. 20, 18:11

YOUR DRIVE AND AMBITION
Mars in Capricorn, Feb. 18, 19:01 - Mar. 20, 18:11

YOUR LUCK MAGNETISM
Jupiter in Capricorn, Feb. 18, 19:01 - Feb. 23, 9:27
Jupiter in Aquarius, Feb. 23, 9:28 - Mar. 20, 18:11

World Events

Feb. 22 – The U.S. and China agree to establish liaison offices in the capital cities of each country.

Feb. 28 – Two hundred and fifty members of the American Indian Movement seize Wounded Knee, demanding that the U.S. Senate opens an inquiry into government treatment of Indians.

Death of painter Pablo Picasso

ARIES
Your Personal Planets

YOUR LOVE POTENTIAL
Venus in Pisces, Mar. 20, 18:12 - Mar. 24, 20:33
Venus in Aries, Mar. 24, 20:34 - Apr. 18, 1:04
Venus in Taurus, Apr. 18, 1:05 - Apr. 20, 5:29

YOUR DRIVE AND AMBITION
Mars in Capricorn, Mar. 20, 18:12 - Mar. 26, 20:58
Mars in Aquarius, Mar. 26, 20:59 - Apr. 20, 5:29

YOUR LUCK MAGNETISM
Jupiter in Aquarius, Mar. 20, 18:12 - Apr. 20, 5:29

World Events

Mar. 26 – British playwright Noël Coward dies.

Apr. 8 – Pablo Picasso dies.

PISCES
From February 18, 19:01 through March 20, 18:11

The Intuitive Warrior

As a 1973 Pisces, you have a strong sense of purpose and are more willing to take direct action than most twentieth-century Pisceans. You tend to prefer a step-by-step approach in life, but when you feel you are spiritually guided, you may be willing to buck authority or challenge the status quo, even if it means making great personal sacrifices. Not the wishy-washy type, you have a fighter's instincts.

On February 28, 1973, members of the American Indian Movement took ten hostages at Wounded Knee and demanded a government investigation into the treatment of Indians. This event reflects the celestial qualities present at the time, which also shape your life—including the warrior's path, when necessary. On March 1, 1973, Robyn Smith became the first female jockey to win at a major horse race, likewise reflecting your willingness to fight for equality and fair treatment.

In your professional life, you have a keen social awareness that can be translated into meaningful work. When this is combined with your strong work ethic, you rise quickly in your chosen field. Your ability to attract the movers and shakers may put you on the fast track, if you don't move too quickly or take unsound risks. You love to be around friendly people, and work provides this outlet.

You are likely to have a highly romantic nature, and enjoy quiet, intimate get-togethers. Another side of you enjoys meeting and socializing with like-minded friends, perhaps over a favorite cause or recreational activity. Getting your desire for friends and intimacy in sync can be a difficult task, but you prefer to let people come and go as they please. In general, you get along best with Cancerians, Scorpios, Capricorns, and Aquarians.

One challenge you might face is in the quality of your thinking. At times you may be flooded by unrealistic fantasies, while at other times you are tuned into mystical messages. You may be highly intuitive, or deluded by false hope. Your gift is that once you have fine-tuned your own mental radio, you may be a constructive force in the evolution of the thinking patterns of others.

ARIES
From March 20, 18:12 through April 20, 5:29

The Team Leader

As a 1973 Aries, you were born during an era of great social change, a time that likely shaped you into an independent thinker with a strong social conscience. You probably have a sharp wit and fiery enthusiasm that can inspire others. You may have unusual, even radical ideas about what needs to be done, and, if you are willing to work with others, may help bring about great changes.

On April 1, 1973, India began a campaign to save the tiger. This important turning point was brought about by the same celestial forces shaping your life, which encourage and favor cause-oriented team efforts. On April 15, 1973, Cesar Chavez led the United Farm Workers' Union to boycott the California grape growers, and this event is likewise a group-oriented movement favored by those born at this time. As for work, you need to be as independent as possible, while still making a living wage. Your "don't fence me in" attitude can work against having a routine job, so working as a freelancer, or owning a small business might suit you best. You may find that an open-minded partnership will also aid you in the business world. You may be very effective as a team player, if you approve of the group's goals.

You probably have a group of friends you like to be with—people who enjoy your feistiness, blunt honesty, and the bold colors you wear. You probably have no trouble charming others by your self-confidence and your amusing remarks. When you are attracted to someone, you usually aren't shy about it. You enjoy the mating game, but then when it's time to make a commitment, you're less sure of yourself. In general, you get along best with Geminis, Leos, Librans, and Sagittarians.

A big challenge for you, Aries of 1973, may be to develop roots and to form long-term relationships. You have a great mental detachment that facilitates your objective view of things, but when it comes to more emotional situations, you can get thrown for a loop. Your strength is that you have great ideas and plenty of enthusiasm to lead others. When you are focused on a cause, you may make significant social progress..

► Read about your Chinese Astrological sign on page 838. ► Read about your Personal Planets on page 826. ► Read about your personal Mystical Card on page 856.

TAURUS

From April 20, 5:30 through May 21, 4:53

The Steady Connoisseur

As a 1973 Taurus, you have good taste, and recognize and appreciate quality when you see it. Born during a politically chaotic era, you are more likely to be interested in real change, not the "maybe-it-will, maybe-it-won't" kind of proposals. Instinctively, you know that for any change to be truly effective, it has to have wide support. Until that happens, you rely on tried-and-true methods.

On May 7, 1973, Bernstein and Woodward of the *Washington Post* were awarded the Pulitzer Prize for their coverage of the Watergate scandal. The astrological themes of your birth month are reflected in this event, and they point to quality, intelligence, and social progress. A similar set of traits can be seen in the May 14 launch of *Skylab*, the first U.S. space station. *Skylab* became the enduring hallmark for space exploration after the series of *Apollo* flights to the Moon.

In your professional life, you have a refreshing practicality about you that your peers lack. While others get whip-lashed by many fanciful ideas or playful escapes, you are the steady one, and may have slowly developed a marketable expertise concerning certain quality goods or services. You still carry the 1973 vibe of wanting social progress, so you may find a work opportunity that helps expand people's awareness.

When you make a friend or become intimately connected to someone, they'll probably be around you for the rest of your life. Even if you separate, you may stay in touch through mutual friends or by sending holiday greetings. You value your people connections, and add a sense of stability and honesty to others' lives. In general, you get along best with Virgos, Capricorns, Aquarians, and Pisceans.

A potential problem area for you can be found in balancing your love life with your circle of friends. You are liable to have a great interest in sharing time with friends of both sexes, and this can be tricky when you are involved with one individual. Your special strength is that you are motivated by anything that has been tested by time. When a revolutionary idea arrives, only you will know if its time is ripe.

GEMINI

From May 21, 4:54 through June 21, 13:00

The Restless Promoter

As a 1973 Gemini, you have diverse skills and interests, and a passionate curiosity for facts and information. You are very likely to be more serious than most Geminis of the twentieth century, perhaps because you have tuned into some important ideas, and want to make an impact on the world. You are also likely to have unusually wide mood swings for a thinker, and may be highly intuitive.

On May 26, 1973, the Supreme Court ruled that radio and television stations were not obligated to sell equal airtime for political issues. This historical event reflects a celestial influence prevalent during your birth month, which also influences your life. Events of June 16 further illustrate this concern about ideas and information. On that day, Soviet Premier Leonid Brezhnev arrived in the U.S. to sign an agreement to promote scientific exchanges between the two Superpowers.

In your career, you may be a promoter of some kind, and may be especially adept at telecommunications or information technology. You have an unusually assertive style and may at times push too fast or too hard, but when you have seen the importance of restraint, you may also wait too long to say your piece. When you have these two tendencies in balance, you will go far in your climb to success.

In your relationships, you have a charming quality about you that others find curiously attractive. Highly sentimental when it comes to romance, you may find that your earlier years were filled with poetry and shared travel experiences. However, you may get easily bored, and are not likely to settle into a more committed relationship until the age of thirty or so. You tend to get along best with Cancerians, Librans, Sagittarians, and Aquarians.

A significant challenge for you is to get grounded. You have such widespread interests that you may find it easy to move on, both in your relationships and in where you call home. Once you have established some roots, your many excellent insights and ambitions will have a chance to grow into your strength, which is your ability to put new ideas into constructive forms.

TAURUS
Your Personal Planets

YOUR LOVE POTENTIAL
Venus in Taurus, Apr. 20, 5:30 - May 12, 8:41
Venus in Gemini, May 12, 8:42 - May 21, 4:53

YOUR DRIVE AND AMBITION
Mars in Aquarius, Mar. 20, 5:30 - May 08, 4:08
Mars in Pisces, May 08, 4:09 - May 21, 4:53

YOUR LUCK MAGNETISM
Jupiter in Aquarius, Apr. 20, 5:30 - May 21, 4:53

World Events

May 7 – *The Washington Post* is awarded the Pulitzer Prize for its coverage of the Watergate affair.

May 14 – The first U.S. space station, *Skylab 1*, is launched.

The staff of The Washington Post discuss developments in the Watergate story

GEMINI
Your Personal Planets

YOUR LOVE POTENTIAL
Venus in Gemini, May 21, 4:54 - June 05, 19:19
Venus in Cancer, June 05, 19:20 - June 21, 13:00

YOUR DRIVE AND AMBITION
Mars in Pisces, May 21, 4:54 - June 20, 20:53
Mars in Aries, June 20, 20:54 - June 21, 13:00

YOUR LUCK MAGNETISM
Jupiter in Aquarius, May 21, 4:54 - June 21, 13:00

World Events

May 24 – British House of Lords leader Earl Jellicoe resigns amidst an escalating sex scandal.

June 16 – Soviet leader Brezhnev arrives in the U.S. and signs agreements to reduce the risk of accidental nuclear war.

➤ Read about your Chinese Astrological sign on page 838. ➤ Read about your Personal Planets on page 826. ➤ Read about your personal Mystical Card on page 856.

1973

CANCER
Your Personal Planets

YOUR LOVE POTENTIAL
Venus in Cancer, June 21, 13:01 - June 30, 8:54
Venus in Leo, June 30, 8:55 - July 22, 23:55

YOUR DRIVE AND AMBITION
Mars in Aries, June 21, 13:01 - July 22, 23:55

YOUR LUCK MAGNETISM
Jupiter in Aquarius, June 21, 13:01 - July 22, 23:55

World Events

June 24 - Eamon de Valera, President of Ireland and the oldest active head of state, retires at ninety years old.

July 10 - The Bahamas becomes independent of Great Britain.

President of Ireland Eamon de Valera

LEO
Your Personal Planets

YOUR LOVE POTENTIAL
Venus in Leo, July 22, 23:56 - July 25, 2:12
Venus in Virgo, July 25, 2:13 - Aug. 19, 1:09
Venus in Libra, Aug. 19, 1:10 - Aug. 23, 6:52

YOUR DRIVE AND AMBITION
Mars in Aries, July 22, 23:56 - Aug. 12, 14:55
Mars in Taurus, Aug. 12, 14:56 - Aug. 23, 6:52

YOUR LUCK MAGNETISM
Jupiter in Aquarius, July 22, 23:56 - Aug. 23, 6:52

World Events

July 28 - Six hundred thousand people attend the largest U.S. rock concert ever held, at Watkins Glen in New York.

Aug. 19 - Greek President Papaudopolos restores the country from its state of marshal law.

598

CANCER
From June 21, 13:01 through July 22, 23:55

The Nurturing Warrior

Cancer of 1973 has a highly dramatic style that may fool others into thinking you're not really a Moon Child. However, those who know you best will recognize your devotion to family, and your sensitivity and concern for the less fortunate. You may have a strong loyalty to an ethnic or national ancestry, and won't back down when you're defending your people or your principles.

On June 24, 1973, Eamon de Valera, President of the Republic of Ireland, resigned at the age of ninety. This event reflects the celestial influence of tradition and ancestry that was venerated during your birth month. On June 22 Soviet Prime Minister Leonid Brezhnev attended a summit conference in the U.S. He signed a pact aimed at avoiding confrontations that could lead to nuclear war. In the same spirit, you can protect your own interests through peaceful means, but can be assertive when necessary.

In your professional life, you have charisma and a fiery enthusiasm that can take you far. You can wow people with your ease in social settings and your self-confidence. You have a great deal of personal power that can create some envy or adversity when working with a team or within an organization.

You have a natural warmth and sense of showmanship that makes you popular and fun to be around. When you get intimately involved, your emotional side emerges, and you may prefer that your partner be the strong one. If your partner doesn't recognize your needs, you may assert them indirectly through strong moods. When you're not involved with one person, you have plenty of friends and family members to entertain. You get along best with Leos, Scorpios, Pisceans, and Ariens.

A major challenge may be to balance your emotional, nurturing side with an inner warrior that desires to be the best. You might find that these divergent interests come out at different times or with different people. When you recognize both of these tendencies as valid and necessary, then you have found your gift. Then you can creatively blend your drives and moods at the most opportune times and for maximum effectiveness.

LEO
From July 22, 23:56 through August 23, 6:52

The Paradigm Buster

As a 1973 Leo, you have a larger-than-life sense of drama, and may be a master of special effects. You may have an attraction for big events that transform not only your personal life, but also the lives of those around you. Like many born during 1973, you may have come from a dysfunctional family, but by following a creative and brave path, you have found a new sense of belonging and community.

On July 28, 1973, the largest rock concert in history was held at Watkins Glen, New York, and this event reflects the planetary forces that also shape your life. The communal experience was a transformative, counter-cultural, and mystically inventive event. In the same way, you have a strong drive to find your own creative path and to have a dynamic impact on the tenor of your times.

As a professional, you have a unique ability to think big. At times, you may be forced to play by what seem like oppressive rules. If you follow this path, you may actually be successful, and become a strong voice for the tried-and-true ways, while feeling inwardly stifled or smothered. Your mission, should you choose to accept it, is to help overcome old structures in favor of deeper truths and new ways. You have the energy, ingenuity, and vision to take this path.

Family means a lot to you, and even if you felt disappointed by the way things developed when you were growing up, those early learning experiences continue to influence your life through your relationship patterns. As a natural paradigm buster, you have it within your abilities to recreate healthy, loving, mutually supportive relationships, and a tribal circle of friends to go along with them. In general, you get along best with Librans, Sagittarians, Aquarians, and Ariens.

A major life challenge for you may be to let go of the past. Your life karma probably includes some deep crisis or transformative experience that has reshaped your worldview. Blaming parents, teachers, or society in general won't help you to grow as an individual. In letting go, you open yourself to your gift, which is your creative power to make a new world.

➤ Read about your Chinese Astrological sign on page 838. ➤ Read about your Personal Planets on page 826. ➤ Read about your personal Mystical Card on page 856.

VIRGO

From August 23, 6:53 through September 23, 4:20

The Practical Mystic

As a 1973 Virgo, you have a strong work ethic, and an unusually high tolerance for risk. With your keen analytical skills, you may be adept at understanding and utilizing the best of the new technologies, putting you on the cutting edge of advances in the workplace, health fields, and communications. You may also be blessed with a great imagination, and are perfectly capable of finding practical solutions to problems.

The same cosmic influences that cause your affinity with the animal kingdom were highlighted on a grand scale the year you were born. On August 30, 1973, Kenya banned the hunting of elephants and commercial trade in ivory. On September 20, the infamous "battle of the sexes" tennis match took place between Bobby Riggs and Billie Jean King—she won—and this event symbolizes your good-natured, imaginative, and competitive spirit.

In your career, you may excel in a field that uses or promotes some new technology. You are instinctively attuned to the daily demands of the job, and you can lighten up, or charm, your co-workers through a touch of magic. Even if you aren't consciously aware of the process, you may have unusual abilities that startle others with their strangeness or mystery. You may have healing gifts, or perhaps even work as a health practitioner.

Your relationship patterns can go through cycles of deep change. Perhaps relocating for a new job, or just personal adjustments, have caused you to re-evaluate your partnership status and your circle of friends. You are motivated by stability, but you also have a constant need to regenerate yourself and therefore your relationships. In general, you get along best with Librans, Scorpios, Capricorns, and Taureans.

A major life challenge for you is to recognize your supernatural talents. You were born during a mystical planetary alignment shaped like a pentagram, and this celestial set-up has great potential for creative, or destructive, force. The better you know yourself, the better you will be able to maximize your potential. Your gift attunes you to the power of the spirit over the material world.

LIBRA

From September 23, 4:21 through October 23, 13:29

The Power Broker

As a 1973 Libra, you were born during an era of social turmoil resulting from major shifts in geopolitical power. Most twentieth-century Librans seek harmony and peaceful co-existence; you, however, came into a world teetering dangerously toward chaos. Through your many social interactions, you are likely to have developed the networking skills and intellectual tools to be on the front lines of collective change.

On October 6, 1973, Syria and Egypt attacked Israel, beginning the Yom Kippur War. Then on October 17, the Arab nations of OPEC began cutting oil production. By the end of 1974, oil prices had quadrupled, leading to rocketing prices for many other goods. The underlying cosmic forces supporting this massive transfer of financial and political power are the same ones that astrologically shape your life path.

In your professional life, you have the shrewdness and work ethic to know how to make a buck. Yet, because you were born during such a transformative month, an "ordinary" job may not satisfy you. By fate or your own conscious efforts, your career is likely to be closely involved with larger social issues. While you're no radical, you would like to help others make radical changes.

A rare pentagram configuration influenced your entire birth month, giving you a cosmic itch that makes it difficult to stay in a traditional partnership. You are likely to seek unusual kinds of connections with people, and you may enjoy experimenting with alternative lifestyles and co-habitation. Above all, you need a great deal of personal freedom within your closest relations. In general, you get along best with Scorpios, Sagittarians, Aquarians, and Geminis.

A major life challenge for you is how to constructively use the incredible cosmic forces at your disposal. The inherent power available to the 1973 Libra can simply be too much to master, and can lead to destructive impulses. Your gift is your sense of harmony, your ability to keep the various psychodynamics in balance. With it, you can become a player in the big games and help mediate a smooth transition to the new..

➤ Read about your Chinese Astrological sign on page 838. ➤ Read about your Personal Planets on page 826. ➤ Read about your personal Mystical Card on page 856.

VIRGO
Your Personal Planets

YOUR LOVE POTENTIAL
Venus in Libra, Aug. 23, 6:53 - Sept. 13, 9:04
Venus in Scorpio, Sept. 13, 9:05 - Sept. 23, 4:20

YOUR DRIVE AND AMBITION
Mars in Taurus, Aug. 23, 6:53 - Sept. 23, 4:20

YOUR LUCK MAGNETISM
Jupiter in Aquarius, Aug. 23, 6:53 - Sept. 23, 4:20

World Events

Aug. 25 - Doctors in London report having made the first CAT scan

Sept. 20 - "The Battle of the Sexes" tennis match is played between Billie Jean King and Bobby Riggs; Billie Jean King emerges the victor.

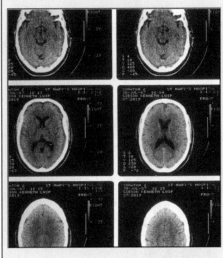

Doctors in London make the first CAT scan

LIBRA
Your Personal Planets

YOUR LOVE POTENTIAL
Venus in Scorpio, Sept. 23, 4:21 - Oct. 09, 8:07
Venus in Sagittarius, Oct. 09, 8:08 - Oct. 23, 13:29

YOUR DRIVE AND AMBITION
Mars in Taurus, Sept. 23, 4:21 - Oct. 23, 13:29

YOUR LUCK MAGNETISM
Jupiter in Aquarius, Sept. 23, 4:21 - Oct. 23, 13:29

World Events

Oct. 6 - The Yom Kippur War begins between Egyptian and Israeli forces.

Oct. 20 - The new opera house in Sydney, Australia is officially opened by Queen Elizabeth II.

1973

SCORPIO
Your Personal Planets

YOUR LOVE POTENTIAL

Venus in Sagittarius, Oct. 23, 13:30 - Nov. 05, 15:38
Venus in Capricorn, Nov. 05, 15:39 - Nov. 22, 10:53

YOUR DRIVE AND AMBITION

Mars in Taurus, Oct. 23, 13:30 - Oct. 29, 22:55
Mars in Aries, Oct. 29, 22:56 - Nov. 22, 10:53

YOUR LUCK MAGNETISM

Jupiter in Aquarius, Oct. 23, 13:30 - Nov. 22, 10:53

World Events

Nov. 13 – Italian fashion designer Elsa Schiaparelli dies.

Nov. 14 – Britain's Princess Anne and Capt. Mark Phillips wed in Westminster Abbey, London.

Princess Anne marries Captain Mark Phillips

SAGITTARIUS
Your Personal Planets

YOUR LOVE POTENTIAL

Venus in Capricorn, Nov. 22, 10:54 - Dec. 07, 21:36
Venus in Aquarius, Dec. 07, 21:37 - Dec. 22, 0:07

YOUR DRIVE AND AMBITION

Mars in Aries, Nov. 22, 10:54 - Dec. 22, 0:07

YOUR LUCK MAGNETISM

Jupiter in Aquarius, Nov. 22, 10:54 - Dec. 22, 0:07

World Events

Nov. 24 – Australia grants the vote to Aborigines.

Dec. 13 – In an unusual move to save fuel, Britain cuts the working week to three days.

SCORPIO
From October 23, 13:30 through November 22, 10:53

The Independent Analyst

As a 1973 Scorpio, you are likely to be keenly attuned to who has power and influence and who doesn't. You may be interested in curtailing the excess or arbitrary use of authority, especially when it weighs on your personal rights. More introspective than many Scorpios, you also have a wider understanding of geopolitical issues, and an interest in the wise and responsible use of power.

On November 7, 1973, the U.S. Congress—over Nixon's veto—passed the War Powers Resolution, and this historical event closely reflects the astrological currents of your birth month. Nixon complained that this law would dangerously restrict the President's ability to send troops into foreign conflicts. The new law demanded congressional approval before troops were committed. Although future Presidents ignored the measure, putting limits on power was its central theme.

In your professional life, you are naturally drawn to those with financial influence and personal prestige, yet at the same time won't long stand being told what to do. Your scope of vision includes awareness of major business cycles, which favors a career as a money analyst or assets manager. You would do best as an independent worker or consultant; you have freedom to take advantage of your insights, then.

You probably think a great deal about your personal relationships, and like many born during 1973, have been forced to deal with major upheavals. For you, making a long-term commitment is connected to having children, and that step would curtail your need for independence. If you find the right partner, you could commit— when your income is secure. In general, you get along best with Capricorns, Pisceans, Cancerians, and Librans.

A big challenge for you may be to handle your urge to confront authority figures, either your parents or bosses, or society in general. Your strong rebellious streak can undermine the lifestyle that you so carefully build. On the other hand, at times you may be totally reasonable in confronting powerful people. Your gift is your sense of justice, and this instinct will tell you when to act.

SAGITTARIUS
From November 22, 10:54 through December 22, 0:07

The Robust Adventurer

As a 1973 Sagittarius, you have an unusually excitable nature, and are always ready for sudden changes. You may not have the time or inclination for a wandering, philosophic quest, such as those that many twentieth-century Sagittarians indulge in, although you may be interested in understanding the nature of crises, especially in relationship patterns. You are likely to have great personal courage, a high tolerance for risk, and a compelling love of thrills and adventure.

The Sagittarian's love for the great outdoors is well known. As a 1973 Archer, you also place great value on public recognition. This combination makes you especially competitive and successful in sports, like the famous Jack Nicklaus. On December 11, 1976, he became the first golfer to earn $2 million in a single year.

In your career, you would do well in any fast-paced or action-oriented venture. You thrive under adverse conditions, and would easily become bored in a routine job. Your enjoyment of action and speed is the temperament of a racecar driver, though you may find the competitive high-tech industry or military service equally rewarding. You probably exhibit a fascination and expertise for specific technologies—areas in which you can gain steady employment.

In the romance department, your robust independence can work against long-term relationships. If you have found a loving, faithful partnership, it's probably characterized by frequent interruptions or separations, often for reasons beyond your control. You are likely to surround yourself with friends who share your worldview, and these ties can become almost familial. In general, you get along best with Aquarians, Ariens, Leos, and Librans.

A significant life challenge for you may be to not get discouraged by the uncertainty and volatility of your lifestyle. Settling into a regular routine is probably not suitable for your intense spontaneity, but being ungrounded, restlessly seeking new challenges, is not satisfying either. Your special gift is your network of friends—it makes you a global citizen, with your home being Planet Earth.

➤ Read about your Chinese Astrological sign on page 838. ➤ Read about your Personal Planets on page 826. ➤ Read about your personal Mystical Card on page 856.

CAPRICORN

From December 22, 0:08 through December 31, 23:59

The Ultimate Survivor

As a Capricorn born in December 1973, you are likely to have a fascination for the unknown, especially if it's potentially dangerous, threatening, or supernatural. Yet your inherently cautious nature finds ways to understand and endure, because you are, above all other things, a survivor. You are likely to have dealt with intense or difficult struggles while growing up, and these family patterns continue to shape your current affairs.

On December 25, 1973, Skylab astronauts photographed the comet Kahoutek, and this event reflects your own ingenuity in understanding the unknown. On December 28, 1973, Alexander Solzhenitsyn's *Gulag Archipelago* was published for the first time in Paris. This chronicle of Stalin's prison camps also characterizes the astrological influences that shape your life, which include personal hardship, survival, and moral courage.

These qualities are superb assets in the business world, and you may go far in whatever career you choose. You may have tremendous resourcefulness to overcome occasionally virulent opposition from rivals, and you have a talent for digging in your heels to outlast any opponent in a showdown. In short, your challenges are great, but also you have the skills and determination to overcome them and rise to the top.

Although your early family life may have been upsetting at times, you have a personal magnetism that attracts friends of both sexes. You are probably well liked in diverse social circles, and have plenty of casual companions. Forming a healthy, intimate relationship may depend on how well you've come to terms with your parents. In general, you get along best with Taureans, Cancerians, Virgos, and Aquarians.

A big problem for you might be to manage your intensity levels. The astrological influences of your birth week include some of the most problematical and most favorable combinations possible. Your challenge is to not lose sight of your cosmic gifts as you work to resolve the complexities that you inevitably attract. Your gifts are many, and include a circle of well-meaning friends and a sense of social justice.

CAPRICORN
Your Personal Planets

YOUR LOVE POTENTIAL
Venus in Aquarius, Dec. 22, 0:08 - Dec. 31, 23:59

YOUR DRIVE AND AMBITION
Mars in Aries, Dec. 22, 0:08 - Dec. 24, 8:08
Mars in Taurus, Dec. 24, 8:09 - Dec. 31, 23:59

YOUR LUCK MAGNETISM
Jupiter in Aquarius, Dec. 22, 0:08 - Dec. 31, 23:59

World Events

Dec. 25 - Astronauts on the Skylab space station make a record-breaking seven-hour space-walk.

Dec. 26 - Long Boret becomes Cambodian premier.

The Findhorn Nature Sanctuary

Special Feature
Findhorn's Magical Garden

(Continued from page 593)

The co-directors created the Findhorn Foundation as a legal trust and Scottish charity. They purchased the caravan park and a nearby cottage and hotel. David went on from his Findhorn experience to become one of the leading luminaries for New Age ideas.

The New Age entrepreneur Paul Hawken also participated around this time, and would later give his eyewitness account in *The Magic Of Findhorn*. Hawken described Findhorn as an organism in itself, and an emergent aspect of the evolution of consciousness. The people who lived there were part of the growing organism, helping to bring it to life and fruition. "Far away from the cities, the pollution, the strange vibrations and cultural forms of civilization, desolate in a way, Findhorn was located where the air, water, and land were pure," he wrote. "I knew that we had not decided anything, nor created anything, but had co-created it."

Today, through synergy and synchronicity, Findhorn has evolved into a center for holistic education. Each year about 4,000 people take part in residential programs lasting from one week to six months. Visitors are welcomed at the rate of 10,000 annually, and cooperation with nature has expanded from gardening to working on a variety of environmental projects. In 1990 the residents began constructing an experimental Ecovillage, designed to combine everything they learned about the divinity of life and cooperation with nature.

The Ecovillage began by replacing the ageing caravans (mobile trailers) with ecological housing. A wind generator now provides twenty percent of Findhorn's electricity needs, and many buildings have solar panels. The most recent addition is a "Living Machine," which is a sewage treatment facility using plant bacteria and animal life to break down waste naturally. The ongoing development of the Ecovillage is intended to provide a model for the twenty-first century, and continues to function as a tool for research and education. The Findhorn Foundation is the heart of a rapidly growing Ecovillage network, which links similar projects worldwide.

Findhorn thrives today as a constantly expanding and diversifying community. About 450 people who live in the local area are linked to thousands of friends and supporters around the world. Findhorn businesses include publishing, a holistic healthcare center, solar panel production, and Findhorn Flower Essences. In 1997 Findhorn was recognized as an official United Nations Non-Governmental Organization, and participated in UN events including the Earth Summit and Habitat II. Findhorn has since become the heart of an international community, connecting environmental, economic, social, and spiritual values. ✪

➤ Read "Gaia's Mystical Power Places" by Ronnie Grishman on page 745. ➤ Read "The Enigma of Crop Circles" by Frank Andrews on page 673.

1974

Difficult Transitions: Saturn and Pluto

Saturn and Pluto are two slow-moving planets that, when they connect, remain in tandem for more than a year. Saturn, the teacher of our most difficult lessons, often instructs us through hardship. Pluto, lord of hidden power, may manifest itself in the desire to exert control. When they combine, problems of both power-grabbing and hardship may arise. This is precisely what happened in 1973–74. Two issues were central: the Arab oil embargo against Israel's allies and the balance of power between branches of government. The latter was exhibited by the battle of U.S. President Richard Nixon versus the legislative and judicial branches related to the Watergate scandal.

In early 1974, as Saturn and Pluto were repeatedly triggered, the courts began their inexorable march toward justice in the Watergate hearings. At the same time, the oil embargo was wreaking its worst on motorists throughout Europe and America, resulting in rationing and skyrocketing prices. Although the embargo was lifted in March, the oil-producing nations refused to cut prices, and the crisis continued to take its economic toll on those countries that had crossed the Arabs. As Saturn and Pluto made their final contact in May, Congress began to push for Nixon's impeachment. In August, activating Jupiter touched off Saturn again, and the scandal reached its climax with Nixon's resignation. Leadership crises in other nations were also resolved this year and new leaders assumed power in Ethiopia, Portugal, Greece, Israel, and West Germany. The cathartic events of 1974 resulted in a more stable world.

Soviet ballet star Mikhail Baryshnikov defects while on tour in Toronto

The vote for Nixon's impeachment

German chancellor Willy Brandt resigns

PSYCHIC SPY

In the summer of 1974, in Langley, Virginia, CIA officers launched the first documented psychic-spying mission in United States history. Pat Price, a "remote viewer" hired on a CIA contract, was given the coordinates of a secret research center in the USSR, about which the CIA would like more information. Price cleared his mind and peered mentally in search of the site, claiming to see "a damn big crane." This is just one observation that proved accurate at the time, though the CIA did not continue the project.

GOVERNMENTS IN FLUX

Several countries experienced changes of leadership. In Greece, seven years of military rule by the colonels ended when Constantine Karamanlis returned from exile to form a civilian government. Argentine President Juan Peron died and wife Isabel succeeded him. France narrowly elected rightist Giscard d'Estaing as President. Israeli Prime Minister Golda Meir was succeeded by Yitzhak Rabin. German Chancellor Willy Brandt resigned in favor of Helmut Schmidt. Portugal's military overthrew dictator Caetano and set the scene for democratic reform. Under threat of impeachment for his part in the Watergate cover-up, U.S. President Nixon resigned. Vice-President Ford succeeded him. The Arab oil embargo continued, forcing stringent rationing on motorists. An attempt was made in London to kidnap the recently married Princess Anne. As kidnap for ransom crimes proliferated, publishing heiress Patty Hearst, captured by the Symbionese Liberation Army, helped raid a San Francisco bank. Russian ballet star Mikhail Baryshnikov emulated Nureyev and Makarova in defecting to the West. Condominiums revolutionized home ownership in the U.S.

➤ Read Elizabeth Taylor and Richard Burton's Star Profiles on page 609.

CAPRICORN
From January 01, 0:00 through January 20, 10:45

The Trusted Partner

As a 1974 January Capricorn, you are likely to have a strong ambition to make something of your life, and are aided by a steady and persevering work ethic. You have an unusually keen understanding of money issues, and a personal sense of authority based on factual evidence and knowledge. While you are naturally conservative in many of your views, you may also have a tough independent streak that occasionally rocks the status quo.

On January 11, two giant insurance companies—Blue Cross and Blue Shield—announced merger plans, setting off a wave of corporate mergers. The underlying astrological influences supporting this deal are the same that shape your life, and include a thorough understanding of financial matters, and the ability to bridge a traditional path with a progressive, new format, especially one that involves partnership.

In your career, you may find the easiest path for you is within an organized structure. However, this may not be fulfilling in the long run, even if it provides you with financial security. To follow your destiny, you probably need to express more of your individuality, and this can be done by forming more egalitarian alliances, as in the insurance merger. Business partnerships are likely to be your key to success and personal fulfillment.

In the romance department, you have a highly sensual nature, and a strong desire for intimacy. You may find that you must compromise in order to balance the needs of your intimate relationships and your sexual desires, but if this can be worked out, then you are likely to have a profound interest in forming a long-term, committed relationship. In general, you get along best with Taureans, Cancerians, Virgos, and Aquarians.

A significant challenge for you is to avoid getting stuck in a professional rut. You may have serious doubts or suspicions about working with a partner, or striking out on your own. When you realize that alliances or working as an equal within a group are both exciting and fulfilling, you will have found your strength. Then you will also have created a model for the twenty-first century.

AQUARIUS
From January 20, 10:46 through February 19, 0:58

The Risk Taker

As a 1974 Aquarius, you are likely to have an unusually active social life, with a network of diverse friends and progressive ideas or causes to keep you busy. You may excel in some technological area, or have an enduring interest in a scholarly pursuit. You have the gift of gab, and can talk yourself into or out of anything. You may also enjoy getting into difficult or even dangerous situations.

On January 25, 1974, Dr. Christiaan Bernard, pioneer of heart transplants in 1967, transplanted a human heart without removing the original organ. This medical breakthrough was experimental and controversial, but typifies the celestial vibes of your birth month: technologically advanced, risky, and supported by a community of like-minded colleagues. Similar cosmic forces were in play when the Symbionese Liberation Army kidnapped Patty Hearst on February 4: the boldness, the group effort, and the cause.

You probably blend these same elements creatively in your career path. You like the new or different, the risk, and the idea of working with like-minded friends. If you don't spend all your time studying, you may enjoy a career in telecommunications or information technology. Since you communicate so effectively, you would do well in sales or as a presenter. You are great at recognizing financial opportunities.

Friendship is a high priority for you, and this is especially true in your most intimate affairs. Your gregarious attitude is great for bringing many different kinds of people together, and since you're rarely at a loss for words, you keep the flow of conversation going. When it comes to forming a committed partnership, however, you may be more shy or a late bloomer. In general, you get along best with other Aquarians, Geminis, Librans, and Capricorns.

A significant challenge for you is to manage your attraction for the bizarre or outlandish. You may enjoy shocking people just to wake them up, but anything that has a lasting importance to you may also be shaken up by this tendency. Your strengths are your communications skills and your understanding of interdependence.

➤ Read about your Chinese Astrological sign on page 838. ➤ Read about your Personal Planets on page 826. ➤ Read about your personal Mystical Card on page 856.

CAPRICORN
Your Personal Planets

YOUR LOVE POTENTIAL
Venus in Aquarius, Jan. 01, 0:00 - Jan. 20, 10:45

YOUR DRIVE AND AMBITION
Mars in Taurus, Jan. 01, 0:00 - Jan. 20, 10:45

YOUR LUCK MAGNETISM
Jupiter in Aquarius, Jan. 01, 0:00 - Jan. 20, 10:45

World Events

Jan. 3 - U.S. Secretary of State Henry Kissinger and Israeli Defense Minister Moshe Dayan meet.

Jan. 9 - Government troops in Cambodia launch a new offensive against members of the Khmer Rouge.

Patty Hearst is abducted by the Symbionese Liberation Army

AQUARIUS
Your Personal Planets

YOUR LOVE POTENTIAL
Venus in Aquarius, Jan. 20, 10:46 - Jan. 29, 19:50
Venus in Capricorn, Jan. 29, 19:51 - Feb. 19, 0:58

YOUR DRIVE AND AMBITION
Mars in Taurus, Jan. 20, 10:46 - Feb. 19, 0:58

YOUR LUCK MAGNETISM
Jupiter in Aquarius, Jan. 20, 10:46 - Feb. 19, 0:58

World Events

Jan. 25 - In South Africa, Dr. Christiaan Barnard transplants the first human heart without removing the defective organ.

Feb. 5 - Patty Hearst, daughter of millionaire publisher Randolph Hearst, is abducted by the Symbionese Liberation Army.

1974

PISCES
Your Personal Planets

YOUR LOVE POTENTIAL
Venus in Capricorn, Feb. 19, 0:59 - Feb. 28, 14:24
Venus in Aquarius, Feb. 28, 14:25 - Mar. 21, 0:06

YOUR DRIVE AND AMBITION
Mars in Taurus, Feb. 19, 0:59 - Feb. 27, 10:10
Mars in Gemini, Feb. 27, 10:11 - Mar. 21, 0:06

YOUR LUCK MAGNETISM
Jupiter in Aquarius, Feb. 19, 0:59 - Mar. 08, 11:10
Jupiter in Pisces, Mar. 08, 11:11 - Mar. 21, 0:06

World Events

Mar. 7 – The first signs of dissatisfaction with Haile Selassie's rule in Ethiopia show in a general strike.

Mar. 18 – OPEC ends the oil embargo begun in 1973 during the Yom Kippur War.

Robert Redford and Mia Farrow in "The Great Gatsby"

ARIES
Your Personal Planets

YOUR LOVE POTENTIAL
Venus in Aquarius, Mar. 21, 0:07 - Apr. 06, 14:16
Venus in Pisces, Apr. 06, 14:17 - Apr. 20, 11:18

YOUR DRIVE AND AMBITION
Mars in Gemini, Mar. 21, 0:07 - Apr. 20, 8:17
Mars in Cancer, Apr. 20, 8:18 - Apr. 20, 11:18

YOUR LUCK MAGNETISM
Jupiter in Pisces, Mar. 21, 0:07 - Apr. 20, 11:18

World Events

Mar. 27 – The film of F. Scott Fitzgerald's *The Great Gatsby*, starring Robert Redford, premières.

Apr. 15 – Patty Hearst helps her captors rob a San Francisco bank.

PISCES
From February 19, 0:59 through March 21, 0:06

The Friendly Psychic

As a 1974 Pisces, you have a deep empathy and compassion—the kind that creates lasting relationships and a friendly work environment. You are likely to feel concern for the disadvantaged or for those who can't fend for themselves in the competitive global economy. Your natural charm and friendly manner make you good company in any social gathering, though you may feel others' pain and become emotionally involved in their situations.

On March 6, 1974, Harold Wilson, the recently elected Labour Prime Minister of Britain, announced his intention to prioritize the settlement of a coalminers' strike with a larger wage increase than the previous Conservative government allowed. This political development was made possible by the astrological influences of your birth month, which also shape your life pattern. You may have the same interest in improving the lives of people, especially those who need protection from social injustice.

Being a caring, socially aware individual can shape your career objectives. And like others born in early 1974, you may have an aptitude for telecommunications or information technologies. You're a people person, and enjoy work that actively involves others. On the down side, you may also be a psychic sponge; if you are feeling depressed or down while on the job, you may be picking up atmospheric conditions.

In relationships, you become confident and strong if you and yours are getting along well. If either you or your partner is disappointed or disillusioned, however, then both of you will suffer. You are likely to have excellent communication skills, but may be less than candid when asked about your feelings. In general, you get along best with Geminis, Cancerians, Scorpios, and Aquarians.

Your challenge is to set up boundaries so that you can develop your own individuality without undue influence by others. You're so sensitive to what others are thinking that you may find it difficult to identify your own feelings and goals. Your gift is your circle of friends and other relations—those who encourage you, and are encouraged by you in return

ARIES
From March 21, 0:07 through April 20, 11:18

The Idealistic Rival

As a 1974 Aries, you are likely to have a healthy dose of self-confidence and strength of character. You may closely identify with a social group or faction, especially one that is opposed by another. The sense of "us" and "them" can become a defining characteristic of your job, personal relationships, and social standing. You have strong ideals or beliefs, and from time to time may become disillusioned when people or circumstances don't measure up.

On March 27, 1974, *The Great Gatsby*, a movie depicting the shallow social elitism of the 1920s, premiered. The celestial vibrations that coincided with this movie's theme are the same that affect your life; in this case, the haves versus the have-nots. On April 10, Israeli Premier Golda Meir resigned due to divisions in her own party. Again, the theme of factions is the underlying influence.

In your career, you may encounter work situations that emphasize intense competition. You may be an independent professional or part of a group that works for a cause or against a system, or you may have tough rivals. The Aries energy provides you with a warrior's discipline in the market economy, though you may face the most difficult challenges due to your idealism or convictions. You could excel at communications, if you aren't too blunt.

In relationships, you are likely to get along best with those who share your beliefs and opinions. At times, you may have to go your own way when what you want isn't allowed within the structure of your partnership. A major factor in the health of your relationships is the quality of your communications. In general, you get along best with Geminis, Leos, Librans, and Aquarians.

A major life challenge for you is to find compromises. All too often you may give or get an ultimatum that leads to separation and hurt feelings. Being willing to forgive and let go is the key to growth. Your strength is in your curiosity and thirst for knowledge. You may enjoy wonderful traveling experiences, and these help to broaden your worldview and expand your appreciation for different cultures and value systems.

➤ Read about your Chinese Astrological sign on page 838. ➤ Read about your Personal Planets on page 826. ➤ Read about your personal Mystical Card on page 856.

TAURUS

From April 20, 11:19 through May 21, 10:35

The Resilient Defender

As a 1974 Taurus, you have unusually strong security needs that are likely to find expression in a healthy drive for financial well-being and domestic safety. You can be ferociously defensive when your home or those you love are threatened, and this makes you a good provider who is sensitive to family concerns. Periodically, you may have to restructure your entire lifestyle, and these experiences are what shape your need for stability.

On May 6, 1974, Willie Brandt, the Chancellor of Germany, was forced to resign due to a large spy scandal. The underlying astrological influences of this historical event are the same forces that shape your life: upheaval, security issues, and rebuilding toward a safer situation. The same cosmic factors were apparent on May 15, 1974 when the Dalkon Shield (IUD) was taken off the market because of serious health concerns.

In your professional life, you may prefer to work out of your home, or in an office situation that approximates a homey atmosphere. Your co-workers may become like family members, or your family members may help you with your career or business. You may be tuned into women's rights in the workplace, and could greatly benefit by securing a place for more women. You may also prosper in the food or health industries.

In your personal relationships, you have a very sympathetic and understanding demeanor. You care for the underdog, and may find that many of your friends come to you for advice because you listen so well. In the home, you are likely to be the one who takes charge, since you have very strong ideas about the way things should be. In general, you get along best with Cancerians, Scorpios, Capricorns, and Pisceans.

A major challenge for you comes up fairly regularly in your life—the testing of your ability to withstand major disruptions. You cherish stability and tradition, and the threat of their disappearance is what makes you the most nervous. Sometimes you just have to let go. Your gift is your spiritual strength. You may be fortunate to have divine protection, perhaps a guardian angel or spirit guide.

GEMINI

From May 21, 10:36 through June 21, 18:37

The Quick Thinker

As a 1974 Gemini, you have a speed and agility that makes you capable of reacting spontaneously and with great effect. You're probably more physically oriented than most Geminis of the twentieth century, and may excel in several areas thanks to your adroitness. This may apply to a musical instrument, recreational sport, or technological tool. You may strongly identify with your family, nation, or ethnic ancestry.

On June 14, 1974, Dr. Henry Heimlich introduced a method for preventing death by choking known as the Heimlich Maneuver. The procedure calls for the strategic placing of the hands round the victim's midriff in order to expel the obstruction. The Heimlich Maneuver was created under the same astrological influences that shape your life, and reflects your ability to react quickly to potentially dangerous situations. Also note the use of precise hand movements.

In your professional life, you may specialize in an area that makes use of your dexterity, or your ability to think and act promptly. You will prosper in your career if you develop more than one marketable talent, especially since you tend to bolt when you get bored, or lack enough personal freedom. Since your lifestyle may undergo complete restructuring from time to time, flexibility becomes even more necessary.

In love, you may it difficult to settle into a committed partnership since you find so many people fascinating. Because of your family or cultural background, you may feel that marriage is appropriate for you. However, you are celestially scheduled for major lifestyle transformations from time to time, and this includes in partnership. In general, you get along best with Cancerians, Librans, Aquarians, and Pisceans.

A life challenge for you may be to manage your anger. You may have a tendency to be emotionally volatile, but you also have a strong faith in a benevolent universe. When you can release control of tense situations to a higher power, then you can get your emotional side under control. Your strength then becomes your ability to let go and move on when fundamental change is inevitable.

➤ Read about your Chinese Astrological sign on page 838. ➤ Read about your Personal Planets on page 826. ➤ Read about your personal Mystical Card on page 856.

TAURUS
Your Personal Planets

YOUR LOVE POTENTIAL
Venus in Pisces, Apr. 20, 11:19 - May 04, 20:20
Venus in Aries, May 04, 20:21 - May 21, 10:35

YOUR DRIVE AND AMBITION
Mars in Cancer, Apr. 20, 11:19 - May 21, 10:35

YOUR LUCK MAGNETISM
Jupiter in Pisces, Apr. 20, 11:19 - May 21, 10:35

World Events

May 6 - German Chancellor Willy Brandt resigns in the midst of a spy scandal.

May 18 - India becomes the sixth nation to possess the atomic bomb.

The atomic bomb

GEMINI
Your Personal Planets

YOUR LOVE POTENTIAL
Venus in Aries, May 21, 10:36 - May 31, 7:18
Venus in Taurus, May 31, 7:19 - June 21, 18:37

YOUR DRIVE AND AMBITION
Mars in Cancer, May 21, 10:36 - June 09, 0:53
Mars in Leo, June 09, 0:54 - June 21, 18:37

YOUR LUCK MAGNETISM
Jupiter in Pisces, May 21, 10:36 - June 21, 18:37

World Events

June 14 - Dr. Henry Heimlich of Xavier University in Cincinnati invents the "Heimlich Maneuver."

June 17 - The IRA bombs the most historic section of the British Houses of Parliament, the 900-year-old Westminster Hall.

1974

CANCER
Your Personal Planets

YOUR LOVE POTENTIAL
Venus in Taurus, June 21, 18:38 - June 25, 23:43
Venus in Gemini, June 25, 23:44 - July 21, 4:33
Venus in Cancer, July 21, 4:34 - July 23, 5:29

YOUR DRIVE AND AMBITION
Mars in Leo, June 21, 18:38 - July 23, 5:29

YOUR LUCK MAGNETISM
Jupiter in Pisces, June 21, 18:38 - July 23, 5:29

World Events

June 30 – Soviet ballet star Mikhail Baryshnikov defects to Canada.

July 19 – Prince Juan Carlos takes over the reigns of power in Spain due to Francisco Franco's deteriorating health.

U.S. President Nixon resigns

LEO
Your Personal Planets

YOUR LOVE POTENTIAL
Venus in Cancer, July 23, 5:30 - Aug. 14, 23:46
Venus in Leo, Aug. 14, 23:47 - Aug. 23, 12:28

YOUR DRIVE AND AMBITION
Mars in Leo, July 23, 5:30 - July 27, 14:03
Mars in Virgo, July 27, 14:04 - Aug. 23, 12:28

YOUR LUCK MAGNETISM
Jupiter in Pisces, July 23, 5:30 - Aug. 23, 12:28

World Events

Aug. 1 – The constitution of 1952 is restored in Greece.

Aug. 8 – U.S. President Nixon resigns in the wake of the Watergate scandal.

CANCER
From June 21, 18:38 through July 23, 5:29

The Reborn Talent

As a 1974 Cancer, you are an unusually deep thinker, especially when it comes to family affairs and your relationships. Your daily moods depend a great deal on how well you're getting along with your family or partner, and from time to time you may be forced to make heroic efforts to keep everyone together. You have tremendous pride and personal strength, and may enjoy many traveling experiences.

On June 30, 1974, Soviet ballet star Mikhail Baryshnikov defected to Canada. This event reflects some of the same astrological influences that shape your life. Baryshnikov was a great talent and a superstar. He loved his country, but not its government. In the same way, you may be a superstar in some sense, and have a deep love for your family or country. However, due to trying circumstances, you may occasionally be forced to take courageous action.

You often have a charm and lightness of spirit that makes work a fun place to be. You also have a more serious side that makes you capable of intense and focused mental effort, perhaps as a creative talent. If you find that your light side is at work, but your mind is at home, then your career path may become unstable. Finding a professional outlet for your mental power is a healthy way to channel this energy.

You have great sex appeal and a winning way that makes you popular in your community of interests. Perhaps you find that the best way to know people is to travel with them. Your quick wit and radiant personality do well in a variety of social settings, but attitudes may change as soon as you share a residence with those friends. In general, you get along best with Leos, Scorpios, Pisceans, and Geminis.

A major challenge for you is to keep perspective on what's important in life. You may have a tendency to get so focused on a particular situation that your relationships or job suffer a lack of attention. Your early family dynamics probably shape most of your current relationships, and when you've come to healthy terms with your parents, then you've found your gift, which is the ability to start fresh with a clean slate.

LEO
From July 23, 5:30 through August 23, 12:28

The Calm Center

Leos of 1974 are graced with a compassion and sensitivity missing in many twentieth-century Leos. Your ability to make grand gestures to others—great gifts of kindness or material help—marks you as a leader and a trusted friend. You are likely to have a strong work ethic and devotion to duty. While you may be known as a caring parent, you may experience bewildering developments or breaks in family unity.

On August 9, 1974, President Nixon resigned because of the Watergate scandal; Vice-President Gerald Ford was sworn in, becoming the first non-elected President in U.S. history. While this important episode has unique correlations to the U.S. horoscope, some of the underlying astrological factors are also present in your personal life. These include startling events, family support, and the following of protocol, even if a cloud hangs over the transfer of power.

In your professional life, you are likely to be a good organizer, and have the creative intelligence to see the big picture. Since only success satisfies you, you may be a risk-taker, but you may be tripped up from time to time by your lack of attention to details. You may prosper in the food industry, as a caretaker, or in a health field. You do best when you're in charge.

When you get romantically involved, it's usually a package deal. Either you or your significant other may come with a lot of close relatives, and these extended ties can have significant influence over your most intimate relationship. You may have a keen sense of order or cleanliness within your home, but are constantly battling against chaos. In general, you get along best with Librans, Sagittarians, Ariens, and Cancerians.

A big challenge for you might be to maintain a sense of independence and autonomy within your network of personal relationships. Your wonderful generosity of spirit makes it difficult to create healthy boundaries. This could lead to co-dependency, resentments, and eventually to serious disruptions. Your strength is in your over-riding trust in the Universe: that no matter what happens, everything is as it was meant to be.

➤ Read about your Chinese Astrological sign on page 838. ➤ Read about your Personal Planets on page 826. ➤ Read about your personal Mystical Card on page 856.

VIRGO

From August 23, 12:29 through September 23, 9:57

The Compassionate Worker

As a 1974 Virgo, you have an unusually strong sense of what is useful and what is pointless. Your natural attention to detail and devotion to duty make you an able and valued worker in any business or profession. Your ability to discriminate between what is healthy and unhealthy, combined with a compassion and sensitivity, gives you an awareness of how every individual's well-being contributes to the whole.

On September 16, 1974, new U.S. President Gerald Ford granted disgraced ex-President Nixon a complete pardon. In this widely criticized act of kindness, Ford realized how futile it would be for the nation to pursue Nixon. The same astrological currents shape your life: you see the value of forgiveness and moving on. You have the rare ability to stand back and see how your actions influence the interests of the larger community.

Your career is greatly enhanced by your strong work ethic, and your holistic view. In your professional life, you may also have an excellent sense of business cycles. On September 8, 1974, New York's Franklin Bank declared bankruptcy and became the biggest bank failure in U.S. history. The planetary cycle in effect as this event unfolded is also dominant in your horoscope, helping you to recognize key turning points.

Unlike many born in 1974, you may greatly benefit from your family connections. You may choose to live near family members, and enjoy each other's interests and network of friends. Your love life is likely to be closely connected to your work environment. Through experience you have probably learned to curb an excessively critical attitude, and now live and let live. In general, you get along best with Capricorns, Pisceans, Taureans, and Cancerians.

A significant challenge for you may be to accurately evaluate risk. You may have a natural tendency to go out on a limb, or contrarily, to stay in an uncomfortable rut and only fantasize about great escapes. Finding the balance between these two extremes may also lead you to financial prosperity. Your gift is your deep sense of compassion, making you a treasured friend or partner.

LIBRA

From September 23, 9:58 through October 23, 19:10

The Realistic General

You have a natural charm and diplomatic attitude 1974 Libra, which serves you well in challenging the status quo. You may be a good strategist, like the general who sees the obstacles to the goal, and has a plan to get safely through them. You are likely to be interested in social progress, and the lifestyle and friends you choose express your desire for change.

During this month, two separate studies reported that the Freon used in refrigerators and aerosol sprays was destroying the ozone layer. This event reflects a basic astrological influence of your birth month—the challenge to business as usual. Anthropologists were few days away from discovering the partial skeleton of the 3.2 million-year-old humanoid *Australopithecus afarensis* in Ethiopia, upsetting prevailing theories. Again, the same celestial influence was present, and that is the challenge to established tradition.

You've probably run up against terrible bosses, or have testily confronted those in charge. This pattern won't break until you have found a job that helps you challenge something outside your paymaster. When your work in some way contributes to social evolution, then you will find a steady career path. You may find that a partnership helps define your professional or business role.

Although Libra is the sign of harmony and balance, you've probably discovered that your personal relationships don't always run smooth. You need a lot of freedom to come and go, and you have friends and other interests that make an intimate, traditional commitment difficult. Family connections can also complicate your affairs. In general, you get along best with Sagittarians, Aquarians, Geminis, and Leos.

A big challenge for you is always right around the corner. Your celestial make-up is geared toward challenges, and you wouldn't be content if life got too easy and comfortable. Accepting that your destiny includes overcoming unhealthy or outmoded traditions is your ticket to success. Then you tune into your strength, and you'll find prosperity, beauty, and able partners as you help humanity advance to a better place.

➤ Read about your Chinese Astrological sign on page 838. ➤ Read about your Personal Planets on page 826. ➤ Read about your personal Mystical Card on page 856.

1974

VIRGO
Your Personal Planets

YOUR LOVE POTENTIAL
Venus in Leo, Aug. 23, 12:29 - Sept. 08, 10:27
Venus in Virgo, Sept. 08, 10:28 - Sept. 23, 9:57

YOUR DRIVE AND AMBITION
Mars in Virgo, Aug. 23, 12:29 - Sept. 12, 19:07
Mars in Libra, Sept. 12, 19:08 - Sept. 23, 9:57

YOUR LUCK MAGNETISM
Jupiter in Pisces, Aug. 23, 12:29 - Sept. 23, 9:57

World Events

Sept. 2 – Dictator Franco resumes control of Spain.
Sept. 12 – Emperor of Ethiopia Haile Selassie is deposed after fifty-eight years.

Ethiopian Emperor Haile Selassie is deposed

LIBRA
Your Personal Planets

YOUR LOVE POTENTIAL
Venus in Virgo, Sept. 23, 9:58 - Oct. 02, 14:26
Venus in Libra, Oct. 02, 14:27 - Oct. 23, 19:10

YOUR DRIVE AND AMBITION
Mars in Libra, Sept. 23, 9:58 - Oct. 23, 19:10

YOUR LUCK MAGNETISM
Jupiter in Pisces, Sept. 23, 9:58 - Oct. 23, 19:10

World Events

Sept. 30 – President Spinola of Portugal resigns, warning of the chaos caused by a leftist revolution.
Oct. 11 – The IRA steps up its terrorist campaign, setting off bombs in central areas of London.

SCORPIO
Your Personal Planets

YOUR LOVE POTENTIAL
Venus in Libra, Oct. 23, 19:11 - Oct. 26, 14:11
Venus in Scorpio, Oct. 26, 14:12 - Nov. 19, 11:55
Venus in Sagittarius, Nov. 19, 11:56 - Nov. 22, 16:37

YOUR DRIVE AND AMBITION
Mars in Libra, Oct. 23, 19:11 - Oct. 28, 7:04
Mars in Scorpio, Oct. 28, 7:05 - Nov. 22, 16:37

YOUR LUCK MAGNETISM
Jupiter in Pisces, Oct. 23, 19:11 - Nov. 22, 16:37

World Events

Oct. 28 – Arab heads of state demand an independent Palestinian state.

Nov. 7 – Britain's Lord Lucan is sought by the police on suspicion of murdering his children's nanny.

Lord Lucan with his wife

SAGITTARIUS
Your Personal Planets

YOUR LOVE POTENTIAL
Venus in Sagittarius, Nov. 22, 16:38 - Dec. 13, 9:05
Venus in Capricorn, Dec. 13, 9:06 - Dec. 22, 5:55

YOUR DRIVE AND AMBITION
Mars in Scorpio, Nov. 22, 16:38 - Dec. 10, 22:04
Mars in Sagittarius, Dec. 10, 22:05 - Dec. 22, 5:55

YOUR LUCK MAGNETISM
Jupiter in Pisces, Nov. 22, 16:38 - Dec. 22, 5:55

World Events

Dec. 8 – Greece votes to abolish its 142-year-old monarchy.

Dec. 11 – Rhodesian premier Ian Smith agrees a ceasefire with black nationalists.

SCORPIO

From October 23, 19:11 through November 22, 16:37

The Passionate Insider

As a 1974 Scorpio, you are likely to have an interest in exploring the hidden side of life, perhaps a fascination with the cryptic, the unknown, or the occult. You have an intensity about you that ignores trivial events and focuses on control and influence. Through your willpower and the unusual facts or knowledge you amass, you can cause deep and sudden changes, and these may be either destructive or creative.

On November 13, 1974, Karen Silkwood died in suspicious circumstances while on her way to meet a *New York Times* reporter. Silkwood had documents proving that a nuclear power plant had falsified quality-control reports. The incident, which coincidentally synchronized with the movie debut of *The China Syndrome*, reveals the planetary influences of your birth month including an interest in secrets, insider information, and the associated danger.

You have a mental edge that could be a great asset in your professional life. Although you may be scattered at times, leaping from one idea to the next, you also have an aptitude for grasping certain technologies that elude others. You may excel at any profession that makes use of your specialized knowledge, and this could include health, biotechnology, criminology, research, or espionage.

You are likely to have a highly charged sex drive, and a magnetic personality that brings plenty of friends and opportunities for love. No doubt you enjoy intense intimacy, but volatile emotions could become an obstacle to a long-term partnership. Your partner needs to understand your intellect and your electric ideas, and this goes a long way in creating harmony. In general, you get along best with Pisceans, Cancerians, Virgos, and Libras.

A big challenge for you may be to avoid falling victim to conspiracy theories or wild ideas that bear no relation to reality. Of course, you may see things that no one else does, and only you may know if they are real or not. The trick is perspective, so that you don't lose sight of what others see as their reality. Then your gift is the ability to share your knowledge and insights with everyone else.

SAGITTARIUS

From November 22, 16:38 through December 22, 5:55

The Philosopher King

As a 1974 Sagittarius, you are likely to have a keen interest in traveling and experiencing foreign cultures first-hand. Your ceaseless desire to expand your horizons probably includes a spiritual quest as much as seeking to understand geopolitical events. You are a global citizen, and may wonder at provincial attitudes, or why people can't see that religion is more a function of geography than spiritual truth.

A number of important turning points occurred during your birth month. On November 26, 1974, Japan's Prime Minister Tanaka resigned in the face of financial scandals. On December 8 Greece abolished its monarchy. And then, on December 6, the Dow Jones bottomed out at 577.6 points. The planetary dynamics corresponding to these transitions tune you into the larger meaning of events.

In your professional life, you may find meaningful work helping people through the really major changes in their lives. Whether this is as a lawyer, consultant, health practitioner, teacher, or writer doesn't matter so much; you have strong convictions and want to have an impact upon people's lives. You may also attract and influence society's movers and shakers, securing not only your own financial well-being, but also facilitating social progress.

In your relationships, you are likely to have an outgoing, entertaining manner that easily attracts friends. You may charm others with great stories, or have a flair for humor. Because you are a natural wanderer, you may find it difficult to settle down in a committed partnership, though part of you would cherish the idea. It could work, though, if you and your mate have similar lifestyles. In general, you get along best with Ariens, Leos, Librans, and Pisceans.

A major challenge for you may be to escape the psychological conditioning of the circumstances of your birth. Since your birth month is colored by significant religious markers, you may have a narrow background to grow out of before you can feel connected to universal truths. Once you have broken free, then you have your gift, which is the experience of being the philosopher king.

➤ Read about your Chinese Astrological sign on page 838. ➤ Read about your Personal Planets on page 826. ➤ Read about your personal Mystical Card on page 856.

CAPRICORN

From December 22, 5:56 through December 31, 23:59

The Odds Player

As a Capricorn born in December 1974, you are likely to have an ambitious drive to be successful and get to the top. You may be preoccupied with financial, corporate, or political power; specifically, what it does, and how to get it for yourself. You may also be highly imaginative, cultivated, and much more of a risk-taker than most Capricorns of the twentieth century.

On December 23, 1974, the U.S. successfully tested its first B-1 bomber. The underlying celestial influences that brought about this event also structure your life pattern, and they include the desire to be the biggest and the most powerful. On December 18, a two million gallon oil spill off Japan polluted 1,600 square miles of inland sea, and this event reflects the magnitude of the forces you are dealing with, and what happens when the risks are miscalculated.

In your professional life, you may be very successful, if you calculate the risks correctly. Your career path may be facilitated by influential people or even spiritual forces, if your goals benefit the larger community or society. You have an intensity about you that can attract powerful rivals, and from time to time you may need to completely restructure your long-range plans. You may have a capacity to discover important secrets.

You're probably a late bloomer in the romance department. This doesn't mean that love is denied to you, just that it may take longer than usual before you can open up your heart. Perhaps you feel you must achieve a certain amount of success or financial security first. Family members can play a large role in shaping your relationship patterns. In general, you get along best with Pisceans, Taureans, Virgos, and Scorpios.

A major challenge in your life is to not push too fast or too hard. You probably want to get ahead quickly in your career (you may even drive too fast), and to make an impact upon the rest of the world. Capricorn's path to success is built slowly, step-by-step, so being patient will help a lot. Since you have a laser-like mental focus, when you put your mind to it, you can accomplish anything.

ELIZABETH TAYLOR – Pisces
RICHARD BURTON – Scorpio

Elizabeth Taylor, born February 27, 1932
Richard Burton
November 10, 1925 - August 5, 1984

Richard Burton was a prominent actor who was propelled into superstardom by his incendiary love affair with Elizabeth Taylor, one of the most celebrated movie stars of all time.

One of the strongest indicators of romantic chemistry in a horoscope is to look at the relative positions of the planets of love and sex, Venus and Mars. When there are contacts between one person's Mars and the other's Venus, or vice versa, even people who don't particularly care for each other feel that exciting undercurrent of sexual attraction. In the case of Elizabeth and Richard, her Mars contacted his Venus.

It takes more than sex to keep a couple interested, however. It takes a sense of resonance. When you have certain planetary combinations and you meet someone whose same planets are connected, you feel "simpatico" with that person and you naturally understand each other. Elizabeth and Richard shared contacts between the Moon, the planet of emotions, and Pluto, the planet of passion, control, and domination. These larger-than-life characters both expected some turbulence in their emotional alliances and each was comfortable with a partner who could be demanding and possessive. In addition, contacts from Neptune, the planet of confusion, to each of their Suns, planet of identity, made these two lovers equally insecure and demanding.

Another important astrological factor is how one person's planets combine with the other person's. Richard's Sun was in Scorpio, a sign noted for its intensity and personal magnetism, while Elizabeth's passionate Scorpio Moon gave them a mutual emotional frame of reference.

Ultimately, though, a liaison will endure if each partner has the capability for constancy. In Richard's chart, challenging aspects between Pluto and expansive Jupiter created the expectation of marital havoc, and Elizabeth's house of foundations was challenged by the presence of Uranus, planet of upheaval. Richard was accurate in his assessment of their problem. They were married and divorced twice and of their union he said, "Our love is so furious that we burn each other out."

➤ Read the Duke of Windsor's Star Profile on page 329.

609

1975

Highlighting Social Change: Saturn and Uranus

The ponderous nature of last year's troubles put other problems in perspective and both individuals and groups were suddenly more open to resolving them. This is the impact of Saturn "square" Uranus that occurred in 1975. Saturn is associated with the old way of doing things, while Uranus represents our need to introduce new approaches, creating more freedom in the process. In a square relationship changes come about with friction or effort. In this context, issues that had faced humanity for many years were cleared. Egypt finally relented and allowed ships to pass through the Suez Canal after eight years of closure. In order to actively desegregate schools, Boston was ordered to bus minority students into Anglo-American neighborhoods. The nations of the West were beginning to free themselves of the Arab monopoly on oil production through self-sufficiency: Britain began tapping its North Sea oil reserves.

Through Saturn's association with science and Uranus's with discovery, scientific discoveries brought new understanding. A human-like footprint four million years old was found near Africa's Olduvai Gorge, while Chinese Emperor Shih Hwang-Ti's life-sized clay army, more than 2,000 years old, was unexpectedly uncovered. Perhaps most important of all developments this year, thirty-five nations gathered in Helsinki, Finland, and signed an agreement affirming human rights and the use of peaceful means to resolve disputes. This change in international consciousness came as Uranus was in its last days in the peace-loving sign of Libra.

Last-minute evacuation at the U.S. embassy in Saigon, Vietnam

Film "Jaws" breaks all box office records

An "army" of life-sized clay warriors are unearthed in a burial mound in China

THE LIGHT AT THE END OF THE TUNNEL

In his book *Life After Life*, Dr. Raymond Moody described "near-death experience" as the mystical phenomena experienced by people who appear to die and then return to life or who come close to death. Eight million Americans claim to have had an NDE. An NDE can include out-of-body experiences, in which the individual floats above the body, feelings of bliss, and of traveling down a tunnel toward a light at the end. Some have reported meeting spirits who glow, dead friends and relatives, or even a Supreme Being, and reviewing their entire life.

A RETURN TO NORMALCY

South Vietnam and Cambodia fell to communist forces. The Suez Canal opened to ocean-going traffic after eight years of closure. Beirut was torn by Muslim-Christian civil war. After dictator Franco died, Spain returned to royal rule with King Juan Carlos on the throne. Australia's Governor General Kerr ended a government crisis by dismissing Prime Minister Whitlam. The U.S. and Russia mirrored their recent accord when the Apollo and Soyuz spacecraft docked for a joint mission in space. Thirty-five countries signed a human rights pact in Helsinki, Finland. In the U.S., Patty Hearst faced charges for aiding her kidnappers. Chinese archeologists uncovered the 'Terracotta Army', a life-sized clay army of 6,000 men buried over three acres with Emperor Shih Hwang-ti in 206 BC. The U.S. TV industry declared 7 to 9 p.m. as family time viewing. A vegetarian diet was declared a protection against breast cancer. Hawaii's Mauna Loa volcano erupted after remaining dormant for twenty-five years. *Jaws*, directed by Steven Spielberg, riveted audiences and soprano Beverly Sills made her debut at the Metropolitan Opera House, New York.

➤ Read Muhammad Ali's Star Profile on page 617.

CAPRICORN

From January 01, 0:00 through January 20, 16:35

The Psychic Healer

Sensitive and compassionate, the January-born 1975 Capricorn has tremendous healing powers. You can tell what's troubling a person just by being in the same room together. Some of your associates think your "hunches" are downright spooky, but the smart ones will heed your advice. You understand what it means to suffer and intend to alleviate other people's pain whenever possible. Quite often, a friend who is in trouble will get a surprise call from you asking if everything is all right. Consequently, your sixth sense may have become a legend among your loved ones.

If there's anybody suited to the caring professions, it's you. You'd make an excellent hospice worker, prison counselor, or psychotherapist. Giving comfort to people in bleak situations gives you a divine sense of purpose. You're also very creative and could earn a living as an artist. Teaching arts and crafts to troubled children or nursing-home patients would be a good way to combine your compassion with your artistry.

A self-sacrificing person like you needs a strong relationship to stay centered. You're not the type to go from one lover to another; in fact, it takes a long time for you to develop romantic feelings. That's because you need to feel absolutely sure of their character before giving your heart away. The year you were born, Olivia Newton-John's "I Honestly Love You" won a Grammy as Record of the Year. You're equally as sincere when it comes to affairs of the heart.

Friends are very important to you. Tender-hearted to the point of naïveté, you need pals who will look after your interests. Ariens, Taureans, Virgos, and Capricorns can drive opportunists from your door, while you happily occupy yourself with genuine people. In love, you would be wise to pair with someone who can lift you out of the melancholy moods that sometimes plague you.

Your greatest challenge is to become more selfish. You're so giving and generous that you may easily burn out. Your biggest strength is your incredible healing power. If you use it selectively, you will leave the world a better place than you entered it.

AQUARIUS

From January 20, 16:36 through February 19, 6:49

The Zealous Truth-Seeker

A true original, the 1975 Aquarius never seeks public approval. Instead, you're determined to challenge authority, shatter taboos, and splinter the status quo. Folks may accuse you of being a rabble-rouser, but what you're really seeking is the truth. If that means exposing people or practices as fraudulent, so be it. The year you were born, John Mitchell, H.R. Haldeman, and John Ehrlichman were found guilty in the Watergate cover-up case in the U.S. If it were up to you, far more officials would pay for their abuse of power. You'd rather face the truth than bury your head in the sand.

Investigative work suits you best. You'd make an excellent auditor, private detective, or consumer reporter. Archeology might also appeal to you; studying ancient civilizations appeals to your analytic side. Blessed with considerable technical ability, you might consider becoming an electrical engineer, computer technician, or repair person. Chances are you will change careers several times as you're easily bored. Doing the same thing day after day simply won't work for you.

Although most Water-bearers aren't physically affectionate, you may be the exception to the rule. You can't help lavishing loved ones with hugs and kisses, and you need these caresses to be returned. Birthdays and holidays may be sacred to you. Your house is always adorned with festive seasonal decorations, and you probably have plenty of gift-wrapping supplies on hand just in case you want to give somebody a present.

Your favorite people are straight-talking, earthy types. Taureans, Virgos, Sagittarians, and Capricorns make up the lion's share of your social circle. When it comes to romance, you need somebody who is willing to come to your aid at a moment's notice. Having a helpmate can be very comforting to you.

Your greatest challenge as a 1975 Aquarius is to rely more on your intuition. Although logic is your strong suit, you possess a highly developed sixth sense, too. Your biggest strength is your realism. If you apply it properly, you can clear away harmful deceptions so the truth is revealed.

1975

CAPRICORN
Your Personal Planets

YOUR LOVE POTENTIAL
Venus in Capricorn, Jan. 01, 0:00 - Jan. 06, 6:38
Venus in Aquarius, Jan. 06, 6:39 - Jan. 20, 16:35

YOUR DRIVE AND AMBITION
Mars in Sagittarius, Jan. 01, 0:00 - Jan. 20, 16:35

YOUR LUCK MAGNETISM
Jupiter in Pisces, Jan. 01, 0:00 - Jan. 20, 16:35

World Events

Jan. 4 - The Khmer Rouge launches a new attack on the Cambodian capital Phnom Penh.

Jan. 16 - The IRA end the ceasefire which had been put into effect in Northern Ireland.

Margaret Thatcher wins the Conservative leadership

AQUARIUS
Your Personal Planets

YOUR LOVE POTENTIAL
Venus in Aquarius, Jan. 20, 16:36 - Jan. 30, 6:04
Venus in Pisces, Jan. 30, 6:05 - Feb. 19, 6:49

YOUR DRIVE AND AMBITION
Mars in Sagittarius, Jan. 20, 16:36 - Jan. 21, 18:48
Mars in Capricorn, Jan. 21, 18:49 - Feb. 19, 6:49

YOUR LUCK MAGNETISM
Jupiter in Pisces, Jan. 20, 16:36 - Feb. 19, 6:49

World Events

Feb. 11 - Margaret Thatcher defeats Edward Heath for the Conservative leadership in Great Britain.

Feb. 11 - Hal Ashby's comic play *Shampoo* opens in New York.

➤ Read about your Chinese Astrological sign on page 838. ➤ Read about your Personal Planets on page 826. ➤ Read about your personal Mystical Card on page 856.

PISCES
Your Personal Planets

YOUR LOVE POTENTIAL

Venus in Pisces, Feb. 19, 6:50 - Feb. 23, 9:52
Venus in Aries, Feb. 23, 9:53 - Mar. 19, 21:41
Venus in Taurus, Mar. 19, 21:42 - Mar. 21, 5:56

YOUR DRIVE AND AMBITION

Mars in Capricorn, Feb. 19, 6:50 - Mar. 03, 5:31
Mars in Aquarius, Mar. 03, 5:32 - Mar. 21, 5:56

YOUR LUCK MAGNETISM

Jupiter in Pisces, Feb. 19, 6:50 - Mar. 18, 16:46
Jupiter in Aries, Mar. 18, 16:47 - Mar. 21, 5:56

World Events

Mar. 4 - Movie icon Charlie Chaplin receives a knighthood.

Mar. 14 - American film actress Susan Hayward dies.

Death of President of Nationalist China Chiang Kai-shek

ARIES
Your Personal Planets

YOUR LOVE POTENTIAL

Venus in Taurus, Mar. 21, 5:57 - Apr. 13, 22:25
Venus in Gemini, Apr. 13, 22:26 - Apr. 20, 17:06

YOUR DRIVE AND AMBITION

Mars in Aquarius, Mar. 21, 5:57 - Apr. 11, 19:14
Mars in Pisces, Apr. 11, 19:15 - Apr. 20, 17:06

YOUR LUCK MAGNETISM

Jupiter in Aries, Mar. 21, 5:57 - Apr. 20, 17:06

World Events

Apr. 5 - President of Nationalist China Chiang Kai-shek dies.

Apr. 17 - Pol Pot's communist Khmer Rouge captures Phnom Penh.

PISCES
From February 19, 6:50 through March 21, 5:56

The Creative Genius

All Pisceans are creative, but the 1975 Fish is especially so. You're loaded to the fingertips with talent. Sometimes you're unsure of which gifts to develop. The key is to obey your intuition—you have true creative genius that sets you apart from the competition. The year you were born, twenty-two-year-old Paul Allen and nineteen-year-old Bill Gates formed a company called Microsoft, which would revolutionize the entire computer industry in years to come. Properly developed, your ideas could have a similar impact on whatever field you choose.

Spirituality will play a great role in your work. You have a strong sense that an invisible thread connects the entire universe. Locating this thread may be the theme of your art. What form your art takes is entirely up to you. Dance, photography, or poetry might be avenues to explore. There's a strong possibility you could be a gifted painter, writer, or sculptor. Whatever form your creativity takes, it is almost sure to have a healing power. Some folks may find your work controversial, but most will be comforted by it. Take your critics with a grain of salt.

You may be reluctant to have children, worrying that they will interfere with your work. Alternately, child-rearing responsibilities could delay your career as an artist. As you get older, it will become easier to balance your personal duties with your creative ones, but some sacrifices will have to be made. Contrary to what you have heard, you can't have it all—at least, not all at once.

Wonderfully idealistic, you need to surround yourself with visionary types who are on your wavelength. Ariens, Geminis, Aquarians, and Pisceans are good companions for you. As far as love is concerned, you'd be wise to select a partner who has both feet firmly planted on the ground. A common-sense Virgo or Capricorn would suit you well.

Your greatest challenge as a 1975 Pisces is to take full advantage of your gifts. Don't put off your dreams for the sake of a practical job or predictable lifestyle. Your biggest strength is your vast imagination. Let it be your ticket to stardom.

ARIES
From March 21, 5:57 through April 20, 17:06

The Relentless Risk-Taker

The 1975 Aries has a deep need to be innovative. That's why you're always trying new things. Risking life and limb makes you feel young and vital. If you don't perform physical feats of courage, you may enact intellectual ones. You're the first one to tell the boss what you really think of their latest pet project. Similarly, you love taking financial risks, and you could have considerable success with speculative investments. Cowardice is a dirty word in your dictionary. The year you were born, the movie *Jaws* kept people away from the beach for an entire summer. You're the type who would have headed for the ocean the second you left the theater.

Naturally, you need a career that involves risks. You'd make a great firefighter, paratrooper, or police officer. Gambling also appeals to you, which probably explains why so many 1975 Rams are stockbrokers and movie producers. If you're looking for an intellectual and physical challenge, try work as an emergency services technician. You're bound to get plenty of stimulation from any of these jobs!

You put a lot of energy into your friendships and probably lead a pack of irrepressible rowdies. Joining an athletic team is a good idea for you as it will provide you with a welcome outlet for your boundless energy as well as an additional source of camaraderie. Fiercely loyal, you would swim the English Channel for the sake of a pal. If someone crosses you though, they're out of your graces forever.

You get along best with folks who are feisty and fun. Ariens, Geminis, Leos, and Sagittarians are entertaining company. Sexually, you may run hot and cold. Ideally, you need a romantic partner who can keep your interest alive. A sexy Libra or a smoldering Scorpio could fit the bill. Just be sure to respect your mate, even if they aren't a daredevil like you.

Your greatest challenge is to maintain your youthful exuberance. Keep exploring new territory and do everything you can to stay mentally and physically active. Your biggest strength is your courage. Use it to champion underdogs who can't defend themselves.

➤ Read about your Chinese Astrological sign on page 838. ➤ Read about your Personal Planets on page 826. ➤ Read about your personal Mystical Card on page 856.

TAURUS

From April 20, 17:07 through May 21, 16:23

The Skillful Contributor

Always in the midst of some project, the 1975 Taurus is rarely bored. You're eager to pitch in whenever and wherever necessary. Whether this means taking on an unpleasant job or additional responsibilities is immaterial. The important thing is that you are contributing in some material way. You've probably performed so many different kinds of work that you've become a jack-of-all-trades. No matter what the economy is like, you'll always manage to find a job thanks to your wide variety of skills.

Blessed with quick reflexes, you may enjoy sports and hobbies that require split-second decisions. The year you were born, Bjorn Borg won the Wimbledon Men's Singles Tournament for the first of five consecutive times. You could prove particularly gifted at this sport, given your speed and agility. The 1975 Bull is a notable exception to the idea that most Taureans are slow and cautious in their movements.

You will probably have a variety of jobs throughout the course of your life. The most satisfying ones will probably be service-oriented. You would make an excellent personal assistant, secretary, or concierge. The healing professions might also appeal to you. You could also have great success as a nurse, homeopath, dietician, or fitness trainer. Chances are you prefer working on the sidelines than assuming a more public role. You don't want to be a star, just appreciated.

You're slow to trust people but once you make a pal, they're with you for life. It's a good idea to surround yourself with rambunctious types who can motivate you to try new things. Ariens, Geminis, Leos, and Sagittarians can bring out the best in you. Romantically, you are more suited to an intense, creative person, like a Cancer or Scorpio.

Hard-working and loyal, your greatest challenge is to develop your imagination. Artistic and intellectual hobbies can help you find creative solutions to persistent problems. Your biggest strength is your desire to do good work. People admire your humble attitude and respect you for it, too.

GEMINI

From May 21, 16:24 through June 22, 0:25

The Optimistic Innovator

Inventive and curious, the 1975 Gemini is always thinking "what if?" You have big dreams and love building castles in the air. You need an outlet for your prodigious imagination, whether it's a hobby or a full-time job. Chances are you are drawn to electronics in some way. Playing electric guitar, designing neon lights, or inventing video games are just some of the ways you can capitalize on your creativity.

You enjoy working as part of a team. Sometimes your thinking gets so conceptual that you have a difficult time putting your thoughts into words. Colleagues can help you present your ideas in lay terms. Working in an advertising agency, television studio, or science lab could appeal to you. You would also make a great comedy writer or set designer. Whatever job you choose, make sure it involves lots of collaboration. The year you were born, American and Soviet astronauts made an orbital link-up in space. You need to make similar connections with your co-workers.

Affluence is important to you. Fortunately, a creative person like you should have no trouble bringing in a sizable income. If you play your cards right and make wise financial decisions, you can retire early. Spending your golden years on leisurely pursuits is a distinct possibility for you, provided you create a nest egg at the earliest possible convenience. You may want to consult a financial manager to devise a strategy for building wealth.

With regard to relationships, you need serene, open-minded friends. Taureans, Cancerians, Leos, and Librans help you slow down and smell the flowers. Romantically, you hit it off best with Sagittarians. Archers can delight in your vivid imagination and have no trouble keeping up with your energetic pace.

Your greatest challenge as a 1975 Gemini is to find peace. Learn to enjoy moments of repose; you don't have to fill all your time with activities. Napping in a hammock is a perfectly wonderful way to spend a few hours' time. Your biggest strength is your imagination. Entertain it at every possible opportunity; somebody else can handle the practical stuff.

➤ Read about your Chinese Astrological sign on page 838. ➤ Read about your Personal Planets on page 826. ➤ Read about your personal Mystical Card on page 856.

TAURUS
Your Personal Planets

YOUR LOVE POTENTIAL
Venus in Gemini, Apr. 20, 17:07 - May 09, 20:10
Venus in Cancer, May 09, 20:11 - May 21, 16:23

YOUR DRIVE AND AMBITION
Mars in Pisces, Apr. 20, 17:07 - May 21, 8:13
Mars in Aries, May 21, 8:14 - May 21, 16:23

YOUR LUCK MAGNETISM
Jupiter in Aries, Apr. 20, 17:07 - May 21, 16:23

World Events

Apr. 30 – The Vietnam War draws to a close as Communist forces seize Saigon.

May 16 – Junko Tabai of Japan becomes the first woman to reach the top of Mt. Everest.

Last-minute evacuation at the U.S. embassy in Saigon, Vietnam

GEMINI
Your Personal Planets

YOUR LOVE POTENTIAL
Venus in Cancer, May 21, 16:24 - June 06, 10:53
Venus in Leo, June 06, 10:54 - June 22, 0:25

YOUR DRIVE AND AMBITION
Mars in Aries, May 21, 16:24 - June 22, 0:25

YOUR LUCK MAGNETISM
Jupiter in Aries, May 21, 16:24 - June 22, 0:25

World Events

May 30 – The European Space Agency (ESA) is established.

June 5 – The Suez Canal reopens after eight years.

1975

CANCER
Your Personal Planets

YOUR LOVE POTENTIAL
Venus in Leo, June 22, 0:26 - July 09, 11:05
Venus in Virgo, July 09, 11:06 - July 23, 11:21

YOUR DRIVE AND AMBITION
Mars in Aries, June 22, 0:26 - July 01, 3:52
Mars in Taurus, July 01, 3:53 - July 23, 11:21

YOUR LUCK MAGNETISM
Jupiter in Aries, June 22, 0:26 - July 23, 11:21

World Events

June 25 - Portugal grants independence to Mozambique.

June 26 - Widespread riots in India cause Prime Minister Indira Gandhi to declare a state of emergency.

Prime Minister of India Indira Gandhi greets members of Parliament.

LEO
Your Personal Planets

YOUR LOVE POTENTIAL
Venus in Virgo, July 23, 11:22 - Aug. 23, 18:23

YOUR DRIVE AND AMBITION
Mars in Taurus, July 23, 11:22 - Aug. 14, 20:46
Mars in Gemini, Aug. 14, 20:47 - Aug. 23, 18:23

YOUR LUCK MAGNETISM
Jupiter in Aries, July 23, 11:22 - Aug. 23, 18:23

World Events

July 29 - Gerald Ford becomes the first U.S. President to visit a Nazi concentration camp, at Auschwitz in Poland.

Aug. 9 - Pioneering Russian composer Dimitri Shostakovitch dies.

CANCER
From June 22, 0:26 through July 23, 11:21

The Support System

Everybody can count on the 1975 Cancer to make things right. That's because you're an expert at fixing other people's mistakes. You're often the one to dispense money or advice to people in need. Normally, helping others gives you a profound sense of fulfillment, but it can also cloud your priorities sometimes. The year you were born, North Vietnamese troops completed an invasion of South Vietnam and united the two countries under Communist rule. Make it your mission to maintain a separate identity from your loved ones or it may be difficult to discern your needs from theirs.

One of the most effective ways to attain distinction is to have a successful career. Blessed with considerable leadership ability, you would make an excellent hospital administrator, chief executive officer, or movie director. You would also do well in a hierarchical professional environment, such as the military or police force. Don't worry if you have to start out at the very bottom of the heap. Talent like yours always rises to the top.

Romance is very important to you, and you may seek to be in a serious relationship at a very early age. Do your best to find a mate who knows how to give as well as receive. Having someone wait on you from time to time will remind you that your own needs are just as important as everybody else's. Don't be shy about pampering yourself, either. Going out for gourmet meals at fine restaurants may be one of your favorite forms of indulgence.

Sharing, caring people are good friendship material for you. Geminis, Cancerians, Librans, and Pisceans should make up the better part of your social circle. Romantically, you are most drawn to Pisceans, who seem to know what you're thinking before you even say a word. Anybody with a strong intuition and compassionate heart would make a good mate for you.

Your greatest challenge as a 1975 Cancer is to form supportive, nurturing relationships. Reach out to folks who are just as giving as you are. Your biggest strength is your likable personality. You should have no trouble attracting a sizable crowd of wonderful friends.

LEO
From July 23, 11:22 through August 23, 18:23

The Thoughtful Speaker

Calm, cool and collected, the 1975 Leo doesn't fill the air with a lot of idle chitchat. You only open your mouth when there is something important to say. This gives your word an added force that is almost intimidating. The year you were born, *The Godfather, Part II* won the Academy Award for best picture. Al Pacino's slow, quiet delivery as Michael Corleone is similar to your own speech. No wonder the room comes to a standstill whenever you clear your throat!

The pursuit of wealth is your first objective when choosing a career. Therefore, you may take a job as a banker, stockbroker, or doctor as a path to financial security. An appreciation for art could draw you to a creative field like architecture, interior design, or antique restoration. Chances are that you will deal with only the highest echelon of society because you enjoy dealing with luxury markets. Whatever job you take, make sure it features elegant surroundings. You are very sensitive to your environment and need a lush decor in which to thrive.

If you do make a lot of money, you won't be miserly. You have a strong philanthropic streak. Giving money to various schools may be your favorite way to promote peace and progress. Education is important to you, as is travel. Your most valuable lessons will probably be learned abroad. You enjoy comparing and contrasting cultures and may spend several years in a foreign country, just soaking up the atmosphere. Your home is probably filled with artwork picked up along your travels.

You have an impressive array of friends, most of whom are over-achievers. Ariens, Taureans, Leos, and Capricorns comprise the greatest part of your social circle. As far as love goes, you'll probably wait to settle down. When you do decide on a partner, try to pick someone who is ambitious and good-humored.

Your greatest challenge as a 1975 Leo is to become more flexible. This will make it easier for you to enjoy life. Your biggest strength is your air of authority. Use it to attract financial and spiritual abundance. Here's a tip: sharing your wealth will always bring you luck.

➤ Read about your Chinese Astrological sign on page 838. ➤ Read about your Personal Planets on page 826. ➤ Read about your personal Mystical Card on page 856.

VIRGO

From August 23, 18:24 through September 23, 15:54

The Idea Person

Brimming with brainstorms, the sheer intellectual power of the 1975 Virgo is astonishing. You're always interested in trying something different, learning the latest skill, and inventing new ways of doing things. The incredible breadth of your expertise has gained you the reputation for being a "know-it-all." People are always calling you to find out the state bird of Maryland, the home cure for hiccups, or the top five Russian-language novels. You're better than an encyclopedia!

The year you were born, the Altair home computer kit allowed consumers to build and program their own personal computers. The advent of PCs was a true blessing for you as it allows you to obtain and process information with a click of a button. Chances are you would have great success as a computer programmer or software developer. You also have considerable writing talent and may want to try your hand at journalism. Whatever career you choose, it should involve gathering and processing lots of information. Such work greatly appeals to your neat, orderly mind.

You are very physically affectionate, and you need a partner who loves to cuddle as much as you do. Chances are you will enjoy a fulfilling sex life well into your golden years. This will keep you strong, healthy, and vigorous. Later in life, folks may tease you about your youthful exuberance and demand to know your secret. Replying with a mysterious smile will give you a delightful kick. One thing is for sure; you will get better as you grow older.

Clever and witty, you like folks with a good sense of humor. Geminis, Leos, Sagittarians, and Capricorns keep you rolling in the aisles. Earth signs are your best bet for romance as these are the only signs that are as sensual and passionate as you. A tender Taurus, virtuous Virgo, or comely Capricorn would make a good mate for you.

Your greatest challenge as a 1975 Gemini is to listen as much as you speak. This will strengthen your reputation as a fabulous conversationalist. Your biggest strength is your inventive mind. Folks like you don't look for solutions—they create them!

LIBRA

From September 23, 15:55 through October 24, 1:05

The Justice Seeker

Adventurous and intellectual, the 1975 Libra is a natural scholar. You could hardly be described as bookish though, you're much too jolly. Still, beneath your merry exterior beats the heart of a crusader. You are deeply committed to the idea of justice and you may devote your entire life to its cause. The year you were born, Indian Prime Minister Indira Gandhi was found guilty of electoral fraud. Rather than stepping down from office, she suppressed civil liberties throughout the country. Such transgressions against democracy make your blood boil, and you may make it your life's work to prevent similar abuses from occurring.

Emotionally intense, you need a job that speaks to your soul. If you don't become a civil rights lawyer, you will probably hold a job that promotes human dignity. You would fit in well with organizations like UNICEF, Amnesty International, or Medecins sans Frontières. Alternatively, you would make a good university professor, war correspondent, or newspaper publisher. As far as you're concerned, a free exchange of information is the best defense against oppression.

You have strong visualization skills, and you should use them at every opportunity. Drawing pictures of your dreams can be a powerful way to achieve your aims. The more detailed the images, the easier it will be for you to turn them into living realities. Guided meditations can also draw you closer to your most cherished wishes.

Your social circle is probably made up of outgoing, opinionated people. Ariens, Geminis, Leos, and Sagittarians are always willing to debate with you. When it comes to romance though, you need somebody with a softer touch. A Taurean or Piscean can bring out your tender instincts.

Passionate about your beliefs, your greatest challenge is to promote them effectively. Your most valuable teachers are people who don't share your convictions. Take the time to understand their beliefs, so you can argue effectively against them. Your biggest strength is your love of justice. Make it your life's mission to bring aid and comfort to the disadvantaged and dispossessed.

➤ Read about your Chinese Astrological sign on page 838. ➤ Read about your Personal Planets on page 826. ➤ Read about your personal Mystical Card on page 856.

VIRGO
Your Personal planets

YOUR LOVE POTENTIAL
Venus in Virgo, Aug. 23, 18:24 - Sept. 02, 15:33
Venus in Leo, Sept. 02, 15:34 - Sept. 23, 15:54

YOUR DRIVE AND AMBITION
Mars in Gemini, Aug. 23, 18:24 - Sept. 23, 15:54

YOUR LUCK MAGNETISM
Jupiter in Aries, Aug. 23, 18:24 - Sept. 23, 15:54

World Events

Sept. 9 - Eighteen-year-old Czech tennis star Martina Navratilova defects to the West.

Sept. 14 - Rembrandt's *The Night Watch* is slashed and damaged in Amsterdam.

Nobel Peace Prize winner Andrei Sakharov

LIBRA
Your Personal Planets

YOUR LOVE POTENTIAL
Venus in Leo, Sept. 23, 15:55 - Oct. 04, 5:18
Venus in Virgo, Oct. 04, 5:19 - Oct. 24, 1:05

YOUR DRIVE AND AMBITION
Mars in Gemini, Sept. 23, 15:55 - Oct. 17, 8:43
Mars in Cancer, Oct. 17, 8:44 - Oct. 24, 1:05

YOUR LUCK MAGNETISM
Jupiter in Aries, Sept. 23, 15:55 - Oct. 24, 1:05

World Events

Oct. 9 - Soviet scientist Andrei Sakharov wins the Nobel Peace Prize.

Oct. 11 - *Saturday Night Live* premieres in the U.S., with guest host George Carlin.

1975

SCORPIO
Your Personal Planets

YOUR LOVE POTENTIAL
Venus in Virgo, Oct. 24, 1:06 - Nov. 09, 13:51
Venus in Libra, Nov. 09, 13:52 - Nov. 22, 22:30

YOUR DRIVE AND AMBITION
Mars in Cancer, Oct. 24, 1:06 - Nov. 22, 22:30

YOUR LUCK MAGNETISM
Jupiter in Aries, Oct. 24, 1:06 - Nov. 22, 22:30

World Events

Nov. 10 – Angola finally wins independence from Portugal.

Nov. 20 – Infamous Spanish dictator Francisco Franco dies.

Spanish dictator Francisco Franco

SAGITTARIUS
Your Personal Planets

YOUR LOVE POTENTIAL
Venus in Libra, Nov. 22, 22:31 - Dec. 07, 0:28
Venus in Scorpio, Dec. 07, 0:29 - Dec. 22, 11:45

YOUR DRIVE AND AMBITION
Mars in Cancer, Nov. 22, 22:31 - Nov. 25, 18:29
Mars in Gemini, Nov. 25, 18:30 - Dec. 22, 11:45

YOUR LUCK MAGNETISM
Jupiter in Aries, Nov. 22, 22:31 - Dec. 22, 11:45

World Events

Nov. 28 – East Timor proclaims independence from Portuguese rule.

Dec. 21 – Six gunmen seize hostages during the OPEC talks in Vienna.

SCORPIO
From October 24, 1:06 through November 22, 22:30

The Free Spirit

The lessons of the sexual revolution are not lost on the 1975 Scorpio. You simply exude sensuality and make no effort to hide it. It feels good to be admired, and you may dress in dark or provocative clothing to invite more attention. The year you were born, the major U.S. broadcasting companies agreed to create a "family-hour" of television, which was devoid of sex and violence. You'd prefer it if such subjects were treated in a more open, honest fashion, instead of swept under the rug.

Deeply ambitious, you want to hold a position of importance in the working world. Putting in long hours at the office makes you feel needed and virtuous. You could have great success in managing large construction crews or coordinating government agencies. You also have a strong love of glamour and could run a successful chain of beauty salons or start your own line of cosmetics. Working for an opera house, dance troup, drama group, or symphony might also appeal to your theatrical spirit.

You're a bit secretive, which only adds to your allure. Spending long periods of time alone allows you to dream freely. You hate being hampered by small-minded people. Some of your favorite times are spent in the privacy of your own home. Having a secluded workspace can allow you to express yourself in the most daring and imaginative ways without fear of censure. You would definitely benefit from keeping a diary. Be sure to keep it under lock and key, though!

Because you are so open-minded, you enjoy the company of people who have similarly liberal views. Geminis, Sagittarians, Aquarians, and Pisceans admire your mysterious allure. When it comes to romance however, you need a partner with a strong personality. An Arien or Leo will provide a delicious challenge when you're feeling feisty.

Directed and determined, your greatest challenge is to yield to other people, at least sometimes. Be sensitive to your loved ones' needs. It can be very gratifying to relieve somebody of pain, heartache, or worry. Your biggest strength is your work ethic. You can realize all your dreams through sheer willpower.

SAGITTARIUS
From November 22, 22:31 through December 22, 11:45

The Easygoing Philosopher

All the 1975 Sagittarius needs to be happy is a backpack and a passport. You love exploring different lands and meeting new people. As far as you're concerned, life is one glorious adventure. If you can't travel, you read. It's the next best thing to taking a trip. Sometimes you prefer a good book to an exotic journey because reading allows you to idealize the images that are presented to you. You have a vivid imagination and enjoy speculating about other people's lives. Human behavior is a constant source of fascination for you.

A career in religion, philosophy, or higher education is likely for you. A natural student, you will probably attain a graduate degree in your desired field. If you don't become a professor or a spiritual advisor, you could go into publishing. Championing good books would seem more like play than work for you. The year you were born, E.L. Doctorow published the masterpiece *Ragtime*, kicking off a long and illustrious career as best-selling author. You would love to pick a struggling writer out of obscurity and set them on the road to fame. There's a strong possibility that you could be a successful author, too.

You always manage to have fun, even when you're broke. Although you may run low on cash at times, you'll never lack for friends. Your natural vivacity attracts people like a flower does bees. Discussing books, movies, and politics with pals gives you tremendous pleasure, and you often go without sleep to prolong a good conversation.

You get along best with open-minded, fun-loving people like yourself. Ariens, Geminis, Leos, and Sagittarians never fail to keep your spirits high. Romantically, you feel a strong connection with intellectuals. However, you should make more of an effort to be physically demonstrative with the one you love. Otherwise, your romance could cool into friendship.

Your greatest challenge is to develop your critical-thinking skills. It's essential for fulfilling your potential as a philosopher. Your biggest strength is your love of fun. No matter what duties you assume, you'll always be a child at heart.

➤ Read about your Chinese Astrological sign on page 838. ➤ Read about your Personal Planets on page 826. ➤ Read about your personal Mystical Card on page 856.

CAPRICORN

From December 22, 11:46 through December 31, 23:59

The Persuasive Pacifist

Fair-minded and persuasive, the December-born 1975 Capricorn can bring humanity to a whole new level. You're always thinking in terms of what is best for the group. It's almost impossible for you to make a selfish decision. That's because you understand that everyone is connected on some cosmic level. When people act as a unit to bring about peace, great things are accomplished. If they fight each other though, disaster ensues. Your mission is to make folks aware of their common condition, so that they can work together in harmony.

Your gift for diplomacy must be expressed through your work. You would make an excellent mediator, social worker, or judge. Working in human resources is also a good possibility for you, as you're able to find workable solutions to seemingly impossible conflicts. Blessed with strong visual talent, you'd be a successful interior designer. Designing relaxing spaces for hospitals and government agencies could be a rewarding career for you. If you put your mind to it, you could revolutionize the way bureaucratic institutions do business, simply by adding beauty to them.

As far as you're concerned, "modern" doesn't necessarily mean "better." The year you were born, "The Way We Were" won Song of the Year at the Grammys. This tune's nostalgic flavor mirrors your own attitude toward the past. You probably have an affinity for antique furnishings and vintage clothes, and you may have lots of framed old photographs around the house.

Strong friendships are important to you. Kind, nurturing people hold a special place in your heart. Taureans, Cancerians, Leos, and Pisceans are among your favorite pals. A true romantic, you need a partner who is affectionate and sentimental. The "touch-me-not" type doesn't impress you; you want somebody who knows how to give love, as well as receive it.

As a December-born 1975 Capricorn, you have a tendency to idealize the past. Your greatest challenge is to live for today. A fundamental belief that people are good is your biggest strength. This faith brings out the best in everybody; you are an inspiration.

CAPRICORN
Your Personal Planets

YOUR LOVE POTENTIAL
Venus in Scorpio, Dec. 22, 11:46 - Dec. 31, 23:59

YOUR DRIVE AND AMBITION
Mars in Gemini, Dec. 22, 11:46 - Dec. 31, 23:59

YOUR LUCK MAGNETISM
Jupiter in Aries, Dec. 22, 11:46 - Dec. 31, 23:59

World Events

Dec. 26 – The first supersonic transport service, USSR-Tupolev-144, goes into action.

Dec. 30 – Golf champion Tiger Woods is born.

Muhammad Ali
Born January 17, 1942

MUHAMMAD ALI
Capricorn

Born Cassius Clay, self-dubbed "the Greatest," Muhammad Ali is an Olympic gold medal winner who became a celebrated boxer. Adroit in the ring, graceful and elegant in his movement, Ali was also adept at self-promotion and stinging verbal rejoinders that put his opponents on the defensive. In a protest against racism in America, he joined the nation of Islam and transformed himself from Clay into Ali. His innovative boxing tactic of languishing on the ropes while his opponent pummeled him helped him win matches but may also have been responsible for his battle in later years with Parkinson's syndrome.

Ali is a Capricorn, a sign known for its devotion to hard work and success. Right from the start of his career, Ali was determined to capture the heavyweight championship and he let everyone know of this goal. Capricorn is one of the money signs, and his horoscope is as precise and elegant as his movements;

most of Ali's planets are placed in the houses of work, career and money. We see in his horoscope a configuration known as a grand trine, in which three planets or groups of planets are placed in a triangular shape, each leg being 120 degrees apart. This is generally considered a lucky configuration. In Ali's chart, this grand trine occurs in the Earth signs, known for their practicality, financial acumen and hardworking nature.

Ali has the Moon, the planet of emotions, in the sign of Aquarius and that is an indication of someone who demands equality and who holds broad humanitarian ideals, something that Ali has demonstrated again and again in his life. In addition, a contact from Mercury, planet of communication, can explain his litany of rhymes in the ring and outside it. A contact from Pluto, planet of manipulation, explains how Ali could get under the skin of his opponents and out-psyche them ver-

bally as part of his overall strategy. Another contact from Mars, planet of aggression, made him passionate in his emotions and gave him the warrior mentality and true grit that allowed him to keep battling away for the championship.

➤ Read about Muhammad Ali in "Science, Champions, and the Mars Effect" on page 625.

1976

Deep Feelings Surface: Uranus in Scorpio

The "square" connection between structural Saturn and awakener Uranus, which began last year, continued for the whole of 1976. Weak structures broke down before an awakening to new possibilities. With Uranus recently in Scorpio, novel perspectives were especially emphasized. Scorpio is associated with a dark, subtle and submerged awareness, especially to the inner workings of life and society. Uranus in Scorpio challenged people to experience their feelings, rather than only relating to events on a mental level. Reactions were stronger and more passionate, and sudden social changes occurred. This was shown in many events in 1976. For example, after the women's rights movement of the early seventies, they found themselves in roles often reserved for men. Lynda Carter played TV's *Wonder Woman*, while Barbara Walters made a $1 million deal to co-host the nightly news, the first woman to do so. Argentina's President Isabel Péron was deposed for corruption, while Patty Hearst could not use her gender to exempt her from a guilty verdict for bank robbery.

The death of China's Chairman Mao ended the Cultural Revolution and resulted in the swift arrest of the remaining "Gang of Four" members. Death, also associated with Scorpio, was on the lips of many, as the issue of mass extinction of plant and animal species around the world received global attention. Pop music also reached new heights of passion, as hard rock musicians like Kiss and AC/DC reached prominence and film examined the dark side of politics in *All the President's Men*.

Romania's Nadia Comaneci performing on the bar at the Montreal Olympic Games

Jimmy Carter wins the U.S. Presidential election

Mao Tse-Tung dies

MIND OVER MATTER

Thanks to mind development techniques, the Russians captured first place in the medal race with forty-seven at the 1976 Montreal Olympics. The East Germans were placed second with forty, using similar techniques. Professor Suin, who developed a mind-training program for the 1976 U.S. Olympic ski team, said that most countries were just beginning to look into the possibilities of mind power sports. According to the mentalist "The Amazing Kreskin," the Russians have experimented with mind power in athletics since the 1940s.

CHINA'S CULTURAL NIGHTMARE ENDS

Argentine President Isabel Péron was deposed by a military junta and replaced by a military government headed by Jorge Videla, while elections in Portugal brought socialist leader Soares to power. Concern grew over the extinction and endangerment of both plant and animal species in the last hundred years due to over-hunting, pollution, and destruction of natural habitats. Chinese leader Mao Tse-tung died at eighty-two and was succeeded by Hua Kuo-feng, who promptly vilified Mao and his "Gang of Four", which included his wife Chiang Ching. The U.S. celebrated its bicentennial with fanfare and fireworks as liberal Jimmy Carter was elected President. The U.S. *Viking* spacecraft landed on the planet Mars and took the first close-up pictures of its surface. Thirty-four men died of Legionnaire's Disease, contracted at an American Legion convention in Philadelphia. American Dorothy Hamill achieved fame as an Olympic skater, taking gold in the freestyle. Romanian Nadia Comaneci, aged fourteen, won three gold medals for gymnastics. Sylvester Stallone achieved stardom in *Rocky*. *All the President's Men* chronicled the events of the Watergate scandal.

➤ Read "Science, Champions, and the Mars Effect" by Sophie Mason on page 625.

CAPRICORN
From January 01, 0:00 through January 20, 22:24

The Bright-Eyed Optimist

Poetic and sensitive, the January-born 1976 Capricorn looks at life through rose-colored glasses. Some folks may call you a hopeless dreamer, but you prefer to think of yourself as a hopeful one. Although you may be frequently disappointed by opportunists and cynics, this doesn't stop you from thinking the best of everyone. When the human race lets you down, you lavish affection on your pets. Animals hold a special place in your heart, as do small children. Perhaps you identify with their vulnerability.

Given your nurturing personality, you'd be wise to enter one of the caring professions. You'd make an excellent nurse, veterinarian, or hospital aide. Being a kindergarten teacher might also appeal to you, although you'd be reluctant to administer discipline. At some point in your life, you may prefer working independently. Solitary work like writing, photography, or film editing could provide the freedom you desire.

Because you soak up the atmosphere like a sponge, you need to be careful about the company you keep. The year you were born, Raymond Carver published *Will You Be Quiet, Please?* You would be wise to pose this question to folks who insist on poisoning you with their negative attitudes. In the event pessimists do overwhelm you, you might try going off on your own. Nature walks, prayer, and meditation can put you back in touch with your spiritual essence, which is as pure as a mountain stream.

You need friends who will form a protective barrier around you. Worldly Taureans, Cancerians, Virgos, and Capricorns can keep the wolves at bay. Your ideal romantic partner will bolster your ego. Steer clear of critical types who seek to correct your mistakes. You may be hard enough on yourself already!

Tender and vulnerable, your greatest challenge is to stick up for yourself. Although it's nice to have friends to run interference for you, it's important to be your own advocate. As you get older, it will be easier for you to speak on your own behalf. Your biggest strength is your relentless optimism. Use it as a shield against those who seek to dim your sunny smile.

AQUARIUS
From January 20, 22:25 through February 19, 12:39

The Incurable Romantic

The 1976 Aquarius is on a constant quest for romance. You consider roses, chocolates, and love letters as necessities, not luxuries. Even your childhood crushes had an all-consuming intensity, and you probably remember your first love with special fondness. The movies fed your fantasies of storybook romance. The year you were born, *Gone with the Wind* first aired on American television, scoring record-breaking ratings. Perhaps the love story made a psychic impression on you. It would account for your own poetic impulses.

Writing romance novels may be a good way for you to earn a living. You may also like to work with your hands. Being a sculptor, mechanic, or carpenter could prove rewarding. Whatever job you take should involve freedom of movement. Although you enjoy hard work, you hate feeling chained to a desk. A regular program of aerobic exercise can ward off the restlessness that frequently undermines your progress. Meditation can help, too.

Intense and unpredictable, people may see you as sort of a wild card. Nobody can predict how you'll feel or what you'll do. Your moods change from moment to moment; you're something of an emotional kaleidoscope. If you have children, you'll lavish them with plenty of love, affection, and presents. You can identify with their exuberant, impulsive spirit and will probably play a very active role in their daily lives. It's entirely possible you'll put your career on hold to be a stay-at-home parent.

Friends play a very important role in your life. You get along best with outgoing, creative people like Ariens, Geminis, Librans, and Sagittarians. When it comes time to pick a partner, be sure to choose somebody who is just as sweet and sentimental as you. There's a good chance you'll end up with a painter, poet, or dancer. You could even become creative partners and decide to make beautiful music together.

Your greatest challenge is to maintain an emotional equilibrium. This will become easier with life experience. A capacity for unconditional love is your biggest strength. Whoever captures your heart is lucky indeed.

CAPRICORN
Your Personal Planets

YOUR LOVE POTENTIAL
Venus in Scorpio, Jan. 01, 0:00 - Jan. 01, 12:13
Venus in Sagittarius, Jan. 01, 12:14 - Jan. 20, 22:24

YOUR DRIVE AND AMBITION
Mars in Gemini, Jan. 01, 0:00 - Jan. 20, 22:24

YOUR LUCK MAGNETISM
Jupiter in Aries, Jan. 01, 0:00 - Jan. 20, 22:24

World Events

Jan. 10 - African states meet to discuss the war in Angola.

Jan. 12 - British mystery writer Dame Agatha Christie dies.

Prolific British mystery writer Agatha Christie

AQUARIUS
Your Personal Planets

YOUR LOVE POTENTIAL
Venus in Sagittarius, Jan. 20, 22:25 - Jan. 26, 6:08
Venus in Capricorn, Jan. 26, 6:09 - Feb. 19, 12:39

YOUR DRIVE AND AMBITION
Mars in Gemini, Jan. 20, 22:25 - Feb. 19, 12:39

YOUR LUCK MAGNETISM
Jupiter in Aries, Jan. 20, 22:25 - Feb. 19, 12:39

World Events

Jan. 30 - George Bush takes up the position of director of the CIA.

Feb. 4 - The 12th Winter Olympics open in Innsbruck, Austria.

➤ Read about your Chinese Astrological sign on page 838. ➤ Read about your Personal Planets on page 826. ➤ Read about your personal Mystical Card on page 856.

1976

PISCES
Your Personal Planets

YOUR LOVE POTENTIAL
Venus in Capricorn, Feb. 19, 12:40 - Feb. 19, 16:49
Venus in Aquarius, Feb. 19, 16:50 - Mar. 15, 0:58
Venus in Pisces, Mar. 15, 0:59 - Mar. 20, 11:49

YOUR DRIVE AND AMBITION
Mars in Gemini, Feb. 19, 12:40 - Mar. 18, 13:14
Mars in Cancer, Mar. 18, 13:15 - Mar. 20, 11:49

YOUR LUCK MAGNETISM
Jupiter in Aries, Feb. 19, 12:40 - Mar. 20, 11:49

World Events

Mar. 19 – Princess Margaret separates from Lord Snowdon after sixteen years of marriage.

Mar. 20 – Millionaire's daughter Patty Hearst is convicted of armed robbery.

Argentine President Isabel Péron is deposed by the military

ARIES
Your Personal Planets

YOUR LOVE POTENTIAL
Venus in Pisces, Mar. 20, 11:50 - Apr. 08, 8:55
Venus in Aries, Apr. 08, 8:56 - Apr. 19, 23:02

YOUR DRIVE AND AMBITION
Mars in Cancer, Mar. 20, 11:50 - Apr. 19, 23:02

YOUR LUCK MAGNETISM
Jupiter in Aries, Mar. 20, 11:50 - Mar. 26, 10:24
Jupiter in Taurus, Mar. 26, 10:25 - Apr. 19, 23:02

World Events

Mar. 24 – Argentine President Isabel Péron is deposed by the country's military.

Apr. 5 – American billionaire tycoon Howard Hughes dies.

PISCES
From February 19, 12:40 through March 20, 11:49

The Haunted Mystic

A strongly developed sixth sense sets the 1976 Pisces apart from the rest of the crowd. You're firmly convinced that there's more to the world than what can be seen with the naked eye. From a young age, you were probably captivated by concepts like telekinesis, astral projection, and mind reading. There is a good chance you were misunderstood as a child and considered offbeat or unusual by authority figures. Maybe that's why you sometimes feel like an outsider, even when you're among friends.

Art is like a religion to you. Movies, music, and books provide you with a welcome escape from the real world. You'd make an excellent artist yourself, although it could take time and patience to develop a productive routine. Feel free to play around with different work methods if a particular one no longer inspires you. The year you were born, Steadicam was used for the first time in the movie *Rocky*. You may find that using innovative techniques uplifts and inspires you. You would also make a good psychotherapist as you're particularly talented at interpreting dreams.

Spirituality could play a big role in your life. You have the power to transcend tremendous hardship, provided your faith is strong enough. Studying world religions can provide you with valuable insight into your own beliefs. At some point, you may take a religious pilgrimage that will change the entire course of your life. Recurring themes and symbols will reveal your personal truth.

You enjoy surrounding yourself with grounded, secure people who can benefit from your whimsical outlook. Taureans, Virgos, Sagittarians, and Capricorns can teach you to become more practical while you show them how to be more creative. Your romantic partner will probably be spiritual and artistic. Together, you can make beautiful music.

Your greatest challenge as a 1976 Pisces is to find ways to fulfil your creative and spiritual urges. Your biggest strength is your appreciation for the unseen world. Continue to search for answers that can't be gleaned through ordinary means. Learn to trust that uncanny intuition of yours.

ARIES
From March 20, 11:50 through April 19, 23:02

The Rooted Ruler

The 1976 Aries is unquestionably the king or queen of his or her castle. Even when you were a baby, your entire family deferred to you. Perhaps you marked a turning point in your household's history. Maybe you had the dominant personality. Whatever the reason, you've always held a prominent position at home and must cope with the strengths and setbacks of this situation. While it's true you have the biggest say in family matters, you probably have the most responsibility, too. The year you were born, Alex Haley's book *Roots* was published. Your roots have a profound affect on everything you do.

It is easy to meet your objectives as you are very directed and ambitious. You have a protective instinct that will probably manifest itself in your career. Teaching or childcare may appeal to you. A job in the military might also suit you. You're also interested in protecting your history. Landmark preservation and antiques restoration could prove satisfying in this respect. There's a good chance you will hold a high position of authority at some point, as you are an obvious leader.

Relationships have the power to transform your life. Fortunately, you're smart enough to look past superficial considerations when choosing friends. It doesn't matter whether your loved ones drive flashy cars or wear fashionable clothes. So long as they have substantive characters, they are good enough for you. If someone betrays your trust, it may take years for you to recover.

Loyal, nurturing people bring out the best in you. Taureans, Cancerians, Sagittarians, and Pisceans respect your authority, while providing you with the tender loving care you need. Don't be afraid to pair with a romantic partner who is just as strong-willed as you. It might actually be good for you to meet with resistance now and again.

Your greatest challenge as a 1976 Aries is to come to terms with your own power. Use it to protect your loved ones. Your biggest asset is your willingness to learn from mistakes. It takes a lot of courage to admit you're wrong. Give yourself a gold star for maturity.

➤ Read about your Chinese Astrological sign on page 838. ➤ Read about your Personal Planets on page 826. ➤ Read about your personal Mystical Card on page 856.

TAURUS

From April 19, 23:03 through May 20, 22:20

The Unabashed Hedonist

Nobody knows how to have a good time like the 1976 Taurus. You try to indulge all five senses whenever possible. A steady stream of sensuous fabrics, beautiful vistas, fragrant perfumes, melodic music, and sumptuous flavors pleases you immensely. Unless you can travel first class, you may not go at all. You know the best places to shop and eat, and folks often ask you for recommendations on where to go and what to do.

It's lucky that your refined taste is accompanied by good business sense. You've got a knack for making money both readily and easily. Investing in the arts could be especially lucrative for you. You'd make an excellent art dealer, movie producer, or talent agent. Whatever you do for a living, it will involve large amounts of money exchanging hands. In May of 1976, the OEEC (Office of European Economic Co-operation) established an $800 million fund for developing countries. As a Taurus born that year, you have the talent to manage large sums of money for others as well as yourself. You're always on the lookout for someone with an unusual outlook. Many of your relationships are with visionaries and you enjoy speculating what the future will be like with such people. When you do get married, it should be to somebody intense, magnetic, and powerful. Such a person will be sure to hold your interest over the long haul. You want an enduring relationship.

Determined, results-oriented people find a kindred spirit in you. Maybe that's why you have so many Leos, Scorpios, and Aquarians as friends. You also enjoy the company of your fellow Bulls, although you can both be very stubborn. Where love is concerned, you get along best with starry-eyed idealists. Their whimsy compliments your stability and vice versa.

Your greatest challenge is to find a pleasing use for your business sense. Don't go into a field just because it's lucrative; find something you love and make it turn a profit. Your biggest strength is your Midas touch—use it to benefit others as well as yourself. Donating money to the arts may be your greatest legacy.

GEMINI

From May 20, 22:21 through June 21, 6:23

The Confident Communicator

Low self-esteem is never a problem for the 1976 Gemini. You know you're something special, and you carry yourself accordingly. Yet somehow, you never seem arrogant. People find your confidence refreshing and are happy to hand you heavy responsibilities. You know how to get the job done and won't waste time with deliberations. Once you decide on a plan of action, you run with it, refusing to look back. Regret is not a word in your vocabulary. This is the secret to your success.

Highly creative, you need a job that allows you to express yourself. You would make a great entertainer. If you become an actor, you'll probably favor dramatic parts. You have a serious air that may not lend itself easily to comedy. Becoming a respected newscaster is also an option for you. The year you were born, media mogul Ted Turner established the WTBS "Superstation" in Atlanta, while newspaper giant Rupert Murdoch added the *New York Post* to his stable of one hundred publications. You could achieve similar success in the communications industry, if you so desired.

You have good instincts about people, and probably have a small circle of close friends as opposed to a huge mob of buddies. Most folks would be surprised to learn what a true romantic you are. When you love someone, you will do everything in your power to make him or her happy. Leaving a successful job for the sake of your partner is not outside the realm of possibility. Although you derive a great sense of satisfaction from work, relationships come first with you.

Spiritually-oriented people find a good friend in you. Geminis, Sagittarians, Aquarians, and Pisceans may be among your closest associates. In love, you are drawn to idealistic, dreamy people who want to feel protected and cherished. You need to be needed by your partner and like to be of service.

Your greatest challenge as a 1976 Gemini is to be more open to other people's ideas. Collaborating with others can only enhance your own good instincts. Your biggest strength is your balanced attitude toward life. It's certain that both your public and private lives will both be rewarding.

➤ Read about your Chinese Astrological sign on page 838. ➤ Read about your Personal Planets on page 826. ➤ Read about your personal Mystical Card on page 856.

➤ Read about your Chinese Astrological sign on page 838. ➤ Read about your Personal Planets on page 826. ➤ Read about your personal Mystical Card on page 856.

TAURUS
Your Personal Planets

YOUR LOVE POTENTIAL
Venus in Aries, Apr. 19, 23:03 - May 02, 17:48
Venus in Taurus, May 02, 17:49 - May 20, 22:20

YOUR DRIVE AND AMBITION
Mars in Cancer, Apr. 19, 23:03 - May 16, 11:09
Mars in Leo, May 16, 11:10 - May 20, 22:20

YOUR LUCK MAGNETISM
Jupiter in Taurus, Apr. 19, 23:03 - May 20, 22:20

World Events

Apr. 22 - Barbara Walters makes an appearance as the first female nightly network news anchor in the U.S.

May 10 - Liberal leader Jeremy Thorpe drops out of the British election campaign amidst rumors of homosexuality.

Former British Liberal leader Jeremy Thorpe

GEMINI
Your Personal Planets

YOUR LOVE POTENTIAL
Venus in Taurus, May 20, 22:21 - May 27, 3:42
Venus in Gemini, May 27, 3:43 - June 20, 13:55
Venus in Cancer, June 20, 13:56 - June 21, 6:23

YOUR DRIVE AND AMBITION
Mars in Leo, May 20, 22:21 - June 21, 6:23

YOUR LUCK MAGNETISM
Jupiter in Taurus, May 20, 22:21 - June 21, 6:23

World Events

May 28 - Ellis Island in New York officially reopens.

June 15 - The Chinese government announces that Mao Tse-Tung will no longer meet other world leaders.

1976

CANCER
Your Personal Planets

YOUR LOVE POTENTIAL
Venus in Cancer, June 21, 6:24 - July 14, 23:35
Venus in Leo, July 14, 23:36 - July 22, 17:17

YOUR DRIVE AND AMBITION
Mars in Leo, June 21, 6:24 - July 06, 23:26
Mars in Virgo, July 06, 23:27 - July 22, 17:17

YOUR LUCK MAGNETISM
Jupiter in Taurus, June 21, 6:24 - July 22, 17:17

World Events

July 2 - North and South Vietnam formally reunify under the name the Socialist Republic of Vietnam.

July 3 - Israel launches the rescue of the Air France crew and passengers being held at Entebbe Airport in Uganda by pro-Palestinian hijackers.

One of the team sent to rescue hostages from a plane at Entebbe Airport is cheered by crowds

LEO
Your Personal Planets

YOUR LOVE POTENTIAL
Venus in Leo, July 22, 17:18 - Aug. 08, 8:35
Venus in Virgo, Aug. 08, 8:36 - Aug. 23, 0:17

YOUR DRIVE AND AMBITION
Mars in Virgo, July 22, 17:18 - Aug. 23, 0:17

YOUR LUCK MAGNETISM
Jupiter in Taurus, July 22, 17:18 - Aug. 23, 0:17

World Events

Aug. 1 - Elizabeth Taylor is granted her second divorce from Richard Burton.

Aug. 2 - German film director Fritz Lang dies.

CANCER
From June 21, 6:24 through July 22, 17:17

The Sentimental Sage

A strong love of history characterizes the 1976 Cancer. You firmly believe that in order to understand the present, you have to know the past. History books probably crowd your library, although you may enjoy biographies too. Feeling linked to your ancestors gives you a sense of power. There's a good chance you can trace your family back for several generations. You're probably quite patriotic, too. The year you were born, the United States celebrated its bicentennial anniversary. National holidays are very close to your heart, and you observe them with great respect.

This interest in the past may influence your career choice. You would make an excellent genealogist, archivist, or historian. A love of children could take you in another direction—family planning, obstetrics, or midwifery may be fields worth exploring. Whether it's preserving old traditions or bringing new life into the world, you want to feel that life has a sense of continuity. You could never hold down a dead-end job for very long.

Friends play a big role in your life. You enjoy folks who are creative and well-heeled. "Slumming it" holds little appeal for you. However, you never hesitate to help a pal who has fallen on hard times. There's a good chance that you are a member of at least one humanitarian group. You firmly believe that everybody has a right to be fed, clothed, and housed, regardless of economic straits. Performing charity work is your way of giving thanks for the abundance you enjoy on a daily basis.

Generous people comprise the greater part of your social circle. That's why there are so many Geminis, Librans, Sagittarians, and Pisceans among your acquaintances. In romance, you want a partner who is romantic and spontaneous. You want to be swept off your feet, not under the carpet!

The greatest challenge you face, 1976 Cancer, is to live in the moment. Pining over the good old days can distract you from all the wonderful things that are unfolding right in front of you. Your biggest strength is your ability to make and keep friends. Companionship will rarely elude you.

LEO
From July 22, 17:18 through August 23, 0:17

The Big Success

The 1976 Leo never does anything by half measures. You do everything on a grand scale and seek to have at least two of everything. Perhaps you had a financially insecure childhood. Maybe flamboyant relatives overshadowed you. Whatever the circumstances of your upbringing, they prompted you to become an outstanding success. Fighting your way to the top comes naturally to you. The year you were born, the movie *Rocky* was released. You've probably felt like a heavyweight fighter many times in your life.

You have a strong artistic streak that could net you a fortune. Selling handmade items is a good possibility for you, as you like to put a personal stamp on everything you do. There's a good chance you will integrate nature's bounty into your work. Running a health food store, flower shop, or gardening service are among the ways you may make a living. You will probably market your wares to high-end clients; an air of exclusivity characterizes everything you do. Eventually, you could even launch your own line of luxury products.

Romance is important to you, although work can get in the way of your love life. At some point, you may have to choose between your personal and public lives. You may decide to take time off to raise your children. Such a decision could add an exciting new dimension to your life. Caring for young people fills a deep need within you. Whether you realize it or not, you're a very nurturing person.

Fun-loving people with a dash of flair have a special hold on your heart. Ariens, Leos, Librans, and Sagittarians have a lot in common with you. As far as your love life is concerned, you need a partner who isn't afraid to take risks. With the support of a loving mate, you can accomplish anything you desire. You need to have someone in your corner.

Your greatest challenge, 1976 Leo, is to scale back work for the sake of love. Although you are capable of great things on the career front, it's more important to build up a loyal circle of friends. Your biggest strength is your caring heart. If you obey its instincts, you'll never go wrong.

➤ Read about your Chinese Astrological sign on page 838. ➤ Read about your Personal Planets on page 826. ➤ Read about your personal Mystical Card on page 856.

VIRGO

From August 23, 0:18 through September 22, 21:47

The Prominent Citizen

First and foremost, the 1976 Virgo wants to be a respected member of the community. You're not interested in living behind a high fence; you want to meet with neighbors and converse with shopkeepers. There's a good chance you know most of the people who live on your street and head several civic committees. Living in a large metropolis won't stop you from making friends with your next-door neighbors; you're an expert at promoting a feeling of community, regardless of your surroundings.

A strong interest in politics could draw you to public office. You'd make an excellent mayor, city planner, or civic booster. Whatever you do, a love of language will probably be evident in your work. Becoming a librarian may also appeal to you, as it would give you a welcome opportunity to mix with locals while being surrounded by books. You would also make a good writer, journalist, or public relations representative.

Although you enjoy holding a respected position in your community, you also want a fulfilling home life. Your expectations of your family may occasionally be a bit unrealistic. Take care not to pressure your relatives to put up a front of perfection. Even the happiest families have an element of pathos. The year you were born, Judith Guest's best-selling novel *Ordinary People* was published. The irony of this title should not be lost on you—keep in mind that there is no such thing as ordinary.

Your friends are probably hard-working, bookish types. Geminis, Virgos, Librans, and Aquarians share your love of ideas and can provide you with plenty of stimulating conversation. With regard to love, you need a partner who will expand your horizons. Don't be so quick to dismiss your mate's ideas in favor of your own.

Taking risks is the greatest challenge you face as a 1976 Virgo. Sometimes you have to look beyond your own experience to fully appreciate your range of choices. Your biggest strength is your strong sense of community. By 21st-century standards, it's a refreshing attitude. Combat isolation by forming strong relationships with the folks in your community.

LIBRA

From September 22, 21:48 through October 23, 6:57

The Centered Soul

A profound sense of calm surrounds the 1976 Libra. "Never hurry and never worry," may be your motto. The wisdom of your attitude is reflected by your youthful appearance. When your contemporaries are sporting gray hair and wrinkles, you'll look fresh as a daisy. You're one of the least competitive people around—you'd rather come together with folks in the spirit of harmony. If you weren't so genuine, lots of people would be envious of you. Chances are, though, you have many loyal friends.

Patient and understanding, you would make an excellent teacher. Any profession that involves putting people at ease would suit you, too. You could run a successful hotel, restaurant, or health spa. A great deal of your success can be chalked up to charm. The year you were born, Dorothy Hamill became an international sensation when she won the gold medal for figure skating in the Winter Olympics. Her wholesome appeal is quite similar to yours, and this should take you far in any career.

You may not be very practical when it comes to money and may outspend what you earn. Ruled by the planet Venus, you may find it hard to resist expensive items like gourmet food, designer clothes, and fine furnishings. If you're not careful, you might have to rely on friends to bail you out of debt. This can be embarrassing, as you put great stock in your pals' opinions. Do yourself a favor and learn how to live within your means. It may be one of the most important lessons you will ever learn.

You like to cultivate friendships with well-established, respectable people. Taureans, Cancerians, Leos, and Capricorns have a sense of dignity that you admire. Romantically, you would be well-suited to someone who is fiery and passionate. Such a mate would serve as a counterbalance to your placid personality.

Your greatest challenge is to be more practical with money. Although you may not worry about material matters, your loved ones probably do. Do you really want them to assume responsibility for your obligations? Your biggest strength is your sense of peace. Use it to comfort people in distress.

➤ Read about your Chinese Astrological sign on page 838. ➤ Read about your Personal Planets on page 826. ➤ Read about your personal Mystical Card on page 856.

VIRGO
Your Personal Planets

YOUR LOVE POTENTIAL
Venus in Virgo, Aug. 23, 0:18 - Sept. 01, 17:43
Venus in Libra, Sept. 01, 17:44 - Sept. 22, 21:47

YOUR DRIVE AND AMBITION
Mars in Virgo, Aug. 23, 0:18 - Aug. 24, 5:54
Mars in Libra, Aug. 24, 5:55 - Sept. 22, 21:47

YOUR LUCK MAGNETISM
Jupiter in Taurus, Aug. 23, 0:18 - Aug. 23, 10:23
Jupiter in Gemini, Aug. 23, 10:24 - Sept. 22, 21:47

World Events

Sept. 3 - The *Viking 2* space shuttle lands on Mars.
Sept. 9 - Chinese Communist Party Chairman Mao Tse-tung dies.

Chairman Mao Tse-Tung's reign ends after more than twenty years

LIBRA
Your Personal Planets

YOUR LOVE POTENTIAL
Venus in Libra, Sept. 22, 21:48 - Sept. 26, 4:16
Venus in Scorpio, Sept. 26, 4:17 - Oct. 20, 17:21
Venus in Sagittarius, Oct. 20, 17:22 - Oct. 23, 6:57

YOUR DRIVE AND AMBITION
Mars in Libra, Sept. 22, 21:48 - Oct. 08, 20:22
Mars in Scorpio, Oct. 08, 20:23 - Oct. 23, 6:57

YOUR LUCK MAGNETISM
Jupiter in Gemini, Sept. 22, 21:48 - Oct. 16, 20:23
Jupiter in Taurus, Oct. 16, 20:24 - Oct. 23, 6:57

World Events

Oct. 6 - The military are called in after clashes between students and police in Bangkok.
Oct. 11 - Mao's widow and her associates, the "Gang of Four," are arrested in Peking for plotting a coup.

1976

SCORPIO
Your Personal Planets

YOUR LOVE POTENTIAL
Venus in Sagittarius, Oct. 23, 6:58 - Nov. 14, 10:41
Venus in Capricorn, Nov. 14, 10:42 - Nov. 22, 4:21

YOUR DRIVE AND AMBITION
Mars in Scorpio, Oct. 23, 6:58 - Nov. 20, 23:52
Mars in Sagittarius, Nov. 20, 23:53 - Nov. 22, 4:21

YOUR LUCK MAGNETISM
Jupiter in Taurus, Oct. 23, 6:58 - Nov. 22, 4:21

World Events

Oct. 26 - After many postponements, the National Theatre is finally opened on London's South Bank.

Nov. 10 - American artist Man Ray dies in Paris at the age of sixty-eight.

Man Ray dies after revolutionalizing photographic art

SAGITTARIUS
Your Personal Planets

YOUR LOVE POTENTIAL
Venus in Capricorn, Nov. 22, 4:22 - Dec. 09, 12:52
Venus in Aquarius, Dec. 09, 12:53 - Dec. 21, 17:34

YOUR DRIVE AND AMBITION
Mars in Sagittarius, Nov. 22, 4:22 - Dec. 21, 17:34

YOUR LUCK MAGNETISM
Jupiter in Taurus, Nov. 22, 4:22 - Dec. 21, 17:34

World Events

Dec. 4 - Bokasso proclaims the Central African Empire.

Dec. 4 - Much-loved British composer Benjamin Britten dies.

SCORPIO
From October 23, 6:58 through November 22, 4:21

The Chivalrous Hero

Passionate and idealistic, the 1976 Scorpio is incredibly focused. Once you set your sights on a goal, you'll do everything in your power to reach it. Drive like yours is only found in the most successful artists, athletes, and anarchists. If you channel your ambition in the proper direction, you can accomplish anything your heart desires. Just keep your eyes on the prize!

Working in a challenging environment gives you a great deal of satisfaction. You could have great success as a hospice worker, family court officer, or special education teacher. Medicine may also appeal to you; you'd make a great surgeon or oncologist. As far as you're concerned, there is no such thing as a hopeless situation. Maybe that's why so many people rely on you at the bleakest moments. Nothing seems impossible in your presence; you can actually will miracles to happen. The year you were born, President Gerald Ford survived two assassination attempts thanks to quick-thinking bystanders who intervened. You're capable of similar acts of heroism.

You will do anything for love and will go out of your way to impress the object of your affection. Anybody who criticizes your beloved has an instant enemy in you. You'll fight for the honor of your sweetheart and go out of your way to make them comfortable. So long as you're around, chivalry will never die. Some folks scoff at your ardor, but others are moved by it. Old-fashioned romantics find your intensity sexy and are irresistibly drawn to you.

Loyalty is your number one priority in friendship. Steadfast Taureans, Cancerians, Leos, and Capricorns make you feel safe and secure. Romantically, you fare best with a partner who is willing to give you the upper hand. Fortunately, you are the kind of person who is incredibly attentive to your beloved's spiritual, physical, and emotional needs.

Your greatest challenge as a 1976 Scorpio is continually to set impressive goals for yourself. Fresh challenges always bring out the best in you. Your biggest strength is your determination. Virtually nothing can stand between you and your goals.

SAGITTARIUS
From November 22, 4:22 through December 21, 17:34

The Boundless Explorer

Here, there, and everywhere—it seems like the 1976 Sagittarius can be in three places at once. That's because you're always on the move. The year you were born Nadia Comaneci won three gold medals in gymnastics at the Summer Olympics. You have the coiled energy of a gymnast and you constantly look for ways to unleash it. If there's anything you hate, it's staying in one spot for long periods of time.

Warm and ebullient, you'd make a great tour guide or cruise director. Working with people gives you tremendous satisfaction, although you enjoy the company of animals too. Grooming pets, giving horseback riding lessons, or running a dog-walking service would give you a chance to play on the job. You're also quite an adventurer and would do well as an archeologist, marine biologist, or anthropologist. One thing is for sure; you should avoid desk jobs like the plague.

You have a strong spiritual side that may prompt you to study world religions. Although you may not follow an organized belief system, you do have core principles that guide your actions. Many people would be surprised to learn how deep and introspective you really are. That's because you use humor as a means to hide your true feelings. On the outside, you're all jokes and smiles, but on the inside, you're reflective and philosophical. At times, you need to go off on your own if only to reconnect with your spiritual core.

Tasteful, refined people make up the majority of your friends. Taureans, Cancerians, Leos, and Librans bring out your gentle side and help soothe your jangled nerves. In love, you need a partner who is outgoing and energetic. You're not the type to stay home on the weekends—you want to be out exploring, preferably with your mate!

Your greatest challenge as a 1976 Sagittarius is to settle down. Having a serious relationship may add stability to your life, provided you don't shy away from commitment in the first place. Your biggest blessing is your zest for life. No matter how many experiences you have, you will always find new territory to explore. Keep that passport current!

➤ Read about your Chinese Astrological sign on page 838. ➤ Read about your Personal Planets on page 826. ➤ Read about your personal Mystical Card on page 856.

CAPRICORN
From December 21, 17:35 through December 31, 23:59

The Successful Dreamer

A strong subconscious leads the December-born 1976 Capricorn in all things. You'd rather act on instinct than intellect. Vivid dreams can shape and guide your decisions, and you put great stock in your hunches. To outsiders, there may seem to be no rhyme or reason to your behavior. What they don't realize is that you are obeying an inner logic that has little to do with the outside world. Amazingly, you rarely make a wrong choice, although it may frequently look like you are moving in a trance.

Your work should have a strong spiritual element to it. Teaching yoga or transcendental meditation would be rewarding for you. You could also be an incredible artist—your creative work has an ethereal quality that is most compelling. The year you were born, Philip Glass released his hypnotic composition, *Einstein on the Beach*. Your art can cast a similar spell over your audience, provided you stay true to your spiritual essence. Pandering to what is new or hot will only hinder your success.

Growing up, you may not have had much opportunity to play. Perhaps an illness in your family prevented you from enjoying childish pursuits. Economic hardships may have forced you to work at a young age. The sadness that may have surrounded your childhood has given you wisdom beyond your years. Use this wisdom to your advantage. Now that you're an adult, you can do the things that make you happy without feeling guilty. Remember, life is not a dress rehearsal—find your bliss while you have the chance!

You feel a kinship with reserved people who are just a little unusual. Offbeat Cancerians, Scorpios, Librans, and Pisceans understand and appreciate your sensitivity. As with everything, instinct will lead you to your romantic partner. You're destined to be with a creative, spiritual type who can read your every thought.

Your greatest challenge is to express your feelings openly and honestly, so that loved ones, friends, and colleagues can meet your needs. Your biggest strength is your pure spirit. Let it lead you to a life filled with joy and abundance. You deserve to be happy.

CAPRICORN
Your Personal Planets

YOUR LOVE POTENTIAL
Venus in Aquarius, Dec. 21, 17:35 - Dec. 31, 23:59

YOUR DRIVE AND AMBITION
Mars in Sagittarius, Dec. 21, 17:35 - Dec. 31, 23:59

YOUR LUCK MAGNETISM
Jupiter in Taurus, Dec. 21, 17:35 - Dec. 31, 23:59

World Events

Dec. 24 – Takeo Fukuda is elected Prime Minister of Japan.

Dec. 28 – Winnie Mandela is released in South Africa.

American tennis players Venus and Serena Williams

Special Feature

Science, Champions, and the Mars Effect

by Sophia Mason

Most of us don't need any convincing that astrology works. However, there are quite a few skeptics in the world who are dedicated to denouncing astrology as mere unscientific superstition. Fortunately, they are wrong, and scientific support for astrology is quite strong, as the research of a French psychologist, the late Michel Gauquelin, shows.

Gauquelin had a passionate interest in astrology as a young man, and when some of his elders criticized this pursuit as a waste of time, he decided to prove them wrong. Birth records in France are easily available from local registries and include the actual time of birth, so in 1949 he began collecting data on famous people. In 1955, he published his first discoveries, continuing his work until his death in 1991. By that time, he had accumulated certified data for well over 20,000 European and American professionals.

Through his research, Gauquelin demonstrated a link between the planetary positions in an individual's horoscope at birth and success in certain occupations in adulthood. For example, actors tend to be born when Jupiter, planet of self-expression, is hovering near the eastern horizon or near the highest point it can reach in the sky each day. These areas are often referred to as "power zones" in a horoscope. His research also found that successful scientists are often born at times when the serious and methodical planet Saturn is in these zones, and there is a similar link between Mars and military men. In fact, Gauquelin found links between five different planets and eleven different professions, using certified birth data from various countries in Europe, as well as the U.S.

The most famous of these discoveries is called *The Mars Effect for Sports Champions* (the Mars Effect for short), meaning that Mars is often found in power zones at a higher than normal rate in the birth charts of champion athletes. Gauquelin felt the Mars link to sports

champions was the easiest of his findings for others to test, and challenged skeptics to use it to check his work. His challenge resulted in a forty-year controversy that left the skeptics red-faced when their tests repeatedly confirmed his discovery. The whole tangled tale is told in a book by Suitbert Ertel and Kenneth Irving called *The Tenacious Mars Effect*, and the title says it all—the Mars Effect could not be beat.

(Continued on page 633)

▶ Read Muhammad Ali's Star Profile on page 617.

1977

Middle East Peace: Jupiter engages the Outer Planets

Jupiter, the planet of expansion, enterprise and optimism, was in top form in 1977, charming each of the outer planets to give its best. Jupiter started the year in stolid Taurus until April, then spread its wings in lively Gemini before ending the year in Cancer. While in Taurus, it recalled abrasive contacts it made last year to limiting Saturn and disruptive Uranus. This pattern was replayed in Egyptian leader Anwar al-Sadat's March vow not to let an inch of Arab territory remain under Israeli rule. But even as he uttered those words, the shape of the future was evident, as U.S. President Carter met with Israeli Prime Minister Yitzhak Rabin on the first step in what was to become the year's grandest enterprise, peace in the Middle East.

April 3, the very day that Jupiter entered communicative Gemini, al-Sadat was more conciliatory as he met with Carter himself. On the twenty-fifth, as Jupiter harmonized with love-centered Venus, Jordan's King Hussein came to Washington to further the peace efforts. More peaceful tones were heard in May as Jupiter made a softening "trine" to transformative Pluto and then a conciliatory contact with Saturn for the first of two times this year. The momentum for peace built, culminating at year's end in al-Sadat pledging "no more war" and sponsoring a peace conference in Cairo as Jupiter and Saturn made their second co-operative contact. Jupiter is also associated with broadcasting and mass appeal. In January, it gave voice to the forgotten history of African Americans through Alex Haley's *Roots*, broadcast to record audiences.

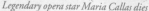

Legendary opera star Maria Callas dies

Israeli premier Menachim Begin with President Anwar al-Sadat of Egypt

Indira Gandhi resigns

CLOSE ENCOUNTERS OF THE THIRD KIND

Steven Spielberg's highly acclaimed sci-fi film *Close Encounters of the Third Kind* departed from decades of other science fiction movies by welcoming alien invaders from outer space. In preparation for the film, Spielberg worked with a team of UFO experts in order to present a story that was realistic. He based the UFO sightings in his film on actual case studies. Even the title is authentic, referring to an actual UFO classification by the U.S. government.

THE KING IS DEAD

Defeated in elections after eleven years of rule, Indira Gandhi resigned, while in Pakistan Prime Minister Ali Bhutto was overthrown in a bloodless coup by General Zia ul-Haq. Pollution in Athens was found to be causing the crumbling of the ancient Acropolis, and Britain's Queen Elizabeth celebrated her Silver Jubilee. Egypt's al-Sadat moved toward peace with Israel, breaking ranks with the rest of the Arab world, which had refused to recognize the existence of Israel since its formation in 1948. In the U.S., murderer Gary Gilmore was the first to die under the restored death penalty. The *Columbia* Space Shuttle made its first flight. The Trans-Alaskan pipeline was opened, so reducing American dependence on foreign oil. Elvis Presley died, a victim of heart disease, which also killed soprano Maria Callas. Two 'jumbo' jets collided on the ground in the Canary Islands, causing 574 deaths. The *Roots* TV mini-series, a chronicle of African American experience from slavery to modern times, drew a record 130-million viewers. CB, or citizens' band, radios became the latest craze. Crooner Bing Crosby and film star Charlie Chaplin died.

➤ Read "Science, Champions, and the Mars Effect" by Sophia Mason on page 625.

CAPRICORN

From January 01, 0:00 through January 20, 4:13

The Smoldering Sensualist

There's a lot more to the January-born 1977 Capricorn than meets the eye. Although you have a "touch-me-not" quality, you're really quite sensual. Lounging in bed with a passionate partner is your idea of a perfect day. You're attracted to passive, sensitive people with colorful imaginations. In order to lure such a mate into your web, you must be the pursuer. Fortunately, you'd rather be the hunter than the prey, at least in the game of love.

Practical and hard-working, you don't mind building a career over time. Get-rich-quick schemes hold little allure for you. Rather, you'd like to establish a business that will grow and prosper long after you retire. You are well-suited to the construction industry because the fruits of your labor would be permanent and substantial. Whatever work you choose, you're sure to experience years of success with it. The year you were born, rock star Elvis Presley died, leaving behind a musical legacy that spanned twenty years.

You're a lot more playful than most Goats. People may accuse you of suffering from the Peter Pan syndrome. While it's true you don't want to grow up that hasn't stopped you from taking on considerable responsibility. "Work hard, play harder," may be your motto. Travel may be your favorite way to unwind. You especially like to visit places that offer lots of great restaurants.

With regard to companionship, you want friends who are successful but fun-loving. Ariens, Taureans, Cancerians, and Capricorns probably comprise most of your social circle. For some reason, you are strongly attracted to foreigners. There's a good chance you will marry someone whose nationality is different than your own.

Your greatest challenge as a January-born 1977 Goat is loyalty in love. Too often, you may be tempted to stray from your partner for the sheer interest of sexual adventure. Make an effort to stay focused on your mate, especially after you settle down in a serious relationship. Your biggest strength is your ability to balance work with play. Nobody could ever accuse you of being a boring workaholic—you're too much fun!

AQUARIUS

From January 20, 4:14 through February 18, 18:29

The Generous Host

Houseguests are a regular part of life for the 1977 Aquarius. That's because you have so many friends, all of whom want to stay at your place. It's no surprise, really. Where else can somebody find such good home cooking, comfortable furnishings, and magnificent conversation? Fortunately, you're fond of entertaining and probably encourage folks to drop in whenever they're passing through your neighborhood. The year you were born, newly inaugurated U.S. President Jimmy Carter pardoned Vietnam draft evaders, thus luring hundreds of men to come home after years of exile. Visiting you is akin to "coming home" again, thanks to your warm hospitality.

Because you're so good at nurturing people, you may want to go into one of the caring professions. You could do well as a hospital aide, kindergarten teacher, or dietician. Working for a non-profit organization is also a possibility as such a job would draw upon your humanitarian instincts. There's a good chance that your methods will be somewhat unorthodox as you put a distinctive personal stamp on everything you do.

Although you enjoy the company of guests, intimate relationships may be a different story. You may wait until you're older before settling down. Perhaps your parents had a difficult marriage, which had a negative impact on you. Maybe you were burned in love at a very early age. Whatever the reason for your hesitation, it will become less compelling with age. You could marry somewhat late in life. Alternately, you could pair up with a person who is much older than you, hoping to benefit from their wisdom and experience.

You like people who value relationships above all else. Cancerians, Leos, Sagittarians, and fellow Aquarians have a lot in common with you. Romantically, you like steady, secure types who want a settled home life. It would also help if they were proficient in the domestic arts, too.

Intimacy is your greatest challenge as a 1977 Aquarius. Share confidences with your closest friends, even if it seems strange at first. Your biggest strength is your warmth. You provide a welcome refuge from the cold, cruel world.

➤ Read about your Chinese Astrological sign on page 838. ➤ Read about your Personal Planets on page 826. ➤ Read about your personal Mystical Card on page 856.

CAPRICORN
Your Personal Planets

YOUR LOVE POTENTIAL
Venus in Aquarius, Jan. 01, 0:00 - Jan. 04, 13:00
Venus in Pisces, Jan. 04, 13:01 - Jan. 20, 4:13

YOUR DRIVE AND AMBITION
Mars in Sagittarius, Jan. 01, 0:00 - Jan. 01, 0:41
Mars in Capricorn, Jan. 01, 0:42 - Jan. 20, 4:13

YOUR LUCK MAGNETISM
Jupiter in Taurus, Jan. 01, 0:00 - Jan. 20, 4:13

World Events

Jan. 1 - A group of Czech intellects begin the human rights group Chapter 77.

Jan. 3 - Steven Jobs and Steve Wozniak launch Apple Computers.

President Idi Amin of Uganda

AQUARIUS
Your Personal Planets

YOUR LOVE POTENTIAL
Venus in Pisces, Jan. 20, 4:14 - Feb. 02, 2:53
Venus in Aries, Feb. 02, 5:54 - Feb. 18, 18:29

YOUR DRIVE AND AMBITION
Mars in Capricorn, Jan. 20, 4:14 - Feb. 09, 11:56
Mars in Aquarius, Feb. 09, 11:57 - Feb. 18, 18:29

YOUR LUCK MAGNETISM
Jupiter in Taurus, Jan. 20, 4:14 - Feb. 18, 18:29

World Events

Feb. 6 - In Britain, the Queen celebrates her Silver Jubilee.

Feb. 16 - In Uganda, the killing of an archbishop heightens Idi Amin's reign of terror.

1977

PISCES
Your Personal Planets

YOUR LOVE POTENTIAL
Venus in Aries, Feb. 18, 18:30 - Mar. 20, 17:41

YOUR DRIVE AND AMBITION
Mars in Aquarius, Feb. 18, 18:30 - Mar. 20, 2:18
Mars in Pisces, Mar. 20, 2:19 - Mar. 20, 17:41

YOUR LUCK MAGNETISM
Jupiter in Taurus, Feb. 18, 18:30 - Mar. 20, 17:41

World Events

Mar. 6 – Israeli Prime Minister Rabin arrives in the U.S. to discuss the Middle East with President Carter.

Mar. 10 – The rings of Uranus are discovered.

Alex Haley, author of "Roots"

ARIES
Your Personal Planets

YOUR LOVE POTENTIAL
Venus in Aries, Mar. 20, 17:42 - Apr. 20, 4:56

YOUR DRIVE AND AMBITION
Mars in Pisces, Mar. 20, 17:42 - Apr. 20, 4:56

YOUR LUCK MAGNETISM
Jupiter in Taurus, Mar. 20, 17:42 - Apr. 03, 15:41
Jupiter in Gemini, Apr. 03, 15:42 - Apr. 20, 4:56

World Events

Mar. 25 - Jacques Chirac is elected mayor of Paris.

Apr. 18 - Alex Haley, author of *Roots*, is awarded a special Pulitzer Prize.

PISCES
From February 18, 18:30 through March 20, 17:41

The Sly Fox

Make no mistake; the 1977 Pisces is no wide-eyed innocent. Contrary to popular belief, you're very worldly and wise. Rather than trumpet your sophistication, though, you hide it beneath a veneer of guileless charm.

Then, when the pressure mounts, you drop the facade and become the ruthless competitor you really are. The year you were born, purged Chinese leader Teng Hsiao-ping made a stunning comeback after the Gang of Four was expelled from the Communist Party. You're capable of similar upsets and frequently astonish onlookers with a sudden show of fierce determination.

Excellent at keeping secrets, you work well in highly private environments. You'd make an excellent personal assistant to a prominent person. Keeping confidential documents like hospital or legal records could also be a possibility for you. Acting as a spiritual advisor might suit you, as you are highly compassionate. Whatever your job, it should involve an element of exclusivity. You love being entrusted with privileged information, and you would probably never use it to your personal advantage.

You are capable of making huge, sudden changes that often stun friends and family. That's because you rarely seek public approval in anything you do. If you feel like switching religions at an advanced age, you will do it. Similarly, you're capable of leaving a successful career for the sake of raising children. One thing is for sure; you never do anything for form's sake. Your whole heart has to be in whatever you are doing, whether it's a job, relationship, or spiritual practice.

In your relationships, you gravitate toward people who don't take things at face value. Geminis, Virgos, Scorpios, and Capricorns both appreciate and respect your secretive ways. Romantically, you are best suited to a partner who is tenacious in their affections, as you have a tendency to be elusive.

Noncommittal and discreet, your greatest challenge is to keep your promises. Try to take others into account before changing your plans. Your biggest strength is your uncanny powers of perception. Not much escapes your attention!

ARIES
From March 20, 17:42 through April 20, 4:56

The Constant Companion

Loyal to the end, the 1977 Aries is an invaluable ally. You choose your friends, lovers, and colleagues with great discrimination and stand by them through thick and thin. The year you were born, the movie *Julia* was released. This story of undying friendship accurately mirrors many of your own relationships. Like Jane Fonda's character in the film, you're willing to expose yourself to danger if it means helping someone close to your heart. Chances are that many people have come to you during their darkest hours. You have a knack for shielding loved ones from danger. No wonder everybody feels safe around you!

Modest and unassuming, you probably enjoy working behind the scenes. You are well suited to charity work, photography, and design. A job that draws on your heroism would also be good for you. You'd make an excellent emergency medical technician, firefighter, or undercover police officer. Assuming a low profile at work allows you an element of freedom that is most rewarding. Although you'd like to be appreciated by your employer, you would hate to be singled out for attention on a daily basis.

You may have a tendency to run hot and cold with your romantic partner. You may be cuddly and affectionate one minute and the next, chilly and aloof. This technique works well with somebody who enjoys a challenge, but it could hurt a person who seeks constant affection and approval. Be aware of your partner's needs. This should be a breeze for a sensitive person like you.

As far as friendships go, you want pals who prize loyalty above all else. Put your faith in Leos, Sagittarians, Scorpios, and Aquarians. With regard to love, you need a partner who is artistic and imaginative. Such a mate will encourage you to develop your own creative talents, which are considerable indeed. Try working on art projects together.

Your greatest challenge as a 1977 Aries is to live and let live. Try to give folks a second chance, particularly when they show genuine remorse for past transgressions. Your biggest strength is your loyalty. Friends like you are more precious than gold.

➤ Read about your Chinese Astrological sign on page 838. ➤ Read about your Personal Planets on page 826. ➤ Read about your personal Mystical Card on page 856.

TAURUS

From April 20, 4:57 through May 21, 4:13

The Big Spender

The 1977 Taurus loves to live large. You have a taste for the finer things in life: gourmet food, designer clothes, and luxury cars. It's important to note, however, that you don't just spend money on yourself. You make a regular habit of buying baubles for friends, too. The year you were born, Britain pulled out all the stops to celebrate Elizabeth II's twenty-fifth anniversary as Queen. Some critics balked at the expensive festivities, but most welcomed the opportunity to celebrate in style. You have the same philosophy about throwing parties: better to spend too much than too little.

Of course, your expensive tastes demand a high-paying job. Fortunately, you've been blessed with considerable intellectual ability. You could do very well in a field that requires lots of study, like medicine or law. You're also a gifted writer and may try your hand at writing a bestseller. If you'd rather sit back and enjoy the good life, learn various investment strategies. You probably have excellent instincts about this field. Maybe it's because you're always talking on the telephone!

When it comes to relationships, you need lots of space. You have your own way of doing things and may resent having to change for the sake of a partner. A long-distance relationship would work well for you. Perhaps shuttling between two homes would prevent you from feeling smothered. At the very least, you and your mate may want separate bathrooms in the interests of domestic harmony.

With regard to friends, you prefer people who are both intense and unusual. Consequently, your social circle is mostly made up of Ariens, Leos, Scorpios, and Aquarians. In terms of romance, you want a partner who is sexy, mysterious, and unpredictable. Knowing too much about each other would only ruin the fun.

Your greatest challenge as a 1977 Taurus is to develop a spiritual practice that brings you peace and contentment. Such a belief system will help you to appreciate all your blessings on a whole new level. Your biggest strength is your keen intellect. Staying mentally active will keep you young.

GEMINI

From May 21, 4:14 through June 21, 12:13

The Quick Student

Blessed with a photographic memory, the 1977 Gemini can master virtually any lesson in a moment. You know a little bit about everything thanks to extensive reading. As a student, you probably excelled at the subjects you loved and struggled in the classes you disliked. This made you somewhat of a puzzle to your teachers. Fortunately, you care very little about impressing others with your intellectual prowess. Learning is a form of entertainment for you. The year you were born, *Annie Hall* won best picture at the Academy Awards. A delicious blend of brains and humor, this movie has a lot in common with your personality.

Your tremendous creative ability may draw you to a profession in the arts. You'd make an excellent film director, music composer, or playwright. Working with children is possible, as you have a very youthful spirit. You may want to consider a career in teaching, childcare, or social work. Ultimately, you need a job that allows you to be expressive and versatile. Following an established routine has very little appeal for you.

As a 1977 Gemini, you say what you mean and you mean what you say. Twins born in other years are prone to exaggeration, but not you. You do, however, gravitate toward people who are dreamy and idealistic. You're wonderful at finding practical ways to make fantastic plans come true. Consequently, you feel right at home with kooky, artistic types.

People who are mystical and meditative comprise the greater part of your social circle. Geminis, Sagittarians, Aquarians, and Pisceans encourage you to think, question, and dream. In love, you're best suited to somebody who is spiritual and artistic. There's a good chance you could meet your mate at a cultural event. Alternately, you could pair up with somebody who introduces you to a new religion.

The greatest challenge you face as a 1977 Gemini is a disdain for structure. Resist the urge to buck the system just for the sake of rebellion. Your biggest strength is your capacity for joy. You're smart enough to know that intelligence has very little to do with happiness.

➤ Read about your Chinese Astrological sign on page 838. ➤ Read about your Personal Planets on page 826. ➤ Read about your personal Mystical Card on page 856.

1977

TAURUS
Your Personal Planets

YOUR LOVE POTENTIAL
Venus in Aries, Apr. 20, 4:57 - May 21, 4:13

YOUR DRIVE AND AMBITION
Mars in Pisces, Apr. 20, 4:57 - Apr. 27, 15:45
Mars in Aries, Apr. 27, 15:46 - May 21, 4:13

YOUR LUCK MAGNETISM
Jupiter in Gemini, Apr. 20, 4:57 - May 21, 4:13

World Events

May 7 – An economic summit opens in London attended by the U.S., West Germany, Italy, France, Japan, and Canada.

May 10 – American actress Joan Crawford dies.

A scene from George Lucas's "Star Wars"

GEMINI
Your Personal Planets

YOUR LOVE POTENTIAL
Venus in Aries, May 21, 4:14 - June 06, 6:09
Venus in Taurus, June 06, 6:10 - June 21, 12:13

YOUR DRIVE AND AMBITION
Mars in Aries, May 21, 4:14 - June 06, 2:59
Mars in Taurus, June 06, 3:00 - June 21, 12:13

YOUR LUCK MAGNETISM
Jupiter in Gemini, May 21, 4:14 - June 21, 12:13

World Events

May 24 – The Soviet Kremlin orders the removal of President Nikolai Podgorny from the Communist Politburo.

May 26 – George Lucas's epic film *Star Wars* opens.

1977

CANCER
Your Personal Planets

YOUR LOVE POTENTIAL

Venus in Taurus, June 21, 12:14 - July 06, 15:08
Venus in Gemini, July 06, 15:09 - July 22, 23:03

YOUR DRIVE AND AMBITION

Mars in Taurus, June 21, 12:14 - July 17, 15:12
Mars in Gemini, July 17, 15:13 - July 22, 23:03

YOUR LUCK MAGNETISM

Jupiter in Gemini, June 21, 12:14 - July 22, 23:03

World Events

June 26 - Elvis Presley gives the last performance of his career.

July 2 - Novelist Vladimir Nabokov dies.

Elvis Presley's funeral

LEO
Your Personal Planets

YOUR LOVE POTENTIAL

Venus in Gemini, July 22, 23:04 - Aug. 02, 19:18
Venus in Cancer, Aug. 02, 19:19 - Aug. 23, 5:59

YOUR DRIVE AND AMBITION

Mars in Gemini, July 22, 23:04 - Aug. 23, 5:59

YOUR LUCK MAGNETISM

Jupiter in Gemini, July 22, 23:04 - Aug. 20, 12:41
Jupiter in Cancer, Aug. 20, 12:42 - Aug. 23, 5:59

World Events

Aug. 16 - Elvis Presley dies at his Memphis, Tennessee home, Graceland.

Aug. 19 - American comedian and member of the Marx Brothers, Groucho, dies.

630

CANCER
From June 21, 12:14 through July 22, 23:03

The Late Bloomer

Although born with considerable talent, the 1977 Cancer may have had a hard time developing it. Perhaps your parents didn't have enough money to get you the proper training. Maybe your family discouraged your interests. Whatever the reason, you probably got a late start in life. The year you were born, Joan Didion's *The Book of Common Prayer* was published. This story of a sheltered woman coming to terms with a politically complex world may reflect your own story in some way. At some point in your adulthood, you will probably look at the world in a whole new way.

A job involving research would probably suit you well. Searching for the truth can help you work through any personal issues that have dogged you since childhood. Consequently, you may be drawn to journalism, science, or detective work. A career related to identity might also speak to some deep inner need. You'd make an excellent actor, cosmetician, or costumer. Don't be surprised if you have a strong urge to switch careers later in life. It's just part of your evolutionary process. So long as you obey your instincts, you will prosper both professionally and personally.

Intensely creative, you need a hobby that allows you to express yourself. Painting, writing, or playing music can help you get in touch with your inner essence. You're probably an inventive cook and create delicious recipes as a means to blow off steam. Friends will cancel previous plans in order to attend your dinner parties.

You prefer the company of people who are artistic but stable. Taureans, Cancerians, Virgos, and Capricorns make up the lion's share of your social circle. In love, you need to be constantly stimulated. You'd be wise to select a partner who acts on their emotions. You've got a weakness for explosive artists. Stiff, repressed types bore you to tears.

Your greatest challenge as a 1977 Cancer is to come to terms with past disappointments. It's never too late to pursue your dreams. Your biggest strength is your tremendous creative energy. Use it to craft a life that gives you a sense of purpose and fulfillment.

LEO
From July 22, 23:04 through August 23, 5:59

The Enthusiastic Dreamer

The 1977 Leo's theme song should be "To Dream The Impossible Dream." You've usually got your head in the clouds, imagining some far-off place where money grows on trees and chocolate makes you slim. You regularly rehearse your Academy Award acceptance speech in the shower and know exactly how you're going to spend your lottery winnings. The year you were born, the movie *Star Wars* was released. You're one of the few people who can create a universe to rival George Lucas's fantastic vision.

A job that's low on practicality and high on whimsy suits you best. You'd make an excellent fashion designer, children's novelist, or actor. Although you love the spotlight, you like working in a big group. Slaving away in a lonely studio is your idea of purgatory. If the arts don't appeal to you, the sciences may. You could have great success working in a lab with a big team of researchers. It's quite possible you could invent a labor-saving device or discover a cure for a disease. The most important thing is that you find work that draws upon your imagination.

Your self-deprecating humor is a defense mechanism. For some reason, you're afraid that people won't like you. Actually, you're one of the most popular people around. You have a tendency to beat yourself up for the smallest mistakes. Learn to replace your critical voice with positive affirmations. This will get easier with age, but it will still take lots of work.

Surrounding yourself with loving, supportive friends can improve your self-image. Ariens, Geminis, Leos, and Sagittarians are quick to point out your many talents. Romantically, you need somebody who is intuitive and artistic. Pair up with somebody who delights in your imagination, rather than disdains it. You need all the encouragement you can get!

Your greatest challenge is to be good to yourself. As a 1977 Leo, you tend to underestimate your abilities and exaggerate your weaknesses. Give yourself some slack. Your biggest strength is your enthusiasm. Don't let the cynics get you down. The world can only benefit from starry-eyed optimists like you.

➤ Read about your Chinese Astrological sign on page 838. ➤ Read about your Personal Planets on page 826. ➤ Read about your personal Mystical Card on page 856.

VIRGO

From August 23, 6:00 through September 23, 3:28

The Tender Idealist

Happy endings really do exist as far as the 1977 Virgo is concerned. You're determined to look at the bright side of things, even when circumstances look bleak. Some folks call you naïve, but you don't care. It comes as a terrible disappointment when your illusions are shattered. When things get really bad, you may prefer to retreat into your own private world. The year you were born, Steven Spielberg's *Close Encounters of the Third Kind* was released. At times, you may wish you could be swept off in a space ship, if only to avoid the harsh realities of planet Earth.

A born nurturer, you would do well in any of the caring professions. You'd make an excellent hospital attendant, chef, or childcare worker. Working in a rehabilitation center might also appeal to you. You could also be a successful social worker. The emotional nature of your job could overwhelm you. Be sure to work a hobby into your daily routine so you won't be consumed by work. Creative writing, sculpting, or painting can keep your mind off job-related stress.

Strong ties to your family could make it difficult for you to break away from home. Carving out your own identity is essential. It's possible that you are very different than your relatives. If that's the case, don't try to emulate their ways for the sake of approval. You need to follow your own path whether that means having an unconventional job, changing your religion, or leading an unusual lifestyle. Never fear, this will become easier as you grow older.

Tender and sensitive, you would be wise to surround yourself with folks who are tough and grounded. Taureans, Cancerians, Leos, and Capricorns can help you make sense of harsh realities, while you can add a touch of whimsy to their lives. In terms of romance, you need a protective, loving partner who can shield you from opportunists.

As a 1977 Virgo, your greatest challenge is to be true to yourself. Don't be swayed by popular opinion; consult your own heart in all matters. Your biggest strength is your optimism. Continue to hope for the best even when the odds are against you.

LIBRA

From September 23, 3:29 through October 23, 12:40

The Nurturing Guide

The 1977 Libra is the embodiment of a perfect parent. It doesn't matter if you have children or not; everybody looks to you for guidance. Kind but firm, you are willing to state painful truths. If someone you love commits a harmful act, you will say so. Similarly, you're willing to give people a second chance, regardless of any past mistakes. Folks respect your judgment and often come to you to provide insight or comfort during times of trial.

Holding a respected position comes naturally to you. You would make an excellent mayor, school principal, or hospital chief. Even if you take time off work to raise a family, you'll still hold a position of authority. You could have great success leading a charitable organization or heading a school committee. One thing is for certain—you are a guiding force wherever you go. Maybe it's because you have a reputation for tempering justice with mercy.

Although you are a powerful figure, you believe strongly in all forms of equality. Race, gender, religion, age, and sexual preference mean nothing to you; humanity is what counts. The year you were born, the first woman Episcopal priest was ordained. You're determined to witness similar breakthroughs throughout the course of your life and may be involved with several civil rights campaigns. Persuasive and forceful in your speech, you have the power to shatter age-old prejudices. At some point, you may decide to lecture on the evils of bigotry.

You enjoy the company of mature, thoughtful people. Taureans, Cancerians, Virgos, and Capricorns make good friends for you. Beware, however, of letting things get too serious with your associates. Take plenty of time for amusement. Going to concerts, plays, and museum exhibits could be a pleasing diversion as you have a passion for the arts. Romantically, you are attracted to forceful, dynamic types.

Serious and responsible, your greatest challenge is to be more joyful. Make more time for creative pursuits that fill you with delight. Your biggest strength is your sense of justice. You can always be trusted to do the right thing.

➤ Read about your Chinese Astrological sign on page 838. ➤ Read about your Personal Planets on page 826. ➤ Read about your personal Mystical Card on page 856.

1977

VIRGO
Your Personal Planets

YOUR LOVE POTENTIAL
Venus in Cancer, Aug. 23, 6:00 - Aug. 28, 15:08
Venus in Leo, Aug. 28, 15:09 - Sept. 22, 15:04
Venus in Virgo, Sept. 22, 15:05 - Sept. 23, 3:28

YOUR DRIVE AND AMBITION
Mars in Gemini, Aug. 23, 6:00 - Sept. 01, 0:19
Mars in Cancer, Sept. 01, 0:20 - Sept. 23, 3:28

YOUR LUCK MAGNETISM
Jupiter in Cancer, Aug. 23, 6:00 - Sept. 23, 3:28

World Events

Sept. 7 - The U.S. and Panama reach an agreement by which the U.S. cedes the Canal to Panama.

Sept. 12 - Civil rights leader Steve Biko dies in police custody in South Africa.

Death of South African dissident Steve Biko

LIBRA
Your Personal Planets

YOUR LOVE POTENTIAL
Venus in Virgo, Sept. 23, 3:29 - Oct. 17, 1:36
Venus in Libra, Oct. 17, 1:37 - Oct. 23, 12:40

YOUR DRIVE AND AMBITION
Mars in Cancer, Sept. 23, 3:29 - Oct. 23, 12:40

YOUR LUCK MAGNETISM
Jupiter in Cancer, Sept. 23, 3:29 - Oct. 23, 12:40

World Events

Oct. 3 - Indian Prime Minister Indira Gandhi is arrested on charges of corruption.

Oct. 14 - American all-round entertainer Bing Crosby dies.

1977

SCORPIO
Your Personal Planets

YOUR LOVE POTENTIAL
Venus in Libra, Oct. 23, 12:41 - Nov. 10, 3:51
Venus in Scorpio, Nov. 10, 3:52 - Nov. 22, 10:06

YOUR DRIVE AND AMBITION
Mars in Cancer, Oct. 23, 12:41 - Oct. 26, 18:55
Mars in Leo, Oct. 26, 18:56 - Nov. 22, 10:06

YOUR LUCK MAGNETISM
Jupiter in Cancer, Oct. 23, 12:41 - Nov. 22, 10:06

World Events

Nov. 2 - Patty Hearst's conviction for bank robbery is upheld by a San Francisco court.

Nov. 19 - Egyptian President Anwar al-Sadat becomes the first Arab leader to visit Israel.

Emperor Jean-Bedel Bokassa

SAGITTARIUS
Your Personal Planets

YOUR LOVE POTENTIAL
Venus in Scorpio, Nov. 22, 10:07 - Dec. 04, 1:48
Venus in Sagittarius, Dec. 04, 1:49 - Dec. 21, 23:22

YOUR DRIVE AND AMBITION
Mars in Leo, Nov. 22, 10:07 - Dec. 21, 23:22

YOUR LUCK MAGNETISM
Jupiter in Cancer, Nov. 22, 10:07 - Dec. 21, 23:22

World Events

Dec. 3 - The U.S. agrees to admit 10,000 South Vietnamese "boat people."

Dec. 4 - Jean-Bedel Bokassa has himself crowned Emperor of the Central African Empire.

SCORPIO
From October 23, 12:41 through November 22, 10:06

The Respected Success

An intense desire for success characterizes the 1977 Scorpio. You're determined to be at the top of your field, no matter how long it takes. Making a name for yourself should be easy as you're willing to use unorthodox methods to meet your goals. You'd rather be called crazy than go unnoticed. If that means breaking the rules or defying authority, so be it. The year you were born, Charlie Chaplin died. For years, the star lived in self-imposed exile to escape the witch-hunting scrutiny of Hollywood. You may have profound respect for misunderstood geniuses like Chaplin and may even seek to become one yourself.

A flair for drama could draw you to the entertainment industry. You'd make a fantastic performance artist or comedian. A dark sensibility pervades everything you do. You're the type of performer who would probably have a cult following rather than a mass audience. You would also do well in any business that involves an element of risk. Real estate development, police work, or commodities trading might appeal to you. Whatever your job, it should be exciting. You aren't suited to the nine-to-five life.

You have a strong sixth sense that should guide you in all things. Resist the temptation to discount your hunches. More often than not, your suspicions will be proved correct. Studying metaphysics can prove enlightening, especially in your later years. Your psychic powers will only improve with time.

Open-minded people make the best companions for you. Geminis, Virgos, Sagittarians, and Pisceans accept your unconventional ways without question. Your ideal romantic partner will be somebody who is loyal, loving, and spiritual. You believe in the concept of soul mates; drifting from one lover to another is not your style. It's possible that you'll fall in love with your mate from across a crowded room. All of your relationships have a karmic quality.

Your greatest challenge is not to take yourself too seriously. Life will become much easier once you learn to laugh at your faults. Your biggest strength is your unique outlook. Nobody could put a label on you.

SAGITTARIUS
From November 22, 10:07 through December 21, 23:22

The Role Model

The 1977 Sagittarius is a born role model. You always put others before yourself and seek to be useful wherever you go. Making great sacrifices is second nature to you. You'd rather do without little luxuries if it means benefiting less fortunate people. Often you're forced to work under difficult conditions. Rather than complaining, though, you'll find ways to make the surroundings more pleasant. You're a master at making the most out of what you've got.

Jobs that involve inspiring others are tailor-made for you. You'd make an excellent sports coach, spiritual advisor, or teacher. You've also been blessed with considerable intellectual ability and would do well in any of the sciences. Medical research may especially appeal to you as it involves helping others. At some point in your life, you may decide to take a leave of absence and work in an impoverished area, providing medical care or housing to needy people. The year you were born, the world's last-known case of smallpox was reported in Somalia. There's a good chance you will devote your life to wiping out physical, emotional, or spiritual disease.

Behind closed doors, you are surprisingly sensual. You love getting lost in your mate's arms. When you aren't in love, you can get very blue. That's because you need an intimate relationship to keep you balanced. When you give so much of yourself on a daily basis, you feel drained. A romantic partner can replenish your spirits through kisses and caresses.

You gravitate toward people who are diplomatic and charming. Geminis, Leos, Librans, and Pisceans are good companions for you, as they put a positive spin on everything. In love, you need somebody who is just as nurturing and supportive as you are. Ideally, your romantic relationship will have a symbiotic quality; you're not interested in being self-sufficient.

Your greatest challenge is to be more selfish. Don't be afraid to ask for more money or assistance if the situation warrants it. Nobility is your biggest strength. You can always be trusted to take the high road, even when temptation is close at hand.

➤ Read about your Chinese Astrological sign on page 838. ➤ Read about your Personal Planets on page 826. ➤ Read about your personal Mystical Card on page 856.

CAPRICORN

From December 21, 23:23 through December 31, 23:59

The Star Attraction

Nobody loves an audience like the December-born 1977 Capricorn. You have considerable star power and command attention wherever you go. You're as graceful as a gazelle and probably move like a dancer. The year you were born, *Saturday Night Fever* jump-started the disco craze. If you haven't learned to dance yet, you should. It would be yet another way to attract attention in a very large crowd. You may also have considerable athletic ability, especially with sports that require precise, fluid movement.

You need a job that puts you before the public in some way. The entertainment industry is a natural fit for you. You would also do well at a public relations firm, government office, or advertising agency. Rising to the top of your profession should be no problem for you, as you're willing to do whatever is necessary to achieve success. There's a good chance you will get an advanced degree in order to gain a more prominent position in the workplace. Learning about the mind-body connection could put you on a new career path. If you ever decide to switch industries, look into alternative medicine.

Strong sexual desires are likely to make you an aggressive suitor. When somebody captures your fancy, you'll do everything possible to make it happen. In relationships, you are generous and kind. Whoever becomes your permanent partner is lucky indeed. There's a good chance you will have a long, happy marriage. You're not impressed by good looks and flashy status symbols; you want somebody who is noble and kind.

You love to be shocked and may surround yourself with unconventional people. Geminis, Scorpios, Aquarians, and Pisceans never fail to delight and surprise you. When it comes to romance, you need somebody who is fun-loving and affectionate. It would also help if your partner shares your interest in spirituality.

Your greatest challenge as a December-born 1977 Capricorn is to be more adventurous. Once you establish a routine, it's hard to break out of it. Your biggest strength is your generous spirit. You truly understand that it is better to give than to receive.

YOUR PERSONAL PLANETS

YOUR LOVE POTENTIAL
Venus in Sagittarius, Dec. 21, 23:23 - Dec. 27, 22:08
Venus in Capricorn, Dec. 27, 22:09 - Dec. 31, 23:59

YOUR DRIVE AND AMBITION
Mars in Leo, Dec. 21, 23:23 - Dec. 31, 23:59

YOUR LUCK MAGNETISM
Jupiter in Cancer, Dec. 21, 23:23 - Dec. 30, 23:49
Jupiter in Gemini, Dec. 30, 23:50 - Dec. 31, 23:59

World Events

Dec. 25 – Charlie Chaplin dies.

Dec. 25 – Israeli Prime Minister Menachem Begin and Egyptian President Anwar el-Sadat meet in Egypt.

Tennis champion Martina Navratilova

Special Feature
Science, Champions, and the Mars Effect

(Continued from page 625)

Psychological studies tell us that people who excel at sports are emotionally stable, vigorous, aggressive, and achievement-oriented— all good keywords for Mars. The person with Mars in a power zone also tends to be focused, competitive, and tireless. Mars people will consider every angle while working toward a chosen objective. When they meet an obstacle, if moving it by brute force fails, they will back off, then come at the problem from all sides until they find just the right approach to move it so they can be on their way again.

Gauquelin demonstrated a link between the planetary positions in an individual's horoscope at birth and success in certain occupations in adulthood.

A prime example of a Mars champion is a man named by many sportswriters as one of the greatest athletes of the last century, Muhammad Ali, who was born January 17, 1942, at 6:30 a.m. in Louisville, Kentucky,

with Mars in the upper power zone. Boxing requires an aggressive and competitive individual with a good deal of stamina. These are powerful Mars traits. Ali's Mars added something extra. On the short list of fifteen all-time great fights listed in *The Ultimate Encyclopedia of Boxing*, Ali is the only boxer listed twice, with each match reflecting a different side of Mars, as described below.

His 1975 "Thrilla in Manilla" against Joe Frazier was a raw test of the skill, courage and strength of two men, as they stood toe-to-toe for fourteen rounds until Frazier's trainer called the fight. Ali's 1974 "Rumble in the Jungle" against George Foreman showed the military, strategic side of Mars. Ali knew that Foreman outclassed him physically, so he hugged the ropes, ducked, and dodged in the early rounds while Foreman thumped away at him, trying to land a telling blow. But Ali's "rope a dope" strategy wore Foreman down, and by the eighth round, Ali waded in and knocked Foreman out.

Tennis great Martina Navratilova (born October 18, 1956, at 4:40 p.m. in Prague) shows Mars at work in a less brutal setting. Born as Mars was rising in her birth chart (a power zone), Navratilova brought power to women's tennis with a well-muscled physique and a tough serve that some found intimidating when she first came on the scene. Despite the fact that her professional career really took off at an age when many women retire from the game, she came to dominate the sport in the 1980s. By the time she had retired, she had won more tournaments (167) and more matches (1,438) than any other professional player, man or woman.

(Continued on page 641)

➤ Read Muhammad Ali's Star Profile on page 617.

1978

Peace Efforts Triumph: Mars and the Eclipses

Although 1977 ended on an optimistic note, the early part of 1978 did not inspire hope for peace in the Middle East. As Mars, which can represent war and aggression, made its biennial Earth fly-by, people were more likely to take action, at times violently. A series of terrorist acts, from the assassination of a Palestinian Liberation Organization (PLO) envoy to disagreements over the disputed Israeli-occupied territories, disrupted the peace process. By the time Mars's orbit took it away from Earth, Israel was attacking PLO bases in the Lebanon to counter Palestinian strikes against civilian targets. At the end of March, the time of a lunar eclipse, Syria, now in charge in Lebanon, provided the PLO and other terrorists with missiles to attack Israel. Eclipses, which occur every six months, signify a dilemma prompting a shift in focus and a consequent change in direction and this is exactly what happened in the Middle East. With the eclipse falling in assertive Aries and co-operative Libra, the emphasis was on war versus peace. Despite agreements with the U.S. that cluster bombs should not be used against civilians, Israeli attacks involved them.

As sanguine Jupiter entered generous, comfort-loving Cancer on April 11, efforts took on a more positive tone. The Israeli Prime Minister, Menachem Begin, met with U.S. President Carter, putting peace efforts back on track by withdrawing troops from Lebanon. Tensions increased in July, however, as Uranus, which may represent insurrection, changed direction, thereby kick-starting events. Not only was the peace process hampered by unwillingness to compromise, but other nations around the world seemed in the midst of change as well. Another eclipse in mid-September came as finally Carter, Egyptian President al-Sadat, and Begin emerged victorious from a peace summit at Camp David, an effort for which Begin and al-Sadat were awarded the Nobel Peace Prize.

Events of social impact were suggestive of the year's planetary picture as well. Jupiter, the planet of entertainment, was in nostalgic Cancer and the nostalgic film *Grease* took responsible adults back to their crazy youth for two hours.

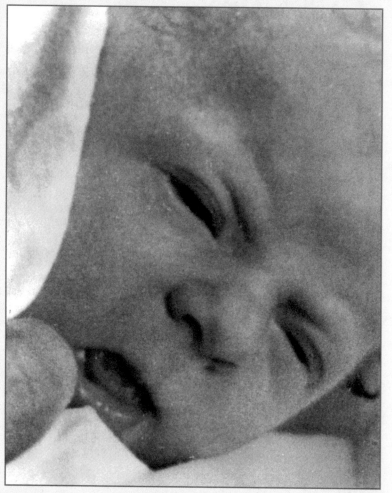

Louise Brown, the world's first test-tube baby, is born

Anwar el-Sadat, Jimmy Carter, and Menachem Begin engage in peace talks

Over 900 members of the People's Temple commit mass suicide in Jonestown, Guyana

JONESTOWN AND MIDDLE EAST PEACE

Despite a seventy-five percent vote of confidence, other nations doubted that dictator Pinochet had the support of the Chilean people. In post-Cultural Revolution China, banned books such as *Hamlet* and *War and Peace* were sold to long queues of people. The oil tanker *Amoco Cadiz* spilled 5,000 tons of oil off the coast of Brittany in France. Iranians demonstrated against their Shah. Rhodesia progressed to majority rule and elected black leaders. Egypt's el-Sadat, Israel's Begin and America's President Carter successfully crafted a peace treaty, earning the Nobel Peace Prize. In Guyana, 913 followers of the Reverend Jim Jones committed suicide. In San Diego, after a mid-air collision, a jetliner crashed into a residential area, killing 150. The Love Canal area of Niagara Falls, New York, was evacuated after illegally dumped toxic chemicals seeped into homes. In Britain, Louise Brown, the first test-tube baby, was born. Argentine footballers won the World Cup. After the deaths of Pope Paul VI and, after only thirty-three days in office, John Paul I, Polish Archbishop Karel Wojtyla, was elected as the first non-Italian pope for 436 years, taking the name John Paul II.

➤ Read "Science, Champions, and the Mars Effect" by Sophia Mason on page 625.

CAPRICORN

From January 01, 0:00 through January 20, 10:03

The Intense Diplomat

A deep desire to succeed motivates the January-born 1978 Capricorn in all things. You are determined to make your mark on the world and will probably achieve success at a very early age. There is no end to your ambition, however. Once you achieve one goal, you set a higher one. Folks marvel at your tireless energy and often come to you when there's a difficult job to be done. You're noted for your diplomacy and can get warring parties to work together in the interest of progress. The year you were born, Egyptian President Anwar Sadat and Israeli Prime Minister Menachem Begin—the leaders of countries that had formerly been sworn enemies—signed an agreement for a peace treaty. You're capable of bringing about similar agreements, if you put your mind to it.

Naturally, someone with your tact would thrive in a career that requires strong inter-personal skills. Working in politics or personnel may prove rewarding for you. You're also adept at putting people at ease; consequently, you could find success as a concierge, maître d'hôtel, or beauty salon owner. There's a good chance you will work your way up from the bottom of your desired industry. This will give you the added advantage of knowing every aspect of your field.

Because you have a tendency to burn out, it's important for you to take long, extended breaks from work. Seasonal work suits you very well, as it requires intense periods of activity followed by prolonged lulls. Hobbies like stenciling, jewelry making, and painting can recharge your batteries. Sports like hiking and biking will also keep you fresh and inspired.

You enjoy having a large group of friends from different walks of life. Geminis, Librans, Scorpios, and Aquarians provide you with plenty of stimulating conversation. Romantically, you need a partner who is sensual and expressive. Reserved intellectuals have little appeal; you'd rather spend the evening cuddling than debating.

A tendency to overwork is your greatest challenge. Learn to put your responsibilities aside for fun, at least once in a while. Your biggest strength is your graceful demeanor. A born diplomat, you can always be trusted to break the ice.

AQUARIUS

From January 20, 10:04 through February 19, 0:20

The Innovative Professional

Original and resourceful, the 1978 Aquarius is an asset to any organization. You can find solutions to the knottiest problems and revel in cutting through red tape. One of the reasons you're so successful is that you're willing to try anything once. Folks have often called your methods crazy, only to eat those words a little later. The first test-tube baby was born in 1978, ushering in a whole new means of conception. Radical procedures like these appeal to the problem-solver in you.

Any job related to the sciences would be good for you. You could find remarkable success in pharmaceutical research. Holistic medicine might also appeal to you because of the unorthodox nature of the field. Alternately, your keen curiosity may lead you to a field like mining, marine biology, or archeology. Digging beneath the surface comes naturally to you! As a 1978 Aquarius, you need work that forces you to constantly question and reassess the facts. You simply hate taking anything at face value.

You gain a great deal of spiritual strength from your friends. Pessimists have no place in your life; you can't abide their negative energy. It's quite possible that you will perform a great deal of humanitarian work with your pals. This is your way of combining the best of both worlds: friendship and service. When you meet with trouble, help is never far away. That's because you associate with folks who are naturally loving and giving.

Altruistic Ariens, Geminis, Aquarians, and Pisceans make up the greater part of your social circle. In love, you seek to be with somebody for life. Casual flirtation is not your style at all. A loyal, passionate mate will suit you best. Be willing to change and grow with your partner over time as your union will probably span many years.

Your greatest challenge is to respect tradition. Although you achieve remarkable success by breaking with convention, it's still important to honor the old ways. Your biggest strength is your need to question everything. Keep searching for deeper truths. The world can only benefit from probing minds like yours.

➤ Read about your Chinese Astrological sign on page 838. ➤ Read about your Personal Planets on page 826. ➤ Read about your personal Mystical Card on page 856.

CAPRICORN
Your Personal Planets

YOUR LOVE POTENTIAL
Venus in Capricorn, Jan. 01, 0:00 - Jan. 20, 10:03

YOUR DRIVE AND AMBITION
Mars in Leo, Jan. 01, 0:00 - Jan. 20, 10:03

YOUR LUCK MAGNETISM
Jupiter in Gemini, Jan. 01, 0:00 - Jan. 20, 10:03

World Events

Jan. 4 - Augusto Pinochet wins the Chilean election with seventy-five percent of the votes.

Jan. 20 - Columbia Pictures pays $9.5 million for the movie rights to *Annie*.

Leon Spinks defeats Muhammad Ali

AQUARIUS
Your Personal Planets

YOUR LOVE POTENTIAL
Venus in Capricorn, Jan. 20, 10:04 - Jan. 20, 18:28
Venus in Aquarius, Jan. 20, 18:29 - Feb. 13, 16:06
Venus in Pisces, Feb. 13, 16:07 - Feb. 19, 0:20

YOUR DRIVE AND AMBITION
Mars in Leo, Jan. 20, 10:04 - Jan. 26, 1:58
Mars in Cancer, Jan. 26, 1:59 - Feb. 19, 0:20

YOUR LUCK MAGNETISM
Jupiter in Gemini, Jan. 20, 10:04 - Feb. 19, 0:20

World Events

Jan. 24 - A Soviet spy satellite crash-lands in Canada.

Feb. 15 - Leon Spinks defeats Muhammad Ali to gain the heavyweight boxing title.

1978

PISCES
Your Personal Planets

YOUR LOVE POTENTIAL
Venus in Pisces, Feb. 19, 0:21 - Mar. 09, 16:28
Venus in Aries, Mar. 09, 16:29 - Mar. 20, 23:33

YOUR DRIVE AND AMBITION
Mars in Cancer, Feb. 19, 0:21 - Mar. 20, 23:33

YOUR LUCK MAGNETISM
Jupiter in Gemini, Feb. 19, 0:21 - Mar. 20, 23:33

World Events

Feb. 24 – Archeologist Mary Leakey discovers a footprint that might prove early human ancestors walked upright.

Mar. 16 – Former Italian President Aldo Moro is kidnapped by the Red Brigade.

Archeologist Mary Leakey

ARIES
Your Personal Planets

YOUR LOVE POTENTIAL
Venus in Aries, Mar. 20, 23:34 - Apr. 02, 21:13
Venus in Taurus, Apr. 02, 21:14 - Apr. 20, 10:49

YOUR DRIVE AND AMBITION
Mars in Cancer, Mar. 20, 23:34 - Apr. 10, 18:49
Mars in Leo, Apr. 10, 18:50 - Apr. 20, 10:49

YOUR LUCK MAGNETISM
Jupiter in Gemini, Mar. 20, 23:34 - Apr. 12, 0:11
Jupiter in Cancer, Apr. 12, 0:12 - Apr. 20, 10:49

World Events

Apr. 9 – A coup in Somalia fails to overthrow the government.

Apr. 18 – The U.S. Senate votes to turn the Panama Canal over to Panama on December 31, 1999.

PISCES

From February 19, 0:21 through March 20, 23:33

The Expansive Idealist

The 1978 Pisces always looks on the bright side. You are a firm believer in utopia and constantly work to make the world a better place. Some folks scoff at your efforts, but most respect them. That's because you are utterly sincere in everything you do. The year you were born, Rhodesia's white Prime Minister agreed to transfer his power to black majority rule. Critics called the move naïve and impractical, but the desire for fairness prevailed. You're similarly determined to do whatever is necessary to bring about truth and justice.

A career in law has probably attracted you from a very early age. You'd make an excellent judge, lawyer, or court clerk. Connecting with people from different walks of life might also appeal to you. Becoming a translator would allow you to achieve this goal while traveling extensively. You could also meet success as a teacher or spiritual advisor because you acquire wisdom so readily. Whatever job you take, it should have a philosophical bent.

You have a great capacity for joy that is evident to everyone you meet. Children especially love your company because you haven't forgotten how to play. Sports probably play a prominent role in your life. Jogging, swimming, and dancing can keep you fit and youthful. You're also quite creative and may enjoy artistic hobbies like woodwork, sewing, or sculpting. You may be famous for making beautiful, personalized gifts for friends and family.

As far as relationships go, you have a nice mix of practical and dreamy friends. Taureans, Cancerians, Virgos, and Scorpios keep your social life varied and interesting. In love, you need an old-fashioned partner who is willing to fight for your honor. Acts of chivalry never fail to win your heart. Your ideal mate is tough on the outside, but tender on the inside.

Your greatest challenge is to take the bad with the good. You have a tendency to turn a blind eye to unpleasantness, which can make you vulnerable. Your biggest strength is your youthful attitude. Somehow, you have retained a sense of wonderment and joy that is rarely found in adults.

ARIES

From March 20, 23:34 through April 20, 10:49

The Luxury Lover

Home is definitely where the heart is for the 1978 Aries. You derive great comfort from familiar surroundings. When you travel, you probably bring your pillow and several framed photographs along, just to remind you of home. Relatives and friends are always eager to stay at your place because it has such a relaxed atmosphere. You prefer soft, sumptuous furnishings that invite you to luxuriate. A red velvet chaise longue perfectly reflects your love of comfortable glamour.

Working from home would suit you very well. Running an online business, daycare center, or pet sitting service may be viable careers for you. You could also be a professional who makes "house calls," like a massage therapist or an interior decorator. Organizing people's work and living spaces could prove profitable as well. Avoid sterile offices as much as possible. You simply can't thrive in an impersonal environment.

You are extremely private and only confide problems to your closest friends. The year you were born, the show *All in the Family* won an Emmy for outstanding comedy series. You prefer to keep personal matters "in the family," and deeply resent it when your trust is betrayed. You're the last person to discuss health troubles, relationship matters, or job worries at a party. You'd rather stick to "safe" topics like movies, books, and music. Folks enjoy talking with you because you always keep the conversation light, upbeat, and interesting.

Friendship means a lot to you. You'd rather have three or four close pals than a huge gang of them. Ariens, Librans, Scorpios, and Pisceans can give you the one-on-one attention you crave. You don't give your heart away easily. It may take years before you settle down, but when you do, it will be with somebody who is passionate, intense, and loyal. It's quite possible that your mate will be several years older than you.

An undue concern for propriety is your greatest challenge. Don't be afraid to commit the occasional gaffe; nobody is perfect. Your biggest strength is your warmth. You have a way of putting folks at ease with just a smile.

➤ Read about your Chinese Astrological sign on page 838. ➤ Read about your Personal Planets on page 826. ➤ Read about your personal Mystical Card on page 856.

TAURUS
From April 20, 10:50 through May 21, 10:07

The Grounded Giver

The energy and enthusiasm of the 1978 Taurus is something to behold. You're in love with life and want to share your passion with everybody. Chances are you entertain a great deal. Opening your home to others gives you tremendous pleasure. Visitors are sure of a fantastic meal and fabulous conversation at your place; you really know how to give a party. Your guestroom is often occupied; you think nothing of hosting pals for weeks or even months. The year you were born, the Eagles' *Hotel California* won the Record of the Year trophy at the Grammys. At times, your place may resemble a chic hotel, though you don't charge for rooms!

Blessed with impeccable taste, you need to work in elegant surroundings to be happy. You'd fare very well in a luxury restaurant, hotel, or boutique. It's possible that you're an excellent cook. If that's the case, you may want to open a catering business. Running an elegant beauty salon or flower shop might also suit you. Ultimately, your work must involve bringing beauty into the world in some material way.

Because you are so giving, you may become easily tired. Invigorating exercise should be a regular part of your life. Swimming, hiking, and biking are all good ways to boost your energy level. Creative pursuits like quilting, carpentry, and pottery can also restore your spirits. Anybody as generous as you are needs to spend quality time alone, at least occasionally.

Intense, artistic types make up the majority of your social circle. You're constantly drawn to Taureans, Cancerians, Scorpios, and Pisceans. In love, you need a partner who is willing to give you some space. Although you are very loving and affectionate, you need lots of freedom to pursue your interests. Having hobbies separate from your mate can actually strengthen your relationship.

As a 1978 Taurus, your greatest challenge is to develop solitary pursuits. While you thrive in the company of others, it's also important to enjoy private moments. Your biggest strength is your sense of grounding. People feel safe and secure in your serene presence; you're a wonderful comfort.

GEMINI
From May 21, 10:08 through June 21, 18:09

The Disciplined Thinker

Smart and insightful, the 1978 Gemini is a determined scholar. You aren't content to take life at face value; you want to know the "how" and "why" of things. Finding solutions to persistent problems gives you great satisfaction. The year you were born, balloon angioplasty was developed to treat coronary heart disease. Such a breakthrough is characteristic of your own thinking. You often use unconventional methods to get around age-old dilemmas.

Serious work of an intellectual nature appeals to you most. You'd make an excellent scientist, surgeon, or lawyer. It may take several years before you reach the pinnacle of your career, but that won't bother you. You're not afraid of hard work, especially if it is performed for a great purpose. A knack for problem-solving could also draw you to a career in government, research, or repairs. So long as you're exercising your brain, your work will be rewarding.

Profoundly romantic, you are destined to have a rich love life. You are willing to go out on a limb to attract the object of your affection. Love has a transformative effect on you; folks can always tell when there is someone special in your life. If you aren't in a relationship, channel your energy into artistic pursuits. You are probably a great writer and could have great success with crafting dark, brooding stories. Restoring antiques and playing chess are also good ways for you to expend your creative energy.

You probably enjoy spending time with friends one-on-one. Big crowds make you uneasy and nervous. Consequently, quiet, reflective people suit you best. Taureans, Librans, Scorpios, and Pisceans put you at ease. Romantically, you need a dreamy, artistic partner with a strong spiritual streak. You like to baby your beloved.

Your greatest challenge is to find work that draws upon your considerable intellect. It may be necessary to change jobs throughout the course of your life as a means to find constant stimulation. Your biggest strength is your creativity. Always look for a new way of doing things; you're too inventive to stick to the tried-and-true.

► Read about your Chinese Astrological sign on page 838. ► Read about your Personal Planets on page 826. ► Read about your personal Mystical Card on page 856.

TAURUS
Your Personal Planets

YOUR LOVE POTENTIAL
Venus in Taurus, Apr. 20, 10:50 - Apr. 27, 7:52
Venus in Gemini, Apr. 27, 7:53 - May 21, 10:07

YOUR DRIVE AND AMBITION
Mars in Leo, Apr. 20, 10:50 - May 21, 10:07

YOUR LUCK MAGNETISM
Jupiter in Cancer, Apr. 20, 10:50 - May 21, 10:07

World Events

May 8 – David Berkowitz pleads guilty to the infamous Son of Sam killings in the U.S.

May 9 – The body of Aldo Moro is discovered in a car in the center of Rome.

Bjorn Borg, French Open winner

GEMINI
Your Personal Planets

YOUR LOVE POTENTIAL
Venus in Gemini, May 21, 10:08 - May 22, 2:02
Venus in Cancer, May 22, 2:03 - June 16, 6:18
Venus in Leo, June 16, 6:19 - June 21, 18:09

YOUR DRIVE AND AMBITION
Mars in Leo, May 21, 10:08 - June 14, 2:37
Mars in Virgo, June 14, 2:38 - June 21, 18:09

YOUR LUCK MAGNETISM
Jupiter in Cancer, May 21, 10:08 - June 21, 18:09

World Events

June 11 – Bjorn Borg wins the French Open tennis championship.

June 21 – Andrew Lloyd Webber and Tim Rice's musical *Evita* premieres in London.

1978

CANCER
Your Personal Planets

YOUR LOVE POTENTIAL
Venus in Leo, June 21, 18:10 - July 12, 2:13
Venus in Virgo, July 12, 2:14 - July 23, 4:59

YOUR DRIVE AND AMBITION
Mars in Virgo, June 21, 18:10 - July 23, 4:59

YOUR LUCK MAGNETISM
Jupiter in Cancer, June 21, 18:10 - July 23, 4:59

World Events

June 24 – U.S. astronomers announce that they have discovered a black hole in space.

July 14 – Soviet dissident Anatoly Scharansky is convicted of anti-Soviet agitation.

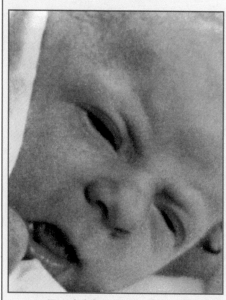

Test-tube baby, Louise Brown, is born

LEO
Your Personal Planets

YOUR LOVE POTENTIAL
Venus in Virgo, July 23, 5:00 - Aug. 08, 3:07
Venus in Libra, Aug. 08, 3:08 - Aug. 23, 11:56

YOUR DRIVE AND AMBITION
Mars in Virgo, July 23, 5:00 - Aug. 04, 9:06
Mars in Libra, Aug. 04, 9:07 - Aug. 23, 11:56

YOUR LUCK MAGNETISM
Jupiter in Cancer, July 23, 5:00 - Aug. 23, 11:56

World Events

July 26 – Louise Brown, the world's first test-tube baby, is born in England.

Aug. 6 – Pope Paul VI dies.

638

CANCER

From June 21, 18:10 through July 23, 4:59

The Compassionate Care-Giver

Kind and intuitive, the 1978 Cancer knows how to put people at ease. You always remember a person's favorite color, drink, and dessert. Pampering and petting your friends gives you a sense of purpose. You probably give away your possessions with alarming regularity, although you will never be poor. You have too many friends who feel indebted to you. If you ever fall on hard times, you can be sure that many people will come to your aid. You don't mind accepting help from others as you understand that relationships are all about give and take. The year you were born, the U.S. Senate voted to turn over the Panama Canal to its native country as a gesture of good will.

You need a job that draws on your nurturing instincts. It doesn't matter if you care for people, pets, or plants so long as you're responsible for their well-being. You'd make an excellent travel guide, veterinarian, or gardener. Because you have a great deal of energy, you could also benefit from work that requires physical exertion. Working as a personal trainer could satisfy both your physical and emotional needs.

Blessed with unusual creative ability, you get a great deal of satisfaction from creative hobbies. It's possible that you were discouraged from developing your artistic talent when you were younger. Seize the opportunity to pursue your interests as soon as you're able. Writing or illustrating comic books may especially appeal to your vivid imagination.

Surrounding yourself with a ragtag group of outcasts gives you great pleasure as this gives you ample nurturing opportunities. Ariens, Geminis, Scorpios, and Pisceans may especially appreciate your pampering ways. In love, you need a passionate, intense partner who is completely devoted to you.

Your greatest challenge is to come to terms with your material desires. Although you value relationships above all else, you like a little luxury, too. That's nothing to be ashamed of; you should treat yourself more often. Your biggest strength is your compassion. People feel understood and comfortable in your presence, and often seek your company.

LEO

From July 23, 5:00 through August 23, 11:56

The Lifelong Student

It's very hard to pin down the 1978 Leo. That's because you're always on the move. You'll try anything once, just on principle. Comparing and contrasting cultures is one of your favorite pastimes. There is a good chance you will travel extensively over the course of your life. Folks admire your adventurous spirit and enjoy hearing stories of your various exploits. The year you were born, Richard Nixon published his memoirs. You may decide to do the same thing after you've amassed a lifetime of interesting experiences.

Work gives you a profound sense of purpose. You enjoy being of service to others who can't help themselves. Attending the sick may appeal to you; you'd make an excellent doctor, nurse, or hospital aide. It's possible you're quite good with tools as well; you could find success repairing machinery. Do your best to take up a profession that can be practiced anywhere. That way, you can feel free to pick up and move whenever the mood strikes you.

You have very little interest in settling down, and probably have a very unusual domestic life. Perhaps you will never own a permanent home, always preferring to move from pillar to post. Maybe you rely on friends to provide you with housing. You may even have several homes all over the world. If you do decide to stay in one place, you should have a living arrangement that involves constant activity. Running a bed and breakfast might suit you as it would allow you to meet different kinds of people without leaving home.

Your friends are a varied bunch, but most of them are brainy. Geminis, Virgos, Librans, and Aquarians provide you with plenty of stimulating conversation. Falling in love is something of a hobby for you. Ideally, you should pick a partner who is very attentive to your needs. In love, you'll settle for nothing less than perpetual courtship.

As a 1978 Leo, your greatest challenge is to find peace within yourself. Your travels will be even more rewarding if you embark on them with a happy heart. Your biggest strength is your adaptability. Wherever you go, you'll always feel at home.

➤ Read about your Chinese Astrological sign on page 838. ➤ Read about your Personal Planets on page 826. ➤ Read about your personal Mystical Card on page 856.

VIRGO

From August 23, 11:57 through September 23, 9:24

The Joyful Perfectionist

Trust the 1978 Virgo to do a good job with everything. You don't take responsibility lightly; work is a religion to you. That doesn't mean, however, that you're incapable of having fun. Quite the contrary! You make a game of work. The year you were born, the sculptor Christo draped saffron-coloured nylon over paths in the Jacob Loose Memorial Park in Kansas City, Missouri. This arduous art project is exactly the kind of task that appeals to you because it comprises equal parts of work and whimsy.

Your job may require an element of sacrifice. Working long hours, acting as an apprentice, or starting at the bottom may be necessary. Fortunately, you don't mind temporary deprivations so long as there is an eventual reward involved. Carrying on old traditions may strongly appeal to you, drawing you to a job as a glass blower, tailor, or metalworker. Farming is also a possibility for you; you could have marvelous success growing organic food. You're a strong believer in getting back to basics and probably disdain modern methods that create inferior products.

You're probably an extensive and adventurous reader. People often seek you out at parties because you're bound to have something interesting to say. You've got a dry sense of humor and frequently make fun of your own shortcomings. Casual acquaintances may not be aware of how accomplished you are because you are so modest. You have a lot in common with the spider in E.B. White's *Charlotte's Web*. While everybody else is bustling around, you're there in the corner, quietly creating masterpieces that only the most sensitive folks can appreciate.

Quiet, introspective people suit you best. You get along very well with Taureans, Virgos, Scorpios, and Capricorns. Romantically, you need a partner who is encouraging and apprecia-tive of your talents. Although you care little about public opinion, it is important to have a mate who understands your work.

Your greatest challenge is to promote yourself, if only to find work that feels meaningful. Your biggest asset is your ability to always live in the moment. Life is a precious gift, and you're able to enjoy it to the fullest.

LIBRA

From September 23, 9:25 through October 23, 18:36

The Pleasant Powerhouse

A force to be reckoned with, the 1978 Libra cuts an impressive figure. Somehow, you manage to be intimidating and charming at the same time. Still, you aim to build consensus and few will refuse your requests. On September 27, 1978, France was finally persuaded to join the UN disarma-ment committee after a seventeen-year absence. Interpersonal relationships of all varieties are your forte, especially romantic unions. In the U.S., first daughter Susan Ford announced her engagement to Charles F. Vance on October 18 in the year of your birth.

Marvelously artistic, you'd make an excellent trendsetter. A career in fashion, hairdressing, or cosmetics could suit you very well. Alternately, you could also write romantic stories that provide folks with a blessed escape from reality. You could even become a motivational speaker. Whatever your job, it should involve setting an example for others. Showing people how to lead a more beautiful or fulfilling life would be a wonderful use of your time.

You enjoy spending money as fast as you make it and probably have an opulent lifestyle. Buying beautiful things for your home may be your favorite hobby; you could be a regular visitor at flea markets and estate sales. Fortunately, you've got great intuition when it comes to money. Profitable investments can keep you afloat, even in difficult times. You would be wise, however, to set something aside for your retirement, just as a safety measure.

People with a spiritual bent have a friend in you. You can spend hours and hours discussing philosophical subjects with Librans, Sagittarians, Aquarians, and Pisceans. In love, you need a mate who is kind, patient, and constant. An impetuous partner would throw you off balance; you need to be secure in the knowledge that your relationship sits on solid ground.

Your greatest challenge is to apply your considerable charm to a positive purpose. You can accomplish great things if you wish, especially in the arts. Your biggest strength is your ability to uplift people. Folks draw inspiration from your vivid imagination, giving you a sense of divine purpose.

➤ Read about your Chinese Astrological sign on page 838. ➤ Read about your Personal Planets on page 826. ➤ Read about your personal Mystical Card on page 856.

VIRGO
Your Personal Planets

YOUR LOVE POTENTIAL
Venus in Libra, Aug. 23, 11:57 - Sept. 07, 5:06
Venus in Scorpio, Sept. 07, 5:07 - Sept. 23, 9:24

YOUR DRIVE AND AMBITION
Mars in Libra, Aug. 23, 11:57 - Sept. 19, 20:56
Mars in Scorpio, Sept. 19, 20:57 - Sept. 23, 9:24

YOUR LUCK MAGNETISM
Jupiter in Cancer, Aug. 23, 11:57 - Sept. 05, 8:29
Jupiter in Leo, Sept. 05, 8:30 - Sept. 23, 9:24

World Events

Sept. 3 - Pope John Paul I is officially installed as the 264th Supreme Pontiff; he dies before the end of the month.

Sept. 18 - The Camp David Agreement is signed between Israel and Egypt.

Pope John Paul II, the first non-Italian in 455 years, is installed

LIBRA
Your Personal Planets

YOUR LOVE POTENTIAL
Venus in Scorpio, Sept. 23, 9:25 - Oct. 23, 18:36

YOUR DRIVE AND AMBITION
Mars in Scorpio, Sept. 23, 9:25 - Oct. 23, 18:36

YOUR LUCK MAGNETISM
Jupiter in Leo, Sept. 23, 9:25 - Oct. 23, 18:36

World Events

Oct. 5 - Isaac Bashevis' *Singer* wins the Nobel Prize for literature.

Oct. 22 - Pope John Paul II is installed as the 265th Supreme Pontiff.

1978

SCORPIO
Your Personal Planets

YOUR LOVE POTENTIAL
Venus in Scorpio, Oct. 23, 18:37 - Nov. 22, 16:04

YOUR DRIVE AND AMBITION
Mars in Scorpio, Oct. 23, 18:37 - Nov. 02, 1:19
Mars in Sagittarius, Nov. 02, 1:20 - Nov. 22, 16:04

YOUR LUCK MAGNETISM
Jupiter in Leo, Oct. 23, 18:37 - Nov. 22, 16:04

World Events

Nov. 6 – The Shah of Iran places the country under military rule.

Nov. 15 – Harold Pinter's *Betrayal* premieres at the National Theatre in London.

The Shah of Iran imposes martial law

SAGITTARIUS
Your Personal Planets

YOUR LOVE POTENTIAL
Venus in Scorpio, Nov. 22, 16:05 - Dec. 22, 5:20

YOUR DRIVE AND AMBITION
Mars in Sagittarius, Nov. 22, 16:05 - Dec. 12, 17:38
Mars in Capricorn, Dec. 12, 17:39 - Dec. 22, 5:20

YOUR LUCK MAGNETISM
Jupiter in Leo, Nov. 22, 16:05 - Dec. 22, 5:20

World Events

Nov. 29 – Followers of the People's Temple cult commit mass suicide in Jonestown, Guyana.

Dec. 5 – An historic treaty of friendship is signed between the USSR and Afghanistan.

SCORPIO
From October 23, 18:37 through November 22, 16:04

The Intense Individualist

The 1978 Scorpio is an exciting person to know. Your approach to life is intense but controlled. On October 27 of the year you were born, the UN military command in South Korea discovered a tunnel that originated in North Korea and passed under the demilitarized zone. You will also reveal your deepest secrets more easily than most of your sign, especially if you can shock folks and shake up the status quo. Unlike most people, you welcome sudden changes and thrive when forced to deal with unforeseen circumstances.

You need a career that involves originality. Scientific research would suit you well, provided you are able to work independently. You'd also make a good character actor, taking on small but memorable parts that get you noticed widely. You might also do well in advertising, devising clever campaigns that have never been seen before. Ultimately, you need a job that allows you to put an unusual spin on your duties. Performing predictable routine work will only dull your enthusiastic spirit.

Quite often, you will retreat to your own private world where friends and family can't reach you. Your reclusive ways help you to regenerate your spirits. An unusual person like you tires easily from mixing with large groups of people. Therefore, you often go off on your own, simply as a means to reconnect with your unique spiritual essence. The people closest to your heart understand this need and will back off when you say the word.

You prefer having a few intimate friends to understand your peculiarities. Taureans, Cancerians, Scorpios, and Pisceans probably receive the lion's share of your affection. In love, you need a partner who is calm, cool, and collected. Anyone who can soothe your restless spirits would make you a fantastic mate.

Your greatest challenge as a 1978 Scorpio is to slow down. You have so many ideas that it's hard for you to rest. At some point, you may have to shelve some of your plans in favor of contentment. Your biggest strength is your originality. There is little threat of you going along with the popular view. You're capable of thinking for yourself and will never fall victim to manipulation.

SAGITTARIUS
From November 22, 16:05 through December 22, 5:20

The Playful Friend

Folks are attracted to the 1978 Sagittarius like moths to a flame. You're so warm, friendly, and sexy that you can't help but be popular. Folks depend on your extravagant compliments and impulsive hugs for spiritual fortification. The year you were born, writer Isaac Bashevis Singer was awarded the Nobel Prize for Literature. His playful, affectionate voice is similar to your own. You're a wonderful representative of the human race.

Writing movies, songs, or books could satisfy your tremendous creative urge. Alternately, a love of travel could lead you to a job in tourism. You would also make a great teacher as you have a knack for presenting even the most boring subjects in a captivating way. Whatever work you perform, it is destined to have an optimistic quality that is immensely popular. Chances are you will reach the pinnacle of success later in life after a slow but enjoyable climb to the top of your profession.

You're frequently on the move and may change addresses quite often. The year you were born, the first Sony Walkman was manufactured. The portable stereo was created for consumers like you. Why invest in an unwieldy sound system when you can just strap a little cassette player to your belt? The best gift anybody could get you is a collapsible suitcase. You simply won't be tied down by possessions.

You're passionate about your friends and will do anything to come to their aid. Outgoing Ariens, Geminis, Leos, and Sagittarians are always good company for you. Sometimes your devotion to friends can interfere with your love life. Ideally, you should marry your best friend. That way, you won't feel torn between your social and personal lives.

As a 1978 Sagittarius, your greatest challenge is to form intimate relationships. Although you prefer to mix with a big gang of friends, you could also benefit from a loving partnership. Don't be so reluctant to devote yourself to one person's pleasure. Your biggest strength is your ability to see the good in all things. Everybody and everything has potential in your eyes; what a wonderful way to view the world!

➤ Read about your Chinese Astrological sign on page 838. ➤ Read about your Personal Planets on page 826. ➤ Read about your personal Mystical Card on page 856.

CAPRICORN

From December 22, 5:21 through December 31, 23:59

The Ardent Sensualist

The December-born 1978 Capricorn simply oozes sensuality. You have a deep appreciation for the physical pleasures of life and seek to indulge yourself at every possible opportunity. Even so, you're a very hard worker. You think nothing of putting in a 14-hour day and following it with a long, languorous massage. You never do anything by half-measures and people respect you for it.

A career that involves a lot of hard work and dedication suits you best. You'd make a marvelous movie director, real estate developer, or anthropologist. Any job that requires vision and courage should bring you pleasure. A natural-born leader, you need to be in charge of operations. You're bound to clash with authority figures that try to pull rank over you. It's better if you can take a job where you call all the shots. If this means working all alone in a studio, so be it. You'd rather be isolated than observed by a critical boss.

You have a strong sex drive that will not be denied. Although most Goats are modest about their desires, you are not. Wearing sexy clothes and musky colognes comes naturally to you. Many people find you irresistible, but you're quite particular when it comes to picking a partner. You'd rather have a single passionate affair than a string of meaningless relationships.

You like to surround yourself with dynamic, aggressive people. Ariens, Leos, Scorpios, and Sagittarians make good friends for you as they're eager to carry out your impressive plans. The year you were born, three Americans made the first transatlantic balloon flight. This kind of excursion is exactly the kind of caper you'd like to hazard. With regard to love, you need a partner who is nurturing but supportive. You wouldn't last long with a worrywart.

Blessed with considerable talent, you are still somewhat unsure of your abilities. Your greatest challenge is to build your self-confidence. A profound appreciation for the finer things in life is your biggest blessing. You'll always take the opportunity to treat yourself, especially after a hard day's work. Continue to revel in life.

CAPRICORN
Your Personal Planets

YOUR LOVE POTENTIAL
Venus in Scorpio, Dec. 22, 5:21 - Dec. 31, 23:59

YOUR DRIVE AND AMBITION
Mars in Capricorn, Dec. 22, 5:21 - Dec. 31, 23:59

YOUR LUCK MAGNETISM
Jupiter in Leo, Dec. 22, 5:21 - Dec. 31, 23:59

World Events

Dec. 25 – Vietnam and Cambodia at war after the former launches an invasion.

Dec. 27 – King Juan Carlos ratifies Spain's first democratic constitution.

Special Feature
Science, Champions, and the Mars Effect

(Continued from page 633)

Of the many fine players in women's tennis since Navratilova retired, the two Williams sisters are the most striking in terms of the power, grace, and discipline they bring to the game. The eldest, Venus, who had Mars rising when she was born on June 17, 1980, at 2:12 p.m. in Lynwood, California, has had her serve clocked as fast as an amazing 127 mph—a speed unmatched by most men let alone women. Both Venus and her younger sister Serena have great tennis gifts and immense discipline, but Venus's power zone Mars suggests she may go the distance longer than her sister.

Perhaps the best example of a "Mars Effect" athlete on the current scene is golfer Tiger Woods, who was born on December 30, 1975, at 10:50 p.m. in Redondo Beach, California. At the time of his birth, Mars was in the upper power zone. His father has said that Tiger does not just hope for victory but rather "expects to win," and win he certainly has, starting with a record-setting string of

amateur victories in his teen years. Woods won his first amateur tournament—the Optimist International—at the tender age of eight, and by the time he had reached the age of twenty, he had become the only person ever to win the U.S. Amateur Championship three consecutive times. In the same year he achieved this, he turned pro, picked up product endorsements worth $60 million, and was named *Sports Illustrated's* Sportsman of the Year. Tiger Woods is truly in a class by himself, and has won major tournaments separated by as many as fifteen strokes from the other competitors.

Mars may not tell us the whole story of any sports champion, but it is a key factor in providing the competitive edge that makes the difference between someone who is merely competent in a sport and the truly great, truly memorable, champion. Though it's easy to find clear examples of the Mars Effect, we should keep in mind the long and difficult process of research that went into its discov-

Golf champion Tiger Woods

ery. Everyone interested in astrology owes a debt to Michel Gauquelin, whose lifelong work and scientific dedication made him a research "champion" in his own right. ❂

➤ Read Muhammad Ali's Star Profile on page 617.

1979

Religious Fervor: Neptune Emphasized

Neptune, the planet of spirituality and imagination, was emphasized as 1979 dawned. Carrying the idealistic and sometimes zealous energy of Sagittarius, Neptune can be associated with high-flying and impractical actions, sometimes based on spiritual or religious ardor. This was seen in a spate of events stemming from this source, from the mass suicide in Jonestown, Guyana, (actually in late 1978) to the rise in popularity of the cleric-leader Ayatollah Khomeini in Iran. However, Neptune is also linked to dissolution of boundaries, such as the alienating walls that have been known to separate warring factions all over the world. Nowhere was this more evident than in the peace agreement between Israel and Egypt that was finally ratified and signed in March of this year. While Neptune was generally more emphasized for the whole of 1979, this particular event occurred as the mid-March eclipse highlighted Neptune. Among the other significant events which coincided with this focus was the trade agreement that was drawn up between China and the U.S., the first one of its kind since the People's Republic had been formed.

Unseen or noxious menaces are Neptune's domain as well and the Three-Mile Island atomic leak also came at the Neptunian eclipse, the same day as the peace agreement was signed. Monty Python's satiric jab at religion in *Life of Brian* carried the religio-spiritual aspect of Neptune into the realms of the absurd. Meanwhile, acts of succor and compassion expressed its highest manifestation: Patty Hearst received a presidential pardon and Mother Teresa won the Nobel Peace Prize. The unseen was also "seen" in films like *Alien*.

Margaret Thatcher becomes the first British woman Prime Minister and celebrates with her son Mark

Armed students hold hostages at the U.S. Embassy in Tehran

American actor John Wayne dies

BIONIC WOMAN

American actress Lindsay Wagner—the Bionic Woman—was scheduled to board an American Airlines flight in Chicago with her mother in May. Overcome by a premonition, she cancelled her reservations. Seconds after clearing the runway, the plane crashed near buildings at the edge of the airport, exploding into a horrific fireball. Everyone on board died instantly. Prior to this, Cincinnati psychic David Booth had called American Airlines with repeated warnings of such a "fireball" disaster although he couldn't pinpoint the exact airport.

THREE–MILE ISLAND AND THE HOSTAGE CRISIS

Iranian cleric Ayatollah Khomeini returned from exile to lead radical Muslims against the Shah, forcing him out of the country. Iranian students stormed the U.S. Embassy and took around ninety hostages in retaliation for U.S. acceptance of the exiled Shah. In Cambodia, the mass graves of Pol Pot's Khmer Rouge victims were revealed. Russian forces invaded Afghanistan to support its weak Marxist regime. Britain elected its first woman Prime Minister, Conservative Margaret Thatcher. The Sandinista rebels took power in Nicaragua. At Pennsylvania's Three-Mile Island nuclear power plant, a radiation leak and partial meltdown nearly caused disaster. Category 5 hurricane David killed 1,000 in the Dominican Republic. Rings were discovered around the planet Jupiter. The science fiction film *Alien* terrified audiences while *Kramer vs. Kramer* showed them the agonies of divorce. Elaine Page shocked the world of biblical history with a daring reinterpretation of *Gnostic Gospels*. Lord Louis Mountbatten, a member of the British Royal Family, was assassinated by an IRA bomb. Film actor John Wayne died of Cancer.

➤ Read Jacqueline Kennedy Onassis' Star Profile on page 649.

CAPRICORN

From January 01, 0:00 through January 20, 15:59

The Protective Parent

Everybody feels safe and secure around the January-born 1979 Capricorn. You feel a great sense of responsibility towards everyone, whether they are children, employees, or close friends. Looking after people's interests gives you a great sense of satisfaction. You have a special weakness for underdogs and may go out of your way to protect them from abuse. The year you were born, Margaret Thatcher became Prime Minister of Britain. Like this imposing authority figure, you don't hesitate to cut your enemies down to size. You will fight tooth and nail to protect the people you love.

You are a born leader, and should find a career that involves serious responsibility. The military would be a good place for you, as it suits your sense of order. You'd also be a good business owner, particularly if you were able to oversee large numbers of employees. Running a large school, hospital, or prison may also appeal to you. Ultimately, you like being responsible for others, and should take a job that draws upon your leadership abilities.

A strong sense of spirituality will help you cope with serious responsibilities. Studying various religions can help you develop your own philosophy. Appreciating nature can become a sort of religion for you, too. Whenever you feel anxious or depressed, you should head for green, leafy vistas. Rustic retreats will restore your spirits, and make your burdens seem less heavy. Yoga and meditation can help when you can't get away from daily stresses.

You need joyful, spirited friends who make you laugh. Geminis, Leos, Librans, and Sagittarians encourage you to let down your hair. Romantically, you need a mate who is tender and caring. Once you fall in love, it is for keeps. You're likely to have a happy marriage.

Your greatest challenge is to take it easy. Just because you have many responsibilities doesn't mean you can't have fun. Make a concerted effort to enjoy yourself, especially when work gets you down. Your biggest strength is your willingness to stand up for the less powerful. The weak and vulnerable have a valuable friend in you.

AQUARIUS

From January 20, 16:00 through February 19, 6:12

The Brazen Noncomformist

Zany and unconventional, the 1979 Aquarius is full of surprises. As far as you're concerned, it's better to be shocking than boring. You're willing to do anything to get a rise out of people, whether it's poking fun at a sacred institution or standing on your head at the dinner table. Setting yourself apart from the crowd is your number one priority. The year you were born, *The Elephant Man* won the Tony award for Best Play. You probably appreciate the message of this drama: great beauty can come from being unique.

Because you are utterly determined to be independent, you need a job that allows you a great deal of freedom. Working with plants or animals may prove rewarding for you. You'd make an excellent botanist, veterinarian, or landscaper. A job that affords lots of travel might also suit you. Joining a music group, theater troupe, or dance company could ward off boredom. Alternately, you could learn a skill that would allow you to pick up and move whenever you crave a change of scenery. If you want to see the world, you could learn how to program computers.

You're a little reserved in your affections, and may wait until you're older to form an intimate partnership. Folks who love a challenge are attracted by your cool. There's something so elusive and mysterious about the way you conduct your personal life; many people assume you have a tragic romance in your past. The truth is you're just reluctant to open up to friends until you know them extremely well.

Offbeat, adventurous people make the best friends for you. No wonder so many Ariens, Geminis, Leos, and Sagittarians make up your social circle! Romantically, you need a warm, effusive partner who can bring out your sensual side. Given enough encouragement, you will be as affectionate as a playful puppy.

Your greatest challenge is to develop your sensual side. Although you are most attracted to the world of ideas, it wouldn't hurt to indulge in physical pleasures from time to time. Your biggest strength is your appreciation for people's differences. You will never lack for varied, interesting company.

➤ Read about your Chinese Astrological sign on page 838. ➤ Read about your Personal Planets on page 826. ➤ Read about your personal Mystical Card on page 856.

CAPRICORN
Your Personal Planets

YOUR LOVE POTENTIAL
Venus in Scorpio, Jan. 01, 0:00 - Jan. 07, 6:37
Venus in Sagittarius, Jan. 07, 6:38 - Jan. 20, 15:59

YOUR DRIVE AND AMBITION
Mars in Capricorn, Jan. 01, 0:00 - Jan. 20, 15:59

YOUR LUCK MAGNETISM
Jupiter in Leo, Jan. 01, 0:00 - Jan. 20, 15:59

World Events

Jan. 8 - Argentina and Chile sign the Beagle Canal accord.
Jan. 16 - Shah Mohammed Reza Pahlavi of Iran flees to Egypt.

Shah Mohammed Reza Pahlavi with his wife

AQUARIUS
Your Personal Planets

YOUR LOVE POTENTIAL
Venus in Sagittarius, Jan. 20, 16:00 - Feb. 05, 9:15
Venus in Capricorn, Feb. 05, 9:16 - Feb. 19, 6:12

YOUR DRIVE AND AMBITION
Mars in Capricorn, Jan. 20, 16:00 - Jan. 20, 17:06
Mars in Aquarius, Jan. 20, 17:07 - Feb. 19, 6:12

YOUR LUCK MAGNETISM
Jupiter in Leo, Jan. 20, 16:00 - Feb. 19, 6:12

World Events

Feb. 1 - Ayatollah Ruhollah Khomeini returns to Iran after fifteen years in exile.
Feb. 7 - Pink Floyd premiere their live version of *The Wall* in Los Angeles.

1979

PISCES
Your Personal Planets

YOUR LOVE POTENTIAL
Venus in Capricorn, Feb. 19, 6:13 - Mar. 03, 17:17
Venus in Aquarius, Mar. 03, 17:18 - Mar. 21, 5:21

YOUR DRIVE AND AMBITION
Mars in Aquarius, Feb. 19, 6:13 - Feb. 27, 20:24
Mars in Pisces, Feb. 27, 20:25 - Mar. 21, 5:21

YOUR LUCK MAGNETISM
Jupiter in Leo, Feb. 19, 6:13 - Feb. 28, 23:34
Jupiter in Cancer, Feb. 28, 23:35 - Mar. 21, 5:21

World Events

Feb. 22 – St. Lucia in the West Indies gains independence from Britain.

Mar. 7 – A photograph sent back by the U.S. *Voyager 1* space probe reveals Jupiter's rings.

Leaders al-Sadat, Carter and Begin sign the peace treaty

ARIES
Your Personal Planets

YOUR LOVE POTENTIAL
Venus in Aquarius, Mar. 21, 5:22 - Mar. 29, 3:17
Venus in Pisces, Mar. 29, 3:18 - Apr. 20, 16:34

YOUR DRIVE AND AMBITION
Mars in Pisces, Mar. 21, 5:22 - Apr. 07, 1:07
Mars in Aries, Apr. 07, 1:08 - Apr. 20, 16:34

YOUR LUCK MAGNETISM
Jupiter in Cancer, Mar. 21, 5:22 - Apr. 20, 16:34

World Events

Mar. 26 – The Camp David peace treaty is signed between Israel and Egypt.

Mar. 28 – Crisis begins at the Three-Mile Island nuclear power station in Pennsylvania.

PISCES
From February 19, 6:13 through March 21, 5:21

The Creative Force

A dreamy, far-away look tends to characterize the 1979 Pisces. You may prefer to build castles in the air than deal with the harsh realities of life. Consequently, you're often engaging in some artistic pursuit, like writing, drawing, or playing music. Art helps to transport you to imaginary lands where there is no cruelty, suffering, or pain. The year you were born, the movie *All That Jazz* was released. Bob Fosse's autobiographical account of his obsession with dance may strike a deep emotional chord in you. You know what it is to be consumed by creativity.

A career in the entertainment industry would suit you very well. You'd make a fantastic actor, singer, or dancer. Because you're a Pisces, you may prefer to be creative in a private setting. Writing, painting, or sculpting may appeal to your reclusive side. At some point, however, you may decide to put your art aside for the sake of raising children. You probably adore kids, and may raise a sizable family, along with a menagerie of adorable pets.

You have the ability to bounce back from incredible adversity. At times folks make the mistake of thinking that you are shy and helpless. Then you astonish them by rallying at the eleventh hour. Overcoming obstacles gives you wisdom beyond your years. Your old soul attracts well-established, successful folks who admire your maturity. There's a good chance you have several friends who are much older than you.

Folks who share your humanitarian spirit make up the greater part of your social circle. Virgos, Librans, Aquarians, and Pisceans are among your closest pals. Chances are, you've met quite a few of your chums while performing volunteer work. In love, you need a partner who is practical and discerning. Such a mate will provide a nice counterbalance to your whimsical ways.

Your greatest challenge is to form relationships with folks who nurture and support your creativity. A sensitive person like you can't afford to have your thinking poisoned by cynics. Your biggest strength is your ability to transcend enormous difficulties. You're much tougher than you appear!

ARIES
From March 21, 5:22 through April 20, 16:34

The Tough Cookie

A fascinating mix of aggression and sweetness, the 1979 Aries can be quite puzzling. One minute you're pushing your way to the front of the line, the next you're bending to comfort a crying child. It's hard to tell when you're going to be sweet or tough, and that's what makes you so compelling. The year you were born, Carroll O'Connor won an Emmy Award for playing the cranky but lovable Archie Bunker. You've got just as many contradictions as this legendary television character. Like Archie, you will probably grow mellow with age, softening your outlook.

Ideally, you should have a job that provides you with an outlet for your boundless energy. You would make a great salesperson, athletic coach, or politician. Any career that involves competition would suit your talents. You could also counsel troubled children, doling out discipline and affection in equal amounts. Whatever job you perform, it should offer plenty of incentives, like bonuses, raises, or promotions. Otherwise, your interest may quickly wane.

As you get older, you may become increasingly interested in guarding your health. Changing your diet, embracing exercise, or practicing meditation could become a regular part of your routine. Forming a stronger connection between your mind, body, and spirit will allow you to lead a long, happy life. There is little chance that you will embark on a leisurely retirement; you'll always be active and vibrant, even in your golden years.

You prefer to surround yourself with people who have plenty of substance. Taureans, Leos, Virgos, and Scorpios comprise the majority of your social circle; you can't abide flighty types. With regard to romance, you need somebody who is strong-willed enough to defy you. Teaming up with a meek, agreeable mate is a bad idea; you want somebody who will challenge your authority from time to time.

Your greatest challenge is to become more discerning. Learning when to be aggressive and when to be nurturing is half the battle for you. Your biggest strength is your sense of healthy competition. Whether you win or lose, you're always a good sport.

➤ Read about your Chinese Astrological sign on page 838. ➤ Read about your Personal Planets on page 826. ➤ Read about your personal Mystical Card on page 856.

TAURUS

From April 20, 16:35 through May 21, 15:53

The Sexy Enigma

Like a great volcano, deep fires burn within the 1979 Taurus. You never know when you're going to erupt, but when you do, look out! The year you were born, a nuclear power plant at Three-Mile Island, Pennsylvania, unexpectedly released radiation into the atmosphere, forcing residents to flee their homes. Your anger can have a similar effect, yet you never lack for admirers. There's something irresistible about those smoldering eyes of yours. Whoever does win your heart has a bumpy but thrilling road ahead!

Hard working and conscientious, you need a job that is utterly absorbing. You would make a remarkable detective, forensic scientist, or mystery writer. Seeking out the truth gives you a profound sense of satisfaction. You'd rather be alone in a quiet studio than operate as part of a team. That's because you hate being watched while you work. Whatever job you take, it should afford you a reasonable level of privacy.

Because you like solitude so much, you need a home that provides a soothing retreat from public life. There's a good chance that your lair is filled with tactile fabrics, soft furnishings, and low lights. Visitors may describe your place as "womb-like." Although you do like your privacy, you also throw a fair amount of parties. It gives you pleasure to feed and entertain friends, and your guest room is often occupied.

You like reserved, creative people who don't wear their hearts on their sleeves. Taureans, Leos, Librans, and Scorpios have the elegance and reserve you admire. In love, you need a partner who is utterly independent; a clinging vine would smother you. If you pick someone who has a few interests that are separate from your own, you could have a rich, rewarding relationship.

Your greatest challenge is to become more spontaneous. A fear of the unknown can make you overly cautious; try to take more chances, especially as you grow older. Your biggest strength is your smoldering passion. Use it to forge relationships with people who are exciting and innovative. Their creative energy can fuel your own, resulting in some very admirable work.

GEMINI

From May 21, 15:54 through June 21, 23:55

The Wistful Homebody

Having a secure home life may be the first priority for any 1979 Gemini. From a very young age, you yearned for a tranquil domain. Perhaps your childhood was disrupted by frequent moves. Maybe you were shuttled between two parents. You might have lived in a messy, chaotic home that conflicted with your need for order. Whatever your background, it had a direct affect on your deep need for a fulfilling domestic life. The year you were born, Jon Voigt and Jane Fonda won Oscars for their performances in the movie *Coming Home*. If you could have one wish, it would probably be to come home to a happy, relaxing household.

Although every Gemini has strong communication skills, yours are particularly strong. You could achieve remarkable success as a journalist, novelist, or radio personality. Becoming a teacher is also a strong possibility for you. Working with small children would probably suit you best. If you don't become a formal school teacher, you could run an extracurricular program devoted to the arts, athletics, or both.

Your subconscious is strongly developed, and you often draw inspiration from dreams. When it comes to hobbies, you prefer working in seclusion. You don't like to be inhibited by critical onlookers; you'd rather develop an idea first, and then show off your work after it's finished. When you do find that dream home of yours, make sure it has a private workspace where you can putter undisturbed.

Rowdy, rambunctious folks have a friend in you. Ariens, Geminis, Leos, and Sagittarians are always willing to go along with your crazy plans. You fall in love often and hard. Ultimately, your life partner should be somebody who is intuitive and spiritual. There's a good chance you can communicate with your mate both verbally and psychically.

Your greatest challenge is to develop realistic expectations of family life. A healthy expression of anger is a necessary component to any happy household; don't be alarmed when arguments break out. Your biggest strength is your sense of fun. Somehow you manage to make a regular trip to the store seem like an adventure.

► Read about your Chinese Astrological sign on page 838. ► Read about your Personal Planets on page 826. ► Read about your personal Mystical Card on page 856.

TAURUS
Your Personal Planets

YOUR LOVE POTENTIAL
Venus in Pisces, Apr. 20, 16:35 - Apr. 23, 4:01
Venus in Aries, Apr. 23, 4:02 - May 18, 0:28
Venus in Taurus, May 18, 0:29 - May 21, 15:53

YOUR DRIVE AND AMBITION
Mars in Aries, Apr. 20, 16:35 - May 16, 4:24
Mars in Taurus, May 16, 4:25 - May 21, 15:53

YOUR LUCK MAGNETISM
Jupiter in Cancer, Apr. 20, 16:35 - Apr. 20, 8:28
Jupiter in Leo, Apr. 20, 8:29 - May 21, 15:53

World Events

May 1 - George Bush announces that he will run for the U.S. presidency.

May 4 - Margaret Thatcher is elected Prime Minister of England.

Jimmy Carter and Leonid Brezhnev during the SALT-2 discussions

GEMINI
Your Personal Planets

YOUR LOVE POTENTIAL
Venus in Taurus, May 21, 15:54 - June 11, 18:12
Venus in Gemini, June 11, 18:13 - June 21, 23:55

YOUR DRIVE AND AMBITION
Mars in Taurus, May 21, 15:54 - June 21, 23:55

YOUR LUCK MAGNETISM
Jupiter in Leo, May 21, 15:54 - June 21, 23:55

World Events

June 11 - Legendary American actor John Wayne dies.

June 18 - Jimmy Carter and Leonid Brezhnev sign the SALT-2 arms treaty.

CANCER
Your Personal Planets

YOUR LOVE POTENTIAL
Venus in Gemini, June 21, 23:56 - July 06, 9:01
Venus in Cancer, July 06, 9:02 - July 23, 10:48

YOUR DRIVE AND AMBITION
Mars in Taurus, June 21, 23:56 - June 26, 1:54
Mars in Gemini, June 26, 1:55 - July 23, 10:48

YOUR LUCK MAGNETISM
Jupiter in Leo, June 21, 23:56 - July 23, 10:48

World Events

June 26 - Muhammad Ali announces his retirement from boxing.

July 16 - Saddam Hussein becomes the President of Iraq.

Iraqui President Saddam Hussein

LEO
Your Personal Planets

YOUR LOVE POTENTIAL
Venus in Cancer, July 23, 10:49 - July 30, 20:06
Venus in Leo, July 30, 20:07 - Aug. 23, 17:46

YOUR DRIVE AND AMBITION
Mars in Gemini, July 23, 10:49 - Aug. 08, 13:27
Mars in Cancer, Aug. 08, 13:28 - Aug. 23, 17:46

YOUR LUCK MAGNETISM
Jupiter in Leo, July 23, 10:49 - Aug. 23, 17:46

World Events

Aug. 8 - Somalia invades Ethiopia in the dispute over the Ogadan.

Aug. 12 - Press censors start a huge series of book burnings in Iran.

CANCER
From June 21, 23:56 through July 23, 10:48

The Gentle Philanthropist

Thoughtful and giving, the 1979 Cancer wants to leave the world a better place. There's a good chance you perform a great deal of volunteer work, and donate a portion of your earnings to charity. Onlookers are constantly amazed by your generosity, but it comes naturally to you. The year you were born, Mother Teresa was awarded the Nobel Peace Prize for taking care of the poor in Calcutta. You are similarly determined to help weak and defenseless people, and will always be involved in some kind of philanthropic endeavor.

Obviously, you need to do work that involves helping others in some way. Rehabilitating criminals, teaching children with learning disabilities, or attending to the sick can give you a great deal of satisfaction. You'd also make a good psychologist, spiritual advisor, or social worker. Any job that allows you to comfort people in distress would appeal to you. You're especially good at work that requires coming up with creative solutions to stubborn problems.

When taking care of everybody else's problems becomes too much, you tend to head straight for home. You love having your family around you, and would rather spend a quiet evening in their company than go out to a big party. Cooking is probably a form of therapy for you. The kitchen is probably the busiest room in your house, because it is where you are most relaxed and happy.

Although you're very selective about the company you keep, the friends you do have are just as important as family. You like folks who are kind, caring, and considerate. Taureans, Cancerians, Librans, and Pisceans probably play significant roles in your life. As far as love is concerned, you need a partner who is in touch with their feelings. There's a good chance your mate will be an artist of some sort.

Your greatest challenge is to emotionally separate your life from your work. People who deal in caring professions can sometimes carry great emotional burdens. Hobbies and sports can help relieve stress. Your biggest strength is your willingness to help others. You can make a positive difference in many people's lives.

LEO
From July 23, 10:49 through August 23, 17:46

The Love Magnet

Nobody has a bigger heart than the 1979 Leo. You are in love with life, and it shows. Even the greatest pessimists feel hopeful in your presence. Children and animals are especially responsive to your warm energy; sometimes you feel like the Pied Piper! The year you were born, *The Muppet Show* was charming children and adults alike with its whimsical, irreverent humor. Your own wit attracts people of all ages to your side. One thing is for sure, you will never lack for loving companionship!

You need a career that involves bringing light and joy into the world. Whether it's entertaining sick people in the hospital, writing comic strips, or working as a circus clown, your work will uplift and inspire folks. You may even opt for a more conventional job, like being a florist, baker, or jeweler. The important thing is that you provide people with services or products designed to lift their spirits. Although you don't care about being rich or famous, chances are you will probably become both, provided you take a job that affords you great happiness.

Your household can be somewhat chaotic, with visitors dropping in and out with alarming regularity. Installing a revolving door might be a good way to cope with the crowds. And while it's gratifying to be so popular, you sometimes need to get off on your own. Taking solitary vacations can keep you centered and balanced. It's also a good idea to turn off your phone for a couple of hours each day.

Not surprisingly, you have friends from all walks of life. Your favorite people, however, are those who are warm and nurturing. Taureans, Cancerians, Leos, and Sagittarians are among your closest chums. Romantically, you need a mate who is dreamy and idealistic. You will thrive in a relationship that is based in faith, love, and hope. Steer clear of status seekers; they're operating on an entirely different level than you.

Your greatest challenge is to carve out a private life for yourself. This can be hard to do when you are in such great demand. Your biggest strength is your capacity for joy. Life is the ultimate high for you.

➤ Read about your Chinese Astrological sign on page 838. ➤ Read about your Personal Planets on page 826. ➤ Read about your personal Mystical Card on page 856.

VIRGO

From August 23, 17:47 through September 23, 15:15

The Reliable Friend

You can't find a better pal than the 1979 Virgo. You're probably the leader of a big pack of friends, all of whom feel like family. Chums see you as a parent figure, because you're always dispensing practical advice or financial assistance. Although you are eminently practical, you like to surround yourself with dreamy, imaginative types. The year you were born, Billy Joel's "Just the Way You Are" won both Record and Song of the Year at the Grammys. This song's sentiment best expresses the attitude of your pals toward you—they love you absolutely and unconditionally.

Because you are so friendly, you are best suited to working with a large group. You would excel at being part of a research or sales team. You're also quite nurturing, and may take a job that involves looking after people, animals, or plants. You'd make a great teacher, animal trainer, or horticulturist. Owning a plant or pet shop would also suit you, as it would allow you to mix with a great variety of people while attending to dependents.

Your modesty and compassion can be quite impressive. You don't mind taking low or menial jobs, so long as your work is for an admirable purpose. Furthermore, you can handle emotionally harrowing situations that would break weaker personalities. Folks know that they can come to you when they are sick or distressed. You make a marvelous nurse and can soothe troubled hearts.

Although you have many friends, they all have one thing in common: kindness. Surrounding yourself with Taureans, Cancerians, Librans, and Pisceans feels enormously comforting. With regard to love, you need a mate who is artistic, spiritual, and just a little impractical. This kind of partner will encourage you to develop your own creative potential.

Your greatest challenge as a 1979 Virgo is to be less demanding of yourself. Resist the urge to berate yourself when you make a mistake; your most valuable lessons could come from committing errors. Your biggest strength is your ability to provide comforting stability to others. In a wild, unpredictable world like this one, that's a welcome trait indeed.

LIBRA

From September 23, 15:16 through October 24, 0:27

The Intense Brooder

Thoughtful and serious, the 1979 Libra is an impressive figure. You have tremendous willpower that is truly awesome. If you weren't so diplomatic, people would be intimidated by you. That's because you can accomplish astonishing amounts of work through sheer determination. The year you were born, revolution broke out in Iran, forcing leader Shah Reza Pahlevi from the country. The odds against vanquishing the Shah and his powerful army were great, but radicals managed to do it through sheer determination. You're capable of forcing similar upsets, thanks to your impressive focus.

You want a job that makes heavy demands on you; otherwise, you'll be easily bored. Emergency medical care, military duty, or police work might appeal to you. Of course, being a Libra, you have considerable talent as a diplomat, too. Learning foreign languages could land you a job as a translator for an important government agency or corporation. Whatever career you choose, it should have an air of importance about it.

A profound love of nature could draw you away from urban landscapes. If you live in a city, there's a good chance you take frequent camping trips to wooded areas. Digging can have a therapeutic effect on you. You may want to take up gardening as a hobby, and may also take an amateur interest in archeology or geology. Researching your family history may also appeal to you, as it's an intellectual form of digging. Your favorite fiction books are probably mysteries.

Your social circle is probably comprised of a great many bigwigs. Ariens, Cancerians, Librans, and Capricorns aren't intimidated by your powerful personality—in fact, they appreciate it. In love, you are best suited to somebody who is both romantic and aggressive. Although you like plenty of peace and quiet, you would be frustrated by a passive partner.

Your greatest challenge as a 1979 Libra is to enjoy your leisure time to the fullest. Having an amusing hobby can bring needed laughter into your life. Your biggest strength is your ability to rise up in the face of adversity. It's practically impossible to keep you down.

➤ Read about your Chinese Astrological sign on page 838. ➤ Read about your Personal Planets on page 826. ➤ Read about your personal Mystical Card on page 856.

VIRGO
Your Personal Planets

YOUR LOVE POTENTIAL
Venus in Leo, Aug. 23, 17:47 - Aug. 24, 3:15
Venus in Virgo, Aug. 24, 3:16 - Sept. 17, 7:20
Venus in Libra, Sept. 17, 7:21 - Sept. 23, 15:15

YOUR DRIVE AND AMBITION
Mars in Cancer, Aug. 23, 17:47 - Sept. 23, 15:15

YOUR LUCK MAGNETISM
Jupiter in Leo, Aug. 23, 17:47 - Sept. 23, 15:15

World Events

Aug. 23 – Bolshoi Ballet dancer Alexander Godunov defects to the U.S.

Sept. 20 – A French coup overthrows the Central African Republic Emperor Bokassa.

Pope John Paul II visits the U.S.

LIBRA
Your Personal Planets

YOUR LOVE POTENTIAL
Venus in Libra, Sept. 23, 15:16 - Oct. 11, 9:47
Venus in Scorpio, Oct. 11, 9:48 - Oct. 24, 0:27

YOUR DRIVE AND AMBITION
Mars in Cancer, Sept. 23, 15:16 - Sept. 24, 21:20
Mars in Leo, Sept. 24, 21:21 - Oct. 24, 0:27

YOUR LUCK MAGNETISM
Jupiter in Leo, Sept. 23, 15:16 - Sept. 29, 10:22
Jupiter in Virgo, Sept. 29, 10:23 - Oct. 24, 0:27

World Events

Sept. 25 – *Evita* opens at the Broadway Theater in New York.

Oct. 1 – Pope John Paul II arrives for a visit to the U.S.

1979

SCORPIO
Your Personal Planets

YOUR LOVE POTENTIAL

Venus in Scorpio, Oct. 24, 0:28 - Nov. 04, 11:49
Venus in Sagittarius, Nov. 04, 11:50 - Nov. 22, 21:53

YOUR DRIVE AND AMBITION

Mars in Leo, Oct. 24, 0:28 - Nov. 19, 21:35
Mars in Virgo, Nov. 19, 21:36 - Nov. 22, 21:53

YOUR LUCK MAGNETISM

Jupiter in Virgo, Oct. 24, 0:28 - Nov. 22, 21:53

World Events

Nov. 4 - Five hundred Iranian "students" seize the U.S. embassy and take ninety hostages.

Nov. 5 - Two men go on trial in Dublin, charged with the murder of Lord Mountbatten.

Students seize the U.S. embassy in Tehran

SAGITTARIUS
Your Personal Planets

YOUR LOVE POTENTIAL

Venus in Sagittarius, Nov. 22, 21:54 - Nov. 28, 14:19
Venus in Capricorn, Nov. 28, 14:20 - Dec. 22, 11:09

YOUR DRIVE AND AMBITION

Mars in Virgo, Nov. 22, 21:54 - Dec. 22, 11:09

YOUR LUCK MAGNETISM

Jupiter in Virgo, Nov. 22, 21:54 - Dec. 22, 11:09

World Events

Nov. 26 - The International Olympic Committee votes to readmit China after twenty-one years.

Dec. 10 - Mother Teresa of India is awarded the Nobel Peace Prize.

SCORPIO
From October 24, 0:28 through November 22, 21:53

The Determined Do-Gooder

The word "can't" doesn't exist in the 1979 Scorpio's vocabulary. You're an eternal optimist, which is why you're so popular. People are attracted to your positive outlook, and gain great inspiration from your company. You dream of a world in which everyone can work together in harmony. Quite often, you launch volunteer projects, bringing your friends along as helpers. You would do very well living on a commune or a kibbutz. Work seems more like play when you're surrounded by friendly, cooperative people

A strong humanitarian streak could draw you to work in the nonprofit field. You would make an excellent fundraiser or grant writer. Building homes for the poor might also appeal to you, as would feeding the homeless. Ultimately, your work should involve making the world a better place for everyone. Performing good works not only makes you feel good, but valued by society. It also allows you to work in an environment that is less adversarial than most industries.

You've got a vibrant personality that can light up a room. Although you have a strong social conscience, that doesn't stop you from having fun. You love parties and dancing. The year you were born, the soundtrack from Saturday Night Fever won a Grammy for Album of the Year. Perhaps the disco craze fueled your own love of dance. If you ever feel blue, head for a club with a group of pals. Troubles seem to melt away after you hit the dance floor.

You have many loyal, kind friends who fill your life with joy. Generous, thoughtful Geminis, Virgos, Sagittarians, and Pisceans have lots in common with you, and make loving pals. With regard to romance, you need a partner who is devoted and down-to-earth. Once you commit to somebody, it will be for keeps. You don't take relationships lightly.

As a 1979 Scorpio, your greatest challenge is to guard your health. Sometimes your zeal to help folks can get in the way of your own self-care. Make a concerted effort to eat nutritious foods and get plenty of exercise. Your biggest blessing is your unselfish nature. A generous spirit like yours is truly precious.

SAGITTARIUS
From November 22, 21:54 through December 22, 11:09

The Class Act

Generous, trusting, and noble, the 1979 Sagittarius is a good person to know. You're always willing to do what's best for the entire group, and frequently put your own needs aside for the sake of others. Although you can be a little absent-minded and even clumsy, you're often described as "classy." That's because you are always acting in the best interests of the public. The year you were born, Tom Wolfe published *The Right Stuff*, a non-fiction account of American test pilots who braved the dangers of space exploration. Like these heroic astronauts, you've always been willing to put yourself on the line for the sake of others.

A civic-minded person like you would thrive in the political arena. You can cut through the red tape that prevents people from leading comfortable, productive lives. If politics doesn't interest you, sports might. You're a firm believer that healthy athletic competition can teach valuable life skills. You would make an excellent coach for young people. Ultimately, you want to provide the public with tools that can improve their lives.

Highly sensitive, you soak up the atmosphere like a sponge. Therefore, it's important to immerse yourself in a healthy environment. Steer clear of pessimists and manipulators, as they will only dim your sunny disposition. Seek out a neighborhood in which people are outgoing and friendly. A snobby, status-oriented area will inhibit you from making pals. Make sure you work with cooperative people, too.

Gracious, artistic people are drawn to your refined ways. You get along especially well with Cancerians, Virgos, Librans, and Pisceans. With regard to romance, you need a partner who shares your interest in justice and mercy. Self-absorbed types have little in common with you.

Your greatest challenge is to be more willing to make exceptions to rules. Although you have a great respect for the law, it's important to recognize when the facts don't support the prescribed course of action. Your biggest blessing is your civility. Regardless of the circumstance, you treat everyone with dignity and respect.

➤ Read about your Chinese Astrological sign on page 838. ➤ Read about your Personal Planets on page 826. ➤ Read about your personal Mystical Card on page 856.

CAPRICORN

From December 22, 11:10 through December 31, 23:59

The Intellectual Ethicist

A love of knowledge inspires the December-born 1979 Capricorn at all times. You're determined to know the "how" and "why" of everything, and may spend many years at institutions of higher learning. Unlike most intellectuals, however, you're not afraid to face unpleasant truths if it means gaining a greater understanding of the world. The year you were born, Norman Mailer published *The Executioner's Song*. This no-holds barred account of a murderer's life is the kind of book you appreciate, as it poses a number of ethical and existential questions without sounding preachy.

You're not afraid of hard work, and may pursue a job that requires an advanced degree. If you do become a doctor, lawyer, or professor, you're sure to be successful, thanks to your warm, humanistic approach. You're also quite spiritual, and may decide to become a religious leader of some sort. Whatever job you take, it should have a strong intellectual aspect. Performing predictable routine work would be a waste of your considerable brainpower.

Creative pursuits afford you welcome relaxation. Activities like woodcarving, needlework, and pottery give you a chance to focus on your hands, rather than your head. Although you're very social, you prefer doing your hobbies in private. You don't want even constructive criticism to inhibit your artistic expression, which accounts for your solitary habits.

Many of your friendships are mentally and spiritually stimulating. You are drawn to people who enjoy discussing art, politics, and religion. Geminis, Virgos, Sagittarians, and Aquarians may make up the majority of your social circle. In love, you are best suited to a mate who is both smart and sensual. Even an intellectual like you likes to be kissed, hugged, and caressed.

Your greatest challenge as a December-born 1979 Capricorn is to serve the public in some practical way. Although you love the world of ideas, you're also very realistic, and want to have something to show for your efforts. Your biggest blessing is your tremendous scholastic ability. Use your knowledge to enlighten and uplift the public.

1979

CAPRICORN
Your Personal Planets

YOUR LOVE POTENTIAL
Venus in Capricorn, Dec. 22, 11:10 - Dec. 22, 18:34
Venus in Aquarius, Dec. 22, 18:35 - Dec. 31, 23:59

YOUR DRIVE AND AMBITION
Mars in Virgo, Dec. 22, 11:10 - Dec. 31, 23:59

YOUR LUCK MAGNETISM
Jupiter in Virgo, Dec. 22, 11:10 - Dec. 31, 23:59

World Events

Dec. 27 – The Soviet Union invades Afghanistan.

Dec. 30 – Composer Richard Rodgers dies.

Jacqueline Kennedy Onassis
July 28, 1929 - May 19, 1994

JACQUELINE KENNEDY ONASSIS
Leo

A socialite and a child of divorce, charming, stylish and accomplished, Jacqueline Kennedy Onassis became one of the most elegant and admired first ladies in the U.S. Her beauty, panache and style made her an international sensation. A devoted wife, she always showed the world a dignified persona, even when rumors of infidelity plagued her marriage to John Kennedy. A second marriage to much-older Aristotle Onassis was widely regarded as unhappy.

Although Jackie was considered to be a shy and private person, her horoscope shows her to be quite well suited for the public life. Leos are generally considered to be natural showmen and with Sun, the planet of identity, and Mercury, the planet of communication, there, Jackie had a flair for expressing herself in a way the public could admire.

Her Moon, the planet of emotions, was in outgoing, impetuous Aries, and this is hardly

a shy placement. Located in the house of work, it was important for Jackie that she make good use of her personal talents and impulses. A contact from Venus, planet of beauty and style, helped Jackie become an enduring fashion icon. A stabilizing contact from responsible Saturn contributed to her desire to work and made her a rock for the people in her life. Her difficult childhood and the emotional power struggles she suffered in both her marriages are described by a challenging contact from Pluto, the planet of domination.

Jackie's Mars, the planet of action, is in practical, hard-working Virgo and its location in her house of career further emphasized her need to work. In the later years of her life, she lived contentedly as a single woman, and rose to success on her own merits in the challenging world of New York publishing. She may have been a first lady for the ages,

but she was also quite successful as a liberated career woman, and chances are that with this dynamic horoscope, she was much happier as an independent in the business world than she was as a beleaguered wife or consort of powerful men in lofty political and international circles.

➤ Read "The Presidential Death Cycle" on page 657. ➤ Read "Cartography and the Planets" on page 505. ➤ Read the Kennedy Family's Star Profile on page 497.

1980

Highs and Lows: Saturn, Uranus, and Neptune

Saturn, the planet of structure, contacted both Uranus and Neptune in 1980. Uranus, representing innovation, received a "sextile" contact from Saturn and was seen in enterprises based on innovative business approaches and scientific breakthroughs, both common for this combination. A possible solution to the mysterious extinction of the dinosaurs was revealed when remnants of an asteroid impact crater were found. In business, Japanese automaker Honda brought innovation to the soil of its biggest market, opening a manufacturing plant in Ohio. World leaders responded to the opportunity by pledging to seek new energy sources, in order to reduce the power of the OPEC oil cartel in world politics and economics.

However, Saturn's contact with Neptune, the symbol of flowing substances such as clouds, gases, and liquids, was more abrasive. After weeks of build-up, Washington State's Mt. St. Helens erupted in a stunning plume of ash and deadly gas. One-third of the volcano disappeared, creating a massive mudflow that destroyed miles of pristine landscape. This contact could also be seen in American weather patterns, as restrictive Saturn emphasized a curtailment in the flow of Neptunian liquids: a summer-long drought and heat wave recalled the disastrous Dust Bowl of the 1930s. In the fall, Saturn moved into relationship-oriented Libra, and marriage and other legal partnership laws were scrutinized. This was evident as Pope John Paul II decreed that, to receive communion, divorced Catholics who remarry must first have a previous marriage annulled.

Former Beatle John Lennon is shot and killed outside his home

Ronald Reagan wins the U.S. Presidency

Polish Solidarity union leader Lech Walesa

ASTEROID EXTINCTION

Geologist Walter Alvarez, along with a team of fellow scientists, offered a theory to explain dinosaur extinction. Because of the discovery of a concentrated layer of iridium in a segment of clay taken from a gorge in Italy, they posited that an asteroid had hit the Earth 65 million years ago with the force of a nuclear explosion. Its impact created a dust cloud that covered the Earth, preventing the Sun's light from shining through and thereby halting the photosynthesis and plant growth that dinosaurs depended on for food.

ERUPTIONS REAL AND SYMBOLIC

Robert Mugabe, the first African to hold the post, was elected Prime Minister of Zimbabwe, formerly Rhodesia. In Saudi Arabia, sixty-three terrorists who seized Mecca's Grand Mosque were executed. Striking shipyard workers in Gdansk, Poland, triumphed when their communist rulers agreed to independent trades unions and their right to strike. Moscow's summer Olympic Games were boycotted by the U.S. and sixty-one other countries in protest against the Russian invasion of Afghanistan. Ex-film star and California Governor Ronald Reagan won the U.S. Presidency. In the U.S., Mt. St. Helens in Washington state erupted, killing fifty-seven, destroying 200 homes and 185 miles of highways and roads, spreading ash over 22,000 square miles. The exiled Shah of Iran, French philosopher Jean-Paul Sartre, film director Alfred Hitchcock, film star Steve McQueen and Sanjay Gandhi, son of former Indian Prime Minister Indira Gandhi, were among those who passed away this year. Former Beatle John Lennon was killed in New York by a deranged fan.

➤ Read "The Presidential Death Cycle" by Rochelle Gordon on page 657.

CAPRICORN

From January 01, 0:00 through January 20, 21:48

The Unswerving Defender

Born during early January 1980, Capricorn, you arrived just as an Islamic Conference in Islamabad voiced its protest against the 1979 Soviet invasion of Afghanistan. On January 4, eight days after the invasion, U.S. President Carter announced sanctions against the Soviet Union. The energies surrounding this formal censure served to infuse you with fixed determination to counter oppression of the weak—by any means necessary.

The astrological factors present as you entered the world show the source of your unyielding dedication to do what's right, fair, and honest—and never compromise what you believe. Three planets—assertive Mars, the ancient warrior; benevolent Jupiter; and Saturn, the astrological "military general"—were keeping very close company in the meticulous sign of Virgo. This powerful fusing of energies combines to conjure the image of an inflexible, unswerving defender who analyzes each and every detail with equal attention, then comes up with a strategy with each of those details in mind. Basically, you were given keen intelligence, strong discriminatory skills, and the ability to take charge of just about any situation. In fact, your strategic talents are extremely potent. Whether you're analyzing a personal or business situation, you'll undoubtedly come up with the perfect solution to just about any problem.

You'll also do what it takes to curb injustice as you see it. Toward that end, you won't be afraid to resist, withhold, or erect roadblocks in the way of your opponent's progress. This makes you a formidable opponent and an extremely sturdy friend or mate.

In relationships, then, you need a partner with an equally strong back-bone—and someone whose determination matches your own. Look to solid, steady-handed Taureans, practical Virgos (who you'll no doubt feel close to immediately), or Cancerians, whose devotion to their dear ones is legendary.

Your challenge is to let go of situations that aren't worthy of your time and energy. Your gift is your ability to know the difference.

AQUARIUS

From January 20, 21:49 through February 19, 12:01

The Daring Dreamer

Born during 1980, Aquarius, you arrived into a time that would beautifully exemplify your sign's love of cheering for the underdog. The U.S. Olympic Ice Hockey Team was in the final stages of training to play against the highly favored Finnish and Russian teams: the U.S. players were said to have virtually no chance of victory. In the event, the U.S. team confounded these predictions and scored a major upset over the USSR, winning the Olympic Gold Medal. This made them national heroes. This event shows the determination and support you show in every situation, regardless of the odds against you—and the fact that belief in oneself makes everything possible.

The astrological factors that fueled this incredible event also endowed you with a zealousness and determination that's undoubtedly displayed itself in your life through your frequent victories in situations that may have initially seemed hopeless. Several planets in your own sign and in Virgo, known for its keen trouble-shooting abilities, describe your resolve to fight against any odds—no matter how overwhelming—as well as the meticulousness with which you conduct your analysis of the opponent.

As such, it's easy to see that when your heart and spirit are involved, you are a virtually unbeatable contender. This reluctance to be intimidated or oppressed shows in every undertaking you pursue, from personal, to competitive, to professional. Your willingness to do your homework to find the chink in your opponent's armor further describes your firmness of mind, tenacity in the face of opposition, and absolute refusal to admit defeat until you've actually been defeated.

In relationships, you'll need someone as determined, focused, and ardent as yourself. As such, optimistic Sagittarians, intense Scorpios, and fiery Leos will appeal to you—and prove to be worthwhile and stoic partners.

Your challenge is never to back down, no matter how devastating the odds stacked against you seem to be. Your gift is your unwavering faith in your purpose.

➤ Read about your Chinese Astrological sign on page 838. ➤ Read about your Personal Planets on page 826. ➤ Read about your personal Mystical Card on page 856.

1980

CAPRICORN
Your Personal Planets

YOUR LOVE POTENTIAL
Venus in Aquarius, Jan. 01, 0:00 - Jan. 16, 3:36
Venus in Pisces, Jan. 16, 3:37 - Jan. 20, 21:48

YOUR DRIVE AND AMBITION
Mars in Virgo, Jan. 01, 0:00 - Jan. 20, 21:48

YOUR LUCK MAGNETISM
Jupiter in Virgo, Jan. 01, 0:00 - Jan. 20, 21:48

World Events

Jan. 6 - Indira Gandhi gains the majority in the legislative elections in India.

Jan. 16 - Scientists use genetic engineering to produce a natural virus-fighting substance they call "interferon."

Indian leader Indira Gandhi

AQUARIUS
Your Personal Planets

YOUR LOVE POTENTIAL
Venus in Pisces, Jan. 20, 21:49 - Feb. 09, 23:38
Venus in Aries, Feb. 09, 23:39 - Feb. 19, 12:01

YOUR DRIVE AND AMBITION
Mars in Virgo, Jan. 20, 21:49 - Feb. 19, 12:01

YOUR LUCK MAGNETISM
Jupiter in Virgo, Jan. 20, 21:49 - Feb. 19, 12:01

World Events

Jan. 22 - Soviet dissident Andrei Sakharov is arrested and exiled.

Jan. 29 - The Islamic Conference, representing thirty-six countries and 900 million Muslims, adopts a resolution asking the Soviets to leave Afghanistan.

PISCES
Your Personal Planets

YOUR LOVE POTENTIAL
Venus in Aries, Feb. 19, 12:02 - Mar. 06, 18:53
Venus in Taurus, Mar. 06, 18:54 - Mar. 20, 11:09

YOUR DRIVE AND AMBITION
Mars in Virgo, Feb. 19, 12:02 - Mar. 11, 20:45
Mars in Leo, Mar. 11, 20:46 - Mar. 20, 11:09

YOUR LUCK MAGNETISM
Jupiter in Virgo, Feb. 19, 12:02 - Mar. 20, 11:09

World Events

Mar. 6 - Marguerite Youcenar becomes the first woman elected to the French Academy since its foundation in 1635.

Mar. 17 - Great Britain votes to boycott the Moscow Olympic Games.

French writer Marguerite Youcenar

ARIES
Your Personal Planets

YOUR LOVE POTENTIAL
Venus in Taurus, Mar. 20, 11:10 - Apr. 03, 19:45
Venus in Gemini, Apr. 03, 19:46 - Apr. 19, 22:22

YOUR DRIVE AND AMBITION
Mars in Leo, Mar. 20, 11:10 - Apr. 19, 22:22

YOUR LUCK MAGNETISM
Jupiter in Virgo, Mar. 20, 11:10 - Apr. 19, 22:22

World Events

Apr. 7 - The U.S. imposes sanctions on Iran after Ayatollah Khomeini sympathizes with the captors of the U.S. hostages in Tehran.

Apr. 15 - French existential novelist and philosopher Jean-Paul Sartre dies.

PISCES
From February 19, 12:02 through March 20, 11:09

The Sanctuary Provider

Born during 1980, Pisces, you made your planetary debut during a period that would serve to show your innate commitment to provide a safe haven to those in search of it—whether needed for personal, political, or religious reasons. The Refugee Act of 1980, signed by President Jimmy Carter during your birth time, was a move that expanded the United States' interpretation of the term "refugee" to include individuals from anywhere in the world. The Act allowed for 50,000 refugees a year, with the President having the discretion to increase this number if circumstances warranted. This strong declaration of that country's belief in "justice for all" is reflected in you through your unswerving determination to help.

The astrological influences of your birth month provide further evidence of your conviction to give refuge and even shelter, if need be, to anyone who needs you, regardless of the reason for their situation. Thoughtful Mercury was in your sign, and loving Venus was in steadfast Taurus—two more indications of your compassion and charity. Three planets also held court in Virgo, the sign that realizes its worth through what it can do to relieve suffering.

You probably have a long list of people and creatures you've taken in, all of whom love and appreciate you unconditionally. The friends and relatives you've helped will also gladly sing your praises, proudly telling others of your kindness and willingness to help.

In relationships, you'll likely pursue others whose selflessness and inclination to provide support rival your own. As such, generous Sagittarians, humanistic Aquarians, and fair-minded Librans will appeal to you. In business relationships, seek out the company of the earth signs, Taureans, Capricorns, and Virgos, whose keen, shrewd ability to dissemble the motives of others will help you to guard against being used.

Your challenge is to only provide refuge and shelter to those who sincerely need it, never allowing yourself to be taken advantage of by manipulative or misleading individuals. Your gift is your unconditional acceptance of anyone, no matter what their background.

ARIES
From March 20, 11:10 through April 19, 22:22

The Dignified Defender

Born during 1980, Aries, you made your entry into a world that was witnessing a major shift in mass consciousness. A regulation prohibiting the sexual harassment of women by their superiors in government or business was issued by the Equal Opportunity Commission of the United States. Although this new ruling pertained specifically to sexual matters, it paved the way for putting an end to many kinds of prejudice and intimidation.

This event served to display your sign's willingness to champion causes near and dear to your heart, even as it gave you a mighty battle to fight. Since Mars, the ancient God of War, is your ruling planet, doing battle comes naturally to you. In fact, your sign is at its very best when it has a noble conflict to undertake. This strong belief in equality and the rights of everyone to do their life work without being intimidated gives you a worthy place to invest your fire and enthusiasm.

The astrological indications of your urge to defend and protect the rights of those you care for and identify with are potent ones. Your own planet, Mars, was in the sign of Leo, long known for its passion and commitment in the face of struggle. Consider the image of a lioness willing to die for her cubs, and you'll have some idea of the relentless protection, entrusted to you by cosmic influences with which you are able to safeguard those dear to you. Add in the presence of several planets in your own assertive sign, and it's easy to see just how involved you'll become in the preservation of the welfare of others—both personally and professionally. In short, you're an indefatigable ally, an impassioned protector, and an ardent supporter—especially when physically threatening situations arise.

In relationships, you'll want someone whose fire and spirit match your own. The other fire signs, Leos and Sagittarians, will often prove to be your best choices.

Your gift is your willingness to compete in combat on many levels when your spirit of fair play is aroused. Your challenge is to only implicate yourself in situations that truly merit your involvement.

➤ Read about your Chinese Astrological sign on page 838. ➤ Read about your Personal Planets on page 826. ➤ Read about your personal Mystical Card on page 856.

TAURUS

From April 19, 22:23 through May 20, 21:41

The Forceful Liberator

Born during 1980, Taurus, you arrived into a time that would reinforce your sign's earthy qualities, including stubbornness, determination, and resolve—not to mention the forcefulness you display in all life situations. An event that demonstrated all these traits and more occurred just as you made your planetary debut. The British SAS stormed the Iranian Embassy in London, freeing hostages who had been held there by an Iranian-Arab minority group. This act of bravery on behalf of those who were imprisoned shows your innate dislike of any situation in which others feel restrained, restricted, or symbolically "held hostage."

Your propensity to break free of limitations or constraints also shows in the astrological influences you inherited. Over half of the planets in the heavens were in earth signs, all of whose motivation include comfort, security, and physical ease. Your love of these circumstances, as well as your willingness to work hard to attain them, is a strong part of the foundation of your personality. Although others who love the finer things in life may become known as materialistic or hedonistic, you, however, likely won't. You'll somehow manage to maintain an even balance between the physical and the spiritual sides of life.

As such, regardless of your occupation, your conviction to attend to both spirit and comfort will allow you to acquire friends from all walks of life—and they'll all undoubtedly admire, appreciate, and learn from the equal consideration you give to both the tangible and the theoretical. In fact, you may be drawn toward joining groups or clubs that investigate either of those subjects.

In relationships, you'll need someone by your side who's just as flexible, multi-faceted, and passionately interested in a variety of topics. As such, Geminis, Sagittarians, and Aquarians will strike your fancy, as will cerebral Virgos.

Your challenge is to devote an equal amount of time to the pursuit of both the sensual and the spiritual sides of life. Your gift is your ability to maintain a fair and equal commitment to physical and spiritual matters.

GEMINI

From May 20, 21:42 through June 21, 5:46

The Equivocal Benefactor

You, 1980 Gemini, arrived during a time that was marked by the need for discrimination and caution—even when it comes to providing safe harbor for those who ask for it. As you entered the world, the United States was in the process of making a difficult decision. Over 125,000 Cuban refugees had fled to the U.S. that year, and concerns were raised over the possibility that Fidel Castro was taking advantage of America's "open-door policy" to empty Cuba's prisons. As a result, steps were taken to slow the tide of immigrants by making screening more rigorous. The dilemma experienced by the United States is one that you may often be posed with in life—to help others, or to refuse, based on the toll your time and attention will take on the welfare of those family and friends who depend on you.

The astrological influences of your birth month describe both your thoughtfulness and your strongly protective character, as well as the indecision you may feel when someone not in your immediate circle comes to you for help. Communicative Mercury and loving Venus were in the sign of Cancer, famous for its predisposition to provide unconditional care and nurturing to anyone who asks. At the same time, three planets were in cautious Virgo, giving you equally strong powers of discrimination. Although you have a tender heart, then, you also have priorities—and family and long-term friends, who you likely consider family, will always come first.

This doesn't mean that you won't go out of your way whenever possible to provide comfort and support to those outside your immediate circle. In fact, even your coworkers probably have stories to tell about your kindness and generosity.

In relationships, you'll do well to seek out a partner who'll provide clear-headed, rational opinions, yet also share your willingness to help. Look to Capricorns, Aquarians, and Librans, whose objectivity and devotion to family is famous.

Your challenge is to keep your emotional priorities squarely in order, never allowing guilt to influence you. Your gift is your eagerness to help others in any way you can.

► Read about your Chinese Astrological sign on page 838. ► Read about your Personal Planets on page 826. ► Read about your personal Mystical Card on page 856.

TAURUS
Your Personal Planets

YOUR LOVE POTENTIAL
Venus in Gemini, Apr. 19, 22:23 - May 12, 20:52
Venus in Cancer, May 12, 20:53 - May 20, 21:41

YOUR DRIVE AND AMBITION
Mars in Leo, Apr. 19, 22:23 - May 04, 2:26
Mars in Virgo, May 04, 2:27 - May 20, 21:41

YOUR LUCK MAGNETISM
Jupiter in Virgo, Apr. 19, 22:23 - May 20, 21:41

World Events

Apr. 30 – Terrorists seize the Iranian embassy in London.

May 4 – Former Yugoslav commander Marshal Tito dies.

British commandos rescue hostages at the Iranian Embassy siege

GEMINI
Your Personal Planets

YOUR LOVE POTENTIAL
Venus in Cancer, May 20, 21:42 - June 05, 5:43
Venus in Gemini, June 05, 5:44 - June 21, 5:46

YOUR DRIVE AND AMBITION
Mars in Virgo, May 20, 21:42 - June 21, 5:46

YOUR LUCK MAGNETISM
Jupiter in Virgo, May 20, 21:42 - June 21, 5:46

World Events

May 24 – Iran rejects a plea by The Hague's World Court to release the U.S. hostages.

May 27 – Former President Milton Obote returns to Uganda.

1980

CANCER
Your Personal Planets

YOUR LOVE POTENTIAL
Venus in Gemini, June 21, 5:47 - July 22, 16:41

YOUR DRIVE AND AMBITION
Mars in Virgo, June 21, 5:47 - July 10, 17:58
Mars in Libra, July 10, 17:59 - July 22, 16:41

YOUR LUCK MAGNETISM
Jupiter in Virgo, June 21, 5:47 - July 22, 16:41

World Events

June 22 – The USSR announces its plans for a partial withdrawal from Afghanistan.

July 19 – The Olympics open in Moscow, but are boycotted by the U.S., West Germany, and Japan.

Russians make a path for Sergei Belov, who carries the torch that holds the Olympic Flame

LEO
Your Personal Planets

YOUR LOVE POTENTIAL
Venus in Gemini, July 22, 16:42 - Aug. 06, 14:24
Venus in Cancer, Aug. 06, 14:25 - Aug. 22, 23:40

YOUR DRIVE AND AMBITION
Mars in Libra, July 22, 16:42 - Aug. 22, 23:40

YOUR LUCK MAGNETISM
Jupiter in Virgo, July 22, 16:42 - Aug. 22, 23:40

World Events

July 27 – The deposed Shah of Iran dies.

Aug. 15 – Divers believe they have located the wreck of the *Titanic* 12,000 ft below the Atlantic Ocean.

CANCER
From June 21, 5:47 through July 22, 16:41

The Steadfast Rebel

Born during 1980, Cancer, you arrived just as the continuing protest against the Soviet invasion of Afghanistan reached a dramatic peak. The 1980 summer Olympic Games, held that year in Moscow, opened without the participation of athletes from the United States and sixty-one other countries. This was a strong statement of the world-wide disapproval of Russia's military actions. The willingness of these nations to stand up so firmly for their beliefs, despite the fact that the Olympic Games have always stood for international friendship and amiable competition, shows your own determination to stand your ground when your beliefs are tested. As such, along with the unconditional acceptance for which your sign is famous, you also have a strong sense of conscience—and you won't be intimidated into acting against it.

The astrological factors of your birth-time illustrate your commitment to doing the right thing in all situations, as well as the fact that you'll undoubtedly take your time when making important choices. Several planets in cerebral air signs and others in cautious Virgo combined forces to give you a sturdy sense of commitment to arrive at a fair and impartial conclusion. You also have the capacity to objectively consider everything that's involved en route to making your decision. In short, when you reach your verdict, it will likely be based on an equal consideration of all factors—and once you've announced that verdict, you won't be convinced otherwise.

These qualities make you an excellent judge, arbitrator, and mediator. Since your sign is so family-oriented, you may often find that you're called on to settle disputes or quarrels—and your advice will always be respected and appreciated by those close to you.

In relationships, you'll probably be drawn to other Cancerians, firm-willed Capricorns, and solid, practical Taureans. In friendships and business matters, perceptive Scorpios and intuitive Pisces will prove worthy and steadfast.

Your challenge is to find a halfway point between your strong emotions and your keen sense of duty. Your gift is your tenacity.

LEO
From July 22, 16:42 through August 22, 23:40

The Revered Entertainer

You, 1980 Leo, arrived during a time that would serve to provide you with a powerful boost to your sign's famous astrological quest: to perform, entertain, and amuse. In New York, the Broadway theater season was marked by a host of revivals, including *West Side Story*, *The Music Man*, *Brigadoon*, and *Camelot*. All over the world, the entertainment industry was experiencing a similar upswing. After many years, it seemed that people were realizing the value of entertainment—quality entertainment.

Being imbued with these potent energies means that you're likely to be quite choosy about your recreational pursuits. If you do find yourself on stage, it will only be in a proud and dignified manner. But those qualities will also find their way into all other aspects of your life. You're likely to be well known among friends, family, and business associates alike for your high standards, honesty, and trustworthiness.

The astrological influences behind your firm sense of principle are potent ones. Fiery Mars, the planet which describes how we take action, was in fair-minded, impartial Libra, a strong statement about your commitment to resolve differences amicably whenever possible. You were also given the blessing of communicative Mercury in your own sign, indicating a flair for the dramatic, and the ability to hold an audience's attention—whether it's an audience of one or one hundred. Added to your theatrical tendencies, all this makes you a natural-born attorney, teacher, and, at times, stand-up comic. In short, 1980 Leo, you're certainly not boring to have around.

When you're choosing a life partner, then, you probably shoot for someone who's as entertaining, interesting, and recreation-oriented as yourself. But on the serious side, you're also looking for someone with extremely high ideals. As such, you'll most probably end up with a Sagittarius or a Libra—and it'll be a good match.

Your challenge is to get serious when the situation calls for it—but not too wrapped up in your ideals to accept a compromise. Your gift is your amazing ability to entertain and amuse.

➤ Read about your Chinese Astrological sign on page 838. ➤ Read about your Personal Planets on page 826. ➤ Read about your personal Mystical Card on page 856.

VIRGO

From August 22, 23:41 through September 22, 21:08

The Safety Enforcer

Born during 1980, Virgo, you entered the world just as an event occurred that signaled a need for effective safety requirements—something with which your sign has always been affiliated. A fuel explosion at a Titan missile site near Damascus, Arkansas, killed one U.S. Air Force employee and injured twenty-one. The blast left a crater 250-feet wide and forced the evacuation of 1,400 people from the area for twelve hours. In the ensuing weeks, the news in many countries focused on calls for tighter inspection policies at similar facilities, as well as at other potentially hazardous occupational sites. Since your sign holds rulership of both work and health, the mood of the times likely reflects your strong concern for issues of safety and security.

The astrological indicators of your birth time also point to a strong proclivity for caution. Several planets made their way through your earthy, practical, flaw-conscious sign, while both fiery Mars and startling Uranus passed through intense, perceptive Scorpio. All of these qualities mean that you hold within you the potential for working in medicine, but regardless of what you choose for a life-path, you'll be an expert trouble-shooter—and the person others turn to when they have a problem that seems irresolvable.

As such, you're probably quite meticulous, and well organized, especially in matters of business. But that attention to detail will show in other aspects of your life, as well. Be careful of a tendency to be critical of yourself. Although you'll always try your hardest to do the right thing by others, they may not always cooperate. If you don't convince someone to make positive changes in their life, remind yourself that you can't control what anyone else does—only yourself. Move on, and let them learn their own lessons.

In relationships, you'll do well to find someone as devoted and settled as you are, like the other earth signs, Taureans and Capricorns.

Your challenge is to be careful of a tendency toward pessimism or over-caution. Your gifts are your strong organizational and analytical skills.

LIBRA

From September 22, 21:09 through October 23, 6:17

The Devoted Partner

Born during 1980, Libra, you entered the world when the qualities your sign represents were being powerfully demonstrated. The Nobel Prizes, which most recently were being given out during the Sun's passage through Libra, were appropriately often awarded to a team—and usually a two-member team. This shows your Sun-sign's affinity with the concept of one-to-one partnerships. In 1980, the Nobel Prize for Physics was awarded to James Cronin and Val L. Fitch for their discoveries concerning the symmetry of subatomic particles. Now, the concept of symmetry is one that's long been associated with your balance-loving sign. As such, the time during which you made your planetary debut served to perfectly illustrate your strongest, most endearing qualities.

Being born during 1980 also gave you other potent traits, however, not the least of which is your innate capacity for investigation and analysis. You own a hefty dose of meticulous Virgo and perceptive Scorpio—the stuff that expert researchers are made of. In your personal life, these energies add to your need for partnership, and show your devotion when you've made a promise.

As a result, the need to comfort and reassure your partner will be your priority above all else—and will likely be reciprocated just as powerfully. This doesn't mean, however, that friends and family members won't be equally important. In truth, the friends you have will likely be in your life forever. Although you may care for them in a different way, your attachment to them is just as deep as the one you feel for your mate.

In relationships, then, you need someone who can make a powerful and long-lasting commitment—someone whose devotion will match your own. Other Librans will fit the bill, as will earthy Taureans, emotionally focused Scorpios, and respectable, responsible Capricorns.

Your challenge is to remember that you have needs of your own, and to never ignore them. Your gift is your capacity for establishing long-term relationships, both romantic and platonic.

➤ Read about your Chinese Astrological sign on page 838. ➤ Read about your Personal Planets on page 826. ➤ Read about your personal Mystical Card on page 856.

VIRGO
Your Personal Planets

YOUR LOVE POTENTIAL
Venus in Cancer, Aug. 22, 23:41 - Sept. 07, 17:56
Venus in Leo, Sept. 07, 17:57 - Sept. 22, 21:08

YOUR DRIVE AND AMBITION
Mars in Libra, Aug. 22, 23:41 - Aug. 29, 5:49
Mars in Scorpio, Aug. 29, 5:50 - Sept. 22, 21:08

YOUR LUCK MAGNETISM
Jupiter in Virgo, Aug. 22, 23:41 - Sept. 22, 21:08

World Events

Aug. 31 - The series of strikes in Poland comes to an end and Solidarity is born.

Sept. 20 - Iraq invades Iran, initiating an eight-year conflict between the two nations.

Solidarity union leader Lech Walesa in Warsaw

LIBRA
Your Personal Planets

YOUR LOVE POTENTIAL
Venus in Leo, Sept. 22, 21:09 - Oct. 04, 23:06
Venus in Virgo, Oct. 04, 23:07 - Oct. 23, 6:17

YOUR DRIVE AND AMBITION
Mars in Scorpio, Sept. 22, 21:09 - Oct. 12, 6:26
Mars in Sagittarius, Oct. 12, 6:27 - Oct. 23, 6:17

YOUR LUCK MAGNETISM
Jupiter in Virgo, Sept. 22, 21:09 - Oct. 23, 6:17

World Events

Sept. 26 - The highest price ever paid to a living artist goes to Jasper Johns, who is paid $1 million for his *Three Flags*.

Sept. 30 - The shekel replaces the pound in Israeli currency.

1980

SCORPIO
Your Personal Planets

YOUR LOVE POTENTIAL
Venus in Virgo, Oct. 23, 6:18 - Oct. 30, 10:37
Venus in Libra, Oct. 30, 10:38 - Nov. 22, 3:40

YOUR DRIVE AND AMBITION
Mars in Sagittarius, Oct. 23, 6:18 - Nov. 22, 1:41
Mars in Capricorn, Nov. 22, 1:42 - Nov. 22, 3:40

YOUR LUCK MAGNETISM
Jupiter in Virgo, Oct. 23, 6:18 - Oct. 27, 10:09
Jupiter in Libra, Oct. 27, 10:10 - Nov. 22, 3:40

World Events

Nov. 9 – President Saddam Hussein of Iraq declares a holy war against Iran.

Nov. 21 – The "Who Shot JR?" episode of *Dallas* is watched by more television viewers than any other program in history.

Saddam Hussein decalres war on Iran

SAGITTARIUS
Your Personal Planets

YOUR LOVE POTENTIAL
Venus in Libra, Nov. 22, 3:41 - Nov. 24, 1:34
Venus in Scorpio, Nov. 24, 1:35 - Dec. 18, 6:20
Venus in Sagittarius, Dec. 18, 6:21 - Dec. 21, 16:55

YOUR DRIVE AND AMBITION
Mars in Capricorn, Nov. 22, 3:41 - Dec. 21, 16:55

YOUR LUCK MAGNETISM
Jupiter in Libra, Nov. 22, 3:41 - Dec. 21, 16:55

World Events

Dec. 8 – Former Beatle John Lennon is shot and killed outside his home by obsessive fan Mark David Chapman.

Dec. 14 – NATO issues a warning to the Soviet Union to stay out of the internal affairs of Poland.

SCORPIO
From October 23, 6:18 through November 22, 3:40

The Mystery-Lover

Born during 1980, Scorpio, you arrived into a world that was held rapt by a fictional murder—and that fascination was experienced in several places. The "Who Shot J.R." episode of *Dallas*, an American television series, was seen by more U.S. viewers than any other television program in history. The show also aired in countries in Europe and elsewhere, and for weeks, the identity of the murderer was the subject of games, theme evenings, and masquerade parties. Although the content was something quite serious—a murder that was probably committed by a family member—the mystery behind it was what kept the world captivated. This light-hearted global obsession beautifully illustrates your sign's affinity with puzzles and secrets—and you're undoubtedly exceptionally good at both.

Your knack for unraveling a riddle shows in the astrological factors of your birth time, as well. Three planets in your own sign combined forces with four in balance-loving Libra. Together, they give you an eye for beauty and harmony, and the ability to perceive what's missing. As such, you have a shrewd business-sense, keen antennae, and an acute ability to interpret clues, all of which make you a natural candidate for work involving any type of research.

In relationships, it's easy for you to immediately grasp the motives of another—and you won't beat around the bush when it comes to telling them what you've discovered. Your bluntness, in fact, may even put some people off. In short, you're not for the feint of heart, 1980 Scorpio—but then, anyone who appeals to you won't be, either.

When it comes to a long-term partner, you'll need to find someone with an equal amount of backbone and mettle. Other Scorpios, as well as Capricorns and Taureans will probably make good choices. In friendships, look to Cancerians and Pisceans, water sign cousins who operate, as you do, through what they sense.

Your challenges are never to become obsessed with petty details or lose sleep worrying about something you can't change. Your gift is your ability to assemble a series of tiny clues into a solution.

SAGITTARIUS
From November 22, 3:41 through December 21, 16:55

The Beloved Philosopher

Born during 1980, Sagittarius, you arrived at a moment in time that served to show your innate respect for accomplishment and experience—in any field. John Lennon, long known for not just his music, but also his strong opinions on peace, pacifism, and brotherly love, was shot and killed outside his apartment building, the Dakota, in New York City, by a deranged fan. The world's response was shock, sadness, and loss. Lennon's music, early on through the Beatles and then solo, was part of the lives of almost anyone who was alive during the sixties and seventies—and his genius in that department was undisputed. As such, the tragedy of his death opened the world's eyes to the fact that it's more important to give honor and appreciation while an individual is still alive, than to do it posthumously.

As a Sagittarius of this year, however, the planets above you also held several planets in Libra, the sign of one-to-one relationships, including your own ruling planet, Jupiter, the ancient Roman Father of the Gods himself. This gives you an additional boost of partner-oriented energies, which makes you a highly devoted, charming, and entertaining spouse—once you decide to settle down, that is. Your search for the right person may last for years—but that doesn't mean it'll be unpleasant. You know exactly what you want, and what you don't want, and while you may not find the right person right away, you'll gain something from each and every encounter.

In all matters, you'll show an integrity, dignity, and nobility that will win you admiration and esteem. Your presence commands respect in many circles, and your friends are likely to be a diverse, interesting crew, all of whom you think of as more like family than acquaintances.

In relationships, you're on the lookout for someone as partner-oriented and capable of commitment as you are. Direct your energies toward Scorpios, Librans, or sturdy Taureans, all of whom share your longing for a long-term situation.

Your gift is your ability to make and keep a promise. Your challenge is to be honest with yourself as well as with your admirers.

➤ Read about your Chinese Astrological sign on page 838. ➤ Read about your Personal Planets on page 826. ➤ Read about your personal Mystical Card on page 856.

CAPRICORN

From December 21, 16:56 through December 31, 23:59

The Scientific Observer

Born during late December 1980, Capricorn, you arrived just as astronomical data sent back from *Voyager 1* was being analyzed. The spacecraft, which flew within 77,000 miles of Saturn, had certainly done its job. Among its discoveries was the fact that there were far more rings around Saturn than had been previously identified through telescopes alone. These amazing discoveries would help scientists at the time to further their theories on the origins of our solar system—and fuel the curiosity of those to come.

Astrologically speaking, you were given the same traits this event reflected; a meticulous eye for detail, and the ability to investigate, research, and dig. As such, you, born in 1980, are a different breed of Capricorn. Although the respect and responsibility of all those born under your sign were instilled very deeply within you, you also received a strong dose of innovation and futuristic thought. Uranus, the ruler of science, space, and the quality of genius, was in penetrating Scorpio—the perfect astrological recipe for the revelation of groundbreaking discoveries. You inherited all these qualities, along with a touch of rebellion against authority—something you have probably turned into a positive trait. After all, most inventions are the end result of someone trying something new and different.

Your ability to learn a variety of techniques, master any subject, and teach what you know to others means you'd make a wonderful scientist yourself—but you'd also do well at instruction, research, and investigation. No matter what you pursue, however, you'll go after it with an eye toward mastering it—and once you've learned the rules, you'll break them, in order to learn more.

In relationships, you'll need someone whose quest for depth and meaning matches your own—and someone who's a bit rebellious, as well. As such, Aquarians, Sagittarians, and Ariens will suit you.

Your challenge is to stay objective, no matter how engrossed you become in a project. Your gift is the ability to connect the lessons of the past with your curiosity about the future.

CAPRICORN
Your Personal Planets

YOUR LOVE POTENTIAL
Venus in Sagittarius, Dec. 21, 16:56 - Dec. 31, 23:59

YOUR DRIVE AND AMBITION
Mars in Capricorn, Dec. 21, 16:56 - Dec. 30, 22:29
Mars in Aquarius, Dec. 30, 22:30 - Dec. 31, 23:59

YOUR LUCK MAGNETISM
Jupiter in Libra, Dec. 21, 16:56 - Dec. 31, 23:59

World Events

Dec. 23 - Former Soviet President Alexei Kosygin is buried in a state funeral.

Dec. 24 - The former Emperor of the Central African Republic, Bokassa, receives the death penalty in absentia.

Abraham Lincoln, 16th U.S. President

Special Feature

The Presidential Death Cycle

by Rochelle Gordon

A curious, almost eerie—and what appears to be predictable—pattern revolves around presiding U.S. Presidents. Since Benjamin Harrison was elected president in 1840, every president elected during a year ending in zero divisible by twenty has died while in office. Ronald Reagan is the exception. However, had it not been for the sophisticated medical treatment available at the time, some feel that the 1981 assassination attempt could easily have proven fatal. In total, eight U.S. sitting presidents have died, four by natural causes and four by assassination. Seven of these eight deaths fall under the twenty-year death cycle.

Could the consistency of these deaths be a coincidence? The superstitious might consider this pattern a curse. But those who follow astrology attribute this historical recurrence to an astrological event, the Jupiter-Saturn conjunction in an earth sign.

As the planets travel through the twelve signs during their revolution around the Sun,

their relationships to one another are constantly changing. In the case of the Jupiter-Saturn conjunction, the two planets meet up in the same sign every twenty years. In the period between 1840 and 1960, every time Jupiter and Saturn met or were conjunct, it occurred in an earth sign (Taurus, Virgo, Capricorn). Interestingly enough, the 1980 Jupiter-Saturn conjunction was in an air sign. Did this air sign conjunction make the difference in Reagan's being able to survive his term, unlike the seven presidents who succumbed to the "curse"?

In 2000, the Jupiter-Saturn conjunction was once again in an earth sign, making President Bush a candidate for this cycle. We will have to wait and see what is written in the stars for him. Incidentally, this is the last time in a long while that these two planets will meet up in an earth sign. In 2020, this troublesome planetary conjunction will occur in an air sign. ☺

Year Elected	Presiding President
1840	William Harrison (died of natural causes)
1860	Abraham Lincoln (assassinated)
1880	James Garfield (assassinated)
1900	William McKinley (assassinated)
1920	Warren Harding (died of natural causes)
1940	Franklin D. Roosevelt (died of natural causes)
1960	John F. Kennedy (assassinated)
1980	Ronald Reagan (survived assassination attempt)
2000	George W. Bush

➤ Read about JFK in the Kennedy Family Star Profile on page 497. ➤ Read about JFK in "Cartography and the Planets" on page 505. ➤ Read about the Reagans in "Astrology in the White House" on page 705.

Transitions in Leadership: Jupiter and Saturn Conjoin

Every twenty years, when Jupiter and Saturn come together in the heavens, their conjunction signals shifts in power and leadership. The planet Jupiter is associated with the entrepreneurial side of success, which must be applied in both business and politics in order to provide effective leadership. Saturn is linked to the restrictions and limitations imposed by structures, laws, and institutions—factors also necessary for the balanced use of power. A new cycle in this arena begins when Jupiter and Saturn conjoin, reflected in an emphasis on leadership. With both planets in Libra, along with explosive Pluto, the events surrounding world leaders were not all graceful, despite the fact that Libra represents peace and cooperation. Pluto's hand was felt in the numerous assassination attempts that occurred throughout the year. In March, John Hinckley gravely wounded U.S. President Reagan in an assassination attempt. Pope John Paul II was the target in May, but, like Reagan, he survived the attack. These two men were lucky—other attempts were successful. The world was horrified when Egyptian President Anwar el-Sadat was brutally gunned down by Muslim fundamentalists who had infiltrated his military guard—retribution for making peace with Israel.

A more peaceful transition captivated audiences with its resplendent pageantry, as Prince Charles married Diana Spencer, heralding a new era for England's ruling family. Planets in balancing Libra are also good for promoting the equality of the sexes, as evidenced by the appointment of Susan Day O'Connor to the U.S. Supreme Court, the first woman to receive this honor.

Prince Charles and Lady Diana Spencer on their wedding day

President Reagan is wounded in an assassination attempt

President Anwar al-Sadat of Egypt is assassinated

TO CATCH A THIEF

Since World War II, psychics have been used in police investigations and jury selections for civic and criminal trials. This year, investigators consulted psychics to help find a child murderer in Atlanta, Georgia, and defense attorneys for Jean Harris, convicted of murdering Dr. Tarnower, the "Scarsdale Diet Doctor," used a psychic in the jury selection. Although psychics' testimony remained inadmissible in court, lawyers interviewed by *The National Law Journal* foresaw continued and even increasing use of psychics in the legal system.

ASSASSINS AND WOULD-BE ASSASSINS

Muslim fundamentalist soldiers assassinated Egyptian peace-maker Anwar el-Sadat during a military display. Two months after inauguration, U.S. President Reagan was seriously wounded by would-be assassin John Hinckley Jr. In Rome, Turkish gunman Mehmet Ali Agca attempted to kill Pope John Paul II. In London, Marcus Sergeant fired blanks at Queen Elizabeth II during a procession and Prince Charles married Lady Diana Spencer in a magnificent ceremony at St. Paul's Cathedral. In Poland, Jaruzelski declared martial law, arresting 14,000 striking workers. France gained its first socialist President, François Mitterand. In the U.S., Reagan announced plans to cut 37,000 Federal jobs as part of government decentralization. Sandra Day O'Connor became the first woman judge of the U.S. Supreme Court. The high-speed TGV electric train was launched in France. Director Steven Spielberg and scriptwriter George Lucas brought *Raiders of the Lost Ark* to the cinema screen. U.S. publisher De Witt Wallace, founder of *Reader's Digest*, passed away, as did World War II commander General Omar Bradley, Nazi architect Albert Speer and film star Natalie Wood.

➤ Read Andy Warhol's Star Profile on page 665.

CAPRICORN

From January 1, 0:00 through January 20, 3:35

The Skeptical Patriot

Born during early 1981, Capricorn, you arrived at a time that was noted for an event that was simultaneously wonderful and a bit too coincidental to some political analysts. Literally minutes after Ronald Reagan was inaugurated President of the United States, Iran released the fifty-two American captives who had been seized at the U.S. embassy in Tehran in November of 1979. Although the relief of the U.S. and its allies at the return of the hostages was palpable, the timing of this event raised doubts regarding the honesty of the government. As such, you inherited the seeds of skepticism, which has probably served you well over time, teaching you the virtues of discrimination and critique. You also have a strong patriotic bent, however, which means you're often torn between being too idealistic and too critical.

The astrological influences of your birth-time also point to a keen sense of discrimination and order. Thoughtful Mercury, the planet of reason, was in your objective, practical sign. In addition, Jupiter, the ruler of wide-angle vision, and Saturn, whose skill at the other side of the coin—detail—is famous, were keeping very close astrological company. The two in fact were "fused," giving you the two-sided ability of equally appreciating the forest and the trees. In short, you have the capacity to see the total picture and to understand how each component makes it complete.

There is also a strongly skeptical side to your personality, however, especially when it comes to the issue of trust in professional and personal relationships, as well as with regard to politics. Your humor and wit are likely to be sharp and well honed, as well.

In relationships, you'll likely turn to Virgos, Taureans, and Scorpios, all of whom will equal you in your longing for long-term commitment and your powers of discrimination. In friendships, you'll enjoy the company of light-hearted Sagittarians and Geminis.

Your challenge is to maintain a balance between your attention to detail and your ability to appreciate the big picture. Your gift is your innate understanding of process.

AQUARIUS

From January 20, 3:36 through February 18, 17:51

The Technological Genius

Your sign has long been connected with its "computer-friendly" skills and demeanor, and its ability to work in concert with just about any type of electronic device. As such, you, 1981 Aquarius, arrived at a time that beautifully displayed that knack and helped to "program" you with the "hardware" necessary to teach others what you know about the world of electronics. IBM announced its introduction of the personal computer this month, a development that lent legitimacy to the growing computer industry and was destined to turn it into a major economic force in just a few short years. In fact, a mere ten years later, over half of the households in the western world owned a personal computer, using it for e-mail, financial records, and a myriad of other tasks. You may or may not be drawn into work with computers in particular, then, but you'll likely come into contact with them on a daily basis. One way or the other, this major event, occurring during your particular year, put you even more under the influence of your innate Aquarian traits.

The astrology behind that time was also quite accommodating to the development of other qualities that aren't often associated with your detached, friendly sign. Three planets in partner-oriented Libra point to the fact that you're likely to be far more interested in a long-term relationship than others born under your sign. In fact, your search for the perfect partner may mean you found him or her early on, and you've stayed together for years.

In other types of relationships, both business and platonic, you'll usually end up being the objective element—the voice of reason. No matter where you go or what you do, you'll also be deeply committed to making sure you give others the knowledge you possess that they need.

In personal relationships, your search for a life partner could lead you to other Aquarians or to Librans, with whom you'll likely feel an automatic affinity.

Your challenge is to stay in close touch with both humans and cutting-edge technology. Your gift is your innate ability to operate just about any electronic device.

➤ Read about your Chinese Astrological sign on page 838. ➤ Read about your Personal Planets on page 826. ➤ Read about your personal Mystical Card on page 856.

CAPRICORN
Your Personal Planets

YOUR LOVE POTENTIAL
Venus in Sagittarius, Jan. 01, 0:00 - Jan. 11, 6:47
Venus in Capricorn, Jan. 11, 6:48 - Jan. 20, 3:35

YOUR DRIVE AND AMBITION
Mars in Aquarius, Jan. 01, 0:00 - Jan. 20, 3:35

YOUR LUCK MAGNETISM
Jupiter in Libra, Jan. 01, 0:00 - Jan. 20, 3:35

World Events

Jan. 10 – A law prohibiting obscene language in the presence of women is lifted by the Supreme Court in Alabama, U.S.

Jan. 16 – The activist Bernadette Devlin is shot and seriously wounded.

Hostages freed from Iran arrive at West Germany's Wiesbaden Airport

AQUARIUS
Your Personal Planets

YOUR LOVE POTENTIAL
Venus in Capricorn, Jan. 20, 3:36 - Feb. 04, 6:06
Venus in Aquarius, Feb. 04, 6:07 - Feb. 18, 17:51

YOUR DRIVE AND AMBITION
Mars in Aquarius, Jan. 20, 3:36 - Feb. 06, 22:47
Mars in Pisces, Feb. 06, 22:48 - Feb. 18, 17:51

YOUR LUCK MAGNETISM
Jupiter in Libra, Jan. 20, 3:36 - Feb. 18, 17:51

World Events

Jan. 23 – U.S. composer Samuel Barber dies.

Jan. 31 – The Indian Point nuclear power plant in New York is closed when leakages are found.

1981

PISCES
Your Personal Planets

YOUR LOVE POTENTIAL
Venus in Aquarius, Feb. 18, 17:52 - Feb. 28, 6:00
Venus in Pisces, Feb. 28, 6:01 - Mar. 20, 17:02

YOUR DRIVE AND AMBITION
Mars in Pisces, Feb. 18, 17:52 - Mar. 17, 2:39
Mars in Aries, Mar. 17, 2:40 - Mar. 20, 17:02

YOUR LUCK MAGNETISM
Jupiter in Libra, Feb. 18, 17:52 - Mar. 20, 17:02

World Events

Feb. 24 – Prince Charles and Lady Diana Spencer announce their engagement.

Feb. 26 – Margaret Thatcher and Ronald Reagan meet for the first time.

President Ronald Reagan and Prime Minister Margaret Thatcher at the White House in Washington

ARIES
Your Personal Planets

YOUR LOVE POTENTIAL
Venus in Pisces, Mar. 20, 17:03 - Mar. 24, 7:42
Venus in Aries, Mar. 24, 7:43 - Apr. 17, 12:07
Venus in Taurus, Apr. 17, 12:08 - Apr. 20, 4:18

YOUR DRIVE AND AMBITION
Mars in Aries, Mar. 20, 17:03 - Apr. 20, 4:18

YOUR LUCK MAGNETISM
Jupiter in Libra, Mar. 20, 17:03 - Apr. 20, 4:18

World Events

Mar. 30 – Ronald Reagan is injured in an assassination attempt by John Hinckley.

Apr. 12 – The space shuttle *Columbia* is launched.

PISCES
From February 18, 17:52 through March 20, 17:02

The Stylish Rebel

There's no sign more connected to the concept of glamour and beauty than yours, Pisces, but being born during 1981 gave you a triple-dose of your sign's allure. The spring fashion season in all the major cities of the world opened with a burst of color, marking the end of the trend toward dullness that had prevailed over fashion shows in recent years. Suddenly, the look everyone wanted was fresh, clean, natural, and bright. This love of simple beauty may mean you were influenced by the tastes of your parents in early years—especially if they were "Flower Children" in the late 1960s. As such, you may be known as the master of disguise in your circles, always game for a costume party whether it's official or you're just heading out with some friends to shock and amaze the masses. Regardless of how you dress, you'll do it with flair.

A look at the astrology of the Pisces of 1981 also reveals someone with a strong sense of style and fashion. Three planets held court in your sign, including Venus, the goddess of beauty herself. Three more planets were in Libra, a sign that's ruled by Venus. In all, it seems impossible to imagine you'll ever be anything less than a statement.

Personality-wise, you were born with an equal sense of glamour—a charm and attraction that are quite uncommon. No matter whom you're with, they're comfortable in your presence, too. You'll see to that immediately. More important than how you look or seem, Pisces of 1981, is the fact that below that well-groomed, personable surface is a warm, loving heart, and a compassionate soul. Make sure it shows through.

In relationships, you'll likely turn to someone who appeals to your discriminating eye for beauty, such as sensual Taureans or graceful Librans. Don't forget to look below the surface too, though—especially in the direction of deep, passionate Scorpios.

Your gifts are your infallible taste and your knack for intuitively knowing everything there is to know about beauty, balance, and harmony. Your challenge is to come out from under your disguises and let the world see you as you really are.

ARIES
From March 20, 17:03 through April 20, 4:18

The Bold Trailblazer

During the time of your Sun sign in 1981, Aries, plans were underway to make the space shuttle *Columbia* the first spacecraft ever to achieve a "wheels-down" landing, rather than a "splash-down" into the ocean. This tremendous feat showed just how advanced the space race was quickly becoming and just how advanced your thinking would be. You have a knack for learning just about anything the very first time it's taught to you and, along with your gift for communication, that would make you a first-rate teacher as well.

The astrological factors behind this event couldn't help but provide you with an equal amount of futuristic energy especially since four planets, nearly half the sky, were in your sign. Since you're known for your fire, passion, and initiative, it stands to reason that invention, exploration, and new experiences would be right up your alley. The urge for excitement could also reach into other areas of your life—recreation, in particular. In fact, you may be drawn irresistibly to danger, craving the adrenaline rush of walking just a bit too closely to the wild side. If that's the case, be very careful not to get too close. Temper your restless, risk-loving side with just a touch of caution.

Although it's fair to say you're a bit of a daredevil, then, you also have a softer side, which comes out in your one-to-one relationships. Your opposite sign, Libra, was also strongly represented in the heavens when you arrived and Libra, more than anything, craves relationship.

You'll likely take the selection of a primary partner very seriously, possibly staying single for years at a time until just the right person comes along. Along the way, you'll likely learn to enjoy your own company, however, and come to relish those quiet hours of solitude. Independent signs like Sagittarians, Aquarians, and Geminis will be only too happy to send you on your way while they enjoy a bit of solitude themselves.

Your challenge is to keep yourself safe and sound so that your dear ones will have you around for a good, long time. Your gift is a never-ending supply of adrenaline.

➤ Read about your Chinese Astrological sign on page 838. ➤ Read about your Personal Planets on page 826. ➤ Read about your personal Mystical Card on page 856.

TAURUS

From April 20, 4:19 through May 21, 3:38

The Lucky Romantic

On May 13 of your birth-year, Taurus of 1981, a near-tragedy occurred that proved to the world that not even prophets were beyond the reach of danger. Pope John Paul II was shot and wounded by a would-be assassin. Although the Holy Father survived the assault, the days of bulletproof vehicles for religious figures as well as politicians had begun. As a result, the importance of physical safety, already one of the keystones of your sign, would become an even larger part of your nature. This strong urge to keep who and what you love safeguarded may also extend into your work. In fact, in your adult years, you may pursue a career that allows you to use your skills in this department, such as security or enforcement.

In addition to this strong sense of caution, however, you also have a highly refined, romantic side. In addition to having been born with so many planets in your own sign, you were also given several in Libra. Now, both these signs are under the rulership of the lady Venus, but for entirely different reasons. While your earthy sign is naturally interested in tending to the practical side of life—such as building a home, a financial future, and a family—you'll likely feel the need for a long-term partner thanks to Libra. Once you've decided on a career, then—which will likely be your first priority, even in youth—you'll probably spend a great deal of time looking for the right partner to lavish with attention, affection, and the fruits of your labors. Once those areas have been secured, you'll feel settled—an absolute necessity for your fixed, earthy nature.

In relationships, you'll likely be searching for someone who shares your concern with both financial and emotional security. As such, the other earth signs, Capricorns and Virgos, would be good choices, as would home and family-oriented Cancerians. No matter who you commit yourself to, however, you'll be in the relationship for the long haul.

Your challenge is to devote your time equally to the pursuit of emotional and material comfort. Your gift is your knack for easily attracting both.

GEMINI

From May 21, 3:39 through June 21, 11:44

The Imaginative Creator

On June 6 of your birth-year, 1981 Gemini, a competition to design a Vietnam War Memorial for Washington, D.C., came to an end. The winner was Maya Yang Lin, a twenty-one-year-old Yale undergraduate who majored in architecture. Her design consisted of two long, low granite walls in the form of an open V, on which the names of all the U.S. war dead from the Vietnam War would be inscribed. Yours is the sign of the twins, a duality that's beautifully demonstrated in the creation of this monument—but other astrological factors for Gemini of 1981 point to a knack for balance, also well-captured by the design of this monument.

As you entered the world, three planets in your sign reinforced all those qualities Gemini is famous for: creativity, flexibility, and mental agility. Three planets were also in Libra, known for its aptitude in establishing balance and harmony. Combining these two cerebral air signs means you're likely to be unparalleled in your inventiveness and imagination. As such, you would make a natural designer or graphic artist. The air signs are also expert communicators as well, however, so you could also have been attracted to a career in counseling or teaching. Regardless of the vocation you eventually settle upon, however, you'll undoubtedly be appreciated among your co-workers for your fleetness of mind and your wonderful wit.

If you were born on or after June 9, you may have been shy in your early years. If that's the case, you probably spent a good amount of time reading, which would mean that in later life, your knowledge in many areas would be substantial. In fact, you may be one of those people that others flat out refuse to play word-games with because there's virtually no chance of competing with you, much less winning!

Your search for a partner would likely lead you to fast thinkers, such as Sagittarians, Aquarians, and others of your own sign. Charming, cooperative Librans, however, would also make a good choice.

Your gift is easy comfort with a variety of individuals. Your challenge is to finish learning one subject before you move on to another.

➤ Read about your Chinese Astrological sign on page 838. ➤ Read about your Personal Planets on page 826. ➤ Read about your personal Mystical Card on page 856.

TAURUS
Your Personal Planets

YOUR LOVE POTENTIAL
Venus in Taurus, Apr. 20, 4:19 - May 11, 19:44
Venus in Gemini, May 11, 19:45 - May 21, 3:38

YOUR DRIVE AND AMBITION
Mars in Aries, Mar. 20, 4:19 - Apr. 25, 7:16
Mars in Taurus, Apr. 25, 7:17 - May 21, 3:38

YOUR LUCK MAGNETISM
Jupiter in Libra, Apr. 20, 4:19 - May 21, 3:38

World Events

May 5 - IRA hunger-striker Bobby Sands dies in prison in Northern Ireland.
May 13 - An assassin wounds Pope John Paul II in St. Peter's Square, Rome.

An assassin (left) aims his pistol at Pope John Paul II

GEMINI
Your Personal Planets

YOUR LOVE POTENTIAL
Venus in Gemini, May 21, 3:39 - June 05, 6:28
Venus in Cancer, June 05, 6:29 - June 21, 11:44

YOUR DRIVE AND AMBITION
Mars in Taurus, May 21, 3:39 - June 05, 5:25
Mars in Gemini, June 05, 5:26 - June 21, 11:44

YOUR LUCK MAGNETISM
Jupiter in Libra, May 21, 3:39 - June 21, 11:44

World Events

June 1 - The first English-language newspaper is published in China.
June 18 - A vaccine derived from genetic engineering is introduced against foot-and-mouth disease.

1981

CANCER
Your Personal Planets

YOUR LOVE POTENTIAL
Venus in Cancer, June 21, 11:45 - June 29, 20:19
Venus in Leo, June 29, 20:20 - July 22, 22:39

YOUR DRIVE AND AMBITION
Mars in Gemini, June 21, 11:45 - July 18, 8:53
Mars in Cancer, July 18, 8:54 - July 22, 22:39

YOUR LUCK MAGNETISM
Jupiter in Libra, June 21, 11:45 - July 22, 22:39

World Events

June 24 - Moshe Dayan announces that Israel has the capacity to build nuclear weapons.

July 7 - Sandra Day O'Connor becomes the first woman appointed to the U.S. Supreme Court.

John McEnroe wins the Wimbledon Men's Singles Tennis Championships

LEO
Your Personal Planets

YOUR LOVE POTENTIAL
Venus in Leo, July 22, 22:40 - July 24, 14:03
Venus in Virgo, July 24, 14:04 - Aug. 18, 13:43
Venus in Libra, Aug. 18, 13:44 - Aug. 23, 5:37

YOUR DRIVE AND AMBITION
Mars in Cancer, July 22, 22:40 - Aug. 23, 5:37

YOUR LUCK MAGNETISM
Jupiter in Libra, July 22, 22:40 - Aug. 23, 5:37

World Events

July 29 - Prince Charles and Lady Diana Spencer marry in a "fairy-tale" wedding.

Aug. 3 - Air traffic controllers begin a strike across the U.S., causing serious disruption.

CANCER

From June 21, 11:45 through July 22, 22:39

The Concerned Intellectual

Born during 1981, Cancer, you came into the world just as two major medical breakthroughs were announced. A vaccine produced by genetic engineering had proved effective against foot-and-mouth disease—the first of its kind to provide protection against the disease in both humans and animals. Just three weeks later, the herpes simplex virus was successfully suppressed by an experimental drug, acyclovir. This discovery, reported in the New England *Journal of Medicine*, was a major step toward controlling this rapidly spreading disease. Although the protective quality of your sign is demonstrated in both these events, the inventiveness behind them also points to a knack for research, which you also likely inherited.

Along with the astrological factors that show your loving heart, then, 1981 Cancer, one would also expect to see indications of acute intellectual capability and the heavens did, indeed, hold that potential. Fiery, assertive Mars was posited in cerebral Gemini, a planet-sign combination that points to an incredibly fast and strong-willed mind—which means you may also be quite the skilled debater, especially when your heart is involved in the subject. Fortunately, several planets in balance-loving Libra would help you to make amends—once you've made your point, of course. These influences add up to a personality with heart, ingenuity, and devotion, making you a welcome addition to any group, whether for friendly or work-related reasons.

In relationships, you'll likely be drawn to others with an equal variety of interests and talents. Other Geminis; humorous, philosophical Sagittarians; and Aquarians, often noted for their capacity for genius, may make good choices.

Your gifts are many. You have a knack for coming up with a solution to just about any problem through thinking "outside of the box." You're able to argue your point deliberately and convincingly, managing to avoid offending your opponent in the process—and often winning them over to your side as well. Your challenge is to use your varied talents to effect change in large-scale ways.

LEO

From July 22, 22:40 through August 23, 5:37

The Lavish Lover

Born during 1981, Leo, you arrived at a time that showed your sign's love of lavish displays—the marriage of Prince Charles, heir to the British throne and Lady Diana Spencer. The royal wedding took place at London's St. Paul's Cathedral. The event was televised worldwide, a grand celebration of what seemed to be the perfect storybook romance. This spectacular ceremony perfectly displayed the fire and passion long associated with Leos, especially you—as well as its connection to royalty.

Several planets came together to arrange this momentous event. One of them, of course, was the Sun, your own proud, fiery planet, in your sign—its favorite place. But three planets in partner-oriented Libra also contributed their charming energies, to both the royal wedding and the astrological foundation of your character. Since there is absolutely no more romantic coupling than Leo and Libra, it stands to reason that you'll likely never spend time alone—unless you want to. You may not settle down with just one person for a while, then, and along the way you'll likely break a few hearts. But once you've made your choice and committed your own heart, you'll be as loyal as the day is long—and your lucky partner will certainly know just how much he or she is cherished.

And speaking of partners, when you finally decide to choose one, you'll likely find yourself in the arms of either a Sagittarian, a Libran, or an Arien, any of whom would happily provide you with the attention and affection you crave. In friendships, you would do well to team up with Taureans, whose love of nothing but the best rivals even your own.

Although your partner will always come first, your life will be full of relationships. In fact, your friends will likely be just as spoiled as your mate. Your work, however, will also be quite important to you, and you'll probably tend to whatever profession you choose with as much love and attention as you give to your dear ones.

Your gift is your ability to make someone feel truly special. Your challenge is never to romance anyone for the sport of it.

➤ Read about your Chinese Astrological sign on page 838. ➤ Read about your Personal Planets on page 826. ➤ Read about your personal Mystical Card on page 856.

VIRGO

From August 23, 5:38 through September 23, 3:04

The Precise Observer

As you entered the world, Virgo of 1981, a major scientific discovery was about to be announced. The unmanned observation spacecraft, *Voyager 2*, flew within 62,600 miles of Saturn—the closest look the world had ever had at the ringed planet. Launched by the United States in 1977, *Voyager 2* transmitted data showing thousands of rings around that planet instead of the several hundred previously believed to exist, as well as evidence of three additional moons.

The long-term and enduring nature of this flight, as well as the accuracy of the information it relayed to the world, perfectly describe your sign's diligence, attention to detail, and absolute dedication to finishing what you've started.

The astrological factors of your birth time also show that you would make an excellent scientist or researcher—and a good detective, as well. This doesn't necessarily mean you'll work for the CIA or Interpol and you may never run into James Bond at a cocktail party, but you will likely be able to extract "evidence" easily from whomever you like without even trying. Several planets in charming Libra point to the fact that others will open up to you quickly and without guile. Two planets in secretive, perceptive Scorpio show that you'll have a keen eye for observation. As such, you may need to be on guard against a tendency to interview other people rather than actually talking with them. Keep in mind that depth in all your associations, both business and personal, will likely be far more fulfilling than superficiality.

Needless to say, you'll likely have no trouble finding romantic company. In fact, your worst problems, during your single years, may be which attractive offer to accept and how to refuse someone without hurting them. When you do say yes to a long-term relationship, you'll probably find yourself in the company of Librans, Taureans, other Virgos, or Capricorns.

Your challenge is to use your powerful intuition in positive ways only, never taking advantage of someone less intellectually gifted than yourself. Your gift is the capacity to bond deeply with others.

LIBRA

From September 23, 3:05 through October 23, 12:12

The Personal Peace-Maker

Born during 1981, Libra, you arrived at a time of strong emotions for the world. Muslim fundamentalist soldiers assassinated Anwar el-Sadat, the peace-maker president of Egypt. Seen as a tragedy by pacifists all over the world, Sadat's untimely death brought his accomplishments to the attention of the international community again. This, after all, was the man who had worked long and hard to make peace between Egypt and Israel and he'd accomplished it.

The sadness of Sadat's death, however, was equaled by his powerful legacy—peace, a very Libran legacy, at that. The effect of this event, then, however sad, served to remind the world of the importance of several traits your sign is famous for: compromise, cooperation, and bargaining.

The astrological influences at the time of your planetary arrival were equally cooperative with a strong dose of depth and intensity. As you entered the world, the heavens hosted several planets in your own sign and in your neighboring sign, Scorpio. This combination is famous for having both charm and profoundness—and for its subsequent ability to create everlasting bonds. As such, you would likely be an expert in any occupation that allows you to deal one on one with others, especially in the capacity of counselor, advisor, or consultant. One way or the other, your skill at personal interaction will bring you friends from a variety of backgrounds—and every one of them will be only too happy to return your devotion.

Your simultaneously intense and enchanting personality will likely crave company that's equally partner-oriented and penetrating and you won't be able to settle for anything less than total commitment. As a result, sturdy Taureans, other Librans, and earthy Capricorns would make good choices. In friendships, Geminis and Aquarians will keep your spirits up and your disposition sunny.

Your challenge is to find a partner who'll return the everlasting devotion you naturally give to others. Your gifts are your perceptive abilities and your knack for finding the common denominator that will bring opponents together.

➤ Read about your Chinese Astrological sign on page 838. ➤ Read about your Personal Planets on page 826. ➤ Read about your personal Mystical Card on page 856.

VIRGO
Your Personal Planets

YOUR LOVE POTENTIAL
Venus in Libra, Aug. 23, 5:38 - Sept. 12, 22:50
Venus in Scorpio, Sept. 12, 22:51 - Sept. 23, 3:04

YOUR DRIVE AND AMBITION
Mars in Cancer, Aug. 23, 5:38 - Sept. 02, 1:51
Mars in Leo, Sept. 02, 1:52 - Sept. 23, 3:04

YOUR LUCK MAGNETISM
Jupiter in Libra, Aug. 23, 5:38 - Sept. 23, 3:04

World Events

Aug. 24 - Mark Chapman is found guilty of the murder of John Lennon and sentenced to life imprisonment.

Sept. 22 - The TGV (Train à Grande Vitesse) is launched in France.

President Anwar al-Sadat of Egypt is assassinated

LIBRA
Your Personal Planets

YOUR LOVE POTENTIAL
Venus in Scorpio, Sept. 23, 3:05 - Oct. 09, 0:03
Venus in Sagittarius, Oct. 09, 0:04 - Oct. 23, 12:12

YOUR DRIVE AND AMBITION
Mars in Leo, Sept. 23, 3:05 - Oct. 21, 1:55
Mars in Virgo, Oct. 21, 1:56 - Oct. 23, 12:12

YOUR LUCK MAGNETISM
Jupiter in Libra, Sept. 23, 3:05 - Oct. 23, 12:12

World Events

Oct. 6 - President Anwar el-Sadat of Egypt is assassinated by Muslim fundamentalist soldiers.

Oct. 9 - The Nobel Prize for medicine goes to Robert W. Sperry of Cal Tech for demonstrating the different functions of the right and left sides of the brain.

1981

SCORPIO
Your Personal Planets

YOUR LOVE POTENTIAL
Venus in Sagittarius, Oct. 23, 12:13 - Nov. 05, 12:38
Venus in Capricorn, Nov. 05, 12:39 - Nov. 22, 9:35

YOUR DRIVE AND AMBITION
Mars in Virgo, Oct. 23, 12:13 - Nov. 22, 9:35

YOUR LUCK MAGNETISM
Jupiter in Libra, Oct. 23, 12:13 - Nov. 22, 9:35

World Events

Oct. 24 – Demonstrators march through London in protest against nuclear weapons.
Nov. 10 – French film director Abel Gance dies.

Death of film star Natalie Wood

SAGITTARIUS
Your Personal Planets

YOUR LOVE POTENTIAL
Venus in Capricorn, Nov. 22, 9:36 - Dec. 08, 20:51
Venus in Aquarius, Dec. 08, 20:52 - Dec. 21, 22:50

YOUR DRIVE AND AMBITION
Mars in Virgo, Nov. 22, 9:36 - Dec. 16, 0:13
Mars in Libra, Dec. 16, 0:14 - Dec. 21, 22:50

YOUR LUCK MAGNETISM
Jupiter in Libra, Nov. 22, 9:36 - Nov. 27, 2:18
Jupiter in Scorpio, Nov. 27, 2:19 - Dec. 21, 22:50

World Events

Nov. 29 – American film star Natalie Wood drowns off the coast of California.
Dec. 11 – Javier Perez de Cuellar of Peru is chosen to be the new Secretary-General of the United Nations.

SCORPIO
From October 23, 12:13 through November 22, 9:35

The Painstaking Detective

Your planetary arrival, Scorpio of 1981, coincided with news of the need for one of your sign's most famous traits: detective work. Just that month, the Burns Detective Agency estimated that white collar crime in the U.S. alone would amount to losses between $1.2 and $1.8 billion—and that only fifteen percent of such crimes would ever be detected. The ability to take stock of a situation such as this, assess tiny clues that others would miss, and deduce what those details mean will all come easily to you. You may not solve any major crimes over the course of your life, but you'll undoubtedly make discoveries from time to time and uncover mysteries that are astounding both to others and to yourself.

The astrological influences that make up your personality, 1981 Scorpio, point to these and other talents. Your special blend of energies includes planets in Libra, famous for its ability to restore balance to any situation. In addition, you were given the fire of Mars filtered through the discriminating eye of Virgo—in short, a gift for precise, specific observation. You may be so good at investigation, it may become an unconscious habit—for example, glancing in a reflection to see what's going on behind you.

When it comes to your choice of work, it's easy to see how you may be drawn into fields of investigation or research. But no matter what profession you decide to pursue, you'll likely be known on the job as the person to see when a clear, blunt explanation is what's needed. Just be sure to warn others not to ask if they don't want the truth because they'll certainly have it.

Your need for a bit of intrigue every now and then will be fulfilled nicely by other Scorpios, but if you're looking for steadiness, seek out the company of earthy Taureans, Virgos, Capricorns, or Cancerians and Pisceans, water-sign cousins who'll share your love of home and family.

Your challenge is to keep an open mind; never believe that your knowledge of the facts is all-encompassing. Your gift is your ability to assimilate information and arrive at a logical conclusion in record time.

SAGITTARIUS
From November 22, 9:36 through December 21, 22:50

The Determined Believer

Your sign has long been connected with the big issues, 1981 Sagittarius, such as politics, religion, law, and philosophy. It's no surprise, then, that you arrived at a time when religious rights were in the news. On December 8, the United States Supreme Court heard a case concerning the constitutionality of religious services at public colleges and universities. The case centered specifically around the legality of services held in campus buildings by student organizations but was considered to be the most significant ruling on the issue of separation of church and state in years. The debate ended with the Court upholding the student's rights—a perfect example of your love of freedom in all areas of your life.

The astrological factors involved in the chart for Sagittarians of your year also show your determination to pursue the lifestyle of your choice. Several planets in your own independent sign joined with mighty Jupiter, your planet, in intense, focused Scorpio. In short, you're willing to do battle for your rights and you absolutely will not give up until you've won.

You will fight with equal fervor when any of your rights are threatened, from the simplest to the most complex. Your skill with words and your capacity to convince others of your point would make you a naturally gifted attorney, orator, or teacher. One way or the other, education will likely be quite important to you. No matter which life path you choose, however, you'll follow it with determination and zeal—and anyone who tries to oppose you will likely give up after they have seen how fixed you are in your beliefs and ways.

In relationships, you may seek out the company of Aquarians, whose determination to live their lives by their own rules rivals your own. You may also be drawn to intense Scorpios, or light-hearted Geminis, but whomever you choose for a life-partner will reap the benefits of your long-lasting love and devotion.

Your challenge is to fight City Hall only when the cause is just, never for the sport of it. Your gift is your ability to persuade, and it's a substantial one.

➤ Read about your Chinese Astrological sign on page 838. ➤ Read about your Personal Planets on page 826. ➤ Read about your personal Mystical Card on page 856.

CAPRICORN

From December 21, 22:49 through December 31, 23:59

The Objective Thinker

Born during 1981, December Capricorn, you arrived into a time when your sign's objectivity and innate fairness would be strongly demonstrated. A federal judge in Arkansas struck down a law requiring the teaching of creationist science. The theory, based on the Bible, led the court to rule that its teaching violated the United States' constitutional requirement that matters of church and state remain separate. The effects of this decision would be long-lasting, paving the way for the teaching of a more scientific theory on the beginnings of life—evolution.

The astrology of your birth-time shows the impartiality of this decision, a trait you've likely inherited by virtue of several planets in fair-minded Libra. But you were also given the ability to plead any case with ease thanks to communicative Mercury, who was posited in your own sign. Basically, you're a no-nonsense speaker, a just-the-facts kind of thinker, and a force to be reckoned with when you're defending your opinion.

This propensity toward realism and practicality would likely continue throughout your life, making you a formidable opponent and a powerful ally. In fact, when you're called on to defend an issue, your determination will probably be unmatched. As such, you'd make an excellent advocate, public defender, or prosecutor. Whether or not you actually choose any of these routes for your career, you may still find that your wisdom and candor will often put you in the position of helping dear ones make serious decisions—and you'll be only too happy to be there for them.

Your dedication to both your beliefs and the welfare of your dear ones means you'll likely seek out the company of the other earth signs—Virgos and Taureans—but Cancerians and Librans would also make good choices. No matter whom you become involved with, their interests will always come first.

Your challenge is to allow others to present their opinions, never arguing just for the sake of arguing. Your gifts are your devotion to family and friends, and your no-nonsense way of handling even the most delicate emotional issues.

CAPRICORN
Your Personal Planets

YOUR LOVE POTENTIAL
Venus in Aquarius, Dec. 21, 22:51 - Dec. 31, 23:59

YOUR DRIVE AND AMBITION
Mars in Libra, Dec. 21, 22:51 - Dec. 31, 23:59

YOUR LUCK MAGNETISM
Jupiter in Scorpio, Dec. 21, 22:51 - Dec. 31, 23:59

World Events

Dec. 27 – American pianist Hoagy Carmichael dies.

Dec. 29 – President Reagan places a limit on trade with the USSR in disapproval at the Soviets' Polish policy.

Andy Warhol
August 6, 1928 – February 22, 1987

ANDY WARHOL
Leo

Andy Warhol, the father of Pop Art, elevated common objects like soup cans into dramatic visual pictorials. His celebrity portraits featured bright colors that suited the psychedelic inclinations of the sixties. He made over sixty films, mostly on topics too outrageous for popular cinema, and created a world of his own in a studio dubbed "The Factory," which was frequented by the glitterati of his day.

Warhol was a Leo, a sign noted for artistic inclinations and showbiz panache. His horoscope featured a lucky configuration called a Grand Trine, which helped him focus so much of his energy on creative endeavor. Another indicator of artistic talent is a contact between Venus, planet of beauty, and Mars, planet of action. Warhol actively expressed this energy, which is sometimes sexual and sometimes creative. It's quite understandable that so many of his movies focused on sexual

topics and some were quite groundbreaking in their exploration of homosexuality, still a cinematic taboo in the sixties.

With his Sun, planet of identity, contacted by hardworking Saturn, it was natural that Warhol would turn his work into the very substance of his life. His identity revolved around the work he did and thus he had to build his life on the foundation of his art. Interestingly, his scandalous diary that was published to great excitement began as a simple record for tax purposes of expenditures, such as taxi fares, and as he worked on it, he began to add the infamous personal details.

With the Moon, planet of emotions, in the creative sign of Aries, Warhol was a natural innovator. A difficult contact from controlling Pluto made him quite magnetic and intense and a natural draw for those who wanted to be pushed to be even more outrageous.

Perhaps that's why he created The Factory and surrounded himself on a constant basis with the people who interested him. With the Sun, Moon, and Saturn all connected, it was natural for him to filter all his various moods and impressions out through his work. He was an eccentric genius whose very life turned into an art form.

➤ Read Pablo Picasso's Star Profile on page 57.

1982

Insidious Force: Saturn and Pluto

When authoritarian Saturn and explosive Pluto come into contact, they may correlate with the rise of powerful but pernicious forces in world events. In 1982 both planets were in the co-operative sign of Libra, but Pluto, the mythological Lord of the Underworld, often suggests hidden influences at work. The most notable example of such a force was AIDS. The disease was first identified as this year opened and the Saturn-Pluto contact was beginning to be felt. Another such force was cocaine, which was first recognized as a major cultural problem when athletes were discovered to be using the drug regularly. The sinister but powerful allure of cults also received attention this year as Rev. Sun Myung Moon, leader of the "Moonies", was in the news for both tax fraud and mass marriages among his impassive flock. Saturn-Pluto can also highlight the use of force for political gain. This was evident in the Argentine assault on the British-governed Falkland Islands, as well as England's aggressive and victorious counterattack.

However, Saturn also made a balancing contact with imaginative and artistic Neptune this year, supporting the many beneficial trends that Saturn and Pluto can also symbolize. The film *Gandhi* provided a moving depiction of how the determined but peaceful efforts of a visionary leader can move mountains—another illustration of Saturn's disciplinary side augmenting the power of Pluto. Finally in this year, Harrison Ford's *Blade Runner* inspired the "cyberpunk" cultural identity, evoking post-modern images suggestive of the dark, stark side of Saturn-Pluto blended with the vivid pictorial creativity of Neptune.

Russian leader Leonid Brezhnev is succeeded by ex-KGB head Yuri Andropov

Princess Diana gives birth to Prince William, heir to the British throne after his father Charles

HMS "Sir Galahad" ablaze after an Argentine air raid during the Falklands conflict

FORENSIC HYPNOSIS

Forensic hypnosis has been accepted by most investigative legal agencies as a valid tool to uncover information, although its use in U.S. courtrooms is allowed only under very strict procedural guidelines. In New York this year, two women witnessed a fatal shooting. Under hypnosis, one of them recalled the tiniest details about the gunman, including the glasses he wore. Meanwhile, in Israel, a terrorist was apprehended after a bus driver under hypnosis remembered seeing a man's palms sweating as he carried a parcel onto the bus.

FALKLANDS WAR AND TROUBLES IN BEIRUT

The Falkland Islands, a British colony, was invaded and occupied by Argentina, who claimed them as Las Malvinas. Britain sent a task force which successfully retrieved the islands in a short war. Soviet leader Brezhnev died of a heart attack and was succeeded by ex-KGB head Andropov. Socialists won a landslide election victory in Spain. Israel invaded Lebanon in reprisal for the state's harbouring of Palestinian terrorists and drove the Palestine Liberation Organization out of Beirut. Tear gas and water cannon were used to break up anti-martial law demonstrations in Poland. In the first case of product tampering, seven people died in Chicago when capsules of the pain reliever Tylenol were poisoned. Diana, Princess of Wales gave birth to her first child, Prince William, who became heir to the throne after his father Charles. Italy beat West Germany to win the football World Cup. E.T., the Extraterrestrial introduced audiences to the softer side of alien life. Film stars Henry Fonda and Ingrid Bergman and U.S. jazz pianist Thelonius Monk died. Princess Grace of Monaco, the former film star Grace Kelly, was killed in a car accident.

➤ Read "The Enigma of Crop Circles" by Frank Andrews on page 673.

CAPRICORN

From January 01, 0:00 through January 20, 9:30

The Family Historian

Born in January 1982, Capricorn, you inherited a healthy dose of your sign's love of history—and the entertainment industry seemed to have fallen in love with it that year, as well. The 1983 Academy Awards paid homage to two films made in 1982: *Gandhi* and *Sophie's Choice*. These movies took audiences back to notable historical times in the twentieth century. The quality of these productions demonstrates your regard for details and your fondness for record-keeping—qualities that you may well cultivate throughout the course of your life. This may mean you've acquired the position of "family historian"—and you have what it takes to be quite good at it.

In addition to your Sun sign's respect for the past, a major astrological combination amply reinforced these traits. Your own planet, Saturn, the ruler of experience and wisdom, was keeping very tight company with Pluto, associated with investigation, research, and "digging"—both figurative and literal. Since these two major planetary super-powers were both in Libra, the sign of partnership, you probably also inherited the ability to "interview," and a knack for knowing where to find the information you need. Others may turn to you when they're after an objective, no-nonsense evaluation of facts, then—and you'll never let them down in that department.

You may be drawn into a career path that allows you to put these substantial skills to use, such as teaching, historical research, or genealogy, all wonderful outlets for your curiosity and shrewd intellectual skills. No matter what vocation you eventually call your own, however, you'll undoubtedly be an expert at it. Your meticulous attention to the specifics of your work will perhaps also garner you the admiration and esteem of your peers.

In relationships, you'll probably be drawn to signs that share your intelligence and analytical insight, such as other Capricorns, Geminis, and Virgos. Deep, incisive Scorpios would make good friends and worthy professional partners.

Your challenge is to express your feelings as easily as you show your intellect. Your gifts are your keen memory and your "people skills."

AQUARIUS

From January 20, 9:31 through February 18, 23:46

The Straight-Shooter

As you entered the world, Aquarius, the Middle East had once again erupted in violence—but strong attempts were underway to quell the conflict. Ronald Reagan, then President of the United States, announced that he had decided to commit U.S. Marines as a peacekeeping force in Beirut—a move that was seen as controversial by many Americans, both private citizens and government officials alike. The President's no-nonsense response to the hostilities, despite criticism, reflects your own determination to do what you believe is right—regardless of the consequences.

As a result, you may become known as a bit of a nonconformist or rebel, but you may well only display these qualities when you're pushed to the end of your patience by what you view as unfairness, prejudice, or discrimination. Until you actually reach that point, you'll do everything that you can to keep the peace—but once your indignation has been roused, you'll likely be unstoppable as an advocate. Needless to say, you're a devoted friend and partner.

The intellectual fire you'll likely become known for is strongly described by the astrological factors you inherited, as well. Seven planets in the heavens above you occupied fire and air signs, known to be "masculine," or "assertive" in nature. These energies beautifully outline both your passion and your substantial cerebral abilities—as well as your innately straightforward and outspoken personality.

This strong propensity to stand your ground and fight for your ideals shows the depth of your integrity and your high moral standards. In short, although you'll undoubtedly live life by your own rules, your respect for the right of others to do the same will win you the admiration and support of many. When it comes time to choose a partner, you'll need to find someone as independent and emotionally determined as yourself. Sagittarians, other Aquarians, and Scorpios would probably make good choices.

Your challenge is to detach yourself from no-win situations, no matter how deeply and emotionally involved you are. Your gifts are your passion and commitment.

CAPRICORN
Your Personal Planets

YOUR LOVE POTENTIAL
Venus in Aquarius, Jan. 01, 0:00 - Jan. 20, 9:30

YOUR DRIVE AND AMBITION
Mars in Libra, Jan. 01, 0:00 - Jan. 20, 9:30

YOUR LUCK MAGNETISM
Jupiter in Scorpio, Jan. 01, 0:00 - Jan. 20, 9:30

World Events

Jan. 8 - Spain agrees to call off its siege of Gibraltar, ending twelve years of feuding.

Jan. 13 - An Air Florida jet crashes in Washington, DC, killing seventy-eight people.

Death of American theater director Lee Strasberg

AQUARIUS
Your Personal Planets

YOUR LOVE POTENTIAL
Venus in Aquarius, Jan. 20, 9:31 - Jan. 23, 2:55
Venus in Capricorn, Jan. 23, 2:56 - Feb. 18, 23:46

YOUR DRIVE AND AMBITION
Mars in Libra, Jan. 20, 9:31 - Feb. 18, 23:46

YOUR LUCK MAGNETISM
Jupiter in Scorpio, Jan. 20, 9:31 - Feb. 18, 23:46

World Events

Jan. 31 - Israel agrees to the presence of a UN peacekeeping force in Sinai.

Feb. 17 - American theater director Lee Strasberg dies.

➤ Read about your Chinese Astrological sign on page 838. ➤ Read about your Personal Planets on page 826. ➤ Read about your personal Mystical Card on page 856.

PISCES

Your Personal Planets

YOUR LOVE POTENTIAL
Venus in Capricorn, Feb. 18, 23:47 - Mar. 02, 11:24
Venus in Aquarius, Mar. 02, 11:25 - Mar. 20, 22:55

YOUR DRIVE AND AMBITION
Mars in Libra, Feb. 18, 23:47 - Mar. 20, 22:55

YOUR LUCK MAGNETISM
Jupiter in Scorpio, Feb. 18, 23:47 - Mar. 20, 22:55

World Events

Feb. 24 – Greenland withdraws from the European Economic Community.

Mar. 5 – American comedian John Belushi dies of drug overdose.

Margaret Thatcher during the Argentine invasion of the Falklands

ARIES

Your Personal Planets

YOUR LOVE POTENTIAL
Venus in Aquarius, Mar. 20, 22:56 - Apr. 06, 12:19
Venus in Pisces, Apr. 06, 12:20 - Apr. 20, 10:06

YOUR DRIVE AND AMBITION
Mars in Libra, Mar. 20, 22:56 - Apr. 20, 10:06

YOUR LUCK MAGNETISM
Jupiter in Scorpio, Mar. 20, 22:56 - Apr. 20, 10:06

World Events

Apr. 1 – Ownership of the Canal Zone is transferred from the U.S. to Panama.

Apr. 2 – Argentina invades the British-governed Falkland Islands, sparking the Falklands War.

PISCES

From February 18, 23:47 through March 20, 22:55

The Compassionate Protector

You, 1982 Pisces, came into a world whose arms were open wide to welcome another "new arrival"—E.T., The Extraterrestrial. This endearing three-foot alien, whose "heart-light" glowed red when he was feeling love, was a product of the genius of Steven Spielberg. E.T. captured the hearts of millions, worldwide—and would continue to do so for at least twenty years. In fact, re-released in 2002 to huge audience response, the tiny creature's popularity continued to soar, showing the love of earthlings everywhere. The vulnerability and childlike trust that were the cornerstones of E.T.'s "personality" are also very apt descriptions of your own, 1982 Pisces—and you'll likely exhibit those qualities throughout your life.

The astrological indicators of the traits you inherited by virtue of your birth time are strong ones, Pisces of 1982. In addition to several planets in fair-minded Libra, you were gifted with two in humanistic Aquarius, the sign that most adores the underdog. Along with your Sun-sign's sensitivity to the small and helpless, a famous Piscean trait, all these aspects point to tenderness, empathy, and an intense commitment to protect whomever—and whatever—needs it.

Throughout your life, then, you'll probably become known as the person to see when an emergency occurs—for both the compassion and the devotion you show at these times. In fact, you may even be drawn to work that allows you to take care of the defenseless. If you choose such a profession, you may well bcome a powerful and quite vocal advocate for the rights and interests of the cause you support.

When searching for the right person for a long-term relationship, you'll probably be attracted to Cancerians, other Pisceans, and Scorpios, as well as solid Taureans. All these signs would make good choices for both romance and friendship.

Your challenge, 1982 Pisces, is to guard your tender heart, only giving out your sympathy when it's truly called for. Your gifts are many, including kindness, sympathy, and the urge to protect who and what you hold dear—at times, even at your own emotional expense.

ARIES

From March 20, 22:56 through April 20, 10:06

The Guardian and Ally

Born during 1982, Aries, you entered the world just as a mighty military conflict was initiated—an apt representation of your sign's connection to Mars, the ancient God of War. In response to Argentina's invasion of the Falkland Islands, which was governed by Britain, the United States, led by President Ronald Reagan, offered British Prime Minister Margaret Thatcher "material support" for the Royal Navy task force that reclaimed the islands within fourteen weeks. Your basic nature was infused with the seeds of protection, alliance, and cooperation—and you'll likely exhibit those traits often throughout the course of your lifetime.

You were astrologically gifted with a mixed bag of energies, Aries of 1982, serving to temper your assertive character with a strong dose of tact and diplomacy. Several planets in Libra, your opposite sign, also point to a strong need for a primary partner. Added together, these qualities combine to produce someone who would be a potent adversary, a devoted spouse, and a dutiful, loving friend. In short, when you're on someone's side, you'll stop at nothing to protect their interests aggressively. On the other hand, when you're opposing someone, your aggression can be formidable. Either way, there's no doubt that your presence will always be noticed.

When you find yourself stressed out by the pressures of daily life, be sure to find a productive outlet for your energy, such as aerobics, dance, or working out in a gym under the supervision of a trainer.

In relationships, you'll need someone whose fire and devotion match your own. Sagittarians and Leos will be naturally attractive to you, but Aquarians and Librans may feel like "kindred spirits," too. No matter whom you choose for a life partner, be sure he or she is as fiercely independent as you are.

Your challenge is to channel your energy in worthy ways. You can affect major change for your pet causes if you can stay calm, objective, and detached. Your gift is your ability to pull out all the stops in the pursuit of providing your help and support to those you love.

➤ Read about your Chinese Astrological sign on page 838. ➤ Read about your Personal Planets on page 826. ➤ Read about your personal Mystical Card on page 856.

TAURUS

From April 20, 10:07 through May 21, 9:22

The Philosophical Partner

During the time of your birth in 1982, Taurus, an important meeting was held in Britain. Pope John Paul II met the Archbishop of Canterbury, aiming to discuss the formation of a study that might ultimately lead to rapport between the Catholic Church and the Anglican Church of England. This conference demonstrated your sign's need for constancy, stability, and foundation, personally and philosophically. In short, you need to know that what you believe in, as well as whom and what you care about, are safely and securely grounded. And speaking of stability, you're likely quite realistic and practical in all matters, able to form valid conclusions, despite even the most confusing or contradictory circumstances.

As such, when you love someone, whether romantically or platonically, you'll do literally anything to see to it that they have no worries. Your dedication to your work is probably on the same par, making you a valuable worker, an appreciated coworker, and a fair-minded and thoughtful supervisor. You're capable of seeing a project through to the very end, no matter how many others have given up on it—and your persistence in all circumstances is likely quite inspiring.

In addition to giving you an intellectual strength of purpose, the astrological influences you inherited include a strong sense of camaraderie and a potent loyalty to those you view as kindred spirits. Three planets in Libra, the sign of partnership, blended their energies with mighty Jupiter, the ruler of philosophy, politics, and education—basically, all the "big issues"—to make you a force to be reckoned with when your convictions are threatened.

When it comes to choosing a mate, you'll be looking for someone who'll be as constant and faithful as yourself—no easy task. Other Taureans, as well as those born under the other earth signs, Virgos and Capricorns, will be your best bets, since they innately share your love of permanence.

Your challenge is to find a partner who'll appreciate your fixed and focused devotion. Your gift is your steadfast devotion to whom and to what you hold dear.

GEMINI

From May 21, 9:23 through June 21, 17:22

The Scholarly Protester

During the time of your arrival, Gemini of 1982, the battle over the nuclear arms race came to a powerful head. More than 800,000 demonstrated in New York City, proving to the world that although many politicians believed the race was valid, thousands did not—and they were more than willing to make their opinion known. This event, and others like it that occurred during the same time frame, beautifully show your sign's keen communicative and intellectual skills—as well as your determination to convey those thoughts.

Your competence at arguing, debating, and proving your point is striking and quite impressive, described in detail by the astrological influences of your birth-time. Five planets held court in air signs like your own, known for their connection to cerebral ability. With half the planets in the heavens above in your element, then, a powerful astrological statement was made concerning both your mental proficiency and your ability to excel in any field you choose. The knack for investigation you also received from Jupiter in intense, inquisitive Scorpio would make you an expert researcher, allowing you to prove your point with hard, solid facts. In short, you're probably quite unbeatable at mental contests—a substantial intellectual opponent gifted with a quicksilver mind.

Your search for the right career may lead you into a profession that will allow you to express your strong opinions and teach others what you've learned over the years, both through education and life experience. In that case, you could prove a mighty force for change in the lives of others, a worthy use for your cerebral abilities.

In relationships, you'll probably be drawn to airy Librans, Aquarians, or other Geminis. The fire signs, Sagittarians, Leos, and Ariens, will also appeal to you, both as friends and lovers, and keep you fascinated with their energy and enthusiasm.

Your gifts are your unparalleled intellectual acuity and your ability to convince others of your point of view. Your challenge is to find the right cause or profession to keep your fast-moving mind occupied.

➤ Read about your Chinese Astrological sign on page 838. ➤ Read about your Personal Planets on page 826. ➤ Read about your personal Mystical Card on page 856.

TAURUS
Your Personal Planets

YOUR LOVE POTENTIAL
Venus in Pisces, Apr. 20, 10:07 - May 04, 12:26
Venus in Aries, May 04, 12:27 - May 21, 9:22
YOUR DRIVE AND AMBITION
Mars in Libra, Apr. 20, 10:07 - May 21, 9:22
YOUR LUCK MAGNETISM
Jupiter in Scorpio, Apr. 20, 10:07 - May 21, 9:22

World Events

May 3 - British forces controversially sink the Argentinean cruiser *Belgrano* in Falkland waters.

May 18 - Rev. Sun Myung Moon, leader of the Unification Church, is found guilty of tax fraud.

Argentines surrender to the British

GEMINI
Your Personal Planets

YOUR LOVE POTENTIAL
Venus in Aries, May 21, 9:23 - May 30, 21:01
Venus in Taurus, May 30, 21:02 - June 21, 17:22
YOUR DRIVE AND AMBITION
Mars in Libra, May 21, 9:23 - June 21, 17:22
YOUR LUCK MAGNETISM
Jupiter in Scorpio, May 21, 9:23 - June 21, 17:22

World Events

May 30 - Spain becomes a member of NATO.

June 14 - Argentina surrenders to the British, ending the Falklands War.

1982

CANCER
Your Personal Planets

YOUR LOVE POTENTIAL

Venus in Taurus, June 21, 17:23 - June 25, 12:12
Venus in Gemini, June 25, 12:13 - July 20, 16:20
Venus in Cancer, July 20, 16:21 - July 23, 4:14

YOUR DRIVE AND AMBITION

Mars in Libra, June 21, 17:23 - July 23, 4:14

YOUR LUCK MAGNETISM

Jupiter in Scorpio, June 21, 17:23 - July 23, 4:14

World Events

July 1 - The Rev. Sun Myung Moon marries thousands of couples in a mass ceremony in Madison Square Garden, New York.

July 7 - Queen Elizabeth II discovers an intruder in her bedroom at Buckingham Palace.

Spiritual leader Sun Myung Moon sprinkles holy water on couples at a mass wedding in New York

LEO
Your Personal Planets

YOUR LOVE POTENTIAL

Venus in Cancer, July 23, 4:15 - Aug. 14, 11:08
Venus in Leo, Aug. 14, 11:09 - Aug. 23, 11:14

YOUR DRIVE AND AMBITION

Mars in Libra, July 23, 4:15 - Aug. 03, 11:44
Mars in Scorpio, Aug. 03, 11:45 - Aug. 23, 11:14

YOUR LUCK MAGNETISM

Jupiter in Scorpio, July 23, 4:15 - Aug. 23, 11:14

World Events

July 24 - Bernard Hinault wins the Tour de France for the fourth time.

Aug. 13 - Police clash with demonstrators in Warsaw, as Poland remains under marshal law.

CANCER

From June 21, 17:23 through July 23, 4:14

The Royal Relation

During the year of your birth, Cancer of 1982, Diana, Princess of Wales of the British gave birth to her first child, Prince William, who became next in line to the British throne after his father, Prince Charles. This royal event shows your sign's connection to partnership—and your discrimination in that department. In fact, your choice of partner will likely be a major part of your life—and until you find him or her, you'll probably not be willing to stop your determined search. Several planets in partner-loving Libra worked together with expansive Jupiter in intense Scorpio to see to that, giving you the resolve and strength of purpose that would keep you going until you find exactly the perfect life-mate.

The astrological chart for 1982 Cancer also points to a strong need for family, as well as your strong bond with the friends you'll probably consider part of your "extended family." In addition to a love of home and family, however, you were also given a strong dose of independence, through two planets in freedom-loving Sagittarius.

You'll likely manage to somehow be both devoted and self-reliant—and you expect your mate to be the same. This is no easy task, but try to be patient with your dear ones, who may become dependent on your care and support. Keep in mind that those you nurture will need more than help to remove themselves from uncomfortable situations—they'll also need guidance, and the benefit of your substantial wisdom.

When it comes to relationships, you'll find yourself drawn to Geminis, partner-oriented Librans, or fun-loving, independent Sagittarians. In friendships, look to the other water signs, Scorpios and Pisceans, who'll provide you with the emotional support you need to fulfill your life-long quest for family stability and a long-term partnership.

Your challenge, 1982 Cancer, is to be understanding of those in your life who may have difficulty separating their feelings from their observations. Your gift is the ability to create a solid, stable home base for yourself and your dear ones.

LEO

From July 23, 4:15 through August 23, 11:14

The Dutiful Enforcer

You, Leo of 1982, arrived into a world of dramatic political events and scientific achievements. Astrologically speaking, you were gifted with a knack for maintaining order and balance in the midst of a flurry of activity. At the time of your birth, Middle Eastern tensions were high and UN peacekeeping troops were being sent to Lebanon. In mid-August, Israel's Ariel Sharon urged the Palestinians to discuss peaceful coexistence. On July 26, 1982, Canada's Anik D1 Comsat, a telecommunications satellite, was launched by U.S. Delta rocket, a fitting expression of Leo's dynamic and innovative talents.

You also were born with the resolute energies of endurance, determination, and firmness of mind necessary to become a forceful protector when you feel that your safety, or that of those close to you, is threatened. You are willing to fight for fairness and what you feel is your "right" to have. It is hard for you to turn a blind eye on any injustice. As such, you would probably make a good law-enforcement agent, mediator, or judge. Regardless of which path you decide to follow and call your life's work, you'll follow it with passion and devotion, never swerving from your purpose and determination. As an employee, you are very loyal. Any boss would be happy to have your contribution to their enterprise. On the flip side, as an employer, you would demand that same loyalty from your employees, while being very generous in showing your recognition of their efforts.

In relationships, you'd do well to pursue the partnership of Librans, Aquarians, or Ariens. Sagittarians will also prove worthy of your enduring emotions, as long you don't let their humor convince you that they're not taking you seriously or are not totally appreciative of your efforts.

One of your gifts is the ability to know exactly when force is necessary, especially in an intellectual sense. Your challenge is to never let your need for safety interfere with the need to express your feelings. Tend equally to both sides of your personality and allow yourself to trust.

➤ Read about your Chinese Astrological sign on page 838. ➤ Read about your Personal Planets on page 826. ➤ Read about your personal Mystical Card on page 856.

VIRGO

From August 23, 11:15 through September 23, 8:45

The Cautious Consumer

Born during 1982, your Virgo Sun sign's natural affinity with health and safety was powerfully highlighted. The makers of Tylenol, the over-the-counter painkiller, were forced to pull their product off the shelves of drugstores and supermarkets worldwide in order to protect consumers against the possibility of being poisoned. Seven individuals in Chicago, Illinois, died after ingesting tablets that had been injected with a poisonous substance by an unknown person, causing a worldwide alert. The killer was never found, raising the concerns of consumers of pharmaceutical products everywhere, and causing even the most trusting to closely examine each and every package. The "tamper-proof seal" was developed as a result of this incident—a built-in safeguard against this type of attempted murder—and likely saved many lives.

The astrology of your birth-time points with equal emphasis to your need for security in an uncertain world. Mars, the God of War and the planet that rules aggression, was posited in intense, perceptive Scorpio, making you a natural detective and giving you the determined, focused ability to scrutinize and arrive at a conclusion based upon what you've garnered. As such, your capacity to examine details and add the facts together to make a sound, grounded decision is unparalleled—even more so than others born under your sign.

Basically, you were born with an innate skill at trouble-shooting, an eye for tracking down flaws before they destroy the end result you're working toward—and the leadership qualities necessary to delegate duties only to those who show the traits needed to get the job done.

In relationships, you'll likely be attracted to the other earth signs, Taureans and Capricorns, both of whom will share your propensity for caution and self-discipline.

Your gift, Virgo of 1982, is your knack for spotting a potential problem before it causes a breakdown—in both personal and professional matters. Your challenge is to overcome a tendency to worry excessively, despite the reassurance of the facts.

LIBRA

From September 23, 8:46 through October 23, 17:57

The Entertainment Expert

Born during 1982, Libra, you arrived at a moment in time that would serve to exemplify your sign's cerebral abilities—something that's often overlooked in astrological descriptions of your character. You're an air sign, which rules the intellectual side of life and makes you every bit as thoughtful as your Gemini and Aquarius cousins. Still, your overwhelming propensity to find and keep a long-term partner is the stuff that legends are made of, most often noted before the keen mental skills evidenced by the astrological factors of your birth in 1982.

You're also quite well-versed and knowledgeable in the fields of entertainment and recreation, and gifted with the discretion to know what's quality and what's not. Home video games had moved from the cocktail lounge to the living room, a global trend that had proved more valuable than even video rentals. In fact, on October 3 of your birth month, it was announced that the sale of video games had nearly surpassed the profitability of the film industry on a global level. While this showed an increased agility of both mind and eye-to-hand reactions in the average consumer, it also pointed to a need for human interaction, especially in family situations.

In short, your birth-year gave you a love of entertainment that equals your appreciation of good company. Several planets held court in fiery, quick-witted Sagittarius, a long-known fan of fun and recreation. Still, four planets wore your partner-oriented, devoted sign, pointing out your need for one-to-one encounters—and your natural comfort in this department.

When it comes to partnership, then, you're the sign that best understands how to make it fair and equal. You'll gladly "switch gears" when necessary to keep the balance between you and your dear one, at times being the leader, and at others being the follower. Sagittarians, other Librans, and objective Aquarians may make your best choices.

Your greatest gift is your cerebral astuteness, second only to your ability to bond with anyone, anywhere. Your challenge is to communicate your need for personal encounters.

➤ Read about your Chinese Astrological sign on page 838. ➤ Read about your Personal Planets on page 826. ➤ Read about your personal Mystical Card on page 856.

1982

VIRGO
Your Personal Planets

YOUR LOVE POTENTIAL
Venus in Leo, Aug. 23, 11:15 - Sept. 07, 21:37
Venus in Virgo, Sept. 07, 21:38 - Sept. 23, 8:45

YOUR DRIVE AND AMBITION
Mars in Scorpio, Aug. 23, 11:15 - Sept. 20, 1:19
Mars in Sagittarius, Sept. 20, 1:20 - Sept. 23, 8:45

YOUR LUCK MAGNETISM
Jupiter in Scorpio, Aug. 23, 11:15 - Sept. 23, 8:45

World Events

Sept. 14 – Princess Grace of Monaco dies in a car accident.

Sept. 22 – Margaret Thatcher arrives on a visit to Peking in China.

Helmut Kohl is sworn in as the new West German Chancellor

LIBRA
Your Personal Planets

YOUR LOVE POTENTIAL
Venus in Virgo, Sept. 23, 8:46 - Oct. 02, 1:31
Venus in Libra, Oct. 02, 1:32 - Oct. 23, 17:57

YOUR DRIVE AND AMBITION
Mars in Sagittarius, Sept. 23, 8:46 - Oct. 23, 17:57

YOUR LUCK MAGNETISM
Jupiter in Scorpio, Sept. 23, 8:46 - Oct. 23, 17:57

World Events

Oct. 1 – Helmut Kohl is elected the new Chancellor of West Germany.

Oct. 7 – The musical *Cats*, by Andrew Lloyd Webber and Tim Rice, is launched on Broadway.

1982

SCORPIO
Your Personal Planets

YOUR LOVE POTENTIAL
Venus in Libra, Oct. 23, 17:58 - Oct. 26, 1:18
Venus in Scorpio, Oct. 26, 1:19 - Nov. 18, 23:06
Venus in Sagittarius, Nov. 18, 23:07 - Nov. 22, 15:22

YOUR DRIVE AND AMBITION
Mars in Sagittarius, Oct. 23, 17:58 - Oct. 31, 23:04
Mars in Capricorn, Oct. 31, 23:05 - Nov. 22, 15:22

YOUR LUCK MAGNETISM
Jupiter in Scorpio, Oct. 23, 17:58 - Nov. 22, 15:22

World Events

Nov. 10 - Soviet leader Leonid Brezhnev dies; ex-KGB chief Yuri V. Andropov takes over.

Nov. 11 - The first flight of the space shuttle *Columbia* is deemed to be a success.

Literature Nobel Prize winner Gabriel Garcia Marquéz

SAGITTARIUS
Your Personal Planets

YOUR LOVE POTENTIAL
Venus in Sagittarius, Nov. 22, 15:23 - Dec. 12, 20:19
Venus in Capricorn, Dec. 12, 20:20 - Dec. 22, 4:37

YOUR DRIVE AND AMBITION
Mars in Capricorn, Nov. 22, 15:23 - Dec. 10, 6:16
Mars in Aquarius, Dec. 10, 6:17 - Dec. 22, 4:37

YOUR LUCK MAGNETISM
Jupiter in Scorpio, Nov. 22, 15:23 - Dec. 22, 4:37

World Events

Dec. 10 - Columbian Gabriel Garcia Marquéz wins the Nobel Prize for literature.

Dec. 20 - Pianist Arthur Rubinstein dies.

672

SCORPIO
From October 23, 17:58 through November 22, 15:22

The Stern Guardian

You, 1982 Scorpio, made your planetary debut into a world fraught with worry—but you somehow managed to make the very best of it. On November 22, construction of the MX missile was proposed by United States President Ronald Reagan, who simultaneously called for the deployment of one hundred of these multiple-warhead missiles in "dense pack mode," in an unknown, relatively small area thought to be easier to defend against an enemy's first strike. Although the American President's proposal would be estimated at a cost of $26 billion, many felt that it was justified—while many did not. As such, you arrived just as citizens all over the world were making a powerful decision—whether or not to support their nations in their aim to become involved in the global arms race.

Your parents may have been influenced by this event, making your upbringing quite possibly a stern one. In fact, you may have seen your parents as "the enemy" in your younger years, viewing them as the reason for all your problems. In later years, however, you would likely come to appreciate their wisdom and experience—and possibly to apologize to them as a result. In short, you may be quite close to your family after your younger years, despite any problems you had in your youth.

Astrologically speaking, you were given several gifts, including four planets in your own emotionally determined, focused sign, reinforcing your Sun sign's traits and instilling you with the stubbornness and tenacity to become a strong and powerful guardian of the rights of those unable to defend themselves.

In relationships, you'll probably find the comfort and stability you crave in the arms of Cancerians or Pisceans, but other Scorpios would make equally good choices. In friendships or business relationships, look to the earth signs, especially Taureans, for strong and enduring support.

You've been gifted with the capacity to provide your dear ones with an endless reservoir of strength and energy, both of which will prove indispensable in difficult times. Your challenge is to only offer your support when it's truly deserved.

SAGITTARIUS
From November 22, 15:23 through December 22, 4:37

The Fortunate Recipient

Born during 1982, Sagittarius, you made your planetary debut just as your Sun-sign's fondness for taking risks—and your luck in those instances—was beautifully demonstrated. The first successful artificial heart transplant was performed at the University of Utah's Medical Center. The recipient, Barney Clark, was sixty-one years old, and very close to death at the time of the surgery. Jupiter, the ruler of last-minute luck and your ruling planet, was in the sign of Scorpio, a focused and determined water-sign. In both emotional and spiritual ways, it's easy to see just how fortunate you'd be in your adult life. In addition, since Scorpio rules the inevitable, you own the propensity for timing necessary events with an eye toward doing what must be done as soon as it must be done—one of the most valuable assets anyone can have.

The astrology of your birth time shows both your tendency to give and to accept—but most of all, the incidence of the "eleventh-hour" intervention of fate. In all situations, then, you're likely optimistic, believing that the Universe will provide—and the high side of this unswerving optimism is that it will always be with you, even in seemingly "no-win" situations. In a nutshell, it will likely always be safe for you to trust fate. In fact, your trust in the future will usually lead you to a safe harbor and the genuine knowledge that what is given out is received and given back tenfold—as they say.

As such, you are likely one of the most genuinely generous people in your peer group or circle, lacking nothing when it comes to faith in others. Just be sure you're as cautious as you are fair-minded. Not everyone is as reputable and full of integrity as you are.

Your best bet for a long-term relationship is probably with one of the two other fire signs, Leos or Ariens, but the air signs, Libra, Gemini, and Aquarius, will also prove worthy partners or enduring friends.

Your gift is your ability to make friends easily—and those friendships will last forever. Your challenge is to never let your guard down when your intuition speaks up.

➤ Read about your Chinese Astrological sign on page 838. ➤ Read about your Personal Planets on page 826. ➤ Read about your personal Mystical Card on page 856.

CAPRICORN

From December 22, 4:38 through December 31, 23:59

The Frugal Provider

Born during December 1982, Capricorn, you arrived into a world that was concerned with the growing threat of poverty—even in nations that had been formerly thought of as prosperous and successful. One of the most seemingly "comfortable" countries in the world, the United States, reported through its Census Bureau that the number of Americans living in poverty had grown from 34 million at the beginning of 1982 to nearly 35,300,000 at the close of that year. This marked the highest increase in poverty in that country in the last eighteen years—and similar statistics were seen on a worldwide level. Despite the somber nature of this subject, the intense attention to detail and concern for the welfare of others that the Census Bureau's results showed pointed to two invaluable attributes you inherited from your birth-time.

First off, you have an appreciation of just how important it is to mete out resources realistically. Three planets in your own sign endowed you with the caution, frugality, and sensibility necessary to take good care of both yourself and your dear ones, no matter what your financial circumstances.

In addition, three planets in generous Sagittarius provided you with an extremely open-minded, charitable side—basically, the ability to accept everyone, no matter how different they are from you and yours. These Sagittarian planets also tempered your innate tendencies toward being over-cautious and hesitant. So, although your sign's fondness for vigilance is legendary, you have the ability to know when it's necessary, and when it isn't.

Your choice of partner will probably lead you to keep company with the other earth signs, sensible Virgos and solid Taureans, but you'll probably also have a host of high-minded Sagittarians and principled Librans in your life

Your gifts are your discrimination and your ability to know just how much you can afford to give to others. Your challenge is to never allow yourself to be fearful about poverty. In one way or another, your willingness to work hard and share what you have means the Universe will always provide for you.

CAPRICORN
Your Personal Planets

YOUR LOVE POTENTIAL
Venus in Capricorn, Dec. 22, 4:38 - Dec. 31, 23:59

YOUR DRIVE AND AMBITION
Mars in Aquarius, Dec. 22, 4:38 - Dec. 31, 23:59

YOUR LUCK MAGNETISM
Jupiter in Scorpio, Dec. 22, 4:38 - Dec. 26, 1:56
Jupiter in Sagittarius, Dec. 26, 1:57 - Dec. 31, 23:59

World Events

Dec. 23 – The South Korean opposition leader Kim Dae Jung arrives in the U.S. after his release from Seoul.

Dec. 31 – Martial law is suspended in Poland, freeing most prisoners, including Lech Walesa.

Crop circles in the Hampshire countryside

Special Feature
The Enigma of Crop Circles

by Frank Andrews

In the early 1980s, a mysterious phenomenon known as crop circles began attracting public attention. Crop circles are large circles and geometric shapes in varying degrees of complexity that are inexplicably pressed into the grain in the middle of grain fields. They are found in numerous countries, including the U.S., but the majority (a number reaching into the thousands) are located in the U.K., with a distinct concentration in southwest England near the ancient monument of Stonehenge, Avebury, and Silbury Hill.

The appearance of crop circles has understandably caused quite a stir, and much research has been done in an attempt to explain them. They most commonly seem to show up in wheat, barley, corn, rapeseed (canola), and rye fields, but they have also appeared on snow, dust, pine needles, grass, and sand. They tend to arrive in the early morning hours of the summer months as farmers, military personnel, scientists, and hundreds of enthusiasts anticipate their appearance.

Despite the many stakeouts and fields rigged with high-tech surveillance equipment, crop circles continue to appear right under the noses of those looking for them. A few eyewitness reports describe an incandescent or brilliantly colored ball of light projecting a golden beam onto the field that will show a new crop circle by the next morning.

There are those who dismiss crop circles as hoaxes, especially since TV documentaries have claimed that the circles discovered up until 1992 were made by two elderly English gentlemen named Doug and Dave. These men were responsible for some interesting formations, which they made by using planks to smash down the wheat with a cord tied to a center pole. Others have copied this technique, but the truth is that none of the human-made circles can even attempt to replicate the intricate designs of many of the unexplained circles.

Crop circles of unknown origin baffle scientists, who simply don't have a theoretical framework to explain them. While pranksters need a physical object to flatten the plants, invariably resulting in the breaking of stems, no stems are broken in the genuine formations. In these mysterious cases, the plants seem to be subjected to a short blast of heat, which causes them to bend ninety degrees at the lowest plant node, and then they re-harden into their new position—with no damage. Researchers suggest that microwaves or ultrasound may be the only way of achieving this effect.

Another way to tell the difference is that often in the genuine circles the floor will have layers of weaving, with each layer flowing in the opposite direction from the one below. This type of intricate weaving is virtually impossible to create by trampling.

(Continued on page 681)

➤ Read more about Stonehenge in "Gaia's Mystical Power Places" on page 745.

1983

Starry-Eyed about Life: Jupiter and Uranus

Jupiter and Uranus danced with each other for almost all 1983 and colored world events and trends. Jupiter, the planet of expansion and enterprise, inhabited the same patch of sky as unruly Uranus—the truth-seeking but often unrestrained sign of Sagittarius. With so much uninhibited energy abounding, people felt unlimited idealism and an adventurous spirit. Enthusiasm and optimism informed people's decisions and directions sometimes unhampered by practical considerations. U.S. President Ronald Reagan proposed his ambitious Star Wars defense plan to shoot down enemy missiles in space. The truthful aspect of Sagittarius and Jupiter was displayed by a painfully honest American commission, which acknowledged that Japanese-Americans interned during World War II had endured a "grave injustice."

Jupiter and Uranus, both ancient sky gods, love to "push the envelope." When they are linked, flight and space travel are often boosted. In 1983, Sally Ride became the first American woman to travel in space. Society also displayed more progressiveness, as Greek women were given an equal voice at home. African-Americans gained two firsts when Vanessa Williams won the Miss America beauty contest, and Chicago elected Harold Washington as mayor.

However, this combination can be volatile, contributing to religious extremism and can result in violence. This was the case when Hindu-versus-Muslim violence erupted in India in February and continued tit-for-tat throughout the year. In addition, Central American nations were ravaged by brutal civil wars exacerbated by heavy-handed U.S. involvement throughout the region. Saturn and Pluto, although no longer tightly linked, still functioned together. Saturn, especially when tied to Pluto, can be seen in an upsurge in authoritarianism, while Pluto lends an obdurate quality to factions in contradictory positions. When Pluto was conjoined by the Sun on October 23, two Palestinians each drove a bomb-laden truck into the compounds of the U.S. Marines and French peacekeepers in Beirut, killing hundreds. While these planets revealed new difficulties in human interactions, Jupiter and Uranus suggested new solutions.

The U.S. Embassy in Beirut is bombed

Britain's Margaret Thatcher wins her second term in office

Australia wins the America's Cup

TROUBLES IN THE MIDDLE EAST AND LATIN AMERICA

In Beirut, sixty-three people were killed when Muslim extremists bombed the U.S. Embassy. This was followed up by a car bomb at the airport, which killed 243 U.S. troops. American leaders called for the U.S. to remove forces and bases from Nicaragua, but a defiant President Reagan covertly aided the Contras fighting the Sandinista government. In the Philippines, popular candidate Benigno Aquino and opponent of President Marcos was assassinated at Manila airport. Claiming it was a spy plane, the Soviet Union shot down a Korean passenger jet, killing everyone on board. The U.S. invaded Grenada in the Caribbean to expel communist rebels and restore democratic government. Iran invaded Iraq. Protests flared throughout Western Europe when the U.S. placed missiles in England and West Germany. President Reagan reviled the USSR and proposed the Star Wars defense plan, designed to shoot down missiles while still in Space. Australia won the America's Cup. Margaret Thatcher was re-elected in Britain. An unknown Mozart symphony, written when the Austrian composer was aged nine, was found in Denmark. U.S. playwright Tennessee Williams and film stars Gloria Swanson and David Niven died.

➤ Read "The Enigma of Crop Circles" by Frank Andrews on page 673.

CAPRICORN

From January 01, 0:00 through January 20, 15:16

The Spiritual Pragmatist

As a Capricorn born in 1983, you are in touch with the fish-tail that is part of your symbol. You are not merely an ambitious goat climbing up the mountain; you also have a hidden emotional, mystical dimension, symbolized by that tail. You may even sense at times that you are part Pisces. It's hard for you to ignore your hunch that there is more to life than meets the pragmatist's eye. In fact, as your life unfolds, this nagging suspicion is likely to become a certainty.

There was a major riot at maximum-security Sing-Sing prison in New York as you came into the world, with inmates taking seventeen officers hostage. You, too, may find yourself at some point in your life attempting to break out of a prison of sorts, more likely the prison of your own mind. You bump up against the artificial ceiling of your rationalistic thinking, and wonder, "Is this all there is?" In a word, the answer is "No." There is much more to life than the linear quantities of time, space, money, responsibility, schedules, and productivity you seem to hold so sacred. And you, 1983 Capricorn, are so much more than your job. You may come to think that your job is your prison, but that is not the case. It is how you are looking at it. But you have every likelihood of discovering new, more independent, liberated approaches to generating income for yourself.

As you were born, the Catholic Church expanded women's rights in an effort to keep up with the times. Growing up in this climate of progress and growing respect for the feminine within traditional religious communities is an advantage for your own spiritual growth. It can help you shift from an overtly ambitious approach to the question of enlightenment, to a gentler process of opening your heart.

An upbeat creative Leo can help uncover new sources of income, and a sexy innovative Aquarius can help you have fun as you maximize the opportunity.

Your greatest challenge is to let go of your bottom-line approach to every aspect of life, and your greatest strength is your ability to boil fluff down to its pure essence.

AQUARIUS

From January 20, 15:17 through February 19, 5:30

The Cooperative Competitor

As a 1983 Aquarius, you come to life in democratic, cooperative group situations even more than most. Group associations bring out your visionary, humanitarian best. You tend to renounce competition and conflict, emphasizing teamwork over leadership. In February, in a clear-cut case of "If you can't beat 'em, join 'em," General Motors announced an unprecedented decision to team up with Toyota. The jointly owned production company planned to build a subcompact car in the United States, using Toyota's highly cooperative and efficient manufacturing methods. You tend to seek out similar opportunities for synergy with the other side rather than fighting it out to the bitter end.

It was announced in early February that a 1765 musical manuscript uncovered in Denmark in 1943 was actually the first symphony ever composed by Wolfgang Amadeus Mozart. He was nine years old when he wrote it. You may not be quite as prodigious as Mozart, but your creativity is one of your greatest resources. Whether your medium is music (a distinct possibility) or business, your creativity could be one of your best money-makers. Your willingness to take reasonable creative and financial risks pays handsome dividends in both sectors, and you continue to hone your technique as you develop.

Because authority issues and power struggles are likely to be a source of irritation to you, you might do well to maintain your independence and work as a freelancer or consultant. You perform best when left to your own devices to design your own structures. This happens best when a unique structure is permitted to emerge naturally and organically out of whatever you are creating, rather than being externally imposed.

If you are ever feeling gloomy, an optimistic Sagittarian points to the light at the end of the tunnel. Sex might be a downright mystical experience with a Piscean mate, while an ambitious Scorpio keeps you on task.

Your greatest asset is your creative approach to turning your enemies into partners, and your greatest challenge is to learn to value and enjoy competition, which can be every bit as productive as cooperation.

► Read about your Chinese Astrological sign on page 838. ► Read about your Personal Planets on page 826. ► Read about your personal Mystical Card on page 856.

CAPRICORN
Your Personal Planets

YOUR LOVE POTENTIAL
Venus in Capricorn, Jan. 01, 0:00 - Jan. 05, 17:57
Venus in Aquarius, Jan. 05, 17:58 - Jan. 20, 15:16

YOUR DRIVE AND AMBITION
Mars in Aquarius, Jan. 01, 0:00 - Jan. 17, 13:09
Mars in Pisces, Jan. 17, 13:10 - Jan. 20, 15:16

YOUR LUCK MAGNETISM
Jupiter in Sagittarius, Jan. 01, 0:00 - Jan. 20, 15:16

World Events

Jan. 8 – Margaret Thatcher arrives on a four-day visit to the Falkland Islands.

Jan. 19 – Women's rights are expanded in the eyes of the Catholic Church, according to a new code introduced in Rome.

Former Gestapo official Klaus Barbie back in Lyon, France

AQUARIUS
Your Personal Planets

YOUR LOVE POTENTIAL
Venus in Aquarius, Jan. 20, 15:17 - Jan. 29, 17:30
Venus in Pisces, Jan. 29, 17:31 - Feb. 19, 5:30

YOUR DRIVE AND AMBITION
Mars in Pisces, Jan. 20, 15:17 - Feb. 19, 5:30

YOUR LUCK MAGNETISM
Jupiter in Sagittarius, Jan. 20, 15:17 - Feb. 19, 5:30

World Events

Jan. 25 – Nazi Klaus Barbie, the "Butcher of Lyons," is arrested in Bolivia.

Jan. 25 – The IRAS space probe is launched to study infra-red radiation in the cosmos.

675

1983

PISCES
Your Personal Planets

YOUR LOVE POTENTIAL

Venus in Pisces, Feb. 19, 5:31 - Feb. 22, 21:34
Venus in Aries, Feb. 22, 21:35 - Mar. 19, 9:50
Venus in Taurus, Mar. 19, 9:51 - Mar. 21, 4:38

YOUR DRIVE AND AMBITION

Mars in Pisces, Feb. 19, 5:31 - Feb. 25, 0:18
Mars in Aries, Feb. 25, 0:19 - Mar. 21, 4:38

YOUR LUCK MAGNETISM

Jupiter in Sagittarius, Feb. 19, 5:31 - Mar. 21, 4:38

World Events

Feb. 20 – More than 600 Muslims are slain in Assam.

Feb. 28 – The final episode of the Korean War medical comedy *M*A*S*H* is watched by the largest television audience in U.S. history.

U.S. President Ronald Reagan with his wife Nancy

ARIES
Your Personal Planets

YOUR LOVE POTENTIAL

Venus in Taurus, Mar. 21, 4:39 - Apr. 13, 11:25
Venus in Gemini, Apr. 13, 11:26 - Apr. 20, 15:49

YOUR DRIVE AND AMBITION

Mars in Aries, Mar. 21, 4:39 - Apr. 05, 14:02
Mars in Taurus, Apr. 05, 14:03 - Apr. 20, 15:49

YOUR LUCK MAGNETISM

Jupiter in Sagittarius, Mar. 21, 4:39 - Apr. 20, 15:49

World Events

Mar. 23 – President Reagan proposes a "Star Wars" defense plan, to build a missile shield for the U.S.

Apr. 18 – The U.S. embassy is bombed in Beirut, killing sixty-eight people.

PISCES
From February 19, 5:31 through March 21, 4:38

The Anti-Materialist

You were born, 1983 Pisces, as the world searched for viable solutions to challenging problems. Always concerned with achieving the greatest good for the largest number of people, you will work for positive changes in society through education, law, and politics. However, if socially sanctioned methods fail, you will not hesitate to engage in peaceful demonstrations for your cause. On March 14, 1983, 2,000 Israeli doctors went on a hunger strike in pursuit of a pay raise. It was not until June 26 of the same year that the government agreed to independent arbitration.

Like all Pisceans, you tend to feel "different," and to empathize with the lot of the outsider and the underdog. You may feel called to do work that rights old wrongs, and heals old wounds. The internment of Japanese-Americans during World War II was finally declared unjust in February 1983. You cannot abide by injustice because you feel other's pain as if it exists in your very own heart. You are ruled by the ethereal planet Neptune, and this gives you a direct connection to the dream world, almost as if there are no boundaries between what is and what can be. You can manifest anything that you imagine, and you probably find yourself caught up in daydreams of saving the world. You can do it, too, 1983 Pisces. Only in America: as you were born, the Supreme Court ruled that Parker Brothers, manufacturers of the board game Monopoly, could not stop another company from marketing a game called Anti-Monopoly. As one who tends to forgo personal wealth in lieu of more altruistic, creative, or spiritual values, you would probably like this game. Even if you do not disdain success, you enjoy the alternative perspective on materialistic values.

You feel grounded and at-home with a cozy Taurus, and inspired to new heights by a lofty-minded Sagittarius. But as they say, nobody truly understands a Pisces like another Pisces.

Your greatest challenge is to use your charismatic charm and favor with the gods for the power of good, and your greatest gift is your sympathy for the ever-shape-shifting scapegoat, the smallest fish of the moment.

ARIES
From March 21, 4:39 through April 20, 15:49

The Guided Missile

Aries is the Greek name for the God of War, and in astrology Aries is said to be ruled by the planet Mars, named for the Roman God of War. At the time of your birth, the planet Mars was in the sign of Aries, an emphasis making 1983 Aries even more bellicose than usual. Indeed, as you were born, American President Reagan unveiled his hi-tech military "vision of the future": Star Wars. Rather than retaliation, the elaborate system would offer a protective shield, involving the defensive use of lasers, microwave devices, particle beams, and projectile beams directed from satellites to shoot down Soviet missiles before they could strike American soil.

In a very different expression of power, in April a human chain fourteen miles long was formed by anti-nuclear protesters in England. If you don't end up using your talent for hi-tech communications serving the military (which did, after all, invent the Internet), you could be a powerful voice for peace. You would also do well as a successful multimedia artist, bringing art and technology together in new ways. Or, you may simply bring it all together in some martial art form in your spare time. It is important to learn constructive ways to direct your fiery energy in order to reach your goals, whatever they may be. In addition to your sheer natural force, you possess the discipline to develop skill and precision.

You also have quite a way with money, generating your own resources and employing those of others. With maturity and the right partners, you are able to combine your courage and boldness with the patience to build your financial structures methodically and steadily. You learn the art of waiting patiently, like a cobra poised to strike, for the right opportunity to present itself. You will know it when it comes.

A far-sighted Sagittarius broadens your horizons, but a focused Scorpio helps you zero in on your targets. A stabilizing Taurus steadies your aim to reach them.

Your greatest challenge is to ask questions before you shoot, and to choose your goals carefully. Your deadly aim becomes your greatest strength.

➤ Read about your Chinese Astrological sign on page 838. ➤ Read about your Personal Planets on page 826. ➤ Read about your personal Mystical Card on page 856.

TAURUS

From April 20, 15:50 through May 21, 15:05

The Creative Accountant

The 1983 Taurus is all about partnership, romantic, financial and otherwise. While it may be argued that all relationships are karmic, yours are bound to palpably feel karmic. This means that you can actually tell that you are learning some of your greatest life lessons in this area of your life, and can look to your relationships for guidance the way a dancer consults a mirror. Indeed, your relationships will be mirrors, showing you at times the back of your own head.

Once you learn to recognize yourself in the reflection, the shadowboxing can become a liberating dance, opening up all kinds of creative possibilities. You may literally form a creative partnership, for instance a writing team, which stands to become extremely successful and lucrative. Being very well coordinated, athletics or dance are distinct possibilities for you. You were born as George Balanchine died. The Russian-born choreographer, considered to be one of the founders of modern dance, was able to combine his agility, creativity, and ability to communicate.

At the end of May, a special commission in Washington called the U.S. standard of education so poor that a "tide of mediocrity" threatened the country. If you felt called to the work, you would make a gifted, loving, and creative teacher. Your communication skills can certainly be put to good use in the classroom, stimulating and motivating your students. Beyond that immediate use, your inspiring way with words can also be applied to the larger purposes of fundraising and awareness-raising. You stand a good chance of helping to direct some creative financing toward your own community's efforts, through innovative partnerships and sponsorships, perhaps with the business sector.

A poetic Gemini inspires your imagination and points out lucrative opportunities. A free-spirited Sagittarius supports your sense of possibility and may even help finance your dreams and schemes.

Your greatest challenge is to recognize your own shadow, and your greatest gift is your ability to combine your creative way with words with your creative way with finances.

GEMINI

From May 21, 15:06 through June 21, 23:08

The Well-Tempered Collaborator

The Gemini crop that came in under 1983 skies is especially innovative and original, as well as daring and adventurous. You have boundless energy, likely at times to take the form of violent outbursts. Once you learn to control this explosive force, it can propel you forward like a rocket. Born as Sally Ride, a physicist, became the first American woman to go into space, you too combine the courage of a warrior in battle with the imaginative vision of an inventor at work. You are able to do pretty much whatever you put your mind to, so the sky may literally be the limit for you guys.

You work best with partners who share or spark your innovative vision, and together you become a whole that is much greater than the sum of your individual parts. By grounding a connection for you between Point A and Point B, partnerships help you channel your incredible power toward a higher ideal, rather than just exploding in mid-air, or worse, right in your own lap. Once you learn to control your inner tensions and hot temper, you develop a nearly mechanical sense of timing and you are capable of great things, especially when working with others.

On May 24, the Brooklyn Bridge celebrated its hundredth birthday, marking the anniversary of what was hailed as the greatest engineering feat of its age.

At the time, it was not only the tallest structure along New York's skyline, it was the longest suspension bridge in the world. Along with brilliant and daring design, it required many years of teamwork to complete. Its Gothic cathedral towers, graceful expanse, and harp-like web of cables inspired the poet Hart Crane to muse, "How could mere toil align thy choiring strings." Like all Geminis, writing is one of your strong suits. Your style is especially forceful and expansive, well-suited for debate and rhetoric.

An inspirational Sagittarius encourages you to reach for the stars, while a caring Cancer keeps you coming home again.

Your greatest challenge is to discover a meaningful purpose to which to dedicate your prodigious talents, and your greatest gift is your genius for synergy with others.

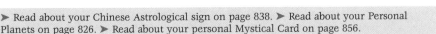

➤ Read about your Chinese Astrological sign on page 838. ➤ Read about your Personal Planets on page 826. ➤ Read about your personal Mystical Card on page 856.

1983

TAURUS
Your Personal Planets

YOUR LOVE POTENTIAL
Venus in Gemini, Apr. 20, 15:50 - May 09, 10:55
Venus in Cancer, May 09, 10:56 - May 21, 15:05

YOUR DRIVE AND AMBITION
Mars in Taurus, Apr. 20, 15:50 - May 16, 21:42
Mars in Gemini, May 16, 21:43 - May 21, 15:05

YOUR LUCK MAGNETISM
Jupiter in Sagittarius, Apr. 20, 15:50 - May 21, 15:05

World Events

Apr. 30 – Russian choreographer George Balanchine dies.

May 4 – The Communist Party in Iran is dissolved; eighteen Soviet diplomats are ordered to leave.

Death of Russian choreographer George Balanchine

GEMINI
Your Personal Planets

YOUR LOVE POTENTIAL
Venus in Cancer, May 21, 15:06 - June 06, 6:03
Venus in Leo, June 06, 6:04 - June 21, 23:08

YOUR DRIVE AND AMBITION
Mars in Gemini, May 21, 15:06 - June 21, 23:08

YOUR LUCK MAGNETISM
Jupiter in Sagittarius, May 21, 15:06 - June 21, 23:08

World Events

June 9 – The Conservative Party is re-elected in Britain.

June 13 – The U.S. probe *Pioneer 10* becomes the first spacecraft to leave the Solar System.

1983

CANCER
Your Personal Planets

YOUR LOVE POTENTIAL

Venus in Leo, June 21, 23:09 - July 10, 5:24
Venus in Virgo, July 10, 5:25 - July 23, 10:03

YOUR DRIVE AND AMBITION

Mars in Gemini, June 21, 23:09 - June 29, 6:53
Mars in Cancer, June 29, 6:54 - July 23, 10:03

YOUR LUCK MAGNETISM

Jupiter in Sagittarius, June 21, 23:09 - July 23, 10:03

World Events

July 3 - John McEnroe takes the men's Wimbledon tennis title.

July 23 - Civil war breaks out between the Tamils and the Singhalese in Sri Lanka.

Benigno Aquino is assassinated in Manila upon his return from exile

LEO
Your Personal Planets

YOUR LOVE POTENTIAL

Venus in Virgo, July 23, 10:04 - Aug. 23, 17:06

YOUR DRIVE AND AMBITION

Mars in Cancer, July 23, 10:04 - Aug. 13, 16:53
Mars in Leo, Aug. 13, 16:54 - Aug. 23, 17:06

YOUR LUCK MAGNETISM

Jupiter in Sagittarius, July 23, 10:04 - Aug. 23, 17:06

World Events

Aug. 12 - Rioters in Chile are viciously attacked by members of the Pinochet regime.

Aug. 21 - Benigno Aquino Jr., the main political rival of Philippine President Ferdinand Marcos, is gunned down at Manila airport on his return from exile.

CANCER
From June 21, 23:09 through July 23, 10:03

The Humanitarian Inventor

The American engineer Buckminster Fuller died around the time you were born, 1983 Cancer, and hopefully your fellow Cancerian passed some of his secrets on to you. The inventor of the geodesic dome had a humanitarian vision to match his ingenuity, and his creations were humble offerings to the average person for a better life. He also sought to empower the impoverished in New York City with simple yet unheard-of alternatives like windmill power and greenhouses on their tenement rooftops.

You are likely to bring a similar caring dimension to your own amazing unconventional creativity, which serves you best when it serves others best. You are likely to excel at using if not inventing high-end communications technology, pushing the envelope wherever the edge is at any given time. You could be called to work behind the scenes on some top-secret project, such as developing military applications or corporate espionage. Or, you could devote your energies to a philanthropic endeavor. You were also born as the U.S. Senate voted in favour of a Partial-Birth Abortion ban. As a nurturing Cancer, you cherish all life, especially human life, and you may grow up to agree, or disagree, with that decision. Whatever your beliefs, you appreciate the democratic process that permits the dialogue to evolve. You may be motivated at some point to put your own considerable argumentative powers to the service of some great debate, and would do well to consider a career in law or even legislature. Again, your mental abilities serve you best when you are serving a larger cause. Your big-picture thinking encompasses multiple perspectives, and you are guided by a profound sense of fairness.

A fiery Leo not only turns you on romantically, but turns you on to great financial opportunities. Scorpio understands your deeply emotional make-up, and helps you focus your creative energies.

Your greatest challenge is to make your actions consistent with your values as you choose to define them, and your greatest gifts are your enormous originality and sense of humanity.

LEO
From July 23, 10:04 through August 23, 17:06

The Covert Operator

As you were born, 1983 Leo, the principal rival of Philippine President Marcos, Benigno Aquino, was assassinated at Manila Airport, as he disembarked from his plane under military escort. After months of controversy, on July 28 the U.S. House of Representatives voted to halt President Reagan's covert aid to the Nicaraguan Contras who were fighting against the Sandinista regime. The President insisted the rebels were "freedom fighters." A poll released on July 1 showed that most Americans didn't even know who the U.S. was supporting in Central America.

If at points in your life you find yourself involved in complex situations that seem like covert warfare, you will have your Mars (the planet of aggression) in your house of hidden enemies to thank. You do have the choice, however, to bring conflicts out into the open, and defuse them. While hopefully you will not be dodging real-life bullets, you may face surprise attacks and underhanded tactics from your rivals. And you may well have rivals, open and hidden, good-natured and hostile. Your subtle strategic ability serves you well in negotiating these touchy situations.

An enormous creativity and a magic wand when it comes to your investments are likely to engender the envy of others. You not only think big, you risk big, and you tend to win big. Your best bet is to exercise your well-known Leonine generosity and share your success with others, even your competitors, if possible. You might even be able to make a pre-emptive strike and head off any ambushes by joining forces with the competition. This might be called covert cooperation.

A wily Cancer can help you scheme behind the scenes. A refined Virgo helps you put the finishing touches on financial proposals, while a fiery Sagittarius ignites your passions, creatively and otherwise.

Your greatest challenge is to acknowledge and express your often hidden anger, which then becomes your strongest ally. Your greatest gift is your lucky King Midas touch in your creative risks.

➤ Read about your Chinese Astrological sign on page 838. ➤ Read about your Personal Planets on page 826. ➤ Read about your personal Mystical Card on page 856.

VIRGO

From August 23, 17:07 through September 23, 14:41

The Disciplined Rebel

With Venus, the planet of beauty, conjunct your Sun, you are likely to be extremely attractive, 1983 Virgo. And with freedom-loving Jupiter buddying up with rebellious Uranus to form a challenging aspect to your Sun and Venus, you are likely to be unusually open-minded for a Virgo. You were born as Vanessa Williams was voted the first African American Miss America. Ms. Williams's reign was short-lived, however, as she was to hand in her resignation—another first in the history of the pageant—in July 1984, when nude photographs of her taken years before were published in *Penthouse* magazine. But then, how many Miss Americas do any of us remember by name? You may have a similar experience of "bad" publicity being better than no publicity; or, maybe even better than good publicity.

You were born as another African American achieved another "first," when Lieutenant Colonel Guion S. Bluford, USAF, became an astronaut aboard the *Challenger* space shuttle. This accomplishment may relate more to the harmonious aspect between your Sun and powerful, focused Pluto conjunct serious, disciplined Saturn. These qualities, favorable for a military officer (which may have helped Bluford to qualify), are in strong evidence in your chart. Your own powers of concentration are likely to be directed toward financial goals with great success.

You are indeed blessed with an interesting mix of discipline and rebelliousness; seriousness and playfulness; conservatism and wildness, 1983 Virgo. You long for freedom, but also for commitment and structure. It may challenge your creativity to blend these qualities into a lifestyle that satisfies all of these needs, but this is by no means impossible. It is a call to individuation, to define oneself in one's own terms.

A Leo may awaken secret passions within you, while an understanding Pisces balances your analytical thinking with sensitive feeling. Your more liberated side feels at home with a freedom-loving Sagittarius.

Your greatest challenge is to weigh your need for freedom of expression against your need for approval, and your greatest asset is your fierce concentration.

LIBRA

From September 23, 14:42 through October 23, 23:53

Ben Lexcen with the America's Cup trophy

The Ecumenical Seeker

When you were born, 1983 Libra, there was a concentration of planets in your house of the intellect. Throughout your lifetime, your thinking is stimulated by three of the "heavies": Jupiter, which rules society, orthodox religion, and law; Uranus, which represents originality, direct inspiration, and radical breaks with tradition; and third, the mysterious planet Neptune, which rules spirituality, mysticism, metaphysics, and transcendence. You may well find yourself pondering questions of theology and the meaning of life professionally.

In October, the National Council of Churches released a new translation of the Bible in which gender references to God were indistinct, and God was referred to as both Father and Mother. The Lutheran and Greek Orthodox Churches refused to use the new translation, citing its inaccuracy and irreverence. Apparently these churches are not familiar with the original Hebrew text, which also does not define God as male. Thankfully, these days direct translations from the Hebrew are simply disdained, and not punishable by death, as was the case in 1536, when William Tyndale was burned at the stake for his unauthorized translation of the New Testament into English. You, too, are likely to show a scholarly disposition, with an interest in and talent for languages, cultures, and world religions. If you don't personally get your hands on the Dead Sea Scrolls, you may still enjoy the questions they raised when they were discovered.

You may also turn your remarkable intellect toward more practical considerations. October 1 marked the seventy-fifth anniversary of Henry Ford's Model T. The inventor displayed not only originality in his mechanical thinking, but an enlightened sense of the larger picture. In addition to developing the first assembly lines, Ford had the win-win common sense to keep his prices reasonable—so that his workers could also afford to be his customers.

An exciting Leo may light your fire, while an Aries can help you zero in on concrete goals and ambitions.

Your greatest challenge is to keep your mind open as it questions, so that your inquiries don't become inquisitions. Your greatest strength is the wisdom to know the difference.

➤ Read about your Chinese Astrological sign on page 838. ➤ Read about your Personal Planets on page 826. ➤ Read about your personal Mystical Card on page 856.

VIRGO
Your Personal Planets

YOUR LOVE POTENTIAL
Venus in Virgo, Aug. 23, 17:07 - Aug. 27, 11:42
Venus in Leo, Aug. 27, 11:43 - Sept. 23, 14:41

YOUR DRIVE AND AMBITION
Mars in Leo, Aug. 23, 17:07 - Sept. 23, 14:41

YOUR LUCK MAGNETISM
Jupiter in Sagittarius, Aug. 23, 17:07 - Sept. 23, 14:41

World Events

Aug. 31 - Western forces come under attack in Beruit.

Sept. 17 - Vanessa Williams becomes the first African American Miss America.

LIBRA
Your Personal Planets

YOUR LOVE POTENTIAL
Venus in Leo, Sept. 23, 14:42 - Oct. 05, 19:34
Venus in Virgo, Oct. 05, 19:35 - Oct. 23, 23:53

YOUR DRIVE AND AMBITION
Mars in Leo, Sept. 23, 14:42 - Sept. 30, 0:11
Mars in Virgo, Sept. 30, 0:12 - Oct. 23, 23:53

YOUR LUCK MAGNETISM
Jupiter in Sagittarius, Sept. 23, 14:42 - Oct. 23, 23:53

World Events

Sept. 26 - Australia defeats the U.S. in the America's Cup, the first nation to do so in 132 years.

Oct. 14 - The National Council of Churches in the U.S. releases a new Bible, admitting God is without gender.

1983

SCORPIO
Your Personal Planets

YOUR LOVE POTENTIAL
Venus in Virgo, Oct. 23, 23:54 - Nov. 09, 10:51
Venus in Libra, Nov. 09, 10:52 - Nov. 22, 21:17

YOUR DRIVE AND AMBITION
Mars in Virgo, Oct. 23, 23:54 - Nov. 18, 10:25
Mars in Libra, Nov. 18, 10:26 - Nov. 22, 21:17

YOUR LUCK MAGNETISM
Jupiter in Sagittarius, Oct. 23, 23:54 - Nov. 22, 21:17

World Events

Oct. 31 – U.S. troops storm Grenada to help restore democratic institutions.

Nov. 4 – An Arab suicide bomber kills thirty-nine Israeli troops.

Harrods after an IRA bomb explodes

SAGITTARIUS
Your Personal Planets

YOUR LOVE POTENTIAL
Venus in Libra, Nov. 22, 21:18 - Dec. 06, 16:14
Venus in Scorpio, Dec. 06, 16:15 - Dec. 22, 10:29

YOUR DRIVE AND AMBITION
Mars in Libra, Nov. 22, 21:18 - Dec. 22, 10:29

YOUR LUCK MAGNETISM
Jupiter in Sagittarius, Nov. 22, 21:18 - Dec. 22, 10:29

World Events

Dec. 17 – An IRA bomb explodes outside Harrods in London's fashionable Knightsbridge.

Dec. 20 – Eight years of military rule ends in Argentina with the inauguration of Paul Ricardo Alfonsin.

SCORPIO
From October 23, 23:54 through November 22, 21:17

The Confident Confidant

"Top Secret" could be the middle name of any Scorpio, but this holds especially true for 1983 Scorpio. You would make an excellent spy or criminal psychologist, loving to probe dark secrets as you do, whether they belong to countries, companies, or individuals. Your character is marked by intense self-restraint and behind-the-scenes strategic ability. You are likely to be recognized in your lifetime for your diplomatic use of power. At worst, you might be accused of hidden agendas and manipulation; but probably not blatant violence or the flagrant misuse of force. It is not clear from your chart where your heart is likely to lie in terms of a higher good; or what your dreams will be.

On October 27, under an international news blackout, U.S. troops stormed the Caribbean Island of Grenada. The ostensible purpose of the invasion was to restore recently overturned democratic institutions, but many observers felt the point was to send an open message to all of Latin America, and the world, that President Reagan would not tolerate Soviet-supported Marxism in the western hemisphere. The Soviets had, for example, been assisting Cuba's Marxist government. The United Nations passed a resolution "deeply deploring" the invasion as a "flagrant violation of international law." You would more likely be involved in the planning of a covert CIA mission than the execution of an outright invasion; unless of course the "open secret" did serve another (hidden) purpose.

In November, U.S. President Reagan signed a bill instituting the first national holiday recognizing an African American—Martin Luther King, Jr., fifteen years after his assassination. King had received the 1964 Nobel Peace Prize for his work as a non-violent civil rights activist. This is also the kind of restrained, diplomatic, strategic, and non-violent use of power of which you are capable, 1983 Scorpio.

An honest Sagittarius prompts you to evaluate your values, while a Libra helps you mastermind your game plan.

Your greatest challenge is to define your ethical beliefs, and your greatest strength is your brilliant strategic ability.

SAGITTARIUS
From November 22, 21:18 through December 22, 10:29

The Two-Party Animal

With five planets in your sign, 1983 Sagittarius, you are truer to your sign than most. With freedom-loving Uranus nestled between the planets representing your identity and your intellect, you are likely to be even more idealistic and open-minded than usual, as well as ingeniously inventive and creative in your thinking. You are more expansive and optimistic than ever, and luck does tend to smile on you. You love a good party as much as a good crusade, and you were born as the Dutch brewery king, Alfred Heineken, was rescued from kidnappers after twenty-one grueling days.

As a Sagittarius born in 1983, you are more egalitarian at heart than the usual Archer. With Uranus on your team, you are also like an honorary Aquarius, meaning that you are likely to be downright utopian in your ideals for humanity. You were born under high hopes as eight years of military rule in Argentina finally came to an end with the inauguration of President Raul Alfonsin. With more than 100,000 in the streets of Buenos Aires cheering in the new era, the new politically moderate leader promised to prosecute the country's former brutal regime.

You may feel called to teach the way some feel called to the cloth—as a mission from God. You may see teaching as an opportunity to, in your own small way, save the world. You see it as much more than a duty to instruct your students in their studies; it is a means to encourage their individual intellectual and spiritual growth toward being worthy citizens of the world. You would not only share your knowledge, you would also inspire them to seek after the ideals of truth, beauty, wisdom, and justice.

You may meet a lovely Libra at a committee meeting who shares your vision of a better humanity sharing a brighter tomorrow, as well as your proclivity for group activities. A visionary Aquarius can certainly share your wavelength, but the two of you might get lost in orbit together.

Your greatest challenge is to remember to check in on Earth occasionally, and your greatest asset is your unbridled optimism.

➤ Read about your Chinese Astrological sign on page 838. ➤ Read about your Personal Planets on page 826. ➤ Read about your personal Mystical Card on page 856.

CAPRICORN

From December 22, 10:30 through December 31, 23:59

The Practical Surrealist

Whatever your religious beliefs, 1983 December Capricorn, with such a packed twelfth house—representing the unconscious and spirituality—spirituality of some kind is likely to be unusually important to you. Your own thoughts on the subject may be somewhat intuitive and difficult to articulate, or simply very private. You may feel that, when it comes to matters of the spirit, the majestic music of Beethoven or Bach expresses more than words ever can. You may feel closer to heaven when looking at an abstract painting's evocation of pure space than within the walls of a religious structure. You are likely to be somewhat unorthodox in your views, even if you are not outspoken about them.

You were born as the Spanish early surrealist painter Joán Miró died. The surrealists were noted for their examination of the workings of the unconscious mind, including dreams and trances. Such inquiries, along with investigations of the occult sciences (such as astrology), no doubt fascinate you. People with strong twelfth houses often experience feelings of alienation. The more you learn to trust and give voice to your own intuitive insights, the less surreal everyday life will seem to you, and the more natural your own exceptional imagination.

Eternal pragmatist that you are, you develop concrete applications for your far-out ideas and inventions. In December 1983, the first photograph was taken of a disc with a black hole at its center. Not so long ago, the idea of black holes was pure abstract theory, and seemed more like science fiction than scientific reality. As you learn to trust your highly original and unorthodox thinking, you are able to bring your conceptions into material forms that are valuable and useful.

A serious-minded Scorpio can arouse surprising passion in the practical old Goat—you are said to get younger as you get older. They also help you ground your visions in reality. A Gemini provides lively companionship on fact-finding missions.

Your greatest challenge is to trust the inherent practicality of your own intuitive imagination, which is your greatest strength.

1983

CAPRICORN
Your Personal Planets

YOUR LOVE POTENTIAL
Venus in Scorpio, Dec. 22, 10:30 - Dec. 31, 23:59

YOUR DRIVE AND AMBITION
Mars in Libra, Dec. 22, 10:30 - Dec. 31, 23:59

YOUR LUCK MAGNETISM
Jupiter in Sagittarius, Dec. 22, 10:30 - Dec. 31, 23:59

World Events

Dec. 25 – Spanish Surrealist painter Joán Miró dies.

Dec. 31 – The EEC lifts the sanctions imposed on the USSR.

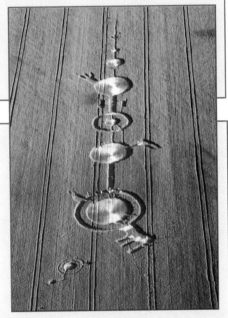

Crop circles in Wiltshire, England

Special Feature
The Enigma of Crop Circles

(Continued from page 673)

Investigators have also discovered a variety of strange phenomena that seems to occur in association with the appearance of crop circles. Often, for example, the electromagnetic field that surrounds the circles is altered, and a compass used in this area is unable to locate north. Another example is that background radiation in crop-circle areas can be up to 300 percent higher than normal, and radio frequencies fall or rise dramatically around the perimeters. Farmers notice that their animals are agitated hours before a circle appears, and dogs will avoid going into the field. Car batteries in nearby villages go dead after a crop circle is found, and in some cases entire towns are left without power.

Genuine crop circles sometimes display obscure theorems based on Euclidean and sacred geometry. The golden ratio pi can be discerned by comparing the angles and sizes of the radiating circles. This same ratio is reflected in the spiral vortex found in shells, sunflowers, and galaxies.

One of the most spectacular crop circles was discovered on July 7, 1996, an enormous spiral of 151 meticulously laid circles. The Julia Set crop circle, named after the computer-generated fractal it resembles, emerged in broad daylight across the main road from Stonehenge. Only a pilot flying overhead could attest to its sudden appearance since the tourists hadn't noticed anything unusual. Thirty minutes earlier he had flown over Stonehenge and seen nothing. On his return trip, the beautiful 900-foot formation was suddenly in place!

> The Julia Set crop circle emerged in broad daylight across the main road from Stonehenge.

Subsequent photographs of the Julia Set revealed an intricate geometric pattern set against the megalithic structures of Stonehenge. The circles and patterns are clearly designed to be viewed from the air since they are all but invisible at ground level.

Who, completely undetected, could have built this beautiful pictogram at one of England's best-guarded national monuments? This extraordinarily complex symbol is one of the most significant to appear in England since the 1970s.

Some people see in crop circles warnings of ecological disaster, while others admire them for their simple beauty. This is a global phenomenon that is showing no signs of slowing down, and the designs are becoming more spectacular every year. Crop circle fans are certain that someone or something is communicating with us! ✪

➤ Read more about Stonehenge in "Gaia's Mystical Power Places" on page 745.

Transitions in Leadership: Jupiter and Saturn Conjoin

Jupiter and Neptune simultaneously entered Capricorn, the sign of regulation and administration, in mid-January, inaugurating new approaches to old problems but enlarging others. Neptune is associated with both imagination and deception, while Jupiter magnifies whatever it contacts. When these planets conjoin, cover-ups may mask illegal behind-the-scenes events. This type of scenario was in its inception in early 1984, when U.S. President Reagan's actions in Central America became more suspect. Protesting America's aggressive actions, Nicaragua asked the International Court of Justice to make a ruling, but before it could act, the U.S. Senate pre-emptively halted funding for the initiative. This did not stop him, however, and for the moment, his actions were beyond the scrutiny of regulating bodies, a prime example of Neptune's deceptive side. Violence was highlighted as rebellious Uranus received emphasis from an activating eclipse in May. When there is an eclipse, people often feel like taking dramatic and final actions. This was seen when, days after this eclipse, Indian Prime Minister Indira Gandhi ordered the attack on the Amritsar Temple to quell a radical Sikh uprising. Unrest continued across India, culminating in Gandhi's assassination by her Sikh bodyguard near the time of the next eclipse in November.

However, there were constructive planetary contacts this year as well. Magnanimous Jupiter was positively bonded with businesslike Saturn, suggesting a stable economy. In America, home prices rose to average $100,000, while consumer inflation hit the lowest level since 1972.

Indira Gandhi is murdered by her own security guards

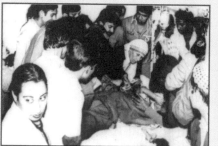

Mother Teresa helps victims of toxic gas poisoning at Bhopal

Desmond Tutu receives the Nobel Peace Prize

IT JUST FEELS RIGHT

By the early 1980s, the existence of psychic abilities was assumed and paranormal research changed its focus to find ways to apply these abilities in business, industry, and science. By 1984, "psionics," or acting on intuition to make decisions, had become an informal part of twenty-eight fields, including: archeology, agriculture, animal training, contests and gambling, environmental improvement, geological exploration, military intelligence, police work, psychotherapy, and weather prediction.

TROUBLES IN INDIA

Indian Prime Minister Indira Gandhi was assassinated by her own Sikh bodyguards for ordering an attack on the Sikhs' Golden Temple at Amritsar. She was replaced by her son Rajiv. British Prime Minister Thatcher escaped unharmed when an IRA bomb exploded at the Conservative Party Conference. Russian leader Andropov died. Britain and China agreed terms for the handover of Hong Kong in 1997. At Bhopal, India, more than 2,000 died when the Union Carbide insecticide plant emitted toxic gas. In Mexico, a gas plant explosion killed 260 and injured 500. Canada and Tunisia got together to improve human resources in Tunisia. In the U.S., Reagan flouted international law by mining Nicaragua's harbors but was re-elected President. British rock stars formed *Band Aid* to help Ethiopian refugees. Bishop Tutu of Johannesburg, South Africa won the Nobel Peace Prize. Stalin's daughter Svetlana returned to Russia after defecting in 1967. The Los Angeles Olympics were boycotted by Eastern Bloc nations. Two sailors, dead for 136 years, were found frozen in the Arctic. Film stars James Mason and Richard Burton and U.S. author Truman Capote died.

➤ Read Princess Diana's Star Profile on page 689.

CAPRICORN

From January 01, 0:00 through January 20, 21:04

The Practical Humanitarian

With five planets in Sagittarius, you may identify more with that sign than your own sign, 1984 January Capricorn. As Sagittarius rules the higher mind, education, philosophy, and law, any of these fields may call to you, although you would still approach them with your well-known Capricornian practicality and good business sense. Sagittarius is also noted for its idealism and concern for humanitarian causes, making an interesting combination.

Events around the world at the time you were born reflected the kind of person you would become. Right at the start of the year Brunei gained independence from Britain, encapsulating your desire for freedom. The U.S. Commission on Civil Rights also voted to discontinue the use of quotas to assure equal employment for African Americans around this time. You are constantly trying to create a balance in your life between getting ahead and making the world a better place. Freedom is your *raison d'etre*, and your Goat-self slogs up the mountain with a zeal that astounds everyone you leave behind in your wake.

Like Indian Prime Minister Indira Gandhi, who died in your birth year, you are a born leader. You are likely to be actively concerned about matters of public debate, on a large or a small scale. You might even become involved in the setting of public policy. While it's hard to say whether you would tend to be liberal or conservative politically, you would almost certainly be one to advocate for the rights of the individual. You might also advocate for the interests of the less privileged members of your community, pointing out the long-term benefits for all concerned. You would also keep a sharp eye on practical considerations, however, such as the bottom line. And you know that one does not necessarily preclude the other.

A Sagittarian or Aquarian mate is likely to share your noble ideals, while a Taurus understands your earthy pragmatism.

Your greatest challenge is to integrate your drive for perfection with your common sense, and your greatest strength is your ability to turn setbacks and limitations into opportunities.

AQUARIUS

From January 20, 21:05 through February 19, 11:15

The Impossible Dreamer

All Aquarians tend to be visionary, and thrive in groups committed to collective aspirations. This is especially true for 1984 Aquarians. With so many planets in your house of groups, including idealistic Jupiter and mystical Neptune, associations and affiliations can take on a nearly religious significance for you. You may face early disappointments of your youthful expectations, which helps you to mature along these lines. Your idealism becomes tempered with realism as you accept that life is an endless negotiation between the possible and the actual.

Despite this, you always keep in mind that it is the dreaming of impossible dreams that sometimes changes the world. What may be science fiction for one generation often becomes reality for the next simply because people dare to dream, and then, working together, bring their visions down to Earth. On February 7, 1984, for the first time in history, two men walked untethered in space, hovering outside the American space shuttle *Challenger*. You are one of these free spirits, and may seem to defy gravity yourself at times.

As a 1984 Aquarius, you are the sort of person that turns fanciful dreams into solid realities. You will strive alone, but only to a point. It's likely that you can better achieve your goals by working with others. Because your intuition is so strong, you know ahead of time what your limits are, and you only push up against them when you sense that you'll leap safely, and in a single bound. Usually you do so without fear, because you have a healthy self-confidence built on past achievements. Your intellect is so strong that others trust you instinctively. You don't even have to speak, because you have an aura of intelligence and determination. Groups are lucky for you, and you tend to lead them.

You find a fellow visionary in a Sagittarius, but a passionate and politically minded Scorpio is realistic, practical, and focused, bringing out your sense of purpose.

Your greatest challenge is to keep just one toe on Earth, and your greatest strength is the sense of possibility you bring to group endeavors.

CAPRICORN
Your Personal Planets

YOUR LOVE POTENTIAL
Venus in Scorpio, Jan. 01, 0:00 - Jan. 01, 1:59
Venus in Sagittarius, Jan. 01, 2:00 - Jan. 20, 21:04

YOUR DRIVE AND AMBITION
Mars in Libra, Jan. 01, 0:00 - Jan. 11, 3:19
Mars in Scorpio, Jan. 11, 3:20 - Jan. 20, 21:04

YOUR LUCK MAGNETISM
Jupiter in Sagittarius, Jan. 01, 0:00 - Jan. 19, 15:03
Jupiter in Capricorn, Jan. 19, 15:04 - Jan. 20, 21:04

World Events

Jan. 4 - Burma gains independent status from Britain.

Jan. 19 - Forty nations attending an Islamic Conference vote to allow Egypt to rejoin.

Yuri Andropov's funeral in Moscow

AQUARIUS
Your Personal Planets

YOUR LOVE POTENTIAL
Venus in Sagittarius, Jan. 20, 21:05 - Jan. 25, 18:50
Venus in Capricorn, Jan. 25, 18:51 - Feb. 19, 4:52
Venus in Aquarius, Feb. 19, 4:53 - Feb. 19, 11:15

YOUR DRIVE AND AMBITION
Mars in Scorpio, Jan. 20, 21:05 - Feb. 19, 11:15

YOUR LUCK MAGNETISM
Jupiter in Capricorn, Jan. 20, 21:05 - Feb. 19, 11:15

World Events

Feb. 7 - President Reagan orders that U.S. peacekeeping forces should be withdrawn from Beirut.

Feb. 13 - Konstantin Chernenko succeeds as General Secretary of the Soviet Union on the death of Andropov.

➤ Read about your Chinese Astrological sign on page 838. ➤ Read about your Personal Planets on page 826. ➤ Read about your personal Mystical Card on page 856.

683

1984

PISCES
Your Personal Planets

YOUR LOVE POTENTIAL
Venus in Aquarius, Feb. 19, 11:16 - Mar. 14, 12:34
Venus in Pisces, Mar. 14, 12:35 - Mar. 20, 10:23

YOUR DRIVE AND AMBITION
Mars in Scorpio, Feb. 19, 11:16 - Mar. 20, 10:23

YOUR LUCK MAGNETISM
Jupiter in Capricorn, Feb. 19, 11:16 - Mar. 20, 10:23

World Events

Feb. 22 – Britain and the U.S. send battleships to the Persian Gulf as Iran attacks Iraq.

Mar. 12 – A nationwide strike of mineworkers goes into effect across Britain.

Death of soul singer Marvin Gaye

ARIES
Your Personal Planets

YOUR LOVE POTENTIAL
Venus in Pisces, Mar. 20, 10:24 - Apr. 07, 20:12
Venus in Aries, Apr. 07, 20:13 - Apr. 19, 21:37

YOUR DRIVE AND AMBITION
Mars in Scorpio, Mar. 20, 10:24 - Apr. 19, 21:37

YOUR LUCK MAGNETISM
Jupiter in Capricorn, Mar. 20, 10:24 - Apr. 19, 21:37

World Events

Apr. 1 – Soul singer Marvin Gaye is shot and killed by his father.

Apr. 17 – WPC Yvonne Fletcher is shot dead during a protest against Libyan leader Gaddafi in London, causing Britain to break diplomatic relations with Libya.

684

PISCES
From February 19, 11:16 through March 20, 10:23

The Open-Minded Professor

You were born, 1984 Pisces, in the midst of a flurry of activity regarding the question of the separation of Church and State in countries as diverse as the United States and Poland. On March 5, the U.S. Supreme Court ruled in favor of communities wishing to continue their traditional displays for religious holidays. Just three days later more than 3,000 Polish youths staged a rally protesting their communist government's removal of crucifixes from their classrooms.

Although you may have supported both these events, you are unlikely to be the kind of person to adhere to any organized religion. You could just as easily find your spirituality in the wonders of nature, in service to humanity, or in great works of art, as within the teachings of a formal religion. Your broad-minded approach to this subject as well as many other areas of life means you demonstrate an exemplary tolerance for those whose ideas may differ from your own. You will never judge anyone; your open mind and "live-and-let-live" attitude draw people to you like a magnet. You would probably endorse the idea of children being exposed to the teachings of all religions in public schools, as well as the concept of no religion. Whether or not you belong to a faith community, your spiritual life is important to you, Pisces of 1984.

The driving force behind this spirituality is the inspired message of unity and compassion that it encapsulates. You would therefore have been pleased later in your life when you heard of the efforts made at reconciliation in Lebanon and the peace accord agreed between South Africa and Mozambique during your zodiac birth month. These developments offered new hope in troubled areas.

You may find a soul mate in a free-thinking Aquarius, and a surprisingly mystical Capricorn helps you read between the lines of formal religion. A Scorpio may be a sexy mentor who spurs you to new philosophical heights.

Your greatest challenge is to communicate your sense of relativity in a way that less open-minded people can relate to. Your greatest strength is your compassion for all points of view.

ARIES
From March 20, 10:24 through April 20, 3:25

The Well-Armed Warrior

As a 1984 Aries, you step up to the plate well armed, not only with your usual iron will, single-mindedness, and individual courage, but also with a powerful ability to finance your endeavors with other people's resources. Whether through grants, loans, prize winnings or investments, you are blessed with abundant opportunities to leverage your own position.

Most Ariens burn through changes and never look back, but you, 1984 Aries, are a little more conservative than your fiery siblings. You still have the unmistakable passion of the Ram, but you know how to use reason and measured perseverance to get what you want. In a bold step that marked welcomed progress for his administration's international relations, U.S. President Reagan signed a new cultural and scientific exchange agreement with China this month. He also signed a tax accord that opened the door for American businesses to operate in China without the penalty of double taxation. You, too, might excel at this kind of "enlightened self-interest," for mutual benefit.

Although you are willing to go to the ends of the Earth to search out your dreams, you are not purely selfish. You'd be willing to go just as far to help a friend or loved one, and you'd probably move just as fast in pursuit of their needs. You are a rare commodity: an altruistic Aries. You can apply your brilliant fire-wisdom to any task, but you especially excel at taking care of others in need. You like to think of yourself as a superhero swooping in with your cape of fire to set everything right again.

A powerful Scorpio helps you locate financing for your dreams. An inspired Capricorn helps you see the big picture and capitalize on your good strokes of luck. You find gentle understanding with a yielding Pisces, and a safe haven with a supportive Cancer.

Your greatest strengths are your determined willingness to maximize your opportunities and to defend yourself and your loved ones ardently and skillfully from any perceived threat. Your greatest challenge is to open your eyes to other points of view, improving the scope of your perceptions.

➤ Read about your Chinese Astrological sign on page 838. ➤ Read about your Personal Planets on page 826. ➤ Read about your personal Mystical Card on page 856.

TAURUS

From April 20, 3:26 through May 20, 20:57

The Logical Positivist

With such a packed ninth house, 1984 Taurus, you are unusually restless and interested in travel, foreign affairs, and higher education. Scientific research may even capture your imagination. You bring your well-known grounded Taurean common sense to all your explorations, whether physical or theoretical, along with an honorary Capricornian logic and ability to see the big picture. You approach a balance of powers in a reasoned and diplomatic way, and you are put off, like Mr. Spock on *Star Trek*, when others behave in ways that strike you as less than rational. You may be learning the hard lessons that life—and humans especially—aren't always predictable, fair, or rational. This has had the benefit of preparing you for some highly illogical situations in life.

In a bizarre shooting spree from inside the Libyan Embassy in London on April 22, ten people were killed while protesting against Colonel Muammar Khadaffi. Britain promptly broke off diplomatic relations with Libya and gave the occupants of the embassy a week to leave England. Just as the British government acted carefully in a grave situation, your Taurean steadfastness informs your sense of diplomacy. You are a rock, grounded by kindness.

On a different battlefront, in April, researchers working concurrently in France and the U.S. located a virus called LAV, which was believed to be the cause of AIDS. While there was still a ways to go and testing would be required to confirm the theory, scientists were hopeful that the discovery would lead to a diagnostic test.

You bring a similar sense of optimism to your search for truth, although tempered by a natural reluctance to jump to premature conclusions. You have a buoyancy that is not common to most Taureans, and your blend of happiness and wisdom encourages a legion of fans to populate around you wherever you go. An affectionate Aries awakens your hidden fire, and you can engage in safe-but-exciting sex with a cautious Scorpio.

Your greatest challenge is to weigh your caution against your optimism, and your greatest strength is your patient perseverance against all odds.

GEMINI

From May 20, 20:58 through June 21, 5:01

The Verbatim Reporter

As a 1984 Gemini, your talents are many. In addition to your natural knack for wielding words like swords, you are not as frenetic as your Mercury-ruled brothers and sisters born in other years. You know how to take a step back, and to get out when the getting is good. As an example of this, on May 7, the Soviet Union withdrew from the summer Olympic Games, being hosted by the United States. Your duality is fierce, and you need to make sure that your more unruly twin speaks only when the moment is right. Your intellect is something wonderful to behold, but you must use it appropriately.

You were born in the year that Bob Geldof created Band Aid, the group that recorded the song, "Do They Know It's Christmas?" This single was a smash hit, and raised a tremendous amount of money to feed the starving in Africa. Because you are a special breed of Gemini, you may find that you'll want to manipulate a new form of media to make a statement. You could work in radio, television, or spread your wisdom through the Web. You have wide-ranging opinions, and you are apt to find a way to get them out into the global village. You are likely to get excellent feedback for your ideas.

Geminis, great lovers of current events and news, excel at board games like Trivial Pursuit and Risk, due to their uncanny ability to keep those facts, names, dates, and relationships straight that the rest of us tend to lose track of. You might put your famed command of language and facts to work as a journalist or political analyst. You also have quite a knack for obtaining "sensitive information." In time, you develop the discrimination to make judicious use of this material.

A stable, quiet Taurus might have a secret crush on your mercurial talents. A health-minded Scorpio discourages your bad habits, and a well-informed Sagittarius can keep up with your insatiable appetite for knowledge.

Your greatest challenge is to focus your inquiring mind on principles as well as data, and your greatest asset is your impartial tape-recorder memory, able to transcribe, store, and retrieve input pretty much verbatim.

➤ Read about your Chinese Astrological sign on page 838. ➤ Read about your Personal Planets on page 826. ➤ Read about your personal Mystical Card on page 856.

1984

TAURUS
Your Personal Planets

YOUR LOVE POTENTIAL
Venus in Aries, Apr. 19, 21:38 - May 02, 4:52
Venus in Taurus, May 02, 4:53 - May 20, 20:57

YOUR DRIVE AND AMBITION
Mars in Scorpio, Apr. 19, 21:38 - May 20, 20:57

YOUR LUCK MAGNETISM
Jupiter in Capricorn, Apr. 19, 21:38 - May 20, 20:57

World Events

Apr. 23 – Researchers in France and the U.S. focus on a virus called LAV, believing it could be the cause of AIDS.

May 8 – The USSR boycotts the Olympics, to be held in Los Angeles.

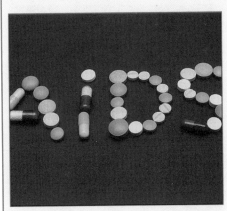

Researchers focus on LAV, a virus thought to be the cause of AIDS

GEMINI
Your Personal Planets

YOUR LOVE POTENTIAL
Venus in Taurus, May 20, 20:58 - May 26, 14:39
Venus in Gemini, May 26, 14:40 - June 20, 0:47
Venus in Cancer, June 20, 0:48 - June 21, 5:01

YOUR DRIVE AND AMBITION
Mars in Scorpio, May 20, 20:58 - June 21, 5:01

YOUR LUCK MAGNETISM
Jupiter in Capricorn, May 20, 20:58 - June 21, 5:01

World Events

May 24 – Iran is accused of aggression by the Arab League; militant Iranian women march in support of Khomeini's Islamic revolution.

June 6 – Four hundred are killed as Indian troops storm the Golden Temple of Amritsar to put down a Sikh uprising.

1984

CANCER
Your Personal Planets

YOUR LOVE POTENTIAL
Venus in Cancer, June 21, 5:02 - July 14, 10:29
Venus in Leo, July 14, 10:30 - July 22, 15:57

YOUR DRIVE AND AMBITION
Mars in Scorpio, June 21, 5:02 - July 22, 15:57

YOUR LUCK MAGNETISM
Jupiter in Capricorn, June 21, 5:02 - July 22, 15:57

World Events

June 24 - French protestors march in Paris against the Socialist government's desire to regulate private schools.

July 17 - Laurent Fabius becomes Prime Minister of France.

Democrat Geraldine Ferraro, the first woman to run for office on a major-party ticket in the U.S.

LEO
Your Personal Planets

YOUR LOVE POTENTIAL
Venus in Leo, July 22, 15:58 - Aug. 07, 19:39
Venus in Virgo, Aug. 07, 19:40 - Aug. 22, 22:59

YOUR DRIVE AND AMBITION
Mars in Scorpio, July 22, 15:58 - Aug. 17, 19:49
Mars in Sagittarius, Aug. 17, 19:50 - Aug. 22, 22:59

YOUR LUCK MAGNETISM
Jupiter in Capricorn, July 22, 15:58 - Aug. 22, 22:59

World Events

July 25 - Soviet Svetlana Savitskaya becomes the first woman to walk in space.

Aug. 5 - British actor Richard Burton dies.

CANCER
From June 21, 5:02 through July 22, 15:57

The Optimistic Feminist

Regardless of your gender, 1984 Cancer, you may tend to be a feminist, favoring the expansion of the feminine role in the world's affairs. Your sign is ruled by the Moon, the ultimate symbol of the nurturing goddess, and you were born with Venus, goddess of love, in your sign as well. Around the time you were born, Svetlana Savitskaya of the Soviet Union became the first woman to walk in outer space. You no doubt appreciate what studies have shown—women possess some qualities that actually qualify them over men as astronauts, including superior patience and endurance under stress.

A line by poet E.E. Cummings could have been written especially for you: "Of love be a little more careful than everything else." You tend to be extremely idealistic in love. While miracles do happen, do double-check anyone who seems too good to be true. They just might be. You may face a thorny dilemma in your partnership selection at some point, calling for a choice between your highest ideals and the facts at hand. In your younger years, you may well have learned the important difference between optimism and wishful thinking. In time, though, you stand an excellent chance of realizing your highest aspirations for true love.

In July 1984, Democrat Walter Mondale was nominated to run for President of the United States against Ronald Reagan. In what some lauded as a daring election move, he chose Geraldine Ferraro as a running mate, the first woman ever to be nominated to run for such a high office. You are the sort that takes risks that may pit you against those who don't trust progressive values and necessary change. Although you love home, hearth, and the status quo, you are unafraid to take the leap of faith needed to embrace new ideas.

A tempting Capricorn warrants a second glance and, if they bear up under scrutiny, could prove to be a faithful partner for life. Fellow water sign Pisces appreciates your appreciation of the feminine.

Your greatest challenge is to assess your most cherished hopes and wishes realistically, and your greatest strength is your capacity to believe the best.

LEO
From July 22, 15:58 through August 22, 22:59

The Multiple Role-Model

Leo is considered to be the sign of the actor, and with three planets in Leo, you are even more likely than usual to be drawn to the stage or screen—or to at least experience a lot of dramatic situations in life. With Venus, the goddess of love, beauty, and art, in conjunction with your Sun, 1984 Leo, you are especially charismatic and attractive—people just seem to enjoy being around you. With imaginative Neptune in a harmonious trine to your Mercury, planet of communication, you also have the mark of a talented writer, and are likely to bring your fiery sense of drama to whatever you write.

The world lost two of its favorite charismatic British actors as you were born. James Mason died on July 27 and Richard Burton died on August 5. You, too, possess the potential to achieve and represent such greatness. On August 25, the American writer Truman Capote passed away. While his chilling *In Cold Blood*—considered to be his masterpiece—was faithfully translated into film, the movie made from his novel *Breakfast at Tiffany's* was less true to his text.

When Capote was asked to explain his technique, he replied that he was just a genius. Perhaps that was his own confident Venus in Leo talking. About Beat writer Jack Kerouac's once-banned novel *On The Road* Capote quipped, "That's not writing, that's typing." You are likely to possess equal measures of talent and chutzpah—luckily the former can pull off the latter. You are also spontaneous and playful, able to ad lib with aplomb, on stage or off. In addition to basking in the limelight, you are known for your courage and sense of honor, and your confidence shows us all a positive example of a healthy sense of self.

Two Leos together are not considered to be a good idea, and you can see why. But in your case it just might work, if you are able to agree to a mutual admiration society. An intense Scorpio can make you feel passionately loved, and safe and secure at home.

Your greatest challenge is to remember the thorn in everyone's paw, including your own, and your greatest strength is your ability to show us all how to roar.

➤ Read about your Chinese Astrological sign on page 838. ➤ Read about your Personal Planets on page 826. ➤ Read about your personal Mystical Card on page 856.

VIRGO

From August 22, 23:00 through September 22, 20:32

The Incredible Voyager

As a 1984 Virgo, you are full of contradictions: in addition to three planets in your own fastidious sign, you have three in Sagittarius, adding a dash of adventurousness—maybe even a wild streak—to your usual sense of propriety. It may take a while for your inner "odd couple" to strike a deal, but they will grow to appreciate each other in time. Your Felix impulses toward purity, exquisite detail, and perfection are truly complementary to your Oscar enthusiasm, big-picture thinking, and expansiveness.

You were born as the first solo crossing of the Atlantic in a helium balloon was accomplished, in a rather Sagittarian feat combining wackiness and adventure. You may surprise yourself at some point, breaking with your normally cautious way of life in a sudden bolt for freedom. And then you may just find yourself feeling more at home in the world at large. You may even trade in your Virgoan microscope for a Sagittarian telescope now and then, just for a change of scene.

Virgo's usual affinity for refining, purification, and healing is enhanced by the extra planets in your sign. You may feel called to medicine or decide to devote your analytical abilities to biological research. Or you may be drawn to environmental work. In August, a French ship carrying 450 tons of uranium sank off the coast of Belgium. After the environmental protection group Greenpeace revealed the fact, the owners of the ship admitted belatedly that it had been carrying nuclear cargo. Experts quickly assured the public that any radiation would be diluted if the uranium came into contact with water. But with your analytical Mercury (ruling the questioning intellect) forming a challenging aspect to Uranus (ruling uranium) in sagacious Sagittarius, you might question the wisdom of transporting nuclear materials by sea.

A rebellious Sagittarius helps you break out of the mold, while a serious Scorpio seems able to read your mind.

Your greatest challenge is to integrate the micro with the macro; the particular with the general. Your greatest gift is the way you transform your cold feet into bold feats.

LIBRA

From September 22, 20:33 through October 23, 5:45

The Diplomatic Alchemist

Libra is said to be the sign of the great diplomat, because you are able to see both sides to every question, and your ancient symbol—the only inanimate symbol in the entire zodiac—is the scales of justice. And while in our hearts we all like to think we know what justice is, in reality it's a rather abstract concept. Like the ancient Chinese curse, 1984 Libra, you were born into interesting times. Your arrival came at a time when many countries were experiencing divisions—ethnic, religious, and political. Despite this, statesmen continued to work towards that elusive goal, peace. You, too, value harmonious relationships and mediating in conflict comes easily to you.

Even as Libya's Colonel Khadaffi announced that he had sent troops and arms to aid the Sandinista government in Nicaragua, the opposing Contras claimed to have raised $10 million in "private aid" from individuals and corporations in the United States, and from the governments of Israel, Argentina, Venezuela, Guatemala, and Taiwan. We now know that these so-called private funds also included diverted U.S. tax dollars. You are the type of person who can stunningly manipulate activities behind the scenes in an effort to achieve a "harmonious" outcome.

In 1984, Britain prepared to observe the terms of the ninety-nine-year lease of its crown colony of Hong Kong from China—a lease that was due to end in 1997. Hong Kong would prove to be a valuable contact with the West for communist China. In a reflection of this, you adore any arrangement that creates peace between opposing forces. You simply cannot abide disharmony, and will go out of your way to avoid it. When your relationships are running smoothly you are on top of the world.

A powerful Scorpio keeps your eye on the ball of bottom-line calculations, while a Sagittarian suggests interesting compromises. A practical but idealistic Capricorn helps you synthesize your options.

Your greatest challenge is to achieve compromise without totally compromising your ethics, and your greatest strength is your ability to combine fire and water to make powerful steam.

➤ Read about your Chinese Astrological sign on page 838. ➤ Read about your Personal Planets on page 826. ➤ Read about your personal Mystical Card on page 856.

VIRGO
Your Personal Planets

YOUR LOVE POTENTIAL
Venus in Virgo, Aug. 22, 23:00 - Sept. 01, 5:06
Venus in Libra, Sept. 01, 5:07 - Sept. 22, 20:32

YOUR DRIVE AND AMBITION
Mars in Sagittarius, Aug. 22, 23:00 - Sept. 22, 20:32

YOUR LUCK MAGNETISM
Jupiter in Capricorn, Aug. 22, 23:00 - Sept. 22, 20:32

World Events

Aug. 25 – The *Mont Louis*, carrying uranium to the USSR, sinks off the coast of Belgium; no radioactivity is discovered in the area because it is diluted by sea water.

Sept. 3 – A typhoon sweeps through the Philippine Islands; up to 1,000 people are feared dead.

Francois Mitterand, left, and Helmut Kohl hold hands during a French-German reconciliation ceremony

LIBRA
Your Personal Planets

YOUR LOVE POTENTIAL
Venus in Libra, Sept. 22, 20:33 - Sept. 25, 16:04
Venus in Scorpio, Sept. 25, 16:05 - Oct. 20, 5:44
Venus in Sagittarius, Oct. 20, 5:45 - Oct. 23, 5:45

YOUR DRIVE AND AMBITION
Mars in Sagittarius, Sept. 22, 20:33 - Oct. 05, 6:01
Mars in Capricorn, Oct. 05, 6:02 - Oct. 23, 5:45

YOUR LUCK MAGNETISM
Jupiter in Capricorn, Sept. 22, 20:33 - Oct. 23, 5:45

World Events

Sept. 26 – Spanish bullfighter Paquirri Rivera dies after being gored by a bull in Cordoba, Spain.

Oct. 12 – The IRA detonate a bomb at a hotel in Brighton during a Conservative Party conference.

1984

SCORPIO
Your Personal Planets

YOUR LOVE POTENTIAL
Venus in Sagittarius, Oct. 23, 5:46 - Nov 13, 23.53
Venus in Capricorn, Nov. 13, 23:54 - Nov. 22, 3:10

YOUR DRIVE AND AMBITION
Mars in Capricorn, Oct. 23 5:46 - Nov. 15, 18:08
Mars in Aquarius, Nov. 15, 18:09 - Nov. 22, 3:10

YOUR LUCK MAGNETISM
Jupiter in Capricorn, Oct. 23, 5:46 - Nov. 22, 3:10

World Events

Oct. 26 – A baboon's heart is tranplanted into a fifteen-day-old infant born with a heart defect.

Oct. 31 – Indira Gandhi is murdered by her own personal security guards who are Sikh extremists.

Two of her security guards gun down Indira Gandi as she walks from her home to her office

SAGITTARIUS
Your Personal Planets

YOUR LOVE POTENTIAL
Venus in Capricorn, Nov. 22, 3:11 - Dec. 09, 3.25
Venus in Aquarius, Dec. 09, 3:26 - Dec. 21, 16:22

YOUR DRIVE AND AMBITION
Mars in Aquarius, Nov. 22, 3:11 - Dec. 21, 16:22

YOUR LUCK MAGNETISM
Jupiter in Capricorn, Nov. 22, 3:11 - Dec. 21, 16:22

World Events

Dec. 3 – A toxic gas leak from a Union Carbide insecticide plant in Phopal, India, kills 2,100 and spreads over an area inhabited by 200,000 people.

Dec. 10 – Bishop Desmond Tutu of South Africa is awarded the Nobel Peace Prize.

SCORPIO
From October 23, 5:46 through November 22, 3:10

The Powerful Ally

With four planets in your sign, including your powerful ruler Pluto, 1984 Scorpios are especially Scorpionic. Scorpio rules death, transformation, power, and sex. It also rules secrecy, mystery, hidden depths, and treachery. As it has been said since ancient times, power is in itself neither good nor evil; it depends for what purposes it is used. Your chart indicates that you are likely to wield power at some point in your life, but how you use it is up to you. Your values tend to be rather idealistic, but that in itself is no guarantee of goodness. As the intensely Scorpionic French writer André Gide pointed out, "Isn't evil always what we do in return?" However, this is unlikely to apply to you, as your Venus in Sagittarius offers hope of kindness.

In a sequence of events rather mysterious to western minds, India's Prime Minister Indira Gandhi was assassinated by two Sikh members of her own security guard on October 31. This was in retaliation for her order to attack the Golden Temple in June—some 300 people were reported to have been killed in the attack on the holiest of Sikh shrines. You have a superior intellect, 1984 Scorpio, and situations like this tend to intrigue you, particularly when something important is at stake, or when people are in any danger—physical or psychological. Trivial pursuits are just plain boring to your searching mind, because pure truth is the only thing worth pursuing. You will always get to the very core and find the deepest meaning.

On the Scorpionic rebirth note, on October 26 a still-beating heart was removed from a baboon and implanted in a fifteen-day-old human born with a heart defect, allowing baby Fae to live a few weeks longer than she would have otherwise; and twenty days longer than the baboon.

An affectionate Sagittarius can steal your heart, while a hard-nosed Capricorn turns out to have one made of gold. A nurturing Libra becomes a hidden ally, despite your initial suspicions.

Your greatest challenge is to open and then follow your heart, and your greatest strength is your ability to exercise your power without fear.

SAGITTARIUS
From November 22, 3:11 through December 21, 16:22

The Maverick Missionary

Always something of a freedom fighter, with liberating Uranus in your sign along with the articulate planet of communication, Mercury, 1984 Sagittarius is a powerful spokesperson for freedom and justice. You believe in the importance of equitable public policy, as much as the power of the individual. As you were born, black South African Bishop Desmond Tutu was accorded the Nobel Peace Prize for his non-violent battle against apartheid in South Africa. You are likely to be called to at least one humanitarian mission in your lifetime; likely many more than one.

Sagittarius is said to be especially suited for teaching and law. A big-picture thinker, you tend to be interested in humanity as a whole, history and the social sciences in general. You are also likely to be concerned about the environment, seeing the overview as you do. You were born during a deadly toxic gas leak from a Union Carbide insecticide plant in Bhopal, India. The poison, methyl isocyanate, escaped into the atmosphere, killing at least 2,100 people. Another 200,000 were injured, many of them blinded—if they were lucky enough to survive. The new Indian Prime Minister Rajiv Gandhi sought damages from Union Carbide, and a $15 billion class action suit was filed against the firm by two American lawyers. You could be exactly the kind of activist attorney to take that kind of case.

You are more than just an impassioned Don Quixote tilting at windmills, though. In addition to your rousing enthusiasm for a good cause, you are also a keen strategist, patient to work behind the scenes with focused intent until your opportunity presents itself. You are also not above secret tactics and plots. In the end, only you can say whether your ends justify your means, and vice versa.

A serious but optimistic Capricorn warms your heart and points you toward lucrative opportunities. An independent Aquarius stimulates your thinking and intrigues you into pursuing them until you are caught.

Your greatest challenge is to keep your methods as above-board as your motives, and your greatest strength is your sense of mission.

➤ Read about your Chinese Astrological sign on page 838. ➤ Read about your Personal Planets on page 826. ➤ Read about your personal Mystical Card on page 856.

CAPRICORN

From December 21, 16:23 through December 31, 23:59

The Creative Pragmatist

Great at management and always one to have at least one eye on the bottom line, 1984 December Capricorn is not likely to be distracted from this factor. With liberating Uranus in your twelfth house, representing institutions, including prisons (literal and figurative), you may develop an interest in the growing prison-reform movement. As you were born, a study revealed that it was costing taxpayers $40,000 every year to keep each prisoner in New York City—more than a lot of taxpayers made in a year—and 10,000 inmates meant a lot of tax dollars. Progressive public service and work-study programs were suggested to reduce costs—the kinds of innovative policies you are capable of conceiving and administering.

In a mind-boggling contrast to the state of the world's economy, you were born as the twenty-six-year-old Michael Jackson's $.5 million *Thriller* video was pronounced a sound investment—the album from which it was spawned broke all music-industry records, with sales topping $37 million. While you may not rack up eight Grammy awards in a single year, you do stand to achieve significant success, in creative terms as well as financial. Your enormous creativity can generate a substantial income. If you are not self-employed, you are at least likely to operate in a highly independent manner.

Four planets in your conservative Sun sign of Capricorn would probably prevent you from ever going completely wild, but you also have two planets in zany Aquarius, plus another two in adventurous Sagittarius, making it impossible to straitjacket you entirely, either. Your thinking is highly intuitive and inspired, rather than merely logical; and your love life is likely to be decidedly unorthodox. How you bring this together with your incredible business sense and gift for organizational overview will be a sight to behold.

An Aquarian excites your affections as well as your passions, while a visionary Sagittarius becomes an encouraging confidant.

Your greatest challenge is to decide what to do with your greatest gifts—your enormous talent, including keen financial and management ability.

1984

CAPRICORN
Your Personal Planets

YOUR LOVE POTENTIAL
Venus in Aquarius, Dec. 21, 16:23 - Dec. 31, 23:59

YOUR DRIVE AND AMBITION
Mars in Aquarius, Dec. 21, 16:23 - Dec. 25, 6:37
Mars in Pisces, Dec. 25, 6:38 - Dec. 31, 23:59

YOUR LUCK MAGNETISM
Jupiter in Capricorn, Dec. 21, 16:23 - Dec. 31, 23:59

World Events

Dec. 25 – Rebels are attacked by government forces in Cambodia, causing many to flee across the border into Thailand.

Dec. 29 – Rajiv Gandhi becomes Prime Minister of India.

Princess Diana
July 1, 1961 – August 31, 1997

PRINCESS DIANA
Cancer

Lady Diana Spencer, later the Princess of Wales, was a young woman who wanted nothing more than to overcome the trauma of her parents' divorce and to find love. Diana was tall, stylish and beguiling, and although she became the most loved woman in the world, that was not enough to secure the ongoing devotion of her husband or the success of her storybook marriage to a prince. After her divorce, she came into her own, working for deserving causes and to establish her separate identity. The world mourned her loss after a tragic auto accident took her life at age thirty-six.

Diana was a Cancer, a sign noted for its emotionality and devotion to home and family. With her Sun, planet of identity, located in her house of partnership, it was quite understandable for Diana to need the sense of belonging that a happy marriage would provide. While this placement would often indicate positive partnerships, her other planets told a different story.

Diana's Moon, the planet of emotions, was in the people-loving sign of Aquarius, inspiring her to work tirelessly for a number of worthy causes. Eventually she became known as "the people's princess," saying after her divorce that she hoped to reign as "queen of people's hearts." A difficult contact from Uranus, planet of upheavals, described her sense of childhood alienation after the divorce of her parents as well as her personal loneliness all during her marriage to Prince Charles, a mate who was widely regarded as inattentive. This discordant energy was filtered out through her Venus, planet of love, making it easier for her to receive love at a distance—from the public, rather than in her personal life.

Mars is the planet of action and, in a woman's chart, it sometimes describes the men to whom she is attracted. With a contact between Mars and controlling Pluto,

Diana was attracted to powerful men, who sometimes dominated her. This is also an aspect of sex appeal and it was often written that she could have succeeded on the silver screen. Another manifestation of this energy is her devotion to humanitarian causes and her tireless work to change the world for the better.

➤ Read about Princess Diana in "An Astrology Family Tree: The British Royal Family" on page 425.
➤ Read Queen Elizabeth's Star Profile on page 449. ➤ Read the Duke of Windsor's Star Profile on page 329.

689

Freedoms are Won: Jupiter Contacts Pluto

A s free-spirited Jupiter entered egalitarian Aquarius in February, oppressed peoples of the world reached out toward rights and freedoms. Jupiter was making an abrasive "square" to power-wielding Pluto and some groups found themselves opposed by force. This was the case in South Africa: as Jupiter and Pluto were making their connection in late February. After years of forced relocations, black squatters rioted and clashed with police over a new scheme to move them to a segregated township on barren sand dunes. However, planetary contacts are not destiny and two other groups won important new rights: women were permitted to become rabbis in U.S. Conservative Judaic communities, while in Ireland contraceptives were made accessible to any adult, an important stride in women's rights. Resistance to change, symbolized by hard-line Saturn in Scorpio, is sometimes released explosively by another astrological contact. When the solar eclipse on May 19 connected with Saturn, soccer matches in Beijing, Brussels and London ended in violence. While this intense energy was still highlighted, radical Muslims shocked the world by hijacking a jet and holding passengers hostage.

Over the rest of the year, adventurous Jupiter made three friendly links to innovative Uranus, fostering more positive events. Progressive Soviet leader Gorbachev made overtures of peace and openness to the U.S. in Geneva and in a feat of Uranian technological gymnastics, a twenty-three-week-old fetus received ex-utero surgery, was returned to the womb and later born healthy.

Two Live Aid concerts are staged to raise money for Ethiopia

Death of actor Yul Brynner

Mikhail Gorbachev is chosen as the new Soviet leader

GORBACHEV ENTERS THE INTERNATIONAL ARENA

After only thirteen months in office, Andropov's successor as Soviet Prime Minister, Chernenko died; fifty-four-year-old radical Mikhail Gorbachev replaced him. Gorbachev called for immediate changes in economic policies and a reduction in arms. In South Africa, police clashed with squatters in Capetown, killing eight and injuring several hundred. A cataclysmic quake struck Mexico City, killing over 2,000 but leaving fifty-eight newborn infants unharmed. In northern Colombia, a volcanic mudflow buried two villages, killing 20,000 people. Terrorists attacked the Israeli El Al airline counters in Rome and Vienna. Three air crashes in Britain, Japan and the U.S. killed 711. Gorbachev and Reagan met in Geneva and agreed on arms reduction. In Brussels, Belgium, forty-one football fans were killed in a hooligan rampage at Heysel Stadium. Aged seventeen, German tennis star Boris Becker became the youngest Wimbledon champion. British rock superstars staged two *Live Aid* concerts to raise £50,000,000 ($72,411,354) for famine-struck Ethiopia. Film stars Rock Hudson, Orson Welles, and Yul Brynner died. *Out of Africa*, starring Robert Redford, won seven Oscars.

➤ Read Salman Rushdie's Star Profile on page 697.

LAND THAT DEFIED SEASON

A narrow strip—1,000 meters long and 15 meters wide—of mysterious land running down a hill to a river was discovered in Huanre County of Liaoning province in China. Amazingly, the temperature of the ground changed in the exact reverse of the seasons. In the winter, it remained at 17 degrees Fahrenheit when the surrounding temperature was -30 degrees and could be used to grow vegetables. During the summer, however, the strip froze to a depth of one meter and was used by the local inhabitants as a refrigerator.

CAPRICORN

From January 01, 0:00 through January 20, 2:57

The Shrewd Organizer

Making order out of chaos is easy for you, January-born 1985 Capricorn. You can look at a complicated job and know which aspects need to be tackled first, second, and last. You've also got a knack for negotiating impressive partnerships. The year you were born U.S. President Ronald Reagan and Soviet Premier Mikhail Gorbachev met to renew cultural contacts for their mutual political benefit. You're capable of similar feats of diplomacy, so long as your interests are being served.

You need a job that comes with lots of responsibility. Overseeing a big team of workers would be an ideal situation for you. You'd make a wonderful leader of a research team, labor union, or military division. Alternately, you could become the head of a prestigious academic institution. You have a love of learning that will surely manifest itself in your career. It's very possible that you will have to start at the bottom of your industry and work your way up the ladder of success. Never fear; your talent will be recognized, provided you work hard.

Status is important to you, but you don't want to be isolated in your success. Rather, you want to preside over a large group of folks who are happy to have you as their leader. Group outings have a special appeal for you. Company picnics, spiritual retreats, and family reunions bring out the best in you. Without question, you rule the roost at both home and work. People respect your authority because you are a fair and generous leader.

You have a small but devoted group of friends. Most of your pals are probably loyal Taureans, Virgos, Scorpios, and Capricorns. You need to know that your loved ones will stick with you through thick and thin, and these signs are among the most devoted in the zodiac. In love, you are best suited to a partner who is nurturing and domestic. Having a comfortable home is very important to you.

Your greatest challenge is to find a job that calls upon your considerable leadership ability. Your biggest strength is your appreciative nature. You make everybody feel valued and important, regardless of their position in society.

AQUARIUS

From January 20, 2:58 through February 18, 17:06

The Respected Authority

A hush comes over the room whenever you enter, 1985 Aquarius. That's because people sense your authority and defer to it. Whether you take advantage of your power is a different story. You don't enjoy bossing folks around, but it does tickle you to know that they will obey your every command. The year you were born, Ronald Reagan was inaugurated as U.S. President for the second time. You have the air of an established leader, too, and your stature will only grow bigger with time.

Chances are you are very ambitious and will pursue a prestigious career. You might find success as a politician; the more prominent the position, the better. Alternately, you could become a doctor or lawyer, specializing in a field that is hot or glamorous. Perhaps you will become the authority on a particular branch of medicine, or a celebrity attorney. Ultimately, you need a job that attracts lots of attention and acclaim. You're not the type who will be content slaving away in a dark little office. You intend to be recognized, respected, and rewarded for your work, and you will do everything in your power to make this happen.

The secret to your success is your strong intuition. You've got wonderful business sense and can detect trends before they become full-blown fads. Taking advantage of these cycles will benefit your career. However, it's a good idea to develop a spiritual practice as a means to stay balanced. Studying world religions can help you develop your own belief system. You're not the type to follow an organized faith; you prefer to puzzle things out on your own.

You like outgoing, entertaining people and probably have a great many Ariens, Geminis, Leos, and Sagittarians as friends. Romantically, you are best suited to an intellectual partner who has many different interests. You prefer stimulating conversation to soulful silences, so make sure your mate is a bit chatty.

Your greatest challenge as a 1985 Aquarius is to develop a fulfilling private life. Resist the temptation to pour all of your energy into career concerns. Your biggest strength is your awe-inspiring aura.

➤ Read about your Chinese Astrological sign on page 838. ➤ Read about your Personal Planets on page 826. ➤ Read about your personal Mystical Card on page 856.

1985

CAPRICORN
Your Personal Planets

YOUR LOVE POTENTIAL
Venus in Aquarius, Jan. 01, 0:00 - Jan. 04, 6:22
Venus in Pisces, Jan. 04, 6:23 - Jan. 20, 2:57

YOUR DRIVE AND AMBITION
Mars in Pisces, Jan. 01, 0:00 - Jan. 20, 2:57

YOUR LUCK MAGNETISM
Jupiter in Capricorn, Jan. 01, 0:00 - Jan. 20, 2:57

World Events

Jan. 10 – Daniel Ortega is sworn in as President of Nicaragua.

Jan. 20 – Ronald Reagan is inaugurated for his second term in office.

Nicaraguan President Daniel Ortega takes the oath of office

AQUARIUS
Your Personal Planets

YOUR LOVE POTENTIAL
Venus in Pisces, Jan. 20, 2:58 - Feb. 02, 8:28
Venus in Aries, Feb. 02, 8:29 - Feb. 18, 17:06

YOUR DRIVE AND AMBITION
Mars in Pisces, Jan. 20, 2:58 - Feb. 02, 17:18
Mars in Aries, Feb. 02, 17:19 - Feb. 18, 17:06

YOUR LUCK MAGNETISM
Jupiter in Capricorn, Jan. 20, 2:58 - Feb. 06, 15:34
Jupiter in Aquarius, Feb. 06, 15:35 - Feb. 18, 17:06

World Events

Feb. 14 – The main Khmer Rouge base at Phnom Malai in Cambodia is besieged by Hanoi troops.

Feb. 14 – The U.S. Assembly of Conservative Judaism votes to permit women to become rabbis.

PISCES
Your Personal Planets

YOUR LOVE POTENTIAL

Venus in Aries, Feb. 18, 17:07 - Mar. 20, 16:13

YOUR DRIVE AND AMBITION

Mars in Aries, Feb. 18, 17:07 - Mar. 15, 5:05
Mars in Taurus, Mar. 15, 5:06 - Mar. 20, 16:13

YOUR LUCK MAGNETISM

Jupiter in Aquarius, Feb. 18, 17:07 - Mar. 20, 16:13

World Events

Mar. 3 – The coal miners' strike over government layoffs in Britain ends after one year, as the National Coal Board forces the National Union of Mineworkers to capitulate.

Mar. 11 – Mikhail Gorbachev is chosen as the new Soviet leader.

Soviet leader Mikhail Gorbachev

ARIES
Your Personal Planets

YOUR LOVE POTENTIAL

Venus in Aries, Mar. 20, 16:14 - Apr. 20, 3:25

YOUR DRIVE AND AMBITION

Mars in Taurus, Mar. 20, 16:14 - Apr. 20, 3:25

YOUR LUCK MAGNETISM

Jupiter in Aquarius, Mar. 20, 16:14 - Apr. 20, 3:25

World Events

Apr. 7 - Pop duo Wham! arrive in China to play two concerts.

Apr. 17 - Lebanese Prime Minister Rashid Karami resigns.

PISCES
From February 18, 17:07 through March 20, 16:13

The Pensive Philosopher

The 1985 Pisces has a hard time seeing the trees for the forest. You're not concerned with what a particular individual did on a certain day; you're interested in what their actions say about humanity as a whole. Your observations have a great deal of wisdom because they are grounded in the belief that all people are essentially the same. The year you were born, Soviet Premier Mikhail Gorbachev came to power, promoting glasnost (cooperation across cultures and political philosophies). This humanitarian philosophy probably matches your own.

Finding links among different cultures has a special appeal for you. You'd make a wonderful art historian, linguist, or travel writer. There's a good chance you will make a dramatic career change at some point in your life. As you get older, working for a humanitarian organization may appeal to you, prompting you to switch jobs quite suddenly. You may even decide to program computers, especially if your work involves helping disadvantaged people. Prepare to undergo a radical but fulfilling career change in your later years.

You're a very spiritual person and enjoy spending time alone. Taking solitary vacations can be very rewarding. At the very least, you need to be by yourself at least one weekend each year. This will give you the opportunity to reflect on your progress, assess your needs, and formulate new goals. It's better to do this without the input of friends and family as these well-intentioned folks can sometimes prompt you to make decisions that are not in your best interests.

Your dreamy idealism attracts practical people who want to add a splash of color to their lives. Taureans, Virgos, Capricorns, and Aquarians appreciate your whimsical ways and make good friends for you. In love, you need a partner who will allow you a strong measure of freedom.

Your greatest challenge as a 1985 Pisces is to listen to your heart, even when it tells you to defy the status quo. A special person like you can't expect to live a conventional lifestyle. Your biggest strength is your ability to find common ground with everybody you meet.

ARIES
From March 20, 16:14 through April 20, 3:25

The Smoldering Sensualist

Born with a healthy appetite for all things pleasurable, the 1985 Aries intends to live life to the fullest. You don't believe in restraint of any sort, which either shocks or delights onlookers. Glamour plays a big part in your life; the year you were born, *Kiss of the Spider Woman* hit movie theaters. Like the characters in the film, you can sympathize with the temptation to retreat into a fantasy of glamour, passion, and romance. There's a good chance your fashion sense runs to vintage items from the thirties and forties. One thing is for sure: you dress to impress.

Because you are so preoccupied with physical pleasure, you would be wise to find work that engages your senses in some way. You'd make an excellent gourmet chef, wine vendor, or chocolatier. Alternately, you could find success as a florist or parfumier. There is even a chance you could create your own fragrance. Whatever your job, it could involve luxury products that are marketed to folks with discerning tastes. Don't be afraid to learn a trade from the bottom up; it will give you the necessary skills to open your own business.

You have a strong sex drive that will not be ignored. Nothing may turn you on more than the sight of an athlete bathed in sweat. Tousled hair is also probably an aphrodisiac for you. You positively can't abide prissy types. If anybody wants to capture your heart, they should defy your wishes. You absolutely love a challenge and like the idea of taming your partner. When you finally settle down, it will be for keeps.

As a 1985 Aries, you can't help but make friends wherever you go. You like sporty, outgoing types like Ariens, Geminis, Leos, and Sagittarians. Romantically, you need a partner who is earthy but gentle. You'll know you've met someone special when you can rest your head in their lap and confide all your fears.

Your greatest challenge is to use your passionate desires in a productive way. Let your wonderful taste fund your own fabulous purchases; you are meant to live the good life. Your biggest strength is your playful attitude. Laughter and you go hand in hand.

► Read about your Chinese Astrological sign on page 838. ► Read about your Personal Planets on page 826. ► Read about your personal Mystical Card on page 856.

TAURUS

From April 20, 3:26 through May 21, 2:42

The Constant Companion

Loyal to the end, the 1985 Taurus is a valuable ally. You like working as a team and seek out partners in both your personal and professional lives. In fact, there's a good chance you could meet your romantic partner at work or form a business with your mate. Work is a pleasure for you when it's performed with a person you love and respect. You even benefit when relationships go sour because you treat broken unions as learning experiences. The year you were born, Tina Turner's *What's Love Got to Do with It?* won Grammys for record and song of the year. The album marked a spiritual and artistic comeback for the singer after allegedly enduring years of abuse from her ex-husband. Whatever the condition of your relationships, they are sure to give you plenty of inspiration too.

Making folks feel and look good may be your specialty. You would make a marvelous beautician, hair stylist, or masseuse. Alternately, you could design clothes or jewelry. Whatever you decide to do, it should involve an element of beauty. Stay away from working environments where the employees are nasty or competitive.

You have a vivid imagination that should serve you well in all walks of life. Your whimsical spirit may make you popular with peers. Your brilliant ideas likely make you a valued employee. And your creative approach to lovemaking wins you the eternal devotion of your partner. You're the type who gets better with age simply because you refuse to stop dreaming.

Although you're quite popular, you prefer seeing friends one-on-one. Quiet but humorous Taureans, Cancerians, Librans, and Capricorns suit you best. In love, you need a partner who is both affectionate and joyous. Ideally, your relationship should feel like an eternal romp at the playground.

Your greatest challenge is to overcome feelings of jealousy. You care so deeply for friends that it's hard for you to share them with others. If you let go just a little bit, your relationships will blossom and grow. Your biggest strength is your imagination. It will prevent you from leading a life that is boring and predictable.

GEMINI

From May 21, 2:43 through June 21, 10:43

The Earth-Bound Angel

Considerate and attentive, the 1985 Gemini is always looking for ways to be of use. You're not terribly concerned about getting credit for your work; you just want to bring a smile to somebody's face each day. Whether that means giving a stranger a sincere compliment or helping an elderly person cross the street, you're always primed for action. Most of your friends program your number on speed dial, knowing they can call on you in any emergency.

The healing professions probably appeal to you. You'd make an excellent doctor, nurse, or emergency medical technician. Medical research is also a strong possibility for you. The year you were born, scientists Michael Brown and Joseph Goldstein were awarded the Nobel Prize for Medicine. Their research shed light on cholesterol metabolism, thereby allowing people to prevent and treat heart attacks more effectively. There's a good possibility that your work could have similar value provided you find a career that is emotionally satisfying.

You're quite adventurous and probably travel a fair amount. Seeing how other people live gives you a profound appreciation for your own culture. There's a good chance that you will work with an overseas volunteer organization at some point in your life. Providing medical care or building homes for people in impoverished countries can give you a profound sense of satisfaction. Alternately, you may provide financial assistance to countries affected by famine, war, or natural disasters.

Open-minded and gregarious, you probably have lots of friends from many different walks of life. Your favorite folks are probably Ariens, Geminis, Leos, and Sagittarians as they share your considerable zest for life. In love, you need more freedom than most people. Make sure your partner is willing to give you lots of space before making a serious commitment.

Your biggest challenge as a 1985 Gemini is learning to relax. Very often, you're so busy doing nice things for other people that you forget to pamper yourself. Your biggest strength is a genuine desire to help humankind. You make the world a better place.

➤ Read about your Chinese Astrological sign on page 838. ➤ Read about your Personal Planets on page 826. ➤ Read about your personal Mystical Card on page 856.

1985

TAURUS
Your Personal Planets

YOUR LOVE POTENTIAL
Venus in Aries, Apr. 20, 3:26 - May 21, 2:42

YOUR DRIVE AND AMBITION
Mars in Taurus, Apr. 20, 3:26 - Apr. 26, 9:12
Mars in Gemini, Apr. 26, 9:13 - May 21, 2:42

YOUR LUCK MAGNETISM
Jupiter in Aquarius, Apr. 20, 3:26 - May 21, 2:42

World Events

May 7 - Muhammad Abdul Aziz, convicted of the assassination of civil rights leader Malcolm X, is released on parole.

May 16 - An anti-alcohol drive begins in Russia.

The remains of the "Angel of Death" of Auschwitz, Dr. Mengela, are found

GEMINI
Your Personal Planets

YOUR LOVE POTENTIAL
Venus in Aries, May 21, 2:43 - June 06, 8:52
Venus in Taurus, June 06, 8:53 - June 21, 10:43

YOUR DRIVE AND AMBITION
Mars in Gemini, May 21, 2:43 - June 09, 10:39
Mars in Cancer, June 09, 10:40 - June 21, 10:43

YOUR LUCK MAGNETISM
Jupiter in Aquarius, May 21, 2:43 - June 21, 10:43

World Events

June 3 - The Vatican and Italy ratify a pact which sees the end of Roman Catholicism as the state religion.

June 21 - The corpse of Dr. Josef Mengele, the "Angel of Death" of Auschwitz, is found in Brazil.

1985

CANCER
Your Personal Planets

YOUR LOVE POTENTIAL
Venus in Taurus, June 21, 10:44 - July 06, 8:00
Venus in Gemini, July 06, 8:01 - July 22, 21:35

YOUR DRIVE AND AMBITION
Mars in Cancer, June 21, 10:44 - July 22, 21:35

YOUR LUCK MAGNETISM
Jupiter in Aquarius, June 21, 10:44 - July 22, 21:35

World Events

June 30 - American hostages of flight TWA 847, hijacked by Hezbollah radical Shiite terrorists in Beirut, are freed after seventeen days.

July 13 - "Live Aid," a world rock festival for famine victims in Ethiopia, is held simultaneously in London, Philadelphia, Moscow, and Sydney.

Freddie Mercury at the Live Aid rock festival

LEO
Your Personal Planets

YOUR LOVE POTENTIAL
Venus in Gemini, July 22, 21:36 - Aug. 02, 9:09
Venus in Cancer, Aug. 02, 9:10 - Aug. 23, 4:35

YOUR DRIVE AND AMBITION
Mars in Cancer, July 22, 21:36 - July 25, 4:03
Mars in Leo, July 25, 4:04 - Aug. 23, 4:35

YOUR LUCK MAGNETISM
Jupiter in Aquarius, July 22, 21:36 - Aug. 23, 4:35

World Events

July 25 - American actor Rock Hudson is hospitalized with AIDS in Paris.

July 28 - A military coup in Uganda sees the overthrow of President Obote.

CANCER
From June 21, 10:44 through July 22, 21:35

The Serious Partyer

The 1985 Cancer takes fun and games very seriously. You're determined to have a good time in life, even if it means putting work by the wayside. Some folks disapprove of your attitude and accuse you of being lazy.

Actually, nothing could be further from the truth. You are a tremendously diligent worker so long as your labors seem like play. The year you were born, Madonna launched her first road show, The Virgin Tour. Nobody can deny that this singer is a hard worker though she always looks like she's having fun on stage. As far as you're concerned, there's no point in taking on a project if it's not amusing.

Naturally, you need a job that is creative and engaging. You'd make a marvelous singer, actor, or stand-up comedian. If the entertainment industry doesn't interest you, the tourism field might. You could find success as a cruise director, tour guide, or travel writer. Playing dress-up was probably one of your favorite games as a child; why not become a makeup artist or costume designer? Whatever career you decide to pursue, it should make people ask with envy, "You mean you get paid to do that?"

Fortunately, you are pushier than most Crabs and can talk your way into virtually any situation. Your daring charm will help you land a plum position, but you will probably have to hustle to get what you want. As a 1985 Cancer, you don't attract luck, you make it. If that means barging into a company president's office and demanding a job, so be it. You manage to make aggression look sexy.

You have a select group of friends who share your love of fun and spontaneity. Ariens, Geminis, Cancerians, and Leos are among your closest pals. In love, you want a partner who is creative but practical. There is a good chance your mate will be a craftsperson of some sort. It will help if your beloved has a healthy sexual appetite to match yours.

Your greatest challenge is to find work that inspires and uplifts you. Resist the social pressure to take a respectable job; social acceptance is not all that it is cracked up to be. Your biggest blessing is your love of fun.

LEO
From July 22, 21:36 through August 23, 4:35

The Passionate Soul-Searcher

The word deep doesn't begin to describe the 1985 Leo. Profound, thoughtful, and reflective, you've always got something important on your mind. From a very early age, you may have been determined to make your mark on the world. You're determined not to be average in any way. Folks sense that you have a special destiny and probably set you apart from the crowd. Sometimes this can feel isolating, sometimes gratifying; it all depends on the situation. As you get older, you will enjoy being treated differently.

The year you were born, *The Breakfast Club* opened in movie theaters around the world. This movie could have a special resonance for you as it involves five students discussing their emotions in a brutally open, honest way. You need a job that requires you to take frequent inventory of your own feelings. Being an actor, writer, or performance artist are all possibilities for you. You would also make an excellent psychotherapist. Whatever career you choose, it should draw on your integrity. Steer clear of advertising and sales like the plague—you're too honest.

Taking a holistic approach to your health is probably wise. Alternative therapies like acupuncture, reiki and reflexology can keep you in top condition. As a 1985 Leo, your mind, body, and spirit are intricately connected. Medical problems can be manifestations of a spiritual issue while emotional anxieties could have their source in a physical injury. Keep an open mind when it comes to combining Eastern and Western approaches to medicine; you'll get benefits from both schools of thought.

You probably have a great many eccentrics among your friends. Ariens, Geminis, Sagittarians, and Aquarians help you appreciate your own unique qualities. With regard to love, you need a mate who is artistic, flamboyant, and spontaneous. Dull, dependable types leave you cold.

Utterly unique, your greatest challenge is to come to terms with your distinction. There's no point for a peacock like you to blend in with a bunch of sparrows. Your biggest strength is your honesty. You mean what you say and say what you mean.

➤ Read about your Chinese Astrological sign on page 838. ➤ Read about your Personal Planets on page 826. ➤ Read about your personal Mystical Card on page 856.

VIRGO

From August 23, 4:36 through September 23, 2:06

The Information Seeker

The 1985 Virgo is on a perpetual quest for knowledge. You probably were the type of kid who asked why? all the time, much to the frustration of adults. You'll never be the kind of person who blindly follows a fad or tradition. The year you were born, the movie *Real Genius* opened in theaters. You probably identify with the story of teen whiz kids who use creative means to combat unethical authority figures. Throughout the course of your life, you may be forced into similar situations. Fortunately, you have the good sense to trust your intuition, even when it defies conventional thought.

Blessed with strong communication skills, you may want to consider working for a newspaper, magazine, or television station. Being a radio talk show host is also a possibility. Teaching gifted children may also appeal to you, as you can appreciate their probing minds. You could also find success as a writer of how-to books, although fiction isn't entirely out of the question for you. Ultimately, you need a job that allows you to share information; you're too outgoing to work in a lonely research lab.

Your home life may be unusual in some way. Perhaps you'll have a job that requires you to live out of a suitcase. Maybe you'll move on a regular basis. You may switch roles with your domestic partner, assuming primary childcare duties if you're a man or being the principal breadwinner if you're a woman. Your household will be anything but average.

Because you are so unique, you need friends who won't feel threatened by your individualism. Quirky Ariens, Geminis, Sagittarians, and Aquarians are among your favorite friends. With regard to romance, you need a partner who has an adventurous, curious mind. You're especially attracted to creative types, and may meet your mate at a cultural event of some kind.

Your greatest challenge is to persist in asking questions, even if it means challenging authority figures. You need to form opinions on your own terms instead of tacitly accepting the established view. Socializing is your greatest strength as you are a fascinating conversationalist.

LIBRA

From September 23, 2:07 through October 23, 11:21

The Enterprising Collector

If shopping were a sport, the 1985 Libran would win a gold medal in it. That's because you equate possessions with security. When you're surrounded by beautiful things, you feel that all is right with the world. If you're confronted with a bare cupboard, though... watch out. Your first instinct may be to grab your wallet and head for the nearest mall. There's a good chance that you have one of the nicest wardrobes around, though you're always eager to add more items to your collection. Perhaps this is a consequence of being born during the acquisitive eighties. The year you were born, the U.S. enacted a budget-balancing bill in a desperate attempt to counteract deficit spending. Take care you don't have to do the same.

Fortunately, you're quite enterprising about getting merchandise at bargain basement prices. You should look for work that draws upon this talent. You'd make an excellent department store buyer, product tester, or music reviewer. Alternately, you could create packaging for luxury items like cosmetics and gourmet foods. You're an expert at making items look luscious and desirable. You may even decide to become a store window designer. Whatever job you take, it should offer plenty of perks and freebies.

An aura of romance surrounds you, luring admirers from near and far. You'll always have the pick of the litter when it comes to love. During the first bloom of youth, you may be attracted to aloof, mysterious types. This will change as you get older, when you'll seek a loving, demonstrative partner.

Bright, original folks comprise your social circle. Consequently, you know a great many Geminis, Librans, Sagittarians, and Aquarians. When you decide to settle down, make sure it is with somebody who has a strong personality. You need a mate who won't be intimidated by your star power.

Your greatest challenge as a 1985 Libra is to enjoy yourself whether you're in or out of a relationship. Loving yourself is the first step toward finding true happiness. Your biggest strength is your knack for bargaining. Nobody pays full price when they're with you.

➤ Read about your Chinese Astrological sign on page 838. ➤ Read about your Personal Planets on page 826. ➤ Read about your personal Mystical Card on page 856.

VIRGO
Your Personal Planets

YOUR LOVE POTENTIAL
Venus in Cancer, Aug. 23, 4:36 - Aug. 28, 3:38
Venus in Leo, Aug. 28, 3:39 - Sept. 22, 2:52
Venus in Virgo, Sept. 22, 2:53 - Sept. 23, 2:06

YOUR DRIVE AND AMBITION
Mars in Leo, Aug. 23, 4:36 - Sept. 10, 1:30
Mars in Virgo, Sept. 10, 1:31 - Sept. 23, 2:06

YOUR LUCK MAGNETISM
Jupiter in Aquarius, Aug. 23, 4:36 - Sept. 23, 2:06

World Events

Sept. 1 – A team of French and American researchers find the *Titanic* 12,000 ft below the surface near Newfoundland.

Sept. 13 – The World Health Organization announces that AIDS is now considered to be of epidemic proportions.

The wreck of the liner "Titanic" is found

LIBRA
Your Personal Planets

YOUR LOVE POTENTIAL
Venus in Virgo, Sept. 23, 2:07 - Oct. 16, 13:03
Venus in Libra, Oct. 16, 13:04 - Oct. 23, 11:21

YOUR DRIVE AND AMBITION
Mars in Virgo, Sept. 23, 2:07 - Oct. 23, 11:21

YOUR LUCK MAGNETISM
Jupiter in Aquarius, Sept. 23, 2:07 - Oct. 23, 11:21

World Events

Oct. 10 – American actor Yul Brynner dies.

Oct. 13 – Physicists at the Fermi National Accelerator laboratory in Illinois switch on the world's largest atom-smasher.

1985

SCORPIO
Your Personal planets

YOUR LOVE POTENTIAL
Venus in Libra, Oct. 23, 11:22 - Nov. 09, 15:07
Venus in Scorpio, Nov. 09, 15:08 - Nov. 22, 8:50

YOUR DRIVE AND AMBITION
Mars in Virgo, Oct. 23, 11:22 - Oct. 27, 15:15
Mars in Libra, Oct. 27, 15:16 - Nov. 22, 8:50

YOUR LUCK MAGNETISM
Jupiter in Aquarius, Oct. 23, 11:22 - Nov. 22, 8:50

World Events

Nov. 9 - Gary Kasparov beats Anatoly Karpov to become the youngest-ever chess champion at the age of twenty-two.

Nov. 21 - President Reagan and Soviet leader Mikhail Gorbachev meet in Geneva.

President Reagan and Soviet leader Mikhail Gorbachev at the Geneva Summit

SAGITTARIUS
Your Personal Planets

YOUR LOVE POTENTIAL
Venus in Scorpio, Nov. 22, 8:51 - Dec. 03, 12:59
Venus in Sagittarius, Dec. 03, 13:00 - Dec. 21, 22:07

YOUR DRIVE AND AMBITION
Mars in Libra, Nov. 22, 8:51 - Dec. 14, 18:58
Mars in Scorpio, Dec. 14, 18:59 - Dec. 21, 22:07

YOUR LUCK MAGNETISM
Jupiter in Aquarius, Nov. 22, 8:51 - Dec. 21, 22:07

World Events

Nov. 27 - Members of the British House of Commons approve the Anglo-Irish Act.

Dec. 5 - Britain withdraws from UNESCO.

SCORPIO

From October 23, 11:22 through November 22, 8:50

The Miracle Worker

Whoever said you can't fight City Hall has obviously never met a 1985 Scorpio. You're a formidable opponent in any arena because you have a will of iron. Working around the clock doesn't faze you so long as you are inching toward a goal. However, you're the first one to oppose senseless, inefficient proposals. Leave it to you to find a cheaper, easier, or more effective solution to a problem. Folks who ignore your proposals usually come to regret it. Thankfully, you're not the type of person to crow, "I told you so" when proven correct.

The year you were born, British scientists reported a hole in the Earth's ozone layer over Antarctica. Thanks to their discovery, humans have been able to start devising strategies to slow the decay of this precious protection. You're also an expert at getting to the root of serious problems. You'd make an excellent psychiatrist, undercover police officer, or environmentalist. You might also want to go into special education, finding ways to make information more comprehensible to folks who are learning-disabled. Whatever your career, it should involve an element of detective work.

Because you live so intensely, you need a home that provides plenty of rest and relaxation. You would probably benefit from living near a body of water. Looking at an ocean, lake, or river has an extremely calming effect on you. When you take time off, you probably prefer staying home with relatives than going on an exotic vacation. Friends and family love staying at your place because you are a warm and generous host.

You need to be very selective about the company you keep as manipulative people can easily drain your energy. Self-reliant Taureans, Cancerians, Scorpios, and Capricorns should make good pals for you. In love, you need a partner who is outgoing and friendly enough to lure you out of your shell.

Your greatest challenge is to create a home that affords you peace and contentment. Living in a secluded area may be very beneficial for you. Your biggest asset is your ability to find innovative solutions to seemingly insurmountable problems.

SAGITTARIUS

From November 22, 8:51 through December 21, 22:07

The Practical Leader

The 1985 Sagittarius is born to make a mark on the world in a significant way. You're passionately committed to improving the condition of humankind. The year you were born, a group of international physicians won the Nobel Peace Prize for their work in preventing nuclear war. With the proper motivation, you could make a similar contribution. It's all a matter of finding a niche for your motivational skills.

A career in religion might suit you, as it would allow you to uplift and inspire large groups of people. You would also make an excellent civil rights lawyer, environmentalist, or ecologist; any job that involves protecting vulnerable beings would give you tremendous satisfaction. You're destined to rise to the top of your profession and make a significant contribution to your field. Whatever job you assume, there is a good chance it will attract a large following as you have a talent for connecting with the public in a profound way.

If you make a lot of money, you will probably give large portions of it away to charity. Material wealth means very little to you, you're more interested in forming rewarding relationships. You have a good sixth sense about people. It's easy for you to tell the difference between loyal friends and hangers-on. Forming a small circle of close pals is important if you become famous. When the pressure gets to be too much, go off on your own for a while. Solitary vacations allow you to reconnect with your soul. Camping trips may be especially gratifying.

Your favorite people are thoughtful, kind, and spiritual. Consequently, you have many Cancerians, Virgos, Sagittarians, and Pisceans among your acquaintance. In love, you need a partner who is nurturing and instinctive. You would thrive in a relationship that is based on mutual spiritual beliefs.

As a 1985 Sagittarius, your greatest challenge is to find hope in even the bleakest situations. If folks see that you are optimistic, they will follow suit. Your biggest strength is your ability to act in the best interests of the group. You are an unselfish and generous leader.

➤ Read about your Chinese Astrological sign on page 838. ➤ Read about your Personal Planets on page 826. ➤ Read about your personal Mystical Card on page 856.

CAPRICORN

From December 21, 22:08 through December 31, 23:59

The Intuitive Healer

The December-born 1985 Capricorn is a natural psychic. You likely know the exact moment to call a friend who is in pain and the precise second when your boss will ask for a certain report. Folks often come to you for comfort because you don't judge or ridicule. The year you were born, Rock Hudson died of complications from the AIDS virus, prompting the public to show more compassion toward the disease. You've always had an innate sympathy for the sick, wounded, and troubled, and you may devote your life to helping such people.

Hands-on health care is the ideal field for someone with your gifts. You'd make an excellent masseuse, chiropractor, or physical therapist. Being a drug counselor or a social worker is also a possibility for you, so long as you could take a small case-load. Because you can anticipate people's needs, you might also do well in the service industry. Running a cozy hotel or restaurant may satisfy your nurturing instincts. Any job that allows you to take a personal approach to clients would suit you very well.

You possess a great deal of creative talent and probably have at least one artistic hobby. Working with earthy materials like sand, clay, and stone can inspire you. If you ever feel like you've reached a dead end, take a pottery class. Getting your hands dirty can be very therapeutic for the 1985 Capricorn.

There's a good chance that you put lots of time and effort into friendships. You especially enjoy the company of constant, reliable people. Taureans, Leos, Virgos, and Capricorns dominate your social circle. In love, you need a mate whom you can respect. Pick a partner who is hard-working and determined. It doesn't matter whether they are successful or not, just so long as they strive toward their goals.

Loneliness is your greatest challenge. Your sensitivity can make you feel isolated; nobody seems to feel things as acutely as you do. Learn to lean on your pals for support when you feel lonely or misunderstood. Your biggest strength is your healing power. Apply it to anybody who is deprived of love, encouragement, or compassion.

1985

CAPRICORN
Your Personal Planets

YOUR LOVE POTENTIAL

Venus in Sagittarius, Dec. 21, 22:08 - Dec. 27, 9:16
Venus in Capricorn, Dec. 27, 9:17 - Dec. 31, 23:59

YOUR DRIVE AND AMBITION

Mars in Scorpio, Dec. 21, 22:08 - Dec. 31, 23:59

YOUR LUCK MAGNETISM

Jupiter in Aquarius, Dec. 21, 22:08 - Dec. 31, 23:59

World Events

Dec. 30 – Palestinian terrorists, aided by Libya, strike Rome and Vienna airports.

Dec. 30 – Martial law is lifted in Pakistan for the first time in eight years.

Salman Rushdie
Born June 19, 1947

SALMAN RUSHDIE
Gemini

Salman Rushdie's incendiary novel, *The Satanic Verses*, which explores religious fanaticism, terrorism and political issues, propelled him to fame when Ayatollah Ruhollah Khomeini, former religious sovereign of Iran and spiritual leader to millions of fundamentalist Muslims worldwide, ordered his death. Rushdie was then forced to write in exile and, torn between the ongoing cultural and religious conflict between India and Pakistan, his political parables explore themes of alienation and poke fun at those whose mindless adherence to religion takes the place of genuinely meaningful faith.

Rushdie is a Gemini, a sign noted for intelligence, communication skills, and clever tongue twisters. In addition, his Moon, planet of emotions, is also in this sign, so his energies are quite coherent and devoted to his writing. With his Moon and Sun, planet of identity, in his house of money, it's natural that Rushdie

would write for a living and also that some of his themes would focus on issues of value.

With a contact from Uranus, planet of upheavals, to both Sun and Moon, Rushdie could be described as a bit of an eccentric genius, a rebel, and someone for whom life is unstable and never dull. He has his own opinions, his own feelings, and he enjoys expressing them, no matter what the consequences.

Rushdie's Mars, the planet of action, is prominently placed as well as located in the durable sign of Taurus, giving him stability and the tenacity that helps him hold fast when others are suggesting he retreat. With a contact from expansive Jupiter, he is courageous and energetic. This is not a man who uses restraint or thinks better of a chosen course of action.

In Rushdie's house of home and emotional foundations we find both Saturn, planet of

limits, and Pluto, planet of oppression. It's not surprising at all that with this placement he was forced from his home. Normally he would feel a sense of limitation because of the teachings of his parents and childhood but, in this case, it's the entire culture associated with his nation that he feels he must challenge.

➤ Read "East Meets Twentieth-Century West" on page 65. ➤ Read "Nostradamus: A Prophet Across Time" on page 785.

Explosions and Silent Killers: Pluto's Dark Power

Two events in 1986 showed the power of the unseen influences symbolized by Pluto. America found out about the dangers of space travel when the space shuttle *Challenger* exploded just after lift-off in January, as Pluto's position was emphasized. Explosions are associated with Pluto, the planet of cathartic transformation. The second event that occurred when Pluto was highlighted was the meltdown of nuclear Reactor 4 in Chernobyl, Ukraine, on April 26, also triggered by an explosion. Pluto is also linked to nuclear power because of the profound transformative power of radioactive elements and their sinister ability to cause decay from within.

However volatile Plutonian substances may be, Pluto can be tied to forces of positive change. For example, the Chernobyl accident prompted more open exchange and support between nations regarding nuclear dangers. Because Pluto stays in a sign for no less than twelve years, as was the case with its sojourn through Scorpio, it is associated with social and political movements. While it was in Scorpio, we saw many changes in the way people thought of economics, one of the macro-sociological subjects associated with this sign. As Pluto was in the early degrees of Scorpio, U.S. President Ronald Reagan imposed a bold economic plan on America, which would influence the social and political systems around the world for years to come. The transformation to stable, independent nations which was taking place in many former colonies was also a part of this momentum, although it did not always take place calmly.

A fire at the Chernobyl nuclear power plant causes a radiation leak in the Ukraine

The President of Haiti Claude Duvalier flees to France

The Duke and Duchess of York outside Westminster Abbey on their wedding day

TELEVISED TELEKINESIS

Parapsychologists define "telekinesis" (also known as "teleportation") as the movement of bodies or objects without any contact or other physical means. In 1986, millions of tennis fans witnessed the short, sharp rebellion of a humble tennis ball against the tyranny of the laws of physics during Wimbledon. "Live" on television, the rogue ball skimmed unaided through the net, not leaving any hole, displaying for every viewer an example of this transference.

CHALLENGER AND CHERNOBYL

In the Ukraine a reactor fire in the Chernobyl nuclear power plant caused a catastrophic radiation leak. After twenty years in power, authoritarian Philippine President Ferdinand Marcos was forced to flee the country and was succeeded by Corazon Aquino, widow of assassinated candidate Benigno Aquino. Self-styled President-for-Life "Baby Doc" Duvalier was thrown out of Haiti and escaped to France. The U.S. launched air strikes against Libya and a state of emergency was declared in South Africa as hundreds of African activists and trade unionists were arrested. In France, four died and forty-four were injured when Arab terrorists threw a bomb into a Paris department store. In the U.S., the space shuttle *Challenger* exploded after lift-off, killing all seven astronauts on board, including schoolteacher Christa McAuliffe. Swedish Prime Minister Olaf Palme was assassinated in Stockholm. Faulty rivets were blamed for the sinking of the *Titanic* in 1912. Prince Andrew, second son of Queen Elizabeth, married Sarah Ferguson in London. The Duchess of Windsor, the former Wallis Simpson, died in Paris. Film star James Cagney died.

➤ Read "Astrology in the White House: The Reagans" by Frank Andrews on page 705.

CAPRICORN

From January 01, 0:00 through January 20, 8:45

The Practical Seeker

The mid-1980s saw materialism grow in the Western world, a trend led by the U.S. where the German BMW automobile became a status symbol, possibly driven by a family wearing Izod shirts. You, January 1986 Capricorn, emerged into a society of rampant consumerism. Coincidentally, Paul Newman won an Oscar award in 1986 for best actor in the film, *The Color of Money*. Though this time of conspicuous consumption could resonate with the Capricorn traits of seeking prestige and material wealth, you are also likely to have the desire to explore the spiritual side of life. Much of your growth could come from trusting the intuitive mind and allowing explorations into the unknown.

The position of luck-bringer Jupiter in otherworldly Pisces could mean that great leaps come for you when you open to the intangible. At times, this might conflict with more practical Capricorn attributes, which often center on what is "real." By opening to both spiritual and material abundance, you can find yourself quite wealthy. Indeed, Saturn, the planet of limitations, was in knowledge-seeking Sagittarius at the time of your birth. This could make it difficult for you to learn simply for the joy of it. With this Saturn placement, you could seek knowledge that also has a practical application.

Mars has been described as the fuel that drives the engine in a person's birth-chart. With Mars in intense Scorpio, you gain a double-dose of determination, focus, and ambition toward any goal. Your work life is likely to be a source of validation and self-respect, and you have what it takes to succeed at anything you try. With your dogged persistence, you could make a fine researcher, investigator, or financial wizard.

You could be drawn to companions that have a philosophical and introspective view of life. Good connections could be made with Sagittarians, Pisceans, or Capricorns.

Your gift is your dynamic presence—both forward moving and deeply rooted in practical realities. Your challenge is not to compromise your sense of stability and self-respect in your effort to forge ahead with your plans.

AQUARIUS

From January 20, 8:46 through February 18, 22:57

The Cosmic Explorer

Those with signs in Aquarius are often equipped with the ability to view life from a removed, even cosmic level. If the 1986 Aquarius seems aloof and detached, it could be that they see things from a distance rather than up close and personal. You might even have an interest in the world beyond Earth, leading you to study astronomy or cosmology. As humans have ventured into space exploration, there have been both incredible triumphs—such as the first moonwalk of 1969—and tragic events. One such tragic event took place around the time of your birth. The space shuttle *Challenger* exploded in a ball of fire seventy-two seconds after lift-off. It was the U.S. space program's worst accident, made all the more tragic as it carried the first civilian into space—Christa McAuliffe. The enthusiasm of McAuliffe, a schoolteacher, inspired many and her loss was mourned around the world. You are likely to have admired the pioneering spirit of her and the other brave souls on board who followed their dreams of venturing into space.

You are a born rebel and also may not follow the expected or easy route. You can be a formidable opponent for those who dare to try to curtail your freedom or resist your urge to discover. With Jupiter, the planet of abundance, in your sign, you could enjoy times of remarkable serendipity—and fortuitous discoveries—throughout your life.

The sciences could appeal to the bright 1986 Aquarius, who is likely to have the ability to absorb concepts and ideas quickly. Such a gift for abstract thinking could also lead you into pioneering ventures in the computer field. Your quicksilver mind likely thrives in areas where your gift for logic and reason can be put to good use.

You are likely to seek companions who understand your need for complete freedom. Some possible mates for the kinds of evolving connections you seek may have signs in Aquarius, Pisces, or Sagittarius.

Your gift is a brilliant mind that is expansive and always curious about the world. Your challenge is discovering the joy of sharing your deepest feelings with others on an intimate level.

➤ Read about your Chinese Astrological sign on page 838. ➤ Read about your Personal Planets on page 826. ➤ Read about your personal Mystical Card on page 856.

CAPRICORN
Your Personal Planets

YOUR LOVE POTENTIAL
Venus in Capricorn, Jan. 01, 0:00 - Jan. 20, 5:35
Venus in Aquarius, Jan. 20, 5:36 - Jan. 20, 8:45

YOUR DRIVE AND AMBITION
Mars in Scorpio, Jan. 01, 0:00 - Jan. 20, 8:45

YOUR LUCK MAGNETISM
Jupiter in Aquarius, Jan. 01, 0:00 - Jan. 20, 8:45

World Events

Jan. 1 – U.S. President Reagan and Soviet leader Gorbachev broadcast New Year's wishes to each other's nations for the first time since 1973.

Jan. 17 – The National Resistance Army battles with government forces in Uganda.

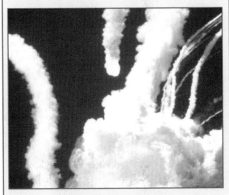

The space shuttle Challenger explodes moments after lift-off

AQUARIUS
Your Personal Planets

YOUR LOVE POTENTIAL
Venus in Aquarius, Jan. 20, 8:46 - Feb. 13, 3:10
Venus in Pisces, Feb. 13, 3:11 - Feb. 18, 22:57

YOUR DRIVE AND AMBITION
Mars in Scorpio, Jan. 20, 8:46 - Feb. 02, 6:26
Mars in Sagittarius, Feb. 02, 6:27 - Feb. 18, 22:57

YOUR LUCK MAGNETISM
Jupiter in Aquarius, Jan. 20, 8:46 - Feb. 18, 22:57

World Events

Jan. 28 – The space shuttle *Challenger*, carrying the first ordinary citizen into space, explodes in a ball of fire seconds after lift-off.

Feb. 10 – Jean-Claude Duvalier, corrupt dictator of Haiti, flees to France.

PISCES

Your Personal Planets

YOUR LOVE POTENTIAL

Venus in Pisces, Feb. 18, 22:58 - Mar. 09, 3:31
Venus in Aries, Mar. 09, 3:32 - Mar. 20, 22:02

YOUR DRIVE AND AMBITION

Mars in Sagittarius, Feb. 18, 22:58 - Mar. 20, 22:02

YOUR LUCK MAGNETISM

Jupiter in Aquarius, Feb. 18, 22:58 - Feb. 20, 16:04
Jupiter in Pisces, Feb. 20, 16:05 - Mar. 20, 22:02

World Events

Feb. 20 – Plans for a Channel Tunnel between England and France are unveiled.

Feb. 25 – President of the Philippines Ferdinand Marcos flees to Hawaii.

Deposed President Ferdinand Marcos

ARIES

Your Personal Planets

YOUR LOVE POTENTIAL

Venus in Aries, Mar. 20, 22:03 - Apr. 02, 8:18
Venus in Taurus, Apr. 02, 8:19 - Apr. 20, 9:11

YOUR DRIVE AND AMBITION

Mars in Sagittarius, Mar. 20, 22:03 - Mar. 28, 3:46
Mars in Capricorn, Mar. 28, 3:47 - Apr. 20, 9:11

YOUR LUCK MAGNETISM

Jupiter in Pisces, Mar. 20, 22:03 - Apr. 20, 9:11

World Events

Apr. 14 – Simone de Beauvoir dies.

Apr. 15 – The U.S. launches an assault on Khadaffi's Libyan base as a punishment for its international "reign of terror."

PISCES

From February 18, 22:58 through March 20, 22:02

The Fiery Dreamer

The 1986 Pisces came into the world as plans for the "Chunnel" between England and France were unveiled. The European world would grow closer with this tunnel built beneath the waters of the English Channel. The 1986 Pisces is able to build such bridges between worlds and often between people as well. You are likely to be a compassionate soul who seeks to better the lives of those around them. Also at this time in history, Ferdinand Marcos, the president of the Philippines, was exiled to Hawaii and replaced by Corazon Aquino. Her desire to diminish the poverty and suffering in her country would likely appeal to the humanitarian heart of the 1986 Pisces.

With many planets in expansive Sagittarius, the 1986 Pisces is a unique blend of Piscean compassion and sensitivity with Sagittarian fire and vitality. Your restless spirit could seem to send you in many different directions. The absorbent mind of the 1986 Pisces requires constant feeding so that the vital imagination does not stray into the realm of worry and fear. In the vast sea of possibilities, your challenge could lie in deciding how to choose the right path. The 1986 Pisces may seem indecisive, but it is simply your reluctance to narrow the choices. With strong choices, however, you can forge a determined path toward success. Once you set your mind to a task, you can show remarkable determination.

Your dynamic creativity demands an outlet and you could thrive in any artistic endeavor. From theater to music to the more solitary pursuits of writing and painting, there is no reason why you can't give it all a try. The 1986 Pisces could thrive in environments that allow ample room to grow along with constant support from trusted companions.

You could shine with loved ones who honor your sensitivity and can inspire you to face your fears. Those with signs in Pisces, Scorpio, or Sagittarius could offer the stimulating company you seek.

Your gift is an intuitive creativity that is inspiring to others. Your challenge is finding ways to give yourself the peaceful solitude you need to recharge your batteries.

ARIES

From March 20, 22:03 through April 20, 9:11

The Incendiary Warrior

At the time you were born, Clint Eastwood enjoyed a landslide victory and became mayor of Carmel, California. A film actor known for his rugged, masculine on-screen persona, he brought this image of the cowboy spirit to governing this small town on the West Coast of the U.S. The 1986 Aries is poised for such success in life and likely to be cut from a similar cloth. Independent and tenacious, the 1986 Aries is here to forge a distinct identity apart from the crowd. This could often be done in a forceful way; the 1986 Aries will not allow other people to stand in the way of legitimate goals. Aries is ruled by Mars, the planet associated with war and aggression. At the time of your birth, the U.S. government sought to undermine Libya's Muammar Khadaffi, for what the administration saw as that leader's international reign of terror. Also in this year, a movie about the Vietnam War, *Platoon*, took home the Oscar award for best picture. Oliver Stone, who also won the Oscar award for best director in this year, had himself been on the front lines as a soldier.

The 1986 Aries can summon the mask of the warrior when necessary in life. Other key planets in Aries can magnify an ego-centered approach that leaves gentler souls quivering in their wake. Your impulse to express your true nature leads, at times, to brutal honesty that unintentionally injures others. When your motivations are honorable, you can trust yourself to give all that fire free reign.

The 1986 Aries could thrive with work that is full of adventure and new thrills. Always charging ahead to new projects, you are probably a true maverick in your own life and a catalyst for those around you.

Your vibrant personality seeks companions who can energize you and inspire you to be your best. You could find harmonious relations with those with planets in Aries, Taurus, or Sagittarius.

Your gift is your "take-no-prisoners" approach to life, which allows you to travel light and keep moving forward. Your challenge is tempering your aggressive thrusts toward action with an ability to respect the feelings of others.

➤ Read about your Chinese Astrological sign on page 838. ➤ Read about your Personal Planets on page 826. ➤ Read about your personal Mystical Card on page 856.

TAURUS

From April 20, 9:12 through May 21, 8:27

The Steady Constructor

Around the time you were born in 1986, there was a major accident at the nuclear power plant in Chernobyl, Ukraine. This was the worst disaster in the history of nuclear power. The earth surrounding the Chernobyl site was poisoned, along with the waters and the skies, something that would likely jar the security-loving 1986 Taurus. This year's Taurus draws comfort from being in the physical world, and you are uniquely tuned in to sensory pleasures. The 1986 Taurus is a master builder of the safe, steady, and solid.

On the other side of the world, South Africa was the scene of a major strike in protest against apartheid in 1986. This was a pivotal point in the effort to dismantle a system in that country that kept wealth and power in the hands of the whites. The 1986 Taurus can be a bit resistant to change too, unless you have methodically planned it down to the last detail. With Mars, the planet of action, in meticulous Capricorn, you can be relied on to have a practical, grounded approach to life. The placement of Jupiter, the planet of abundance, in mystical Pisces tempers that practicality with a side that seeks answers beyond the visible world. Lucky breaks could come in ways that open you to a sense of oneness with the world. Thus, the 1986 Taurus can have a unique perspective on how to create solid structures that support people in mind, body, and spirit.

Careers that give you the chance to design and build, such as architecture, could offer the challenge you crave. You are uniquely able to take abstract ideas and bring them to reality on the physical plane. The 1986 Taurus could enjoy such pursuits as gardening, designing for theater and movies, or building homes.

Your relationships should offer you a sense of continuity and loyal support. You know how to have a good time and can really let your hair down with those who have planets in Taurus, Gemini, or Capricorn.

Your gift is your ability to translate dreams into reality and, through careful planning, to reach your goals. Your challenge is to avoid getting fixed in place and remain open to change.

GEMINI

From May 21, 8:28 through June 21, 16:29

The Truth-Seeking Wordsmith

When you emerged into the world, 1986 Gemini, the United Nations reported that 50,000 people in Africa were infected with the AIDS virus. The 1986 Gemini is gifted with a natural curiosity for facts and figures, along with a deeply compassionate heart. Also at this time, the U.S. Embassy in Moscow advised pregnant women not to drink milk due to the increase in radiation in Russia following the Chernobyl disaster. The 1986 Gemini is likely to have an idea of what is going on beyond your sphere and take an active interest in world politics. If you chose to, you could write eloquently and passionately on social issues, perhaps motivating others to take action.

The presence of Mars, the planet of action, in methodical Capricorn brings your Gemini traits of mercurial flightiness back down to the ground. You are likely to work toward goals that bring you the admiration and respect of others. The 1986 Gemini can harness nervous energy through decisive and well-planned actions that lead to sure success. With Saturn, the planet of discipline, in philosophical Sagittarius you could find that you seek knowledge with a practical application. This nicely tempers the more restless Gemini traits, likely giving you a more settled temperament.

With such an affinity for the spoken word, you could be drawn into careers where you can shape, shift, and manipulate words on the page. Writing is an obvious choice and it could take many forms, from fiction to public relations. Adding a financial acumen to your mix of traits, you could write for a newspaper or run it as publisher. You might be drawn to the theater as well.

You are likely to gravitate toward those who understand your chameleon nature and accept your many sides. You may also seek companions who are loyal and consistent, enhancing your own potential to feel secure. You might hit it off with Cancerians, Leos, or Sagittarians.

Your gift is your aptitude for engaging and stimulating conversation with people from all walks of life. Your challenge is to channel your restless energy into activities that feel meaningful to you.

➤ Read about your Chinese Astrological sign on page 838. ➤ Read about your Personal Planets on page 826. ➤ Read about your personal Mystical Card on page 856.

1986

TAURUS
Your Personal Planets

YOUR LOVE POTENTIAL
Venus in Taurus, Apr. 20, 9:12 - Apr. 26, 19:09
Venus in Gemini, Apr. 26, 19:10 - May 21, 8:27

YOUR DRIVE AND AMBITION
Mars in Capricorn, Apr. 20, 9:12 - May 21, 8:27

YOUR LUCK MAGNETISM
Jupiter in Pisces, Apr. 20, 9:12 - May 21, 8:27

World Events

Apr. 26 – A major accident at a nuclear plant in Chernobyl in the Ukraine releases radioactivity into the atmosphere; it is the worst accident in the history of nuclear power.

May 1 – South Africa is hit by the biggest strike ever to protest against apartheid.

AIDS orphans in Kampala, Uganda

GEMINI
Your Personal Planets

YOUR LOVE POTENTIAL
Venus in Gemini, May 21, 8:28 - May 21, 13:45
Venus in Cancer, May 21, 13:46 - June 15, 18:51
Venus in Leo, June 15, 18:52 - June 21, 16:29

YOUR DRIVE AND AMBITION
Mars in Capricorn, May 21, 8:28 - June 21, 16:29

YOUR LUCK MAGNETISM
Jupiter in Pisces, May 21, 8:28 - June 21, 16:29

World Events

June 5 – The UN releases a report estimating AIDS cases in Africa to be at the 50,000 mark.

June 8 – Kurt Waldheim is elected to a six-year term as President of Austria.

CANCER
Your Personal Planets

YOUR LOVE POTENTIAL

Venus in Leo, June 21, 16:30 - July 11, 16:22
Venus in Virgo, July 11, 16:23 - July 23, 3:23

YOUR DRIVE AND AMBITION

Mars in Capricorn, June 21, 16:30 - July 23, 3:23

YOUR LUCK MAGNETISM

Jupiter in Pisces, June 21, 16:30 - July 23, 3:23

World Events

June 29 - Argentina wins the soccer World Cup.

July 23 - Prince Andrew weds Sarah Ferguson at Westminster Abbey, London.

Prince Andrew and his bride Sarah Ferguson

LEO
Your Personal Planets

YOUR LOVE POTENTIAL

Venus in Virgo, July 23, 3:24 - Aug. 07, 20:45
Venus in Libra, Aug. 07, 20:46 - Aug. 23, 10:25

YOUR DRIVE AND AMBITION

Mars in Capricorn, July 23, 3:24 - Aug. 23, 10:25

YOUR LUCK MAGNETISM

Jupiter in Pisces, July 23, 3:24 - Aug. 23, 10:25

World Events

Aug. 1 - The U.S. Senate votes for sanctions against South Africa.

Aug. 6 - A patient who had lived 620 days with an artificial heart dies.

CANCER

From June 21, 16:30 through July 23, 3:23

The Generous Leader

The 1986 Cancer arrived into the world as festivities were underway to celebrate the hundred-year anniversary of the Statue of Liberty in the harbor of New York City. Since 1886, this landmark had stood as a beacon of hope for immigrants seeking a new way of life and a new home in the United States. The 1986 Cancer emerged into this scene with a unique way of seeking their "home" in this world too. With emotional security a high priority, you, 1986 Cancer, thrive in an environment where you are valued and loved for who you are. The extreme sensitivity of the 1986 Cancer gives you a compassion for others that knows no bounds. Also at this time in history, Parliament in Britain abolished corporal punishment in state-supported schools and Sarah Ferguson wed Prince Andrew in what looked to be the beginning of marital bliss. Though bonds may not always be forever, as turned out to be the case of the Duke and Duchess of York, the 1986 Cancer is likely to seek as much stability in relationships as is humanly possible.

The fueling planet of Mars in the sign of determined Capricorn gives structured focus to the make-up of the 1986 Cancer. Once you've set your course in a particular direction, you can be quite persistent at reaching your goal. You might, however, find it helpful to enlist the help of others rather than always trying to make it on your own.

The 1986 Cancer can be a formidable leader who understands the motivations of others on a deeply intuitive level. You could rise to the top with positions in finance, education, or the arts. You probably thrive in a work place where you are given ample space to work alone. You may need time to "hide" occasionally, periods during which you can go within and recharge your batteries.

The 1986 Cancer will likely employ a strategic caution in deciding whom they draw into their life. Some possible matches are with Virgos, Leos, or Pisceans.

Your gift is the emotional richness and imagination you can draw on to fulfill your potential. Your challenge is learning to balance self-protection with a need to be open to change.

LEO

From July 23, 3:24 through August 23, 10:25

The Transcendent Performer

At the time when you were born, 1986 Leo, medical history was being made. Artificial heart recipient William Schroeder died at this time, but he had lived a record 620 days, almost two years. This was the most successful heart transplant in history. The 1986 Leo is a big-hearted sort with the ability to energize everyone around them. With a practical way of channeling your exuberance, you can "reach for the stars, with your feet on the ground," as the saying goes. It's always showtime for the 1986 Leo and you probably love to take center stage. Like Marlee Matlin, winner of the Oscar for best actress in 1986, your dramatic flair is likely a delight to others.

The placement of the action planet of Mars in methodical Capricorn gives the 1986 Leo a way to harness those sudden bursts of excitement. You are likely to seek respect and status through your work and can thrive in environments that support your impulsive spontaneity. But you can find harmony by engaging in consistent activities that allow you to build continually toward solid achievement. With Saturn, the planet of limitations, in restless Sagittarius, you could benefit from a structured approach to your creativity. A desire to rush ahead toward your goals could be tempered by an equally powerful need to create strong foundations.

Though it may seem paradoxical, a disciplined artistic life could be a fulfilling career choice for you. Careers in the performing arts could validate your need to be in the limelight. You might be drawn to dance, theater, or music and find that you have the discipline to go far in these pursuits. You could also be drawn to other careers in the public eye, such as motivational speaker or teacher. The 1986 Leo can radiate a transcendent energy that seems to raise everyone around them.

You can shine with people who encourage you to be your most outrageous self. Good matches could be made with those who have planets in Virgo, Libra, or Sagittarius.

Your gift is an unflagging enthusiasm and zest for life. Your challenge is to find stable environments within which you can grow and change.

➤ Read about your Chinese Astrological sign on page 838. ➤ Read about your Personal Planets on page 826. ➤ Read about your personal Mystical Card on page 856.

VIRGO

From August 23, 10:26 through September 23, 7:58

The Practical Sage

The mid-1980s was the height of the jogging and aerobics craze in America with people such as Jane Fonda and Richard Simmons leading the way to physical fitness. Simmons expressed an unusually caring demeanor in his popular television show; it became an inspiration to some and a target for derisive humor to others. The 1986 Virgo, like other Virgos, is likely to be concerned with health and staying fit. Consistent physical activity could be a regular and necessary part of the life of the energetic 1986 Virgo.

Your earth sign, Virgo, is complemented by the position of Mars, the planet of "getting things done," in grounded Capricorn. Your talent lies in knowing how to make things happen, down to the details. The 1986 Virgo leaves little to chance. Everything is meticulously thought out and plans usually lead to success. With steady Capricorn also influencing Neptune, the planet of dreams and visions, the 1986 Virgo is unlikely ever to be accused of flakiness or lack of substance. Your unique search for meaning could manifest in the way you live day to day. Your sense of harmony with the universe could come from simply staying engaged by what others may consider the mundane. Your complete commitment to daily life gives you all the oneness you need to feel part of things.

The 1986 Virgo is well suited to be of service to others, possibly through the helping professions, including medicine, counseling, or teaching. You are likely energized by being actively involved in consistent activities that lead to growth in those around you. Your joy could come from improving the lives of others in practical ways. Because you radiate an air of authority, people could look to you for advice on issues big and small.

You could benefit from seeking those with whom you can engage in thoughtful, analytical discussions. Your best bet for compatibility comes from those who have planets in Libra, Scorpio and Virgo.

Your gift is your ability to use reason and logic to achieve your goals. Your challenge is to avoid the restraint that comes with a tendency toward perfectionism.

LIBRA

From September 23, 7:59 through October 23, 17:13

The Balanced Activist

At the time of your birth, an International Committee for Prostitutes' Rights ended a three-day conference in Brussels. In this unprecedented meeting, a list of human rights abuses was cited, including lack of civil liberties and harassment by pimps. The committee urged the use of condoms to protect the women against disease and pregnancy. The 1986 Libra is a humanitarian and one who is likely to desire peace and justice for all people. Though perhaps more of a one-on-one person in your private life, it is possible that you emerge as a public authority or leader to champion a cause of some kind.

Your natural Libran tendency to seek out the balance of equal partnerships is likely to be knocked askew at times by a drive toward passionate and dramatic entanglements. With Venus, the planet of relationships, in deeply inward Scorpio you are likely to seek transformative connections that engage your mind, body, and spirit. The presence of Mars, the planet of action, in ambitious Capricorn can temper that intensity with a motivation to seek stability and status. You may have many ideas along with an awareness of the best route to making them a reality. Others will likely recognize your insightful, yet viable ideas and support you in your goals. You could find that your best self is expressed by working in a partnership.

A disciplined seeker of the truth, you could be rewarded by study in fields such as law, philosophy, or religion. You have the makings of a courageous activist, working on behalf of the downtrodden, disempowered, and disenfranchised. You might find fulfillment in the non-profit world. With your gift for language, you may also be drawn toward writing or some other form of communication.

Though it may be hard for you to be simply social and light, you likely enjoy many meaningful relationships. You could find rewarding connections with those with the sign of Scorpio, Cancer, or Aquarius.

Your gift is the innate sense of harmony and balance that keeps your life moving forward. Your challenge is to stay emotionally independent, so that you can achieve your goals.

➤ Read about your Chinese Astrological sign on page 838. ➤ Read about your Personal Planets on page 826. ➤ Read about your personal Mystical Card on page 856.

1986

VIRGO
Your Personal Planets

YOUR LOVE POTENTIAL
Venus in Libra, Aug. 23, 10:26 - Sept. 07, 10:14
Venus in Scorpio, Sept. 07, 10:15 - Sept. 23, 7:58

YOUR DRIVE AND AMBITION
Mars in Capricorn, Aug. 23, 10:26 - Sept. 23, 7:58

YOUR LUCK MAGNETISM
Jupiter in Pisces, Aug. 23, 10:26 - Sept. 23, 7:58

World Events

Aug. 31 - British sculptor Henry Moore dies.
Sept. 6 - Two Arab gunmen kill twenty-one people in a synagogue in Istanbul.

Death of British artist and sculptor Henry Moore

LIBRA
Your Personal Planets

YOUR LOVE POTENTIAL
Venus in Scorpio, Sept. 23, 7:59 - Oct. 23, 17:13

YOUR DRIVE AND AMBITION
Mars in Capricorn, Sept. 23, 7:59 - Oct. 09, 1:00
Mars in Aquarius, Oct. 09, 1:01 - Oct. 23, 17:13

YOUR LUCK MAGNETISM
Jupiter in Pisces, Sept. 23, 7:59 - Oct. 23, 17:13

World Events

Oct. 12 - Queen Elizabeth II becomes the first British monarch to visit China.

Oct. 22 - Four American firms, General Motors, Honeywell, Warner, and IBM, withdraw from South Africa because of apartheid policies.

1986

SCORPIO
Your Personal Planets

YOUR LOVE POTENTIAL
Venus in Scorpio, Oct. 23, 17:14 - Nov. 22, 14:43

YOUR DRIVE AND AMBITION
Mars in Aquarius, Oct. 23, 17:14 - Nov. 22, 14:43

YOUR LUCK MAGNETISM
Jupiter in Pisces, Oct. 23, 17:14 - Nov. 22, 14:43

World Events

Oct. 28 - Sheikh Yamani is removed by the King of Saudi Arabia, who wants control of the oil fields.

Nov. 10 - Thousands of tons of chemicals pollute the Rhine River after a fire in a chemical warehouse in Basle, Switzerland.

Death of film star Cary Grant

SAGITTARIUS
Your Personal Planets

YOUR LOVE POTENTIAL
Venus in Scorpio, Nov. 22, 14:44 - Dec. 22, 4:01

YOUR DRIVE AND AMBITION
Mars in Aquarius, Nov. 22, 14:44 - Nov. 26, 2:34
Mars in Pisces, Nov. 26, 2:35 - Dec. 22, 4:01

YOUR LUCK MAGNETISM
Jupiter in Pisces, Nov. 22, 14:44 - Dec. 22, 4:01

World Events

Nov. 29 - American actor Cary Grant dies.
Dec. 9 - The Musée D'Orsay opens in Paris.

SCORPIO
From October 23, 17:14 through November 22, 14:43

The Mysterious Investigator

By 1986, the corporate greed of the 1980s was beginning to wear thin with the public in America. In a scandal on Wall Street, Ivan Boesky pleaded guilty to insider trading before a New York City judge. This was the beginning of what would be a series of revelations of white collar crimes. The 1986 Scorpio comes equipped to investigate, to interrogate, and to probe for the truth. You have enormous energy reserves and the desire to dive below the surface to experience the deeper realties of life. In other world events of that year, a king who wanted full control of oil reserves in the Middle East removed Sheikh Yamani, the man behind OPEC's rise to power. The 1986 Scorpio can struggle with issues of control, which are often at odds with the radically transformative nature of the sign. The 1986 Scorpio knows that change comes with letting go, but for them, it is often a Herculean task.

The 1986 Scorpio has many planets in his or her own sign, including Mercury, the planet of communication. You, 1986 Scorpio, may long to express your unfathomable depths to others and could feel frustrated when words fall short. A longing to share the hidden mysteries of the self with others can lead to many interesting connections. The position of Mars, the planet of action, in detached Aquarius brings the welcome influence of logic to the emotionally charged Scorpio. With this influence, your greatest achievements could come by working with a group.

The 1986 Scorpio requires a work life that allows for diving and resurfacing on many levels. You could find happiness as an artist of some kind. You could also enjoy fields that involve intense investigative work, such as journalism or scholarship.

The 1986 Scorpio is not a casual acquaintance, but one who seeks connections full of depth and intensity. Those with signs such as Scorpio, Pisces, and Cancer could hold their own in these deep waters.

Your gift is the ability to express the dark and mysterious in an intuitive, creative way. Your challenge is avoiding the kinds of passionate intrigues that could lead you down the wrong path.

SAGITTARIUS
From November 22, 14:44 through December 22, 4:01

The Diligent Traveler

Around the time when you were born, Elie Weisel, the author who survived the concentration camp at Auschwitz, won the Nobel Prize for his books on the Holocaust. In his celebrated book entitled *Night*, he gave an account of a father and son in the camps together and their desperate effort to survive. The 1986 Sagittarius is here to explore his or her relationship to the universe. Like Weisel, you are on a quest for the truth of your experience. You are discovering your identity by exploring the vast unknown territories outside yourself. Also at this time, French Prime Minister Jacques Chirac yielded to student protesters and gave up on a plan to reform the university system. The 1986 Sagittarius is full of strong opinions and ready to take on a challenge for a cause they believe is right. Your optimism and idealism can spark the energy of a group situation.

The time of your birth also coincided with the opening of the Musée d'Orsay in Paris. The 1986 Sagittarius would likely enjoy roaming large art galleries and other cultural institutions. You might also like to visit the planetarium so that you might be able to travel the cosmos. A desire to roam the world could also lead you on many adventures and enable you to explore different cultures. With Saturn, the planet of structure and order, in your sign, you might insist on a disciplined approach to what appears to others to be aimless wandering. The way you go about things is utterly unique, and only you will know when you are making the most of your time and talent.

Your focus on the big picture could lead you into work that satisfies your desire to ponder concepts, rather than getting to grips with details. You might find happiness as an author or professor in a university.

The 1986 Sagittarius can flourish when given unrestricted freedom within stable relationships. You could find harmony with those with planets in Sagittarius, Pisces, or Scorpio.

Your gift is your cheerful outlook and inspiring quest for your own personal truth. Your challenge is developing tact and being aware of the feelings and sensitivities of others.

➤ Read about your Chinese Astrological sign on page 838. ➤ Read about your Personal Planets on page 826. ➤ Read about your personal Mystical Card on page 856.

CAPRICORN

From December 22, 4:02 through December 31, 23:59

The Ambitious Advocate

At the time of your arrival, 1986 December Capricorn, the scandal of the Iran-Contra affair was coming to light in America. The Reagan presidency was revealed to have sold arms to Iran in exchange for the release of hostages held in Lebanon. The money from these arms sales was then allegedly diverted to Nicaraguan rebels, the contras. The 1986 Capricorn was destined to live in a world where things are not always as they appear. Trusted leaders were exposed as having secret agendas and deals were being forged with questionable allies. Also at this time, the *Voyager*, a super-light plane that carried five times its weight in fuel, circled the globe in a non-stop flight. This was expected to lead to more fuel-efficient air transport. The 1986 Capricorn is similarly able to navigate in life in a "fuel-efficient" manner.

If Mars is the planet that fuels the engine, then its presence in sensitive Pisces gives the 1986 Capricorn the desire to act on the behalf of others. A strong interest in the fate of humanity could lead you to engaging your Capricorn traits of determination and creating structures that alleviate suffering. You might feel unusually motivated to dedicate your life to a cause. Intuitive Pisces also makes its mark on Jupiter, the planet of abundance, shining on the 1986 Capricorn and giving you a tendency toward lucky breaks that propel you forward. This aspect brings ease in your affairs, once you decide on a course to follow.

You are likely to be energized by a career that is the center of your life. It is possible that you could rise to some level of status and prestige. You could be motivated by work that involves bringing practical improvements to the lives of others.

You seek to surround yourself with loyal, stable people who can give you a sense of continuity. You could find fulfilling connections with those who have planets in Scorpio, Pisces, or Cancer.

Your gift is the compassion for others that drives your ambitions. Your challenge is overcoming any tendency toward melancholy that threatens to prevent you from cultivating your potential.

1986

CAPRICORN
Your Personal Planets

YOUR LOVE POTENTIAL
Venus in Scorpio, Dec. 22, 4:02 - Dec. 31, 23:59

YOUR DRIVE AND AMBITION
Mars in Pisces, Dec. 22, 4:02 - Dec. 31, 23:59

YOUR LUCK MAGNETISM
Jupiter in Pisces, Dec. 22, 4:02 - Dec. 31, 23:59

World Events

Dec. 23 – A super-light plane circles the globe non-stop; the *Voyager* can carry five times its weight in fuel.

Dec. 29 – Former British Prime Minister Harold Macmillan dies.

The Reagans on the White House lawn

Special Feature
Astrology in the White House: The Reagans

by Frank Andrews

Many actors have had the opportunity to play the President of the United States, but only in the case of Ronald Reagan did an actor actually become President. "Lights, camera, action"—in Washington, not Hollywood—began when Reagan was sworn in as the fortieth U.S. President in 1980. It has long been known that the Hollywood community is big on astrology and other forms of prognostication, such as psychic predictions, and has many followers. So it came as no surprise to longtime friends of the Reagans when it was learned that Nancy Reagan had consulted both psychics and astrologers during her time in the White House.

Before Reagan's successful election, Nancy had regularly consulted the famed psychic Jeanne Dixon. Those in the know have speculated that Nancy ended her long association with Dixon when her predictions did not include a White House career for Reagan.

With eyes on the White House, Nancy decided to look for a new consultant. Shortly after, Joan Quigley came into the picture. A San Francisco socialite and celebrity astrologer, Quigley eventually wrote a tell-all book about the many ways in which she'd helped the Reagans achieve their political goals and find their way to the White House.

Unlike psychics, who are notoriously incorrect where timing is concerned, astrologers can be wonderfully helpful in the fortuitous timing of future events—something both Ronald and Nancy Reagan knew, and which they used to their advantage. During the campaign, they consulted Quigley to help schedule political affairs, such as debates. When these events went in Reagan's favor, it only seemed to prove that astrology was a dependable way of guiding their presidential campaign and later the scheduling of events during his time in office.

Amusing case in point: Ronnie, prepared to announce his candidacy for re-election, was persuaded to postpone his speech until a more propitious time. Joan's choice was January 29, 1985, at the peculiar hour 10:55 p.m. This is something that few but the initiated could understand. He followed her advice, and it appears not to have done him any harm; in fact, it turned out to have been very good timing!

(Continued on page 713)

➤ Read about another influential astrologer in "Astrology Goes on Trial" on page 185.
➤ Read "Astrology Reigns Through the Ages" on page 25. ➤ Read "The Presidential Death Cycle" on page 657.

1987

A World Unravels: A Planetary Cycle Ends

In 1987, several cycles were completing and earthly events reflected these processes. Saturn, planet of structure, was closing in on Uranus, the prophet of change and planet of group leadership. This suggests that some old structures were about to come apart at the seams. In the U.S., a stunned legislature watched agog as the details of "Iran-Contragate" were revealed. In this debacle the President and his advisors traded arms to terrorist state Iran and used the proceeds to fund the Nicaraguan contra rebels, despite an explicit ban by Congress. This called into question the balance of power between the basically Saturnian presidency and Congress, a symbolically Uranian body. Meanwhile, Soviet Premier Mikhail Gorbachev gave more consistent signals that his nation's economy was flagging, if not failing. He called for a change in the old regime, linked to Saturn, to greater democracy, a Uranus concept—a glimpse of what was to come.

Because Saturn and Uranus had not yet completed their old cycle, these initiatives did not reach a satisfactory conclusion in 1987. However, active, adventurous Jupiter made a resonant "trine" to both planets later in the year, encouraging cooperation and progress in breaking down old barriers. This was seen in the warming of relations between the U.S. and USSR, culminating in their first nuclear arms reduction treaty in December, as Jupiter's optimistic energy was highlighted. An international treaty to protect the ozone layer was also signed this year, another illustration of the Jupiter-Saturn spirit of cooperation.

Wall Street during the Black Monday stock market crash

Van Gogh's "Sunflowers" brings in $32 million at Christie's

Lt. Col. Oliver North is sworn in before the Iran-Contra committee in Washington

GREAT WEALTH IS IN THE STARS

The financial world began to accept the validity of astrology after astrologers correctly predicted the stock market crash of 1987. Many financial astrologers, including Englishman Charles Harvey, had predicted the crash up to a full year before it happened. Wall Street took notice and the role of astrology in predicting financial futures was taken seriously even by the press. The *New York Times* requested American financial astrologer Henry Weingarten to write an op-ed piece in its business section, the first such invitation ever extended to any astrologer.

IRAN–CONTRAGATE AND PERESTROIKA

Loosening the grip of Marxist principles and authoritarian government, Premier Gorbachev called for *glasnost* (openness), *perestroika* (restructuring) and other democratic reforms to revive Russian culture and economy. The U.S. lifted economic sanctions against Poland after the end of martial law. Conservative British Prime Minister Margaret Thatcher won a third term of office. During the yearly Haj pilgrimage, Iranians in Mecca demonstrated against Saudi Arabia's support for Iraq in the Iran-Iraq war and scores died when police opened fire on protestors. U.S. President Reagan was criticized for involvement in the Iran-Contra scandal, but escaped legal repercussions. In the U.S., minister Jim Bakker tearfully apologized on TV when his sexual infidelities were revealed. The 'Black Monday' market crash, the highest one-day loss in history, caused an economic downturn around the globe. A severe storm hit southeast England, killing seventeen. Pope John Paul II visited the U.S. Van Gogh's *Sunflowers* sold for £22 million ($32 million) in London and his *Irises* sold for the highest ever price for a painting, $54 million (£37 million) in New York.

➤ Read "Astrology in the White House: The Reagans" by Frank Andrews on page 705.

706

CAPRICORN

From January 01, 0:00 through January 20, 14:39

The Moral Entrepreneur

The Oscar award for best picture went to *The Last Emperor* in 1987 with top directing honors going to Bernardo Bertolucci. The 1987 January Capricorn stars in his or her own epic life with the personality of a regal monarch. It is likely that you enjoy the finer things of life and could be devoted to financial gain. The actor Michael Douglas personified the ruthless greed of the 1980s, and took best actor honors for the movie *Wall Street*. Also in this year, McDonald's, the biggest employer of unskilled labor in the U.S., announced it had expanded to forty countries. The hamburger chain with humble beginnings was now reporting the opening of a new store every seventeen hours. The 1987 January Capricorn may have the business sense to be a leader in the corporate world, but you are also graced with a sense of integrity.

In 1987, the ice-cream company, Ben & Jerry's, became the third largest producer of ice cream in the U.S. These two former hippies founded the company with the goal of using products and production methods that are in harmony with the Earth. Similarly, you are likely to strive to undertake only those projects that are in harmony with their deepest values. The presence of Saturn, the planet of restrictions, in moral Sagittarius gives the 1987 January Capricorn a drive to succeed with a clear conscience.

The business world could use your dynamic ability to create stable structures. You could rise quickly to leadership positions in any field. An emphasis on form and building could lead you into architecture or construction. As a leader, you are likely to be generous and able to seize opportunities without hesitation. Your success and wealth could come later in life after much hard work and many challenges.

You could gravitate toward stable, reliable people who also have exuberant creative sides. Some possible matches for you are those who have planets in Aquarius, Pisces, and Virgo.

Your gift is the integrity and vision you bring to any project you undertake. Your challenge is to be open to the opinions of others while trying not to become too sanctimonious.

AQUARIUS

From January 20, 14:40 through February 19, 4:49

The Cool Activist

As a 1987 Aquarius, you are often involved in cutting edge cultural events. Your sign is associated with aircraft so the timing was just right for British Airways to begin trading stocks in February of 1987. To bring a corporation public takes great teamwork and that's your specialty. Whether working in large groups or small ones, you definitely share your team's spirit. Aquarians of 1987 often enjoy taking part in organized sports. On February of that year, England beat Australia 2-0 to win the World Series Cup.

Also in 1987, U.S. Surgeon General Dr. C. Everett Koop spoke on television about the use of condoms to stem the spread of AIDS. You are probably not afraid to stir up controversy and have the courage to challenge any resistance to meeting your goals. The 1987 Aquarius has a progressive and entirely original mind; you may be unafraid to express extreme views.

Some might find you a bit serious at first and you might be more at ease in groups rather than intimate situations. The presence of Mercury, the planet of communication, in detached Aquarius gives your mind an unemotional view on things. You are likely to bring objectivity to confusing situations since you are blessed with an unbiased view of things. The influence of Jupiter, the planet of expansion, in impulsive Aries could give you the tendency to dive right into things. The 1987 Aquarius is quick to take advantage of opportunities but may also be quick to change courses.

The 1987 Aquarius could gravitate toward careers in the sciences, possibly finding fulfillment in being at the leading edge of technology. Any work should offer complete freedom and this could lead to working independently, such as in an artistic pursuit.

You could thrive by surrounding yourself with intellectually stimulating companions who activate your mind. Those with planets in Gemini, Sagittarius, or Aries could be harmonious companions.

Your gift is your broad perspective, which gives you a rich imagination and vibrant personality. Your challenge is to find ways to make deeper connections that still allow you room to grow.

► Read about your Chinese Astrological sign on page 838. ► Read about your Personal Planets on page 826. ► Read about your personal Mystical Card on page 856.

CAPRICORN
Your Personal Planets

YOUR LOVE POTENTIAL
Venus in Scorpio, Jan. 01, 0:00 - Jan. 07, 10:19
Venus in Sagittarius, Jan. 07, 10:20 - Jan. 20, 14:39

YOUR DRIVE AND AMBITION
Mars in Pisces, Jan. 01, 0:00 - Jan. 08, 12:19
Mars in Aries, Jan. 08, 12:20 - Jan. 20, 14:39

YOUR LUCK MAGNETISM
Jupiter in Pisces, Jan. 01, 0:00 - Jan. 20, 14:39

World Events

Jan. 96 – A new galaxy, 12 billion light years away is discovered by Californian astronomers.

Jan. 16 – Communist Party leader Hu Yao-Bang resigns after six weeks of student protests urging free expression in China.

Gorbachev talks to factory workers near Moscow

AQUARIUS
Your Personal Planets

YOUR LOVE POTENTIAL
Venus in Sagittarius, Jan. 20, 14:40 - Feb. 05, 3:02
Venus in Capricorn, Feb. 05, 3:03 - Feb. 19, 4:49

YOUR DRIVE AND AMBITION
Mars in Aries, Jan. 20, 14:40 - Feb. 19, 4:49

YOUR LUCK MAGNETISM
Jupiter in Pisces, Jan. 20, 14:40 - Feb. 19, 4:49

World Events

Jan. 29 – Gorbachev makes another call for greater democracy in the USSR.

Feb. 19 – Trade sanctions against Poland are lifted after the Communists free political prisoners.

1987

PISCES
Your Personal Planets

YOUR LOVE POTENTIAL
Venus in Capricorn, Feb. 19, 4:50 - Mar. 03, 7:54
Venus in Aquarius, Mar. 03, 7:55 - Mar. 21, 3:51

YOUR DRIVE AND AMBITION
Mars in Aries, Feb. 19, 4:50 - Apr. 20, 14:43
Mars in Taurus, Apr. 20, 14:44 - Mar. 21, 3:51

YOUR LUCK MAGNETISM
Jupiter in Pisces, Feb. 19, 4:50 - Mar. 02, 18:40
Jupiter in Aries, Mar. 02, 18:41 - Mar. 21, 3:51

World Events

Mar. 6 - The British ferry *Herald Of Free Enterprise* capsizes off the coast of Zeebrugge, killing hundreds.

Mar. 15 - Fifteen hundred people march in Budapest to demand liberal reforms across Hungary.

Van Gogh's "Sunflowers" being auctioned at Christie's

ARIES
Your Personal Planets

YOUR LOVE POTENTIAL
Venus in Aquarius, Mar. 21, 3:52 - Mar. 28, 16:19
Venus in Pisces, Mar. 28, 16:20 - Apr. 20, 14:57

YOUR DRIVE AND AMBITION
Mars in Taurus, Mar. 21, 3:52 - Apr. 05, 16:36
Mars in Gemini, Apr. 05, 16:37 - Apr. 20, 14:57

YOUR LUCK MAGNETISM
Jupiter in Aries, Mar. 21, 3:52 - Apr. 20, 14:57

World Events

Mar. 30 - Vincent Van Gogh's *Sunflowers* is sold for $32 million in London.

Mar. 30 - The Vietnam War movie *Platoon* takes four Oscars at the Academy Awards.

PISCES
From February 19, 4:50 through March 21, 3:51

The Ambitious Dreamer

American pop artist Andy Warhol died at age 58 during routine gall bladder surgery around the time of your birth. The prolific Warhol experimented with the ideas of mass production and popular culture in his work. The 1987 Pisces is also graced with the imagination of an artist, along with the determination to bring their imaginings to life. The 1987 Pisces is a dreamer, but also a highly motivated doer. Like Warhol, you are likely to mass produce your art for appreciative audiences.

With Neptune, the planet of imagination and spiritual yearnings, in practical Capricorn, the 1987 Pisces may be less likely to have trouble focusing his or her energy than Pisces of other years. When you came into the world, "yuppies" were replacing "hippies" in the neighborhoods of San Francisco. Many of the yuppies were hippies who had decided that their progressive ideals could be channeled into money-making ventures. They had reconciled their counter-culture values with the social system and found harmony as well as, in some cases, great wealth. The prevalent Capricorn influence in your chart perhaps makes it hard for you to "lose touch with reality"—a common complaint about the hippies who "dropped out" of life. For the determined 1987 Pisces, common sense paired with an unlimited imagination could bring the ability to achieve any ambition desired.

A life in the arts could satisfy the endless creative urges of the 1987 Pisces. You could be drawn to telling stories, perhaps through movies or painting. If you are lured into the limelight, it is likely that you have keen insight into what audiences want to see. Your sensitivity can be a blessing, when protected and nurtured by those around you.

The 1987 Pisces is likely to desire steadfast companions who can understand his or her sensitive nature. Those with planets in Taurus, Cancer, or Scorpio are possible good matches.

The gift of the 1987 Pisces is the extraordinary ability to access the magic of the imagination. Your challenge is to strive to maintain an individual sense of identity, even in long-term partnerships.

ARIES
From March 21, 3:52 through April 20, 14:57

The Sensible Innovator

A major U.S. scandal hit the tabloids when you were born: evangelist Jim Bakker resigned from his successful television ministry after revealing that he had an affair. At the same time, the Republic of Ireland was experiencing a "brain drain"—30,000 of the Emerald Isle's brightest were leaving that country every year due to a poor economy. The 1987 Aries might welcome such adventures as a leap into the unknown of infinite possibility, but not at another's expense. Full of optimism and courage, the 1987 Aries also brings a desire to better his or her quality of life and gain material wealth. They are not chasing rainbows but probably making daring moves to achieve tangible rewards.

Also at this time, jewels that once belonged to the late Duchess of Windsor were sold at auction in Switzerland, bringing $33.5 million to benefit the Pasteur Institute in Paris. Though you are compassionate, your generosity may be motivated more by a desire to fill a need than by sympathy. With Jupiter, the planet of expansion, in practical Taurus, you are likely to be drawn only to ideas that have everyday application. Some of the luckiest events in your life could be related to money or other tangible assets.

The 1987 Aries could thrive in environments where the atmosphere is experimental and unrestricted. However, your practical side will likely lead you into areas of tangible productivity. Seeking the best of both worlds could lead to careers that enhance the daily lives of others. The 1987 Aries might find fulfillment in teaching, medicine, or politics. You could find yourself in leadership positions where your ability to outline a realistic plan will make others want to take part. The 1987 Aries surely radiates an air of confidence that others will find intoxicating.

You could find yourself in the company of other adventurous, impulsive spirits who also seek ways of manifesting their visions in practical ways. Some possible matches are Taureans, Geminis, or Sagittarians.

Your gift is your boldness and enthusiasm, which inspires and energize others. Your challenge is to cultivate the patience to bring projects to completion.

➤ Read about your Chinese Astrological sign on page 838. ➤ Read about your Personal Planets on page 826. ➤ Read about your personal Mystical Card on page 856.

TAURUS

From April 20, 14:58 through May 21, 14:09

The Diligent Dreamer

At this time in history, Japan revealed the findings of its study of American work habits—the U.S. was turning into a hamburger stand economy due to ineffective management and poor labor relations. Meanwhile, Japan had become the leading manufacturer, which was attributed to high productivity, low labor costs, and plain old hard work. The 1987 Taurus is also focused on diligently creating a stable life, full of material comforts. You probably also exhibit a surprisingly unpredictable nature that needs much personal freedom. This is the balance you must walk in life to feel fulfilled. In addition, Taurus, ruled by Venus, the planet of love and beauty, might have mourned the loss of wholesome screen goddess Rita Hayworth, who died this year.

With Mars, the planet of personal action, in eccentric Aquarius, you may be expressive in unexpected ways. You may seek stable environments that also allow unlimited growth. There is much potential for innovative achievement thanks to your unique diligence and perseverance. The addition of Saturn, the planet of restrictions, in truth-seeking Sagittarius brings a discipline to any quest for knowledge. Your mind is open to the infinite and finding order in that is a big task. You will need your vast stores of determination to focus and harness all your potential.

You might enjoy a disciplined life in the arts. If the inclination for music is there, you could become a prodigious talent. You possess the ability to stay committed to one activity, which can lead to mastery in any field you choose. Paradoxically, you are likely to thrive in a field that holds the universe of possibilities within it. Some examples are science, technology, or, as mentioned before, the arts.

You seek loyal companions who have proven themselves trustworthy and nonjudgmental in the past. You could find harmony with those who have planets in the signs of Gemini, Cancer, or Aquarius.

Your gift is the ability to find security while remaining flexible during change. Your challenge is to balance the desire for stability with the continual need for innovation.

GEMINI

From May 21, 14:10 through June 21, 22:10

The Empathic Observer

At the time of your birth, 1987 Gemini, scandal erupted in the U.S. when Gary Hart, Democratic candidate for president, had to withdraw from the race after being caught with twenty-nine year old model Donna Rice. His reputation for "womanizing" tarnished the senator's image beyond repair. Geminis are notorious investigators, researchers, and gossips, and many have found success in the world of investigative reporting. While the 1987 Gemini may enjoy keeping up-to-date on world events and local intrigue, you also have an equally powerful desire to escape the outer world and rest in solitude. The 1987 Gemini can be quite the homebody and a wonderful host for parties or gatherings in his or her home.

The lively 1987 Gemini is a surprising mix of influences, some of which bring more emotional sensitivity to the usually intellectual and detached Gemini. With Venus, the planet of relationships, in home-loving Cancer, the 1987 Gemini likely craves the warmth and companionship of family and friends. Many of your activities could be centered on your home life. With the addition of Mars, the planet of action, in sensitive Pisces, you could find that your best work happens in quiet, calm environments. You can also find inspiration by connecting with people who are intuitive and soothing.

With your big heart and talent for communication, you could find yourself in fields of work that involve communicating about people's lives. As a writer, you could experience the feelings of your characters, which would bring them to life. You could also find fulfillment as a voice for the downtrodden, such as writing for a non-profit organization.

The 1987 Gemini may seem coolly detached at times, but there is a sensitive underbelly that seeks trustworthy souls with which to build connections. Some possible ties could be formed with those whose planets are in Cancer, Pisces, or Scorpio.

Your gift, 1987 Gemini, is the ability to express yourself in an articulate, intuitive way bordering on the profound. Your challenge is to cultivate the discipline to make the most of these communication skills.

➤ Read about your Chinese Astrological sign on page 838. ➤ Read about your Personal Planets on page 826. ➤ Read about your personal Mystical Card on page 856.

1987

TAURUS
Your Personal Planets

YOUR LOVE POTENTIAL
Venus in Pisces, Apr. 20, 14:58 - Apr. 22, 16:06
Venus in Aries, Apr. 22, 16:07 - May 17, 11:55
Venus in Taurus, May 17, 11:56 - May 21, 14:09

YOUR DRIVE AND AMBITION
Mars in Gemini, Apr. 20, 14:58 - May 21, 3:00
Mars in Cancer, May 21, 3:01 - May 21, 14:09

YOUR LUCK MAGNETISM
Jupiter in Aries, Apr. 20, 14:58 - May 21, 14:09

World Events

May 11 – The trial of Klaus Barbie begins in Lyons.

May 14 – American actress Rita Hayworth dies.

Death of American actress Rita Hayworth

GEMINI
Your Personal Planets

YOUR LOVE POTENTIAL
Venus in Taurus, May 21, 14:10 - June 11, 5:14
Venus in Gemini, June 11, 5:15 - June 21, 21:10

YOUR DRIVE AND AMBITION
Mars in Cancer, May 21, 14:10 - June 21, 21:10

YOUR LUCK MAGNETISM
Jupiter in Aries, May 21, 14:10 - June 21, 21:10

World Events

June 10 – Riots break out in Seoul and South Korean cities after Pres. Chun Doo-Hwan refuses to hold direct presidential elections.

June 12 – Margaret Thatcher wins a third general election in Britain.

1987

CANCER
Your Personal Planets

YOUR LOVE POTENTIAL
Venus in Gemini, June 21, 21:11 - July 05, 19:49
Venus in Cancer, July 05, 19:50 - July 23, 9:05

YOUR DRIVE AND AMBITION
Mars in Cancer, June 21, 21:11 - July 06, 16:45
Mars in Leo, July 06, 16:46 - July 23, 9:05

YOUR LUCK MAGNETISM
Jupiter in Aries, June 21, 21:11 - July 23, 9:05

World Events

June 22 - American dancer and actor Fred Astaire dies.

July 5 - Martina Navratilova wins her record-breaking sixth straight Wimbledon title.

Martina Navratilova celebrates her win

LEO
Your Personal Planets

YOUR LOVE POTENTIAL
Venus in Cancer, July 23, 9:06 - July 30, 6:48
Venus in Leo, July 30, 6:49 - Aug. 23, 13:59
Venus in Virgo, Aug. 23, 14:00 - Aug. 23, 16:09

YOUR DRIVE AND AMBITION
Mars in Leo, July 23, 9:06 - Aug. 22, 19:50
Mars in Virgo, Aug. 22, 19:51 - Aug. 23, 16:09

YOUR LUCK MAGNETISM
Jupiter in Aries, July 23, 9:06 - Aug. 23, 16:09

World Events

July 31 - Four hundred people are gunned down during riots in Mecca when Shiite Muslims protest against Sunni Muslims who back Iraq in the Iran-Iraq war.

Aug. 7 - Five central American countries sign a peace plan to bring about democracy in the region.

CANCER
From June 21, 22:11 through July 23, 9:05

The Vivacious Care-Giver

Around the time of your birth, 1987 Cancer, a young German pilot flew a small plane from Helsinki, Finland through 400 miles of Soviet airspace and landed his small craft in Moscow's Red Square. Even though his feat of daring was not politically motivated, he was arrested and jailed for one year. Like this boy pilot, you are probably not as homebound as many of your sign tend to be. Your other planetary factors may make you quite the social butterfly and give you a desire to soar beyond your usual sphere. You emerged into the world when the political climate in the U.S. was reeling from a series of revelations about the Iran-contra affair. Col. Oliver North implicated the White House in testimony before a congressional panel. Across the ocean in Britain, Margaret Thatcher and the Conservative Party won an unprecedented third general election. Whatever your political beliefs, the 1987 Cancer is likely to favor a conservative approach to taking actions in life.

With Neptune, the planet of spiritual aspirations, in austere Capricorn, the 1987 Cancer could steer toward the safe, sure bets in life. Jupiter, the planet of expansion, also appears in restrained Capricorn, adding a sense that growth in life often comes through material gains. Your tendency toward a vibrant social life comes with Venus, the planet of relationships, in lively Gemini. Your connections with others could be the one area where you take risks to broaden your sphere. You need variety and excitement to truly thrive.

Your yearning for an eclectic social life along with a need for security could lead to a career with continuity that is also based on social interaction. Your compassion for others could lead to working as a therapist or teacher.

Though you seek security in your connections, you are also likely to seek the company of witty, fun-loving types. You may well be drawn to those with planets in Gemini, Taurus, or Scorpio.

Your gift is the warmth and compassion of your personality that enhances your vivacious demeanor. Your challenge is to cultivate the self-confidence to move in the direction of your highest dreams.

LEO
From July 23, 9:06 through August 23, 16:09

The Exuberant Warrior

At the time of your arrival, 1987 Leo, two world events showed the violent and peace-loving sides of humanity. In the Islamic holy city of Mecca, 400 people, mainly Iranian shiite Muslims were killed and hundreds injured during anti-West demonstrations. Meanwhile, across the globe, Guatemala, Honduras, Nicaragua, El Salvador, and Costa Rica signed a peace plan for democracy in the region. The 1987 Leo emerged as a warrior with the energy to fight and win any battle, including building peace. Proud and regal, you may thrive on competition and challenge. When you compete against your own limitations instead of with other people, you can avoid the trap of egotism that allows you to feel either superior or inferior to others.

The placement of Mars, the planet of action, in aggressive Aries may make the 1987 Leo a vital, action-oriented person. You need to keep moving to feel fully alive. You can be exuberant and fiery. Your intense drive can even be destructive sometimes if not guided through the cultivation of discipline and discernment. You can flourish when you learn which battles lead to growth. With Jupiter, the planet of expansion, in clever Gemini, you can find opportunities when you delve into a field of study.

Though you could find much growth in higher education, you'll have to balance book learning with physical activities. You could enjoy pursuing a sport as a hobby or more seriously. The theater world is a welcoming environment for a persona as big as yours, and you could thrive in such an electrified setting. Whether or not you choose entertainment as a career, you are likely to find yourself drawn to the limelight of a public life.

With your luminous personality, you are likely to be quite popular. You seek other souls who are generous of spirit, and might find that those with signs in Aries, Gemini, or Cancer are a good match.

Your gift is your infectious enthusiasm for life and your boundless physical energy. Your challenge is having self-confidence without becoming arrogant or egocentric.

➤ Read about your Chinese Astrological sign on page 838. ➤ Read about your Personal Planets on page 826. ➤ Read about your personal Mystical Card on page 856.

VIRGO

From August 23, 16:10 through September 23, 13:44

The Refined Intellect

The 1987 Virgo arrived when the U.S. was celebrating the bicentennial of its constitution. This document protected the individual rights of citizens against certain government intrusions. It secured the right of American 1987 Virgos to broadcast opinions to the world without fearing persecution. Certain planetary influences give this year's Virgo a balance to the restrained modesty that is often attributed to the sign. The presence of Jupiter, the planet of expansion, in fiery Aries brings the ability to seize the day and make the most of opportunities. You are likely to create your own luck through your own ingenuity.

However, the 1987 Virgo gains a double dose of the sign's traits, possibly more, as a multiple alignment was occurring at this time in this constellation. With Mars, the planet of action, in orderly Virgo, the 1987 Virgo's yearning for purity of mind, body, and spirit was accentuated. You might be well-suited to certain forms of exercise, such as yoga, that emphasize a union of all three. Your pursuit of knowledge could be unusually disciplined. With Saturn, the planet of discipline, in truth-seeking Sagittarius, you probably seek practical applications for the wisdom you acquire. The 1987 Virgo is also likely to be well-groomed and conscious of the image he or she presents. In some areas, you may seem conservative or restrained. You are likely to shield your private life from all but those closest to you.

The 1987 Virgo is meticulous and detail-oriented, and would thrive in an environment that is stimulating intellectually. Some might enjoy working in a university setting, while others might be drawn toward careers as writers. Working in a library or doing research of some kind could keep the 1987 Virgo mentally engaged.

These discerning souls have high ideals when it comes to the company they keep. You would be well-suited to those with signs in Virgo, Libra, or Taurus.

The gift of the 1987 Virgo is the care and quality you bring to even the smallest tasks. The challenge is to let go of perfectionism and accept themselves and others as they are.

LIBRA

From September 23, 13:45 through October 23, 23:00

The Passionate Balance

The 1987 Libra arrived on the world stage as destabilizing tremors shook both Wall Street financial markets and the state of California. A crash of the markets in New York City sent the Dow plunging 508 points, far worse than the Great Crash of 1929. Along the Pacific coast, two violent earthquakes, measuring 6.1 and 6.7 on the Richter scale shook California. The 1987 Libra finds transformation through both balance and the occasional "shake-up" of the deepest foundations. Relationships are an area where this balance and turbulent passion give the 1987 Libra an opportunity to refine his or her character and grow.

The 1987 Libra embodies the grace and refinement of the sign. You can be charming and witty, and the party guest who can keep the conversation flowing. With Jupiter, the planet of expansion, in aggressive Aries, your people-pleasing tendency is tempered by an impulsive, passionate side that can lead to new growth. There could be times when this composed, fair person turns into a reckless, selfish entity. The 1987 Libra needs the chance to be outrageously self-centered so he or she can return to the harmony of connection. You are seeking to maintain a sense of identity and exploring the nature of fairness in relationships. The 1987 Libra is likely to move into uncharted waters and be transformed before returning to find harmony and balance.

A talent for language could lead the 1987 Libra into the communication fields. Your natural diplomacy skills could lead you into politics or other careers in the public eye. The 1987 Libra could be an inspiring public speaker, a talent that could be useful in many careers including teaching. Your skill in one-on-one encounters could make you a highly effective counselor.

The 1987 Libra needs the company of others to find balance and thrives when there is intellectual rapport. You could find the right chemistry with those whose signs are in Virgo, Libra, or Gemini.

Your gift is your unique blend of both gracious charm and fiery passion. Your challenge is to keep your own sense of identity, while growing in a relationship.

➤ Read about your Chinese Astrological sign on page 838. ➤ Read about your Personal Planets on page 826. ➤ Read about your personal Mystical Card on page 856.

VIRGO
Your Personal Planets

YOUR LOVE POTENTIAL
Venus in Virgo, Aug. 23, 16:10 - Sept. 16, 18:11
Venus in Libra, Sept. 16, 18:12 - Sept. 23, 13:44

YOUR DRIVE AND AMBITION
Mars in Virgo, Aug. 23, 16:10 - Sept. 23, 13:44

YOUR LUCK MAGNETISM
Jupiter in Aries, Aug. 23, 16:10 - Sept. 23, 13:44

World Events

Sept. 7 - Erich Honecker becomes the first East German head of state to visit West Germany.

Sept. 16 - Twenty-four countries sign the Montreal Protocol to help preserve the Earth's ozone layer.

Wall Street during the Black Monday stock market crash

LIBRA
Your Personal Planets

YOUR LOVE POTENTIAL
Venus in Libra, Sept. 23, 13:45 - Oct. 10, 20:48
Venus in Scorpio, Oct. 10, 20:49 - Oct. 23, 23:00

YOUR DRIVE AND AMBITION
Mars in Virgo, Sept. 23, 13:45 - Oct. 08, 19:26
Mars in Libra, Oct. 08, 19:27 - Oct. 23, 23:00

YOUR LUCK MAGNETISM
Jupiter in Aries, Sept. 23, 13:45 - Oct. 23, 23:00

World Events

Oct. 1 - A violent earthquake ravages Los Angeles, California.

Oct. 19 - Black Monday on the stock exchange brings fears of another Depression.

1987

SCORPIO
Your Personal Planets

YOUR LOVE POTENTIAL
Venus in Scorpio, Oct. 23, 23:01 - Nov. 03, 23:03
Venus in Sagittarius, Nov. 03, 23:04 - Nov. 22, 20:28

YOUR DRIVE AND AMBITION
Mars in Libra, Oct. 23, 23:01 - Nov. 22, 20:28

YOUR LUCK MAGNETISM
Jupiter in Aries, Oct. 23, 23:01 - Nov. 22, 20:28

World Events

Nov. 8 - Eleven are killed by an IRA bomb at Enniskillen in Northern Ireland, during a parade in memory of Britain's war dead.

Nov. 18 - President Reagan is blamed by Senate and House panels for the Iran-contra affair, but escapes illegality.

An IRA bomb kills eleven at Enniskillen in Northern Ireland

SAGITTARIUS
Your Personal Planets

YOUR LOVE POTENTIAL
Venus in Sagittarius, Nov. 22, 20:29 - Nov. 28, 1:50
Venus in Capricorn, Nov. 28, 1:51 - Dec. 22, 6:28
Venus in Aquarius, Dec. 22, 6:29 - Dec. 22, 9:45

YOUR DRIVE AND AMBITION
Mars in Libra, Nov. 22, 20:29 - Nov. 24, 3:18
Mars in Scorpio, Nov. 24, 3:19 - Dec. 22, 9:45

YOUR LUCK MAGNETISM
Jupiter in Aries, Nov. 22, 20:29 - Dec. 22, 9:45

World Events

Nov. 29 - The first democratic elections in Haiti are prevented by riots.

Dec. 8 - Gorbachev and Reagan sign the first treaty to reduce the size of their nuclear arsenals.

SCORPIO
From October 23, 23:01 through November 22, 20:28

The Solitary Investigator

The 1987 Scorpio entered the world the same year that Cher won the best actress award for her role in the movie *Moonstruck*. With your desire to explore all things hidden or passionate, you might have appreciated this darkly comic romance. Also in this year, the U.S. Congress officially blamed President Ronald Reagan for the Iran-contra affair. Though his actions were not deemed illegal, his image was sullied. The 1987 Scorpio is a talented investigator and tries to get to the bottom of things. You seek to find the real, multi-layered truths behind the façade.

The 1987 Scorpio may maintain a cautious reserve until a course of action has been decided. But with Jupiter, the planet of opportunities, in impulsive Aries, the 1987 Scorpio can seize on something if the timing is right. You can be confident, enthusiastic, and enjoy healthy competition with others. This influence could also give you the desire to expand your horizons through travel. The position of Mars, the planet of action, in fair Libra may make the 1987 Scorpio less argumentative than others in this combative sign. You are likely to crave harmony and balance in your relationships.

The 1987 Scorpio has enormous reserves of energy and should seek continually for challenging projects. You should avoid work that is too routine. Your work should engage your imagination rather than merely being a detail-oriented job. Working alone for long periods of time may often be energizing for you. This could lead to careers in art, such as painting, writing, or making music. You could likely find fulfillment as a detective or investigative reporter. Another possibility is the field of engineering. You have the discipline to become adept at whatever you try.

The 1987 Scorpio can develop all-consuming friendships and partnerships, which can be dramatically transformative. Those with signs in Scorpio, Sagittarius, or Cancer are possible compatible matches.

Your gift is your ability to stick with a task long enough to see it come to fruition. Your challenge is to avoid possessiveness and jealousy in relationships.

SAGITTARIUS
From November 22, 20:29 through December 22, 9:45

The Exuberant Thinker

At the time of your birth, 1987 Sagittarius, the Soviet Union's Mikhail Gorbachev and U.S. President Ronald Reagan signed an historic treaty. Both of the superpowers agreed to reduce the size of its arsenal of nuclear weapons. Also at this time, a violent protest halted the first democratic elections in Haiti. The 1987 Sagittarius is opinionated about worldly concerns but might find it challenging to express them. This is because you may see both sides of any issue. The 1987 Sagittarius is likely committed to his or her own education, whether it occurs in a classroom setting or out in the real world. You learn best through direct experience, and are often the most energetic and exuberant person around.

The 1987 Sagittarius seeks total freedom to wander, to explore, and to travel. With Jupiter, the planet of opportunities, in vital Aries, the 1987 Sagittarius is prone to sudden outbursts of enthusiasm. You should surround yourself with hearty, fun-loving people who can support your dynamic expansiveness. With Saturn, the planet of limitations, in your sun sign, the 1987 Sagittarius will have plenty of internal obstacles to dismantle. The key is facing the fears that arise when you go beyond your known limits.

A career that allows travel, both literal and symbolic, would probably suit the 1987 Sagittarius. You could enjoy work that brings out your talent for philosophizing, such as counseling or teaching. There could be athletic prowess in the 1987 Sagittarius make-up. Trying different sports could satisfy a natural competitive drive. A career as a coach or physical therapist could be rewarding. You have the ability to inspire others, which can translate to success in many fields.

Though you may enjoy a wide circle of acquaintances, it could be harder for you to make close friends. You may be drawn to those whose planets are in Sagittarius, Gemini, or Aquarius.

Your gift is your endless curiosity and the desire to try new things continually. The challenge is to learn the discipline necessary to become a master in one area rather than simply a hobbyist in many.

➤ Read about your Chinese Astrological sign on page 838. ➤ Read about your Personal Planets on page 826. ➤ Read about your personal Mystical Card on page 856.

CAPRICORN

From December 22, 9:46 through December 31, 23:59

The Methodical Opportunist

At the time of your birth, 1987 December Capricorn, one second was added to the year to compensate for the precession of the Earth's axis. This gave you another moment in which to share your gifts and talents with the planet. You may be an ambitious sort who can appear uninterested or emotionally detached. Inwardly, you are probably planning and plotting and, when the right moment comes, you seize it with lightning speed. You probably have the patience and determination to achieve success.

With Mercury, the planet of communication, also in rational Capricorn, the 1987 December Capricorn is doubly influenced by the methodical reasoning ability for which the sign is known. You are likely to have a disciplined mind. You may radiate a confidence and self-respect that could propel you into a leadership role. You are the one who can keep a cool head in times of chaos. With Mars, the planet of action, in intense Scorpio, your logical brain is tempered by a fiery, emotional impulsiveness to take action. The presence of Venus, the planet of relationships, in unconventional Aquarius gives you a non-judgmental openness to all kinds of people. You have an offbeat humor that delights and surprises others.

You could find success in the business world. Working as your own boss, perhaps starting your own entrepreneurial venture, could satisfy your need for authority and independence. Your ability to build on solid ground can translate into excellence as a manager or architect. Your work life should be filled with an eclectic assortment of people. This could mean establishing a business with a social atmosphere. You also might be drawn to teaching or writing.

The 1987 December Capricorn may feel a conflict between a desire to form lasting bonds and an equal desire to remain completely independent. Some satisfying relationships could be formed with those whose signs are in Aquarius, Gemini, or Scorpio.

Your gift is your determination and focus, which is strengthened by a strong will to take action. Your challenge is to allow your quirkiness and humor to shine through all the time.

CAPRICORN
Your Personal Planets

YOUR LOVE POTENTIAL
Venus in Aquarius, Dec. 22, 9:46 - Dec. 31, 23:59

YOUR DRIVE AND AMBITION
Mars in Scorpio, Dec. 22, 9:46 - Dec. 31, 23:59

YOUR LUCK MAGNETISM
Jupiter in Aries, Dec. 22, 9:46 - Dec. 31, 23:59

World Events

Dec. 29 - Col. Yuri Romanenko breaks the record for time spent in space—326 days.

Dec. 31 - One second is added to the year to make up for the precession of Earth's axis.

Ronald and Nancy Reagan at their ranch

Special Feature
Astrology in the White House: The Reagans

(Continued from page 705)

However, there is more to the Reagans' consulting of astrologers and psychics than just good political strategy. It is said that the greatest need for astrological assurances was Nancy's. There was, first of all, the "twenty-year death cycle" to consider. Some people believe that a sitting President who is elected in a year divisible by twenty will die in office. For more information, read "The Presidential Death Cycle."

Nancy, a Cancer born on July 6, 1921, is a sensitive woman: with five planets in this emotional sign, her need for security is intense. She loves her husband and has always been willing to take any and all necessary steps to ensure his safety. Reagan, a broad-minded Aquarian, born February 6, 1911, was willing to go along with whatever would make Nancy happy. Many people even claim that his interest in astrology was as strong as his wife's. Just like the rest of the Hollywood community, they wisely agreed that it didn't hurt, might help, so why not!

On March 30, 1981, it appeared that the cycle might repeat itself. John Hinckley, Jr., made an unsuccessful attempt on Reagan's life. Nancy learned from a friend that an astrologer of her acquaintance had consulted had said she could have predicted that date as a very bad one for the President. Nancy picked up the phone and called Joan Quigley, who became Nancy's first line of defense against any further threats on the life of her beloved husband.

"I wasn't about to take any chances," Nancy reveals in her memoirs My Turn. "Very few people can understand what it's like to have your husband shot at and almost die, and then have him exposed all the time to . . . tens of thousands of people, any one of whom might be a lunatic with a gun. I have been criticized and ridiculed for turning to astrology . . . I was doing everything I could think of to protect my husband . . . ."

A discrete woman, Nancy had private phone lines installed in the White House and at Camp David so that her calls to Quigley would remain secret. And as Quigley worked on Reagan's chart and gave her pronouncements, they were used to fine-tune his schedule, something nobody minded and which brought a great deal of comfort to Nancy. Not until Donald Regan was appointed White House Chief of Staff—and was ultimately fired—did this secret get out. Some people believe it was revealed because Regan held no love for the First Lady.

(Continued on page 721)

➤ Read about another influential astrologer in "Astrology Goes on Trial" on page 185. ➤ Read "Astrology Reigns Through the Ages" on page 25. ➤ Read "The Presidential Death Cycle" on page 657.

Birth of a New World: Saturn and Uranus

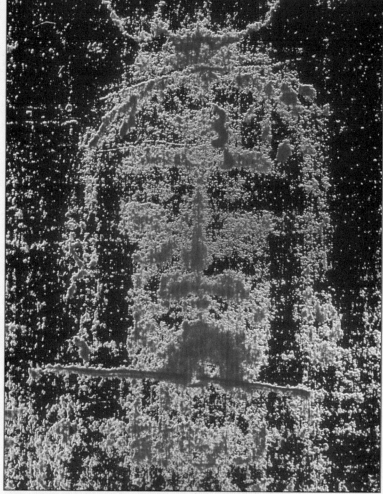

The Shroud of Turin is found to date from the Middle Ages

A major planetary cycle was about to begin as 1988 opened and the earth and sky rumbled with portents of what was to come. Saturn and Uranus were about to conjoin in late Sagittarius, then meet Neptune in early Capricorn over the next five years. This would be the triple "conjunction" of these planets, which happens about once every 680 years. Saturn is associated with the form and structure of governments and civilizations, and Uranus is linked with the renewal that keeps those structures fresh and responsive to the needs of the populations they serve. Imaginative Neptune provides the vision that informs the new structures, often expressed as a religious or spiritual movement. Together, they symbolize transition periods in civilizations when the forms as they are known previously are substantially changed.

This was evident in world events during 1988. The Soviets introduced a policy of *perestroika*, or "openness", moving away from centuries of isolationism, correlating with the first Saturan-Uranus connection. On May 26, while Saturn and Uranus were making their second of three exact contacts, Ronald Reagan was in Moscow and on June 2, he and Soviet leader Mikhail Gorbachev completed more agreements on arms control, high-school student exchange and cooperation on space exploration. It seemed as though the Cold War was ending.

Saturn and Uranus were not the only planets making waves this year. Mars was on the warpath, too, as its fiery nature was expressed mainly from August through October, as the Red Planet made its closest swing past Earth. At the beginning of that time, lightning hit drought-famished brush and lit wildfires across the U.S. However, attention soon focused on Yellowstone National Park, where Forest Service officials followed a non-interference policy for naturally ocurring fires. The flames became a firestorm and threatened to devastate the park as Mars reached its closest proximity to Earth. As Mars "cooled off", rains drenched the fires and saved most park structures and many forests.

Dr. Kurt Waldheim is faced with his Nazi past

George Bush wins the U.S. Presidential election

TURMOIL AND RESTRUCTURING

Haiti held its first presidential election in thirty years. Zimbabwe became a one-party state while Surinam, Cyprus, South Korea, Italy, and Ecuador saw changes in leadership. In the U.S., former Vice-President George Bush was elected President. Austrian President Kurt Waldheim came under pressure for his alleged Nazi past. Three members of the IRA were killed in Gibraltar by the SAS. Soviet forces prepared to withdraw from Afghanistan. There was a cease-fire in the Iran-Iraq war. Major earthquakes struck China, Armenia, and the Himalayan Mountains. Following a report by U.S. Surgeon General Dr. C. Everett Koop, pointing to the addictive and harmful nature of tobacco products, smoking was banned in many places, including on airline flights of under two hours. The Olympic Games were held in Seoul, despite fears of political unrest. A terrorist bomb on board Pan Am Flight 103 caused it to crash at Lockerbie, Scotland, killing 270. The U.N. peacekeeping forces received the Nobel Peace Prize for supervising cease-fires and moderating conflicts. The Turin Shroud was revealed as a medieval fake. Greek shipowner Christina Onassis died.

➤ Read "Astrology in the White House: The Reagans" by Frank Andrews on page 705.

CAPRICORN

From January 01, 0:00 through January 20, 20:23

The Generous Authority

Your arrival coincided with the era of perestroika in the Soviet Union. This promised to bring a new openness between Russia and other nations and increase freedoms for the Soviet people. The 1988 January Capricorn insists upon complete personal freedom, and you would find it difficult to live in a restrictive society. You have a refined sensibility and exude a quiet dignity. You create opportunities rather than waiting for them, working toward achievement in a methodical, steady manner. You are a doer, who cannot be rushed. Like the tortoise, you'll get there at your own pace. You probably seek a sense of stability in this often chaotic and, at times, dangerous world. At the time of your birth, a new report from the U.S. National Academy of Sciences linked radon gas and lung cancer, and Israeli soldiers battled with Palestinians outside the Al Aqsa mosque in Jerusalem. While you cannot control chaos, you are likely to work toward a solid career with a sense of continuity.

With Neptune, the planet of spiritual yearnings, in practical Capricorn, it is unlikely that you'll venture too far into the metaphysical or "new age." Your own search for enlightenment could be more rooted in the way you live your daily life. Your dreams to better the world could manifest in projects that are of service to others. The presence of Saturn, the planet of limitations, in knowledge-seeking Sagittarius may give you an interest in assimilating knowledge in practical ways.

The 1988 Capricorn is a high-achiever and can persevere to achieve long-term goals. You could gravitate toward leadership positions that offer prestige and status. The 1988 Capricorn could succeed in business, and would probably enjoy the competition of the financial world.

The 1988 Capricorn is a loyal companion, who seeks steadfast, yet unconventional friends and relations. Good companions for you are those with planets with signs in Pisces, Aquarius, or Taurus.

Your gift is a focused ambition that inspires you to blaze your own trail. Your challenge is to balance your need for stability with a desire for freedom within relationships.

AQUARIUS

From January 20, 20:24 through February 19, 10:34

The Nimble Intellect

The medical establishment announced two "happy accidents" at the time of your birth. The first was the discovery that Retin-A, the anti-acne medicine, could also reduce wrinkles. Plus, in a study by the American National Heart, Lung and Blood Institute, aspirin had been shown to reduce the risk for heart attacks. The 1988 Aquarius is also a cosmic coincidence, bringing together all the elements for potential genius. Those around you learn to accept and appreciate your unpredictable nature. You will not tolerate being reigned in, or pigeonholed into one way of acting. You are a social creature who sees the essence of people, and you would rarely judge someone based on external, social yardsticks. Others appreciate this and you may find they open up to you in unexpected ways.

With Mercury, the planet of communications, in unconventional Aquarius, the mind of the 1988 Aquarius is electrified with the quirky, detached energy of the sign. It is as if you are an observer of human maneuverings, often finding compassion for the frailties of others. It is likely more challenging for you to engage in intimate encounters than in-group situations. You are likely in the center of interesting and unusual social circles. The presence of Mars, the planet of action, in knowledge-seeking Sagittarius helps the unsettled mental Aquarian energy. It brings the discipline to find practical ways to harness the brilliance of the 1988 Aquarian mind.

You could find challenges in the world of new technology. You could find happiness doing work that allows you complete freedom to follow your own strong intuitive hunches. You could be an inspiring teacher, particularly in the sciences. With your humanistic views, you might be drawn to activism, as well.

You thrive with companions who are joyful, spontaneous, and intellectually stimulating. You could find harmony with those whose planets are in the signs of Pisces, Aries, or Gemini.

Your gift is a nimble mind that finds connections with most of the people who cross your path. Your challenge is to avoid a detached, moralistic attitude that can alienate others.

➤ Read about your Chinese Astrological sign on page 838. ➤ Read about your Personal Planets on page 826. ➤ Read about your personal Mystical Card on page 856.

1988

CAPRICORN
Your Personal Planets

YOUR LOVE POTENTIAL
Venus in Aquarius, Jan. 01, 0:00 - Jan. 15, 16:03
Venus in Pisces, Jan. 15, 16:04 - Jan. 20, 20:23

YOUR DRIVE AND AMBITION
Mars in Scorpio, Jan. 01, 0:00 - Jan. 08, 15:23
Mars in Sagittarius, Jan. 08, 15:24 - Jan. 20, 20:23

YOUR LUCK MAGNETISM
Jupiter in Aries, Jan. 01, 0:00 - Jan. 20, 20:23

World Events

Jan. 15 – Arab-Israeli clashes spread to the holy mosques in Jerusalem.

Jan. 17 – President Ortega of Nicaragua offers U.S. troops a ceasefire.

Finish athlete Matti Nykanen

AQUARIUS
Your Personal Planets

YOUR LOVE POTENTIAL
Venus in Pisces, Jan. 20, 20:24 - Feb. 09, 13:03
Venus in Aries, Feb. 09, 13:04 - Feb. 19, 10:34

YOUR DRIVE AND AMBITION
Mars in Sagittarius, Jan. 20, 20:24 - Feb. 19, 10:34

YOUR LUCK MAGNETISM
Jupiter in Aries, Jan. 20, 20:24 - Feb. 19, 10:34

World Events

Jan. 21 – Nikolai Bukharin and other victims of Stalin's regime are honored.

Feb. 13 – The winter Olympics open in Calgary, Canada.

1988

PISCES
Your Personal Planets

YOUR LOVE POTENTIAL
Venus in Aries, Feb. 19, 10:35 - Mar. 06, 10:20
Venus in Taurus, Mar. 06, 10:21 - Mar. 20, 9:38

YOUR DRIVE AND AMBITION
Mars in Sagittarius, Feb. 19, 10:35 - Feb. 22, 10:14
Mars in Capricorn, Feb. 22, 10:15 - Mar. 20, 9:38

YOUR LUCK MAGNETISM
Jupiter in Aries, Feb. 19, 10:35 - Mar. 08, 15:43
Jupiter in Taurus, Mar. 08, 15:44 - Mar. 20, 9:38

World Events

Feb. 24 – Scientists in Utah identify the oldest-known dinosaur embryo.

Mar. 9 – Anthropologists working in Chile discover charcoal remains that prove humans existed on Earth 33,000 years ago.

A Soviet military convoy in Afghanistan

ARIES
Your Personal Planets

YOUR LOVE POTENTIAL
Venus in Taurus, Mar. 20, 9:39 - Apr. 03, 17:06
Venus in Gemini, Apr. 03, 17:07 - Apr. 19, 20:44

YOUR DRIVE AND AMBITION
Mars in Capricorn, Mar. 20, 9:39 - Apr. 06, 21:43
Mars in Aquarius, Apr. 06, 21:44 - Apr. 19, 20:44

YOUR LUCK MAGNETISM
Jupiter in Taurus, Mar. 20, 9:39 - Apr. 19, 20:44

World Events

Mar. 24 – The war in Nicaragua comes to an end.

Apr. 7 – Mikhail Gorbachev agrees terms for a Soviet withdrawal from Afghanistan.

PISCES
From February 19, 10:35 through March 20, 9:38

The Timeless Realist

There were two discoveries in archeology that coincided with your birth, 1988 Pisces. On the mesas of Utah in the U.S., scientists discovered a dinosaur egg with an embryo inside. At the same time, in the South American country of Chile, 33,000-year-old charcoal remains were found, indicating the earliest human presence on that continent. The 1988 Pisces is similarly a timeless creature, connected in a mysterious way to the collective imagination of human history. But your otherworldly Piscean traits are rooted in a realistic notion of how to make things happen. You are practical when it comes to making your dreams come true and you carry a respect for tradition. This is a nice complement to your Piscean compassion and sensitivity, making it easier for you to turn your visions into reality.

The presence of many planets in determined and practical Capricorn tempers your dreamy Piscean personality with a grounded outlook. With Saturn, the planet of limitations, in steady Capricorn you may have the unique ability to reorganize and restructure things that have outlived their usefulness. You bring an intuitive, almost otherworldly wisdom to all you undertake. Coincidentally, at the time you were born, "otherworldly" Superman, created by cartoonists José Shuster and Jerry Siegel, turned fifty years old. The influence of Jupiter, the planet of opportunities, in adventurous Aries gives you the vitality of a superhero. At times, you may be like Superman, surprising everyone with your daring and courage.

You could find fulfillment in fields where you canm express artistic freedom. You are surprisingly organized and disciplined, which can bring success in many fields. With your ability to stabilize weak structures, you could lead an arts organization or a business to a more stable foundation.

You can shine in environments where your sensitivity is valued. Some possible companions for you are those with signs in Scorpio, Cancer, or Taurus.

Your gift is a strong intuition and a vivid, purposeful imagination. Your challenge is building the self-confidence you need to put forth your plans.

ARIES
From March 20, 9:39 through April 19, 20:44

The Cautious Competitor

The arrival of the 1988 Aries coincided with pivotal events that brought peace to two regions of the world. The war in Nicaragua ended and, across the globe, Mikhail Gorbachev agreed to a Soviet withdrawal from Afghanistan. The 1988 Aries is a warrior, who also knows when to bring conflicts to an end. Your desire to create a stable, secure life may conflict with your impulsive, reckless Arien temperament. The 1988 Aries can thrive being a pioneer within the context of a structured daily routine. It's the kind of innovative spirit that led to Harvard scientists' patent for a genetically altered mouse, the first for a life form, at this time. The 1988 Aries has the potential to cultivate the discipline and perseverance to complete projects, a trait that is not always attributed to this sign.

With Saturn, the planet of limitations, in cautious Capricorn, the innate impulsiveness of the 1988 Aries is balanced with a tendency to "look before you leap." With many other planets in practical Capricorn as well, you have the ability to plan your actions in a methodical way. Your progressive thinking and confidence, along with a realistic vision, give you the qualities of an effective leader. The presence of Jupiter, the planet of opportunities, in steady Taurus means the 1988 Aries is intimately bound with the physical world, its pleasures, and material abundance. You are possibly influenced by a desire to build wealth around you and to live comfortably.

The 1988 Aries has a competitive nature that can be channeled into fields such as business, entertainment, sports, or journalism. Though you are likely to seek secure positions that lead to financial wealth, the 1988 Aries also seeks thrills and adventure in the work place.

The 1988 Aries is dynamic and engaging company, and usually the life of the party. You could find it stimulating to be in the company of those with signs in Leo, Taurus, or Gemini.

Your gift is your ability to act as an inspiring catalyst to others. Your challenge is to avoid becoming so attached to material gain that you compromise your values to attain it.

➤ Read about your Chinese Astrological sign on page 838. ➤ Read about your Personal Planets on page 826. ➤ Read about your personal Mystical Card on page 856.

TAURUS

From April 19, 20:45 through May 20, 19:56

The Collaborative Creator

Soviet *perestroika* led to airtime being sold to Pepsi-Cola on Soviet television when you were born, 1988 Taurus. The showing of a Michael Jackson ad was the first time that the hand of corporate America had been able to reach Soviet viewers. Also at this time, socialist François Mitterand was elected to a second term as president of France. In other landmark events, smoking was banned on airline flights shorter than two hours by order of U.S. law. The 1988 Taurus emerged into a world becoming more health conscious in general. With a strong physical constitution and interest in health, the 1988 Taurus might not mind such trends.

With Mars, the planet of action, in social Aquarius, the 1988 Taurus could find that fulfillment comes from working in collaboration with others. You have a talent for translating ideas into actions and can be a thoughtful communicator of complex ideas. With Jupiter, the planet of "good luck," in your sign of Taurus at the time of your birth, you could consider yourself born under a lucky star. This could mean that opportunities come your way in abundance. Many planets in disciplined Capricorn, including Saturn, the planet of restrictions, make sure that you, 1988 Taurus, keep your feet on the ground.

The 1988 Taurus works best in group situations, and you can bring a stability to even the most chaotic situations. You could be drawn to teaching, especially in an environment in which you can collaborate with fellow educators. A possible talent for the culinary arts could lead to a career in catering. You could thrive in work that offers a chance to coordinate large events. You might also be drawn to artistic pursuits that involve collaboration, such as theater or the creation of murals.

The 1988 Taurus is likely to have a wide circle of acquaintances but only a few close friends. You could find compatibility with those whose signs are in Gemini, Cancer, or Aquarius.

Your gift is the steady, clear-eyed way you plan things, which often leads to success. Your challenge is breaking out of your routine to allow new possibilities to unfold.

GEMINI

From May 20, 19:57 through June 21, 3:56

The Agile Communicator

At the time of your birth, 1988 Gemini, the United Kingdom celebrated the 400th anniversary of the defeat of the Spanish Armada. U.S. President Ronald Reagan paid his first visit to the Soviet Union, a country he once called the evil empire. And in Northern Ireland, six British soldiers were killed in an IRA attack. The 1988 Gemini emerged into this changing world blessed with an agile mind and a gentle spirit. You are poised for success with your ability to turn abstract concepts into reality. Though your curiosity could lead you in many directions, you also seek solid growth that is real and tangible. The 1988 Gemini seeks to translate words into deeds and very often will succeed.

With Mercury, the planet of communication, also in Gemini, you are doubly endowed with the curiosity for which your sign is famous. You have flexibility in your thinking that allows you to see many sides of one issue. This can lead to scattered thinking if you don't harness the mind. You can be a skeptic until you've convinced yourself that something is true through logic and facts. The presence of Mars, the planet of action, in inspirational Pisces brings an intuitive quality to the way you initiate things. You might have interests in spiritual philosophies, particularly inspired writings. With Venus, the planet of relationships, in loving Cancer, the 1988 Gemini shows a strong nurturing tendency as well.

The 1988 Gemini is fluent in the language of emotion and could find fulfillment in work that employs this talent. You might be drawn to the expressive arts of theater or working with children. A career in psychology and counseling could also satisfy your desire to articulate the inner life. You could be an inspiring teacher or public speaker.

The 1988 Gemini is likely someone who finds it enjoyable to connect through sharing their feelings. You could find that kind of atmosphere with people whose signs are in Cancer, Scorpio, or Gemini.

Your gift is a social ease that makes you the perfect host or hostess. Your challenge is to focus your mental energies so that you can fulfill your vast potential.

➤ Read about your Chinese Astrological sign on page 838. ➤ Read about your Personal Planets on page 826. ➤ Read about your personal Mystical Card on page 856.

1988

TAURUS
Your Personal Planets

YOUR LOVE POTENTIAL
Venus in Gemini, Apr. 19, 20:45 - May 17, 16:25
Venus in Cancer, May 17, 16:26 - May 20, 19:56

YOUR DRIVE AND AMBITION
Mars in Aquarius, Apr. 19, 20:45 - May 20, 19:56

YOUR LUCK MAGNETISM
Jupiter in Taurus, Apr. 19, 20:45 - May 20, 19:56

World Events

May 8 - François Mitterand is elected for a second term as President of France.

May 15 - The USSR begins its withdrawal from Afghanistan.

Ronald Reagan with Mikhail Gorbachev in Moscow

GEMINI
Your Personal Planets

YOUR LOVE POTENTIAL
Venus in Cancer, May 20, 19:57 - May 27, 7:35
Venus in Gemini, May 27, 7:36 - June 21, 3:56

YOUR DRIVE AND AMBITION
Mars in Aquarius, May 20, 19:57 - May 22, 7:41
Mars in Pisces, May 22, 7:42 - June 21, 3:56

YOUR LUCK MAGNETISM
Jupiter in Taurus, May 20, 19:57 - June 21, 3:56

World Events

May 31 - Ronald Reagan visits the Soviet Union, the country he once referred to as an "evil empire."

June 9 - Students and police clash in Seoul during demonstrations for unification with North Korea.

1988

CANCER
Your Personal Planets

YOUR LOVE POTENTIAL
Venus in Gemini, June 21, 3:57 - July 22, 14:50

YOUR DRIVE AND AMBITION
Mars in Pisces, June 21, 3:57 - July 13, 19:59
Mars in Aries, July 13, 20:00 - July 22, 14:50

YOUR LUCK MAGNETISM
Jupiter in Taurus, June 21, 3:57 - July 21, 23:58
Jupiter in Gemini, July 21, 23:59 - July 22, 14:50

World Events

July 7 - The *Piper Alpha* oil rig explodes in the North Sea, the worst accident of its kind in history.

July 20 - Ayatollah Khomeini calls an end to the war in the Gulf.

The "Piper Alpha" oil rig explodes

LEO
Your Personal Planets

YOUR LOVE POTENTIAL
Venus in Gemini, July 22, 14:51 - Aug. 06, 23:23
Venus in Cancer, Aug. 06, 23:24 - Aug. 22, 21:53

YOUR DRIVE AND AMBITION
Mars in Aries, July 22, 14:51 - Aug. 22, 21:53

YOUR LUCK MAGNETISM
Jupiter in Gemini, July 22, 14:51 - Aug. 22, 21:53

World Events

July 31 - Jordon's King Hussein announces he will relinquish his country's claim to the West Bank.

Aug. 8 - A ceasefire between Iran and Iraq comes into effect.

CANCER
From June 21, 3:57 through July 22, 14:50

The Social Homebody

An oil rig exploded in the North Sea, killing all but seventy of the rig's 227 workers. It was one of the worst industrial accidents at sea. The U.S. was suffering its worst drought in fifty years; scientists claimed it was the result of the "greenhouse effect." As you have grown, 1988 Cancer, environmental awareness has brought other, similar new concepts. Many people are trying to protect the ecosystem of this planet we call home. You would thrive and grow in a protected, nurturing "home." You instinctively draw people toward you who can value your sensitivity and offer understanding. You may be a highly social "homebody" who is likely to enjoy family life.

The placement of Venus, the planet of relationships, in lively Gemini gives you a mercurial inconsistency. The flightiness of Gemini combines with the moodiness of Cancer to give you a personality that changes with each passing moment. Others may find you difficult to figure out or occasionally a bit superficial in your interests. With Jupiter, the planet of opportunities, in stabilizing Taurus, growth could come when you settle into your physical surroundings and root yourself in one activity. The presence of Saturn, the planet of limitations, in truth-seeking Sagittarius means you may strive for practical applications for any education you receive.

You could find fulfillment in the business world, where your ability to socialize could work in your favor. Your fluency with figures could also lead to the initiation of your own entrepreneurial project. Your intuitive understanding of hidden motivations could be an asset in fields such as psychology, teaching, or the arts. A home-based business could suit you just fine. You could also be effective as a leader, even in politics.

You could seek variety in your social connections, along with the depth of emotional understanding you crave. You could find harmony with Pisces, Gemini, or Scorpio.

Your gift is the empathic understanding you offer, which brings rich emotional connections. Your challenge is to find a consistency in your personality, so that you might pursue a focused path.

LEO
From July 22, 14:51 through August 22, 21:53

The Regal Initiator

At the time of your birth, 1988 Leo, the last of the Playboy Clubs in the U.S, at Lansing, Michigan closed down. Jordan's King Hussein announced that he would relinquish his country's claim to the West Bank. And in other world news, Sarah, the Duchess of York, gave birth to a baby girl. The 1988 Leo might have shouted, "Look at me!" upon arrival. You have energy to spare, and you are likely to attract plenty of the attention you crave. The 1988 Leo also has the potential to cultivate a disciplined intellect, which can be a significant benefit to your career. You are likely to seek environments that encourage enthusiastic competition. Not one to sit on your hands, you are likely to jump on every opportunity that comes your way. And your pride and ambition will lead you into positions of leadership and authority. Others will likely respond favorably to your regal bearing.

With Mars, the planet of action, in fiery Aries, you are poised for immediate action at any time. This gives you an edge in environments where decisive action is needed. There could be a recklessness to your actions that could benefit from the company of practical minds. The presence of Jupiter, the sign of expansion, in fluent Gemini means some opportunities could come through communication or writing. You may have a lifelong interest in language, and find enjoyment in expressing yourself.

Your affinity for children could lead you into teaching or school counselor positions. The 1988 Leo will no doubt rise to become a respected colleague and eventually leader in any field they choose. A career in the performing arts could give the 1988 Leo a channel for all that exuberant vitality. You could be a formidable executive in the business world, as well.

The 1988 Leo needs to be around equally exuberant souls, who can also provide an anchor with sound, realistic advice. Those whose signs are in Cancer, Gemini, or Aries could create the sparks you seek.

Your gift is your warmth and natural self-confidence that leads to respect from others. Your challenge is to stay flexible to the opinions of others.

➤ Read about your Chinese Astrological sign on page 838. ➤ Read about your Personal Planets on page 826. ➤ Read about your personal Mystical Card on page 856.

VIRGO

From August 22, 21:54 through September 22, 19:28

The Meticulous Crusader

The arrival of the 1988 Virgo coincided with the beginning of a thirteen-nation benefit tour, which brought together a group of rock stars to sing for the cause of human rights. In Poland, Lech Walesa led a series of strikes. And in the Caribbean, the fiercest storm of the century rocked residents and caused havoc. The 1988 Virgo may be stirred to action when others are in need. Your help may come often in the form of easing the burdens of everyday life for those around you. But the 1988 Virgo also rushes in where others fear to tread, especially to aid your fellow humans. You are endowed with a curious mind and a voracious appetite for knowledge.

With Jupiter, the planet of expansion, in diversified Gemini, the 1988 Virgo is likely to enjoy a wide variety of intellectual interests. There's a good chance that you enjoy the written word, whether in the form of books or newspapers. The presence of Saturn, the planet of limitations, in disciplined Capricorn gives the 1988 Virgo a keen sense of what constitutes a solid foundation. The 1988 Virgo values tradition and you could thrive in settings where you can engage your meticulous mind in ways that uphold and honor such traditions.

The 1988 Virgo could find fulfillment in writing or research fields. A library setting could suit you just fine. You have a talent for minding the details that could be an asset in many fields. You could be energized by a daily routine that offers growing challenges in the same environment. As long as your mind is stimulated, you could find rewards in any field that you choose. But the 1988 Virgo has a desire to be of service, and you could best bring your analytical mind to bear for organizations whose causes inspire you.

The 1988 Virgo has high standards for company, and you may seek those with similar intellectual interests. You could find pleasing relations with people whose signs are in Cancer, Libra, or Aquarius.

Your gift is the dedication and integrity you bring to whatever you do. Your challenge is accepting people for who they are, not who you want them to be.

LIBRA

From September 22, 19:29 through October 23, 4:43

The Peace-Loving Intellectual

When you arrived, 1988 Libra, Naguib Mahfouz became the first Arab writer to win the Nobel Prize. At the same ceremony, the Nobel Peace Prize went to the United Nations peacekeeping forces. The 1988 Libra values harmony and abhors conflict, making you and your brethren natural peacekeepers. You know when to take risks and can surprise people with your impulsive decisions. You can see both sides of an issue, making you a natural diplomat. The 1988 Libra is probably well respected and you may quickly rise to leadership positions.

With Mercury, the planet of communication, also influenced by your sign of Libra, your mind often strives for balance and objectivity. The 1988 Libra could have trouble with extreme views, both within themselves and in others. The placement of Mars, the planet of action, in decisive Aries brings vital fire to your constitution. The 1988 Libra may be challenged to balance the need to weigh options thoughtfully before acting with the need to dive in. At times, you can reveal your own attraction to extremes in thought and action. When you trust your own motives, you can blend your intuitive hunches with your logical decision-making.

The 1988 Libra has the energetic disposition to keep long hours, especially if you believe in what you are doing. With your natural talent for communication, you could find success in public speaking. This could lead to politics or success in business management. Your mediation skills could be well suited to any work that involves conflict resolution. This could lead you to a legal career or working in education. You could also make a fine writer. The 1988 Libra gravitates toward work that engages the mind, rather than some kind of physical endeavor.

The 1988 Libra is likely to thrive in partnerships, both in work and romance. You could be drawn particularly to people whose signs are in Leo, Virgo, or Pisces.

Your gift is the grace and refinement that you exude, which draws to you a large circle of admirers. Your challenge is to avoid cultivating a "people-pleasing" personality and seek to discover your own truths.

VIRGO
Your Personal Planets

YOUR LOVE POTENTIAL
Venus in Cancer, Aug. 22, 21:54 - Sept. 07, 11:36
Venus in Leo, Sept. 07, 11:37 - Sept. 22, 19:28

YOUR DRIVE AND AMBITION
Mars in Aries, Aug. 22, 21:54 - Sept. 22, 19:28

YOUR LUCK MAGNETISM
Jupiter in Gemini, Aug. 22, 21:54 - Sept. 22, 19:28

World Events

Sept. 3 - Lech Walesa calls for Polish workers to end their strike.

Sept. 17 - The summer Olympics open in Seoul.

Egyptian writer Naguib Mahfouz Nobel Prize-winner

LIBRA
Your Personal Planets

YOUR LOVE POTENTIAL
Venus in Leo, Sept. 22, 19:29 - Oct. 04, 13:14
Venus in Virgo, Oct. 04, 13:15 - Oct. 23, 4:43

YOUR DRIVE AND AMBITION
Mars in Aries, Sept. 22, 19:29 - Oct. 23, 4:43

YOUR LUCK MAGNETISM
Jupiter in Gemini, Sept. 22, 19:29 - Oct. 23, 4:43

World Events

Sept 29 - United Nations peacekeeping forces are awarded the Nobel Peace Prize.

Oct. 13 - Naguib Mahfouz becomes the first Arab writer to win the Nobel Prize for literature.

➤ Read about your Chinese Astrological sign on page 838. ➤ Read about your Personal Planets on page 826. ➤ Read about your personal Mystical Card on page 856.

1988

SCORPIO
Your Personal Planets

YOUR LOVE POTENTIAL
Venus in Virgo, Oct. 23, 4:44 - Oct. 29, 23:19
Venus in Libra, Oct. 29, 23:20 - Nov. 22, 2:11

YOUR DRIVE AND AMBITION
Mars in Aries, Oct. 23, 4:44 - Oct. 23, 22:00
Mars in Pisces, Oct. 23, 22:01 - Nov. 01, 12:56
Mars in Aries, Nov. 01, 12:57 - Nov. 22, 2:11

YOUR LUCK MAGNETISM
Jupiter in Gemini, Oct. 23, 4:44 - Nov. 22, 2:11

World Events

Nov. 8 – Ronald Reagan is re-elected in the U.S.

Nov. 10 – The President of the Bundestag, Phillip Jenniger, delivers a pro-Nazi speech that forces his resignation the following day.

An earthquake in Armenia kills 100,000

SAGITTARIUS
Your Personal Planets

YOUR LOVE POTENTIAL
Venus in Libra, Nov. 22, 2:12 - Nov. 23, 13:33
Venus in Scorpio, Nov. 23, 13:34 - Dec. 17, 17:55
Venus in Sagittarius, Dec. 17, 17:56 - Dec. 21, 15:27

YOUR DRIVE AND AMBITION
Mars in Aries, Nov. 22, 2:12 - Dec. 21, 15:27

YOUR LUCK MAGNETISM
Jupiter in Gemini, Nov. 22, 2:12 - Nov. 30, 20:53
Jupiter in Taurus, Nov. 30, 20:54 - Dec. 21, 15:27

World Events

Nov. 30 – Yasser Arafat is denied a visa to address the United Nations in New York.

Dec. 10 – A huge earthquake devastates Armenia, killing an estimated 100,000 people.

SCORPIO
From October 23, 4:44 through November 22, 2:11

The Powerful Revealer

The arrival of the 1988 Scorpio with coincided the discovery of a fossil in Quebec, Canada, that scientists dated at 390 million years old, the oldest remains of a creature yet found. In other historical events, PLO Chairman Yasser Arafat declared the creation of the state of Palestine. There was also a powerful digital virus, which infected thousands of computers across the U.S. The 1988 Scorpio is deep thinking and able to dig through the layers to get to what is wanted, whatever the medium. You crave great intensity and depth in your career and relationships. The 1988 Scorpio seeks the truth in a disciplined, often solitary way.

The position of Jupiter, the planet of expansion, in objective Gemini can bring the balance of rational thinking to your intense emotionality. The 1988 Scorpio enjoys lively social engagements and can be talkative when the conversation stimulates them. You work best alone and can be known to go deep within for long periods of time. The 1988 Scorpio finds richness in the interior corridors of his or her own imagination. With Pluto, the planet of power to create new life, also in your sign, the 1988 Scorpio can be a powerful person, who has a dynamic ability to transform and grow.

The 1988 Scorpio could be drawn into artistic fields that give your solitary imagination a chance to flourish. You are likely to be a good investigator, researcher, or scientist. You have the ability to dive deep into something and re-emerge transformed. The 1988 Scorpio may change careers many times in life to accommodate radical growth. A career as a performer could satisfy this need to discover the truth behind what is hidden. Your intuitive understanding of human nature could lead to success in psychology as well.

Though the 1988 Scorpio can appear reserved, you enjoy many rich, passionate connections. Those with signs in Virgo, Libra, or Cancer could be good matches.

Your gift is the inwardly directed productivity that allows you, 1988 Scorpio, to unearth your talents and share them with others. Your challenge is to avoid getting lost in your own murky depths.

SAGITTARIUS
From November 22, 2:12 through December 21, 15:27

The Candid Philosopher

Big shifts occurred at the time of your birth, shaking up the world. PLO Chairman Yasser Arafat, who had recently announced the creation of the Palestinian state, was denied a visa to address the United Nations in New York. Margaret Thatcher and other leaders of Europe viewed the removal of Soviet troops and weapons from Eastern Europe as a sign that the Cold War was over. And a huge earthquake devastated the country of Armenia. The 1988 Sagittarius can navigate such chaotic times, often coming to profound philosophical truths that resonate with those around them. You are the ultimate truth-seeker and sometimes your search may take you into spiritual realms. You may be highly creative, and you bring passion and intensity to everything you try. Vital and alive, you are constantly looking for new challenges.

With Mars, the planet of action, in aggressive Aries, the 1988 Sagittarius has ample fire to stay inspired. Your outward focus is enhanced by this placement, making you gregarious and social. The 1988 Sagittarius could be drawn to competitive sports and thrive on vigorous physical activity. The placement of Venus, the planet of relationships, in passionate Scorpio probably attracts stormy relationships to the 1988 Sagittarius. You could struggle with issues of jealousy and possessiveness, which interfere with your Sagittarian trait of desiring complete independence.

The 1988 Sagittarius could find joy as a philosopher or educator. You may seek work that gives you the opportunity to continually try new things. A career involving travel could suit this explorer of new worlds. You might also be drawn to a job in publishing or the art world. There could also be athletic prowess in your make-up.

You are a "friend of the zodiac," 1988 Sagittarius, and could have a wide circle of acquaintances. Closer connections could be made among those with planets whose signs are in Scorpio, Aries, or Sagittarius.

Your gift is your open-minded curiosity to explore and experience the world. Your challenge is avoiding detrimental entanglements that steer you off your course.

➤ Read about your Chinese Astrological sign on page 838. ➤ Read about your Personal Planets on page 826. ➤ Read about your personal Mystical Card on page 856.

CAPRICORN

From December 21, 15:28 through December 31, 23:59

The Social Achiever

The arrival of the 1988 December Capricorn coincided with the first days in office of Pakistan's Benazir Bhutto, the first woman to rule an Islamic country. In an historic agreement, Canadian Parliament approved a trade pact with the United States. And tragedy struck when a terrorist bomb exploded on board a Pan Am jet, killing all 259 passengers and 11 people on the ground when it crashed in Lockerbie, Scotland. The 1988 Capricorn is a practical being with a mind geared toward turning knowledge or tragedy into tangible rewards. You can spend long hours hard at work, but you are also quite social and usually have a wide variety of acquaintances. Your serious outlook is tempered with a wry humor and blunt honesty. The 1988 December Capricorn has the ambition to achieve success, and you are likely to do that in the company of many others.

The presence of Mars, the planet of action, in outgoing Aries brings a fiery impulsiveness to the 1988 Capricorn's usually austere demeanor. There is ample energy to set a determined path and you are quick to take advantage of open doors. With Venus, the planet of relationships, in optimistic Sagittarius, you attract many friends and acquaintances. You enjoy being in the middle of the excitement, especially if it is competitive in nature. Your opinions can come forward in a blunt manner, which may at times step on the toes of others.

The 1988 December Capricorn has vast stores of energy, and you require work that is secure, while allowing plenty of room to move. You could enjoy work with a physical component, such as architecture or home construction. You are not afraid to make big changes that improve an organization, which would make you an excellent manager in the financial world.

Although you are open-minded in your search for companions, you likely are attracted to others who have similar ambitious streaks. You could be drawn to those whose signs are in Sagittarius, Aries, or Taurus.

Your gift is your ability to inspire others to work together toward constructive goals. Your challenge is curbing a tendency to ignore the sensitivities of others.

CAPRICORN
Your Personal Planets

YOUR LOVE POTENTIAL
Venus in Sagittarius, Dec. 21, 15:28 - Dec. 31, 23:59

YOUR DRIVE AND AMBITION
Mars in Aries, Dec. 21, 15:28 - Dec. 31, 23:59

YOUR LUCK MAGNETISM
Jupiter in Taurus, Dec. 21, 15:28 - Dec. 31, 23:59

World Events

Dec. 24 - Canada and the U.S. reach a trade agreement.

Dec. 30 - Japanese-American sculptor Isamu Noguchi dies.

Ronald and Nancy Reagan

Special Feature
Astrology in the White House: The Reagans

(Continued from page 713)

When the astrology scandal broke, Nancy was upset that more people didn't empathize and understand her great need. She writes, "It didn't seem to matter that nothing other than Reagan's schedule was affected by astrology. Or that tens of millions of Americans really believed in astrology. Or that almost every newspaper that ridiculed me for taking astrology seriously also featured a daily horoscope column."

Joan Quigley recounts her version of this time in her own book, *What Does Joan Say?* Quigley immodestly declares that she knew Nixon would come to ruin, was sure Reagan would win, and that she was the one responsible for transforming Nancy from an overdressed Hollywood wife to the caring and involved First Lady people came to admire.

"I was the Teflon in what came to be known as the 'Teflon Presidency'," Quigley writes. She felt that it was her scheduling derring-do that

helped Reagan evade all crises and appear in his most positive light. She also felt that it was her choice of timing for Reagan's visit to concentration-camp site Bergen-Belsen that defused the political ramifications of an American president laying a wreath where Nazi soldiers were buried.

There is more to the Reagans' consulting of astrologers and psychics than just good political strategy.

The timing may have helped, but most people regard this gesture as a presidential mistake. By May 1988, the President was in definite trouble: embroiled in the Iran-Contra affair, wrestling with fiscal problems throughout the country, and ignoring suspicions that his mental acuity was faltering could not have been easy. Then it came out that an *astrologer* was in charge of the President's schedule!

When the scandal erupted, and astrologers

everywhere were giving sound bites to local news stations, Nancy counseled Quigley to deny her connection with the Reagans, keep their involvement confidential, and to act with discretion. Quigley refused. She felt it was her prerogative to answer any and all questions put to her, and in the way that seemed most appropriate to her. It was her decision to speak out that caused Nancy to end their relationship. Now that both women have written memoirs about the matter, it is left to readers to decide which one's recollection is the most accurate and relevant. ✪

➤ Read about another influential astrologer in "Astrology Goes on Trial" on page 185. ➤ Read "Astrology Reigns Through the Ages" on page 25. ➤ Read "The Presidential Death Cycle" on page 657.

1989

Freedom Returns: Jupiter meets the Triple Conjunction

The twentieth century world cracked open in 1989 and the international balance of power would be completely different by the end of the year. These dramatic changes coincided with the continued "triple conjunction" of Saturn, Uranus, and Neptune, where all three planets are found in the same part of the heavens. The pattern was put in the spotlight by Jupiter, opposing them from across the skies from August. Saturn is linked with government and societal structures, while Uranus is expressed by the changing of outmoded forms. Neptune represents the images and ideals that provide motivation for the structures; Jupiter is expansionary, magnifying whatever it contacts. As the planets began their heavenly dance, the failing forms of the old system began to collapse.

The most potent expression of this pattern was the loosening of Communism's grip on Eastern bloc countries. The connections began in March, when the USSR had its first competitive elections since 1917. The next contact came in June, as idealistic Chinese students demonstrated for democracy in Tiananmen Square, then were brutally massacred by military forces. While this cry for freedom was quashed, it was the beginning of a revolutionary tide that would not be turned, signaled by continuous connections between these planets for the rest of the year. In Poland, the communist government was diluted when a Solidarity labor union member became Premier in August, as Jupiter touched off Uranus. In October, Hungary declared itself independent and democratic. In November, East Germany's communist government opened its borders and citizens jubilantly tore down the Berlin Wall, while revolutions sparked democratic changes in Czechoslovakia and Rumania.

The core contact of the year was between Saturn and Neptune. Their combination coincided with an unfortunate accident. The oil tanker *Exxon Valdez* broke up on a reef and spoiled the pristine Prince William Sound with eleven million gallons of oil, the accident attributed to its drunken captain's "pilot error." Oil, oceans, spills, toxins, and alcohol are all linked to Neptune, while Saturn represents the reef and the harsh lessons that ensued.

The tanker Exxon Valdez leaks oil off the coast of Alaska

East Germany opens its borders as the Berlin Wall is demolished

Tanks in Tiananmen Square in Beijing, China

THE IRON CURTAIN COLLAPSES

In Beijing's Tiananmen Square, hundreds of pro-democracy protesters were shot dead by the Chinese army. The USSR's first competitive elections in seventy-two years ousted many communists. Poland's Communist Party agreed to share power with the workers union Solidarity. Communist rule came to an end in Hungary, Bulgaria, and Czechoslovakia. In Romania, communist dictator Ceauscescu and his wife were executed. East Germany opened its borders as its citizens tore down the twenty-eight-year old Berlin Wall. Soviet leader Gorbachev and U.S. President Bush pronounced the end of the Cold War. U.S. troops ousted Panama's dictator Manuel Noriega. In Iran, the Ayatollah Khomenie, who died this same year, pronounced a fatwa, an Islamic death sentence, on British author Salman Rushdie for blasphemy in his novel *The Satanic Verses*. The worst oil spillage in U.S. history occurred when the 987ft. supertanker *Exxon Valdez* ran aground off the Alaskan coast. Satellite TV was launched in Britain. A violent quake in San Francisco killed 273. Emperor Hirohito of Japan, actor Laurence Olivier, former Philippines President Marcos and film star Bette Davis died.

➤ Read Nelson Mandela's Star Profile on page 729.

CAPRICORN

From January 01, 0:00 through January 20, 2:06

The Cool Customer

The January-born 1989 Capricorn is a good person to have around during an emergency. That's because you're always calm under pressure. No matter what the situation, you can be trusted to handle it in a controlled, dignified way. The year you were born, Kazuo Ishiguro's book *The Remains of the Day* was published. This tale of a dedicated but impassive butler reflects your own story in some way. You never let emotions get in the way of doing a good job.

A great deal of your identity is wrapped up in the work you perform. Therefore, you need a job that fills you with pride. You would do very well as a store manager, hotel concierge, or town planner. Giving other people direction and focus is your strong suit. If you'd like work that is a little more creative, you may want to become an event planner or wedding coordinator. Whatever position you hold, it should give you lots of autonomy. You dislike having your decisions questioned at every turn; you'd rather have your excellent work speak for itself.

When you're not working, you're luxuriating at home. Having a comfortable domestic life is very important to you. There's a good chance you have a flair for decorating and may constantly revamp various rooms. You are definitely the head of your household, which can create power struggles from time to time. However, if you maintain your sense of humor while laying down the law, you will avoid major blow-ups. Be willing to bend the rules to accommodate special circumstances or unusual situations.

You're attracted to people with strong personalities. Consequently, most of your friends are probably Ariens, Leos, Scorpios, and Capricorns. In love, you should look for a partner who is comforting and nurturing. You need plenty of tender loving care.

Your greatest challenge as a January-born 1989 Capricorn is to laugh at yourself. There's nothing undignified about making mistakes. In fact, people will admire you more for laughing at your own follies. Your biggest strength is your ability to remain calm under pressure. You're an enormous comfort during times of trial.

AQUARIUS

From January 20, 2:07 through February 18, 16:20

The Contented Recluse

It's very rare that a 1989 Aquarius makes a public appearance. That's because you're so happy at home. Enjoying a big dinner with your family, puttering around in the garden, curling up in bed with a good book—these are your favorite forms of recreation. If your best friends aren't your relatives, they are probably treated like family. Your upbeat attitude makes you a popular figure, though you'd rather throw an informal dinner party than attend a swanky soiree. The year you were born, Bobby McFerrin's "Don't Worry, Be Happy" was awarded Grammy Awards for Best Song and Best Record. This cheerful tune nicely sums up your own attitude toward life.

Ideally, you should find creative work that can be performed away from prying eyes. You would make a great writer, radio personality, or photographer. Working in a big office filled with people may not suit you very well. You'd rather operate in a quiet studio somewhere, surrounded by familiar sights, sounds, and scents. Ideally, you should have your own workspace that can be decorated any way you choose. Operating a business out of your own home is a strong possibility for you.

You have a strong spiritual side and may be deeply interested in the unconscious mind. Subjects like E.S.P., metaphysics and psychology could play an important part in your life. Although you are very logical, you rely on your intuition more than your intellect. As a 1989 Aquarius, this is a very wise decision. By trusting your unconscious, you will feel bliss that most people will never experience.

Spiritual but mischievous people have a friend in you. That's why there are so many Geminis, Sagittarians, Aquarians, and Pisceans among your acquaintances. As far as romance is concerned, you need a partner who loves home and family just as much as you do. There is a good chance that your mate will have a playful, childlike spirit.

Your greatest challenge as a 1989 Aquarius is to carve out an enriching home life. Everything after that will be icing on the cake. Your biggest strength is your unconscious mind; let it be the primary guiding force in your life.

➤ Read about your Chinese Astrological sign on page 838. ➤ Read about your Personal Planets on page 826. ➤ Read about your personal Mystical Card on page 856.

CAPRICORN
Your Personal Planets

YOUR LOVE POTENTIAL
Venus in Sagittarius, Jan. 01, 0:00 - Jan. 10, 18:07
Venus in Capricorn, Jan. 10, 18:08 - Jan. 20, 2:06

YOUR DRIVE AND AMBITION
Mars in Aries, Jan. 01, 0:00 - Jan. 19, 8:10
Mars in Taurus, Jan. 19, 8:11 - Jan. 20, 2:06

YOUR LUCK MAGNETISM
Jupiter in Taurus, Jan. 01, 0:00 - Jan. 20, 2:06

World Events

Jan. 4 – The U.S. shoots down two Libyan jets.

Jan. 7 – Japanese Emperor Hirohito dies.

Death of Surrealist painter Salvador Dali

AQUARIUS
Your Personal Planets

YOUR LOVE POTENTIAL
Venus in Capricorn, Jan. 20, 2:07 - Feb. 03, 17:14
Venus in Aquarius, Feb. 03, 17:15 - Feb. 18, 16:20

YOUR DRIVE AND AMBITION
Mars in Taurus, Jan. 20, 2:07 - Feb. 18, 16:20

YOUR LUCK MAGNETISM
Jupiter in Taurus, Jan. 20, 2:07 - Feb. 18, 16:20

World Events

Jan. 23 – Spanish artist Salvador Dalí dies.

Jan. 24 – U.S. serial killer Theodore Bundy is executed in the electric chair.

1989

PISCES
Your Personal Planets

YOUR LOVE POTENTIAL
Venus in Aquarius, Feb. 18, 16:21 - Feb. 27, 16:58
Venus in Pisces, Feb. 27, 16:59 - Mar. 20, 15:27

YOUR DRIVE AND AMBITION
Mars in Taurus, Feb. 18, 16:21 - Mar. 11, 8:50
Mars in Gemini, Mar. 11, 8:51 - Mar. 20, 15:27

YOUR LUCK MAGNETISM
Jupiter in Taurus, Feb. 18, 16:21 - Mar. 11, 3:25
Jupiter in Gemini, Mar. 11, 3:26 - Mar. 20, 15:27

World Events

Mar. 2 - The European Community vows a ban on chlorofluorocarbons (CFCs), believed to adversely affect the Earth's atmosphere.

Mar. 8 - Protests against Chinese rule in Tibet lead to the region being placed under marshal law.

An oil-covered bird is examined after the "Exxon Valdez" disaster

ARIES
Your Personal Planets

YOUR LOVE POTENTIAL
Venus in Pisces, Mar. 20, 15:28 - Mar. 23, 18:31
Venus in Aries, Mar. 23, 18:32 - Apr. 16, 22:51
Venus in Taurus, Apr. 16, 22:52 - Apr. 20, 2:38

YOUR DRIVE AND AMBITION
Mars in Gemini, Mar. 20, 15:28 - Apr. 20, 2:38

YOUR LUCK MAGNETISM
Jupiter in Gemini, Mar. 20, 15:28 - Apr. 20, 2:38

World Events

Mar. 30 - The *Exxon Valdes* supertanker spills vast amounts of oil, severely damaging the Alaskan coastline.

Apr. 5 - A Polish accord is signed, making Poland the first Communist state to become a democracy.

PISCES
From February 18, 16:21 through March 20, 15:27

The Hopeful Humanitarian

Despite all its faults, nobody loves the human race more than the 1989 Pisces. You are passionately committed to improving people's lives. The year you were born, tens of thousands of Chinese students took over Beijing's Tiananmen Square in a rally for democracy, despite powerful military opposition. You're willing to take similar chances for the sake of civil rights. There's a good chance that you will be involved with several protest movements throughout the course of your life. Fighting for your principles is as natural as breathing for you.

Being an advocate for the poor or disadvantaged may prove satisfying. You'd make an excellent civil rights lawyer, social worker, or welfare administrator. Alternately, you may want to be a fundraiser for a non-profit organization. Working for a group such as Amnesty International or Doctors without Borders might also appeal to you. Whatever job you perform, make sure that it is geared toward helping society's underdogs.

When you aren't working for some humanitarian cause, you are probably exploring. You love to visit different places and read about exotic lands. The older you get, the more you will realize that people everywhere are essentially the same. This knowledge will help you form bonds with folks who, on the surface, seem to have very little in common with you. As the years go by, your parties may become famous, because they'll include so many different types of fascinating people.

As far as friends are concerned, you are drawn to folks who are both adventurous and spiritual. Consequently, you may have a great many Ariens, Sagittarians, Aquarians, and Pisceans among your acquaintances. Romantically, you need a partner who is tender and nurturing. Sometimes you get so busy taking care of others that you forget to attend to your own needs! This is where the right mate can prove tremendously helpful.

Your greatest challenge as a 1989 Pisces is to pick your causes carefully. It's hard to do justice to a particular issue when your energies are scattered. Your biggest strength is your genuine love of people. It's a gift.

ARIES
From March 20, 15:28 through April 20, 2:38

The Gifted Speaker

The ideal gift for a 1989 Aries is a microphone. You may love talking to the public, whether at an informal party or a business meeting. Having an audience makes you come alive; you're never more attractive than when you're standing behind a podium. You probably have a distinctive way of talking that both charms and disarms people. The year you were born, George Bush was inaugurated as the 41st President of the United States. Like Bush, you are the frequent target of affectionate mimics. Folks can't resist copying your memorable gestures and mannerisms.

Without a doubt, you are a born salesperson. You're one of those rare folks who can achieve great success with cold calls. If a career in sales doesn't interest you, tourism might. You would make a great travel agent, cruise director, or tour guide. Alternately, you could go into the entertainment industry. You would do well at virtually any job that puts you before the public, whether it's as a news anchor or stand-up comedian. The job field is wide open for a forceful, charming person like you.

You have a remarkable intuition that should serve you well in virtually every area of life. You're especially good at picking up romantic vibes. While others stumble and fumble in the game of love, you breeze through it with an air of calm assurance. Although some folks might take advantage of this situation, you won't. Romance is a serious business to you. Pursuing someone just for the sake of a challenge simply isn't your style.

Because you have such powerful magnetism, you may find that you attract receptive, responsive friends. Geminis, Cancerians, Librans, and Pisceans probably make up the biggest part of your social circle. In love, you are likely to seek out a partner who is tactful, artistic, and flexible. Such a mate will smooth over your rough edges, while you add a bit of force to their personality.

Your biggest challenge as a 1989 Aries is to develop your listening skills. Being open to other people's input will only strengthen your effective speaking talent. Your greatest strength is your self-confidence.

➤ Read about your Chinese Astrological sign on page 838. ➤ Read about your Personal Planets on page 826. ➤ Read about your personal Mystical Card on page 856.

TAURUS

From April 20, 2:39 through May 21, 1:53

The Cautious Optimist

Planning ahead is a specialty of the 1989 Taurus. You love to consider the future, weigh your options, and create agendas. Quite often, you not only meet but also surpass your goals. You're the type who enjoys the process just as much as the results. The year you were born, the Berlin Wall was toppled, sending shockwaves throughout the world. Although it was a gradual process, the results made a sizable tear in the Iron Curtain. You're similarly willing to inch toward a goal, even if it takes years before you finally reach it.

You possess admirable intellectual ability and may decide to go into the education field. You'd make an excellent college professor, probably specializing in a field like history or anthropology—the past holds a certain fascination for you. Alternately, you might like to go into publishing, editing or acquiring interesting new books. Whatever your career, it should constantly expose you to all sorts of interesting information. You can't afford to let your brain stagnate once you leave school.

Earning and spending money come easily to you. You know how to attract lucrative jobs that will allow you to live in style. Creature comforts are very important to you, although you don't hoard your riches. Chances are you will spend a great deal of time entertaining friends in your sumptuous home. Guests know that they will be treated to gourmet food and fine wine whenever they visit. Consequently, your house may be the most popular place in town.

It's important for you to have very close friendships. You enjoy the company of intense, driven people who have a sense of destiny about them. Ariens, Taureans, Leos, and Scorpios are among your favorite friends. Romantically, you need a mate who is strong-willed but tender. Wishy-washy types leave you cold and you like lots of cuddling.

Your greatest challenge as a 1989 Taurus is to take time out of your busy schedule to have fun. Resist the urge to put off fun for the sake of work; you need to strike an even balance. Your biggest blessing is your brain power. Learning will be a lifelong process.

GEMINI

From May 21, 1:54 through June 21, 9:52

The Lifelong Student

Reading is an obsession for the 1989 Gemini. Chances are you've always got your nose in a book. That's because you're always trying to learn something new. As soon as you digest new bits of information, you're eager to share them. You're probably famous for your party chatter and folks often cross the room for the express purpose of talking to you. You enjoy discussing controversial subjects that lead to spirited debates. The year you were born, Salman Rushdie's novel *Satanic Verses*, published in September 1988, incurred the wrath of Islamic militants. It probably fascinates you to think that ideas can move people to incredible acts of courage or violence, and you may explore this phenomenon throughout the course of your life.

A born communicator, you need a job that involves delivering information. You'd make an excellent writer, political commentator, or news anchor. Alternately, your fascination with human nature may lead you to a career in psychology, psychiatry, or criminology. Whatever job you take, it should allow you to be opinionated and independent.

Your love life can have some interesting ups and downs. You will probably go through periods when you will feel intensely amorous, followed by stages when you are shy and reserved. These changes in behavior can bewilder your partner. When you do fall in love, make a concerted effort to assure your mate of your affection both verbally and physically.

Witty, talkative people comprise the greater part of your social circle. You probably have many pals who are Ariens, Geminis, Librans, and Sagittarians. Romantically, you need a partner who is smart, sensual, and demonstrative. With a little encouragement from your mate, you can balance your physical and intellectual sides.

Your greatest challenge as a 1989 Gemini is to decide on a career. This can be difficult for you, because you have so many different interests. Go with the discipline that most captures your imagination—financial considerations shouldn't enter into your decision. Your biggest strength is your quick mind. Mastering skills should be a snap for you.

► Read about your Chinese Astrological sign on page 838. ► Read about your Personal Planets on page 826. ► Read about your personal Mystical Card on page 856.

TAURUS
Your Personal Planets

YOUR LOVE POTENTIAL
Venus in Taurus, Apr. 20, 2:39 - May 11, 6:27
Venus in Gemini, May 11, 6:28 - May 21, 1:53

YOUR DRIVE AND AMBITION
Mars in Gemini, Mar. 20, 2:39 - Apr. 29, 4:36
Mars in Cancer, Apr. 29, 4:37 - May 21, 1:53

YOUR LUCK MAGNETISM
Jupiter in Gemini, Apr. 20, 2:39 - May 21, 1:53

World Events

Apr. 25 - Japanese Prime Minister Takeshita resigns amid allegations that he traded political favors for the Recruit Company.

May 3 - Unions in the USSR are granted the right to strike.

Death of Ayatollah Khomeini

GEMINI
Your Personal Planets

YOUR LOVE POTENTIAL
Venus in Gemini, May 21, 1:54 - June 04, 17:16
Venus in Cancer, June 04, 17:17 - June 21, 9:52

YOUR DRIVE AND AMBITION
Mars in Cancer, May 21, 1:54 - June 16, 14:09
Mars in Leo, June 16, 14:10 - June 21, 9:52

YOUR LUCK MAGNETISM
Jupiter in Gemini, May 21, 1:54 - June 21, 9:52

World Events

June 4 - Chinese Communist troops kill students in Tiananmen Square in Beijing.

June 4 - Ayatollah Khomeini dies.

CANCER
Your Personal Planets

YOUR LOVE POTENTIAL
Venus in Cancer, June 21, 9:53 - June 29, 7:20
Venus in Leo, June 29, 7:21 - July 22, 20:44

YOUR DRIVE AND AMBITION
Mars in Leo, June 21, 9:53 - July 22, 20:44

YOUR LUCK MAGNETISM
Jupiter in Gemini, June 21, 9:53 - July 22, 20:44

World Events

July 9 - Boris Becker and Steffi Graf become Wimbledon champions.

July 14 - France celebrates the bicentenary of the French Revolution.

Bastille Day fireworks over the Eiffel Tower in Paris

LEO
Your Personal Planets

YOUR LOVE POTENTIAL
Venus in Leo, July 22, 20:45 - July 24, 1:30
Venus in Virgo, July 24, 1:31 - Aug. 18, 1:57
Venus in Libra, Aug. 18, 1:58 - Aug. 23, 3:45

YOUR DRIVE AND AMBITION
Mars in Leo, July 22, 20:45 - Aug. 03, 13:34
Mars in Virgo, Aug. 03, 13:35 - Aug. 23, 3:45

YOUR LUCK MAGNETISM
Jupiter in Gemini, July 22, 20:45 - July 30, 23:49
Jupiter in Cancer, July 30, 23:50 - Aug. 23, 3:45

World Events

Aug 9 - Japan's Prime Minister appoints two women to the Japanese Cabinet.

Aug. 13 - The space shuttle *Columbia* returns from a five-day secret mission.

CANCER
From June 21, 9:53 through July 22, 20:44

The Devoted Partner

The 1989 Cancer is rarely alone. You're usually arm-in-arm with your best friend or sweetheart, finishing their sentences. When you're not in the company of someone special, you feel just a little bit vulnerable. Maybe it's because you're so kind and sensitive. You want a shield from the harsh realities of life and often enlist loved ones to perform this task. In exchange, you provide them with a constant supply of tender loving care. The year you were born, comedienne Lucille Ball died at the age of seventy-eight. Like Lucy, there is a good chance you will form a significant partnership at some point in your life.

Your ideal job would involve pleasing others. You'd make an excellent confectioner, florist, or decorator. Alternately, you could find a job caring for people in need of personal services. You could find success as a private chef, nurse, or companion. Be very selective about the people for whom you work, however. You're too tender hearted to sustain abuse from an unfeeling employer.

Although you're constant and loyal in love, you are a bit of a gambler in other areas. You don't think twice about leaving a secure job for one that's less stable but more exciting. You're also willing to experiment with unusual creative techniques, and you are eager to defy conventions and social trends in your art. At some point, you may decide to take time away from your job in order to write, paint, or play music.

Earthy, practical types make you feel safe and secure. Consequently, you have a great many friends who are Taureans, Virgos, and Capricorns. You also enjoy the company of Scorpios because they are so fiercely protective. In love, you need a mate who is reserved, dignified, and accomplished. You want to look up to your partner.

Your greatest challenge as a 1989 Cancer is to develop a greater sense of independence. Learn to enjoy solitary pursuits like reading and meditating. This will help you establish healthy boundaries among you and your loved ones. Your biggest blessing is your generous instincts. You are firmly convinced that it is better to give than to receive.

LEO
From July 22, 20:45 through August 23, 3:45

The Rescue Worker

The 1989 Leo is famous for bailing out friends, relatives, and strangers from distressing situations. That's because you're always looking to be of service. You're the person who learns CPR, just to be on the safe side. If somebody gets a flat tire, you pull over to help. And if a friend needs a shoulder to cry on, you're there with the tissues. A lot of weight can rest on your capable shoulders and it is often put there. The year you were born, Amy Tan published *The Joy Luck Club*. This story of dutiful daughters may strike a chord with you.

You are perfectly suited to any of the healing professions. You'd make a marvelous doctor, psychologist, or spiritual counselor. Because you can also master endless detail, you could also get a job as a film director, wedding coordinator or school administrator. While others would buckle under handling so many different aspects of a job, you remain cool as a cucumber. Maybe that's why you're always entrusted with serious responsibilities.

From a very early age, you probably earned a special position in your family. Perhaps you had to parent the adults in your home. Maybe you were the only child and given prodigious amounts of attention. It's possible that you didn't fit in with the other members of your family and were a source of concern or perplexity. Whatever the circumstance, you were singled out in a way that gave you both power and pressure. This feeling could continue into your adult life unless you're willing to delegate responsibilities to others. Give yourself permission to be carefree, at least once in a while!

You're very selective about the company you keep. Generally, you are drawn to Taureans, Leos, Scorpios, and Capricorns, thanks to their sense of duty toward others. In love, you need a partner who is witty and irreverent. Having a mate who can make you laugh will add a great deal of levity to your life.

Your greatest challenge as a 1989 Leo is to develop hobbies. Doing things for sheer pleasure can be a lovely revelation for you. Your biggest strength is your desire to help others in any way possible.

➤ Read about your Chinese Astrological sign on page 838. ➤ Read about your Personal Planets on page 826. ➤ Read about your personal Mystical Card on page 856.

VIRGO

From August 23, 3:46 through September 23, 1:19

The Late Bloomer

Born with tremendous potential, the 1989 Virgo may be slow to find a calling. That's because you're good at so many different things. Never fear; you can plant the seeds for future success simply by dreaming. There's a good chance that your life's work will involve the arts. The year you were born, the movie of Christy Brown's *My Left Foot* received popular and critical acclaim all over the world. This true life-story of an artist with cerebral palsy may give you tremendous inspiration.

Working with your hands may have great appeal for you. You'd make an excellent carpenter, jewelry maker, or sculptor. Alternately, you might like to learn a craft that is becoming increasingly rare, like glassblowing or weaving. Whatever practice you decide to take up, you're sure to put an unusual twist on it. Your artwork is destined to be utterly unique and may challenge the status quo in some ways. Unlike Virgos born in other years, you enjoy creating controversy. Don't be afraid to part from tradition—it's the best way to get your work noticed.

You are hard-working and conscientious, and you are willing to do whatever is necessary to meet your goals. Even if you get a late start in life, it won't take long for you to catch up with the competition. That's because you are blessed with incredible drive. You're also quite a perfectionist and will practice for hours and hours to master a particular skill. Edison's observation that "success is five percent inspiration, ninety-five percent perspiration" perfectly applies to you.

Friends are as important as family to you. Surrounding yourself with caring, nurturing people is essential to your emotional health. Consequently, it would be a good idea to befriend Taureans, Cancerians, Leos, and Pisceans as a general rule. In love, you are best suited to a partner who is intuitive and spiritual.

Your greatest challenge as a 1989 Virgo is to turn your setbacks into advantages. If you come to your calling late in life, let your early frustrations fuel your success. Your biggest strength is your determination. Little stands between you and your dreams, provided you work hard.

LIBRA

From September 23, 1:20 through October 23, 10:34

The Soothing Peace-Maker

The 1989 Libra positively radiates serenity. You possess an inner calm that is very difficult to shake. Folks gravitate to you when they need comfort or reassurance. Even during the most chaotic times, you are placid and steady, providing needed perspective to those who can't handle sudden changes. The year you were born, the Dalai Lama won the Nobel Prize for Peace. Like this respected spiritual leader, you too have learned to live in the moment, accepting whatever comes with quiet dignity.

There is a good chance you will achieve prominence in your profession, mainly because people respect you so much. You need to be emotionally involved with your work and may choose a career in law. You'd make an excellent judge. You also possess considerable writing ability and may choose to write books on subjects like spirituality, kindness, or etiquette. Working in human resources or diplomacy are other possibilities for you. Whatever your job, it should involve getting people to treat each other in a gracious, generous, and fair manner.

You have the potential to make a great deal of money over the course of your life. Part of this is because you can attract high-paying positions, but another part of it is because you are so resourceful. You buy possessions for quality and durability, not status. Furthermore, you're able to stretch funds to the breaking point. In your spare time, you may decide to do some fundraising for your favorite charities.

Many of your friends are sensitive and emotional. You probably get along very well with Cancerians, Librans, Scorpios, and Pisceans. Romantically, you are best suited to a partner who is energetic, enthusiastic, and direct. You need a dynamic mate who can shake you out of complacency every now and again. The best relationships involve a little friction.

Your greatest challenge as a 1989 Libra is to connect with folks on an emotional level. Share your feelings with others during the few times when you are nervous or afraid. Your biggest strength is your sense of inner peace. It's so strong that it rubs off on everybody you meet.

➤ Read about your Chinese Astrological sign on page 838. ➤ Read about your Personal Planets on page 826. ➤ Read about your personal Mystical Card on page 856.

1989

VIRGO
Your Personal Planets

YOUR LOVE POTENTIAL
Venus in Libra, Aug. 23, 3:46 - Sept. 12, 12:21
Venus in Scorpio, Sept. 12, 12:22 - Sept. 23, 1:19

YOUR DRIVE AND AMBITION
Mars in Virgo, Aug. 23, 3:46 - Sept. 19, 14:37
Mars in Libra, Sept. 19, 14:38 - Sept. 23, 1:19

YOUR LUCK MAGNETISM
Jupiter in Cancer, Aug. 23, 3:46 - Sept. 23, 1:19

World Events

Aug 24 – Drug lords declare war on the government in Columbia.

Sept. 11 – Thousands of East German refugees in Hungary begin to emigrate to West Germany.

Death of actress Bette Davis

LIBRA
Your Personal Planets

YOUR LOVE POTENTIAL
Venus in Scorpio, Sept. 23, 1:20 - Oct. 08, 15:59
Venus in Sagittarius, Oct. 08, 16:00 - Oct. 23, 10:34

YOUR DRIVE AND AMBITION
Mars in Libra, Sept. 23, 1:20 - Oct. 23, 10:34

YOUR LUCK MAGNETISM
Jupiter in Cancer, Sept. 23, 1:20 - Oct. 23, 10:34

World Events

Oct. 1 – Gay marriages are permitted in Denmark.

Oct. 6 – Hollywood legend Bette Davis dies.

1989

SCORPIO

Your Personal Planets

YOUR LOVE POTENTIAL

Venus in Sagittarius, Oct. 23, 10:35 - Nov. 05, 10:12
Venus in Capricorn, Nov. 05, 10:13 - Nov. 22, 8:04

YOUR DRIVE AND AMBITION

Mars in Libra, Oct. 23, 10:35 - Nov. 04, 5:28
Mars in Scorpio, Nov. 04, 5:29 - Nov. 22, 8:04

YOUR LUCK MAGNETISM

Jupiter in Cancer, Oct. 23, 10:35 - Nov. 22, 8:04

World Events

Nov. 10 – The Berlin Wall is brought crashing down in the greatest symbol of the new order in Europe.

Nov. 16 – South African President F. W. de Klerk orders that the beaches be desegregated.

Olympic gymnast Nadia Comaneci

SAGITTARIUS

Your Personal Planets

YOUR LOVE POTENTIAL

Venus in Capricorn, Nov. 22, 8:05 - Dec. 10, 4:53
Venus in Aquarius, Dec. 10, 4:54 - Dec. 21, 21:21

YOUR DRIVE AND AMBITION

Mars in Scorpio, Nov. 22, 8:05 - Dec. 18, 4:56
Mars in Sagittarius, Dec. 18, 4:57 - Dec. 21, 21:21

YOUR LUCK MAGNETISM

Jupiter in Cancer, Nov. 22, 8:05 - Dec. 21, 21:21

World Events

Nov. 27 – The first live-donor liver transplant is performed in Chicago.

Dec. 9 – Rumanian gymnast Nadia Comaneci defects to the West.

SCORPIO

From October 23, 10:35 through November 22, 8:04

The Thoughtful Sage

Quiet, reserved, and dignified, the 1989 Scorpio can be an intimidating figure. You're always sizing up people, but you usually keep your opinions to yourself. Talking with you is a little like sitting in a psychiatrist's couch while the doctor busily scribbles notes. After a while, one can't help but wonder what's being written. What most folks don't realize is that you are quite generous and compassionate in your assessments. You have a very philosophical outlook, and you don't feel the need to judge. Rather, you're just interested in observing human behavior.

Any work that involves constant study and analysis would suit you perfectly. You'd make an excellent psychologist, psychiatrist, or zoologist. As a Scorpio, there's a good chance you're interested in crime. Consequently, you may feel moved to write mystery novels with a psychological bent. The sciences also hold a special attraction for you, and you may be drawn to a career in medical research.

You are a very spiritual person, and you may need to retreat from the public periodically in order to nourish your soul. Taking nature walks, listening to music, and meditating are all ways you can restore harmony and balance to your life. On November 10, 1989, the Berlin Wall was opened, having been in place since 1961. You have a similar talent for breaking down barriers and bringing people together.

Although you have many acquaintances, you prefer keeping a small circle of friends. People who are on the intellectual side appeal to you most. That's why you have so many Geminis, Librans, and Aquarians among your acquaintances. You also like spending time with spiritual Pisceans. In love, you need a partner who is sensual and charming.

As a 1989 Scorpio, your greatest challenge is to know when to analyze a situation and when to abandon yourself to it. You weren't meant to sit on the sidelines and take notes all the time; allow yourself to have a little fun. Your biggest blessing is your ability to see the truth in any deceptive situation.

SAGITTARIUS

From November 22, 8:05 through December 21, 21:21

The Centered Soul

Having an identity crisis is highly unlikely for the 1989 Sagittarius. From a very early age, you knew who you were and where you were going. That's because you came into the world with a highly developed soul. There's a good chance you have a special gift of some kind, one that gives you a sense of purpose and belonging. Despite your self-assurance, folks could never call you smug. You're too friendly and accepting for that.

You don't care whether you are working with your head or hands, so long as your job gives you a sense of accomplishment. You're very skilled at containing disasters. The year you were born, the ruptured tanker *Exxon Valdez* sent eleven million gallons of crude oil into Prince William Sound off Alaska. You're the type who could have handled the massive clean-up effort with great efficiency. Consequently, you may want to think about going into emergency surgery, international politics, or environmental work. You're well suited to any job that involves sudden emergencies.

Being entrusted with other people's secrets is par for the course for the 1989 Sagittarius. Folks sense that you are a caring, empathetic person and confess their darkest feelings to you. You're flattered to be so trusted among your friends, but they can drain you of energy if you're not careful. Learn to draw personal boundaries early in life. You need to attend to your own needs before anyone else's.

Most Archers have a huge gang of friends with whom they meet regularly. You're a bit different in this respect. You'd rather have three or four close friends. Quiet, considerate Taureans, Virgos, Librans, and Capricorns find favor with you. Romantically, you need a partner who provides you with both emotional and intellectual support.

Your greatest challenge is to overcome a fear of poverty. Although you're secure about your abilities, you may worry that you won't make enough to get by. Remember that if you do what you love, the money will follow. Your biggest strength is your balanced perspective on life. You always manage to take the bad with the good and still remain happy.

➤ Read about your Chinese Astrological sign on page 838. ➤ Read about your Personal Planets on page 826. ➤ Read about your personal Mystical Card on page 856.

CAPRICORN

From December 21, 21:22 through December 31, 23:59

The Ambitious Protector

Always watching after others, the December-born 1989 Capricorn is a comforting presence. You're willing to put your own needs aside for the sake of friends and family. Although you are generous, you are discriminating about those you help and how you assist them. You're not the type to throw money at a problem, hoping it will go away. Rather, you discover the exact nature of a person's dilemma and the best way to treat it.

You are probably very ambitious and need a career that confers both responsibility and respectability. You'd make a wonderful CEO, university president, or hospital administrator. Politics may also interest you, and you may decide to run for office at some point in your life. You're also very creative and may pursue a career in the arts. You have the makings of a great orchestra conductor, lead singer, or principal dancer.

Although you have both feet planted firmly on the ground, you rely on your intuition a great deal. You're not afraid to break the rules if you think there's a better way of doing things. This can get you into trouble with authority figures, especially in your early years. However, as you grow older, folks will see the wisdom of your ways. The year you were born, George Michael's *Faith* won the Grammy for Album of the Year. That's all you need to accomplish your objectives—faith.

It's possible you are the member of several social and professional organizations, making friends in both camps. Your favorite folks are accomplished, thoughtful Taureans, Leos, Scorpios, and Aquarians. In love, you are best-suited to a mate who is generous in their affections. Too often, you deprive yourself of the tender loving care you deserve. Your mate can rectify this imbalance.

Your greatest challenge as a December-born 1989 Capricorn is to learn when to delegate responsibilities to others. It's not healthy to carry the entire weight of the world on your shoulders all the time. Be willing to farm out jobs to folks who are eager to prove themselves to you. Your biggest strength is your ability to set goals and meet them, whatever the odds.

CAPRICORN
Your Personal Planets

YOUR LOVE POTENTIAL
Venus in Aquarius, Dec. 21, 21:22 - Dec. 31, 23:59

YOUR DRIVE AND AMBITION
Mars in Scorpio, Dec. 21, 21:22 - Dec. 31, 23:59

YOUR LUCK MAGNETISM
Jupiter in Cancer, Dec. 21, 21:22 - Dec. 31, 23:59

World Events

Dec. 22 – The Brandenburg Gate between East and West Germany is opened.

Dec. 29 – Vaclav Havel is sworn in as Czech President.

Nelson Mandela
Born July 18, 1918

NELSON MANDELA
Cancer

Nelson Mandela, a soft-spoken but determined man, has spent his entire life in service of justice within his homeland of South Africa. A country populated largely by Black Africans, it remained under the thumb of white minority leaders who instituted a policy of extreme racial separation known as "apartheid." It was this injustice that Mandela was unwaveringly committed to redress, even during a twenty-seven year period of imprisonment. Only a worldwide outcry and an economic boycott could bring about his release, which resulted in more humane policies in his nation, his ascension to its presidency and his receipt of a Nobel Prize.

There is no question that the sign Cancer is known for its sensitivity and emotionality, but it's also important to realize that, like a mother fighting for the survival of her young, Cancerians will bravely put their lives on the line to assure the safety of what matters most

to them. In addition to having his Sun, planet of identity, in this sensitive sign, Mandela's Moon, planet of emotions, is in another intense sign, Scorpio. He is a man of deep feeling, intense, and passionate, who is driven by those feelings rather than by mere intellectual rhetoric.

Mars is the planet of action and of war, and with Mars in the congenial sign of Libra, Mandela strives to get along with all people. He will not tolerate any form of racism from anyone, no matter to what race they belong. Interestingly, more generals have Mars in Libra than in any other sign, so perhaps that is what makes him such a skilled and respected leader. In addition, a contact from Venus, planet of affection, prominently placed in his horoscope gives him physical grace and universal appeal.

Mandela remained married during his long incarceration, only to discover after his release that his wife was guilty of criminal

wrongdoings that resulted in her exile and their divorce. With Pluto, the planet of power struggles, and Jupiter, planet of expansion, in his house of marriage, we can see that he could have turbulent partnerships that are both challenging and rewarding.

➤ Read Martin Luther King's Star Profile on page 537 ➤ Read Mahatma Ghandhi's Star Profile on page 377. ➤ Read Mother Teresa's Star Profile on page 777.

1990

Changes Continue: Jupiter and Saturn

In 1987, Saturn, Uranus, and Neptune began coming together in an unusual "triple conjunction", or meeting in one place in the skies. Saturn, the ruler of governments and laws, first contacted Uranus, the planet of insurrection and independence, in 1987-88. In 1989, Saturn linked up with Neptune, planet of religion and spirituality. When they combine, a transition in society and its perspectives takes place, often radically changing the forms of government and its ideals. As they began to conjoin this time, the worst of the old system's oppressions were challenged and many were overturned. This was seen in the astonishing transformation that took place in the USSR and the Eastern bloc countries, as they began to open up and regain their autonomy. In 1990, the focal point of the triple conjunction was Saturn, which was "opposed" from across the heavens by expansive Jupiter. The spotlight on Saturn emphasized the manifestation aspect of its nature. This was seen in the continuing transformation in the Soviet Union and its satellites. Poland, Rumania, and Hungary instituted democratic reforms, Lithuania declared its independence and Germany was unified after forty-five years of separation into east and west.

As Jupiter entered bold and proud Leo toward the end of August, Iraqi leader Saddam Hussein invaded neighboring Kuwait and threatened Saudi Arabia, initiating the Persian Gulf War. Most of the international community was united in its condemnation of the attack and demanded immediate withdrawal, but in the Arab world, he was a hero to poorer nations and people.

East and West Germany are reunited

French and U.S. troops are deployed to Saudi Arabia   *Margaret Thatcher resigns*

CROP CIRCLES

In 1990, 400 crop circles, or large spiral-shaped formations, had been found in the middle of grain fields in England. Most appeared overnight, sometimes preceded by amber lights hovering above the Earth. The grain was crushed horizontally suggesting an external force was responsible, such as a UFO. Some shapes resembled pictograms, leading British psychical researchers to conclude that some degree of intelligence—perhaps even of a divine nature—had been at work in an attempt to communicate with humankind.

IRAQ INVADES KUWAIT

Saddam Hussein, ruler of Iraq, invaded Kuwait and took over its oil fields. The French, whose embassy in Kuwait was looted by Iraqi forces, sent 4,000 men to Saudi Arabia, while the Saudi forces went on full alert. The UN gave Saddam notice that he must pull his forces out of Kuwait by January 15, 1991 or face attack by a U.S.-led alliance. East and West Germany were reunited. The Baltic states of Latvia, Lithuania and Estonia pressed for independence from Russia, but economic problems arose throughout the former Eastern Bloc countries as the painful business of moving from a communist to a capitalist system got under way. Nelson Mandela was freed after being imprisoned for twenty-seven years for his opposition to apartheid in South Africa. In Nicaragua, voters removed the ruling leftist Sandinista party and elected moderate Violeta Barrios de Chamorro to the presidency. Opposed within her own Conservative Party, British Prime Minister Margaret Thatcher resigned and was succeeded by John Major. Around the world, increasing attention was drawn to environmental concerns, particularly habitat destruction and global warming.

➤ Read Bill Gates' Star Profile on page 737.

CAPRICORN

From January 01, 0:00 through January 20, 8:01

The Unprejudiced Politician

As a Capricorn born in January of 1990, you arrived at the beginning of a year that would see major triumphs in the struggle for freedom and racial equality. The first, which occurred in the U.S., was the swearing in of David Dinkins as the first African American to be elected mayor of New York City. These and subsequent events of a similar nature showed that after many years of struggle, judging individual capability based on race or religion might have some hope of losing its grip.

The astrological influences of your birth-month were equally momentous. The heavens played host to five planets in your own objective sign, which could have given you the ability to see past physical and philosophical differences, and to make choices based on an unprejudiced evaluation of the facts. As such, you may be drawn to work with groups or organizations that foster equality, and you'd be a mighty advocate for those and any causes you chose to champion.

It's likely that your unbiased, fair-minded manner will win you friends from all walks of life—all of whom would value your wisdom, tolerance, and nonpartisan opinions. As a result, you may be often called upon to negotiate, mediate, and help adversaries to reach a peaceful agreement. Whether or not you choose to undertake this work as a profession, you'll probably be responsible for inspiring many compromises throughout your life, simply by offering a fair evaluation of the situation at hand.

In love relationships, you may be drawn to partners who share your open-mindedness, compassion, and tolerance. As such, an abundance of Sagittarians, Aquarians, and Librans may find their way into your life and if you don't give your heart to another Capricorn, one of them could win your lifelong affection.

You've been gifted with the innate fairness of a judge and the wisdom of a philosopher, qualities that are much sought-after and hard to come by. Your greatest challenge is to treat yourself as gently as you treat others.

AQUARIUS

From January 20, 8:02 through February 18, 22:13

The Unwavering Believer

Born during 1990, Aquarius, you made your planetary debut at the moment that after twenty-seven years of political imprisonment Nelson Mandela was finally freed. In less than three years from that historic day, Mandela would be elected President of South Africa—a far cry from being locked away for his adamant refusal to renounce his fight against apartheid. The same month, the ban on anti-apartheid parties was lifted. Although all natives of your sign are famous for their love of freedom and independence, being born at this particular time may have heightened these qualities in you, and fostered your determination to be yourself at all cost.

The astrological factors of your birth-time perfectly describe the seeds of your freedom-oriented, autonomous personality and provide clues as to just how strongly you'll stand up for your principles throughout life. The heavens held an unprecedented gathering of planets in Capricorn, a sign that rivals your own when it comes to integrity, self-respect, and honor. You were also given a strong dose of Cancerian energy, accounting for your devotion to family and friends.

It's likely that your respectful attitude in the presence of elders gives you wisdom beyond your years, and may mean that you'll pursue a career that allows you to put what you've learned from them into action. You may also feel a need to do what you can to help rid the world of all forms of prejudice. By example, you'll influence others to put aside pettiness and seek out the self-respect that comes from being true to themselves.

In love relationships, you'll often be drawn to Capricorns, who'll feel like kindred spirits. You may also find yourself with Librans and Sagittarians, whose constant optimism, open-minded manner, and steady support will help you to stay on your chosen path. Look to other Aquarians and Geminis, as well as spiritually advanced Pisceans, for friendship.

Your challenge is to take a firm stance with regard to your personal convictions, never allowing others to force you to buckle to what society considers appropriate. Your gifts are your innate integrity and your staunch and unwavering devotion to what you know is right.

► Read about your Chinese Astrological sign on page 838. ► Read about your Personal Planets on page 826. ► Read about your personal Mystical Card on page 856.

1990

CAPRICORN
Your Personal Planets

YOUR LOVE POTENTIAL
Venus in Aquarius, Jan. 01, 0:00 - Jan. 16, 15:22
Venus in Capricorn, Jan. 16, 15:23 - Jan. 20, 8:01

YOUR DRIVE AND AMBITION
Mars in Sagittarius, Jan. 01, 0:00 - Jan. 20, 8:01

YOUR LUCK MAGNETISM
Jupiter in Cancer, Jan. 01, 0:00 - Jan. 20, 8:01

World Events

Jan. 1 – David Dinkins is sworn in as the first African American Mayor of New York City.

Jan. 3 – Panama's leader Gen. Manuel Noriega surrenders to U.S. authorities.

Nelson Mandela with his wife Winnie after his release from prison

AQUARIUS
Your Personal Planets

YOUR LOVE POTENTIAL
Venus in Capricorn, Jan. 20, 8:02 - Feb. 18, 22:13

YOUR DRIVE AND AMBITION
Mars in Sagittarius, Jan. 20, 8:02 - Jan. 29, 14:09
Mars in Capricorn, Jan. 29, 14:10 - Feb. 18, 22:13

YOUR LUCK MAGNETISM
Jupiter in Cancer, Jan. 20, 8:02 - Feb. 18, 22:13

World Events

Jan. 29 – *Exxon Valdez* Captain Joseph Hazelwood goes on trial for his accountability in the oil spill.

Feb. 11 – Nelson Mandela is freed in South Africa after twenty-seven years of imprisonment.

1990

PISCES
Your Personal Planets

YOUR LOVE POTENTIAL
Venus in Capricorn, Feb. 18, 22:14 - Mar. 03, 17:51
Venus in Aquarius, Mar. 03, 17:52 - Mar. 20, 21:18

YOUR DRIVE AND AMBITION
Mars in Capricorn, Feb. 18, 22:14 - Mar. 11, 15:53
Mars in Aquarius, Mar. 11, 15:54 - Mar. 20, 21:18

YOUR LUCK MAGNETISM
Jupiter in Cancer, Feb. 18, 22:14 - Mar. 20, 21:18

World Events

Mar. 11 - Lithuania declares its independence from the USSR.

Mar. 14 - Mikhail Gorbachev becomes President of the Soviet Congress.

Death of Greta Garbo

ARIES
Your Personal Planets

YOUR LOVE POTENTIAL
Venus in Aquarius, Mar. 20, 21:19 - Apr. 06, 9:12
Venus in Pisces, Apr. 06, 9:13 - Apr. 20, 8:26

YOUR DRIVE AND AMBITION
Mars in Aquarius, Mar. 20, 21:19 - Apr. 20, 8:26

YOUR LUCK MAGNETISM
Jupiter in Cancer, Mar. 20, 21:19 - Apr. 20, 8:26

World Events

Apr. 11 - Constantine Mitsotakis is sworn in as Prime Minister of Greece.

Apr. 15 - Legendary film star Greta Garbo dies.

PISCES
From February 18, 22:14 through March 20, 21:18

The Spiritual Diplomat

You, 1990 Pisces, arrived around the time Mikhail S. Gorbachev, a man many believed would be able to reunite Russia with the world community, became President of the Soviet Union. Famous for the liberal beliefs, which were in stark contrast to many of his predecessors, Gorbachev's election seemed to herald a time of new cooperation with the West. Although he would remain in office for less than two years—his influence on the world would last far longer. In fact, his policy of *perestroika* became virtually synonymous with efforts to end the Cold War, not just in name, but in a spiritual sense as well.

The astrological influences in effect when you were born were geared toward the collective, unconditional acceptance of all races, creeds, and philosophies. Your own sign and visionary Aquarius among whose common denominators are humanitarianism, equality, and the unqualified embracing of individuals of all faiths each hosted an abundance of planets at the time you arrived. This could have given you the tools to become a spiritual diplomat, and help to unite others under the broad canopy of humanity.

As such, you're probably quite spiritual yourself. Whether that means you follow a devout religious path, or you simply believe that we are all part of one universal being, your belief in a higher power is probably the foundation you build your life upon. Regardless of the philosophy you follow, you may be an inspirational leader to others, both by the power of your words and the power of your example.

In love relationships, you may want to surround yourself with others whose faith in a higher power is as strong as your own. As such, you'll probably seek out the company of Scorpios and Cancerians, whose depth and keen intuition will provide you with a solid emotional home base. In friendships, look to Aquarians, Sagittarians, Capricorns and, of course, members of your own mystical sign.

Your challenge is to accept those who refuse to believe in anything they can't actually see or touch. Your gift is your innate sureness that everything happens for a reason.

ARIES
From March 20, 21:19 through April 20, 8:26

The Bold Rebuilder

You were born, Aries of 1990, as the continent of Africa was finally bringing the last chapter in its 105-year history of colonialism to a close. On March 21, 1990, Namibia became an independent country. It was the last African nation to break away from colonial rule, following years of fighting against South African occupation. Namibia's independence provided a shining moment of hope and promise, for a continent that had been ripped apart for centuries by Great Power colonialism, economic exploitation, and racial oppression. Independence and self-rule are only one happy milestone in the story. Your generation will bear the responsibility of helping the Dark Continent and its inhabitants to heal from the many wounds and scars remaining from the ravages of colonialism.

You have the energy and will to make a new and better beginning. You can be force to be reckoned with when you see the need for change, and because your ruling planet is Mars, the Roman god of war, you won't shy away from aggressively plowing through any obstacles.

Indicators in your birth chart serve to reinforce those character traits. In addition to the planets that were in your own sign, the heavens hosted several Capricorn energies. Now, Capricorn is famous for its love of structure, walls, and boundaries, while Aries is known for fast action—which includes taking apart, knocking down, or razing those structures. This symbolically includes your immediate, spontaneous tendency to let go of behavior, beliefs, or habits that are no longer constructive. You may often have the unpleasant task of bearing bad news, but your personal strength of character will help you to perform that duty during even the most difficult of times.

In love relationships, you'll probably want others by your side who are as fond of new beginnings as you are—and just as unafraid to initiate them. Seek out Sagittarians, Aquarians, and Leos, who'll match you in courage and adventurousness.

Your gift is your ability to take swift and decisive action. Your challenge is to fight off any doubt or hesitancy that threatens to stop you.

➤ Read about your Chinese Astrological sign on page 838. ➤ Read about your Personal Planets on page 826. ➤ Read about your personal Mystical Card on page 856.

1990

TAURUS
From April 20, 8:27 through May 21, 7:36

The Discriminating Connoisseur

You may have been born with an appreciation for perseverance, diligence, and hard work, Taurus of 1990. Although these traits are common among Taureans, it's likely that your birth-time gave you even more determination to develop them than Taureans born in other years possess. Around the time you were born, in a testament to the immortality of mastery in a chosen field, a painting by Vincent Van Gogh, one of the most respected and revered artists of all time, was sold for a record-breaking price at auction: $82.5 million. In his lifetime, Van Gogh had not earned enough by his art to support himself and he relied on his brother Theo for money to live on and buy his paints and brushes.

The astrological influences of your birth-time show your diligence, industry, and application as well as your taste for the aesthetic. In addition to two planets in your own quality-conscious sign, the heavens held several planets in Pisces, the sign that shares your artistic, musical, and performing talents. You've probably become quite the connoisseur in each of those categories, and you can be absolutely insistent when it comes to excellence.

That thirst for nothing but the best extends into your relationships, too, whether they're business or personal. You may admire individuals with high moral and ethical standards and its likely that you've worked hard to develop those qualities within yourself. As such, your personal integrity can be stainless, as is the reputation you'll earn among co-workers and authority figures alike. Your attention to detail will probably put you at the very top of your field, regardless of what career path you choose to follow.

In romance, you'll probably seek out the company of Virgos and Capricorns, your fellow earth signs who also reach for high standards and share your enjoyment of fine food and wine, beautiful art, and good music.

Your challenge is to develop tolerance with others whose tastes may not be quite as discriminating as your own and to show them the better things in life. Your gift is the ability to spot a fake or phony a mile away.

GEMINI
From May 21, 7:37 through June 21, 15:32

The Non-Partisan Truth-Seeker

You, 1990 Gemini, arrived into a world that heard the news of a major progress in the spread of freedom and democracy throughout the world. In June of 1990, Czechoslovakia held its first free elections following the fall of the Iron Curtain. Celebrated author and dissident, Vaclav Havel, was elected to lead the new government. In America, anti-apartheid hero and statesman, Nelson Mandela, recently freed from imprisonment in South Africa, received a ticker tape parade to mark his first visit to New York City. Havel and Mandela represented ideals that are precious to Gemini: freedom, equality, and the right to open expression.

Gemini is an inherently democratic sign. Because members of this sign have a dual-sided personality, you have an intuitive appreciation for the value of debate. Even when you agree with an opening assertion, your speedy mind can immediately anticipate an opposing view. To say that you can appreciate both sides of an issue may actually insult your intelligence. A Gemini is likely to see many sides to any given issue. Throughout life, you've probably found yourself playing the devil's advocate, striving to present each side of an argument with impartial enthusiasm.

Your goal is to arrive at the concrete truth. Fortunately, your lack of attachment to either side would have allowed you to develop the qualities of fairness, objectivity, and candor—without which true justice would never be attained. You are likely to care deeply about applying your excellent ideas to the real world, to make conditions better for those who are suffering.

In love, you may be after someone who's as open-minded and cerebral as you are. As such, broad-minded Sagittarians and visionary Aquarians could suit you just fine. However, other Geminis could provide you with a sounding board and a worthy adversary at the same time—maybe even besting you in debate every now and then, as well!

Your challenge is to surround yourself with those who, like you, will not pass judgment on others. Your gifts are your innate fairness, and the ability to see both sides of every story.

TAURUS
Your Personal Planets

YOUR LOVE POTENTIAL
Venus in Pisces, Apr. 20, 8:27 - May 04, 3:51
Venus in Aries, May 04, 3:52 - May 21, 7:36

YOUR DRIVE AND AMBITION
Mars in Aquarius, Apr. 20, 8:27 - Apr. 20, 22:08
Mars in Pisces, Apr. 20, 22:09 - May 21, 7:36

YOUR LUCK MAGNETISM
Jupiter in Cancer, Apr. 20, 8:27 - May 21, 7:36

World Events

Apr. 25 - The Hubble Space Telescope is placed into orbit by the U.S. shuttle *Discovery*.

Apr. 29 - Wrecking cranes begin tearing down the Berlin Wall at the Brandenburg Gate.

The Hubble Space Telescope in orbit

GEMINI
Your Personal Planets

YOUR LOVE POTENTIAL
Venus in Aries, May 21, 7:37 - May 30, 10:12
Venus in Taurus, May 30, 10:13 - June 21, 15:32

YOUR DRIVE AND AMBITION
Mars in Pisces, May 21, 7:37 - May 31, 7:10
Mars in Aries, May 31, 7:11 - June 21, 15:32

YOUR LUCK MAGNETISM
Jupiter in Cancer, May 21, 7:37 - June 21, 15:32

World Events

June 11 - The U.S. Supreme Court decrees that the law prohibiting the desecration of the U.S. flag is unconstitutional.

June 21 - An earthquake with hundreds of aftershocks hits Iran; an estimated 50,000 people are believed to be killed in the disaster.

➤ Read about your Chinese Astrological sign on page 838. ➤ Read about your Personal Planets on page 826. ➤ Read about your personal Mystical Card on page 856.

1990

CANCER
Your Personal Planets

YOUR LOVE POTENTIAL
Venus in Taurus, June 21, 15:33 - June 25, 0:13
Venus in Gemini, June 25, 0:14 - July 20, 3:40
Venus in Cancer, July 20, 3:41 - July 23, 2:21

YOUR DRIVE AND AMBITION
Mars in Aries, June 21, 15:33 - July 12, 14:43
Mars in Taurus, July 12, 14:44 - July 23, 2:21

YOUR LUCK MAGNETISM
Jupiter in Cancer, June 21, 15:33 - July 23, 2:21

World Events

July 1 - The Deutschmark becomes the official currency of the new united Germany.

July 12 - Boris Yeltsin quits the Soviet Communist Party.

Boris Yeltsin resigns

LEO
Your Personal Planets

YOUR LOVE POTENTIAL
Venus in Cancer, July 23, 2:22 - Aug. 13, 22:04
Venus in Leo, Aug. 13, 22:05 - Aug. 23, 9:20

YOUR DRIVE AND AMBITION
Mars in Taurus, July 23, 2:22 - Aug. 23, 9:20

YOUR LUCK MAGNETISM
Jupiter in Cancer, July 23, 2:22 - Aug. 18, 7:29
Jupiter in Leo, Aug. 18, 7:30 - Aug. 23, 9:20

World Events

July 24 - U.S. warships in the Persian Gulf are placed on alert after Iraq amasses nearly 30,000 troops near its border with Kuwait.

Aug. 7 - The U.S. deploys troops to Saudi Arabia.

CANCER
From June 21, 15:33 through July 23, 2:21

The Fierce Supporter

You, Cancer of 1990, were born during a time when Russian President Boris Yeltsin resigned from the Communist Party. When you consider the impact of Russia's takeover by the Communists in 1917 and the devastating loss of life and freedom in the decades that followed—only when you roll back in your history book to remember the famines, the purges, the forced collectivization, and the gulag—only then can you appreciate the astonishing significance of a Russian President abandoning the Communist Party. Because your birth-time coincided with this milestone, your personality may be infused with the seeds of peaceful, but meaningful change.

The astrological influences of your birth-time were equally rebellious. Several planets in your own tenacious sign were directly opposite to three powerful outer planets in Capricorn—the sign that's famous for resisting change and holding on to the past. This astrological opposition of energies perfectly explains the tug of war that caused such major change in the former Soviet Union, but it probably also describes a familiar pattern in your life.

In short, you may sometimes find it necessary to make your point through issuing ultimatums. This trait will emerge most dramatically when you're acting in defense of your dear ones—who are likely to look to you often for support—and you'll never let them down. Your unwillingness to back down from your position, regardless of pressure from authority figures or society in general, probably means you're also a strong, uncompromising champion of the disadvantaged. Once your heart is involved, you'll stop at nothing to protect who and what you love. Home and family will always be at the very top of that list, along with lifelong friends, whom you no doubt also consider family.

Your choice of partner should be someone just as protective, nurturing, and fiercely loyal as you are, and you can look to Pisceans, Taureans, and other Cancerians for all these traits and more.

Your challenge is to rebel only when your cause is just. Your gift is your unconditional, loving support of your dear ones.

LEO
From July 23, 2:22 through August 23, 9:20

The Underdog's Champion

You were born when the United States began preparations for Operation Desert Storm, its military campaign against Iraq's seizure of Kuwait. This tiny, oil-rich nation had been overrun by Saddam Hussein's army in a mere twelve hours, giving the Iraqi president control over some ten percent of the world's known oil reserves. Although it seemed initially that Hussein would be unchallenged, Kuwait called on the world for help and the United States answered. The same energy that inspired a superpower to go to the defense of a nation totally unable to protect itself probably inspired you with a strong urge to champion the underdog, Leo of 1990, and it's likely that the more powerless they are, the more fiercely determined you'll be to protect them.

The astrological factors that influenced your birth-time also show your intense resolve to defend the helpless and your capacity to do just that. The heavens hosted several planets in protective earth signs, not the least of which was Mars, the ancient god of war, who was storming through stubborn, determined Taurus, giving you the ability to be a fierce and faithful advocate.

In addition to your fiery loyalty and fierce determination, you may also have an innate kindness and compassion. When those feelings are stirred, especially if someone or something is being taken advantage of or bullied, you'll probably take their side and never leave it. As such, you may often be called on to defend and protect your dear ones, and you'll gladly do so. You may also be drawn to work that allows you to counsel those you see as victims. One way or the other, you'll have the capacity to do good for others, and gain the respect and gratitude of everyone whose life you touch.

In love relationships, your search for the right partner will probably lead you into the arms of someone as compassionate and tender yet strong as you are, and you'd do well to seek out Cancerians, Ariens, and other Leos.

Your challenge is to avoid putting yourself in harm's way when protecting someone else. Your gift is your loyalty, which knows no bounds.

➤ Read about your Chinese Astrological sign on page 838. ➤ Read about your Personal Planets on page 826. ➤ Read about your personal Mystical Card on page 856.

VIRGO

From August 23, 9:21 through September 23, 6:55

The Cooperative Ambassador

Virgo of 1990, you made your planetary debut during a time that saw the leaders of two former enemy nations come together with a single goal to bring about a peaceful solution to the military conflict in Kuwait. On September 9, U.S. President George Bush and Soviet leader Mikhail Gorbachev met in Helsinki, Sweden, to urge Iraq to leave Kuwait. Although their trip would prove to be futile, the cooperation demonstrated by that meeting showed the world that even old adversaries could put aside their differences in favor of effecting peace.

The astrological factors that influenced your birth-time also show that urge for compromise. Holding court in the heavens were several planets in solid, responsible earth signs, all of whom share a common mission: to maintain the status quo through keeping the peace and following the rules. As such, you may have been given an equally peaceful and respectful nature, along with the ability to inspire cooperation. You'll probably often be summoned by your dear ones when they find themselves in no-win situations, confident that you'll be able to bring about a happy ending if anyone can. You may also be known as a true team player, someone who's intent on working for the good of the many without allowing your personal agenda to interfere.

Since you know the value of a smile and a pleasant disposition, you'd make an excellent go-between in any situation. In fact, when an ambassador is needed, you'll probably offer your services. Still, your easy smile and gentle manner belie your inner firmness and resolute determination. When you're placed in a position of authority, you can be a capable judge and a wise advisor.

In love, quick-thinking Gemini may fascinate you, but in the end, you'll probably prefer the solid, stable manner of Taureans and Capricorns, your fellow earth signs, who'll never fail to provide you with emotional and spiritual support.

Your gift is your ability to find common ground and effect compromise in difficult situations through your keen analysis of any situation. Your challenge is to avoid taking on problems that don't belong to you.

LIBRA

From September 23, 6:56 through October 23, 16:13

The Good Listener

You may have been born with a knack for bringing reason and objectivity to even the most unbalanced situations, Libra of 1990. Around the time you arrived, Mikhail Gorbachev, the Soviet President, was awarded the Nobel Peace Prize. This soft-spoken, seemingly mild-mannered man had quietly effected a great change in his own country and as a result, in the entire world ushering in a period of democratic reform in the USSR that helped to bring the Cold War to an end.

The fact that this remarkable man's gifts were recognized while the Sun was in Libra may reflect your sign's natural talent for restoring balance, which could make you an equally competent advocate for peace and equality within your own circle of family, friends, and co-workers. You could work long and hard to learn how to intervene and settle disputes amicably, but your innate gift for inspiring others to find a middle ground should make it easy for you to perfect your talents.

The astrological influences of your birth-time may show just how capable you are in situations of unrest, agitation, and turmoil. The skies hosted an equal number of planets in solid earth and communicative air signs, a combination that fosters reason, rationality, and fairness. These qualities probably will be put to good use over the course of your lifetime, as your dear ones may turn to you when circumstances seem irresolvable. Since you were probably given a big helping of compassion and understanding as well, you could find that just listening to what they have to say helps the situation immeasurably.

In love, you may want someone by your side who is willing to put aside their personal feelings in favor of bringing about peace and harmony. As a result, other Librans, broadminded Sagittarians, and objective Aquarians could be your best bet, but the friendship of a few intuitive Pisceans will also help you hone your skills.

Your greatest challenge is to be as fair to yourself as you are to others. Your gift is the ability to recognize exactly where two opponent similarities lie and to help them reach that common ground.

➤ Read about your Chinese Astrological sign on page 838. ➤ Read about your Personal Planets on page 826. ➤ Read about your personal Mystical Card on page 856.

VIRGO
Your Personal Planets

YOUR LOVE POTENTIAL
Venus in Leo, Aug. 23, 9:21 - Sept. 07, 8:20
Venus in Virgo, Sept. 07, 8:21 - Sept. 23, 6:55

YOUR DRIVE AND AMBITION
Mars in Taurus, Aug. 23, 9:21 - Aug. 31, 11:39
Mars in Gemini, Aug. 31, 11:40 - Sept. 23, 6:55

YOUR LUCK MAGNETISM
Jupiter in Leo, Aug. 23, 9:21 - Sept. 23, 6:55

World Events

Aug. 31 - East and West Germany agree terms by which their legal and political systems will be joined.

Sept. 9 - President George Bush and Mikhail Gorbachev meet in Helsinki and urge Iraq to leave Kuwait.

President Gorbachev wins the Nobel Peace Prize

LIBRA
Your Personal Planets

YOUR LOVE POTENTIAL
Venus in Virgo, Sept. 23, 6:56 - Oct. 01, 12:12
Venus in Libra, Oct. 01, 12:13 - Oct. 23, 16:13

YOUR DRIVE AND AMBITION
Mars in Gemini, Sept. 23, 6:56 - Oct. 23, 16:13

YOUR LUCK MAGNETISM
Jupiter in Leo, Sept. 23, 6:56 - Oct. 23, 16:13

World Events

Oct. 6 - A military coup to overthrow the Philippine government fails.

Oct. 15 - Soviet President Mikhail Gorbachev is offered the Nobel Peace Prize.

1990

SCORPIO
Your Personal Planets

YOUR LOVE POTENTIAL

Venus in Libra, Oct. 23, 16:14 - Oct. 25, 12:02
Venus in Scorpio, Oct. 25, 12:03 - Nov. 18, 9:57
Venus in Sagittarius, Nov. 18, 9:58 - Nov. 22, 13:46

YOUR DRIVE AND AMBITION

Mars in Gemini, Oct. 23, 16:14 - Nov. 22, 13:46

YOUR LUCK MAGNETISM

Jupiter in Leo, Oct. 23, 16:14 - Nov. 22, 13:46

World Events

Nov. 12 – Iraq delivers an ultimatum to Kuwaiti citizens: they must all bear Iraqi identity cards within forty-eight hours.

Nov. 18 – Saddam Hussein announces his intention of releasing his hostages.

The French and English flags are exchanged through the Channel Tunnel

SAGITTARIUS
Your Personal Planets

YOUR LOVE POTENTIAL

Venus in Sagittarius, Nov. 22, 13:47 - Dec. 12, 7:17
Venus in Capricorn, Dec. 12, 7:18 - Dec. 22, 3:06

YOUR DRIVE AND AMBITION

Mars in Gemini, Nov. 22, 13:47 - Dec. 14, 7:45
Mars in Taurus, Dec. 14, 7:46 - Dec. 22, 3:06

YOUR LUCK MAGNETISM

Jupiter in Leo, Nov. 22, 13:47 - Dec. 22, 3:06

World Events

Nov. 25 – Lech Walesa wins Poland's first popular election.

Dec. 2 – U.S. composer Aaron Copland dies.

SCORPIO
From October 23, 16:14 through November 22, 13:46

The Emergency Specialist

Born during the turbulent fall of 1990, you may have been given a double dose of the intensity, determination, and focus your sign is famous for, Scorpio. In response to Saddam Hussein's invasion of Kuwait, U.S. President George Bush announced plans to send an additional 100,000 troops to the Persian Gulf, joining the 210,000 American soldiers already there, to further strengthen the coming offensive against Iraq. This was a major indication of the United States' determination to restore Kuwaiti independence and stop future Iraqi aggressions. The cost of the conflict there, both financially and psychologically, would amaze the world.

Power struggles and conflict may have marked your arrival, but these are situations you could be especially well-equipped to deal with. Along with the turbulence of the time came the astrological components necessary to handle it. The heavens hosted several planets in your own rugged, enduring sign, all of which never fail to see an undertaking through to the very end for better or worse. As a result, your already intense nature could have been heightened along with your ability to handle crises.

The ultimate strategist, you were probably gifted with the ability to out-think, out-plan, and out-maneuver your peers. As a result, you could be the person everyone turns to when urgent or emergency situations arise, due to your competency, calmness, and capacity to take charge immediately. You may be drawn to medical or military occupations that allow you to use these skills, but regardless, it's likely that your strong backbone will always make others feel safe and secure in your presence. No matter how desperate the times, you'll have a solution ready and the presence of mind to put it into action.

In love relationships, you'll want someone who's equally brave, focused, and steady-handed. For that reason, other Scorpios may attract you, as will rock-solid Capricorns, nurturing Cancerians, and intuitive Pisceans.

Your challenge is to find an outlet for stress. Your gift is your calmness during even the most challenging times.

SAGITTARIUS
From November 22, 13:47 through December 22, 3:06

The Optimistic Opponent

You may have been born with the ability to stay positive during even the most stressful times, 1990 Sagittarius. Within days of your birth, Lech Walesa was elected by a landslide victory to the presidency of Poland, in his country's first free election. Walesa's campaign actually began in 1980, when he defied the Communist government of Poland by founding the independent labor union, Solidarity. Rapidly gaining the support of ten million members in the early 1980s, Solidarity evolved into a national freedom movement. In 1983 Walesa won the Nobel Peace Prize.

This type of optimism against all odds is characteristic of your sign, known for its high spirits, upbeat attitude, and unsinkable confidence. But it's likely that the astrological influences in effect at your birth-time gave you an even hardier dose of all these positive qualities. Several planets in your own sign and in Scorpio, the most famously tenacious of all the signs, added to your ability to hold on no matter how bad things look. This powerful combination gives you the best of both worlds: diligence, focus, and persistence under pressure, as well as confidence and optimism. In short, you're very well equipped to handle anything—and your enthusiasm is contagious.

As a result, you're probably the person your family and friends will turn to when they are feeling frightened, pessimistic, or desperate. Your happy demeanor, upbeat attitude, and cheerful outlook could also make you the center of attention in any social circle. It's likely that your friends are a varied and interesting crew, many of whom you may have met under unusual circumstances—in far-off places on one of your many long-distance adventures, perhaps.

In love relationships, you may look for someone as optimistic, lighthearted, and jovial as you. As such, Leos and Ariens, the other fire signs, could suit you just fine. In friendships and business relationships, you may look to Capricorns and Taureans for solid advice and counsel.

Your gift is your never-ending faith in the Universe. Your challenge is to know when it's time to give up and give in.

➤ Read about your Chinese Astrological sign on page 838. ➤ Read about your Personal Planets on page 826. ➤ Read about your personal Mystical Card on page 856.

CAPRICORN
From December 22, 3:07 through December 31, 23:59

The Happy Laborer

As a Capricorn born in December of 1990, it's likely that you were blessed with a rare gift: the capacity to make a hobby into a job you'll love. A shining example of this was illustrated during your birth month, when *Time* magazine announced the results of a poll. Former Mr. Universe Arnold Schwarzenegger, who always talked enthusiastically about his work, was the number one movie star not just in the country of his residence, the United States, but in the world! The publicity and acclaim this action film star earned worldwide at the end of 1990 reflects an ability you too may possess to turn something you enjoy doing into your road to success.

The astrological factors in place in the heavens may also show your capacity to spend each and every hour of your life doing what you love. Although many people spend their days doing a job that simply pays the bills, you may have been born with the knowledge that if you follow your bliss, as Joseph Campbell once said: "The doors will open for you that wouldn't have opened for anyone else." Whether you earn a six-figure salary or just barely get by probably won't matter to you. The quality of the hours you spend on the planet is what will make you a happy, fulfilled individual.

You could have a knack for networking and finding just the right people to help you further your goals. And if you focus first on finding the one thing that gives you joy, then make connections, you'll undoubtedly find work in the field you desire. As an ambitious Capricorn, your success in your chosen field is all but guaranteed, as is the inspiration you'll give to those who know you.

In love, you may want to be in the company of someone whose *joie de vivre* is as strong as your own. As such, Sagittarians, Aquarians, and Librans could appeal to you. For help in grounding your dreams in reality, however, look to Taurus and Virgo, your fellow earth signs.

Your challenge is to pursue your dreams, even if life seems intent on distracting you with promises of a large salary for doing work that's pure drudgery to you. Your gift is the inspiration you'll give others by your example.

CAPRICORN
Your Personal Planets

YOUR LOVE POTENTIAL
Venus in Capricorn, Dec. 22, 3:07 - Dec. 31, 23:59

YOUR DRIVE AND AMBITION
Mars in Taurus, Dec. 22, 3:07 - Dec. 31, 23:59

YOUR LUCK MAGNETISM
Jupiter in Leo, Dec. 22, 3:07 - Dec. 31, 23:59

World Events

Dec. 22 - Prince Charles makes a trip to Saudi Arabia to visit British troops serving there.

Dec. 26 - Garry Kasparov beats Anatoly Karpov to retain the world chess championship title.

Bill Gates
Born October 28, 1955

BILL GATES
Scorpio

Bill Gates, America's wealthiest man, is the Harvard dropout whose Windows software came along at the perfect time. Before Windows, computing was complicated and user-unfriendly. Now, eighty-five percent of the computers across the globe use this operating system. A shy computer nerd since high school, his first contacts with computers were with the room-sized ones used by scientists, machines less powerful than the ones now in kindergartens around the world! His company, Microsoft, gained an early lead in the software market and endeavored to dominate every corner of the software industry, which resulted in an antitrust suit against the giant corporation.

Gates is a Scorpio, a sign known for its intensity and tenacity. With Uranus, the planet of technology—and computers—contacting his Sun, the planet of identity, his choice of career makes perfect sense. In addition to that contact, Uranus is prominently placed in his horoscope, making Gates impatient and a law unto himself.

Gates's Moon, the planet of emotion, is in the headstrong sign Aries, in his house of career. It was quite natural for him to marry an employee with this placement. In addition, his Moon is also contacted by Uranus, further adding to his technological mentality and headstrong, independent nature. Another contact comes from Mars, the planet of action, making him determined to have his own way. And a contact from Mercury, planet of communication, adds to Gates's desire for speedy intellectual connections.

The real story about Gates's need to amass such a huge fortune lies in his house of home and family. Neptune, the planet of insecurity, is there, and that generally produces a sense that he won't get enough of what he needs. In addition, with Venus, the planet of affection, contacted by Saturn, the planet of limitations, Gates feels he must keep trying, working harder and faster, or else others will gain on him and he will lose out. In his house of money lies Jupiter, the planet of expansion, tightly connected to Pluto, the planet of big business. Gates is a spectacular example of how someone with personal insecurities can use them as motivation to achieve much more than a contented person might.

▶ Read J. P. Morgan's Star Profile on page 49. ▶ Read Henry Ford's Star Profile on page 89.

1991

Major Transitions: Spotlighting Eclipses

With Saturn, Uranus, and Neptune clustered in one part of the skies, many dramatic changes had taken place over the last four years. Now, although the pattern was dispersing, the eclipses of 1991 would bring a wave of turbulence with them. When eclipses contact a planet, they highlight it and events are filled with phenomena symbolized by that planet. This was seen as reforms continued in the Soviet world. At the time of January's eclipses, the Baltic States—Lithuania, Latvia, and Estonia—wanted their independence, dissolving Soviet control of their states, but the USSR resisted with military force. This eclipse triggered Neptune, which symbolizes dissolution (as of states), as well as oil, oceans, and poisons. At the same time, the U.S. spearheaded Operation Desert Storm and UN efforts to recover Kuwait from Iraqi occupation began. Iraq retaliated by "poisoning the well," destroying the oil fields that they were forced to give up and soiling the Persian Gulf by releasing huge quantities of oil into it.

The disintegrating energy of the Neptune-focussed eclipse continued to be felt as the old Eastern bloc agreed to dissolve their military alliance, the Warsaw Pact, after thirty-six years. In June, a second eclipse highlighted Uranus and the calls for independence became more strident. When hard-line Communists tried to oust Soviet Premier Gorbachev, thousands of citizens at the Kremlin thwarted the take-over. By the year's end, the Soviet Union was dissolved, and a new Commonwealth of Independent States formed in its place.

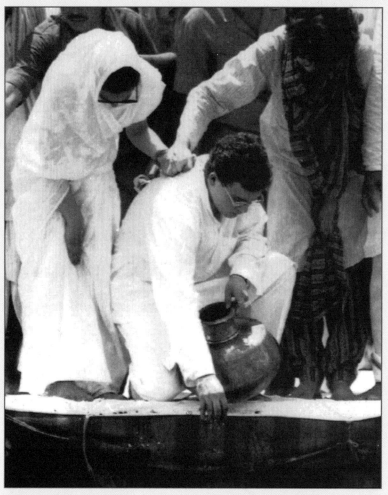

The ashes of Rajiv Gandhi, former Indian Prime Minister, are scattered into the Ganges by his son

Gorbachev is ousted by Boris Yeltsin

Kuwaiti soldiers celebrate the liberation of Kuwait

WATER OF LIFE

In May, millions of people lined up to drink the water of Jean Chahin's well in the little town of Tlacote, Mexico. Some traveled from as far away as Europe and Russia. The miracle water was said to have cured everything from AIDS and cancer to obesity and high cholesterol. When water was sent to a nearby army hospital, 600 sick soldiers were cured. Microbiological studies found that the water caused changes on a cellular level. Chahin called the phenomena a "new creation of God on Earth."

THE PERSIAN GULF WAR

After Saddam Hussein refused to withdraw troops from Kuwait in response to the UN ultimatum, the U.S.-led allied forces launched Operation Desert Storm against him: within six weeks, Kuwait was liberated and the war ended. The U.S. and Russia signed the first Strategic Arms Reduction Treaty. In Russia, communists staged a coup against Gorbachev, but were foiled by Yeltsin, the Russian Republic's president. Subsequently, Yeltsin ousted Gorbachev. Seven republics of the former Soviet Union claimed their independence. As Yugoslavia broke up, civil war threatened. Western European nations moved toward closer political union. Israelis and Arabs met in Madrid to discuss peace in the Middle East. Seven million Africans were feared to be at risk from famine while Bangladesh suffered catastrophic floods. Liberal African American U.S. Supreme Court Justice Thurgood Marshall retired and was replaced by African American conservative Judge Clarence Thomas, despite allegations of sexual harassment. Prime Minister Rajiv Gandhi of India was assassinated by a suicide bomber. Freddie Mercury, lead singer of the rock group Queen, died of AIDS.

➤ Read "Gaia's Mystical Power Places" by Ronnie Grishman on page 745.

CAPRICORN

From January 01, 0:00 through January 20, 13:46

The Gallant Knight

January Capricorn of 1991, you arrived at a moment in history that called for courage, reliability, and trustworthiness. After giving time for Iraqi leader Saddam Hussein to remove his troops from invaded Kuwait, which he failed to do, a U.S.-led coalition of states embarked on war with Iraq on January 16: the campaign was named "Operation Desert Storm" and it was going to be very brief.

The astrology of your birth-time also shows your patience, self-discipline, and resourcefulness—traits your sign has long been associated with. Six planets took turns passing through your own sensible, respectful sign, heightening the sense of duty and responsibility you're best known for. This startling emphasis of astrological energy gifted you with certainty and sureness, the ability to know when extreme action is merited, and the presence of mind to take that action without guilt or hesitation. As a result, you may often find yourself in a position of leadership, regardless of whether you want to be. Still, your innate sense of responsibility will see you through, winning you many long-term friends in the process.

You've also inherited a knack for politeness and tact. This can make you an excellent diplomat or politician, and a welcome addition to any gathering. Although you're an expert at negotiation, you also understand when talking isn't enough. In times of irresolvable conflict, whether business or personal, you won't be afraid to take steps to set things right, whether that means ending an unhealthy relationship or challenging an authority figure who's unfair or prejudiced.

In love, you may delight in the softness of Cancerians, Pisceans, and Scorpios, the water signs, but you could be most comfortable with Taureans and Virgos, the other earth signs.

Your challenge is to use your power only when necessary—and not to be provoked into action by someone with a less than honest agenda. Your gift is your completely impartial manner, allowing you to move quickly and confidently against the root of any problem.

AQUARIUS

From January 20, 13:47 through February 19, 3:57

The Independence Advocate

Aquarius of 1991, you made your entrance during a time that would serve to reinforce your sign's love of freedom, independence, and liberty. Around the time you were born, Kuwait, the tiny oil-rich country that had been invaded by Iraq in 1990, was liberated. The United States and its allies drove Iraqi troops back across the border after less than six weeks of a very one-sided conflict, in which Iraq responded to the attacks made upon it only by firing Scud missiles against Israel and Saudi Arabia. However, the war in the Persian Gulf concerned more than oil reserves or Saddam Hussein's aggression. The conflict alerted the world to the dangerous potential of any rogue nation, especially a nation like Iraq which had stockpiled chemical warfare weapons, whose activities were left unchecked.

The astrological factors that affected your birth-time would also have instilled in you the quality of bravery in the face of tyranny. Saturn, the symbolic "military general" of the heavens, set off for your freedom-oriented sign during this period, giving you persistence, boldness, and unwavering conviction. The strength of character you inherited from this planet can help you to pursue your quest for personal independence, pursuing it with steely resolve. But you may also become an agent for change on behalf of others. And when your beliefs are tested, you'll undoubtedly step up to the challenge without hesitation.

You may often find yourself involved in movements or causes that support freedom—and the more oppressed those you're defending have been, the harder you'll work to change their situation. In the process, you'll teach others just how important it is to follow their own truth.

It's likely that your search for a partner will lead you to those signs who are determined to retain their own independence even when involved in a relationship—something that's absolutely essential to you. Sagittarians, Geminis, and other Aquarians could suit you just fine, as will focused, self-sufficient Capricorns.

Your challenge is to stay involved with your causes, but never at the expense of your personal needs. Your gift is your ability to allow others their freedom, even as you offer them your love and commitment.

➤ Read about your Chinese Astrological sign on page 838. ➤ Read about your Personal Planets on page 826. ➤ Read about your personal Mystical Card on page 856.

CAPRICORN
Your Personal Planets

YOUR LOVE POTENTIAL
Venus in Capricorn, Jan. 01, 0:00 - Jan. 05, 5:02
Venus in Aquarius, Jan. 05, 5:03 - Jan. 20, 13:46

YOUR DRIVE AND AMBITION
Mars in Taurus, Jan. 01, 0:00 - Jan. 20, 13:46

YOUR LUCK MAGNETISM
Jupiter in Leo, Jan. 01, 0:00 - Jan. 20, 13:46

World Events

Jan. 14 - Abu Iyad, deputy leader of the PLO, is assassinated in Tunis.

Jan. 15 - An allied coalition, led by the U.S., makes a series of air attacks on Iraq.

Iraq deliberately pumps oil into the sea during the Gulf War

AQUARIUS
Your Personal Planets

YOUR LOVE POTENTIAL
Venus in Aquarius, Jan. 20, 13:47 - Jan. 29, 4:43
Venus in Pisces, Jan. 29, 4:44 - Feb. 19, 3:57

YOUR DRIVE AND AMBITION
Mars in Taurus, Jan. 20, 13:47 - Jan. 21, 1:14
Mars in Gemini, Jan. 21, 1:15 - Feb. 19, 3:57

YOUR LUCK MAGNETISM
Jupiter in Leo, Jan. 20, 13:47 - Feb. 19, 3:57

World Events

Feb. 9 - A leak of radioactive water causes a nuclear plant 220 miles west of Tokyo to release about eight percent of the plant's annual radioactive emissions in a single day.

Feb. 16 - Over 7,000 gay rights activists march through London.

1991

PISCES
Your Personal Planets

YOUR LOVE POTENTIAL

Venus in Pisces, Feb. 19, 3:58 - Feb. 22, 9:01
Venus in Aries, Feb. 22, 9:02 - Mar. 18, 21:44
Venus in Taurus, Mar. 18, 21:45 - Mar. 21, 3:01

YOUR DRIVE AND AMBITION

Mars in Gemini, Feb. 19, 3:58 - Mar. 21, 3:01

YOUR LUCK MAGNETISM

Jupiter in Leo, Feb. 19, 3:58 - Mar. 21, 3:01

World Events

Feb. 28 - Kuwait is liberated, ending the Gulf War.

Mar. 7 - Saddam Hussein begins releasing prisoners of war.

The great white shark reaches the brink of extinction

ARIES
Your Personal Planets

YOUR LOVE POTENTIAL

Venus in Taurus, Mar. 21, 3:02 - Apr. 13, 0:09
Venus in Gemini, Apr. 13, 0:10 - Apr. 20, 14:07

YOUR DRIVE AND AMBITION

Mars in Gemini, Mar. 21, 3:02 - Apr. 03, 0:48
Mars in Cancer, Apr. 03, 0:49 - Apr. 20, 14:07

YOUR LUCK MAGNETISM

Jupiter in Leo, Apr. 21, 3:02 - Apr. 20, 14:07

World Events

Apr. 11 - The great white shark is registered as an endangered species.

Apr. 16 - British film director David Lean dies.

PISCES
From February 19, 3:58 through March 21, 3:01

The Compassionate Guardian

You, 1991 Pisces, arrived into a time whose events would serve to reinforce the qualities those born under your Sun sign are here to learn: compassion, unconditional acceptance of others, and the willingness to put personal agendas aside in favor of doing good for the needy. Around the time you were born, thousands of Kurds fled from Iraq, seeking safety across the Turkish border. Within two weeks, as word of the refugees' desperate plight became evident, the British and American governments responded with food, medicine, and other necessary supplies. This show of concern and compassion mirrors your sign's consideration and regard for those in trouble. However, unlike Pisceans born in other years, you can be quite willing to confront the oppressors, and even fight them, in order to pursue the interests of those who need your help.

The astrological influences of your birth-time further serve to exemplify the distinctive personal quest you're here to accomplish. Several planets in your own sign, as well as in action-oriented fire signs, contain the astrological recipe for not just empathizing with the helpless, but also defending their interests—even if it means going into battle to do it.

This mixed bag of astrological attributes has given you the courage necessary to protect the ones you love, and even to put yourself in the line of fire when necessary. This unconditional willingness to defend and protect the people and causes near and dear to you might have led you to work in the field of law or social work, and could make you a hero in the eyes of the people you defend.

In love relationships, you may look for a mate who'll stand by you without hesitation when you find yourself called upon to help those in need. Tenderhearted Cancerians, strong-willed Capricorns, and emotionally sturdy Scorpios can prove worthy partners, but a detail-oriented Virgo may be the one whose ability to budget around the sacrifices wins your heart.

Your challenge is to act on behalf of those who really deserve your efforts, without allowing yourself to be exploited or "used." Your gift is your strength of purpose.

ARIES
From March 21, 3:02 through April 20, 14:07

The Energetic Combatant

Born during 1991, Aries, your sign's natural bravery, assertiveness, and fearlessness were reflected in the events of that time. You arrived during a time of crippling labor strikes in Russia, an effort by disappointed Russian workers to force the economic changes they felt their government had failed to achieve with sufficient speed. As prices skyrocketed and everyday provisions became scarce, calls were heard for the resignation of the President of the Soviet Congress, Mikhail Gorbachev. The Duma (Parliament) in Moscow also granted Boris Yeltsin, President of the Russian Federation, the special power to implement economic reform by official decree, so challenging Gorbachev's authority. This set the stage for a huge confrontation between Yeltsin and Gorbachev, a conflict that would eventually bring about the dissolution of the Soviet Union.

The astrological factors that influenced your birth-time show the courageousness your sign is famous for—but they also provide clues to a more specific side of your character. The heavens hosted several oppositions, the astrological recipe for initiating necessary conflict, which lies at the core of your Sun sign's warrior spirit. But the fact that a strong dose of Aquarius energy was also present shows your capacity to rebel, resist, and refuse to conform to what you view as unfair societal rules.

It's likely that you may have become known as a bit of a rebel yourself, a trait that may have surfaced in your early years. As time passed, however, you probably learned to be discriminating in the battles you fight, opting to pass on those that aren't worthy of your time and effort, and channeling your energy into more productive endeavors.

In love, you may look for a partner who isn't intimidated by your fire and passion. As such, Leos and Sagittarians, the other fire signs, could be good choices, as would Aquarians, those famous non-conformists.

Your challenge is to channel your energy into only those circumstances that merit it. Your gift is your seemingly limitless reserves of energy, strength, and boldness.

➤ Read about your Chinese Astrological sign on page 838. ➤ Read about your Personal Planets on page 826. ➤ Read about your personal Mystical Card on page 856.

TAURUS

From April 20, 14:08 through May 21, 13:19

The Worldly Investor

As a Taurus born in 1991, you were strongly endowed with all the traits your sign is known for, including a keen business sense and the willingness to work hard for financial security. Around the time you were born, the world received news of a global sale of state-owned assets. From Europe to Asia to Latin America, finance ministers offered up assets ranging from airlines to phone companies to state-owned factories. Putting these huge corporations up for sale on the open market was done in the hope that privatization would help to alleviate their countries' debt-burdened economies. And in several cases, the effort proved successful. As such, on both a personal level and in matters of business, your acuity, insight, and perceptiveness can make you a natural investor. And whether you use this talent in your career or simply "play the market" in your spare time, your uncanny investment instinct all but guarantees your success.

The astrological factors that appeared in the heavens above you during your birth-time perfectly show the source of this financial acumen—but they also show your wisdom in many other areas of life. The skies hosted several planets in your own sign and in shrewd, judicious Capricorn, another sign famous for its keen antennae and uncanny knack for timing. In short, regardless of your goal, you were born with an instinct for taking action at exactly the right time.

This patience and discretion makes you a powerful ally—as well as emotionally available to those you love. In fact, in times of distress or sadness, your family and friends will probably turn to you first, confiding their fears and seeking the reassurance of your wisdom.

Your search for a partner who's self-confident and experienced will probably lead you to Capricorns and Virgos, the other earth signs, but shrewd, perceptive Scorpios could also appeal to you.

Your challenge is to keep in mind that the best things in life truly are free, and not allow your quest for the finer things in life to become an obsession. Your gift is your knack for recognizing the potential for success in all situations.

GEMINI

From May 21, 13:20 through June 21, 21:18

The Thoughtful Uniter

You were born during a period that saw a remarkable example of your sign's ability to combine two perspectives into one final result, Gemini of 1991. On June 21 (the cusp between Gemini and Cancer), the governments of East and West Germany announced that they had chosen Berlin to serve as the capital of a newly reunited Germany. This final step in the effort to restore unity to a once-divided country mirrors your own ability to take the best of seeming opposites and blend them into a solid, cooperative common entity.

The astrology behind this rare skill involves the unusual balance of energies the heavens hosted at that time. All three astrological qualities were equally represented, including change-oriented cardinal signs, sturdy fixed signs, and flexible mutable signs. This perfect astrological equilibrium can give you an innate, enviable skill: the knack for determining which course of action is appropriate in any set of circumstances. It also gives you the gift of sound reasoning, a trait that means you can easily excel in intellectual pursuits and gamesmanship.

This adaptability has probably made you quite successful over the years, since you can always make choices based on present conditions, rather than on any emotional or psychological past attachments. You're probably quite well-adjusted, able to see the rhyme and reason behind everything that's happened to you over the course of your lifetime. The ability to assimilate the best of every circumstance makes you a wise and versatile counselor, an open-minded friend, and a respected colleague. In work as well as in personal relationships, you'll undoubtedly enjoy the admiration and respect you deserve.

In love relationships, you may be drawn to fair and flexible Librans, broad-minded Sagittarians, and wise, objective Aquarians, all of whom will appreciate your honesty, candor, and intellectual keenness.

Your challenge is to allow your feelings to emerge as confidently as you show your intellectual side. Your gift is inspiring others by showing them just how important it is to "go with the flow."

► Read about your Chinese Astrological sign on page 838. ► Read about your Personal Planets on page 826. ► Read about your personal Mystical Card on page 856.

TAURUS
Your Personal Planets

YOUR LOVE POTENTIAL
Venus in Gemini, Apr. 20, 14:08 - May 09, 1:27
Venus in Cancer, May 09, 1:28 - May 21, 13:19

YOUR DRIVE AND AMBITION
Mars in Cancer, Apr. 20, 14:08 - May 21, 13:19

YOUR LUCK MAGNETISM
Jupiter in Leo, Apr. 20, 14:08 - May 21, 13:19

World Events

May 16 – Edith Cresson becomes France's first female Prime Minister.

May 21 – Rajiv Gandhi is assassinated while campaigning near Madras.

Edith Cresson, France's first woman Prime Minister

GEMINI
Your Personal Planets

YOUR LOVE POTENTIAL
Venus in Cancer, May 21, 13:20 - June 06, 1:15
Venus in Leo, June 06, 1:16 - June 21, 21:18

YOUR DRIVE AND AMBITION
Mars in Cancer, May 21, 13:20 - May 26, 12:18
Mars in Leo, May 26, 12:19 - June 21, 21:18

YOUR LUCK MAGNETISM
Jupiter in Leo, May 21, 13:20 - June 21, 21:18

World Events

May 24 – India mourns the death of a ruling dynasty, as the body of Rajiv Gandhi is cremated.

June 17 – The South African Parliament repeals the last of its apartheid laws.

1991

CANCER
Your Personal Planets

YOUR LOVE POTENTIAL
Venus in Leo, June 21, 21:19 - July 11, 5:05
Venus in Virgo, July 11, 5:06 - July 23, 8:10

YOUR DRIVE AND AMBITION
Mars in Leo, June 21, 21:19 - July 15, 12:35
Mars in Virgo, July 15, 12:36 - July 23, 8:10

YOUR LUCK MAGNETISM
Jupiter in Leo, June 21, 21:19 - July 23, 8:10

World Events

June 25 - The USSR signs a treaty officially concluding its military involvement in Czechoslovakia.

July 7 - King Hussein of Jordan restores most of the freedoms removed during the period of marshal law.

King Hussein of Jordan

LEO
Your Personal Planets

YOUR LOVE POTENTIAL
Venus in Virgo, July 23, 8:11 - Aug. 21, 15:05
Venus in Leo, Aug. 21, 15:06 - Aug. 23, 15:12

YOUR DRIVE AND AMBITION
Mars in Virgo, July 23, 8:11 - Aug. 23, 15:12

YOUR LUCK MAGNETISM
Jupiter in Leo, July 23, 8:11 - Aug. 23, 15:12

World Events

July 31 - The French government is forced to abandon plans for two dams across the Loire River.

Aug. 7 - Canada's premier, Bob Rae, signs an agreement giving indigenous Canadians the right to govern themselves.

742

CANCER
From June 21, 21:19 through July 23, 8:10

The Concerned Sympathizer

You, 1991 Cancer, were born during a time that displayed the qualities your sign is famous for: nurturing, caregiving, and selflessness. Despite the fact that scientists had long suspected that vast reserves of oil lay beneath the surface, the U.S. signed the Protocol on Environmental Protection to the Antarctic Treaty which banned mining there for at least fifty years. This move to protect part of the world's wilderness for the children of the future mirrors your own concern for them—and for the animals whose survival depends on the protection of their native habitat.

The astrological influences of your birth-time show the strong urge you may have to put your sympathy to use on behalf of small creatures. The skies hosted several planets in your own tender-hearted sign, as well as some in Leo, also known for its love of children and animals. As such, you may become involved with groups or organizations that seek to protect the rights of these beings, as well as those that safeguard the care of the elderly and infirm. You may also be drawn to the medical profession, or to work that involves helping others to make the most of their lives.

Regardless of the field you choose, it's likely that your relationships with others will be protective and caring—and that you'll make a wonderful parent, should you choose to have children of your own. Your home will undoubtedly also be a top priority, and you'll probably strive to make it a safe, secure nest for you and your loved ones. "Home" to you also includes the country of your birth, so you may develop a strong sense of patriotism, as well. Although you won't hesitate to take a public stand to help further the causes that appeal to your heart, you should never forget your sign's intense need for privacy.

When choosing a partner, you may look for someone equally gentle and humane, such as other Cancerians, emotional Scorpios, sensitive Pisceans, or earthy Taureans, whose love of security and comfort rivals your own.

Your challenge is to respect your need for privacy as much as you respect the needs of others. Your gift is your strong intuitive nature.

LEO
From July 23, 8:11 through August 23, 15:12

The Health-Minded Authority

You may have been born with a strong urge to safeguard the health and safety of those you love, Leo of 1991. And this trait was reflected through a telling and important event that occurred around the time you were born. After years of research, the United States initiated steps to protect its citizens when health authorities announced that a new, firmer stance would be taken to keep the deadly AIDS virus from spreading. Everyone who sought to immigrate to the U.S. would be tested for AIDS, and those found carrying it would not be allowed to enter. While controversial, this policy showed the genuine concern health officials felt regarding the need to stem the spread of this modern-day plague.

The astrological influences of your birth-time even further show your determination to safeguard the well-being of those you care about. Several planets were passing through Virgo, the most health-conscious sign in the heavens. This concern for freedom from disease and the soundness of both mind and body may have brought you into association or employment with groups and causes who stand for those interests, and it's likely that your contemporaries and co-workers can benefit from your knowledge and experience.

But even if you don't take an active stance beyond caring for yourself and those close to you, your lifestyle probably reflects your concern for habits and behavior that are beneficial to physical wellness. Indeed, the people closest to you may be the ones who are equally meticulous in that department.

In love relationships, your best bet will always be Virgos, who'll feel very much like kindred spirits to you, equally conscious of living healthily and productively. In addition, Taureans and Capricorns, both earth signs like yourself, will be likely to share your concerns about health and wellness.

Your challenge is to continue your attention to health matters without overreacting to what you see as "symptoms." When in doubt, seeking out the advice of a health professional is always best. Your gift is your innate knowledge of what's good for you, and what's not—in all ways.

➤ Read about your Chinese Astrological sign on page 838. ➤ Read about your Personal Planets on page 826. ➤ Read about your personal Mystical Card on page 856.

VIRGO

From August 23, 15:13 through September 23, 12:47

The Quicksilver Competitor

Born during 1991, Virgo, you arrived at a time that showed just how valuable quick, well-planned action is to winning—whether it's winning a battle or winning a reward. On August 25, star sprinter and Olympic athlete Carl Lewis accomplished something he had been trying to do for quite some time. He created a new record: the 9.86-second 100-meter dash.

Appropriately enough, at the time of this momentous athletic achievement, your ruling planet, Mercury, who rules speed (cerebral and physical), was in Leo, the sign that's most often associated with showmanship and a love of applause for genuine accomplishments. The pride that Leo possesses, however, was tempered by your sign's innate humility, making this a powerful blend of natal energies. This and other planetary placements show the talents your birth-time gave you, as well as the goals all those of your Sun sign share: efficiency, expediency, and methodical action. Specifically, with Mars, the ruler of energy, in balanced Libra, you intuitively know how much effort to expend and how much to reserve.

The combination of qualities your birth-time bestowed can make you a natural debater, a tireless competitor, and a worthy opponent. You love challenge and adventure, and probably aren't afraid to participate in contests of any kind. If you're defeated, you have the presence of mind and keen social skills to concede cheerfully, as you applaud your competitor. As such, you inspire others to go after their goals, forgetting the risk of failure in the process of learning what it's like to pursue their dreams.

In relationships, you may be best-suited to partners who possess strong Capricorn, Leo, and Gemini qualities—those who'll be able to keep up with your quickness in thought as well as movement. In friendship and group situations, your skill for cooperation with everyone means you're quite capable of bonding with every sign.

Your greatest challenge is to retain your speed while maintaining your sign's careful attention to detail. Your gift is your ability to move swiftly and confidently in both mental and physical tasks.

LIBRA

From September 23, 12:48 through October 23, 22:04

The Dispassionate Judge

Around the time you were born, Libra of 1991, your sign's symbol, the scales of justice, took center stage in news that was broadcast all over the world. Although the event that inspired it occurred in the United States, the issue extended well past societal and national concern: should someone accused of a crime be put in a position of being a judge himself? In Washington, DC, Judge Clarence Thomas was nominated for a seat on the U.S. Supreme Court. Shortly afterwards however, Professor Anita Hill accused Thomas of sexual harassment. Nevertheless, after a stormy series of Senate hearings, in which he was exonerated, Thomas' appointment was confirmed.

Your sign's association with the delicate balance behind this and all major decisions was outlined in keywords that appeared on magazine covers and in the opinions that were voiced repeatedly in the international media coverage of this issue. And contrary to popular opinion, this unbalanced situation is an example of Libra's quest: to restore balance. As such, the above event, as well as the astrological influences that held court in the heavens above you, aptly describe your special gifts: impartiality, consideration, and diplomacy.

You may also have been blessed with graciousness, sociability, and refinement—invaluable assets in any life situation. Whether you choose to use these skills in career or personal situations, you'll always be able to moderate, intercede, and help warring factions find their common ground. In short, making peace and instituting fair solutions is your business—and since you would never buckle under peer pressure, it's likely that you can usually bring those conditions about.

In love, your search for a partner who'll share your fair-mindedness and assist you in your never-ending search for equality will probably bring you to Sagittarians, Aquarians, and other Librans.

Your challenge is to maintain an impartial and unbiased approach, even if you're emotionally tied to one side or the other. Your gifts are your knack for finding an equitable solution to every dispute, and for providing others with the inspiration to meet in the middle.

➤ Read about your Chinese Astrological sign on page 838. ➤ Read about your Personal Planets on page 826. ➤ Read about your personal Mystical Card on page 856.

VIRGO
Your Personal Planets

YOUR LOVE POTENTIAL
Venus in Leo, Aug. 23, 15:13 - Sept. 23, 12:47

YOUR DRIVE AND AMBITION
Mars in Virgo, Aug. 23, 15:13 - Sept. 01, 6:37
Mars in Libra, Sept. 01, 6:38 - Sept. 23, 12:47

YOUR LUCK MAGNETISM
Jupiter in Leo, Aug. 23, 15:13 - Sept. 12, 5:59
Jupiter in Virgo, Sept. 12, 6:00 - Sept. 23, 12:47

World Events

Aug. 25 – Lithuania, Estonia, and Latvia win independence from the USSR.

Sept. 5 – Former President of Panama Gen. Manuel Noriega goes on trial in Miami.

Soviet economic sanctions after Lithuania's declaration of independence result in petrol shortages

LIBRA
Your Personal Planets

YOUR LOVE POTENTIAL
Venus in Leo, Sept. 23, 12:48 - Oct. 06, 21:14
Venus in Virgo, Oct. 06, 21:15 - Oct. 23, 22:04

YOUR DRIVE AND AMBITION
Mars in Libra, Sept. 23, 12:48 - Oct. 16, 19:04
Mars in Scorpio, Oct. 16, 19:05 - Oct. 23, 22:04

YOUR LUCK MAGNETISM
Jupiter in Virgo, Sept. 23, 12:48 - Oct. 23, 22:04

World Events

Oct. 1 – The Soviet city of Leningrad becomes St. Petersburg.

Oct. 15 – The U.S. Senate confirms Judge Clarence Thomas for U.S. Supreme Court despite accusations of sexual harassment.

1991

SCORPIO
Your Personal Planets

YOUR LOVE POTENTIAL
Venus in Virgo, Oct. 23, 22:05 - Nov. 09, 6:36
Venus in Libra, Nov. 09, 6:37 - Nov. 22, 19:35

YOUR DRIVE AND AMBITION
Mars in Scorpio, Oct. 23, 22:05 - Nov. 22, 19:35

YOUR LUCK MAGNETISM
Jupiter in Virgo, Oct. 23, 22:05 - Nov. 22, 19:35

World Events

Nov. 18 - Anglican Church envoy Terry Waite is released from captivity.

Nov. 21 - Boutros Boutros-Ghali of Egypt is declared Secretary-General of the United Nations.

Death of Freddie Mercury

SAGITTARIUS
Your Personal Planets

YOUR LOVE POTENTIAL
Venus in Libra, Nov. 22, 19:36 - Dec. 06, 7:20
Venus in Scorpio, Dec. 06, 7:21 - Dec. 22, 8:53

YOUR DRIVE AND AMBITION
Mars in Scorpio, Nov. 22, 19:36 - Nov. 29, 2:18
Mars in Sagittarius, Nov. 29, 2:19 - Dec. 22, 8:53

YOUR LUCK MAGNETISM
Jupiter in Virgo, Nov. 22, 19:36 - Dec. 22, 8:53

World Events

Nov. 24 - British pop icon Freddie Mercury dies of AIDS.

Dec. 21 - The USSR is formally dissolved.

SCORPIO
From October 23, 22:05 through November 22, 19:35

The Deep Realist

The headlines during your birth year were not for the faint of heart, 1991 Scorpio. The transforming energies of your sign ruler, Pluto, were extremely active. Middle Eastern tensions remained high following the Gulf War. The collapse of the Communist system in Europe and the disintegration of the USSR were momentous events. A civil war broke out in Iraq and Yugoslavia came to the brink the same year.

Although these topics aren't easy ones, they reflect the traits and issues your sign is associated with. The fact that Pluto, your own ruling planet, was in your sign during 1991—the most potent, influential, and perfect placement for it—may account for the fact that such transformations became part of the mass consciousness in such an insistent way. But Mars, the ruler of assertion, was also posited in your sign, and these powerful factors may explain the added depth, intensity, and profundity that Scorpios born in 1991 can possess.

As such, you'll never back away from the issues that need to be faced and reckoned with. It's likely that your work might involve informing people in some way, and you could be drawn to teaching, journalism, or the law. In your spare time, games of strategy like chess or bridge may occupy your attention, and with the depth and intensity you bring to them, it's possible that you will make a name for yourself when you enter and do well in tournaments or competitions later in life.

In love, you may want to partner up with someone who's equally unafraid of tackling the tough topics—someone who'll stand by you when you feel that you need to broach the issues that others may not be comfortable with. It's likely that other Scorpios, blunt, truth-wielding Sagittarians, and objective Capricorns will prove worthy of your depth and allow you to express your personal convictions.

Your challenge is to express yourself tactfully, with an understanding of how hesitant others may be to think about these topics, much less discuss them. Your gift is your ability to impel others to face their fears.

SAGITTARIUS
From November 22, 19:36 through December 22, 8:53

The Philosophical Explorer

Around the time you were born, 1991 Sagittarius, the news was full of the reports of religious sightings purported to have begun occurring the world over. In Lourdes, France, many new visitors reported seeing the Virgin Mary—and their descriptions were similar to reports from the past. In Knock, Ireland, the faithful also noted appearances of the Blessed Virgin. And in Fatima, Portugal, Czestochowa, Poland, and San Bruno, California, attendance at shrines where Mary was said to have recently appeared was recorded as doubling, tripling, and even quadrupling. The news of these apparitions caused a worldwide restoration of belief among the faithful—and a new wave of skepticism among non-believers.

Since you're here to learn and perfect an objective respect and understanding of all belief systems, it's probably no surprise that religion was in the headlines at the time you arrived. The issues of faith and belief have long been associated with your sign, where several planets were stationed during your birth-time. Therefore, the events of this time probably served to encourage you to reconsider the big questions, and you may have spent a substantial amount of time gathering information on these and other subjects, furthering your soul in its search for truth.

Being born during this time may have reinforced your hunger for understanding of other kinds as well. It's likely that everything you learn along the way will afford you with the ability to confidently voice the opinions you form. As a result, you probably defend whatever you believe in with passion, intensity, and animation—and without hesitation. You might also be drawn to philosophy, comparative religion, or world literature as subjects to learn and teach.

In love relationships, you may look for others whose curiosity and thirst for knowledge match your own. As such, Geminis, Aquarians, and other Sagittarians may prove to be your best mates.

Your challenge is to honor everyone, regardless of their convictions. Your gifts are your investigative powers, and your relentless thirst for knowledge.

➤ Read about your Chinese Astrological sign on page 838. ➤ Read about your Personal Planets on page 826. ➤ Read about your personal Mystical Card on page 856.

CAPRICORN

From December 22, 8:54 through December 31, 23:59

The Confident Commander

Capricorn, your arrival in December of 1991 coincided with the resignation of Mikhail Gorbachev and the dissolution of the world's first and most powerful socialist nation. The Soviet Union was formally disbanded, replaced by a Commonwealth of Independent States composed of the twelve former Soviet republics. This move put former Russian Federation President Boris Yeltsin in control, and signaled the end of an important political era. At the same time, there was a renewed push to unify the European nations into a powerful political and economic bloc. As a result, you grew up in a time that saw an unprecedented consolidation of power worldwide.

The astrological factors in effect at this time influenced you on a personal level as well. In fact, the heavens were perfectly arranged to increase your potential for developing several qualities your sign has always been associated with—devotion to family and friends, and the ability to take charge when the situation warranted it. At a very early age, you may have displayed the ability to take control when it became clear that the current leaders had shirked or fallen short of their responsibilities.

Your immediate circle of friends may look to you as the leader in all situations, whether recreational or professional. In both cases, you'll undoubtedly handle the mantle of authority well, aiming for decency, virtuousness, and equal justice for everyone. Because of the varied planetary influences you were born with, you could have many interests, pursuing several different careers in the course of your life.

In romance, it's likely that your search for an equally responsible, practical, and integrity-filled partner will lead you to other Capricorns, high-minded Sagittarians, and devout Scorpios. The family-loving side of you may also be drawn to Cancerians, long known for their devotion to family, children, and home.

Your challenge is to remain objective and cordial in all situations, even when you've defeated an adversary and he or she is less than civil. Your gift is your willingness to take on responsibilities, both personal and professional, with an eye toward fairness.

1991

CAPRICORN
Your Personal Planets

YOUR LOVE POTENTIAL
Venus in Scorpio, Dec. 22, 8:54 - Dec. 31, 15:18
Venus in Sagittarius, Dec. 31, 15:19 - Dec. 31, 23:59

YOUR DRIVE AND AMBITION
Mars in Sagittarius, Dec. 22, 8:54 - Dec. 31, 23:59

YOUR LUCK MAGNETISM
Jupiter in Virgo, Dec. 22, 8:54 - Dec. 31, 23:59

World Events

Dec. 27 - Algeria's militant fundamentalist Islamic Salvation Front wins the first round of free elections.

Dec. 25 - Mikhail Gorbachev resigns as Soviet Premier.

Comet Hale-Bopp above Stonehenge

Special Feature
Gaia's Mystical Power Places
by Ronnie Grishman

Since ancient times, certain locations on our planet have become quietly famous for the powerful energy that invisibly—but tangibly—emanates from them. Some are natural formations, such as caves, healing springs, or waterfalls, known primarily to those who live near them. Others are man-made—burial structures like the Egyptian Sphinx, the great pyramids, or Tibetan temples, and other places of ancient worship, such as Stonehenge. While the energies of these magical places cannot be seen, their effects can certainly be felt.

It's also believed that different sites are endowed with different spiritual powers—some of them quite specific: it is thought that they may enhance health, enlighten the soul, or spark creativity. The waters of the Chalice Well in Glastonbury, England, for example, have been proven to be amazingly beneficial in myriad ways, but are especially renowened for their restorative powers and their capacity for enhancing natural psychic abilities. The many stone circles—large and small—that are scattered throughout Great Britain are all amazingly potent sources of both psychic and spiritual energy.

Among the most famous stone circles are Stonehenge and Avebury Circle, long venerated, fascinating, and mystifying to spiritual pilgrims for centuries. Stonehenge has several circles of giant upright megaliths, holding huge cross-stones on top. The arrangement of the stones creates a natural "astronomical observatory." The most famous pointer at Stonehenge is the heel stone, which lines up directly with sunrise on Midsummer Day. This ancient place of worship and ritual, the focus of year-round visitors, but particularly during the solstices, dates back to 3000 B.C. and has sparked spiritual insight in thousands.

A similar sacred place, called "Newgrange"—located just outside of Dublin, Ireland—is an ancient Celtic burial mound. For five days, during the time of the Winter Solstice, this three-sided chamber is illuminated by the sun—for just seventeen minutes per day.

Thousands flock to Newgrange during this time of astrological rebirth to see the golden sunlight creep down the ancient stone pathway. It is believed that the Celtic people of this time placed their loved ones' remains in these chambers, where they awaited their "rebirth." Appropriately, the Winter Solstice, the darkest day of the year, was thought to bring the "return of the light," since each day's daylight hours would gradually increase from that point on. The "rebirth" of the light, was said to symbolize the reincarnation of all life forms.

(Continued on page 753)

➤ Read "Ancient Secrets of the Egyptian Pyramids" on page 305. ➤ Read "The Enigma of Crop Circles" on page 673.

1992

A New Dawn: Uranus and Neptune

After four years of startling changes on the international map, the world was ready to settle down into a new normal. A new 680-year cycle was beginning, as Saturn, Uranus, and Neptune were completing their rare triple "conjunction" all in one small area of the sky. In 1992, Uranus and Neptune began their linkage, starting the third and final stage of the pattern, with correlating events in worldly affairs. Uranus, symbolizing innovation and upheaval, suggested that the year would bring more astonishing events. Neptune, representing visionary dreams and subtle influences, implied that new ideals and dreams would inspire people wherever they were. This was seen in the ceaseless reforms continuing in the old Soviet states and Eastern Europe. U.S. citizens felt new confidence in their military as the cease-fire in the Persian Gulf War held. A new wave of social awareness seemed to be growing, as both Israel and the U.S. elected more liberal leaders. Yitzhak Rabin won leadership from the Knesset, while Democrat Bill Clinton, with environmentalist Al Gore as his Vice President, was the first of the "yuppie" generation to take the helm of the U.S.

Mars, the planetary agitator, stirred up the stew toward the end of the year. In India, 800 people died in the fighting when Hindus destroyed the Babri mosque. The potential for nuclear disaster was highlighted when police recovered four pounds of uranium originating in the old USSR. "Nannygate" plagued a Clinton nominee but he was still able to put together a Cabinet that "wore the face of America".

A young famine victim in Somalia

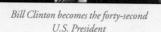

Bill Clinton becomes the forty-second U.S. President

A last farewell between father and son as a fourteen-bus convoy gets ready to leave Sarajevo

AURA Z

Along with the introduction of democracy, the Eastern Bloc in Europe experienced an outbreak of paranormal events. Romanians and Russians reported frequent sightings of angels. Some believed this was a divine sign supporting the end of Communism. Crop circles, bizarre disappearances, spacenappings, and UFO sightings happened throughout Eastern Europe as well. In 1992, members of the Academy of Sciences in Moscow launched a privately funded research project called "Aura Z" to study such strange phenomena.

A LIBERAL ERA BEGINS

Tribal fighting and famine persisted in Somalia and the U.S. sent marines to facilitate humanitarian aid. In Britain, John Major and the Conservative party won the general election. Nineteen European countries created the world's largest trade bloc. Moderate Yitzhak Rabin won the Israeli parliamentary election. In Afghanistan, radical Muslims overthrew President Najibullah and captured Kabul. Bosnia-Herzegovina seceded from Yugoslavia, presaging ethnic conflict. In the U.S., Democrat Bill Clinton and Independent candidate Perot challenged incumbent Republican George Bush Sr. for the presidency: Clinton won. In Peru, Shining Path guerrilla leader Guzman was arrested. Los Angeles suffered savage race riots, but in Germany, a wave of racist violence produced strong protests. Anti-Mafia Judge Falcone was murdered in Sicily. Britain suffered its worst drought for 247 years. The Big Bang theory of the origin of the Universe was confirmed by NASA. In Britain, Princess Anne divorced, but remarried at the end of the year. The marriages of her brothers, Prince Charles and Prince Andrew, broke down. British comedian Benny Hill died.

➤ Read "Gaia's Mystical Power Places" by Ronnie Grishman on page 745.

CAPRICORN

From January 01, 0:00 through January 20, 19:31

The Communication Specialist

You, 1992 January Capricorn, were born during a very special month—one that forever affected communication as we know it. Just as you entered the world, the "information super-highway" got underway, allowing schools, homes, hospitals and businesses to connect with a single keystroke. The creators of this "fiber-optic spinal cord" promised to do for the world's communication systems what the interstate highway system did for transport in the United States in the 1950s—to make computer travel as easy as the highways made physical travel. This major expansion to an already ingenious invention called the Internet served to illustrate beautifully the thirst for speed and knowledge personified by your particular breed of Capricorn.

The astrological indicators of that period were equally astounding. Several planets in Sagittarius—famous for long-distance travel and mass communication—perfectly showed how easily you could become proficient at this new development in data transmission. And if all those merry communicators weren't enough to inspire you to perfect your computer skills and learn your way around the Web, Saturn, the "Cosmic School-Teacher" himself, was in computer-literate Aquarius. Long known for its affiliation with computer technology, this planet can teach you to teach others the ins and outs of computers.

Since Sagittarius and Aquarius have charge over the future, they also have a strong connection to the development of new ideas. As such, it's not very difficult to picture you taking all this knowledge a step further, into the realm of inventing something electronically new yourself. One way or another, you'll undoubtedly be a force to be reckoned with once you take your seat behind the keyboard.

In partnerships, you'd do well to stay close to Sagittarians, Aquarians, and cerebral Geminis, all of whom will stimulate your keen mind.

Your gifts are your wizardry and your ability to learn anything quickly as it's taught to you. Your challenge is never to forget to relate to "real" people—no matter how much you enjoy your virtual connections.

AQUARIUS

From January 20, 19:32 through February 19, 9:42

The Determined Digger

Aquarians of 1992 entered the world as an amazing discovery was made. Just outside Salalah, Oman, a team of archeologists uncovered an octagonal fortress containing more than forty campsites—a fact consistent with classical accounts of a place known as Ubar. This city, labeled the "Atlantis of the Sands" and "the lost city," was mentioned in the classic tale *Arabian Nights* but never discovered, which led many to believe it was as fictional as the 1,001 tales of the work in which it was described. The first artifacts found were identified as Egyptian, Syrian, Chinese, Roman, and Greek, some of them Roman, dating back to 2800 BC. Although it was estimated that total excavation could take as much as forty years to complete, archeologists were certain their efforts would unearth a wealth of artifacts to rival those of Pompeii in Italy.

This incredible find reflects your own determination to unearth secrets, information, and knowledge—and perhaps even archeological treasures. You came along during a birth-time that witnessed planets primarily in your own inventive sign of Aquarius as well as in Capricorn, long associated with its love of unearthing and its appreciation for treasure. In short, Aquarius, you probably arrived with an innate love of "digging" on many levels.

This could extend into the area of research, at which your skills would be unparalleled. But adding the discipline and application of Capricorn to the fixed determination of your own sign means that you'll excel at any task you choose, especially if your curiosity is aroused. As a result, your expertise in your field will surely be the stuff of which legends are made.

In relationships, you'd do well to seek out the company of Capricorns, Sagittarians, and Virgos, all of whom have an innate inquisitiveness to rival your own.

Your greatest gifts are your inventiveness and your dogged determination to get to the bottom of things. Your challenge is to allow yourself time to enjoy life in between career accomplishments.

➤ Read about your Chinese Astrological sign on page 838. ➤ Read about your Personal Planets on page 826. ➤ Read about your personal Mystical Card on page 856.

CAPRICORN
Your Personal Planets

YOUR LOVE POTENTIAL
Venus in Sagittarius, Jan. 01, 0:00 - Jan. 20, 19:32

YOUR DRIVE AND AMBITION
Mars in Sagittarius, Jan. 01, 0:00 - Jan. 09, 9.46
Mars in Capricorn, Jan. 09, 9:47 - Jan. 20, 19:32

YOUR LUCK MAGNETISM
Jupiter in Virgo, Jan. 01, 0:00 - Jan. 20, 19:32

World Events

Jan. 11 – Musician Paul Simon begins an international tour in South Africa.

Jan. 15 – The European Community recognizes the independence of the states of Croatia and Slovenia.

Boris Yeltsin with President George Bush

AQUARIUS
Your Personal Planets

YOUR LOVE POTENTIAL
Venus in Sagittarius, Jan. 20, 19:33 - Jan. 25, 7:13
Venus in Capricorn, Jan. 25, 7:14 - Feb. 18, 16:39
Venus in Aquarius, Feb. 18, 16:40 - Feb. 19, 9:43

YOUR DRIVE AND AMBITION
Mars in Capricorn, Jan. 20, 19:33 - Feb. 18, 4:37
Mars in Aquarius, Feb. 18, 4:38 - Feb. 19, 9:43

YOUR LUCK MAGNETISM
Jupiter in Virgo, Jan. 20, 19:33 - Feb. 19, 9:43

World Events

Feb. 1 – George Bush and Boris Yeltsin proclaim a formal end to the Cold War at Camp David.

Feb. 14 – A ceasefire begins in Somalia.

1992

PISCES
Your Personal Planets

YOUR LOVE POTENTIAL

Venus in Aquarius, Feb. 19, 9:44 - Mar. 13, 23:56
Venus in Pisces, Mar. 13, 23:57 - Mar. 20, 8:47

YOUR DRIVE AND AMBITION

Mars in Aquarius, Feb. 19, 9:44 - Mar. 20, 8:47

YOUR LUCK MAGNETISM

Jupiter in Virgo, Feb. 19, 9:44 - Mar. 20, 8:47

World Events

Feb. 26 - The Irish Supreme Court rules that a fourteen-year-old rape victim may have an abortion.

Mar. 9 - Former Israeli Prime Minister Menachem Begin dies.

General Noriega is convicted in a U.S. court and sentenced on drugs charges

ARIES
Your Personal Planets

YOUR LOVE POTENTIAL

Venus in Pisces, Mar. 20, 8:48 - Apr. 07, 7:15
Venus in Aries, Apr. 07, 7:16 - Apr. 19, 19:56

YOUR DRIVE AND AMBITION

Mars in Aquarius, Mar. 20, 8:48 - Mar. 28, 2.03
Mars in Pisces, Mar. 28, 2:04 - Apr. 19, 19:56

YOUR LUCK MAGNETISM

Jupiter in Virgo, Mar. 20, 8:48 - Apr. 19, 19:56

World Events

Apr. 9 - Gen. Manuel Noriega, former leader of Panama, is convicted in a U.S. court and sentenced to forty years on drug charges.

Apr. 9 - The Conservative Party in Britain, under the leadership of John Major, sweeps to victory in the general election.

PISCES
From February 19, 9:43 through March 20, 8:47

The Discriminating Disciple

Pisces born during 1992 came into the world just as *Pravda*, the official newspaper of the defunct Communist Party in the Soviet Union, had lost ninety percent of its readership. Publishers finally decided to stop the presses and the paper was said to be completely and utterly broke. At the same time, the Christian Science Church, a worldwide "self-help" religion with an estimated fortune in the millions of dollars, faced legal problems, the disillusionment of thousands of members, and financial woes of its own. As such, your "being" was most likely infused with the roots of skepticism, something your ingenuous, trusting sign doesn't ordinarily possess.

The astrological influences of your sign's arrival in 1992 could also help make you prone to question authority and organized belief systems of all kinds. Your innocent nature was tempered by a host of planets in Aquarius—a logical, cerebral, and objective sign that's famous for doubting what it can't see, touch, or prove on paper. Far from distancing you from your strong Piscean faith in belief, however, this equal distribution of astrological energies gave you a healthy balance of traits. In short, you'll do your homework to find the truth and, if you find it, you'll be completely devoted. If you're disappointed, however, you'll move quickly to your next investigation, spurred on by your desire to find what is true.

This seeming contradiction of qualities really just serves to make you a steadfast defender of what you find to be solid. In fact, once you settle on something, you'll want to let the world know you've found it—and you'll keep trying to convince others of the truth in what you've discovered.

Your never-ending search for the real and genuine will lead you to the company of other Pisceans, Aquarians, and Sagittarians who share your hunger for knowledge.

Your greatest challenge is not to become jaded or disappointed before you find your truth. Your gift is your relentless determination to keep at your investigations until you discover something to believe in that is logical and well-grounded in reality.

ARIES
From March 20, 8:48 through April 19, 19:56

The Adamant Authority

Ariens of 1992 arrived on the planet just as a major playground was unveiled in Europe. EuroDisney opened outside Paris during the month of your Sun sign's passage. Although its opening wasn't without a bit of battle, your feisty sign never shied away from that sort of thing, adding perhaps to the symbolic quality of this event for those Rams born at this time. It seems that the president of EuroDisney had some criticisms and made some suggestions to the architect, Aldo Rossi. Instead of giving in, however, Rossi responded by penning a letter that let the higher-ups know his determination to have things his way, or else. He told of a king of France who commissioned an architect named Bernini to build a palace and then asked for modifications. Bernini quit. As Rossi wrote in his letter, "I realize that I am not Bernini, but you are also not the king of France. I quit."

This amusing anecdote perfectly shows your fiery sign's resolve to do things your own way—and that determination is a quality you may have exhibited throughout your life both personally and professionally in business relationships. With several planets traveling through independent, unconventional, and rebellious Aquarius during your birth-time—including Saturn, the patron planet of construction—it's not hard to imagine that this trait extends into far more than career matters.

You're probably known among your circle of friends for your outright refusal to buckle under when you know you're right. That trait will win you a group of admirers who will respect your innate courage and bravery as well as your maverick personality. Those you win over will steadfastly remain by your side, which is really all you ask and something you'll happily reciprocate for your friends.

In relationships, you'd do best to seek out open-minded Sagittarians, fiery Leos, and witty Geminis, each of whom will be delighted to stand by you no matter which authority you may challenge.

Your gift is your strong determination to do things your way. Your challenge is to know when it's right to give in—and that's a hefty one.

➤ Read about your Chinese Astrological sign on page 838. ➤ Read about your Personal Planets on page 826. ➤ Read about your personal Mystical Card on page 856.

TAURUS

From April 19, 19:57 through May 20, 19:11

The Stubborn Survivor

You, 1992 Taurus, are gifted with the potential for longevity—both in the doggedness with which you pursue your interests and the actual length of your life. During the time of your arrival, a poll noted that the number of humans now living to more than one hundred years had tripled, a statistical fact consistent with your sign's reputation for stubbornness and refusal to give up the ghost or anything else that you want.

The astrological factors of your birth-time were equally determined and perfectly display your love of life. Several planets in feisty Aries and in your own solid sign held court in the heavens along with Jupiter, the planet of abundance, in health-conscious Virgo. As such, you will probably spend a good deal of your life concentrating on how to keep your "machinery" running well—that is, concentrating on maintaining your health, wellness, and the physical fitness of your body.

This determination to enjoy every possible moment here on the planet makes sense, considering your likely love of physical pleasures. After all, what better vehicle is there to enjoy the world's creature comforts than a human body? For that matter what other vehicle do we know of for that purpose? This relentless resolve to reap the best from each and every moment and event will make you an expert on living life to its fullest. And that trait will probably win you the respect and admiration of others who may look to you for an example of how to make the most of every last bit of life. Just don't forget to treat yourself to a bit of excess every now and then—in the name of comfort, of course.

You'd do well to pursue the company of like-minded signs, such as health-conscious Virgos, Capricorns—the sign of longevity—and Sagittarians, all of whose personal philosophies likely include a *joie de vivre* that's contagious.

Your challenge is to allow yourself to enjoy just a bit of indulgence in life and not to worry about whether or not it will remove five minutes from your life span. Your gift is the example you'll provide to others of how life really should be lived.

GEMINI

From May 20, 19:12 through June 21, 3:13

Death of film actress Marlene Dietrich

The Cause Communicator

Born during 1992, Gemini, you arrived as final plans were made for The Earth Summit in Rio de Janeiro, Brazil. This meeting of world leaders included representatives from 172 nations. Its mission was to help save the planet from pollution, deforestation, and the extinction of endangered animal and plant species. Since you were born during this time, you may carry the seeds of powerful causes, possibly even including this one with its need to prove to industry and the public that environmentalism can be sensible and even potentially profitable—not to mention that protecting the Earth's resources benefits everyone.

You also received the astrological factors necessary to make your case. The skies hosted a pack of planets in your own cerebral sign and Jupiter—the king of the gods and the ruler of mass communication—was in earthy, conservative Virgo. These energies endowed you with the ability to give a precise and fervent voice to any cause you believe in, to say the least. You are also likely to be a convincing speaker and writer no matter what your topic, able to convey what is on your mind to just about anyone, anywhere.

As such, you're particularly well-suited to occupations that require strong communication skills and you may be drawn to them early in your working years. You may also feel that your mission in life is to make the case for worthy causes, such as the safety and conservation of the environment. One way or the other, you'll undoubtedly affect far more than just your own future through the power of your words and your commitment to your cause.

In relationships, look to freewheeling Leos, Sagittarians, and Aquarians for fun, easygoing, and light-hearted company. In friendships, seek out the earth-signs: sturdy Taureans, Virgos, and Capricorns who will share your probable enjoyment of the great outdoors.

Your challenge is to convince others that there truly is a happy medium between enjoying the physical pleasures and comforts of the Earth and squandering them. Your gift is your ability to present a case for compromise with a clear and respectable voice.

➤ Read about your Chinese Astrological sign on page 838. ➤ Read about your Personal Planets on page 826. ➤ Read about your personal Mystical Card on page 856.

1992

TAURUS
Your Personal Planets

YOUR LOVE POTENTIAL
Venus in Aries, Apr. 19, 19:57 - May 01, 15:40
Venus in Taurus, May 01, 15:41 - May 20, 19:11

YOUR DRIVE AND AMBITION
Mars in Pisces, Apr. 19, 19:57 - May 05, 21:35
Mars in Aries, May 05, 21:36 - May 20, 19:11

YOUR LUCK MAGNETISM
Jupiter in Virgo, Apr. 19, 19:57 - May 20, 19:11

World Events

Apr. 23 - McDonald's opens its first fast-food restaurant in Beijing, China.

May 6 - German-born film star Marlene Dietrich dies.

GEMINI
Your Personal Planets

YOUR LOVE POTENTIAL
Venus in Taurus, May 20, 19:12 - May 26, 1:17
Venus in Gemini, May 26, 1:18 - June 19, 11:21
Venus in Cancer, June 19, 11:22 - June 21, 3:13

YOUR DRIVE AND AMBITION
Mars in Aries, May 20, 19:12 - June 14, 15:55
Mars in Taurus, June 14, 15:56 - June 21, 3:13

YOUR LUCK MAGNETISM
Jupiter in Virgo, May 20, 19:12 - June 21, 3:13

World Events

June 5 - Waldemar Pawlak becomes Prime Minister of Poland.

June 17 - Presidents Bush and Yeltsin sign an agreement outlining arms reduction in their nations.

1992

YOUR LOVE POTENTIAL

Venus in Cancer, June 21, 3:14 - July 13, 21:06
Venus in Leo, July 13, 21:07 - July 22, 14:08

YOUR DRIVE AND AMBITION

Mars in Taurus, June 21, 3:14 - July 22, 14:08

YOUR LUCK MAGNETISM

Jupiter in Virgo, June 21, 3:14 - July 22, 14:08

World Events

June 23 - Yotzhak Rabin wins the Israeli parliamentary election.

July 15 - Pope John Paul II is hospitalized for three weeks after having a tumor removed.

Yitzhak Rabin wins the Israeli parliamentary election

LEO
Your Personal Planets

YOUR LOVE POTENTIAL

Venus in Leo, July 22, 14:09 - Aug. 07, 6:25
Venus in Virgo, Aug. 07, 6:26 - Aug. 22, 21:09

YOUR DRIVE AND AMBITION

Mars in Taurus, July 22, 14:09 - July 26, 18:58
Mars in Gemini, July 26, 18:59 - Aug. 22, 21:09

YOUR LUCK MAGNETISM

Jupiter in Virgo, July 22, 14:09 - Aug. 22, 21:09

World Events

July 22 - Colombian drug baron Pablo Escobar escapes from his prison near Medellin.

July 23 - Former Emperor of Ethiopia Haile Selassie is buried.

CANCER
From June 21, 3:14 through July 22, 14:08

The Ingenious Teacher

Born during 1992, Cancer, you arrived during the same month that the electronic book made its debut. This innovative source of entertainment and education was aimed primarily at the children throughout the world who had developed a fascination with television, video games, and hand-held electronic toys over preceding decades. Generally, anything of an electronic nature appeared to be more alluring to these youngsters than the "old-fashioned" book and manufacturers sought to capitalize on that trend. The easy availability and access this medium provided to readers of all ages could represent a tremendous step toward helping improve literacy levels, making education more appealing, and bringing the gift of reading to those who were home-bound or unable to obtain books.

The astrological factors that influenced both this amazing brainchild and your own thirst for knowledge were powerful ones. Saturn, the "Cosmic Schoolteacher" himself, was posited in cerebral, computer-savvy Aquarius, the sign that shares rulership of mass communication with its intellectual cousin, Sagittarius. Mercury, the "Messenger of the Gods" and the purveyor of knowledge and information, was in showy, lavish Leo, a theatrical sign-planet combination.

Basically, you were astrologically endowed with the ability to be an entertaining and informative speaker—and since your sign has a natural affiliation with children, you may use your talents in occupations that involve them. Even if you choose another line of work, you may be quite computer-savvy yourself. You may possess an affinity with other types of electronic devices as well.

Your search for the perfect partner will probably lead you to someone who will keep your mind occupied—well before you consider giving up your heart. As such, Aquarians, Sagittarians, and Scorpios will likely always be in your life.

Your gift is your ability to understand exactly how to communicate with anyone—but particularly with youngsters. Your challenge is never to become so involved in the cerebral side of life that you lose your real, personal connection with others.

LEO
From July 22, 14:09 through August 22, 21:09

The Entertainment Expert

Born during 1992, Leo, you arrived at a time that would powerfully heighten your love of entertainment in all its forms—and your own innate ability to perform. All over the world, a new trend in literature took shape. "summer readers" were treated to a veritable buffet of biographies—some authorized and some not—that opened up the private lives of celebrities whose names were already famous in every corner of the globe. Some of the subjects that made the top of the lists of book readers and reviewers all over the world included Frank Sinatra, Noël Coward, Marlene Dietrich, Marilyn Monroe, and Sean Connery.

This sudden interest in the makings of a star may have given you the urge to make your mark on the entertainment world or it simply may have piqued your curiosity to learn the secrets of the rich and famous. But one way or the other, you'll probably be quite the historian—and quite the entertainer, regardless of which social circle you call your own. With Jupiter, the "Great Expander," in precise, discriminating Virgo, you may also find your niche in critique or analysis.

Astrologically speaking, your birth-time was a splashy one. Several planets hovered in your own dramatic, theatrical sign, perhaps giving you a love of the spotlight and the applause of the crowd. The planet Mars, the bravest energy in all our charts, was in intelligent Gemini, the sign that's famous for its "gift of gab." As such, you may be naturally comfortable with speaking in front of groups, acting in the theater, or teaching. Needless to say, your communication skills are likely quite substantial.

Your perfect partner necessarily will be someone who will amuse and entertain you, as much as you'll be able to charm and delight him or her. Look to Sagittarians, Ariens, and other Geminis for just that quality—as well as for adventurousness that will match your own.

Your challenge is to allow your star to shine—to find a spotlight you feel comfortable in and let your talents show. Your gift is your capacity to intuit exactly what an "audience" sees as quality entertainment.

➤ Read about your Chinese Astrological sign on page 838. ➤ Read about your Personal Planets on page 826. ➤ Read about your personal Mystical Card on page 856.

VIRGO

From August 22, 21:10 through September 22, 18:42

The Quality-Conscious Manager

Virgos of 1992 arrived into a time that would serve to exemplify the sign's affinity with work, details, and trouble-shooting. A technique known as "Total Quality Management," developed by the Japanese, had recently made its debut in American and European industries. This cerebral import involved training seminars to educate managers and low-level employees alike on the virtues of trouble-shooting procedures, the assessment of work habits, and regularly scheduled performance evaluations. Goal-oriented at its very roots, this system promised to be the key to improving production in major international corporations, such as Xerox, Motorola, Federal Express, and Harley-Davidson, as well as smaller companies whose very existence depended on efficiency. You too understand the value of such detailed analysis and you have the skills to carry it out with success.

The astrology of the time provided a potent boost to your innate knack for discrimination and sharpened your already keen critical skills. Several planets were in your own sign, known for its ability to sniff out potential trouble through seeing the flaws in any process. The most powerful of all included Jupiter, who naturally expands the qualities of the sign he inhabits.

All this means is you'll excel in any occupation you choose, probably becoming known as the person to help when a project is failing for reasons others can't quite see. In personal relationships, however, you may need to temper your natural ability to critique with a good dose of consideration for the feelings of others. Otherwise, what you may intend as a helpful suggestion could be interpreted as fault-finding or criticism.

Your choice of partner should necessarily be someone who is self-confident, astute, and pragmatic. Look to the other earth signs—Taureans and Capricorns—for just those qualities.

Your challenge is to temper your insight with tact and diplomacy, always keeping the other person's point of view in mind. Your gift is your ability to spot a small and seemingly insignificant problem before it snowballs into a major disaster.

LIBRA

From September 22, 18:43 through October 23, 3:56

The Expert Conciliator

You, 1992 Libra, arrived into a time when the world's news was full of debates and reconciliation—topics your sign is quite familiar with and well equipped to handle. The animosity between Russian President Boris Yeltsin and the former leader of the Soviet Union Mikhail Gorbachev heated up substantially, highlighting once again the old rift between not just the two men but the forms of government they supported for that country. At the same time, 600 Japanese military engineers and other personnel joined the United Nations peacekeepers in Cambodia, hoping to end the bad feelings that had existed between the two countries since the Japanese Imperial Army had occupied the region in 1941 during World War II.

Since your sign's knack for restoring balance is legendary, it makes sense that you might feel an affinity with these events—after all, how would you ever learn balance if you never experienced imbalance? Debates and disagreements give you a chance to put your talents to work, honing your skills and developing an even keener sense of what's fair and what's not. As such, you'll probably often be put in a position of mediation, negotiation and peace-making—and the older you get, the better you'll be at achieving those ends.

Those born under the sign of Libra during your year, however, were particularly well endowed with these abilities. The heavens played host to generous Jupiter's arrival into your sign during this time and Jupiter never fails to expand the qualities of the sign it inhabits. As such, you were gifted with a tremendous capacity for overseeing negotiations, arranging conferences, and facilitating the arbitration of differences between just about any two entities.

With regard to relationships, you'll likely prefer the company of those who are equally peace-oriented, such as other Librans, merry, optimistic Sagittarians, and appreciative Leos.

Your gift is the ease, comfort, and grace you show in the company of anyone, from any walk of life. Your challenge is to learn to disagree when it becomes necessary and never sell out or concede your opinions for temporary peace.

➤ Read about your Chinese Astrological sign on page 838. ➤ Read about your Personal Planets on page 826. ➤ Read about your personal Mystical Card on page 856.

1992

VIRGO
Your Personal Planets

YOUR LOVE POTENTIAL
Venus in Virgo, Aug. 22, 21:10 - Aug. 31, 16:08
Venus in Libra, Aug. 31, 16:09 - Sept. 22, 18:42

YOUR DRIVE AND AMBITION
Mars in Gemini, Aug. 22, 21:10 - Sept 12, 6:06
Mars in Cancer, Sept. 12, 6:05 - Sept. 22, 18:42

YOUR LUCK MAGNETISM
Jupiter in Virgo, Aug. 22, 21:10 - Sept. 22, 18:42

World Events

Sept. 12 – The first married couple go into space together in the shuttle *Endeavor*.

Sept. 22 – Serbian-dominated Yugoslavia is banned from the UN.

A Serbian soldier in Sarajevo, Yugoslavia

LIBRA
Your Personal Planets

YOUR LOVE POTENTIAL
Venus in Libra, Sept. 22, 18:43 - Sept 25, 3:30
Venus in Scorpio, Sept. 25, 3:31 - Oct. 19, 17:46
Venus in Sagittarius, Oct. 19, 17:47 - Oct. 23, 3:56

YOUR DRIVE AND AMBITION
Mars in Cancer, Sept. 22, 18:43 - Oct. 23, 3:56

YOUR LUCK MAGNETISM
Jupiter in Virgo, Sept. 22, 18:43 - Oct. 10, 13:25
Jupiter in Libra, Oct. 10, 13:26 - Oct. 23, 3:56

World Events

Sept. 28 – Speculation is raised about the existence of a tenth planet in the Solar System.

Oct. 12 – An earthquake in Cairo kills 540 people.

1992

SCORPIO
Your Personal Planets

YOUR LOVE POTENTIAL
Venus in Sagittarius, Oct. 23, 3:57 - Nov. 13, 12:47
Venus in Capricorn, Nov. 13, 12:48 - Nov. 22, 1:25

YOUR DRIVE AND AMBITION
Mars in Cancer, Oct. 23, 3:57 - Nov. 22, 1:25

YOUR LUCK MAGNETISM
Jupiter in Libra, Oct. 23, 3:57 - Nov. 22, 1:25

World Events

Nov. 3 - Democrat Bill Clinton wins the U.S. presidential election over President Bush.

Nov. 20 - Fire breaks out at the royal residence Windsor Castle, causing millions of dollars worth of damage.

U.S. President Bill Clinton celebrating his election victory with his runningmate Al Gore.

SAGITTARIUS
Your Personal Planets

YOUR LOVE POTENTIAL
Venus in Capricorn, Nov. 22, 1:26 - Dec. 08, 17:48
Venus in Aquarius, Dec. 08, 17:49 Dec. 21, 14:42

YOUR DRIVE AND AMBITION
Mars in Cancer, Nov. 22, 1:26 - Dec. 21, 14:42

YOUR LUCK MAGNETISM
Jupiter in Libra, Nov. 22, 1:26 - Dec. 21, 14:42

World Events

Nov. 24 - Queen Elizabeth II recalls her "annus horribilis."

Dec. 20 - Slobodan Milosevic is re-elected as President of Serbia.

SCORPIO
From October 23, 3:57 through November 22, 1:25

The Charming Investigator

Born during 1992, Scorpio, you were given the ability to conduct your sign's primary business—the unearthing of information—with a charm not many of your fellow Sun-sign members possess to such a grand extent. You may manage to draw others out, persuade them to reveal their deepest selves to you and become their personal confidante, making you a wonderful detective, analyst, or researcher, no matter what arena you put those skills to work in. You could also find yourself involved in other occupations that require counseling or one-on-one communication.

The aptitudes you may possess were put on display for the world in grand fashion during your birth-time. Globally published and broadcast, interviews with Syria's President Hafez Assad and Israeli Prime Minister Yitzhak Rabin—two nations that had been bitter foes for decades—showed the world how honest answers could be obtained from anyone, even two men as politically and emotionally different and defensive as these two. Although the interviews were conducted at separate times, both men knew the other was answering similar questions—and both were won over by the objective, impartial tone of the interviewer.

The astrological factors that influenced this event gave you the same qualities that were needed to make it possible. Jupiter, the "Great Expander," was in charming, sociable Libra, the sign that's most famous for its ability to mingle with anyone. Other planets in broad-minded, friendly Sagittarius—including Mercury, the planet of communication—also gave you a knack for candor, blunt honesty, and chatting comfortably with others from a variety of backgrounds.

In relationships, aim to partner yourself with those born under signs that have the same type of depth, intensity, and friendliness. Other Scorpios, Pisceans, Capricorns, and Sagittarians would make wise choices, as would concise, humble Virgos.

Your challenge is never to extract information from anyone for a less than above-board reason. Your gift is the ability to provide an empathetic ear to those who feel there's no one in whom they can confide.

SAGITTARIUS
From November 22, 1:26 through December 21, 14:42

The Unprejudiced Leader

Born during 1992, Sagittarius, you entered the world as an historic event was taking place—one that would serve to infuse you with even more of the open-mindedness and impartiality that makes your sign famous. The Anglican Church or Church of England, voted to ordain women to the priesthood. The announcement was delivered by the Archbishop of Canterbury, Dr. George Carey, but was made by the church's three governing houses—bishops, clergy, and laity. Although the decision had yet to be ratified by Parliament and the Queen, this monumental step toward removing gender as a prerequisite for religious leadership served as a leap toward ending discrimination of all kinds, once and for all.

Your equally unprejudiced nature received a mighty boost through the influence of your ruling planet, Jupiter, as well. Posited in fair-minded Libra, this planet is in charge of religion, politics, and philosophy—basically all the "big issues." Also, during your birth-time, cerebral Mercury, the planet of reason, had made his way into your own broad-minded sign. In short, Sagittarius, you probably can't imagine how—or why—anyone would choose to harbor bad feelings toward any group of people.

This unprejudiced objectivity will probably win you friends from many social, religious, and ethnic backgrounds—and every one of them will appreciate your color—and class-blind attitude. You also may be quite the advocate on behalf of those who find themselves stigmatized or unfairly judged by others, or put in disadvantaged situations. Whether you choose to pursue this cause as a career or just live your life by these standards, you'll benefit greatly from the variety of experiences you'll be able to enjoy as a result.

In relationships, you'll most likely seek out someone who is equally unprejudiced, impartial and fair-minded, such as Librans, Geminis, other Sagittarians, or Aquarians.

Your gift is your immediate acceptance of everyone. Your challenge is to learn to distinguish between those who deserve your kindness and those who would seek to take advantage of you.

➤ Read about your Chinese Astrological sign on page 838. ➤ Read about your Personal Planets on page 826. ➤ Read about your personal Mystical Card on page 856.

CAPRICORN

From December 21, 14:43 through December 31, 23:59

The Committed Protector

Born during late 1992, Capricorn, you entered the world just as the human-rights abuses in Bosnia had reached crisis proportions. After months of deliberation, the United States opted to stop the Serbs and their "ethnic cleansing" of the portions of that country in which some Serbs lived. Options discussed included establishing a no-fly zone, expanding relief operations, arming the Bosnians, and sending ground forces into the area to enforce a peace. The fact that this situation was horribly reminiscent of the Nazi's campaign to completely exterminate the Jews of Europe helped the plight of the Bosnians and added to the international outrage stirred.

This worldwide fury and call for justice, as well as the measures in the works to put a stop to them, reflect your innate kindness, concern for others, and willingness to do what it takes to protect those who are victims of hatred or brutality. The astrological factors that contribute to your probable resolve include fiery Mars, the angry god of war, posited in Cancer—the sign that rivals your own in its urge to defend the helpless.

As such, you may well be a serious and powerful "guardian angel" of the unfortunate, no matter who or what preys upon them. You may actually be drawn into work that allows you to vocalize your unbiased views or into law enforcement or counseling victims. No matter what career path you choose, your internal commitment to champion the weak will remain strong. You may be in charge of a group or movement that espouses these causes. Even in your personal life your likely passionate commitment to the well-being of those you love will reflect your strongly protective nature.

When searching for a life partner, you'll probably find yourself often in the company of other Capricorns, Cancerians, or Scorpios.

Your challenge is to offer your help only to those who legitimately deserve it, never allowing yourself to be used by anyone who refuses to take responsibility for the consequences of their actions. Your gifts are your innate compassion, sensitivity, and unyielding defense of what's right.

1992
CAPRICORN
Your Personal Planets

YOUR LOVE POTENTIAL
Venus Aquarius, Dec. 21, 14:43 - Dec. 31, 23:59

YOUR DRIVE AND AMBITION
Mars in Cancer, Dec. 21, 14.43 - Dec. 31, 23:59

YOUR LUCK MAGNETISM
Jupiter in Libra, Dec. 21, 14:43 - Dec. 31, 23:59

World Events

Dec. 24 - President Bush pardons the former Reagan administration officials implicated in the Iran-contra affair.

Dec. 29 - President Daniel arap Moi wins the first multi-party elections held in Kenya in twenty-six years.

Machu Pichu, Peru

Special Feature
Gaia's Mystical Power Places

(Continued from page 745)

Not surprisingly, all these places, great and small, famous and virtually unknown, exert a magnetic "pull" that inspires millions to visit them every year. Scientists have attempted to define and label what is happening in these energy centers for decades—but try as they might, there are some things that simply cannot be explained. Still, magnetic fields and electrical impulses have been measured in and around these sites, shedding light on their workings and leading to the discovery of actual biochemical changes that take place in visitors' bodies. These centers—regardless of the climate or geographical region in which they are located—have also been found to be heavily charged with negative ions (electrical charges in the air which have "positive" effects on living beings). According to both ancient legends and current reports, what the energy actually "does" varies with each individual. Some people find themselves awakened, while others travel into the past in a dreamy, trance-like state. Some experience actual physical reactions, such as weightlessness, lack of coordination, or an overwhelming sense of joy. Regardless of the effects, however, everyone seems to feel "something"—much to the bewilderment of the scientific community.

> Scientists have attempted to define and label what is happening in these energy centers for decades—but try as they might, there are some things that simply cannot be explained.

Scientific or not, our early ancestors were well aware of these and other sensations experienced by visitors to these power places. They believed that "ley" lines—invisible Earth grids and vortexes "buried" deep within the Earth—were wells of holy power. They respected the strength of these unseen powers and felt that the lines allowed them to commune with their Creator, to uplift their consciousness and fortify their souls.

In the United States, a people known as the Anasazi created a civilization stretching from New Mexico and Arizona to Utah. Anasazi is a Pueblo name meaning Ancient Ones. The Anasazi showed their respect for the sacred in their kivas, temples lying beneath the floors of their pueblos. The walls of the kiva were decorated with paintings (called petroglyphs), the precise meanings of which are unknown. The best-known Anasazi sites are in Arizona and New Mexico, sacred to the Southwestern American tribes. Another creation of the Anasazi similar to that of other sacred sites is an arrow-straight, thirty-mile road originating at Kutz Canyon in New Mexico.

(Continued on page 761)

➤ Read "Ancient Secrets of the Egyptian Pyramids on page 305. ➤ Read "The Enigma of Crop Circles" on page 673.

1993

Growing Pains: Saturn and Pluto

After the political landscape had been transformed over the past few years, stability had yet to be achieved in many locales. This was symbolized in the heavens by the Uranus and Neptune link, which persisted through 1993. In global politics, Uranus represents pressures to split apart but also to renew, while Neptune suggests disintegrating forces but also ideals and visions of the future. As 1993 began, the states of the old Soviet Union were struggling to exist autonomously, jumpstarting their economies without financial fuel. Long suppressed cultural groups felt a need to express their own identity independently, leading several former republics to fragment further. For example, Czechoslovakia split into two states and unrest was recorded among ethnic groups in Yugoslavia.

However, another powerful planetary connection occurred this year, as Saturn made a challenging square to Pluto starting in February. Saturn, the planet of manifestation, was in stubborn Aquarius, while Pluto, the planet of deep transformation, was in recalcitrant Scorpio. When these planets came together many were resistant to change. In the U.S., the religious extremist Branch Davidians, engaged in a disastrous siege with federal agents, then committed mass suicide. The World Trade Center in New York City was bombed by Muslim terrorists who were part of an international network that was also planning other attacks. However, a great good came out of this year's impetus toward renewal: South Africa finally gave up its apartheid policy and agreed to multi-racial elections.

Actress Audrey Hepburn dies

Aborigines playing the didgeridoo in Queensland, Australia

Peace agreement between Israelis and Arabs

THE TERRORIST FRINGE EMERGES

Czechoslovakia split peacefully into the Czech Republic and Slovakia. In Cambodia, Prince Sihanouk returned to his throne after thirty-eight years. U.S., French, and British planes bombed targets in Iraq in answer to Saddam Hussein's violations of UN resolutions. A Northern Ireland peace was signed by the British and Irish prime ministers and U.S. President Clinton brokered a peace between Israelis and Arabs. The U.S. midwest suffered severe flooding. Australian aborigines won land rights when parliament passed the Native Title Bill. After a fifty-one-day siege, David Koresh and the eighty-seven members of his Branch Davidian cult committed suicide at Waco, Texas. At New York's World Trade Center, five died in a bomb blast. Canada and Turkey acquired their first women prime ministers. Mafia 'boss of bosses' Salvatore Riina was captured in Sicily and India's Bandit Queen, Phoolan Devi, was released after eleven years in prison. In Britain, Buckingham Palace was opened to tourists. Deaths included Russian-born ballet star Nureyev, jazzman Dizzy Gillespie, film stars Audrey Hepburn and Lillian Gish and U.S. press magnate William Randolph Hurst.

➤ Read "Gaia's Mystical Power Places" by Ronnie Grishman on page 745.

CAPRICORN

From January 01, 0:00 through January 20, 1:22

The Shrewd Professional

Born in early 1993, January Capricorn, you arrived into a world that witnessed the toppling of several international business icons. The chairmen of the U.S.-based companies IBM and Westinghouse resigned followed later that same week by James Robinson of American Express. In addition, Delta Airlines, Boeing, and Sears reported layoffs and massive financial losses. These corporate shake-ups perfectly showed the need for the two qualities your sign is famous for mastering: business acuity and financial planning.

In addition to the influence of the Sun, a look at the astrology of your entry into the world this year reveals that you were born with three other planets in your own sign, strongly reinforcing the practicality and thoughtfulness for which Capricorn is known. As such, you could possibly make a keen executive, a shrewd administrator, or a devoted employee. You also may find yourself placed in a position of authority at work, probably after very little time on the job. You have the ability to learn quickly, described by the position of Saturn, your own equally business-oriented planet, in Aquarius—the sign of genius.

In short, Capricorn of 1993, you probably have a take-charge personality that will earn you the respect and appreciation of higher-ups, friends, and your primary partner alike. Your dedication to keeping your commitments will also probably be quite strong, so whether you're deciding on a partner or a career, you'll probably do it just once. In fact, once you've made just about any choice, your determination to stick to your path will be quite firm and unwavering.

When it comes time to find yourself a partner, you would do well to pursue one of the other earth signs, Taureans or Virgos, but the importance you place on family could mean that home and family-oriented Cancerians would also make a good choice.

Your challenge is to allow yourself to relax and enjoy what you've accomplished as it happens. Your gifts are persistence, responsibility, and the willingness to work hard to build a solid, unshakable foundation for yourself and your loved ones.

AQUARIUS

From January 20, 1:23 through February 18, 15:34

The Eternal Activist

As you entered the world, Aquarius of 1993, Germany had to deal with a vast amount of Neo-Nazi violence: among 2,000 acts of violence in 1993, there were seven murders and twenty attempted murders. Among the weapons the German government chose were: bans on four known neo-Nazi groups, the proposed criminalization of symbols and phrases known to be used by "skinheads," and police raids on the homes and offices of those who produced or performed "skinhead" music. These strong steps showed the determination of the German government to eradicate racial and religious hatred once and for all—a legacy that country has worked long and hard to overcome.

This event perfectly outlined your sign's affinity with brotherhood, humanitarianism, and freedom for all—as it also displayed your willingness to take sudden, drastic steps to achieve those aims. The astrological factors you inherited point to your firm conviction that each and every individual deserves the right to live life as they see fit. Three planets in your own sign point to the fact that you could make a strong and stubborn champion of the underdog, regardless of how he or she came to be in that position.

Throughout life, then, you'll probably often find yourself debating these issues, or actually even becoming an active advocate for people less fortunate than yourself. Whether or not you pursue this path as a career, you still may often be put in the position of being the on-the-job defender, activist, and rebel. Fortunately, your sign's skill at fighting City Hall is famous—and that reputation is well deserved.

In relationship matters, you'd do well to seek out the company of other Aquarians, fair-minded Librans, and friendly, adaptable Geminis. You may also gain pleasure from the fire and passion of Sagittarians or Ariens—especially when you're looking for a worthy ally for your current cause.

Your gifts are your openness, tolerance, and unconditional acceptance of others, no matter how different their beliefs are from your own. Your challenge is to understand that restrictions of many kinds are often necessary to maintain order and civility.

➤ Read about your Chinese Astrological sign on page 838. ➤ Read about your Personal Planets on page 826. ➤ Read about your personal Mystical Card on page 856.

CAPRICORN
Your Personal Planets

YOUR LOVE POTENTIAL
Venus in Aquarius, Jan. 01, 0:00 - Jan. 03, 23:53
Venus in Pisces, Jan. 03, 23:54 - Jan. 20, 1:22

YOUR DRIVE AND AMBITION
Mars in Cancer, Jan. 01, 0:00 - Jan. 20, 1:22

YOUR LUCK MAGNETISM
Jupiter in Libra, Jan. 01, 0:00 - Jan. 20, 1:22

World Events

Jan. 1 - The twelve-member European Economic Community sets up a vast free-trade zone.

Jan. 1 - Czechoslovakia separates into the Czech Republic (Bohemia) and Slovakia.

Flags of the EEC members outside the new European Parliament building

AQUARIUS
Your Personal Planets

YOUR LOVE POTENTIAL
Venus in Pisces, Jan. 20, 1:23 - Feb. 02, 12:36
Venus in Aries, Feb. 02, 12:37 - Feb. 18, 15:34

YOUR DRIVE AND AMBITION
Mars in Cancer, Jan. 20, 1:23 - Feb. 18, 15:34

YOUR LUCK MAGNETISM
Jupiter in Libra, Jan. 20, 1:23 - Feb. 18, 15:34

World Events

Feb. 10 - President Clinton agrees to deploy U.S. troops in Bosnia if necessary to implement the peace process.

Feb. 11 - British Prime Minister John Major announces that the Queen will pay taxes like everyone else.

1993

PISCES
Your Personal Planets

YOUR LOVE POTENTIAL
Venus in Aries, Feb. 18, 15:35 - Mar. 20, 14:40

YOUR DRIVE AND AMBITION
Mars in Cancer, Feb. 18, 15:35 - Mar. 20, 14:40

YOUR LUCK MAGENTISM
Jupiter in Libra, Feb. 18, 15:35 - Mar. 20, 14:40

World Events

Feb. 24 – A painting bought for three dollars by an American tourist at a junk sale in London is found to be worth $40,000.

Feb. 26 – Islamic fundamentalists bomb the World Trade Center in New York.

Terrorists plant a bomb in the World Trade Center

ARIES
Your Personal Planets

YOUR LOVE POTENTIAL
Venus in Aries, Mar. 20, 14:41 - Apr. 20, 1:48

YOUR DRIVE AND AMBITION
Mars in Cancer, Mar. 20, 14:41 - Apr. 20, 1:48

YOUR LUCK MAGNETISM
Jupiter in Libra, Mar. 20, 14:41 - Apr. 20, 1:48

World Events

Mar. 25 – President de Klerk admits that South Africa had constructed six nuclear bombs, but states that they have been disarmed and dismantled.

Apr. 7 – The former Yugoslav republic of Macedonia becomes a member of the United Nations.

PISCES
From February 18, 15:35 through March 20, 14:40

The Tenacious Peace-Lover

Born during 1993, Pisces, you arrived at a time that would serve to demonstrate the need for your sign's most famous quality: compassion. Thousands of Bosnians continued to live in terror of the "ethnic cleansing" being attempted by their neighbors, the Serbians. This was an echo of something Europeans had hoped would never happen again: the racial and religious hatred that marked the Nazi attempt to exterminate the Jews. As such, your arrival coincided with a huge, worldwide outpouring of rage and opposition to these heinous acts, showing the humanity inherent in most people.

From an astrological point of view, you were gifted with a potent dose of gentleness and sympathy—more so, perhaps, than many of your Piscean cousins born during other years. Thoughtful Mercury, the ruler of reason, was posited in your tender-hearted sign, and fiery Mars, the ancient warrior-god, wore equally sympathetic Cancer. These factors would serve to make you a powerful defender of the weak, possibly leading you into work that allows you to publicly champion the group or groups you support most strongly. Whether or not you choose a vocation such as this, however, you'll probably always be willing to extend your hand to help someone—whether that someone is a friend or a stranger.

Regardless of your urge to help everyone, however, your family will likely come first. In addition to fire and aggression, Mars is astrologically known as the purveyor of energy and initiative. In Cancer, this describes the strong urge to create a family—and to protect them. As a result, you're probably quite close to your relatives and your long-term friends, and a fierce defender when their safety or well-being is threatened.

In relationships, you would do well to keep company with the other water signs, Scorpio and Cancerians, who'll feel like kindred spirits almost immediately. In friendships, look to the earth signs, Taureans, Capricorns, and Virgos, whose solid support and loyalty will never waver.

Your gift is your total compassion for one and all. Your challenge is to never take on responsibility for the actions of another.

ARIES
From March 20, 14:41 through April 20, 1:48

The Fearless Debater

You, 1993 Aries, arrived into a world that was watching as Boris Yeltsin did battle with the Russian Duma (Parliament). Yeltsin's dismissal of a provincial chief from Siberia infuriated many potentates throughout the country, forcing Yeltsin to publicly apologize and promise to punish the aides who had recommended that the individual be fired. In addition, in exchange for a promise that he would not be impeached, Yeltsin agreed to create a federation council of regional leaders to supervise and control the decisions of the president. Needless to say, this substantially reduced the amount of power a Russian president would wield, a strong statement of the power of collective opinion and democratic expression.

The astrology of your birth-time shows your Sun sign's innate willingness to argue, defend, and engage in fierce verbal battle over what you believe in—but you were also given a strong dose of intuition. As such, you know what to say and how to say it and can drive home your point with force and accuracy. In fact, when you're angry, you would do well to temper your rhetoric with a touch of tact, diplomacy, and concern for the feelings of others. Learn that lesson early on, and you'll earn a reputation as a determined but fair-minded opponent— something that will come in handy throughout life, both personally and professionally.

When it comes to the subject of choosing a profession, you may be drawn into work that allows you to use your substantial energy and enthusiasm, either physically or intellectually. Whether it's with your mind or body, however, you'll undoubtedly work hard and be a welcome addition to any team.

Those born under the other two fire signs, Sagittarians and Leos, will likely always be in your life, both for romantic and platonic reasons. But don't discount the charm of Geminis or the independence of Aquarians, whose energies will blend well with yours.

Your challenge is to learn to think before you speak, especially when you know you're tired, angry, or stressed. Your gift is your ability to express yourself powerfully and convincingly.

➤ Read about your Chinese Astrological sign on page 838. ➤ Read about your Personal Planets on page 826. ➤ Read about your personal Mystical Card on page 856.

TAURUS

From April 20, 1:49 through May 21, 1:01

The Reluctant Celebrity

Born during 1993, Taurus, you were given the ability to lead and the personal resolve to finish what you've started. These qualities may make you successful and possibly also quite famous—but you may not be fond of the kind of celebrity status you'll earn.

As you arrived, a woman working at a simple desk job in Japan's Ministry of Foreign Affairs was preparing to become a Crown Princess. Crown Prince Naruhito, the eldest son of the current emperor, had proposed to Masako Owada—and she had accepted. Owada was looking forward happily to spending the rest of her life with her prince but she was, all the same, not eager to assume a role in the spotlight.

The astrological influences of your birth-time were evenly distributed between planets in solid, determined fixed signs and planets in action-oriented, initiative cardinal signs. These energies give you the qualities necessary to become known as a self-starter—but you'll also be quite good at finishing what you start. As such, your skill at planning and executing, as well as the freshness of your ideas will probably be unparalleled, along with your ability to attract the attention of your supervisors unconsciously. Whether or not you deliberately seek out notice, then, you'll likely have it. You'll need to adjust yourself to the concept of fame, which usually goes hand-in-hand with success. Since your sign has long been affiliated with the urge to achieve material success, it's your attitude toward that fame that you will need to handle carefully. Keep in mind that the more notice you achieve, the more lives you'll be able to touch. As such, the ability to do your job well may bring you less personal privacy, but the good you will do for the world will appeal to you far more than your own personal needs.

Look to Virgos and Capricorns for the solidity you absolutely require in relationships. Earth signs like yourself, they will always give you the loyalty and honesty you absolutely require.

Your gift is your ability to finish—thoroughly—the job you were given. Your challenge is to know when it's time to quit.

GEMINI

From May 21, 1:02 through June 21, 8:59

The Comforting Communicator

As you made your planetary debut, Gemini of 1993, the world heard news of a significant technological innovation—something for which your cerebral sign has always been famous. The ability to make computers interactive had been perfected, beautifully portraying your sign's skill at two-way communication and your love of new information. Although this invention would primarily be used for business, it opened the world's eyes to an entirely new way to meet others—"on line."

This new and incredibly popular computerized means of introduction spread across the world in a flash, allowing those who might not ever have met otherwise to become e-pals—a relationship based on a meeting of the minds, that some said took the shallowness out of initial encounters. As such, it's easy to see that before your heart can become involved, you likely need to feel an intellectual attraction.

The astrological influences of your birth-time point to a substantial amount of air energies. Since this is the element that rules communication, it's easy to see that you would easily become an expert at your sign's job—one-to-one discussion. Adding to your ease in social situations is another quality you inherited by virtue of being born during this year, Gemini of 1993—Jupiter in friendly Libra, the "cruise director" of the heavens. Basically, you're an expert at making everyone in the room feel comfortable and included.

All these wonderfully cerebral, communicative energies suggest that you would make an excellent coordinator, especially with regard to recreation. Fiery Mars, the planet of taking action, was posited in Leo, famous for its love of enjoying life to the fullest. In short, you probably have an unquenchable appetite for having fun and your enthusiasm in that department is likely to be quite contagious.

In relationships, seek out the company of the signs who most notoriously share your love of leisure and adventure, such as Sagittarians and Leos.

Your challenge is to get serious every now and then. Your gift is your infectious knack for enjoying each and every minute.

➤ Read about your Chinese Astrological sign on page 838. ➤ Read about your Personal Planets on page 826. ➤ Read about your personal Mystical Card on page 856.

TAURUS
Your Personal Planets

YOUR LOVE POTENTIAL
Venus in Aries, Apr. 20, 1:49 - May 21, 1:01

YOUR DRIVE AND AMBITION
Mars in Cancer, Apr. 20, 1:49 - Apr. 27, 23:39
Mars in Leo, Apr. 27, 23:40 - May 21, 1:01

YOUR LUCK MAGNETISM
Jupiter in Libra, Apr. 20, 1:49 - May 21, 1:01

World Events

Apr. 23 – The World Health Organization in Geneva declares that tuberculosis is now a global emergency.

Apr. 24 – The IRA sets off a series of bombs in the City of London.

IRA bombings in London

GEMINI
Your Personal Planets

YOUR LOVE POTENTIAL
Venus in Aries, May 21, 1:02 - June 06, 10:02
Venus in Taurus, June 06, 10:03 - June 21, 8:59

YOUR DRIVE AND AMBITION
Mars in Leo, May 21, 1:02 - June 21, 8:59

YOUR LUCK MAGNETISM
Jupiter in Libra, May 21, 1:02 - June 21, 8:59

World Events

June 1 – Guatemalan President Jorge Elias is overthrown by the military.

June 13 – At opposite sides of the world, two women are elected head of their parties and designated premier: Kim Campbell in Canada and Tansu Ciller in Turkey.

1993

CANCER
Your Personal Planets

YOUR LOVE POTENTIAL

Venus in Taurus, June 21, 9:00 - July 06, 0:20
Venus in Gemini, July 06, 0:21 - July 22, 19:50

YOUR DRIVE AND AMBITION

Mars in Leo, June 21, 9:00 - June 23, 7:41
Mars in Virgo, June 23, 7:42 - July 22, 19:50

YOUR LUCK MAGNETISM

Jupiter in Libra, June 21, 9:00 - July 22, 19:50

World Events

July 9 - British scientists assert that the bones discovered in Russia in 1991 are indeed those of the murdered Russian Czar Nicholas II and his family.

July 18 - Afghan President Ishaq Khan and premier Nawaz Sharif resign.

Csar Nicholas II and his family

LEO
Your Personal Planets

YOUR LOVE POTENTIAL

Venus in Gemini, July 22, 19:51 - Aug. 01, 22:37
Venus in Cancer, Aug. 01, 22:38 - Aug. 23, 2:49

YOUR DRIVE AND AMBITION

Mars in Virgo, July 22, 19:51 - Aug. 12, 1:09
Mars in Libra, Aug. 12, 1:10 - Aug. 23, 2:49

YOUR LUCK MAGNETISM

Jupiter in Libra, July 22, 19:51 - Aug. 23, 2:49

World Events

Aug. 7 - Buckingham Palace opens its doors to paying guests for the first time.

Aug. 12 - Pope John Paul II begins a visit of the U.S

CANCER
From June 21, 9:00 through July 22, 19:50

The Diligent Negotiator

Just as you entered the world, Cancer of 1993, the world was applauding Canada's nineteenth Prime Minister, Kim Campbell. Sworn in on June 25, 1993, she was the first woman to hold this post. On the other side of the ocean, two great female athletes met on the courts at Wimbledon on July 3 of the same year. Steffi Graf of Germany defeated Jana Novotna of the Czech Republic to win her third consecutive title. As a 1993 Cancer, male or female, your connection with high achieving women is strong. You have all the valuable Cancer nurturing qualities and domestic skills plus the ability to succeed in the outer world.

Being born during this particular year also gave you the communicative blessings of loving Venus in conversational Gemini and outgoing Jupiter in sociable Libra, planetary allies that would add their energies to make you the perfect spokesperson or negotiator for any group—especially if your emotions are involved. In short, you have an equal dose of heart and intellect, a powerful combination that will undoubtedly serve you well throughout life, both personally and professionally. Several planets in earth signs also point to a propensity to work hard to accomplish your goals. As such, you're a devoted spouse, a committed friend, and a diligent, dutiful worker.

When it comes to career, you should search out a vocation that allows you to use all these traits but regardless of which path you choose, you'll be completely intent on it. Just be sure to allot equal time for your mate and family, whose support and affection will keep your tender heart feeling safe and appreciated.

Your choice of life-partner may lead you into the arms of the other water signs, Pisceans and Scorpios, whose equally emotional natures will blend nicely with your own. In friendships and business, however, the earth signs, Taureans, Capricorns, and Virgos, will prove worthy allies.

Your challenge is to find a profession that allows you to use your substantial blend of talents. Your gift is your determination to keep the promises you've made.

LEO
From July 22, 19:51 through August 23, 2:49

The Competitive Entertainer

Born during 1993, Leo, you arrived into a time when the world heard news of war—but not in a military sense. This war concerned the dominance of American late-night television and the combatants were celebrities. After Johnny Carson's retirement, five men stepped up to compete for the place he'd held in the world's living rooms for nearly thirty years. David Letterman, Jay Leno, Conan O'Brien, Arsenio Hall, and Chevy Chase were all given late-night talk shows in the United States and the battle for Carson's audience was on. This conflict beautifully reflected your sign's association with recreation and entertainment, as well as your pride—especially when leadership and authority are involved.

The astrological influences that held court as you entered the world were equally fiery and equally entertaining. Conversational Mercury in your own captivating sign probably gave you the ability to talk your way in or out of any situation with grace, charm, and enthusiasm, and Mars, the warrior god himself, headed off into attractive Libra, joining Jupiter, the ruler of mass communication. All this adds up to a personality that's built for the spotlight as your friends and admirers have no doubt often told you.

In addition to being comfortable—and appealing—onstage in one form or another, you're probably also known for your originality and humor. As such, you're probably a much sought-after guest at a variety of gatherings, and you'll do your best to make an appearance no matter where you've been invited.

Your busy social calendar likely means you've also had the opportunity to meet folks from many different backgrounds so when it comes time to choose a partner, you'll definitely have options. But your humor and knack for amusing the masses will be most appreciated by Sagittarians and Ariens, the other fire signs, who are also famous for loving the playful side of life.

Your challenge is never to spread yourself too thin—that is, to only give the pleasure of your company to those you genuinely enjoy in return. Your gift is your ability to turn the lackluster into the spectacular.

➤ Read about your Chinese Astrological sign on page 838. ➤ Read about your Personal Planets on page 826. ➤ Read about your personal Mystical Card on page 856.

VIRGO

From August 23, 2:50 through September 23, 0:22

The Careful Navigator

Born during 1993, Virgo, you arrived just as a major discovery was made, one that would serve to make air travel safer for passengers throughout the world. The Federal Aviation Administration in the United States released the news that some electronic devices, including cell phones and laptop computers, held the potential to cause problems with the navigation and communication systems of airplanes. This revelation brought an end to a mystery that had baffled investigators worldwide: why certain planes strayed off course or lost vital flight information displays during and after takeoff.

At that time, planes had basically become computers with wings, leading scientists to investigate the possibility that other computerized devices might be the problem. Their efforts—and this substantial discovery—reflect several of your sign's qualities, including attention to detail, strong research abilities, and the urge to fix something, traits you're likely to have inherited as a result of your birth during this year.

Four planets were posited in safety-oriented earth signs as you entered the world, including Mercury, the ruler of transportation and communication. As such, you may become involved in work or leisure pursuits that allow you to learn, share that knowledge, and make improvements to existing systems. In fact, you would make an excellent trouble-shooter at virtually any occupation, but your love of details may mean you particularly enjoy working with electronics and computers. Even if you never pursue this type of vocation, however, you'll likely have a personal computer of your own and use it often.

In relationships, look to Aquarians, Geminis, and other Virgos, whose love of specifics and capacity for genius rivals your own. In friendships, the other earth signs, Capricorns and Taureans, will prove deserving of your devotion and be more than willing to aid you in achieving your goals as well.

Your challenge is to put your clever mind to good use by finding creative, positive outlets. Your gift is your knack for finding your way, both physically and intellectually.

LIBRA

From September 23, 0:23 through October 23, 9:36

The Even-Tempered Ally

Born during 1993, Libra, your planetary arrival coincided with the news that several recently approved prescription drugs had been found to combat chemical imbalances in the brain, allowing many to feel comfortable inside themselves for the first time in years. On that list was Prozac, labeled "a medical breakthrough" by the American Medical Association. Recent research had shown that when prescribed to patients who suffered from severe depression, phobias, obsessions, or compulsions the drug had "miracle results." People with milder problems, such as simple social discomfort, also used the drug increasingly. The newfound popularity of Prozac and similar drugs reflected your sign's affinity with the concept of restoring balance—as well as your love of feeling peaceful.

The astrological influences of your birth-time included three planets in your own sign, one of which was mighty Jupiter, the king of the gods, long known for his ability to expand and enlarge the qualities of the sign he inhabits. As such, you were given a very strong urge to fix what's out of kilter—to bring balance and harmony to unstable situations. In addition, three planets in deep, intense Scorpio pointed to your need to get at the truth—you are well aware that in order to make repairs, one must first uncover the problem.

Throughout life, you may often be placed in a position that's less than comfortable for you—you may be asked to detect the flaw in the system, even if it happens to be an individual who's not doing his or her job adequately. At that point, your desire to maintain friendships with most everyone may conflict with the side of you that promotes equality and fairness, but your ability to keep your perspective will always get you through any situation.

Your search for a partner will likely lead you to other Librans, Sagittarians, or Aquarians, but Geminis will also prove worthy companions.

Your challenge is never to blame yourself for the actions of others, no matter how involved you've become in their situation. Your gift is your ability to establish relationships that last.

➤ Read about your Chinese Astrological sign on page 838. ➤ Read about your Personal Planets on page 826. ➤ Read about your personal Mystical Card on page 856.

VIRGO
Your Personal Planets

YOUR LOVE POTENTIAL
Venus in Cancer, Aug. 23, 2:50 - Aug. 27, 15:47
Venus in Leo, Aug. 27, 15:48 - Sept. 21, 14:21
Venus in Virgo, Sept. 21, 14:22 - Sept. 23, 0:22

YOUR DRIVE AND AMBITION
Mars in Libra, Aug. 23, 2:50 - Sept. 23, 0:22

YOUR LUCK MAGNETISM
Jupiter in Libra, Aug. 23, 2:50 - Sept. 23, 0:22

World Events

Sept. 9 – The Palestinian Liberation Organization recognizes the state of Israel.

Sept. 13 – Israel and the Palestinian Liberation Organization sign a peace accord.

General Colin Powell

LIBRA
Your Personal Planets

YOUR LOVE POTENTIAL
Venus in Virgo, Sept. 23, 0:23 - Oct. 16, 0:12
Venus in Libra, Oct. 16, 0:13 - Oct. 23, 9:36

YOUR DRIVE AND AMBITION
Mars in Libra, Sept. 23, 0:23 - Sept. 27, 2:14
Mars in Scorpio, Sept. 27, 2:15 - Oct. 23, 9:36

YOUR LUCK MAGNETISM
Jupiter in Libra, Sept. 23, 0:23 - Oct. 23, 9:36

World Events

Sept. 30 – General Colin Powell steps down as Chief of Staff of the U.S. armed forces; he is awarded an honorary knighthood by Queen Elizabeth II.

Oct. 7 – Toni Morrison is awarded the Nobel Prize for literature, the first African American woman to receive the honor.

1993

SCORPIO
Your Personal Planets

YOUR LOVE POTENTIAL
Venus in Libra, Oct. 23, 9:37 - Nov. 09, 2:06
Venus in Scorpio, Nov. 09, 2:07 - Nov. 22, 7:06

YOUR DRIVE AND AMBITION
Mars in Scorpio, Oct. 23, 9:37 - Nov. 09, 5:28
Mars in Sagittarius, Nov. 09, 5:29 - Nov. 22, 7:06

YOUR LUCK MAGNETISM
Jupiter in Libra, Oct. 23, 9:37 - Nov. 10, 8:14
Jupiter in Scorpio, Nov. 10, 8:15 - Nov. 22, 7:06

World Events

Nov. 14 - Puerto Rico votes against becoming the 51st U.S. state.

Nov. 18 - Black and white leaders in South Africa approve the new breakthrough democratic constitution.

Former U.S. President George Bush, Knight of the Order of the Bath

SAGITTARIUS
Your Personal Planets

YOUR LOVE POTENTIAL
Venus in Scorpio, Nov. 22, 7:07 - Dec. 02, 23:53
Venus in Sagittarius, Dec. 02, 23:54 - Dec. 21, 20:25

YOUR DRIVE AND AMBITION
Mars in Sagittarius, Nov. 22, 7:07 - Dec. 20, 0:33
Mars in Capricorn, Dec. 20, 0:34 - Dec. 21, 20:25

YOUR LUCK MAGNETISM
Jupiter in Scorpio, Nov. 22, 7:07 - Dec. 21, 20:25

World Events

Nov. 30 - Former U.S. President George Bush is created an honorary Knight of the Order of the Bath.

Dec. 6 - American animal-rights activists demand a halt in the foie gras trade driven by the French.

SCORPIO
From October 23, 9:37 through November 22, 7:06

The Fascinated Observer

Born during 1993, Scorpio, you entered the world just as it was revealed that multi-billionaire Pablo Escobar had been killed in Colombia during an attempted capture by the police. His wealth, obtained through his iron rule over an international drug empire, had bought him a mansion in Miami and a ranch stocked with giraffes, camels, and a kangaroo. In the end, however, it was not enough to save him from a death he was alleged to have earned. The striking finality of this man's end, as well as the lavish life he lived, served to exemplify the power of secret organizations—both legal and illegal—and aptly reflected your fascination with intrigue, mystery, and secrets.

In addition to that love of secrets, however, you were given keen powers of observation, outlined by the factors that influenced your birth-time. A powerful group of planets held court in your intense, curious sign, including cerebral Mercury, fast-acting Mars, and intense Pluto, your own planet. If you were born after November 10, you were also endowed with Jupiter in your sign—the planet that elaborates and enlarges the signs it wears.

All this means is that you would make an excellent detective, researcher, or examiner. Your ability to scrutinize any situation with an eye toward understanding the inner workings is unparalleled. Regardless of which profession you choose your keen powers of observation will probably make you an expert at it, quickly. In all situations, your ability to analyze, understand, and focus are likely to prove to be your most invaluable attributes.

In relationships, you would do best to focus your substantial energy in the direction of other Scorpios, Cancerians, Pisceans, or Taureans. No matter whom you choose for a life partner, however, your devotion and commitment will likely be unmatched and your lucky mate will consider him or herself quite fortunate to have you.

Your challenge is to channel your intensity and depth into projects that merit your interest and never to allow yourself to be pulled into any less than above board activities. Your gift is your keen mind for investigation.

SAGITTARIUS
From November 22, 7:07 through December 22, 20:25

The Well-Traveled Enthusiast

You entered the world in 1993, Sagittarius, an arrival that coincided with the launch of the space shuttle *Endeavour 5*. Like the scientists and crew responsible for this project, you keep moving forward into unknown territory. Always questing, your journeys may be literal—the kind that lead you to travel in foreign countries. It's also possible that your searching is conducted on the spiritual plane: you love to explore various faith communities and forms of mysticism.

The astrological factors that appeared during your birth-time also show your propensity for long-distance communication, mingling with new and different people, and pursuing new experiences. In fact, the quote from the original Star Trek series—"to boldly go where no man has gone before"—quite beautifully exemplifies your pioneering spirit, both personally and professionally. When it comes to career, you may search out a vocation that's unusual, something that will allow you to find your own special niche in life while you're expressing your own unique talents.

Your knack for bonding means you'll likely be put in contact with others who'll be more than happy to help you further your goals. In short, your friendly, outgoing personality shows the potential to become number one in any field you choose—but it will probably be an unusual one. You probably revel in amazing others but just make sure that your love of being different doesn't lead you to rebel when there's really nothing to rebel against. Your substantial independence can be put to far better use.

Your choice of partners will likely lead you into the arms of the other fire signs, Leos and Ariens, whose adventurousness and enthusiasm will keep you happy and interested long-term. Still, you'll need to tell whomever you end up with that your love of freedom comes first.

Your challenge is to involve yourself only with others who will prove to be positive influences in your life. Your gift is your capacity to make and keep friends from all backgrounds.

➤ Read about your Chinese Astrological sign on page 838. ➤ Read about your Personal Planets on page 826. ➤ Read about your personal Mystical Card on page 856.

CAPRICORN

From December 22, 20:26 through December 31, 23:59

The Political Peace-Maker

Born during late 1993, December Capricorn, you arrived into a year of events that brought special meaning to religious communities in Europe and the Middle East. On December 25 of that year, full-fledged Christmas celebrations returned to Bethlehem. They had been suspended for six years following a Palestinian uprising. On December 30, Israel and the Vatican agreed to recognize one another, bringing together two well-established powers. As a 1993 Capricorn, you have a gift for meeting challenges with tolerance and the ability to compromise without forsaking your highest ideals. Yours is one of the parental signs of the zodiac and your special projects become your "babies" that you nurture until it's time for them to be launched.

Your sign, long known for its affinity with government, rules, and law, was well represented by the news of your birth-time, but the astrological factors you inherited were also quite telling. Six planets made their way into your sign during late December, reinforcing all your sign's qualities. In addition, an active square between Saturn, your own serious planet, and Pluto, the ruler of intensity, endowed you with the ability to lead with force, firmness and steely determination. In short, you were given the capacity to become a worthy leader, a responsible co-worker, and a devoted friend or partner.

Your skills at peace-making, negotiation, and mediation are likely to be unparalleled, possibly leading you into a career in politics, social work, or business administration—all of which you could excel at if you chose. But no matter which vocation you choose, you'll strive long and hard to be an expert at it, and you'll likely become known for your professionalism, responsibility, and dutiful attention to detail.

Your search for the right life partner will probably lead you into relationships with the other earth signs, Taureans and Virgos, whose attention to detail and meticulous regard for following the rules will rival your own.

Your gift is undoubtedly your ability to lead, and lead well. Your challenge is to let the rules slide for extenuating circumstances.

CAPRICORN
Your Personal Planets

YOUR LOVE POTENTIAL
Venus in Sagittarius, Dec. 22, 20:26 - Dec. 26, 20:08
Venus in Capricorn, Dec. 26, 20:09 - Dec. 31, 23:59

YOUR DRIVE AND AMBITION
Mars in Capricorn, Dec. 22, 20:26 - Dec. 31, 23:59

YOUR LUCK MAGNETISM
Jupiter in Scorpio, Dec. 22, 20:26 - Dec. 31, 23:59

World Events

Dec. 22 – Australian Aborigines celebrate their victory over rights to land lost when Europeans colonized Australia more than 200 years ago.

Dec. 31 – Barbra Streisand gives her first public concert in twenty-two years.

Uluru (Ayers Rock), Australia

Special Feature
Gaia's Mystical Power Places

(Continued from page 753)

This road has been viewed as a spiritual line, not unlike "ley" lines, and sometimes also known a telluric pathway. Ancient peoples knew of these lines, and worked out how to amplify the energy contained within them. Native Americans called them "the spirit path." The Chinese understood them to be the flow of chi—the "life force"—while the Aborigines of Australia called them "song lines."

The tiny village of Lourdes in France, is one of the most famous centers of healing energy, and it has been the most visited pilgrimage site in Christendom for the last 140 years. In 1858, a fourteen-year-old girl, Bernadette Soubirous, saw apparitions of "a white-robed lady," who announced herself as Mary, the Mother of Jesus. According to Bernadette, the Holy Virgin Mother instructed her to "Go and tell the village priest to build a chapel here," and throngs of people would soon come to pray in the holy grotto.

Bernadette dug in the earth until she found the source of a spring—the holy waters for which Lourdes is now famous.

The island of Kauai in Hawaii features several heiau (ancient temple sites), where Hawaiian priests and ruling chiefs performed spiritual ceremonies. Kauai is the northernmost of the main Hawaiian Islands. Ancient Hawaiian legends associate it with the lost continent of Mu and with the star cluster called the Pleiades. There are a number of other sacred sites around the island, all equally powerful—and equally inspirational.

Despite the impossibility of explaining these phenomena—or, perhaps, because of it—incredible "power places" continue to be among the most venerated and visited locations on the planet. With so many sites in so many different countries, you can probably find one in your vicinity. Or you could make a special pilgrimage to one. Go to the United Kingdom and visit Stonehenge, the Tor,

Newgrange, or Sillbury. Hike through the desert and sit before a wall of Native American petroglyphs—or simply sit beside an eloquent stream. One way or the other, be sure to take time to experience the gifts of the Earth—and the magic and inspiration it holds. ☉

➤ Read "Ancient Secrets of the Egyptian Pyramids" on page 305. ➤ Read "The Enigma of Crop Circles" on page 673.

1994

Easier Times: Jupiter Trine Saturn

After tough times with Saturn and Pluto last year, jolly Jupiter lightened up events in 1994. Jupiter, the planet of optimism and expansion, made a harmonious "trine" to Saturn, the planet of constriction until the end of August. When they blend sonorously, they lend support to wise business and government plans and projects. At this time, the global community had a window of opportunity to work out adversarial situations. This was evident in many ways, as the long-contested North Atlantic Free Trade Agreement (NAFTA) went into effect. In a spirit of international generosity, U.S. President Clinton opened trade with Vietnam, while the Vatican acknowledged the sorrow of the Holocaust. Progressive new structures were initiated when the Church of England ordained its first female priests, and the Channel Tunnel linking England and France was opened.

As the year ended, this planetary pattern faded in favor of a challenging contact made by Jupiter to revolutionary Pluto. This could be experienced as greed or an expansion of power. This was shown on a small scale when a struggle between striking players and baseball owners could only be ended by canceling the season after a long stalemate in negotiations. On a larger scale, this was seen in U.S. politics when the conservative movement won a majority in the U.S. Congress for the first time in decades. In the international arena, powerful changes were made when South Africa was readmitted to the United Nations. The crowning glory of the year, however, was the recognition that Yasser Arafat, Yitzhak Rabin, and Shimon Peres received for forging Middle Eastern peace.

Refugees in Rwanda

Russian forces enter Chechnya

Nelson Mandela is elected President of South Africa

THE BIRTH OF MIRACLE

A rare white buffalo was born on a Wisconsin farm in 1994. The birth carried great cultural significance for the Great Plains Native American tribes as a symbol of hope, rebirth, and unity. These Native Americans believe the calf's birth was an important sign of well being and would "bring purity of mind, body, and spirit and unify all nations—black, red, yellow, and white." The odds of a white buffalo calf birth were one in six billion so the calf was named "Miracle."

O.J., NAFTA, AND A COMET

Ethnic conflict raged in Rwanda and the former Yugoslavia. Right-wing media tycoon Berlusconi won an election in Italy, but fell from power by the year's end. The North American Free Trade Agreement joined the U.S., Canada, and Mexico as a trading unit. Nelson Mandela became President of South Africa. Carlos the Jackal, the world's most wanted terrorist, was captured. The long-awaited thirty-one-mile Channel Tunnel linked England and France under the English Channel. Comet Shoemaker-Levy collided spectacularly with the planet Jupiter. A major earthquake struck Los Angeles, measuring 6.6 on the Richter Scale. Football hero and film star O.J. Simpson went on trial for double murder. Singer-dancer Michael Jackson married Elvis Presley's daughter Lisa Marie. Outstanding films of the year were *The Shawshank Redemption* and *Forrest Gump*, which earned Tom Hanks his second consecutive Best Actor Oscar. Deaths included former President Nixon, Greek film actress and politician Melina Mercouri and Theatre of the Absurd dramatist Eugene Ionesco. Brazilian Formula One racing champion Ayrton Senna was killed during the Grand Prix at Imola, Italy.

➤ Read Oprah Winfrey's Star Profile on page 769.

CAPRICORN

From January 01, 0:00 through January 20, 7:06

The Orderly Executive

Born during early 1994, Capricorn, you arrived into a world that was paying homage to the peace-making efforts of several politicians, among them American President Bill Clinton. The year before, Clinton had skillfully arranged a meeting of the minds and a never before seen display of promise between the leaders of two countries notorious for their inability to reach a consensus: Palestine's Yasser Arafat and Israel's Yitzhak Rabin. "The handshake," as it came to be known, occurred on the lawn of the White House in Washington, D.C. and, although it was arranged, the feeling that greeted it internationally was not. To demonstrate this, *Time* magazine named Rabin, Arafat, F.W. de Klerk and Nelson Mandela its "Men of the Year," for 1993, showing the world's heartfelt wish for peace everywhere.

Although your sign is not ordinarily connected with the peace process, it is affiliated with governance. Good governments keep the peace among their citizens. Professionally, you also know that there's no better way to create a productive team than to foster loyal, emotional ties between them. As such, your management abilities are probably quite keen, as well as your ability to delegate duties to those most aptly qualified.

The astrology behind your birth-time points to what you share on a personal level with these events and with the peace-making process in general: your need for order. Appropriately, half of the planets in our solar system were in your own sign, known for its love of order. As such, the skills you inherited from your year of birth include a strong dose of leadership, responsibility, and integrity, and the ability to take charge of literally any situation.

In relationships, you may often find yourself in the company of someone either much younger or much older than yourself but no matter who you choose for a partner, you'll be devoted and faithful, which will earn you the same in return.

Your challenge is never to allow yourself to feel guilty over the shortcomings or failures of others. Your gifts are your unparalleled ability to organize, lead, and provide support.

AQUARIUS

From January 20, 7:07 through February 18, 21:21

The Peaceful Rebel

During the time of your birth in early 1994, Aquarius, Nelson Mandela, freed in 1992 after twenty-seven years of imprisonment in South Africa, was nearing the end of his campaign for president. And, as *Newsweek* magazine said, "no public figure this side of Mother Teresa had ever enjoyed such a forgiving press." Mandela's newfound fortune, so entirely different from the life he'd lived behind bars, is a perfect example of the qualities your sign is famous for: sudden change and unswerving humanitarianism.

Mandela's success, especially after so many years of defending his ideals despite imprisonment, reflects several other Aquarian traits, as well. First off, your stubbornness, which although not nearly as famous as Taureans, is just as fixed. Then there's your love of causes, which may draw you into a career that allows you to be as radical and rebellious as you please. Finally, it's interesting to note that the sudden shifts in direction that occur frequently in your life that may sometimes make you feel as if you've just been assigned to a whole new lifetime are also perfectly mirrored by Mandela's complete and total reversal of fortune. In fact, abrupt change is likely to be the thing you enjoy most, since it allows you to really feel alive.

With all that said it's easy to see that there's likely a strong dose of Aquarian energy in your birth chart in addition to the Sun. And that's exactly what was happening in the heavens above you. Four planets had entered your sign over the past few weeks, famous for all the above-mentioned traits, but also for its love of freedom and individuality. So needless to say, fear of repression and the urge to buck the system are also characteristics you possess. Channel that fear into determination, however, and you'll have all the confidence you need to face any situation.

Given these qualities, you may keep a Sagittarian or Libran by your side to keep your optimism high and your heart full.

Your gift is your ability to stand by your ideals no matter what. Your challenge is to surround yourself with those who'll support your independence.

➤ Read about your Chinese Astrological sign on page 838. ➤ Read about your Personal Planets on page 826. ➤ Read about your personal Mystical Card on page 856.

CAPRICORN
Your Personal Planets

YOUR LOVE POTENTIAL
Venus in Capricorn, Jan. 01, 0:00 - Jan. 19, 16:27
Venus in Aquarius, Jan. 19, 16:28 - Jan. 20, 7:06

YOUR DRIVE AND AMBITION
Mars in Capricorn, Jan. 01, 0:00 - Jan. 20, 7:06

YOUR LUCK MAGNETISM
Jupiter in Scorpio, Jan. 01, 0:00 - Jan. 20, 7:06

World Events

Jan. 6 – Olympic figure skater and silver medal winner Nancy Kerrigan is attacked by competitor Tonya Harding's bodyguard.

Jan. 11 – NATO nations approve President Clinton's Partnership for Peace plan.

"The Scream" by Edvard Munch

AQUARIUS
Your Personal Planets

YOUR LOVE POTENTIAL
Venus in Aquarius, Jan. 20, 7:07 - Feb. 12, 14:03
Venus in Pisces, Feb. 12, 14:04 - Feb. 18, 21:21

YOUR DRIVE AND AMBITION
Mars in Capricorn, Jan. 20, 7:07 - Jan. 28, 4:04
Mars in Aquarius, Jan. 28, 4:05 - Feb. 18, 21:21

YOUR LUCK MAGNETISM
Jupiter in Scorpio, Jan. 20, 7:07 - Feb. 18, 21:21

World Events

Jan. 25 – Accused of molesting a thirteen-year-old boy, Michael Jackson settles a civil lawsuit out of court.

Feb. 12 – Edvard Munch's painting *The Scream* is stolen from a museum in Oslo.

PISCES
Your Personal Planets

YOUR LOVE POTENTIAL
Venus in Pisces, Feb. 18, 21:22 - Mar. 08, 14:27
Venus in Aries, Mar. 08, 14:28 - Mar. 20, 20:27

YOUR DRIVE AND AMBITION
Mars in Aquarius, Feb. 18, 21:22 - Mar. 07, 11:00
Mars in Pisces, Mar. 07, 11:01 - Mar. 20, 20:27

YOUR LUCK MAGNETISM
Jupiter in Scorpio, Feb. 18, 21:22 - Mar. 20, 20:27

World Events

Feb. 28 – NATO fires its first shots over Bosnia.
Mar. 12 – The Church of England ordains thirty-three women priests.

A woman priest waits to be ordained into the Church of England

ARIES
Your Personal Planets

YOUR LOVE POTENTIAL
Venus in Aries, Mar. 20, 20:28 - Apr. 01, 19:19
Venus in Taurus, Apr. 01, 19:20 - Apr. 20, 7:35

YOUR DRIVE AND AMBITION
Mars in Pisces, Mar. 20, 20:28 - Apr. 14, 18:01
Mars in Aries, Apr. 14, 18:02 - Apr. 20, 7:35

YOUR LUCK MAGNETISM
Jupiter in Scorpio, Mar. 20, 20:28 - Apr. 20, 7:35

World Events

Apr. 5 – American rock star Kurt Cobain, of the group Nirvana, commits suicide.
Apr. 7 – Rwanda descends into civil war.

PISCES
From February 18, 21:22 through March 20, 20:27

The Caring Specialist

Born during 1994, Pisces, you entered the world just as it was discovered that taking antibiotics too often would lessen their helpful effects, a revelation that would change the face of medicine forever. Your sign, under the rulership of sensitizing Neptune, is often associated with the concept of vulnerability, and with what's hidden or unseen, including secrets of all kinds.

As a result, since many diseases work behind the scenes, going virtually undetected until they cause a problem, they are also under the rulership of Neptune. But your sign's affiliation with medicine means you've been gifted with the ability to soothe and cure and that quality will probably show itself over and again through your life in many ways. The power of your compassionate touch alone is magical and healing, in fact, but your intuitive understanding of what's wrong and hidden makes you an extraordinary healer. Your counseling skills are also quite amazing, making you an understanding confidante and a wise advisor.

The astrology behind Pisces of 1994 further describes your capacity to find solutions in many departments. First off, you were given three planets in your own sign, reinforcing your kindness and empathy. But the influence of cerebral Mercury and Mars, the Great Initiator, both of them in dazzling Aquarius, lend you the ingenuity and brilliance necessary to put that compassion to use to help in solid, realistic ways. In addition, the presence of expansive Jupiter in shrewd Scorpio gives you the ability to dig and to come up with answers.

In relationships, the other water signs will likely prove invaluable to you, both for the emotions you share and their equal concern with helping others. The earth signs, Taureans, Virgos, and Capricorns, will also prove worthy allies and hard working co-workers.

Your challenges are to learn to combine your substantial intellect with your caring heart and tenderness. Your gift is your knack for bonding easily with others, so much so that they're often willing to reveal their deepest, darkest secrets, their fears, and their hopes.

ARIES
From March 20, 20:28 through April 20, 7:35

The Intuitive Warrior

Born during 1994, Aries, you arrived just as the debate over cigarette smoking reached a new peak in the United States. Although smoking was quite accepted in other parts of the world, a battle had been waged in America and the lines were clearly drawn. Smokers were heavily segregated, often restricted to indulging their habit in sealed, separately ventilated rooms or, in some cases, out of doors, which seemed to satisfy both sides, however grudgingly. But during the time of your arrival, the uneasy truce between smokers and non-smokers was crumbling. The state of California would lead the campaign by making it illegal to smoke in any public facility including cocktail lounges, once famous for their smoky atmospheres.

This battle waged appropriately over "fire" reflects your sign's reputation for confrontation, but the astrology of your planetary debut points to an even more assertive personality than that of many of your Aries cousins born in other years. Four planets passed through your sign this month, including your own fiery planet, Mars, the ancient god of war.

It's easy to see that making your point and fighting non-stop for what you believe in would serve to make you a force to be reckoned with throughout your life. In fact, when you firmly believe in something, there's literally no way you'll stop doing battle for it—until you've won, that is. Needless to say, this makes you someone everyone wants on the team, but you may need to be careful not to alienate others without meaning to simply because the force of your personality can be quite intimidating.

When it comes time to settle down and have a committed relationship, you'll definitely need to find someone with as much fire, independence, and determination as yourself, otherwise you'll likely become bored. The other fire signs, Sagittarians and Leos, would make fine choices, as would freedom-loving, rebellious Aquarians.

Your challenge is to find positive outlets for your energy and your warrior-like nature. Your gift is your keen intuition, which will help you perfect the skills of strategy. If you can put the brakes on with a little tact and diplomacy when needed, you will truly be a force to be reckoned with.

➤ Read about your Chinese Astrological sign on page 838. ➤ Read about your Personal Planets on page 826. ➤ Read about your personal Mystical Card on page 856.

TAURUS

From April 20, 7:36 through May 21, 6:47

The Privacy Lover

Born during 1994, Taurus, you arrived just as news of the death of Jacqueline Kennedy Onassis made headlines worldwide. The elegant former First Lady of the United States passed away just as she had lived, privately and quietly, with her family and long-time partner by her side. Often described by the press who adored her as an enigma, this lovely, refined woman had achieved a kind of icon status. She rarely granted interviews and made public appearances only when they would benefit one of her favorite causes. In short, like a fine work of art, she was considered by many of her admirers to be rare and beautiful but too valuable and delicate to ever dare to touch.

The dignity of both the life and the passing of the former "Queen of Camelot" beautifully reflected several qualities your sign is famous for, including grace under pressure, elegance, and integrity. But her clean, natural beauty, her appreciation for silence, and her insistence on absolute privacy are also well represented by the astrology of your arrival. Two planets in intensely private Scorpio point to the similarity you share with Jackie O, as she was dubbed by many, when it comes to leading your life out of the spotlight. Two more in your own sign, however, as well as fiery Mars in assertive, noticeable Aries, show that your passion for your own causes and your substantial personal magnetism may make that hard to do.

In fact, you may often find yourself in the spotlight, both for personal and professional reasons. The quiet power you naturally exude may put you on the receiving end of a veritable parade of admirers, but once you're happily attached, you'll probably be quite skilled at fending off unwanted attention.

Speaking of partners, your love of solitude and beauty may make aesthetically inclined Pisceans good choices, along with others of your own sign. Earthy Virgos and Capricorns could also prove worthwhile, devoted companions.

Your challenge is to enjoy your solitude, but never to become reclusive. Your gift is your ability to establish bonds with others that will last a lifetime.

GEMINI

From May 21, 6:48 through June 21, 14:47

The Honorable Achiever

Your sign's cerebral abilities made international news during the time of your arrival, 1994 Gemini. Appropriately, the subject was education. In a study released in the month of your birth, it was found that college students all over the world were increasingly concerned with achieving good grades—something more than one parent of a college freshman was delighted to hear.

Another interesting factor also surfaced during that time, however, one that would point to the insistence of Geminis born during your year in particular to receive only what they've earned, nothing more, and nothing less. Oddly enough, students at Stanford University made headlines by fighting for the right to receive an "F," something Stanford's esteemed faculty actually had to vote to restore. The high principles, integrity, and determination to honestly succeed that were reflected in this unusual movement would possibly become part of your character. In fact, at a very early age, you may have displayed signs of the development of these qualities.

Your sign's quick-witted, often playfully mischievous side was tempered by several planets in water signs, famous for their skill at tuning in to the feelings of others. In addition, Mars, the planetary purveyor of initiative, was in quietly focused Taurus, giving you the ability to channel your energies into only the most worthwhile of projects. As such, you likely won't be prone to scattering your energies, preferring instead to concentrate on just one thing at a time until it's completed, perfected, or memorized.

In relationships, you'd do well to seek out the company of the earth signs: Virgos, Capricorns, and most especially fixed, devoted Taureans. In friendships and professional relationships, however, look to Sagittarians and Aquarians for the inspiration you'll need to reach your goals.

Your challenge is to let your innate integrity lead you, never giving in to the temptation of an easy win, especially if winning involves being less than honest. Your gift is your ability to concentrate in even the most distracting environments.

➤ Read about your Chinese Astrological sign on page 838. ➤ Read about your Personal Planets on page 826. ➤ Read about your personal Mystical Card on page 856.

TAURUS
Your Personal Planets

YOUR LOVE POTENTIAL
Venus in Taurus, Apr. 20, 7:36 - Apr. 26, 6:23
Venus in Gemini, Apr. 26, 6:24 - May 21, 1:25
Venus in Cancer, May 21, 1:26 - May 21, 6:48

YOUR DRIVE AND AMBITION
Mars in Aries, Apr. 20, 7:36 - May 21, 6:48

YOUR LUCK MAGNETISM
Jupiter in Scorpio, Apr. 20, 7:36 - May 21, 6:48

World Events

Apr. 26 – The top quark, the missing link of the atom and one of the building blocks of matter, is discovered by physicists after a twenty-year search.

Apr. 29 – South Africa holds its first interracial national election and Nelson Mandela is elected President.

Nelson Mandela, President of South Africa

GEMINI
Your Personal Planets

YOUR LOVE POTENTIAL
Venus in Cancer, May 21, 6:49 - June 15, 7:22
Venus in Leo, June 15, 7:23 - June 21, 14:47

YOUR DRIVE AND AMBITION
Mars in Aries, May 21, 6:49 - May 23, 22:36
Mars in Taurus, May 23, 22:37 - June 21, 14:47

YOUR LUCK MAGNETISM
Jupiter in Scorpio, May 21, 6:49 - June 21, 14:47

World Events

May 23 – Roman Herzog is elected President of Germany.

June 15 – Full diplomatic relations are resumed between The Vatican and Israel.

1994

CANCER
Your Personal Planets

YOUR LOVE POTENTIAL
Venus in Leo, June 21, 14:48 - July 11, 6:32
Venus in Virgo, July 11, 6:33 - July 23, 1:40

YOUR DRIVE AND AMBITION
Mars in Taurus, June 21, 14:48 - July 03, 22:29
Mars in Gemini, July 03, 22:30 - July 23, 1:40

YOUR LUCK MAGNETISM
Jupiter in Scorpio, June 21, 14:48 - July 23, 1:40

World Events

July 1 – PLO-leader Yasser Arafat returns to Gaza after twenty-seven years.

July 22 – Comet *Shoemaker-Levy 9* impacts with the planet Jupiter.

Yasser Arafat after crossing the border from Egypt to Gaza

LEO
Your Personal Planets

YOUR LOVE POTENTIAL
Venus in Virgo, July 23, 1:41 - Aug. 07, 14:35
Venus in Libra, Aug. 07, 14:36 - Aug. 23, 8:43

YOUR DRIVE AND AMBITION
Mars in Gemini, July 23, 1:41 - Aug. 16, 19:14
Mars in Cancer, Aug. 16, 19:15 - Aug. 23, 8:43

YOUR LUCK MAGNETISM
Jupiter in Scorpio, July 23, 1:41 - Aug. 23, 8:43

World Events

Aug. 1 – The Rolling Stones begin their "Voodoo Lounge" world tour.

Aug. 15 – The world's most wanted terrorist, the man known as Carlos the Jackal, is captured in Khartoum, Sudan.

CANCER
From June 21, 14:48 through July 23, 1:40

The Home-Loving Adventurer

As you entered the world in 1994, Cancer, steps were being taken to leave it, but not for a simple walk on the Moon, a feat already accomplished at that time by six previous teams of astronauts and cosmonauts. This time out, the goal of an international team of scientists was to reach Mars and to see whether the "Red Planet" might be capable of sustaining human life—of being a new home, in the event that Earth someday was no longer habitable.

It may seem a bit odd that a mission to leave Earth was being planned at this time, given your famous love of home and family. But the foresight, advanced thinking, and concern for the future this project necessarily entailed, traits you no doubt possess, were all well described by the astrology of your birth in 1994. Jupiter, the planet of higher understanding, was in deep, intense Scorpio, the sign of the detective, researcher, and analyst. This alone points to a highly inquisitive nature, but fiery Mars in curious Gemini also contributed its energy. In short, although you were given no less love for domesticity than other Cancerians, your curiosity and adventurousness may make it tough for you to stay put for long.

As such, you'll ptobably do more traveling than the average Cancer, allowing you to make contact with all kinds of interesting and unusual individuals, many of whom will remain in your life forever. But after the adventure is through, you'll always want a solid home base to return to, and you'll doubtless find an innovative way to somehow balance your love of freedom and experience with your sign's innate need for security.

In relationships, you are likely to find the air signs to be your favorite companions. You may enjoy cerebral Geminis and genius-like Aquarians in particular, but settling down with a partner-oriented Libran could be wise, since this sign's devotion is famous. For friendships and professional success, look to shrewd Scorpios and fiery Leos.

Your gift is your perpetual hunger for knowledge and new experiences. Your challenge is to maintain a home and family even as you pursue your dreams.

LEO
From July 23, 1:41 through August 23, 8:43

The Expert Mediator

Born during 1994, Leo, you arrived as the world's hopes for global peace were raised by a promising sight. As viewers gathered around their televisions, Jordan's King Hussein and Israel's Prime Minister Rabin shook hands on the lawn of the White House, warmly pledging an end to war and the beginning of an era of cooperation. This display of the intention to compromise, appropriately arranged by a man born under your own sign, U.S. President Bill Clinton, would spread an encouraging message to far more than just the citizens of the two nations involved. In fact, it seemed to be the answer to a prayer the world had shared for decades that the continuing violence in the Middle East might come to an end.

Despite the fact that this would be only one of many such meetings and that peace was not yet to be a reality in that region, this powerful meeting of the minds will hopefully one day become known as the first step taken toward peace, something those of you born during this year are keenly interested in seeing. In fact, the even balance of astrological energies you were given, 1994 Leo, make you quite Libran in many ways. Libra is the sign of harmony and balance, known for its expertise at gently tapping the scales of any situation back toward equilibrium, qualities you may share.

This knack for achieving equality likely shows in your ability to help warring parties resolve their differences peaceably. You might do well to pursue a career that allows you to negotiate, mediate, or bargain. Regardless of the work you do, however, you'll probably be the person everyone will come to when a happy medium is needed. Your personal relationships will also reflect this innate skill, possibly from an early age.

In relationships, you would do well to keep company with Librans, since your energy is so similar to their own, but Sagittarians and Pisceans will also appeal to you.

Your gift is your instinctive knowledge of just what it would take for any adversaries to reach a common ground. Your challenge is never to become involved in disputes that don't directly concern you.

➤ Read about your Chinese Astrological sign on page 838. ➤ Read about your Personal Planets on page 826. ➤ Read about your personal Mystical Card on page 856.

VIRGO

From August 23, 8:44 through September 23, 6:18

The Disciplined Preventer

Born during 1994, Virgo, you arrived into a time that would serve to reinforce several qualities your sign is here to perfect, among them self discipline, research ability, and a knack for trouble-shooting. Doctors and the public, long concerned over the growing resistance of many infectious diseases to prescribed antibiotics, could finally breathe a sigh of relief. Rather than giving up, drug companies all over the world fought back against resistant contagion. Pharmaceutical researchers employed several new strategies that they hoped would put medicine back in the battle and it was announced this month that their efforts were proving quite successful.

This determination to triumph over disease and illness, as well as the meticulous, careful research it took to create new vaccines and remedies beautifully shows your sign's affinity with health, details, and fixing what's broken.

Cerebral Mercury held court in your painstaking, fastidious sign, giving you the ability to weigh every detail of a project and the understanding of just how much influence each of those details would have over the final outcome. This makes you an excellent trouble-shooter, able to see potential problems well before they surface and well before they can wreak havoc on the big picture. Far-sighted Jupiter in shrewd Scorpio also aided you for this is a sign-planet combination that promises depth, strong perceptive ability, and the capacity to foresee difficulties before they materialize. As such, you may find work in the health fields quite rewarding, but no matter what path you choose you'll be dutiful, diligent, and devoted.

In relationships, you may be instinctively drawn to other Virgos, whose attention to detail and discriminating eye will make them feel like kindred spirits. But the other earth signs, Capricorns and Taureans, also hold the capacity for the stable, grounded partnership that you'll likely find essential.

Your challenge is to allow yourself to give up when it's absolutely impossible or pointless to pursue a project. Your gift is the ability to know the difference.

LIBRA

From September 23, 6:19 through October 23, 15:35

The Intuitive Combatant

Born during 1994, Libra, you inherited a double-dose of your sign's knack for restoring balance to unbalanced situations and its drive to help anyone whose physical challenges or "imbalances" seem to make achieving their dreams impossible. You were born within days of the Miss America pageant. This winner was different from the ones that had walked the runway in prior years. Miss Alabama, Heather Whitestone, was completely deaf in one ear and had only five percent hearing in the other. Her victory in the seventy-fourth annual Miss America Pageant, in mid-September, 1994, gave hope to physically challenged individuals all over the world, allowing them to see that anything was indeed possible as long as they were willing to dare.

The courage, hard work, and spirit Ms. Whitestone had shown, simply by virtue of entering the contest, perfectly exemplified several qualities that Librans born in 1994 tend to possess. Jupiter, the planet that expands the qualities of the sign he inhabits in fixed, focused, never-say-die Scorpio, describes your determination. In addition, serious, disciplined Saturn, the ruler of the concept of mastery, was in intuitive Pisces, giving you keen antennae, capable of sensing problems well before they surface. In short, you're equal parts cerebral and psychically sensitive.

This capacity just to know without having access to any factual evidence shows the potency of your insight and would make you a shrewd businessperson, a gifted counselor, or an instinctive healer. But no matter which profession you choose to follow your dedication to doing it right will probably be unparalleled.

In relationships, you would do well to seek out the company of other Librans, Aquarians, or Geminis, all of whom are of the air element and just as cerebrally tuned in as yourself. In addition, the water signs, Cancerians, Scorpios, and Pisceans, will be able to back up your intuition and help you to develop your psychic awareness.

Your challenge is to listen to the voice of your subconscious. Your gift is your unwavering determination to reach your goals no matter how difficult.

VIRGO
Your Personal Planets

YOUR LOVE POTENTIAL
Venus in Libra, Aug. 23, 8:44 - Sept. 07, 17:11
Venus in Scorpio, Sept. 07, 17:12 - Sept. 23, 6:18

YOUR DRIVE AND AMBITION
Mars in Cancer, Aug. 23, 8:44 - Sept. 23, 6:18

YOUR LUCK MAGNETISM
Jupiter in Scorpio, Aug. 23, 8:44 - Sept. 23, 6:18

World Events

Aug. 31 – A Pentium computer beats the world chess champion Garry Kasparov.

Sept. 8 – The last Allied soldiers bid farewell to Berlin after spending fifty years guarding the city.

Gary Kasparov plays chess against a computer

LIBRA
Your Personal Planets

YOUR LOVE POTENTIAL
Venus in Scorpio, Sept. 23, 6:19 - Oct. 23, 15:35

YOUR DRIVE AND AMBITION
Mars in Cancer, Sept. 23, 6:19 - Oct. 04, 15:47
Mars in Leo, Oct. 04, 15:48 - Oct. 23, 15:35

YOUR LUCK MAGNETISM
Jupiter in Scorpio, Sept. 23, 6:19 - Oct. 23, 15:35

World Events

Oct. 14 – The Nobel Peace Prize is awarded to Yasser Arafat, Yitzhak Rabin, and Shimon Peres.

Oct. 14 – The space probe *Magellan* burns up in the atmosphere around Venus.

➤ Read about your Chinese Astrological sign on page 838. ➤ Read about your Personal Planets on page 826. ➤ Read about your personal Mystical Card on page 856.

1994

SCORPIO
Your Personal Planets

YOUR LOVE POTENTIAL
Venus in Scorpio, Oct. 23, 15:36 - Nov. 22, 13:05

YOUR DRIVE AND AMBITION
Mars in Leo, Oct. 23, 15:36 - Nov. 22, 13:05

YOUR LUCK MAGNETISM
Jupiter in Scorpio, Oct. 23, 15:36 - Nov. 22, 13:05

World Events

Nov. 10 - Chandrika Kumaratunga is elected President of Sri Lanka.

Nov. 11 - Bill Gates buys Leonardo da Vinci's *Codex* for $30,800,000.

Chechnyan armed women

SAGITTARIUS
Your Personal Planets

YOUR LOVE POTENTIAL
Venus in Scorpio, Nov. 22, 13:06 - Dec. 22, 2:22

YOUR DRIVE AND AMBITION
Mars in Leo, Nov. 22, 13:06 - Dec. 12, 11:31
Mars in Virgo, Dec. 12, 11:32 - Dec. 22, 2:22

YOUR LUCK MAGNETISM
Jupiter in Scorpio, Nov. 22, 13:06 - Dec. 09, 10:53
Jupiter in Sagittarius, Dec. 09, 10:54 - Dec. 22, 2:22

World Events

Dec. 3 - Three-times Tour de France winner Greg LeMond announces his retirement from the sport.

Dec. 11 - Russian forces enter Chechnya.

SCORPIO
From October 23, 15:36 through November 22, 13:05

The Secretive Defender

Born during 1994, Scorpio, you arrived just as your sign's love of secrecy was given a whole new slant. In fact, the need for your discretion and love of privacy was beautifully exemplified by one event in particular. Just that month, a kiss-and-tell book about Britain's Princess Diana was released, an unauthorized look at the princess's personal life that many found offensive, intrusive, and totally inappropriate.

Former army Major James Hewitt of Britain had told the story of his alleged relationship with Diana to Anna Pasternak, who penned a book entitled *Princess in Love*. Described as "absolute rubbish," "sleazy," and "grubby and worthless" by spokespersons for Buckingham Palace, the book became subsequently famous not for its content but for its intent: to make money from prostituting the personal life of someone who was as intensely private as your sign is known to be.

The astrological factors of your birth-time alluded to your innate distaste for exposés as well as your reluctance to discuss your personal affairs with anyone you deem untrustworthy. Four planets in your own sign, long known for its connection to secrets, mysteries, and concealment, reinforced your fierce defense of the right to carry on your life as you see fit without the intrusion of outside parties. Loving Venus, the ruler of relationships, was posited in your deeply confidential sign, giving you the need to maintain the sanctity of your private life at all costs. In addition, assertive Mars in fiery Leo bestowed the ability to protect yourself and your dear ones with as much fury as that of a lioness protecting her cubs.

In partnerships, you'll probably seek others as ardently tight-lipped as you are, especially when it comes to the intimate details of your relationship. This means that other Scorpios, as well as Cancerians and Pisceans, will always be your best bets.

Your challenge is never to avoid the spotlight when professional appreciation is the reason for it. Your gift is to carry on your business quietly and confidently with an eye toward keeping intimate details intimate.

SAGITTARIUS
From November 22, 13:06 through December 22, 2:22

The Perpetual Optimist

As you entered the world in 1994, Sagittarius, the Beatles were once again making international news, this time not for their haircuts but for their attitudes. A new two-CD set of the "Fab Four's" live British radio performances culled from recordings made on Britain's BBC had been released. Some of these recordings, made years before the group had even released their first single, contained something even more valuable to Beatles fans than the music itself: actual excerpts of dialogue. The fun and high spirits displayed by the four young men on the recording beautifully demonstrate your sign's capacity to enjoy each and every moment of life as well as the sense of humor you're famous for.

The astrology of your birth-time points to a keen wit, a strong optimistic streak, and an extremely generous heart. Cerebral Mercury, the planet of communication, was posited in your own sign, very close to the Sun. This pair gives you the ability to waltz into any social situation with confidence, amaze the masses with your stories and jokes, and leave with even more friends than you had when you arrived. If you were born after December 10, you were also given a rare gift: your planet, benevolent Jupiter, moved into your sign, a "costume-change" that planet makes only once every twelve years.

As if all this weren't enough to make you a welcome addition to any group, you also have a flair for the dramatic in your astrological tool-kit. Fiery Mars, the planet that describes our capacity for action, wore entertaining Leo, the sign of the performer. In all, your presence at any gathering, large or small, turns the atmosphere of the event into a celebration of life.

When it comes time to choose a partner, you'll likely choose one of the other fire signs, Leos or Ariens, or someone born under your own sign. These passionate folks will share your love of life, your sense of adventure, and your sparkling sense of humor.

Your challenge is to get serious when the situation calls for it. Your gift is your ability to bring a smile to anyone, no matter how dire his or her circumstances seem.

➤ Read about your Chinese Astrological sign on page 838. ➤ Read about your Personal Planets on page 826. ➤ Read about your personal Mystical Card on page 856.

CAPRICORN

From December 22, 2:23 through December 31, 23:59

The Esteemed Philosopher

During the time of your birth, December Capricorn, Pope John Paul II was named as *Time* magazine's "Man of the Year." Long known for his morality, integrity, and unwavering insistence that Roman Catholics adhere strictly to the church's dogma, this fixed, focused man born Karol Wojtyla in Wadowice, Poland had been the head of the Roman Catholic Church for the past sixteen years. He was the first Pole ever to assume that revered office, and the first Pope ever to receive the annual award. Writer Paul Gray penned perhaps the most apt description of the Pope's global influence in that issue, the last of 1994. Gray wrote, "His appearances generate an electricity unmatched by anyone else on earth;" and "When he talks, it is not only to his flock of nearly a billion; he expects the entire world to listen." People did and they still do.

Just as this man was honored for his piety as well as his brilliance and determination to maintain old traditions in modern times, your arrival shows an equally fixed resolve. Three planets in Scorpio, famous for depth and intensity, gave you the conviction and emotional tenacity necessary to see all your projects through to the very end. Five planets in solid earth signs also gave you a strong capacity for leadership and a quiet, yet powerful wisdom. As such, you're probably called on often by loved ones to advise, negotiate for, or defend them and it's easy to see that you won't refuse.

Along with the intelligence your birth-time shows, you were given a sense of humor and a rather philosophical bent. Jupiter, the planet of higher understanding, was happily posited in its own sign, Sagittarius, an indication of confidence and the ability to see the big picture.

When it comes to a life partner, the other earth signs, Virgos and Taureans, might make good choices for you. No matter who you commit yourself to, you'll undoubtedly prove a faithful and devoted mate.

Your challenge is to avoid the tendency to become self-righteous. Remember: others have as much right to their beliefs as you do. Your gift is your quiet power.

CAPRICORN
Your Personal Planets

YOUR LOVE POTENTIAL
Venus in Scorpio, Dec. 22, 2:23 - Dec. 31, 23:59

YOUR DRIVE AND AMBITION
Mars in Virgo, Dec. 22, 2:23 - Dec. 31, 23:59

YOUR LUCK MAGNETISM
Jupiter in Sagittarius, Dec. 22, 2:23 - Dec. 31, 23:59

World Events

Dec. 31 – Austria, Finland, and Sweden join the European Union, bringing its membership total to fifteen.

Dec. 31 – The World Organization replaces the General Agreement on Tariffs and Trades (GATT).

Oprah Winfrey
Born January 29, 1954

OPRAH WINFREY
Aquarius

Oprah Winfrey is the media mogul who has been on the air almost constantly for well over two decades. Despite a childhood marred by emotional pain and sexual abuse, she once confessed to Barbara Walters in an interview that she always knew she was "born for greatness."

As an Aquarius, the sign of friendship, Oprah knows how to reach out and connect with all sorts of people. Her Sun, the planet of identity, is joined in her house of career by Venus and Mercury, the planets of affection and communications, respectively. When Oprah started her book club, America started reading again and many unknown authors got the platform they needed. In her house of work we find Saturn, the planet of striving and responsibility, as well as Neptune, the planet of film. In addition, Uranus, the planet of television, is in her house of communication. Her career as a talk-show host and actress is perfect for her!

Oprah is more than just a friendly face on TV. Her determined personality and drive to go straight to the top is defined by dynamic contacts to her Sun from both Pluto, the planet of intensity, and Mars, the planet of action. That explains her interest in all forms of self-help programs, psychological awareness, and anything geared to help people take charge of and improve their lives.

Oprah's Moon, the planet of emotions, is in her house of partnerships, and perhaps that's why she seems like everyone's best pal. Although she has a decade-long relationship, so far she has never chosen to marry. A contact from expansive Jupiter, prominently placed, demands freedom and independence. Closeness without too much pressure is perfect for her.

The Moon can also reflect domestic issues and food. In Oprah's case, her Moon receives a contact from Jupiter as well as Venus, the planet of pleasure, so her well-documented struggle with weight makes a lot of sense. It is her ability to confront her personal obstacles on her TV talk show that has helped her viewers handle their own serious life issues and has made her show a success.

➤ Read Josephine Baker's Star Profile on page 217. ➤ Read Princess Diana's Star Profile on page 689.

1995

Shifting Forces: Mars and Pluto

Mars and Pluto squared off with each other in 1995, marking major changes in the world. Mars, the planet of energy and aggression, was in a strident "square" angle to Pluto, the planet of intense and often suppressed explosive force, through the end of May. As suggested by this relationship, events during that time were often cataclysmic. Most outstanding among them was January's massive earthquake in densely populated Kobe, Japan, which killed around 5,000. At the same time, in the U.S., Newt Gingrich became Speaker of the House and Conservative spokesman. His outspokenness epitomized the Mars persona. In addition, television audiences watched the O.J. Simpson murder trial, which focused on aggression—Mars—resulting in death—Pluto. Both U.S. events had originally been set in motion in late 1994, when Mars and Pluto first challenged each other. These planets were again in the limelight in April, when the tragic Oklahoma City bombing was carried out by enraged white supremacists.

However, in other ways the year was full of opportunity. Economies were booming around the world and it seemed a more peaceful place as Israel stopped patrolling the West Bank while freeing hundreds of Palestinian prisoners. These events were tied to Saturn's pleasant contact with Neptune. Saturn is associated with sustaining, sobering forces, while Neptune with ideals, imagination and the arts. Business flourished under this connection and people sought entertainment from more serious sources. Movies, such as *Dead Man Walking*, had a more thoughtful tinge.

Israeli Prime Minister Yitzhak Rabin is assassinated

Victims of the nerve gas attack on the Tokyo subway

The aftermath of the Federal Building bombing in Oklahoma City

FENG SHUI

Throughout the 1990s Westerners developed a growing interest in the ancient Chinese practice of harmonious design called feng shui. In 1995, Donald Trump employed a feng shui specialist to inspect a building site before beginning construction after his Hong Kong partners insisted. In Hong Kong, business tycoons are known to regularly consult feng shui masters in the course of business. Several Western companies with Hong Kong subsidiaries implemented feng shui principles as well, including Citibank, N.M. Rothschild, Shell, and Sime Darby.

PEACE—AND EXPLOSIVE ANGER

U.S. President Clinton masterminded another Arab-Israeli agreement, this time to give self-determination to Palestinians on the West Bank of the River Jordan. Bosnian Serbs captured the Muslim enclave of Srebrenica. At least 5,000 people were killed in a quake in Kobe, Japan. Rogue trader Nick Leeson, who bankrupted Barings Bank through risky deals, was sentenced to over six years' imprisonment for fraud. In Japan, the Supreme Truth religious sect killed and injured around 5,000 people by releasing the toxic gas Sarin in the Tokyo underground. A department store in Seoul, Korea collapsed, killing sixty-three, injuring 850. White supremacist Timothy McVeigh bombed a federal building in Oklahoma City, killing 168. The British Antarctic Survey reported that the hole in Earth's ozone layer was widening. France exploded a nuclear bomb at the Pacific atoll of Mururoa. Israeli Prime Minister Rabin was assassinated by a Jewish extremist. After a year-long televised trial, O.J. Simpson was found not guilty of murder. Jo Salter became the first woman bomber pilot in Britain's Royal Air Force. Film stars Ginger Rogers and Lana Turner died.

➤ Read Mother Teresa's Star Profile on page 777.

CAPRICORN

From January 01, 0:00 through January 20, 12:59

The Technological Wizard

Born during 1995, Capricorn, you arrived as the digital satellite system was gaining substantial popularity. This technological innovation surpassed even the wonders of cable television, which were substantial for that time, by making consumers an offer they couldn't refuse: digital perfection on literally hundreds of channels. The dishes themselves were sleeker and more attractively designed than their larger, yard-sized predecessors, yet these relatively tiny structures guaranteed laser disc quality pictures and compact disc quality sound. In short, this product was a dream come true for admitted television addicts, occasional viewers, and video rental aficionados alike.

The very act of mainstreaming and marketing this device, previously considered strictly for military and corporate use, showed the world the value of two qualities your birth in 1995 instilled in you: a capacity for genius and a strong dose of business sense. This invaluable blend of energies will undoubtedly serve you well, regardless of the career path you choose, enabling you to grasp the future.

You are gifted in other ways as well. The astrology of your birth-time points to a substantial and varied bag of talents. You are the proud owner of a tight bundle of planets in several different signs—an indication that you'll be a specialist at whatever profession you choose. You're also quite capable of leading or following, depending on what's necessary, making you the perfect addition to any staff and a wonderful playmate as well.

And speaking of playmates, when it comes time for you to choose one for life, you may be surprised to find that he or she isn't one of the earth signs as many Sun sign books will suggest. Your strongly cerebral nature means that you'll likely be far more comfortable in the company of the air signs, Librans, Geminis, and especially Aquarians. A light-hearted Sagittarian may also steal your heart.

Your gift is your capability to perform well in all situations, even the most stressful. Your challenge is to choose a career that will allow you to use all your talents.

AQUARIUS

From January 20, 13:00 through February 19, 3:10

The Stubborn Humanitarian

Born during 1995, Aquarius, you arrived in the same month as *Shadows of the Mind: A Search for the Missing Science of Consciousness* by Roger Penrose was published. The focus of this book is the theory that the human mind does not function like a computer program and that there can be no electronic substitute for the mind. Aquarius is one of the human signs of the zodiac, having a glyph that depicts the figure of a water-bearer. Your sign also has a strong connection with the mind and modern technology. In Penrose's book, humanity is superior to technology, a theory you would agree with.

Two of the most famous Aquarian qualities are intellectual curiosity and objectivity. The subject of this book will doubtless be one that you will happily debate in later years.

The release of this eye-opening study is described aptly by the astrological qualities of the time—factors you also inherited. Communicative Mercury was in your unbiased, humanistic sign and Jupiter, the king of the gods himself and the planet that rules incorporation rather than segregation, was in open-minded Sagittarius. In short, it's next to impossible for you to hold a grudge against anyone or anything—unless a dear one's safety and security are threatened. In that case, your Mars, in lavish, dramatic Leo, will literally leap to the defense via a very public display, most likely, regardless of where you happen to be when your fire erupts.

While the fire and passion you have for who and what you hold dear may be intimidating to some, anyone worthy of your companionship long-term will appreciate it and respect your strong ideals as well. Just be sure to keep your mind open by enjoying the company of a variety of individuals, not just those who share and support your beliefs.

In partnerships, you may be drawn to other Aquarians, Librans, or Geminis, but fiery, fun-loving Sagittarians will probably also find a place in your heart.

Your challenge is to respect the opinions of others, never imposing your own upon them. Your gift is your capacity to learn something from everyone you meet.

➤ Read about your Chinese Astrological sign on page 838. ➤ Read about your Personal Planets on page 826. ➤ Read about your personal Mystical Card on page 856.

1995

CAPRICORN
Your Personal Planets

YOUR LOVE POTENTIAL
Venus in Scorpio, Jan. 01, 0:00 - Jan. 07, 12:06
Venus in Sagittarius, Jan. 07, 12:07 - Jan. 20, 12:59

YOUR DRIVE AND AMBITION
Mars in Virgo, Jan. 01, 0:00 - Jan. 20, 12:59

YOUR LUCK MAGNETISM
Jupiter in Sagittarius, Jan. 01, 0:00 - Jan. 20, 12:59

World Events

Jan. 1 – A four-month ceasefire goes into effect in Bosnia.

Jan. 17 – An earthquake hits Japan, causing widespread damage and loss of life.

A lone farm flooded by the river Waal in the Netherlands

AQUARIUS
Your Personal Planets

YOUR LOVE POTENTIAL
Venus in Sagittarius, Jan. 20, 13:00 - Feb. 04, 20:11
Venus in Capricorn, Feb. 04, 20:12 - Feb. 19, 3:10

YOUR DRIVE AND AMBITION
Mars in Virgo, Jan. 20, 13:00 - Jan. 22, 23:47
Mars in Leo, Jan. 22, 23:48 - Feb. 19, 3:10

YOUR LUCK MAGNETISM
Jupiter in Sagittarius, Jan. 20, 13:00 - Feb. 19, 3:10

World Events

Feb. 7 – Josef Olensky becomes Prime Minister of Poland.

Feb. 2 – A mass evacuation from eastern and central regions of the Netherlands is carried out due to a flood scare.

1995

PISCES
Your Personal Planets

YOUR LOVE POTENTIAL
Venus in Capricorn, Feb. 19, 3:11 - Mar. 02, 22:10
Venus in Aquarius, Mar. 02, 22:11 - Mar. 21, 2:13

YOUR DRIVE AND AMBITION
Mars in Leo, Feb. 19, 3:11 - Mar. 21, 2:13

YOUR LUCK MAGNETISM
Jupiter in Sagittarius, Feb. 19, 3:11 - Mar. 21, 2:13

World Events

Mar. 7 - New York becomes the 38th state to have the death penalty.

Mar. 17 - Sinn Fein leader Gerry Adams visits the White House.

British Prime Minister John Major with President Bill Clinton

ARIES
Your Personal Planets

YOUR LOVE POTENTIAL
Venus in Aquarius, Mar. 21, 2:14 - Mar. 28, 5:09
Venus in Pisces, Mar. 28, 5:10 - Apr. 20, 13:21

YOUR DRIVE AND AMBITION
Mars in Leo, Mar. 21, 2:14 - Apr. 20, 13:21

YOUR LUCK MAGNETISM
Jupiter in Sagittarius, Mar. 21, 2:14 - Apr. 20, 13:21

World Events

Apr. 4 - John Major and Bill Clinton affirm old ties as the two men express agreement on the Irish question.

Apr. 19 - Scores are killed as a terrorist's car bomb blows up the block-long Oklahoma City federal building.

PISCES
From February 19, 3:11 through March 21, 2:13

The Mystery Solver

Born during 1995, Pisces, you arrived just as two real-life murder mysteries made headlines throughout the world. First off, more than a year after her death, friends and employees of the Beverly Hills billionaire Doris Duke filed a suit in an attempt to prove that she had not died of natural causes as her death certificate read, but rather that she had been murdered. They alleged that this eccentric woman, whose two pet camels, "Baby" and "Princess," were quite literally given the run of her thirty-room mansion, had been drugged to death and the accusers pointed their fingers, believe it or not, at her butler of eight years, Bernard Lafferty.

This Agatha Christie-like tale strongly reflects your sign's love of intrigue, as does a second story that captured the imagination of the world at the time. Ramzi Ahmed Youssef, the alleged mastermind of the World Trade Center bombing in 1993, was captured and brought to trial. He was eventually found guilty but even then Youssef refused to reveal the names of those for whom he had been working.

Despite the tragic quality of both events, the questions surrounding them reflect your Sun sign's affinity for secrets and mysteries. Fortunately, the astrological influences of your birth in 1995 gave you the shrewdness necessary to solve these puzzles—in fact, to solve puzzles and riddles of all kinds. You're the proud owner of several planets in your own sign that joined forces during your birth month with Pluto, the planet that most loves to dig, both literally and figuratively. This should make you an expert detective.

In relationships, you'll likely find the shrewdness and depth of Scorpios to be quite alluring, but fact-loving Capricorns and Virgos would also make fine choices. You may also be drawn to other Pisceans, whose love of mystical knowledge and capacity for long-term bonds will rival your own, keeping your curious mind sparked and your tender heart secure.

Your challenge is to put your substantial problem-solving skills to good use. Your gift is the ability to combine observation and perception to arrive at valid, well-grounded conclusions.

ARIES
From March 21, 2:14 through April 20, 13:20

The Cautious Realist

Born during 1995, Aries, you arrived just as the world heard news of a terrifying event—one that would serve to remind everyone of the need for two qualities your sign is famous for: bravery and survival instinct. At the peak of the morning rush hour in Tokyo, Japan, the deadly nerve gas Sarin was released on five trains in the Tokyo underground system. Ten people died and more than 5,000 were treated for injuries in what Japanese authorities called "an assault against society." The weapon—invisible but quite potent—was a nerve poison called Sarin. To the Supreme Truth cult, which was alleged to have unleashed it, the word Sarin symbolized the end of the world—and that's exactly what they tried to create.

The use of a chemical weapon highlighted the fears of citizens the world over with regard to cults, biochemical warfare, and terrorism. But the determination, fearlessness, and audacity it took for Tokyo's nine-to-five population—as well as commuters throughout the world—to resume their normal daily activities also strongly reflected your sign's affiliation with the planet Mars

Mars, otherwise known as the "Red Planet," is the ruler of assertion, aggression, and adrenaline—facts you're probably not surprised to hear, since yours is the sign Mars rules. At the time of the attack, this fiery fellow was in the sign of Leo—a fire sign itself, famous for its love of adventure, charm, and courage. Leo is lion, the "King of the Jungle" and the bravest of all creatures so, needless to say, you received a double dose of the bravery your sign already owns.

As such, you're likely quite popular, both for your charm and your devotion to your dear ones. Add in the tender touch of loving Venus in wistful Pisces, however, and it's easy to see that you're also quite the romantic. In fact, you may be drawn to Pisceans, solid Taureans, or Leos, a wonderful choice of playmate for you.

Your challenge is to keep your temper in check. Your gifts are your open-minded approach to new experiences and the bravery with which you face any dangers or setbacks.

➤ Read about your Chinese Astrological sign on page 838. ➤ Read about your Personal Planets on page 826. ➤ Read about your personal Mystical Card on page 856.

TAURUS

From April 20, 13:21 through May 21, 12:33

The Steadfast Leader

Your arrival in 1995, Taurus, coincided with Nelson Mandela's first anniversary as president of South Africa and its National Congress—and he'd gotten rave reviews from one and all. When he took office, Mandela promised to create "a rainbow nation at peace with itself and with the world" and he was rapidly en route to realizing that goal. Even "rightists" in the government were said to speak with great reverence and respect about the president. Mandela managed to make several powerful changes in society. Economic growth in the nation had gone up three points, an appealing lure to foreign investors, and state-run schools were being peacefully integrated.

The peace and prosperity Mandela gave his country is a wonderful example of your sign at its very best. Mandela's rock-solid determination and steadfast devotion to his ideals are also apt descriptions of Taureans. But you inherited several other astrological factors that show inner strength, a sense of purpose, and quite a sense of humor as well.

Saturn, the planet of rules, self-discipline, and responsibility, was in an easy conversation with Neptune, whose job duties include inspiration, dedication, and unconditional love. The energy of these two planets will likely fuel you with the urge to be as protective of your dear ones as Mandela was of each and every citizen he led—a lovely trait. Cerebral Mercury was in fast-moving, curious Gemini, giving you a keen wit to say the very least. But since you were also given fiery Mars in proud, dramatic Leo, you're likely to be quite the performer, no matter what type of gathering you're attending.

Speaking of gatherings, you may be drawn to group situations throughout life, since your astrological energies make you a very social creature. At one of those gatherings, you may cross paths with an independent Aquarian, a glib Gemini, or a fun-loving Sagittarius, all good choices for you.

Your challenge is to keep your own needs in mind, as well as those of your dear ones. Your gifts are your wisdom, stability, and determination.

GEMINI

From May 21, 12:34 through June 21, 0:33

The Adaptive Mind

Born during 1995, Gemini, you arrived just as a convention of Southern Baptists came together in Mississippi. The stated goal of the convention was to make peace between the Southern Baptist Church and African Americans in the southern United States. During the conference, several ministers rose to publicly apologize, extending their arms and their hearts to those they had shut out for so very long. More than 219 years after the Declaration of Independence declared that all men were created equal, 132 years after President Lincoln signed the Emancipation Proclamation, and forty-one years after the U.S. Supreme Court banned segregation, Baptist church officials finally admitted that slavery was sinful. They asked forgiveness from black Christians for the historic role their church had played in defending segregation.

Although many blacks returned the sentiment, only too happy to put an end to the animosity, others were not quite so forgiving—understandably so after so many years of discrimination from a religious institution. The duality of your sign is described aptly by both the 360-degree shift in the Baptist's sentiment as well as the mixed reaction the Baptist's apology received.

Gemini is the sign of the twins, so the ability to shape-shift on an intellectual level means you're probably good at defending both sides of an issue with equal intensity. In career and professional ventures, this adaptability will serve you well, as will your gift of gab. You also have a knack for handling details. Action-oriented Mars was in meticulous Virgo at the time of your birth, giving you a keen eye, a sharp mind, and the capacity to see potential problems before they surface—invaluable traits both personally and professionally.

When it comes to relationships, concentrate your energies on the other air signs, Librans and Aquarians, who'll actually be able to keep up with you on an intellectual level.

Your challenge is to learn to take a stand when the situation requires it—no matter who you are afraid of alienating in the process. Your gift is your fleet-footed mind.

➤ Read about your Chinese Astrological sign on page 838. ➤ Read about your Personal Planets on page 826. ➤ Read about your personal Mystical Card on page 856.

TAURUS
Your Personal Planets

YOUR LOVE POTENTIAL
Venus in Pisces, Apr. 20, 13:22 - Apr. 22, 4:06
Venus in Aries, Apr. 22, 4:07 - May 16, 23:21
Venus in Taurus, May 16, 23:22 - May 21, 12:33

YOUR DRIVE AND AMBITION
Mars in Leo, Apr. 20, 13:22 - May 21, 12:33

YOUR LUCK MAGNETISM
Jupiter in Sagittarius, Apr. 20, 13:22 - May 21, 12:33

World Events

May 14 - President Carlos Menem is re-elected in Argentina.

May 16 - Japanese police arrest cult leader Shoko Asahara and charge him with a nerve-gas attack on Tokyo's subways two months before.

The Winter Olympic flame of 2002 after Salt Lake City was chosen as venue

GEMINI
Your Personal Planets

YOUR LOVE POTENTIAL
Venus in Taurus, May 21, 12:34 - June 10, 16:18
Venus in Gemini, June 10, 16:19 - June 21, 20:33

YOUR DRIVE AND AMBITION
Mars in Leo, May 21, 12:34 - May 25, 16:08
Mars in Virgo, May 25, 16:09 - June 21, 20:33

YOUR LUCK MAGNETISM
Jupiter in Sagittarius, May 21, 12:34 - June 21, 20:33

World Events

June 16 - Salt Lake City is awarded the 19th Winter Olympics in 2002.

June 17 - British actor Hugh Grant is arrested on a prostitution charge in Los Angeles.

1995

CANCER
Your Personal Planets

YOUR LOVE POTENTIAL
Venus in Gemini, June 21, 20:34 - July 05, 6:38
Venus in Cancer, July 05, 6:39 - July 23, 7:29

YOUR DRIVE AND AMBITION
Mars in Virgo, June 21, 20:34 - July 21, 9:20
Mars in Libra, July 21, 9:21 - July 23, 7:29

YOUR LUCK MAGNETISM
Jupiter in Sagittarius, June 21, 20:34 - July 23, 7:29

World Events

June 23 – Biologist Jonas Salk dies.

July 9 – Jack Nicklaus wins golf's British Open, making him only the fourth golfer to win all four majors.

American golfer Jack Nicklaus, British Open winner

LEO
Your Personal Planets

YOUR LOVE POTENTIAL
Venus in Cancer, July 23, 7:30 - July 29, 17:31
Venus in Leo, July 29, 17:32 - Aug. 23, 0:42
Venus in Virgo, Aug. 23, 0:43 - Aug. 23, 14:34

YOUR DRIVE AND AMBITION
Mars in Libra, July 23, 7:30 - Aug. 23, 14:34

YOUR LUCK MAGNETISM
Jupiter in Sagittarius, July 23, 7:30 - Aug. 23, 14:34

World Events

July 27 – Monica Seles beats Martina Naratilova in her return to tennis.

July 27 – Evidence emerges that man's ancestors were walking upright 3.7 million years ago.

774

CANCER
From June 21, 0:34 through July 23, 7:29

The Assertive Peace-Maker

Born during 1995, Cancer, you arrived into a time of reconciliation—the long-overdue peacemaking between the United States and Vietnam. Years after the end of the Vietnam War, which officially closed with the fall of Saigon, America reached out to Vietnamese citizens, hoping to normalize diplomatic communications and relations. President Bill Clinton, had once again put a substantial amount of time and energy into forging a compromise. This time out, his goal was to establish a new relationship with the small Asian country and he was off to a good start. Mending fences has long been a trait your tender-hearted sign is famous for but you were also born with an added dose of conciliatory energies.

At the time of your planetary arrival, fiery Mars, the ancient god of war, was preparing to make his way into Libra, the sign that is best qualified to restore balance and harmony. As such, in addition to being born with three planets in compassionate Cancer, you were given the initiative to use your natural empathy and cooperation to push for compromise—and push hard, when necessary.

This trait may put you in the position of peace-maker over the course of your life, most likely in family and domestic situations. If you do find this quality being brought into play on a career level, it may be through counseling families. Regardless of which professional path you choose, however, you'll likely be the person to talk to when no-win situations present themselves—and you'll be more than happy to lend your talents to come up with a solution that is acceptable to all parties concerned.

In relationships, you'll probably enjoy the company of cooperative Librans or benevolent Sagittarians, but the other water signs, Scorpios and Pisceans, will provide you with emotional support, loyalty, and reassurance.

Your challenge is to back off when it's obvious that the peace you're working toward is impossible for the moment, at least. Your gift is your ability to make everyone feel comfortable and appreciated in your presence.

LEO
From July 23, 7:30 through August 23, 14:34

The Charming Combatant

Born during 1995, Leo, you arrived just as one of the world's best-known fashion designers was forced to drop several advertisements deemed inappropriate by feminists, parents, and consumers alike—even among the teen-age consumers his advertisements were aimed to attract. For the past fifteen years, Calvin Klein had built a successful international fashion empire, largely by tapping into images of youthful sexuality. Although several organizations had insisted that the concept of free speech should allow Klein to continue along this path, the pressure he received from other groups was enough to convince the designer to end the campaign.

This successful battle to bring back modesty, respect, and protection of the innocent was a perfect description of many of the traits you inherited by entering the world during this time. One of the most powerful of these traits is your willingness to boycott or openly protest what you see as the exploitation of the undeserving or benighted.

You were given several planets in Virgo, the sign most concerned with humility and modesty. In addition, war-like Mars had just entered Libra and contrary to what's usually written about its peace-loving qualities, Libra is the sign of open enemies. Libra's tactics in battle, while not as openly aggressive as its opposite counterpart Aries, are equally potent. Libra attracts what it wants through charm and cooperation. But its motivation, determination, and strength of purpose are the reasons Libra has long been known as the iron hand in the velvet glove. This potent astrological gift will likely make you a determined advocate for those who you see as being unfairly exploited, both personally and professionally.

When it comes to relationships, you'll need a partner who's also concerned with fairness, integrity, and common decency, such as Librans, Sagittarians, or Aquarians—but don't rule out members of your own sign.

Your challenge is to adhere firmly to your strong principles, no matter who you're afraid you'll alienate in the process. Your gift is your ability to push gently but firmly until you attain your goals.

➤ Read about your Chinese Astrological sign on page 838. ➤ Read about your Personal Planets on page 826. ➤ Read about your personal Mystical Card on page 856.

VIRGO

From August 23, 14:35 through September 23, 12:12

The Balanced Care-Giver

Your health-oriented sign, 1995 Virgo, has long been connected to medicine, hygiene, and the development of new treatments for illnesses. As such, your arrival this year coincided beautifully with discoveries that were wonderfully appropriate examples of those traits. Scientists working on the Human Genome Project at the National Cancer Institute in North Carolina had recently released the news that they had identified more than 3,200 genetic defects, many linked to diseases, including colon cancer, Huntington's disease, and cystic fibrosis. Even better, they announced that they were also working on developing new drugs that might eventually make it possible to substitute good genes for bad ones, finally putting an end to these diseases.

This major breakthrough went hand-in-hand with the availability of a drug called Imitrex that was designed to give migraine sufferers relief from symptoms that sometimes lasted several consecutive days, rendering many virtually unable to perform even the most simple tasks. Your entry into the world just as these findings were revealed illustrate the astrological qualities you inherited as a 1995 Virgo.

First off, you were given two planets in your own sign and two in Libra, long known for its ability to restore balance. Adding Virgo and Libra together aptly describes a personality that is equally skilled at finding problems, no matter how seemingly small and insignificant, and solving them. Also, assertive Mars was in Scorpio, the sign that most loves to dig, both literally and figuratively. When applied to the health industry, all this means you're likely quite well suited to work in these fields, whether through one-to-one care-giving or research.

In relationships, you're likely to find yourself drawn to other Virgos or Scorpios, whose love of investigation and research will make you feel immediately as if you're in the presence of a kindred spirit.

Your challenge is not to become so involved with the problems of others that you take them on yourself. Your gift is to keep at a project until you achieve the end you're after.

LIBRA

From September 23, 12:13 through October 23, 21:31

The Dedicated Friend

Ever since the murder of former Beatle John Lennon outside his New York apartment at the Dakota Building in 1980, fans of the "Fab Four" had been resigned to the fact that, outside of past recordings, they would never hear the reunion of their four favorite voices. Your 1995 arrival, however, coincided with that seemingly impossible dream becoming a reality, Libra. The three remaining Beatles, Paul McCartney, George Harrison, and Ringo Starr, came together in a recording studio to finish "Free as a Bird," a song Lennon had started shortly before his death, which would then appear on The Beatles Anthology set to be released this month.

Since your Sun sign is so closely connected with the concept of partnerships, most especially long-term partnerships, this was a beautiful example of the endless devotion and all-out adoration for which your sign is famous—in addition to being a real treat for fans. In other words, once you give your heart, you've given it for good and the astrology of your arrival shows all this and more.

Your were born with three planets in your sign, including Mercury, the planet of communication, and loving Venus, the planet that most loves reconciliation and reunion. Whether or not this reunion happened posthumously, it was just as tender and just as endearing to fans. In addition, mighty Jupiter was in Sagittarius, the sign that knows no boundaries when it comes to extravagance, excess, and all-out generosity. As such, you were given not just the charm and loyalty necessary to be a devoted friend, but also the benevolence required to be fair, impartial, and wise—all invaluable gifts, no matter which path you pursue in life.

When you're after a long-term partner, then, you'd do well to turn your attention to other Librans, Taureans, or Capricorns, good choices for the myriad of astrological traits you possess. Family-oriented Cancerians also might work well.

Your challenge is to let go of relationships that are no longer productive, no matter how difficult it is for you. Your gift is the ability to stay dedicated to the ones you love forever.

➤ Read about your Chinese Astrological sign on page 838. ➤ Read about your Personal Planets on page 826. ➤ Read about your personal Mystical Card on page 856.

1995

VIRGO
Your Personal Planets

YOUR LOVE POTENTIAL
Venus in Virgo, Aug. 23, 14:35 - Sept. 16, 5:00
Venus in Libra, Sept. 16, 5:01 - Sept. 23, 12:12

YOUR DRIVE AND AMBITION
Mars in Libra, Aug. 23, 14:35 - Sept. 07, 6:59
Mars in Scorpio, Sept. 07, 7:00 - Sept. 23, 12:12

YOUR LUCK MAGNETISM
Jupiter in Sagittarius, Aug. 23, 14:35 - Sept. 23, 12:12

World Events

Aug. 24 – The Windows 95 computer operating system is launched.

Sept. 1 – NATO air strikes against the Bosnian Serbs are suspended for twenty-four hours while peace talks are underway.

O.J. Simpson stands trial for murder

LIBRA
Your Personal Planets

YOUR LOVE POTENTIAL
Venus in Libra, Sept. 23, 12:13 - Oct. 10, 7:47
Venus in Scorpio, Oct. 10, 7:48 - Oct. 23, 21:31

YOUR DRIVE AND AMBITION
Mars in Scorpio, Sept. 23, 12:13 - Oct. 20, 21:01
Mars in Sagittarius, Oct. 20, 21:02 - Oct. 23, 21:31

YOUR LUCK MAGNETISM
Jupiter in Sagittarius, Sept. 23, 12:13 - Oct. 23, 21:31

World Events

Oct. 3 – In the "trial of the century," the jury finds O. J. Simpson not guilty of double murder, as millions watch on television worldwide.

Oct. 10 – Millions of public-service workers go on strike in France.

1995

SCORPIO
Your Personal Planets

YOUR LOVE POTENTIAL

Venus in Scorpio, Oct. 23, 21:32 - Nov. 03, 10:17
Venus in Sagittarius, Nov. 03, 10:18 - Nov. 22, 19:00

YOUR DRIVE AND AMBITION

Mars in Sagittarius, Oct. 23, 21:32 - Nov. 22, 19:00

YOUR LUCK MAGNETISM

Jupiter in Sagittarius, Oct. 23, 21:32 - Nov. 22, 19:00

World Events

Oct. 30 – The people of Quebec narrowly reject an independence referendum.

Nov. 20 – Princess Diana attacks the monarchy in a candid interview on television program *Panorama*.

The symbol of the "Euro," the new European monetary system

SAGITTARIUS
Your Personal Planets

YOUR LOVE POTENTIAL

Venus in Sagittarius, Nov. 22, 19:01 - Nov. 27, 13:22
Venus in Capricorn, Nov. 27, 13:23 - Dec. 21, 18:22
Venus in Aquarius, Dec. 21, 18:23 - Dec. 22, 8:16

YOUR DRIVE AND AMBITION

Mars in Sagittarius, Nov. 22, 19:01 - Nov. 30, 13:57
Mars in Capricorn, Nov. 30, 13:58 - Dec. 22, 8:16

YOUR LUCK MAGNETISM

Jupiter in Sagittarius, Nov. 22, 19:01 - Dec. 22, 8:16

World Events

Dec. 15 – European community leaders meeting in Madrid decide on "Euro" as the name for the single currency.

Dec. 21 – Cheers greet the Palestinian police as they enter the holy city of Bethlehem, where the first Christmas as part of Palestine is being celebrated.

SCORPIO
From October 23, 21:32 through November 22, 19:00

The Eternal Philosopher

Your sign is associated with urgent or critical times, Scorpio. No easy task, but one you were given the mettle to handle quite well. Your planet is Pluto, the ruler of regeneration, immortality, and posthumous recognition for good deeds, and a sad but noble event that occurred during the time of your arrival in 1995 perfectly showed all those honorable qualities. Moments after leaving a peace rally in Tel Aviv, Yitzhak Rabin was gunned down by a right-wing Jewish assailant. This great man shared the same fate as other peace-makers who had also been assassinated for their efforts, including Mahatma Gandhi and Anwar Sadat. Although their physical selves had been destroyed, the legacies of these peace-makers will live on forever.

The astrological factors of this month point to the immortality of Rabin's influence on the world and to qualities you no doubt possess, as well. Cerebral Mercury was in your own sign, keeping quite close company with the Sun, showing your intensity and thoughtfulness, as well as your long-term devotion to those you love. In addition, three planets in outgoing, benevolent Sagittarius, including mighty Jupiter himself, the owner of that sign, point to a strong and never-ending faith in the future and a knack for understanding the necessity of each and every event that occurs to you, no matter how wonderful or terrible that event happens to be.

As such, you are quite probably perceptive and philosophical and aware of the value of respect, appreciation, and honor. In short, you're a good friend, and in committed relationships, your devotion is likely unparalleled.

Speaking of relationships, you'd do well to keep company with the other water signs, Cancerians and Pisceans, or other Scorpios, all of who will share your intensity and passion for causes. But look to Taureans and Aquarians for understanding and support of this same intensity and passion.

Your challenge is never to obsess on the past. Your gift is the ability to remain faithful to dear ones, no matter how irreconcilable your lifestyles or opinions happen to be.

SAGITTARIUS
From November 22, 19:01 through December 22, 8:16

The Happy Home-Maker

Just as you entered the world, Sagittarius of 1995, the Walt Disney Corporation was preparing to create a new, utopian-like community. The company opened a town called Celebration, just fifteen miles south of Disney World in Orlando, Florida. The idealism and broad goals your sign is famous for are perfectly described by the opening of this new community—and some of the rules for living there are also quite appropriate examples of other astrological qualities you possess. For example, the types of homes planned included Victorian, Colonial, French, and Mediterranean, all associated with either foreign or period housing—and your sign has long been known for its fondness for other times and far-off places.

Future street names read like a list of Sagittarian key words as well: Zip-a-Dee-Doo-Dah Drive, Hip-Hip-Hooray Highway, and Cinderella Lane, for example. In addition, your sign's long connection with education was also well represented by this ambitious project. An on-campus school system covered children from kindergarten through high school, complete with an on-site teacher training academy financed by Disney and included in the price of this covenant-bound community.

In short, the happiness and optimism represented by the creation of this "ideal community" perfectly reflects your Sagittarian qualities, as well as a few others your birth in 1995 afforded you. First off, thoughtful Mercury and no-holds barred Jupiter, your ruling planet and the owner of the concepts of extravagance and abundance, were both in your sign. The restrictions—hidden, but nonetheless quite present—involved in living in a place like this were shown by the presence of four planets in Capricorn, the sign of rules, regulations, and strict adherence to what's "normal."

In relationships, the blend of Sagittarian and Capricorn energies you possess would mix quite well with those born under these signs, as well as peace-loving Librans, who are also quite fond of "ideal" and aesthetic surroundings.

Your greatest challenge is to face reality when necessary. Your gift is your perpetual faith in the future.

➤ Read about your Chinese Astrological sign on page 838. ➤ Read about your Personal Planets on page 826. ➤ Read about your personal Mystical Card on page 856.

CAPRICORN

From December 22, 8:17 through December 31, 23:59

The Private Extrovert

Born during late 1995, Capricorn, you have a rather unusual talent for being an authority figure that identifies strongly with the masses. You were born around the time of a groundbreaking interview by a member of the British monarchy, when Diana, Princess of Wales, broke her silence on many issues, both personal and with regard to the royal family. The unprecedented openness and candor of Princess Diana during this interview served to increase her affection with the public. Diana became a popular spokesperson for many causes that benefited the less fortunate of society.

You too will use your position in life to bring aid and comfort to others and occasionally this will involve restoring needed structure into situations that are problematic. On December 31, 1995, the first U.S. tanks moved from Croatia to Bosnia under NATO command. This began the deployment of 20,000 U.S. troops as an Implementation Force that intervened in that area's war.

Astrologically speaking, this mixed bag of energies is aptly described by your chart. Five planets held court in your own reputable, responsible sign, showing a strong backbone, a strict adherence to propriety, and an innate integrity. At the same time, however, two planets were posited in blunt, truthful Sagittarius, including expansive Jupiter—a planet that's never been famous for his ability to keep a secret. In addition, loving Venus, the ruler of who and what we adore, most especially our dear ones, was in radical, rebellious Aquarius, long known to be just as blunt and honest—to a fault at times—as Sagittarius. All of this does, indeed, break down into "bravery and vulnerability" and makes you a worthy partner, friend, and business associate.

In relationships, you'll probably find yourself in the arms of either other Capricorns or Aquarians, both of whom will feel immediately like kindred spirits to you.

Your gift is the ability to find a happy medium between honesty and privacy. Your challenge is to find the courage to let the world see you as you truly are.

CAPRICORN
Your Personal Planets

YOUR LOVE POTENTIAL
Venus in Aquarius, Dec. 22, 8:17 - Dec. 31, 23:59

YOUR DRIVE AND AMBITION
Mars in Capricorn, Dec. 22, 8:17 - Dec. 31, 23:59

YOUR LUCK MAGNETISM
Jupiter in Sagittarius, Dec. 22, 8:17 - Dec. 31, 23:59

World Events

Dec. 25 – American actor Dean Martin dies.

Dec. 25 – The Pope curtails his traditional Christmas address in St. Peter's Square, due to a bout of flu.

Mother Teresa
August 26, 1910 - September 5, 1997

MOTHER TERESA
Virgo

Agnes Gonxha Bojaxhiu grew up in Skopje, in what is now Macedonia. At the age of eighteen, she joined a community of Irish nuns with a mission in Calcutta and took the name "Sister Teresa." After teaching for seventeen years, she felt a call to serve God in the slums, among the poorest of the poor. Receiving permission to leave the order and work on her own, after taking a medical training course, she went into the slums of Calcutta to start a school for children. She founded the Missionaries of Charity, which grew from twelve members to more than 4,000 running orphanages, AIDS hospices and other charity centers worldwide. She established a home for the dying poor and received the Nobel Peace Prize in 1979 for her work.

Mother Teresa was a Virgo, a sign known for an interest in health and the desire to help others. With her Sun, planet of identity, in her eighth house of transformation and death in close contact with Mars, the planet of action, also in Virgo, it is not so surprising that she would feel called to work with the extremely poor and incurably ill. With an easy contact from Mars to her Moon (emotions) in practical Taurus, she no doubt found great satisfaction and fulfillment in her work. With a dynamic aspect from her Moon to Uranus, the planet of the unusual, in her public first house, she used her creative energies to make her unique work known to all.

With idealistic Sagittarius rising, she traveled widely and set up her missions around the globe. This international theme is echoed by her ninth house, the "natural" home of Sagittarius. There she has Jupiter, the planet of growth and expansion, and Mercury, the planet of communication. By 1996, she was operating 517 missions in more than one hundred countries. And when her funding methods or personal attitudes to abortion and divorce were questioned, she had one practical Virgo response: "No matter who says what, you should accept it with a smile and do your own work."

➤ Read Dalai Lama's Star Profile on page 809. ➤ Read Nelson Mandela's Star Profile on page 729. ➤ Read Martin Luther King, Jr's Star Profile on page 537. ➤ Read Princess Diana's Star Profile on page 689.

777

1996

Opportunities Abound: Saturn, Uranus, and Pluto

Ease and flow were the by-words as Saturn, Uranus and Pluto made harmonious contacts with each other throughout the year. Saturn is associated with manifestation and staying power, while Uranus's feeling is short and sudden. Pluto represents deep, often hidden, long-term influences. When these three harmonize, we have the opportunity to balance these often inimical energies within and around us. This was seen in the de-escalation of two major conflicts. Israel and Palestinians became more cooperative with each other and the Israelis released more Palestinian prisoners. The ethnic war in Bosnia reached a peace agreement and war tribunals began in May. In the U.S., voters were happy enough with their lives to re-elect President Clinton, despite barbed attacks from Newt Gingrich and the conservative House of Representatives. With the activating energies of eclipses in relationship-oriented Libra, sentimental feel-good movies like *The Full Monty*, and *Good Will Hunting* topped the box office.

However, Uranus and Neptune were still close enough to each other in the heavens to pack a punch when triggered by other planets. Neptune, representing gases, waters and insidious influences, when coupled with Uranus often suggests sudden, sometimes catastrophic, events from these sources. This was the case when TWA Flight 800 crashed into the ocean off New York's coast for mysterious reasons. The Atlanta Olympic Games were marred by a bomb blast in a late-night crowd, initiated by a renegade anti-abortionist.

Prince Charles and Princess Diana are divorced

Taliban guerrillas capture Kabul in Afghanistan

U.S. President Bill Clinton is re-elected

WAR IN THE BALKANS ENDS

Following last year's Paris peace accord ending the war, NATO troops arrived in Bosnia on their peacekeeping mission. Palestinian leader Yasser Arafat took office as new President of the Palestinian Authority. In the UN, Cuba was denounced for shooting down two unarmed planes belonging to a Cuban exile group. In Afghanistan, Taliban guerrillas captured Kabul. Tamil separatists in Sri Lanka bombed the Central Bank in Colombo. President Clinton won re-election. Two cloned sheep were displayed by the Roslin Institute, Edinburgh. Longest-serving monarch in the world King Bhumiphol of Thailand celebrated his Golden Jubilee. In Britain, the Queen's sons Prince Charles and Prince Andrew were divorced. Singer Madonna gave birth to her first child, Lourdes. The Summer Olympic Games in Atlanta, Georgia were marred by a bomb exploding in Centennial Olympic Park. The 500-year-old mummified corpse of an Inca girl found in the Andes went on display in Washington. A 4.5-billion-year-old meteorite yielded clues to life on the planet Mars. Mel Gibson triumphed at the Oscars, winning Best Picture and Best Director awards for *Braveheart*.

CIA PSYCHICS EXPOSED

In 1996, the U.S. government released a classified CIA report on their mid-1970s project "Operation Star Gate." The project used psychics and remote viewing techniques as an aid in intelligence gathering. By the time the program ended, the Department of Defense had invested $20 million in parapsychology and the development of psychic spying skills. The release revealed D. Kenneth A. Kress, a CIA engineer dubbed paranormal project officer, as the "father of America's remote-viewing program."

➤ Read "Nostradamus: A Prophet Across Time" by Skye Alexander on page 785.

CAPRICORN

January 01, 0:00 through January 20, 18:51

The Rebellious Leader

Born in 1996, January Capricorn, you arrived just as communism was making a comeback in Russia and the Communist Party leader, Gennady Zyuganov ran for the presidency against the incumbent, Boris Yeltsin. The current leader of Russia's Communist Party, Gennady Zyuganov, had just announced his intention to seek that seat in the upcoming elections and, interestingly enough, the platform he was planning to run on sounded like a chain of Capricorn keywords. Zyuganov stated that he would "re-nationalize" all Russian industries, "rebuild" the armed forces, and "re-create" either the Soviet Union or "a great Russian state." He also hastened to mention that all this would be done "in a consistent, step-by-step manner, on the basis of official elections, and legal referendums." The aspiring candidate's announcement during the time of your planetary arrival perfectly reflected the substantial number of planets that were posited in your sign, showing your textbook Capricorn qualities. In the election, held in August, Yeltsin won by a narrow majority.

In fact, a total of six planets—out of ten, including the Moon—passed through your sign as you entered the world. One of them was Jupiter, which expands and exaggerates the qualities of any sign it inhabits. Needless to say, your sign's most famous traits—caution, self-discipline, and responsibility—will probably be quite obvious in your character.

In addition, however, you were given a strong dose of Aquarius energies, including cerebral Mercury, relationship-oriented Venus, and assertive Mars. These three planets in this famously non-conformist sign might ordinarily point to someone who was a rebel. In your case, you'll probably only rebel if you feel justified, righteous, and certain of the outcome.

In relationships, you'd do well to spend time with the other earth signs, Virgos and Taureans, but home-oriented Cancerians will also probably appeal to you.

Your challenge is to manage a happy medium between fighting City Hall and running it entirely on your own. In other words, you may need to learn to delegate. Your gift is your ability to concentrate all your energies on one project at a time.

AQUARIUS

From January 20, 18:52 through February 19, 9:00

The Curious Observer

Born during 1996, Aquarius, you entered the world just as astronomers announced several major discoveries. First, they detected water-bearing planets around several nearby stars—"nearby" meaning only as close as the Big Dipper constellation. Still, the fact that other planets were capable of supporting the existence of water in liquid form raised scientist's expectations of finding other Earth-like worlds, something amateur and professional astronomers alike had been excitedly awaiting for decades. At the same time, two more planets were discovered. The first, orbiting the star 47 Ursae Majoris, was a mere 200 trillion miles from Earth and appeared to be twice the size of Jupiter. The second, circling the star 70 Virginis, possibly hosted weather conditions even more extreme than stormy Jupiter.

The sudden changes in astronomical thought that these discoveries fueled, including new theories about the creation of the Universe, show your capacity for intellectual rebellion. Long known as the sign of "The Observer", in addition to the Sun, you were given a potent pack of energies in Aquarius, beautifully outlining your fondness for science, space, and futuristic thinking.

Your own planet, Uranus, had just arrived into your sign for the first time in eighty-four years. This radical, rebellious planet in your own equally unconventional sign provided you with a double-dose of typically Aquarian qualities. Fiery Mars, the ruler of assertion, aggression, and taking action, was also in your sign. Added together, these two planets alone point to a preponderance of your Sun sign's traits for those of you born during this time, including a strong urge to break the rules—especially when you're certain that rebellion is the only way to usher in a new wave of thinking or understanding.

In relationships, you'll likely need a partner who's as cerebral and intellectual as yourself, such as other Aquarians, keen-minded Geminis, or broad-minded Sagittarians.

Your challenge is to learn the rules before you go ahead and break them. Your gift is your unwavering determination to make the future happen.

▶ Read about your Chinese Astrological sign on page 838. ▶ Read about your Personal Planets on page 826. ▶ Read about your personal Mystical Card on page 856.

1996

CAPRICORN
Your Personal Planets

YOUR LOVE POTENTIAL
Venus in Aquarius, Jan. 01, 0:00 - Jan. 15, 4:29
Venus in Pisces, Jan. 15, 4:30 - Jan. 20, 18:52

YOUR DRIVE AND AMBITION
Mars in Capricorn, Jan. 01, 0:00 - Jan. 08, 11:01
Mars in Aquarius, Jan. 08, 11:02 - Jan. 20, 18:52

YOUR LUCK MAGNETISM
Jupiter in Sagittarius, Jan. 01, 0:00 - Jan. 03, 7:21
Jupiter in Capricorn, Jan. 03, 7:22 - Jan. 20, 18:52

World Events

Jan. 2 – U.S. ground forces flood into Bosnia as part of NATO's peacekeeping exercise.

Jan. 18 – Lisa Marie Presley, daughter of Elvis, files for divorce from superstar Michael Jackson in New York.

The Council of Europe admits Russia as a member

AQUARIUS
Your Personal Planets

YOUR LOVE POTENTIAL
Venus in Pisces, Jan. 20, 18:53 - Feb. 09, 2:30
Venus in Aries, Feb. 09, 2:31 - Feb. 19, 9:00

YOUR DRIVE AND AMBITION
Mars in Aquarius, Jan. 20, 18:53 - Feb. 15, 11:49
Mars in Pisces, Feb. 15, 11:50 - Feb. 19, 9:00

YOUR LUCK MAGNETISM
Jupiter in Capricorn, Jan. 20, 18:53 - Feb. 19, 9:00

World Events

Jan. 25 – Meeting in Strasbourg, Europe's leading human rights organization, the Council of Europe, admits Russia as a member.

Feb. 12 – Yasser Arafat becomes President of the Palestinian Authority.

PISCES
Your Personal Planets

YOUR LOVE POTENTIAL
Venus in Aries, Feb. 19, 9:01 - Mar. 06, 2:00
Venus in Taurus, Mar. 06, 2:01 - Mar. 20, 8:02

YOUR DRIVE AND AMBITION
Mars in Pisces, Feb. 19, 9:01 - Mar. 20, 8:02

YOUR LUCK MAGNETISM
Jupiter in Capricorn, Feb. 19, 9:01 - Mar. 20, 8:02

World Events

Feb. 21 - Jean Calment celebrates his 121st birthday, making him the oldest person alive.

Feb. 22 - President Jacques Chirac announces that France will be abolishing conscription and dismantling all ground-based nuclear weapons.

Reports circulate that Madonna is pregnant

ARIES
Your Personal Planets

YOUR LOVE POTENTIAL
Venus in Taurus, Mar. 20, 8:03 - Apr. 03, 15:25
Venus in Gemini, Apr. 03, 15:26 - Apr. 19, 19:09

YOUR DRIVE AND AMBITION
Mars in Pisces, Mar. 20, 8:03 - Mar. 24, 15:11
Mars in Aries, Mar. 24, 15:12 - Apr. 19, 19:09

YOUR LUCK MAGNETISM
Jupiter in Capricorn, Mar. 20, 8:03 - Apr. 19, 19:09

World Events

Mar. 25 - France, Britain, and the U.S. sign a treaty banning nuclear weapons from the South Pacific.

Apr. 16 - Reports circulate that Madonna is pregnant by Carlos Leon, her Cuban fitness instructor.

PISCES
From February 19, 9:01 through March 20, 8:02

The Secret Star

Born during 1996, Pisces, you arrived just as two of your sign's qualities—secrecy and mystery—were made public for rather notorious reasons.

Holidaymakers in the Caribbean were shocked to learn that a series of drug-related crimes had rocked the island of St. Kitts for the past two years. In fact, a former St. Kitts ambassador who had been implicated in money-laundering and receiving gifts bought with "drug money" had recently disappeared while on a Sunday fishing trip with his wife and four friends. All this—going on in secret while life on this and other resort islands continued as usual—superficially, at least—took the world quite by surprise, making us wonder what else might be going on behind the scenes, even in our own backyards.

Again, while these events point to the seamier side of life, they were perfect examples of several qualities your sign is known for, qualities whose higher side would serve your evolving soul quite well. You're capable of living one life in the spotlight and another, entirely different one behind closed doors, a trait that will likely come in handy throughout your life, especially if you eventually find yourself with a fair amount of fame—and you may.

In addition to a fondness for mystery however, the four planets that passed through your sign as you entered the world also gave you other famous Piscean talents—a love of the spiritual, mystical, and unseen, for example. You may find that you're drawn to work with local theaters or movie houses, actual performing, or even investigation, all of which should leave you feeling fulfilled and happy.

In relationships, you'll probably need someone as privacy-oriented as yourself, such as intrigue-loving Scorpios or home-loving Cancerians. Other Pisceans will also understand your mission to be simultaneously famous and nondescript.

Your challenge is to use your sign's love of mystery for constructive purposes, never allowing yourself to be drawn into anything unsavory or even illegal. Your gift is your ability to know just what's coming around the next corner.

ARIES
From March 20, 8:03 through April 19, 19:09

The Honest Citizen

Born during 1996, Aries, you arrived as a major battle was being waged that rang bells around the world in general: whether to put family ties or duty to one's country first. The family members in question were the Kaczynski brothers, Theodore and David, and the issue revolved around a recent conversation between David and the Federal Bureau of Investigation in the United States.

After years of unsuccessfully attempting to find the man who called himself "the Unabomber" and the author of the *Communist Manifesto*, the FBI received information from David Kaczynski. This eventually incriminated his brother in a series of mail-bombings that killed and maimed leaders of several large corporations whose policies Theodore openly disagreed with. David's willingness to put aside personal feelings to save the lives of strangers, obviously a difficult decision, shows the true bravery and honesty inherent in your fast-moving sign.

Although Capricorns are usually described as the most honest sign in the zodiac, Aries, your commitment to integrity rivals that of this respectable sign. First off, your planet, Mars, is the astrological equivalent of a bullet. Mars prefers moving directly from point A to point B at all times, regardless of what may lie in between. Such "straight-line" movement is the only way you're really capable of moving at all. That leaves no time for lies, distortions, or anything remotely resembling deception—only straightforward, blunt truth and direct action. Mars and Aries are respectively the Roman and Greek gods of war, so you're here to learn the attributes of assertion, aggression, and proper expression of anger—and without conflict, you'd never be able to do that.

In all, you're not for the faint of heart, Aries, so your mate needs to be equally strong, determined, and blunt. As such, you'd do well to find a Sagittarian or Leo partner, whose fire and passion will match your own.

Your challenge is to remain true to your ideals, no matter that who or what you love is at odds with them. Your gifts are your bravery and all-out determination to present yourself as you truly are.

➤ Read about your Chinese Astrological sign on page 838. ➤ Read about your Personal Planets on page 826. ➤ Read about your personal Mystical Card on page 856.

TAURUS

From April 19, 19:10 through May 20, 18:22

The Extravagant Consumer

Born during 1996, Taurus, you arrived just as a true display of your sign's love of opulence was put on for the entire world to see. An auction of extremely high-priced objects was held at Sotheby's Auction House, their value due not to quality or value, but to the mystique of the former owner Jacqueline Kennedy Onassis. The former First Lady of the U.S., known for qualities that echo your own, including style, taste, and magnetism, left her children virtually all of her personal possessions with instructions to "keep what they wanted and sell everything else."

What ended up on the auction-house floor was an odd collection. It included "three cushions" (purchased for $25,300), a heart-shaped silver candy-dish, (worth $150-$200 but actually sold for $29,900), and a humidor that once belonged to Jackie's first husband, John F. Kennedy, which sold to the publisher of the magazine *Cigar Aficionado* for $574,500. The humidor was given to the former president by actor Milton Berle, who'd spent "approximately $800 to $1,000" on it in 1961. Possibly the most valuable of all the 1,300 lots was a single item: the forty-carat diamond ring Jackie had been given by her second husband, Aristotle Onassis. Estimated at $500,000 to $600,000 by Sotheby's, it was bought by a bidder who'd been only too happy to pay $2.6 million for it.

Astrologically, you were given an equally rare and varied blend of energies, including prestige-loving Saturn in impulsive Aries, three planets in sturdy Capricorn—famous for its respect of "the elders" and their antique possessions—and three planets in your own quality-conscious sign. In short, you're an expert when it comes to assessing value—and monetary worth likely has a very little part to play in that assessment.

In relationships, you'll probably find that other Taureans and Capricorns, as well as Virgos, will share your love of nothing but the best, as will lavish Leos.

Your challenge is not to overspend simply for the thrill of the purchase. Your gift is your instinctive ability to know how valuable both objects and personal relationships really are.

GEMINI

From May 20, 18:23 through June 21, 2:23

The Fair Thinker

You, 1996 Gemini, arrived at an extremely appropriate moment in time. Touted in the press as "Russia's favorite guessing game," the question of whether or not Boris Yeltsin would run in the upcoming presidential election was a popular debating point. What was the dual-sided dilemma Yeltsin faced? To hang on to power at all costs, or to go down in history as the father of Russian democracy. Ideally, of course, he'd probably have preferred to have both but forced into a choice, which would it be?

Appropriately, the key to Yeltsin's dilemma involved a very Gemini array of options. He could form a government of national unity with the Communist Party and its candidate, Gennady Zyuganov, a partnership of sorts that reflects your sign's two-sided nature. A second choice would be either to postpone the election or go ahead with it, assuming that his accomplishments would compel the Russian people to reward him with the presidency. On the other hand, Yeltsin could also go to Chechnya, to "sit around the negotiating table and talk" with two other non-Communist candidates, Aleksandr Lebed and Svyatoslav Fyodorov—and chatting, of course, is also a Gemini specialty.

Yeltsin's situation showed the substantial astrological influence of your own sign and of two others as well. The Sun and loving Venus spent most of the month in your sign, where Mars arrived on June 12 and Mercury the following day. But several other planets spent time in sturdy, stubborn Taurus, the sign of determination. At the same time, Jupiter, the planet of optimism, and Saturn, the planet of caution, were "wearing" each other's signs—a strong connection between two quite opposite energies. In short, your duality is quite a bit more pronounced than that of Geminis born in other years.

In relationships, you'd do well to seek out Librans or Sagittarians, who are as prone to seeing both sides of an issue as yourself.

Your challenge is to pay equal respect to both sides of a subject you're debating. Your gift is the ability to do just that—as long as you're not emotionally attached to the outcome.

TAURUS
Your Personal Planets

YOUR LOVE POTENTIAL
Venus in Gemini, Apr. 19, 19:10 - May 20, 18:22

YOUR DRIVE AND AMBITION
Mars in Aries, Apr. 19, 19:10 - May 02, 18:15
Mars in Taurus, May 02, 18:16 - May 20, 18:22

YOUR LUCK MAGNETISM
Jupiter in Capricorn, Apr. 19, 19:10 - May 20, 18:22

World Events

May 7 - The Bosnian war crimes trial opens at The Hague.

May 21 - A 500-year-old Incan mummy of a young girl, discovered in Peru and named Juanita, goes on display in Washington, DC.

King Bhumibol and Queen Sirikit of Thailand

GEMINI
Your Personal Planets

YOUR LOVE POTENTIAL
Venus in Gemini, May 20, 18:23 - June 21, 2:23

YOUR DRIVE AND AMBITION
Mars in Taurus, May 20, 18:23 - June 12, 14:41
Mars in Gemini, June 12, 14:42 - June 21, 2:23

YOUR LUCK MAGNETISM
Jupiter in Capricorn, May 20, 18:23 - June 21, 2:23

World Events

May 30 - The Duke and Duchess of York receive a decree absolute.

June 9 - King Bhumibol of Thailand becomes the world's longest-serving monarch as he celebrates fifty years on the throne.

➤ Read about your Chinese Astrological sign on page 838. ➤ Read about your Personal Planets on page 826. ➤ Read about your personal Mystical Card on page 856.

1996

CANCER
Your Personal Planets

YOUR LOVE POTENTIAL
Venus in Gemini, June 21, 2:24 - July 22, 13:18

YOUR DRIVE AND AMBITION
Mars in Gemini, June 21, 2:24 - July 22, 13:18

YOUR LUCK MAGNETISM
Jupiter in Capricorn, June 21, 2:24 - July 22, 13:18

World Events

June 23 - South Africa's leading Anglican clergyman, Archbishop Tutu, leads a farewell service in Cape Town to mark his retirement.

July 12 - Prince Charles and Princess Diana agree on a divorce settlement.

Archbishop Desmond Tutu greets Nelson Mandela before the farewell service to mark his retirement

LEO
Your Personal Planets

YOUR LOVE POTENTIAL
Venus in Gemini, July 22, 13:19 - Aug. 07, 6:14
Venus in Cancer, Aug. 07, 6:15 - Aug. 22, 20:22

YOUR DRIVE AND AMBITION
Mars in Gemini, July 22, 13:19 - July 25, 18:31
Mars in Cancer, July 25, 18:32 - Aug. 22, 20:22

YOUR LUCK MAGNETISM
Jupiter in Capricorn, July 22, 13:19 - Aug. 22, 20:22

World Events

July 30 - *Pravda*, Lenin's revolutionary newspaper is relaunched in Moscow as a tabloid.

Aug. 3 - Muhammad Ali is awarded an honorary gold medal to replace the one he rejected from the 1960 Olympics in Rome.

CANCER
From June 21, 2:24 through July 22, 13:18

The Determined Patriot

Your home-loving sign isn't often connected with the issue of patriotism, Cancer of 1996, but it should be. After all, once you've decided to put down roots, your choice of where to settle is just as important. So the fact that the land where you choose to nest—in other words patriotism itself—was an important topic the month you were born had everything to do with your Sun sign and with several other astrological factors that you inherited by being born during 1996.

Benjamin Netanyahu had just won a razor-thin victory in Israel's recent election for Prime Minister, but the victory was marked by three distinctly troubling issues, especially since it came during a month when land was such a highly-contested topic. Three factors that marked Netanyahu's campaign rhetoric included three "no's"—"no" to a Palestinian state, "no" to any compromise on Israel's sovereignty over a united Jerusalem, and "no" to a surrender of the Golan Heights to Syria. But Netanyahu's comments also revealed a more hopeful approach. He was willing to negotiate, compromise, and leave open the question of trading land for peace—both peace and home are Cancerian topics. In fact, as he was quoted, "What good is peace if not for the achievement of tranquillity? If peace involves continued bus bombings, violence and terrorism, that is not peace."

Your love of home, family, and the earth beneath your feet is beautifully exemplified by the astrological influences you inherited in your birth-year, Cancer of 1996. One of the most telling was sedate, grounded Saturn in aggressive Aries—a very powerful and defensive placement for this tradition-loving, family-oriented planet.

Your personal urge to set down roots points to the need to establish all those qualities and more for yourself and your family. As such, you'll likely do well with another earth sign as a partner, such as Virgo or Capricorn.

Your challenge is to give yourself the chance to explore new places and new people. Your gift is your dedication to family, friends, and dear ones that will likely win you equal devotion from others.

LEO
From July 22, 13:19 through August 22, 20:22

The Imaginative Playmate

Members of your sign have a connection with both recreational activities and children's affairs. As a Leo born in 1996, you would have been delighted to learn of the strange incident that took place at the Brookfield Zoo in Illinois on August 16, 1996. A three-year-old boy fell into a concrete area of the zoo's guerilla exhibit and was rescued by Binti, a seven-year-old gorilla. With your upbeat outlook, you find many occasions to celebrate life. Whether you're the host or guest of honor, when you're at a party, it becomes very special. On August 18, 1996, on the eve of his fiftieth birthday, President Clinton was guest of honor at a trio of events in New York that combined celebrating with fund-raising.

Youthful exuberance is occasionally directed towards political causes. In South Korea, 7,000 students protested for reunification with North Korea and the removal of 37,000 U.S. troops. With Saturn in red-hot Aries at the time of your birth, rebellion against perceived limitations would naturally be a primary theme in the headlines and, later on, in your own life. This is the cosmic equivalent of a bullet and the kind of sign-planet combination that points to swift and disciplined reasoning—and even swifter action.

Uranus recently entered Aquarius, its own sign, the sign of genius—a perfect representation of a scientist at work in his or her laboratory. As such, in addition to the fire and passion of two planets in your own sign, you were given the ability to build mechanical and electronic inventions that are specially designed for creating good times. This innately fun-loving bent to your personality shows in far more than just your creations. In fact, anyone who's ever spent time with you knows that you're a bit of a "Sensor" yourself, tuned into having a good time—and that it's contagious. This is how life becomes art and how your sign becomes famous, as it often does.

When it comes to relationships, you'd do well to search out someone as creative and inventive as yourself, such as Aquarians, Sagittarians, or Geminis.

Your challenge is to give your creativity free reign. Your gift is the capacity for genius.

➤ Read about your Chinese Astrological sign on page 838. ➤ Read about your Personal Planets on page 826. ➤ Read about your personal Mystical Card on page 856.

VIRGO

From August 22, 20:23 through September 22, 17:59

The Truthful Care-Giver

During the time of your birth, 1996 Virgo, the world heard the news that cigarette smoking had been proven not only harmful but also addictive. The results of a research project conducted by a team of Italian researchers were published in the journal *Nature*—and their findings were astonishing. Rats were injected intravenously with a small dose of nicotine, about as much as a smoker receives from one drag of a cigarette. The team found that levels of the brain chemical dopamine dramatically increased in the amygdala, an important emotional center. The results proved that the brain makes no distinction between addictive drugs—in other words, that nicotine had just as much effect on the brain as cocaine.

This finding, revealed just as the Sun made its way through your zodiacal sign, shows your natural affiliation with health and wellness as well as other qualities you inherited by virtue of being born this year. Your determination to speak your truth, especially with regard to issues of health, is shown in several ways. First off, mighty Jupiter, the planet that rules mass communication, was in steady-handed, responsible Capricorn, showing your absolute insistence on telling the truth in blunt and honest fashion. In addition, Saturn, the cosmic authority-figure, was in fast-moving Aries—a sign that's never been known for being deceitful.

In short, you were given the capacity to let your truth be known, regardless of the consequences, in a very big way. This makes you a wonderful employee or employer, an honest businessperson, and a devoted friend. In one-to-one relationships, you're also quite dedicated. In fact, you'll likely take a partner early in life and remain committed to that person for your entire life.

When searching out that partner, then, you'll need to find someone just as practical, honest, and trustworthy as yourself. You'd do well to look to the other earth signs, Capricorns, Taureans, and other Virgos.

Your gift is your absolute dedication to honesty and integrity. Your challenge is to resist the urge to compel others to adhere to your beliefs.

LIBRA

From September 22, 18:00 through October 23, 3:18

The Team Player

Born during 1996, Libra, you arrived into a world that saw an amazing display of teamwork—one that many thought would never happen. Two famous long-time rivals had put aside their differences and the urge to beat each other in a race conducted in outer space. In this post-Berlin wall, pre-International Space Station era, the race to Mars suddenly became a team effort and the United States and Russia, far from competing, were actually pooling their efforts to get to that planet. And it wasn't just these two countries that had decided to work together. In fact, an upcoming Japanese mission to Mars was planning to carry U.S.-made instrumentation. The efforts shown by these events perfectly reflect your sign's connection to partnership, and the astrology of your birth-time reveals even more insights about your cooperative, compromising character.

You entered the world with several planets in earth signs, the most respectable and responsible of all the four elements, an indication that you would be equally dutiful to your friends, family, and career—in short, to anyone or anything to which you've promised yourself. You were also given the gift of fiery Mars in Leo, a showy, lavish sign that loves displays of affection. As such, your devotion in all your relationships is unparalleled as is your absolute insistence on keeping your promises, making you a good friend, a dedicated partner, and a committed worker.

Your steady-handed approach to all situations will probably gain you many good friends, a solid one-to-one relationship, and the ability to create a name for yourself in the career of your choice. In fact, once you've given your word, it will be next to impossible to get you to renege on it.

This serious, dutiful side of your personality means you may find what you're searching for in the company of the earth signs, Virgos, Capricorns, and Taureans, all of whom will share your need to make a solid home-base.

Your challenge is to live your life as you see fit, never allowing the opinions of others to affect your decisions. Your gift is your emotional solidity.

➤ Read about your Chinese Astrological sign on page 838. ➤ Read about your Personal Planets on page 826. ➤ Read about your personal Mystical Card on page 856.

VIRGO
Your Personal Planets

YOUR LOVE POTENTIAL
Venus in Cancer, Aug. 22, 20:23 - Sept. 07, 5:06
Venus in Leo, Sept. 07, 5:07 - Sept. 22, 17:59

YOUR DRIVE AND AMBITION
Mars in Cancer, Aug. 22, 20:23 - Sept. 09, 20:01
Mars in Leo, Sept. 09, 20:02 - Sept. 22, 17:59

YOUR LUCK MAGNETISM
Jupiter in Capricorn, Aug. 22, 20:23 - Sept. 22, 17:59

World Events

Aug. 25 – Tiger Woods wins the 96th U.S. Golf Amateur Championship.

Aug. 30 – Controversial U.S. Nation of Islam leader Louis Farakhan is offered a Human Rights award from the Libyan government.

Tiger Woods wins the 96th U.S. Golf Amateur Championship

LIBRA
Your Personal Planets

YOUR LOVE POTENTIAL
Venus in Leo, Sept. 22, 18:00 - Oct. 04, 3:21
Venus in Virgo, Oct. 04, 3:22 - Oct. 23, 3:18

YOUR DRIVE AND AMBITION
Mars in Leo, Sept. 22, 18:00 - Oct. 23, 3:18

YOUR LUCK MAGNETISM
Jupiter in Capricorn, Sept. 22, 18:00 - Oct. 23, 3:18

World Events

Oct. 10 – Islamic Taliban guerillas are forced to surrender positions in the mountains around Kabul by troops loyal to the former Afghan President Rabini.

Oct. 16 – After the massacre of schoolchildren at Dunblane in Scotland, Britain plans to abolish the right to the possession of handguns.

1996

SCORPIO
Your Personal Planets

YOUR LOVE POTENTIAL
Venus in Virgo, Oct. 23, 3:19 - Oct. 29, 12:01
Venus in Libra, Oct. 29, 12:02 - Nov. 22, 0:48

YOUR DRIVE AND MAGNETISM
Mars in Leo, Oct. 23, 3:19 - Oct. 30, 7:12
Mars in Virgo, Oct. 30, 7:13 - Nov. 22, 0:48

YOUR LUCK MAGNETISM
Jupiter in Capricorn, Oct. 23, 3:19 - Nov. 22, 0:48

World Events

Oct. 23 – O. J. Simpson is back in court to face questioning in the civil trial brought against him by the Brown and Goldman's families.

Nov. 18 – Romania abolishes its Communist government.

Kofi Annan, the new Secretary General of the United Nations

SAGITTARIUS
Your Personal Planets

YOUR LOVE POTENTIAL
Venus in Libra, Nov. 22, 0:49 - Nov. 23, 1:33
Venus in Scorpio, Nov. 23, 1:34 - Dec. 17, 5:33
Venus in Sagittarius, Dec. 17, 5:34 - Dec. 21, 14:05

YOUR DRIVE AND AMBITION
Mars in Virgo, Nov. 22, 0:49 - Dec. 21, 14:05

YOUR LUCK MAGNETISM
Jupiter in Capricorn, Nov. 22, 0:49 - Dec. 21, 14:05

World Events

Dec. 12 – Madeleine Albright becomes the first female U.S. Secretary of State.

Dec. 13 – Kofi Annan of Ghana replaces Egypt's Boutros Boutros-Ghali as Secretary-General of the United Nations.

784

SCORPIO
From October 23, 3:19 through November 22, 0:48

The Determined Sleuth

Born during 1996, Scorpio, you arrived just as a great mystery was unearthed. The body of the great explorer Meriwether Lewis—who had died in 1809, and had been the first white man to see and describe most of North America—was about to be exhumed in Tennessee in 1996. The purpose was to discover whether he had been murdered, died in an accidental shooting, or committed suicide as the prevailing legend said. James Starrs, a law professor from George Washington University and a forensic expert, was heading a committee bent on unearthing Lewis's remains to find the truth. The hotly debated subject made headlines in magazines and newspapers all over the world. Over one hundred of Lewis's descendants had been contacted to obtain their support and almost half that number had already responded positively.

The mysterious nature of Lewis's death, as well as the emotional battle behind the exhumation, points to several major qualities of your Sun sign. First off, your innate need to know the facts, and your willingness to "dig" in every manner possible to find them. You were also given the determination to convince others of your opinion, well described by both this event and the astrology of your birth.

At the time of your planetary arrival, cerebral Mercury held court in your sign, giving you the mind of an analyst, detective, and researcher. Fiery Mars, the planet that shows how we take action, was in meticulous Virgo, a sign whose love of analyzing details rivals your own. In short, you were given a strong curiosity, an even stronger determination to quench it, and the intellectual powers necessary to reach a valid conclusion.

When it comes to relationships, then, you'll probably find that you're drawn to others whose energies are as focused as your own. As such, other Scorpios, earthy Taureans, and detail-oriented Virgos would all make fine choices.

Your challenge is to ignore those who would hold you back from finding the answers you need to make your point and quell the amazingly inquisitive side of your personality. Your gift is your capacity to keep at a project until you discover absolutely everything that you need to know.

SAGITTARIUS
From November 22, 0:49 through December 21, 14:05

The Perceptive Communicator

Born during 1996, Sagittarius, you arrived into a world whose attention was focused on something your sign is famous for: a courtroom trial. O. J. Simpson was on trial again for the murder of his ex-wife, Nicole, and Ronald Goldman—this time in civil court. He was about to decide whether or not to take the stand himself to testify in his defense. Unlike the first trial however, which was televised in its entirety, the judge in this trial, Hiroshi Fujisaki, banned cameras from the courtroom, hoping to avoid the media circus the criminal trial had attracted.

Producers at the E! Television Network however, figured out a way to give viewers what they were looking for every day. They created a nightly one-hour "news" program called *The O.J. Civil Trial*, a "dramatic re-enactment" of the day's courtroom events. The huge media attention this second trial attracted worldwide, as well as the sensationalism that surrounded it, perfectly exemplify your sign's connection to Jupiter, the planet of mass communication, exaggeration, and extravagance.

The astrology of your birth year also points to a fondness for mysteries and a love of analysis. Venus, the ruling planet of relationships, was in Scorpio, the sign that most loves to dig, both figuratively and literally. Mars, the planet of action, was in detail-oriented Virgo. In short, you were given the perfect astrological recipe for doing detective work and for making the results of your analysis public knowledge. Add in the touch of cerebral Mercury in Capricorn, a no-nonsense, just-the-facts-ma'am, kind of sign, and it's easy to see that you would make a good detective, producer, or researcher. No matter which career path you choose however, you'll likely become quite well-known. In fact, fame may actually be difficult for you to avoid.

Your love of drama may find you in relationships with Leos, other Sagittarians, or fiery Aries, but rebellious Aquarians would also make good choices.

Your gift is the ability to assimilate details into the big picture. Your challenge is to avoid becoming involved in sensational situations.

► Read about your Chinese Astrological sign on page 838. ► Read about your Personal Planets on page 826. ► Read about your personal Mystical Card on page 856.

CAPRICORN

From December 21, 14:06 through December 31, 23:59

The Realistic Dreamer

Born during late 1996, Capricorn, you arrived at a time that showed both your connection to realism as well a love of imagining. This combination of cosmic energies is well represented by news that surfaced that month in Washington, D.C.—a secret program called "Star Gate". That was the actual code name—not a post-scandal tabloid headline—of a secret program that had cost $20 million over the past ten years. Psychics had been employed to help the Defense Intelligence Agency solve crimes—at least, that was the hope of the agency.

According to statisticians at the University of California, the psychics were right "about twenty-five percent of the time." Typically, the reports included "a large amount of irrelevant, erroneous information," the study said and when the reports did seem on target, they were "vague and general." The fact that the CIA itself had dabbled in the use of parapsychologists for the past few years didn't help "Star Gate's" reputation. In fact, what the report really found was that people want to believe in the paranormal—a trait you may have inherited by virtue of being born during this period of 1996.

You entered the world with the planet Uranus, the ruler of space travel, Star Wars, and science fiction in its own sign, Aquarius. As such, you were given an especially potent dose of imagination, more so than many born under your Sun sign in other years. Jupiter, the planet of expansion, was also keeping very close company with Neptune, the planet of dreams. Still, your Sun in Capricorn would provide a sturdy anchor for all this imagining, allowing you to be both inventive and well-grounded—and the results of that combination might have given you the capacity for genius.

In relationships, you'll need someone just as cerebral and imaginative as yourself, such as Geminis or Aquarians. Sagittarians, however, would also make good choices since their wide-angle view of the world may be very close to your own.

Your challenge is to maintain a happy balance between imagination and reality. Your gift is the capacity for combining those traits into genius.

1996
CAPRICORN
Your Personal Planets

YOUR LOVE POTENTIAL
Venus in Sagittarius, Dec. 21, 14:06 - Dec. 31, 23:59

YOUR DRIVE AND AMBITION
Mars in Virgo, Dec. 21, 14:06 - Dec. 31, 23:59

YOUR LUCK MAGNETISM
Jupiter in Capricorn, Dec. 21, 14:06 - Dec. 31, 23:59

World Events

Dec. 26 - Thousands march in Belgrade in continuing protest against the President's annulment of the election results.

Dec. 30 - The last Russian troops withdraw from Chechnya, surrendering the territory to rebel forces.

Astrologer and seer Nostradamus

Special Feature
Nostradamus: A Prophet Across Time
by Skye Alexander

The French mystic and healer Nostradamus is perhaps the most celebrated seer of all time. The prophecies he wrote in poetic quatrains have captured the interest of scholars and the curious for centuries, and recently sparked renewed interest as the millennium drew near.

From his vantage point in the sixteenth century, Nostradamus offered a narrative of the human timeline that saw the rise and fall of monarchs, empires, and those he referred to as "Antichrist" figures. He chronicled wars between nations, and the assassinations of world leaders. A pioneer time traveler through history, he also caught glimpses of the technological marvels of the future, such as the first moonwalk.

He will come to take himself to the corner of Luna (the Moon),
Where he will be taken and placed on alien land.

In his own lifetime, his legendary status grew as his predictions came true, bringing admiration from some and suspicion from others. Nostradamus had to balance his desire to share his gift with the world with his need to shield himself from the probing eye of the Inquisition. An enigma to his contemporaries, this gifted seer, who could see centuries ahead, was also fully immersed in the trials and triumphs of his particular time in history.

Michel de Nostradamus was born on December 14, 1503, in Southern France, emerging from an idyllic rural childhood to become a true "Renaissance Man." He was a respected and courageous physician who risked his own life to rid entire towns of the bubonic plague. His innovative mind and culinary mastery led to the creation of the first fruit preservatives. He also created and refined cosmetics, and eventually produced and sold his own line of products.

From early in his life, it was clear to his grandfathers that the young Michel also had a remarkable gift of prophecy. The first of five sons in a Jewish family, he was educated by the two elder patriarchs, who passed on a knowledge of classical literature, history, mathematics, and medicine. They also secretly instructed him in the mysteries of the mystical Kabbalah and metaphysical alchemy.

As an adolescent, he was already versed in the disciplines of mathematics and what was then known as the "celestial science," or astrology. Often seen with both his books and his instruments to navigate the heavens, he soon earned the nickname "the little astrologer" at his school in Avignon. He went on to study medicine at a prestigious university in Montpellier.

(Continued on page 793)

➤ Read "Predictions, Eclipses, and September 11" by Rochelle Gordon on page 825.

1997

The Sky's the Limit: Mars, Jupiter, and Uranus

The three liveliest planets in the solar system, Mars, Jupiter and Uranus, were all in air signs in the early part of the year, with powerful Pluto also in the mix. Mars represents action, while Jupiter is expansive and opportunistic. Uranus prickles with electricity, stimulating novel approaches and unexpected results. All their connections were harmonious and stirring. People became more adventurous and sometimes challenged the boundaries of respectability and lawfulness. Amid scandal, Woody Allen, sixty-two, married twenty-seven-year-old Soon-Yi, the adopted daughter of his ex-wife, Mia Farrow. These energies were also at a peak when Andrew Cunanan went on a murder spree across America, avenging imagined slights and killing Gianni Versace before turning the gun on himself. Later in the year, we felt powerful emotions as Princess Diana and Mother Teresa died within days of each other when an eclipse in contact with Pluto was cresting. Eclipses emphasize the planets that they contact and Pluto in this instance, represented death. The eclipse was in Virgo, sign of the servant of humanity. In a sense, each of these women worked their power in service of humankind, as Diana produced England's heirs and lobbied for an anti-land mine treaty, while Mother Teresa ministered to the destitute in India.

More happily, two comets, linked to heavenly Uranus, kept early risers amazed in February and March, while the long-anticipated return of capitalist stronghold Hong Kong to China went off without an economic hitch as Jupiter was strong in July.

Tony Blair is elected Prime Minister of Britain

The funeral of Diana, Princess of Wales

Italian fashion designer Gianni Versace is murdered by Andrew Cunanan

THE GREAT COMET

On March 22, members of a cult called "Heaven's Gate" committed mass suicide, believing that they would join a spaceship traveling in the wake of the comet Hale-Bopp. When the comet neared Earth and became visible, the eagerly anticipated Hale-Bopp was said to be the brightest "naked-eye" comet of the century and called "The Great Comet." Cult members believed that the Virgin Mary had been impregnated by aliens on a spacecraft that was returning with this comet to beam up believers to the "level above human."

TITANIC BOX OFFICE, AND DEATH OF PRINCESS DI

Following the death of Princess Diana in a Paris car crash, a cause for which she had campaigned succeeded when more than one hundred nations, though not the U.S. or China, signed a treaty banning anti-personnel land mines. Britain relinquished Hong Kong to China after 200 years of colonial rule. The charismatic Tony Blair became British Prime Minister when his New Labour Party won a landslide election victory. In the U.S., Oklahoma City bomber Timothy McVeigh was found guilty and sentenced to death. Thirty-nine members of the Heaven's Gate cult committed suicide in California. Islamic extremists killed seventy people at Luxor, Egypt. The African state of Zaire ceased to exist and was replaced by the Democratic Republic of Congo. An Italian-led multinational peacekeeping force arrived in chaotic Albania. A year after being cleared in a criminal court, O.J. Simpson was found guilty of 'causing wrongful death' after a private prosecution case was brought against him. Andrew Cunanan murdered fashion designer Gianni Versace in Miami. In the cinema, *As Good As It Gets*, *Titanic* and *Men In Black* were big box- office hits.

➤ Read "Nostradamus: A Prophet Across Time" by Skye Alexander on page 785.

786

CAPRICORN

From January 01, 0:00 through January 20, 0:41

The Respectful Communicator

Your planet, 1997 Capricorn, is Saturn, the ruler of maturity, experience, and respect. As the property of this practical, sturdy entity, members of your sign are known as the super-achievers of the zodiac who achieve success in traditional occupations. Capricorns born in 1997, however, can also excel in more pioneering endeavors. On January 18 of that year, Norwegian Boerge Ousland completed a solo crossing of Antarctica that began on November 15. He used a parachute and skis to help pull himself across the 1,695 miles from Berkner Island to Scott Base. You also show no fear when facing the unknown and, with rugged determination, will go the extra mile to reach your goals.

Another adventurer, Balloonist Steve Foster, ended his attempt to circle the globe on January 19, 1997. His balloon, *Solo Spirit*, ran out of gas and landed in India after covering 9,000 miles and floating for over six days. One of your best Capricorn qualities is that, while you recognize your limitations, you do not become discouraged by life's challenges. Instead, you are energized by them and never give up until you reach your objectives.

Whether you find success in business, government, or other unexpected areas of life, you believe strongly in contributing to society. On January 16, 1997, Maurice Strong, Canadian millionaire businessman and environmentalist, was appointed by Kofi Annan to coordinate UN reform for a salary of $1 per year.

Four planets held court in your refined, cultured sign, including cerebral Mercury and Venus, the ruler of art, love, and beauty. As if this isn't enough astrological proof that you would probably be quite dutiful and responsible, you were also given the gift of imagination courtesy of expansive Jupiter and dreamy Neptune. You'd make a wonderful writer, storyteller, or lecturer, but whichever profession you choose, you're likely a skilled and enthralling speaker.

Your choice of partner may lead you to aesthetically inclined Taureans and Librans, but the quiet power of Capricorns may also attract you.

Your challenge is to learn to appreciate the new as much as you love things that are old. Your gifts are responsibility and devotion.

AQUARIUS

From January 20, 0:42 through February 18, 14:50

The Natural Inventor

Born during 1997, Aquarius, you arrived just as your sign's connection with excitement, discovery, and rapid-fire technical change were highlighted worldwide. More practical uses of satellites were being found at that time. On January 30, 1997, Global Positioning System (GPS) satellites detected unusual crustal movements of the Kilauea volcano in Hawaii, alerting that area to possible eruptions. Aquarians have an affinity for all cutting-edge technology. Further in deep space, *Discovery*'s astronauts performed a one billion mile tune-up of the Hubble Space Telescope on February 13 of that year. This enabled Hubble to peer more deeply into the Universe.

Whether in outer space or terra firma, you value your own liberty and individual rights and will protect those of others. On January 22, 1997, Canada and Cuba announced a fourteen-point agreement. They pledged cooperation on human rights and sought to shield foreign investors targeted for punishment by Washington. You will frequently take up special causes or directly intervene when you know people are suffering. The UN World Food Program announced a six-month $19.4 million food aid operation in Sierra Leone on January 29 the year of your birth.

The fact that so many of your sign's qualities are shown through these events is astrologically explained by the fact that five of the ten planets astrologers use were in your own inventive, intellectual sign. As such, you're a "super-Aquarius" and it's likely very easy for you to identify with classic descriptions of your Sun sign. But there's more to your nature. In addition, as a 1997 Aquarian, you work well as part of a team but you frequently take a leadership role within your group. You also have a very strong need to balance relationships and career, and you would likely be very good at doing just that, quite naturally.

Speaking of relationships, when you're ready to settle down, be sure to choose a sign as inventive, curious, and open-minded as yourself, such as Geminis, Sagittarians, or other Aquarians.

Your challenge is to express your creative side, no matter how unusual your works are. Your gift is your ability to interpret meaning from symbols.

► Read about your Chinese Astrological sign on page 838. ► Read about your Personal Planets on page 826. ► Read about your personal Mystical Card on page 856.

1997

CAPRICORN
Your Personal Planets

YOUR LOVE POTENTIAL
Venus in Sagittarius, Jan. 01, 0:00 - Jan. 10, 5:31
Venus in Capricorn, Jan. 10, 5:32 - Jan. 20, 0:42

YOUR DRIVE AND AMBITION
Mars in Virgo, Jan. 01, 0:00 - Jan. 03, 8:09
Mars in Libra, Jan. 03, 8:10 - Jan. 20, 0:42

YOUR LUCK MAGNETISM
Jupiter in Capricorn, Jan. 01, 0:00 - Jan. 20, 0:42

World Events

Jan. 7 - The British public votes in favor of retaining the monarchy after a television phone-in.

Jan. 9 - Yachtsman Tony Bullimore is rescued five days after his boat capsized in the Southern Ocean.

A television phone-in poll shows that the British public want to keep the monarchy

AQUARIUS
Your Personal Planets

YOUR LOVE POTENTIAL
Venus in Capricorn, Jan. 20, 0:43 - Feb. 03, 4:27
Venus in Aquarius, Feb. 03, 4:28 - Feb. 18, 14:51

YOUR DRIVE AND AMBITION
Mars in Libra, Jan. 20, 0:43 - Feb. 18, 14:51

YOUR LUCK MAGNETISM
Jupiter in Capricorn, Jan. 20, 0:43 - Jan. 21, 15:12
Jupiter in Aquarius, Jan. 21, 15:13 - Feb. 18, 14:51

World Events

Jan. 25 - Martina Hingis of Switzerland becomes the youngest tennis player to win a Grand Slam tournament, at the age of sixteen.

Feb. 13 - Debbie Rowe and Michael Jackson have a baby boy.

1997

PISCES
Your Personal Planets

YOUR LOVE POTENTIAL
Venus in Aquarius, Feb. 18, 14:52 - Feb. 27, 4:00
Venus in Pisces, Feb. 27, 4:01 - Mar. 20, 13:54

YOUR DRIVE AND AMBITION
Mars in Libra, Feb. 18, 14:52 - Mar. 08, 19:49
Mars in Virgo, Mar. 08, 19:50 - Mar. 20, 13:54

YOUR LUCK MAGNETISM
Jupiter in Aquarius, Feb. 18, 14:52 - Mar. 20, 13:54

World Events

Feb. 23 - Scientists in Scotland announce they have succeeded in cloning an adult mammal, producing a lamb named "Dolly."

Mar. 13 - Ex-Beatle Paul McCartney receives a knighthood from Queen Elizabeth II.

Sir Paul McCartney

ARIES
Your Personal Planets

YOUR LOVE POTENTIAL
Venus in Pisces, Mar. 20, 13:55 - Mar. 23, 5:25
Venus in Aries, Mar. 23, 5:26 - Apr. 16, 9:42
Venus in Taurus, Apr. 16, 9:43 - Apr. 20, 1:02

YOUR DRIVE AND AMBITION
Mars in Virgo, Mar. 20, 13:55 - Apr. 20, 1:02

YOUR LUCK MAGNETISM
Jupiter in Aquarius, Mar. 20, 13:55 - Apr. 20, 1:02

World Events

Mar. 25 - The wreck of a seventeenth-century Spanish galleon is discovered, complete with a cargo worth approximately $4 billion.

Apr. 7 - Liam Gallagher marries Patsy Kensit in a registry office ceremony.

PISCES
From February 18, 14:51 through March 20, 13:54

The Scientific Dreamer

Born during 1997, Pisces, you arrived just as two major scientific events occurred. First off, cognitive scientists Roger Schank and Christopher Owens revealed that computers were as apt a canvas as any made of paper, and that creating with this "cyber-palette" had become a reality. The two found that art and music were being produced on computers on a regular basis, and that the creations were amazingly aesthetic. An invention that debuted during your birth-month also points to the marriage of technology and imagination, two rare astrological gifts of your birth-year. The "interactive theater" made its debut, allowing audiences to actually vote on the plot line they'd like to see next by pressing a button on a joystick. A twenty-minute interactive movie, *Mr. Payback*, could be experienced by the viewer at least twenty-five times before it became repetitive.

These events, blending science with creativity, were predecessors of virtual reality, and both perfectly exemplify both your sign's affinity with make-believe and your ability to make the unreal into the real.

The Sun, Mercury, and Venus, keeping very close company at the time, gave you a gift for fiction, creativity, and imagination. In addition, mind-expanding Jupiter and Uranus, the planet of invention, were traveling together, the perfect astrological recipe for big ideas—in a nutshell, the capacity for genius. Add in the influence of quick-moving Mars in detail-oriented Virgo and it's easy to see that you would probably possess an amazing array of talents, affording you the luxury of excelling at virtually anything you do. You may work with computers, in science, or be a teacher, but regardless of the profession you decide to follow, you'll probably become quite well-known for your accomplishments.

In relationships, you'll need the company of those as keen-minded, versatile, and prone to flashes of brilliance as yourself, such as Aquarians, Sagittarians, or Geminis.

Your challenge is to combine science and art into your own special brand of creativity. Your gift is the ability to connect the factual with the fantastical.

ARIES
From March 20, 13:55 through April 20, 1:02

The Stubborn Believer

Born during 1997, Aries, you arrived just as one of the world's most revered religious leaders, Pope John Paul II, released his eleventh papal letter entitled "Evangelium Vitae," or the "Gospel of Life." This summoned the world's one billion Catholics to "resist crimes which no human law can claim to legitimize," such as abortion, euthanasia, and capital punishment. It was seen by many as the signature statement of this Pope, the Roman-Catholic pontiff for the past nineteen years. However, it was also seen by many as quite controversial.

The papal pronouncement, addressing the most undeniably incendiary moral issues of the moment, was a rare document in church history since in it the Pope actually invoked the full teaching authority of the church to declare certain acts, specifically abortion and euthanasia, as inherently evil. The work was so bold that both supporters and dissenters agreed that it was akin to "the roaring of a lion in winter." Your sign, of course, is synonymous with bravery and assertion, which this latest papal missive perfectly shows.

The volatility of the issues Pope John Paul II tackled in this papal letter was shown by the astrology of the time, which also reveals the mixed blend of energies you inherited by being born an Aries during this particular year. The Sun, Venus, and Saturn—the "Cosmic Schoolteacher"—were all in your fiery, assertive sign. Mars, your own equally assertive planet, was in intellectual Virgo, demonstrating your knack for details and your innate precision in speech and writing.

In relationships, you'll feel most comfortable with the earth signs, especially Taureans and Virgos. In friendships, however, look to the other fire signs, Leos and Sagittarians, who'll help you to access the passion and flare for the extravagant your element is known for—not to mention the playfulness you three also share.

Your challenge is to lighten up—to take life seriously but not too seriously. Your gift is the capacity for producing meticulously detailed, incredibly accurate verbal and written works, the stuff of which genius can be made.

➤ Read about your Chinese Astrological sign on page 838. ➤ Read about your Personal Planets on page 826. ➤ Read about your personal Mystical Card on page 856.

TAURUS

From April 20, 1:03 through May 21, 0:17

The Elegant Individual

Born during 1997, Taurus, you arrived as the fashion industries of New York, Paris, and Milan turned out a season of pretty, practical clothing—quite a change from the preceding years that were seen by many as gimmicky, excessive, and unrealistic. Leading designers the world over created a trend that was new but classic—elegant, "wearable" clothes. Heralded by many who follow the fashion world as "the season of sexy and classy," the very words they chose to describe the season's collective style are apt descriptions of your Sun sign, which played a very prominent astrological role in your birth month.

Thoughtful Mercury and Venus, the planet of love and beauty, both shared much of the Sun's month-long passage through your sign. This was a strong indication that our collective thinking, as well as our collective interpretation of what was currently "beautiful," was quite strongly affected by traits you're famous for—quiet opulence and simple beauty in particular. In addition, Mars, the planet of assertion and pursuit, was in meticulous, earthy Virgo, a humble, practical, and modest sign, showing that what was currently appealing was neatness—in short, a well-groomed appearance and personality. Needless to say, then, you arrived at an optimum moment to help hone your personal astrological mission.

Along with all this modesty and humility, however, you were also given a strong dose of individuality, as evidenced by both extravagant Jupiter and unique Uranus, both traveling through startling Aquarius. In all, you're capable of being equal parts rebel and conformist, depending on which is required, in your mind, at any given moment.

In relationships, you'll need to partner up with someone who's equally fashion-conscious, well-mannered, and refined. As such, you'd do well to seek out the company of other Taureans, Capricorns, and Virgos, all of whom will feel immediately like kindred spirits.

Your challenge is to look beneath the surface for the real beauty, especially in your encounters with others. Your gift is your appreciation for both simplicity and opulence.

GEMINI

From May 21, 0:18 through June 21, 8:19

The Intellectual Connoisseur

Born during 1997, Gemini, you arrived just as a highly-touted book that perfectly reflects your sign's most famous qualities made the top of book lists all over the world. *The Bible Code*, a controversial work written by journalist Michael Drosnin, outlined what the author believed to be a highly complex code in the Hebrew Bible. Among the striking revelations: "economic collapse" and "1929" were encoded as were "Hitler," "Nazi and enemy" and "slaughter," all found in Genesis along with "Wright Brothers" and "airplane."

In addition to politics and mechanical discoveries, other subjects were decoded. For example, "Shoemaker-Levy" and "will pound Jupiter" were also found; the comet had slammed into the giant planet in 1994. Possibly most striking was the fact that one full year before the Israeli prime minister was killed, Drosnin apparently found an encrypted warning for Yitzhak Rabin: "Assassin will assassinate."

The mystery, the quality of genius with words and figures, and the unraveling of this mega-puzzle all coincide beautifully with your Sun sign's fondness for riddles, word games, and knowledge. These traits are also well-described by the astrology of your birth-month, which shows the capacity for genius, an innate knack for problem-solving, and the ability to easily assimilate information to obtain a sturdy conclusion. You were given the gift of having assertive, initiator Mars in Virgo, the sign with whom you share a ruling planet—thoughtful, quicksilver Mercury. Both mind-expanding Jupiter and Uranus, the planet of genius, were in Aquarius, Uranus's own sign, and the astrological purveyor of brilliance. In short, Gemini of 1997, your cerebral gifts are many and your ability to use them all to come up with the perfect solution to any dilemma is unparalleled.

In relationships, you'll need to find someone as intellectually apt and mentally fast as yourself, such as other Geminis, Aquarians, or Sagittarians.

Your gift is your incredible mind. Your challenge is never to lose touch with the physical world, no matter how appealing you find the intellectual side of life.

► Read about your Chinese Astrological sign on page 838. ► Read about your Personal Planets on page 826. ► Read about your personal Mystical Card on page 856.

1997

TAURUS
Your Personal Planets

YOUR LOVE POTENTIAL
Venus in Taurus, Apr. 20, 1:03 - May 10, 17:19
Venus in Gemini, May 10, 17:20 - May 21, 0:17

YOUR DRIVE AND AMBITION
Mars in Virgo, Mar. 20, 1:03 - May 21, 0:17

YOUR LUCK MAGNETISM
Jupiter in Aquarius, Apr. 20, 1:03 - May 21, 0:17

World Events

May 1 - The Labour Party sweeps to victory in Britain, ending eighteen years of Conservative government.

May 12 - Russia and Chechnya sign a peace deal after 400 years of conflict.

The first all-female British team to walk to the North Pole

GEMINI
Your Personal Planets

YOUR LOVE POTENTIAL
Venus in Gemini, May 21, 0:18 - June 04, 4:17
Venus in Cancer, June 04, 4:18 - June 21, 8:19

YOUR DRIVE AND AMBITION
Mars in Virgo, May 21, 0:18 - June 19, 8:29
Mars in Libra, June 19, 8:30 - June 21, 8:19

YOUR LUCK MAGNETISM
Jupiter in Aquarius, May 21, 0:18 - June 21, 8:19

World Events

May 29 - The Democratic Republic of Congo is established.

June 13 - Oklahoma bomber Timothy McVeigh is found guilty and sentenced to the death penalty.

1997

CANCER
Your Personal Planets

YOUR LOVE POTENTIAL
Venus in Cancer, June 21, 8:20 - June 28, 18:37
Venus in Leo, June 28, 18:38 - July 22, 19:14

YOUR DRIVE AND AMBITION
Mars in Libra, June 21, 8:20 - July 22, 19:14

YOUR LUCK MAGNETISM
Jupiter in Aquarius, June 21, 8:20 - July 22, 19:14

World Events

July 1 - Britain hands back Hong Kong to the Chinese in a spectacular ceremony.

July 15 - Fashion designer Gianni Versace is shot by serial killer Andrew Cunanan.

Cathy Freedman of Australia holds her national flag

LEO
Your Personal Planets

YOUR LOVE POTENTIAL
Venus in Leo, July 22, 19:15 - July 23, 13:15
Venus in Virgo, July 23, 13:16 - Aug. 17, 14:30
Venus in Libra, Aug. 17, 14:31 - Aug. 23, 2:18

YOUR DRIVE AND AMBITION
Mars in Libra, July 22, 19:15 - Aug. 14, 8:41
Mars in Scorpio, Aug. 14, 8:42 - Aug. 23, 2:18

YOUR LUCK MAGNETISM
Jupiter in Aquarius, July 22, 19:15 - Aug. 23, 2:18

World Events

Aug. 4 - Australian Cathy Freedman becomes the first athlete of Aboriginal origin to win a gold medal.

Aug. 8 - Ramzi Yousef, mastermind of the World Trade Center bombing, goes on trial.

CANCER
From June 21, 8:20 through July 22, 19:14

The Instinctive Companion

Born during 1997, Cancer, you entered the world just as it heard news of a major discovery concerning estrogen, the hormone under the rulership of the Moon that is naturally produced by females of all species. Touted as the "closest science has ever come to putting the fountain of youth in a little oval tablet," the pill was gaining reputability as the pharmaceutical fulfillment of a dream not merely by adding years to life, but by adding life to years. That same study also revealed that scientists were hot on the trail of new forms of estrogen that would bring virtually all of the benefits but none of the risks of taking it, according to endocrinologists at Columbia University in New York.

The fact that estrogen basically increases fluidity and lubrication in an organism—and that your sign is ruled by the Moon, the astrological patroness of water—points to your innate connection with this discovery, made during the Sun's trek through your sign in 1997.

In addition to the Sun in Cancer, however, you were given two very charming planets in two very charming signs, a strong indication that it's probably quite easy for you to have what you wish for, especially when it comes to companions. Venus, the goddess of love and beauty, was posited in lavish, showy Leo, the irresistible sign of the performer. Mars, Venus's ancient lover and the planet that rules passion and initiative, was in cooperative, sociable, partner-oriented Libra. You were also given the cooperative efforts of outgoing Jupiter and respectful Saturn, a pair that, when working in concert, give the owner a knack for relating with anyone, from any social background, at any time, as the astrology of your personality suggests.

Your choice in relationships will probably be one of the water signs, either another Cancerian, a Piscean, or a Scorpio—all of whom possess antennae as keen and highly-tuned as your own.

Your challenge is never to ignore your intuition, no matter what you're told by others or what you believe is normal. Your gifts are your compassion, ease in social situations, and magnetic charm.

LEO
From July 22, 19:15 through August 23, 2:18

The Influential Egoist

Yours is the sign of the performer, 1997 Leo. In fact, some of history's all-time biggest celebrities were born while the Sun passed through your section of the heavens. The fame many of you fiery folks have earned isn't surprising, considering your ruling planet is the Sun, the ruler of fame—and of fortune and success. Basically, the Sun is the force inside each of us that drives us to become what we know we're destined to become and since yours is the sign he most adores, your urge to fulfill your destiny is the strongest and most undeniably mandatory of all the signs.

This is beautifully evidenced by the fact that Robert Redford, Madonna, Robert DeNiro, Mae West, Melanie Griffith, and Antonio Banderas are just a few of the stars with whom you share your ruling planet. You also share your affinity with the lion, the king of beasts, with Elvis Presley, "The King" of rock and roll himself.

Appropriately, during the trek of the Sun through your sign in 1997, it was revealed that Elvis, dead for twenty years, had amassed even more of a fortune after his death than while he was alive. The company that kept the King's legacy alive by marketing products bearing his name, image, or music, was called, not coincidentally, Elvis Presley Enterprises. It controlled much of the half-billion dollar global Elvis industry, which strictly limited the world's supply of singing hound-dog dolls, Heartbreak Hotel matchboxes, and pink Cadillac key chains—not to mention visits to the Graceland mansion in Memphis, "Elvis Headquarters."

In relationships, you'll need to seek out the company of someone with an equally strong and confident personality. As such, the fire signs, including other Leos, Sagittarians, and Aries, will probably often be by your side, but steady, focused Scorpios and Aquarians may also prove quite appealing.

Your gifts are your ability to turn wherever you are into a stage built for a star and to always amaze and amuse your audience. Your challenge is to allow others their fifteen minutes of fame. Remember, sharing the spotlight is the true measure of confidence.

➤ Read about your Chinese Astrological sign on page 838. ➤ Read about your Personal Planets on page 826. ➤ Read about your personal Mystical Card on page 856.

VIRGO

From August 23, 2:19 through September 22, 23:55

The Unconditional Believer

Born during 1997, Virgo, you arrived just as the most timeless feminine example of your sign was receiving a new wave of adoration. A growing movement in the Roman Catholic Church asked the Pope to proclaim a new, controversial dogma: that Mary, the Mother of Jesus, was the "co-Redeemer." Regardless of whether or not this would come to pass, the effort, unconditional love, and unwavering belief of those who spearheaded the movement perfectly portray several of your sign's qualities, including spiritual devotion, love of perfection, and the willingness to help.

The astrological indicators of your birth month also point to an innate respect for the sacred in all its forms, from a rose petal to a newborn child. The combination of your Sun in Virgo and the fact that strong-willed Mars was posited in intense, perceptive Scorpio show a knack for doing research, working with details, and assimilating bits of knowledge into a cohesive, practical solution. As such, you would likely make an excellent researcher or scientist, but your more spiritual, nurturing side could also be called to work in counseling, psychology, psychiatry, or the health professions.

In addition, the fact that both expansive Jupiter and cautious Saturn were in an easy, cooperative astrological relationship during the time of your birth show your innate knack for being in the right place at the right time, with all the right allies. You may seem lucky to some, then, but whatever you're given is what you deserve. Your integrity and honesty are also quite notable, making you a trustworthy friend and a devoted partner.

When choosing a life-partner, however, you may find that you're disappointed initially, but not forever. Your capacity to see the best in everyone could mean you're often disillusioned with those you've placed your unconditional faith in, but eventually you'll find your prince or princess—and he or she may well be a Taurean, Capricorn, Scorpio, or another Virgo.

Your challenge is to trust your intuition and practicality equally. Your gift is the ability to learn from your experience.

LIBRA

From September 22, 23:56 through October 23, 9:14

The Generous Socialite

Born during 1997, Libra, you arrived just as the world heard news of that year's Nobel Peace Prize and it's inspiring recipient. On October 10, 1997, the prize went to Jody Williams and the International Campaign to Ban Land Mines (ICBL). Thanks to this organization, progress was being made towards eliminating millions of anti-personnel mines buried around the world. As a 1997 Libra you highly value peaceful solutions to conflict, especially where individuals may incur physical harm. You also value interpersonal relationships and marital harmony. The Promise Keepers' "Sacred Assembly of Men," a group of Christians devoted to maintaining their marital vows met in Washington DC on October 4, 1997. The numbers were estimated at 500,000, making it one of the largest religious gatherings in U.S. history.

On a lighter note, because you value all kinds of relationships, you are adept at bringing unusual groups of people together, either professionally or socially, and in very creative ways. Who would have anticipated that Bob Dylan would ever be invited to perform at a religious congress in Bologne? Even Pope John Paul II attended this event, along with a crowd of 200,000, on September 26, 1997. When you throw a party, everyone wants to be there, just because you make it so special.

Astrologically speaking, you were built for giving in many ways. Your Sun and cerebral Mercury, both in your sign, are as partner-oriented as possible. In short, once you give your word, make a promise, or commit yourself to a person or belief, you'll likely never waver from that path. As such, you would certainly make a wonderful friend, co-worker, or partner, since your devotion is never-ending.

And speaking of devotion, when you're deciding whom to choose for a lifelong partner, you'll possibly find that you're in the company of other Librans, Taureans, or Capricorns, who'll share your fondness for solidity and stability.

Your challenge is to find the happy medium between socializing and giving yourself the time alone you so profoundly need. Your gift is your lifelong ability to establish relationships that last.

1997

VIRGO
Your Personal Planets

YOUR LOVE POTENTIAL
Venus in Libra, Aug. 23, 2:19 - Sept. 12, 2:16
Venus in Scorpio, Sept. 12, 2:17 - Sept. 22, 23:55

YOUR DRIVE AND AMBITION
Mars in Scorpio, Aug. 23, 2:19 - Sept. 22, 23:55

YOUR LUCK MAGNETISM
Jupiter in Aquarius, Aug. 23, 2:19 - Sept. 22, 23:55

World Events

Aug. 31 – Diana, Princess of Wales and her closest companion, Dodi Fayed, are killed in a car crash in Paris.

Sept. 5 – Mother Teresa dies.

Death of Mother Teresa and Princess Diana

LIBRA
Your Personal Planets

YOUR LOVE POTENTIAL
Venus in Scorpio, Sept. 22, 23:56 - Oct. 08, 8:24
Venus in Sagittarius, Oct. 08, 8:25 - Oct. 23, 9:14

YOUR DRIVE AND AMBITION
Mars in Scorpio, Sept. 22, 23:56 - Sept. 28, 22:21
Mars in Sagittarius, Sept. 28, 22:22 - Oct. 23, 9:14

YOUR LUCK MAGNETISM
Jupiter in Aquarius, Sept. 22, 23:56 - Oct. 23, 9:14

World Events

Sept. 28 – Seve Ballesteros leads Europe's golfers to a Ryder Cup triumph in Valderama in southern Spain.

Oct. 15 – British-made ThrustSSC, driven by Andy Green, breaks the land speed record in Nevada.

➤ Read about your Chinese Astrological sign on page 838. ➤ Read about your Personal Planets on page 826. ➤ Read about your personal Mystical Card on page 856.

SCORPIO
Your Personal Planets

YOUR LOVE POTENTIAL

Venus in Sagittarius, Oct. 23, 9:15 - Nov. 05, 8:49
Venus in Capricorn, Nov. 05, 8:50 - Nov. 22, 6:47

YOUR DRIVE AND AMBITION

Mars in Sagittarius, Oct. 23, 9:15 - Nov. 09, 5:32
Mars in Capricorn, Nov. 09, 5:33 - Nov. 22, 6:47

YOUR LUCK MAGNETISM

Jupiter in Aquarius, Oct. 23, 9:15 - Nov. 22, 6:47

World Events

Oct. 30 - British au pair Louise Woodward is sentenced to life imprisonment for the death of eight-month-old Matthew Eappen.

Nov. 3 - French truck drivers strike over pay; disruption follows as blockades are set up around the country.

Kim Dae Jung gives a speech in Korea

SAGITTARIUS
Your Personal Planets

YOUR LOVE POTENTIAL

Venus in Capricorn, Nov. 22, 6:48 - Dec. 12, 4:38
Venus in Aquarius, Dec. 12, 4:39 - Dec. 21, 20:06

YOUR DRIVE AND AMBITION

Mars in Capricorn, Nov. 22, 6:48 - Dec. 18, 6:36
Mars in Aquarius, Dec. 18, 6:37 - Dec. 21, 20:06

YOUR LUCK MAGNETISM

Jupiter in Aquarius, Nov. 22, 6:48 - Dec. 21, 20:06

World Events

Dec. 4 - The EU votes against the promotion of tobacco.

Dec. 18 - Kim Dae Jung becomes President of South Korea.

SCORPIO
From October 23, 9:15 through November 22, 6:47

The Mysterious Solver

Born during 1997, Scorpio, you arrived just as your sign's connection to mystery and intrigue made headlines all over the world. Since the recent death of Britain's Princess Diana, the world had come face-to-face with an irrefutable fact: that we will all eventually leave this planet, no matter how beautiful, successful, or well-loved we are. The fact that both the paparazzi and "an underground royal plot" were rumored to have been involved in the tragic crash, which Parisian authorities had labeled accidental, perfectly portray your affiliation with intrigue and mystery.

Although the Princess's death was unbelievably sad, it inspired a lot of thought. When the blunt reality of mortality comes home to rest, it often reveals a path that hadn't been noticed, basically, what one really needs to do. Your sign is ruled by Pluto, the ruler of inevitable changes, so you know that major change is rejuvenating and impossible to do without, from a spiritual perspective.

Each and every experience we have contributes to who we are—right here, right now—something else you've always understood. The rest of the world, however, often feels fear regarding the subject of death. As such, your understanding and wisdom are sorely needed. That communicative edge you also possess comes to you courtesy of the Sun and cerebral Mercury, posited in your own detective-like, perceptive sign, and always ready, willing, and able to help you unravel a puzzle. Your love of interpreting clues is also shown through a connection between Pluto, your own intense planet, and Uranus, the ruler of all things unpredictable.

In relationships, you'd probably do well to pursue the company of those who share your fondness for secrets, intrigue, and solving mysteries. Other Scorpios, Pisceans, and quick-witted Geminis would make good choices, as would cerebral Virgos.

Your challenge is never to become obsessed with tiny details, always reminding yourself to consider the big picture before you make a decision. Your gift is the ability to understand the deepest meaning of each and every event that happens to you.

SAGITTARIUS
From November 22, 6:48 through December 21, 20:06

The Generous Humanitarian

Born during 1997, Sagittarius, you arrived just as a major show of your sign's affiliation with generosity, mass communication, and philanthropy was put on display for the entire world. Ted Turner, the television mogul who had founded CNN, the Cable News Network, as well as TNT and Court TV, had donated $1 billion to the United Nations. Turner put Tim Wirth in charge of the foundation he created. Wirth served as Turner's spokesman to the citizens of the world at large, all of whom wondered why—why someone would give this amount of money to an organization whose duties were so far-reaching it would be difficult to actually see the results. The answer to that question, however, was a Sagittarian one—the gift was given out of the generosity of Turner's heart to a group for which he obviously had strong feelings.

This display of benevolence and charity perfectly exemplifies your sign's innate kindness and altruism, traits you doubly inherited by virtue of being born during this particular year. The history and astrology of this time also perfectly describes your association with the planet Jupiter, the benevolent, kind-hearted king of the gods, and with the concept of humanitarianism.

You entered the world with Jupiter, your own planet, loving Venus, and Uranus, the ruler of the odd, unusual, and erratic, all in Aquarius, a sign whose radical, rebellious traits are famous. In short, you were given a double-dose of outgoing, sociable astrological energies, all of which would serve you well throughout life no matter which career path you choose.

In relationships, seek out the company of the three fire signs—other Sagittarians, Leos, and Aries—all of whom are your kindred spirits, perfectly ready, willing, and able to support and assist you in achieving your goals. Never, however, ignore Aquarians, whose freedom-loving, independent qualities rival your own.

Your gift is the ability to convey your message with strength and confidence. Your challenge is never to allow yourself to fall prey to "users," those who would seek to take advantage of your tender, generous heart.

➤ Read about your Chinese Astrological sign on page 838. ➤ Read about your Personal Planets on page 826. ➤ Read about your personal Mystical Card on page 856.

CAPRICORN
From December 21, 20:07 through December 31, 23:59

The Blunt Communicator

Born during late 1997, Capricorn, you arrived into a world that heard news of the declining health of Boris Yeltsin, the president of Russia. Long rumored to have been failing due basically to heart trouble, it was announced during your birth-month that Yeltsin, "an actuarial accident waiting to happen," was, indeed, suffering from heart pains. In fact, one of his closest aides told *Newsweek* magazine that Yeltsin's condition was "very serious." This close scrutiny, especially concerning the life of a public figure, reflects your sign's connection to no-nonsense communication—or your ability to shoot straight from the hip, with no sugar-coating allowed.

The astrology of your birth-month also shows your commitment to honesty and integrity, and your fondness for bluntness. While the Sun, the center of our corner of the galaxy, held court in your sign, four planets in Aquarius, the sign of rebelliousness, gave you the ability to break the rules you took so long to diligently learn—all in favor of the advancement of knowledge, your personal quest. In addition, cerebral Mercury was in wide-angle Sagittarius, the sign most famous for its fondness for foreign, exotic places and people—and its ability to ignore meaningless details in favor of envisioning the big picture.

In all, you were given the gifts of foresight, wisdom, and futuristic imagining, all quite valuable traits which will no doubt come in handy as you pass through life, seeking information and intelligence. All of this will serve you well in both work and personal encounters.

In relationships, you'll probably turn to others who are as open-minded, optimistic, and outgoing as you, including Ariens, Leos, and Aquarians. Geminis, however, will also prove to be good friends, courtesy of the fact that you share an unquenchable thirst for knowledge of all kinds.

Your challenge is to learn when the time is right to tell the truth but also when holding back the facts is the right thing to do. Your gift is your innate capacity for telling the unvarnished truth, no matter how unpopular that truth might be.

CAPRICORN
Your Personal Planets

YOUR LOVE POTENTIAL
Venus in Aquarius, Dec. 21, 20:07 - Dec. 31, 23:59

YOUR DRIVE AND AMBITION
Mars in Aquarius, Dec. 21, 20:07 - Dec. 31, 23:59

YOUR LUCK MAGNETISM
Jupiter in Aquarius, Dec. 21, 20:07 - Dec. 31, 23:59

World Events

Dec. 24 – The first commercial spy satellite, *Early Bird 1*, is launched from Russia.

Dec. 29 – Daniel Arap Moi is elected for his fifth term as President of Kenya following an election rumored to have been rigged.

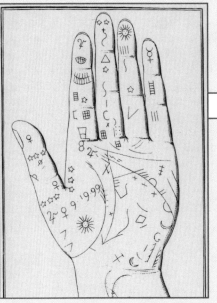

The Lines of Unity: the hand of Napoleon Bonaparte

Special Feature
Nostradamus: A Prophet Across Time

(Continued from page 785)

As a physician, he was ahead of his time in prescribing a regimen of herbal remedies, cleanliness, and fresh air, rather than the more common practice of "bleeding" patients. His "rose pills," and knowledge of the astrological makeup of his patients, helped rid many French towns of the deadly bubonic plague.

In a tragic irony, he was shunned by his patients and accused of heresy after he was unable to cure his own wife and two young children of the deadly plague. In his grief, he wandered through Europe for a few years, during which time his gift of foresight reportedly deepened and grew.

He eventually settled in Salon, France, where he remarried and created an alcove study so he could delve deeply into the mysteries of his unique psychic gifts. By candlelight, he would study the ever-changing sky and open his mind to receiving visions. To peer into the future, he used the technique known as "scrying." He would perform a magical ritual using methods of the prophetesses of ancient Greece, quiet his mind and gaze into a bowl of water set on a brass tripod. A voice he believed to be a divine presence spoke to him, along with "the subtle spirit of fire."

Many of the predictions in his ten-volume work *The Centuries* are startling in their specific accuracy, with names and places woven into the quatrains. Others seem open to many possible interpretations, mysteriously presented as anagrams, wordplay, or riddles. Always aware of the watchful eye of the Inquisition of his day, Nostradamus disguised his prophecies in a mixture of languages and cryptic messages.

Some of his images seem to offer a poetic impression of an event. Could the following quatrain possibly be, as many scholars say, his vision of the D-Day Invasion, with a haunting account of the amphibious tanks that came ashore on the beaches of Normandy?

When the fish, that is both terrestrial and aquatic,
By a strong wave shall be cast upon the shore,
With his strange, fearful, horrid form,
Soon after the enemy shall come to the walls by the sea.

Among his predictions is the naming of three tyrants through history, whom he called "Antichrist" figures. The first is presumed by scholars to be Napoleon, who Nostradamus described as "less a prince than a butcher." He accurately predicted a fourteen-year reign for the "crophead" Napoleon, whose hairstyle resembled that of his hero, Julius Caesar.

(Continued on page 801)

➤ Read more about Hitler on page 353 ➤ Read more about Nostradamus in "Astrology Reigns Through the Ages on page 25 ➤ Read "Predictions, Eclipses and September 11" on page 821.

1998

Progress and Apocalypse: Uranus and Neptune

Uranus, the planet of change and disruption and the energy it represents were emphasized in 1998, as the eclipses moved near its position in Aquarius, the sign of social activism and futuristic approaches. A brave new world began as California banned smoking in bars and clubs and Viagra revolutionized the lives of impotent men. However, as the eclipse highlighted Uranus in early August, more disruptive events occurred. Two U.S. Embassies in Africa were suddenly struck by Osama bin Laden's suicide bombers, killing hundreds. A month later, Swissair Flight 111 crashed in the ocean near Nova Scotia, leading to questions of more terrorist involvement. Saturn and Neptune were interacting in a challenging way, suggesting trends and long-term issues rather than discrete events. Saturn, the planet of leaders, regulations and governments, was "square" to Neptune, planet of undermining and dissolving influences. These were seen in the progression of events surrounding the Monica Lewinsky scandal in the U.S., which undermined the ability of President Clinton to lead the country.

Governments of Europe felt the dissolving influence of Neptune, as the European Economic Union became more of a reality with the minting of the first Euros and the disintegration of divergent regulations between states. Neptune also symbolizes films and visual images and with the strident tie to Saturn, some dark subjects made it to the screen. Among the best were Roberto Benigni's tragi-comedy *Life is Beautiful* and the realistic *The Thin Red Line*.

The first Euros are minted

Former Chilean dictator Augusto Pinochet is arrested in London

Frank Sinatra dies

ABORIGINE SPACE PORTRAIT

In July 1998, an enormous line drawing of an Aborigine man holding a spear was discovered in the Australian desert north of Adelaide. Well-proportioned and beautifully drawn into the Earth with a twenty-foot-wide gouged line, the image was visible only from 3,000 feet in the air. A deep rust color against the pale sand, it measured three miles long with a perimeter of ten miles. The mysterious figure was thought to be the work of extraterrestrials since the shape could not be recognized from the ground.

THE EUROPEAN UNION EMERGES

The first Euros, future currency of the Common Market, were minted. In Africa, the American embassies in Kenya and Tanzania were simultaneously bombed by terrorists led by Osama bin Laden, who had declared a personal war on the U.S. While in London for medical treatment, the eighty-three-year-old former Chilean dictator Augusto Pinochet was arrested on charges of crimes against humanity. The U.S. and Britain launched Operation Desert Fox against Iraq after Hussein refused to cooperate with U.N. arms inspectors. Swissair Flight 111, flying from New York to Geneva, crashed in the Atlantic, killing 229. In Israel, Arabs rioted on the West Bank after a Palestinian terrorist was killed and mudslides killed eighty-one people near Naples in Italy. In Cambodia, Khmer Rouge dictator Pol Pot died: he was responsible for over one million deaths. Facing possible impeachment, President Clinton gave testimony on TV in the Monica Lewinsky sex scandal. Chep Lap Kok, the world's largest airport, opened in Hong Kong. Viagra, a cure for impotence, became available. Ex-Beatle Paul McCartney's wife Linda died of cancer at fifty-six. Crooner Frank Sinatra died at eighty-two.

➤ Read "Nostradamus: A Prophet Across Time" by Skye Alexander on page 785.

CAPRICORN

From January 01, 0:00 through January 20, 6:45

The Inventive Pragmatist

As a Capricorn born near the end of the twentieth century, you bring the wisdom of the old millennium into the new, combining the best of both eras. You respect the past, knowing that we are all part of a long tradition, but you won't allow yourself to be limited by what's gone before nor will you cling to old ideas and attitudes.

Instead, you look to the future and want to do your part to make the new world a better place. In the truest sense, you will be a practical idealist, for you want to resolve the struggles of previous generations. Born as the European nations were continuing to work toward establishing economic unity and cooperation, you understand the benefits of putting aside personal differences for the good of all.

Like all Capricorns, you will be a hard worker and good at business. Born during a period when sophisticated computer technology was linking the world through the Internet and expanding our vision with special effects in movies such as *Titanic*, you'll see technology as an asset and a necessity.

In your relationships with other people you will probably be firm but fair. You respect honesty and forthrightness, but also want to keep your private life private. Perhaps the publicity that surrounded President Bill Clinton's relationship with Monica Lewinsky had an impact on your attitudes. You believe in commitment and responsibility in partnerships, but you also will uphold the rights of the individuals involved to have some autonomy. You know that a relationship that encourages its members to grow and develop themselves is likely to be more fresh and exciting. Some of your favorite companions might be independent and fair-minded Aquarians, though you might also get along with Virgos and Taureans.

Although you realize that rules are necessary and you usually play by them, you also know when to break rules that have outlived their usefulness. Your strength will be your ability to take the plans and structures developed by others and improve them by putting your own spin on them. Your challenge will be to use your heart as well as your head to connect with other people.

AQUARIUS

From January 20, 6:46 through February 18, 20:54

The Compassionate Reformer

Like all water bearers, you are a visionary with a dream. In your world plan, everyone will play a role and everyone's welfare will be taken into consideration. You won't believe that only the richest and most powerful should determine matters that affect all of us. Instead, you will feel a certain responsibility toward the less fortunate and will want to help them to achieve more.

Born at a time when leaders abused their power—such as South Africa's President Botha and Chile's dictator Pinochet—you may dedicate yourself to restoring justice and righting wrongs of all sorts. A champion of the underdog, you stand up for what you believe. Your humanitarianism may lead you to a career in politics or social services where you can put your ideals to work. Or you might prefer to help others by working in the fields of health, science, or technology, where your special combination of inventiveness and compassion could bring you the respect of your peers.

Although you might not put financial gain at the top of your list of priorities, you do possess a capacity for earning money. Consequently, you will probably be more successful in your professional life if you ally yourself with a partner or group of like-minded individuals. That way you can inspire your associates while the more down-to-earth members of the group can help you keep a realistic perspective.

In your personal relationships, you will be a romantic, yet you understand that everyone has feet of clay. Therefore, you may be willing to forgive a partner's foibles, while at the same time encouraging him or her to follow a course of self-improvement. Like all Aquarians, you will have a strong independent streak, but you also will be a loyal partner and friend. You tend to enjoy the company of Capricorns and Pisceans, though you might also be compatible with Ariens, Geminis, and Librans.

Your optimism, creativity, and enthusiasm will be strengths you can use to help change the world and bring about the long prophesied "Age of Aquarius." Your challenge will be to combine your idealism with common sense.

➤ Read about your Chinese Astrological sign on page 838. ➤ Read about your Personal Planets on page 826. ➤ Read about your personal Mystical Card on page 856.

1998

CAPRICORN
Your Personal Planets

YOUR LOVE POTENTIAL
Venus in Aquarius, Jan. 01, 0:00 - Feb. 09, 21:02
Venus in Capricorn, Feb. 09, 21:03 - Jan. 20, 6:45

YOUR DRIVE AND AMBITION
Mars in Aquarius, Jan. 01, 0:00 - Jan. 20, 6:45

YOUR LUCK MAGNETISM
Jupiter in Aquarius, Jan. 01, 0:00 - Jan. 20, 6:45

World Events

Jan. 7 - The Canadian government apologizes for its former racism against the Native American population.

Jan. 9 - British composer Michael Tippett dies.

Death of Michael Tippett

AQUARIUS
Your Personal Planets

YOUR LOVE POTENTIAL
Venus in Capricorn, Jan. 20, 6:46 - Feb. 18, 20:54

YOUR DRIVE AND AMBITION
Mars in Aquarius, Jan. 20, 6:46 - Jan. 25, 9:25
Mars in Pisces, Jan. 25, 9:26 - Feb. 18, 20:54

YOUR LUCK MAGNETISM
Jupiter in Aquarius, Jan. 20, 6:46 - Feb. 04, 10:51
Jupiter in Pisces, Feb. 04, 10:52 - Feb. 18, 20:54

World Events

Jan. 26 - Intel launches the 333 MHz Pentium II computer chip.

Jan. 26 - President Clinton vehemently denies a sexual relationship with White House aide Monica Lewinsky.

PISCES
Your Personal Planets

YOUR LOVE POTENTIAL

Venus in Capricorn, Feb. 18, 20:55 - Mar. 04, 16:13
Venus in Aquarius, Mar. 04, 16:14 - Mar. 20, 19:54

YOUR DRIVE AND AMBITION

Mars in Pisces, Feb. 18, 20:55 - Mar. 04, 16:17
Mars in Aries, Mar. 04, 16:18 - Mar. 20, 19:54

YOUR LUCK MAGNETISM

Jupiter in Pisces, Feb. 18, 20:55 - Mar. 20, 19:54

World Events

Feb. 20 - Fifteen-year-old Tara Lipinski becomes the youngest gold medallist in the history of the Winter Olympics, for her ice-skating performance.

Feb. 25 - Switzerland's first legal brothel opens in Zurich.

Leonardo di Caprio and Kate Winslet star in Titanic

ARIES
Your Personal Planets

YOUR LOVE POTENTIAL

Venus in Aquarius, Mar. 20, 19:55 - Apr. 06, 5:37
Venus in Pisces, Apr. 06, 5:38 - Apr. 20, 6:56

YOUR DRIVE AND AMBITION

Mars in Aries, Mar. 20, 19:55 - Apr. 13, 1:04
Mars in Taurus, Apr. 13, 1:05 - Apr. 20, 6:56

YOUR LUCK MAGNETISM

Jupiter in Pisces, Mar. 20, 19:55 - Apr. 20, 6:56

World Events

Mar. 23 - The most expensive film ever made, *Titanic*, wins eleven Oscars at the Academy Awards.

Apr. 15 - Reports reach the world of the death of Khmer Rouge leader Pol Pot.

PISCES
From February 18, 20:55 through March 20, 19:54

The Unconventional Artist

Whether or not you consider yourself an artist in the usual sense, you will have a vivid imagination and a unique vision that will enrich your life and the lives of those around you. Whatever you do, you do it with flair and originality.

Art and music that utilize new technology or make some sort of political statement might appeal to you. In your opinion, art can be used as an instrument for change. You might even choose to earn your living in a creative field. For you, making lots of money won't be as important as being able to express yourself in an independent, imaginative way. In fact, you might even be a bit impractical about your work and expectations. Because you will be individualistic and private, you might be more content working alone rather than in a conventional, structured environment.

Spiritual or philosophical ideas may also interest you, offering you the possibility for continued growth. You may have much to offer others in this area, too, for you probably will possess a certain vision and teaching ability. But your independent side probably will keep you from following one of the organized religions as you need to find the truth for yourself.

Creativity and spiritual awareness likely will influence your personal relationships. Many of the people you will know may be involved in artistic pursuits and/or be of a spiritual mindset. You and a partner may share a special empathy that sets you apart from the rest of the world. Easily bored, you will need romance, excitement, and stimulation and should seek a partner who is as idealistic and imaginative as you will be. You tend to get along best with Cancers and other Pisceans, though Capricorns and Aquarians might be good choices too.

Traveling could be an eye- and mind-opening experience for you. Your greatest happiness may come through expanding your horizons beyond the here and now, whether you journey in the outer or inner world. Your greatest strength will be your imagination that lets you see things in a fresh way. Your challenge will be to harness your visions and bring them down to Earth.

ARIES
From March 20, 19:55 through April 20, 6:56

The Practical Pioneer

In typical Aries fashion, you will be an adventurer and a pioneer, although in the physical sense, there will be fewer frontiers available to you. As a result, you may choose to push the outside of the envelope in meta-physical areas, as did Arien psychiatrist and cosmo-biologist Wilhelm Reich. Because you were born during a period of unprecedented advances in computers and medical technology, you may decide to explore these areas' unrealized possibilities.

You possess a special blend of daring and pragmatism that many Ariens lack. This combination will be a great asset in virtually every area of life, from playing sports to earning a living. With your courage, curiosity, and enthusiasm, you will eagerly take on challenges that would intimidate other less confident individuals. But you won't rush ahead blindly, rather, you will take time to plan your strategy so that you often come out on top.

Your independent spirit, however, may sometimes bump against the walls of authority. Enterprising and individualistic, you will want to do things your own way, at your own pace—which is quite rapid—and won't want anyone else to interfere. You may find that your ideas will be ahead of their time. For this reason, you might be successful going it alone, so to speak, as you possess an entrepreneurial nature that thrives on competition and risk-taking.

This doesn't mean that you will be anti-social, though certainly you are quite content being alone—in the great outdoors, for instance. You will be attracted to people who are unusual, forthright, and outgoing, and your ideal companions might be Aquarians, Sagittarians, and Leos. In relationships, you will require a good deal of freedom and a bit of a challenge. Although you do have a serious side, your upbeat, optimistic temperament will make you a fun person to be around.

You will always be in search of the new, the different, and the exciting; chances are good that you will find it. Your greatest strengths will be your vitality and pioneering spirit. Your challenge will be to break new ground without stepping on too many toes.

➤ Read about your Chinese Astrological sign on page 838. ➤ Read about your Personal Planets on page 826. ➤ Read about your personal Mystical Card on page 856.

TAURUS

From April 20, 6:57 through May 21, 6:04

The Beauty Lover

No one enjoys the good life more than you will. You will have a deep appreciation for all things bright and beautiful and see the world with an artist's eye. You probably will have more than your share of creative ability too, which you will probably express in tangible ways. Whatever you put your hand to will become a thing of beauty.

Your wonderful imagination and love of fine things could be well-used in one of the decorative arts fields. You possess a natural sense of color and rhythm, and probably will enjoy many forms of artistic expression including music, gardening, photography, cooking, or sculpture. It will be important for you to be able to see the results of your efforts in a physical way—and to be amply rewarded for your abilities.

You will place a high value on money and what it can buy. You need to have a good income so that you can surround yourself with the beautiful things that you adore. A true lover of luxury and sensory pleasures, you might even be a bit of a hedonist at times.

Born during a time when health-consciousness was not only fashionable but also fostered by laws such as those that limited smoking, you may face a dilemma choosing between enjoying earthly delights and maintaining a responsible lifestyle. Even your relationships with other people may center on sharing good times and a few indulgences. Your friends and partners might also share your interest in art, music, and other creative endeavors. Best matched with Capricorns, Cancers, Pisceans, and other Taureans, you will have no trouble attracting companions.

While you display a relaxed, gentle, and unassuming nature, there will be a determined side to you too. Once you make your mind up to do something, you won't quit until you've accomplished your aims. Of course, you will have your ups and downs, like everyone, but you know that success means being able to roll with the punches. Your creativity will be your greatest strength and asset. Your challenge will be to use good judgment in terms of the people you let into your life, making sure your values are similar to theirs.

GEMINI

From May 21, 6:05 through June 21, 14:02

A Beautiful Mind

The entire world will be grist for your mental mill, Gemini of 1998. Hungry for knowledge and experience of all kinds, you will be a lifelong student. Your range of interests will be second to none, but there will always be more to discover. You will possess an insatiable curiosity that may take you from the ocean's depths to the furthest reaches of outer space—at least intellectually. Collecting information and sharing what you know may be among your favorite pastimes.

You were born when the Internet and computer technology had expanded the communications field dramatically. The media's ability to influence public opinion was also increasing. As a result, you will see knowledge as power. With your natural proclivity for communication, you may succeed at a career in one of the communications fields or in a job that involves sharing knowledge, such as teaching or writing. You might even pursue more than one vocation simultaneously, for you won't like to limit your options.

Not just another clever "nerd," you will have a creative vision that gives your ideas richness and beauty. Your imagination will let you see things in a way that other people won't and you may be able to express yourself in a truly artistic manner.

Your diverse interests and facility with speech will make you a fascinating, sought-out conversationalist. Gregarious and good-natured, you probably will have many friends from all walks of life. Easily bored, however, you won't waste time with people who don't stimulate you or can't keep up with your fast-paced lifestyle. Therefore, Ariens, Aquarians, and other Geminis are good companions for you, though Taureans could help you keep your feet on the ground. Because you don't want to miss out, you might not limit yourself to one significant other.

At times, however, your curiosity and expansiveness may cause you to overextend yourself. Although your strength will be your ability to keep many balls in the air simultaneously, you need to be realistic about your capabilities. Your challenge will be to say "no" so that you don't take on more than you can handle.

➤ Read about your Chinese Astrological sign on page 838. ➤ Read about your Personal Planets on page 826. ➤ Read about your personal Mystical Card on page 856.

1998

TAURUS
Your Personal Planets

YOUR LOVE POTENTIAL
Venus in Pisces, Apr. 20, 6:57 - May 03, 19:15
Venus in Aries, May 03, 19:16 - May 21, 6:04

YOUR DRIVE AND AMBITION
Mars in Taurus, Apr. 20, 6:57 - May 21, 6:04

YOUR LUCK MAGNETISM
Jupiter in Pisces, Apr. 20, 6:57 - May 21, 6:04

World Events

Apr. 30 – British adventurer David Hempleman-Adams reaches the geographic North Pole in fifty-six days.

May 11 – The first Euro coins are minted near Bordeaux.

British adventurer David Hempleman-Adams

GEMINI
Your Personal Planets

YOUR LOVE POTENTIAL
Venus in Aries, May 21, 6:05 - May 29, 23:31
Venus in Taurus, May 29, 23:32 - June 21, 14:02

YOUR DRIVE AND AMBITION
Mars in Taurus, May 21, 6:05 - May 24, 3:41
Mars in Gemini, May 24, 3:42 - June 21, 14:02

YOUR LUCK MAGNETISM
Jupiter in Pisces, May 21, 6:05 - June 21, 14:02

World Events

June 4 – Terry Nichols, Oklahoma City bomber, is sentenced to life in prison.

June 12 – Japan announces that it is suffering a recession.

1998

CANCER

Your Personal Planets

YOUR LOVE POTENTIAL

Venus in Taurus, June 21, 14:03 - June 24, 12:26
Venus in Gemini, June 24, 12:27 - July 19, 15:16
Venus in Cancer, July 19, 15:17 - July 23, 0:54

YOUR DRIVE AND AMBITION

Mars in Gemini, June 21, 14:03 - July 06, 8:59
Mars in Cancer, July 06, 9:00 - July 23, 0:54

YOUR LUCK MAGNETISM

Jupiter in Pisces, June 21, 14:03 - July 23, 0:54

World Events

June 30 – Linda Tripp gives her testimony to the grand jury about the Clinton sex scandal.

July 2 – The world's largest international airport, Chep Lap Kok, opens in Hong Kong.

Monica Lewinsky

LEO

Your Personal Planets

YOUR LOVE POTENTIAL

Venus in Cancer, July 23, 0:55 - Aug. 13, 9:19
Venus in Leo, Aug. 13, 9:20 - Aug. 23, 7:58

YOUR DRIVE AND AMBITION

Mars in Cancer, July 23, 0:55 - Aug. 20, 19:15
Mars in Leo, Aug. 20, 19:16 - Aug. 23, 7:58

YOUR LUCK MAGNETISM

Jupiter in Pisces, July 23, 0:55 - Aug. 23, 7:58

World Events

Aug. 2 – Marco Pantani of Italy wins the Tour De France.

Aug. 6 – Monica Lewinsky testifies before a federal grand jury for eight and a half hours.

CANCER

From June 21, 14:03 through July 23, 0:54

The Deep Care-Giver

No one is more sensitive than you, 1998 Cancer. You may be so sensitive, in fact, that you might even seem psychic at times. Other people may be surprised that you know intuitively what's going on inside their heads. You will feel a deep connection to the world around you.

Your compassionate nature and your ability to empathize with other people could serve you well in a career in medicine, social services, or psychology. Not only do you make others feel safe and secure, you possess a special talent for understanding what's really troubling them and how to correct it.

One of the ways you show you care is through feeding your loved ones. From a very young age, you may well like to cook. Your innate talents in this area could even express themselves in a career as a chef, baker, or restaurateur. With your natural appreciation for beauty, you will put your creative touch on everything in your personal environment and make it aesthetically pleasing. Interior design might be a special interest. As a result, other people will like to gather in your home, which is a good thing because you will be a real homebody.

Your kindness and personal warmth will attract people of all ages, and you rarely will turn away anyone. Family will be very important to you. Your immediate family members as well as your ancestors will give you a sense of belonging to something larger than yourself. Your friends will form an extended family for you and you will be especially fond of children. Taureans and Pisceans will be good signs for you to be with, though you might also enjoy the carefree nature of Geminis.

Because you will have such deep feelings and can be easily hurt, you may try to hold on to the people you care about too tightly. Born during highly publicized sex scandal involving President Clinton, you may have been influenced by attitudes and actions that you feel undermine security and family values. Your strength will be your loyalty and devotion to those you care about. Your challenge will be to find security within yourself, instead of looking to others to provide it.

LEO

From July 23, 0:55 through August 23, 7:58

The Responsible Leader

People immediately see you as a born leader, Leo of 1998. Not only do you exude a natural charisma and style, you also will know how to take charge of situations and manage them in a responsible way. Whether you become captain of your athletic team or head of a business venture, you will do what's necessary to get the job done.

Of course you may be aware of your own abilities and may be a bit self-centered at times. That innate self-confidence will serve you well in your role as leader. But you shall rarely let your own interests overshadow your sense of responsibility. To your family, friends, and loved ones, you will be a caring and loyal person who can be trusted. Fiercely protective of those you love, you may go to great lengths to ensure that the people close to you are secure. You could even assume a protector role on a larger scale for you probably have a strong sense of patriotism.

Self-expression may be important to you and you probably possess the lion's share of talent. Most likely, you could enjoy movies and the theater, where everything is bigger than life— like the blockbuster film *Titanic*, which won so many Oscars the year you were born. With your imagination and creativity, you might excel in the arts, perhaps as an actor or filmmaker yourself. Advertising, fashion design, or architecture might also appeal to you.

In one-to-one relationships, you will tend to enjoy a bit of drama. This won't mean you are superficial, however. Quite the opposite—you will have deep feelings and take partnerships quite seriously. Although you may see eye-to-eye with Sagittarians and Ariens, you probably prefer the soothing company of Cancers or Pisceans.

Naturally, you will like attention and want to be respected—and rewarded—for your efforts. Born when the global economy generally stagnated, you may have gained an awareness of the need for financial security. Your strength will be your ability to combine creativity with determination. In both personal and group endeavors, you can achieve a great deal—your challenge will be to help others to do the same.

➤ Read about your Chinese Astrological sign on page 838. ➤ Read about your Personal Planets on page 826. ➤ Read about your personal Mystical Card on page 856.

VIRGO

From August 23, 7:59 through September 23, 5:36

The Capable Fixer

Whenever something goes wrong, you are probably the one who steps in to save the day. You have the skills and willingness to fix anything, from a broken copy machine to a broken heart. At an early age, you may start taking things apart to see how they work, then improve upon the original design. In a neat, orderly fashion, you will put things right so they operate more efficiently than before.

You shall approach life in a methodical way. At home, school, or in the workplace, your diligence and careful attention to detail will enable you to excel at the tasks you undertake. Unlike some of your peers, who rush in without much forethought, you consider all angles and take it one step at a time. As a result, you won't make many mistakes. While you could expect to be thanked and appreciated for your efforts, you will accept a role as the power behind the throne.

Your abilities could be well-suited to jobs that require precision and patience, such as auto repair, editing, or computer programming. Healthcare fields and social services could also be good choices for you, because you will be as competent at fixing people as you are at repairing objects. Like fellow Virgo Mother Teresa of Calcutta, you will be concerned about the well being of others, particularly those who are hurt or disadvantaged. Your kind-heartedness will extend to all creatures, and you probably will bring home stray or injured animals.

You will always be willing to help out friends and loved ones. The saying "a friend in need is a friend indeed" certainly describes you. However, you will have high expectations of others. In relationships, you will your companions with great care, but once a partner passes your test for perfection, you will him or her your complete devotion and loyalty. Taureans, Capricorns, and Cancers should be good companions for you.

Your strength will be your special combination of imagination and practicality that can help you succeed in virtually anything you set your mind to. Your challenge will be to be more tolerant of others' limitations.

LIBRA

From September 23, 5:37 through October 23, 14:58

The Determined Diplomat

You will have a talent for smoothing troubled waters, 1998 Libra. Born when the nations of Europe were attempting to put old rivalries behind them, you see the value in cooperation. From an early age, you will probably be the one who tries to solve problems between friends and family members. You dislike conflict and strive to balance and order your life.

Despite your graceful demeanor, you won't be a pushover. To some extent, your strength could lie in your ability to remain detached from emotionally charged situations. Because you can see both sides of an argument, you will often come up with a solution that is acceptable to all concerned. This valuable skill may be useful in law, psychology, politics, or business. You also will be quite flexible so that you bend rather than break under stress.

Beauty may be important to you and you will have an appreciation for the finer things in life. Your natural sense of harmony probably will make you fond of music as well as art. You also possess a good imagination that could be utilized in many creative fields including fashion design, architecture, or graphic arts. Cooking, too, may appeal to you—you put a touch of artistry into even the simplest meals.

However, your dispassionate nature may make you seem rather aloof, particularly in close relationships. Relationships will certainly be important to you—you might maintain a large network of friends. You may get along well with other outgoing types, including Geminis, Sagittarians, Leos, and Aquarians. In one-to-one partnerships, you will be considerate and eager to please. A true social animal, you will enjoy entertaining. With your charm, you can be the perfect host and a welcome guest at any gathering.

Like other Librans, you may tend to be rather conservative, however, you will have an unconventional side that keeps you from being boring or predictable. When you let yourself go, you should really sparkle. Your strength will be your ability to restore harmony to stressful situations. Your challenge will be to stick to your decisions once you've made them.

VIRGO
Your Personal Planets

YOUR LOVE POTENTIAL
Venus in Leo, Aug. 23, 7:59 - Sept. 06, 19:23
Venus in Virgo, Sept. 06, 19:24 - Sept. 23, 5:36

YOUR DRIVE AND AMBITION
Mars in Leo, Aug. 23, 7:59 - Sept. 23, 5:36

YOUR LUCK MAGNETISM
Jupiter in Pisces, Aug. 23, 7:59 - Sept. 23, 5:36

World Events

Sept. 3 - President Clinton makes a visit to Northern Ireland.

Sept. 6 - Japanese film director Akira Kurosawa dies.

British police arrest former Chilean dictator Augusto Pinochet

LIBRA
Your Personal Planets

YOUR LOVE POTENTIAL
Venus in Virgo, Sept. 23, 5:37 - Sept. 30, 23:12
Venus in Libra, Sept. 30, 23:13 - Oct. 23, 14:58

YOUR DRIVE AND AMBITION
Mars in Leo, Sept. 23, 5:37 - Oct. 07, 12:27
Mars in Virgo, Oct. 07, 12:28 - Oct. 23, 14:58

YOUR LUCK MAGNETISM
Jupiter in Pisces, Sept. 23, 5:37 - Oct. 23, 14:58

World Events

Oct. 16 - The Nobel Peace Prize is awarded to Northern Ireland politicians John Hume and David Trimble.

Oct. 17 - Chilean dictator Augusto Pinochet is arrested in London on charges of crimes against humanity.

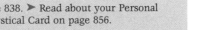 ➤ Read about your Chinese Astrological sign on page 838. ➤ Read about your Personal Planets on page 826. ➤ Read about your personal Mystical Card on page 856.

1998

SCORPIO
Your Personal Planets

YOUR LOVE POTENTIAL

Venus in Libra, Oct. 23, 14:59 - Oct. 24, 23:05
Venus in Scorpio, Oct. 24, 23:06 - Nov. 17, 21:05
Venus in Sagittarius, Nov. 17, 21:06 - Nov. 22, 12:33

YOUR DRIVE AND AMBITION

Mars in Virgo, Oct. 23, 14:59 - Nov. 22, 12:33

YOUR LUCK MAGNETISM

Jupiter in Pisces, Oct. 23, 14:59 - Nov. 22, 12:33

World Events

Oct. 29 - British Poet Laureate Ted Hughes dies.

Nov. 20 - The first section of the International Space Station is launched in Russia.

Senator John Glenn preparing to launch into space

SAGITTARIUS
Your Personal Planets

YOUR LOVE POTENTIAL

Venus in Sagittarius, Nov. 22, 12:34 - Dec. 11, 18:32
Venus in Capricorn, Dec. 11, 18:33 - Dec. 22, 1:56

YOUR DRIVE AND AMBITION

Mars in Virgo, Nov. 22, 12:34 - Nov. 27, 10:09
Mars in Libra, Nov. 27, 10:10 - Dec. 22, 1:56

YOUR LUCK MAGNETISM

Jupiter in Pisces, Nov. 22, 12:34 - Dec. 22, 1:56

World Events

Dec. 9 - Switzerland votes in its first female Jewish President Ruth Dreifuss.

Dec. 13 - The electorate of Puerto Rico votes against U.S. statehood for the third time in eight years.

800

SCORPIO

From October 23, 14:59 through November 22, 12:33

The Attentive Watcher

Nothing will escape your careful scrutiny, 1998 Scorpio. You will examine everything deeply, looking beneath the surface to see what lies at the core. Hence, you will be able to discover what causes certain conditions and what motivates people. Because you will be such an attentive observer, you may appear psychic at times. Friends, family members, and even casual acquaintances may feel that you know their most intimate secrets—if you don't, you'll soon ferret them out. But woe to anyone who investigates your private affairs.

Your keen analytical abilities could serve you well if you become a police officer, psychiatrist, surgeon, detective, or financial analyst. Your innate shrewdness will be combined with a unique ability to sense what lies ahead—you won't be the type to miss the forest for the trees. This special talent could be a valuable asset when it comes to making investments. In fact, you will probably be good at handling money and you may work to earn your own from an early age, squirreling it away.

Born at a time when international terrorism posed a threat to even the strongest nations, you may have a profound skepticism that causes you to distrust people until they prove their worthiness. Even then, you will believe nothing you hear and only half of what you see. You will choose your friends and partners carefully, allowing only a select few to get close to you. No one will know your heart of hearts, however.

To the people you let into your inner circle, you will be loyal, loving, and fiercely protective. Once engaged, your strong emotions may win out over common sense. Particularly in romantic relationships, you may be rather jealous and possessive. You will usually be most compatible with Cancers, Pisceans, Virgos, and other Scorpios.

Whether you operate on a small or grand scale, you will want to keep your hand on the wheel so you can carefully maneuver everything around you. Your greatest strength will be your ability to manage situations and people—wielding power comes naturally to you. Your challenge will be to use your power wisely.

SAGITTARIUS

From November 22, 12:34 through December 22, 1:55

The Curious Optimist

Your thirst for knowledge may take you to the far corners of the globe or even into the metaphysical realm, Sagittarius of 1998. Infinitely curious, you will want to gain as much information and experience as possible. As a young person, you probably will be a quick student with varied interests. In adulthood, you will likely continue studying, either in a formal or informal manner. Everyone you meet and everything you do will offer possibilities for personal growth.

With your wealth of ideas and interests, you could be an excellent teacher or writer. A fascinating conversationalist, you will always have something entertaining to add to any discussion. You possess a unique sense of humor and can be both funny and insightful, often making connections that others miss.

Most of the time, you will be a cheerful individual who enlivens any gathering. You will also have your serious side, though you will tend to be something of a social butterfly. You will surround yourself with eclectic, gregarious people with whom you can share ideas and activities—like the characters on the popular television comedy sitcom, *Seinfeld*, which stopped production the year you were born. With your restless nature, you might have some difficulty settling down one-to-one and probably get along best with other free spirits: Ariens, Leos, and Aquarians.

Your search for truth may involve a sojourn into the areas of philosophy, psychology, or religion. Whether or not you subscribe to an organized theology or theory, you will probably have an interest in spiritual matters. You will seek explanations for the mysteries of life, and in the process you could arrive at some original discoveries of your own.

If you choose to travel to distant lands—and you probably will—you might come into contact with people whose beliefs have a strong impact on you. You also will tend to have a profound influence on those you encounter and you might even transform a few lives along the way. Your greatest strength will be your optimism. Your challenge will be to develop self-discipline so you can achieve your lofty goals.

➤ Read about your Chinese Astrological sign on page 838. ➤ Read about your Personal Planets on page 826. ➤ Read about your personal Mystical Card on page 856.

CAPRICORN

From December 22, 1:56 through December 31, 23:59

The Practical Idealist

Although you will tend to be rather conservative, you won't be stodgy, 1998 December Capricorn. You will have a special blend of idealism and practicality that lets you dream big and make those dreams realities. Born as the twentieth century was drawing to a close, you look to the future. You realize there will be challenges to face—you came into the world when the have-nots of the planet were challenging the haves—but you will feel up to them.

Even as a young child, you will be known for your responsibility and your determination. Ambitious and hard-working, you may make steady progress because you manage your time and resources wisely. Your quick mind will let you see the big picture, even as you address the necessary details at hand. With your expansive imagination, you will know that the possibilities are infinite, but you always will keep your feet on the ground.

You will appreciate the security and material goods money can provide. Most likely, you will have a knack for earning and handling it. You won't be selfish, however, and might even be something of a philanthropist. Business partnerships and managing other people's resources could be profitable for you, but with your head for business and your drive to get ahead, you could succeed in any area. You know that success is "ten percent inspiration, ninety percent perspiration."

Although you may be a bit pushy at times, you generally will get along well with people. You will value relationships and take your commitments to other people seriously. You will also realize that it's not just what you know but who you know, and your connections may help you to advance. You will usually get along well with Taureans, Virgos, and Pisceans.

Fundamentally a practical person, you also will possess a creative side. Perhaps you will dabble in art or music or give money to support the arts. You definitely will believe that one of the reasons for working hard is to surround yourself with beauty. One of your greatest strengths will be your hard-working, responsible nature. Your challenge will be to learn how to have a good time too.

1998
CAPRICORN
Your Personal Planets

YOUR LOVE POTENTIAL
Venus in Capricorn, Dec. 22, 1:57 - Dec. 31, 23:59

YOUR DRIVE AND AMBITION
Mars in Libra, Dec. 22, 1:57 - Dec. 31, 23:59

YOUR LUCK MAGNETISM
Jupiter in Pisces, Dec. 22, 1:57 - Dec. 31, 23:59

World Events

Dec. 29 – A U.S. yacht wins the Sydney-Hobart yacht race after storms that killed six competitors.

Dec. 30 – Two former leaders of the Khmer Rouge movement in Cambodia surrender and apologize for the atrocities they have committed.

Special Feature
Nostradamus: A Prophet Across Time

(Continued from page 793)

The second Antichrist was named by Nostradamus as "Hifter," and he documented his rise and fall, naming warring countries, alliances (including Imperial Japan), opponents, and finally, his mysterious death.

> *From the deepest part of Western Europe*
> *A young child will be born to poor people:*
> *Who by his speech will seduce a great multitude,*
> *His reputation will increase in the Kingdom of the East.*

Was such a window on the suffering of humanity also a burden for this humble and gentle healer? In anguished verse he wrote of a future weapon that would "make the sun appear double." He foretold "two scourges the like of which was never seen before," which would take place "near the harbors within two cities" (Hiroshima and Nagasaki).

> *Famine, pestilence within, people put out by the sword.*
> *They cry for help from the great immortal God!*

Some interpreters claim that Nostradamus might have had foreknowledge of the September 11, 2001 attack on New York City. In one quatrain, he writes that "the great King of Terror will come from the sky."

> *The sky will burn at forty-five degrees latitude,*
> *Fire approaches the great new city.*
> *Immediately a huge, scattered flame leaps up*
> *When they want to have verification from the Normans.*

Nostradamus named the third Antichrist as Mabus, a man emerging from the Middle East, whose terrorist aggressions would trigger a global conflict to last over two decades. Has the Armageddon that he predicted already been set in motion? Do we face an uncertain future of continued war and violence between nations, and possible ecological catastrophes? Along with his apocalyptic visions of the future, Nostradamus also spoke of a strong desire for peace among the people:

Hiroshima: a watch stopped at 8.15am when the bomb was dropped

> *Many people will want to come to terms,*
> *With the great world leaders who will bring war upon*
> *them: The political leaders will not want to hear anything of their message,*
> *Alas! If God does not send peace to the Earth.*

The genius of the life and work of Nostradamus is that it continues to generate thoughtful discussion about the fate of humanity. What does the future hold? He may very well have been asking us to reflect on the many possible outcomes. ✪

➤ Read more about Hitler on page 353 ➤ Read more about Nostradamus in "Astrology Reigns Through the Ages on page 25 ➤ Read "Predictions, Eclipses and September 11" on page 825.

Awaiting the Millennium: Saturn and Uranus

Fears and joyous anticipation grew as 1999 dawned. Y2K threatened to crash the global computer system and manufacturers feared running short of champagne. Systems were stretched to the limit as Saturn, the great lord of systems, made a strident connection with the disruptive planet of electronics, Uranus. Other events and trends this year were also suggestive of this connection. Stealthy hackers sent out pernicious email-borne viruses like Melissa and Chernobyl, overburdening corporate mail servers and bringing record revenues to anti-virus software companies. Tragedy struck and no school was ever the same again after Columbine High School was savaged by two alienated teens in Goth garb. This event exploded onto the world scene as Uranus's rebelliousness was expanded by Jupiter's penchant for magnification.

But there was much to be optimistic about as a new age dawned. The Internet had a new high of 150 million users—a marketer's dream audience. Everyone rushed to capture this consumer base. The planets that signified this process were Mars, Jupiter, and Neptune, all making stimulating but enriching contacts with each other. Mars, the activator was linked to Jupiter mid-year and entrepreneurs prospered. Venture capitalists, Jupiterians at heart, wanted to cash in on the "cyber-market" and the rush was on to gain a niche before someone else got it. Also on this wave of liberating energy, President Clinton was acquitted of impeachable offenses, and the Dow Jones Industrials broke the 10,000-point limit for the first time.

Huge anti-WTO protests lead to a police crackdown

Russian President Yeltsin resigns

A total eclipse of the Sun takes place on August 11

THE GREAT PLANETARY CROSS

A significant celestial event, called the most potent planetary event in 2,000 years, took place on August 11. The last total solar eclipse of the century occurred with the Sun and Moon in conjunction forming a grand square with the planets Mars, Saturn, and Uranus. In astrology, this pattern is known as a "Grand Cross" and is an archetypal chart of massive and fundamental change. Some called it an earthquake chart. Since a similar sky existed when Mohammed was born, a great effect on Islamic nations was predicted.

MILLENNIUM FEARS IN THE DIGITAL AGE

There was worldwide panic over the possibly disastrous, but actually non-existent, year 2000 effect on computers. The viruses Melissa and Chernobyl infected computers all over the world. In his campaign of ethnic cleansing, Yugoslav President Milosovic sanctioned the murder of forty-five Albanians in Kosovo. John Kennedy Jr., his wife and her sister died in a plane crash off Martha's Vineyard, Massachussets. In Britain, a racist bomb attack injured six in east London. Russian president Yeltsin resigned on the last day of the year, naming Putin as his successor. U.S. President Clinton escaped impeachment when acquitted by the Senate of perjury and obstructing justice. The Dow Jones index reached its highest, 10,000 points and in the U.S., two students killed thirteen and injured twenty-three at Columbine High School, Colorado. In Britain, Prince Edward married Sophie Rhys-Jones. Carcinogens in Belgian food products caused a scare. Some 350 million people worldwide watched the solar eclipse on August 11. *Shakespeare in Love*, set in sixteenth-century England, won seven Oscars. *The Blair Witch Project* terrified movie audiences. King Hussein of Jordan died.

➤ Read the Dalai Lama's Star Profile on page 809.

CAPRICORN

From January 01, 0:00 through January 20, 12:36

The Optimistic Realist

When you were born, January Capricorn of 1999, investigations into the scandal surrounding President Clinton were about to reach an end. His impeachment trial began and your family may have resolved to set you a positive example of responsibility. While you honor this emphasis on duty, you may occasionally be tempted to rebel against it. Naturally self-contained, your rebellion may consist of carefully constructed arguments lightened by dry humor.

Your ambition will be aided by your clear and strategic thinking. Success in your chosen profession may be a major goal but you will also know how and when to take recreational breaks. All work and no play makes for a dull companion. Competitive sports may be a physical outlet and satisfy your need to match yourself against your peers. The retirement of basketball ace, Michael Jordan, brought to an end a spectacular sporting career at this time.

The launch of the Euro, the new European Union single currency, was a bold move in plans to unify the continent and reinforce its position as a major economic force. You may come to admire the enterprise of the European politicians when you are plotting your professional path. Capricorns are often linked to banking and you will become aware that solid financial foundations are vital if individuals and nations are to thrive. Being your own boss may become a cherished goal but going it alone may be delayed until you have built your nest egg.

Courtesy and consideration could be two of your most attractive traits. You may not be one of life's extroverts but you will probably prefer partnership to being single. Witty in private, someone that shares your conventional take on relationships and your love of conversation would be an ideal mate. It will help if they have a zany slant on life and can see the funny side of difficulties. You are likely to be most comfortable with Virgos, Taureans, Pisceans, and Scorpios.

One of your challenges could be learning how to express your feelings rather than bottling them up. Your strength will be your cheerful acceptance of life's downs as well as ups.

AQUARIUS

From January 20, 12:37 through February 19, 2:46

The Gentle Anarchist

Aquarius of 1999, you were born equipped with more than your fair share of chutzpah. At this time U.S. President Bill Clinton emerged from his impeachment trial acquitted of perjury and obstruction of justice. You will come to detest all forms of restriction and may sometimes find yourself in hot water after a cheeky confrontation. You could learn on early that you must sometimes use your charm to defend your position. Naturally friendly, you may find that you just can't help assuming a leadership role.

Freedom and independence are Aquarian watchwords. On February 3, 1999 in Kosovo, members of the KLA demanded that peace talks include a guaranteed vote for independence. You may find that your hatred of oppression grows as you mature and encompasses both large-scale political bigots and everyday mini-tyrants. Your own family may have encouraged your natural spirit of enterprise and independence. In addition, your distaste for hypocrisy will usually be equaled by your sympathy to human folly. Jordan's King Hussein, mourned this month by his people, learned how to walk the fine line between appeasing the Islamic world while remaining a friend to the West.

You may become less impulsive as you grow up and learn how to channel your energy more efficiently. You may want to put every idea immediately into practice but as time goes on you will begin to focus on what is most relevant. You could become a technological whiz-kid but your interest may lay in its application to everyday life. The emphasis on mundane detail could discourage you from mainstream politics and you may be a romantic rather than a realist.

Love for you may mean a mental connection above all. You will be able to zero in on the hidden beauty of even the plainest of mates—so long as they stimulate your mind and allow a very long leash. Swapping ideas may come easily with Librans, Geminis, Ariens, and Sagittarians.

Commitment when faced with so much choice may be one of your trickiest challenges, Aquarius of 1999. Your strength could be sticking to your principles regardless of circumstances.

➤ Read about your Chinese Astrological sign on page 838. ➤ Read about your Personal Planets on page 826. ➤ Read about your personal Mystical Card on page 856.

1999

CAPRICORN
Your Personal Planets

YOUR LOVE POTENTIAL
Venus in Capricorn, Jan. 01, 0:00 - Jan. 04, 16:24
Venus in Aquarius, Jan. 04, 16:25 - Jan. 20, 12:36

YOUR DRIVE AND AMBITION
Mars in Libra, Jan. 01, 0:00 - Jan. 20, 12:36

YOUR LUCK MAGNETISM
Jupiter in Pisces, Jan. 01, 0:00 - Jan. 20, 12:36

World Events

Jan. 1 – The new single European currency, the Euro, is launched.

Jan. 7 – President Bill Clinton's impeachment trial officially begins.

The "Los Angeles Times" announces the beginning of Bill Clinton's impeachment trial

AQUARIUS
Your Personal Planets

YOUR LOVE POTENTIAL
Venus in Aquarius, Jan. 20, 12:37 - Jan. 28, 16:16
Venus in Pisces, Jan. 28, 16:17 - Feb. 19, 2:46

YOUR DRIVE AND AMBITION
Mars in Libra, Jan. 20, 12:37 - Jan. 26, 11:58
Mars in Scorpio, Jan. 26, 11:59 - Feb. 19, 2:46

YOUR LUCK MAGNETISM
Jupiter in Pisces, Jan. 20, 12:37 - Feb. 13, 1:21
Jupiter in Aries, Feb. 13, 1:22 - Feb. 19, 2:46

World Events

Feb. 8 – The funeral of King Hussein of Jordan draws world leaders from all over the globe.

Feb. 12 – The 2002 Winter Olympics Committee hires a new chief, millionaire businessman Mitt Romney, after a three-month corruption scandal involving bribery charges against Olympic officials.

803

1999

PISCES
Your Personal Planets

YOUR LOVE POTENTIAL

Venus in Pisces, Feb. 19, 2:47 - Feb. 21, 20:48
Venus in Aries, Feb. 21, 20:49 - Mar. 18, 9:58
Venus in Taurus, Mar. 18, 9:59 - Mar. 21, 1:45

YOUR DRIVE AND AMBITION

Mars in Scorpio, Feb. 19, 2:47 - Mar. 21, 1:45

YOUR LUCK MAGNETISM

Jupiter in Aries, Feb. 19, 2:47 - Mar. 21, 1:45

World Events

Mar. 7 – Film director Stanley Kubrick dies.

Mar. 9 – Iranian President Khatami visits Italy in his first visit to Europe since the Islamic revolution in 1979.

Death of experimental film director Stanley Kubrick

ARIES
Your Personal Planets

YOUR LOVE POTENTIAL

Venus in Taurus, Mar. 21, 1:46 - Apr. 12, 13:16
Venus in Gemini, Apr. 12, 13:17 - Apr. 20, 12:45

YOUR DRIVE AND AMBITION

Mars in Scorpio, Mar. 21, 1:46 - Apr. 20, 12:45

YOUR LUCK MAGNETISM

Jupiter in Aries, Apr. 21, 1:46 - Apr. 20, 12:45

World Events

Mar. 31 – NATO announces an increase in air strikes over the Federal Republic of Yugoslavia.

Apr. 15 – Former Chilean dictator Augusto Pinochet faces extradition to Spain.

PISCES

From February 19, 2:47 through March 21, 1:45

The Happy Wanderer

Your creative potential, Pisces of 1999, will be marked by a determination to achieve concrete results untypical of your sign. Creative success may only measure up in your eyes if it has a lasting value. Your dedication and self-containment may impress your family. Film director Stanley Kubrick, who died this month, shared your independence, your reliance on your own vision, and your painstaking attention to detail.

During your lifetime you may wish to explore the laws and beliefs of value systems and religious beliefs. You will be adept at reconciling opposing viewpoints. You will also excel at unifying people in conflict. Tapping into similar planetary energies on March 8, 1999, Britain and Ireland signed four treaties for the Northern Ireland peace accord. Possibly uncomfortable adhering to one belief system you may prefer to take a little from each as your unique spirituality will not be the "One Size Fits All" variety.

Material gains may be more important to you than the typical Pisces but you could strive to develop a laid-back attitude to money. You may believe that the world will provide and act accordingly. Generous to a fault when cash is available, you could be convinced that fate takes care of the lean times. You may also discover early on that your career follows many twists. So long as you remain true to yourself, you will soon learn each fork in the road is an opportunity not a setback. You could be most comfortable working in the arts but you may also excel at encouraging others to fulfill their creative potential.

Capable of intense passion, you may sometimes lack confidence in relationships. You will be unlikely to make the first move until you are certain of a positive response. Cancerians, Scorpios, Capricorns, and Taureans will all be signs well-equipped to stimulate your senses while understanding your sensitivity.

Curtailing your extravagance may be your challenge, Pisces of 1999. A little prudence when flush will see you through the hiccups in income. Your strength will be the ease with which you make your ideas into reality.

ARIES

From March 21, 1:46 through April 20, 12:45

The Dependable Companion

Your birth, Aries of 1999, came when the U.S. Dow Jones Industrial Average reached an all-time high, breaking 11,000 points. That barriers are there to be broken will be one concept that you may take to heart. Most Ariens are dynamic characters but you will have an impact on your environment throughout your life. It may be your stubborn refusal to take no for an answer or the passionate way you'll expound on your pet theories. You could sometimes be a little too blunt as you will revere honesty. Your family may attempt to teach you a measure of tact.

You may become aware that your personal power and unflagging energy will best be used positively. You may come to appreciate the maxim "Stop and Think" before you go ahead and act as you gradually learn to exercise self-discipline. One sad example of acting in haste occurred when NATO personnel attacked an Albanian refugee convoy, mistakenly confusing them for Serbian troops. Another, when two disgruntled students opened fire on their classmates at Columbine High School.

Your energy will be easy to harness and you may work long and tirelessly for desired results. Success may come more sluggishly than you anticipate but your optimism will be of great assistance when you encounter setbacks. Bricks and mortar will be as attractive as money in the bank and you could find you are a genius at dealing in real estate. Behind your bluff and confident exterior will lurk a sharp and perceptive mind. Big-hearted and generous, you exude infectious confidence.

A kind-hearted and trusting soul, you may sometimes be disappointed at other's behavior. You could be too idealistic about relationships and may sometimes suffer when others prove to be less than candid. In your closest relationship your passion will be quickly unleashed. The thrill of the romantic chase will be of the utmost enjoyment for you and an ideal partner could be a Leo, Sagittarian, Gemini, or Aquarian.

Developing patience when in sight of your goal may be one challenge you need to grapple with, Aries of 1999. One of your strengths will be your child-like confidence in the goodness of others.

➤ Read about your Chinese Astrological sign on page 838. ➤ Read about your Personal Planets on page 826. ➤ Read about your personal Mystical Card on page 856.

TAURUS

From April 20, 12:46 through May 21, 11:51

The Shy Romantic

When you were born, Taurus of 1999, a law was passed in California limiting the size of handguns, and in Chicago and elsewhere, regulation of handgun ownership was being discussed. Paradoxically, at Chinese embassies across the globe, demonstrations were taking place to protest the accidental bombing by NATO forces of the Chinese Embassy in Belgrade. These events could reflect the difficulties you may have knowing when to assert yourself and when to pull back. Like others of your sign you will not be aggressive but you will be capable of digging in your heels to make a point. You will hate rocking the boat but sometimes it'll be necessary.

Conservative you may be but when you turn toward career opportunities you may find it difficult to make a choice. One thing is certain: you will be less satisfied with routine than the traditional Taurean. You may also find that you get a thrill from surprising and sometimes shocking others. While your family will most likely encourage you to be a go-getter, their main concern could be that you are happy in your chosen field. Material security may come to be one of your requirements but not if your integrity is compromised.

Shyness and a desire for privacy could obscure your sweet nature. However, when you let your guard down in the security of your own home or with trusted friends, a more quirky and mysterious personality could be revealed. You will have an ability to draw others out of their shells and you could make an excellent counselor or human resources manager. Your patience and willingness to listen and keep confidences will be great assets.

Ever discreet, you may find that you prefer to spend time with one important person rather than hang out with the crowd. Your desire for emotional security could far outstrip your interest in success. You will be adept at making others feel special and Virgos, Capricorns, Pisceans, and Cancerians will probably head the line-up vying for your attention.

One challenge, Taurus of 1999, will be to be less suspicious—the world is not such an unfriendly place. Your strength will be your absolute dependability, especially in a crisis.

GEMINI

From May 21, 11:52 through June 21, 19:48

The Comical Comrade

Your birth, Gemini of 1999, came when one of the greatest of all international statesmen retired from active politics. Nelson Mandela, who had fought a long and often lonely battle for the emancipation of his people, handed over the reigns of government to his successor. He represented those ideals of equality, justice and brotherhood that you may come to value above all. You may share with others of your sign an eternally child-like curiosity and a sparkling wit that draws others toward you. However, you also possess gravity not immediately obvious to casual acquaintances.

Your family may need to help you develop confidence in your own intellect and you may be more prepared to explore one interest thoroughly rather than moving from project to project. The restoration of Leonardo Da Vinci's *Last Supper* was completed and revealed this month, demonstrating the value of painstaking craftsmanship.

You may come to value those friendships based on mental compatibility, but you could also enjoy active pursuits. You may be an enthusiastic if sometimes outspoken friend, and competitive sport could help to dissolve any build-up of tension. In possession of an admirable spirit of enterprise you may become confident in your own initiative early on in life. Working for yourself or at least being the boss may suit you, as cooperation may be more preferable socially than professionally. The stock market could attract you but so could your own book or antique store.

Endlessly fascinated by humanity's variety you may find it difficult to settle on one life partner. There will be so much choice: how could you possibly choose one at the expense of all the rest. However, you may be surprised when you fall in love that it really will be easy to remain faithful. Aquarians, Librans, Leos, and Ariens could keep pace with your passion for new and diverse interests.

Quick-acting and sometimes rash, your challenge, Gemini of 1999, is to control your temper. Your strength is your unshakeable loyalty to your friends and your humor in times of need.

➤ Read about your Chinese Astrological sign on page 838. ➤ Read about your Personal Planets on page 826. ➤ Read about your personal Mystical Card on page 856.

TAURUS
Your Personal Planets

YOUR LOVE POTENTIAL
Venus in Gemini, Apr. 20, 12:46 - May 08, 16:28
Venus in Cancer, May 08, 16:29 - May 21, 11:51

YOUR DRIVE AND AMBITION
Mars in Scorpio, Apr. 20, 12:46 - May 05, 21:31
Mars in Libra, May 05, 21:32 - May 21, 11:51

YOUR LUCK MAGNETISM
Jupiter in Aries, Apr. 20, 12:46 - May 21, 11:51

World Events

May 9 - Demonstrations break out at U.S. embassies all over the world, after the Chinese embassy in Belgrade is accidentally bombed.

May 17 - Ehud Barak, leader of the One Israel party, wins the election and becomes the new Israeli Prime Minister.

Ehud Barak, the new Israeli Prime Minister

GEMINI
Your Personal Planets

YOUR LOVE POTENTIAL
Venus in Cancer, May 21, 11:52 - June 05, 21:24
Venus in Leo, June 05, 21:25 - June 21, 19:48

YOUR DRIVE AND AMBITION
Mars in Libra, May 21, 11:52 - June 21, 19:48

YOUR LUCK MAGNETISM
Jupiter in Aries, May 21, 11:52 - June 21, 19:48

World Events

June 16 - Nelson Mandela resigns as President of South Africa.

June 19 - Prince Edward and Sophie Rhys-Jones marry at St. George's Chapel, Windsor.

CANCER
Your Personal Planets

YOUR LOVE POTENTIAL
Venus in Leo, June 21, 19:49 - July 12, 15:17
Venus in Virgo, July 12, 15:18 - July 23, 6:43

YOUR DRIVE AND AMBITION
Mars in Libra, June 21, 19:49 - July 05, 3:58
Mars in Scorpio, July 05, 3:59 - July 23, 6:43

YOUR LUCK MAGNETISM
Jupiter in Aries, June 21, 19:49 - June 28, 9:28
Jupiter in Taurus, June 28, 9:29 - July 23, 6:43

World Events

July 4 - Pete Sampras beats Andre Agassi to take the Wimbledon men's singles trophy for the sixth time in seven years.

July 7 - The tobacco industry is found guilty of conspiring to conceal the addictive properties of cigarettes by a jury in Miami.

Pete Sampras with Andre Agassi after the men's final at Wimbledon

LEO
Your Personal Planets

YOUR LOVE POTENTIAL
Venus in Virgo, July 23, 6:44 - Aug. 15, 14:11
Venus in Leo, Aug. 15, 14:12 - Aug. 23, 13:50

YOUR DRIVE AND AMBITION
Mars in Scorpio, July 23, 6:44 - Aug. 23, 13:50

YOUR LUCK MAGNETISM
Jupiter in Taurus, July 23, 6:44 - Aug. 23, 13:50

World Events

Aug. 2 - The Taliban seizes the capital of the northern Parwan province.

Aug. 11 - A total eclipse of the Sun is watched by 350 million people worldwide.

CANCER
From June 21, 19:49 through July 23, 6:43

The Quiet Campaigner

Family will be important to you, Cancer of 1999, but you may find that early independence from them also appeals. You will always value and appreciate their contribution to your growth but you may find that you need to gain recognition in your own right. You may have strong ambition and you will be protective of your reputation. Success will be irrelevant if you compromise your integrity.

However, maintaining family links will be vital to your sense of security as will a few long-lasting friendships, sometimes with older people. The American public shared one famous family's loss this month. John F. Kennedy, Jr., while piloting his own plane, crashed into the sea killing all on board. Americans may have been saddened at his death because it symbolized the final end to the golden Kennedy era.

You may share your sign's natural intuition and sensitivity but you may also develop shrewd financial skills. Handling both your own and other people's money could be one way of making a living. You could also find that you have an affinity with the public and serving them could give you satisfaction. Working in healthcare or bringing to light information that is in the public interest may both be attractive options. Your family may have been following the trial of the tobacco giants; these companies were found guilty of actively concealing the addictive properties of their product. Taking responsibility for your own health may have been one of the values your parents tried to teach you.

Relationships will be precious to you but your independent streak may mean that you are in no hurry to settle down. Both financial and emotional security will be crucial and you could find that an older and wiser partner meets your requirements. Both earth and water signs supply the stability you will prefer. You may feel most at home with Scorpios, Pisceans, Virgos, or Taureans.

One challenge, Cancer of 1999, could be that you sometimes find it difficult to adapt to changing circumstances. Your strength could be that you are never prepared to weaken your commitment to the best interests of the public.

LEO
From July 23, 6:44 through August 23, 13:50

The Popular Altruist

You, Leo of 1999, were born when 350 million people witnessed a total eclipse of the Sun. All babies are special, but Leos often come with a solid sense of their own individuality. You'll be no exception to that rule but you could also recognize the need for continual improvement. You may love the praise heaped on you by others but your own opinion will be far more important. Your family could seek to make your home life just as rewarding and diverse as the outside world, reinforcing your confidence in your own worth.

Somewhat of a perfectionist, you may be discriminating and exacting in pursuit of your objectives. You may never lose sight of your principles and you will defend them even in the teeth of formidable opposition. Born into the sign of royalty, you are honorable in your dealings and you do appreciate worldly recognition of your talents. On August 9, 1999, the Japanese parliament adopted the Rising Sun flag as its national symbol and an ode to the emperor.

Not all Leos can become film stars, but you could lend a touch of glamour to all your undertakings. The death of Joe DiMaggio this month may have made many recall his short-lived marriage to that eternal symbol of glamour, Marilyn Monroe. When you choose a career, try to keep in mind that your greatest asset is yourself. You may gain most satisfaction if you utilize your powers of self-expression for the benefit of others.

Ever charming, Leo of 1999, you could be surrounded by admirers. This will probably delight you, as solitude may not be to your taste. You may only be truly content when in the throes of an intense and passionate relationship. However, you may find that your passion can disappear as suddenly as it appeared. Ariens, Sagittarians, Librans, or Geminis may be the ones to kindle and maintain the glow of romance.

Others may be unable to match your high standards and dealing philosophically with their shortcomings could present your challenge. A willingness to consider the needs of others could be your strength. Your convictions will not impair your sense of fair play.

➤ Read about your Chinese Astrological sign on page 838. ➤ Read about your Personal Planets on page 826. ➤ Read about your personal Mystical Card on page 856.

VIRGO

From August 23, 13:51 through September 23, 11:30

The Confident Analyst

You were born, Virgo of 1999, with the potential to become a courageous seeker after truth regardless of the consequences. Your parents could believe strongly that deception is usually uncovered no matter how deeply buried. Mafia "Godfather", John Gotti, Jr. began a seventy-seven month prison sentence for his crimes. Two years after Princess Diana's death, Henri Paul, the driver of the car in which she was travelling was officially blamed for that fatal accident in Paris.

While sharing the tendency toward self-analysis typical of your sign, you may find that you come to possess a quiet confidence in your own talent and abilities. You may be able to communicate your opinions and ideas with force and dynamism, dispelling Virgo's reputation as the astrological "Shrinking Violet." Your family may seek to encourage your ever-expanding self-confidence.

As you begin to struggle to make sense of life's mysteries, Virgo of 1999, you may come to find that compartmentalizing information will be less important than viewing the big picture. You may find that your intuition becomes a tool just as valuable as your talent for discrimination. It could guide you to make radical contributions in your career, whether in traditional fields such as education or healthcare or more adventurous pursuits such as journalism. Writing professionally or for personal reasons could be of lifelong importance to you.

Idealistic in relationships, you may also display fiery and passionate instincts. But you are unlikely to be attracted to a partner less frank and open than you are and you may learn early on to rely on your own good judgment. You could find that you are most comfortable relating to Capricorns, Taureans, Cancerians, or Scorpios.

Positive and assertive, your challenge may be to temper your bluntness a little. Sometimes you will be tempted to wade in with your opinions and ideas when letting others have their say could achieve far better results. One of your strengths will be your tenacity when delving into the heart of anything important. You will never give up on a project until you have exhausted every possibility and angle.

LIBRA

From September 23, 11:31 through October 23, 20:51

The Wise Interpreter

You were born, Libra of 1999, as global belligerence appeared to be increasing. As you mature you could become more and more aware that words have the power to heal as well as wound. You may quickly learn how to express your opinions with tact but without pulling your punches. Your family may encourage lively debate and you could become expert at fighting from your corner.

Librans often have an aptitude for rational thought but you also will grow up to appreciate the power of the subconscious and the importance of intuition. You could find pleasure in artistic and creative activities. Everything you do will be stamped with your own individualism. You may also understand that right and wrong are not always as clear cut as they appear. On September 29, 1999, U.S. President Clinton offered to forgive all the official debts to the U.S. by as many as thirty-six of the world's poorest nations. The write-off could total as much as $5.7 billion. You may prefer unusual solutions to pressing problems, ones that enhance peaceful relationships.

Your unconventional sense of drama will infiltrate all areas of your life. New technology will hold few fears and you may love the way that science and art combine. An example of the creative use of the new media was the NetAid series of rock concerts transmitted live on the Web. Even better, they were fundraisers for charity. Using your fine judgment may be the career path you will wish to follow. Your gift for communications could be an asset in business but you could prefer to work in the service sector where the greatest use can be made of your humanitarian ideals.

Love makes the world go round and you will be one of life's charmers. Always happier with a partner to bounce your ideas off of, you may also make material gains from marriage. You may enjoy the mental agility of Aquarians and Geminis and the spontaneity of Leos and Sagittarians.

Your challenge, Libra of 1999, may be to overcome a tendency toward self-indulgence—you relish luxury. Your strength will be your versatility and talent for coherent communication.

➤ Read about your Chinese Astrological sign on page 838. ➤ Read about your Personal Planets on page 826. ➤ Read about your personal Mystical Card on page 856.

VIRGO
Your Personal Planets

YOUR LOVE POTENTIAL
Venus in Leo, Aug. 23, 13:51 - Sept. 23, 11:31

YOUR DRIVE AND AMBITION
Mars in Scorpio, Aug. 23, 13:51 - Sept. 02, 19:28
Mars in Sagittarius, Sept. 02, 19:29 - Sept. 23, 11:31

YOUR LUCK MAGNETISM
Jupiter in Taurus, Aug. 23, 13:51 - Sept. 23, 11:31

World Events

Sept. 3 – The inquiry into the death of Princess Diana officially blames Henri Paul, the driver of the Mercedes limousine in which she was traveling.

Sept. 13 – A large-scale evacuation begins along America's East Coast, as Hurricane Floyd heads toward the region.

Augusto Pinochet

LIBRA
Your Personal Planets

YOUR LOVE POTENTIAL
Venus in Leo, Sept. 23, 11:32 - Oct. 07, 16:50
Venus in Virgo, Oct. 07, 16:51 - Oct. 23, 20:51

YOUR DRIVE AND AMBITION
Mars in Sagittarius, Sept. 23, 11:32 - Oct. 17, 1:34
Mars in Capricorn, Oct. 17, 1:35 - Oct. 23, 20:51

YOUR LUCK MAGNETISM
Jupiter in Taurus, Sept. 23, 11:32 - Oct. 23, 5:48
Jupiter in Aries, Oct. 23, 5:49 - Oct. 23, 20:51

World Events

Oct. 8 – A court in London rules that human rights criminal August Pinochet should be extradited to Spain to face charges there.

Oct. 15 – Constant rain causes severe flooding in central and southern Mexico; serious damage is done to land and property.

1999

SCORPIO
Your Personal Planets

YOUR LOVE POTENTIAL
Venus in Virgo, Oct. 23, 20:52 - Nov. 09, 2:18
Venus in Libra, Nov. 09, 2:19 - Nov. 22, 18:24

YOUR DRIVE AND AMBITION
Mars in Capricorn, Oct. 23, 20:52 - Nov. 22, 18:24

YOUR LUCK MAGNETISM
Jupiter in Aries, Oct. 23, 20:52 - Nov. 22, 18:24

World Events

Nov. 13 – Briton Lennox Lewis defeats American Evander Holyfield to become the heavyweight boxing champion.

Nov. 15 – China joins the World Trade Organization.

World Trade Organization protesters in Seattle are teargased by police

SAGITTARIUS
Your Personal Planets

YOUR LOVE POTENTIAL
Venus in Libra, Nov. 22, 18:25 - Dec. 05, 22:40
Venus in Scorpio, Dec. 05, 22:41 - Dec. 22, 7:43

YOUR DRIVE AND AMBITION
Mars in Capricorn, Nov. 22, 18:25 - Nov. 26, 6:55
Mars in Aquarius, Nov. 26, 6:56 - Dec. 22, 7:43

YOUR LUCK MAGNETISM
Jupiter in Aries, Nov. 22, 18:25 - Dec. 22, 7:43

World Events

Dec. 4 – In Seattle, thousands of activists take to the streets to protest against the World Trade Organization.

Dec. 16 – The Russians launch an unsuccessful attempt to capture the Chechnyan capital of Grozny.

SCORPIO
From October 23, 20:52 through November 22, 18:24

The Loyal Fighter

It may be a cliché that Scorpios like control, but born now, Scorpio of 1999, you may be encouraged to develop more flexibility. Your family may be closet eccentrics and your early home life could be a tad unconventional. However, you will soon learn to go with the flow and your background could balance your orderly outlook. You could grow up to have a healthy respect for money and a shrewd ability for financial gain. China's admission to the World Trade Organization at this time symbolizes your recognition that the pooling of resources can help the most people.

Your eyes may come to be firmly fixed on the future but your tendency to rush there could mean that you sometimes miss vital detail. George W. Bush, interviewed on television during his election campaign, illustrated this point when he was unable to name important international leaders. But you will be nothing if not strong willed and you could easily assimilate the information and action required to reach your chosen objectives.

You could appear somewhat self-contained or even detached and that will be misleading because you'll love company. You could also enjoy argument and debate and will put across your key points with gusto. Choosing a career in the military or civilian armed forces could supply the comradeship and sense of duty that will appeal to you. You will commit your energy wholeheartedly to your chosen career and might sometimes overdo it as you strive to succeed.

Loyalty will be one of your main considerations when picking a partner. You may especially appreciate a lover that appreciates you. You will be willing to lavish affection on one that matches your commitment. Your passion could grow stronger the longer you remain together. Cancerians, Pisceans, Virgos, and Capricorns could all be signs with the qualities you desire.

Your challenge, Scorpio of 1999, may be to learn how to share the load. Never one to shirk responsibility, you might sometimes find yourself overwhelmed by the amount you have taken on. Cheerful acceptance of the lion's share of the work could be your strength.

SAGITTARIUS
From November 22, 18:25 through December 22, 7:43

The Wise Explorer

Sagittarius of 1999, you may become an eternal seeker after knowledge. You might develop a sharp and probing intellect, but when your interest begins to diminish you may drift toward indolence. Your family could try to ensure that you enjoy constant mental stimulation. When your imagination and your humanitarian instincts come together you could be a formidable spokesperson with original and unexpected strategies. The anti-capitalists demonstrating in Seattle against the vast power of the World Trade Organization applied tactics you might come to appreciate.

Your expertise could be most obvious, however, in the fields of recreation and leisure. You could excel at sport, and games of chance may entrance you. Your commitment to pleasure may only be equaled by the thrill found in risk-taking. With an endearing ability to bounce back from disappointments you will cheerfully shrug off any gambles that fail. Writer Joseph Heller, author of *Catch-22* died this month. His most famous work told the story of World War II airmen constantly pitting their wits against unfair obstacles and institutions.

Working for the sake of it just won't be your style, Sagittarius of 1999, but when you find your niche you will be capable of diligence and unexpected attention to detail. You might make an excellent educator as you could develop a unique and appealing way of attracting your student's interest. Broadcasting may also allow you to expound on your favorite subjects. Your interest in exchanging ideas could draw you toward publishing. The most important criteria will be the opportunity to grow intellectually.

Your happy-go-lucky attitude and your thirst for new vistas could make you a tricky person to pin down. While your warmth will be obvious you may have a tendency to ignore others' feelings. You might feel most at home with freedom-loving Aquarians and Librans or robust and fiery Leos and Ariens.

Your challenge could be to empathize with more timid souls that could also have something to contribute. Your strength will be your eternal quest to understand humanity in all its forms.

➤ Read about your Chinese Astrological sign on page 838. ➤ Read about your Personal Planets on page 826. ➤ Read about your personal Mystical Card on page 856.

CAPRICORN

From December 22, 7:44 through December 31, 23:59

The Secret Healer

Like most Capricorns you could recognize the importance of honesty but you will also love intrigue, December Capricorn of 1999. You may come to understand that what goes on in private may have public consequences. You may make a point of thoroughly investigating any given situation before you draw your conclusions. Your family may have suspected that the public is often purposefully kept in ignorance. Anxiety was high at the time of your birth that the so-called "Millennium Bug" in computers would disrupt almost every area of life.

You could have a healthy respect for power but you also may develop an interest in spiritual values. You might be happiest far from the corridors of power, preferring to spend time in contemplation. One task may be to unite your spiritual ideals with your material goals. You will be confident enough to march to the beat of a different drum and you will relish your independence. Your nickname could be "The Lone Ranger", and Clayton Moore, the actor that played him for so many years, died this month.

Traditionally, Capricorns enjoy big business but you might prefer another direction. Your interest could be aroused by conditions in institutions and you could work in a hospital or prison administration. Osteopathy and chiropractic could also benefit from your hands-on approach and candid manner. Your dry wit will do much to allay your clients' fears. Whatever area you find yourself working in, others will warm to your sympathetic personality.

While you might not fear solitude, your relationships will still be precious to you. Your dignified but humorous demeanor will attract many admirers but you may like to look around before taking the marital plunge. Physical attraction could be a draw but above all you may prize commitment to family life. You could find what you seek with Taureans, Virgos, Pisceans, or Scorpios.

Your challenge, December Capricorn of 1999, could be to learn not to be so suspicious—every secret does not mean a conspiracy. Your strength may be your understanding that everyone needs a little more love.

1999
CAPRICORN
Your Personal Planets

YOUR LOVE POTENTIAL
Venus in Scorpio, Dec. 22, 7:44 - Dec. 31, 4:53
Venus in Sagittarius, Dec. 31, 4:54 - Dec. 31, 23:59

YOUR DRIVE AND AMBITION
Mars in Aquarius, Dec. 22, 7:44 - Dec. 31, 23:59

YOUR LUCK MAGNETISM
Jupiter in Aries, Dec. 22, 7:44 - Dec. 31, 23:59

World Events

Dec. 29 - Paris is named a "natural disaster area" after a four-day hurricane hits France.

Dec. 31 - President Yeltsin announces his resignation live on television.

Dalai Lama
Born July 6, 1935

DALAI LAMA
Cancer

The Dalai Lama is a man chosen to teach and lead because he is identified by Buddhist monks as the reincarnation of all previous Dalai Lamas. Lhamo Dhondrub, the 14th Dalai Lama, was discovered at age three and was installed as spiritual leader of Tibet at age five. For decades, Tibet has fought against occupation by China and the conflict got so extreme that the Dalai Lama was forced to live in exile in India. His interests are broad and his humanitarian efforts and devotion to peace, goodness, and love have earned him a Nobel Prize.

The Dalai Lama is a Cancer, a sign noted for sensitivity and emotionality. With his Sun, the planet of identity, prominently placed in his birth chart, the Dalai Lama makes a strong, immediate impression. Six of the remaining nine planets contact his Sun, making him a multi-dimensional man with a great deal of energy.

The first contact is from the Moon, planet of emotions, creating a sense of harmony between his inner self and the work he must do out in the world. The Moon is in practical Virgo, and a contact to both Moon and Sun from Neptune, the planet of idealism, enhances the Dalai Lama's psychic and spiritual inclinations.

Mars, the planet of action, creates a bit of turmoil as it is placed in his horoscope's house of home and foundations and in part explains the chaos in his homeland that forced his exile. A challenging contact from Mars to his Sun gives him dynamism and energy. A contact from expansive Jupiter helps in his religious and spiritual pursuits and gives him optimism and courage. Saturn, the planet of hard work, provides another contact, resulting in stamina and determination. And finally, Uranus, the planet of innovation provides those modern inclina-

tions that have encouraged him to travel the globe and share his message of love.

His Moon, the planet of one's deepest feelings as well as roots and foundations, receives a challenging aspect from Saturn, the planet of restrictions and limitations. This can explain the early removal from his mother as well as the loss of his beloved homeland.

➤ Read about the Dalai Lama in "East Meets Twentieth-Century West" on page 65.

2000

The Wealth Game: Jupiter-Saturn in Taurus

The Supreme Court awards the presidency to George W. Bush

The world made it to the new millennium without an electronic meltdown and there seemed to be no limit on success. Capitalism was in a new heyday and the Internet was the vehicle for retirement by age thirty. An adventurous spirit, typified by expansive and speculative Jupiter in bold and pioneering Aries, propped up "Cyber-success". In 1999 and the first part of 2000, venture capitalists poured millions into web enterprises. However, when Jupiter went into security-conscious Taurus on February 14, they wanted a return on their dollars. This motion was seconded by the fact that stodgy Saturn was already inhabiting Taurus, adding to that I-want-money-in-the-bank urge.

Before Jupiter went into Taurus, the world's stock markets, particularly New York's NASDAQ, were racing to an unknown heaven. Once Jupiter entered this earth-bound sign, the stock market got wobbly, fluctuating more wildly until the "May bubble," when tech stocks reached their peak. As the bubble built, Jupiter was rushing toward Saturn, the other planets crowding around to get some of the action. By the end of May, when Jupiter finally caught Saturn, the bubble had burst, and a dose of sobering Saturnian reality had brought the market down to solid ground and halved many fortunes.

While half-fortunes were a lasting testament to the overall beneficence of this planetary combination, political events also bore this out. Jupiter's progressive touch was seen as liberal reformers won control of Iran's parliament, the first time since the 1979 Islamic revolution.

The Queen Mother celebrates her one-hundredth birthday

A nationwide uprising overthrows Yugoslavian President Slobodan Milosevic

THE AGE OF AQUARIUS

"When the moon is in the Seventh House and Jupiter aligns with Mars..." What does the song from the musical *Hair* mean? The Seventh House in astrology indicates a change. The person who once was your partner now becomes your open enemy. Jupiter is the planet of brotherhood and Mars is the planet of war and action. When these two align, they balance each other and work together toward peace and love. Every 2,000 years humanity enters a new zodiacal age. Aquarius is the age of brotherhood, bright ideas, and innovation.

YUGOSLAV PEACE AND ELECTION TURMOIL

Year 2000 was greeted on January 1 by celebrations worldwide. Vicente Fox Quesada was elected President of Mexico, ending seventy-one years of Revolutionary Party rule. U.S. President Clinton hosted peace talks between Syria and Israel but they failed to reach agreement. In Yugoslavia, Milosevic was voted out in favour of Kostunica and was forced to accept defeat. After twenty-two years, Israel withdrew from Lebanon. A Concorde airliner crashed near Paris, killing 113. Former Indonesian president Suharto and his son were tried for corruption and his grandson was arrested on weapons charges. The furor over Elian Gonzalez' return to Cuba ended when he was retrieved from his Miami relatives and reunited with his father. After recounts in the closest-ever presidential election, the Supreme Court declared Bush the winner over Gore. Thalidomide, long banned for causing birth defects, but on sale again since 1998, was pronounced a possible treatment for leprosy, AIDS, and some cancers. Britain's Queen Elizabeth, the Queen Mother celebrated her centenary, the first British royal to reach this milestone.

➤ Read George W. Bush's Star Profile on page 817.

CAPRICORN

From January 01, 0:00 through January 20, 18:22

The Inspirational Builder

Born at the start of the last year of the twentieth century, January Capricorn of 2000, your realistic outlook will combine with a sense of innovation. Aware that there is no substitute for hard work, you will not forget that without a clear vision, no progress is ever made. Beneath your practical surface beats a heart of passion and innate spirituality. Naturally creative, you will never lose sight of the need to utilize that creativity.

Capricorns may be conservative by nature but your family may have noticed that the world was undergoing a quiet revolution. The World Wide Web became reality as Time-Warner and America Online united, creating a truly mass media company encompassing a variety of platforms. Acting president Vladimir Putin brought a sense of order to troubled Russia. This mirrors your nature, as your will to break down barriers will be tempered by your respect for tradition.

You have a foot in both centuries and you will be at home with new technology as well as old-fashioned craftsmanship. Capricorns are known for their acute business sense but you may bring a touch of artistic flair to your chosen field. You will be a self-starter and motivational to others. Sympathetic to emerging talent and the needs of others, you may find yourself working for a prestigious art institution or major charity. You could find that you get most satisfaction from expanding on the foundation already laid by others.

Loyalty and stability may be two of your requirements in relationships but you will also demand fun and romance. Your earthy nature will know that the spark of physical attraction must always be nurtured or love can die. You may also be the one that maintains the sense of romance in your relationships. You could feel happiest when linked with Taureans, Virgos, Pisceans, or Scorpios.

One challenge for you, January Capricorn of 2000, is to balance your artistic side and your clear-sighted business sense. Your strength will be your unwavering commitment to excellence. You will never give less than your best and will know that your contribution is inspirational to others.

AQUARIUS

From January 20, 18:23 through February 19, 8:32

The Unconventional Samaritan

Above all, you, Aquarius of 2000, will strive to maintain your individualism while remaining aware of humanity's need to join together for everyone's sake. Your parents may be unconventional and encourage you to think for yourself and challenge the status quo when necessary. You were born when Communist China attempted to apply the brakes to the growing availability of information on the Internet. Like other Aquarians, new technology and its uses will be fascinating to you. You arrived when the NEAR spacecraft made the first orbit of an asteroid.

You may well have a sixth sense and an awareness of trends in the collective consciousness; this will give you the ability to be in the right place at the right time. Your humanitarian ideals will be easily aroused and you may find your niche working for the underdog. Direct action may appeal to you but you'll soon understand that throwing the baby out with the bath water is unlikely to bring about lasting changes for the good. You could be well-placed to work from within the establishment to reform radically some outmoded attitudes and institutions.

You will be unafraid to question received wisdom, never letting go of a subject until you have unearthed the truth however much this unsettles those around you. Your unique thought processes could lead you toward a career in politics or the law. In either case, you are a formidable opponent and not easily diverted from your objectives. The quest for truth runs like a river through all areas of your life.

Relationships will undoubtedly be important to you but not when they conflict with your ideals. Friendships will be maintained through thick and thin and you will be unimpressed with partners that want you all to themselves. You may find an affinity with fellow air signs, Geminis and Librans, along with fiery Sagittarians and Ariens.

Your challenge may be to learn how to listen to others and concede ground gracefully. Your strength will be your commitment to the elevation of your fellow man as well as your knowledge of how to cut through the endless red tape that impedes progress.

➤ Read about your Chinese Astrological sign on page 838. ➤ Read about your Personal Planets on page 826. ➤ Read about your personal Mystical Card on page 856.

CAPRICORN
Your Personal Planets

YOUR LOVE POTENTIAL
Venus in Sagittarius, Jan. 01, 0:00 - Jan. 20, 18:22

YOUR DRIVE AND AMBITION
Mars in Aquarius, Jan. 01, 0:00 - Jan. 04, 3:00
Mars in Pisces, Jan. 04, 3:01 - Jan. 20, 18:22

YOUR LUCK MAGNETISM
Jupiter in Aries, Jan. 01, 0:00 - Jan. 20, 18:22

World Events

Jan. 3 – Acting Russian President Putin dismisses Kremlin advisor Tatyana Dyachenko, daughter of former President Yeltsin.

Jan. 10 – America Online agrees to buy Time Warner in the biggest merger in U.S. history.

Russian President Vladimir Putin

AQUARIUS
Your Personal Planets

YOUR LOVE POTENTIAL
Venus in Sagittarius, Jan. 20, 18:23 - Jan. 24, 19:51
Venus in Capricorn, Jan. 24, 19:52 - Feb. 18, 4:42
Venus in Aquarius, Feb. 18, 4:43 - Feb. 19, 8:32

YOUR DRIVE AND AMBITION
Mars in Pisces, Jan. 20, 18:23 - Feb. 12, 1:03
Mars in Aries, Feb. 12, 1:04 - Feb. 19, 8:32

YOUR LUCK MAGNETISM
Jupiter in Aries, Jan. 20, 18:23 - Feb. 14, 21:38
Jupiter in Taurus, Feb. 14, 21:39 - Feb. 19, 8:32

World Events

Jan. 26 – China announces controls on the Internet over fears of state secrets being leaked through the medium.

Feb. 14 – The *NEAR* spacecraft is sent into orbit around the asteroid Eros.

2000

PISCES
Your Personal Planets

YOUR LOVE POTENTIAL
Venus in Aquarius, Feb. 19, 8:33 - Mar. 13, 11:35
Venus in Pisces, Mar. 13, 11:36 - Mar. 20, 7:34

YOUR DRIVE AND AMBITION
Mars in Aries, Feb. 19, 8:33 - Mar. 20, 7:34

YOUR LUCK MAGNETISM
Jupiter in Taurus, Feb. 19, 8:33 - Mar. 20, 7:34

World Events

Feb. 26 - Reformists win control of the Iranian Parliament for the first time since the 1979 Islamic revolution.

Mar. 12 - Pope John Paul II delivers an unprecedented apology for Church errors over the last 2,000 years.

Pope John Paul II deep in prayer

ARIES
Your Personal Planets

YOUR LOVE POTENTIAL
Venus in Pisces, Mar. 20, 7:35 - Apr. 06, 18:36
Venus in Aries, Apr. 06, 18:37 - Apr. 19, 18:39

YOUR DRIVE AND AMBITION
Mars in Aries, Mar. 20, 7:35 - Mar. 23, 1:24
Mars in Taurus, Mar. 23, 1:25 - Apr. 19, 18:39

YOUR LUCK MAGNETISM
Jupiter in Taurus, Mar. 20, 7:35 - Apr. 19, 18:39

World Events

Apr. 4 - Yoshiro Mori is elected Prime Minister of Japan.

Apr. 14 - Russia ratifies its arms reduction treaty, START II.

PISCES
From February 19, 8:33 through March 20, 7:34

The Divine Dreamer

Pisces of 2000, you were born with a deep sense of yourself as a spiritual being. You may be unable to pinpoint exactly how or why this is but your family may have helped to foster the attitude that we are all brothers and sisters under the skin. Radical changes in fundamentalist Iran this month must have seemed one small step toward better understanding among religions and subsequently among nations.

The stock market crash at this time, dampening the optimism generated by the Internet boom, could have made your parents acutely aware that money can never be an end in itself. You may be happier in the realm of the senses as you are possibly the least materialistic of the signs. Nevertheless, you will know that poverty is self-defeating. Your talent for communication and your powerful intuition could help you make your mark in the media. You will spot a trend a hundred miles away and know instinctively how to exploit it. You may also strive constantly to combine your creativity and highly developed aesthetic sense with your everyday, mundane life.

You may find that while you will enjoy interacting with colleagues and friends, quiet periods are essential for your emotional and spiritual well-being. In fact some of your best ideas could emerge after a spell of contemplation. Your sensitivity to your environment could mean that you absorb the emotions and ideas of others, which you must periodically shed.

You could be ardent and unconventional in relationships, Pisces of 2000, but potential lovers must share your spiritual outlook. They must also understand and honor your need for privacy. You will require a partner that values emotional commitment but allows you room to breathe. You may find this with Cancerians, Scorpios, Capricorns, or Taureans.

How to balance the demands of the real world with your need to experience the divine is one challenge you may face. You will strive to shake off any negative vibrations that surround you. Your strength will be your awareness of how we human beings seldom measure up and you will be willing to give others a second chance.

ARIES
From March 20, 7:35 through April 19, 18:38

The Sensitive Warrior

With your reputation as a fighter, Aries of 2000, you could be surprised by your sensitivity. While your instincts will encourage you to stand up for yourself, you will sometimes hold back if others could be hurt. The dispute between Cuba and the U.S. surrounding little Elian Gonzalez was finally resolved at your birth. Your family would have seen that the stand-off could have damaged the child. They may encourage you to think of the consequences before acting. This is not to say that you will be a pushover—just that you will be aware of others' feelings.

You may be more of a team player than other Ariens. Russia finally ratified the outstanding arms reduction treaty, signaling a desire for partnership rather than confrontation. This could have symbolized to your parents a more positive attitude toward those of differing beliefs. While you may find that you develop strongly held convictions you may also respect those who are equally convinced of the opposite.

You will soon come to recognize that if you want something badly enough, it is up to you to go out and get it. You will understand the power of money and while you know it's not everything you will always ensure that you have enough for your needs. This won't discount a desire for risk-taking and you could find you have an interest in the stock market or speculation in general.

While you may be subject to sudden infatuations and a touch more sentimental than most Ariens, when you find the person you want to spend your life with, nothing will deter you. You will be unafraid of the realities of any relationship. The marriage vow "for better or for worse" strikes a real chord and your partner will know that your commitment will be unconditional. Leos, Sagittarians, Aquarians, or Geminis could match your wit and warmth.

Your personal challenge may be to keep material objectives in mind while retaining your empathy with others. You will know that riding roughshod over others could mar your achievements. Your strength will be your honesty and willingness to cooperate. You will wish to shine but not at the expense of others.

➤ Read about your Chinese Astrological sign on page 838. ➤ Read about your Personal Planets on page 826. ➤ Read about your personal Mystical Card on page 856.

TAURUS

From April 19, 18:39 through May 20, 17:48

The Cheerful Realist

Dynamic planetary emphasis heralded your birth, Taurus of 2000. Always described as a steady plodder, you will be eager to make a lasting impact during your lifetime. Rigid thinking was being challenged continually by unexpected wrenches hurled into the works. Thalidomide, once spoken of with such terror for the birth defects it caused, was found to have unexpected healing properties for modern day scourges such as cancer and AIDS. The "I Love You" computer virus indicated that our dependence on current technology could easily be disrupted by mischievous hackers.

Your family may want to make you aware that the best-laid plans can become obsolete in the face of unfolding events. While tenacity can be an asset they may encourage you to be flexible and willing to go with the flow. They are most likely aware that taking a risk is sometimes the best option. As you mature you may find that you possess an astounding sense of timing, knowing just when to move and when to stand still.

You will grow up knowing that a secure foundation is the best basis for building your dreams. Rather than remaining behind the scenes, you will desire recognition for your achievements. You will be ready to work tirelessly for your goals but could become discouraged by negative feedback. A career in the arts could beckon as you seek to increase the quality of our lives. Interior design and even architecture are fields that could bring both personal and financial rewards.

You will probably form relationships easily and will have little difficulty relating to your peers. Initially bashful, you will quickly open up when you realize how much fun others can be. When love comes calling, it may be with a Capricorn, Virgo, Cancerian, or Piscean. Nothing will restore your sunny disposition quicker than a loving word from your partner.

You could find that you have a slight tendency to resist new ideas and this could be your challenge, Taurus of 2000. You will however be prepared to incorporate these new ideas if you can see their validity. Your strength will be your ability to bounce back from setbacks.

GEMINI

From May 20, 17:49 through June 21, 1:47

The Iron Butterfly

Far from being the butterfly of the zodiac, you, Gemini of 2000, will become adept at seeing projects through to their conclusion. While you may grow to possess all the Gemini qualities of wit, curiosity, and playfulness, you will also learn to appreciate the importance of self-control. Your family may foster the idea that you could have the power to initiate great changes in your lifetime but they may never let you forget that with power comes responsibility. One individual that abused his personal and political power, former President Suharto of Indonesia, was under house arrest at this time, awaiting the outcome of corruption charges.

Your vivid imagination and interest in the world around you will be apparent early in life. You will adore interaction with others and your family could be delighted with your quirky outlook and unorthodox attitude to learning. They may have been following the ongoing development of a new stroke treatment incorporating innovative therapy that can assist recovery from paralysis. They may continue to encourage your unconventional approach into adulthood.

The exchange of information will become a vital aspect of your development. You may find that you wish to take this to its logical conclusion and seek a career in the media or education. Your clever knack with words could make you a popular and respected figure in any career requiring good communication skills.

As you grow you will continue to be fascinated by humanity in all its diversity. You will never cease to be amazed that you can learn something from everyone. You may come to learn that emotional commitment does not have to mean that you lose contact with new people. Those born under Libra, Aquarius, Aries, or Leo may provide the compatibility and space that you desire.

Your ability to charm others into your way of thinking may be a trait you come to take for granted as you reach maturity. Your challenge could be to use your power over others wisely. Your strength will be to assimilate the abundance of data surrounding you and then distribute it where it can do the most good.

➤ Read about your Chinese Astrological sign on page 838. ➤ Read about your Personal Planets on page 826. ➤ Read about your personal Mystical Card on page 856.

2000

TAURUS
Your Personal Planets

YOUR LOVE POTENTIAL
Venus in Aries, Apr. 19, 18:40 - May 01, 2:48
Venus in Taurus, May 01, 2:49 - May 20, 17:48

YOUR DRIVE AND AMBITION
Mars in Taurus, Apr. 19, 18:40 - May 03, 19:17
Mars in Gemini, May 03, 19:18 - May 20, 17:48

YOUR LUCK MAGNETISM
Jupiter in Taurus, Apr. 19, 18:40 - May 20, 17:48

World Events

May 12 - War breaks out between Eritrea and Ethiopia.

May 20 - Chen Shui-bian is sworn in as the new President of Taiwan.

Former Indonesian President Suharto

GEMINI
Your Personal Planets

YOUR LOVE POTENTIAL
Venus in Taurus, May 20, 17:49 - May 25, 12:14
Venus in Gemini, May 25, 12:15 - June 18, 22:14
Venus in Cancer, June 18, 22:15 - June 21, 1:47

YOUR DRIVE AND AMBITION
Mars in Gemini, May 20, 17:49 - June 16, 12:29
Mars in Cancer, June 16, 12:30 - June 21, 1:47

YOUR LUCK MAGNETISM
Jupiter in Taurus, May 20, 17:49 - June 21, 1:47

World Events

May 29 - Former Indonesian President Suharto is held under house arrest, charged with corruption and abuse of power.

June 14 - The Presidents of North and South Korea sign a peace accord, ending half a century of antagonism.

CANCER
Your Personal Planets

YOUR LOVE POTENTIAL

Venus in Cancer, June 21, 1:48 - July 13, 8:01
Venus in Leo, July 13, 8:02 - July 22, 12:42

YOUR DRIVE AND AMBITION

Mars in Cancer, June 21, 1:48 - July 22, 12:42

YOUR LUCK MAGNETISM

Jupiter in Taurus, June 21, 1:48 - June 30, 7:33
Jupiter in Gemini, June 30, 7:34 - July 22, 12:42

World Events

June 26 – The human genome is mapped.

July 2 – Vicente Fox Quesada is elected President of Mexico, ending seventy-one years of one-party rule.

Vicente Fox Quesada is elected President of Mexico

LEO
Your Personal Planets

YOUR LOVE POTENTIAL

Venus in Leo, July 22, 12:43 - Aug. 06, 17:31
Venus in Virgo, Aug. 06, 17:32 - Aug. 22, 19:48

YOUR DRIVE AND AMBITION

Mars in Cancer, July 22, 12:43 - Aug. 01, 1:20
Mars in Leo, Aug. 01, 1:21 - Aug. 22, 19:48

YOUR LUCK MAGNETISM

Jupiter in Gemini, July 22, 12:43 - Aug. 22, 19:48

World Events

July 25 – The Camp David summit between Israeli and Palestinian leaders concludes without a compromise being reached over the issue of Jerusalem.

July 25 – The Concorde crashes near Paris, killing 113 people.

CANCER
From June 21, 1:48 through July 22, 12:42

The Determined Homebody

At the time of your birth, Cancer of 2000, the dramatic deciphering of the human genome inspired scientists the world over. While your family may have had some concerns about how far science was progressing they could have been comforted by the thought that during your lifetime great strides were being made in the field of healing. Family life will become your touchstone but you may find that as you grow the traditional set-up gives way to more unusual groupings. Two events at your birth illustrate how the status quo can change in an instant. Mexico over-turned seventy years of one-party rule when Vicente Fox Quesada was elected President. The African Methodist Episcopal Church elected the Rev. Vashti McKenzie as its first female head.

Learning how to embrace change will be part of your education as you grow to adulthood. Your sense of security will not be threatened so long as you remember that you have the power to control your everyday life. Your family may encourage you to take an interest in personal health and help you explore ways of maintaining wellness. You may find that while there is enough to fascinate you within your immediate environment your family will gently encourage you to come out of your shell and explore the infinite opportunities on offer.

You may gradually become more adept at dealing with group activities the more you are exposed to them. You could be drawn toward medicine or social work as a career, particularly when it involves children.

Security and stability may be two qualities you most value in relationships. Your loyalty and humor will be given the opportunity to thrive when you know that you are safe. Fellow water signs, Pisceans and Scorpios, as well as earthy Taureans and Virgos provide the prime partnership candidates.

Your challenge, Cancer of 2000, may be to learn that while it is crucial to have control of your personal surroundings and your daily routine, allowing space for the unexpected is also important. You may come to understand that not all change is bad. Your strength will be your loyalty to family and friends and your desire to support them.

LEO
From July 22, 12:43 through August 22, 19:47

The Glamorous Negotiator

You were born, Leo of 2000, with the potential to develop very strong willpower and a desire to do things your way. England's indomitable Queen Mother celebrated her one hundredth birthday this month—an example of someone who overcame obstacles by sheer courage. Charming and deter-mined you may be—but your family may attempt to demonstrate the importance of compromise. The miserable stalemate achieved at the Camp David summit this month indicated there was still a vast distance to go before Palestinians and Israelis were prepared to agree on terms. Your family may understand that without compromise, there can never be progress.

You may find that you begin to develop a taste for the limelight. Nothing could please you more than to be close to the center of the action. You may learn to accept compliments easily but your family could also recognize that a touch of modesty is not out of place. You enjoy both formal and impromptu celebrations. On August 20, 2000 at the Vatican, two million young people closed the six-day World Youth festival that came to be known as the Catholic Woodstock.

Your ability to take center stage and at the same time spur others into action could turn you toward entertainment. Not everyone can be the star but you may discover that being the main protagonist on your own personal stage could satisfy your ego needs. You may retain your playfulness well into adulthood and your affinity with children could open up opportunities in childcare.

While you may discover that you are attracted to a tremendous variety of people, when you fall in love you may want it to be all-consuming. You could steadfastly hold out for the right partner, as your affections will be too precious to waste on also-rans. Ariens, Sagittarians, Geminis, and Librans all combine the spontaneity and burning warmth you will adore. Your desire to organize life to suit you may often be challenged as you grow to maturity.

Your learning curve may be how to incorporate meeting others halfway while hanging on to your vision. You could bring a touch of glamour to everything you touch and that will be your strength.

➤ Read about your Chinese Astrological sign on page 838. ➤ Read about your Personal Planets on page 826. ➤ Read about your personal Mystical Card on page 856.

VIRGO

From August 22, 19:48 through September 22, 17:27

The Quiet Genius

Your arrival, Virgo of 2000, coincided with spectacular developments in stem cell research. Leading to dramatic implications for the treatment of a variety of diseases and conditions, this research may have the potential to change the face of medicine. Typically, Virgos are characterized as having an interest in healing and you were born as the links between space-age science and medicine became even closer.

As you progress through your life both your care and attention to detail will become more apparent. You display, however, an unconventional attitude to everyday matters that can sometimes result in noisy tiffs with your family. Far from being malleable, you will be willing to go out on a limb if your sense of fair play is activated. You may have a particular interest in the less able members of society. This concern for the underdog is symbolized by this month's Olympic Games. Held in Australia, the Aborigines were encouraged to take a prominent role where once they may have been sidelined.

You may grow into an adult who despite a demure demeanor holds a steely determination to clarify issues and separate the wheat from the chaff. You may not wish to court confrontation but will have no truck with tradition for its own sake. You may prefer to work away from the public eye but your original contributions will eventually be given due recognition. Medicine, both alternative and orthodox, science, or education may all attract you when the time is right.

Your symbol, Virgo of 2000, is of a virginal maiden but this does not indicate any lack of relationships. After all, you are a sensual earth sign but you must be sure that a partner is worth your while before you relinquish your independence. Both body and mind will need to be aroused for you to be tempted. You may be most in tune with Taureans, Capricorns, Cancerians, and Scorpios.

You may relish most challenges but sometimes you will be faced with situations when rational thought will not provide the answers. Your intuition will be a valuable tool. Your main strength will be your ability to create order from chaos.

LIBRA

From September 22, 17:28 through October 23, 2:46

The Charming Adversary

You were born, Libra of 2000, with an unshakeable and solid sense of justice. Right and wrong will be clearly defined for you and you will be comfortable defending your beliefs even in the face of formidable opposition. Your parents may have been struck by the idea that evil is eventually punished. At the time of your birth, President Milosevic of Yugoslavia was finally deposed by the very people in whose name he had perpetrated his atrocities.

You will be aware, Libra of 2000, that firmly held convictions must be balanced by an ability to see other points of view. The approval in the U.S. of the controversial abortion pill, RU-486, illustrated the need for rational thought. Your family may have taught you that cooperation and conciliation will serve you better as you proceed through life than bigotry and mistrust.

Your passions will be aroused by injustice and you could fight like a terrier for your favorite causes, especially if they involve personal freedom. Quick-thinking and articulate, you will be a match for anyone. But you may find you prefer to surround yourself with joy and beauty. Your exquisite taste could even lead you to work in some aspect of design. You will understand the effect of the immediate environment on mood and behavior. An ability to pour oil on troubled waters could also make you an excellent counselor or arbitrator.

Relationships are of great importance to most Librans and you'll be no exception. Your desire to share life's ups and downs may sometimes be hard to marry with your need for individual freedom. A meeting of minds will allow you to develop your potential as an individual while loving and being loved. Compatibility could be found with Geminis, Aquarians, Sagittarians, or Leos. You constantly try to take care of the details while keeping the big picture in focus.

Your challenge, Libra of 2000, will be to retain your ideals while acknowledging the shackles of reality. Diplomacy will be one of your main strengths and you can achieve spectacular results with persuasion and charm rather than by the drawing up of battle lines.

VIRGO
Your Personal Planets

YOUR LOVE POTENTIAL
Venus in Virgo, Aug. 22, 19:49 - Aug. 31, 3:34
Venus in Libra, Aug. 31, 3:35 - Sept. 22, 17:27

YOUR DRIVE AND AMBITION
Mars in Leo, Aug. 22, 19:49 - Sept. 17, 0:18
Mars in Virgo, Sept. 17, 0:19 - Sept. 22, 17:27

YOUR LUCK MAGNETISM
Jupiter in Gemini, Aug. 22, 19:49 - Sept. 22, 17:27

World Events

Aug. 30 - Pres. Bill Clinton visits Columbia, offering military aid to assist anti-drug efforts being made by the country.

Sept. 15 - The summer Olympic Games open in Sydney, Australia.

Professor Emile Baulieu, inventor of the RU-486 abortive pill

LIBRA
Your Personal Planets

YOUR LOVE POTENTIAL
Venus in Libra, Sept. 22, 17:28 - Sept. 24, 15:25
Venus in Scorpio, Sept. 24, 15:26 - Oct. 19, 6:17
Venus in Sagittarius, Oct. 19, 6:18 - Oct. 23, 2:47

YOUR DRIVE AND AMBITION
Mars in Virgo, Sept. 22, 17:28 - Oct. 23, 2:47

YOUR LUCK MAGNETISM
Jupiter in Gemini, Sept. 22, 17:28 - Oct. 23, 2:47

World Events

Sept. 28 - The abortion pill RU-486 is approved in the U.S.

Oct. 5 - A nationwide uprising overthrows the Yugoslavian President Slobodan Milosevic.

➤ Read about your Chinese Astrological sign on page 838. ➤ Read about your Personal Planets on page 826. ➤ Read about your personal Mystical Card on page 856.

SCORPIO
Your Personal Planets

YOUR LOVE POTENTIAL
Venus in Sagittarius, Oct. 23, 2:48 - Nov. 13, 2:13
Venus in Capricorn, Nov. 13, 2:14 - Nov. 22, 0:18

YOUR DRIVE AND AMBITION
Mars in Virgo, Oct. 23, 2:48 - Nov. 04, 1:59
Mars in Libra, Nov. 04, 2:00 - Nov. 22, 0:18

YOUR LUCK MAGNETISM
Jupiter in Gemini, Oct. 23, 2:48 - Nov. 22, 0:18

World Events

Nov. 8 – The closest-run presidential election campaign ever causes confusion across the U.S.; a recount is called for in some states.

Nov. 14 – Demonstrations are held in Manila in the Philippines, demanding the overthrow of President Estrada.

Israeli leader Barak resigns

SAGITTARIUS
Your Personal Planets

YOUR LOVE POTENTIAL
Venus in Capricorn, Nov. 22, 0:19 - Dec. 08, 8:47
Venus in Aquarius, Dec. 08, 8:48 - Dec. 21, 13:36

YOUR DRIVE AND AMBITION
Mars in Libra, Nov. 22, 0:19 - Dec. 21, 13:36

YOUR LUCK MAGNETISM
Jupiter in Gemini, Nov. 22, 0:19 - Dec. 21, 13:36

World Events

Dec. 9 – Israeli Prime Minister Barak resigns.

Dec. 12 – The Supreme Court awards the presidency to George W. Bush.

SCORPIO
From October 23, 2:47 through November 22, 0:18

The Undercover Revolutionary

Alarming reports of the danger of global warming may have overshadowed your birth, Scorpio of 2000. Your family may know that their protection counts for very little if the planet is in danger of self-destruction. Optimistically, however, they probably recognize that during your lifetime you may have the opportunity to contribute something to halt this trend. They may instill in you the importance of responsibility for your own waste. With mad cow disease rampant in Europe they could also have been more aware than ever of the old maxim: "you are what you eat.

"While intensity is Scorpio's middle name you may come to realize as you mature that your focus shifts from your personal concerns to the resources that we all share on this Earth. You will learn quickly that money represents power and that those who have the most seem to have the biggest say. You may not turn into a disciple of Karl Marx but you are likely to believe that a more even distribution of wealth affords a more harmonious atmosphere.

You will have a clear idea of your priorities as you grow up. You may sometimes faze less robust souls with your approach but you could be an expert at organizing disparate groups into efficient teams. Management could be your forte and you could use this to great effect in local or national politics. The upcoming U.S. election, in which George W. Bush would ultimately be declared the winner, was closer than a whisker. Your desire to expose cover-ups could even lead you into investigative journalism.

The intrigue and mind games involved in the pursuit of love will be endlessly fascinating to you. Quality rather than quantity may be more important when it comes to choosing a mate. Shared values are at the top of your wish list and you could find compatibility with Cancerians, Pisceans, Virgos, or Capricorns.

Driven by a hatred of greed and waste, you may confront it wherever it appears. Your challenge could be to allow others to add their contribution to your fight against these twin evils. Your strength will be never to relinquish your principles no matter what inducements are offered.

SAGITTARIUS
From November 22, 0:19 through December 21, 13:36

The Impatient Philosopher

You, Sagittarius of 2000, were born just as an environmental gathering came to a close. On November 25, 2000, the last day of the Global Warming conference in the Hague, Netherlands ended. Although less than successful—a compromise between U.S. and E.U. negotiators failed—it did result in a declaration of intent to reduce greenhouse gas emissions. On this issue and others, you will follow the adage to "think globally but act locally."

You may share many characteristics with other Sagittarians, such as good humor, a sense of the ridiculous, and faith in human nature. Your instincts may be more refined as you could also set great store by old-fashioned virtues like courtesy and constancy. However, individual freedom is one belief that you may never relinquish. America, Russia, and many other countries were deeply concerned at this time when the Taliban continued to impose their harsh, extremist interpretation of Islam on the citizens of Afghanistan.

In the future, you may come to highly prize cooperation with friends, family, and colleagues. You will value your friendships and take more care than many of your sign to maintain them. You will soon come to realize that life's journey is much more pleasant when not traveled alone. You may be drawn to travel as a career, either writing about foreign lands or organizing trips for others. You could also explore the far reaches of human thought and ideas. Teaching or research at the highest levels could excite you.

Relationships will be the spice of life for you, Sagittarius 2000. Playing the field holds many attractions but you will be capable of commitment when you meet a partner that shares your lust for life and love of freedom. Woe unto them, though, if they try to clip your wings through lack of trust. You may find that Leos, Ariens, Aquarians, and Librans are most able to match your boundless enthusiasm.

One challenge you may often face is to maintain a sense of perspective. The myriad ideas that compete for space in your mind may sometimes lead to impatience and frustration. Your strength will be that you are unafraid to face setbacks and obstacles head on.

➤ Read about your Chinese Astrological sign on page 838. ➤ Read about your Personal Planets on page 826. ➤ Read about your personal Mystical Card on page 856.

CAPRICORN

From December 21, 13:37 through December 31, 23:59

The Dutiful Eccentric

As you were born at year's close, December Capricorn of 2000, outgoing President Bill Clinton made one final attempt before his presidency came to an end to secure a peace deal in the Middle East. His plan involved both Israelis and Palestinians conceding to unpopular and unexpected demands. This could symbolize the contrasts in your personality as you begin to grow up. You may cherish traditional values but you could also be intrigued by more radical ways of thinking. The original "Material Girl," Madonna, previously notorious for her outlandish appearance and behavior, chose the most formal of settings when she married her film director husband this month.

While you will always be capable of handling the practical side of life, you will not lose sight of the more intangible qualities that improve life. You may believe that what you send out often comes back to you. You will try to treat everyone with respect regardless of their status—a long way from the regular description of power-hungry Capricorns. You may often seem serious but a dry sense of humor and an ability to see the funny in any situation increases as you get older.

While you may well be attracted to a career in finance, your approach will be far from standard. You may find that you won't be overly ambitious and clawing your way to the top interferes with a more relaxed lifestyle. Your eye for design could steer you toward antiques or art. And if the nine-to-five doesn't suit you, it won't indicate you are lazy. It's just that you will prefer working on your own timetable.

When you're ready to choose a partner you may discover that this is one area where traditional values rule. You may want mutual pampering and your innate sensuality could mean that looks are important to you. Virgos, Taureans, Pisceans, and Scorpios may all share characteristics that fit your particular bill.

Your challenge, December Capricorn of 2000, may be to drop your guard and allow others a peep into your world. You may be quaking inside but you will never appear less than self-assured. Your strength will be your dependability, which is prized by others.

2000

CAPRICORN
Your Personal Planets

YOUR LOVE POTENTIAL
Venus in Aquarius, Dec. 21, 13:37 - Dec. 31, 23:59

YOUR DRIVE AND AMBITION
Mars in Libra, Dec. 21, 13:37 - Dec. 23, 14:36
Mars in Scorpio, Dec. 23, 14:37 - Dec. 31, 23:59

YOUR LUCK MAGNETISM
Jupiter in Gemini, Dec. 21, 13:37 - Dec. 31, 23:59

World Events

Dec. 22 - Pop star Madonna and film director Guy Ritchie marry in a ceremony in Scotland.

Dec. 31 - The U.S. government signs a World Criminal Treaty.

George W. Bush
Born July 6, 1946

GEORGE W. BUSH
Cancer

The forty-third president of the United States came to power after a tumultuous election the likes of which had never been seen in America. Despite the fact that he had been a successful businessman, earning millions in savvy deals, and a popular two-term governor of Texas, there were doubts expressed about his ability to lead the nation, perhaps because his maladroit verbal misfires made him seem ill-prepared. But when the terrorist-driven tragedies of September 11, 2001 occurred, Bush stepped forward and showed his mettle as a strong and determined leader, and at last he gained the respect not only of a nation but the world.

Bush is a Cancer, a sign known for tenderness, sensitivity and a love of home. His often-repeated bit of advice, "Listen to your mother," might as well be the Cancer theme song. With his Sun, planet of identity, lacking prominent placement in his horoscope, he might easily

have been overlooked. A contact from Neptune, planet of insecurity, gives him a tentative quality and a certain modesty. It's also probably responsible for Bush's well-publicized bouts with alcohol. But Neptune also grants inspiration and idealism, and Bush comes across as a man who trusts his heart.

Known as a popular politician who gets along well with everyone, Bush has the Moon, planet of emotions, in people-loving Libra. A contact from expansive Jupiter gives him the ability to relate to those who are different from himself and is also responsible for that merry twinkle in his eye.

Prominently placed in his horoscope is Pluto, planet of force and big business. Because it contacts Mercury, planet of communication, Bush's method of speaking is to be precise rather than glib. Pluto can also give a powerful, swashbuckling quality and Bush radiates physical strength and athletic skill.

His Mars, the planet of assertiveness, in practical Virgo, explains his constant references to himself as a patient man as well as his methodical approach to the task of defeating terrorism. Despite the fact that he is an emotional man, he is one who understands his limitations, curbs his ego, and surrounds himself with people whose counsel he can trust.

➤ Read "The Presidential Death Cycle" on page 657. ➤ Read Nixon's Star Profile on page 577.
➤ Read Roosevelt's Star Profile on page 257. ➤ Read the Kennedy Family's Star Profile on page 497.

Fury Unleashed: Jupiter and Saturn Oppose Pluto

The World Trade Center before its collapse

Jupiter and Saturn continued to be the major players in 2001 but as they both entered dualistic Gemini, there was another force to reckon with. Pluto, planet of revolutionary change, was in the belief-oriented, sometimes fanatical Sagittarius. Pluto's entry, in 1995, signalled escalation in conflicts based on beliefs. As expansive Jupiter opposed Pluto from across the heavens, it heralded a period of unrestrained use of power. This was seen in the ruthless control that power companies wielded over consumers in the energy crisis first felt in deregulated California. When authoritarian Saturn entered Gemini in April, power struggles around the world became more obdurate. U.S. President Clinton was unsuccessful in crafting an Israeli-Palestinian peace accord, as a wave of conservatism ushered hard-liner Ariel Sharon in as Israeli Prime Minister. In the ultimate manifestation of fanatic violence, the al Qa'eda terrorist network engineered a gruesome attack on the United States, downing the World Trade Center in New York as Saturn and Pluto made their exact contact.

But all was not lost to the horrors of hatred as human kindness rose to the top. A deluge of volunteers assisted those besieged by loss and grief. Many people found solace in lofty expressions of human nature in the arts, where fantasy was king as *Harry Potter* and *The Lord of the Rings* broke box office records. These were signified in the heavens by Jupiter's sojourn in caring Cancer, magnifying the search for healing and nurture, as well as its fulfillment.

Europe suffers its worst-ever foot-and-mouth disease crisis

The Lord of the Rings is a box office success

PLANETS OPPOSED

In August and November, the planets Saturn and Pluto aligned 180 degrees apart, opposing each other. This astrological configuration, which occurs about every thirty-five years, indicated a difficult and challenging time for the world. Astrologically, Pluto connotes power and transformation while Saturn resists change. It was expected that this opposition would bring an unanticipated event that would force movement in a different direction. In the past, this configuration coincided with recession, war, and conflicts in the Middle East.

SEPTEMBER 11 AND ITS AFTERMATH

Suicide pilots of Osama bin Laden's terrorist Al Qa'eda network crashed two planes into the twin towers of New York's World Trade Center and another into the Pentagon: a fourth, believed to be on its way to Camp David, crashed in Pennsylvania. Over 3,000 people were thought to have died. Fears of biological terrorist warfare followed when anthrax was found in the U.S. postal system. U.S. President Bush pronounced a worldwide war on terrorism and first attacked Afghanistan, where the Taliban were protecting bin Laden. The Taliban were defeated, but bin Laden escaped. Milosevic appeared before UN war crimes tribunal at The Hague. Sino-American relations became strained when a Chinese jet and U.S. spy plane collided over Chinese territory: the Chinese pilot died. Europe suffered its worst-ever foot-and-mouth crisis, costing Britain, worst hit by the animals' disease, an estimated $4 billion. Fantasy movies topped the box office, as *Harry Potter and the Sorcerer's Stone* and *The Lord of the Rings: the Fellowship of the Ring* delighted audiences. *Gladiator* and its star, controversial New Zealand actor Russell Crowe, won Oscars.

➤ Read "Predictions, Eclipses, and September 11" by Rochelle Gordon on page 825.

CAPRICORN

From January 01, 0:00 through January 20, 0:16

The Hasty Achiever

You were born, January Capricorn of 2001, as George W. Bush assumed his presidency and many hoped this was the start of a new and sleaze-free era. The outgoing president Bill Clinton issued 140 pardons as his final presidential act. Your family may resolve to stress the necessity of honesty and probity.

Ambition could be essential, January Capricorn of 2001, but it may be wise to keep in mind the old maxim: "more haste, less speed." In your hurry to reach your objectives you might overlook vital details. Your parents could try to teach you that time spent laying the foundation is never wasted. Nevertheless you should be able to dismiss most obstacles strewn in your path by sheer willpower and the conviction that you will be able to succeed under any circumstances.

Capricorn labors under a cold reputation but you will have a huge streak of compassion running through your personality. It will touch your personal relationships but you may be able to combine your idealism and your dynamism in your professional life. Medicine, both human and animal, will be an obvious example of a career where both job satisfaction and financial rewards coexist. Engineering or construction could also be a way of benefiting others and at the same time having something concrete to show for your effort. Buildings don't always have to be multi-story representations of greed.

You may approach your relationships in the direct manner you approach business. However, the complexities of love will not always be so clear cut. In your eagerness to relate you could find you overpower some people and could be the one left wondering why you are so misunderstood. Taureans, Virgos, Pisceans, and Scorpios will be best placed to appreciate your honesty and emotional simplicity.

Your challenge, January Capricorn of 2001, may be to reign in your gung-ho impulses in both love and work. Time spent with a metaphorical map and compass could mean you reach your destination in double-quick time. Your strength will be that you never give up on anyone or anything until each angle has been explored.

AQUARIUS

From January 20, 0:17 through February 18, 14:27

The Friendly Persuader

You were born, Aquarius of 2001, with the potential to become a very forceful and charismatic character. Your desire to lead could become apparent to your family while you are still small. While not deliberately willful you could also make it very clear that once your mind is made up nothing will change it. Nothing, that is, except your own sudden reversals of opinion. Your family may have held strong and clear political and philosophical opinions and will try to nurture your interest in the wider world and its problems. A new player entered the turmoil in the Middle East when the Likud party, headed by Ariel Sharon, won the election in Israel. However, many Israelis felt that Sharon's hardline right-wing stance offered little chance of peace with the Palestinians.

You could be a diligent pupil but only if your imagination is fully engaged. Boredom could be your ultimate enemy and your ingenious mind could lead to disruptive behavior. As you mature, your enterprise and will to succeed will begin to develop apace. You may be capable of leadership but you will also know intuitively when cooperation will bring the desired results. Your career could by marked by sudden reversals of fortune—once your interest wanes you could quickly move on. Remaining stuck in a limiting and stale situation could lead to nervous irritation. Tom Cruise and Nicole Kidman, regarded as a golden Hollywood couple, announced that they were parting, surprising a public which had been convinced that they had a happy marriage.

A passionate mind and a passionate heart—you, Aquarius of 2001, will come to possess both. You may loathe restriction but you might also be fearful of betrayal and rejection. You will prefer to know that your chosen partner has eyes for no other and may be endearingly sincere in your declarations of love. You may feel most comfortable with Geminis, Librans, Ariens, and Sagittarians.

Your challenge, Aquarius of 2001, could be to learn how to see your undertakings through to their conclusion. A catalogue of half-finished projects could lead to frustration. Your strength will be your ability to convince others that black really is white if necessary.

➤ Read about your Chinese Astrological sign on page 838. ➤ Read about your Personal Planets on page 826. ➤ Read about your personal Mystical Card on page 856.

CAPRICORN
Your Personal Planets

YOUR LOVE POTENTIAL
Venus in Aquarius, Jan. 01, 0:00 - Jan. 03, 18:14
Venus in Pisces, Jan. 03, 18:15 - Jan. 20, 0:16

YOUR DRIVE AND AMBITION
Mars in Scorpio, Jan. 01, 0:00 - Jan. 20, 0:16

YOUR LUCK MAGNETISM
Jupiter in Gemini, Jan. 01, 0:00 - Jan. 20, 0:16

World Events

Jan. 20 – On his last day as President, Bill Clinton issues a number of controversial pardons, including one for Marc Rich, the billionaire fugitive financier.

Jan. 20 – George W. Bush is inaugurated as U.S. President.

Bill Clinton issues controversial pardons

AQUARIUS
Your Personal Planets

YOUR LOVE POTENTIAL
Venus in Pisces, Jan. 20, 0:17 - Feb. 02, 19:14
Venus in Aries, Feb. 02, 19:15 - Feb. 18, 14:27

YOUR DRIVE AND AMBITION
Mars in Scorpio, Jan. 20, 0:17 - Feb. 14, 20:06
Mars in Sagittarius, Feb. 14, 20:07 - Feb. 18, 14:27

YOUR LUCK MAGNETISM
Jupiter in Gemini, Jan. 20, 0:17 - Feb. 18, 14:27

World Events

Feb. 6 - Ariel Sharon wins the election in Israel, becoming the nation's fifth Prime Minister in as many years.

Feb. 7 - Film star Tom Cruise files for divorce from Nicole Kidman, citing irreconcilable differences.

2001

PISCES
Your Personal Planets

YOUR LOVE POTENTIAL
Venus in Aries, Feb. 18, 14:28 - Mar. 20, 13:31

YOUR DRIVE AND AMBITION
Mars in Sagittarius, Feb. 18, 14:28 - Mar. 20, 13:31

YOUR LUCK MAGNETISM
Jupiter in Gemini, Feb. 18, 14:28 - Mar. 20, 13:31

World Events

Feb. 20 - FBI agent Robert Hanssen is charged with spying for Russia for fifteen years.

Mar. 12 - Six people die when the U.S. navy drops a 500-lb missile during a training exercise, hitting an observation post in Kuwait, filled with military personnel.

A U.S. maritime patrol aircraft collides with a Chinese fighter jet

ARIES
Your Personal Planets

YOUR LOVE POTENTIAL
Venus in Aries, Mar. 20, 13:32 - Apr. 20, 0:36

YOUR DRIVE AND AMBITION
Mars in Sagittarius, Mar. 20, 13:32 - Apr. 20, 0:36

YOUR LUCK MAGNETISM
Jupiter in Gemini, Mar. 20, 13:32 - Apr. 20, 0:36

World Events

Mar. 25 - The film *Gladiator* wins five Oscars at the Academy Awards.

Apr. 2 - A U.S. surveillance plane and Chinese jet collide, sparking a Sino-American standoff.

PISCES
From February 18, 14:28 through March 20, 13:31

The Undercover Agent

Pisces of 2001, you could share those qualities usually associated with your sign such as creativity and sensitivity but also possess a strong sense of your own personal power. You may be so keen to advance that your family marvels at your headstrong personality. The only problem could be that you'll tend to act first and think later. A tragic example was the U.S. Navy bombing of one of their own observation posts in Kuwait, killing several personnel.

As you begin to grow up you could be intrigued by life's mystery rather than what is presented as fact. The motivations behind human behavior will always amaze you. Expert at reading between the lines you may have an uncanny ability to home in on lies. You could also be adept at disguising your own plans and objectives. These could be ideal for work in psychology. A good listener and very discreet, you could excel at any form of therapy. It would be preferable than some other uses of these talents. It was disclosed that Robert Hanssen, an FBI agent, had in fact been spying for the Russians for the past fifteen years.

Unusually for a Piscean, you may have a high regard for status and even money. The money will most likely be important for the beautiful objects it can buy rather than itself alone. You may have an artist's eye but your exacting standards could mean that you fear missing the mark with your own work. Rather than torture yourself with the creative process, you could find you gain more satisfaction from being a collector.

You may have high standards where love and relationships are concerned. More passionate and assertive than is typical, you could home in like an Exocet missile on your chosen partner—although they'll be taken unawares. That dreamy exterior will conceal an ardent lover. You may feel most comfortable with Cancerians, Scorpios, Taureans, or Capricorns.

Your challenge, Pisces of 2001, may be to learn to accept people for who they are rather than what their position in life indicates. A book should never, ever be judged by its cover. Your strength could be that you never betray a confidence.

ARIES
From March 20, 13:32 through April 20, 0:36

The Curious Traveler

You may come to possess the natural confidence and assertion so typical of your sign but you will soften it with tact, Aries of 2001. Your family might instill in you virtues such as courtesy and cooperation as ways to achieve your ends. On April 11, 2001, China released the twenty-four U.S. spy plane crew members detained since April 1 after a U.S. text was released with the words "sincerely regret" and in China, the text was translated to "deeply sorry." While stressing the importance of compromise, your parents may also encourage you to maintain your beliefs through thick and thin.

You could develop a restless and versatile mind and may continue to be a self-educator, endlessly bewitched by foreign culture and scientific advances. Ongoing stem cell research revealed exciting possibilities for the repair of damaged heart tissue this month. Your mental agility could be directed toward the sciences but you could also display a flair for languages or even mimicry. In later life, long-distance travel could become a passion and each trip should provide a chance to further expand your knowledge.

While you may appear to be a mental butterfly, flitting from one interest to another, you will possess a high level of concentration and when necessary you may exhibit powerful self-discipline. You may become an expert tactician knowing just how to conserve your energy to exploit it to the full. Your commitment to knowledge could direct you toward a career in education. Diplomacy could provide opportunities to indulge in your fascination for all things foreign.

Your flirtatious and sociable personality indicates that you'll be unlikely to spend your life alone. Passionate about all your interests, Aries of 2001, relationships will be no exception. Confident about your power to attract, you may take an optimistic and open approach to the game of love. Leos, Sagittarians, Aquarians, and Geminis are all signs that will share your curiosity and warmth.

Your challenge could be to maintain your independence—you may sometimes put others' needs above your own. Your strength will be your capacity to take in and assimilate vast quantities of information.

► Read about your Chinese Astrological sign on page 838. ► Read about your Personal Planets on page 826. ► Read about your personal Mystical Card on page 856.

TAURUS

From April 20, 0:37 through May 20, 23:44

The Cautious Spendthrift

You were born, Taurus of 2001, when American viewers were gripped by the prospect of Tina Wesson, a forty-year-old nurse, winning $1 million on the *Survivor* television show. It was a wonderful symbol of your innate ability with money. Your parents may instill in you the idea that without secure finances, life is potentially a struggle. You could grow up supremely confident that you know when to conserve your resources and when to speculate. However, you may find that you also veer from extreme extravagance to petty economies within minutes.

While money will undoubtedly be important you won't lose sight of spiritual ideals. You could be adept at finding imaginative uses for your wealth and may always be relied on to give assistance to the less fortunate. But if your generosity is abused you might turn off the financial flow without any second thoughts. Your financial acumen could be put to good use by charities or public services. Your good taste might mean that an artistic career would appeal.

You will come across as a sweet-natured and slow-to-anger sign, but you might be capable of ruthless determination when the need arises. It will be crucial that you maintain your integrity in both personal and professional dealings. Louis J. Freeh, head of the FBI, announced his impending resignation this month. While he expanded the agency's sphere of operations, some of his methods were questionable.

Sensual and kind, you will be at your happiest when in love. Relationships will provide the secure base from which to construct your empire. You could be conservative in your attitude to romance and allow the passion to build gradually rather than explode like a rocket only to fizzle out quickly. Fellow earth signs Virgo and Capricorn may take the same approach and Cancerians and Pisceans could share your emotional outlook.

Your challenge, Taurus of 2001, could be to curb the temptation to impress others with your material wealth. You should know that it's not what you have but how you use it that counts for the most. Indeed, that could be your greatest strength.

GEMINI

From May 20, 23:45 through June 21, 7:38

The Intuitive Intellectual

You were born, Gemini of 2001, crystallizing many charming qualities associated with your sign. You could, however, develop a maddening tendency to argue the point from a very early age. Your family could soon learn the benefits of using reverse psychology as gentle persuasion might fail dismally. This ability to assimilate myriad possibilities might be one of your strongest attributes. You will never take anything at face value. While you may also be adept at forcefully stating your opinions you could sometimes confuse others with your sudden reversals. Actress Anne Heche, for so long one half of a famous gay couple, suddenly announced she was engaged to a man. Like her, you could change your direction with surprising ease and speed.

You will be a useful employee in any organization that requires a confident public face. Your mental agility and verbal skill could be put to good use in politics or a court of law. Not only will you be unafraid of picking holes in your opponents' argument, you will be adroit at moving the goalposts if it advances your case. One politician that dared to change sides was Republican Senator Jim Jeffords. His switch to Independent changed the Senate balance from Republican to Democrat.

While first impressions indicate the attractive flippancy and enthusiasm of your sign, this could mask a more serious mind. Your craving for knowledge might be matched by a need to understand each subject in detail. You'll learn to be armed with all information before you launch your argument. Your dazzling verbal dexterity could overcome most opposition.

Variety may be the spice of your social life, Gemini of 2001, but you might still be capable of genuine devotion to your chosen partner. What may appeal most to you is the mental connection with someone that also values intellectual softball. You could be compatible with Aquarians, Librans, Leos, or Ariens.

Your challenge may be to use your humor to illustrate your arguments. Obstinacy could win the battle but lose the war. Your strength could be your ability to let past clashes remain in the past.

➤ Read about your Chinese Astrological sign on page 838. ➤ Read about your Personal Planets on page 826. ➤ Read about your personal Mystical Card on page 856.

TAURUS
Your Personal Planets

YOUR LOVE POTENTIAL
Venus in Aries, Apr. 20, 0:37 - May 20, 23:44

YOUR DRIVE AND AMBITION
Mars in Sagittarius, Apr. 20, 0:37 - May 20, 23:44

YOUR LUCK MAGNETISM
Jupiter in Gemini, Apr. 20, 0:37 - May 20, 23:44

World Events

Apr. 25 - Former Philippine President Estrada is sentenced to imprisonment for corruption.

May 4 - The United Nations Security Council raises sanctions against Liberia because of its support of rebels in Sierra Leone.

Terrorist Timothy McVeigh

GEMINI
Your Personal Planets

YOUR LOVE POTENTIAL
Venus in Aries, May 20, 23:45 - June 06, 10:25
Venus in Taurus, June 06, 10:26 - June 21, 7:38

YOUR DRIVE AND AMBITION
Mars in Sagittarius, May 20, 23:45 - June 21, 7:38

YOUR LUCK MAGNETISM
Jupiter in Gemini, May 20, 23:45 - June 21, 7:38

World Events

May 24 - The floor of a hall collapses during a wedding in Jerusalem, killing more than twenty-five people.

June 11 - Oklahoma bomber Timothy McVeigh is executed by lethal injection in Indiana.

2001

YOUR LOVE POTENTIAL
Venus in Taurus, June 21, 7:39 - July 05, 16:44
Venus in Gemini, July 05, 16:45 - July 22, 18:26

YOUR DRIVE AND AMBITION
Mars in Sagittarius, June 21, 7:39 - July 22, 18:26

YOUR LUCK MAGNETISM
Jupiter in Gemini, June 21, 7:39 - July 13, 0:03
Jupiter in Cancer, July 13, 0:04 - July 22, 18:26

World Events

June 29 - Former Yugoslav President Slobodan Milosevic is delivered to a UN tribunal in The Hague to await a war-crime trial.

July 16 - Russia and China sign a friendship treaty, binding their nations in opposition to the U.S.-proposed missile shield.

Former Yugoslav President Slobodan Milosevic awaits a war-crime trial

LEO
Your Personal Planets

YOUR LOVE POTENTIAL
Venus in Gemini, July 22, 18:27 - Aug. 01, 12:18
Venus in Cancer, Aug. 01, 12:19 - Aug. 23, 1:27

YOUR DRIVE AND AMBITION
Mars in Sagittarius, July 22, 18:27 - Aug. 23, 1:27

YOUR LUCK MAGNETISM
Jupiter in Cancer, July 22, 18:27 - Aug. 23, 1:27

World Events

Aug. 10 - A temporary suspension of Home Rule in Ireland is imposed by the British government.

Aug. 15 - NATO authorizes the first draft of peacekeeping troops to enter Macedonia.

CANCER
From June 21, 7:39 through July 22, 18:26

The Shy Fanatic

Cancer of 2001, you may have your sign's preference for tradition but you will also understand that it is possible to maintain principles while assimilating new attitudes and ideas. World events, however, did not mirror your spirit of compromise. America's non-attendance at the UN conference aimed at cutting pollution meant that while the majority of industrialized nations were prepared to cut emissions, the U.S. was unwilling to curb its own contribution to global warming. It illustrated that stubborn tenacity to fly in the face of fashion that is typical of Cancer.

You could be protective if you feel that you or those that you love are at risk from any source. On June 26, 2001 in China, seven members of a North Korean family were given refuge in the Beijing office of the UN High Commissioner for Refugees, claiming fear of deportation. The aid and comfort you will provide others may be on a smaller scale—a cup of tea and a sympathetic ear—but they will be memorable to the people involved.

You may become more adaptable than many of your sign and you could develop an intuitive ability to comprehend shifts in the collective consciousness. Your sensitivity to atmospheric undercurrents could provide you with the ideal qualities to work with or on behalf of the public. You may find that your protection extends further than your close circle and you could put your formidable energy to use for environmental or social reform. Patience will be an asset as you slowly edge toward your goals.

A solid relationship may be of vital importance, serving as a springboard from which to launch your worldly goals. In public you could be a stern taskmaster but behind closed doors you may like to be cosseted. You may be subject to sudden and unexpected attractions and infatuations but when you meet your soul mate you won't be keen to stray. Pisceans, Scorpios, Virgos, and Taureans all contain the required stability and sensitivity.

Your challenge, Cancer of 2001, might be to overcome your shyness and let the world hear your voice. Your strength could be your willingness to make tradeoffs.

LEO
From July 22, 18:27 through August 23, 1:27

The Creative Dynamo

Leo of 2001, you were born with the innate confidence that "the Earth will provide." Your family may be convinced that the way to make progress is to remain true to yourself. You could develop a powerful presence while lacking the need to overtly draw attention to yourself. Creative self-expression is vital to most Leos but you may also have an uncanny ability to tap into the collective consciousness and produce work that speaks to humanity. You may have unshakable faith in life's goodness. The Chinese released American scholar Gao Zhan this month from a ten-year prison sentence—possibly as a good-will gesture.

Creative growth could be your main objective and while you may welcome worldly success you might not actively pursue it. One politician that certainly pursued success was fellow Leo, Bill Clinton. Now out of office he was paid a record amount to write his memoirs and spill some of his fascinating beans.

While you will be both sociable and popular you could equally value periods of solitude. Encouragement and praise from others may be welcome but not crucial for your confidence. A perfectionist, you might be quietly prepared to destroy your creations if they don't reach your exacting standards. You'll hope for a career that makes use of your creativity, but may settle for undemanding work that allows time that can be devoted to your own pursuits.

But making do with undemanding relationships just won't be your style, Leo of 2001. All or nothing is a phrase that springs to mind to describe your needs and you may be less concerned with long-term prospects than the immediate expression of love. You might be prepared to remain alone if all-consuming passion is not on offer. However, when love appears, you will be prepared to sacrifice almost everything to keep the flame burning. Ariens, Sagittarians, Geminis, and Librans all have the qualities that will press your buttons.

Your challenge might be to differentiate between confidence and complacency. You may occasionally suffer from a touch of smugness. Your main strength could be your childlike faith in life's rich bounty.

➤ Read about your Chinese Astrological sign on page 838. ➤ Read about your Personal Planets on page 826. ➤ Read about your personal Mystical Card on page 856.

VIRGO

From August 23, 1:28 through September 22, 23:05

The Rigorous Perfectionist

Far from hiding in the background, you, Virgo of 2001, were born with the urge to make a difference. Your willingness to serve might bear direct proportion to your belief in the cause. Articulate and discriminating, you will hold firm convictions and a will to express them. Your family may encourage your talent for debate and help you to develop self-confidence. You might contain Virgo's critical streak with continual self-improvement being one aim. Sometimes you may be a little too hard on yourself—no one is perfect.

You may develop deep concern for the state of our planet and environmental issues could be of great interest to you. U.S. President Bush sanctioned $1.27 billion in funding for 2002 to the U.S. fish and Wildlife Service. You may become a tireless and efficient worker for the preservation of what remains of our natural bounty. You might also be an implacable enemy of hypocrisy, trying to always act consistently and with conviction while hanging on to your humanity. Fanatical beliefs can be dangerous. The terrorist attacks on New York's World Trade Center and the Pentagon in Washington on September 11 were horrifying examples of how ideals can lead to wicked malevolence.

Professional success may be slow in coming but you could show little concern for external plaudits or even a fat paycheck. Your main motivation could be to improve conditions for the greatest number of people. Working in health or education could provide the sort of challenges you will relish.

Straightforward and generous in your responses to others you could be a witty and entertaining companion. Never short on company you may, however, be extremely discriminating when it comes to your intimate relationships. Honesty and good conversation might win out over wealth and good looks. You may feel most comfortable with Capricorns, Taureans, Cancerians, and Scorpios.

You may find that your challenge is to soften your opponents up rather than browbeat them into submission. While your forcefulness may be an asset it could sometimes be self-defeating. Your strength will be your willingness to learn from your mistakes.

LIBRA

From September 22, 23:06 through October 23, 8:26

The Cautious Dancer

You were born, Libra of 2001, in troubled times. Britain and the U.S. began their battle to oust the hated Taliban regime from Afghanistan. The opposing ideologies had no common ground. You may find that gaining emotional and spiritual equilibrium will be a lifelong quest. Your family may encourage you to cultivate balance. While you will be a thinker as you grow, you may sometimes struggle to make sense of the conflicting information that bombards you. You may like to mull things over rather than make snap decisions.

The threat of anthrax infection via the mail caused great concern at this time. Learning healthy caution while not succumbing to irrational fear could be another lesson for you. Your parents could work hard to help you develop a positive outlook. You'll be an eager student and crave the broadening of your horizons and approach each new challenge with glee. Your ambition and thirst for knowledge may only be matched by your love of family oriented activities. Your home life could be constantly stimulating and entertaining.

You may possess good business acumen and excellent timing, making finances or negotiating two possible careers. Mentally sharp as well as practical, many fields could attract you. But you may find that you yearn to make a more personal contribution to society. Intense but controlled, your method of communicating could lead you toward writing or broadcasting. However, modesty may find you behind the scenes rather than in the public eye.

Mental stimulation combined with a love of romance could describe your requirements in a partner. While you'll be sought after and sociable, it's the one-on-one that you'll really appreciate. Possessive types need not apply for the position, but you will be capable of deep passion. You may feel most at home with Aquarians, Geminis, Leos, and Sagittarians.

One challenge you may face could be to maintain your balance during periods of chaos. You could be easily upset when things don't go according to plan. Your main strength might be your readiness to go the extra mile in another man's shoes.

➤ Read about your Chinese Astrological sign on page 838. ➤ Read about your Personal Planets on page 826. ➤ Read about your personal Mystical Card on page 856.

VIRGO
Your Personal Planets

YOUR LOVE POTENTIAL
Venus in Cancer, Aug. 23, 1:28 - Aug. 27, 4:12
Venus in Leo, Aug. 27, 4:13 - Sept. 21, 2:09
Venus in Virgo, Sept. 21, 2:10 - Sept. 22, 23:05

YOUR DRIVE AND AMBITION
Mars in Sagittarius, Aug. 23, 1:28 - Sept. 08, 17:51
Mars in Capricorn, Sept. 08, 17:52 - Sept. 22, 23:05

YOUR LUCK MAGNETISM
Jupiter in Cancer, Aug. 23, 1:28 - Sept. 22, 23:05

World Events

Sept. 11 – Terrorist attacks on the U.S. shock the world, as the twin towers of the World Trade Center are razed to the ground.

Sept. 22 – Violinist Isaac Stern dies.

The collapse of the World Trade Center

LIBRA
Your Personal Planets

YOUR LOVE POTENTIAL
Venus in Virgo, Sept. 22, 23:06 - Oct. 15, 11:42
Venus in Libra, Oct. 15, 11:43 - Oct. 23, 8:26

YOUR DRIVE AND AMBITION
Mars in Capricorn, Sept. 22, 23:06 - Oct. 23, 8:26

YOUR LUCK MAGNETISM
Jupiter in Cancer, Sept. 22, 23:06 - Oct. 23, 8:26

World Events

Oct. 11 – V. S. Naipaul wins the Nobel Prize for literature.

Oct. 7 – U.S. and British air forces launch an attack on Taliban military installations and terrorist training camps in Afghanistan.

2001

SCORPIO
Your Personal Planets

YOUR LOVE POTENTIAL
Venus in Libra, Oct. 23, 8:27 - Nov. 08, 13:28
Venus in Scorpio, Nov. 08, 13:29 - Nov. 22, 6:01

YOUR DRIVE AND AMBITION
Mars in Capricorn, Oct. 23, 8:27 - Oct. 27, 17:19
Mars in Aquarius, Oct. 27, 17:20 - Nov. 22, 6:01

YOUR LUCK MAGNETISM
Jupiter in Cancer, Oct. 23, 8:27 - Nov. 22, 6:01

World Events

Nov. 10 – After a fifteen-year debate, the World Trade Organization admits China.

Nov. 12 – The Northern Alliance captures Herat and Kabul and the Taliban flee from the Afghan capital.

Death of George Harrison

SAGITTARIUS
Your Personal Planets

YOUR LOVE POTENTIAL
Venus in Scorpio, Nov. 22, 6:02 - Dec. 02, 11:12
Venus in Sagittarius, Dec. 02, 11:13 - Dec. 21, 19:22

YOUR DRIVE AND AMBITION
Mars in Aquarius, Nov. 22, 6:02 - Dec. 08, 21:52
Mars in Pisces, Dec. 08, 21:53 - Dec. 21, 19:22

YOUR LUCK MAGNETISM
Jupiter in Cancer, Nov. 22, 6:02 - Dec. 21, 19:22

World Events

Nov. 27 – The UN hosts a meeting to create a new broad-based government in Afghanistan.

Nov. 29 – Former Beatle George Harrison dies.

SCORPIO
From October 23, 8:27 through November 22, 6:01

The Moral Magician

Scorpio of 2001, you could come to possess a fierce ability to unearth the truth, no matter how well concealed. As you mature you may find yourself drawn to psychology, research, and even astrology. Underneath your cool facade you might nurture a restless quest for knowledge. Your family may stress the importance of exploring all aspects of anything that interests you. Early bedtime reading might have included the *Harry Potter* books. The film, released this month, may not have impressed the critics but it gathered $93.5 million at the box office in its first weekend alone.

Along with an interest in religion and philosophy, distant lands and foreign culture may intrigue you. It is sad to think that when you were born, Afghanistan, a fascinating country, was still suffering the disruption of war. The major Afghan cities of Herat and Kabul were both seized from the Taliban this month. You might come to feel moral outrage that Afghan's ancient culture was overtaken and subsumed by aggressive folly.

Expanding your physical and mental horizons could give you the most pleasure, Scorpio of 2001. However, your underlying restlessness could indicate that you wouldn't be content with an "ivory tower" existence. You will want to make concrete use of your knowledge and will happily bury yourself in research so long as the results come to serve a purpose. Medicine is an obvious area where your diligent perfectionism could be of great use.

While you share in common with others of your sign the need for emotional security, you, Scorpio of 2001, may also require room to maneuver. Both a love of freedom and a desire for partnership will co-exist within your heart. A partner who can stimulate your mind, reciprocate your passion, and also have a life of his or her own could be a hard package to find. You may find these qualities with Cancerians, Pisceans, Virgos, or Capricorns.

Your ability to concentrate could be marred by your restlessness. Your challenge might be to harness and direct your nervous energy. Your strength could be your morality and your insistence on behaving with dignity.

SAGITTARIUS
From November 22, 6:02 through December 21, 19:22

The Controlled Enthusiast

At the time of your birth, Sagittarius of 2001, many were mourning the death of George Harrison, the most spiritual of the Beatles. Your parents may be a little young to recall the Beatles' heyday but they may still feel sadness at his passing. The sense that the past was a simpler time may be true for some, but Sagittarians generally prefer to look forward. While you might be outwardly more controlled than is typical, you could still become completely carried away by your latest enthusiasm.

You could grow up with a natural sense of justice and a desire to share your ideas with your peers. You will always be happy to listen to other viewpoints, as your thirst for knowledge will be unquenchable. The UN hosted a summit this month to thrash out plans for the new government in Afghanistan. Many conflicts of interest had to be united if the plan was to succeed. You may grow to have a cheerful but realistic attitude and this approach could make you a natural leader.

Your early life could be characterized by endless curiosity and your family could struggle to answer your questions. You could evolve your own very idiosyncratic way of looking at things. You could be the one who, with a flash of inspiration, solves problems that others toil over. You could outstrip your teachers and may find that boredom will be your worst enemy. Blessed with huge energy, a desk-bound job will be sure to drive you crazy.

A fascinating companion, you might flit from friend to friend, never settling long enough to really connect. You could long for a committed relationship but your impatience may prevent you from really getting to know people. However, once you do stand still long enough for someone to touch your heart, you will be a loyal and entertaining lover. You might be most attracted to Leos, Ariens, Aquarians, and Librans.

Your challenge, Sagittarius of 2001, could be to acquire self-knowledge. You could have your eyes fixed on such distant horizons that you overlook what's right in front of you. Your strength could be your ability to come up smiling no matter how tough life gets.

➤ Read about your Chinese Astrological sign on page 838. ➤ Read about your Personal Planets on page 826. ➤ Read about your personal Mystical Card on page 856.

CAPRICORN

The Virtuous Comedian

December Capricorn of 2001, you were born when the Afghan peace-keeping agreement took shape. A spirit of optimism prevailed after months of anxiety. Your parents may have breathed a sigh of relief along with many in the West. Dignity, duty, and self-control are words frequently applied to Capricorn. You will own all these qualities, but you will also display good humor, a willingness to cooperate, and an upbeat attitude. You will soon come to appreciate that life is far more enjoyable when surrounded by friends.

Nevertheless, you may display the ambition and fortitude that is typical of your sign, Capricorn. You will come pre-programmed to work tirelessly to reach your goals, both at school and in your career. Your orderly outlook will mean that you learn early the benefit of sticking to suitable routines. But you will also know how to lighten up and enjoy your leisure. You will appreciate luxurious surroundings and may be keen to constantly upgrade your home. There's no denying that you could have an acute interest in financial affairs but you may value a loving relationship more highly than a well-paid but lonely career.

The pleasures of the senses could also attract you. The American Diabetes Association announced that diabetics could eat sweets, as long as they kept their blood sugar levels on an even keel. You too will enjoy the taste of good food but luckily you will have the ability to keep your appetites balanced.

Your sensuality will be a vital part of your personality, enticing many potential lovers. Where you could differ from typical Capricorns may be in your mischievous sense of fun and open approach to others. That and your calmness under pressure could make you a very attractive individual. You may find a soul mate among Virgos, Taureans, Pisceans, or Scorpios.

Your challenge, December Capricorn of 2001, could be to love yourself as much as you appreciate others. Generous to a fault, remember that charity begins at home. Your strength could be your cheerful willingness to shoulder more than your share of the load.

2001

CAPRICORN
Your Personal Planets

YOUR LOVE POTENTIAL
Venus in Sagittarius, Dec. 21, 19:23 - Dec. 26, 7:25
Venus in Capricorn, Dec. 26, 7:26 - Dec. 31, 23:59

YOUR DRIVE AND AMBITION
Mars in Pisces, Dec. 21, 19:23 - Dec. 31, 23:59

YOUR LUCK MAGNETISM
Jupiter in Cancer, Dec. 21, 19:23 - Dec. 31, 23:59

World Events

Dec. 30 – Argentinean President Saa resigns after just one week in office.

Dec. 28 – Australian bush fires reach within twelve miles of Sydney.

A total eclipse of the Sun

Special Feature

Predictions, Eclipses, and September 11

by Rochelle Gordon

The astonishing and horrifying tragedy of September 11, 2001, transformed our global village as we collectively entered the twenty-first century. Astrologers have looked at this incident from many different angles to put it in perspective. Probably the single, most notable astrological event that explains its significance was the Summer Solstice Solar Eclipse of June 21, 2001.

Since ancient times, most astrologers have seen solar eclipses as harbingers of misfortune, especially for reigning kings. John Milton expressed a common feeling in *Paradise Lost*: "As when the Sun new ris'n looks through the horizontal misty air shorn of his beams, or from behind the Moon in dim eclipse, disastrous twilight sheds on half the Nations, and with fear of change perplexes monarchs."

The Solar Eclipse of June 21, 2001, was especially ominous because it took place exactly as the Sun reached its highest latitude on its annual journey around the zodiac. At that time, the Sun as seen from the Earth is at zero degrees of the sign Cancer, which is the point of the Summer Solstice. Astrologically the solstices are powerful annual events. Astrologers often draw up horoscopes for the solstices and equinoxes to judge the nature of the political climate. An eclipse landing on the same day as the solstice is a rare event, and the influence is exceptionally strong and possibly ominous.

The awesome potential in a Solar Eclipse is stored up like a coiled snake ready to strike. The red planet Mars is one planet that can trigger such a strike. Violence or military events are associated with Mars, the war planet. For most of 2001 Mars was in the sign of Sagittarius. On September 8, Mars entered Capricorn, which occurs at zero degrees of that sign. This was an opposition astrological aspect to the Solar Eclipse/Summer Solstice degree of zero Cancer. On that day, the hijackers were well into their plans. By September 11, 2001, Mars acted as the astrological catalyst that changed our world.

I remember studying that Solar Eclipse chart on the Solstice point and feeling a chill. I did not know what would occur, yet I knew it would be something big and probably not good! I knew it would be a world event, but never bothered to research where that might be. Like most Americans prior to September 11, 2001, I was living in denial about the real world. ☉

➤ Read "Nostradamus: A Prophet Across Time" by Ske Alexander on page 785.

Your Personal Planets

VENUS ♀
Your Love Potential

"Love makes the world go round," or so they say. As humans, we tend to love the qualities that we value most when we see them in other people, whether or not we can claim these qualities as our own. Often, what we appreciate in others is what we feel we lack ourselves. Sometimes we may try to absorb these qualities, almost as if by osmosis, through our relationships with the people close to us. At other times, our partners may serve as mirrors for us, reflecting our own special qualities. Through our close ties with other people, we gain new appreciation for the talents and qualities that make life worthwhile, and which help us to achieve a greater sense of personal balance.

In the birth chart, the planet Venus indicates your love potential. It reveals much about your personal love nature, how you give and receive love, and what you value in relationships. It also shows the kinds of people you are attracted to and with whom you are likely to be most compatible. Venus not only indicates who you love, but what you love as well.

VENUS IN ARIES
Do I See a Daredevil?
You value excitement and want lots of stimulation in love. Honesty and directness are also important to you—you have no desire to be involved with people who are not forthright and open with you. You probably don't have much patience with people who don't know what they want or who know but are too afraid to go after it. In fact, you can be quite impulsive at times. Your impatience with others may cause you consternation at times, when you forget that not everyone is as clear about their wants and desires as you are.

Your personality has an edgy and original quality that makes you stand out in a crowd. It may also cause you to rock a few social boats at times, when things seem to be getting too dull or routine. You know that actions speak louder than words, and you want to be with people who are actively involved in many areas of life. Generally speaking, you tend to get along best with other outgoing, independent, and fun-loving individuals such as Sagittarians, Leos, Aquarians, and Geminis. You enjoy the dynamic aspect of meeting people who can spark new ideas and bring new experiences into your life. However, you may sometimes be too interested in the thrill of the chase, which consequently can lead you to undervalue stability and commitment in a relationship.

VENUS IN TAURUS
Consistency Is One of Your Best Features
The old saying "slow and steady wins the race" could very well be one of your favorites because it really applies to your social style in many ways. One of your best qualities is your ability to be consistent with those you love. You like to build upon a solid foundation to strengthen your bonds, and you are very generous to those you love when you feel that they deserve a helping hand. Once you commit to a relationship, you play to stay, and would probably be best matched with Cancers, Virgos, or Capricorns.

You appreciate the best of everything, and you may even have been born into a family that gave you a leg up in that direction. If not, it seems your cheery disposition could help you attract people who offer you "the good life." You also have a deep appreciation for sensual delights and nature's bounty and beauty. As a result, you probably have a wonderful "green thumb" and can grow just about anything. You have such flair and taste that anything you grow—whether it's flowers or a bank account—you do with style. You would probably be happiest owning your own property and living where you are surrounded by nature and beauty. Beauty is high on your list in relationships, too, and you prefer a physically attractive partner who has an attractive personality as well.

Marilyn Monroe—Venus in Aries

VENUS IN GEMINI
You Like Variety

You are usually willing to try anything once and maybe even twice, just to make sure that you get to experience all the glorious possibilities that you might have missed the first time around. And occasionally you may even like to juggle more than one relationship at the same time, since you thrive on social stimulation and feel the urge to connect with a wide range of people. You are keenly observant about people—it may amaze others how quickly you pick up on their little idiosyncrasies and how much you can tell them about themselves. You also enjoy talking and prefer the company of friends who know how to carry their side of the discussion.

You love language. Being able to communicate with others is high on your list of priorities in friendships as well as romantic relationships. Therefore, you tend to get along well with Aquarians, Librans, and Ariens. Good looks are not as important to you as a really good mind. Remember, Marilyn Monroe described Albert Einstein as the sexiest man she'd ever met. You may even like to participate in many different social circles, since one is hardly likely to be enough. You are impatient with people who get stuck in routines or are unwilling to try something different. The "good life" for you means a steady diet of variety, after all.

VENUS IN CANCER
Your Heart Is at Home

Your favorite place in the whole world could be your very own home, and for many good reasons. A well-stocked kitchen and a comfortable, inviting environment make you and the people you care about feel welcome in your home. However, just because you like being home so much doesn't mean you like being alone. Your family, friends, and neighbors find that your door is always open to them. You take great pleasure in having visitors in your home and like to fuss over them a little.

You may be attracted to people who remind you of your parents in some significant way, such as a personal quality, character trait, physical attribute or a talent. This is because the sense of familiarity gives you an idea of what to expect, and brings a sense of security and comfort. Often you're attracted to people who share your strong love of family and have a background that's similar to yours. Since you prefer to build on what makes you comfortable, you may keep many of the same friends that you've known "forever." Forever is how you see love relationships, too, and you are a very dedicated partner. Once you make a commitment to someone, you keep it and value it. Therefore, you would probably be happiest with a Taurus, Scorpio, or Pisces partner who shares your sensitivity and devotion.

The Dalai Lama—Venus in Leo

VENUS IN LEO
You Thrive on Creativity

You have an abundance of creativity, which you express on many levels, and you value artistic and outgoing friends who know and appreciate how special you are. No doubt the first people you are likely to notice are those who are also involved in some form of creative expression. You are not afraid to express your true affections to the people you love. Even the way you approach love and relationships is a form of creative expression—you do it with dramatic flair. Lively, fun-loving partners such as Ariens, Geminis, and Sagittarians are generally good matches for you. Children are likely to play an important role in your choice of a partner, for you enjoy children's vitality—and your natural joyfulness is highly attractive to young people, too.

In many ways, you are truly pure at heart, as the saying goes, because you have a genuine optimism about love and you trust in the basic goodness of people in general. However, you do have your share of pride and you expect loved ones to treat you with the respect and dignity that you deserve. You are willing to give love another chance, even if you have been hurt or disappointed. You know that love is the greatest gift of all, and that you must be willing to love yourself before you can really accept it from others.

VENUS IN VIRGO
Love Is in the Details

You take pleasure in doing whatever you do well and always try to perform at your highest level. Not surprisingly, you are attracted most strongly to people

Marlene Dietrich — Venus in Aquarius

who are also looking to become "the best that they can possibly be." You know that, although none of us is perfect, it is the striving for perfection that counts. Although you don't expect a partner to be a "perfect 10," there is just something about neat clothes, a good haircut and a general quality of good grooming that catches your eye. You may also find that you enjoy the company of "diet buddies" or "exercise buddies" who share your desire to celebrate good health in a pleasant way.

You take an interest in diet and exercise because you know that your body can only serve you as well as you serve it. On those occasions where you are looking for an extra push, remember that taking care of the little things all adds up to a feeling of wellness and "everything in its place." Your desire for order extends into love relationships too, since you like others to know their "place" and to behave in a way that is appropriate for whatever the social occasion requires. Good manners are more likely to endear you to a partner than a flashy, bold style. Tauruses, Cancers, and Capricorns could be your best love matches.

VENUS IN LIBRA
Are You in Love with Love?
Because you see the good qualities in others, you attract people of all kinds and you probably have a vast array of people in your life who love you in different ways. You have a way of bringing out the best in the people you care about and can encourage them to rise to meet your positive expectations of them. Naturally sociable and diplomatic, you really like being around other people. You're quite charming and have a talent for being able to converse with a broad spectrum of people from many walks of life.

Your keen sense of beauty is expressed with good taste and style in all you do—through your choices in fashion, interior décor, entertaining, and manners. You have an artistic temperament and could benefit from exploring one or more artistic outlets, either professionally or simply for your own pleasure. You also appreciate balance and fair play in your personal relationships and usually make a concerted effort to keep from rocking the boat. However, you may be a bit too willing to compromise in order to keep peace in a relationship and may place a partner's wishes above your own. You are attracted to partners who share your refinement, creativity, social and intellectual interests. As a result, you would tend to get along best with Geminis, Aquarians, and Leos.

VENUS IN SCORPIO
A Touch of Mystery
When it comes to friendship, you are seeking two distinct characteristics in the people you choose as your companions. First and foremost, they have to be willing to respect and honor your privacy and not ask too many probing questions that you feel are no one else's business. Second, they must exude an "air of mystery." People who are too easy to figure out just won't hold your interest over the long haul, since you thrive on social challenges and enjoy a bit of intrigue. The same is true in your love relationships—you want a partner who has a lot going on beneath the surface. Consequently, you're likely to be attracted to Cancers, Capricorns, and Pisceans, as well as other Scorpios.

You understand the value of change and you realize that people can and do change over time, yourself included. It would be a serious mistake for anyone else to presume that they know the "real" you—since this is subject to change without notice. Nonetheless, you are a devoted mate and once you give your love to someone, you do it totally. This can result in jealousy and possessiveness, however, especially if you are involved with a more free-spirited type. That can hurt you in the long run, and you may need to learn to "lighten up" a bit and develop a more trusting attitude toward others.

VENUS IN SAGITTARIUS
Love Is an Adventure!
You have a broad capacity to love on many levels. You tend to be very generous with the people who are fortunate enough to find favor in your eyes, and you lavish friends and loved ones with blessings in abundance. Outgoing and fun-loving, you are usually the life of the party. One of your best traits is your vivacious sense of humor that allows you to laugh at yourself as well as others. You would become easily bored with people who can't laugh at themselves, too.

You enjoy sharing ideas and advice with just about

anyone. You may not care if your friends choose to ignore your suggestions as long as they are willing to admit how right you were when it turns out the way you called it, as it so often does. Just being able to express your insights is a lot of fun and is one way to show others that you care. You probably find yourself attracted to people who share your casual outlook and great sense of humor. You also look for someone who has opinions and is willing to discuss them with you—in a friendly, impartial way, of course. Your sense of personal liberation extends into matters of the heart as well as to your friendships, and you require a lot of freedom in relationships. Other independent and outgoing sorts, such as Aquarians, Ariens, and Leos, are good matches for you.

VENUS IN CAPRICORN
You Take Love Seriously

You tend to set pretty high standards in love. This is because you know what you want and you are not willing to compromise on what really matters most to you. You appreciate and expect other people to have good manners and to know how to behave correctly in different situations and places. While some may say that image shouldn't matter, you have a different slant on that—you know from personal experience that the way you present yourself to others certainly does make a difference in the way that they relate to you. Because of that, you strive to make your appearance and your conduct a source of pride to yourself and to those you love.

Known for your practicality in all areas of life, you realize that, while love is terrific, love alone isn't enough to pay the bills and put food on the table. Therefore, you strive for the most productive and stable lifestyle possible to ensure your long-range security and comfort. So you'd probably be most content with a Taurus or Virgo partner—or another Capricorn. At times, you can even seem rather business-like in your approach to love. You expect your friends and loved ones to be mature and responsible about their commitments. You certainly are, so why shouldn't they be? Love for you, like fine wine, may improve with age.

VENUS IN AQUARIUS
Marching to Your Own Beat

Your love is certainly not confined to one or two individuals. On the contrary, it comes very naturally to you to love on a far more universal scale. You have a strong desire to have a positive influence on causes related to social justice and equality between the sexes, and you expect your friends and associates to also embrace tolerance and brotherly love as their ideals. This, however, does not make you a conformist by any means!

On the contrary, you thrive on novelty and variation in social relations and in close love connections. Independence, too, is vital to you. Therefore, you'd be happiest with other free-spirited people, such as Geminis and Sagittarians. You want to express your affections in unusual ways that can show your loved ones that you are not just following the crowd, but that you are perhaps even setting new trends. Among the values that you cherish most dearly are independence, freedom of expression, and unconventional ways of relating in social settings. You tend to remain detached and objective, so that your emotions do not get in the way of your ability to judge people and situations with impartiality and fairness. Your knack for knowing how to collaborate in a team or group makes you the perfect person to coordinate a range of social functions.

VENUS IN PISCES
Romance Is in Your Heart

You seem to have an endless reservoir of goodwill toward your fellow humans. Although this is especially true in close relationships, you show kindness even toward perfect strangers. Your compassionate nature draws people to you who need understanding and help, and you can make a difference in their lives simply by offering them acceptance and empathy. Your generosity of spirit can cause you not to discriminate against others for their flaws and failings, but you may need to guard against a tendency to be too forgiving of others' bad behavior.

In love, you are idealistic and may search for the perfect partner. Your deep affinity for music, art, and theater can also be carried over into your relationships, giving them a touch of glamour. As a result, love may have caused you some disappointments from time to time. But you know that it is important to get back on the horse that has thrown you, and you continue to open your heart to romance, never giving up on the possibility of true love and living happily ever after. You have a shy quality that is very refreshing. You are usually best matched with someone who is equally sensitive and emotional, such as a Cancer or Scorpio. However, you can also be happy with a more stable and practical partner, such as a Taurus or Capricorn.

Winston Churchill—Venus in Sagittarius

MARS ♂
Your Drive and Ambition

Just as different kinds of vehicles may run best on different types of fuel, so are people "fueled" by different kinds of drives and motivations. In your birth chart, the planet Mars tells a great deal about your special drives, your ambitions, and how you tend to assert yourself in the world. This dynamic, energetic planet reveals what gets you going and what motivates you to keep on going until you are satisfied that you have achieved the results that you are after.

Because Mars represents pure energy and desire, it also shows how you express your desires, particularly those of a sexual nature. Mars also suggests what excites you in a partner and how you are likely to pursue the object of your desires. The symbol for Mars is the familiar symbol for masculinity but, of course, this energy is not limited to men. In some cases, though, Mars can indicate the type of man a woman is drawn to, especially if she is inclined to project her own desire nature onto her partners.

MARS IN ARIES
You're Anything But Slow!
You are ready to spring into action at a moment's notice and this quick-reflex response can work to your advantage or disadvantage. Impulsive and impatient, you are inclined to jump into action as the spirit moves you, rather than waiting to see how things develop on

John F. Kennedy—Mars in Taurus

their own. Two of your best attributes are daring and courage—you aren't afraid to act on your convictions. However, it is really important that you know the reasons for your actions, even if other people do not. Try to think before you leap, even though this is not always easy.

You have a tremendous drive for independence, and you want to feel that whatever you have accomplished, you've done it on your own terms. You may react strongly, though, if you feel you are obligated or forced into something by external pressures. Because you have a wonderful reserve of energy at your command most of the time, you can probably run circles around nearly everyone else in your life. But, like the hare in the story of the tortoise and the hare, you may be better at starting things than finishing them, so it is in your best interest to pace yourself for the long haul. Your boundless enthusiasm is wonderful and can amaze people who are more content to keep things as they are. Thus, you can be a catalyst for change.

MARS IN TAURUS
Steady as You Go
You are not intimidated by obstacles. In fact, your determined nature thrives on doing what others might think is impossible. Some may consider you to be stubborn, but you are probably the first person who comes to mind when they are thinking of who would be most reliable and steadfast for a job. You aren't likely to leap into a situation—you need time to evaluate what you are getting into, how much it will cost, and how much time it should take before you commit. Once you begin, however, you have more than enough patience to see it through to the end. This can be true even after others have long since given up on a cause. While this is an asset, you might also want to remember that old gambler's motto "know when to fold 'em!"

Your persistence and patience pay off, as you create long-term security for yourself and for those who matter most to you. Material and worldly things play a prominent role in motivating you. Whether your intention is to acquire an object or a relationship, practicalities are a primary concern to you. You have a highly constructive style of doing things, and once you are on a path, you stick with it until you are satisfied with the results. The key to your success, however, is that you have to want to get started, for you will not be pushed.

MARS IN GEMINI
You Are a Master at Juggling
You know the saying "two heads are better than one"? This certainly describes you, as you have a talent for being able to look at a situation as if you really do have two minds. You are such a keen observer of people and ideas that you are able to see things from more than

Martin Luther King—Mars in Gemini

one point of view. This helps you decide which course is the best to follow. Little escapes your attention and your sharp mind is always busy. This is terrific when it comes to activities or problems that require quick thinking. You can run into trouble, however, when you try to pay attention to too many things at once and you need to guard against letting yourself become distracted.

Most people enjoy your quick wit, but sometimes you need to recognize when your "teasing" may not always be appreciated. Your words can become like a sword, so it's best if you attempt to tell the truth to the best of your ability, when and where it is appropriate. Having fun with people is a big motivator for you and this makes you a lively and entertaining companion. You can be on the nervous and restless side, though, every now and then. Take a deep breath whenever you start to have that hemmed-in feeling and remember why you chose your present path in the first place. You are rarely, if ever, stuck without choices.

MARS IN CANCER
Feeling Your Way

Do you know the phrase "what's eating you?" That one question says a lot about the way you approach situations when you are not sure if you are ready to move forward. It is very important that you safeguard your energy supply by following a reasonable and healthy, nutritious pattern of eating. Your motivation to work or play can be strongly affected by whether or not you have fed yourself well. If you feel emotionally upset with your situation or your prospects, you can fall into a pattern of poor eating habits. On the positive side, you enjoy cooking for yourself and others. Your

instinct is to nurture and protect yourself and others, and you make certain the people you care about are safe and secure. This instinct is so strong that you may try to achieve peace at all costs.

You are quite sensitive and your emotions can get the better of you at times, causing you to jump into situations without forethought. You'll want to try to curb that and be more objective. This, of course, does not mean that you shouldn't take action when you feel strongly about something. Just don't act out of anger or when you are upset. Give yourself the time you need to collect your thoughts before you react. You have to feel up to something before you can do it, so listen to what your feelings are saying!

MARS IN LEO
Your Pride Is Your Guide

You don't just walk into a room—you command attention as you enter. You have a way of doing things that makes others take notice and admire your energy, style, and enthusiasm. You have a natural flair for the dramatic that must be expressed. If you have not yet done any formal acting, you might enjoy joining a community theater group, even if it is just to help with set design or costumes. Your creative drive is a strong motivating factor, and this allows you to look at any situation as an opportunity to express your individuality in a unique way. You are happiest and most fulfilled when you are doing something creative, where you can express your own individuality and have fun in the process.

These qualities are terrific as long as you are also willing to share the stage with others. Your leadership qualities are excellent and chances are other people ask you for guidance and direction. You are bold in your ability to act on your convictions, and it may take you by surprise when others do not have the courage to also act on theirs. You know how to run the show and make an excellent teacher, guide or model for others to follow. It may not be easy for you to take directions and accept guidance from others, however, unless you feel that it is a win-win situation.

MARS IN VIRGO
You Leave No Stone Unturned

When it comes to getting the job done right, you are the right person for the job! You have an uncanny ability to see the proverbial "trees" in the forest, and others know that you can always be counted upon when details must be taken into account. Your analytical approach means that you take it one step at a time in the most efficient manner possible, and move forward only after you have figured out the best method or strategy for doing so. You thrive on working in a systematic way. This is fine, as long as you can accept that others may not have your devotion to details and may not understand your dedication to the job.

Service is your motto and you want to feel that what you do is useful. You have a terrific knack for assessing problems and finding solutions that make sense. This problem-solving ability makes you the perfect person for jobs and projects where precision and a strong work ethic are needed. You may have a tendency to be too serious in your pursuit of perfection, however, and may need to remember to pause long enough to smell the proverbial roses every so often. Set aside time for leisure and relaxation, too, rather than devoting yourself entirely to your work. Eating meals at a relaxed, leisurely pace is important to your digestion and overall good health.

MARS IN LIBRA
You Seek to Achieve Balance and Beauty

You have an artistic temperament, whether or not you consider yourself to be an artist. This quality comes through in how you dress and the care that you take with your appearance, so that you always make a good first impression. You have a strong awareness of what is likely to please other people and how to best go about it. You are so talented at understanding what motivates others that you could even help them to realize their full potential, especially in areas that involve artistic expression.

Fairness, equality and justice are enormously important motivations for you. Thus, you can be very persuasive when there is a cause you feel you must champion. You are happy to engage in an argument when you feel that issues of fairness are at stake, and your ability to use logic and reason usually wins the day. But sometimes you might continue the argument too long, just to make your point. You put lots of energy into a relationship and expect the other person to be equally willing to make compromises that are necessary in order to resolve any problem. Your diplomacy skills are so well developed that others come to you when they need an objective opinion about what to do. You not only "don't rock the boat," you know how to reposition everyone for better balance all around.

MARS IN SCORPIO
Your Desires Hold the Key

You can take whatever life tosses your way and turn it into something no one else would have thought to create. You are terrific when it comes to reinventing new wheels from old ones and turning raw materials into something useful. This makes you a natural catalyst for change. You aren't afraid of getting into what others may consider to be a messy situation, in order to transform it into something better. You know

there are times when you have to dig deep to find the treasures you seek and you are willing to probe beneath the surface to get to the bottom of things.

You possess many strengths that other people can only dream about. When you desire something (or someone!) there is virtually no stopping you. This works both ways, however—when you don't want to do something, or don't want to be with someone, you refuse to be forced into the situation against your will, and you let others know when they are expecting too much from you. Quite likely you have a natural instinct to heal, and you may sometimes become involved with partners upon whom you have a healing, transforming effect. Your passionate nature and intensity can make you prone to extremes and you might overreact a bit now and then. Not surprisingly, others may respond to you very strongly at times as well.

MARS IN SAGITTARIUS
You Need Room to Explore

People should stand back and give you plenty of room, as you have energy to spare. You also have many great ideas about how to use your talents, time and resources. You possess a natural gift of persuasion and can usually convince others to follow your lead. This gift can help you obtain material things, but you can also be very influential when it comes to your philosophy or principles. Others often seek your advice because you have a knack for projecting into the future and envisioning how trends will develop.

When you take action, you use broad strokes—your strength lies in being able to see the big picture and believing in your lucky hunches. You know that life is too precious to waste time worrying about the past or crying over missed opportunities. Usually you make

Janis Joplin—Mars in Sagittarius

George Harrison—Mars in Capricorn

the most of the opportunities that arise, although you are better at starting things than finishing them. Always eager to have fun, you are gregarious and optimistic—the life of the party. Restless and curious, you would greatly enjoy exploring distant cultures and places if the opportunity presents itself. When it comes to expressing your sexuality, you are equally restless and curious and may have a hard time limiting yourself to a single partner. In this, as in other areas, you need room to explore.

MARS IN CAPRICORN
Like Cream, You Rise to the Top

When it comes to drive, you have plenty to spare. You have a strong sense of purpose and focus, and you manage your time in such a way that you waste very little of it. You are so determined that you may feel that other people are unmotivated. You take a great deal of pride in your competence and in your ability to figure things out for yourself. But if you can't, you don't mind delegating responsibility. Whether or not you have ever owned your own business, you have a natural business instinct and chances are you would do quite well being in business for yourself. You could be very comfortable in the public eye, in a political role or other context.

Because you are so time conscious, you don't mind taking a short cut here or there if you think it will get you to your destination faster or easier. Your ambitions keep you busy and there is always another mountain to climb after you've reached each pinnacle of success. Share your knowledge with others, either in a formal way or by mentoring others who admire and respect your talents and are willing to learn from you. You are no stranger to responsibility and you expect other people to accept and live up to their own responsibilities, too. Don't be too hard on them if they can't or won't meet your standards. You are exceptional.

MARS IN AQUARIUS
Follow Your Ideals

Freedom is one of your greatest motivators. You cherish your right to determine your own course and to walk your path in your own way, despite others' expectations of you. Some people may even consider you to be a bit of a rebel in this respect. Your urge to invent and innovate leads you to explore and discover the unknown. You are not afraid to ask the big questions and to go where you need to go to uncover the truth. Friends often look to you for advice. When they are thinking about making a change, you encourage them to take their destinies into their own hands. It's also natural for you to want to become involved in group endeavors and activities, as you are great at planning special events.

Your drive for freedom is likely to express itself mentally as well as physically. You are happiest when you can work in a situation where you can apply your mind to a task or challenge as part of a team effort. You grow bored if you must stay in a situation where there is no room for change. It is important for you to have lots of variety and to stimulate new thinking in other people. You work so well independently that others may seek your services as an independent consultant in those areas where you have a specialized skill. Satisfaction comes from following your ideals.

MARS IN PISCES
Compassion Is Your Guide

You are highly sensitive and compassionate. You are strongly motivated to help others, especially those who are less fortunate than yourself—you really bend over backwards to make yourself available whenever the need arises. You probably do far more than you get credit for, but you give because it is your nature to give, not because you are counting the favors you will get in return. Your sincerity and generosity make others feel as though you are a very wise person. You are so very sensitive that others hardly have to say a word before you sense that they are troubled or upset. And you are ever ready to offer the bandage, cup of tea or sympathy that is needed for the occasion.

In fact, you may be better able to do things for others than for yourself. You need to be good to yourself, too, and do something special just for yourself once in a while. Your psychic sensitivity is well developed, too. Your sensitivity may also show itself in the areas of art, poetry, or music, and you are inclined to devote a great deal of energy and effort to your creative endeavors. As a result, your art is likely to be an expression of the passion you feel for beauty. A romantic at heart, you bring a touch of magic and a sense of excitement to your relationships, which keep things from ever becoming dull.

JUPITER ♃
Your Luck Magnetism

Life presents each of us with many opportunities to advance materially, mentally, emotionally and spiritually. Understanding luck goes far beyond thinking about a winning ticket or bingo card, however. Your attitude and your approach to life have a significant impact on how lucky you are. Part of being lucky is being open and receptive to opportunities that come your way, so that you can take advantage of the abundance that exists all around you. In your birth chart, the planet Jupiter indicates what areas are likely to be lucky for you, and where you possess a sense of optimism and self-confidence that can help you make your own luck.

Three attributes are especially important when it comes to attracting good fortune: trust, hope and faith. Without trust, you wouldn't take a chance when luck comes knocking. Hope allows you to recognize opportunities when they present themselves. Most importantly, your personal faith allows you to believe that you deserve all the good things life has to offer. Your expansiveness and your faith in yourself are instrumental in attracting fortunate people and situations to you. Jupiter's position shows how you approach trusting in the goodness of the world, as well as those areas in which you tend to see the glass as half-full rather than half-empty.

John Lennon—Jupiter in Taurus

JUPITER IN ARIES
You Have Faith in Yourself

Your enthusiasm for life is bountiful and it's contagious to people whose spirits need a lift. Thus, you are a very pleasant and vibrant companion. Luck arises out of your willingness to live in the moment, and to trust that all will work out in the end, no matter what happened before. You realize that to a large degree you make your own luck with your enterprising nature and your willingness to take a chance. Other people may feel reluctant to try new things that no one else has done before because they fear the risk of failure or embarrassment. However, your daring can enable you to win the prize long before others know that one exists. Even on the gloomiest of days, the strength of your hope will brighten your life.

You have great confidence in yourself, which is one of your best strengths. This encourages others to believe in you as well and to be willing to accept your ideas and suggestions. Your ability to enjoy the varied experiences in your life is another way in which you are lucky. Other people find your independent thinking and your optimistic and open intention to be a real source of strength. They are therefore willing to put their trust and faith in you, knowing you can show them the way. You also tend to be lucky when traveling and your experiences create wonderful memories.

JUPITER IN TAURUS
Life Showers You with Abundance

You may not feel as though you were born with the proverbial "silver spoon" in your mouth, but other people may see you that way anyhow. This is because you have a great appreciation for the good things in life and you attract many of them. One key to your luck is your ability to preserve those valuable things by taking good care of them, so that they last a long time. You lavish love and attention on your cherished possessions. You can turn a simple item into a work of art by treating it with care and featuring it to the best advantage in your home. Your fortune is expressed in simple elegance, and your good taste makes others feel at home in your home. Because you hope for the best, you are very likely to attract it.

When it comes to money, you have the Midas touch. No matter what seed you plant, it bears beautiful fruit. You also are quite fortunate in areas that involve cooking and food, mainly because you enjoy all aspects of the dining experience. Other people are amazed at what you can create from simple ingredients by combining them thoughtfully and presenting them sensuously. One of your greatest attributes—your persistence in those areas that matter to you—attracts luck to you. Your faith that there will always be more allows you to be generous with what you have.

JUPITER IN GEMINI
It's Who You Know

The saying it's "who you know"—as well as what you know—really applies to you. You are blessed with many social graces that enable you to talk with anyone from any background. This versatile social skill opens many doors for you. You are lucky when it comes to meeting new people and your social circle is an ever-expanding adventure. Each new person brings a gift of connection and meaning. Your luck comes from the excellent way in which you so naturally "network" in your community and within your various social circles — one small group of acquaintances would never be enough for you!

Your acquaintances know that if they want to spread the word about something important, all they have to do is tell you! You can also have good luck with the written word, for you have much to say. Trust your mental powers. Your good fortune comes from your keen wit, your capacity to see various points of view before judging a situation, and through sharing information with others. Whether in private notes or in public journals, magazines, newspapers, or special publications, you always have something relevant to say. Teaching could be fortunate for you, too, for you enjoy sharing ideas. Your faith in the power of language to educate and entertain makes other people trust you to excel at both.

JUPITER IN CANCER
Because You Care So Much

Your luck is the result of your sensitive and caring nature. You nurture and protect other people in ways that make them feel as though you are "family" to them. Because they know that you genuinely care about their welfare, you gain others' trust easily—you do not stand in judgment of them, knowing that we are all human after all. When others get too caught up in the hustle and bustle of pursuing material gain or status, they can always return to you and feel accepted for who they are, not just because of what they own or how high on the ladder of worldly success they have climbed. Your warm and personable nature makes everyone who knows you want to take care of you as well. You are lucky in the way others show how much they appreciate your basic goodness.

In the areas of real estate, money, and family life, good fortune is likely to shine on you as well. Your faith in life's goodness attracts security—both emotional and financial—and helpful people to you. The value that you place on your possessions is sentimental more than monetary. Your home conveys a strong sense of warmth and belonging that is missing elsewhere, and this makes others feel comfortable. All who love you know they are welcome in your life because of the room you have made for them in your heart.

JUPITER IN LEO
All the World's Your Stage

You are enormously bighearted toward everyone you love. This, in turn, creates an enormous amount of luck and good fortune for you—especially in love's many forms of expression and in all sorts of creative pursuits. Because you enjoy life so much, you set a wonderful example for other people who need a dose of your joy, confidence and encouragement—you help them put their own lives in order. You have a can-do quality that inspires others to follow your lead. Your willingness to be a guide, teacher or leader for others is one of the ways that you create and spread great luck and good fortune.

With the people you care about, you are amazingly generous. You take great pride in your capacity to give to others and to bring happiness and joy to family and friends alike. In turn, your generosity attracts good things to you, because others trust you and want to make you happy, too. Therefore, they may present you with fortunate opportunities. Being able to pursue happiness is truly fundamental to your nature. This gives you a quality of warmth and enthusiasm that earns you much affection and popularity. Your good character wins others over. Your faith in people's basic goodness tends to bring out the best in others and they want to rise to meet your expectations of them.

JUPITER IN VIRGO
By Your Works

Your special blend of luck stems often from the careful attention you give to practical matters and as a result of your concern for the well-being of others. You have many remarkable problem-solving skills and you put these to work with joy and enthusiasm. Other people often marvel at how easy you make it all look, but they don't realize how much attention you have paid to the

Oprah Winfrey—Jupiter in Gemini

Madonna—Jupiter in Libra

small details. You have a lot of faith in the old Boy Scout motto "be prepared." Because you make sure you are ready for almost any eventuality, you seem to be fortunate at never getting caught off-guard or never lacking what you need.

Because you have faith that diligent effort rather than random luck will produce positive results, you make your good fortune through your own hard work. You savor most of the good things that come to you because you know you have earned them. Your competence can, in fact, become one of your mixed blessings. Not surprisingly, you can find yourself loaded with work that others delegate to you because they know how very capable and competent you are. If you hope to gain more leisure time, however, you might have to show others that you trust them to do the job. Thus, you demonstrate that you care and have faith in them— even if you secretly know that you could do it better.

JUPITER IN LIBRA
The Gift of Beauty and Appreciation
Your blessings are many and your luck comes through relationships with people who love and admire you. Social contacts bring you much pleasure and many happy experiences, as you thrive on personal interactions and intellectual stimulation. You are also gifted when it comes to the arts, music, fashion, literature or theater. In fact, some of your happiest times may stem from being involved with some form of artistic expression. And you express your artistic sensibility in every facet of life, from the way you dress with taste and style to decorating your home with aplomb.

You have many social graces. Consequently, people tend to be on their best behavior around you because they know that you are a refined person of excellent taste. In fact, you may be asked for advice on many matters that pertain to good manners, social protocol,

and entertaining. You have a great knack for making matches in love, not only in terms of attracting fortunate partners for yourself, but also for helping others to do so. People may often ask for your advice about whether or not you think they are well suited to be with the partners they are considering. You also are a very good judge of character, which gives others so much faith in your opinion that they may ask you to mediate in a dispute.

JUPITER IN SCORPIO
Desire Is the Pearl in Your Oyster
You have an abundance of intuition and your sixth sense brings you lucky hunches that often prove correct. You have an uncanny knack for knowing who is on the phone before picking it up and which corner to turn to find the perfect parking space. But your lucky hunches extend to more important matters, too. You can sense when someone needs your help and when to put your hand on someone's shoulder to give encouragement and support that keeps them going in rough times. Your wishes and desires are powerful enough to make them come true, so put your faith and trust in them.

Good fortune smiles on your financial ventures, especially when handling others' assets. People trust you to steer them in the right direction and they reward you—in cash or in kind—with the support that you need. You are gifted as a natural psychological counselor, as your insights into human nature and motivation are reliable and sincere. If anyone needs a confidant, you are the perfect candidate. You are great at keeping secrets and this attribute can bring you good luck, especially if you are inclined toward doing investigative work or research. You have a healing touch as well. People recognize your magnetic, charismatic qualities and hope that you will spice up their lives with a touch of your magic.

JUPITER IN SAGITTARIUS
The Sky's the Limit
Luck is your middle name and you probably have far more lucky hunches than most other people. Your uncanny knack for correctly guessing what the future holds makes others seek your advice in a variety of personal and business situations. You are actually quite a visionary, and this gives you the ability to sense when something is a good idea, with serious potential for success. By investing in those things or allying yourself with people whom you perceive to be "going places," you are often successful, too.

Speaking of going places, a great deal of your happiness and luck comes through traveling, so expand your horizons and see as much of the world as your interests, resources and time allow. You have such a wonderfully optimistic nature and forthrightness that others trust you implicitly. They know that if you are willing to take a chance on something, it must be good. Your ability to "get to the point" and see what's really important is very liberating, leaving you plenty of time for other pursuits. Your luck also comes from being a good judge of character. You know when a person is—or is not—worth cultivating a relationship with and thus make many fortunate associations. Your faith in the power of your own judgment and convictions will see you through every time.

JUPITER IN CAPRICORN
The Blessings of Tradition

While other people may want to escape reality, you are the opposite. Your clear sense of knowing what's what is the source of your greatest luck and good fortune. You are blessed with an uncanny ability to know what is needed in any situation. Your respect for your own and others' limitations allows you to find the resources and tools you need to stretch those limits a little further. You have a reputation for reliability and others trust you to deliver when you make a promise or a commitment. Mature and responsible, you seek first and foremost to act out of personal and/or professional integrity.

Your conscience is an excellent guide. This stems from the earliest lessons that you learned from elders, for whom you have much respect. Carrying on traditions that you were taught means a great deal to you. You know that the torch of wisdom must be passed from generation to generation and you are up to the challenge. Your faith in time-tested traditions inspires others to ask you to represent them in public situations—your dignity and sincerity could bring you awards as well as social approval. You are also lucky in business matters, earning trust and confidence as a result of your reliable track record of success. You know what works and you put that knowledge to good use.

JUPITER IN AQUARIUS
The Gift of Knowledge

The pursuit of knowledge and truth is the source of your greatest luck and good fortune. Because you recognize and understand the basic truth that life is a school in which we are all students, you make the most of every opportunity, problem or challenge to learn something valuable from it. You also have a special skill for making learning fun. For this reason, you could be very lucky working in an educational environment, or wherever new trends are being developed. Always in the vanguard, you seem to know what the future holds and can use your forward-thinking nature to attract good fortune.

You are lucky at making friends and know how to connect with different kinds of people from all walks of life. You are terrific at coordinating large groups of people and bringing them together to pursue a common goal or objective. Other people trust that they can rely on you to shape the clearest vision of where they should go. Speaking of going, you can have excellent luck when you are traveling—you enjoy exploring new places without having to stick to a rigid agenda or schedule. You are highly inventive, which makes others seek your advice when they have tried everything else and need a fresh perspective or idea. Your freethinking ability and your faith in the truth renew hope.

JUPITER IN PISCES
Your Faith Is Great

You are so very softhearted that the phrase "he ain't heavy, he's my brother" rings especially true for you. Your compassion is as boundless as the ocean, and this quality brings you the greatest luck and good fortune. Generous with your time and compassion, you make an enormous difference in the lives of those upon whom you shower love. Your willingness to forgive is also a source of good fortune, more than you may imagine. You can be lucky in romance, as you have a great capacity to love unselfishly and to open your heart to others, seeing the best in them. Your faith in human goodness and in a higher good is stronger than most people's.

Because you know that love is more than a matter of give-and-take—it is who you are at heart—you look beyond the surface when choosing partners. They respond by being good to you, which brings everyone good fortune. Your quiet and humble nature allows you to make a difference in many small but significant ways. Your psychic sensitivity is enormous, too, and if you trust it, it can bring you plenty of luck. Your sensitivity to beauty also causes you to be fortunate in creative areas. Whether or not you achieve professional success in art or music, you derive great personal pleasure from artistic pursuits—your own and other people's.

The Queen Mother—Jupiter in Sagittarius

Chinese Astrology

Your Animal Sign and Element

Like Western Astrology, Chinese Astrology is a centuries-old method of forecasting the future and analyzing character, however, the Chinese system relies on the year of birth rather than the day.

In the Chinese Zodiac, there are twelve signs which are represented by animals and each sign lasts one year. The Chinese new year begins and the astrological sign changes in January or February, which on our Western calendar is the day of the first New Moon in the sign of Aquarius.

According to Chinese legend, thousands of years ago before Buddha left this world, he called all the animals together for a meeting. However, only twelve animals showed up. The first to arrive was the Rat, then the Ox, followed by the Tiger, Rabbit, Dragon, Snake, Horse, Sheep, Monkey, Rooster, Dog and finally the Pig. They were each rewarded with a year named after them in the order in which they arrived. Their characteristics are said to influence worldly events for that year and the personality and fate of each human born during that time.

Also, according to Chinese philosophy, we are all influenced by the five elements of nature—Water, Wood, Fire, Earth, and Metal. Each year is assigned an element and they have the power to modify or enhance the quality of whatever or whomever they represent.

Another energy influence taken into account in Chinese Astrology is the Yin-Yang polarity. Yin energy is passive and receptive, while Yang energy is outgoing and active. Yin and Yang balance each other—you can't have one without the other. They can be likened to two sides of one coin. Each Chinese astrological year is either Yin or Yang.

It is important to bear in mind that, as your complete Chinese Astrological makeup is made up of many influences and factors, you are not all Yin or all Yang. You are a mixture of both with a predominance of Yin.

Yin and Yang people complement each other. Yang people are the movers and shakers—they act and do. A Yin person is easily able to receive the active, outgoing energy of a Yang person. Yin people naturally create environments where ideas, circumstances, and people can thrive and grow. They are the nurturers of the Universe. Yin individuals are willing to accept what is happening without necessarily feeling the need to make changes; they provide comfort, peace, and harmony. While Yang energy starts, Yin is able to conclude.

Express your total nature and enjoy life to the fullest.

Rat

Water Rat

If you are a Water Rat, it's likely you love the written word and are probably never without a good book to read. Because you love exploring new interests, you are able to educate yourself when you wish and may enroll in continuing education classes. You will want to have a nice, big easy chair for comfortable reading and a large desk on which to spread out your writing materials and papers.

Since you're so knowledgeable and perceptive, you know how to make your way in the world. You always find the cleverest way of getting a job done and, because you can see so far into the future, you often spot trends before they happen. You are well-respected by your associates. You can be accommodating and compassionate, and your diplomatic nature always senses what would please others.

You are a great believer in the value of following tradition. You're not too interested in change. In fact, you're quite happy with things the way they are, thank you. Others count on your stability and may turn to you in times of need to be their rock.

Although you do have your quiet moments, you can be very chatty and will talk to anyone and everyone you meet. Strangers can become friends very quickly.

Wood Rat

As a Wood Rat, you are quite capable of attaining any goal you set for yourself, and you will not stop until you are successful. You probably have a well-thought-out plan of action for what you want and how you're going to go about getting it. It's all a matter of following the logical steps on the path.

You love security and comfort and will not mind having to work very hard to ensure that you get them. There is no need for you to worry about the future. You know where you want to get to and have the energy to reach your destination.

Henri Toulouse Lautrec—Wood Rat

You are the backbone of any group endeavor, and others can depend on you to support the structure of an existing organization and also come up with creative ideas of your own to help it progress. Everything goes like clockwork when you're around. You have an amiable personality and can be very popular. Others will gladly support your efforts, not only because they have respect for your ideas, but because they like you. You exude confidence and know-how and warmth.

You are one of those lucky individuals who will find a way to make an experience enjoyable no matter what. You're a born communicator and delight in letting others in on the great things you've discovered. You want them to have the best, too!

Fire Rat

Being a Fire Rat, you can be a real attention-getter because of your style. Your energy is sparkling. Your refinement is seen in your courtly nature, and you love being the one to step in and save the day. Justice is important to you and you've probably fought for many an underdog just because you thought it was the right thing to do. Others love you because you are sincerely interested in their happiness.

You're always dashing somewhere because travel thrills you. You have a lot of energy to give to others and to projects you're involved in—and meeting new people, being involved in new activities, and championing new causes feeds your passionate, idealistic nature. You can also be very competitive. Whatever position or goal you set your sights on, you'll do everything that you can to attain. You'd make an excellent teacher because you love to talk about all that you've learned. Others enjoy listening to you, so don't hold back—although you're never shy when you have something to say!

Through all the ups and downs of life, you can be counted on to maintain your optimistic, forward-looking spirit. There is always the next great adventure that life has to offer, and you want to experience it. Your generosity in sharing your good fortune endears you to all who know you.

Earth Rat

Because you are an Earth Rat, you tend not to be a risk-taker. Rather, you prefer to work slowly but surely toward getting the things you have planned for yourself. And what you want is a comfortable, orderly existence, for your feet are very firmly planted on the ground. Everything around you must be shipshape and organized to satisfy you. You also appreciate art and good design and want to live in comfortable, attractive surroundings.

Your friends contribute to an overall feeling of security. Others definitely would say you're a loyal soul who is always there for them when they need your help. You like getting along with everyone, and this attracts the companions you need and the support you want for your ideas.

Your reputation is important to you. Not only do you want to be a success for what it brings, but because the respect of your peers means a lot to you. Others recognize your talents and admire your integrity very much, so you don't have to worry about that.

You can be very warm and protective of those close to you. You love being surrounded by people you care about and providing them with what they need to be happy.

Metal Rat

Being a Metal Rat, you are very idealistic and want the best for yourself and those close to you. Having comfortable and aesthetic surroundings is very important to you. Since you are so adaptable and clever, you could probably transform any residence into a cozy, comfortable spot. Your home is definitely your castle!

You love having nice things, and you work hard to get them. You can be a whiz with money if you put your mind to it and you usually invest well. You appreciate value and quality, and you always know how to choose what's classic and best.

Your personality is quite cheerful and pleasant, although you may hide your true feelings just to be sociable. Making sure that others are comfortable makes you appreciated by all who know you. People can tell your interest in them is real.

You love inviting people over and entertaining. The food is usually wonderful because you have a very sensual nature that you love to indulge. Cheery, festive surroundings please you and your guests, especially if you're celebrating a holiday—and you love celebrating holidays! You make friends easily and probably have a great many who deeply appreciate your kindness and love your companionable, positive spirit. Since you are so lovable, the "good life" is yours for the asking!

Ox

Water Ox

You possess the strength and stamina characteristic of the Ox combined with the fluid nature of the Water Element. As a Water Ox, you are likely to view the world as a realist, not a romantic. You understand that, in order to be successful, you may need to work hard—and you don't really mind this, do you? You move methodically toward your goals. Whatever you set your mind on, you plan to reach eventually.

However, while on the road to attaining your ambitions, you are willing to change course if it will help you. Your fluid nature allows you to see other possibilities and you are prepared to make concessions to attain your goals. You will flow with the tide if necessary and easily absorb useful suggestions.

A Water Ox is very congenial. You enjoy participating in group activities and are valued for the contribution you make to any project or gathering. You are an extremely kind person by nature and very sympathetic to others' feelings. This trait makes you quite popular with those who know you and easily attracts new friends.

Your hardworking, patient, and loving nature will take you very far toward creating a secure and happy life.

Wood Ox

Being a Wood Ox gives you a little more daring than your fellow Oxen. Your character is still wonderfully steady and reliable, but the Wood Element adds a bit of showmanship. You are exceptionally gregarious and not afraid to introduce yourself to a stranger. Communication is important and you make sure that your ideas are understood by all who will listen. You are likely to be interested in progressive ideas. Many Wood Oxen are drawn to become teachers because a Wood Ox loves the pursuit of knowledge.

You are also the type of individual who makes a wonderful executive, or the person in charge, as you are able to handle anything and make snap decisions when necessary. You could reach any goals you set for yourself. Many Wood Oxen are found in the corporate world. You like being part of something larger than yourself and appreciate the value of teamwork and cooperation. Also, you tend to be very lucky with money!

Because you reach out eagerly to befriend others, you can be lucky with people, too. You attract many fond friends, as you are very considerate of other people's feelings. All those you are close to have the deepest respect for your integrity and strong character. They also appreciate your loving, giving nature.

Fire Ox

Being a Fire Ox gives you a much more ardent personality than your fellow Oxen. You possess all the wonderful Ox qualities of stability, honesty, and loyalty, but your step is a little quicker, your temper a little hotter, and your emotions a little more volatile. You want to be the center of attention and will express yourself so passionately and enthusiastically that others can't help but give you the stage. What a thrill to watch you in action!

You are usually found leading a brigade defending a cause you truly believe in. In fact, a lot of Fire Oxen

are found in the military. You are in control, very determined, and proudly march toward your goals. Your dynamic presence is able to rally round you supporters for your causes, no matter how big or small. Success is there waiting for you to seize it!

Those you care for can count on your loyalty and fierce protection and they rely very much on your strength. Although you may have a load of responsibilities on your shoulders, you always remember to stop and show those you love the tender, loving feelings that burn in your heart.

Earth Ox

As an Earth Ox, you can be counted on in any situation. Of course, you can—because you're so very down-to-earth! Others look up to you because you're sensible, reliable, and honest. Because you possess a lot of common sense, your judgment is solid. You exhibit a keen sense of how the world works, particularly in financial matters.

Whatever you attempt, you are almost guaranteed to have success. Even if you have to work extra hard and it takes a long time, eventually you will get there. You will continue to work long past the point where many others might have given up, and you will step over any and all obstacles to your success.

In all your relationships, you tend to be there for the long haul. Affectionate and faithful, you are much loved by those close to you for the emotional security you offer them. You are exceptionally loyal to friends. There is nothing anyone can do to lose your friendship once you've given it. This trait can definitely make you a popular person!

Metal Ox

You will let nothing stand in the way of your getting what you want! Your nature combines the stamina and integrity of the Ox with a very strong will. You are the hardest worker on the face of the earth and very conscientious. Others will want to be on your team because they know it will be the winning one. Your tenacity and ambition are greatly respected and admired.

When pursuing a goal, though, you often forget to take time to relax! Remember to recoup your energy with a break every once in awhile, so that you are always ready for the next challenge. No one would ever accuse you of ignoring your duties, so taking frequent naps may be just what you need.

Your sensibilities tend to be refined and you are likely to appreciate the finer things, like music and art. Pursue these interests even if they are not on your list of things to do. It is a good way for you to enjoy yourself. Perhaps, you may even want to try your hand at a creative hobby.

Since you're so determined to get where you're

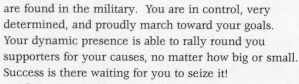

going, you may need to remind yourself to take a little time to notice what others around you are thinking. Rest assured that they admire you very much—and you have such a lot to offer them. So, give a smile to someone new today and engage them in conversation.

Tiger

Water Tiger

Water has a calming effect on the energetic Tiger. Because you are a Water Tiger, you could be called a cool cat! Your nature is to stand back and watch what's going on around you. You'll act only after you have sized up the situation. You have excellent judgment because you are not impulsive like other Tigers. Sometimes you may just choose not to do anything, and that's fine, too. You have this wonderful ability to go with the flow.

Your open-mindedness affords you many different experiences and, coupled with your joy in communicating, you are a pretty interesting person to have around. You probably enjoy telling stories of the many people you've met and new ideas you've encountered. You're quite an eloquent speaker, and you can easily command an audience's attention with your thoughts on everything around you. There are probably quite a few TV newscasters who are Water Tigers.

Since you are so kind and sensitive to others' feelings, it's easy for you to gather a roomful of people who adore you. You are pleasant company and love entertaining. Intuitive and perceptive, you know just the right things to do and say to make those you care about feel loved.

Wood Tiger

Because you are a Wood Tiger, you thrive on being part of a group. Although Tigers usually function well independently, you are practical enough to realize that, with the cooperation of others, you can often attain success faster. You are quite willing to share any attention you get for your excellent contribution. Of course, this makes you a very welcome member of any organization. Wood Tigers are often found in the corporate world.

The Wood Element adds solidity and stability to your commanding Tiger presence and grants you managerial skills. People trust your advice and guidance. You are also quite adept at negotiating and delegating responsibilities. Because others like your affable and practical personality, they will gladly follow your lead.

Your interests are quite varied and you can enjoy many hobbies. You like to plan your leisure activities very carefully and take full advantage of the time that's

your own. You also enjoy mingling with different groups of people. Being a democratic Wood Tiger, you can get along with people from all walks of life.

Anywhere you go, you are usually quite popular with others. You easily attract many friends and supporters with your warm and sincere nature. Being a Wood Tiger makes you such a pleasant and easygoing companion.

Fire Tiger

Being a Fire Tiger, you are an enthusiastic adventurer by nature. You love meeting new people, seeing different places, having new experiences. All this moving around delights you. You have so much energy and you enjoy every exciting new opportunity that comes your way. Of course, this can make you a little unpredictable, because others never know what daring adventure you'll be pursuing next!

Added to your commanding Tiger presence is the Fire of drama and expressiveness. You definitely know how to impress! You are gifted with leadership abilities and can accomplish just about anything you set your mind to. Others are easily inspired because you are so optimistic about the outcome of any of your projects. Success is there just waiting for you to grab it.

Not only are you compelling and charismatic, but your terrific sense of humor draws people to you as if by magnetism. Others always know that, when you're around, something exciting is sure to be happening or, if not, you will create it! Your colorful, positive personality is a delight to all who know you. Now, all you may need is to slow down long enough to let someone love you.

Earth Tiger

The Earth Element creates a more realistic Tiger. Most Tigers are prone to springing into action without thinking, but you are quite practical and give a lot of thought to your actions. You have the Tiger abundance of energy and enthusiasm, but are content to take a steady, sure path to success. Others admire your fortitude, your sense of responsibility, and your sensible nature.

With a steadier emotional makeup, you are easily able to concentrate your mind and work hard for long periods. You can be proud of what you have accomplished. Your dreams are attainable, so keep pursuing them with that characteristic Tiger passion. You will proceed quietly, without show or fanfare, to make your mark. You know where you are going and have the talent and vision to get there. Stop worrying! Your mind may be working overtime needlessly. Think less, feel more.

Your genuine concern for others attracts people who admire your thoughtfulness and maturity. A warm, loving nature makes you very likable, although you may tend to be serious and quiet at times. You may want to try to find occasions that give you the opportunity to laugh a little more with your dear friends.

Metal Tiger

If you are a Metal Tiger, you are sharp, perceptive, direct, and to-the-point. There is nothing shy about you! A lightning quickness characterizes your thought and communication. You pursue your dreams with a tremendous amount of energy, passion, and determination.

You are a freedom-lover, a truly unusual individual who finds new and different ways of doing things. When your thoughts are directed toward a goal, you know exactly what you want to accomplish and how, and often your ideas are quite innovative. Others depend on you to find creative solutions to difficult problems. You may even have considerable artistic talent, as many Tigers do.

You tend to be a hard worker. Slow down for a few minutes to get a little more enjoyment out of your experiences. Look before you leap. You will eventually get where you are going! Definitely an attention-getter, whatever you do usually does not go unnoticed.

Of course, like most Tigers, you are quite sociable. Even when you are competing, you are able to turn it into a social occasion. Your many friends enjoy your exuberant spirit and you always find it easy to welcome people into your life and heart.

Rabbit

Water Rabbit

You are a very sweet, sensitive soul. There's nothing you want more than for everyone to be happy and content. Any kind of disagreement can upset your soft nature, so you have become very good at keeping the peace. Don't be afraid to speak up when you need to, though. Others will be more than willing to support you.

You would be surprised at how many fans you have that you are unaware of! People really appreciate how supportive you can be. Since the Water Element makes you very emotional, it is easy for you to sympathize with others' feelings. Some may say you understand them so well, you must be psychic!

Your loving nature is very attractive and helps you make friends easily. Stay away from negative people, though, as you are not likely to be happy under their influence. Bright, positive friends are the kind of people you need around you. You especially love reminiscing about the past and the happy times you have spent together with old friends.

Often, you may find yourself seeking a quiet place to meditate. There is certainly nothing wrong with

Oscar Wilde — Wood Tiger

wanting to be alone to rejuvenate your spirit. Generally, though, you are friendly and easygoing, and enjoy the company of those you hold dear.

Wood Rabbit

The Wood Rabbit's basic nature is peace-loving and kind. Sometimes, though, you may be so concerned that everything go smoothly that you don't say what you want for fear of upsetting someone. Go ahead and speak up. You have valuable insights that can be helpful to all around you. Being as good-hearted as you are, you are not likely to ever hurt anyone's feelings.

The Wood Element helps you to function very well as part of a group, and any team would be happy to have your valuable assistance. Also, you tend to find having a group's support important to your own security and happiness. You can thrive in large organizations where you steadily build a reputation for cooperation and diplomacy. Success is yours for the asking.

You have no trouble at all making new friends wherever you go. Your generous spirit and understanding nature make you very attractive, and you are always ready to give of yourself and your time. Those close to you depend a lot on your support and loyalty, you take care of them so lovingly.

Fire Rabbit

You are a bolder, more decisive and adventurous Rabbit, for your Fire Element eliminates any Rabbit shyness from your nature. You are not afraid to express your opinions—and quite passionately, too. Your emotions can be a bit fiery, but your Rabbit gift for diplomacy helps you control any unruly feelings for the sake of peace and harmony. Basically, you have a sparkling personality and are a lot of fun, Fire Rabbit!

Others are drawn to your strength of character,

honesty, and enthusiasm, giving you exceptional leadership abilities. Display the abundance of charm and intelligence you were blessed with. Your talent for diplomacy and a pleasant way with words could take you anywhere you want to go in life. Success is almost guaranteed with hard work. Be sure to follow your intuition, as it is highly sensitive. You may even think of yourself as psychic!

Your enthusiasm for life is very attractive and an outgoing and positive nature wins you friends easily. Enjoy many good times in their company. You are graced with their good will and wholehearted support and you quite generously return it.

Earth Rabbit

As an Earth Rabbit, your personality is serious, steady, and practical. Your dreams are realistic and you work hard to attain them. Since you are careful to make well-laid plans and you persevere beyond any obstacles, you should be a success at whatever you set your sights on. Such wonderful qualities help to earn the trust and support of all who know you.

Because you possess such an even temperament, you create an atmosphere around you that is quite tranquil. You love the good things in life and enjoy accumulating beautiful material things. You strive to overcome any shortcomings in your character and are constantly pursuing some sort of self-improvement regimen. Redecorating and making your surroundings as pleasant as possible may be a favorite pastime, too.

A comfortable home and loving friends are necessities for your happiness. You are able to attract companions easily because of your refined sensibilities and many other sterling qualities. Others depend on you for your solid advice and clear thinking. Your constancy makes you greatly loved by those close to you.

Metal Rabbit

Being a Metal Rabbit, you are a Rabbit with a stronger presence than most. Rabbits are often timid, but the Metal Element adds a certain resiliency to your nature and makes you tougher. You are able to handle any problem, for you are sure of yourself and your own abilities. Although you're not afraid of taking on heavy responsibility, sometimes you like to hide your ambitious nature.

In your surroundings and clothing, your impeccable taste and love of beautiful things is evident. A Rabbit personifies refinement, and a Metal Rabbit always notices the best and will want to have it. You are very cultured, appreciating all kinds of art and music. You may even be artistically talented yourself. If so, you are likely to be very involved in your creative pursuits.

Friendship inspires you and you enjoy sharing your love of beauty with others. It is an honor to be chosen as your friend, because your demure and discerning nature reaches out only when you feel someone is very special. You prefer sharing your deepest thoughts and longings with only a few close companions whom you always try to make happy in your elegant way.

Dragon

Water Dragon

A Water Dragon breathes less fire than other Dragons. Water gives you a calm and especially pleasing personality. Even though a strong moral character guides you, you are still open to seeing the other person's point of view. Any organization would be proud to have you as a member.

You're good at keeping your wits about you, particularly in a tough negotiating situation. You have the ability to step back and review the situation objectively. Therefore, you are able to make superior decisions for the good of all. You are also great at promoting ideas that you believe in. Doesn't everyone usually agree with you that your ideas are brilliant!

You are ambitious in true Dragon fashion but, if things don't go as planned, you don't get dejected—you just pick yourself up by the bootstraps and try again. You are optimistic about your own powers and can be assured of a successful outcome in your endeavors.

Although you may prefer to remain in the background and quietly make your mark, you eventually will cause others to sit up and take notice. Do you find that friends often come to you for advice? You may not know how much others admire and depend on your wisdom, but it's probably a lot!

Wood Dragon

As a Wood Dragon, you are more practical and logical than other Dragons. The Wood Element also makes you very inquisitive about the world around you. You want to know "why?" and "how?" before making any kind of a decision. Only then do you decide what course of action would be best. Therefore, you display great intelligence and forethought. You can accomplish much with these excellent traits.

Add to these qualities a talent for being creative and imaginative and you see that your gifts are considerable! "Necessity is the mother of invention" is probably one of your mottoes. You find creative solutions to problems that stump others. Explore artistic avenues that interest you, too, because you may have yet to discover the depth of your creativity.

Your magnanimous personality endears you to those close to you. You're not as focused on yourself as other Dragons sometimes are. Other people and discussions about their ideas interest you more. You really get a big kick out of meeting new people, don't you? They feel your kindness and interest right away, and are likely to respond warmly to you. All these wonderful qualities help you create a contented life for yourself.

Fire Dragon

Because you are a Fire Dragon, you are a real powerhouse! Your enthusiasm and energy are huge assets in accomplishing what you want and getting the things that you need to be happy. You have quite a lot to offer.

There is a definite air of authority about you and your leadership abilities are considerable. You can easily obtain a following or supporters for any of your causes. Sometimes, though, you may expect too much from yourself as well as from others. However, those around you see that you are understanding and open to their ideas. Your humanity shines through everything you do and makes you quite a charismatic individual. Performing in front of an adoring public would be nice, wouldn't it?

You leave no stone unturned in your quest for the truth. Quite the perfectionist in everything you attempt, you could build a brilliant empire if you wanted to or, perhaps, lead the whole world to a more ideal way of life. It goes without saying that you must be very important to a lot of people who depend on you.

Your delightful, vivacious personality inspires those who know you. Because you are a Dragon full of fire, perhaps you sometimes have to control your temper! You're getting better at it though, aren't you?

Earth Dragon

Being an Earth Dragon, you take your responsibilities very seriously and surely earn everything you acquire. Of all the Dragons, you are the most realistic. You work quietly and unhurriedly toward your goals. No matter how long it takes, though, you always get where you're going.

You are also a born leader. In true Dragon style, an air of authority surrounds you. Many Earth Dragons tend to be executives. You have tiptop managerial ability and are able to organize projects and people very well. You definitely deserve the respect given you, for you work hard for the benefit of all on any project you're involved in.

Others find you easy to get along with because you are fair and appreciate their ideas. You especially value cooperation in those you have around you and, in turn, you will pitch in where you're needed. There isn't a selfish bone in your body.

You can enjoy a rich social life because you are well liked by those you meet. Parties and all sorts of get-togethers amuse you and you should accept all invitations! On an intimate level, you take your

friendships just as seriously as your goals. Your kind and considerate nature and even temperament are cherished. Friends can always count on you to be level-headed and ready to be helpful.

Metal Dragon

A Metal Dragon can best be described as brave and forceful. You have strong opinions on just about every subject and express them easily. Your honesty and high moral character are admirable.

Never one to sit back and let life come to you, you go out and make it happen! And why not? When you want something, isn't it just simpler to go after it? You can easily obtain your most secret desires, Metal Dragon, when you focus your tremendous energy on your goals. Others will be amazed by your fervor, and follow.

When you have a worthwhile cause to champion, you are at your best and happiest. A true warrior, you cannot tolerate any injustice to others. Of course, this makes everyone want you on their side because you can win any battle and save the day. You like being the hero, don't you? Well, you often are.

Finding time to relax in your home is something you must do to regenerate! You like being at the center of the action so much, and you have so many projects going at once, that you may find this the one and only difficult thing to do. Since you enjoy the company of others like yourself—high-energy, intelligent people— your home could be a center for many lively discussions. Have the time of your life!

Salvador Dali—Wood Dragon

Snake

Water Snake

Being a Water Snake, gives you a lot of charisma and makes you very influential wherever you go. You have good old-fashioned common sense which others find comforting. Always trust your hunches because they are right on target. Some may even call you psychic!

Being very practical, you can manage anything with ease. Whether it's handling a multitude of tasks or a room full of people, you are the one in charge. You're adept at planning because of your ability to concentrate and your iron determination. When you have set a goal for yourself, you head for it with blinders on and ignore unimportant things. When Water Snakes go into business for themselves, they're usually quite successful because of these traits.

You may have a tendency to hold things in—to just "grin and bear it." Let your feelings out! If you have things on your mind that bother you, others will understand and be even more eager to help. If you discuss problems openly, it's easier to do something about them, right?

You are loved greatly by everyone who knows you because of your kindness and your sweet, loving ways. And, most of all, if someone becomes your friend, you are loyal through thick and thin.

Wood Snake

A Wood Snake is quite a charming, intelligent, and lucky individual! Interesting and alluring only begin to describe you. You have so many positive qualities that just being yourself should easily attract to you what you want in life!

First of all, you express yourself beautifully. Not only are you an eloquent speaker, but you're most likely a snappy dresser too. Most Wood Snakes enjoy having beautiful things around, and are well-read and cultured individuals. Also, your wisdom and understanding of life accentuate your brilliant character. You're very practical about learning, however. Whatever you study must have a purpose and somehow advance you or apply to your everyday life.

You like to be free to make your own decisions and chart your own course without too much interference from those around you. In fact, your only fault may be trying to handle difficult tasks on your own without bothering anyone else for their help.

Your friends (and *everyone* who meets you) probably call you "a real sweetheart," as there is nothing you wouldn't do for them. You enjoy their company and want to have their admiration and support. All in all, a quiet, stable, emotionally-satisfying life is the one for you!

Fire Snake

Being a Fire Snake gives you a tremendous amount of energy and ambition. The Fire Element makes you a born leader. Blessed with loads of charisma, you've probably been voted president of something at least once so far! You have many talents, and the confidence you feel in yourself gives others faith in your abilities. Your basic honesty also easily wins people to your side.

Fire Snakes have tremendous drive and determination. With perseverance, you should be able to succeed in whatever you attempt. Your aspirations are always high, but you're quite capable of attaining them. The desire for power and riches is very strong in you. You want to feel more than just comfortable, don't you? Once you win power or wealth, it would be difficult to take it away from you because you like being King of the Hill!

A very private person, you prefer having only one or two really close friends that you share your most intimate thoughts with. Most people probably don't know the real you. But those close to you feel loved and protected. You're quite an exciting friend to have. A great sense of humor makes you a fun companion, too.

Earth Snake

If you're an Earth Snake, you're the warmest Snake of all! Your manner is easygoing, honest, considerate, and quite charming.

You have a practical, logical mind. Earth Snakes are often very successful in financial matters. You are sensible, hardworking, and reliable. Taking risks is not your natural way of doing things. You prefer a steadier, more systematic approach. With sustained effort and by calculating your moves ahead of time, you can succeed in building a stable and comfortable life. Like all Snakes, you derive much pleasure from possessing beautiful material things.

Once you've made up your mind about someone or something, you rarely change your opinion because you've given the matter very careful thought. Actually, you are quite a forward-thinker and can predict the future with a fair bit of accuracy based on your observations. Trust your excellent hunches and you can satisfy your ambitions.

People gravitate to you because you naturally try to form a good opinion of everyone. Group activities, or memberships in social or sport clubs, suit your |convivial, sociable nature. Your friends particularly appreciate the loyalty and support you readily offer. A basic trust in others and yourself can guarantee easy relationships and a peaceful, happy existence.

Metal Snake

Being a Metal Snake makes you a strong personality with enormous willpower. Because you're very clever, you know exactly how to get what you want, don't you? You are very dedicated to whatever project you are involved in and refuse to accept defeat or failure in attaining your goals. A very generous and cooperative spirit also guides you. These are the qualities that can lead to success in whatever you attempt.

Of course, you love having nice things, but you don't mind working hard or saving your pennies so you can enjoy them. Snakes have excellent taste. You plan very well toward the attainment of your material desires, so it's fine to indulge in small luxuries occasionally. Many Metal Snakes work extra hard to attain great wealth just because they need to have the very best of everything they see!

Snakes are often loners. You tend to be a very private person, choosing your friends carefully. People are apt to have great admiration for you even if you are unaware of it. You may want to open up more to others, as you'll find that things are even easier with their support. Also, it can mean more fun for you!

Horse

Water Horse

Lucky you! You're a Water Horse, which makes you a lot more easygoing and adaptable than other Horses. Not much bothers you—you just take things as they come, and deal with them. Always cheerful and optimistic, you are concerned with maintaining a comfortable place for yourself. You head straight for your goals.

Of course, sometimes you can change your mind at the drop of a hat and leave everyone around you wondering which way you're going! Changing your direction is easy for you, if you think another path would be more productive—or simply more fun. Your spontaneity is refreshing and can stimulate others to follow you.

Aretha Franklin—Water Horse

Possessing the Horse's love of travel, you are likely to take many short trips. You enjoy being on the go, meeting new people, and selling your ideas. Being sociable as well as hardworking, a Water Horse can be a very successful business person. You're also a stylish dresser, so you make quite an impressive picture!

You have a great sense of humor and the gift of gab, so you can make friends easily wherever you go. There may be a few pals who share your love of sports, and you enjoy many outings with them or happy gatherings around the TV watching a game. Have fun and pass the popcorn!

Wood Horse

Being a Wood Horse can make you less skittish than other Horses. The desire for adventure is there, but your travels have a definite purpose—they must further your goals. You are capable of accomplishing a lot and achieving much success because of your tranquil nature.

You do not like being dominated by others, like a true Horse, but you will not seek to dominate them either. You are friendly to everyone you meet and quite a good conversationalist. A cooperative spirit makes you a welcome member of any group or organization, where your logical approach to solving problems is valued. You work hard and can focus for long periods of time. Always one to fulfill your responsibilities first, your gait is measured and usually wins the race!

Your interests are varied and you probably want to know what is current and new so that you can get involved in it or use it for your benefit. Most Wood Horses tend to be modern thinkers and possess all the latest technology.

A genuinely happy disposition draws many friends to you. You can have a rich social life, enjoying many hours of lively conversation about the state of the world. You can be counted on to be there when you're needed, and you are very much loved by all.

Fire Horse

Being a Fire Horse makes you a lively and quite daring thoroughbred! There is nothing shy about you. Flamboyant and passionate, you make things happen by sheer force of will. You can be a lot to handle, even for yourself sometimes!

You like living on the edge, don't you? A wild streak can cause you to take chances others wouldn't. Of course, this makes you very exciting to know. There's always plenty of action whenever you're around. But, just as everyone starts marveling at your brilliant mind and charismatic personality, suddenly you're racing off in another direction! You need new adventures and new challenges and often juggle several projects all at once.

You can deal with anything that comes your way. You are resourceful and possess the intellect to quickly grasp any situation, then make a decision where needed. This makes you an excellent person to put in charge. Combine this with the ability to get along with just about anyone you meet and you become a vital cog in the machinery.

Your friends are likely to be in awe of your romantic individualism. You can enthrall them with the stories of your exciting travels and adventures. Others see you as a charming and very lucky person.

Earth Horse

As an Earth Horse, you can be very steady and practical. You tend to be a bit tamer than other Horses, liking a calmer existence and your feet firmly planted on the ground. You will work hard to ensure your comfort no matter how long it takes.

Before making any kind of decision, you like to look at the situation from all different sides. You grasp things quickly, but you will always deliberate very carefully on what course of action to take. Sometimes, you may even have a bit of trouble making up your mind because your research is so thorough.

One of your biggest assets is your ability to turn things around and make a success of tough situations. You work very hard to obtain security and are able to adapt to anything. Be careful not to bite off more than you can chew, though. You can be very smart about where you put your money, only investing where you're sure to come out ahead.

Others are attracted to your happy disposition and terrific sense of humor. You also show great sensitivity and kindness to those close to you, taking your personal commitments very seriously. These wonderful qualities draw people to you easily.

Metal Horse

A Metal Horse is the liveliest, most independent Horse of all. Every new adventure is a thrill for you. With a boundless energy and spirit, you gallop through life, loving wide-open spaces and the feel of the wind in your hair!

Your roving spirit creates a need for a great deal of activity on a daily basis. You are always on the go, even if it means just taking short trips around town or dropping by to visit many different people. A mobile home would likely be your idea of a comfortable and ideal place to live. You could just pick up and go when the spirit moved you!

Because you need more freedom than the average person, it may be difficult for you to concentrate on one project for long. You need constant new challenges along with ever-changing scenery. Be sure to give yourself the freedom you crave and also to let others know this is what you want. When you are happy, brilliant ideas

just flow out of you and you make valuable contributions to any project or group association. When you feel hemmed in, your productivity lags.

Others find your daring spirit very attractive and exciting. You're a great friend to have because you are so optimistic and genuinely warm. Of course, you're also a lot of fun!

Sheep

Water Sheep

A Water Sheep can be quite a lovable character. If ever you're in need of help, a lot of people would wait in line, hoping to be the one who assists you! You're a very special person in many ways, and you deserve every bit of the admiration you receive.

The Water Element gives you various interests and you mix easily with different kinds of people. Water tends also to make you adaptable and compliant. You usually go with the flow. Of course, this can make you a welcome guest everywhere, and others dream of having you as an associate. Getting involved with groups is your best bet for happiness and success.

Whatever endeavors you pursue, you approach them with determination and a healthy sense of humor. Although a bit on the shy side, at times you can be very articulate and outgoing. Be confident in your abilities and you'll do well wherever you go because of your pleasant nature and ability to fit in anywhere.

You like to feel safe and protected in your home and will opt for a secure, quiet existence. There is an aura about you that makes people want to take care of you, and, of course, you revel in their nurturing. Those close to you see just how special you are and will always be there for you.

Wood Sheep

If you're a Wood Sheep, you're a person who gets very involved with others. Everyone is your friend! Always willing to extend a helping hand to those who need it, you are quick to offer comfort and support to those around you. Your friends all depend on you very much. Of course, these qualities make you quite popular.

Your compassion for your fellow man runs very deep. The thoughtfulness you display is usually rewarded, but be careful that others don't take advantage of your giving nature. The Wood Element makes you very eager to please others. But you must be sure to spend time on yourself and put your own needs first sometimes. It's okay to turn down requests for your time every now and then. People will understand that you can't be everywhere at once.

In your many different projects, you always

display high moral principles. And you trust the good faith of others in return. You are respected for your steady, thoughtful, good-humored demeanor. If you put all your wonderful qualities to work for you in financial matters, you should come out ahead. Others will probably be very willing to give you what you want, if you ask for it!

Fire Sheep

Being a Fire Sheep can make you the most courageous and individualistic of all Sheep. You're more willing to take chances, and you care a lot less about the approval of others. The Fire Element gives you a lot of confidence in your own abilities. You're more comfortable being a leader than a follower.

Quite creative and with a dramatic personality, many Fire Sheep are attracted to the theater. With your liveliness and charm, you can find many admirers and friends to cheer on any of your artistic endeavors. You can be quite outspoken in your opinions and always ready to express your feelings on any subject. The people close to you admire your energy and enthusiasm for your projects. You believe anything is possible!

But underneath all the excitement you generate, you are still a peace-loving Sheep. You love quiet and calm, and are most content when you're in comfortable surroundings. Spend time making your home a place where you can relax and get away from it all. But also be ready to throw open the doors and show it off to the people you'd like to entertain. Remember to take time off from pursuing your dreams to appreciate the wonderful things you already have and the many friends who care about you.

Earth Sheep

Being an Earth Sheep, you are sensible and conservative. The Earth Element gives you a firm grounding, making you more self-reliant than other Sheep. You know what you want and you don't waste any time going after it. You appreciate the finer things in life. And, since you're an industrious and resourceful Earth Sheep, you know that you'll always find a way to have them!

There is nothing more important to you than your domestic life and you work hard to ensure that you have a comfortable, secure existence. You're very reliable and tend to err on the side of caution with your finances. Part of the reason why is that you take your responsibilities so seriously. You are very devoted to those close to you, and there is practically nothing you wouldn't do to help out a friend in need.

Others appreciate your quiet yet commanding presence. You may not like to be the acknowledged leader of a group, preferring to put your ideas forward

behind the scenes. But your ideas are sure to be the ones that are put into action.

People gravitate to your sunny disposition and find you nice to be around. Your optimism guarantees success wherever you go, so don't worry for a minute that you aren't making a good impression. Have a little more confidence in yourself. Others can't help but notice all your admirable qualities.

Metal Sheep

Since you're a Metal Sheep, you can seem a little tougher on the outside than other Sheep. You present a very calm and commanding exterior. But underneath is that wonderful heart of gold and soft nature that endears you to others. Sensitive and artistic, your main goals focus on creating an idyllic, harmonious existence for yourself and others.

You possess a great deal of pride and are well aware of how talented and deserving you are, aren't you? Well, you are the very best! You also don't mind working hard to ensure your financial security.

Metal Sheep are often artistically inclined. You can appreciate beauty all around you. Comfortable, attractive surroundings are important to your happiness. Spend extra time decorating your home if you wish. You would enjoy the process of picking out colors and furnishings according to your wonderful taste. You can provide a beautiful showcase for all to enjoy.

A harmonious emotional life is very necessary for you to maintain a feeling of balance. You prefer having a small circle of friends that understand your sensitive and vulnerable nature and make you feel secure. Friends can help you enjoy your life and prosper, and you love to coddle them and make them happy, too.

Monkey

Water Monkey

Being a Water Monkey, you're a little more sensitive than other Monkeys. Not only is your heart easily touched, but your feelings are so tender that you often try to hide them for protection. Others rarely know just what is going on beneath your dignified exterior. You conceal there a very kind and decent soul that you should share with others often!

You have many wonderful qualities that can lead you to success. You're a cooperative person with original ideas who prefers to pursue your goals quietly and methodically. Have patience and all will work out in your favor. Chart your path carefully and do not veer off course once you've made a decision. Work around any barriers to success with your usual Monkey flair and imagination. Surprise yourself with how ingenious you can be when it comes to solving problems. Your determination can be an inspiration to all around you.

You have a good understanding of what makes relationships successful and you'll do your best to insure that you get along with everyone. Your graceful manner and pleasant personality win you many friends who think you're simply brilliant!

Wood Monkey

Being a Wood Monkey, you're a born communicator. The Wood Element makes you a veritable genius at getting along with people! You love the spoken word and your Monkey sense of humor and charm give you a leg up on the competition. You can go very far in any organization with your hard work and diplomatic skills.

Your integrity is admirable. There is no one with a higher set of standards than a Wood Monkey. You will work very hard to improve yourself, always looking for new ways of doing things or learning different skills. You love a challenge, and your highly evolved intuition allows you to know which step to take next for a favorable outcome.

Your curious nature is always leading you in new directions. Wherever your ambition takes you, you will manage to fit in. It's easy for you to figure out how things work and carve out a place for yourself. Projects involving any new computer technology may excite you. Or, one of your hobbies may be surfing the Net. You are a forward thinker and very interested in the future.

In your personal life, you enjoy the affection and admiration of all who know you. You respect the privacy of others and expect the same, but you are always ready to lend a helping hand to those who need it. You are a warm and loyal friend.

Fire Monkey

As a Fire Monkey, you possess an abundance of positive energy. You are a person of action and a real leader. Confident in your abilities and determined to succeed, you blaze through life!

The Fire Element makes you the most forceful of all Monkeys. It's important to you that you make your mark on the world in a big way, and you'll work overtime to insure that your ambition is satisfied. You have a lot of talent and are quite knowledgeable in many subjects. You can sometimes seem opinionated, but it's just your positive desire to learn and share your knowledge. Not everyone will always agree with you, but that's what makes life fun for you Fire Monkeys. It's fine with you for others to have their own independent thoughts — you just love arguing with them!

Your honesty is appreciated by all who know you. Since it's easy for you to express yourself in words,

you can make friends easily. Most of all, you're curious and interested in everyone. You're eager to make new contacts and learn new things that may help you. You are charming and a lot of fun to have around, because wherever you are there is sure to be a whirlwind of activity. Others find you both attractive and entertaining.

Earth Monkey

An Earth Monkey is reliable, calm, cool, and collected. Your quiet and dignified personality commands respect and admiration. Highly intelligent and knowledgeable, you are likely to have many intellectual interests, as the Earth Element directs the Monkey curiosity into serious, even academic, pursuits.

You're full of inventive ideas. To some, an Earth Monkey's thinking may even seem a little unconventional. That may sound funny to you because you pride yourself on following well-trodden paths. Well, you may just be a deeper thinker than everyone else!

Any organization would welcome you as a member because you're so thorough in your efforts and honest in your dealings with others. You can always be counted on to follow through with promises made and support offered. Your reputation is solid and your devotion to any group's success is appreciated.

When you care for someone, you would move mountains for them. You can attract many loving friends because of this. They like knowing they have someone they can count on. Friends admire your many wonderful qualities but, above all, they appreciate your unselfish and very understanding nature. In your own quiet way, you can enjoy much kindness, loyalty, and love reflected back to you.

Metal Monkey

Being a Metal Monkey, you're passionate about everything you do. Determined and ambitious, it shouldn't be too difficult for you to attract success. The Metal Element gives you a strength of will that enables you to put in long hours pursuing your goals. Financial security is very important to you, and you're always looking for wise investments.

Although you may prefer going it alone, your charm and warmth help you to make friends and persuade others to assist you. Your nimble wit delights and entertains those around you. Gifted with such an outgoing personality, you could sell anything to anyone! Your sophistication and positive attitude win you many friends and admirers.

You are loyal and devoted to those you love. Your passionate nature is evident in the way you express your affections. Those close to you know just how much you care, and love you very much for it. You are always trying to better yourself and your situation, for which your friends respect you greatly. Hardworking and practical, you provide for your own security, as well as that of those you care for.

Rooster

Water Rooster

Because you are a Water Rooster, you are gifted with a tremendous amount of energy that you are able to apply wherever you wish. The Water Element makes you quieter, calmer, and more intellectual than other Roosters. But you're still a very practical, organized person who knows how to get things done. And, if you can't do something yourself, you don't hesitate to ask for help.

Your major interests can lie in the areas of science and communications. You may enjoy reading about health and nutrition or finding out about the latest contraption in the area of new technology. You enjoy being a well-rounded person, which is why you are such an avid reader. Writing can also give you much pleasure, and you can excel at it. Others probably remark on what a compelling speaker you are. You can command the attention of a room full of people if you want, and inspire them to jump on your bandwagon.

Although you have an exceptional talent for focusing on details, you don't get lost in trivialities that do not support your practical goals. You get along easily with people because the Water Element makes you less critical than other Roosters. You are more apt to see the other person's point of view and opt for a compromise whenever you can. As you know, a sweet disposition attracts many friends.

Wood Rooster

As a Wood Rooster, you're a real team player. You have a great deal of energy and a profound social conscience that guides your life. You love to share your forward-looking ideas, hoping to make things better for all. You are conscientious and devoted to duty, and you can excel at whatever organizational task you set your mind to.

Others respect your integrity and enthusiasm for your various causes and are amazed at your stamina. Go easy on everyone, as they may not have the same amount of energy and dedication as you do! At the same time, you should avoid taking on more than you can handle. When others see just how reliable you are, they may have a tendency to give you more responsibility. You take your duties very seriously and would never let anyone down, but you need to make time for yourself, too!

Security is important to you, and you will work hard to insure your comfort. Your congenial nature allows you to get along easily with everyone you come in contact with. You treat people equally, showing great consideration for everyone's feelings.

Those who are especially close to you know that you always have their happiness in mind and wish them nothing but the best. You are devoted to those you love and give unstintingly of your time and attention.

Fire Rooster

Being a Fire Rooster, you are a born leader, chock-full of star quality! Your aura commands respect before you even say anything. You have the potential to go far in life because your talents are considerable. You are blessed with exceptional willpower, motivation, energy, and style.

Your image is extremely important to you, and you're probably thought of as a snappy dresser. You are very conscious of the impression you make and spend lots of time and money on your appearance and clothes. It's fun for you to be dramatic!

Whenever you are in charge of a project—and Roosters usually are in charge—you conduct it with great skill and precision. You want correct facts and a predictable outcome. Others' opinions never affect you. You work tirelessly until you achieve your goals in your own way. All of your actions spring from the noblest of intentions, and associates can count on your honesty in any dealings with you.

You can have a tendency to be overly critical, especially of those close to you. Try to be more understanding. Not everyone can measure up to your high expectations at all times. Show your genuine affection. It will make those close to you happy, which is really what you want.

Earth Rooster

As an Earth Rooster, you possess many qualities that can lead you to success. You are honest, mature, hard-working, and responsible. A clear and organized mind makes you super-competent and able to handle any task. Most organizations would find you quite valuable because you do what's needed to get a job accomplished.

You like a neat and tidy space around you. It allows you to be more efficient and focuses your powers of concentration. Inviting people into your home is one of your favorite activities. You have many gatherings there, which can be geared toward promoting your pet projects. You take on social causes and like to get your friends involved in helping you. A work party is your idea of fun.

Your standards are usually quite high regarding whatever you are doing. Others are easily inspired by your dedication. Remember to throw a few compliments their

Enrico Caruso—Water Rooster

way when they've made contributions you appreciate. Also, remember to praise yourself for your accomplishments.

You may like living a simple life, but guard against getting too austere. Enjoy your success more. At the end of the day, remind yourself to relax!

Metal Rooster

Because you are a Metal Rooster, you are industrious and passionate. When you're involved in a project, you throw yourself totally into it. With your optimistic attitude, you easily achieve the success you hope for.

Metal Roosters are well-respected and often hold a place of importance in their communities. Your energies are usually split between pursuing your material goals and working for the good of others. The world around you is very important and you can be quite idealistic about how you think things should be organized. Your opinions are strong and you communicate your ideas forcefully.

You have analytical gifts that would best be channeled into your projects rather than turned onto yourself or others. Your powers of deduction and rational mind would be assets in any organization. Others admire your reasoning abilities, and, if you are ever called on to speak in front of a crowd, you can easily sway them to your way of thinking with your talent for oratory. Roosters are often brilliant performers.

Your appreciation for order and tidiness can be reflected in a pleasant and orderly home. Take a little time off from all your projects to relax there. Rather than letting your mind rule the roost all the time, try to let your emotions lead you a little more often. Those who care about you really want to know your feelings. Follow your heart!

Dog

Water Dog

Lucky you! You are a Water Dog, which makes you a very desirable companion. Water Dogs are usually quite attractive with lovely manners and pleasing personalities. More easygoing than other Dogs, your motto is "Live and let live." The Water Element gives you your graceful demeanor. Think of a quiet lapdog with large soulful eyes and that may describe your inner nature.

However, added to this is a keen eye for what's going on around you, and a contemplative stance. You have a good "take" on people and can be counted on to understand just how they're feeling.

Because you're able to step back and judge a situation fairly, you see the other person's point of view easily. You know instinctively what to do and say in any situation to make them feel good. Others may often come to you seeking your counsel and wise advice. In fact, many Water Dogs are drawn to the legal and counseling professions. You can impress others quite easily with your composure and quiet self-confidence.

All these wonderful qualities attract many friends, so Water Dogs can be very popular. Many social invitations could come your way, which you should always accept, because you truly enjoy and blossom in the company of others. People trust you and feel comforted with you by their side.

Wood Dog

Being a Wood Dog, you have a sweet, warm-hearted, even-tempered disposition. The Wood Element makes you a bit more intellectual than other Dogs. Money and success are important to you, and your goals tend to focus on bettering yourself and your environment.

More than anything, you like feeling part of a group. You know you have wonderful ideas, but you feel even better about them when others support them. You have many interests and lots of energy, making you a fascinating person to have around. It should be very easy for you to gain entry into any association you desire.

At times, you may be a little shy when meeting new people. Don't hold yourself back. You present yourself as a very pleasant and refined individual, which can only serve to make you very well liked. With your talent for getting along with people, you are able to deal famously with just about anyone from any walk of life.

Whether it's a weekly bridge game or a book discussion group, you enjoy yourself most when you have pals who share your interests. Your friends appreciate your generosity and loyalty. They admire your knowledge and refinement, and may even try to emulate your enchanting ways.

Fire Dog

Fire Dogs possess sparkling personalities that attract attention and applause. You Fire Dogs are the show dogs of the Zodiac—you love making an impression. Go out and wow 'em! Others can hardly resist your power to enchant.

Because of your friendly, outgoing nature, you could accomplish anything you want and you easily gain the support of anyone you meet. Charming, independent, and high-spirited, you're a born leader. Others respect and admire you and know they can rely on your honesty. You say what you mean and mean what you say. However, it is never a good idea to cross you—your bark can be as fierce as your bite!

The Fire Element blesses you with great creativity and courage. You thrill to each new challenge you encounter. Sometimes a childlike enthusiasm seems to govern what you do—however, your feet are always firmly planted on the ground. Although you are idealistic, your ideals are based in reality. Your faith and ambition help you overcome any barriers. And, success doesn't spoil you at all.

Your friends can count on your exceptional loyalty. And they always feel they're on an exciting ride, being close to you. You're the life of any party. Your sense of humor and joie de vivre magnetize everyone around you!

Earth Dog

Being an Earth Dog, you're one of the wisest and kindest people in the whole wide world! In practical matters, your instincts are impeccable. It is the "slow but sure" that wins the race—and that's you!

You possess strong beliefs and will fight for them if you must. But, you'd prefer to go along with the majority when you can. The most democratic of all Dogs, you are a welcome addition to any group. You can easily handle a leadership role and will delegate responsibility fairly. You like to take care of business without any unnecessary fanfare. You are practical, unsentimental, and exceptionally honest—a real treasure in anyone's book! The respect you receive is definitely well earned.

Nothing will ever get you down, because you know how to survive. You can think constructively and find a positive solution to any problem. Of course, this comes from your work on building a healthy sense of self. Thoroughly dependable, others turn to you often for your sound and valuable advice.

Your quiet powers of persuasion can guide others to setting higher standards for themselves. Those close to you are inspired to be better people just by knowing you. They feel cared for, loved, and, most of all, safe. What a gift you give to those you love!

Metal Dog

You're a Metal Dog, the most loyal, alert, and tenacious Dog of all. The ultimate "social animal," you care deeply about maintaining the health and stability of relationships on personal, social, and political levels. Likely to hold strong political views, you may feel obliged to get involved in public service.

Devotion to the cause of justice is a cornerstone of your character, and upholding principles of fair play is essential to your sense of security. People who violate the "social contract" may be profoundly offensive to you. When someone presumes to operate by his or her own set of rules, you may feel threatened. Such a person may appear to present a danger not only to you, but to the stability of your family and community.

Heaven help any person or institution who endangers loved ones or those who are weak, vulnerable or powerless. You are fiercely protective of friends and family and the ultimate champion of the underdog. Because you see issues in terms of right-and-wrong, black-and-white, you are not afraid to call things as you see them.

Others find your certitude stabilizing and comforting, but you may need to watch out for excessive rigidity. You are a rock of reliability and a font of inexhaustible and unconditional love!

Pig

Water Pig

A Water Pig believes in miracles—and so you're more likely to attract them! You are kind and loving, and always try to see the best in others. This, of course, makes you very good at dealing with people, and can also attract many friends who care deeply for you.

You have a talent for persuading others to see your point of view because you are so adept at understanding theirs. Blessed with the qualities of a fine diplomat, you can often be entrusted with the task of negotiating on behalf of a group. You can be quite resourceful when it comes to bargaining. Any organization would be happy to have you as its emissary.

The Water Element makes you more flexible than other Pigs, although it is already in the Pig nature to be basically easygoing. There are many directions you could go in because you have a variety of interests beckoning you. Wherever you put your energy, you should be successful. Perseverance and hard work will get you what you're after.

You love meeting new people and are blessed with the ability to talk to anyone. Your friends enjoy your good company and generosity. Happy gatherings with lots of good food and fun conversation could be a constant occurrence, but you are happiest spending time relaxing at home with those you love.

Wood Pig

Being a Wood Pig, you are one of the most generous people around! Always ready to see the positive side of things, you can draw people to you easily with your happy disposition. A great sense of humor also helps to make you especially attractive to others.

The Wood Element gives you more drive and ambition to get to the top than other Pigs. And since you are so kind-hearted, the "top" may include being the chief organizer of charity functions. You have a real flair for managing any kind of social function or club activity. Your "hail-fellow-well-met" attitude lends homespun comfort to an affair. Money should flow easily to the causes you champion.

You Wood Pigs will always stand by those you believe in. You can often be rewarded for the faith you put in people by being placed in important positions. And, since you have a remarkable talent for helping everyone to get along, you're likely to meet many interesting acquaintances along the way.

In your circle of friends, you're known for being understanding and helpful. Your loving nature is evident in the way you cheer everyone up when they need inspiration. You're an excellent entertainer, and an invitation to your home is eagerly anticipated. You love a good party!

Fire Pig

As a Fire Pig, you are exceptionally courageous, and capable of heroic feats that astound those watching! So determined are you to succeed, you put all your passion behind every plan you commit to. The Fire Element gives you a lot of energy and also makes your emotions more powerful than in other Pigs. This can take you to the highest levels of achievement.

You are a risk-taker by nature. The lure of adventure is strong, and you are not one to sit on the sidelines and watch others have all the fun. You are a striver and a doer. Sometimes, things work to your favor in a big way. Other times, you may see meager returns for your efforts. But either way you have a lot of fun trying! You are a person who knows how to enjoy life and all its pleasures.

Your home can be all-important to you. After all, it is both a "base camp" and a place to showcase your achievements. Chances are it's filled with souvenirs and mementos of your adventures.

The great motivator for you is love, and you will do anything to protect and provide a good life for those close to you. Within your circle of friends, you are famous for helping out those who need you, both emotionally and financially. It's that big heart of yours!

Earth Pig

Being an Earth Pig, you can always find ways to make yourself feel happy and content. You are a peaceful, comfort-loving person. Easygoing and sensible, you go through life allowing very little to ruffle you. Others look to you as an example of how to make things run smoothly for themselves.

The Earth Element adds real solidity of character to the cheerful Pig disposition. Your practicality is evident in the way you take care of your affairs. You're well-organized and patient, and you will pursue your goals until you reach them. Success is yours for the asking. Try not to push yourself too hard, though. Slow and steady wins the race.

You may find yourself in a leadership position quite often because of your reliability, and you're sure to treat others fairly. Always ready to be helpful, you are kind and respectful of everyone you meet. Tranquility is your main goal and you always find ways of steering things in that direction.

Your social life can be as active as you want it to be. Of course, you love parties. Good food, pleasant conversation, and the people you love to enjoy them with... that's all you need to make you happy!

Metal Pig

Being a Metal Pig gives you tremendous strength and power. Even if no one has ever told you, everyone who knows you is probably in awe of your energy and endurance. You are a real powerhouse who puts your heart into everything you do. You love to win!

Having a good reputation is important to you and you will work hard to insure that you keep yours intact. You deserve the respect others have for you because you have certainly earned it. You're cheerful and industrious, and you get along well with most people. You have a good word to say to everyone to brighten up their day. Encouraging others comes easily to you. Any organization or association would welcome your participation.

Your passionate nature seeks out fine things and comfortable living. You may even have to guard against a tendency to overindulge in the easy life. You love parties because you like socializing with people. If you reach for the healthy snacks, like carrot and celery sticks, you can save yourself a bit of dieting later on.

To those who are close to you, you are faithful and true. You think the world of them and can lavish them with affection. Your friends all recognize your worth and think you're as good as gold!

Chinese Astrology Dates 1900–2001

(All times are GMT in military format)

Year	From – To	Chinese Sign	Yin/Yang
1900	Jan. 31, 1900 at 1:23 – Feb. 19, 1901 at 2:44	Metal Rat	Yang
1901	Feb. 19, 1901 at 2:45 – Feb. 8, 1902 at 13:20	Metal Ox	Yin
1902	Feb. 8, 1902 at 13:21 – Jan. 28, 1903 at 16:37	Water Tiger	Yang
1903	Jan. 28, 1903 at 16:38 – Feb. 16, 1904 at 11:04	Water Rabbit	Yin
1904	Feb. 16, 1904 at 11:05 – Feb. 4, 1905 at 11:05	Wood Dragon	Yang
1905	Feb. 4, 1905 at 11:06 – Jan. 24, 1906 at 17:08	Wood Snake	Yin
1906	Jan. 24, 1906 at 17:09 – Feb. 12, 1907 at 17:42	Fire Horse	Yang
1907	Feb. 12, 1907 at 17:43 – Feb. 2, 1908 at 8:35	Fire Sheep	Yin
1908	Feb. 2, 1908 at 8:36 – Jan. 22, 1909 at 0:11	Earth Monkey	Yang
1909	Jan. 22, 1909 at 0:12 – Feb. 10, 1910 at 1:12	Earth Rooster	Yin
1910	Feb. 10, 1910 at 1:13 – Jan. 30, 1911 at 9:43	Metal Dog	Yang
1911	Jan. 30, 1911 at 9:44 – Feb. 18, 1912 at 5:43	Metal Pig	Yin
1912	Feb. 18, 1912 at 5:44 – Feb. 6, 1913 at 5:21	Water Rat	Yang
1913	Feb. 6, 1913 at 5:22 – Jan. 26, 1914 at 6:33	Water Ox	Yin
1914	Jan. 26, 1914 at 6:34 – Feb. 14, 1915 at 4:30	Wood Tiger	Yang
1915	Feb. 14, 1915 at 4:31 – Feb. 3, 1916 at 16:04	Wood Rabbit	Yin
1916	Feb. 3, 1916 at 16:05 – Jan. 23, 1917 at 7:39	Fire Dragon	Yang
1917	Jan. 23, 1917 at 7:40 – Feb. 11, 1918 at 10:03	Fire Snake	Yin
1918	Feb. 11, 1918 at 10:04 – Jan. 31, 1919 at 23:06	Earth Horse	Yang
1919	Jan. 31, 1919 at 23:07 – Feb. 19, 1920 at 21:33	Earth Sheep	Yin
1920	Feb. 19, 1920 at 21:34 – Feb. 8, 1921 at 0:35	Metal Monkey	Yang
1921	Feb. 8, 1921 at 0:36 – Jan. 27, 1922 at 23:47	Metal Rooster	Yin
1922	Jan. 27, 1922 at 23:48 – Feb. 15, 1923 at 19:06	Water Dog	Yang
1923	Feb. 15, 1923 at 19:07 – Feb. 5, 1924 at 1:37	Water Pig	Yin
1924	Feb. 5, 1924 at 1:38 – Jan. 24, 1925 at 14:44	Wood Rat	Yang
1925	Jan. 24, 1925 at 14:45 – Feb. 12, 1926 at 17:19	Wood Ox	Yin
1926	Feb. 12, 1926 at 17:20 – Feb. 2, 1927 at 8:53	Fire Tiger	Yang
1927	Feb. 2, 1927 at 8:54 – Jan. 22, 1928 at 20:18	Fire Rabbit	Yin
1928	Jan. 22, 1928 at 20:19 – Feb. 9, 1929 at 17:54	Earth Dragon	Yang
1929	Feb. 9, 1929 at 17:55 – Jan. 29, 1930 at 19:06	Earth Snake	Yin
1930	Jan. 29, 1930 at 19:07 – Feb. 17, 1931 at 13:10	Metal Horse	Yang
1931	Feb. 17, 1931 at 13:11 – Feb. 6, 1932 at 14:44	Metal Sheep	Yin
1932	Feb. 6, 1932 at 14:45 – Jan. 25, 1933 at 23:19	Water Monkey	Yang
1933	Jan. 25, 1933 at 23:20 – Feb. 14, 1934 at 0:42	Water Rooster	Yin
1934	Feb. 14, 1934 at 0:43 – Feb. 3, 1935 at 16:26	Wood Dog	Yang
1935	Feb. 3, 1935 at 16:27 – Jan. 24, 1936 at 7:17	Wood Pig	Yin
1936	Jan. 24, 1936 at 7:18 – Feb. 11, 1937 at 7:33	Fire Rat	Yang
1937	Feb. 11, 1937 at 7:34 – Jan. 31, 1938 at 13:34	Fire Ox	Yin
1938	Jan. 31, 1938 at 13:35 – Feb. 19, 1939 at 8:27	Earth Tiger	Yang
1939	Feb. 19, 1939 at 8:28 – Feb. 8, 1940 at 7:44	Earth Rabbit	Yin
1940	Feb. 8, 1940 at 7:45 – Jan. 27, 1941 at 11:02	Metal Dragon	Yang
1941	Jan. 27, 1941 at 11:03 – Feb. 15, 1942 at 10:02	Metal Snake	Yin
1942	Feb. 15, 1942 at 10:03– Feb. 4, 1943 at 23:28	Water Horse	Yang
1943	Feb. 4, 1943 at 23:29 – Jan. 25, 1944 at 15:23	Water Sheep	Yin
1944	Jan. 25, 1944 at 15:24 – Feb. 12, 1945 at 17:32	Wood Monkey	Yang
1945	Feb. 12, 1945 at 17:33 – Feb. 2, 1946 at 4:42	Wood Rooster	Yin
1946	Feb. 2, 1946 at 4:43 – Jan. 22, 1947 at 8:33	Fire Dog	Yang
1947	Jan. 22, 1947 at 8:34 – Feb. 10, 1948 at 3:01	Fire Pig	Yin
1948	Feb. 10, 1948 at 3:02 – Jan. 29, 1949 at 2:41	Earth Rat	Yang

Year	From – To	Chinese Sign	Yin/Yang
1949	Jan. 29, 1949 at 2:42 – Feb. 16, 1950 at 22:52	Earth Ox	Yin
1950	Feb. 16, 1950 at 22:53 – Feb. 6, 1951 at 7: 53	Metal Tiger	Yang
1951	Feb. 6, 1951 at 7:54 – Jan. 26, 1952 at 22: 25	Metal Rabbit	Yin
1952	Jan. 26, 1952 at 22:26 – Feb. 14, 1953 at 1:09	Water Dragon	Yang
1953	Feb. 14, 1953 at 1:10 – Feb. 3, 1954 at 15:54	Water Snake	Yin
1954	Feb. 3, 1954 at 15:55 – Jan. 24, 1955 at 1:06	Wood Horse	Yang
1955	Jan. 24, 1955 at 1:07 – Feb. 11, 1956 at 21:37	Wood Sheep	Yin
1956	Feb. 11, 1956 at 21:38 – Jan. 30, 1957 at 21:24	Fire Monkey	Yang
1957	Jan. 30, 1957 at 21:25 – Feb. 18, 1958 at 15:37	Fire Rooster	Yin
1958	Feb. 18, 1958 at 15:38 – Feb. 7, 1959 at 19:21	Earth Dog	Yang
1959	Feb. 7, 1959 at 19:22 – Jan. 28, 1960 at 6:14	Earth Pig	Yin
1960	Jan. 28, 1960 at 6:15 – Feb. 15, 1961 at 8:09	Metal Rat	Yang
1961	Feb. 15, 1961 at 8:10 – Feb. 5, 1962 at 0:09	Metal Ox	Yin
1962	Feb. 5, 1962 at 0:10 – Jan. 25, 1963 at 13:41	Water Tiger	Yang
1963	Jan. 25, 1963 at 13:42 – Feb. 13, 1964 at 13:00	Water Rabbit	Yin
1964	Feb. 13, 1964 at 13:01 – Feb. 1, 1965 at 16:35	Wood Dragon	Yang
1965	Feb. 1, 1965 at 16:36 – Jan. 21, 1966 at 15:45	Wood Snake	Yin
1966	Jan. 21, 1966 at 15:46 – Feb. 9, 1967 at 10:43	Fire Horse	Yang
1967	Feb. 9, 1967 at 10:44 – Jan. 29, 1968 at 16:28	Fire Sheep	Yin
1968	Jan. 29, 1968 at 16:29 – Feb. 16, 1969 at 16:24	Earth Monkey	Yang
1969	Feb. 16, 1969 at 16:25 – Feb. 6, 1970 at 7:12	Earth Rooster	Yin
1970	Feb. 6, 1970 at 7:13 – Jan. 26, 1971 at 22:54	Metal Dog	Yang
1971	Jan. 26, 1971 at 22:55 – Feb. 15, 1972 at 0:28	Metal Pig	Yin
1972	Feb. 15, 1972 at 0:29 – Feb. 3, 1973 at 9:22	Water Rat	Yang
1973	Feb. 3, 1973 at 9:23 – Jan. 23, 1974 at 11:01	Water Ox	Yin
1974	Jan. 23, 1974 at 11:02 – Feb. 11, 1975 at 5:16	Wood Tiger	Yang
1975	Feb. 11, 1975 at 5:17 – Jan. 31, 1976 at 6:19	Wood Rabbit	Yin
1976	Jan. 31, 1976 at 6:20 – Feb. 18, 1977 at 3:36	Fire Dragon	Yang
1977	Feb. 18, 1977 at 3:37– Feb. 7, 1978 at 14:53	Fire Snake	Yin
1978	Feb. 7, 1978 at 14:54 – Jan. 28, 1979 at 6:19	Earth Horse	Yang
1979	Jan. 28, 1979 at 6:20 – Feb. 16, 1980 at 8:50	Earth Sheep	Yin
1980	Feb. 16, 1980 at 8:51 – Feb. 4, 1981 at 22:13	Metal Monkey	Yang
1981	Feb. 4, 1981 at 22:14 – Jan. 25, 1982 at 4:55	Metal Rooster	Yin
1982	Jan. 25, 1982 at 4:56 – Feb. 13, 1983 at 0:31	Water Dog	Yang
1983	Feb. 13, 1983 at 0:32 – Feb. 1, 1984 at 23:45	Water Pig	Yin
1984	Feb. 1, 1984 at 23:46 – Jan. 21, 1985 at 2:27	Wood Rat	Yang
1985	Jan. 21, 1985 at 2:28 – Feb. 9, 1986 at 0:54	Wood Ox	Yin
1986	Feb. 9, 1986 at 0:55 – Jan. 29, 1987 at 13:44	Fire Tiger	Yang
1987	Jan. 29, 1987 at 13:45 – Feb. 17, 1988 at 15:53	Fire Rabbit	Yin
1988	Feb. 17, 1988 at 15:54 – Feb. 6, 1989 at 7:36	Earth Dragon	Yang
1989	Feb. 6, 1989 at 7:37 – Jan. 26, 1990 at 19:19	Earth Snake	Yin
1990	Jan. 26, 1990 at 19:20 – Feb. 14, 1991 at 17:31	Metal Horse	Yang
1991	Feb. 14, 1991 at 17:32 – Feb. 3, 1992 at 18:59	Metal Sheep	Yin
1992	Feb. 3, 1992 at 19:00 – Jan. 22, 1993 at 18:26	Water Monkey	Yang
1993	Jan. 22, 1993 at 18:27 – Feb. 10, 1994 at 14:29	Water Rooster	Yin
1994	Feb. 10, 1994 at 14:30 – Jan. 30, 1995 at 22:47	Wood Dog	Yang
1995	Jan. 30, 1995 at 22:48 – Feb. 18, 1996 at 23:29	Wood Pig	Yin
1996	Feb. 18, 1996 at 23:30 – Feb. 7, 1997 at 15:05	Fire Rat	Yang
1997	Feb. 7, 1997 at 15:06 – Jan. 28, 1998 at 6:00	Fire Ox	Yin
1998	Jan. 28, 1998 at 6:01 – Feb. 16, 1999 at 6:38	Earth Tiger	Yang
1999	Feb. 16, 1999 at 6:39 – Feb. 5, 2000 at 13:03	Earth Rabbit	Yin
2000	Feb. 5, 2000 at 13:04 – Jan. 24, 2001 at 13:07	Metal Dragon	Yang
2001	Jan. 24, 2001 at 13:08 – Feb. 12 2002 at 7:41	Metal Snake	Yin

Mystical Card

Many psychics use the playing card deck to see into the future. It is a little known fact that these cards have a mystical significance, much like a tarot deck. Some esoteric schools believe the playing cards predate the tarot. When the secret language of the cards is decoded, it is discovered that each card relates to a date–a date of birth.

The mystical meanings for each card are derived from an ancient esoteric system that combines the knowledge gleaned from astrological and numerological influences. Some say this came down to us from the lost continent of Atlantis. All we know for sure is that the cards are uncannily accurate. They reveal the inner essence of a particular moment in time and can interpret the meaning of your birth date.

Each card represents a planet in that date's horoscope, which can be used for compatibility and predictive uses. The complete system of card interpretation is too complicated to go into here. So for our purposes, we will describe the general meanings of the suits and numbers, and reveal a birth date's personality profile. You can compare your own card's characteristics with that of others to see how compatible you are or to discover more about yourself and others.

Each suit represents a different personality type and each number has its own symbolic significance. These combine to give a unique meaning to each card, which can have both a positive and a negative expression. The meanings of each card are outlined briefly below.

Hearts thrive on love. Relationships are the most important thing in the world to them. Hearts are in tune with the arts: music, poetry, and the pursuit of beauty. They can be kind, affectionate and friendly, or selfish and self-seeking.

Clubs thrive on intellect. Learning, seeking knowledge and communicating are their strengths. Clubs will do well in education, legal matters, and publishing. They can be brilliant, helpful and aggressive, or tricky and unreliable.

Diamonds thrive in the material world. Money, finance and business are their forte. They can be generous, powerful and influential, or miserly and avaricious.

Spades know how to overcome obstacles through wisdom. This can come from trial and error or innate ability. They make excellent healers and are drawn to the service professions. They can be self-disciplined and a tireless worker or a tyrant.

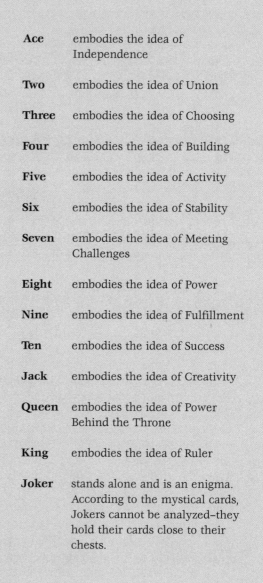

Ace	embodies the idea of Independence
Two	embodies the idea of Union
Three	embodies the idea of Choosing
Four	embodies the idea of Building
Five	embodies the idea of Activity
Six	embodies the idea of Stability
Seven	embodies the idea of Meeting Challenges
Eight	embodies the idea of Power
Nine	embodies the idea of Fulfillment
Ten	embodies the idea of Success
Jack	embodies the idea of Creativity
Queen	embodies the idea of Power Behind the Throne
King	embodies the idea of Ruler
Joker	stands alone and is an enigma. According to the mystical cards, Jokers cannot be analyzed–they hold their cards close to their chests.

To Determine Your Card

To find the card for any birthday, refer to the chart opposite. Locate the month of birth across the top. Then, locate the date of birth in the far left column. From this date column move your finger across to the month column to pinpoint the card in question. Then look up the meaning of the card on the pages which follow.

	Jan.	Feb.	Mar.	Apr.	May	June	July	Aug.	Sept.	Oct.	Nov.	Dec.
1	K♠	J♠	9♠	7♠	5♠	3♠	A♠	Q♦	10♦	8♦	6♦	4♦
2	Q♠	10♠	8♠	6♠	4♠	2♠	K♦	J♦	9♦	7♦	5♦	3♦
3	J♠	9♠	7♠	5♠	3♠	A♠	Q♦	10♦	8♦	6♦	4♦	2♦
4	10♠	8♠	6♠	4♠	2♠	K♦	J♦	9♦	7♦	5♦	3♦	A♦
5	9♠	7♠	5♠	3♠	A♠	Q♦	10♦	8♦	6♦	4♦	2♦	K♣
6	8♠	6♠	4♠	2♠	K♦	J♦	9♦	7♦	5♦	3♦	A♦	Q♣
7	7♠	5♠	3♠	A♠	Q♦	10♦	8♦	6♦	4♦	2♦	K♣	J♣
8	6♠	4♠	2♠	K♦	J♦	9♦	7♦	5♦	3♦	A♦	Q♣	10♣
9	5♠	3♠	A♠	Q♦	10♦	8♦	6♦	4♦	2♦	K♣	J♣	9♣
10	4♠	2♠	K♦	J♦	9♦	7♦	5♦	3♦	A♦	Q♣	10♣	8♣
11	3♠	A♠	Q♦	10♦	8♦	6♦	4♦	2♦	K♣	J♣	9♣	7♣
12	2♠	K♦	J♦	9♦	7♦	5♦	3♦	A♦	Q♣	10♣	8♣	6♣
13	A♠	Q♦	10♦	8♦	6♦	4♦	2♦	K♣	J♣	9♣	7♣	5♣
14	K♦	J♦	9♦	7♦	5♦	3♦	A♦	Q♣	10♣	8♣	6♣	4♣
15	Q♦	10♦	8♦	6♦	4♦	2♦	K♣	J♣	9♣	7♣	5♣	3♣
16	J♦	9♦	7♦	5♦	3♦	A♦	Q♣	10♣	8♣	6♣	4♣	2♣
17	10♦	8♦	6♦	4♦	2♦	K♣	J♣	9♣	7♣	5♣	3♣	A♣
18	9♦	7♦	5♦	3♦	A♦	Q♣	10♣	8♣	6♣	4♣	2♣	K♥
19	8♦	6♦	4♦	2♦	K♣	J♣	9♣	7♣	5♣	3♣	A♣	Q♥
20	7♦	5♦	3♦	A♦	Q♣	10♣	8♣	6♣	4♣	2♣	K♥	J♥
21	6♦	4♦	2♦	K♣	J♣	9♣	7♣	5♣	3♣	A♣	Q♥	10♥
22	5♦	3♦	A♦	Q♣	10♣	8♣	6♣	4♣	2♣	K♥	J♥	9♥
23	4♦	2♦	K♣	J♣	9♣	7♣	5♣	3♣	A♣	Q♥	10♥	8♥
24	3♦	A♦	Q♣	10♣	8♣	6♣	4♣	2♣	K♥	J♥	9♥	7♥
25	2♦	K♣	J♣	9♣	7♣	5♣	3♣	A♣	Q♥	10♥	8♥	6♥
26	A♦	Q♣	10♣	8♣	6♣	4♣	2♣	K♥	J♥	9♥	7♥	5♥
27	K♣	J♣	9♣	7♣	5♣	3♣	A♣	Q♥	10♥	8♥	6♥	4♥
28	Q♣	10♣	8♣	6♣	4♣	2♣	K♥	J♥	9♥	7♥	5♥	3♥
29	J♣	9♣	7♣	5♣	3♣	A♣	Q♥	10♥	8♥	6♥	4♥	2♥
30	10♣		6♣	4♣	2♣	K♥	J♥	9♥	7♥	5♥	3♥	A♥
31	9♣		5♣		A♣		10♥	8♥			4♥	Joker

MYSTICAL CARD INTERPRETATIONS

A ♥

You are a lover at heart. Without love, or at least the idea of romance in your life, you feel incomplete, and this saddens you. You have wonderful leadership abilities and are always ready to move forward and start something new. Although you don't hesitate to delegate projects to others, you like to have full control over everything. In your book, only your decisions are valid.

A ♣

Attaining knowledge is very important to you. As an Ace of Clubs, you desire food for your mind and love for your heart. You are attracted to those who have new ideas and you enjoy communicating with them. Relationships play a big role in your life and you need to fully understand all of their ins and outs. You can get hung up in looking after your own interests.

A ♦

You are a person who is concerned about your reputation and the impression you make. You enjoy starting new endeavors and making progress, but can sometimes find yourself caught up in procrastination. As an Ace of Diamonds, you strive to achieve financial success and determine your self-worth by that. Your popularity and status spell happiness for you.

A ♠

As a busy person, you can get more done in one day than someone else may choose to do in a week. Your mind is always active as well, and you want to delve into secrets. You desire to know what makes the world go round. There may be times when you feel you have many burdens to carry, but you bear them well. You don't mind burdens or responsibility as long as you have control.

2 ♥

Love in a strong partnership is extremely important to you. Your relationships are always a big part of your life. Cooperation and friendliness mark all that you do. These attributes make you a good and loyal friend to have. Sometimes a fear of hurting friends' or loved ones' feelings can cloud your judgment. You're good at blending sensitivity with logic.

2 ♣

Sharing knowledge motivates you like nothing else. Friends and lovers alike must be able to communicate clearly with you; otherwise, you are likely to feel left out and confused. You excel at finding the source of a conflict, talking things out, and diplomatically finding solutions. You can use these special skills to discover the truth about anything that happens.

2 ♦

Partnerships are essential for you when it comes to achieving the wealth and security you desire. Your success has much to do with how well you get along with people. If anticipated rewards do not come as quickly as you would like, you might be tempted to break off relationships. Using diplomacy and maintaining patience are the things that reap the most gains for you.

2 ♠

Fulfillment in life for you is found in stable and compatible relationships. You thrive when your work and love are intimately connected and are happiest when sharing projects with someone as enthusiastic as you. At times, you may expect too much of others. To make things work, you allow others their own space and freedom to make their own decisions.

3 ♥

Your strongly affectionate tendencies and social nature can at times make it hard for you to make choices about people or situations. That's because your happiness depends on freely expressing your feelings and experiencing many things all at the same time. You may believe you'll find happiness by not binding yourself to one person or thing until you are certain of your choice.

3 ♣

Seeking knowledge and sharing it with others are what turns you on. You excel in expressing your ideas, whether to one person or a group. You can, however, be indecisive—which may get the best of you at times. You are happiest when you're optimistic and know that conveying your enthusiasm helps you avoid worrying, which usually turns out to be unnecessary anyway.

3 ♦

Keeping productive is your life's motto. If you don't have a means for making money, you feel you're wasting time and are likely to fall prey to undue concern over finances. Finding new and creative ways to build a nest egg ensures you happiness and optimism, while making certain that you have choices and that you don't feel boxed in keeps you free from worry and concerns.

3 ♠

Three of Spades Happiness for you means channeling your creative wisdom in a variety of ways. If you're not working on at least two different things at once, you may feel deeply dissatisfied, be indecisive, and your morale might suffer a setback. You like to pursue a number of diverse positive outlets for your artistry and share your talents with as many people as possible.

4 ♥

Permanence and compatibility in an exclusive relationship are of paramount importance to you. You must have a partner who is able to express affection and be a steadfast helpmate. Family and social life center around your home. You do all you can to keep close bonds viable and strong. There are times when you tend to be somewhat overprotective of loved ones.

4 ♣

Your active mind is a vast storehouse of knowledge with almost instant recall, thanks to your organized thinking. By analyzing situations, you bring about better understanding that helps you and others achieve peace of mind. Sound judgment and the ability to concentrate make you a good advisor. However, inflexibility in your attitude can sometimes distance you from others.

4 ♦

You equate security with money. In your estimation, creating a sound financial base is the first step toward achieving your desires. You possess the organizational ability and discipline needed to earn a prestigious position and to get what you want in life. You dislike being restricted, and if you feel you can't be your own person, you may turn your back on situations.

4 ♠

You seek security in all areas of your life. You want the results of your labors to be a source of satisfaction, and you do not rest easy unless you have everything in order. You are accustomed to helping others and are happiest when you have a lot to occupy yourself with. Hard work is no stranger to you. You can be careless at times in not finishing what you start.

5 ♥

Changes of heart tend to cause upheavals in your life. You often seek greener pastures, to your detriment. You have been separated from at least one important person in your life. You are convivial, reaching out to others and befriending those who are accepting of your life-style. If you get overwhelmed, there's a chance that your emotions may get the best of you.

5 ♣

You have a driving need to "know it all" and to seek out whatever is new, or different, or will make your life better. You like to be on the go—if not traveling, then considering new areas of exploration. It's difficult to satisfy your restless spirit. When it comes to others' private affairs, you try not to cross the line separating concerned interest and being nosy. You respect intelligence in others.

5 ♦

Perhaps more than once in your life you have changed direction because of a shift in goals or because the grass seemed greener elsewhere. What you had originally decided was just right for you was left by the wayside and replaced by something better. You are still learning to deal with fluctuations in your finances. Getting stuck in trivialities has set you back on a number of occasions.

5 ♠

Changes in your daily routine, your work, and social activities are something that you are used to. You let nothing stand in your way from reaching an objective. If conditions are not improving the way you would like them to, you tend to become easily frustrated and dissatisfied. Others may not appreciate your independent ways and can consider you aloof at times.

6 ♥

You want everyone around you to be happy and you do what you can to bring it about. Compromising and helping out are a way of life for you. You often put others before yourself. Your strength lies in being certain about your mission in life, which is fostering love. You are prone to bouts of anxiety when your expectations aren't met. You often feel responsible for keeping peace in relationships.

3 ♣

You have a deep inner sense of where you are going. You are careful in conveying information and speaking your mind to avoid any misunderstandings or problems. As a romantic at heart, you take pleasure in being around artistic creations, and the strains of fine music appeal to your cultured sensibilities. You often fear criticism resulting from past deeds.

6 ♦

You are conscientious when it comes to looking after responsibilities (especially financial obligations) and reciprocating favors. In the back of your mind you want to know your true purpose in life. You feel there is something special, perhaps unique to you alone, that you need to accomplish. You are careful not to interfere with the wishes of others, just as you want your own desires honored.

6 ♠

You wisely recognize the connection between what you've done and the consequences, positive or negative. You have reaped just rewards, but you are also accustomed to paying the piper. After reluctantly taking up opportunities, unaware of their value, you're surprised by your good fortune that results. You're prone to being apprehensive about fulfilling obligations.

7 ♥

You are subjected to emotional challenges involving those close to you. Your good nature is likely to be taken advantage of. Your love is put to the test when the object of your affection doesn't meet your expectations and especially when their ideas or actions are not in everyone's best interests. Having a loving heart, you are most fulfilled when helping others. You can be too skeptical at times.

7 ♣

You have a very sensitive nature that keeps you attuned to everything around you. At times, you can fall prey to the negative moods and thoughts of others, causing you to be pessimistic. Your goals can turn to spirituality and higher endeavors to counteract melancholy. Because of your sensitivity, you are highly attuned to music, beauty, and even mysticism. You find joy in peace and quiet.

7 ♦

Your inclination to get into social or creative endeavors could be thwarted by an attachment to material things, especially money. Due to your keen mental ability, you are good at managing your finances. But your intuition tells you that money is not your main purpose in life. There is a skeptical streak in you that can work toward your benefit or can turn you off to people or situations.

7 ♠

Keen intuition helps you to overcome challenges, especially in the areas of work and health. You are prone to holding on to negative thoughts and resentments, which often affect your physical and emotional life. However, your intuition, inner strength, and innate power can conquer any restrictions or hurdles that life throws in your way, especially when you release the past.

8 ♥

Your charm and charisma win you friends and allies and allow you to be adept at dealing with groups, too. You have a powerful emotional strength that helps you to make things happen by "wishing it so." Your magnetic personality attracts many people to you. There are times when you may succumb to being manipulative or being heavy-handed, but your loving nature keeps this in check.

8 ♣

You have the ability to focus your mind with laser-beam accuracy. When you aim to achieve what you set your sights on, you stay with it until you succeed. You're used to overcoming many obstacles. A good memory is your forte. Because your inner vision is so sharp, you might see your way as the only one and get into schemes if others don't agree with you.

8 ♦

A lot of what you do centers around accumulating and managing money. You recognize the power that goes with having financial control. Freedom to have what you want and do what you like is high on your priority list. However, among the many hats you wear is that of the philanthropist. You are a magnificent dreamer, but you do have a tendency to be a schemer as well.

8 ♠

Hard work is a way of life for you. You learn all you can about your work and all you do. You know what it takes to achieve a position equal to your expertise. You like to keep physically fit. Your overall strength is a combination of innate power and brains. Determination and willpower are what got you where you are today. Your relentless drive can sometimes cause a clash of wills with others.

9 ♥

Your friends are very important to you. Their support gets you through tough emotional situations. Your love runs deep, and your affections know no bounds. You are no stranger to disappointments in life, but this has made you that much more compassionate and understanding of others and their hardships. You know the benefits of deep trust, faith, and inner strength, all of your own making.

9 ♣

You have an innate wisdom that you willingly share with others. It is not unusual for people to come to you for advice. Sometimes you need to heed your own counsel, as life's school of hard knocks has given you much wisdom. Because of knowledge gained from your deep understanding, you know how to see the good in all situations, especially when you encounter a loss.

9 ♦

Although you are well versed in matters of finance, you are not exempt from suffering losses, which could be substantial. You have had your share of ups and downs. However, setbacks never stop you. You have the wonderful ability to think big. You see the larger picture and set out to get the best for yourself and those you care about. At times it is as though you are "divinely inspired."

9 ♠

You have played the part of the phoenix, making a comeback and assuming a whole new way of life after something important to you is over with—whether it be job, life-style, or a close relationship. You are often faced with major challenges, but find ways to overcome them. Because you're so accustomed to fending for yourself, you sometimes may not see the needs of others.

10 ♥

You know the true meaning of love. It is as if you were born knowing the power of this universal force. And you try to live your life with this principle in the forefront of all you do. Those who know you are sure that they can depend upon you to make them feel better, no matter what their situation; but who is there to comfort you? Others may see you as selfish at times.

10 ♣

Wisdom and knowledge are the main tools that help you get ahead. You are a natural communicator and teacher. Your sharp mind makes you a good speaker and/or writer. You have received happiness from and take pride in using your talents to benefit many people. However, winning the admiration of your peers and others who look up to you can cause you to be egotistical.

10 ♦

Money means a great deal to you, and you tend to rate things according to their monetary value. You are a financier at heart. This can take the form of an avid interest in global endeavors, some sort of money dealings with groups, or perhaps actually managing or handling significant sums. You could be tempted to exploit situations to your benefit.

10 ♠

You have a driving need to succeed, and, rather than sit back and enjoy the fruits of your labors, you keep going after more and more. It's as though you build up a momentum and don't know how to quit. Obstacles generally don't faze you. When you're obsessed with reaching your goal, you stop at nothing to attain it. You get what you aim for in any area that is of great interest to you.

J ♥

You give your all to those you love, others who need you, or for the ultimate good of whomever or whatever you deem worthy. When the opportunity appears for you to come to the rescue, you rise to the occasion. Your love is not just a matter of being humane but aspires to the higher levels of spirituality. As generous as you are, you are prone to idle away your valuable time.

J ♣

You have what seems like a never-ending supply of creative and innovative ideas. Your knowledge and understanding are a source of inspiration to yourself and others. Sometimes you can become very lazy and choose not to implement any of your thoughts and projects. At other times, you can use fancy footwork to cajole others into doing what you want, without taking into consideration their needs.

J ♦

Your main strength lies in your business abilities. You can be a master at making money. This comes easily to you. Others are attracted to you because of your optimistic way of thinking, which in turn motivates them to move forward on their own. There are times when you become your own worst enemy through laziness or taking the easy way out. Yet you always manage to succeed.

J ♠

You are the Great Pretender—you know how to play a role, get the part, and succeed through the magnificence of your imagination. You don't let anything stop you once you make up your mind about something. However, there are times when you can be lazy, letting things fall by the wayside. Yet your wonderful creative abilities carry you through any situation.

Q ♥

Your warm and loving ways, combined with your true nurturing spirit, endear you to those who know you. Expressing affection and taking care of others come naturally to you. You enjoy the company of the opposite sex and like to indulge in romantic fantasies. You tend to gain weight easily. You can pursue the free and easy life, sometimes even to the extent of shirking responsibilities.

Q ♣

You have a strong desire to help others and you do this best by giving them the information and knowledge that they need to solve their problems. Your intelligence serves you well. You have a very strong intuitive side that is a part of everything you do. Sometimes this ability can be disconcerting, as you tend to be high-strung. As an aside, patience is not your strong suit.

Q ♦

You aspire to have the finer things in life, regardless of your finances. So you have a tendency to spend beyond what you can afford. You might acquire status symbols for their prestige value. You have good business sense, and financial success comes through sales or marketing. Although you are a nurturer, there is a part of you that can be withholding at times.

Q ♠

You are master of your own destiny. You know who you are and where you are going. You are a natural leader, a good organizer and set an example for others by your own hard work. You also have the ability to inspire others in spiritual ways. You achieve success by virtue of your experiences in life. Being overly devoted to your work can cause life to be tedious for you at times.

K ♥

Because you are good at understanding the world of emotions, others look to you for guidance. Love and compassion come easily to you, and you make it a point to express them to all and in all you do. This is your strength and your gift to the world. Your creative and artistic abilities bring joy to you as well. Your innate wisdom about the power of love carries you through all of life's travails.

K ♣

Leadership responsibility is bestowed upon you because of your extensive knowledge in your chosen field, most likely related to communications. You are considered an authority and have received recognition for your career achievements. Your keen intuition helps you size up people and situations. You often struggle to maintain your high standards and don't wish to compromise your principles.

K ♦

Financial success in business is the driving force behind
your ambition. You are more likely to have your own
business than to work for someone else. Regardless
of whether you are independent or not, you do well
managing money and in foreign investments. Integrity
and a strong sense of values are important to you. You
can become preoccupied with things working out the
way you want them to.

K ♠

Your wisdom is of a practical bent and comes from
personal experience, both in business and in matters
of the heart. You strive to achieve and maintain
mastery over your environment and yourself. It is
for these reasons that you are valued as a leader. You
hold yourself with confidence and assurance. However,
you can get stuck sometimes, which can hamper your
progress.

Joker

You have a very serious nature, and the words
"lighten up" are not foreign to you. You take your
responsibilities very seriously and can be counted on
to accomplish anything you set out to do. Some people
may consider you mysterious, as you keep your cards
close to your vest. When you commit, especially in
love, you take your promises to heart. Your wisdom
comes from personal experience.

About the Editors

Rochelle Gordon
EDITOR-IN-CHIEF

An expert with more than thirty years experience in astrology, tarot, and acrophonology, Rochelle Gordon is the author of several books, including *Body Talk* and *Personal Power Is In Your Name*. A former editor of *Body Mind Spirit* magazine, she is a member of the American Federation of Astrologers and past President of the Astra Guild for Education. Rochelle lives in Connecticut, and has a grown son, a Scorpio like herself.

Nadia Stieglitz
GENERAL EDITOR

Managing Editor for the Pasteur Publishing Group, Nadia Stieglitz has been the creative force behind many successful titles such as *Supermarket Remedies*, *OmniForce*, *Feng Shui Solutions*, *Your Spirit Animal Helpers and Enchanted Secrets* and *Magickal Spells*. An experienced feng shui practitioner, Nadia lives with her husband and three children in London, England.